"一带一路"
沿线国家法律
环境国别报告

(中英文对照)

第四卷
VOLUME IV

LEGAL ENVIRONMENT REPORT OF
THE "BELT AND ROAD" COUNTRIES

中华全国律师协会 编
ALL CHINA LAWYERS ASSOCIATION

北京大学出版社
PEKING UNIVERSITY PRESS

图书在版编目（CIP）数据

"一带一路"沿线国家法律环境国别报告. 第四卷/中华全国律师协会编. — 北京：北京大学出版社，2018.12
ISBN 978-7-301-30003-9

Ⅰ.①一… Ⅱ.①中… Ⅲ.①国际投资法学—指南 Ⅳ.①D996.4-62

中国版本图书馆CIP数据核字（2018）第240663号

书　　　名	"一带一路"沿线国家法律环境国别报告（第四卷） "YI DAI YI LU" YANXIAN GUOJIA FALÜ HUANJING GUOBIE BAOGAO（DI-SI JUAN）
著作责任者	中华全国律师协会　编
责任编辑	陈晓洁　田　鹤
标准书号	ISBN 978-7-301-30003-9
出版发行	北京大学出版社
地　　　址	北京市海淀区成府路205号　100871
网　　　址	http://www.pup.cn　http://www.yandayuanzhao.com
电子信箱	yandayuanzhao@163.com
新浪微博	@北京大学出版社　@北大出版社燕大元照法律图书
电　　　话	邮购部 010-62752015　发行部 010-62750672　编辑部 010-62117788
印　刷　者	南京爱德印刷有限公司
经　销　者	新华书店
	720毫米×1020毫米　16开本　70.25印张　2271千字
	2018年12月第1版　2018年12月第1次印刷
定　　　价	398.00元

未经许可，不得以任何方式复制或抄袭本书之部分或全部内容。
版权所有，侵权必究
举报电话：010-62752024　电子信箱：fd@pup.pku.edu.cn
图书如有印装质量问题，请与出版部联系，电话：010-62756370

出版说明

共同建设"丝绸之路经济带"和"21世纪海上丝绸之路"（以下简称"一带一路"）是中国主动适应全球经济形势深刻变化提出的重大合作倡议。为推进律师行业投身"一带一路"建设，中华全国律师协会于2016年启动中国律师服务"一带一路"建设项目，着手编写了《"一带一路"沿线国家法律环境国别报告》（以下简称《报告》）第一卷、第二卷。2017年12月，中华全国律师协会又启动了《报告》第三卷、第四卷的编写工作。

《报告》旨在介绍"一带一路"沿线国家的基本法律制度和法律环境。本次出版的是《报告》的第三卷、第四卷，含"一带一路"沿线38个国家的投资法律环境报告。报告内容涉及投资、贸易、劳动、环境保护、知识产权、争议解决等领域。具体包括相关国家的法律制度及基本法律环境概述，相关国家的市场准入、外汇管理、融资、土地政策、公司设立与解散、并购、竞争管制、税收政策、证券交易、投资优惠、贸易法律规定及管理、工会与劳动组织、劳动争议解决、知识产权保护、环境保护、争议解决方式及机构等具体法律制度。

本书编写特点及特别声明：

一、《报告》由中华全国律师协会国际业务专业委员会委员和中华全国律师协会涉外律师领军人才联手"一带一路"沿线国家律师事务所的律师共同撰写。"一带一路"沿线国家参与撰稿的律师事务所的选择，是按照国际著名法律评级机构评定前五名的律师事务所。中国律师两人一组作为一个国家的国别协调人，负责联络该国家的律师事务所，请他们指定本所律师根据中华全国律师协会拟定的写作提纲及要求，撰写本国英文版法律环境报告。报告在规定的时间完成后，中国律师将英文稿翻译成中文稿，交中华全国律师协会编审汇总后，交付出版机构。

二、《报告》真实反映了"一带一路"沿线国家实际法律环境状况，具有很强的实用性、权威性和可操作性，可以为社会各界与"一带一路"沿线国家开展官方与民间交流提供科学准确的法律环境参考，同时《报告》在附录部分收录了参与写作的境内外律师事务所、律师介绍，可以为参与"一带一路"建设的中国企业聘请中外律师提供相关参考信息。

三、《报告》编写所依据的法律及实践截至2018年1月31日，包含了"一带一路"沿线国家所适用、已颁布并且现行有效的当地投资法律及参与撰写《报告》的"一带一路"沿线国家律师事务所的实践。中华全国律师协会并未调查、未明示或暗示地运用上述日期以后的"一带一路"沿线国家投资法律和实践或除"一带一路"沿线国家以外其他任何国家的法律和实践。

四、《报告》中对于"一带一路"沿线国家投资法律概念的解释均以中文直译。有关的法律概念也许不会与在其他司法管辖区内对应的英语术语表达的法律概念完全等同。因此，《报告》只可能在其明确表达下对基于"一带一路"沿线国家投资法律管辖下产生的解释或法律责任问题负责。中华全国律师协会不对外国司法体系下法官、仲裁员等如何解释"一带一路"沿线国家投资法律概念及法律表述提供任何意见。

五、《报告》中引用及使用的术语或概念的中文翻译，在"一带一路"沿线国家投资法律中可能不具有完全等同的术语或概念。《报告》仅为社会各界了解"一带一路"沿线国家的相关投资法律和实践时参考使用，不代表中华全国律师协会、相关律师事务所和律师对其中所述任何事项的法律意见。受限于客观条件，中华全国律师协会并未核查《报告》中相关内容的真实性、合法性和有效性，参与撰写《报告》的"一带一路"沿线国家的律师事务所对其所撰写的内容独自承担责任。

六、《报告》的相关知识产权归中华全国律师协会所有，包括但不限于著作权、邻接权与标识，非经中华全国律师协会事先书面同意和批准，《报告》不得用于营利或据以向中华全国律师协会追究任何责任。对《报告》解释和修改的权利归中华全国律师协会所有。

由于各个国家的社会制度不同，法律环境各异，作者来自不同国家，在撰稿、编译及编辑过程中难免出现各种不同理解及错误遗漏，希望各位读者及时反馈，以便我们在后续的项目中日臻完善。

七、本说明中文文本与英文文本不一致的，以中文文本为准。

中华全国律师协会
2018 年 12 月

NOTIFICATION OF PUBLICATION

Joint construction of the "Silk Road Economic Belt" and the "21st Century Maritime Silk Road" (hereinafter referred to as the "Belt and Road Initiative") is a milestone cooperative initiative proposed by China to actively adapt to profound changes in the ever-changing global economic environment. To more effectively integrate the legal profession/industry into the establishment of the "Belt and Road Initiative", All China Lawyers Association (ACLA) launched the "Belt and Road Initiative" developmental project for Chinese attorneys in 2016, and initiated the composition of the First and Second Volume of the "National Legal Environment Report along the 'Belt and Road Initiative'"(hereinafter referred to as the "Report"). In December 2017, the All China Lawyers Association initiated preparation of the Third and Fourth Volume of the Report.

The tenet of the "Report" aims at introducing the fundamentals of legal system and legal environment of countries along the "Belt and Road Initiative". The most recent publication of both the Third and Fourth Volume of the "Report" contains detailed descriptions of investment legal environment of the 38 countries along the "Belt and Road Initiative". Scope of the report covers issues such as investment, trade, labor, environmental protection, intellectual property right, as well as dispute resolution. The "Report" includes overviews of the legal system and basic legal environment of pertinent countries along the "Belt and Road Initiative". More specifically, it includes these countries' legal organization on issues such as requirement/standard of market access, foreign exchange regulations, finance, land policy, company establishment and dissolution, mergers and acquisitions, competition control, taxation policies, securities transactions, investment preferences, legal regulation and management of trade, trade unions and labor organizations, labor dispute resolution, intellectual property protection, environmental protection, as well as methods and institutions of dispute resolution.

Unique features and special announcements of the "Report":

1. The "Report" is co-authored by Members of the International Business Professional Committee of the All China Lawyers Association and Leading Lawyers for Foreign Related Issues from the All China Lawyers Association, in cooperation with lawyers of law firms from countries along the "Belt and Road Initiative". Law firms that participated in drafting of the "Report" are selected from top five law firms of corresponding countries pursuant to ratings from internationally renowned legal rating agencies. Two attorneys from China are assigned to a team, with each team designated as a particular country's

national coordinator; each team is responsible for liaising with that country's law firms and inquire from them English version of legal environment reports in accordance with the written outlines and requirements of the All China Lawyers Association. After the report is completed within the prescribed time, the attorneys from China then translate the English text into a Chinese manuscript. The manuscript is then submitted to ACLA for review, and is eventually delivered to the publishing agency.

2. The "Report" truthfully reflects actual legal environment of countries along the "Belt and Road Initiative", it is highly practical, authoritative, and operable. The "Report" serves the purpose of promoting communications between various sectors of the society (world) and countries along the "Belt and Road Initiative" as an accurate scientific standard of reference, on both governmental and private-sector levels. Meanwhile, provided in the appendix are the introductions of domestic and foreign law firms and lawyers that participated in the composition of the "Report". For Chinese companies that participate in the construction of the "Belt and Road Initiative", the "Report" can provide relevant referential information for those companies that are interested in hiring domestic and foreign attorneys.

3. As of January 31st, 2018, laws and legal practices on which the Report is based on include local investment laws that have been adopted, promulgated, and are currently in force along the "Belt and Road Initiative" countries, as well as actual practice experiences of law firms that participated in the composition of the "Report" from countries along the "Belt and Road Initiative" countries. The All China Lawyers Association has not investigated, nor explicitly or implicitly incorporated, laws and practices of countries along the "Belt and Road Initiative", or laws and practices of countries not included in the "Belt and Road Initiative", subsequent to the above date.

4. Within the "Report", interpretations of legal investment concepts (and or definitions) of all countries along the "Belt and Road Initiative" are translated directly (verbatim) into Chinese. There is a possibility that such legal concepts or definitions of one particular jurisdiction do not exactly/precisely correspond to a suitable legal concept or definition within the realm of legal English in a different jurisdiction. Thus, unless a statement is made clearly in the "Report", the "Report" shall not be legally responsible or liable for issues arising out of such interpretations. Among the countries along the "Belt and Road Initiative", the All China Lawyers Association did not and will not provide suggestions or recommendations to professionals such as judges or arbitrators from a foreign judicial system on interpretations of legal investment concepts and relevant laws.

5. There is the possibility that the Chinese translation of professional terms or concepts cited and used in the "Report" do not correspond precisely/exactly to a suitable and equivalent professional term or concept in a country along the "Belt and Road Initiative". The "Report" is composed only for purpose of reference to aid various sectors of the society/world to better understand relevant investment laws and legal practices of countries along the "Belt and Road Initiative". Any issues within the "Report" shall not be considered in any way as legal opinions presented by the All China Lawyers Association, nor any law firms or lawyers participated in the composition of the Report. Subject to practical limitations, the All China Lawyers Association did not verify the authenticity, legitimacy, and validity of the relevant contents of the "Report". Law firms from various countries along the "Belt and Road Initiative" shall be solely responsible for the contents to which it participated in drafting.

6. Relevant intellectual property rights of the "Report" are retained by the All China Lawyers Association, including but is not limited to copyright, its neighboring rights, and logos. Without prior written consent/approval from the All China Lawyers Association, the "Report" shall not be used for purposes of generating profits, or as evidence of any liability perused against the All China Lawyers Association. The All China Lawyers Association retains the right to interpret and amend this "Report".

Taking into consideration of the differences among socio-political system, legal environment, and diverse background of the authors (of the "Report"), it is reasonably foreseeable that there might exist various (subjective) interpretations and/or mistakes within the "Report". It is our sincerest hope that the readers conveniently provide us with timely feedbacks, so that we can follow up and make appropriate adjustments in our subsequent projects.

7. Should there be any inconsistencies in between the Chinese text of this notification and its English translation, the Chinese text shall prevail.

All China Lawyers Association
December 2018

总目录
SUMMARY OF CONTENTS

（以国家名称英文字母排序）
LISTED BY ALPHABETICAL ORDER

第四卷
VOLUME IV

- **L** 黎巴嫩 ··· 1
  Lebanon ·· 32

  立陶宛 ··· 66
  Lithuania ··· 88

- **M** 马其顿 ··· 115
  Macedonia ··· 137

  马耳他 ··· 163
  Malta ··· 179

  墨西哥 ··· 197
  Mexico ··· 218

  摩尔多瓦 ··· 241
  Moldova ··· 264

  黑山 ·· 289
  Montenegro ·· 314

  摩洛哥 ··· 342
  Morocco ··· 370

- **N** 新西兰 ··· 401
  New Zealand ·· 427

  尼日利亚 ··· 454
  Nigeria ··· 490

P	巴勒斯坦	530
	Palestine	561
	巴拿马	597
	Panama	625
	秘鲁	655
	Peru	682
S	斯洛文尼亚	711
	Slovenia	741
	南非	777
	South Africa	798
T	东帝汶	821
	Timor-Leste	847
	土库曼斯坦	875
	Turkmenistan	898
V	委内瑞拉	922
	Venezuela	944
Z	津巴布韦	971
	Zimbabwe	1004
	附录	1041
	APPENDIX	1041

目录
CONTENTS

L

黎巴嫩 / Lebanon

中文	页码	English	Page
一、概述	1	I. Overview	32
二、投资	3	II. Investment	34
三、贸易	18	III. Trade	50
四、劳动	21	IV. Labour	54
五、知识产权	22	V. Intellectual Property	56
六、环境保护	25	VI. Environmental Protection	58
七、争议解决	26	VII. Dispute Resolution	60
八、其他	28	VIII. Others	62

立陶宛 / Lithuania

中文	页码	English	Page
一、概述	66	I. Overview	88
二、投资	69	II. Investment	91
三、贸易	78	III. Trade	102
四、劳动	79	IV. Labour	104
五、知识产权	82	V. Intellectual Property	108
六、环境保护	84	VI. Environmental Protection	109
七、争议解决	85	VII. Dispute Resolution	111
八、其他	85	VIII. Others	112

M

马其顿 / Macedonia

中文	页码	English	Page
一、概述	115	I. Overview	137
二、投资	116	II. Investment	138

三、贸易 …………………………………… 126
四、劳动 …………………………………… 128
五、知识产权 ……………………………… 130
六、环境保护 ……………………………… 131
七、争议解决 ……………………………… 133
八、其他 …………………………………… 134

III. Trade …………………………………… 151
IV. Labour ………………………………… 152
V. Intellectual Property ……………………… 155
VI. Environmental Protection ……………… 156
VII. Dispute Resolution …………………… 158
VIII. Others ………………………………… 160

马耳他 / Malta

一、概述 …………………………………… 163
二、投资 …………………………………… 165
三、贸易 …………………………………… 172
四、劳动 …………………………………… 173
五、知识产权 ……………………………… 176
六、环境保护 ……………………………… 176
七、争议解决 ……………………………… 177
八、其他 …………………………………… 177

I. Overview ………………………………… 179
II. Investment ……………………………… 181
III. Trade …………………………………… 189
IV. Labour ………………………………… 191
V. Intellectual Property ……………………… 193
VI. Environmental Protection ……………… 194
VII. Dispute Resolution …………………… 194
VIII. Others ………………………………… 195

墨西哥 / Mexico

一、概述 …………………………………… 197
二、投资 …………………………………… 198
三、贸易 …………………………………… 209
四、劳动 …………………………………… 211
五、知识产权 ……………………………… 212
六、环境保护 ……………………………… 214
七、争议解决 ……………………………… 215
八、其他 …………………………………… 216

I. Overview ………………………………… 218
II. Investment ……………………………… 219
III. Trade …………………………………… 231
IV. Labour ………………………………… 233
V. Intellectual Property ……………………… 234
VI. Environmental Protection ……………… 236
VII. Dispute Resolution …………………… 237
VIII. Others ………………………………… 238

摩尔多瓦 / Moldova

一、概述 …………………………………… 241
二、投资 …………………………………… 242
三、贸易 …………………………………… 252
四、劳动 …………………………………… 254
五、知识产权 ……………………………… 256
六、环境保护 ……………………………… 259
七、争议解决 ……………………………… 260
八、其他 …………………………………… 262

I. Overview ………………………………… 264
II. Investment ……………………………… 265
III. Trade …………………………………… 275
IV. Labour ………………………………… 277
V. Intellectual Property ……………………… 280
VI. Environmental Protection ……………… 283
VII. Dispute Resolution …………………… 285
VIII. Others ………………………………… 287

黑山 | Montenegro

中文	页码	English	Page
一、概述	289	I. Overview	314
二、投资	291	II. Investment	317
三、贸易	304	III. Trade	330
四、劳动	305	IV. Labour	331
五、知识产权	307	V. Intellectual Property	333
六、环境保护	308	VI. Environmental Protection	335
七、争议解决	310	VII. Dispute Resolution	337
八、其他	311	VIII. Others	339

摩洛哥 | Morocco

中文	页码	English	Page
一、概述	342	I. Overview	370
二、投资	344	II. Investment	372
三、贸易	356	III. Trade	385
四、劳动	359	IV. Labour	389
五、知识产权	362	V. Intellectual Property	392
六、环境保护	364	VI. Environmental Protection	394
七、争议解决	366	VII. Dispute Resolution	396
八、其他	368	VIII. Others	398

N

新西兰 | New Zealand

中文	页码	English	Page
一、概述	401	I. Overview	427
二、投资	402	II. Investment	428
三、贸易	415	III. Trade	442
四、劳动	417	IV. Labour	444
五、知识产权	419	V. Intellectual Property	446
六、环境保护	422	VI. Environmental Protection	449
七、争议解决	423	VII. Dispute Resolution	450
八、其他	424	VIII. Others	451

尼日利亚	Nigeria
一、概述 ……………………454	I. Overview …………………… 490
二、投资 ……………………457	II. Investment …………………… 493
三、贸易 ……………………477	III. Trade …………………… 516
四、劳动 ……………………479	IV. Labour …………………… 518
五、知识产权 ………………483	V. Intellectual Property …………………… 522
六、环境保护 ………………484	VI. Environmental Protection …………………… 524
七、争议解决 ………………485	VII. Dispute Resolution …………………… 525
八、其他 ……………………486	VIII. Others …………………… 526

P

巴勒斯坦	Palestine
一、概述 ……………………530	I. Overview …………………… 561
二、投资 ……………………532	II. Investment …………………… 563
三、贸易 ……………………547	III. Trade …………………… 580
四、劳动 ……………………549	IV. Labour …………………… 582
五、知识产权 ………………553	V. Intellectual Property …………………… 587
六、环境保护 ………………555	VI. Environmental Protection …………………… 590
七、争议解决 ………………557	VII. Dispute Resolution …………………… 592
八、其他 ……………………559	VIII. Others …………………… 594

巴拿马	Panama
一、概述 ……………………597	I. Overview …………………… 625
二、投资 ……………………598	II. Investment …………………… 626
三、贸易 ……………………611	III. Trade …………………… 640
四、劳动 ……………………613	IV. Labour …………………… 642
五、知识产权 ………………616	V. Intellectual Property …………………… 645
六、环境保护 ………………619	VI. Environmental Protection …………………… 648
七、争议解决 ………………620	VII. Dispute Resolution …………………… 649
八、其他 ……………………623	VIII. Others …………………… 652

秘鲁	Peru
一、概述 655	I. Overview 682
二、投资 655	II. Investment 682
三、贸易 666	III. Trade 694
四、劳动 669	IV. Labour 697
五、知识产权 673	V. Intellectual Property 702
六、环境保护 675	VI. Environmental Protection 704
七、争议解决 676	VII. Dispute Resolution 705
八、其他 677	VIII. Others 706

S

斯洛文尼亚	Slovenia
一、概述 711	I. Overview 741
二、投资 712	II. Investment 742
三、贸易 725	III. Trade 757
四、劳动 728	IV. Labour 761
五、知识产权 731	V. Intellectual Property 764
六、环境保护 735	VI. Environmental Protection 769
七、争议解决 736	VII. Dispute Resolution 770
八、其他 738	VIII. Others 773

南非	South Africa
一、概述 777	I. Overview 798
二、投资 778	II. Investment 799
三、贸易 787	III. Trade 809
四、劳动 788	IV. Labour 810
五、知识产权 790	V. Intellectual Property 813
六、环境保护 792	VI. Environmental Protection 815
七、争议解决 793	VII. Dispute Resolution 816
八、其他 793	VIII. Others 816

T

东帝汶 / Timor-Leste

中文	页码	English	Page
一、概述	821	I. Overview	847
二、投资	826	II. Investment	852
三、贸易	838	III. Trade	865
四、劳动	839	IV. Labor	867
五、知识产权	842	V. Intellectual Property	870
六、环境保护	843	VI. Enviromental Protection	871
七、争议解决	843	VII. Dispute Resolution	871
八、其他	844	VIII. Others	872

土库曼斯坦 / Turkmenistan

中文	页码	English	Page
一、概述	875	I. Overview	898
二、投资	876	II. Investment	899
三、贸易	886	III. Trade	910
四、劳动	888	IV. Labour	911
五、知识产权	890	V. Intellectual property	914
六、环境保护	892	VI. Environmental Protection	916
七、争议解决	893	VII. Dispute Resolution	917
八、其他	895	VIII. Others	919

V

委内瑞拉 / Venezuela

中文	页码	English	Page
一、概述	922	I. Overview	944
二、投资	924	II. Investment	947
三、贸易	935	III. Trade	960
四、劳动	936	IV. Labour	962
五、知识产权	938	V. Intellectual Property	964
六、环境保护	939	VI. Environmental Protection	964
七、争议解决	940	VII. Dispute Resolution	966
八、其他	940	VIII. Others	967

Z

津巴布韦	Zimbabwe
一、概述 …………………………… 971	I. Overview …………………………… 1004
二、投资 …………………………… 971	II. Investment ………………………… 1004
三、贸易 …………………………… 981	III. Trade …………………………… 1015
四、劳动 …………………………… 985	IV. Labour ………………………… 1019
五、知识产权 ……………………… 989	V. Intellectual Property …………… 1024
六、环境保护 ……………………… 992	VI. Environmental Protection ……… 1027
七、争议解决 ……………………… 994	VII. Dispute Resolution …………… 1030
八、其他 …………………………… 999	VIII. Others ………………………… 1035

附录 ………………………………………………………………………………… 1041

APPENDIX …………………………………………………………………………… 1041

黎巴嫩

作者：Chadia El Meouchi、Carine Farran
译者：陈健斌、茆宇

一、概述

（一）政治、经济及法律环境概述

黎巴嫩历史悠久，在 1943 年 11 月 22 日法国殖民结束时独立。作为中东动荡地带的中心，黎巴嫩以其自身的文化及经济的多元化而著称，具有极强的适应能力和发展能力。事实上，黎巴嫩丰富的自然资源和人民的主观能动性使得该国蓬勃发展。在社会层面上，黎巴嫩具有独特的社会环境，其融合了不同文化、宗教、种族及社会形态。在经济层面上，尽管黎巴嫩作为发展中国家挑战不断，且难民的大量涌入对国家经济造成了严重负担，但黎巴嫩努力发展金融行业，并从银行保密业务中受益。

这个 10452 平方公里的国家自独立以来，虽然一直处于繁荣与动荡交替的状态，但总能在其侨民的帮助下渡过难关。这极大地促进了该国国际化的发展，并且黎巴嫩侨民已遍布世界各地。

黎巴嫩的官方语言是阿拉伯语，大部分人亦对英语或法语都非常精通。黎巴嫩的官方货币是黎巴嫩镑（LBP），而私营企业普遍使用美元（USD）进行交易。

黎巴嫩经历了漫长的内战。然而，黎巴嫩在内战结束之后是相对稳定的，它已经并将继续努力在政治、社会、经济和法律层面上进行自我重建。

1. 政治

根据黎巴嫩宪法，黎巴嫩是一个在尊重公众自由的基础上建立的议会民主共和国，其信奉自由，并在所有公民不受歧视的前提下做到尊重社会正义和权利与义务平等。该国遵循的一个关键原则是分权、平衡和合作。

黎巴嫩通过批准《塔伊夫协定》采取了具有本国特色的权力制衡制度，以持续维持该国稳定。这个政治改革的原则是"相互共存"——即不同的宗教团体平衡分配权力。

在更国际化的层面上，黎巴嫩以自身是一名遵守协定和盟约的阿拉伯联盟创始成员和积极成员为荣，同时，黎巴嫩也是联合国创始成员，以遵守盟约和《世界人权宣言》为傲。

2. 社会

从社会层面上来说，黎巴嫩官方认可 19 个宗教团体。黎巴嫩人具有国际化视野，能包容外国市场的融入，这促使黎巴嫩成为中东地区的主要旅游目的地。

而且，由于黎巴嫩人具有强大的适应能力和创业精神，是世界各国非常受欢迎的发展人才。黎巴嫩的教育系统通过鼓励学习语言（主要是法语或英语或两者兼而有之），并允许黎巴嫩人在获取黎巴嫩学士学位的同时，获取多种国际公认的学位，促进黎巴嫩人融入世界。

由于目前邻国内部发生动乱，尤其是叙利亚战争导致黎巴嫩持续接纳大量难民，而这些难民虽然从国内和国际方面都得到一定的安置及援助，但仍从经济、社会和其他方面对黎巴嫩造成了沉重的负担。

3. 经济

黎巴嫩的经济以服务业为主，并高度依赖银行业和旅游业。根据世界银行的数据，黎巴嫩的 GDP 增长率将继续保持平稳，预计未来 3 年将达到约 2.6%。[①]

[①] 黎巴嫩的经济展望，参见 http://www.worldbank.org/en/country/lebanon/publication/lebanon-economic-outlook-october-2017。

黎巴嫩的经济鼓励自由市场。黎巴嫩政府通常不限制外国投资。

在中央银行（BDL）的严格监管下，黎巴嫩境内的银行机构高速发展，并因其财务状况良好而声誉在外。黎巴嫩资本市场已于2011年随着资本市场管理局（CMA）的成立而重建。

黎巴嫩经济的一个重要方面是《银行保密法》（BSL）的存在，其使得黎巴嫩成为少数受益于这种法律的国家之一。此外，截至2001年，银行有义务遵守随后修订的关于反洗钱的2001年第318号法令。

不久前在黎巴嫩离岸处能源的发现，标志着黎巴嫩石油部门的发展，这既能创造就业机会，又能吸引外国投资。此外，黎巴嫩还通过不同的举措和政府招标的方式进行可再生能源的开发。

4. 法制

黎巴嫩属于大陆法系，且黎巴嫩已经起草了自己的一套准则，其中最著名的是"义务和合同准则"。然而，与个人事务相关的事宜，如就婚姻和继承来说，各教派社区由其专门的法律管辖。

根据《塔伊夫协定》修正的1926年黎巴嫩《宪法》规定，国家的政治制度是建立在行政、立法和司法权力分立与平衡的原则基础之上的。

黎巴嫩的以下人士拥有行政管理权：①以议会议员2/3多数选出的国家元首即总统，任期6年；一旦当选，总统也负责监督国防高级理事会，并且被视为军队的首席指挥官。②由总统任命的总理。总理与总统配合负责尤其是挑选部长及制定内阁政策提交给议会的事务。

议会组建立法部门，并负责立法和法律的发布。

司法部门由宪法委员会、行政法院，包括商事法庭在内的民事法庭、刑事法庭和个人事务法庭组成。

（二）在"一带一路"倡议下与中国企业合作的现状和方向

"中国近年来的开放使得人与人之间的交流显著增加"，中国驻黎巴嫩大使馆宣布在贝鲁特开设中国签证申请中心时表示。① 这个中国方面的小而重要的举动是两国关系愈发密切的证据。事实上，为了在平等互利的基础上加强两国间的经济合作，黎巴嫩与中国于1996年达成了一项关于鼓励和相互保护投资的协定，该协定于1997年生效。此外，黎巴嫩还被中国贸促会选为中东和北非地区总部。根据黎巴嫩外交部的说明，中国贸促会的重点是实施国家发展战略，鼓励外贸、双边投资和经济技术合作。②

此外，自从"一带一路"倡议开始以来，中国已决定将黎巴嫩列入新丝绸之路国家之一。事实上，中国认为黎巴嫩不仅是这一政策实施的理想地点，它还是该地区在安全和政治层面上最稳定的国家之一。③

考虑到黎巴嫩2016年的主要进口伙伴是中国，且其11.2%的进口来自中国④，预计黎巴嫩将成为中国"一带一路"建设的密切合作伙伴。事实上，"一带一路"这一倡议因其能够提高参与国之间的经济、文化和社会交流水平而受到赞扬。

此外，在国家层面，黎巴嫩的黎波里热衷于积极参与"一带一路"建设。⑤ 黎波里市长表示，他"会为促进黎波里的地位和对中国市场的开放而不遗余力付出任何努力"⑥。

---

① 中华人民共和国驻黎巴嫩共和国大使馆2017年11月2日关于在贝鲁特开设中国签证申请中心的通知，参见http://lb.china-embassy.org/eng/xwdt/t1506865.htm。
② 中国的贸易机构选择黎巴嫩作为中东、北非地区总部，参见http://www.xinhuanet.com/english/2018-01/16/c_136900363.htm。
③ Lorient Le Jour, Adnan Kassar: les entreprises chinoises prêtes à investir au Liban, 2018年1月29日。来自Lorient Le Jour's，参见https://www.lorientlejour.com/article/1096789/adnan-kassar-les-entreprises-chinoises-pretes-a-investir-au-liban.html。
④ 参见https://www.cia.gov/library/publications/the-world-factbook/fields/2061.html#le。
⑤ 黎巴嫩的黎波里热衷于积极参与"一带一路"建设，参见http://www.xinhuanet.com/english/2017-11/26/c_136779409.htm。
⑥ 同上注。

二、投资

（一）市场准入

1. 投资行业的法律及法规

关于鼓励在黎巴嫩投资的最重要的法律是 2001 年第 360 号法（以下简称"投资法"）。投资法设立了黎巴嫩投资发展局（IDAL）并强调 IDAL 的任务是为规范黎巴嫩投资活动制定一个框架，并向投资者提供一定范围的激励措施和商务支持服务。

投资法将投资者定义为依照投资法在黎巴嫩投资的黎巴嫩籍、阿拉伯籍或其他国籍的自然人或法人。投资法适用于所有希望根据投资法规定在工业、农业、旅游业、信息、通信、技术、媒体和其他由内阁会议根据总理要求确定的行业获益的投资项目。

投资法规定，黎巴嫩可以缔结一揽子协议，即由 IDAL 代表黎巴嫩，给予愿意在特定项目投资的投资者激励、豁免和减免（由 IDAL 董事会成员通过）而签订的合同，但规定投资者应根据合同条件来执行该项目。这种一揽子协议可以使投资者从最大限度的激励、减免或豁免政策中明显受益，包括但不限于豁免所得税和土地登记、外国雇员的工作许可、居留许可费的减免等。

还有以下与黎巴嫩投资有关的法律：

① 2017 年政府和社会资本合作法（以下简称"PPP 法"）：PPP 法主要涉及 PPP 的一般定义、PPP 项目的所有阶段以及提议和选择项目的程序。

② 2000 年私有化法：该法规定了一般的私有化框架，明确了私有化运作的条件及其实施范围。该法还建立了一个负责启动、实施和执行私有化运作的私有化高级委员会。

③ 1969 年第 11614 号法令关于外国人取得在黎巴嫩的不动产权利及其随后关于黎巴嫩境内不动产的外资所有权的修正案（以下简称"外资所有权法"）。

④ 此外，央行 2013 年致银行和其他金融机构的第 331 号通知（以下简称"331 号通知"）规定，通过保证黎巴嫩商业银行在初创公司中的投资高达 75%，来激励黎巴嫩商业银行直接向初创公司、基金、风险投资公司和孵化器投资。此类实体应采用 SAL①的形式注册，且不能是金融公司或离岸公司。

2. 监督投资的部门

在黎巴嫩，没有一个单独的部门负责监督和管理投资。

3. 投资的形式

（1）外国投资可以通过在黎巴嫩设立的各种法律实体来完成。将在"公司的设立和解散"部分讨论在黎巴嫩的主要设立形式。

（2）外国投资也可以通过在黎巴嫩设立的外国公司的分支机构完成。除了一些例外情形，外国公司的分支机构通常可以进行与其母公司经营活动相同的商业活动。

该分公司没有独立于其母公司的法人资格，因此分公司的责任原则上由母公司承担。根据黎巴嫩《商业法典》（LCC），每个在黎巴嫩设有分支机构的外国商业公司都应在商业登记处登记。在商业登记处登记之前，该分支机构还应在经济贸易部（MoET）进行登记。

根据实际利润计算方法，分支机构应按照 17% 的税率缴税，此外还有 10% 的股息分配税。

4. 市场准入和检验标准

以下是对外国投资的一些主要限制：

（1）1955 年《抵制法》中关于贸易限制的法规规定了与以色列建立任何联系是受到禁止的。根据《抵制法》，禁止直接或通过任何中介机构与住所地在以色列境内的机构或人员，或与代表以色列或其利益而行事的个人或实体签订任何协议，并且禁止任何关于以色列货物、财务文件和证券的交易，否则，按照《抵制法》和黎巴嫩《刑法》的规定，会受到处罚，包括监禁、罚款、工作禁令或解散公司。MoET 负责执行抵制法规。

---

① SAL 为黎巴嫩企业的一种形式，下文详述。——译者注

（2）对黎巴嫩某些行业的外资所有权和／或许可要求有一些额外的限制，例如但不限于不动产、保险、媒体和民航行业。

（二）外汇管理

1. 监管外汇的部门

原则上，黎巴嫩没有任何部门监管外汇。

然而，BDL 的其中一项任务是稳定汇率；的确，按照适用的法律和法规，BDL 有权在财政部部长的同意下在市场上进行经营活动。

2. 外汇法律法规的简要介绍

在黎巴嫩，除了限制涉及以色列当事方或涉及货币的交易外，一般没有明确限制或强加外汇管制的法律法规。

货币兑换行业受到监管，且除了银行、其他金融机构和在 BDL 注册的金融中介机构，任何法律实体均不得在未经 BDL 事先批准的情况下进行外汇交易操作。

此外，黎巴嫩法律一般要求，任何人亲自或以行李或以任何其他方式运输可流通票据的，无论是进入或是出黎巴嫩，只要可流通票据价值超过 15 000 美元或与 15 000 美元等价的其他货币价值的，必须向海关当局申报该可流通票据。

（三）财政

1. 主要的金融机构

（1）BDL 是根据 1963 年的《货币和信用法典》（CMC）建立的。BDL 是享有财务和行政自主权的公共法人，它不受适用于公共部门的行政和管理规定的约束。BDL 的资金完全由国家拨付。

BDL 的职能之一是授予在黎巴嫩设立银行、其他金融机构、货币交易商、外国银行和租赁公司的许可证。银行控制委员会（BCC）负责管理和监督这些机构。

BDL 发布管理银行与客户关系的通告和决议。

（2）黎巴嫩金融机构协会（AFIL）成立于 1971 年。2001 年，为维护金融机构的权利，AFIL 恢复授权许可的权力。

金融机构受 CMC 和 BDL 通告（包括已修订的 1998 年第 7136 号决定）的规定管辖，且其设立必须经 BDL 批准。

（3）在黎巴嫩境内设立伊斯兰银行或外国伊斯兰银行的分行需要得到 BDL 中央委员会的授权。BCC 伊斯兰银行部门成立于 2012 年，其使命是建立一个健全、良好、有效的符合国际最佳实践并遵守伊斯兰银行业务活动和黎巴嫩的适用法律法规的监管政策、标准、管理机制和方法的框架。

（4）黎巴嫩保险协会（ACAL）成立于 1971 年。ACAL 的目标主要是在技术和健全的基础上建立保险行业，制定规章制度以提高保险行业的水平，并维护公共利益。

根据 1968 年第 9812 号法令（以下简称"保险法"），所有在黎巴嫩从事保险法中提及的任何业务的黎巴嫩公司和外国公司都应遵守保险法，并且必须获得许可。

2. 外国企业的融资条件

（1）银行账户：在黎巴嫩，没有关于外国人或非本国居民在黎巴嫩以本地货币或外币开立和经营银行账户的具体明确限制。银行有严格的查询机制来确保国际和国内法规得到遵守；银行重点执行黎巴嫩的反洗钱和打击恐怖主义融资法律，并赞成以"了解你的客户"制度和其他法规打击逃税。所有黎巴嫩银行都必须遵守外国账户税务合规法案。

（2）融资：银行是黎巴嫩企业信贷的主要提供者。无论外国企业是否位于黎巴嫩，原则上获得融资不受任何限制，只需遵守通常的信用审查。

（3）来自外国实体的贷款服务：贷款服务只能由黎巴嫩银行、其他金融机构和贷款实体（被称为商行）在黎巴嫩进行。

（4）贝鲁特数码区（BDD）：BDD 旨在建立和发展黎巴嫩的技术集群和联系。该空间旨在为本地和外国信息通信技术公司提供服务，包括以较低的价格获得先进的信息技术服务和光纤基础设施。BDD 是由电信部领导的与 ZRE 和 Berytech 合作的公私合作企业。①

（四）土地政策

黎巴嫩一般认可房地产及不动产上的所有权和财产权。

两部主要的、与土地有关的法律是：

① 1930 年黎巴嫩财产法及随后的修正案（以下简称"物权法"）；

② 1969 年立法令及其随后的修正案，尤其是关于不动产资产的外资所有权的第 296/2001 号法（以下简称"外资所有权法"）。

物权法主要管辖黎巴嫩国民的所有财产权的收购和处置。与不动产资产有关的所有权利必须在不动产登记处正式登记；特别是通行权、征用权、抵押权、诉讼权、扣押权和任何其他权利。

外资所有权法管理非黎巴嫩籍人购买不动产的行为。

根据外资所有权法，非黎巴嫩籍人在整个黎巴嫩领土内一般可以获得不超过 3 000 平方米的面积，而无需采取任何额外措施。非黎巴嫩籍人的任何超过 3 000 平方米的收购行为须经内阁会议根据财政部部长的建议给予事先批准。

根据外资所有权法，获得不动产权利的非黎巴嫩籍人应在收购后或获得上述授权后自在不动产登记处注册之日起 5 年内，在土地上完成建筑物的建设或实现其所宣称拥有所有权的目的。这个期限经内阁会议决定只能延长一次。

（五）公司的设立和解散

1. 企业的形式

在黎巴嫩，公司主要有两种类型：民事公司和商业公司。

商业公司应有一个商业目标，主要由 LCC 管辖，有以下主要类型：

- SAL；
- 黎巴嫩控股公司；
- 黎巴嫩离岸公司；
- 有限责任公司；

这些商业公司具有法人资格。

（1）SAL

SAL 是由若干股东组成的，他们对超出其资本认购金额部分的公司债务不承担责任。无论是否有任何相反规定，SAL 必须有在黎巴嫩的注册办事处和黎巴嫩国籍。如果公司的目标是开发一项公共服务，1/3 的资本必须由黎巴嫩人持有的记名股票组成，并且这种记名股票只能转让给黎巴嫩人，如转让给非黎巴嫩籍人，则转让无效。

SAL 股东的责任限于他们持有的股本。

SAL 最少必须由 3 个发起人建立，并且必须始终保持至少有 3 个股东。

SAL 股本最少必须达到 30 000 000 黎巴嫩镑，也就是大约 20 000 美元。SAL 的全部股本可以由非黎巴嫩籍人持有，但担保股本除外，担保股本必须由黎巴嫩籍的董事会成员持有。

SAL 的财务报表每年必须由股东指定的审计人员进行审计。有关的商事法庭也会指定另一名审计员。SAL 还需要每年聘请一名律师。

原则上，股份在生前转让给第三方是不受任何限制的，除非 SAL 的章程有诸如现有股东优先权这样的限制规定。

SAL 的管理是委托给董事会的，董事会由至少 3 名最多 12 名成员组成，大多数的成员都是黎巴嫩人，一般他们的任期最多为 3 年（可连任）。总经理可以是外国人，但需要工作和居住许可证。

SAL 的股东每年必须至少召开一次年度常规大会（及/或在任何时候应董事会的要求召开），大会

---

① 参见 http://investinlebanon.gov.lb/en/doing_business/financing_a_business/loans_other_facilities。

的召开要符合法定人数及遵守法定的决策门槛，大会的目的是核准上一财政年度的账目。

SAL 章程的修改只能通过特别大会的决议作出，特别大会由符合法定人数的股东召开，要遵守法定的决策门槛。只要 SAL 的国籍没有改变，特别大会可以修改章程中的所有条款。股东的责任不会增加，且第三方的权利不会受到影响。

关于董事会会议：
- 为使董事会的决议有效，至少一半的董事会成员必须亲自出席或派代表出席；
- 决议要由大部分亲自出席或派代表出席的董事会成员作出。

至于适用的税收制度，在高级别基础上，SAL 尤其应该遵守：
- 所得税税率 17%；
- 股息预扣所得税税率 10%。

（2）黎巴嫩控股公司

控股公司是以 SAL 的形式注册的，因此承担有限责任；然而，修正过的 1983 年第 45 号法令（DL45）对控股公司还有一些特殊规定。LCC 中涉及 SAL 的条款，尤其是上述提及的那些条款，只要它们不与 DL45 的规定相矛盾，也适用于控股公司。

① 公司发行的所有文件、证件、出版物和任何其他印刷文件中，公司的名称后面必须明确提及"控股公司"。

② 控股公司的目标被法律加以以下严格限制：
- 收购股份或份额或参股设立黎巴嫩或外国合资公司或有限责任公司；
- 向其持有股份或份额的公司发放贷款，且为该公司向第三方借款提供担保；
- 对其持有股份或份额的公司进行管理；
- 收购专利、发明专利、特许使用权、注册商标和所有其他私人的权利，并授予在黎巴嫩的公司或国外的公司许可；
- 仅为满足经营活动需求而收购动产或不动产，且符合法律中涉及在黎巴嫩拥有不动产权利的非黎巴嫩籍国民的收购行为的规定。

一家控股公司不能在两个以上在黎巴嫩境内从事同一工业、商业或非商业活动的公司中投资超过 40%，否则上述投资违反了 1967 年第 32 号法令规定的限制条款。上述规定不适用于在黎巴嫩境外的投资。

如上述限制，控股公司禁止直接从事任何不属于其经营范围的活动。

公司成立时发起人的数量最少为 3 名，股东的数量最少亦为 3 名。

最低股本是 30 000 000 黎巴嫩镑，也就是大约 20 000 美元；控股公司的股本可以是外币的形式，并且它的账簿和资产负债表可以用同一种外币形式编制。

董事会必须由最少 3 名、最多 12 名成员组成，成员由年度常规大会选举产生，任期最多为 3 年，可以连任。根据 2006 年 DL45 修正案规定，不要求控股公司董事会大部分成员国籍为黎巴嫩国籍。董事会指定其中一名成员作为董事长兼总经理。董事长兼总经理可以是外国人，而且如果他不居住在黎巴嫩，也不需要他获得工作和居住许可。为保证董事会决议有效，至少一半的董事会成员必须亲自出席或派代表出席。决议由亲自出席或派代表出席的董事会多数成员作出。

控股公司必须至少任命一名拥有黎巴嫩国籍并且居住在黎巴嫩的审计员，且必须每年聘用一名律师。

控股公司的办事处/总部，也就是公司的住所所在地和保存文件的地方，必须在黎巴嫩。然而，如果在公司章程中另有规定，除了少数例外情况，公司的大会和董事会会议可以在黎巴嫩以外的地方举办。

控股公司受益于多种税收优惠。事实上，控股公司每年应缴纳相当于其股份资本总额 6% 的一次性税收，当股份资本总额不超过 50 000 000 黎巴嫩镑时，将增加储备基金；当股本总额在 50 000 000 黎巴嫩镑到 80 000 000 黎巴嫩镑之间时，每年的一次性税收的比率将会减少至 4%；当总额超过 80 000 000 黎巴嫩镑时，比率将减少至 2%。

在任何情况下，适用于控股公司的年度税收将不会超过 5 000 000 黎巴嫩镑，即大约每年为 3 335

美元。

此外，控股公司还受益于其他免税政策，且有具体可适用的税收制度。

（3）黎巴嫩离岸公司

黎巴嫩离岸公司是以 SAL 的形式设立的，因此承担有限责任；然而，修正后的 1983 年第 46 号法令（DL46）对离岸公司还有一些特别的规定。LCC 中有关 SAL 的条款，尤其是上述提及的那些条款，只要它们不与 DL46 的规定相矛盾，也适用于离岸公司。

黎巴嫩离岸公司的经营严格限于以下活动：

• 对涉及交易和买卖的合同和协议的谈判和签署，这些交易应在黎巴嫩领土之外进行的，并且与在海外或者在海关免税区的资产有关；

• 管理公司和机构，公司和机构的活动仅限于在黎巴嫩境外开展业务，这些业务包括出口技术、管理服务和组织服务之外，及向住所在黎巴嫩境外并且有此方面需求的机构出口与任一种信息技术相关的软件和程序；

• 发生在黎巴嫩境外的三方或多方外国商业经营活动；

• 承担海上运输业务和活动；

• 持有外国和非本地机构和公司的股份、份额、债券和参股外国及非本地机构和公司，及向其持股超过 20% 的非本地机构发放贷款；

• 因进行与代理机构相关活动而获益，以及代表外国公司在海外市场进行活动；

• 在黎巴嫩境外开设分支机构和代表处；

• 除了 DL46 第 2 条（第 2 条的规定如下文）所禁止的情形，所有类型的经济项目的构成、投资、管理和拥有；

• 开设债权人账户，向住所在黎巴嫩或国外的银行和其他金融机构借款，来为上述列举的活动和交易供给资金；

• 在黎巴嫩租用办事处及拥有经营活动所需的不动产，遵守外国人在黎巴嫩有关持有不动产所有权的规定。

禁止黎巴嫩离岸公司：

• 从事各种类型的保险活动，从事银行、其他金融机构和所有应受黎巴嫩中央银行控制的机构所从事的活动和交易；

• 在黎巴嫩从事任何其他未在 DL46 第 1 条规定的活动；

• 从位于黎巴嫩境内的动产或不动产中，或从提供给在住所地位于黎巴嫩的公司的服务中赚取利润、收入或收益，除了公司银行账户中所得的收入，还有自黎巴嫩国债的认购和交易中产生的收入。

黎巴嫩离岸公司的发起人最少应该有 3 名。发起人/股东和董事会成员可以全部是外国人。

如果黎巴嫩离岸公司的董事长兼总经理是非黎巴嫩籍人，他将免予获得工作许可和居住许可。实践中，这样的规定也适用于董事长兼总经理在黎巴嫩领土之外承担职责、从事活动，并且凭借旅游签证来到黎巴嫩的情况。然而，如果总经理将在黎巴嫩领土上承担职责，并且居住于此地，他就必须遵守劳工部的要求。

黎巴嫩离岸公司的最低股本是 30 000 000 黎巴嫩镑，即大约 20 000 美元；如果公司账户是用同一种外币持有的，则股本可以固定用该种外币。

如黎巴嫩离岸公司的资本超过 50 000 000 黎巴嫩镑或其年度资产负债表总额超过 500 000 美元，则其免予聘请一位律师。公司的审计员可以只有一个，但是其应该是黎巴嫩国民且有权在黎巴嫩进行专业审计活动。

离岸公司须每年一次性缴税 1 000 000 黎巴嫩镑，即大约 666 美元。离岸公司也可以从免税和特殊的税收制度中获益。

（4）有限责任公司

有限责任公司（SARL）是商业公司，由合伙人组成，合伙人对公司债务中超出其认购数额的部分不承担责任，且合伙人资本被划分为份额而不是股份。SARL 受到贸易法律法规以及 1967 年第 35 号法令（DL35）规定的约束。SARL 不会从事某些活动，即保险、航空运输，还有所有银行和基金管理业务。SARL 应该在黎巴嫩有一个注册办公地。

SARL 的合伙人不需要是黎巴嫩国民，原则上，他们的数量最少为 3 名，最多为 20 名；如果有超过 20 位的合伙人的情况，合伙人大会应该决定将公司从 SARL 转换为 SAL。

SARL 所需的最低资本是 5 000 000 黎巴嫩镑（即大约 3 333 美元），在公司设立时必须全部付清。SARL 被禁止用自己的账户通过公开认购方式发行可转让证书（不论是无记名还是记名）、动产、股票、债券和股份。

SARL 不需要任命审计员，除非在以下情况：
- 如果合伙人的数量超过 20 名；
- 如果资本达到 30 000 000 黎巴嫩镑；和／或
- 如果一个或更多代表至少 1/5 的资本的合伙人，要求任命一名审计员。

然而，财政部通常要求 SARL 每年审计一次，并且汇给财政部的 SARL 的账目应是经过审计的。

SARL 应每年聘用一名律师。

合伙人生前向第三方转让份额的，须经代表至少 3/4 资本的合伙人同意。除此之外，现有的合伙人在购买转让份额时享有优先权。此外，这种转让行为应负缴税义务，包括基于转让部分价值的印花税（税收原则上如下：①印花税税率为 3‰；②律师协会的费用为 1‰；③公证费用为 1‰）且对转移份额收 10% 的资本收益税。

SARL 由一名或几名经理管理，这些经理有可能是在合伙人中选出的，但他们不可以是法人。这些管理人员不要求是黎巴嫩人，需要注意的是任何外国管理人员都需要工作和居住许可。

经理认为有必要的，根据其要求，年度常规大会必须每年举行一次普通大会，以批准前一财政年度的 SARL 账目以及经理的业务行为。

合伙人大会必须召开特别大会以修正 SARL 的章程，例如增加和减少资本、改变法律形式。

关于适用的税收制度，在一个高层次的基础上，SARL 尤其应负以下缴税义务：
- 总计为 17% 的公司所得税；
- SARL 的股息分配应缴 10% 的预扣所得税。

2. 设立的程序

除未申报的合伙企业外，所有商业公司的组建行为都必须通过完成下面详述的手续进行公布，否则将无效。

（1）SAL

成立一家 SAL 的步骤可以总结如下：

① SAL 的发起人必须在公证人面前签署其章程，并自签署章程之日起 5 日内向黎巴嫩财政部按股本缴纳股本的印花税费用（在这方面应缴纳两种类型的费用：股本总额的 3‰ 的印花税费用，以及一次性支付 1 000 000 黎巴嫩镑，即大约 666 美元）。

② 其后，发起人必须以 SAL（筹备中）的名义开设一个银行账户，以存入资本金。然后，银行将出具 SAL 的股本已被股东们认购的证明。

③ 股东必须召开第一次大会（即创立大会）来批准建立 SAL 并任命第一届董事会成员。上述第一届董事会将召集并选举出 SAL 的董事长兼总经理。

④ 一旦准备并签署完上述所有文件后，则为了在商业登记处登记 SAL，必须向商业登记处提交一份申请以及法律规定的随附文件。

⑤ 在商业登记处登记之后（即一经商业登记处审查了上述提交的文件并确认所有必要文件已经备妥和提交之后）以及在公司注册证书出具之后，SAL 应在其成立后的两个月内告知财政部其活动的开始。

（2）黎巴嫩控股公司

控股公司是以 SAL 的形式设立的，并且和 SAL 适用同样的法律法规，除非这些法律法规与有关控股公司的具体规定有任何程度的抵触。

关于控股公司的成立，正如上述对 SAL 的详细说明那样，控股公司根据 LCC 的规定在商业登记处进行注册。此外，控股公司的特别登记处将设立在一审法院，与其相关的所有文件和信息也被记录在那里。

（3）黎巴嫩离岸公司

离岸公司是以 SAL 的形式设立的，并且和 SAL 适用同样的法律法规，除非这些法律法规与有关离岸公司的具体规定有任何程度的抵触。

关于离岸公司的成立，正如上述对 SAL 的详细说明，离岸公司根据 LCC 的规定在商业登记处进行了注册。离岸公司的特别登记处将设立在一审法院，与其相关的所有文件和信息也被记录在那里。

（4）有限责任公司

成立一家 SARL 的步骤可以总结如下：

① SARL 的发起人必须在公证人面前签署 SARL 的章程，并自签署章程之日起 5 日内向财政部按股本缴纳印花税费用（原则上，应缴纳两种类型的费用：①股本的 3‰ 的印花税费，以及②一次性支付 750 000 黎巴嫩镑，即大约 500 美元）。

② 在获得经过正式公证的章程的正本之后，发起人必须以 SARL（筹备中）的名义开设一个银行账户，以存入资本金。一旦开立了账户并存入资本金，银行将出具资本已被合伙人认购的证明。

③ 然后，合伙人必须召开第一次大会（被称为"创立大会"）来正式批准 SARL 的设立并任命管理者。

④ 一旦准备并签署完上述所有文件后，则为了在商业登记处登记 SAL，必须向商业登记处提交一份申请以及法律规定的随附文件。

⑤ 在商业登记处登记后（即一经商业登记处审查了上述提交的文件并确认所有需要的文件已经备妥和提交）以及出具了公司注册证书后，SARL 应在成立后的两个月内告知财政部其活动开始。

3. 解散的路径和要求

所有商业企业解散的主要原因如下，这其中不包括破产程序（破产程序有一套独立的程序）：

- 公司成立的期限届满；
- 公司正常结束/完成运营；
- 企业的目标不再存在。

此外，在合伙人的请求下，法院通常还可以以它认为的合理理由宣布解散公司，或者决定逐出不履行其合伙人义务的某个合伙人。

（1）SAL

除了上述常见的解散原因之外，SAL 还有以下主要的解散原因：

- 事先已决定的期限到期或者合同规定的企业已完成，或者该企业不可能继续经营（上述常见的原因）；
- 合伙人在特别大会期间表达的意愿；
- 公司资本损失 3/4。在这种情况下，董事必须召集一次大会，决定是否需要提前解散公司、减少资本或采取其他适当的行动；
- 如果董事未能召集会议、董事会未满足法定人数召开，或董事会会议驳回解散的决定，则每位合伙人均有权向法院提出解散。

由此作出的决定，无论是特别大会的决议还是法院的命令，都必须按照法律的要求予以公布。

（2）黎巴嫩控股和离岸公司

控股公司和离岸公司应遵守有关 SAL 的法律法规进行解散。

（3）有限责任公司

除了上述常见的解散原因之外，有限责任公司还有以下主要的解散原因：

- 在该公司未能在两年内转为 SAL 的情况下，公司成员人数超过 30 名；
- 在该公司成立未满一年或公司形式没有变更的情况下，公司的资本已低于法定最低值 5 000 000 黎巴嫩镑；
- 损失 3/4 的资本，值得注意的是，如果合伙人尚未决定解散，他们必须将资本减少到损失后的数额。

（六）并购交易

1. 黎巴嫩法律所规定的兼并和收购的方式和程序

（1）在实践中，收购通常包含：
- 购买另一家公司的股份；及/或，
- 购买另一家公司的资产；

根据具体情况的不同，通常是借助资产转让或股份购买协议的形式。

根据 LCC 的规定，采取吞并的方式兼并和采取结合的方式兼并，两者是有区别的，这两种机制都在黎巴嫩法律著作中有所分析和详述。

从总体上看，兼并是指两个或更多的公司再联合起来组成一个公司；需要注意的是，这种联合意味着那些加入的公司都会解散，成为一个新的独一无二的法人。根据兼并是采取吸收、并吞还是结合的方式，兼并可能牵涉：

① 解散的公司/被兼并方公司的构成要件/净资产向吸收方或新兼并方公司的转移；
② 被兼并方公司的股东向兼并方公司或由兼并而形成的新公司的股东的转换；
③ 被兼并方公司的解散，由兼并方公司受益。

（2）LCC 只规定了 SAL 的兼并；尽管如此，适用于上述公司的兼并规则也同样适用于其他类型的公司，只要不与它们的性质相矛盾。

（3）LCC 规定，为了使数个公司结合为一个公司时能遵守兼并程序。LCC 亦规定，兼并是由特别大会所决定的。然而，董事会（或总经理）在获得年度常规大会授权后可以在预并购协议（即"初步协议"）中代表公司；只要这种批准是限于提出兼并且未决定兼并事项的执行，这种批准就是有效的。

年度常规大会可能会批准这一初步协议（考虑到这个协议将被提交给年度常规大会）或者拒绝按照其中约定的条款来兼并。

在每个涉及的公司中，批准最终兼并的决议都必须在特别大会这一级别作出。

（4）LCC 还明确规定了兼并的程序，当一家新公司是由多家旧公司兼并而成立时，需要遵守公司设立的法律规则，且必须执行有关旧公司在"期限之前"的解散程序和新公司设立的发布程序。另外，当任何一家公司并吞到另一家公司时，被并吞方公司必须公布其在"期限之前"的解散，并且并吞方公司必须遵守与资本增加相关的基本规则和正式规则。

（5）如果采取并吞或吸收方式来兼并，而这导致被兼并方公司的解散及兼并方公司的资本增加，需要作出以下决定：

① 必须在期限届满之前，根据法定人数和大多数人的决定解散公司的表决，作出同意兼并和被兼并方公司的决定。
② 兼并方公司的特别大会作出的、因兼并而增加资本的决定，该决定需要在符合法定人数参加的组织大会上作出。

公布要求也必须得到保证。兼并方公司的章程将在兼并后加以修改，并应在商业登记处公布。

（6）如果兼并是通过结合完成的，那结果将是两方被兼并方公司的解散以及另一个新公司的成立。因此，两方公司同意兼并的决议都必须在特别大会期限届满前、由特别大会按照法定人数和大多数人的决定解散公司的要求下作出。另外，兼并后的新公司将遵守与设立程序（包括公布的要求）相关的所有规则。

2. 兼并的特征和影响

（1）对股东和/或合伙人的影响

一经兼并，被兼并方公司的股东就从兼并方公司或从两家公司兼并而创建的新公司中，按照他们在被兼并方公司中拥有的权利的比例取得股份。

（2）对相关公司的债权人的影响

① 对被兼并方或被吸收方公司的债权人来说，兼并可以被认为是债务从被合并方或被吸收方公司续期或转让给新的公司或者吸收方公司。就本身而言，债务从一位债务人（即被兼并方公司）转让给另一位债务人（即兼并方公司）的这种兼并影响不适用于被兼并方公司的债权人，除非债权人同意。

此外，就 SAL 而言，所述债权人在兼并的情况下根据法律有权享有特殊担保／保证。对于被兼并方公司的特别大会作出的同意兼并的决定，债权人有权在该决定公布之日起 3 个月内向有管辖权的法院提起反对／质疑。

照此类推，原则上同样的程序也适用于合伙企业之间的兼并。

② 兼并方或吸收方公司的债权人无权反对兼并，因为兼并已增加了该公司的债务和义务，债权人处于普通债权人的地位，不得不承担债务人的行为导致的增加其自身债务的后果，只要法律没有给予他们任何对兼并方公司的继承财产的优先权或引起被兼并方公司继承财产的独立性的权利。

（3）对被兼并方或被吸收方公司的债务人的影响

被兼并方公司或被吸收方公司的权利转移给兼并方或吸收方公司，因此被兼并方或被吸收方公司的债务人成为兼并方或吸收方公司的债务人；同样的，兼并方公司可以向被兼并方公司的债务人主张这些权利。

（4）兼并对第三方的影响

根据黎巴嫩法律体系，第三方与被吸收方或被兼并方公司之间正在进行的、不考虑当事方"个人方面"或"属人性"（如采购和运输合同）的合同继续有效，并且赋予兼并方公司由此产生的权利，并使第三方受上述合同条款的约束，除非存在控制权变动条款或其他明确规定了相反规定的条款。

值得注意的是，除了遵守 LCC 相关适用条款之外，在一些业务领域的并购交易中，特别是关于公众公司（即在证券交易所上市的公司）的交易和与黎巴嫩的银行有关的交易，也受到一些特殊法律法规的管辖。

3. 有关公众公司（即在证券交易所上市的公司）的并购交易

（1）除 LCC 相关适用条款外，上市公司的并购交易还须遵守关于实施贝鲁特证券交易所（BSE）章程的 1995 年第 7667 号法令和确立于 2011 年的 CMA 的适用法规。

（2）除了上述的、所适用的所有方式和程序，从并购交易的一般法律角度来看，收购一家上市公司通常由投标人的要约收购构成；注意到根据 1995 年 12 月 16 日颁布的、关于实施 BSE 章程的第 7667 号法令，任何希望在官方或二级市场报价的公司中拥有 10% 以上投票权，或希望在该公司中获得绝对多数①或合格多数的投资者或投资者群体，应该通过金融经纪人提交公开要约收购或以物易物的草案。

（3）此外，在并购交易中，在黎巴嫩上市的公司应在黎巴嫩证券交易所（目前只有一家黎巴嫩证券交易所，就是 BSE）在以下时间点作出公告：在签署兼并协议时；在召集股东批准时；在关闭公司时。

（4）而且，规范黎巴嫩资本市场的 2011 年第 161 号法律特别规定了，任何因各种类型的业务而直接或间接获得发行实体或公众公司中的等于或超过 5% 的有表决权的股份的法人，必须在执行导致该所有权比例的操作之前向 CMA 披露。该法律实体还会在向 BSE 提交报告之前详细说明发行实体以及后者的股票是否在 BSE 上市。该法律实体还必须披露会导致达到或超过 5% 限制的所有采购操作。

（5）另一方面，对在 BSE 上市的公司所进行的任何报价都必须提交给 BSE 委员会审批。

（6）所有在 BSE 上市的公司都是 SAL。应该注意的是，如果同一投资者持续两年持有 SAL 的股份，则根据黎巴嫩法律，那些股份所附带的表决权将自动加倍；这是归属于股份持有人的个人权利。当投资者的表决权加倍时，如果因此触发了披露要求（根据第 161 号法律或 BSE 制度），则需要按照通常方式作出通告。

4. 关于黎巴嫩银行的并购交易

（1）BDL 的中央委员会制定了有关黎巴嫩银行的并购和购买黎巴嫩银行股票的规定。它监督所有在银行和金融服务部门的收购行为，并确保所有受监管的实体会遵守适用的法律和法规。黎巴嫩银行的并购主要由：① CMC；② 1993 年第 192 号法令中的条款（以下简称"银行兼并法"）；③ 2001 年第 308 号关于组织发行和交易股票、债券以及银行收购不动产的法令（以下简称"第 308 号法"）进行规范。

---

① 绝对多数意味着 50% 加 1 股，而规定的多数是指适用于该公司的可能会被规定的其他多数，它可能会根据具体情况而有所不同，需要注意的是这些定义并非法律明文规定的，而是被人们所普遍接受的对于这些术语的定义。

（2）银行兼并法适用于出让银行向受让银行出售其全部资产、权利、债务和义务，该受让银行将购买出让银行的资产和权利并承担其所有债务和义务的情形。

银行兼并法规定，它将适用于从另一家希望清算其业务并从银行名单中除名的银行处购买所有资产和权利，并承担其所有债务和义务的银行；因此银行兼并法将此类收购交易视为兼并。

（3）根据银行兼并法的规定，两家或两家以上银行之间的兼并业务需经 BDL 中央委员会批准，而 BDL 中央委员会拥有全权决定批准或拒绝银行和金融服务部门里的任何收购的权力。上述兼并业务必须遵守一套详细的程序。

在中央委员会最终决定批准兼并的一个月内，兼并银行必须在官方公报和至少两家当地报纸上发布相关银行的特别大会所作出的兼并决策的摘要，以及 BDL 中央委员会的最终决定。

（4）根据第 308 号法律的相关规定，认购和交易黎巴嫩银行的股份需经 BDL 中央委员会事先批准：

• 如果这导致认购人或受让人直接或通过信托合同获得银行总股份的 5% 以上或获得与此类股份有关的 5% 以上表决权，以较高者为准。

• 股份转让时，受让人持有银行总股份的 5% 或以上或与此类股份相关的 5% 或以上表决权，以较高者为准。

• 不论转让股份的数量是多少，当转让人或受让人是银行董事会的成员或当选成员时。

（1）黎巴嫩银行并购交易的方式和程序

为了获得 BDL 批准，必须遵循以下程序：

• 董事会和（如果需要）各银行的股东将批准交易；

• 兼并协议将由各方执行；

• 银行将向 BDL 申请对交易的暂时批准；

• BDL 中央委员会的暂时决定将被发布，而且如果暂时批准兼并，将"列明要获得其最终决定所需要的条件、期限和保证"；

• 如果买方接受 BDL 要求的任何条件或担保，则要满足 BDL 的要求，并在必要时获得股东的批准；和

• 在满足这些条件和担保（如果有的话）之后，银行将向 BDL 申请获得其最终批准兼并的决定，其中包括满足了相关条件/担保的证据，并提供股东批准的会议记录。

（2）银行部门兼并的特征和影响

因此，被兼并的银行将从 BDL 公布的银行名单中被除名，并将在公司注册处将公司登记状态申请登记为公司清算。

总之，银行兼并法规定了一系列好处，尤其包括：

• 根据法律规定的在银行间自动转移资产和债务的操作，原则上不需要取得交易对方的同意（即适用于整个交易）；

• 对两家银行实行某些税收豁免；

• 关于交易的税收豁免；

• 在某些情况下，BDL 中央委员会可以向受让银行授予贷款奖励。

此外，银行兼并法特别明确规定了，兼并方银行在 BDL 中央委员会作出最终决定后，将立即依法取代被兼并银行（一家或多家）的所有权利和义务。

5. 专门部门的并购交易

黎巴嫩的其他部门也可能是受保护部门，例如保险和媒体部门。这些部门也受黎巴嫩特别规章制度的约束。

根据不同部门的情况，可能需要有关监管机构或部门的管制批准。

（七）竞争管制

1. 监督竞争管制的部门

在黎巴嫩，MoET 是监督和管理贸易的主要政府机构；它根据 1973 年 12 月 28 日第 6821 号法令

（明确了 MoET 的职责和功能）所赋予的任务处理经济和商业事务。MoET 还特别从事反垄断事务并采取措施，这些措施为综合经济利益提供了最广泛的商业竞争。

根据 1942 年 11 月 18 日第 1523 号法令，1942 年成立了一个控制高价格和垄断的部门（现在设在 MoET 内部），其主要任务是从整体上搜索和调查所有与贸易和价格有关的犯罪。

2. 竞争法和规范竞争措施的简要介绍

（1）黎巴嫩目前没有任何专门的反竞争或反垄断法律。一个关于竞争的法律草案旨在通过在黎巴嫩建立一个自由贸易区来实施《欧洲—地中海协议》（黎巴嫩于 2006 年加入）的规定，将在条约生效起 12 年内准备好。该法律草案于 2007 年发给内阁会议，并得到内阁会议的批准，然后根据法令传达给议会。但自那时以来，该草案既未颁布也未送交主管议会委员会进行进一步研究。

（2）但是有几部法律涉及黎巴嫩某些领域的竞争问题，例如：

① 规定货物、产品和农作物的持有和贸易的 1983 年 9 月 9 日第 73 号法令第 4 章（经修正）包含了有关企业联盟、垄断和不正当竞争的条款。

② 关于工业和商业财产权利的 1924 年 1 月 17 日第 2358 号决定，明确规定以下几种情形将被视为不正当竞争：通过不适用第 2358 号决定第 6 章（举例说明，第 6 章包括商标和品牌名称、工业设计）中规定的适用条件中的任何一条，从而违反了第 2358 号决定，以及任何受法院自由管辖并被认定为不正当竞争的行为。一般诉讼可以不正当竞争行为为由主张请求停止竞争行为、停止损害行为和请求损害赔偿，除非这些行为被视为违反且应根据《刑法典》或第 2358 号决定的规定受到处罚。

③ 根据 LCC 的相关规定，如发现任何人有歧视行为导致他人受到不法伤害的，其应承担所有赔偿责任。主张不正当竞争或垄断行为的一方可以依赖于这个一般规定。

④ 黎巴嫩《刑法典》明确规定，任何以欺诈或虚假指控的方式，或为了转移其他人的客户而暗示其不诚信的人，将在受害人的控诉的基础上受到处罚，被处以罚金。

⑤ 除上述之外，还有某些专门法律处理特定情形和特定部门的竞争：这些法律包括：2000 年 5 月颁布的第 228 号私有化法，该法设立了黎巴嫩投资发展局，并给予信息技术项目最高优先权；促进黎巴嫩投资有关的 2001 年 8 月 13 日第 360 号法律；2006 年 2 月 4 日第 659 号消费者保护法。

（八）税收

1. 税收制度和规则

在黎巴嫩，只有黎巴嫩议会才有权决定征收国家税和市政税。一方面，国家税由财政部的理事会，即国家税务总局根据 1959 年 12 月 16 日颁布的第 2868 号法令收取。另一方面，市政税由市政府自行收取。

税收分为直接税收或间接税收。直接税收包括 1959 年 6 月 12 日颁布的第 144 号法令及其修正案（以下简称"所得税法"）中所规定的所得税。所得税法分为三个章节，所得税由下列征收的税收组成：①从工业、商业和非商业行业获取的收益（"营业利润税"）；②薪酬、工资和福利；③来自动产的收入。因此，应纳税人的每种类型的收入都应根据其所属的所得税法章节来进行计算。

（1）营业利润税

除特定豁免，特别是对社会团体和非政府组织的豁免外，这项税收原则上应对居住在黎巴嫩境内或境外的所有自然人和法人在黎巴嫩所取得的应税利润进行征收。

应税利润是扣除所有从事商业、工业或某一行业所需的开支和债务之后，纳税人应纳税的收益总和。根据实体的法律地位和/或其规模，所得税是根据实际利润、定额利润或核定/估算的利润计算的。实际利润算法包括调整会计利润以确定基于税收规则计算的收益，其中，应税收入的确定应扣除前几年的损失。

根据定额算法，财政部每年根据应纳税人申报的销售额来确定销售额百分比，以计算出应税所得额。

最后，根据核定/估算利润算法，财政部直接通过对纳税人进行实地审计来确定应纳税所得额。

关于非居民的营业利润税，根据所得税法的有关规定，在黎巴嫩取得营业收入但不在黎巴嫩居住或没有营业注册地的自然人或法人,应根据他们从黎巴嫩获得的核定利润征收预扣所得税,即从服务中获得的收入按7.5%的税率征收,且从供应商品中获得的收入按2.25%的税率征收。

(2)对薪酬、工资和福利的征税

雇主代表其雇员代扣代缴该税款。但是,纳税人在一年中应缴纳营业利润税的,和/或由不止一个雇主雇用的,必须提交自己的纳税申报表。

应纳税所得额是通过从年度总收入中扣除符合条件的开支和家庭部分的减免来确定的。

(3)动产所得税

无论该动产的名称、生产公司的国籍或该动产收益的受益者的居住地是什么,当该动产出现在黎巴嫩或者应归属于黎巴嫩居民时,该动产所产生的收益,应适用10%的所得税征收。所得税法规定了本项税收的某些豁免情况,其中包括最常见的是对银行账户利息和黎巴嫩政府国库券利息的免税。动产所得税应由应报税的缴纳实体预扣。

2. 主要税种和税率

黎巴嫩的主要税种主要包括所得税,可将其分为三类,包括公司利润税、工资税和动产所得税。

(1)在某些获得豁免的情况下,企业的利润税率为17%,个人的税率范围在4%至21%之间逐渐递增。

(2)工资税一般在2%至20%的范围之间。最后,动产所得税的税率等于7%。

(3)在某些获得豁免的情况下,雇主及雇员一般应缴纳的社会保障基金的税率分别为21.5%、2%。

(4)房产需缴纳的房产税范围为0至14%,具体取决于租金收入。

(5)关于印花税,可能根据需要征收印花税费的手续和文件,征收不同数额的印花税费。在这方面,在合同、协议或契据在黎巴嫩境内成立或签署时应支付5 000黎巴嫩镑的固定印花税以及合同或协议或契据规定的0.4%比例的印花税费;或者即使合同、协议或契据是在黎巴嫩境外签署或成立的,但是在黎巴嫩境内实施的情况也同样应征收印花税费。

(6)11%的增值税(VAT)适用于涉及商品和服务的大多数交易。

(7)黎巴嫩还根据上述法律实体的类型和法律性质,为法人实体提供各种税收和免税政策。

3. 税务申报和税收优惠

(1)税务申报

黎巴嫩的税务申报如下:

① 商业利润税	
个人	
•实际利润算法	5月31日
•定额利润算法	1月31日
•核定利润算法	不需提交税务申报
法人	5月31日
② 薪酬工资和福利税	
个人	
•核定利润算法	1月31日
•多种收入来源	3月31日
法人	5月31日
免除营业利润税的纳税人	1月31日
③ 动产所得税	
所有应纳税人	付款到期或被宣布后一个月的月末

（2）税收优惠
① 营业利润税的豁免
在免征营业利润税的部分实体中，主要实体如下：
- 教育机构；
- 精神病院和结核病诊所；
- 并非商业性质的消费者合作社、企业联合组织、农业合作社；
- 在一定条件下的农业投资者；
- 不与私人机构竞争的公用事业；
- 具有手工艺性质的旅游机构。

② 薪水、工资和福利税的豁免
除其他豁免外，免交薪水、工资和福利税：
- 给神职人员执行宗教仪式的拨款；
- 外国大使、外交代表、领事、领事代表和在互惠的条件下雇用的外籍人员所获得的工资和报酬；
- 盟国的军人，不论其军衔、所赚取的薪酬；
- 农业工人的工资；
- 根据黎巴嫩的适用法律支付的遣散费；
- 根据适用的法律和法规支付的家庭赔偿金。

③ 动产所得税的豁免
除其他豁免外，可免除对动产所得收入征税：
- 并非从利润、损失和储备金中扣除的，为偿还债权人和股东而支付的金额；
- 在银行开设的所有活期账户的利益和收入；
- 黎巴嫩国库债券的收益。

④ 增值税的豁免
a. 获得豁免的活动
在黎巴嫩境内进行的与以下任何活动有关的交易都免征增值税：
- 医生或从事医疗活动的人员提供的服务；
- 医院费用；
- 教育；
- 雇主和相关服务；
- 银行和金融服务；
- 旅客集体运输，包括出租车运输；
- 打赌、彩票和其他形式的赌博；
- 建筑物的销售；
- 建筑物的居住出租；
- 农民的农业生产供应活动。

b. 获得豁免的商品
特别是下列货物免收增值税：
- 某些食品；
- 邮政邮票和印花税邮票和纸币；
- 家用燃气（丁烷）；
- 种子、肥料、饲料和农药；
- 农业机械；
- 药剂、药品和药用物品以及医疗工具、设施和装备；
- 宝石和半宝石，用于镶嵌或更新的宝石和半宝石、珍珠、钻石、金、银和其他贵金属。
- 纸币或硬币形式的可流通的钱。

此外，黎巴嫩还签订了多项为鼓励外国投资而豁免某些税收或免去双重征税的条约，例如，1997

年中华人民共和国和黎巴嫩之间的双边条约。此外,黎巴嫩的一些经济部门受益于本文未涉及的具体税收豁免。

(九) 证券

1. 证券相关法律法规简介

BDL 和 CMA 负责监督黎巴嫩银行和金融部门。因此,根据具体情况的不同,所有的银行和金融活动以及与金融工具、金融产品和证券相关的交易都由 BDL 和/或 CMA 的规定进行管制。

我们在此只讨论了 CMA 的作用,鉴于除少数例外情况外,它是管理证券交易的主要监管机构。CMA 是依据第 161 号法令设立的独立机构。

CMA 的主要目的是管理和监督黎巴嫩资本市场、确保金融工具的投资安全性和鼓励黎巴嫩的金融市场。

CMA 已经发布了数个决定,尤其是关于:①某些公司应该采取的披露政策;②众筹规定;③集体投资基金和伊斯兰集体投资基金的许可和授权要求。

此外,CMA 在 2016 年 11 月 10 日至 2017 年 8 月 7 日期间颁布了若干实施细则,特别是:

(1) 关于许可和注册的 2000 系列细则,其目的是规范证券市场的交易行为。其尤其建立了在黎巴嫩开展证券业务所需的注册功能的类别,并确定对适用的许可要求适用的豁免情形。

(2) 关于商业行为监管规定的 3000 系列细则,主要是:①制定被核准的机构在进行证券业务及与客户打交道时必须遵守的规则和行为准则;②制定被核准的机构必须建立、实施和保持更新的政策、程序、系统和控制措施。

(3) 关于市场行为监管规定的 4000 系列细则,其适用于交易有价证券和与买卖可交易证券相关的行为。4000 系列细则的主要目的是:①规范证券市场的行为;②列出禁止内幕交易和市场操纵的细节;③列出被核准机构在证券市场进行交易的职责。

(4) 关于证券发行规定的 6000 系列细则,其旨在概述与在黎巴嫩证券发行有关的要求,并确定豁免于适用更严格的公开发行要求的证券发行类型。

关于在黎巴嫩市场上金融产品的销售和分销,CMA 原则上对于在黎巴嫩分销复杂和创新型金融产品、金融工具和证券保持灵活和开放的态度,前提是这种行为符合其监管要求和应适用的法律法规。

2. 证券市场监管和规范

(1) CMA 是监督和管理证券市场的主要监管部门。CMA 的管理工作是由 BDL 的主管人员所主持的董事会来担任的。CMA 董事会的主要特权是鼓励和保护投资,以及执行金融市场的一般规定。CMA 董事会特别授予合并集体投资计划和金融中介机构的许可证,以及在黎巴嫩市场销售和分销金融产品的预先核准。

第 161 号法律还规定设立一个特殊的资本市场法院,以解决投资者与金融工具推销商之间产生的任何争端或冲突。然而,该法院至今尚未建立。

(2) 黎巴嫩也有正式的市场。2017 年 9 月 15 日,根据第 161 号法律的规定颁布了 1404 号法令,目的是解散之前的交易所并以贝鲁特证券交易所 SAL (BSE SAL)(基于 SAL 的所有权利、义务和活动)取代之。该 BSE SAL 的建立即将完成,并且取代 BSE 的程序在第 1404 号法令某些程序完成后将予以执行。

BSE SAL 的目标主要包括:①管理、调控、开发、交易和定价与金融权利、金融工具、原材料和黑色金属相关的市场;②保护在 BSE 交易的投资者的利益;③上述金融工具的上市、交易和定价;④调控和监督在 BSE 上市的公司的工作;⑤为在 BSE 上市的金融工具开发电子和非电子的交易和定价系统。

3. 外国企业参与证券交易的要求

第 161 号法律明确允许非黎巴嫩籍的公司和实体根据有关特别条例的规定在黎巴嫩从事有关证券的业务。

根据黎巴嫩的法律和法规,任何人在黎巴嫩开展证券业务,都必须成为获得 CMA 许可的被核准机构，除非该人根据 CMA 2000 系列细则和应适用的豁免规定被免予获得许可。简而言之，在符合某些条件的情况下，有一些可被容忍的执业行为和明确规定的豁免情况是可以适用的；而原则上，在获得 CMA 许可之前，任何人不得开展证券业务或继续开展证券业务。

申请许可（成为被核准的机构）的申请人必须在黎巴嫩成立：

① 一家在 CMA 或 BDL 合法注册的银行、其他金融机构或金融中介公司；

② 一个外国金融实体的分支机构，其母公司从事证券业务并获得有公认的管辖权的主管部门的许可。

此外，申请许可证时，申请人必须仅从事于证券业务，或者如果申请人是经过 BDL 许可的公司，仅从事于许可范围内的业务。申请人的总部必须是在黎巴嫩。

CMA 对与黎巴嫩的交易对手开展金融交易的外国实体采取了极其限制性的措施，无论这些外国实体是银行、其他金融机构、经纪机构或是任何其他实体。相应的，CMA 法规规定，任何人不得向黎巴嫩人制作或传播证券广告[①]，除非该人为被核准的机构，一旦 CMA 发现有将证券广告发送给黎巴嫩人的，将视做向黎巴嫩人制作或传播证券广告的行为。

BDL 于 2016 年 11 月 8 日发布了一项 2017 年 12 月 21 日修正的金融中介决定，规定限制向专业银行和金融中介机构，或由专业银行和金融中介机构开展的对所有金融工具和产品的经营活动，这项决定于 2018 年 6 月 30 日生效。

（十）投资优惠和投资保护

1. 优惠政策的架构

在黎巴嫩，没有任何优惠政策。

尽管如此，从国有化优惠的角度来看，根据劳动部部长于 2013 年 2 月 2 日提出的第 19/1 号决定，某些活动只能由黎巴嫩国民开展，特别是银行、保险和任何类型的行政活动，尤其是担任董事、副董事、主任、出纳、会计师、秘书、档案工作者、工匠、IT 工作者、贸易代表、营销代表、监督员、仓库管理员、销售人员、机械师和维护人员、监护人等类似职位，以及一般可以由具有所需的专门知识和技能的黎巴嫩人从事的所有活动和职业。

但是，黎巴嫩致力于鼓励外国投资，尤其是与各主要国家签署若干协议以促进和保护投资以及签署协定来避免双重征税和防止偷漏税，这些协定加强了签署方之间的投资合作，签署方包括但不限于中国、意大利、科威特、俄罗斯。例如，黎巴嫩议会于 1997 年 2 月 28 日颁布了第 614 号法律，根据第 614 号法律，黎巴嫩政府授权批准了黎巴嫩政府与中国在 1996 年 6 月 13 日在北京签署的关于促进和保护相互投资的协定。

2. 对特殊行业和地区的支持

黎巴嫩境内对各个部门和行业的投资都在不断增长，无论是在工业、农业和农业产业、旅游、信息、通信、技术、媒体还是其他由部长会议根据总理的要求下颁布的法令所决定的任何其他部门。

此外，房地产和技术领域在黎巴嫩一贯受到大力推广。

3. 特殊经济区

根据 2000 年 12 月 15 日第 4461 号法令（以下简称《海关法》）规定，将允许在关税区内建立免税区和免税商店，该关税区不受海关制度管辖，而是受到海关法下特殊规定管辖。

在这方面，黎巴嫩政府经营 3 个自由贸易区，这些自由贸易区位于贝鲁特港、的黎波里港和塞拉塔港。

《海关法》规定，可以通过分配港口和内部空间的区域来建立自由贸易区和自由工业区，并将其视为关税区范围之外的区域。

除了《海关法》规定的某些禁止类型的货物，所有类型的货物不论是来自当地的还是来自外国的，

[①] 根据 CMA 的解释，如果一则证券广告指向在黎巴嫩的人，那么它可以被制作和传播给在黎巴嫩的人。证券广告是指为了邀请或引导某人从事证券活动而在业务过程中以任何口头、电子、广播或书面形式作出的传播。

都可以进入免税区，除了为免税区经营者的利益而强加的费用外，不必在进入、储存、出口和再出口时被征收关税和其他税收、费用。货物在转运到关税区外时也不受任何行政限制。

除上述所有内容外，BDD 接待外国 ICT 公司并为他们提供先进的设施，包括获得先进的 IT 服务和以优惠的价格获得光纤基础设施。

4. 投资保护

初步来说，黎巴嫩 1926 年《宪法》规定了在黎巴嫩，所有权是宪法赋予的权利。就这方面来说，《宪法》第 15 条规定，财产受到法律的保护，且除非财产是公共设施、有法律规定及事先得到公平的补偿的，任何人不得被剥夺其财产。

黎巴嫩与许多主要国家签署了一系列协议以及《关于避免双重征税和防止偷漏税的协定》，这加强了签署国之间就投资和财政层面的合作。

此外，举例来说，黎巴嫩签署了《欧盟—地中海协议》(2006 年 4 月 1 日开始实施)。该协议在欧洲共同体及其会员国之间建立了联系，另一方面在欧洲共同体及其会员国和黎巴嫩之间建立了联系。该协议尤其逐渐建立了货物、服务及资本的贸易自由化，推动了黎巴嫩和欧洲共同体会员国之间的贸易发展、和谐经济的展开及社会关系的发展。

另外，黎巴嫩与欧洲自由贸易联盟国家（冰岛、列支敦士登、挪威及瑞士）签署了《自由贸易协定》，主要目标是在这些领域内建立一个自由贸易区促进经济活动，由此提升生活质量和改善用工环境并促进欧盟—地中海地区的经济融合。

黎巴嫩也是世界贸易组织（WTO）的观察国，有志于成为其会员。

三、贸易

(一) 贸易监管部门

MoET 是负责黎巴嫩贸易的主要政府机构，它的职责是负责经济和商业事务，特别是：①与其他部委合作发展该国的经济设施和国家财富；②在经济发展和采取必要措施的情况下，在该国的商业、供应和消费条件下受益；③反垄断和采取反垄断措施，为正常经济利益提供最广泛的商业竞争环境；④照顾和发展贸易，促进服务部门的振兴；⑤发展经济研究，特别是与对外贸易、贸易平衡和与此有关的统计资料的传播；⑥授予货物进出口许可证。

(二) 贸易法和法规简介

以下是黎巴嫩贸易法和条例的举例说明：

(1) 黎巴嫩已采取贸易自由化政策，作为其综合经济战略的一部分，使黎巴嫩进一步融入全球经济。它与阿拉伯国家和欧洲联盟签署了贸易协定，包括但不限于欧盟—地中海合作倡议[①]和欧洲自由贸易协会的自由贸易协定[②]。黎巴嫩也是大阿拉伯自由贸易区（GAFTA）的成员[③]，贸易与投资框架协议（TIFA）[④]的成员，阿拉伯联盟投资协议[⑤]成员，伊斯兰会议投资协议[⑥]组织成员。

(2) 对于商业代理机构，1967 年 8 月 5 日颁布的第 34 号法令（DL 34）被视为公共政策组成部分，

---

① 根据欧盟委员会官方网站，其于 2006 年 4 月 1 日在黎巴嫩生效，并在欧盟官方刊物上发表，参见 http://ec.europa.eu/trade/policy/countries-and-regions/regions/euro-mediterranean-partnership/。
② 根据联合国贸易和发展会议官方网站，其于 2007 年 1 月 1 日在黎巴嫩生效，参见 http://investmentpolicyhub.unctad.org/IIA/CountryOtherIias,116#iiaInnerMenu。
③ 根据黎巴嫩经济贸易部官方网站，其于 1998 年 1 月 1 日在黎巴嫩生效，参见 http://economy.gov.lb/en/what-we-provide/trade/foreign-trade-department/international-agreements/gafta/。
④ 参见美国贸易代表办公室官方网站与联合国贸易和发展会议官方网站，https://ustr.gov/trade-agreements/trade-investment-framework-agreements。
⑤ 根据联合国贸易和发展会议官方网站，其于 1981 年 9 月 7 日在黎巴嫩生效，参见 http://investmentpolicyhub.unctad.org/IIA/treaty/3087。
⑥ 根据联合国贸易和发展会议官方网站，其于 1988 年 2 月 5 日在黎巴嫩生效，参见 http://investmentpolicyhub.unctad.org/IIA/treaty/3092。

因此，一旦存在适用该法令的情形，将强制适用该法令，而不适用任何可能与之相反的条约协定。DL 34 将商业代理定义为：

① 通过其惯常和独立的职业而不受服务租金合同约束的授权人，进行谈判，以签订销售和购买、租赁或提供服务交易的生产者或交易商名义的账目；或

② 买卖以他的名字和他自己的账户的交易者，他已经购买了凭借合同授予他的拥有独家代理或经销商的能力。

（3）此外，为了确保在黎巴嫩市场上销售、交易和分发的货物和产品的安全和质量，第659号《消费者保护法》于2005年2月4日颁布。除管制黎巴嫩市场内的贸易活动外，其主要目的是在黎巴嫩维持一个现代的消费者保护框架，保障消费者的利益，并确保给消费者一个安全、公平和公正的环境。简言之，《消费者保护法》主要旨在概述关于保护消费者和货物和服务的安全和质量的一般规则；维护消费者权利，保证经济交易的透明度，其中消费者可以参与；保护消费者免遭欺诈和误导性广告，并防止其被欺诈和误导。

（4）2015年11月24日关于打击洗钱和资助恐怖主义的第44号法律，禁止特别是非法武器贩运、内幕交易、腐败，包括但不限于影响贸易。

（5）根据2016年10月27日第75号法律，与取消持票人股份和本票有关，业务员禁止发行无记名股票；而已经拥有无记名股票的公司则被迫以记名股票取代它们。

（6）原则上，没有任何一般性法律限制或规范黎巴嫩投资者对涉及以色列当事方或货币的交易的上述限制的兑换、转让或过境。

然而，根据2015年11月24日关于宣布跨境运输货币的第42号法律（"第42/2015号法律"），原则上任何人在通过境外运输货币或流通票据时，进出境通过以人身或行李或任何其他方式携带货物，或进行集装箱运输或通过邮寄，只要其价值超过15 000美元或其他货币的等值金额，必须通过填写包含完整和所需信息的表格向海关提交书面证明。

（7）此外，MoET第277/1号决议于1972年6月15日通过，并与确定商业利润百分比有关，管制贸易商（例如批发商和零售商）从某些商品（如谷物、油、糖、盐、蔬菜和水果等，获得的最大利润。

（8）黎巴嫩海运法典的规定丰富了黎巴嫩的立法，该法典扩大了领土内贸易活动的范围，并确保了经济层面上的全球海运贸易。

（9）除以上所有内容外，《竞争条例》概述了黎巴嫩的竞争法和规范竞争的措施。

（三）贸易管理

黎巴嫩一直保持着对私人投资的普遍不干预立场，以鼓励外国投资。[①] 黎巴嫩在传统上是一个自由开放的国家。通过区域或国际、双边或多边贸易协定改善市场准入而强调贸易制度，需要强调的是黎巴嫩在努力实现贸易自由化的同时，着重于欧盟、世界贸易组织和阿拉伯国家。因此，黎巴嫩的贸易自由，允许外国投资者自由地进口和出口资本，但受与贸易有关的法律和条例规定的限制，特别是《抵制法》和《海关法》的规定。

黎巴嫩还通过《欧盟—地中海协定》管理贸易关系（黎巴嫩于2002年签署并于2006年4月生效）[②] 主要旨在提供对大多数工业品进行互惠自由贸易，并在一系列农产品上实现贸易自由化；特别致力于建立地中海区域的自由贸易区。

黎巴嫩签署的自由贸易协定在吸引外国贸易投资和鼓励开放贸易环境方面发挥着重要作用，特别是1997年签署的《大阿拉伯自由贸易协定》，于1998年生效[③]，逐渐取代与阿拉伯国家签署的双边自由贸易协定。

[①] 请参阅标题为"市场准入"和"投资保护和投资保护"这两部分内容。
[②] 根据欧盟委员会官方网站，其于2006年4月1日在黎巴嫩生效，并在欧盟官方刊物上发表，参见http://ec.europa.eu/trade/policy/countries-and-regions/regions/euro-mediterranean-partnership/。
[③] 1998年1月1日在黎巴嫩生效，参见http://economy.gov.lb/en/what-we-provide/trade/foreign-trade-department/international-agreements/gafta/。

黎巴嫩于2016年与南方共同市场国家发起了自由贸易协定谈判[1]，并与几个国家签署双边投资协议[2]：包括但不限于2010年与卡塔尔，2004年与荷兰，2002年与奥地利，1999年与法国、德国和英国，1997年与加拿大、俄罗斯和中国。

（四）进出口商品检验检疫

（1）贸易壁垒可能会影响某些进口和出口货物，其中包括禁止进口或出口商品，或限制此类活动。黎巴嫩《海关法》规定，除其外，限制商品只能进口或出口，但须经有关当局签发的许可证、执照、证书、事先批准或签证。

（2）在有关当局的法律、条例和决定，或黎巴嫩作为缔约方或成员的国际协定中严格规定禁止进口的，特别是包括：①非法药物、武器、炸药和弹药；②文物；③假币和货物；④以色列制造或原产的货物以及其他产品，值得注意的是，所有受进口和出口禁令限制的货物也可禁止过境黎巴嫩。应当指出的是，在进出口时，垄断和受限制的货物必须与违禁货物同等对待。

（3）此外，某些货物可能会受到特别临时许可证的规范和限制，并应在授权的临时入境期结束时，在自由区或公共仓库中重新出口或储存。此类货物包括：①在公共工程、考古、电影院和新闻业使用的设备和机器；②用于保养和维修的物品；③临时进口的物品，用于在公共或私人展览、季节性集市、论坛、剧院、艺术表演和操场上展出或使用；④拟在公众展览展出的首饰及装饰品。

（4）黎巴嫩在这方面不受具体的出口管制或特别制裁；需注意的是，原则上，所有出口都需要许可证。

（5）根据《海关法》的规定，任何有意向黎巴嫩进口或出口的自然人或法人，任何类型的货物，均应在主管海关处进口或出口，并缴纳关税。

（6）在相关说明中，MoET还检查食品装运，以确保遵守《消费者保护法》规定的标签要求和规定。法律对专业人士的规定参见脚注。[3]

（7）与工业部相连的是，黎巴嫩标准机构（LIBNOR）是黎巴嫩唯一负责颁布、出版和修订黎巴嫩标准的机构，其目的是设置尺寸、标准、符号和定义产品质量，并给予黎巴嫩合格标记NL证明产品符合黎巴嫩标准。

（五）海关管理

黎巴嫩海关管理局是黎巴嫩负责征收海关关税和控制进出该国的货物流动的政府部门。它在财政部下运作，并与在内政和城镇部下运作的公安总局合作。

黎巴嫩遵循其统一的关税制度。

海关已积极推出自动通关系统的在线业务，从而使交易商和报关员可以在线输入和追踪报关单。

此外，一般而言，欧洲货物根据《欧盟—地中海协定》和欧洲自由贸易联盟《自由贸易协定》免征关税。此外，来自几个阿拉伯国家的货物也根据《大阿拉伯自由贸易协定》免除关税。

关于海关的价值，世界贸易组织的关税价值已在黎巴嫩实施。在1995年，所有进口关税都被统一在一个关税称为"单一关税"。如上所述，关税的计算是根据职责的类型，并可能因比例或固定的职责而有所不同。

根据《海关法》，某些货物可在某些条件下免除关税，包括但不限于公共行政机构和市政当局进口的车辆、设备、材料、附件和备用件，或授予他们用于灭火和救援目的的飞机，在黎巴嫩机场的房舍内使用的设备。

---

[1] 参见 http://www.itamaraty.gov.br/images/documents/Documentos/Fact_Sheet_Mercosur_English.pdf.

[2] 根据黎巴嫩经济贸易部官方网站、欧洲委员会官方网站和黎巴嫩投资发展局正式网站，这些协定已获得批准并生效，参见 http://economy.gov.lb/en/what-we-provide/trade/foreign-trade-department/international-agreements/bilatera/, http://investmentpolicyhub.unctad.org/IIA/CountryBits/116#iiaInnerMenu, http://investinlebanon.gov.lb/Content/uploads/SideBlock/161219112515166~Investment%20Protection%20Agreements.pdf.

[3] 根据《消费者保护法》第2条，专业人士是指私人或公共部门中代表他自己，或者是为了别人的利益而从事分发、销售或租赁货物或提供服务的自然人或法人。专业人士亦指在其专业活动范围内，以分发、销售或租赁该等货品为目的而进口货品的人。

此外，根据《海关法》可设立的自由区和免税商店，不受关税制度的制约，而是根据《海关法》具体条文的规定。

四、劳动

（一）劳动法和条例简介

（1）管制黎巴嫩就业部门的主要法律是 1946 年 9 月 23 日颁布的黎巴嫩《劳动法》。为保护雇员的权益，《劳动法》的条款和规定均属于维护公共利益的强制性规定。《劳动法》规定雇主应向雇员提供的最低权利，由雇主决定是否愿意为《劳动法》规定的最低权利之上规定任何额外权利。

（2）黎巴嫩是若干与劳动和就业领域有关的阿拉伯条约和国际公约的成员；这些协定往往针对《劳动法》未予处理的任何就业方面，或向雇员提供额外的《劳动法》中没有规定的利益和权利。

（3）有关社保安全方面，它是根据 1963 年 9 月 26 日颁布的第 13955 号法令（国家社会保险法，或 NSSF 法律）规定的。下面将详细介绍。

（4）1964 年 9 月 2 日颁布的第 17386 号法令（CLCL）规定集体劳动合同、调解和仲裁。根据 CLCL 的有关规定，集体劳动合同是一项协议，其目的是组织代表集团（或多个集团）的一方或工会（或多个联合体）之间的工作条件。集体协议的一方可以是一个单独雇主（或一个以上雇主），也可以是一个专业委员会（或一个以上的委员会）的代表，还可以是雇主的专业工会（或多个专业工会）。黎巴嫩的几个部门（例如银行部门、移动电信运营商）缔结了集体劳动协定等。

（二）雇用外籍雇员的要求

1. 工作许可证

希望在黎巴嫩工作的外国人应首先获得劳工部（MoL）的工作许可证以及来自黎巴嫩公安总局（LGS）的派驻许可证。

2. 申请程序

在某些情况下，获得工作许可证和居留许可的程序可能会非常耗时，但并非总是如此。这实际上是个案问题，并取决于许多因素，例如外籍员工所在的单位。

如果外国人已经根据旅游签证逗留在黎巴嫩，则为获得 MoL 和 LGS 颁发的该项工作和居留许可而采取的程序如下：

（1）请求应由相关外国人的"雇主"提交给要求签发"初步批准"的 MoL，需要提及的是，雇主应在 MoL 就业部门登记过。

（2）在获得"初步批准"后，如果外国人使用旅游签证或提交工作签证申请进入黎巴嫩领土，雇主应向 LGS 提出请求，以便将外国人的签证状况从"旅游签证"改为"工作签证"连同由雇主在公证人面前签字的承诺。

（3）一旦外国人获得工作签证，应将"事先批准"所需的费用结算给 MoL，因此，应在向 MoL 提交要求之前，并附上各种文件。

（4）最后，在获得工作许可后，应向 LGS 提出申请，以获得居留许可。请注意，在此期间，LGS 将再次拿到外国人的护照，并提供给他证明程序已启动的证明。

（5）当外国雇员还未进入黎巴嫩工作时，就需要启动申请程序，雇主应在向劳工部申请之前获得初步批准，然后在同一主管当局面前请求"事先批准"。根据上述批准，外国雇员将获准进入黎巴嫩领土，并在一定的时间内获得 LGS 的工作许可证。

（6）最后，工作许可和居留许可通常被授予一年的期限，因此每年需缴纳相关费用以换取新的许可。

3. 国家社会保险基金

雇主必须在其开始工作之日起 15 天内在 NSSF 登记。获得有效工作许可和居留许可的外籍雇员也应在 NSSF 登记，但不受益于 NSSF 提供的任何福利；他们只能享有服务赔偿金的福利。

（三）出境和入境

1. 签证类型

在黎巴嫩，有几种类型的签证（如过境签证、居留签证、礼遇签证等），如上所述，为了让外国人在黎巴嫩工作，最终获得工作和居留许可需要工作签证。

2. 出境和入境的限制

外籍雇员一旦获得居留许可，就不会受到限制。

（四）工会和劳工组织

在黎巴嫩，工会得到承认，并与世界各地的工会一样，发挥着类似的作用，即在相关行业维护工人和雇员的权利。《劳动法》特别对工会及其承认、组成、权利和义务提出以下规定：

① 对于任何职业，雇主和雇员，都可以成立一个特别的工会。工会具有法人人格，可以提起诉讼；

② 成立工会的唯一目的，是保护、促进和维护行业利益，提高其标准，并参与该行业的经济、工业和商业进步。

③ 雇主或雇员的工会，在没有获得 MoL 事先授权的情况下，不得成立。

④ 每一个工会都必须有内部规章，由大会上 2/3 的出席成员批准通过。

⑤ 任何雇主或雇员均可自由加入或不加入工会。

⑥ 任何人如欲加入工会，必须符合下列条件：
- 具有黎巴嫩国籍并享有所有公民权利；
- 在申请时正从事该职业；
- 年满 18 岁；
- 无犯罪记录。

⑦ 外国人如果符合《劳动法》中列举的某些条件，并有工作许可证在黎巴嫩工作，则可以加入工会。外国成员没有资格投票；他们有权授权加入工会的成员在工会委员会面前捍卫自己的利益。

⑧ 每个工会由至少 4 名成员组成的委员会管理，最多有 12 名成员。

（五）劳资纠纷

个别劳资纠纷及因适用 NSSF 法而产生的纠纷，完全属于仲裁劳动委员会的权力范围。仲裁劳动委员会有权审查因下列事项引起的争端：
- 最低工资的确定；
- 在适用法律中明确规定的职业事故；
- 因适用劳动法而产生的雇主与雇员之间的纠纷，包括被解雇及离职、处以罚款及一般的所有争议。

此外，在没有代理律师代理的情况下，可以提起诉讼并参加仲裁劳动委员会的听证会。

五、知识产权

（一）知识产权法律法规简介

黎巴嫩颁布了几项旨在规范和保护知识产权的法律和条例，除此之外，它是世界知识产权组织成员，适用世界知识产权组织公约。

黎巴嫩也是 WIPO 管理的许多条约的成员，特别是 1924 年 9 月 1 日《保护工业产权巴黎公约》（《巴黎公约》），其适用于最广泛意义上的工业产权，包括专利、商标、工业设计、实用新型、服务商标、厂商名称、地理标志和制止不正当竞争。

黎巴嫩还批准了关于商品和服务的国际分类的《尼斯协定》，以注册商标。

（二）商标

1. 商标保护

商标由于1924年1月17日2385/LR号修订的法国高级专员关于"黎巴嫩商业、工业、文学、艺术和音乐财产的条例和制度"（以下简称"2385条例"）以及黎巴嫩《刑法》的某些规定所保护。

第2385号条例将工厂或贸易的商标定义为：和别人不同的名称、标题、符号、邮票、字母、突出的标记和图案等，即任何一种旨在给消费者、工厂所有者和经销商带来利益的标志。这些标志通过与其他事物区别开来，显示出商品的身份、来源、原产地以及属性（工业、商业、农业、森林或金属产品）。

在黎巴嫩也承认服务商标，可以在MoET登记。服务商标应用程序与商标的应用相同，并且，服务商标适用于所提供的服务，除了应用程序所涉及的服务的详细信息。

商标注册是可选的，除非有相反的法律规定；也就是说，除非事先向MoET的保护署提交了商标的个人所有权权属证明，否则不得索赔。因此，注册商标赋予其作者主张其商标的个人所有权，出售、转让并继承商标的权力。

2. 商标注册程序

黎巴嫩商标注册制度是一种登记注册制度。商标注册过程简述如下：

（1）商标注册程序通过MoET在其网站上提供的服务在线提交，但该过程的费用和其他剩余程序将必须在MoET内亲自完成。

（2）在收到该注册程序和随附的文档后，MoET保护署的署长将对其进行检查，以决定是否接受该商标的注册。以色列审核部门还核实申请人是否在抵制名单上。

（3）在不接受注册的情况下，保护部门主任连同他的报告将该文件提交给工商部部长。部长可以在15天内通过一项决定接受或拒绝登记。在被拒绝的情况下，在工商部门向申请人发出通知之日起30天内，可对该决定提出异议。

（4）如果接受商标注册，则必须在商标注册表（在MoET的保护部门）中记录所有必要的信息；注册证书将在注册之日起15天内移交。

（5）注册商标通常需要两个星期。商标备案有效期为登记日起15年，并可在类似期间内续期，但须缴付所需款项。

（6）希望注册商标的外国人必须由居住在黎巴嫩的人代理。在黎巴嫩，商标申请的使用不是强制性的，以便提出商标申请、维护或更新。但是，在有争议的情况下，使用是确定商标所有权的主要标准。

（三）专利

1. 专利保护

第240号专利法于2000年8月7日颁布（以下简称"专利法"）。该法规定了发明和植物品种的专利保护，以及对集成电路布局设计的特殊保护。专利法主要对未披露的信息提供保护，根据WIPO的规定，专利法完全符合《与贸易有关的知识产权协定》（TRIPs）。任何可申请专利的发明，如下所述，授予其所有者及其后继者使用该发明的专有权利。

根据专利法，专利保护被授予一项发明，如果它具备新颖性、创造性，并可以应用于工业。

发明是否被授予，将从以下几个方面考察：①新颖性，即它不是现有技术的一部分；②创造性，即一个正常的专业人员不能根据现有技术获得它（现有技术包括专利申请的日期或《巴黎公约》要求的优先权申请日期之前的所有技术），而该技术不能由公众在任何地点或时间，不论是以手稿、口头或实际使用或以任何其他手段获得；③在工业中的可应用性，即它可以在任何类型的工业中被制造或使用（"工业"一词将被广泛解释为经修正的《巴黎公约》第1条所界定的内容）。一项发明如果违反了公共秩序或道德，就不能被授予专利权。

2. 专利注册程序

（1）黎巴嫩专利登记制度是登记注册制度。申请人必须向MoET的保护署署长提交专利申请。申请书必须采用阿拉伯文,并包括一项发明、数字、图纸的说明和摘要。需要指出的是,如果申请人不是黎巴嫩国民或居民,他必须任命一名居住在黎巴嫩的代理人。对法律规定的专利申请不予审查。

(2)注册程序可能不包含多个发明或多个相互关联的发明,形成一个一般的创造性概念。否则,本发明将被视为一项复杂的发明,在这种情况下,申请人将不得不为发明提出新的单独申请。

(3)专利注册一般需要两个星期。专利保护有效期为授予之日起20年,之后专利就会公开。

(四)工业设计

1. 工业设计保护

WIPO 将工业设计定义为一件物品的装饰性或美学特征。该设计可能包括三维特征,如物品的形状或曲面,或二维特征(如图案、线条或颜色)。

工业设计适用于各种工业产品和手工艺品。

根据 2385 条例第 48 条,任何图纸或设计的发明者,或有关的权利人,均可单独享有其使用权,并有权售卖或要约出售,并授权售卖,但该图纸或设计需在 MoET 的保护局备案过。

工业设计也根据黎巴嫩《刑法》的某些规定进行保护。

2. 工业设计保护程序

(1)图纸或设计的发明者或其代理人或官方代理人必须将申请送交保护署署长。

(2)保护署署长将在为此目的指定的特别登记册上登记申请许可证,并在其中注明提交日期、时间和编号。

(五)版权

1. 版权保护

第 75 号《版权法》于 1999 年 4 月 3 日颁布;版权保护现在适用于文学、艺术、音乐和科学作品、计算机软件和各种视听作品,以及作品形式的表达。《版权法》还加重了对罪犯的处罚,扩大了侵犯版权的案件范围,并对其权利受到侵害的人提供了更好的赔偿。

根据《版权法》,任何艺术或文学作品的作者都将因作品的创作而对其作品拥有绝对产权,并保留其所有权利,而无须考虑作品的载体形式。

根据《版权法》给予提交人的经济权利的保护期限,将是作者终生及其死后 50 年,从死亡发生之年年底开始计算。

2. 版权保护程序

(1)作品、录音、表演、广播或电视节目将存入 MoET 知识产权保护办公室。存储将构成对储户对工作、录音、表演或广播或电视节目所有权的推定。

(2)版权持有人、相关权利持有人或其特定或普遍继承人如希望提存,必须向知识产权保护局提交其或其代理人签署的申请。

(3)除非该费用为《版权法》特别规定,否则不接受提存申请。

(4)提存申请将在知识产权保护办公室登记。将向申请人提交一份证书,提及申请中所述的信息,并附上存放在该办公室的三份副本之一。

(六)域名

1. 域名保护

域名是标识网站的唯一名称。在黎巴嫩,域名不受特别法律保护。然而,黎巴嫩域名有 35 类登记为商标保护,贝鲁特美国大学的黎巴嫩域名登记处是黎巴嫩域名的当地登记处。因此,不需要普通的域名保护方式。

2. 域名应用程序

为在黎巴嫩注册域名,申请人必须提供下列文件和资料:

（1）申请表；
（2）35 类黎巴嫩域名注册证书复印件；
（3）由黎巴嫩领事馆公证和合法化的授权委托书；
（4）如果申请人在黎巴嫩没有合法的申请资质，则由黎巴嫩领事馆办理公证和合法化的授权信。

（七）IP 保护的主要措施

（1）如上所述，黎巴嫩现有的知识产权法律涵盖版权、工业设计、专利、商标和地理要素。

（2）MoET 知识产权保护办公室是保护 IP 的中心机构，其设立目的是为了建立保护知识产权的法律框架，尽管到目前为止它拥有的资源非常有限。MoET 起草了关于工业设计、商标和地理标志的新法律和修正案，以加强知识产权制度；这些仍有待议会批准。

（3）此外，知识产权案件主要由内部安全部队特别刑事调查司以及知识产权网络犯罪股和黎巴嫩海关执行。

六、环境保护

（一）环境保护监督部门

（1）环境部成立于 1993 年，负责管理所有环境问题，特别是在保护和可持续保护自然资源，以及启动和激活黎巴嫩参与全球环境公约方面。

环境部制定了国家的总体政策，为环境安全和自然资源的可持续性制定了短期、中期和长期的项目和计划，并提出了执行措施，以监测其执行情况。它还提请注意重要的、新兴的全国性和国际性环境问题。①

（2）2002 年，环境部设立了黎巴嫩清洁生产中心。该中心为中小型企业采取清洁生产措施和可持续的工业生产模式提供援助，以减少用水、能源等方面的消耗，减少废水等污染物的排放及资源浪费。②

（3）2005 年，环境部设立了条件和机制，向非营利组织（非政府组织）提供捐款，目的是开展环境活动。这使得国家和国际非政府组织发挥了新的作用，而它们在提高公众对环境和可持续发展问题和活动的认识方面发挥着越来越重要的作用。例如，1960 年以来在黎巴嫩开展工作的联合国开发计划署制定了"环境与能源方案"，除了与当地社区和民间组织合作，该方案与政府密切合作，为更有效的环境和能源管理提供政策支助，通过改进环境管理改善生计。③

（4）2014 年，在 6 个省（贝鲁特、黎巴嫩山、北方、南方、贝卡和纳巴蒂耶）任命了专职环境检察长，并在两个省（贝鲁特和南方）任命了检查法官，目的是强制执行任何违反环境法律法规的行为。

（二）环境保护法律法规简介

（1）1926 年通过的黎巴嫩《宪法》，虽然之后进行过修正，但没有明确将在清洁和健康的环境中生活的权利，作为黎巴嫩公民的宪法权利。黎巴嫩于 1948 年通过了《世界人权宣言》。《世界人权宣言》特别规定，人人有权享有为维持他本人和家属的健康和福利所需的生活水准，以满足自己及其家庭的健康和福祉，可将这一规定视为确保黎巴嫩公民享有同样权利的依据。

事实上，黎巴嫩制定了相当数量的法律和条例来管理和规范环境保护，但它们的可执行性仍然是一个需要解决的问题。

以下是直接或间接管制黎巴嫩环境保护的主要法律：

• 216/93 法，日期为 1993 年 4 月 2 日，建立了环境部并确定了其任务，这是黎巴嫩环境保护管理法中的一座重要里程碑。

• 在 2002 年 7 月 26 日，黎巴嫩议会颁布了第 444 号法律，即《环境法》，这是制定关于环境保护

---

① 参见 http://www.moe.gov.lb/The-Ministry/History.aspx?lang=en-us。
② 参见 http://www.biodiv.be/liban/implementation/national-legislation-and-policies。
③ 参见 http://www.lb.undp.org/content/lebanon/en/home/environmental-governance.html 和 http://www.lb.undp.org/content/lebanon/en/home/about-us.html。

和环境管理的基本原则和一般规定的里程碑。它呼吁保护和可持续地利用生物多样性、建立自然保护区及规定了遗传资源的管理部门和获取方式。该法还规定了对滥用环境资源和造成环境污染的人的责任和处罚。①

· 根据 2005 年 7 月 1 日颁布的第 14865 号法令，非政府组织的作用应运而生，这部法令规定环境部为开展环境活动而给予非政府组织捐款的条件和机制。

· 如上文所述，2014 年 4 月 15 日通过的第 251 号法令要求任命专职环境检察官和检查法官；以及司法部 2014 年 10 月 9 日 1837 号通知，要求环境专家参加法庭宣誓的专家名册。②

（2）除上述情况外，在每个环境领域都有规章，如规定：①减少运输部门的空气污染；②固体废物管理；③森林保护；④狩猎做法；⑤监督和控制黎巴嫩近海石油活动的环境方面、环境风险、保护环境的义务等。

（3）此外，双边和多边环境公约和条约对环境保障具有重大影响。黎巴嫩批准并加入了与环境有关的许多公约和条约。

黎巴嫩已批准的一些主要环境条约是：① 2008 年 10 月 16 日批准加入的《卡塔赫纳生物安全议定书》；② 2001 年 5 月 22 日签署的《关于持续性有机污染物的斯德哥尔摩公约》；③ 1994 年 12 月 21 日批准加入的联合国《防治荒漠化公约》；④ 1993 年 3 月 31 日加入的《关于消耗臭氧层物质的蒙特利尔议定书》；⑤ 1977 年 6 月 30 日加入的《保护地中海海洋环境和沿海地区公约》《巴塞罗那公约》；⑥ 1966 年 11 月 16 日加入的《防止石油污染海洋国际公约》；⑦ 1964 年 12 月 30 日批准的《禁止在大气层、外层空间和水下进行核武器试验条约》。

（三）环境保护评估

黎巴嫩有基本法律框架，如果这些法律始终如一地适用，将使环境受到保护。

毫无疑问，国际和国家非政府组织正在与黎巴嫩政府一道努力实现基本的环境保护，如废物回收、减少空气污染水平、海岸和森林的保护，以及保护遗产。

然而，黎巴嫩仍有很长的路要走，还有许多障碍要克服，包括近期的垃圾危机。环境法的可执行性是过去几十年的主要问题。然而，最近通过的有关环境起诉和调查的法律为颁布的环境保护法带来了一些法律公信力。

七、争议解决

国内法没有强制性的争议解决程序。合同双方可以自由选择在发生冲突时解决争议的方法。

根据黎巴嫩法律，当事各方可向外国法律提交协议，除非一项具体规定禁止选择外国法或对后者不给予法律效力，而且只要此类实质性规定不违反黎巴嫩的公共政策，那么，在这种情况下，黎巴嫩法院将不适用与黎巴嫩的公共政策背道而驰的具体规定，同时坚持外国法律的其余规定。事实上，黎巴嫩法律的有关规定规定，合同的当事方可以根据其认为合适的条件确定其法律关系，只要它们符合公共秩序、公共道德和强制性法律规定。

此外，原则上，没有任何条款禁止当事方将其协定/合同提交外国法院管辖，只需满足以下两个条件即可：①黎巴嫩管辖权承认该其他管辖权的管辖权；②黎巴嫩法律中没有规定黎巴嫩为主管管辖权的具体条款。

（一）黎巴嫩法律制度/黎巴嫩法院

黎巴嫩的法律制度主要由下列机构组成：

· 司法法院；

· 行政法院；

· 宗教法庭；

---

① 参见 http://www.moe.gov.lb/The-Ministry/History.aspx?lang=en-us。

② 参见 http://www.biodiv.be/liban/implementation/national-legislation-and-policies/environmental-legislation。

- 特别法庭；
- 特殊法庭；
- 司法委员会；
- 宪法委员会。

1. 司法法院

黎巴嫩的司法管辖制度如下：
- 第一级管辖权是一审法院。一审法院可以是一名法官或由三名法官组成的法庭。
- 第二级管辖权是上诉法院。上诉法院有权审查下级法庭作出的判决。它实际上和法律上都是第二次裁判争议。索赔人有权全面重新开庭。上诉追索权必须在黎巴嫩《民事诉讼法》（LCCP）规定的期限内提交。
- 第三级（和特别）管辖权是最高法院。如果上诉法院向最高法院提出上诉，则在法律严格确定的具体情况下，最高法院有可能作出不利的判决。最高法院（位于贝鲁特）可在任何一方的追索权下审查法官处理案件实质的裁决。它仅解决法律或适用法律的问题，它不审查案件的事实。但是，当最高法院撤销了这一项法院裁决后，它将审查整个事件，并将其替换为发出质疑性决定的法院。

2. 行政法院

司法法院管辖个人、协会、公司之间的争端，行政法院管辖私人和公共实体之间的诉讼及公共实体的诉讼。

在黎巴嫩，国务院将行政冲突的管辖分为初审法院、上诉法院和最高法院三级；在黎巴嫩行政冲突的实践中不适用双重管辖权原则。但是，如果满足某些条件，国务院的决定有时会受到挑战（例如反对、重新审理程序的申请）；国务院还在发布一些行政决定前向黎巴嫩政府提出建议。

3. 宗教法院

由黎巴嫩19个公认教派的法院系统组成，涉及三个主要宗教，即基督教、伊斯兰教和犹太教。这些法院的管辖权仅限于根据法律授权的个人案件和家庭法事项。

4. 特别法庭

在这两种制度（司法和行政）中，都有一些根据具体法律设立的特别法庭。在这种情况下，一般法院的管辖权被排除在外。在这方面可以举出的一些例子包括司法制度中的仲裁劳动理事会和行政制度中的征用委员会。

5. 特殊法庭

特殊法庭是在特殊情况下设立的，比如军事法庭。特殊法庭因特殊情况而存在，当特殊情况消失，特殊法庭通常也会撤销。当然，也存在因为某些原因（主要是政治原因）而继续维持的。

6. 司法委员会

司法委员会是一个有权对敏感的刑事事项进行限制性和明确规定的刑事法院，在黎巴嫩《刑事诉讼法》（主要是针对国家安全的罪行）中规定的。司法委员会通过部长理事会颁布的一项法令予以受理。它的决定是终局的，不能受到挑战，除非申请重开诉讼程序（注意到这种程序受某些条件的限制）。

7. 宪法委员会

根据1993年7月14日第250号法律，黎巴嫩成立了宪法委员会。其存在的主要目的是为了控制法律的合宪性；宪法委员会的所有决定都对公共当局和司法、行政法院具有约束力。

（二）仲裁

（1）根据黎巴嫩法律，诉诸仲裁是有效的。黎巴嫩的仲裁程序由LCCP管辖。

（2）关于黎巴嫩的仲裁程序，对仲裁庭的选择和仲裁条款受LCCP的条款的管辖，除非合同另有规定。在这方面，根据黎巴嫩《民事诉讼法》，当事人可以直接或参照确定的仲裁规则在仲裁协议中指定仲裁员或仲裁人，也可以在其中确定其任用方法。

（3）关于国内仲裁，简而言之，LCCP 规定：①订立商业或民事协议的缔约方可选择将仲裁条款（特别是应予书面）作为争端解决办法；②黎巴嫩共和国以及任何公法实体可适用仲裁解决任何争端，无论他们订立的合同的性质，但仲裁条款或仲裁协议的公共合同（即在私法人和公法人之间的合同）只会在部长理事会获得批准后，根据有关部长的建议生效。

（4）关于国际仲裁，在国外发生的仲裁程序中提起的外国裁决由 LCCP 负责。当请求方正式证明存在裁决并且裁决不违反国际公共政策时，这些裁决被认可并被授予豁免权。此外，黎巴嫩还是 1958 年《承认及执行外国仲裁裁决公约》（《纽约公约》）的签署国，必须指出，只有在适用《纽约公约》的国家，黎巴嫩才会承认和执行在另一缔约国领土上作出的裁决。

（5）此外，在黎巴嫩，商业、工业和农业都有仲裁和调解中心分庭。黎巴嫩仲裁和调解中心是为黎巴嫩的仲裁程序提供管理和监督服务的唯一机构。该中心自 1995 年成立以来一直活跃于仲裁领域；它向企业界、私营和公共机构以及政府提供服务。

该中心监督仲裁程序，负责：
- 指定仲裁员或确认当事人提名的仲裁员；
- 决定对仲裁员的质疑；
- 固定和延长时限；
- 审议和批准所有仲裁裁决；
- 修正仲裁员的费用，考虑到争议的金额。

（三）调解

目前，没有关于在黎巴嫩明确调解的法律或条例，因为这种调解是由当事方之间的协定所应用的私人纠纷解决机制；需要注意的是，当事人可以在调解程序中选择黎巴嫩仲裁与调解中心的规则。

LCCP 指出调解是黎巴嫩法官的特权。

八、其他

（一）反商业贿赂

1. 反商业贿赂法律法规简介

（1）黎巴嫩《刑法》规定了反贿赂条款和贿赂罪的后果。根据《刑法》的有关规定，简而言之，贿赂罪被认为是在任何雇员、当选或指定为公职人员的个人以及负责公务的个人（例如专家，法官等），接受或寻求为本人或第三方提供的礼物、许诺或任何其他利益，以承担他职务说明中的行为，采取违背其职能的行为或假装这种行为属于他的职责范围之内，或在他的工作描述中忽略或延迟履行其任何职责。

（2）1959 年 6 月 12 日第 112 号法令《关于雇员条例的黎巴嫩法令》特别规定，公职人员不得直接或通过中介人寻求或接受不正当利益。

（3）1999 年 12 月 27 日发布的第 154 号法令《非法财富法》定义了非法获得的资金，例如，雇员获得的资金、公共服务提供者、法官或其亲属或合伙人通过贿赂、使用影响、剥削自己的工作或任何其他非法手段。

（4）反腐败斗争的另一个基本步骤是，2017 年 2 月 16 日发布的法律是反腐败斗争的里程碑事件，因为它强制性地规定信息公开的程度。

（5）关于主要国际反腐败公约，黎巴嫩于 2009 年 4 月 22 日通过 58/4 号决议批准了《联合国反腐败公约》。此外，黎巴嫩是阿拉伯联盟反腐败公约的成员，由黎巴嫩内政部部长和司法部部长签署，于 2010 年 12 月 21 日由 21 个阿拉伯国家签署。

2. 部门监管反商业贿赂

内政部于 2011 年 3 月 19 日设立了反腐败委员会，其目的是打击各部门和各种形式的腐败，不公开地谴责各级的腐败行为，并恢复违反法律和宪法而颁布的公民权利。

在2016年12月，黎巴嫩政府首次设立了一个打击腐败的国家部门，从而委托一个指定的部门来建立一个有效的机制，以便在黎巴嫩打击腐败。

此外，公共卫生部还推出了一条热线（1214）以及一个在线平台，以便为公民向该部提供欺诈行动报告。MoET还推出了热线（1739）和在线申请，这两项服务都允许消费者提出投诉并跟进。

同样，黎巴嫩透明协会（LTA）在2008年发起了黎巴嫩反贿赂网络，以打击在黎巴嫩的贿赂行为。LTA还设立了黎巴嫩宣传和法律咨询中心（LALAC），目的是向公民通报他们的合法权益，并鼓励受害者和证人对腐败案件采取行动。在这方面，LTA还提供了一条热线电话（9613-868-303）。

3. 惩罚性措施

以下是可能的刑事和惩戒制裁的措施（未尽）。

（1）刑事制裁

根据《刑法》，主要的刑事制裁如下：

① 任何雇员、当选或指定为公职人员的个人以及负责公务的个人（如专家、法官等），为自己或任何第三方需求不正当利益而接受馈赠或事后利益及任何其他利益，可按照下列情况处理：

·属于他的职责范围，将被判处的刑期从3个月到3年不等，罚款等于至少两倍的贿赂，他索取或收到的数额。

·违背他的职能或假装这种行为属于他的职能范围，或在其职务说明中忽视或推迟任何职责，将被判处暂时强迫劳动并处以至少等同于他拿走或收到的贿赂价值的3倍。

② 在私营部门雇用的任何工作人员，不论是有报酬的雇员、专家还是顾问，以及与雇主有报酬的就业协议有关的任何工人，他们寻求或接受礼物、许诺或任何其他利益，无论是为本人或第三方，为了披露对业务有害的机密或信息，以作为或者不作为的方式，意图对雇主或对后者的利益造成物质或非物质损害，将受监禁两个月至两年，并处100 000～200 000黎巴嫩镑罚款（即约66美元到132美元）。

③ 向根据第①项所述的人提供或承诺提供或许诺给予的任何人的礼物或任何其他福利作为不正当利益，为了让其承诺疏忽或者迟延履行其法庭范围内的工作职责。如果上述请求被拒绝，他将被判处至少3个月的监禁，并处以至少两倍于要约或诺言的罚款。

④ 此外，第①项所述的任何个人，如接受对他已经采取并属于其工作范围内的行为的不正当奖励，将被判处监禁1个月至1年，罚款等于至少他收受或收受的贿赂的价值两倍。

与贿赂有关的规定在个人和公司之间，不区分行贿者。但是，根据《刑法》的规定，法律实体对其经理、董事、代表和雇员在代表公司执行此类行为时所犯罪行负有刑事责任。在此情况下，公司将受到对外公示、罚款或者没收资产的处罚。

（2）惩戒制裁

根据《雇员条例》第54条，雇员如故意或疏忽违反现行法律及规章所规定的职责，将会受到纪律处分。这一纪律起诉并不妨碍雇员在必要时对民事或刑事法院进行起诉。

（二）项目承包

（1）关于颁发公共（行政）合同的主要法律和条例是：

① 根据14969号法令颁布的《公共会计法》（PAL）；

② 根据1959年12月16日2866法令颁布的招标条例。

黎巴嫩还颁布了《公私合伙法》（PPP法），其在2017年9月9日正式公报中发表。PPP法主要论述PPP的一般定义、PPP项目的所有阶段以及建议和选择项目的程序。它还规定，由国家、公共机构、市镇和市镇工会执行的项目均受PPP法的规限。

（2）一个合同当满足以下条件时为行政合同：

·合同缔约方之一是公法实体；

·合同的目的或宗旨是提供公共服务或履行公共利益；

·该合同规定了公法缔约方为其自身利益所包括的例外条款。

行政合同的特点是，国家/公共当局（公法缔约方）具有这种酌处权（在执行合同时），是否在协议文件中明确规定，以及这样酌处原则上不可能存在争议。然而，尽管公约缔约方对是否执行合同及是否只执行部分合同内容具有酌处权，但国务院通过控制公法缔约方是否使用了其酌处权来监督此种自由裁量权权力滥用的方式。国务院通常会审查公法缔约方是否超过了拥有此类酌处权的理由，或者在没有任何有效的事实或法律理由的情况下拒绝执行合同关系。

1. 许可制度

一般而言，在黎巴嫩，在公法缔约方与私法个人和实体（私法缔约方）之间缔结的涉及竞争过程的公共合同或先前的招标程序中，黎巴嫩政府请有关的私人当事方按照预定的条款和条件，在公开招标中提出投标。

公共合同的执行或履行须征得黎巴嫩政府的批准，通常由有关部门代表，这取决于所设想项目的性质。

这就是说，审批过程没有特定的程序。一般而言，在私法人缔约方提出提案之后，黎巴嫩政府和有关部门研究此种提议，或者签字接受，或者要求修正。在某些情况下，可能还需要颁布一项法令。项目不同，审批程序的时间也不尽相同，这取决于项目的具体情况。

并非所有的公共合同都是在竞争过程或以前的招标程序之前进行的。有时，公共合同是由私法人缔约方和公法人缔约方之间的谈判或黎巴嫩政府直接裁决的结果缔结的，但是，这种公共合同必须与明确列出的具体项目有关。该谈判或缔结对象，例如仅通过不能成为公共采购对象的用品、工程和服务等，要么是因为它们必须保密，要么是由于公共安全要求，但须经有关部委的批准。

谈判合同应遵守合同双方规定的条款和条件，并应在裁决时有自己的招标文件。

2. 禁止区域

PAL 和招标条例没有明确规定禁止任何地方或外国个人或实体与黎巴嫩政府签订公共合同的任何条款。

然而，根据每个项目的需要，这些条例给公法缔约方提供了相当大的自由，以组织其投标，特别是私法缔约方的甄选标准。因此，某些具体项目可能禁止外国人员和产品，并严格授予黎巴嫩国民或当地生产的产品。其他国家可能允许外国参加者与黎巴嫩实体联合。

需要提及的是，尽管有相反的规定，LCC 规定，即在黎巴嫩设立的 SAL 必须在黎巴嫩拥有其注册办事处，并在法律上享有黎巴嫩国籍，但注意到，如果 SAL 的目的是利用公共服务，其资本必须由将由黎巴嫩国民拥有的名义股组成。这些股份只能在无效罚款的情况下转让给黎巴嫩股东。

3. 招标和竞标的邀请

根据 PAL 和招标条例的规定所有投标书必须在合同签订之日起 15 天内，在官方公报和至少 3 份当地报纸上公布。

每项投标的投标文件必须明确说明，包括：①项目的目标和将要进行的工作；②候选人的资格要求；③选择和奖励标准（公法缔约方可能不会遵循最低价格，只要它明确在招标文件的招标优惠标准中说明招标方在必要时可以单方解释标准）；④项目的执行条件及其执行的截止日期；⑤债券参与投标要求的保证金；⑥履约保证书，保证对私法当事人义务的正确执行。投标保证金和履约保证金都可以是货币或由可接受的银行发行。

申请必须符合标书的要求，每份标书最少须提交 2 份申请。如果只提交了 1 份申请，除非所提供的价格至少低于投标文件所述的价格，否则该项目将不会授予给该申请人。

此外，可向在黎巴嫩制造的特定产品提供 10% 的优惠保证金，条件是这些产品及其规格由部长会议的一项法令确定。

PAL 和招标章程只包含主要原则，并没有解决投标阶段的数量、时间表、与申请人沟通的方式和选择标准等问题，因此留下了相当大的自由度，以根据项目的需要组织投标。

根据 PPP 法的规定，PPP 项目包括任何公共项目由国家或市镇所属的政府或公共行政部门进行的公共事业，在这些机构中，私营部门对项目的筹资和管理作出贡献，并至少有下列阶段之一：设计、建立、施工、开发、翻新、装备、维修、操作。

根据 PPP 法的规定，启动招标程序须遵守招标透明、参与自由及所有候选人（包括黎巴嫩人和外国人）一律平等原则，并应在必要的宣传之前，以便收到多项报价。招标程序的步骤如下：

① 招标程序开始于启动公开邀请，其中说明根据 PPP 项目的规模和性质规定的资格标准决定；

② PPP 委员会向候选人提供必要的信息和建议，并根据这些资料提出他们的要求；

③ PPP 委员会审查和评估上述要求，并向最高私有化合作理事会（SCPP）提出一份经证实的报告，其中载有建议的预审候选人的姓名和被取消资格的候选人的姓名。必须至少有 3 个建议的预审候选人；

④ PPP 委员会起草投标书。PPP 委员会随后通知所有预审候选人投标；

⑤ PPP 委员会随后将最后投标书提交部长会议核准；

⑥ PPP 委员会随后通知投标人预审候选人。预审候选人向 PPP 委员会提出他们的技术和财务提议；

⑦ PPP 委员会决定提出的技术提议。不符合投标要求的技术报价将被拒绝；

⑧ PPP 委员会评估剩余的技术报价并根据投标要求确定合格的产品，PPP 委员会根据上述评价设立合格的候选人。如果至少有两项技术要约不被接受，该项目将会重新投标，以确保竞争性；

⑨ PPP 委员会展示合格参与者的财务报价，并从技术和财务角度对报价进行分类，并将报告发送给 SCPP；

⑩ PPP 委员会在 SCPP 的授权下，可以与首选申请人进行谈判，目的是从技术角度改进报价。该项目根据投标书中所列的要求，并在 SCPP 的批准下，按照 PPP 委员会的选择，授予申请人最优惠的报价。

⑪ 在决策过程结束后，PPP 委员会将公布结果。

Lebanon

Authors: Chadia El Meouchi, Carine Farran
Translators: Chen Jianbin, Mao Yu

I. Overview

A. General Introduction to the Political, Economic, Social and Legal Environment

The Lebanese Republic, known as Lebanon, rich in history gained its independence at the end of the French mandate on the 22nd of November 1943. Lebanon has become notorious for its culture, diversity and economy and, although in the eye of the storm with the general unrest in the middle-east, has proven its resilience and capacity to develop. Indeed, Lebanon's natural richness and the readiness of its people have allowed the country to prosper. On a social level, Lebanon benefits of a unique society which has become a melting pot and point of intersection of multiple cultures, whether religious, ethnic, social or other. On an economic level, despite the troubles associated with the developing world, and the heavy onset of refugees weighing on the country's economy, Lebanon manages to maintain an active financial sector, benefiting from banking secrecy.

This small country of 10452 square kilometres has, ever since its independence, known periods fluctuating between prosperity and turmoil, and has persevered, with the help of its expatriate community. This phenomenon has greatly increased the already major international aspect of the country, and the Lebanese diaspora can be found in all corners of the world.

The official language in Lebanon is Arabic, a large part of the population is also proficient in most notably either English or French. The official currency is the Lebanese Pound (LBP), and the United States Dollar (USD) is commonly accepted in the private sector.

Lebanon has suffered a lengthy civil war. However, the end of the civil war was followed by a relative stability in which the country has and continues to commit serious efforts in reconstructing itself on a political, social, economic and legal level.

a. Political

According to its constitution, Lebanon is a parliamentary democratic republic, founded on the respect of public freedoms at the forefront of which are the freedom of opinion and belief, and the respect for social justice and equality of rights and duties among all citizens without discrimination. A key principle followed by the country is that of the separation of powers, their balance and cooperation.

Lebanon adopted a unique consociational system through the ratification of the Taif Agreement that continues to lend stability to the country. This political reform anchors the principle of "mutual coexistence" within the political structure of the country in itself—the seats of power are distributed in a seemingly balanced way between the different religious groups.

On a more international level, Lebanon prides itself in being a founding and active member of the Arab League abiding by its pacts and covenants, as well as a founding member of the United Nations abiding by its covenants and the Universal Declaration of Human Rights.

b. Social

On a social level, Lebanon is home to 19 officially recognized sectarian communities. The Lebanese are a cosmopolitan people that have generally welcomed foreign markets' integration in the country. This helped Lebanon become a prime tourist destination in the Middle East.

Moreover, due to their strong adaptability, and entrepreneurial drive, the Lebanese people have often been sought after as human resources across the world. The educational system in Lebanon facilitates this integration by encouraging the learning of languages, mainly either French or English or both, and allowing the development of a myriad of internationally recognized school degrees alongside the Lebanese baccalaureate.

With the current unrest within neighbouring countries, and most notably the war in Syria, Lebanon continues to take in a large number of refugees who are being partly supported through national and international initiatives and aids but still represent a heavy burden for Lebanon, from economic, social and other perspective.

c. Economic

Lebanon's economy is predominantly service oriented and relies highly on the banking and tourism sectors. Lebanon continues to average a somewhat steady GDP growth rate which is estimated to reach approximately 2.6% during the next 3 years according to the World Bank.[1]

Lebanon's economy embraces the liberal free-market in which the government generally does not restrict foreign investments.

The banking sector within Lebanon, strictly regulated by the Central Bank (the "BDL"), is highly developed and reputable for its financial standing. The Lebanese capital market (the "CMA") has been reshaped with the creation of the Capital Markets Authority in 2011.

An important aspect of the Lebanese economy is the presence of the banking secrecy law, (the "BSL"), making Lebanon one of the few remaining countries to benefit from such a law. Moreover, as of 2001, the banks have an obligation to abide by Law no 318 of 2001 as amended subsequently regarding Anti-Money Laundering.

The recent discovery of energetic resources in the Lebanese offshore, marks the development of the Lebanese petroleum sector in a way that is both job creating and attractive for foreign investments. Furthermore Lebanon has also been engaged in the development of renewable energy through different initiatives and governmental tenders.

d. Legal

Lebanon is a "Civil Law" jurisdiction, and Lebanon has drafted its own set of codes, the most notable of which is the Code of Obligations and Contracts. However, matters relating to the personal status including for example marriage and inheritance are regulated by another set of laws drafted specifically for every sectarian community.

The Lebanese constitution of 1926, as amended by the Taif Agreement, provides that the country's political system is established on the principle of separation and balance of the executive, legislative and judicial powers.

The executive power in Lebanon is formed by (i) the President Head of State who is elected at a two-thirds majority of the deputies in the Parliament for a six-year term; once elected, the President also presides over the high council for national defence and is regarded as the chief commander of the armed forces, and (ii) the Prime Minister who is named by the President. In coordination with the President, the Prime Minister, inter alia, selects the ministers and sets the Cabinet's policies to be presented to the Parliament.

The Parliament forms the legislative branch and is responsible for the legislation and the issuance of laws.

The judicial branch is formed of the Constitutional Council, the Administrative Court, the civil courts including the commercial courts, the penal courts, and the personal status courts.

B. The Status and Direction of the Cooperation with Chinese Enterprises Under the B&R

"The rapid opening up of China in recent years has led to a remarkable increase in its people-to-people exchanges with other countries" states the Chinese embassy in Lebanon at the announcement of the opening of the China Visa application centre in Beirut.[2] This, small but significant move on the part of the Republic of China is proof as to the ever increasing relationship between the two countries. Indeed, desiring to intensify the economic cooperation between them on the basis of equality and mutual benefits the Lebanese Republic and China have concluded in 1996 an agreement which came into force in 1997 concerning the encouragement and reciprocal protection of investments. Furthermore, Lebanon has been chosen as the regional headquarters in the Middle East and North Africa for the China Council for the promotion of International Trade which focuses on implementing national strategies for development, encouraging foreign trade, bilateral investment and economic and technological cooperation according to the Lebanese Foreign Ministry.[3]

Also, China had ever since the start of the B&R initiative decided to include Lebanon among the countries of the new Silk Road. Indeed, China considers that Lebanon is not only geographically ideally located for this initiative, it is also one of the most stable countries within the region both on a security and political level.[4]

Considering that Lebanon's main import partner in 2016 was China, from which 11.2% of the imports were

---

[1] The World Bank, Lebanon's Economic Outlook – October 2017, 11 October 2017.From the World Bank's website available at: http://www.worldbank.org/en/country/lebanon/publication/lebanon-economic-outlook-october-2017.

[2] Embassy of the people's Republic of China in the Republic of Lebanon, Notice on the Opening of the China Visa Application Center in Beirut, 2 November 2017.From the Embassy of the People's Republic of China in the Republic of Lebanon's website available at: http://lb.china-embassy.org/eng/xwdt/t1506865.htm.

[3] XinhuaNet, China's trade body chooses Lebanon as Mideast, North Africa headquarters, 16 January 2018.From XinhuaNet's website at:http://www.xinhuanet.com/english/2018-01/16/c_136900363.htm.

[4] Lorient Le Jour, Adnan Kassar: les entreprises chinoises prêtes à investir au Liban, 29 of January 2018.From Lorient Le Jour's website available at :https://www.lorientlejour.com/article/1096789/adnan-kassar-les-entreprises-chinoises-pretes-a-investir-au-liban.html.

provided[1], it was to be expected that Lebanon would be an enthusiastic partner of China's Belt and Road initiative. Indeed, this initiative has been praised for the effect it is hoped it will have to boost the level of economic, cultural and social exchange between the participant countries.

Moreover, on a national level Lebanon's Tripoli is keen for active role in Belt and Road initiative.[2] Effectively the mayor of Tripoli stated that he "will not spare any effort in boosting Tripoli's standing and its openness on Chinese markets"[3].

II. Investment

A. Market Access

a. Laws and Regulations of Investment Industry

The most significant law is Law No.360 of 2001 regarding the encouragement of investments in Lebanon (the "Investment Law"). The Investment Law established the Investment Development Authority of Lebanon (IDAL) and reinforced IDAL's mission by providing a framework for regulating investment activities in Lebanon, and providing investors with a range of incentives and business support services.

The Investment Law defines, inter alia, the investor as a physical or legal Lebanese, Arab or foreign person who invests in Lebanon in accordance with the Investment Law. The Investment Law applies to all investments belonging to investors, who wish to benefit from its provisions in the fields of industry, agriculture, tourism, information, communication, technology, media and other sectors that the council of minister will determine by decree upon request of the Prime Minister.

The Investment Law provides that Lebanon may conclude a package deal, i.e.a contract by virtue of which the Lebanon represented by IDAL, grants the investor willing to invest in a specific project, incentives, exemptions and reductions (adopted by the board member of the IDAL) provided that the investor executes the project in accordance with the conditions in the contract. Such package deal can benefit from a maximum of incentives, reductions or exemptions expressly, including but not limited to, exemptions from income taxes and land registration, work permits for foreign employees, reductions on residence permit fees, and so forth.

We also have the following laws which also relate to investment in Lebanon:

- The Private Public Partnership Law of 2017 (the "PPP Law"). The PPP Law addresses mainly the general definitions of PPP, all of the phases of a PPP project as well as the procedures of proposing and choosing a project.

- The Privatization Law of 2000; This law sets out the general privatization framework specifying the conditions of privatization operations and their scope of implementation. It also establishes a Higher Council for Privatization responsible for the initiation, implementation, and execution of the privatization operations.

- The Decree 11614 of 1969 on acquisition of real estate rights of foreigners in Lebanon and its subsequent amendments regarding the foreign ownership of real estate assets in Lebanon (the "Foreign Ownership Law").

- Also, the Central Bank's circular 331 of 2013 addressed to banks and financial institutions (the "Circular 331") provides incentives for Lebanese commercial banks to directly invest in start-ups, funds, venture capital companies, and incubators by guaranteeing up to 75% of their investments in start-ups. Such entities should be under the form of an SAL, and should not be a financial company or an Offshore Company.

b. Department Supervising Investment

In Lebanon, there is no single department in charge of supervising and controlling investments.

c. Forms of Investment

(i) Foreign investment can be done through various legal entities established in Lebanon. See the part titled "The Establishment and Dissolution of Companies" in which we address the key forms of establishment in Lebanon.

(ii) Foreign investment can also be done through a branch of a foreign company established in Lebanon. A branch of a foreign company may generally undertake the same commercial activity as the activity of its mother

---

[1] Central Intelligence Agency, World Fact Book - Imports Exports Partners (2016).From the Central Intelligence Agency's website available at :https://www.cia.gov/library/publications/the-world-factbook/fields/2061.html#le.
[2] XinhuaNet, Lebanon's Tripoli keen for active role in Belt and Road initiative, 26 November 2017.From XinhuaNet's website at:http://www.xinhuanet.com/english/2017-11/26/c_136779409.htm.
[3] Op.cit.XinhuaNet.

company, save some exceptions.

The branch does not have a separate legal personality from that of its mother company and therefore the liability of the branch will in principle be borne by the mother company. According to the Lebanese Code of Commerce (the "LCC"), every foreign commercial company having a branch in Lebanon should be registered with the commercial registry. Prior to its registration at the Commercial Registry, the branch should also be registered with the Ministry of Economy and Trade ("MoET").

A branch is taxed at the rate of 17%, in addition to the dividends distribution of 10% based on the real profit method of calculation.

d. Standards of Market Access and Examination

Below are some of the main restrictions with regards to foreign investment:

(i) A restriction on trade under the Boycott Law of 1955 (the "Boycott Law") prohibits the establishment of any relations with Israel. According to the Boycott Law, any agreements either directly or through any intermediary with institutions or persons having residence in Israel, or with persons or entities acting on behalf of Israel or its interest are forbidden and any trade of Israeli goods, financial documents, and securities is prohibited, subject to criminal penalties, including imprisonment, fines, work prohibitions or the dissolution of a company, as set out in the Boycott Law and the Lebanese Criminal Code. The MoET is responsible for enforcing the boycott regulations.

(ii) There are additional restrictions with respect to foreign ownership and / or licensing requirements for certain sectors in Lebanon such as by way of example only and without limitation, real estate, insurance, media and civil aviation.

B. Foreign Exchange Regulation

a. Department Supervising Foreign Exchange

In principle, there is no department per se supervising foreign exchange in Lebanon.

However, one of the BDL's missions is to stabilize the exchange rates; indeed, the BDL is notably entitled to operate in the market, in agreement with the Minister of Finance, in compliance with applicable laws and regulations.

b. Brief Introduction of Laws and Regulations of Foreign Exchange

In Lebanon, there are in general no laws and regulations that expressly restrict or impose foreign exchange controls, to the exception of restrictions on transactions involving Israeli parties or currency.

The money exchange profession is regulated and it is prohibited for any legal entity, other than banks, financial institutions and financial intermediary institutions registered at the BDL, to undertake exchange operations, without the prior approval of the BDL.

Furthermore, Lebanese laws require in general that any person transporting negotiable instruments in person or in a luggage or by any other means, whether into or out of Lebanon, must declare the negotiable instruments to the customs authorities whenever their value exceeds USD /15,000/ or its equivalent in other currencies.

C. Financing

a. Main Financial Institutions

(i) The BDL was established by the Code of Money and Credit of 1963 (the "CMC"). BDL is a legal public entity enjoying financial and administrative autonomy. It is not subject to the administrative and management rules applicable to the public sector. Its capital is totally appropriated by the State.

One of the BDL's functions is granting licenses for the establishment of banks, financial institutions, money dealers, foreign banks, and leasing companies in Lebanon. The Banking Control Commission the ("BCC") controls and supervises these institutions.

The BDL issues circulars and resolutions governing the relations of banks with their customers.

(ii) The Association of Financial Institutions ("AFIL") in Lebanon was established in 1971. In 2001, the licensing of AFIL was revived to safeguard the rights of the financial institutions.

Financial Institutions are governed by the provisions of the CMC and of the BDL's circulars including Decision No.7136 of 1998 as amended ("Decision 7136"), and their establishment must be approved by the BDL.

(iii) The establishment, in Lebanon, of an Islamic bank or a foreign Islamic bank's branch requires an authorization from the Central Council of the BDL. The Islamic Banking department at the BCC was established in 2012. Its mission is to put in place a sound and effective framework of supervisory policies, standards, controls and instruments that conform to international best practices and comply with Islamic banking activities and applicable laws and regulations in Lebanon.

(iv) The "Association des Compagnies d'Assurance au Liban" ("ACAL") was established in 1971. ACAL aims mainly at building the insurance profession on technical and sound bases, instituting rules and regulations to raise the level of the insurance industry, and safeguarding the public interest.

According to Decree No.9812 of 1968 (the "Insurance Law"), all Lebanese and foreign companies that undertake in Lebanon, any of the activities mentioned the Insurance Law are subject to the Insurance Law and must be licensed to do so.

b. Financing Conditions for Foreign Enterprises

(i) Bank accounts: There are no specific express restrictions in Lebanon regarding a foreigner or non-resident's ability to open and operate a bank account in local currency or foreign currencies in Lebanon. Banks have stringent inquiry mechanisms to ensure compliance with international and domestic regulations; they notably implement Lebanon's anti-money laundering and combating terrorism financing laws and uphold Know-Your-Customer requirements and other regulations to combat tax evasion. Lebanese banks are all obliged to comply with the Foreign Account Tax Compliance Act.

(ii) Financing: Banks are the major providers of credit to businesses in Lebanon. There are in principle no restrictions on foreign enterprises, without or with a presence in Lebanon, to obtain financing, subject to usual credit checks.

(iii) Lending services from foreign entities: Lending services may only be undertaken in Lebanon by Lebanese banks, financial institutions and lending entities (called comptoirs).

(iv) The Beirut Digital District (the "BDD"): the BDD aims at building and developing technology clusters and linkages in Lebanon. The space is designed to host local as well as foreign ICT companies, including access to advanced IT services and fiber optics infrastructure at reduced rates. The BDD is a Public Private Partnership led by the Ministry of Telecommunications in collaboration with ZRE and Berytech.①

D. Land Policy

Lebanon recognizes ownership and property over real estate and immovable assets in general.

The two main land-related laws are:

(i) The Lebanese property law of 1930 and its subsequent amendments (the "Property Law"); and,

(ii) The Legislative Decree of 1969 and its subsequent amendments notably Law No.296/2001 regarding the foreign ownership of real estate assets (the "Foreign Ownership Law").

The Property Law governs mainly the acquisition and disposition of all property rights by Lebanese nationals. All rights related to real estate assets must be duly registered at the real-estate registry; notably rights of way, expropriation, mortgage, lawsuits, seizures and any other right.

The Foreign Ownership Law governs the acquisition of real estate by non-Lebanese.

Non-Lebanese as defined under the Foreign Ownership Law may in general acquire up to /3 000/ square meters in the entire Lebanese territory without having to undertake any additional measures. Any acquisition by such Non-Lebanese in excess of /3 000/ square meters is subject to prior authorization granted by the Council of Ministers upon the Minister of Finance's suggestion.

A non-Lebanese individual that has acquired real estate rights under the Foreign Ownership Law should finalize the construction of a building on the land or achieve the purpose of the ownership as declared upon acquisition or upon obtaining the aforementioned authorization, within 5 years as of the time of registration in the real estate registry. This term can be extended only once by decision of the Council of Ministers.

E. The Establishment and Dissolution of Companies

a. The Forms of Enterprises

In Lebanon, there are two main types of corporations, civil and commercial.

Commercial corporations have a commercial object and are governed mainly by the LCC, the main ones being as follows:

- SAL;
- Lebanese Holding Company;
- Lebanese Offshore Company;
- Limited liability company;

These commercial corporations are endowed with legal personality.

---

① Invest in Lebanon, Financing your business - loans and other facilities.From Invest in Lebanon's website available at:http://investinlebanon.gov.lb/en/doing_business/financing_a_business/loans_other_facilities.

a) The SAL

The SAL is formed by a number of shareholders who are not liable for the company's debts beyond the amount of their capital subscription. An SAL must have its registered office in Lebanon and Lebanese nationality, notwithstanding any provision to the contrary. In the event the object of the company is the exploitation of a public service, one third of its capital must be composed of nominal shares that will be owned by Lebanese and only transferred to Lebanese under penalty of nullity if transferred to non-Lebanese.

The liability of the shareholders of an SAL is limited to their participation in the share capital.

An SAL must be founded by a minimum of three founders, and must maintain a minimum of three shareholders at all times.

The minimum share capital of an SAL must amount to LBP/30,000,000/, i.e.approximately USD/20,000/. The entire share capital of the SAL may be owned by non-Lebanese nationals, to the exception of the guarantee shares, which must be held by Lebanese board members.

The financial statements of an SAL must be audited on an annual basis by an auditor appointed by the shareholders. An additional auditor is appointed by the concerned commercial court. The SAL is also required to retain a lawyer on an annual basis.

In principle, the transfer of shares inter vivos to third parties is free from any restrictions, unless the SAL's by-laws provide for restrictions such as priority rights to existing shareholders.

The management of an SAL is entrusted to a board of directors composed of a minimum of three and a maximum of twelve members, the majority of which should be Lebanese, duly appointed for a maximum period of three years (renewable) in general. The Chairman-General Manager may be a foreign national but will require work and residency permits.

The shareholders of the SAL must hold at least one annual ordinary general assembly meeting (the "OGA") in compliance with the quorum and decision making threshold provisions in the law for the purpose of approving the accounts of the preceding fiscal year, and / or at any time upon the request of the board of directors.

The amendment of the SAL's bylaws can only be done by a resolution of an extraordinary general assembly meeting (the "EGA") of shareholders held in compliance with the quorum and decision making threshold provisions in the law. An EGA may amend all clauses of the bylaws provided that the SAL's nationality is not changed, the shareholders' liabilities are not increased and third parties' rights are not affected.

For board of directors' Meetings:

- At least half of the members of the board must be present or represented in order for the board's resolutions to be valid;
- Decisions are taken by a majority of the board members present or represented.

Concerning the applicable tax regime, and on a high-level basis, the SAL is subject notably to:

- Income tax of 17%; and
- Distribution of dividends' withholding tax of 10%.

b) The Lebanese Holding Company

Holding companies are incorporated under the form of an SAL, and therefore have limited liability; however, there are special rules governing holding companies by virtue of Decree Law No.45 of 1983, as amended ("DL 45"). The provisions of the LCC concerning the SAL, notably those mentioned here-above, also apply to holding companies when they do not contradict the provisions of DL 45.

- The expression "Holding Company" must be clearly mentioned next to the company's name on all documents, papers, publications, and any other printed document issued by the company.

- The object of the Holding Company is strictly restricted by law to the following:

• The acquisition of shares or parts or the participation in the establishment of Lebanese or foreign Joint-Stock companies or Limited Liability companies;

• The granting of loans to the companies in which it owns shares or parts, and providing guarantees for such companies vis-à-vis third parties;

• The management of companies in which it owns shares or parts;

• The acquisition of patents, rights over inventions, concessions, registered trademarks and all other privative rights, and granting licenses thereon to companies in Lebanon or abroad; and

• The acquisition of movable or immovable assets provided that they are exclusively destined to the needs of its activities, and are in compliance with the provisions of the law concerning the acquisition by non-Lebanese of real estate rights in Lebanon.

A Holding Company cannot invest more than 40% in more than two companies operating in the same industrial, commercial or non-commercial activity in Lebanon, if the said investments contravene the restrictions provided for in Decree Law No.32 of 1967. The provisions mentioned do not apply to investments outside

Lebanon.

A Holding Company is prohibited from undertaking directly any activity which does not fall under the scope of its object as restrictively defined here-above.

The minimum number of founders at the time of incorporation is three and the minimum number of shareholders is three.

The minimum share capital is LBP/30,000,000/, i.e.approximately USD/20,000/; the share capital of a Holding Company can be fixed in a foreign currency and its accounts and balance sheets can be held and organized in the same foreign currency.

The board of directors must be composed of a minimum of three and a maximum of twelve members elected by the OGA for a maximum period of three years in general renewable. It is no longer required for Holding companies, by virtue of the amendment brought to DL 45 in 2006, that the majority of the members of the board of directors be of Lebanese nationality. The board of directors designates one of its members as Chairman-General Manager. The Chairman-General Manager may be a foreign national and is not required to obtain a work and residency permit if he is not resident in Lebanon. At least half of the board members must be present or represented in order for the board's resolutions to be valid. Decisions are taken by a majority of the board members present of represented.

The Holding Company is required to appoint at least one auditor, of Lebanese nationality and resident in Lebanon, and to retain a lawyer on an annual basis.

The Holding's main office / headquarters, where the company's registries and documents are held and kept, must be in Lebanon. However, if provided for in its Articles of Association, the company's general assembly and board meetings can be held outside of Lebanon, save for a few exceptions.

Holding companies benefit from several tax advantages. Indeed, the Holding Company is subject to an annual lump-sum tax equivalent to 6 % of the total value of its share capital, to which will be added the reserve funds, when the total does not exceed LBP /50,000,000/; the rate of the annual lump-sum tax will be reduced to 4 % when the total ranges between LBP/50,000,000/ and LBP/80,000,000/, and to 2 % when the total exceeds LBP /80,000,000/.

In any event, the annual tax applicable to Holding companies will not exceed LBP /5,000,000/, i.e.approximately USD /3,335/ per annum.

Furthermore, Holding companies benefit from other tax exemptions and has a specific tax regime that apply.

c) The Lebanese Offshore Company

Lebanese offshore companies are incorporated under the form of an SAL, and therefore have limited liability; however, there are special rules governing Offshore companies by virtue of Decree Law No.46 of 1983, as amended ("DL 46"). The provisions of the LCC regarding the SAL, notably those mentioned here-above, also apply to offshore companies when they do not contradict the provisions of DL 46.

The object of a Lebanese Offshore Company is strictly limited to the following activities:

• The negotiation and signature of contracts and agreements in respect of transactions and deals, the implementation of which is undertaken outside of the Lebanese territory and which are relevant to assets located abroad or in the customs free zones;

• The management from Lebanon of companies and institutions, the activities of which are restricted to those undertaken outside of Lebanon, in addition to the export of technical, administrative and organizational services as well as software and programs relating to information technology of any kind to institutions domiciled outside of Lebanon and upon the request of such institutions;

• Tri-partite or multi-partite operations of foreign commerce occurring outside of Lebanon;

• The undertaking of sea shipping operations and activities;

• The ownership of shares, parts, bonds and participations in foreign and non-domiciled institutions and companies, and the granting of loans to the non-domiciled institutions in which the company owns more than 20% of the share capital;

• The appropriation and / or benefit of rights related to products agencies and merchandise, and the representation of foreign companies in foreign markets;

• Opening branches and representative offices outside of Lebanon;

• Constituting, investing, managing, and owning economical projects of all kinds to the exception of the prohibitions mentioned under Article 2 of DL 46 (the provisions of Article 2 are mentioned below);

• Opening creditor accounts and borrowing from banks and financial institutions domiciled in Lebanon or abroad to finance the activities and transactions enumerated here-above; and

• Renting offices in Lebanon and owning the real estates required for its activity, all in compliance with the law regulating the ownership by foreigners of real estate rights in Lebanon.

- The Lebanese Offshore Company is prohibited from:
• Engaging in insurance activities of all kinds, and in activities and transactions that are undertaken by banks, financial institutions, and any and all institutions that are subject to the control of the Central Bank of Lebanon;
• Undertaking in Lebanon any activity other than the activities mentioned under Article 1 of DL 46; and
• Making any profit, income or proceeds from moveable or immoveable assets located in Lebanon, or from services provided to establishments domiciled in Lebanon, except income from the company's bank accounts, as well as income generated by the subscription to and the trading of Lebanese treasury bonds.

The minimum number of founders of the Lebanese Offshore Company should be at least three. The founders /shareholders and board members may all be foreigners.

If the Chairman – General Manager of the Lebanese Offshore Company is a non-Lebanese person, he will be exempted from obtaining a work permit and a residence. In practice, such provisions apply if the Chairman – General Manager will undertake his duties and activities from outside the Lebanese territory and will come to Lebanon by virtue of a tourist visa. However, in the event where the Chairman – General Manager will undertake his duties from the Lebanese territory and will reside therein, it will be compulsory to abide by the requirements of the Ministry of Labour.

The minimum share capital of the Lebanese Offshore Company is LBP /30,000,000/, i.e.approximately USD /20,000/; the share capital can be fixed in a foreign currency provided that the company's accounts are held in the same foreign currency.

The Lebanese Offshore Company is exempted from the obligation of retaining a lawyer, unless its capital exceeds LBP /50,000,000/ or the total of its annual balance sheets exceeds the equivalent of USD /500,000/. The auditor of the company can be only one but should be a Lebanese national and authorized to exercise the professional audit activity in Lebanon.

The Offshore Company is subject to an annual lump sum tax of LBP /1,000,000/, i.e.approximately USD /666/. The Offshore Company also benefits from tax exemptions and a specific tax regime.

d) The Limited Liability Company

The limited liability company (the "SARL") is a commercial corporation formed by partners who are not liable for the company's liabilities beyond the amount of their contribution, and whose capital is divided into parts rather than shares. The SARL is subject to the laws and regulations of trade as well as to the provisions of Decree-Law No.35 of 1967 ("DL 35"). The SARL will not engage in certain activities, namely insurance, air transport, as well as all banking and fund management operations. The SARL should have a registered office in Lebanon.

The partners of an SARL are not required to be Lebanese nationals, and their number must range between a minimum of three and a maximum of twenty partners in principle; in the event that it exceeds twenty partners, the partners' assembly should resolve the transformation of the SARL into a SAL.

The minimum capital required is LBP /5,000,000/ (i.e.approximately USD /3,333/) which must be entirely paid-up upon incorporation of the SARL. The SARL is prohibited from issuing, for its own account, negotiable certificates (whether bearer or registered) and, by way of public subscription, movable assets, stocks, bonds or shares.

The SARL is not required to appoint an auditor, except in the following cases:
• If the number of partners exceeds twenty;
• If the capital reaches LBP /30,000,000/; and / or
• If one or more partners, representing at least 1/5 of the capital, request that an auditor be appointed.

Nevertheless, the MoF usually requires that the SARL be audited yearly and that the SARL's accounts, when remitted to the MoF, be audited.

Also, the SARL is required to retain a lawyer on an annual basis.

The transfer of parts to third parties inter vivos is subject to the approval of the partners representing at least three-quarters of the capital. Moreover, existing partners possess a priority right in the purchase of parts subject of the transfer. Furthermore, such transfer is subject to taxes, including notably stamp duty taxes on the value of the parts' transfer (which taxes are in principle the following: (i) 3 per mil as stamp duty fees, (ii) 1 per mil as bar association fees, and (iii) 1 per mil as notary public fees and a 10% tax on the capital gains of the parts being transferred.

The SARL is managed by one or several managers who may or may not be selected among the partners and who must not be legal entities. The managers are not required to be Lebanese, noting that any foreign managers will require work and residency permits.

The OGA must hold an ordinary meeting of members annually, and upon request of the manager(s) when deemed necessary, in order to approve the accounts of the SARL for the preceding fiscal year as well as the manager's conduct of business.

The general assembly of partners must hold an EGA in order to amend the SARL's statutes, e.g.for the increase and reduction of capital, the change of its legal form.

Concerning the applicable tax regime, and on a high-level basis, the SARL is subject notably to the following taxes:
• A corporate income tax amounting to 17%; and,
• Distribution of dividends in the SARL is subject to a withholding tax of 10%.

b. The Procedure of Establishment

The constituent acts of all commercial companies, with the exception of undeclared partnerships, must be published through the completion of the formalities detailed below, under the penalty of being null and void.

a) The SAL

The steps to incorporate an SAL can be summarized as follows:

(i) The founders of the SAL must sign its bylaws before a notary public and pay the stamp duty fees on the share capital (there are two types of fees payable in this respect: (i) a 3 per mil stamp duty fee on the amount of the share capital, and (ii) a lump sum fee of LBP/1,000,000/, i.e.approximately USD/666/ before the Lebanese MoF within 5 days as of the date of signature of the bylaws.

(ii) Thereafter the founders must open a bank account in the name of the SAL (under formation) in order to deposit the amount of the share capital. The bank will then issue an attestation that the SAL's share capital has been subscribed to by the shareholders.

(iii) The shareholders must then hold the first general assembly (i.e.the constituent general assembly) to ratify the establishment of the SAL and appoint the members of the first board of directors. The said first board of directors will then convene and elect the Chairman-General Manager of the SAL.

(iv) Once all the above-mentioned documents are prepared and signed, and in order to register the SAL before the Commercial Registry, an application must be submitted to the Commercial Registry along with accompanying documents as set out in the law.

(v) Upon registration before the Commercial Registry (i.e.once the Commercial Registry reviews the submission mentioned above and confirms that all required documents have been duly prepared and submitted) and after the issuance of the certificate of incorporation, the SAL should inform the MoF of the commencement of its activities within two months as of the incorporation.

b) The Lebanese Holding Company

Holding companies are established under the form of SALs and are subject to the same laws and regulations governing the SALs, except to the extent of any contradiction with the specific regulations related to the Holding Company (mentioned above).

Regarding its establishment, the Holding Company is registered at the Commercial Registry in accordance with the provisions of the LCC as detailed above for the SAL. In addition, a special registry for holding companies will be kept at the Registry of the Court of First Instance, in which the Holding Company is registered and all documents and information related to it are recorded.

c) The Lebanese Offshore Company

Offshore companies are established under the form of SALs and are subject to the laws and regulations governing the SALs, except to the extent of any contradiction with the specific regulations related to the Offshore Company (mentioned above).

Regarding its establishment, the Offshore Company is registered at the Commercial Registry in accordance with the provisions of the LCC as detailed above for the SAL. A special Registry for offshore companies will be kept at the Registry of the Court of First Instance, in which the Offshore Company is registered and all documents and information related to it are recorded.

d) The Limited Liability company

The steps to incorporate an SARL can be summarized as follows:

(i) The founders of the SARL must sign the SARL's bylaws before a notary public and pay the stamp duty fees on the share capital (there are, in principle, two types of fees payable: a 3 per mil stamp duty fee on the capital, and an lump sum of LBP/750,000/, i.e.approximately USD/500/) before the MoF within 5 days as of the date of signature of the bylaws.

(ii) Having obtained a true copy of the bylaws duly notarized, the founders must open a bank account in the name of the SARL (under formation) in order to deposit the amount of the capital. Once the account is opened and the amount of the capital is deposited, the bank will issue an attestation that the capital has been subscribed to by the partners.

(iii) The partners must then hold the first general assembly (called the "constituent general assembly") to ratify the establishment of the SARL and appoint the manager(s).

(iv) Once all the above-mentioned documents are prepared and signed, and in order to register the SARL before the Commercial Registry, an application must be submitted to the Commercial Registry along with the necessary documents as set out on the law.

(v) Upon registration before the Commercial Registry (i.e.once the Commercial Registry reviews the submission mentioned above and confirms that all required documents have been duly prepared and submitted) and issuance of the certificate of incorporation, the SARL should inform the MoF of the commencement of its activities within two months as of the incorporation.

c. Routes and Requirements of Dissolution

The main causes of dissolution common to all commercial enterprises, not including bankruptcy which has a procedure of its own, are the following:
- The expiration of the duration for which the company had been formed;
- The normal end / accomplishment of the contemplated enterprise;
- The very object of the enterprise no longer exists.

In addition, the Court may always, upon partners' request, either declare the dissolution of the company on justified grounds as it may appreciate, or decide the exclusion of a partner who does not meet his partnership obligations.

a) The SAL

SALs are subject to the main following causes of dissolution, in addition to the common causes of dissolution abovementioned:
- The end of the predetermined duration or the completion of the enterprise for which they were contracted, or the impossibility to continue the said enterprise (common causes abovementioned);
- The will of the partners, expressed during an EGA;
- The loss of 3/4 of the company's capital. In that case, the directors must convene a general assembly that will decide whether the situation requires the premature dissolution of the company, a capital decrease or any other appropriate action;
- Every partner has the right to present the dissolution to the court if the directors have failed to convene a meeting, if the quorum has not been met or if the meeting has dismissed the dissolution.

The decision issued thereof, whether a resolution of the EGA a court order, must be published according to the requirements of the law.

b) The Lebanese Holding and Offshore Companies

Dissolution of Holding and Offshore companies is subject to the SALs laws and regulations.

c) The Limited liability Company

Limited liability companies are subject to the main following causes of dissolution, in addition to the common causes of dissolution abovementioned:
- The number of members of the company exceeds thirty, provided that the company has not been transformed into an SAL within two years;
- The capital of the company has fallen below the legal minimum of LBP /5,000,000/, provided that it has not been completed within one year or that the form of the company has not been changed;
- The loss of three quarters of the capital, noting that if the partners have not decided the dissolution, they must reduce the capital to the amount of the loss.

F. M&A Transactions from a General Lebanese Law Perspective

a. Forms, Modalities and Procedure of Mergers and Acquisitions Under Lebanese Law

(i) In practice, an acquisition usually entails:
- The purchase of another company's shares; and / or,
- The purchase of another company's assets;

Usually by virtue of an asset transfer or a share purchase agreement, as the case may be.

According to the provisions of the LCC, a distinction is made between mergers by annexation and mergers by combination, both mechanisms being analyzed and detailed in Lebanese legal writings.

From a general perspective, the merger is composed of the reunion of two or more companies into one company; noting that such reunion implies the dissolution of the joined companies that melt into a new unique legal person. Depending on whether a merger is by absorption or annexing or by combination, a merger may entail:
- The transfer of the constitutive elements / net assets of the dissolved / merged company to the absorbent or new merging company.
- The conversion of the shareholders of the merged company or companies into shareholders in the merging

company or new company emerging from the merger.

- The dissolution of the merged companies to the benefit of the merging company.

(ii) The LCC only addresses mergers of SALs; nonetheless, the rules applicable on the mergers of said companies also apply to other types of companies as long as it does not contradict with their nature.

(iii) The LCC provides that, for the merger procedure to be respected in the event of a combination of several companies; pursuant to relevant provisions of the LCC, the merger is decided by EGA. However, the board of directors – or the general manager – may represent the company in a Pre-Merger Agreement ("Preliminary Agreement") after having obtained an authorization to do so from the OGA; such an approval would suffice as long as it is limited to introducing the merger without deciding its execution.

The OGA may either ratify the Preliminary Agreement (given it would be submitted to the OGA) or reject the merger at the terms determined therein.

The decision of approving the final merger, in each concerned company, has to be taken at the level of the EGA.

(iv) The LCC also regulates the merger's procedure by expressly providing that when a new company is established by the merger of old companies, the legal rules for the establishment of companies will be observed, and publication procedures regarding the "prior to the term" dissolution of the old companies and the establishment of the new company must be carried out. Also, when any of the companies annexes another one, the annexed company must publish its "prior to the term" dissolution and the annexing company must be subject to the basic and formal rules related to capital increases.

(v) In case of merger by annexation / absorption, which would lead to the dissolution of the merged company and the increase of capital of the merging company, the following decisions need to be taken:

- The decision of approval on merger of the merged company must be issued in accordance with the quorum and majority determined for dissolution of the company prior to the expiration of its term; and,

- A decision by the EGA of the merging company for increasing the capital in consequence of the merger would be taken at the quorum determined for a constitutive assembly.

Publishing requirements must also be undertaken. The bylaws of the merging company are to be modified following the merger and should be published at the Commercial Registry.

(vi) In case the merger is by combination, the consequences would be the dissolution of both merged companies and the establishment of another new company. Therefore, the decision with approval on merger in both companies must be taken by the EGA at the quorum's and majority's requirements determined for the dissolution of the company prior to the expiration of its terms. On another hand, the new merged company will adhere to all rules related to establishment procedures (including the publishing requirement).

b. Characteristics and Implication of a Merger

a) Effects on Shareholders and / or Partners

The shareholders of the merged company receive, upon the merger, shares from the merging company or the new merging company created upon the merger of two companies, pro rata to the rights they had in the merged company.

b) Effects on the Creditors of the Concerned Companies

(i) Towards the creditors of the merged or absorbed company, the merger can be analyzed as a renewal or an assignment of debt by the merging or absorbed company to the new or absorbing company. As such, the merger's effect of assignment of debt by one debtor (i.e.merged company) to another (i.e.merging company) would not apply to the creditors of the merged company unless they approve it.

Furthermore, the said creditors are entitled by the law in case of mergers – in the case of SALs to a special guarantee / security which is the right to object / challenge the decision issued by the EGA of the merged company approving the merger before the competent courts within 3 months from the date of this decision's publishing.

By analogy, same procedure would in principle apply in case of merger among partnerships.

(ii) Creditors of the merging or absorbent company are not entitled to object the merger on the basis that it has increased the debts and obligations on this company, as they are in the position of regular creditors who have to incur the results of their debtor's behaviors that lead to increasing his debts, as long the law does not give them any priority right on the patrimony of the merging company or the right to provoke the independence of its patrimony from the merged company.

c) Effects on the Debtors of the Merged or Absorbed Companies

The rights of the merged or absorbed company are transferred to the merging or absorbent company, hence the debtors of the merged or absorbed become debtors to the merging or absorbent company; as such, the merging company can claim these rights from the debtors of the merged company.

d) Effects of the Merger Towards Third Parties

According to Lebanese jurisprudence, ongoing contracts between third parties and absorbed or merged company which do not take into consideration the "personal aspect" or "intuitus personae" of the party therein (such as purchase and transportation contracts), continue to have effect, and so confer to the merging company the rights resulting therefrom, and to bind the third party to the terms of the said contracts, unless there exist change of control provisions or other provisions which would expressly provide otherwise.

It is important to note that in addition of being subject to the relevant applicable provisions of the LCC, M&A transaction in some areas of practice, notably (i) in transactions regarding public companies (i.e.companies listed on a stock exchange); and (ii) in transactions regarding Lebanese banks, are also governed by some special laws and regulations.

c. M&A Transactions Regarding Public Companies (i.e.Companies Listed on a Stock Exchange)

(i) In addition to the relevant applicable provisions of the LCC, M&A transactions regarding listed companies are also subject to Decree 7667 of 1995 regarding the implementation of the Beirut Stock Exchange's ("BSE") bylaws; and the applicable regulations of the CMA that was established in 2011.

(ii) In addition to all forms, modalities and procedures mentioned here above, and applicable, from a general law perspective to M&A transactions, an acquisition of a publicly listed company is usually structured as a tender offer by the bidder; noting that according to Decree 7667 issued on 16 December 1995 regarding the Implementation of the by-laws of the BSE any investor or group of investors wishing to own more than 10% of the voting rights in a company quoted in the official or secondary market, or wishing to acquire the absolute or qualified[①] majority in this company, should present a draft for a tender public offer or bartering via a financial broker.

(iii) Furthermore, in the context of an M&A transaction, a company listed in Lebanon will be required to make announcements on the Lebanese Stock Exchange (in the current time there is only one Lebanese Stock exchange and that is the BSE) upon signing of the merger agreement; upon convening a shareholder approval; and on closing.

(iv) Also, Law 161 of 2011, regulating the Capital Markets in Lebanon ("Law 161") provides notably that any legal entity that acquires directly or indirectly, as a result of any type of operation, a share in the issuing entity or public company equal to or exceeding five percent (5%) of the shares with a voting right in the said company or in the issuing entity has to disclose to the CMA prior from the execution of the operation which led to such percentage of ownership. The legal entity will also specify the issuing entity and whether the latter's shares are listed on the BSE before submitting a report to the BSE. The legal entity must also disclose, all purchase operations that result in reaching or exceeding the five percent (5%) limit.

(v) On another hand, any offer for a company listed on the BSE has to be submitted to the Committee of the BSE for approval.

(vi) All companies listed on the BSE are SALs. It should be noted that when the shares of an SAL are held by the same investor continually for two years, the voting rights attaching to those shares will automatically double under Lebanese law; this is a personal right attributable to the holder of the shares. When the investor's voting rights double, if, as a result, a disclosure requirement is triggered (either under the Law 161 Regime or the BSE Regime) then notifications will be required to be made in the usual manner.

d. M&A Transactions Regarding Lebanese Banks

i) The Central Council of the BDL sets the regulations concerning the Lebanese banks' M&A and the purchases of shares in Lebanese banks. It supervises all takeovers in the banking and financial services sector, and ensures that all regulated entities comply with applicable laws and regulations. M&A of Lebanese banks are mainly regulated by the CMC; the provisions of Law no.192 of 1993 ("Banking Merger Law"); Law no.308 of 2001 organizing the issuance and trade of stocks and bonds and acquisition of real estate by banks ("Law 308").

(ii) The Banking Merger Law applies to a transferring bank selling all of its assets, rights, liabilities and obligations to a transferee bank that will purchase the assets and rights and assumes all liabilities and obligations of the transferring bank.

The Banking Merger Law stipulates that it will apply to a bank that buys all the assets and rights and bears all the liabilities and obligations of another bank that wishes to liquidate its operations and strike off its name from the list of banks; hence the Banking Merger Law has treated such acquisition transaction as a merger.

---

① An absolute majority means 50% plus one share, and a prescribed majority means such other majority as may be prescribed as applying to the company, which may vary on a case by case basis, noting that these definitions are not expressly provided for by law and are the generally accepted definitions of such terms.

(iii) According to the provisions of the Banking Merger law, a merger operation between two banks or more is subject to the approval of the Central Council of the BDL which has all discretionary powers to approve or reject any takeover within the banking and financial services sector. A detailed procedure must be complied with.

Within one month from the Central Council's final decision approving the merger, the merging bank must publish in the Official Gazette, and in two local newspapers at least, a summary of the merger decisions taken by the EGA of the concerned banks, together with the BDL Central Council's final decision.

(iv) Pursuant to the relevant provisions of Law 308, subscribing to and trading in Lebanese banks' shares are subject to prior approval by the Central Council of the BDL:

- If this results in the subscriber or the assignee acquiring, directly or through a fiduciary contract, more than 5% (five percent) of the total shares of the bank or of the voting rights relating to such shares, whichever is higher.
- When, upon assignment of the shares, the assignee holds 5% (five percent) or more of the total shares of the bank or of the voting rights relating to such shares, whichever is higher.
- Regardless of the number of assigned shares, when the assignor or the assignee is a member or member-elect of the bank's board of directors.

a) Forms, Modalities and Procedures of M&A Transactions Regarding Lebanese Banks

The following procedure must be followed for BDL approval:

(i) the board of directors and, if required, the shareholders of each bank would approve the transaction;

(ii) the merger agreement would be executed by the parties;

(iii) the banks would apply to the BDL for its provisional approval for the transaction;

(iv) the provisional decision of the Central Council of the BDL would be issued and, if provisionally approving the merger, will "specify the conditions, deadlines and guarantees required for its final decision";

(v) any conditions or guarantees requested by the BDL would, if acceptable to the buyer, then be met to the satisfaction of the BDL and, if necessary, shareholder (or further shareholder) approval would be obtained; and

(vi) following satisfaction of such conditions and guarantees (if any), the banks would apply to the BDL for its final approval of the merger, including with such request evidence of the satisfaction of the relevant conditions / guarantees and providing minutes of the shareholder approvals.

b) Characteristics and implication of a merger in the banking sector

(i) As a result, the merged bank would be removed from the list of banks as published by the BDL and would apply for the corporate registration of its corporation to be liquidated at the corporate registry.

(ii) Overall, the Banking Merger Law provides a number of benefits, including inter alia, :

- The automatic transfer of assets and liabilities between the banks by operation of law and, in principle, without the need to obtain counterparty consent (i.e.application to the entirety of the business);
- Certain tax exemptions with respect to both banks;
- Tax exemptions with respect to the transaction;
- Loan incentives may be granted by the BDL Central Council to the transferee bank in certain circumstances.

(iii) Furthermore, the Banking Merger Law provides notably that the merging bank will immediately replace by law the merged bank(s) in all of its (their) rights and obligations, upon the issuance of a final decision by the Central Council of the BDL.

e. M&A Transactions Regarding Specialized Sectors

Other sectors in Lebanon may also be protected sectors, such as insurance and media for example. These sectors are also governed by Lebanese special rules and regulations.

Depending on the sectors, regulatory approvals may be required from the relevant supervisory authorities or Ministries.

G. Competition Regulation

a. Department Supervising Competition Regulation

The MoET is the main governmental body supervising and regulating trade in Lebanon; it is concerned with economic and commercial affairs in accordance with the tasks entrusted to it by virtue of Decree No.6821 of December 28, 1973 (specifying the duties and functions of the MoET). The MOET is also notably concerned with anti-monopoly in general and with taking measures that provide the broadest commercial competition for the general economic interest.

A department to control high prices and monopoly was established in 1942 by virtue of under Decree No.1523 dated 18 November 1942, (today in the MoET), and its main mission is to search and investigate all crimes related to trade and prices in general.

b. Brief Introduction of Competition Law and Measures Regulating Competition

(i) Lebanon does not currently have any specific anti-competition or anti-trust laws. A draft law on competition, aiming to implement the provisions of the Euro-Mediterranean Agreement (to which Lebanon adhered in 2006) by creating a Free Trade Area in Lebanon, will have to be prepared within 12 years as of its entry into force. The draft law was sent to the Council of Ministers in 2007 and was approved by the Council of Ministers, and then transmitted to the Parliament by decree. However, since then, the draft was neither promulgated nor sent for further studies to the competent Parliamentary Commissions.

(ii) However, there are several laws that deal with the competition issues in Lebanon; by way of example only we have set out the following:

- Section IV of Decree Law No.73 of September 9, 1983 regarding the possession and trade of merchandise, products and crops" (as amended) (the "DL no.73") contains provisions relating to cartels, monopolies and unfair competition.

- Decision 2358 dated 17 January 1924 ("Decision 2358") regarding the rights of industrial and commercial property, provides notably that will be considered as unfair competition any violation of Decision 2358 by which any one of the requirements for the application of the provisions of Section 6 of Decision 2358 is not applied (such Section 6 includes by way of example only trademark and brand names, industrial designs); and any act subject to the free jurisdiction of courts and determined to be unfair competition. Acts of unfair competition may only be the subject of a lawsuit requesting cessation of competition or damaging act, and claim for damages, except where such acts are considered violations subject to penalties under criminal codes or under the provisions of Decision 2358.

- According to relevant provisions of the LOC any action by a person that results in unlawful harm to others will be liable for full compensation, if he / she is found guilty of discrimination. This general provision could be relied upon by a party alleging acts of unfair competition or monopoly.

- The Lebanese Criminal Code provides notably that any person who, by means of fraud or false allegations, or suggesting bad faith as to the transfer of the clients of others, will be punished on the basis of a complaint by the victim, of a fine.

- In addition to the above, certain specific laws address competition in specific contexts and sectors; these include: the Privatization Law No.228 of May 2000, which establishes the Investment Development Authority of Lebanon and accorded to highest priority of information technology projects; Law No.360 dated 13 August 2001 related to promoting investments in Lebanon; Consumer Protection Law No.659 dated 4 February 2006.

H. Tax

a. Tax Regime and Rules

In Lebanon, there are both national and municipal taxes that may only be levied by the Lebanese Parliament. On one hand the national taxes are collected by the Tax Administration which is a Directorate of the MoF by virtue of Decree-Law number 2868, dated 16 December 1959, and on the other, municipal taxes are collected by the municipalities themselves.

Taxes may be levied either directly or indirectly. Direct taxes include the income tax which is governed by Decree-Law number 144 dated 12 June 1959 and its amendments (the "Income Tax Law"). The Income Tax Law is divided into three chapters comprising the taxes on (i) the gains from industrial, commercial and non-commercial professions (the "Tax on Business Profits"), (ii) the salaries, wages and benefits, and (iii) the income derived from movable capital. Consequently, each type of income of a taxable person is to be calculated according to the chapter of the Income Tax Law under which it falls.

a) The Tax on Business Profits

Except for certain exemptions including most notably public entities and non-governmental organizations, this tax is due, in principle, by all physical and legal persons residing within the Lebanese territory or abroad, on their taxable profit made in Lebanon.

The taxable profit is the sum of the taxpayer's returns that may be subject to the tax after the deduction of all expenses and obligations required for engaging in the commerce, the industry, or in a profession. In accordance with the legal status of the entity, and / or its size, the income tax is calculated on a real profit, lump-sum profit or deemed / estimated profit basis. The real profit method consists of adjusting the accounting profit in order to determine an income measure based on tax rules, from which the losses of prior years are deducted in order to determine the taxable income.

Under the lump-sum method, the MoF determines annually a percentage of sales depending on the sales figures declared by the taxable person in order to represent the taxable income.

Finally, under the deemed / estimated profit method, the MoF determines the taxable income directly through a field audit of the taxpayer.

Concerning the Tax on Business Profits made by non-residents, in accordance with of the relevant applicable provisions of the Income Tax Law, physical or legal persons that earn business income in Lebanon, but do not reside nor have a registered place of business therein, are subject to a withholding tax on the basis of the deemed profit of the income that they receive from Lebanon at an effective tax rate of 7.5% on the income derived from services and 2.25% if derived from the supply of goods.

b) The Tax on Salaries, Wages and Benefits

This tax is withheld and paid by the employer on behalf of his employee. However, taxable people who are subject to the Tax on Business Profits, and / or that have been employed by more than one employer during the year, must file their own tax returns.

The taxable income is determined through the deduction of eligible expenses and family abatements from the gross income made during the year.

c) The Tax on Income Derived from Movable Capital

An income tax of 10% is applicable on the revenues, income and interest generated on moveable capitals, regardless of their denomination or the nationality of the company that generated them or the domicile of the beneficiary of the revenues, when they have occurred in Lebanon or are due to a Lebanese resident. Certain exemptions to this tax are provided for in the Income Tax Law, including most notably interest on current bank accounts and on treasury bills of the Lebanese government. The tax on income derived from movable capital is to be withheld by the paying entity which is required to file a tax form in this respect.

b. Main Categories and Rates of Tax

The main categories of taxes in Lebanon include notably the income tax which may be divided into three categories encompassing the corporate tax on profits, the tax on wages, and the taxes on income made from movable capital.

- Subject to certain exemptions, the corporate tax on profits amounts to 17% for corporations and ranges progressively between 4 and 21% for individuals.
- The tax on wages generally ranges between 2 and 20%. Finally the taxes on income made from movable capital is equal to 7%.
- Subject to certain exemptions, the taxes paid as contributions to the social security fund amount in general to 21.5% for employers and 2% for employees.
- Properties are subject to the property tax which ranges between 0 to 14% depending on the profit made from rent.
- With regard to stamp duty, a stamp duty fee may be levied in various amounts depending on the procedure and document on which the stamp duty fee needs to be levied. In this respect a fixed stamp duty of LBP /5,000/ as well as a proportionate stamp duty fee of 4 per mil (0.4%) of the amount of the contract or agreement or deed, is notably due as of the moment the contract, agreement or deed is established or signed in Lebanon; or if it is signed or established outside of Lebanon as of the moment it is used in Lebanon.
- Value Added Tax (VAT) of 11% is applicable to most transactions involving goods and services.
- Lebanon also provides for sets of taxes and exemptions specific to legal entities depending on the said legal entity's type and legal nature.

c. Tax Declaration and Preference

a) Tax Declaration

Tax declarations in Lebanon are due as follows:

i.Taxes on Business Profits	
Individuals	
-Real profit method	March 31st
-Lump-sum profit method	January 31st
-Estimated profit method	Are not require to file tax declarations
Legal persons	May 31st

ii. Taxes on Salaries Wages and Benefits	
Individuals	
-Estimated profit method	January 31st
-Multiple income sources	March 31st
Legal entities	May 31st
Taxable persons exempt from the taxes on Business Profits	January 31st
iii. Taxes on Income Derived from Movable Capital	
All taxable persons	End of the month following that when a payment is due or announced

b) Tax Preferences
(i) Exemptions from the Tax on Business Profits
Amongst certain entities that are exempted from the tax on business profits, we have listed the following main ones:
- Educational institutions.
- Mental hospitals and tuberculosis clinics.
- Consumer cooperatives, syndicates, agricultural cooperatives, if not of a commercial nature.
- Agricultural investors under certain conditions.
- Public utilities that do not compete with private institutions.
- Touristic institutions of an artisanal nature.
(ii) Exemptions from the tax on salaries, wages and benefits
Amongst other exemptions, are exempt from the tax on salaries, wages and benefits:
- The allocations given to clergy men for the execution of religious rites.
- The salaries, and indemnities earned by foreign country's ambassadors, diplomatic representatives, consuls, and consular representatives, and foreign nationals in their employ, on the condition of reciprocity.
- The salaries, indemnities and wages earned by military men no matter their rank if belonging to allied countries.
- Wages of agricultural workers.
- Severance indemnities paid in accordance with applicable laws in Lebanon.
- Family indemnities paid in accordance with the applicable laws and regulations.
(iii) Exemptions from the tax on income derived from movable capital
Among other exemptions, are exempt from the tax on income derived from movable capital:
- The amounts paid in order to repay creditors and shareholders, if they are not taken from the profits, losses and reserves account.
- Interest and proceeds of all current accounts open at banks.
- Bond revenues on the Lebanese treasury.
(iv) Exemption from the value added tax
- Concerning the exempted activities
Are exempted from the value added tax transactions carried out within the Lebanese territory which relate to any of, inter alia, the following activities:
• Services offered by medical doctors or persons performing a medical activity.
• Hospital fees.
• Education.
• Employers and related services.
• Banking and financial services.
• Collective transport of persons, including transport by taxicabs.
• Betting, lotteries and other forms of gambling.
• Sale of built properties.
• Residential letting of built properties.
• Farmer's activities concerning the supply of their agricultural production.
- Concerning the exempted goods
Are exempted from the value added tax, inter alia, the following goods:

- Certain food items;
- Postal and fiscal stamps and paper money;
- Gas for household consumption (butane);
- Seeds, fertilizers, feeds and agricultural pesticides;
- Agricultural machinery;
- Medicines, drugs and pharmaceutical products and medical tools, installations and equipment;
- Precious and semi-precious stones, precious and semi-precious stones destined for mounting or renewed, pearls, diamonds, gold, silver and other precious metals.
- Negotiable money in paper or coins.

Also, Lebanon has concluded a multitude of treaties which, for the encouragement of foreign investments, have provided for certain tax related exemptions or protections from double taxation, an example of such a treaty being the bilateral treaty between the People's Republic of China and the Lebanese Republic of 1997. Furthermore, some economic sectors in Lebanon benefit from specific tax exemptions not addressed herein.

I. Securities

a. Brief Introduction of Securities-related Laws and Regulations

The banking and financial sector in Lebanon is monitored by the BDL and the CMA. Hence, all banking and financial activities as well as transactions related to financial instruments and products and to securities are regulated by the BDL's and / or the CMA's regulations, as the case may be.

We have only addressed herein the role of the CMA, given that it is, save a few exceptions, the main competent regulatory body governing trading in securities. It is an independent authority established by virtue of Law 161.

The CMA's main purpose is the regulation and supervision of the Lebanese capital markets, ensuring the safe investment in financial instruments and encouraging the financial markets in Lebanon.

The CMA has issued several decisions, regarding notably: (i) the disclosure policies that should be adopted by certain companies, (ii) crowd funding regulations, and (iii) the licensing and authorization requirements notably regarding collective investment funds and collective Islamic investment funds.

Moreover, it has recently issued several implementation regulations between 10 November 2016 and 7 August 2017, notably:

- Series 2000 regarding licensing and registration which aims to regulate the conduct of trading in the securities markets. It notably establishes the categories of registered functions required to carry on securities business in Lebanon and identifies applicable exemptions to applicable licensing requirements.

- Series 3000 regarding business conduct regulation which mainly (i) establishes the rules and code of conduct that an approved institution must comply with in carrying out securities business and dealing with clients, and (ii) defines the policies, procedures, systems and controls that an approved institution must establish, implement and keep up to date.

- Series 4000 regarding market conduct regulation which applies to trading in, and conduct related to dealing in, traded securities. The main purpose of Series 4000 is to: (i) regulate conduct in the securities markets, (ii) set out the details of the prohibitions on insider trading and market manipulation, and (iii) set out the details of approved institutions' obligations in carrying out transactions in the market.

- Series 6000 regarding regulations on offers of securities aims at outlining the requirements related to offers of securities in Lebanon and determining the types of offers that are exempted from the more stringent requirements applicable on public offers.

With respect to the marketing and distribution of financial products on the Lebanese market, the CMA is in principle, flexible and open to the distribution of sophisticated and innovative financial products, instruments and securities in Lebanon, provided that this is done in compliance with its regulatory requirements and applicable laws and regulations.

b. Supervision and Regulation of Securities Market

(i) The CMA is the main competent regulatory body supervising and governing the securities market.

The management of the CMA is undertaken by a board presided by the governor of the BDL. The main prerogatives of the board of the CMA are the encouragement and protection of investments, as well as the implementation of general regulations for the financial markets. The board of the CMA notably grants (i) licenses for the incorporation of collective investment schemes and financial intermediation institutions, and (ii) prior-authorization for the marketing and distribution of financial products on the Lebanon market.

Law 161 also provides for the creation of a special capital markets court that settles any dispute or conflict arising between investors and promoters of financial instruments. This court however has not been established to date.

(ii) Lebanon also has a formal market. On 15 September 2017, a decree no.1404 was issued in compliance with provisions of Law 161 to dissolve the previous exchange and replace it with the Beirut Stock Exchange SAL ("BSE SAL"), an SAL in all its rights, obligations and activities. The establishment of this BSE SAL will be completed and its replacement to the BSE will be enforced upon the fulfillment of certain procedures mentioned in decree 1404.

The object of the BSE SAL covers mainly (i) managing, regulating, developing, trading and pricing the markets related to financial rights and financial instruments and raw materials and ferrous metals; (ii) protecting the interests of investors trading in the BSE; (iii) listing, trading and pricing the abovementioned financial instruments; (iv) regulating and supervising the work of companies listed in the BSE; and (v) developing electronic and non-electronic trading and pricing systems for financial instruments listed on the BSE.

c. Requirements for Engagement in Securities Trading for Foreign Enterprises

Law 161 expressly allows non-Lebanese companies and entities to undertake operations related to securities in Lebanon in accordance with its provisions and the provisions of the relevant special regulations.

According to Lebanese laws and regulations, in order to carry on securities business in Lebanon, any person must be an approved institution licensed by the CMA (an "Approved Institution"), unless such person is excluded from the requirement to be licensed under notably CMA Series 2000 and the applicable exemptions, noting that in very brief there are a number of tolerated practices and expressly regulated exemptions that may apply if certain conditions are met; and in principle, a person must not carry on, or hold itself out as carrying on, securities business prior to obtaining approval for a license from the CMA.

To apply for a license (to become an Approved Institution) an applicant must be established in Lebanon as:

- a bank, a financial institution or a financial intermediation company duly registered with the CMA or the BDL,
- a branch of a foreign financial entity whose parent company is engaged in securities business and is licensed by a competent authority in a recognized jurisdiction.

Furthermore, to apply for a license, an applicant must be engaged solely in securities business, or in the case of a company licensed by the BDL, solely in business covered by that license. His head office must be in Lebanon.

The CMA has adopted a very restrictive approach regarding foreign entities that are undertaking financial transactions with Lebanese counterparties, whether these entities are banks or financial institutions or brokerage institutions or any other entities. Accordingly, CMA regulations provide that a person must not make or communicate any securities advertisement[1] to a person in Lebanon unless the first person is an Approved Institution, and it considers that a securities advertisement is made or communicated to a person in Lebanon if it is directed to persons in Lebanon.

BDL issued on 8 November 2016 an intermediary decision amended on 21/12/2017 restricting carrying on operation on all financial instruments and products to and by specialized banks and financial intermediary institutions to be effective as of 30/6/2018.

J. Preference and Protection of Investment

a. The Structure of Preference Policies

There are no preference policies per se in Lebanon.

That being said, and from a nationalization preference perspective, according to decision number 19/1, rendered on February 2, 2013 by the Minister of Labor, certain activities can only be undertaken by Lebanese nationals, notably banking, insurance and administrative activities of any kind and especially occupying the positions of director, vice-director, chief of staff, treasurer, accountant, secretary, archivist, craftsman, IT, trade delegate, marketing delegate, supervisor, warehouse keeper, seller, mechanics and maintenance, guardian and the like, and in general all the activities and professions that can be occupied by Lebanese persons having the required expertise and skills.

However, Lebanon is committed to encouraging foreign investments notably by signing a certain number of agreements with various key nations for the promotion and protection of investments as well as conventions for the avoidance of double taxation and the prevention of fiscal evasion which enhance the collaboration on investments between the signatories, including but not limited to China, Italy, Kuwait, Russia.

---

[1] According to the interpretation of CMA, a securities advertisement is made or communicated to a person in Lebanon if it is directed to persons in Lebanon. A securities advertisement means any form of verbal, electronic, broadcast or written communication made in the course of business for the purpose of inviting or inducing a person to engage in securities activity.

In this respect, and by way of example only, law number 614 was enacted by the Lebanese Parliament on 28 February 1997, by virtue of which the Lebanese government granted the authorization to ratify the convention on the promotion and protection of mutual investments signed between the governments of Lebanon and China (the "Contracting Parties") in Beijing on 13 June 1996 (the "Convention").

b. Support for Specific Industries and Regions

Investment in various sectors and industries is constantly promoted throughout the territory of Lebanon, whether in the fields of industry, agriculture and agriculture industry, tourism, information, communication, technology, media or in any other sectors that the council of minister will determine by virtue of a decree issued upon the request of the Prime Minister.

Furthermore, the real estate as well as the technology fields are always highly promoted in Lebanon.

c. Special Economic Areas

Decree 4461 dated 15 December 2000 (the "Customs Law"), provides inter alia that it will be allowed to establish free zones and duty-free stores within the customs territory, which will not be subject to the customs regime but to specific provisions set forth under the Custom Law.

In this respect, the Lebanese government operates three free trade zones, which are located at the port of Beirut, port of Tripoli, and Selaata.

The Customs Law, provides that free trade zones and free industrial zones may be established by allocating areas of the ports and the internal spaces and consider them to be outside the Customs territory.

Subject to the prohibition on certain types of goods provided for in the Customs Law, all types of goods will be admitted into free zones, whether of local or foreign origin, without being subject upon entry, storage, export and re-export, to customs duties and other taxes and charges other than those imposed for the benefit of the party operating the free zone. Goods will also not be subject to any administrative restrictions when transferred other than to the Customs territory.

In addition to all of the above, the BDD hosts foreign ICT companies and provide them with art facilities, including access to advanced IT services and fiber optics infrastructure at reduced rates.

d. Investment Protection

On a preliminary note, the ownership right in Lebanon is a constitutional right provided in the Lebanese Constitution of 1926. In this respect, Article 15 of the Constitution provides that the property is under the protection of the law and that no one may be deprived of his property except for reasons of public utility, in the cases established by law, and with just and prior compensation.

Lebanon has signed a certain number of agreements for the Promotion and Protection of Investments as well as conventions for the Avoidance of Double Taxation and the Prevention of Fiscal Evasion on Taxes from Income and Capital with many key nations, which enhance the collaboration on investments and fiscal level between the signatories.

Furthermore, by way of example, Lebanon signed the Euro-Mediterranean Agreement (which entered into force on 1 April 2006) establishing an association between the European Community and its Member States, on one hand, and the Republic of Lebanon, on the other. This Agreement establishes, inter alia, the conditions for the gradual liberalization of trade in goods, services and capital and promotes the trade and the expansion of harmonious economic and social relations between Lebanon and the member states of the European Community.

In addition, Lebanon signed the Free Trade Agreement with the EFTA States (being Iceland, Liechtenstein, Norway and Switzerland), which main objective is to establish a free trade area with a view to spurring economic activities in their territories, thereby raising standards of living and improving employment conditions and contributing to Euro-Mediterranean economic integration.

Lebanon is also an observer to the World Trade Organization with an objective to become a member thereof.

III. Trade

A. Department Supervising Trade

The MoET is the main governmental body regulating trade in Lebanon; it is concerned with economic and commercial affairs , notably with: (i) working with other ministries on the development of economic facilities and national wealth in the country; (ii) following the economic developments and taking the necessary measures to benefit from them in the country's commercial, supply and consumption conditions; (iii) anti-monopoly and taking measures that provide the broadest commercial competition for the general economic interest; (iv) taking care of and developing trade and contributing to the revitalization of the services sector; (v) the development of economic studies, particularly those related to foreign trade, trade balance and the dissemination of statistics related thereto; and (vi) granting licenses for the import and export of goods.

B. Brief Introduction of Trade Laws and Regulations

Below are only a few examples of trade laws and regulations in Lebanon:

(i) Lebanon has adopted trade liberalization policies as part of its comprehensive economic strategy to integrate Lebanon further into the global economy. It has signed trade agreements with Arab countries and the European Union, including but not limited to the Euro- Mediterranean Partnership Initiative[1], and the Free Trade Agreement with the European Free Trade Association[2]. Lebanon is also a member of the Greater Arab Free Trade Area (GAFTA)[3], the Trade and Investment Framework Agreement (TIFA)[4], the Arab League Investment Agreement[5], and the Organization of Islamic Conference Investment Agreement[6].

(ii) Decree Law No.34 of August 5, 1967 (The "DL 34")) regarding commercial agency and representations, is considered of public policy, and therefore, where applicable, such decree will be of mandatory application, superseding any agreement to the contrary between the parties. DL 34 defined the commercial representative as either:

- The mandated person who through his usual and independent profession and without being bound by a contract for the rent of services, undertakes negotiations to conclude sales and purchase, or lease or provide services transactions as the case may be, in the name of producers or traders and for the latter's account; or,

- The trader who sells in his name and for his own account what he has bought by virtue of a contract granting him / her the capacity of exclusive representative or distributor.

(iii) Furthermore, in order to ensure the safety and quality of goods and products that are being sold, traded and distributed on the Lebanese market, the Consumer Protection Law number 659 was enacted on February 4, 2005 (the "Consumer Protection Law"). Its main purpose, in addition to regulating trading activities within the Lebanese market, is to maintain a modern consumer protection framework in Lebanon that safeguards consumer's interest and to ensure that a safe, fair and equitable environment exists for consumers. In brief, the Consumer Protection Law mainly aims to outline the general rules concerning the protection of consumers and the safety and quality of goods and services, assert consumer rights and guarantee the transparency of economic transactions in which the consumer may engage, and protect consumers from fraud and misleading advertisements and prevent their exploitation.

(iv) Law No 44 of November 24, 2015 related to Fighting Money Laundering and Terrorism Financing prohibits notably illicit arms trafficking, insider trading, corruption, including but not limited to trading in influence.

(v) Pursuant to Law No.75 dated October 27, 2016, related to cancelling bearer shares and promissory notes, SALs are forbidden from issuing bearer shares; and companies who already have bearer shares are compelled to replace them with nominal shares.

(vi) In principle, there are no general laws that restrict or regulate the conversion, transfer or transit of currency undertaken by investors in Lebanon to the exception of the aforementioned restriction on transactions involving Israeli parties or currency.

However, pursuant to Law No.42 dated 24 November 2015 on declaring the cross-border transportation of

---

[1] Entered into force in Lebanon as of April 1st, 2006 according to the European Commission official Website and published in the EU's official Journal No.L 143 of 30.5.2006.From Europa's website, available at: http://ec.europa.eu/trade/policy/countries-and-regions/regions/euro-mediterranean-partnership/.
[2] Entered into force in Lebanon as of January 1st 2007 according to the United Nations Conference on Trade and Development official website, available at:http://investmentpolicyhub.unctad.org/IIA/CountryOtherIias/116#iiaInnerMenu.
[3] Entered into force in Lebanon January 1st, 1998, according to the Ministry of Economy and Trade official website, available at:http://economy.gov.lb/en/what-we-provide/trade/foreign-trade-department/international-agreements/gafta/.
[4] According to the Office of United States Trade Representative official Website and the United Nations Conference on Trade and Development official website, available at:https://ustr.gov/trade-agreements/trade-investment-framework-agreements .
[5] Entered into force in Lebanon September 7, 1981, according to the United Nations Conference on Trade and Development official website, available at:http://investmentpolicyhub.unctad.org/IIA/treaty/3087 .
[6] Entered into force in Lebanon February 1988, according to according to the United Nations Conference on Trade and Development official website, available at: http://investmentpolicyhub.unctad.org/IIA/treaty/3092 .

money ("Law 42/2015"), in principle, any person, when transporting physically currency or negotiable instruments[1] across the border, in or out, by mean of carrying it in person or in luggage, or by any other means, or by containerizing it in cargo or any other means of shipping, or through the post, must submit a written declaration thereon to the customs authorities, whenever their value exceeds the amount of USD /15 000/ or its equivalent in other currencies, by filling out a form that includes the complete and requested information.

(vii) Moreover the MoET's resolution No.277/1 issued on June 15, 1972, reinstated in 2010 by resolution 196/1, and related to the determination of the percentages of commercial profits, regulates the maximum amount of profits that traders (for example wholesalers and retailers) can make from certain goods and commodities such as grains, oils, sugar, salt, vegetables and fruits.

(viii) On a final note, the Lebanese legislation is also enriched by the provisions of the Lebanese Code of Maritime Commerce, which expands the scope of trading activities in the territory and ensures an economic dimension in global sea trade.

(ix) In addition to all the above, we also refer you to the "Competition regulations" section which summarizes competitions laws in Lebanon and measures regulating competition.

C. Trade Management

Lebanon, having maintained a generally non-interventionist position towards private investment in order to encourage foreign investment[2], has traditionally been a country with a free and open trade regime emphasized by the improved market access through regional or international, bilateral or multilateral trade agreements, noting that within its efforts towards trade liberalization, Lebanon has focused on the European Union (EU), the World Trade Organization (WTO), and the Arab world. Thus, the freedom of exchange in Lebanon allows foreign investors to import and export capital freely subject to the restrictions set out in laws and regulations related to trade, and notably to the provisions of the Boycott Law and of the Custom Law.

Lebanon also manages trade relationships through Euro-Mediterranean Partnership agreement (signed by Lebanon in 2002 and entered into force in April 2006)[3] mainly aiming to providing for reciprocal free trade on the majority of industrial goods and liberalizing trade on a large basket of agricultural goods; and notably by establishing a free trade area for the Mediterranean region.

The free trade agreements signed by Lebanon, play a major role in attracting foreign trade investments and encouraging an open trade environment, notably the Greater Arab Free Trade Agreement signed in 1997 and brought into force in 1998[4], which gradually replaced the bilateral FTAs signed with Arab countries.

Lebanon launched free trade agreement negotiations with MERCOSUR countries in 2016[5], and has signed bilateral investment agreements[6] with several countries including but not limited to Qatar in 2010, Netherlands in 2004, Austria in 2002, France, Germany and the United Kingdom in 1999, Canada, Russia and China in 1997.

D. The Inspection and Quarantine of Import and Export Commodities

(i) Trade barriers may affect some of the imported and exported goods by either prohibiting the importation or exportation of merchandise, or restricting such activities. The Lebanese Custom Law provides inter alia that restricted merchandise may only be imported or exported subject to a permit, license, certificate, prior approval or

---

[1] Law 42/2015 defines Currency/Negotiable Instruments as follows:- Banknotes and coins in circulation, whether in Lebanese pound or any other currency.- Commercial papers, securities, means of payment and other types of negotiable movable assets, in case they are not made out or endorsed to the benefit, or to the order of a designated payee (drawing bonds, promissory notes, checks, payment orders, bearer shares, prepaid cards, etc.).

[2] Please refer to the section titled "Market Access" and "Preference and Protection of Investment".

[3] Entered into force in Lebanon as of April 1st, 2006 according to the to the European Commission official website and published in the EU's official Journal No.L 143 of 30.5.2006, available at: http://ec.europa.eu/trade/policy/countries-and-regions/regions/euro-mediterranean-partnership/.

[4] Entered into force in Lebanon January 1st, 1998, according to the Ministry of Economy and Trade official website, available at:http://economy.gov.lb/en/what-we-provide/trade/foreign-trade-department/international-agreements/gafta/.

[5] According to Brazilian Ministry of Foreign Affairs' official website, available at: http://www.itamaraty.gov.br/images/documents/Documentos/Fact_Sheet_Mercosur_English.pdf.

[6] According to the Lebanese Ministry of Economy and Trade official Website, the European Commission official Website; and the Investment Development Authority of Lebanon's official website, noting that these agreements were ratified and brought into force, respectively available at:

http://economy.gov.lb/en/what-we-provide/trade/foreign-trade-department/international-agreements/bilatera/;

http://investmentpolicyhub.unctad.org/IIA/CountryBits/116#iiaInnerMenu;

http://investinlebanon.gov.lb/Content/uploads/SideBlock/161219112515166~Investment%20Protection%20Agreements.pdf.

visa issued by a relevant authorities.

(ii) Prohibited imports that are strictly provided in laws, regulations, and decisions of relevant authorities or by virtue of the international agreements to which Lebanon is a party or a member include notably illegal drugs, weapons, explosives and ammunition, archaeological pieces, counterfeit money and goods, goods manufactured in or originating from Israel, and other products, noting that all goods subject to import and export prohibitions could be also prohibited from transiting Lebanon. It is to be noted that monopolized and restricted goods must be treated similarly to prohibited goods upon import and export.

(iii) Also, certain goods may be subject to a special temporary permit and should be re-exported or stored in the free zone or a public warehouse at the end of the authorized period of temporary entry status. Such goods include equipment and machinery used in public works, archeology, cinema, and journalism; items intended or used for maintenance and repair; items temporarily imported for display or use in public or private exhibitions, seasonal fairs, forums, theaters, artistic shows, and playgrounds; and, jewelry and ornaments intended for display in public exhibitions.

(iv) Lebanon is not subject to specific export controls or special sanctions in this respect; noting that in principle, all exports require a license.

(v) According to the provisions of the Custom Law, any physical or legal person that intends to import to or export from Lebanon, any goods, items or things, of any type whatsoever should mandatorily declare them before the competent customs office of import or export, and pay customs duties.

(vi) On a related note, food shipments are also inspected by the MoET to ensure compliance with labelling requirements and regulations set out in the Consumer Protection Law. Said law sets on professionals.[1]

(vii) Attached to the Ministry of Industry, the Lebanese Standards Institution (LIBNOR) is the only authority in Lebanon in charge with issuing, publishing, and amending Lebanese standards by setting the dimensions, conventions, symbols, and the definition of products quality, as well as granting the Lebanese Conformity Mark NL proving the compliance of products to Lebanese standards.

E. Customs Management

Lebanese Customs Administration is the government authority in Lebanon responsible for collecting custom duties and controlling the flow of goods in and out of the country. It operates under the MoF, and works together with the General Security, which operates under the Ministry of Interior and Municipalities.

Lebanon follows the harmonized system for its tariff regime.

Customs have actively introduced online operations for its automated clearance system, thereby allowing traders and custom brokers to enter and track customs declarations online.

Furthermore, in general, European goods are exempted from customs fees in accordance with the European Mediterranean Association Agreement and the European Free Trade Association (EFTA) agreement. In addition, goods from several Arab countries are also exempted from customs fees in accordance with the Greater Arab Free Trade Area (GAFTA) Agreement.

As for the value of the customs, the customs value of World Trade Organization (WTO) known by the GATT has been implemented in Lebanon. In 1995, all import customs duties were unified under one customs duty known as the " Single Customs Duty". As mentioned above, the calculation of the customs duties is based on the type of the duty and may vary between proportional or fixed duties.

Under the Custom Law some goods may be exempted of custom duties under certain conditions, including but not limited to cars, vehicles, equipment, materials, accessories, and spare parts imported by public administrations and institutions and municipalities or granted to them for firefighting and rescue purposes, airplanes, equipment used within the premises of Lebanese airports.

Furthermore, free zones and duty-frees that can be established under the Custom Law, will not be subject to the customs regime but to specific provisions set forth under the Custom Law.

---

[1] As per Article 2 of the Consumer Law Protection Law, Professional will mean a natural or legal person, from the private or the public sector, engaged in the distribution, sale, or rent of goods or in the provision of services, on his behalf, or in the interest of someone else.Professional will also mean a person who imports goods with the aim of selling, renting or distributing such goods, within the scope of his professional activity.

IV. Labour

A. Brief Introduction of Labour Laws and Regulations

(i) The principal law that regulates the employment sector in Lebanon is the Lebanese Labour Law issued in September 23, 1946 (the "Labour Law"). The articles and provisions of the Labour Law are considered of public order and of mandatory application and are applied and interpreted to the benefit of the employee. The Labour Law provides for the minimum rights that should be granted by the employer to the employee and it is up to the employer to decide whether he would like to provide for any additional rights above and over the minimum rights provided for in the Labour Law.

(ii) Moreover, Lebanon is a member of a number of Arab and international conventions related to the labor and employment field; such conventions are often relied upon on to cover any employment aspect not addressed in the Labour Law or to provide the employee with additional benefits and rights not provided for in the Labour Law.

(iii) As for the social security aspect, it is regulated by virtue of Decree Law No 13955 issued on September 26, 1963 (the National Social Security Law, or the "NSSF Law"); which are detailed here below.

(iv) Also, Decree Law No 17386 issued on September 2, 1964 governs the Collective Labour Contracts, Mediation and Arbitration ("CLCL"). Pursuant to the relevant provisions of the CLCL, a collective labour contract is an agreement by virtue of which are organized the conditions of work between a party representing a syndicate (or more than one syndicate), or a union (or more than one union) of the union of syndicates of employees, and a party who may be one individual employer (or more than one employer), a representative of a professional committee (or more than one committee), or a professional union for the employers (or more than one professional union). Several sectors in Lebanon have concluded collective labour agreements [e.g.the banking sector, the mobile telecoms operator (MTC and Alfa) and so forth].

B. Requirements of Employing Foreign Employees

a. Work Permit

Foreigners who wish to work in Lebanon should first obtain a work permit from the Ministry of Labour (the "MoL") as well as a residency permit from the Lebanese General Security ("LGS").

b. Application Procedure

The procedure to obtain the work permit as well as the residency permit may, in certain cases, but not always, be time consuming; this really is a case by case issue and depends on many factors such as for example the position to be held by the foreign employee.

In case the foreigner is already in Lebanon based on a tourist visa, the procedures to be undertaken before the MoL and the LGS in order to obtain the work and the residency permits are the following:

(i) A request should be submitted by the employer of the concerned foreigner (the "Employer") to the MoL requesting the issuance of a "preliminary approval"; noting that the Employer should be registered before the Employment Department at the MoL.

(ii) After obtaining the "preliminary approval", a request should be submitted by the Employer to the LGS in order to change the status of the foreigner's visa from "tourist visa" to "work visa", if the foreigner has entered the Lebanese territory using a tourist visa or submit for a work visa (if the employees has not entered yet to the Lebanese territory as will be detailed here below), along with an undertaking signed by the Employer before the notary public.

(iii) Once the foreigner obtains the work visa, the fees required for the "prior approval" should be settled to the MoL and accordingly a request should be submitted before the MoL to obtain the work permit accompanied by various documents.

(iv) Finally, after having obtained the work permit, a request should be submitted before the LGS in order to obtain the residency permit. Kindly note that the LGS will again take the passport of the foreigner during this period and provide him with an attestation proving that the procedure has been initiated.

(v) The above-mentioned process is started while the foreigner is still abroad, a request will have to be submitted before the MoL to obtain the preliminary approval, followed by the request before the same authority for the "prior approval". Based on the said approvals, the foreign employee will be granted permission from the LGS to enter the Lebanese territory and to obtain a work permit form the MoL within a certain period of time.

(vi) Finally, work permit and residency permits are generally granted for a period of one year and should be therefore renewed every year by settling the required expenses.

c. National Social Security Fund

Employers are required to register in NSSF all employees working for local and international firms within 15 days as of the date they start their work. Foreign employees with a valid work permit and residency permit should also be enrolled within the NSSF however they do not benefit of any of the benefits provided by the NSSF; they can only be entitled to the end of service indemnity benefit.

C. Exit and Entry

a. Visa Types

In Lebanon, there are several types of visa (e.g.transit visa, residence visa, courtesy visa....), noting that as mentioned here above, in order for a foreigner to work in Lebanon a work visa is required to eventually obtain the work and residency permit.

b. Restrictions for Exit and Entry

There are no restrictions to the entry and exit of the foreigner employee once the latter receives a residency permit.

D. Trade Union and Labour Organizations

In Lebanon unions are recognized and have a similar role to all unions across the world, i.e.defending workers and employees' rights in their relevant industry. The Labour Law provides notably the following as to the unions, their recognition, their composition and their rights and obligations:

(i) Every category of professions, employers on one hand, and employees on the other, may set up a special trade union. This trade union has a legal personality and may initiate legal proceedings;

(ii) Trade unions are established for the sole purpose of protecting, promoting and defending the profession's interests, to raise its standard, and to participate in the economic, industrial and commercial progress of the profession.

(iii) Trade unions whether for employers or employees, may not be established without having obtained a prior authorization from the MoL.

(iv) Every trade union must have internal regulations, duly approved at the general meeting by a majority of two-third of the attending members.

(v) Any employer or employee is free to join or not to join the trade union.

(vi) Any person who wishes to join a trade union must meet the following conditions:
- Have the Lebanese nationality and benefit from all civil rights;
- Exercise the profession at the time of application;
- Be eighteen years of age; and
- Not be convicted of any crime or offense.

(vii) Foreigners may join a trade union if they meet certain conditions enumerated in the Labour Law and if they have a work permit to work in Lebanon. Foreign members are not eligible or qualified to vote; they are however entitled to appoint one of them to defend their interests before the committee of the trade union.

(viii) Every trade union is managed by a committee composed of a minimum of four members and a maximum of twelve members.

E. Labour Disputes

The individual labor disputes and the disputes arising from the application of the NSSF Law are exclusively within the power of the Arbitral Labour Councils. The Arbitral Labour Council is competent to examine the disputes arising out of:
- The determination of the minimum wage.
- The occupational accidents, expressly stipulated in applicable laws.
- The dismissal from service and leaving work, and imposing fines, and in general all the disputes arising between employers and employees stemming from the application of the Labour Law.

Moreover, filing lawsuits, and attending hearings before the Arbitral Labour Councils, is possible without being represented by an attorney.

V. Intellectual Property

A. Brief Introduction of IP Laws and Regulations

Lebanon has enacted several laws and regulations meant to standardize and protect Intellectual Property rights, in addition to the fact that it is part of the WIPO Convention, the constituent instrument of the World Intellectual Property Organization ("WIPO").

Lebanon is also a member of many WIPO-Administered Treaties, notably the Paris Convention for the Protection of Industrial Property (the "Paris Convention") of September 1, 1924. The Paris Convention applies to industrial property in its widest sense, including patents, trademarks, industrial designs, utility models, service marks, trade names, geographical indications and the repression of unfair competition.

Lebanon has also ratified the Nice Agreement concerning the international classification of goods and services for purposes of the registration of marks.

B. Trademark

a. Trademark Protection

Trademarks are provided protection by virtue of the High French Commissioner's Ordinance regarding "Regulations and Systems of Commercial, Industrial, Literary, Artistic and Musical Property in Lebanon" No.2385/LR of January 17, 1924, as amended ("Ordinance No 2385") as well as under certain provisions of the Lebanese Criminal Law.

Ordinance No 2385 has defined trademarks for factories or trade, as names written in a way which distinguishes them from others, titles, nomenclatures, symbols, stamps, letters, protruding marks and drawings, small drawings and figures, in general, any sign of any kind intended to bring benefit to the consumer, the factory owner and the dealer, by distinguishing between things and showing the identity, source, origin of goods, and the industrial, commercial or agricultural product, or the products of forests and metals.

Service marks are also recognized in Lebanon and can be registered at the MoET. The service mark application is the same as that of the trademark, with the mention that the mark applies to services rendered, in addition to the details of the services concerned by the application.

A trademark registration is optional, unless there are legal provisions to the contrary; that being said, personal ownership of a trademark may not be claimed unless such a trademark has been previously filed with the Protection Bureau the MoET. Thus, a registered trademark confers to its author the right to claim personal ownership of the trademark, sell it, assign it, as well as transfer it by inheritance.

b. Trademark Application

The Lebanese trademark registration system is a deposit system. The trademark registration process is briefly as follows:

(i) Trademark applications are submitted online through a service provided for by the MoET on its website, but the fees and the remaining of the procedure will then have to be completed in person at the MoET.

(ii) After having received the application and the documents enclosed therewith, the Director of the Protection Department at the MoET examines them in order to decide whether or not to accept the registration of the trademark. The Israeli Boycott Department also verifies whether the applicant is on the boycott list or not.

(iii) In the case of non-acceptance of the registration, the director of the Protection Department refers the file to the Minister of Commerce and Industry, along with his report. The Minister may then accept or reject the registration by a decision he issues within fifteen days. Such decision may be objected in case of rejection, before the State Council within thirty days as of the date of notification to the applicant.

(iv) In case the trademark registration is accepted, it must be recorded in the register of trademarks (at the Protection Department of the MoET) with all necessary mentions; the registration certificate will be handed over within fifteen days as of the date of its registration in the register.

(v) The registration of a trademark generally takes two weeks. A trademark filing is valid for fifteen years as of the registration date, and is renewable for similar periods, provided that the required payments are made.

(vi) A foreigner who wishes to register a trademark must be represented by a person residing in Lebanon. In Lebanon, the use of a trademark is not mandatory in order to file a trademark application, maintaining it or renewing it. However, the use constitutes the main criteria in order to determine the proprietorship of the trademark in the case of a dispute.

C. Patent

a. Patent Protection

A Patent Law No.240 was enacted on August 7, 2000 (the "Patent Law"). The law provides for patent protection for inventions and plant varieties and a sui generis protection for layout designs of integrated circuits. The Patent law provides mainly protection for undisclosed information, noting that according to the WIPO, the Patent Law is in complete conformity with the Agreement on Trade Related Aspects of Intellectual Property Rights (the "TRIPS"). Any patentable invention as detailed hereinafter grants its owner and his successors the exclusive right to use the said invention.

Pursuant to the Patent Law, patent protection is granted to an invention if it is novel, creative and can be applied in industry.

An invention will be considered (i) novel, if it is not part of previous technique; (ii) creative, if it is not obvious for a normal professional to obtain it based on previous technique (previous technique includes everything up to the date of filing of the patent application or of the priority requested by the Paris Convention) available to the public at any place or time whether manuscript, verbal or utilized or by any other mean; (iii) can be applied in industry, if it can be manufactured or utilized in any type of industry (the term "industry" will be broadly interpreted as defined in Article 1 of the Paris Convention as amended). An invention is not patentable if it violates the public order or morality.

b. Patent Application

(i) The Lebanese patent registration system is a deposit system. The applicant must file a patent application to the Director of Protection Department at the MoET. The application must be in Arabic and include a description and abstract of the invention, figures, drawings, noting that if the applicant is not a Lebanese national or resident, he has to appoint an agent residing in Lebanon. There is no examination of the patent application provided for by the law.

(ii) The application may not include more than one invention or a multiple interrelated inventions forming one general creative concept. Otherwise, the invention will be considered a complex invention in which case the applicant will have to file new separate applications for the inventions.

(iii) The registration of a patent generally takes two weeks. Patent protection is valid for twenty years as of the acceptance date, after which the patent becomes public.

D. Industrial Design

a. Industrial Design Protection

The WIPO defines an industrial design as being the ornamental or aesthetic aspect of an article. The design may consist of three-dimensional features, such as the shape or surface of an article, or of two-dimensional features, such as patterns, lines or color.

Industrial designs are applied to a wide variety of products of industry and handicraft.

According to article 48 of Ordinance No 2385, any inventor of a drawing or a design, or those who have rights thereon, will alone have the right of usufruct thereto, and the right to sell, or offer it for sale, and to authorize its sale, provided that such drawing or design had been previously filed at the Protection Bureau of the MoET.

Industrial designs are also provided by virtue of certain provisions of the Lebanese Criminal Law.

b. Industrial Design Application

(i) The inventor of a drawing or design or his agent or official proxy must send the filing application to the Director of the Protection Bureau.

(ii) The Director of the Protection Bureau will register the filing permit in a special register designated for that purpose, in which he will mention the date, hour and serial number of the filing.

E. Copyright

a. Copyright Protection

A Copyright Law No.75 was enacted on April 3, 1999 (the "Copyright Law"); copyright protection now applies to literary, artistic, musical and scientific works, to computer software and all kind of audio-visual works, and to utilitarian forms of expression. The Copyright Law also aggravated the penalties for offenders, extended the cases of copyright breach and provided better compensation to the persons whose rights have been infringed.

According to the Copyright Law, the author of any artistic or literary work will, as a result of the creation of the work, have an absolute property right over his work and will reserve all his rights without having to follow any formality.

The term of protection granted under this Law to the economic rights of the author, will be the life of the author and 50 years after his death, to be computed from the end of the year in which the death has occurred.

b. Copyright Application

(i) Works, sound recordings, performances, and radio or television programs will be deposited with the Intellectual Property Protection Office at the MoET. The deposit will constitute a presumption as to the ownership by the depositor of the work, the sound recording, the performance or the radio or television program.

(ii) Copyright holders, holders of related rights or their particular or universal successors who wish to make a deposit must submit to the Intellectual Property Protection Office an application signed by them or their agent.

(iii) The application for deposit will not be accepted unless it is accompanied by the fees set out by the Copyright Law.

(iv) The application for deposit will be registered at the Intellectual Property Protection Office. A certificate will be delivered to the applicant mentioning the information stated in the application and it will be accompanied by one of the three copies deposited with the Office.

F. Domain Names

a. Domain Names Protection

A domain name is a unique name that identifies a website. Domain names are not protected under a special law in Lebanon. However, Lebanese domain names are registered as a Trademark protection in class 35 and the Lebanese Domain Registry in the American University of Beirut (LB-DOM) is the local registry for domain names in Lebanon. The domain name does not have to be used in order to be protected.

b. Domain Names Application

In order to register a domain name in Lebanon, the applicant must provide the following documents and information:
- The application form;
- A copy of the Lebanese trademark registration certificate in class 35;
- A Power of Attorney notarized and legalized by the Lebanese Consulate;
- An authorization letter duly notarized and legalized by the Lebanese Consulate if the applicant does not have a legal local presence in Lebanon.

G. Main Measures for IP Protection

(i) As detailed above, the existing intellectual property rights' laws in Lebanon cover copyrights, industrial designs, patents, trademarks, and geographical elements.

(ii) The Intellectual Property Protection Office of the MoET is the central organ which rallies efforts, though with modest resources up until now, in order to improve the legal framework of intellectual property rights. The MoET has drafted new laws and amendments regarding industrial design, trademark, and geographical indications, in order to enhance the intellectual property rights system; these are still pending parliamentary approval.

(iii) In addition, Intellectual Property rights' cases are primarily enforced by the Special Criminal Investigation Division of the Internal Security Forces, as well as by the Cybercrime and Intellectual Property Unit and the Lebanese Customs.

VI. Environmental Protection

A. Department Supervising Environmental Protection

(i) The MoE, established in 1993, manages all environmental issues, specifically in terms of protection and sustainable conservation of natural resources, and of initiation and activation of Lebanon's participation in the global environmental conventions.

The MoE develops the general policy of the country, sets projects and plans on the short, medium and long term for the environmental safety and sustainability of natural resources, and proposes implementation steps to monitor their execution. It also draws attention to the important emerging environmental national and international issues.[1]

---

[1] The MoE, History, from the MoE's website available at: http://www.moe.gov.lb/The-Ministry/History.aspx?lang=en-us.

(ii) The Lebanese Cleaner Production Center was established in 2002 by The MoE. The center provides assistance to small and medium sized enterprises in adopting cleaner production measures and sustainable industrial production modes that will reduce consumption of water, energy, and so forth., decrease pollutants emissions, effluent loads and waste.[1]

(iii) In 2005, conditions and mechanisms were set for the MoE to grant contributions to non-profit organizations (the "NGOs") for the purpose of undertaking environmental activities. This lead to an emerging role of national and international NGOs, which are assuming an increasingly important role in raising public awareness regarding environmental and sustainable development issues and activities. By way of example, the United Nations Development Program, operating in Lebanon since 1960, has set the "Environment and Energy Programme", which works closely with the Government to provide policy support for more effective environment and energy management, in addition to working with local communities and civil sector organisations to improve livelihoods through improved environmental management.[2]

(iv) In 2014, full-time environmental attorney generals were appointed in six governorates (Beirut, Mount Lebanon, the North, the South, the Bekaa, and Nabatieh) and inspection judges in two governorates (Beirut and the South), with the aim to enforce any infringement of the environmental laws and regulations.

B. Brief Introduction of Laws and Regulations of Environmental Protection

(i) The Lebanese Constitution, adopted in 1926, and amended subsequently, does not mention explicitly the right to live in a clean and healthy environment as a constitutional right of the citizens of Lebanon. Lebanon has adopted the Universal Declaration of Human Rights of 1948. The Declaration notably provides that everyone has the right to a standard of living adequate for the health and well-being of himself and of his family, which provision may be considered as a support to ensure that same right to Lebanese citizens.

In fact, Lebanon has enacted a fair amount of laws and regulations that govern and regulate environment protection, but their enforceability remains, often times, an issue that needs to be solved.

Below are some of the main laws that regulate directly or indirectly the environment protection in Lebanon:

- Law 216/93, dated of April 2, 1993, founded the MoE and identified its tasks, which was a major step in environmental management.

- On July 26, 2002, the Lebanese Parliament enacted Law 444, the "Environment Law", which is believed to be the milestone that set the basic principles and general provisions regulating the environmental protection and management of environmental basins. It calls for the protection and sustainable use of biodiversity, the establishment of nature reserves and for regulating access to genetic resources. This law also defines the responsibilities and penalties for those who abuse the environmental resources and cause environmental pollution.[3]

- The role of NGOs emerged pursuant to the issuance of Decree 14865 on July 1, 2005, which determines the conditions and mechanism for the MoE to grant NGOs contributions in order to undertake Environmental Activities.

- Law 251 dated April 15, 2014 appointing full-time environmental attorney generals and inspection judges, as mentioned above; as well as Notice No.1837 dated October 9, 2014 by the Ministry of Justice calling for environmental experts to join the roster of sworn experts at courts[4].

(ii) In addition to the above there are regulations in each environmental field such as, laws regulating the reduction of air pollution from the transport sector, solid waste management, forests protection, hunting practices, and the supervision and control of the environmental aspect of the offshore petroleum activities in Lebanon, its risks on the environment, the obligation to protect the environment, and so forth.

(iii) Moreover, bilateral and multilateral environmental conventions and treaties have a significant impact on the environment safeguard and protection. Lebanon has acceded to and ratified numerous conventions and treaties related to the environment.

Some key environmental treaties Lebanon has ratified are: the Cartagena Protocol on Biosafety, ratified on 16 October 2008, the Stockholm Convention on Persistant Organic pollutants, signed on 22 May 2001, the United Nations Convention to Combat Desertification, ratified on 21 December 1994, the Montreal Protocol on Substances that deplete the Ozone Layer, adhered to on 31 March 1993, the Barcelona Protocol Concerning

---

[1] Le Centre d'échange d'information de la Convention sur la diversité biologique, Republic of Lebanon, National Legislation and policy.From biodiv.be's website at:http://www.biodiv.be/liban/implementation/national-legislation-and-policies.

[2] United Nations Development Program in Lebanon (UNDP), Environmental governance.From the UNDP's websites available at:http://www.lb.undp.org/content/lebanon/en/home/environmental-governance.html and http://www.lb.undp.org/content/lebanon/en/home/about-us.html.

[3] Op.Cit. The MoE, History, from the MoE's website available at:http://www.moe.gov.lb/The-Ministry/History.aspx?lang=en-us.

[4] Op.Cit. Le Centre d'échange d'information de la Convention sur la diversité biologique, Republic of Lebanon, National Legislation and policy.From biodiv.be's website at:http://www.biodiv.be/liban/implementation/national-legislation-and-policies/environmental-legislation.

Co-operation in Combating Pollution of the Mediterranean Sea by Oil and Other Harmful Substances in Cases of Emergency, acceded on 30 June 1977, the International Convention for the Prevention of Pollution of the Sea by Oil, adhered to on 16 November 1966, and the Treaty Banning Nuclear Weapons Tests in the Atmosphere, in Outer Space and in Underwater, ratified on 30 December 1964.

C. Evaluation of Environmental Protection

Lebanon has the basic legal framework that would enable the environment to be protected if such laws were applied consistently.

There is no doubt that international and national NGOs are working along with the Lebanese Government to achieve basic environmental protections, such as waste recycling, reduction of air pollution levels, coasts' and forests' protection, and preservation of the heritage.

There is still however a long way for Lebanon to go and there are a number of obstacles to overcome, including the most recent garbage crisis. The enforceability of the environmental laws was mainly an issue for the past decades. However, the adoption of laws related to environmental prosecution and investigation recently adopted brought some credibility to the enacted Environment Protection Laws.

VII. Dispute Resolution

There is no mandatory dispute resolution process under domestic law. The parties to a contract are free to choose the method for their dispute resolution in the event of conflict.

According to Lebanese laws, the parties may submit their agreement to a foreign law, unless a specific provision prohibits the choice of the foreign law or does not give legal effect to the latter, and also as long as such substantive provisions are not contrary to public policy in Lebanon, noting that in such event Lebanese courts will not apply the specific provision(s) which is / are contrary to public policy in Lebanon, while upholding the remaining provisions of the foreign law. Indeed, relevant provisions of the Lebanese laws provide that the parties to a contract can determine their legal relationship as they deem fit provided that they comply with public order, public ethics and mandatory legal provisions.

Furthermore, and in principle, nothing prohibits the parties from submitting their agreements / contracts to a foreign jurisdiction provided (i) the Lebanese jurisdiction recognizes the jurisdictional competence of that other jurisdiction; and, (ii) there are no specific provisions in Lebanese law that imposes Lebanon as being the competent jurisdiction.

A. Legal System in Lebanon/Courts in Lebanon

The legal system in Lebanon is mainly composed of the following bodies:
- The judicial courts;
- The administrative courts;
- The religious courts;
- The special courts;
- The exceptional courts;
- The judicial council; and,
- The constitutional council.

a. The Judicial Courts

The judicial court system in Lebanon is composed as follows:
- A first level of jurisdiction is the First Instance Court. The First Instance Court can be a single judge or a tribunal composed of three judges.
- A second level of jurisdiction is the Court of Appeal. The Court of Appeal has jurisdiction to review a judgment rendered by a tribunal of lower level. It judges the dispute for the second time, in fact and in law. The claimant is entitled to fully reopen the case. The appeal recourse must be submitted within a time limit set by the Lebanese Code of Civil Procedure ("LCCP").
- A third (and extraordinary) level of jurisdiction is the Court of Cassation. It is possible, in specific cases strictly determined by law, if an unfavorable judgment is rendered by the Court of Appeal to appeal to the Court of Cassation. The Court of Cassation (situated in Beirut) has the role of reviewing, upon recourse of either parties, the ruling rendered by judges dealing with the substance of a case. It settles only questions of law or of application of the law: it does not review the facts of the case. However, when the Court of Cassation revokes the challenged decision, it reviews the whole matter and is substituted to the court that issued the challenged decision.

b. The Administrative Courts

If the judicial system settles the disputes between persons (individuals, associations, companies), the administrative system has jurisdiction to settle the litigations between a private person and a public entity, or a litigation between public entities themselves.

In Lebanon, the State Council hears and rules on administrative conflicts as a first instance court, an appeal court and a cassation court: the principle of double degree of jurisdiction is not applied in practice in administrative conflicts in Lebanon. However, the decisions of the State Council can be sometimes challenged (e.g.opposition; application to reopen proceedings) if certain conditions are met; the State Council also gives advices to the Lebanese Government before the issuance of some administrative decisions.

c. The Religious Courts

The religious court system is composed of the court systems of the 19 recognized denominations in Lebanon pertaining to the three main religions, i.e.Christianity, Islam and Judaism. The jurisdiction of these courts is limited to personal status and family law matters, as authorized by law.

d. The Special Courts

In both systems (judicial and administrative), there are a number of special courts established by virtue of specific laws. In such cases, the jurisdiction of the ordinary courts is excluded. Some examples that can be cited in this respect include the Arbitral Labor Council in the judicial system and the Commissions of expropriation in the administrative system.

e. The Exceptional Courts

Exceptional courts are tribunals established in exceptional circumstances, such as the Military tribunal; their denomination means that the existence of such courts should cease when the exceptional circumstances disappear. However, such courts are sometimes maintained for various reasons, mainly political ones.

f. The Judicial Council

The Judicial Council is a criminal Court empowered to rule on sensitive criminal matters restrictively and expressly set out in the Lebanese Code of criminal procedure (mainly crimes against State security). The Judicial Council is seized through a decree issued by the Council of Ministers. Its decisions are final and cannot be challenged, except in the case of an application to reopen the proceedings (noting that such procedure is subject to certain conditions).

g. The Constitutional Council

The Constitutional Council was established in Lebanon by virtue of law No 250 dated 14 July 1993. It is not a judicial tribunal; its main attribution is to control the constitutionality of laws; all decisions of the Constitutional Council are binding to public authorities and to judicial and administrative courts.

B. Arbitration

(i) The recourse to arbitration is valid under the laws of Lebanon. Arbitration proceedings in Lebanon are governed by the LCCP.

(ii) Regarding arbitration procedures in Lebanon, the choice of forum and the arbitration clauses are governed by provisions of the LCCP, unless the contract provides otherwise. In this respect, according to he LCCP the parties may appoint in the arbitral agreement directly or by reference to determined arbitration rules the arbitrator or arbitrators, or may determine therein the method of their appointment.

(iii) Regarding domestic arbitration, inbrief, the relevant provisions of the LCCP provide that parties entering into a commercial or civil agreement may choose to include an arbitration clause (which notably should be written) as a dispute resolution, and the Republic of Lebanon, as well as any public law entities, may elect to resolve to arbitration to settle any dispute whatever the nature of the contract they enter into, noting however that the arbitration clause or arbitration agreement in public contracts (i.e.entered into between a private law party and a public law entity) will only be effective once the approval of the Council of Ministers is granted by a decree, based upon the recommendation of the relevant minister.

(iv) Regarding international arbitration, foreign awards that are rendered in arbitration proceedings occurring abroad are governed by the LCCP. They are recognized and are granted exequatur when the requesting party duly proves the existence of the award and provided that the award does not contravene the international public policy. Moreover, Lebanon is a signatory of the 1958 New York Convention on the Recognition and Enforcement of Foreign Arbitral Awards ("New York Convention"), noting that Lebanon will only apply the New York Convention to recognition and enforcement of awards made in the territory of another contracting State.

(v) Also, in Lebanon, there is the Lebanese Arbitration and Mediation Center at the Chamber of Commerce, Industry and Agriculture. The Lebanese Arbitration and Mediation Center is the sole institution that provides administration and monitoring services for arbitration proceedings in Lebanon. The Center has been active in the arbitration field since its establishment in 1995; it offers its services to the business community, to private and public institutions and to the government.

The Center oversees the arbitration process and is responsible for:
- Appointing arbitrators or confirming, as the case may be, arbitrators nominated by the parties;
- Deciding upon challenges of arbitrators;
- Fixing and extending time limits;
- Scrutinizing and approving all arbitral awards;
- Fixing the arbitrators' fees taking into consideration the amount in dispute.

C. Mediation

Currently, there are no laws or regulations governing expressly mediation in Lebanon, and as such mediation is a private business regulated by the agreement between the parties; noting that parties may opt to have their mediation proceedings under the rules of the Lebanese Arbitration and Mediation Center.

The LCCP adresses conciliation, noting that conciliation is of the prerogative of Lebanese judges.

VIII. Others

A. Anti-commercial Bribery

a. Brief Introduction of Anti-commercial Bribery Laws and Regulations

(i) The Lebanese Criminal Code (the "Criminal Code") provides for anti-bribery provisions and the consequences of bribery offences. According to the relevant provisions of the Criminal Code and in short, a bribery offence is considered as having been committed whenever any employee, any individual elected or designated for a public service and any individual in charge of an official duty (e.g.expert, judge, etc.), accepts or seeks, for himself / herself or for a third party, a gift, a promise or any other benefit in order to undertake an act that falls within his / her job description, undertake an act that is contrary to his / her function or to pretend that such act falls within his / her function, or to neglect or delay any duty within his / her job description.

(ii) The Lebanese Decree Law No.112 dated 12 June 1959 concerning employees' regulations provides notably that it is forbidden for a public official to seek or accept advantages or to solicit or accept, directly or through an intermediary due to the position that he or she occupies, gifts or gratuities of any kind.

(iii) The Illicit Wealth Law No.154 issued on December 27, 1999, (the "Illicit Wealth Law") defines funds acquired illicitly as, inter alia, funds acquired by an employee, a provider of public services, a judge or their relatives or partners through bribery, use of influence, exploitation of their job or any other illegal means.

(iv) Another fundamental step in the fight against corruption in general, is the Law to Access Information, published on 16 February 2017, as it imposes and allows a level of transparency.

(v) With respect to the main international anti-corruption conventions, the United Nations Convention against Corruption adopted by the General Assembly's resolution 58/4 on 31 October 2003 has been ratified by Lebanon on 22 April 2009. Moreover, Lebanon is member of the Arab Convention to Fight Corruption of the Arab League, signed on 21 December 2010 by 21 Arab countries, which was signed by the Lebanese Minister of Interior and Minister of Justice.

b. Department Supervising Anti-commercial Bribery

On 19 March 2011, the Ministry of Interior has established the Anti-Corruption Commission, which aims to combat corruption in all of its forms in various sectors and departments, and to condemn corruption at all levels without exposing or defaming, and to restore the citizens' rights that have been issued in violation of the law and the constitution.

In December 2016, the Lebanese Government established for the first time a State Ministry for Combatting Corruption, thus entrusting a designated individual with the mission of establishing an efficient mechanism in order to fight corruption in Lebanon.

In addition, the Ministry of Public Health has introduced a hotline (1214) as well as an online platform in order to facilitate for citizens the report of fraudulent actions to the Ministry. The MoET has also launched a hotline (1739) and an online application, both of which allow consumers to deposit complaints and follow up with them.

Similarly, the Lebanese Transparency Association (the "LTA") has launched the Lebanon Anti-Bribery Network in 2008, then in 2013 for specific periods, in order to combat bribery in Lebanon. The LTA has also established the Lebanese Advocacy and Legal Advice center (the "LALAC"), with the purpose of informing citizens about their legal rights and encouraging victims and witnesses to take action against cases of corruption. In this respect, a hotline was also provided for by the LTA (+9613-868-303).

c. Punitive Actions

Below are examples (non-exhaustive) of possible criminal and disciplinary sanctions.

a) Criminal sanctions

According to the Criminal Code, the main criminal sanctions are the following:

(i) Any employee, any individual elected or designated for a public service and any individual in charge of an official duty (e.g.expert, judge, etc.), who accepts or seeks, for himself / herself or for a third party, a gift, a promise or any other benefit in order to undertake an act that:

- falls within his / her job description, will be condemned to a prison sentence varying from three months to three years and to a fine equal to at least twice the amount of the bribe he took or received.

- is contrary to his / her function or to pretend that such act falls within his / her function, or to neglect or delay any duty within his / her job description, will be condemned to temporary forced labour and to a fine equal to at least three times the value of the bribe he took or received.

(ii) Any worker employed in the private sector, whether a remunerated employee, an expert, or an adviser, and whomever is related to an employer by virtue of a remunerated employment agreement, who sought or accepted a gift, a promise or any other benefit, whether for himself / herself or for a third party, in order to reveal secrets or information prejudicial to the business or to undertake or refrain from any action with the intent to cause material or non-material damage to the employer or to the latter's interest, will be subject to imprisonment from two months to two years, and to a fine between 100,000 and 200,000 Lebanese Pounds (i.e.approximately US$ 66 and US$132).

(iii) Any person who offers or promises to offer to one of the persons mentioned under paragraph (i), a gift or any other benefit as an undue wage in order to undertake, to neglect or to delay any lawful act within his / her job description. He / she will be subject, in the event the said offer has been refused, to an imprisonment of a minimum of three months and to a fine of a minimum of twice the value of the offer or the promise.

(iv) Moreover, any of the individuals mentioned in paragraph (i) who accepts an undue reward for an act already undertaken by him and falling within his / her job description, will be condemned to imprisonment from one month to one year, and to a fine equal to at least twice the value of the bribe he took or received.

The provisions related to bribery do not distinguish, in the case of the person committing bribery, between individuals and companies. However, and according to the provisions of the Criminal Code, legal entities will be criminally responsible for the criminal acts committed by their managers, directors, representatives and employees when such acts have been performed on behalf of the companies or by any of its means. In this event, the company will be subject to a fine, the confiscation of its assets and the publication of the judgment.

b) Disciplinary sanctions:

According to Article 54 of the Employees' Regulations, the employee will be held liable from a disciplinary point of view and be subject to disciplinary sanctions if he / she deliberately or negligently breaches the duties imposed by the laws and regulations in force. This disciplinary prosecution does not prevent the employee's prosecution, when necessary, before competent civil or criminal courts.

B. Project Contracting

(i) The main laws and regulations regarding the award of public (administrative) contracts are:

- The Public Accounting Law promulgated by virtue of Decree number 14969 issued on 30 December 1963 (the "PAL"); and,

- The tender regulations promulgated by virtue of Decree 2866 dated 16 December 1959 (the "Tender Regulations");

Lebanon also enacted the Lebanon Public Private Partnership Law published in the Official Gazette, on September 9, 2017 (the "PPP Law"). The PPP Law addresses mainly the general definitions of PPP, all the phases of a PPP project as well as the procedures of proposing and choosing a project. It also specifies that projects which are carried out by the State, public institutions, municipalities and the unions of municipalities are subject to the provisions of the PPP Law.

(ii) A contract is considered to be an administrative contract when the following conditions are met:

- One of the parties to the contract is a public law entity;

- The object or the purpose of the contract is to render a public service or fulfill a public interest;

- The contract provides for exceptional clauses included by the public law party for its own benefit.

Administrative contracts are characterized by the fact that the State / public authority (the "Public Law Party") has such discretionary power (in enforcing the contract or not), whether this is expressly stated in the agreement documents or not, and such discretionary power cannot in principle be disputed. However, despite the fact that the Public Law Party has a discretionary power in enforcing a contract or not or elect to enforce a part thereof, the State Council monitors such discretionary power by controlling whether the Public Law Party has used its discretionary power in an abusive manner. The State Council usually examines whether the Public Law Party has exceeded the reason for having such discretionary power, or refused to enforce the contractual relationship without any valid factual or legal grounds.

a. Permission System

In general, the conclusion of a public contract in Lebanon between the Public Law Party and private law individuals and entities (the "Private Law Party") involves a competition process or previous tender procedures. The Lebanese Government invites the interested private parties to submit their bid in a public tender, according to predetermined terms and conditions.

The execution or the performance of the public contract is subject to the approval of the Lebanese Government, often represented by the relevant Ministry, depending on the nature of the contemplated project.

This being said, there is no particular procedure for the approval process. In general, following the submission of the proposal by the private law party, the Lebanese Government and the relevant Ministry study such proposal and either accept it as is or request amendments prior to its signature. In some cases, the issuance of a Decree might also be necessary. The timing differs from one project to another, depending on the surrounding circumstances.

That being said, not all public contracts are preceded by competition process or previous tender procedure. Sometimes, a public contract is concluded as a direct result of negotiations between the Private Law Party and the Public Law Party or by the direct award by the Lebanese Government - however, such public contracts must be related to specific items expressly listed in the PAL, such as by way of example only, supplies, works and services that cannot be the object of public procurement, either because they have to remain secret or because of public safety requirements, subject to the relevant ministries' approval.

Negotiated contracts should abide to the terms and conditions set out by the parties to the contract and should have its own tender documents upon adjudication.

b. Prohibited Areas

The PAL and Tender Regulations do not expressly include any provision prohibiting any local or foreign person or entity from entering into a public contract with the Lebanese Government.

These regulations however leave considerable freedom to the Public Law Party to organize its tenders, notably the selection criteria of the Private Law Party, in accordance with each project's needs. Therefore, some specific projects might be prohibited to foreign persons and / or products, and awarded strictly to Lebanese nationals or to products manufactured locally. Others may allow foreign participants in consortium with Lebanese entities.

We remind you also of the provisions of the LCC, according to which an SAL incorporated in Lebanon must have its registered office in Lebanon and will have de jure the Lebanese nationality, notwithstanding any provision to the contrary, noting that in the event the object of the SAL is the exploitation of a public service, one third of its capital must be composed of nominal shares that will be owned by Lebanese nationals. These shares can only be transferred to Lebanese shareholders under penalty of nullity.

c. Invitation to Bid and Bidding

According to the provisions of the PAL and the Tender Regulations, all tenders must be published in the Official Gazette and in at least 3 local newspapers, 15 days prior to the date of contracting.

The tender documents for each tender must clearly state, inter alia, (i) the object of the project and the work to be undertaken, (ii) the qualification requirements for the candidates, (iii) the selection and award criteria (the Public Law Party may intent to not abide by the lowest price, as long as it clearly includes in the tender preferential criteria, with a rate for each one when necessary), (iv) the project's implementation conditions, the deadline for its execution, (vi) the bid bond required to participate in the bid, and (vii) the performance bond to guarantee the right execution of the Private Law Party obligations. Both the bid bond and the performance bond could be either monetary or issued by an acceptable bank.

Applications must comply with the tender's requirements, and a minimum of 2 applications must be submitted for each tender. In the event only 1 application was submitted, the project will not be granted to this one applicant unless the price offered is at least 10% lower than the price stated in the tender documents.

Moreover, a margin of preference of 10% may be provided to specific products manufactured in Lebanon, on the condition that such products and their specifications are determined by a decree from the council of ministers.

The PAL and Tender Regulations only contains the main principles and does not address such questions as the number of tender stages, timeline, communication modalities with applicants and selection criteria, thereby leaving considerable freedom to organize the tender in accordance with the project's needs.

According to the provisions of the PPP Law, a PPP Project includes any public project of public utility carried out by the State or the public administrations affiliated to the State or the municipalities, in which the private sector contributes to the financing and administration of the project and to at least one of the following phases: the design, the establishment, the construction, the development, the renovation, the equipping, the maintenance, and / or the operation.

According to the provisions of the PPP Law, the launching of the tender proceedings is subject to the principles of transparency, freedom of participation and equality between all the candidates, Lebanese or foreign, and should be preceded by the necessary publicity in order to receive multiple offers which will be competing to win the contract. The steps of the tender proceedings are, briefly, as follows:

- The tender proceedings start by the launching of an open invitation in which are stated the criteria for qualification in accordance with the size and nature of the PPP project;

- The PPP committee provides the candidates with the necessary information and recommendations, on the basis of which they will submit their requests;

- The PPP committee, examines and evaluates the aforementioned requests and raises a substantiated report to the Supreme Counsel for Privatization and Partnership (the "SCPP") containing the names of the suggested prequalified candidates and the names of the disqualified candidates. There has to be at least 3 suggested prequalified candidates;

- The PPP committee drafts a tender. The PPP committee then notifies all prequalified candidates of the tender;

- Subsequently, the PPP committee raises the final tender to the Council of Ministers for approval;

- The PPP committee then notifies the tender to the prequalified candidates. The prequalified candidates present their technical and financial offers to the PPP committee;

- The PPP committee decides on the technical offers presented. The technical offers that do not correspond with the tender's requirements are rejected;

- The PPP committee evaluates the remaining technical offers and determines the qualified ones in accordance with the tender's requirements, and the PPP committee establishes the eligible candidates in light of the said evaluation. If at least two technical offers are not accepted, the project is reissued in order to insure competitiveness;

- The PPP committee unfolds the financial offers of the qualified participants and provides a classification of the offers from a technical and financial perspective and sends its report to the SCPP;

- The PPP committee, with the SCPP's authorization, can negotiate with the preferred applicant, aiming to improve the offer from a technical perspective. The project is awarded to the applicant with the most favorable offer as selected by the PPP committee, based on the requirements listed in the tender, and with the SCPP's approval.

- At the end of the decision process, the PPP committee will announce the results.

立陶宛

作者：Vilius Bernatonis、Donatas Šliora、Jonas Saladžius、Neringa Bubnaitytė
译者：张云燕、王勇

一、概述

（一）概况

立陶宛共和国位于欧洲北部，波罗的海东南部。它是波罗的海三国（另两个国家是拉脱维亚和爱沙尼亚）中最大的一个国家。常住人口约290万人，国土面积为65 300平方公里。立陶宛是欧盟发展最快的经济体之一。它为投资者提供多元化经济，高技能劳动力，低企业税率，该地区最发达的公路网以及稳定、民主的政治和法律体系。

立陶宛自2004年以来成为欧盟的成员国，因此它是单一市场的一部分，同时也得到了进入东欧国家市场的机会。立陶宛北与拉脱维亚接壤，东邻白俄罗斯，南邻波兰，西南与俄罗斯加里宁格勒州相邻。海岸线长90.66公里。位于波罗的海东部海岸最北端的不冻港，可以被认为是立陶宛最重要的交通枢纽之一。铁路货运服务直接将立陶宛与俄罗斯、白俄罗斯、拉脱维亚、波兰、德国、乌克兰和亚洲（包括中国）相连接。此外立陶宛还有3个为了方便进入欧洲主要地区的国际商业机场。

立陶宛的法律为国外投资者提供与国内投资者同等保护，它同时是双边和多边投资保护协定的缔约国，立陶宛在投资环境方面排名一直很靠前，是国外投资者的理想投资区域。该国在确保外国投资者权利和改善商业环境方面有着出色的记录。

（二）政治环境

1. 政治体系

立陶宛是一个稳定独立的民主议会共和国。立陶宛《宪法》（1992年通过）规定了国家实行立法、司法、行政三权分立的政治体制。

最高立法权由141名议员（任期4年）组成的一院议会（立陶宛议会）行使，其中71名议员在单一选区以绝对多数票选出，其余70名议员则通过公开名单比例代表制选举产生。

行政权力主要由政府行使，总统办事处行使某些具体职权。总统的权力和职能包括外交政策、国防、国家代表权；此外还拥有立陶宛《宪法》和其他相关法律规定的其他具体权力。立陶宛总统由民众直接选举产生，任期5年。政府由总理和14位部长组成，总理经议会批准后，由立陶宛总统任命。

立陶宛法院系统包括三级民事法院和刑事法院、专门行政法院和立陶宛宪法法院。民事和刑事法院系统包括12个区法院、5个地区法院、上诉法院和最高法院。立陶宛宪法法院对议会、总统和政府通过的立法进行宪法监督。所有其他规范行为都是由行政法院系统管辖。行政法院系统包括5个地区行政法院和最高行政法院；行政法院系统不包括上诉审。

2. 行政区划和市政管理

立陶宛划分为60个直辖市，均为真正的自治政府。

直辖市由市长和市议会领导，宪法规定通过直辖市进行地方自治，并且由相关法律进一步作出具体规定。立陶宛宪法规定了包括独立国家预算和独立市政预算组成的预算制度以及市政当局设立地方税的权力，直辖市可以行使任何未明确保留给立陶宛国家的权力。

3. 参加国际组织

立陶宛是一些国际组织的成员国。立陶宛于2001年5月31日加入世界贸易组织（WTO）；2004年3月29日加入了北大西洋公约组织（北约）；2004年5月1日加入欧盟（EU），欧盟法案涉及消费者保护、安保和防务等多个政策领域。此外，立陶宛还于 2007 年 12 月 21 日加入了申根区。

立陶宛于 2015 年收到经济合作与发展组织（经合组织）的正式邀请，并开始着手加入该组织的进程。立陶宛当局正在积极准备加入进程，预计将在 2018 年年底前完成。

（三）法律环境

立陶宛法律体系的特点与欧洲大陆的传统相一致。国家立法体系基于等级体系原则，即在层级体系中处于较低级别的法律行为不得与层级体系内的高级别法律行为相冲突。

立陶宛宪法具有最高法律效力，其后效力从高到低分别为宪法性法律、法律、议会（Lith. Seimas）或立陶宛共和国政府决议、总统法令以及其他政府机构和地方市政当局的法案。下位法必须服从上位法。

议会批准的所有国际条约和公约是立陶宛法律制度的组成部分，即国际条约经议会批准即具有法律效力。如果国家法案（立陶宛宪法除外）的规定与国际条约的条款相冲突，则适用后者。

自 2004 年加入欧盟以来，立陶宛的法律制度在很大程度上受欧盟法律的影响。欧盟法是立陶宛法律制度的组成部分，包括欧盟的创始条约，欧盟法的规范必须直接适用，但是如果法律规范之间存在冲突，欧盟法优先于国家法律和其他法律得以适用。

虽然立陶宛的法律主体是法定的，但司法判例也被视为立陶宛的法律渊源之一。

（四）经济和社会环境

立陶宛在波罗的海国家中经济数据居首位，也是对外国投资者最具吸引力的波罗的海国家。2013—2018 年期间的主要宏观经济指标（期末指标基于预测）详情如下[①]：

	名义国内生产总值（GDP）（欧元 10 亿）	国内生产总值（GDP）增长率（%）	年均通胀率（%）	失业率（%）
2013 年	35.0	3.5	1.2	11.8
2014 年	36.6	6.0	0.2	10.7
2015 年	37.3	1.7	−0.7	9.1
2016 年	38.6	2.3	0.8	8.0
2017 年	40	3.3	3.2	7.3
2018 年	41.3	2	2.2	7.1

立陶宛在各种国际排名中均居前列：在世界银行对 190 个国家在商业环境方面所做的评估中名列第 16 位；在传统基金会编制的 180 个国家经济自由指数排名中名列第 19 位。

立陶宛全民接受高等教育占总人口比率位列欧盟第一。有 84% 的人精通英语，而 50% 的人至少会说两种外语。[②]

立陶宛的地理位置优越，交通运输十分便利。与拥有现代集装箱码头的克莱佩达不冻海港连接的铁路系统，为通往俄罗斯、白俄罗斯、拉脱维亚、波兰、德国、意大利、乌克兰，以及哈萨克斯坦、中国等亚洲国家提供了高效的多式联运货物的机会。此外，立陶宛拥有发达的高速公路网络以及 4 个国际机场。

立陶宛积极改善商业环境以吸引各行业和领域的投资。最受欢迎的是全球商业服务、制造业、技术和金融科技。

金融科技行业是立陶宛最有前途和增长最快的行业之一。政府部门新近采取的政策导向促使金融市场参与者（主要是电子货币机构和支付机构）大幅增加。立陶宛还引入了专门的银行制度，可以胜任大多数传统的银行业务，初始资本要求却相对较低（100 万欧元）。预计后者的发展将大大增加银行

---

① 参见 https://www.lb.lt/uploads/publications/docs/18367_de2b496c8a7462db1ed8c67b92ac89a2.pdf。
② 参见 https://investlithuania.com/wp-content/uploads/2017/09/Invest-Lithuania-general-presentation.pdf。

业的竞争力,并且目前已经吸引本地以及境外的投资者前来投资。

可再生能源的发展对立陶宛的出口也变得愈发重要。新兴清洁技术行业的未来发展依靠当地科学家和研究人员、电子工业取得的世界级成就以及该行业发展的递增利率的共同推进。立陶宛力求到2020年使用可再生能源的比例提高到该国能源消耗平衡总量的23%。

立陶宛的生物技术领域被认为是中欧和东欧最发达的国家之一。激光技术是立陶宛的另一个高科技行业,信息通信技术也是一个高度发达的行业。①

1. 累计境外直接投资投资国②

	31/12/2016	
	欧元(百万)	占比(%)
合计	13 066.24	100.0
瑞典	2 496.73	19.1
荷兰	1 585.68	12.1
德国	1 315.42	10.1
波兰	957.82	7.3
挪威	919.18	7.0
爱沙尼亚	696.41	5.3
塞浦路斯	660.88	5.1
丹麦	591.06	4.5
芬兰	588.29	4.5
马耳他	405.42	3.1
其他国家	2 849.35	21.9

2. 对外直接投资累计经济活动③

	31/12/2016	
	欧元(百万)	占比(%)
合计	13 066.24	100.0
金融保险业	3 077.07	23.5
制造业	2 602.11	19.9
批发零售业、运输车辆和摩托车维修业	1 795.51	13.7
房地产交易	1 671.24	12.8
信息通信业	1 100.51	8.4
科学技术领域	765.86	5.9
运输和存储行业	407.87	3.1
房产私人交易	367.97	2.8
行政和支持服务	345.29	2.6
其他行业	932.81	7.3

---

① 参见 https://www.pwc.com/lt/lt/assets/publications/PwC_Business_Guide_Lithuania_2018.pdf。
② 参见 https://www.lb.lt/en/statistics-database。
③ 参见 https://www.lb.lt/en/statistics-database。

（五）"一带一路"倡议下与中国企业合作的现状与方向

立陶宛与中国的经济关系日益密切。立陶宛不仅交通系统发达，而且物流快速发展，因此中国企业家对投资立陶宛十分感兴趣，并正与立陶宛的公司建立贸易联系，包括筹备中立贸易论坛。中立贸易委员会于2014年1月成立，其主要任务是发展和促进中国与立陶宛之间的商业关系。

在中立两国的双边努力下，立陶宛已成为中国在波罗的海国家中最大的经济合作伙伴，同时中国也是立陶宛最大的亚洲贸易伙伴。近几年来，立陶宛和中国的贸易关系得到加强和扩大。立陶宛对中国的产品出口增长近四倍，贸易额增加近两倍。[①]

二、投资

（一）市场准入

1. 投资监管部门

立陶宛吸引和促进投资领域的职责主要归属于经济部（Lith. Lietuvos Respublikos ūkio ministerija）。经济部成立了立陶宛投资促进局（Lith. Investuok Lietuvoje），该局积极推动外商在立陶宛投资，并向潜在投资者提供有关投资环境以及在立陶宛实际投资（如创业）方面的建议。

2. 投资法律和法规

外商投资企业由立陶宛国家立法和一些国际协议进行规范和保护。立陶宛目前是55个双边投资条约（包括与中国签订的双边投资条约）和诸如《能源宪章条约》（该条约规定了额外投资保护措施和机制）等国际协议的缔约方。

立陶宛《投资法》确立了投资领域的主要原则。该部法律的核心是平等对待和保护投资的原则，这意味着外国投资者在商业活动方面享有与立陶宛投资者相同的权利并履行相同的义务，且外国投资者的合法权益也与境内投资者受到立陶宛当地法律同样的保护。同时平等待遇制并不妨碍投资者受国际协议的保护。

此外，考虑到投资立陶宛，可能还有一些法律与此相关。立陶宛《特许经营权法》也与考虑投资公私合作伙伴（PPP）的外商投资者有关。当选择商业领域时，外国投资者还应考虑立陶宛有关自由经济区基本法的法律，该法规定，在自由经济区设立和经营的某些企业以及在这些区域的投资将得到更有利的待遇。

3. 投资形式

立陶宛的投资体系基于个人自由经济原则，这意味着在立陶宛，无论是否设立法律实体，任何人均可参与经济活动。一般而言，境外投资者可投资所有合法的商业活动，但在土地所有权，以及与国家安全和防务有关的领域，投资会有一些限制。

《投资法》规定，投资可以通过以下方式进行：①成立经济主体，在立陶宛注册的经济主体中取得资本或股份；②购买所有类型的证券；③创立、取得或增加长期资产价值；④向经济主体提供资金或其他资产，投资者因此持有股权，目的是为了能够对经济主体进行控制或产生重大影响；⑤实施特许经营权合同、融资租赁合同（租赁）以及 PPP 合同。

实际上，外国投资者也可以通过在立陶宛设立的分支机构和代表处进行投资。

4. 市场准入和检验标准

外资在立陶宛投资不需要政府当局的特别许可。但在国家安全和国防领域，立陶宛《投资法》禁止外国投资者投资该领域（除非外商投资符合立陶宛选择的欧洲大西洋一体化标准，该投资需经国防委员会批准）。

立陶宛《国家安全法》也规定了特别程序和特殊情形。当被认定对具有国家战略重要性的公司或在具有国家战略重要性的经济领域（比如能源、军事装备等部门）运行的公司进行投资时，要求委员

---

① 参见 https://osp.stat.gov.lt/uzsienio-prekyba1。

会批准协调保护重点对象以确保国家安全。

某些受监管的行业如金融、能源、医疗保健的经济活动均需获得许可，且该许可对境内投资者也同样适用。

（二）外汇管理

1. 外汇管理部门

立陶宛目前没有具体的外汇管理规定或限制可供执行。因此，不存在任何监管外汇的部门或政府机构。

2. 外汇管理法律法规简介

如前所述，立陶宛没有具体的外汇管理条例或限制。但是，欧盟实行现金控制——凡携带 10 000 欧元（或任何其他等值货币）或 10 000 欧元以上现金入境或离境的必须申报。

3. 外资企业的外汇管理要求

立陶宛对外资企业没有外汇管理的要求，因此实行自由宽松的汇款政策。

（三）融资

1. 主要金融机构

立陶宛金融机构稳定，符合欧盟标准，并且发展迅速。立陶宛银行和财政部已制定了致力于使立陶宛在成为现代金融科技中心的同时促进传统金融业改革的目标并采取实施措施。

目前，立陶宛的金融体系主要由提供零售银行服务、租赁和保险服务的银行主导。持牌的有 6 家境内银行及 7 家境外分行；欧盟有 340 家银行在立陶宛提供跨境服务，但未设立分行。按总资产计算，银行业市场占有率如下：

银行	总资产	市场份额
Swedbank, AB	EUR 7 027 479 000	24.44 %
Luminor Bank AB	EUR 6 884 488 000	23.94 %
AB SEB bankas	EUR 7 643 625 000	26.59 %
AB Šiaulių bankas	EUR 1 861 114 000	6.47 %
AB "Citadele" bankas	EUR 523 189 000	1.82 %
UAB Medicinos bankas	EUR 270 601 000	0.94 %
Foreign bank branches	EUR 4 540 864 000	15.79 %

立陶宛银行业的集中度在欧洲最高，这就是为什么在立陶宛可以看到新兴强劲的市场参与者的积极参与。[1]

欧洲投资银行（EIB）、北欧投资银行（NIB）和欧洲复兴开发银行（EBRD）等国际金融机构在立陶宛也非常活跃。各金融机构通常为重大项目提供融资（如克莱佩达液化天然气终端的实施、立陶宛跨欧洲东西铁路走廊的现代化等），并积极参与各种基金和融资计划的设立。

2. 外资企业的融资条件

法律体系对于外资企业融资条件虽然没有歧视性规定，但金融机构有完善的风险管理政策和程序，从某种意义上说，这可能阻碍境外融资进程。实际上，金融机构要求潜在客户提供其有关股权结构和股权行为的详细信息及其相关证明，以满足反洗钱和反恐怖融资的要求。

当然，在某些情况下，由于客户风险或地理风险可能被考虑在内（如：金融机构与客户没有长期

---

[1] 参见 https://www.lb.lt/en/publications/financial-stability-review-2017-1。

合作关系），实际融资条件可能不太理想。影响境外企业总体融资状况还可能与可供担保的物或替代措施有关，以确保境外企业履行融资约定的义务。

（四）土地政策

1. 土地相关法律法规简介

与外资企业有关的主要立法是关于执行立陶宛共和国宪法第47条第（3）款的宪法性法律，该法在立陶宛设立了取得土地的规则和限制。

其他关于在立陶宛取得、租赁土地的国家立法主要规定在立陶宛《关于取得农用地法》《土地法》《民法》以及立陶宛政府批准的《国有农用地块销售规则》和《国有农用地块租赁规则》。

2. 外资企业取得土地规定

（1）外资企业取得土地的限制

宪法规定，允许符合欧盟跨大西洋一体化标准的国外主体取得对土地、内部水域和森林的所有权。

前述国外主体属于下列工会、协定或组织成员之一的外国法人实体及其他外国组织（苏联为基础建立的政治、军事、经济或其他联盟或其他国家联合体除外）：①欧盟；②北大西洋公约组织；③欧洲经济区协定；④符合立陶宛实施的欧洲大西洋一体化标准的经济合作与发展组织。

实际上，取得土地的条件取决于企业的设立地，而非法律实体的受益人的国籍或居住地。

（2）对农用地的获取和使用的一般限制

最新立陶宛监管体系明确了对取得农用地主体的具体要求不再适用，尽管如此，某些一般限制（与国内外实体相关）依然存在。

农用地取得受《农用地取得法》和其他相关法律的管辖。自然人和法人都有权取得立陶宛的农用地，但有下列几种限制：①已经取得农业地的人在取得该土地后必须确保用于农业活动不得少于5年（除非上述期限届满前将地块转让第三方）；②已取得农用地不得超过最大面积限制（如下所述）；③个人及其利害关系人（配偶、父母/养父母、未成年子女/收养子女及其他相关法律实体等）取得的农用地数量将予以整体考虑。

根据《农用地取得法》，只有经农业部国土局批准，才能依据地块位置取得面积10公顷以上的农用地。国土局核实登记记载的有关人员或股权控制的农用地的面积后予以批准，以对前述人员所有的法律实体进行监管。

此外，在寻求获得拥有超过10公顷的农用地的法律实体控制权时（在法人实体参与者会议上获得至少25%的股份或投票权），国土局进行数据核实和批准的要求也同样适用。

《农用地取得法》第3条规定了可以获得农用地所有权的最大面积，即：①个人或其利害关系人可以在立陶宛境内从国家取得农用地的面积不超过300公顷；②个人或其利害关系人可以在立陶宛境内通过国家和其他人员受让取得其持有的农用地总面积不超过500公顷。

如果农用地用于畜牧业发展并且获得土地不超过个人所持牲畜单位公顷（1牲畜单位/1公顷），则不适用上述取得农用地所有权最大面积限制。《农用地取得法》第3条第2款还规定，如果过去3年牲畜单位数量下降（个人无法控制的情况而减少的除外）或个人有意将土地转让第三方的，国家必须回购畜牧业发展取得的超过市场均价允许限度内的土地面积。

（3）农地租赁

私人农业用地的租赁适用《民法》中土地租赁一般条件的规定，没有特别（专门）规定。

国有土地租赁也是根据《民法》的规定，而《土地法》中对具体条款和程序规则作了具体规定。根据有关立法，立陶宛和外国或其他外国组织的自然人和法人有权租赁国有农用地。土地租赁期由出租人与承租人协议确定，但不得超过25年。国有土地租赁期限届满后，如果未预见有其他用途，承租人适当履行合同义务并希望续约的，须在协议终止前3个月提交续租申请，并有权不遵守优先购买权而续约。同时，承租人完全履行合同义务的，在国家租赁协议届满前3个月内，可申请延期一次，但期限不得超过合同约定，且根据国土规划文件该地块无其他用途。

地块租金按市议会批准的费率计算。出租人有权根据议会每3年评估一次的费率重新调整地块租金。

(五) 公司设立和解散

1. 企业形式

（1）最普遍的企业形式

不同形式的私人和公共法律实体都各有其益处。但立陶宛最普遍的企业形式是私人有限责任公司（Lith. uždaroji akcinė bendrovė）和公共有限责任公司（Lith. akcinė bendrovė）。规范各种形式法律实体的法律主要是立陶宛公司法，自然人和法人都可以成为公司股东。

在立陶宛是根据公司财产独立于个人财产的原则设立有限责任公司的，各类型公司之间的差异主要如下：

	私人有限责任公司	公共有限责任公司
最低法定资本	2 500 欧元	40 000 欧元
股东数量	上限 250 人	无限制
公开市场股票交易	不可交易	上市公司即可交易
管理结构	股东大会 总经理 董事会（可选） 监事会（可选）	股东大会 总经理 董事会（可选） 监事会（可选） 公司内至少须组建一个治理机构

公众有限责任公司须进行强制审计，但私人有限责任公司的审计不是强制性的，除非满足以下至少两项标准：①一个财务年度内销售收入超过 350 万欧元；②资产负债表中资产总价值超过 180 万欧元；③财务年度内平均雇员人数达 50 人或以上。

（2）其他外国投资者企业形式

在立陶宛进行商业活动还可以其他类型设立公司，这些公司包括普通和有限合伙企业、农业公司、一人公司以及欧洲公司、欧洲合作社①等。

一人公司（Lith. individualij monė）是一个无限责任的法人。所有者应以其所有财产对公司承担责任。由于其没有最低法定资本要求，并且适用的财务会计规则简易，因此这种公司形式在立陶宛非常普遍。

普通合伙企业（Lith. tikroji ū kinė bendrija）是根据若干自然人或法人之间的合伙合资协议建立的承担无限责任的一种企业形式。这种合伙关系是通过将个人财产转移为合伙企业的共同财产实现，其目的是以共同的企业名义进行商业活动。普通合伙的所有合伙人均应以其个人财产对合伙企业承担连带责任，但是合伙企业对合伙人在不因合伙企业所产生的义务时，不承担责任。

有限合伙企业（Lith. komanditinė ū kinė bendrija）拥有无限责任的普通合伙人和仅以其认缴的出资额为限承担有限责任的有限合伙人，这些合伙人仅以其对合伙的贡献承担责任。有限合伙企业必须至少有一名普通合伙人和一名有限合伙人。

还有可能根据欧盟法的规定成立合法企业，主要形式为欧洲合作社（SCE）和欧洲公司（Societas Europaea，SE）。欧洲公司类似于资本划分为股份的公共有限责任公司。欧洲公司最低认购股本不低于 120 000 欧元。欧洲合作社旨在满足其成员的利益并发展他们的经济和社会活动，特别是与他们就商品供应、提供服务或履行义务达成协议。最低法定资本不低于 30 000 欧元。欧洲合作社社员可承担有限责任，也可承担无限责任。

2. 设立程序

成立不同类型企业需要采取的步骤也不同。建立私人有限责任公司和公众有限责任公司的程序包括以下步骤：①选择和预留公司名称；②准备设立公司的文件；③开设银行账户；④将股本转入累计银行账户；⑤在公证处办理文件公证；⑥向公司登记处注册法人实体。

---

① 企业形式并未全部列举。

如果创办人拥有合格电子签名并符合法律规定的其他条件,某些类型企业(包括私营有限责任公司)可以通过电子方式设立。

当然,设立公司前还需办理相关手续,包括向国家税务监察局(立陶宛税务局)进行税率登记,再向国家社会保险基金董事会(SODRA)登记注册并完成增值税登记。

应该强调的是,从事某些行业(如医疗保健、金融服务领域)需要获得许可证和/或执照。

3. 解散途径和条件

根据立陶宛法律,只有当法人不存在未清偿债务或所有债务在清算程序中最终解决时,法人才可通过清算程序得以注销。法人实体所有成员可以就清算公司和清算人任命作出决定。一旦决定作出,公司的所有机构都无权清算,并且只有清算人才可以代表公司进行清算工作。

(六)兼并和收购

立陶宛关于兼并和收购(以下简称"并购"或"M&A")的主要法律规范是《民法》《公司法》《竞争法》《证券法》以及《金融工具市场法》。考虑到交易的复杂性和具体情况,也可能涉及其他相关法律规定。所有相关法律均与欧盟相一致。

《民法》为大部分并购交易类型奠定法律基础。它提供了至少三种商业销售的替代模式:①股票交易;②资产交易;以及③企业交易(这种转让包括相关特定业务的资产、权利和义务)。根据《民法》的规定,通过合并(加入或联合)进行的重组也被视为一种商业收购模式。重组程序非常复杂且耗时;因此,它很少被选择作为收购手段,而是通常被用于收购后优化目标公司的机制。

关于转让公共和私人有限责任公司股份以及公司管理机构的权限和义务的条款由《公司法》规定。

《竞争法》也适用于并购交易。在法律规定的情况下〔如下第(七)部分"竞争管制"所述〕,竞争委员会评估潜在并购交易并作出决议:①关于集中批准;②关于批准某些条件下由合并公司或其管理机构履行集中;或③拒绝集中许可。

《证券法》还规定了其他相关规定〔详见下文第(九)部分"证券"〕。

根据并购交易类型及其复杂性适用其他法律。

(七)竞争管制

1. 反不正当竞争法律规定

立陶宛竞争理事会是国家监督机构和竞争监督机构。竞争理事会执行立陶宛竞争政策,并监督规则遵守情况。竞争理事会由1名主席和4名理事会成员组成,所有成员都是由立陶宛总统根据总理提名任命。

2. 竞争法简介

《竞争法》是立陶宛竞争法的主要规定。立陶宛的竞争制度与欧盟模式基本一致。另外,竞争委员会的二级立法也符合欧盟竞争规则和其他规定。

3. 规范竞争法的措施

反竞争协议。《竞争法》和《欧盟运行条约》第101条禁止公司之间的协议妨碍、限制或扭曲竞争,并且违反这些法律可能导致重罚。反竞争协议包括价格操纵或市场垄断,它们保护参与此类协议的公司免于开发新产品、提高质量和降低价格的竞争,从而导致消费者更高的价格购买产品。以下协议通常被认为是反竞争的:①关于操纵价格的协议;②关于限制生产的协议;③关于分享市场或客户的协议;④关于分享商业秘密的协议;⑤串标协议;⑥关于操纵转售价格的协议(制造商和分销商之间)。

尽管如此,这一制度对于反竞争协议也有排除适用。各自的规则适用于因不可预见的影响而能限制竞争(法律规则)的经营者之间的协议。据推测,下列协议因无足轻重而无法限制竞争:①总市场份额不超过相应市场10%的企业之间的横向或混合协议;②单个市场份额不超过相应市场15%的企业之间的纵向协议。

此外,排除的情形有:有关协定促进投资、技术或经济进步或改善货物分配的;以及协议不对缔约方的活动施加对于达到上述目标不是不可缺少的限制的,且协议并未给予缔约方限制主要市场竞争的可能性。无须获得竞争理事会的事先批准来确保此类协议的有效性。但按照有关规定，举证责任由希望享有豁免权的一方承担。

滥用支配地位。具有市场支配地位并不被禁止，但占有市场支配地位的企业必须遵守与不具备市场支配力的竞争对手相比的更为严格的要求。禁止采取限制或可能限制竞争的行为，排挤其他经营者的可能性，或者损害消费者权益的行为，滥用相关市场的支配地位。市场支配地位被定义为一个或多个企业在相关市场中处于没有直接竞争的地位，或者是能够单独通过有效限制竞争在该市场施加决定性影响的地位。

下列情况推定为支配和共同支配：①一个经营者在相关市场的市场份额达到 40%；②三个或三个以下经营者中每个经营者单独在相关市场占有最大份额并共同占有市场份额达到 70% 的。

《竞争法》还列举了可能构成滥用支配地位行为的情形。这种行为包括：①直接或间接地设定不公平的购买或销售价格的，或其他不公平的交易条件的；②限制生产、市场或技术发展，损害消费者利益的；③在相同的交易情形下，对交易对方当事人实行不同的交易条件，因而置其于不利的竞争地位的；④要求对方当事人接受与合同主体在本质上或商业惯例上无关联的附加义务，作为签订合同的前提条件的。

不公平竞争。禁止经济主体采取任何违背公平商业惯例和良好做法的行为，这可能会对另一经济主体的竞争潜力产生负面影响。《竞争法》规定了可能被认为构成不正当竞争行为的非详尽清单，其中包括：①未经许可，使用与其参考标记相同或近似的名称、注册商标或未注册的知名商标或其他经济主体具有显著特征的参考标记的，导致或容易导致混淆的；或者为寻求滥用该经济主体（标记或参考标记）声誉或可能损害该经济主体（标记或参考标记）声誉；或者可能降低该经济主体使用的标记或参考标记的显著特征；②通过向经济主体提供关于生产的数量、质量、成分、使用性能、地点以及制造方法和价格或者隐瞒商品的消费量、加工或其他用途的风险的错误或未证实的信息，误导经济主体的；③为了争夺市场份额，未经其他经济主体许可以及从无权转让人处获取信息，使用、转让、披露经济主体商业秘密信息，获取利益或损害该经济主体等。

根据适用法律，竞争委员会仅在不正当竞争行为违反大多数经济主体或消费者利益的情况下才进行调查。

合并控制。竞争委员会履行监管市场集中度的职能。在立陶宛法律条文中，集中度是指：①当一个或多个企业终止其单独经营活动而合并共同继续经营业务，或者一个或多个企业终止其单独经营活动而新设一个企业的合并；②当同一自然人或已经控制一个或多个企业的自然人或一个或多个企业，通过协议共同设立新企业时获得控制权（除非新企业不能独立承担责任），或者通过合同或任何其他方式收购整个或部分企业，企业的全部或部分资产、股份或其他证券以及投票权，从而获得对另一企业的控制权。

计划并购之前必须通知竞争委员会，如果合并集中前一个财年企业合并总收入超过 20 000 000 欧元，且合并集中前一财年至少两个企业中各自的总收入超过 2 000 000 欧元。尽管总收入不超过《竞争法》规定的限制，竞争委员会在可能导致产生或加强支配地位或实质限制竞争相关市场的情况下启动兼并控制程序，合并必须获得许可。

在通知之前实施合并，以及在暂停期间继续合并，并且违反既定的合并条件或义务，可能会对企业处以上一个业务年度总收入的 10% 的罚款。未能提供信息或提供合并审查所需的不正确和不完整的信息，可能会对企业处以上一个业务年度全年总收入最高 1% 的罚款。对于未及时履行竞争委员会的指示的承诺，可对企业处以前一个业务年度平均每日总收入 5% 的罚款。

（八）税收

1. 税制和规则

立陶宛《税收管理法》第 13 条规定了构成立陶宛税收制度的法律清单。以下为主要税费：个人所得税、企业所得税、增值税、消费税、房地产税、土地税、遗产税以及彩票博彩税。

立陶宛税制由立陶宛税务局、海关当局、社会保险局和立陶宛环境部授权的机构管理。

2. 主要税种和税率

企业所得税（CIT）。外国实体驻立陶宛的居民企业和常设机构（包括分支机构）须缴纳全球所得税（包括股息、获得的援助/捐赠未用于所述目的等）的企业所得税。

非居民企业的常设机构缴纳与居民企业相同税率的企业所得税。

企业所得税税率一般为15%。下列企业，企业所得税税率可减征5%：①符合特定条件的小型企业；②参与农业活动且符合一定条件的公司。以下企业可将税率降低至零：①在自由经济区（FEZ）设立的前6年内（接下来10年，税率为7.5%）；②雇用有资格获得社会支持的特定群体。

资本收益。立陶宛经济实体从证券交易或其他金融工具中获得的收入构成应纳税所得额，须按照一般税率缴纳企业所得税。

但是，如果从在欧洲经济区注册或以其他方式成立的法人的股权转让中获得收益，且该实体通常缴纳利润税，立陶宛的实体至少连续2年持有该实体10%以上的股份的，该资本收益不应纳税。

股息。一般来说，从立陶宛或外国实体收取的股息红利中代扣15%的所得税。如果一个立陶宛实体支付股息给另一个立陶宛实体并代扣15%的所得税，利息付款人可将所扣税款抵缴自己应缴的企业所得税。

根据立陶宛加入的免税规则，从立陶宛实体至少持有12个月达10%以上股份的当地或外国实体（免税地区的实体除外）所收取的股息红利，免征所得税，立陶宛实体的收入不包括在内。

立陶宛实体向外国股东（实体或个人）支付的股息红利须代扣15%的所得税；但根据国家加入的免税规则，支付给外国股东（法人、免税地区实体）的股息红利，该股东持有立陶宛实体10%以上的股份至少12个月（包括股息红利分配期间）的，免征所得税。

社会税。除支付员工工资外，雇主还有义务每月计算并支付社会税。社会税率为31.18%至32.80%，强制性医疗保险9%，员工需缴纳9%的社会税，且雇主必须代扣代缴。

增值税。增值税是对在立陶宛经营活动过程中提供商品和服务实现的增值额征收的一个税种。

历年应纳税所得额达45 000欧元需进行强制纳税登记，未达45 000欧元可自愿登记。

增值税税率一般为21%。企业从事下列项目的所得，减征9%增值税税率：①书籍和非定期信息出版；②报纸、杂志和期刊（除色情、暴力或不符合职业道德要求的出版物外）；③定期航线客运服务和旅客行李运输；④住宿服务；⑤为住宅供暖和为消费者供应热水所供热能。

企业从事下列项目的所得，增值税税率减征5%：①残疾人辅助器具和维修残疾人辅助器具；②根据《医疗保险法》有权全额或部分偿还购置费用的人提供药品和医疗援助。

增值税零税率适用于从立陶宛运到另一欧盟成员国或欧盟以外的货物供应。

个人所得税。立陶宛居民需对其全球范围内的收入纳税。如果个人居住地或社会经济利益中心在立陶宛的，或者在立陶宛居住至少183天，则为立陶宛居民。应纳税所得额主要包括工资、营业收入、租金收入、股息。

非居民在立陶宛境内或境外取得个人所得的，如果收入与非居民在立陶宛的永久性财产有关，包括利息、股息、不动产租金、特许权使用费、工资、体育活动收入、表演收入、出售或交换依法登记的不动产或动产、侵犯版权或邻接权赔偿费，则需缴纳个人所得税。

个人所得税平均税率为15%，收入源于个人行为的除外——5%或15%（取决于收入水平）。

不动产税。不动产税应由立陶宛不动产（各种用途的建筑物）所有者支付。

这些税由公司和自然人支付。对自然人而言，非征税限额为220 000欧元。

如果房产通过融资租赁的方式购买，不动产税由该购房者支付，而非由注册为房产的官方所有人的金融机构支付。适用税率为0.3%至3%不等，具体取决于房产所在地政府。市议会有权使用市政预算而完全给予减税或免税；通常，在相关市镇开展业务的投资者享受该利益和例外。

（九）证券

1. 证券相关法律法规简介

立陶宛证券市场主要受《证券法》监管。当一家公司的股票被允许在立陶宛证券交易所进行交易时，他们将受到所有强制性收购要约以及《证券法》规定的排除规则和出售规则的约束。根据《证法》，一人单独或与他人共同收购，获得由其或与他人一致行动使其在公司股东大会上获得超过 1/3 的投票权的股票，他必须或转让股份超过这一比例，或宣布强制要约收购获取表决权的剩余公司股份和确认授予表决权股份的证券。所赋予职责也适用于对持有公司股份的实体取得控制权的人，就其股份而言，收购要约将使其获得股东大会 1/3 以上的表决权。在挤出的情况下，当一个主体单独或与他人一致行动而获取不低于资本表决权的 95% 以及不低于发起人大会总数的 95%，有权要求所有剩余发起人股东出售其所持有的有表决权的股份，且股东有出售义务。在出售情况下，任何小股东均有权要求，单独或与他人一致行动时获得的股份不少于资本表决权的 95% 和不少于股东大会总票数的 95% 的主体购买属于小股东并授予表决权的股份，而且该主体有购买义务。

此外，《市场滥用条例》（MAR）也是立陶宛（以及欧盟其他任何成员国）直接适用的法律，适用的立陶宛法律没有在《市场滥用条例》所涵盖的监管领域附加任何规定。

2. 监管证券市场

立陶宛银行。立陶宛证券市场由立陶宛银行监管。在其权限范围内，立陶宛银行致力于确保国内金融服务和证券市场体系的安全性、健全性和透明度。

纳斯达克。立陶宛金融工具交易市场由纳斯达克运作。它根据适用的法律开展业务，包括《金融工具市场法》及纳斯达克内部规定，其中包括纳斯达克组织章程、纳斯达克上市规则等。

纳斯达克运作的交易市场构成了相关欧盟立法和《金融工具市场法》规范的受监管市场。纳斯达克还组织并运营一个非监管市场的另类交易系统（First North）。纳斯达克经营的交易市场提供了在主板市场和二板市场上市的可能性。

根据纳斯达克的网站（www.nasdaqbaltic.com），迄今，68 家公司的股票在纳斯达克波罗的海上市。截至 2018 年 2 月 14 日，纳斯达克上市公司的总资本为 73.16 亿欧元。

证券交易所交易机制。根据纳斯达克规则，纳斯达克定期于周一至周五的维尔纽斯时间每天上午 10 点开盘至下午 4 点收盘，除非纳斯达克管理委员会另有决定。在交易时间（上午 10 点至下午 4 点）内，会员可以订购、更改、暂停、恢复或取消订单。与收益率、交易量和其他条件下对应的买卖订单通过自动对盘进行配对交易。在这个交易阶段可能会报告手动交易。会员在交易前或交易后不得订购或更改订单或报告手动交易。有关证券的价格、交易量和任何特定权利（优先权或分红权）的信息可在纳斯达克官方网站上获取。纳斯达克或其他监管机构并未确定立陶宛的经纪佣金，其由执行交易的经纪行设定。

3. 外资企业从事证券交易的要求

外国企业在立陶宛享有平等进入证券市场的权利。请注意，力求在立陶宛进行公开发行的潜在外国企业必须遵守立陶宛法律（主要根据《证券法》）规定的最低标准。

（十）投资的优先和保护

1. 优惠政策的结构

没有具体既定的优惠政策。但是立陶宛是欧盟成员国也因此是欧洲单一市场的一部分，该欧洲单一市场旨在消除欧盟内部货物和服务自由流动的内部边界和其他监管障碍。此外，立陶宛是一些双边投资条约的缔约方，这些条约授予这些特定国家的投资者额外的保护，并因此具有优势。

2. 支持特定行业和地区

各个部门均有支持措施，实施这些措施是为了促进出口、再生能源、研发和创新等。

通过各种措施促进可再生能源的生产，其中包括但不限于税收优惠（如再生能源免除消费税）、补贴和贷款。在立陶宛，来自可再生能源的电力主要通过滑动馈电技术增强。除此之外，用于运输部门的可再生能源通过多种支持计划得到推广。

三项主要的促进出口措施包括：①立陶宛的政府代理商和电子商务网络提供的咨询支持；②旨在鼓励企业更积极地寻求外国合作伙伴并增加在国外市场的销售的欧盟支持；③由英维格（Invega）机构提供的出口信贷保险。不应将出口促进措施视为向出口商给予不符合欧盟和世界贸易组织的补贴、财政援助或直接支付的行为。①

立陶宛在研究开发以及技术创新领域提供了一系列直接和间接支持措施。这些措施主要分为三类，即：①税收优惠；②科技园区、立陶宛创新中心、科技创新机构；③能使中小企业有权从研究教育机构购买研发专业知识的创新券（小额信贷（固定资金））。

3. 特殊经济领域

（1）区域政策的修订

立陶宛当局最近推出了旨在促进立陶宛和谐、可持续发展的区域政策白皮书。拟议政策的核心原则之一是区域专业化，这是整个区域发展优先事项及其实施措施，把人力资本和金融资本集中于最具效率和潜力的经济特区。②例如，从 2018 年起，克莱佩达地区将致力于支持海上海事领域可持续发展的长期战略，帕涅韦日斯市力图成为机器人的中心，马里扬泊列市寻求吸引木材、食品和金属等行业的投资者。预计修订政策的实施将对潜在投资环境产生重大积极影响。

（2）自由经济区

自由经济区（FEZ）被指定用于商业、金融或工业活动的区域，其中适用的是税收优惠制度。在立陶宛，被允许在区域进行的活动可能仅限特定的自由经济区。一般而言，任何不被禁止的经济活动均可进行，除国防工业（包括生产、储存或销售武器和爆炸物）、烟草，烈酒生产，证券，钱币，邮票的制作，生产、储存或销售药物或有毒物品，博彩业等。

不同的税收优惠适用于位于自由经济区的企业。该区域企业无须缴纳房地产税，外国投资者赚取的股息红利也是免税的。此外，目前法律规定，从事工业、仓储、航空或 IT 领域运营的投资者超过 100 万欧元的，在公司设立前 6 年免缴企业所得税，接下来的 10 年适用 50%的企业税率。100 万欧元投资额是免税起点；它也适用于雇员不少于 20 名且投资不低于 10 万欧元的商业服务公司。

税	自由经济区	立陶宛（一般）
公司税	0%（前 6 年）	15%
公司税	7.5%（后 10 年）	15%
房地产税	0%	1%

目前在立陶宛建立了 7 个自由经济区（分别为 Akmenė, Kaunas, Kėdainiai, Klaipėda, Marijampolė, Panevėžys, Šiauliai）。③自由经济区交通便利地理位置优越，每个自由经济区都有与该地区相关的额外优势。

4. 投资保护

立陶宛与包括中国④在内的 54 个国家签有双重征税条约，从而为外国投资创造了有利的税收环境。

根据国家法律和国际协定，投资受到保护。立陶宛目前是 55 个双边投资条约（包括与中国签订的双边投资条约）的缔约国以及如《能源宪章条约》《解决投资争端国际中心（ICSID）公约》等国际协定的缔约方。

《投资法》规定，国家和地方政府和官员均无权干涉投资对象的管理、使用和处置。国家或地方当局及其官员的非法行为对投资者造成损害的，将按照立陶宛法律规定的程序予以赔偿。

外国投资者与立陶宛投资者之间的投资争议可以通过双方协商、立陶宛法院的判决或国际仲裁机构仲裁的方式解决。如果发生投资争议，外国投资者有权直接向 ICSID 提起仲裁。

---

① 参见 https://ukmin.lrv.lt/en/sector-activities/export/export-promotion-measures。
② 参见 https://vrm.lrv.lt/uploads/vrm/documents/files/LT_versija/Veikla/Veiklos%20sritis/Region%C5%B3%20pl%C4%97tra/Lithuanian%20Regional%20Policy%20(White%20Paper).pdf.
③ 参见 https://ukmin.lrv.lt/lt/veiklos-sritys/investiciju-veiklos-sritis/pramoniniai-parkai-ir-lez。
④ 参见 http://www.vmi.lt/cms/en/tarptautines-dvigubo-apmokestinimo-isvengimo-sutartys。

三、贸易

（一）贸易监管机构

立陶宛经济部负责创造良好的法律及经济环境以促进经济增长。经济部负责监管国内贸易、出口、投资、创新、特许经营、国有企业及欧盟对于商业、公共采购、旅游等领域的支持。此外，经济部与立陶宛外交部合作，制定立陶宛的对外贸易政策。经济部还密切管理军民两用物品[①]、技术及军事装备的出口、进口、过境及经纪活动。

严格来讲，对贸易的监督和控制权并不完全掌握在经济部手中。具体就某个产品而言，不同的产品可能牵涉不同的主管部门。例如食品贸易，监管当局可能包括：立陶宛政府、立陶宛经济部、立陶宛卫生部、立陶宛农业部、立陶宛国家食品兽医局和国家消费者权益保护局。

（二）贸易法律法规简要介绍

在立陶宛，规制贸易的最重要的法律是立陶宛《民法》，《民法》包含了适用法律合集，包括买卖、消费者权利、特许经营、分销、货运代理及贸易其他重要领域的基本要求。另一个值得提及的法律是立陶宛《竞争法》，该法保障立陶宛的公平竞争自由。如果贸易涉及消费者商品，则应注意立陶宛《关于禁止对消费者不公平贸易的商业实践法》《禁止零售商不公平行为法》和《消费者权益保护法》。就贸易而言，重要立法包括立陶宛《产品安全法》《包装及包装废料管理法》《商品标签及价格指示规定》（由经济部长命令批准），以及《零售贸易规定》（由立陶宛政府决议批准）。

其他适用的立法及二级法律应根据商品的种类、贸易性质及业务类型而决定。

（三）贸易管理

为了创造条件使欧盟的出口商在向第三国出口农产品及食品的全球市场上更具竞争优势，适用的立法允许支付出口退税，以在一定程度上弥补全球和欧盟市场价格之间的差异。此外，也有某些特定措施（例如进口许可及进口税）用于阻止来自第三国的廉价产品侵入欧盟内部市场。例如，在农业领域，欧盟已对某些农产品实行进口关税配额。在某些情况下，在进口关税配额下进口的产品须按照2006年8月31日第1301/2006号委员会条例的规定，实行进口许可制度，该条例规定了在进口许可证体系管理下农产品进口关税配额管理的一般规则。在立陶宛，负责管理农产品进出口许可证和证书的政府当局是立陶宛农业部下属的国家支付机构，该机构实行预先补偿机制。根据国家支付机构公布的数据，登记在该机构市场监管部门的《贸易商登记册》中的公司数目已从2005年的156家增加到2013年的310家。同样，由国家市场监管部签发的进口许可证数量也从2005年的231个增加到2013年的348个。

（四）进出口商品检验检疫

根据欧洲议会及理事会于2013年10月9日通过的欧盟第952/2013号条例中制定的联合海关代码，海关当局可进行他们认为必要的海关管制。具体而言，海关管制可能包括货物检验、采样，检查报关单或通知单上信息的准确性及完整性，是否具备文件及文件的真实性、准确性及有效性、检查运营者的账户及其他记录，检查运输工具，查验被检查人携带的行李及其他物品及进行官方询问或类似手段。优先控制区包括某些特定的海关程序、货物种类、运输路线、运输方式或在一定时期内受到更高级别的风险分析及海关管制（但不影响海关当局通常进行的其他管制）的经济经营者。

海关查验货物、取样、检验运输工具，并可以随时要求卸下货物并拆箱。经运输工具装载或需卸货的货物须经海关当局授权，在这些当局指定或批准的地点卸货或转运。

为了海关管控的目的，海关可以检查报关单、暂时存放声明、出入境摘要报关单、再出口报关单或再出口通知上信息的完整性及准确性，以及是否具有相关证明文件及该等文件的真实性、准确性及

[①] 军民两用物品是指可用于民用和军用目的的物品，包括软件和技术，也包括所有可用于非爆炸性用途和以任何方式协助制造核武器及其他核爆装置的物品。

有效性，且可以查验报关人账户及与问题货物经营相关的其他记录或该等货物放行前或放行后的商业运营相关记录。如可能，当局也可以检查货物或取样。该等管控措施可以在货物持有人、货物代理人、其他以商业身份而直接或间接地参与到前述运营的人或任何为商业目的而拥有上述文件及数据的人的住所进行。

海关应采取必要措施（包括没收、出售或销毁）以处理下列货物：
① 未履行海关立法中规定将非欧盟货物引入欧盟关税区的任一义务，或由海关监管扣留的货物；
② 货物因以下任一原因而不能被放行：
- 由于报关员的原因，海关当局无法在规定期限内进行或继续货物检查；
- 未能提供货物应有的或放行所必须提供的海关手续文件；
- 在规定期限内未能缴纳进口或出口关税费用或提供担保（视情况而定）；
- 货物受到禁止或限制。
③ 货物在放行后的合理期限内未被移走。
④ 在货物放行后，发现货物不符合该放行的条件。
⑤ 被遗弃给国家的货物。

根据立陶宛《海关法》，如达成了某一决定并根据该决定将归还在民事、行政、刑事案件或审前调查中或由立陶宛其他相应的主管部门决定而没收的货物，但若货物的所有者没有在相应通知/决定的生效之日起30个工作日内取回货物，这些货物将被出售。销售货物的收益，在扣减进口及其他税费（若有）及储存、运输及销售费用后应退还给货主。不能出售的货物（以及应销毁的货物）必须销毁。

（五）海关管理

欧盟单一市场运作的关键要素是关税同盟。它运用一套通用的规则和程序来运行一个单一的货物进出口系统。关税同盟意味着，成员国之间的所有货物贸易没有国界和关税，欧盟内的货物自由流动。在欧盟边界外，共同关税及一体化税率（TARIC）适用于非欧盟国家的货物。

由于立陶宛是欧盟的成员国，其关税规则和程序直接由适用于整个欧盟内国家的欧盟海关代码（欧洲联盟议会及理事会第952/2013号条例制定的欧盟海关代码）规定。欧盟海关代码是欧盟海关规定和程序的框架规则。欧盟海关代码的主要目标是转变为完全使用电子系统，利用电子数据处理技术处理海关当局间、海关当局与经济经营者间的所有信息交换及该等信息的存储。大多数适用于欧盟海关编代码条款的新的或升级后的电子系统将于2020年年底前投入使用，但有些电子系统可能直到2025年年底才能全部完成。

立陶宛的边境国际贸易由立陶宛海关控制。立陶宛海关系统包括立陶宛财政部海关部门、海关刑事部门、海关培训中心、海关检测中心、海关信息系统中心及三个位于维尔纽斯、考纳斯及克莱佩达的区域性海关办公室。

四、劳动

（一）劳动法律法规简介

在立陶宛，规制劳动关系的主要法律是立陶宛《劳动法》。相比以前的《劳动法》（在2017年6月30日前有效），现行的《劳动法》允许自由订立固定期限劳动合同，且允许根据雇主意愿终止劳动关系，显著降低雇主主动终结劳动关系时的遣散费及通知期限，放宽了加班的最大限制，引入了新的劳动合同类型（工作共享、同时为多家雇主工作、学徒制、基于特定项目的劳动关系），放开了高薪雇员的合同自由，并采取了其他重要措施以在雇佣关系方面建立更灵活的监管规定，增强立陶宛劳动市场对外国投资者的吸引力。

除了《劳动法》，劳动关系也受立陶宛政府的法令（其中最值得注意的是《员工健康及安全法》《外国人法律地位法》《国家社会保险法》）及决议，以及社会劳动保障部部长、卫生部部长、首席劳动督察长的命令及其他法令的监管。违反劳动法律的责任在《劳动法》《行政违法法》《刑法》以及其他法律中均有规定。

(二) 雇用外国人的规定

欧盟国民可以不受任何限制地在立陶宛工作。欧盟国民不必取得工作许可证和/或居留证，但在立陶宛于任意半年内工作或停留超过 3 个月以上的欧盟国民必须取得证书，证明其在立陶宛共和国拥有居留权。

意图在立陶宛工作的非欧盟国民必须满足两项要求：

① 在立陶宛的停留必须合法，即为了进入和停留在立陶宛，他们必须获得签证或暂住证，除非适用免签证制度；

② 必须获得工作许可证或劳动交换决定，确认雇员的工作满足立陶宛劳动力市场的需要，除非他们被相应豁免。

立陶宛的法律规定了多种可以在立陶宛雇用非欧盟国民的方式。

1. 工作许可

为了使非欧盟国民在立陶宛根据劳动合同工作，雇主需要首先向立陶宛劳动交换部门申请并获得工作签证，或获得劳动交换部门的决定（以下简称"劳动交换决定"），确认雇员的工作满足立陶宛劳动市场的需求，除非该规定不适用。

立陶宛法律规定了多种非欧盟国民可以豁免持有工作签证或劳动交换决定的义务的情形：

① 非欧盟国民来立陶宛处理涉及协商合同及履行合同、培训人员或安装设备的事宜，每年最多不超过 3 个月；

② 非欧盟国民是成立于欧盟/欧洲自由贸易联盟成员国的公司的永久员工，该员工被派来立陶宛临时工作且他在该成员国具有社会保险；

③ 非欧盟国民来立陶宛从事需要高资质的工作（即所谓"欧盟蓝卡"），且其月薪不低于立陶宛平均月薪总额的 3 倍，或不低于立陶宛平均月薪总额的 1.5 倍且其职业在立陶宛劳动市场职业需求列表中；

④ 非欧盟国民具有立陶宛永久居民身份；

⑤ 非欧盟国民的职业在立陶宛劳动市场职业需求列表中；

⑥ 非欧盟国民来立陶宛的外国公司代表处、分公司或外国集团公司的立陶宛关联方作为董事或专家工作不超过 3 年，但该非欧盟国民需在该外国公司已工作超过 6 个月且立陶宛相关单位非常需要他的专业技能或高级专业资格；

⑦ 非欧盟国民是立陶宛私人单位的股东或董事（该单位的经营期限、最低股本值及人员数量方面都有特定要求）；

⑧ 其他法律规定的情形。

工作许可及劳动交换决定由立陶宛劳动交换处签发。工作许可最长可签发 1 年，劳动交换决定最长可签发 1 年或 2 年，且以后可以延长。

劳动交换处向外国人颁发了允许其在立陶宛工作的文件后，该外国人应当申请合法居留在立陶宛的证件。如外国人已经获发工作许可，他应当申请国家 D 类签证。如果获发劳动交换决定，应领取暂时居留许可。

2. 申请程序

申请工作许可/劳动交换决定具有以下程序步骤：

① 向高等教育质量评估中心提交学历证书以获得职业资格推荐（如适用）；

② 在地区劳动交换处登记空缺；

③ 向劳动交换处提交工作许可/劳动交换决定申请；

④ 在地区劳动交换处登记劳动合同。

雇主需对该程序负责。

暂时居住许可程序：

① 向立陶宛境内的移民当局或立陶宛驻外使馆或领事馆提出申请；

② 正式确定暂时居住许可；

③ 领取暂时居住许可。

如需获得国家 D 类签证，程序包括下列步骤：
① 向立陶宛驻外使馆或领事馆提出申请；
② 获得签证。

3. 社会保险

在立陶宛与雇主订立雇佣合同时，雇主必须在正式工作开始前至少 1 个工作日通知国家社会保险基金并提供一份标准表格。

一般来说，如果个人与立陶宛的公司签订雇佣合同，他就必须缴纳个人所得税、健康保险和社会保险。但是，由于可能会适用某些豁免，适用的税费需根据个案来评估。

（三）出入境

1. 签证类型

签证具有两种类型，即申根签证及国家签证。

申根签证：
① 机场过境签证 (A) —— 在申根成员国境内一个或多个机场的国际中转区域中转的有效签证；
② 短期停留签证 (C) —— 从第一次入境申根成员国的领土起算，任意 180 天内可在申根成员国的领土内中转或停留不超过 90 天的签证。

国家签证 —— 允许来到并在立陶宛停留 1 年的签证。

对在立陶宛获得临时或永久居留许可的非欧盟国民，可以签发单一入境签证。

多次入境签证可以签发给要在立陶宛长期停留的非欧盟国民［例如非欧盟国民前来立陶宛工作且持有工作许可，或他的职业是列在立陶宛劳动市场职业需求清单内的，非欧盟国民基于当地公司与外国公司的服务合同或工作合同被借调到立陶宛的客户的公司工作（由外国公司派出）等］。

暂住许可：如果非欧盟国民打算在立陶宛于 180 天内停留超过 90 天，该非欧盟国民可以申请暂住许可。暂住许可授予一个非欧盟国民在该许可规定的期限内在立陶宛临时居住的权利。通常，暂住许可的期限是 1 年，但其期限也可以更短。立陶宛法律提供了多种非欧盟国民可以申请暂住许可的依据（例如，非欧盟国民获发劳动交换决定；非欧盟国民打算从事需要高资质的工作；非欧盟国民由隶属于同一集团的公司被派遣来工作等）。

欧盟蓝卡：值得一提的是欧盟蓝卡，该卡是一种签发给来立陶宛从事高资质要求工作的非欧盟国民的暂时居住许可。

为了符合申请该卡的资格，非欧盟国民需要具有由高等教育（如大学）文凭证明的高专业资格或不少于 5 年专业经验，且该专业经验对于雇主根据劳动协议承诺雇用他的职位或者劳动协议本身而言非常重要。此外，为了符合欧盟蓝卡的资格，应满足每月薪金的要求（每月不低于 1.5 倍或 3 倍立陶宛平均月薪）。

如果外国人的月薪不低于立陶宛平均月薪的 3 倍或不低于立陶宛平均月薪的 1.5 倍且其职业被列入立陶宛需求职业清单，该外国人不需要履行工作许可或者劳动交换决定相关的手续，而应当直接申请暂时居住许可，该许可足以使其在立陶宛工作及居住。

如果该外国人的月薪低于立陶宛平均月薪的 3 倍，但高于立陶宛平均月薪的 1.5 倍，且该外国人的职业不在立陶宛需求职业清单中，该外国人需要获得劳动交换决定，确认其高资质要求的工作符合立陶宛的劳动市场需求。

2. 出入境限制

为了进入和停留在立陶宛，一个非欧盟国民需要持有签证或临时居留证，除非他适用免签制度，没有其他的出入境限制。

（四）工会和劳工组织

在立陶宛，员工可通过一个工会和 / 或劳资委员会（或小企业中的员工代表而非劳资委员会）而被集体代表。劳资委员会是雇主层级的员工代表机构。劳资委员会的主要职能是参与信息和咨询程序。它也可提起集体劳动诉讼,向雇主提供有关经济、社会和劳动问题的建议,自雇主和国家或市政机构处获得为履行劳资委员会职能而需获取的信息等。

大型雇主必须实施劳资委员会选举制度,除非存在一个公司层级的工会且超过1/3的员工是该工会的成员。根据法律,如果员工的平均数量达到或超过20人,雇主必须在2周内发布有关任命选举委员会的指令。雇主的员工的平均数量意指订立有效的超过3个月的劳动合同的员工的数量。如果公司通过临时员工中介机构雇用了临时员工,且该等临时员工已在公司工作超过3个月,其也应被计算在内。

但是,劳资委员会的权限和职权是有限的。拥有全部职权的员工代表机构是工会。工会有权依法代表其全体成员和个别成员(在劳动关系,法院和行政程序中)以及保护他们的劳动、经济和社会权利和利益。工会是独立的组织,在自愿的基础上组建,且受《劳动法》《工会法》和其他规制工会的法律以及工会章程规制。

法律授予工会广泛的职权。工会最重要的职能之一是拥有开展集体磋商、达成集体劳资谈判协议和提起集体劳动利益纠纷诉讼的排他性权利。为维护其成员的权利,工会有权举行罢工。

工会可由立陶宛共和国的公民和依法有权工作的外国国民组建。组建一个在雇主层级运作的工会最少需要的创建者人数是20人或雇主员工的1/10,但不少于3名员工。在一份劳动合同项下或基于其他法定理由在立陶宛共和国地域内被合法雇用的人士有权自由加入工会并参与其活动。雇主不得以员工同意不加入或退出工会为条件而进行招聘或保留工作。雇主的授权代表不能是在其企业、机构和组织发挥作用的工会成员。

工会有权设立和参与在行业或地域层级运作的工会组织,前提是该等组织由至少5家公司工会组成。行业或地域层级的工会组织可在国家层级联合。

(五)劳动争议

劳动争议分为两种类型:权利争议和利益争议。

权利争议可能是个人的或集体的。个人的权利争议是员工(以及前员工或求职者)和雇主(以及前雇主或招聘公司)之间有关劳动合同的订立、修改、履行或终止和/或未履行/未完全履行劳动法律的规定的争议。集体的权利争议是员工代表和雇主(或雇主组织)之间有关未履行/未完全履行劳动法律或双方协议的规定的争议。权利争议由劳动争议委员会和法院审查。如果争议各方在争议发生后同意,权利争议也可提交仲裁。

如果侵害一项权利,一般要求受害方在3个月内向劳动争议委员会寻求救济。如果是违法中止、终止或违反集体劳动合同的情形,前述期限缩短为1个月。劳动争议委员会对争议进行快速审理是快速的且不应长于1个月。如果争议的任一方对劳动争议委员会的裁决不服,该方可在1个月内向法院提起诉讼。如果未向法院提起诉讼,劳动争议委员会的裁决生效且须被遵从。

集体的劳动利益争议指的是员工代表和雇主(或雇主组织)之间有关双方权利和义务规则或设立合法的劳工规则的争议。集体的劳动利益争议需首先由争议双方组成的集体劳动利益争议委员会审理。除非委员会设定了不同期限,争议必须在10个自然日内被审理。如果未能就争议事宜达成协议,委员会可寻求调解人的协助或可进一步将争议提交劳动仲裁。

如果一个工会或工会组织宣布罢工,雇主或雇主组织有权在收到罢工通知的5个工作日内就罢工的合法性向法院提起诉讼。同样地,如果一个雇主宣布停工,工会或工会组织有权在收到停工通知的5个工作日内就停工的合法性向法院提起诉讼。有关罢工或停工合法性的问题,法院必须非常迅速地在5个工作日内作出判决。

五、知识产权

(一)知识产权法律法规简介

在立陶宛1990年3月11日重新宣布独立后,立陶宛国家专利局于1991年4月12日设立。国家专利局负责专利、商标、半导体拓扑图和设计的注册。国家专利局不负责版权的注册或保护。在立陶宛，版权不被注册，版权的保护由协会进行，例如于1990年由立陶宛的作者和创新联合会设立的LATGA-A，是一个集体版权管理协会。

立陶宛在很多国际组织中获得成员资格，且成为一些国际条约的缔约方：1992年4月30日，《建立世界知识产权组织（WIPO）公约》；1994年5月22日，《保护工业产权巴黎公约》；1994年7月5日，《专利合作条约》；1994年7月5日，《立陶宛政府和欧洲专利组织的合作协议》；1997年2月22日，《商标注册用商品和服务国际分类尼斯协定》；1997年11月15日，《马德里议定书》；1998年4月27日，《商标法条约》（TLT）；1998年4月9日，《国际承认用于专利程序的微生物保存布达佩斯条约》；2004年12月1日，《欧洲专利公约》；2008年9月26日，《工业品外观设计国际保存海牙协定》。

自2004年5月1日起，立陶宛成为欧盟成员国。由于法律融合进程，加入欧盟导致所有知识产权法律的修订。

（二）专利注册

立陶宛《专利法》规制了专利专有权。根据法律，所有的技术领域的任何发明均可申请专利，前提是具有新颖性、独创性且实用性。提交一项专利注册申请的费用是86欧元。该费用包含最多14项发明权利要求。超过14项权利的每项权利要求的费用是14欧元。授予一项专利的费用是52欧元。

对以下各项，不授予专利权：
① 发现、科学理论和数学方法；
② 产品设计；
③ 比赛方案、规则和方法，智力或经济活动，以及电脑程序；
④ 信息展示；
⑤ 人体或其要素，包括基因序列或部分序列、各阶段的构造和发育。

一项注册专利的有效期是20年（受限于年费的支付），自申请日起算。

（三）商标注册

注册商标和未注册知名商标的保护受立陶宛《商标法》规制。

商标注册申请可提交纸质版或电子版。初始申请费是69欧元（每一项额外的商品和服务类别应另外支付34欧元）。注册、公告和登记费是69欧元。立陶宛国家专利局完成商标专家评审且确认申请符合法律要求（非描述性，符合最低要求的独特性，不违反道德要求和公共秩序，不包含地理标志等）时应支付第二笔费用。通常，一项商标将在申请日后的9个月内被注册。

立陶宛国家专利局不核查其他人的在先权利（商标、版权、商号）的潜在侵权。在先权利的任何所有者可在注册公告日后的3个月内就注册商标提出异议，并要求撤销注册。商标的注册可能被驳回，且针对其无效和撤销行为也可能基于其他理由而启动，例如，未使用、成为通用商标、丧失显著特征等。

根据适用法律，注册商标必须在注册证书颁布之日起的5年期限内开始使用，注册商标的有效期是10年，在提交续展请求且支付续展费用后，注册商标可续展。

（四）知识产权保护措施

根据适用法律，注册商标、专利和设计的所有人（申请人、所有者、权利继受者）在行使其权利时，排他性许可的被许可人在保护被授予给他们的权利时，应有权根据法律所规定的程序向法院提起诉讼，并寻求：
① 权利的承认；
② 拟终止侵权活动的禁令；
③ 禁止实施活动，理由是权利可能被实际侵犯或被损害；
④ 物质损失的赔偿，包括收入损失和支付的其他开支；
⑤ 立陶宛《商标法》和其他法律所规定的其他救济申请。

其他救济可能包括向法院提出申请并要求侵犯知识产权的产品被召回，从商业渠道中被移除，以该种方式避免对前述人士造成任何损害并确保其权利的保护（例如，将侵权产品重制成其他产品或采取类似措施），或要求将法院已查明是侵犯依法已赋予的权利的产品和（在适当的情况下）用于创作或制造特定物品的主要材料和工具予以销毁。

如果存在涉及域名的注册和使用的争议，且域名被认定为侵犯在先知识产权，经要求通常该等域名会无偿转让给原告。因为不存在特别的仲裁机构专门解决域名争议，所以该等争议由普通法院予以解决。

知识产权相关的普通争议由立陶宛国际专利局或维尔纽斯地区法院解决，维尔纽斯地区法院是该等争议的一审法院及立陶宛国家专利局作出的决定的上诉法院。

六、环境保护

（一）环境保护监管部门

环境部是制定立陶宛的环境保护、林业、自然资源利用、地质和水文气象、国土规划、建设、居民公共设施供给和住房供给的国家政策以及协调政策实施的主要监管机构。有若干下属机构协助环境部履行其职责：地区环保部门、国家公园理事会、国家严格自然资源保护区、环境保护局、国家国土规划和建设督查局、住宅能源效率局、地质测量局、林业局、国家保护地区服务局和许多其他机构。

（二）环境保护法律法规简介

同很多其他国家一样，立陶宛已经采取了可持续发展模式。立陶宛已确认接受签署联合国环境和发展会议宣言，且认可二十一世纪议程（Agenda 21）的实施。作为欧盟成员国，立陶宛有义务使其法律和其他规定与欧盟的法律要求接轨。

在环境保护领域，国家主要的法律是立陶宛《环境保护法》《环境保护国家控制法》《环境监控法》《国土规划法》《土地和森林利用特别条款》《计划经济活动环境影响评价法》《废弃物管理法》《废弃物管理条例》《国家废弃物管理战略规划》《噪音管理法》《核能法》《放射性废弃物管理法》《气候变化金融工具管理法》《水法》《野生生物法》。除了大量国家法律外，立陶宛的环境保护还受限于国际条约和公约，例如：《气候变化框架公约》《京都议定书》《保护臭氧层公约》(《维也纳公约》)《关于消耗臭氧层物质的蒙特利尔议定书》《生物多样性公约》《保护欧洲野生生物和自然栖息地公约》(《伯尔尼公约》)、《在环境问题上获得信息、公众参与决策和诉诸法律的公约》(《奥尔胡斯公约》)，以及许多其他国际条约和公约。

（三）环境保护评价

立陶宛环境保护战略的主要目标是确保国家可持续发展，保护健康的环境、生物多样性和风景以及优化自然资源的利用。在实施归属于其权限的任务时，环境部遵循将环境政策纳入经济及部门的总体规划原则、污染预防原则、"污染者支付"原则、合作和分工负责原则、信息公开原则以及其他原则。公众有权获取有关环境保护政策的制定信息，表达意见，以及提出有关急迫问题的建议书。

根据立陶宛计划经济活动环境影响评价法，环境影响评价自1996年起在立陶宛实施，这是对于计划经济活动的潜在环境影响的识别、描述和评价程序。负责环境影响评价的主管部门是环境保护局。除计划经济活动的组织者（承包机构）和准备环境影响评价文件的人员外，环境影响评价程序还涉及负责医疗保健、消防、文物保护、经济发展和农业发展的公共机构、地方政府机构和社会。

计划经济活动的环境影响评估法根据环境影响评估是否即刻被认定为强制要求，还是首先要进行筛选程序，将计划经济活动分为两个清单（见计划经济活动的环境影响评估法的附录1和2）。

附录1列出必须要进行环境影响评估的计划经济活动。另外，在以下情况时环境影响评估是强制性的：①决定程序中规定该计划经济活动必须进行环境影响评估时；②该计划经济活动的实施可能对欧洲生态网络（Natura 2000）所覆盖的地区产生影响，且主管保护区安全及管理组织的部门（保护区国家服务部）认定该等影响可能重大时，应履行环境部规定的程序。

如果一项计划经济活动被列入附录2，相关部门将决定是否有必要对具体的计划经济活动进行环境影响评估，以确保活动计划的下一阶段能通过实施减少影响的技术措施及提供防止不利影响的综合手段来处理环保方面的问题。计划经济活动组织者提供的关于拟议经济活动地址的信息,以及计划经济活动的详情也会被适当纳入考虑。决定程序将包括与环境影响的评估主体和相关公众磋商、采纳关于环境影响评估决定的合理结论及其公告。

七、争议解决

(一)争议解决方法及机构

立陶宛的司法仅由法院管理。立陶宛的法院系统由宪法法院、一般管辖权法院及特殊管辖权法院组成。一般管辖权法院是指最高法院、上诉法院、地区法院及地方法院。他们负责处理民事、刑事案件及行政违法案件(除了上诉法院)。立陶宛最高行政法院及地区行政法院是审理行政法律关系争议的特殊管辖法院。

应注意,在某些案件中,根据法律,要求于法院外进行初步的争议解决(例如,劳动争议中,受害一方应将争议提交到劳动争议委员会)。在其他案件中,如消费合同争议,争议双方可以利用法院外初步争议解决程序,或选择直接到法院解决争议。

到法院诉讼并非解决争议的唯一路径,除法院外,争议双方可以选择仲裁。在立陶宛,仲裁由商事仲裁法所规制。除了很少的特例,所有争议都可以通过仲裁解决,仲裁可能无法解决或审理某些争议案件,即受限于行政程序的争议,或属于立陶宛宪法法院的移交听证案件。家事法律关系引起的争议以及与专利、商标及设计注册有关的争议也不能提交仲裁。劳动争议、消费合同争议不得提交仲裁,除非在争议出现后,争议双方达成仲裁协议。

另一个代替争议解决的选择是调解。民事争议中,各方可以将其国内或跨国的争议在公共或私营部门进行非司法的和/或司法调停、调解。如争议各方约定通过调停调解解决争议,各方必须在提交法院或仲裁庭之前,尝试通过这一程序解决争议。如果调停调解协议设定了终止调停调解的时间限制,争议各方仅当该时间限制期满后才可将争议提交法院或仲裁庭。

(二)法律适用

立陶宛《民法》第1.37章第一部分规定了各方的自治权原则,即合同责任应由双方约定的法律所规制。该约定可以在合同中通过单独条款约定,或者考虑案件的实际情况来确定。缔约各方指定的国家法律可以用于整个合同或合同的一部分。如果各方在选择准据法时行使了他们的权利,法院(在处理争议时)必须要根据各方选择的准据法来确定各方的权利及义务。

但是,在选择准据法时,各方并非享有绝对的自由。根据立陶宛《民法》,当立陶宛加入的国际条约或是立陶宛法律有规定时,外国法也应用于民事关系。例如,立陶宛《民法》规定:保险合同应由保险人经营场所或住所地国家法律所管辖。不动产保险合同应由不动产所在地国家法律所管辖;不动产交易的形式或是权利应由不动产所在地国家法律所管辖;消费合同的形式应由消费者住所所在地法律所管辖。

另外,不论各方是否约定适用其他国家法律,应适用与争议有最紧密联系的立陶宛或其他国家法律的强制性规定。法院在确定这些问题时,应考虑这些规定的性质、目的以及适用或不适用的后果。如果适用外国法律会让协议各方避开立陶宛或协议各方联系最紧密的另一国法律中的强制性规定的适用,法院可以拒绝适用该等外国法。立陶宛《民法》明确规定,如果适用外国法律条款不符合立陶宛《宪法》或其他法律所建立的公共秩序,则不得适用该等外国法律。在该情形下,应适用立陶宛《民法》。

八、其他

(一)反商业贿赂

1. 反商业贿赂法律法规简介

主要的反商业贿赂法律包括立陶宛《刑法》和《刑事诉讼法》。贪污腐败的责任规定于立陶宛《刑法》。主要的贪污腐败犯罪活动包括（但不限于）贿赂、影响力交易、贪污、滥用职权。

2. 监控反商业贿赂的部门

主要的立陶宛反商业贿赂机构是立陶宛特殊调查服务部。该部门建立于1997年，并向总统及议会汇报。特殊调查服务部有三个主要目的：调查贪污腐败犯罪、防止贪污腐败及向公众进行反腐败教育。特殊调查服务部还领导实施国家反腐败计划，可以向特殊调查服务部正式、秘密或匿名地举报索贿及其他贪污腐败犯罪活动，也可以向警察或检察官办公室举报索贿或其他贪污腐败犯罪活动。

3. 惩罚性措施

根据立陶宛《刑法》第230章，有权代表私营实体行事，且为该实体工作的个人，具有等同于公务员的地位，因此，由商人向私营商人贿赂（B2B贿赂）是刑事犯罪，可能被认定为下列罪行：贿赂、影响力交易、贪污或滥用职权。

犯贿赂或影响力交易罪行的自然人所面临的最高刑罚是8年有期徒刑。贪污或滥用职权的最高刑罚是7年有期徒刑。

应注意贪污腐败犯罪活动的刑事责任不仅及于自然人，还及于法人实体。法人实体可能因贿赂、影响力交易、贪污、滥用职权及其他犯罪而承担刑事责任。通常而言，公司仅因其自身行为承担责任。但是，在某些案例中，一个法人实体可能会因另一个由该实体所控制或代表该实体的法人实体的犯罪行为承担刑事责任，前提是该犯罪行为是为前一法人实体的利益所为，且该行为是受前一法人实体的高管（或其授权代表）所指示或所允许的，或由于前一法人的监管或控制不足所导致的。

根据立陶宛《刑法》以及法官的自由裁量权，针对贪污腐败的法人实体的制裁之一可能是限制它们的活动。同时，根据《政府采购法》，如果在过去5年内，供应商（法人实体）被判罪名成立（罪名包括贿赂、影响力交易或贪污），或者外国供应商被判罪名成立，且该等罪名被列入欧盟议会及欧盟理事会于2004年3月31日颁布的协调公共工程合同、公共供应合同及公共服务合同裁决程序的2004/18/EC指令第45章第(1)部分的欧盟法案，则缔约机构应拒绝该等供应商参与及投标的请求。应注意，上述法律的禁止性规定具有强制性。

（二）项目缔约

1. 许可系统

为了确保所有公司及所有自然人有平等的机会将产品、服务或工作成果出售给国家，组建了政府采购部。政府采购是缔约机构根据那些主要列于公共采购法中的规则，采购物资、服务或工作成果。政府采购的目的是签订公共售购合同。公共采购的益处不仅有合理使用资金购买所需商品、服务和/或工作成果，还有质量保证，并与可靠的商品服务供应商签订合同。为了达到此目的，感兴趣的投标者及他们的商品/服务必须满足缔约机构为特定采购准备的合同文件中所列的特定要求。

缔约机构是：

① 任何国家或地方机构；

② 全部或部分活动的目的是满足大众利益的非商业或非工业需求的公共或私营法人实体，且符合如下至少一种情形：

- 法人实体的活动资金50%以上来源于国家或市政预算或其他国家或市政基金；
- 法人实体由国家或地方机关控制，或由其他具有资质的公共或私营法人实体控制；
- 法人实体有行政、管理或监督委员会，其中过半数委员是由国家或当地机关或由有资质的公共或私营法人实体所委任。

由缔约机构进行采购，通过公开宣传或只向选中的供应商发出邀请进行采购。取决于采购的种类及价值、购买商品及服务的数量，采购要遵守不同的程序：公开程序、限制程序、提前公开的协商程序、竞争性谈判、没有公开的协商程序、协作创新程序。

2. 禁止领域

如下内容不适用《公共采购法》，且不开展公共采购：

① 劳动合同；

② 仲裁及调解服务；
③ 某些法律服务，如必须由公证员进行的文件证明及认证服务；
④ 与发行、出售、购买或转让证券或其他金融票据相关的金融服务；
⑤ 贷款，不论是否与证券或其他金融票据的发行、出售、购买或转让有关；
⑥ 由非营利组织或协会提供的民防、群众防护及危险预防服务，及涵盖在特定通用采购词汇法令内的服务（除了转移病人的救护车服务）；
⑦ 火车或地铁公共客运交通服务；
⑧ 某些政治竞选服务（竞选广告服务等）；
⑨ 基于法律法规或与欧盟运作条约相一致的已公布的行政规定所赋予的独占权利，由缔约机构授权另一缔约机构或缔约机构的一个协会的公共服务合同。

除了一些特例，《公共采购法》并不适用于签订公共合同或在防护或安全领域组织的设计竞赛。军事设备、保密设备、其零件及组成部件、组件以及相关工作成果、商品及服务，以及保密工作成果及服务，都根据防护与安全领域的《公共采购法》进行采购。由立陶宛政府审批通过的特殊规则，也适用于通过各种财政手段进行的土地、现有建筑或其他不动产或其上相关权利的收购或租赁，以及由视听或电台媒体服务提供者授权的、用于视听媒体服务或电台媒体服务的节目类素材的购买、开发、生产或共同生产，或授予视听或电台媒体服务提供者关于广播时间或节目准备的合同。

3. 投标邀请及投标

缔约机构必须根据《公共采购法》、其他法案（立陶宛政府的决议、部长的命令等）及简化的采购法规进行采购。

采购之前，缔约机构必须确定采购的价值并选择一个适当的采购类别。可选择下述国际阈值的采购种类：公开或限制程序、竞争性谈判、提前公开的协商程序或没有公开的协商程序。对于简化的采购（包括小额采购），可以适用下述类别：简化公开程序、简化限制程序、提前公开的简化协商程序、简化的竞争性谈判、简化的公开设计竞赛、简化的限制设计竞赛以及基于调查的采购。

当缔约机构提前公开进行采购，合同文件及采购公开必须在公共采购中央入口（由中央采购办公室管理的信息系统）公布。根据《公共采购法》，缔约机构（除了外交代表团、立陶宛在外国的领馆、立陶宛在国际组织的代表团）必须通过中央采购办公室进行采购，或者从中央采购办公室购买商品、服务或工作成果。

缔约机构必须起草符合《公共采购法》的合同文件。合同文件必须精确、清晰、明白，以使供应商能够投标且缔约机构能够购买所需物品。合同文件必须以立陶宛语拟订，此外，合同文件也可以具有其他语言版本。

缔约机构有义务在合同文件中提供所有合同条件及签约程序的信息。合同文件必须包括：关于投标书的说明；供应商资质要求；产品、服务或相关工作成果的标准、数量、公共供应合同附带服务的性质、提交产品、提供服务或工作成果的时间限制；技术指标；投标评价标准及条件；由缔约机构向其他方提出的公共合同的条款及条件，和/或草拟的合同（如有）；投标保证书（如需）要求；提交参加请求并投标的截止日期；及其他信息。政府采购中央入口必须确保各方能够自由、直接且没有任何限制地访问公开文件。

每名投标人可投标一次。通过政府采购中央入口电子提交申请及投标。收到投标后，缔约机构评估供应商的资质及其投标。总的原则是，如果投标信息符合合同文件中提出的要求、条件及标准，且根据法律没有必须将该投标人排除在外的情形，则最具有经济优势的投标胜出。在确定胜出投标之后，缔约机构必须通知供应商。采购程序以与获胜供应商签约告终。

Lithuania

Authors: Vilius Bernatonis, Donatas Šliora, Jonas Saladžius, Neringa Bubnaitytė
Translators: Zhang Yunyan, Wayne Wang

I. Overview

A. General Introduction

The Republic of Lithuania is situated in Northern Europe on the south-eastern shore of the Baltic Sea. Lithuania is the largest of the three Baltic States (other two being Latvia and Estonia) by a permanent population of approximately 2.9 million people and an area of 65,300 square kilometres. Lithuania is ranked among the fastest growing economies in the European Union. It offers investors a diversified economy, a skilled workforce, low corporate taxation, the best developed road network in the region and a stable and democratic political and legal system.

Since 2004 Lithuania is a member of the European Union, thus, is part of a single market and at the same time offers access to countries in Eastern Europe. Lithuania borders with Latvia to the north, Belarus to the east and south as well as Poland and Kaliningrad region of the Russian Federation to the southwest. Lithuania has 90.66 kilometres of seashore with the northernmost ice-free port on the eastern coast of the Baltic Sea which can be considered as one of the most important Lithuanian transport hubs. Rail cargo services directly connect Lithuania to Russia, Belarus, Latvia, Poland, Germany, Ukraine, and Asia (including China). Lithuania also has 3 international commercial airports allowing for access to key European locations.

Lithuanian legislation offers equal protection for both foreign and domestic investments. Lithuania is also a party to bilateral and multilateral international agreements in the field of investment protection. Lithuania consistently scores very high in rankings on investment climate and is an excellent location for foreign investment. The country has an excellent record of ensuring foreign investors' rights and ease of doing business.

B. Political Environment

a. Political System

Lithuania is a stable independent democratic parliamentary republic. The Constitution of the Republic of Lithuania (adopted in 1992) prescribes for separation of powers between the legislature, the executive, and the judiciary.

The supreme legislative power is vested in the one-chamber Parliament (Lith.Seimas) consisting of 141 members elected for a term of four years. 71 members of the Parliament are elected by an absolute majority vote in single-member constituencies and the other 70 members are elected through an open-list proportional representation system.

Executive powers are primarily vested in the Government (Lith.Vyriausybė), with some specific powers vested in the office of the President of Lithuania. The powers and functions of the President of Lithuania are in the fields of foreign policy, national defence, and representation of the state; the President of Lithuania also has other specific powers prescribed under the Constitution of the Republic of Lithuania and other relevant laws. The President of Lithuania is directly elected by popular vote for a term of five years. The Government is comprised of the Prime Minister and 14 ministers. The Prime Minister is appointed by the President of Lithuania with the assent of the Parliament.

The system of courts in Lithuania includes a three-level civil and criminal court system, a specialised administrative court system, and the Constitutional Court of the Republic of Lithuania. The civil and criminal court system comprises twelve district courts, five regional courts, the Court of Appeal, and the Supreme Court of Lithuania. The Constitutional Court of the Republic of Lithuania carries out constitutional control of the legislation adopted by the Parliament, the President of Lithuania, and the Government. The legitimacy of all other normative acts is enforced by the administrative court system. The administrative court system consists of five regional administrative courts and the Supreme Administrative Court; the administrative court system does not include a cassation instance.

b. Administrative Division and Municipal Governance

Lithuania is divided into 60 municipalities (Lith.savivaldybė) which are genuine self-governing authorities.

Municipalities are led by mayors and municipal councils. Local self-government through municipalities is provided for by the Constitution and is further specified in relevant laws. The Constitution of the Republic of Lithuania provides for a budgetary system consisting of an independent state budget as well as independent municipal budgets and the right for municipalities to establish local levies. By virtue of the law on municipal councils, local authorities have general administrative competence. They can exercise any task not explicitly reserved for the Lithuanian state.

c. Participation in International Organizations

Lithuania is a member of a number of international organisations. Lithuania has been a member of the World Trade Organization (WTO) since 31 May 2001. On 29 March 2004, Lithuania joined the North Atlantic Treaty Organization (NATO). Lithuania became a full-fledged member of the European Union (EU) on 1 May 2004. The EU acts in a variety of policy areas, from consumer protection to security and defence. Lithuania also joined the Schengen Area on 21 December 2007.

In 2015 Lithuania received an official invitation to start the process of accession to the Organisation for Economic Cooperation and Development (OECD). The Lithuanian authorities are actively preparing for the process of accession, which is expected to be completed by the end of 2018.

C. Legal Environment

The Lithuanian legal system is characteristically aligned to the tradition of continental Europe. The system of national legislation is based on the principle of hierarchy, i.e.a legal act allocated a lower position in the hierarchy must not conflict with a superior legal act within the hierarchical system.

The Constitution of the Republic of Lithuania is the supreme legal act followed by constitutional laws, laws, resolutions of the Parliament (Lith.Seimas) or the Government of the Republic of Lithuania (Lith.Vyriausybė), decrees of the President of the Republic of Lithuania, and acts of other governmental institutions and local municipal authorities.

All international treaties and conventions ratified by the Parliament (Lith.Seimas) are a constituent part of the legal system of the Republic of Lithuania, namely, international treaties which are ratified by Parliament acquire the power of law. In cases where a national legal act (except for the Constitution of the Republic of Lithuania) establishes the regulation which competes with that established under the international treaty, the latter is to be applied.

Since the accession to the European Union in 2004, Lithuania's legal system has been largely influenced by European Union law. European Union law is a constituent part of the Lithuanian legal system and where it concerns the founding treaties of the European Union, the norms of European Union law must be applied directly, while in the event of collision of legal norms, they have supremacy over the national laws and other legal acts.

Although the principal body of law in Lithuania is statutory, the judicial precedent de jure is also considered as a source of law in Lithuania.

D. Economic and Social Environment

Lithuania demonstrates the best economic figures among the Baltic States and is the most attractive Baltic country for foreign investors. The main macroeconomic indicators for the period of 2013-2018 (the indicators for the end of the period are based on forecasts) are provided below.[1]

	Nominal GDP (EUR billion)	GDP growth rate, %	Average annual inflation, %	Unemployment rate, %
2013	35.0	3.5	1.2	11.8
2014	36.6	6.0	0.2	10.7
2015	37.3	1.7	-0.7	9.1
2016	38.6	2.3	0.8	8.0
2017	40	3.3	3.2	7.3
2018	41.3	2	2.2	7.1

Lithuania is highly ranked in various international rankings – it is ranked 16 out of 190 countries evaluated for ease of doing business by the World Bank, it is placed 19 out of 180 countries in the Index of Economic Freedom

---

[1] https://www.lb.lt/uploads/publications/docs/18367_de2b496c8a7462db1ed8c67b92ac89a2.pdf.

prepared by Heritage Foundation, etc.

Lithuania is No.1 in the European Union by percentage of population with higher education. 84 per cent of the population are proficient in the English language, and 50 per cent of the population speak at least two foreign languages.[1]

The geographical position of Lithuania is convenient for transit. The railway system linked to the ice-free Seaport of Klaipėda with a modern container terminal opens opportunities for efficient intermodal shipments to Russia, Belarus, Latvia, Poland, Germany, Italy, Ukraine, Kazakhstan, China and other Asian countries. The Republic of Lithuania also has a wide network of motorways. Lithuania also has 4 international airports.

Lithuania's business environment is primed for investments in a range of sectors. The most popular are global business services, manufacturing, technology, fintech.

The Fintech sector is one of the most promising and fastest growing sectors in Lithuania. Recently the policy direction taken by governmental authorities has led to a significant increase of financial market participants (mostly e-money institutions and payment institutions). Lithuania has also introduced a regime for specialized banks which may engage in most of the traditional banking activities, however, are subject to a lower initial capital requirement (EUR 1 million). The latter development is expected to significantly increase competition in the banking sector and has already attracted local and foreign investors.

Renewable energy development is becoming increasingly important for Lithuania's export, too. Emerging potential of a clean technology industry is supported by the pool of local scientists and researchers, world-class achievements in electronics, and increasing interest of businesses with respect to the development of this industry. Lithuania seeks to increase energy consumption from renewable sources up to 23% of the country's total energy balance by 2020.

Lithuania's biotechnology sector has been recognised as one of the most developed in Central and Eastern Europe. Another high-tech sector in Lithuania is laser technologies. The information and communication technology sector also is a highly prioritised sector in Lithuania.[2]

a. Cumulative FDI by Investing Country[3]

	31/12/2016	
	EUR millions	structure, %
Total	13,066.24	100.0
Sweden	2,496.73	19.1
The Netherlands	1,585.68	12.1
Germany	1,315.42	10.1
Poland	957.82	7.3
Norway	919.18	7.0
Estonia	696.41	5.3
Cyprus	660.88	5.1
Denmark	591.06	4.5
Finland	588.29	4.5
Malta	405.42	3.1
Other countries	2,849.35	21.9

---

[1] https://investlithuania.com/wp-content/uploads/2017/09/Invest-Lithuania-general-presentation.pdf.
[2] https://www.pwc.com/lt/lt/assets/publications/PwC_Business_Guide_Lithuania_2018.pdf.
[3] https://www.lb.lt/en/statistics-database.

b. Cumulative FDI by Economic Activity[①]

	31/12/2016	
	EUR millions	**structure, %**
Total	13,066.24	100.0
Financial and insurance activities	3,077.07	23.5
Manufacturing	2,602.11	19.9
Wholesale and retail trade, repair of transport vehicles and motorcycles	1,795.51	13.7
Real estate transactions	1,671.24	12.8
Information and communication	1,100.51	8.4
Professional, scientific and technical activities	765.86	5.9
Transportation and storage	407.87	3.1
Private purchases and sales of real estate	367.97	2.8
Administrative and support service activities	345.29	2.6
Other activities	932.81	7.3

E. The Status and Direction of Cooperation with Chinese Enterprises Under the B&R

Economic relations between Lithuania and China are growing stronger. Lithuania is a transit-friendly country with its sophisticated transportation system and rapidly developing logistics. Chinese entrepreneurs are interested in opportunities to invest in Lithuania and are establishing business contacts with Lithuanian companies, including organization of Lithuanian–Chinese business forums. In January 2014, the Lithuania–China Business Council was founded; the main task of the council is the development and promotion of business relations between Lithuania and China.

With bilateral efforts of Lithuania and China, Lithuania has become China's largest economic partner in the Baltic States, while China is the largest Asian trading partner of Lithuania. Over the past few years, trade relations between Lithuania and China have strengthened and expanded. Lithuanian production exports to China have increased by almost four times, and the trade turnover has increased almost twice.[②]

II. Investment

A. Market Access

a. Department Supervising Investment

The main responsibilities in the field of attracting and promoting investments lie with the Ministry of Economy of the Republic of Lithuania (Lith. Lietuvos Respublikos ūkio ministerija). The Ministry of Economy has established an agency, Invest Lithuania (Lith. Investuok Lietuvoje), which actively promotes foreign investment in Lithuania and advises potential investors on the investment environment as well as practical aspects of making investments (e.g. setting up a business) in Lithuania.

b. Laws and Regulations Governing Investments

Foreign investments in Lithuania are regulated and protected by national legislation and a number of international agreements. Lithuania is currently a party to 55 bilateral investment treaties (including a bilateral investment treaty with China) and to international agreements such as the Energy Charter Treaty which provides for additional investment protection measures and mechanisms.

The Law of the Republic of Lithuania on Investments establishes main principles in the field of investments. At

---

[①] https://www.lb.lt/en/statistics-database.
[②] https://osp.stat.gov.lt/uzsienio-prekyba1.

the core of this legal act is the principle of equal treatment and protection of investments meaning that Lithuanian and foreign investors are granted the same rights and obligations relating to commercial activities, and that the rights and lawful interests of Lithuanian and foreign investors are equally protected by Lithuanian laws. Naturally, the equal treatment regime does not in any way prevent the investors from taking advantage from the protection provided by international agreements.

There are a number of legal acts which may be of relevance when considering making an investment in Lithuania. The Law of the Republic of Lithuania on Concessions is also of relevance to foreign investors considering investments in public–private partnerships. When choosing the area for activities, foreign investors should also take into account the Law of the Republic of Lithuania on the Fundamentals of Free Economic Zones which stipulates that certain enterprises established and doing business in the free economic zones as well as the capital invested in such zones will be treated more favourably.

c. Forms of Investment

Lithuania's investment system is based on the principle of personal freedom to engage in economic activities, meaning that in Lithuania any person may engage in economic activities with or without establishing a legal entity. Generally, foreign investment is permitted in all legitimate commercial activities, however, some restrictions on investment are applied in relationship to ownership of land and areas relating to national security and defence.

The Law on Investments stipulates that investments can be made by: (i) setting up an economic entity; acquiring the capital of an economic entity registered in the Republic of Lithuania or a share therein; (ii) acquiring securities of all types; (iii) creating, acquiring long-term assets or increasing the value thereof; (iv) lending funds or other assets to economic entities, in which the investor owns a share in the capital enabling it to control the economic entity or to exert a considerable influence over the economic entity; (v) implementing concession contracts, contracts of financial lease (leasing), and public–private partnership contracts.

In practice, foreign investors may also make investments through branches and representative offices established in Lithuania.

d. Standards of Market Access and Examination

No special permit is required from government authorities to invest foreign capital in Lithuania. Nonetheless, the Law of the Republic of Lithuania on Investments prohibits foreign investments in the sector of national security and defence (with an exception for investments by foreign entities meeting the criteria of European and Transatlantic integration which Lithuania has opted for, provided such investments are approved by the State Defence Council).

The Law of the Republic of Lithuania on the Protection of Objects of Importance to Ensuring National Security also prescribes a special procedure and, in certain cases, a requirement of approval from the Commission for Coordinating Protection of Objects of Importance to Ensuring National Security when investing into companies which are considered to be of national strategic importance or companies which carry out activities in the economy sectors of national strategic importance (such as energy, military equipment sector, etc.).

Some economic activities in certain regulated sectors, for example, financial, energy, healthcare sectors, are subject to licensing. The licensing requirements are equally applicable to foreign and local investors.

B. Foreign Exchange Regulation

a. Department Supervising Foreign Exchange

There are no specific foreign exchange regulations and / or restrictions in force in Lithuania. Therefore, there is no department or any governmental authority supervising foreign exchange.

b. Brief Introduction of Laws and Regulations of Foreign Exchange

There are no specific foreign exchange regulations and / or restrictions in force in Lithuania. Nonetheless, there are certain cash controls applicable in the entire European Union – a person entering or leaving the European Union with EUR 10,000 (or its equivalent in any other currency) or more in cash must declare it.

c. Requirements of Foreign Exchange Management for Foreign Enterprises

There are no requirements of foreign exchange management for foreign enterprises in force in Lithuania. Lithuanian remittance policies allow free and unrestricted transfers.

C. Financing

a. Main Financial Institutions

The financial sector is stable and conforms to the standards of the European Union. The financial sector in

Lithuania is rapidly developing as the Ministry of Finance of the Republic of Lithuania and the Bank of Lithuania (the financial supervisory authority in Lithuania) have set an objective and are implementing measures to make Lithuania a hub for fintech as well as to become more attractive for traditional players in the financial market.

Currently, the Lithuanian financial system is dominated by banks offering retail banking services, leasing and insurance services. There are 6 banks holding a licence from the Bank of Lithuania and 7 foreign branches; there are 340 European Union banks that provide cross-border services in Lithuania without having established a branch. The banking sector market share by total assets is as follows:

Bank	Total assets	Market share
Swedbank, AB	EUR 7,027,479,000	24.44 %
Luminor Bank AB	EUR 6,884,488,000	23.94 %
AB SEB bankas	EUR 7,643,625,000	26.59 %
AB Šiaulių bankas	EUR 1,861,114,000	6.47 %
AB "Citadele" bankas	EUR 523,189,000	1.82 %
UAB Medicinos bankas	EUR 270,601,000	0.94 %
Foreign bank branches	EUR 4,540,864,000	15.79 %

The level of concentration in the Lithuanian banking sector is among the highest in Europe, which is why the entry of new and strong market players that are capable of intensifying competition in the market is seen in a positive light.[1]

International financial institutions such as the European Investment Bank (EIB), the Nordic Investment Bank (NIB) and the European Bank for Reconstruction and Development (EBRD) are also very active in Lithuania. The respective financial institutions often finance major projects (such as implementation of the Liquefied Natural Gas terminal in Klaipėda, modernization of Trans European east-west railway corridors in Lithuania, etc.) and also actively participate in establishment of various funds and financing schemes.

b. Financing Conditions for Foreign Enterprises

The legal framework does not provide for different treatment of foreign enterprises in relation to financing conditions. Nonetheless, financial institutions have risk management policies and procedures which may, in a sense, impede the process of getting financing from foreign entities. In practice, financial institutions require potential clients to provide extensive information regarding their ownership structure and activities as well as documents supporting such information; the information is requested in order to comply with applicable anti-money laundering and terrorist financing prevention requirements.

Naturally, in some cases the actual financing conditions may be less favourable as the client risk or geographical risk may be taken into consideration (e.g.where a financial institution does not have a long-term relationship with a client). Other circumstances having effect on the overall financing conditions of a foreign enterprise could be related to the available collateral or alternative measures to secure the performance of the foreign enterprise's obligations under the financing arrangements.

D. Land policy

a. Brief Introduction of Land-related Laws and Regulations

The main legislative act establishing provisions relevant to foreign enterprises is the Constitutional Law of the Republic of Lithuania on the Implementation of Article 47(3) of the Constitution of the Republic of Lithuania establishing rules and restrictions on acquisition of land in the Republic of Lithuania.

Other principal national provisions on acquisition and lease of land in the Republic of Lithuania are set out in the Law of the Republic of Lithuania on the Acquisition of Agricultural Land, the Law of the Republic of Lithuania on Land, the Civil Code of the Republic of Lithuania, as well as the Rules for the Sale of State-Owned Agricultural Land Plots and the Rules for the Lease of State-Owned Agricultural Land Plots, approved by the Government of the Republic of Lithuania.

---

[1] https://www.lb.lt/en/publications/financial-stability-review-2017-1.

b. Land Acquisition Rules for Foreign Enterprises

a) Restrictions on the Acquisition of Land by Foreign Enterprises

The respective constitutional law establishes that acquisition into ownership of land, internal waters and forests may be permitted to foreign subjects meeting the criteria of European and transatlantic integration embarked on by Lithuania.

Foreign legal entities, as well as other foreign organisations, established in states that are excluded from political, military, economic or other unions or commonwealths of states created on the basis of the former Union of Soviet Socialist Republics, and are a party to one of the following unions, agreements or organisations: (i) the European Union; (ii) the North Atlantic Treaty Organisation; (iii) the Agreement on the European Economic Area; (iv) the Organisation for Economic Cooperation and Development meet the criteria of European and transatlantic integration embarked on by Lithuania.

In practice, the status of the acquiring enterprise is determined by the place of establishment of the enterprise rather than by the citizenship or residence of the beneficial owner of such legal entity.

b) General Restrictions on the Acquisition and Use of Agricultural Land

Recent developments in the regulatory framework of Lithuania determine that specific requirements to the acquirers of agricultural land are no longer applicable. Nonetheless, some general (relevant to both domestic and foreign entities) restrictions and limitations still exist.

Acquisition of agricultural land. Acquisition of agricultural land is regulated by the Law on the Acquisition of Agricultural Land and other relevant legislation. Both natural and legal persons have rights to acquire agricultural land in Lithuania, however, several restrictions apply: (i) persons who have acquired agricultural land must ensure that this land is used for agricultural activities for at least five years after its acquisition (except for the cases where a land parcel is transferred to third parties before the expiry of the above-mentioned time limit); (ii) the maximum quantity of the agricultural land acquired may not exceed maximum limits (as described below); (iii) the amount of the agricultural land acquired by both the persons and the "associated persons" (spouses as well as their parents / adoptive parents and their minor children / adopted children; associated legal entities, etc.) is taken into account.

According to the Law on the Acquisition of Agricultural Land, persons may acquire agricultural land with an area of 10 ha or more only having obtained a permission from a division of the National Land Service under the Ministry of Agriculture (hereinafter, the National Land Service) according to the location of their land. A permission to acquire agricultural land is issued after the National Land Service verifies the data contained in registers concerning the areas of agricultural land managed by persons and / or shares in agricultural land managing legal entities possessed by the said persons.

Besides, the same requirements for data verification and issuing of a permission of the National Land Service are applicable when seeking to acquire control in a legal entity (by gaining at least 25% of shares or voting rights at the meeting of participants of the legal entity) which holds more than 10 hectares of agricultural land by the right of ownership.

Maximum area of agricultural land being acquired into ownership. The Law on the Acquisition of Agricultural Land (Article 3) specifies the maximum area of agricultural land that could be acquired into ownership, i.e.: (i) a person or associated persons may acquire such quantity of land within the territory of Lithuania that the total surface area of agricultural land acquired by them from the State does not exceed 300 ha, (ii) a person or associated persons may acquire such quantity of land within the territory of Lithuania that the total surface area of agricultural land held by them and acquired from the State and other persons does not exceed 500 hectares.

The above-described restrictions on the maximum area of agricultural land which could be acquired into ownership are not applicable if agricultural land is acquired for livestock farming development and the quantity of acquired agricultural land does not exceed the number of hectares per livestock unit held by the person (1 livestock unit/1 hectare). The Law on the Acquisition of Agricultural Land (Article 3(2)) also provides that if the number of livestock units decreases over the last three years (with the exception of decrease due to circumstances beyond the person's control) or the person intends to transfer the land to third parties, the state must buy out the area of land which was acquired for livestock farming development and which exceeds the permissible limits at the average market value.

c) Lease of Agricultural Land

There is no specific (exclusive) regulation regarding lease of private agricultural land – general conditions of land lease as set in the Civil Code are applicable.

State-owned land lease is also regulated in accordance with the Civil Code and certain specific provisions are set in the Law on Land and the applicable rules specifying the procedure. According to the relevant legislation, natural and legal persons of the Republic of Lithuania and foreign countries or other foreign organizations have the right to lease state-owned agricultural land plots. The land lease term is determined by an agreement between the lessor and the lessee, but may not exceed the period of 25 years. After the expiry of the term of the state land lease, if the land plot is not foreseen for other uses, the lessee, having carried out the obligations undertaken in accordance with the relevant lease agreement in an orderly manner and wishing to renew the lease, must submit an application for renewal of the lease agreement 3 months before the termination of the agreement and has the right to renew it without observing the pre-emptive right. Also, upon expiry of the term of the state lease agreement, but not later than 3 months before the expiry of the agreement, the lessee, who has performed the obligations undertaken in accordance with the agreement in an orderly manner, may apply for one extension thereof for a period not longer than the term specified in the contract if, according to the territorial planning documents, the land plot is not intended to be used for other purposes.

The land plot rent rate is calculated according to the rate approved by the municipal council. The lessor is entitled to recalculate the value of the land plot from the basis of which the land rent is calculated every three years.

E. Establishment and Dissolution of Companies

a. Forms of Enterprises

a) Most Popular Forms of Enterprises

There is a number of forms of private and public legal entities each having its benefits. Nonetheless, the most popular forms of enterprises for doing business in Lithuania are a private limited liability company (Lith. uždaroji akcinė bendrovė) and a public limited liability company (Lith. akcinė bendrovė). The main legal act governing the respective forms of legal entities is the Law of the Republic of Lithuania on Companies. Both natural and legal persons are allowed to be shareholders in the respective companies.

Limited liability companies in Lithuania are organized based on the principle of separation of assets of the shareholder(s) and the company itself. Main differences between the respective types of companies are as follows:

	Private limited liability company	**Public limited liability company**
Minimum authorized capital	EUR 2,500	EUR 40,000
Number of shareholders	Up to 250	Unlimited
Trading shares on a public market	Unavailable	Available, if listed
Management structure	General meeting of shareholders General manager Board (optional) Supervisory Board (optional)	General meeting of shareholders General manager Board (optional*) Supervisory Board (optional*) *at least one of the collegial management bodies must be formed in the company

Public limited liability companies are subject to mandatory audit. Meanwhile, the audit for private limited liability companies is not mandatory, save for cases where at least two of the following criteria are met: (i) the sales income exceeds EUR 3.5 million in the financial year; (ii) the total value of assets in the balance sheet exceeds EUR 1.8 million, (iii) the average number of employees during the financial year is 50 or more.

b) Other Forms of Enterprises Used by Foreign Investors

There are also other types of companies which are used for carrying out business activities in Lithuania. Such companies include general and limited partnerships, agricultural companies, one-person companies as well as European companies, a European Cooperative Society,[1] etc.

The one-person company (Lith. individuali įmonė) is a legal person with unlimited liability. The owner is liable for the obligations of the company with all of his / her property. This is a very popular form of business in Lithuania as there is no minimum authorized capital requirement and simplified financial accounting rules apply.

The general partnership (Lith. tikroji ūkinė bendrija) is an enterprise with unlimited liability established on the basis of a partnership and joint venture agreement between several natural and / or legal persons. Such a partnership is created through the transfer of the individual property to property co-ownership in the partnership, with the purpose of carrying out business activities under a common name of the enterprise. All partners of a general partnership are jointly liable with their personal property for the obligations of the partnership. However, the partnership is not liable for the obligations of its partners if such obligations arise in their activity that is unrelated to

---

[1] The list is non-exhaustive.

the activities of the general partnership itself.

The limited partnership (Lith. komanditinė ūkinė bendrija) has general partners with unlimited liability and limited partners which are liable only to the extent of their contributions to the partnership. It is mandatory that the limited partnership has at least one general partner and one limited partner.

Establishing legal enterprises specified under European Union law is also possible. Main forms of enterprises in this category are a European Cooperative Society (SCE) and a European Company (Societas Europaea) (SE). The European Company is similar to a public limited liability company, which capital is divided into shares. The minimum subscribed share capital of the European Company is set to be not less than EUR 120,000. The European Cooperative Society aims to satisfy the interests of its members and develop their economic and social activities, especially by concluding agreements with them regarding the supply of goods, provision of services or performance of works. The minimum authorized capital is set to be not less than EUR 30,000. The liability of European Cooperative Society's members may be either limited or unlimited.

b. Procedure of Establishment

Establishing different types of enterprises requires different steps to be taken. The procedure of establishing both a private limited liability company (Lith. uždaroji akcinė bendrovė) and a public limited liability company (Lith. akcinė bendrovė) consists of the following steps: (i) selecting and reserving a company's name, (ii) preparing founding documents, (iii) opening an accumulative bank account, (iv) transferring the share capital to the accumulative bank account, (v) notarising the founding documents at the notary's office, (vi) registering the company with the Register of Legal Entities.

Certain forms of enterprises (including a private limited liability company) may be established electronically if the founder has a qualified electronic signature and other necessary conditions determined by legislation are fulfilled.

Naturally, some additional actions are required to be taken prior to initiating activities of a company, such actions include registration with the State Tax Inspectorate (Lithuanian Revenue Authority) for corporate income tax purposes, and the State Social Insurance Fund Board (SODRA) and completion of VAT registration.

It should be stressed that engaging in certain activities (e.g.in the field of healthcare, financial services) requires licences and / or permits to be acquired.

c. Routes and Requirements of Dissolution

According to the Lithuanian laws, legal entities may be closed down through the liquidation procedure only if the legal entity has no outstanding debts or provided that all of its debts would be finally settled during the liquidation procedure. Members of a legal entity may adopt a decision on the liquidation of the company and appointment of a liquidator. Once such a decision is made, all bodies of the company are deprived of their rights and only the liquidator may represent the company and carry out its winding-up.

F. Mergers and Acquisitions

The main legislative acts on mergers and acquisitions (hereinafter, M&A) in Lithuania are the Civil Code of the Republic of Lithuania, the Law of the Republic of Lithuania on Companies, the Law of the Republic of Lithuania on Competition, the Law of the Republic of Lithuania on Securities as well as the Law of the Republic of Lithuania on Markets in Financial Instruments. Other legislative acts may also be relevant taking into consideration the complexity and specifics of the transaction. All the relevant legislative acts are aligned with European Union legislation.

The Civil Code sets the basis for most M&A transaction types. It provides at least three alternative models of sale of a business: (i) share deals, (ii) asset deals, and (iii) enterprise deals (such transfer includes assets, rights and obligations related to the particular business). Reorganization by way of merger (either joining or consolidation) which may also be considered as a business acquisition model is also regulated pursuant to the provisions of, inter alia, the Civil Code. The reorganization procedure is quite complex and time-consuming; therefore, it is rarely chosen as means of acquisition but is used as a mechanism for optimising activities of the target company after the acquisition.

Certain provisions relating to share transfers in public and private limited liability companies, as well as competencies, rights and duties of the management bodies of the companies are prescribed under the Law on Companies.

The Law on Competition is also relevant in the context of M&A transactions. In cases prescribed by law (as specified in Section G below), the Competition Council assesses a potential M&A transaction and issues a resolution: (i) on the approval of the concentration, (ii) on the approval of the concentration with certain conditions to be fulfilled by the merging companies or the management bodies thereof, or (iii) on the refusal of a clearance of the concentration.

Other relevant rules are also prescribed under the Law on Securities (for more information please see Section I (Securities) below).

Other legal acts are applicable based on the M&A transaction type and complexity thereof.

G. Competition Regulation

a. Department Supervising Competition Regulation

The national supervisory authority and competition watchdog is the Competition Council of the Republic of Lithuania (hereinafter, the Competition Council). The Competition Council implements the Lithuanian competition policy and supervises compliance with competition rules. The Competition Council consists of its Chairperson and four Council Members, all of whom are nominated by the President of the Republic of Lithuania upon proposal by the Prime Minister.

b. Brief Introduction to Competition Law

The primary source of competition law in Lithuania is the Law on Competition. The Lithuanian competition regime is largely aligned with the EU model. In addition, the Competition Council's secondary legislation also complies with the EU competition rules and other regulations.

c. Measures Regulating Competition Law

Anti-Competitive Agreements. The Law on Competition and Article 101 of the Treaty on the Functioning of the European Union prohibit agreements between companies which prevent, restrict or distort competition, and the breach of these laws may result in heavy fines. Anti-competitive agreements include, for example, price-fixing or market-sharing cartels which protect companies participating in such agreement from competitive pressure for launching new products, improving their quality and decreasing prices, which leads to higher prices for consumers. The following agreements are generally considered anti-competitive: (i) agreements on fixing prices; (ii) agreements on limiting production; (iii) agreements on sharing markets or customers; (iv) agreements on sharing commercially sensitive information; (v) agreements on bid rigging; (vi) agreements on fixing resale prices (between manufacturers and distributors).

Nonetheless, there are also certain exemptions to the regime in respect of anti-competitive agreements. The respective rules are not applicable to agreements between undertakings which, due to their non-appreciable influence, cannot substantially restrict competition (de minimis rule). It is presumed that the following agreements are incapable of restricting competition owing to their insignificance: (i) horizontal or mixed agreements between undertakings, the aggregate market share of which does not exceed 10 per cent of the respective market; and (ii) vertical agreements between undertakings, the separate market share of which does not exceed 15 per cent of the respective markets.

Another exemption is applicable in case where the relevant agreement promotes investment, technical or economic progress or improves the distribution of goods, and also where the agreement does not impose restrictions on the activities of the parties thereto, which are not indispensable to the attainment of the above-mentioned objectives, and the agreement does not afford the contracting parties the possibility of restricting competition in the major part of the market concerned. No prior approval of the Competition Council is required to ensure the effectiveness of such agreement. Nonetheless, the burden of proof concerning the compliance with the respective provisions lies with the party that wishes to benefit from the exemption.

Abuse of dominant position. Holding a dominant position is not prohibited, however, dominant undertakings must comply with stricter requirements as opposed to their competitors that do not exercise such market power. It is prohibited to abuse a dominant position within a relevant market by performing any acts which restrict or may restrict competition, limit the possibilities of other undertakings to act in the market, or violate the interests of consumers. A dominant position is defined as a position of one or more undertakings that face no direct competition in a relevant market or a position that enables them to exert unilaterally a decisive influence in that market by effectively restricting competition therein.

Dominance and collective dominance is presumed in the following cases: (i) an undertaking has a market share of not less than 40 per cent; and (ii) each undertaking in a group of three or fewer undertakings has the largest share of and jointly hold 70 per cent or more of the relevant market.

The Law on Competition also lists cases of conduct likely to constitute abuse of a dominant position. Such conduct includes: (i) directly or indirectly imposing unfair purchase or selling prices or other unfair trading conditions; (ii) limiting production, markets or technical development to the prejudice of consumers; (iii) applying dissimilar (discriminative) conditions to equivalent transactions with other trading parties, thereby placing them at a competitive disadvantage; or (iv) making the conclusion of contracts subject to acceptance by the other parties of supplementary obligations, which, by their nature or according to commercial usage, have no connection with the subject of such contracts.

Unfair competition. Economic entities are prohibited from performing any actions contrary to fair business practices and good usages and which may negatively affect the competitive potential of another economic entity. The Law on Competition provides for a non-exhaustive list of actions which may be considered to constitute unfair competition practices, which includes: (i) unauthorised use of a reference mark identical or similar to the name, registered trade mark or unregistered well known trade mark or any other reference mark having a distinguishing feature of another economic entity, if this causes or is likely to cause confusion with that economic entity or its activity, or where it is sought to take undue advantage of the reputation of that economic entity (its mark or reference mark) or where this may be detrimental to the reputation (mark or reference mark) of that economic entity, or where it may reduce the distinguishing feature of the mark or reference mark used by that economic entity; (ii) misleading of economic entities by providing them with incorrect or unsubstantiated information about the quantity, quality, components, properties of usage, place and means of manufacturing and price of its goods, or concealing the risks associated with the consumption, processing or other usage of those goods; (iii) usage, transfer, disclosure of information representing a commercial secret of another economic entity without its consent as well as obtaining of such information from persons having no right to transfer such information, in order to compete, seeking self-benefit or inflicting damage on that economic entity, etc.

In accordance with applicable legislation, the Competition Council investigates the actions of unfair competition only in those cases where these actions violate the interests of the majority of economic entities or consumers.

Merger control. The Competition Council carries out the functions of the supervisor of concentrations. In the context of Lithuanian legislation, concentration means: (i) a merger when one or more undertakings which terminate their activity as independent undertakings are joined to the undertaking which continues its operations, or when a new undertaking is established from one or more undertakings which terminate their activities as independent undertakings; (ii) acquisition of control when the same natural person or natural persons already controlling one or more undertakings, or one or more undertakings, by agreement, jointly set up a new undertaking (except the cases when such new undertaking does not perform the functions of an independent undertaking) or gain control over another undertaking by acquiring an enterprise or part of it, all or part of the assets of the undertaking, shares or other securities, voting rights, by contract or by any other means.

An intended merger must be notified to the Competition Council prior to its implementation and its permission must be obtained if the combined aggregate income of the undertakings concerned in the business year preceding the concentration exceeds EUR 20,000,000 and the aggregate income of each of at least two undertakings concerned in the business year preceding the concentration exceeds EUR 2,000,000. Even though the aggregate income does not exceed the limits entrenched in the Law on Competition, the Competition Council may initiate merger control proceedings in those cases where the intended merger is likely to result in the creation or strengthening of a dominant position or a substantial restriction of competition in a relevant market.

Implementing a merger prior to its notification, as well as continuing a merger during the period of its suspension and infringing the established merger conditions or obligations may impose on undertakings a fine of up to 10 per cent of the gross annual income in the preceding business year. Failure to provide information or providing incorrect and incomplete information required for merger examination may impose on undertakings a fine of up to one per cent of the gross annual income in the preceding business year. A fine of up to five percent of the average gross daily income in the preceding business year may be imposed on undertakings for the failure to comply in a timely manner with the instructions given by the Competition Council.

H. Tax

a. Tax Regime and Rules

A list of laws forming the Lithuanian taxation system is provided in Article 13 of the Law of the Republic of Lithuania on Tax Administration. The following taxes and duties are considered to be the main ones: income tax of individuals; corporate income tax; value added tax; excise duties; real estate tax; land tax; inheritance tax; and lottery and gambling tax.

The Lithuanian tax system is administered by the Lithuanian Tax Authority, the Customs Authority, the Social Insurance Authority, and institutions authorised by the Lithuanian Ministry of Environment.

b. Main Tax Categories and Rates

Corporate Income Tax (CIT). Resident companies and permanent establishments of foreign entities (including branches) in Lithuania are subject to corporate income tax of worldwide income (including dividends, received assistance / donations which were used not for stated purposes, etc.).

Permanent establishments of non-resident companies are subject of corporate income tax on the same grounds as resident corporations.

A standard CIT rate is 15%. A reduced CIT rate of 5% applies to: (i) small companies which meet certain conditions; (ii) companies involved in agricultural activities and which meet certain conditions. A reduced CIT rate of 0% applies to the companies that: (i) are established in a free economic zone (FEZ) for the first 6 years (and 7.5 % for the next 10 years); (ii) employ certain groups of people eligible for social support.

Capital gains. Income earned by a Lithuanian entity from trade in securities or other financial instruments constitutes taxable income, which is subject to corporate income tax at an ordinary tax rate.

However, capital gains are not taxable if the gain is received from the transfer of shares of the legal entity, which is registered or otherwise organized within the European Economic Area and is generally subject to taxes on profit and the Lithuanian entity has continuously held more than 10% of the shares in such entity for at least 2 years.

Dividends. As a general rule, 15% withholding tax is applied on dividends received from Lithuanian or foreign entities. In case one Lithuanian entity pays out dividends to another Lithuanian entity and withholds 15% tax, the payer of interest may credit the amount of the tax withheld against its own payable corporate income tax.

Under Lithuanian participation exemption rules, dividends received from a local or foreign entity (other than a tax heaven entity), where a Lithuanian entity holds more than 10% of shares for a period of at least 12 months, are tax exempt and are not included in income of the Lithuanian entity.

Dividends paid by a Lithuanian entity to a foreign shareholder (entity or individual) are subject to 15% withholding tax; however, under national participation exemption rules, dividends paid to a foreign shareholder (legal person, not a tax heaven entity), which holds more than 10% shares of the Lithuanian entity for a period of at least 12 months (including the moment of distribution of dividends) are tax exempt.

Social Tax. Employers are obliged to calculate and pay social tax monthly in addition to the wages payable to the employee. A general social tax rate is approx. 31.18% to 32.80%, compulsory health insurance contributions – 9%. Employed individuals are subject to social tax at a rate of 9%, and employers are required to withhold and pay the social tax contribution.

VAT. VAT is charged on supplies of goods and services in the course of business activities in Lithuania, which generate any income.

The threshold for obligatory registration as a taxable person is EUR 45,000 of taxable supply from the beginning of the calendar year. Voluntary registration is possible before reaching the threshold.

A standard VAT rate is 21%. A reduced 9% VAT rate is applicable to: (i) books and non-periodical informational publication; (ii) newspapers, magazines, and periodical publications (except for those of erotic, violent nature or publications that do not comply with professional and ethical requirements); (iii) passenger transportation services by regular routes as well as transportation of passenger luggage; (iv) accommodation services; (v) heat energy supplied for residential heating and for hot water supplied to consumers.

A reduced 5 % VAT rate is applicable to: (i) technical aids for disabled persons and repairs of such technical aids; (ii) supply of pharmaceuticals and medical aids to persons who have the right to full or partial reimbursement of acquisition expenses pertaining to such goods in accordance with the Law on Health Insurance.

A 0% VAT rate applies to supply of goods transported from Lithuania to another EU Member State or outside the EU.

Personal Income Tax. Lithuanian residents pay tax on their worldwide income. An individual is a Lithuanian resident if his or her place of residence is in Lithuania, his or her centre of social and economic interests is in Lithuania or the individual stays in Lithuania for at least 183 days over the course of 12 calendar months. Taxable income includes, in particular, wages, business income, rental income, dividends.

Individual income generated or earned by a non-resident in Lithuania and abroad is subject to personal income tax if the income is associated with the non-resident's permanent base in Lithuania, including the following income: interests, dividends, rent of immovable property, royalties, wages, income from sports activities, income from performance, sold or exchanged immovable or movable property subject to legal registration, compensations for infringements of copyright or neighbouring rights.

A general flat rate of personal income tax is 15%, with exception of income from individual activities – 5% or 15% (depending on income level).

Immovable Property Tax. Immovable property tax is payable by the owner of a particular property (buildings of various purposes) which is located in Lithuania.

The tax is payable by companies and natural persons. For natural persons, a non-taxable limit of EUR 220,000 is set.

In case a property is bought by way of financial leasing, immovable property tax is paid by the buyer of such property and not by the financial institution, which is registered as an official owner of the property. The applicable tax rate is 0.3% to 3%, depending on the municipality where the property is located. Municipal councils have the right, at the expense of the municipal budget, to reduce the tax or to release from it altogether; normally the benefits and exceptions are applicable to investors which start they business in the territory of the relevant municipality.

I. Securities

a. Brief Introduction of Securities-Related Laws and Regulations

The securities market in Lithuania is regulated mainly under the Law on Securities. When shares of a company are admitted to trading on a stock exchange in Lithuania, they become subject to all mandatory takeover bids and squeeze-out and sell-out rules specified in the Law on Securities. Following the Law on Securities, in the event of a takeover bid, where a person, acting independently or in concert with other persons, acquires shares that in connection with the holding held by him or by other persons acting in concert entitles him to more than 1/3 of votes at the general meeting of shareholders of the company, he must either transfer shares exceeding this threshold, or announce a mandatory takeover bid to buy up the remaining shares of the company granting the voting rights and the securities confirming the right to acquire shares granting the voting rights. The given duty also applies to a person who has acquired control over an entity holding shares of the company in respect of whose shares a takeover bid is to be submitted that entitle him to more than 1/3 of votes at the general meeting of shareholders. In the squeeze-out situation, a person, when acting independently or in concert with other persons and having acquired not less than 95 percent of the capital carrying voting rights and not less than 95 percent of the total votes at the general meeting of the issuer, has a right to require that all the remaining shareholders of the issuer sell the voting shares owned by them, and the shareholders are obligated to sell the shares. In the sell-out situation, any minority shareholder, owning equity securities, has a right to require that a person, who, when acting independently or in concert with other persons, has acquired the shares comprising not less than 95 per cent of the capital carrying the voting rights and not less than 95 per cent of the total votes at the general meeting of shareholders, would buy the shares belonging to the minority shareholder and granting the voting rights, while the said person is obligated to purchase those shares.

Furthermore, the Market Abuse Regulation (MAR) is also a directly applicable legal act in Lithuania (as well as in any other Member State of the European Union). The applicable Lithuanian laws do not provide for any additional provisions of regulation in the field of regulation covered by the MAR.

b. Supervision and Regulation of the Securities Market

Bank of Lithuania. The securities market in Lithuania is supervised by the Bank of Lithuania. Within the range of its competence, the Bank of Lithuania seeks to ensure the security, soundness, and transparency of the domestic system of financial services and securities market.

Nasdaq. The Lithuanian financial instruments exchange market is operated by Nasdaq. It runs its business pursuant to applicable laws, including the Law on Markets in Financial Instruments and its internal regulations, including the Articles of Association of Nasdaq, the Listing Rules of Nasdaq, etc.

The exchange market operated by Nasdaq constitutes a regulated market for the purposes of the relevant EU legislation and the Law on Markets in Financial Instruments. Nasdaq also organizes and operates an Alternative Trading System (First North) which is a non-regulated market. The exchange market operated by Nasdaq offers listing possibilities on the Main List and the Secondary List.

According to Nasdaq's website (www.nasdaqbaltic.com), as of today, shares of 68 companies are listed on Nasdaq Baltic lists. The total capitalization of the companies listed on Nasdaq was EUR 7.316 billion as of 14 February 2018.

Stock exchange trading mechanisms. Pursuant to the Nasdaq rules, Nasdaq sessions are held regularly from Monday to Friday from 10:00 a.m.to 4:00 p.m.Vilnius time, unless the management board of Nasdaq decides otherwise. During the trading hours (10:00 a.m.to 4:00 p.m.) members may place, change, suspend, resume or cancel orders. Sell and buy orders that correspond in yield, volume and other conditions are matched into trades via automatic order matching. Manual trades may be reported during this trading phase. Members may not place or change orders or report manual trades during the pre-trading session or the post-trading session. Information as to price, trading volume and any specific rights (pre-emption or dividend rights) attached to the relevant securities is available on the Nasdaq's official website at www.nasdaqbaltic.com.Brokerage commissions in Lithuania are not fixed by Nasdaq or other regulatory bodies and are set by the brokerage house executing the transaction.

c. Requirements for Engagement in Securities Trading for Foreign Enterprises

Foreign enterprises in Lithuania have equal rights for access to securities market. Please note, that a prospective foreign enterprise seeking to make a public offering in Lithuania must comply with minimum standards set out in Lithuanian legislation (specified mainly under the Law on Securities).

J. Preference and Protection of Investment

a. Structure of Preference Policies

There are no specific preference policies in place. Nonetheless, Lithuania is a Member State of the European Union and thus a part of the European Single Market which seeks to remove internal borders and other regulatory obstacles to the free movement of goods and services within the European Union. Moreover, Lithuania is a party to a number of bilateral investment treaties granting investors of those particular countries additional protection and, as a result, an advantage.

b. Support for Specific Industries and Regions

There is a number of support measures in various sectors. Such measures are implemented for the purpose of promoting export, producing energy from renewable sources, research and development and innovation, etc.

Production of energy from renewable sources is promoted by various measures, including, but not limited to, tax incentives (e.g.energy produced from renewable sources is exempt from excise duty), subsidies and loans. In Lithuania, electricity from renewable sources is mainly promoted through a sliding feed-in premium. In addition to that, renewable energy use in the transport sector is promoted through several support schemes.

Three major groups of export promotion measures include: (i) counselling-support, provided by the government agency Enterprise Lithuania and the network of Commerce Attachés; (ii) the European Union support intended to encourage enterprises to seek foreign partners more actively and increase sales in foreign markets; (iii) guarantees for export credit insurance, provided by the agency Invega. The export promotion measures should not be considered as granting of subsidies, financial aid or direct payments to exporters, which is a non-compliance with the European Union and the World Trade Organisation.[①]

Lithuania offers a range of measures of direct and indirect support in the area of research and development as well as technological innovation. Such measures may be categorized in three main groups, namely: (i) tax incentives; (ii) counselling by science and technology parks, the Lithuanian Innovation Centre, the Agency for Science, Innovation and Technology; (iii) innovation vouchers [a small credit (a fixed sum of money) that entitles small and medium enterprises to buy research and development expertise or knowledge from research and educational institutions].

c. Special Economic Areas

a) Revision of Regional Policy

The Lithuanian authorities have recently introduced the Lithuanian Regional Policy Whitepaper for harmonious and sustainable development. One of the core principles of the proposed policy is regional specialization, which is the entirety of regional development priorities and their implementing measures, concentrating human and financial capital into the most productive and promising areas of economic development of a specific functional region.[②] For instance, from 2018, Klaipėda region focuses on the long-term strategy to support sustainable growth in the marine and maritime sectors, Panevėžys aims at becoming the hub of robotics, Marijampolė seeks to attract investors in wood, food and metal industries, etc. The implementation of the revised policy is expected to have a significant positive effect on the conditions for potential investors.

b) Free Economic Zones

A free economic zone (FEZ) is an area designated for commercial, financial or industrial activities, in which a preferential tax regime is applicable. In Lithuania, the activities allowed to be pursued in the FEZ may be limited to a specific FEZ. In general, any not forbidden economic activity may be carried out there, except for the defence industry (including production, storage of or trade in weapons and explosives), tobacco, strong alcohol production, production of securities, coins, postal stamps, production, storage of or trade in medicines or poisonous materials, casino and lottery activities, etc.

Different tax incentives are applicable to the companies located in the FEZ. The companies in the FEZ do not pay real estate taxes, the dividends earned by foreign investors are also tax-free. Additionally, current regulation provides that investors of over EUR 1 million, operating in industrial, warehousing, aviation or IT areas, are exempt from corporate tax for the 6 first years, and a 50% corporate tax rate is applicable for the next 10 years.

---

① https://ukmin.lrv.lt/en/sector-activities/export/export-promotion-measures.
② https://vrm.lrv.lt/uploads/vrm/documents/files/LT_versija/Veikla/Veiklos%20sritis/Region%C5%B3%20pl%C4%97tra/Lithuanian%20Regional%20Policy%20(White%20Paper).pdf.

The tax exemption is applicable from the moment the investment amount reaches EUR 1 million threshold; it is also applicable to the business service companies, which employ not less than 20 employees and made capital investments of not less than 100 thousand euros.

Tax	In FEZ territory	In Lithuania (generally)
Corporate tax	0 % (first 6 years)	15%
Corporate tax	7.5% (other 10 years)	15%
Real estate tax	0%	1%

There are currently 7 (seven) FEZs established in Lithuania (in Akmenė, Kaunas, Kėdainiai, Klaipėda, Marijampolė, Panevėžys, and Šiauliai).[1] FEZs are located in geographically convenient locations and each of the FEZs offers additional benefits coherent to that particular location.

d. Investment Protection

Lithuania has double taxation treaties with 54 (fifty-four) countries including China,[2] thus creating a favourable tax environment for foreign investments.

Investments are granted protection under national legislation as well as international agreements. Lithuania is currently a party to 55 bilateral investment treaties (including a bilateral investment treaty with China) and to international agreements such as the Energy Charter Treaty, ICSID Convention.

The Law on Investments establishes that state and local authorities and officers have no right to interfere with the management and use as well as disposal by the investors of the object of investment. Damage inflicted upon the investor by unlawful acts of state or local authorities and their officers is compensated according to the procedure established by the laws of the Republic of Lithuania.

Investment disputes between foreign investors and Lithuania may be resolved by way of mutual agreements, by the courts of Lithuania, or international arbitration institutions. In case of investment disputes, foreign investors have the right to refer directly to the International Centre for Settlement of Investment Disputes.

III. Trade

A. Department Supervising Trade

In Lithuania, the task of developing positive legal and economic environment for economic growth has been entrusted to the Ministry of Economy of the Republic of Lithuania (hereinafter the Ministry of Economy). The Ministry of Economy is in charge of supervising domestic trade, export, investment, innovation, concessions, state-owned enterprises, EU support to business, public procurement, tourism, and other areas. In addition, the Ministry of Economy, in cooperation with the Ministry of the Republic of Lithuania of Foreign Affairs, shapes Lithuania's foreign trade policy. Moreover, the Ministry of Economy closely manages activities in the field of export, import, transit and brokering activities of dual use goods[3] and technologies as well as military equipment.

It must be said that supervision and control over trade is not solely in the hands of the Ministry of Economy. Depending on a product, there may be a chain of authorities involved. For example, if one trades in foodstuffs, the supervising authorities will include: the Government of the Republic of Lithuania, the Ministry of Economy, the Ministry of Health of the Republic of Lithuania, the Ministry of Agriculture of the Republic of Lithuania, the State Food and Veterinary Service, and the State Consumer Rights Protection Authority.

B. Brief Introduction of Trade Laws and Regulations

The most significant legal act regulating trade in Lithuania is the Civil Code of the Republic of Lithuania (hereinafter the Civil Code) which contains provisions regarding applicable law and sets, inter alia, the most general requirements for sale and purchase, consumer rights, franchise, distribution, freight forwarding, and other

---

[1] https://ukmin.lrv.lt/lt/veiklos-sritys/investiciju-veiklos-sritis/pramoniniai-parkai-ir-lez.
[2] http://www.vmi.lt/cms/en/tarptautines-dvigubo-apmokestinimo-isvengimo-sutartys.
[3] Dual use goods are items, including software and technology, which can be used for both civil and military purposes, and include all goods which can be used for both non-explosive uses and assisting in any way in the manufacture of nuclear weapons or other nuclear explosive devices.

aspects significant for trade. Another notable legal act is the Law of the Republic of Lithuania on Competition, which safeguards the freedom of fair competition in the Republic of Lithuania. If trade involves goods for consumers, attention should be paid to the Law of the Republic of Lithuania on the Prohibition of Unfair Business-to-Consumer Commercial Practices, the Law of the Republic of Lithuania on the Prohibition of Unfair Practices of Retailers and the Law of the Republic of Lithuania on the Protection of Consumer Rights. For trade, very important legislation includes the Law of the Republic of Lithuania on Product Safety, the Law of the Republic of Lithuania on the Management of Packaging and Packaging Waste, the Regulations for the Labelling of Goods and Indication of Prices (approved by an order of the Minister of Economy), the Regulations for Retail Trade (approved by a resolution of the Government of the Republic of Lithuania).

Other applicable legislation and secondary legal acts should be consulted taking into consideration the type of commodity, the nature of trade, and type of business.

C. Trade Management

In order to create conditions for EU exporters to better compete on the global market in exporting agricultural products and foodstuffs to third countries, applicable legislation allows payment of export refunds to compensate, to an extent, for the difference between global and EU market prices. Moreover, certain measures, such as import licenses and import duties, are used to keep off an invasion of cheaper products from third countries into the internal EU market. In the field of agriculture, for example, the European Union has opened import tariff quotas for certain agricultural products. In some cases imports of products under such import tariff quotas are subject to an import licensing system, as provided for by Commission Regulation (EC) No 1301/2006 of 31 August 2006, laying down common rules for the administration of import tariff quotas for agricultural products managed by a system of import licences. In Lithuania, the government authority which administers the system of licences and certificates for import and export of agricultural products with pre-established compensation is the National Paying Agency under the Ministry of Agriculture of the Republic of Lithuania. According to the data publicly announced by the National Paying Agency, the number of companies registered in the register of traders of the Market Regulation Measures Department of the National Paying Agency has grown from 156 in 2005 to 310 companies in 2013. Similarly, the number of import licences issued by the Market Regulation Measures Department of the National Paying Agency has increased from 231 import licences in 2005 to as many as 348 licences in 2013.

D. The Inspection and Quarantine of Import and Export Commodities

Pursuant to the Regulation (EU) No 952/2013 of The European Parliament and of the Council of 9 October 2013 laying down the Union Customs Code, the customs authorities may carry out any customs controls they deem necessary. Customs controls may in particular consist of examining goods, taking samples, verifying the accuracy and completeness of the information given in a declaration or notification and the existence, authenticity, accuracy and validity of documents, examining the accounts of economic operators and other records, inspecting means of transport, inspecting luggage and other goods carried by or on persons and carrying out official enquiries and other similar acts. Priority control areas shall cover particular customs procedures, types of goods, traffic routes, modes of transport or economic operators which are subject to increased levels of risk analysis and customs controls during a certain period, without prejudice to other controls usually carried out by the customs authorities.

For the purpose of examining the goods, taking samples or examining the means of transport carrying the goods, the customs authorities may at any time require goods to be unloaded and unpacked. Goods shall be unloaded or trans-shipped from the means of transport carrying them solely with the authorisation of the customs authorities in places designated or approved by those authorities.

For the purpose of customs controls, the customs authorities may verify the accuracy and completeness of the information given in a customs declaration, temporary storage declaration, entry summary declaration, exit summary declaration, re-export declaration or re-export notification, and the existence, authenticity, accuracy and validity of any supporting document and may examine the accounts of the declarant and other records relating to the operations in respect of the goods in question or to prior or subsequent commercial operations involving those goods after having released them. Those authorities may also examine such goods and / or take samples where it is still possible for them to do so. Such controls may be carried out at the premises of the holder of the goods or of the holder's representative, of any other person directly or indirectly involved in those operations in a business capacity or of any other person in possession of those documents and data for business purposes.

The customs authorities shall take any necessary measures, including confiscation and sale, or destruction, to dispose of goods in the following cases:

(i) where one of the obligations laid down in the customs legislation concerning the introduction of non-Union goods into the customs territory of the Union has not been fulfilled, or the goods have been withheld from customs supervision;

(ii) where the goods cannot be released for any of the following reasons:
• it has not been possible, for reasons attributable to the declarant, to undertake or continue examination of the goods within the period prescribed by the customs authorities;
• the documents which must be provided before the goods can be placed under, or released for, the customs procedure requested have not been provided;
• payments or a guarantee which should have been made or provided in respect of import or export duty, as the case may be, have not been made or provided within the prescribed period;
• the goods are subject to prohibitions or restrictions;
(iii) where the goods have not been removed within a reasonable period after their release;
(iv) where after their release, the goods are found not to have fulfilled the conditions for that release; or
(v) where goods are abandoned to the State.

In accordance with the Law of the Republic of Lithuania on Customs, if upon coming into force of a decision, according to which seized goods must be returned to the owner and which is taken in a civil, administrative, administrative offences, criminal case or pre-trial investigation, or which is another decision of an authority of the Republic of Lithuania, competent to seize goods, the owner of the goods does not take the goods back within 30 working days of a relevant notice / the effective date of the said decision, the goods shall be sold. Proceeds from the sold goods, less import and other duties (if applicable) as well as costs for storage, transportation and selling, shall be returned to the owner. The goods which may not be sold (as well as goods subject to destruction) must be destroyed.

E. Customs Management

An essential element in the functioning of the EU's single market is the Customs Union. It applies one common set of rules and procedures to run one single system for importing and exporting goods. The Customs Union means that in relation to the trade of all goods between member states there are no borders and no customs duties, and that goods within the EU move freely. At external borders of the EU, the Common Customs Tariff, along with the Integrated Tariff (TARIC), are applied to goods from non-EU countries.

As Lithuania is a Member State of the European Union, its customs rules and procedures are directly regulated by a European Union-wide regulation on the Union Customs Code (Regulation EU No.952/2013 of the European Parliament and of the Council laying down the Union Customs Code). The Union Customs Code is a framework regulation on the rules and procedures for customs throughout the EU.A major goal of the Union Customs Code is the shift to a complete use of electronic systems with the goal that all exchanges of information between customs authorities, and between economic operators and customs authorities, as well as storage of such information are to be made using electronic data-processing techniques. Most of the new or upgraded electronic systems that are necessary to apply the provisions of the Union Customs Code will be operational by 2020, although some electronic systems may not be fully completed until 2025.

International trade at the borders in Lithuania is controlled by the Lithuanian customs. The Lithuanian customs system comprises the Customs Department under the Ministry of Finance of the Republic of Lithuania, Customs Criminal Service, Customs Training Center, Customs Laboratory, Customs Information System Centre and three territorial customs offices in the cities of Vilnius, Kaunas, and Klaipėda.

IV. Labour

A. Brief Introduction of Labour Laws and Regulations

In Lithuania, the main legal act regulating labour relationships is the Labour Code of the Republic of Lithuania (hereinafter the Labour Code). Compared to the previous Labour Code, which was valid until 30 June 2017, the current Labour Code liberalized conclusion of fixed-term employment contracts, gave way for employment termination at the employer's will, significantly reduced severance payments and notice periods for employment termination on the employer's initiative, increased maximum overtime limits, introduced new types of employment contracts (job sharing, work for several employers, apprenticeship, project-based employment), opened freedom of contract for highly paid employees, and made a number of other large steps in building more flexible regulation of employment relations to make the Lithuanian labour market more attractive for foreign investors.

In addition to the Labour Code, the employment relationships are additionally regulated by laws (of which the most notable are the Law on Employee Health and Safety, the Law on the Legal Status of Foreigners, the Law on the State Social Insurance), resolutions of the Government of the Republic of Lithuania, orders of the Minister of Social Security and Labour, orders of the Minister of Health, orders of the Chief State Labour Inspector, and other legal acts. Liability for breaches labour laws is provided in the Labour Code, the Code of Administrative Offences of the Republic of Lithuania, the Criminal Code of the Republic of Lithuania, and in other laws.

B. Requirements for Employing Foreign Employees

EU nationals can work in Lithuania without any limitations. EU nationals do not have to obtain a work permit and / or residence permit, however an EU national working and staying in Lithuania for more than 3 months in any half-year must obtain a certificate proving the right of residence in the Republic of Lithuania.

Non-EU nationals intending to work in Lithuania must meet 2 requirements:

(i) Their stay in Lithuania must be legal, i.e.in order to enter and stay in Lithuania they are required to have a visa or a temporary residence permit, unless a visa free regime is applicable to them; AND

(ii) They have to obtain a work permit or Labour Exchange decision confirming that employee's work meets the needs of the Lithuanian labour market (hereinafter Labour Exchange decision), unless they are exempt from this obligation.

Lithuanian laws provide a number of different grounds based on which a non-EU national can be employed in Lithuania.

a. Work Permit

In order a non-EU national could work in Lithuania under employment contract, the employer shall firstly apply to Lithuanian Labour Exchange and obtain a work permit or Labour Exchange decision confirming that employee's work meets the needs of the Lithuanian labour market (hereinafter – Labour Exchange decision), unless this requirement is not applicable.

Lithuanian laws provide some exceptions when a non-EU national is relieved from the obligation to have work permit or Labour Exchange decision:

(i) a non-EU national is coming to Lithuania to handle matters relating to the negotiation of the contract and the performance of the contract, to train personnel or install equipment, for a maximum of 3 months per year;

(ii) a non-EU national is a permanent employee of a company established in a EU / EFTA member state and he is sent for temporary work in Lithuania and covered by social insurance in that Member State;

(iii) a non-EU national is coming to Lithuania to perform work which requires high qualification (the so-called EU blue card) in case his / her monthly salary is not lower than 3 average monthly gross salaries in Lithuania (currently approx. 2552 EUR) or not lower than 1,5 average monthly gross salaries in Lithuania (currently approx.1276 EUR) and his / her profession is in the list of the professions in demand to the Lithuanian Labour Market;

(iv) a non-EU national has the status of a permanent resident in Lithuania;

(v) a non-EU national's profession is in the list of the professions in demand to the Lithuanian Labour Market;

(vi) a non-EU national is coming to Lithuania to work in a foreign company's representative office or a branch or in a Lithuanian affiliate of a foreign group company as the director or a specialist for up to 3 years, provided that the non-EU national has worked in that foreign country's company for at least 6 months and his expertise or high professional qualification is absolutely necessary for the relevant entity in Lithuania;

(vii) a non-EU national is a shareholder or the director in a private Lithuanian entity, which is subject to certain requirements in respect of the duration of operation, minimum value of equity, number of personnel;

(viii) other cases provided by laws.

Work permits and Labour Exchange decisions are issued by Lithuanian Labour Exchange. Work permit can be issued for a maximum period of 1 year, Labour Exchange decision can be issued for 1 or 2 years, later it can be extended.

Once the Labour Exchange issues a document authorizing the foreigner to work in Lithuania, the foreigner shall apply for the document allowing him / her legally stay in Lithuania. In case the foreigner has work permit issued, he / she shall apply for the national visa D. In case of Labour Exchange decision a temporary residence permit shall be obtained.

b. Application Procedure

Work permit / Labour Exchange decision procedure consists of the following steps:

(i) Submission of diploma(s) to the Centre for Quality Assessment in Higher Education for the recommendations regarding professional qualification (if applicable);

(ii) Registration of the vacancy with the territorial labour exchange;

(iii) Submission of application to the Labour Exchange for the work permit / Labour exchange decision;
(iv) Registration of the employment contract at the territorial labour exchange.
The employer is responsible for the procedure.
Temporary residence permit procedure:
(i) Submission of application at Migration authorities in Lithuania or diplomatic mission or consular post of Lithuania abroad;
(ii) Formalisation of the temporary residence permit;
(iii) Collection of the temporary residence permit.
In case national visa D shall be obtained, the procedure consists of the following steps:
(i) Submission of application at diplomatic mission or consular post of Lithuania abroad.
(ii) Collection of visa.

c. Social Insurance

In case an employment contract is concluded with the employer in Lithuania, the employer must give a standard form notice to the State Social Insurance Fund about employment of an employee at least 1 working day before the actual work commences.

As a general rule, if a person concludes an employment contract with Lithuanian company, he / she is required to pay tax in Lithuania, i.e.personal income tax, health insurance and social security contributions. However, applicable tax considerations shall be assessed on case to case basis, as some exemptions might be applicable.

C. Exit and Entry

a. Visa Types

There are 2 types of visa: a Schengen visa and a national visa.
Schengen visa:
(i) airport transit visa (A) – a visa valid for transit through the international transit areas of 1 or more airports of the Schengen Member States;
(ii) short-stay visa (C) – a visa valid for transit through or an intended stay in the territory of the Schengen Member States of a duration of no more than 90 days in any 180-day period from the date of first entry in the territory of the Schengen Member States.
National visa – a visa which allows coming to Lithuania and staying in it for a period up to 1 year.
(i) A single entry national visa may be issued to a non-EU national who has been granted a temporary or permanent residence permit in Lithuania.
(ii) A multiple entry national visa may be issued to a non-EU national whose purpose of entry into Lithuania is a long term stay in Lithuania [e.g., a non-EU national is coming to work to Lithuania and (s)he holds a work permit, a non-EU national is coming to Lithuania to work and his / her profession is in the list of the professions in demand to the Lithuanian Labour Market, a non-EU national is seconded to the client company in Lithuania on the ground of contract on providing services or performing jobs between a local company and a foreign company sending an employee, etc.].
Temporary residence permit:
In case a non-EU national intends to stay in Lithuania for a period longer than 90 days during a period of 180 days, a non-EU national can apply for a temporary residence permit. Temporary residence permit is a document granting a non-EU national the right to temporary reside in Lithuania for a period specified in the permit. It is usually issued for a period of 1 year, though it may also be issued for a shorter period. Lithuanian laws provide a number of grounds based on which non-EU nationals can apply for temporary residence permits (e.g.a non-EU national is issued a Labour Exchange decision; a non-EU national intends to perform a work requiring high professional qualification; a non-EU national is sent from the company that belongs to the same group of companies, etc.).
EU Blue Card:
It is worth to mention the so-called EU Blue Card – a temporary residence permit that can be issued for the non-EU nationals that are coming to Lithuania to perform work which requires high qualification.
In order to qualify for this, the non-EU national shall have high professional qualification evidenced by a higher education (e.g.university) diploma or no less than five years of professional experience that is essential for the profession or sector specified in the employer's commitment to hire him according to the employment agreement or in the employment agreement itself. Furthermore, in order to qualify for the EU Blue Card the provided monthly salary requirement (not lower than 1.5 or 3 average monthly gross salaries in Lithuania) shall be met.
In case foreigner's monthly salary is not lower than 3 monthly average salaries in Lithuania or his / her monthly salary is not lower than 1.5 monthly average salaries in Lithuania but his / her profession is in the list of

professions in need in Lithuania, no further formalities are required in relation to a work permit or Labour Exchange decision – the foreigner shall apply just for the temporary residence permit and this is sufficient for work and residence in Lithuania.

If the monthly salary is higher than 1.5 monthly average salaries but lower than 3 monthly average salaries in Lithuania, and foreigner's profession is not in the list of professions in need in Lithuania, the foreigners is required to obtain a decision of the Lithuanian Labour exchange, confirming the fact that the foreigner's high qualification work meets the demands of the Lithuanian labour market.

b. Restrictions for Exit and Entry

In order to enter and stay in Lithuania a non-EU national is required to have a visa or a temporary residence permit, unless a visa free regime is applicable to him / her. No other exit or entry restrictions are applicable.

D. Trade Union and Labour Organizations

In Lithuania, employees may be collectively represented through a trade union and / or a works councils (or, instead of a works council, an employee representative in small enterprises). A works council is an employee representative body on the employer's level. The primary function of a works council is participation in the information and consultation procedures. It can also initiate a collective labour dispute, make suggestions to the employer regarding economic, social and employment issues, receive information, required for performance of the works council functions, from the employer and state and / or municipal institutions, etc.

It is a must for a sizeable employer to initiate election of the works council, unless there is a company-level trade union and more than 1/3 of the employees are members of this trade union. By law, if the average number of employees reaches or exceeds 20, no later than within 2 weeks the employer must issue an order regarding appointment of the election committee. The employer's average number of employees means the number of employees who have an employment contract valid for more than 3 months. If a company hires a temp through a temporary work agency, such a temp must be also counted in, if he / she has worked at the company for more than 3 months.

The competence and the powers of a works council are, however, limited. An employee representative body with a full scope of powers is a trade union. A trade union is entitled by law to represent its members collectively and individually (in employment relationships, in court and administrative procedures) and to protect their labour, economic and social rights and interests. Trade unions are independent organisations, formed on a voluntary basis, and governed by the Labour Code, the Law of the Republic of Lithuania on Trade Unions, other laws regulating trade union activities as well as the articles of association of a trade union.

The law confers a wide range of powers upon trade unions. One of the most important functions of a trade union is an exclusive right to conduct collective bargaining, conclude collective bargaining agreements and initiate collective labour disputes of interests. In defending the rights of their members, trade unions have a right to go on strike.

A trade union may be founded both by citizens of the Republic of Lithuania and by foreign nationals who are legally entitled to work. The minimum required number of founders of a trade union, operating on the employer' level, is 20 or 1/10 of an employer's employees, but no fewer than 3 employees. Persons who are legally employed under an employment contract or on other statutory grounds in the territory of the Republic of Lithuania have the right to freely join trade unions and participate in their activities. Employers are prohibited from making employment or retention of a job conditional upon the employee's consent to refrain from joining or to withdraw from a trade union. An employer, his authorised representative may not be a member of trade unions functioning in his enterprise, establishment, organisation.

Trade unions have a right to found and participate in trade union organizations, operating on a sectoral or territorial level, provided that such an organization consists of at least 5 company-level trade unions. Sectoral or territorial level trade union organizations may make unions on a national level.

E. Labour Disputes

Labour disputes are divided into two types: disputes of right and disputes of interest.

Disputes of right may be individual or collective. An individual dispute of right is a dispute between an employee (as well as a former employee or a job applicant) and an employer (as well as a former employer or a hiring company) over conclusion, amendment, implementation or termination of an employment contract and / or over failure to implement / duly implement provisions of labour legal acts. A collective dispute of right is a dispute between employee representatives and an employer (or employer organizations) over failure to implement / duly implement provisions of labour legal acts or mutual agreements. Disputes of right are examined by labour dispute commissions and courts. If parties to a dispute so agree after a dispute arises, a dispute of right may be also referred to arbitration.

In case of breach of a right, the aggrieved party is generally required to go to a labour disputes commission within three months. In case of illegal suspension, illegal termination or breach of the collective bargaining agreement, the term is shortened to one month. Hearing of the dispute in a labour disputes commission is quick and should not last longer than one month. If either party to the dispute disagrees with the judgement of the labour disputes commission, the party can make a claim to the court within one month. If no claim to the court is made, the judgement of the labour disputes commission comes into force and must be complied with.

A collective labour dispute of interest means a dispute between employee representatives and an employer (or employer organizations) over regulation of mutual rights and duties or setting legal labour rules. A collective labour dispute of interest must be heard, first of all, by a commission on collective labour dispute of interest, made up by both disputing parties. Unless the commission sets a different term, the dispute must be heard within 10 calendar days. In case of failure to achieve an agreement over the disputed matter, the commission may resort to the assistance of a mediator or may further refer the dispute to labour arbitration.

If a trade union or an organization of trade unions declares a strike, an employer or an organization of employers has a right to go to court regarding legitimacy of the strike within five working days of receipt of a strike notice. Likewise, if an employer declares a lockout, a trade union or an organization of trade unions has a right to go to court regarding legitimacy of the lockout within five working days of receipt of a lockout notice. The matter over legitimacy of the strike or the lockout must be decided by the court very promptly, within five working days.

V. Intellectual Property

A. Brief Introduction of IP Laws and Regulations

After re-establishment of independence of the Republic of Lithuania on 11 March 1990, the State Patent Bureau of Lithuania was established on 12 April 1991. The Bureau is in charge of registration of patents, trademarks, topography of semiconductors and design. The Bureau is not in charge of registration or protection of copyrights. In Lithuania, copyrights are not registered and protection of copyrights is given to associations, like LATGA-A which is a collective copyright management association, established by Lithuanian authors and creative unions back in 1990.

The Republic of Lithuania gained membership in many international organizations and became party to a number of international treaties: on 30 April 1992, Convention establishing the World Intellectual Property Organization (WIPO); on 22 May 1994, Paris Convention for the Protection of Industrial Property; on 5 July 1994, the Patent Cooperation Treaty; on 5 July 1994, the Co-operation Agreement between the Government of the Republic of Lithuania and the European Patent Organisation; on 22 February 1997, Nice Agreement Concerning the International Classification of Goods and Services for the Purposes of the Registration of Marks; on 15 November 1997, the Madrid Protocol; on 27 April 1998, the Trademark Law Treaty (TLT); on 9 April 1998, the Budapest Treaty on the International Recognition of the Deposit of Microorganisms for the Purposes of Patent Procedure; on 1 December 2004, the European Patent Convention; on 26 September 2008, the Hague Industrial Design Convention.

As of 1 May 2004, the Republic of Lithuania is a member of the European Union. Joining the European Union resulted in amendment of all intellectual property legal acts due to the process of harmonization of the laws.

B. Patent Registration

Exclusive right to patents are regulated by the Law of the Republic of Lithuania on Patents. According to the law, patents shall be available for any inventions in all fields of technology, provided that they are new, involve an inventive step and are capable of industrial application.

Filing of a patent application costs 86 EUR. This fee encompasses up to 14 invention description claims. Each claim in excess of 14 claims costs 14 EUR. Granting of a patent costs 52 EUR.

The following cannot be patented:
(i) discoveries, scientific theories and mathematical methods;
(ii) design of products;
(iii) schemes, rules and methods of games, intellectual or economic activities, as well as programmes for computers; and
(iv) presentations of information;

(v) the human body or its element, including the sequence or partial sequence of a gene, at the various stages of its formation and development.

A registered patent is valid for 20 years as from the date of filing the application (subject to the payment of an annual fee).

C. Trademark Registration

Protection of registered trademarks, as well as non-registered well-known trademarks is regulated by the Law of the Republic of Lithuania on Trademarks.

Trademark registration can be executed by filing either a hardcopy or electronic application. Fee for the application starts from 69 EUR (additional fee of 34 EUR shall be paid for each additional class of goods and services). Registration, publication and certificate fee is 69 EUR. This second fee shall be paid when the State Patent Bureau of Lithuania executes expertise of the trademark and confirms that the application meets requirements of the law (is not descriptive, has minimal distinctiveness, does not contradict requirements of morality and public order, does not contain geographical indication, etc.). Usually a trademark is registered within a 9-month period from the date of the application.

The State Patent Bureau of Lithuania does not check potential infringements of earlier rights (trademarks, copyrights, business names) of other persons. Any holder of earlier rights can file an opposition against registered trademark within a 3-month period from the date of the publication of the registration and seek cancelation of the registration. Registration of the trademark may be challenged, and invalidation and cancellation actions against it may be started on other grounds as well, for example, for lack of usage, for becoming generic, for loss of distinctive character, etc.

According to applicable legislation, the usage of the registered trademark must start within a 5-year period from the date of issuance of the registration certificate. Registered trademark is valid for a period of 10 years. The registration can be renewed after a renewal request has been filed and the renewal fee has been paid.

D. Measures for IP Protection

According to applicable legislation, the owners (the applicants, the proprietor, successors in title) of registered trademarks, patents and design, when enforcing their rights, and the licensees of exclusive licences, when protecting the rights granted to them, shall be entitled to apply to the court in accordance with the procedure laid down by the law and to seek:

(i) recognition of the rights;

(ii) an injunction intended to terminate the continuation of infringing activities;

(iii) prohibition to carry out activities by reason of which the rights may be actually infringed or the prejudice suffered;

(iv) compensation for the material damage, including lost income and other incurred expenses;

(v) application of other remedies set out by the Law of the Republic of Lithuania on Trademarks and other laws.

Other remedies may include application to the court and requesting that goods infringing intellectual property rights be recalled, removed from the channels of commerce in such a manner as to avoid any harm being caused to the said persons and to ensure the protection of their rights (for example, to remake the infringing goods into other goods or to apply similar measures), or to request that the goods, which the court has found to be infringing the rights established by the laws and, in appropriate cases, the materials and implements principally used in the creation or manufacture of the specified objects be destroyed.

If a dispute concerns registration and usage of a domain name, which was recognized to be infringement of earlier IP rights, such a domain name is usually transferred free of charge to the plaintiff upon request. There is no special arbitration body, which would specialize in solution of domain name disputes, thus such disputes are solved in general courts.

General intellectual property-related disputes are solved by State Patent Bureau of Lithuania or Vilnius Regional Court, which is the first instance court for such disputes and appeal instance for decisions of the State Patent Bureau of Lithuania.

VI. Environmental Protection

A. Department Supervising Environmental Protection

The Ministry of Environment is the main managing authority which forms Lithuania's state policy of environmental protection, forestry, use of natural resources, geology and hydrometeorology, territorial planning, construction, provision of residents with utilities and housing, as well as coordinates its implementation. In its mission, the Ministry of Environment is assisted by a number of subordinate institutions: regional environmental protection departments, directorates of national parks, state strict nature reserves, the Environmental Protection Agency, the State Territorial Planning and Construction Inspectorate, the Housing Energy Efficiency Agency, the Lithuanian Geological Survey, the General Forest Enterprise, the State Protected Areas Service, and many others.

B. Brief Introduction of Laws and Regulations of Environmental Protection

As many other countries, Lithuania has accepted a sustainable development model. It has confirmed the acceptance signing the Declaration of the United Nations Conference on Environment and Development and acknowledging the implementation of the Agenda 21. Being a member state of the European Union, Lithuania is obliged to approximate its laws and other legal acts with legal requirements of European Union.

In the field of environmental protection, the major national laws are the Law of the Republic of Lithuania on Environmental Protection; the Law of the Republic of Lithuania on State Control of Environmental Protection; Law of the Republic of Lithuania on Environmental Monitoring; the Law of the Republic of Lithuania on Territorial Planning; Special Conditions for the Use of Land and Forests; the Law of the Republic of Lithuania on Environmental Impact Assessment of Planned Economic Activities; the Law of the Republic of Lithuania on Waste Management; the Regulations for Waste Management; the State Strategic Plan for Waste Management; the Law of the Republic of Lithuania on Noise Management; the Law of the Republic of Lithuania on Nuclear Energy; the Law of the Republic of Lithuania on the Management of Radioactive Waste; the Law of the Republic of Lithuania on the Financial Instruments for Climate Change Management; the Law of the Republic of Lithuania on Water; the Law of the Republic of Lithuania on Wildlife. In addition to a multitude of national legal acts, environment protection in Lithuania is also subject to international treaties and conventions, such as Framework Convention on Climate Change, Kyoto Protocol, Convention for the Protection of the Ozone Layer (Vienna Convention), Protocol on Substances that Deplete the Ozone Layer (Montreal Protocol), Convention on Biological Diversity, Convention on the Conservation of European Wildlife and Natural Habitat (Bern convention), Convention on Access to Information, Public Participation in Decision-Making and Access to Justice in Environmental Matters (Aarhus Convention), and many others.

C. Evaluation of Environmental Protection

The main goal of Lithuania's environmental protection strategy is to ensure sustainable development of the country and thus conserve healthy environment, biodiversity and landscape as well as optimize use of natural resources. In implementation of the tasks designated to its competence, the Ministry of Environment follows such principles as integration of environmental policy into overall planning of the economy and its sectors, pollution prevention, "polluter-pays" principle, partnership and division of responsibility, information publicity, and other principles. The public have a right to receive information on the formation of environmental protection policy, express their opinion, and submit proposals on acute issues.

The environmental impact assessment is performed in Lithuania since 1996 pursuant to the Law on the Environmental Impact Assessment of Planned Economic Activities. It is the process for the identification, description and assessment of the potential environmental impact of the planned economic activity. The competent authority in charge of environmental impact assessment is the Environmental Protection Agency. Besides the organizer of the planned economic activity (contracting authority) and the person preparing environmental impact assessment documents, the environmental impact assessment process also involves public authorities responsible for health care, fire protection, protection of cultural valuables, economic development and agricultural development, local municipal authorities, and the society.

The Law on the Environmental Impact Assessment of Planned Economic Activities divides planned economic activities into two lists (Annex 1 and Annex 2 to the Law on the Environmental Impact Assessment of Planned Economic Activities) depending on whether the environmental impact assessment is obligatory right away or whether the planned economic activities are first subject to a screening and selection process.

Annex 1 lists the planned economic activities in respect of which the environmental impact assessment must be done. Additionally, the environmental impact assessment is mandatory 1) when it is established during the selection process that the planned economic activity has to be subject to the environmental impact assessment or 2) when the implementation of the planned economic activity may have an impact on the areas of the European Ecological Network Natura 2000, and the authority in charge of the organization of the security and management of protected areas (the State Service for Protected Areas) establishes that such impact may be significant, following the procedure prescribed by the Ministry of Environment.

If a planned economic activity is listed in Annex 2, the competent authority will decide whether it is necessary to perform the environmental impact assessment of the specific planned economic activity and to ensure that environmental aspects will be considered during further stages of the activity planning not only by applying technical measures reducing the impact but also by providing complex measures for the prevention of adverse impact. Due consideration will be given to information provided by the organizer of the planned economic activity about the site for the intended economic activity and to the details of the planned economic activity. The selection process will include consultations with environmental impact assessment subjects and with the interested public, adoption of a reasoned finding regarding the selection for environmental impact assessment and its public announcement.

VII. Dispute Resolution

A. Methods and Bodies of Dispute Resolution

Justice in the Republic of Lithuania is administered only by courts. The court system of the Republic of Lithuania is made up of the Constitutional Court, the courts of general jurisdiction and courts of special jurisdiction. The courts of general jurisdiction are the Supreme Court of Lithuania, the Court of Appeals of Lithuania, regional and district courts. They deal with civil and criminal cases as well as with cases of administrative offences (save for the Court of Appeals of Lithuania). The Supreme Administrative Court of Lithuania and regional administrative courts are courts of special jurisdiction hearing disputes arising from administrative legal relations.

It should be noted that in certain cases provided for by laws preliminary dispute resolving out of court is required (for example, in labour disputes the aggrieved party should refer the dispute to a labour disputes commission). In other cases, such as in disputes arising out of consumer contracts, parties to a dispute may make use of the procedure for preliminary dispute resolution out of court, or opt to go straight to court.

Litigation in court is not the only way to solve a dispute. Instead of going to court, parties to a dispute may choose to go to arbitration. In Lithuania, arbitration is governed by the Law on Commercial Arbitration. With very few exceptions, all disputes may be settled by arbitration. Arbitration may not settle disputes that are subject to the administrative procedure or hear cases that fall within the remit of the Constitutional Court of the Republic of Lithuania. Disputes arising from family legal relations and disputes concerning registration of patents, trademarks and design may not be submitted to arbitration. Disputes arising from employment and consumer contracts may not be submitted to arbitration except for the cases where an arbitration agreement is concluded after the dispute has arisen.

Another option of alternative dispute resolution is mediation. In civil disputes, parties may refer their national and cross-border dispute for extrajudicial and / or judicial conciliatory mediation both in the public and private sectors. Where parties to a dispute agree to settle the dispute through conciliatory mediation, they must attempt to settle the dispute by this procedure before referring to court or arbitration. If a conciliatory mediation agreement sets time limits for the termination of conciliatory mediation, the party to the dispute may refer to court or arbitration only after the expiry of these time limits.

B. Application of Laws

Part 1 of Article 1.37 of the Civil Code of the Republic of Lithuania establishes the principle of autonomy of parties, according to which contractual obligations shall be governed by the law agreed by the parties. Such agreement of the parties may be expressed in the form of separate provisions in the concluded contract or it may be determined taking into consideration the factual circumstances of the case. The law of the state designated by the agreement of the contracting parties may be applied to the whole contract or only to a part or parts thereof. If parties have exercised their right in choosing the governing law, the court (in case of dispute) must determine the rights and duties of the parties according to the governing law chosen by the parties.

However, the parties do not have absolute freedom in choosing the governing law. Pursuant to the Lithuanian Civil Code, foreign law shall also apply to civil relationships where it is so provided for by the international treaties of the Republic of Lithuania or the laws of the Republic of Lithuania. For example, the Lithuanian Civil Code provides that: a contract of insurance shall be governed by the law of the state where the domicile or the place of business of the insurer is located; a contract of insurance in respect to an immovable thing shall be governed by the law of the state in the territory of which the thing is located; the form of transactions regarding an immovable thing or the rights therein shall be governed by the law of the state in which the immovable thing is located; the form of consumer contracts shall be governed by the law of the place of the consumer's domicile.

Moreover, mandatory provisions of laws of the Republic of Lithuania or those of any other state most closely related with a dispute shall be applicable regardless of the fact that other foreign law has been agreed upon by the parties. In deciding on these issues, the court shall take into consideration the nature of these provisions, their purpose and the consequences of application or non-application thereof. The court may refuse to apply foreign law of if the application of such law would allow the parties to an agreement to escape application of mandatory rules of the law of the Republic of Lithuania or of another state with which the relationships between the parties are most closely related. It is clearly stated in the Lithuanian Civil Code that the provisions of foreign law shall not be applied where the application thereof might be inconsistent with the public order established by the Constitution of the Republic of Lithuania and other laws. In such instances, the civil laws of the Republic of Lithuania shall apply.

VIII. Others

A. Anti-commercial Bribery

a. Brief Introduction of Anti-commercial Bribery Laws and Regulations

The main anti-bribery laws are the Criminal Code of the Republic of Lithuania and the Criminal Procedure Code of the Republic of Lithuania. Liability for corruption activities is provided in the Criminal Code of the Republic of Lithuania. The major corruption criminal activities include (but are not limited to) bribery, trading in influence, graft, and abuse of office.

b. Department Supervising Anti-commercial Bribery

The major Lithuanian anti-corruption institution is the Special Investigation Service of the Republic of Lithuania. It was established in 1997 and reports to the President and the Parliament. The Special Investigation Service operates in three directions: investigation of corruption crimes, prevention of corruption and education of the public about anti-corruption. The Special Investigation Services also controls the implementation of the National Anti-corruption Programme. Requests for bribes and other corruption criminal activities can be reported to the Special Investigation Service officially, confidentially or anonymously. Requests for bribes and other corruption criminal activities can also be reported to the police or the public prosecutor's office.

c. Punitive Actions

Bribery of private businesspeople ("B2B bribery") by businesspeople is a criminal offence may qualify as, for example, bribery, trading in influence, graft, or abuse of office, as under Article 230 of the Criminal Code of the Republic of Lithuania the status of a person who works for a private legal entity and is entitled to act on behalf of the legal entity equals the status of a civil servant.

The maximum penalty that a natural person may face for bribery or trading in influence is 8 years' imprisonment. Maximum penalty for graft or abuse of office is 7 years' imprisonment.

It should be noted that criminal liability for corruption criminal activities may be imposed not only on natural persons, but also on legal entities. Legal entities can be held criminally liable for bribery, trading in influence, graft, abuse of office, and other crimes as well. As a general rule, companies will only be held responsible for their own conduct. However, in certain cases, a legal entity may be held criminally liable for criminal acts committed by another legal entity which is controlled by or represents the former legal entity, if such criminal acts were committed in favour of the former legal entity under instruction or with permission of a managing officer (or his authorized representative) of the former legal entity or as a result of insufficient supervision or control.

According to the Criminal Code of the Republic of Lithuania and upon discretion of the judge, one of the sanctions for legal entities convicted for corruption may be restriction of their activities. Also, according to the Law on Public Procurement, the contracting authority shall reject requests to participate and tenders if a judgment of conviction was passed and became effective against the supplier (legal entity) during the last five years for bribery, trading in influence, or graft, or if a judgment of conviction was passed and became effective against the suppliers of other countries for the crimes defined in the legal acts of the European Union listed in Article 45(1) of Directive 2004/18/EC of the European Parliament and of the Council of 31 March 2004 on the coordination of procedures for the award of public works contracts, public supply contracts and public service contracts. It should be noted that debarment on the above-mentioned legal grounds is mandatory.

B. Project Contracting

a. Permission System

In order to ensure that all companies and all natural persons have equal possibilities to sell their goods, services or works to the state, public procurement is organized. Public procurement (hereinafter referred to as "procurement") is the procurement of supplies, services or works performed by a contracting authority subject to the rules set forth mainly in the Law on Public Procurement. The goal of procurement is to award a public purchase and sales contract. The benefits of public procurement are not only reasonable use of finances for required goods, services and / or works, but also warranty of quality, and conclusion of contracts with reliable suppliers of goods and services. In order to achieve this, interested tenderers and their goods / services must meet certain requirements which are set in contract documents prepared for specific procurement by a contracting authority.

A contracting authority is:

(i) any state or local authority;

(ii) a public or private legal entity if all or part of its activities are especially intended for meeting non-commercial and non-industrial needs of general interest and meet at least one of the following conditions:

• more than 50% of financing for the activities of the legal entity is granted from state or municipal budget or from other state or municipal funds;

• the legal entity is controlled by the state or local authorities, or by other qualifying public or private legal entities;

• the legal entity has an administrative, managerial or supervisory board, more than half of whose members are appointed by the state or local authorities or by qualifying public or private legal entities.

Procurement is carried out by a contracting authority. Procurement may be carried out by announcing about it publicly or only by sending invitations to selected suppliers. Depending on the type and value of the intended procurement, the quantities of purchased goods and services, procurement may be subject to different procedures: open procedure, restricted procedure, negotiated procedure with prior publication, competitive dialogue, negotiated procedure without publication, innovation partnership.

b. Prohibited Areas

The Law on Public Procurement does not apply, and public procurement is not carried out in respect of the following:

(i) employment contracts;

(ii) arbitration and conciliation services;

(iii) certain legal services, such as document certification and authentication services which must be provided by notaries;

(iv) financial services in connection with the issue, sale, purchase or transfer of securities or other financial instruments;

(v) loans, whether or not in connection with the issue, sale, purchase or transfer of securities or other financial instruments;

(vi) civil defence, civil protection, and danger prevention services that are provided by non-profit organisations or associations, and which are covered by certain Common Procurement Vocabulary codes (except patient transport ambulance services);

(vii) public passenger transport services by rail or metro;

(viii) certain political campaign services (advertising campaign services, etc.);

(ix) public service contracts awarded by a contracting authority to another contracting authority or to an association of contracting authorities on the basis of an exclusive right which they enjoy pursuant to a law, regulation or published administrative provision which is compatible with the Treaty on the Functioning of the European Union.

With a few exceptions, the Law on Public Procurement does not apply either to the awarding of public contracts and to design contests organised in the fields of defence and security. Military equipment, secret equipment, their parts and constituent elements, units as well as related works, goods and services and secret works and services are procured in accordance with the Law on Public Procurement in the Fields of Defence and Security. Special rules, approved by the Government of the Republic of Lithuania, also apply to the acquisition or rental, by whatever financial means, of land, existing buildings or other immovable property or concerning rights thereon as well as to the acquisition, development, production or co-production of programme material intended for audiovisual media services or radio media services, that are awarded by audiovisual or radio media service providers, or contracts for broadcasting time or programme provision that are awarded to audiovisual or radio media service providers.

c. Invitation to Bid and Bidding

A contracting authority must carry out procurement in accordance with the Law on Public Procurement, other legal acts (resolutions of the Government of the Republic of Lithuania, orders of ministers, etc.), and simplified procurement regulations.

Before commencing procurement, a contracting authority must decide on the value of procurement and choose a due procurement type. The following types of procurement of international threshold value may be chosen: an open or restricted procedure, competitive dialogue, negotiated procedure with prior publication or negotiated procedure without publication. For simplified procurement (including small value procurement), the following types apply: simplified open procedure, simplified restricted procedure, simplified negotiated procedure with prior publication, simplified competitive dialogue, simplified open design contest, simplified restricted design contest, and procurement performed on the basis of survey.

When a contracting authority carries out procurement with prior publication, contract documents and publication about procurement must be published on the Central Portal of Public Procurement (an information system managed by the Central Procurement Office). Under the Law on Public Procurement, contracting authorities (with the exception of diplomatic missions, consular posts of the Republic of Lithuania abroad and missions of the Republic of Lithuania to international organisations) must either carry out procurement via the Central Procurement Office or acquire goods, services or works from the Central Procurement Office.

The contracting authority must draft contract documents in compliance with the provisions of the Law on Public Procurement. The contract documents must be precise, clear, and unambiguous so that the suppliers could submit tenders and the contracting authority could purchase what it needs. Contract documents must be drawn up in Lithuanian. In addition, the contract documents may also be drawn up in other languages.

In contract documents, the contracting authority is obliged to give all the information about contract conditions and award procedures. The contract documents must include: instructions on the drawing up of tenders; supplier qualification requirements; indication of the products, services or works concerned, amounts, the nature of services incidental to the public supply contract, time limits for delivery of products, rendering of services or performance of works; technical specifications; tender evaluation criteria and conditions; the terms and conditions of the public contract proposed to the parties by the contracting authority and / or a draft contract (if available); tender security (where required) requirements; a deadline for submission of requests to participate and tenders; and other information. The Central Portal of Public Procurement must ensure free, direct and unlimited access to publications.

Each tenderer may submit only one tender. Requests and tenders are submitted electronically, via the Central Portal of Public Procurement. Upon receipt of tenders, the contracting authority assesses qualification of suppliers and evaluates their tenders. As a general rule, the winning tender is the most economically advantageous tender if the data of the tender meets the requirements, conditions and criteria provided for in contract documents and if there are no other circumstances provided by law due to which the tenderer must be excluded. After the winning tender is clear, the contracting authority must notify suppliers. The procurement procedure ends by awarding a contract to the winning supplier.

马其顿

作者：Bojana Paneva、Ljupka Noveska Andonova、Veton Qoku
译者：马笑匀、冯帆

一、概述

（一）政治、经济、社会和法律环境的总体介绍

马其顿位于东南欧的巴尔干半岛。马其顿作为南斯拉夫分裂后产生的几个国家之一，于1991年宣布独立。马其顿北与塞尔维亚接壤，东与保加利亚接壤，南面紧邻希腊，西边与阿尔巴尼亚相邻。马其顿首都是斯科普里。2018年，马其顿人口约209万人，在世界上位列第144。①

马其顿自从独立后就不断地努力通过外商直接投资的方式来吸引外国资本。国家从经济和法律方面持续采取了一系列措施来建立良好的国际投资环境，获得有利的国际投资地位。为了提升外国投资者对马其顿的投资兴趣，马其顿通过修改法律，给予国内外投资者同等的权利和待遇，并且通过给予外国投资者更大的保护来保障其权利。马其顿政府最重要的目标是加入欧盟和北约。

1. 政治方面

马其顿1991年宪法设立了共和国议会（Sobranie）。立法权、司法权和行政权之间有明确的划分。总统是国家元首和军队总司令。马其顿议会是公民的代表，掌握国家立法权。议会由123名成员组成，均由全民公投选出，任期4年。行政权由政府行使。为了确保政府的有效运作，公民权利得到保障，每个部门都有其自己的职权和责任，并且要和其他部门一起合作。

2. 经济方面

独立以来，马其顿在经济自由化和鼓励经济发展上取得了进步，为投资者提供了新的投资机会。较低的税率和自由经济区帮助其吸引外资。在技术工业区内，政府特别注重在国内企业和外国企业之间建立联系。最终目标是在2017—2020年间平均经济增长率高于5%。

3. 社会方面

社会政策方面，政府的主要目标是到2020年将贫困比例降到16%以下。政府将设立有效运行的社会保护机构网络，这些机构贴近市民，能够满足其需要，其中部分的功能由当地的自治组织承担，它们与市民联系更为紧密，可以快速根据需求作出调整。该网络将包括为老年人提供支持和缓解性治疗的社会服务、护理中心、收容护理中心、残疾人中心，为26岁以上的残疾人提供住所，保护相关人员免受基于性别的暴力行为，为面临一定社会风险、需要保护的人群提供服务。

4. 法律方面

马其顿法律体系基于大陆法系。马其顿法院行使司法权。法院是独立自治的国家机关。司法部门由27个基层法院、4个上诉法院（负责审理不服基层法院判决而提起的上诉案）、最高法院、行政法院和高等行政法院组成。此外还有一个宪法法院，负责维护宪法和法定权利。

（二）"一带一路"倡议下与中国企业的合作情况和合作方向

马其顿和中国的关系以友好互利、相互理解并尊重主权、领土完整，以及平等对待为原则。马其顿和中国在1993年10月12日建立了大使级外交关系。②

马其顿政府支持"一带一路"倡议（即"16+1"合作项目），换言之，中国在未来将与马其顿建立

---

① 参见 http://worldpopulationreview.com/countries/macedonia-population/。
② 参见 http://mfa.gov.mk/index.php?option=com_content&view=article&id=260&catid=84&Itemid=349&lang=en。

更好的经济贸易伙伴关系。其目标是完成两条高速公路的建设，该项目由中国公司与马其顿公司共同负责。马其顿计划与该区域内几家中国公司签署几份有关能源和铁路运输的合作备忘录。这表示，马其顿视中国为重要的经济合作伙伴。双方同意为两个国家的企业提供支持，促进经济贸易合作，以及在其他重要领域为两国国民提供支持。①

2017年，在布达佩斯召开的第六次中东欧国家与中国政府首脑峰会期间，马其顿总理在论坛上告诉与会者，马其顿将举办几场与中国合作进程有关的重要活动，比如成立"中国和中东欧国家文化合作协调中心"。"作为马其顿文化部门的一个组成部分，文化合作协调中心将在2018年设立。马其顿也将在2018年举办第五届中国与中东欧国家合作研讨会、2018高级别智囊团会议，并将在2019年举办第四届文化合作部长级会议"。基于与中国的合作精神，马其顿总理指出，双方已经在保健和医疗等领域展开合作，并且根据《替代和补充药物法》，政府决定在马其顿成立中医药中心。②

二、投资

（一）市场准入

1. 投资主管部门

马其顿外国投资与出口促进机构是根据关于法律成立的主要政府机构③，主要负责吸引新的外商投资者以及支持已在马其顿投资的外商投资者扩大经营规模。此外，该机构（作为国家补助的提供者）代表马其顿政府为马其顿的出口企业提供国际贸易、出口程序、税务与法律规定的相关信息，协助提供行政许可证及执照，以及为了帮助出口企业寻找国外合作伙伴提供国际市场准入信息。除以上工作外，该机构还在马其顿国内以及境外开展出口推广活动并为马其顿出口企业与国外买家牵线搭桥，为国外公司提供马其顿国内潜在出口企业的信息。

另外一个对于外国投资比较重要的机构是根据相关法律成立的技术工业开发区委员会。④该机构设立的目的是创造、发展以及处理工业发展园区的相关活动，包括监管园区的使用者活动以及对开始、发展、完成相关活动进行审批。技术工业开发区为企业发展提供优厚条件，例如提供被管理的工业区域、事先建好的工厂、完备的法律和基础设施以及税务、关税以及其他福利。

2. 投资行业规定

马其顿国内未制定直接监管外国投资的法律。

马其顿《宪法》保证了市场上的所有实体拥有平等的地位，保证外国投资者的投资资本以及利润可以自由流动并汇往他国。法律框架包括多种法律：《贸易公司法》《证券法》《利润税法》《增值税法》《控股公司收购法》《外汇法》《银行法》《劳动法》《所有权及其他物权法》等。

"投资资金支持法"作为第一部投资监管法律，目前仍在编制中，尚不确定何时会获得批准。该部法律规定了向满足条件的公司批准资金支持和拨款方面的标准和程序。"投资资金支持法"将规定向受托在马其顿开展投资的实体给予资金支持的类型、资金支持额度、条件、方式及程序。

该部法律的目的旨在通过投资支持增强马其顿经济与就业的竞争力来促进马其顿经济增长与发展。能够得到资金支持的受益者为开展生产活动且从生产活动中获得收入增加，并提供相同的平均就业人数，即与前3年的平均数相比，上一年度的就业平均数增加。或者如果该实体在提交资金支持申请时，在马其顿注册并开展业务的时间不足4年，则对比的基准时间可少于3年。

在该部法律中，投资资金支持的种类如下：

（1）支持创造新就业；

（2）支持建立并促进马其顿供应商的合作；

（3）支持建立科技发展与研究的组织形式；

---

① 参见 http://vlada.mk/node/13547。
② 参见 http://vlada.mk/node/13780。
③ 参见 http://www.investinmacedonia.com。
④ 参见 http://www.dtirz.com。

（4）支持具有巨大经济利益的投资项目；
（5）支持资本投资与收入的增长；
（6）支持企业在困难情况下购买资金。
提供提高竞争力的金融资金种类：
（1）支持已经提高市场竞争力的企业实体；
（2）支持正在拓展市场并增加销售额的企业实体。

3. 投资方式

在马其顿，外资投资形式可以是现金、设备以及原材料。

根据《外汇法》，直接投资是指投资者旨在建立一种永久的经济联系以及/或管理其投资的公司或其他法律实体的投资。在《外汇法》中，直接投资为：

（1）成立一家公司，或投资者通过增加初始资本获得对公司的完全所有权，成立子公司或通过收购获得现有贸易公司的完全所有权；

（2）参股新公司或现有公司，且投资者拥有或购买超过10%的公司初始资本，或获得超过10%的决定权；

（3）签订为期5年或以上的长期贷款协议，且贷款来自投资者并计划全部用于某家贸易公司；

（4）签订为期5年或以上的长期贷款协议，且贷款用于在已有经济利益关系的实体之间建立永久性利益关联。

《技术工业开发区法》为投资自由贸易区的投资者提供优厚的条件。首先，技术工业开发区的投资者在10年内免缴个人所得税和企业所得税。投资者可免缴增值税和货物、原材料及设备机器的进口关税。其次，建筑成本补贴最高达50万欧元，具体金额根据投资额和雇用员工数量决定。马其顿技术工业开发区的土地租赁期最长可达99年。除税收激励政策外，该法还免除了一些惯常费用，包括：完整的配套设施，免费接通天然气、水、电以及准入国际主要公路网等服务。投资者还无需缴纳建设场地准备费。技术工业开发区提供快捷的营业登记手续办理流程，进一步降低了开设公司的成本。此外，国外投资者如果根据《外汇法》规定进行了直接投资登记，并依法履行了在马其顿纳税和缴纳社会保障费用的全部相关义务，即可自由转移其利润。

4. 准入条件及审查

国外投资者可直接投资受法律限制以外的所有行业和业务。投资武器制造和麻醉药剂需获得政府批准。此外，部分业务部门的投资者，如银行业、保险活动和投资基金，必须满足某些许可要求，该要求对国内外投资者一视同仁。

（二）外汇管理

1. 外汇主管部门

外汇管理机制在《外汇法》中进行了规定，对《外汇法》及其相关法规实施情况的监管由马其顿国家银行、财政部国家外汇监察署、财政部海关监察署、经济部和证券交易委员会共同负责。

马其顿国家银行对其颁发工作许可证的银行、储蓄所和外汇办事处的运营实施直接监管。

财政部国家外汇监察署对在马其顿领土范围内开展经营活动的居民和非居民的工作进行监管。在进行监管时应适用《监督管理法》的规定。

财政部海关监察署对进出马其顿的有效国内外货币以及从马其顿出口的支票以及货币性黄金（即由马其顿领土范围内的居民和非居民从国外进口或通过邮寄方式寄送）进行监管。

居民和非居民有义务使外汇监察员能够实施监管工作、了解业务情况，并应监察员要求准备或提交一切必要的文件和数据。

为开展监察工作，居民和非居民开设账户的银行有义务在收到监察员的书面请求后，提供通过账户开展业务的所有文件记录。工作监察和文件监察意味着监管局将了解居民和非居民与监察相关的文件和账户情况。

2. 外汇法律法规简介

《外汇法》的规定包括：居民和非居民之间进行的经常交易和资本交易，以及与之相关的支付和转移；在工作中使用国外支付方式或经营范围为国外支付方式的居民之间的经常交易和资本交易；单方面从马其顿向外转移资金或单方面从外部将资金转移到马其顿（不代表居民和非居民之间进行交易）；以及外汇监管和管制。

经常交易指居民和非居民之间不以资本转移为目的的交易。经常交易的支付和转移包括：基于交换货物和服务的支付、家庭生活开支的适度汇款等。

资本交易指居民和非居民之间以转移资本为目的的交易，如：直接投资、房地产投资、证券交易、信贷业务、担保、存款业务、投资（投资型）黄金的交易等。

直接投资指投资者有意向成立贸易公司，或通过追加初始资本获得贸易公司完全所有权，或参股新公司或现有贸易公司，或签订5年及以上的长期贷款协议等。国外投资者到马其顿投资时，需要到非居民直接投资登记处办理登记。

证券交易，就外汇业务的货币而言，是指对资本市场和货币市场上的证券进行交易，将马其顿国内证券在国外发行、登记或出售，在马其顿境内发行、登记和出售国外证券，非居民在马其顿境内投资证券，以及马其顿居民在境外投资证券。

投资基金股票（即非居民投资基金的股票）可在马其顿境内出售，前提是该投资基金管理公司按照《投资基金法》的要求在马其顿境内成立国外投资基金管理公司的子公司。

信贷业务是指为签订贷款协议而进行的交易。

国际支付业务是指由马其顿国家银行授权开展的国际支付业务。

为满足马其顿的需求，国际支付业务由马其顿国家银行实施。马其顿国家银行应规定开展国际支付业务的方式。

本法律规定的国外支付市场包括在马其顿境内在内的进行国外支付方式的所有买卖国交易。根据本法规定，国外支付方式是指外币、外币现金、支票、信用证和其他以外币计价并可以兑换成外币的支付工具。

3. 外资企业外汇管理要求

外国公民的法律地位决定其可在马其顿自由投资，前提是必须在投资前60天内向马其顿中央登记局报告。马其顿中央登记局设直接投资登记处，外国投资者在马其顿境内以资本或实物的形式作出的所有投资都必须在此登记。不报告直接投资是追究违法责任的依据，而报告直接投资则让投资者获得转移利润和金融资产以及清算的机会。

在马其顿境内按照专门法或批准的国际协议条款收购马其顿房地产的非居民、国外银行支行、国外贸易公司子公司，有义务在获得马其顿房地产所有权法律依据之日起60天内，向中央登记局报告该项资产投资以及所有房地产投资方面的变化情况。

中央登记局应将该项房地产投资资产和任何其他房地产投资变化情况记录在马其顿非居民房地产投资登记项下。

在马其顿发行和登记国外证券必须获得证券交易委员会的批准。证券交易委员会决定获得证券发行和登记的条件和方式。期限在3年以上的国外债务性证券不得在马其顿境内发行和登记。

非居民可在马其顿内订立证券交易协议或交易证券，但仅能通过获得授权的证券市场参与者进行。获得授权的证券市场参与者有义务向马其顿国家银行提交报告，说明非居民在马其顿境内的所有证券投资情况，以及这些投资的变更情况，包括转让情况。马其顿国家银行规定非居民在马其顿境内开展证券业务的方式和条件。

对于投资基金单位的销售即封闭式投资基金的股票份额，非居民投资的基金必须获得证券交易委员会的批准。证券交易委员会通过管理条例确定获得批准的条件和方式。

非居民可以在获得授权的银行开设和拥有外币及马其顿代纳尔（MKD）账户。在开设账户时，授权银行必须确认非居民的身份。马其顿国家银行规定开设和持有账户的方式和条件。

非居民可根据专门法规定，在马其顿境内投资并交易投资型黄金。

基于资本交易的支付和资金转移可自由实现，前提是该交易的达成、报告和登记符合《外汇法》规定，且所有向马其顿的纳税义务和社会保障费缴纳义务均已履行。

转移或资金转移应指投资者为了行使参与所投资法律实体破产或清算后的利润分成或剩余财产分配的权利而进行的为实现资本交易的资金转移。

（三）金融融资

1. 主要金融机构

银行系统是马其顿整体金融系统最重要的组成部分。马其顿的金融系统由马其顿国家银行（央行）[1]、商业银行[2]、储蓄所[3]、外汇办事处[4]、斯科普里银行间同业小额支付清算所[5]、斯科普里存款保险基金所[6]和马其顿证券交易所（MSE）[7]组成。

银行是主要的融资来源。根据马其顿《国家银行法》和《银行业法》，马其顿国家银行是负责马其顿境内银行和储蓄所执照许可和监管的唯一监管当局。马其顿国家银行的主要监管职能是维护银行系统的安全稳健运行，并保护存款人和在银行业进行金钱投资的其他债权人的利益。国家银行的主要目标是实现和保持价格稳定性。另外一个服从于主要目标的次要目标是致力于维护稳定、具有竞争力并且以市场为中心的金融体系。

2. 外资企业融资条件

《外汇法》及其配套法规对于非居民在马其顿进行直接投资未设置监管限制条件。非居民可以在不受限制的情况下在马其顿银行开设外币和代纳尔的非居民账户。在开设账户时，获得授权的银行有义务确认非居民的身份。

居民和非居民之间可自由开展信贷业务。唯一的要求是所达成的信贷业务必须向央行报告。

央行规定开设和持有非居民账户的方式和条件，以及与非居民达成信贷业务的报告方式和条件。[8]

（四）土地政策

1. 土地法律法规概况

外国人获得财产权的法律依据是马其顿《宪法》，其规定："在马其顿的外国人在法律规定的条件可获得财产所有权。"同时，马其顿《宪法》还保了国外投资者自由转移所投资的资本和利润的权利。此外，《所有权及其他物权法》对外国人获得所有权和其他物权的情形进行了详细规定。马其顿土地相关法律法规的其他法律问题参见《建筑法》《建设用地法》《国有建设用地私有化和租赁法》《房地产地籍法》《农业用地法》《债法》和《技术工业开发区法》。

2. 外资企业获得土地规定

马其顿有两种土地所有权：公有和私有。

公共财产以及指定作为公共用途和服务公共职能的财产如国家道路、森林和公园、街道、广场、学校、博物馆等属于国家所有，所有法律实体和个人均可使用。这些财产在符合法律规定的情况下可通过特许权或长期租赁转让给第三方。

根据《所有权及其他物权法》，来自欧盟成员国和经济合作与发展组织成员国的外国个人和法律实体可获得马其顿领土范围内的建设用地所有权和长期租赁权（最长可达99年），所享受的条件与国内法律实体和个人完全相同。非欧盟和非经济合作与发展组织成员国的外国个人、法律实体和居民可在互惠条件下获得马其顿领土范围内的建设用地所有权和长期租赁权。

---

[1] 参见 http://www.nbrm.mk/pocetna-en.nspx。
[2] 参见 http://www.nbrm.mk/banki-en.nspx。
[3] 参见 http://www.nbrm.mk/stedilnici-en.nspx。
[4] 参见 http://www.nbrm.mk/mienuvacnici.nspx。
[5] 参见 http://www.kibs.com.mk/en/default.aspx。
[6] 参见 http://www.fodsk.org.mk/Default。
[7] 参见 http://www.mse.mk/en/。
[8] 参见 http://www.nbrm.mk/decisions_from_the_area_of_foreign_exchange_operations-en.nspx。

《建设用地法》详细规定了与建设用地相关的权利义务、建设用地开发、建设用地管理条件和方式以及建设用地领域的其他法律事宜。国内和国外个人及法律实体可获得建设用地的长期租赁权,且该权限最高可持续 99 年。根据该法规定,国内和国外个人及法律实体可获得马其顿公有建设用地的短期租赁权,且期限可长达 5 年,期满后还可再续租 3 年。

根据《所有权及其他物权法》的规定,外国自然人和法人无法获得马其顿领土范围内的农业用地所有权。

在马其顿,国外个人和法律实体可根据互惠条件获得马其顿领土范围内农业用地的长期租赁权,但必须获得司法部长的同意,且在此之前必须征求农业、林业和水资源管理部部长以及财政部部长的意见。互惠条件是否成立应由司法部部长根据法律规定的条件和程序确定。

此外,法律要求取得所有权或其他限制物权必须在马其顿房地产地籍管理机构进行登记,经登记后方对第三方有效。

然而,为保护国家权益,几乎每个国家都会对部分地区设置限制条件。马其顿在《所有权及其他物权法》中作出了限制:外国人不得获得"固定财产"的所有权,该"固定财产"是为保护马其顿权益由法律宣布外国人无权拥有的土地区域。

(五)企业设立与解散

1. 企业形式

《贸易公司法》是马其顿规范商业活动的主要法律。《贸易公司法》规定了马其顿公司的组建、经营、转型和终止。根据《贸易公司法》,马其顿有五种类型的经济组织:普通合伙企业(JTD)、有限合伙企业(KD)、有限责任公司(DOO–LLC)、股份公司(AD)和股份有限公司(KDA)。根据《贸易公司法》,马其顿和外国个人或公司均可设立上述五种类型的经济组织。外国投资者最常设立的经济组织是有限责任公司和股份公司。

普通合伙企业是指由两个或两个以上个人或法律实体联合组建,合伙人以全部资产就公司的债务对债权人承担无限责任的实体。普通合伙企业所有股东之间的关系建立在"个人属性"(intuitu personae)原则之上,即每位合伙人对公开发行证券的公司的设立、经营和终止都拥有决定权。《贸易公司法》未规定普通合伙企业的最低注册资本金额度,因为此规定对于此种形式的贸易公司来说缺乏必要性和重要性,它之所以不重要,是因为公司对债权人的债务也由合伙人承担。普通合伙企业的成立只需创始人之间签订一份合伙协议。该合伙协议应连同其他要求提供的文件在商业登记之前提交。

有限合伙企业是指由两个或两个以上的个人或法律实体联合组建,至少其中的一位合伙人(普通合伙人)应以其全部资产对企业的债务负责,即承担无限责任,而至少有另外一位合伙人(有限合伙人)应以其在有限合伙企业资本中的认缴出资额为限对企业债务负责。

股份有限公司是一种有限合伙形式,其资本被分成等额股份。

有限责任公司是最常见的企业形式,可由一人或多人组建。股东不对公司债务负责,也就是说此类公司仅以其资产为限对债权人负责。法律规定此类公司的股东人数不得超过 50 人。注册资本金最低必须等于与 5 000 欧元等价的马其顿代纳尔(根据马其顿国家银行在支付当天公布的平均汇率计算)。法律规定的资本金必须是 100 的整数倍。如果出于任何原因导致资本金减少,应在年度账目设立当天起 60 天内将资本金补齐到法律规定的金额,除非该公司在此期间转变为其他类型的公司。个人注资不得少于与 100 欧元等价的马其顿代纳尔柜台交易价,且如果以实物资产出资,则应由有资质的资产评估单位对资产进行评估。公司应由一位经理或多位经理管理,且由股东任命。如果有两个或两个以上的投资人,该公司成立时应制定公司章程。如果是独资有限责任公司(DOOEL),则公司成立时仅需制定声明书而无须制定公司章程。

股份公司是指全部资本分成等额股份的公司。股东不就股份公司的债务对债权人承担责任。公司可以有一位或多位股东。成立股份公司有两种方式:发起设立和募集设立。发起设立的股份公司未通过公开发行公告募集股份,其资本金的最低名义金额不得低于与 25 000 欧元等价的马其顿代纳尔柜台交易价(按照马其顿国家银行发布的平均汇率计算)。募集设立的股份公司通过公开发行公告募集股份,其资本金的最低名义金额不得低于与 50 000 欧元等价的马其顿代纳尔金额(按照马其顿国家银行发布的平均汇率计算）。对于保险公司、投资公司和银行，法规要求的最低资本金会更高一些。公司资本被分为普通股和优先股。每股最低价值不得少于 1 欧元。公司管理层级可按照单层制（董事会）或两层制（管理层或经理、监事会）构建。管理层成员不得担任监事会成员。

2. 设立程序

设立公司的第一步是订立公司章程，必须涵盖：公司名称和住所、公司经营范围、公司管理层及法定代表人、合伙人或公司所有者的身份（股份公司除外）、合伙人出资方式（现金或实物）和金额（适用于普通合伙企业和有限合伙企业）、公司注册资本金额（适用于有限责任公司、股份公司和股份有限公司），以及《贸易公司法》中规定的视具体公司类型而定的其他事项。

马其顿中央登记局是负责新设本地公司或外国公司本地办事处注册登记的唯一授权机构。新设立的公司只有在商业登记处录入信息后才视为在法律意义上已经成立，也就是说，在注册前，该公司不存在。法律框架包括一站式服务系统，通过该系统可在提交申请后 4 小时内完成公司注册。使用一站式服务系统的另一好处是其电子分发服务允许潜在投资人或第三方获得该国家公司经营的全部电子信息，从而可以在线注册公司、管理和关闭业务，而无需到场处理或聘请马其顿第三方中介机构。注册公司的申请文件连同其他需要提交的文件可向马其顿中央登记局指定的当地登记机构提交电子版。

3. 解散方式及要求

根据《贸易公司法》，公司终止有几种方式，包括公司经营期限到期或公司章程中规定的其他情形、公司破产、公司被合并或分立、根据法院最终判决及法律规定的其他情形。

当发生以上任何一种情况时，除非公司已启动破产程序，否则公司应进行清算。在商业登记处删除信息后，公司失去其法律地位。

（六）合并收购

根据马其顿立法规定，企业的合并可以通过收购、改变企业状态（加入、兼并和分立）、跨境兼并以及改变法律形式来实现。

收购可以通过购买股票、股份或资产的形式开展，然后按照《贸易公司法》履行相关程序。一个或多个公司（被加入的公司）可在不进行清算的情况下通过向另外一家公司（收购方）转移其全部资产和负债，以此成为收购方的组成部分或拥有收购方的股份。

两个或两个以上的公司可实行兼并，无需清算，而是通过成立一家新的受益公司，向其转移被兼并公司的全部资产和负债，以此成为新受益公司的组成部分或拥有收购方的股份。

根据《贸易公司法》，马其顿股份公司及有限责任公司可以与在欧盟注册的有限责任公司进行跨境兼并。跨境兼并只能在有限责任公司之间进行，管理投资基金的公司和主营业务为集资进行金融投资的公司不得进行跨境兼并。

公司可通过分立的形式，同时将其全部资产和负债转移给两个或两个以上的新公司，或两个或两个以上的现有公司，在此种情况下，进行分立的公司应在不进行清算的情况下清盘。公司可通过分立的形式，将其部分资产和负债转移给一个或更多的新公司，或一个或更多的现存公司，此种情况下，该公司不需清盘。

加入公司的决定应获得被加入的公司和收购标的公司（被收购公司）的同意。兼并的决定应获得被兼并公司的同意。

在派生分立和新设分立两种形式分立公司时，该决定应经被分立的公司同意。当公司接管派生分立出去的公司和接管新设分立出去的公司时，该决定应获得被分立的公司以及接受部分资产和负债转移的公司（收购公司）同意。公司分立的两种形式详述如下：

新设分立指的是除了现存的公司外，再成立另外一家公司。接管新设分立出去的公司是指将新设的公司股份转让，例如：被另外一个现存的贸易公司收购。

派生分立指的是母公司将自己的子公司（商业单元）剥离，然后被剥离的单位成为一家独立的公司。另外，接管派生分立出去的公司是指另外一家贸易公司收购被剥离的单元。

加入、兼并和分立应获得作为加入、兼并和分立对象的每家公司股东大会通过，并应当符合《贸易公司法》有关章程修订所规定的条件和方式。

如果在兼并或分立过程中成立了新公司,则成立该新公司应符合《贸易公司法》有关成立相关类型公司的规定,《贸易公司法》章节中另有规定的除外。

如果由于加入、兼并或分立导致一个或多个公司的股东负债增加,则加入、兼并或分立的决定应获得全体股东的同意。

董事长,即管理层总裁应在公司加入股份公司(兼并)或股份公司分立当日起8天之内,向中央证券存管机构通报有关章程修订事宜,并下令将章程修订情况记入股东账簿,即对股东账簿进行更新。意思是,现存的合资企业的股东名册反映了分立、合并或者收购等交易行为。但为了在法律上合规,股东名册需要进行修改。基于分立、合并或者收购等交易行为,新成立的合资公司的股东名册需要进行更新。

加入、兼并或分立公司(派生分立公司被接管或新设公司被接管)时,目标公司应终止经营但不进行清算,且将其全部资产和负债转移给新公司以及收购方,转移时间应为协调加入、兼并或分立条件的协议中明确的日期,或计划开展派生分立和新设分立的日期。

因兼并、加入或分立(派生分立公司被接管或新设公司被接管)而新成立的公司,应作为被加入、兼并或分立的公司的债权人的连带债务人。

股票的发行,或股份的收购和提取应根据协议或公司分立计划实施。

股票,例如为了反映公司与其他各方的相关交易,基于分立、合并或者收购等交易行为的公司股票需要根据分立计划进行划分。这也意味着,新股票,例如新的合资公司或者有限责任公司的股票需要在公司成立之时发行,或者,公司现有的股票,在合资公司解散后被收回(例如:有限责任公司由于分立、合并或者收购等交易行为而解散)。

被加入公司的管理机构,收购方公司的管理机构,被兼并公司的管理机构即被分立公司(派生分立公司被接管或新设公司被接管)的管理机构,以及被收购方公司的管理机构应签署一份协议,协调加入、兼并或分立的条件。该协议应进行公证。

在股东同意此种决定,或在召开股东会或全体股东大会以通过此种协议,或公司分立计划完成制订之时最晚1个月之前,已签署协议的公司管理机构或已签署协议的被分立公司(派生分立公司被接管或新设公司被接管)管理机构应就所签署的协议发布联合公告,或者在马其顿《官方公报》上公布已获通过的分立计划,且至少是在一份日报上予以公布。

协议或分立计划在获得参与加入、兼并和分立的公司股东或股东会或公司全体股东大会接受后立即生效。

股东会作出的决议,例如,股东大会批准分立计划。如果股份交换比例过低,加入、兼并和成立的公司协议无法得到批准,法院可根据股东或持股人员的请求,裁决予以不超过股份的股票票面金额10%的补充支付。

(七)竞争管制

1. 竞争管制主管机构

在马其顿,与保护竞争相关的法律框架主要是《竞争保护法》及为促进上述法律实施的配套法规。

竞争权的确立是为了确保马其顿国内市场的自由竞争,以提升经济效益并保障消费者权益。适用竞争规定的目的是建立一个让所有企业实体都在同等条件下享受同等待遇的市场,且他们的市场地位根据所提供的商品和服务质量而定。为此,竞争法的核心理念是监管企业实体的市场活动,而竞争法的核心目标则是建立具有竞争性的市场。

保护竞争委员会负责监管《竞争保护法》的实施。保护竞争委员会的基础职能是:管控《竞争保护法》条款的应用;一定程度上监测和分析市场条件,以便促进市场的自由发展和有效竞争;根据法律规定执行程序并作出决策。保护竞争委员会的职能涵盖以下方面:评估实体之间的协议;防止和消除滥用市场主导地位,并防止经营者集中。保护竞争委员会是具有法律实体地位的独立国家机构,根据法律授予的职能有权独立工作和作出决策。保护竞争委员会由马其顿议会任命的1名主席和4名成员组成,任期为5年,可以连选连任。

2. 竞争法概况

《竞争保护法》适用于：企业实体、企业实体的联合组织、附属或独立的企业实体、国家行政单位、公众利益实体，以及受托提供具有一般经济利益的服务的实体，这些实体在获得收入方面具有天然的垄断地位或者被授予专门和专属的权利或优惠条件，除非该法律的规定将阻碍这些实体行使法律授予其的能力或这些实体成立之时旨在获得的能力。

《竞争保护法》明确了可能阻止、限制或扭曲马其顿市场竞争情况的三种基本形式，即禁止签订的协议、滥用市场主导地位、禁止的营业者集中。

根据《竞争保护法》，企业实体之间签订的所有协议、企业实体联合组织所作出的决策，以及一致采取的商业行为，如果其目的或效果导致竞争关系扭曲，则应被禁止，尤其是以下情形：直接或间接固定购买或销售价格或任何其他交易条件；限制或控制生产、市场、技术开发或投资；分享市场或供应来源；针对同等或类似的交易向其他交易合作伙伴提出不同的条件，从而使其陷入不利的竞争地位，或签订受制于其他签约方接受补充性义务的协议，而这些补充性义务根据其性质或根据商业惯例与协议的主题无关。

在相关市场具有主导地位的企业实体是指作为特定商品和/或服务的潜在卖方或买方：在相关市场上没有竞争对手，或与其他竞争对手相比，在相关市场上占据领先地位，尤其是在以下方面：

- 市场份额及地位；
- 经济实力；
- 获得供应来源或市场的能力；
- 与其他实体之间的联系；
- 其他企业实体进入该市场会受到法律上或实际上的障碍；
- 考虑到其供应或者需求情况，具有决定市场情况的能力；
- 通过采取针对其他企业实体的行动，而将其他竞争对手挤出市场的能力。如果某企业实体所占市场份额超过40%，则应假定其具有市场主导地位，除非该企业实体能够提供相反的证明。两个或多个法律上相互独立的企业实体如果在相关市场上联合行动或联合参与市场，则应假定其联合起来具有市场主导地位。

禁止一个或多个企业实体在相关市场或其重要领域滥用其市场主导地位。此种滥用尤其存在于以下情形：直接或间接强迫他人接受不公平的买卖价格或其他不公平的交易条件；限制生产、市场或技术开发从而损害了消费者权益；针对同等或类似的交易向其他商业合作伙伴提出不同的条件，从而使其陷入不利的竞争地位；或签订受制于其他签约方接受补充性义务的协议，而这些补充性义务根据其性质或根据商业惯例与协议的主题无关；无正当理由拒绝交易，或鼓励和要求其他企业实体或企业实体的联合组织不要与某一特定实体进行商品和/或服务的买卖，且其意图为以不诚信的行为对该实体形成伤害，以及无正当理由拒绝另外一个企业实体进入其自己的网络系统或其他基础设施以获得适当补偿，前提是如果该企业无法获得使用网络系统和其他基础设施的同意，会由于法律上或实际上的原因，无法参与相关市场的竞争。

根据《竞争保护法》，通过以下方式会长期改变企业控制权而造成营业者集中：两个或两个以上之前独立存在的业务实体或实体的部分组织机构被兼并，或一个或多个实体（已借助协议或法律规定的其他方式，通过购买证券或资产，至少控制一个实体或一个或多个企业实体）获得对一个或多个实体的整体或部分的直接或间接控制权。

3. 竞争管制措施

保护竞争委员会应制定保护竞争的规定和措施，以及建立有效竞争机制的措施。

不当行为管理委员会应在保护竞争委员会之前启动不当行为管理程序，并对法律规定的不当行为予以处罚，在确定罚款金额时，不当行为管理委员会应考虑：不当行为的严重性、不当行为持续的时间、竞争关系的扭曲程度，以及不当行为造成的影响。

法律对此种行为规定了多种处罚措施，如经济处罚，以及在罚款的基础上，不当行为管理委员会还可在一定时期内禁止该实体从事某一职业、开展某一活动或行使某一职责。

(八)税收

1. 税收体系与制度

马其顿的税务体系由可满足税收政策的不同种类的税合理组合而成。

税收体系包括三个税种:①所得税(利润税和个人所得税);②消费税(增值税、货物税和关税);③财产税。负责征收公共收入的国家行政管理机构是公共收入办公室。

2. 主要税赋与税率

在马其顿,个人所得税(PIX)是向个人就其国内外各种收入来源征收的税。马其顿居民纳税人根据他们来源于全球的总收入纳税,非居民纳税人根据他们在马其顿境内产生的收入缴税。个人所得税计税收入的形式不仅包括收到的现金、证券、实物,也包括任何其他形式的补偿。个人所得税实行10%的统一税率。

马其顿公司应依据全球收入缴纳企业所得税。外国公司在马其顿的计税依据是他们通过在马其顿建立常设机构开展活动所产生的利润,以及来自马其顿的收入。企业所得税税率为10%。《利润税法》规定征收利润税的方式、利润税费率、利润税的纳税人、利润税计费的税基、利润税缴纳期限,以及其他有关利润税的确定和支付的重要事项。

《增值税法》对增值税(VAT)以及增值税的计算和缴纳作出了规定。增值税征内容为在马其顿境内有供应地的产品或服务供应,以及进口到马其顿境内的货物。纳税人如果营业收入超过每年100万马其顿代纳尔,必须登记缴纳增值税。也可基于自愿纳税。大多数应税供货的一般增值税税率为18%。适用5%增值税优惠税率的主要为以下货物和服务的供应和进口:供人类消费的食物、公共供水系统提供的饮用水、出版物、农业使用的种子和种植材料、农业机械和塑料薄膜、医药和医疗器械、计算机、个人交通工具、软件、太阳能供热系统及其部件、供残障人士个人使用的可为其提供协助和治疗的医疗设备和其他装置、人类消费食物烹制所需的原油、公共废物处理服务、酒店住宿服务、牲畜饲料、牲畜饲料添加剂、牲畜、婴儿产品及文具等。

3. 纳税申报与优惠

根据《个人所得税法》,应税的个人所得由以下几种收入组成:个人收入(工资或投资)、独资经营收入、销售自有农产品的收入、来源于财产和产权的收入、来源于版权和工业产权的收入、资本利得、博彩收入及其他收入。自2018年1月1日起,马其顿精简了法律实体和个人申报和缴纳个人所得税的程序。法律实体有义务编制并通过公共收入办公室的新电子个人纳税系统提交电子计算表,并在收到个人收入的同时缴纳个人所得税。提交电子计算表后,税收当局将针对同时获得的个人收入和缴纳的个人所得税生成电子支付单。

根据《利润税法》,企业所得税计算依据是纳税人根据会计规则和标准所确定总收入和总支出金额的差额。税基(总收入和总支出之间的差额)应在发生未确认费用时调增。当上年度利润进行投资(将利润用于再投资)时,应将该部分利润从税基中扣除。

对利润再投资部分免于征税是最常见的税收激励措施,企业可利用该项政策扩大经营活动,创造新的就业机会。利润再投资是指出于企业发展的目的用于再投资的利润,即为扩大纳税人的经营活动而有形资产(不可移动的财产、厂房和设备)以及无形资产(计算机软件和专利)。乘用车、家具、地毯、视听设备、大型家电、纯艺术品和实用艺术品及其他行政性投资除外。同时,纳税人还必须满足一个条件。纳税人必须对再投资利润购买的资产保有5年的所有权。如果纳税人在购买之日起的5年内将用再投资利润购买的资产的所有权转让出去,则纳税人必须补缴被免征的税款。

根据《利润税法》和《公共活动捐赠和赞助法》,向体育联盟、马其顿奥委会、足球俱乐部、篮球俱乐部、手球俱乐部和其他体育运动的俱乐部捐款可享受减税。前提条件是这些体育俱乐部必须参与有组织联盟的国家竞赛体系内的赛事,还需要注册过初级体育学校,而且纳税人应持有青少年体育运动机构签发的证书。从此种捐赠中受益的实体是那些符合《体育法》规定可行使减税权的实体。向上述体育俱乐部捐款的纳税人,通过专用指定账户捐款,视不同的体育俱乐部类型而定,在计税时将扣除捐赠金额的35%~50%。

根据《利润税法》,对马其顿境内或境外向外国法律实体支付的收入,且这些收入不属于在马其顿领土范围内外国法律实体常设机构业务框架之内的，应征收预提所得税，前提是避免重复征税的国际协议①中未作其他规定。如果接收收入而应缴纳预提所得税的一方为已与马其顿共和国签订避免重复征收利润和资本税的外国居民，则所签订协议的规定将优先于马其顿法律适用，意味着如果有特定的协议，则可对收入按照低税率征收；如果没有特定协议，则应适用《利润税法》。

根据《增值税法》，部分供应品可免缴增值税但不可免缴输入增值税，包括住宅物业租金、邮票、邮政服务、特定银行及金融业务、保险及再保险服务、健康服务及教育服务等。部分供应品可免缴增值税且免缴输入增值税，包括商品出口、向央行供应黄金及其他贵重金属等。

然而，在自由贸易区（又称"技术工业开发区"），事实上可适用大多数税收激励政策。与上文所述相反，自由贸易区外的增值税率为18%，而在自由贸易区内则为零；自由贸易区外的企业所得税和个人所得税税率为10%，而自由贸易区内同样是零。

（九）证券交易

1. 证券法律法规概况

监管资本市场的立法相当复杂，这是因为该法需要监管参与资本市场实体之间的具体关系。证券立法包括众多法律法规，但其中最重要的法律有：《贸易公司法》《证券法》《收购股份公司法》《投资基金法》，马其顿在1995年成立了马其顿证券交易所，为监管投资组合创造了条件。

2. 证券市场监管

对证券交易业务和交易参与者的监督由马其顿证券交易委员会负责实施。马其顿证券交易委员会是具有法律实体地位及自主性和独立性的组织，其公共授权来自《证券法》《收购股份公司法》和《投资基金法》。委员会负责证券市场的合法运转及投资者权益保护。

中央证券存管机构是马其顿资本市场的另一个重要机构。中央证券存管机构的任务是向所有市场利益相关方提供高质量和及时的服务，侧重于促进创新性和可持续的技术解决方案，以便可快速、持续、简便地获得服务，同时确保所有参与方的利益。根据《证券法》，中央证券存管机构履行以下职能：马其顿境内以电子记录（保管证券登记记录）形式进行的证券发行和转让登记；为所有的证券发行提供国际证券识别编码；证券持有人登记；根据"货银对付"原则进行交易结算；非贸易转让（执行赠与协议、继承决定、法院判决等）；为证券借贷创造条件；监测成员的财务状况，以便管理可能无法结算交易以及为证券发行人提供额外服务的风险。

3. 外资企业参与证券交易要求

财政部（代表马其顿）、马其顿国家银行、直辖市及斯科普里市、股份公司、股份有限公司和其他国内外法律实体可根据法律规定的条件发行证券。

在一级市场发行证券（包括自己的股票），均应提前获得证券交易委员会批准。

在一级市场发行证券可以公募也可以私募。

总金额不超过与25 000欧元等价的马其顿代纳尔柜台价的公募或私募证券的发行，无需获得证券交易委员会的批准。此种情况下的证券发行者有义务将此募股行为告知证券交易委员会，并向证券交易委员会提交发行证券行为的报告，并公开刊登通知让公众知晓其募股行为。证券发行者每两个日历年内未经证券交易委员会批准而发行证券的行为不得超过一次。

违反《证券法》规定的证券发行将被视为无效。

证券经过登记、贸易交易成立及对证券进行非贸易转让，均意味着证券账户开设。证券存管所是根据《贸易公司法》和《证券法》设立的总部位于马其顿的股份公司。证券存管所可成立经纪行、银行、保险公司或资金管理公司。证券存管所必须在任何时候持有和保持最少等价于500 000欧元的马其顿代纳尔基础资本（按照自取得成立证券存管所执照之日起马其顿国家银行的中间汇率换算）。证券交易委员会应详细规定证券存管所本金的结构和计算方式。

证券的二级交易通过证券交易委员会委托的证券交易所进行。证券交易所是根据《证券法》和

---

① 参见 http://www.ujp.gov.mk/en/plakjanje/category/137。

《贸易公司法》设立的总部位于马其顿的股份公司。证券交易所可由国内外的法人和自然人成立。证券交易所必须在任何时候持有和保持最少等价于 500 000 欧元的马其顿代纳尔基础资本（按照自取得成立证券交易所执照之日起马其顿国家银行的中间汇率换算）。证券交易委员会将具体规定证券交易所必须具备的资产结构和计算方式。

可开展《证券法》所规定的证券服务的单位包括：取得委员会所颁发工作许可的经纪行、根据《银行法》获得授权且取得委员会所颁发工作许可的银行、取得委员会所颁发工作许可的外国经纪行子公司。

经授权可在任何经济合作与发展组织成员国开展所有或部分证券服务的外国经纪行，可通过获得委员会所颁发营业执照的子公司，在马其顿领土范围内提供相同的服务。

与执行客户订单相关的服务，以及与通知买方或证券买方相关的服务（但不构成在经纪行咨询投资），仅能由经授权的经纪人提供。

（十）投资优惠及保护

1. 优惠政策框架

在 2018 年的预算中，马其顿政府预计经济发展项目的预算达到 31 亿马其顿代纳尔（约 5 000 万欧元），较 2017 年增长了 46%。通过《经济增长计划》，马其顿为国内外投资者提供同等透明条件，并将通过两种方式促进国内外投资者的合作：一是鼓励外国投资者与国内投资者合作；二是支持国内投资者成为外国投资者的合格供应商。此外，该计划还制定了"绿地投资"和"棕地投资"这两种投资措施。

2. 特定行业与地区鼓励

《经济增长计划》的措施将被转化为一项具体的法规——"投资资金支持法"（目前仍在就通过该法律进行讨论），通过该项法规，2018年的资金将得到系统分配，公司自3月份或4月份即可开始使用。

根据《马其顿政府计划（2017—2020）》，马其顿政府将采取积极和透明的政策来吸引外国直接投资。政府将侧重于建造基础设施，并将通过中国和中东欧 "16+1" 合作机制启动 3 个优先级基础设施项目的融资谈判，项目总金额达 100 亿美元。①

3. 特别经济区

对寻求进入马其顿市场的外国投资者来说，自由贸易区是最具吸引力的选择。

外商拥有 100% 的所有权，增值税、企业所得税、个人所得税、关税、地税全免，仅需象征性地缴纳少量土地租赁税，且享受可高达 500 欧元的直接国家补助，是该地区采取打造最具竞争力的经营环境的多种价值主张之一。

4. 投资保护

马其顿签署了多个双边投资协定（BITs）。② 马其顿和中国之间的双边投资协定于1997年11月1日生效，该协定旨在为投资者创造有利条件，激发投资者的创业积极性，促进两国经济发展。③

三、贸易

（一）贸易主管部门

继贸易部和商务部后，经济部目前负责监督和促进马其顿国内外贸易，特别是在经济部内部有一个独立的国际贸易合作机构，负责处理有关国际贸易体制和双边及多边合作的问题。经济部在这一领域的工作重点是与外国和跨国机构进行沟通，以便达成和执行国际贸易协定、完善国家立法以及颁发某些贸易许可证。

---

① 参见 http://vlada.mk/programa。
② 参见 http://investmentpolicyhub.unctad.org/IIA/CountryBits/124#iiaInnerMenu。
③ 参见 http://investmentpolicyhub.unctad.org/Download/TreatyFile/757。

此外，该部还负责为产业的发展创造条件，刺激商业活动和投资增长的经济环境，发展能源行业，开发天然矿产资源，增加和促进出口，发展公共－私人合伙等。

（二）贸易法律法规概况

《贸易法》（2004年）规定了内外部市场的一般贸易条件和贸易方式、限制贸易的措施以及该领域的保护措施。考虑到需要保护环境、个人健康和安全以及与某些金属的贸易，《贸易法》还以一般方式列出了进口和出口商品的许可证类型，以此作为武装和保护公共安全的手段。马其顿政府可以对特定商品的大量进口采取包括反倾销措施在内的安全措施，以保护国内产业。其他一些法律也规定了马其顿的贸易，例如《消费者保护法》（2004年）、《产品安全法》（2006年）、《建筑产品法》（2015年）等。

此外，一些法律针对的是更为具体和受到严格监管的贸易，例如：

- 《控制双重用途货物和技术出口管制法》（2005年）规定买卖可用于民用和军事目的的这类货物需获得经济部颁发特别许可证；
- 《军备和军事装备制造和贸易法》（2002年）规定了批准这类装备贸易的要求和程序。为了获得必要的批准，外国投资者必须在马其顿境内有相应的业务。

（三）贸易管理

马其顿试图通过为贸易、海关和贸易的各个方面提供具有竞争力的条件，来建立自己在该地区的贸易中心地位。具体而言，基于签署的双边和多边自由贸易协定，在马其顿的企业可以免费获得超过6.5亿的消费者，具体如下：

- 与欧盟成员国达成稳定和结盟协议（SAA）；
- 与欧洲自由贸易联盟（EFTA）签署的自由贸易协定；
- 与阿尔巴尼亚、波斯尼亚和黑塞哥维那、摩尔多瓦、塞尔维亚、黑山的中欧自由贸易协定；
- 与土耳其的自由贸易协定；
- 与乌克兰的自由贸易协定。

大部分贸易是通过技术工业开发区（TIDZ）的企业实现的，这些开发区是免税区。客观地说，2016年，TIDZ的出口占马其顿出口总额的47.1%。[①] TIDZ是马其顿关税区的一部分，但与此同时，也是一个与关税区的其余部分分隔且被单独隔开，在此区域内需根据TIDZ的法律和其他适用法律规定的条款和条件开展活动。这些活动包括生产、提供服务、科学研究活动、仓储、银行和其他金融活动、财产和人身的保险和再保险；而TIDZ企业不能从事有腐败或变质商品、放射性物质、药物、化学和有机材料、武器和弹药贸易的活动。

TIDZ建立了详细具体的关税税收制度，该制度是该地区最有利的投资减免和激励措施之一。其中一些奖励措施包括从开始活动后10年内免除企业所得税和免除企业雇员的个人所得税、海关法规定的关税豁免和减免、对员工进行培训和改进的援助、建筑成本补助、公用事业税豁免等。

（四）进出口商品检验检疫

根据马其顿立法，马其顿在进出口商品的检验和检疫方面采取了以下保护措施：

（1）保护环境：保护植物、动物、真菌、臭氧层、废物、电池和蓄电池以及电子设备。属于上述类别的所有商品均需要特定的检查、检疫、许可证和执照；

（2）检疫植物：在马其顿海关进口植物、花卉、水果和蔬菜时，必须获得农林水事管理部——植物检疫总局的批准。

（3）监管食品和兽医：受《食品安全法》（2010年）、《兽医卫生法》（2007年）、《动物副产品法》（2007年）和《兽药管理法》（2010年）监管。所有涉及本条例的商品必须获得适当的许可证和执照并接受具体的海关检查。马其顿在很大程度上一直使其食品安全立法与欧盟保持一致，例如，考虑欧洲食品安全局的意见，马其顿规定了标签要求和风险分析。此外，畜产品可能从欧盟国家进口，或者一

[①] 参见马其顿国家银行编制的《新出口型公司对国内经济的影响分析》第10页，载 http://www.NBRM.mk/content/publikacii/Analiza-na-efektite-od-novite-izvozno-orientirani-kompanii-vo-domasnata-ekonomija.pdf。

般从欧盟委员会或国家主管部门批准的第三国进口。

（五）海关管理

依照2006年的马其顿《海关法》，该国海关法规的执行标准是与欧盟规定一致的，其中包括对自由区治理和运作的规定。此外，对于入境加工适用更为简化的程序，如"更简易的申报"。且这些规则制定了海关债务的担保、对某些特定类别货物的关税分级制度，以及确定特定商品的原产地声明，以明确可享受关税优惠待遇或不享受关税优惠待遇的预见性。2010年12月修订的《海关法》还规定了海关工作人员须有执业许可。

关税规定适用于绝大多数进口到马其顿的产品，且大多产品受到海关市场调查部门工作人员的质量监控。这些工作人员受雇于经济部以保证进口货物符合国内标准。受管控的产品主要包括农产品、汽车、电器或可能对消费者构成健康风险的未达标产品，而且产品必须通过卫生、植物病理学或兽医系统的管控。根据马其顿和欧盟成员国之间的稳定及联盟协议，通常情况下马其顿作为原产地的产品出口到欧盟国家可享受免关税待遇。

四、劳动

（一）劳动法律法规概况

马其顿的《劳动法》（2005年）规定了最低限度的福利标准和对雇员的最低保护，不能因为集体谈判协议或雇佣合同或雇主的任何内部行为而降低该最低保障。该领域的立法和规章制度规范了员工和雇主之间的劳动关系必须以合同的形式建立，尤其是规定了合同的终止、免受歧视和骚扰、明确工资和工作时间、假期等。《劳动法》与其他很多相关的法律和劳动法共同形成了劳动力市场中的特定规范，譬如：

- 《就业和失业保障法》中规定了失业情况下的雇主权利和义务、失业者和其他就业相关问题；
- 《劳动调查法》规定了国家劳工观察部门的组织和执行细则；
- 临时就业机构的法规规定了临时就业机构的设立条件和方式，以及设立临时工作的条件和方式，还包括一名人员同时为两名雇主提供临时工作的情形；
- 《外国人就业法》规定在马其顿雇用外国人工作的条件和流程；
- 《工作安全和健康法》保障员工工作中的安全和健康事宜，包括规定了在工作安全领域雇主的义务和受雇佣人的权利义务。

劳动领域中最重要的是劳动和社会政策部，其负责监管包括劳动关系、工作期间的劳动者保护，以及与国家劳工观察部门合作的其他劳动事项。

（二）外国人在当地工作规定

1. 工作许可

马其顿国在2006年的《外国人法》中提及了外国人入境的要求、驱逐和在马其顿国内停留的事项，以及外国人享有的权利和义务，同时《外国人就业法》涉及在马其顿国雇用外国人时所需要的条件和程序。

外国人，依照《外国人就业法》可以被雇用，从事自由职业或在马其顿工作，但须具备内政部签发的以工作为目的的临时居留证或由就业服务机构签发的工作许可证。在为工作目的颁发的暂住证程序中，就业服务机构根据人员配额的限制和当前马其顿劳动力市场的需要提出意见。签发的工作许可证可以是一年有效并可以延展的，或者是永久有效的形式，在该有效期内外国人被允许进入劳动力市场。

某些境内活动可不需获得工作许可证就在马其顿进行，适用的情况仅限于：

- 文化领域的创意服务；
- 商业博览会的相关服务；
- 短期的由外国人提供的服务；

- 由居住在马其顿的外国人发起的以研究为目的的工作；
- 紧急服务。

这些活动的开始和结束时都需要登记，就业服务局向需要登记的人员发放一份表格。

2. 申请程序

申请需向就业服务机构或其他该机构授权的机构提交，由一名在该国非因工作目的而居住的外国人提出。这份申请须包括外国人的简历，资质（比如特长），以及从事的工作类别。如果外国人没有合法停留在马其顿国，则还需要内政部出具意见。之后工作许可就由就业服务机构签发，并根据相关法律法规可以对该工作许可时限进行延长。

获得工作许可的必要文件根据许可的类型会有不同，通常包括：已经填写完毕的表格，雇主的公司信息，雇用外国人的必要性的简要说明，已签订的劳动合同，护照复印件和被雇用的外国人居住处的租房合同。内政部和就业服务机构在签发许可证上有权限的划分，由内政部先受理申请，然后再转给负责签发许可的就业服务机构。

3. 社会保险

在马其顿，养老保险和基本的医疗保险都是强制的，而且必须由雇主支付。雇主不能通过让受雇人员支付来豁免掉这些强制的义务。强制性社会保障的缴款主要受《强制社会保障贡献法》（2008年）的规定，其中强制性社会保险包括：

- 基于目前收入所享有的养老和残疾保险；
- 强制缴足的养老保险；
- 随服务年数增加而增长的保障；
- 医疗保险；
- 失业保险。

（三）出入境

1. 签证类型

在马其顿需要签证入境的外国人，必须在入境前获得签证。但将被当地雇主雇用的外国人只有签证是不够的，因为在马其顿的领土只允许外国人从事签证类型许可的活动。与此一致，签证可以被分类为"过境签证"或"居留签证"。一般来说，前者是机场的过境签证（A签证）和过境签证（B签证），后者包括短期的逗留签证（C签证）和长期逗留签证（D签证）。

外国旅客在机场不离开国际机场区域不需要任何签证，除非政府发现有必要为某些特定国家的公民提供签证A。相对的，签证B是从其他国家来去往其他国家而在马其顿过境有效期为1年的签证。但是，以签证B过境的话，该外国人在马其顿实际停留的时间不能超过5天。短期和长期逗留签证是为商业、个人、旅游、教育和其他目的签发的。在签证C的基础上，外国人可以在6个月的有效期内在马其顿停留不超过90天。持签证D的外国人则可以在6个月的有效期内停留不超过30天。

持有第三国家有效旅行证件，且根据马其顿签证制度需要签证进入马其顿的外国人，可以在以下情况下没有签证就入境：

- 在欧盟成员国或《申根协议》的签订国拥有一个有效的永久居民身份；
- 持有有效的多次出入的申根签证，该签证有效期比在马其顿停留的日期长5天以上。

每次进入马其顿，这样的外国人最多可逗留15天，而在马其顿连续逗留的总时间不得超过3个月，总时间不得超过6个月，从第一次入境的日期起算。

欧盟成员国和申根缔约国的公民可凭本国主管当局签发的有效身份证进入马其顿。

2. 出入境限制

如上所述，在马其顿连续逗留期间的总时间不得超过3个月，总时间不得超过6个月，从第一次入境日起算。由外交部[①]保留一份需要签证入境及不需签证入境的世界各国的名单。

---

① 参见 www.mfa.gov.mk。

（四）工会与劳工组织

根据《劳动法》，受雇人员有权依照其自由意志，根据工会条例的相关规定组成工会。工会被描述为"自主、民主和独立的受雇人员自愿组成，旨在代表、提出、促进和保护他们的经济、社会及其他个人和集体的利益"[①]。雇主也可以根据自己的意愿选择组织自己的协会。雇主可以自由决定受雇人员的加入和离开工会，即雇主协会可以决定工会的雇员去留。

（五）劳动争议

根据《劳动法》，个人和集体的劳动争议都可能发生。个人争议可以是由雇员或雇主主动发起，而集体争议则由集体协议签署各方之间产生。当雇主对员工在工作中的特定要求不给予积极的回应，或在用工关系中雇主侵犯了受雇人员的权利时，员工会启动个人劳动争议，他会在雇主处用尽法律的救济之后，要求获得特定机关的保护。

根据《劳动法》，个人或集体劳动争议可以通过友好协商解决或通过仲裁或法庭程序解决。

五、知识产权

（一）知识产权法律法规概况

知识产权（IP）是一个相当广泛的法律范畴，结合了国内和国际上适用的各种法律渊源。具体来说，国家知识产权法是指 2009 年的《工业产权法》，它是规定专利、工业设计、商标、原产地和地理标志的一揽子法规。此外还有 2010 年《版权和衍生权利法》，该法对版权作出了规定。此外，还有关于《保护集成电路法》（1998 年）和《保护知识产权的海关实施法》（2015 年）两个单独的法律。除了主要的立法之外，还采用了许多细则，特别是针对上述 IP 相关问题（例如工业设计的规则手册和商标保护细则）。同时，该法律渊源还包括众多该领域的国际公约和欧盟协定[②]，例如《WIPO 公约》《与贸易有关的知识产权协定》《保护工业产权巴黎公约》等。

尽管保护知识产权的权力机构很多，负责 IP 的确权和保护的国家工业产权办公室（SOIP）是主要机构。此外还有海关总署和国家市场检查部门也是知识产权保护体系的重要组成部分。后者的主要职责是监督国内和国外市场的货物销售和国际贸易。

（二）专利申请

从国家立法的角度来看，专利主要受 2009 年的《工业产权和专利条例》的规制。根据该法，申请人可以在所有技术领域就一项新的、包含有创造性的、可以适用于工业的发明寻求保护。所受的专利保护是以国土为界，可由 SOIP 的程序实现或通过依据《专利合作条约》《欧洲专利公约》和《马其顿与欧洲专利局专利领域合作协议》设立的机构实现。例如，欧洲专利局认可的欧洲专利，在权利范围方面，能在马其顿获得与该国家专利产品的同等力度的专利保护；并在某些特定情况下，对覆盖相同领域的发明来说，欧洲专利比国家专利更有优先权。

通常本土申请的要素包括发明的请求和说明，以及一份摘要和图纸（如果需要的话）。尽管国家申请可以使用外语文本，但必须有马其顿文的翻译。必要的文件包括：
- 如果由专利代理人提交，需有委托书；
- 支付给行政机构的缴费证明；
- 其他申请人的信息以及联合申请中的几个申请人共同的陈述书；
- 公开给其他发明人的数据；
- 如果有发明人不希望被列在申请表上，需要有他本人的声明；
- 若声称享有优先权则需提供的依据等。

首先，SOIP 会审核申请材料的完整性。在满足所有材料要求后，其确定一个申请日期，然后登记

[①] 参见《劳动法》第 184 条第 2 段。
[②] 根据《稳定与结盟协定》，马其顿有义务使其立法与欧盟共同体包括欧盟的相关知识产权立法协调一致。

在专利申请登记簿上。申请人可以要求在现有的国际机构中作出全面审核,也可以要求由 SOIP 来进行专利请求的审核。根据所进行的审核和结果,SOIP 会要求申请人支出相应的费用,然后就是否授予专利的权利作出决定。该决定的相关资料会在专利登记册上登记,并刊登在 SOIP 的官方公报上。

(三) 商标注册

工业产权法将商标定义为工业中保护有辨识度的商业标识、认证标志、集体商标和商品标记所享有的权利。商标保护的主体是一种图形化的标志,它可以区分出不同市场参与者的商品和服务。这些符号包括:单词、字母、数字、图片、图画、特定颜色组合、三维形式(包括物品的形状或包装),及以上的所有符号的组合。有一些绝对和相对的因素会导致某些标志无法得到商标保护。

获取商标权保护的程序可以在 SOIP 前启动或根据《商标国际注册马德里协定》和马德里协议议定书相关规定启动。申请商标需包括的材料有:

- 主张商标权的申请书;
- 申请人信息;
- 寻求保护的标志外观描述;
- 寻求保护的商品和服务清单、所属类别;
- 商标规则手册中规定的其他适用的信息和文件(如共同所有人的信息、集体商标的行为或它的一般使用规则、优先权的依据、向行政机关的缴费凭据和委托书)。

正如专利认证的程序一样,SOIP 必须审核申请资料的完整性,然后将其登记在商标申请的名册中。此外,该登记程序会在 SOIP 官方公报上发布。任何第三方可凭绝对理由提出异议,使 SOIP 可以据此拒绝授予商标权,而其他一些特定主体(譬如商标持有人或在先前已提出申请的申请人)可以根据相对的理由提出异议。若商标的识别没有任何问题,并且申请人已经支付了相应的费用,SOIP 将作出肯定的决定并将该商标权登记在商标注册簿中。该商标也会在 SOIP 的官方公报上发布。

(四) 保护知识产权措施

对已获得工业产权的司法保护进一步加强了对于工业产权的认可和注册形式的保护。为了启动任何工业产权侵权的诉讼程序,相关人员须在知道或应当知道此类侵权行为的 3 年内提起诉讼。在诉讼中,工业产权持有人可以要求颁发禁令以禁止违反其权利,赔偿损失,没收和销毁产品等行为。

依据《马德里协定》向国家工业产权局提交请求也是在国际层面上对工业产权的一种保护。如果国家工业产权局认定该请求符合商标规则手册,则将其转交给日内瓦世界知识产权保护组织国际局。

考虑到海关当局对马其顿进口及出口货物的监管,国家制定了一项单独的《知识产权海关保护法》,以加强对知识产权侵权的预防和侦查。根据该法,海关当局有权依职权或应有关方的要求行事。如果涉嫌侵权,海关当局可能会扣留相关商品。如果当局未发现任何人可能请求实施侵犯知识产权的行为或此类请求遭到拒绝或从未提交过,则会放行商品。该法规定在一定条件下可对商品做出潜在破坏行为。

最后,《反不正当竞争法》(1999 年)也规定了对知识产权侵权的罚款和制裁,从而保护知识产权。例如,罚款范围约在 500 欧元至 2 500 欧元或两年以下监禁均可用于处罚不当竞争或个人获利的情形,未经授权任何人不得使用或转让未受知识产权保护的图纸、计划、蓝本或其他此类文件。

六、环境保护

(一) 环境保护主管部门

在马其顿,环境保护系统由各国家级机构和地方各级机构组成。环境和自然规划部(以下简称"环境部")有权制定二级立法、执行环境立法和监测环境保护。市级单位[①]被授予特定权限,他们主要有权采纳当地的计划和战略,颁发适当的批准和许可,并从地方管辖权角度监督环境法的实施。环境

---

① 马其顿的市级单位是当地的市政府和斯科普里市。

部和市级单位都可以发布保护措施。例如，环境部可以禁止某些商品的生产、交易和使用，而双方都可以禁止可能危害环境或个人生命和健康的活动的进行。

检查监督也分为国家和地方组织，分别由国家环境监察局和相关市级单位的视察团执行。此外，其他国家机构可以监督特定的环境问题，例如国家市场监察局、国家卫生和健康检查局、植物检疫管理局和国家农业监察局。在其权限范围内，环境检查员有权采取必要的措施或命令行动来预防或消除有可能造成污染的源头。根据潜在不端行为的类型，可以在环境部或主管法庭进行的程序中发布轻罪裁决（例如罚款 3 000 欧元或最多 200 000 欧元）。另外，根据造成的生态破坏，污染者可能会面临刑事指控并要求恢复原状或赔偿损失。

（二）环境保护法律法规概况

环境保护是马其顿宪法下的一项基本价值，同时也保证了每个人享有健康环境的权利。这种担保是通过特定于该领域的若干法律提供的，其中 2005 年的《环境法》是主要的环境立法法案。《环境法》规定了国家和地方当局的权利和义务，以及法人和自然人在保护和改善环境条件方面的权利和义务，以便公民可以行使健康环境权。根据该法，在进行环境影响评估研究或获得相关综合环境许可证后，可以实施某个项目或特定工厂内的生产。例如，此类许可证包含操作员和安装的数据，以及与排放限值有关的强制性条件，各种介质和环境区域的保护措施，包括设备操作员的监测方式。其他相关的环境法律是：

- 《废物管理法》①（2004 年），《包装和废旧包装管理法》（2009 年），《电池、蓄电池和废旧电池、蓄电池管理法》（2010 年），《电子设备及废电子设备管理法》（2012 年），这些法律规定了不同种类废物的管理；
- 《水资源法》（2008 年），规定地表水和地下水及其处理、水资源管理设施和服务以及水资源可以使用和排放的条件和程序；
- 《环境空气质量法》（2004 年），规定避免、预防及减少空气污染对人体健康和整体环境有害影响的措施；
- 《防环境噪音保护法》（2007 年），规范各机关、法人及自然人关于环境噪音的管理及防范措施的权利及义务；
- 其他包含环境保护条例的法律［例如《农业用地法》（2007 年），《森林法》（2009 年），《能源法》（2011 年）及《矿物资源法》（2012 年）等］。

2004 年，马其顿批准了《联合国气候变化框架公约京都议定书》，其中规定了成员国必须遵循的有约束力的减排目标。为了执行国家气候变化减缓计划并让马其顿参与到全球减少气候变化的努力中，环境部根据《京都议定书》所设清洁发展机制对开展的项目进行评估和批准。此外，马其顿还批准了环境领域的许多其他国际协定，如《巴黎协定》《跨境环境中的环境影响评估公约》（埃斯波公约）、《生物多样性公约》《维也纳保护臭氧层公约》，以及《关于持久性有机污染物的斯德哥尔摩公约》等。

（三）环境保护评估

上述监管框架显示，马其顿的环境保护受到广泛监管。然而，由于一些法律与欧洲立法不完全一致，特别是在工业污染和风险管理、水和空气质量、化学品和气候变化等领域，某些领域仍有进一步改进的空间。②欧盟委员会强调，当局应该更有效地执行国家空气质量保护计划，进一步改善环境影响评估程序和执行《巴黎协定》。③未来的立法要求实施更严格的标准和执法，增加对违规行为的罚款及处罚，而且公司、管理层和员工要承担更大的责任。公众意识不断增强，公众迫使当局从国家和市政府的预算拨出更多资金用于环保。环境检查越来越频繁地进行，对不合格情况采取卫生措施。大公司投资于环境保护和一些组织，比如创新和技术开发基金，为减少污染的技术解决方案提供资金支持。

---

① 正在制定新的废物管理法，以便适应欧盟法律在这方面的新变化。
② 《前南斯拉夫马其顿共和国 2016 年报告》第 73 页，由欧盟委员会编写，载 https://ec.europa.eu/neighbourhood-enlargement/sites/near/files/pdf/key_documents/2016/20161109_report_the_former_yugoslav_republic_of_macedonia.pdf。
③ 同上注。

七、争议解决

(一) 争议解决方式及机构

各方可以自由地就纠纷的争议解决机制达成一致，该纠纷需涉及可自由处置的权利且不属于马其顿法院的专属管辖权。一般而言，如果有关各方不愿意友好调解纠纷，可以选择以下其中一种方法：①法庭诉讼程序；②仲裁；或③调解。

1. 法庭诉讼程序

马其顿司法机构是一个三级法院系统，基层和上诉法院是民事和刑事事务的一审和二审法院，以及行政法院和高等行政法院有权审理一审和二审行政案件。终审法院有权审理各种纠纷（民事、刑事和行政），是马其顿最高法院。基层法院是为一个或多个直辖市设立的，具有基本或扩展的权限，而上诉法院覆盖几个基层法院的管辖范围。目前，斯科普里、比托拉、斯托普和戈斯蒂瓦尔市有4个上诉法院，行政法院、高等行政法院和最高法院位于首都斯科普里，对马其顿全境具有管辖权。

在基层法院提起诉讼开始民事诉讼程序需附有相关证据以证明陈述的主张和事实。之后，尊重平等的原则，程序通常分两个阶段进行，即初步审判和主要审理。与基层法院进行的诉讼相比，通常上诉法院裁决争议不需开庭审理。上诉权利由马其顿宪法保护。由于法律制度是以大陆法系为基础的，所以先例对法院不具约束力。此外，还有一些权限被委托给其他机构，例如公证机构和执法机构。例如，前者被授权根据债权人的要求发布付款指令，后者则对债务人执行这些付款指令。

除有针对政府当局行为提供司法保护的权限，行政法院有权处理因特许权协议、政府采购合同和政府当局为追求公共利益或提供公共服务作为签署方的任何其他协议产生的争议。在发生行政纠纷的情况下，有权上诉到高等行政法院。一般而言，两个法院的诉讼程序都是在书面陈述的基础上进行的，无需开庭审理。

马其顿民事法院处理国际争端的权限需由法律或国际协议明确规定。如果对有关争议没有明确规定，且该争议管辖权适用马其顿法院的地域管辖权规则，则马其顿法院将有权限管辖该争议。如果至少其中一方是马其顿公民或住所地在马其顿的法人实体，则当事方可以约定马其顿法院享有管辖权。与此相反，为了约定外国法院享有管辖权，其中一方必须是外国公民或法人实体，且马其顿法院对争议不享有专属管辖权。

2. 仲裁

双方可约定仲裁解决已经产生的纠纷，或者解决因法律关系产生的所有未来争议。在马其顿有权进行仲裁的机构是附属于经济商会和其他组织的常设法院，例如马其顿经济商会和马其顿商业商会附属的常设法院。这些机构可以管辖国内和国际仲裁，这取决于争端是否包括国际因素。必须满足下列条件之一，才可以约定国际仲裁机构的管辖权：

- 在缔结仲裁协议时至少有一方当事人居住在境外或位于马其顿境外；
- 应履行主要义务的地方或与争议的标的物有最密切联系的地方在马其顿境外。

马其顿经济商会常设仲裁法院有一份仲裁员名单，但双方也可以选择不在名单上的仲裁员。常设仲裁法院的程序是一步式的程序，其通过的决定是最终的，对当事方具有约束力。根据马其顿《国际商事仲裁法》(2006年)，通过的仲裁裁决的法定补救办法是向管辖法院提起撤销诉讼。最后，还有一些特定的部门进行仲裁，例如马其顿的授权建筑师和授权工程师协会。

3. 调解

若当事人书面同意，在发生纠纷后启动司法或其他诉讼程序前，他们愿意尝试通过直接谈判或调解的方式解决纠纷，则可以启动调解程序。但是，即使启动了法庭审理程序，在某些情况下，法院有义务在一审程序中向当事人推荐调解的方式。在这种情况下，当事人可以书面声明他们自愿参与调解。作为例外，因标的额不超过1 000 000代纳尔（大约16 300欧元）的商业纠纷提起的诉讼，当事人有义务尝试通过调解解决纠纷。

调解由调解员目录中登记的持牌调解员进行。他们由马其顿调解员协会组织，这是一个非营利的法律实体，协会确保他们按照法律和《调解员的道德准则》确立的原则进行调解。调解程序在发出程序启动声明之日起 60 天内结束，无论结果如何。根据争议中是否存在外国因素，调解可以是国内的或国际的。

（二）法律适用

法院根据宪法、根据宪法批准的国家法律和国际协议决定诉讼各方的权利和义务。

《国际私法》（2008 年）规定了具有国际因素的民事、劳工和商业事项适用法律的规则。关于协议，除非法律或国际协议没有另行规定，当事人可以选择适用的法律。上述法律还包含承认外国法院裁决和外国其他当局裁决的规则。关于承认和执行外国仲裁裁决，应适用 1958 年《承认及执行外国仲裁裁决公约》的条件。

不同的法律规范不同类型的争议解决机制和程序。关于调解程序，主要适用《调解法》（2013 年）。就国际仲裁而言，有关的程序法是主要以《贸易法委员会国际商事仲裁示范法》为基础的《国际商事仲裁法》。《民事诉讼法》（2005 年）规范民事诉讼程序和国内仲裁。根据《刑事诉讼法》（2010 年）进行刑事诉讼。最后，行政纠纷依据《行政纠纷法》（2006 年）进行处理。

八、其他

（一）反商业贿赂

1. 反商业贿赂法律法规概况

反腐败和贿赂的主要法律是 2002 年《反腐败法》。《反腐败法》规定，公司或其他法人实体的负责人不得利用其地位获得任何奖励或任何其他利益或承诺此类利益，不得为了自己或他人而：
- 在市场上建立垄断；
- 歧视其他公司或其他法人实体；
- 对市场造成干扰；
- 因市场上不公平竞争对其他自然人或其他法人实体造成损害。

腐败导致的法律行为无效。所有具有合法利益的实体都可以通过提交确认腐败存在的最终法院裁决来要求其撤销。此外，遭受任何损害的当事方可要求赔偿。打击反商业贿赂的监管框架也包括：
- 《防止利益冲突的法律》（2007 年）规定关于防止滥用公职人员的公权力和职务以谋取个人或关系人利益的规则。
- 《举报人保护法》（2015 年），规定了举报应受惩罚或非法行为的制度、举报人的权利、机构和法人实体在保护举报过程中的职责。受保护的举报即以告发一个合理的怀疑或告知其了解关于应受惩罚的或其他非法或不可接受的行为，这些行为侵犯或威胁公众利益。可以通过在机构或公司内部举报，也可以通过当局或通过公开信息来举报。
- 《游说法》（2008 年）规定了游说和说客的原则，对游说的监督以及由于违反法律而对游说者施加的措施。根据这项法律，说客必须遵守包括反贿赂在内的反腐败条款。
- 根据《刑法》（1996 年）规定，官员不得为了作出不应从事的公务行为，或为了不作出应该从事的公务行为，而直接或间接地要求或收受礼物或其他好处，包括提供贿赂的承诺等。给予、承诺或提供上述好处的行为也是应受处罚的。最后，《刑法》对因非法干预而给予和接受奖励的行为给予制裁。

2. 主管部门

国家预防腐败委员会（以下简称"国家委员会"）是一个由 7 名成员组成的独立自主的法人实体。它有许多权限，包括：
- 与主管机构共同提出举措控制政党、工会、公民协会和基金会的财务和实质运作；
- 在主管机构前，对针对处置国家资本的选举或委任人员、公权力机构或其他法人实体负责人提出可能的处理程序，这些可能程序包括解雇、调任、开除或其他追究他们责任的程序；
- 发起追究处置国家资本的选举或委任人员、公权力机构或其他法人实体负责人刑事责任的倡议；

- 在法律规定的公共和私人利益冲突的情况下采取行动；等等。

国家委员会鼓励检察官和有组织犯罪和腐败检察官办公室启动基于怀疑犯下腐败行为的刑事诉讼程序。它还从所有相关机构收集必要的信息和文件，以便在特定情况下确定事实。

3. 惩处措施

现有的反商业贿赂法律框架含有广泛的轻罪条款。此外，《刑法》除了规定没收犯罪所得和禁止从事专业活动和担任相应职位 1 至 10 年，还规定了若干制裁措施。这些制裁包括：

（1）受贿：①作出不应从事的公务行为或不作出应该从事的公务行为，处有期徒刑 4 至 10 年；②如果犯罪获得重大财产利益，处至少 5 年有期徒刑。

（2）行贿：①贿赂官员使其作出不应作出的公务行为，或不作出必须作出的公务行为，或任何在这种关系中斡旋的人，处 1 至 5 年有期徒刑；②对犯下此罪的法人实施罚款等。

（3）因非法因素给予和接受奖励：罪犯将根据具体情况受到惩罚，而对这种罪行的最高处罚是 5 年的有期徒刑。如斡旋贿赂人在因非法因素给予和接受奖励中斡旋而获得奖励或其他利益的，处 1 年以上 10 年以下有期徒刑。法人判处罚金。

除了上述对受贿和行贿的制裁之外（包括因非法干预接受奖励），如果该行为是代表法人实施的，《反腐败法》规定对法人实施 4 000 至 5 000 欧元的轻罪罚款。

最后，《反不正当竞争法》规定，为了获得某些产品或服务的特权地位，向雇员或法人实体的代理人提供或承诺给予贿赂的，罚款金额介于 3 300 欧元至 16 300 欧元之间。请求或接受贿赂的人应被监禁 3 个月至 3 年。赃款赃物即收到的礼品或者其他物质利益应予没收。

（二）工程承包

1. 许可制度

《政府采购法》（2007 年）规定签订政府采购合同（即购买商品、服务和工程）和建立公私合作伙伴关系（PPP）的程序。本法根据欧盟指令 2004/18/EC[①] 制定，规定了签订政府采购合同的方式和程序（PP 合同），并规定处理政府采购问题的机构框架，主要是政府采购局和国家上诉委员会。与政府采购制度发展有关的活动以及保证政府采购合同履行中的合理性、效率和透明度由政府采购局负责，该机构是财政部范围内的一个法人实体机构，而上诉委员会负责在授标程序中提供法律保护。公私合作伙伴关系的监管框架还包括《特许权和 PPP 法》（2012 年），该法除了对某些 PPP 方面的规定外，还涉及授予普遍利益商品特许权。

签订 PP 合同是为了建设施工、交付货物或提供某些服务，因此可以是建设施工、提供商品或服务等多种形式。相比之下，PPP 被定义为公私伙伴之间的长期契约协作，私人伙伴承担在公共伙伴权限范围内为最终用户提供公共服务的义务和/或为公共合作伙伴能提供这种公共服务提供必要的先决条件。出于这些目的，私人伙伴可以融资、设计、建造、开发或维护公共基础设施等。根据公共合作伙伴因市政工程/服务支付报酬的资金用途以及现存关键风险的分配，PPP 可以为：市政工程/服务特许权或 PP 市政工程/服务合同。

2. 招投标

一般而言，政府采购是通过所谓的"标准程序"即公开或限制招标完成的，而其他程序在法律确定的特定情况下则为例外。公开招标、限制招标和简化招标必须通过由政府采购局管理的电子公共采购系统使用电子方式进行。《公共采购法》规定了下列法定程序：

（1）公开招标：每个利益相关方都有权提交投标。在对收到的投标进行评估之后，电子拍卖被用于招标的最后阶段。

（2）限制招标：每个利益相关方可以要求参加，但只有选定的候选人被邀请提交标书。该程序通过以下三个阶段进行：①资格预审阶段（选择候选人）；②评标；③电子拍卖。

---

① 欧洲议会和理事会 2004 年 3 月 31 日关于签订市政工程合同、政府采购合同和政府服务合同的协调程序，载 http://eur-lex.europa.eu/legal-content/EN/TXT/PDF/?uri=CELEX:32004L0018&from=en。

（3）竞争性对话：每个相关方都可以要求参与对话阶段，为采购当局的要求制订适当的方案，而采购当局只与选定的候选人进行对话。确定最佳解决方案后，所选候选人将提交报价。竞争对话采购在 PP 合同特别复杂并且不允许使用公开或限制招标签订合同时使用，且也以电子拍卖程序终结。

（4）协议采购：是订约当局咨询选定的候选人并与其中一个或多个候选人谈判合同条款的程序。谈判程序有两种类型：事先公布合同通知的协议采购和不公布合同通知的协议采购。

（5）签订 PP 合同的简化程序：该程序适用于签订价值高达 20 000 欧元的商品和服务 PP 合同，以及价值高达 50 000 欧元的市政工程 PP 合同。

任何经济运营商有权在签订 PP 合同的程序中单独或作为一组经济运营商的成员共同参与。提交共同参与申请或联合投标的运营商不需要以法律形式进行关联。在同一程序中，候选人/投标人只能参加一个投标，尽管它可能有参与多个投标的能力。

为确保给潜在投标人明确指示，招标文件规定了关于签订 PP 合同程序的方式的要求、条件、标准和其他必要信息。招标文件必须通过技术对话进行市场测试。在公开和限制招标中，为签订估价超过等值于 130 000 欧元的马其顿代纳尔的商品和服务的 PP 合同时，上述步骤是强制性的，并且在公共采购决定通过之后和公告的发布前执行。采购当局可能要求以银行担保或存入资金的形式提供投标担保。其他表示投标人严肃性的手段也适用。为了保证合同的高质量履行，采购主管部门可以进一步要求最优投标方提供银行保函的担保。签约程序的透明度通过发布事先指示性通知、签订 PP 合同的公告、已签订 PP 合同和/或撤销签订合同程序的通知来确保。

《公共采购法》对行业 PP 合同作出了单独规定，这些合同是为从事以下一项或多项活动而签订的：供水、能源、运输、邮政服务和其他活动。

关于 PPP 合同，签订程序规则由《公共采购法》规定。特别是，可以通过公开或限制招标、竞争性对话或通过事先公开合同通知的协议采购签订 PPP 合同。与这一解决办法相比，一般利益商品的特许权授予程序由《特许权和 PPP 法》规定。特许权授予人即政府伙伴进行授予一般利益商品特许权和 PPP 合同的准备活动。它们包括以下内容的准备：①对以前基本项目要素进行分析的报告；②可行性研究；③环境影响评估；④其他必要的活动。

Macedonia

Authors: Bojana Paneva, Ljupka Noveska Andonova, Veton Qoku
Translators: Ma Xiaoyun, Feng Fan

I. Overview

A. General Introduction to the Political, Economic, Social and Legal Environment

The Republic of Macedonia is a country in the Balkan Peninsula in Southeast Europe. Macedonia declared its independence in 1991, as one of the successor states of the former Yugoslavia. The Republic of Macedonia is bordered to the north by Serbia, to the east by Bulgaria, to the south by Greece, and to the west by Albania. The capital is Skopje. In 2018, the estimated population of Macedonia is 2.09 million, which ranks 144th in the world. [1]

The Republic of Macedonia, has been constantly making efforts to attract foreign capital through foreign direct investments since its independence. A number of measures from an economic and legal point of view are constantly being undertaken to create a favourable international investment climate and to achieve a favourable international investment position. In order to increase the interest of foreign investors in investing their capital in the Republic of Macedonia, the legislation has undergone changes and was designed to provide equal rights and conditions for domestic and foreign investors, as well as to protect their rights, through greater protection of foreign investments. The European Union (EU) integration of the Republic of Macedonia and the North Atlantic Treaty Organization (NATO) integration are the most important goal of the Government.

a. Political

Macedonia's 1991 constitution established a republican Assembly (called The Sobranie). There is an explicit separation of powers between the legislature, the judiciary, and the executive. The President is the Head of State and Commander-in-Chief of the army. The Assembly of the Republic of Macedonia is a representative body of the citizens and holder of the legislative power of the Republic. The Assembly is composed of 123 members elected by popular vote who serve a four-year term. Executive power rests with the Government. To ensure the government is effective and citizens' rights are protected, each branch has its own powers and responsibilities, including working with the other branches.

b. Economy

Since its independence, Macedonia has made progress in liberalizing its economy and encouraging economic development, providing new opportunities for investors. Its low tax rates and free economic zones have helped in attracting foreign investment. The government pays special attention in linking domestic enterprises with foreign ones in technological-industrial zones. The ultimate goal is to achieve an average rate of growth of the economy higher than 5% in the period 2017-2020.

c. Social

The key goal of the government in the field of social policy is to reduce the poverty rate below 16% in 2020. The government will establish a functional network of social protection institutions close to the citizens and appropriate to their needs, with part of the competence being transferred to the local self-government that is closer to them and can quickly adjust to their needs. The network will include social services for support and palliative care for the elderly, care centers, care and inclusion (including people with disabilities in everyday activities and encouring them to have roles similar to their peers who do not have a disability). centers for persons with disabilities, housing communities for persons with disabilities over 26 years of age, services for protection against gender-based violence and services for the protection of other groups of citizens in need, who are at some social risk.

d. Legal

The Macedonian legal system is grounded in civil law. The judicial power is exercised by the courts in

---

[1] http://worldpopulationreview.com/countries/macedonia-population/.

the Republic of Macedonia. The courts are autonomous and independent state bodies. The judicial branch is comprised of twenty-seven Basic Courts, four Courts of Appeal (that decides upon appeals against decision issued by the Basic Courts), the Supreme Court, the Administrative Court and the Higher Administrative Court. Also, there is Constitutional Court, responsible for the protection of constitutional and legal rights.

B. The Status and Direction of the Cooperation with Chinese Enterprises Under the B&R

Relations between the Republic of Macedonia and the People's Republic of China are developing in the spirit of friendship, mutual understanding and respect for the sovereignty, territorial integrity and equality of these two countries. Republic of Macedonia and People's Republic of China established diplomatic relations on 12th October 1993 on the ambassadorial level.[1]

The Government of the Republic of Macedonia supports the Belt and Road (the 16 + 1 project), in other words, the People's Republic of China will have an even better partner in the Republic of Macedonia in the economic and trade relations in the future. The goal is to fully implement the two highways, built by a Chinese company in cooperation with domestic firms. There are plans to sign several memorandums with several other Chinese companies present in the region, in the field of energy and rail transport. This shows that we see a great economic partner in the People's Republic of China. Both sides agreed to provide support to the business communities of both countries for enhanced cooperation in the economy and trade, but also in other important areas for the citizens of both countries.[2]

As part of the Summit of Heads of Government for Cooperation of Central and Eastern European Countries with the People's Republic of China, held in Budapest, the Prime Minister of the Republic of Macedonia informed the participants at the forum that the Republic of Macedonia will host several important events related to the process of cooperation with the People's Republic of China such as the "China SEEC Coordination Center for Cultural Cooperation". "The Coordination Center for Culture Cooperation will be established in 2018 as part of the Ministry of Culture of the Republic of Macedonia. The Republic of Macedonia will also host the 5th Chinese Symposium for Cooperation of Central and Eastern European Countries, High Rank of Think Tank Organizations in 2018 and the 4th Ministerial Meeting on Cultural Cooperation in 2019". In the spirit of cooperation with the People's Republic of China, the Prime Minister of the Republic of Macedonia pointed out that cooperation, among other things, is taking place in areas such as health and medicine and, with the decision of the government, in accordance with the Law on Alternative and Complementary Medicine, the Center was established for traditional Chinese medicine in Macedonia.[3]

II. Investment

A. Market Access

a. Department Supervising Investment

The Agency for Foreign Investments and Export Promotion of the Republic of Macedonia-Invest Macedonia[4], established in accordance with the Law on Establishment of the Agency for Foreign Investments and Export Promotion of the Republic of Macedonia is the primary government institution, which is in charge of attracting new foreign investments in the country and supporting the expansion of the foreign companies with already established operations. In addition to the other activities, the Agency concludes an agreement on behalf of the Government of the Republic of Macedonia, as a state aid provider, providing information services to exporters from the Republic of Macedonia in relation to foreign trade, export procedures, customs, taxes and legal regulations, as well as assistance in providing administrative licenses and permits, providing information on access to international markets for facilitating exporters in finding foreign business partners, performing activities for export promotion in the country and abroad and connecting Macedonian exporters with foreign buyers, providing information services to foreign companies for export potentials in the Republic of Macedonia.

Another entity of importance to foreign investments is the Directorate for Technological Industrial Development Zones[5], established in accordance the Law on Technological Industrial Development Zones in order to create, develop and take care of the activities related to industrial development zones, including monitoring and regulating

---

[1] http://mfa.gov.mk/index.php?option=com_content&view=article&id=260&catid=84&Itemid=349&lang=en.
[2] http://vlada.mk/node/13547.
[3] http://vlada.mk/node/13780.
[4] http://www.investinmacedonia.com.
[5] http://www.dtirz.com.

the activities of the users of the zones and issuing approvals for starting, developing and completing user activities. Technological industrial and development zones provide favourable conditions for development of business activities through the supply of regulated industrial sites and pre-built factories, with fully prepared legal and physical infrastructure for investment, with services and tax, customs and other benefits.

b. Laws and Regulations of Investment Industry

There are no laws directly regulating foreign investments.

The Constitution of the Republic of Macedonia guarantees equal position for all entities in the market and provides for free transfer and repatriation of investment capital and profits for foreign investors. The legal framework is comprised of several laws including: the Trade Companies Law; the Securities Law; the Profit Tax Law; the Value Added Tax Law; the Law on Acquiring Shareholding Companies; the Foreign Exchange Operations Law; the Banking Law; the Labor Law, the Law on Ownership and other Property Rights, etc.

The Law on Financial Support of Investments, as the first investment regulatory law is in the phase of preparation and it is unknown when the law will be ratified in the foreseeable future. It provides a legal framework that stipulates the criteria, the procedure for granting and payment of financial support to the companies that will meet the set conditions. The Law on Financial Support of Investments will regulate the types of financial support for investments, the amount of the financial support, the conditions, the manner and the award procedure of financial support to the entrusted entities that will invest in the Republic Macedonia.

The purpose of this law is to encourage economic growth and development in the Republic Macedonia through support of investments to increase the competitiveness of Macedonian economy and employment. Entities that can be beneficiaries of financial support are business entities that perform production activities and who have increased the income from the activity and provide the same average number i.e.increase in the average number of employees in the last year in relation to the average of the previous three years or shorter period if the business entity is registered and started its activity within a period shorter than four years from the date of submission of the request for granting financial support.

In this law, as types of financial support for investments are provided:
- Support for creating new employments;
- Support for establishing and promoting collaboration with suppliers from Republic of Macedonia;
- Support for the establishment of organizational forms for technology;
- development and research;
- Support for investment projects of significant economic interest;
- Support for growth of capital investments and revenues; and
- Support for the purchase of funds from enterprises in difficulty.

Types of financial support for competitiveness are provided:
- Support for business entities that have increased their competitiveness on;
- market;
- Support for business entities expanding into markets and increasing sales.

c. Forms of Investment

In our country, foreign investment may be in the form of money, equipment, or raw materials.

Direct investment according to the Law on Foreign Exchange Operations are investments with which the investor intends to establish a permanent economic connection and / or to manage the company or other legal entity in which it invests. In the said law, direct investments foresee:

- establishment of a company or increase of the initial capital of the company into full ownership of the investor, establishment of a subsidiary or acquisition of full ownership over the existing trade company;

- participation in a newly formed or already existing company, if the investor owns or acquires more than 10% of the initial capital of the company, or more than 10% of the right to decide;

- a long-term loan with a maturity period of five years or more, when it is a loan from an investor and which is intended for a trading company in its entirety;

- a long-term loan with a maturity period of five years or more, when it is a loan intended for establishing a permanent economic connection and if it is given among economically connected entities.

The Law on Technological Industrial Development Zones provides for an exceptional treatment for investors who invests within the free zones. First the investors in TIDZ are entitled to personal and corporate income tax exemption for the first 10 years. Investors are exempt from payment of value added tax and customs duties for goods, raw materials, equipment and machines. Moreover, up to €500.000 can be granted as incentive towards building costs depending on the value of the investment and the number of employees. Land in a TIDZ in Macedonia is available under long-term lease for a period of up to 99 years. In addition to the tax incentives, this

Law also provide for certain customs exemptions including completed infrastructure that enables free connection to natural gas, water, electricity and access to a main international road network. Investors are also exempt from paying a fee for preparation of the construction site. Fast procedures for business activity registration are provided in TIDZ that further reduce the costs of setting up. Besides, foreign investors can freely transfer profit, if they have registered their direct investments according to the Law on Foreign Exchange and have paid all legal obligations relating to taxes and contributions in the Republic of Macedonia.

d. Standards of Market Access and Examination

Foreign investors are allowed to invest directly in all industry and business sectors except those limited by law. Investment in the production of weaponry and narcotics is subject to government approval. Also, investors in some sectors such as banking or insurance activities and investment funds, must meet certain licensing requirements that apply equally to both domestic and foreign investors.

B. Foreign Exchange Regulation

a. Department Supervising Foreign Exchange

The foreign exchange regime is governed by the Law on Foreign Exchange Operations. The supervision over the implementation of the Law on Foreign Exchange Operations and over the accompanying regulations, is performed by the National Bank of the Republic of Macedonia, the Ministry of Finance - the State Foreign Exchange Inspectorate, the Ministry of Finance - the Customs Administration, the Ministry of Economy and the Securities and Exchange Commission.

The National Bank of the Republic of Macedonia performs direct supervision over the operations of the banks, savings houses and exchange offices to which they have issued a work permit.

The Ministry of Finance - State Foreign Exchange Inspectorate performs inspection supervision over the work of residents and non-residents who perform activities on the territory of the Republic of Macedonia. The provisions of the Law on Inspection Supervision shall apply in the procedure of performing the inspection supervision.

The Ministry of Finance - the Customs Administration supervises the exportation from the Republic of Macedonia and the importation into the Republic of Macedonia of the effective domestic and foreign money, checks and monetary gold that are exported from the Republic of Macedonia, ie they are imported by residents and nonresidents in the Republic of Macedonia or sent by post way.

Residents and non-residents shall be obliged to enable the foreign exchange inspector to perform the inspection supervision, insight in the operation and upon his request, to make available or submit all the necessary documentation and data.

For the purposes of the inspection supervision, the banks where the accounts of residents or non-residents are kept shall be obliged, upon a written request from the inspector, to provide the whole documentation for their operations through the accounts. The inspection in the work and in the documentation implies an insight into the documentation and accounts of residents and non-residents related to the supervision.

b. Brief Introduction of Laws and Regulations of Foreign Exchange

The Law on Foreign Exchange Operations regulates: the current and capital transactions and their realization in the form of payments and transfers between residents and non-residents, among residents if they work with foreign means of payment or if the subject of operations are foreign means of payment and unilateral transfer of funds from and to the Republic Macedonia which do not represent transactions between residents and non-residents, as well as foreign exchange supervision and control.

Current transactions are transactions between residents and non-residents whose purpose is not transfer of capital. Payments and transfers of current transactions include: payments received based on the exchange of goods and services, moderate remittances for family living expenses, etc.

Capital transactions are transactions between residents and non-residents whose purpose is transfer of capital, such as: direct investments, real estate investments, securities transactions, credit operations, guarantees, deposit operations, investment in investment gold, etc.

Direct investments are investments with which the investor intends to found a trading company or increase the initial capital of a trading company in full ownership of the investor, a participation in a newly formed or already existing trading company, a long-term loan with a maturity period of five and more years, etc. When a foreigner invests in our country, registration in the Register of direct investments of non-residents follows.

Securities transactions, in terms of the currency for foreign exchange operations, are transactions with securities on the capital market and the money market, such issuance, registration and sale of domestic securities abroad, issuance, registration and sale of foreign securities in the Republic of Macedonia, investment in securities in the Republic of Macedonia by non-residents, as well as investment of securities abroad by a resident.

Shares of investment funds, i.e.shares of non-resident investment funds may be offered for sale in the Republic of Macedonia only if the investment fund management company has registered a subsidiary of a foreign investment fund management company in the Republic of Macedonia in accordance with the Investment Funds Act.

Credit operations are transactions for concluding loan agreements.

The international payment operations are performed by banks authorized by the National Bank of the Republic of Macedonia for performing international payment operations.

For the needs of the Republic of Macedonia, the international payment operations are performed by the National Bank of the Republic of Macedonia. The National Bank of the Republic of Macedonia shall prescribe the manner of performing the international payment operations.

The foreign payment market under this Law, covers all transactions for the purchase and sale of foreign means of payment in the Republic of Macedonia. According to the law, foreign means of payment are foreign currencies, foreign currency cash, checks, letters of credit and other payment instruments that are denominated in foreign currency and can be converted into foreign currency.

c. Requirements of Foreign Exchange Management for Foreign Enterprises

The legal position leads to the conclusion that foreign citizens can freely invest in Macedonia, provided that such investment is reported to the Central Register of the Republic of Macedonia within 60 days of the investment made. The Central Register of the Republic of Macedonia maintains a Register of Direct Investments in which all investments in the form of money and items invested by a foreign investor in the Republic of Macedonia are registered. Non-reporting of the direct investment is the basis for submitting liability for an offense, while the reporting assumes and acquiring a range of opportunities for the investor regarding the transfer of profits and financial assets, as well as part of the liquidation mass.

Non-residents, branches of foreign banks and subsidiaries of foreign trade companies in the Republic of Macedonia that acquired ownership of real estate in the Republic of Macedonia under conditions determined by a special law or ratified international agreements shall be obliged, within 60 days from the date of occurrence of the legal basis for acquiring ownership of real estate in the Republic of Macedonia to report the investment of assets and all changes in the investment in real estate in the Central Register.

The Central Register shall record the assets invested in real estate and any changes in the investment in the registry of investments in real estate of non-residents in the Republic of Macedonia.

The issuance and registration of foreign securities in the Republic of Macedonia requires the approval of the Securities and Exchange Commission. The Securities and Exchange Commission determines the conditions and the manner under which an approval for issuance or registration of securities can be obtained. Issuance and registration of foreign debt securities with a maturity of over three years in the Republic of Macedonia is not allowed.

Non-residents may enter and trade securities in the Republic of Macedonia only through authorized participant. The authorized participant is obliged to submit a report to the National Bank of the Republic of Macedonia for all investments of non-residents in securities in the Republic of Macedonia, as well as for modification of these investments, including their alienation. The National Bank of the Republic of Macedonia prescribes the manner and conditions for the operation of non-residents with securities in the Republic of Macedonia.

For the sale of units of investment funds, ie shares of closed-end investment funds, non-resident investment funds must obtain approval from the Securities and Exchange Commission. The Securities and Exchange Commission, by means of a by-law, determines the conditions and the manner in which the approval can be obtained.

Non-residents may open and have accounts with authorized banks in foreign currency and in MKD. When opening the account, the authorized bank shall mandatorily determine the identity of the non-resident. The National Bank of the Republic of Macedonia prescribe the manner and conditions for opening and maintaining accounts.

Non-residents could perform investment and trading with investment gold in the Republic of Macedonia in accordance with a special law.

The realization of payments and transfer of funds on the basis of capital transactions is free if it is a transaction that is concluded, reported and registered in accordance with the Law on Foreign Exchange Operations, and if all liabilities based on taxes and contributions towards the Republic of Macedonia are settled.

Transfer or transfer of funds shall mean the transfer of funds for the realization of capital transactions for the exercise of the right of the investor on the basis of participation in the profit or the balance of the property after the bankruptcy or liquidation of the legal entity in which he invested.

C. Financing

a. Main Financial Institutions

The banking system is the most important part of the overall financial system of Macedonia. The institutional framework of the financial system in Macedonia is composed of the National Bank of the Republic of Macedonia (Central Bank)[1], commercial banks[2], savings houses[3], exchange offices[4], the Clearing House KIBS A.D.Skopje[5], the Deposit Insurance Fund Skopje[6] and Macedonian Stock Exchange (MSE).[7]

Banks are the main source of financing. According to the Law on the National Bank of the Republic of Macedonia and the Banking Law, the National Bank of the Republic of Macedonia is the only supervisory authority responsible for licensing and supervision of banks and savings houses in the Republic of Macedonia. The main purpose of the supervisory function performed by the NBRM is the maintenance of a safe and sound banking system and protection of depositors and other creditors that invest their money in the banking sector. The main goal of the National Bank is to achieve and maintain price stability. Another goal of the National Bank, which is subordinate to the main goal, is to contribute to maintaining a stable, competitive and market-oriented financial system.

b. Financing Conditions for Foreign Enterprises

According to The Law on Foreign Exchange Operations and other bylaws originating from this Law, there are no regulatory restrictions on foreign direct investments by non-residents in Macedonia. Non-residents can without restraint open foreign currency and Denar non-resident accounts in Macedonian banks. When opening an account, the authorized bank is obliged to identify the non-resident.

Credit operations between residents and non-residents can be freely arranged. The only requirement is that the concluded credit operations must be reported to the Central Bank.

The Central Bank prescribe the method and the conditions for opening and keeping non-residents accounts and the conditions and the method of reporting on the concluded credit operations with non-residents.[8]

D. Land Policy

a. Brief Introduction of Land-Related Laws and Regulations

The basis for the acquisition of property rights for foreigners are contained in the Constitution of the Republic of Macedonia: "A foreigner in the Republic of Macedonia may acquire the right to ownership under conditions determined by law". Also, the Constitution of the Republic of Macedonia guarantees a foreign investor the right to the free transfer invested capital and profits. Furthermore, the Law on Ownership and Other Property Rights in detail regulates the acquisition of the right to ownership and other real rights of foreign persons. Other legal issues pertaining to land-related law and regulations in Macedonia are: the Construction Law, the Law on Construction Land, the Law on privatization and Lease of Construction Land on State Property, the Law on Real Estate Cadastre, Law on Agricultural Land, the Law on Obligations and the Law on Technological Industrial Development Zones.

b. Rules of Land Acquisition for Foreign Enterprises

There are two types of land ownership in Macedonia: public and private.

Public properties as well as those designated for public use and public functions such as national roads, forests and parks, streets, squares, schools, museums are state owned and can be used by all legal entities and individuals. These properties can be ceded to third parties through concession or long-term lease upon fulfillment of the conditions provided for in the law.

Pursuant to the Law on Ownership and Other Property Rights, foreign individuals and legal entities resident in member states of the European Union and the OECD may acquire the right to ownership and the right to long-term lease of construction land (up to 99 years) on the territory of the Republic of Macedonia under the same conditions as domestic legal entities and individuals. Foreign individuals and legal entities, residents of non-EU and OECD countries may acquire the right to ownership and long-term lease of construction land on the territory of the Republic of Macedonia under reciprocity conditions.

The Law on Construction Land in more detail regulates the rights and obligations regarding the construction land, the construction land development, the conditions and the manner of managing the construction land, as

---

[1] http://www.nbrm.mk/pocetna-en.nspx.
[2] http://www.nbrm.mk/banki-en.nspx.
[3] http://www.nbrm.mk/stedilnici-en.nspx.
[4] http://www.nbrm.mk/mienuvacnici.nspx.
[5] http://www.kibs.com.mk/en/default.aspx.
[6] http://www.fodsk.org.mk/Default.
[7] http://www.mse.mk/en/.
[8] http://www.nbrm.mk/decisions_from_the_area_of_foreign_exchange_operations-en.nspx.

well as the other issues in the field of construction land. A right to a long-term lease may be established over construction land for the benefit of domestic and foreign individuals and legal entities and the lease may last for a maximum of 99 years. A right to a short-term lease for the benefit of domestic and foreign individuals and legal entities which may last up to five years and which may be extended for additional three years, may be established on construction land in ownership of the Republic of Macedonia, in accordance with the provisions of this Law.

Pursuant to the Law on Ownership and Other Property Rights, foreign natural and legal persons cannot acquire the right to ownership of agricultural land on the territory of the Republic of Macedonia.

In Macedonia, foreign individuals and legal entities may, under conditions of reciprocity, acquire the right to long-term lease of agricultural land on the territory of the Republic of Macedonia, on the basis of the consent of the Minister of Justice, upon previously obtained opinion of the Minister of Agriculture, Forestry and Water Economy and the Minister of Finance. The existence of reciprocity shall be determined by the Minister of Justice, under conditions and procedure determined by law.

Furthermore, the law requires that the acquisition of the ownership title or other limited property rights must be registered in the Real Estate Cadastre Agency of the Republic of Macedonia and by virtue of this registration, it becomes effective with regard to third parties.

However, due to the protection of the interests and security of the state, almost every state provides restrictions on certain areas. Our state in the Law on Property and Other Property Rights makes a limitation, that a foreign person cannot be an owner of a fixed property, which, due to the protection of the interests and security of the Republic of Macedonia, is declared by law as an area where foreign persons are not entitled to ownership.

E. The Establishment and Dissolution of Companies

a. The Forms of Enterprises

The Trading Company Law is the primary law regulating business activity in Macedonia. The Trading Company Law governs the formation, operation, transformation and termination of companies in the Republic of Macedonia. There are five forms of business association in Macedonia under the Trading Company Law: General partnership (JTD), Limited partnership (KD), Limited liability company (DOO-LLC), Joint-stock Company (AD) and Limited partnership with shares (KDA). In accordance with the Trading Company Law, both Macedonian and foreign individuals or companies can establish those types of business association. The most common forms of business association for foreign investors are the Limited Liability Company (DOO-LLC) and the joint-stock company (AD).

A General partnership (JTD) is an entity formed by two or more individuals or legal entities, that join together and who are liable to the creditors for the obligations of the company unlimitedly and with their entire asset. All relations between the shareholders in the General partnership are based on the principle of intuitu personae, ie the fact that the person of each of the partners has a decisive role in the establishment, operation and termination of the public company. Trading Company law does not prescribe a minimum amount of the basic capital of the General partnership since it is not necessary and significant for this type of trading company, and it is not important because the obligations of the company towards the creditors are also answered by the partners. The General partnership is established simply with a partnership agreement between the founders. The partnership agreement shall be submitted before the Trade register along with the other required documents.

Limited partnership (KD) is an entity formed by two or more individuals or legal entities that join together and at least one of the partners (general partner) shall be responsible for the obligations of the company personally with all of its assets, ie unlimitedly and also at least one of the partners (limited partner) shall be liable for the obligations of the company only up to the amount of their subscribed contribution in the capital of the limited partnership.

Limited partnership with shares (KDA) is a limited partnership, whose capital is divided in shares.

Limited liability Company (LLC - DOO) is the most common form of business entity and it can be formed by one or more persons. Shareholders are not liable for the obligations of the company, so it means that this type of company is liable to its creditors only to the extent of its own assets. The law provide that the maximum number of shareholders shall not exceed 50. The basic capital assets shall be at least EUR 5,000 expressed in MKD equivalent, according to the average exchange rate, which is announced by the National Bank of the Republic of Macedonia, applicable for the day on the payment. The amount of the statutory capital shall be expressed in a round number divisible by 100. If the basic capital is reduced for any reason, the amount must be increased to the amount provided for in this Law within six months from the day of the adoption of the annual account, unless the company has been transformed into another form of company within that period. The individual deposit cannot be less than EUR 100 in MKD counter value and if the capital is invested in assets, a qualified appraiser must perform the appraisal. The company is managed by a manager or managers, and they shall be appointed by the

Shareholders. If there are two or more investors, the company is established with an Articles of Association. In the case of a DOOEL (solely-owned limited liability company), the company is established only with a Statement, instead of Articles of Association.

A Joint stock company is a company whose capital is divided into shares. Shareholders are not liable to the creditors for the obligations of the joint stock company. The company may have one or more shareholders. There are two ways on establishing a joint-stock company: simultaneously or successively. The minimum nominal amount of the basic capital, when the company is founded simultaneously, without a public offering notice for subscription of shares, is EUR 25,000 in MKD counter value, according to the average exchange rate of the National Bank of the Republic of Macedonia. When the company is established successively, through a public offering notice to subscribe for shares, the minimum nominal amount of the capital shall be at least EUR 50,000 in MKD equivalent value according to the average exchange rate of the National Bank of the Republic of Macedonia. A higher statutory minimum is required for insurance, investment companies and banks. The capital of the company is divided into ordinary and preference shares. The minimum amount of the share may not be less than 1 EUR. The management of the company can be organized according to a one-tier system (board of directors) or by a two-tier system (management board or manager and supervisory board). A member of the Management Board shall not be a member of the Supervisory Board.

b. The Procedure of Establishment

The first step in the establishment of the company is the adoption of the Articles of Association and it must contain: trade name and address of the company, the company's activities, management and representation of the company, identity of the partners or owners of the company (except for AD), type (cash or in-kind) and amount of partner contributions(for JTD and KD), and the amount of the company's capital (for LLC-DOO, AD and KDA) and other matters as regulated by the Law on trade companies, which are different for each form of company.

The Central Register of Republic of Macedonia is the only body authorized to carry out the registration of a new local company or a branch office of a foreign company. A newly established company comes into legal existence with its entry into the Trade Register, which means that before the enrollment, the company does not exist. The legal framework includes the One-Stop-Shop system through which the registration of the company can be completed within 4 hours of submitting of an application. Another benefit of the One-Stop-Shop is the electronic distribution service that allows any potential investor or third party to obtain complete electronic information about the operations of companies in the country, so you could complete on-line registration, administrate and close the business without the need of physical presence or engagement of intermediaries in Macedonia. Applications for registration of a company along with the other required documents can be submitted in electronic form through local registration agents appointed by the Central Register of the Republic of Macedonia.

c. Routes and Requirements of Dissolution

According to the Trading Company Law, there are several ways for termination of a company, including expiration of the term of the company or other circumstances provided for in the Articles of Association, bankruptcy of the company, by merger or division of the company, upon a final court judgment and in other cases prescribed by law.

When something of the above happened, the company undergoes liquidation proceedings unless a bankruptcy procedure has already been initiated. Upon deletion from the Trade Register, the company loses its legal status.

F. Merger and Acquisition

According to Macedonian legislation, a business combination can be achieved through an acquisition, status changes (accession, merger and division), cross-border mergers and changes of legal form.

An acquisition can be made in the form of purchasing shares, stakes or assets, which is followed by a respective procedure pursuant to the Trade Companies Law. One or more companies may be acquired (company subject to accession) by another company (acquiring company) by transferring its entire assets and liabilities, without conducting a liquidation procedure, in exchange for parts or share in the acquiring company.

Two or more companies may merge without conducting a liquidation procedure, by founding a new company beneficiary, to which the entire assets and liabilities to the merging companies are transferred, in exchange for parts or shares of the new company beneficiary.

Pursuant to the Trade Company Law, a cross-border merger can be made between Macedonian joint-stock companies and limited liability companies, and limited liability companies registered in the European Union. A cross-border merger is possible only for limited liability companies, excluding companies managing investment funds and companies with the main business of acquiring funds for financial investment.

A company may, by way of division, simultaneously transfer its entire assets and liabilities to two or more newly founded companies, or two or more existing companies, whereby the company subjected to division shall be wound up without conducting a liquidation procedure. A company may, by way of division, transfer part of its assets and liabilities to one or more newly founded companies, or one or more existing companies, whereby the company shall not be wound up.

The decision on accession shall be adopted by the company being accessed and the company being the subject to acquisition (acquiring company).

The decision on merger shall be adopted by the companies being merged.

In the event of division of the company by separation with incorporation and spin off with incorporating new companies, the decision shall be adopted by the company being divided. When the division of the company is carried out by separation with takeover and spin-off with takeover, the decision shall be adopted by the company being divided and the company to which a part of the assets and liabilities of the company subject to division are transferred (acquiring company). As further clarification on the set opinions for division of one company it should be noted the following.

By means of separation with incorporation it refers to the situation when one company is divided in a way that other than the existing one, another one is incorporated. On the other hand by means of eparation with takeover, it refers to the situation when one company is divided in a way that part of the existing company is being transferred, i.e. is being acquired by another existing trade company.

By means of spin-off with incorporation, it refers to the situation when a parent company spins off its subsidiary (business unit) and the divested unit becomes an independent company. On the other hand, by means of spin-off with takeover, it refers to a situation when the divested united is being acquired by another trade company.

A decision on accession, merger and division shall be adopted by the members' meeting that is the assembly of each company subject to accession, merger and division in accordance with the conditions and the manner anticipated by the Trade Companies Law regarding the amendment to the articles of association, that is, the statute.

If a new company is incorporated by a merger or division, the incorporation shall be carried out in accordance with the provisions of this Law referring to the incorporation of the respective type of a company, unless otherwise determined by the provisions of this chapter.

If due to the accession, merger or division, the liabilities of the members or the stockholders of one or more companies increase, the decision on accession, merger or division shall be adopted with the consent of all members that is stockholders.

The president of the board of directors, that is the president of the management board shall, not later than eight days as of the day of entry of the accession of a company to a joint stock company, that is the merger, or the division of a joint stock company, shall inform the Central Securities Depository about the performed statutory amendment and shall give an order for the amendments to be entered into the stockholders book, that is the stockholders book to be opened. Namely, the stockholders book of the already existing joint stock company that was part of any transaction referring to division, merger or acquisition, but still has its legal presence, it shall be amended. And the stockholders book of a newly incorporated joint stock compant out of any transaction referring to division, merger or acquisition shall be opened.

In case of accession, merger or division of the company by separation with incorporation and separation with takeover, the company shall terminate without liquidation and a general transfer of its entire assets and liabilities shall be made to the newly incorporated companies and to the acquiring companies, as of the day determined in the agreement harmonizing the terms for accession, merger, or division or the plan on division by separation with incorporation and spin-off with incorporation.

The newly incorporated companies that have been incorporated with the merger, accession or division by separation with takeover and spin-off with takeover shall be joint debtors to the creditors of the companies subject to accession, merger or division.

The issuance that is the withdrawal of the stocks, that is the takeover and withdrawal of shares shall be carried out in accordance with the agreement that is the division plan. The stocks, i.e. the shares of the companies that are subject to the relevant transaction on the basis of the division, merger or acquisition, shall be divided accordingly with the division plan, which presents the relevant agreement between the companies that are parties of the relevant transaction. This may also mean that, new stocks, i.e. shares may be issued upon incorporation of new joint stock company or limited liability company. Or already existing stocks, i.e. shares may be withdrawn upon the termination of existing joint stock company, i.e. limited liability company, as resuit of the relevant tansaction on the basis of the division, merger or acquisition.

The management body of the company that is being accessed and the management body of the acquiring company, the management bodies of companies subject to merger, that is the management body of the company subject to division by separation with takeover or spin-off with takeover and the management body of the acquiring company shall conclude an agreement wherein the conditions for accession, merger or division shall be harmonized. The agreement shall be composed in a form of a notary act.

Not later than one month prior to the decision adoption by the members, that is before convening the members' meeting or the assembly at which a decision on the adoption of the agreement, that is the division plan shall be made, the management bodies of companies that having concluded the agreement or the management body of the company subject to division by separation with incorporation and spin-off with incorporation shall jointly publish a notification on the concluded agreement, that is the adopted division plan in the "Official Gazette of the Republic of Macedonia" and in at least one daily newspaper.

The agreement that is the division plan shall become effective once the members, the members' meeting that is the assembly of the companies participating in the accession, merger, and division shall accept it.

The Decision adopted by the shareholders meeting, i.e. the assembly meeting to approve the division plan, i.e. the agreement for accession, merger or division cannot be contested if the exchange ratio for conversion of shares, i.e. stocks is determined to be too low. Further to this, if the exchange ratio has been determined too low, the court can, upon a proposal of the shareholders, i.e. the stockholders, order additional payment that cannot exceed 10% of the nominal amount of the given shares, i.e. stocks.

G. Competition Regulation

a. Department Supervising Competition Regulation

In Republic of Macedonia, the legal framework for protection of competition relates primarily to the Law for Protection of Competition and the by-laws for the implementation of the above mentioned law.

The right of competition is established to ensure free competition on the domestic market with the aim of stimulating economic efficiency and consumers' welfare. The application of competition rules has as a purpose establishing a market on which all business entities are equal under equal conditions and their position on the market is rated according to the quality of the goods and services they offer. In that matter, the central idea of competition law is the regulation of market activities of the entities and the central aim of competition law is the achievement of a competitive market.

The Commission for Protection of Competition shall supervise the implementation of the Law on Protection of Competition. The basic competencies of the Commission for Protection of Competition are the control of the application of the provisions stipulated in the Law on Protection of Competition, to monitor and analyze the conditions on the market to the extent necessary for the development of free and efficient competition, to conduct procedures and make decisions according to the provisions of the Law. The Commission for protection of competition covers the following areas: evaluation of agreements between entities; prevention and elimination of the abuse of dominant position, and control of concentrations. The Commission is an independent state body with a status of a legal entity, independent in its work and decision making process within the competencies provided by the Law. The Commission consists of President and four members appointed and dismissed for a five-year period by the Assembly of the Republic of Macedonia, with the right to reappointment.

b. Brief Introduction of Competition law

The Law on protection of Competition applies to: business entities, associations of business entities, associated or dependent business entities, state administration entities, and public entities, entities that are entrusted with rendering services of general economic interest, which by their nature constitute monopolies collecting revenues, or are granted special and exclusive rights or concessions, except in the cases where the application of the provisions of this Law would hinder the exercise of the competencies determined by law or the competencies for which those entities have been established.

The Law on protection of Competition establishes three basic forms of action of undertakings that may prevent, restrict or distort competition in Macedonian market, such as prohibited agreements, abuse of dominant positions, and prohibited concentrations.

According to the Law on protection of competition, all agreements concluded between business entities, decisions of associations of business entities and concerted practices which have as their object or effect the distortion of competition shall be prohibited, and in particular those which: directly or indirectly fix purchase or selling prices or any other trading conditions; limit or control production, markets, technical development or investments; share markets or the sources of supply; apply dissimilar conditions to equivalent or similar transactions with other trading partners, thereby placing them in less favorable competitive position, or make the conclusion of the agreements subject to acceptance of supplementary obligations by the other contractual parties, which by their nature or according to the commercial customs are not connected with the subject of the agreement.

A business entity shall have a dominant position on the relevant market if, as a potential seller or purchaser of certain kinds of goods and / or services: it does not have competitors on the relevant market, or compared to its competitors, it has a leading position on the relevant market, and especially in relation to:
- the market share and position and / or
- the financial power and / or
- the access to sources of supply or the market and / or
- the connection with other entities and / or
- the legal or factual barriers for entry of other business entity to the market and / or
- the ability to dictate the market conditions taking into consideration its supply or demand, and / or
- the ability to exclude the other competitors from the market by directing towards other business entities. It shall be presumed that a business entity has a dominant position if its share on the relevant market is more than 40%, unless the business entities proves the opposite. It shall be presumed that two or more legally independent business entities have a joint dominant position on a relevant market if they act or participate jointly on the relevant market.

Any abuse of the dominant position by one or more business entity on the relevant market or its substantial part shall be prohibited. The abuse shall in particular exist in the case of: direct or indirect imposition of unfair purchase or selling prices or other unfair trading conditions; limitation of the production, markets or technical development to the detriment of consumers; application of different conditions for equivalent or similar legal activities with other commercial partners, thereby placing them in a less favorable competitive position; making the conclusion of agreements subject to acceptance of additional obligations by the other contractual parties which, by their nature or according to the commercial customs, are not connected with the subject of the agreement; unjustified refusal to trade or encouraging and requesting from the other business entities or associations of entities not to purchase or sell goods and / or services to a certain entity, with an intention to harm that entity in a dishonest manner, and unjustified refusal to allow another entity access to its own network or other infrastructure facilities of another entity for an adequate compensation, provided that the other entity, without such concurrent use, due to legal or factual reasons, is hindered to act as a competitor on a particular relevant market.

Pursuant to the Law on protection of competition, concentration shall be created by the change of the control on a long-term basis, and as a result of: merger of two or more previously independent business entities or parts of entities or acquisition of direct or indirect control over the whole or parts of one or more entities by: one or more entities that already control at least one entity or one or more business entities, by purchasing securities or assets, by an agreement or in any other manner prescribed by law.

c. Measures Regulating Competition

The Commission for Protection of Competition shall determine rules and measures for protection of competition and measures for establishment of effective competition.

The Misdemeanor Commission shall conduct the misdemeanor procedure before the Commission for Protection of Competition and shall impose a misdemeanor sanction for the misdemeanors determined by the Law. When setting the fine, the Misdemeanor Commission shall take into account: the gravity of the misdemeanor; the duration of the misdemeanor, and the degree of distortion of competition and the effects caused by the misdemeanor.

There are various sanctions provided in the Law, such as financial penalties and in addition to the fine, the Misdemeanor Commission may impose a ban on performing a profession, activity or duty for a certain period.

H. Tax

a. Tax Regime and Rules

The tax system of Republic of Macedonia is a rational combination of different kinds of taxes that are suitable for achieving the goals of the tax policy.

The tax system includes three types of taxes: (i) Income taxes (Profit tax and Personal Income tax); (ii) Consumption taxes (Value added tax, excises and customs); (iii) Property taxes. The state administration body responsible for collection of public revenues is the Public Revenue Office.

b. Main Categories and Rates of Tax

In Macedonia, the Personal Income Tax (PIT) is a tax collected from individuals and is imposed on different sources of income generated in the country and abroad. Macedonian tax residents are taxed on their worldwide income. Non-residents are taxed on their income derived in the Macedonian territory. PIT is payable on income irrespective of whether received in money, securities, in kind, or any other type of compensation. Personal income is subject to a flat 10% tax rate.

Macedonian companies are subject to corporate tax (CIT) on their worldwide income. Foreign companies are taxed in Macedonia on their profits generated from activities conducted through a permanent establishment in the country and on income from Macedonian sources. The corporate income tax rate is 10%. The Law on profit tax regulate the manner of profit taxation, the rate for profit tax calculation, the taxpayers of profit tax, the tax base for profit tax calculation, the deadlines for profit tax payment, as well as other issues of importance for determination and payment of the profit tax.

The Law on value added tax (VAT) introduce the value added tax and regulate its calculation and payment. Value added tax (VAT) is levied on supplies of goods or services with a place of supply in Macedonia and import of goods into Macedonia. A taxpayer must register for VAT purposes if its turnover exceeds MKD 1 million per year. Voluntary registration is allowed as well. The general VAT rate that applies to most VAT taxable supplies is 18%. A preferential VAT rate of 5% applies mainly to the supply and import of the goods and services including: food products for human consumption, drinking water provided from public systems, publications, seeds and planting materials, agricultural mechanization and plastic foils for use in agriculture, pharmaceutical and medical devices, computers, transportation of persons, software, solar heating systems and their components, medical equipment and other devices for the purpose to facilitate or treatment of a disability which are for personal use by disabled persons, crude oil for production of food for human consumption, communal and waste disposal services, hotel accommodation services, livestock feed, livestock feed additives, and livestock, baby products, school supplies etc.

c. Tax Declaration and Preference

According to the Personal Income Tax, the taxable income comprises of the following types of revenues: personal earnings; income from sole proprietorship; income from sale of own agricultural products; income from property and property rights; income from copyrights and industrial property rights; capital income; capital gains; gains from games of chance; and other incomes. Starting from 1 January 2018, the procedure for reporting and payment of personal income tax (PIT) has been simplified both for legal entities and individuals. Legal entities are obliged to prepare and submit an electronic calculation for PIT through an online portal – the new e-personal tax system by the Public Revenue Office and pay PIT at the same time with the payment of the income. Upon submitting the calculations, the tax authority will generate an electronic payment order for simultaneous payment of income and PIT.

According to the Law on profit tax, the base for calculating of Corporate Income Tax is the difference between the total income and the total expenditures of the taxpayer in amounts determined in accordance with accounting regulations and standards. The tax base (the difference between the total income and expenditures) shall be increased of the amount of unrecognized expenses and the tax base shall be decreased by the amount of the investments made from the previous year profit (reinvested profit).

Non taxation of reinvested profit is seen as most popular tax incentive with which you could expend the business activities and produce new employments. Reinvested profit mean the investments made from the profit for development purposes, that is, investments in material assets (immovable property, plants and equipment) and in non-material assets (computer software and patents) for the purpose of expanding the activity of the taxpayer. There is an exception for the investments in passenger vehicles, furniture, carpets, audio visual devices, white goods, pieces of fine and applied art, and other investments that serve administrative purposes. Also, there is a condition that the taxpayer must satisfy. The taxpayer must maintain ownership over the assets purchased with the reinvested profit for a period of five years. If the taxpayer transfers the right of ownership of the assets which it has acquired by reinvesting the profit within a period of five years as of the day of their acquisition, the taxpayer must pay the tax saved.

According to the Law on profit tax and Law on Donations and Sponsorship of Public Activities, there are some tax reduction for donation funds to sports federation, the Macedonian Olympic Committee, football clubs, basketball clubs, handball clubs and sports clubs in other sports. The condition is that the sports clubs have to compete in a national competition system where there is an organized league, need to have also a registered active junior school and the taxpayer should possess a certificate from the Agency for Youth and Sports that the entities that are beneficiaries of the donations are entities that meet the requirements for using the right of tax reduction in accordance with the Law on Sports. The taxpayer who has donated funds to the said sports clubs, paid at a special dedicated account will reduce the calculated tax for the amount of the given donation, that varies from 35%, up to 50% regarding the type of the sport club.

According to the Law on profit tax, the withholding tax is made on revenues paid in the Republic of Macedonia or abroad to the foreign legal entities, and which are not realized in the frames of the business of the permanent establishment of the foreign legal entity on the territory of the Republic of Macedonia, provided it is not otherwise determined by the International Agreements for avoiding double taxation.[1] If the income recipient to which the withholding of tax is applied is a resident of a foreign country that has signed an agreement with the Republic of

---

[1] http://www.ujp.gov.mk/en/plakjanje/category/137.

Macedonia for the avoidance of the double taxation in relation to profit and capital taxes, the provisions of the Agreement will prevail over the Macedonian legislation, meaning that lower rates can be applied on the income if provided by a particular Agreement. If not, the provisions of the Law on profit tax will apply.

According to the Law on Value Added Tax, certain supplies are VAT exempt without the right to deduct input VAT, including residential property rentals, postage stamps, postal services, certain banking and financial operations, insurance and reinsurance services, health services, and educational services etc. Certain supplies are VAT exempt with the right to deduct input VAT, including exports of goods, supplies of gold and other precious metals to central banks etc.

However, the free trade zones, known as Technological Industrial Development Zones are actually the pool where most of the tax incentives exist. Contrary to the above, the VAT rate applied outside the zones is 18%, in comparison with the 0% applied within the zones and the corporate and the personal income tax rates applied outside the zones are 10% in comparison with 0% applied within the zones.

I. Securities

a. Brief Introduction of Securities-Related Laws and Regulations

The legislation regulating the capital market is quite complex due to the regulation of certain specific relations between the entities that participate in the capital market. The legislation consists many laws and regulations, but the most important are the Trading Company Law, the Securities Law, the Law on Takeover of Joint-Stock Companies and the Investment Funds Law. The establishment of the Macedonian Stock Exchange (MSE) in 1995 made it possible to regulate portfolio investments.

b. Supervision and Regulation of Securities Market

Supervision over the operations of the stock exchange and over the participants in transaction is carried out by the Macedonian Securities and Exchange Commission. The Commission is an autonomous and independent organization with the status of a legal entity, which has public authorizations established by the Securities Law, the Law on Takeover of Joint-Stock Companies and the Investment Funds Law. It is responsible for the legal functioning of the securities market, as well as the protection of investors rights.

The Central Securities Depositary is another important institution of the capital market infrastructure in our country. The mission of the Central Securities Depositary is to provide quality and timely services to all market stakeholders, giving special focus to stimulating innovative and sustainable technological solutions in order to provide fast, continuous and simple access to its services, at the same time ensuring protection of the interest of all parties involved. According to the Law on Securities, the Depository performs the following functions: registration of the issuance and transfer of securities in the Republic of Macedonia in the form of electronic records (keeping a register of securities); provision of international identification number of securities (ISIN) for all securities issues; registration of holders of securities; settlement of trade transactions according to the principle "delivery versus payment"; execution of non-trade transfers (implementing gift agreements, inheritance decisions, court decisions, etc.); creation of conditions that enable the borrowing of securities; monitoring of the financial condition of its members, in order to manage the risks associated with the possibility of failure to settle the trade transactions, and performance of additional services for the issuers of securities.

c. Requirements for Engagement in Securities Trading for Foreign Enterprises

Securities may be issued by the Ministry of Finance on behalf of the Republic of Macedonia, the National Bank of the Republic of Macedonia, the municipalities and the City of Skopje, joint stock companies and companies with shares and other domestic and foreign legal entities under conditions determined by law.

The issuance of securities on the primary market, including its own shares, shall be made upon prior approval by the Commission.

The issuance of securities on the primary market can be performed by means of a public offer and through a private offer.

Approval by the Securities and Exchange Commission is not required for the issuance of securities by public or private offering, the total amount of which is not more than 25.000 Euros in MKD counter-value. The issuer of securities in this case shall be obliged to notify the Commission of such a bid, to submit to the Commission the act on issuance of securities and to publish a notice for informing the public about such a bid. The issuer of securities may issue securities without approval from the Commission, not more than once in two calendar years.

The offer of securities made contrary to the provisions of the Securities Law will be considered void.

For the registration of securities, the establishment of trade transactions and the performance of non-trade transfers with securities, securities are established. The depositary is established as a joint-stock company with headquarters in the Republic of Macedonia in accordance with the Law on Trade Companies and this Law. The depositary may establish brokerage houses, banks, insurance companies or fund management companies. The depositary must at all times hold and maintain a basic capital in the amount of at least EUR 500,000 in MKD equivalent calculated according to the middle exchange rate of the National Bank of the Republic of Macedonia from the date of obtaining the license for the establishment of a depositary. The Commission shall prescribe in detail the structure and the manner of calculation of the principal of the depositary.

Secondary trading in securities is carried out through a stock exchange of securities commissioned by the Commission. Stock exchange is established as a joint-stock company with headquarters in the Republic of Macedonia in accordance with the Law on Securities and the Law on Trade Companies. The stock exchange may be established by domestic and foreign, legal and natural persons. Stock exchange must hold and maintain at all times the basic capital in the amount of at least EUR 500,000 in MKD counter value, calculated according to the middle exchange rate of the National Bank of the Republic of Macedonia, starting from the date of obtaining the license for founding a stock exchange. The Commission shall specify the mandatory structure and the method of calculating the equity of the stock exchange.

In the sense of the Law on Securities may perform: a brokerage house with a work permit obtained by the Commission, an authorized bank in accordance with the Banking Law, with a work permit obtained by the Commission and a subsidiary of a foreign brokerage house that has received a work permit from the Commission.

A foreign brokerage house authorized to perform all or some of the services of securities in any of the member countries of the Organization for Economic Cooperation and Development may perform the same services on the territory of the Republic of Macedonia through its subsidiary having a license for operations obtained by the Commission.

Services related to the execution of client orders, informing buyers or buyers of securities that do not constitute investment counselling in a brokerage house can only be performed by authorized brokers.

J. Preference and Protection of Investment

a. The Structure of Preference Policies

In the Budget for 2018, the Government of the Republic of Macedonia predicted in the economic development program 3.1 billion MKD, that is, about 50 million EUR, which is 46% more funds compared to 2017. With the Economic Growth Plan, the Government of the Republic of Macedonia offered the same transparent conditions for domestic and foreign investors and will work on raising the cooperation between domestic and foreign investors in two ways, by encouraging foreign investors to cooperate with domestic and supporting domestic ones suppliers for abroad. Also, the Plan offers measures for new Greenfield and Brownfield investments.

b. Support for Specific Industries and Regions

The measures from the Economic Growth Plan will be transferred into a specific law – Law for Financial Support of Investments (which is still in procedure for adoption), through which the funds for 2018 will be systematically distributed and companies will be able to start using them from March or April.

According to the Government Program of the Republic of Macedonia (2017-2020), the Government will conduct an active and transparent policy of attracting foreign direct investments. The government will focus on building infrastructure and will initiate negotiations to finance 3 priority infrastructure projects through the initiative of 16 European countries plus China, over $ 10 billion.[①]

c. Special Economic Areas

The free trade zones, known as Technological Industrial Development Zones are the most attractive option for foreign investors looking to enter the Macedonian market.

- 100 % foreign ownership, 0% tax and customs duties, no municipality taxes, symbolic land lease rate and direct State Aid in the amount of up to 500.000 EUR are only one segment of the value proposition that provides the most competitive operating environment in the region.

d. Investment Protection

Republic of Macedonia signed various bilateral investment treaties (BITs).[②] The BIT between Republic of Macedonia and People's Republic of China which entered into force on 01 November 1997 aimed of creating favorable conditions for investing investors, which will stimulate the business initiative of investors and will promote the economic development of both countries.[③]

---

① http://vlada.mk/programa.
② http://investmentpolicyhub.unctad.org/IIA/CountryBits/124#iiaInnerMenu.
③ http://investmentpolicyhub.unctad.org/Download/TreatyFile/757.

III. Trade

A. Department Supervising Trade

As successor of the former Ministry of Trade and Ministry of Commerce, the Ministry of Economy is currently in charge with monitoring and enhancing the internal and foreign trade in Republic of Macedonia. In particular, within this governmental body there is a separate sector for international trade cooperation which deals with questions regarding international trade regime and bilateral and multilateral cooperation. The predominant focus of the Ministry of Economy in this area is put on communication with foreign national and multinational authorities for the purpose of entering and implementing international trade agreements, improving of the national legislation, as well as issuing certain trade licences.

In addition, the Ministry is tasked with creating conditions for development of the industry, stimulating the economic climate for growth of business activities and investments, development of the energy sector, exploitation of natural mineral resources, increase and promotion of exports, development of public-private partnership, etc.

B. Brief Introduction of Trade Laws and Regulations

The Trade Law (2004) sets the general trade conditions and manner of conducting trade in the internal and external market, the measures for limiting trade and the protective measures in this area. The Trade Law also lists in a general manner the types of licences for import and export of goods, having in mind the need for protection of the environment, health and safety of individuals, as well as the trade with certain metals, as means for arming and protection used for public safety. Safety measures in terms of mass import of certain products may be imposed by the Government of Macedonia ("Government") to protect the domestic industry, including anti-dumping measures. A number of other laws regulate trade in Macedonia, such as the Law on Consumer Protection (2004), Law on Safety of Products (2006), the Law for Construction Products (2015), etc.

In addition, several laws address more specific and heavily regulated trade, such as the:

- Law on Control of Export of Goods and Technologies with Dual Use (2005), regulating the trade of such goods which can be used for civil and military purposes, for which the Ministry of Economy issues a special permit; and

- Law on Manufacture and Trade of Armament and Military Equipment (2002), governing the requirements and the process for approving trade with this kind of equipment. Foreign investors need to have local presence in Macedonia in order to receive the necessary approvals.

C. Trade Management

Macedonia has attempted to establish itself as a trade centre in the region by offering competitive conditions on all aspects of trade, customs and generally doing business. Specifically, undertakings based in Macedonia have duty free access to more than 650 million consumers based on the signed bilateral and multilateral Free Trade Agreements, as follows:

- Stabilization and Association Agreement (SAA) with the EU Member States;
- Free Trade Agreement with the European Free Trade Association (EFTA) states;
- Central European Free Trade Agreement (CEFTA) with Albania, Bosnia and Herzegovina, Moldova, Serbia, Montenegro;
- Free Trade Agreement with Turkey; and
- Free Trade Agreement with Ukraine.

Significant portion of the trade is achieved through companies from the Technological Industrial Development Zones ("TIDZ"), which are free zones in terms of customs and tax laws. To put it in perspective, in 2016 the export from the TIDZs participated with 47.1% of the total export from Macedonia[1]. The TIDZs are part of the customs area of the territory of Macedonia, but at the same time a separately fenced and marked area separated from the remaining part of the customs area, in which activities are performed under the terms and conditions prescribed by the Law on TIDZ and other applicable laws. Such activities include production, rendering services, scientific and research activities, warehousing, banking and other financial activities, insurance and reinsurance of property and persons; while TIDZs companies cannot perform activities related to trade of decayed or spoiled goods, radioactive materials, drugs, chemical and organic materials, weapons and ammunition.

---

[1] Analysis of effects of new export-oriented companies in domestic economy, prepared by National Bank of Republic of Macedonia, p.10, Available from: http://www.nbrm.mk/content/publikacii/Analiza-na-efektite-od-novite-izvozno-orientirani-kompanii-vo-domasnata-ekonomija.pdf .

Specific customs and tax regime is established in the TIDZ, being one of the most favourable sets of reliefs and incentives for investment in the region. Some of these incentives include exemptions from corporate income tax and personal income tax for the incomes of the employees for a period of ten years after the start with the activity, customs exemptions and reliefs specified in the Law on Customs, aid for training and improvement of employees, grant for construction costs, exemption from utility taxes, etc.

D. The Inspection and Quarantine of Import and Export Commodities

In accordance with Macedonian legislation, the following protective measures are applied in Macedonia with regards to inspection and quarantine of import and export commodities:

- Protection of environment: protection of plants, animals, fungi, ozone layer, waste, batteries and accumulators and electronic equipment. Specific inspections, quarantine, permits and licences are required for all commodities that fall into the above categories;

- Phytosanitary inspection: When importing plants, flowers, fruits and vegetables in the customs area of Macedonia, it is mandatory to have an approval issued by the Ministry of Agriculture, Forestry and Water Management - Phytosanitary Directorate.

- Food and veterinary control: regulated by the Law on Food Safety (2010), Law on Veterinary Health (2007), Law on animal by-products (2007) and Law on Veterinary Medicinal Products (2010). All commodities concerned with this regulation must obtain the appropriate permits and licenses and undergo specific customs inspections. Macedonia has, in a large part, harmonized its legislation regarding food safety with that of the European Union, for example, regarding labelling requirements and risk analysis which are carried out by taking into consideration the opinions from the European Food Safety Authority. In addition, products of animal origin may be imported from countries within the European Union and generally from third countries for which the European Commission or the national authority has given approval for.

E. Customs Management

The current Customs Law is applicable from 2006 and is used to further align the Macedonia's customs regulations with EU standards. The law includes provisions for the governance and operation of free zones. Also, simplified procedures are introduced for inward processing such as easier-to-use declarations. Furthermore, such rules provide for the guarantee of customs debt, the issuance of binding statements for tariff classification of certain goods, and binding origin statements for specific goods in determining the predictability of preferential and non-preferential tariff treatment. The amendments of the Customs Law in December 2010 introduced licenses for customs agents.

Customs duties generally apply to most products imported into Macedonia. A number of products are subject to quality control by market inspection officials at customs offices. These officials are employed by the Ministry of Economy to ensure that imported goods are in compliance with domestic standards. The products subject to quality control include mostly agricultural products, cars and electrical appliances or products in which failure to meet set standards may pose a health risk to consumers. Where applicable, products also must pass sanitary, phytopathologic or veterinary control. According to the Stabilization and Association Agreement between Macedonia and the EU Member States, generally, products with Macedonian origin can be exported into EU countries free of customs duties.

IV. Labour

A. Brief Introduction of Labour Laws and Regulations

Macedonia's Labour Law (2005) provides the minimal standard of entitlements and protections for the employees which cannot be diminished by Collective Bargaining Agreements or employment contracts or any internal acts of the employer. This legislative piece, along with a number of bylaws, regulates the labour relations between the employees and the employers established by entering into employment contracts, especially the termination, protection from discrimination and harassment, wages and working hours, vacations etc. Together with the Labour Law, there are a number of other laws regulating specific areas of the labour market, such as the:

- Law on Employment and Insurance in Case of Unemployment which regulates the rights and obligations of the employers, the unemployed persons and other employment related issues;

- Law on Labour Inspection which governs the organization and the operation of the State Labour Inspectorate;

- Law on Agencies for Temporary Employment which regulates the conditions and the manner of setting up agencies for temporary employment, as well as the conditions and the manner of providing temporary employment for the purpose of performing temporary work with another employer;

- Law on the Employment and Work of Foreigners which provides the conditions and the procedure for employment or work of foreigners in Macedonia;

- Law on Safety and Health at Work which regulates the measures for safety and health at work, including the employer's obligations and the employees' rights and obligations in the field of safety and health at work.

Key authority in the field of labour is the Ministry of Labour and Social Policy, which oversees labour relations, employment and protection of workers during work, as well as other aspects of labour matters in cooperation with the State Labour Inspectorate.

B. Requirements of Employing Foreign Employees

a. Work permit

The Macedonian Law on Foreigners (2006) regulates the conditions for entry, abandonment and stay of foreigners in Macedonia, as well as their rights and obligations, while the Law on Employment and Work of Foreigners ("Law on Employment of Foreigners") regulates the conditions and procedure under which foreigners are employed or work in the country.

Foreigners, who in accordance with the provisions of the Law on Employment of Foreigners may be employed, self-employed, or work in Macedonia, should possess: (i) a temporary residence permit for work purposes issued by the Ministry of Interior or (ii) a work permit issued by the Employment Service Agency and regulated residence on any other ground. During the procedure for granting a temporary residence permit for work purposes, the Employment Service Agency issues an opinion based on the quota fulfilment and the current needs of the Macedonian labour market. Work permit which is issued for a definite period of time of up to one year shall be a renewable or permanent form of a work permit, which allows the foreigner free access to the labour market during its validity period.

Certain onshore activities can be performed in Macedonia without the need to obtain a work permit. This applies to a limited scope of activities, such as:
- creative services in the field of culture;
- services related to commercial fairs;
- short-term services provided by foreigners;
- work performed by foreigners residing in Macedonia for the purpose of studying; and
- emergency services.

The beginning and the end of these activities need to be registered for which the Employment Service Agency issues a form to the responsible person for registration.

b. Application Procedure

An application for issuance of a work permit is submitted at the Employment Service Agency or in other premises determined by the Agency, by a foreigner who has a regulated stay in the country on grounds other than work. The application shall contain data on the foreigner, his qualifications (i.e.its speciality), and the type of work he wants to engage in. If the foreigner has not regulated stay in Macedonia, an opinion from the Ministry of Interior shall also be needed. The work permit is then issued by the Employment Service Agency by adopting a decision for issuance of a work permit or extension of the work permit, under the conditions from the relevant law.

The necessary documentation for obtaining of a work permit, depending on the type of permit, will usually consist of: filled-out prescribed form, company excerpt of the employer, short explanation on the need of employing a foreigner, signed employment agreement, copy of the passport and a lease agreement for the place of stay of the employee. There is a split competence for issuance of the work permit between the Ministry of Interior, who receives the application and forwards it to the Employment Service Agency, who issues the work permit.

c. Social Insurance

Pension insurance, as well as basic healthcare insurance are obligatory in Macedonia, and must be paid by the employer. The employer cannot waive its obligation to make these contributions on behalf of employees. Contributions for compulsory social security are primarily governed by the Law on Compulsory Social Security Contributions (2008), whereby the mandatory social insurance consist of contributions for:
- pension and disability insurance on the basis of a current payment,
- mandatory fully funded pension insurance,
- years of service which are calculated with increased duration,
- health insurance and
- insurance in case of unemployment.

C. Exit and Entry

a. Visa Types

Foreigners who need to have a visa for their stay in Macedonia, have to obtain it before their arrival. Having a visa is not enough for the foreigner to be employed at a local employer since the presence on the Macedonian territory is allowed only for the purpose stated in the visa. In line with this, there are several types of visas which can be categorised as 'transit visas' or 'visas for stay'. In general, the former are the airport transit visa (Visa A) and the transit visa (Visa B), while the latter include the short stay visa (Visa C) and the long stay visa (Visa D).

In particular, foreign passengers which do not exit from the international zone in an airport do not need any visa, except when the Government finds appropriate to require Visa A for citizens of certain countries. In contrast, Visa B is required for travel from one country to another by transiting through the territory of Macedonia and can have an expiry period of up to one year. However, the actual stay of the foreigner based on Visa B cannot last longer than five days. The short stay and long stay visas are issued for business, personal, touristic, educational and other purposes. Based on Visa C, the foreigner can stay up to 90 days during a six-month period, while under the terms of Visa D the foreigner is entitled to stay up to 30 days with the right to obtain a permit for temporary residence.

Foreigners, holders of a valid travel document of a third country, for which a visa for entry into Macedonia is required under the Macedonian visa regime, may enter into Macedonia without a visa if they:

• have a regulated permanent residence in an EU Member State or in a signatory to the Schengen Agreement, and

• hold a valid multiple Schengen C visa with a validity period longer than five days of the planned stay in Macedonia.

At each entry on Macedonian territory, such foreigner may stay up to 15 days, while the total duration of the successive stays in Macedonia must not be longer than three months during each six-month period, counting from the day of the first entry.

Citizens of EU Member States and Schengen Contracting States may enter into Macedonia with a valid identity card issued by the competent authorities of their country.

b. Restrictions for Exit and Entry

As stated above, the total duration of the successive stays in Macedonia must not be longer than three months during each six-month period, counting from the day of the first entry. The Ministry of Foreign Affairs[1] keeps a list of countries around the world whose citizens need or do not need a visa for traveling to Macedonia.

D. Trade Union and Labour Organizations

In accordance with the Labour Law, employees have a right to constitute a trade union and become its members by their own free choice, under the conditions set forth by the statute or by the rules of that trade union. Trade unions are described as "autonomous, democratic and independent organization of employees which they join voluntarily for the purpose of representing, presenting, promoting and protecting their economic, social and other individual and collective interests."[2] Employers may also organise associations of their own by their own free choice. The employee, that is, the employer may freely decide on his joining and leaving the trade union, that is, the employers' association.

E. Labour Disputes

According to the Labour Law, individual and collective labour disputes may occur. Individual disputes can be initiated at the initiative of the employee or of the employer, while collective disputes arise between the signatory parties to a collective agreement. The employee usually initiates an individual labour dispute, when the employer does not respond positively to a particular request of the employee related to the right to work, or when the employer violated the employee's rights from the employment relationship, so he, after exhausting the legal protection at the employer, requires protection before the competent authority.

Under the Labour Law, the individual or collective labour dispute can be resolved amicably or through (i) an arbitration or (ii) a court proceeding.

---

[1] www.mfa.gov.mk.
[2] Article 184, Paragraph 2 of the Labour Law.

V. Intellectual Property

A. Brief Introduction of IP Laws and Regulations

Intellectual Property ("IP") is set out under quite extensive legislation considering the number of applicable domestic and international legal sources. In particular, key national IP laws are the 2009 Law on Industrial Property, as an umbrella law for patents, industrial design, trademarks, appellation of origin and geographical indications, and the 2010 Law on Copyright and Related rights, which regulates copyrights. There is also a separate Law on Protection of Topographies of Integrated Circuits (1998) and a Law on Customs Measures for Protection of Intellectual Property Rights (2015). Apart from the primary legislation, many bylaws have been adopted, especially for addressing matters related to the mentioned IP rights (like the Rulebook on Industrial Design and the Rulebook on Trademarks). At the same time, important element of the relevant legal framework are the numerous sector specific international and EU instrument[1]. For example, the WIPO Convention, the Agreement on Trade-Related Aspects of Intellectual Property Rights, the Paris Convention for the Protection of Industrial Property and many other.

Despite the various authorities included in the protection of IP rights, leading role has the State Office of Industrial Property ("SOIP") as a body in charge with matters related to the process of acquiring and protecting IP rights. Along with SOIP, significant part of the IP protection system are the Customs Administration and the State Market Inspectorate, with their competences to monitor sale and trade with goods for the domestic and foreign market.

B. Patent Application

From the aspect of the national legislation, patents are primary governed by the Law on Industrial Property and the Rulebook on Patents (2009). Under the Law, applicants may seek protection for inventions in all technology areas, if they are new, contain inventive contribution and have industrial applicability. Such protection can be established nationally, during procedures before the SOIP or through international bodies based on the Patent Cooperation Treaty, the European Patent Convention and the Agreement for Cooperation in the Field of Patents between Macedonia and the European Patent Office. As an example, European patents recognised by the European Patent Office, which include protection for Macedonia are levelled with the national patents with respect to the scope of rights. Also, under certain circumstance, the European patents override the national patents that cover same scope of invention.

General elements of the national applications include the claim and the specification of the invention, together with an abstract and drawings (if needed). Even though national applications can be submitted on a foreign language, they have to be accompanied by a translation in Macedonian. The necessary documentation that is required encompasses:
- power of attorney, if the application is submitted through an agent;
- proof of paid appropriate administrative fee;
- data for other applicants and a statement of joint representative if the application is submitted by several applicants;
- data for other inventors;
- a statement from the inventor if he does not want to be listed in the application;
- proof of the priority right if there is a request for such right; etc.

As a first step, SOIP examines the completeness of the application. Upon satisfaction of all requirements it determines the date of application and registers the application in the Register of Patent Applications. The applicant can chose between a complete examination at the available international institutions or examination of the claim by SOIP. Based on the outcome of the carried out examination SOIP invites the applicant to pay the applicable fees and costs and afterwards issues a decision for granting the right to a patent. Relevant information from the decision are registered at the Register of patent and are published in the official gazette of SOIP.

C. Trademark Registration

The Law on Industrial Property defines trademarks as a right of industrial property that protects the trade sign, by making a distinction between a service mark, certification mark, collective mark and a mark for goods. Subject of protection under a trademark is a sign that can be shown graphically and which is suitable for distinguishing

---

[1] Under the Stabilization and Association Agreement, Macedonia is obliged to harmonise its legislation with the acqui communautaire, including with the relevant IP legislation of the European Union.

goods and services from different market participants. These signs include: words, letters, numbers, pictures, drawings, combinations of colours, three-dimensional forms, including shapes of goods or their packaging, as well as combinations of all of the mentioned signs. There are absolute and relative grounds for refusing to protect a specific sign.

Procedure for recognising a trademark can be initiated before the SOIP or in accordance with the Madrid Agreement Concerning the International Registration of Marks and the Protocol Relating to the Madrid Agreement. The trademark application must include:
- claim for recognition of the trademark right;
- data for the applicant;
- the appearance of the sign for which protection is sought;
- a list of the goods and services for which protection is sought; and
- other applicable data and documents regulated with the Rulebook on Trademarks (such as data for the joint representative, general act for collective mark or rules for using a certification mark, proof of priority right, proof for paid administrative fee and a power of attorney).

As in the case of the procedure for recognition of patents, SOIP has to determine the completeness of the application after which registers it in the Register of Trademark Applications. Also, the application is published in the official gazette of SOIP. Any third party may argue that there are absolute grounds for SOIP to refuse the recognition of the trademark, while certain parties (like a holder of a trademark or applicants with prior application) can object the application based on existence of relative grounds for refusal. If there are no obstacles for recognition of the trademark and the applicant has paid the applicable amounts, SOIP will issue a positive decision and shall register the trademark right in the Register of Trademarks. The Trademark is also published in the official gazette of SOIP.

D. Measures for IP Protection

The protection in the form of a recognition and registration of IP rights is further strengthened with judicial protection for the acquired IP rights. To initiate a court proceeding for any IP infringement the concerned person has to file a lawsuit within three years from the moment of becoming aware of such infringement. With the lawsuit, the holder of the IP rights may request issuance of a ban on the actions that breach its rights, compensation of damages, confiscation and destruction of products, etc.

Protection of the IP rights can be also achieved on international level by submission of a request to SOIP in accordance with the Madrid Protocol. If SOIP determines that the request is in accordance with the Rulebook on Trademarks, it forwards it to the International Bureau of the World Organization for Protection of Intellectual Property in Geneva.

Considering the competences of the Customs Administration to supervise the goods that enter and exit from Macedonia, a separate Law on Customs Measures for Protection of Intellectual Property Rights was enacted in order to improve the prevention and detection of IP infringements. Under this Law, the Customs Administration is authorised to act ex officio or upon a request from a concerned party. In case of suspicion for potential IP infringement, the Customs Administration may retain the respective goods. The release of the goods will follow if (i) the authority did not identified any person that can potentially request carrying out actions due to IP infringements or (ii) such request was rejected or never filed. Certain conditions are stipulated for potential destruction of the goods.

Finally, the Law against Unfair Competition (1999) also provides protection of IP rights through stipulating fines and sanctions for IP infringements. As an example, a fine in the range between approx. EUR 500 and EUR 2,500 or imprisonment up to two years can be issued when for the purposes of competition or personal benefit, a person uses or transfers, without an authorization, drawings, plans, prototypes or other such documents, which are not protected IP rights.

VI. Environmental Protection

A. Department Supervising Environmental Protection

Separate authorities on state and local level comprise the system for protection of the environment in Macedonia. Crucial role in such set-up has the Ministry of Environment and Physical Planning ("Ministry of Environment"), who is empowered to enact secondary legislation, implement the environmental legislation and monitor the environment protection. Certain competences have been delegated to the municipal units[1], who are primary entitled to adopt local plans and strategies, issue appropriate approvals and permits, as well as to supervise the implementation of the environmental laws from the aspect of the local competences. Both the Ministry of Environment and the municipal units can issue protective measures. For example, the Ministry can ban the production, trade and usage of certain goods, while both authorities can ban the carrying out of certain activities that can harm the environment or the life and health of the individuals.

The inspection supervision is organised also on state and local level, carried out by the State Environmental Inspectorate and by authorised inspectors of the relevant municipality unit. Additionally, other state bodies can supervise specific environmental issues, such as the State Market Inspectorate, the State Sanitary and Health Inspectorate, the Phytosanitary Administration and the State Agriculture Inspectorate. Within their competences, the environmental inspectors are entitled to impose measures or order actions that have to be performed for prevention or elimination of the causes for the environmental pollution. Depending on the type of the potential misdemeanour, a misdemeanour sanction (e.g.a fine in the amount of EUR 3,000 or up to EUR 200,000) can be issued within a procedure carried out by the Ministry of Environment or the competent court. Also, depending on the caused ecological damage, the polluter could face criminal charges and claims for restitution or compensation of damages.

B. Brief Introduction of Laws and Regulations of Environmental Protection

Environmental protection represents a fundamental value under the Macedonian Constitution, which at the same time guarantees the right to a healthy environment to each individual. Such guarantee is provided through several laws specific to this area, with the Law on the Environment ("Environment Law") from 2005 as main environmental legislative act. The Environmental Law regulates the rights and duties of the state and local authorities, as well as the rights and duties of the legal entities and natural persons in providing conditions for protection and improvement of the environment, so that the citizens can exercise their right to a healthy environment. Under this Law, the implementation of a certain project or the production within specific factories can be done after conducting an Environmental Impact Assessment Study or obtaining relevant integrated environmental permit. Such permit for instance contains data for the operator and the installation, as well as mandatory conditions related to the emission limit values, the protection measures of individual media and areas of the environment, including the manner of monitoring by the operator of the installation. Other relevant environmental laws are the:

- Law on Waste Management[2] (2004), the Law on Management of Packaging and Packaging Waste (2009), the Law on Management with Batteries and Accumulators and Waste Batteries and Accumulators (2010), and the Law on Management with Electrical and Electronic Equipment and Waste Electrical and Electronic Equipment (2012), regulating the management of different type of waste;

- Law on Waters (2008), governing the issues pertaining to surface and ground waters, their management, water resources management facilities and services, as well as conditions and procedures under which the waters can be used and discharged;

- Law on Quality of Ambient Air (2004), addressing measures for avoiding, preventing or reducing the harmful effects of ambient air pollution on human health, as well as the environment as a whole;

- Law on Protection against Environmental Noise (2007), regulating the rights and obligations of the authorities and all legal entities and natural persons in relation to environmental noise management and protection against environmental noise;

- other laws which contain environmental protection provisions (such as the Law on Agricultural Land (2007), the Law on Forests (2009), the Energy Law (2011), the Law on Mineral Resources (2012), etc.).

In 2004 Macedonia ratified the Kyoto Protocol to the United Nations Framework Convention on Climate Change which sets binding emission reduction targets which have to be followed by the member states. In order to implement the National Climate Change Mitigation Plan and involve Macedonia in the global efforts for reduction of climate change, the Ministry of Environment evaluates and approves projects under the clean development mechanism established in the Kyoto Protocol. In addition, Macedonia has ratified many other international agreements in the field of environment, like the Paris Agreement, the Convention on Environmental Impact Assessment in a Transboundary Context (Espoo Convention), the Convention on Biological Diversity, the Vienna Convention for the Protection of the Ozone Layer, the Stockholm Convention on Persistent Organic Pollutants, etc.

C. Evaluation of Environmental Protection

The above presented regulatory framework shows that environmental protection is widely regulated in

---

[1] Municipal units in Macedonia are the local municipalities and the City of Skopje.
[2] New Law on Waste Management is being prepared in order to comply with the new changes to EU law in this area.

Macedonia. However, there is still space for further improvement in certain areas since some of the laws are not fully aligned with the European legislation, especially in the areas of industrial pollution and risk management, water and air quality, chemicals and climate change[①]. The European Commission emphasizes that, the authorities should work on more effective implementation of the national plan for air quality protection, further improvement of the environmental impact assessment process and the implementation of the Paris Agreement.[②] The legislation that is planned to be adopted will require stricter standards and enforcement, increased fines and penalties for non-compliance, and bigger responsibility for companies, their management and employees. Public awareness increases constantly and the public pressure the authorities to allocate more funds from the state and municipalities' budget for environmental protection. Environmental inspections are conducted more and more often and incompliances are sanitized. Large companies invest in environment protection and some organizations like the Fund for Innovation and Technological Development finance technological solutions for reducing pollution.

VII. Dispute Resolution

A. Methods and Bodies of Dispute Resolution

Parties are free to agree the dispute resolution mechanism for disputes which concern rights that can be freely disposed with and which are not under exclusive jurisdiction of the Macedonian courts. Generally, if the parties concerned are not willing to solve the dispute amicably, they can opt for one of the following available methods: (i) a court proceeding; (ii) an arbitration; or (iii) a mediation.

a. Court Proceedings

The Macedonian judiciary is structured as a three-tier court system organised through basic and appellate courts, as first and second instance courts for civil and criminal matters, and with the Administrative Court and the Higher Administrative Court with competence to solve administrative disputes in first and second instance. Third and final court instance for all kinds of disputes (civil, criminal and administrative) is the Supreme Court of the Republic of Macedonia. Basic courts are established for one or more municipalities as courts with basic or expanded competence, while the appellate courts cover the territory of several basic courts. Currently, there are four appellate courts in the cities of Skopje, Bitola, Stip and Gostivar, while the Administrative Court, the Higher Administrative Court and the Supreme Court are situated in the capital city of Skopje and perform their authority on the entire territory of Macedonia.

Civil law proceedings are initiated before the basic courts by submitting a lawsuit, accompanied by relevant evidence for the stated assertions and facts. Afterwards, respecting the principle of equality of arms the proceedings are generally carried out through two phases, preliminary and main hearing. In contrast to the proceedings before the basic courts, Appellate courts usually rule on the dispute without holding a hearing. The right to appeal is guaranteed by the Macedonian Constitution. Since the legal system is based on civil law principles, precedents are not binding for the courts. In addition, several competences have been delegated to other authorities, like the public notaries and the enforcement agents. For example, the former being authorised to issue payment orders upon request of the creditors and the latter to enforce such payment orders against the debtors.

Together with the competences to provide judiciary protection against the acts of the public authorities, the Administrative Court is empowered to solve disputes which arise from concession agreements, public procurement contracts and any other agreement with a public authority as a signatory party, entered for the purpose of pursuing a public interest or exercising public service. In case of an administrative dispute, the right to an appeal is exercised before the Higher Administrative Court. In general, the proceedings before both courts are carried out based on written submissions, without holding a hearing.

Disputes with an international element are solved by Macedonian civil courts when the competence for such dispute is explicitly determined by law or by an international agreement. When there is no such explicit provision for the respective dispute, then a Macedonian court will be competent if its jurisdiction arises from the rules for territorial jurisdiction of Macedonian courts. Parties may agree jurisdiction of a Macedonian court if at least one of

---

① The former Yugoslav Republic of Macedonia 2016 Report, prepared by the European Commission, pg.73.Available from: https://ec.europa.eu/neighbourhood-enlargement/sites/near/files/pdf/key_documents/2016/20161109_report_the_former_yugoslav_republic_of_macedonia.pdf.
② Ibidem.

them is a Macedonian citizen or a legal entity seated in Macedonia. Contrary to this, in order to agree jurisdiction of a foreign court, one of the parties has to be a foreign citizen or a legal entity based abroad, subject to not having an exclusive jurisdiction of a Macedonian court for the dispute.

b. Arbitration

Arbitration can be agreed for resolving disputes which have already arisen between the concerned parties or for all future disputes arising from a legal relationship between them. Competent institutions to conduct arbitration in Macedonia are the permanent courts attached to the economic chambers and other organizations, such as the permanent court before the Economic Chamber of Macedonia and the one before the Macedonian Chambers of Commerce. These institutions can administer both domestic and international arbitrations, depending whether the dispute includes an international element. In order to agree jurisdiction of an international arbitration, one of the following conditions have to be met:

• at least one of the parties has residence or is based outside of Macedonia at the time of conclusion of the arbitration agreement; or

• the place where a significant part of the obligations should be performed, or the place which has the closest connection with the subject matter of the dispute is outside of Macedonia.

The permanent court before the Economic Chamber of Macedonia has a list of arbitrators, but the parties can also choose arbitrators which are not on that list. The procedure before the permanent courts is a one-step procedure and the decision adopted by them is final and binding on the parties. As a legal remedy against the arbitral award adopted in accordance with the Law on International Commercial Arbitration of the Republic of Macedonia (2006) is the lawsuit for annulment, which is submitted to the competent court. Finally, there are also certain sector specific bodies which conduct arbitration such as the Chamber of Authorized Architects and Authorized Engineers of the Republic of Macedonia.

c. Mediation

Mediation can be initiated if the parties have agreed in writing that in the event of a dispute they will try to resolve it by means of direct negotiation or mediation before commencing judicial or other proceedings. However, even if court proceedings are initiated, in certain cases the court has an obligation to recommend mediation to the parties in the first instance proceedings. In that case, the parties can give a written statement that they accept to participate in mediation. As an exception, for commercial disputes concerning a monetary claim which does not exceed MKD 1,000,000 (approx.EUR 16,300) and for which proceedings are initiated with a lawsuit, before filing the lawsuit, the parties are obliged to attempt to solve the dispute through mediation.

Mediation is conducted by licenced mediators registered at the Directory of Mediators. They are organised in the Chamber of Mediators of the Republic of Macedonia, which is a non-profit legal entity that ensures that they carry out the mediation in accordance with the principles established, by law and the Code of Ethics of Mediators. The mediation procedure ends within 60 days from the date of giving a statement for initiation of the procedure, regardless of its outcome. Depending on the fact whether there is a foreign element in the dispute, mediation can be domestic or international.

B. Application of Laws

Courts decide upon the rights and obligations of the parties to the proceedings based on the Constitution, the national laws and international agreements ratified in accordance with the Constitution.

The International Private Law (2008) contains rules for determining the applicable law for civil, labour and commercial matters with an international element. When it comes to agreements, parties can choose the governing law if it is not otherwise determined by law or by an international agreement. The mentioned law also contains rules for the recognition of foreign court decisions and decisions of other authorities of a foreign country. With respect to the recognition and enforcement of foreign arbitral award, the conditions from the 1958 New York Convention on the Recognition and Enforcement of Foreign Arbitral Awards, shall apply.

Separate laws govern the different types of dispute resolution mechanisms and procedures. With respect to mediation proceedings, the main applicable law is the Law on Mediation (2013). For international arbitration the relevant procedural law is the Law on International Commercial Arbitration which is generally based on the UNCITRAL Model Law on International Commercial Arbitration. The Law on Civil Proceedings (2005) governs civil court proceedings and domestic arbitrations. Criminal proceedings are conducted in accordance with the Law on Criminal Proceedings (2010). Finally, administrative disputes are regulated with the Law on Administrative Disputes (2006).

VIII. Others

A. Anti-commercial Bribery

a. Brief Introduction of Anti-commercial Bribery Laws and Regulations

Main law governing anti-corruption and bribery is the 2002 Law on Prevention of Corruption ("Anti-Corruption Law"). The Anti-Corruption Law envisages that the responsible person in a company or other legal entity must not use his / her position, for the purpose of receiving any reward or any other benefit or promising such benefit, for himself / herself or for others in order to:
- create a monopoly on the market;
- discriminate other companies or other legal entities;
- cause disturbance to the market; and
- cause damage to other natural person or other legal entity not resulting from fair competition at the market.

Legal acts which result from corruption are null and void. All entities which have a legal interest can request their annulment by submitting a final court decision which confirms the existence of corruption. In addition, parties who suffered any damage can request compensation. The regulatory framework for fighting anti-commercial bribery is also consisted of the:

- Law on Prevention of Conflict of Interests (2007), regulating the rules for prevention against abuse of public authorisations and duties of an official for self-interest or interest of affiliated persons.

- Law on Whistle-blowers Protection (2015), setting out the system for informing on punishable or illegal actions by whistle-blowers, their rights, as well as actions and duties of institutions and legal entities regarding the process of protected reporting (i.e.whistleblowing). Protected reporting represents informing on a reasonable suspicion or knowledge for punishable or otherwise unlawful or unacceptable actions that violates or threatens the public interest. The reporting can be done by informing within the institution or the company, to the authorities or by making the information publicly available.

- Law on Lobbying (2008) which gives out the principles of lobbying and lobbyists, supervision of the lobbying and measures that can be imposed on a lobbyist due to noncompliance with the law. According to this law, the lobbyist must comply with the anti-corruption provisions which include anti-bribery.

- Criminal Code (1996), according to which, an official may not directly or indirectly request or receive a gift or another benefit, including a promise for such bribery, in order to perform an official activity which should not be performed, or does not perform an official activity which should be performed, etc. Punishable is also the act of giving, promising or offering the mentioned benefits. Finally, the Criminal Code sanctions the actions of giving and receiving a reward for unlawful influence.

b. Department Supervising Anti-commercial Bribery

The State Commission for Prevention of Corruption ("State Commission") is an autonomous and independent legal entity composed of seven members. It has many competences including:

- Raising initiatives with competent bodies for conducting control of the financial and material operation of political parties, the labour union, and citizens associations and foundations;

- Raising initiatives for potential procedure before competent bodies for dismissal, transfer, removal or undertaking other measures for liability against elected or appointed persons, responsible persons in public enterprises or other legal entities which dispose with state capital;

- Raising initiative for criminal prosecution against elected or appointed persons, officials or responsible persons in public enterprises, public institutions and other legal entities which dispose with state capital;

- Acting in cases of conflict of public and private interests, defined by law; etc.

The State Commission raises an incentive to the Public Prosecutor of the Republic of Macedonia and the Public Prosecutor's Office for Organized Crime and Corruption for initiating a criminal prosecution procedure based on a suspicion for committing an act of corruption. It also collects necessary information and documents from all relevant institutions for the purpose of establishing the facts in a specific case.

c. Punitive Actions

The presented legal framework for anti-commercial bribery contains broad misdemeanor provisions. In addition, the Criminal Code envisages several sanctions besides seizing the benefit obtained with the crime and ban on practicing a profession, carrying out an activity or duty for a period of one to ten years. These sanctions include:

a) Taking bribe: (i) imprisonment between four and ten years for performing an activity which should not be performed, or not performing an official activity which should be performed; (ii) imprisonment of at least five years if significant property benefit is obtained with the crime, etc.

b) Giving bribe: (i) imprisonment between one and five years for giving bribe to an official in order to perform an official activity, which otherwise should not be performed, or not to perform an official activity which must be performed, or whosoever mediates in such relation; (ii) a fine to the legal entity who has committed this crime, etc.

c) Giving and receiving a reward for unlawful influence: the offender will be punished in accordance with the specific circumstances, whereas the maximum punishment for this crime is imprisonment of up to five years. If the mediator has received a reward or other benefit for mediating in the receiving of a reward for unlawful influence, it shall be sentenced to imprisonment of one to ten years. Legal entities are sentenced with monetary fines.

In addition to the mentioned sanctions for taking and giving bribe, including for receiving a reward for unlawful influence, if the action is carried out on behalf of a legal entity the Anti-Corruption Law stipulates a misdemeanour fine for the legal entity in the amount between EUR 4,000 and 5,000.

Finally, the Law against Unfair Competition stipulates a fine in the amount between EUR 3,300 and EUR 16,300 for given or promised bribery to an employee or to an agent of a legal entity for the purpose of obtaining a privilege position regarding certain products or services. The person requesting or accepting the bribe, shall be imprisoned in duration between three months and three years. The object of the bribe i.e.the received gift or any other material benefit shall be confiscated.

B. Project Contracting

a. Permission System

Awarding public procurements contracts (i.e.purchasing of goods, services and works) and establishing of public private partnerships ("PPP") is done through the procedures regulated by the Public Procurement Law (2007). Drafted in accordance with the EU Directive 2004/18/EC[①], this Law regulates the manner and procedures for awarding public procurement contracts ("PP Contract") and provides the institutional structure that deals with public procurement issues, primary the Public Procurement Bureau ("Bureau") and the State Appeals Commission on Public Procurement ("Appeals Commission"). Activities related to the development of the public procurement system, as well as the provision of rationality, efficiency and transparency in the implementation of the public procurements is carried out by the Bureau, as a legal entity in scope of the Ministry of Finance, while the Appeals Commission is responsible for providing legal protection during the awarding procedures. The regulatory framework for PPPs is consisted also with the Law on Concessions and PPP (2012) which in addition to the regulation of certain PPP aspects, it also addresses the awarding of concessions for goods of general interest.

PP Contracts are concluded for the purpose of performing works, delivery of goods or provision of certain services. Accordingly, the PP Contract can be in the form of a PP Contract for work, goods or services. In comparison, the PPP is defined as a long-term contractual collaboration between the public and the private partner where the private partner assumes the obligation to provide a public service for end users in fields of competence of the public partner and / or the obligation to provide the necessary prerequisites for the public partner to provide such public service. For these purposes, the private partner may finance, design, build, exploit or maintain a public infrastructure facility, etc. Depending on the purpose of the funds for compensation by the public partner for the provision of public works / services, as well as the allocation of key existing risks, the PPP may be established as: public works / services concession or PP Contract for public works / services.

b. Invitation to Bid and Bidding

Generally, the public procurement is done through the so-called "standard procedures" i.e.the open or restricted procedure, while other procedures are used as an exception in specific cases determined by law. The open, restricted and the simplified procedure, have to be conducted by using electronic means through the Electronic System for Public Procurement which is managed by the Bureau. The Law on Public Procurement provides the following awarding procedures:

a) Open procedure: every interested party has a right to submit a bid. After evaluation of the received bids, an electronic auction is used as a final phase of the procedure.

b) Restricted procedure: every interested party may request to participate, but only the selected candidates are invited to submit a bid. This procedure is conducted through the following three stages: (i) pre-qualification phase (selection of the candidates); (ii) evaluation of bids and (iii) an electronic auction.

c) Competitive dialogue: every interested party may request to participate in the dialogue phase for developing

---

[①] Directive 2004/18/EC of the European Parliament and of the Council of 31 March 2004 on the coordination of procedures for the award of public works contracts, public supply contracts and public service contracts.Available from: http://eur-lex.europa.eu/legal-content/EN/TXT/PDF/?uri=CELEX:32004L0018&from=en.

an appropriate solution for the requirements of the procuring authority, whereby the procuring authority conducts a dialogue only with selected candidates. After identifying the best solution, the selected candidates submit their bids. This procedure which also ends with an electronic auction is used when the PP Contract is particularly complex and the use of the open or restricted procedure will not allow the award of the contract.

d) Negotiated procedure: is a procedure in which the contracting authority consults the selected candidates and negotiates the terms of the contract with one or more of them. There are two types of negotiated procedure: negotiated procedure with prior publication of a contract notice and a negotiated procedure without publication of a contract notice.

e) Simplified procedure for awarding a PP Contract: is a procedure which is implemented for awarding PP Contracts with a value up to EUR 20,000 for goods and services and up to EUR 50,000 for works.

Any economic operator has the right to participate, individually or as a member in a group of economic operators, during the procedure for awarding a PP Contract. Economic operators who act as a group for the purpose of submitting a joint request for participation or a joint bid are not required to be connected in a legal form. Within the same procedure, the candidate / bidder is allowed to participate only with one request for participation / bid, while it may have a capacity of a subcontractor in more than one request for participation / bid.

In order to ensure clear instructions for the potential bidders, the tender documentation provide the requirements, conditions, criteria and other necessary information regarding the manner of conducting the procedure for awarding the PP Contract.The tender documentation has to be put on a market test by carrying out a technical dialogue. This phase is mandatory in case of an open and restricted procedure for awarding a PP Contract for goods and services with an estimated value exceeding EUR 130,000 in MKD counter-value, and is carried out after the adoption of the decision on public procurement and before the publication of the announcement. The procuring authority may require a tender guarantee in a form of a bank guarantee or deposited funds. Other instruments for expressing seriousness of the bidder are also applied. The procuring authority may further require from the bidder whose bid is chosen as most favorable one to provide a guarantee for quality contract performance in a form of a bank guarantee. The transparency in the awarding procedure is ensured by publishing a prior indicative notice, announcement for awarding a PP Contract, notification of a concluded PP Contract and / or notification of annulment of the awarding procedure.

The Law on Public Procurement stipulates separate provisions for sector PP Contracts which are awarded for performing one or more of the following activities: water supply, energy, transport, postal services and other activities.

When it comes to PPP Contracts, the procedural rules of the awarding procedure are regulated with the Law on Public Procurement. In particular, a PPP Contract can be awarded through an open or restrictive procedure, a competitive dialogue procedure or by a negotiated procedure with prior publication of a contract notice. Compared to this solution, the awarding procedure for concession of goods of general interest is shaped with the Law on Concessions and PPP. The preparatory activities for awarding a concession for goods of general interest and a PPP Contract are carried out by the concession grantor i.e.the public partner. They include a preparation of: (i) a report for previous analysis of the basic project elements; (ii) a feasibility study; (iii) an assessment of the environmental impact; and other necessary activities.

马耳他

作者：Joseph Camilleri、Stephen Muscat、Jonathan Abela Fiorentino、Christine Calleja
译者：刘志刚、熊代琨

一、概述

（一）政治、经济、社会和法律环境概述

马耳他实行自由议会民主制度，由拥有普选权的公民进行选举。宪法捍卫公民的基本人权，确保行政、司法和立法三权分立。马耳他的历史丰富多变，其文明可以追溯至公元前5200年。考古遗迹显示公元前6世纪这里曾存在腓尼基人或者迦太基人。公元前218年马耳他受罗马统治。马耳他先后被阿拉伯人、诺尔曼人和一些封建主统治。在1530年至1798年期间，耶路撒冷圣约翰骑士团（医院骑士团）接管该岛。马耳他骑士团，这是为后人所知的名字，在岛上留下了丰富的文化遗产。该岛被拿破仑•波拿巴治下的法国统治两年（1798—1800）后，转由英国统治。马耳他在1964年脱离英国独立。1964年，马耳他独立宪法确立马耳他为君主立宪制国家。1974年，马耳他通过修改宪法变更为共和国，总统是国家元首。行政权力归首相和内阁。马耳他属于英联邦成员。

马耳他是世界上最小的经济体之一。2015年以市场价格计算的马耳他国民生产总值（GDP）大约为87.965亿欧元，约等于欧盟（EU）国民生产总值的0.05%，大约是欧元区国民生产总值的0.07%。马耳他于2004年5月加入欧盟。2015年马耳他的人均国民生产总值约为20400欧元，因此马耳他被世界银行列为高收入国家，被联合国开发计划署列为人类发展指数极高的国家（位列前四分之一）。

马耳他的社会结构、态度和价值观正在快速改变。土地开发、大众旅游、信息技术、新型工作和休闲模式以及高等教育的迅速扩张正在逐渐渗透紧密交织的传统天主教社会。在诸多方面，马耳他已经成为现代欧洲城市。不过，与邻近的其他欧洲国家相比，马耳他仍然是没有明显的种族、民族或宗教分裂的相对同质化社会。

马耳他的法律体系是所谓的混合法律体系。

数百年来，马耳他的法律体系以罗马法为基础，罗马法是由查士丁尼皇帝编纂并在欧洲大陆大部分地区重新发现、发展和施行的法律。

鉴于马耳他法律体系的历史和根源，其法律根植于罗马法（大陆法）系并吸收了普通法（英国法）传统的许多特征。换言之，是混合法律体系。虽然马耳他刑法典关于盗窃的规定是受罗马法（大陆法）启发，但是英国法律的陪审团制度也被吸收进马耳他刑法典。因此马耳他法律体系是将两大法系进行融合的早期尝试。

马耳他成文法可以进行四种主要划分：
- 民法和刑法；
- 公法和私法；
- 实体法和程序法；
- 国内法和国际公法。

民法关注人之间的权利和义务，并提供救济手段，比如赔偿金或实际履行。

刑法关注违反公共秩序和反社会的故意或疏忽行为，规定诸如监禁或罚金等处罚措施。

因此民事违法和刑事犯罪的区别并不在于行为的性质，因为同样的行为既可以构成刑事犯罪也可以构成民事违法。

公法主要由以下法律组成：
- 宪法；

- 行政法；
- 刑法。

私法包括民法和商法，目的是保护私人利益。

（二）"一带一路"倡议下与中国企业合作的现状和方向

马耳他外交部网站列举的下述清单，清楚地证明马耳他与中国政府的合作长久、深入而广泛：
- 中国外交学院与马耳他地中海外交学院合作协议；
- 马耳他共和国政府与中华人民共和国政府关于马耳他给予中国长期贷款的协议；
- 马耳他共和国政府与中华人民共和国政府关于中国给予马耳他长期无息贷款的协议；
- 马耳他共和国政府与中华人民共和国政府避免双重征税和防止逃税的协议；
- 马耳他共和国政府与中华人民共和国政府促进和保护投资协议；
- 马耳他共和国政府与中华人民共和国政府在旅游领域进行合作的协议；
- 马耳他共和国教育和就业部与中华人民共和国教育部协议；
- 马耳他共和国国防部与中华人民共和国国防部协议；
- 马耳他共和国与中华人民共和国在传统中药领域合作的协议；
- 马耳他大学与中国孔子学院总部在马耳他大学设立孔子学院的协议；
- 马耳他青年和运动部与中华全国青年联合会在青年领域合作的协议；
- 马耳他共和国政府与中华人民共和国政府打击跨国犯罪的协议；
- 马耳他共和国政府与中华人民共和国政府文化合作的协议；
- 马耳他共和国政府与中华人民共和国政府海运协议；
- 马耳他共和国政府与中华人民共和国政府科学技术合作协议；
- 中华人民共和国政府拨款五百万元人民币给马耳他政府的协议；
- 马耳他地中海外交学院与中国外交学院合作协议；
- 马耳他共和国政府与中华人民共和国政府文化合作执行计划；
- 马耳他共和国政府与中华人民共和国政府建立外交关系的联合公报；
- 马耳他共和国卫生部与中华人民共和国卫生部在卫生和医药领域的合作计划；
- 马耳他共和国政府与中华人民共和国政府文化交流计划；
- 马耳他共和国政府与中华人民共和国政府2009—2012年文化交流计划；
- 马耳他共和国政府与中华人民共和国政府关于中国向马耳他提供技术援助和开发项目的协议；
- 马耳他共和国卫生、老龄和社区关怀部与中华人民共和国卫生部协议；
- 武器贸易条约；
- 建立友好城市关系协议（姊妹城市协议）；
- 民用航空运输协议；
- 在中国香港地区维持名誉领事职位的协议；
- 马耳他共和国政府与中华人民共和国政府关于打击非法运输和滥用麻醉药物和精神类物质的合作协议；
- 马耳他共和国武装力量与中华人民共和国人民解放军关于中国向马耳他无偿提供军事援助的协议；
- 马耳他共和国国防部与中华人民共和国国防部关于中国向马耳他无偿提供军事援助的协议；
- 马耳他共和国政府与中华人民共和国政府关于2002—2005年教育合作的协议；
- 外交护照和公务护照持有者相互豁免签证协议；
- 贸易和经济合作协议；
- 2005—2008年教育合作执行计划；
- 中国向马耳他提供无偿军事援助协议；
- 避免双重征税协议；
- 传统中药领域合作协议；

- 中国向马耳他提供完整项目和技术援助协议;
- 为马尔萨什洛克港防浪堤项目提供技术援助协议;
- 中国向马耳他提供开发项目和技术援助协议;
- 在传统中药领域合作协议续约;
- 马耳他共和国教育和就业部与中华人民共和国体育总局体育合作谅解备忘录;
- 马耳他共和国经济、投资和小企业部商务部与中华人民共和国知识产权局在知识产权领域的谅解备忘录;
- 马耳他共和国政府与中华人民共和国政府电影共同生产协议;
- 马耳他共和国司法、文化与地方政府部与中华人民共和国文化部关于共同支持欧洲文化城市与东亚文化城市文化交流与合作谅解备忘录;
- 马耳他共和国卫生部与中华人民共和国卫计委关于在传统中药领域合作协议。

二、投资

(一)市场准入

1. 投资监管部门

马耳他的投资监管主体是马耳他企业局(以下简称"企业局"),系依据《企业法》(《马耳他法》第463章)设立,以履行上述法律赋予的职能。

总体上,企业局具有如下职能:

(1)按照马耳他政府制订的目标、政策和目的启动、引导和促进马耳他经济和社会的发展;

(2)引导与各种企业相关的马耳他战略,并通过与其他政府机构、国家部门和私营部门协调一致地共同发展和施行以保证战略的执行;

(3)发展马耳他企业,并为其提供所需的协助和支持服务;

(4)将马耳他作为企业注册地进行推广,对该等推广提供协助和协调;

(5)促进、协助和发展马耳他企业的设立、竞争力和国际化;

(6)发展技术、人力资源和技能基础,加强从事战略评估和规划、进行创新和开展研究、开发和设计活动的能力;

(7)为企业提供和管理土地、场所、房产、服务和设施;

(8)管理需要资金支付的计划、补助和其他金融工具,包括来源于国外的资金支付;

(9)就涉及本法实施与目的的事务为马耳他政府提供咨询;

(10)行使马耳他政府赋予的其他职能。

在行使上述职能时,企业局还有权:

(1)进行各种形式的投资,包括单独持股或与他人合伙,向企业贷款,认购、承销或买卖公司股票和债券,向他人贷款,向企业发放补助,管理和控制企业,但是在上述交易中应合理管控企业局投资或负债的风险;

(2)收购、出售或租赁土地、工厂、机器设备和其他资产,和以其他方式将资产给予第三方使用;

(3)经营、开发土地,实施土地工程,维护工程或协助维护工程;

(4)提供与其功能相关的咨询、其他服务或设施,或协助前述提供行为;

(5)一般性地从事与其功能一致或有利于其功能实现的其他事项。

2. 与投资相关的法律法规

除了前文已提及的《企业法》,规范投资的法律法规主要有四部,即:

- 《商业促进法》(《马耳他法》第325章);
- 《开发公司法》(《马耳他法》第202章);
- 《工业援助条例》(《马耳他法》第159章)及相关规定;
- 《商业促进规定》,依据上述《商业促进法》制定。

3. 投资形式

企业局将下述产业作为马耳他的经济支柱产业而给予特别关注：①高端制造；②生命科学；③通信；④航空；⑤教育；⑥旅游和医疗；⑦医疗保健。

4. 市场准入和审查标准

企业如希望通过"投资优惠与保护"部分介绍的企业局管理的项目而在马耳他经营并享受鼓励措施，其市场准入和审查标准，与在马耳他设立公司（或其他商业合伙）相同。

（二）外汇法规

1. 外汇监管部门

马耳他的外汇监管部门是根据《中央银行法》(《马耳他法》第204章）而建立的马耳他中央银行。

2. 外汇法律法规简要介绍

马耳他相关的外汇立法是《对外交易法》(《马耳他法》第233章）。

《对外交易法》建立了所谓"外部交易"的自由化框架。该框架包括居民与非居民自然人或其他实体之间的资本交易和经常项目交易，而无论该交易是否在马耳他境内。同时，还包括居民或者居民之间的外汇业务操作。①

为上述法律之目的，外汇被定义为以任何纸币、硬币、支票、汇票、旅行支票、信用证、本票、汇票、单据、信用卡、借记卡、其他银行卡或任何通过电子、磁方式记入价值的，使不特定个人代替货币用作支付的方式；或者，以马耳他法定货币之外的任何国家货币体现的其他支付方式。上述法律中提到的外汇包括任何即期收取在任何信贷机构的信贷或余额外汇的权利。

3. 对外国公司外汇管理的要求

除非另有规定，或者财政部部长根据《对外交易法》发出命令，所有对外交易和有关付款均不受限制。

但是在例外情况出现时，财政部部长可根据马耳他中央银行的建议，制定对资本交易和相关付款的限制，至于该限制的性质是特定的还是普遍的，则视需要而定：

前提是该限制不得向任何欧盟成员国实施。

基于上述规则目的，当财政部部长根据马耳他中央银行的建议行事并宣布：①马耳他国际收支差额出现危机；或②进出马耳他的资本流动给金融体系稳定性造成了严重困难或产生了造成严重困难的威胁，此时视为出现了例外情况。

如限制的基础不再存在，上述的任何外汇限制法规将会被财务部长立即撤销，在任何情况下，外汇限制法规有效期将不会超过6个月。但是基于《联合国宪章》《欧盟加入条约》或者对马耳他国家利益进行单方保护而产生的国家义务而对任何国家、个人或组织对资本、交易以及相关支付进行控制或者限制的权力例外。

（三）金融

在马耳他，许多金融机构的名声良好，多年来表现非常出色，包括汇丰银行、隆巴德银行、APS银行、BNF银行以及瓦莱塔银行。上述银行均有国际业务。相关监管立法为《银行法》(《马耳他法》第371章）。

企业局也提供和／或促进某些金融业务，将在下文予以介绍。

---

① "资本交易"是指因资本转移或者流动而产生的外部交易，包括：不动产的转让；直接投资；发行、出售或者购买有价证券，包括公司股份、债券、存单或者其他类似的负债的行为；在集体投资计划、人寿保险和年金长期政策中（无论是否和指数挂钩），以单位形式进行发行、出售或者购买的行为；贷款、借款、支付或分期偿还贷款；提供担保或者任何其他形式的担保付款；认股权证、期权、期货和其衍生品，以及其他用于投资目的的金融工具；信贷机构存款；礼物和捐赠基金；在与中央银行协商后，由财政部部长基于政府宪报公告而决定的其他类型交易。

(四）土地政策

1. 与土地有关的法律法规简介

概括而言，规制土地（或任何不动产）权属取得的法律是《民法典》(《马耳他法》第 16 章)，土地权属一般而言包括所有权、永佃权和租赁权等，这些都是权利人的专属权利。对于前两种权属，《民法典》要求由公证员起草一份公开契据；对于第三种权属，要求一份不公开的书面文书（不需要公证员介入），除非授予权属的期限少于 2 年，此种情形下不需要书面形式。

在马耳他购买土地（无论是所有权还是永佃权）涉及的技术性细节，可以在《公共注册法》(第 56 章) 找到，这些细节都由受托发表公开契据的公证员处理。值得一提的是，公证员被认为是公职人员，对普通民众负有责任。公证员的作用是在契据中确认、核实在马耳他取得土地的人取得完整有效的所有权。

2. 外国企业取得土地的规定

外国企业，不得在马耳他购买土地（或任何其他不动产），但取得国内税收局资本转移税部许可的除外。

该部应该在收到申请之日起 35 日内颁发许可，但是否颁发许可取决于按照其质量服务章程提交的申请是否正确无误。

除在对取得不动产绝对没有限制的指定地区外，非居民只允许在马耳他购买一处不动产。

马耳他或欧盟成员国居民的配偶可与其一起购买不动产，因其均属于"马耳他居民"。

在欧盟成员国成立、经营的公司也可以自由购买不动产，前提是其股权的 75% 或更多份额由一名或多名欧盟公民持有。

在任何其他情形下，都不允许法律实体购买不动产。但若工业或旅游项目需要用地，或该项目有利于马耳他的经济发展，主管部长可颁布特别许可，甚至可以向非欧盟实体颁发许可。

在后一种情况下，企业局及相关部门，需要在促进并维持投资方面发挥重要作用，下文将予以解释。

（五）公司的成立和解散

1. 企业的形式

用专业术语表达，公司被视为一种商业合伙。根据马耳他法律，商业合伙可以采取以下形式：

（1）合伙；
（2）合伙或有限合伙；
（3）公司。

2. 成立程序

公司通过将资本划分为股份由股东持有的方式成立。股东的责任限于各自持有股份的未出资金额。需要至少两名股东签订章程并认缴出资，公司方能依据该法有效成立，一人公司除外。

3. 解散的路径和要求

出现下列情形的，公司应予解散并清算：

（1）公司通过特别决议由法院解散并进行清算；
（2）公司通过特别决议自行解散并进行清算。

除上述解散方式外，出现下列情形的，可由法院解散公司并进行清算：

（1）公司停止营业达连续 24 个月的；
（2）公司不能清偿债务的，且出现下列情形的，应当由法院解散公司：

- 公司股东人数少于两人并持续 6 个月以上的；
- 董事人数少于《企业法》第 137 条规定的最低人数并持续 6 个月以上的；
- 法院认为有充足理由准许解散公司并进行清算的；
- 公司章程规定的存续期间（若有）届满，或公司章程规定的清算事由（若有）出现，且期限届满或事由出现前,公司股东大会未通过自行解散的决议的。

(六)公司合并

公司合并可以采取下列方式:
(1)吸收合并;
(2)新设合并。

吸收合并是一个公司向另一个或另几个被吸收公司的股东发行股票并支付部分现金(若有),以换取这个(些)公司的所有资产和负债,现金不得超过所发行股票票面价值的10%。

新设合并是两个或两个以上公司新设一个公司,并将其全部资产和负债交付给该公司,换取新公司的股份和部分现金(若有),现金不得超过所发行股票票面价值的10%。

(七)竞争规制

1. 竞争规制监管部门

马耳他监管竞争规制的主体是依据《竞争与消费者事务局法》设立的马耳他竞争与消费者事务局(《马耳他法》第510章)。

2. 竞争法简介

马耳他规制竞争并保障公平交易的法律是《竞争法》(《马耳他法》第379章)。

3. 规制竞争的措施

依据前述法律,禁止下列情形,也就是说,以在马耳他阻止、限制或扭曲竞争为目的或具有此种效果的任何企业间的协议、企业协会的任何决定和企业间的任何协同行为均予禁止。尤其是,在不影响本款规定的普遍适用性的情况下,任何下列协议、决定或做法均予禁止:

(1)直接或间接固定购销价格或其他交易条件的;
(2)限制或控制生产、市场、技术发展或投资的;
(3)分割市场或供应来源的;
(4)对协议之外的相同交易的相对人,在交易条件上实行差别待遇,使其处于不利的竞争地位;
(5)订立合同时强迫对方接受依合同性质或商业惯例与合同标的无关的附加义务的。

依照前述规定禁止的协议或决定依法无效并不得强制履行。

但前述规定不适用于下列情形:
(1)企业间的任何协议;
(2)企业协会作出的任何决定;
(3)任何协同行为,如果其有利于改进产品或服务的生产或分配,或推动技术或经济发展,并可以使消费者公平分享利益,并且不:

- 向相关企业强加任何对于实现该目的并非必不可少的限制;
- 就协议、决定或协同行动所涉的大部分产品,使相关企业消除或明显减少竞争成为可能。

此外,若企业间的协议、决定或协同行动对于相关市场的影响微不足道,则不在上述禁止之列。

禁止企业在马耳他滥用市场支配地位。

企业有下列情形的,应被视为滥用市场支配地位:
(1)直接或间接地强加过分的或不公平的购销价格或其他交易条件的;
(2)限制生产、市场或技术发展,损害消费者利益;
(3)对相同交易的不同相对人,在交易条件上实行差别待遇,包括价格歧视,从而使任何或部分交易相对人处于不利的竞争地位;
(4)订立合同时强迫对方接受依合同性质或商业惯例与合同标的无关的附加义务的。

相关企业或企业协会针对局长作出的侵权判定、停止侵权令或守法令、行政罚款和/或按日计算的罚金,可根据《竞争法》规定于收到通知后20日内向上诉法庭提交上诉申请。

上诉不停止命令、行政罚款和/或按日计算的罚金的执行。除非上诉法庭,应上诉方合理的请求,并考虑局长提交的意见后，在其认为适当的条件下，中止命令、行政罚款和/或按日计算的罚金的执行，并陈述理由，以待最终的上诉决定。

上诉法庭考虑侵权的严重性及持续时间以及任何加重或减轻情节，可以全部或部分确认或撤销局长的决定和/或命令，撤销或变更局长作出的行政罚款和/或按日计算的罚金。

局长及任何向上诉法庭上诉的当事方对上诉法庭决定不服的，可自上诉法庭决定之日起20日内，向上诉法院登记处提出申请，就法律问题提起上诉。

（八）税收

1. 税制和规定

马耳他成为众多公司青睐的住所地有诸多原因，包括：
- 施行完全归属制；
- 广泛的双重征税条约系统，加上即使没有有效双边条约时也可享受的优惠；
- 退还税收优惠政策——无论股东为居民或非居民，公司盈利均向股东分红；
- 对于个人而言理想的税收居民地位；
- 遵守欧盟不歧视制度。

2. 主要的税种和税率

广义上说，马耳他的主要税种有两个：个人税和公司税。

马耳他个人税的基本规定是：如果个人的住所地在马耳他或经常居住在马耳他，应当就自己的（包括配偶及受抚养的子女的）任何来源的全部收入进行申报。如果个人的住所地不在马耳他，或不在马耳他经常居住，应当对自己（包括配偶及受抚养的子女）在马耳他取得的或来源于马耳他的全部收入，以及汇入马耳他的任何收入进行申报。

在马耳他，个人所得税实行累进税，即收入越高，缴税越多。个人税主要通过暂缴系统、最终结算系统或自我评估的方式进行缴纳。就暂缴系统而言，某一特定年度的税负在取得收入的相同期间征收，主要适用于收入来源于贸易、商业、受聘等的人。最终结算系统主要适用于雇员和领退休金者，是为了精确计算报酬的扣税金额。该方法确保在取得报酬时，从中扣除准确的税额，从而减少大额退税或税收申报的发生。不通过这两种系统征收的税而以通过自我评估的方式，于税收结算到期日，即收入年度次年的6月30日缴纳。

根据所得税立法，马耳他居民公司就其全球所得和资本利得缴税，公司税率为35%。设立于马耳他境外但在马耳他境内从事商业活动的外国公司应就来源于马耳他境内的收入缴税。值得注意的是，如果公司的管理和控制位于马耳他，则在税收上作为居民公司对待。

当公司按照35%的标准税率缴税时，公司分红后，股东有权就公司缴纳的部分或全部税款申请退税。该减免制度的目的是消除在分红时可能发生的双重征税。这样公司利润只需在公司层面缴税。

3. 税收申报与优惠

纳税申报程序如上所述。

在税收优惠方面，马耳他采用基于收入来源和国别的避免双重征税办法。

避免双重征税的马耳他税制不仅包括条约豁免而且包括单方豁免，从而确保即使没有避免双重征税协议，来源于海外的收入也不会被双重征税。

按照国内立法，只要符合一系列条件，支付给非居民的分红、利息和许可费无需预扣税。另外，只要符合相关条件，尤其是被转让股份的公司的唯一或主要资产不包括马耳他的不动产，非居民转让公司证券所得无需交税。

而且，对某些重要经营实体实行优惠税率或免征税：
- 银行和金融机构、基金经理/基金管理人：与在马耳他注册的所有公司同等征税。
- 保险公司：对于保险业务总收入的确定实行特别规定。
- 保险经理：与在马耳他注册的所有公司同等征税。
- 投资基金：一般而言，在马耳他注册的基金，只要其位于马耳他的资产不超过85%，免征所得税和资本利得税。

- 信托：若并非所有的信托受益人都以马耳他为住所或居住在马耳他，且信托资产位于马耳他境外，无需缴纳所得税（或过户税）。
- 基金会：基金会可视为马耳他公司，并受益于马耳他的完全归属制。基金会也可选择与信托同样的方式缴税。
- 退休计划：获批准的退休计划免于征收所得税和资本利得税，但免税范围不包括位于马耳他境内的不动产。

为吸引高素质人士到金融服务业，马耳他于2011年启动了一个以高收入外国行政管理人员为对象的激励计划。对于获得相关部门许可或承认在马耳他境内从事金融业务的公司，受雇于该类公司担任高级职务但住所位于马耳他境外的个人，可以享受税率15%的所得税。

（九）证券

1. 与证券有关的法律法规简介

上述《银行法》和《金融服务法》（包括依据该两部法律制定的任何法规）是规制监管在马耳他从事金融服务的银行和其他机构的主要立法，构成该领域的法律框架。根据这些主要法律还发布了众多的规制银行交易特定方面的法令和规制信贷机构的规定。民法典和商法典提供了规制借贷、存款、付款、抵销、财产的质押和抵押交易的各种基本原则。

2. 证券市场的监管

《银行法》包括两条非常重要的规则，即：

- 除持有有权部门依据银行法授予许可的公司外，任何公司不得在马耳他境内开展银行业务。
- 除持有有权部门依据本法授予许可的信贷机构外，任何获得境外许可或持有相同授权的信贷机构不得在马耳他境内开设分支机构、代理处或代表处，不得设立附属机构。

根据《金融服务主管机构法》，依据该法设立的主管机构在行使其职权时，有权以合理的方式进入被许可人的任何经营场所和/或办公场所，有权取得被许可人的任何相关文件和/或记录，包括任何电话或其他记录，有权取得与该主管机构许可的或属于其监管职能范围内活动有关的任何其他信息。

主管机构还有权发布命令，按照该主管机构书面规定的冻结期限和条件，冻结被许可人，或命令上指明的任何第三方名下的资金和/或包括银行账号在内的其他资产。命令也可以禁止被许可人转移、处置或放弃对任何此类资金或资产的占有。命令也可应外国执行或监管机构的请求而发布。

该主管机构的权力十分宽泛。

3. 外国企业从事证券交易的要求

证券业是高度专业化的行业，受诸多法规约束，法律规定的意图是为外国企业从事该行业提供便利。

（十）投资优惠与保护

1. 优惠政策的体系

为了提振工业和发展创新企业，企业局制定了各种激励措施。
企业局为致力于成长、增加附加值和提供就业的企业提供各种临时的激励措施。

2. 对特定产业和地区的支持

从事制造业、信息通信技术、客户服务中心、医疗保健、药店、生物科技、航空和水运服务、教育培训、物流等的企业可以享受这些激励措施。

3. 投资保护

企业局不时发布很多临时激励计划，以下是一些值得关注的：

（1）中小企业创新扶助

该措施向所有符合激励条件的中小企业开放，允许这些企业以税额减免的方式收回向大型企业和研究与知识传播组织借用高素质人才产生的部分费用。

扶助采用税额减免的方式给予，金额不超过符合条件的费用的50%。

（2）投资扶助税额减免（2014—2020）

投资扶助税额减免旨在保持马耳他地区工业和经济的发展。该措施通过鼓励新企业的设立和现有企业的扩大、发展促进初始投资。

（3）研发项目扶助（税额减免）

该项激励措施允许公司就开展的与公司业务有关的研发项目所直接或间接产生的费用申请税额免除。符合条件的项目应当以解决科技难题、实现科技领域的进步为目的。

（4）商业发展和持续

商业发展和持续计划旨在促进有望推动马耳他地区发展、支持现有企业在重组期间持续经营的增值项目。

（5）创新和发明行业符合条件的就业（个人税）

该措施通过财务激励暂时减少税务支出，促进在目前本地劳动力市场不能满足的岗位上雇用非居民。

（6）研发可行性研究（2014—2020）

鉴于研发计划通常伴有较高风险，建议企业进行研发可行性研究，以确定拟进行的研发项目的关键因素系建立在稳健性原则基础上。

（7）研发（2014—2020）

该措施扶持为获取可产生创新产品和解决方案的知识而进行的行业研究或试验开发。

（8）启动融资（2017—2020）

该措施的目标是通过扶持在启动和早期发展阶段即展示出可行商业概念的小型初创企业，帮助创新企业在其发展的初级阶段融资。

（9）研发创新税额减免

任何企业，只要雇用一名获得或正在攻读科学、信息技术或工程博士学位的人士至少12个月，即可享受该措施。受益者将被授予10 000欧元的税额减免，若申请人超过了单个企业的可分配限额，税额减免的上限将相应调整。

（10）商业启动

企业局通过商业启动措施向启动阶段的马耳他企业提供种子基金。该措施旨在扶持在初级发展阶段具有可行性商业概念的小型初创企业。

（11）对高效能热电联产的投资扶助

企业局与能源水利部合作，帮助企业投资热电联产设备（即同时产生热能和电能和/或机械能的能效方案）。

（12）知识转化

该激励计划通过支持对现有及新员工的培训和再培训为解决技术短缺提供框架，旨在支持知识转化、获取与产业知识技术要求相一致的新技能。

（13）微投资

该计划的目标是鼓励企业投资业务，创新、扩张、实施遵循指令或发展运营。

（14）软贷款

软贷款通过对符合条件的部分金融投资提供低利率的贷款从而扶持企业。

（15）对Ta' Qali和Ta' Dbieġi工艺村的车间、相关零售店的扶助

该激励措施旨在帮助位于Ta' Qali和Ta' Dbieġi工艺村的企业。

（16）小型商业场地申请

（17）商会扶助

商会一般从事支持特定行业的企业共同发展和成长的活动。此类活动包括建立关系网、信息收集研究和制定行业标准。

（18）餐饮服务能力建设

该计划的范围是协助餐饮企业雇用厨师以支持服务能力建设、创新及经营发展。企业（包括个体

经营者）通过对一定比例的符合条件的支出和具有国际经验厨师的工资进行税额减免的方式得到扶持。

（19）取得资格（2014—2020）

取得资格是一项扶持个人发展、取得产业要求的资格和证书的计划。该激励措施适用于参加可以获得证书、文凭、学位或研究生学位课程学习的个人。

（20）Gozo 地区运输费补助计划

该计划通过削减岛际运输费用，扶持在 Gozo 地区经营的生产企业。

（21）利率补贴

贷款利率补贴旨在扶持制造企业进行的新投资项目。

（22）贷款担保

贷款担保帮助企业获取融资以协助企业收购资产实现更有效和高效的生产和服务提供。该激励计划的主要目标是扶持制造企业进行的新投资项目。

（23）微担保计划（2017—2020）

资金获得的限制常常阻碍小型企业进行新投资项目，从而可能导致商业机会的丧失。微担保计划的目标是通过便利小型企业获得债务融资来加速发展。

（24）租金补贴

该计划扶持从事符合要求的业务而需要临时或永久性工业场所的小型企业。

（25）贸易促进

该激励措施旨在扶持愿意开创新市场或在现有国际市场上推出新服务或产品的企业。[①]

三、贸易

（一）贸易主管部门

根据《贸易许可法》（《马耳他法》第 441 章），由商务部部长或该部长指定的人或机构负责对贸易的管理。

（二）贸易法律法规简介

关于贸易的立法主要参看《贸易许可法》（《马耳他法》第 441 章），其对规范商业活动和与商业活动相关的事宜作出了规定。

在该法中，"商业活动"的定义是任何贸易或经济行为，包括商品买卖、提供规定的服务，不论该等商业活动是否在商业营业场所进行，但不包括由其他法律所规范的商业活动。

（三）贸易管理

前法详细规定了进行前文所定义之商业活动的条件，即：

（1）商业营业场所内部及其外部附近区域应一直保持干净整洁状态。任何从事商业活动的人应负责人行道、人行道下方空间和商业营业场所门口街道空间的清洁。营业时间结束后，禁止（商业活动）持证人在人行道、人行道下方空间和商业营业场所门口街道空间遗留任何垃圾或物品。

（2）在商业营业场所进行的商业活动或其中储存的物品不应当：

对邻居造成干扰；可能引发火灾或爆炸；散发蒸发物、烟、蒸汽、气体、粉尘或向大气排放可能有害健康的有毒或刺鼻气味；发出噪音。

（3）将物品摆放到营业场所外部进行展示销售时，该商业活动的负责人应当保证该等行为不会妨碍路上的行人，且该展示物品的摆放不应超越人行道的 50 厘米范围。

（4）对于包含交通工具销售或修理的商业活动，不得在街道上展示、修理或清洗交通工具。任何种类的交通工具，不论是商业还是其他类别，不论是崭新还是二手，均不得以展示出售为目的，标注"待售"或任何类似表达（包括展示电话和 / 或手机号码）停放在公共区域。

---

① 参见马耳他企业局官网。

（5）杂志、任何不适宜未成年人使用或消费的物品或物资或任何不适宜通常使用的物品，不应当售卖给未成年人或以任何能被未成年人或普通大众接触到的方式展示在商业营业所中。

（6）不得向未满17岁的人出售酒类或烟草。

（7）①自晚上9点到次日凌晨4点，酒类饮品只能在下列场所以店堂内享用的方式进行销售或提供：

- 经正式许可为会所的营业场所；
- 结婚礼堂；
- 经马耳他旅游主管部门许可为餐饮机构的商业营业场所，其首要目的是销售食物和店堂内享用的酒类饮品。

②任何时间都禁止沿街小贩和市场小贩销售或提供酒类饮品。

③不得在不允许销售酒类饮品的商业营业场所储存酒类饮品。

（8）每日下午1点至4点，晚上7点至次日早上7点之间，禁止在商业营业场所使用锤子或机械发出噪音，使得噪音外泄，造成对邻居的干扰。

（9）每日晚上11点至次日早上9点，下午1点至4点之间，禁止在市区内的商业活动通过现场乐队或扩音等方式演奏音乐发出噪音，使得噪音外泄，造成对邻居的干扰。

（10）在经营场所中的商业活动包括制造活动的，可在该经营场所零售该场所所制造的产品。

（11）禁止沿街售卖、车载售卖或在学校附近进行售卖，除非是售卖冰激凌或餐饮。

（四）进出口商品检验检疫

《马耳他法》中包含一系列关于检疫的规则，主要与植物源的进口相关。这些规则是基于久经考证的欧盟规则而制定。

（五）海关管理

作为欧盟成员国，马耳他海关承担着保护欧洲外部边界的重大责任。欧盟成员国需废除欧盟内部边界的日常管控，然而威胁欧盟社会和公民安全的有组织的跨境犯罪活动日益增加，需要有效控制。

无用的贸易壁垒期结束后，当今的马耳他海关和所有现代海关一样，通过结合欧共体和国家层面上商业和经济政策中贸易流动更顺畅的需求来行使其职责，持续对新的和不同的事物保持开放态度，同时保护马耳他和其他欧盟公民的利益以及文化特征。

欧盟的海关政策是鼓励和支持贸易和公平交易的重要工具，其通过发展欧盟内的产业来增加就业和商业竞争力。马耳他海关代表马耳他一致实施了这项政策，与欧盟实体展开紧密合作。

此外，通过征收包括生产和消费税在内的税赋，海关代表马耳他公众和消费者履行重要而敏感的职责。总而言之，马耳他海关作为马耳他和共同体需求的国家和国际代表，对提高马耳他和共同体系统的质量和竞争力都作出了贡献。

除了所有海关机构一直以来履行的传统职责，最近海关新增了十分重要的职责。除了与其他当地主管机关（如警察局）合作，海关一直位于打击走私、新旧非法运送武器、毒品、烟草、洗钱、假冒商品、濒危保护物种和艺术品的前线。马耳他海关也一直在前线打击放射性物质、有害废物、非法或过期药物、对健康和环境造成损害的物品的运输。

四、劳动

（一）劳动法律法规简介

马耳他法律中包含一整套与雇佣相关的法律法规，很多是保护雇员的条件，其尝试在雇主和雇员各自的权利义务之间寻得平衡。

《雇佣和劳资关系法》（《马耳他法》第452章）中包含一系列最基本就业条件。换句话说，如雇主和雇员签订的合同中约定的条件低于前法规定的最基本条件，则该等行为违法，这将导致合同无效。

与雇佣相关的法律法规有：

- 养老金就业条例令；
- （女性回归就业）税收减免规则；
- （个人税）创新和创意合格就业规则；
- （就业或养老金收入）扣减规则；
- （个人税）航空合格就业规则；
- 就业条件（规定）法；
- 残疾人士（就业）法；
- 雇用残疾人士标准百分比令；
- 残疾人士指定雇用令；
- 残疾人士兼职雇用规定；
- 公共交通（就业规则）法；
- 居留许可费和就业许可费规定；
- 第三国国民高端就业人才入境和居留条件规定；
- 第三国国民季节性工人入境和逗留条件规定；
- 商船运输（青年人就业）规定；
- 就业委员会法；
- 就业和培训服务法；
- 就业申请人登记令（第二部分）；
- 劳动力记录（就业开始或结束）规定；
- 职业介绍所规定；
- 兼职就业登记规定；
- 雇用和劳资关系法；
- 集体裁员（保护就业）规定；
- 企业转让（保护就业）规定；
- 雇用和劳资关系解释令；
- 孕妇保护（就业）规定；
- 青年人（就业）规定；
- 就业平等待遇规定；
- 政府服务适用性展期（就业平等待遇）规定；
- 政府服务适用性展期（保护孕妇就业）规定；
- 就业状况国家标准令；
- 政府服务适用性展期（就业状况）规定；
- 自主创业平等待遇命令；
- 议会成员（公职人员就业）规定。

（二）雇用外国员工的要求

1. 工作许可

非欧盟成员国公民需取得工作许可才能在马耳他工作。

2. 申请步骤

申请"居留就业许可"，申请人应向相关主管部门提交一系列材料如下：
- 申请人护照；
- 申请人彩色护照照片；
- 疾病保险一切险；
- 健康检查证明原件（"健康检查同意表"）；
- （外国）银行流水；

- 租赁协议；
- 租金申报表；
- 个人简历；
- 工作职位描述；
- 申请人的工作推荐信或证明；
- 资质证明和认证／认可；
- 雇主注明工作地点的说明信；
- 马耳他签证／居留许可；
- 进入申根区和马耳他的机票；
- 雇用合同。
- 不予退还的受理费280.5欧元。

3. 社会保险

根据《社会保险法》(《马耳他法》第318章)，该法第一附表第一部分中规定的雇佣关系均应当购买保险，第二部分排除的情形除外。

前法中的"雇用"是指在马耳他以书面或口头方式明示或暗示的任何服务合同或学徒合同所形成的雇佣关系。雇主从雇员工资中代扣一部分用于缴纳社保。

（三）出入境

1. 签证类型

和大多数欧盟成员国一样，马耳他也加入了申根条约。

要入境申根区国家，申请人应当向其访问的主要目的地国家的使领馆递交欧洲签证申请。当申请人准备访问多个申根成员国（在每个国家停留时间长短差不多）时，申请人应当向其入境申根区的首个国家的使领馆提交签证申请。因此，如申请人将马耳他作为主要目的地或申根区的首次入境国，其必须向马耳他使领馆或其代理机构提交申请。

签证申请必须通过书面形式提出，并提供签证申请表中所要求的全部材料。签证申请表可从马耳他大使馆、领事馆或网上免费获得。

签证申请表必须完整并清楚地填写，由申请人签名，并附上如下材料：
- 有效的旅行证件（护照），有效期不得少于3个月；
- 两张护照尺寸的白底彩色照片，面部应清晰可见；
- 签证费。

申请申根短期停留签证，可于计划行程日的前3个月内进行申请。一般来说，申请会在7～15天内审核。个别情况下，审核期会被延长到最多30天，例外情况下，审核期会被延长至最多60天。建议至少在计划行程日前15天提出签证申请，因为签证的审核时间不能保证。申根国家多次短期停留签证持有者可在该签证过期前提出签证申请，前提是该签证已生效至少6个月。欧盟公民的家庭成员提出的签证申请会在尽可能短的时间内进行审核。

2. 出境限制

马耳他对于出境没有限制。

（四）工会和劳工组织

马耳他的工会由《承认工会条例》中一系列具体的法规来进行规范，其中规定了授予和撤销承认工会作为在工作单位中唯一集中谈判机构为员工提供更多保护的情形。

（五）劳动争议

非司法途径上，劳动争议通过经认可的工会和用人单位谈判解决；司法途径上，劳动争议在名为劳资裁判庭的特别法庭解决。可在上文提到的《雇佣和劳资关系法》中找到规定劳动争议的法条。

五、知识产权

(一)知识产权法律法规简介

总体来说,所谓的"知识产权"由《著作权法》《商标法》《专利和设计法》提供保护,这些法律包含了详细而复杂的保护原则。

(二)专利申请

当某项发明属于《专业和设计法》(《马耳他法》第 417 章)规定的可申请专利的情形,专利申请人可通过规定的形式提出专利申请,并提交工业产权审核办公室,申请材料应包含:①申请授予专利的申请书;②发明的说明书;③一项或多项权利要求;④说明书或权利要求中提到的图纸;⑤发明的摘要;⑥发明的名称,名称需清楚准确地描述该发明的技术。前述①到⑥还适用于本段生效时仍在进行中的申请。申请应当列明其全部发明者。如果申请人不是发明者,或不是唯一发明者,则应当说明他有权提起该申请的法律依据。申请还应当支付规定的申请费。

(三)商标注册

工业产权审核办公室接受通过电子形式提交商标申请。该流程很直接,通过"wizard"工具对申请者进行全程指导,向申请者发出电邮申请确认函和分配商标申请号。

此外,通过电子形式提交申请的申请人或代理人,可见到其后续申请信息已储存于系统中。为同一个商标申请多种分类时,申请人可提交一个商标申请(不用像人工申请时提交多个申请),每个类别都会被分配到一个不同的商标号码,工业产权审核办公室会对各个类别的申请分开处理。款项通过信用卡或银行转账即时支付。

(四)知识产权保护措施

组成知识产权法的一系列法律,包含了十分具体且复杂的规定,充分保护知识产权权利人免受侵害,保护方式包括相当于或接近等于禁止令的禁止性命令、认定保护和包括精神损害赔偿等在内的赔偿措施。

六、环境保护

(一)环境保护主管部门

负责监管环境保护的部门是环境和资源局,独立于行政部门,其成立的法律依据是《环境保护法》(《马耳他法》第 549 章)。

(二)环境保护法律法规简介

上述法律,除了规定成立上述环境和资源局外,还对环境保护作出了非常全面的规定,并赋予环境和资源局权力,并规定了其他相关事项。

尤其是,前法项下颁布的《环境保护(预防和补救措施)规定》授权环境和资源局局长本人或通过其下属公务员,在持有主管环境的部长签署的身份证明的情况下,检查马耳他任何地点、车辆、船只、平台、飞机或其他航天器,或任何在马耳他领海外但属于马耳他国籍的车辆、船只或飞行器的权力,以此查明环保等级,调查涉嫌违反前法、其项下规定或操作规程的行为,对该等违法行为进行证据保全。

(三)环境保护评价

鉴于马耳他有限的国土面积,要平衡开发商和环境保护主义者各自的合法权益不是一件容易的事。至少原则上,每任政府都力求在进行更多环保举措的同时,给予开发商和土地所有者最大限度发挥其资产价值的空间。时任政府也正考虑在宪法中确立环境保护的地位，这项修改需要众议院 2/3 多数表决通过。

七、争议解决

（一）争议解决的方式和机构

总体上讲，马耳他的法院既有刑事管辖权也有民事管辖权。而民事法律还能再细分为调整人与人（既包括自然人也包括法人）之间或人与行政政府之间法律关系的不同法律领域，即民法、商法、行政法和宪法。

除了极少数例外，每个判决都可上诉。

如争议双方选择通过仲裁解决争议，不论是事前协议还是事后一致同意，均可提交仲裁。在特定情况下，马耳他法律允许对仲裁裁决进行上诉，除非双方一致排除上诉权。

在特定有限的情况下，仲裁是强制的。

（二）适用法律

所有在马耳他的人，无一例外均享有宪法对以下基本自由赋予的完整保护：
- 生存权保护；
- 保护免受擅自逮捕或羁押；
- 保护免受强制劳动；
- 保护免受不人道待遇；
- 保护免受无偿剥夺财产；
- 保护家庭和其他财产的隐私权；
- 保障法律保护的规定
- 保护宗教信仰自由；
- 保护言论自由；
- 保护集会结社自由；
- 禁止出逐出境；
- 保护迁徙自由；
- 保护免受种族歧视等。

八、其他

（一）反商业贿赂

1. 反商业贿赂法律法规简介

《马耳他法》第 326 章中确立了反腐败常务委员会作为监管反商业贿赂的主管机构。重要的是，该委员会在履行其职责时无需受其他任何人或机构的指导或控制。

前述委员会的职责是：

（1）对于（2）和（3）段中提到的人被指控或涉嫌进行或参与的腐败行为，当委员会认为已有证据足以提起调查时，对该等指控或嫌疑进行调查并作出报告；

（2）当委员会认为公职人员（包括部长和政务次官）的行为可能存在腐败、与腐败行为有关联或有牵连时，对该等公职人员的行为进行调查并作出报告；

（3）当委员会认为如下人员的行为可能存在腐败、与腐败行为有关联或有牵连时，对该等公职人员的行为进行调查并作出报告：该人员被合伙或其他主体授权，或具有与该合伙或其他组织行政有关的职能（马耳他政府、一个或多个政府主管机关、当地政府部门、法定团体、前述合伙或其结合体对该等合伙或其他主体享有控制权或实施有效控制）。

（4）对（3）段提到的政府部门、当地政府主管部门、法定团体或其他主体的行为和流程进行检查，以更好地发现腐败行为，对可能导致腐败行为的工作方式或流程提出修改建议，并作出报告；

（5）根据部长，或被（3）段提到的政府部门、当地政府主管部门、法定组织或其他主体所授权的人员要求，就消灭腐败行为的方法向该等人员进行指导、建议和协助。

2. 惩罚性措施

前法对"腐败行为"的定义参照了《刑法典》(《马耳他法》第9章）中的一些规定，用于惩处违反公众信任的犯罪，其中包含刑罚/惩罚性措施。

（二）工程承包

1. 许可系统

根据《开发规划法》(《马耳他法》第552章），必须取得开发许可方可进行开发。

前述规定中的"开发"是指进行建筑、工程、采石、采矿或其他在陆地或海域上方、中间、内部、下方进行的建筑、拆除、改建、广告投放，或对土地用途、建筑物用途或海域用途做任何重大改变，其中有一系列的技术例外，该等技术例外是以个案形式来决定的。

2. 禁止区域

马耳他国土大致被分为所谓的"开发区"和"非开发区"。在"开发区"，允许进行前文定义的开发活动，而"非开发区"仅能用于十分有限的用途，特别是和农业相关的用途，不允许在该区域内开展真正意义上的开发。

3. 招标和投标

《政府采购规定》中规定了政府采购的规则，并提供了一系列主张透明性的十分详尽的规定。总的来说，经济上最有竞争力、技术上全部符合的投标就是成功的投标。任何认为自身权益受到合同负责人侵害的利益相关方均可向特别委员会提交申诉，委员会将审查整个过程并作出决定。

Malta

Authors: Joseph Camilleri, Stephen Muscat, Jonathan Abela Fiorentino, Christine Calleja
Translators: David Liu, Xiong Daikun

I. Overview

A. General introduction to the Political, Economic, Social and Legal Environment of Malta

Malta is a liberal parliamentary democracy, with regular elections based on universal suffrage. Its constitution safeguards the fundamental human rights of citizens, and guarantees a separation between the executive, judicial and legislative powers. The Maltese Islands have a rich and varied history, and traces of civilisation on the Islands date back to about 5200 BC. Archaeological remains indicate that there was a Phoenician / Carthaginian presence during the 6th century BC. In 218 BC Malta fell under Roman rule. The Islands were subsequently ruled by Arabs, Normans, and a number of feudal lords. The Order of St. John of Jerusalem (the Knights Hospitaliers) took over the Islands between 1530 and 1798. The Knights of Malta, as they came to be known, left a rich cultural heritage on the Islands. Following a two-year rule by the French (1798-1800), under Napoleon Bonaparte, the Islands passed under British rule. Malta gained independence from Britain in 1964. The Malta Independence Constitution of 1964 established Malta as a Constitutional Monarchy, but in 1974 the Constitution was modified to the effect that Malta became a Republic with the President of Malta as Head of State. Executive power lies with the Prime Minister and the Cabinet of Ministers. Malta forms part of the Commonwealth of Nations.

The Maltese economy is one of the smallest in the world. In 2015 the Maltese gross domestic product (GDP) at market prices amounted to approximately €8,796.5m, equivalent to around 0.05% of the GDP of the European Union (EU), which Malta joined in May 2004, and around 0.07% of that of the eurozone. Malta's average GDP per head in 2015 amounted to approximately €20,400, leading to Malta being classified as a high-income country by the World Bank, and as a country with very high human development (in the top quartile) by the UN Development Programme.

Maltese society is changing at a rapid rate in terms of structure, attitudes and values. Land development, mass tourism, overseas travel, information technology, new work and leisure patterns and a rapid expansion of higher education are permeating the closely knit traditional Catholic society. In many respects, the Maltese Islands have become one modern European city. In comparison with other neighbouring European countries, however, Malta remains a relatively homogenous society with no marked racial, ethnic or religious divisions.

The Maltese legal system is what is known as a mixed legal system.

Malta's legal system for many centuries was based on the Roman law as codified by the Emperor Justinian and as rediscovered and developed and practiced by the greater part of continental Europe.

Given the history and sources of the Maltese legal system, we may say it has its roots in the Civil Law (continental) family but which has absorbed many features of the Common Law (British) tradition. In other words, it is a mixed legal system. While the rules on theft in the Maltese Criminal Code are inspired by the Civil Law (continental) approach, the English law institution of the jury system has been grafted onto the Maltese Criminal Code. The Maltese legal system thus represents an early attempt to fuse together two great families of law.

Written Maltese Law may be divided in four main sub-divisions:
- Civil Law and Criminal Law;
- Public Law and Private Law;
- Substantive Law and Procedural Law;
- Municipal Law and Public International Law.

Civil Law is concerned with the rights and obligations of persons towards one another and provides a system of remedies, such as damages or specific performances.

Criminal Law, on the other hand, is made up of rules of law concerned with acts or omissions which are contrary to public order and society as a whole and prescribe punishment such as imprisonment or a fine.

Hence the distinction between civil and criminal wrongs does not lie in the nature of the offence, since the same act may be both a criminal offence and a civil wrong.

Public Law comprises mainly:

- Constitutional Law;
- Administrative Law; and
- Criminal Law.

Private Law includes both Civil and Commercial Law, aiming to protect private interests.

B. The Status and Direction of the Cooperation with Chinese Enterprises Under the B&R

The level and extent of cooperation with Chinese enterprises is long-standing and very strong, as clearly evidenced by the following list, taken from website of the Maltese Ministry of Foreign Affairs:

China Foreign Affairs College - MADS Cooperation Agreement;

China - Agreement between the government of the republic of Malta and the government of the people's republic of China on a long term loan by malta to China;

China - Agreement between the Government of Malta and the Government of Malta and the Government of the people's republic of China on a long-term and interest-free loan by China to Malta;

China - Agreement between the Government of Malta and the Government of the People's Republic of China for the Avoidance of Double taxation and the prevention of fiscal evasion;

China - Agreement between the Government of Malta and the Government of the people's Republic of China on the promotion and protection of investments;

China - Agreement between the government of the people's Republic of China and the Government of the Republic of Malta on co-operation in the field of tourism;

China - Agreement between the Ministry for Education and Employment of the Republic of Malta and the Ministry of Education of the People's Republic of China;

China - Agreement between the Ministry of Defense of the Republic of Malta and the Ministry of National Defense of People's Republic of China;

China - Agreement between the republic of Malta and republic of China concerning co-operation in the field of traditional chinese medicine;

China - Agreement between the University of Malta and Confucius Institute headquarters of China on the establishment of Confucius institute at the University of Malta;

China - Agreement of co-operation in the field of youth between the department of youth and sport of Malta and the all China youth federation;

China - Agreement on cooperation between the Government of Malta and the Government of the People's Republic of China in Combating Transnational Crime;

China - Agreement on cultural cooperation between the government of the republic of Malta and the government of the people's republic of China;

China - Agreement on maritime transport between the government of Malta and the government of people's republic of China;

China - Agreement on Scientific and Technological co-operation between the Government of Malta and the Government of the People's Republic of China;

China - Agreement to extend to the government of Malta a grant totalling Five Million RMB Yuan by the Government of the People's Republic of China;

China - Cooperation agreement between the Mediterranean Academy of Diplomatic Studies of Malta and the Foreign Affairs College of China;

China - Executive programme on cultural co-operation between the government of Malta and the Government of China;

China - Joint communique of the government of China and the government of Malta on the establishment of diplomatic relations between China and Malta;

China - Plan of co-operation in the fields of Health and Medicine between the Ministries of Health of Malta and the People's Republic of China;

China - Programme of cultural exchanges between the Government of Malta and the Government of the People's Republic of China;

China - Programme of the cultural exchanges between the government of Malta and the government of the people's republic of China for the period 2009-2012;

China - Protocol between the government of Malta and the government of China on the development projects and technical assistance to be provided by China to Malta;

China - Protocol between the Ministry for health, the elderly and community care of Malta and the Ministry of health of the people's republic of China;

China - The arms trade treaty;

China - Agreement on the Establishment of the Friendly-City relation (Twinning Agreement);
China - Agreement relating to Civil Air Transport;
China - Agreement on the Maintenance of post of Honorary Consul in Hong Kong (China);
China - Agreement between the Government of Malta and the Government of the People's Republic of China on Co-operation against Illicit Traffic In and Abuse of Narcotic Drugs and Psychotropic Substances;
China - Agreement between the People's Liberation Army of the People's Republic of China and the Armed Forces of Malta on China's Provision of Military Assistance Gratis to Malta;
China - Agreement between the Ministry of Defence of the Republic of Malta and the Ministry of National Defence of the People's Republic of China on China's Provision of Military Assistance Gratis to Malta;
China - Agreement on Educational Co-operation between the Government of Malta and the Government of the People's Republic of China for the Period 2002-2005;
China - Mutual Visa Exemption for Holders of Diplomatic and Service Passport Holders;
China - Agreement on Trade and Economic Cooperation;
China - Education Cooperation Executive Programme (2005 -2008);
China - Protocol on China's provision of military assistance gratis to Malta;
China - Avoidance of Double Taxation Agreement;
China - Cooperation in the field of Traditional Chinese Medicine;
China - Protocol on the provision of complete projects and technical assistance by China to Malta;
Protocol on the Provision of Technical Assistance for a Break-water project at Marsaxlokk Harbour;
Protocol on the development projects and Technical Assistance to be provided by China to Malta;
China - Renewal of the Co-operation in the field of Traditional Chinese medicine;
Memorandum of Understanding on Sports Cooperation between the Ministry of Education and Employment of the Republic of Malta and the General Administration of Sport of the People's Republic of China;
Memorandum of Understanding on Cooperation in the Field of Intellectual Property between the Commerce Department of the Ministry for the Economy, Investment and Small Business of the Republic of Malta and the State Intellectual Property Office of the PRC;
Film Co-Production Agreement between the Government of the Republic of Malta and the Government of the People's Republic of China;
MoU between the MJCL of the Republic of Malta and the Ministry of Culture of the People's Republic of China on Jointly Supporting Intercultural Exchange and Cooperation between the European City of Culture (Valletta 2018) and the East Asia City of Culture;
Protocol between the Ministry for Health of the Republic of Malta and the National Health and Family Planning Commission of the People's Republic of China on Cooperation in the Field of Traditional Chinese Medicine.

II. Investment

A. Market Access

a. Department Supervising Investment

The entity supervising investment in Malta is Malta Enterprise (hereinafter referred to as 'the Corporation'), which is a corporation established under the Malta Enterprise Act (Chapter 463 of the Laws of Malta), in order to perform the functions assigned to it under the said Act.

In general, the Corporation has the following functions:

a) to originate, lead and further initiative the economic and social development of Malta in line with the objectives, policies and goals set out by the Government of Malta;

b) to lead Malta's strategy as relates to all forms of enterprise, ensuring the implementation of such activity through a co-ordinated and coherent approach developed and implemented with other Government bodies, national constituted bodies and the private sector;

c) to develop, and to provide the required assistance and support services to enterprise in Malta;

d) to promote Malta as a location for enterprise, to assist and co-ordinate its promotion as such a location;

e) to promote, assist and develop the establishment, competitiveness and internationalisation of enterprise in Malta;

f) to develop the technological, human resource, and skills bases, and to strengthen the capacity of undertakings, to undertake strategic assessment and formulation, to innovate, and to undertake research, development and design activities;

g) to provide and manage land, sites, premises, services, and facilities for business enterprises;

h) to administer schemes, grants and other financial facilities requiring the disbursement of funds, including funds originating from foreign sources;

i) to advise the Government of Malta on any matter relating to the operations and purposes of this Act; and

j) to carry out such other functions as may be assigned to it by the Government of Malta from time to time.

In the exercise of the above functions, additionally the Corporation shall have power to:

a) make all forms of investment, including direct ownership of undertakings in its own right or in partnership with other persons, grant loans and advances to undertakings, subscribe, underwrite or deal in shares and debentures of companies, guarantee loans and advances to other persons, make grants to undertakings, and manage and control undertakings: provided that in any such transaction as aforesaid the investment or liability of the Corporation shall be made or assumed at fair risk;

b) acquire, sell or lease land, plant, machinery and equipment, and other property, and otherwise make available property for use by other persons;

c) manage land, develop land, and carry out works on land, and maintain works or assist in their maintenance;

d) provide advisory or other services or facilities in relation to any of its functions, or assist in their provision; and

e) generally do all such things as may be incidental or conducive to the performance of its functions.

b. Laws and Regulations of Investment Industry

Apart from the Malta Enterprise Act, referred to in the foregoing paragraphs, the laws and regulations that regulate the investment industry are essentially four (4) in number, namely:
- The Business Promotion Act (Chapter 325 of the Laws of Malta);
- The Malta Development Corporation Act (Chapter 202 of the Laws of Malta);
- The Aids to Industry Ordinance (Chapter 159 of the Laws of Malta) and regulations made thereunder; and
- The Business Promotion Regulations, promulgated under the Business Promotion Act, referred to above.

c. Forms of Investment

The types of investment which are considered by the Corporation as a mainstay of the Maltese economy and which deserve particular attention are the following: (i) Advanced Manufacturing, (ii) Life Sciences, (iii) ICT, (iv) Aviation, (v) Education, (vi) Tourism and Hospitality and (vii) Healthcare.

d. Standards of Market Access and Examination

The standards of market access and examination in the case of an entity that wants to do business in Malta and benefit from the incentives on offer, through schemes managed by the Corporation that will be referred to under Part J below, are no different from the standards required to set up a company (or other commercial partnership) in Malta.

B. Foreign Exchange Regulation

a. Department Supervising Foreign Exchange

The entity supervising foreign exchange in Malta is the Central Bank of Malta established under the Central Bank of Malta Act (Chapter 204 of the Laws of Malta).

b. Brief Introduction of Laws and Regulations of Foreign Exchange

The relevant legislation regulating foreign exchange in Malta is the External Transactions Act (Chapter 233 of the Laws of Malta).

The External Transactions Act, inter alia establishes a framework for the liberalisation of so-called 'external transactions' which include both capital[①] and current transactions involving operations between resident and non-resident persons or other entities, whether in or outside Malta, and may also include operations involving foreign exchange by a resident or between residents;

For the purposes of the aforesaid Act, "foreign exchange" is defined as any note, coin, cheque, draft,

---

[①] "capital transactions" means external transactions arising from the transfer or movement of capital and includes: (a) transfers of immovable property; (b) direct investments; (c) the issue, sale or purchase of securities including shares and stock in the capital of a company, debentures, certificates of deposit and any other similar instrument acknowledging indebtedness; (d) the issue, sale or purchase of units in a collective investment scheme, life and annuity long-term insurance policies whether index-linked or not; (e) lending, borrowing and payment or receipt of amortisation on loans; (f) granting of guarantees or any other form of security for payment; (g) warrants, options, futures and other derivatives as well as any other financial instrument entered into for investment purposes; (h) deposits with credit institutions; (i) gifts and endowments; and (j) any other type of transaction which the Minister responsible for finance may, after consultation with the Central Bank, determine by notice in the Government Gazette.

travellers' cheque, letter of credit, promissory note, bill of exchange, voucher, credit or debit card or other card or means in which value is inputted through electronic or magnetic methods and which any unspecified person is able to use for payment in lieu of currency, or other means of payment expressed in the currency of any country which is not legal tender in Malta and references in the said Act to foreign exchange include references to any right to receive on demand foreign exchange in respect of any credit or balance at any credit institution anywhere.

c. Requirements of Foreign Exchange Management for Foreign Enterprises

Unless otherwise specified by means of regulations or orders issued by the Minister responsible for finance under the External Transactions Act all external transactions and related payments may be carried out without restriction.

However, where exceptional circumstances arise, the Minister responsible for finance may, on the recommendation of the Central Bank of Malta, make regulations imposing such restrictions on capital transactions and related payments, whether of a specific or a generic nature, as may be deemed necessary:

Provided that such restrictions shall not be imposed in relation to a State which is a member of the European Union.

For the purposes of the foregoing rule, exceptional circumstances shall be deemed to exist, where the Minister responsible for finance, acting upon the recommendation of the Central Bank of Malta, declares that: (a) there is a sudden crisis in Malta's balance of payments; or (b) movements of capital to or from Malta cause or threaten to cause serious difficulties for the stability of the financial system.

Any regulations restrictive of foreign exchange made, as aforesaid, will be revoked by the Minister responsible for finance, without delay as soon as the grounds which gave rise to such restrictions cease to exist and, in any case, shall not remain in effect for a period exceeding six months, save the power to impose controls or restrictions on capital or other transactions or related payments in respect of any state, person or group of persons whether arising from Malta's international obligations under the United Nations Charter, the European Union Accession Treaty or otherwise unilaterally to defend Malta's national interests.

C. Financing

There are a number of financial institutions in Malta which are of impeccable repute and have experienced a strong financial performance over the years, amongst them HSBC Bank, Lombard Bank, APS Bank, BNF Bank and Bank of Valletta. Each one of the said banks has had international business exposure. The regulating legislation is the Banking Act (Chapter 371 of the Laws of Malta).

The Corporation also provides and / or facilitates certain finance, as will be described below.

D. Land Policy

a. Brief Introduction of Land-Related Laws and Regulations

In general terms, the law regulating the acquisition of a given title over land (or, as it were, any immovable property), broadly-speaking ownership, emphyteusis and a lease which are all possessory titles in favour of whosoever they are granted, is the Civil Code (Chapter 16 of the Laws of Malta). The Civil Code requires a public deed, drawn up by a notary public, in the case of the first two (2) titles referred to here and a private writing (that does not require the intervention of a notary public) in the case of the latter title referred here, unless the title is granted for less than two (2) years in which case no written formality would be required.

The technical details involved when one comes to purchase land in Malta, whether by ownership or emphyteusis, may be found in the Public Registry Act (Chapter 56), details which are invariably handled by the notary public who would be entrusted with the publication of the public deed. Crucially, the role of the notary public who is considered at law as a public officer, as it were owing a duty to the public at large, is to confirm and certify in the deed itself that whosoever acquires a property in Malta does so under a good title.

b. Rules of Land Acquisition for Foreign Enterprises

A foreign enterprise cannot purchase land (or any other immovable property) in Malta, unless it obtains a permit in this regard from the Capital Transfer Duty Department of the Inland Revenue Division.

The said Department is committed to issue the requested permit within thirty-five (35) days, subject to whether the application submitted is correct as per its Quality Service Charter.

Non-residents are allowed to purchase only one (1) immovable property in Malta, unless it is situated in Special Designated Areas where there are absolutely no restrictions on acquisition.

The spouse of a citizen of Malta or of a Member State of the European Union, may acquire immovable property together with his or her spouse as they fall within the definition of a "resident of Malta".

Commercial partnerships which are established, and operate from an EU member state may freely acquire immovable property as well, provided that 75% or more of its shareholding is held by one or more EU citizens.

In all other cases, purchase of property by legal entities is not allowed. However, specific permits may be issued by the Minister in question, even to non-EU entities, where the property is required for an industrial or touristic project, or if the project contributes to the economic development of Malta.

In the latter situation, The Corporation and other entities acting in conjunction with the Corporation, has a very important role to play in favouring and maintaining investment, as shall be explained below.

E. The Establishment and Dissolution of Companies

a. The Forms of Enterprises

In technical terms, a company is termed as a commercial partnership. Under Maltese law, commercial partnerships may be of the following kinds:

a) a partnership en nom collectif;
b) a partnership en commandite or limited partnership; and
c) a company.

b. The Procedure of Establishment

A company is formed by means of a capital divided into shares held by its members. The members' liability is limited to the amount, if any, unpaid on the shares respectively held by each of them.

A company shall not be validly constituted under this Act unless a memorandum of association is entered into and subscribed by at least two persons, save the case of a single member company.

c. Routes and Requirement of Dissolution

A company shall be dissolved and consequently wound up in the following cases:

a) the company has by extraordinary resolution resolved that the company be dissolved and consequently wound up by the court;

b) the company has by extraordinary resolution resolved that the company be dissolved and consequently wound up voluntarily.

In addition to the modes of dissolution referred to above, a company may be dissolved and wound up by the court in the following cases:

a) if the business of the company is suspended for an uninterrupted period of twenty-four months;

b) the company is unable to pay its debts; and Moreover, a company shall be dissolved by the court in the following cases:

• the number of members of the company is reduced to below two and remains so reduced for more than six months;

• the number of directors is reduced to below the minimum prescribed by article 137 and remains so reduced for more than six months;

• the court is of the opinion that there are grounds of sufficient gravity to warrant the dissolution and consequent winding up of the company;

• when the period, if any, fixed for the duration of the company by the memorandum or articles expires, or the event occurs, if any, on the occurrence of which the memorandum or articles provide that the company is to be wound up, and the company in general meeting has not before such expiry or event passed a resolution to be wound up voluntarily.

F. Merger and Acquisition

Amalgamation of two or more companies may be effected by:

a) merger by acquisition; or
b) merger by formation of a new company.

Merger by acquisition is the operation whereby a company acquires all the assets and liabilities of one or more other companies, in exchange for the issue to the shareholders of the companies being acquired of shares in the acquiring company and a cash payment, if any, not exceeding ten per cent of the nominal value of the shares so issued.

Merger by formation of a new company is the operation whereby two or more companies deliver to a company which they set up all their assets and liabilities in exchange for the issue to the shareholders of the merging companies of shares in the new company and a cash payment, if any, not exceeding ten per cent of the nominal value of the shares so issued.

G. Competition Regulation

a. Department Supervising Competition Regulation

The entity in Malta supervising competition regulation is the Malta Competition and Consumer Affairs Authority set up in terms of the Malta Competition and Consumer Affairs Authority Act (Chapter 510 of the Laws of Malta).

b. Brief Introduction of Competition Law

The law that regulates competition and provides for fair trading in Malta is the Competition Act (Chapter 379 of the Laws of Malta).

c. Measures Regulating Competition

In terms of the aforesaid Act, the following is prohibited, that is to say any agreement between undertakings, any decision by an association of undertakings and any concerted practice between undertakings having the object or effect of preventing, restricting or distorting competition within Malta or any part of Malta and in particular, but without prejudice to the generality of this subarticle, any agreement, decision or practice which:

a) directly or indirectly fixes the purchase or selling price or other trading conditions; or

b) limits or controls production, markets, technical development or investment; or

c) shares markets or sources of supply; or

d) imposes the application of dissimilar conditions to equivalent transactions with other parties outside such agreement, thereby placing at a competitive disadvantage; or

e) makes the conclusion of contracts subject to the acceptance by the other parties of supplementary obligations which, by their nature or according to commercial usage, have no connection with the subject of such contracts.

Agreements or decisions prohibited in accordance with the aforesaid rule shall be ipso jure, null and unenforceable.

However, the aforesaid rule does not apply in the case of:

a) any agreement between undertakings; or

b) any decision by an association of undertakings; or

c) any concerted practice, which contributes towards the objective of improving production or distribution of goods or services or promoting technical or economic progress and which allows consumers a fair share of the resultant benefit and which does not:

(i) impose on undertakings concerned any restriction which is not indispensable to the attainment of the said objective; or

(ii) give the undertakings concerned the possibility of eliminating or significantly reducing competition in respect of a substantial part of the products to which the agreement, decision or concerted practice refers.

Moreover, agreements, decisions or concerted practices between undertakings shall not be subject to the prohibition referred to above, if the impact of the agreement, decision or practice on the relevant market is minimal.

Any abuse by one or more undertakings of a dominant position within Malta or any part of Malta is prohibited.

One or more undertakings shall be deemed to abuse of a dominant position, where it or they:

a) directly or indirectly impose an excessive or unfair purchase or selling price or other unfair trading conditions;

b) limit production, markets or technical development to the prejudice of consumers;

c) apply dissimilar conditions, including price discrimination to equivalent transactions with different trading parties, thereby placing any or some of the trading parties at a competitive disadvantage;

d) make the conclusion of contracts subject to the acceptance by the other party of supplementary obligations which, by their nature or according to commercial usage, have no connection with the subject of such contracts.

The undertaking or association of undertakings concerned may appeal by application filed before the Appeals Tribunal from any infringement decision, cease and desist or compliance order, administrative fine and, or daily penalty payment adopted or imposed by the Director General in accordance with the provisions of the competition Act within twenty days of notification thereof The appeal shall be notified to the Director General and the Director General shall file his reply thereto within twenty days from the date of notification of the appeal.

An appeal shall not have the effect of suspending the order, administrative fine and, or daily penalty payment appealed from unless the Appeals Tribunal ,upon a reasoned request by a party to the appeal, and after considering the submissions of the Director General, suspends the order, administrative fine and, or daily penalty payment under such conditions as it may deem fit, stating its reasons therefor, pending the final determination of the appeal.

The Appeals Tribunal may either confirm in whole or in part or quash the decision and, or order of the Director

General and may confirm, revoke or vary the administrative fine and, or daily penalty payment imposed by the Director General, taking into account the gravity and duration of the infringement as well as any aggravating or attenuating circumstances.

The Director General and any party to an appeal before the Appeals Tribunal who feels aggrieved by a decision of the Appeals Tribunal may appeal on a question of law to the Court of Appeal by means of an application filed in the registry of that court within twenty days from the date of the decision of the Appeals Tribunal.

H. Tax

a. Tax Regime and Rules

Malta is a preferred choice of domicile for companies for various reasons, including:
• With full imputation system applying;
• Extensive network of double taxation treaties, plus benefits even when no bilateral treaty in force;
• Refundable tax credit scheme – on revenues as dividends to shareholders, resident & non-resident;
• Ideal tax residency status for individuals;
• Compliant with EU non-discrimination system.

b. Main Categories and Rates of Tax

Broadly-speaking, the main categories of tax, in Malta are two (2), that is personal tax and corporate tax.

The general basis of personal taxation in Malta is that if, you are domiciled and ordinarily resident in Malta you should declare all your income (including that of your spouse and dependent children) from whatever source. If you are either not domiciled or not ordinarily resident in Malta you should declare all income accruing to you in Malta or derived from Malta (including that of your spouse and dependent children), as well as any income which was remitted to Malta.

In Malta the taxation of an individual's income is progressive; i.e.the higher an individual's income, the higher the tax paid. Payment of personal tax is mainly effected either through the Provisional Tax system, the FSS (Final Settlement System) or by means of the Self-Assessment. In the case of the Provisional Tax, the tax due for a particular year is collected during the same period in which income is earned. It applies mostly to persons whose sources of income include trade, business, profession or vocation. The FSS (Final Settlement System) which mainly caters for employees and pensioners is designed to produce accurate tax deductions from emoluments. This methodology ensures that the correct amount of tax is deducted from gross emoluments as they are received, thus reducing the incidence of large refunds or tax claims. Any tax due not collected by these two systems is to be paid by the tax-settlement due date, i.e the 30th June of the year following the year in which income was earned by means of the Self-Assessment.

According to the income tax legislation, Maltese-resident companies are subject to corporate tax at the rate of 35% on their worldwide income and capital gains. Foreign companies, incorporated outside Malta carrying out business activities in Malta are liable to tax on income arising in Malta. It is worth noting that a company is considered to be resident for tax purposes in Malta when the management and control of the company is exercised in Malta.

When companies are taxed at the standard rate of 35%, following the distribution of dividends, shareholders are entitled to a refund of part or of all the tax paid by the company. The purpose of this imputation system is to eliminate any double taxation that might arise on the distribution of such dividends. Thus company profits will only be subject to tax at corporate level.

c. Tax Declaration and Preference

The procedure to declare income for the purposes of tax has been dealt with above.

By way of preference, Malta grants relief from double taxation under the credit method on source-by-source and country-by-country bases. The Maltese tax regime governing double taxation relief includes not only treaty relief but also unilateral relief, and thereby ensures that income arising from overseas is not subject to double taxation, even if there is no double taxation agreement in existence.

In terms of domestic legislation, no withholding taxes are imposed on dividends, interest and royalties paid to non-residents, as long as various conditions are complied with. In addition, no Maltese tax is imposed on gains realised from transfers of corporate securities by non-residents, again as long as the relevant conditions are complied with, particularly that the sole or main assets of the company whose securities are being transferred do not consist of Maltese immovable property.

Moreover, certain key vehicles are taxed favourably or not taxed at all:
• Banks and Financial Institutions & Fund Managers / Fund Administrators: Taxed like all companies registered in Malta;
• Insurance Companies: Special provisions apply to the determination of total income from the business of

insurance;
- Insurance Managers: Taxed like all companies registered in Malta;
- Investment Funds: Malta-domiciled funds are, as a general rule, exempt from Maltese income and capital gains tax as long as they do not have over 85% of their assets situated in Malta;
- Trusts: When all the beneficiaries of a trust are not domiciled / resident in Malta and where the trust assets are situated outside Malta, no Maltese income tax (or transfer duty) is payable;
- Foundations: A foundation may be treated as a Maltese company and benefit from Malta's full imputation system. Foundations may also opt to be taxed in the same manner as a trust;
- Retirement Schemes: Licensed retirement schemes are exempt from tax on income and capital gains but this does not apply to immovable property situated in Malta.

To attract highly qualified personnel to the financial services industry, Malta introduced an incentive scheme in 2011 targeting well-paid foreign executives. Individuals who have their domicile outside of Malta and are employed in senior positions with a company licensed or recognised by the relevant authority to conduct financial business in or from Malta, can benefit from a flat personal income tax rate of 15% on his income.

I. Securities

a. Brief Introduction of Securities-Related Laws and Regulations

The Banking Act referred to above and the Malta Financial Services Act (and any regulations made thereunder), are the main pieces of legislation presenting a framework for the regulation and supervision of banks and other players in the financial services sector in Malta. A variety of legal notices regulating specific aspects of banking transactions and the regulation of credit institutions has also been issued under these main Acts. One also finds that the Civil Code and the Commercial Code present various basic principles regulating transactions such as borrowing and loans, deposits, payments, setting off, pledges and hypothecation of property.

b. Supervision and Regulation of Securities Market

The Banking Act contains two (2) very important rules, namely:
- No business of banking shall be transacted in or from Malta except by a company which is in possession of a licence granted under the Banking Act by the competent authority.
- No credit institution licensed or holding an equivalent authorisation outside Malta may open a branch, agency or representative office or set up any subsidiary in Malta unless it is in possession of a licence granted under this Act by the competent authority.

Under the Malta Financial Services Authority Act, cited above, the Authority set up under the said Act shall, in the exercise of its functions and powers have the right to reasonable access and entry to any business premises and, or offices of a licence holder, access to any relevant documentation and, or records of a licence holder, including access to any telephonic or other records and access to any other information relating or pertaining to the activities licensed or authorised by the said Authority or otherwise falling under its supervisory or regulatory functions.

The Authority shall also have the right to issue orders for the freezing of funds and, or other assets including bank accounts in the name of the licence holder or any other third party or parties as may be indicated and for such time and under such conditions as the Authority may set out in writing. The order may also prohibit a licence holder from transferring, disposing or losing possession of any such funds or assets. These orders may also be issued at the request of a foreign enforcement or supervisory authority.

Indeed, the powers of the said Authority are extensive and far-reaching.

c. Requirements for Engagement in Securities Trading for Foreign Enterprises

The legislative requirements are meant to favour the engagement of foreign enterprises in the industry which is a highly specialized industry and subject to a number of regulations, as aforesaid.

J. Preference and Protection of Investment

a. The Structure of Preference Policies

The Corporation has developed various incentives for the promotion and expansion of industry and the development of innovative enterprises.

The Corporation provides on an ad hoc basis, incentives for enterprises demonstrating commitment towards growth, an increase in value added and employment.

b. Support for Specific Industries and Regions

Enterprises engaged in manufacturing, ICT development activities, call centers, healthcare, pharmaceuticals, biotechnology, aviation and maritime services, education and training, logistics and more may benefit from these incentives.

c. Investment Protection

Again, on an ad hoc basis, the Corporation has issued, from time to time, incentive schemes, which are worthy of mention here:

a) Innovation Aid for SMEs

This measure is open to all SMEs that qualify for this incentive and shall allow these undertakings to recover in the form of tax credits, part of the costs incurred for the loan of highly qualified personnel from large undertakings and Research and Knowledge-dissemination Organisation.

The aid shall be granted in the form of tax credits and shall be capped at 50% of the eligible costs.

b) Investment Aid Tax Credits 2014 - 2020

Investment Aid Tax Credits are intended to sustain the regional industrial and economic development of Malta. This measure facilitates initial investments by encouraging the setting up of new establishments and the expansion and development of existing businesses.

c) Aid for Research and Development Projects (Tax Credits)

This incentive measure allows companies to claim tax credits on costs incurred directly or indirectly in carrying out an R&D project or projects relevant to the company's trade. Eligible projects should seek to achieve an advance in a field of science or technology through the resolution of scientific or technological uncertainty.

d) Business Development and Continuity

The Business Development & Continuity Scheme is intended to facilitate value added projects that are expected to contribute to the regional development of Malta and to support existing undertakings sustain operations during restructuring.

e) Qualifying Employment in Innovation and Creativity (Personal Tax)

This measure facilitates employment of non-residents in roles which are currently not addressed by the local labour market by temporarily easing the tax expenses incurred by such persons through a fiscal incentive.

f) R&D Feasibility Studies 2014 - 2020

Since Research & Development initiatives are associated with high risk, it is advisable that undertakings undertake R&D Feasibility studies to determine that the key elements of the proposed research project are based on sound principles.

g) Research and Development 2014 - 2020

This measure supports industrial research or experimental development carried out for the acquisition of knowledge leading to the development of innovative products and solutions.

h) Start-Up Finance 2017 - 2020

The aim of this measure is to finance innovative undertakings in their early stages of development by supporting Small Start-up Undertakings that demonstrate a viable business concept in the setting-up and initial growth phases.

i) Tax Credits for R&D and Innovation

This measure is open to all undertakings that employ for a period of at least twelve (12) months a person holding or reading for a doctoral degree in science, information technology or engineering. Beneficiaries shall be awarded a tax credit of €10,000 which shall be capped accordingly if the applicant exceeds the de minimis limited allocated to the single undertaking.

j) Business Start (B. Start)

Malta Enterprise, via Business Start is offering a seed funding for start-ups. The measure is intended to support Small Start-up Undertakings that have a viable business concept and are in the early stage of its development.

k) Investment Aid for High-Efficiency Cogeneration

In collaboration with the Energy and Water Agency, Malta Enterprise is assisting undertakings to invest in cogeneration equipment (ie energy efficient solutions that simultaneously generate thermal energy and electrical and/or mechanical energy).

l) Knowledge Transfer

This Incentive provides a framework for addressing skill shortages by supporting training and re-skilling of existing and new employees. The aim is to support knowledge transfer, and the acquisition of new competences in line with the knowledge and skill requirements of industry.

m) Micro Invest

The objective of this scheme is to encourage undertakings to invest in their business, innovate, expand, and implement compliance directives or to develop their operations.

n) Soft Loans

Soft Loans support enterprises through loans at low interest rates for part financing investments in qualifying expenditure.

o) Aid for the Development of Workshops and Associate Retail Outlets at the Ta' Qali and Ta' Dbieġi Crafts Village

This incentive is aimed at assisting undertakings based in the Ta' Qali Crafts Village and the Ta' Dbieġi Crafts Village.

p) Application for Industrial Space for Small Business Activities

q) Business Associations Grant

Business Associations typically perform activities that support collective development and growth of undertakings within a specific sector. Such activities include networking, information gathering, research, and establishing industry standards.

r) Catering Capacity Building

The scope of this scheme is to assist hospitality and catering establishments that engaging a chef to support in capacity building, innovation, and in the development the operations. Undertakings (including self-employed operators) will be supported through a tax credit representing a percentage of the eligible expenditure and wages of the international experienced chefs.

s) Get Qualified 2014 - 2020

Get Qualified is an initiative that supports the personal development of individuals for the achievement of qualifications and certifications required by industry. The incentive is applicable to individuals following a course of studies leading to a certification, diploma, degree or post-graduate degree courses.

t) Gozo Transport Grant Scheme

This scheme supports manufacturing undertakings operating from Gozo by reducing their inter-island transport costs.

u) Interest Rate Subsidies

Loan Interest Rate Subsidies to support new investment projects undertaken by enterprises engaged in manufacturing.

v) Loan Guarantees

Loan Guarantees facilitate access to finance to assist enterprises in the acquisition of capital assets that will lead to a more effective and efficient production and supply of service/s. The main objective of this incentive is to support new investment projects undertaken by enterprises engaged in manufacturing.

w) Micro Guarantee Scheme 2017-2020

Limited availability of funds many times prohibits small business from carrying out new investment projects and may consequently lead to the loss of business opportunities. The Micro Guarantee Scheme has the objective to accelerate growth by facilitating access to debt finance for smaller business undertakings.

x) Rent Subsidy

This scheme supports small undertakings engaged in eligible activities that require industrial space as a temporary, or permanent solution.

y) Trade Promotion

This incentive aims to support undertakings that are willing to establish new markets, or to introduce a new service or product in an existing international market.[1]

III. Trade

A. Department Supervising Trade

In terms of the Trading Licences Act (Chapter 441 of the Laws of Malta), the administration of trade shall be vested in the Minister responsible for commerce or such other person or authority designated by the said Minister for any of the purposes of the same said Act.

B. Brief Introduction of Trade Laws and Regulations

The main body of legislation in this respect is the Trading Licences Act (Chapter 441 of the Laws of Malta) which makes provision for the regulation of commercial activities and for matters ancillary to or connected with

---

[1] Information taken from the official website of Malta Enterprise.

such activities.

In this Act, "commercial activity" is defined as the exercise of any trading or economic activity including the sale of goods, and the provision of any services as may be prescribed, irrespective of whether such commercial activity is exercised from commercial premises or otherwise but shall not include any commercial activity regulated under any other law.

C. Trade Management

The said Act prescribes in great detail, the conditions for carrying out a commercial activity, as defined above, namely:

a) The commercial premises are at all times to be kept in a clean and wholesome manner both within the premises and in the immediate vicinity outside the premises. Any person carrying out a commercial activity should be responsible for the cleaning of the pavement, the space beneath the pavement and of the street space in front of the commercial premises. After the opening hours the licensee is forbidden from leaving any waste or any objects on the pavement, the space beneath the pavement and the street space in front of his commercial premises.

b) The commercial activity carried out in the premises or things stored with in the premises shall not:

cause annoyance to neighbours; be likely to occasion any fire or explosion; emit exhalation, fumes, vapours, gases, dust or emit noxious or offensive odours into the atmosphere that may cause damage or are injurious to health; cause annoyance by way of noise.

c) When a commercial activity expose for sale any article or any other thing placed outside the premises, the person responsible for the commercial activity shall see that these do not cause an obstacle to the pedestrians and that these should never exceed 50 cm of the same pavement.

d) Where the commercial activity comprises the sale or repair of vehicles, no vehicles shall be displayed for sale, repaired or else be washed in any part of the street. No vehicles of whatever kind, commercial or otherwise, brand new or second hand, can be parked in any public place for the intention of exhibiting for sale the vehicle, marked by the words "For Sale" or any other words that indicate the aforesaid intention, including the display of any telephone and / or mobile numbers.

e) Magazines, or any other items or materials which by their nature are objectionable for use or consumption by minors, or any items which by their nature are objectionable by general use, shall not be sold to minors or displayed in any manner within the commercial premises where they will be accessible to or within the reach of such minors or general public.

f) No alcohol and no tobacco products shall be sold to persons under the age of seventeen (17) years.

g) (i) Between 9.00p.m. and 4.00a.m. of the following day, alcoholic beverages shall only be sold or served for consumption on the premises where they are sold as follows:

• by premises duly licensed as clubs;

• at wedding halls;

• by commercial premises licensed by the Malta Tourism Authority as catering establishments where the primary purpose is the sale of food and alcoholic beverages to be consumed on the premises.

(ii) The sale or serving of alcoholic beverages by street hawkers and by market hawkers is prohibited at all times.

(iii) The storing of alcoholic beverages is prohibited at commercial premises which by their nature shall not sell such products.

h) No noise shall be generated from any commercial premises and be heard from outside the premises that causes annoyance and disturbance to neighbours by hammering or by the use of machinery between 1.00p.m.and 4.p.m.of the same day and between 7.00.p.m. and 7.00.a.m. of the next following day.

i) No commercial activity located in an urban area can generate noise that can be heard from outside the premises that causes annoyance and disturbance to neighbours by playing of music by live bands or amplified music or other means between the hours of 11.00 p.m.and 9.00 a.m.of the following day and between 1.00 p.m.and 4.00 p.m.

j) Where the commercial activity in any premises involves manufacturing activities, the retail sale of products manufactured therein may also be carried out from such premises.

k) The sale from street hawkers or the sale from any vehicle or in the vicinity of a school is prohibited except the sale of ice-cream or catering units.

D. The Inspection and Quarantine of Import and Export Commodities

Maltese law contains a set of rules on quarantine that are mostly concerned with imports of plant-origin. These rules, transpose well-tested European Union rules.

E. Customs Management

With Malta's membership of the EU, Maltese customs has immense responsibilities for the protection of the external border of the EU. Membership involves the abolition of routine controls at the internal borders of the EU, but this did not diminish the increasing threats to society resulting from activities of cross-border organised crime which threaten the security of the Union's citizens.

Finished the period of useless barriers to trade, today Maltese Customs, like all modern Customs administrations, goes on to perform its role by adapting to the needs for a smoother flow of trade to the commercial and economic policy at the European Community and national level, in a constant effort to keep an open mind on what is new and different while protecting the interests and cultural identities particularly of Maltese and other EU citizens.

The EU customs policy is an important tool to encourage and support trade and fairness of transactions by developing industries within the Union in order to increase employment and competitiveness of business. Maltese customs coherently implements this policy on behalf of Malta and in close cooperation with EU bodies.

Furthermore, the Department of Customs carries out on behalf of the Maltese community and consumers, important and sensitive tasks through the collection of duties and taxes including excise duties on production and consumption. Above all, as national and international representative of Maltese and Community needs, the said Department contribute towards the improvement in the quality and competitiveness of Maltese and Community systems.

Next to the traditional tasks which are historically well-grounded in all customs institutions, other very important tasks have been included in recent times. Besides the cooperation with other local authorities such as the police, Customs are in the front line in the fight against smuggling, new and old illicit traffic of weapons, drugs, cigarettes, money laundering, counterfeit of goods, endangered protected species and works of art. Customs in Malta is also front line in the fight against the traffic of radioactive materials, hazardous waste, illegal or expired drugs, and goods which cause harm to health and environment.

IV. Labour

A. Brief Introduction of Labour Laws and Regulations

Maltese law contains a whole body of legislation relating to employment, concerned very much with protecting the conditions of employees in a way that it tries to create a balance between the respective rights and obligations of employers on the one hand and employees on the other hand.

Incidentally, the Employment and Industrial Relations Act (Chapter 452 of the Laws of Malta) contains a set of conditions of employment which cannot be derogated from. In other words, it would be illegal for an employer and employee to contract on conditions which are less favourable than the minimum conditions prescribed by the said Act, as aforesaid, which would effectively render such a contract null and void.

The Laus and regulations of employment:
- Employment for the purposes of the Pensions Ordinance Order;
- Tax Credit (Women Returning to Employment) Rules;
- Qualifying Employment in Innovation and Creativity (Personal Tax) Rules;
- Deduction (Income from Employment or Pension) Rules;
- Qualifying Employment in Aviation (Personal Tax) Rules;
- Conditions of Employment (Regulation) Act;
- Disabled Persons (Employment) Act;
- Standard Percentage of Employment of Persons with Disability Order;
- Designated Employment of Persons with Disability Order;
- Part-time Employment of Persons with Disability Regulations;
- Public Transport (Regulation of Employment) Act;
- Fees payable for Residence Permits and Employment Licences Regulations;
- Conditions of Entry and Residence of Third-Country Nationals for the purpose of Highly Qualified Employment Regulations;
- Conditions of Entry and Stay of Third Country Nationals for the purpose of Employment as Seasonal Workers Regulations;
- Merchant Shipping (Employment of Young Persons) Regulations;
- Employment Commission Act;
- Employment and Training Services Act;

- Register of Applicants for Employment (Part Two) Order;
- Manpower Records (Commencement or Termination of Employment) Regulations;
- Employment Agencies Regulations;
- Register of Part-Time Employment Regulations;
- Employment and Industrial Relations Act;
- Collective Redundancies (Protection of Employment) Regulations;
- Transfer of Business (Protection of Employment) Regulations;
- Employment and Industrial Relations Interpretation Order;
- Protection of Maternity (Employment) Regulations;
- Young Persons (Employment) Regulations;
- Equal Treatment in Employment Regulations;
- Extension of Applicability to Service with Government (Equal Treatment in Employment) Regulations;
- Extension of Applicability to Service with Government (Protection of Maternity Employment) Regulations;
- Employment Status National Standard Order;
- Extension of Applicability to Service with Government (Employment Status) Regulations;
- Equal Treatment in Self Employment and Occupation Order;
- Members of Parliament (Public Employment).

B. Requirements of Employing Foreign Employees

a. Work Permit

Nationals of non-European Union Member States require a formal work permit to be able to engage in employment in Malta.

b. Application Procedure

An Application for a so-called 'Residence Permit Employment', together with a number of documents, is required to be submitted with the relevant authorities, as follows:
Passport of Applicant/s;
Colour Passport Photos of Applicant/s;
Sickness Insurance Coverage for all risks;
Original Health Screening Certificate ('Health Screening Approval Form');
Bank (foreign) Statements;
Lease Agreement;
Rent Declaration Form;
Curriculum Vitae;
Job position description;
Applicant's Work Reference or Testimonials;
Qualification Certificates and Accreditations / Recognitions;
Covering Letter by the Employer indicating site of work;
VISA / Residence permit for Malta territory ;
Flight ticket for entry into Schengen Area and Malta;
Contract of Employment;
Non-refundable fee of €280.50 (two hundred eighty and fifty euros).

c. Social Insurance

For the purposes of the Social Security Act (Chapter 318 of the Laws of Malta), every employment specified in Part I of the First Schedule to that Act, unless excepted under Part II of that Schedule, shall be an insurable employment:

In terms of the said Act, 'Employment' is defined as employment in Malta under any contract of service or apprenticeship, written or oral, and whether expressed or implied. On the income that is paid to the employee, the employer pays a social security contribution, which is thus deducted at source.

C. Exit and Entry

a. Visa Types

Malta, like the majority of European Union Member states, forms part of the Schengen treaty.

For entry in a state that forms part of Schengen, a European visa application is required which must be lodged at the diplomatic mission of the country which is the main destination of the visit. In the event, therefore, that an applicant intends to visit several Schengen Member States (with stays of approximately the same duration), the application must be lodged at the diplomatic mission of the country of first entry into Schengen. Thus, applicants wishing to visit Malta as the main destination, or being the country of first entry into the Schengen area, must lodge their applications at Malta's diplomatic missions or its representations

Visa applications must be in writing, giving all details required on the Visa Application Form which can be acquired free of charge from Malta's diplomatic missions and consular posts or online.

The Visa Application Form must be wholly and legibly completed, and signed by the applicant, and accompanied by:
- a valid travel document (passport) validity of which must not be less than three (3) months;
- two (2) passport-size photographs, in colour and taken against a white background, with face clearly visible;
- the visa fee.

Applications for Schengen short-stay visas can be lodged within 3 months prior to the planned trip. Applications are in most cases reviewed within 7-15 days. In individual cases, the review period can be extended up to 30 days and in exceptional cases up to 60 days. It is recommended not to lodge a visa application later than 15 days prior to the planned trip, as it cannot be otherwise guaranteed it will be reviewed in time. Holders of multiple-entry Schengen short-stay visas can lodge a visa application before this visa has expired, provided it has been valid for at least 6 months. Visa applications of family members of EU citizens will be reviewed in the shortest possible period of time.

b. Restrictions for Exit

There are no restrictions for leaving the territory of Malta.

D. Trade Union and Labour Organizations

Trade unions, as they are commonly known in Malta, are regulated by a specific set of regulations, namely the Recognition of Trade Unions Regulations, which regulate the award and revocation of the recognition of a union, as the sole collective bargaining union at the place of work, affording greater protection to employees.

E. Labour Disputes

Labour disputes are decided non-judicially through negotiation between the recognised trade unions and the employers and judicially, before a specialized tribunal called the Industrial Tribunal. The body of legislation regulating labour disputes can be found in the Employment and Industrial Relations Act, referred to above.

V. Intellectual Property

A. Brief Introduction of IP laws and Regulations

So-called "intellectual property rights" in general, are afforded protection under the Copyright Act, the Trademarks Act and the Patents and Designs Act, each one of these pieces of legislation containing detailed and sophisticated rules of protection.

B. Patent Application

Where an invention is susceptible of a patent in terms of the Patent and Designs Act (Chapter 417 of the Laws of Malta), an application for a patent shall be made in the prescribed form and shall be filed at the Office of the Comptroller of Industrial Property and shall contain: (i) a request for the grant of a patent; (ii) a description of the invention; (iii) one or more claims; (iv) any drawings referred to in the description or the claims; (v) an abstract of the invention; and (vi) the title of the invention, which shall clearly and concisely state the technical designation of the invention, provided that the requirements stated in paragraphs (i) to (vi) shall also apply to applications which are still pending at the time when this paragraph comes into force. The application shall designate the inventor or, where there are several inventors, all of them. If the applicant is not the inventor, or is not the sole inventor, the applicant shall indicate the legal grounds for his entitlement to file the application. The application shall be subject to the payment of a filing fee as may be prescribed.

C. Trademark Registration

The Comptroller of Industrial Property allows the electronic filing of a Trademark application. It is a straight forward process which uses a 'wizard' tool that guides the appliacnty through the whole process, against an acknowledgement of filing by email and the assignment of a Trademark application number;

Moreover, an applicant or representative who files electronically, can find his / her details already in the system for their subsequent applications. In cases of multiple classes for the same mark, the applicant can fill in one trademark application (instead of multiple applications in case of manual applications) – a different Trademark number for each class is assigned and the office of the Comptroller of Industrial Property will then process each class as a separate application. Finally, payment is effected immediately using a credit card or via bank transfer.

D. Measures for IP Protection

The set of laws making up the whole of intellectual property legislation, contain very detailed and sophisticated provisions that fully protect owners from infringements, including by means of prohibitory injunctions, equivalent or nearly equivalent to stop and desist orders, recognition of protection, damages, including moral damages etc.

VI. Environmental Protection

A. Department Supervising Environmental Protection

The entity supervising environmental protection is the Environment and Resources Authority established as an authority, independent of the executive government, under the Environment Protection Act (Chapter 549 of the Laws of Malta).

B. Brief Introduction of Laws and Regulations of Environmental Protection

The said Act, which apart from establishing the said Environment and Resources Authority, makes a very extensive provision for the protection of the environment, in pursuance of the powers vested in that Authority to that effect and for matters connected therewith or ancillary thereto.

In particular, the Environment Protection (Preventive and Remedial Measures) Regulations, promulgated under the aforesaid Act, grants the Director for the Protection of the Environment the power, personally or through his officers, carrying identification attestations signed by the Minister responsible for the environment, to inspect any place in Malta, or any vehicle, ship, platform, airplane or other craft existing therein, or any such vehicle, vessel or aircraft belonging to Malta outside the territorial waters of Malta, in order to ascertain the levels of protection of the environment as well as to investigate suspected violations of the provisions of the Act (referred to above) or of regulations made thereunder, or codes of practice issued under the Act, and to secure proof of any such violation.

C. Evaluation of Environmental Protection

Given the limited space of the Maltese territory, it is never easy to balance the respective legitimate interests of developers and environmentalists. At least in principle, every successive governments have strived to afford a greater measure of protection to the environment while giving developers and landowners the space to maximize their assets. The Government of the day is also thinking in terms of entrenching environmental protection in the Constitution which would require a 2 / 3 majority of the House of Representatives to change.

VII. Dispute Resolution

A. Methods and Bodies of Dispute Resolution

Broadly-speaking, courts in Malta can either have a criminal competence or a civil competence. The latter is further sub-divided into the different spheres of laws that regulate the relationship between persons (whether natural or legal) or between persons and the executive government, namely civil law, commercial law and administrative / constitutional law.

Save for very few exceptions, every judgment is subject to an appeal.

Arbitration is also available, if the parties to a dispute choose to determine their dispute by means of arbitration, whether by prior agreement or successively. Unless, the parties exclude the right of appeal, Maltese law allows an appeal from an arbitral award under certain cases.

In certain limited case, arbitration is mandatory.

B. Application of Laws

All persons in Malta, without any distinction, are afforded full protection under the Constitution which contains the following fundamental freedoms:
- Protection of right to life;
- Protection from arbitrary arrest or detention;
- Protection from forced labour;
- Protection from inhuman treatment;
- Protection from deprivation of property without compensation;
- Protection for privacy of home or other property;
- Provisions to secure protection of law;
- Protection of freedom of conscience and worship;
- Protection of freedom of expression;
- Protection of freedom of assembly and association;
- Prohibition of deportation;
- Protection of freedom of movement;
- Protection from discrimination on the grounds of race, etc.

VIII. Others

A. Anti-commercial Bribery

a. Brief Introduction of Anti-commercial Bribery Laws and Regulations

Chapter 326 of the Laws of Malta, has established the Permanent Commission against Corruption as the authority supervising anti-commercial bribery. Significantly, in the exercise of its functions, the Commission shall not be subject to the direction or control of any other person or authority.

The functions of the said Commission are:

a) to consider alleged or suspected corrupt practices committed by or with the participation of any person mentioned in paragraphs (b) and (c) and, where the Commission determines that there are sufficient grounds for holding an investigation, to investigate any such allegation or suspicion and to make a report thereon;

b) to investigate the conduct of any public officer, including any Minister or Parliamentary Secretary, which in the opinion of the Commission may be corrupt or may be connected with or may be conducive to corrupt practices and to report thereon;

c) to investigate the conduct of any person who is or has been entrusted with, or has or has had functions relating to the administration of a partnership or other body in which the Government of Malta, or any one or more of any other authority of the Government, a local government authority, a statutory body, or a partnership as aforesaid or any combination thereof, has a controlling interest or over which it has effective control, where such conduct, in the opinion of the Commission may be corrupt or connected with or conducive to corrupt practices, and to report thereon;

d) to examine the practices and procedures of government departments, local government authorities, statutory bodies or other bodies referred to in paragraph c) in order to facilitate the discovery of any corrupt practices and to recommend the revision of methods of work or procedures which may be conducive to corrupt practices, and to report thereon; and

e) to instruct, advise and assist any person, on his request, on ways in which corrupt practices may be eliminated, provided that such request may only be made by a person who has ministerial responsibility or who is entrusted with, or has functions relating to, the administration of a government department, local government authority, statutory body or other body referred to in paragraph c).

b. Punitive Actions

The aforesaid Act, defines 'corrupt practices' with reference to a number of provisions in the Criminal Code (Chapter 9 of the Laws of Malta), amongst others, dealing with crimes against public trust and contain, as it were, penal / punitive measures.

B. Project Contracting

a. Permission System

In terms of the Development Planning Act (Chapter 552 of the Laws of Malta), no development shall be carried out except with development permission.

For the purposes of the aforesaid rule, "development" means the carrying out of building, engineering, quarrying, mining or other operations for the construction, demolition or alterations in, on, over, or under any land or the sea, the placing of advertisements or the making of any material change in use of land or building and sea, subject to a number of technical exceptions that are invariably determined on a case by case basis.

b. Prohibited Areas

The Maltese territory is broadly divided into so-called 'development zones', where development, as defined above is permitted and 'non-development zones' where only very limited uses are allowed, typically, related to agriculture but no development in the true sense of the word.

c. Invitation to Bid and Bidding

Public procurement rules can be found in the Public Procurement Regulations and provide for a very detailed and extensive set of regulations that favour transparency. Generally-speaking, the most economically-competitive technically compliant bid is successful. Any interested party who may feel aggrieved by a decision of the Director of Contracts may file an appeal before a specialized Board that reviews the whole process, leading to the decision.

墨西哥

作者：Manuel Galicia Romero、Juan Pablo Cervantes
译者：连铮、杨闰

一、概述

墨西哥是一个代表制民主联邦共和国。根据墨西哥《宪法》（Constitución Política de los Estados Unidos Mexicanos），公共权力在行政、立法和司法部门之间分配。

立法部门由墨西哥国会领导，国会以两院制国民议会的形式组建，由参议院与众议院构成。众议院由 500 名当选议员组成，任期 3 年。在此 500 名众议员中，300 名直接选举产生，200 名由比例代表制方式选举产生；众议员不能连任。参议院有 128 名议员，其中 96 名直接选举产生（在 32 个 3 议席选区中，得票最多的政党取得 2 席，得票居次的政党获得 1 席），32 名由比例代表制方式选举产生，任期 6 年；参议员不能连任。

根据墨西哥《宪法》明确规定的权力，总统领导行政部门，通过直接、不记名和全民性投票选举产生，任期 6 年。《宪法》禁止总统有第二个任期、连续任期或交替任期。总统有权任命和罢免国务部长。

墨西哥联邦司法部门由最高法院（Suprema Corte de Justicia de la Nación）、联邦司法委员会（Consejo de la Judicatura Federal）、选举法庭（Tribunal Electoral）以及合议庭、单一法庭和地区法庭组成。最高法院由总统经参议院批准任命的 11 名法官组成，其主要职责是解释墨西哥法律和国际条约，并就宪法事项作出裁决。

各州均有众议院，就有限的问题与该州自身的宪法进行立法。截至 2017 年年底，墨西哥城宪法正在审议当中，该宪法预计自 2018 年起生效。

墨西哥是一个混合型经济体，私人投资极为活跃。制造业、采矿业、贸易业、建筑业及服务业是私营经济的最大贡献者。墨西哥的国内生产总值于 2017 年第二季度达 145 868.19 亿比索[1]，根据国际货币基金组织的估算，在未来几年将继续增长。

2017 年，墨西哥境内的外国直接投资达 156.452 亿美元。[2] 墨西哥经济由对外贸易驱动。虽然石油、旅游业、农业及采矿业也为收入作出了贡献，但出口收入主要来自于制造业。该国的外国投资主要依靠制造业、矿业及金融行业。

墨西哥与世界各国建立了富有成效的关系，但因地理位置相邻，同时受益于《北美自由贸易协定》（NAFTA），美国一直是墨西哥最大的贸易伙伴。墨西哥于 1993 年成为北美自由贸易协定成员。除北美自由贸易协定外，墨西哥还与世界各经济体建立了充满希望、富有成效的关系，与中美洲（哥斯达黎加、萨尔瓦多、危地马拉、洪都拉斯及尼加拉瓜）、秘鲁、玻利维亚、乌拉圭、哥伦比亚、智利、欧盟、以色列、日本、美国及加拿大签署了自由贸易协定。此外，墨西哥还与阿根廷、巴西、秘鲁、巴拉圭、古巴、厄瓜多尔及巴拿马签署了经济互补协定。

墨西哥是世界贸易组织（WTO）成员，已取消了大多数出口许可证，大幅消减了出口税和直接出口补贴，并取消了对出口的财政激励。为鼓励出口销售，墨西哥实施了各种出口激励计划，包括特殊的临时进口计划。

2012 年 4 月，智利、哥伦比亚、秘鲁及墨西哥签署了太平洋联盟协定，旨在建立一个政治诉求、经济和商业一体化并向世界投射的平台，其重点在于亚太地区。该商业协定正在考虑降低出口税，解

---

[1] 参见 http://www.banxico.org.mx/SieInternet/consultarDirectorioInternetAction.do?accion=consultarCuadro&idCuadro=CR142&locale=es。
[2] 参见 https://www.gob.mx/cms/uploads/attachment/file/255232/Carpeta_IED.pdf。

决争端，并减少商业障碍。

此外，墨西哥是经济合作与发展组织（OECD）与二十国集团（G20）成员。

二、投资

（一）市场准入

1. 投资监督部门

（1）外国投资委员会

负责监督墨西哥境内投资的主要部门是外国投资委员会（Comisión Nacional de Inversión Extranjera），该委员会是墨西哥经济部的一个机构。外国投资委员会的主要职能包括：① 发布外国投资准则，并建立促进墨西哥境内的外国投资机制；② 决定外国人参与具体活动的条款及条件。

（2）国家外国投资登记处

外商直接或间接投资的墨西哥公司应在国家外国投资登记处进行登记，并有义务在某些情况下（即股权结构、公司名称、税务地址等变更）更新其登记信息。

（3）墨西哥投资贸易促进局

虽然墨西哥投资贸易促进局本身并不是一个政府职能机构，但该局是墨西哥联邦政府（经济部）的一个实体，负责促进国际贸易与投资。该局成立于2007年，在31个国家设有48个办事处，包括北京、上海、香港、首尔及东京办事处。

2. 投资法律与规章

（1）法律

墨西哥《外国投资法》设定了墨西哥境内外国投资的总体框架。其主要目的是制定规则以在墨西哥境内引导外国投资，并促使国家利用外资加强自身发展。具体而言，墨西哥《外国投资法》规定了：①某些活动仅能由墨西哥人开展，不允许外国投资（无论直接或间接）；②某些活动受管制，即允许外国投资，但受到某些限制（即股比限制或需经外国投资委员会批准）；③关于购置不动产（对物）财产、开发某些资源、建立信托以及成立外商投资实体的条例；④外国投资委员会与国家外国投资登记处的监管框架。

（2）规章

墨西哥《外国投资法实施条例》具体阐明了墨西哥《外国投资法》中规定的一些普遍性准则与标准，以及外国投资应向外国投资委员会与国家外国投资登记处履行的某些程序。

3. 投资形式

（1）直接投资

关于通过特定企业形式在墨西哥进行直接投资的信息，请参阅"公司的设立与解散"部分。

（2）分支机构

非墨西哥公司可以在墨西哥设立子公司，根据相关法律，此等子公司在法律上独立于总部而存在。

相反，设立分支机构的外国公司却会因一些原因遭受不利。分支机构不得拥有不动产，不得扣除向总部支付的利息、特许权使用费、收费或其他服务款项。设立分支机构比成立公司花费更多的时间和金钱，而分支机构章程通常比公司章程包含更多的限制。由于分支机构在法律上不与总部分开，因此总部会被要求对分支机构的负债承担责任。此外，根据墨西哥《外国投资法》，所有开展商业活动的外国公司都应获得经济部的许可证。

4. 市场准入与审查标准

总体来说，墨西哥境内的外国投资不受限制，外国投资者享有与国内投资者相同的权利。然而，墨西哥《外国投资法》罗列了外国投资受到限制的三种主要活动类型：

- 只有墨西哥政府才能从事的活动：①（截至目前，如下文所述，根据墨西哥《宪法》[①]第27条和第28条）石油勘探、开采、输电及配电；②核能发电；③放射性矿物；④电报；⑤邮寄；⑥钞票发行；⑦硬币铸造；⑧港口、机场及直升机机场的控制与监视。
- 只有墨西哥公民或具有外国人排除条款的墨西哥公司才能从事的活动，其中不得有外国直接或间接参与：旅客与货物的陆路运输。
- 特殊管制且外国投资比例（10%至49%，取决于具体活动）受到限制和/或需要审批的活动与收购。

尽管如此，外国资本仍可通过"中性投资"投资于前述后两款所述活动（"中性投资"指的是对墨西哥实体或信托进行投资，投资者持有无表决权或有限表决权股份，此等股份优先获得一定比例的股息，并需获经济部批准）。

由于最近的宪法改革，墨西哥现允许外资在电信和卫星通信行业中最高持有100%的股权，在广播行业中最高持有49%的股权。

墨西哥"能源改革"启动了石油、天然气及电力部门的转型进程。在石油与天然气方面，改革为该部门引入了竞争。墨西哥石油公司，即前国营石油公司（Pemex），成为一家生产力较强的国有企业，能够与其他国内和国际私营企业竞争。2014年颁布的二级立法适用于上中下游市场，这些市场也对私营部门开放。

此外，针对电力工业，"能源改革"中制定的新条例允许私营部门更积极地参与发电，而墨西哥政府则保持对输电和配电活动的控制。系统运行以及电力传输和分配完全由国家专营，但可以与个人签订合同。

（二）外汇监管

1. 外汇监管部门

墨西哥中央银行（Banco de México）是墨西哥负责监督墨西哥境内外汇的机构。

2. 外汇法律法规简介

目前，墨西哥对非居民在当地持有本国或外国货币没有任何限制，官方也没有对保持货币可兑换作出保证。请注意，如果在墨西哥提起诉讼，要求履行墨西哥比索以外货币的付款义务，则根据墨西哥《货币法》（Ley Monetaria de los Estados Unidos Mexicanos），债务人可按付款当日墨西哥比索的汇率，以墨西哥比索支付任何到期款项，从而履行其义务。

（三）融资

1. 主要金融机构

（1）信贷机构

墨西哥金融市场的主要参与者是信贷机构，受《信贷机构法》（Ley de Instituciones de Crédito，LIC）管辖。墨西哥的信贷机构总体上分为两大类：①私人银行（banca multiple），由私人管理，受其章程与《信贷机构法》管辖，其主要目的是从私人与实体获得资金，并向私营部门提供服务（例如，发放贷款、维持银行账户等）；②开发银行（banca de desarrollo），为联邦公共行政之一部分，由公法管辖，其主要目的是支持生产性活动。

建立和经营一家商业银行之前，必须获得国家证券与银行委员会（Comisión Nacional Bancaria y de Valores，CNBV）的批准。

一般来说，信贷机构只能从事《信贷机构法》允许的业务，其中包括：①接收存款；②接受贷款；③发放银行奖金；④发行次级债务；⑤发行信用卡；⑥管理证券（受《信贷机构法》与其他条例约束）；⑦提供安全存款服务；⑧担任可转让票据持有人的代理；⑨订立金融租赁；⑩根据信托协议担

[①] 在最近的宪法改革中，墨西哥《宪法》与二级立法对能源领域的规定作了修改。该改革包含一项新的法律制度，允许私营部门（国内和国际）参与石油工业生产链的每一项活动，并参与发电。

任受托人；⑪执行衍生产品交易。

（2）保险

墨西哥金融市场的另一个主要参与者是保险公司（aseguradoras），受《保险机构法》（Ley de Instituciones de Seguros y Fianzas）与《保险机构通用准则》（Circular Única de Seguros y Fianzas）管辖。

（3）退休储蓄基金

墨西哥金融市场的另一个参与者是养老金基金（administradoras de fondos para el retiro，AFOREs），受《退休储蓄系统基金法》（Ley de los Sistemas de Ahorro Para el Retiro）管辖。养老金基金是私营金融机构，负责管理和投资墨西哥社会保障局（Instituto Nacional del Seguro Social）或国家工作人员保障与社会服务局（Instituto de Seguridad y Servicios Sociales de los Trabajadores del Estado）关联雇员的退休储蓄。

2.外国企业融资条件

总的来说，外国企业与国内企业在融资条件上没有差别。

（四）土地政策

1.土地相关法律与法规简介

（1）不动产（对物）权利类型

在墨西哥，个人或公司对不动产享有下列权利：①所有权；②使用权；③用益权；④通行权；⑤担保权（即抵押、工业抵押等）。

（2）不动产的购置与登记

为了根据墨西哥法律取得不动产，并使此等购置相对于第三方有效，此等购置应在财产公共登记处（Registro Público de Comercio）进行登记。此外，此类协议应有公开契据（escritura pública）予以证明。

2.外国企业土地购置规则

（1）直接购置

外国法人实体与个人可以直接在墨西哥购置并拥有土地［限制区域（专属经济区，zona económica exclusiva）除外，该区为沿国界与海岸线分别长达100公里和50公里的狭长地带］，前提是放弃在相关不动产资产方面援引其国籍国保护的权利，并就该购地事宜接受视同墨西哥国民身份（即受墨西哥土地和财产条例与法院的约束）；此等权利放弃通常被称为"卡尔沃条款"（cláusula Calvo）。

（2）间接购置

外国法人实体与个人可通过参与或设立墨西哥法人实体，向墨西哥外交部备案接受"卡尔沃条款"的文件，并在此后60天内发出购置公告，从而间接购置并拥有墨西哥限制区域之外的土地（以居住为目的的除外）。

（3）使用权

外国法人实体与个人可以通过经核准的金融机构担任托管人的墨西哥信托，间接取得在墨西哥限制区域内以居住为目的的土地使用权，之后再向墨西哥外交部申领这方面的许可证。

除遵守适用于墨西哥国民的一般性的本地法与民事法律外，外国人在墨西哥租赁土地没有其他限制。

（五）公司的设立与解散

1.企业形式

（1）总则

《商业公司普通法》（Ley General de Sociedades Mercantiles，LGSM）与《证券市场法》（Ley del Mercado de Valores，LMV）规定了墨西哥的企业形式。《商业公司普通法》认可七种形式的企业：①集体名义合伙；②有限合伙；③有限责任公司（SRL）；④股份有限公司（S.A.）；⑤股份有限合伙；⑥合作社；⑦简化股份公司（SAS）。此外，《证券市场法》还提供了三种额外股份有限公司形式：

①可变资本股份制公司（S.A.P.I.）；②上市有限公司；③证券交易所投资公司。在实践中，国内与外国投资者趋向于采用"有限责任公司""股份有限公司"或"可变资本股份制公司"形式进行直接投资。

（2）股份有限公司与可变资本股份制公司

股份有限公司是国内与外国投资者最普遍使用的法人实体类型，也是与美国公司最相似的形式。其主要特征包括：①公司法人的独立人格；②成立公司需要最低固定资本（该规定刚经过修订）；③公司的权益应由公司发行的股票代表；④无对股份转让的法律限制（虽然此类限制可能反映在公司章程中）；⑤股本增加时，股东有优先购买股份的权利；⑥在任何时候至少有两名股东。

根据最近对《商业公司普通法》的修订，可变资本股份制公司和股份有限公司与有限责任公司相比具有一定的优势和灵活性，即在股东协议和/或章程中体现某些约定的可能性，而在《商业公司普通法》修订之前，此类约定受到限制（例如，跟售权、拖售权、优先报价权、优先取舍权、看跌期权、看涨期权等）；在最近的修订之前，此类约定只允许实施于可变资本股份制公司。

尽管最近对《商业公司普通法》的修订缩小了可变资本股份制公司与股份有限公司之间的区别，上述两种公司形式之间仍然存在一定的差别，主要包括：①可变资本股份制公司有权购买本公司股份；②允许可变资本股份制公司订立协议，将一位或多位股东排除在利润分成之外；③允许可变资本股份制公司的股东设立适用于上市公司的监督部门；④允许股份有限公司由单一董事进行管理（而可变资本股份制公司必须由董事会进行治理）；⑤降低行使某些少数股权事项的门槛（下文将进一步详细说明）；⑥可变资本股份制公司通常是股份有限公司与上市公司之间的一个过渡（虽然可变资本股份制公司没有在证券交易所上市和交易其股票的义务）。

可行使少数股权的事项	行权要求的股份比例	
	股份有限公司	可变资本股份制公司
在符合一定条件的前提下，向公司总经理或者法定审计师提起民事权利请求。	25%	15%
要求董事会召开股东大会。	33%	10%
如果股东没有收到有关议程上任何要点的完整信息，则推迟股东大会。	25%	10%
在符合一定时间和程序要求的前提下，对股东大会通过的决议提出异议。	25%	20%
任命总经理或法定审计师。	25%	10%

（3）有限责任公司

有限责任公司是一种合伙制结构，也是墨西哥第二常用的商业实体形式。有限责任公司的主要特点包括：①其股本由合伙人拥有的股权（合伙权益）代表；②合伙人的限额为50名；③合伙人转让其股权有法定限制。

（4）简化股份公司

最近，为了促进小型企业的设立，《商业公司普通法》进行了修订，简化股份公司这一公司形式被纳入了该法；简化股份公司可由一名或多名个人成立，并可根据适用于此类公司的法律规定持有可变股份。设立简化股份公司的主要目的是使公司的成立程序更为简便，从而促进公司的成立；其主要特点包括：①简化股份公司可以由一名股东注册成立（这一点与所有其他公司形式不同，所有其他公司形式在任何时候都至少需要两名股东/合伙人）；②简化股份公司可以通过电子方式在不需要公证人协助的情况下成立。③简化股份公司的章程需依照经济部提供的一种格式，因此在股东协议方面的灵活性较小；④如果简化股份公司收入达到了一定的水平，则应转变为另一类型的商业实体（在未进行这种转变之前,否认公司法人的独立人格);⑤简化股份公司的股东不得持有任何其他类型商业实体的股本。

2. 设立程序

在墨西哥成立公司的程序简单明了,通常仅需要 4 至 6 周(除非在此过程中出现某些复杂情况)。

除简化股份公司外,公司成立必须有墨西哥公证人或公共经纪人(corredor público)在场,证明公司注册的文书必须在商业公共登记处进行登记。此外,必须向经济部申领公司名称的使用许可证;处理此类申请和获得公司名称许可证大约需要两个工作日。

如果创始股东或合伙人(或就公司而言,其法定代理人)居住在国外,无意前往墨西哥在公证人面前签署公司成立文书,则可就签署公司成立文书事项向墨西哥境内的第三人出具授权委托书。任何此类委托书必须符合墨西哥法律,并且必须获得委托书出具所在国的法律认可,然后在墨西哥公证人面前进行公证。

公司章程及细则取决于将采用的公司形式,并应与指定公司经理或董事会或唯一管理人以及审查员与实际代理人的股东或合伙人的最初决议一起拟定。

3. 解散途径与要求

墨西哥公司的解散与清算受《商业公司普通法》管辖。发生以下情况时,公司可以解散:①经营期限届满;②公司目的已经实现或无法实现;③经全体股东/合伙人协商一致;④公司在任何时候只有一个股东/合伙人(简化股份公司除外的所有类型的公司);⑤股本损失达 2/3;⑥法院判决(此类强制性解散根据其他适用法律进行)。

自愿解散由股东/合伙人会议决议,会议记录应在公共商业登记处进行登记;在作出相关决议后,解散中的公司启动清算程序,由一名或多名清算人(在作出解散决议的会议上指定)进行清算;清算人将:①终止未决交易;②收取公司的所有应收账款,并支付所有应付账款;③出售公司资产;④将公司所有现金分配给股东/合伙人;⑤公布期末资产负债表(须经股东/合伙人会议批准,并在公共商业登记处登记,且在经济部的电子系统上公布);⑥撤销公司在公共商业登记处及其他适用的登记处(例如联邦纳税人登记处)的登记。

最近修订的《商业公司普通法》纳入了公司解散和清算的简易程序,但公司必须满足某些要求(例如,股东/合伙人只能是个人,且在预定解散日期之前未进行交易,也未在预定解散日期前 2 年内出具发票,严格遵守税收、劳工及社会保障义务,无针对第三方的尚未履行之义务等)。该简易程序也降低了对公告的要求,且规定在商业公共登记处登记解散和清算环节可获得经济部的协助。

(六)兼并与收购

1. 兼并

墨西哥公司的兼并通常由《商业公司普通法》规定(虽然某些公司,如银行实体,应遵循其他适用法律规定的特别程序),但也须遵守本文所述的某些法律。

兼并程序如下:

1	兼并应获得被兼并实体与兼并后拟存续实体的特别股东会议/合伙人会议批准,并获准执行兼并协议。
2	执行兼并协议。
3	在公共商业登记处登记批准兼并的特别股东会议记录。
4	在经济部设立的电子系统中公布:①兼并协议;②被兼并实体与兼并后存续实体的资产负债表(通常由批准兼并的会议批准);③被兼并实体的资产与负债的消灭安排。

2. 收购

除上文第（一）部分"市场准入"概述的限制外，外国投资者收购墨西哥实体不受任何限制。尽管如此，在某些收购交割之前，可能需要获得某些政府审批：

（1）兼并许可

根据《联邦反垄断法》（Ley Federal de Competencia Económica，FCA）的规定，超过某些门槛的兼并与收购须向墨西哥反垄断委员会和/或联邦电信局通报并获其批准。有关此等门槛的更多信息，请参阅下文第（七）部分"竞争监管"。

（2）联邦电信局批准

如果墨西哥公司的资产价值超过联邦电信局每年确定的一定数额①，有意收购此等公司股权的外国投资者应获得联邦电信局的批准。

（3）其他政府机构批准

根据具体行业与适用于墨西哥实体的法规，在某些合并与收购交割之前，可能需要得到其他政府机构批准（例如，拥有特许权的基础设施相关公司、银行实体等）。

（4）公司授权与批准

如上文所述，就有限责任公司而言，第三方收购股权须经有限责任公司合伙人批准。此外，还应对公司章程和/或股东/合伙人的安排进行彻底审查，以确定是否应在并购交易交割之前获得更多的公司授权与批准。

（七）竞争监管

1. 竞争管制监督部门

（1）墨西哥反垄断委员会（Comisión Federal de Competencia Económica，COFECE）

墨西哥反垄断委员会是一个独立的宪法性机构，负责确保自由竞争，防止和调查垄断、垄断做法、非法合并及对自由市场的其他限制，并执行措施。

（2）联邦电信局（Instituto Federal de Telecomunicaciones，IFT）

与墨西哥反垄断委员会一样，联邦电信局也是一个独立的宪法性机构，在竞争监管方面与墨西哥反垄断委员会的职责相当，具体负责电信行业。

2. 竞争法律简介

（1）墨西哥《宪法》

墨西哥《宪法》第28条赋予墨西哥反垄断委员会与联邦电信局防止、调查垄断并执行惩罚措施的权力，为反垄断权威部门的行动与决策规定了一个总体框架。

（2）《联邦反垄断法》（Ley Federal de Competencia Económica）

《联邦反垄断法》对墨西哥《宪法》第28条概述的反垄断事项条款作出了具体的规定。其主要目的为促进、保护和确保自由竞争，防止、调查、惩罚和消除垄断做法、非法合并、准入壁垒及对自由市场的其他限制。

（3）软法

墨西哥反垄断委员会与联邦电信局业已公布《联邦反垄断法》的实施准则与意见；虽然这些准则与意见不具约束力，但在与墨西哥反垄断权威部门打交道时，建议遵循此等准则与意见以避免任何调查或惩罚措施。

（4）判例

墨西哥法院在解决反垄断问题时发布的判例在某些情况下可能具有约束力，而在另一些情况下则充当解释标准；因此，建议了解墨西哥法院在这方面发布的适用标准。

---

① 目前相当于 16 816 200 000 墨西哥比索。

3. 竞争监管措施

（1）在墨西哥进行并购前备案的义务

根据《联邦反垄断法》，如果并购超过了某些法定门槛中的至少一项，则无论这类交易是否引起排除或限制竞争的关切，该并购均须向墨西哥反垄断委员会提交通知。《联邦反垄断法》规定的法定门槛如下：

门槛	描述	金额
分配给墨西哥实体或资产的价格（《联邦反垄断法》§ 86-I）①	不论其执行地为何处，如果该交易（或一系列交易）为该交易涉及墨西哥的部分提供超过每日计量及更新单位（Unidad de Medida y Actualización, UMA）1 800 万倍的应付对价②。	1 450 800 000 墨西哥比索，大约 77 900 000 美元
墨西哥标的之资产/销售额（《联邦反垄断法》§ 86-II）	如果交易（或一系列交易）导致在墨西哥至少获得经济代理人总资产或总股本的 35%，而该经济代理人在墨西哥的总资产或销售额超过 UMA1 800 万倍。	1 450 800 000 墨西哥比索，大约 77 900 000 美元
标的资产/股本和参与者的全球资产/销售额（《联邦反垄断法》§ 86-III）	如果交易（或一系列交易）导致在墨西哥获得的资产或股本超过 UMA 的 840 万倍，且该交易（或一系列交易）所涉经济代理人在墨西哥的共同资产或年销售额至少为 UMA 的 4 800 万倍或更多。	（标的）677 040 000 墨西哥比索，大约 36 300 000 美元（参与者）3 868 800 000 墨西哥比索，大约 207 000 000 美元

根据联邦反垄断委员会的现行标准，上述计算应以相关公司经审计的最新财务报表确定的数额为基础。

关于上述情况，《联邦反垄断法》规定，"符合条件的交易"（即必须向墨西哥反垄断委员会备案或提交合并控制通知的交易）的当事方在墨西哥反垄断委员会签发有关授权之前，不得交割。

（2）其他措施

如上所述，根据墨西哥《宪法》与《联邦反垄断法》，墨西哥反垄断委员会与联邦电信局也是负责调查、防止和惩罚影响自由市场的活动和/或交易的权威部门（例如，垄断做法、准入壁垒及基本投入的控制）。因此，墨西哥反垄断委员会与联邦电信局也可以开展调查，以确定是否存在垄断做法，并对此实行惩罚。

（八）税收

1. 税务部门

税务管理局（Servicio de Administración Tributaria 或根据西班牙语首字母缩写为"SAT"）是负责管理、征收和执行联邦税收的联邦机构。

在州市两级，设有地方税务局，负责地方税收的管理、征收和执行。根据协调方案，在某些情况下，地方税务局有权执行和征收联邦税收。

2. 企业所得税

根据墨西哥《所得税法》（Ley del Impuesto Sobre la Renta 或"MITL"），下列人员须在墨西哥缴纳所得税：

（1）墨西哥居民的全球收入均需纳税。

（2）在本国境内有常设机构（establecimiento permanente 或"PE"）的外国居民，为归属于该常设

---

① 墨西哥反垄断委员会只针对以下交易运用这一门槛：仅涉及收购墨西哥公司或资产的交易；当事方（在相关收购协议中或谈判期间）将价格或对价的一部分具体分配给墨西哥公司或资产的全球或国际交易。

② UMA 类似于记账单位、费率、基数、计量单位或参考单位，旨在确定联邦、地方及墨西哥城法律以及这些法律产生的其他条例中规定的付款义务。2018 年，UMA 的价值为每日 80.60 墨西哥比索。

机构的收入纳税。

墨西哥税收条例规定了引力原则的适用标准，根据该标准，外国居民的收入也可视为归属于其在墨西哥的常设机构，其比例为墨西哥常设机构的费用占外国居民的全部费用的比例。

外国居民在墨西哥境内实际或合法存在时，可以被视为在墨西哥设有常设机构。外国居民在本国境内有营业场所，供其开展全部或部分商业活动或提供独立个人服务时，则视为在本国境内有实体存在。在下列情形中，法律存在视为形成：当外国居民通过非独立代理人在本国行事，如果该代理人以外国居民的名义或代表该外国居民行使订立协议的权利，以便为该外国居民在墨西哥开展活动的话；或通过独立代理人在本国境内行事，如果该代理人不在其正常营业范围内行事。

（3）在墨西哥无常设机构的外国居民，但收入来源于墨西哥境内的财产。

如果外国公司无常设机构，或收入不归属于该机构，在法律具体规定的个案中，来自墨西哥境内的财产的相关收入将在本国纳税。一般来说，如果一项收入被认为来于墨西哥，将根据收入的具体项目征收预扣税，例如：

- 处分股权所产生的资本收益（总收入的25%；如果满足某些要求，则为净收入的35%）[1]；
- 处分不动产（总收入为25%；如果满足某些要求，则为净收入的35%）[2]；
- 在墨西哥提供服务的收入（预扣税为总收入的25%）[3]；
- 利息支付（税率从4.9%至35%不等，视个案的具体情况而定）[4]；
- 特许权使用费支付（5%或25%，视个案的具体情况而定）[5]；
- 股息支付（相关股息总额的10%）[6]。

可以使用《双重税务协定》(DTT)降低或取消预扣税，前提是必须符合相应的使用条件。

（1）应税利润

墨西哥常驻公司对其全球收入负有纳税义务，而且必须通过按照企业所得税税率（目前为30%），就其在纳税年度获得的"应税利润"计算所得税负债。应纳税利润的计算如下：

	总收入
减	核准抵扣
等于	净利润
减	向员工支付的分红
减	结转亏损
等于	应税利润

一般来说，所得税按权责发生制征收；但在某些情况下，可适用现金制，详见下文。

墨西哥公司有权扣除或折旧《所得税法》允许的具体项目（即销售成本、有形和无形资产投资、某些支出与其他项目），并必须遵守《所得税法》及其条例中规定的某些要求。

墨西哥纳税人只有在有发票证明和根据税法准备书面证据（"税收证明"）的情况下，才能扣除进行其活动所绝对必要的费用。与其他司法管辖区一样，墨西哥法律规定了极为严格的费用扣除要求。除其他要求外，税收证明必须明确包括任何适用的增值税。

关于分红问题，墨西哥《宪法》规定雇员有权按照一定的比例，参与分享墨西哥公司在每个纳税

---

[1] 出售股份所得的资本收益须缴纳国内税。
[2] 处置不动产的资本收益须缴纳国内税。
[3] 无常设机构的外国居民在墨西哥提供服务所得的收入，可能适用中国与墨西哥之间订立的《双重税务协定》中的商业利润条款，因此可能无须在墨西哥纳税。
[4] 运用中国与墨西哥之间订立的《双重税务协定》，预扣税税率可降至5%，前提是利息的受益所有者持有付款公司至少10%的资本或投票权。
[5] 运用中国与墨西哥之间订立的《双重税务协定》，预扣税税率可降至10%，前提是特许权的收益所有者是另一缔约国的居民。
[6] 运用中国与墨西哥之间订立的《双重税务协定》，预扣税税率可降至5%，前提是股息的收益所有者是另一缔约国的居民。

年度获得的利润。这一比例目前按《所得税法》计算为应税利润的10%。分红必须在提交年度所得税申报表后60天内支付给雇员。在某些情况下（例如新公司的第一年内），公司可以免于向员工分红。最近，严格规范以外包方式规避向员工分红的条例已得到实施。

亏损可在10年期间结转，并须予以更新。

（2）通胀调整

墨西哥公司必须在纳税年度结束时进行通胀调整。为此，纳税人必须在纳税年度结束时计算其贷项与借项的月平均余额。如果贷项的年平均余额超过借项的年平均余额，则差额乘以年度调整系数，其结果即为可扣除的通胀损失。如果借项的年平均余额超过贷项的年平均余额，则差额乘以年度调整系数，其结果即为应税通胀利润。

（3）纳税申报与预缴税款

墨西哥居民纳税人必须提交年度纳税申报表以及相应的应付所得税款。此外，他们还须按月预付税款，此等款项可记入其年度所得税负债的贷项。

（4）转移定价

关联方交易受转移定价规定的约束。作为一项一般性主张，墨西哥法律遵循经济合作与发展组织《跨国企业与税务管理之转移定价准则》规定的标准。

3. 增值税

根据墨西哥《增值税法》（Ley del Impuesto al Valor Agregado 或 "VAT 法"），以下人士均有义务缴纳增值税：①在墨西哥境内供应商品或服务的，②准予在墨西哥境内临时使用或享有资产的，或③为墨西哥进口商品或服务的。增值税是一种基于消费的税收，适用于供应链的各个环节。其抵免制度（见下文）只允许每个环节增加值的增值税付款（避免级联效应）。

在某些情况下，商品与服务的出口税率为零。适用零税率的行为或活动所产生的法律效力，与增值税按16%缴纳的行为或活动所产生的法律效力相同。

（1）触发事件

《增值税法》定义了纳入商品或服务供应、资产临时使用或享有以及商品或服务进口等范畴的行为与活动，并提供了某一具体活动是否应视为在本国领土内进行的判定规则。此外，增值税以收付实现制为原则进行计算。

（2）责任方

责任方是商品与服务的供应商、商品临时使用与享有的授予者，以及商品或服务的进口商。增值税申报表应由被认定为责任方的公司每月提交。

一般来说，外国居民在墨西哥境内直接或通过常设机构从事应税活动时，将征收增值税。

从事应缴纳增值税的活动，如果输入增值税符合《增值税法》规定的"可抵扣的"（或可扣减的）条件的话，纳税人应当向税务管理局支付其输入增值税（供货商收入的增值税）与输出增值税（该公司的交易中向客户收取的增值税）之间的差额所产生的增值税数额。

输入增值税符合可抵扣的条件：①输入增值税应当对应于商品、服务或开展活动所"绝对必需"的商品临时使用或享受，且上述事项应支付增值税或适用零税率；②应在发票中注明增值税数额；③增值税应在对应月份实付。

（3）适用税率

一般情况下适用16%的增值税税率；然而，有些活动是零税率并免征其他税收。按零税率征税的商品与服务的例子包括非工业化蔬菜的供应、药品的供应、某些基本食品的供应、农业机械的供应，以及此等商品的相关服务，包括再保险服务以及《增值税法》规定的具体情况下的商品与服务出口。

免征商品与服务税的例子包括土地处置、预定用于施工出售的住宅、书籍、报纸、杂志、股票及证券，在某些情况下，还包括教育服务、国际货物海洋运输服务以及金融供应（如贷款）。

4. 消费税

消费税也是一种基于消费的税收，对某些特定产品进行征收，如烟草、含酒精饮料、能量与风味饮料、农药、非基本类食品（"垃圾食品"）和燃料，或与所述商品有关的经纪或代理服务，以及博彩和电信服务。

在墨西哥境内提供上述产品和/或服务，或将上述产品和/或服务进口至墨西哥境内，即触发消费税纳税义务。此外，消费税应在实际收取应税事项的商定对价时，按照收付实现制进行计算。

商品或服务供应商或进口商是必须向税务管理局缴纳特许权税的人士。消费税按月计算与缴纳。外国居民在墨西哥境内直接或通过常设机构从事应税活动时，将被征收消费税。

（1）消费税抵免制度

一般来说，消费税是不可抵免的。然而，作为一种例外，购买含酒精饮料、燃料、能量与风味饮料、农药以及垃圾食品等方面产生的输入消费税，可与同一活动产生的输出消费税相抵消。

（2）适用税率

适用的消费税税率因具体活动而异：
- 酒类饮品及有关服务从 26.5% 至 53% 不等；
- 烟草和香烟及相关服务从 30.4% 到 160% 不等；
- 农药从 6% 至 9% 不等；
- 加糖饮料，每升 1 墨西哥比索；
- 能量食品 25%；
- 垃圾食品 8%；
- 博彩 30%；
- 通过公共网络提供电讯服务 3%；
- 矿物燃料的消费税，按每升征收，税率视燃料种类而定。

5. 不动产购置税（ISAI）

购置房地产需缴纳地方税，具体特征可能因各州或市的具体规定而异。一般来说，购置土地和/或建筑物时会产生税费。以下是地方法规认定为购置行为的例子：
- 不动产处分行为或任何其他导致不动产转移的行为，包括捐赠、继承和向公司出资；
- 由于合并和分拆导致的不动产购置；
- 实物支付的购置行为；
- 通过信托进行购置而不授予不动产出让方归复权。

纳税义务人是相关不动产的购入方。外国居民在墨西哥购买不动产时应缴纳不动产购置税。

墨西哥各州的不动产购置税税率各有不同；但是，税率范围介于 0.5% 至 5% 之间，通常按不动产实际交易价格或价值、市场价或市政府注册的价值（valor catastral）之间的最高价值征收。

6. 社会保险费

用人单位应当每月报告并为所有参与公司产品生产和服务提供的员工支付社会保险费。

7. 纳税人的主要义务

（1）联邦纳税人登记（RFC）

在任何情况下，公司一旦设立即需在税务管理处登记，获得联邦纳税人注册表或税号以注册成为纳税人。出于此目的，总经理或被公司正式授权的人员必须提交申请并出于税务目的指定一个地址，有时公证人将负责这个过程。税务机关应当在两天内授予税号。公司还需获得电子签名。

除非存在特定情况，否则公司法定代表人、股东和合伙人也应当在税务管理处获得税号和电子签名。如果符合某些条件，则外国股东和合伙人无需承担这项义务。外国居民可通过提交其国内税号来申请其在墨西哥的税号。

（2）文件、记账凭证和发票

公司必须保留下列公司文件的相关记录：①股票登记簿，②股东或合伙人会议记录簿，③董事会或经理会议记录簿，以及④在公司资本可变的情况下，资本增加和减少的账目。

纳税人必须通过电子方式在税务管理局保存和提交会计记录，并且必须签发电子税务发票，每年提交其企业所得税申报单并保持对商品库存的控制。

（3）强制披露

涉及以下事项，纳税人必须披露：
- 关联方之间的交易；
- 资本投入和纳税居所的变化；
- 公司重组和改组；
- 资产出资和处置；
- 与居住地在避税天堂或适用领土税收体系的公司的交易；
- 资本赎回；
- 股息付款。

根据经济合作与发展组织发布的税基侵蚀和利润转移行动计划，墨西哥颁布了法规，要求"大型纳税人"提交披露其业务信息的信息报告，以便确认潜在的激进税收筹划和获取有关关联方交易的信息。

墨西哥是《外国账户税务合规法案》和《通用报告标准》的签署国，并在此方面制定了相应的国内法。

（九）证券

1. 证券相关法律法规简介

墨西哥的证券法主要框架包括以下：
- 《证券市场法》；
- 由国家证券与银行委员会发布的适用于证券发行人和交易市场其他参与者的一般性规定（Disposiciones de carácter general aplicables a las emisoras y a otros participantes del Mercado de Valores）；
- 墨西哥证券交易所内部条例（Reglamento Interior de la Bolsa Mexicana de Valores，Mexican Stock Exchange Regulations）；
- 由国家证券与银行委员会发布的适用于经纪交易商的一般性规定（Disposiciones de carácter general aplicables a las Casas de Bolsa）。

2. 证券市场监督和管理

在墨西哥，证券市场的监督和管理主要由财政和公共信贷部通过国家证券与银行委员会负责。

3. 外国企业从事证券交易的要求

在墨西哥，只有墨西哥银行机构和墨西哥经纪交易商被授权进行证券承销业务。

（十）投资优惠和保护

1. 优惠政策的结构

（1）补助

墨西哥政府可通过各部委、委员会、公共基金和研究机构提供政府补助，以促进和发展特定的活动和行业（例如创业、基础设施、运输、移民、技术和创新等）。[①]

此外，墨西哥还有诸如墨西哥投资贸易促进基金（Fondo Promexico）等计划，旨在通过提供资金以创建和开发有助于国家经济增长的项目，从而吸引外国的直接投资。

（2）双边投资条约

在墨西哥，对投资的优惠和保护通常通过双边投资条约（BITs）来实现。墨西哥拥有广泛的贸易网络，与来自拉丁美洲、欧洲、亚洲和东欧等各个国家签署了多达32个双边投资协定。墨西哥也已加入了一些区域性或多边条约，如《北美自由贸易协定》、TPP等条约都包含保护和促进对墨西哥投资的章节。

---

① 参见由内政部出版的政府补助名录，载https://www.gob.mx/cms/uploads/attachment/file/135614/Catalogo_programas_fondos_subsidios_2016.pdf。

2. 对特定行业和区域的支持

墨西哥制定了一系列覆盖范围广泛的优惠方案,重点集中在推动与特定行业和地区有关的产品的生产和出口。例如 IMMEX 方案,该方案旨在允许新设或已成立的公司临时进口原材料、机器、设备、运输工具和包装材料而无需支付本应适用的一般进口税。这些货物将在其后被以工业化标准进行加工,最终产品将出口(回到)国外。该等方案还包括可能允许上述公司推迟缴纳增值税。

另一个例子是行业促进计划(PROSEC),该计划的目的,是允许公司进口那些用于生产并随后出售的产品所必需的、特定的基础商品、机器和设备。上述进口行为可享受对特定行业的进口关税优惠。只有某些行业或领域可以享受 PROSEC 计划的优惠措施,如能源、电力、汽车工业、化工等。

3. 经济特区

在现行行政系统下,享受到经济优惠的区域被设立为经济特区(zonas económicas especiales),旨在促进墨西哥最不发达地区经济的可持续增长。设立特区的行政命令指出,这些经济特区应该有助于减少贫困并缩短欠发达地区与国内其他区域的经济发展水平差距。经济特区旨在推动投资、生产、竞争、就业等领域发展和使得收入被更好地分配。

上述领域将被视为国家的优先发展领域,国家将为其提供条件和激励措施,使其能在私营经济和公共部门的参与下,促进其所在地区的经济和社会发展。

在经济特区经营的个人或公司将获得税收、海关、金融优惠,以及享受包括行政设施和优越的基础设施在内的便利条件。优惠措施包括在经营的首个 10 年内,现金、货物、服务或信贷收入产生的税减免 100%;其后的 5 年,上述收入产生的税减免 50%。此外,如果积分管理人或投资者在经济特区境内获取资产,则在依据出售资产的价值计算增值税率时,他们可据此申请零增值税税率。若获取的资产原本是在经济特区之外,但随后被引进经济特区,则买方将获得增值税退税优惠。

4. 投资保护

如前所述,在墨西哥,对投资的优惠和保护通常通过双边投资条约来实现。墨西哥拥有广泛的贸易网络,与来自拉丁美洲、欧洲、亚洲和东欧等多个国家签署了多达 32 个双边投资协定。墨西哥也已加入一些区域或多边条约,如北美自由贸易协定、TPP 等条约都包括保护和促进墨西哥投资的章节。

双边投资条约是关于外国直接投资(FDI)的国际协议,旨在促进生产部门的资本流动并为之提供法律保护。因双边投资条约有助于建立有利的环境从而刺激生产性投资并最终推动墨西哥的经济发展,所以它们被公认为是外国投资者的信心源泉。

值得一提的是,墨西哥和中国都是世界贸易组织的成员国,双方所加入的条约包括《与贸易有关的投资措施协定》(TRIMS)。"本协议承认,某些投资措施可能会限制和扭曲贸易。它规定世贸组织成员不得采用任何歧视外国产品或导致数量限制的措施,采用上述措施均违反 WTO 的基本原则。TRIMS 协议所附的禁止投资措施清单,例如当地成分要求,也是 TRIMS 协议的一部分。TRIMS 委员会监督协议的运作和实施,并允许成员就与之相关的任何事宜进行磋商。"[1]

三、贸易

(一)贸易监管部门

墨西哥进出口法规的实施情况由经济部与财政和公共信贷部共同监督。凡涉及推广方案的授权与推进,或涉及进出口条例、进口关税缴纳及审计程序的执行,上述各部委都将根据具体情况定期对公司税务进行核查。

有关新的贸易机会或投资协议的谈判事项由经济部对外贸易秘书处管理。它是联邦政府的办事处,获得联邦授权,致力于推动墨西哥对外贸易多元化发展并巩固墨西哥作为出口大国和投资目的地的地位。该秘书处的另一个主要任务是管理墨西哥签署的贸易和投资协议从而支持经济的增长。它负责捍卫墨西哥在海外的商业利益,包括在争端解决场合中为国家辩护。最后,该秘书处会在多边及区域贸

---

[1] 《与贸易有关的投资措施协定》,载 https://www.wto.org/english/tratop_e/invest_e/invest_info_e.htm。

易机构和论坛中代表墨西哥，并监督与国际贸易政策有关的国际承诺的实施情况。

（二）贸易法律法规简介

在墨西哥，与贸易方面有关的法律、法规和规章有许多，最具关联性的概括如下：

• 《墨西哥海关法》（Ley Aduanera）：制定适用于货物进出口的规定以及进出口商必须支付的税费。该法还包含了对违规行为的处理准则及处罚。

• 《墨西哥海关法实施条例》（Reglamento a la Ley Aduanera）是为海关法提供解释和说明的法律文件。

• 《对外贸易法》（Ley de Comercio Exterior）和《对外贸易法实施条例》（Reglamento de la Ley de Comercio Exterior）：这些法律条款规定了原产地的确定原则、贸易救济原则及促进公平贸易原则。

• 《联邦财政法典》（Código Fiscal de la Federación）：确定了纳税人在该国的所有纳税原则、规则和规定。

• 《对外贸易规则》：由税务管理局制定的年度法规汇编而成，为外贸业务以及有政府授权的外贸相关项目提供切实可行的标准。

• 《进出口税通则》（Ley de los Impuestos Generales de Importación y de Exportación）：规定了运用于产品分类中的每一个关税代码对应的进出口税率。其关税分类系统遵循世界海关组织制定的规则（HTS 代码）。

（三）贸易管理

如上所述，在墨西哥，贸易管理由税务管理局负责监督，具体体现为监督落实税收及海关法律法规，以便个人和公司可按比例公平地为公共开支作出贡献。该机构同样负责纳税人审计，以确保税收和海关法规能得到遵守；它还负责促进和鼓励纳税人自愿遵守上述法规，并为税收政策的制定和税收效率的评估提供必要的信息。

因我们的信息系统近期正进行现代化优化，现大部分进出口数据都由进出口商以电子方式向该机构提交。这使得有关部门可以更快、更高效地完成税务及海关的审查。

（四）进出口商品检验检疫

在墨西哥，负责对进出口商品进行监督、检查和检疫的有如下机构：

• 联邦环境保护局（Procuraduría Federal de Protección al Ambiente），其主要任务是促使环境法规得到遵守，从而推动环境法律法规的执行及可持续发展。

• 全国农业食品健康、安全、质量服务中心（Servicio Nacional de Sanidad, Inocuidad y Calidad Agroalimentaria），负责保护农业、水产养殖和畜牧资源免受检疫性和（对受威胁地区）具有经济重要性的病虫害及疾病的威胁。

• 联邦卫生风险防范委员会（Comisión Federal Para la Protección Contra Riesgos Santiarios）力求保护人们免受因使用和购买商品、服务、健康用品以及由环境和劳动力因素造成的健康风险。

• 过程控制和监督使用农药及有毒物质内部秘书委员会（Comisión Intersecretarial para el Control del Proceso y Uso de Plaguicidas y Sustancias Tóxicas）的主要活动涉及发放农药、化肥和有毒物质的登记证书及进口许可证。

• 环境和自然资源部（Secretaría de Medio Ambiente y Recursos Naturales）是负责保护、恢复墨西哥生态系统、自然资源及保护环境产品和服务，从而推动其使用和可持续发展的联邦政府部门。

• 农业、畜牧业、农村发展、渔业和食品部（Secretaría de Agricultura, Ganadería, Desarrollo Rural, Pesca y Alimentación）的目标之一是鼓励实施一项支持政策，该政策能提高生产率，进一步利用农业部门的比较优势并将农村活动与其他经济部门的生产链结合起来。

• 能源委员会（Comisión Reguladora de Energía）负责确定进出口石油、天然气、电力和其他资源的要求。

(五)海关管理

为了使货物能顺利进出墨西哥,进出口商有必要聘请海关经纪人。海关经纪人属于私营部门,具有商业特征,他们从税务管理局获得执照,能代表进出口商协助海关办理清关手续。他们还能代表他们的客户向海关证明其已支付货物税款,非关税条例和限制已被遵守,从而确保货物能以快速、合法和安全的方式被进口或出口。海关经纪人常常和运输公司、货运代理商、仓库、监管机构、海关当局和进出口商等保持良好互动,以协调物流链条和商品流动。

海关总署(Administración General de Aduanas)负责实施规范海关清关的法律法规以及进出口清关应遵循的系统、方法和程序。此外,还有一些其他机构会参与到海关监管中来,所有这些机构都从属于税务管理局。

四、劳动

(一)劳动法律法规简介

以下是主要规范劳动事项的墨西哥法律法规:
- 墨西哥《宪法》;
- 《联邦劳动法》。

(二)雇用外籍员工的要求

1. 工作许可

临时居住在墨西哥的外国人可以申请在墨西哥逗留期间的工作许可证[如下面的第(三)部分"出入境"所述]。该工作许可证由国家移民协会(Instituto Nacional de Migración, INM)授予:如果未获得工作许可证,外国人可能无法从在墨西哥从事的工作活动中获得报酬。

2. 申请程序

为了获得工作许可,居住在墨西哥的外国人必须:①填写并打印提交相关文件(可在INM的网页上查阅);②向国家移民协会办公室提交要求的文件;以及③接收相应的决定书(由国家移民协会在20个工作日内颁发)。如果该协会认为在颁发决定书前,申请人需满足额外要求,则申请人需在7日内完成相应的要求。

3. 社会保障

根据墨西哥相关法律,如上文第二部分"投资"所述,如果个人(无论是墨西哥人还是外国人)被认为在墨西哥境内有劳动关系(因此在墨西哥境内参加劳动并在墨西哥境内获得报酬),则此人的雇主有义务在国家社会保障协会(Instituto Mexicano del Seguro Social)登记该雇员,并每月支付社会保险费。

(三)出入境

经过近期的移民改革后,墨西哥现有三种出入境许可类型。第一种针对游客访问者,游客访问者可以在墨西哥连续停留180日。游客访问者若未能获得工作许可证,便不能参加有报酬的活动,并须证明他们在逗留墨西哥期间的食宿资金充足。若游客访问者希望在逗留期间参加有薪工作,他们须拥有一份工作邀请或文化或艺术邀请才能获得工作许可。如果该游客访问者来自邻国,则他们可以在墨西哥与该国接壤的地区停留长达一年,还可以自由出入境并获得工作许可证。

临时居民可以在墨西哥停留不超过4年,在此期间临时居民可自由出入境,可获得工作许可证,并能携带子女、父母、妻子或丈夫和事实上的妻子或丈夫入境。

永久居民可在墨西哥无限期停留。这种身份许可通常授予难民、与墨西哥籍家庭成员一起生活的个人、有足够生活资金的退休人员、连续4年在墨西哥的临时居民、在墨西哥出生的个人的长辈或后裔以及因与墨西哥人结婚而连续居住墨西哥满两年的临时居民。

(四)工会与劳动组织

拥有超过20名员工的机构可以成立一个工会。联邦法律规定,集体谈判协议每两年至少进行一次修订。员工薪酬必须每年审核一次。

罢工只有在雇主拒绝遵守法律或合同义务时才是合法的(例如,制定或修改工会合同,接受仲裁委员会的裁决或支付法定利润分成)。只要大多数工人同意,他们可以实施罢工以支持另一场罢工。工会必须按照特定程序进行罢工。

签订劳动合同可能会涉及的季节性合同、试用期合同及初期培训合同也已被包含在最新修订版的劳动法中。此外,分包合同以及通过电子方式支付工资现已被允许。

此外,此次修订规定了"外包"制度,这是一种过去常用于规避支付员工分红所常用的方式。目前,若要合法使用外包制度,一般而言,必须遵守以下规定:①不能覆盖公司100%的经营活动;②必须能够证明外包具有专业性这一正当理由;③不能将与其自身工人从事的活动相类似的活动进行外包。

这些规定及最高法院确定的标准会对劳动、税收和反洗钱产生影响。如果外包不符合上述要求,则公司应被视为雇主,有义务遵守所有关于社会保障福利的规定,并不能将支付给员工的工资作为增值税的抵扣项。

最后,外包很可能因违反反洗钱法规而受到质疑,因此,公司必须在反洗钱网页上进行注册,准备一本指南并向金融情报单位提交报告。

(五)劳动争议

尽管有调解或私下协商等替代机制可以用来解决劳动争议,但在墨西哥,大多数劳动争议都由劳动委员会解决。

墨西哥国会最近在讨论通过改变立法以取消劳动委员会,由墨西哥法院来解决劳动争议。

五、知识产权

(一)知识产权法律法规简介

墨西哥的知识产权制度是在《北美自由贸易协定》(NAFTA)和《与贸易有关的知识产权协定》(TRIPs)等条约中规定的国际标准的基础上制定的。《知识产权法》(Ley de Propiedad Industrial,IPL)是关于发明、实用新型、工业设计、商标和商业广告或口号(每个均为"IPR",当统称"IPRs"时,还应包括著作权)的联邦法规。因此,该法确立了此类权利的获取、无效和实施的准则和要求。

墨西哥承认具有新颖性、创造性和实用性的发明[①]的可专利性。专利自申请起20年内受保护,该期限不可延长且须缴纳一定的政府费用。[②]根据尼斯国际分类,商标和服务标志授予与单个国际分类有关的特定商品或服务。商标和服务标志自申请日起被授予10年保护期,该期限可延展,且可按意向使用的方式提交,或说明首次在墨西哥使用的具体时间。单词、字母、数字、设计和三维图形可以注册为标识。《知识产权法》还为墨西哥驰名商标提供特殊保护。

墨西哥的原始计算机程序受作者权利分类的保护。墨西哥的作者权利包括一系列精神权利和经济权利,作者和开发人员因作品为其创作的简单原因而享有该等权利,其保护范围分为两部分权利:①精神或非继承性权利,在墨西哥作者权利体系下为了作者利益被承认且永久受保护[③];②允许著作权作品的专有使用和利用的经济权利或"继承性权利"。

---

① 发明,在《知识产权法》中的定义为:"任何满足具体需要的使自然界发现的物质或能量转化为人类应用的人类创造。"
② 发明者有获得相应专利的权利,无论是自然人还是企业。
③ 从广义上讲,精神权利是与作者的荣誉、声望和声誉相关的一系列权利或特权,以及授权或拒绝对其作品的任何修改或改动的可能性。

墨西哥作者权利的保护由联邦立法[①]专属管辖。目前的著作权管理法规是《联邦作者权利法》(Ley de Derechos de Autor，著作权法）。它规定国家作者权利机构，即国家著作权登记处，对大部分与墨西哥著作权体系相关的事项有管辖权。

（二）专利申请[②]

专利申请必须包括：对发明的描述，该描述必须足够清楚和完整，以使读者充分理解，并在适当的情况下指导具有专业技能和一般知识的人员完成该项发明。同样的，当本专利的描述不清楚时，它还必须介绍申请人已知的实施本发明的最佳方法，以及说明本发明的工业应用的信息。

专利审查过程包括将专利文件根据与该发明相关的技术领域分配给审查员时的实质审查。审查员需要确定该申请是否符合《知识产权法》第16条规定的新颖性、创造性和实用性的要求，并且确认该发明不属于知识产权法中规定被排除在外的情况。《知识产权法》及其实施条例授权墨西哥专利和商标局（IMPI）作出最多4次官方行动，以便将所有对特定申请的异议或任何技术层面上的澄清要求通知申请人。法律还规定，申请人应当拥有两个月的期限及额外两个月的延长期，以遵从每项官方行动。[③] 在此过程中专利和商标局的第五次官方行动必须是驳回专利申请或者发出专利授权通知（称为"支付邀请"）。

（三）商标注册[④]

整个商标注册流程所需的平均时间为6个月至1年。在收到申请后，专利和商标局将进行正式的审查以验证申请是否完整。商品或服务的分类正确性审查亦于此阶段进行。此后，专利和商标局开展新颖性审查，专利和商标局将搜索相似或相同的在先注册或未决申请。该搜索将在国际领域和国内领域内一起进行。

（四）知识产权保护措施

任何国内或国外的个人或实体均有权根据《知识产权法》和《著作权法》提交专利申请或注册申请（如适用），或者行使权利以防止对其在墨西哥境内知识产权的任何不合法行为。实际上，墨西哥必须保护在墨西哥已加入的国际条约的成员国境内注册的所有知识产权，例如《WIPO公约》《保护工业产权巴黎公约》和《专利合作条约》。

根据墨西哥知识产权法律和司法判例，为了能在民事诉讼中就损害知识产权行为进行索赔，原告须先在行政侵权诉讼中获得最终决定。侵权行为由专利和商标局判定，并可处以最高20 000日墨西哥城最低工资（约75 000美元）的罚款，并且在某些情况下，暂时或最终关闭设备或侵权者的企业。

通过行政侵权诉讼行使一项知识产权的条件是权利人必须：①证明其具有启动诉讼程序的法定理由（在专利/商标侵权的情况下，这可以通过提供知识产权证书来证明）和②已经按知识产权法规定在受知识产权保护的产品中插入了《知识产权法》规定的注册说明和声明，如专利号或™、® 符号，或者以其他方式公开宣布相关产品或方法受知识产权保护。根据墨西哥的法律和惯例，知识产权的使

---

① 在墨西哥，获得作者权利保护的基本要求如下：(a) 固定：法律规定墨西哥作者权利自 "……作品被固定在物质基础之上，独立于其艺术价值、定数或表达方式"起受到保护。固定的定义为："可用于表达看法、复制或以任何形式的交流的，以字母、符号、声音、图像和其他元素的组合的作品表达形式，或者该等元素以任何形式或物质基础的数字方式的体现，包括电子方式。"《著作权法》明确规定了获得作者权利无需办理手续。该法律规定 "作者权利和邻接权的认定不取决于事先注册，也不取决于任何文件或形式"。(b) 作者：根据墨西哥《著作权法》规定，只有个人可能被授予作者权利。该法明确规定，法人（公司）只能作为原作者代理人或代表人持有作者权利，并且只能利用或获得作品的 "家长权利"。(c) 原创性：根据《著作权法》的规定，作品必须是原创才能符合获得作者权利保护的要求。该法明确规定："受本法保护的作品是可以通过任何方式发表或复制的原创作品。"如上所述，作品不需要履行任何手续即可获得保护。此外，"版权声明"在墨西哥是非强制性的。版权声明的遗漏并不意味着作者权利的丧失，但未遵守规定在作品上声明保留权利或版权保留（原文为：derechos reservados）或未在所写 "D.R."后加上由字母 "c"及圆圈组成的符号的，可能被除以罚金（罚金仅适用于作品的编辑）。
② 若专利在墨西哥申请时已经在国外申请专利的，只要在国际条约中规定的时限内在墨西哥提交，或者在国外提交后的12个月内在墨西哥申请的，可以确认其优先权。
③ 参见《知识产权法》第55、58章。
④ 根据《保护工业产权巴黎公约》，墨西哥也承认商标优先权。在国际条约规定的时限内，或于在其他国家提交申请后6个月内在墨西哥提出商标注册申请的，应将第一个申请日认定为优先权日。

用行为并非行使知识产权的必要条件。

一旦专利和商标局最终确认某行为侵权,知识产权所有者有权向民事法院[①]提出民事诉讼中的损害赔偿[②],或向刑事法院提请刑事诉讼,如果侵权人继续实施已被认定为侵权的侵犯知识产权的行为。

除了专利和商标局判处的行政罚款,以及民事法庭判定的不少于侵权人出售的产品的销售价格40%的赔偿金之外,墨西哥的知识产权法律并未规定其他专利或知识产权侵权(包括法律费用赔偿)的救济。

六、环境保护

(一)环境保护监管部门

环境与自然资源部(Secretaría de Medio Ambiente y Recursos Naturales 或 SEMARNAT)是负责实施联邦环境法律、法规的联邦主管部门。此外,该部门还负责授予开展特定活动所需的许可证,而环境保护总检察长办公室(Procuraduría Federal de Protección al Ambiente 或 PROFEPA)是与该许可证相关的执法机构。环境与自然资源部及其他附属机构如国家水资源委员会(Comisión Nacional del Agua 或 CONAGUA)。

其他政府机构可能通过实施与环境事项密切相关的法律法规、授予开展特定活动所需的许可证的方式参与项目和活动的开展。与此最具关联的政府机构包括隶属于能源部(Secretaría de Energía 或 SENER)的国家核安全与保障措施委员会(Comisión Nacional de Seguridad Nuclear y Salvaguardias 或 CONASENUSA)和隶属于文化部(Secretaría de Cultura)的国家人类历史研究所(Instituto Nacional de Antropología e Historia 或 INAH)。

如果某些活动属于当地环境保护部门(无论是州政府还是市级政府)的管辖范围,这些活动必须获得当地环境保护部门的许可并符合当地法规。

(二)环境保护法律法规简介

《生态平衡和环境保护法》(Ley General del Equilibrio Ecológico y la Protección al Ambiente 或 LGEEPA)是墨西哥联邦环境保护领域的框架法。该法制定了绝大部分在墨西哥开发的项目和活动需遵守的环境政策。

尽管有这样的框架法,在墨西哥开展特定项目,还有许多其他关于环境保护方面的规则、条例和规范需遵守,具体包括:①《森林可持续发展通则》(Ley Federal de Desarrollo Forestal Sustentable);②《国家水域法》(Ley de Aguas Nacionales);③《预防与综合管理废弃物通则》(Ley General para la Prevención y Gestión Integral de los Residuos 或 LGPGIR)等。

最具关联性的联邦环境政策是:①环境影响评估;②领土与海洋生态规划;③建立自然保护区。

在墨西哥,从环保角度来说,开发任何项目或活动的可行性将很大程度上取决于该项目与相应的生态环境规划以及当地城市发展规划的兼容性,这主要通过环境影响评估程序进行评估。

(三)其他有关的环境事项

1. 土壤污染/补救责任

《预防与综合管理废弃物通则》对危险废弃物的处理进行了规定,并建立了对污染场所的购置所产生的环境责任及场地修复规则。

最相关的是:
- 受有害物质或废物污染的场所所有者/卖方有义务通知购置方有关污染物的存在。

---

① 在专利侵权案件中,有权向民事法院申请相关赔偿的专利权人必须已经获得专利权,损害赔偿包括自申请公开之日起的所有损失。
② 墨西哥的损害赔偿具有补偿性,且应在不低于侵权人可证实的销售价格(销售总额)的40%来合理地确定赔偿额。但是,由于墨西哥法律体系中的举证责任受否定者不应证明(affirmanti incumbit probatio)的原则约束,这就意味着举证责任由提出索赔的一方承担,原告在提出损害赔偿的民事诉讼中必须合法地证明导致其损失的侵权行为的范围以获得相应赔偿。

- 受危险废物污染的场所的所有权转移需经环境与自然资源部授权。
- 受有害物质或废物污染的场所所有者和经营者或拥有人对进行任何必要的补救措施负有连带责任。

2. 对海岸的使用

联邦海区（Zona Marítima Federal 或 ZOFEMAT）海滨属于公有财产，因此使用联邦海区只能经过环境与自然资源部特别授权。使用联邦海区的特许权期限通常为 15 年，到期可续，使用者需就使用支付政府费用。上述费用根据《联邦权利法》（Ley Federal de Derechos）制定，并很大程度上取决于特许经营的联邦海区地表位置和特许权人对其使用情况。

总而言之，前文概括地提出了可能对项目开发产生影响的最常见的环境监管部门和相应许可证；然而，每个企业都面临着不同的挑战，需根据具体案例的特点来制定具体的监管策略。

七、争议解决

（一）诉讼

墨西哥的诉讼程序首先是由宪法规定的，根据宪法规定，民事法律事项属于地方管辖，因此每个州都有自己的《民法典》（Código Civil）和《民事诉讼法》（Códigos de Procedimientos Civiles）；尽管如此，墨西哥也有一部适用于民事冲突的《联邦民事诉讼法》（Código Federal de Procedimientos Civiles）。墨西哥的法院分为联邦法院和地方法院。

诉讼程序通常开始于一方向有管辖权的法院起诉；诉讼主要包括以下阶段：开始阶段（提交起诉书与答辩状）、庭前会议、庭前和解、质证阶段和结束阶段。除少数例外情况外，所有下级法院的裁判都可能被上诉或被请求维持。

审判必须以符合墨西哥法定诉讼程序的方式自由、迅速地进行。

（二）仲裁

鉴于中大型交易各方会签署仲裁协议，墨西哥商业仲裁数量已显著增长。任何有资格行使民事权利的主体均可签署仲裁协议；然而，由于法律明文禁止，公共秩序事项（如环境、家庭、刑事、税务、劳动、反垄断、知识产权和消费者）不能提交仲裁解决。

仲裁由《商法典》规范，《商法典》基本上采用了《联合国国际贸易法委员会国际商事仲裁示范法》，并附加了一些规定，例如：①存在一个特别司法程序，使得当地法院可以介入和协助仲裁程序；②确定仲裁成本与费用的章节。

根据《商法典》（Código de Comercio），仲裁程序中的各方必须得到平等对待，并给予充分的机会来主张他们的权利。

墨西哥主要的争议解决机构如下：墨西哥仲裁中心（Centro de Arbitraje de México 或 CAM）、墨西哥城国家商会（Cámara Nacional de Comercio de la Ciudad de México 或 CANACO）、国际商会（ICC）和国际争议解决中心（ICDR）。

（三）其他替代纠纷解决机制

民事诉讼程序在墨西哥被广泛运用，案件数量巨大；因此墨西哥法院和当局最近一直提倡使用调解等替代性争议解决方式；这些替代方式只有在各方达成一致的情况下才能使用，且适用情况并不普遍。

八、其他

（一）反商业贿赂

1. 反商业贿赂法律法规简介

尽管墨西哥在过去几年颁布了对公职人员的一般反贿赂强制性法律和法规，但墨西哥目前尚未实施反商业贿赂法律和法规。但在最近，一些针对公职人员（servidores públicos）贿赂行为的宪法修正案得到了实施。2015 年 5 月 27 日，宪法修正案通过并设立了国家反贿赂系统（Sistema Nacional Anticorrupción，NAS），据此，2016 年 7 月 18 日，一些二级法规随之颁布，其中包括全国反贿赂系统法（Ley General del Sistema Nacional de Anticorrupción）和行政责任法（Ley General de Responsabilidades Administrativas）。此外，为了制裁与公职人员有关的贿赂行为，联邦刑法典（Código Penal Federal）也作出了一些修改。

国家反贿赂系统的主要目的是建立一个行政机构，负责颁布政府部门之间就鉴定、调查和执行相关行政及刑事惩罚措施的协调工作的政策及程序。上述行政及刑事措施意在惩罚公职人员在履行职责时实施相关贿赂活动的行为。

除设立和运行国家反贿赂系统外，相应的二级法规依据行为的严重程度对是否可适用刑法进行了分类。

无论是个人还是企业，当其参与或涉及实施贿赂行为时，上述反贿赂规定和惩罚措施将根据具体情况适用。但是，上述法规中提及的行为均源于公职人员或与公职人员有关，而不是由私人商业关系中的个人或公司实施。

2. 监督反商业贿赂的部门

如上所述，国家反贿赂系统及其相关规定不适用于商业关系中的行为。因此，这些规定所描述的行为仅与行政行为或公职人员有关。

负责落实该等法规和运作国家反贿赂系统的政府机关如下：
- 联邦行政监察部门（Secretaría de la Función Pública）；
- 州行政监察部门；
- 联邦审计部（Auditoría Superior de la Federación）；
- 州监察部门（entidades de fiscalización superior de las entidades federativas）；
- 政府生产企业的责任代表单位（Unidades de Responsabilidades de las Empresas productivas del Estado）；
- 联邦行政法院（Tribunal Federal de Jusiticia Adminsitrativa）。

3. 惩罚性措施

实施下述行为将可能会受到惩罚：
- 贿赂：个人和公司不得直接或通过第三方向公职人员承诺、提供或者交付任何礼品或利益，以要求公职人员根据其职责作为或不作为。
- 非法参与行政程序：个人和公司被禁止参与行程序时则不得参与该等行政程序。此外，他们不得为了被禁止参与行政程序的第三方的利益参与该等行政程序。
- 利用影响力交易：无论结果如何，个人和公司均不得利用其对任何公职人员影响力、经济或政治权利为其自身或第三方谋取利益。
- 使用虚假信息：个人和公司不得使用虚假或被篡改的信息以获取授权或获得某些利益。
- 共谋：个人和公司不得为了在公共采购中获得利益而实施共谋行为。

适用于个人和公司的惩罚措施如下：

（1）个人
- 处以相当于非法所得两倍的罚款，若没有获取任何利益的，处约 410 000 美元以上、约 615 000 美元以下的罚款；

- 暂时不得参与采购、租赁、服务或者公共项目，持续时间为 3 个月到 8 年；
- 赔偿联邦或地方财政遭受的损失和损害。

（2）公司
- 处相当于非法所得两倍的罚款，若没有获取任何利益的，处 1 000 UMAs（约 4 100 美元）以上、1 500 000 UMAs（约 6 150 000 美元）以下的罚款；
- 暂时不得参与采购、租赁、服务或者公共项目，持续时间为 3 个月到 10 年；
- 暂停与被处罚行为相关的商业、经济、合同或商业活动，持续时间为 3 个月到 3 年；
- 解散公司；
- 赔偿联邦或地方财政遭受的损失。

（二）项目承包

1. 权限系统

为了确保在价格、质量、融资、时间安排和其他有关方面获得最佳条件，墨西哥《宪法》规定，所有公共采购，包括采购、租赁和销售货物，以及提供服务和工程承包，都应当通过公开招标程序进行。

墨西哥《宪法》还规定，每当公开招标程序无法确保墨西哥政府在上述方面获得最佳条件时，二级法规应确定适用于此种情况的程序、规则和要求（如直接选择或限制邀请）。

因此，《公共部门采购、租赁和服务法》（Ley de Adquisiciones, Arrendamientos y Servicios del Sector Público，LAASSP）规定，所有公共采购通常应通过公开招标程序进行，限制邀请和直接选择作为补充。《公共部门采购、租赁和服务法》允许通过公开程序以外的两种方式进行采购：①限制邀请；②直接选择。采用这些例外方式必须是出于经济标准、有效性、公正性、可接受性和透明性的考虑，且是合同主体获得可取得的最佳条件的可用、必要的方式。此外，在前述任一情况下，采用该等方式的理由及正当性应以书面形式证明并由负责人员签字。

除了《公共部门采购、租赁和服务法》及其条例中规定的条款外，有关部门还颁布适用于其采购流程的内部政策和指导方针。

2. 招标和招标邀请

采购货物或服务时，在进入上述三种程序前，有关部门应当向指定的合同集中管理部门提交采购申请。

除了采购申请外，《公共部门采购、租赁和服务法》规定在进入投标过程前，合同主体应当准备一项调研以确定所需商品或服务的市场条件，例如所需数量商品或服务的可获得性、国内供应商、国际供应商所在地以及此类商品或服务的价格。此外，这项研究还可以用于确定最合适该情形的公共采购程序类型。

最后，根据参与者和产品的原籍国，《公共部门采购、租赁和服务法》规定了三种公开招标程序：
- 国内公开招标程序，本程序仅适用于墨西哥自然人或企业，其产品在墨西哥制造，且由经济部门（Secretaría de Economía）确定其产品至少 65% 的生产花费，如劳动成本、原材料和其他花费是发生在国内的；
- 国际条约下的国际公开招标程序，本程序适用于墨西哥和国外参与者，后者住所地需在已与墨西哥签订自由贸易协议且该协议包括公共采购内容的国家；
- 国际公开招标程序用于采购任何产地的产品，适用于所有国家的个人和公司。此类程序适用于下列情况：此前的国内公开招标程序被取消（如没有投标人或参与者或产品不符合投标规则），或在向联邦政府提供外国信贷资助的合同中有所约定（通常是多边组织，如世界银行）。

Mexico

Authors: Manuel Galicia Romero, Juan Pablo Cervantes
Translators: Lian Zheng, Rene Yang

I. Overview

The United Mexican States ("Mexico") is a representative, democratic and federal Republic. Under the Mexican Constitution (Constitución Política de los Estados Unidos Mexicanos), public power is divided between the Executive, Legislative and Judiciary Branches.

The Legislative Branch is headed by the Mexican Congress, which is organized as a bicameral National Congress, formed by the Chamber of Senators and the Chamber of Deputies. The Chamber of Deputies (the House of Representatives) is composed of 500 members elected for three-year terms. Of these 500 members, 300 are directly elected and 200 are elected by proportional representation. Deputies cannot serve two consecutive terms. The Chamber of Senators has 128 members, of whom 96 are directly elected (two for each state, two for the Mexico City and one for the first minority group) and 32 are elected by proportional representation for six-year terms. Senators cannot be reelected.

With powers clearly defined in the Mexican Constitution, the President heads the Executive Branch and is elected by direct, secret and universal vote for a six-year term. The Federal Constitution does not allow the President to serve a second, consecutive or alternate term. The President appoints and dismisses Ministers of State.

Mexico's federal Judiciary Branch is comprised by the Supreme Court of Justice (Suprema Corte de Justicia de la Nación), the Council of the Federal Judiciary (Consejo de la Judicatura Federal), the Electoral Tribunal (Tribunal Electoral) and collegiate, unitary and district courts. The Supreme Court of Justice is comprised by eleven justices appointed by the President with Senate approval, and its main role is to interpret Mexican laws and International treaties as well as render rulings with respect to constitutional matters.

Each state has its own House of Representatives which legislates on limited matters and an individual constitution. As of 2017, the constitution of Mexico City is being discussed by a constituent Congress, which is intended to be effective as of 2018.

Mexico has a mixed economy, extremely rich in private investment. Manufacturing, mining, trade, construction and service industries are the strongest contributions of private entities. The Gross Domestic Product (GDP) in Mexico was worth $14,586,819 million pesos for the second quarter of 2017[1], and is expected to be increased in the upcoming years, based on estimations of the International Monetary Fund.

Foreign direct investments in Mexico for 2017 reached USD$15,645.2 million dollars.[2] Mexico's economy is driven by external trade. Export earnings are fueled by manufacturing, although oil, tourism, agriculture and mining also contribute to revenue. The country's foreign investment relies mainly on manufacturing, mining and the financial sectors.

Mexico has established productive relations with countries all over the world; however, the US remains Mexico's largest trading partner, due to its geographical proximity and the benefits of the North American Free Trade Agreement (NAFTA). Mexico became a member of NAFTA in 1993. Besides NAFTA, Mexico has established promising productive relationship with various economies around the world, taking part in free trade agreements with Central America (Costa Rica, El Salvador, Guatemala, Honduras and Nicaragua), Peru, Bolivia, Uruguay, Colombia, Chile, The European Union, Israel, Japan, The United States and Canada. Mexico has signed Economic Complementation Agreements with Argentina, Brazil, Peru, Paraguay, Cuba, Ecuador and Panama.

Mexico is a member of the World Trade Organization (WTO) and has eliminated most export permits, substantially reduced export taxes and direct export subsidies, and eliminated fiscal incentives for exports. A variety of export-incentive programs, including special temporary import programs, are in place to encourage export sales.

---

[1] Mexican Institute of Statistics and Geography (available at http://www.banxico.org.mx/SieInternet/consultarDirectorioInternetAction.do?accion=consultarCuadro&idCuadro=CR142&locale=es).

[2] Mexican Ministry of Economy (available at https://www.gob.mx/cms/uploads/attachment/file/255232/Carpeta_IED.pdf).

Additionally, in April 2012, Chile, Colombia, Peru and Mexico signed the Pacific Alliance (PA) in order to build a platform of political articulation, economic and commercial integration and projection to the world, with emphasis on the Asia-Pacific region. The commercial agreement considers a decrease of export taxes, a settlement of disputes, and a reduction of the commercial obstacles.

Furthermore, Mexico is member of the Organization for Economic Co-operation and Development (OECD), and the Group of Twenty (G20).

II. Investment

A. Market Access

a. Department Supervising Investment

a) Foreign Investments Commission

The main department in charge of supervising investment in Mexico is the Foreign Investments Commission (Comisión Nacional de Inversión Extranjera) ("FIC"), which is an agency of the Mexican Ministry of Economy. Main functions of the FIC include (i) issuing guidelines for foreign investments and creating mechanisms to promote foreign investment within Mexico; and (ii) resolving on the terms and conditions for foreigners to participate in specific activities.

b) National Registry of Foreign Investments

Mexican Companies with direct or indirect foreign investments shall be registered in the National Registry of Foreign Investments (Registro Nacional de Inversiones Extranjeras) ("RNIE") and are obliged to update their registration information in certain scenarios (i.e.changes within shareholding structure, corporate name, tax address, among others).

c) Promexico

Promexico, while not an authority per se, is an entity of the Federal government of Mexico (Ministry of Economy) that promotes international trade and investment. Founded in 2007, it has a network of 48 offices in 31 countries, including Beijing, Shanghai, Hong Kong, Seoul, and Tokyo.

b. Laws and Regulations of Investment

a) Laws

The Mexican Foreign Investment Law (Ley de Inversión Extranjera) ("LIE") lays down the general framework for foreign investments within Mexico. Its main purpose is to establish rules to channel foreign investment within Mexico and promote national development derived therefrom. Specifically, the Mexican Foreign Investment Law sets forth (i) certain activities reserved to the Mexican State, in which foreign investment is not allowed (whether directly or indirectly); (ii) certain regulated activities, in which foreign investments are allowed subject to certain restrictions (i.e.percentage limits or approval by the FIC); (iii) certain regulations for the acquisition of real (in rem) property, the exploitation of certain resources and the creation of trusts and the incorporation of Mexican entities with foreign investments; and (iv) the regulatory framework of the FIC and the National Registry of Foreign Investments.

b) Regulations

The Regulations of the Mexican Foreign Investment Law (Reglamento de la Ley de Inversión Extranjera) specifies some general guidelines and criterion set forth in the Mexican Foreign Investment Law, as well as certain procedures to be followed before the FIC and RNIE.

c. Forms of Investment

a) Direct Investments

For information regarding direct investments in Mexico through specific forms of enterprises, please refer to Section E. Below.

b) Branches

Non Mexican companies can establish subsidiaries in Mexico, under applicable laws, which have distinct legal existence separate from the head office.

On the other hand, although some foreign companies have established branches in Mexico, they are at a disadvantage for several reasons. Branches may not own real estate, and they may not deduct payments to the head office for interest, royalties, fees or other services. Establishing a branch takes more time and money than establishing a corporation, and branch charters usually contain more restrictions than corporation charters. Because branch offices are not legally separate from the head office, the head office can be held responsible for the liabilities of a branch. Additionally, pursuant to the LIE, all foreign companies that carry out commercial activities shall obtain a permit from the Ministry of Economy.

d. Standards of Market Access and Examination

Generally, foreign investments within Mexico are not restricted and foreign investors enjoy the same rights as domestic investors. Nonetheless, the LIE lists three main types of activities in which foreign investment is restricted:

- Activities that only the Mexican government can perform: (i) until recently and as described below, oil exploration and extraction and transmission and distribution of electricity, in terms of articles 27 and 28 of the Mexican Constitution (Constitución Política de los Estados Unidos Mexicanos)[①]; (ii) nuclear energy generation; (iii) radioactive minerals; (iv) telegraphs; (v) mail delivery; (vi) issuance of banknotes; (vii) coin minting and (viii) control and surveillance of ports, airports and heliports.

- Activities only Mexican citizens or Mexican companies with foreigner-exclusion clause can perform, and in which no foreign participation, direct or indirect, is allowed: land transportation of passengers and goods.

- Activities and acquisitions that are specifically regulated and in which the percentage of foreign investment (from 10% to 49%) depending on the activity, is limited and/or requires approval.

Notwithstanding the above, foreign capital may be invested in the activities mentioned in the last two paragraphs through "neutral investment" (i.e.investment in a Mexican entity or trust, in which non-voting or limited voting shares are held that have priority to receive a certain percentage of dividends, and which is authorized by the Ministry of Economy).

Due to recent constitutional reforms, participation of up to 100% of foreign investment is now permitted in telecommunications and satellite communications and up to 49% in broadcasting.

The Energy Reform initiated a process of transformation of the oil& gas and electricity sectors. Regarding Oil & Gas, the reform opened the sector to competition. Petroleos Mexicanos, the former State run Oil Company (Pemex) became a Productive State Enterprise, capable of competing with other domestic and international private players. The secondary legislation enacted in 2014, is applicable to the upstream, midstream and downstream markets, was opened to private sectors too.

In addition, and concerning the electrical industry, the new regulation established in the Energy Reform allows the private sector to participate more actively in the generation of electricity, while the Mexican State maintains control of the activities of transmission and distribution of electricity. The operation of the system and transmission and distribution of electric power is reserved exclusively for the State, being able to contract for it with individuals.

B. Foreign Exchange Regulation

a. Department Supervising Foreign Exchange

The Central Bank of Mexico (Banco de México) is the Mexican institution in charge of overseeing the exchange in Mexico.

b. Brief Introduction of Laws and Regulations of Foreign Exchange

As of this date, there are no restrictions on domestic or foreign currency held locally by nonresidents, and no official guarantees against inconvertibility. Please take into consideration that in the event proceedings are brought in Mexico seeking performance of payment obligations denominated in a currency other than Mexican Pesos, pursuant to the Mexican Monetary Law (Ley Monetaria de los Estados Unidos Mexicanos), the obligor may discharge its obligations by paying any sum due in Mexican Pesos at the rate of exchange prevailing in Mexico on the date when payment is made.

C. Financing

a. Main Financial Institutions

a) Credit Institutions

The main participants in the Mexican financial market are credit institutions, governed by the Credit Institutions Law (Ley de Instituciones de Crédito or "LIC"). In general terms, credit institutions in Mexico are divided into two main groups: (i) private banking (banca multiple), which is managed by private individuals, is governed by its bylaws and by the LIC and which main purpose is to obtain funds from private individuals and entities and provide

---

① Due to recent constitutional reforms, the Mexican Constitution and the Secondary Law was amended in the field of energy. The reform contains a new legal regime that allows the private sector (domestic and International) to participate in each activities of the production chain of the oil industry; and in the generation of electricity.

services to the private sector (e.g.by granting loans, maintaining bank accounts, etc.) and (ii) development banking (banca de desarrollo), which are part of the federal public administration, governed by public law and which main purpose is to support productive activities.

In order to create and operate a commercial bank, prior approval by the National Securities and Banking Commission (Comisión Nacional Bancaria y de Valores or "CNBV") shall be obtained.

In general terms, credit institutions may only perform the actions permitted under the LIC, which include, among others, (i) receiving deposits; (ii) accepting loans; (iii) issuing banking bonuses; (iv) issuing subordinated debt; (v) issuing credit cards; (vi) managing securities (subject to the LIC and other regulations); (vii) providing safe deposit services; (viii) acting as representatives of holders of negotiable instruments; (ix) entering into financial leases; (x) acting as trustees under trust agreements; and (xi) executing derivatives transactions.

b) Insurance

Another main participant in the Mexican financial market are insurance companies (aseguradoras), governed by the Law of Insurance Institutions (Ley de Instituciones de Seguros y Fianzas) and the General Guidelines for Insurance Institutions (Circular Única de Seguros y Fianzas).

c) Retirement Savings Funds (AFOREs)

Another participant in the Mexican financial market are mutual pension funds (administradoras de fondos para el retiro or "AFOREs"), governed by the Retirement Savings Systems Funds (Ley de los Sistemas de Ahorro Para el Retiro), private financial institutions in charge of managing and investing retirement savings of employees affiliated to the Mexican Social Security Institute (Instituto Nacional del Seguro Social) or the Institute of Security and Social Services for State Workers (Instituto de Seguridad y Servicios Sociales de los Trabajadores del Estado).

b. Financing Conditions for Foreign Enterprises

In general terms, there are no differences in financing conditions between domestic enterprises and foreign enterprises.

D. Land Policy

a. Brief Introduction of Land-Related Laws and Regulations

a) Types of Real Property (in rem) Rights

In Mexico, individuals or companies may have the following rights over real property: (i) ownership; (ii) use; (iii) usufruct (usufructo); (iv) rights of way (servidumbres); and (v) security rights (i.e.mortgage, industrial mortgage, etc.).

b) Acquisition and Registration of Real Properties

In order to acquire a real property under Mexican law and for such acquisition to be valid vis-à-vis third parties, such acquisition shall be registered in the Public Registry of Property (Registro Público de Comercio). In addition, such agreements shall be evidenced in a public deed (escritura pública).

b. Rules of Land Acquisition for Foreign Enterprises

a) Direct Acquisition

Foreign legal entities and individuals may directly acquire and own land in Mexico (other than in the restricted area (zona económica exclusiva) which conforms a strip of land of one hundred kilometers along national borders and fifty kilometers along coasts) by waiving the right to invoke the protection of their country of citizenship in connection with the relevant real estate asset and, therefore, being deemed Mexican nationals for that purpose only (i.e.subject to Mexican regulations and courts on land and property); such waiver is commonly known as "Calvo clause" (cláusula Calvo).

b) Indirect Acquisition

Foreign legal entities and individuals may indirectly acquire and own land in Mexico in the Restricted Area (other than for residential purposes), by participating in or setting up a Mexican legal entity that files acceptance of the Calvo clause with the Mexican Ministry of Foreign Affairs and providing notice of the acquisition within 60 days thereafter.

c) Rights of Use

Foreign legal entities and individuals may indirectly acquire rights to use land in Mexico for residential purposes in the restricted area (zona económica exclusiva), through a Mexican trust with a Mexican authorized financial institution as trustee, prior obtaining a permit with the Mexican Ministry of Foreign Affairs to that effect.

No restrictions for foreigners to lease land in Mexico other than observance of the usual local and civil laws also applicable to nationals are in force.

E. The Establishment and Dissolution of Companies

a. The Forms of Enterprises

a) General

The General Law of Commercial Companies (Ley General de Sociedades Mercantiles) ("LGSM") and the Securities Market Law (Ley del Mercado de Valores) ("LMV") regulate the corporate forms in Mexico. The LGSM recognizes seven forms of enterprises: (i) sociedad en nombre colectivo; (ii) sociedad en comandita simple; (iii) sociedad de responsabilidad limitada ("SRL"); (iv) sociedad anónima ("S.A."); (v) sociedad en comandita por acciones; (vi) sociedad cooperativa; and (vii) sociedad por acciones simplificada ("SAS"). In addition, the LMV provides three additional forms of S.A.: (i) sociedad anónima promotora de inversion de capital variable ("S.A.P.I."); (ii) sociedad anónima bursátil; and (iii) sociedad anónima promotora de inversión bursátil. In practice, domestic and foreign investors prefer incorporating SRLs, S.A.s or SAPIs to effect direct investments.

b) S.A. and S.A.P.I.

The S.A. is the most common type of legal entity used by national and foreign investors, and is the most similar form to a U.S. corporation. Among others, its main features are (i) corporate veil; (ii) minimum fixed capital is required to incorporate the company, (provision recently amended); (iii) equity interests in the company shall be represented by stock issued by the company; (iv) no statutory limitations on the transfer of shares are applicable (although such restrictions may be reflected within the bylaws of the company); (v) shareholders have a preemptive right to acquire shares in the event of a capital stock increase; and (vi) a minimum of two shareholders at all times.

Pursuant to recent amendments to the LGSM, both the S.A.P.I. and the S.A. allow certain benefits and flexibility compared to the SRL, namely, the possibility to reflect certain agreements in shareholders' agreements and/or bylaws were restricted prior to such amendments (e.g.tag along, drag along, preemptive rights, rights of first offer, rights of first refusal, put options, call options, among others); prior to recent amendments, such agreements were only allowed for S.A.P.I.s.

Although recent amendments to the LGSM have diminished differences between S.A.P.I.s and S.A.s, certain relevant differences among these corporate forms include: (i) the right for S.A.P.I.s to acquire their own shares; (ii) the permission for shareholders of S.A.P.I.s to enter into agreements to exclude one or more shareholders from receiving profits; (iii) the permission for shareholders of S.A.P.I.s to create surveillance bodies applicable to publicly traded companies; (iv) the permission for S.A.s to be directed by a sole director (while S.A.P.I.s shall be governed by a board of directors); (v) lower thresholds for the exercise of certain minority rights (described in further detail below); and (vi) typically, S.A.P.I.s are intended to be a step between a normal S.A. and a publicly traded company (although there are no obligations for S.A.P.I.s to go public and trade their shares in a stock exchange).

Minority Right	% of shares required for exercise	
	S.A.	S.A.P.I.
File a civil claim against the general manager or statutory auditor of the company, provided that certain conditions are met.	25%	15%
Request the board of directors to call a shareholders' meeting.	33%	10%
Postpone the shareholders' meeting if they have not received complete information regarding any of the points on the agenda.	25%	10%
Contest resolutions adopted by the shareholders' meeting, provided that certain temporal and procedural requirements are met.	25%	20%
Appoint a general manager or statutory auditor.	25%	10%

c) SRL

The SRL is a partnership type structure, and it is the second most commonly used form of commercial entity in Mexico. Main features of SRL include: (i) their capital stock is represented by equity interests (partes sociales), owned by partners; (ii) a limit of 50 partners; and (iii) statutory restrictions for partners to transfer their equity interests.

d) SAS

Recently, and with the purpose of promoting the creation of small enterprises, the LGSM was amended to include the corporate form of SAS, which may be incorporated by one or more individuals and may have variable stock according to the applicable legal provisions for such kind of companies. The main purpose for the creation of SAS was to facilitate the incorporation procedure of companies in order to promote such incorporation; its main features include, among others: (i) the possibility for SAS to be incorporated by one shareholder (unlike all other corporate forms, which require at least two shareholders/partners at all times); (ii) the possibility to incorporate SAS electronically and without the need of the assistance of a Notary Public; (iii) bylaws of SAS derive from a form provided by the Ministry of Economy and thus, less flexibility on shareholders' agreements is allowed; (iv) in the event a SAS reaches certain revenues, it shall be transformed into another type of business entity (piercing the corporate veil until such transformation is not effected); and (v) shareholders of SAS may not participate in the capital stock of any other types of business entities.

b. The Procedure of Establishment

The process to incorporate a company in Mexico is a straight forward procedure which normally takes about four to six weeks (unless certain complications occur within such process).

Except for SAS, companies must be incorporated in Mexico before a Mexican Notary Public or Public Broker (corredor público) and the instrument evidencing such incorporation must be registered in the Public Registry of Commerce. In addition, a permit for use of a corporate name must be obtained from the Ministry of Economy ("ME"); it takes approximately two business days to process such application and obtain the corporate name permit.

If the founding shareholders or partners (or in the case of companies, their legal representatives) reside abroad and do not wish to travel to Mexico to appear before the Notary Public to sign the deed of incorporation, each may grant a power of attorney to a third person in Mexico for such purposes. Any such powers of attorney must comply with Mexican law and be legalized in the country in which they are granted and further notarized before a Mexican Notary Public.

The charter and by-laws of the company depend on the corporate form that will be used and should be prepared together with the initial resolutions of the shareholders or partners designating the managers or a board of directors or sole administrator, the examiners and the attorneys-in-fact of the company.

c. Routes and Requirements of Dissolution

Dissolution and liquidation of Mexican companies are regulated in the LGSM. Companies may be dissolved (i) due to the expiration of their term; (ii) if their corporate purpose has been fulfilled or is impossible to be undertaken; (iii) by agreement of the shareholders/partners; (iv) for all types of companies, excepting SAS, if such companies have only one shareholder/partner at any time; (v) due to the loss of two thirds of their capital stock; and (vi) by court resolution (such mandatory dissolution is conducted in terms of other applicable law).

Voluntary dissolution is resolved by the shareholders'/partners' meeting and minutes of such meeting shall be registered before the Public Registry of Commerce; following the corresponding resolution, a company in dissolution initiates a liquidation process, to be carried out by one or more liquidators (appointed in the meeting that resolved on the dissolution), who will (i) terminate pending transactions; (ii) collect all accounts receivable and pay all accounts payable of the company; (iii) sell the company's assets; (iv) distribute all cash of the company to the shareholders/partners; (v) issue a closing balance sheet (which shall be approved by the shareholders'/partners' meeting, registered in the Public Registry of Commerce and published in the electronic system of the ME); and (vi) cancel the registration of the Company in the Public Registry of Commerce and other applicable registries (e.g.the Federal Taxpayers' Registry).

Recent amendments to the LGSM have included a simplified procedure for the dissolution and liquidation of companies, provided such companies fulfill certain requirements (e.g.shareholders/partners shall only be individuals, do not conduct transactions prior to the intended dissolution date, nor have issued invoices within 2 years prior to the intended dissolution date, are in strict compliance with tax, labor and social security obligations, do not have pending obligations before third parties, among others). Such simplified procedure includes easier publication requirements and the assistance of the ME in the registration of dissolution and liquidation steps in the Public Registry of Commerce.

F. Mergers and Acquisitions

a. Mergers

Mergers of Mexican companies are typically governed by the LGSM (although certain companies, such as banking entities, shall follow special procedures set forth in other applicable law), subject also to certain laws, as mentioned herein.

Outline of Merger Procedure:

1	The merger shall be approved by the extraordinary shareholders' meetings/partners' meetings of the merging entity and the surviving entity, along with the approval to execute a merger agreement.
2	Execution of merger agreement.
3	Registration of minutes to the extraordinary shareholders' meetings in which the merger was approved within the Public Registry of Commerce.
4	Publication in the electronic system established by the ME of (a) the merger agreement, (b) the balance sheets of the merging entity and the surviving entity immediately prior to the merger (typically approved by the meetings that approved the merger) and (c) the mechanism for the extinction of assets and liabilities held by the merging entity.

b. Acquisitions

Except for the limitations outlined in section A.above, foreign investors may acquire Mexican entities without any restrictions. Nonetheless, certain governmental authorizations may need to be obtained prior to the closing of certain acquisitions:

a) Merger Clearance

The Federal Antitrust Law (Ley Federal de Competencia Económica or "FCA") requires for mergers and acquisitions that exceed certain thresholds to be communicated and approved by the Mexican Antitrust Commission (Comisión Federal de Competencia Económica) and/or the Federal Telecommunications Institute (Instituto Federal de Telecomunicaciones). For more information regarding such thresholds, please refer to Section G.below.

b) FIC Approval

In the event the value of the assets of Mexican companies exceed certain amount determined annually by FIC[①], foreign investors that intend to acquire stake of such companies shall obtain FIC approval.

c) Other Governmental Approvals

Depending on the sector and regulation applicable to Mexican entities, other governmental approvals may be required prior to the closing of certain mergers and acquisitions (e.g.infrastructure related companies which hold concessions, banking entities, etc.).

d) Corporate Authorization and Approvals

As stated above, in the particular case of a SRL, the acquisition of equity interests by third parties are subject to approval by the partners of an SRL. In addition, a thorough review of the bylaws and/or shareholders'/partners' arrangements should be conducted to determine whether additional corporate authorization and approvals should be obtained prior to the closing of an M&A transaction.

G. Competition Regulation

a. Department Supervising Competition Regulation

a) Mexican Antitrust Commission (Comisión Federal de Competencia Económica or "COFECE")

COFECE is an autonomous constitutional body (organismo constitucional autónomo) in charge of ensuring free competition and preventing, investigating and enforcing measures against monopolies, monopolistic practices, illicit mergers and other restrictions to free market.

b) Federal Telecommunications Institute (Instituto Federal de Telecomunicaciones or "IFT")

As COFECE, IFT is also an autonomous constitutional body (organismo constitucional autónomo) which responsibilities in connection with competition regulation are equal to those of COFECE, with specific responsibilities over the telecommunications sector.

b. Brief Introduction of Competition Law

a) Mexican Constitution

Article 28 of the Mexican Constitution establishes the capacities of COFECE and IFT to prevent, investigate

---

① Currently, equivalent to $16,816,200,000.00 Mexican Pesos.

and enforce measures to prevent and punish monopolistic practices, setting forth a general framework for the actions and decision-making of both antitrust authorities.

b) Federal Antitrust Law (Ley Federal de Competencia Económica)

The Federal Antitrust Law provides specific regulations for the provisions generally outlined in article 28 of the Mexican Constitution for antitrust matters. Its main purpose is to promote, protect and ensure free competition and to prevent, investigate, punish and eradicate monopolistic practices, illicit mergers, barriers to entry and other restrictions on free market.

c) Soft Law

COFECE and IFT have published guidelines and opinions on the application of the Federal Antitrust Law; while these instruments are not binding, it is advisable to follow such guidelines and opinions while interacting with Mexican antitrust authorities and to prevent any investigations or punitive measures.

d) Jurisprudence

Jurisprudence issued by Mexican Courts while resolving antitrust matters may be binding in certain scenarios, while used as an interpretative standard in others; thus, it is advisable to be aware of criteria issued by Mexican Courts on this regard.

c. Measures Regulating Competition

a) Obligation to Make a Pre-merger Filing in Mexico

Pursuant to the Federal Antitrust Law (Ley Federal de Competencia Económica), mergers and acquisitions are subject to the filing of a notice with the Mexican Antitrust Commission in the event that the same exceed at least one of certain statutory thresholds, regardless of whether such transactions present a competitive concern or not. The statutory thresholds set forth in the Federal Antitrust Law (Ley Federal de Competencia Económica) are as follows:

Threshold	Description	Amount
Price allocated to the Mexican entities or assets (FCA §86-I). ①	If the transaction (or series of transactions), regardless of the place of execution thereof, provide a consideration payable for the Mexican portion of the Transaction in excess of 18 million times the daily unit of measurement and update (Unidad de Medida y Actualización "UMA"). ②	MXP$1,450,800,000.00 Approx. US$77,900,000.00
Assets/sales of target in Mexico (FCA §86-II)	If the transaction (or series of transactions) result in the acquisition in Mexico of at least 35 percent of the total assets or capital stock of an economic agent whose total assets or sales in Mexico are in excess of 18 million times the UMA.	MXP$1,450,800,000.00 Approx. US$77,900,000.00
Assets/capital stock of target and global assets/sales of participants (FCA §86-III)	If the transaction (or series of transactions) result in the acquisition in Mexico of assets or capital stock in excess of 8.4 million times the UMA provided that the joint assets or annual sales in Mexico of the economic agents involved in the transaction (or series of transactions) amount to at least 48 million times the UMA or more.	(Target) MXP$677,040,000.00 Approx. US$36,300,000.00 (Participants in Mexico) MXP$3,868,800,000.00 Approx. US$207,000,000.00

Pursuant to prevailing criteria of the Federal Antitrust Commission, the foregoing calculations shall be made based on amounts established on the most recent audited financial statements of the relevant companies.

In connection with the above, the FCA provides that the parties to a "qualifying transaction" (that is, a transaction which requires the filing or a merger control notice before the COFECE), must refrain from closing until the relevant authorization has been issued by the COFECE.

---

① The COFECE applies this threshold exclusively to (i) Transactions involving only the acquisition of Mexican companies or assets and (ii) global or international Transactions in which the parties have allocated (in the relevant acquisition agreement or during the negotiations) specifically to the Mexican companies or assets a portion of the price or consideration.

② The UMA is employed like unit of account, rate, base, measurement, or reference to determine the payment of the obligations established in the federal, local and the Mexico City laws, and in the other regulations that emerge of these laws. In 2018, the value of the UMA are daily MXP$80.60.

b) Other Measures

As stated above, under the Mexican Constitution and the Federal Antitrust Law, COFECE and IFT are also the authorities responsible for investigating, preventing and punishing activities and/or transactions that affect free market (e.g.monopolistic practices, barriers to entry and control of essential inputs). Thus, COFECE and IFT may also conduct investigations to determine whether such monopolistic practices have been undertaken and impose sanctions in connection thereto.

H.Tax

a. Tax Authorities

The Tax Administration Service (Servicio de Administración Tributaria or "SAT" as per its acronym in Spanish) is the federal agency responsible for the administration, collection and enforcement of federal taxes.

At the State and Municipal levels, there are local revenue offices, which are responsible for the administration, collection and enforcement of local taxes. Under coordination programs, local revenue offices are entitled to enforce and collect federal taxes in certain circumstances.

b. Corporate Income Tax ("IT")

Under Mexican Income Tax Law (Ley del Impuesto Sobre la Renta or "MITL"), the following persons are subject to income tax ("IT") payable in our jurisdiction:

(i) Residents in Mexico pay taxes on a universal income basis;

(ii) Foreign residents with a permanent establishment (establecimiento permanente or "PE") within national territory, pay taxes with regards to the income attributable to said PE.

Mexican tax provisions set forth a force of attraction standard under which income of the foreign resident is also deemed as attributable to its Mexican PE, in the proportion that the foreign resident's overall expenses are comprised by expenses of the PE in Mexico.

Foreign residents could be deemed have a PE in Mexico, when they have a physical or legal presence within the country. Foreign residents have physical presence in national territory when they maintain a place of business in which they undertake, totally or partially, business activities or render independent personal services. Legal presence arises when foreign residents: (i) act in the country through a dependent agent, if such agent exercises powers to conclude agreements in the name or on behalf of the foreign resident, with purposes of carrying out the activities of such foreign resident in Mexico; or, (ii) act within national territory through an independent agent, if such agent does not act in the ordinary course of its activity.

(iii) Foreign residents without a PE in Mexico, with regards to income derived from a source of wealth located within the country.

Where foreign companies do not have a PE or income is not attributable thereto, relevant income will be taxed in Mexico when derived from a source of wealth located within the country, in the cases specifically set forth in Law. Generally, if an income is deemed to be sourced in Mexico, it will be subject to a withholding tax depending on the specific item of income, for example:

- Capital gains from shares disposal (25% on the gross income or alternatively 35% on the net income if some requirements are fulfilled)[1];
- Immovable property disposal (25% on the gross income or alternatively 35% on the net income if some requirements are fulfilled)[2];
- Income from services rendered in Mexico (25% withholding rate on the gross income)[3];
- Interest payments (rates range from 4.9% up to 35% depending on the particularities of each case)[4];
- Royalties' payment (5% or 25% depending on the particularities of each case)[5]; and
- Dividends payments (10% on the gross amount of the relevant dividend)[6].

Withholding tax can be reduced or eliminated through the application of Double Taxation Treaty ("DTT"),

---

[1] Capital gains from shares disposals are subject to domestic taxation.
[2] Capital gains from immovable property disposals are subject to domestic taxation.
[3] Income from services rendered in Mexico by foreign residents with no PE, might be subject to the DTT entered into between China and Mexico's (the "CH-MX DTT") business profits clause treatment and, therefore, not subject to taxation in Mexico.
[4] Withholding rate might be reduced to 5% through the application of the CH-MX DTT, provided the interests' beneficial owner participate of at least 10% of capital or voting power of the paying company.
[5] Withholding rate might be reduced to 10% through the application of the CH-MX DTT, provided the royalties' beneficial owner is a resident of the other Contracting State.
[6] Withholding rate might be reduced to 5% through the application of the CH-MX DTT, provided the dividends' beneficial owner is a resident of the other Contracting State.

provided the corresponding requirements for its application are fulfilled.

a) Taxable Profits

Mexican resident corporations are liable to tax on their worldwide income and must calculate their IT liability by applying to the "taxable profits" obtained during the tax year, the corporate income tax rate, which currently is 30%. The computation of taxable profits is as follows:

	Gross income (ingresos acumulables)
Less:	Authorized deductions(deducciones autorizadas)
Equals:	Net profits (utilidad fiscal)
Less:	Employees' profit sharing paid (participación de los trabajadores en las utilidades, PTU)
Less:	Carried-forward losses (pérdidas fiscales)
Equals:	Taxable profits (resultado fiscal)

Generally, the income tax is levied on an accrual basis; however, in certain cases a cash basis might be applicable as detailed below.

Mexican corporations are entitled to deduct or depreciate exclusively the items allowed by the Income Tax Law "ITL" (i.e., cost of sales, investments in tangible and intangible assets, certain expenses and other items) and must comply with certain requirements specified in the ITL and its regulations.

Mexican taxpayers may only deduct expenses that are strictly necessary to perform their activities, as long as invoices support them and documentary evidence is prepared in accordance with the tax laws ("tax support"). As in other jurisdictions, Mexican law imposes very strict requirements to allow for the deductibility of expenses. Among other things, tax support must expressly include any applicable value added tax.

Regarding profit sharing (participación de trabajadores en las utilidades or PTU), the Mexican Constitution provides that employees have the right to participate in a certain percentage on the profits obtained by Mexican corporations during each tax year. Such percentage is currently 10% of the taxable profits calculated in terms of the ITL. PTU must be paid to the employees within the 60 days following the filing of the Annual Income Tax Return. There are certain cases of exemption to pay the PTU (e.g.new companies, within their first year). Recently, strong regulations have entered into force against PTU avoidance outsourcing schemes.

Losses may be carried forward during a 10-year period and are subject to update.

b) Inflationary Adjustment

Mexican corporations are required to make adjustments for inflation, at the end of the tax year. For these purposes, taxpayers must calculate their monthly average balance of credits and debts at the end of the tax year. If the annual average balance of credits exceeds the annual average balance of debts, the difference must be multiplied by the annual adjustment factor; the result is a deductible inflationary loss. If the annual average balance of debts exceeds the average balance of credits, the difference is multiplied by the annual adjustment factor; the result is a taxable inflationary profit.

c) Tax Returns and Advance Payments

Mexican resident taxpayers are required to file an annual tax return, together with the corresponding IT payment. In addition, they are required to make monthly advance payments that may be credited against their annual IT liability.

d) Transfer Pricing

Related-party transactions are subject to transfer pricing provisions. As a general proposition, Mexican law follows the standards set forth by the OECD Transfer Pricing Guidelines for Multinational Enterprises and Tax Administrations.

c. Value Added Tax ("VAT")

In terms of the Mexican Value Added Tax Law (Ley del Impuesto al Valor Agregado or "VAT Law"), persons who (i) supply goods or services within Mexican territory, (ii) grant the temporary use or enjoyment of assets within

Mexican territory or (iii) import goods or services into Mexico, are obliged to pay VAT. VAT is a consumption-based tax applicable in each of the stages of the supply chain. Its crediting system (see below) allows VAT payment only on the value added in each stage (avoiding a cascade effect).

Exports of goods and services are zero-rated in certain cases. Acts or activities to which 0% rate is applicable produce the same legal effects than those produced by those for which VAT shall be paid at 16% rate.

a) Triggering Events

The VAT Law contains a definition of acts and activities that are included into the categories of supply of goods or services, grant of temporary use or enjoyment of assets and imports of goods or services and provides rules for determining whether a specific activity is deemed to be carried out within national territory. Further, VAT should be paid on a "cash basis" at the moment considerations agreed for taxable events are actually charged.

b) Liable Parties

The liable party is the supplier of goods and services, the grantor of the temporary use and enjoyment of goods and the importer of goods or services. VAT returns should be filed on a monthly basis by the company considered as liable party.

Generally, foreign residents will be subject to VAT in Mexico to the extent they perform taxable activities within national territory, directly or through a PE within national territory.

Taxpayers which carry out activities for which VAT is due shall pay to the SAT the amount of VAT resulting from the difference between its input VAT (VAT received from providers) and output VAT (VAT charged to customers on company's transactions), as long as the input VAT qualifies as "creditable" (or deductible) under the terms set forth in the VAT Law.

In order for the input VAT to qualify as creditable: (i) it should correspond to goods, services or temporary use or enjoyment of goods "strictly necessary" for the carrying out of activities, for which VAT should be paid or to which 0% rate is applicable; (ii) the amount of VAT charged should be expressly mentioned in an invoice; (iii) the VAT should be actually paid in the corresponding month.

c) Applicable Rates

Generally, 16% VAT rate is applicable; however, some activities are zero-rated and other tax exempt. Examples of goods and services taxed at a 0% rate include supplies of non-industrialized vegetables, supplies of medicines, supplies of certain basic foods, supplies of agricultural machinery, services related with such goods, including reinsurance services, and exports of goods and services in the specific cases indicated under the VAT Law.

Examples of exempt goods and services include land disposals, dwelling destined for building disposals, books, newspapers and magazines, shares and securities, in certain cases, education services, maritime international goods transport services, and financial supplies (such as lending money).

d. Excise Tax (Impuesto Especial Sobre Producción y Servicios "IEPS")

IEPS is also a consumption-based tax levied on certain specific products such as tobacco, beverages with alcohol content, energized and flavoured beverages, pesticides, non-basic foods ("junk food") and fuel or the rendering of broker or agency services related to the referred goods, as well as gambling and telecommunications services.

The activities considered as triggering events are the supply within national territory or import of the specific products and/or services detailed above. Further, IEPS should be paid on a "cash basis" when considerations agreed for taxable events are actually charged.

The supplier of goods or services or the importer are the persons that must remit IEPS to the SAT. IEPS is computed and paid on monthly basis. Foreign residents will be subject to IEPS in Mexico to the extent they perform taxable activities within national territory directly or through a PE within national territory.

a) IEPS Crediting System

As a general rule IEPS is not creditable. However, as an exception input IEPS generated on the acquisition of alcoholic beverages, fuel, energizing and flavoured beverages, pesticides and junk food can be offset against output IEPS generated on the same activities.

b) Applicable Rates

The applicable IEPS rates vary depending on the relevant activity:

- Alcoholic beverages and related services range from 26.5% up to 53%;
- Tobacco and cigarettes and related services range from 30.4% up to 160%;
- Pesticides range from 6% up to 9%;
- Sugar-sweetened beverages MXP$1.00 per litre;
- Energizers 25%;
- Junk food 8%;

- Gambling and lotteries 30%;
- Rendering of telecommunications services through public networks 3%; and
- For fossil fuels IEPS rate is assessed through a fee per litre, which may vary depending on the type of fuel.

e. Acquisition of Immovable Property Tax ("ISAI")

The acquisition of real estate is subject to a local tax, which particular characteristics may vary depending on the particular provisions of each State or Municipality. Generally, the tax is triggered on the acquisition of land and/or constructions. The following events are examples of what local codes deem as an act of acquisition:

- Acts derived from the disposal of immovable property or any other act having as effect the transfer of immovable property including donations, inheritance and capital contributions to companies;
- Acquisitions derived from mergers and spin-offs;
- Acquisitions from payments in kind;
- Acquisitions carried out through trusts where reversion rights were not granted to the transferor of the immovable property.

The liable party is the acquirer of the relevant immovable property. Foreign residents will be subject to ISAI when they acquire immovable property located in Mexico.

The applicable tax rate varies depending on the State; however, rates range between 0.5% and 5%, and are usually imposed over the highest value among: (i) the transaction price or value, (ii) the fair market value, or (iii) registered municipality value (valor catastral).

f. Social Security Institute Contributions

Employers are obliged to report and pay every month the social security contributions triggered for all the employees involved in the production of the company's products or services.

g. Taxpayer's Main Obligations

a) Federal Taxpayer Registry ("RFC")

In any case, upon incorporation, companies must be registered before the SAT in order to obtain its Federal Tax Payer Registry ("RFC", as per its acronym in Spanish) or tax identification number to be registered as a taxpayer. For such purposes, the General Manager or a person duly authorized by the corporation must file an application and appoint an address for tax purposes. In some cases, the notary public takes care of this procedure. The tax authorities shall issue the RFC during the following two days. Companies are also required to obtain an electronic signature (e.firma).

Except under certain circumstances, companies' legal representatives, shareholders and partners are also obliged to request its RFC and e.firma before the SAT. Provided certain conditions are met, foreign shareholders and partners will not have this obligation. Foreign residents are able to request for their RFC by providing their domestic tax identification number.

b) Books, Accountability Records and Invoicing

Corporations are required to maintain relevant records in the following corporate books: (i) stock registry book; (ii) minutes book for shareholders' or partners' meetings; (iii) minutes book for board of directors or managers' meetings; and (iv) ledger for the records of capital increases and decreases, in the case of variable capital corporations.

Taxpayers must keep and file their accounting records before the SAT through electronic means, they also must issue electronic tax invoices, file their IT return on an annual basis and keep a merchandise inventory control.

c) Mandatory Disclosures

Among others, the following events are classified as "relevant" and must be disclosed by taxpayers:
- Transactions between related parties;
- Capital contributions and changes in tax residency status;
- Corporate reorganizations and restructures;
- Asset contributions and disposals;
- Transactions with companies residing in tax havens or with a territorial taxation system;
- Capital redemptions; and
- Dividends payment.

In line with Base Erosion Profit Shifting action plan issued by the Organization for the Economic Cooperation and Development (OECD), Mexico enacted regulations which oblige "large taxpayers" to file informative statements disclosing information regarding their operations in order to identify potentially aggressive tax planning and to obtain information regarding related party transactions.

Mexico is signatory of Foreign Account Tax Compliance Act and Common Reporting Standard instruments, and has enacted domestic provisions in this regard.

I. Securities

a. Brief Introduction of Securities-Related Laws and Regulations

The main Mexican legal framework comprises the:
- LMV;
- General regulations applicable to issuers of securities and other participants of exchange markets (Disposiciones de carácter general aplicables a las emisoras y a otros participantes del Mercado de Valores), issued by the CNBV (CNBV Regulations);
- Mexican Stock Exchange Internal Regulations (Reglamento Interior de la Bolsa Mexicana de Valores) (Mexican Stock Exchange Regulations);
- General regulations applicable to broker-dealers (Disposiciones de carácter general aplicables a las Casas de Bolsa), issued by the CNBV.

b. Supervision and Regulation of Securities Market

In Mexico, the main supervision and regulation of the securities market is responsibility of the Ministry of Finance and Public Credit through the CNBV.

c. Requirements for Engagement in Securities Trading for Foreign Enterprises

In Mexico, only Mexican banking institutions and Mexican broker-dealers (casas de bolsa) are authorized to carry out any underwriting of securities.

J. Preference and Protection of Investment

a. The Structure of Preference Policies

a) Grants

Mexican government, through Ministries, Commissions and Public Funds and Institutes, may provide state grants to promote and develop specific activities and sectors (e.g., entrepreneurship, infrastructure, transportation, immigration, technology and innovation, among others)[1].

In addition, certain initiatives such as Promexico Fund (Fondo Promexico) are aimed to attract foreign direct investment in Mexico, by providing funds to create and develop projects that contribute to national economic growth.

b) Bilateral Investment Treaties

Preferential treatment and protection of investments are conducted in Mexico usually through Bilateral Investment Treaties (BITs). Mexico has a network of 32 BITs entered into with a diverse range of countries from Latin America, Europe, Asia and East Europe. Some regional or multilateral treaties are also in place, such as NAFTA, TPP that also include chapters protecting and promoting investments in our Country.

b. Support for Specific Industries and Regions

Mexico has established a broad range of programs focused on promoting the production and exportation of products related to specific industries and regions. As examples, we can mention the IMMEX Program, intended to allow new or established companies the temporary importation of raw material, machinery, equipment, transportation gear and packaging materials without paying the general import duty otherwise applicable to any other importation. Those goods are then subjected to an industrial process or service to manufacture a final product that will later be exported (returned) abroad. Such program also includes the possibility of deferring the payment of VAT.

Another example is the Sectoral Promotion Program (PROSEC) whose purpose is to allow companies to import on definitive basis goods, machinery and equipment that is necessary to produce other products that will later on be sold. This importation is done under preferential import duty tariff, and is sector-specific. Only some industries or areas are subject to the PROSEC Program benefits, such as energy, electric, auto industry, chemical, etc.

c. Special Economic Areas

Under the current administration, preferential economic areas were created as Special Economic Zones (zonas económicas especiales), with the purpose of promoting sustainable economic growth in the least-developed parts of the Country. The mandate states that such SEZs should help to reduce poverty and shorten the breach

---

[1] Catalogue of State Grants published by the Ministry of Internal Affairs (available at https://www.gob.mx/cms/uploads/attachment/file/135614/Catalogo_programas_fondos_subsidios_2016.pdf).

between less prosperous regions and the rest of the national territory. They are intended to promote investment, productivity, competitiveness, employment and a better distribution of income among the population.

These areas will be considered priority areas of national development and the State will promote the conditions and incentives so that, with the participation of the private and social sectors, it contributes to the economic and social development of the regions in which they are located.

Individuals or corporations that operate in the SEZs will receive tax, customs and financial benefits, as well as administrative facilities and competitive infrastructure, among other special conditions. Some of the benefits include tax cuts on income in cash, goods, services or credit generated in 100% during the first 10 years and 50% in the 5 subsequent years. In addition, they can apply a 0% VAT rate to the value of the sale of the assets if the integral managers or investors acquire assets in the territory of the SEZs. In case of acquiring the assets outside this zone and later introduce them into a SEZ, buyer will obtain the refund of the VAT transferred to it.

d. Investment Protection

As mentioned before, preferential treatment and protection of investments in Mexico is usually covered BITs. Mexico has a network of 32 BITs entered into with a diverse range of countries from Latin America, Europe, Asia and East Europe. Some regional or multilateral treaties are also in place, such as NAFTA, TPP that also include chapters protecting and promoting investments in our Country.

BITs are international agreements on Foreign Direct Investment (FDI) that are designed for the promotion and legal protection of capital flows destined to the productive sector. They are recognized as a generator of confidence for foreign investors, since they allow the establishment of a favorable climate that may stimulate productive investment and, simultaneously, promote the economic development of Mexico.

It is also important to mention that both Mexico and China are part of the WTO, which includes the Agreement on Trade-Related Investment Measures (TRIMS). "This agreement recognizes that certain investment measures can restrict and distort trade. It states that WTO members may not apply any measure that discriminates against foreign products or that leads to quantitative restrictions, both of which violate basic WTO principles. A list of prohibited TRIMS, such as local content requirements, is part of the Agreement. The TRIMS Committee monitors the operation and implementation of the Agreement and allows members the opportunity to consult on any relevant matters."[1]

III. Trade

A. Department Supervising Trade

Mexico's compliance with import and export regulations is supervised jointly by the Ministry of Economy (Secretaría de Economía) and the Ministry of Finance and Public Credit (Secretaría de Hacienda y Crédito Público). Depending on the specific issue, whether it is related to the authorization and continuation of promoting programs, or compliance with the import and export regulations, payment of import duties and taxes, as well as the auditing process, each of the mentioned Ministries will act upon regular verifications in the tax domicile of the companies.

Relate to the negotiation of new trade and investment agreements, the Under Secretariat of Foreign Trade of the Ministry of Economy is the office of the Federal Government empowered to diversify foreign trade and consolidate Mexico as an exporting power and investment destination. Another main objective is to administer trade and investment agreements signed by Mexico in order to support economic growth. They are in charge of defending Mexico's commercial interests abroad, including the defense of our Country in dispute settlement situations. Finally, they represent Mexico in multilateral and regional trade bodies and forums and monitor compliance with international commitments related to international trade policy.

B. Brief Introduction of Trade Laws and Regulations

In Mexico, there are several laws, codes and rules regulating trade aspects. The most relevant are described below:

- Mexican Customs Law (Ley Aduanera): sets up the rules applicable to the importation and exportation of goods to and from the country, as well the taxes and fees that importers and exporters must pay. It also includes

---

[1] World Trade Organization.(2018).Agreement on Trade Related Investment Measures.February 19th 2018, de WTO Sitio web: https://www.wto.org/english/tratop_e/invest_e/invest_info_e.htm.

the operational guidelines and sanctions for non-compliance.

- Mexican Customs Law Regulations (Reglamento a la Ley Aduanera): additional instrument that provides with interpretation and clarification in the application to the Customs Law.

- Foreign Trade Law (Ley de Comercio Exterior) and Foreign Trade Law Regulations (Reglamento de la Ley de Comercio Exterior): these legal provisions deal with the principles of origin determination, trade remedies and promotion of equity and fair trade.

- Federal Fiscal Code (Código Fiscal de la Federación): establishes the tributary principles, rules and provisions of all contributions (taxes) by the taxpayers in the country.

- Rules of Foreign Trade: Annual compendium of regulations established by SAT providing with practical standards applicable to foreign trade operations and the programs authorized by the authority related to those activities.

- General Import and Export Taxes Law (Ley de los Impuestos Generales de Importación y de Exportación): indicates the import and export duty rate applicable to each tariff code used in the classification of the products. Our tariff classification system follow the rules stablished by the World Customs Organization (HTS code).

C. Trade Management

As established above, in Mexico, the trade management is supervised by SAT, which is responsible for applying tax and customs legislation, so that individuals and corporations contribute proportionally and fairly to public spending. This agency is in charge of auditing taxpayers to secure compliance with tax and customs provisions; to facilitate and encourage voluntary compliance, and to generate and provide the necessary information for the design and evaluation of tax policies and efficiencies.

Because of recent attempts to modernize our information system, most of the import and export data is filed with the agency electronically by importers and exporters. This allows for a faster and more effective review process on tax and customs regulation.

D. The Inspection and Quarantine of Import and Export Commodities

In Mexico, there are different agencies involved in the supervision, inspection and quarantine of import and export commodities, such as:

- The Federal Agency for Environmental Protection (Procuraduría Federal de Protección al Ambiente) whose main task is to increase the levels of compliance of environmental regulations, in order to contribute to sustainable development and enforce environmental laws.

- The National Service of Health, Safety and Quality of Agricultural Food (Servicio Nacional de Sanidad, Inocuidad y Calidad Agroalimentaria) protects agricultural, aquiculture and livestock resources from pests and diseases of quarantine and economic importance.

- The Federal Commission for Protection against Sanitary Risks (Comisión Federal Para la Protección Contra Riesgos Santiarios) seeks to protect the population against health risks caused by the use and consumption of goods and services, health supplies, as well as exposure to environmental and labor factors.

- The Inter-secretarial Commission for the Control of the Process and Use of Pesticides and Toxic Substances (Comisión Intersecretarial para el Control del Proceso y Uso de Plaguicidas y Sustancias Tóxicas) main activity is related to the issuance of registrations and import authorizations of pesticides, fertilizers and toxic substances.

- The Ministry of Environment and Natural Resources (Secretaría de Medio Ambiente y Recursos Naturales) is the federal government agency responsible for promoting the protection, restoration and conservation of ecosystems and natural resources and environmental goods and services of Mexico, in order to promote their use and sustainable development.

- The Ministry of Agriculture, Livestock, Rural Development, Fisheries and Food (Secretaría de Agricultura, Ganadería, Desarrollo Rural, Pesca y Alimentación), has among its objectives to encourage the exercise of a support policy that allows better production, better use of the comparative advantages of agricultural sector and integrate the activities of the rural environment with the productive chains of the rest of the economy.

- The Energy Commission (Comisión Reguladora de Energía) is in charge of determining the requirements applicable for the importation and exportation of oil, gas, electricity and other resources.

E. Customs Management

In order to import and export goods into and from Mexico it is necessary to use custom brokers, who are members of the private sector -with business character- that receives a patent from SAT to assist and carry out the clearance of the goods from the customs offices on behalf of importers and exporters. They represent their clients before the customs authorities, in order to prove payment of taxes and compliance with non-tariff regulations and restrictions, assuring that goods can be imported or exported in an agile, legal and safe way. Usually customs brokers interact with carriers, shipping agents, warehouses, regulatory authorities, customs authorities, importers and exporters, to coordinate the logistics chain and flows of merchandise movement.

The General Customs Administration (Administración General de Aduanas) applies the legislation regulating the customs clearance, as well as the systems, methods and procedures to be followed to clear imports and exports. There are several other agencies involved in the supervision of customs regulations, all deriving from SAT.

IV. Labour

A. Brief Introduction of Labour Laws and Regulations

Among others, the following are the main Mexican laws and regulations that regulate labour matters:
- Mexican Constitution (Constitución Política de los Estados Unidos Mexicanos);
- Federal Labour Law (Ley Federal del Trabajo).

B. Requirements of Employing Foreign Employees

a) Work Permit

Foreigners residing in Mexico temporarily may apply to be granted with a work permit during their stay in Mexico (as further described in section C.below). Such work permit is granted by the National Migration Institute (Instituto Nacional de Migración) ("INM"): in the event such work permit is not granted, foreigners may not receive payments from activities developed in Mexico.

b) Application Procedure

In order to receive a work permit, foreigners residing in Mexico must (i) fill out and print a submission (available in the webpage of the INM; (ii) deliver such submission in the offices of INM; and (iii) receive the corresponding resolution (issued by INM within a term of 20 business days). In the event INM determines additional requirements are required to issue a resolution, the applicant will be granted with a term of 7 days to fulfill the corresponding requirement.

c) Social Security

Under Mexican applicable Law, as outlined in Part II, Section H above, in the event an individual (whether Mexican or foreigner) is deemed to have a labor relationship within Mexico (and thus, performs her/his activities in Mexico and receives payments in Mexico), the employer of such individual is obliged to register the corresponding employee before the National Institute of Social Security (Instituto Mexicano del Seguro Social) and pay social security contributions on a monthly basis.

C. Exit and Entry

As a result of recent immigration reforms, there are now three immigration permits in Mexico. The first one is for Visitors. Visitors may stay in Mexico for 180 continuous days. If they don't have a working permit, they may not partake in remunerated activities and must attest sufficiency of funds for room and board during their stay. If, however, visitors wish to participate in salaried activities during their stay, they must have a job offer or a cultural or artistic invitation to obtain a work permit. If the foreigner is from a bordering country, they may stay in the bordering states for up to one year, being able to leave and re-enter the country freely as well as obtain a working permit.

Temporary residents may stay in Mexico up to four years, while allowed to leave the country and re-enter as they please, they may have a working permit and bring with them children, parents, wives, husbands and common law wives or husbands.

Permanent residents may stay in Mexico indefinitely. This status is awarded to refugees, individuals living with Mexican family members, retired individuals with enough funds for living, temporary residents who have been in Mexico for four consecutive years, ascendants or descendants of any Mexican born individual or temporary residents who have stayed in Mexico for two consecutive years as a result of marrying a Mexican individual.

D. Trade Union and Labour Organizations

Establishments with more than 20 employees can have a union. Federal law requires that collective-bargaining agreements be revised at least once every two years. Salaries must be reviewed annually.

Strikes are legal only when employers refuse to comply with a legal or contractual obligation (for example, to make or revise a union contract, to accept an award by an arbitration board or to make mandatory profit-sharing payments). A strike may also be called to support another strike, provided the majority of workers agree. Unions must follow specific procedures to go on strike.

In the latest reform to the labour law, the possibility of a seasonal contract, a contract for a trial period and an initial training period contract were included. Furthermore, subcontracting is now permitted as well as electronic payment of wages.

Additionally, the reform regulated "outsourcing", which used to be a common practice and was used in the past as a way to avoid the payment of PTU. At present and in order for such outsourcing regime to be legally used, in general terms, it has to comply with the following: (i) it may not cover 100% of the activities of the company; (ii) it has to be duly justified because of its specialty and (iii) it may not include the performance of activities that are similar to those performed by workers.

Such regulation, and the criteria set forth by the Supreme Court of Justice, has labor, tax and anti-money laundering consequences. If outsourcing does not comply with the applicable requirements, the company shall be considered as employer and is obliged to comply with all social security benefits and may not credit the payments for employees against the VAT.

Finally, outsourcing is considered a vulnerable activity for purposes of the anti-money laundering legislation. Therefore, the company has to be registered before the anti-money laundering webpage, prepare a manual and file reports before Financial Intelligence Units (Unidades de Inteligencia Financiera).

E. Labour Disputes

Although alternative mechanisms such as mediation or private arrangements may be used to solve labour disputes, most labour disputes in Mexico are solved before Labour Boards (Juntas de Conciliacion y Arbitraje).

Recent discussions in the Mexican Congress could derive on legislative changes to eliminate Labour Boards for labour dispute resolution to be solved by Mexican courts.

V. Intellectual Property

A. Brief introduction of IP Laws and Regulations

The intellectual property system in Mexico is based on the international standards set forth in treaties such as the North American Free Trade Agreement ("NAFTA") and the Agreement on Trade-Related Aspects of Intellectual Property Rights ("TRIPS"). The Industrial Property Law (Ley de Propiedad Industrial) (or "IPL") is the federal statute governing inventions, utility models, industrial designs, trademarks and commercial ads or slogans (each an "IPR" and, when used conjunctively "IPRs", which shall include copyrights) in Mexico, and as such, it establishes the guidelines and requirements to obtain, invalidate, or enforce any such rights.

Mexico recognizes the patentability of inventions[1] that are new, the result of an inventive step, and susceptible of industrial application. Patents shall be protected for a non-extendable term of 20 (twenty) years as of the filing date of the application and subject to the payment of specific government fees.[2] Trademarks and service marks are granted for specific goods or services pertaining a single international class, according to the Nice International Classification. They are granted for renewable terms of ten years as of the filing date, and can be filed on an intent-to-use basis, or indicating the exact date of the first use in Mexico. Words, letters, numbers, designs or three-dimensional figures can be registered as marks. The IPL also provides special protection for well-known marks in Mexico.

Original computer programs in Mexico are protected under the author's rights classification. An author's right in Mexico includes a set of moral and pecuniary prerogatives that creators or developers of a work possess for the simple reason of its creation, and which scope of protection is divided into mainly two types of rights: (i) moral or non-patrimonial rights, which under the author's rights system in Mexico are recognized and perpetually protected in benefit of the author[3]; and, (ii) economic or "patrimonial rights", which permit the exclusive use and exploitation of the copyrighted work.

---

[1] Invention, as defined by the IPL, is "any human creation that allows the transformation of matter or energy found in nature for human application and for satisfying concrete needs."
[2] The right to obtain a patent corresponds to the inventor, whether individual or corporation.
[3] Broadly defined, moral rights are a set of rights or prerogatives related to the honor, prestige and reputation of the author and the possibility of the same to authorize or deny any modification or alteration to its work.

The protection of author's rights in Mexico is governed exclusively by federal legislation[1]. The current copyright governing statute is the Federal Law of Author's Rights (Ley de Derechos de Autor) (the "Copyright Act"). It contains provisions that grant jurisdiction to the National Institute of Author's Rights for most of the matters relating to the Mexican copyright system and, also, to act as the National Copyrights Registry.

B. Patent Application[2]

A patent application shall be accompanied by: The description of the invention, which must be sufficiently clear and complete to enable a full understanding of it and, where appropriate, to guide its accomplishment for a person who possesses know-how and average knowledge in the matter. Likewise, when it is not clear from the description of the invention, it must also include the best method known to the applicant to implement the invention, as well as information that illustrates the industrial application of the invention.

The patent examination process consists of a substantive examination during which the patent file is assigned to an examiner based on the technical field to which the invention relates. The examiner is required to determine whether the application meets the requirements of novelty, inventive step, and industrial application set forth in Article 16 of the IPL, as well as to verify and determine that the invention does not fall under one of the grounds for exclusion laid down in the IPL. The IPL and its Regulations empower the Mexican Patent and Trademark Office (or "IMPI") to issue a maximum of four official actions, so as to inform the applicant of all the objections to a particular application or to require clarification of any technical aspect. The law also provides that the applicant shall have a period of two months, extendable by two more months, to comply with every official action.[3] The fifth official action issued by IMPI during the proceeding must either deny the application or give notice of the grant (called an "invitation to pay").

C. Trademark Registration[4]

The process of registration has an average timeframe of 6 (six) months to 1 (one) year. Upon receiving the application, IMPI performs a formal examination in which it verifies if the application is complete. The correct classification of the goods or services covered by the mark is also reviewed within this stage. The following stage consists of a novelty examination in which IMPI searches for similar or identical prior registrations or pending applications. This search is carried out in both the International class and the corresponding National classes.

D. Measures for IP Protection

Any national or foreign individual or entity is entitled to submit applications for patents or registrations under the IPL or the Copyright Act, as applicable, or to exercise rights in defense of any breach to their intellectual property in Mexican territory. In fact, Mexico is bound to protect any intellectual property registered in any other country signatory of any of the international treaties executed by Mexico, such as the WIPO Convention, the Paris Convention for the Protection of Industrial Property and the Patent Cooperation Treaty.

---

[1] In Mexico, the basic requirements for obtaining author's rights protection are the following: (a) Fixation: Author's right protection exists in Mexico as a matter of law from the moment that "....the works have been fixed in a material base, independently of their artistic merit, destiny or way of expression." Fixation is defined as "[t]he incorporation of letters, signs, sounds, images and others elements in which the work has been expressed, or the digital embodiment of said elements, which in any form or material base, including electronic means, permits its perception, reproduction or any form of communication." The lack of formalities required to obtain author's rights protection is expressly mentioned in the Copyright Act.The statute provides that the "[r]ecognition of authors' rights and neighboring rights does not depend on prior registration nor on any document or formality." (b) Authorship: The authorship in Mexico states under the contents of the Copyright Act that only individuals are susceptible of being granted an author's right.The statute makes clear that legal persons (corporations) may only be holders of author's rights as agents or representatives of the original author, and may only exploit or acquire the "patrimonial rights" of a work.(c) Originality: Under the Copyright Act, a work must be original in order to qualify for author's rights protection.The Act makes clear that "[w]orks protected by this law are works of original creation that can be divulged or reproduced by any means".As noted above, a work does not require the fulfillment of any formality in order to be protected.Furthermore the "copyright notice" is optional in Mexico.The omission of the copyright notice does not imply the loss of the author's rights, but failure to comply with the requirements of stating that the work in question has reserved rights or derechos reservados or its acronym "D.R." followed by a symbol comprised of a letter "c" within a circle, may be subject to a pecuniary penalty (this penalty only applies to the Editor of the work).
[2] When a patent is filed in Mexico after being filed abroad, the priority filing date can be recognized, so long as it is submitted in Mexico within the timeframes set forth in International Treaties or, otherwise, within the 12 (twelve) months following the filing abroad.
[3] Article 55 and 58 of the IPL.
[4] Mexico also recognizes priority rights according to the Paris Convention in the case of trademarks.When a trademark registration is requested in Mexico within the timeframes provided by the international treaties or, otherwise, within the 6 (six) months following the application in another country, the first application date shall be acknowledged as priority date.

According to the Mexican IP legislation and judicial precedents, in order to be in possibility of enforcing an IPR before a Court throughout a civil action for compensatory damages, it is necessary for the plaintiff to have obtained a definitive decision in an administrative infringement action. Infringement actions are decided by IMPI, and are administratively punished with fines that can amount up to 20,000 days of minimum salary effective in Mexico City (approximately USD $75,000.00) and, in some cases, with the temporary or definitive closure of the facilities or the infringer's establishment.

The only conditions required to enforce an IPR through an administrative infringement action are for the holder to (i) prove the legal standing that it has to commence the litigation proceeding (in case of patent/ trademark infringement this can be proved through the offering of the IPR certificate), and (ii) have had inserted in the products protected by the IPR the indications and statements of registration foreseen in the IPL, such as the number of patent or the symbols ™, ®, or to have otherwise publicly announced that the relevant product or process is protected by an IPR. The use of the IPR is not required to enforce it under Mexican law and practice.

Once an infringement action is definitely decided by IMPI, the IPR's holder is entitled to claim (i) compensatory damages[1] under a civil action before a Civil Court[2], or (ii) a criminal action before a Criminal Court, if the infringer insists in violating the IPR subject of the firmly declared infringement action.

Other than the deterring punishment of paying the administrative fine imposed by IMPI, and the compensatory payment awarded by a Civil Court of no less than a 40% of the sale price of the product sold by the infringer, Mexico's IP laws do not foresee other form of relief that can be obtained for patent or other IPR's infringement (including reimbursement of legal fees).

VI. Environmental Protection

A. Departments Supervising Environmental Protection

The Ministry of Environment and Natural Resources (Secretaría de Medio Ambiente y Recursos Naturales or "SEMARNAT") is the federal authority in charge of executing the federal environmental laws and regulations. Among other duties, it grants the permits required for the development of specific activities, with the General Attorney's Office for the Protection of the Environment (Procuraduría Federal de Protección al Ambiente or the "PROFEPA") acting as the enforcement agency. There are other entities attached to the SEMARNAT that execute the federal environmental regulations in particular fields, such as the National Water Commission (Comisión Nacional del Agua or the "CONAGUA").

Other government agencies may be involved in the development of projects and activities, by executing regulations in subjects that are closely related to environmental matters and by granting permits for the development of specific activities. The most relevant ones are the National Nuclear Safety and Safeguards Commission (Comisión Nacional de Seguridad Nuclear y Salvaguardias or the "CONASENUSA"), which is attached to the Ministry of Energy (Secretaría de Energía or the "SENER"), and the National Institute of Anthropology and History (Instituto Nacional de Antropología e Historia or the "INAH"), which is attached to the Ministry of Culture (Secretaría de Cultura).

Certain activities fall under the jurisdiction of local environmental authorities, whether state or municipal, and thus these must obtain local permits and comply with local regulations.

B. Brief Introduction of Laws and Regulations of Environmental Protection

The General Law for Ecological Equilibrium and Environmental Protection (Ley General del Equilibrio Ecológico y la Protección al Ambiente or the "LGEEPA") is the framework law in federal environmental matters in Mexico. This law establishes environmental policy instruments that are applicable to most projects and activities developed in Mexico.

Notwithstanding this framework law, there are many other regulations, statutes and norms that regulate

---

[1] Damages in Mexico are of a compensatory type, and shall be determined on a reasonable royalty basis of no less than 40% of the sale price (gross sales) of the products which were proved to be sold by the infringer.However, because in the Mexican legal system the burden of proof is governed by the principle affirmanti incumbit probatio, which means that the burden of proof shall be on the person asserting a claim, the plaintiff in a civil action for damages has to legally prove the scope of the infringement vis-à-vis the damage suffered, to be awarded with the payment of any compensatory sum.

[2] In cases of infringed patent applications, the damages that the relevant holder would be entitled to claim before a Civil Court should the application matures into a Patent, would be comprehensive of any damages caused during the period of time running from the moment the application was published.

different environmental aspects of a specific project to be developed in Mexico, including: (i) the General Law for Sustainable Forestry Development (Ley Federal de Desarrollo Forestal Sustentable); (ii) the National Waters Law (Ley de Aguas Nacionales); and (iii) the General Law for the Prevention and Integral Management of Wastes (Ley General para la Prevención y Gestión Integral de los Residuos or the "LGPGIR"), among others.

The most relevant federal environmental policy instruments are: (i) environmental impact assessment; (ii) the territorial and marine ecological ordainment; and (iii) the establishment of natural protected areas.

The feasibility of developing any project or activity from an environmental standpoint in Mexico will depend greatly on the compatibility of such project with the applicable ecological ordainment program and local urban development programs, which is evaluated mainly through the environmental impact assessment procedure.

C. Other Relevant Environmental Matters

a. Liability for Soil Contamination / Remediation

The LGPGIR regulates the handling of hazardous waste and establishes the rules for environmental liability resulting from the acquisition of contaminated sites, as well as the rules for site remediation.

The most relevant are:
- The owner/seller of a site contaminated with hazardous materials or wastes is obligated to inform the acquirer about the existence of the contamination;
- The transfer of ownership of a site contaminated with hazardous wastes requires an authorization from SEMARNAT;
- Owners and operators or possessors of a site contaminated with hazardous materials or wastes are jointly and severally liable for conducting any required remediation.

b. Use of Coasts

The Federal Maritime Zone (Zona Marítima Federal or "ZOFEMAT") (beachfront) is public domain property and thus its use can only be conducted by means of a concession granted by the SEMARNAT. Concessions for the use of the ZOFEMAT area are usually granted for 15-year renewable terms and its use results in the obligation to pay governmental fees. The fees are established in the Federal Law of Rights (Ley Federal de Derechos) and vary depending on the location of the surface area of ZOFEMAT under concession and the use given to it by the concession titleholder.

In sum, the foregoing presents, in general terms, the most usual environmental authorities and permits that may yield influence in the development of a project; however, each venture presents its own challenges and a particular regulatory strategy should be tailored to the merits of the specific case.

VII. Dispute Resolution

a. Litigation

Litigation proceedings in Mexico are governed firstly by the Constitution which establishes that civil law matters are of local jurisdiction consequently each state has its own Civil Code (Código Civil) and Code of Civil Procedures (Códigos de Procedimientos Civiles); notwithstanding, there is also a Federal Code of Civil Procedures (Código Federal de Procedimientos Civiles) which applies to civil conflicts. Mexico's courts are divided into federal and local courts.

Proceedings start when a claim is filed before a court that has jurisdiction over the matter, usually; the main stages of the proceedings are as follows: opening stage (statement of claim and statement of response), pretrial conference and pretrial settlement, evidentiary stage and closing stage. All lower courts decisions are subject to challenge by appeal or an amparo claim with a few exceptions.

Justice must be delivered in a free and expedited manner compliant to the due process requirements under Mexican law.

b. Arbitration

Commercial arbitration in Mexico has significantly grown since in both, medium and large transactions, parties have been including an arbitration agreement. Anyone qualified to exercise his civil rights can enter an agreement submitting to arbitration for dispute resolution; however, matters of public order (such as environmental, family, criminal, tax, employment, antitrust, intellectual property and consumer) cannot be resolved via arbitration as it is expressively prohibited by law.

Arbitration is governed by the Commercial Code, which fundamentally adopted the United Nations Commission on International Trade Law Model Law on International Commercial Arbitration with some additional provisions such as: (i) the existence of a special judicial proceeding where a local court can intervene and assist an arbitration proceeding; and, (ii) a chapter determining costs and fees of the arbitral tribunal.

Pursuant to the Commerce Code (Código de Comercio) all parties in an arbitration proceeding must be treated equally and be granted with sufficient opportunity to express given the chance to express their rights.

The principal organizations used in Mexico for dispute resolution are: the Arbitration Centre of Mexico (Centro de Arbitraje de México or CAM), the National Chamber of Commerce of Mexico City (Cámara Nacional de Comercio de la Ciudad de México or CANACO), the International Chamber of Commerce (ICC), and, the International Center for Dispute Resolution (ICDR).

c. Other Alternative Dispute Resolution Proceedings

Civil litigation is extensively used in Mexico and therefore, the caseload is substantial; thus, Mexican courts and authorities have recently been endorsing the use of alternative dispute resolution proceedings such as mediation; these alternative methods can only be utilized if all parties agree upon them and are not commonly applied.

VIII. Others

A. Anti-commercial Bribery

a. Brief Introduction of Anti-commercial Bribery Laws and Regulations

Although general bribery laws and regulations mandatory for public officers have been enacted in the past few years, no anti-commercial bribery laws and regulations are currently in force in Mexico. However, certain constitutional amendments were executed recently regarding public official's (servidores públicos) bribery practices. The National Anti-bribery System (Sistema Nacional Anticorrupción) (the "NAS") was established through a Constitutional amendment dated May 27, 2015 and, therefore, certain secondary regulations were issued as of July 18, 2016, including the General Law for the National Anti-bribery System (Ley General del Sistema Nacional de Anticorrupción) and the General Law for Administrative Responsibilities (Ley General de Responsabilidades Administrativas). Furthermore, certain amendments were made to the Federal Criminal Code (Código Penal Federal) in order to sanction bribery actions related with public officials.

The main purpose of the NAS is the creation of an administrative body in charge of the issuing of policies and procedures for the coordination between government authorities in matters related to the identification, investigation and the enforcement of administrative and criminal punitive actions of certain bribery activities executed mainly by public officials in the execution of their corresponding responsibilities.

In addition to the incorporation and operation of the NAS, the applicable secondary regulation sets forth a list of conducts classified based on their severity to the extent that its execution may be considered to be enforced by the criminal laws.

The foregoing anti–bribery regulations and punitive actions may be applicable to particulars, whether individuals or companies, when they participate or are involved with the execution of certain relevant conducts. However, the conducts described by the regulation are in any case derived from or in connection with public officials and may not be incurred by individuals or companies in private commercial relations.

b. Department Supervising Anti-commercial Bribery

As mentioned above, the NAS and the regulation in connection thereto does not foresee conducts carried out under commercial relations. Thus, the conducts described by such regulations are in all cases related to or in connection with an administrative action or public official.

The authorities in charge of the application of the regulations and the operation of the NAS are the following:
- The Federal Ministry for the Administrative Surveillance (Secretaría de la Función Pública).
- The state´s local Ministries for the Administrative Surveillance.
- The Federation's Audit Department (Auditoría Superior de la Federación).
- State local surveillance Departments (entidades de fiscalización superior de las entidades federativas).
- The responsibility representation units of Government Production Companies (Unidades de Responsabilidades de las Empresas productivas del Estado).
- Federal Court of Administrative Justice (Tribunal Federal de Jusiticia Adminsitrativa).

c. Punitive Actions

Among the conducts that are susceptible to punitive actions are the following:

- Bribery: individuals and companies may not promise, offer or deliver any type of gift, either directly or through third parties, to public officials, when such gifts or benefits require the public official to act or refrain from acting according to their official obligations.

- Illegal participation in administrative procedures: individuals and companies may not participate in administrative procedures when they are banned from doing so. Furthermore, they may not participate in administrative procedures for the benefit of a third party that is banned from doing so.

- Traffic of influence: individuals and companies may not use their influence, economic or political power, over any public official, in other to obtain a benefit for themselves or for a third party, or in order to cause damages to any person, regardless of the result of such actions.

- Use of false information: individuals and companies may not use false or altered information in order to receive an authorization or obtain certain benefits.

- Collusion: individuals and companies may not execute actions in order to obtain benefits in public procurements.

The punitive actions applicable to the individuals and companies are the following:

For individuals:

- Penalties equivalent to up to twice the benefit obtained from conduct, or, if no benefit was obtained, sanctions range from 100,000 UMAs (approximately USD $410,000.00) to 150,000 UMAs (approximately USD$615,000.00).

- Temporary suspension regarding the possibility to take part in acquisitions, leasing, services or public projects, for a term ranging from three months up to eight years.

- Indemnity for loss and damages incurred by the federal o local Public Finance.

For companies:

- Penalties equivalent to up to twice the benefit obtained from conduct, or, if no benefit was obtained, sanctions range from 1,000 UMAs (approximately USD $4,100.00) to 1,500,000 UMAs (approximately USD$6,150,000.00);

- Temporary suspension regarding the possibility to take part in acquisitions, leasing, services or public projects, for a term ranging from three months up to ten years;

- Suspension commercial, economic, contractual or business activities related to the sanctioned conduct, for a term ranging from three months up to three years;

- Dissolution of the company;

- Indemnity for loss and damages incurred by the federal o local Public Finance.

B. Project Contracting

a. Permission System

In order to ensure the best conditions available in terms of price, quality, financing, timing and other relevant circumstances, the Mexican Constitution states that all public procurement, including the acquisition, lease and sale of goods, as well as the provision of services and contracting of works, shall be subject to public bidding procedures.

The Mexican Constitution, however, also states that whenever public bidding procedures are not suitable to ensure such conditions for the Mexican Government, secondary laws shall determine the procedures, rules and requirements that shall apply (i.e.direct awards or restricted invitations).

Consequently, the Public Sector Acquisitions, Leases and Services Law (Ley de Adquisiciones, Arrendamientos y Servicios del Sector Público) ("LAASSP") provides that all public procurement shall, as a general rule, be performed through public bidding procedure, restricted invitations and direct awards are to be used as an exception. The LAASSP allows for procurement through two options other than the public bidding procedures: (i) restricted invitations; and (ii) direct awards. These exceptions must be based and motivated on economic criteria, efficacy, impartiality, honorability and transparency as applicable, necessary to offer the best conditions available to the contracting entity. Furthermore, in each case, such reasons and their justification must be evidenced in writing and signed by a responsible officer.

In addition to the provisions set forth in the LAASSP and its Regulations, public entities issue internal policies and guidelines applicable to its procurement processes.

b. Invitation to Bid and Bidding

Prior to engaging in any of the three abovementioned procedures, the acquisition of goods or services, the area in question shall file a purchase request to the designated centralized contracting area of the relevant entity.

In addition to the purchase requests, the LAASSP provides that prior to engaging in a bidding process, the contracting entity shall prepare a study that allows it to determine existing market conditions for the items or services required, such as the availability of goods or services in the required amount, the existence of domestic suppliers, or the location of international suppliers and to know the price of such goods or services. This research may also be used to, among others things, to determine the type of public procurement procedure that is most appropriate for the case in question.

Finally, based on the nation of origin of the participants and products involved, the LAASSP provides for three types of public bidding procedures:

- National Public Bidding Procedures, which involve only Mexican individuals or companies, with products made in Mexico and have at least 65% of national content, considering labor costs, raw materials and other aspects determined by the Ministry of Economy (Secretaría de Economía);

- International Public Bidding Procedures Under International Treaty Coverage, which are directed to Mexican and foreign participants, where the latter must reside in a country with which Mexico has entered into a free trade agreement with a public procurement chapter; and

- Open International Public Bidding Procedures include individuals and companies of all nationalities for the procurement of products of any origin. These procedures may be initiated provided that (a) a previously called national public bidding procedure has been cancelled (i.e., no bidders showed up or the participants or products did not qualify under the bidding rules), or (b) it is stipulated under a contract to be financed by foreign credits granted to the federal government (typically multilateral organizations such as the World Bank).

摩尔多瓦

作者：Alexander Turcan、Andrei Caciurenco
译者：卞栋樑、李黎

一、概述

（一）政治、经济、社会和法律环境概述

摩尔多瓦（全称为摩尔多瓦共和国）是一个与罗马尼亚和乌克兰接壤的东南欧国家。摩尔多瓦于1991年8月27日宣布独立，自苏联解体后始终是一个主权国家。

根据2014年全国人口普查的初步数据显示，摩尔多瓦全国人口约为300万。摩尔多瓦的官方语言是罗马尼亚语。虽然俄语不是摩尔多瓦官方语言，但被认为是大部分人口通用的跨族群语言。英语的使用主要分布在商业区和城市地区。

摩尔多瓦目前划分为37个一级行政区域，包括32个区、3个直辖市（基希讷乌、伯尔兹、本德尔），以及2个地方行政区（加告兹自治行政区、德涅斯特河左岸行政区）。摩尔多瓦的首都和最大的城市是基希讷乌。

摩尔多瓦有66个市（城）和917个市镇。

根据1994年通过的现行《宪法》，摩尔多瓦是单一制的代议制民主共和国。宪法将国家权力分为三个独立的部门—立法、行政和司法。

1. 政治

摩尔多瓦立法机关实行一院制，由选举产生的101名代表（议员）组成，议员作为各自政党的代表，任期为4年。根据2017年7月的立法修改，摩尔多瓦在2018年11月的议会选举中引入混合选举制度，具体将按照下列条件选出议员：51名议员将从政党名单中选举产生，50名议员将从各个独立选区选举产生。摩尔多瓦公民具有的投票权最低年龄是18岁。

行政权力由政府（内阁）行使。政府（内阁）包括总理、副总理、部长和其他阁员。政府推行国内外各项议程，并管理公共行政事务。总理由议会中的多数派指定，并经与少数派议员协商后由总统批准。

总统以直接选举的方式产生，任期4年。

司法机关包括最高法院、4个地区上诉法院和各个地方法院。最高法院是摩尔多瓦的最高司法机关，有权审查下级法院作出的判决。摩尔多瓦宪法法院是摩尔多瓦共和国唯一的宪法司法管辖机构。

2. 经济

摩尔多瓦是一个新兴市场，摩尔多瓦国民生产总值基本上每年实现稳步增长。

摩尔多瓦经济很大程度上受制于海外劳工收入的对内汇入（占国内生产总值的24%）、向独联体和欧盟出口、海外捐助（约占政府支出的10%）的情况。

2014年，摩尔多瓦与欧盟签署《联盟协议》以及包括在内的《深入而全面的自由贸易协议》。

《联盟协议》包含有约束力的监管规定和更广泛的合作安排，涉及各个领域（例如公司法、劳动力、消费者保护、竞争、税收、关税、公共采购等）。《联盟协议》特别规定了关于有效履行和执行的内容，包括设定了10年执行期限。

《深入而全面的自由贸易协议》设想在相互贸易中逐步取消对商品和服务的关税和配额，以及消除非关税壁垒。

此举旨在促进摩尔多瓦融入欧盟内部市场。

摩尔多瓦货币是摩尔多瓦列伊（MDL）。摩尔多瓦在国际贸易中广泛接受并使用美元和欧元。

3. 社会

除了不享有选举权外，外国人和摩尔多瓦海外侨民基本上享有与本国人同等的权利。摩尔多瓦海外侨民问题备受关切，并且对摩尔多瓦的人口和经济有着重大影响。根据不同的数据统计，大约100万的摩尔多瓦公民占人口总数的将近25%在国外工作。

4. 法律

摩尔多瓦的法院体系包括宪法法院和具备一般管辖权的三级法院。该三级法院有权审理所有刑事、行政和民事案件。宪法法院解释宪法并审查法律法规的合宪性。

具备一般管辖权的法院包括地方法院体系、4个地区上诉法院和最高法院。最高法院是一般管辖权法院的终审法院。

（二）"一带一路"倡议下与中国企业合作的现状与方向

尽管摩尔多瓦目前没有签署有关"一带一路"倡议的正式协议。然而，在不同的论坛场合，摩尔多瓦政府代表赞扬并表示了他们对这项倡议的兴趣。

二、投资

（一）市场准入

1. 政府监管投资

摩尔多瓦投资和出口促进机构，是致力于投资推广的摩尔多瓦政府部门——该公共机构旨在促进竞争力协调政策的实施，推动摩尔多瓦出口以及吸引投资。

2. 投资产业有关的法律法规

根据摩尔多瓦法律，外商投资者可以在摩尔多瓦设立混合资本公司（摩尔多瓦和外国参与者的合资公司）和外资公司。公司可以完全由外国投资者拥有。法律禁止基于原籍国、居住地、经营地/登记地或者任何其他理由对投资进行任何形式的歧视。法律为外国投资者和本国投资者提供了几乎相同的条件。例如，办理登记手续、开展经营活动的程序和外商投资公司解散的程序与内资公司相同。对投资的管理、经营、维护、利用、获取、延期或处置没有歧视性的要求。

3. 投资形式

摩尔多瓦允许外国公司：
① 参加合资公司（对最低/最高份额无限制）；
② 设立100%由外商投资的公司；
③ 购买现有公司的股份；
④ 设立分支机构和/或子公司；
⑤ 在自由经济区内建立企业，并获得区内居民身份；
⑥ 设立IT园区内建立企业，并获得区内居民身份。

4. 市场准入和审查标准

对来自某些不执行国际有关透明度标准的地区（如离岸地区）的投资者，存在准入限制（例如禁止持有银行股份、保险公司等）。

外国公司和外商投资的摩尔多瓦公司不得拥有自己的农场和林地。

（二）外汇监管

1. 外汇监管机构

摩尔多瓦在外汇监管领域设有数家地方监管机构，如摩尔多瓦国家银行、国家金融市场委员会、海关总署、国家税务局等。

2. 外汇监管相关法律法规简介

摩尔多瓦的官方货币是摩尔多瓦列伊（MDL）。在摩尔多瓦进行结算时，摩尔多瓦列伊必须不受任何限制地被使用。除在免税商店消费以及缴付公司股本出资外，摩尔多瓦列伊是摩尔多瓦境内唯一的法定支付货币。

摩尔多瓦居民之间无法利用银行进行外币转账。居民向非居民的转账只有在特定的情况下可以实现。

对于摩尔多瓦公司股份的买卖，如果是在外国卖方和外国买方之间进行，则可使用外币进行现金结算。

根据相关规定，摩尔多瓦居民仅限在特定目的下，可以利用其境内账户向境外汇出外币。该等付汇视情况可能需要（也可能不需要）获得摩尔多瓦国家银行的许可。

摩尔多瓦境内法律实体可向获得许可的摩尔多瓦商业银行申购外汇，并且购汇的用途仅限于跨境交易的对外支付。

基于反洗钱目的，摩尔多瓦有关政府机构将对所有超过 500 000 摩尔多瓦列伊（约合 30 000 美元）的跨境电汇或超过 100 000 MDL（约合 6 000 美元）的现金出入境进行监管。该等机构有权对任何认为可疑的交易进行调查。

3. 外资公司外汇管理要求

摩尔多瓦法律在外汇操作上的管理对本土和外国投资公司没有差别。

一般来说，法律允许居民和非居民之间不同类型的交易以本币及外币进行交易，但同时存在一定的约束和限制。在摩尔多瓦境内的大部分支付，比如采购和工资的支付，必须使用摩尔多瓦列伊。

居民和非居民之间在跨境贸易中的付款可以用外币进行。

摩尔多瓦银行可以向非居民进行支付为目的，向摩尔多瓦居民提供外币贷款。

摩尔多瓦居民的对外金融义务（即向境外举借贷款/信贷、签订租赁协议、提供担保、开设境外银行账户等），应当向摩尔多瓦国家银行履行通知或申请授权程序。

（三）金融

1. 主要金融机构

摩尔多瓦国家银行是摩尔多瓦共和国的中央银行，其作为一个依法、公开并自主行使其职责的实体，向议会负责。国家银行定期向公众通报宏观经济分析结论、金融市场动态和统计信息，包括货币供应量、国际收支和外汇市场情况。国家银行许可和监督不同类型的活动，并有权设定摩尔多瓦列伊对主要外币的汇率。

国家银行独立行使摩尔多瓦《国家银行法》规定的职能。国家银行有权发布决定、规章、指示和命令。国家银行的规范指令对金融机构、其他法人和自然人是强制性的。国家银行负责对金融机构活动的授权、监督和管理。在不久的将来，摩尔多瓦银行系统计划引入《巴塞尔协议 III》标准。

目前摩尔多瓦有 11 家商业特许银行。

2. 外国企业融资条件

银行账户：基于反洗钱法规的要求，所有摩尔多瓦注册实体应当在摩尔多瓦一个或多个银行开设账户。各类公司开设摩尔多瓦列伊、美元和欧元账户在摩尔多瓦很常见。虽然摩尔多瓦很大程度上是以现金为基础的经济体，但摩尔多瓦政府鼓励各类实体在商业交易中通过银行转账方式进行付款，而不提倡以现金方式进行结算支付。

融资：一般而言，本国商业银行会按照惯常市场商业条款提供授信。然而，大型基础设施建设项目通常都由国际金融机构提供融资，例如欧洲复兴开发银行（EBRD）、欧洲投资银行（EIB），黑海贸易与发展银行（BSTDB）、国际金融公司（IFC）以及其他类似机构。

(四)土地政策

1. 土地相关法律法规简介

摩尔多瓦土地主要相关法令为《土地法》以及若干有关土地地块购买的法律和条例。

国有土地（中央或者地方政府所有）仅限以公开拍卖的方式出售或者出租。此外，不动产可在市场自由交易。不动产买卖合同必须进行公证。不动产可以抵押用作履行融资义务的担保。

不动产权利登记于公共地籍登记处，私人当事人可在线获取不动产登记信息。

2. 外国企业土地收购规则

一般来说，外国公司与当地公司一样享有土地买卖权。但是，外国公司和外资公司不得拥有农业和林地。此类地块只能租赁。

(五)公司的设立与解散

1. 公司形式

投资者在摩尔多瓦可以选择单独设立商业实体进行商业活动。该等商业实体应当按照摩尔多瓦法律规定的公司形式设立，并且只有在摩尔多瓦政府部门正式注册后方可运营。

摩尔多瓦《民法》规定，该国商业实体包括以下各种法定形式：
- 有限责任公司（LLC）；
- 股份公司（JSC）；
- 普通合伙（GP）；
- 有限责任合伙（LP）；
- 合作企业（COOP）。

一般而言，商业组织的形式不影响其作为法律实体可参与之活动的类型。在某些情况下，商业组织的具体形式是取得许可证的特殊要求（例如，只有股份公司才可以获得银行与保险业务许可证等）。外国投资者在摩尔多瓦开展业务时最常用的公司形式是有限公司，因其具有简单灵活的注册、管理和营运准则。

外国法人和个人可在摩尔多瓦设立公司（包括有限责任公司和股份公司），既可以是持有100%的法定资本，也可以与当地公司或个人合伙设立合资公司。

即使是本地企业也很少采用普通合伙、有限合伙和合作企业的形式。

外国公司在摩尔多瓦的分支机构一般采取的形式是外国公司在摩尔多瓦设立全资子公司。

一般认为，外国公司的代表机构仅限于在摩尔多瓦境内从事营销、推广和协助外国公司的各项活动。

（1）有限责任公司

有限责任公司设立：有限责任公司一般是由数量不多的股东设立，由于其设立所需的登记与管理简便，摩尔多瓦最为常见的公司形式即为有限责任公司。有限责任公司可以由一个或一个以上的发起人设立，发起人包括外国（非摩尔多瓦）单位或者个人。有限责任公司的股东人数限制在50人以下。只有在摩尔多瓦国家公司登记部完成登记的有限责任公司方能开始营业。

有限责任公司的业务活动范围：根据《民法》和《有限责任公司法》的规定，有限公司有权从事任何不受法律禁止的活动。

为了合法地从事某些业务活动，有限责任公司需要持有公共机构颁发的许可。多数与国家许可有关的业务类型包括：电力市场活动、建筑、药品、电视和无线电台、电信和其他业务。有限责任公司禁止从事某些经营，比如银行和保险活动。只有注册成立的股份公司才可持有银行或保险活动许可证。

股本：有限责任公司的资本体现为各股东参与并持有的股权。通常，公司章程中应当对股本有所规定。有限责任公司的股本没有法定最低限额。

资本公积：有限责任公司有义务维持其股本的10%作为法定资本公积。资本公积可用于弥补亏损或增加有限责任公司的股本。

有限责任公司股东的权利和义务：有限责任公司的股东有权按照摩尔多瓦法律的规定，享有最低限度的权利。有限责任公司也可以通过章程设定股东的权利。有限责任公司章程记载的股东权利不得减损法律规定赋予的权利范围，亦不得设立任何与法律要求不一致的股东权利。

优先购买权：股东可自由出售其持有的有限公司股权。但是，根据摩尔多瓦《公司法》规定，同等条件下有限公司的原股东对其他股东拟转让的股权享有优先购买权，第三方只有在有限责任公司其他原股东拒绝受让拟转让的股权的情况下，方可受让该等股权。

股东责任：一般而言，股东对有限责任公司仅承担限于其在有限责任公司所占股权的价值的责任。股东只有在公司破产清算等特殊情况下，方才承担额外责任。

损益：除非公司设立文件中另有规定，有限责任公司可在缴纳税款和其他应付款项后，每年分配净利润。

决定向股东分配净利润比例的决议由公司股东通过股东会议确定。净利润应当按（股东在）公司核定资本中所占的比例进行分配。经公司全体股东通过股东会一致同意，可以改变净利润分配顺序。

有限责任公司的治理结构：根据法律规定，有限责任公司的组成结构包括：

① 股东会（如果有限责任公司只有一个股东，则为股东）；
② 董事会；
③ 经理（执行机构）；
④ 审计。

有限责任公司股东会的专有权力：根据《有限责任公司法》，下列事项属于股东会的专有职权范围：

① 批准有限责任公司的章程的修改；
② 批准有限责任公司变更注册资本；
③ 选举和在任期结束前罢免有限责任公司董事会成员和审计师；
④ 向有限责任公司董事会成员和审计师提出索赔，要求赔偿其对有限责任公司造成的损失；
⑤ 批准有限责任公司董事会规章；
⑥ 批准有限责任公司董事会和审计员报告；
⑦ 批准有限责任公司年度资产负债表；
⑧ 通过关于有限责任公司利润分配的决定；
⑨ 批准有限责任公司重组以及重组计划；
⑩ 批准有限责任公司清算事项，任命清算组成员以及批准资产清算表；
⑪ 批准有限责任公司的基金设立；
⑫ 批准有限责任公司董事会成员与审计的报酬；
⑬ 对有限责任公司以合同方式进行股权变更或者将权利转让给包括股东在内的某些第三方（包括股东）进行批准；
⑭ 有限责任公司分公司和代表处的设立；
⑮ 批准有限责任公司设立其他法律实体；
⑯ 决定有限责任公司作为共同创始人设立其他法律实体。

董事会：有限责任公司董事会的设立与否不作强制规定。一般来说，当有限责任公司拥有较多数量的股东时，会成立董事会。在董事会没有设立时，董事会的部分权力由公司的股东会（如果有限责任公司只有一个股东，则为股东）或经理代为执行。

经理：除专属于股东大会和/或董事会职权范围内的事务外，有限责任公司的经理或行政机构必须处理公司所有事务。有限责任公司的经理无需授权即可以公司名义行事，并在与第三方交易中代表公司利益。经理违反公司章程规定权限所达成的交易应继续有效，且不得取消，但经理本人将对违反权限所为事项承担个人责任。

有限责任公司审计师：有限责任公司审计师的设立，其目的在于监督有限责任公司的商业与财务活动。审计需要核验公司的年度资产负债表和财务报表，并且需要就该等事项出具审计报告。

（2）股份公司

股份公司设立：股份公司可以由摩尔多瓦或非摩尔多瓦的自然人或法律实体设立。股份公司的发起人数量不受限制。股份公司可以只有一个发起人,前提是该发起人本身不得为一个自然人创立的公司。公司发起协议应当确定:发起人信息、公司名称、预期股本、初始认购人数、股份类别和发起人会议日期。

股份公司的业务活动范围:根据《民法》和《股份公司法》的规定,股份公司有权从事任何不受法律禁止的活动。为了合法地从事某些业务活动,股份公司需要持有公共机构颁发的许可证。

股本:股份公司的股本被划分为股东所持有的股份。股份公司所需的最低股本为20 000摩尔多瓦列伊(约1 200美元)。原始股份将由发起人进行分配,其价格不得低于股票的票面价值。发起人可用现金或其他有价物认购。对于特定类型的股份公司来说,法律可能会要求更高的最低股本(例如银行、保险公司等)。

资本公积:股份公司有义务维持其股本的10%作为法定资本公积。资本公积可用于弥补亏损或增加股份公司的股本。

股份公司股东的权利和义务:股份公司的股东有权享有摩尔多瓦法律规定的最低限度的权利。公司章程同样会为股东创设该等权利。章程记载的股东权利不得减损法律规定赋予的权利范围,亦不得设立任何与法律要求不一致的股东权利。

股东责任:一般而言,股东对股份公司责任承担仅限于其持有股份的价值。股东只有在公司破产清算等特殊情况下,方才承担额外责任。

损益:股份公司的损益由法律决定。净利润应当在缴纳税款和其他应付款项后确定,并由公司决定如何处分。

每财年净利润分配决议由公司董事会根据公司股东大会核准的分配比例确定。年度净利润分配决议由公司董事会提议,经由股东大会决定。

股份公司的治理结构:
① 股东大会;
② 董事会;
③ 总经理(执行机构);
④ 审计委员会。

股份公司股东大会的专有权力:根据股份公司有关法律,下列事项属于股东大会的专有职权范围:
① 修订公司章程(或批准新的章程)修正案;包括授权更改股份配售的类别和数量、股份转换、合并或拆分;
② 批准和修改公司治理守则;
③ 批准股东查阅公司文件的方式;
④ 改变股本;
⑤ 批准董事会有关规章,选举董事会成员和终止董事任期,确定董事的薪酬机制、年度薪酬和补偿,以及确定董事会成员的责任或免责;
⑥ 批准审计委员会的规章,选举审计师和终止其任期,确定其薪酬规模、年度薪酬和补偿,以及确定审计委员会成员的责任或免责;
⑦ 选择一个审计机构,并决定支付该审计机构的服务费用;
⑧ 参与决定大额交易的决策,这些大额交易包括销售或采购的标的、设定抵押或接受抵押的抵押物以及出租或承租租赁物的价值超过按最新资产负债表记载公司资产的50%;
⑨ 核准配售债券的类别及数目;
⑩ 审查公司的年度财务报告;批准董事会与审计委员会各自的年度报告;
⑪ 批准公司利润分配规则;
⑫ 决定年度利润分配,包括支付年度股息,或补偿公司亏损;
⑬ 决定公司的转制、重组或清算;
⑭ 批准公司的分拆、合并或余额清算;
⑮ 决定将未发股份向公司股东和/或雇员进行授予或者转让。

股东大会可以将其下述权力全部或部分授予董事会:

①批准公司业务的优先方向；
②批准管理委员会的条例，任命公司董事，终止其职务，确定其薪金、年度薪酬和补偿的数额，并就公司董事的责任或责任免除作出决定；
③批准季度报告；
④批准公司分支机构和代表机构的设立、转制和清算，任命和解聘其董事。

董事会：董事会成员的任期为4年。董事会必须由至少3名成员组成。如果公司的股东人数超过100人，董事会必须由至少5人组成。

股份公司总经理：总经理或执行机构必须处理股份公司所有的日常事务，但属于股东大会和董事会专属权限的事务除外。总经理无需授权即可以公司名义行事，并在与第三方交易中代表公司利益。总经理必须向董事会提交公司经营情况的季度报告。

股份公司审计委员会：审计委员会的任务是监督股份公司的业务和财务活动，隶属于股东大会。审计委员会成员的任期为2～5年。审计委员会的成员人数必须是单数。

2. 设立过程

在摩尔多瓦，公司由公共服务局办理登记。

每个公司必须至少有一个注册经理（管理员）和一个注册地址。注册地址将决定新公司的财政管辖权。

如果一个公司是由一家或多家外国公司（发起人）设立的，则需要以译文形式提供关于每个公司发起人的信息。

一旦所有文件准备完毕并提交，公共服务局将在24小时内登记新公司。该局还可以提供4小时内快速登记的服务。

新摩尔多瓦公司可以选择印刻一枚公司印章（但不是强制性要求）。

摩尔多瓦公司登记的印花税不超过100美元。

在摩尔多瓦注册公司的命名中使用国名"摩尔多瓦"须经一个政府特别委员会批准，并须缴纳约6 000美元的一次性印花税。这种命名方式也大大减缓了整个登记过程。

3. 解散的步骤和要求

法律实体的解散意味着清算程序的开始。即使在解散之后，只要有必要对财产进行清算，该法律实体在解散后仍然存在。经理从解散之时起不得继续对公司进行经营。

关于解散的决议，股份公司至少应以2/3的票数通过，有限责任公司则应以3/4的票数通过。

解散该实体的资料应当在摩尔多瓦《官方监测》上公布。必须通知债权人解散，并允许他们在两个月内对解散的公司申报债权。

解散程序可长达12个月。

（六）兼并和收购

2017年的情况表明，在历经2009—2016年期间并购活动相对减缓的情况后，摩尔多瓦未来时期的特点是公司并购和资产剥离领域的活动将更为活跃。

1. 投资摩尔多瓦私营公司

由于摩尔多瓦公司大多数都是有限责任公司（共有约10万家有限责任公司，4 500家股份公司），买卖摩尔多瓦有限责任公司的股权，其方式和要求与大多数国家或地区类似。因为只要现有股东放弃或不行使优先购买权，股权转让的各方当事人在出售和购买交易的架构设计方面就享有很大的自由。比较常见的做法是对股权的收购设定一些前提条件。股权买卖的交易需要公证，并且需要在公共服务机构所属公共服务局进行产权转让登记。外国公司可以获得摩尔多瓦公司资本中100%的股份。摩尔多瓦没有本国股东最低（数量/股份）要求的限制。

2. 通过摩尔多瓦证券交易所收购公司

摩尔多瓦的股份制大企业以及受监管的股份企业，在大多数情况下，其股份是通过摩尔多瓦证券交易所（证交所）进行交易的。因为任何一项证交所的交易是通过买卖双方的报价匹配从而达成交易，在这种情况下，再另行协商任何先决条件是不可能的。因此，在决定在证券交易所进行交易之前，一般而言交易参与方就必须满足股票买卖所需的大多数先决条件。

（在证交所交易下）如果已经持有超过摩尔多瓦股份公司50%的股份（至少超过1股），那么该投资者须对其余股东的股票发出强制收购要约。

虽然摩尔多瓦法律允许少数股东明确拒绝排斥收购，但如果某一股东已经持有摩尔多瓦股份公司90%股份，则其有权可以向其余股东提出进一步的排斥收购要约。

3. 私有化：从国家收购公司

在过去几年中，摩尔多瓦已出售国有银行部门的全部股份，出售了电力经营公司、一家天然气运输公司、一家大型水泥厂、多家酒店物业和全国最大的百货商店。

摩尔多瓦仍有许多国有资产待售，包括国家拨号电话网络运营商和一些能源公司等战略资产。

摩尔多瓦采用不同的方法出售其国有资产。有时是进行国际招标，并与中标人谈判以及协商买卖协议，中标人不仅需要提供有竞争力的价格，也必须提供最具吸引力的对目标公司的投资方案。在许多情况下，摩尔多瓦通过国家证券交易所将其所拥有的公司股份进行出售，由出价最高者中标。

4. 对受监管企业的投资

对银行、保险和能源部门公司进行投资，必须事先获得监管机构的同意。只有声誉长期良好的企业，才有希望获得监管机构关于对该等公司进行投资的批准。因为监管机构的同意可能需要几个月的时间，为了在收购之前获得监管机构的同意，故选择合适的时机很重要。

（七）竞争条例

1. 摩尔多瓦竞争理事会

摩尔多瓦竞争理事会是一个根据《竞争法》设立的自主公共机构，负责确保市场主体遵守《竞争法》。竞争理事会的决定由5名成员组成的合议机构全体会议通过。

2.《竞争法》简介

《竞争法》规定了摩尔多瓦竞争管理的一般框架。该法律还得到各种附属规章的进一步补充。这些法律转用了大多数欧盟竞争规定，禁止反竞争和不公平竞争，对市场的经济集中设立管控制度。

因此，《竞争法》禁止缔结反竞争协议和协同做法。旨在：①直接/间接固定价格；②限制生产或销售；③划分市场、供应来源；④投标操纵以及其他形式的行为之相关协定均被禁止并且应当无效。

此外，禁止相关市场上的具有支配地位的主体通过以下方式滥用其支配地位：①直接或间接实行不公平的购买或销售价格；②限制生产、分销或技术研发；③对同等交易适用不同条件，从而使贸易伙伴处于竞争劣势；④收取过高或掠夺性价格；⑤无理拒绝订立合同或供应等。如果企业占据的市场份额超过50%，则推定该企业为具有市场支配地位。

对其他竞争者的不公平竞争也是被禁止的。这些行动包括：①诋毁竞争者；②煽动终止与竞争者的合同；③获取和/或非法使用竞争者的商业秘密；④窃取竞争者的客户；⑤与竞争者、其产品或经济活动混淆。不正当竞争行为的类型仅限于以上几种。

关于经营者集中，《竞争法》规定，在满足适用的法律门槛时，收购其他公司的股份/资产，将控制权授予收购方，或将收购前独立的公司或公司的一部分合并，以及设立全面运作的合资企业，必须事先通知竞争理事会，并由竞争理事会批准这类交易。有关的法律规定，如果计划集中的有关公司在交易前一年的营业总额超过约120万欧元，并且参与集中的两家以上相关公司中的任何一家公司，在交易前一年内在摩尔多瓦获得超过约48万欧元的累计营业额，则该次经营者集中交易应当事先通知竞争理事会并获得其批准。

3. 对违反竞争法行为的制裁

竞争理事会可对公司缔结反竞争协议（也应视为无效）、滥用市场支配地位、未经通知进行的经营者集中或实施被认为与竞争环境不相容的经济集中的行为，处以最高营业额5%的罚款。主管部门还规定，可指令当事方将被认为与竞争环境不相容的经营者集中予以解散，或要求通过法院予以解散。

对不公平竞争行为，最高可处以公司营业额 0.5% 的罚款。

对违反程序性规定的行为，如不提供当局要求的信息、反对突击调查等，也可对公司实行营业额 0.5% 的处罚。

（八）税收

20 世纪 90 年代，摩尔多瓦的税收法律散见于各种法律和条例。20 年来，大多数税法规定都已编纂入《税法》，涉及个人和企业所得税、增值税、货物税、房地产税、地方税、公路税、自然资源税和财政管理等问题。

摩尔多瓦与下列国家建立了大约 50 个日益完善的避免双重征税条约的网络：阿尔巴尼亚、亚美尼亚、奥地利、阿塞拜疆、白俄罗斯、比利时、波斯尼亚和黑塞哥维那（简称"波黑"）、保加利亚、加拿大、中国、捷克、塞浦路斯、克罗地亚、芬兰、德国、希腊、爱沙尼亚、瑞士、爱尔兰、以色列、日本、哈萨克斯坦、科威特、吉尔吉斯斯坦、立陶宛、拉脱维亚、卢森堡、马其顿、英国、马耳他、黑山、阿曼、波兰、葡萄牙、罗马尼亚、俄罗斯、塞尔维亚、斯洛伐克、斯洛文尼亚、西班牙、塔吉克斯坦、土耳其、土库曼斯坦、荷兰、乌克兰、匈牙利、乌兹别克斯坦、意大利。

1. 对摩尔多瓦公司利润征税

从历史上看，摩尔多瓦在 1992 年开始对公司利润征税，税率为 32%。多年来，当局持续将该税率降低到 28%、25% 等，直到 2007 年方才确定用于再投资的利润，其税率可被确定为零。2012 年对企业利润征税的税率降到 12% 的新水平，并沿用至今。

通常允许扣除营业费用，公司必须准备证明其具备特定业务所需的常见及必要特性。

2. 股息所得税

在摩尔多瓦，股息不视为应税收入的观点持续了大约 20 年，但这种待遇已然不再。根据摩尔多瓦《税法》，公司在缴纳 12% 的利润税后，应将支付给摩尔多瓦财政居民和非居民的股息上再预提 6% 的税。

2000 年《中摩税收协定》将摩尔多瓦公司向中国股东分配的股息预扣税从 6% 降至 5%，条件是中国股东是股息的受益所有人，并直接持有摩尔多瓦公司至少 25% 的资本。

3. 利息税

至于利息所得，根据摩尔多瓦《税法》，向非居民债权人支付的利息将按 12% 的比例预扣税款。根据《中摩税收协定》，对摩尔多瓦借款人向中国商业银行支付的利息预扣所得税可从 12% 降至 10%。

此外，根据《中摩税收协定》，由中国政府、中国政府全资拥有的金融机构或中国任何其他居民全资拥有的金融机构基于中国政府资助的债务，在摩尔多瓦所产生的利息应免征预扣税。

4. 在摩投资的税收优先管辖

有经验的投资者会选择以荷兰私人有限公司和公众有限公司作为平台投资摩尔多瓦。摩尔多瓦与荷兰的税务条约可能是最好的。两国之间关于 5% 利息预扣税，2% 特许权使用费预扣，以及大型投资获利零税收的政策所吸引了很多投资者。塞浦路斯条约规定股息、利息和特许权使用费的税率仅为 5%，而这也在投资者中相当流行。

5. 增值税

摩尔多瓦的增值税标准税率为 20%。对社会大众敏感的需求品（如面包、奶制品、糖、某些医药产品、天然气和其他物品），其增值税降至 8%。企业应在其年销售额达到 120 万摩尔多瓦列伊（约合 70 000 美元）之前登记为增值税纳税人。此外，在符合法律规定的条件下，可以自愿登记为增值税纳税人。某些用品可免征增值税。摩尔多瓦增值税制度在广义上与大多数欧洲国家的做法相同。增值税领域中最具挑战性的问题仍然是如何从多付的增值税中准确退税。

6. 薪资所得税

年薪低于 33 000 摩尔多瓦列伊（约合 2 000 美元）的，所得税降至 7%。收入超过前述指定标准的，其征税税率为 18%。雇员还享有若干与个人、家庭和社会地位有关的所得税减免。

除所得税外，薪金还应包括下列社会和医疗缴款：

（1）社会保障缴款

①雇主支付（相当于工资的）：23%；

②员工从工资中扣缴（相当于工资的）：6%。

（2）强制性医疗保险缴款

①雇主支付（相当于工资的）：4.5%；

②员工从工资中扣缴（相当于工资的）：4.5%；

③雇员还可享受雇主支付的免税餐券。

对在信息领域经营的公司还有一些特别的税收优惠。

（九）证券

1. 证券相关法律法规简介

摩尔多瓦资本市场的立法框架正在不断进行改革。现行的《资本市场法》于2013年生效。该法试图遵循欧盟法律，从而转用与资本市场有关的11项欧盟指令，其中包括《金融工具市场指令》《招投标指令》《投资者赔偿计划指令》《市场滥用指令》《资本充足率指令》和《统一货币与投资指令》。

摩尔多瓦证券交易所（MSE）是摩尔多瓦唯一的经营证券交易所。

2. 对证券市场的监督和管理

证券交易受《资本市场法》和有关条例的制约。主要管理机构是：财政部、国家金融市场委员会和摩尔多瓦国家银行。

国家金融市场委员会负责监督市场，并进行与市场舞弊有关的调查。视调查结果而定，国家融资机制可禁止市场参与者使用金融交易工具或提供投资服务和活动，暂停或撤销授权，扣押相关资产或处以罚款。执法机构调查有关操纵和内幕交易的刑事案件。

3. 外国公司参与证券交易的要求

摩尔多瓦证券交易所的官方网址为：http://www.moldse.md/。

摩尔多瓦证券交易所于1994年设立，至今只有在摩尔多瓦注册的公司才能进行股票交易。虽然法律并不禁止，但是外国企业从未参与证券交易所的股票发行。

摩尔多瓦私人企业进行股票公开发行不太常见。

摩尔多瓦企业进行债券的公开发行也比较罕见。

摩尔多瓦政府经常会在摩尔多瓦证券交易所对正在进行私有化的公司的股票进行销售。

从规定上而言，外国投资者可以聘用摩尔多瓦当地的经纪人购买摩尔多瓦证券交易所上市公司的股票。

如果一家公司在银行的股票拟进行交易，股票的买方需要事先获得摩尔多瓦国家银行签发的事先授权后方能交易。

（十）投资优惠与保护

1. 优惠政策的结构

摩尔多瓦本地公司不享有官方优惠政策，它们享有与外国公司相同的权利。尽管如此，摩尔多瓦仍然致力于支持投资，已与不同国家签订双边条约，并不断就开展商业活动修订法律。根据摩尔多瓦《宪法》，国家必须确保外国投资不可侵犯。政府渴望制定协调的政策和平衡良好的立法，以刺激国内和外国投资。

2. 对特定行业和区域的支持

政府倾向于以国家援助支持特定行业，即农业和葡萄酒部门。欧盟向设在摩尔多瓦的公司提供了一笔赠款，用于提高能源效率、改组葡萄酒部门、吸引青年和妇女（特别是来自农村地区的妇女）参与商业活动。

对某些领域有若干税收奖励办法，例如：农业领域税收奖励办法（如社会保障缴款减少、降低增值税税率）；信息技术产业个人所得税与社会保障保险激励措施；根据进关手续协定提供服务的轻工业公司增值税为零；为自由经济区的居民（企业）降低所得税率和增值税激励措施；为朱朱列什蒂国际自由港的一些供应品免征所得税和零增值税；为马尔古列什蒂国际自由空港的一些供应品征收零增值税。

根据摩尔多瓦加入的自由贸易安排，摩尔多瓦对来源于特定原产地的货物给予优惠关税待遇。摩尔多瓦迄今与大多数独立国家联合体（独联体）国家缔结了自由贸易协定，也是中欧自由贸易协定的缔约国。与欧盟的《联盟协议》包括一项《深入而全面的自由贸易协议》，规定对某些货物实行优惠关税税率配额。

3. 特别经济区域

摩尔多瓦划定了特定区域，在该类区域内，摩尔多瓦国内和外国投资者能够在优惠条件下（即优惠税收、海关和其他制度）开展创业活动。

自由经济区是摩尔多瓦海关管辖区域的一部分，但在经济领域单独区分，当地和外国投资者可在该区域内以优惠制度开展创业活动。在自由经济区设立的实体，凡从自由经济区向摩尔多瓦共和国海关境外出口货物和服务，或将所生产的货物交付给其他自由经济区居民（企业）用于出口的，摩尔多瓦政府有权对这类收入适用50%的所得税税率。在其他情况下，所得税税率为标准税率的75%。对于原产自由经济区的货物（服务）向摩尔多瓦海关领土之外出口货物（服务）获得的收入，以及原产自由经济区向其他自由经济区居民供应但最终用于出口的货物所获得的收入，可免征3年税款，但前提是自由经济区居民（企业）在其企业的固定资产和/或在开发区基础设施的发展方面投资了至少100万美元。如果其投资资本至少为500万美元，则可在5年内免征所得税。

从增值税的角度来看，从国外向自由经济区提供的货物和服务、从自由经济区向摩尔多瓦海关外地区提供的货物和服务、从摩尔多瓦其他地区向自由经济区提供的货物和服务，以及向其他自由经济区居民供应的货物和服务需缴纳的增值税为零。

工业园区可在国有或私有企业的区域内，通过绿色领域投资或以政府和社会资本合作（PPP）的方式建立，为期30年。在实践中，工业园区是企业根据政府的决定取得工业园区的（土地）所有权而创建的。工业园区的居民（企业）和管理部门可从下列与不动产有关的措施及政府支持中获益：

- 免费变更农用土地使用用途；
- 有权以法律规定的地价将公共财产土地连同建筑物私有化；
- 根据业主的决定为工业园区的设立而免费对公共动产和不动产进行转让；
- 管理企业可申请将减让系数降至公共土地年租赁费征收标准的0.3%；
- 优化政府监管。

信息产业科技园：摩尔多瓦的信息技术产业在不断成长。最近，摩尔多瓦议会批准了一项关于信息技术工业园的法律，其目的是为刺激信息技术工业的发展（包括进出口交易）创造必要条件。立法对信息产业科技园的创建和运作有特定的规范和监管要求。对信息产业科技园的激励包括将其他税收（如公司所得税、地方税等）合并的优惠单一税收制。

4. 双边投资保护

摩尔多瓦与各国签署了39项双边投资协定，为投资者提供了更多的保障和支持。

摩尔多瓦于2011年批准加入《关于解决国家和其他国家国民之间投资争端公约》（即《ICSID公约》），从而确保承认国际投资争端解决中心（ICSID）作出的任何决定（裁决）是强制性的，并承诺确保该等裁定中包含的经济方面的制裁内容在摩尔多瓦领土内得以执行。

摩尔多瓦还是《承认及执行外国仲裁裁决公约》（1958年《纽约公约》）的签署国，这意味着地方法院必须执行符合某些条件的国际仲裁裁决。

摩尔多瓦1994年批准了《中华人民共和国政府和摩尔多瓦共和国政府关于鼓励和相互保护投资协定》。该协定允许在摩尔多瓦的中国投资者在被指控侵犯投资者受保护权利的情况下向国际裁判机构提起诉讼。

三、贸易

(一) 贸易主管部门

摩尔多瓦政府是批准贸易法规的政府当局。然而,负责制定国家贸易政策和法规,履行行政管理职责的中央专门机构是经济部。

经济部在贸易领域的主要职责为:制定贸易发展的国家计划和战略;制定相关领域的规范性文件;为商品和服务生产和销售创造有利条件;制定和推广旨在保护国内市场的措施;提交关于在商业贸易领域负有管理职责的国家机构的职能优化方案。

经济部在对外贸易领域推行的政策主要与欧洲一体化的总体目标相联系。核心重点是履行2013年11月28日在维尔纽斯启动的《摩尔多瓦共和国与欧盟之间建立深度和综合自由贸易区的协定》。

经济部推行的各项商业贸易政策旨在巩固摩尔多瓦与其主要贸易伙伴国家的商业关系,以及促进与潜在合作伙伴的国际商贸交流活动。

(二) 贸易法律法规概况

自2001年7月26日起,摩尔多瓦成为世界贸易组织(WTO)的正式成员,致力于消除贸易壁垒,制定新规则,促进货物和服务贸易的自由化。

摩尔多瓦自2007年起成为《中欧自由贸易协定》(CEFTA)的缔约方。其主要目标是增加商品和服务贸易,推动CEFTA成员国之间的投资,消除贸易壁垒和扭曲,促进跨境货物的流通以及缔约国之间货物和服务的跨境交流。

《独联体自由贸易区协定》于2011年10月18日签署,旨在促进区域贸易便利化,改善缔约国之间的商业关系。

《摩尔多瓦共和国与欧盟和欧洲原子能共同体及其成员国之间的合作协定》(2014年6月27日签署)是自由贸易协定,要求在摩尔多瓦与欧盟之间建立深度和综合的自由贸易区(DCFTA)。自由贸易协定旨在开放货物和服务贸易市场,并逐步接受欧洲关于产品和服务的质量标准和规范。

摩尔多瓦与许多国家签署了双边自由贸易协定,其中包括克罗地亚、塞尔维亚、马其顿、波黑、阿尔巴尼亚、保加利亚、黑山、乌克兰、俄罗斯和土耳其等国。

目前,摩尔多瓦与中国以及与阿拉伯、埃及之间的自由贸易协定草案正在谈判中。

摩尔多瓦与中国的主要经济协议包括:《经济贸易协定》(1992年1月18日在基希讷乌签署)、《关于鼓励和相互保护投资的协定》(1992年11月6日在北京签署),以及《避免双重征税和防止偷漏税的协定》(2000年6月7日在北京签署)。

任何通过海关进出口的产品,都受到2000年7月20日颁布的《海关法》管理,并适用于每个通关口岸的海关管理。

战略物资的通关受2000年7月26日制定的《控制战略物资出口、转口、进口和运输法》规范。战略物资清单包括:①具有双重用途(民用和军用)的产品、技术和服务;②武器、弹药、军事装备,及相关技术和服务;③可用于制造和使用核武器、化学武器、生物武器和导弹,或上述武器携带者的产品、技术和服务;④根据摩尔多瓦加入的国际协定和安排,为了国家安全或外交政策而需要进行特殊管控的其他产品、技术和服务。

国内贸易受2010年9月23日的《国内贸易法》规范。

(三) 贸易管理

除上述协定外,摩尔多瓦还广泛参与区域性组织。摩尔多瓦是黑海地区经济合作组织(BSEC)的正式成员,多瑙河合作进程、民主与经济发展组织(GUAM)及其所属机构成员,即"古阿姆"集团(指格鲁吉亚、乌克兰、阿塞拜疆和摩尔多瓦四国),欧洲理事会和欧洲安全与合作组织(OSCE)的成员。摩尔多瓦还是中欧倡议(CEI)、区域合作委员会(RCC)、东南欧合作进程(SEECP)、东南欧合作倡议（SECI）和《东南欧能源条约》的成员。①

摩尔多瓦还批准加入了 20 项联合国、欧洲经济委员会的运输公约和协定。自从与欧盟签署相关协议以来，摩尔多瓦已在海关管理、过境贸易、食品安全、植物保护和检疫、动物管制、技术标准、认证和合格评定等领域，根据欧盟法令调整国内立法。

通过精准的国内立法调整，取得了提高管理水平和无纸化管理系统的并行效果，同时引进了 ISO 9001：2008 质量管理体系标准。此外，还启动了电子许可证和证书提交系统，允许企业在线提交申请，上传相关文件，并通过电子邮件接收许可证和证书。以简化的贸易活动通知程序取代了原有的审批程序。

1995 年，摩尔多瓦推出了自由经济区立法。从那时起，已经建立了 7 个自由经济区。在区内经营的公司享受特殊的税收和海关制度，旨在促进出口和招商引资。

（四）进出口商品的检验检疫

一般来说，依照商品安全的法律规定，禁止危险商品流入市场。

受国家动物卫生监管的货物进出口、过境，应在海关内部的动物监控部门进行。

如果没有取得动物监控部门的通行许可，海关将不允许向摩尔多瓦境内运送活体动物、动物源性材料和受动物监管的产品。

活体动物、动物源性材料、受动物监管产品的出口应在与进口许可类似的条件下进行，并应遵守动物健康管理规定，提供进口国所要求的动物进口许可，以及接受进口的证明和过境国动物监管机构的许可。

只有提前 24 小时取得"签发检查证书信息系统"（TRACES）的通知，方可进行活体动物、动物源性胚胎细胞、受动物监控产品的进出口和过境业务。

进口动物应接受预防性检疫，最长期限为 30 天。

摩尔多瓦境内植物、植物产品和接受植物检疫的相关产品，应在出口国主管机构出具植物检疫证书后方可办理。植物检疫证书的有效期为自签发之日起 14 天。

（五）海关管理

自 2017 年起，摩尔多瓦启用了新的海关管理结构，并优化海关结构。海关还推出了《授权经营计划》（AEO）。该计划采用欧盟模式对 AEO 组织进行认证（符合特定标准），以期达到：①简化海关手续（不完全申报程序、简化申报程序、就地清关程序）；②安全和保障；③简化安全和保障手续。②

摩尔多瓦海关还将联合国贸易和发展会议（UNCTAD）的电子海关数据平台（ASYCUDA）作为海关综合信息系统（CIIS）的基础。

因此，建立了进出口和过境贸易一站式系统（SW），贸易商可以在线提交进出口报关单（通过 ASYCUDA World），并上传所有的相关文件。

摩尔多瓦同意取消所有的关税，但也采取一些过渡期和保护性措施，逐步取消一些关税，或给予免税配额。在海关电子数据平台启用之后，摩尔多瓦进口的许多欧盟产品已经实现免税。在欧盟进口的商品中，近 46% 的商品已享受到零关税进口的最惠国待遇。另外 47% 的货物在海关电子数据平台启用后也立即降低关税。除免税配额所涉及的货物外，2024 年 1 月 1 日起摩尔多瓦将全面解禁欧盟进口产品。③

---

① 参见 http://mei.gov.md/sites/default/files/all_study_for_publication.with_comments_integrated.final.pdf。
② 参见 http://mei.gov.md/sites/default/files/all_study_for_publication.with_comments_integrated.final.pdf。
③ 参见 http://documents.worldbank.org/curated/en/566151468196761047/pdf/ACS17523-WP-P148369-Overview-MDA-TradeStudy-PUBLIC.pdf。

四、劳动

(一) 劳动法律法规概况

摩尔多瓦规范劳动关系的主要法律是 2003 年 3 月 28 日的第 154 号《劳动法》。《劳动法》规定了所有劳动方面的规范,例如劳动合同的基本原则、工作时间、解雇理由、休息日、薪酬和补偿、担保和责任、针对某些类别雇员的特别保护措施,以及劳动争议解决等。《劳动法》适用于所有在摩尔多瓦工作的雇员,无论是本国人还是外国人。《劳动法》也适用于所有经济领域以及公共服务领域。

除了《劳动法》之外,各立法机构还制定了下列规范性法规:
- 摩尔多瓦议会制定的就业管理方面法规(例如,2002 年 2 月 14 日的第 847 号《工资法》;2012 年 3 月 22 日的第 48 号《公务员工资法》等);
- 摩尔多瓦政府制定的法规(例如 2012 年 3 月 22 日制定的第 48 号《关于实体经济部门最低工资保障的决议》);
- 卫生劳动和社会保障部制定的法规(例如《工作岗位命名修正案》)。

摩尔多瓦的雇主必须遵守其签订的集体谈判协议。此外,摩尔多瓦雇主需详细制定和实施内部就业政策及其规定,以规范与其经营活动相关的劳动问题。

卫生劳动和社会保障部是负责劳动就业的主要政府机构和政策制定者。摩尔多瓦雇主履行法律的情况由国家劳动监察局监管,该局系卫生劳动和社会保障部的一个下属部门。国家劳动监察局有权对摩尔多瓦雇主进行检查,发现侵权案件时有权向摩尔多瓦法院提起行政诉讼。

(二) 外国人在当地工作规定

1. 工作许可

只有在当地人力资源匮乏的情况下,摩尔多瓦雇主才被允许雇用外国公民。因此,在雇用外国人之前,摩尔多瓦的雇主将被要求证明其已在当地宣布了现有的职位空缺,且无摩尔多瓦公民提出工作申请。

为了能够在摩尔多瓦就业,外国公民必须与雇主一起从主管政府机构获得工作许可证。

未经许可的雇用,摩尔多瓦雇主和外国雇员都面临着行政法律责任。

除国际协议另有规定,外国公民可以持摩尔多瓦承认或接受的文件和签证等有效文件,进入和离开摩尔多瓦。此外,打算进入摩尔多瓦并停留的外国公民,必须证明他们每天至少有 30 欧元的旅费,住宿期限不超过 10 天的,应不少于 300 欧元。

2. 申请程序

为了获得工作许可,摩尔多瓦雇主应采取以下步骤:

(1) 职位空缺的登记和公布

摩尔多瓦雇主应向当地就业局登记空缺职位,并在当地报刊上刊登职位空缺广告。

(2) 申请工作许可

为了获得工作许可,雇主应与外国公民一起向摩尔多瓦移民局提交下列文件:

① 移民局核准的格式申请书;
② 拟聘用外国公民护照的复印件;
③ 职位空缺广告的复印件;
④ 劳动合同文本,包含摩尔多瓦雇主应付的工资情况;
⑤ 文凭证书(学位)或其他证明外国公民学历的文件副本;
⑥ 由其本国政府主管部门签发的外国公民无犯罪记录证明;
⑦ 在规定期限拥有住房的证明(房主证明/租赁协议/买卖协议);
⑧ 覆盖摩尔多瓦行程的国际医疗保险或当地医疗保险;
⑨ 血型确认;
⑩ 3 厘米 ×4 厘米大小的 2 张彩色照片。

国家移民局有 20 天的时间审查提交的文件，并颁发工作许可证。通常情况下，工作许可为 1 年期限，并可延长 1 年。

3. 社会保险

1999 年 7 月 8 日的第 489-XIV 号《公共社会保险制度法》，适用于根据劳动合同在摩尔多瓦就业的本国人和外国人。摩尔多瓦社会保险的监管主体是国家社会保险委员会（Casa Nationala pentru Asigurari Sociale）。

根据摩尔多瓦社会保险条例的规定，居住在摩尔多瓦的人应享受社会保险，如达到退休年龄、失去支持者、失去工作能力、由于疾病或意外事故造成残疾无法工作、职业病、儿童保育、疾病预防、职业康复、生育、分娩、失业和丧葬等。

社会保险缴纳主体包括拥有摩尔多瓦永久居留权的人和受雇于劳动合同的个人。如果该公民是企业根据劳动合同、服务或其他协议聘用的，则社会保险费由雇主缴纳。

因此，摩尔多瓦雇主必须支付强制性的国家社会保险费，并从雇员的工资中扣除个人应承担的社会保险费。每年应付的社会保险费由《社会保障预算法》确定。例如，根据 2017 年 12 月 15 日发布的第 281 号《2018 年社会保险预算法》规定，摩尔多瓦雇主有义务计算和支付国家社会保险费预算：①企业缴费率为 23%，按每月其雇员、其他雇员的工资或其他类似协议约定，作为雇主缴费部分；②个人缴费率为 6%，按每月雇员的工资和其他就业所得计算。

根据 2002 年 12 月 26 日颁布的第 1593-XV 号《强制医疗保险费金额、计算方式和支付期限法》，摩尔多瓦也建立了医疗强制保险制度，由国家强制医疗保险公司（Compania Nationala a Asigurarilor Obligatorii in Medicina）负责监管。因此，雇主和雇员都必须向国家支付强制医疗保险费。个人企业主、商业专利持有人、律师、公证员和其他个人应当按照《强制医疗保险预算法》，每年支付固定金额的医疗保险费。例如，根据 2017 年 12 月 15 日颁布的第 280 号《2018 年强制医疗保险基金法》，摩尔多瓦雇主有义务计算和支付国家强制医疗保险费：①企业缴费率为 4.5%，按每月其雇员、其他雇员的工资或其他类似协议约定，作为雇主缴费部分；②个人缴费率为 4.5%，按每月员工的工资和其他就业所得计算。

（三）出入境

1. 签证类型

个人进入摩尔多瓦所需的签证类型取决于多种因素，如个人国籍、访问目的和访问期限。

根据访问目的和期限的不同，外国人可以获得以下类型的签证进入并在摩尔多瓦停留：

（1）A 类——机场过境签证：A 类签证允许外国人在摩尔多瓦机场的国际过境区过境，且无需进入摩尔多瓦领土。

（2）B 类——过境签证：B 类签证是向有意经过摩尔多瓦进入第三方国家的外国人而签发的。B 类签证由目的地国签发，签证期限不超过 1 年。此类签证允许外国人以过境为目的在摩尔多瓦的领土上停留不超过 5 天。

（3）C 型——短期居留签证（用于传教、旅游、访问、商业、运输、体育活动、文化、科学和人道主义活动、短期医疗和其他不违反摩尔多瓦法律的活动等目的）。C 类签证的签发时间为固定期限，最近 6 个月内一次或多次签证的停留时间不超过 90 天。

（4）D 类——长期逗留签证（用于企业经营活动、就业、学习、家庭团聚、宗教和人道主义活动、外交和服务活动以及医疗等）。D 类签证颁发期限不超过 12 个月，最近 6 个月内在摩尔多瓦一次或多次签证的停留时间不超过 90 天。D 类签证允许外国人在摩尔多瓦申请工作许可。

下列国家的公民可免签进入摩尔多瓦：欧盟成员国、美国、加拿大、瑞士、挪威、爱尔兰、日本、安道尔、以色列、列支敦士登、摩纳哥和梵蒂冈。

2. 出入境限制

外国公民进入或在摩尔多瓦停留的，受 2010 年 7 月 16 日第 200 号《外国人管理法》规范。

下列人员禁止进入摩尔多瓦：

（1）未按照摩尔多瓦法律的要求提交正式、内容有效的入境文件，或在履行入境手续时提供虚假信息；

（2）存在个人参与资助、筹备、支持或实施恐怖主义行为的情形，或者为跨国犯罪组织提供支持，参与或可能参与摩尔多瓦加入的国际条约中所规定的危害和平与人类罪、战争罪或危害人类罪；

（3）违反国家边境的管理规定或边境通关规定；

（4）在摩尔多瓦境内或停留期间，向摩尔多瓦及其公民实施犯罪，并有犯罪记录；

（5）介绍或企图介绍外国人非法进入摩尔多瓦，或参与外国人口走私；

（6）违反规定、无合法理由取得签证进入摩尔多瓦，或先前离开摩尔多瓦时未偿还相关费用，或在摩尔多瓦逾期滞留，或有其他禁止进入摩尔多瓦的情形。

根据摩尔多瓦刑事或民事诉讼法律规定，在某些的情况下个人被禁止离开摩尔多瓦，特别是基于下列原因：

（1）根据刑事法院的判决被囚禁在摩尔多瓦，或者在摩尔多瓦的刑事起诉或审判中，被列入通缉名单或被禁止离开当地和出境，受监管或居家监禁，或受防范性拘留，或因司法保释而临时释放，但不得离开当地的；

（2）根据《刑法》的规定，外国公民在摩尔多瓦接受强制医疗措施的约束；

（3）法院根据《执行法》作出决定，禁止外国公民离开摩尔多瓦的。

（四）工会和劳工组织

根据摩尔多瓦《劳动法》和2000年7月7日第1129-XIV号《工会法》，允许雇员创立或加入工会，以促进雇主、政府机构和其他实体对雇员权益的保护。

工会可由3人创设。它根据章程运作，并须在摩尔多瓦司法部注册。任何在摩尔多瓦合法居留的公民或外国公民，有权创立或加入工会。

创设工会是非强制性的。在股东大会上，雇员可以委派一人或多人代表他们的利益，处理与雇主的关系。此种委托无需任何形式的注册。

（五）劳动争议

雇员与雇主之间的劳动争议，受《劳动法》、2003年5月30日第225号《民事诉讼法》，以及雇员与雇主之间劳动合同的约束。《劳动法》规定了员工索赔的特殊限期，取决于具体的索赔理由。因此，非财产性的索赔从雇员知道或应该知道其权利受侵害之日起3个月内提出；雇员提出财产性索赔的时限为3年。

集体劳动争议应当由数量相等的雇主和雇员代表组成的调解委员会来解决。如果一方当事人不同意委员会作出的决定，或者委员会无法就集体争议达成调解协议，则各方可在委员会就争议作出决定之日起10天内向有关法庭起诉。

五、知识产权

（一）知识产权法律法规概况

摩尔多瓦已建立符合国际标准和规则的现代知识产权体系（IP）。摩尔多瓦的知识产权法律框架涵盖商标、专利发明、地理标志、原产地证明、传统特色保护、新植物品种、工业品外观设计、集成电路布图、版权及相关权利。在摩尔多瓦共和国加入世贸组织的过程中，不断加强知识产权领域立法，以达到TRIPs协定的要求。由于摩尔多瓦是国际知识产权组织的主要成员和一些重要国际条约的缔约方，因此摩尔多瓦的知识产权注册和保护程序便捷而又透明，并符合通行的国际规则。摩尔多瓦国家知识产权局（AGEPI）经授权建立国内知识产权保护体系，负责注册和促进知识产权保护，并维护知识产权所有者的权利。

1. 专利保护

摩尔多瓦的专利保护受 2008 年 3 月 7 日颁布的第 50-XVI 号《发明保护法》规范。此外，由于摩尔多瓦是《专利合作条约》(PCT)、《国际承认用于专利程序的微生物保存布达佩斯条约》《国际专利分类斯特拉斯堡协定》(PLT) 的成员，因此，在摩尔多瓦申请专利符合通行的国际标准。

摩尔多瓦建立了必要的法律框架，适用《欧洲专利公约》，1992 年 6 月 18 日的理事会（EEC）第 1768/92 号《关于创建药物产品的辅助保护证书条例》，1996 年 7 月 23 日欧洲议会和理事会（EC）第 1610/96 号《关于植物保护产品的辅助保护证书条例》，1998 年 7 月 6 日的欧洲议会和理事会第 98/44/EC 号《关于生物技术发明的法律保护指令》，2004 年 4 月 29 日欧洲议会和理事会第 2004/48/EC 号《关于知识产权执法指令》等。

2. 商标保护

商标保护受新修订的 2008 年 2 月 29 日第 38-XVI 号《商标保护法》《商标法条约》(TLT)、《商标法新加坡条约》和《商标国际注册马德里协定》规范。

摩尔多瓦的商标申请遵循《商标注册用商品和服务国际分类尼斯协定》和《建立商标图形要素国际分类维也纳协定》的规定。

3. 版权保护

摩尔多瓦的版权立法包括 2010 年 7 月 2 日的第 139 号《版权与相关权利法》，这是最新的知识产权立法之一，依照《欧盟关于版权保护的指令》制定。摩尔多瓦签署了《保护文学和艺术作品伯尔尼公约》《保护表演者、音像制品制作者和广播组织罗马公约》《保护录音制品制作者禁止未经许可复制其录音制品公约》《世界知识产权组织版权条约》《世界知识产权组织表演和录音制品条约》，以及《视听表演北京条约》。

4. 工业设计保护

2007 年 7 月 12 日第 161-XVI 号《工业品外观设计法》是关于创造程序、新颖性、注册和工业品外观设计保护标准的主要国内立法。摩尔多瓦是《工业品外观设计国际注册海牙协定》和《建立工业品外观设计国际分类洛迦诺协定》的缔约方。

（二）申请专利

摩尔多瓦专利授予任何涉及产品、生产过程和所有的科技领域内具有新颖性和创造性的发明（即发明对于本领域在艺术、科技、实践中经验丰富的人员而言不是显而易见的），并可应用于工业和农业领域。发明受到保护的权利包括：

（1）发明专利；
（2）短期发明专利；
（3）辅助保护证书；
（4）欧亚专利；
（5）经过验证的欧洲专利。

任何自然人或法人都有权向国家知识产权局（AGEPI）提交专利申请。

除非合同另有规定，雇员在履行其职务或经书面委托的特定任务时（职务发明），发明的专利权属于雇主。

发明专利期限自申请专利之日起 20 年。短期专利的期限应自提出短期专利申请之日起 6 年，并可延长 4 年。

专利申请应以罗马尼亚语向 AGEPI 提交。它可以用其他语言提交，但须翻译成罗马尼亚语。

专利申请应包含：

（1）颁发专利申请书；
（2）发明描述；
（3）一项或多项申请；
（4）说明书或权利要求书中涉及的任何附图；

(5)摘要。

专利申请须缴纳约 500 欧元的正式和实质审查费用。

专利申请应仅涉及一个发明或相互联系形成总构思的一组发明。

AGEPI 应审查专利申请和发明形成的主题是否符合法律的要求。AGEPI 应进行正式和预备审查，并应要求对专利申请进行实质性审查。

在正式审查中，AGEPI 应审查专利申请是否符合正式要求，之后应进行预备审查。

如 AGEPI 发现申请中存在缺陷应予纠正时，将给予申请人进行更正的机会。

专利申请自申请之日起届满 18 个月的，或者自优先权日起主张优先权的，应当予以公布。

在实质审查中，AGEPI 应审查发明是否可以获得专利，并且符合新颖性、创造性、工业实用性和应用性。申请人有机会在整个审查过程中修改和说服持反对意见的审查人员。

在完成专利申请的实质性审查并出具审查报告后，AGEPI 应决定是否授予专利。AGEPI 的决定应在提出异议期限届满时公布。除公布决定外，还应公布专利说明书，包含权利描述、检索报告，以及所附图纸。

自公布后 6 个月内，任何人均可对专利提出异议。如果没有提交书面反对意见，或异议被争议委员会驳回，AGEPI 应向权利人颁发专利，但须缴纳国家税费，并应在《工业产权公报》(BOPI) 发布有关颁发专利的通知。

专利需要支付年费。

(三) 注册商标

商标是任何标志或任何易于用图形表示的标志组合，用于本人与他人的商品或服务。

以下内容可能被注册为商标：文字（包括人名）、字母、数字、图纸、颜色组合、图形元素、三维形式，特别是产品或其包装的形式，以及任何符号组合。

对不具有独特性，以产品或服务的地理来源、质量或性质误导消费者，违反公共秩序或商业道德，或损害国家形象和利益的商标不予注册。使用国家或地区名称的商标需经国家批准。

商标所有人拥有处置和使用商标的专属权利，并且在商标有效期内有权禁止他人在摩尔多瓦境内使用该商标。

任何自然人、法人、自然人或法人团体都可以注册商标。外国人应通过授权的专利代理人在摩尔多瓦注册商标。

商标注册申请书应当包括：

(1) 申请人的身份证明；
(2) 代理人证明；
(3) 清晰的商标图样及其说明；
(4) 根据尼斯商品和服务分类所确定的商品和服务清单。

在多数情况下，外国人可向其在摩尔多瓦的授权代表颁发授权书，提供商标说明并支付商标注册费，也可以聘请专利律师在线提交商标注册申请。在某些特定情况下，申请应附以下文件：

(1) 优先权文件（适用于 6 个月优先）；
(2) 使用集体商标的规定（适用于集体商标）；
(3) 使用认证标志的规定（适用于认证标志）；
(4) 确认有权在商标中使用地理标志或原产地名称；
(5) 确认有权在商标中使用工业品外观设计；
(6) 授权使用国家标志、官方或历史名称以及国际政府间组织的全称或简称；
(7) 授权使用当地行政机构的官方名称或标志、构成国家文化遗产的名称、标志、形象、标牌，或政府管理、维护和标记的印意，使用名人姓名。

如果申请人证明其为公司的所有人，公司名称也可注册为商标。

申请日期起 1 个月内，AGEPI 将根据要求审查商标的注册申请。

如果发现申请文件不合理或缺失，申请人应自 AGEPI 通知起 2 个月内纠正不合规之处；否则视为撤回申请。

如果商标注册申请符合要求，AGEPI 应在 3 个月内在《工业产权公报》（BOPI）上公布注册商标的申请。申请人也会收到通知。

商标注册申请公布之日起 3 个月内，任何人均可提出异议，权利人也可对商标注册提出异议。如果无异议或通过实质审查，AGEPI 应当作出商标注册或拒绝注册的决定。任何关于商标注册申请的决定都可以向 AGEPI 的竞争委员会提出上诉。在缴纳国家注册费后，将颁发商标注册证书。

商标自申请日起注册期限为 10 年。商标注册期在 10 年期满后可续展。商标注册费用为 40 欧元，审查费用 200 欧元，颁发商标证书 250 欧元，每次延期费 250 欧元。

（四）保护知识产权措施

权利受到侵犯的人可以在法定时效期内向摩尔多瓦民事法庭申请保护其权利，法定时效为 3 年。

侵犯知识产权的物品越过国境时，也可以要求摩尔多瓦海关介入加以保护。

海关保护措施旨在保护国内市场免受假冒和盗版商品的侵害，避免权利人的权益受损，引起不正当竞争，并对国家的经济安全和当地消费者权益构成威胁。

知识产权权利人应向海关提交申请，说明其所寻求保护的知识产权。接受申请后，在发现涉嫌侵犯知识产权的货物时，海关应当实行保护措施。海关应暂停通关程序，通知权利人和货物的申报人或收货人，并启动司法程序。这些措施由海关依职权行使。如果权利人未在规定的期限内提起诉讼，海关当局会放行货物，但应遵守其他法律规定。

六、环境保护

（一）环境保护主管部门

农业、区域发展和环境部（Ministry）是摩尔多瓦负责环境保护和合理利用自然资源的主管部门，制定和推动保护环境和合理利用资源领域内的国家政策，旨在创造有利的生活条件，保持国家的可持续发展，加强国际合作，推进国内立法与欧盟法律的融合。

在该部的隶属和直接监督下，若干政府机构和部门在水质、废物和资源管理、环境影响评价和环境质量监督方面行使管理职权。

主要的二级政府机构包括：国家环境保护局、国家水文气象局、国家地质和矿产资源局、国家水利局、国家原子能机构、环境地理和渔业研究院。

上述政府机构拥有广泛的管理权，涵盖了环境政策实施、生态和地质国家监督、自然资源管理和水资源保护。

如果发生环境违法行为，国家环境保护局会采取积极行动，行使禁止和停止违反环境保护条例的建筑施工等权力，并暂停影响环境状况的经济活动。

此外，联合国在摩尔多瓦共设立了永久性机构，在生物多样性保护、气候变化条例的实施，以及联合国环境规划署制定的"绿色经济"概念等方面，无疑产生了的重大影响，如"摩尔多瓦可持续发展绿色城市项目""氢氯氟烃逐渐淘汰管理计划项目"和"生物多样性保护纳入摩尔多瓦的国土规划和土地管理实践项目"。

（二）环境保护法律法规概况

摩尔多瓦环境保护的法律和监管框架主要来源于 2014 年缔结的《欧盟—摩尔多瓦合作协定》。该协定确定了摩尔多瓦的环境保护政策，并明确了未来几年的工作目标。在签署合作协定后，摩尔多瓦开始本国法律与欧盟法律融合的进程。因此，这是摩尔多瓦实现包括环境法在内的所有政策法规与欧盟统一的主要法律手段。

此外，摩尔多瓦迄今已批准了若干与环境保护有关的国际公约，实现国内法律与国际规范相结合，并确保环境保护的可持续性。摩尔多瓦还是以下协约的缔约国，包括《跨界环境影响评价公约》《埃斯波公约》）、《奥胡斯公约》、在里约热内卢通过的《气候变化框架公约》《京都议定书》《保护世界文化和自然遗产公约》等。

除了已批准的国际公约外，摩尔多瓦的环境保护监管框架还描绘出一个全方位的法律和法规体系，其法律效力遍及所有的环保领域。国家环境立法的基石是《环境保护法》，规定了在空气质量、水保护、废物管理、污染防控、气候变化、环境影响评估等方面的主要法律义务。

环境影响评估对摩尔多瓦和其他国家的环境保护计划和活动具有里程碑的意义，已经有两项重要立法来防止社会经济活动对环境的潜在影响。

因此，根据《环境影响评估法》和《环境鉴定法》的规定，对拟实施的经济活动进行强制性的事前影响评价，以减轻对环境带来的不利后果，并在环境决策过程中确立"公众参与"的约束性机制，以保障公民在环境影响评估过程中的必要参与度。

（三）环境保护评估

环境可持续性问题是摩尔多瓦的重点关注和优先事项，因为它直接关系到人们的生活和健康状况，关系到经济利益和社会的可持续发展的实现。

摩尔多瓦认为，可持续发展是增强社会凝聚力和确保经济增长的重要途径。

《2014—2023年国家环境战略》中列明了未来几年的主要环境保护目标。

摩尔多瓦的内在目标是确保国家和地方层面的环境保护，在公民、经济和环境之间创造和谐的状态。摩尔多瓦也试图改革目前的法律框架，融合欧盟法律，为法人实体、自然人和政府机构制定明确的环境保护义务，确保将环境保护程序扩展到所有的环境可持续发展领域，并保障摩尔多瓦公民享受未受污染和健康的环境，与经济发展和社会福祉相协调。

七、争议解决

（一）解决争端的方法及机构

1. 摩尔多瓦管辖民事争议的法律制度

根据《宪法》的规定，摩尔多瓦是一个主权独立、统一和不可分割的国家。法院根据法律开展司法活动。

摩尔多瓦的司法制度建立在三层结构的基础之上，包括最高法院、4个上诉法院和15个普通法院（初审法院）。上级法院的裁决对下级法院具有约束力。在具体法律程序中的法官人数可能会有所不同，取决于案件的复杂程度和具体情况，以及主管法院的层级。尽管具有约束性的先例并未被视为直接法律渊源，但遵循法律关系安全和确定性的原则，一般倾向于追求判例的统一性。

摩尔多瓦的法律制度沿袭大陆法系，即传统民法。它主要影响到法律编纂、实体法与程序法的区别，以及法学理论研究。

法律程序中使用的语言是国家官方语言。不使用国家官方语言的诉讼参与者，有权在翻译的帮助下熟悉案卷文件和在庭审中陈述。法庭的各类决定须以民事程序中的使用语言或以国家官方语言发布。经裁判法官许可，可使用所有诉讼参与者都可接受的语言进行庭审；但是，判决应以国家官方语言发布。

目前，某些形式和内容的诉讼可以直接向主管法官提交，也可以在损害发生后邮寄诉讼申请。正在修订的《民事诉讼法》，允许提交电子形式诉讼申请。但是，修订尚未获得批准。法庭会通知被告第一次庭审时间，法官会限定提交答辩意见和所有必要证据的时间。

除非法律另有规定，各方当事人均应证明案件事实，作为其主张和抗辩的依据。如有必要，法官有权要求当事人和其他诉讼参与者提供补充证据，并应核实其真实性。法院应当仅对与案件有关的证据进行审查和调查，确认或否定案件事实，或就现有或缺失的案件事实进行说明，作出适当裁决。

此外，法院庭审是公开的（通过SRS FEMIDA音频系统录音），但法律明确规定不公开的情形除外（例如涉及国家机密、青少年出庭的）。经合议庭审判长的许可，允许诉讼参与者录制庭审过程。

作为案件审理的结果，要公布判决结果。如果出现以下情况，法院会发布完整的判决：①庭审参与者提出要求；②对判决提出上诉；③涉及承认和执行程序。在这些情况下，法院会在申请提出后15天内作出完整的判决。除非法律另有规定，对法院判决可在公布之日起30日内提出上诉。在上诉案件中对案件进行审查后，法院判决为终审决定并可强制执行。对法院终审判决可申请再审撤销原判。

以下法院判决应视为不可撤销：①未在法定期限内提出上诉；②上诉法院作出的判决后，未在法定期限内提起再审；③再审法院作出的判决。

在判决不可撤销之后，案件当事人和其他参与者及其继承人不能以同样的理由和案件事实向法院申请撤销原判，也不能就不可撤销判决向不同法院提出事实和法律异议。不可撤销的判决对个人或与案件利益有关的个人和组织，均具有约束力。

2. 仲裁

仲裁受2003年5月30日第225-XV号《民事诉讼法》（第XLII-XLIV章）、2008年2月22日第23-XVI号《仲裁法》和2008年2月22日第24-XVI号《国际商事仲裁法》规范。

摩尔多瓦批准了一系列国际条约，其中最重要的是《欧洲仲裁公约》《欧洲国际商事仲裁公约》（1998年3月5日生效），1958年在纽约缔结的《承认及执行外国仲裁裁决公约》（1998年9月18日生效）和1965年在华盛顿缔结的《关于解决国家和他国国民之间投资争端公约》（2011年6月4日生效）。

主要的仲裁机构如下：摩尔多瓦工商会国际商事仲裁院、摩尔多瓦国家知识产权局调解和仲裁中心、摩尔多瓦民航航空仲裁院、摩尔多瓦国际运输协会仲裁院，以及基希讷乌国际商事仲裁院。

根据契约自由原则，双方可选择仲裁作为解决争议的条款，仲裁适用法律和机构、仲裁员以及其他相关的事项。

3. 专家法庭

在2016年重组之前，曾有专门的法庭，如商业巡回法庭和军事法庭，现均已被撤销。

4. 调解

调解受2015年7月3日第137号《调解法》规范。申请调解可以导致自调解协议签署后中止民事或仲裁程序。双方在调解员的协助下达成协议，决定调解程序的规则和期限。在和解协议签署之前，经征得双方同意可暂停程序，征询专家的意见并得出结论。

此外，2003年5月30日第225-XV号《民事诉讼法》第XIII章规定了某些类型案件的司法调解程序：消费者权益保护、劳动争议、货物所有权纠纷、标的低于200列伊的案件。经当事人的要求，亦可在其他案件中申请司法调解。

司法调解的期限不得超过第一次庭审日期后的45天。通过调解程序可以和解案件。如果一方或双方拒绝通过调解解决争议，或者争议在法律规定的时间范围内未能解决，或者各方尚未就所有的争议达成共识，法院作出裁决（不能对其提出异议）。在拒绝调解或调解期限届满起3日内，调解程序终止，并将案件材料送交法院。

（二）适用法律

有关民事和商事案件的审理程序受2003年5月30日第225-XV号《民事诉讼法》规范。对于某些类别的案件，可以根据法律规定或由当事人约定，适用初步庭外争端解决的法定程序。

各方当事人遵守有关法院管辖权的规定也是非常重要的。需要注意的是，法院对具有外国因素案件管辖权的特殊性，特别是摩尔多瓦法院的专属管辖权（例如，对位于摩尔多瓦境内的不动产主张权利；根据运输协议提出的诉讼，其中承运人出发地或到达地位于摩尔多瓦；总部设在摩尔多瓦的外国商业实体启动破产程序或其他终止付款程序等）。

摩尔多瓦可以执行外国仲裁裁决和外国判决。如前所述，摩尔多瓦于1998年12月17日开始执行《承认及执行外国仲裁裁决公约》。

八、其他

(一) 反商业贿赂

1. 反商业贿赂法律法规概况

摩尔多瓦《刑法》第 324—335 条涵盖了政府和私人领域贿赂犯罪的刑事责任范围。根据法律规定，贿赂是指无论是否为本人或他人利益，以任何形式的商品、服务、特权或优惠，向公务人员提议给予或承诺履行、延迟或加快履行其职责相悖的行为。

《刑法》将以下与贿赂有关的罪行定为犯罪：主动和被动腐败、渎职（政府部门）、收受贿赂（私营部门）。外国政府官员也被视为犯罪主体。此外，公务员选任也受到 2017 年 5 月 25 日颁布的第 82 号《诚信法》（如礼品制度）和 2013 年 12 月 23 日第 325 号《机构诚信评估法》的规范。

摩尔多瓦于 2007 年 10 月 1 日通过第 158/2007 号《联合国反腐败公约》，并于 2003 年 12 月 26 日通过了第 542/2003 号《反腐败民事公约》，由政府与总检察长办公室行使管理职责。

2003 年 3 月 14 日第 122 号《刑事诉讼法》，不仅规定了国家反腐败中心和反腐败检察官办公室的权限，还规定了刑事调查的启动、执行程序、终止程序、案件移送法院、初审案件审理条件、普通或特别上诉程序等相关方面。

2. 反商业贿赂主管部门

负责调查贿赂行为的机构是国家反腐败中心和反腐败检察官办公室。反腐败检察官办公室负责起诉由国家反腐败中心刑事调查机构所进行刑事调查的案件。

向警方提交举报或揭发贿赂行为将启动刑事调查。即使案件不在其职权范围内，刑事调查机构也会接受投诉，然后协助调查。不论是否启动调查程序，应立即对举报人进行询问，并在调查过程中进一步核实。从传唤罪犯到将案件送交法院的整个程序，都受到法律的严格规范，并由法院作出适当的裁决和刑罚。

3. 惩处措施

根据犯罪的严重程度，反商业贿赂行为适用的刑罚包括罚款和监禁。

贿赂犯罪的最高处罚如下：

- 被动腐败的，处 15 年有期徒刑、500 000 列伊的罚款，以及剥夺担任某些公职的权利，或在 15 年的时间内禁止从事特定活动。
- 主动腐败的，处 12 年有期徒刑、400 000 列伊的罚款，对法人处以 900 000 列伊的罚款，剥夺担任某些公职的权利，或禁止从事特定活动，或担任清算人。
- 渎职的，处 7 年有期徒刑，对自然人处以 300 000 列伊的罚款，对法人处以 600 000 列伊罚款，禁止从事特定活动或担任清算人。
- 受贿的，处 7 年有期徒刑、317 500 列伊的罚款，剥夺担任某些公职的权利，或在 7 年的时间内禁止从事特定活动。
- 行贿的，处 7 年有期徒刑、415 500 万列伊的罚款，对法人处以 750 000 列伊的罚款，剥夺从事某些特定活动或担任清算人的权利。

(二) 工程承包

摩尔多瓦涉及政府采购的主要法律是 2015 年 7 月 3 日第 131 号《政府采购法》。该法最近已生效，旨在适用欧盟 2004/18/EC《关于协调政府采购货物、工程和服务程序的指令》，还部分适用了 2014/24/EU 和 89/665/EEC 欧盟指令。

1. 许可制度和限制

根据摩尔多瓦法律，任何经营者，无论是本国人或外国居民，注册为公法或私法上的个人或法人实体，都有权参与政府采购程序。

外国企业有权参与摩尔多瓦的招投标程序，同样，摩尔多瓦企业在该国也作为外国企业，对等参与该国的招投标活动。

一些投标人在先前的投标程序中不履行义务（例如，未履行其合同义务或在投标中提交错误或不正确的信息），可能会被限制参与政府采购机构的下一步投标。政府采购机构有权限制经营者3年内不准参与政府采购程序。被限制参加公开招标的实体名单是公开的，并公布在政府采购署的官方网站上。

2. 招标和邀请招标

在政府采购中采用的招标程序取决于政府采购部门的选择。摩尔多瓦《政府采购法》规定了以下投标程序：

（1）公开招标；
（2）邀请招标；
（3）竞争性谈判；
（4）谈判程序；
（5）报价；
（6）项目方案评判（解决方案）；
（7）在补贴住房项目中的政府采购工程。

公开招标和邀请招标是主要的招投标程序。其他程序只适用于法律明文规定的情况。此外，还可以采用其他特别招投标程序，即框架协议、动态采购系统和电子拍卖。

摩尔多瓦招标程序的阶段如下：

（1）资格预审阶段：在这个阶段，由政府采购部门确定选择潜在投标人的标准。潜在投标人将提交包含详细信息的资料，允许政府采购部门根据采购要求选择最合适的投标人进入下一阶段。

（2）邀请招标：政府采购部门将向资格预审阶段的候选投标人发出邀请，或者将通过在采购公告和政府采购部门的网站上公开招标，启动招标程序。招标公告必须包含但不限于投标规则、采购部门的信息和投标的有效期等。投标人可能会对采购部门的要求提出质疑，政府采购部门应以书面形式予以回应。

（3）提交投标书：在此阶段，投标人将被要求提交完整的技术方案，其中包括但不限于报价、交付时间表、服务等级。技术方案必须完全符合政府采购部门的所有要求。投标人还必须同意拟签订的合同条款和条件，以最终确认为准。招标文件应以罗马尼亚语提交，除非招标文件明确可使用其他语言。

（4）评标：假设政府采购部门已收到必需数量的投标书，符合招标条件规定和经济利益考量的投标方案中标采购合同。中标人将被通知与有关政府采购部门签署最终合同。

（5）采购合同签订和履行：在法律规定的期限内，中标人有义务签署合同并开始履行合同。由政府部门出资的采购合同必须在摩尔多瓦财政部下属的地方财政局进行强制性登记。

Moldova

Authors: Alexander Turcan, Andrei Caciurenco
Translators: Bian Dongliang, Lily Li

I. Overview

A. General Introduction to the Political, Economic, Social and Legal Environment of the Country Receiving Investment

Moldova (officially the Republic of Moldova) is a country situated in South Eastern Europe, which borders Romania and Ukraine. Moldova declared independence and has been a sovereign state since 27 August 1991 following the dissolution of the Soviet Union.

According to the preliminary data from the 2014 national census the population of Moldova is approximately 3 million people. The official language in Moldova is Romanian. Although Russian is not an official language, it is considered as a language of inter-ethnic communication and is spoken by the vast majority of the population. The use of English is spread mainly in the business areas and in the urban regions.

Moldova is currently divided into 37 first-tier territorial units, including 32 districts, three municipalities (Chişinău, Bălţi, Bender), one autonomous territorial unit (Gagauzia) and one territorial unit (Transnistria). The capital and largest city of Moldova is Chisinau.

Moldova has 66 cities (towns) and 917 communes.

Under the current Constitution adopted in 1994, Moldova is a unitary parliamentary representative democratic republic. The Constitution divides the state powers into three separate branches – legislative, executive and judicial.

a. Political

Moldova's legislative branch is represented by a unicameral Parliament. It consists of 101 deputies (MPs), elected for a 4-year term and which are representatives of political parties. Due to the amendment to the legislation in July, 2017, a mixed electoral system was introduced and the 2018 elections to the Parliament shall be conducted according to the following terms – 51 MPs will be elected from political party lists, and 50 MPs will be elected from single mandate electoral districts. The voting age in Moldova is 18.

The executive power is represented by the Government (Cabinet of Ministers). It consists of the Prime-Minister, deputy prime ministers, ministers and other members. The Government exercises domestic and foreign agenda, as well as controls the activity of public administration. Prime Minister is designated by the majority of the Parliament, and is approved by the President after the consultation with the parliamentary fractions.

The President is elected for a 4-year term by way of direct elections.

The judicial branch encompasses the Supreme Court of Justice, four regional Courts of Appeal and a number of local district courts. The Supreme Court of Justice is the highest court and has the power to review decisions made by lower courts. The Constitutional Court of Moldova is the sole authority of constitutional jurisdiction in the Republic of Moldova.

b. Economic

Moldova is considered an emerging market. Moldova has shown moderate GDP growth almost every year.

Moldova remains highly vulnerable to fluctuations in remittances from workers abroad (24 percent of GDP), exports to the CIS and EU, and donor support (about 10 percent of government spending).

In 2014 Moldova has signed an Association Agreement and a Deep and Comprehensive Free Trade Agreement with the European Union.

The Association Agreement contains binding regulatory provisions and broader cooperation arrangements in all sectors of interest (e.g.corporate law, labour force, consumer protection, competition, tax, customs duties, public procurement etc.). Special attention is given to the effective implementation and enforcement of the Association Agreement, including by stipulating deadlines of up to 10 years.

The DCFTA agreement envisions gradual abolition of duties and quotas in mutual trade of goods and services, as well as the elimination of non-tariff barriers.

This is intended to enhance the integration of Moldova into the EU internal market.

The local currency is Moldovan leu (MDL). The US Dollar and Euro are commonly used and well-accepted in international trade.

c. Social

The foreigners and expatriates have basically the same rights as locals, except for election rights. The issue of emigration of Moldovans abroad poses a serious concern for Moldova and has a major impact on the country's demographics and economy. According to different sources, around one million of Moldovan citizens (almost 25% of the population) are working abroad.

d. Legal

Moldova's legal system comprises a Constitutional Court and three tiers of courts of general jurisdiction having general authority to hear all criminal, administrative and civil matters. The Constitutional Court interprets the Constitution and controls the constitutionality of laws and regulations.

The courts of general jurisdiction include a network of local district courts, four regional appellate courts, and one national Supreme Court of Justice. The Supreme Court of Justice acts as the court of final review for the courts of general jurisdiction.

B. The Status and Direction of the Cooperation with Chinese Enterprises Under the B&R

At present Moldova does not have official agreements under the Belt and Road Initiative. However during the different forums the governmental representatives of Moldova praised and showed their interest in the initiative.

II. Investment

A. Market Access

a. Department Supervising Investment

The Moldovan Governmental department dedicated to promotion of investments in Moldova is the Moldovan Investment and Export Promotion Organization (http://MIEPO.md/) – a public institution coordinating policy implementation for competitiveness, export promotion and investment attraction in Moldova.

b. Laws and Regulations of Investment Industry

According to Moldovan law, companies with foreign investments can be established in Moldova in the form of companies with mixed capital (joint ventures between Moldovan and foreign participants) and companies with foreign capital. Companies can be fully owned by foreign investors. The law prohibits any form of discrimination against investments based on country of origin, residence, places of activity / registration or any other grounds. The law provides almost the same conditions for the foreign investors as for the local ones. For example, the registration procedure, the procedure for carrying out activities and the procedure for dissolving an enterprise with foreign investments are identical to those for domestic enterprises. There are no discriminatory requirements regarding the management, operation, maintenance, utilization, acquisition, extension or disposal of investments.

c. Forms of Investment

In Moldova the foreign companies are allowed to:
a) participate in joint ventures (no limit on min / max share);
b) create enterprises with 100% foreign capital;
c) buy shares in existing companies;
d) establish branches and / or subsidiaries;
e) establish enterprises that become residents in Free Economic Zones;
f) establish enterprises that become residents of the IT Park Zone.

d. Standards of Market Access and Examination

Certain market access restrictions exist for residents of zones that do not implement international standards of transparency, like off-shore areas (e.g.prohibition to hold shares in banks, insurance companies, etc.)

Foreign companies and Moldovan companies with foreign capital are not allowed to own farm and forestry land.

B. Foreign Exchange Regulation

a. Department Supervising Foreign Exchange

There are several local regulators in the area of foreign exchange control, such as the National Bank of

Moldova, National Commission on Financial Markets, customs service, tax service.

b. Brief Introduction of Laws and Regulations of Foreign Exchange

The official currency of Moldova is the Moldovan Lei (MDL). It must be accepted, without any limitations, in the settlement of obligations in Moldova. The MDL is the only legal instrument for payments in the territory of Moldova, with some exceptions like payments in duty-free shops and contributions to the share capital of corporations.

Bank transfers in foreign currency between Moldovan residents are not possible. Payments by residents in favor of non-residents are possible only in specifically established cases.

Cash settlements for shares of Moldovan companies between a foreign seller and a foreign purchaser may be carried out in foreign currency.

Moldovan residents may transfer abroad monies in foreign currency from their accounts in Moldova only for certain purposes set forth in the related regulations. Such transfers may or may not require an authorization issued by the NBM.

A resident Moldovan legal entity may acquire foreign currency in Moldova only through a duly licensed Moldovan commercial bank, and only in order to make a foreign currency payment under a cross-border transaction.

For purposes of detecting money laundering, the appropriate Moldovan governmental agency monitors all transfers of funds out of Moldova and into Moldova that exceed 500,000 MDL by wire transfer (approximately USD 30,000) or 100,000 MDL in cash (approximately USD 6,000). This agency has the right to inquire about such a transaction, in the event it deems it to be suspicious.

c. Requirements of Foreign Exchange Management for Foreign Enterprises

The law does not make distinctions between local and foreign investment enterprises for the purposes of the foreign exchange operations.

Generally the law allows different types of transactions between residents and non-residents in local as well as in foreign currency, however there are certain restrictions and limitations. Most payments on the territory of Moldova must be made in Moldovan Lei, such as local purchases and local salaries.

Payments between residents and non-residents in the context of cross-border trade can be done in foreign currencies.

Moldovan banks may provide loans in foreign currency to Moldovan residents for the purpose of making payments in favor of non-residents.

External financial undertakings of Moldovan residents (i.e.external loans / credits, lease agreements, guarantees, opening accounts in the banks abroad) are subject to notification or authorization procedures with the National Bank of Moldova.

C. Financing

a. Main Financial Institutions

The National Bank of Moldova is the central bank of the Republic of Moldova and exercises its functions as a legal, public, autonomous person responsible to the Parliament. The National Bank periodically informs the public on the macroeconomic analysis results, the financial market dynamics and statistical information, including on money supply, the balance of payments and the situation within the foreign exchange market. The National bank licenses and supervises different types of activities and is entitled to set the exchange rate of Moldovan lei towards major foreign currencies.

The National Bank is independent in exercising its functions established by the Law on the National Bank of Moldova. The National Bank has the right to issue decisions, regulations, instructions and orders. The normative acts of the National Bank are compulsory for financial institutions and other legal and physical persons. The National Bank is responsible for the authorization, supervision and the regulation of financial institutions' activity. In the near future the banking system of Moldova plans to introduce Basel III standards.

Currently there are eleven commercial licensed banks in Moldova.

b. Financing Conditions for Foreign Enterprises

Bank accounts: Subject to compliance with the money laundering regulations, all Moldovan registered entities should have bank accounts with one or more banks. It is customary for companies to open bank accounts in Moldovan Lei, US Dollars and Euros. Moldova is largely a cash-based economy, the Government stimulates payments by bank transfers and discourages payments in cash in the context of commercial transactions between businesses.

Financing: Local credit is generally available from local banks on customary market-level commercial terms.

However, large infrastructure development projects are usually funded by international financial institutions such as the European Bank for Reconstruction and Development (EBRD), the European Investment Bank (EIB), the Black Sea Trade and Development Bank (BSTDB), the International Finance Corporation (IFC) and other similar organizations.

D. Land Policy

a. Brief Introduction of Land-Related Laws and Regulations

The main legal acts in the area are Land Code and several laws and regulations dealing with the purchase of land plots.

The land plots that are state owned (by central or local administration) can be sold or leased only on the basis of public auctions. Otherwise, immovable property is freely transacted on the market. The agreements on sale and purchase of immovable property must be notarized. Immovable property can be mortgaged to secure financial obligations.

The rights to immovable property are registered in a public cadastral registry that is accessible online to private parties.

b. Rules of Land Acquisition for Foreign Enterprises

Generally foreign enterprises enjoy the same rights for land acquisition as local enterprises. However it is forbidden for foreign enterprises and for enterprises with foreign capital to own the agricultural or forest lands. Such land plots can only be leased.

E. The Establishment and Dissolution of Companies

a. The Forms of Enterprises

An investor may select to incorporate a separate business entity to perform business activity in Moldova. Such business entity will be able to operate only if duly registered with Moldovan public authorities, and if created according to one of the incorporation forms regulated by Moldovan law.

Moldovan Civil Code regulates the following legal forms for incorporation of business entities:
- Limited Liability Company ("LLC");
- Joint Stock Company ("JSC");
- General Partnership ("GP");
- Limited Partnership ("LP");
- Co-operative ("Coop").

In general, the form of business organization does not influence the type of activity to be carried out by a legal entity. In some cases, the specific form of business organization is regarded as a special requirement for obtaining a license (e.g. only JSC may obtain licenses for banking, insurance activities, etc.). The most popular form used by foreign investors when opening a business in Moldova is the LLC form, due to the simple and flexible registration, management and business conduct.

Foreign legal entities and individuals may incorporate companies in Moldova (both LLC and JSC), either as sole shareholders owning 100% of the statutory capital or in partnership with a local company or individual.

GP, LLP, and Coop are rarely used even by the local enterprises.

Branch offices of the foreign companies are organized in Moldova as fully-owned subsidiaries of foreign companies.

Representative offices of the foreign companies are generally contemplated to be restricted to marketing, promoting, and assisting the foreign company's activities in Moldova.

a) Limited Liability Company

LLC Creation: LLCs are generally incorporated by a small number of shareholders and are also the most common legal form of incorporation in Moldova due to simplicity of their registration and management. An LLC can be incorporated by one or more founder(s), including foreign (non-Moldovan) entities or individuals. The number of shareholders of an LLC is restricted to fifty (50). An LLC may start its operation only after is duly registered with the Moldovan State Registry of Companies.

Business objects of LLC: According to the provisions of the Civil Code and the Law on Limited Liability Companies, an LLC is entitled to carry out any activity that is not legally prohibited.

In order to lawfully conduct certain business objects an LLC shall need to hold a license issued by a public authority. Most relevant business objects subject to state licensing include: electricity market activity, construction, pharmaceuticals, TV and Radio, telecommunications, and other businesses. Some activities are prohibited to be performed by an LLC, namely banking and insurance activities. Only companies incorporated as joint stock companies may hold banking or insurance activity licenses.

Share Capital: The share capital of an LLC is divided into participation stake(s) held by the shareholder(s). As a rule, the share capital should be provided in the Charter of the company. There is no statutory minimum for the share capital of LLC.

Reserve Capital: A LLC is under obligation to maintain a statutory reserve equal to 10% of its share capital. The reserve capital may be used to cover for losses or to increase the LLC's share capital.

Rights and obligations of LLC shareholders: The participation stakes in the capital of an LLC grant to their holders statutory minimum of rights established by the Moldovan laws. Such rights are established also by the Charter of the LLC. The shareholders' rights listed into the LLC's Charter cannot diminish the scope of shareholders' rights established by law or provide for rights which are inconsistent with the legal requirements.

Pre-emption Rights: Any shareholder is free to sell its stake held in an LLC. However, a third party may purchase interest in a LLC only after the refusal of the other stakeholders to purchase such interest, since under Moldovan company laws the stakeholders enjoy pre-empting rights over third parties in respect to purchase of stakes.

Liability of shareholders: As a general rule, the shareholders' liability for the activity of the LLC shall be limited to the value of their shares in the LLC's capital. Additional liability may arise in cases such as insolvency, in particular situations.

Profit and Losses: LLC annually distributes net profit registered after payment of taxes and other mandatory payments, unless otherwise provided by the constituent document.

The decision to determine the portion of the net profit that will be distributed among the shareholders is taken by the general meeting. Net profit is distributed in proportion to the share in the authorized capital of the company. The order of distribution of net profit can be changed by decision of the general meeting unanimously accepted by all shareholders of the company.

Governing Bodies of an LLC: In accordance with the provisions of the law, the corporate bodies of an LLC are:
• General Meeting of Shareholders (Sole Shareholder, if the LLC has only one shareholder);
• Board of Directors;
• Manager (Executive Body);
• Auditor.

Exclusive powers of LLC General Meeting of Shareholders: Pursuant to the Law on Limited Liability Companies, the following matters shall be within the exclusive competence of the General Meeting of Shareholders:
• approval of amendments to the Constituting Act of LLC;
• approval of change of the share capital of LLC;
• election of members of LLC Board of Directors and of the Auditor, the ending of its office before its term expires;
• claiming against the members of the LLC Board of Directors and the Auditor for damage caused to the LLC;
• approval of the regulation of the LLC Board of Directors;
• approval of the LLC Board of Directors and Auditors reports;
• approval of the LLC Annual Balance Sheet;
• adoption of the decision on LLC profit distribution;
• approval of the decision on LLC's reorganization and approval of the reorganization plan;
• approval of the decision on LLC's liquidation, appointing of the liquidator and approval of liquidation balance sheet;
• approval of the LLC funds formation;
• approval of the remunerations for the members of the LLC's Board of Directors, and for the Auditor;
• prior approval of the contracts by which the LLC convey into ownership or assigns gratuitously the rights to some third parties, including to the shareholders;
• formation of LLC's branches and representative offices;
• approval of foundation by LLC of other legal entities;
• decision over LLC participation as co-founder to other legal entities.

Board of Directors: The existence of the Board of Directors is not mandatory. As a rule, the Board of Directors is created when the LLC has a larger number of shareholders. When no Board of Directors is created, some of its powers are vested in the General Meeting of Shareholders (Sole Shareholder) of LLC and in the Manager of the LLC.

Manager of LLC: The Manager or the Executive Body of the LLC must deal with all issues of LLC, except for those that are within the exclusive competence of the General Meeting of Shareholders and / or the Board of Directors. The manager may act in the name of the LLC without any proxy and represent the LLC's interests in relations with third parties. Transactions entered into by the Manager in breach of limitations of its powers, as stipulated by the LLC's Charter shall remain to be valid and may not be cancelled, while the Manager may be personally held liable for such a breach of limitation.

Auditor of LLC: The Auditor is appointed for monitoring the business and financial activity of the LLC. It verifies the annual balance sheet and financial report of LLC and prepares an audit report on these issues.

b) Joint Stock Company

JSC Creation: A JSC may be created by natural persons or legal entities, both nationals of Moldova or foreigners. The number of founders of a JSC is not limited. A joint stock company can have a single founder, if that founder is not in its turn a company founded by one person. The founding agreement will provide: information on the founders, company name, envisaged share capital, number and class of shares for the initial subscription, date of the founders' meeting.

Business objects of JSC: According to the provisions of the Civil Code and the Law on Joint Stock Companies, a JSC is entitled to carry out any activity that is not legally prohibited. In order to lawfully conduct certain business objects a JSC shall need to hold a license issued by a public authority.

Share Capital: The share capital of a JSC is divided into shares held by the shareholder(s). The minimum required share capital for a joint stock company is 20,000 MDL (about $1,200). Shares will be placed only with the founders at a price that shall be not lower than the nominal value. The founders can pay the subscription price in cash or in kind. For certain categories of JSC the law may require higher minimum capital (banks, insurance companies, etc.).

Reserve capital: A JSC is under obligation to maintain a statutory reserve equal to 10% of its share capital. The reserve capital may be used to cover for losses or to increase the JSC's share capital.

Rights and obligations of JSC shareholders: The shares held in the capital of a JSC grant to their holders statutory minimum of rights established by the Moldovan laws. Such rights are established also by the Charter of the JSC. The shareholders' rights listed into the JSC's Charter cannot diminish the scope of shareholders' rights established by law or provide for rights which are inconsistent with the legal requirements.

Liability of shareholders: As a general rule, the shareholders' liability for the activity of JSC shall be limited to the value of their shares in the JSC's capital. Additional liability may arise in cases such as insolvency, in particular situations.

Profit and losses: Profit (loss) of the company is determined in accordance with the procedure provided for by law. Net profit is formed after the payment of taxes and other mandatory payments and remains at the disposal of the company.

The decision on the distribution of net profit during the fiscal year is made by the company's board on the basis of the distribution ratios approved by the general meeting of shareholders, and the decision on the distribution of net profit for the year by the annual general meeting of shareholders upon the proposal of the company's board.

Governing Bodies of a JSC:
• General Meeting of Shareholders;
• Board of Directors;
• General Director (Administrative Board);
• Audit Committee.

Exclusive powers of the General Meeting of Shareholders: Pursuant to the Law on Joint Stock Companies, the General Meeting of Shareholders enjoys exclusive authority to:

• amend the company's charter (approve a new version of it), including as regards changes of classes and number of shares authorized for placement, shares conversion, consolidation or splitting;

• approve and amend the corporate governance code;

• approve the manner of provision of shareholders' access to company documents;

• change the share capital;

• approve the regulations of the board of directors, elect directors to the board and terminate their office, establish the size of their salary, annual compensations and indemnifications, as well as decide on liability or exemption from liability of the members of the board of directors;

• approve the regulations of the audit committee, elect auditors and terminate their office, establish the size of their salary, annual compensations and indemnifications, as well as decide on liability or exemption from liability of the members of the audit committee;

• select an auditing organization and decide on the amount of payment for its services;

• adopt the decisions on entering into the large transactions, which involve sale or purchase, granting of

collateral or accepting of collateral, lease or rent of goods with a value exceeding 50 per cent of the company's assets according to the last balance sheet;
  • approve the classes and number of the bonds authorized for placement;
  • review the annual financial report of the company; approve the annual report of the board of directors and the annual report of the audit committee;
  • approve the norms of distribution of the company's profit;
  • decide on the distribution of annual profit, including payment of annual dividends, or on compensation of the company losses;
  • decide on conversion to another type of company, on company's reorganization or liquidation;
  • approve the spin off, consolidation or liquidation balance of the company;
  m) decide on alienation or transfer of treasury shares to shareholders and / or employees of the company.

The shareholders' meeting may delegate, in whole or in part, to the Board of Directors the powers to:
  • approve the priority directions for the company's activity;
  • approve the regulations of the management board, appoint the company's director(s) and terminate his / her office, establish the size of his / her salary, annual compensations and indemnifications, as well as decide on liability or exemption from liability of the company's director (s);
  • approve the quarterly reports;
  • approve the creation, conversion and liquidation of the company's branches and representations, appoint and dismiss their directors.

Board of Directors: The members of the Board of Directors are elected for a term of 4 years. The Board of Directors must consist of at least 3 members. If the number of shareholders of the company exceeds 100 members, the Board of Directors must consist of at least 5 members.

General Director of JSC: The General Director or the Executive Body of the JSC must deal with all current issues of JSC, except for those that are within the exclusive competence of the General Meeting of Shareholders and of the Board of Directors. It may act in the name of the JSC without any proxy and represent the JSC's interests in relations with third parties. The General Director must submit quarterly reports to the Board of Directors on the results of company's activity.

Audit Committee of JSC: The Audit Committee is appointed for monitoring the business and financial activity of the JSC and is subordinated to the general meeting of shareholders. The members of the Audit Committee may be appointed for the term of 2 to 5 years. The number of members in the Audit Committee must be odd.

b. The Procedure of Establishment

In Moldova companies are registered by the Public Services Agency.

Each company must have at least one registered manager (administrator) and a registered address. The registered address will determine the fiscal jurisdiction of the new company.

If a company is established by one or more foreign companies (founders), then the company information about each founder needs to be provided in a translated form.

Once all filings are prepared and submitted, the Public Services Agency registers a new company within 24 hours. Expedited registration in 4 hours is also available.

New Moldovan companies do not have to have a company seal, but may choose to have one.

The stamp duties for registering a Moldovan company do not exceed $100.

Use of the country name 'Moldova' in the naming of Moldovan registered companies is subject to approval by a special Governmental commission and will require payment of a one-time stamp duty of about $6,000. Such naming also significantly slows down the total registration process.

c. Routes and Requirements of Dissolution

Dissolution of a legal entity entails the opening of a liquidation procedure. The legal entity continues to exist even after the dissolution to the extent that it is necessary to liquidate the property. From the moment of dissolution, the manager is not allowed to continue operations.

Resolution on dissolution should be adopted by at least 2/3 of the votes in case of JSC and ¾ of votes in case of LLC.

The information on dissolution of the entity should be made public through the publication in the Official Monitor of the Republic of Moldova. Creditors must be notified of dissolution and are allowed up to two months to files their claims against the company subject to dissolution.

The procedure of dissolution may last for up to 12 months.

F. Mergers and Acquisitions

After a relative slowdown in M&A activity in Moldova during 2009-2016, the year 2017 showed that the future period may be marked by a more active movement in the area of corporate consolidations and divestitures.

a. Investing in Moldovan Private Companies

As most Moldovan companies are organized as LLCs (a total number of 100,000 LLCs vs 4,500 JSCs), buying and selling shares in a Moldovan LLC is very similar to doing the same in most jurisdictions. For as long was preemptive rights of existing shareholders are waived or not exercised, the parties enjoy plenty of freedom in how to structure a sale and purchase transaction. Buying shares subject to fulfillment of certain conditions precedent is very common. Sale and purchase transactions need to be notarized and transfer of title registered in the public registry held by the Public Services Agency. Foreign companies can acquire up to 100% in the capital of a Moldovan company. Moldova does not have minimum national shareholder requirements.

b. Buying Companies on the Moldovan Stock Exchange

Larger and regulated Moldovan businesses are organized as JSCs, and, in most cases, shares of JSCs are transacted via the Moldovan Stock Exchange (MSE). Because an MSE transaction is a matching of orders to buy and sell shares at a particular price, negotiating conditions precedent in such situations is not possible. Therefore, it is customary to require that most of conditions precedent to a purchase be fulfilled before the parties decide to transact on the stock exchange.

Investors who acquire 50%+1 share in a Moldovan JSC must make a mandatory takeover bid to the remaining shareholders.

Investors who acquire 90% in a Moldovan JSC are allowed to make a further squeeze out offer to the remaining shareholders, even though the Moldovan law allows the minority shareholders to expressly refuse a squeeze out sale.

c. Privatization: Buying Companies from the State

In the past years the state has disposed of all of its shares in the banking sector, has sold electricity distribution companies, a gas transport company, a major cement plant, a number of hotel properties and the largest department store in the country.

The state has a number of assets that it still wishes to sell, including strategic assets such as the national telephony operator and some energy companies.

The state employs different methods to sell its property. Sometimes is announces international tenders and negotiates sale and purchase agreements with the winning bidder, who not only offers a competitive price, but also the most attractive investment program for the target company. On many occasions, the state puts the shares in the companies it owns on sale via the MSE, and the highest bidder wins.

d. Investing in Regulated Businesses

Investing in companies from the banking, insurance and energy sector requires prior regulatory consent. Only businesses with good long-standing reputation may expect to obtain regulatory consent for investing in these sectors. Because regulatory consent may take months, working out the right timing for obtaining the consent prior to the purchase is always important.

G. Competition Regulation

a. Moldovan Competition Council

The Moldovan Competition Council was established by the Competition Law, as an autonomous public authority that ensures compliance with Competition Law. Decisions of the Competition Council are adopted by the Plenum, a collegial body comprised of 5 members.

b. Brief Introduction to Competition Law

Competition Law provides the general framework of competition regulation in Moldova. The law was further supplemented by various subordinated regulations. These legal acts transpose most EU competition provisions, and prohibit anticompetitive and unfair competition, as well as institute a control regime for economic concentrations.

As such, Competition Law prohibits the conclusion of anticompetitive agreements and concerted practices. Agreements aiming at (i) direct / indirect fixing of prices, (ii) limiting of production or sale, (iii) sharing the market, the sources of supply, (iv) bids rigging, as well as

Further, dominant undertaking(s) on the relevant markets are prohibited to abuse their dominant position by way of (i) directly / indirectly imposing unfair purchase or selling prices, (ii) limiting production, distribution, or technical development, (iii) applying of dissimilar conditions to equivalent transactions, thereby placing trading partners at a competitive disadvantage, (iv) charging excessive or predatory prices, (v) unjustified refusal to contract or supply, etc.. If the market share of the dominant undertaking(s) exceeds 50%, such undertaking(s) is/are presumed dominant.

Unfair competition towards other competitors is also prohibited. Such actions include (i) discrediting of competitors, (ii) incitement to termination of contract with competitor, (iii) acquiring and / or illegal use of competitor's commercial secret, (iv) stealing competitor's clients, and (v) creating confusion with a competitor, its products or economic activities. The types of unfair competition behaviors are limited to the above.

In relation to economic concentrations, Competition Law provides that an acquisition of shares / assets in other company(ies) that grants control to the acquirer(s) over the respective company(ies), as well as mergers of previously independent companies or parts of companies, and creation of fully-functional joint ventures are subject to prior notification and clearance of such transactions by the Competition Council, in case the applicable legal thresholds are met. The relevant legal thresholds require that economic concentrations shall be notified and authorized by the Competition Council in case the overall turnover of the companies concerned in the year prior to the transaction exceeds about EUR 1.2 million, and each of at least two companies concerned have an aggregate turnover obtained in Moldova in the year prior to the transaction exceeding about EUR 480,000.

c. Sanctions for Breaches of Competition Law

Competition Council may impose fines of up to 5% from the turnover of the company for conclusion of anticompetitive agreements (that shall also be deemed void), abuse of dominant position, non-notification of economic concentrations, or implementation of an economic concentration that was deemed incompatible with the competition environment. The authority may also impose that a concentration that was deemed incompatible with the competition environment is dissolved by the parties, or request such dissolution in court.

Unfair competition actions may be sanctioned with a fine of up to 0.5% from the turnover of the company.

Sanctions of up to 0.5% from the turnover of the company may also be imposed for procedural breaches, such as not providing the information requested by the authority, opposing dawn raids, etc.

H. Tax

In the 90s' Moldova's tax laws were spread throughout a large variety of laws and regulations. For two decades now most of the tax laws have been codified into a Tax Code, which deals with issues of personal and corporate income tax, VAT, excises, real estate taxes, local taxes, road taxes, natural resources taxes and fiscal administration.

Moldova has a growing network of about 50 double taxation avoidance treaties with the following countries: Albania, Armenia, Austria, Azerbaijan, Belarus, Belgium, Bosnia and Herzegovina, Bulgaria, Canada, China, Czech Republic, Cyprus, Croatia, Finland, Germany, Greece, Estonia, Switzerland, Ireland, Israel, Japan, Kazakhstan, Kuwait, Kyrgyzstan, Lithuania, Latvia, Luxemburg, Macedonia, UK, Malta, Montenegro, Oman, Poland, Portugal, Romania, Russia, Serbia, Slovakia, Slovenia, Spain, Tajikistan, Turkey, Turkmenistan, Netherlands, Ukraine, Hungary, Uzbekistan, Italy.

a. Taxation of Corporate Profits in Moldova

Historically, in 1992, Moldova started with a tax on corporate profits of 32%. For many years the authorities were reducing this rate down to 28%, 25% and so on, until in 2007 it was established at zero percent on reinvested profits. In 2012 the tax on corporate profits was reinstated at a new rate of 12%, which continues to apply.

Deduction of business expenses is generally allowed, but companies need to be prepared to justify their ordinary and necessary character for the particular business.

b. Taxation of Dividends

For about 20 years dividends were not deemed taxable income in Moldova, but not any longer. After paying 12% tax on profits, according to the Moldovan Tax Code, the dividend-paying company will withhold an additional 6% tax on dividends paid out to both the fiscal residents of Moldova as well as non-residents.

The 2000 China-Moldova tax treaty reduces the withholding tax on dividends distributed by Moldovan companies to Chinese shareholders from 6% to 5%, provided the Chinese shareholder is the beneficial owner of the dividends and holds directly at least 25% of the capital of the Moldovan company.

c. Taxation of Interest Payments

As to interest payments, pursuant to the Moldovan tax legislation, payments made to non-resident creditors will be subject to a final interest withholding tax at the rate of 12%. Under the China-Moldova tax treaty, withholding tax on interest paid by the Moldovan borrower to a commercial Chinese lender can be reduced from 12% to 10%.

Further, under the China-Moldova tax treaty, interest arising in Moldova and derived by the Government of China or any financial institution wholly owned by the Government of China or by any other resident of China with respect to debt financed by the Government of China shall be exempt from withholding tax in Moldova.

d. Preferred Tax Jurisdictions to Invest in Moldova

Experienced investors choose Dutch B.V.s and N.V.s in order to invest in Moldova. Moldova's tax treaty with the Netherlands is probably the best one. Investors seem to be attracted by the 5% withholding tax on interest, 2% withholding on royalties and zero percent on dividends derived from larger investments. The Cypriot treaty offering 5% on dividends, interest, and royalties is also quite popular among investors.

e. Taxation on Added Value (VAT)

The standard rate of VAT in Moldova is 20%. The reduced VAT rate for socially-sensitive supplies (e.g.bread, dairy, sugar, certain pharmaceutical products, natural gas and other) is 8%. Businesses should register as VAT-payers before their annual sales reach the level of 1.2 million MDL (circa USD 70,000). Also, voluntary registration as a VAT payer is possible, subject to conditions stipulated by law. Certain supplies are subject to VAT exemptions. The system of Moldovan VAT, in broad terms, operates in the same manner as in most European countries. The most challenging issue in the area of VAT continues to be recovery from the state of VAT paid in excess.

f. Payroll Taxation in Moldova

Annual salaries below MDL 33,000 (USD 2,000) are subject to a reduced rate of income tax of 7%. Income above the named threshold is taxed at 18%. Employees also enjoy a number of personal, family and social status-related income tax deductions.

In addition to income tax, salaries are also subject to social and medical contributions as follows:
- social security contributions:

Employer pays on top of salary:	23%
Employee pays from salary:	6%

- mandatory medical insurance contributions:

Employer pays on top of salary:	4.5%
Employee pays from salary:	4.5%

Employees may also enjoy tax-free meal vouchers payable by employers.
A number of particular tax incentives exists for companies operating in the IT sector.

I. Securities

a. Brief Introduction of Securities-Related Laws and Regulations

The capital market legislative framework of Moldova is in a constant process of reform. The current Law on Capital Market is in force from 2013. The Law seeks to follow the acquis communautaire and thereby transposes 11 EU Directives related to capital markets, including MiFID, the Directive on Takeover Bids, the Investor Compensation Scheme Directive, the Market Abuse Directive, the Capital Adequacy Directive and the UCITS Directive.

The Moldova Stock Exchange (MSE) is the only operating stock exchange in Moldova

b. Supervision and Regulation of Securities Market

The trading in securities is governed by the Law on Capital Market and relevant regulations. The primary regulatory institutions are: the Ministry of Finance, the National Commission of Financial Market (NCFM) and the National Bank of Moldova.

The NCFM supervises the market and carries out investigations related to market abuses. Depending of the results of an investigation, the NCFM may prohibit market participants to trade financial instruments or provide investment services and activities, suspend or withdraw the authorisation, seize related assets or impose a fine. The law enforcement bodies investigate criminal cases on manipulation and insider trading.

c. Requirements for Engagement in Securities Trading for Foreign Enterprises

The official website of the MSE is http://www.moldse.md/.

The MSE was established in 1994, but to date only Moldovan registered companies have traded shares on it. Although it is not prohibited, foreign companies have never made securities offerings on the MSE.

Public offerings of shares by Moldovan private companies are infrequent.

Public offerings of bonds by Moldovan companies are very rare.

The Government often sells on the MSE shares of companies that are undergoing privatization.

As a rule, foreign investors are allowed to engage Moldovan brokers and to buy shares of Moldovan companies on the MSE.

When shares in banks are transacted, then the purchaser needs to hold a prior authorization of the National

Bank of Moldova in order to buy the respective shares.

J. Preference and Protection of Investment

a. The Structure of Preference Policies

There are no official preference policies for local companies, which benefit from the same rights as foreign-owned companies. However Moldova remains committed to supporting the investment by entering in the bilateral treaties with different countries and constantly adapting the legislation for conducting the business activity. According to the Moldovan Constitution, the state must ensure the inviolability of foreign investments. The Government is keen to establish coordinated policies and well-balanced legislation in order to stimulate both domestic and foreign investments.

b. Support for Specific Industries and Regions

Government tends to support specific industries with state aid and namely agricultural and wine sectors. European Union provides an amount of grants for Moldovan based companies related to energy efficiency, restructuring the wine sector, attracting the youth and women (especially from rural areas) for the implication in the business activity.

There is a number of tax incentives for some areas, like: tax incentives (e.g.diminished social security contributions, reduced VAT rate) for agricultural industry; personal income tax and social security insurance incentives for the IT industry; zero rate VAT for light industry companies providing services based on agreements on inward customs processing; reduced income tax rate and VAT incentives for the residents of Free Economic Zones; income tax exemption and zero rate VAT for some supplies in the Giurgiulesti International Free Port; zero rate VAT for some supplies in the Marculesti International Free Airport.

A preferential tariff treatment is granted for specific categories of goods depending on their origin and in accordance with the free trade arrangements (FTAs) to which Moldova is a party. Moldova has concluded FTAs to date with most of the Commonwealth of Independent States (CIS) countries and is also a Central European Free Trade Agreement (CEFTA) contracting state. The Association Agreement with the European Union, which includes a Deep and Comprehensive Free Trade Agreement (DCFTA), provides for preferential tariff rate quotas on certain goods.

c. Special Economic Areas

Moldova has designated areas where domestic and foreign investors can carry out entrepreneurial activities under preferential terms and conditions (i.e.favorable tax, customs and other regimes).

Free Economic Zones (FEZ) are parts of the Moldovan customs territory, separate from the economic perspective, in which local and foreign investors may carry out entrepreneurial activities under a preferential regime. Entities established in the FEZ and which export goods and services from FEZ to outside the customs territory of the Republic of Moldova or deliver the produced goods to other FEZ residents for goods to be exported are entitled to apply 50% of the applicable income tax rate on such income. For other cases, the income tax is 75% of the standard rate. The income obtained from exports of goods (services) originating from the FEZ to outside the customs territory of the Republic of Moldova or from supply of the produced goods to other FEZ residents for goods to be exported is exempted from tax for a period of three years, provided the FEZ residents invested a capital equivalent of at least USD 1 million in the fixed assets of their enterprises and / or in the development of the infrastructure of the FEZ, and is exempted from income tax for a period of five years, where the invested capital is of at least USD 5 million.

From a VAT perspective, goods and services supplied in the FEZ from abroad, from FEZ outside the customs territory of the Republic of Moldova, in the FEZ from other areas of Moldova and those supplied to residents of other FEZ are subject to 0% VAT.

Industrial parks (IP) may be created for 30 years either on the territory of state or private enterprises, through green field investments or by means of public private partnerships. In practice, an industrial park is created by means of obtaining the title of industrial park by an enterprise on the basis of Government decision. IP Residents and IP Administration may benefit from the following real estate facilities and Government support:

• free of charge change of the category of land with agricultural destination;

• entitlement to privatize public property land associated with constructions, at the price land established by law;

• free of charge transfer of public property assets with the purpose of industrial parks establishment upon owner's decision;

• application, by the administrating enterprise, of the reduction coefficient down to 0.3% of the tariff set for the annual lease payment for the public property land;

• optimization of state inspections.

IT Park: The IT sector is continuously growing in the Republic of Moldova. Recently, the Moldovan Parliament approved a law on IT industry parks, which aims at creating the necessary conditions for stimulating the development of IT industry, including import / export transactions. There are specific conditions regulating the process of IT industry parks creation and their operation established by the legislation. Incentives for IT park include single reduced tax that combine other taxes (such as corporate income tax, local taxes, etc.)

d. Bilateral Investment Protection

Additional guarantees and support to investors are offered by 39 bilateral treaties signed between Moldova and various countries for the mutual protection of investments.

By ratifying the Convention on the Settlement of Investment Disputes between States and Nationals of Other States (ICSID Convention) in 2011, Moldova undertook to recognize any decision (award) issued by the International Center for Settlement of Investment Disputes (ICSID) as being mandatory and committed to ensuring the enforcement of the pecuniary sanctions imposed by the award on its territory.

Moldova is also a signatory to the convention on the Recognition and Enforcement of Foreign Arbitral Awards (1958 New York Convention), meaning local courts must enforce international arbitration awards that meet certain conditions.

The bilateral treaty on mutual investment protection between Moldova and China was ratified in 1994. The treaty allows Chinese investors in Moldova to bring claims before an international tribunal in case of an alleged infringement of protected investor rights.

III. Trade

A. Department Supervising Trade

The Government of the Republic of Moldova is the authority that approves trade regulations. However, the central specialized body of the public administration responsible for the elaboration of the state policy on trade and the regulation of this field is the Ministry of Economy.

The main tasks of the Ministry of Economy in the trade field are as follows: elaboration of state programs and strategies for the trade development; elaboration of the normative acts in the respective field; creation of the favorable conditions for the production and marketing of goods and services; elaboration and promotion of the measures aimed to protect the internal market; submission of proposals on the competence optimization of the state bodies empowered with control functions in the field of commerce, etc.

The policy promoted by the Ministry of Economy in the field of foreign trade is linked mainly to the general objective of European integration. The core efforts are focused on the fulfilment of the Agreement on establishment of the Deep and Comprehensive Free Trade Area between the Republic of Moldova and the European Union (DCFTA), initiated on November 28, 2013 in Vilnius.

The commercial policies fostered by the Ministry of Economy aim at consolidating the commercial relations with the countries that are the key commercial partners of the Republic of Moldova, as well as promoting foreign commercial exchanges with potential partners.

B. Brief Introduction of Trade Laws and Regulations

Since July 26, 2001 the Republic of Moldova is a full member of the World Trade Organization (WTO) that fosters the liberalization of trade with goods and services by removing the obstacles and developing new rules in trade-related areas.

The Republic of Moldova is party to the Central European Free Trade Agreement (CEFTA) since 2007. The main objective of it is to increase the trade with goods and services and impel the investments between the CEFTA member states, as well as eliminate obstacles and distortions from the way of trade and facilitate the circulation of goods in transit and the trans-border circulation of goods and services between the Parties' territories.

The Agreement on the Trade Area in the CIS is signed on October 18, 2011. It stipulates the facilitation of regional trade by improving commercial relations between signatory states.

Part of the Association Agreement between the Republic of Moldova, on the one side, and the European Union and the European Atomic Energy Community and its Member States, on the other side (signed on June 27, 2014) is the free trade agreement. Its requires creation of the Deep and Comprehensive Free Trade Area between the Republic of Moldova and the European Union (DCFTA). The Free Trade Agreement goes for the opening of markets for goods and services trade, gradually taking over European standards and norms governing the quality of products and services.

Moldova has signed bilateral Free Trade Agreements with a number of countries, among which are Croatia, Serbia, Macedonia, Bosnia-Herzegovina, Albania, Bulgaria, Montenegro, Ukraine, Russian Federation, Turkey.

Currently the drafts of the Free Trade Agreement between the Republic of Moldova and the People's Republic of China as well with the Arab Republic of Egypt are being negotiated.

The main Economic Agreements between the Republic of Moldova and People's Republic of China include: Commercial and Economic Agreement (signed in Chisinau, January 18, 1992); Agreement on the stimulation and reciprocal protection of investments (signed in Beijing, November 6, 1992); and Agreement for the avoidance of double taxation and the prevention of tax evasion with respect to taxes on income (signed in Beijing, June 7, 2000).

Any products, as well as means of transportation crossing the customs line, whether at import or export, are subject to the Customs code of the Republic of Moldova dated July 20, 2000. It also provides for the customs regimes applicable to each crossing.

Crossing of the customs border with the strategic goods is regulated by a special regulation, which is Law on the control of the export, re-export, import and transit of strategic goods dated July 26, 2000. The list of the strategic goods includes: (i) products, technologies and services that have dual (civil and military) use; (ii) armaments, ammunition, military equipment, related technologies and services; (iii) products, technologies and services which may be used in the manufacture and use of nuclear, chemical, biological and missile weapons which may be carriers of such weapons; (iv) other products, technologies and services requiring special control in the interest of national security or foreign policy in accordance with the international agreements and arrangements to which the Republic of Moldova is a party.

Internal trade is regulated by the Law on internal trade dated September 23, 2010.

C. Trade Management

Along with the above-mentioned agreements the Republic of Moldova has an active participation in the regional organizations. Moldova is a fully-fledged member of the Organization of the Economic Cooperation of the Black Sea region (BSEC); all the structures of the Danubian Cooperation Process and the Organization for Democracy and Economic Development, commonly referred to as GUAM (Georgia, Ukraine, Azerbaijan and the Republic of Moldova); and, the Council of Europe and the Organization for Security and Co-operation in Europe (OSCE). Moldova is also a member of the Central European Initiative (CEI), the Regional Cooperation Council (RCC), South-East European Cooperation Process (SEECP), South-East European Cooperative Initiative (SECI) and South-East European Energy Treaty[1].

Moldova has also ratified 20 of UNECE's transport conventions and agreements, and the period since signing the Associated Agreement with the EU has made the country to harmonize national legislation with the EU directives in the field of customs administration, transit trade, food safety, plant protection and quarantine, veterinary measures, technical standards, accreditation, and conformity assessment.

Regulatory harmonization has been paralleled by targeted efforts to improving management practices and migrating to paperless systems. Thus, ISO 9001:2008 quality management system standard was introduced. Also, an electronic submission system for permits and licenses was launched. It allows enterprises to submit applications on-line, upload the support documents, and receive the permits and licenses via e-mail. A simplified procedure of notification on the trade activity replaced the procedure of obtaining the authorization for the respective activity.

In 1995 Moldova introduced free economic zone legislation. Since then, seven zones have been established. Companies operating in the zones enjoy special tax and customs regimes, which are specifically aimed at supporting export promotion and investment attraction.

D. The Inspection and Quarantine of Import and Export Commodities

The law on general product safety prohibits dangerous products from being placed on the market.

The sanitary-veterinary supervision of goods subject to state veterinary control under import, transit or export regime shall be carried out at the veterinary control posts organized within the customs posts.

The customs authorities shall not allow transporting live animals, germinating material, products subject to veterinary supervision and control on the territory of the Republic of Moldova if these have not received the free passage from the veterinary control post in the customs post.

The export of live animals, germinal material of animal origin, products subject to veterinary supervision and

---

[1] Regulatory and Procedural Barriers to trade in the Republic of Moldova.Need Assessment.United nations, New York and Geneva, 2017 // http://mei.gov.md/sites/default/files/all_study_for_publication.with_comments_integrated.final.pdf.

veterinary control shall be carried out under conditions similar to importation, plus compliance with the animal health conditions, the veterinary certification required by the importing country and the existence of the acceptance of import by the importing country and by the competent veterinary authorities of the transit countries.

The import, export and transit operations of live animals, germ-line of animal origin, products subject to veterinary supervision and control may only be carried out if prior notice has been given through the TRACES information system at least 24 hours prior to the operation import, export or transit.

Animals from import shall be subject to prophylactic quarantine for a maximum period of 30 days.

The import or transit on the territory of the Republic of Moldova of plants, plant products and associated products subject to the phytosanitary quarantine regime shall be admitted upon presentation of the phytosanitary certificate issued by the competent authorities of the exporting state. The period of validity of the phytosanitary certificate shall be 14 days from the date of its issuance.

E. Customs Management

As of 2017, Moldovan Customs Service has been operating under a new organizational structure, with optimized customs houses. Customs has also introduced an Authorized Economic Operator (AEO) scheme, which, drawing on the EU model, certifies AEOs (subject to certain criteria) for: (i) customs simplification (Incomplete Declaration Procedure, Simplified Declaration Procedure, Local Clearance Procedure); (ii) security and safety; or, (iii) for simplification, security and safety.[1]

The Moldovan Customs has also integrated the United Nations Conference on Trade and Development (UNCTAD) web-based Automated System for Customs Data (ASYCUDA) World to serve as the backbone for the Customs Integrated Information System (CIIS).

As the result of establishing a Single Window (SW) facility for exports, imports and transit trade, traders can submit customs declarations for exports and imports online (via ASYCUDA World) and upload all the support documents.

Moldova agreed to eliminate all its customs duties. However, a number of transition periods and protectionist measures apply in its case. Elimination of some duties will take place gradually, while others are subject to duty-free quotas. As of the AA's entry into force, many of the EU products imported by Moldova were already duty-free. Almost 46 percent of the goods imported from the EU were already covered by zero percent MFN import duty. For another 47 percent of the traded goods, there was an immediate reduction of tariffs as of the date of entry into force of the AA. Aside from the goods covered by tariff–free quotas, January 1, 2024, is the latest date when full liberalization of EU products imported by Moldova needs to be achieved[2].

IV. Labour

A. Brief Introduction of Labour Laws and Regulations

The main legal act regulating the employment relations in the Republic of Moldova is the Labour Code No 154 of 28 March 2003. The Labour Code regulates all employment aspects such as basic rules on employment agreements, working hours, grounds for dismissal, days-off, salaries and compensations, guarantees and responsibilities, special protection measures for certain categories of employees and employment disputes resolution. The Labour Code is applicable to all employees performing work in Moldova, notwithstanding whether the employees are Moldovan or foreign nationals. The Labour Code is applicable to all area of economic activity, as well as to the public service.

Besides the Labour Code, the employment legislation is also represented by normative acts approved by:

- the Parliament of the Republic of Moldova, governing specific employment issues (such as, for instance, Law on Salary No 847 of February 14, 2002; Law on Public Servants Salary No 48 of March 22, 2012, etc.);

- Moldovan Government (such as, for instance Government Resolution No 48 of March 22, 2012 on Guaranteed Minimum Salary in the Real Sector);

- the Ministry of Health, Labour and Social Protection (such as, for instance, amendments to the Nomenclature of Job Positions in the Republic of Moldova).

---

[1] Regulatory and Procedural Barriers to trade in the Republic of Moldova.Need Assessment.United nations, New York and Geneva, 2017 // http://mei.gov.md/sites/default/files/all_study_for_publication.with_comments_integrated.final.pdf.

[2] Moldova trade Study Overview elaborated by the World Bank // http://documents.worldbank.org/curated/en/566151468196761047/pdf/ACS17523-WP-P148369-Overview-MDA-TradeStudy-PUBLIC.pdf .

Moldovan employers are also required to comply with the collective bargaining agreements to which they are party. In addition, Moldovan employers are required to elaborate and put in place internal employment policies and regulations, governing the employment issues specific to their activity.

The Ministry of Health, Labour and Social Protection is the main governmental authority and policy maker in employment. The control over the correspondence of Moldovan employers to Moldovan law requirements is performed by the Labour State Inspectorate, representing a structural subdivision of the Ministry of Health, Labour and Social Protection. The Labour State Inspectorate is authorized to perform inspections at Moldovan employers and initiate administrative proceedings in Moldovan courts in case of discovered infringements.

B. Requirements of Employing Foreign Employees

a. Work Permit

Moldovan employers are allowed to employ foreign citizens only when local human resources cannot fill the vacancies. Therefore, prior to employ foreigners, Moldovan employers will be requested to prove that they announced locally about the existent vacancies, and that no correspondent Moldovan candidate applied for the job.

In order to be employed in Moldova, foreign citizens will have to obtain, together with the Moldovan employer, the work permit from Moldovan authorities.

Employment without such authorization is subject to administrative liability for both the Moldovan employer and foreign employee.

Foreign citizens may enter and leave Moldova based on valid documents required to cross the state border, which are recognized or accepted by the Republic of Moldova and a visa, if international agreements do not stipulate otherwise. In addition, foreign citizens who intend to enter and stay in Moldova must prove that they have at least EUR 30 per day of stay, but not less than EUR 300 for an up to 10 days stay.

b. Application Procedure

In order to obtain a work permit, the Moldovan employer shall take the following steps:

a) Registration and Publication of Vacancies

The Moldovan employer shall register the offer of its job vacancies with the Local Employment Agency and advertise such job vacancies in local press.

b) Application for Work Permit

In order to obtain a work permit, the Employer, together with the foreign citizen to be employed shall submit to the Moldovan Bureau of Migration the following documents:

• application according to the form approved by the Moldovan bureau of Migration;
• copy of the national passport of the foreign citizen to be employed;
• copy of the job vacancies advertising;
• draft of the employment agreement, containing the information on foreign citizen's salary to be paid in Moldova;
• copy of study documents (diploma) or other documents confirming the qualification of the foreign citizen;
• criminal record of the foreign citizen to be employed in Moldova issued by the competent authority of their home jurisdiction;
• document confirming the existence of living premises for requested period (declaration of owner / lease agreement / sell and purchase agreement);
• international medical insurance covering the Republic of Moldova or local medical insurance;
• confirmation of blood type;
• 2 color photos 3x4 size.

The National Bureau of Migration will have 20 days to review the submitted documents and issue the work permit as requested. As a rule, the work permits are granted for 1-year period, with right to extension for additional 1-year periods.

c. Social Insurance

The Law on the Public System of Social Security No 489-XIV of July 8, 1999 is applicable both to Moldovan and non-Moldovan individuals that are employed in the Republic of Moldova under employment agreements. The supervising public authority of social securities in Moldova is the National Social Insurance Commission (Casa Nationala pentru Asigurari Sociale).

According to the Moldovan social security rules an individual, domiciled in Moldova, shall be insured for social risks, such as retirement age, loss of supporter, invalidity, temporary disability to work caused by illness or accidents, professional diseases, child care, illness prevention, rehabilitation of work capacity, maternity, child birth, unemployment, and burial.

The subjects of taxation include persons who have permanent residence in Moldova, and are employed under individual employment agreements. If the individual is employed by a Moldovan employer based on employment, service or other similar agreement, the social security contribution is paid by the employer.

Thus, Moldovan employers are required to pay its mandatory state social insurance contribution and withhold from the pay of the individuals the mandatory state social insurance contribution of its employees. The exact social security contribution to be paid is determined on yearly basis by the social security budget law for the respective year. For instance, in 2018, according to the Law on Social Securities' Budget for 2018 No 281 of December 15, 2017, Moldovan employers have the obligation to calculate and pay to the State social securities' budget (i) the corporate contribution of 23% per month from the payroll for its employees and other individuals employed under service or other similar agreements as employer's contribution; and (ii) the individual contribution for each employee of 6% per month withheld from salary and other employment payments.

A similar system has been created in Moldova for the medical mandatory insurance of individuals according to the Law on Amount, Manner and Period of Payment of Medical Mandatory Insurance Contributions No 1593-XV of December 26, 2002, supervised by the National Medical Mandatory Insurance Company (Compania Nationala a Asigurarilor Obligatorii in Medicina). Thus, both the employer and the employee are required to pay mandatory medical insurance contributions to the state budget. The individual entrepreneurs, holders of business patents, lawyers, notaries, and other individuals shall pay the medical insurance contribution in a fixed amount, as determined on yearly basis by the medical mandatory insurance budget law for the respective year. For instance, in 2018, according to the Law on Medical Mandatory Insurance Fund for 2018 No 280 of December 15, 2017, Moldovan employers have the obligation to calculate and pay to the State medical mandatory insurance budget (i) the corporate contribution of 4.5% per month from the payroll for its employees and other individuals employed under service or other similar agreements as employer's contribution; and (ii) the individual contribution for each employee of 4.5% per month withheld from salary and other employment payments.

C. Exit and Entry

a. Visa Types

The type of visa required for an individual to enter the Republic of Moldova depends on several factors, such as the individual's nationality, the purpose of the visit, and the intended duration of the visit.

Depending on the purpose and the intended visit duration, the following types of visas may be obtained by the foreigners to enter and stay in Moldova:

a) type A - airport transit visa: bthe type A visa allows the foreigner to transit the international transit area of an airport in the Republic Moldova, without entering the Moldovan territory.

b) type B – transit visa: the type B visa is issued upon the request of the foreigner who intends to enter a third-party state by transiting the Republic of Moldova. The type B visa is issued for the term of the visa issued by the state of destination, and for a term not exceeding 1 year. This type of visa allows the foreigner to stay on Moldovan territory for the purpose of transit for a period not exceeding 5 days.

c) type C – short stay visa (for such purposes as mission, tourism, visit, business, transport, sport activities, cultural, scientific and humanitarian activities, medical treatment for short period and other activities that do not contradict to Moldovan laws). The type C visa is issued for a determined period, with the right of one or more stays not exceeding 90 days during the last 6 months.

d) type D – long stay visa (for such purposes as entrepreneurial activity, employment, study, family reunification, religious and humanitarian activities, diplomatic and service activities and medical treatment). The type D visa is issued for a period not exceeding 12 months, for one or more stays in Moldova with a duration not exceeding 90 days during the last 6 months. The type D visa allows the foreigners to apply for the work permit in the Republic of Moldova.

Citizens of the following countries may enter Moldova without a visa: EU member states, United States of America, Canada, the Swiss Confederation, the Norwegian Kingdom, the Republic of Ireland, Japan, Andorra, Israel, Liechtenstein, Monaco and The Holy Seat.

b. Restrictions for Exit and Entry

The entry and / or exist of foreign citizens in / from Moldova is regulated by the Law on Foreigners Regime in the Republic of Moldova No 200 of July 16, 2010.

An individual will be prohibited to enter Moldova if:

a) he failed to present entry documentation of due form, validity and content, as required by Moldovan law; or filed false information when executing the entry documentation;

b) information exists that the respective individual is involved in financing, preparing, supporting or committing of terrorist acts; or is part of or support transnational criminal organized groups; or might participate or participated at crimes against peace and humanity or war crimes, or crimes against humanity regulated by international treaties to which Moldova is a party;

c) he infringed the regime of State frontier or the regime of the passing point at the State frontier;

d) he committed crimes against the Republic of Moldova or its citizens during other stays in the Republic of Moldova or abroad and has outstanding criminal record;

e) he illegally introduced or attempted to introduce in the Republic of Moldova other foreigners or is involved in the traffic of human beings;

f) he has infringed, without any grounds, the purpose for visa obtainment or upon entry on the territory of the Republic of Moldova; or was previously removed from the territory of the Republic of Moldova and did not reimburse the associated costs; have exceeded the stay period on the territory of the Republic of Moldova under the law; or has other prohibitions to enter Moldova.

An individual will be prohibited to exit Moldova only in limited cases as regulated by criminal or civil proceedings law of the Republic of Moldova, in particular due to the following reasons:

a) he is imprisoned in Moldova based on a criminal court judgement; or, in a criminal prosecution or trial on Moldovan territory, he is put on a wanted list or has prohibition not to leave the locality or country; is subject to conveyance of the minor under supervision, or home arrest, or preventive arrest, or temporary release under judicial bail, with the obligation not to leave the town;

b) the foreign citizen is subject to medical coercive measures in Moldova under the criminal law;

c) the foreign citizen is prohibited to leave Moldova based on a court decision under the Moldovan Enforcement Code.

D. Trade Union and Labour Organizations

Moldovan Labour Code and the Law on Trade Unions No 1129-XIV of July 7, 2000 allows employees to create and be part of trade unions to promote their employment rights and interests in relation with employers, public authorities and other entities.

A trade union may be created upon the initiative of at least 3 persons. It operates based on its charter and is subject to registration with the Ministry of Justice of the Republic of Moldova. Any individual – Moldovan or foreign citizen who legally stays in Moldova – is entitled to create or adhere to a trade union.

The creation of trade unions is not mandatory. The employees, in general meeting, may appoint one or more representatives who will represent their interests in relations with the employer. Such representation does not require any form of registration.

E. Labour Disputes

The individual labour disputes between a specific employee and employer are regulated by the Labour Code, Civil Proceeding Code No 225 of May 30, 2003, and the employment agreement with the respective employee/employer. The Labour Code regulated special limitation periods for the employee's claims, depending on the claimed subject matter. Thus, the non-pecuniary employee claim is subject to 3 months limitation period from the day when the employee knew or should have known about his right infringement; or 3 years limitation period for pecuniary claims of employee.

Collective labour disputes shall be settled by a commission of conciliation, represented by equal members of employer and employees. If the parties do not agree with the decision issued by the commission, or the commission could not reach to an agreement regarding the collective dispute, each party has 10 days as of the date of commission's respective decision to defer the dispute for settlement to the competent court.

V. Intellectual Property

A. Brief Introduction of IP Laws and Regulations

The Republic of Moldova has established a modern Intellectual Property (IP) system, compatible with the international standards and regulations. The legislative framework of Moldova covers trademarks, patent inventions, geographical indications, appellations of origin, traditional specialities guaranteed, new plant varieties, industrial designs, topographies of integrated circuits, copyright and related rights. Within the process of accession of the Republic of Moldova to the WTO, the legislation in the field of intellectual property was strengthened for the purpose of compliance with the requirements imposed by the TRIPS Agreement. As the Republic of Moldova is a member of major international IP organizations and a party to key international treaties, the procedures for registration and protection of IP in Moldova are rather straightforward and transparent, as well as streamlined with the applicable international rules. The State Agency on Intellectual Property of the Republic of Moldova (AGEPI) is the authority vested with the right, inter alia, to organize national IP protection system, promote and register IP rights and maintain IP registers.

a. Patent Protection

Patent protection in Moldova is regulated under the Law on Protection of Inventions No 50-XVI of March 7,2008. Moreover, since Moldova is a party to Patent Cooperation Treaty (PCT), Budapest Treaty on the International Recognition of the Deposit of Microorganisms for the Purposes of Patent Procedure, Strasbourg Agreement Concerning the International Patent Classification and Patent Law Treaty (PLT) filing patent applications in Moldova is rather harmonised and meets most of the international standards.

The Moldovan law establishes the necessary framework for the application of the Convention on the Grant of European Patents (European Patent Convention), Council Regulation (EEC) No.1768/92 of June 18, 1992 Concerning the Creation of a Supplementary Protection Certificate for Medicinal Products, Regulation of the European Parliament and of the Council (EC) No.1610/96 of July 23, 1996 Concerning the Creation of a Supplementary Protection Certificate for Phytopharmaceutical Products, Directive of the European Parliament and of the Council 98/44/EC of July 6, 1998 on the Legal Protection of Biotechnological Inventions, Directive of the European Parliament and of the Council 2004/48/EC of April 29, 2004 for the Enforcement of Intellectual Property Rights.

b. Trademark Protection

Trademark protection is regulated under the renewed Law on the Protection of Trademarks No 38-XVI of February 29, 2008, Trademark Law Treaty (TLT), Singapore Treaty on the Law of Trademarks and Protocol Relating to the Madrid Agreement Concerning the International Registration of Marks.

Trademark applications in Moldova follow the classifications set by Nice Agreement Concerning the International Classification of Goods and Services for the Purposes of the Registration of Marks and Vienna Agreement Establishing the International Classification of the Figurative Elements of Marks.

c. Copyright Protection

Moldovan copyright legislation includes the Law on Copyright and Related Rights No 139, of July 2, 2010 which is one the most recent pieces of IP legislation transposing the provisions of EU directives governing copyright protection. Moldova is a party to Berne Convention for the Protection of Literary and Artistic Works, Rome Convention for the Protection of Performers, Producers of Phonograms and Broadcasting Organizations, Universal Copyright Convention, signed in Geneva, Convention for the Protection of Producers of Phonograms Against Unauthorized Duplication of Their Phonograms, signed in Geneva, WIPO Copyright Treaty, signed in Geneva, WIPO Performances and Phonograms Treaty, signed in Geneva and Beijing Treaty on Audiovisual Performances.

d. Industrial Design Protection

The Law on Protection of Industrial Designs No 161-XVI of July 12, 2007 is the main national legislation governing the procedure of creation, criteria of novelty, registration, and protection of industrial designs. Moldova is a party to Hague Agreement Concerning the International Deposit of Industrial Designs and Locarno Agreement Establishing an International Classification for Industrial Designs.

B. Patent Application

Patent protection in Moldova shall be granted for any invention having as subject a product or a process, in all fields of technology if the invention is novel, involves an inventive step (that is the invention is not obvious to a person skilled in the art or presents a technical or practical advantage) and can be applied in industry, including agriculture. Inventions are protected by a title of protection, which could be:
    a) patent for invention;
    b) short-term patent for invention;
    c) supplementary protection certificate;
    d) Eurasian patent;
    e) validated European patent.

Any natural or legal person shall be entitled to apply for a patent by filing a patent application with the AGEPI.

The right to a patent for an invention made by an employee in the exercise of his duties or specific tasks entrusted to him in writing (service invention) shall belong to the employer, unless otherwise provided by contract.

The term of a patent for invention shall be 20 years from the date of filing of the patent application. The term of a short-term patent for invention shall be 6 years from the date of filing of the short-term patent application with the possibility of extension for additional 4 years.

A patent application shall be filed with the AGEPI in the Romanian language. It may be filed in other language as well with translation into Romanian language.

A patent application shall contain:
a) a request for the issuance of a patent;
b) a description of the invention;
c) one or more claims;
d) any drawings referred to in the description or the claims; and
e) an abstract.

The patent application shall be subject to the payment of the filing fee which is around EUR 500 for formal and substantive examination.

The patent application shall relate only to one invention or to a group of inventions so linked as to form a single general inventive concept.

AGEPI shall examine whether the patent application and the invention which forms its subject-matter meet the requirements of the law. AGEPI shall undertake a formal and a preliminary examination and, upon request, a substantive examination of the patent application.

In the formal examination, AGEPI shall check whether the patent application meets the formal requirements and afterwards shall proceed to a preliminary examination.

Where AGEPI notes that there are deficiencies in the application which may be corrected, it shall give the applicant an opportunity to correct them.

A patent application shall be published after the expiry of a period of eighteen months from the date of filing or, if priority has been claimed, as from the date of priority.

In the substantive examination, the AGEPI shall check whether the invention can be patented and meets the novelty, inventiveness and industrial utility and applicability. The applicant is provided an opportunity to amend and overcome the objections of the examiner throughout the examination process.

Upon completion of the substantive examination of the patent application and based on the examination report, the AGEPI shall decide either to grant a patent or to refuse the patent application. The decision of AGEPI shall be published upon expiry of the term for filing an opposition. Along with decision it shall also publish a specification of the patent containing the description, the claims, the search report and, where appropriate, any drawings.

Within 6 months from the publication any person may file an opposition to the patent. If the opposition was not filed or subsequently rejected by the Contestation Commission, AGEPI shall issue a patent to the entitled person, subject to payment of the state duty, and shall publish in BOPI a note on issuance of respective patent.

Maintenance of a patent requires payment of the annual fees.

C. Trademark Registration

A trademark is any sign or any combination of signs susceptible of graphic representation serving to distinguish the goods or services of one persons from the others.

The following may be registered as trademarks: words (including names of persons), letters, figures, drawings, combinations of colours, figurative elements, three-dimensional forms, in particular the form of a product or its package, and any combinations of signs.

Trademarks that are devoid of distinctive character, misleading the consumer in relation to the geographical origin, quality or nature of the product or service, trademarks which are contrary to public order or good morals or harmful to the state image and interests may not be registered. Trademarks including the name of the state or localities require special state approval.

The holder of a trademark has the exclusive right to dispose of and use the trademark, and the right to prohibit other parties from making use of the trademark on the territory of the Republic of Moldova throughout the validity period of the trademark.

Any natural or legal person or group of natural and / or legal persons may register a trademark. Foreign persons should be represented in Moldova through authorized patent attorneys.

The application for the registration of a trademark shall include:
a) identification of the applicant;
b) identification of its representative;
c) sufficiently clear trademark reproduction and the description thereof;
d) the list of goods and services according to the Nice Classification of Goods and Services.

In most ordinary cases a foreign person issues a power of attorney to its authorized representative in Moldova, provides a description of the trademark and pays the state duty. This is enough for a patent attorney to

file an application for trademark registration which can be done online. In certain specific cases, the application may be accompanied by the following documents:
   a) the priority document (6 months priority applies)
   b) regulations on use of the collective mark (in case of a collective mark);
   c) regulations on use of the certification mark (in case of a certification mark);
   d) confirmation of the right to use geographical indication or an appellation of origin in a trademark;
   e) confirmation of the right to use industrial design in a trademark;
   f) consent to use state symbols, official or historical state names and the full or abbreviated names of international intergovernmental organizations;
   g) consent to use the official names or symbols of the local administrative units and the names, symbols or images that constitute the national cultural heritage, signs, official seals of control, warranty or marking, use of names of famous persons.

Company names may also be registered as trademarks if the person who submits application confirms its ownership in the company name.

Within one month of the filing date AGEPI examines the trademark registration application on the formalities requirements.

Where certain irregularities are found in the application documents or some of the documents are missing, the applicant shall remedy such irregularities within two months from the notification by AGEPI. Otherwise, the application shall be deemed withdrawn.

If the requirements of filing an application for the registration of a trademark are met AGEPI shall within 3 months publish the application for the registration of a trademark in the Official Bulletin of Industrial Property (BOPI). The applicant shall be duly notified.

Within 3 months from the publication of the application for trademark registration any person may submit observations and titleholders can submit oppositions to the trademark registration. In case no objections were raised and the application passed substantive examination AGEPI shall issue a decision on the trademark registration or refusal thereof. Any decision on the applications for registration of trademarks may be appealed to Contestation Commission of AGEPI. Upon payment of the state duty the certificate of trademark registration will be issued.

A trademark shall be registered for a 10 year-period starting from the filing date. Trademark registration may be renewed for consecutive 10-year periods whenever required. State fee for filing of the application is EUR 40, for examination – EUR 200, for issuance of a trademark certificate – EUR 250 and EUR 250 for each subsequent renewal.

D. Measures for IP Protection

A person whose rights have been infringed may apply to the civil courts in Moldova for protection of its rights within the period of legal limitation established by the law and constituting not less than three years.

IP rights may also be protected by means of customs intervention at border of the Republic of Moldova when goods infringing IP rights cross the state border.

Customs protection measures are aimed at protecting internal market from import of counterfeit and pirated goods, marketing of which causes damages to the right holders and sets the grounds for unfair competition, and represents a threat to economic security of the country and health of the local consumer.

The IP rights holder shall submit an application to the customs authorities describing the intellectual property the protection of which is sought. Upon acceptance of the application customs authorities shall enforce the protection measures when detect the goods suspected of infringing an intellectual property right. Customs authorities shall suspend customs clearance procedure and notify the right holder and the declarant / consignee of goods in order to initiate judicial proceedings. These measures can also be applied ex officio. If the rights holder does not bring an action within the envisaged time-limit, the customs authority orders to release the goods, provided that other legal provisions are observed.

VI. Environmental Protection

A. Department Supervising Environmental Protection

The Ministry of Agriculture, Regional Development and Environment ("Ministry") is the Moldovan central authority in charge with environmental protection and rational use of natural resources. It is the governmental body which elaborates and promotes the state policy in the field of environmental protection and rational use of natural resources, aimed at creating beneficial conditions for life, sustainable development of the country, international collaboration, approximation of national legislation to the European Union acquis.

Under the subordination and direct supervision of the Ministry, several governmental agencies and services are vested with powers and competences with regards to water quality, waste and resource management, environmental impact assessment and the environmental state quality supervision.

The main subordinated governmental structures are: the State Inspectorate for Environment Protection, the State Hydro Meteorological Service of the Republic of Moldova, the Agency for Geology and Mineral Resources, the Agency "Waters of Moldova", the Agency "Moldsilva", the Institute of Environment and Geography and the Fisheries Service.

The above mentioned governmental bodies are empowered with wide attributions which cover the scope of environmental policy implementation, ecological and geological state supervision, management of natural resources and the preservation of water resources.

In case of environmental breaches, the State Inspectorate for Environment Protection may react adequately, being attributed with the right to prohibit and stop construction works that infringe environmental protection regulations and suspend any economic activity that affects the state of environment.

Additionally, the United Nations entities exercise a permanent presence in the Republic of Moldova, having an undoubtedly significant impact on biodiversity conservation, implementation of climate change regulations and development of the "Green Economy" concept through the United Nation Environment Program, the "Moldova Sustainable Green Cities" Project, "HCFC Phase-Out Management Plan" Project, "Mainstreaming biodiversity conservation into Moldova's territorial planning policies and land use practices" Project.

B. Brief introduction of Laws and Regulations of Environmental Protection

The legal and regulatory framework of environmental protection of Republic of Moldova is mainly determined by the EU-Moldova Association Agreement concluded in 2014 that defines Moldova's policy and sets clear-cut objectives to be achieved in the following years. Upon signing the Association Agreement Moldova embarked upon a process of legal alignment to EU acquis. Hence, this is a central legal tool on which Moldova relies all its policies and norms for achieving more convergence, including in the environmental sector.

Additionally, Republic of Moldova has ratified until today several international conventions related to environment protection, aligning its legal provisions to requirements established internationally, and ensuring environmental sustainability. Republic of Moldova is a party to such instruments as: Convention on Environmental Impact Assessment in a Transboundary Context (the Espoo Convention), the Aarhus Convention, the Climate Change Convention adopted at Rio de Janeiro, the Kyoto Protocol, the Convention Concerning the Protection of the World Cultural and Natural Heritage.

Besides the international conventions ratified, the national regulatory framework for environmental protection in the Republic of Moldova depicts a comprehensive structure of sectoral laws and regulations, whose action extends to all the main areas of environment. The basis of the national environmental legislation is the Law on Environmental Protection which provides for the main statutory obligations in relation to air quality, water protection, waste management, pollution control, climate change, environmental impact assessment and others.

The assessment of environmental impact is an important milestone to be considered in the management of programs and activities that may have an impact on the environment in the Republic of Moldova or in other states. Two important pieces of legislation have been adopted to prevent the potential environmental impacts of social-economic activities.

Thus, the Law on Environmental Impact Assessment and the Law on Environmental Expertise provide for a mandatory prior impact assessment of proposed economic activities for mitigating their eventual negative consequences and establish the binding rule of "public participation" in environmental decision-making process for ensuring the necessary level of inclusiveness of citizens in the environmental impact assessment process.

C. Evaluation of Environmental Protection

Environmental sustainability is a major concern and a priority for the Republic of Moldova as it directly regards the living and health conditions of the population, the achievement of economic interests, sustainable development of the society.

Moldova believes that sustainable development is the pathway to social cohesion and economic growth.

The main objectives for environment protection envisaged in the following years are included in the National Environmental Strategy for the years 2014-2023.

Moldova's intrinsic objective is to ensure environment protection both at national and local levels creating a state of harmony between its citizens, economy and the environment. Moldova, also seeks to reform its current legal frameworks and transpose the EU acquis, establishing clear-cut obligations for legal entities, natural persons and public authorities, ensuring the extension of environment protection process to all key areas of environmental sustainability, and guaranteeing the access of the population of the Republic of Moldova to an unpolluted and healthy environment, in harmony with economic development and social well-being.

VII. Dispute Resolution

A. Methods and Bodies of Dispute Resolution

a. Civil Law System Governing Disputes in the Republic of Moldova

In accordance to the Constitution, the Republic of Moldova is a sovereign and independent, unitary and indivisible state. Justice is carried out in the name of law by the Courts.

The judicial system of the Republic of Moldova is based on a three-tier structure which is comprised of: one Supreme Court of Justice, four Courts of Appeal and fifteen Ordinary Courts (First Instance Courts). The decision of a higher court is binding upon lower courts. The number of judges in legal proceedings may vary depending on the complexity and specificity of the case, as well as on the competent court hierarchy level. Even though the binding precedent is not recognized as a direct source of law, there is a general tendency to pursue a uniform jurisprudence, following the principle of the security and certainty of legal relations.

The legal system is of continental orientation, in other words of civil law tradition. It primarily involves codification, the distinction between substantive and procedural law and the (doctrine) writings of legal scholars have a certain influence.

The language of procedure in a due process is the state official language. The participants who do not speak the state official language have the right to get acquainted with the case files and speak during hearings with the assistance of an interpreter. The acts of disposition of the court are being issued in the language of the process or at request in the state official language. By means of a ruling the judge, may conduct the hearings in a language acceptable to all participants in the process. However, the judgement shall be issued in the state official language.

Currently, the claims bearing a certain form and content are submitted either directly to the Court Chancellery or by post with the date of expenditure applied. There is a project to amend the Code of Civil Procedure in order to allow the electronical submission of the claim. However, it has not been approved yet. The respondent is notified about the first hearing and the judge sets a date for the submission of the statement of opposition and of all the necessary evidence.

Each party shall prove the facts which are invoked as a basis for their claims and defenses, unless the law provides otherwise. The judge is entitled to ask the parties and other participants in the process, if necessary, to provide additional evidence and prove the facts which are the subject of probation to verify their authenticity. The court shall take into examination and investigation only that evidence which is relevant to the case, that confirms or refutes the findings or cast doubts on the existence or absence of circumstances relevant to the proper resolution of the case.

In addition, the Court hearings are public (audio recorded through the "SRS FEMIDA" system), except for limited situations explicitly provided by law (e.g.cases dealing with state secret, attending by juveniles etc.). The participants are allowed to record the hearings with the permission of the Chairman of the Court panel.

As a result of the case hearing the operative part of the judgement is issued. The court issues the complete court judgment, if: a) participants in the process demanded this right; b) the court judgement was appealed; c) the judgment is subject to the procedure for recognition and enforcement. In these cases, the court issues a complete judgment within 15 days from the date of the request. The court judgement may be appealed within 30 days from the date of the announcement of the operative part of the judgment, unless the law provides otherwise.

The court judgment shall be deemed final and enforceable after the case was examined in the appellate procedure. The final court judgement may be challenged in order of cassation.

The following court judgments shall be deemed irrevocable: a) judgment was not appealed within the legal terms; b) judgment made in Appellate Court was not challenged within the legal terms; c) judgment made in Cassation Court.

After the judgment becomes irrevocable the parties and other participants in the process, as well as their successors cannot apply to the court with the same claims on the same grounds, as well as to challenge in a different court the facts and legal relations established in the judgment of the court, which became irrevocable. Irrevocable judgment is binding for the person in whose interest the case was filed by persons or authorities.

b. Arbitration

Arbitration is regulated by the provisions of the Code of Civil Procedure No 225-XV of May 30, 2003 (Chapter XLII- XLIV), by the Law on Arbitration No 23-XVI of February 22, 2008 and by the Law on International Commercial Arbitration No 24-XVI of February 22, 2008.

The Republic of Moldova has ratified a range of international instruments, amongst most important: the European Arbitration Convention and the Arrangement on the Application of the European Convention on International Commercial Arbitration (in force as of March 5, 1998), the Convention on the Recognition and Enforcement of Foreign Arbitration Awards concluded in New York 1958 (in force as of September 18, 1998) and the Convention on the Settlement of Investment Disputes between States and Nationals of other States, Washington 1965 (in force as of June 4, 2011).

The major institutions on arbitration are as it follows: the International Commercial Arbitration Court of the Chamber of Commerce and Industry of the Republic of Moldova; Mediation and Arbitration Center of the State Agency on Intellectual Property of the Republic of Moldova; the Aeronautical Court of Arbitration of the Civil Aviation Patronage of the Republic of Moldova; the Arbitration Court of the Moldova International Transporters Association; and the Chisinau International Court of Commercial Arbitration.

By virtue of contractual freedom, the parties may conclude a clause through which they agree upon the choice of arbitration as means of dispute settlement, along with the governing law and the institution / arbitrators, other details as deemed pertinent.

c. Specialist Tribunals

Before the reorganization in 2016, there were specialized tribunals like the Circuit Commercial Court and the Military Court, which were ultimately excluded.

d. Mediation

Mediation in the Republic of Moldova is regulated namely by the Law on Mediation No 137 of July 3, 2015. The initiation of mediation constitutes grounds for the suspension of the civil or arbitration proceedings from the date of signing the mediation contract. The parties decide by common agreement and with the assistance of a mediator, over the rules and the duration of the mediation process. Before the settlement is signed, the parties are entitled, by common agreement to take a pause in order to consult the opinion of experts and to formulate commentaries, in order to express their free and informed consent.

Also, the Code of Civil Procedure No 225-XV of May 30, 2003, Chapter XIII, regulates the judicial mediation procedure for certain categories of cases: consumer protection, labor disputes, right of ownership over goods, including cases of a value less than MDL 200.000 etc. At the parties' request judicial mediation can be applied in other cases as well.

The term of the judicial mediation cannot exceed 45 days form the day set for the first hearing. The outcome of these procedure results the conclusion of the settlement. If one party or both refuse to settle the dispute by mediation, or the dispute is not settled within the timeframe provided by law, or the parties have not reached a consensus on all the claims, the Court issues a ruling (which cannot be challenged) within 3 days from the receipt of the refusal or expiration of the mediation term, on the termination of the mediation procedure and conveys the case file to Court.

B. Application of Laws

Court procedures regarding civil and commercial matters are governed by the Code of Civil Procedure No 225-XV of May 30, 2003. For certain category of cases there is the legal obligation to respect the preliminary extrajudicial dispute settlement procedure, which can be either provided by the law or stipulated by the agreement of the parties.

It is important for the parties to observe the legal rules on the jurisdiction of the Courts. One should note the peculiarities of the jurisdiction of the Courts in matters having a foreign element, in particular the exclusive jurisdiction of the Courts in the Republic of Moldova (e.g.the claim following from the right to immovable property located on the territory of the Republic of Moldova; the claim following from a carriage agreement, where the carriers or the points of the embarkation and disembarkation are located in the Republic of Moldova; the purpose of the proceedings is the commencement of insolvency or of any other proceedings on termination of payments in respect to a foreign business entity, headquartered in the Republic of Moldova etc).

Enforcement of both foreign arbitral awards and of the foreign judgements is possible in Moldova. As already mentioned the Republic of Moldova has ratified on December 17, 1998, the New York Convention on the Recognition and Enforcement of Foreign Arbitration Awards.

VIII. Others

A. Anti–commercial Bribery

a. Brief Introduction of Anti-commercial Bribery Laws and Gegulations

The Criminal Code of the Republic of Moldova, under Articles 324 to 335, covers the scope of criminal liability for bribery both in the public and private sphere. In accordance with the law, a bribe represents goods, services, privileges or advantages of any form whatsoever, not due to the person itself, for the person itself or other person, or the acceptance of an offer or a promise to fulfill, or not to delay, or speeding the performance of an act in the exercise of employee's function or contrary to it.

The Criminal Code criminalizes the following offences associated to bribery: passive and active corruption, influence peddling (public sector); taking and giving bribes (private sector). Foreign public officials are also exposed as subjects of the crimes. Moreover, public service employment is also governed by the Law No 82 of May 25, 2017 on Integrity (e.g.gifts regime), Law No 325 of December 23, 2013 on the Assessment of the Institutional Integrity.

The Republic of Moldova has ratified on October 1, 2007 the United Nations Convention against Corruption through the Law No 158/2007, as well as the Civil Convention on Corruption dated December 26, 2003, through the Law No 542/2003, instruments which will be implemented by the Government in collaboration with the General Prosecutor's Office.

Code of Criminal Procedure No 122 of March 14, 2003 regulates not only the competence of the National Anticorruption Center and of the Anticorruption Prosecutor's Office, but also the procedure of initiation and unfolding of the criminal investigation, termination, sending the case to court, general conditions for a case trial in the first instance, ordinary / extraordinary means of appeal, and other related aspects.

b. Department Supervising Anti-commercial Bribery

Authorities competent for investigating bribery practices are the National Anticorruption Center and the Anticorruption Prosecutor's Office. The Anticorruption Prosecutor's Office leads the investigation in the cases in which the criminal investigations were carried out by the criminal investigative body of the National Anticorruption Center.

Filing of a complaint or denunciation of the bribery practice to the police is sufficient to launch the criminal investigation. The criminal investigative body will accept complaints even if the case is not within its competence and then coordinates it. The person filing the complaint shall be immediately issued the minutes and furtherly provided a response on the course of the investigation, whether it was or not initiated. The entire procedure from summoning the offender, to sending the case to court is exhaustively regulated by law. The court decides on the applicable sanctions and individualization.

c. Punitive Actions

The applicable penalties linked to anti-commercial bribery practices range from fines to imprisonment based on the gravity of the crime.

The maximum penalties for bribery offences are as follows:
- 15 years of imprisonment, a fine in the amount of MDL 500,000, for passive corruption, and the deprivation of the right to accede to some public positions or to carry a certain activity during a period up to 15 years.
- 12 years of imprisonment, a fine in the amount of MDL 400,000 and for the legal person of MDL 900,000, for active corruption, and the deprivation of the right to accede to some public positions or to carry a certain activity or liquidation of the legal person.
- 7 years of imprisonment, or a fine in the amount of MDL 300,000 for natural person and a fine of MDL 600,000 for the legal person, for influence peddling, with the deprivation of the right to accede to carry certain activity or with the liquidation of the legal person.
- 7 years of imprisonment or with a fine in the amount of MDL 317,500, for taking bribe, in both cases with the deprivation of the right to accede to certain positions or to carry certain activity for a period of 7 years.
- 7 years of imprisonment or with a fine in the amount of MDL 417,500, for giving bribe, for the legal person a fine in the amount MDL 750,000 with the deprivation of the right to carry certain activity or with the liquidation of the legal person.

B. Project Contracting

The main legal act regulating public procurement in the Republic of Moldova is the Law on Public Procurement No 131 of July 3, 2015. The Law has been recently enacted and aims to transpose the European Directive 2004/18/EC on the Coordination of Procedures for the Award of Public Works Contracts, Public Supply Contracts and Public Service Contracts. It also partially transposes Directives 2014/24/EU and 89/665/EEC.

a. Permission System and Restrictions

Any business operator, Moldovan or foreign resident, registered as individual or legal entity of private or public law, or any group thereof have the right to participate to public procurement procedure under the Moldovan law.

A foreign business will have same right to participate in tender proceedings in the Republic of Moldova as the Moldovan businesses have in the country of home jurisdiction of the respective foreign business.

Some bidders that did not correspond to their obligation in previous tender procedures (for instance, failed to perform their contractual obligations or filed false or erroneous information in their bids) may be restricted to participate in further bids by the Public Procurement Agency. The Public Procurement Agency may restrict the right of business operators to participate in public procurement proceedings for a period not exceeding 3 years. The list of entities that are restricted to participate in public tenders is public and is placed on the official web site of the Public Procurement Agency.

b. Invitation to Bid and Bidding

The bidding procedure to be applied in public procurement depends on the exact awarding procedure to be selected by the contracting authority. Moldovan Public Procurement Law regulates the following awarding procedures:

 a) open tender;
 b) restricted tender;
 c) competitive dialogue;
 d) negotiated procedure;
 e) reference of price offers;
 f) contest of project proposals (solutions);
 g) procurement of public works within subsidized housing schemes.

Open and restricted tenders represent the main award procedures. Other procedures may be applied only in the cases expressly provided by law. In addition, other special award procedures may be applied, namely the framework agreement, dynamic purchasing system, and electronic auctions.

The phases of a tendering process in Moldova are as follows:

a) pre – qualification phase: at this phase, the contracting authority establishes the criteria upon which prospective tenderers will be selected. Prospective tenderers will submit information containing details and capabilities, allowing the contracting authority to select the most suitable bidders to proceed to the next phase as per the contracting authority's requirements.

b) invitation to tender: contracting authorities will issue an invitation to either the shortlisted bidders selected from the pre-qualification phase, or will initiate the process by publicly advertising the tender in the Public Procurement Bulletin and on the web site of the Public Procurement Agency. The advertisements must contain information such as, but not limited to, the rules for submitting the tender, information about the contracting authority, and the tender's validity period. Tenderers may raise queries regarding the requirements of the contracting authority, which the contracting authority should respond to via written clarification.

c) submission of bids: at this phase, the bidding company will be required to submit a complete technical proposal, which includes but is not limited to pricing, delivery timescales, service levels. Such a proposal must comply fully with all the requirements specified by the contracting authority. The bidder must also agree to the proposed contract terms and conditions, subject to final clarifications. The tenders are to be submitted in Romanian language, unless the tender documentation explicitly indicates that other language is applicable.

d) tenders evaluation: assuming the contracting authority has received the requisite number of bids, the contract will be awarded on the basis of economic benefits of the proposal, provided it conforms to tender conditions and specifications. The selected bidder will be notified prior to being invited to sign the final contract with the concerned contracting authority.

e) contract signing and performance: within the term specified by law, the selected bidder has the obligation to sign the awarded contract and to start its performance. The public procurement contract financed from public funds is subject to mandatory registration at the correspondent territorial treasury department of the Moldovan Ministry of Finance.

黑山

作者：Marko Ivković、Savo Jasnić、Nikolina Kažić、Sonja Guzina
译者：陈学斌、罗民

一、概述

（一）黑山政治、经济、社会及法律环境简介

黑山在 2006 年经公投重获国家全面独立，结束了近九十年的南斯拉夫联邦成员身份。根据其 2007 年《宪法》[1]，黑山是一个实行政府共和制的国家，国家权力被分为三个部分，分别为立法权、行政权和司法权。立法权由议会行使，政府行使行政权，司法系统即法院行使司法权。

议会是由 81 名议会成员组成的一院制机构。议员通过平等的选举权直选产生，任期 4 年。议会拥有包括通过宪法和法律、批准国家预算、选举总理及其内阁成员及其他权力在内的权力。

黑山政府是行政机构，由议会中多数议员选举产生，经黑山总统提名的总理是政府首脑。黑山政府目前拥有 3 名副总理和 19 名部长。政府的职责包括管理国家内部及外交政策、向议会提交法律议案、执行法律、通过法令和其他法规、签订国际条约等。

黑山司法体系设有普通法院和特别法院。最高法院是黑山的终审法院，其主要职责在于确保各法院在法律执行上的统一性。宪法规定审判委员会的任命及罢免法院的法官和院长。

黑山总统通过无记名投票直选产生，任期 5 年。总统的主要职能包括在国内外事务上代表黑山、向议会提名总理和颁布法律。黑山总统还有权根据国防安全委员会的决定向黑山军队发号施令。

黑山是联合国成员，同时还是世界贸易组织、欧洲安全与合作组织以及欧洲理事会成员。政治领导（包括反对党的主要领导）均致力于使黑山成为欧盟成员国。这一努力获得公众广泛承认和支持。自 2007 年签署《成员结盟与稳定协议》后，黑山获得了正式的候选国地位，且欧盟于 2012 年 6 月 29 日启动了正式入盟谈判。该谈判最初聚焦欧盟法律第 23 章和第 24 章涉及基本自由、司法、反腐败和集团犯罪的内容。黑山于 2017 年 6 月 5 日成为北约成员国。

虽然不在欧元区，但黑山还是单方面批准欧元作为永久外币。黑山 2016 年 GDP 为 39.54 亿欧元，增长 2.9%，人均 GDP 为 3 354 欧元。[2] 根据前 9 个月输出量和最近 3 个月可得到的数据，黑山政府预计 2017 年 GDP 增长可达 4%，或者 GDP 总量可达 42.021 亿欧元。[3]

2017 年 12 月 31 日黑山政府负债总额达 26.479 亿欧元，其中 62.75% 与国内的 GDP 有关[4]，低于欧洲平均水平，但近几年负债累积迅速。在全球债务方面，自 2006 年起，国债攀升，其时负债额为 7.011 亿欧元，占其时 GDP 百分比为 38.3%。[5]

2017 年 12 月黑山人均总收入达 768 欧元，而同时期人均净收入（不含税费及供款）达 512 欧元。[6] 目前黑山的失业率为 20.71%，即失业人口为 48 040 人。[7]

---

[1] 参见 2007 年 10 月 25 日黑山政府公告 01/07。
[2] 截至 2017 年 9 月 29 日的黑山 2016 年国内生产总值，可查询：https://www.monstat.org/userfiles/file/GDP/bdp2016/Annual%20GDP%202016_eng_29_09_2017.pdf（访问时间：2018 年 2 月 12 日）。
[3] 截至 2018 年 1 月的 2018—2020 年黑山经济改革方案，可查询：http://www.gov.me/en/homepage/Montenegro_Economic_Reform_Programme/（访问时间：2018 年 2 月 12 日）。
[4] 截至 2018 年 1 月 15 日的投资者更新，可查询：http://www.mif.gov.me/en/news/180802/Investor-update.html?alphabet=lat（访问时间：2018 年 2 月 6 日）。
[5] 截至 2006 年 12 月 31 日黑山共和国的国债，可查询：http://www.mif.gov.me/en/sections/state-debt/88175/20157.html（访问时间：2018 年 2 月 7 日）。
[6] 截至 2018 年 1 月 26 日的平均收入（工资），可查询：http://monstat.org/eng/novosti.php?id=2429（访问时间：2018 年 2 月 12 日）。
[7] 可查询：http://www.zzzcg.me/（访问时间：2018 年 2 月 14 日）。

自私有化进程开始后，近 90% 的黑山公司已私有化，包括银行、电信公司和石油分销公司。黑山电力行业的私有化流程还未完成，因为意大利公司 A2A 在 2009 年收购了黑山电力行业 47.3% 的股份并于 2017 年行使卖出期权，而该等已出售的黑山电力行业股份变为国有财产。国家仍掌握着黑山最重要的公司，诸如黑山机场、黑山航空、巴尔港、黑山铁路和 Plantaže 葡萄庄园。

2016 年外国直接投资净额达 6.87 亿欧元（较 2015 年减少 7 000 万欧元）。2016 年黑山的最大投资来自挪威，其投资额占全部外国直接投资的 30%，第二大和第三大投资分别来自意大利和俄罗斯联邦。黑山与俄罗斯联邦、土耳其、乌克兰、欧盟、中欧自由贸易联盟和欧洲自由贸易联盟签订了自由贸易协议。

2014 年，黑山政府选择了两家中国公司——中国交通建设股份有限公司和中国路桥工程有限责任公司参与重点基础公路项目——建设 Bar-Boljare 高速公路的主干道。

黑山的房地产市场曾一直呈上升趋势，但因 2008 年全球金融危机等其他原因房地产贸易及发展遭受重挫。同时，市场展现出明显的复苏迹象，目前靠机构投资人推动。

黑山领土面积不到 14 000 平方米，西临亚得里亚海，拥有约 629 000 名居民。房地产投资客选择黑山主要是为了建设旅游设施，诸如开发度假酒店及第二故乡。黑山到所有欧洲主要国家首都的航行时间为 2 小时。其亚得里亚海岸线长达 250 公里，沿途拥有海滩和可追溯至罗马、奥斯曼、威尼斯和奥匈统治时期的历史遗迹。被称为欧洲最南湾的托尔湾整体列入联合国教科文组织世界遗产名录。除了世界最古老的国家公园之一的 Biogradska Gora 国家公园、欧洲最陡峭的峡谷塔拉河谷以及各类其他自然景观，黑山还拥有独特且人迹罕至的山区。

黑山的法律体系属于基于罗马法的大陆法系。在黑山，法院判决不是正式的法律渊源，但下级法院可以援用上级法院的判决作为指导。

（二）"一带一路"倡议下与中国企业合作的情况及方向

黑山政府在 2017 年与中国政府正式签署在丝绸之路经济带和 21 世纪海上丝绸之路倡议框架下的谅解备忘录，从而成为"一带一路"的组成部分。该谅解备忘录于 2017 年 5 月 14 日生效，有效期长达 5 年，至 2022 年 5 月 14 日。到期后，倘若任何一方均未在有效期届满前 3 个月终止的，该谅解备忘录将自动延长 5 年。

黑山与中国签订了一系列双边协议，这些协议共同构成双方在若干机构合作和金融合作项目上的法律框架，诸如 Bar-Boljare 高速公路（黑山从进出口银行贷款 6.8816 亿欧元）和重建久尔杰维恰塔拉桥（捐赠 265 万欧元）。

黑山已公布了其通过的自 2012 年 12 月 28 日至 2012 年 12 月 31 日间通过与中国的外交照会而签订的巩固合约关系协议。下表罗列了两国已签署的一系列双边协议。[①]

1	1972 年 4 月 14 日南斯拉夫社会主义联邦共和国政府和中华人民共和国政府在贝尔格莱德签署的有关民航空运的协议；
2	1978 年 2 月 3 日南斯拉夫社会主义联邦共和国运输和通信联邦委员会代表团和中华人民共和国民航代表团在贝尔格莱德签署的协定；
3	1979 年 3 月 2 日南斯拉夫社会主义联邦共和国政府和中华人民共和国政府在北京签署的有关兽医领域合作的协定；
4	1979 年 4 月 19 日南斯拉夫社会主义联邦共和国政府和中华人民共和国政府在北京签署的有关外交护照、公务护照及普通商务护照相互免签及免签证费的协定[②]；
5	1980 年 10 月 16 日南斯拉夫社会主义联邦共和国民航代表团和中华人民共和国民航代表团在北京签署的协定；
6	1980 年 11 月 8 日南斯拉夫社会主义联邦共和国政府和中华人民共和国政府在北京签署的有关海运合作协定；

---

① 参考该协议第 1 条，免签证仅适用于外交护照及公务护照持有人；参考协议第 2 条，双方同意删除全条内容。

7	1982年2月4日南斯拉夫社会主义联邦共和国和中华人民共和国在北京签署的领事公约；
8	1989年1月23日南斯拉夫社会主义联邦共和国议会的联邦行政委员会和中华人民共和国政府在贝尔格莱德签署的海关事务合作协议；
9	1997年3月21日南斯拉夫联盟共和国联邦政府和中华人民共和国政府在贝尔格莱德签署的避免双重征税协议；
10	2000年2月3日南斯拉夫联盟共和国联邦政府和中华人民共和国政府在北京签署的通信和邮政服务领域合作的协议；
11	2006年7月6日黑山共和国与中华人民共和国在北京签署建立外交关系联合声明；
12	2006年7月6日黑山政府与中华人民共和国政府在北京签署的谅解备忘录；
13	2006年8月29日黑山政府与中华人民共和国政府在圣斯特凡签署的经济贸易合作协议；
14	2007年9月5日黑山共和国外交部与中华人民共和国外交部在波德戈里察签署的合作协定；
15	2009年4月14日黑山政府与中华人民共和国政府在北京签署的文化、教育、社会科学及体育领域合作协议；
16	2010年9月24日黑山政府和中华人民共和国政府在布德瓦签署的经济与技术合作协议；
17	2011年4月24日黑山卫生部与中华人民共和国卫生部在波德戈里察签署的谅解备忘录；
18	2011年5月16日黑山政府与中华人民共和国政府在波德戈里察签署的科技合作协议。

二、投资

（一）市场准入

1. 投资监管部门

（1）黑山促进外商投资机构

黑山促进外商投资机构负责促进外商投资。该机构执行下述任务：协调和执行黑山促进外商直接投资战略；向外籍投资者提供专业服务；为目标公司开发数据库；向投资者展示黑山投资优势；安排外籍投资者与国内企业直接联络；为促进外商投资与相关国际机构合作；监管外国投资项目的实现；为促进和支持投资项目的实现与黑山国家机关、当地自治政府机构和国家机构合作等。

黑山在共同促进和保护投资方面已签署26份协议，该等协议的缔约国分别为奥地利、斯洛伐克、塞尔维亚、捷克、芬兰、丹麦、卡塔尔、比利时、卢森堡、马其顿、马耳他、法国、荷兰、以色列、塞浦路斯、罗马尼亚、乌克兰、匈牙利、德国、波兰、西班牙、土耳其、瑞士、阿塞拜疆、摩尔多瓦、希腊和阿联酋。

（2）外商投资委员会

外商投资委员会通过政策调整来指导对外商投资活动的鼓励和促进。

2. 投资法律法规

（1）法律

考虑到黑山作为投资目的地国家外来投资进入私人领域，黑山议会于2011年年中通过了《外商投资法》。根据《外商投资法》，外商投资形式可以是钱款、实物、服务、财产权和证券投资。外籍投资者可设立公司、外商合法分支机构以及收购公司股权或按与黑山国民相同条件（国民待遇）购买公司。

（2）法规

《促进直接投资法案》本着鼓励新就业、增加产能及提升竞争力的目的，为绿地和棕地投资者提供金融支持。

3. 投资形式

根据《促进直接投资法案》，投资项目被分成有形资产投资和无形资产投资两大类。

有形资产投资有以下两个组成部分：

- 绿地投资，指通过建设工厂、机器和设备来设立全新的公司；
- 棕地投资，指在租期不短于 10 年（自签订资金使用协议之起算）的条件下于承租的附带基础设施的土地（通常这些土地指的是废弃的军事设备、营房，空置的未被使用的大厅和仓库）上开始建设，投资者将之恢复到原先状态。

无形投资指根据管辖国家资助的有关法规对专利和许可证进行投资，投资金额分期计算，资金受益人对投资资金的使用记录在前述受益人的资产负债表中。

4. 市场准入标准及审核

如上文所述，外籍投资者可设立公司，并且在设立公司的同时按黑山国民的同等待遇投资该公司。然而，对特定行业的投资，诸如武器和军用设备的投资须事先获得管理外商贸易事务的国家行政机构的批准。根据《所有权法案》之规定，外籍人士不得拥有自然资源、公共产品、农业土地、森林及林地、具有特别重大作用的文化场馆、宽度达一公里的边界区域内的房产及岛屿、不得拥有位于法律以保护国家利益和安全为目的禁止外籍人士拥有所有权的区域内的房产。但例外是外籍人士可收购覆盖面积不超过 5 000 平方米的农业用地、森林及林地，且该土地上坐落有作为合同（出售、赠予、交换等合同）标的物的住宅建筑。

（二）外汇监管

1. 外汇监管部门

黑山中央银行作为黑山的主要货币机构监管银行外汇支付的执行情况及其他机构的外汇支付操作。黑山中央银行同时还收集黑山居民与非居民直接的外汇和资本运作数据，并根据该等数据进行国际收支统计。

2. 外汇法律法规简介

《外汇及资本运作法》（黑山政府公告，编号 45/05、62/08、40/11、32/13、70/17）管辖跨境支付交易并区分资本运作和外汇交易。资本运作指以进行跨境资金转移为目的的运作，诸如直接投资、房产投资、证券运作及货币市场工具运作。另外，外汇交易指黑山国民与非国民之间不以资本转让为目的而进行的交易。通常情况下，外汇交易和资本运作以及从黑山向国外或国外向黑山进行资产转让均可自由进行。

3. 外资企业的外汇管理要求

《外汇及资本运作法》管辖居民与非居民欧元及其他货币的直接支付交易、向黑山及从黑山进行财产转账方式以及居民享有的支付欧元以外其他货币的权利。

在黑山，外汇交易和资本运作（包括从黑山及向黑山进行财产转让）均可自由进行，因此《支付系统法》（政府公告，编号 62/13 和 06/14）在支付服务上的一般规则同样适用于国际交易。

（三）融资

1. 主要金融机构

黑山的主要金融机构包括：黑山中央银行、商业银行、保险公司、租赁公司和养老基金公司。

黑山宪法将中央银行定义为负责银行业货币和金融稳定性及功能性的独立机构。中央银行的主要目标是完全按照自由开放的市场原则及创业和竞争自由的原则促进和维持金融系统的稳定、健全的银行体系和安全且高效的支付体系，并尽力实现和维持物价的稳定。

银行作为金融市场的主要参与者受《银行法》的监管。《银行法》监管银行、小额信贷金融机构和信用社的设立、管理、运营及运营控制，同时还管辖从事信贷和担保行业的人士的运营条件及经营控制。银行从事下述活动：①签发保函并承担其他资产负债表外债务；②购买、出售和催收债权（保理和滞纳金业务等）；③签发、处理和记录支付票据；④根据管辖支付系统的相关法规管理国内及国际支付交易；⑤融资租赁；⑥根据相关证券交易法律经营涉及证券的业务；⑦代表银行自身及其账户或客户的账户与外国支付渠道进行交易，包括外汇操作及金融衍生品；⑧存款业务；⑨就法人及企业家的贷款信誉度及公司运营方面的其他事项提供分析、沟通信息及建议；⑩提供安全的保险箱；⑪属于银行业务的其他活动、与该银行经营有关的附属性质的活动以及按该银行章程之规定与其业务直接相关的其他活动。

银行仅可设立为股份有限公司，可由黑山境内或境外的自然人和/或法人创立。银行的初始资本不得少于5 000 000欧元，且必须在向商业实体注册中心登记注册前全额缴清。外资银行可通过分支机构在黑山经营，但必须事先获得中央银行书面的经营许可。此外，在获得中央银行批准的情况下，外资银行还可在黑山设立其代表处。外资银行的代表处代表该外资银行的利益，不得从事境内银行活动。目前有15家银行在黑山市场经营。①

黑山的另一类金融机构是保险公司。保险业务分为保险活动、共同保险活动及再保险。位于黑山的保险或再保险公司在获得黑山保险监管机构这一独立监管机构的许可后可从事保险、共同保险和再保险业务。但例外情形是：①空运和海运必须购买强制运输险；②拥有黑山永久或暂时居留权的外籍自然人及其财产可向外籍保险公司投保。外资公司可从事保险经纪业务、保险代理业务和提供附属保险服务。保险服务可分为以下险种：

（1）非人寿险种；

（2）人寿险种；

（3）强制保险险种。

根据《黑山融资租赁法》之规定，出租人按承租人要求的规格及其认可的条款条件，同意向供货商购买租赁物的所有权的，则该融资租赁交易即为合法交易。出租人进一步同意，承租人在约定期间内以分期支付费用为对价有权占有和使用租赁物。该法律的缺陷在于并未规范租赁服务的设立、运营和监管以及保理服务。

在加入欧盟过程中，黑山应完全将其银行经营法规与欧盟指令相融合。因此，黑山议会已经通过《融资租赁、保理业务、购买应收账款、小额信贷及信贷担保业务法》，该法律于2018年5月11日生效，先行的《融资租赁法》将不再适用。新法将租赁及保理业务提供者定义为在黑山有经营场所的公司，因而非黑山企业将不得从事该类业务。中央银行对该类业务拥有完全的控制管理权。租赁和保理公司可设立为股份公司或有限责任公司，其初始资金为125 000欧元。此外，新法还认可了下述保理类型：①附追索权保理；②无追索权保理；③国内保理；④国际保理；⑤反向保理。

在养老基金方面，自黑山议会2006年通过《自愿养老基金法》后，自愿养老储蓄已成为养老金改革的第三支柱。黑山证券委员会作为资本市场的监管机构发展了附带的规章制度，该规章制度与相关法律一同为养老金改革的执行奠定了良好的基础。《自愿养老基金法》明确了养老基金管理公司的设立条件及自愿养老基金的管理。截至目前，黑山证券委员会已授权DZU Atlas Penzija和DZU Market Investto来运营养老基金，此外还有两家自愿养老基金公司，分别是Penzija Plus和Market Penzija。

2. 外资企业的融资条件

外资企业（即外籍法人）与黑山国内企业在融资条件上享有相同的权利和义务。任何银行或其他外汇支付业务供应商的任何客户（无论黑山籍还是外籍）在每次支付的外币超出中央银行规定的限额时均须表明其支付目的。

---

① 参见 http://www.bankar.me/banke-u-crnoj-gori-lokacije-ekspoziture-bankomati/。

(四)土地政策

1. 相关土地法律及法规简介

(1) 黑山房地产法律渊源

①《所有权法》——约束所有权及其他财产权、动产及不动产的占有以及该等权利的收购、转让、保护和让与方式、设置抵押的规则和流程、抵押的类型和登记,同时还规定外籍实体在黑山获得财产的条件。

②《国有财产法》——约束属于黑山或地方自治政府的物品及其他产品的使用、管理及处置。

③《国家不动产丈量及地籍法》——规定基于不动产的权利的登记。

④《空间规划及建设法》——规定空间规划系统、建筑施工方式及条件、非法建筑合法化及其他空间规划和设施建设方面的重要事项。

⑤《不动产税及不动产交易税法》——规定不动产税及其支付义务和不动产交易税计算方式。

⑥《土地征用法》——规定因公共利益征收私有财产并支付公平补偿款的流程。

(2) 所有权类型及其他财产权

黑山法律中规定的所有权类型包括单独所有权、共同所有权、联合所有权和共同所有。单独所有人对不动产享有排他性的权利,包括处置权、设置抵押和留置的权利。两名或两名以上所有人对某一未分割的财产共同享有地产权的即为共同所有人。该所有权与全部财产的非物理可分部分有关。联合所有权即平均享有未分割财产,但不同于共同所有权,其所有部分是可分的,只是尚未确定。公共持有是指对某建筑或该建筑所在的某土地的公共区域的所有权。可根据法律、私人协议及司法或行政机构的判决或通过继承获得房产。所有权通常是永久持有的,不受时间限制。仅当为满足公共利益之需要并获得公平对价时征用才是合法的。

地役权是一种在未占有的情况下得以使用和/或进入他人不动产的非占有性质的权利。黑山法律将他役权和自役权予以区分。某不动产的所有人(需役地)获得有关另一不动产(供役地)的权利,通常是为了进行特定活动。受制于地役权可能存在这样的情况,即供役地所有人禁止特定活动,而这就可能影响到需役地。黑山《所有权法》并未对不动产地役权进行最终的分类。然而该法律也规定了大多数常见的权属类型,诸如路权、公用线路安装权、窗户权、在供役地上保留部分建筑的权利及类似权利。不动产地役权可通过合法交易、法院或行政判决和事实占有的方式设立。私人地役权的规定类型包括用益权、使用权和居住权。

财产的收费、产权负担及所有权的限制均应根据《国家不动产丈量及地籍法》之规定向土地登记处进行登记。在黑山,房产抵押是房产上设立担保的最常见形式。抵押物可以是有货币价值及可以货币交易的任何房产。抵押通常基于:①协议;②留置声明,以第三人为受益人单方设立抵押;③司法判决;④法律规定设置抵押。

2. 外资企业土地收购法规

根据《所有权法》之规定,外籍人士(包括自然人及法人)可按黑山国民享有的相同条件购买不动产。但是还存在一些例外情况。外籍人士不得享有以下所有权:①自然资源;②通用设施;③农业用地;④森林及林地;⑤重要和特定用途的文化场馆;⑥国境一公里范围内及岛屿上的不动产;⑦为保护国家安全利益之目的被法律禁止外籍人士拥有所有权的特定区域内的不动产。但特例是,外籍人士可获得不超过 5 000 平方米的农业用地、森林和林地,前提是该土地上坐落有作为收购标的物的住宅建筑。尽管存在前述限制,外籍人士仍然有权签署短期和长期租赁协议、让与协议、建造、经营和转让安排及类似的公共——私有安排。

然而,根据 2007 年黑山与欧盟签署的《成员结盟与稳定协议》之规定,在不动产购买事宜上,来自欧盟成员国的外籍人士有权要求获得与黑山国民同等的待遇。

(五)公司的设立和解散

1. 企业形式

根据《商业实体法》之规定,黑山存在六种公司组织形式:企业家、普通合伙企业、有限合伙企业、股份公司、有限责任公司及外国公司合法分支机构。

（1）企业家

企业家是以营利为目的独立经营业务的自然人。企业家以自身的全部财产对其所从事的业务经营承担责任。如企业家不以自身名义从事经营活动的，必须向商业实体注册中心登记。倘若名称或所有权变更的，企业家必须在变更发生后的30日内向商业实体注册中心汇报其变更情况。为统计之目的，企业家须以提交登记声明的方式向商业实体注册中心进行登记。企业家将获得一份登记证书。然而，该证书并不是其有资格从事业务经营的背书。

（2）普通合伙企业

普通合伙企业由两名或两名以上的自然人或法人（普通合伙人）组成，相互承担无限连带责任。普通合伙企业的设立不以向商业实体注册中心登记为前提条件。

（3）有限合伙企业

有限合伙企业是由一名或多名被称为普通合伙人的自然人或法人及一名或多名被称为有限合伙人的自然人或法人组成的合伙企业。普通合伙人对有限合伙企业的全部债务和义务承担无限连带责任。而有限合伙人仅在其出资范围内对有限合伙企业的债务和义务承担责任。有限合伙人可以现金或经评估的实物或权益出资。有限合伙企业必须向商业实体注册中心先行登记方可设立。否则应视为是普通合伙企业，在此情况下，每一名有限合伙人则成为普通合伙人。

（4）股份有限公司

股份有限公司是指有一名或多名创始人（自然人或法人）的公司。一家股份有限公司的股本被分成若干股份。股份有限公司的最低股本为25 000欧元。创始人须现金支付初始股本。股东应在其出资范围内对股份有限公司承担责任。仅当股份有限公司严重违规的情况下才承担无限责任。①

股份有限公司的组织构架包括股东大会（强制性）、董事会（强制性）、执行董事（强制性）、公司秘书（强制性）及公司审计师（强制性）。执行董事和公司秘书可由同一人担任。倘若该股份有限公司仅有一名股东的，则该名股东行使股东大会的职能。

（5）有限责任公司

有限责任公司可由一名或多名自然人或法人（最多不超过30名）以资金或非资金向公司供款的方式组成。各股东的持股比例与其出资额成比例。每一股东拥有一个单独的持股比例（以百分比代表）。可以授权持有公司一股股份的股东享有超过一票表决权的权利。有限责任公司的最低资金股本为1欧元。创始人应在其出资范围内对有限责任公司承担责任。如出现重大违规情形，应承担无限责任。

有限责任公司的组织构架包括股东大会（非强制性）、执行董事（强制性）和董事会（非强制性）。倘若该有限责任公司仅有一名股东的，则该名股东行使股东大会的职能。该名股东可担任公司的执行董事或任命其他人士担任该执行董事职位。

（6）外国公司合法分支机构

外国公司合法分支机构是在黑山国以外设立注册的公司的一部分，且该分支机构在黑山领土内经营业务。与股份有限公司和有限责任公司不同的是，外国公司合法分支机构不具有法律实体的地位，这就是其设立流程区别于前两者的原因。

外国公司合法分支机构未被强制要求设立执行董事，这大幅降低了投资者在此方面的成本。外国公司合法分支机构仅需任命一名授权代表且该代表必须为黑山国籍，但该名代表无需受聘于公司。虽然根据黑山的法律规定至少一名授权代表须是黑山国籍，但仍可通过任命其他授权代表对所有主要事项作决定的方式来限制该黑山国籍的授权代表的权力。该等任命的其他授权代表仅需提供护照复印件及任命同意函而无需拥有黑山国籍或工作许可，这一举措大大地简化了相关流程。

2. 公司设立流程

鉴于有限责任公司是在黑山最为常见的公司形式，故本节仅讨论有限责任公司的设立。一家有限责任公司的设立包括以下程序：

---

① 所有人及公司资产或资金合并；虚假和欺诈登记；未按规定保存记录；未向商业实体注册中心提交信息和出资不足或发行的股份不符合公司所从事的业务领域附带的风险；《商业实体法》第4条规定的其他情形。

（1）于商业实体注册中心登记注册

在申请人提交所有必要文件的情况下，注册流程较简单，最多不超过 4 天。所需的文件包括：
- 经公证的创设决定 / 创设协议；
- 章程备忘录；
- 任命执行董事和授权代表（如适用）的书面同意函；
- 商业实体注册中心提供的完整的注册表；
- 注册费缴付证明——向商业实体注册中心支付 10 欧元注册费，再支付 12 欧元用于在政府公告上刊登说明；
- 中央存托机构有关创始人证券的摘录；
- 有限责任公司的创始人 / 执行董事 / 授权代表（如适用）的身份证件复印件；
- 如该创始人在黑山的其他公司还持有超过 30% 的股权的，须提供证明该等公司良好存续且无犯罪记录的确认函；
- 授权委托书，授权律师在公司设立过程中采取所有法律及程序性行为（倘若该等流程由该名律师管理的）。

（2）开设银行账户

公司登记后，为完成其基本经营，公司应在其选择的银行开设银行账户。因此，获得授权进行金融交易的执行董事及其他人士需在黑山公证处对签字进行公证。但特例是，一些银行接受该等签字的外国公证书。

（3）向税务机构登记

为使公司获得增值税编号，公司应向税务机构进行登记。增值税登记不是必须的，但当公司的年营业额超过 18 000 欧元时，须进行增值税登记。增值税登记可与公司的注册登记同时进行。

（4）税务行政机关进行员工登记

雇主必须在聘用关系成立后的 8 天内向税务行政机关进行员工登记。

（5）刻制印章

虽然印章的刻制不是法定义务，但在黑山刻制印章属行业惯例。可由专门从事该行业的企业刻制印章。公司印章的制作耗时一天，花费不超过 20 欧元。

3. 公司解散方式及要求

在黑山，公司的解散受到《商业实体法》的监管。公司的解散流程被称为"自愿清算"。仅当公司处于资产超出其负债的情况下方才进入自愿清算。这是一个简单的流程，由公司自行操作，与国家机构关系不大。

（1）清算人角色及清算流程概述

公司决定清算后，股东大会任命一名清算人，该清算人由董事会提名，负责公司的清算工作。清算人起草所有资产清单及自清算流程开始有关业务的财务报告，特别是清算资产负债表。如清算人认为公司的资产不足以清偿债权人的所有债权的，清算人应根据管辖商业实体资不抵债的相关法律申请破产程序。在清算过程中，未经清算人同意的任何股份转让、资产处置或负债均系无效。

（2）清算完成

当所有正在进行中的业务都完成时，清算人起草一份说明清算流程如何进行以及公司资产如何处置的最终报告。清算人按各股东所持股份附带的权利向各位股东分配公司的剩余资产（如果这些剩余资产仍可利用）。清算人就其行为造成的损害对公司和第三人负责。

（3）简易清算

《商业实体法》提到，在公司不存在剩余负债且其所有股东均同意公司进入清算的情况下，可启动简易清算程序。在此类情形下，股东自公司从商业实体注册中心注销后的 3 年内对公司的所有债务及责任承担无限连带责任。

（4）结论

在黑山公司清算流程将持续若干周（简易清算）至若干年（如对债权提出质疑或发生其他情形）。

清算步骤
• 股东大会作出公司不再继续经营并自愿进入清算的决定。
• 公司决定清算,须由其管理层自作出该决定之日后的 5 日内向商业实体注册中心登记。
• 于作出清算决定的股东大会上须指定清算人来完成清算流程。该清算人的具体信息须向商业实体注册中心登记。
• 清算人向债权人发出有关公司清算的通知。
• 通常情况下索赔的提交期限不少于发布公告后的 60 天。
• 截止日期后提交的所有索赔须在按时提交的所有其他索赔理赔后方才予以处理。所有剩余资产均在有权股东之间分割。
• 在最后一次股东会议上须提交与清算执行的方式及公司所有资产的资产负债表有关的最终报告。该报告获得批准后,于股东会议后的 7 天内须向商业实体注册中心提交该报告的复印件和注销申请。在商业实体注册中心向政府公告发布公司注销通知后公司不复存在。

(六)兼并和收购

黑山的兼并和收购交易受到《商业实体法》(黑山政府公告编号 06/02、17/07、80/08、40/10、36/11 和 40/11)和对股份公司收购作出详细规定的《股份有限公司收购法》(黑山政府公告编号 18/11 和 52/16)的约束。

1. 兼并

股份有限公司的兼并是黑山法律项下公司重组的一种形式。[①]《商业实体法》认可以下两种兼并形式:

(1)一家或多家公司通过向一家现有公司转让资产及债务的方式并入该公司,同时该现有公司向被并入的公司股东发行股份;

(2)两家或多家公司合并共同形成一家全新的实体,由该新实体向被合并的公司股东发行股份。

兼并,作为另一种公司重组方式,只有当公司资产超出其负债的情况下方可进行。兼并所需的文件包括:管理层和股东大会决定、兼并协议及其他公司文件(新章程备忘录及财务报表等)。

兼并将于注册中心登记之日完成,同时注册中心将在黑山政府公告上公布兼并协议。

《商业实体法》还规定了简易的兼并模式,适用于接收公司联合持有被并购公司至少 90% 的股份。倘若交易受制于兼并审查,兼并所涉及的公司有义务向竞争保护机构披露详细的文件清单。

2. 收购

法律并未对外国的所有权进行限制,在收购的情况下,境外投资者和黑山投资者并无区别。

收购交易通常通过购买股份的方式进行。《商业实体法》规定,公司不得向该公司股份的潜在买家提供贷款、担保或提供任何其他形式的财务支持。该限制不适用于金融组织的运营,亦不适用于以向相关公司的员工提供股份激励为目的的股份收购。根据《执行法》(黑山政府公告,编号 36/11、28/14、20/15、22/17 和 76/17)之规定,还可在公开拍卖上购买股份,但这种收购股份的方式较少见。

对于某些特定行业(诸如银行业、保险业、媒体、电信、特许经营、能源等),黑山法律就目标公司股份收购事宜制定了特别的条件(批准)。例如,根据《银行法》之规定,如收购黑山银行的合格股权或表决权的,须事先获得黑山中央银行的批准;或根据《保险法》之规定,如收购黑山保险公司的

---

① 公司重组的其他形式有:分拆、反兼并和公司组织形式变更。

合格股权或表决权的，须事先获得黑山保险监管机构的批准。

在黑山，收购交易涉及的公司实体主要是有限责任公司和股份有限公司。

（1）有限责任公司

涉及有限责任公司的交易较涉及股份有限公司的交易更为灵活。根据《商业实体法》之规定，有限责任公司在出售股份时须受到该有限责任公司股东及公司本身的优先购买权的限制。仅当有限责任公司的其他股东及公司本身在售股要约后的 30 天内拒绝购买待售股份的，该待售股方可转让给第三方，但出售条件不得优于给该公司及其股东的出售条件。倘若发生股份转让的，转让人及受让人将对与其股东身份有关的债务向有限责任公司承担连带责任。

根据已签署并经公证的股份购买协议、优先购买权弃权书（如有）及新的公司章程备忘录进行股份转让。每次交易必须向商业实体注册中心登记。

（2）股份有限公司

股份有限公司的收购受《股份有限公司收购法》的约束，该法律规定了公开收购的过程。该收购流程有两种类型，分别是强制收购和自愿收购。

根据《股份有限公司收购法》之规定，收购上市公司不超过 30% 股份的可直接或间接地在要约程序之外进行。倘若受让人自行或与其关联方一同直接或间接收购某股份有限公司之股份且因该次收购受让人持有目标股份有限公司超过 30% 的表决权股份的，则该受让人必须公告其对目标股份有限公司的股份收购。倘若受让人将获得少于 30% 的表决权的，其可公告自愿收购，但非必须。《股份有限公司收购法》已规定了公开收购的强制流程和自愿流程的相关细节，且收购人必须满足一定的条件。

《股份有限公司收购法》同时还规定了收购流程的一些豁免情形。

在收购中，所有股东均获得相同的条款和条件，且取得相同的收购交易信息。涉及股份有限公司的交易须向商业实体注册中心和中央存托机构登记。

3. 国有公司

《经济私有化法案》（黑山政府公告 编号 23/96、06/99、59/00 和 42/04）规定了收购国有公司的流程。根据该法律，黑山政府设立了私有化及资本项目委员会。

根据《经济私有化法案》之规定，私有化进程必须按照私有化及资本项目委员会提议并经黑山政府通过的年度私有化方案执行。

（七）竞争规则

1. 监管竞争法规的部门

（1）竞争保护机构

竞争保护机构是一个成立于 2013 年的独立行政机构，负责监管黑山的竞争法规的执行。竞争保护机构执行竞争保护，包括评估两家公司之间的限制性协议、调查和证明可能存在滥用市场支配地位的情形以及评估和监控并购交易。

（2）国家援助监管委员会

经黑山政府任命的国家援助监管委员会负责监管报告及认可国家援助的合规性。但根据《竞争保护法》之法律修改议案（该议案已提交议会[①]），竞争保护机构将从国家援助监管委员会处接管国家援助。

2. 竞争法简介

（1）《竞争保护法》

为与欧盟的相关法规相统一，黑山制定并通过了《竞争保护法》（黑山政府公告，编号 44/12），该法涵盖了与限制性协议、滥用市场支配地位及兼并控制有关的基本规则。

---

① 参见 2017 年 12 月 28 日的《竞争保护法》之法律修改议案，载 http://zakoni.skupstina.me/zakoni/web/dokumenta/zakoni-i-drugi-akti/341/1628-10215-08-1-17-1.pdf（访问时间：2018 年 2 月 14 日）。

（2）《国家援助监管法》

《国家援助监管法》（黑山政府公告，编号 74/09 和 57/11）载明了在市场经济和竞争保护原则下授予国家援助及其对使用监管方面的条款及流程。

（3）特别领域法律

在某些领域的专门法律涵盖反垄断和竞争的某些方面，诸如《媒体法》《电子通信法》《能源法》，另外因《国家援助监管法》不约束以下领域，因而还存在一些有关农业、渔业国家援助的特别规定。

（4）国际渊源

黑山与欧盟在 2007 年签订了《成员结盟与稳定协议》，该协议规定了黑山在竞争和国家援助及其监管方面的义务。黑山《宪法》确定了国际法律效力优先于国内法律的原则。根据该原则，经修改和公布的国际协议及普遍认可的国际条约均是国内法令的组成部分，其效力也优于国内立法，并在与国内立法相冲突时可直接适用。根据该原则，倘若《成员结盟与稳定协议》与国内立法存在冲突，抑或相关国内立法在竞争和国家援助领域内未作规定，直接适用《成员结盟与稳定协议》。

（5）附属规则

黑山政府在国家援助领域内已通过许多具有法律约束力的法规，但主要还是在提供国家援助上的具体标准、条件及方式的法令（黑山政府公告，编号 27/10、34/11 和 16/14）。根据该法律，财政部已公布国家援助规则清单手册（黑山政府公告，编号 35/14、02/15、38/15 和 20/16），涵盖欧盟成员国援助立法的公开翻译版。该欧盟次级立法直接适用于黑山法律体系。

黑山政府在竞争领域通过了众多法律法规，诸如集体豁免的纵向协议禁止法令（黑山政府公告，编号 13/14）；道路和铁路交通及内陆水域交通阻隔豁免协议及海上航道交通联盟协议法令（黑山政府公告，编号 59/14）；个人豁免限制性协议之适用内容及方式的程序规则（黑山政府公告，编号 18/13）；相关市场定义的方式及标准规则（黑山政府公告，编号 18/13）。

3. 竞争约束措施

（1）反垄断和竞争

黑山的竞争保护机构负责评估两家公司之间的限制性协议、调查和证明可能存在滥用市场支配地位的情形以及评估和监控并购交易。该机构无处罚权，仅可向轻罪法庭提起诉讼。

① 限制性协议

根据黑山法律规定，预防、限制或扭曲相关市场竞争的协议[①]，诸如市场分享协议、定价协议、供应资源分享或供应限制安排，均被禁止且属无效协议。

限制性协议可以是横向协议（处于同一生产或经销链水平的两家现有和/或潜在公司之间的协议）和纵向协议（处于不同生产或经销链水平的两家现有和/或潜在公司之间就供应、购买、出售或转售条件达成的协议）。

倘若竞争保护机构在双方要求的情况下允许个人特例，倘若协议满足了黑山政府规定的集体豁免条件，抑或根据法律规定的条件该协议的重要级别较低，限制性协议可免受禁令约束。

② 滥用支配地位

根据《竞争保护法》之规定，如某公司在相关市场的市场份额超过 50% 的，则推定该公司在产品市场中占有支配地位。倘若两家或多家公司之间不存在显著竞争且彼等在相关市场内的总共份额超过 60% 的，则进一步推定存在集合支配地位。在所有其他情况下，当相关市场份额低于上述比例的，竞争保护机构须证明某公司占有市场支配地位。

《竞争保护法》禁止处于市场支配地位的公司滥用其市场支配地位，包括强行施加不公平的买卖价格或其他不公平的交易条件，对有偏见的消费者限制生产、限制市场或技术发展、在与其他公司的同等交易中适用不同条件从而使得该等公司处于竞争不利地位、强制要求接受补充义务条款（就该等条款之性质或就商业用途而言，与拟签订合同标的无关联的）方才签署合同。

③ 兼并控制

根据黑山法律，兼并控制集中于：

---

① 限制性协议包括书面或口头安排、合同、协议的单独规定、明示或默示协议、联合行为以及公司合营决定。

- 在相关市场内两家或多家独立公司或其部分进行的兼并；
- 由一名或多名已控制至少一家公司的自然人，或由直接或间接控制另一家公司全部或部分业务的一家或多家公司进行的并购；
- 设立新公司的或取得长期独立经营且履行作为一家自治公司的所有职能的现有公司联合控制权的两家或多家独立公司（合资）。

倘若发生下述情形之一的，经相关公司请求，在竞争保护机构批准的前提下方可执行集中度，且必须提交：

- 至少两方于上一财年在黑山市场的合并年营业总额超过 500 万欧元的；
- 双方在上一财年的合并全球年营业总额汇总超过 2 000 万欧元的，假定至少一方同期于黑山的营业额达到 100 万欧元的。①

所提及的请求应于下述活动后的 15 天内提交：签署协议或合同；公开招标或投标公布或公开投标结束；取得控制，以时间较早的为准。

在特例情况下，竞争保护机构可独立启动兼并控制程序，如果该兼并未申报（并购之前根据金融阈值标准到申报标准），但结果导致并购后的公司占据市场份额的 60%。

双方须中止集中度执行直至竞争保护机构决定批准拟定的集中度。如竞争保护机构未在法律规定的截止日期前作出决定，该交易视为正常交易。

基于公开信息，竞争保护机构于 2017 年作出了 37 项兼并决定。

（2）国家援助

《国家援助监管法》将国家援助定义为"通过授予特定经济实体、产品或服务更为优惠的市场地位的方式干扰或可能干扰市场自由竞争且影响黑山和欧洲共同体或中欧自由贸易协定的成员国之间的贸易的支出、收入或国家或市政府资产的减少"。

根据法律规定，干扰或可能干扰市场自由竞争的国家援助是被禁止的，除非经法律允许或该援助不被视为国家援助。被认可的国家援助的形式有：补贴，财务救济，国家或市政府担保，贷款利率补贴，就授予人开发项目而向经济实体提供国家或市政府的收益或分红，债务解除，国家或市政府以低于市场价的价格出售不动产或以高于市场价的价格购买不动产。

在授予国家援助前，授予人须就任何国家援助的授予通知国家监管委员会。②该通知可提及个人援助（为特定目的或特定项目而向特定受益人授予的援助）或国家援助计划（该行动规定基于国家援助的条件可授予潜在受益人）。

国家监管委员会有义务自通知提交日后的 30 天内按法律之规定就国家援助是否合规作出决定。

（八）税

1. 税制及规定

（1）适用法律

① 《个人所得税法》；
② 《公司利润税法》；
③ 《增值税法》；
④ 《不动产税法》；
⑤ 《不动产交易税法》；
⑥ 《税务管理法》；
⑦ 《强制性缴纳社会保险法》；
⑧ 《消费税法》；
⑨ 《关税法》。

---

① 对于银行、保险公司和其他金融机构的营业额适用其他特别规则。
② 国家援助可在国家及地区层面从国家机构、当地自治政府机构和负责管理国家资源的法律实体取得。

（2）一般规则

财政部根据《税务管理法》代表黑山政府的机构进行收税和税务监管。税务年度与自然年度保持一致，每个纳税人均有义务在年底提交纳税申报表。

在黑山领土取得应纳税收入的居民或非居民自然人须缴纳个人所得税。此处居民是指在黑山有居所或营业所或在税务年度内在黑山停留超过183天的自然人。

在黑山从事以营利为目的的活动的居民或非居民法人须缴纳企业所得税。此处的盈利系指居民/非居民在黑山或居民法人在黑山以外获得的利润。黑山中央银行、公募基金和由黑山政府及当地市政府资助的公共机构免于缴纳企业所得税。

（3）双重征税协定

黑山已经与包括中国在内的43[①]个国家签署了双重征税协定。2014年4月3日，黑山政府与中华人民共和国政府签订了有关合约情势巩固方面的协议，就此黑山在其以联盟成员身份签订的18份协议中的主体地位均获得巩固加强。其中一份协议便是南斯拉夫联邦政府与中华人民共和国政府于1997年3月21日在贝尔格莱德签订的避免双重征收所得税和房产税协议。根据黑山《宪法》，该等经确认并修改的国际条约的效力优于该等条约约束事项相关的国内法律。

2. 主要税种及税率

税　种	税　率		
个人所得税 （个人收入；个体经营活动；财产及基于财产的权利；资本；资本收益[②]）	9%和11% （11%适用于月平均收入高于黑山上一年度月平均总收入的情形）		
社会保险供款		养老	医疗	失业
	个人	15%	8.5%	0.5%
	雇主	5.5%	4.3%	0.5%
企业所得税	9%		
增值税	标准税率——21% 较低税率——7%和0%		
财产税	0.25%~1.0%，但当地政府可决定适用更高或更低的税率		
财产交易税	3%		
根据中黑双重征税协定	股息——5% 权益和特许使用费——10%		

3. 纳税申报及优惠

为自身业务而投资固定资产的企业家有权获得投资金额50%的税收减免，而减免最高不超过该税期总赋税的70%。倘若纳税人在税费已定（或计划营收）年度的上一年的营业收入总额少于18 000欧元的，税务管理机构可授权该纳税人每年一次性支付税费。

就企业所得税而言，在经济欠发达省市新设立的且在设立后的前3年内从事生产活动的法律实体可享受税费豁免及税费优惠。

（九）证券

1. 证券及相关法律法规简介

为了使本国法律与欧盟法律保持一致，2017年12月，黑山通过了《资本市场法》。《资本市场法》规定了资本市场设立及运作的条件；金融工具类型；证券发行；投资公司组建及业务经营；资本市场

---

① 与印度签署《双重征税协定》时黑山还是塞尔维亚和黑山国家联盟的成员，且在签约前黑山亦参与了相关谈判，独立后该协定并未修改。（来源：黑山财政部，http://www.mif.gov.me/biblioteka/ugovori）
② 非居民个人权益收入按5%纳税。

的规范；证券二级市场交易；金融工具登记、金融工具交易的清算、结算及登记；公开金融及其他数据并向发行人及资本市场的其他参与者报告；禁止资本市场滥用；对资本市场而言具有重要作用的其他发行工作。资本市场通过多边体系［包括多边交易平台（MTP）、有组织的交易平台（OTP）和场外交易市场（OTC）］运作。

中央存托机构作为主要的登记和证券存托机构。该机构执行证券登记、已完结的证券交易或与证券有关的其他交易的结算工作。向中央存托机构提交有关已签署的购买协议的信息，其中每一笔交易均已登记，且证券所有权转让均已执行。要购买证券，均须向中央存托机构注册证券账户。源自中央存托机构登记处的摘录是证券所有权的唯一证据来源。

证券交易所从事证券市场活动。证券交易所旨在高效解决证券供需关系及公开告知有关证券市场的信息。证券的交易严格按照法律对每一市场参与人所规定的规则进行。卖方及消费者之间的关系是间接的，是接通过投资经纪人（即股票经纪公司和资金托管银行）进行的。

为证券买卖之目的必须用到投资经纪人（即股票经纪公司和资金托管银行）服务。投资中介机构负责根据《资本市场法》之规定执行证券买卖及其他证券交易的中介活动。投资中介机构提供的中介服务将产生费用，而中介机构以收取费用的方式作为其提供服务的对价。该笔费用包括证券交易费和中央存托机构交易费用。①

2. 证券市场的规则及监管

黑山的资本市场由负责黑山资本市场的委员会管理，黑山证券委员会是一个独立的管理机构。市场组织者必须向证券委员会提出申请从而获得履行职责的授权。

3. 外资企业从事证券交易的要求

就在黑山资本市场买卖证券而言，外籍自然人和法人享有同黑山国民同等的权利，不受任何限制。外国自然人和法人在证券交易上的条件和流程详见《资本市场法》《证券交易所规则》和《经纪规则》。

（十）投资优惠政策和投资保护

1. 投资优惠政策

（1）国家补贴

根据《促进直接投资法令》的规定，对投资额在 250 000 欧元或 500 000 欧元以上且雇用至少 10 名或 20 名员工的投资项目可以提供制造和服务补贴。适用条件具体取决于项目所在地，越是欠发达地区，严苛的要求越少。投资项目和新员工雇用均须在资金使用协议签署后的 3 年期内完成。该期间最长可延长至 5 年，但必须获得政府批准。

拟根据《促进直接投资法令》授予的鼓励投资补贴额占总投资额的 50%、60% 或 70% 不等，具体取决于受益人被归为大型商业实体还是中型或小型商业实体。授予资本投资项目的金额最高不得超过投资项目总额的 17%。此外，受益人有权获得补贴用以支付新招募员工的工资。每一笔授予的补贴均根据鼓励投资补贴授予标准执行。

需留意的是，只有注册在黑山的公司才有资格获得鼓励投资的补贴。

（2）黑山投资优势

投资者在黑山投资益处颇多，包括：

- 政治和经济稳定；
- 欧元为全国通用货币；
- 优惠的税务环境；
- 已达到私有化水平；
- 高水准的经济改革和新设立机构；
- 完善的私有化银行体系；
- 发达的电信基础设施；

---

① 投资中介机构的信息可从证券委员会网址 www.scmn.me 和证券交易所网址 www.scmn.me 查询。

- 受教育程度相对较高的劳动力及相对低廉的劳动力成本；
- 在劳动关系领域不断改进的劳动力市场；
- 自由进入欧盟市场；适用中欧自由贸易协定、黑山与欧洲自由贸易区国家之间的自由贸易协议以及与俄罗斯和土耳其的自由贸易协定；
- 设立新公司流程简易（4天的设立时长及1欧元的设立资本）；
- 相对较低的关税税率；
- 赋予外籍投资者的国民待遇；
- 财政激励、监管和金融措施达到一定水平；
- 再投资收益及款项自由转向国外；
- 在欠发达地区设立法律实体，可豁免缴纳所得税（8年）；
- 避免双重征税（与40多个国家签署避免双重征税协定）；
- 世界贸易组织（WTO）成员国；
- 北大西洋公约组织（NATO）成员国。

此外，一些地方政府机构还规定了其他豁免和扣减优惠政策。

2. 对特定行业和地区的支持

鼓励投资补贴用于制造业和服务业的投融资项目，但不包括主要农业生产、合成纤维制造、运输（包括航空客运、海运、公路或铁路运输及通过内陆河流或货运业务的商业运输）、赌博、贸易、煤及钢材的主要生产、发电、石油和天然气、烟草及烟草制品、武器和弹药、转基因生物体和危险废料生产。

鼓励投资人以较低资格要求获得国家补贴进行投资的地区系国家的北部及中部地区的自治政府，不包括波德戈里察首府。

3. 特别经济区

（1）商业区

黑山的几个当地自治政府已进行了商业区开发（诸如贝拉内、比耶洛波列、科拉欣、莫伊科瓦茨、尼克希奇、采蒂涅、乌尔齐尼和波德戈里察），在该等商业区内投资者可获得的优惠条件包括：

- 按优惠条件支付公共事业或其他费用；
- 在商业区内就场地租赁/购买商议价格；
- 个人所得附加税减免；
- 房地产税费降低；
- 确定公私合伙优惠模式的可能性；
- 为缺少发达基础设施的区域装备基础设施。

（2）自由区

就外贸、外汇、税收、海关及外商投资而言，在自由区内的经营体制与国家的一般商业条件有所不同。在自由区工作的最重要的优势在于：

- 所有经营活动均可在自由区进行（但不包括那些危害环境、人民健康、主要商品和土壤安全的活动）；
- 保障海外投资者在投资权利、自由区内已建设施和活动组织的所有权收购上享有完全平等的权利；
- 自由区内场地和设备的使用均按固定条件以长期租赁的方式获得；
- 进口至自由区的商品无需缴纳关税及增值税，无论该等进口商品的类型及其进入自由区的目的；
- 进口至自由区的商品可无限期停留；
- 商品可暂时带离自由区至黑山其他地方或从其他地方进口至自由区做进一步加工、安装、检测、调查、维修或商用展示等；
- 分派至黑山其他地方待进一步销售的商品在离开自由区时须缴纳的关税和增值税仅限商品的海外组成部分；

- 自由区使用人无需为法律实体支付利润税；
- 在自由区内投资和转让利润均免费。

三、贸易

（一）贸易监管部门

黑山目前由经济部负责监管并推动国内外贸易。经济部下设国际贸易合作事务处、区域合作和多边合作事务处。国际贸易合作事务处负责处理国际贸易相关问题。

（二）贸易法律法规概述

国内贸易法规范国内贸易，规定贸易规则和贸易形式，保护贸易行为免受不正当竞争的侵害，并监督法律的实施。外贸法规范外贸事务，包括四部分：①总则；②对外货物贸易；③服务贸易；④贸易救济。

下面两项是对外贸法的补充：
（1）外贸法补充法令；
（2）货物进出口监管清单。

除上述法律法规外，黑山还制定了其他法律进一步监管贸易事务，包括：消费者保护法、产品安全法及建筑产品法等。

（三）贸易管理

2006年12月，黑山签订了中欧自由贸易协定（CEFTA），旨在到2010年在各成员国之间彻底取消工业和农产品的海关限制。2007年，议会批准加入中欧自由贸易协定，黑山正式成为中欧自由贸易协定成员国。同时，阿尔巴尼亚、马其顿、摩尔多瓦等也正式成为贸易协定新成员国。中欧自由贸易协定原成员国包括：保加利亚、捷克共和国、匈牙利、波兰、罗马尼亚、斯洛伐克和斯洛文尼亚。欧洲自由贸易协定（EFTA）成员国（包括瑞士、挪威、冰岛和列支敦士登）于2011年签署了自由贸易协定（FTA）。虽然均为小国，但瑞士、挪威、冰岛和列支敦士登在全球经济的多个重要领域处于领先地位。

黑山同欧盟签署了特惠贸易协定。欧盟通过建立自主贸易优惠（ATP）制度，对超过95%的货物免除进口关税，从而鼓励欧盟成员国之间的货物贸易。免税的货物包括酒水、肉类和钢铁。黑山的产品可不限量地向欧盟成员国出口并可免除海关关税和费用，但农产品、嫩牛肉制品和纺织品除外。

（四）进出口货物的检验检疫

对于进出口货物的检验检疫，黑山根据其法律实施下列保护性措施：环境保护方面（动植物保护、电池、蓄电池、电子设备，所有属于上述类别的货物应通过特定的检验、检疫并取得许可和执照）；植物检疫方面（从黑山的关税区域进口植物、花卉、水果和蔬菜，应取得农业、林业和水资源管理部植物检疫部门的许可）；食品和动物监管方面（所有相关货物应取得相应的许可和执照，并接受特定的海关检查）。

（五）海关管理

黑山的海关法律体系主要包括海关法和关税法。另外，除了海关法和关税法，黑山还有一系列二级法规，用以规定关税、海关手续以及通关费用。

进入黑山市场之前，外来进口货物应办理海关进口手续。此类货物应当进行关税申报，报关单应符合黑山法规。报关单应列明详细信息（货物种类、数量、价值等）以便计算关税。另需提供的相关文件包括：协议书、发票、采购订单、运单等，以证明报关单所列信息。

备案的进口商仅限黑山实体。外国实体需办理海关手续的，应当指定其在黑山的代理人代为办理。

海关税率由关税法规定，但货物的种类和用途不同，海关税率亦不同。若黑山和进口货物的原产国之间存在自由贸易协定，海关税则可能根据协定减少或被免除。黑山已与欧盟、周边中欧国家以及俄罗斯缔结了自由贸易协定。根据这些协定，成员国的货物可享受关税优惠。

黑山的进口制度包括永久进口和临时进口两种主要方式。

永久进口货物与国内货物一样可进入黑山市场进行交易。经过备案的进口商，应就符合一般规定的货物进口足额缴纳关税和进口增值税。

临时进口适用于从黑山购买并拟在不变条件下出口的货物。临时进口的期限由海关部门决定，一般不超过24个月。但必要时，为了实现货物进口，此期限可延长。

四、劳动

（一）劳动法律法规概述

黑山的劳动法律法规分若干级别，包括：黑山统一适用劳动法、通用集体协商协议、各行业各自适用的特殊集体协商协议以及适用于特殊雇佣者的集体协商协议。

劳动法：劳动法是调整劳动关系和统一规定劳动权益的一般性法律，适用于所有劳动者，包括所有为黑山境内的国内实体、外资法人实体或个体工作的本国公民和外国公民。

通用集体协商协议：黑山2015年颁布的一般性劳动协议，适用于所有雇主。

特殊集体协商协议：特殊集体协商协议有很多种，分别适用于某一特定行业的所有雇主，由具有代表性的工会和经营者协会共同执行。

公司集体协商协议：适用于特定的公司，基于特定公司的雇佣关系调整权利和义务。

（二）雇用外籍员工的要求

1. 工作（许可）

若外籍人员拟在黑山工作，他需要根据预计的工作时间，取得相应的居住证和工作许可证（或工作登记确认书）。

2. 申请程序

国内雇佣、季节性劳动或借调至黑山境内（可能与在黑山境内提供服务相关，或可能与公司之间进行的外籍人员借调相关），需要申请签发居住证和工作许可证。

工作许可证统一由黑山内务部签发。工作许可证申请书和其他文件应一并提交给内务部，用以证明该外籍人员具有足够的资产支持其在黑山的生活、住宿、健康保险，以及其在黑山居住的正当理由（如工作/季节性工作邀约、借调协议等）。内务部在必要时可酌情要求增补相关文件。

文件提交后，警方将自提交之日起约20日内签发工作许可证，外籍劳动人员应在签发后5日内领取工作许可证。若外籍劳动者在上述期限内未领取工作许可证，则被视为放弃工作许可证申请。

工作许可证自签发之日起有效期最长1年，之后可延期2年。季节性劳动工作许可证1年内有效期最长为6个月。

3. 社会保险

取得工作许可证后，劳动者应签订劳动合同。自劳动合同签订之日起8日内，本地雇佣者应前往黑山税务机关，对该外籍劳动者进行备案登记，以便为其购买强制性社会保险。

注意：黑山的工作许可证签发每年有不同的配额限制。一旦满额，工作许可证的签发将不再进行，但向在黑山备案的董事或管理人员签发工作许可证的情况除外。

（三）出入境

一般情况下，外国公民应就近前往黑山领事馆或大使馆办理签证后方可入境黑山，除非其本国适用黑山的特定免签制度。比如，根据黑山的免签制度，持有效护照的欧盟成员国公民和塞尔维亚公民可免签进入黑山，但180天内在黑山累计居留时间不得超过90天。

1. 签证类型

机场过境签证（A）：外籍人士搭乘国际航班需要在黑山通过机场国际中转区转机而无需进入黑山境内，可予以签发机场过境签证，有效期最长3个月。一般情况下，外籍人士在黑山机场转机时，若不离开国际中转区，则无需申请签证。但为了维护国家安全和法律秩序，黑山政府规定特定国家的公民必须办理机场过境签证。

过境签证（B）：过境签证用于在黑山单次过境、往返过境或多次过境，有效期最长6个月。根据过境签证，外籍人士每次旅程可在黑山停留不超过5天。持有入境担保的外籍人士可予以签发过境签证。此签证可向个人签发，也可向集体签发。

短期居留签证（C）：短期居留签证用于因旅游、商务、个人或其他目的单次、两次或多次入境。自首次入境之日起6个月内，持有短期居留签证的人员在黑山境内持续或累计停留不得超过90天。可多次入境的C类签证有效期最长1年，特殊情况下此类签证的有效期可延长，但不得超过5年。短期居留签证可签发给外国团体（即团体签证）。团体签证可附于团体护照，有效期不得超过30天。

长期居留签证（D）：外籍人士持有长期居留签证可单次、两次或多次入境黑山。自首次入境之日起，该外籍人士可在黑山境内居留90天以上，但一年内停留时间不得超过6个月。此类签证可向符合下列条件的外籍人士签发：

- 根据商业和技术合作协议、长期生产合作协议、技术转让和外方投资协议，进行商业或其活动并提供专业咨询，需在黑山居留的；
- 在黑山境内工作的外国驻黑山外交机构和领事代表机构成员，黑山认可的国际组织成员、经济与文化代表机构成员，以及各成员的家属（如该成员的持有外交护照或公务护照的家庭成员）。

2. 出入境限制

有下列情形的外籍人士不得入境黑山：使用他人护照、无效（如虚假）护照或其他证件的；不符合法律要求的；侵害国家安全、公共秩序和公共健康的；其属国采取保护性措施或安全措施宣告该人员被驱逐出境且该宣告仍然有效，黑山采取保护性措施将该外籍人士驱逐出境，或其居留被撤销的；等等。

（四）工会和劳动组织

为保证劳动者的权利，提高劳动者的职业和经济利益，公司应保障劳动者加入工会、参加工会活动的自由。公司设立工会应在劳动事务管理部门进行登记备案。

（五）劳动纠纷

黑山不设专门的劳动法院，劳动纠纷由常规民事法院受理，即初级法院、上级法院以及作为终审法院的最高法院。最高法院决定同意或驳回上级法院对特别案件作出的判决。对劳动纠纷裁决有异议的劳动者，或劳动权益受到侵害的劳动者，有权自收到裁决之日或发现其权益被侵害之日起15日内向有管辖权的法院提起诉讼。因雇佣引起的金钱诉讼不受上述期限的限制，员工可随时提起诉讼。

劳动者可决定是否通过向劳动争议和平解决机构提出仲裁申请的方式和平解决劳动争议。仲裁员由劳动争议双方共同决定，仲裁程序快捷。仲裁员所作仲裁决定为最终决定，且对双方均有约束力。在黑山，个人劳动纠纷通常由劳动者向法院提起诉讼解决，通过仲裁解决劳动纠纷的情况极少。对于工会与雇佣者之间的群体性劳动争议，争议和平解决机构仅作为中间人对纠纷进行调解，并不作最终和有约束力的裁定。

劳动部可通过劳动监察部门对劳动法规的适用进行监督。根据劳动者个人提出的申请（可匿名申请），劳动监察部门可开展实地监察，实地监察通常分定期监察和特别监察。若劳动监察发现雇佣者有违法行为，劳动部门可启动针对该雇佣者的违法审查程序。

另外，一些权力机构的职权范围亦可涉及雇佣关系的某些方面（尽管其职权不仅仅包括对雇佣关系的管辖），例如监察专员（负责管理歧视类案件）。监察专员的决定虽无法律约束力，但相关权力机关会重视其意见。

五、知识产权

（一）知识产权法律法规概况

关于知识产权，国内和国际已有相当广泛的适用法律。具体而言，黑山知识产权法律包括：2015 年《专利法》、2010 年《商标法》、2010 年《工业品外观设计保护法》、2011 年《版权及相关权利法》、2008 年《地理标志法》和 2010 年《半导体拓扑图保护法》。

除主要立法外，黑山又制定若干规章制度专项规范知识产权注册事宜。同时，知识产权的注册还需遵守相关行政程序规定。

尽管黑山有多个部门均涉及知识产权保护事宜，但只有黑山知识产权局（MIPO）是主管部门，负责知识产权的获得和保护。除黑山知识产权局外，知识产权保护体系的重要组成部分还包括：

- 经济部：在行政程序中提出的与知识产权注册相关的请求，由经济部负责处理（www.mek.gov.me）；
- 行政法院：与知识产权注册相关的行政纠纷，由行政法院管辖（sudovi.me）；
- 波德戈里察商业法院：负责处理涉及各方（不分身份地位）的知识产权侵权案件（sudovi.me）；
- 波德戈里察商业上诉法院：负责处理上诉阶段的知识产权侵权案件（sudovi.me）；
- 海关管理局：财政部下属的国家权力机关，负责监管国家边境上侵犯知识产权的商品（www.upravacarina.gov.me）；
- 市场监察局：贸易、旅游和电信部下属的国家权力机关，负责对商标侵权商品进行内部市场控制（www.uip.gov.me/kontakt）。

（二）专利申请

在国家立法层面，专利申请主要由 2015 年《专利法》规范。根据该法规定，申请人可以在所有技术领域内为其发明寻求保护。在黑山境内，申请人可向黑山知识产权局申请保护；在国际上，申请人可根据专利合作协定、欧洲专利公约、黑山与欧洲专利局之间的专利合作协定，向国际机构申请保护。例如，欧洲专利局同样保护黑山的专利，其认可的欧洲专利与国家专利在权利范围方面是一致的。同时，在某些情况下，发明涵盖的范围相同时，欧洲专利与国家专利相比，其权利范围更为广泛。

专利认可程序的第一步是提交申请。专利申请应一式三份，使用黑山语以书面形式直接提交或邮寄。每个发明需提交一份申请书。专利认可申请应包括以下内容：

- 由黑山知识产权局提供的申请表；
- 该项发明的具体描述；
- 专利请求；
- 草图；
- 摘要。

注册国家级专利所需的文件包括：

- 申请书由代理人提交的，需提供授权委托书；
- 管理费支付证明；
- 提交申请书的申请人为多人时，需提供所有申请人的资料及共同委托代表的声明书；
- 若发明人不愿被列为申请人，需提供发明人的声明书。

若满足法律规定的条件，自专利申请提交之日起期满 18 个月，专利申请应尽快在专利局公报中公告，专利许可决定应作出，有关专利认可的资料应在黑山专利登记簿中记录。否则，专利申请将被驳回。

（三）商标注册

商标注册的优点很多，但其最主要的优点在于保护商标免受侵权。商标权所有人享有将商标用以标明商品和/或服务的排他权，并有权禁止他人在市场上擅自使用相同或相似的标志来标记相同或相似的商品或服务，从而避免可能引起的商业混淆。此外，《商标法》特别规定，在故意侵犯商标权的情况下，被侵害方不仅可以要求侵害方赔偿其金钱损失，还可以要求侵害方支付相当于被侵权商标授权费最多3倍的赔偿款。

如果申请注册商标的标识没有与之前其他注册商标相冲突，商标注册流程通常需要2至6个月的时间，包含因黑山知识产权局可能提出的任何审查报告而延长的时间。

若申请注册的标识涉及法院在审的侵权案件，则在法院作出判决前，该注册程序将被暂停，注册程序可能会被延长至几年。

注册程序的平均总费用（不含括回复审查报告可能产生的任何额外费用）约为177欧元。

注册程序的审查报告仅包含商标注册的形式审查。

形式审查包括审核商标申请书是否有效（包括对商标申请表、申请注册的商标、商标所适用的商品及服务项目的审核；商标注册由他人代为申请的，还包括对授权书的审核）。若发现申请不符合规定，审查人员将发送审查报告详细告知申请人，并要求申请人于30日内补正。申请人未能在指定的期限内补正或未足额支付相关费用，审查人员将作出预审裁定，驳回其申请。

除非有关方面要求进行材料审查，否则该项审查不作为黑山知识产权局职权范围内的常规审查。

注册商标的有效期为10年，自核准注册之日起算。按规定缴纳行政费用后，商标有效期可续展10年，如此可无限期延长。

（四）知识产权保护措施

对知识产权，尤其是商标权的保护措施，包括以下几个方面：

一方面，海关管理局可以通过边境管控机制保护商标权；即商标所有人、申请人及专有许可证持有人，可以请求相关部门在国家边境保护其商标权。根据权利人的请求或依据职权，有关部门在掌握侵犯知识产权的初步证据时，可暂时扣押侵权货物（该货物可以是知识产权的侵权对象或手段）。缉获之后，海关人员应立即向权利人、黑山知识产权局（如需获得相关信息）以及已知的任何其他利害关系方通知海关方已经采取的措施。

此项通知至关重要，因为知识产权权利人据此可向法院提出诉讼，寻求知识产权保护，并将诉讼进程或法院发出的临时禁令告知海关。

另一方面，当认为其标识/商标受到侵犯时，申请人或商标所有人可通过内部市场控制措施保护自己的权利。根据商标所有人的请求或者依职权，市场监察机构可采取市场控制措施扣押侵犯知识产权的商品（该商品可为侵权对象或手段）。该程序本身与海关管理局所执行的程序非常相似。除非诉讼解决机制达成庭外和解，该程序往往会伴随法院诉讼。

法院诉讼为第三种执法手段，权利人可向有管辖权的法院提出请求。侵权诉讼通常伴有预先禁令请求。收到请求后，法院将尽快决定是否颁发禁令。此外，在对诉讼作出最终判决前，法院将安排开庭，听取各方陈述。在作出裁决前，审判人员将根据需要安排相应数量的庭审。

诉讼费取决于诉讼请求的金额或价值、诉讼时间以及庭审的数量。在黑山，诉讼费用包括案件受理费，其中包括一审费用和上诉费用。由于个案差异较大，具体侵权案件的费用，难以根据一个特定的标准确定。

六、环境保护[①]

（一）环境保护监管部门

环境保护局是可持续发展与旅游部的下属部门，负责环境保护监管事宜，其根据黑山政府2008年

---

① 为保护自然资源及其领土的特性，黑山于1991年9月20日通过了《生态国宣言》，从而成为世界上第一个生态国家，这一地位在2007年黑山《宪法》中正式确立。在整个地区动荡不安的时期，黑山议会在北部镇扎布利亚克通过了这一宣言，这标志着公众的环保意识开始增强。次年，这项宣言被载入1992年黑山《宪法》。在过去10年中，特别是2006年黑山独立后，这些想法重新被重视，黑山加入重要的国际环境保护论坛，设立环境保护机构，在当地适用当代法律规范，并宣布建立第五国家公园（Prokletije）。宣言链接：www.mgreens.co.me/declaration.htm。

一项法令设立。

环境保护局负责与环境保护相关的专业事务及行政工作,如:
- 进行环境监测;
- 进行环境分析并出具报告;
- 签发许可文件;
- 与相关的国内外组织以及公众交流沟通等。

环境保护局[①]已加入欧盟内部的专业交流机构等国际机构,负责与国际环境保护组织之间的合作,特别是与欧洲环境局和国际原子能总局的合作。

黑山的环境保护工作由检查管理部门负责。检查管理部门是根据一项关于公共管理组织及运作的法令而成立的国家机关。该法令于2012年1月20日生效,为联合检查机构的设立提供了法律依据,环境保护属于联合检查机构的职能之一。

可持续发展与旅游部有权制定二级立法,实施相关的环境立法并负责监督环境保护。其部分职权已经委托给市政单位[②],市政单位的基本职权包括制定地方规划和战略,并在地方职权范围内对环境法的实施进行监督。

其他国家机关,如市场监督机关以及卫生和健康监督机构,亦可对环境保护进行监督。环境监察员可在其职权范围内采取强制措施,预防或消除可能对环境造成不良影响的行为。根据不良行为的类型,行为人可能被处以轻罪处罚(如处以现金罚款或责令停止经营);另外,根据行为造成的生态破坏及相关的法律规定,行为人也可能面临刑事起诉或损害赔偿。

(二)环境保护法律法规概述

根据2007年黑山《宪法》,环境保护体现了宪法的基本价值,宪法保障人人拥有健康生活环境的权利。除宪法外,黑山在环境保护领域还有多项法律规定。2016年颁布的《环境法》为主要的环境立法。《环境法》规定了国家和地方机构、各企业组织及自然人在环境保护及环境改善方面的权利和义务,以此保障公民享有健康良好的环境。该法还规定:对环境有影响的项目建设或生产活动,应当在完成环境影响评价分析或取得环境保护许可证后方可进行。《环境法》还就环境保护和可持续发展原则、环境保护参与实体与手段、公众参与义务及其他对黑山环境有重要意义的问题作出相关规定。其他相关的环境法律还包括:

- 2005年《环境影响评价法》(不定期修订):该法规定对环境有重大影响的项目应当进行环境影响评价,并规定了环境影响评价分析的内容,相关机关、组织和公众的参与义务,环境影响评价及审批/许可流程以及信息交流等。
- 2005年《战略环境影响评价法》(不定期修订):该法规定了对特定方案或规划进行战略性环境评价的条件、方法和程序,将环境保护原则贯彻在对环境有重大影响的方案或规划中。
- 2005年《污染综合防治法》(不定期修订):针对可能对健康、环境和货物带来不利影响的设施及活动,本法规定了综合许可证签发的条件和程序,同时还规定了有关环境污染防治和监测的相关事宜。
- 2011年《废物管理法》(不定期修订)、2016年《化学品法》、2014年《环境损害赔偿责任法》(不定期修订)、2007年《海洋法》(不定期修订)、1992年《海岸带法》(不定期修订)。
- 2007年《水法》(不定期修订):对地表水和地下水及其管理、水资源管理设施和服务以及水资源利用和排放的条件和程序等相关问题作出规定。
- 2010年《空气保护法》(不定期修订):规定了避免、防止或减轻空气污染对人类健康以及整个环境造成不利影响的措施。
- 2007年《环境噪声防治法》:规定了各机关、法人实体和自然人在环境噪声管理与防护方面的权利和义务。

---

① 其直属部门包括:自然保护、监测、分析和报告部门;许可证颁发部门;环境保护领域信息系统管理部门;综合事务、法律事务和财务部;放射和核安全及电离和非电离辐射防护部;化学品管理部。
② 黑山市政单位包括地方市政府及波德戈里察市政府。

• 其他包含环境保护条款的法律,如:1992 年《农业用地法》(不定期修订),2010 年《森林法》(不定期修订),2016 年《能源法》(不定期修订)等。

2007 年,黑山签署《联合国气候变化框架公约京都议定书》。该议定书规定了成员国应遵守的具有法律约束力的减排目标。此外,黑山也签署了《巴黎协定》(2017 年)等环境领域的其他多项国际协定。

(三)环境保护评估

以上现行法律体系及《生态国宣言》均表明:黑山正在积极开展环境保护工作。尽管如此,由于部分法律与欧洲立法并不完全一致,黑山在某些领域的实践方面,仍有待改进;特别是在工业污染和风险管理、水和空气质量、化学品和气候变化等领域,这一点尤为重要。黑山即将通过的立法提出更加严格的标准及更强的执行力度,对违规违法行为提高罚款额度及惩处力度,要求公司、管理层及其员工承担更大的责任。公众环保意识不断增强,在公众压力下,相关权力机关在国家及市政预算中安排越来越多的资金用于环境保护。另外,黑山的环境监察活动日渐频繁,相关违法行为日渐杜绝。但是,任重而道远,黑山目前仍未达到欧盟在环境保护方面的最低标准。

七、争议解决

(一)争议解决的方法及机构

争议所涉及的相关权利可由争议双方自行处置的,或不受黑山法院专属管辖的,争议双方(包括公司和自然人)有权通过协商确定争议解决方式。争议双方不同意和解的,通常可选择以下任一种方式解决争议:①法院诉讼;②仲裁;③调解(在实践中很少使用)。

1. 法院诉讼

一般而言,黑山司法系统是指由基层法院、上级法院和上诉法院组成的三级法院体系,负责民事和刑事案件的一审和二审。行政法院负责解决行政争议。最高法院是所有争议(包括民事、刑事和行政争议)的终审法院。基层法院具有基本或扩展的权限,为一个城市或多个城市提供司法裁判,但上诉法院和商事法院仅有一个。

民事诉讼程序首先在基层法院提起而启动,起诉时应提交与诉讼请求和事实相关的证据/文件。根据平等对抗原则,民事诉讼一般分为预审和正式审两个阶段。与基层法院诉讼程序不同,上诉法院通常不开庭直接作出裁决,而最高法院从不开庭。黑山《宪法》以及引入的欧盟和其他公约,均保障公民上诉权。由于黑山法律制度以民法原则为基础,所以判例对法院无约束力。此外,法院已将部分职权委托给其他机构,包括公证和执法等机构。

行政法院受理起诉政府机关的案件。此外,为保护公共利益、提供公共服务,公共机关签署一些特许协议、政府采购合同和其他协议;因这些协议(合同)产生的争议,也由行政法院受理。一般情况下,行政法院根据所提交的文件进行书面审理,通常无需开庭,但也有例外,视具体情况而定。

若争议涉及涉外因素,且相关法律或国际协定明确规定此类争议的受理权限时,该类争议由规定的黑山民事法院解决;若无相关的明确规定,则根据黑山法院地域管辖权的规定,该涉外争议由有地域管辖权的黑山法院解决。若争议一方或多方为黑山公民或在黑山设立的法人实体,争议双方可选择向黑山法院起诉。相反,若争议方拟向外国法院起诉,则争议一方应为该国公民或在该国设立的法人实体,且黑山法院对该争议没有专属管辖权。

2. 仲裁

争议双方可通过仲裁的方式解决现有的或未来可能产生的法律纠纷。黑山经济商会仲裁院是黑山的仲裁机构,负责国内及国际仲裁,具体取决于纠纷是否含有涉外因素。

黑山经济商会仲裁院为自主独立的机构,根据《黑山经济商会仲裁院仲裁规则》及争议双方的约定,处理国内商事争议和有涉外因素的争议。争议双方有权选择仲裁员。任何具有订约能力的自然人,不分国籍,皆可担任仲裁员。

除《黑山经济商会仲裁院仲裁规则》外,争议双方可商定根据《联合国国际贸易法律委员会仲裁规则》在仲裁院解决争议。

仲裁院仲裁的目的在于确保公平有效地解决争议，避免不必要的延误和费用。法律框架如下：2015 年《仲裁法》、2015 年《黑山经济商会仲裁院仲裁规则》《联合国国际贸易法律委员会仲裁规则》和《仲裁员道德准则》。

黑山的仲裁法和仲裁规则已与国际规定（特别是《联合国国际贸易法律委员会国际商事仲裁示范法》）一致。

3. 调解

当事人可事先达成书面协议，约定：一旦发生争议，在启动司法或其他程序前，他们将尝试通过直接谈判或调解的方式解决争议。即使向法院提起诉讼，法院也有义务在一审程序期间建议当事人进行调解。当事人若同意调解，应当提交接受调解的书面声明。

为了推动调解工作，确立调解员的地位，成立了黑山调解员协会。调解员为中立的第三方，帮助当事人进行协商沟通，寻找双方共同的可接受的解决方案。根据所调解的争议类型，调解员可由法官、律师、心理学家、医生、经济学家、工程师及其他各领域的知名专家担任。调解员应当为黑山公民，具有大学学历和 5 年专业经验，且应接受专业培训。培训完成后，经司法部委员会提议，调解员由司法部部长委任。司法部委员会经司法部部长授权成立，由法官、调解员和司法部工作人员组成。

调解员也可不具备上述条件，前提是其必须在特定调解领域具有专业知识或实践经验。在黑山，含有涉外因素的争议，可由在他国有调解权的外国公民调解。

（二）法律适用

法院根据宪法、法律及国际条约的规定，确定诉讼双方的权利与义务。

2014 年《国际私法》（不定期修订）对含有涉外因素的民事、劳动及商业事件所适用的法律作出了规定。法律或国际条约没有特别规定的，当事人可自行选择适用的法律，包括承认外国法院判决和外国其他机构裁决的相关规定。对外国仲裁裁决的承认和执行，适用 1958 年《承认及执行外国仲裁裁决公约》。

不同的法律对应不同类型的争议解决机制和程序。调解程序主要适用的法律为 2005 年《调解法》；国际仲裁适用的诉讼规则一般是以《联合国国际贸易法律委员会国际商事仲裁示范法》为基础的《国际商事仲裁法》；民事诉讼适用 2004 年《民事诉讼法》（不定期修订）；刑事诉讼适用 2009 年《刑事诉讼法》（不定期修订）；行政争议适用 2016 年《行政争议法》。

八、其他

（一）反商业贿赂

1. 反商业贿赂法律法规概况

反贪污贿赂主要适用 2014 年的《预防腐败法》(《反腐败法》)。《预防腐败法》在预防潜在利益冲突、公共职权限制、举报人保护等方面作了全面规定。

《反腐败法》将"腐败"定义为：任何滥用职权或凭借商业（或社会）地位（或影响），谋取个人利益或为他人谋取利益的行为。鉴于腐败现象在社会各个领域普遍存在，《反腐败法》通过各种措施最大可能地预防和减少任何形式的腐败行为。在这一方面，《反腐败法》引入了一项重要的具有创新性的规定；根据该项规定，所有国家机关有义务制定"诚信计划"。诚信计划包括：国家机关披露的腐败信息、腐败高发岗位以及减少腐败发生风险的措施和活动。诚信计划公开，并由反腐局认真监督落实。

向公共机关赠与、赞助和捐赠的行为已受到特别关注。就赠与而言，不论价值多少，公职人员均不得收受金钱、证券或贵重金属。在黑山，公职人员仅允许接受礼仪和/或价值不超过 50 欧元的礼品。超过规定价值的礼品一律不得保留。若公职人员一年之内多次收受来自同一人的礼品，所有礼品的价值总和应为赠与人礼品的价值，该价值不得超过 50 欧元。另外，若代表公职人员签署赞助协议，以及公职人员代表国家机关签署赞助协议、接受捐赠等行为，影响了或可能影响国家机关的合法性、客观性及公正性,则此等行为应被禁止。违反此项规定,所签协议无效。黑山另有单独的法律条款,规定国家权力机关有义务向反腐败局报告所收到的赞助和捐赠的情况,保留相关记录并将这些记录在其官网上进行公示。

在保护举报人方面,黑山近年来取得了卓有成效的进展。举报人是指有正当理由怀疑公共利益受到危害的人,即怀疑存在腐败行为(即:违反法律法规、道德准则的行为,或可能对环境和人的生命、健康和安全造成威胁,对人身权利造成侵害,对国家或法人及自然人造成金钱或非金钱损失的行为,以及掩盖此类侵害行为的举动)的人。除举报人外,《反腐败法》还为举报协助人员和所有因与举报人关联而可能遭受损害的人提供保护。

就更广泛意义而言,打击反商业贿赂的制度还包括:

2014 年《游说法》——制定了游说和说客的原则,规定了游说监管办法和对违反法律的说客所采取的可行措施。

2014 年《政治实体融资和竞选法》——本法适用范围包括:对政治实体的日常工作或竞选活动的资金作出规定,对国家财产和资金在竞选期间的处置进行约束,并对此类融资和财产/资金处置进行监督。

2003 年《刑法》——根据该法,贿赂是指:请托人向公职人员送礼或提供其他好处,使公职人员在其职权范围内执行不应执行的公务或不执行应当执行的公务,或为请托人介绍贿赂的行为。贿赂还存在另一种形式,即:请托人向公职人员送礼或提供其他好处,使公职人员执行其本应执行的公务或不执行其不应执行的公务,或为请托人介绍贿赂的行为。

2. 反商业贿赂监督部门

黑山反腐局是黑山议会成立的自主独立的法律实体,其职能众多,包括:

① 在公共利益与个人利益发生冲突时发挥作用,并在公共职能执行方面进行约束;
② 审查公职人员提交的收入和财产报告;
③ 处理举报人的投诉等。

黑山反腐局由委员会和局长组成。委员会成员共 5 名,由黑山共和国议会选任,而局长则由议会通过公告选任。

3. 惩罚措施

现行的反商业贿赂法律框架包含大量轻罪规定。此外,《刑法》还规定了许多制裁措施:

(1)受贿
① 执行不应执行的公务,不执行应当执行的公务,最高处 12 年监禁;
② 对于涉及刑事案件等的受贿人,最高处 15 年监禁。

(2)行贿
通过行贿使公职人员执行不应执行的公务或放弃执行应执行的公务的,最高处 8 年监禁。

(二)项目承包

1. 许可制度

黑山规范公私合作伙伴关系的法律包括:2009 年《特许权法》(《特许权法》)和 2002 年《私营部门参与执行公共权力法》(《PPS 法》)。在撰写本文时,尽管关于公私合作伙伴关系的法律草案正在拟定中,但在黑山并没有规定公私合作伙伴关系的具体立法。因此,在相关部门的特定法律生效前,公私合作伙伴关系一直按特许经营管理。

公私合作伙伴关系领域的主管部门:

黑山特许权委员会——其职权包括:裁决与投标人评估和排名相关的申诉,保管登记册,批准延长特许经营期限,以及在没有实施特许程序的情况下,特许相关单位在经批准的开采领域内开采附生矿产资源(www.komisijazakoncesije.me/cg);

黑山议会——其职权为:根据 2009 年《国家物权法》(以下简称《物权法》)批准其管辖范围内的特许权(www.skupstina.me);

黑山政府——其职权为：根据《物权法》批准其管辖范围内的特许权（www.gov.me）；

地方市政府——其职权为：根据《物权法》批准其管辖范围内的特许权（uom.me）。

2. 招标和投标

国家政府或市政府（具体由《物权法》规定的资产处置权确定）制定的年度计划是授予特许权的依据。年度计划在国家政府或市政府的网站上公布。

国家政府及市政府授予的特许经营期限可长达 30 年，议会授予的特许经营期限可长达 60 年。特许经营可延长的最长期限，为最初授予期限的一半。

授权机构通过颁布特许令来启动特许程序。特许令内容包括：特许区域地理位置的相关信息，评估投资成本效益的基本参数、技术文件，特许权申请人在特许经营活动开始前应提交的批准文件、许可证明、同意书和执照清单，特许经营人获得特许经营权所应符合的资金和技术条件的清单，以及特许经营的最长或最短期限等。

特许权可根据按照如下规则执行的招标程序授予：

① 开放性公开竞争程序；

② 两阶段竞标程序，即：投标人筛选阶段和封闭竞标阶段；

③ 授予 3 年特许期限的，可采用加速竞标程序。

在上述所有程序中，授予部门将组成招标委员会来管理特许程序并对投标人进行排名。投标人有权对招标委员会的决定提出异议，特许委员会对申诉程序中的异议进行裁决。

即使特许计划中没有规定特许范围，利害关系方也可要求启动特许授予程序。如果授予单位认为其请求依据充分，利害关系方应缴纳颁发特许令（包括提交招标文件和起草特许权合同）所需的资金，支付招标委员会的工作费用及开展公开辩论所需的费用。若利害关系方未获得特许，除去购买特许行为的费用外，所缴纳的其他资金将被退还。

授予机关以黑山语公布特许活动（国际招标则使用英文），而投标书则应以招标文件中规定的语言提交。价格应以欧元为单位。

Montenegro

Authors: Marko Ivković, Savo Jasnić, Nikolina Kažić, Sonja Guzina
Translators: Chen Xuebin, Luo Min

I. Overview

A. General Introduction to the Political, Economic, Social and Legal Environment of Montenegro

Montenegro regained full national independence in 2006, on the merit of its citizens' decision, after it had constituted part of former Yugoslavia for nearly 90 years. Under its Constitution from 2007[1], Montenegro is a state with the republican form of government and the power is divided into three branches: legislative, executive and judicial power. The legislative power is performed by the Parliament, the executive by the Government and the judicial by the judiciary system – the courts.

The Parliament is a unicameral body that has 81 Members of Parliament (MPs). MPs are elected directly, on the basis of the general and equal electoral right and for the period of four years. The Parliament, among other things, adopts the Constitution, passes laws, approves the state budget and elects the Prime Minister and his cabinet.

The Government is the executive organ, chosen by the majority members of the Parliament and headed by the Prime Minister who is proposed by the President of Montenegro. The Government of Montenegro currently has three Deputy Prime Ministers and 19 ministers. The Government, inter alia, manages internal and foreign policy, submits the proposal of the laws to the Parliament, implements laws and adopts decrees and other regulations and concludes international treaties.

In Montenegrin judiciary system, there are courts of general jurisdiction and the specialized courts. The Supreme Court is the court of last resort in Montenegro and its main role is to secure uniform enforcement of laws by the courts. The Constitution provides that the Judicial Council appoints and revokes judges and presidents of the courts.

The President of Montenegro is elected in direct elections and by secret ballot, for the period of five years. His main competencies are to represent the country home and abroad, to propose the Prime Minister to the Parliament, to promulgate the laws. President of Montenegro also commands over the Montenegrin Army, on the basis of the Defence and Security Council's decisions.

Montenegro is member of the United Nations, the World Trade Organization, the OSCE and the Council of Europe. The political leadership, including main parts of the opposition, strive for EU membership. This is backed by a stable public acknowledgement. After concluding the Stabilization and Association Agreement in 2007, Montenegro gained official candidate status and on 29 June 2012 the EU launched the official accession negotiations. The talks initially focus on Chapters 23 and 24 of the EU Acquis, covering topics such as fundamental freedoms, judiciary, fight against corruption and organised crime. Montenegro also became member of NATO on 5 June 2017.

Although not part of the Eurozone, Montenegro has adopted the Euro unilaterally as a permanent foreign currency. In 2016, Montenegrin GDP was 3,954 million EUR with an actual GDP growth of 2.9% and GDP per capita was 3,354 EUR.[2] The Government of Montenegro, on the basis of the first nine months of output and the available indicators for the last three months, expects that GDP growth will reach 4.0 percent in 2017 or that GDP will reach 4,202.1 million EUR.[3]

Gross government debt of Montenegro on 31 December 2017 was 2,647.9 million EUR, 62.75% relative to

---

[1] Official Gazette of Montenegro 01/07 of 25 October 2007.
[2] Gross domestic product of Montenegro in 2016 as of 29 September 2017, availabe at: https://www.monstat.org/userfiles/file/GDP/bdp2016/Annual%20GDP%202016_eng_29_09_2017.pdf (last visited: 12 February 2018).
[3] Montenegro Economic Reform Programme 2018-2020 as of January 2018, availabe at: http://www.gov.me/en/homepage/Montenegro_Economic_Reform_Programme/(last visited: 12 February 2018).

the national GDP①, which is below European average, but debts were accumulating rapidly in the recent years. The public debt has risen since 2006 in global debt terms, when it was 701.1 million EUR, as well as in terms of GDP percentage, when it amounted to 38.3%.②

The average earnings (gross) in Montenegro in December 2017 were 768 EUR, while the average earnings without taxes and contributions (net) were 512 EUR.③ Unemployment rate in Montenegro is currently 20,71% or 48.040 unemployed persons.④

From the beginning of the privatization process nearly 90% of Montenegrin companies have been privatized, including banking, telecommunications and oil distribution. Privatisation procedure of the Electric Power Industry of Montenegro ("EPCG") has not been completed, because the Italian company A2A, which in 2009 acquired 47,3% of EPCG, activated the put option in July 2017, by which previously sold shares of EPCG became state property. The most important companies which still remain in the hand of the state are the Airports of Montenegro, Montenegro Airlines, Port of Bar, Montenegro Railways, Plantaže Vineyards.

The net Foreign Direct Investments in 2016 were 687 million EUR (70 million EUR less in comparison to 2015) and the largest investor in 2016 was Norway, whose investments represents 30% of total FDI, second place was taken by Italy and third place by Russian Federation. Montenegro has free trade agreements with the Russian Federation, Turkey, Ukraine, the EU, CEFTA, EFTA.

In 2014 the Government of Montenegro selected two Chinese companies – China Communications Construction Company (CCCC) and China Road and Bridge Corporation (CRBC) for the key infrastructure highway project – construction of the priority section of the national highway Bar-Boljare.

The real estate market in Montenegro was on rise, until amongst other causes the global financial crisis of 2008 led to a major setback in both property trade and development. Meanwhile, the market shows clear signs of recovery and is now driven by institutional investors.

With a territory of less than 14,000 m² alongside the western coast of the Adriatic Sea, it is home to 629,000 inhabitants. Property investors choose Montenegro mainly for the construction of tourist facilities, such as resort hotels and second home developments. With an average flight distance of two hours from all main European capitals, Montenegro offers 250 kilometres of Adriatic coast, lined with beaches and historic sites dating back to Roman, Ottoman, Venetian and Austrian-Hungarian reigns. The Bay of Kotor, known as the southernmost fjord of Europe, is in its entirety a UNESCO World Heritage site. Along with Biogradska Gora, one of the oldest national parks worldwide, Europe's steepest canyon, Tara, and various other natural settings, Montenegro also possesses a uniquely untouched mountain region.

Montenegro's legal system is a civil, continental type based on Roman law. In Montenegro, court decisions are not formal source of law, but lower courts may use higher court decisions as guidance.

B. The Status and Direction of the Cooperation with Chinese Enterprises Under the B&R

Montenegro has become part of the B&R since 2017, by concluding the Memorandum of Understanding between the Government of Montenegro and the Government of the People's Republic of China ("MoU") within the framework of Silk Road Economic Belt and 21st Century Maritime Silk Road Initiative. The MoU came into force on 14 May 2017 with a validity period of five years from its signing date, i.e.14 May 2022. The MoU will be automatically extended to additional five-year period provided that none of the parties terminates it three months before the expiry date.

There are number of bilateral agreements between Montenegro and China which constitute a legal framework for institutional and financial cooperation on several projects, such as the construction of Bar-Boljare highway (EUR 688,16 million loan from Exim bank) and reconstruction of Djurdjevica Tara bridge (EUR 2,65 million donation).

Montenegro has published the Agreement on consolidation of contractual relationship between Montenegro and the People's Republic of China, that had been concluded by exchange of diplomatic notes from 28 December 2012 and 31 December 2012. A list of concluded bilateral agreements is presented in the table below.

---

① Investor update as of 15 January 2018, available at http://www.mif.gov.me/en/news/180802/Investor-update.html?alphabet=lat (last visited: 6 February 2018).
② Public Debt of the Republic of Montenegro as of December 31st 2006, available at: http://www.mif.gov.me/en/sections/state-debt/88175/20157.html (last visited: 7 February 2018).
③ Avarage Earnings (wages) Decembar 2017 as of 26 January 2018, avaliable at http://monstat.org/eng/novosti.php?id=2429 (last visited: 12 Febrary 2018).
④ Available at: http://www.zzzcg.me/ (last visited: 14 February 2018).

1	Agreement between the Government of the Socialist Federal Republic of Yugoslavia and the Government of the People's Republic of China on Civil Air Transport, signed on 14 April 1972 in Belgrade
2	Protocol between delegation of the Federal Committee for Transport and Communications of the Socialist Federal Republic of Yugoslavia and the Civil Aviation delegation of the People's Republic of China, signed on 3 February 1978 in Belgrade
3	Agreement between the Government of the Socialist Federal Republic of Yugoslavia and the Government of the People's Republic of China on cooperation in the veterinary field, signed on 2 March 1979 in Beijing
4	Agreement between the Government of the Socialist Federal Republic of Yugoslavia and the Government of the People's Republic of China on the abolition of visas for holders of diplomatic, official and ordinary passports with a clause "business" and the abolition of visa fees, signed on 19 April 1979 in Beijing [①]
5	Protocol between the Civil Aviation Delegations of the Socialist Federal Republic of Yugoslavia and the Civil Aviation of the People's Republic of China, signed on 16 October 1980 in Beijing
6	Agreement on cooperation in maritime transport between the Government of the Socialist Federal Republic of Yugoslavia and the Government of the People's Republic of China, signed on 8 November 1980 in Beijing
7	Consular Convention between the Socialist Federal Republic of Yugoslavia and the People's Republic of China, signed on 4 February 1982 in Beijing
8	Agreement between the Federal Executive Council of the Assembly of the Socialist Federal Republic of Yugoslavia and the Government of the People's Republic of China on Cooperation in Customs Matters, signed on 23 January 1989 in Belgrade
9	Agreement between the Federal Government of the Federal Republic of Yugoslavia and the Government of the People's Republic of China on the avoidance of double taxation in relation to income and property taxes, signed on 21 March 1997 in Belgrade
10	Agreement between the Federal Government of the Federal Republic of Yugoslavia and the Government of the People's Republic of China on cooperation in the field of telecommunications and postal services, signed on 3 February 2000 in Beijing
11	Joint Statement on the Establishment of Diplomatic Relations between the Republic of Montenegro and the People's Republic of China, signed on 6 July 2006 in Beijing
12	Memorandum of Understanding between the Government of Montenegro and the Government of the People's Republic of China, signed on 6 July 2006 in Beijing
13	Agreement on economic and trade cooperation between the Government of Montenegro and the Government of the People's Republic of China, signed on 29 August 2006 at Sveti Stefan
14	Protocol on Cooperation between the Ministry of Foreign Affairs of the Republic of Montenegro and the Ministry of Foreign Affairs of the People's Republic of China, signed on 5 September 2007 in Podgorica
15	Agreement on Cooperation in the Field of Culture, Education, Social Sciences and Sport between the Government of Montenegro and the Government of the People's Republic of China, signed on 14 April 2009 in Beijing
16	Agreement on economic and technical cooperation between the Government of Montenegro and the Government of the People's Republic of China, signed on 24 September 2010 in Budva
17	Memorandum of understanding in the field of health between the Ministry of Health of Montenegro and the Ministry of Health of the People's Republic of China, signed on 24 April 2011 in Podgorica
18	Agreement on Scientific and Technological Cooperation between the Government of Montenegro and the Government of the People's Republic of China, signed on 16 May 2011 in Podgorica

---

① With reference to Article 1 of the Agreement, the visa exemption will only apply to holders of diplomatic and official passports; with reference to Article 2 of the Agreement, both parties agree to delete the entire article.

II. Investment

A. Market Access

a. Department Supervising Investment

a) Montenegrin Agency for the Promotion of Foreign Investments

Promotion of foreign investments is conducted by the Montenegrin Agency for the Promotion of Foreign Investments ("the Agency"). The Agency performs the following tasks: coordination and implementation of the Strategy for encouraging foreign direct investments in Montenegro; providing professional services to foreign investors; developing a database of targeted companies; presenting the advantages that Montenegro offers to investors; arranging direct contacts between foreign and domestic enterprises; cooperation with relevant international institutions for boosting foreign investments; monitoring the realization of foreign investments, cooperation with state agencies, local self-government bodies and state institutions in Montenegro with the aim to promote and support the realization of investments, etc.

Montenegro has signed 26 agreements on the mutual promotion and protection of investments. Agreements are signed with Austria, the Slovak Republic, Serbia, the Czech Republic, Finland, Denmark, Qatar, Belgium, Luxemburg, Macedonia, Malta, France, Netherlands, Israel, Cyprus, Romania, Ukraine, Hungary, Germany, Poland, Spain, Turkey, Switzerland, Azerbaijan, Moldova, the Hellenic Republic and the United Arab Emirates.

b) The Council for Foreign Investments

Guidance of strategic activities towards promotion and incitement of foreign activities are conducted by the Council for Foreign Investments.

b. Laws and Regulations of Investment

a) Laws

Having in mind that presentation of the Country as an investment destination transferred into individual sectors, the Parliament of Montenegro adopted the Foreign Investment Law in the middle of 2011. According to the Foreign Investment Law, a foreign investment may be a pecuniary investment, investment in goods, services, property rights and securities. A foreign investor may establish a company, a foreign legal branch, as well as acquire shares in the company, or purchase the company under the same conditions provided for nationals (national treatment).

b) Regulations

The Decree of Fostering Direct Investmentsoffers financial support to green-field and brown-field investors with the aim of encouraging new employment, increasing capacity and improving competitiveness.

c. Forms of Investment

Under the Decree of Fostering Direct Investments, investments are divided to investments in tangible assets and investments in intangible assets.

Investments in tangible assets consist of:

• Green-field investments, which include establishment of entirely new business, through construction of factories, plants, machines and equipment;

• Brown-field investments, which start on leased land with accompanying infrastructure (usually this implies abandoned military facilities, barracks, empty unused halls, warehouses) which the investor then restores back to their previous state, under condition that the period of lease is not shorter than ten years as of the day of concluding the agreement on use of funds.

Intangible investments are investments in patents and licenses in accordance with the regulations governing the state aid, for which amortization is calculated and which are used by the beneficiary of the funds and recorded in the balance sheets of the mentioned beneficiary of funds.

d. Standards of Market Access and Examination

As mentioned above, foreign investor may establish a company and invest in the company under the same conditions provided for national when establishing companies. However, investment in certain industries, such as armament and military equipment are subject to approval from the State Administration Body in charge of Foreign Trade Affairs. According to the Law on Ownership Rights, a foreigner cannot own natural resources, public goods, agricultural land, forests and forest land, cultural monuments of great and special importance, real estate in a land-border area up to a depth of one kilometer and islands, real estate located in an area which was declared by law as an area in which foreigners cannot have right of ownership in view of protecting the interests and security of the country. Exceptionally, foreigners may also acquire the right of ownership on agricultural land, forests and forest land having a surface area of up to 5,000m^2, only if a residential building located on that land is subject of the contract (sale, gift, exchange, etc.).

B. Foreign Exchange Regulation

a. Department Supervising Foreign Exchange

Central Bank of Montenegro ("CBM"), as the main monetary authority in Montenegro, controls the performance of foreign payment operations by banks and other providers of foreign payment operations. CBM also collects data on foreign current and capital operations between residents and non-residents and, on the basis of these data, produces balance of payments statistics.

b. Brief Introduction of Laws and Regulations of Foreign Exchange

The Law on foreign current and capital operations (Official Gazette of Montenegro no. 45/05, 62/08, 40/11, 32/13, 70/17) regulates cross-border payment transactions and makes a distinction between capital and current operations. Capital operations are those which aim is to make a cross-border transfer of capital, such as direct investments, investments in real estate, operations in securities and operations in money market instruments. On the other hand, current operations are operations between residences and non-residences which aim is not transfer of capital. Generally, the performance of current and capital operations, as well as the transfer of assets from Montenegro to abroad and from abroad to Montenegro, is under free regime.

c. Requirements of Foreign Exchange Management for Foreign Enterprises

Law on Foreign Current and Capital Operations regulates the performance of payment operations between residents and non-residents in euro and currency other than euro, the manner for transfer of property to Montenegro and out of Montenegro, as well as the capacity of residents to have ownership over means of payment denominated in currency other than euro.

In Montenegro, current and capital operations, including transfers of property from and to Montenegro, are under free regime, so the general provisions on payment services, prescribed by the Payment System Law (Official Gazette of Montenegro no.62/13, 06/14), apply on international transactions as well.

C. Financing

a. Main Financial Institutions

Main financial institutions in Montenegro are: the Central Bank of Montenegro, commercial banks, insurance companies, leasing companies and pension funds.

The Constitution of Montenegro defines the Central Bank as an independent organization which is responsible for the monetary and financial stability and functionality of the banking sector. The main objective of the Central Bank is to foster and maintain the financial system stability, a sound banking system, safe efficient payment system and to contribute to achieving and maintaining price stability, all in accordance with the principles of free and open market and freedom of entrepreneurship and competition.

Banks, as the main participants in the financial market, are regulated under the Banking Law. This law regulates the establishment, management, operation and control of the operations of banks, microcredit financial institutions and credit unions and regulates the conditions and control of the operations of persons engaged in credit and guarantee operations. Banks engage in the following activities: (i) issue guarantees and assume other off-balance sheet obligations; (ii) purchase, sell and collect claims (factoring, forfeiting, etc.); (iii) issue, process and record payment instruments; (iv) domestic and international payment transactions pursuant to the regulations governing payment systems; (v) financial leasing; (vi) operations involving securities, in accordance with the law governing the securities transactions; (vii) trade on its own behalf and for its own account or for a client's account with foreign means of payment, including exchange operations and financial derivatives; (viii) depositary operations; (ix) drafting analysis and communicating information and advice on creditworthiness of legal persons and entrepreneurs, and other issues with respect to the business operations; (x) offer safe deposit boxes; and (xi) activities that are part of banking operations, activities that are of ancillary nature in relation to the operations of that bank, and other activities directly related to the operations of that bank in accordance with the bank's articles of association.

Banks can only be established as a joint stock company, by natural and / or legal persons, both Montenegrin and foreign. The initial bank's capital cannot amount to less than EUR 5,000,000, and must be paid in full before registering the establishment of the bank before the Central Registry of Business Entities. A foreign bank may operate in Montenegro through a branch, with acquiring a prior approval for operation from the Central Bank. Furthermore, a foreign bank can, with approval from the Central Bank, establish its representative office in Montenegro. The foreign bank's representative office represents the interests of that foreign bank and cannot perform bank activities. There are currently 15 banks operating in the Montenegrin market.[1]

Another financial institution in Montenegro is insurance company. Insurance business consists of insurance activities, co-insurance activities, and reinsurance. Insurance, coinsurance and reinsurance activities may be performed by insurance or reinsurance company with their seat in Montenegro, and which are licensed by the independent regulatory authority–Insurance Supervision Agency of Montenegro. Exceptionally, (i) aircraft and maritime transportation above compulsory traffic insurance and (ii) foreign natural persons with permanent and temporary residence in Montenegro and their property may be insured with a foreign insurance company. Insurance brokerage activities, insurance agency activities and provision of ancillary insurance services may also be performed by foreign companies. Insurance services are classified into the following groups:

(i) group of non-life insurances;
(ii) group of life insurances; and
(iii) compulsory insurances.

According to the Montenegrin Law on Financial Leasing, financial leasing transaction is a legal transaction where the lessor agrees with the supplier acquisition of the ownership right on the leased object, pursuant tothe specification provided by and under the terms approved by the lessee. The lessor further agrees with the lessee the right to possess and use the leased object for the agreed period of time in return for payment of a fee in certain instalments. The disadvantages of this law are that the conditions for establishment, operation and control of leasing services, as well as of factoring services are not regulated.

In the process of EU accession, Montenegro shall fully harmonize regulations in the area of banking operations with the EU directives. Consequently, Montenegrin Parliament has adopted the Law on Financial Leasing, Factoring, Purchase of Receivables, Microcredit and Credit-Guarantee Operations which will be applied as of 11 May 2018 when the existing Law on Financial Leasing shall cease to apply. The new Law defines leasing and factoring providers as companies with their business seats in Montenegro, thus disabling non-residential companies to engage in these services, so that the Central Bank could have a full control of this business. Leasing and factoring providers may be established as joint stock or limited liability companies, with the initial capital amounting to EUR 125,000. Furthermore, the new Law recognizes the following types of factoring: (i) recourse factoring; (ii) non-recourse factoring; (iii) domestic factoring; (iv) international factoring; and (v) reverse factoring.

With regards to pension funds, after the Parliament of Montenegro adopted the Law on Voluntary Pension Funds in 2006, the third pillar of the pension reform was established, as a form of voluntary pension savings. The Securities Commission of Montenegro, as the supervisory authority on the capital market, developed the accompanying bylaws, which together with the law represent a good basis for the implementation of the reform. The Law on Voluntary Pension Funds sets out the conditions for the establishment of pension fund management companies and the organization of voluntary pension funds. So far, the Securities Commission of Montenegro, granted permission to DZU Atlas Penzija and DZU Market Investto operate pension funds, as well as to two voluntary pension funds: Penzija Plus and Market Penzija.

b. Financing Conditions for Foreign Enterprises

Foreign enterprises, i.e.foreign legal persons enjoy the same rights and obligations as domestic persons regarding the financing conditions. Any client (both domestic and foreign) of a bank or other provider of foreign payment operations is obliged to state the purpose of the payment for every payment made in foreign payment currency that exceeds the amount prescribed by the Central Bank.

D. Land Policy

a. Brief Introduction of Land-Related Laws and Regulations

a) Sources on Real Estate Law in Montenegro

(i) Law on Ownership Rights–regulates ownership rights and other property rights, possession of movable and immovable property, as well as the manner of acquisition, transfer, protection and cessation of these rights, the rules and procedures for establishing a mortgage, the types and registrations of mortgages, and stipulates the conditions under which foreign entities may acquire property in Montenegro.

(ii) Law on State Property - regulates the use, management, and disposal of things and other goods belonging to Montenegro or a local self-government.

(iii) Law on State Surveying and Cadastre of Immovable Property–regulates registration of immovable property-based rights.

(iv) Law on Spatial Planning and Construction–regulates the system of spatial planning, the manner and

---

[1] http://www.bankar.me/banke-u-crnoj-gori-lokacije-ekspoziture-bankomati/.

conditions for the construction of buildings, the legalization of illegal buildings and other issues of importance for the planning of space and the construction of facilities.

(v) Law on Immovable Property Tax and Law on Tax on Immovable Property Transactions—regulate the elements of tax on immovable property and obligation of payment and the manner of calculation of the tax on immovable property transactions, respectively.

(vi) Law on Expropriation – regulates the procedure on the expropriation of privately owned properties based on public interest against a fair compensation.

b) Types of Ownership and Other Property Rights

Types of ownership described by the Montenegrin law are single ownership, co-ownership, joint ownership and common hold. A single owner has exclusive control over a real estate, including the right of disposal and the establishment of mortgages and liens. Two or more owners sharing the freehold title to an undivided property are co-owners. The ownership relates to an ideal part of the whole property. Joint ownership evenly relates to undivided property, but unlike in case of co-ownership, the ownership parts are determinable, but not defined. Common hold pertains to the ownership of common areas of a building and the land, on which such building is situated. Real estate may be acquired on the basis of the law, private agreements, and decisions of judicial or administrative state bodies or by inheritance. Ownership rights are generally perpetual and not limited in time. Expropriations are legal only to the extent necessary for satisfying of the public interest and require fair compensation.

An easement is a non-possessory right to use and / or enter onto the real property of another without possessing it. The Montenegrin law distinguishes between easements in favour of another property and private easements. With the real easement in favour of another property, the owner of one property (dominant estate) is granted a right in respect of another property (servient estate), usually the performance of certain activities. Subject to the easement right may also be that the owner of the servient estate refrains from certain activities, which would affect the dominant estate. The Montenegrin Law on Ownership Rights does not give a final catalogue of real easements. The law does, however, regulate the most common types, such as the right of way, installation of utility lines, right to a window, the right to remain with a part of a building on the servient estate and similar. The real easement may be established by (i) legal transaction, (ii) court or administrative decision, and (iii) adverse possession. Regulated types of private easements are usufruct, right of use and right of dwelling.

Charges, meaning encumbrances on a property and restrictions of ownership rights, are registered with the Land Registry in accordance with the Law on State Surveying and Cadastre of Immovable Property. Mortgages are the most common means of security established on real estate in Montenegro. The subject of a mortgage may be any real estate property that can be monetarily valued and traded. A mortgage is established on the basis of (i) an agreement, (ii) a lien statement, which is the unilateral establishment of a mortgage in favour of a third person, (iii) a judicial decision, or (iv) by law.

b. Rules of Land Acquisition for Foreign Enterprises

Under the Law on Ownership Rights, foreign persons, both natural and legal, may acquire real estate in Montenegro under the same conditions as Montenegrin persons. However, there are a few exceptions. Foreigners may not acquire the ownership over (i) natural resources, (ii) goods in general use, (iii) agricultural land, (iv) forests and forest land, (v) cultural monuments of high importance and particular significance, (vi) immovable property within one kilometre of the national border and islands, and (vii) immovable property located in an area in which foreign ownership is prevented by law in order to protect national security interests. Exceptionally, a foreign natural person may acquire agricultural land, forests and forest land of up to 5,000 square meters, for as long as a residential building on such land constitutes part of the acquisition. Non-withstanding these restrictions, foreign persons remain entitled to short and long-term lease agreements; concessions; build, operate and transfer arrangements; and similar public-private arrangements.

However, under the Stabilization and Association Agreement that was concluded between the EU and Montenegro in 2007, foreigners originating from a EU member state have right to claim equal treatment with Montenegrin citizens in respect to the acquisition of real estates.

E. The Establishment and Dissolution of Companies

a. The Forms of Enterprises

On the basis of the Law on Commercial Entities, six forms of business organizing are possible: Entrepreneur; General Partnership (GP); Limited Partnership (LP); Joint Stock Company (JSC); Limited Liability Company (LLC) and Foreign Legal Branch.

a) Entrepreneur

An Entrepreneur is a natural person who performs independent business activities for the purpose of gaining profit. An entrepreneur is liable by his entire property for all the activities that he undertakes when doing business. If entrepreneurs do not perform activities under their name or title, they are obliged to register that name or title at the Central Registry of Commercial Entities ("the CRCE"). In case of changing the name or title, entrepreneur is obliged to report a change to the CRCE within 30 days as of the date when a change has been made. An entrepreneur has to be registered at the CRCE for statistical purposes by submitting a registration statement. The entrepreneur is issued a certificate of registration. However, this certificate is not an endorsement of eligibility for the business activity performance.

b) General Partnership ("GP")

General Partnership consists of two or more natural or legal persons (general partners) which have unlimited joint and individual liability. The existence of GP is not conditioned by its registration with the CRCE.

c) Limited Partnership ("LP")

A Limited Partnership is a partnership of one or more natural or legal persons called general partners, and one or more natural or legal persons called limited partners. General partners are, without limit, jointly and individually liable for all debts and obligations of the LP. Limited partners are liable for debts and obligations of the LP only to the extent of their contributions. The contributions of limited partners may be in money or in kind and in rights that are assessed. The existence of the LP is conditioned by its registration with the CRCE. Otherwise it shall be deemed to be a general partnership, in which case every limited partner becomes a general partner.

d) Joint Stock Company ("JSC")

A Joint Stock Company is a company of one or more founders, natural or legal persons. A JSC's share capital is divided into shares. A JSC's minimum share capital amounts to EUR 25,000. The founders are obliged to pay the initial capital in cash. Shareholders shall be liable for the obligations of the JSC to the extent of their contributions. Unlimited liability exists only in the case of gross violations of the provisions on JSC[①].

Organizational structure of JSC includes Shareholder's Assembly (mandatory), Board of Directors (mandatory), Executive Director (mandatory), Secretary of company (mandatory), and Auditor of company (mandatory). Executive director and Secretary of company may be the same person. In case of Sole Member JSC, the shareholder performs the function of the Shareholder's Assembly.

e) Limited Liability Company ("LLC")

A Limited Liability Company may be formed by one or two natural or legal persons (up to 30), by giving a pecuniary or non-pecuniary contribution in the company. A stake/quota of each shareholder is proportionate to the amount of his contribution. Each shareholder owns a single stake/quota (represented by percentages) in the company's share capital. A share in the company may entitle a member to have more than one vote. An LLC's minimum pecuniary share capital is EUR 1. Founders shall be liable for the obligations of the LLC to the amount of their contributions. Unlimited liability exists in the case of gross violations of the provisions on LLC.

Organizational structure of LLC includes Shareholder's Assembly (not mandatory), Executive Director (mandatory) and Board of Directors (not mandatory). In case of Sole Member LLC, the shareholder performs the function of the Shareholder's Assembly. Sole member may choose to be an Executive Director of the company or appoint another person to be an Executive Director.

f) Foreign Legal Branch ("FLB")

A Foreign Legal Branch is part of a company established and registered outside of Montenegro, which performs business on the territory of Montenegro. Unlike stock and limited liability companies, a FLB does not have the status of a legal entity, which is why the procedure for establishing a FLB is different to a certain extent.

The Executive Director is not a mandatory body of a FLB, which significantly reduces the costs that the Investor would have in that regard. In the FLB it is only necessary to appoint an authorized representative who must be a Montenegrin citizen, but that person does not have to be employed in the company. Although at least one authorized representative must be from Montenegro in accordance with our legal regulations, his powers may be limited by appointing other authorized representatives who would decide upon all major issues. Authorized representatives do not have to possess a residence or work permit, which significantly reduces the procedures for their appointment, but they must provide only a copy of the passport and give their consent to the appointment.

b. The Procedure of Establishment

This section deals only with the establishment of an LLC, since this is the most common form of registration in Montenegro. The incorporation of an LLC includes:

a) Registration Before the CRCE

The registration procedure is simple and it may last maximum four days, provided that the applicant submitted all the necessary documents. The documentation required for incorporation comprises the following:

---

① Comingling of assets or funds of the owners and the company; false and fraudulent registration; failure to keep the prescribed records; failure to submit information to CRCE and inadequate capitalization or insurance that are not proportionate to the risk associated with the type of business engaged; Law on Commercial Entities, article 4.

- Founding Decision / Founding Agreement, notarized;
- A Memorandum of Association ("MoA");
- Written consent to appointments of Executive Director and Authorized Representative (if applicable);
- Completed registration form provided by the CRCE;
- Evidence on payment of the registration fees – EUR 10 for registration before CRCE and EUR 12 for publication in the Official Gazette;
- Extract from the Central Depository Agency on securities of the founders;
- A copy of an identification document of the LLC's Founders / Executive Director / Authorized Representative (if applicable);
- If the Founder holds simultaneously more than 30% stake in other local companies, confirmation on good-standing and absence of criminal record of such companies is required.
- Power of Attorney, authorizing the Attorney/s to take all legal and procedural actions in the process of establishing a company, if the procedure is managed by him / them.

b) Opening of a Bank Account

Upon the registration of the company, in order to fulfil its elementary operations, the company shall open the bank account with the bank of the its choice. For this purpose the Executive Director and other persons, who shall be authorized for undertaking financial transactions are supposed to have their signatures verified before a Montenegrin public notary. Exceptionally, some banks accept a foreign notarization of the signatures.

c) Registration with the Tax Authority

Registration with the Tax Office is necessary in order to provide the company with its VAT Number (PDV). The VAT registration is not obligatory, but only when the company's yearly trade exceeds 18,000 Euro. Vat registration may be performed simultaneously with the registration of the company.

d) Registration of Workers at the Tax Administration

The employer must register workers at the Tax administration within eight days from the day of establishment of employment.

e) Making a Seal

Although there is no legal obligation of making a seal, such practice is commonly used in Montenegro. Making of seals is conducted by enterprises specialized for this activity. The production time for a stamp is one day, and it costs up to 20 EUR.

c. Routes and Requirements of Dissolution

The dissolution of a company in Montenegro is regulated by the Law on Commercial Entities. The process of dissolution of a company is called "Voluntary liquidation", which may be conducted only in the case when the financial resources of the company exceed its debts. It is a simple procedure, conducted by the company itself, with the minimal contact with state authorities.

a) Role of the Liquidator and Procedure Overview

Following the adoption of decision on liquidation of the company, the Shareholder's Assembly appoints a liquidator, nominated by the Board of Directors, whose task is to liquidate the company. The liquidator prepares the list of all assets and an accounting report on business from the beginning of the liquidation procedure, in particular the liquidation balance sheet. The liquidator shall file a request for a bankruptcy procedure in accordance with the law governing the insolvency of commercial entities, if he determines that the assets of the company are not sufficient to satisfy all claims of the creditors. During liquidation, any transfer of shares, disposal of assets or indebting without liquidator's consent is without any effect.

b) Completion of Liquidation

When all the ongoing businesses have been completed, the liquidator prepares a final report showing how the liquidation procedure has been conducted and how the assets of the company have been disposed of. The liquidator carries out the distribution of the remaining assets (if applicable) of the company to shareholders, in accordance with the rights attached to their shares. The liquidator is liable to the company and third persons for the damage resulting from his own actions.

c) Shorter Voluntary Liquidation

The Law on Commercial Entities foresees the shorter voluntary liquidation which can be initiated if there are no liabilities left and the liquidation decision was approved by all the members of the company. In such case, shareholders are without limit, jointly and severally liable for all debts and obligations of the company for the period of three years after the removal of the company from the CRCE.

d) Conclusion

The process of company liquidation in Montenegro can take from a few weeks (in case of a shorter voluntary liquidation) to several years if the claims are contested or other issues occur.

Liquidation Steps
• The Shareholder's Assembly makes a decision that the company should not continue the business and that it should be voluntarily liquidated.
• The decision of liquidation of a company must be registered with the CRCE by the company's management no later than five days since it was taken.
• During the general meeting where the decision is taken, a liquidator must be appointed in order to complete the process of liquidation. His details must also be registered at the CRCE.
• The liquidator delivers a notification related to liquidation to the creditors.
• The usual term of submitting the claims is not shorter than 60 days since the publication of the announcement.
• All the claims submitted after the expiration of the deadline must be satisfied after all the other claims submitted in time are fulfilled. All the remaining assets are divided between the entitled shareholders.
• A final report related to the way the process was performed and a balance sheet with all the company's assets must be presented in front of a final meeting of the shareholders. After being approved, a copy of the final report and a request of de-registration must be sent to the CRCE, but not later than 7 days from the meeting. The CRCE is sending a notification of de-registration to the Official Gazette and the company ceases to exist.

F. Merger and Acquisition

Merger and acquisition transactions in Montenegro are regulated by the Law on Commercial Entities (Official Gazette of Montenegro no.06/02, 17/07, 80/08, 40/10, 36/11, 40/11) and the Law on Takeover of Joint Stock Companies (Official Gazette of Montenegro no.18/11, 52/16) which prescribes specific rules for acquisition of JSC.

a. Merger

Merger of the JSC is one of the forms of corporate restructuring, under Montenegrin law.[1] The Law on Commercial Entities recognises two forms of merger:

(i) joining one or more companies to another existing company by transferring the entire assets and liabilities to that company which, in exchange, issues shares to shareholders of the companies being merged or

(ii) combining two or more companies and forming an entirely new entity which, in exchange, issues shares to shareholders of the companies being merged.

Merger, as every other form of corporate restructuring, may only take place when the assets of a company exceed its liabilities.

Documents required for merger are: decisions of the management boards and general shareholder meeting, the Merger Agreement and other corporate documents (new Memorandum of Association, financial statements etc.).

A merger is considered to be completed on the day of its registration with the Central Registry, which publishes the Merger Agreement in the Official Gazette of Montenegro.

The Law on Commercial Entities also prescribes simplified form of merger in case of merged company with the recipient company holding at least 90% of shares of that company.

If the transaction is subject to merger clearance, the companies involved in merger are obliged to disclose an exhaustive list of documents to the Agency for the Protection of Competition ("APC").

b. Acquisition

There is no foreign ownership restriction provided by these Laws, thus there are no differences between conditions for acquiring shares in Montenegrin companies for foreign investors and Montenegrin investors.

Acquisition transactions are usually done through a share purchase, and the Law on Commercial Entities prescribes that company cannot give loans, guarantees or provide any other form of financial assistance to a potential buyer of shares in that company. Such restriction does not apply to operations of the financial organisations, as well as to the acquisition of shares in order to give those shares to the employees of the relevant company. Shares could also be acquired on public auction, under the Law on Enforcement (Official Gazette of Montenegro no.36/11, 28/14, 20/15, 22/17, 76/17), but this method of acquisition is rare.

In certain industries (e.g.banking, insurance, media, telecommunications, concessions, energy etc.), Montenegrin law prescribes specific conditions (approvals) for acquiring shares in target company. For example, pursuant to the Law on Banks, CBM issues a prior approval for acquisition of a qualified shareholding or voting rights in Montenegrin banks or pursuant to the Law on Insurance, Insurance Supervision Agency of Montenegro issues a prior approval for

---

[1] Other form of corporate restructuring are: spin-offs, demergers and change of organisation form of the company.

acquisition of a qualified shareholding or voting rights in Montenegrin insurance companies.

In Montenegro, the main corporate entities involved in acquisition are LLCs and JSCs.

a) LLC

Transactions involving LLC are more flexible than those involving JSC. Pursuant to the Law on Commercial Entities, the sale of shares of an LLC is subject of pre-emptive rights of the LLC's members and LLC itself. Only if other LLC's members and LLC itself have declined to purchase the proposed share within 30 days from the day when the share was offered, the share may be transferred to a third party, but under no more favourable terms than those offered to LLC and its members. In the event of the share being transferred, the transferor and transferee will be jointly and severally liable to the LLC for the obligations associated with the membership.

The share is transferred by the signed and notarised Share Purchase Agreement, waiver of pre-emption rights (if applicable); and new Memorandum of Association. Each transaction must be registered before the Central Registry of Business Entities.

b) JSC

Takeover of the JSC is regulated by the Law on Takeover of Joint Stock Companies, which foresees the procedure of a public takeover bid. There are two types of this procedure: obligatory and voluntary.

Pursuant to the Law on Takeover of Joint Stock Companies, shares of up to 30% of the share capital of a listed JSC can be directly or indirectly acquired outside the offer process. In case an acquirer, alone or together with its related parties, directly or indirectly, acquires shares of a JSC, as a result of which the acquirer holds more than 30% of total voting shares of the target JSC, he is obliged to announce a takeover bid of shares of the target JSC. If the acquirer intends to acquire less than 30% of voting rights, he may announce a voluntary takeover bit, but he is not obliged to do so. A detailed obligatory and voluntary procedure of the public takeover bid are set in the Law with number of requirements that the acquirer must fulfil.

The Law on Takeover of Joint Stock Companies also prescribes certain exemptions from the takeover bid procedure.

In a takeover bid, all shareholders must be offered the same terms and conditions and receive the same information about the deal. Transactions involving JSC must be registered with the Central Registry of Commercial Entities and the Central Depositary Agency.

c. State-owned Company

The procedure for acquisition of state-owned company is regulated by the Law on Privatisation of Economy (Official Gazette of Montenegro no.23/96, 06/99, 59/00, 42/04), under which the Government of Montenegro established Council for Privatisation and Capital Projects.

Pursuant to the Law, privatisation shall be made in accordance with annual privatisations plans adopted by the Government of Montenegro, on the proposal of the Council for Privatisation and Capital Projects.

G. Competition Regulation

a. Department Supervising Competition Regulation

a) The Agency for the Protection of Competition

Agency for the Protection of Competition ("APC") supervises competition regulation in Montenegro, as an independent administrative body since 2013. APC performs competition protection, which includes assessment of restrictive agreements between undertakings, investigation and establishment of potential abuses of dominant position and assessment and control of mergers and acquisitions.

b) State Aid Control Commission

State Aid Control Commission ("SACC"), appointed by the Government of Montenegro, controls the compliance between reported and granted state aid. However, pursuant to the Proposal of the Law on Amendments to the Law on Protection of Competition, which has already reached Parliament[1], APC will soon take over the control of state aid from the SACC.

b. Brief Introduction of Competition Law

a) The Law on Protection of Competition

The Law on Protection of Competition (Official Gazette of Montenegro no.44/12) was adopted as a result of harmonization with relevant EU rules and contains the basic rules on restrictive agreements, abuses of dominant positions and merger control.

---

[1] Proposal of the Law on Amendments to the Law on Protection of Competition, as of 28 December 2017, available at: http://zakoni.skupstina.me/zakoni/web/dokumenta/zakoni-i-drugi-akti/341/1628-10215-08-1-17-1.pdf (last visited: 14 February 2018).

b) The Law on State Aid Control

The Law on State Aid Control (Official Gazette of Montenegro no.74/09, 57/11) prescribes the conditions and the procedure for granting and controlling the use of state aid, on the principles of market economy and preservation of competition.

c) Sector-specific Laws

Certain sector specific regulations cover some aspects of antitrust and competition: i.e.The Media Act, the Electronic Communications Act, the Energy Act, while laws on agriculture and fisheries prescribed special state aid rules, since The Law on State Aid Control does not regulates these areas.

d) International Sources

The Stabilisation and Association Agreement between Montenegro and the EU, which has been concluded in 2007, contains the obligations of Montenegro in the area of competition and state aid, as well as in the area of state aid control activities. The Constitution of Montenegro prescribes the principle of supremacy of international law over national law, according to which the ratified and published international agreements and general accepted rules of international law are an integral part of the national legal order and they have supremacy over the national legislation and are directly applicable when differing from national legislation. According to this principle, the Stabilization and Association Agreement prevails or is directly applicable in case of conflict with national legislation, or in the absence of relevant national legislation in the area of the competition and the state aid.

e) By-laws

The Government of Montenegro has adopted many legally binding regulations in the area of the state aid, but the main is the Decree on detailed criteria, conditions and manner on granting state aid (Official Gazette of Montenegro no.27/10, 34/11, 16/14). On the basis of this Decree, Ministry of Finance has adopted Rulebook on the List of State Aid Rules aid (Official Gazette of Montenegro no.35/14, 02/15, 38/15, 20/16) which contains published translations of the EU secondary state aid legislation. In this manner EU secondary legislations were directly implemented into the Montenegrin legal system.

In the area of competition there are also many regulations adopted by the Government, such as: Decree on group exemption of vertical agreements from prohibition (Official Gazette of Montenegro no.13/14); Decree on block exemption of agreements in road and railroad traffic and traffic in inland waters and consortium agreements in maritime shipping lanes traffic (Official Gazette of Montenegro no.59/14); Rules of procedure on content and manner of application for individual exemption from restrictive agreements (Official Gazette of Montenegro no.18/13); Rules of procedure on manner and criteria for definition of relevant market (Official Gazette of Montenegro no.18/13).

c. Measures Regulating Competition

a) Antitrust and Competition

Montenegro's APC performs assessment of restrictive agreements between undertakings, investigation and establishment of potential abuses of dominant position and assessment and control of mergers and acquisitions. It not authorised to impose fines, it may only initiate proceedings before a misdemeanour court.

(i) Restrictive agreements

Pursuant to the Montenegrin law, agreements[1] preventing, restricting or distorting competition on the relevant market, such as market sharing agreement, price fixing agreement, and arrangement on sharing sources of supply or on limitation of supply, are prohibited, null and void.

The restrictive agreements may be horizontal (agreements between existing and / or potential undertakings operating at the same level of the production or distribution chain) and vertical (agreements on conditions of supply, purchase, sale or resale, between existing and / or potential undertakings operating at a different level of the production or distribution chain).

Restrictive agreements may be exempted from the prohibition if the APC allows individual exception on the request of the parties, if the agreement fulfils the conditions for the "block exemption", prescribed by the Government or if the agreement is of minor importance in accordance with the Law prescribed conditions.

(ii) Abuse of dominance

According to the Law on Protection of Competition, there is a presumption of dominant position in the market of products, if a company's market share in the relevant market exceeds 50%. There is also a presumption of collective domination if there is no significant competition between two or more companies and if their aggregate share in the relevant market exceeds 60%. In all other cases, when the share in the relevant market is lower than above mentioned percentages, the APC must prove that a company is dominant.

---

[1] Restrictive agreements shall include written or verbal arrangements, contracts, single provisions of agreements, explicit or tacit agreements, concerted practice, as well as decisions by associations of undertakings.

Law on the Protection of Competition prohibits dominant company from abusing its market power, which includes imposing unfair purchase or selling prices or other unfair trading conditions, limiting production, markets or technical development to the prejudice of consumers, applying dissimilar conditions to equivalent transactions with other undertakings, thereby placing them at a competitive disadvantage, making the conclusion of contracts subject to acceptance of supplementary obligations which, by their nature or according to commercial usage, have no connection with the subject of such contracts.

(iii) Merger control

Pursuant to the Montenegrin law, concentrations for the purposes of merger control present the following:

• a merger of two or more independent undertakings or parts thereof in the relevant market;

• an acquisition, by one or more natural persons already controlling at least one undertaking, or by one or more undertakings, of indirect or direct control of the whole or a part of another undertaking;

• two or more independent undertakings establishing a new undertaking or acquiring joint control of the existing undertaking that operates independently on a lasting basis and performs all the functions of an autonomous undertaking (joint venture).

A concentration must be implemented only on the basis of the approval that is issued by the APC on the request of the undertakings involved, which must be submitted if:

• the combined aggregate annual turnover of at least two parties to the concentration achieved in the market of Montenegro exceeds 5 million EUR in the preceding financial year; or

• the combined aggregate annual worldwide turnover of the parties to the concentration achieved in the preceding financial year exceeds 20 million EUR, if at least one party's turnover in Montenegro achieved 1 million EUR in the same period. [1]

The request referred to shall be submitted no later than 15 days from the first of the following actions: conclusion of the agreement or contract; announcement of the public call or bid or closing of the public bid; or the acquisition of control.

In exceptional circumstances, the APC may independently initiate a merger control procedure if a concentration that had not been notified (and was not notifiable, according to the financial thresholds criteria), results in the merged undertakings having a market share above 60%.

The parties are obliged to suspend the implementation of concentration until the APC issues the decision approving the intended concentration. If the APC does not render a decision in deadlines prescribed in the Law, the transaction is deemed to be clear.

Based on published information, in 2017 the APC rendered 37 merger decisions.

b) State Aid

The Law on State Aid Control defines state aid as "expenditures, reduced revenues or reduced assets of the State or municipality that distort or may distort free competition in the market and that may affect the trade between Montenegro and the European Community or a member state of the CEFTA, by conferring a more favourable market position on certain economic entities, products or services."

Pursuant to the Law, state aid which distorts or may distort free competition in the market is prohibited, unless it is permitted under the law or unless the aid is not considered to be the state aid. Forms of granted state aid are: subsidies, fiscal reliefs, state or municipal guarantee, subsidy of loans' interest rate, giving gain or dividends of the State or municipality for grantor's development projects to economic entities, discharge of debt, sale of immovable property by the State or municipality at a price lower than the market price or purchase at a price higher than the market price.

The SACC must be notified about any state aid, by the state aid grantor[2], prior the state being awarded. The notification may refer to an individual aid (granted to a certain beneficiary for a certain purpose or certain project) or to a state aid scheme (the act which stipulated the conditions on the basis of which state aid may be granted to potential beneficiaries).

The SACC is obliged to adopt the decision on compliance of the state aid with the Law within the 30 days from the day of submission the notification.

H. Tax

a. Tax Regime and Rules

a) Applicable Regulations

(i) Law on Personal Income Tax;

---

[1] There are special rules for turnover which apply on banks, insurance companies and other financial institutions.

[2] State aid may be granted on national and local levels, from the state authorities, local self-government authorities and legal entities in charge of the management of state resources.

(ii) Law on Corporate Profit Tax;
(iii) Law on Value Added Tax;
(iv) Law on Immovable Property Tax;
(v) Law on Tax on Immovable Property Transactions;
(vi) Law on Tax Administration;
(vii) Law on Contributions for Compulsory Social Insurance;
(viii) Law on Excise Taxes;
(ix) Customs Law.

b) General Rules

Ministry of Finance, through Tax Administration, is the acting body of the Montenegrin Government in regulating and collecting taxes. Tax year corresponds to the calendar year, and a taxpayer is obliged to file a tax return at the end of the year.

The taxpayer of personal income tax is a resident or non-resident natural person who realizes taxable income on the territory of Montenegro. The resident is a natural person who has a residence or business seat in Montenegro, or is staying in the territory of Montenegro for more than 183 days during the tax year.

Taxpayer of corporate income tax is a resident, or a non-resident legal person performing an activity for the purpose of gaining profit. This profit can be realized in Montenegro by a resident / non-resident or outside of Montenegro by a resident legal person. The Central Bank of Montenegro, public funds and public institutions founded by Montenegro or local Municipalities are exempted from paying the corporate income tax.

c) Double Taxation Treaty

Montenegro has concluded Double Taxation Treaties with 43[1] countries, including People's Republic of China. On 3 April 2014 the Government of Montenegro and People's Republic of China have concluded an Agreement on consolidation of the contractual situation by virtue of which 18 agreements that have been concluded while Montenegro was a part of the Union and Federation have been consolidated. One of those agreements is the Agreement between the Federal Government of the Federal Republic of Yugoslavia and the Government of the People's Republic of China on the Avoidance of Double Taxation in Relation to Income Tax and Property Tax, signed on March 21, 1997 in Belgrade. As per the Montenegrin Constitution, confirmed and ratified international treaties supersede national laws in the matters regulated by the treaties.

b. Main Categories and Rates of Tax

Tax	Tax Rate			
Personal Income Tax (personal earnings; self-employment activity; property and property-based rights; capital; capital gains[1])	9% and 11% (11% is applicable when monthly average earnings exceed the average monthly gross salary realized in the previous year in Montenegro)			
Social Contributions		Pension	Health	Unemployment
	Individuals	15%	8.5%	0.5%
	Employers	5.5%	4.3%	0.5%
Corporate Income Tax	9%			
Value Added Tax	Standard rate–21% Lower rate–7% and 0%			
Property Tax	0.25%–1.0%, but the local municipalities may determine a higher or a lower rate			
Property Transaction Tax	3%			
Under Chinese - Montenegrin Double Taxation Treaty	5%–dividends 10%–interest and royalties			

---

[1] Double Taxation Treaty with India was concluded while Montenegro was still part of Serbia and Montenegro union, and while Montenegro did partake in the negotiations preceding the Treaty, after gaining independence the Treaty was not ratified (source: Ministry of Finance, http://www.mif.gov.me/biblioteka/ugovori).

c. Tax Declaration and Preference

Entrepreneurs who make investments in fixed assets for their own business have the right to calculate the tax deduction in the amount of 50% of these investments, and up to 70% of the total tax liability for a certain tax period. The Tax Administration may authorize the tax to be paid in an annual lump sum for the taxpayer whose total turnover (revenue) in the year preceding the year for which the tax is determined (or planned turnover) is less than EUR 18,000.

Tax exemptions and benefits in view of corporate income tax are granted to newly-established legal entities in economically underdeveloped municipalities that perform production activities during the first three years from the beginning of those activities.

I. Securities

a. Brief Introduction of Securities-Related Laws and Regulations

In December of 2017 Montenegro adopted the Capital Markets Law for the purpose of harmonizing domestic legislation with the EU acquis. The Capital Markets Law regulates the conditions for the establishment and operation of the capital market; types of financial instruments; issuance of securities; organization and business of investment companies; regulated capital market; secondary trading of securities; registration of financial instruments, clearing, settlement and registration of transactions of financial instruments; publication of financial and other data and reporting of issuers and other participants in the capital market; ban on abuses in the capital market; as well as other issues of importance for the work of the capital market. The capital market operates through a multilateral system which includes the (i) Multilateral Trading Platform – MTP; (ii) Organized Trading Platform – OTP, and (iii) Off Stock Market (OTC).

Central Depository Agency (CDA) acts as a central register and securities depository authority. The Central Depository Agency performs registration of securities, clearing and settlement operations of concluded transactions with securities and other transactions related to securities. Information on concluded purchase agreements is submitted to the Central Depository Agency, where each transaction is registered and transfer of ownership of securities is carried out. In order to become owner of securities, one must register for the securities account with the CDA. An excerpt from CDA registry is the sole and exclusive evidence of ownership of securities.

The Stock Exchange performs the activities of the securities market. The Exchange operates in a way that enables efficient connection of supply and demand for securities and public dissemination of information about the securities market. Securities are traded in accordance with the strict rules required for each market participant. The relationship between sellers and customers is indirect–through investment brokers (broker-dealer companies and custodian banks).

In order to sell or purchase securities, services of an investment broker, such as broker-dealer companies and custodian banks must be used. Investment intermediaries perform mediation activities in the purchase and sale of securities and other securities transactions in accordance with the Capital Markets Law. Investment intermediaries have costs related to the activities they perform and cover them by charging fees for their services. This fee includes both a stock exchange fee and a Central Depository Agency fee for the transaction.[2]

b. Supervision and Regulation of Securities Market

Management of the capital market is performed by the Commission for the Capital Market of Montenegro – Securities Commission as an independent regulatory body. Organizers of market must apply with the Commission for the authorization to perform their duties.

c. Requirements for Engagement in Securities Exchange for Foreign Enterprises

Regarding the purchase and sale of securities on the Montenegrin capital market, foreign natural and legal persons enjoy the same rights as Montenegrin persons, without any restrictions. The conditions and procedure for foreign natural and legal persons for securities exchange are set out in the Capital Markets Law, the Rules on Stock Exchange and the Rules on Brokerage.

J. Preference and Protection of Investment

a. The Structure of Preference Policies

a) State Grants

According to the Decree of Fostering Direct Investments, subsidies in manufacturing and services sector may

---

[1] Tax on interest income earned by a non-resident individual amounts to 5%.
[2] Information on the investments intermediaries may be found on the web sites of Securities Commission www.scmn.me, and stock exchange www.scmn.me.

be granted for investment projects with a minimum investment value of EUR 250,000 or 500,000 and which enable the employment of at least 10 or 20 employees. The applicable condition in both cases depends on the location of the project – less demanding requirements are applied for the less developed municipalities. Investment project and employment of new employees must be completed within the period of three years from the conclusion of the agreement on use of funds. Such period may be extended up to five years at most, subject to approval from the Government.

Amount of funds for fostering investments that may be granted pursuant to the Decree of Fostering Direct Investments is limited to 50%, 60% or 70% of the total value of investment, depending on whether the beneficiary is classified as a large, medium or small business entity. Maximum amount of allocated funds for capital investments must not exceed 17% of the total value of investment project. In addition, the beneficiary is entitled to subsidies to cover the cost of newly hired employees' salaries. The amount of each grant depends on the criteria for granting of funds for fostering investments.

It should be noted that only companies registered in Montenegro are eligible to receive funds for fostering investments.

b) Advantages of Investing in Montenegro

There are number of benefits available to investors. These include the following:
- Political and economic stability;
- Euro as the national currency;
- Favourable tax environment;
- The achieved level of privatization;
- High level of realized economic reforms and created new institutions;
- Restructured and privatized banking system;
- Developed telecommunication infrastructure;
- Relatively highly educated workforce and relatively low wages;
- Continuous improvement of the labour market in the field of labour relations;
- Free access to EU markets; application of the CEFTA agreement; Free Trade Agreement between Montenegro and EFTA countries; and the FTA with Russia and Turkey;
- Simple procedure for creating a company (four days and founding capital of EUR 1);
- Relatively low customs rates;
- National treatment of foreign investors;
- Achieved level of incentive fiscal, regulatory and financial measures;
- Free transfer of reinvested earnings and payments abroad;
- Exemption from paying income tax (8 years) for the establishment of a legal entity in less developed municipalities;
- Avoidance of double taxation (Double Taxation Avoidance Treaty with over 40 countries); and
- Membership in the WTO;
- Membership in NATO

In addition, some local government units have defined additional exemptions and deductions.

b. Support for Specific Industries and Regions

Funds for fostering investments are used for financing investment projects in manufacturing and services sector, except for primary agricultural production, manufacturing of synthetic fibers, transport including the transport of passengers in air, maritime, road or railroad traffic and via inland waterways or commercial transport of cargo services, games of chance, trade, primary production of coal and steel, production of electric power, oil and gas, tobacco and tobacco products, weapons and ammunition, production of genetically modified organisms and hazardous waste.

Regions where investors are encouraged to invest by way of lower eligibility requirements to benefit from state funds are local self-government units from the northern or central region of the country, apart from the Capital city of Podgorica.

c. Special Economic Areas

a) Business Zones

Several local self-governments in Montenegro have developed business zones (Berane, Bijelo Polje, Kolašin, Mojkovac, Nikšić, Cetinje, Ulcinj and Podgorica),in which investors may invest under favourable terms such as:
- Payment of utility or other charges under the favorable conditions;
- Bargain price of lease / purchase of premises within business zones;
- Reduction or exemption from surtax on individual income;

- Lowering tax rates on real estate;
- The possibility to define a favorable model of public-private partnership; and
- Equipping with infrastructure areas which do not have a developed infrastructure.

b) Free zones

The regime of performing activities in free zones differs from the general conditions of business in the Country in the field of foreign trade regime, foreign exchange regime, tax regime, customs regime and foreign investment regime. Some of the most significant advantages for the work in free zone are:
- All business activities can be carried out in the Free zone (except for those jeopardizing environment, people's health, material goods and soil safety);
- Complete equality of investors from abroad is secured in terms of investment rights, acquisition of ownership of the built facilities and activities organization in them;
- The use of ground and facilities in the free zone is enabled on the basis of long term lease in accordance with fixed conditions;
- Customs, customs duties, and value added tax are not paid for the goods imported into the Zone, regardless of the type of imported goods and their purpose in the Zone;
- Goods imported in the zone can stay there indefinitely;
- Goods can be temporarily taken out from the Zone to the remaining part of the country or imported in the Zone from the remaining part of the Country to be processed, installed, tested, surveyed, repaired, commercially presented etc;
- The goods dispatched to the remaining part of Montenegro to be further traded are subject to payment of customs, customs duties and VAT at the moment of leaving the Zone, where the customs and customs duties are paid only for the foreign components in the goods;
- Zone user does not pay profit tax for legal entities; and
- Investing the capital in the Zone area and transfer of profit are free.

III. Trade

A. Department Supervising Trade

The Ministry of Economy is currently in charge of monitoring and enhancing internal and foreign trade in Montenegro. In particular, within this governmental body there is a separate sector for international trade cooperation which deals with questions regarding the international trade regime and the sector for regional and multilateral cooperation.

B. Brief Introduction of Trade Laws and Regulations

This Law on Internal Trade regulates internal trade, trade requirements and forms, protection against unfair competition in trade, and supervision over the application of such a law. On the other hand, the Law on Foreign Trade deals with foreign trade and is divided into 4 parts i.e.(i) general provisions, (ii) foreign trade in goods, (iii) foreign trade in services and (iv) trade remedies.

The following was adopted under the Law on Foreign Trade:
(i) the Decree for the implementation of Law on foreign trade; and,
(ii) the Control List for Export and Import of Goods.

In addition to the mentioned, there are several laws which further regulate trade in Montenegro, such as the Law on Consumer Protection, Law on the Safety of Products, the Law for Construction Products, etc.

C. Trade Management

In December 2006, Montenegro signed the Central European Free Trade Agreement (CEFTA), intended to eliminate all customs restrictions for industrial and agricultural products in member states by 2010. The Parliament ratified CEFTA in 2007, and it took effect in Montenegro (and simultaneously in Albania, Macedonia, Moldova, etc.). Bulgaria, the Czech Republic, Hungary, Poland, Romania, Slovakia, and Slovenia were already parties to the Agreement. A Free Trade Agreement (FTA) with the European Free Trade Association (EFTA) countries (Switzerland, Norway, Iceland, and Liechtenstein) was signed in November 2011. Although the four EFTA countries are small, they are the leaders in several sectors vital to the global economy.

Montenegro signed a Preferential Trade Agreement with the EU. The European Union has taken steps to stimulate the export of goods among the countries in the region through the establishment of autonomous trade preferences (ATP), which provide duty-free entry for over 95 percent of goods. Exemptions include wine, meat, and steel. Products originating from Montenegro are generally admitted into the EU without quantitative restrictions and are exempted from custom duties and charges. The products exempted from the free import regime are agricultural products, "baby beef " products, and textile products.

D. The Inspection and Quarantine of Import and Export Commodities

In accordance with Montenegrin legislation, the following protective measures are applied in Montenegro with regard to the inspection and quarantine of import and export commodities:

the Protection of environment (protection of plants, animals, waste, batteries and accumulators and electronic equipment, specific inspections, quarantine, permits and licences are required for all commodities that fall into the above categories);

Phytosanitary inspection (when importing plants, flowers, fruits and vegetables in the customs area of Montenegro, it is mandatory to have an approval issued by the Ministry of Agriculture, Forestry and Water Management - Phytosanitary Directorate);

and, the Food and veterinary control, where all commodities concerned with this regulation must obtain the appropriate permits and licenses and undergo specific customs inspections.

E. Customs Management

The system of customs in Montenegro is governed by the Customs Law and the Law on Customs Tariffs, and a number of secondary regulations with customs laws governing the customs tariffs, customs procedures and payment of customs which have been issued on the basis of these laws.

In order to be placed on Montenegrin market, foreign goods have to be imported in Montenegro and go through customs import procedure. The goods have to be included in the customs declaration, on the form prescribed by the Montenegrin regulations. The declaration should contain sufficient information (type of goods, quantity, value, etc.) for the calculation of customs duties. Information in the customs declaration has to be supported by appropriate documents, such as agreements, invoices, purchase orders, waybills, etc.

The importer on record may only be a Montenegrin entity. Foreign entities participating in the customs procedure have to appoint their representative in Montenegro.

Applicable customs rates are established by the Law on Customs Tariff, and depend on the type and purpose of the goods. The customs rates may be lower or eliminated on the basis of the free trade agreement between Montenegro and the country of origin of the goods which are being imported. Montenegro has several free trade agreements, including ones with the EU, regional countries (CEFTA) and Russia which provide for the preferential treatment of goods originating from these countries.

Two main modalities of the import regime in Montenegro are the permanent import and temporary import.

Permanently imported goods are granted the status of domestic goods and therefore may be placed on the Montenegrin market. The importer on record is required to pay the full amount of customs duties and import VAT due on the import of goods under the general rules.

Temporary import is allowed for goods which are brought in Montenegro with intention to be exported in unchanged condition. The customs authorities decide about the duration of the temporary import, provided that it cannot exceed 24 months. As an exemption, this deadline may be extended if it's necessary to realize the purpose of import.

IV. Labour

A. Brief Introduction of Labour Laws and Regulations

Under Montenegrin law there is a hierarchy of labour regulations which starts with the Labour Law, the General Collective Bargaining Agreement–for the territory of Montenegro as a whole, the Special Collective Bargaining Agreement for the respective business branch, and the Collective Bargaining Agreement applicable for specific employer.

The Labour Law establishes a general framework for the legal regime applicable to labour relationships and a number of nominal employment rights and entitlements. The Labour Law applies to all employees–nationals and non-nationals–who work in the territory of Montenegro for domestic or foreign legal entities or individuals.

The General Collective Bargaining Agreement–In Montenegro, there is the GCBA in place, enacted in 2015, which is applicable equally to all employers.

The Special Collective Bargaining Agreement–there are a number of Special CBAs, which are applicable to all employers within a certain industry. They are executed between the representative trade unions and employers' associations.

Company's Collective Bargaining – is executed at the level of a specific company and regulates rights, obligations and responsibilities based on employment in the respective company.

B. Requirements of Employing Foreign Employees

a) Work Permit

In case a foreigner intends to work in Montenegro, he / she should obtain the Residence and Work Permit or the Confirmation of Work Registration, depending on the planned period of the work.

b) Application Procedure

The Residence and Work Permit is issued for the purpose of local employment, seasonal works or secondment to Montenegro (secondment can be in relation to the services provided in Montenegro or in relation to an inter-company move of the seconded foreigner).

The permit is one overall document issued by the Ministry of Internal Affairs, upon the submission of certain documents, which, amongst other, prove that the foreigner has sufficient assets for life, accommodation, health insurance and a justified reason for residing in Montenegro (e.g.the offer for employment / seasonal works, the agreement on secondment etc.). The Ministry for Internal Affairs is supplemented with discretion rights and may require some additional documents it deems necessary.

Once the documents are submitted, the police will issue the Permit within approximately 20 days from the date of submitting the documents and the foreigner is obliged to take over the issued Permit within 5 days afterwards. If the foreigner fails to take the Permit in the mentioned deadline it will be considered that he / she has given up on the submitted application.

The Permit can be issued for no longer than one year, after which it can be prolonged for additional two years (the Permit for seasonal works is issued for up to 6 months within one year).

c) Social Insurance

Upon obtaining the Permit the employer is required to conclude the employment contract. Afterwards, the local employer is obliged to register the foreigner as its employee with the Montenegrin Tax Authority for mandatory social security insurance within 8 days from the conclusion of the employment agreement.

Note that in Montenegro there is a changeable annual quota for Permits that may be issued within one calendar year. Once the quota is reached, no additional Permits can be issued – except for a director registered in Montenegro or for managerial positions.

C. Exit and Entry

In general, foreign citizens are required to obtain a visa in the nearest consular office or embassy of Montenegro in order to be able to enter Montenegro, unless a specific non visa regime is applied to their country of origin. For example, non-visa regime applies to citizens of EU countries, Serbia etc. who may enter Montenegro freely without visa, with a valid passport and reside in it up to 90 days within a 180 days period.

a) Visa Types

Airport transit visa (A) may be issued to a foreigner for one or several transits through the airport international transit area, between internationals flights, without entry into the territory of Montenegro, with a validity period of up to 3 months. As a general rule, a foreigner who does not leave the international transit area in between flights at a Montenegro airport or on international flights does not require a visa. The Government of Montenegro may stipulate that nationals of certain countries, for national security and legal order reasons, shall require an airport-transit visa.

Transit visa (B) may be issued for one, two or exceptionally several transits through the territory of Montenegro, with a validity period of up to 6 months. On the basis of a transit visa, a foreigner may stay in Montenegro for a period of up to 5 days upon each journey. A transit visa may be issued to a foreigner if he / she has secured entry into the state to which he / she is traveling. This visa may be individual and collective.

Short stay visa (C) may be issued for one, two or multiple entries into Montenegro for tourist, business, personal or other purposes. Continuous stay or the total duration of consecutive stays may not exceed 90 days in the period of 6 months, counting from the date of first entry. The validity period of Visa C for multiple entries is up to one year. Exceptionally this type of visa may be issued for a longer period of validity, but no longer than five years. Short stay visas may be issued to a group of foreigners (a collective visa). The validity period of a collective visa cannot exceed 30 days and it may be affixed to a group passport.

Long stay visa (D) may be issued to a foreigner for one, two or multiple entries into Montenegro, intending to stay in the territory of Montenegro over 90 days, but no longer than 6 months in the period of one year, counting from the date of first entry. This type of visa may be granted to a foreigner:

- intending to stay in Montenegro in order to perform business or other activities, provide advisory expert activities as agreed by the Agreement on business and technical cooperation, on a long-term production cooperation, and on transfer technologies and foreign investments; and,

- coming to serve in Montenegro as a member of a foreign diplomatic and consular representative office to Montenegro or an international organizations accredited to Montenegro, a member of economic and cultural representative office, as well as to the members of his family, i.e.members of his household holding diplomatic or official passports.

b) Restrictions for Exit and Entry

A foreign person shall not be permitted to enter Montenegro, if, inter alia, he / she uses another person's, invalid, i.e.false passport or other document; he / she fails to satisfy the requirements stipulated in the law; this is required by reasons of national security, public order and public health; a pronounced protective measure of expulsion is in force, or a security measure of deportation of a foreign citizen from the state, protective measure of deportation of a foreign citizen from the territory of Montenegro or his / her stay is cancelled; etc.

D. Trade Union and Labour Organizations

Freedom to organize in trade unions and free trade union activity is guaranteed to employees, in order to protect the rights and promote professional and economic interests of employees. Trade unions are established by making a relevant entry into the trade union register kept by the ministry in charge for labour affairs.

E. Labour Disputes

In Montenegro there are no special labour courts, but labour disputes are dealt with by the regular civil courts –Basic Courts, Higher Court and the Supreme Court as the final court instance. The Supreme Court is in charge on deciding on extraordinary legal remedies against the rulings of the Higher Court. An employee who finds that his employment right was violated is entitled to submit a claim before the competent court within 15 days as of the receipt of the disputable resolution or as of the date when he / she finds out on the breach of right. Monetary claims deriving from employment are not subject to the statute of limitation and can be submitted at any time.

Employees may choose to peacefully resolve their labour dispute by way of arbitrage before the Agency for Peaceful Settlement of Labour Disputes. The arbitrator is determined by the parties jointly and the arbitrage process is urgent. The arbitrator's decision is final and binding for the parties. Arbitrage on individual labour disputes is quite rare in Montenegro, as employees usually refer to courts. This Agency for Peaceful Settlement of Labour Disputes also resolves collective disputes related to trade union relations with the employer – but in this case the role of the Agency is only to be a mediator and does not provide for final and binding decision.

The Ministry of Labour supervises the application of the labour regulations through the Labour Inspection, which often performs field controls – regular or extraordinary controls, based on an individual's application (which can also be anonymous). If the labour inspection identifies a certain failure of the employer to abide by the laws, it may initiate a misdemeanour procedure against the employer.

In addition, there are certain authorities whose field of activity may include some aspects of employment relations (though not exclusively), such as the Ombudsman (for discrimination cases). The Ombudsman does not have the power to enact binding decisions, but his recommendations are observed by the authorities.

V. Intellectual Property

A. Brief Introduction of IP Laws and Regulations

Intellectual Property ("IP") is set out under quite extensive legislation considering the number of applicable domestic and international legal sources. In particular, key national IP laws are the 2015 Law on Patents, 2010 Law on Trademarks, 2010 Law on Legal Protection of Industrial Design, 2011 Law on Copyright and Related Rights, 2008 Law on Geographical Indications and 2010 Law on the Protection of Topographies of Semiconductors.

Apart from the primary legislation, many bylaws have been adopted, especially for addressing matters related to the registration of mentioned IP rights, while the process of registration is governed by general administrative procedure rules.

Despite the various authorities included in the protection of IP rights, the leading role is held by the Montenegrin Intellectual Property Office ("MIPO"), as the body in charge of matters related to the process of acquiring and protecting IP rights. Along with MIPO, a significant part of the IP protection system are:

- Ministry of Economy: the authority that rules based on the appeal from the administrative proceedings related to the registration of IP rights (www.mek.gov.me);

- Administrative court: the authority that leads administrative disputes related to the registration of IP rights (sudovi.me);

- Commercial Court in Podgorica: competent for handling cases of IP rights infringement involving parties regardless of their status (sudovi.me);

- Commercial Court of Appeals in Podgorica: Competent for handling cases of IP rights infringement on the appellate level (sudovi.me);

- Customs Administration: the state authority under the Ministry of Finance, appointed to monitor state borders for goods used for IP rights infringement (www.upravacarina.gov.me); and,

- Market Inspectorate: the state authority under the Ministry of Trade, Tourism and Telecommunications, appointed to perform controls of internal markets for goods used for trademark infringement (www.uip.gov.me/kontakt).

B. Patent Application

From the national legislation aspect, patents are primary governed by the Law on Patents (2015). Under the Law, applicants may seek protection for inventions in all areas of technology, if they are new, contain inventive contribution and have industrial applicability. Such protection can be established nationally, during procedures before the MIPO or through international bodies based on the Patent Cooperation Treaty, the European Patent Convention and the Agreement for Cooperation in the Field of Patents between Montenegro and the European Patent Office. As an example, European patents recognized by the European Patent Office, which include protection for Montenegro, are levelled with the national patents with respect to the scope of rights. Also, under certain circumstance, the European patents override the national patents that cover same scope of invention.

The procedure for patent recognition begins with the submission of application. The patent application is submitted in written form, in three copies, in Montenegrin language, directly or by post. A separate application is submitted for each invention. The application for the recognition of a patent must include:

- an application in form provided by MIPO;
- the description of the invention;
- patent requests;
- draft; and,
- abstract.

The necessary documentation for the registration of a patent on a national level encompasses:

- the power of attorney, if the application is submitted through an agent;
- proof of payment of the appropriate administrative fee;
- data for other applicants and a statement of joint representative if the application is submitted by several applicants; and,
- a statement from the inventor if he does not want to be listed in the application; etc.

If the conditions prescribed by the law are fulfilled, the patent application shall be published in the official gazette as soon as possible after the expiration of 18 months from the date of filing the patent application, the decision on the recognition of the patent will be rendered and the data on the recognition of the patent in the Register of Patents of Montenegro shall be entered. Otherwise, the patent application will be rejected.

C. Trademark Registration

The benefits of registering a trademark are multiple, but the main one lies in the protection it grants. Thus, the trademark holder has the exclusive right to use the trademark for goods and / or services to which it relates, and to prohibit others from unauthorized use of an identical or similar mark for marking identical or similar goods or services on the market, should such use be likely to cause confusion in commerce. Additionally, the Trademark Law specifically governs that, in the event of intentional infringement of a trademark, the injured party may, instead of simply being remunerated pecuniary damage, request from the infringing party compensation of up to three times the usual license fee it would have obtained for the use of the infringed trademark.

The trademark registration procedure, where a mark is not found to be in opposition to any other previously registered trademark, usually takes somewhere from two to six months, thereby comprising any potential examination reports rendered by the MIPO leading to the extension of the procedure.

However, should there be a parallel court procedure initiated for the infringement involving a filed mark, the registration procedure might be extended to several years as the registration procedure would be suspended until the decision is rendered in the court proceedings.

The average total cost for the registration proceedings excluding any potential additional costs for responses to the examination report amounts to approximately EUR 177.

The examination report of the registration procedure consists solely of formal requirements for the trademark registration.

Formal examination consists of verifying the validity of the filed trademark application (consisting of the trademark application form, the mark claimed, list of goods and services to which the mark applies, and power of attorney, should the applicant be represented by someone). Should the examiner find that an application is improper, he / she will notify the applicant by dispatching an examination report to him specifying the irregularities noted and inviting the applicant to remedy the deficiencies within a 30-day time limit. If the applicant fails to remedy the deficiencies in the application within the time limit assigned, or if he / she fails to pay an adequate administrative fee for remedying such deficiencies, the examiner will issue a procedural order rejecting the application.

Material examination is no longer performed ex officio by the MIPO, but only upon the request of the interested parties.

The trademark lasts for 10 years as of the date of the filing of the application for registration, and is indefinitely renewable for further 10-year periods upon the payment of prescribed administrative fees.

D. Measures for IP Protection

Measures for the protection of IP rights and, particularly, trademarks are performed on several different levels.

On the one hand, border control mechanisms are available via the Customs Administration, allowing for trademark holders, applicants or exclusive license holders to file a demand for trademark protection at the state borders. Acting upon the right holders' request, or ex officio, the authorities are empowered to temporally seize all goods that are either the object or means of an IP rights infringement, whenever there is prima facie evidence establishing that an IP right has been infringed. Following the seizures, the customs officers notify without delay the rights' holders, the MIPO (if it is necessary to obtain relevant information) and any other interested parties (if any such parties are known) about the measures taken.

The notification is crucial as it includes an invitation to the holder of the IP rights to initiate the proceedings for the protection of its rights in the court proceedings and to inform the customs authorities about such proceedings or of the preliminary injunction issued by the court.

On the other, control of the internal markets is also at hand to the applicants or trademarks holders suspecting that their marks / trademarks are being infringed. Controls are performed via Market Inspectorate either upon holders request or ex officio, resulting in the seizure of goods that are either the object or means of an IP rights infringement. The procedure itself is very similar to the one performed by the Customs Administration and is usually followed by court proceedings, unless an out-of-court settlement was reached through the ADR mechanisms.

Court proceedings, as the third means of enforcement, are initiated by filing a complaint with the competent court. The infringement complaint is usually filed with a demand for preliminary injunction. After receiving such a complaint, the court quickly decides on the preliminary injunction. Furthermore, before rendering the final decision on the complaint, the court schedules a hearing to receive the statements from the parties. The judge will schedule as many hearings as is deemed necessary before rendering a decision.

Litigation costs depend on the value of the claim, length of the proceedings and number of hearings. In Montenegro, litigation costs comprise the costs of filing of the complaint, to which are added the costs of rendering the decision of the first instance court, and in case of appeal, for rendering the decision on the appellate level. As the range between cases can be very different, it is impossible to determine a typical range of costs in an infringement action.

VI. Environmental Protection[①]

A. Department Supervising Environmental Protection

The main role in supervising environmental protection is embodied in the Agency for the Protection of

---

① In order to protect natural resources and preserve the identity of its unique territory, Montenegro adopted the Declaration on the Ecological State (20 September 1991), thus becoming the world's first ecological state, the status Montenegro legally confirmed by the Constitution in 2007.The Montenegrin Parliament adopted the Declaration in the northern town of Žabljak, amidst turbulent times for the whole region, which marked the beginning of the increased public awareness of the need to preserve the environment.The following year, the commitment expressed in this declaration became part of the Montenegrin Constitution of 1992. In the past decade and particularly since the restoration of Montenegro's independence in 2006, the revival of these ideas comes about and Montenegro joins main international fora on environmental protection, introduces environmental protection institutions, adopts contemporary legal norms in this area and proclaims fifth national park (Prokletije).Link to the declaration: www.mgreens.co.me/declaration.htm.

Environment ("Agency"), which is a part of the multi-competent Ministry of Sustainable Development and Tourism. It was founded back in 2008, by a decree from the Government of Montenegro.

The Agency carries out various expert and related administrative tasks in the field of environmental protection, such as:
- environmental monitoring;
- it produces analyses and reports;
- it issues permits; and,
- the Agency conducts communication with the relevant domestic and international bodies and organizations, as well as with the public; etc.

The Agency[①] cooperates with international bodies and organizations of other countries dealing with environmental protection, in particular with the European Environment Agency, the International Atomic Energy Agency, and participates in the professional networks within the European Union, as well as with similar agencies in other countries.

Inspection regarding environmental protection is given to the Administration for Inspection Affairs, which is a state body founded by a Decree on Organization and Functioning of Public Administration, which entered into force on 20 January 2012. This created a legal basis for the establishment of united inspection body–and one of the sectors it supervises is environment protection.

The Ministry of Sustainable Development and Tourism is entitled to enact secondary legislation, implement environmental legislation and also monitor environment protection. Certain competences have been delegated to the municipal units[②], who are primary entitled to adopt local plans and strategies, as well as to supervise the implementation of the environmental laws from the aspect of the local competences.

In addition, other state bodies can supervise specific environmental issues, such as the Market Inspectorate and Sanitary and Health Inspectorate. Within their competences, the environmental inspectors are entitled to impose measures or order actions that have to be performed for the prevention or elimination of the causes for the environmental pollution. Depending on the type of the potential misdemeanour, a misdemeanour sanction (e.g.monetary fines or cease of production) may be issued. Also, depending on the caused ecological damage, the polluter could face criminal charges and claims for restitution or compensation of damages, in accordance with the law.

B. Brief Introduction of Laws and Regulations of Environmental Protection

Environmental protection represents a fundamental value under the Montenegrin Constitution (2007), which at the same time guarantees the right to a healthy environment to each individual. Such a guarantee is provided through several laws specific to this area, with the Law on the Environment ("Environment Law") from 2016 as main environmental legislative act. The Environmental Law regulates the rights and duties of the state and local authorities, as well as the rights and duties of the legal entities and natural persons in providing the conditions for the protection and improvement of the environment, so that the citizens can exercise their right to a healthy environment. Under this Law, the implementation of a certain project or the production within specific factories can be done after conducting an Environmental Impact Assessment Study or obtaining the relevant integrated environmental permit. Further, this Law governs: the principles of environmental protection and sustainable development entities and instruments for environmental protection, public participation on environmental issues and other issues of major importance for the Montenegro environment. Other relevant environmental laws are:

- The Law on Environmental Impact Assessment (2005, amended from time to time), which regulates the impact assessment procedure for projects that may have significant impact on the environment, contents of the Environmental Impact Assessment Study, participation of authorities, organizations and the public concerned, evaluation and procedures for approvals / permits, exchange of information etc.

- The Law on Strategic Environmental Impact Assessment (2005, amended from time to time), which stipulates the conditions, methods and procedures for undertaking of strategic environmental assessment of certain plans or programs through the integration of environmental protection principles into the procedures of preparation, adoption and implementation of plans or programmes that have significant impact on the environment.

- The Law on Integrated Pollution Prevention and Control (2005, amended from time to time) which governs

---

① Its separate units are the following: Sector for Nature Protection, Monitoring, Analysis and Reporting; Sector for issuing permits; Sector for information system management in the field of environmental protection; Department for General, Legal and Financial Affairs; Department for Radiological and Nuclear Safety and Security and Protection against Ionizing and Non-Ionizing Radiation; Department of Chemicals Management.

② Municipal units in Montenegro are the local municipalities and the City of Podgorica.

conditions and procedures for issuing integrated permit for facilities and activities which may have a negative impacts on health, environment or goods, surveillance and other issues of importance for the prevention and control of environmental pollution.

- The Law on Waste Management (2011, amended from time to time), Law on Chemicals (2016), Law on Liability for Damages in Environment (2014, amended from time to time), Law on Sea (2007, amended from time to time), Law on Coastal Zone (1992, amended from time to time);
- The Law on Waters (2007, amended from time to time), governing the issues pertaining to surface and ground waters, their management, water resources management facilities and services, as well as conditions and procedures under which the waters can be used and discharged;
- The Law on Air Protection (2010, amended from time to time), governing measures for avoiding, preventing or reducing the harmful effects of ambient air pollution on human health, as well as the environment as a whole;
- The Law on Protection against Environmental Noise (2007), regulating the rights and obligations of the authorities and all legal entities and natural persons in relation to environmental noise management and protection against environmental noise;
- other laws which contain environmental protection provisions (such as the Law on Agricultural Land (1992, amended from time to time), the Law on Forests (2010, amended from time to time), the Energy Law (2016, amended from time to time), etc.;

In 2007, Montenegro ratified the Kyoto Protocol to the United Nations Framework Convention on Climate Change which sets binding emission reduction targets which have to be followed by the member states. In addition, Montenegro has ratified many other international agreements in the environment field, like the Paris Agreement (in 2017).

C. Evaluation of Environmental Protection

The above presented regulatory framework, together with the Declaration on the Ecological State, indicates that environmental protection is widely regulated in Montenegro. In spite of this, there is still room for further improvement in certain areas, especially improvements in practice, since some of the laws are not fully aligned with European legislation. This is specifically important to the areas of industrial pollution and risk management, water and air quality, chemicals and climate change. The legislation which is planned to be adopted requires stricter standards and enforcement, increased fines and penalties for non-compliance, and bigger responsibility for companies, their management and employees. Public awareness increases constantly and the public pressure the authorities to allocate more funds from the state and municipalities' budget for environmental protection. Environmental inspections are conducted more and more often and incompliances are sanitized. However, there is still a lot of work to be done, even to reach the minimal EU standards in this area–which is very important.

VII. Dispute Resolution

A. Methods and Bodies of Dispute Resolution

Parties (both companies and natural persons) are entitled to mutually reach the dispute resolution mechanism for disputes which concern rights that can be freely disposed with and which are not under exclusive jurisdiction of the Montenegrin courts. Generally, if the parties are not willing to solve the dispute amicably, they can opt for one of the following available methods: (i) a court proceeding; (ii) an arbitration; or (iii) a mediation (used very rarely in practice).

a. Court Proceedings

In general, the Montenegrin judiciary system is structured as a three-tier court system organized through basic, higher and appellate courts, as first and second instance courts for civil and criminal matters, and with the Administrative Court with competence to solve administrative disputes. The final court instance for all kinds of disputes (civil, criminal and administrative) is the Supreme Court of Montenegro. The basic courts are established for one or more municipalities as courts with a basic or expanded competence, while there is only one Appellate and only one Commercial Court.

Civil law proceedings are initiated before the basic courts by submitting a lawsuit, accompanied by the relevant evidence / documents for the stated allegations and facts. Afterwards, respecting the principle of equality of arms, the proceedings are generally carried out through two phases, the preliminary and main hearing. In contrast to the proceedings before the basic courts, Appellate courts usually rule on the dispute without holding a hearing. Supreme Court never holds hearings. The right to appeal is guaranteed by the Montenegrin Constitution, as well as with the introduced EU and other conventions. As the legal system is based on civil law principles, precedents are not binding for the courts. Further, several competences have been delegated to other authorities, like the public notaries and the enforcement agents.

Together with the competences to provide judiciary protection against the acts of the public authorities, the Administrative Court is empowered to solve disputes which arise from concession agreements, public procurement contracts and any other agreement with a public authority as a signatory party, entered for the purpose of pursuing a public interest or exercising public service. In general, the proceedings before this court are carried out on the basis of written submissions, without holding a hearing - which may happen depending on the circumstances of a specific case.

Disputes with an international element are solved by the Montenegrin civil courts when the competence for such dispute is explicitly determined by law or by an international agreement. When there is no such explicit provision for the respective dispute, then a Montenegrin court will be competent if its jurisdiction arises from the rules for territorial jurisdiction of Montenegrin courts. Parties may agree jurisdiction of a Montenegrin court if at least one of them is a Montenegrin citizen or a legal entity seated in Montenegro. Contrary to this, in order to agree the jurisdiction of a foreign court, one of the parties has to be a foreign citizen or a legal entity based abroad, subject to not having an exclusive jurisdiction of a Montenegrin court for the dispute.

b. Arbitration

Arbitration can be agreed for resolving disputes which have already arisen between the concerned parties or for all future disputes arising from a legal relationship between them. The competent institution to conduct arbitration in Montenegro is the Arbitration Court at the Chamber of Economy of Montenegro. This institution may administer both domestic and international arbitrations, depending whether the dispute includes an international element.

The Arbitration Court at the Chamber of Economy of Montenegro is an autonomous and independent institution before which domestic commercial disputes and disputes with an international element are resolved in accordance with the Arbitration Rules of the Arbitration Court at the Chamber of Economy of Montenegro and other rules and procedures agreed by the parties. The parties have the right to choose arbitrators. Any natural person with a capacity to contract may act as an arbitrator, regardless of his or her nationality.

Apart from the Arbitration Rules of the Arbitration Court at the Chamber of Economy of Montenegro, the parties may agree that the Arbitration Rules of the United Nations Commission on International Trade Law (UNCITRAL) be applicable conducting a dispute before the Arbitration Court.

The Arbitration Court conducts the proceedings so as to ensure a fair and efficient resolution of disputes and to avoid unnecessary delay and costs. The legal framework is the following: Law on Arbitration (2015), Arbitration Rules of the Arbitration Court at the Chamber of Economy of Montenegro (2015), Arbitration Rules of the United Nations Commission on International Trade Law (UNCITRAL), Code of Ethics of Arbitrators.

The Law on Arbitration and the Arbitration Rules have been harmonized with the international rules, and in particular with the provisions of the UNCITRAL Model Law on International Commercial Arbitration.

c. Mediation

Mediation may be initiated if the parties have agreed in writing that, in the event of a dispute, they will try to resolve it by means of direct negotiation or mediation before commencing judicial or other proceedings. However, even if court proceedings are initiated, in certain cases the court has an obligation to recommend mediation to the parties in the first instance proceedings. In that case, the parties can give a written statement that they accept to participate in mediation.

In order to promote mediation and to recognize the role of a mediator, placed mediators formed the Association of Mediators of Montenegro. A mediator is a third, neutral person who helps parties communicate and find a common, acceptable solution for their dispute. Mediators may be judges, lawyers, psychologists, doctors, economists, engineers and other prominent experts from various fields depending on the type of dispute they mediate in. Mediators may be all persons who are citizens of Montenegro, have a University degree and five years of professional experience. In order to become a mediator, one must undergo special training and become a certified mediator. After the successful completion of the training, mediators are appointed by the Minister of Justice, which is initiated by proposal from the Committee of the Ministry of Justice. The Committee is formed by the Minister of Justice, and it consists of judges, mediators and the Ministry of Justice.

Notwithstanding, a mediator may be a person who does not meet the above criteria, if he / she has professional knowledge and practical experience for a particular area of mediation. The mediation procedure in Montenegro in some cases concerning disputes with a foreign element can lead to a foreign national who is authorized to conduct mediation activities in another country.

B. Application of Laws

The courts decide upon the rights and obligations of the parties to the proceedings based on the Constitution, the national laws and international agreements ratified in accordance with the Constitution.

The International Private Law (2014, amended from time to time) contains rules for determining the applicable law for civil, labour and commercial matters with an international element. When it comes to agreements, parties can choose the governing law if it is not otherwise determined by law or by an international agreement. The mentioned law also contains rules for the recognition of foreign court decisions and decisions of other authorities of a foreign country. With respect to the recognition and enforcement of a foreign arbitral award, the conditions from the 1958 New York Convention on the Recognition and Enforcement of Foreign Arbitral Awards apply.

Separate laws govern the different types of dispute resolution mechanisms and procedures. With respect to mediation proceedings, the main applicable law is the Law on Mediation (2005). For international arbitration the relevant procedural law is the Law on International Commercial Arbitration which is generally based on the UNCITRAL Model Law on International Commercial Arbitration. The Law on Civil Proceedings (2004, amended from time to time) governs civil court proceedings. Criminal proceedings are conducted in accordance with the Law on Criminal Procedure (2009, amended from time to time). Administrative disputes are governed by the Law on Administrative Disputes (2016).

VIII. Others

A. Anti-commercial Bribery

a. Brief Introduction of Anti-commercial Bribery Laws and Regulations

The main law governing anti-corruption and bribery is the 2014 Law on Prevention of Corruption ("Anti-Corruption Law"). The aim of this Law is to comprehensively regulate the area of potential conflicts of interests and restrictions on the exercise of public functions, as well as the protection of whistle-blowers.

The Anti-Corruption Law defines corruption as any abuse of official, business or social position or influence for personal benefit or the benefit of other. Considering that this phenomenon is widespread in various spheres of society, the Anti-Corruption Law seeks to prevent and reduce to a minimum level any form of corruptive behaviour through numerous measures. In this regard, an important innovation introduced by the Law is the obligation of all state authorities to have so-called "integrity plan". The integrity plan contains information on the exposure of state authority to corruption, work positions that are highly exposed to corruption and measures and activities focused on reducing the risk of corruption. The plans are be publicly available and their implementation in practice is carefully monitored by the Agency for Prevention of Corruption ("Agency").

A special focus has been placed on the gifting, sponsorships and donations to public authorities. With respect to gifting, public officials cannot receive money, securities or precious metals, regardless of their value. A public official in Montenegro is only allowed to receive protocol and / or gifts of minor value—which does not exceed EUR 50. Gifts exceeding the stated value cannot be kept. If a public official receives several gifts from a single donor within one year, the sum value of all gifts shall be deemed the gift value and cannot exceed EUR 50. A prohibition is also prescribed for concluding sponsorship agreements on behalf of the public official and for sponsorship agreements and receiving donations by the public official on behalf of a state authority, if such an act has an effect or could have an effect on legality, objectivity and impartiality of the state authority. Agreements concluded contrary to the mentioned restrictions will be null and void. A separate law provision also imposes an obligation to state authorities to submit annual reports on the received sponsorships and donations to the Agency, to maintain respective records and to make such records publicly available on their website.

In the recent years the most significant progress has been made on the field of protection of whistle-blowers. A whistle-blower is a person who has justified reasons to suspect an endangering of public interest which indicates the existence of corruption (i.e.a violation of regulations, ethical rules or the possibility of such a violation which causes, has caused or threatens to cause danger to life, health and safety of people and environment, violation of human rights or monetary and non-monetary damages to state or legal and natural person, and act whose aim is to hide such violation). In addition to whistle-blowers, the Anti-Corruption Law also provides protection for persons who assist whistle-blowers, as well as all persons that probably suffered damage as a result of their connection with a whistle-blower.

In a broader sense the regulatory framework for fighting anti-commercial bribery is also consisted of:
- The Law on Lobbying (2014)—which sets out the principles of lobbying and lobbyists, supervision of the

lobbying and measures that can be imposed on a lobbyist due to noncompliance with the law.

- The Law on Financing of Political Entities and Election Campaigns (2014)–which governs the financing of political entities for regular work and election campaigns, restrictions on the disposal with state property and funds during the campaign and supervision of such financing and disposal.

- The Criminal Code (2003)–according to which, a bribery is the making or offering a gift or other benefit to an official to perform, within his or her official competence, an official act that should not be performed or not to perform an official act that should be performed, or as intermediation in such bribing of an official. Another form of bribery exists if making or offering a gift or another benefit to the official is undertaken in order for him or her to perform an official act that he or she is obliged to perform or not to perform an official act that he or she may not perform, or if intermediation in such bribing of an official is undertaken.

b. Department Supervising Anti-commercial Bribery

The Agency is an autonomous and independent legal entity founded by the Montenegrin Parliament. It has many competences including:

i. acting in cases of conflict of public and private interests, as well as cases concerning restrictions in the performance of public functions;

ii. review of the income and property reports submitted by public officials; and,

iii. acting upon the whistle-blower's complaint etc.

The Agency consists of the Council and the Director. The Council has five members elected by the Montenegrin Parliament, while the Director is elected by the Council based on a public announcement.

c. Punitive Actions

The presented legal framework for anti-commercial bribery contains broad misdemeanor provisions. In addition, the Criminal Code envisages several sanctions:

(i) Taking bribe: imprisonment up to twelve years for performing an activity which should not be performed, or not performing an official activity which should be performed; imprisonment up to fifteen years if bribe is related to criminal proceedings, etc.

(ii) Giving bribe: imprisonment up to eight years for giving bribe to an official in order to perform an official activity, which otherwise should not be performed, or not to perform an official activity which must be performed,

B. Project Contracting

a. Permission System

Public-private partnerships are regulated by the 2009 Law on Concessions ("Concessions Law") and the 2002 Law on participation of private sector in performing public authority ("PPS Law"). At the time when this was written, there is no specific PPP legislation in place in Montenegro, even though a draft law on PPPs is in the pipeline.

For this reason PPPs are regulated as concessions until entry into force of the sector specific law.

The competent authorities with powers in PPP field are:

The Concession Commission of Montenegro ("Concession Commission")–with the authority to decide on appeals related to the evaluation and the ranking of the bidders, maintenance of the register, approving extension of the concession terms, as well as awarding concessions for the exploitation of accessory mineral resources within approved exploitation field without conducting concession procedure (www.komisijazakoncesije.me/cg);

The Parliament of Montenegro - with the authority to approve concession within its jurisdiction in accordance with 2009 State Property Law ("SP Law") (www.skupstina.me);

Government of Montenegro–with the authority to approve concessions within its jurisdiction in accordance with SP Law (www.gov.me); and,

Local municipalities–with the authority to approve concessions within their jurisdiction in accordance with SP Law (uom.me).

b. Invitation to Bid and Bidding

Concessions are awarded on a basis of an annual plan which is devised either by the Government or the municipalities, depending on their right to dispose with assets in accordance with SP Law. Plans are published on websites of the Government or municipality.

The term of the concession may be 30 years for a concession granted by the Government and municipalities or 60 years for a concession granted by the Parliament. The term may be extended for a maximum period of one half of the originally awarded concession term.

An awarding authority initiates the concession procedure by rendering the concession act. This act comprises of, among others, information related to the geographical location of the concession area, basic parameters for evaluation of the cost-effectiveness of the investment, technical documentation and a list of approvals, permits, consents and licenses that a prospective concessionaire must obtain prior to the commencement of the concession activity, a list of financial and technical requirements a concessionaire must meet in order to be awarded concession rights, maximum or minimum term of the concession etc.

A concession may be awarded on the basis of a tendering procedure, which may be conducted as:

(i) Open public competitive procedure;

(ii) Two-stage competitive procedure where bidders are shortlisted before entering into closed competitive procedure; and

(iii) Accelerated competitive procedure for concession granted for a period of up to three years.

In all of the above cases, the awarding authority forms a tender committee which manages the concession procedure and ranks the bidders. Bidders have the right to object to a decision of the tender committee, while the Concession Commission decides on objections in appellate proceedings.

An interested party may request the initiation of the concession awarding procedure, even if the area of concession is not provided for in the concession plan. In case that the awarding authority finds the request well-grounded, the interested party must deposit funds required for the rendering of the concession act, including the rendering of tender documentation and the draft concession contract, costs for the work of the tender committee and the costs for carrying out a public debate. In case the interested party is not awarded the concession, the deposited funds will be repaid, reduced for the expenses of purchasing the concession act.

In regards to the language, the awarding parties announce concession acts in the Montenegrin language (and in English when the tenders are internationally published), while the bids must be submitted in the language specified in tender documents. Prices must be expressed in euros.

摩洛哥

作者：Amin Hajji, Nihma El Gachbour, Asmae El Khaier, Rachid Benzakour
译者：徐步林、刘蓉

一、概述

（一）摩洛哥政治、经济、社会和法律环境概述

摩洛哥王国是一个二元制君主立宪制国家。[①]

根据 2011 年通过的现行摩洛哥《宪法》，国王是国家元首。国王从众议院大选获胜的政党中选任政府首脑，并根据政府首脑的提议任命政府成员。国王有权罢免大臣、解散议会并组织新的选举。国王通过 Dahir（皇家法令）进行统治。

摩洛哥的政治体系由立法机关（议会）、行政机关（政府）和司法机关三个分支机构组成。

政府由政府首脑（首相）和大臣组成，他们对国王和议会负责。政府负责实施政府计划，保障法律实施，安排行政事务，提出立法建议，监督公共机构的活动。

议会由众议院和参议院两院组成。众议院议员共 395 名，通过直接选举产生，任期 5 年；参议院议员共 120 名，由间接选举产生，任期 6 年。议会拥有立法权，对包括《财政法案》(the Finance Bill) 在内的法案进行表决，控制政府和评估公共政策。

摩洛哥的司法部门独立于立法部门和行政部门。最高司法委员会（Le Conseil Supérieur du Pouvoir Judiciaire）负责法官的任命、晋升、退休和纪律监管，并保证他们的独立性。

法律是摩洛哥国家意志的最高体现。摩洛哥法律主要在名为 Dahir formant Code des Obligations et des Contrats（下称"1913 年 8 月 12 日 DOC"）的《摩洛哥民法典》(Moroccan Civil Code) 及穆斯林与犹太传统教法的基础上产生。

在摩洛哥，法律（皇家法令）是由国王、首相或议员提出法案，然后由议会两院（众议院和参议院）进行批准。

而且，所有立法必须由皇家法令颁布，然后便取得优于任何其他相关文本的效力。议会法案以及根据宪法规定应以"基本法"形式颁布的某些立法类型，应以皇家法令颁布。

此外，关于个人身份、行为能力和继承的法律关系受 2004 年 2 月 3 日第 70-03 号法律的规制，该法是在伊斯兰法典（Malékite School 马利基学派）的基础上成立的新《家事法》(the Family Code)。

关于合同、义务和不动产的立法受 1913 年 8 月 12 日 DOC 的规制。

宪法是摩洛哥的最高法律形式。并且，它还阐释了君主制内各种机构的地位和相互关系，并涵盖多种法律原则。

此外，1974 年《民事诉讼法》(the Code of Civil Procedure) 限制了司法机关的作用，规定法院不得对法律或法令的合宪性作出审查，同样司法机关也不得审查行政行为。

因此，1993 年在行政法院设立的同时成立了宪法法律顾问部门。2011 年新宪法颁布后，宪法法律顾问部门变为宪法法院。

最后，宪法于 2011 年 7 月 29 日进行最新修订，认可由摩洛哥王国正式批准的国际条约优于摩洛哥法律法规，具有最高效力。

关于司法机构，摩洛哥最高级别的法院是终审上诉法院（最高法院）。其他法院包括初审法院、上诉法院和专门法院如商业法院、商业上诉法院、行政法院和行政上诉法院。摩洛哥还有一些例外的司法管辖区和宪法委员会。

[①] 2011 年《摩洛哥宪法》第 1 条。

近年来，摩洛哥经济的特点是宏观经济稳定和低水平的通货膨胀（2015年为1.5%）。2015年，摩洛哥的国内生产总值（GDP）接近1 010亿美元，GDP增长4.6%；2016年的GDP增长率放缓至1.6%；得益于非农活动的持续增长，2017年GDP预计增长4.8%。

2015年，政府总债务额占国家GDP的63.7%，政府预算赤字达到GDP的-4.3%。近年来，失业率一直上升，2015年达到9.7%。①

摩洛哥经济以农业为主导，农业领域雇用了近40%的劳动力。然而，2017年和2018年财政法案的目标是加速经济结构转型，重点在工业化和可再生能源（摩洛哥蕴藏2600千瓦时/㎡/年的太阳能资源）。2016年2月，摩洛哥启动瓦尔扎扎特太阳能发电站项目，建成之后将成为世界上最大的太阳能发电厂。

在进出口和投资方面，西班牙和法国是摩洛哥主要的对外贸易伙伴，占据了摩洛哥44%的出口和28.2%的进口。②

截至2017年11月，摩洛哥吸引了将近23.5亿美元的外商直接投资（FDI），并将通过一项新的《投资宪章》，以便分别在该国的12个区域内发展自由贸易区。

摩洛哥是阿拉伯自由贸易区的成员，与美国、欧洲自由贸易联盟（EFTA）和土耳其签订了自由贸易协定。

摩洛哥还与欧盟签署了一项联盟协定，与超过15个非洲国家签订双边协定并以此方式尤其活跃在非洲大陆上，使其成为非洲的主要投资国之一。

摩洛哥的官方货币是摩洛哥迪拉姆（MAD）。2018年1月，摩洛哥扩大了迪拉姆兑欧元和美元的汇率浮动区间，兑换价格由上下浮动0.3%扩大到上下浮动2.5%。

（二）"一带一路"倡议下与中国企业合作的现状及趋势

摩洛哥于2017年11月17日签署《中华人民共和国政府和摩洛哥王国政府关于共建"一带一路"的双边谅解备忘录》（以下简称"备忘录"），正式参与"一带一路"项目。

摩洛哥和中国在经济、工业、文化和政治领域有着长期的交流。2016年，摩洛哥从中国的进口额约39亿美元，使中国成为摩洛哥第四大贸易伙伴。

摩洛哥和中国签订了许多双边协定，这些协定构成与中国投资者进行合作的法律框架，例如：

• 1995年3月27日中摩签署的《关于鼓励和相互保护投资协定》，于2000年8月14日在摩洛哥生效；

• 1996年4月16日中摩签署的《关于民事和商事司法协助的协定》，于2000年5月3日在摩洛哥生效；

• 2002年8月27日中摩签署的《关于对所得税避免双重征税和防止偷漏税的协定》，于2009年2月18日在摩洛哥生效。

2016年5月，摩洛哥王国和中国在银行业、旅游、经济、工业和投资领域签署15个双边协定。15个双边协定的详细清单见下表：

No.	双边协定名称
1	《摩洛哥王国与中国海特集团关于在摩洛哥建立工业和住宅园区项目的谅解备忘录》
2	《摩洛哥政府与中国工商银行股份有限公司在投资和金融领域的合作协议》
3	《摩洛哥政府与中国港湾工程有限公司关于北水南调工程的谅解备忘录》
4	《摩洛哥国家电力水利局（ONEE）与山东电力建设第三工程公司协议草案》

---

① IMF：《世界经济数据库》，2017年。
② 参见《摩洛哥贸易摘要（2016）》，载世界银行网站（https://wits.worldbank.org/CountrySnapshot/en/MAR）。

续表

No.	双边协定名称
5	《摩洛哥旅游局与中国国际旅行社（CITS）伙伴关系协议》
6	《扬子江汽车集团与摩洛哥能源投资公司（SIE）、玛丽塔集团和中央银行（Banque Centale Populaire）就购置和建造电动公共汽车生产车间的伙伴关系协议》
7	《力诺瑞特、摩洛哥能源投资公司、Cap控股公司和阿提扎利瓦法银行在摩洛哥创建太阳能热水器统一工业生产中心的伙伴关系协议》
8	《海润太阳能、摩洛哥能源投资公司、Jet承建商集团和阿提扎利瓦法银行之间就开发光伏电池生产单元的伙伴关系协议》
9	《中国非洲发展基金（CAD基金）和阿提扎利瓦法银行之间就通过完成贷款发放和为摩洛哥—中国在非洲的投资机会开辟新前景以支持非洲企业的谅解备忘录》
10	《海特集团、摩洛哥—中国国际和摩洛哥外贸银行（BMCE）关于在摩洛哥设立中国—摩洛哥工业园和针对航空、金融、工业园和基础设施行业的中国—摩洛哥十亿美元投资基金的谅解备忘录》
11	《非洲摩洛哥外贸银行（BMCE）与中非发展基金（CAD基金）之间就为非洲关键行业的发展项目提供资金及在非洲公私债务市场投资的谅解备忘录》
12	《在摩洛哥建造水泥厂的融资协议》
13	《四川华铁高科建筑工程有限公司、摩洛哥国家运输和物流协会（SNTL）与阿提扎利瓦法银行间关于发展铁路、汽车和航空业零配件生产的工业物流中心的谅解备忘录》
14	《在非洲发展物流园区的谅解备忘录》
15	《"可为中国"（Clevy China）、摩洛哥国家运输和物流协会与阿提扎利瓦法银行之间就中非跨境电子贸易的谅解备忘录》

2016年6月，摩洛哥准许中国公民免签证入境摩洛哥。

2017年12月，中国电动汽车制造商比亚迪公司签署一项在摩洛哥建造工厂的协议，以在丹吉尔生产电动汽车。

二、投资

（一）市场准入

1. 投资主管部门

（1）全球性的投资监管

在摩洛哥的投资由投资贸易与信息经济部（the Ministry of Industry, Investment, Trade and Digital Economy）监管，该部主要通过下属的几个部门（工业、贸易和分销、先进技术、质量和市场监督等部门）对与投资有关的事项进行监管。

其中，该部确保完成以下任务：确认贸易、分销、发展投资和提高与中小企业（SMEs）竞争力有关策略的效力，为与工商业和新技术领域的国内和国际机构、组织之间的关系处理提供帮助，发展伙伴关系，协调和实施合作计划，为工商业、技术及竞争中心拓展和协调对接空间，诚邀、告知和引导工商业和分销领域的投资者，为工商业和新技术制定立法和组织框架，以及在上述领域提升质量和安全。

（2）投资发展和实践

摩洛哥国家投资和出口发展署（AMDIE）是摩洛哥负责发展和推动在该国投资的主要部门。

AMDIE 受投资贸易与信息经济部的监督，系具有法人资格和财务自主权的公共机构。

AMDIE 的创立是为支持新工业加速计划（the new Industrial Acceleration Plan）设定的王国新的投资愿景，它由之前负责投资、出口、展览交易会的三个部门合并产生，旨在解决三机构履行职责不协调的问题，以达更好的连贯性和更高的标准化效率。

根据设立 AMDIE 的法律，该机构的主要职能是确保发展、鼓励和促进国内外投资的国家战略的实施。在此背景下，该机构应主要通过采取行动来预估潜在的国内外投资者的发展前景，在与有关当局协调下，通过交流和成熟的贸易促进政策实施，在政府设定的国家出口发展战略的框架内，提升摩洛哥的出口报价，并推进交易博览会行业的发展。

（3）经商环境全国委员会

为保护国内外经营者的利益，并保证有益投资框架的清晰度和透明度，经商环境全国委员会（CNEA）于 2009 年 12 月创建。这个高级别机构由政府首脑担任主席，由公共和私营部门的代表组成。其主要任务是确定和实施旨在提升摩洛哥投资吸引力的措施。

2. 投资行业法律法规

（1）法律

1995 年 10 月 3 日第 18-95 号《蓝图法》以标准文本形式规定了摩洛哥的《投资宪章》作为标准文本适用于所有行业，目的在于通过改善投资环境和条件并提供旨在推动国内外投资发展（直接和组合投资）的激励措施来鼓励和推动投资。

除了某些未禁止准入但又受当局管制的特定领域如农业、磷酸盐和保险业外，不论经营的行业为何，《投资宪章》给予本国人和外国人同等优惠。因此，《投资宪章》就税收、关税和注册费规定了激励措施，亦为投资于硬通货的投资者提供转移利润和资本的自由，为实施项目的投资者提供建议和协助，并减少与投资有关的行政手续。

最后，摩洛哥在近几十年中建立了一个健全的法律规范体系，包括劳动、版权、个人信息保护、价格和竞争自由、消费者保护、工业产权、公司和仲裁等。这些新的法律法规旨在改善投资条件，从而产生大量的国内和外国私人资本流动。

（2）法规

第 2-00-895 号法令是为适用《蓝图法》第 17 条和第 19 条关于实施《投资宪章》的规定，且该法令适用于经济活动受到国家特殊支持的省、县和地区。

（3）新修订的法律

到 2014 年，摩洛哥采取新的做法并实施了"2014—2020 工业加速计划"（IAP）。该计划以建立高效的生态系统为基础，旨在整合价值链，巩固当地大公司和中小企业的关系，并改善外国投资者的进入条件。

IAP 还规定通过一项新的《投资宪章》，其中一些措施已经由 2017 年和 2018 年的财政法草案实施。

《投资宪章》的修订引入了新的激励措施，以巩固在工业加速政策框架内就促进投资吸引力方面所取得的进步。例如为新工业企业规定 5 年期的零公司税，建立区域性的自由贸易区，扶持受重视较少的地区推动产业投资，促进区域间均衡发展并承认间接出口商（主要出口集团的分包商）的地位。

3. 投资形式

《投资宪章》根据持有项目的公司的重要性、投资数额或项目实施区域对投资做了区分。因此《投资宪章》规定了在摩洛哥投资的一般形式，通过给予投资者特殊的财政、税收、海关和管理费优惠等激励措施，并在投资者符合所需标准的情况下，将此优惠纳入欲缔结的公共协定或投资合同中。

此外，摩洛哥还为具有高附加值的有关特定领域、技术和活动的项目提供投资费用的资助。因此，2015 年，通过财政法设立了工业和投资发展基金（the Industrial and Investment Development Fund），为工业生态系统提供直接的财政支持或直接援助，并在"2014—2020 工业加速计划"的施行期间将此纳入《投资宪章》的一部分。

4. 市场准入和检验标准

外国投资者可以在大多数领域进行自由投资，并持有摩洛哥公司的全部资本，甚至建立一个没有公司架构的永久性机构。原则上，投资市场准入自由，并给予国内外投资者相同的准入条件。

因此，投资法律框架在金融、不动产、行政管理、税收、海关和设立投资项目所需的一切必要程序方面坚持公平和非歧视原则。此外，国家还实施企业合并奖励措施，通过创建区域投资中心（Regional Investment Centers）简化若干行政管理和登记程序，使商业注册过程清晰且完整。

但是，某些行业如农业、渔业、磷酸盐、碳氢化合物、银行和保险业等限制外国人进入，且受到特定部门的管制。

市场进入可通过不同的公司形式实现，而它们或多或少都得益于《投资宪章》所提供的同样的激励措施。

最后，与外国缔结伙伴关系协定能够使双方在自由贸易、开放边界和投资保护方面互利互惠。

（二）外汇管制

1. 外汇监管部门

摩洛哥外汇局（ODC）负责外汇管理和控制。ODC是个公共机构，受经济与财政部（the Ministry of Economy and Finance）的监督。

外汇局负责制定外汇管制措施，统计编制对外贸易和国际收支数据。

ODC特别负责授权经批准的银行中介机构进行资金和资本的境外转移，并保证必要的可转让资产（如出口货物和服务）的调回，以及登记并惩处违反外汇管理规定的违法行为。

2. 外汇法律法规概况

2013年12月31日发布的《外汇交易指南》（the General Instruction on Foreign Operations）是规范摩洛哥外汇交易和跨境流动的主要法规。

根据该指南，摩洛哥迪拉姆不能任意出口和自由兑换，所有免征税的资本输出均须ODC事先批准。

然而，摩洛哥发起了一项自由化改革——实施自由兑换的迪拉姆制度，旨在为国际贸易和金融交易提供便利。在某些条件下，该制度保证了经ODC授权的银行中介机构能够进行股息、资产清算产品等的自由转移。

关于违反外汇管理规定的行为，1949年8月30日的皇家法令规定了外汇管理违法行为的认定、追诉和制裁条件。

此外，外汇管理规定还包括若干法令、部长级命令和备忘录，规定了所有与外贸相关的国内外交易业务，涉及私法甚至公法上的自然人和法人。最后，《投资宪章》还规定可向外国投资者自由转移资金。

3. 外资企业外汇管理要求

ODC授权经摩洛哥批准的银行中介机构自由实行与下列事项有关的结算：投资、进口、出口、国际运输、保险和再保险、外国技术援助、技术转让、分销、特许经营、保理、担保、旅游、学校教育、医疗保健、收入节余和由《外汇交易指南》所规定的所有其他现行操作。

跨境付款应以马格里布银行（BAM），即摩洛哥中央银行，所指定的外币支付，而来自境外的结算可通过BAM所指定的外币调回或通过特定借记账户来作出。因此，外国人可以在摩洛哥开立银行账户，这些账户可以是外币账户、可兑换迪拉姆的外国账户、远期可兑换账户和适用于某类外国实体（外国采购承包商和外交代表）的特别账户。

资本交易需要ODC的授权。这些授权常在与商业有关的交易上作出。无论哪种方式，ODC都可以要求获得授权和声明。而是否要求，具体取决于需要授权和声明的外汇交易类型，并应遵守与其他国家签订的协议。

（三）融资

1. 主要金融机构

根据摩洛哥法律，主要金融机构是贷款机构（Etablissement de crédit），主要为银行和融资公司。

还可以是支付机构、小额信贷协会、离岸银行和金融公司。

根据摩洛哥《银行法》（2014 年 12 月 24 日第 103-12 号法律），贷款机构可提供以下服务：①接收公众存款，②贷款业务，③发放付款卡，④投资服务，⑤外汇业务，⑥租赁业务，⑦担保和证券业务，⑧保理业务，⑨黄金、贵金属和货币业务，⑩保险经纪，⑪其他与前述事项相关或类似的活动。

贷款机构须取得摩洛哥中央银行"马格里布银行"（BAM）颁发的许可证。中央银行还负责银行业的监管。

自 2015 年，摩洛哥引入一种被称为"公众参与制银行"（banques participatives）的新型金融机构，用来提供符合伊斯兰教法规则的产品和服务。公众参与制银行提供不产生任何利息的参与性投资产品和服务。

保险公司是摩洛哥第二大金融机构。目前摩洛哥市场有 21 家保险和再保险公司，1873 家保险中介机构（1427 家代理商和 446 名经纪人）。

2. 外资企业融资条件

一般而言，外资企业与国内企业的融资条件相同。但应当指出，外资企业应在其融资活动开始实施的 6 个月内通知（连同融资合同副本或银行财务报表）摩洛哥外汇局（ODC）。

（四）土地政策

1. 土地法律法规概况

（1）根据摩洛哥法律，土地可以公有，也可以私有。公有土地为摩洛哥国家所有，不得出售。私有土地由自然人或法人实体私人所有。私有土地有两种类型：登记土地和未登记土地。

① 登记土地

登记土地受 1913 年关于土地登记的皇家法令的调整，该法已由 2011 年第 14-07 号法律修订。登记制度保证了土地交易的安全。因此，任何交易或土地上的任何权利，如所有者权利、承租人权利和抵押权人权利等，必须登记在摩洛哥土地登记册（the Moroccan land register）上才有效、合法并产生约束第三人的效力。

与登记土地有关的交易应履行一些手续来确保其效力并在摩洛哥土地登记处进行登记。例如，摩洛哥登记土地的取得应以书面契约的形式作出，并由公证员进行公证。后者在未事先调查土地现有权利和事后告知买方（如有）的情况下，不能进行契约公证。

公证员还应在出售前清理土地上的所有欠缴税款和税收管理权。最后，公证员将自行完成土地取得登记并支付所有的登记费。该登记将授予买方由摩洛哥土地登记官颁发的所有权证。

② 未登记土地

根据摩洛哥法律，未登记土地被归为"私有"土地，意味着认可因占有而取得土地，因为任何人通过证明其以所有者身份占有和使用未经登记土地超过十年，便可优先取得对该未登记土地的所有权。

未登记土地受伊斯兰教法律传统规则的调整，可以出售、出租、扣押或征用。相比登记土地，未登记的土地并不保证所有者能够安全地保有权利。但需要注意的是，任何未登记的土地均可根据所有权人的要求履行登记手续。

（2）不动产权。

不动产权由 2011 年 11 月 22 日第 39-08 号法律规制。不动产权有两种类型：主不动产权和从属不动产权。

主不动产权即所有权。从属不动产权依赖于个人权利而存在并以其作为该个人权利实现的担保。产生于不动产之上的从属不动产权有三种：留置权、质押权和抵押权。

法定留置权（Privilège）源于法律的单独规定。它因债务人对债权人所负担的债务而授予债权人对债务人财产的优先权利。该法定留置权可以是一般留置权或特定留置权。

由合同约定的留置权可以是质押权（antichrèse）或抵押权（hypothèque）。质押权是一种不动产的质押，债务人脱离对其财产的占有以作为对债权人的担保。

依据摩洛哥法律，抵押是一种债务人准予债权人对其不动产享有权利的合同。债务人违约时，债权人便有权向摩洛哥法院请求履行抵押合同，从而出售抵押的不动产并从销售价格中获得偿付。抵押合同是一种担保权益，无需债务人脱离对抵押财产的占有。

2. 外资企业取得土地的规定

一般而言，除农地外，摩洛哥企业和外资企业在获得土地方面没有差别。外国人无论是自然人或法人都无法获得摩洛哥的农地。就其他土地，无论登记与否，外国人均能以与本国国民相同的条件取得。然而，仍建议外国人获取登记的土地，以保护其土地权利并保有其所有权。

（五）公司设立和解散

1. 公司形式

摩洛哥《商业公司法》（the Moroccan Business Companies' Code）规定了几种公司形式：

（1）股份有限公司（SA）

股份有限公司形式通常适用于较大的公司。实际上，设立股份有限公司需要至少 5 个股东和最低 30 万迪拉姆的出资。公司若寻求公众投资，则最低需出资 300 万迪拉姆。

股份有限公司可以发行很多种记载不同权利的股票，这些权利涉及投票权、股息和企业清算时的分配权。不同类别的股票可以有不同的票面价值，唯一限制是，股份有限公司的股票是报价出售的，股票票面价值不得低于 100 迪拉姆。

股份有限公司有两种管理形式可供选择。股份有限公司可由董事会管理或者由监事会和管理委员会共同管理。

在此类公司中，股东的责任限于股东所持股份的数额。公司成立时，若以现金出资，须预付 1/4 的股本金。若以实物出资，则须全额缴付。

（2）有限责任公司（SARL）

有限责任公司由较少的人员组成，所需资本较少，通常更容易设立、管理和运营。因其转化为股份有限公司相对容易，通常被用作成长中企业的过渡形式。

有限责任公司可由 1—50 个合伙人组成。如果超过 50 个合伙人，公司必须在两年内改制为股份有限公司。此类公司没有最低资本额，然而公司章程必须表明股份的价值以及任何实物出资的价值。

有限责任公司由一个或多个经理人（Gérant or cogérants）管理，他们无需成为股东但必须是个人而非公司。这些经理人由合伙人任命。

经理人员管理不善时亦适用民事和刑事责任。有限责任公司的股东以其出资额为限承担责任。

（3）分支机构（Succursale）

分支机构不视为独立的法人实体，须遵守摩洛哥及原籍国的法律。

分支机构没有法定最低资本限制，也没有股东。这类公司须任命至少一个经理人且仍须服从母公司的决策。

财务方面，它属于常设性机构，且需缴纳所得税和公司税。

（4）代表处（Bureau de representation）

代表处是一种非完整实体，并非独立法人，完全由总公司所有。代表处无权从事营利性商业活动。从法律角度说，没有备案登记要求。代表处将根据所产生的收入上缴商业税和可能的所得税。

（5）合伙公司（SNC）

普通合伙是合伙的一种形式，所有的合伙人都分别对合伙债务承担连带责任。

所有合伙人都可以代表公司从事商业活动，并对合伙公司债务负无限连带责任。合伙的名称为所有或一个或多个合伙人的姓名后加以"和公司"（and company）的字样。

（6）有限合伙（SCS）

有限合伙有两类合伙人，一类是普通合伙人（associés commandités）：可代表公司从事商业活动，对合伙债务承担无限连带责任；一类是有限合伙人（associés commanditaires）：以其出资额为限对合伙债务承担责任。

（7）股份制有限合伙（SCA）

这类公司的资本被划分为可自由流通转让的股份，并以持股证明为代表。

有两类合伙人：普通合伙人，被视为可代表公司从事商业活动的人，对股份制有限合伙的债务承担连带责任；有限合伙人，被视为股东，仅以其出资为限承担损失。有限合伙人的人数不少于3人。

2. 设立程序

本节仅涉及有限责任公司和股份有限公司的设立，因为这两种公司类型在摩洛哥最为普遍。

在摩洛哥设立公司在区域投资中心（CRI）进行，这些区域投资中心设在摩洛哥最重要的城市（即卡萨布兰卡、拉巴特、马拉喀什、阿加迪尔、丹吉尔等），这样操作便利了公司设立进程。

为进行企业设立，投资者应取得并准备下列文件：

① 由摩洛哥工业和商业产权局（the Moroccan Industrial and Commercial Property Office）颁布的可在公司存续期间持续保留商号的商号证书（certificate négatif）；

② 与有固定住所的当地公司签订的租赁协议或注册地址协议；

③ 载有法定事项的公司章程；

④ 法语或阿拉伯语文本的章程和登记文件；

⑤ 资金冻结证书；

⑥ 向区域投资中心提出的本地实体的设立申请。

对于有限责任公司，若资本不足10万迪拉姆，则并不强制要求在企业设立前开立银行账户或取得资金冻结证书。

此外，股东/合伙人若为公司的，还应提供商业登记证、公司章程和法定代表人的护照。股东是自然人的，只需提供护照复印件。

一旦所需文件入档备案，CRI将颁发全套的登记证书（税务证、与社会保险有关的证书、商业登记号）。

3. 解散方式及要求

摩洛哥公司进行解散/清算的，应由股东/合伙人特别大会决定公司的预期解散，任命一个或多个清算人，并决定该一个或多个清算人的职权范围及清算总部的设置。

清算人可在股东或任何其他个人/公司中选定。清算的总部可以设在摩洛哥的任何地点，但该处必须保留会计。

公司解散决定作出后的30日内，清算人必须将决定公司解散的股东特别会议的会议纪要向税务登记服务处和商业登记处送并存档，并在《摩洛哥司法制报》和《摩洛哥政府公报》上发布公司解散的决定。

在解散决定做出后的45日内，根据《摩洛哥税法》（the Moroccan Tax law）第150条第1项的规定，由股东/合伙人特别会议选任的清算人须明确公司资产和平衡公司债务。

该项工作完成后，公司清算人须召集股东/合伙人特别会议，批准由清算人拟备的清算报告和会计报告，终结清算程序并组织清算人退场。

在上述解散决定作出后的30日内，清算人必须将批准公司清算的股东/合伙人特别会议的会议纪要向税务登记服务处和商业登记处送并存档，并且将公司批准清算的事项公布在摩洛哥报纸和《摩洛哥政府公报》上。

然而，在下列特别情况下，公司解散是被迫的：

• 有限责任公司：如果公司资本损失达3/4，经理人必须就是否对公司解散进行表决并征求股东的意见。

• 股份有限公司：如果股东人数减至不足5人并持续1年以上，则商事法院可应任何利害关系人的请求而宣布公司解散。在公司资产减至不足其资本的1/4时，也可能被解散。在此情况下，董事会须召集一次特别大会来决定是否解散。

• 合伙公司：除非公司章程有相反规定，合伙公司将于合伙人之一死亡时终止。在企业破产、歇业或合伙人之一丧失行为能力的情况下，除非公司章程规定此种情况下延续或全体合伙人一致同意，否则合伙公司将被解散。

（六）兼并收购

在摩洛哥，根据 2014 年《价格自由与竞争法》（the Law on the Freedom of Price and Competition）的规定，每项兼并行为均应在正式实施之前，由参与兼并的相关主体应事先通知竞争委员会（Conseil de la Concurrence）。

通知义务由取得对一个公司全部或部分控制权的个人和公司履行，或在兼并或创建共同公司的情况下，须向所有相关方发出共同通知。

此外，满足下列三项条件的，便需作出通知：

- 参与兼并的全部公司或公司集团或个人的全球不含税总营业额超过 7.5 亿迪拉姆（约 6 900 万欧元）；
- 参与兼并的至少两家公司或集团公司或个人在摩洛哥所实现的不含税总营业额超过 2.5 亿迪拉姆（约 2 300 万欧元）；
- 公司当事方（或受兼并，或与其有经济上的关联）在过去一个日历年内，在国内同类可互换的货物、产品或服务市场上共实现超过 40% 销售额、购买额或任何其他交易额，或在上述市场上占据可观的地位。

最后，竞争委员会有权对负有事先通知义务的主体进行罚款，最高数额为最近财政年度内在摩洛哥所实现的不含税营业额的 5%。符合条件的，还会随着被其收购的公司所实现的营业额而增加。对个人来说，最高罚款额为 500 万迪拉姆（约 45 万欧元）。

（七）竞争管制

1. 竞争管制主管机构

摩洛哥竞争委员会是一个独立的行政机构，负责监督竞争管制和竞争规则的施行。政府首脑对竞争委员会就有关集中交易的公共利益事项所作的决定保留最后的诸如撤销的权力。

在摩洛哥，一些特定行业由该行业主管部门进行规制，如电信行业由国家电信管理局（ANRT）进行规制；视听市场行业由高级视听传媒管理委员会（HACA）进行规制；银行业由马格里布银行即摩洛哥中央银行进行规制；资本市场由摩洛哥资本市场管理局（AMMC）进行规制；港口由国家港口局（ANP）进行规制；保险由保险和社会福利管理局（ACAPS）进行规制。

2. 竞争法概况

摩洛哥竞争管理的主要法律是 2014 年 6 月 30 日第 104–12 号《价格自由和竞争法》[1]和 2014 年 6 月 30 日与竞争委员会有关的第 20–13 号法律[2]。

其他法律法规可以是某些特定行业部门所适用的部门条例，如电信、视听、资本市场、银行、港口和保险等。

此外，不公平竞争由下列法律规范：

- 1913 年 8 月 12 日《摩洛哥民法》（the Moroccan Civil Law）；以及
- 由第 23–13 号法律修订的第 17–97 号《工业产权保护法》（the Law on the Protection of Industrial Property）。[3]

3. 竞争管制措施

摩洛哥的竞争管制常通过禁止反竞争行为和兼并管制来保护价格自由和竞争自由。

（1）反竞争行为

摩洛哥竞争法禁止并惩处下列各种集体或个人行为：

- 反竞争协定或协同行为（Les ententes anticoncurrentielles）：限制、歪曲或妨碍摩洛哥市场竞争的

---

[1] 由 2014 年 6 月 30 日第 1-14-116 号皇家法令公布。
[2] 由 2014 年 6 月 30 日第 1-14-117 号皇家法令公布。
[3] 由 2000 年 2 月 15 日第 1-00-91 号皇家法令公布。

协定、公约和协同行为，特别是控制生产、限制进入市场或共享市场、限制供应来源的行为；

摩洛哥竞争法为法律或法规文本中的禁止性协议规定了某些豁免，以促进经济进步或不在实质上限制竞争。

• 滥用市场支配地位：摩洛哥竞争法禁止滥用支配地位或对没有任何同等替代性选择的供应商或客户的经济依赖地位。可表现为拒绝销售、搭售、歧视性的销售条件，因拒绝不公平的销售条件而终止商业关系或因最低转售价和最低利润率而终止商业关系。

• 滥用低定价和其他限制竞争行为（pratiques restrictives de la concurrence）。

竞争委员会可着手进行调查、扣押文件、下令采取临时措施并根据违法严重程度处以罚款，数额可达涉案公司在全球或国内统一最高营业额的10%（行为主体是自然人的，为400万迪拉姆）。理事会也可决定其他处罚措施，如在民事上认定无效、发布停止反竞争行为的禁止令或公开理事会的决定等。

（2）兼并管制

摩洛哥竞争法规范三种类型的交易：

• 两个或多个独立企业的合并；

• 通过获取资本份额、收购资产、订立合同或任何其他方式，由一个（单独控制）或多个（共同控制）企业取得对另一企业或多个企业的全部或部分控制权；

• 设立长期履行独立企业职能的合资企业。

符合下列条件之一的，当事人依法必须将任何上述交易事先通知竞争委员会：

• 集中交易各方在全球范围内的税前总计营业额等于或大于7.5亿迪拉姆；

• 集中交易中至少两方在摩洛哥的税前总计营业额等于或大于2.5亿迪拉姆；

• 集中交易的各方或被集中的对象，在过去一个日历年内，在国内市场上的销售、采购或其他交易中共产生40%以上的应计价值。

关于通知程序，一旦有关当事方能够出具充分具体的文件以便于进行案件调查，尤其在当事人已经签订协议、签署意向书或宣布公开要约时，就必须在交易执行前通知竞争委员会。

如果没有提交通知，除非恢复至交易前的状态，否则竞争委员会将以按日收取罚款的形式迫使当事人提交交易行为的通知。

竞争委员会的决定可以上诉至摩洛哥有管辖权的法院。

（八）税收

针对所得税避免双重征税和禁止偷税、漏税，中摩双方于2002年8月27日缔结一项避免双重征税的双边协定。

摩洛哥的税收制度规定在《摩洛哥税法通则》（the General Tax Code 或 OGI）中，主要税种有：

• 个人和私有公司收入和盈利的所得税；

• 公司和其他法律实体赚取收入和盈利的公司税；

• 适用于消费支出的增值税（VAT）；

• 注册税和印花税。

此外，为鼓励投资和推动某些部门发展，现有关于税收优惠的法律规定，预想在一般法和部门法的层面实行税收豁免。

（1）所得税（IT）

所得税适用于未选择适用公司税的自然人和法律实体的收入和利润。有关的收入为：

• 工资收入；

• 专业收入；

• 土地收入和利润；

• 动产和利润所得；

• 农业收入。

收入组别（迪拉姆）	税率
0～30 000	0%
30 001～50 000	10%
50 001～60 000	20%
60 001～80 000	30%
80 001～180 000	34%
＞180 000	38%

（2）公司税

公司税强制适用于资本公司、公共机构和其他开展营利性业务的公司取得的收入和利润，并以不可撤销的方式适用于合伙公司。

公司收入（迪拉姆）	税率
0～300 000	10%
300 001～1 000 000	20%
＞1 000 000	31%

（3）增值税（VAT）

增值税适用于工业、手工业、商业和自由职业活动及进口业务，税率为20%。还有三档较低税率，7%和10%的税率专门适用于消费品和某些食品、饮料及旅店行业，14%的税率适用于其他产品。

税 率	产 品
14%	•可以抵扣的品名有茶叶、黄油、运输、电力、商用轻型车辆和轻便摩托车、太阳能热水器等； •抵扣不适用于保险代理商或经纪人提供的服务。
10%	可以抵扣的品名： •酒店和其他旅馆住宿或翻修活动； •为餐馆现场消费提供的以及服务商向公司雇员提供的食品和饮料销售服务； •食用油； •太阳能热水器； •渔业人员用的渔具和渔网； •大米、意大利面和食用盐； •石油天然气和其他烃类气体，以及石油和页岩油； •银行和信贷业务（包括向当地社区发放预付款和贷款相关的业务和利益以及投机类替代金融产品）及外汇佣金； •与共同基金发行股票或股份有关的交易； •经纪公司开展的与证券有关的交易； •公共设施基金开展的业务及与为该基金发放贷款和预付款相关的业务； •持照专业人员开展的业务（律师、口译员、公证员、兽医等）； •公司直接向员工置办的餐饮活动； •家畜和低产动物饲料； •农业专用设备。
7%	可以抵扣的品名： •某些消费品（提供给公共配售系统的水、沙丁鱼罐头、奶粉、学校用品及投入，医药产品及投入等）； •精制或结块糖； •奶粉； •经济型汽车及其制造所需的所有产品和材料，以及按照监管条件提供的装配服务。

（九）证券

1. 证券法律法规概况

2012年12月28日第44-12号关于公开发行（appel public à l'épargne）的法律所界定的金融工具

包括：证券、集合投资基金股份和衍生品。

（1）证券

证券是可以在证券交易所上市交易、互换的金融工具，受股份有限公司第 17-95 号法律的规制。证券有两类：股票和债券。

股票是一种证券，是公司股份的所有权单位，是对公司资产和收益的一种请求权。持有人享受与股票相关的权利（知情、投票权、股息等）。股票可以是记名或不记名，不记名股票的股东身份对发行人公开。

债券是一种债务担保，代表对发行人的请求权。债券持有人在债券到期前有权获取定期利息。债券工具可由发行人根据资金结构和意图达成的目标采取很多种形式（固定利率、浮动利率、可转换债券等）。

（2）集合投资基金

集合投资基金有三种类型：共同基金、风险投资基金和证券化信托。

共同基金是一家投资公司，其资金投资于证券和/或其他流动金融资产，并由第 53-01 号法律修订后的 1993 年 9 月 21 日皇家法令进行规制。其存在两种合法的公司形式：开放式共同基金（SICAV）和共同基金。

• 开放式共同基金是拥有可变资本的有限责任公司，唯一目的是管理证券和现金投资组合。

• 共同基金是证券和现金的共同所有权。

风险投资基金（VCF）是一种进行风险投资的基金，受经由 2015 年 2 月 19 日第 18-14 号法律修订的第 41-05 号法律的规制。VCF 有两种：风险投资公司和风险投资中的集合投资基金（CIF）。

风险投资人预计将以股权、可转换证券/债券以及给股东预付保证金的形式为中小型企业提供融资。风险投资 CIF 的法律形式有：

• 风险投资公司：以合伙为典型组织形式，普通合伙人担任公司经理；

• 风险投资中的 CIF：以有限责任公司为组织形式。

证券化信托并非法律实体，而是一种共有权，受经由第 05-14 号法律修订的 2004 年 4 月 21 日第 33-06 号法律的规制。证券化是一种金融交易，在此交易中证券化信托通过发行股份和/或发行债券从一个或多个发起人处获得合同债务。

（3）金融行业工具

金融行业工具由 2014 年 5 月 14 日第 42-12 号法律规制。金融行业工具可以是期货、掉期或期权。然而，金融行业工具市场在摩洛哥还未发挥作用。

2. 证券市场的监管

摩洛哥资本市场由依据 2013 年 3 月 13 日第 43-12 号法律设立的摩洛哥资本市场管理局（AMMC）监管。其任务是：

• 确保投资于金融工具的储蓄款得到保护；

• 确保投资者的公平待遇、资本市场以及投资者信息的透明度和完整性；

• 确保资本市场的正常运作，并确保法律和规章规定的执行；

• 确保对受其控制的不同组织和个人的活动进行控制；

• 确保受其控制的个人和机构遵守反洗钱相关的法律法规；

• 推动对储蓄者的金融教育；

• 协助政府管理资本市场。

为完成上述任务，AMMC 有权采取下列行为：

（1）详情通告

通过详情通告，AMMC 设定专业实践操作规则、道德规范和法律法规在技术上和实践中的应用规则。拟定详情通告的过程应与专业人士合作进行，并在规制证券市场的国际标准方面采用最佳做法。

详情通告由政府批准并在《摩洛哥政府公报》上发表"官方公告"。

（2）利害关系方的授权

AMMC 授权个人在其控制的法人中履行某些职能。

授权形式是在审查后授予专业卡,并根据履行职能的性质确定其有效期。

AMMC 保留已向公众披露的获得授权人士的登记册。

(3)产品有关的签证、认证和意见

在适当情况下,AMMC 就集体储蓄产品进行认证或对其情况发表意见,并对提供给投资者的招股说明书授予签证。所涉产品有可转换证券的集合投资公司(UCITS)、风险投资基金和证券化信托。

通过这一特权,AMMC 通过确保利害关系方遵守金融产品和投资者信息的法律法规要求,及证实利害关系方具备管理哪些产品的能力来保证投资安全。

(4)审查利害关系方的批准文件

批准程序中的利害关系方是经纪公司、风险投资基金和证券化信托管理公司。AMMC 审查批准文件后,向财政大臣发出准予或不予批准的通知。AMMC 应证实被认可的利害关系方能够提供充分的保证,尤其是在组织、技术、财务资源和管理人员的经验方面。

(5)金融交易招股说明书签证

AMMC 审查了发布给投资者的信息的充分性和一致性之后,批准发行人关于公开发行、回购计划的招股说明书。目的是确保投资者掌握所有相关信息以作出在知情基础上的决定。经 AMMC 批准的招股说明书可在交易开始前向公众自由告知。

(6)发行人财务报告控制

该制度控制的目标是确保投资者定期收到有关发行人的信息。因此,AMMC 确保发行人履行公布年度、半年度和季度财务报表的义务,并披露可能影响其股价或影响证券持有人储蓄金的所有重要信息。

发行人确保信息简明、真实、准确,并及时向全体金融界披露。

(7)专业人员控制

受 AMMC 控制的专业机构和人员有经纪公司、证券交易所、账户持有人、中央储备库和管理公司。

该控制采用两种互补方式:通过在中介机构营业场所进行检查的现场控制,以及通过由 AMMC 确定了内容和频次的报告所进行的文件控制。

该项控制的主要目的是确保专业机构和人员,尤其在组织、技术、财务和人力资源方面,能够长久性地拥有充分的保障措施,并确认其递交申请获批的条件得以维持。

(8)投诉处理

AMMC 收到投资者关于可疑的证券交易投诉的,会核查投诉与事实是否一致,并据此采取适当行动。

(9)监督、调查和制裁

AMMC 确保证券市场交易符合规则,以保证市场完整性。AMMC 在必要时可进行调查。

调查证实后,AMMC 有权对违法或违反规范其活动或规范市场运行之规则的当事方发布制裁。制裁措施需要在尊重相关方权利的基础上作出。

3. 外资企业参与证券交易的要求

外资企业在摩洛哥金融市场上公开发行股份或债券需要 AMMC 的事先批准。此外,外资企业投资摩洛哥金融市场还需要通知摩洛哥外汇局(ODC)。该声明将准予 ODC 控制投资收益的调回。

(十)投资优惠及保护

1. 优惠政策框架

实施先进的区域化政策并采取"2014—2020 工业加速计划",以及升级有益于投资的行业部门,目的是支持工业生态系统,以实现长期可持续的经济增长。

在此框架内,根据项目类别,投资者可在符合申请条件和资格标准的情况下得到好处。

一方面,"战略性"和"结构化"项目能够将财政支助指向工业生态系统。"战略性"投资项目按其经济影响分为以投资创造永久性工作机会的"持久运转"项目和涉及公共秩序的"承包商"项目。"结构化"投资项目分为"首创型""资源增值型""地方一体化""采购型"项目和"工程与研发中心"项目。

另一方面,工业和投资发展基金(the Industrial and Investment Development Fund)涉及向满足具体

标准并符合《投资宪章》及其适用法令的投资者提供直接财政支持的相关业务。

值得注意的是，该基金提供的利益可以累积，但援助或支持不能超过投资项目总额的5%，或者当项目在某些地域实施或涉及特定领域的投资时，不能超过项目总额的10%。

2. 对特定行业与地区的支持

对特定行业和地区的工业投资由以下机构通过他们之间达成的协议提供支助：哈桑二世经济与社会发展基金（FHII），投资贸易和信息经济部的工业司，以及经济与财政部。

为了从上述部门提供的支持中获益，投资者应与FHII签订合同。新的投资项目（新建或扩展）若符合以下所有要求的，均可得益于FHII的资助：不含税投资总额超过1 000万迪拉姆；生产资料投资超过500万迪拉姆（不包括进口关税和税收）；并且投资公司须从事汽车制造业、航空航天业、电子业、化工业和制药业，以及与纳米技术、微电子和生物技术相关的生产制造活动。

此外，特殊经济区域和满足工业与投资发展基金提供财政支助条件的投资者，亦有资格从中获益。

3. 特殊经济区域

（1）免税出口区

免税出口区按照免税出口区域有关的法律执行，该法将其定义为这样一种关税区：有资格在此区域设立的公司就其所有以工业或商业为目的的出口活动以及相关服务活动，可免受海关、对外贸易和外汇方面的管制。

每个区域都是由一项法令创建和划界分隔的，该法令决定了可能设立于此的公司的性质和活动。主要的免税出口区域分布在丹吉尔、Tangier Med Ksar el Majaz Mellousa的1号和2号免税区①、达赫拉、阿尤恩、Kebdana②、纳祖尔（碳氢化合物储存地）及盖尼特拉。出口加工区的承租人确保区域开发和管理，以及为获得主管该区域的地方委员会的批准而呈递投资者档案。

（2）卡萨布兰卡金融城

根据2010年12月的第44–10号法律，卡萨布兰卡金融城（CFC）是为符合法律、经济和财务标准的公司所创建的标签城市，并给予他们巨大的税收优惠、外汇管制便利和利用商业设施的便利。

4. 投资保护

在摩洛哥促进和保护外国投资不仅限于《投资宪章》的规定、国家投资和出口发展署（AMDIE）的职责，还包括其加入的、作为加强与主要合作伙伴关系的一部分的多边国际公约和双边条约的约定。这些公约和条约规定了各方之间的同等待遇和相互保护。这些条约和公约的主要条款基于以下几个方面的内容：

• 对投资待遇承认"最惠国待遇"原则；
• 资本和收入的自由转移；
• 除因公用利益且经过司法决定（在非歧视的基础上，并及时给予充分赔偿）征用之外不得征用投资；
• 损害赔偿的保证；
• 经由投资者选择通过国内法院或国际仲裁机构进行争端解决。

（1）国际公约

摩洛哥已批准关于担保和保护投资的国际公约，包括设立国际投资争端解决中心（ICSID）、多边投资担保机构（MIGA）和阿拉伯国际投资担保公司（the Inter-Arab Organization for Investment Guarantee Corporation）的协定。

（2）双边条约

摩洛哥还通过国家投资委员会（Commission Nationale des Investissements）与阿拉伯、非洲、欧洲、亚洲和美洲国家签署了六十多项双边投资协定，该投资委员会由政府首长担任主席，由AMDIE保障秘书处工作，以确保投资者保护和投资，并协调国内规定与国际标准。

---

① Tangier Med是直布罗陀海峡沿岸的物流门户和工业区，Ksar el Majaz是摩洛哥西水部临近地中海沿岸的一个小城镇，Mellousa是位于丹吉尔东南部的一个城市，三个区域共同组成一个自由贸易区。——译者注。
② Kebdana是位于摩洛哥北部、纳祖尔市东部的一个地方。——译者注。

三、贸易

（一）贸易主管部门

在摩洛哥，贸易方面的主要监管部门是摩洛哥工业投资贸易和信息经济部。

该部没有中央行政机构。分管以下 9 个方面：工业、贸易和分配、信息经济、统计和监测、质量和市场监督、先进技术与创新研发、接待、合作与沟通、资源和信息系统。

摩洛哥工业投资贸易和信息经济部有以下职责：
- 制定与工业、贸易、新技术和邮政部门有关的发展战略并将其转化为实施方案；
- 批准发展投资和提高中小企业竞争力的战略并将其转化为实施方案；
- 指导并实施与工业、贸易、新技术以及邮政部门有关的发展战略；
- 管理摩洛哥在工业、贸易、新技术领域与其他国家和国际组织的关系；
- 在工业，贸易和新技术领域开展研究工作并编制统计数据；
- 获取、保存并评估工业、贸易和新技术部门的发展战略和商业情报；
- 促进和发展工业和新技术领域的创新；
- 发展和协调工业，商业、技术接待以及创新产业园区的工作；
- 协助制定工业、贸易和新技术领域的培训计划并促进其实施；
- 制定工业，贸易和新技术部门的法律和组织框架；
- 对工业、贸易和新技术领域的规章制定提出建议；
- 对邮政部门进行监管；
- 发展伙伴关系、合作并推进合作项目；
- 促进工业、贸易和新技术领域的质量和安全；
- 确保对计量、认证、质量、公司安全的控制，监测摩洛哥市场以及保护消费者权益；
- 确保工业、贸易和新技术领域的交流。

（二）贸易法律法规概况

摩洛哥与贸易相关的主要法律法规如下：
- 1996 年 8 月 1 日颁布的第 15-95 号法律，构成《商法典》（经修订和完成）（及其法令），主要涉及适用于商人和商业公司的条款，商业资产，支票，汇票和类似票据（商业票据），商业合同（例如抵押贷款、租赁、银行合同等）和经营困难（特别是破产程序）；
- 1996 年 8 月 30 日颁布的第 17-95 号法律是关于联合股份公司的（SA）（经修订和完成）（其法令编号为 2-09-481），该法令主要规范摩洛哥的联合股份公司和简化联合股份公司（SAS）；
- 1997 年 2 月 13 日颁布的关于合伙关系的第 5-96 号法律主要规范合伙制企业（SNC），有限合制企业（SCS），股份有限合伙制企业（SCA），有限责任公司（SARL）和未申报的合作伙伴关系（合资企业）（经修订和完成）；
- 1999 年 2 月 5 日颁布的关于经济利益集团（GIE）的第 13-97 号法律（经修订和完成）；
- 2014 年 6 月 30 日颁布的第 104-12 号法律（及其法令），规定了价格和竞争自由的有关内容；
- 2011 年 2 月 18 日颁布的第 31-08 号法律颁布消费者保护措施（及其法令和命令）；
- 2014 年 12 月 24 日颁布的关于信贷机构和同类机构的第 103-12 号法律；
- 2000 年 2 月 15 日关于保护工业产权的第 17-97 号法律（经修订和完成）（及其法令和命令）；
- 2000 年 2 月 15 日关于著作权和类似权利的第 2-00 号法律（经修订和完成）（及其法令和命令）；
- 1984 年 10 月 5 日颁布的关于反商品欺诈的第 13-83 号法律；
- 皇家法令颁布的 1977 年 10 月 9 日第 1-77-339 号法律，颁布了海关和间接税管理局主管的海关和海关间接税收管理法（经修订和完成）（及其法令和命令）；
- 1919 年 3 月 31 日颁布的《海商法》（经修订和完成）（及其法令）。

除此之外，摩洛哥还根据上述法律制定了许多次级法规，详细规定了与特定贸易有关的事项。

(三) 贸易管理

1. 一般贸易规定和反不正当竞争

在摩洛哥,《贸易法》是管理贸易和贸易商行为的法律文本。

贸易法中包含了进行贸易活动的一般要求,例如贸易商地位的取得、商业能力、贸易商的义务等。

贸易商的地位是通过开展贸易法中列举的通常或专业的商业活动获得的。例如:

- 购买家具进行转售或租赁;
- 租赁家具用于转租;
- 购买不动产后在国内转售或加工后在国内转售;
- 工业或手工活动;
- 运输;
- 银行、信贷和金融交易;
- 保险业务;
- 通过任何形式或媒介进行的印刷和出版;
- 建筑和公共工程;
- 商务、旅行、信息和广告的办公室和机构;
- 提供产品和服务。

摩洛哥的贸易活动受到有关价格和竞争自由(及其法令)的第 104-12 号法律的规制。

本法适用于:

① 任何个人或法人实体无论在摩洛哥境内是否拥有注册办事处或营业场所,只要是其经营或行为对摩洛哥全部或部分市场的竞争产生影响或者是有产生影响的目的;

② 所有生产、分销和服务活动;

③ 出口协议对摩洛哥国内市场相应领域的竞争产生影响。

该法主要规定了自由定价、反不正当竞争、控制兼并和限制竞争的原则和规定。

根据该法规定,下列以限制或妨害市场竞争为目的的行为是被禁止的:一致的行动、协议、公约或联盟,无论基于何种理由和形式建立,当它们倾向于:

① 限制其他公司进入市场或者自由竞争;

② 人为地推动市场价格上涨和下跌来阻碍市场自由调整价格;

③ 限制或控制生产、销售、投资或技术进步;

④ 划分市场,供应来源或公共市场。

下列以防止、限制或妨碍竞争为目的的行为是被禁止的:

公司或者集团滥用:

- 国内市场的主导地位;
- 客户或供应商存在经济依赖情况,并且没有任何其他等同的替代方案。

同时,向消费者的报价或者实际出售的价格不允许不合理地低于成本,如果上述产品优惠价格的目的是为了垄断市场、阻碍其他企业或者产品进入市场,则该产品将被禁止加工和销售。

此外,法律还规定了经营者集中制度。以下情况需要进行审核:

- 两个或更多的独立公司合并;
- 已经控制一家企业的个人通过直接或者间接的形式包括但不限于通过股权收购、资产收购、合同等形式控制另一家企业或多家企业的全部或部分业务;
- 当一家或多家企业直接或者间接通过收购股权、购买资产、合同或任何其他形式控制另一家或者多家企业的全部或部分业务。

新的兼并控制制度规定,在满足下列条件之一时,向竞争委员会发出通知是强制性的:

- 所有相关方(企业、自然人或法人团体)的全球税前总营业额超过 7.5 亿迪拉姆(约合 7 000 万欧元);
- 至少两方主体(企业或自然人或法人团体)在摩洛哥取得的税前营业额超过 2.5 亿迪拉姆(约合

2 200 万欧元）；

• 在摩洛哥的市场份额合计等于或超过 40%。

2. 电子贸易和消费者保护

摩洛哥的电子贸易不受具体法律的约束。唯一颁布的法律主要规定了法律数据的电子传输问题。上述法律规定了电子数据交换的制度以及纸质和电子文件、纸质签名和电子签名的效力一致。

它还确定了适用于电子认证服务提供者进行操作的法律框架，以及电子认证服务提供者和电子证书持有者需遵守的规则。

另外，摩洛哥通过颁布关于保护个人信息处理方面的第 09-08 号法律来加强专门保护私人数据的法律制度。该文本的制定旨在保护互联网用户免遭可能影响其隐私的数据滥用。

有关法律数据电子传输的法律规定了以电子形式制定或以电子方式传送的文件的有效性，以及适用于确保电子签名、加密和电子认证有效的法律制度。

在摩洛哥，消费者权益由 2011 年 2 月 18 日颁布的第 31-08 号法律规定，该法规定了消费者保护措施及其相关的法令和命令。

该法的目的为：

① 确保消费者对其可能获得或者使用的产品、商品或者服务可以获得准确、清楚的信息；

② 保障消费者在其签订的合同中的权利，特别是不公平条款、与金融服务有关的条款、消费者和房地产贷款的条款、远程销售和门到门销售的条款；

③ 确保在产品出售和售后服务中有缺陷时有法律和合同上的保护，并确定消费者权益受侵害时的损害赔偿的条件和程序；

④ 确保依据本法运行的消费者保护协会代表并保护消费者利益。

（四）进出口商品检验检疫

进出口商品的检验检疫由摩洛哥海关进行。

皇家法令 1977 年 10 月 9 日颁布的第 77-339 号法律，批准了海关和间接税收管理局颁布的海关和间接税收法典（经修订和完成）（及其法令和命令），规定了海关服务和征收间接税的基本原则，货物的清关，行政部门征税及相关权力，海关的管理体系、特殊制度、对外关系，监督对外贸易及其变化态势，间接税，适用于饮料、酒精和酒精类产品的国内消费税，适用于石油产品、铂金和白银材料及工序的担保，人造烟草等的国内消费税。

此外，针对不同类型的商品，海关处理上还有一些二级法律和规定，例如：

• 第 24-89 号法律规定了进口动物、动物产品、动物繁殖产品以及海鲜和淡水生鲜的动物健康措施；

• 第 2-01-2689 号法令规定了在公共假期期间和海关管理局关闭时间，边防哨所执行兽医管制特别措施的条件；

• 第 2-01-2690 号法令规定了在公共假日期间和海关管理局关闭期间，边防哨所执行对植物进行控制、卫生和检疫处理特别措施的条件；

• 第 2-16-535 号法令禁止进口用于农业生产的塑料信封和毯子；

• 农业和农业发展部部长第 2249-94 号令规定了用于动物副产品加工的进口动物产品应满足的卫生条件和相应处理措施；

• 农业和农业发展部部长 514-94 号令，规定了进口牛、绵羊、山羊和马科动物的畜牧标准；

• 农业部部长与财政和外国投资部部长联合第 1726-96 号令，确定对进口动物、食品和动物产品开放的边境站的名单。

（五）海关管理

1. 适用的法律、法规和国际协议概述

（1）海关法

摩洛哥关于管理摩洛哥海关的主要法律是皇家法令 1977 年 10 月 9 日颁布的第 1-77-339 号法律，

批准了海关和间接税收管理局颁布的海关和间接税法典（经修订和完成）（及其命令和法令）。

（2）海关关税税则

海关关税取决于产品的性质（可分为动物、植物产品、动植物油脂及其分离产品、食品、饮料、烟草和人造烟草、矿物产品、化学或相关工业产品、塑料等）以及是否存在自由贸易协定。

（3）海关业务协定

摩洛哥在全球开放和自由化战略的框架内，在过去10年中建立了一个通过双边或区域性缔结自由贸易协定与其潜在合作伙伴发展商业关系的法律框架。摩洛哥随后缔结了多个贸易协定，其中包括：摩洛哥—欧盟关联协定、摩洛哥—美利坚合众国自由贸易协定、摩洛哥—欧洲自由贸易区自由贸易协定、摩洛哥—土耳其自由贸易协定，阿拉伯自由贸易区。

2. 海关管理和程序

进口时，共分为3个通关阶段：

① 货物在海关阶段：在此阶段进口货物直接进入第一办事处或者由海关邮政部门进行报关；

② 货物清关：向清关服务提供者提供简要声明及其他文件，由清关服务提供者代替承运人承担清关责任；

③ 货物结算：申报文件指定了货物适用的海关制度（释放消费、经济制度等），并作为所申报货物所有海关手续（而非海关）履行情况的证明。

出口时，共分为3个通关阶段：

① 货物出口清关手续：这一阶段包括将出口货物转移到海关或到政府指定的地点进行详细申报。这些货物应是原产于摩洛哥或者在摩洛哥主权领土及经济制度下自由流通的。作为出口商，只要相应海关对有关业务开放办理，就可以自由选择出口办事地点；

② 货物清关：在进口时，货物通关需要提交简要声明，出口时则不需要此类声明。货物必须在抵达离境办公室时详细申报；

在仓库和清关区域，用于出口的商品将在清关期间被一个特殊的登记处接管，并被送往离境办公室。

③ 出口通关：这一阶段的完成需提交货物适用的海关制度（简单出口、经济制度等）明确规定的申报文件。该申报文件详细说明已经完成了申报货物应提交的所有海关手续。

3. 统计

在进口方面，欧盟是摩洛哥的主要供应来源，约占进口量的47%，细分如下：

- 半成品（化学品、塑料、铜、钢铁等），占从欧盟进口商品总量的绝大部分；
- 工业设备（机械及其他设备、电线电缆、工业车辆、电气开关设备、发电机和电动机、研磨设备等）；
- 消费成品（乘用车、药品、乘用车零部件、织物等）。

从阿拉伯国家的进口数据来看，从这些地区的进口量占摩洛哥进口总量的15%左右。它们主要包括能源产品（原油和石油天然气），约占从这些国家进口量的67%，其次是半成品。

来自中国、美国和土耳其的进口约占总量的15%。

关于出口，欧盟仍然是摩洛哥主要出口客户。摩洛哥向欧盟市场销售包括完成消费品（成衣、针织品、乘用车、鞋类等），工业资本货物和用于切割或连接电路和食品的设备。

所有阿拉伯国家所占的出口市场份额仅达到出口商品的5%左右，主要侧重于半成品（原料银、板材、磷酸、肥料等）以及消费成品（乘用车、汽车、药品、香水等）。

四、劳动

（一）劳动法律法规概况

摩洛哥的主要劳动法律和法规如下：

- 2003年9月11日颁布的关于劳动法（及其法令）的第65–99号法律；

· 2004年12月29日关于单方面终止无限期雇佣协议通知期限的第2-04-469号法令。

无限期合同是基本的合同形式。

除非员工犯下严重的错误，否则无限期雇佣合同不能由雇主在没有支付赔偿的情况下终止。

在下列情况下允许签署固定期限雇佣合同：

- 在一名雇员的合同被中止的情况下由另一名雇员替换该名雇员；
- 暂时增加活动；
- 季节性工作；
- 首次开业或在公司内开设新公司或推出新产品。

固定期限合同的最多可签署1次，时限为1年，可续期1次。

如果员工在固定期限合同到期后继续工作，该合同到期后自动成为无限期合同。

劳动合同试用期如下：

对于固定期限雇佣合同：

- 签订合同的时间少于6个月时，试用期为15天；
- 签订合同的时间超过6个月时，试用期为1个月。

对于无限期雇佣合同：

- 高管试用期为3个月；
- 员工为1.5个月；
- 劳工为15天。

（二）外国人在当地工作规定

1. 工作许可

首先，应该指出的是，在摩洛哥工作的外国人与摩洛哥人一样，需要遵守国家调查劳动关系的相关法律：规定了《劳动法》的第65-99号法律。

《劳动法》规定，任何希望招聘外籍员工的雇主必须获得负责劳务的政府部门的授权。

因此，为了聘请外国人，应从摩洛哥劳动部获得授权。

授权日期表明工作许可的开始和结束时间。对合同的任何后续修改（工资、工作条件，尤其是修改合同期限、辞职、终止、解雇甚至更改雇主）也需要从劳动部获得签证。

因此，涉及外国人的雇用合同必须符合负责劳动的政府部门制定的模板。

如果摩洛哥雇主雇用外国雇员时未履行上述义务，根据《劳动法》第521条，雇主可能会被罚款2000至5000迪拉姆。

雇佣关系在签证到期时终止，当事人（雇主和雇员）互相不再承担义务。外籍雇员在签证到期后继续工作将被认为是不合法的。

2. 申请程序

申请获得工作许可所需的文件如下：

- 完成包括雇佣合约在内的申请；
- 毕业证书和工作证明（以法文翻译）；
- 护照复印件；
- 国家促进就业和竞争力机构（ANAPEC）颁发的证书，证明没有本国人选填补提议给外国雇员的职位。

但是，以下候选人免除ANAPEC申请程序和证书：

- 在摩洛哥出生的外国人，连续居住至少6个月；
- 摩洛哥公民的配偶；
- 公司的所有者、授权人员和管理人员；
- 公司的合伙人和股东；
- 合作框架内的代表或代表，任期不超过6个月；

- 教练和运动员；
- 外国艺术家；
- 政治难民和无国籍人士；
- 与摩洛哥达成协议的国家（阿尔及利亚、突尼斯和塞内加尔）的国民。

3. 社会保险

每名员工都有社会保险，其中包括健康保险、养老保险和伤残保险。社会保障缴费是强制性的。每月社会保障缴款的一部分由雇主支付，另一部分由雇员支付（通过扣缴机制）。

（三）出入境

1. 签证类型

2016年6月，摩洛哥穆罕默德六世国王访华，进一步取消了赴摩洛哥的中国游客签证要求。

对于国民没有获得摩洛哥入境签证豁免的国家，摩洛哥主管当局可以颁发四种入境签证：

- 短期签证，允许任何外国人由于移民以外的原因进入摩洛哥境内不间断的短期住宿或多次入境的短期住宿。每次停留的时间可以在 1～90 天之间。
- 长期签证有效期超过 3 个月，经摩洛哥外交和领事代表处事先与外交和合作部磋商后签发。该签证的有效期不得超过 1 年，每次停留期限可以在 1～90 天之间。

持有长期签证并希望在摩洛哥停留超过 3 个月的外国人必须向国家安全总局的主管部门申请获得居留证。

- 过境签证，授权外国人为前往第三国过境摩洛哥。这种签证可以为 1 或 2 次过境签发，而每次过境的持续时间不超过 72 小时。
- 在边境签发的签证：在特殊情况下，安全部门可以向边防哨所签发短期停留和过境签证。

签证可以是①普通的（即旅游、工作、商业、投资者、会议、学生、学员或研究人员、家庭团聚、记者、访客、医疗居留、难民和无国籍人士、机组人员、水手、技术人员援助、文化或体育赛事和艺术动画）或②官方（即认证签证、外交签证或服务签证）。

2. 出入境限制

相关规定有 2003 年 11 月 11 日颁布的第 2-03 号关于外国人在摩洛哥的入境和居留的移民和非正规移民的法令以及第 2-09-607 号关于外国人越过边界接受摩洛哥当局的控制的法令。后者要求对护照和签证进行有效性检查。相关限制还涉及对移民财政资源的核实，进入摩洛哥的原因以及他们返回本国的承诺。

如果外国人不符合上述条件，他可能会被拒绝进入摩洛哥。但是，被拒绝入境的外国人也享有一定的权利，例如通知本应该接待他的人、通知他的领事馆并与律师联系。

符合入境条件的外国人在签证有效期内可以留在摩洛哥境内。外国人逗留时间超过 3 个月的，其应在签证有效期届满前或者已经获得豁免签证外国人则在 90 天期限内，去其居留城市的警察局办理居留许可手续。第一次入境摩洛哥的，在申请居留许可时应提交体检证明和犯罪记录证明。

未能提交所要求的行政文件或证明文件的人、被下达驱逐令的人或者被法院命令禁止入境的人将被拒绝进入摩洛哥领土。

如果外国人在摩洛哥境内的停留对公共秩序构成严重威胁，摩洛哥政府可能会下达驱逐令。

（四）工会和劳工组织

目前，摩洛哥有 20 个专业工会。

1957 年 7 月 16 日关于职业工会的第 1-57-119 号皇家法令（经修正和补充）构成了工会权利和自由的法律基础。

根据这一法令：

- 工会负责组织和代表摩洛哥公民；
- （雇员）有创造和加入职业工会的自由；

- 罢工权利得到保证；
- 除"负责确保摩洛哥国家安全和维护公共秩序的代理人"之外，公务员还有权组建工会组织；
- 除提交章程和工会办公室成员名单外，摩洛哥政府不要求组建工会必须获得事先授权；
- 职业工会具有法人资格和起诉权；
- 工会有权创造、获得财产，建立共同基金和养老金，并签署集体协议。

（五）劳动争议

摩洛哥法院解决当事方或劳动监察员无法解决的劳资纠纷。

关于终止劳动合同，在存在严重不当行为的情况下，永久性劳动合同可以不经通知终止。

通知的应提前的期间如下：

① 对于高管们：
- 如果资历不足一年：提前 1 个月通知或直接支付 1 个月工资；
- 如果资历在 1 年至 5 年之间：提前 2 个月通知或直接支付 2 个月工资；
- 如果资历超过 5 年：提前 3 个月通知或直接支付 3 个月工资。

② 对于普通员工：
- 如果资历不到 1 年：提前 8 天通知或直接支付 8 天工资；
- 如果资历在 1 至 5 年之间：提前 1 个月通知或直接支付 1 个月工资；
- 如果资历超过 5 年：提前 2 个月通知或直接支付 2 个月工资。

如果员工没有发生严重错误，应支付遣散费。

遣散费根据雇员的资历和薪水计算如下：

① 法定赔偿：
- 工龄不满 5 年，支付 96 小时工资；
- 工龄从 6 年到 10 年，支付 144 小时工资；
- 工龄从 11 年到 15 年，支付 192 小时工资；
- 工龄超过 15 年，支付 240 小时工资。

② 不公平解雇补偿：每工作一年支付 1.5 个月薪水。

③ 无偿休假的补偿。

④ 通知期间的费用。

五、知识产权

（一）知识产权法律法规概况

在摩洛哥，知识产权法律框架由许多国内颁布的法律以及摩洛哥批准的国际公约组成。

摩洛哥的主要知识产权法律法规如下：

- 2000 年 2 月 15 日关于保护工业产权（经修订和完成）（及其法令和命令）的第 17-97 号法律，其中规定了专利、集成电路布局设计、工业品外观设计、商标、工业产权顾问的专业名称、地理标志、原产地标签和不正当竞争、临时展览保护、行业奖励和创作约会和实践条件；
- 2000 年 2 月 15 日关于著作权和类似权利（经修订和完成）（及其法令和命令）的第 2-00 号法律，该法调整版权、表演者权、录音制品制作者和广播组织的权利、版权和类似权利的集体管理，针对盗版行为和其他刑事犯罪的措施，起诉和法律制裁以及服务提供者的责任；
- 2000 年 2 月 15 日第 13-99 号法律设立的摩洛哥工业和商业产权局（OMPIC）（及其法令），是摩洛哥负责保护工业产权（商标、专利和工业品外观设计）的机构，以及记入摩洛哥中央贸易登记册并记入国家工业财产/产权（商标、专利、工业品外观设计、地理标志和原产地名称）登记册；
- 1965 年 3 月 8 日创建摩洛哥版权局（BMDA）的第 2-64-406 号法令（经修订和完成）。

摩洛哥批准的主要国际公约有：

- 《国际承认用于专利程序的微生物保存布达佩斯条约》（2011 年 7 月 20 日）；
- 《世界知识产权组织版权条约》（《WIPO 版权条约》）（2011 年 7 月 20 日）；
- 《世界知识产权组织表演和录音制品条约》（2011 年 7 月 20 日）；
- 《商标法条约》（TLT）（2009 年 7 月 6 日）；
- 《商标国际注册马德里协定有关议定书》（1999 年 10 月 8 日）；
- 《专利合作条约》（1999 年 10 月 8 日）；
- 《建立世界知识产权组织公约》（1971 年 7 月 27 日）；
- 《商标注册用商品和服务国际分类尼斯协议》（1966 年 10 月 1 日）；
- 《工业品外观设计国际注册海牙协定》（1930 年 10 月 20 日）；
- 《商标国际注册马德里协定》（1917 年 7 月 30 日）；
- 《制止商品来源虚假或欺骗性标记马德里协定》（1917 年 7 月 30 日）；
- 《保护工业产权巴黎公约》（1917 年 7 月 30 日）；
- 《保护文学和艺术作品伯尔尼公约》（1917 年 6 月 16 日）。

（二）申请专利

任何个人或法人都可以向摩洛哥工商业财产管理局（OMPIC）提出专利申请。

关于在摩洛哥提交的任何专利，专利申请应包括：

① 填写完整的专利申请的专门表格；

② 对该发明的描述：其所属领域、现有技术的状态、对本发明提供的技术问题和解决方案的描述以及可能的工业应用；

③ 界定所要求保护的目的和限制的一项或多项权利要求；

④ 必要时附图，以解释该发明；

⑤ 总结发明技术内容的摘要；

⑥ 支付费用（约 1 200 美元）。

程序如下：

为了评估本发明的新颖性、创造性和工业实用性，附有可专利性意见的初步检索报告由该发明所处技术领域的专利审查员专家确定。上述报告提到了现有技术（现有技术指与该发明有关的，并且在专利申请的提交日期之前，已经向公众公布的发明和文件的专利清单）。

审查员将初步报告通知申请人。

自申请之日起 18 个月期满后，如果专利申请未被撤回或拒绝，则应予以公布。

在确认没有拒绝理由后，专利可以在支付所需费用后授予。

授予的专利与最终检索报告一起发布。因此，OMPIC 根据申请给予持有人或其代表专利权。

（三）注册商标

关于在摩洛哥提交的任何商标注册申请，文件申请必须在提交之日包含：

① 申请人填妥的申请表格；

② 两个商标黑白模型的复制品；

③ 两个商标颜色模型的复制品（如果后者是彩色的）；

④ 各种授权书，视情况而定；

⑤ 支付所需费用（约 240 美元）。

商标注册申请需经过正式的审查，即对完成的表格的有效性和其他文件进行审查。商标注册申请的审查须包含实质性审查。

该商标须在"商标正式商品目录"中公布 2 个月。

两个月的公布期届满且没有异议，商标可以注册。行政部门须通知申请人或其代理人，并发放"商标注册证书"。

（四）保护知识产权措施

1. 专利保护

专利是一项工业产权，赋予其拥有者一项临时专有权（最多 20 年）以利用其所有的发明。术语"专利"还指技术文件，其对发明进行了描述。

任何具有独创性和工业实用性的新发明都可申请专利。因此，在提交专利申请之前，有必要进行现有技术检索。

对于未居住在摩洛哥的外国人来说，在摩洛哥通过专利代理来申请专利非常重要。

2. 商标保护

商标有许多类型，包括：商标、服务商标和集体商标（例如由协会使用）。

商标可以采用多种形式：公司名称、数字、口号、字母、图形或颜色组合。事实上，商标承载着公司的形象和声誉，并因此具备了可观的价值，并成为公司能够被识别的一个重要因素。

商标的利益在于授予其所有者的保护期限，其期限为 10 年，可无限期延长。

商标的有效性条件：

① 商标必须与众不同；

商标不能指定产品的特性，也不能指出其质量或组成；其图形、语音或颜色必须是原创的；

② 商标必须合法；

③ 商标不得含有任何可能误导消费者的有关产品或服务特性或质量的成分；

④ 不得含有法律禁止的标志，例如国家或政府间组织的旗帜、武器和官方标志，且不得违反公共秩序和道德；

⑤ 商标必须可用。

第三方不得将该商标用于相同的产品或服务。但是，如果相同的商标涉及两件不可能产生混淆的产品，则不会被法律禁止。

六、环境保护

（一）环境保护主管部门

摩洛哥环境保护工作由隶属于能源、矿山与可持续发展部下属的秘书处承担，负责环境的可持续发展。

针对太阳能资源的开发利用，摩洛哥还专门根据 2010 年 2 月 11 日的第 57-09 号法律设立了一家由公益资金支持的私人公司，即"摩洛哥太阳能公司"（MASEN），这家公司一直引领着摩洛哥可再生能源的开发利用工作。作为全国再生能源开发项目的一部分，MASEN 致力于在 2020 年之前至少完成总装机量达 3000MW 的发电项目，并争取在 2030 年之前达到 6000MW。

摩洛哥还依据 2010 年 2 月 11 日的第 16-09 号法律设立了称为"摩洛哥能源效率署"（AMEE）的政府部门，在能源、矿山与可持续发展部的指导下工作。

AMEE 的职能包括：

- 为提高摩洛哥能源利用效率，向摩洛哥管理部门提出全国性或区域性、地域性的方案建议；
- 设计、实施与监督能效项目；
- 监管与协调能效领域的相关措施和行动；
- 监管和协调能效普查，支持能效建议的实施；
- 为有效实现 AMEE 的职能而筹集必要的资金；
- 设计与普及能效设施设备的标准化。

（二）环境保护法律法规概况

摩洛哥有关环保方面的法律法规如下：

- 2003 年 5 月 12 日第 11-03 号法律，主要涉及环境保护与改善；

- 2003 年 5 月 12 日第 12-03 号法律，主要涉及环境影响研究；
- 2014 年 3 月 6 日第 99-12 号框架方案，环境保护与可持续发展国家宪章；
- 2010 年 2 月 11 日第 16-09 号法律，设立了可再生能源与能效署，自 2016 年开始更名为能效署；
- 2010 年 2 月 11 日第 57-09 号法律，设立了摩洛哥太阳能公司。

第 11-03 号法律的目的是制定全国性的环保规章制度的基本原则和规则，这些原则和规则的目标是：
- 防止各种形式的环境污染；
- 改善人民居住环境与条件；
- 为环境保护与治理确立基本的立法原则、技术与资金扶持政策；
- 建立环境污染责任制度，确保环境损害赔偿金和受害者赔偿金。

第 99-12 号法律设定了环境保护和可持续发展的国家行动的基本目标。该法律致力于：
- 加强对自然资源和环境、生物多样性、文化遗产的保护，防止和控制污染与破坏行为；
- 将可持续发展纳入部门公共政策并通过国家可持续发展战略；
- 将摩洛哥环保法律体系与有关环境保护和可持续发展的国际公约和标准统一起来；
- 加强对气候变化的缓解和应对措施，防治荒漠化；
- 决定环境治理的体制、经济、金融和文化改革；
- 确定国家、地方当局、公共机构和国有公司、私营企业、民间社会组织和公民在环境保护和可持续发展方面的承诺；
- 建立环境破坏责任制度和环境监测体系。

（三）环境保护评估

2014 年 12 月 23 日第 2-14-758 号法令赋予了环保部关于环境监测的部分职权，特别是该法令第 10 条规定，控制、评估和法律事务局（DCEAJ）负责通过与有关部门合作定期进行检查，确保环境法律和法规得以顺利实施。

环境保护是政府的责任，这主要包括技术上的和法律上的工作，以检查对环境保护法规所设立各项标准的遵守情况以及对法律设立的技术要求的执行情况。

很多因素对环境监测工作都起到了巨大的推动作用，其中包括：
- 皇家就制定国家环境与可持续发展宪章的指示表达了政治意愿；
- 法律和监管框架已经相对完善（制定法律和法规）；
- 第 12-03 号法律对已经提交环境影响评价报告的新的投资项目签发环境许可决定，并推进项目的实施；
- 环境部有权授予一系列行政许可，尤其是在废弃物和化学品的出口领域；
- 启动和实施由环境部资助的几个项目（FODEP、PAN、PNDM、PER、NGOs、试点项目）；
- 摩洛哥致力于实现环境保护努力的国际承诺。

环境保护评估按照以下原则进行：

（1）政府把握方向

由于其法律后果，环境保护控制取决于政府，甚至，政府决定哪个领域的活动需要被控制，并制定框架以规定哪些领域必须注意、哪些控制手段必须采取。环境监测的实施部门应被告知其被支持和批准的环境监测程序，反之，受环境监测的主体要被告知相应的环境监测主管部门以及他们的权责。

（2）咨询

咨询是环保工作中的重要一环，通过上下游、内外部共同完成。许多主体都会参与其中。

（3）计划

环保行动需要精心策划并遵循预定时间表。计划也可以确保各项行动按步实施。同时，良好的计划还能使组织者制定好工作方案，并采取可行的步骤与预案确保行动成功。

（4）适应

由于环境监测活动非常多样化，特性在各种形式的环境监测活动中广泛存在。因而环境监测必须适应每一种不同的情况，并针对不同的环境监测活动采用不同的监测技术。根据适应原则，特殊的环境监测手段可以基于国际或国内的其他部门层级的专业意见实施。

（5）实地监测

监测是实地的实践活动，不可局限于对文件或者是被监测方的解释的收集。环境监测部门必须进行实际勘察、记录并进行审查。如实反映现场的实际情况确保监测工作的可靠性和严肃性。

（6）报告

环境保护控制工作需要一份详细的追踪报告支持，包括所有已采取的环保措施与流程。尤其是，报告需要披露环保工作中所存在的法律法规障碍。此外，还需要提出针对污染者的惩处建议。

另一方面，建立了国家环保基金。

这一基金的活动是在国家相关环保部门监管下进行的。

国家环保基金意在资助环保项目。

七、争议解决

（一）争议解决方式及机构

1. 诉讼

在摩洛哥，诉讼方面的法律包括：
- 1974 年 7 月 15 日第 1–74–338 号皇家法令（经修订和完成），主要涉及摩洛哥王国司法体系；
- 1974 年 9 月 28 日第 1–74–447 号皇家法令（经修订和完成），批准了民诉法文本；
- 1997 年第 53–95 号法律（经修订和完成），设立了商事法法院；
- 1993 年 9 月 10 日第 41–90 号法律（经修订和完成）（以及落实法令），设立了行政法院。

摩洛哥法院系统主要由一审法院、二审法院、最高法院组成。

除普通管辖之外，还有专门的管辖区和其他所谓的"特殊"管辖区。

普通管辖可处理专属管辖外的所有其他案件。

（1）一审法院

一审法院的管辖权非常宽泛，它可以审理除专属管辖外的所有案件。

一审法院一般由合议庭审理案件（3 名法官），但对某些特定案件也可以由一名法官独任审理。

（2）二审法院（上诉法院）

二审法院审理对一审法院判决不服的上诉案件。

二审法院内部设立了民事、行政、刑事等不同审判庭，并由合议庭（3 名法官）审理案件。

（3）最高法院

最高法院对摩洛哥全境享有管辖权。最高法院内部设立了民事、商事、行政、刑事等不同审判庭，每个审判庭由庭长与顾问组成。

理论上，对一审法院或上诉法院所作判决均可上诉至最高法院。但最高法院并不构成第三级审判机关，它仅就案件的法律适用问题进行审查，而不会审理案件事实。

就专属管辖而言，摩洛哥设立了商事法院与行政法院。

（1）商事法院

商事法院包括基层商事法院与商事上诉法院。

基层商事法院管辖与下列事项有关的全部商事纠纷：
- 商事合同纠纷；
- 商事主体之间基于商行为所发生的纠纷；
- 票据纠纷（诸如支票、汇票等）；
- 商业公司之间的纠纷；

· 与商业资产相关的纠纷。

（2）行政法院

行政法院由行政裁判所与行政上诉法院组成。

行政法院管辖与选举、行政权滥用、行政决定、行政合同、行政赔偿等相关的纠纷，但不包括行政机关所属车辆所产生的交通事故纠纷。

行政法院还管辖且有权解决因适用公务员、地方当局、公共机构和人员的退休金和死亡福利规定而产生的争议，还包括税务争议、行政征用、国债纠纷、国家与地方公务员个人纠纷。

2. 仲裁

非仲裁机构仲裁受《民事诉讼法调整》（第306条及后续条文）。

《民事诉讼法》第306条和后续条文将仲裁分为国内仲裁与国际仲裁。

民事诉讼法既有关于国内，也有关于国际仲裁的相关规定。

此外，《纽约公约》于1959年6月7日对摩洛哥生效，摩洛哥是该公约的第二个签署国。

在摩洛哥可以向法院申请承认与执行外国仲裁裁决。但是，只有在满足如下条件的情况下，摩洛哥法院才会准许：

· 有关仲裁裁决由相关司法管辖区内适格的法庭作出；
· 有关仲裁裁决可依据作出裁决的法律强制执行；
· 仲裁双方当事人均获得了妥当的代理；
· 仲裁裁决不违背摩洛哥公共政策。

3. 常规调解

摩洛哥《民事诉讼法》第327—355条及其后续文件创建了新的争议解决程序。

为了防止或解决争议，当事人可以同意任命一名调解员来解决争议。与仲裁的区别在于，调解员并未接受当事人的委托来处理争议，而是以达成和解为目的主持与当事人的相关会议。

调解协议可以包含在主协议（调解条款）中，也可以在纠纷发生后达成。调解也可能直接介入法庭诉讼，在这种情况下，需要尽快提请法院中断诉讼。

调解协议必须始终以书面形式作出，并在调解协议无效的情况下，当事人需指定调解员或规定其任用条件。

意图应用调解条款的一方应立即通知另一方并依据调解条款提名调解员。

（二）适用法律

合同当事人可以就潜在问题的管辖权达成一致。

另一方面，拖延执行国家判决并诉诸外国管辖权以取得不同判决的行为构成对国家主权的侵犯。

摩洛哥最高法院曾对此类案件作出裁决，其在2006年10月18日的判决中确认："被告人拒绝履行摩洛哥法院对他作出的判决，并将其移交外国司法管辖区来获得离婚判决的行为是对摩洛哥公共秩序的侵犯，因此有必要否定前述判决的执行力。

摩洛哥承认与执行外国判决有三个条件：

· 外国判决必须符合其所属国的程序规则，本国法院不对事实、相关性、原因真实性和证据内容进行任何的审查；
· 外国法院必须有作出有关判决的管辖权；
· 外国判决必须尊重摩洛哥的公共秩序。

由于公共秩序的概念是相对的，法官有自由裁量权审查外国判决与本国公共秩序是否一致。

值得注意的是，如果判决的一部分违反摩洛哥公共秩序，法院可以判决部分执行外国判决。

为此增加了另一个条件，即：

· 外国判决必须是最终判决，并且能够在判决作出的国家适用：

最终判决是指相关判决根据它所在的国家的法律不再有任何救济措施，这保证了相关判决所述当事人权利的确定性。

但是，某些国际公约中规定的这一原则也有例外。

摩洛哥司法机构实际控制着对外国判决的承认与执行，对外国判决的承认与执行的控制主要是外部的，控制的目的只是确保承认与执行的判决不违反公共秩序和善良风俗，而摩洛哥也不适用互惠制度。

关于执行外国判决的法院问题，外国法院作出的法院判决只有在被告的住所或居住地的有权行使执行权的一审法院批准后才能在摩洛哥执行。

尽管摩洛哥法律对外国判决的承认与执行有上述规定，但国际合作仍然是解决这些跨国界冲突所造成的问题的最佳途径。

基于对上述合作重要性的肯定，摩洛哥通过批准几项公约来加强其合作。举例说明：
- 法国与摩洛哥法律协助、引渡和执行公约，1957年10月5日签署；
- 摩洛哥王国与法兰西共和国关于个人和家庭地位以及司法合作的公约，签署于1981年10月8日，通过1998年10月7日颁布的BGB公布；
- 2002年6月26日摩洛哥王国与比利时王国就承认和执行有关赡养费判决达成协议；
- 2002年6月26日摩洛哥王国与比利时王国关于司法合作的公约，承认和执行关于监护权和访问权的决定。

摩洛哥还通过与若干国家（主要是法国和西班牙）相互交换法官以及与其他国家建立联合委员会的形式来保障上述公约及双边条约的实施。

外国判决只有生效后才能在摩洛哥执行。这些判决基本上是在民事、商业、家庭和刑事等领域内作出的。

八、其他

（一）反商业贿赂

1. 反商业贿赂法律法规概况

在摩洛哥，反商业贿赂方面主要有以下方面的法律规范：
- 2007年4月17日关于打击洗钱的第43-05号法律（经修订和完善）；
- 1962年11月26日颁布的第1-59-413号刑法；
- 2015年6月9日颁布的关于国家廉洁、预防和打击腐败的第113-12号法律。

第113—12号法律规定了预防和打击腐败的国家权力机构，并规定了其目标、组成和运作规则。

就本法立法目的而言，腐败是指按现行法律规定的一切受贿罪行、影响力交易、贪污或勒索罪行以及任何其他特定立法规定的腐败罪行。

根据刑法，腐败是指任何人承诺、征求、索取或接受捐赠、礼物或其他好处，并且：
- 作为地方法官，公职人员或有选举权的人，利用其职权或虽在其职权范围外但协助其他有职权的人做出或拒绝做出一定行为，而不考虑该行为是否公平；
- 作为行政或司法机关任命的仲裁员或专家，作出决定或给予有利或不利的意见；
- 作为地方官、评税审查员或审判人员，决定是否偏袒歧视某方；
- 作为医生、外科医生、牙医、助产士，提供虚假证明隐瞒疾病、疾病的存在或怀孕状态，或提供病源、虚弱或死亡原因的虚假迹象。

2. 主管部门

负责监督反商业贿赂的部门是国家廉政，预防和打击腐败部门，其任务主要是：
- 接收和审查与腐败案件有关的所有报告、投诉和信息，核实其中提及的事实真相，并酌情将其转交主管当局；
- 开展对其关注的腐败案件的调查；
- 制定反腐败犯罪预防方案，促进公共生活道德化，确保其执行；
- 努力传播和宣传善政规则；

· 拟定传播、沟通和认知廉洁价值观的方案并确保其实现；
· 应政府的要求，表达其旨在防止或打击腐败的任何计划、措施、项目或举措。

3. 惩处措施

根据刑法的规定，犯有腐败罪的人将被处以 2—5 年徒刑以及 2 000 至 5 万迪拉姆的罚款处罚。如果腐败总额高于 10 万迪拉姆，处以 5—10 年监禁，并罚款 5 000 迪拉姆至 10 万迪拉姆。

（二）工程承包

1. 许可制度

公共采购（公开采购）遵循以下原则：
· 获取公共订单的自由；
· 平等对待竞争对手；
· 保证竞争者的权利；
· 客户选择的透明度。

公共采购也需要服从善政的规则。
公共采购考虑到尊重环境和可持续发展的目标。

2. 禁止领域

对国内外企业没有具体的禁止性规定。

3. 招投标

招标邀请可以是开放的或受限制的。当任何竞争主体可以获得咨询文件并提交申请时，此种情况被称为"开放"。当只有开发商决定的竞争主体才可以提交的投标文件时，被称为"受限"。

招标委员会在征询委员会的意见后，只有从技术和财务角度来看有足够能力的投标者，才能被授权提交投标书，这被称为"预选"。

竞争使竞争方在同一个项目上竞争，以达到需要对技术，审美或财务进行特殊研究的服务要求。

公开或受限投标邀请遵循以下原则：
· 鼓励竞争；
· 公开招标；
· 投标人委员会审查投标书；
· 由招标委员会选择最有利的报价；
· 进行招标的招标方有义务告知招标委员会成员预算数额。

Morocco

Authors: Amin Hajji, Nihma El Gachbour, Asmae El Khaier, Rachid Benzakour
Translators: Xu Bulin, Liu Rong

I. Overview

A. General Introduction to the Political, Economic, Social and Legal Environment of Morocco

The Kingdom of Morocco is a constitutional, democratic, parliamentary and social monarchy[①].

According to 2011 Moroccan Constitution, the King is the Head of State. The King appoints the Head of Government from the political party which won the general election of the House of Representatives' members and appoints the members of the Government on the Head of Government proposal. The King may dismiss ministers, dissolve parliament and call for new elections. The King rules by Dahir (Royal Decree).

The Moroccan political system is made up of three branches: the legislative branch (Parliament), the executive branch (Government) and the judiciary branch.

The Government consists of the Head of Government and Ministers which are responsible before both the King and Parliament. The Government implements its governmental program, ensures the implementation of laws, arranges the administration, propose laws and supervises the activities of public institutions.

The Parliament consists of two chambers, the House of Representatives and the House of Councilors. The 395 members of the House of Representatives are elected for a five-year term of office by direct public vote and the 120 members of the House of Councilors are indirectly elected for a six-year term of office. The Parliament have legislative powers, vote on bills including the Finance Bill, control the government and evaluate public policies.

The Judiciary in Morocco is independent from the legislative and executive powers. The High Judicial Council (Le Conseil Supérieur du Pouvoir Judiciaire) is responsible of the appointment, the promotion, the retirement and the discipline of judges and guarantees their independence.

The law is the supreme expression of the will of the Moroccan Nation. Moroccan law is mainly based on Moroccan Civil Code named "Dahir formant Code des Obligations et des Contrats" (hereinafter "DOC" of 12 August 1913) and a combination of Muslim and Jewish traditions.

In Morocco, laws (Dahirs) are bills proposed by the King, the Prime Minister or by a Member of Parliament and then subsequently approved by both houses of Parliament ("Chambre des Représentants" and "Chambre des Conseillers").

Furthermore, all legislation must be promulgated by Royal Dahir, which is then accorded precedence over any other related texts. This applies to Acts of Parliament as well as to certain types of legislation that must be enacted, as "organic laws", according to the Constitution.

Besides, the laws on personal status, capacity, and inheritance are submitted to the law No.70-03 of 3 February 2004 establishing the new Family Code, which is based on an Islamic codification (Malékite School).

Legislation on contracts, obligations, and real property is submitted to the DOC promulgated in 1913.

The Constitution is the highest form of law in Morocco. Besides, it sets out the role and interrelationship of the various organs of the Monarchy and contains various principles of law.

Besides, the Code of Civil Procedure of 1974 limits the role of the judiciary providing that courts are forbidden to judge the constitutionality of a law or decree and the judiciary is equally reluctant to review administrative acts.

Thus, a Constitutional Counsel has been established together with administrative Courts in 1993. The Constitutional Counsel became the Constitutional Court from the promulgation of the new Constitution in 2011.

Finally, the Constitution was lately amended in 29 July 2011 and now recognizes the supremacy of international treaties duly ratified by the Kingdom of Morocco over Moroccan laws and regulations.

Regarding the judicial organization, the highest court in Morocco is the Court of Cassation (The Supreme Court). There are other courts including First Instance Courts, Appeal Courts and specialized jurisdictions as the Commercial Courts, the Commercial Courts of Appeal, the Administrative Courts and the Administrative Courts of

---

① Article 1 of the 2011 Moroccan Constitution.

Appeal. Morocco has also some exceptional jurisdictions as well as a Constitutional Council.

In recent years, the Moroccan economy has been characterized by macro-economic stability and low levels of inflation (1.5% in 2015). In 2015, Morocco's GDP was approximately USD 101 billion with a GDP growth of 4.6% which slowed to 1.6% in 2016 and is estimated to 4.8% in 2017 thanks to the continued growth of non-agricultural activity.

The General Government Gross debt was amounted to 63.7% of the national GDP and the government budget deficit reached −4.3% of GDP in 2015. The unemployment rate has been rising in recent years and reached 9.7% in 2015[1].

The Moroccan economy is dominated by the agricultural sector which employs nearly 40% of the workforce. However, the objectives of the 2017 and 2018 Finance Bills are to accelerate the structural transformation of the economy with a focus on industrialization and renewable energies (a potential of 2,600 kW · h/m²/year of solar resources). In February 2016, Morocco inaugurated the Ouarzazate Solar Power Station, which will ultimately be the largest of its kind in the world.

With respect to export-import activities and investment, Spain and France are the main partners in foreign trade representing 44% of Moroccan exports and 28.2% of imports[2].

Morocco attracted nearly 2.35 billion U.S.dollars of foreign direct investment (FDI) in the first 11 months of 2017. A new investment charter is to be adopted in order to develop free-trade zones in each of the 12 regions of the country.

Morocco is a member of the Arab Free Trade Zone and has free trade agreements with the United States of America, EFTA and Turkey.

Morocco has also an Association agreement with the European Union and is particularly active on the African continent through bilateral agreements with more than fifteen African countries which makes Morocco one of Africa's major investors.

Morocco's official currency is the Moroccan Dirham (MAD). On January 2018, Morocco widened the fluctuation band in which the dirham is traded against the Euro and U.S.dollar from 0.3 percent to 2.5 percent either side.

B. The Status and Direction of the Cooperation with Chinese Enterprises Under the B&R

Morocco has officially been part of the B&R since November 17, 2017 date of the execution of a bilateral Memorandum of Understanding (MoU) between the Kingdom of Morocco and the People's Republic of China on joint construction of the Belt and Road.

The Kingdom of Morocco and the Republic of China have a long history of exchange in several fields: economic, industrial, cultural and political. In 2016, Morocco imported some 3.9 billion U.S.dollars from China making China the fourth largest trading partner of Morocco.

There are a number of bilateral agreements between Morocco and China which constitute a legal framework for the cooperation with Chinese investors, such as:

• The agreement on the encouragement and mutual protection of investments executed between Morocco and China on March 27, 1995 and entered into force in Morocco on August 14, 2000;

• The agreement on mutual legal assistance in civil and commercial matters executed between Morocco and China on April 16, 1996 and entered into force in Morocco on May 3, 2000; and

• The bilateral agreement to avoid double taxation and to prohibit tax evasion with respect to income taxes executed between Morocco and China on August 27, 2002 and entered into force in Morocco on February 18, 2009.

On May 2016, the Kingdom of Morocco and the Republic of China executed fifteen (15) bilateral agreements in the sectors of banking, tourism, economy, industry and investment.

A detailed list of the fifteen (15) bilateral agreements may be found in the table below:

No.	Bilateral Agreements
1	MoU to set up an industrial and residential park in Morocco between the Kingdom of Morocco and the Chinese group HAITE.
2	Cooperation agreement on the sector of investment and finance between the Moroccan government and the Industrial and Commercial Bank of China Limited.

---

[1] IMF - World Economic Database - 2017.
[2] Trade summary for Morocco, 2016, World Bank, available at: https://wits.worldbank.org/CountrySnapshot/en/MAR.

(continued)

No.	Bilateral Agreements
3	MoU on the transfer of North-South waters between the Moroccan government and China Harbour Engineering Company Ltd.
4	Draft agreement between "Office National de l'électricité et de l'eau potable" (ONEE) and China's SEPCO III Electric Power Construction.
5	Partnership agreement between the Moroccan Tourism Office and China International Travel Service (CITS).
6	Partnership agreement between YANGTSE, the "Société d'Investissement Energétique" (SIE), Marita Group and the "Banque Centale Populaire" for purchasing and building a unit for manufacturing electric buses.
7	Partnership between Linuo Ritter, SIE, Cap Holding and Attijariwafa Bank for the creation of an industrial production unity for solar water-heaters in Morocco.
8	Partnership agreement between Hareon Solar, SIE, Jet Contractor and Attijariwafa Bank for the development of a photovoltaic cells production unit.
9	MoU between China Africa Development Fund (CAD Fund) and Attijariwafa Bank to back up African enterprises by completing the loan offer and opening new prospects for Moroccan-Chinese investment opportunities in Africa.
10	MoU between Haite Group, Morocco-China International and BMCE Bank of Africa on the setting up in Morocco of a Chinese-Moroccan Industrial Park and a Chinese-Moroccan one billion dollars investment fund targeting the sectors of aeronautics, finances, industrial parks and infrastructure.
11	MoU between BMCE Bank of Africa and China Africa Development Fund (CAD Fund) on the funding of development projects in key-sectors in Africa, investment in public and private debt markets in Africa.
12	Agreement on financing the construction of a cement plant in Morocco.
13	MoU for the development of an industrial and logistical hub for manufacturing spare parts for railway, car and aeronautics industries between the Sichuan Huatie hi-tech Construction Engineering, the SNTL and Attijariwafa Bank.
14	MoU for the development of logistical zones in Africa.
15	MoU for China-Africa cross-border E-Trade between Clevy China, the SNTL and Attijariwafa Bank.

On June 2016, Morocco granted Chinese citizens visa-free entry to Morocco.

On December 2017, the Chinese leading electric vehicle manufacturer BYD signed an agreement in order to build a plant in Morocco to produce battery-powered vehicles in Tangier.

II. Investment

A. Market Access

a. Department Supervising Investment

a) Global supervision of investments

Investments in Morocco are supervised by the Ministry of Industry, Investment, Trade and Digital Economy, acting mainly, regarding investments, through its several Departments (Industry, Trade and Distribution, Advanced Technologies, Quality and Market Surveillance, etc.).

The Ministry ensures among other missions: to validate the strategies for trade, distribution and developing investment and enhancing the competitiveness of small and medium-sized enterprises (SMEs), to contribute to the management of relations with national and international institutions and organizations in the sectors of industry, commerce and new technology, to develop partnerships, coordinate and implement cooperation programs, to develop and coordinate reception spaces for industry, commerce and technology, as well as competitive hubs, to welcome, inform and guide investors in the industrial, commercial and distribution sectors, to define the legislative and organizational framework for industry, commerce and new technologies, and to promote quality and safety in those sectors.

b) Development and performance of investments

The Moroccan Agency for Investments' and Exports' Development or the "AMDIE" (In French: l' "Agence Marocaine de Développement des Investissements et des Exportations") is Morocco's primary agency responsible for the development and promotion of investment in Morocco. The Agency is a public institution endowed with legal personality and financial autonomy, under the supervision of the Ministry.

The Agency was created for the support of the Kingdom's new investment vision, set by the new Industrial Acceleration Plan, and was born by the merger of prior agencies in charge of investments, exports, fairs and exhibitions. The creation of the new Agency aims to concentrate the non-harmonized efforts of the three bodies for more efficiency of coherence and standardization.

Under the law establishing the AMDIE, the main functions of the Agency are to ensure the implementation of the national strategy for the development, encouragement and promotion of domestic and foreign investment. In this context, the Agency shall mainly pilot the prospection of potential national and foreign investors through several actions, promote, in coordination with the authorities, the Moroccan exportable offer through a policy of communication and mastered promotion, within the framework of the national strategy of exports development fixed by the government, and develop the promotion of fairs and exhibitions.

c) The National Committee for the Business Environment

In order to guarantee a clear and transparent framework conducive to investment for the benefit of national and international operators, the National Committee for the Business Environment (in French: "Comité National de l'Environnement des Affaires", "CNEA") was created in December 2009. This high-level body is chaired by the Chief of the Government and composed of representatives of the public and private sectors. Its main mission is to identify and implement measures designed to enhance the attractiveness of investments in Morocco.

b. Laws and Regulation of Investment Industry

a) Laws

The blueprint law No.18-95 of 3 October 1995 sets Morocco's Investment Charter in the form of a standard text applicable to all line of businesses, aiming at the encouragement and promotion of investment by improving its climate and conditions and offering incentives designed to simulate the development of both domestic and foreign investments (direct and portfolio).

The Charter gives the same benefits to national and aliens regardless of the industry in which they operate, with the exception of certain sectors such as agriculture, phosphates and insurance which are not forbidden access but remain subject to the regulation of specific authorities. The Charter thus provides incentives on taxes, custom duties and registration fees. It also grants freedom for the transfer of profits and capital of the persons who make investments in hard currencies, the advising and assistance for investors in carrying out their projects and the alleviation of the administrative procedure relevant to investments.

Finally, Morocco has put in place in recent decades a robust legal and regulatory framework including labor, copyrights, personal data protection, freedom of pricing and competition, consumer protection, industrial property, corporation and arbitration. These new laws and regulations are aimed to improve investment conditions and, thus, to generate significant domestic and foreign private capital flows.

b) Regulations

The Decree No.2-00-895 was taken for the application of articles 17 and 19 of the blueprint law implementing the Investment Charter and is related to the provinces, prefectures and regions whose economic activity justifies a special support from the State.

c) New amendments

By 2014, Morocco has adopted a new approach and undertook the implementation of the "2014—2020 Industrial Acceleration Plan" (IAP) based on the establishment of efficient ecosystems aiming at the integration of value chains, the consolidation of the local relations between big firms and SMEs, and the improvement of the foreign investor's path in Morocco.

The IAP also provides for the adoption of a new Investment Charter, some of whose measures have already been implemented by the draft Finance laws for 2017 and 2018.

The amendments of the Charter introduce new incentives to consolidate the progress made in the industrial acceleration policy framework on investment attractiveness, such as the provision of a 0% corporation tax for a duration of five years for new industrial enterprises, the establishment of regional free zones, the support for the less favored regions to boost industrial investment, promote balanced territorial development and recognize the status of the indirect exporter (the subcontractors of the major exporting groups).

c. Forms of Investment

The Investment Charter makes the difference between investments depending on the importance of the companies holding the projects, the amounts of investments or the regions in which the projects will take place. The Charter thus sets the general forms of investments in Morocco, by offering incentives granting specific financial, tax, customs and registration fees advantages to investors, as part of public agreements or investments contracts to be concluded, provided that they meet the required criteria.

Furthermore, Morocco contributes to certain investments' expenses regarding specific sectors, technologies and activities, as well as depending on projects with high added value. Thus, in 2015, the Finance law created the Industrial and Investment Development Fund offering direct financial support to industrial eco-systems or direct aid as part of the Charter during the establishment of the "2014—2020 Industrial Acceleration Plan".

d. Standards of Market Access and Examination

Foreign investors have the possibility to invest freely in most areas and hold up the whole capital of a Moroccan company, or even create a permanent establishment without a corporate structure. In principle, the access to the investment market is free and grants the same access conditions for both domestic and foreign investors.

The investment legal framework thus guarantees the principles of equity and non-discrimination on financial, real-estate, administrative, tax, customs and all the necessary procedures needed for the establishment of investments projects. Moreover, the State has implemented a corpus of business incorporation incentives leading to eliminate several administrative and registration steps by creating Regional Investment Centers (in French: "Centre Régional d'Investissement") making the business registration process clear and complete.

However, certain sectors such as agriculture, fishing, phosphates, hydrocarbons, banking and insurance are restricted from access to aliens and remain subject to regulation of specific authorities.

The access to the marketplace may be materialized by different corporation forms and they all benefit more or less from the same incentives provided by the Investment Charter.

Finally, the forming of partnership agreements with foreign countries allows the two parties to benefit from reciprocal advantages in terms of free trade, open borders and protection of investments.

B. Foreign Exchange Regulation

a. Department Supervising Foreign Exchange

The Moroccan Foreign Exchange Office (the "Office des Changes" or "ODC") is the office in charge of the control and regulation of foreign exchanges. The ODC is a public institution subject to the supervision of the Ministry of Economy and Finance.

The Office is responsible for providing exchange control measures and compiling statistics on foreign trade and the balance of payments.

The ODC is in particular responsible to authorize foreign transfers of funds and capitals delegated to approved banking intermediaries and guarantees the repatriation of the necessarily transferable assets such as the exports of goods and services, as well as to register and punish offenses and infringements against foreign exchange regulations.

b. Brief Introduction of Laws and Regulations of Foreign Exchange

The General Instruction on Foreign Operations of 31 December 2013 (In French: "Instruction Générale des Opérations de Change") is the main statute regulating foreign exchanges and cross-border flows with Morocco.

Under the General Instruction, the Moroccan Dirham is not freely exportable and convertible and all exports of capitals abroad which are exempted from taxation are submitted to the prior authorization of the ODC.

However, Morocco has initiated a liberalization program by putting in place a system of freely convertible Dirhams, designed to facilitate international trade and financial transactions. The system allows, under certain conditions, a guarantee of free transfers (dividends, products of assets' liquidations, etc.) through banking intermediaries approved by the ODC.

Regarding infringements against foreign exchange regulations, the Dahir of 30 August 1949 lays down the conditions under which breaches and infringements to the foreign exchange regulations are established, prosecuted and repressed.

Furthermore, the exchange regulations include several decrees, ministerial orders and memorandums regulating all to foreign trade aspects for both domestic and foreign exchange operations, regarding natural and legal persons of private and even public laws. Finally, the Investment Charter also provides free transfer of funds to foreign investors.

c. Requirements of Foreign Exchange Management for Foreign Enterprises

The ODC delegated to Moroccan approved intermediaries banks the authority to freely carry-out settlements relating to investments, imports, exports, international transport, insurance and reinsurance, foreign technical assistance, transfer of technologies, distribution, franchising, factoring, guaranties, travel, schooling, medical care, savings on income and all others current operations provided by the General Instruction.

Under the latter, Cross-border payments abroad shall be made by a foreign currency quoted by Bank Al-Maghrib ("BAM"), the central bank of Morocco, whereas settlements coming from abroad can be made either through the repatriation of a foreign currency quoted by BAM or through a debit of a specific account. Therefore, foreigners have the possibility to open their banking accounts in Morocco which may be foreign currency accounts, foreign accounts in convertible dirham, forward convertible accounts and special accounts for certain categories of foreign entities (foreign contractors of procurements and diplomatic representations).

Capital transactions require authorization from the ODC and are usually granted for business-related transactions. Either way, the ODC may require an authorization and declaration depending on the type of exchange transaction for which the authorization or declaration is required, subject to agreements entered into with other countries.

C. Financing

a. Main Financial Institutions

Under Moroccan law, the main financial institutions are the loan institutions "Etablissement de crédit" which are mainly banks and funding companies. They could be also (i) payment institutions; (ii) associations of micro-credit; (iii) offshore banks and (iv) finance companies.

Pursuant to Moroccan banking law (Law No.103-12 of December 24, 2014) the loan institutions could undertake the following services: (i) receiving deposits from the public; (ii) loan operations; (iii) issuance of payment cards; (iv) Investment services; (v) foreign-exchange operations; (vi) leasing operations; (vii) guaranties and securities operations; (viii) factoring operations; (iv) gold, precious metals and coins operations; (x) insurance brokerage and (xi) other activities that are connected or are similar to the aforementioned.

The loan institutions are subject to a license issued by the Moroccan central bank "Bank Al-Maghrib" (BAM) which is also the responsible of banking supervision.

Since 2015, Morocco has introduced a new category of financing institution called participatory banks "banques participatives" which offer products and services in compliance with Sharia (Islamic) rules. The participatory banks provide participatory investment products and services which do not give rise to any payment of interest.

The insurance companies are the second largest financial institutions in Morocco. There are currently 21 insurance and re-insurance companies in the Moroccan market and 1873 insurance intermediaries (1427 agents and 446 brokers).

b. Financing Conditions for Foreign Enterprises

In general, the foreign enterprises are subject to the same financing conditions of domestic enterprises. However, it should be noted that the foreign enterprises should notify the Moroccan Exchange Office-ODC "Office des Changes" of the financing operation (with financing contract's copy or Bank's statement of the financing) within the six (6) months of its execution.

D. Land Policy

a. Brief Introduction of Land-Related Laws and Regulations

a) Under Moroccan Law, the lands are either public or private. The public lands are owned by Moroccan State and could not be subject to sale. The private lands are owned by private persons either a natural person or a legal entity. There is two type of private lands: registered lands and unregistered lands.

(i) Registered lands

The registered lands are governed by Royal Decree of 1913 relating to lands registration as amended by Law No.14-07 of 2011. The registration system grants the safety of lands transactions. Thus, any transaction or any rights over the lands such as the owner's right, the lessee's right and the mortgagee's right must be registered with the Moroccan land register to be valid, legal and having binding effect on third persons.

The transactions relating to registered lands should respect some formalities to ensure their effectiveness and registration with the Moroccan land register. For example, the acquisition of a Moroccan registered land should be prepared in the form of a written deed and should be notarized before a public notary. This latter, could not proceed with the notarization of the deed before a prior investigation on the existing rights over the land and after informing the buyer, if any.

The public notary should also proceed to purge the land before its sale of all unpaid taxes and tax administration rights. Finally, the public notary would himself proceed to the registration of the land acquisition and the payment of all registration fees. Such registration would grant to the buyer the title of ownership which is issued by the Moroccan land registrar.

(ii) Unregistered lands

The unregistered lands are called under Moroccan law "Melk" lands which mean "possession" lands since any person could prevail of the ownership of an unregistered land by proving that he possessed and enjoyed the land as an owner within more than ten (10) years.

The unregistered lands are governed by traditional rules of the Islamic law and could either be sold, leased, seized or expropriated. In comparison to registered lands, the unregistered lands do not grant a safety rights to the owner. However, it should be noted that any unregistered land could be subject to the registration process on the owner's request.

b) Real property rights.

The real property rights are governed by Law No.39-08 of November 22, 2011. There are two types of real property rights: principal real property rights and accessory real property rights.

The principal real property is the ownership right. The accessory real property right is a right which depends on the existence of a personal right and stands as a security for its performance. There are three types of accessory real property rights which could arise over an immovable property: liens, antichresis and mortgages.

A statutory lien (Privilège) is a lien which arises solely by force of law and it grants to the creditor a preferential right over the debtor's property which arises due to his debt obligation to the creditor. Such a statutory lien can be a general or a specific lien.

A contractual lien could be either an antichresis (antichcrèse) or a mortgage (hypothèque). An antichresis is a pledge of an immovable by which the debtor is dispossessed of his property which is given as a security to the creditor.

A mortgage under Moroccan Law is a contract in which a debtor gives to its creditor a right over its immovable property. In case of the default of the debtor, the creditor, then, has the right to seek before Moroccan Courts the performance of the mortgage contract and, thereby, to sell the mortgaged real estate and be paid out from the sale price. A mortgage contract is a security interest without any dis-possession of the debtor of the property concerned by the mortgage.

b. Rules of Land Acquisition for Foreign Enterprises

In general, there is no differences between land acquisition by Moroccan enterprises and foreign enterprises except for the agriculture lands. The foreigners either natural person or legal entity could not acquire a Moroccan agriculture lands. The other lands either registered or unregistered could be acquired by foreigners in the same conditions of nationals. However, it is recommendable that the foreigner acquires a registered land to protect his rights on the land and preserve his ownership.

E. The Establishment and Dissolution of Companies

a. The Forms of Enterprises

The Moroccan business companies' code provides for several forms of Companies:

a) The joint stock company (in French: Société anonyme SA)

The joint stock company is typically used for larger corporations. Indeed, it requires a minimum of five (5) shareholders and a minimum capital contribution of Dirham (MAD) 300,000 or three (3) million if the corporation seeks public investment.

A joint stock company can issue a number of different shares carrying different rights relating to voting, dividends and entitlement to a distribution on a winding-up. Shares of different classes can have different par values, the only restriction being that if the shares of a joint stock company are to be quoted they have to carry a minimum par value of MAD 100.00 at least.

There are two alternative forms of management of the joint stock company that can be adopted by the Corporation. The joint stock company can be managed by the board of directors or by both the supervisory board and the management board.

In such a corporation, the shareholders' liability is limited to the amount of share equity the shareholder holds. Upon incorporation of the corporation, a quarter of the equity capital must be paid in advance if paid in cash contributions. If it is paid in contributions in kind, it must be fully paid upon corporation.

b) The Limited Liability Company (in French: Société à responsabilité limitée SARL)

The Limited Liability Company is organized by fewer persons, with less capital and is generally easier to incorporate, manage and operate and as it is relatively easy to transform it into a joint stock company, it is often used as an intermediate vehicle for growing businesses.

The Limited Liability Company may be formed by one partner at least and fifty at the most. If more than fifty partners, the company must be transformed in Joint Stock Company in the time allowed of two years. There is no minimum capital for this company, however the articles of association must indicate the value of shares and value of any contribution in kind.

The Limited Liability Company is managed by one or more managers (in French: "Gérant or cogérants") who do not need to be shareholders but must be individuals rather than companies. Said managers are appointed by the partners.

Civil and criminal liability is applicable to managers in case of mismanagement. Shareholders investing in a SARL are liable to the extent of the capital they have contributed.

c) Branch (in French: Succursale)

The branch office is not considered a separate legal entity and must abide by the laws of both Morocco and its country of origin.

The Branch has no legal required minimum capital and has no shareholders. Said company must appoint at least one manager but still subject to the decision of the mother company.

Fiscally, it is a permanent establishment and is subject to the income tax and the corporate tax.

d) Representative office (in French: Bureau de representation)

A representative office is a non-full entity, it is not a separate legal entity and it is wholly owned by head office. The representative office is not entitled to perform revenue-generating commercial activities.

From a legal standpoint there is no filing registration requirement. The representative office would be submitted to business tax and possibly income tax depending on the generated revenue.

e) The partnership company (in French: Société en nom collectif, SNC)

The general partnership is a form of partnership whereby all of the associates are jointly and severally liable for the partnership's liabilities.

All partners have the quality of tradesmen and are indefinitely and jointly responsible for company debts. The partnership style includes either the names of all partners or the name of one or several partners followed by the words "and company."

f) The limited partnership (in French: Société en commandite simple, SCS)

The Limited Partnership has two categories of associates, the general partners: (in French: associés commandités) which are tradesmen and are jointly and severally liable without limitations for the partnership debts and limited partners: (in French: associés commanditaires) they are liable for the partnership debts to the extent of the amount of their capital contribution.

g) The limited stock partnership (in French: Société en commandite par actions, SCA)

This is a company whose capital is divided into shares that are freely negotiable and represented by stock certificates.

There are two categories of associates, the general partners which are considered as tradesmen and are jointly and severally liable for the limited stock partnership's liabilities and the limited partners which are considered as shareholders and bear the losses only to the extent of their contributions. The number of limited partners may not be less than three.

b. The Procedure of Establishment

This section deals only with the establishment of a Limited Liability Company and the Joint Stock Company, since these are the most popular corporate form in Morocco.

The establishment in Morocco is undertaken by the Regional Center for Investments (in French: Centres Régionaux d'Investissement CRI) based in the most important cities of Morocco (i.e.Casablanca, Rabat, Marrakech, Agadir, Tanger...) which have been implemented to facilitate the establishment process.

In order to proceed with the incorporation, the investors should obtain and prepare the following documentation:

(i) The trade name certificate (in French: certificate négatif delivered by the Moroccan Industrial and Commercial Property Office reserving the trade name during the company life;

(ii) A lease agreement or a domiciliation agreement with a domiciliation company;

(iii) The articles of association containing the legally required mentions;

(iv) The constitutional and registration documents in French or Arabic version;

(v) A certificate of the blocking of the funds; and

(vi) The application for the incorporation of the local entity before the Regional Center for Investments.

Regarding the Limited Liability Company, if the capital is lower than MAD 100,000 it is not compulsory neither to open a bank account before the incorporation nor to obtain a certificate of the blocking of the funds.

Besides, the shareholders / partners being companies should provide with a trade registry certificate, articles of association and passport of the legal representative. For shareholders being natural persons a simple copy of the passport is sufficient.

Once the required documentation filed, the CRI issues a full set of registration certificates (tax certificate, affiliation certificate to the social security, trade registry numbers).

c. Routes and Requirement of Dissolution

In order to proceed with the dissolution / liquidation of a Moroccan company, the extraordinary general meeting of the shareholders / partners should decide the anticipate dissolution of the company, the appointment of one or more liquidator, the power of one or more liquidator and the setting of the head office of the liquidation.

The liquidator can be chosen among the shareholders or any other individual / company. The head office of the liquidation can be set anywhere in Morocco in which the accountancy must be kept.

Before the end of the 30th days following the dissolution decision, the liquidator must issue and file in the minutes of the extraordinary meeting of the shareholder(s) deciding the dissolution of the company at the tax registration duties service, at the trade registry and publish in a Moroccan legal newspaper and in the Moroccan Official Gazette the decision of the company's dissolution.

Before the end of the 45th days of the decision of the dissolution in accordance with the article 150 point I of the Moroccan Tax law, the liquidator appointed by the extraordinary meeting of the shareholders / partners has to realize the assets and balance the liabilities of the company.

After the performing of this operation, the liquidator of the company has to convoke an extraordinary meeting of the shareholders / partners in order to approve the report and accountancy prepared by the liquidator, close the liquidation and clear the liquidator.

Before the end of the 30th days of the aforesaid decision of the dissolution, the liquidator must issue and file in the minutes of the extraordinary meeting of the shareholders / partners approving the liquidation of the company at the tax registration duties service and the trade registry and publish in a Moroccan newspaper and in the Moroccan Gazette the liquidation approval of the company.

However, there are cases where the dissolution is imposed, particularly in the following cases:

• The Limited Liability Company: in the event of the loss of three-quarters of the capital of the company, the managers must consult the shareholders as to whether or not they must vote the dissolution of the company;

• The Joint Stock Company: the commercial court may, upon request by any person having an interest, pronounce dissolution of the corporation, if the number of shareholders has been reduced to less than five for more one than a year. The corporation may also be dissolved in the event its assets are reduced to less than a quarter of its capital. In such case, the Board of Directors must convene an Extraordinary General Meeting to decide upon its dissolution; and

• The partnership: it is terminated on the death of one of the partners, unless a clause to the contrary is in the articles of association. In case, of bankruptcy, suspension from carrying on business or incapacity of one of the partners, the partnership is dissolved unless its continuance is provided for by the articles of association or unanimously decided by the partners.

F. Merger and Acquisition

In Morocco, every merger operation is subject to a prior notification to the Competition Council (in French "Conseil de la Concurrence") by the entities involved in the operation before entering into the operation pursuant to the provisions of the law on the freedom of price and competition of 2014.

The obligation of notification is the responsibility of the individuals and companies which acquire the control of all or a part of a company or, in case of a merger or if a common company is created, to all parties concerned that have thus to make a common notification.

Furthermore, the notification condition is required when the following three (3) conditions are fulfilled:

• the total worldwide turnover, tax excluded, of the entire companies or groups of companies or individuals involved in the merger exceeds the amount of MAD 750,000,000 (approx.69,000,000 €);

• the total turnover, tax excluded, realized in Morocco by at least two of the companies or groups of companies or individuals involved in the merger exceeds the amount of MAD 250,000,000 (approx.23,000,000 €); and

• the companies' parties or subject to the merger or economically related to it have realized together, during the previous civil year, more than forty percent (40%) of the sales, purchases or any other transaction in a national market of goods, products or services of same nature or interchangeable, or in a substantial part of said market.

Finally, the Competition Council is entitled to fine the entities subject to the prior notification obligation for a maximum amount of five percent (5%) tax excluded of the turnover realized in Morocco during the latest financial year, increased by, if applicable, the turnover realized by the acquired company, and, for the individuals, five million

MAD (MAD 5,000,000—approx.450,000 €).

G. Competition Regulation

a. Department Supervising Competition Regulation

The Moroccan Competition Council "Conseil de Concurrence" is an independent administrative body responsible for supervising competition regulation and enforcement of competition rules. The Head of Government retains residual powers as the revocation power on the decisions of the Competition Council for matters of public interest regarding the concentration transactions.

Some specific sectors are regulated in Morocco by sectoral authorities such as the telecommunications (Agence Nationale de Réglementation des Télécommunications or ANRT), the audiovisual market (Haute Autorité de la Communication Audiovisuelle or HACA), banking sector (Bank Al-Maghrib, the Moroccan central bank) the capital market (L'Autorité Marocaine du Marché des Capitaux or AMMC), ports (l'Agence Nationale des Ports or ANP) and insurance (Autorité de contrôle des Assurances et de la Prévoyance Sociale or ACAPS).

b. Brief Introduction of Competition Law

The main texts governing competition in Morocco is the Law No.104-12 of 30 June 2014[1] on free pricing and competition and the Law No.20-13[2] relating to the Competition Council 30 June 2014.

Other legal and regulatory provisions may apply in certain specific industry sectors subject to sectoral regulations such as telecommunications, audiovisual, capital markets, banking, ports and insurance.

In addition, the unfair competition is regulated by the following texts:
• The Moroccan Civil Law named Dahir des Obligations et Contrats of 12 August 1913; and
• Law No.17-97 on the Protection of Industrial Property[3] as amended by Law No.23-13.

c. Measures Regulating Competition

The Moroccan competition regulation tends to protect the freedom of prices and competition through the prohibition of (i) anticompetitive practices; (ii) and merger control.

a) Anticompetitive practices

The following various collective or individual behaviors are prohibited and punishable under Moroccan competition law:

• Anticompetitive agreements or concerted practices (Les ententes anticoncurrentielles): Agreements, conventions and concerted actions which restrict, distort or prevent the competition on the Moroccan market are prohibited in particular when they control the production, limit access to the market or share markets and sources of supply;

Certain exemptions are provided for by the Moroccan competition law for the prohibited agreements resulting from a legal or regulatory text, contributing to economic progress or do not substantially restrict the competition;

• Abuse of dominance: The Moroccan competition law prohibits the abuse of a dominant position or a situation of economic dependence towards a supplier or customer that does not have any equivalent alternative option, it may consist in refusal to sell, tie-in sales, discriminatory conditions of sale, termination of commercial relationships based on a refusal of unjustified conditions of sale or minimum resale prices and minimum margin; and

• Abusively low pricing and other restrictive practices (pratiques restrictives de la concurrence).

The Competition Council could proceed to investigations, seize documents, order interim measures and impose fines proportionate to the seriousness of the offence and up to 10 per cent of the highest worldwide or national consolidated turnover of the involved company (or 4 million MAD if the author of the practices is a natural person). Other penalties may be decided such as civil nullity, injunctions to cease the anticompetitive practice or the publication of the Council's decision.

b) Merger control

The Moroccan competition law refers to three types of transactions:
• Mergers of two or more independent undertakings;

---

[1] Promulgated by Dahir (Royal Decree) No.1-14-116 of June 30, 2014.
[2] Promulgated by Dahir (Royal Decree) No.1-14-117 of June 30, 2014.
[3] Promulgated by Dahir (Royal Decree) No.1-00-91 of February 15, 2000.

• The acquisition of control by an undertaking (sole control) or several undertakings (joint control) over all or part of another undertaking or undertakings by acquiring a share in capital, purchasing assets, entering into a contract or any other means; and

• The establishment of a joint venture which is performing functions of an independent undertaking on a long-term basis.

A prior mandatory notification of any of the aforementioned transactions should be done by the parties before the competition council, when one of the following conditions is fulfilled:

• The combined aggregate worldwide pre-tax turnover of all the parties to the concentration is equal to or more than 750 million dirhams;

• The aggregate Moroccan-wide pre-tax turnover of at least two of the parties concerned by the concentration is equal to or more than 250 million dirhams; or

• The parties to a concentration, or which are the subject to a concentration have generated altogether during the previous calendar year an accrued value of more than 40 % of the sales, purchases or other transaction on a national market.

Regarding the procedure, the transaction must be notified to the Competition Council before its completion as soon as the parties concerned are able to present a sufficiently concrete file allowing the investigation of the case and, in particular, when the parties have entered into an agreement, signed a letter of intent or as of the announcement of a public offer.

Upon failure to file a notification, the Competition Council compels the parties, subject to a daily penalty payment, to notify the operation unless they revert to the previous state of affairs.

The decisions of the competition council may be appealed before the Moroccan competent courts.

H. Tax

Morocco and China had signed a non-double taxation bilateral agreement to avoid double taxation and to prohibit tax evasion with respect to income taxes, and it was concluded between Morocco and China on August 27, 2002.

The Moroccan tax system has been codified under the General Tax Code (CGI). The main taxes in the Moroccan system are:

• Income Tax concerning income and profits of individuals and private companies;
• Corporate Tax concerning income and profits earned by companies and other legal entities;
• Value added tax (VAT), which applies to consumer spending;
• Registration fees and stamp duties.

Moreover, in order to encourage investment and promote certain sectors, the existing legislative provisions relating to tax incentives envisage tax exemptions in terms of common law and at the sectoral level.

a) The Income Tax (IT)

The IT applies to income and profits of natural persons and legal entities that have not opted for Corporate Tax. The concerned incomes are:

• Wage income;
• Professional income;
• Land income and profits;
• Income from movable capital and profits; and
• The agricultural income.

Income Groups (In DH)	Rate
0–30,000	0%
30 001–50,000	10%
50 001–60,000	20%
60 001–80,000	30%
80 001–180,000	34%
> 180 000	38%

b) The Corporate tax

The Corporate tax applies mandatorily to income and profits of capital companies, public institutions and other corporations that carry out lucrative transactions and on an irrevocable basis to partnerships.

Company Income (In DH)	Rate
0–300,000	10%
300 001–1 000,000	20%
> 1,000,000	31%

c) The Value added Tax (VAT)

The Value added Tax applies to industrial, craft, commercial and liberal activities, as well as import operations of 20%. There are reduced rates of 7% and 10% on consumer products and certain food products, beverages and hostelry industry in particular and 14% for other products.

Rate	Products
14%	• With a right to deduct for tea, butter, transportation, electricity, commercial light-duty vehicles and mopeds, solar water heaters… • Deductions not applicable for services supplied by insurance agents or brokers.
10%	With a right to deduct, namely for: • Accommodation or renovation operations carried out by hotels and other touristic lodging; • Sales of foodstuffs and beverages consumed on-site in restaurants and those supplied by service providers to employees of companies; • Food oils; • Solar water heaters • Fishing gear and nets for fishing professionals • Rice, pasta, and kitchen salt; • Petroleum gas and other hydrocarbon gases, as well as petroleum or shale oil; • Bank and credit operations (including operations and interests pertaining to advances and loans granted to local communities and the Mourabaha alternative financial product) and commissions on foreign exchange; • Transactions related to stocks or shares issued by mutual funds; • Transactions related to securities carried out by brokerage firms; • Operations carried out by the Fonds d'Équipement Communal, and those pertaining to loans and advances granted to said Fund; • Operations carried out by licensed professionals (lawyers, interpreters, notaries, veterinarians, etc.); • Catering operations provided directly by the company to its employees. • Feed for livestock and low-yield animals • Agricultural equipment for use exclusively in agriculture
7%	With a right to deduct, namely for: • Certain consumer products (water delivered to public distribution networks, canned sardines, powdered milk, school supplies and their inputs, pharmaceutical products and their inputs, etc.); • Refined or agglomerated sugar; • Milk powder • Economic cars and all products and materials needed for their manufacturing, as well as assembly services under the conditions prescribed by the regulatory way.

I. Securities

a. Brief Introduction of Securities-Related Laws and Regulations

The financial instruments as defined by Law No.44-12 of December 28, 2012 relating to public offering "appel public à l'épargne" cover: (i) securities; (ii) collective investment funds shares and (iii) derivatives.

a) Securities

Securities are marketable and fungible financial instruments that can be listed on the stock exchange and are governed by Law No.17-95 relating to Join Stock companies. There are two categories of securities: stocks and bonds.

A Stock is a security representing a unit of equity ownership in a company. It represents a claim on the company's assets and earnings. The holder enjoys the rights associated with the shares (information, voting rights, dividend etc.). Stocks can be registered shares or bearer shares. In the latter case the identity of the shareholder is known to the issuer.

A bond is a debt security, representing a claim on the issuer. The bondholder is entitled to receive regular interests' payments until the maturity of the bond. Bond Instrument can take many forms defined by the issuer depending on the funding structure and the intended target (fixed rate, floating rate, convertible bonds ...).

b) Collective investment funds

There are three types of collective investment funds: mutual funds, venture capital funds and securitization trust.

A Mutual fund is an investment company whose funds are invested in securities and / or other liquid financial assets and are governed by Royal Decree of September 21, 1993 as amended by Law No.53-01. Two legal corporate forms could be found: open ended mutual funds (SICAV) and mutual funds.

• Open ended mutual funds (SICAV) area limited company with variable capital whose sole purpose is to manage securities and cash portfolio.

• Mutual Fund is a joint ownership of securities and cash.

Venture capital funds (VCF) are investment funds that makes venture investments and are governed by Law No.41-05 as amended by Law No.18-14 of February 19, 2015. There are two kinds of VCF: venture capital companies and collective investment fund (CIF) in venture capital.

The venture capitalists are expected to bring financing to small and medium enterprises, under the form of equity, convertible / debt securities as well in advance deposits to shareholders. The legal forms for CIF in Venture capital are:

• Venture Capital companies: typically structured as partnerships, the general partners serve as managers of the firm;

• CIF in Venture Capital: structured as limited liability companies.

The securitization trust is not a legal entity but a joint ownership and are governed by Law No.33-06 of April 21, 2004 as amended by Law No.05-14. Securitization is a financial transaction throughout which a securitization trust acquires contractual debts from one or more originators through the issuance of shares and / or via debt issuance.

c) Derivatives

Derivatives are governed by Law No.42-12 of May 14, 2014. Derivatives could be futures, swaps or options. However, the derivatives market is still not effective in Morocco.

b. Supervision and Regulation of Securities Market

The Moroccan capital market is supervised by the AMMC "Autorité Marocaine du Marché des capitaux" which was established by Law No.43-12 of March 13, 2013 and whose mission is to:

• Ensure the protection of savings invested in financial instruments;

• Ensure equal treatment of investors, transparency and integrity of the capital market and of the investors information;

• Ensure proper functioning of the capital market and ensure the implementation of legislative and regulatory provisions;

• Ensure control of the activity of different organizations and persons subject to its control;

• Ensure compliance with laws and regulations related to the fight against money laundering by individuals and institutions subject to its control;

• Contribute to promoting financial education for savers;

• Assist the government in the regulation of the capital market.

To fulfill these missions, The AMMC is empowered to the following:

a) Circulars Elaboration

Through circulars, the AMMC sets rules of professional practices, ethics codes and technical and practical applications of laws and regulations. The process of drawing up circulars is conducted in cooperation with professionals and relies on best practices with regard to international standards in regulating securities markets.

The circulars are approved by the government and published in the Moroccan Official Gazette "Official Bulletin".

b) Stakeholders Empowerment

The AMMC empowers individuals to perform certain functions within legal persons subject to its control.

Empowerment takes form through granting a professional card following a review, and whose validity period is determined according to the nature of the function performed.

The AMMC keeps a register of authorized persons, the list of which is disclosed to the public.

c) Visa, Accreditation and Opinions Related to Products

As appropriate, the AMMC accredits collective savings products or issue an opinion in their regards and grants visa to prospectuses meant to investors. The products in question are the Undertakings for the Collective Investment in Transferable Securities, UCITS, Venture capital funds and securitization trusts.

Through this prerogative, the AMMC ensures secure investment by ensuring compliance with legal and regulatory requirements for financial products and investors' information, verifying the ability of stakeholders to manage those products.

d) Examination of Stakeholders' Approvals Files

Stakeholders subject to the approval procedure are brokerage firms, Venture capital funds and securitization trusts management companies. The AMMC examines approval files and sends a notice to the Minister of Finance that grants or denies the approval. The AMMC verifies that the stakeholders to be accredited offer sufficient guarantees, particularly with regard to their organization, technical and financial resources and their managers' experience.

e) Financial Transactions Prospectuses Visa

The AMMC approves issuers' prospectuses on public offerings, Buyback programs, after reviewing the adequacy and consistency of information issued to investors. The objective is to ensure that investors have all the relevant information to make informed decisions. The approved prospectuses by the AMMC are freely available to the public prior to the transaction start.

f) Control of Issuers Financial Reporting

The objective of this control is to ensure that investors receive regular information about issuers. Thus, the AMMC ensures that issuers meet their obligations to publish annual, semiannual, and quarterly financial statements and disclose all material information that may affect the share price of their securities or affect the savings of Securities holders.

It ensures that information is concise, truthful, accurate and disclosed on a timely basis to the entire financial community.

g) Control of Professionals

Professionals subject to the AMMC control are the brokerage firms, the stock exchange, the account holders, the central depository and the management companies.

This control comes in two complementary ways: On-site control, through inspections conducted in the premises of the intermediaries, and document control, through reportings whose content and frequency are fixed by the AMMC.

The main purpose of this control is to ensure that professionals have permanently adequate safeguards, particularly with regard to organization, technical, financial and human resources and to verify that the conditions for delivering Application approval are maintained.

h) Complaints Processing

The AMMC receives complaints from investors concerning suspicious trading transactions in securities, and verifies the consistency of the complaint and takes appropriate action accordingly.

i) Surveillance, Investigations and Sanctions

The AMMC ensures compliance of securities market transactions with the rules in order to guarantee market integrity. The AMMC conducts investigations when necessary.

When facts are proven, the AMMC is empowered to issue sanctions against parties that committed the violations or breached the rules regulating their activities or the functioning of the market. Sanctions are pronounced following a procedure that respects the rights of the concerned parties.

c. Requirements for Engagement in Securities Exchange for Foreign Enterprises

The public offerings related to equity or debt securities in the Moroccan financial market by foreign enterprises would require a prior approval from the AMMC. In addition, the investment on Moroccan financial market by foreign enterprises would also require to notify the OdC of the investment. This declaration would permit to the OdC to control the repatriation of the investment proceeds.

J. Preference and Protection of Investment

a. The Structure of Preference Policies

The implementation of advanced regionalization and the adoption of the "2014—2020 Industrial Acceleration Plan", as well as the upgrading of conducive sectors to investment are aiming to support industrial ecosystems laying to a sustainable long-term economic growth.

Within this framework, investors may enjoy benefits when responding to application conditions and eligibility criteria depending on the categories of projects.

On the one hand, "Strategic" and "Structuring" projects are eligible to direct financial support to industrial eco-systems. "Strategic investments projects" are categorized, depending in their economic impact, in "Locomotive" projects with investments creating permanent jobs and "Contractor" projects which concern public order. "Structuring investments projects" are categorized in "Pioneer", "Added value resource", "Local Integration", "Sourcing" projects and projects for "Engineering and Research and Development centers".

On the other hand, the Industrial and Investment Development Fund covers transactions relating to direct financial support granted to investors responding to specific criteria and conform to the Investment Charter and its application decrees.

It is worth noting that the advantages offered by the Fund can be accumulated, however the aid or support cannot go beyond 5% of the overall amount of the investment program, or 10% when the project implemented in certain areas or when it involves investments in specific sectors.

b. Support for Specific Industries and Regions

Industrial investments for specific industries and regions are supported by the Hassan II Fund for Economic and Social Development ("FHII"), the Industry Department of the Ministry of Industry, Trade, Investment, and Digital Economy, and the Ministry of Economy and Finance, by agreements concluded between them.

For beneficiating of the support, investor shall firm an investment contract with the FHII. New investment projects (creation or extension) can benefit from a contribution from the FHII if they comply with all of the following requirements: a total amount of investment of over MAD ten million (MAD 10 million) tax excluded, an investment in capital goods of over MAD five million (MAD 5 million) (excluding import duties and taxes), and the investing company must operate in the automotive, aerospace, electronics, chemical and pharmaceutical industries, as well as manufacturing activities linked with nanotechnologies, microelectronics and biotechnologies.

Besides, special economic areas and investors meeting criteria for receiving financial support from the Industrial and Investment Development Fund are also eligible for beneficiating from advantages offered to them.

c. Special Economic Areas

a) Duty-free export zones

Duty-free export zones were implemented by the law on duty-free export zones which defines them as areas of the custom territory where the companies that were eligible to settle there are exempted from the application of customs, foreign trade and foreign exchange regulations, for all export activities for industrial or commercial purposes, as well as related service activities.

Each zone is created and delimited by a decree that determines the nature and activities of the companies that may be established there. The main active duty-free export zones in Morocco are located in Tangier, Tangier Med Ksar el Majaz Mellousa (1 and 2), Dakhla and Laayoune, Kebdana and Nador (for hydrocarbons storages), and Kenitra. The lessee of the export processing zone ensures the development and management of the area as well as the presentation of the investors' files for the approval of the local board in charge of the zones.

b) Casablanca Finance City

Under the law No.44-10 of December 2010, the "Casablanca Finance City" or "CFC" is a label created for companies meeting legal, economic and financial criteria and granting them a number of significant tax incentives, exchange control facilitations and doing business facilities.

d. Investment Protection

The promotion and protection of foreign investment in Morocco is not only limited to the Investment Charter and the missions assigned to the AMDIE but extends to its adherence to international multilateral conventions and the bilateral treaties, as part of strengthening relations with key partners. These conventions and treaties provide for an equal treatment and reciprocal protection between the parties. The main provisions of these treaties and conventions are based on the following aspects:

• Admission of the principle of the " most favored nation" for the treatment of investments;

• Free transfer of capital and income;

• Non-expropriation of investment, except for public utility interest and following a judicial decision (on a nondiscriminatory basis and to pay a prompt and adequate compensation);

• Guarantee of compensation for damages; and

• Disputes resolution through domestic courts or international arbitration at the choice of the investor.

a) International conventions

Morocco has ratified international conventions relating to the guarantee and protection of investment including agreements on the establishment of the International Center for Settlement of Investment Disputes "ICSID", the

Multilateral Investment Guarantee Agency "MIGA" and the Inter-Arab Organization for Investment Guarantee Corporation.

b) Bilateral treaties

Morocco has also signed, through its National Investments Commission (in French: la "Commission Nationale des Investissements") which is chaired by the Chief of the Government and which Secretariat is ensured by the AMDIE, more than sixty bilateral investment treaties with Arab, African, European, Asian and American countries, ensuring investors protection and investment, and coordination of national regulations with international standards.

III. Trade

A. Department Supervising Trade

The Moroccan competent authority for supervising trade in Morocco is the Ministry of Industry, Investment, Trade and Digital Economy.

This Ministry includes a central administration which has the following nine (9) directions: Direction of Industry, Direction of Trade and Distribution, Direction of Digital Economy, Direction of Statistics and Monitoring, Direction of Quality and Market Surveillance, Direction of Advanced Technologies, Innovation and Research and Development, Direction of Reception Areas, Direction of Cooperation and Communication and Direction of Ressources and Information Systems.

The Moroccan Ministry of Industry, Investment, Trade and Digital Economy is in charge of:
• Preparation of development strategies relating to the industry, trade, new technologies and post office sectors and their conversion into operational programs;
• Validation of the strategies for developing investment and enhancing the competitiveness of SMEs as well as their conversion into operational programs;
• Direction and implementation of the development strategies related to the industry, trade, new technologies and post office sectors;
• Contribution to the management of relations with national and international institutions and organizations in the industry, trade and new technologies sectors;
• Conducting studies and producing statistics in the industry, trade and new technologies sectors;
• Furniture of strategic intelligence / monitoring and evaluation of strategies for the industry, trade and new technologies sectors;
• Promotion and development of innovation in the industry and new technologies sectors;
• Development and coordination of industrial, commercial and technological reception areas as well as innovation centres (pôles de compétitivité);
• Contribution to the definition of training plans in the industry, trade and new technologies sectors and taking part in following up their implementation;
• Definition of the legal and organizational framework for the industry, trade and new technologies sectors;
• Making proposals for the regulation of the industry, trade and new technologies sectors;
• Regulation of the postal sector;
• Development of partnerships, coordination and implementation of cooperation programs;
• Promotion of quality and safety in the industry, trade and new technologies sectors;
• Ensuring control in the sectors of metrology, certification, quality, safety within companies, surveillance of the Moroccan market and consumer protection;
• Ensuring communications in the industry, trade and new technologies sectors.

B. Brief Introduction of Trade Laws and Regulations

Main Moroccan laws and regulations regulating trade in Morocco are the following:
• Law n°15-95 of 1st August 1996 forming the Commercial Code (as amended and completed) (and its Decrees) dealing mainly with provisions applicable to businessmen and commercial companies, business assets (fonds de commerce), checks, bills of exchange and similar deeds (effets de commerce), commercial contracts (such as for example, mortgage, leasing, banking agreements, etc.) and companies difficulties (in particular, bankruptcy proceedings);
• Law n°17-95 of 30 August 1996 relating to joint stock companies (sociétés anonymes—SA) (as amended and completed) (and its Decree n° 2-09-481) which regulate Moroccan joint stock companies and Moroccan simplified joint stock companies (sociétés anonymes simplifiées—SAS);

• Law n°5-96 of 13 February 1997 relating to partnerships (sociétés en nom collectif—SNC), limited partnerships (sociétés en commandite simple—SCS), partnerships limited by shares (sociétés en commandite par actions - SCA), limited liability companies (sociétés à responsabilité limitée—SARL) and undeclared partnerships (sociétés en participation) (as amended and completed) which regulates such forms of Moroccan companies;

• Law n°13-97 of 5 February 1999 relating to economic interest groups (groupements d'intérêt économique - GIE) (as amended and completed);

• Law n°104-12 of 30 June 2014 relating to freedom of prices and competition (and its Decrees);

• Law n°31-08 of 18 February 2011 enacting measures of consumer protection (and its Decrees and Orders);

• Law n°103-12 of 24 December 2014 relating to credit institutions and similar institutions;

• Law n°17-97 of 15 February 2000 relating to the protection of industrial property (as amended and completed) (and its Decrees and Orders);

• Law n°2-00 of 15 February 2000 relating to copyrights and similar rights (as amended and completed) (and its Decrees and Orders);

• Law n°13-83 of 5 October 1984 relating to repression of fraud on merchandises;

• Dahir enacting Law n°1-77-339 of 9 October 1977 approving the Code of Customs and Indirect Taxes Coming Under the Authority of the Customs and Indirect Taxes Administration (as amended and completed) (and its Decrees and Orders);

• Law dated 31 March 1919 forming Maritime Commercial Code (as amended and completed) (and its Decrees).

Other than that, there are many secondary legislation enacted based on the laws mentioned above and governing specific trade related matters in details.

C. Trade Management

a. General Trade Requirements and Unfair Competition

In Morocco, the Trade Law is the legislative text governing acts of trade and traders.

General requirements in order to perform trade activities, such as the acquisition of the status of trader, commercial capacity, obligations of the traders, are contained in the Law of Trade.

The status of trader is acquired by the usual or professional exercise of commercial activities listed in the Trade Law. We quote as an example:

• Purchase of furniture for resale or renting;
• Renting furniture for subletting;
• Purchase of immovable property for resale in the state or after processing;
• Industrial or craft activity;
• Transportation;
• Banking, credit and financial transactions;
• Insurance operations;
• Printing and publishing whatever form and medium;
• Building and public works;
• Offices and agencies for business, travel, information and advertising;
• Supply of products and services;

Trade activities in Morocco are regulated by provisions of Law n°104-12 relating to freedom of prices and competition (and its Decrees).

This Law shall apply to:

(i) any individuals or legal entities whether having or not their registered office or establishment in Morocco, provided that their operations or behaviors have as a purpose or which may have an effect on competition in the Moroccan market or a substantial part of it;

(ii) all production, distribution and services activities;

(iii) exportation agreements to the extent that their application has an impact on competition in the internal Moroccan market.

This Law deals mainly with the principle of freedom of prices, anti-competitive practices, merger control rules and practices restrictive of competition.

According to this Law, are prohibited, where their purpose is preventing, restricting or distorting competition in a market: concerted actions, conventions, agreements or coalitions, in whatever form and for whatever reason, when they tend:

(i) to limit access to the market or the free exercise of competition by other companies;

(ii) to hinder the formation of prices by the free play of the market by artificially favoring their rise or fall;

(iii) to limit or control the production, outlets, investments or technical progress;

(iv) to divide markets, sources of supply or public markets.

Is prohibited, where its purpose is to prevent, restrict or distort competition: the abuse by a company or group of companies of:

• a dominant position in the internal market;

• a situation of economic dependence in which a customer or supplier is found and does not have any another equivalent alternative.

Also, are prohibited price offers or price selling practices to consumers that are unreasonably low in relation to the costs of production, processing and marketing are prohibited where these offers or practices have as their object eliminating a market, or to prevent access to a market, a business or any of its products.

Moreover, the law regulates economic concentration. A concentration operation is carried out:

• When two or more previously independent companies merge;

• where a person, who already has control of at least one enterprise, acquires, directly or indirectly, whether through the acquisition of equity interests or the purchase of assets, contracts or any other means, control of all or part of another company or all or parts of several other enterprises;

• when one or more companies acquire, directly or indirectly, whether through the acquisition of equity interests or the purchase of assets, contracts or any other means, the control of all or part of the 'another enterprise or the whole or parts of several other enterprises.

The new merger control regime provides that a notification to the competition council is mandatory when one of the following conditions is met:

• the aggregate worldwide pre-tax turnover of all of the parties concerned (undertakings or group of natural or legal persons) exceeds MAD 750 million (around Eur 70 million);

• the pre-tax turnover achieved in Morocco by at least two of the parties concerned (undertakings or groups of natural or legal persons) exceeds MAD 250 million (around Eur 22 million); or

• the combined market share in Morocco is equal or exceeds 40%.

b. Electronic Trade and Consumer Protection

Electronic trade in Morocco is still not governed by a specific law; the only law that was enacted concerns electronic exchange of legal data.

The above-mentioned law establishes the regime applicable to electronic data exchanged the equivalence of paper-based and electronic documents and electronic signatures.

It also determines the legal framework applicable to the operations performed by electronic certification service providers, as well as the rules to be observed by electronic certification service providers and the holders of electronic certificates issued.

Also, Morocco has strengthened its legal system dedicated to the protection of private data by the enactment of law 09-08 on the protection of individuals with regard to the processing of personal data. The adoption of this text aims to protect Internet users against abuses of data use that may affect their privacy.

The law concerning electronic exchange of legal data foresees the validity of documents drawn up in electronic form or transmitted electronically, as well as the legal regime applicable to secure electronic signature, cryptography and electronic certification.

In Morocco, the consumer protection is regulated by provisions of Law n°31-08 of 18 February 2011 enacting measures of consumer protection and its related Decrees and Orders.

The purpose of this Law is:

(i) to ensure the appropriate and clear information of consumers on the products, goods or services they may acquire or use;

(ii) to guarantee the protection of consumers regarding clauses provided for in consumer contracts, notably, unfair clauses, clauses relating to financial services, consumer and real estate loans and clauses relating to advertising, distance selling and door-to-door sales;

(iii) to determine the legal and contractual guarantees of the defects of sold products and the after-sales service and to precise the conditions and procedures for the compensation of damages that may harm consumers;

(iv) to ensure the representation and defense of consumers' interests through consumer protection associations operating in accordance with the provisions of this Law.

D. The Inspection and Quarantine of Import and Export Commodities

The inspection and quarantine of import and export commodities is made by the Moroccan customs service.

The Dahir enacting Law n°1-77-339 of 9 October 1977 approving the Code of Customs and Indirect Taxes Coming Under the Authority of the Customs and Indirect Taxes Administration (as amended and completed) (and its Decrees and Orders) regulates the general principles concerning the action of the customs Service and indirect taxes, the clearance of goods, the rights and taxes perceived by the administration, the economic regimes in customs, special regimes, external relations, control of external trade and changes, indirect taxes, domestic consumption taxes applicable to beverages, alcohols and alcohol-based products, domestic consumption taxes applicable to petroleum products, guarantee of materials and works of platinum gold and silver, manufactured tobacco, etc.

Also, there are several secondary laws and regulations which regulate customs treatment of different types of commodities, such as for example:

• Law n°24-89 on Animal Health Measures for the Importation of Animals, Animal Products, Animal Products, Animal Propagating Products and Seafood and Freshwater Products;

• Decree n°2-01-2689 laying down the conditions for carrying out, as an exceptional measure, veterinary control operations at frontier posts during public holidays and outside the opening hours of the customs administration;

• Decree n°2-01-2690 laying down the conditions for carrying out, as an exceptional measure, control and sanitary and phytosanitary treatment of plants at border posts during public holidays and outside the legal opening hours of the plant.

• Decree n°2-16-535 prohibiting the import of plastic envelopes and blankets that have been used in agricultural production;

• Order of the Minister of Agriculture and Agricultural Development n°2249-94 laying down the sanitary conditions and treatment to be met by imported animal products intended for the animal by-products industry;

• Order of the Minister of Agriculture and Agricultural Development n°514-94 fixing the zootechnical standards for the importation of breeding animals of the bovine, ovine, caprine and equine species;

• Joint Order of the Minister of Agriculture and the Minister of Finance and Foreign Investment n°1726-96 determining the list of border posts open for the importation of animals, foodstuffs and animal products.

E. Customs Management

a. Overview of the Applicable Laws, Regulations and International Agreements

a) Customs Law

The main Moroccan Law regulating customs in Morocco is the Dahir enacting Law n°1-77-339 of 9 October 1977 approving the Code of Customs and Indirect Taxes Coming Under the Authority of the Customs and Indirect Taxes Administration (as amended and completed) (and its Decrees and Orders).

b) The Customs Tariff

The Customs tariffs depend on the nature of the product (animals, vegetable products, animal or vegetable fats and oils; products of their dissociation; food products; beverages; tobacco and manufactured tobacco, mineral products, products of the chemical or allied industries, plastics…) and also the existence or not of a Free Trade Agreement.

c) Agreements on Customs Operations

Within the framework of its global openness and liberalization strategy, Morocco has set up during the last decade a legal framework conducive to developing its commercial relations with some of its potential partners through the conclusion of free trade agreements either bilaterally or regionally. Morocco has then concluded multiple trade agreements, among which for example: the Morocco—European Union Association Agreements, the Morocco-United States of America Free Trade Agreement, the Morocco-EFTA Free Trade Agreement, the Morocco-Turkey Free Trade Agreement, the Arab Free Trade Zone.

b. Customs Management and Procedures

On importation, three (3) phases of customs clearance should be distinguished:

(i) the conduct of goods in customs: such phase concerns the direct movement of imported goods to the first office or customs post of entry for reporting;

(ii) the customs clearance of goods: it is carried out by depositing in the hands of the service a summary declaration or any other document in lieu of which the burden is on the carrier;

(iii) the accounting of goods: the filing of the declaration in detail assigns to the goods a definitive customs regime (release for consumption, economic regimes, etc.). This declaration in detail serves as a support for the fulfillment of all the customs formalities (and not customs) to which the declared goods are submitted.

On exportation, three (3) phases of customs clearance should be distinguished:

(i) customs clearance of goods for export: such phase consists of moving the goods for export to a customs office or to the places designated by the Administration to be declared in detail. These goods are either of

Moroccan origin or free circulation on the subject territory or under economic regimes. As an exporter, one is free to choose its export office as long as it is open to the intended operations;

(ii) the customs clearance of goods: if on import, the customs clearance of goods results in the filing of a summary declaration, on export, this type of declaration is not required. Goods must be declared in detail as they arrive at the export office.

In stores and customs clearance areas (MEAD), goods intended for export are taken over in a specific register while awaiting customs clearance and driving to the office of exit.

(iii) customs clearance for export : such phase is concretized by the deposit of a declaration in detail assigning to the merchandise a definitive customs regime (simple exportation, economic regimes, etc.). This declaration in detail serves as a support for the accomplishment of all the customs formalities to which the declared goods are submitted.

c. Statistics

As regards imports, the European Union remains Morocco's leading supplier with around 47% of imports, broken down as follows:
• semi-finished products (chemicals, plastics, copper, iron and steel, etc.), accounting for around of imports from these countries;
• industrial equipment (machinery and miscellaneous equipment, electrical wires and cables, industrial cars, electric switchgear, generator and electric motor, grinding equipment, etc.);
• finished products of consumption (passenger cars, medicines, parts and spare parts for passenger cars, fabrics, etc.).

From the Arab countries, purchases accounted for around 15% of all Moroccan imports. They consist mainly of energy products (crude oil and petroleum gas), which account for around 67% of purchases from these countries, followed by semi-finished products.

Imports from the United States, China and Turkey constituted around 15% of the total.

Regarding exports, the European Union remains at the top of Morocco's customers. Sales in this market are finished consumer goods (made-up clothing, knitwear, passenger cars, footwear, etc.), industrial capital goods and equipment for cutting or connecting electrical circuits and foodstuffs.

The market share of all the Arab countries reached only around 5% of the exported goods, which focused mainly on semi-finished products: (raw silver, plate, phosphoric acid, fertilizers, etc.) as well as finished products from consumption (passenger cars, medicines, perfumeries, etc.).

IV. Labour

A. Brief Introduction of Labour Laws and Regulations

The main Moroccan labour laws and regulations are the following:
• Law n°65-99 of 11 September 2003 relating to the Labour Code (and its Decrees and Orders);
• Decree n°2-04-469 dated 29 December 2004 relating to the notice period regarding the unilateral termination of indefinite term employment agreements.

Indefinite term contracts are the ordinary form of contracts.

An indefinite employment contract cannot be terminated by the employer without payment of compensation, unless the employee commits a serious fault.

Fixed-term employment contracts are allowed under the following circumstances:
• Replacement of an employee by another in case of suspension of his contract;
• Temporary increase of the activity;
• Seasonal work;
• Opening of a business for the first time or opening of a new establishment within the company or launching a new product.

Maximum number and timeframe of fixed term contracts is one (1) year, renewable once.

If the employee continues working past expiration date of a fixed term contract, the latest becomes automatically an indefinite term contract.

The probationary period for employment contracts is as follows:
For fixed-term employment contracts:
• up to fifteen (15) days when contracts are concluded for a period of less than 6 months;
• one (1) month when the contracts exceeds six (6) months.

For indefinite term employment contracts:
- three (3) months for executives;
- one month and half (1,5) months for employees;
- fifteen (15) days for laborers.

B. Requirements of Employing Foreign Employees

a. Work Permit

In the first place, it should be noted that foreigners that are working in Morocco are, like Moroccans, subject to the national legislation governing labor relations: the law n° 65-99 forming the Labor Code.

The Labor Code provides that any employer wishing to recruit a foreign employee must obtain an authorization from the governmental authority responsible for labor.

Thus, in order to hire expats, an authorization shall be obtained from the Moroccan Labor Ministry.

The dates of the authorization indicate the beginning and the end of the work permit. Any subsequent modification of the contract (wages, working conditions and, above all, modification of the duration of the contract, resignation, termination, dismissal or even change of employer) is also subject to the same formalities for obtaining a visa from the Ministry of Employment.

The employment contract for foreigners must therefore conform to the model set by the governmental authority responsible for labor.

In the event that a Moroccan employer would employ a foreign employee without having complied with the obligations described above, the employer is punished with a fine of 2,000 to 5,000 dirhams per contract non authorized, in accordance with article 521 of the Labor Code.

The employment relationship ends when the visa expires and makes the parties (employers and employees) free from each other at that time. The foreign employee who continued to work after the expiry date of the visa, is considered to be in an irregular situation.

b. Application Procedure

The documents requested to obtain work permits are the following:
- Completion of an application including employment contract;
- Diplomas obtained and certificates of work (with their translation in French language);
- Copy of passport;
- Certificate issued by the National Agency for the Promotion of Employment and Competence (ANAPEC), certifying the absence of national candidates to fill the position proposed to the foreign employee;

However, the following candidates are exempted from the ANAPEC procedure and certificate:
- Foreigners born in Morocco who are residents in a continuous way for a period of at least six (6) months.
- Spouses of nationals;
- The owners, authorized officers and managers of the company;
- The partners and shareholders of the company;
- Delegates or representatives in the framework of cooperation for a period not exceeding six months;
- Coaches and athletes;
- Foreign artists;
- Political refugees and stateless persons;
- Nationals of countries with which Morocco has concluded an establishment agreement (Algeria, Tunisia and Senegal).

c. Social Insurance

Every employee has social insurance which consists in the health insurance, pension and disability insurance. Social security contributions are mandatory. Part of the monthly social security contribution is payable by the employer and another part is payable by the employee (through a salary deduction mechanism—système de retenue à la source).

C. Exit and Entry

a. Visa Types

Visa for Chinese tourists coming to Morocco was abolished further to Mohammed VI King of Morocco's visit to China on June 2016.

For countries which nationals are not exempted from entry visa to Morocco, the Moroccan competent authorities may issue four (4) types of entry visas:

• A short-term visa, which allows any Foreigner to enter the territory of Morocco for reasons other than immigration for a short uninterrupted stay or several short stays in the case of multiple entries. The duration of each stay may be between one (1) and ninety (90) days.

• A long-term visa, which is valid for more than three (3) months and is a multiple entry visa issued by the Moroccan diplomatic / Consular representations after prior consultation with the Ministry of Foreign Affairs and Cooperation. The duration of validity of such visa can not exceed one (1) year and the duration of each stay may be between one (1) and ninety (90) days.

A Foreigner who has a long-term visa and wishes to stay in Morocco for more than three (3) months must ask the competent services of the General Direction of National Security to obtain a residence card.

• A transit visa, which authorizes a Foreigner traveling to a third State to cross the territory of Morocco. Such visa may be issued for one (1) or two (2) transits without the duration of stay of each transit exceeding 72 hours.

• A visa issued at the border: in exceptional cases, the Security Services may issue short-stay and transit visas to the Border Posts.

Visas granted may be either (i) ordinary (i.e.for tourism, work, business, investors, conferences, students, trainees or researchers, family reunification, journalists, visitors, medical stay, refugees and Stateless persons, aircraft crew members, sailors, technical assistance, cultural or sporting events and artistic animations) or (ii) official (i.e.accreditation visas, diplomatic visas or service visas).

b. Restrictions for Exit and Entry

Law n°02-03 of 11 November 2003 relating to the entry and stay of Foreigners in Morocco, emigration and irregular immigration and its Decree n°2-09-607 submits Foreigners crossing Moroccan borders to the Moroccan authorities' control. A validity check of the passport and the visa is then carried out by the latters. The control concerns also the verification of immigrants' financial resources, their reasons for entry in Morocco and guarantees of their return to their country.

If the Foreigner does not fulfill these conditions, he may be refused entry in Morocco. However, there are certain rights granted to foreigners whose entry to the territory is refused, such as to inform the person who should host him, notify his Consulate and contact a lawyer.

The Foreigner fulfilling the entry requirements is allowed to stay in the Moroccan territory during the validity of his visa. When his stay lasts more than three (3) months, he must before the expiry of his visa or before the expiry of ninety (90) days if he is exempted from visa to go to the police of his city of residence to accomplish the formalities for the establishment of a residence permit. At the first entry to Morocco, the medical certificate and criminal record of the Foreigner are required to apply for a residence permit.

Entry into the Moroccan territory may be refused to any person who does not submit the administrative documents or supporting documents requested or who is the subject of a deportation order or a Court order prohibiting entry into the Moroccan territory.

The expulsion may be pronounced by the Moroccan administration if the presence of a Foreigner on the Moroccan territory constitutes a serious threat for the public order.

D. Trade Union and Labour Organizations

Today, there are about twenty (20) professional unions in Morocco.

The Dahir n°1-57-119 of 16 July 1957 relating to professional unions (syndicats professionnels) (as amended and completed) is the legal basis of trade union's rights and freedoms.

According to this Dahir:

• Trade union organizations participate in the organization and representation of Moroccan citizens;
• There is a freedom to create and join professionnal unions;
• The right to strike is guaranteed;
• Civil servants (fonctionnaires) also enjoy the right to establish trade union organizations with the exception of "agents who are responsible for ensuring the security of the Moroccan State and the defense of public order";
• No prior authorization is required by the Moroccan State for the constitution of unions with the exception of the deposit of the articles of association and the list of members of the union office;
• Professional unions have legal personality and the right to sue;
• Trade unions have the right to establish, acquire property, constitute mutual funds and pensions and sign collective agreements,

E. Labour Disputes

Labor disputes which cannot be settled by the parties or the Labor Inspector are settled by Moroccan Courts.

Regarding the termination of an employment contract and in case of serious fault, indefinite term employment contracts can be terminated without any notice period.

The notice period is as follows:

(i) For executives:
• if seniority is less than one year: 1 month salary;
• if seniority is between one year to 5 years: 2 months salary;
• if seniority is more than 5 years: 3 months salary;

(ii) For employees and workers:
• if seniority is less than 1 year:8 days salary;
• if seniority is between 1 to 5 years: 1 month salary;
• if seniority is more than 5 years: 2 months salary.

In case of absence of a serious fault committed by the employee, severance shall be paid.

Severance is calculated upon employee's seniority and salary as follows:

(i) Legal compensation:
• 96 hours of salary for the first 5 years of seniority,
• 144 hours of salary from 6 to 10 years seniority,
• 192 hours of salary from 11 to 15 years seniority,
• 240 hours of salary for the seniority exceeding 15 years.

(ii) Compensation for unfair dismissal: 1.5 months of salary per year of work,

(iii) Compensation for unpaid vacation leave,

(iv) Severance pay for notice period.

V. Intellectual Property

A. Brief Introduction of IP Laws and Regulations

In Morocco, the intellectual property legal framework consists of many enacted laws, as well as international conventions ratified by Morocco.

Main Moroccan IP laws and regulations are the following:

• Law n°17-97 of 15 February 2000 relating to the protection of industrial property (as amended and completed) (and its Decrees and Orders) which regulate patents, integrated circuits layout designs, industrial designs, trademarks, commercial names, geographical indications, labels of origin and unfair competitition, temporary protection to exhibitions, industrial awards and datation of creations and conditions of exercice of the profession of advisors on industrial property;

• Law n°2-00 of 15 February 2000 relating to copyrights and similar rights (as amended and completed) (and its Decrees and Orders) which regulate copyrights, rights of artists, interpreters or performers, phonogram producers and broadcasting organizations, collective management of copyrights and similar rights, measures, lawsuits and legal sanctions of piracy and other criminal offences and responsabily of service providers;

• Law n°13-99 of 15 February 2000 creating the Moroccan Office of Industrial and Commercial Property (OMPIC) (and its Decree) which is the Moroccan organism in charge of the protection of industrial property rights (trademarks, patents and industrial designs) and the keeping of the central trade register in Morocco and the keeping of national registers of industrial property titles / rights (trademarks, patents, industrial designs, geographical indications and labels of origin);

• Decree n°2-64-406 of 8 March 1965 creating the Moroccan Copyright Office (BMDA) (as amended and completed).

The main international conventions ratified by Morocco are:

• Budapest Treaty on the International Recognition of the Deposit of Microorganisms for the Purposes of Patent Procedure (July 20, 2011);

• WIPO (World Intellectual Property Organization) Copyright Treaty (July 20, 2011);

• WIPO Performances and Phonograms Treaty (July 20, 2011);

• Trademark Law Treaty (TLT) (July 6, 2009);

• Protocol Relating to the Madrid Agreement Concerning the International Registration of Marks (October 8, 1999);

• Patent Cooperation Treaty (October 8, 1999);

• Convention Establishing the World Intellectual Property Organization (July 27, 1971);

• Nice Agreement Concerning the International Classification of Goods and Services for the Purposes of the Registration of Marks (October 1, 1966);
   • Hague Agreement Concerning the International Registration of Industrial Designs (October 20, 1930);
   • Madrid Agreement Concerning the International Registration of Marks (July 30, 1917);
   • Madrid Agreement for the Repression of False or Deceptive Indications of Source on Goods (July 30, 1917);
   • Paris Convention for the Protection of Industrial Property (July 30, 1917);
   • Berne Convention for the Protection of Literary and Artistic Works (June 16, 1917).

B. Patent Application

Any individual or legal entity may file a patent application before the Moroccan Office of Industrial and Commercial Property (OMPIC).

Regarding the filing of any patent in Morocco, the patent application shall include:
(i) completion of a specific form for the patent application;
(ii) a description of the invention: its field, the state of the prior art, a description of the technical problem and the solution provided by the invention as well as the possible industrial applications;
(iii) one or more claims defining the purpose and limits of the protection requested;
(iv) the drawings, if they are necessary for the understanding of the invention;
(v) an abstract that summarizes the technical content of the invention;
(vi) payment of fees (around USD 1,200).

The procedure is as follows:

A preliminary search report accompanied by an opinion on patentability in order to assess the novelty, the inventive step and the industrial application of the invention is established by a patent examiner specialist in the technical field of the invention. Such report mentions the state of the art (i.e.it establishes a patent list of inventions and documents relating to the invention and which have been made accessible to the public before the filing date of the patent application).

The examiner notifies the preliminary report to the applicant.

After expiry of an eighteen (18) month-period from the date of filing and if the patent application has not been withdrawn or rejected, it shall be published.

After verification of the absence of rejection grounds, the patent may be issued after payment of the required fees.

The granted patent is published with the definitive search report. Thus, the OMPIC gives the title of the patent granted to the holder or his representative on request.

C. Trademark Registration

Regarding the filing of any trademark in Morocco, the file application must contain on the date of its deposit:
(i) The application form duly completed by the applicant;
(ii) Two (2) reproductions of the black and white model of the trademark;
(iii) Two (2) reproductions of the colour model of the trademark (if the latter is in colours);
(iv) Any power of attorney, as the case may be;
(v) Payment of the required fees (around USD 240).

The application for trademark registration goes through a formal examination, namely the study of the validity of the form to be completed and other documents. The application also goes through a substantive examination.

The trademark is published for a period of two (2) months in the "Official Catalogue of Trademarks".

After two (2) months of publication and if no opposition has arisen, the trademark may be registered. A "certificate of registration of the trademark" is then delivered or notified to the applicant or its agent.

D. Measures for IP Protection

a. Protection of Patents

A patent is an industrial property right which confers to its owner a temporary exclusive right (for 20 years maximum) to exploit the invention of which it is the object. The term "patent" also refers to the technical document in which the invention is described.

Any new invention involving an inventive step and capable of industrial application is patentable. It is therefore necessary to perform a prior art search before filing a patent application.

For Foreigners which are not resident in Morocco, it is essential to have a representative domiciled in Morocco to file the patent application.

b. Protection of Trademarks

Regarding trademarks, there are many types: trademarks, service trademarks and collective trademarks (used by associations for example).

Trademarks can take the most varied forms: name of the company, numbers, slogan, letters, drawing or color combination. In fact, a trademark carries an image and reputation that gives it a value that is sometimes considerable, an essential factor in the recognition of the company.

The interest of a trademark lies in the duration of the protection conferred on its owner, which consists of a period of ten (10) years, renewable indefinitely.

Conditions of validity of any trademark:

(i) It must be distinctive;

It must not designate a characteristic of the product nor indicate its quality or composition. It must be original by its graphics, phonetics or colors;

(ii) It must be lawful;

(iii) The trademark must not contain any misleading elements that could mislead the consumer as to the characteristics or the quality of the product or service;

(iv) It must not contain signs prohibited by law such as flags, arms, official emblems and hallmarks of countries or intergovernmental organizations or be contrary to public order or morality;

(v) It must be available;

The trademark must not be used by a third party to designate the same product or service. However, there is nothing to prevent two identical trademarks from coexisting legally if they concern different products between which there is no likelihood of confusion.

VI. Environmental Protection

A. Department Supervising Environmental Protection

The Moroccan Department supervising environment protection in Morocco is the State Secretariat under the Minister of Energy, Mines and Sustainable Development, in charge of Sustainable Development.

With respect to solar energy, there is a private company with public funds dedicated to solar energy called the "Moroccan Agency For Solar Energy—MASEN" which has been created by Law n°57-09 dated 11 February 2010 (as amended and completed) and is in charge of piloting renewable energies in Morocco. As part of the National Renewable Energy Development Program, MASEN aims to carry out a program of development of electricity generation projects with an additional minimum total capacity of 3,000 MW by 2020 and 6,000 MW by 2030.

There is also an agency called "The Moroccan Agency for Energy Efficiency—AMEE" created by Law n°16-09 of 11 February 2010 (as amended and completed) which is a public institution under the supervision of the Minister of Energy, Mines and Sustainable Development.

The AMEE's missions are:

• To propose to the Moroccan Administration a national plan and sectorial and regional plans for the development of energy efficiency;

• To design and carry out energy efficiency programs;

• To monitor, coordinate and supervise development actions in the sector of energy efficiency;

• To monitor and coordinate completion of energetic due diligence and support the implementation of their recommendations;

• To mobilize the financial resources necessary for the completion of the AMEE's missions;

• To propose and popularize standards and labels in energy efficiency of equipments and devices.

B. Brief Introduction of Laws and Regulations of Environmental Protection

Main Moroccan laws and regulations relating to environmental protection in Morocco are the following:

• Law n°11-03 dated 12 May 2003 relating to the protection and enhancement of the environment;

• Law n°12-03 dated 12 May 2003 relating to the environmental impact studies;

• Framework Law n°99-12 dated 6 March 2014 the National Charter for the Environment and Sustainable Development;

• Law n°16-09 dated 11 February 2010 creating the "National Agency for the Development of Renewable Energy and Energy Efficiency (ADEREE) which has become since 2016 the "Moroccan Agency for Energy Efficiency—AMEE" as amended and completed);

• Law n°57-09 dated 11 February 2010 creating the company "Moroccan Agency For Solar Energy" (MASEN) (as amended and completed);

The purpose of Law n°11-03 is to lay down basic rules and principles of national policy in the field of protection and enforcement value of the environment. These rules and principles aim:
• to protect the environment against all forms of pollution and degradation from any source;
• to improve the environment and the living conditions of man;
• to define the basic guidelines of the legislative, technical and financial framework concerning the protection and management of the environment;
• to put in place a specific liability regime to ensure compensation for environmental damage and compensation to victims.

Law n°99-12 sets the basic objectives of state action in environmental protection and sustainable development.

It aims to:
• strengthen the protection and preservation of natural resources and environments, biodiversity and cultural heritage, prevent and combat pollution and nuisances;
• integrate sustainable development into sectoral public policies and adopt a national strategy for sustainable development;
• harmonize the national legal framework with international conventions and standards related to environmental protection and sustainable development;
• strengthen mitigation and adaptation measures to climate change and combating desertification;
• decide on institutional, economic, financial and cultural reforms in environmental governance;
• Define the commitments of the country, local authorities, public institutions and state-owned companies, private enterprise, civil society associations and citizens with regard to environmental protection and sustainable development;
• establish an environmental liability regime and an environmental control system.

C. Evaluation of Environmental Protection

As part of the mission of environmental control assigned to the Ministry of the Environment by Decree No.2-14-758 of 23 December 2014 on the organization and attributions of the Ministry of the Environment, in particular Article 10 of the decree which provides that the Directorate of Control, Environmental Assessment and Legal Affairs (DCEAJ) is responsible for ensuring the application of environmental legislation and regulations by regularly carrying out inspections in collaboration with the relevant departments.

The environmental control is a mission of the Government; it is about a technical-legal operation which aims at checking the respect of the provisions of the environmental laws of the standards and the technical requirements envisaged by the laws. The control is used for the application of the regulations, it results in inspection actions, scheduled or unannounced, conducted according to a well-defined process.

Many factors give great importance to the mission of environmental control including:
• political will expressed by the royal directives concerning the elaboration of the national charter of the environment and sustainable development;
• advanced stage of completion of the legal and regulatory framework (enactment of laws and regulations);
• issuance of the environmental acceptability decision for the projects submitted to the environmental impact study under the law 12-03 and realization of the new investment projects;
• granting by the Environment Department of a number of authorizations, particularly in the field of import and export of waste and chemicals;
• launching and implementation of several projects funded by the Department of the Environment (FODEP, NAP, PNDM, PER, NGOs, pilot projects);
• Morocco's commitment to international governance in the field of the environment.

The environment protection evaluation operates according to a well defined method that can be broken down into 6 key concepts listed below:

a) Hierarchical orientation

Due to their legal consequences, environmental control operations are triggered by the hierarchy. Indeed, it is up to the hierarchy to set the area of activity to control, to draw the framework in which the control must be carried out and the aspects on which it must focus. The hierarchy is informed of the control program that it approves and supports, in turn the control teams are informed of the agreement of the hierarchy and its commitment.

b) Consultation

Consultation is an important requirement of the environmental control operation. It is done upstream and downstream, internally and externally. Many parties are involved in the control.

c) Programming

Any environmental control operation must be scheduled and follow a timetable communicated to the parties directly concerned. The programming ensures the progress of the control action. It also allows the controllers to plan their work and to take all the necessary measures and precautions in order to succeed in their mission.

d) Adaptation

The activities to be controlled are very diversified and the peculiarities are very widespread. Therefore, control operations must be adapted to each situation and use the relevant control methods required by each activity. According to this principle of adaptation, certain control operations can rely on external expertise at the departmental level, both national and international.

e) Field inspection

Environmental control is exercised in the field. It is never limited to the verification of the file or the collection of explanations collected from the controlled party. The environmental controller must always go on site to check, record, take and review the situation. The contact with the reality of the ground assures the credibility and the seriousness with the operation of control.

f) Reporting

The control is sanctioned by a report which retraces in detail, all the steps of the control process. In particular, the report gives a summary of the dysfunctions found in relation to the requirements laid down in the legislation or regulations governing the controlled activity. It also identifies recommendations and measures against parties who have committed.

On another note, a National Fund for the Protection and Enhancement of the Environment is established.

The activities and tasks of such fund are monitored by the government responsible for the environment.

The resources of the national fund are intended to finance the incentives provided for by this law and exceptionally to finance environmental and experimental pilot projects.

VII. Dispute Resolution

A. Methods and Bodies of Dispute Resolution

a. Litigation

In Morocco, litigation is governed by the following main laws:
• Dahir enacting Law n°1-74-338 of 15 July 1974 relating to judicial organization of the Kingdom of Morocco (as amended and completed);
• Dahir enacting Law n°1-74-447 of 28 September 1974 approving the text of the Civil Procedure Code (as amended and completed);
• Law n°53-95 of 12 February 1997 creating the Commercial Courts (as amended and completed);
• Law n° 41-90 of 10 September 1993 creating the Administrative Courts (as amended and completed) (and its implementing Decree).

The Moroccan judiciary system is based on the so-called first-instance and second-level courts (courts of appeal) and, at the top of this organization, the Court of Cassation.

In addition to common law jurisdictions, there are specialized jurisdictions and other so-called "exceptional" jurisdictions.

A common law jurisdiction is in principle competent for any dispute not specifically assigned by law to another jurisdiction.

a) Courts of First Instance

The field of competence of the Courts of First Instance is very varied. It judges all cases which have not been specially assigned to another jurisdiction.

The court of first instance rules in collegiality (three magistrates). Nevertheless, it may also decide by a single judge for certain cases.

b) Courts of Appeal

There are Courts of Appeal which role is to review appeals from decisions rendered by the Courts of First Instance.

They are composed of magistrates divided into chambers (civil, social, criminal, etc.) and judge in collegiality (three magistrates).

c) Court of Cassation

It exercises jurisdiction over the entire Moroccan territory. It is divided into chambers (civil, commercial, administrative, criminal, etc.) each composed of a President and advisers.

Theoretically, any decision finally rendered by the Courts of First Instance or the Courts of Appeal may be appealed. The Court of Cassation does not constitute a third degree of jurisdiction, it only checks the conformity to the law without re-examining the facts and determines the meaning in which the rule of law must be applied.

Concerning specialized jurisdictions, there are Commercial Courts and Administrative Courts.

d) Commercial Courts

Commercial Courts include Commercial Courts and Commercial Courts of Appeal.

Commercial Courts are competent to settle all commercial disputes relating:
- to commercial agreements;
- between businessmen or commercial entities in the context of their commercial activities;
- actions relating to effets de commerce (such as checks, bills of exchange, etc.);
- disputes between partners of any commercial company;
- disputes relating to business assets (fonds de commerce).

e) Administrative Courts

The Administrative Courts include administrative tribunals and administrative appeals courts.

The Administrative Courts are competent to settle disputes relating to electoral disputes, actions for annulment for abuse of authority / power against the decisions of the administrative authorities, disputes relating to administrative contracts and actions for compensation for damages caused by acts or activities of public persons, excluding those caused on the public highway by any vehicle belonging to a public entity.

The Administrative Courts are also competent to settle disputes arising from the application of the legislation and the regulation of pensions and death benefits of State employees, local authorities, public institutions and staff, tax disputes, expropriation for reasons of public utility, contentious actions relating to recoveries of treasury claims, disputes relating to the individual situation of civil servants and agents of the State, local authorities and public institutions.

b. Arbitration

Non institutional arbitration is governed by the Civil Procedure Code (articles 306 and subsequent).

Articles 306 and subsequent of the Civil Procedure Code distinguish between internal arbitration and international arbitration.

The Code of Civil Procedure contains rules governing arbitration for domestic and Foreign awards.

Also, the New York Convention on the Recognition and Enforcement of Foreign Arbitral Awards is in force in Morocco since 7 June 1959, as Morocco was the second signatory country of such Convention.

It is possible to enforce a Foreign arbitral award in Morocco by leave of Moroccan Courts. However, Moroccan courts will not grant leave to enforce such arbitral awards unless:
- it was made by a competent court in the relevant jurisdiction;
- the award is enforceable under the law in which judgment was rendered;
- the parties have been properly represented; and
- the decision is not contrary to Moroccan public policy.

c. Conventional Mediation

Articles 327-55 and subsequent of the Civil Procedure Code create a new dispute resolution process.

In order to prevent or resolve a dispute, the parties may agree to the appointment of a mediator to facilitate the conclusion of a transaction. Compared to arbitration, the difference lies in the fact that the parties do not entrust the mediator with the decision to settle the dispute but to officiate with the parties in order to reach a settlement.

The mediation agreement may be contained in the main agreement (mediation clause) or concluded after the dispute has arisen (mediation agreement). It can also intervene during a legal proceeding. In this case, it is brought to the attention of the Court as soon as possible and interrupts the procedure.

The mediation agreement must always be in writing and, subject to nullity, appoint the mediator or provide for the terms of his appointment.

The party intending to apply the mediation clause shall immediately inform the other party and refer the mediator named in the clause.

B. Application of Laws

Parties of a contract can agree on the jurisdiction that is deemed to handle the potential issues.

On the other hand, the removal from the execution of a national judgment and the recourse to a foreign jurisdiction to obtain a judgment contrary to it constitutes an attack on the sovereignty of the State.

The Supreme Court ruled on this matter, confirming in its judgment of 18/10/2006 that: "the removal of the respondent from the execution of the judgment rendered against him by a Moroccan court and the referral to a foreign jurisdiction to obtain the divorce constitutes an attack on Moroccan public order; therefore, it is necessary to break the judgment which has rendered the judgment enforceable".

Three conditions are required for exequatur:

• The foreign judgment must comply with the procedural rules of the State to which it belongs, without any examination by the national Court of the characterization of the facts, the relevance and the sincerity of the reasons and the means of proof;

• The foreign Court must be competent to make the judgment in question;

• The foreign judgment must respect Moroccan public order.

Since the notion of public order is relative, the judge has a discretionary power to review the conformity of the foreign judgment with national public order.

It must be remembered that the Court may order the partial exequatur of a foreign judgment if the other part of the judgment is contrary to Moroccan public order.

To this is added another condition, namely

• The foreign judgment must be final and capable of application in the State where it was rendered:

A final judgment is a judgment that is not subject to any remedy under the law of the country from which it emanates, which ensures a guarantee of the rights of the parties.

However, there are exceptions to this principle set by certain international conventions.

Moroccan justice exercises control over foreign judgments. The system adopted is that of control is the control of the external conditions of the foreign judgment by excluding the system of reciprocity.

As regards to the authority responsible for exequatur, Court decisions rendered by foreign Courts are enforceable in Morocco only after having been granted by the Court of first instance of the domicile or residence of the defendant or failing that, the place where the execution is to take place.

Even though the Moroccan legislator has regulated the matter of foreign judgments and their exequatur, international cooperation remains the best way to overcome the problems created by these overlapping cross-border conflicts.

Believing in the importance of this cooperation, Morocco has worked for its strengthening through the ratification of several conventions. We can cite as examples:

• Franco-Moroccan Convention on Mutual Legal Assistance, Execution of Judgments and Extradition, signed on 5 October 1957;

• Convention between the Kingdom of Morocco and the French Republic on the status of persons and the family, and judicial cooperation, dated 10/08/1981, published in the BGB of 07/10/1987;

• Agreement of 26/06/2002 between the Kingdom of Morocco and the Kingdom of Belgium on the recognition and enforcement of judgments relating to alimony;

• Convention of 26/06/2002 between the Kingdom of Morocco and the Kingdom of Belgium on judicial cooperation, recognition and enforcement of judgments on the right of custody and access;

Morocco has also adopted new mechanisms for international cooperation through the mutual exchange of judges with several countries, mainly France and Spain, and the establishment of joint commissions with foreign countries to follow up the conventions. bilateral ties that bind them.

Foreign judgments can be executed in Morocco only if they are enforced. These judgments are essentially rendered in civil, commercial, family and criminal matters.

VIII. Others

A. Anti-commercial bribery

a. Brief Introduction of Anti-commercial Bribery Laws and Regulations

Anti-commercial bribery is mainly governed in Morocco by:

• Law n°43-05 dated 17 April 2007 relating to the fight against money laundering (as amended and completed);

• Criminal Code No 1-59-413 dated 26 November 1962 ;

• Law n°113-12 on 9 June 2015 relating to the National Instance of Probity, Prevention and Fight Against Corruption.

The law N° 113-12 establishes the missions, the composition, the organization and the operating rules of the National Authority for Probity, Prevention and the Fight against Corruption.

For the purposes of this law, corruption means any crime of bribery, trading in influence, embezzlement or extortion, as provided by the law in force and any other crime of corruption provided for by specific legislation.

According to the criminal law, is guilty of corruption a person who solicits or approves offers or promises, solicits or receives donations, present or other advantages, for:

• Being a magistrate, public official or having an elective office, perform or abstain from performing an act of office, fair or not, but not subject to remuneration or an act which, although outside of his personal attributions, is, or could have been facilitated by his function;

• Being an arbitrator or expert appointed either by the administrative or judicial authority or by the parties, render a decision or give a favorable or unfavorable opinion;

• Being a magistrate, assessor-juror or member of a jurisdiction, to decide either in favor or to the prejudice of a party;

• Being a doctor, surgeon, dentist, midwife, falsely certifying or concealing the existence of diseases or infirmities or a state of pregnancy or providing false indications of the origin of a disease or infirmity or the cause of a death.

b. Department Supervising Anti-commercial Bribery

The department supervising anti-commercial bribery is the National Instance of Probity, Prevention and Fight Against Corruption which mission is mainly:

• receive and examine all reports, complaints and information relating to corruption cases, verify the truth of the acts and facts they mention and forward them, where appropriate, to the competent authorities;

• to carry out investigation of the cases of corruption brought to its attention;

• to develop prevention programs against corruption crimes and contribute to the moralization of public life, ensuring their execution;

• to work to disseminate and publicize the rules of good governance;

• to establish programs of communication, awareness and dissemination of probity values and ensure their realization;

• to give its opinion, at the request of the Government, on any program, measure, project or initiative aimed at preventing or combating corruption;

c. Punitive Actions

According to Criminal Law, those guilty of corruption are punished by imprisonment from two (2) to five (5) years and a fine of MAD 2,000 to MAD 50,000.

When the sum of corruption is greater than MAD 100,000, the punishment is five (5) years to ten (10) years' imprisonment and MAD 5,000 to MAD 100,000 fine.

B. Project Contracting

a. Permission System

Public procurement (passation des marches publics) follows the principles:
• freedom of access to the public order;
• equal treatment of competitors;
• guaranteeing the rights of competitors;
• transparency in the client's choice.

It also obeys the rules of good governance.

Public procurement takes into consideration respect for the environment and the objectives of sustainable development.

b. Prohibited Areas

There is no specific prohibitive rules on national and foreign enterprises.

c. Invitation to Bid and Bidding

The invitation to bid may be open or restricted. It is said "open" when any competitor can obtain the consultation file and submit his application. It is said "restricted" when only bids that can be submitted are the competitors that the developer has decided to consult.

The call for bidders is said to be "preselected" when only those who have sufficient capacity, in particular from a technical and financial point of view, are allowed to submit tenders, after consulting an admission committee.

The competition puts competitors in competition, on the basis of a program, for the realization of a service requiring special research of a technical, aesthetic or financial nature.

The open or restricted invitation to bid follows the following principles:

(i) a call for competition;
(ii) the opening of bids in public session;
(iii) the examination of tenders by a bidder commission;
(iv) the choice by the tender commission of the most advantageous offer to be offered to the client;
(v) the obligation for the contracting authority that conducts the call for tenders to communicate to the members of the tender commission the amount of the estimate.

新西兰

作者：Chris Gordon、Dean Alderton、Dan Jones、Mei Fern Johnson
译者：韦金记、辜超平

一、概述

（一）新西兰政治、经济、社会与法律环境介绍

1. 新西兰的监管框架

新西兰在经济方面管制的解除和分权，使其直接面对国际竞争。在过去30年中，历届新西兰政府都致力于消除进口障碍，取消大部分补贴，确保有关海外投资的规则，旨在鼓励在新西兰的海外投资，实现贸易规则改革。新西兰一直被世界银行和其他组织列为世界上最为商业友好的国家之一。

2. 新西兰的政治体系

新西兰作为独立主权国家和英联邦成员国，没有成文宪法。

新西兰并非联邦国家。所有的立法均由唯一的议会——众议院表决通过，众议院是新西兰的最高立法机构。新西兰采用"混合代表制"（MMP）作为其选举制度。议会每3年举行一次民主选举。

3. 新西兰的法律制度

新西兰是普通法系国家，法律包括判例法（法院判决）和新西兰议会制定的成文法，后者可以取代前者。

（二）"一带一路"倡议下与中国企业合作的现状及趋势

1. 两国关系

新西兰与中国于1972年首次建立外交关系，自此两国关系迅猛发展。

2. 中国与新西兰的双边协定

中国是新西兰最大的商品贸易伙伴，也是包括服务贸易在内的全球第二大合作伙伴。[①]

2008年签订的《中国—新西兰自由贸易协定》（NZCFTA）是中国首次与发达国家签订自由贸易协定，巩固了两国的贸易关系，为出口商、服务业和投资者打开了贸易的大门。[②]

《中国香港与新西兰紧密经贸合作协定》（CEPA）是中国香港特别行政区与新西兰于2010年3月签订的双边自由贸易协定，是中国香港特别行政区首次与外地经济体系签订双边货物和服务贸易协定，该协定是对自由贸易协定的补充，使得香港更有望成为与中国内地贸易往来的平台。[③]

2017年3月，中国总理李克强访问新西兰，代表多个政府机构与新西兰签署了一系列协议，其中包括：

- 《中华人民共和国政府和新西兰政府关于加强"一带一路"倡议合作的安排备忘录》；
- 《中华人民共和国商务部和新西兰外交贸易部关于电子商务合作的安排》；
- 《中华人民共和国商务部和新西兰外交贸易部关于加强国际发展合作交流的安排》。[④]

[①] "Our Relationship with China" New Zealand Foreign Affairs and Trade <www.mfat.govt.nz>.
[②] https://www.mfat.govt.nz/en/countries-and-regions/north-asia/china#Trade.
[③] "Hong Kong and New Zealand sign Closer Economic Partnership Agreement" (29 March 2010) Hong Kong Government News Press Release <http://www.info.gov.hk/gia/general/201003/29/P201003290114.htm>.
[④] "Our Relationship with China" New Zealand Foreign Affairs and Trade <https://www.mfat.govt.nz/en/countries-and-regions/north-asia/china#Trade>.

3. 安排备忘录——"一带一路"倡议

中国和新西兰签订《关于加强"一带一路"倡议合作的安排备忘录》反映了两国加强合作交流，支持"一带一路"倡议的共同愿望。备忘录阐明了中国和新西兰相互理解[①]：

"实现两国共同发展目标，将紧密的政治关系、经济互补、人文交流的优势转化为务实合作、持续增长的优势，使两国政治关系持续友好，经济纽带更加牢固，人文联系更加紧密，更好造福两国人民。"

二、投资

近年来，中国（包括香港地区）和新西兰两国（地区）之间的投资一直强劲增长，在 2016 年达到了 62 亿新西兰元[②]，中国在新西兰的投资横跨多个行业。

（一）市场准入[③]

1. 投资主管部门

海外投资办公室（OIO）负责批准海外人士在新西兰的投资申请。2005 年的《海外投资法》和《海外投资条例》赋予了海外投资办公室广泛的自由裁量权，无论申请人是否满足条件，其均可决定同意或拒绝投资申请。海外投资办公室由财务部部长负责，同时土地信息部部长和渔业部部长分别负责涉及"敏感土地"和渔业的投资申请。

2. 投资行业法律法规

（1）投资激励

新西兰没有针对批准项目或特定地区的投资激励举措，也没有自由贸易区鼓励海外投资。新西兰吸引海外投资者的原因在于其健全、一致的经济政策，良好的经济增长率和稳健的政治体系。

（2）海外投资管控

新西兰的海外投资管控要求，海外个体在投资特定种类资产前应当获得同意。对于在新西兰设立或收购企业的海外个体，主要的限制源于《海外投资法》和《海外投资条例》。

从广义上讲，"海外个体"包括非新西兰公民也非新西兰普通居民的个人，在新西兰境外注册成立的公司，或是 25%（或以上）的所有权或控制权由海外人员所有的公司、合伙企业或其他实体。

（3）一般管控

同新西兰国内投资者一样，海外投资者必须遵守新西兰的一般法律。举例来说，《公司法》（1993年）、《合伙法》（1908年）、《有限合伙法》（2008年）、《商业法》（1986年）和《新西兰储备银行法》（1989年）在同等程度上影响着新西兰国内投资者和海外投资者。

3. 投资方式

《海外投资法》和《海外投资条例》适用于所有类型的投资，并规定了海外个体在投资新西兰前需经政府同意的情形。是否需经同意取决于所涉及的投资额、拟投资类型和拟投资行业。

《海外投资法》规定，海外投资交易涉及以下三个方面的，需要取得同意：

- "重大商业资产"；
- "敏感土地"（包括农田）；
- 捕捞配额。

对于需要取得同意的情形，必须在交易生效前取得认可/同意。即使另外存在收购要约，经海外投资办公室同意后，投资者也可以签订股份收购协议。

[①] Memorandum of Arrangement on Strengthening Cooperation on the Belt and Road Initiative between the Government of New Zealand and the Government of The People's Republic Of China https://www.mfat.govt.nz/assets/FTAs-agreements-in-force/China-FTA/NRA-NZ-China-Cooperation-on-Belt-and-Road-Initiative.pdf.

[②] New Zealand Foreign Affairs and Trade, 'China' https://www.mfat.govt.nz/en/countries-and-regions/north-asia/china

[③] 本文出版之日，《海外投资法》和《海外投资条例》可能因《海外投资修正案》的出台而有所变更。

4. 海外投资"重大商业资产"

如果海外个体有意收购新西兰企业的证券，在新西兰设立公司，或购买资产，又或海外个体享有新西兰公司25%及以上的所有权益或控制权益，并希望提高所有权益或控制权益的，那么在不涉及"敏感土地"或捕捞配额权益的情况下，如果存在以下情形，交易将需经海外投资办公室同意：

- 用于收购证券的金额超过1亿新西兰元；
- 已发行股票的总价值超过1亿新西兰元；
- 目标公司资产总值超过1亿新西兰元。

如果拟投资额超过1亿新西兰元（不论是通过一次还是多次相关投资），经海外投资办公室同意后该投资将被视为海外投资"重大商业资产"。

5. 海外投资"敏感土地"

海外个体购买或取得（3年以上，不含3年）"敏感"土地权益的，无论是直接购得，还是通过购买享有土地权益的公司的证券取得（海外个体持有或控制公司25%以上份额），均需取得同意。前述公司所持有的土地，及其任何相关土地应满足以下列出的任意条件。

"敏感土地"是指满足以下条件的土地（或任何相关土地）：

① 超过5公顷且非城市土地（即农田或非位于市区的商业用地、工业用地或住宅用地）；
② 是，或包括前滩和/或海床，或特定已命名岛屿；
③ 超过4 000平方米，且：

- 是湖床的一部分；
- 是特定已命名岛屿的一部分；
- 出于保护目的的保护区、公园，出于娱乐目的的私人开放空间；
- 受《资源管理法》（1991年）规定的遗产令或相关规定限制，或依照《新西兰文化遗产法》（2014年）属于新西兰文化遗产；又或属于遗产令或相关规定内容，是历史遗迹、历史区域、（毛利人的）圣地遗址，或是依照《新西兰文化遗产法》（2014年）申请或提议登记的遗址；
- 超过2 000平方米且毗邻前滩；
- 超过4 000平方米且毗邻湖床等特定土地。

是否同意取决于各种条件。海外投资者必须通过投资者测试，综合考量其性格、商业头脑和财务承受能力。希望购得"敏感土地"的海外投资者得有意成为新西兰永久居民，或证实这一投资对新西兰有利。

（二）外汇管制

新西兰早已取消全部外汇管制。因此，在新西兰转入或转出资本、收益、股息、特许权使用费或利息均不受限制。

（三）金融融资

1. 主要金融机构

新西兰储备银行是新西兰的中央银行，独立于新西兰政府，自主运作，主要是制定和实施货币政策，维持价格稳定，促进维护健全高效的金融体系，满足公众货币需求的政策组织机构。储备银行有两个关键职责，负责银行注册和监管，以及在银行财务状况对金融体系造成严重威胁时，应对金融困境或银行倒闭。

2. 外资企业融资条件

（1）银行账户

在新西兰金融机构开设银行账户的程序各不相同。但是，银行通常会要求提供认证过的身份信息和地址证明。海外投资者可能还需提供其他信息，比如主要的税收居住国，以便银行履行新西兰法律规定的反洗钱义务。

（2）融资

外资企业可以在新西兰进行融资。但是，2016 年部分主要的新西兰金融机构对海外购房者实施了新的贷款限制，针对取得海外收入的非居民贷款人，限制甚至停止向非居民提供住房抵押贷款。

3. 反洗钱和反恐怖主义资助

在新西兰运作或与新西兰有关的实体同样受到新西兰反洗钱和反恐怖主义资助相关法律的约束。

（四）土地政策

1. 土地法律法规概述

（1）商业用地

一般而言，海外个体无需取得监管机关同意即可在新西兰自由购买商业建筑。但是，如果该商业建筑（单独或其他收购资产一起）的价值或支付的对价超过 1 亿新西兰元，或者，如果该商业建筑建造于或毗邻"敏感土地"，那么依照《海外投资法》和《海外投资条例》须经海外投资办公室同意。

海外个体可以在新西兰自由租赁或出租商业建筑。若该商业建筑建造于或毗邻"敏感土地"，且租约在 3 年及以上（包括续约权），那么依照《海外投资法》和《海外投资条例》须经海外投资办公室同意。

（2）住宅用地[①]

无需取得事前同意，海外个体即可在新西兰自由购买住宅或度假屋，但不得涉及"敏感土地"（尤其是 2 000 平方米以上的沿海土地或特定岛屿上的土地）。

（3）土地买卖

依照新西兰法律，土地买卖协议必须书面，并经各方或其代表签署。土地买卖协议可不附条件，也可出于某一方利益考虑约定条件。

土地所有权的变更需要在电子财产登记系统——"新西兰土地信息"（LINZ）进行登记。公众可以在这一中央系统上查阅相关信息。

在产权办理转让登记时也会登记税务信息，在特定情形下，如海外个体在购得土地后 2 年[②]内将其售出，出售时可能需要缴纳住宅用地预提税。

（4）土地租赁

土地租赁必须以书面形式约定，并由各方或其代表签订租约。租赁通常无需在"新西兰土地信息"登记。

（5）《资源管理法》（1991 年）

新西兰的环境立法主要是 1991 年《资源管理法》（RMA），其中规定，地方和地区政府机关负责管理土地、空气或水资源的使用。

任何开发计划都需经过预先审批同意。根据《资源管理法》规定，必须向地方当局申请资源同意书。之后，相关地方当局可以（附条件或不附条件）同意。申请人，或任何提交申请的个人（如该申请已公告），均有权向环境法院申诉。

（6）《建筑法》（2004 年）

《建筑法》（2004 年）和《建筑法典》规定房屋和其他建筑的修建问题。其中规定，在新建建筑（包括住宅和商业建筑）和改建现有建筑时，必须取得地方当局的修建许可。

《建筑法》包括旨在提高现有建筑抗震可能性的条款。《建筑法》规定，如果一栋新建建筑的抗震强度不足现行标准规定的 1/3，那么一般会将该建筑视为"易震"建筑。地方当局可以要求易震建筑所有人提高建筑的抗震强度，使其不再属于易震建筑。一般来说，此类花销由土地所有人自行负担。

（7）《怀唐伊条约》（1975 年）

根据《怀唐伊条约》（1975 年），怀唐伊法院审理历史上国王或王后违反《怀唐伊条约》的有关土地请求。一般而言，毛利人的土地请求只限于国王王后或皇家拥有的土地。

---

① 引入《海外投资修正案》后，下述意见可能会有所不同。
② 新西兰政府表示，购买土地后 5 年内出售土地的人在出售时可能需要支付住宅用地预扣税。

（8）《个人财产担保法》（1999年）

《个人财产担保法》（1999年）规定，优先权并非由个人财产所有权人确定，而是在"创设"或"完善""担保权益"时确定。依照《个人财产担保法》，"个人财产"定义宽泛，企业所有或使用的大多数资产均可能产生担保权益（不包括土地权益）。

《个人财产担保法》的基本机制是，试图购买个人财产的个体可以卖方名义在"个人财产担保登记"（PPSR）系统进行查询，确认该出售财产上是否有担保负担。"个人财产担保登记"的在线维护和搜索地址为 www.ppsr.govt.nz。

根据《个人财产担保法》，当对个人财产持有担保权益的一方在"个人财产担保登记"系统上登记"财务说明"以对抗债务人时，该担保权益即已"完善"。

2. 外资企业获得土地的规定

《海外投资法》和《海外投资条例》规定了对在新西兰获得土地的海外个体的主要限制。

2017年年底，新的"政府联盟协定"作出了一系列针对海外投资和林业的政策变化。新西兰政府于2017年12月发布了第一个旨在加强《海外投资法》的政策变化，即向海外投资办公室发布新的指令函。新的指令函承认海外投资对新西兰经济增长而言仍然重要，但在考虑海外投资申请时，应当转变海外投资办公室的关注点和重点。新的指令函适用于2017年12月15日起所有的新申请和现有申请。

3.《海外投资修正案》

《海外投资修正案》于2017年12月出台。《海外投资修正案》建议修改《海外投资法》，将"住宅用地"作为需要海外投资办公室批准的新型敏感土地。住宅用地将参照财产评级状况进行界定，为评级之便，其将包括"住宅"和"生活方式"用地。

《海外投资修正案》规定，如果海外个体通过以下任一测试，其仍可购买住宅用地：
- 承诺在新西兰居住测试；
- 在住宅用地上增加新房供应测试；
- 有利于新西兰测试。

《海外投资修正案》提议，公司取得住宅用地，并将其作为业务一部分的，在购买住宅用地之前应当经海外投资办公室同意。这将要求他们关注新房供应测试或现有的有利于新西兰测试。

《海外投资修正案》还建议，持有居民（而非工作）签证的移民，在新西兰居住时间达12个月的，可以购买敏感土地。移民者以投资人身份申请购买的，无需满足在新西兰居住满12个月这一条件。

（五）企业设立与解散

1. 企业形式

在新西兰可以通过以下任一架构开展业务：
- 公司（有限责任或无限责任）；
- 普通合伙和有限合伙；
- 合资企业；
- 信托；
- 个体经营者。

合理架构的选择有赖于事实本身，包括业务或投资性质，以及在新西兰或其他地区的税务后果等。应当根据实际情况寻求有关合理架构的具体建议。

（1）公司

《公司法》（1993年）规定了有限责任或无限责任公司的设立，以及在新西兰设立的公司的管理、运作和清算问题。《公司法》并未区分上市公司和非上市公司。最常见的公司类型是股份有限公司。

除非公司章程另有规定，否则有限责任公司的股东责任以其承诺的出资额为限。如果一个股东已经全部出资到位，那么该股东对公司资本再无其他责任。

《公司法》对公司股东人数及其向公众募集资金的能力并无限制。[1] 从商业角度，公司可以分为上市公司［即股份在新西兰交易所（NZX）主板、NXT市场或其他持牌市场挂牌的公司］和非上市公司（即公司股份并未挂牌的公司）。

公司设立登记详情见《公司法》。

（2）普通合伙和有限合伙

合伙企业在新西兰的某些行业中很常见，依合伙人之间的合伙协议设立。有限合伙企业是一种合伙形式，涉及普通合伙人和有限合伙人，普通合伙人承担有限合伙企业的所有债务和责任，有限合伙人则在出资额范围内对合伙企业承担责任。

新西兰有限合伙企业根据《有限合伙企业法》（2008年）登记设立。有限合伙企业和海外有限合伙企业的登记由新西兰公司注册处管理。海外有限合伙企业必须于新西兰开展业务后10个工作日内申请注册。

（3）合资企业

合资企业是指两个或以上个体共同设立法人或非法人企业的情形。

（4）信托

信托是新西兰常见的财产保护和资产管理方式。《受托人法》（1956年）是新西兰规制信托的法律。

（5）个体经营者

个体经营者是独自创业或承包的个人，无需进行公司注册。很多小企业家、承包商、自雇人士一开始也是个体经营者。个体经营者需要就工作所得的全部收入缴纳税款，但可以主张从工作成本中扣除。

2. 企业设立程序

在新西兰注册设立公司，必须向公司注册处提交在线申请。如果公司名称经同意保留，申请人需在20个工作日内完成公司注册申请，包括提交所有董事和股东签署的同意书。

公司详细信息包括注册办公地址、服务范围和通讯信息必须提供。也可进行税务登记，包括税务局（IRD）号码注册、货物和服务税号码注册，和/或雇主身份注册。

如果公司最终由一家控股公司控制，那么还须提供控股公司的类型、名称、注册国家、注册号码或代码（如有）和注册办公地址。

公司注册处同意注册申请后，将颁发公司设立证书，公众也可查询公司信息。

3. 在新西兰开展业务

海外公司可以通过以下方式在新西兰开展业务：

- 在新西兰设立分支机构；
- 依照《公司法》新设子公司；
- 收购新西兰公司的股份，或成立合资企业。

4. 注册分支机构

《公司法》也是规范海外公司在新西兰运作的主要法律，其要求，"在新西兰开展业务"的每家海外公司均应依照《公司法》完成海外公司登记注册。

"海外公司"是指在新西兰以外成立的公司。一般而言，《公司法》关于新西兰公司的规定并不适用于海外公司（部分财务报告规定除外）。

除非海外公司的名字（其在设立国注册的名字）在新西兰已有备案，否则该海外公司不得在新西兰开展业务。一经登记注册，其将受到新西兰法律管辖。

5. 设立子公司

新西兰全资子公司（由海外控股公司控制的公司）可按照《公司法》8.2节规定的程序设立，完成公司登记。

---

[1] 尽管2013年《金融市场行为法》（FMCA）（见11节）规定了这一程序。

6. 解散方式和要求

申请从新西兰公司注册簿上涂销登记可以通过股东间的特别决议，或在公司章程允许的情况下，由董事会或其他人员完成。

公司解散前，在公司登记簿上的备案信息需要保持更新。如果依照《公司法》或其他法律规定，公司应当提交财务审计报表的，公司在申请从注册簿上涂销登记前必须提交此类报表。

公司解散或清算时，必须完成税务局的备案要求，包括自公司停止运营之日起用公司的最新账户进行纳税申报。公司也可能有缴纳营业税和货物与劳务税、注销雇主身份登记和货物与劳务税注册的其他义务。在个人或公司提交最终的纳税申报表之前，应视为没有履行其营业税义务（这种情况下公司将无法解散）。

个人申请涂销公司登记前，必须保证：
- 该公司已不再运营；
- 其所有债务都已偿清；
- 公司已按照符合《公司法》和其章程（如有）的方式分配资产；
- 无任何债权人采取措施使公司进入清算程序；
- 已向在"个人财产担保登记"系统中登记"财务说明"的任何当事人发出计划解散公司的通知。

（六）兼并收购

在新西兰，兼并收购受一系列法律、法规、法典和条例的规范。但实质上，非公开兼并收购依然是以双方买卖股份/资产协议达成的条款和条件为基础。

1.《商业法》

《商业法》（1986年）就兼并收购对新西兰市场竞争的影响作出了规定。

2. 涉及私营企业的兼并收购

《公司法》高度规范了兼并收购问题，规定了股票转让和发行的特定行政程序（诸如获得股东同意和签署文件等）。

3. 收购

收购主要由2000年新西兰收购委员会经《收购法批准令》批准施行的《收购法》规管。不得违反《收购法》订立合同。

《收购法》的目的在于确保股东得到平等对待，且在适当的信息披露后，股东可以就接受还是拒绝"目标公司"的控制权交易作出知情决定。

"目标公司"指在新西兰设立，且有或在过去12个月中有以下行为的公司：
- 持有在NZSX、NZAX或NXT市场挂牌的投票证券；
- 有50名或以上股东和50份以上股份份额。

《收购法》的根本规则是，一方有意为以下行为的，必须遵守《收购法》：
- 取得一家目标公司20%以上的投票权；
- 增加持有现有的一家目标公司20%以上的投票权。

收购规则规定了以下收购机制：

（1）场外收购

"场外收购"指收购方在要约文件中以相同条款向目标公司的所有股东提出要约。该要约必须以收购方接受同意表为条件，这将导致其持有50%以上的有表决权股份，并且通常要求收购方持股达到90%。股东通过签署并交还他们的同意表接受要约。

场外收购导致收购方持有目标公司90%股份的，收购方可以通过强制收购程序收购剩下10%的股份。

（2）同意发行新股

通过目标公司发行新股或收购其他股东股份，股东可以同意取得投票证券的收购方跨越20%的门槛，或增加持有现有的20%以上的投票证券。收购方或其相关人员不得就该交易投票。（在收购时，卖方及其相关人也无投票权。)

（3）5%的增长

已经持有或控制一家目标公司50%到90%的投票权的股东，可以在任何12个月内收购最高5%的额外股份（以12个月内的最低持股量为准）。

（4）强制收购

股东持有目标公司90%或以上股份的，可以强制收购剩余股份。

4. 安排方案

新西兰上市公司的另一种收购架构是安排方案。安排方案即希望重组的各方向法院申请同意该方案的条款细节。

安排方案可能应用于更大范围的公司重组，包括向收购方转让股东的全部（或特定比例）证券，取消现有证券，以及向收购方发行新证券。安排方案的性质使收购方额外增加了方案的复杂性（诸如转让或分拆特定资产或责任，或减少目标公司资本）。

安排方案总是在友好而非敌对的基础上进行，目标公司和收购方签署正式的实施协议，列明将向证券持有人提出并将得到目标方案公司董事支持的方案条款。

（1）流程

在安排方案中，目标公司、股东或债权人均可向法院提出申请。但是，由于目标公司和董事会在召集其证券持有人会议方面的中心作用，通常认为目标公司提出和支持该方案是至关重要的。法院拥有批准、修改或拒绝安排方案的广泛权力。如果法院认为该方案可能会损害证券持有人、债权人或其他方，即使该方案在会议上获得了必要的证券持有人同意，法院也可以拒绝该方案。

方案将产生"全有或全无"的效果，收购方将明确知道其要么成功，取得100%的控制权，要么失败，空手而归。法院的任何决定都对公司和任何其他个人（诸如股东和债权人）具有约束力。

正如收购要约一样，安排方案可以将出现或不出现特定事件或情形为条件。常见的条件是，提出的方案应当取得必要的监管批准，或目标公司的财务状况无重大不利变化。

（2）须取得股东同意

经法院同意的安排方案将影响上市公司（或其他目标公司）投票权的，该方案应当：

- 经各有投票权的权益股东小组75%多数同意，且经有权投票的股东简单多数同意；
- 由收购委员签发"无异议声明"，或目标公司应当向法院承诺，其股东不会因该交易以安排方案形式而非其他收购形式收购受不利影响。

（七）竞争管制

1. 竞争管制主管机构

《商业法》管辖新西兰市场的商业竞争。商务委员会是新西兰主要的竞争监管机构，负责监督《商业法》的遵守情况——包括调查《商业法》（现在或未来）的潜在违规情况，作出与拟议的兼并和收购有关的决策，识别和调查反竞争实践，教育公众遵守《商业法》。

2. 竞争法概述

新西兰的竞争法将重点放在维护新西兰消费者的长期利益、促进市场竞争上。为此，如果某个收购行为将或可能导致企业"实质上降低市场竞争力"，那么《商业法》将禁止收购该企业的股份或资产。换句话说，收购能否提高买方的市场竞争力。但这一禁令存在一个例外，即收购带来的公共利益超过了市场竞争力降低导致的损害。

（1）"市场"

要确定收购行为是否会"实质上降低市场竞争力"，首先要判断货物和服务市场为何。判定市场是个技术活，应当包括对产品/服务、产品/服务所销往的地理位置、产品/服务的功用（如是否用于制造、批发、零售等）以及消费者层面和时间的分析。

从更高层面上讲，市场是那些用收购的产品/服务替代的产品/服务。如果消费者在特定产品/服务的价格小幅上涨时转向其他产品/服务，那么产品/服务通常会相互替代。例如，如果黄油价格小幅上涨，消费者转而使用人造黄油，那么黄油和人造黄油将被视为处于同一市场。

（2）收购可能的影响

收购对市场竞争力可能造成的影响必须是可估测的。如果收购行为很可能大幅提高收购者的市场支配力，那么这一收购很可能会被禁止。

（3）集中指标

市场份额是决定收购是否会被禁止的初步指南，委员会根据市场份额发布了"集中指标"。举例来说，委员会认为，以下收购行为不太可能会违反《商业法》：

- 占市场份额最大的三家公司的份额总计低于70%，其中一家收购另一家后所占市场份额低于40%；
- 占市场份额最大的三家公司的份额总计高于70%，其中一家收购另一家后所占市场份额低于20%。

（4）其他考量

一个收购行为即使不满足集中指标，也可能不会在相关市场大幅降低竞争力。比如，如果市场准入或扩张的门槛较低，或市场参与者之间的协调机会有限或没有机会（例如市场支配和市场规范机会有限），那么将仍允许进行收购。

（5）公共利益

在少数情形下，如果公共利益高于对市场的不利影响，那么即使收购很可能大幅降低市场竞争力，也可能继续进行。公共利益标准较高，通常不会依赖这一点取得成功。

3. 竞争管制措施

（1）违反《商业法》

委员会监督并调查收购行为，确保不存在违反《商业法》的行为。包括公司在内的任何社会成员认为有违反《商业法》行为的，均可向委员会投诉。

（2）寻求委员会许可或授权

对于收购是否应当通知委员会并无强制要求。相反，企业可以自愿将拟收购计划提交委员会审查。如果收购可能会违反《商业法》，尤其建议如此，因为这样可以预防收购完成后出现问题。

委员会因为认为收购不可能大幅降低市场竞争力，或公共利益高于市场竞争力的降低，从而认定不会违反《商业法》的，将"许可"收购。许可为公开许可，公众可以查阅。委员会作出决定的法定时限是10个工作日。然而，委员会可以要求延长这一时间，近来的实践表明，至少应当需要40到60个工作日。

在颁发许可或授权之日起12个月内进行收购的，收购行为将不受委员会或第三方依《商业法》提出的质疑。

（八）税收

1. 税收体系和制度

《所得税法》（2007年）管辖新西兰的税收。个人和公司纳税人的所得税是以所有来源的年度总收入，减去年度总扣除和任何结转损失后征收的。这一净额为应纳税所得额。"总收入"包括在商业条款中被视为收入的科目，包括金融工具的所有收益，以及土地或股份交易中的短期或计划利润。允许扣除额是指为取得收入或在经营活动中产生的所有开支。个人、公司和信托采用不同的征税制度。

居民和非居民企业、个人以及信托适用不同的税率和规则。这些实体所适用的税率和其他税收规则的概述如下：

新西兰不存在资本利得税。但是，某些交易，即使实质上是资本也可能需要纳税，包括：

- 土地和个人财产的特定销售；
- 任意财务安排收益，包括免除债务的情形；
- 新西兰居民所有的某些海外投资的价值的特定比例。某些情形下，此类投资价值的年度增长也应征税。

2. 主要税赋和税率

（1）企业所得税

① 企业税率

企业满足以下条件的，应当向新西兰缴税：

- 是新西兰居民企业的，新西兰可对其全球所得征税；
- 非新西兰居民企业，但有来源于新西兰境内的所得的，新西兰仅可对源于其境内的所得征税；
- 非新西兰居民企业，也无来源于新西兰境内的所得，但是被视为由新西兰居民企业控制的，此类企业可能因来源于该外国实体的被动收入而被征税。

企业所得税税率为28%。为确保海外公司对来源于新西兰的利润缴纳适当的税款，存在转让定价制度。

如适用，新西兰允许支付的外国税款抵免税额相当于所支付的外国税款和应纳新西兰所得税在总收入的相关部分中的较低者。这些规则可以通过适用新西兰与其他国家签订的特定双重税收协定（DTA）进行修改。

包括有限合伙企业在内的合伙企业本身不征税，合伙人按其合伙所得的份额征税。

非居民公司在新西兰成立分支机构运营的，其分支机构的收益应当按28%的税率缴纳税款。分支机构向非居民总部汇出的利润或该总部向公司股东支付的股息不征收预提税。

② 股息

新西兰拥有完整的股息归集系统，根据该系统，新西兰居民企业缴纳的税款可以分配到股东的股息处归集抵免，新西兰居民股东可以此抵消与这些股息相关的纳税义务。

根据非居民在新西兰居民企业所享有权益的百分比，归集抵免额可能会将部分或全部股息的非居民预提税税率降至零，或者减少非居民所得股息的其他应纳预提税款。支付给非居民的全额抵免股息可以实际支付，不用缴纳非居民预提税。

新西兰居民企业取得海外公司股息的，一般可以在新西兰免税。

③ 资本弱化规则

对于在新西兰运营的海外控股公司（比如控制50%或以上所有权），也存在资本弱化规则。此外，不论何种信托，只要该信托50%或以上的结算由非居民企业完成，将同样适用这一规则。通常情况下，债务资产比率不超过60%的，利息可以全额扣除。

④ 结转税款损失

满足特定条件时，企业可以结转税款损失，并用于抵扣未来应纳税所得。为维持损失结转权，必须满足所有权持续测试。测试要求，从出现损失年度的年初到损失用于抵扣应纳税所得年度的年末：

- 居民企业保持66%的共同所有权；
- 非居民企业保持44%的共同所有权。

（2）个人所得税

① 应纳税个人

新西兰居民应就全球所得缴纳税款。非居民只需就来源于新西兰境内的所得向新西兰纳税。出于税务考虑，下列情况下个人将被视为"新西兰居民"：

- 在新西兰有永久居住地，而不论其在新西兰以外是否有永久居住地（一般而言，永久居住地指固定或习惯住所）；
- 在任意12个月内，其在新西兰停留累计超过183天；
- 因为为新西兰政府服务而不在新西兰境内。

多数情况下，若一个人同时是多个国家居民的，将按照双重税收协定从税务角度判断其应被视为哪个国家的"居民"。

短期借调人员可以免征新西兰税，如果：

- 他们并未在任意12个月内在新西兰累计停留超过183天；
- 他们的海外雇主所在国与新西兰签有双重税收协定；
- 他们的薪酬并非由非居民在新西兰的营业地承担。

雇主所在国与新西兰之间并不存在双重税收协定的，个人如果想在新西兰免税，那么其在任意12个月内不得在新西兰累计停留92天以上。

② 个人税率

新西兰的税率采取分层制度，应纳税额取决于个人所得额。

税率如下：

所得额	税率
0~14 000 新西兰元	10.5%
14 001~48 000 新西兰元	17.5%
48 001~70 000 新西兰元	30%
70 001 新西兰元及以上	33%

新西兰也有一个"新移民"税收体系，在新移民成为新西兰税收居民的4年内，可以就其来源于境外的收入（职业收入除外）免税。不过，此期间来源于新西兰境内的收入仍应纳税。

制定归属规则意在确保，在特定情况下，个人服务的收入属于该个人，而不是转移给以较低税率支付税款的关联方（例如税率为28%的公司）。

（3）信托所得

信托所得包括受托人所得和受益人所得。受托人所得指受托人取得的所有所得，而非作为受益人所得分配给受益人的所得。信托保留的所得和受托人所得征税的税率是33%。

受益人所得，即在信托产生所得的同一所得年度内，或在该所得年度结束后以及受托人进行（或应当进行）该所得年度所得税申报之日起的6个月内，分配给受益人的所得。受益人所得适用特别税率。未成年受益人所得统一适用33%的固定税率。

如果外国信托的信托人是新西兰居民，那么该外国信托也受新西兰税收规则约束。来自某些外国信托（即不合规信托）的应税利润分配按45%的罚款率征税，以防止新西兰居民信托人转移本应税的收入。外国信托的非居民受益人仅对来自新西兰的收入征税。

（4）非居民预提税

① 税率

新西兰居民企业向非居民支付的股息、利息和特许权使用费应当缴纳非居民预提税（NRWT），税率如下：

收入类型	税率
股息	30%
	对于从持有的投资组合（即低于10%）取得的全额抵免股息，为15%
	对于从非投资组合取得的全额抵免股息，为0%
利息	15%
特许权使用费	15%

新西兰居民公司向非居民承包商支付价款的，必须在支付时按15%的税率代扣代缴非居民承包商税（NRCT）。非居民承包商税是一种临时责任，非居民必须提交纳税申报表，以确定其最终的纳税义务。任何非居民承包商税的代扣代缴均可抵扣。举例来说，如果依照双重税收协定最终不存在应纳税额，税务局将就此颁发免税证明。如果非居民发行证券，或证明其至少在两年内税务合规，并无过错的，也可免税。

② 其他细则

就支付给非关联方的股息、文化特许权使用费和利息征收的非居民预提税是该收入的最终税收。其他情形下，非居民预提税为最低税额，收款人必须就收到的所得填报新西兰纳税申报表。该所得涉及的支出可以扣除，所得余额按标准税率征税。

如果非居民持有一家新西兰公司 10% 以下股份，新西兰公司支付时对股息进行了全额抵免，那么公司可以支付补充股息，有效返还股息应纳的 15% 的非居民预提税。

根据核准发行人制度注册的债券应当支付利息的，则可以支付等于借款人应付利息 2% 的核准发行人税以代替非居民预提税。在某些情况下，对于广泛持有的债券，这一税率会降至零。核准发行人制度只适用于非关联方之间的贷款，且这些贷款不被视为关联方债务的情形。

（5）雇主的纳税义务

① 一般义务

雇主必须从支付给员工的薪酬或工资中扣缴 PAYE 税额（按收入缴税）。PAYE 税额因员工负有收入年度的最终纳税义务而被扣除。根据扣除的金额，员工可能获得退款，也可能需要支付额外的税额。

新西兰的意外事故赔偿和康复保险计划 ACC 废除了诉请获得意外伤害赔偿金的权利。雇主和雇员均须向这一计划支付税费。目前，雇员按照年收入的 1.45% 支付保费。雇主缴纳的部分根据支付给雇员的总工资计算。每位雇员的最高征税收入为 118 191 新西兰元。不同行业，雇主的税率不同。

② 附加福利

雇主因雇佣向雇员提供非现金福利的，需要支付附加福利税（FBT）。这些福利包括公司汽车、低息贷款和补贴货物。附加福利税按季支付，在相关日历季度内根据提供给雇员的附加福利的应税价值按照 49.25%、42.86%、21.21% 或 11.73%（取决于雇员的边际税率）的税率支付。附加福利税可以扣除，从而雇员的最高税后支出仅为所得的 33%。

雇主可以选择在所得年度的前三个季度按照固定税率 49.25% 支付附加福利税，或者就提供的全部附加福利按照 42.86% 的税率支付附加福利税。第四季度的附加福利将会进行调整，附加福利税税率以福利所属雇员的边际税率为基础计算。

③ 养老金（KiwiSaver 计划）

雇主缴纳的注册养老金计划款项均可扣除，但须根据雇员的年薪或酬劳分别按 10.5%、17.5%、30% 或 33% 的税率进行代扣代缴。

从税务的角度，符合《金融市场行为法》规定的退休计划的计划被视为信托。该计划的收入通常按 28% 的税率征税，目前向受益人支付的福利——无论是一次性付款还是养老金，均可免税。雇主必须在支付雇员工资和薪酬时扣除参与 KiwiSaver 计划的雇员的应纳款（除非雇员此时不用缴纳款额）。现有雇员可以随时选择加入 KiwiSaver 计划。新员工将自动注册 KiwiSaver 计划，但可能会在指定的时间段内退出。

雇员自身也必须强制缴纳 KiwiSaver 计划款额，雇主缴纳的 KiwiSaver 计划款额，或雇主向合规的养老金基金缴纳的款项可以扣除，雇主同时应代扣代缴上述税款。

（6）货物与劳务税（GST）

提供大多数货物和劳务服务都需按照 15% 的税率缴纳货物与劳务税。可以免交货物与劳务税的主要是金融服务和住宅租赁服务。货物与劳务税应当由货物和劳务服务的最终消费者承担。

企业可以进行货物与劳务税登记，并在销售货物或服务被征税（销项税）时主张用其开展业务缴纳的税款（进项税）抵扣。销项税大于进项税的，应当向税务局支付差额。相反，进项税大于应付销项税的，税务局应退还差额。

满足特定标准时，向非居民出口货物、提供劳务服务的货物与劳务税税率为零。新西兰海关向所有进口货物征收 15% 的货物与劳务税。

某些土地供应的货物与劳务税税率为零。企业间提供某些商业金融服务（及其他商品和服务）的货物与劳务税税率也为零，但不是免征货物与劳务税。反向收费机制意味着提供某些已进口服务也会对进口商征收货物与劳务税。

个人实施或有意实施应税活动的，可以进行货物与劳务税登记。应税活动指持续或定期向他人提供货物和劳务以换取金钱或相应价值的行为。在任意 12 个月内，在新西兰实施的应税活动超过或可能超过 60 000 新西兰元的，必须进行登记。

非居民向新西兰个体消费者提供远程服务，年服务价值超过 60 000 新西兰元的，非居民的货物与劳务税税率为 15%。这些规则也适用于向新西兰提供跨境数字内容和其他数字服务的情形。但是，非居民向货物与劳务税登记人提供远程服务后，登记人在应税活动中使用这些服务的，非居民无需缴纳货物与劳务税。

所有进行货物与劳务税登记的实体都应当定期提交货物与劳务税纳税申报表。多数情形下，每两个月需要进行一次申报。年供应价值超过 2 400 万新西兰元的，应当按月申报。

3. 纳税申报和优惠

纳税人应当自愿遵循新西兰税收制度，鼓励作出诚实准确的收入申报。纳税人一般在每年 3 月 31 日前完成前一年度的年度收入申报。因商业原因，（非个人）纳税人获得 IRD 批准在其他日期申报的除外。

进行纳税申报的纳税人必须在其新西兰收入纳税申报表中披露所有应当纳税的收入。纳税人还须披露特定相关的财务安排。此外还应披露在海外控股公司、海外投资基金和海外信托中的权益。

个人收入来自工资或薪酬，已经依照 PAYE 规则正确扣缴税款的，一般无需进行年度纳税申报，但对包括利息和股息在内的其他来源收入，超过最低限度收入的，个人仍需进行年度纳税申报。

（九）证券

1. 证券法律法规概述

《金融市场行为法》和《金融市场行为条例》（2014 年）是新西兰规管证券的法律法规。

违反《金融市场行为法》中的披露义务将会导致刑事和民事后果。

（1）发行金融产品

无论该金融产品是由新西兰发行人发行还是海外发行人发行，《金融市场行为法》和《金融市场行为条例》均规管新西兰所有金融产品的供应。"金融产品"一词非常宽泛，包括债券、股权、管理投资产品和衍生品。

通常情况下，金融产品的发行人应当向潜在投资者提供产品披露说明书（PDS），使得他们可以就该投资作出知情决定，要约存在相关排除条款除外。

《金融市场行为法》和《金融市场行为条例》规定了一个规范要约的产品披露说明书的内容、形式和长度，其依所提供的金融产品类型的不同而不同。不需要在产品披露说明书中披露的重大信息必须同产品披露说明书一起在在线要约登记系统登记（披露登记）。

《金融市场行为法》规定了发行人不用提供产品披露说明书的几种例外情况：

• 向批发投资者发出的要约，批发投资者包括主营业务是"投资业务"的个人、"大型"个人，或订购 750 000 或以上新西兰元的个人；

• 向"密切商业伙伴"发出的要约；

• "小型要约"，即债券或股权证券的要约对象在 12 个月内不超过 20 名投资者，募资额不少于 200 万新西兰元。

《金融市场行为法》采用合理灵活的方法促进规范化要约。但是，在向披露登记提交产品披露说明书前后仍然有一些适用于广告的具体规则。《金融市场行为法》还包含对金融产品自发要约的限制。

就债券或管理投资产品而言，规范要约发行人必须遵守《金融市场行为法》规定的管理和许可义务。

（2）在市场上市

新西兰有三个主要的金融产品交易市场：

• NZX 主板（NZSX）：这是新西兰股权证券交易的主要市场，为大型成熟公司设计，有着最为严苛的准入和持续义务的要求；

• NXT 市场：低成本市场，专为价值在 1 000 万新西兰元到 1 亿新西兰元的中小型公司设计；

• NZX 债券市场（NZDX）：NZDX 挂牌多种投资债券，包括公司和政府债券，以及固定收益证券。

有意上市并在 NZX 运营的市场挂牌证券的公司必须（通过组织经纪人）向 NZX 申请上市。公司上市前，必须同意遵守 NZX 相关市场的上市规则（NZX 上市规则）。

海外公司满足在新西兰设立公司条件的，可以在 NZX 进行第一上市。在特定情形下，公司已经在"认可的"海外交易所上市的，也可在 NZX 作为"两地上市发行人"或"海外上市发行人"上市。两地上市公司应当遵守 NZX 上市规则和海外交易所的相关规定。海外上市发行人应当优先遵守所在国交易所规则，且可豁免大部分 NZX 上市规则。

（3）披露上市公司的重大股权

根据《金融市场行为法》规定，投资者直接或间接取得一家在 NZSX 或 NZAX 上市的公司 5% 以上股份的，投资者应当向该公司和 NZX 提交一份规定格式的重大产品持有人通知。通知应当包括投资者和其所持有的股权信息。通知提交之后，投资者持股变化在总发行股票的 1% 或以上的，应当公开披露。公众可以在 NZX 的网站上查阅投资者提交给 NZX 的通知。

2. 证券市场监管

《金融市场行为法》和《金融市场行为条例》受金融市场机构（FMA）监管。因此，金融市场机构负责证券、财务报告和公司法的执行，因为这些也适用于金融服务和证券市场，并负责管理证券交易所、财务顾问和经纪人、审计师、受托人和发行人。

3. 外资企业参与证券交易的要求

外资企业在新西兰从事任何证券交易都将受到《金融市场行为法》和《金融市场行为条例》约束。海外发行人无需满足《金融市场行为法》规定的发布产品披露说明书这一要求。潜在的例外情形包括，要约：

• 是收购招标或安排方案的对价的一部分；
• 是向现有的新西兰证券持有人发出（比如依照供股或权利要约）。

然而，即使在这些例外情形下，发行人可能仍需遵守《金融市场行为法》和《金融市场行为条例》规定的特定义务，包括与要约有关的任何文件或其他行为不得具有误导性、欺骗性，或包含任何虚假陈述。

（十）投资优惠和投资保护

1. 优惠政策结构

新西兰官方未曾发布任何优惠投资政策。但是，新西兰和澳大利亚之间签署了促进澳大利亚人在新西兰投资的协议。《海外投资法》规定收购"重大商业资产"的门槛便是一个例子。澳大利亚非政府投资者作为买方时，货币门槛则更高。

新西兰也有一些现行有效的公平贸易协议（FTA），近来也签署了《全面与进步跨太平洋伙伴关系协定》（CPTPP）。

2. 特定行业和地区的鼓励投资

新西兰不鼓励人们投资获批项目或特定地区。新西兰政府认为，新西兰稳健、一贯的经济政策，良好的经济增长率和稳定的政治体系足以吸引海外投资者前来投资。

3. 特别经济区

新西兰国内没有自由贸易区或类似经济区以鼓励海外投资。

4. 投资保护

（1）新西兰与澳大利亚之间更紧密的经济关系

新西兰与澳大利亚签署了一份有关"更紧密经济关系的协议"（CER），两国之间设有自由贸易区。"更紧密经济关系的协议"被公认为全球最全面的双边公平贸易协定，其产生的一个重要影响就是新西兰和澳大利亚投资者现在更加确定他们的投资将得到保护。

（2）WTO、APEC 和 ASEAN 自由贸易协定

新西兰积极推动世界贸易组织、亚太经济合作组织和东南亚国家联盟（ASEAN）等国际组织的自由贸易。《新西兰、澳大利亚与东南亚国家联盟之间的自由贸易协定》（AANZFTA）促进了新西兰、澳大利亚、文莱、柬埔寨、印度尼西亚、老挝、马来西亚、缅甸、菲律宾、新加坡、泰国和越南之间的自由贸易。

《新西兰、澳大利亚与东南亚国家联盟之间的自由贸易协定》还规定了一系列投资保护措施和有约束力的投资者—国家仲裁程序，从而为东盟经济体的投资者提供更好的安全和保护。

（3）中国、马来西亚和韩国自由贸易协定

新西兰与中国、马来西亚和韩国签署了双边自由贸易协定，向投资者提供保护，确保一个更确定的投资环境。①

具体来说，就中国而言，自2008年双边协定签署并生效以来，新西兰对中国的商品出口翻了两番。中国现在是新西兰的第二大贸易伙伴，双边贸易额超过220亿新西兰元，其中包括出口额123亿新西兰元（货物出口额94亿新西兰元和服务出口额29亿新西兰元），进口额约105亿新西兰元（货物进口额100亿新西兰元和服务进口额5.38亿新西兰元）。②

近年来，中国已经成为新西兰第九大海外直接投资来源国。两国之间的旅游、教育和其他人文联系也日益强烈。③

（4）《全面与进步跨太平洋伙伴关系协定》（CPTPP）

《全面与进步跨太平洋伙伴关系协定》增加了11个国家之间的优惠市场准入——新西兰、澳大利亚、加拿大、智利、文莱、日本、马来西亚、墨西哥、新加坡、秘鲁和越南。它规定了一系列事宜，包括货物和服务市场准入、劳动法、环境政策、知识产权保护和药品法规。

三、贸易

（一）贸易主管部门

新西兰负责贸易立法执行的监管机构是商业委员会。

（二）贸易法律法规简介

与企业日常经营相关的主要贸易立法包括：
- 《公平贸易法》（1986年）；
- 《消费者权益保障法》（1993年）；
- 《隐私权法》（1993年）；
- 《合同法和商法》（2017年）；
- 《反垃圾邮件法》（2007年）；
- 《有害数字通信法》（2015年）。

新西兰颁布的所有法律均可通过 www.legislation.govt.nz 在线查询。

（三）贸易管理

相关贸易立法各部分涵盖的范围如下：
- 《公平贸易法》（1986年）是一部保护消费者的法律，内容包括了禁止实施及代理可能误导或欺骗消费者行为的大量条款。根据该法，企业不可能免除自身义务，除非双方当事人都从事贸易（且免除义务公平合理）。《公平贸易法》（1986年）也禁止与消费者订立的格式合同中包含不平等条款。

---

① 新西兰与马来西亚自由贸易协定（新西兰外交贸易部），新西兰与中国自由贸易协定（新西兰外交贸易部）以及新西兰与韩国自由贸易协定指南（新西兰外交贸易部，2015年1月）。
② https://www.mfat.govt.nz/en/trade/free-trade-agreements/free-trade-agreements-in-force/nz-china-free-trade-agreement.
③ https://www.mfat.govt.nz/en/trade/free-trade-agreements/free-trade-agreements-in-force/nz-china-free-trade-agreement.

•《消费者权益保障法》(1993年)也是保护消费者权益的法律,对通常用于个人/家庭的产品和服务的供应商、生产商规定了一系列义务。该部立法规定了产品和服务必须遵守若干法定"保证",包括所有权、可接受的质量、符合产品描述/样品、价款和符合缔约目的等内容。只有以"商业目的"购买产品和服务而缔结的合同才属于该法律调整的范围(而且合同内容必须公平合理)。

•《隐私权法》(1993年)保护被商业组织收集的个人信息。该部立法规定了商业组织在收集、使用及运用个人信息时需要承担的法律义务,以及应当如何存储个人信息(包括存储期限)。《隐私权法》(1993年)还规定了个人享有获取、更正商业组织所持有的其信息的权利。所有在新西兰境内收集可识别个体信息的商业行为均需要按本法履行法定程序。

•《合同法和商法》(2017年)包含了若干技术性事项,如合同的订立、货物销售的特别条款(包括《联合国国际货物销售合同公约》的生效条款)、电子交易、货物运输及其他商业事项。

•《反垃圾邮件法》(2007年)禁止通过新西兰网络链接(例如访问邮件的电脑、服务器、设备位于新西兰境内,或收件人人身在新西兰)发送商业垃圾邮件,除非收件人同意接收上述邮件信息。商业电子邮件必须包括发送人的准确信息以及实际可用的拒绝接收选项。

•《有害数字通信法》(2015年)对发布有害数字通信(泛指用来造成严重情绪困扰的通信)的行为进行了规制。

外国实体在新西兰开展商事业务无需事先在新西兰境内成立一个机构。境外投资者及其在新西兰境内的商事业务和国内投资者及其公司及商事业务适用相同的法律法规。

其同样适用特定行业的消费者法,如基于《信贷合同与消费者金融法》(2003年)缔结的消费者信贷合同约定的相关义务。

(四)进出口商品的检验检疫

1. 进口

进口商必须确保所有商品货物通关并取得第一产业部许可。进口商必须进行电子的进口申报或货物报关,并承担一切相关手续费及税费。农产品、化学品、食品、药品及危险品等物品可能需要另行获得进口许可,或者在其他政府部门进行登记,其中部分物品被完全禁止进口(详情参考 https://www.customs.govt.nz/business/import/prohibited-and-restricted-imports/prohibitions-and-restrictions)。货物或外包装容器可能需要经过检查或处理才能通关。

2. 出口

出口商必须确保所有商品货物通关。出口商必须提交电子的出口申请或货物信息,并承担一切相关手续费及税费。野生动物、化学品、特定农产品及有害废物/化学品等物品可能需要另行获得出口许可,或者在其他政府部门进行登记,其中部分物品被完全禁止出口。(详情参考 https://www.customs.govt.nz/business/export/prohibitions-and-restrictions/)

(五)海关管理

1. 适用法律

新西兰的海关规定是由行政长官/审计长官根据《海关和货物税法1996》制定的。所有规定均可通过 https://www.customs.govt.nz/about-us/legislation/customs-rules/ 查询。关税征收依《关税法》(1988年)进行。

2. 关税

进口到新西兰的大多数货物不征收进口关税。对于新西兰本土也制造的一些进口商品,包括纺织品、加工食品、机械、钢和塑料制品等,适用5%的关税。

新西兰是《商品名称及编码协调制度的国际公约》(又称"协调关税制度")的缔约国,该公约由《关税法》(1988年)颁布。

新西兰是《关税及贸易总协定》的成员国,也是世界贸易组织关于贸易技术壁垒、补贴和反补贴、反倾销、海关估价和知识产权协定的缔约国。

3. 自由贸易协定

新西兰与亚太地区、美国及欧盟保持着稳健的贸易合作关系。

2008年4月，新西兰成为首个与中国协商订立自由贸易协定的国家，并且于2017年4月开展升级谈判。

新西兰同时是下列自由贸易协定与经贸合作协定的缔约方：
- 《东盟—澳大利亚—新西兰自由贸易协定》（2010年）；
- 《新西兰—马来西亚自由贸易协定》（2010年）；
- 《中国香港与新西兰紧密经贸合作协定》（2011年）；
- 《新西兰—韩国自由贸易协定》（2014年）。

目前，新西兰正与下列国家商谈签订自由贸易协定：
- 2018年3月9日在智利签订的《全面与进步跨太平洋伙伴关系协定》的10个缔约国（澳大利亚、文莱、加拿大、智利、日本、马来西亚、墨西哥、秘鲁、新加坡和越南）；
- 《区域全面经济伙伴关系协定》的15个缔约国（东盟十国及澳大利亚、中国、印度、日本、韩国）；
- 印度；
- 欧盟；
- 俄国、白俄罗斯、哈萨克斯坦；
- 《太平洋紧密经贸关系协定》太平洋岛国论坛的全部成员（澳大利亚、库克群岛、密克罗尼西亚联邦、斐济、基里巴斯、瑙鲁、纽埃、帕劳、巴布亚新几内亚、马绍尔群岛共和国、萨摩亚、所罗门群岛、汤加、图瓦卢、瓦努阿图）。

4. 报关及关务管理

请阅读上文第（四）部分有关新西兰进口的说明。

除此之外，新西兰与中国海关总署签订了互认协定，这意味着两国均承认对方的供应链安检程序，并向获得批准的出口商提供更为快捷的边检通道，使其在贸易市场和在经济复苏形势下占据优势地位。

在新西兰和中国海关友好合作过程中，新西兰海关还建立了联合电子核查系统，通过向中国海关提供出口货物的电子化相关信息加速货物通关。

四、劳动

（一）劳动法律法规简介

新西兰劳动法受一系列成文法及习惯法影响。《雇佣关系法》（2000年）是行业的核心立法，要求雇佣关系的各方主体（包括雇员、雇主及工会）均应诚实守信。

此外，《工作健康与安全法》（2015年）是新西兰保障工作环境健康与安全的法律。

（二）聘用外国雇员的要求

1. 工作许可

（1）签证主要有三种类别：

① 开放式工作签证，包括：
- 工作度假计划——持有者可以从事全职工作，但不得长期从事同一工作。一些国家对于其公民的限制更为严格。
- 学生签证——持有者通常每周最多工作20小时，但有些持有者可在主要节假日全职工作。
- 配偶签证——新西兰工作签证持有者的配偶享有全职工作权利，签证有效期限与配偶的签证一致（新西兰公民或永久居民的配偶享有最多2年的签证期限）。
- 毕业开放式工作签证——持有该签证的国际毕业生可以为任一雇主工作12个月，以便找到符合其资质的工作。

② 雇主担保工作签证：该签证与特定工作挂钩，并且有固定期限。常见类型包括工作转永居留签证、普通工作签证、季节性工作签证、特殊用途工作签证，以及毕业后雇主担保工作签证。如果要留在新西兰，签证持有人必须在现有签证到期前申请新签证。

③ 居留签证：持有者可以为任何新西兰雇主工作。居留签证的常见类型包括技术移民、投资者、家庭，或太平洋配额这几类。

通常而言，在招聘外国雇员之前，新西兰雇主必须优先招聘能够或经培训能够胜任同一岗位的新西兰公民或居民，例外情形如下：

· 雇主经新西兰移民局认证，并且根据优才（认可雇主）工作签证评判标准雇用外国劳工；

· 该工作在重要技能需求清单上，且申请人满足清单的资质要求和/或工作经验要求。

雇主雇用已在新西兰且持有如工作度假签证等开放工作签证的外籍劳工，或取得工作许可的国际学生的，无需优先在当地招聘。

（2）短缺职业

长期短缺职业清单（LTSSL）指在新西兰持续紧缺技术人员的职业。如果雇主招聘的工作岗位在长期短缺职业清单上，则其无需提供其有意雇用新西兰公民或居民的证明。如果外籍劳工符合要求并能够胜任该工作，则可能取得普通工作签证或长期短缺职业清单工作签证；有意申请工作转居留签证的，可以在两年后提出居留申请。

即时短缺职业清单（ISSL）以地域为基础，确认在某一地区存在技能短缺的职业。由于雇主无需证明其曾试图招聘新西兰公民或居民，这类工作签证也更容易得到支持。

如果雇主招聘的工作岗位列于即时短缺职业清单，且外籍劳工满足该工作的具体要求，他们可获发普通工作签证，并被允许暂时在新西兰工作。

坎特伯雷短缺职业清单（CSSL）包含在坎特伯雷地区极度短缺的职业，包括与坎特伯雷重建相关的工作。如果雇主招聘的工作岗位列于坎特伯雷短缺职业清单且位于坎特伯雷地区，则外籍劳工可获得普通工作签证。

（3）配额

任何时候，总共有1 000名中国居民可以基于中国技术工人政策在新西兰从事特定职业，每个职业最多可提供100个名额。申请人必须取得该特定职业的真实工作邀请，并符合健康、品格等方面的基本要求。职业清单详情可见 https://www.immigration.govt.nz/new-zealand-visas/apply-for-a-visa/about-visa/china-skilled-workers-visa。

2. 申请流程

需要注意的是，海外求职者无需签证就可申请或获得一份工作，并且多数情况下，求职者要成功申请签证，必须有一份工作邀请。

3. 社会保险

（1）意外事故赔偿计划

"新西兰意外事故赔偿计划"（ACC）为所有新西兰居民和新西兰游客提供全面、无过失的人身伤害保险。该计划涵盖了（居民或非居民）发生在新西兰或（常居新西兰的个人）发生在海外的伤害事故。

如果该伤害属于"人身伤害"的范畴，它将通过"新西兰意外事故赔偿计划"获得赔偿。然而，"完全或实质上由于逐渐演变、疾病或传染"导致的伤害不属于上述计划的赔偿范围，但这一伤害与工作相关，是治疗伤害，由可预估的人身伤害导致，或由人身伤害治疗引起的除外。

"新西兰意外事故赔偿计划"制度的核心特征是，如果某一人身伤害已经由"新西兰意外事故赔偿计划"赔偿，那么索赔人不得再提起损害赔偿之诉。

（2）雇主义务

在"新西兰意外事故赔偿计划"制度下，雇主的主要经济义务是支付每位雇员的相关税款，以囊括他们的工伤事故费用，以及因工伤离职的雇员离职后首周工资的80%。

雇主须支付税款，税率由支付的工资总额、预计支付额，或视为雇主已向其雇员支付的金额来确定。自由职业者、独立承包商或私人家庭佣工亦须纳税。

失业保险在新西兰不属于强制责任保险。

KiwiSaver 计划是所有雇主都必须向雇员提供的一项自愿性养老金计划。该计划源于《储蓄法案》（2006 年），根据该计划，参加 KiwiSaver 计划的雇员必须将其薪金或工资总额的至少 3% 用于他们选择的养老金计划。雇主也必须为每名参与的雇员缴纳 3% 的款额。

（三）出入境

1. 签证类型

除了上文所列签证，新西兰针对一些国家推出了免签计划（详情请见 https://www.immigration.govt.nz/new-zealand-visas/apply-for-a-visa/about-visa/visa-waiver#https://www.immigration.govt.nz/new-zealand-visas/apply-for-a-visa/tools-and-information/general-information/visa-waiver-countries/slider）。这些国家的居民有权在没有旅游签证或短期学习签证的情况下进入新西兰。

其他所有类型的签证都有特定的申请要求，详情请见 https://www.immigration.govt.nz/new-zealand-visas/apply-for-a-visa。

2. 出入境限制

外国人进入新西兰必须持有签证或享受免签政策。大多数签证在有效期内都允许持有人多次出入境，从签证上可以获知是否可以持该签证多次入境。

（四）工会及劳工组织

《雇佣关系法》促进了集体谈判，支持工会在新西兰劳工关系中的重要地位，但是劳动者无加入工会的义务，任何人亦不得强制其加入。只有工会才有权（代表其组成成员）与雇主达成集体谈判协议。工会和雇主在谈判时均负有诚实信用的义务，尽管谈判破裂可能导致罢工或在其他罕见情形下的行业活动。

新西兰的工会集中在公共部门，私营部门参与度较低。在新西兰，只有不足 20% 的雇员是工会成员。

（五）劳动争议

在新西兰，劳动争议可以通过调解（私下进行且免费）和／或向雇佣关系局提起申诉等非正式途径解决。雇佣关系局作出的裁决可能会被劳动法庭所推翻。

当事人各方就劳动争议解决办法达成一致的，可以作出正式的调解记录。

五、知识产权

（一）知识产权法律法规简介

1. 专利

专利授予的依据是《专利法》（2013 年）。专利一旦被授予，将对一项新发明的专有权利持续长达 20 年的保护。某些发明不得授予专利，例如，对其的商业利用有悖于"公共秩序"或伦理的发明。

2. 商标

《商标法》（2002 年）允许进行商标及服务商标注册。

商标注册只对相同或类似商品上已经注册的商标提供保护。新西兰的商品和服务分类遵循尼斯分类系统。

对那些被认为仅具有描述性质的商标和服务商标，因其缺乏注册所必需的独特性，新西兰知识产权局（IPONZ）通常不予许可注册。

3. 外观设计

根据《外观设计法》（1953年）注册外观设计可保护产品的视觉设计并及于通过任何工业流程应用于产品的新型或原始形状、结构或图案。设计注册有效期可长达15年，申请注册必须向新西兰知识产权局提交申请表，内容包括设计图纸及对设计独创性的说明。

4. 著作权

著作权法不保护思想本身，而是禁止他人复刻表达思想的特定方式。和其他类型的知识产权不同，著作权在新西兰无需登记注册，这一点也与著作权经注册才受保护的其他国家不同。

在新西兰，按照《著作权法》（1994年）的规定，创作、出版或表演的原创作品受到著作权保护。作品类型包括文学、音乐、戏剧或艺术作品；录音和电影；广播和有线电视节目；以及任何数字或纸质出版物。包括说明书、手册、保证、设计、包装、标志和广告。软件的著作权也受保护，即将源代码视为"文学作品"。著作权保护期为50年，自作品可为公众使用或被广播当年年末起算。文学作品的著作权保护期限自作者去世之日起计算。

通常，作品的创作者即为著作权所有人，但作品系他人雇佣或委托并支付报酬而创作的除外（故著作权将重新分配）。

（二）申请专利

申请专利必须依据《专利法》（2014年）向新西兰知识产权局提交专利申请，申请必须内附对发明进行书面描述的"说明书"，包括如何制造和使用该发明的详细信息（可能包含图纸），以及关于该发明的声明。与完整说明书相比，临时说明书要求填写的内容更少，目的在于使当事人从专利申请日起获得优先权。提交临时说明书的，则必须在提交专利申请之日起12个月内提交完整说明书。

一旦提交完整说明书，将在5年内接受专利审查。发布审查报告是审查程序的一部分，报告将说明完成申请所需要处理的事项。

向《巴黎公约》和《专利合作条约》成员国提出申请的，也可向新西兰提出申请。《巴黎公约》规定的时限为自第一次提交到向新西兰提交完整说明书止间隔12个月内；《专利合作条约》规定则必须在最早的优先日期后31个月内向新西兰提交申请。

申请人无须在新西兰有营业地点，但必须有送达地址和通讯地址（电子邮件地址）。送达地址可以是位于新西兰境内的营业或居住地址、邮局信箱或文件交换箱。

（三）商标注册

商标注册应当向新西兰知识产权局提出申请，其中必须包括将使用该标记的所有商品和/或服务的列表。在向新西兰知识产权局提交申请后，经审查，新西兰知识产权局将发出受理通知书或合规报告。商标申请受理后，将在官方月刊上进行3个月公示，公示期间第三方可以提出反对注册的意见。如无反对意见，商标注册完成。

商标注册人及持有人在较长的期间内（目前为连续3年）未在有关类别的商品中使用该商标的，可能面临该商标因长期不使用而被从注册商标中移除的风险。

如果在向新西兰提出商标申请之日起6个月内又向海外申请注册该商标的，可以就该申请主张公约优先权。但这仅适用于《巴黎公约》成员国。

（四）知识产权保护措施

1. 雇员和承包商

任何新西兰企业都面临的一个主要风险是，当其雇员或第三方承包商在工作中可能开发新的知识产权时，如何保护知识产权权益。

就雇员而言，劳动合同中应当明确约定在工作过程中创造的一切知识产权均属于企业。

就第三方承包商而言，在企业与承包商之间的合同中，约定自动将承包商向企业履行合同服务而创造的所有知识产权自动归属于企业十分重要，否则，默认该知识产权归创造者即承包商所有。

2. 专利

一旦专利被授予，可能发生的侵权情形有：

（1）从事任何只有专利持有人才有权从事的行为，如当发明为：

① 一种产品时，

A. 制造、租用、出售或以其他方式处置该产品；

B. 承诺制造、租用、出售或以其他方式处置产品；

C. 使用或进口该产品；

D. 为进行 A 到 C 节所述行为而持有该产品；

② 一种制造方法时，使用该制造方法或对使用该制造方法制造的产品实施上述任一行为的。

（2）向他人提供或提出提供关于发明的基本要素的任何方法，以使该发明可供实施。

如侵权行为成立，法庭可发出强制令，并可根据原告的选择，支持损害赔偿或侵权利益。但在非有意侵权的情况下，不会判令偿付损害赔偿或侵权利益。

3. 商标

商标注册后，商标权通过下列方式得到保护：

· 使用 ® 标志；

· 保持最新的所有权及地址详述；

· 监控商标以对抗侵权行为。

侵权行为包括：

· 在交易过程中使用相同或近似的标记；

· 违反关于允许使用商标的合同要求。

根据《商标法》和普通法的规定，法院有大量的民事救济措施赔偿注册商标所有人因注册商标受到侵犯而遭受的损失，包括损害赔偿、禁止令、解释收益的命令、将侵权商品移交权利人的命令。

《商标法》（2002 年）也包含为商业利益侵犯著作权作品和伪造注册商标的刑事罪名。因上述行为被定罪者可被判处最高 5 年的监禁或 150 000 新西兰元的罚款。新西兰警方可对注册商标伪造者进行调查并提出控告。

此外，商业、创新和就业部有权对《商标法》和《著作权法》规定的制造、进口和销售假冒商品、盗版作品的罪行提起诉讼。

企业可在高等法院就使用具有误导性或欺诈性的商标等违反《商标法》及《公平交易法》的行为提起诉讼。该诉讼将在小额仲裁法庭、地方法院或高等法院进行（视情况而定）。

在注册商标产品的侵权复制品进口时，注册商标所有人及特许使用人可要求新西兰海关在疑似侵权商品被其控制时对该产品进行扣押。注册商标所有人 / 特许使用人应随后在 10 个工作日内启动诉讼程序，否则上述商品将被放行。

4. 著作权

实践中有多种保护著作权的方法，包括：

· 在作品上使用著作权指示标记 "©"，后接著作权所有人名称及该享有著作权的作品最早创作出来的年份；

· 保存关于作品创作及所有权的信息记录；

· 确保企业拥有（或至少有权使用）已付费的任何知识产权；

· 确保企业拥有其雇员在工作中创作的作品的所有著作权（如上所述）。

著作权可能因实体的以下行为受到侵犯：

· 复制作品；

· 向公众发布复制的作品；

· 在公众场合表演文学、戏剧或音乐作品；

· 在公众场合播放或展示录音、电影或书信作品；

· 向公众传播作品；

- 改编文学、戏剧或音乐作品；
- 进口、拥有或买卖侵权作品；
- 提供制作侵权作品的方法；
- 同意为侵权行为提供房屋使用权或器械。

根据《著作权法》和普通法的规定，法院有大量的民事救济措施赔偿受著作权保护作品的所有人因著作权受到侵犯而遭受的损失，包括损害赔偿、禁止令、解释收益的命令、将侵权作品移交权利人的命令。

5. 外观设计

根据《外观设计法》，外观设计经登记获得著作权，并适用前述关于著作权的规定。

六、环境保护

（一）环境保护监管部门

环境保护署（EPA）是负责管理影响新西兰环境的活动的政府机构。该机构向环境部长报告，其职能包括：
- 向部长提出建议；
- 依照《资源管理法》（1991年），就具有全国性意义的申请向决策机构提供行政协助；
- 批准或拒绝在新西兰进口或制造农药、危险品、家用化学品和其他有害物质；
- 管理在新西兰专属经济区和大陆架的某些海事活动；
- 管理新西兰碳排放交易计划；
- 就向新西兰引入新生物的申请作出决定；
- 向政府环境政策、立法和规章提出建议；
- 强制执行某些规则。

根据《资源管理法》（1991年），地方和区域理事会有权制定政策及规划文件，管理其所在区域的资源利用及开发。理事会负责颁发资源许可，批准实施可能对环境产生影响的活动（有时视条件而定），并强制执行前述资源许可。

（二）环境保护法律法规简介

环境保护署依《环境保护署法》（2011年）成立，但《资源管理法》（1991年）才是新西兰环境管理的主要立法。

《资源管理法》规定了新西兰自然和物质资源（包括土地、水和空气）的使用、开发和保护，并且寻求促进对这些资源的可持续管理，使其能被居民和社区用来为社会、经济、文化福祉服务。

（三）环境保护评估

2017年经济合作与发展组织（以下简称"经合组织"）对新西兰的环境性能进行了评估。经合组织认为新西兰人享有高质量的生活环境，并可触及未经开发的地区。尽管如此，新西兰主要依靠开采自然资源的增长模式，随着温室气体排放和水污染的持续增加，已经开始显现出环境极限。

经合组织的报告同时指出：
- 尽管新西兰80%的电力来自可再生资源，为经合组织可再生资源占比最高的国家之一，但人均国内生产总值单位排放量占经合组织第二位，人均排放量为第五位。农业占排放量的49%。
- 新西兰城市注重绿色环保，环境质量好，但人口增长、城市扩张使住房、交通、废物处理和水利基础设施的压力不断增加。

经合组织在报告中总结道：
- 《资源管理法》是一项非常全面的环境立法，但效力有待加强；
- 农业排放亟待解决；

- 国家淡水政策施行需迅速、有效；
- 必须有向低碳、绿色经济过渡的长期愿景。

七、争议解决

（一）争议解决的方式和主体

1. 诉讼

在新西兰最常见的解决纠纷的司法途径是诉讼。诉讼在本质上必然是对抗性的（即涉及对抗双方或相对的利益集团为争取对自身最有利结果而进行的竞争）、严格正式的，并且受规则约束。诉讼各方随时可在判决作出前另行解决争议。

可向以下法院起诉：
- 小额仲裁法庭（诉讼标的额在 15 000 新西兰元以下）；
- 地方法院（诉讼标的额在 350 000 新西兰元以下）；
- 高等法院（诉讼标的额在 350 000 新西兰元及以上）；
- 在专门法院之一，如就业法庭。

上诉可从：
- 小额仲裁法庭到地方法院；
- 地方法院或专门法院到高等法院（或某些情况下到上诉法院）；
- 高等法院到上诉法院（如向该法院提起上诉是被准许的）；
- 上诉法院到最高法院（如向该法院提起上诉是被准许的）。

根据《司法审查程序法》（2016 年），也可向高等法院提出司法审查申请。该法为司法审查是否使用法定权利规定了一个单一程序。

上级法院的判决对下级法院具有约束力，作为上诉的终审法院，最高法院的判决对其他所有法院具有约束力。

相关法院的诉讼程序规定如下：
- 地方法院——《地方法院法》（2016 年）和《地方法院法规》（2014 年）规定了地方法院的组成和管辖权、工作内容和程序，以及司法和其他官员的选择、任命、免职和条件。
- 高等法院——《高级法院法》（2016 年）及《高等法院法规》（2016 年）。《高级法院法》（2016 年）设立了高等法院、上诉法院和最高法院，并明确了其管辖权及程序。而《高等法院法规》（2016 年）则规定了如何启动程序，指明必须提交的文件及其内容，以及文件如何提交；同时为案件管理、临时救济、发现和调查等审前事项提供了详细指导。案件管理程序旨在确保案件通过系统有效推进。
- 上诉法院——《高级法院法》（2016 年）和《上诉法院（民事）法规》（2005 年）。《上诉法院（民事）法规》（2005 年）规定了提起民事上诉的程序要求。
- 最高法院——《高级法院法》（2016 年）和《最高法院法规》（2004 年）。《最高法院法规》（2004 年）规定了提起上诉的程序要求。

新西兰解决纠纷的其他常见方式如下。

2. 调解

调解是一种经各方同意、保密且相对不正式的协商程序。争议各方在被称作调解人的具备相关技能的独立第三方的协助下，明确争议事项，开发探寻解决方案，评估各方案的影响，协商出一个各方都能接受并满足他们的利益和需求的方案。

通常，达成的任何协议都将以书面形式记录并对各方具有约束力。协议任何一方均可通过启动法院诉讼程序强制执行协议条款。

3. 专家决定

专家决定是一种具有约束力的简便的争议解决方式。该方式系经各方同意的、保密的并且相对非正式的程序，由合同各方同意将争议事项提交独立人员决定。选择该独立人员则是因为其在各方所争议事项方面具有专门的知识技能，受人尊敬。

专家决定可提供具有约束力或不具有约束力的决定（视当事人约定而定），作出专家决定不涉及仲裁和诉讼等更正式的程序中的许多手续。

经当事人同意，决定对其具有约束力的，一方当事人可通过启动法院诉讼程序强制执行。

4. 仲裁

仲裁是一种正式的争议解决程序，由两方或两方以上当事人将所有或部分争议提交被称为仲裁员的独立人员以获得一个有约束力的决定。仲裁通过协议约定，仲裁程序由《仲裁法》（1996年）及《仲裁修正案》（2007年）（或其他经各方同意的仲裁规则）规定。

仲裁员的决定称为裁定，对各方均具有约束力，并和法院的判决一样具有强制执行力。

（二）法律适用

1. 诉讼

如前所述，上级法院的判决对下级法院具有约束力，作为终审法院，最高法院的判决对其他所有法院具有约束力。法律由此一致适用。

2. 仲裁

根据《仲裁法》，仲裁一般保密。因此，在新西兰无法得出关于仲裁裁定的结论。

3. 调解和专家决定

调解和专家决定程序一般保密。因此，在新西兰无法得出关于该类程序的结论。

八、其他

（一）反商业贿赂

1. 反商业贿赂法规简介

在严格的反腐败法律规定下，新西兰被誉为全世界最不腐败国家之一。

新西兰是各项条约的签约国：

- 经合组织《国际商务交易反对行贿外国公职人员公约》；
- 联合国《反腐败公约》；
- 联合国《打击跨国有组织犯罪公约》。

新西兰有关反贿赂及腐败的关键立法有：

- 《刑法》（1961年）；
- 《秘密佣金法》（1910年）；
- 《反洗钱及反恐怖主义资助法》（2009年）。

（1）《刑法》

对于给予、提供或同意给予他人任何贿赂以期对他人履行公务产生影响的行为，《刑法》针对以下人员，规定了多项罪名：

- 司法官员；
- 国家部长；
- 议会成员；
- 执法官员；
- 公务人员，指任何服务于新西兰最高政权当局的人（无论该等服务是否有偿，也无论该等行为发生在新西兰内或境外），任何地方当局或公共团体的成员或雇员，或任何在《国家部门法》（1988年）所指的教育服务行业中任职的人员。

按照《刑法》规定，任何官员被确认腐败地（要求明知相关事项）接受或获取贿赂也是一种犯罪。

贿赂被广泛定义为直接或间接的金钱、有价值的报酬、职位、工作或任何利益。

(2)《秘密佣金法》

《秘密佣金法》旨在防止在新西兰发生贿赂及腐败行为。该法比《刑法》适用范围更加广泛，涵盖在公私领域与贿赂及腐败相关的罪行，包括代理人、委托人及第三方之间的交易和优惠。该法规定的罪行有：

- 提供或接受礼物或其他报酬形式的贿赂；
- 未披露合同中的经济利益；
- 提供和交付虚假收据；
- 介绍一方订立合同从而收取秘密报酬；
- 协助和教唆犯罪。

这些罪行包括给予或收受礼物或任何其他形式的报酬。报酬系指任何类型的有价值的报酬，特别是折扣、佣金、回扣、奖金、扣除、手续费、雇佣金、金钱支付（无论以贷款、礼物或其他方式），及（应当要求而）未要求其他金钱或有价物品。

建议任何人与第三方订立合同，不经其知晓和同意从第三方处收受或同意收受利益，且以该利益（无论是礼物还是其他形式的利益）作为提出立约建议或促成合同的诱因或报酬的，也被认定为犯罪。

2. 反商业贿赂监督部门

严重欺诈办公室（SFO）负责对严重或复杂的经济犯罪（包括贿赂和腐败）进行调查和提起诉讼。严重欺诈办公室与其他执法机构建立了合作网（国内和国际的合作），可对新西兰公民、居民及在新西兰组建的企业完全发生在新西兰之外的贿赂和腐败行为提起公诉，包括通过外国中间人支付贿赂的行为。

严重欺诈办公室的重点案件集中于：

- 多名受害人的投资欺诈案件；
- 涉及在信托方面处于重要地位的人的欺诈（如律师）案件；
- 贿赂及腐败案件；
- 对新西兰公平自由的经济市场有重大潜在损害的案件。

3. 惩处措施

《刑法》规定的惩罚包括对最严重的罪行处以最高14年的监禁。

目前，根据《秘密佣金法》，对任何犯罪的惩罚为不超过7年的监禁。①

如果新西兰警方怀疑个人从贿赂或腐败行为中受益，《犯罪收益（追回）法》（2009年）允许国家追回来源于前述罪行的金钱或财产。该法允许警方向法庭申请冻结或追回来源于犯罪的金钱或财产。这些财产包括来源于犯罪的直接利益（如从贿赂中收受的金钱），或间接利益（如使用欺诈获取的金钱购买的车辆）。这一制度的目的在于收取犯罪收益，去除犯罪工具，并利用追回的犯罪所得对受害者进行潜在赔偿。根据该法，无论个人是否被定罪，公诉人均可追回犯罪收益。如果法庭确信财产来源于犯罪行为，该财产可被没收。

（二）工程承包

政府部门、新西兰警方、新西兰国防军和大多数国企的采购受新西兰政府采购部（隶属于商业、创新和就业部）颁布的《政府采购规则》管辖。

1. 许可制度

不存在一般许可制度，每一份采购通知（或类似文件）可指定参与采购的条件。

2. 禁止领域

政府机构在有合理理由的情况下，可排除某一供应商参与投标。这些理由包括：

- 破产、破产管理或清算；
- 作虚假声明；

---

① Secret Commissions Act 1910, s 13.

- 此前合同存在严重履约问题；
- 对严重罪行或违法行为的定罪；
- 职业不端行为；
- 对供应商商业信用产生不良影响的行为或不作为；
- 不缴纳税款和其他征收的费用；
- 涉及政府敏感信息的机密性，威胁国家安全；
- 供应商被新西兰警方认定为恐怖分子的个人或组织。

除上述规定外，对特定行业还存在法定的监管限制。在初级产品领域、能源、渔业、林业、保险业、银行业、航空服务及自然资源开发领域均可找到实例。其他产业群如汽车经销商、房地产经纪及私家侦探也受到法律监管。

3. 招标和投标

投标人的条件和投标要求（包括时间）将在有关项目的采购通知（或类似文件）中列明。

政府机构可不时建立供应商名单，包括已登记的供应商名单、通过初审的供应商名单及供应商小组。这些名单的建立将公开宣告，并且除供应商小组外，所有采购也将继续公开通告。

政府机构可规定投标人须满足某些先决条件方可参与采购流程。这些条件限定于以下关键范围：
- 法律行为能力；
- 经济能力；
- 商业或运营能力，或交付能力；
- 适当的技术技能、专门知识或相关经验。

New Zealand

Authors: Chris Gordon, Dean Alderton, Dan Jones, Mei Fern Johnson
Translators: Wei Jinji (Glen), Gu Chaoping

I. Overview

A. Introduction to New Zealand's Political, Economic, Social and Legal Environment

a. New Zealand's Regulatory Framework

New Zealand has a deregulated and decentralised economy which is directly exposed to international competition. Over the past three decades, successive New Zealand Governments have reformed New Zealand's trade rules by removing many barriers to imports, ending most subsidies and ensuring that the rules relating to overseas investment are designed to encourage overseas investment in New Zealand. New Zealand is consistently ranked by the World Bank and others as one of the most business-friendly countries in the world.

b. New Zealand's Political System

New Zealand is an independent sovereign state and a member of the Commonwealth and does not have a written constitution.

New Zealand is not a federal state. All legislation is passed by a single chamber, the House of Representatives, which is the highest law-making body in the country. The New Zealand electoral system is a "Mixed Member Proportional" (MMP) representation system. Parliament is triennially democratically elected.

c. New Zealand's Legal System

New Zealand is a common law jurisdiction. The law is developed from case law (the decisions of the courts) and from statutes enacted by the New Zealand Parliament. Case law may be superseded by statute.

B. Status and Direction of Cooperation with Chinese Enterprises Under the Belt and Road Initiative

a. Relationship Between the Countries

New Zealand and China first established diplomatic relations in 1972, and the relationship between the two countries has since expanded rapidly.

b. China and New Zealand Agreements

China is New Zealand's largest trading partner in goods and second largest overall, including trade in services. [1]

The New Zealand–China Free Trade Agreement (NZCFTA) signed in 2008 was China's first fair trade agreement with a developed country. The NZCFTA cements the trading relationship between China and New Zealand, and frees up business for exporters, the service sector and investors. [2]

The Hong Kong–New Zealand Closer Economic Partnership Agreement (CEPA) is a bilateral free trade agreement that was signed between the Hong Kong Special Administrative Region of China and New Zealand in March 2010. It was the first bilateral free trade agreement on goods and services that Hong Kong SAR signed with a foreign country. The CEPA complements the FTA and enhances the potential for Hong Kong to be used as a platform for trade into Mainland China. [3]

Chinese Premier Li Keqiang visited New Zealand in March 2017. During this visit several initiatives between China and New Zealand were signed on behalf of a number of government agencies, including:

• a Memorandum of Arrangement on Strengthening Cooperation on the Belt and Road Initiative between the

---

[1] "Our Relationship with China" New Zealand Foreign Affairs and Trade <www.mfat.govt.nz>.
[2] https://www.mfat.govt.nz/en/countries-and-regions/north-asia/china#Trade.
[3] "Hong Kong and New Zealand sign Closer Economic Partnership Agreement" (29 March 2010) Hong Kong Government News Press Release <http://www.info.gov.hk/gia/general/201003/29/P201003290114.htm>.

Government of New Zealand and the Government of The People's Republic of China;

• an arrangement between the Ministry of Foreign Affairs and Trade of New Zealand and the Ministry of Commerce of The People's Republic of China on Cooperation on Electronic Commerce; and

• an arrangement between the Ministry of Foreign Affairs and Trade of New Zealand and the Ministry of Commerce of the People's Republic of China on Strengthening Exchanges on International Development Cooperation. [1]

c. Memorandum of Arrangement-Belt and Road Initiative

New Zealand and China's entry into the Memorandum of Arrangement on Strengthening Cooperation on the Belt and Road Initiative reflects the countries' common desire to promote cooperation and exchanges to support the Belt and Road initiative. The memorandum sets out China and New Zealand's mutual understanding of: [2]

"achieving the goal of common development, translating advantages of close political relations, economic complementarities and cultural exchanges into practical cooperation and sustainable growth, pushing for continued friendly bilateral political ties, stronger economic ties, closer people-to-people relations and greater benefit amongst the two peoples."

II. Investment

Investment between New Zealand and China, including Hong Kong, has been growing strongly in recent years, reaching NZ$6.2 billion in 2016[3]. Chinese investment in New Zealand exists across a diverse range of sectors.

A. Market Access[4]

a. Department Supervising Investment

The Overseas Investment Office (OIO) is responsible for approving applications by overseas persons to invest in New Zealand. The Overseas Investment Act 2005 (OI Act) and the Overseas Investment Regulations 2005 (OI Regulations) confer a broad discretion on the OIO to grant consent, with or without conditions, or to refuse consent to an application. The OIO operates under the Minister of Finance. The Minister of Land Information and the Minister of Fisheries are also responsible for applications involving "sensitive land" and fisheries respectively.

b. Laws and Regulations of Investment Industry

a) Investment Incentives

New Zealand does not provide incentives for people to invest in approved activities or in specific geographic areas, and there are no internal free trade zones for the encouragement of overseas investment. Overseas investors are attracted to New Zealand because of its sound, consistent economic policies, good rates of economic growth and a stable political system.

b) Overseas Investment Controls

New Zealand's overseas investment controls require overseas persons to obtain consent before they can invest in certain types of assets. The principal restrictions on an overseas person setting up or acquiring a New Zealand business are contained in the OI Act and the OI Regulations.

Broadly speaking, an "overseas person" is a person who is not a New Zealand citizen nor ordinarily resident in New Zealand, a company that is incorporated outside of New Zealand or a company, partnership or other body corporate that is 25% (or more) owned or controlled by an overseas person or persons.

c) General Controls

An overseas investor is required to comply with the general law of New Zealand in the same way as a New Zealand investor. For example, the Companies Act 1993, the Partnership Act 1908, the Limited Partnerships Act 2008, the Commerce Act 1986 and the Reserve Bank of New Zealand Act 1989 affect overseas and New Zealand

---

[1] "Our Relationship with China" New Zealand Foreign Affairs and Trade <https://www.mfat.govt.nz/en/countries-and-regions/north-asia/china#Trade>.

[2] Memorandum of Arrangement on Strengthening Cooperation on the Belt and Road Initiative between the Government of New Zealand and the Government of The People's Republic Of China https://www.mfat.govt.nz/assets/FTAs-agreements-in-force/China-FTA/NRA-NZ-China-Cooperation-on-Belt-and-Road-Initiative.pdf.

[3] New Zealand Foreign Affairs and Trade, 'China' https://www.mfat.govt.nz/en/countries-and-regions/north-asia/china

[4] As at the date of this publication, the OI Act and the OI Regulations may be subject to change under the Overseas Investment Amendment Bill.

investors in the same way.

c. Forms of Investment

The OI Act and the OI Regulations apply to all types of investment and prescribe the circumstances where an overseas person is required to obtain consent before investing in New Zealand. Whether or not consent is required will depend on the amount of money involved, the type of investment proposed and the sector in which the investment is to be made.

The OI Act requires consent for a transaction if it involves an overseas investment in:
- "significant business assets";
- "sensitive land" (including farm land); and
- fishing quota.

If consent is required, it must be obtained before a transaction is given effect. An agreement for the acquisition of shares, including under a takeover offer, can be entered into provided that it is conditional upon OIO consent being obtained.

d. Overseas Investment in "Significant Business Assets"

If an overseas person plans to acquire securities in a New Zealand business, set up a New Zealand business or purchase assets in New Zealand, or if an overseas person has a 25% or more ownership or control interest in a New Zealand company and wishes to increase that ownership or control interest, then provided the transaction does not involve the acquisition of "sensitive land" or an interest in fishing quota, OIO consent will be required if:
- the amount to be paid for the securities exceeds NZ$100 million;
- the total value of the shares on issue exceeds NZ$100 million; or
- the gross value of the target company's assets exceeds NZ$100 million.

If the proposed investment is expected to exceed NZ$100 million (whether by one transaction or through a series of related transactions), the investment will be considered an overseas investment in "significant business assets" and OIO consent will be required.

e. Overseas Investment in "Sensitive Land"

Consent will be required for an overseas person to purchase or acquire an interest (for greater than three years) in land which is "sensitive", either directly or through the purchase of securities in a company that owns land (with the overseas person owning or controlling more than 25% of the company) which, together with any associated land, meets any of the thresholds set out below.

"Sensitive land" is land (or any associated land) that:

(i) exceeds five hectares and is non-urban land (being farm land or any land other than land in an urban area that is used for commercial, industrial or residential purposes);

(ii) is or includes the foreshore and / or seabed or certain named islands;

(iii) exceeds 4,000 m² and:
- is part of the bed of a lake;
- is part of certain named islands;
- is held for conservation purposes, is provided as a reserve, a public park, for recreation purposes or as a private open space;
- is subject to a heritage order or a requirement for a heritage order under the Resource Management Act 1991 or by Heritage New Zealand Pouhere Taonga under the Heritage New Zealand Pouhere Tanonga Act 2014; or is subject to a heritage order or a requirement for a heritage order, is an historic place, historic area, wahi tapu (sacred to Māori) site or for which there is an application or proposal for registration under the Heritage New Zealand Pouhere Taonga Act 2014;
- exceeds 2,000 m² and adjoins the foreshore; or
- exceeds 4,000 m² and adjoins certain land, such as a lake bed.

Consent may be granted subject to conditions. Overseas investors must pass an investor test that considers character, business acumen and level of financial commitment. Overseas investors wishing to purchase "sensitive land" must either intend to reside permanently in New Zealand or demonstrate that the investment will benefit New Zealand.

B. Foreign Exchange Regulation

New Zealand has revoked all foreign exchange controls. Accordingly, there are no such restrictions on the transfer of capital, profits, dividends, royalties or interest into, or from, New Zealand.

C. Financing

a. Main Financial Institutions

The Reserve Bank of New Zealand is New Zealand's central bank. Operating autonomously from the New Zealand government, it is primarily a policy organisation which formulates and implements monetary policy to maintain price stability, promotes the maintenance of a sound and efficient financial system and meets the public's currency needs. There are two key elements to the Reserve Bank's purpose, undertaking bank registration and supervision, and maintaining a capacity to respond to financial distress or bank failure where a bank's financial condition poses a serious threat to the financial system.

b. Financing Conditions for Foreign Enterprises

a) Bank Accounts

The process for opening a bank account varies between financial institutions in New Zealand. However, generally banks will require a certified form of identification and proof of address. Overseas investors may be required to provide additional information, including the main country of their tax residence, in order for banks to meet their obligations under New Zealand's anti-money laundering legislation.

b) Financing

Finance is available to foreign enterprises in New Zealand. However, in 2016 some of the main New Zealand financial institutions introduced new lending restrictions for overseas property buyers. The restrictions are directed at non-resident borrowers with overseas income and restrict or stop the offer of residential mortgages to non-residents.

c. Anti-money Laundering and Countering Financing of Terrorism

Entities operating in, or in connection with, New Zealand are also subject to New Zealand's anti-money laundering and countering of financing of terrorism laws.

D. Land Policy

a. Brief Introduction of Land-Related Laws and Regulations

a) Commercial Properties

Generally, overseas persons are free to purchase a commercial building in New Zealand without any need for consent from a regulatory body. However, if the value of, or consideration to be paid for, the commercial building (either alone or together with other assets to be acquired) exceeds NZ$100 million, or if the commercial building is situated on, or adjoins, "sensitive land", OIO consent is required under the OI Act and the OI Regulations.

Overseas persons are free to lease or rent commercial buildings in New Zealand. If the commercial building is situated on, or adjoins, "sensitive land" and the lease is for a term of three years or more (including rights of renewal), OIO consent is required under the OI Act and the OI Regulations.

b) Residential Properties[1]

An overseas person is free to purchase a residence or holiday house in New Zealand without any prior regulatory consent, provided the property does not fall within the definition of "sensitive land" (particularly in relation to coastal land over 2,000m² or land on certain islands).

c) Sale and Purchase of Land

Under New Zealand law, agreements for the sale and purchase of land must be in writing and signed by the parties or their representatives. An agreement for the sale and purchase of land may be unconditional or subject to conditions for the benefit of either party.

Changes in land ownership are registered on an electronic property registration system Land Information New Zealand (LINZ). This is a centralised system which can be searched by the public.

Tax information is also collected at the time of registration of the property transfer, and in certain limited circumstances an overseas person who is selling land within two years[2] of purchasing it may be required to pay residential land withholding tax at the time of the sale.

d) Leasing of Land

Leases of land must be in writing and signed by the parties or their representatives. Leases are not typically registered at LINZ.

---

[1] The following comments may be subject to change following the introduction of the Overseas Investment Amendment Bill.

[2] As at the date of this publication, the New Zealand Government has indicated that a person who sells land within five years of purchasing it may be required to pay residential land withholding tax at the time of the sale.

e) Resource Management Act 1991

Environmental law in New Zealand is regulated primarily by the Resource Management Act 1991 (RMA). Under the RMA, all uses of land, air and water are regulated by local and regional government.

A consent process has been established for approval of any development proposal. Applications for resource consents must be made to local authorities in accordance with the RMA. Following the consent process, the relevant local authority may grant consent (with or without conditions). Applicants, or any person who makes a submission in relation to an application (if an application is publicly notified), have a right of appeal to the Environment Court.

f) Building Act 2004

The Building Act 2004 (Building Act), in conjunction with the Building Code, regulates the building of houses and other buildings. It requires building consent to be obtained from local authorities for the construction of new buildings (residential and commercial) and alterations of existing buildings.

The Building Act includes provisions designed to improve the likelihood of existing buildings withstanding earthquakes. Under the Building Act, a building is generally considered to be "earthquake prone" if it has less than one third of the seismic strength required for a new building constructed under current standards. The local authority can require the owner of an earthquake prone building to carry out seismic upgrade works to the building so that it is no longer earthquake prone. The cost of such work is typically for the land owner's account.

g) Treaty of Waitangi Act 1975

Under the Treaty of Waitangi Act 1975, the Waitangi Tribunal hears land claims relating to historical breaches by the Crown of the Treaty of Waitangi. Generally, Maori land claims only relate to land owned by the Crown or Crown entities.

h) Personal Property Securities Act 1999

The Personal Property Securities Act 1999 (PPS Act) provides that priority is determined not by whom holds title to personal property but by the timing of "creation" and "perfection" of "security interests". Under the PPS Act, "personal property" is broadly defined and most assets owned or used by a business can become subject to a security interest (excluding interests in land).

The general scheme of the PPS Act is that a person looking to acquire personal property is able to search the Personal Property Securities Register (PPSR) under the name of the vendor(s) to check whether or not the property being sold is encumbered by a security interest. The PPSR is maintained and searchable online at www.ppsr.govt.nz.

Under the PPS Act, a security interest in personal property is "perfected" when the party holding the security interest registers a "financing statement" on the PPSR against the debtor.

b. Rules of Land Acquisition for Foreign Enterprises

The principal restrictions on an overseas person acquiring land in New Zealand is contained in the OI Act and the OI Regulations.

At the end of 2017, a range of changes targeted at overseas investment and the forestry industry were outlined in the new Government's Coalition Agreement. The New Zealand Government published the first of its changes aimed at strengthening the OI Act by issuing a new Directive Letter (the Directive Letter) to the OIO in December 2017. The Directive Letter acknowledges that overseas investment remains important for New Zealand's economic growth, but shifts the OIO's focus and emphasis when its considers overseas investment applications. The new Directive Letter applies to all new and existing applications from 15 December 2017.

c. Overseas Investment Amendment Bill

The Overseas Investment Amendment Bill was introduced in December 2017. The Bill proposes to change the OI Act to include "residential land" as a new category of sensitive land requiring OIO approval. Residential land will be defined by reference to a property's rating status, and will cover land classified as "residential" and "lifestyle" for rating purposes.

The Bill provides that an overseas person will still be able to buy residential land if they can pass one of the following tests:
- a commitment to reside in New Zealand test;
- an increased housing on residential land test; or
- the benefit to New Zealand test.

The Bill proposes that corporates which acquire residential land as part of their business will have to obtain OIO consent to buy residential land. This will require them to focus on the "new housing supply" test or the existing "benefit to New Zealand" test.

The Bill suggests that migrants who hold residence (as opposed to work) visas will be able to buy sensitive land provided they have lived in New Zealand for 12 months. Migrants who have applied under the investor categories are not required to have lived in New Zealand for 12 months.

E. The Establishment and Dissolution of Companies

a. The Forms of Enterprises

Business in New Zealand may be conducted through any of the following structures:
- companies (limited or unlimited);
- partnerships and limited partnerships;
- joint ventures;
- trusts; and
- sole proprietorships.

The choice of an appropriate structure will depend upon the facts, including the nature of the business or investment and the resulting tax consequences in New Zealand or otherwise. Specific advice as to the appropriate structure should be sought on a case-by-case basis.

a) Companies

The Companies Act 1993 (Companies Act) provides for the incorporation of a limited or unlimited liability company and regulates the management, operation and liquidation of companies incorporated in New Zealand. The Companies Act does not distinguish between public and private companies. The most common type of company is a company limited by shares.

Unless the constitution of a company specifies otherwise, the liability of each shareholder of a limited company is limited to the amount of share capital that the shareholder has agreed to contribute to the company. When a shareholder has paid all of the money payable on its shares, that shareholder has no additional liability to contribute to the capital of the company.

Under the Companies Act, there is no limitation on the number of shareholders a company may have, or on its ability to raise money from the public [although this process is regulated under the Financial Markets Conduct Act 2013 (FMCA)]. Commercially, companies can be classified as listed [i.e., their shares are quoted on a licensed market such as the New Zealand Exchange (NZX) Main Board or the NXT Market] or unlisted (i.e., their shares are not quoted).

See the Companies Act for details on company registration.

b) Partnerships and Limited Partnerships

Partnerships are common in certain professions in New Zealand, and are established by a partnership agreement between the partners. Limited partnerships are a form of partnership involving general partners, who are liable for all the debts and liabilities of the partnership, and limited partners, who are liable to the extent of their capital contribution to the partnership.

Limited partnerships in New Zealand are registered under the Limited Partnerships Act 2008. The registers of limited partnerships and overseas limited partnerships are administered by the New Zealand Companies Office (Companies Office). An overseas limited partnership must apply to register within 10 working days of commencing to carry on business in New Zealand.

c) Joint Ventures

Joint ventures, where two or more persons enter into a business venture together, can be incorporated or unincorporated.

d) Trusts

Trusts are popular in New Zealand as a means of protecting property and managing assets. The Trustee Act 1956 is the governing trust legislation in New Zealand.

e) Sole Proprietorships

Sole traders are individuals who start in business or contracting on their own, without registering as a company. Many small business owners, contractors and self-employed people begin as sole traders. A sole trader will pay tax on all the income they earn from their work, but will be able to claim work expenses.

b. The Procedure of Establishing a Company

To register and incorporate a company in New Zealand, an online application must be made to the Companies Office. Where a company name has been reserved, the applicant will have 20 working days to complete the incorporation application. This includes filing signed consent forms for all directors and shareholders.

Details of the company, including the address of the registered office, service and correspondence, must be provided. Tax registration options will also be available, including registering for an Inland Revenue Department (IRD) number, a Goods and Services Tax number and / or as an employer.

If a company is controlled by an ultimate holding company, the type of the holding company, its name, country of registration, registration number or code (if any) and registered office address must also be provided.

Where an application is approved by the Companies Registrar, a certificate of incorporation will be provided and the company details will become publicly available.

c. Setting Up Business in New Zealand

Overseas companies can operate in New Zealand by:
- registering a branch in New Zealand;
- incorporating a new subsidiary company under the Companies Act; or
- acquiring shares in, or entering into a joint venture with, a New Zealand company.

d. Registering a Branch

The Companies Act is also the main legislation governing overseas companies operating in New Zealand. The Companies Act requires every overseas company that "carries on business in New Zealand" to register as an overseas company under the Companies Act.

An "overseas company" is a company that is incorporated outside New Zealand. Generally, the provisions of the Companies Act relating to companies incorporated in New Zealand do not apply to overseas companies (with the exception of some of the financial reporting requirements).

An overseas company may not commence business in New Zealand unless the name of the overseas company (as it is registered in its country of incorporation) has been reserved. Once registered, it will be governed by New Zealand law.

e. Establishing a Subsidiary

A wholly owned New Zealand subsidiary, being a company controlled by an overseas holding company, can be incorporated and registered on the Companies Register in accordance with the process set down in section 8.2.

f. Routes and Requirements of Dissolution

An application to remove a company from the New Zealand Companies Register can be made either by the shareholders through a special resolution or, if permitted by the constitution of the company, by the board of directors or another person.

Before a company can be closed, its company filing requirements need to be up to date on the Companies Register. If a company is due to file audited financial statements under the Companies Act or other legislation, these must be completed before applying for the removal of a company from the Register.

When a company is dissolved or liquidated, it must fulfil its IRD filing requirements. This involves filing a tax return with up-to-date company accounts from the date the company stopped operating. A company may also have other obligations, ranging from business tax and GST payments to cancelling employer and GST registrations. Until a person or company files their final tax return, they will be deemed to have not complied with their business tax obligations (and in the case of a company will be unable to dissolve).

Before a person can apply to remove a company from the Companies Register, they must ensure that:
- the company is no longer in business;
- all business debts are paid;
- the company has distributed its assets in ways that comply with the Companies Act and its constitution (if it has one);
- there are no creditors who have taken steps to put the company into liquidation; and
- a notice of intention to remove the company has been given to any parties that have registered a financing statement over the company on the PPSR.

F. Merger and Acquisition

In New Zealand, mergers and acquisitions are governed by a variety of laws, regulations, codes and rules. However, the substance of private mergers and acquisitions is based on the terms and conditions agreed between the parties pursuant to a sale and purchase of shares / assets agreement.

a. Commerce Act

The Commerce Act 1986 (the Commerce Act) regulates mergers and acquisitions with respect to their effect on competition in the New Zealand market.

b. Mergers and Acquisitions Involving Private Companies

The Companies Act governs mergers and acquisitions at a high level, prescribing certain administrative processes for the transfer and issue of shares (e.g., such as obtaining shareholder consent and signing documentation).

c. Takeovers

Takeovers are primarily regulated by the Takeovers Code approved by the Takeovers Code Approval Order 2000 (Takeovers Code), which is enforced by the New Zealand Takeovers Panel (Takeovers Panel). It is not possible to contract out of the Takeovers Code.

The aim of the Takeovers Code is to ensure that shareholders are treated equally and, after appropriate disclosure, are able to make informed decisions on whether to accept or reject a control transaction for a "code company".

A "code company" is New Zealand-incorporated company that has, or in the last 12 months had:
• voting securities quoted on the NZSX, the NZAX or the NXT Market; or
• has 50 or more shareholders and 50 or more share parcels.

The fundamental rule in the Takeovers Code is that a party must comply with the Takeovers Code if it wishes to:
• obtain more than 20% of the voting rights in a code company; or
• increase an existing holding of 20% or more of the voting rights in a code company.

The takeover rules provide the following takeover mechanisms:

a) Off-market Takeover

An "off-market takeover" is where a bidder makes an offer to all shareholders of the target code company on the same terms in an offer document. Such offer must be conditional on the bidder receiving acceptances which will result in it holding more than 50% of the voting shares, and is often conditional on the bidder reaching 90%. Shareholders accept the offer by signing and returning their acceptance form.

Where an off-market takeover results in the bidder holding 90% of the shares in the code company, the bidder can acquire the further 10% of shares through compulsory acquisition.

b) New Issue Approval

Shareholders can approve a bidder acquiring voting securities to cross the 20% threshold or to increase an existing holding above 20% either pursuant to a new issue by the target or by acquisition from other shareholders. Neither the bidder nor its associates can vote on that transaction (nor the seller or its associates in an acquisition).

c) 5% Creep

A shareholder who already holds or controls between 50% and 90% of the voting rights in a code company is permitted to acquire up to an additional 5% in any 12-month period (based on its lowest holding at the start of that 12-month period).

d) Compulsory Acquisition

If a shareholder holds 90% or more of a code company, it can compulsorily acquire the balance.

d. Schemes of Arrangement

An alternative acquisition structure for a New Zealand listed company is a scheme of arrangement. A scheme of arrangement is where parties wishing to restructure apply to the court for its approval with the particulars of the terms of that proposed scheme.

Schemes of arrangement may be used to effect a wide range of corporate restructures including transfers of all (or a specified proportion) of shareholders' securities to a bidder, cancellations of existing securities and issues of new securities to a bidder. The nature of a scheme of arrangement enables a bidder to incorporate additional complexities into a scheme (such as the transfer or demerger of specified assets or liabilities or the reduction of a target's capital).

Schemes of arrangement invariably proceed on a friendly rather than hostile basis, with targets and bidders entering into a formal implementation agreement setting out the terms upon which a scheme will be proposed to security holders and supported by a target's directors.

a) Process

The target company, a shareholder or a creditor can apply to the court under a scheme of arrangement. However, because of the central role of the target and its board in convening the meeting of its security holders, it is generally considered essential for a scheme to be proposed and supported by the target company. The court has broad powers to sanction, amend or reject a scheme of arrangement. A court may reject a scheme of arrangement if it considers the scheme will potentially prejudice security holders, creditors or other parties, even if the requisite levels of security holder approval have been obtained at the scheme meeting.

A scheme has an "all or nothing" outcome, and a bidder will have the certainty of knowing that it will either acquire 100% control if successful, or nothing if it is not successful. Any order that a court makes is binding on the company and any other person (e.g., shareholders and creditors) that the court thinks fit.

As with takeover offers, schemes of arrangement can be made conditional upon the occurrence or non-occurrence of specified events or circumstances. It is common for schemes to be proposed subject to the receipt of necessary regulatory approvals, or there being no material adverse change in the financial position of the target.

b) Subject to Shareholder Approval

Where a court-approved scheme of arrangement would affect the voting rights in a listed company (or any other code company), the scheme requires:

• approval by 75% of the votes cast by shareholders in each interest class entitled to vote and voting and approval by a simple majority of the votes of shareholders entitled to vote; and

• either the Takeovers Panel must issue a "no objection statement" or the target company must satisfy the court that its shareholders will not be adversely affected by the transaction being undertaken by way of scheme rather than takeover.

G. Competition Regulation

a. Department Supervising Competition Regulation

The Commerce Act governs commercial competition in the New Zealand market. The Commerce Commission (Commission) is New Zealand's primary competition regulatory body that oversees compliance with the Commerce Act, including investigating potential breaches (either present or future) of the Commerce Act, undertaking decision-making exercises relating to proposed mergers and acquisitions, identifying and investigating anti-competitive practices and educating the public on the Commerce Act.

b. Brief Introduction of Competition Law

Competition law in New Zealand is focused on promoting competition in markets for the long-term benefit of consumers within New Zealand. To this effect, the Commerce Act prohibits the acquisition of the shares or the assets of a business if that acquisition would have, or would be likely to have, the effect of "substantially lessening competition in a market". In other words, is the acquisition likely to result in an increase of the market power of the purchaser? The only exception to this prohibition is where the public benefits resulting from the acquisition outweigh the detriment that results from the lessening of competition in the market.

a) The "Market"

Whether an acquisition has the effect of "substantially lessening competition in a market" firstly requires a determination of what the market of the goods and services is. Determining the market is a technical exercise that includes the analysis of the product / service, the geographical area being serviced by the product / service, the functional level of the good / service (e.g., manufacture, wholesale, retail etc.) and the consumer dimension and time.

At a high level, the market will be those goods / services that are substitutable with the goods / services being acquired. Goods / services will generally be substitutes to one another if consumers would switch to the other good / service if there was a small increase in the price of the particular good / service. For example, if there is a small increase in the price of butter and consumers switch to margarine, butter and margarine will be deemed to be in the same market.

b) The Likely Effect of the Acquisition

Secondly, the likely impact of the acquisition on competition in the market must be assessed. If the impact of the acquisition is likely to increase the market power of the acquirer in a substantial manner, it will likely be prohibited.

c) Concentration Indicators

The Commission has published "concentration indicators" based on market shares that are a preliminary guideline as to whether an acquisition will be likely to be prohibited. For example, in the Commission's view, an acquisition is unlikely to breach the Commerce Act:

• where the combined market share of the three largest firms is below 70% and the market share of the company once it has acquired the other company is less than 40%; or

• where the combined market share of the three largest firms is above 70% and the market share of the company once it has acquired the other company is less than 20%.

d) Other Considerations

Even if an acquisition falls outside the concentration indicators, it still may not substantially lessen competition in the relevant market. For example, if there are low barriers to entry or expansion in the market or there is limited or no opportunity for co-ordinated behaviour between market participants (such as limited opportunities for collusion and discipline in the market), the acquisition may still be permissible.

e) Public Benefit

In limited circumstances, an acquisition may proceed even where the effect of the acquisition is likely to substantially lessen competition in a market if the benefit to the public is likely to outweigh the detrimental effect on the market. The public benefit requirement is a high standard, not often successfully relied upon.

c. Measures Regulating Competition

a) Breach of the Commerce Act

The Commission monitors and investigates acquisitions to ensure there is no breach of the Commerce Act. Any member of the public, including a company, can make a complaint to the Commission if it feels that the Commerce Act has been breached.

b) Seeking Clearance or Authorisation from the Commission

There is no compulsory requirement to notify the Commission of acquisitions. Instead, businesses can voluntarily submit proposed acquisitions to the Commission for review. This is the recommended course of action if there is the possibility that the acquisition will breach the Commerce Act as it prevents issues post-completion of the acquisition.

The Commission will provide "clearance" to an acquisition if it is satisfied that it does not breach the Commerce Act – either because it is unlikely to have the effect of substantially lessening competition in a market or the public benefit outweighs the lessening of competition in the market. Such clearance is publicised and accessible to the public. The statutory timeframe for the Commission to make a decision is 10 working days. However, this period may be extended at the Commission's request, and recent experience suggests a period of at least 40 to 60 working days should be provided for.

If an acquisition proceeds in accordance with a clearance or authorisation within 12 months from the date on which it is issued, the acquisition is protected from challenge under the Commerce Act by either the Commission or a third party.

H. Tax

a. Tax Regime and Rules

The Income Tax Act 2007 governs tax in New Zealand. Income tax for individual and corporate taxpayers is levied on annual gross income from all sources, less annual total deductions and any losses carried forward. This net amount is the taxable income. "Gross income" includes items that would be regarded as income in commercial terms, including all gains on financial instruments and short-term or planned profits on land or share transactions. Allowable deductions are all expenses incurred in deriving the income or in carrying on business for the purpose of deriving income. Individuals, companies and trusts are subject to different taxing regimes.

Different tax rates and rules apply to resident and non-resident companies, individuals and trusts. An overview of these rates, and additional taxation rules applying to these entities, is provided below.

There is no capital gains tax in New Zealand. However, some transactions, which could be capital in nature, are subject to tax. These include:

• particular sales of land and personal property;
• gains on any financial arrangement, including forgiveness of debt; and
• a specified percentage of the value of certain foreign investments owned by New Zealand residents (in some cases annual increases in the value of such investments are taxable).

b. Main Categories and Rates of Tax

a) Corporate Income Tax
(i) Company Tax Rates
To be subject to tax in New Zealand, a corporate entity must be:
• resident in New Zealand, in which case their worldwide income is taxable in New Zealand;
• non-resident in New Zealand but deriving income from a source in New Zealand, in which case it is taxed on the income it derives in New Zealand; or
• non-resident in New Zealand, not deriving income from a source in New Zealand, but is considered to be under the control of New Zealand residents, in which case the New Zealand residents may be taxed on the passive income of that foreign entity.

The corporate income tax rate is 28%. To ensure that overseas-owned companies pay the appropriate level of tax on their New Zealand-sourced profits, a transfer pricing regime exists.

Where applicable, New Zealand allows a tax credit for foreign tax paid equal to the lesser of that foreign tax paid and the New Zealand income tax payable on the relevant portion of the total income. These rules may be modified by the application of particular Double Tax Agreements (DTAs) that New Zealand has with other countries.

Partnerships, including limited partnerships, are not taxed in their own right but individual partners are taxed on their share of partnership income.

Where a non-resident company operates a branch in New Zealand, it is subject to tax on branch profits at the rate of 28%. No withholding tax is imposed on profits remitted by a branch operation to its non-resident head office or on dividends paid by that head office to the company's shareholders.

(ii) Dividends

New Zealand has a full dividend imputation system under which tax paid by New Zealand-resident companies can be allocated as imputation credits to dividends paid to shareholders. New Zealand-resident shareholders are able to offset these imputation credits against their tax liability in respect of those dividends.

Depending on a non-resident's percentage interest in the New Zealand-resident company, these imputation credits may either reduce the rate of non-resident withholding tax on some or all of the dividend to 0%, or reduce non-resident withholding tax otherwise payable on dividends. Fully imputed dividends paid to non-residents can be effectively paid free of non-resident withholding tax.

Where a New Zealand resident company receives dividends from a foreign company, the dividend is usually exempt from New Zealand tax.

(iii) Thin Capitalisation Rules

There are also thin capitalisation rules for foreign-controlled (e.g., 50% or more ownership) companies operating in New Zealand. These rules also apply to all types of trusts, where 50% or more of the trust's settlements are made by non-residents. Generally, interest will be fully deductible where the debt-to-asset ratio does not exceed 60%.

(iv) Carrying forward tax losses

When certain conditions are met, a company can carry forward its tax losses and set them off against future taxable income. To maintain the right to carry forward losses, a continuity of ownership test must be satisfied. The test requires:

• New Zealand resident companies to maintain 66% commonality of ownership; and

• non-resident companies to maintain 49% commonality of ownership,

from the beginning of the year in which the loss was incurred to the end of the year in which the loss is offset against taxable income.

b) Personal Income Tax

(i) Individuals that are taxed

New Zealand residents are taxed on their worldwide income. Non-residents are liable to New Zealand tax only on income deemed to be derived from New Zealand. Individuals will be "resident in New Zealand" for tax purposes if:

• they have a permanent place of abode in New Zealand, whether or not they have any permanent place of abode outside New Zealand (in general terms, a permanent place of abode is a fixed or habitual home);

• they are physically present in New Zealand for more than 183 days in aggregate in any 12-month period; or

• they are absent from New Zealand in the service of the New Zealand government.

In most situations, if an individual is resident in more than one country at the same time, DTAs will determine the country that the person will be deemed "resident" for tax purposes.

Individuals on short-stay secondments may be exempt from New Zealand tax if:

• they are not personally present in New Zealand for more than 183 days in aggregate in any 12-month period;

• their overseas employer is resident in a country with which New Zealand has a DTA; and

• their remuneration is not borne by the non-resident's place of business in New Zealand.

Where New Zealand does not have a DTA with the employer's country of residence, the individual cannot be in New Zealand for more than 92 days in aggregate in any 12-month period if they wish to remain exempt from New Zealand tax.

(ii) Tax rates for individuals

New Zealand has a tiered tax rate system whereby the amount of tax is dependent on the income derived by that individual.

The tax rates are as follows:

Income Amount	Rate of Tax
NZ$0 to NZ$14,000	10.5%
NZ$14,001 to NZ$48,000	17.5%
NZ$48,001 to NZ$70,000	30%
NZ$70,001 or more	33%

New Zealand also has a "new migrants" tax regime, which effectively exempts new migrants who become New Zealand tax residents from tax on their foreign sourced income (other than employment income) for a four year period. However, New Zealand sourced income is taxable during this period.

An attribution rule is in place to ensure that, in defined circumstances, the income from the personal services of an individual is attributed to that individual, rather than being diverted to an associated person that pays tax at a lower rate (such as a company that is taxed at 28%).

c) Income Derived from Trusts

Income derived by trusts is separated into trustee and beneficiary income. Trustee income is defined to mean all income derived by a trustee other than income distributed to beneficiaries as beneficiary income. Income retained by the trust and taxed as trustee income is taxed at the rate of 33%.

Beneficiary income is income that is distributed in the same income year in which it is derived by the trust, or within the later of six months from the end of that income year and the date by which the trustee files (or should have filed) the income tax return for the income year. Beneficiary income is taxed at the particular rate of tax applying to the beneficiary concerned. Income of minor beneficiaries is taxed at a flat rate of 33%.

Foreign trusts are also subject to New Zealand tax rules if the settlor is resident in New Zealand. Taxable distributions from certain foreign trusts (i.e., non-complying trusts) are taxed at a penal rate of 45%, so as to discourage New Zealand resident settlors from diverting what would otherwise be taxable income. Non-resident beneficiaries of foreign trusts are only taxed on income derived from New Zealand.

d) Non-resident Withholding Tax

(i) Rates

Dividends, interest and royalties paid by a New Zealand resident company to non-residents are subject to non-resident withholding tax (NRWT). NRWT is levied at the following rates:

Income Type	Rate of Tax
Dividends	30%
	15% for fully imputed dividends derived from portfolio holdings (i.e., less than 10%); or
	0% for fully imputed dividends derived from non-portfolio holdings
Interest	15%
Royalties	15%

Where a payment is made by a New Zealand resident company to a non-resident contractor, non-resident contractors tax (NRCT) must be withheld, at the rate of 15% of the payments. NRCT is an interim liability and the non-resident must lodge a tax return to determine its final tax liability. Credit will be given for any NRCT withheld. The Inland Revenue Department will issue an exemption from this liability if, for example, by operation of a DTA no New Zealand tax is ultimately payable. An exemption can also be obtained if the non-resident posts a bond or demonstrates that it has at least two years' tax compliance without default.

(ii) Additional nuances

NRWT on dividends, cultural royalties and interest paid to a non-associated person is a final tax on that income. In other cases, NRWT is a minimum tax in which case the recipient must file a New Zealand tax return in respect of the income received. Expenses attributable to that income are deductible and the balance of income is then subject to tax at standard rates.

If a non-resident owns less than 10% of the shares in a New Zealand company that pays a fully imputed dividend, a supplementary dividend can be paid by the company. This effectively refunds the 15% NRWT payable on the dividend.

If interest is payable on debt which is registered under the Approved Issuer Regime, an approved issuer levy equal to 2% of the interest payable by the borrower can be paid in lieu of NRWT. In certain circumstances in respect of widely-held bonds, this levy will be reduced to 0%. The approved issuer regime only applies where loans are between non-associated parties and those loans are not otherwise treated as related party debt.

e) Tax Obligations of Employers

(i) General obligations

Employers must deduct PAYE tax (pay as you earn) from payments of wages or salaries made to employees. PAYE is deducted on account of the employee's final tax liability for an income year. The employee is able to obtain a refund, or may be required to pay additional tax depending on the amount deducted.

New Zealand has an accident compensation and rehabilitation insurance scheme, ACC, which abrogates the right to sue for damages for accidental injuries. Both the employer and employee must pay a levy towards this compensation scheme. Employees pay an earners' premium which is currently 1.45% of earnings per annum. The employer levy is calculated on the total salaries paid to employees. The maximum levied earnings per employee is NZ$118,191. Different industries have different employer levy rates.

(ii) Fringe Benefit Tax

Employers who provide non-cash benefits to employees by reason of employment pay Fringe Benefit Tax (FBT). These benefits include company vehicles, low-interest loans and subsidised goods. FBT is payable quarterly at the rate of 49.25%, 42.86%, 21.21% or 11.73% (depending on the employee's marginal tax rate) on the taxable value of fringe benefits provided to employees during the relevant calendar quarter. FBT is deductible, resulting in a maximum after-tax expense to the employer of 33%.

Employers have the option of paying FBT for the first three-quarters of the income year at either a 49.25% flat rate or a 42.86% rate on all fringe benefits provided. There is an adjustment in the fourth quarter for attributed fringe benefits, with the FBT rate based on the marginal tax rate of the employee to whom the benefits have been attributed.

(iii) Superannuation (KiwiSaver)

Any contributions made by an employer to a registered superannuation scheme is deductible to the employer but subject to a withholding tax levied at the rate of 10.5%, 17.5%, 30% or 33% depending on the employee's annual salary or wages.

Schemes that are retirement schemes under the FMCA are treated as trusts for tax purposes. Earnings of the scheme are generally taxed at the rate of 28% and benefits paid to beneficiaries are currently exempt, whether they are in the form of a lump sum or a pension. Employers must deduct KiwiSaver employee contributions from payments of wages and salaries made to employees who are members of a KiwiSaver scheme (unless the employee is taking a contribution holiday). Existing employees may opt into KiwiSaver at any time. New employees are automatically enrolled in KiwiSaver but may opt out within a specified time period.

Employers must also make a compulsory employer KiwiSaver contribution. KiwiSaver employer contributions, or contributions to a complying superannuation fund made by an employer, are deductible to the employer and are subject to the withholding tax described above.

f) Goods and Services Tax (GST)

GST is charged at a rate of 15% on the supply of most goods and services. The supply of financial services and the supply of residential rental accommodation are the principal exemptions from GST. GST is intended to be borne by the final consumer of goods and services.

Businesses are able to register for GST and claim a credit for any GST they incur in conducting their business (input credits) while charging GST on their sales (output tax). Where output tax exceeds input credits, the difference is payable to the IRD. Conversely, where the credit claimed on inputs exceeds the GST payable on outputs, the IRD refunds the difference.

GST is charged on exported goods and the provision of services to non-residents at 0%, provided certain criteria are satisfied. GST is levied by New Zealand Customs at 15% on all goods imported into New Zealand.

Certain supplies of land are charged with GST at a rate of 0%. Certain supplies of business-to-business financial services (among other goods and services) are also charged with GST at a rate of 0%, as opposed to being exempt from GST. A reverse charge mechanism means that certain supplies of imported services give rise to a charge, in respect of GST, levied on the importer.

A person can register for GST provided that they conduct or intend to conduct a taxable activity. A taxable activity is any activity carried on continuously or regularly involving the supply of goods and services to another person for money or money's worth. Registration is compulsory when taxable supplies made in New Zealand have exceeded or are likely to exceed NZ$60,000 in any 12-month period.

GST is imposed at a rate of 15% on the supply of remote services by non-residents to private New Zealand consumers, if the value of the non-resident's New Zealand supplies exceeds NZ$60,000 per annum. These rules apply to supplies of digital content and other digital services provided cross border into New Zealand. However,

GST is not imposed on supplies of remote services by non-residents to GST registered persons that use those services in the course of their taxable activity.

All GST-registered entities are required to file regular returns of the GST collected by them. In most situations, returns are made every two months. Where supplies are in excess of NZ$24 million per annum, returns are required monthly.

c. Tax Declaration and Preferences

Taxpayers are required to comply voluntarily with the New Zealand tax system. They are encouraged to make honest and accurate returns of income. Taxpayers will generally make an annual return of income for a year ended 31 March. The exception to this balance date is where the taxpayer (other than an individual) is given approval by the IRD to adopt a different balance date for business reasons.

Taxpayers who are required to file tax returns must disclose all income liable to tax in their New Zealand income tax returns. Taxpayers must also disclose certain inter-related financial arrangements. There are also requirements to disclose interests in controlled foreign companies, foreign investment funds and foreign trusts.

Individuals who derive their income from salary or wages that have been subject to the correct deductions under the PAYE rules are not generally required to file annual tax returns. There are exceptions for individuals who earn over a de minimis threshold amount of income from other sources, including interest and dividends.

I. Securities

a. Securities-Related Laws and Regulations

The FMCA and the Financial Markets Conduct Regulations 2014 (FMC Regulations) govern securities in New Zealand.

There are both criminal and civil consequences for breaches of the disclosure obligations in the FMCA.

a) Issuing Financial Products

The FMCA and the FMC Regulations regulate all offers of financial products in New Zealand, whether or not the financial products are issued by a New Zealand issuer or an overseas issuer. The term "financial products" is very broad and covers debt, equity, managed investment products and derivatives.

Generally, issuers of financial products are required to provide prospective investors with a product disclosure statement (PDS) to allow them to make an informed decision about the investment, unless a relevant exclusion applies to the offer.

The content, format and length of a PDS for a regulated offer are prescribed by the FMCA and the FMC Regulations, and must be tailored to the particular type of financial products being offered. Material information relating to the offer that is not required to be in the PDS must be lodged on an online offer register (the Disclose Register) together with the PDS.

There are some exemptions under the FMCA which do not require issuers to provide a PDS. These include:

• offers to wholesale investors, which includes a person whose principal business is an "investment business", a person who is "large" or a person who is subscribing to an offer of NZ$750,000 or more;

• offers to "close business associates"; and

• "small offers", where debt or equity securities are being offered to no more than 20 investors in a 12-month period, raising less than NZ$2 million.

The FMCA has a reasonably flexible approach to the promotion of regulated offers. However, there are some specific rules that apply to advertisements both before and after a PDS has been lodged on the Disclose Register. The FMCA also contains restrictions on unsolicited offers of financial products.

Issuers of regulated offers of debt securities or managed investment products must comply with governance and licensing obligations under the FMCA.

b) Listing on a Market

In New Zealand there are three principal markets for trading financial products:

• NZX Main Board (NZSX): this is New Zealand's principal market for equity securities. It is designed for large and established companies, and carries the most stringent admission and continuing obligations requirements;

• NXT Market: this is a lower cost market designed for small to medium sized companies worth between NZ$10 million to NZ$100 million; and

• NZX Debt Market (the NZDX): a range of investment debt securities, such as corporate and government bonds and fixed income securities, are listed on the NZDX.

A company that wishes to be listed and to have its securities quoted on the markets operated by the NZX must apply (through an organising broker) to the NZX for listing. Before a company is listed, it must agree to comply with the listing rules of the relevant NZX market (NZX Listing Rules).

Overseas companies can have a primary listing on the NZX by meeting the same requirements that apply to New Zealand incorporated companies. In certain situations, a company which is already listed on a "recognised" overseas exchange can also list on the NZX as a "Dual Listed Issuer" or an "Overseas Listed Issuer". Dual listed companies are required to comply with the NZX Listing Rules and the rules applicable to the overseas exchange. Overseas Listed Issuers must comply primarily with the rules of their home exchanges and are exempt from most of the NZX Listing Rules.

c) Disclosure of Substantial Shareholdings in Listed Companies

Under the FMCA, if an investor directly or indirectly acquires 5% or more of the shares in a company whose shares are quoted on the NZSX or NZAX, the investor must file a substantial product holder notice in the prescribed form with the company concerned and with the NZX. The notice must include information about the investor and the shares in which it has the interest. After a substantial product holder notice is filed, public disclosure of changes in the investor's shareholding equal to 1% or more of the total shares on issue is also required. A notice given to the NZX will be available to the public through the NZX website.

b. Supervision and Regulation of Securities Market

The FMCA and the FMC Regulations are supervised by the Financial Markets Authority (FMA). Consequentially, the FMA is responsible for enforcing securities, financial reporting and company law as they apply to financial services and securities markets and regulating securities exchanges, financial advisers and brokers, auditors, trustees and issuers.

c. Requirements for Engagement in Securities Trading for Foreign Enterprises

Foreign enterprises will be subject to the FMCA and the FMC Regulations in undertaking any securities trading in New Zealand.

Overseas issuers may be exempt from the requirement in the FMCA to issue a PDS. Potential exclusions include where the offer is:

- part of the consideration for a takeover bid or scheme of arrangement; or
- to existing New Zealand security holders (e.g., under a rights issue or an entitlement offer).

However, even where one of these exclusions applies, the issuer may still have specific obligations which it must comply with under the FMCA and the FMC Regulations, including that any document or other conduct in relation to the offer must not be misleading or deceptive or contain any false statements.

J. Preference and Protection of Investment

a. The Structure of Preference Policies

New Zealand does not have any official preference policies. However, there are agreements between New Zealand and Australia that facilitate Australian investment in New Zealand. An example of this is the thresholds prescribed under the OI Act for the acquisition of "significant business assets". Where an Australian non-government investor is the purchaser, the monetary threshold is higher.

New Zealand also has several fair trade agreements (FTA) in place and recently become a signatory to the Comprehensive and Progressive Agreement on the Trans-Pacific Partnership (CPTPP).

b. Support for Specific Industries and Regions

New Zealand does not provide incentives for people to invest in approved activities or in specific geographic areas. The New Zealand Government believes that overseas investors will be attracted to New Zealand because of sound, consistent economic policies, good rates of economic growth and a stable political system.

c. Special Economic Areas

There are no domestic free trade zones or similar economic areas that encourage overseas investment.

d. Investment Protection

a) Closer economic relations between New Zealand and Australia

New Zealand and Australia have an agreement prescribing closer economic relations (the CER) and a free trade zone between the two countries. The CER is widely recognised as the most comprehensive bilateral FTA in the world. One of the key outcomes from the CER was that both New Zealand and Australian investors now have more certainty that their investments will be protected.

b) WTO, APEC and ASEAN FTAs

New Zealand is active in promoting free trade at international bodies such as the World Trade Organisation, Asia-Pacific Economic Co-operation and Association of South East Asian Nations (ASEAN). The FTA between New Zealand, Australia and Association of South East Asian Nations (AANZFTA) promotes free trade between

New Zealand, Australia, Brunei, Cambodia, Indonesia, Laos, Malaysia, Myanmar, Philippines, Singapore, Thailand and Vietnam.

The AANZFTA also provides for a range of investment protection measures and binding investor-state arbitration procedures, which results in better security and protection for investors in ASEAN economies.

c) China, Malaysia, and Korea FTAs

New Zealand has entered into bilateral FTA's with China, Malaysia and the Republic of Korea. Each of these FTAs offers protection for investors, to ensure a more certain investment environment.[①]

Specifically, in relation to China, goods exports from New Zealand to China have quadrupled since the FTA was signed and entered into force in 2008. China is now New Zealand's second-largest trading partner, with two-way trade valued at over NZ$22 billion in 2016. This is made up of NZ$12.3 billion in exports (NZ$9.4 billion in goods and NZ$2.9 billion in services), and NZ$10.5 billion in imports (NZ$10 billion in goods and NZ$538 million in services).[②]

In recent years, China has risen to become New Zealand's ninth-largest source of foreign direct investment. Tourism, education and other people-to-people links between the two countries have also grown strongly.[③]

d) CPTPP

The CPTPP increases preferential market access between 11 countries—New Zealand, Australia, Canada, Chile, Brunei, Japan, Malaysia, Mexico, Singapore, Peru and Vietnam. It covers a range of matters, including goods and services market access, labour laws, environmental policies, intellectual property protection and pharmaceutical regulations.

III. Trade

A. Department Supervising Trade

The regulatory body responsible for the enforcement of trade legislation in New Zealand is the Commerce Commission.

B. Brief Introduction of Trade Laws and Regulations

The key pieces of trade legislation that may be relevant to the day-to-day operations of a business include the:
- Fair Trading Act 1986;
- Consumer Guarantees Act 1993;
- Privacy Act 1993;
- Contract and Commercial Law Act 2017;
- Unsolicited Electronic Messages Act 2007; and
- Harmful Digital Communications Act 2015.

All New Zealand legislation is available online at www.legislation.govt.nz.

C. Trade Management

The broad areas which each of the relevant pieces of trade legislation cover are described below.

• The Fair Trading Act 1986 is consumer protection legislation and contains broad provisions prohibiting conduct and representations which are likely to mislead or deceive consumers. It is not possible for a business to contract out of its obligations under this Act, other than certain sections where both of the parties are "in trade" (and the contracting out must be fair and reasonable). The Fair Trading Act also prohibits unfair contract terms in standard form consumer contracts.

• The Consumer Guarantees Act 1993 is also consumer protection legislation and it contains a number of obligations on both suppliers and manufacturers in relation to goods or services which are ordinarily purchased for personal or household use. The Consumer Guarantees Act sets out a number of statutory "guarantees" that the goods or services must comply with including as to title, acceptable quality, compliance with a description /

---

① New Zealand-Malaysia Free Trade Agreement (New Zealand Ministry of Foreign Affairs and Trade) and New Zealand-China Free Trade Agreement (New Zealand Ministry of Foreign Affairs and Trade), and New Zealand-Korea FTA Guide (New Zealand Ministry of Foreign Affairs and Trade, January 2015).
② https://www.mfat.govt.nz/en/trade/free-trade-agreements/free-trade-agreements-in-force/nz-china-free-trade-agreement.
③ https://www.mfat.govt.nz/en/trade/free-trade-agreements/free-trade-agreements-in-force/nz-china-free-trade-agreement.

sample, price and fitness for purpose. It is not possible for businesses to contract out of this Act unless the goods or services have been purchased for "business purposes" (and the contracting out must be fair and reasonable).

• The Privacy Act 1993 protects individuals where personal information about them is collected by a business. The Privacy Act sets out various obligations on businesses, including regarding how personal information may be collected, used and processed and how (and for how long) personal information may be stored. The Privacy Act also provides individuals with the right to access, and correct, personal information that a business may hold about them. All businesses in New Zealand collecting personal information about identifiable individuals need to have processes in place to comply with this Act.

• The Contract and Commercial Law Act 2017covers a number of technical matters, including the formation of contracts, specific provisions relating to sale of goods (including giving effect to the United Nations Convention on Contracts for the International Sale of Goods), electronic transactions, the carriage of goods and other commercial matters.

• The Unsolicited Electronic Messages Act 2007prohibits the sending of unsolicited commercial electronic messages with a New Zealand link (eg the computer, server or device that accesses the message is located in New Zealand, or the recipient is in New Zealand) unless the recipient has consented to the receipt of those messages. Commercial electronic messages must also include accurate sender information and a functioning unsubscribe facility.

• The Harmful Digital Communications Act 2015 regulates the sending of harmful digital communications (broadly being communications designed to cause serious emotional distress).

There is no requirement for a foreign entity to have a presence in New Zealand prior to commencing business in the country. An overseas investor and its New Zealand business are subject to the same regulations and legislation that apply to New Zealand investors and to their companies and businesses.

Industry specific consumer law may also apply, such as obligations relating to consumer credit contracts under the Credit Contracts and Consumer Finance Act 2003.

D. The Inspection and Quarantine of Import and Export Commodities

a. Import

Importers must get all shipments of business and commercial goods cleared by Customs and approved by the Ministry for Primary Industry. Importers must submit an electronic import entry or electronic cargo entry, and pay all relevant fees and taxes. Some goods, including agricultural products, chemicals, foods, medicines and unsafe goods may require additional import permits or registrations with other Government departments, or may be banned entirely (see https://www.customs.govt.nz/business/import/prohibited-and-restricted-imports/prohibitions-and-restrictions / for a list of such items). Goods or containers may need to be inspected or treated before they can be 'cleared' for entry into New Zealand.

b. Export

Exporters must get all shipments of business and commercial goods cleared by Customs. Exporters must submit an electronic export entry or electronic cargo information, and pay all relevant fees and taxes. Some goods, including wildlife, chemicals, some agricultural products and hazardous waste / chemicals may require additional export permits or registrations with other Government departments, or may be banned entirely (see https://www.customs.govt.nz/business/export/prohibitions-and-restrictions/ for a list of such items).

E. Customs Management

a. Laws

Customs rules in New Zealand are created by the Chief Executive / Comptroller under the Customs and Excise Act 1996. All such rules can be found at https://www.customs.govt.nz/about-us/legislation/customs-rules/. Tariffs are imposed under the Tariff Act 1988.

b.Tariffs

Most goods imported into New Zealand have no import tariffs. Tariffs of five percent apply to some imported goods that are also made in New Zealand including textiles, processed foods, machinery, steel, and plastic products.

New Zealand is a signatory to the International Convention on the Harmonized Commodity Description and Coding System Nomenclature, commonly known as the Harmonised System Tariff, which is enacted by the Tariff Act 1988.

New Zealand is a member of the General Agreement on Tariffs and Trade and is a signatory to the World

Trade Organisation's agreements on technical barriers to trade, subsidies and countervailing duties, anti-dumping, customs valuation and intellectual property.

c. Free Trade Agreements

New Zealand has strong trade relationships with Asia, the Pacific, the Americas and the European Union.

Significantly, in April 2008 New Zealand became the first country to negotiate a free trade agreement with China, and negotiations to "upgrade" that agreement commenced in April 2017.

New Zealand is also a party to the following free trade agreements and economic partnerships:
- ASEAN-Australia-New Zealand Free Trade Agreement (2010);
- New Zealand-Malaysia Free Trade Agreement (2010);
- Closer Economic Partnership with Hong Kong (2011); and
- New Zealand-Korea Free Trade Agreement (2014).

New Zealand is currently in the process of negotiating free trade agreements with:
- 10 countries (Australia, Brunei, Canada, Chile, Japan, Malaysia, Mexico, Peru, Singapore and Vietnam) in the Comprehensive and Progressive Agreement for Trans-Pacific Partnership in Chile on 9 March 2018;
- 16 countries (being the 10 ASEAN countries along with Australia, China, India, Japan, Korea, and New Zealand) in the Regional Comprehensive Economic Partnership;
- India;
- the European Union;
- Russia, Belarus and Kazakhstan; and
- all members of the Pacific Islands Forum (being Australia, Cook Islands, Federated States of Micronesia, Fiji, Kiribati, Nauru, New Zealand, Niue, Palau, Papua New Guinea, Republic of Marshall Islands, Samoa, Solomon Islands, Tonga, Tuvalu, Vanuatu) in the Pacific Agreement on Closer Economic Relations.

d. Customs Management and Procedures

Please see section D above in respect of importing into New Zealand.

In addition, New Zealand has a Mutual Recognition Agreements with the General Administration of China Customs. This means that each country recognises each other's supply chain security programme, providing approved exporters with a market advantage through swifter processing with fewer border checks, and priority in trade recovery situations.

The Joint Electronic Verification System has also been developed by New Zealand Customs in partnership with China Customs. This system accelerates clearance of New Zealand exports by electronically providing relevant information to China.

IV. Labour

A. Brief Introduction of Labour Laws and Regulations

Employment law in New Zealand is governed by a number of statutes and by common law. The Employment Relations Act 2000 is the central piece of industrial legislation, and requires all parties to employment relationships (including employees, employers and unions) to deal with each other in good faith.

In addition, the Health and Safety at Work Act 2015 is New Zealand's workplace health and safety law.

B. Requirements of Employing Foreign Employees

a. Work Permit

a) There are three major categories of visas:

(i) Open work visas, including:
- Working Holiday Scheme–holders can work full-time, but cannot take up a permanent role. Some countries have stricter restrictions applied to their citizens.
- Student visa–holders may usually work for a maximum of 20 hours each week, though some may work full time during major holiday breaks.
- Partnership visas–partners of visa holders with work rights may be eligible to work for the duration of their partner's visa (or for up to two years for partners of resident visa holders or New Zealand citizens).
- Post Study work visa–open visa–allows former international students to work for any employer for 12 months to give them time to find a job relevant to their qualification.

(ii) Employer Supported work visas: these visas are tied to specific jobs and have a set duration. Common types include Work to Residence visas, Essential Skills Work Visa, Recognised Seasonal Employer Limited Visa, Specific Purpose Work Visa, and Post Study Work Visa - Employer Assisted. To remain in New Zealand, the visa holder must apply for a new visa before their current visa expires.

(iii) Residence visas: residence visa holders are able to work for any New Zealand employer. Common types of residence visa include the Skilled Migrant, Investor, Family and Pacific Quota categories.

In general, before recruiting offshore, a New Zealand employer will be required to first offer the role to a New Zealand citizen or resident who can do the job or be readily trained to do it. The only exceptions are if:

• an employer is an Accredited Employer with Immigration New Zealand and employs a migrant worker under the Talent (Accredited Employer) Work Visa criteria; or

• the occupation is on one of the Essential Skills in Demand Lists and the applicant meets the qualification and/or work experience requirements of the list.

An employer can hire migrant candidates already in New Zealand with open work visas, such as Working Holiday Work Visas, or international students with permission to work, without advertising locally.

b) Skills Shortages

The Long Term Skill Shortage List (LTSSL) identifies occupations where there is a sustained shortage of highly skilled workers throughout New Zealand. If the job an employer is recruiting for is on the LTSSL, the employer is not required to provide evidence of its attempts to recruit a New Zealand citizen or resident. If the migrant worker is qualified for the job and meets the requirements specified for that occupation, they may be granted either an Essential Skills Work Visa or a LTSSL Work Visa. If they apply for a Work to Residence visa, they can apply for residence after two years.

The Immediate Skill Shortage List (ISSL) is regionally based and identifies occupations for which there is a skill shortage within a region. This makes it easier to support a work visa as an employer is not required to provide evidence of its attempts to recruit a New Zealand citizen or resident.

If the job an employer is recruiting for is on the ISSL, and its migrant worker meets the requirements specified for that occupation, they may be granted an Essential Skills Work Visa. This means that they are permitted to work in New Zealand temporarily.

The Canterbury Skill Shortage List (CSSL) contains occupations in critical shortage in the Canterbury region. It includes skill shortages in occupations relevant to the Canterbury rebuild. If the job an employer is recruiting for appears on the CSSL and is located in Canterbury, its migrant worker may be granted an Essential Skills Work Visa.

c) Quota

At any one time, a total of 1000 citizens of the People's Republic of China can work in New Zealand in certain occupations under the China Skilled Workers Instructions, with up to 100 places available for each occupation. Such persons must have a genuine New Zealand job offer in that occupation and meet normal requirements relating to health and character. The current list of relevant occupations can be found at https://www.immigration.govt.nz/new-zealand-visas/apply-for-a-visa/about-visa/china-skilled-workers-visa.

b. Application Procedures

Note that overseas candidates for a job do not need a visa to be able to apply for, or be offered, a job. However, in many cases, candidates must have a job offer to support their visa application.

c. Social Insurance

a) Accident Compensation Scheme

New Zealand's Accident Compensation Scheme (ACC) provides comprehensive, no-fault personal injury cover for all New Zealand residents and visitors to New Zealand. It covers physical injuries sustained in New Zealand (by residents or non-residents) or sustained overseas (by persons ordinarily resident in New Zealand).

If the injury falls within the scope of "personal injury" it will be covered by ACC. However, injuries caused "wholly or substantially by gradual process, disease, or infection" are specifically excluded unless they are work-related, a treatment injury, or consequential on personal injury for which the person has cover, or are caused by treatment given for a personal injury.

The key feature of the ACC regime is that, if the personal injury is covered by ACC, the claimant is barred from suing for compensatory damages.

b) Employer's Obligations

An employer's main financial obligations under the ACC regime are the payment of levies in respect of every employee to cover the cost of work accidents and the payment of 80% of wages for the first week an employee has off work as a result of a work-related personal injury.

An employer is required to pay a levy, at a rate determined by the amount of earnings paid, estimated to be paid, or deemed to have been paid by that employer to its employees. Self-employed persons, independent contractors and private domestic workers must also pay a levy.

Unemployment insurance is not compulsory in New Zealand.

KiwiSaver is a voluntary superannuation scheme that all employers must offer to their employees. The scheme is governed by the KiwiSaver Act 2006. Under the scheme, employees who participate in KiwiSaver must contribute at least 3% of their gross salary or wages to the superannuation scheme of their choice. Employers must also contribute 3% on behalf of each participating employee.

C. Exit and Entry

a. Visa Types

In addition to the visas referred to above, New Zealand has visa waiver programme with a number of other countries (listed here https://www.immigration.govt.nz/new-zealand-visas/apply-for-a-visa/about-visa/visa-waiver#https://www.immigration.govt.nz/new-zealand-visas/apply-for-a-visa/tools-and-information/general-information/visa-waiver-countries/slider). This entitles residents of those countries to enter New Zealand without a visa for tourist or short term study purposes.

All other visas have specific application requirements, details of which can be found at https://www.immigration.govt.nz/new-zealand-visas/apply-for-a-visa.

b. Restrictions for Exit and Entry

Every foreign person who enters New Zealand must have a visa or be eligible for the visa waiver programme. Most visas allow for multiple entries into, and exits from, New Zealand during the period of that visa—whether a visa allows for multiple entries will be specified on that visa.

D. Trade Union and Labour Organizations

The Employment Relations Act promotes collective bargaining and supports the role of trade unions in labour relations in New Zealand, however there is no obligation on an employee to join a union and no pressure is permitted to be put on an employee to do so. Only unions are able to negotiate collective agreements (on behalf of their members) with employers. There is an obligation on employers and unions to negotiate in good faith, though break-downs in negotiations can lead to strikes and other industrial action in rare circumstances.

Unions in New Zealand are concentrated in the public sector, with low participation in the private sector. Less than 20% of employees in New Zealand are members of a union.

E. Labour Disputes

In New Zealand, employment disputes may be resolved informally, by mediation (which is free and private) and / or by bringing a proceeding with the Employment Relations Authority. Decisions of the Employment Relations Authority may be challenged in the Employment Court.

Where the parties reach a resolution to an employment dispute, they can formally record it in a record of settlement.

V. Intellectual Property

A. Brief Introduction of IP Laws and Regulations

a. Patents

Patents are granted pursuant to the Patents Act 2013. Once granted, the patent protects the exclusive right for a new invention for up to 20 years. Certain inventions may not be patented, such as where the commercial exploitation of the invention is contrary to "public order" or morality.

b. Trademarks

The Trade Marks Act 2002 allows registration of trade marks and service marks.

Trade mark registration only affords protection in respect of the same goods and similar goods to those in which a mark is registered. New Zealand follows the Nice classification system for classes of goods and services.

The Intellectual Property Office of New Zealand (IPONZ) will not generally permit registration of trade marks and service marks which are considered to be of a purely descriptive nature, as such marks are considered to lack the distinctiveness necessary for registration.

c. Designs

Registering a design under the Designs Act 1953 protects the visual design of a product and can relate to the new or original shape, configuration or pattern applied to a product by any industrial process. Design registrations can last up to 15 years. To register a design, application must be made to IPONZ, including drawings of the design and statements regarding what is novel about the design.

d. Copyright

Copyright law does not protect ideas, rather it prevents others from copying the particular way in which an idea is expressed. Unlike other forms of intellectual property, it is not necessary to register copyright in New Zealand. This position is different to other countries, where copyright needs to be registered in order to be protected.

In New Zealand, copyright protection is afforded to original works when they are created, published or performed in accordance with the Copyright Act 1994. The types of works in which copyright subsists include literary, musical, dramatic or artistic works; sound recordings and films; broadcasts and cable programmes; and any digital or hardcopy publications. This includes manuals, brochures, warranties, designs, packaging, logos and advertising. Copyright in software is protected by treating the source code as a "literary work". Copyright protection lasts for 50 years from the end of the year in which the work was made available to the public or was broadcast. In the context of literary works, copyright lasts fifty years from the end of the year in which the author dies.

The person who created the work is usually the copyright owner unless the work is created in the course of someone's employment or someone commissions and agrees to pay for it (therefore reassigning rights).

B. Patent Application

An application must be made to IPONZ to register the patent in accordance with the Patent Regulations 2014. It must include a "specification", which contains a written description of the invention, including detailed information on how to make and use the invention (which may include drawings), as well as claims made in respect of that invention. A provisional specification requires much less information than a complete specification, but may be filed in order to establish a priority filing date. A complete specification will still be required to be filed within 12 months.

Once a complete specification is submitted, an examination must be requested within five years. An examination report will be issued as part of the examination process, which will indicate matters that need to be addressed to progress the application.

Applications can also be made in New Zealand in respect of applications made in Paris Convention countries (a 12 month time limit applies between first filing and when an application in New Zealand with a complete specification must be made) and Patent Cooperation Treaty countries (entry into New Zealand must be requested within 31 months of the earliest priority date).

Applicants are not required to have a place of business in New Zealand, but must have an address for service in New Zealand and communication address (email address). The address for service can be a business or residential address, post office box or document exchange box located in New Zealand.

C. Trademark Registration

An application must be made with IPONZ to register the mark, which must include a list of all goods and / or services that the mark will be used for. After filing the mark with IPONZ, the application is reviewed and IPONZ will either provide notification of acceptance or a compliance report. If the mark is accepted, then it is advertised for three months in the official monthly journal and third parties may oppose its registration. If there is no opposition, then the mark is registered.

Failure of the registered proprietor and its licensees to use the mark itself over an extended period (currently being three continuous years) in the relevant class of goods, may make the mark vulnerable to being removed from the trade marks register for non-use.

If a trade mark is filed overseas, convention priority can be claimed on applications that are based on the New Zealand trade mark application filing date, if done within six months. This only applies in countries that have joined the Paris Convention.

D. Measures for IP Protection

a. Employees and Contractors

A key risk for any New Zealand business is protecting proprietary interests when engaging individuals who are likely to be developing new intellectual property in the course of their employment or as a third party contractor.

For employees, provisions should be included in employment agreements to make it clear that all intellectual property created in the course of employment belongs to the business.

For third-party contractors, it is important that the contract between the business and the contractor automatically assigns all intellectual property created by the contractor in the course of performing services under that contract to the business, otherwise the default position is that the contractor will own the intellectual property s/he creates.

b. Patents

Once a patent is granted, potential infringements include:
a) Doing anything which the patentee has the exclusive right to do if the invention is:
• a product, to:
(i) make, hire, sell, or otherwise dispose of the product; or
(ii) offer to make, hire, sell, or otherwise dispose of the product; or
(iii) use or import the product; or
(iv) keep the product for the purpose of doing any of the things referred to in subparagraphs (i) to (iii); or
• a process, to use the process or to do any act mentioned above in respect of a product resulting from that use.

b) Supplying or offering to supply another person with any of the means, relating to an essential element of the invention, for putting the invention into effect.

If an infringement is established, the Court may grant an injunction and, at the option of the plaintiff, damages or an account of profits (though damages or an account of profits will not be awarded for innocent infringement).

c. Trademark

Following registration, trade mark rights should be protected by:
• using the ® symbol;
• maintaining up-to-date ownership and address details;
• Monitoring the trade mark against infringements.

Infringements include:
• Using an identical or similar sign in the course of trade;
• Breach of contractual requirements which would otherwise allow the use of the mark.

The courts have a wide range of civil remedies available to them (under the Trade Marks Act and under common law) to compensate aggrieved owners of registered trade marks for infringement of their trade marks. These include damages, injunctions, orders to account for profits, and orders to deliver up infringing goods to right holders.

The Trade Marks Act 2002 also contains criminal offences for the infringement of copyright works and counterfeiting of registered trade marks for commercial gain. A person convicted for such activity may be imprisoned for up to five years or fined up to NZ$150,000. The New Zealand Police are able to investigate and prosecute trade mark counterfeiters.

In addition, the Ministry of Business, Innovation and Employment is empowered to prosecute the offences of manufacturing, importing and selling counterfeited goods and pirated works prescribed in the Trade Marks Act and the Copyright Act.

Business may take action in the High Court for breach of the Trade Marks Act and also in relation to breaches of the Fair Trading Act ie using a mark in a way that is likely to mislead or deceive. Such action would be taken through the Disputes Tribunal, District Court or High Court (depending on the circumstances).

Trade mark owners and licensees may, where infringing copies of trade marked goods are being imported, request the detention of suspected infringing goods while they are subject to the control of New Zealand Customs. The mark owner / licensee then has 10 working days to commence proceedings otherwise the goods are released.

d. Copyright

From a practical perspective, there are various methods to protect copyright. These include:
• using a copyright indicator (©) on the work, followed by the name of the copyright owner and the year the copyright work was first created;
• keeping records of information about the creation and ownership of the work;
• ensuring the business owns (or at least has a right to use) any intellectual property paid for; and
• ensuring the business owns all copyright in works created by employees as part of their employment (as described above).

Copyright may be infringed by an entity:
• copying the work;
• issuing copies of the work to the public;
• performance of a literary, dramatic, or musical work in public;

- playing or showing a sound recording, film, or communication work in public;
- communicating a work to the public;
- making an adaptation of a literary, dramatic, or musical work;
- importing, possessing or dealing with an infringing work;
- providing the means for making infringing copies; and
- permitting the use of premises, or providing apparatus, for an infringing performance.

The courts have a wide range of civil remedies available to them (under the Copyright Act and under common law) to compensate aggrieved owners of copyrighted works for infringement of their copyright. These include damages, injunctions, orders to account for profits, and orders to deliver up infringing works to right holders.

e. Designs

On registration of a design under the Designs Act, copyright in the design is granted and the provisions relating to copyright above apply.

VI. Environmental Protection

A. Department Supervising Environmental Protection

The Environmental Protection Authority (EPA) is the government agency responsible for regulating activities that affect New Zealand's environment. It reports to the Minister for the Environment and its role includes:
- Advising the Minister;
- Providing administrative assistance for decision making bodies in relation to applications under the Resource Management Act 1991 where such applications are of national significance;
- Approving or declining applications to import or manufacture pesticides, dangerous goods, household chemicals and other hazardous substances in New Zealand;
- Regulating certain marine activities in New Zealand Exclusive Economic Zone and Continental Shelf;
- Administering the New Zealand Emissions Trading Scheme;
- make decisions on applications to introduce new organisms to New Zealand;
- advising on government environmental policy, legislations, and regulations; and
- undertaking enforcement of certain rules.

Local and regional councils have powers under the Resource Management Act 1991 to formulate policy and planning documents which govern the use and development of the resources within their areas. Councils have the ability to issue resource consents, which give permission (sometimes subject to conditions) for an activity that might affect the environment, and to enforce compliance with such resource consents.

B. Brief Introduction of Laws and Regulations of Environmental Protection

The Environmental Protection Authority is established under the Environmental Protection Authority Act 2011, while the Resource Management Act 1991 is New Zealand's principal legislation for environmental management.

The Resource Management Act determines how natural and physical resources in New Zealand (including land, water and air) can be used, developed or protected, and seeks to promote the sustainable management of those resources in a way which enables people and communities to provide for their social, economic and cultural wellbeing.

C. Evaluation of Environmental Protection

In 2017, New Zealand's environmental performance was assessed by the Organisation for Economic Cooperation and Development (OECD). It found that New Zealanders enjoy a high environmental quality of life and access to pristine wilderness. However, New Zealand's growth model, based largely on exploiting natural resources, is starting to show its environmental limits with increasing greenhouse gas emissions and water pollution.

The OECD Report also noted that:
- Despite generating 80% of its electricity from renewable sources, among the highest in OECD countries, New Zealand has the second-highest level of emissions per GDP unit in the OECD and the fifth-highest emissions per capita. Agriculture accounts for 49% of emissions.
- New Zealand cities are green and environmental quality is good, however population growth and urban expansion are posing increasing pressures on housing, transport, waste and water infrastructure.

The OECD report concluded that:
- the Resource Management Act is a remarkably comprehensive piece of environmental legislation, but could be made more effective;
- emissions from agriculture need to be addressed;
- the national freshwater policy needs to be swiftly and effectively implemented; and
- a long-term vision for the transition towards a low-carbon, greener economy is necessary.

VII. Dispute Resolution

A. Methods and Bodies of Dispute Resolution

a. Litigation

The most common form of judicial dispute resolution in New Zealand is litigation. By necessity, litigation is adversarial in nature (ie a contest involving antagonistic parties or opposing interests competing for an outcome most favorable to their positions) technically formal, and constrained by rules. The parties to litigation may settle their dispute at any time prior to a judgment being issued.

Litigation may commence in:
- The Disputes Tribunal (for claims of up to NZ$15,000);
- The District Court (for claims of up to NZ$350,000);
- The High Court (for claims of NZ$350,000 or more);
- In one of the specialist courts eg the Employment Court.

Appeals can be made from:
- the Disputes Tribunal to the District Court;
- the District Court or a specialised court to the High Court (or the Court of Appeal in certain circumstances);
- the High Court to the Court of Appeal (if leave to appeal to that Court is granted); and
- the Court of Appeal to the Supreme Court (if leave to appeal to that Court is granted).

An application for judicial review may also be made to the High Court under the Judicial Review Procedure Act 2016. This Act provides a single procedure for the judicial review of the use or non-use of statutory powers.

A decision by a higher court is binding on lower courts and decisions of the Supreme Court, as the final court of appeal, are binding on all other courts.

Proceedings in the relevant court are regulated as follows:
- District Court—District Court Act 2016 and District Court Rules 2014. The Act and the Rules govern the constitution and jurisdiction of the court, the practice and procedure of the court and the selection, appointment, removal, and conditions of the judicial and other officers of the court.
- High Court—Senior Courts Act 2016 and High Court Rules 2016. The Act constitutes the High Court, Court of Appeal and Supreme Court, and determines jurisdiction and procedure. The Rules set out how proceedings are started and specify the documents that must be filed, the content of those documents and how they are to be served. The Rules also provide detailed guidance on pre-trial matters such as case management, interim relief, discovery and inspections. The case management procedure aims to ensure that cases are processed through the system efficiently.
- Court of Appeal—Senior Courts Act 2016 and Court of Appeal (Civil) Rules 2005. The Rules set out the procedural requirements for pursuing civil appeals.
- Supreme Court—Senior Courts Act 2016 and Supreme Court Rules 2004. The Rules set out the procedural requirements for pursuing appeals.

Other common forms of dispute resolution in New Zealand are set out below.

b. Mediation

Mediation is a consensual, confidential and relatively informal negotiation process in which parties to a dispute use the services of a skilled and independent third party called a mediator to assist them to define the issues in dispute, to develop and explore settlement options, to assess the implications of settlement options and to negotiate a mutually acceptable settlement of that dispute which meets their interests and needs.

Generally, any agreement reached will be recorded in writing and will be binding on the parties. Any party to such an agreement may enforce its terms by issuing court proceedings.

c. Expert Determination

Expert Determination is a simple means of binding dispute resolution. Expert determination is a consensual, confidential and relatively informal process whereby parties to a contract agree to refer matters in dispute to an independent person to decide. The independent person is selected because the person is respected as having expertise relevant to the matters in dispute between the parties.

Expert Determination can provide either a binding or non-binding determination (subject to agreement by the parties) without involving many of the formalities that can beset more formal processes such as arbitration and litigation.

A Determination which the parties have agreed shall be binding on them may be enforced by a party to the process issuing court proceedings.

d. Arbitration

Arbitration is a formal dispute resolution process whereby two or more parties agree to submit all or certain disputes between them to an independent person called an arbitrator for a binding decision. Arbitration is entered into by agreement and the process is governed by the Arbitration Act 1996 and the Arbitration Amendment Act 2007 (or such other set of arbitral rules as agreed between the parties).

An arbitrator's decision, called an award, is binding on the parties and is enforceable as a judgment of the Court.

B. Application of Laws

a. Litigation

As mentioned above, a decision by a higher court is binding on lower courts and decisions of the Supreme Court, as the final court of appeal, are binding on all other courts. Laws are therefore consistently applied.

b. Arbitration

Proceedings under the Arbitration Act are generally confidential. Accordingly, no conclusion can be reached in relation to arbitral awards in New Zealand.

c. Mediation and Expert Determination

The mediation and expert determination processes are generally confidential. Accordingly, no conclusion can be reached in relation to such processes in New Zealand.

VIII. Others

A. Anti-commercial Bribery

a. Brief Introduction of Anti-commercial Bribery Laws and Regulations

New Zealand has a reputation for being one of the least corrupt countries in the world with strict anti-corruption laws.

NZ is a signatory to various treaties:
• OECD Convention on Combating Bribery of Foreign Public Officials in International Business Transactions;
• United Nations Convention Against Corruption; and
• United Nations Convention against Transnational Organised Crime.

Key pieces of New Zealand legislation dealing with bribery and corruption include the:
• Crimes Act 1961;
• Secret Commissions Act 1910; and
• Anti-Money Laundering and Countering Financing of Terrorism Act 2009 (AML Act).

a) Crimes Act

The Crimes Act creates a number of offences for corruptly giving, offering or agreeing to give any bribe to any person with intent to influence, in the exercise of their official duties, any:
• judicial officer;
• Minister of the Crown;
• Member of Parliament;
• law enforcement officer; or
• official (being any person in the service of the Sovereign in right of New Zealand, whether that service is honorary or not, and whether it is within or outside New Zealand, or any member or employee of any local authority or public body, or any person employed in the education service within the meaning of the State Sector Act 1988).

It is also an offence under the Crimes Act for any of the identified officials to corruptly (which requires knowing engagement in the relevant action) accept or obtain a bribe.

A bribe is widely defined as any money, valuable consideration, office, or employment, or any benefit, whether direct or indirect.

b) Secret Commissions Act

The Secret Commissions Act seeks to prevent acts of bribery and corrupt practices in New Zealand. It has a broader application than the Crimes Act, covering offences relating to bribery and corruption in both the public and private sectors. It covers transactions and favours between agents, principals and third parties. The Act sets out offences for:

- providing or accepting bribes in the form of gifts or other consideration;
- failing to disclose a financial interest in a contract;
- giving and delivering a false receipt;
- receiving a secret reward for procuring a party to enter a contract; and
- aiding and abetting an offence.

The offences cover both the acts of giving and receiving gifts or other consideration. Consideration is defined as valuable consideration of any kind, and particularly includes discounts, commissions, rebates, bonuses, deductions, percentages, employment, payment of money (whether by way of loan, gift, or otherwise), and omission to demand any money or valuable thing.

It is also an offence to advise any person to enter into a contract with a third person and receive or agree to receive from that third person, without the knowledge and consent of the person so advised, any gift or consideration as an inducement or reward for the giving of that advice or the procuring of that contract.

b. Department Supervising Anti-commercial Bribery

Serious or complex financial crimes (including bribery and corruption) are investigated and prosecuted by the Serious Fraud Office (SFO). The SFO partners with a network of other law enforcement agencies (nationally and internationally) and can prosecute New Zealand citizens, residents, and entities incorporated in New Zealand for acts of bribery and corruption that occur wholly outside of New Zealand, including when the bribe is paid through a foreign intermediary.

The SFO's priority cases focus on:
- multi-victim investment fraud;
- fraud involving those in important positions of trust (e.g.lawyers);
- bribery and corruption; and
- significant potential damage to New Zealand's reputation for fair and free financial markets.

c. Punitive actions

Penalties under the Crimes Act include terms of imprisonment of up to 14 years for the most serious offences.

Currently, the penalty for conviction for any offence under the Secret Commissions Act is imprisonment for a term not exceeding 7 years[①].

If the New Zealand Police suspect that an individual has benefitted from a bribe or corrupt activity, the Criminal Proceeds (Recovery) Act 2009 allows the Crown to recover the money or property derived from this crime. The Criminal Proceeds (Recovery) Act allows the Police to apply to the court to freeze or recover money or property derived from crime. This may include the immediate profits of crime (such as the money obtained from accepting a bribe) or the indirect benefits (such as a car purchased using money obtained through fraud). The purpose of the regime is to take the profit out of crime, remove the tools of crime, and potentially compensate victims using recovered criminal proceeds. Under the Act, the proceeds of crime may be recovered by the Crown regardless of whether the individual has been convicted for criminal offending. Assets can be forfeited if the court is satisfied on the balance of probabilities that the assets were acquired as a result of criminal activity.

B. Project Contracting

Procurement by government departments, New Zealand Police, the New Zealand Defence Force and most Crown entities is governed by the Government Rules of Sourcing as published by the New Zealand Government Procurement Department (part of the Ministry for Business, Innovation and Employment).

a. Permission System

There is no general permission system, however each notice of procurement (or similar document) may specify conditions for participating in the procurement process.

---

① Secret Commissions Act 1910, s 13.

b. Prohibited Areas

A government agency may exclude a supplier from participating in a bid if there is a good reason for the exclusion. Such reasons include:
- Bankruptcy, receivership or liquidation;
- Making a false declaration;
- A serious performance issue in a previous contract;
- A conviction for a serious crime or offence;
- Professional misconduct;
- An act or omission which adversely reflects on the commercial integrity of the supplier;
- Failing to pay taxes duties or other levies;
- A threat to national security of the confidentiality of sensitive government information;
- The supplier is a person or organisation designated as terrorists by New Zealand Police.

In addition to the above, there are also statutory and regulatory controls imposed in respect of specific industry types. Examples can be found in the primary products field, energy resources, fisheries, forestry, insurance, banking, air services and the development of natural resources. Other industry groups are also governed by legislation, e.g. motor vehicle dealers, real estate agents and private investigators.

c. Invitation to Bid and Bidding

Details of who is permitted to bid and the bid requirements (including timing) will be set out in the notice of procurement (or similar document) for the relevant project.

Certain lists of suppliers may be established by a government agency from time to time, including registered suppliers lists, pre-qualified suppliers lists and a panel of suppliers. The establishment of such lists will be openly advertised and, apart from in respect of a panel of suppliers, all procurement will continue to be openly advertised.

A government agency may provide for certain pre-conditions to be met by bidders in order to participate in the procurement process. This are limited to the following critical areas:
- legal capacity;
- financial capacity;
- commercial or operational capacity or capability to deliver; and
- appropriate technical skills or expertise or relevant experience.

尼日利亚

作者：Ken Etim、Toba、Ozofu'Latunde Ogiemudia、Mary Ekemezie
译者：谢湘辉、赵荣蓉

一、概述

（一）尼日利亚政治、经济、社会与法律环境概述

1. 主要的社会经济指标

尼日利亚的统计数据证实了该国处于全球经济的前沿，具有高投资回报率。最新的国家数据包括：

① 2017 年，全国人口 1.82 亿人，其中半数以上年龄在 30 岁以下。[①]
② 2050 年，预计人口将达到 4 亿人，超过美利坚合众国人口。[②]
③ 拥有非洲大陆最大的消费品和服务市场，预计将在 2025 年底前成为非洲最大的消费市场。[③]
④ 拥有非洲大陆最多的互联网用户，移动电信普及率非常高。[④] 截至 2017 年 12 月，尼日利亚共有 98 391 456 名网络和移动电信用户，占全部人口的 50.2%。该数据已被 IWS（全球互联网数据统计）证实。
⑤ 是非洲最大原油生产国[⑤]和世界第十三大原油生产国（2015）。
⑥ 拥有非洲最大探明储量的天然气，该储量排名世界第九。[⑥]
⑦ 储存了大量种类繁多的固体矿产资源。[⑦] 尼日利亚拥有丰富的固体矿产资源，约有 44 种不同的非石油矿物的沉积物遍布全国各地。
⑧ 拥有未开垦的大片耕地。[⑧] 尼日利亚的土地总面积约为 8 200 万公顷，自 1990 年以来，其中已发现可耕地面积 910 770 公顷，但仅有 42% 已被种植。
⑨ 是非洲的区域经济中心。[⑨] 拉各斯是尼日利亚人口最多的城市之一，也是一个正在崛起的大型城市，是许多国际企业和商业活动的所在地。

2. 地理、文化与政治

尼日利亚是一个有着丰富多彩文化的国家，共有 250 多个民族和多种类型宗教，并拥有复杂的视觉艺术。尼日利亚的古典艺术作品主要由在不同地点出土的雕塑构成。[⑩]

伴随着一些新兴城市的兴起，尼日利亚多次被评为地球上最幸福人的家园[⑪]，如期望的那样，也是

---

① 尼日利亚国家人口委员会（NPC），2017 年 5 月，详见 http://population.gov.ng/nigerias-population-now-182-million-npc/。
② 联合国："World Population Prospects（2012 版）"，2013 年 6 月，详见 http://www.un.org/en/development/desa/publications/world-population-prospects-the-2012-revision.html。
③ 麦肯锡全球研究所："Lions on the move II: Realizing the potential of Africa's economies"，2016 年 9 月，详见 https://www.mckinsey.com/global-themes/middle-east-and-africa/lions-on-the-move-realizing-the-potential-of-africas-economies。
④ 尼日利亚通信委员会（NCC）：全球互联网数据统计（IWS）报道 "Africa 2018 Population and Internet Users Statistics"，详见 https://www.ncc.gov.ng/stakeholders/statistics-reports/industry-overiveww-graphs-tables-5；https://www.internetworldstats.com/stats1.htm。
⑤ 非洲库：《非洲 20 大石油生产国》，详见 https://www.africanvault.com/oil-producing-countries-in-africa/。
⑥ 世界能源理事会："Gas in Nigeria"，详见 https://www.worldenergy.org/data/resources/country/nigeria/gas/。
⑦ 尼日利亚矿业钢铁发展部："Roadmap for the Growth and Development of the Nigerian Mining Industry"，2016 年，详见 http://www.minesandsteel.gov.ng/wpcontent/uploads/2016/09/Nigeria_Mining_Growth_Roadmap_Final.pdf。
⑧ 尼日利亚事实的报导（FAN）："Agriculture in Nigeria"，详见 https://total-facts-about-nigeria.com/agriculture-in-nigeria.html。
⑨ 世界银行："Global Economic prospects: Sub-Saharan Africa"，2018 年 1 月；Quartz Africa：《拉各斯是非洲第七大经济体并要伴随它的第一处石油的发现壮大》，详见 https://www.worldbank.org/en/region/afr/brief/global-economic-prospects-sub-saharan-africa-2018；https://qz.com/676819/lagos-is-africas-7th-largest-economy-and-is-about-to-get-bigger-with-its-first-oil-finds/。
⑩ 尼日利亚联邦信息文化部，详见 https://fmic.gov.ng/culture/。
⑪ 盖洛普全球情绪报告："尼日利亚人在 2010 年被评为地球上最幸福的人"，2010 年，详见 Gallup 2010 Global Emotions Report @ www http://news.gallup.com/reports。

多样化娱乐方式的汇集之地：激动人心的音乐、欢乐的舞蹈、丰富的食物和饮料，还有剧院。瑙莱坞是仅次于美国好莱坞和印度宝莱坞的世界第三大电影制作商。尼日利亚被广泛视为"非洲音乐心脏"，一直处于世界音乐的先锋地位，产生了许多世界级的歌星，比如已故的费拉库提。[①]

作为一个旅游胜地，该国迅速吸引了众多的游客，成为他们旅游的目的地。尼日利亚的旅游业也得益于吸引人的优惠措施，政府已将其列为优先部门。尼日利亚的美食根植九千年的非洲传统并深受部分欧洲传统的影响。[②]

尼日利亚位于非洲西海岸几内亚湾最内部的角落，面积 923 768 平方公里，其东北部隔乍得湖与乍得接壤，东部接壤喀麦隆，南部紧邻大西洋几内亚湾，西部接壤贝宁共和国，西北部接壤尼日尔共和国，边界总长度达到 4 900 公里，其中海岸线长度达到 853 公里[③]；尼日利亚的地理位置使得它成为丝绸之路经济带和 21 世纪海上丝绸之路的一个重要的国际贸易通道和战略要地。

尼日利亚实行宪政、多党制以及自由民主，使其有一个相对和平稳定的政治空间。自 1999 年以来，在其政府的军事过渡期后，尼日利亚再度回归到民主政体。因其有着连续地、和平地由一个政府转变为另一个政府，由一个执政党更迭为另一个执政党的政治经验，该国已成为非洲其他国家政治建设的参考。

希望在一个繁荣、和平的国际社会中实现国家发展的决心深深影响着尼日利亚的外交政策，为此，其与世界上大多数国家保持友好关系，成为许多双边、多边和全球条约的积极缔约国。尼日利亚宪法[④]，是这个民族的根本准则，也是该国其他所有法律的效力来源，规定了国家的外交政策目标[⑤]：

① 促进和保护国家利益；
② 促进非洲一体化和支持非洲团结一致；
③ 促进国际合作，巩固各国间的普遍和平与相互尊重，消除一切形式的歧视；
④ 尊重国际法和条约义务，寻求通过谈判、协商、调解、仲裁和裁决解决国际争端；
⑤ 促进建立公正的世界经济秩序。

3. 法律环境

尼日利亚拥有高效、务实的司法机构，充满活力的法律行业和建立在法治和最优的国际制度实践基础上的法律制度。尼日利亚法律体系是一个由各种不同来源的法律和规则组成的集合体，其中包括国内法和由立法机构借鉴并转化自外部法律和条约的法律、判例法（司法当局或上级法院的判决），以及被承认的英国法律。

多年来，尼日利亚的法律和监管框架通过制定支持自由的规则、保护财产私有制、向私人参与者（包括外国人）开放重要经济部门、设立各行业质量奖励机制，以及建立与世界其他国家的跨境、互惠或者外交联盟等方式的合作来吸引外来投资。

在有着共同利益与合作的诸多领域，尼日利亚与许多其他国家签订了双边和多边协定，如避免双重征税、贸易的促进和保护、司法引渡协议、移交被判刑人，以及关于刑事和商事的司法互助，等等。[⑥]例如，2017 年 8 月，尼日利亚总统穆罕默杜·布哈里与其他国家签署了九项条约，即：① 与阿拉伯联合酋长国（阿联酋）的刑事事项司法互助协定；② 与阿联酋的民事和商业事务司法互助协议；③ 与阿联酋的移交被判刑者协议；④ 与阿联酋的引渡条约；⑤ 尼日利亚、喀麦隆、中非共和国、利比亚、尼日尔和乍得共和国之间的《乍得湖流域宪章》；⑥《非洲税务管理协议》；⑦《世界知识产权组织表演和录音制品条约》；⑧《世界知识产权组织视听表演条约协定》；⑨《马拉喀什条约》，为盲人、视障者或其他人士获取已出版作品提供便利。

尼日利亚立法机构不断与行政部门合作，确保与其他国家签署的所有条约都在尼日利亚国内法化，

---

① 《经济学家》："Nigerian music: The immortal FelaKuti"，2012 年 11 月 9 日，详见 https://www.economist.com/blogs/baobab/2012/11/nigerian-music.。
② 联邦信息文化部，详见上文。
③ Encyclopedia.com："尼日利亚"，详见 https://www.encyclopedia.com/places/africa/nigeria-political-geography/Nigeria。
④ Constitution of the Federal Republic of Nigeria，1999（经修订）。
⑤ 同上注，第 19 节。
⑥ 《卫报》："Buhari tightens noose on graft war, signs extradition, economic treaties"，详见 https://guardian.ng/news/buhari-tightens-noose-on-graft-war-signs-extradition-economic-treaties/。

以便根据宪法的规定在尼日利亚适用和执行这些条约。① 为进一步落实这一宪法要求，在 2018 年 1 月 26 日，尼日利亚总统穆罕默杜·布哈里同意了早前由立法通过的《尼日利亚联邦共和国和西班牙王国之间避免双重征税协定（归化和执行）法》。②

个人的劳动权或合法经营权是私人取得和财产私有制的必然结果，这是尼日利亚宪法所载的基本人权之一。尼日利亚法院有权裁决在本国内违反这些权利规定的有关事项。具体而言，任何人宣称他的任何权利在该国没有受到侵犯，均可向高等法院申请寻求赔偿。③ 尼日利亚也有专门的法院／法庭，专属管辖一些法律领域，如证券和投资④、劳资关系⑤、税务纠纷⑥等。

（二）"一带一路"倡议下与中国企业合作的现状及趋势

中国和尼日利亚建立外交关系已有近半个世纪之久，给两国带来了诸多利益。两国也有很多相似之处：中国是亚洲乃至世界上人口最多的国家，尼日利亚是非洲人口最多的国家；中国是亚洲最大的经济体，尼日利亚也是非洲最大的经济体；两个国家都以其丰富的历史悠久的文化遗产为豪，对于其他国家和地区而言，两国都有着重要的战略利益；巧合的是，两国的国庆日都是 10 月 1 日。

除了这些相似之处，在双赢的基础上，中国和尼日利亚在贸易、经济和发展领域保持了近五十年的合作伙伴关系，实践证明尼日利亚是宣传"一带一路""政策沟通、设施联通、贸易畅通、货币融通、民心相通"五大主要目标⑦的理想伙伴。

据报道，在深化共同发展、开放和区域经济合作的愿景下，中国正在推进实施"一带一路"在非洲的建设，支持非洲实施 2063 议程和可持续发展 2030 议程，并计划在未来几年集中进口价值约 10 万亿美元的商品和服务，对外投资达到 7 500 亿美元，出境旅游人数达到 7 亿人次⑧。作为非洲的区域大国，尼日利亚将协助中国实现其与非洲共同发展的承诺。

中国的技术、创新、资金正在与尼日利亚丰富的自然资源、廉价的劳动力、巨大的市场和热情好客的人民相结合，共同建设了重要的基础设施，例如中国和尼日利亚近期合作的成果：阿布贾的轻轨、拉各斯的轨道交通系统、阿布贾卡杜纳铁路、曼比拉的发电项目、莱基深水港、拉各斯卡拉巴沿海铁路。在贸易、信息技术、农业和文化领域⑨两国也有着互利合作。

在持续的双边贸易和两国间经济合作协议的推动下，2017 年，中尼双边贸易额达到了 137.8 亿美元。⑩ 2016 年，中国和尼日利亚达成货币互换协议，使得两国之间的贸易可以直接使用当地货币结算，而不再依赖美元，并允许人民币（元）在尼日利亚银行体系内自由流通。几年前，尼日利亚政府将其外汇储备的很大一部分从美元兑换成人民币，目的就是减小尼日利亚经济对美元的依赖并促进与中国的贸易发展。

在国际舞台上，尼日利亚一向认同中国的外交政策和全球志向。尼日利亚与非洲、亚洲、拉丁美洲的其他发展中国家一道，顶住外界压力，恪守"一个中国"政策，并且完全支持中华人民共和国恢复联合国安理会的合法席位。⑪

---

① 《卫报》："Buhari tightens noose on graft war, signs extradition, economic treaties"，第 12 节，详见 https://guardian.ng/news/buhari-tightens-noose-on-graft-war-signs-extradition-economic-treaties/。
② 尼日利亚德勤税务预警，2018 年 1 月 30 日。详见 https://blog.deloitte.com.ng/nigeria-signs-double-tax-treaty-with-spain-into-law/。
③ 《尼日利亚联邦宪法》，第 46 节，详见上文。
④ 投资和证券法庭根据 2007 年《投资证券法案》，第 274 节至 297 节设立。
⑤ 尼日利亚国家工业法院根据 1997 年修订的《尼日利亚联邦宪法》设立。
⑥ 税务上诉法庭根据 2007 年《联邦内陆税收法》设立。
⑦ 中华人民共和国国家发展与改革委员会，外交部、商务部联合出版的《丝绸之路经济带与二十一世纪海上丝绸之路联合建设的构想与行动》，2015 年 3 月，详见中华人民共和国驻尼日利亚大使馆经济商务参赞处网站（http://nigeria2.mofcom.gov.cn/article/c hinanews /201504 /20150400936317.shtml）。
⑧ 晁晓亮，中华人民共和国驻拉各斯办事处总领事，2017 年 11 月 9 日，详见 https://www.Vanguardngr.com /2017/11/china-trade-volume-nigeria-hits-8-94bn/。
⑨ 晁晓亮：《尼日利亚：一个不仅与中国国庆日相同的国家》，2016 年 10 月 1 日，详见 https://www.vanguardngr.com/2016/10/nigeria-beyond-sharing-national-day-with-china/。
⑩ 晁晓亮，中华人民共和国拉各斯办事处总领事，2018 年 2 月 7 日，详见 https://www.vanguardngr.com/2017/11/china-trade-volume-nigeria-hits-8-94bn/。
⑪ 晁晓亮：《尼日利亚：一个不仅与中国国庆日相同的国家》。

15世纪，中国的郑和率领300艘船组成的舰队到达非洲，随后，友谊的种子即被播种在中国和非洲人民的心中。非洲与"一带一路"倡议①有着自然与传统的联系，并且尼日利亚信守其作为非洲大陆门户的诺言。

通过中国合作论坛和其他的外交和互利联盟等平台，尼日利亚作为非洲颇受欢迎的投资目的国，提供了独特的机会，协助实现"一带一路"更紧密地连接亚洲、欧洲、非洲的各个国家和共同繁荣的目标。

二、投资

（一）市场准入

1. 投资监督部门

尼日利亚的主要投资监管部门有：

（1）证券交易委员

证券交易委员会是在财政部的监督下运作的尼日利亚资本市场的最高监管机构。证券交易委员会的职能还包括颁布各种形式的投资规则和准则，规范资本市场，以保护投资者，提高其投资效率，并为私营部门主导的经济铺平道路。②

（2）尼日利亚中央银行

尼日利亚中央银行是尼日利亚金融系统最高管理者，全面控制和管理尼日利亚联邦政府货币和金融部门政策，尼日利亚中央银行不仅负责所有银行和其他金融机构的经济运行工作，而且也分管尼日利亚的法定货币汇率事务；尼日利亚中央银行通过监测和记录货币流通量，促进国内金融体系的健全；尼日利亚中央银行管理国家的外汇储备，控制信贷、对外贸易和外汇③。外国投资者在尼日利亚经营企业需要一定的资本投入，包括将尼日利亚公司纳入为联营公司/子公司、向尼日利亚公司进行股权投资、向当地联营公司/子公司贷款的外国投资者必须将投资资金转移到尼日利亚。在尼日利亚法律中，外国资本的意思是"可自由兑换的货币、厂房、机械、设备、零部件、原材料和其他商业资产，但不包括商誉"，其进入尼日利亚时的初始支出中不包括外汇，并且这些外资将用于那些遵守尼日利亚投资促进委员会法案的相关企业用来生产产品以及提供服务。④法律还规定，外国投资者应通过由尼日利亚中央银行⑤许可授权的经销商将所需资金汇入尼日利亚。授权的经销商在收到用以投资的外资后有义务在24小时内向投资者发放资本输入证明书，并在48小时内向外汇监管机构的尼日利亚中央银行⑥反馈。资本输入证明书赋予投资者在任何授权经销商处开设本国外汇账户和一种特殊的非居民的奈拉账户的资格，并保证在投资者退出尼日利亚市场时无条件地转移和返还资金（包括资本和收益）⑦。

（3）尼日利亚投资促进委员会

尼日利亚投资促进委员会是由尼日利亚联邦政府设立的用来吸引外资的机构。它就政策问题向政府提出建议，包括财政措施，旨在促进尼日利亚的工业化和经济的全面发展。其通过向商业实体提供必要的成长援助和指导，协调、监测和鼓励所有投资活动的建立和运作。

尼日利亚投资促进委员会扮演投资者、政府相关部门和机构、贷款机构以及投资行业的其他部门之间沟通桥梁的角色。尼日利亚投资促进委员会的部分工作包括向投资者宣传最新的投资优惠信息，

---

① 晁晓亮，中华人民共和国拉各斯办事处总领事："The Belt and Road: New Opportunities for China-Nigeria Cooperation"，2017年4月1日，详见中华人民共和国拉各斯办事处总领事网站（http://lagos.china-consulate.org/eng/xwfb/zxhd/t1450672.htm）。
② 尼日利亚证券交易委员会（SEC），详见www.sec.gov.ng/about。
③ 尼日利亚中央银行（CBN），详见www.cbn.gov.ng/AboutCBN。
④ 2004年《尼日利亚联邦法律》第N117章《尼日利亚投资促进委员会法案》第31节。
⑤ 2004年《尼日利亚联邦法律》第F34章《外汇监管法》第15节。
⑥ 同上注，第15节(2)。
⑦ 同上注，第13节和第15节(4)。详见2013年《证监会综合规定》第408(2)，载http://sec.gov.ng/se c-nigerias-consolidated-rules-and-regulations-as-at-2013/。

以及对潜在的和现有的投资者[①]提供支持服务。

在公司成立后开始营业前,外国投资者必须在尼日利亚投资促进委员会进行登记,以此来获得尼日利亚政府对企业的某些特定的优惠,包括减税、降低在退出该国市场时资本撤出的门槛,以及对符合条件的企业给予投资保护和特殊地位称号[②]。

在所有相关注册材料都已备齐并全部提交的情况下[③],尼日利亚投资促进委员会在收到相关材料后14日内向企业单位发放注册证书。向尼日利亚投资促进委员会提交的商业实体注册申请必须具备的文件,包括公司的注册文件、股权结构文件、合资企业股东协议或者合伙协议,以及授权书。

为了进一步实现尼日利亚投资促进委员会的宗旨,政府在尼日利亚投资促进委员会设立了一个一站式投资中心,为在尼日利亚的投资及商业活动提供更多的便利并鼓励他们的投资活动。

一站式投资中心通过便利化的投资机制,将相关政府部门整合到一个办公地点,进行相应的协调和简化,以向投资者提供高效、透明的服务。它为投资者提供了在一个地点就能把所有在尼日利亚设立投资项目所需的法定文件收集齐完整获得批准的便利。一站式投资中心的目标包括消除投资者在设立公司和经营时需要面对的困难和不必要的官僚主义。它提供有关尼日利亚经济、投资环境、法律法规,以及工业及各行业的统计数据和信息,以帮助现有和潜在投资者作出明智的商业决定。一站式投资中心为投资者提供的服务涵盖:

① 关于尼日利亚经济的基本信息和数据,以帮助做出明智的投资决策;
② 提高商业准入审批、许可和授权的效率,使投资者能够及时地设立投资实体;
③ 根据现有的监管要求,政府机构便利简化事后审批、许可和特定部门许可的程序;
④ 考虑投资者的利益,所有政府部门都要向投资项目提供全面的便利和帮助;
⑤ 在尼日利亚为众多利润丰厚的投资机会设立一般咨询服务,包括根据投资者的需求匹配在尼日利亚36个州的投资机会。

以下事项可在一站式投资中心可得到处理和获悉,无需分别到访不同的监管机构[④]:

① 公司注册和登记;
② 营业证可和登记;
③ 税务登记/清关;
④ 工作许可证和其他移民设施;
⑤ 促进投资项目通关;
⑥ 关于尼日利亚经济部门和工业的信息和数据;
⑦ 熟悉尼日利亚的监管环境;
⑧ 解决当地和外国投资者面临的任何行政障碍。

(4)尼日利亚技术引进与推广办公室

尼日利亚技术引进与推广办公室是尼日利亚联邦政府的下属机构,肩负着评估和登记技术转让协议、促进知识产权的发展、提供技术咨询和支持服务等职责。若转让的是一项国外的技术,比如专业技术、厂房、机器设备、工程机械、训练设施、商标和专利权等,有关国外技术的商业合同或协议依法应当在合同签订后60天内在尼日利亚国家技术引进与推广局登记备案。[⑤]

《国家技术引进与推广办公室法案》规定了不予登记技术(资本)转让协议的几种情形,其中包括转让在尼日利亚可以免费获得的技术,以及报酬与已获得的技术或将要获得的技术不相称的。若技术转让协议规定受让方必须就该协议争议提交外国法院管辖,该协议在尼日利亚也无法登记。

2. 投资行业法律法规

参与调整在尼日利亚经济领域投资的法律法规如下:

---

① 尼日利亚投资促进委员会(NIPC),详见 http://www.nipc.gov.ng/about.html。
② 《尼日利亚投资促进委员会法案》,第20节(1)。详见上文。
③ 同上注,第20节(2)。
④ 尼日利亚证券交易委员会—一站式投资中心(NIPC OSIC),详见 http://www.nipc.gov.ng/onestop.html。
⑤ 2004年尼日利亚联邦法律第N62章《国家技术引进和推广办公室法案》第5(2)节。

（1）《公司及相关事务法》（1990年）[①]

该法主要管理尼日利亚的企业以及企业从开业到清算的经营，它规定了企业需要定期出具的法定文件（如企业年报），并设立了公司事务委员会，作为管理尼日利亚公司设立和运营的政府机构。[②]

（2）《公司法》（2012年）[③]

该法是一套根据公司及相关事务法[④]制定并由公司事务委员会实施的法律。该法将一些既定的惯例、习俗以及实体法未妥善处理的问题成文化，还规定了公司设立、管理和解散的法定形式和标准。

（3）《投资与证券法》（2007年）[⑤]

投资与证券法规定设立的证券交易委员会是尼日利亚资本市场最高的监管机构，该法授权其在尼日利亚制定投资和证券业务的规章制度，尤其是在并购、收购和接管领域，以及集合投资计划。该法还规定了尼日利亚的资本市场运营商的许可。

（4）《证券交易委员会规则》[⑥]

有关尼日利亚经济投资的规则是由证券交易委员会颁布和实施。该规则涉及的内容包括：有关公司治理和行为准则的规定，有关固定收入证券的相关规定，有关于基金/投资经理、资本市场运营、证券交易、全球存托凭证、集体投资计划、基础设施建设资金、债券、并购以及收购的规定，等等。[⑦]

（5）尼日利亚《中央银行法》[⑧]

该法设立了尼日利亚中央银行，授权它在尼日利亚管理货币事务和发行法定货币，维持外部储备，促进货币稳定和维护健全的金融体系。除此之外，尼日利亚中央银行还负责调控国内的货币流通量和流入量、投资以及外资外流。

（6）《银行和其他金融机构法》[⑨]

该法授权尼日利亚中央银行为尼日利亚非银行金融业和所有其他金融机构的管理者，负责他们的许可、经营管理、组成以及清算等。

（7）《外汇监管法》[⑩]

外汇法用于规范在尼日利亚设立一个自主外汇市场，监测和监督在市场上进行的交易，管制流入国内用于投资的外国资本。

（8）《货币、信贷、对外贸易和外汇政策准则》[⑪]

这一准则规定了国家在任何特定年份将采取的措施，包括货币措施、信贷、外贸和外汇管理，这在很大程度上决定了在每个财政年度外资流入的水平。

（9）《其他尼日利亚中央银行公报及指引》[⑫]

尼日利亚中央银行对外贸、外汇、投资等规定经常在该公报或者指引上发布，这些公告及指引在很大程度上指导了外国资本的流入或流出。这些公告涉及在财政和投资领域进入外汇市场后外资遇到的所有监管问题，包括进口外汇登记、外资、外国投资遣返以及正当的投资。

（10）《国家技术引进和推广办公室法案》[⑬]

《国家技术引进和推广办公室法案》规定国家技术引进和推广办公室为尼日利技术转让协议和知识产权协议的登记机构。该法案授权国家技术引进和推广办公室规定技术转让申请费和申请人不履行责

---

① 2004年《尼日利亚联邦法律》第C20章。
② 公司事务委员会（CAC），详见 http://new.cac.gov.ng/home/about-us/。
③ 详见 http://new.cac.gov.ng/home/wpcontent/uploads/2013/11/Companies _ Regulations _As _Ammended.pdf 和 http://new.cac.gov.ng/home/wp-content/uploads/2017/04/Amendment-to-Companies-Regulation-2012.pdf。
④ CAMA，第16节、第585节、第609节。
⑤ 尼日利亚中央银行（SEC），ISA，详见 http://sec.gov.ng/investment-and-securities-act/。
⑥ 证券监管规则，详见 http://sec.gov.ng/regulation/rules-codes/。
⑦ 同上注。
⑧ 2007年《尼日利亚中央银行组织法》。
⑨ 2004年《尼日利亚联邦法律》第B3章。
⑩ 2004年《尼日利亚联邦法律》第F34章《外汇监管法》。
⑪ 尼日利亚中央银行（CBN），详见 https://www.cbn.gov.ng/documents/Monetarycreditguide.asp。
⑫ 尼日利亚中央银行（CBN）："All Circulars"，详见 https://www.cbn.gov.ng/documents/circulars.asp。
⑬ 《国家技术促进及推广办公室法案》，详见上文。

任时的罚款。① 有关的合同或协议在签订之日起 30 内未向国家技术引进和推广办公室提出登记的，国家技术引进和推广办公室将课以罚金。②

（11）尼日利亚《投资促进委员会法案》③

尼日利亚《投资促进委员会法案》通过设立尼日利亚投资促进委员会公司鼓励和促进尼日利亚经济投资，并授权它在这方面负责对在尼日利亚企业注册企业和经营予以优惠；指定某些投资"优先领域"应给予特别优惠；帮助在尼日利亚的外资撤出不受阻碍的同时对外国企业的征用提供担保。④

（12）尼日利亚《联邦内陆税收组织法案》⑤

该法案设立了联邦税务服务局并授权它来评估和汇总收益提交给联邦政府。该法案规定，其目的是控制和管理不同的税收和法律法规、国会制定的任何其他法律或根据该法案作出的其他规定，以及向政府说明所征收的所有税款。⑥本质上，这囊括了所有企业预计在尼日利亚开展商业业务所需支付的税款的法律。

3. 投资形式

愿意在尼日利亚投资的外国投资者，可以外国直接投资、外国有价证券投资，或国际商业贷款和资本流动的形式进行投资。正如上文所言，无论选择何种形式，用于投资外国资本的流入必须及时登记在尼日利亚当局，然后取得资本输入证书。

4. 市场准入和审查标准

在外国投资者已取得资本输入证书并且在尼日利亚投资促进委员会注册后，可以自由投资企业或证券，并享受先前声明给予投资领域的所有补贴、优惠以及保证。⑦但是，对在尼日利亚经营要求必须成立公司的，外国投资者必须要遵守。在某些行业或企业中，有特定的行业监管机构规定了准入标准的，外国投资者遵守了相应准入要求后应向其颁发营业许可证。⑧除了获得特定行业的经营许可证，根据《联邦税务服务（设立）法案》，尼日利亚所有的企业都必须登记并取得税务识别号码作为开始营业的先决条件。

（二）外汇管制

1. 外汇监管部门

负责监管尼日利亚外汇市场的主要机构是尼日利亚中央银行。

2. 外汇法律法规简介

尼日利亚外汇管理的主要法规是《外汇监管法》⑨。该法在 1995 年通过引入自由外汇市场放宽了对尼日利亚外汇市场的限制，从由尼日利亚中央银行管理的外汇销售到终端用户，通过指定的授权经销商决定汇率。此外，外汇管理局经授权许可外汇市场的买家和卖家为外汇小额用户提供外汇买卖服务，扩大官方外汇市场。外币兑换所的汇率是由市场决定的。随着银行间外汇市场的引入，外汇市场在 1999 年 10 月进一步自由化。然而，连续几年国际油价持续下跌导致严峻的经济形势，外汇市场自由化影响了当地货币的价值，外汇储备和通货膨胀的压力随之而来，使得尼日利亚中央银行不得不花费几年的时间重新实行外汇管制和采用固定/官方汇率来应对。

---

① 《国家技术促进及推广办公室法案》，第 2 节。
② NOTAP: "Schedule of Applicable Fees for Registration of Technology Transfer Agreements"，详见 http://notap.gov.ng/sites/default/files/schedule_of_applicable_fees_for_registration_of_technology_transfer_agreements.pdf.
③ 《尼日利亚投资促进委员会法案》，详见上文。
④ 同上注，第 22 节至 25 节。
⑤ 2007 年《尼日利亚联邦内陆税收组织法案》。
⑥ 同上注，第 2 节。
⑦ 《外汇监管法》，详见上文，第 15 节。
⑧ 例如，对银行业有意的外国投资者必须遵守尼日利亚中央银行颁发的具体规定，并在经营开始前获得正式许可。其他行业也有相应的监管机构和授权者。
⑨ 同上注。

2016年6月，随着《尼日利亚银行间外汇市场运行准则（经修订）》的推出[①]，尼日利亚中央银行重新回到尼日利亚外汇市场自由化的政策，但是以周期性干预的方式来保持汇市稳定，为所有最终用户引入单一的自治外汇市场和无需交割的外汇期货，并保留了先前尼日利亚外汇市场的41项禁入规定[②]。因此涉及该41项禁止规定的跟单信用证无法开具，除非2015年6月前已开具。[③] 为了进一步提高外汇市场的流动性，确保在尼日利亚的合格交易及时执行和结算，其他许多举措还包括尼日利亚中央银行在2017年设立了投资者和出口商外汇窗口[④]。许多符合规定的交易从中获益包括：偿还贷款、利息支付、股息/收入汇款、资本汇出、托收汇票以及在尼日利亚中央银行外汇手册中指定的其他杂项付款。

3. 外资企业外汇管理的规定

外国企业需要通过尼日利亚中央银行授权的特许经销商，并取得了上述的资本进口证书才能引进投资资本。在这之后，外国投资者才可在授权经销商处或者其他银行开户、保留、使用他们被指定的用于国际可兑换外币的本地账户。如果外国投资者严格遵守了关于输入资本的法律规定和要求，除非法律另有规定，法律保护其存放在本地财产上的资本不被强制披露。这类引入资本也同样受法律保护以免于被政府没收或征用。[⑤] 外国资本的一般管理办法通常在尼日利亚中央银行的公报和指引中发布。[⑥]

（三）融资

1. 主要金融机构

尼日利亚的主要金融机构如下：
① 尼日利亚中央银行——金融系统的最高监管机构；
② 商业银行；
③ 工业银行；
④ 尼日利亚出口银行；
⑤ 农业银行；
⑥ 其他金融机构：初级抵押贷款银行、尼日利亚按揭贷款公司、折扣商店、金融发展机构、金融机构、外汇管理局、微型金融银行等；
⑦ 保险公司；
⑧ 尼日利亚农业保险公司。

2. 外国企业的融资条件

尼日利亚外国企业的融资条件正如上文所述。在大多数情况下，外国投资者借款给尼日利亚企业通常需要经过获得进口资本证书的授权经销商渠道，确保遵守投资、业务和运营管理监督规定。

（四）土地政策

1. 土地法律法规简介

尼日利亚主要的土地政策规定在1978年的《土地使用法》中[⑦]，该法规定联邦任何州的土地均由州长为尼日利亚人民托管，并为其利益进行管理（主要是用于给个人和组织分配土地；用于住宅、农业、商业和其他用途及与之有关的收租）。土地使用法主要规定尼日利亚的土地所有权归属和使用，以及土

---

① 尼日利亚中央银行（CBN）："Revised Guidelines for the Operation of the Nigerian Inter-bank Foreign Exchange Market"。详见 https://www.cbn.gov.ng/out/2016/ccd/revised%20guidelines%20for%20flexible%20exchange%20rate%20marketjune%202016%20v1.pdf.
② 在制定这个指南时规定的41项不适用于在尼日利亚的外汇分配的物品，详见 https://www.cbn.gov.ng/out/2015/ccd/tedcircular062015.pdf.
③ 尼日利亚中央银行（CBN）通告，详见 https://www.cbn.gov.ng/Out/2015/TED/TED.FEM.FPC.GEN.01.021.pdf.
④ 尼日利亚中央银行（CBN）通告："Establishment of Investors' & Exporters' FX Window"，详见 https://www.cbn.gov.ng/out/2017/fmd/establishment%20of%20investors%27%20&%20exporters%27%20fx%20window.pdf.
⑤ 《外汇监管法》，第17节，详见上文。
⑥ 同上，第20节。详见 "CBN's Revised Guidelines for the Operation of the Nigerian Inter-bank Foreign Exchange Market"，载 https://www.cbn.gov.ng/out/2016/ccd/revised%20guidelines%20for%20flexible%20exchange%20rate%20marketjune%202016%20v1.pdf.
⑦ 2004年《尼日利亚联邦法》第15章。

地综合管理。土地使用法第一章①规定联邦州的州长仅对其州领土内所有土地享有所有权（除了属于联邦政府或其机构的土地）（有关农村土体所有权被授予地方政府，在第二章中予以规定②）。土地使用法规定，任何人（个人或公司）在土地上所能享有的最高权益就是"居住权"，这等于是租赁权益，期限通常不超过99年。

根据土地使用法第五章第1条（a）款的规定③，联邦州的州长有权授予居住权，签发入住证明书证明了这一点。任何对土地的后续交易（即居住权的标的），必须征得土地所在州州长同意。

根据土地使用法的规定，未经土地所在州的州长的同意在尼日利亚不得进行转让、抵押土地，占有权转移、转租或其他影响土地权属的交易。④违反本条款而完成的任何交易，任何声称被授予的文书，或在土地上赋予任何人的任何权利和利益，均属无效。⑤然而，尼日利亚最高法院认为，这些交易在没有得到必要的州长同意的情况下成立，并非无效，只是未生效⑥，但有一点很重要需要留意的是，投资者可能无法执行未生效土地交易产生的抵押、收费或任何形式的证券交易。除了土地使用法，联邦的所有州都有各自的土地登记法，规范其州界范围内的房地产交易。在拉各斯州（尼日利亚的商业资本和金融中心），土地所有权登记（其他与此有关的）受2015年拉各斯州《土地登记法》的管辖。拉各斯州《土地登记法》的主要条款如下：

（1）土地交易、转租或抵押必须以契约的方式进行，在地政局备案后生效；
（2）所有土地租赁、抵押贷款、交易的契据都需登记；
（3）需登记的文件必须在获得州长的同意（如适用）之后60天内进行；
（4）授权第三方进行交易的委托书也需登记；
（5）颁发相应的土地证书，其中载有按照要求已经登记的与土地有关的所有交易的详细资料，土地证书是所有权的初步证据；
（6）经登记的土地拥有者经州长的同意后有权处分土地并享有土地产生的任何权益；

所有权的完善主要包括三个阶段：①获得州长的同意；②相关交易单据盖章和缴纳印花税；③有关交易文件在地政局登记。目前在拉各斯州实施三个主要阶段的程序，其中包括一个30天指南（含10个步骤，旨在30天内实现土地权益登记，以提高在该州和全国开展业务的便利性）。

投资者还需要了解，尽管土地所有权是由土地所在州的州长授予，但法律赋予尼日利亚联邦政府的任何土地、领海和专属经济区之下或之上的所有矿物、矿物油和天然气的所有权和控制权⑦。

2. 外国企业土地获得规则

外国企业在尼日利亚获得土地必须依据《尼日利亚联邦共和国宪法》（1999年）（经修订）、《土地使用法》、土地所在州的《国家土地登记法》《尼日利亚矿物与采矿法》（2007年）等法的有关规定进行。

总的来说，想要在尼日利亚经营的外国企业可以依法取得土地，但是根据其取得方式不同会有不同的当地限制要求。在拉各斯州，土地由国家政府分配给外国公司和个人，使用年限最长可达到25年⑧。然而，在实践中，这种规定往往没有得到严格执行。对于外国投资者来说特别重要的是，银行和其他金融机构通常需要不动产作为贷款的担保。这使得一个公司实体必须一直持有其土地/不动产的居住证，因为这通常是为了转让土地交易的顺利进行而必须取得州长许可时要求出具的。

（五）公司的设立和解散

1. 企业形式

在尼日利亚投资者可设立的企业形式有：独资企业、合伙企业和法人公司。法人公司可以是私营

---

① 2004年《尼日利亚联邦法律》第15章。
② 同上注。
③ 同上注。
④ 同上注，第21节和第22节。
⑤ 同上注，第26节。
⑥ Awojugbagbe Light Industries Ltd.Vs.P.N.Chinukwe& Anor [1995] 5 NWLR [Pt.390] 409。
⑦ 1999年修订的《尼日利亚联邦宪法》；Nigerian Minerals and Mining Act, 2007。
⑧ 根据 Aliens Law 获得的土地，详见1994《拉各斯州法》第2章。

有限责任公司，也可以是上市股份有限公司。想要设立非营利组织的外国投资者，必须根据其设立企业的目的注册担保有限公司或信托有限公司。

在尼日利亚投资者最常使用的企业形式是有限责任公司，因为它具有独立于其发起人/股东的独立法人地位的优势。投资者以其出资金额为限对有限责任公司承担责任。该公司的法律人格也确保不限制任何想在尼日利亚对其注册公司进行权益变现的外国投资者。

在尼日利亚设立公司的最低人数为2人。私营公司有不超过50名成员的限制，但上市公司的成员数量没有上限。

外国投资者尤其是私募基金，在尼日利亚设立的另一种常见的企业形式是有限合伙企业。联邦法律对有限合伙企业没有专门的规定，《公司及相关事务法》也仅对企业名称的登记作了规定。然而，私募基金有限合伙企业通常在公司事务委员会以商业名义注册。然而，在拉各斯州，由根据拉各斯州《合伙企业法》设立的有限合伙企业登记处来负责这些事务。①

2. 设立程序

在尼日利亚设立企业实体的程序如下：

（1）拟用名称的保留

在尼日利亚设立公司的第一步是在公司事务委员会进行"可用性查询"，确认拟用的公司名称是可以使用的，即该名称不与现有公司的名称或现有的商品的商标名称相同、类似或者是公司事务委员会规定的其他不可使用的名称。通常，会提交2—3个备选名称进行可用性搜索，若可用，该名称则被保留60天，并可延长60天时间进行修改。在保留期内，任何其他公司不得注册与被保留名称相同的名称或者根据公司事务委员会规定与其近似的名称。

（2）公司的宗旨

外国投资者或单位可以在尼日利亚从事除武器弹药的生产、生产经营麻醉药品和精神药物、与军事和准军事服装和饰品生产有关业务以外的任何业务。如本公司设立的目的包括提供专业服务，则在注册之前，公司事务委员会可能会要求申请人具备相应的水平证书。

（3）公司注册文件

在公司名称已核准并被保留后，申请人应按照公司事务委员会要求的格式提交下列文件：

① 公司章程

公司章程是公司的宪法性文件，规定了其主要目标，同时规定了公司的内部管理和行政程序。章程必须经由至少2个实体（个人或公司）签署。2008年12月，公司事务委员会规定了章程的标准形式，基本上适用了《公司及相关事务法》的规定。不过，公司的发起人可以在章程中附加一页列出任何公司认为必要的条款。

公司章程必须由至少两个实体（个人和/或公司）签署，这两个实体可以是非尼日利亚人，并且必须共同占据本公司至少25%的法定股本。每个签署者必须提交一份认可的身份证明，例如其国际护照、驾照或身份证的信息页复印件；若签署者为公司，则需公司营业执照。

若成立的新公司的发起人中有公司，公司事务委员会要求这类发起人除了加盖该发起公司的印章，还必须有一个代表人来签署公司文件。该发起人通过董事会决议授权该公司作为发起人并提名该代表签署公司文件或作为公司董事会的代表，相关的材料也应与公司设立文件一起提交给公司事务委员会。该授权决议必须放在董事签署的发起人文件上，并盖上公司印章。对于那些提供专业服务的公司，公司事务委员会也可能要求这些公司提交相应的资格证书。

② 法定股本结算单和股份分配收益表（公司事务委员会表2）

本表格载明该公司已授权、已发行及已缴股本的详情（参见下文"股本"部分关于股本法定要求的意见）。

③ 董事的详细情况（公司事务委员会表7）

拟设立公司的董事姓名、地址和职务说明，该公司董事必须至少有两人，必须以这种表列出。董事不必是尼日利亚人但必须已满18岁。必须提交一份认可董事身份证明文件，每个董事的国际护照、

---

① 2003年修订的《拉各斯州法》第P21章。

驾照或身份证的信息页复印件。如果任何董事是在尼日利亚居住的外国人,须同时向公司事务委员会提交居住证明。

④ 登记办公地址通知书(公司事务委员会表 3)

每一个公司在成立时都要求在尼日利亚有一个注册办事地址。

⑤ 公司秘书的详情(公司事务委员会表 2.1)

凡在尼日利亚注册的公司都必须设有公司秘书。①

⑥ 对《公司及相关事务法》规定的合规宣言(公司事务委员会表 4)

该表格是一份由律师作出的法定声明,证明其已符合尼日利亚公司登记的法定要求。

(4)股本

① 法定股本

根据《公司及相关事务法》,一家私营企业的法定股本最少为 ₦ 10 000(一万奈拉),上市公司最低法定股本为 ₦ 500 000(五十万奈拉)。然而,对于公司发起人为境外的单位或者个人的,根据证券交易委员会的规定,公司的法定股本最少为 ₦ 10 000 000(一千万奈拉)。

② 已发行股本

在一家企业的存续期间,其已发行的股本不得少于其法定股本的 25%。也就是说,该公司法定股本中至少有 25% 必须由股东持有。一般来说,尼日利亚法律没有限制外国企业独资拥有一个尼日利亚公司。②然而,某些特定行业限制外国企业独资拥有某些类别的尼日利亚公司。例如,根据沿海和内陆航运法案,任何寻求注册船舶公司的,必须由尼日利亚人拥有 60% 的股份。需要注意的是,《公司及相关事务法》第十八章规定每个尼日利亚公司最少要有 2 个股东(不需要一定是尼日利亚人)。但是,外国公民在尼日利亚从事任何形式的商业活动之前,必须取得商业登记证和营业执照。

③ 实缴股本

法律没有规定公司发行股本中实缴股本的最低限额。

(5)官方费用

公司成立时须根据其法定股本估算应缴纳的官方费用,其中包括:

① 印花税——应向联邦税务局缴纳其法定股本的 0.75% 的印花税;

② 公司事务委员会申请费③——应向公司事务委员会缴纳其股本的 1% 的申请费;

③ 支付公司事务委员会约 ₦ 11 000(一万一千奈拉)获得公司章程和公司事务委员会表 2、表 3、表 7 以及表 2.1 正本。

公司的设立程序通常在向公司事务委员会提供了所有相关文件及支付费用之后的 14 个工作日内完成。

3. 公司解散的途径和规定

在尼日利亚,企业可以通过不同的途径被解散。根据《公司及相关事务法》第 401 条的规定解散是公司破产的后果之一,一个公司可能会因法院的裁判而破产清算,也可能有公司成员或债权人自主申请进入破产程序,或者因法院监管而解散。它也可能是公司事务委员会监管制裁的结果。

《公司及相关事务法》和《公司清算规则》是尼日利亚的公司破产程序相关的法律和法规。尼日利亚的破产制度主要规定在《公司及相关事务法》第十四、十五、十六章中,分别是破产清算和管理者、公司清算整顿和和解的规定。

(1)法院清算

根据《公司及相关事务法》第 408 条,公司可能会基于下列理由被法院要求清算:

① 经特别决议决定公司由法院负责清算;

② 未能向委员会提交法定报告或举行法定会议;

③ 成员人数减少到 2 人以下;

④ 公司无力偿还债务;

---

① 《公司及相关事务法》,第 293 节。
② 2004 年《尼日利亚联邦法律》第 C51 章。
③ 上市公司收取 2% 比例的费用。

⑤ 法院认为清算该公司是合理且公正的。

必须注意的是，公司对债权人负有债务，在以下情况下，该公司应被视为无力偿债：

① 所负债务超过 2 000 奈拉，且在收到法定通知后 3 周内仍无法偿还部分的债务；
② 反对判决的执行，对其全部或部分不满意；
③ 法院考虑到该公司所负债务且认为该公司无力偿还其债务。

如果申请人以公司无力偿还债务为由，向法院提起清算程序且要求由法院和申请人负责执行的，必须表明该申请书是善意提出的，并基于上述任何一个或多个理由提出。此外，根据《公司及相关事务法》第 410 条的规定，下列人员可以为公司清算向的法院单独或联合地提出申请：

① 公司；
② 债权人（包括公司的预期债权人，根据《公司及相关事务法》第 410 条第 2 款第 3 项，法院不会听取预期债权人提出的清算呈请，直至有足够的费用保证金且清算的初步证据达到令法院满意的状态）；
③（破产公司）财产管理人（联邦高等法院副总书记官或由联邦高等法院首席法官指定的管理人，以便清算公司）①；
④ 连带债务人②；
⑤ 破产管理人、债权人或连带债务人的代理人；
⑥ 公司事务委员会。

法院有权为清算程序的进行任命一个财产管理人和一个清算人。根据《公司及相关事务法》相应的规定少数股东有资格作为连带债务人，基于认为对公司的清算是公平合理的，他们可以向法院提出清算申请。

根据《公司及相关事务法》第 407 条到第 410 条以及《公司清算规则》第 15 条到第 41 条的规定，由法院负责执行的公司破产程序如下：

① 由少数股东提交清算申请书；
② 提交一份证明申请书的宣誓书；
③ 经法院同意，在听证日前 15 日内，在报纸和公报上刊登公司清算申请书；
④ 刊登申请书要写明申请人和申请人律师的姓名和地址；
⑤ 听取申请书和作出清算令；
⑥ 法院书记员应在同一天或不迟于清算令作出后的 5 天内，通知财产管理人，告知其清算令已宣布；
⑦ 将三份已盖章的清算令复印件发送给财产管理人③，财产管理人同样发送给公司事务委员；
⑧ 由被授权人向财产管理人提交两份公司事务声明复印件，一份副本用于宣誓，另一份将由财产管理人提交给法院书记员；
⑨ 由法院任命的清算人；
⑩ 在报纸和公报上刊登清算人，并将名单提交给公司事务委员；
⑪ 由清算人负责组织清算；
⑫ 向法院申请并批准解散公司的命令；
⑬ 在 14 天内将解散命令提交给公司事务委员会。

公司一旦被完全清算和解散，就丧失了作为法人的地位，其在法律上的相应权利也不再存在。然而，应当指出，法院有权决定是否批准公司清算，可以批准清算、拒绝清算申请或在同意上述规定同时提出的额外要求。

（2）自愿清算

公司可能（如有的话）因其章程规定经营期届满或公司章程规定公司解散事由（若有）发生或公司股东大会上通过自愿解散的决议而被解散。此外，如果公司通过了自愿清算的特别决议，公司也可

---

① 《公司及相关事务法》，第 419 节（1）。
② 连带债务人是在公司破产清算时要负连带清偿责任的人。
③ 联邦高等法院副总书记官或者由联邦最高法院首席法官为清算而指定的公司的管理人员。

能会自动清算。清算可能通过成员／股东自愿清算程序实现，按照《公司及相关事务法》的规定清算程序主要包括以下步骤：

① 由董事出具一份偿付能力声明书，确认公司有能力偿付其未清偿债务和其他债务（若有）；
② 在股东大会上拟由股东通过的一项特别决议，批准公司清算；
③ 由股东任命清算人（可以在批准清算的股东大会上作出）；
④ 清算人进行公司清盘（即清点公司资产、确认未偿债务和履行到期债务）；
⑤ 召开最后一次股东会议，批准清算人提交的最终报告（有关清算过程）和公司的决算；
⑥ 在公司事务委员会处进行清盘的最后报告和决算的登记；
⑦ 由公司事务委员会负责公司解散和注销公司名称的登记（在公司事务委员会对清算最后报告和决算进行登记后的 3 个月内进行）。

需要注意的是，清算的效果是：清算开始后，公司停止营业。在清算决议通过后的 14 天内，该决议的公告必须在公报或两份日报上刊登并提交给委员会。

（3）在法院的监督下解散

关于在法院的监督下清算，如果一个公司通过自愿清算的决议，经由任何有权可以提出清算申请的人提出①，法院可以命令自愿清算继续进行，但须接受法院的监督。这种清算的效果是，它被视为法院清算。另外，《公司及相关事务法》第 519 条第 1 款规定，有关公司清算的所有事项，法院可召集债权人开会，并应考虑个人债务。完成清算后，法院工作人员要向委员会反馈。

如果公司不再经营，公司事务委员会也可以将公司注册的名称注销。然而，权利受到侵害的成员可以在 20 年内申请恢复该公司名称。②

值得注意的是，通常情况下，在破产程序中法定优先权利将先于担保债权人的债权受偿。在一个公司被清算的过程中，《公司及相关事务法》规定了一个优先制度③，用来指导清算人对公司资产的分配。优先事项可分为以下几类：

① 清算的成本和费用；
② 当地利率和收费，缴纳个人所得税、估定税、土地税、企业所得税；
③《国家住房基金法》项下的扣费项目；
④ 为公司提供服务人员的工资和薪金；
⑤ 因清算令或决议而终止雇佣关系的职员、雇工、工人或劳工累积的假期薪酬；
⑥ 根据雇员补偿法在清盘开始前累积的任何赔偿或赔偿责任的应付款额；
⑦ 债务（有担保债权人优先于无担保债权人受偿）；
⑧ 根据公司的权利和利益向成员分配公司净资产，公司章程有另外规定的遵循章程的规定。

除上述法定优先受偿的费用，所有的无担保债权人在破产程序中将享有同等权利。④

（4）重整或和解

重整或者和解是一种公认的业务整合或重组的模式，有关的规定在《公司及相关事务法》第十六章中。第 538 条重整制度允许公司通过公司清算的特别决议并授权一个清算人出售公司资产，其报酬通常是由被清算公司的股东根据分配给受让公司的股份来决定的。

《公司及相关事务法》第 539 条允许公司和其债权人或股东成员之间协商重整或者和解（或其他有关类别的人员）。该程序以公司向法院提交申请书请求法院组织重整会议的方式进行。会议通知将发出并且附有对重整有重大利益关联的股东或者债权人产生何种影响的说明（任何的公告都必须包含上述说明）。如果被批准同意，会议将被举行。

在法院批准的会议上，重整计划最少需得到代表 3/4 票数的股东（或其一类）或者代表 3/4 债权额（或其一类）的票数才能通过。第 539 条第 2 款进一步规定了重整方案必须提交到证券交易委员会，证券交易委员会必须指派一名或多名检查员调查重整或者和解的公平性，并向法院提交书面报告，如果

---

① 《公司及相关事务法》，第 487 节和第 490 节 (2)："要求由法院监督的清算申请书在大多数情况下被视为由法院来清算。"
② 《公司及相关事务法》，第 525 节 (6)。
③ 《公司及相关事务法》，第 494 节。
④ 《公司及相关事务法》，第 480 节。

法院对重整或者和解的公平性感到满意，可以批准重整方案，该方案对双方有约束力。除了上述提到的，由法院批准实施方案的经认证的副本需提交给公司事务委员会，待公司事务委员会登记后该方案得以正式生效。①

（六）兼并与收购

尼日利亚《投资与证券法》（2007年）是规范兼并和收购（并购）的主要法律文件。交易主要由证券交易委员会②颁布的规则和条例来调整。若并购涉及上市公司，证券交易规则也适用。③

公司在尼日利亚的所有业务（企业合并包括在内）都由《公司及相关事务法》④规范及其根据其制定的2012年《公司条例》⑤规范。根据印花税法，并购的文件需要交纳印花税。根据合并公司所属的经济部门，也可以适用其他法律和法规，银行、保险、电信、电力、广播、石油、天然气等行业专门的法规和规章可能影响到与之相关的并购交易。

在尼日利亚，并购的主要监管机构是证券交易委员会，它审查并批准所有公司整合业务；并购交易需纳的税（包括印花税在内）由其他金融机构管理；公司事务委员会负责审查合并是否符合2012年《公司条例》的规定。

按照法律规定，联邦高级法院可以作出命令，要求双方召开合并前期会议或批准一项完成的合并。根据每个合并案例具体的情况，尼日利亚股票交易所或其他合适的交易所、尼日利亚中央银行或国家保险委员会等机构也会参与。

根据《投资与证券法》的定义，合并指的是任何一个或两个以上公司和一个或多个公司团体⑥承诺整体合并或部分利益的合并，而收购意味着一家公司接管另一家公司足够多的股份从而对其享有控制权。⑦

并购的条件和类别：

证券交易委员会规定了尼日利亚市场的并购门槛，并有权不定期审议小型、中型和大型企业并购的金额标准。⑧在尼日利亚进行并购的法定要求如下⑨：

① 要求有意合并的企业，单独或一起向联邦高级法院提交并购申请；
② 联邦高级法院指令有意合并的企业分别召开会议用以批准并购计划
③ 投资并购决议需要参与并购公司中持有公司股份3/4以上的成员决议批准通过；
④ 通过的决议随后提交证券交易委员会审批；
⑤ 在证券交易委员会批准该并购方案后，双方或其中一方必须向联邦高级法院申请司法批准；
⑥ 在取得并购申请的司法批准后的7天内向公司事务委员会递交法院的指令；
⑦ 联邦高级法院批准并购的指令必须刊登在两份公报和至少一家全国性报刊上。

除上述规定外，《投资与证券法》和《证券交易规则》还规定了在获得所需批准后一旦违约的违约金。证券交易委员会认为符合以下条件则会批准合并：

① 兼并或收购，不论是直接或间接地涉及整个或任何部分的公司股本或其他公司的资产，不会造成实质性的竞争限制，也不会轻易地导致任何企业的垄断；
② 以投票或授权代理或其他方式使用此种股票，不会造成实质性的竞争限制，也不会导致任何企业的垄断；
③ 尽管提议合并看起来似乎是为了限制竞争，但合并的一方已经证明了其意不在此。⑩

证券交易委员会规定的兼并限额如下：

---

① Nelson C.S.Ogbuanya: "Essentials of Corporate Law Practice in Nigeria".
② 证监会规则。详见 http://www.nse.com.ng/regulation-site/Pages/The-Rulebook-of-The-NSE.aspx.
③ 《尼日利亚证券交易所规则》。详见 http://www.nse.com.ng/regulation-site/Pages/The-Rulebook-of-The-NSE.aspx.
④ 2004年《尼日利亚联邦法律》第C20章。
⑤ 详见上文批注39。
⑥ 第119节。
⑦ 证券交易委员会（SEC）第227条规则。
⑧ 《投资与证券法》，第120节。详见上文。
⑨ 《公司及相关事务法》，第591节；ISA，第100节。
⑩ 《投资与证券法》。

① 小型兼并

小型兼并的资金门槛较低，低于 100 万奈拉，既可以是合并资产也可以是合并公司的营业额。

② 中型兼并

中型兼并的资金门槛 100 万～500 万奈拉，既可以是合并资产也可以是合并企业的营业额。

③ 大型兼并

大型兼并的门槛资金是 500 万奈拉以上，既可以是合并资产也可以是合并公司的营业额。

（七）竞争规制

1. 部门竞争监督规则

尼日利亚市场的竞争管制最初仅限于证券交易委员会的职权范围。《投资与证券法》授权证券交易委员会作为可以批准所有形式的商业合并（合并、收购或接管）的机构，并确保兼并计划或任何拟议收购或接管计划不破坏竞争机制或获得不公平的市场优势。其他涉及竞争倾向的行业如电信、银行和保险行业等，有相应的法规规定了专门的行业反竞争检查机制。

2. 竞争法概述

尼日利亚目前没有单独的竞争/反垄断法，2015 年《联邦竞争及消费者保护法》似乎是该国有关竞争立法的第一大步，这部法由尼日利亚联邦参议院通过，但是目前仍在等待联邦众议院的通过。目前，尼日利亚的竞争受《投资与证券法》的管辖，禁止会造成垄断、带来不公平竞争或滥用主导地位的商业行为。

任何形式的实质性禁止或者减少竞争的企业合并都是被禁止的，不能够取得证券交易委员会的法定许可，除非这种反竞争方案将带来任何技术效率的提高或其他有利于竞争的收益，并且这将大于或抵消任何兼并可能带来的对禁止或者限制竞争的影响，或者说，这种减少竞争的安排从公共利益角度上来说是正当的。①

在确定合并是否有可能实质性地禁止竞争或减少竞争的情况下，证券交易委员会有权去评估相关市场的竞争力，以及公司并购后在市场上表现出竞争性或合作性的可能性，将所有与该市场竞争有关的任何因素纳入考虑②，包括：

① 市场上进口竞争的实际与潜在水平；
② 进入市场的便捷性，包括关税和监管壁垒；
③ 市场集中的水平和趋势，以及共谋经历；
④ 市场反补贴的程度；
⑤ 市场的动态特征，包括增长、创新和产品差异化；
⑥ 市场纵向一体化的性质和范围；
⑦ 合并或拟合并的一方的业务或部分业务是否失败或是否有失败的可能性；
⑧ 合并是否会导致有效竞争对手的被排除。

在竞争激烈的行业中，造成不公平市场优势如垄断或滥用优势地位等商业安排通常不被行业特定监管机构所允许。③此外，在企业合并（合并、收购或接管）计划提交给证券交易委员会审批之前，行业监管机构通常会审查他们的任何反竞争动机，并可能拒绝同意这些计划，在此情况下这类计划是没有资格被提交给证券交易委员会的。

3. 规范竞争的措施

目前尼日利亚规范竞争的一些措施主要是检测反竞争行为的监管制度，涉及定价、串通投标、赞助竞争对手的虚假或误导信息、制造垄断、滥用市场支配地位等反竞争行为。

除了证券交易委员会有权阻止不利于任何经济领域健康竞争的商业安排，许多管理机构以规范性文件例如公报、指引和规则的方式禁止反竞争的商业行为。

---

① 《公司及相关事务法》，第 121 节（1）。
② 同上注，第 121 节（2）。
③ 比如银行业的尼日利亚中央银行（CBN）；保险行业的国家保险委员会（NAICOM）；广播行业的国家广播委员会。

以尼日利亚电信业为例，国家通信委员会是公平竞争的监管者。根据尼日利《亚通信法》第 4 条第 4 款[①]，国家通信委员会负责促进通信行业的公平竞争，保护通信服务提供者和设施供应商不受其他服务或设施供应商滥用市场权力或反竞争和不公平行为的影响。同样地，根据尼日利亚《通信法》第 90 条，国家通信委员会拥有专属职权，决定、宣布、管理、监督和强制所有人遵守竞争法律和法规，无论是一般的原则还是具体的规定。具体而言，是为了确保行业内竞争的存在，尼日利亚《通信法》第 91 条第 1 款禁止被许可人参与任何意图或已实质性减少尼日利亚通信市场竞争的行为。

尼日利亚《通信法》第 91 条第 3 款，禁止被许可人订立有关固定利率、市场共享或任何抵制竞争对手、供应商或者其他被许可人的协议或者安排。同时尼日利亚《通信法》第 91 条 4 款，禁止被许可人要求任何获得通信产品或者服务的人去获取其他产品或者服务，无论是从被许可人还是其他人处，或者要求他们不得从被许可人或者其他人处获得任何其他产品或者服务。最后，第 92 条第 1 款允许由国家通信委员会来认定一个被许可人在尼日利亚通信市场的任何方面是否处于支配地位。

尼日利亚《通信法》第 91 条第 2 款和 92 条第 2 款分别授权国家通信委员会颁布尼日利亚通信市场"实质性减少竞争"的定义以及如何认定被许可人"支配地位"的准则和规定。为促进尼日利亚《通信法》第 91 条第 2 款和第 92 条第 2 款的实施，国家通信委员会颁布了竞争规则，规定了国家通信委员会在认定一个特定行为构成尼日利亚《通信法》所规定的实质性减少竞争以及认定一个被许可人是否在一个或者多个通信市场占据"支配地位"的标准和程序。

（八）税收

1. 税收制度和规则

尼日利亚目前的税收环境是由 2017 年《国家税收政策》所设定的。《国家税收政策》及其目标：
① 指导税务系统的运作和审查；
② 为今后的税收立法和管理提供依据；
③ 为所有利益相关者提供一个关于税收的参考；
④ 提供利益相关者承担责任的基准；
⑤ 明确利益相关者在税务系统中的作用和责任。

正如《国家税收政策》所设想的，所有现有和未来的税收都符合以下基本特征[②]：
① 公平和公正——尼日利亚的税收制度应公平、公正、不歧视，应按照纳税人的能力收取；
② 简单、明确和清晰——税法和行政程序应当简单、清晰和易于理解；
③ 便利——履行纳税义务的时间和方式应考虑到纳税人的便利，避免不必要的困难；
④ 低遵守成本——要保持纳税人遵守相关规定所需财务和经济成本是最低限度的；
⑤ 管理费用低——尼日利亚的税务管理应符合国际最佳做法，效率高、成本低；
⑥ 灵活性——税收灵活多变，以不妨碍经济活动的方式应对经济变化；
⑦ 可持续性——税收制度应促进可持续收入、经济增长和发展。税收政策和政府的其他经济政策应该有协同作用。

2. 主要的税收类别和税率

（1）企业所得税

2004 年《企业所得税法案》C21（由 2007 年第 11 号《企业所得税法修正案》修正），在扣除所有免税支出、损失和资本津贴后，对在尼日利亚注册的公司征收的所得税税率为 30%。

根据《企业所得税法案》，每个公司应缴的税必须要进行自我评估和归档，在会计期结束后的 6 个月内审定账目并进行所得税计算。在新公司成立的情况下，收益应在公司成立之日起 18 个月内，或在第一个会计期间后 6 个月内提交，以先出现的为准。

（2）教育税

2004 年根据《教育税法》E4，在尼日利亚注册的公司，必须支付其应税利润的 2% 作为教育税。

---

① 2003 年第 19 号。
② 联邦财政部："Guiding Principles of Nigeria Tax System"，2017 年 2 月 1 日。详见 http://www.finance.gov.ng/。

（3）行业培训基金

《行业培训基金法》（2004年）（由2011年《行业培训基金法修正案》修正）建立了行业培训基金，该基金的目的是促进在工业或商业方面相关技能的取得，建立一个本地的人力资源库，以满足经济发展的需要。符合《行业培训基金法》要求的雇主都有义务向该基金缴纳其年度工资总额的1%，应纳税主体包括：

① 在公司成立时有5个或更多的员工的雇主；
② 有少于5人的员工，但每年的平均营业额有5 000万奈拉或者以上的雇主；
③ 竞标任何联邦政府机构或国营企业或民营企业的合同的供应商、承包商或顾问；
④ 在自由贸易区运作的，寻求批准移民配额或使用海关服务的企业。

在确定缴付金额时，所有雇员，包括兼职和临时雇用的雇员都应包括在内。此外，在评估雇员的工资总额时发放给员工的津贴和补贴，无论是在境内还是境外的，都要计算在内。

《行业培训基金法》还进一步规定雇主有责任为本地员工提供培训以提高他们的工作技能。此外，《行业培训基金法》还规定，在基金理事会认为该雇主培训充分且其感到满意的情况下，基金理事会可以退还高达50%的由雇主支付的费用。

在规定的年度内没有按期缴纳基金的，自超期日起按每月或部分月拖欠金额5%的标准支付罚金。

（4）信息技术税

根据2007年《国家信息技术发展机构法》，对营业额在1 000万奈拉或者以上的下列公司收取其税前利润1%的税收：

① 全球移动通信服务提供商和所有电信公司；
② 网络公司和因特网供应商；
③ 养老金管理人员和与养老金有关的公司；
④ 银行和其他金融机构；
⑤ 保险公司。

（5）个人所得税

雇员的所得按累进税率征收，详见下表。2014年《个人所得税法》第八章建立了所得税预扣法系统，雇主需作为税务机关的代理人，代扣和代缴雇员的个人所得税。预扣的所得税需要在被扣缴后14天内汇出，在每年的年底，雇主须提交所有扣税卡及雇主汇款卡。

超过起征点30万奈拉以内	7%
超过起征点30万奈拉至60万奈拉部分	11%
超过起征点60万奈拉至110万奈拉部分	15%
超过起征点110万奈拉至160万奈拉部分	19%
超过起征点160万奈拉至320万奈拉部分	21%
超过起征点320万奈拉部分	24%

每位雇员扣除的税款的汇总表将显示在雇主的年度申报表上，并提交税务机关。这项工作应在次年1月30日或之前完成。

（6）预扣税

尼日利亚税法（《企业所得税法》和《个人所得税法》）规定，当一个人向另一个人支付款项的时候，相应的代扣所得税税款要被扣除，付款人应按适用税率扣除税款，并在合理期间内将税款汇至有关税务机关，最迟不超过扣税后的30日。需要扣除预扣税的活动以及服务和目前适用的税率的如下：

交易	企业	个人
股息、利息及租金	10%	10%
特许使用费	10%	5%
租用设备、汽车、工厂和机械	10%	10%
佣金、顾问费、技术费、管理费、法律服务费、审计费和其他专业费用	10%	5%
建设项目	5%	5%
除正常业务过程中的销售以外的所有类型的合同和代理协议	5%	5%
董事费	N/A	10%

当向与尼日利亚签订了双重征税条约国家的居民支付股息、利息和特许使用费时相应的预扣税税率减至 7.5%。

（7）资本收益税

资本收益税是对个人处置资产时获得的资产收益所征收的税，不论资产是否位于尼日利亚境内，该税项适用于所有公司，包括先锋公司及所有个人及非法人团体，税率目前为 10%。

（8）转让定价

一般来说，在尼日利亚以外地区使用关联公司进行业务没有任何限制。然而，这种交易可能被视为转让定价从而受 2012 年《所得税（转让定价）条例》约束。转让定价发生在两个属于同一个跨国公司的公司相互贸易的过程中，通常手段是订立水平服务协议。

《所得税（转让定价）条例》第 3 条规定，转让定价条例适用于与不符合正常交易原则有关联的应税人之间的交易，包括：①销售和购买货物和服务；②有形资产的销售、购买或租赁；③转让、购买或使用无形资产；④提供服务；⑤借款；⑥制造协议；⑦任何可能会影响上述①到⑥交易的利润、损失或者其他附带事项的交易。

转让定价条例旨在防止与"有关联的应税人"进行不符合正常交易原则的交易。这些人中的一方要么控制另一方，要么与对方有联系，或者两者都由其他人控制，从事税务机关认为未按照规定进行其他人通常会按照的正常交易原则进行的相同或类似交易。

基本上，其他金融机构的目标是确保关联公司之间进行的交易符合正常交易原则。在确定一个交易或一系列交易的结果是否符合正常交易原则时，其他金融机构会适用以下转让定价方法：①可比较无管制价格法；②转售价格法；③成本加成法；④交易净利润法；⑤交易利润分割法。是否违反正常交易原则和适用哪种转移定价方法要基于个案确定。

3. 税收申报与优惠

纳税申报由纳税义务人按照规定的形式定期向其他金融机构缴纳税款并用以评估，通常为每年一次。《企业所得税法案》在尼日利亚对企业的利润征税（除了石油公司），为此，根据《企业所得税法案》规定应纳税的所有企业需要在其他金融机构进行登记并取得一个纳税识别号，纳税识别号必须体现在与其他金融机构所有的申报和往来文件上。税务登记必须在公司成立后立即进行。

基于所得税预扣法的要求，每个雇主需要在其业务所在州的税务局分区办事处进行登记，此登记必须在公司成立后立即进行。

增值税是根据 2004 年的《增值税法》（经 2007 年第 12 号《增值税修正案》修订）的基础上实施的，根据该法规定，所有制造商开始营业 6 个月内都必须在其他金融机构处登记。

(九) 证券

1. 证券相关法律法规简介

尼日利亚涉及证券投资事项由《投资与证券法》和证券交易委员会的各类规则[1]管辖。2013年《证券交易委员会统一规则》[2]制定了有关在尼日利亚各种形式投资的规定，包括外资和跨国证券交易[3]，将外国投资定义为由外国人（公司或者个人）或者由境外尼日利亚人所做的任何形式的对证券的投资。根据《证券交易委员会统一规则》，外国投资者应当包括外国机构投资者，例如养老基金、单位信托基金、投资信托基金、机构投资经理、委托公司、资产管理公司或任何其他法人团体，以及用外资进行投资的外国人和境外的尼日利亚人等个体投资者。同样，统一规则将所有初级证券市场和二级市场上的证券交易（股票、政府股票、工业贷款股票、债券、单位信托基金、投资信托基金、衍生性金融商品或证券交易委员会登记的任何其他证券）纳入其监管范围内的投资类别。[4]

尼日利亚的证券法律包括下列规定和规章：

① 《投资与证券法》2007年；
② 《公司及相关事项法》1990年（见2004年尼日利亚联邦法律第C20章）；
③ 《中央银行（制定）法》2007年；
④ 《银行和其他金融机构法》1991年，第25条（见2004年尼日利亚联邦法律第B3章）；
⑤ 《投资促进署法》1995年，第16条（见2004年尼日利亚联邦法律第N117章）；
⑥ 《外汇（监督及杂项规定）法》1995年，第17条（见2004年尼日利亚联邦法律第F34章）。

2. 证券市场监管

上述法律共同为尼日利亚证券市场的监管提供了框架。依据《投资与证券法》设立的证券交易委员会作为尼日利亚资本市场的最高监管机构，监督所有证券交易。证券交易委员会与法律规定的金融系统内其他监管机构一起履行其监管职能。例如，证券交易委员会、尼日利亚中央银行和尼日利亚投资证券委员会合作管理资本输入并确保将资本转移到尼日利亚用以投资的外国投资者获得资本输入证明，使他们能够安全地在尼日利亚证券、货币市场产品和企业进行投资，从激励措施中获益、享受投资保护，并在退出时将其资本与收益无缝地返还。[5]

3. 外国企业参与证券交易的要求

希望在尼日利亚境内投资证券业务的外商投资企业，应当遵守外汇市场外汇进口、业务合并、纳税的各项法律并在有关机构进行登记。他们还需要通过在证券交易委员会[6]注册认证的资本市场运营商进行投资。从本质上讲，需要在以下机构进行登记：尼日利亚中央银行（通过授权经销商审核投资者的资本输入证书）、尼日利亚移民服务（审核居民和商业许可证）以及尼日利亚投资证券委员会。

(十) 投资优惠与投资保护

1. 优惠政策框架

被尼日利亚投资证券委员会认定为投资尼日利亚"优先领域"的企业或者产业将享受投资优惠。尼日利亚投资证券委员会发布可以给予与政府政策相符合的鼓励措施和优惠行业的具体指引。一些相关的法律法规规定的各种投资优惠措施包括：免税期、税收抵免、资金补贴、投资补贴、税收减免、退税、出口补贴、扩大补贴、出口发展基金、双重税收减免、促进和保护投资协定等。以下是根据尼

---

[1] 根据《投资与证券法》第313节制定的规则。
[2] 证监会综合规则包含602个规则，适用于市场上的人员及交易在不同的资本市场的投资模式、行为规范模式以及市场上的交易模式。详见 http://sec.gov.ng/sec-nigerias-consolidated-rules-and-regulations-as-at-2013/。
[3] 同上注，H部分。
[4] 同上注，第405节。
[5] 《外汇监管法》第15节和第26节；2013年《证监会综合规则》第408条规则；《尼日利亚投资促进委员会法案》第21节和第24节。
[6] 2013年《证监会综合规则》第406条（2）规则，同上注。

日利亚投资证券委员会的公告可以享受优惠的产业[1]：

① 新兴产业——在尼日利亚处于初始阶段的工业被授予新兴产业的地位。给予一个行业免税期，旨在使有关行业在其形成期内获得合理的利润，且该利润被鼓励再投入企业以促进增长。新兴产业企业地位的授予期限最长为5年（即从首次生产之日起的最初3年期限，对于继续经营尼日利亚经济优先领域的公司，可以再延长2年）。授予新兴产业企业地位的条件是，合资公司或独资公司必须有至少1 000万奈拉股本以及不少于500万奈拉的资本支出，而符合条件的本土企业则不应少于15万奈拉。申请公司必须向尼日利亚投资促进委员会支付其估计节省的2%的服务费。此外，申请公司必须在商业生产开始之日起1年内提交关于新兴产业地位的申请，否则申请会因过期而失效。[2] 新兴地位的法律框架，包括《产业发展（所得税减免）法案》[3]和《新兴地位优惠条例》。根据《产业发展（所得税减免）法案》，如果行业满足以下条件，联邦执行委员会可以宣布一个行业是新兴产业或行业中的产品是一个新兴产品：其一，该行业未在尼日利亚兴起；其二，尼日利亚没有以适合经济的规模经营该行业；其三，该行业在尼日利亚有进一步发展的良好前景；其四，通过宣布其为新兴产业，鼓励在尼日利亚发展或建立该行业，符合公众利益。

② 对从尼日利亚出口的货物，只要收益回流至尼日利亚，并专门用于购买原材料、工厂设备和零部件，公司可以享受免税。

③ 对于那些原材料完全来自出口加工生产企业的，公司利润可以免税。

④ 所有新的工业实体包括出口加工区的外资企业和个体经营户可以享受连续3年免税。

⑤ 作为鼓励工业技术的发展，从事商业化研发活动的公司和其他组织享受20%的投资税收抵免。

⑥ 单位分配的股息无需纳税，也无需缴纳扣所得税，因为该收入一开始就已纳税。

⑦ 凡完全从事用于本地消费或出口的工具、零配件及简单机械制造的公司，均享有25%的投资税收抵免。凡购买当地制造的机器和设备的纳税人，同样可获得所购固定资产15%的投资抵税。

⑧ 厂内培训——适用于设立了厂内培训设施的工业场所，可以享受5年2%的减税优惠。

⑨ 基础设施投资——作为一种奖励措施，给予那些通常应该由政府提供的基础设施的产业，这些设施包括道路、管道供水和电力。提供这些基础设施的成本的20%是免税的。

⑩ 劳动密集型生产方式——劳动密集度/资本比率高的产业有权在尼日利亚享受减税优惠。这些产业配有的工厂、设备和机械，基本上是自动化程度最低的。即便是有自动化的操作，这种自动化在生产过程中不应超过一个生产流程。按比例计算，从业人员1 000人以上的享受15%的税收优惠，从业人员200人以上的享受7%税收优惠，从业人员100人以上的享受6%税收优惠。

⑪ 当地增值——享受个5年的10%的税收减让优惠，适用于其生产投入部分为进口成品的尼日利亚工程产业。特许经营的目的是鼓励当地制造业发展，而不是单纯组装完全分散的部件。

⑫ 再投资补贴——在尼日利亚，奖励那些用合理的资本支出进行企业扩张的从事制造业的公司。奖励是以津贴的形式发放给因下列原因而进行资本支出的企业：生产能力的扩大、生产设施的现代化、相关产品的多样化。

⑬ 最低当地原材料利用率——对达到当地原材料采购和利用的最低水平要求产业可以享受5年20%年税收抵免，地方原材料采购和利用的最低水平是：农业联盟70%、工程60%、化学品60%、和石化70%。

2. 对特定行业的支持

尼日利亚对投资某些特定行业给予奖励措施，特别是对投资在指定优先领域的经营者，以下为给投资者提供的相关产业支持[4]：

（1）农业

农业和农业联合产业的投资者享有以下奖励：

---

[1] 尼日利亚投资促进委员会（NIPC）。详见 http://www.nipc.gov.ng/investment.html。
[2] 同上注。
[3] 2004年《尼日利亚联邦法律》第17章。
[4] 2013年《证监会综合规则》第406条第（2）项。

① 充分和不受限制（100%）的农业联合企业的资本津贴；
② 低利润或无利润公司缴纳的最低税额不适用于农业联盟企业；
③ 农业联合厂房和设备享有高达 50% 的资本津贴；
④ 农产品加工作为一个被授予新兴地位的产业获得为期 5 年的 100% 免税期；
⑤ 涉及农产品以及用于生产农产品和农业联合产品加工的机械和设备的所有农业项目享有 1% 的关税；
⑥ 给投资者向商业银行申请的用于农业生产和加工项目的贷款提供来自于农业信贷担保计划基金高达 75% 的担保；
⑦ 借贷来自于农业信贷担保计划基金的企业和投资者按期还款的，可从利息退税项目基金获得已付贷款利息 60% 的返还。

（2）固体矿物
固体矿物领域享有以下激励：
① 3～5 年的免税期；
② 20%～30% 的低所得税；
③ 根据投资的规模和项目的战略性质，推迟支付特许使用费；
④ 勘探和测量支出的可能资本化；
⑤ 将道路和电力等基础设施铺设到采矿地点；
⑥ 凡符合条件的，采矿租约持有人有权享有下列权利：
• 发生在投资年度经核证的真实资本支出 75% 的资产折旧或者资本减免，下一年为 50%；
• 5% 的投资津贴；
• 免除出口关税和进口关税；
• 移民配额和经核准外籍人员居留证；
• 除了在资本利得税下的滚转冲抵，更换厂房和机器设备的公司将在第一年享受一次性 95% 的资本津贴，保留 5% 的资产价值直到资产被处置；更换其他资产的公司享受 15% 的资本津贴。

（3）石油
与尼日利亚国家石油公司合资经营并签订了《谅解备忘录》的企业可以享受这一领域的优惠政策，这些优惠有：
① 加速资本冲减（税项折旧），使资本冲减无限期地结转。这是授予合格资本支出每年固定 20% 的比例（第 5 年 19% 且余额保留在账簿中直到合格资本支出被处理）；
② 经营石油业务所得的股息免征代扣所得税①；
③ 批准 10% 专利权使用率给在深海作业的石油公司（根据作业水深 0%～12% 不等）。

（4）天然气
鉴于这一部门的巨大潜力，政府已批准了以下财政优惠措施：
① 在天然气生产阶段：
• 适用税率与公司所得税相同；
• 在前 4 年每年的资本冲减率为 20%，第 5 年为 19%，其余年限为 1%；
• 投资税收抵扣，目前是 5%；
• 岸上开采 7% 的许可费和离岸开采 5% 的许可费。
② 在天然气的传输和分配：
• 享有上述生产阶段的资本冲减；
• 享有上述生产阶段的税率；
• 新兴产业地位的免税期。②
③ 液化天然气项目：

---

① 2007 年修订的《汽油利得税法》第 60 节。
② 根据《尼日利亚联邦政府公告》第 63 号令第 102 条的规定，天然气的加工和传输是新兴行业。

- 适用 45% 的石油利润税；
- 在前 3 年中，每年的资本免税额为 33%，而其余 1% 则在账目中；
- 许可费享受 10% 的投资税收抵扣，岸上开采享受 7% 的投资税收抵扣，离岸开采享受 5% 的投资税收抵扣 %。

④ 天然气开采（上游作业），财政安排如下：
- 需要将石油从天然气中分离而不是储存进相应的产品中的所有投资都被认为是油田开发的一部分；
- 资本投资在使用或转移点的设施用于输送相关气体的，在财务用途上将会被作为石油开发资本投资的一部分；
- 资本减免、业务费用和评估依据将按照《石油利得税法》和经修订的《谅解备忘录》的规定执行。

⑤ 天然气利用（下游操作）：
- 从事天然气的利用的企业适用《企业所得税法》；
- 最初的免税期为 3 年，可再延长 2 年；
- 免税期后以 90% 的形式加速资本减免，10% 保留在账目中；
- 享受 15% 投资资本冲减，且不降低资产价值。

⑥ 政府批准的支持天然气产业发展的额外激励措施适用以下领域：
- 所有天然气开发项目，包括从事发电、液体厂、化肥厂、配气/输气管道都要根据《企业所得税法》而不是《石油利得税法》的规定征收税款；
- 自 1997 以来，所有针对天然气利用的下游业务的财政优惠措施将扩大到使用燃气的工业项目，即发电厂、液化天然气厂、化肥厂、气体分配/传输厂；
- 最初的免税期将从 3 年延长到 5 年；
- 天然气的传输无需支付石油利润税和许可费；
- 投资资本冲减从 5% 增加到 15%；
- 对天然气项目的贷款利息可享受税收减免，前提是在获得贷款之前获得联邦财政部事先批准；
- 在免税期分配的所有股息不得征税。

（5）电信

政府为私人投资者提供非财政优惠，除了确保投资者在合理时间内收回投资的税收架构，同时也考虑到了城乡差别税收的必要性。电信监管部门尼日利亚通信委员会批准的税收安排，也为城市营利干线和市内电话以及农村非营利性经营提供了足够的交叉补贴。其他尚在执行的优惠措施还有：

① 制造和安装与电信有关的设备将获得新兴产业地位，并享受 3～5 年的免税期；
② 所征收的税和关税不超过基本电器产品所征收的税额。

（6）能源（电）

政府鼓励电力行业投资者的激励措施有：

① 对于被授予新兴产业地位的制造变压器、仪表、控制面板、开关装置、电缆和其他与电气有关的设备的公司给予 3～5 年的免税期；
② 对使用天然气的发电厂公司所得税以低税率进行评估。

（7）旅游

为鼓励国内和外国投资者参与尼日利亚的旅游业，实施了以下优惠措施：

① 旅游业在 1999 年获得优先行业地位。这使得该部门有资格获得优惠（适用于类似的行业），例如免税期、更长的延缓偿付期和与旅游有关的设备免进口税；
② 提供基本的基础设施，如道路、水、电、通信等，以吸引游客为中心，一些州将特定的地区规划为旅游开发区以便可以更快捷地征用土地；
③ 以更优惠地价为旅游业的发展提供土地；
④ 可获得有更长的延缓偿付期的软贷款。

（8）运输

以下是用来鼓励运输部门投资的优惠措施：

船舶修造、船舶维修、船舶、驳船、潜水和水下工程服务、飞机维修和制造业均被授予新兴产业的地位，因此享有 3～5 年的免税期，具体时限视位置而定。

（9）经济困难地区的投资

无论新兴产业地位法律规定如何，投资位于尼日利亚经济落后地方行政区域的新兴产业可以享受 7 年的 100% 免税期，并可在最初的资本折旧额基础上再增加 5% 的资本折旧津贴。①

3. 经济特区

为鼓励工业化和本土化的发展，吸引外国直接投资和促进经济发展的公私合作伙伴关系（尤其是出口导向型行业），尼日利亚政府指定特定区域作为免税区、出口加工区，这些特定区域里的企业可享受免税和其他财政优惠措施以及规模经济和基础设施集中带来的便利和好处。

（1）尼日利亚出口加工区

1992 年尼日利亚《出口加工区法案》第二章②设立的尼日利亚出口加工管理局负责该法案第四节项下的尼日利亚出口加工区的一般管理、监督和协调事务。尼日利亚《出口加工区法案》第一章授权总统根据尼日利亚出口加工管理局的推荐批准尼日利亚的任何区域作为出口加工区。

（2）石油和天然气免税区

根据 1996 年《石油和天然气免税区法》③，尼日利亚在河流州的恩纳港设立石油和天然气免税区，由石油和天然气免税区管理局管理。《石油和天然气免税区法》规定给免税区内的石油和天然气公司提供优惠措施，这些优惠措施同样适用免税区内为这些石油天然气公司提供相应设备和服务的企业。适用于石油和天然气免税区的监管和操作指南与适用于其他（一般的）出口加工区相似，只是前者是专门为石油和天然气业务而作出的规定，后者则为满足多产业的发展需要。

（3）对免税区内投资者的奖励措施

免税区内的企业登记一般比较容易和快捷，外籍人员的居住和工作许可证的处理和取得无缝衔接。另外，在石油和天然气免税区货物清关的程序通常不会像在普通港口一样，托运人和经营者要经历繁琐的官僚程序。④

在石油和天然气免税区可以享受到的其他优惠措施包括："M 表"中的装运前免责；将散装货物置换成更小的元件进行重新包装出售甚至进行陈列展出的可能性；从石油和天然气免税区出口货物和在石油和天然气免税区内消费免征关税；免除投资者进出口许可证；个人所得税纳税免除；100% 资本和利润的返还；进口到保税区的货物无装运前检验。⑤

值得注意的是，在这方面，适用于免税区的外汇管制条例放宽了，尼日利亚中央银行⑥在 2016 年规定了在尼日利亚所有自由贸易/出口加工区可进行无缝外汇交易。具体而言，政府已向区内投资者提供下列优惠措施：

① 免除所有联邦政府、州政府和地方政府的税收、收费、关税和其他征税；

② 对所有许可证、经营许可证和公司设立文件进行一站式批准；

③ 对用于再出口而进口的货物原材料免税；

④ 引进的资本货物、消费品、零部件、机械、设备和家具全部免税；

⑤ 准许向国内市场销售 100% 在区内制造、装配或进口的货物；

⑥ 当向国内市场销售时，在自由区制造的货物进口关税的进口额是根据原材料或在组装中使用的零部件的价值而不是制成品的价值计算的；

⑦ 100% 外国投资所有权；

---

① 2007 年修订的《汽油利得税法》。
② 2004 年《尼日利亚联邦法律》第 N107 章。
③ 2004 年《尼日利亚联邦法律》第 O5 章。
④ Banwo 和 Ighodalo: "Doing Business in Nigeria: Some of the Incentives Available to Investors"，2015 年 12 月。详见 http://www.banwo-ighodalo.com/grey-matter/doing-business-in-nigeria-some-of-the-incentives-available-to-investors?leaf=3。
⑤ 同上注。
⑥ 尼日利亚中央银行（CBN）: "Guidelines for Banking Operations in the Free Zones in Nigeria"，2016 年 2 月。详见 https://www.cbn.gov.ng/Out/2016/BPSD/GUIDELINES%20FOR%20BANKING%20OPERATIONS%20IN%20THE%20FREE%20ZONES.pdf。

⑧ 资本、利润和股息的 100% 返还；
⑨ 免除所有进出口许可证；
⑩ 免除在区内经营的公司的所有移民配额；
⑪ 禁止罢工和停工；
⑫ 在建设的最初 6 个月内免收地租。

4. 投资保护

（1）双边投资促进与保护协定

作为为增强外国投资者对尼日利亚经济信心所做出的努力的一部分，尼日利亚联邦政府和一些与其有商业来往的国家签订了双边投资促进与保护协定。①这有助于保证缔约方的投资在战争、革命、征用或国有化进程中的安全。这也为投资者的利益、红利、利润、其他收入的转移以及对征用和损失的补偿提供了保障。目前，尼日利亚与法国、英国、荷兰、罗马尼亚、瑞士、西班牙、南非等国家签署了保护协定，与美国、比利时、瑞典、俄罗斯和其他国家的双边投资促进与保护协定的谈判也在开展中。

（2）所有制结构的自由化

政府废除了 1972 年的尼日利亚《企业促进法》，颁布了 1995 年尼日利亚《投资促进委员会法案》，开放了尼日利亚的企业所有制结构。外国人现在可以在任何一家公司拥有 100% 股份，而不再像早前需要由尼日利亚人持股 40%～60%。

（3）利润返还

根据《外汇监管法》②与尼日利亚《投资促进委员会法案》③，外国投资者可以通过可自由兑换货币的授权交易商，将其纳税后净额利润和股息汇出。

（4）保证不征用

尼日利亚《投资促进委员会法案》保证在尼日利亚的任何企业不被政府国有化或征用，任何拥有企业（全部或者部分）资产的个人不被法律强制将其对资本所享有的权益转让给他人。④在尼日利亚和大多数司法管辖区，关于征用的禁令一般都必须具备向国民/投资者支付适当补偿的非歧视措施的条件。无论如何，这项禁令须符合任何征用措施必须具备的条件⑤：

① 符合公共利益和并按照正当法律程序；
② 不违反或者区别对待任何尼日利亚联邦政府规定的明确义务；
③ 具备反映受影响投资的真正价值的公正赔偿的条件；
④ 赋予受影响的投资者有权向法院申请确定投资者的权益，以及其有权获得的赔偿额。

三、贸易

（一）贸易主管部门

尼日利亚工业、贸易与投资部，在财政部、尼日利亚中央银行的协同下，负责尼日利亚贸易政策的制定和执行。在履行其职权过程中，工业、贸易与投资部会参考其他政府部门的意见，如尼日利亚出口促进委员会、尼日利亚投资促进委员会、尼日利亚海关、公共企业管理局；也会听取私营部门组织的意见，如全国商业协会、工业矿石及农业协会、私有企业协会以及尼日利亚劳动者咨询协会等。

（二）贸易法律法规概况

在尼日利亚，与贸易相关的主要法律法规如下：

---

① 尼日利亚投资促进委员会（NIPC）。详见 http://www.nipc.gov.ng/investment.html。
② 第 15 节 (4)。
③ 《尼日利亚投资促进委员会法案》第 24 节和第 25 节。详见上文。
④ 同上注，第 25 节 (1)。
⑤ 同上注，第 25 节 (2)。

①《公司及相关事务法》①，规定了在尼日利亚运营的公司、非公司制组织、慈善机构等的框架；

②《海关和消费税管理法》②，规定了关税和消费税的管理和收取；

③《外汇（监督与杂项规定）法》③，对于外汇交易，建立了自治外汇市场，并规定了在尼日利亚外汇市场进行外汇输入和输出的相关管理和监管措施；

④《投资促进委员会法》④，设立了尼日利亚投资促进委员会，以鼓励和促进对尼日利亚经济和投资；

⑤《出口促进委员会法》⑤，设立了尼日利亚促进委员会，该机构负责管理尼日利亚出口事务，推动、记录和指导尼日利亚的出口工作，并执行和落实尼日利亚相关出口政策；

⑥《进出口银行法》⑥，设立了尼日利亚进出口银行，该机构主要负责提供出口信贷担保和出口信贷保险业务；

⑦《出口加工区法》⑦，设立了尼日利亚出口加工区管理局，该机构负责出口加工区的建立、许可、管理和运营，并监管和协调尼日利亚出口加工区内国营企业和私营部门组织的职能分工；

⑧《标准组织法》⑧，设立了尼日利亚国家标准局，该机构是尼日利亚最主要的标准制定机构；

⑨《沿海和内地船运（沿海运输）法》⑨，规定了外国拥有和使用的船舶在尼日利亚进行沿海交易的相关事项；

⑩《出口（鼓励和杂项规定）法》⑩，规定了出口本国货物的出口商所享有的多种鼓励措施；

⑪《港口管理局法》⑪，设立了尼日利亚港口管理局，该机构管理和运营尼日利亚各港口；

⑫《海事管理和安全局法》⑫，设立了尼日利亚海事管理和安全局，并对加强海事安全、保护海商环境、加强船舶注册、商船和海员管理等相关事宜进行了相关规定；

⑬《国家食品和药品管理控制局法》⑬，设立了尼日利亚国家食品和药品管理控制局，该机构负责管控食品、药品、化妆品、化学药品、洗涤剂、医学设备、包装水的生产、进口、出口、销售、宣传和使用等。

（三）贸易管理

参见上文"贸易主管部门"部分。

（四）进出口商品检验检疫

进出口商品检验检疫由尼日利亚海关、农业部以及国家食品和药品管理控制局负责。

1. 海关

根据尼日利亚海关关于货物进口指南的有关规定，所有的进口物品均应附有特定的证明文件，包括：估价和原产地联合证明书、最终发票/商业发票、装箱单、提单、生产证明/制造商证明等，有时还需要提供检验证明。不符合尼日利亚海关相关规定的物品，将在入境时被没收。被列入进出口禁止清单的物品，不能被进口至尼日利亚，也不能从尼日利亚出口。部分禁止被进口的物品如下：冷冻肉、可可脂、面粉和蛋糕、意大利面/面条、散装果汁、水、啤酒、袋装水泥、驱蚊水等。禁止出口的

---

① 2004 年《公司及相关事务法》第 C20 章。
② 2004 年《尼日利亚联邦法律》第 C44 章《海关法》。
③ 2004 年《尼日利亚联邦法律》第 F35 章《外汇监管法》。
④ 2004 年《尼日利亚联邦法律》第 N117 章《尼日利亚投资促进委员会法》。
⑤ 经 1992 年第 64 号法案修订的 1990 年《尼日利亚联邦法律》第 306、C44 章《尼日利亚出口促进委员会法》。
⑥ 1991 年第 38 号法案《尼日利亚进出口银行法》。
⑦ 2004 年《尼日利亚联邦法律》第 N107 章《尼日利亚出口加工区法》。
⑧ 2015 年第 14 号法案《尼日利亚标准组织法》。该法案废除了 2004 年《尼日利亚联邦法律》第 S9 章规定的《尼日利亚标准组织法》。
⑨ 2003 年第 5 号法案《沿海和内地船运（沿海运输）法》。
⑩ 2004 年《尼日利亚联邦法律》第 E19 章《出口（鼓励和杂项规定）法》。
⑪ 2004 年《尼日利亚联邦法律》第 N126 章《尼日利亚港口管理局法》。
⑫ 《尼日利亚海事管理和安全局法》。
⑬ 2004 年《尼日利亚联邦法律》第 N1 章《尼日利亚国家食品和药品管理控制局法》。

物品包括木材、动物生皮、废金属、未加工的乳胶及橡胶凝块、文物与古董、珍稀野生动物及制品等。

2. 农业检疫局

尼日利亚农业检疫局负责保护尼日利亚农业经济的发展，对进口植物、动物、水产等颁发进口许可证明、卫生证明和植物检疫证书等。

进口植物和植物制品必须进行检查，且应附上进口许可证，特定情况下需附上出口国的植物检疫证。如通过检查，将获颁发植物检查检疫证；如检查报告不符合相关规定，将按照以下方式处理此进口植物或植物制品：实验室化验、适当的消毒、杀菌/灭虫处理、进行转口贸易、没收、以指定方式进行销毁并由进口商承担销毁费用。

如从尼日利亚出口植物或植物制品，或在尼日利亚对植物或植物制品进行转口贸易的，应取得植物检疫证书。

如向尼日利亚出口动物或动物制品，相关货物在入境时必须进行检查。活动物需送往检疫站进行观察，存疑动物制品应进行检测。

如从尼日利亚出口动物或动物制品，应取得出口许可证。

3. 国家食品和药品管理控制局

如进口食品、药品、化妆品、洗涤剂、医学设备、瓶装水和化学药品（管制物品）至尼日利亚，需向国家食品和药品管理控制局申请注册，注册成功后，将获颁注册证明。

（五）海关管理

尼日利亚海关主要负责尼日利亚的海关管理，海关管理包括关税征收（进口关税和其他税种）。进口关税税率最低为进口货物价值的 0%，最高为 35%；进口物品的增值税税率为 5%。

四、劳动

（一）劳动法律法规概况

尼日利亚调整劳动关系的主要法律是 2004 年《尼日利亚联邦法律》第一章之《劳动法》，及尼日利亚判例所确立的裁判规则。《劳动法》及其他法律，均根据 1999 年《尼日利亚联邦共和国宪法》（修订）而制定，任何违反宪法的规定均属无效。《劳动法》的适用范围仅限该法所规定的"劳工"，即体力劳动者或文员工作者。雇主和其他不属于"劳工"范畴的"被雇佣者"（如从事行政管理、执行、技术和专业等工作）的关系，由双方签订的雇佣合同及尼日利亚相关判例裁判规则进行调整。由此可见，从法律关系上来说，尼日利亚有两大类"被雇佣者"：一种是《劳动法》所规定的"劳工"，另一种是从事行政管理、执行、技术和专业人员等工作的被雇佣者（"非劳工"）。

严格来说，虽然《劳动法》仅适用于"劳工"，但在实践中，雇主们在处理与"非劳工"的雇佣关系时，也参照适用《劳动法》来确定最低雇佣标准的情况并不少见，如产假时间、合同终止的通知期限等。

尽管每类"被雇佣者"有特定的内涵，但雇佣合同的组成部分还包括员工手册、服务手册或其他相关文件。如果雇员所加入的工会与雇主签订了集体劳资协议，而雇佣合同中约定集体劳资协议的相关条款是雇佣合同的组成部分，则此雇佣合同条款还应受到集体劳资协议相关条款的约束。

调整雇佣关系的法律还有：

①《退休金改革法》（2014 年），规定了退休金缴纳的相关问题；

②《劳工补偿法》（2010 年），规定了雇员患职业病，或因在工作场合、在工作工程中发生的事故而受伤时所能享受到的赔偿；

③《个人所得税法修正案》[①]，规定雇员获得劳动报酬的应缴税款，以及雇主的代扣和代缴义务；

[①] 经 2011 年《个人所得税法修正案》修订的 2004 年《尼日利亚联邦法律》第 P8 章《个人所得税法》。

④《国民健康保险法》[①]，旨在建立国民健康保险体系，使所有的尼日利亚居民通过多种预缴方式，在自身经济承受范围内得以享受便捷的医疗保障；

⑤《行业培训基金法》(修订)[②]，该法案要求雇主缴纳其年度员工工资总额的1%至由该法创设的行业培训基金。该法适用于以下两类雇主：拥有5个或5个以上雇员的雇主；营业额超过5千万奈拉的雇主（折合美金约143 000元）；

⑥《国家住房基金法》[③]，该法设立了国家住房基金，并规定雇主有义务扣取雇员每月工资的2.5%，并将此款缴付至尼日利亚联邦抵押银行，以代劳动者缴纳国家住房基金款；

⑦《工会法》(2004年)[④]，由《工会法修正案》(2005年)修正，规定了尼日利亚工会的管理、会员及工会相关活动的开展；

⑧《移民法》(2015年)，调整与外国劳动者雇佣关系的相关事宜；

⑨《反歧视HIV和AIDS法》(2014年)，规范了涉及HIV及AIDS人员的雇佣关系的相关事宜，以及雇主对此类雇员的相关义务。

除了上述联邦法律规定，雇主还应遵守雇主经营地所在州制定的其他相关法律规定。

（二）外国人在当地工作规定

1. 工作许可

尼日利亚《移民法》规定，对于拟聘请外国公民作为其雇员的雇主，须向移民局总局长提出申请，未经移民局总局长批准不得雇佣外国劳动者。在实践中，公司申请的雇佣外籍员工审批，也称外国雇员配额审批，由尼日利亚联邦内政部负责审批。获得配额后，该公司便可按照被批准的特定工作岗位和工作期限，雇佣外国劳动者。外国雇员配额的被许可单位是公司，而非外籍员工，因此，当外籍员工离开此公司时，公司仍然享有此配额，并有权在配额有效期内，另行聘请其他外籍人员。

外国雇员配额存在期限限制，首次申请时限一般为2年，可以申请续期5次，特殊情况下可直接批准不超过10年的有效期。配额所批准的具体职位数量，根据公司的经营性质予以确定。由于尼日利亚政府实施鼓励雇用及培训尼日利亚国民培训的政策，因此，雇主在配额到期后申请新的配额工作岗位，必须满足至少有2名尼日利亚本国雇员替代了原外国雇员的工作岗位条件。

部分情况下，公司可获得"免续期申请"配额。此配额一般是给予公司的首席执行官职位，并需要缴纳一定数额的可兑换外汇作为手续费。申请"免续期申请"配额的前提条件是：公司运营超过2年；公司已成功申请普通外国雇员配额。

如果雇主拟雇佣外国雇员提供短期（1~6个月）的、特定的专业技术服务，但是其又尚未获得外国雇员配额的，其可代外国雇员申请临时工作许可。获得临时工作许可的外国雇员在许可规定期限内，无需办理其他移民许可或批准。临时工作许可的有效期一般为3个月，并可申请续期3个月。

申请了外国雇员配额后，公司还需向尼日利亚移民局为外国雇员申请居住和工作许可证（西非国家经济共同体国家的公民除外）。此许可被称为"侨民居留许可与外国人综合卡"，凭此卡，非尼日利亚公民可获准在尼日利亚居住，并可从事上述许可证中涵盖的相关活动。外国雇员的相关随行人员，也须申请该卡。该卡的有效期为每次12个月，期满后可申请续期。

2. 申请程序

① 外国雇员配额许可证：由尼日利亚公司向内政部常任秘书提出申请。申请时须提交如下材料：正确填写的申请表；银行证明；公司营业地、机械设备证明；在尼日利亚的出资证明（证明该公司存在外资情况）；外国雇员职业资格要求、工作岗位、薪酬方案等；该公司对尼日利亚籍员工的培训计划；公司完税证明及增值税登记证；其他内政部认为需要提交的文件。提交申请并缴纳完毕相关费用后的3~4个月内，内政部会对清单进行审核并向符合条件的公司颁发外国员工配额许可证。

[①] 2004年《尼日利亚联邦法律》第N42章《国民健康保险法》。
[②] 2004年《尼日利亚联邦法律》第I9章《行业培训基金法》。
[③] 2004年《尼日利亚联邦法律》第N45章《国家住房基金法》。
[④] 经2005年《工会法修正案》修订的2004年《尼日利亚联邦法律》第T14章《工会法》。

② 临时工作许可证：由尼日利亚公司向尼日利亚移民局总局长提交申请，同时提交外国雇员的护照信息和复印件，以及移民局要求的其他相关资料，如公司设立证明、公司章程。如果申请通过的，尼日利亚移民局将在2～3周内发放临时工作许可证。许可证的首次申请的有效期为3个月，到期后可由公司代为申请续期3个月。续期申请由尼日利亚移民局进行严格审核。

③ 侨民居留许可与外国人综合卡：申请此卡时，雇主须获得外国雇员配额，且外国雇员需持有长期工作签证。办卡申请须在外国雇员入境尼日利亚的3个月内提出。按规定，办卡申请应由外国雇员提出，但事实上，雇主可代外国雇员申请。申请此卡时，应向移民局总局长提交办卡申请书、外国雇员护照、长期工作签证及移民局要求的其他材料。申请外国人居留卡的费用为1200美金，一般申请程序需耗时1～2周。

3. 社会保险

尼日利亚没有社保系统。2005年1月1日，一项自费退休金计划开始实施，目前，该计划根据《退休金改革法》（2014年）相关规定进行运作。根据《退休金改革法》（2014年），拥有15名以上雇员的雇主，应至少按照雇员工资的10%为雇员缴付退休金，雇员自行按照月薪的8%预存退休金，如此，缴纳总额相当于18%雇员工资。雇主应在向雇员发工资后的7日内，将相当于工资总额18%（雇员承担部分由雇主从工资中予以扣除和代缴），存入雇员的退休金账户，该账户由雇员自行选择的退休基金管理人管理。雇主仅对尼日利亚籍雇员有缴纳退休金义务，外国雇员未被要求加入此计划，除非其自愿选择加入。

2014年《退休金改革法》还规定，雇主应该为所有雇员购买人寿险，保险金额为至少雇员年收入的3倍。

（三）出入境

1. 签证类型

根据前往尼日利亚的不同原因、目的，尼日利亚签证可分为以下几种：

① 过境签：适用对象是为了前往其他国家而从尼日利亚过境的外国人。西非国家经济共同体成员国公民，以及其他与尼日利亚签订免签协议的国家公民，无需申请该类签证即可直接入境。

② 旅行签：适用对象是前往尼日利亚旅游、探亲的外国人。西非国家经济共同体成员国公民，以及其他与尼日利亚签订了免签协议的国家公民，无需申请该类签证即可直接入境。

③ 商务签：适用对象是短期前往尼日利亚参加会议、研讨会或其他商务活动的外国人。持有商务签进入尼日利亚的外国人，不得在尼日利亚缔结任何形式的雇佣关系。西非国家经济共同体成员国公民，以及其他与尼日利亚签订了免签协议的国家公民，无需申请该类签证即可直接入境。

④ 长期工作签：适用对象为已经获得尼日利亚雇主的工作要约并决定接受雇佣的外国人。外国人申请长期工作签证时，需向其经常居住地所属国的尼日利亚大使馆或高级专员署提出申请，获得批准后，方能以受雇为目的进入尼日利亚从事雇佣工作。取得该签证后，外国人需在入境之日起3个月内，申请并取得侨民居留许可与外国人综合卡，取得该卡后，便能依法在尼日利亚居住和工作。

⑤ 外交签：适用对象为外国国家领导人、国家高级政府官员、政府任命的外交官、持有联合国工作人员外交护照的人员、持有国际机构外交护照的人员等。

2. 出入境限制

各类签证限制如下：

① 过境签：如系落地过境签，有效期为48小时；如系抵达尼日利亚之前向尼日利亚外交机构申领的，有效期为7日；

② 旅行签：有效期为90日；

③ 商务签：有效期为90日，如确有必要，经尼日利亚移民局批准，可以延期；

④ 长期工作签：有效期为3个月，持有此签证的外国人须在此有效期内申领侨民居留许可与外国人综合卡；

⑤ 外交签：有效期为90日。

(四) 工会与劳工组织

《工会法》①对尼日利亚工会的管理、会员及相关活动的开展进行了规定。在尼日利亚，工会代表工会成员，积极与雇主协商并签订集体劳资协议，该合同内容通常也视为雇员与雇主签订的雇佣合同的一部分。根据《工会法》规定，为了更好地与雇主开展谈判，所有注册的工会均应设立选举制度，以便选举工会代表、与雇主进行谈判。

尼日利亚工会的权利包括：
① 代表工会成员与雇主协商、洽谈雇佣合同的相关条款；
② 组织行业罢工；
③ 进行和平纠察；
④ 在工会成员可能受裁员影响的情况下，向雇主了解裁员理由、裁员力度等。

(五) 劳动争议

1. 关于劳动争议：

在尼日利亚，调整劳动争议的主要法律是《劳动争议法》②，所谓"劳动争议"，需符合以下条件：
① 争议须与劳动争议相关，且争议双方须为雇主与雇员之间，或均为雇员；
② 争议须与是否构成雇佣关系、雇佣合同条款或工作条件相关。③

《劳动争议法》中"劳工"的定义，比《劳工法》中对"劳工"的定义要宽泛得多，指所有劳动者，包括所有国家公务员，以及因与雇主订立合同而从事相关工作的其他人（国家公务员除外）。该合同内容可以是体力劳动、普通公司文员或其他种类工作，合同形式可以是直接告知或间接暗示、口头约定或书面约定，即可以是正式入职合同，也可以是实习协议。

根据《劳动争议法》，劳动争议解决机制如下：

（1）内部协商：如当事人就争议解决方式已有约定，如集体劳资协议中的相关约定，当事人应首先尝试按照合同约定的方式先尝试处理争议。通过该程序，当事人通过协商和沟通，可以开诚布公，化解不满情绪和矛盾。

（2）调解：如当事人没有上述约定，或无法通过上述内部协商方式解决争议的，采用调解方式解决争议。当事人应在各方共同选择和委托的调解员的监督下，进行友好协商。

（3）行政调停：如果调解失败，当事人应在调解时效期满后3日内，将争议事项提交至劳动部长。劳动部长将引导双方进行更多些协商，但如果当事人还是无法协商解决争议，劳动部长将在14天内将此争议移交正式调解。

（4）正式调解：如果正式调解员在接受指派后7天内仍然无法解决争议，或者正式调解员在组织当事人进行洽谈后认为无法达成和解的，正式调解员须向劳动部长报告。

（5）劳动仲裁庭：劳动部长须在收到正式调解员无法调解成功的通知后14天内，将争议提交劳动仲裁庭。劳动仲裁庭主席须组成仲裁合议庭，并应在21日内作出裁决，经劳动部长同意后可以延期；仲裁庭作出裁决后应将裁决提交给劳动部长，不能告知当事人裁决内容。劳动部长收到仲裁裁决后，如在其认为无需发回仲裁合议庭对裁决进行修改，则向当事人送达通知，告知以下事项：
① 告知仲裁裁决；
② 当事人有权在仲裁裁决公布后7日内，向劳动部长提出异议；
③ 如在规定时间内，各方当事人均未按照规定方式向劳动部长提出异议，则劳动部长将确认仲裁裁决。劳动部长将在《联邦公报》上发布通知，确认裁决生效，此裁决对相关的雇主和雇员均具有约束力。

（6）国家劳动法庭：任何一方当事人或双方当事人均对仲裁裁决不服，且向劳动部长送达异议通知的，劳动部长应立即将争议提交国家劳动法庭受理。国家劳动法庭的裁判对双方当事人均有法律约

---

① 经2005年《工会法修正案》修订的2004年《尼日利亚联邦法律》第T14章《工会法》。
② 2004年《尼日利亚联邦法律》第T8章《劳动争议法》。
③ NURTW v. Ogbodo (1998) 2 N.W.L.R (Pt.537) at 189.

束力，如不服该裁决，只能向上诉法院提起上诉。上诉法院作出的判决是终局的，双方当事人均应遵守。

2. 其他与劳动者相关的纠纷

对于与劳动者有关的民事案件和刑事案件，国家劳动法庭享有专属管辖权，所谓"与劳动者有关"，包括工会和劳资关系、工作环境和工作条件、劳动者的人身健康和安全、劳动者福利以及其他与劳资关系相关事项。除了劳动争议之外的其他雇佣合同相关纠纷，均由国家劳动法庭管辖。针对国家劳动法庭裁决所提出的上诉，由上诉法院管辖，上诉法院作出的民事案件裁决为终局裁决。但是，上诉法院就国家劳动法庭关于刑事案件作出的上诉裁决，还可向尼日利亚最高人民法院上诉。国家劳动法庭的法官，对于该法庭受理的案件，均可提交由国家劳动法庭设立的替代性纠纷解决中心进行调解。如当事人无法和解，国家劳动法庭将依法组织开庭。

五、知识产权

（一）知识产权法律法规概况

尼日利亚有两类知识产权：版权和工业产权。工业产权是一个大类，包括商标、专利和工业设计。知识产权受到以下法律保护：

①《版权法》（2004年《尼日利亚联邦法律》C28章）对版权和邻接权进行了相关规定；

②《商标法》（2004年《尼日利亚联邦法律》T13章），以及1967年的《商标条例》，对商标权进行了相关规定；

③《专利和设计法》（2004年《尼日利亚联邦法律》P2章），以及1971年《专利规则》，对专利和工业设计进行了相关规定。

上述法律规定了知识产权的保护范围、注册程序（如果需要注册）、具体实施，以及其他相关事项。

（二）版权

在尼日利亚，版权无需注册，享有版权的作品在创作时自动受法律保护。虽然《版权通知计划》鼓励版权人将他们的版权告知尼日利亚版权委员会，但是，告知不等同于注册，只是为了记录版权归属。

（三）申请专利

专利，是指授予一项发明的独占性、排他性权利。根据《专利和设计法》，一项发明如需注册专利，必须符合以下三点：是一项全新的发明或者对已有发明进行的改进；有创造性；能够投入工业应用。

如需注册专利，应当向专利和设计注册局（以下简称"注册局"）提交申请书。申请书需要具备以下文件或资料：

①专利申请人的全名和地址，如果发明地是在尼日利亚以外的，需提供在尼日利亚的送达地址；

②说明书，并附有相关步骤或图示。说明书应当对此项发明作出清楚、完整的说明，以该技术领域的技术人员能够实现为准；

③权利要求书，对相关发明的功能和用途的详细描述，该权利要求书不能超过前述说明书所列范围；

④当申请人不是实际发明人时，需要实际发明人出具一份声明，注明在专利中其是实际发明人，并在声明中留下姓名和地址；

⑤授权委托书，授权尼日利亚的专利代理人代为提交文件、处理相关申请事宜；

⑥专利注册处规定的其他事项。

满足上述条件并缴纳规定的费用后，该项发明将会被授予专利权。

(四)商标注册

根据《商标法》第67条,商标是指:"使用或者打算使用在商品上指示来源的标志,或在交易过程中表明商品与所有权人及商标注册人之间的关系的标志,无论是否有该人的任何身份迹象。"

商标的注册程序如下:

① 在尼日利亚商标注册处(以下简称"商标注册处")进行查询,以便确定申请注册的商标是否可用于注册(即确认是否该商标已经被注册)。

② 如果该商标可用于注册,申请人应提交申请书到商标注册处进行商标注册。申请书应当包含以下文件或资料:申请人的全名或全称、国籍和住址;拟注册图案/标志的复制件;拟注册商标所涵盖的商品、服务的种类;授权委托书,授权尼日利亚的商标代理人代为提交文件及处理申请事宜。

为注册之目的而对商品的分类,依据《商标法》制定的《商标条例》的第5条和附表4进行了相关规定。目前一个商标可以注册的商品种类共有45个。尼日利亚法律仅对商标在已注册过的商品种类范围内给予保护,如商标在某一商品种类上未注册,不会发生商标侵权。

③ 在申请人提交商标注册申请书后,商标注册处出具一份收件函,以证实确已收到申请书。其后,商标注册处将审查申请书,搜索注册记录,以排查在此之前没有类似图案、标志已被申请或注册过。

④ 当注册处认为没有类似图案、标志被申请或注册过,其向申请人出具一份核准函,表明该商标已被核准注册商标;如果当注册处认为已有类似图案、标志已被申请或注册,将向申请人出具一份驳回函,并在函件中注明驳回的理由。

⑤ 在出具核准函后,该商标将在商标日报上公告,公告期为2个月。在公告期内,任何第三人有权对此商标注册申请提出异议。公告期内如无异议(或异议被驳回),予以核准注册,发给商标注册证;公告期内如有异议,先处理异议再决定是否予以核准注册。对于异议,申请人有义务对异议进行答辩。答辩的内容取决于提出的异议的性质。

(五)知识产权保护措施

相关知识产权法律不仅规定了知识产权在相关注册登记处的注册程序,也规定了知识产权所有权人的权利保护机制。

1. 工业产权(即商标、专利和工业设计)

工业产权在登记注册后,最大的好处是知识产权所有权人在遭受侵权时,享有向联邦高等法院提起诉讼的权利。此种侵权,包括侵犯知识产权所有权人专有权的行为,以及其他与知识产权所有权人相关权利相冲突的行为。

对于上述情况,知识产权所有权人可获得的救济包括损害赔偿、停止侵害和要求侵权人赔偿因侵权所获得的利益。此外,可在审判开始之前采取一项临时措施,即申请诉前调查令,可帮助知识产权所有权人在法警和执法部门的帮助下,到被告的经营场地查封、扣押侵权产品。

2. 版权

跟前述工业产权所有权人类似,版权所有权人也可以在联邦高等法院对侵犯版权的行为提起诉讼。版权人也有权申请诉前调查令这一临时措施。根据《版权法》第17条第1款,版权人在他人违反了相关法定义务、侵犯版权人的专有权时,也享有提起诉讼的权利。

依据《版权法》,制作、销售、分销、进口获得版权保护的作品,构成刑事犯罪,并可判处一定刑期,或单处一定罚金,或两者并处。同时,就同一侵权行为可以同时提起民事诉讼和进行刑事追责。

六、环境保护

(一)环保主管部门

国家环境标准和管理执行局是负责环境保护和发展、执行环境法律法规及标准,阻止个人、企业和其他组织污染和破坏环境的主要部门。

石油资源局负责与石油和天然气相关的环境法规的实施，国家对石油和天然气出台了相关特别规定，此项不在国家环境标准和法规执行局的职责范围之内。

（二）环保护法律法规概况

相关法律法规如下：

（1）《国家环境标准和管理执行局（设立）法案》（2007年）。该法建立了国家环境标准和管理执行局，是尼日利亚关于环境保护的主要法律。该法主要规定如下：空气排放、地下排放和水体排放、噪音污染、污染治理，空气和水土其他形式的恶化防治、臭氧保护、水质标准、污水限制、环境卫生、公共卫生、土地资源、流域质量，以及超标排放有害物质等。

（2）《环境影响评价法》（《尼日利亚联邦法律》2004年，E12章）。根据该法，个人、公司或机构在未事先评估这些项目和活动对环境影响的情况下，不得从事或许可任何项目、活动。此外，相关项目或活动的发起人，需要对此项目或活动进行环境影响评估。该法还规定了环境影响评估必须涵盖的最低限度的内容，包括：

① 对活动及该活动可能造成的环境影响的说明，内容应该详尽、具体，以满足评估环境影响之需；

② 该活动以及该活动备选方案环境评估报告，内容包括直接影响和间接影响、短期影响和长期影响；

③ 减轻或应对环境影响的有效措施，以及对上述措施的作用；

④ 准备相关资料中所遇到的知识差异和不确定因素的说明，以及该活动及备选方案对尼日利亚之外的其他地方可能造成的环境影响。

（3）国家环境标准和管理执行局颁布的条例。《国家环境和标准管理执行局（设立）法案》第7章第（h）条和第（j）条，授权国家环境和标准管理执行局通过合规监测执行噪音、空气、土地、海洋和其他水体相关环保法规和标准，并通过注册登记、许可和许可证制度的环保控制措施来贯彻环境控制措施。就此，该局颁布了许多条例，包括：

①《国家环境（湿地、河岸和湖岸）条例》（2009年），规定了保护和合理使用尼日利亚的湿地及其资源；

②《国家环境（卫生和废物管制）条例》（2009年），规定了在环境卫生和废物管理中采用可持续和无害环境的做法的法律框架，以使污染最小化；

③《国家环境（许可和许可证制度）条例》（2009年），该条例旨在确保环境法律、法规和标准的贯彻执行；

④《国家环境（沙漠化防治和抗旱）条例》（2010年），旨在为已受沙漠化影响地区的可持续利用提供一个有效、务实的框架，并对易受环境不良影响的土地精心保护。

⑤《国家环境保护（保护濒危物种国际贸易）条例》（2010年），旨在保护濒危野生动物。

（三）环保评估

国家环境标准和管理执行局和石油资源局努力履行环境保护相关职责，公民环保意识和守法水平也日益提高。

七、争议解决

在尼日利亚，最常见的纠纷解决方式是诉讼和仲裁。仲裁方式包括临时仲裁和机构仲裁。国际商事交易中，一般根据《国际商会仲裁规则》《英国伦敦国际仲裁院仲裁规则》《英国皇家特许仲裁员协会仲裁规则》等，约定机构仲裁。

交易方仅涉及尼日利亚本国当事人的，一般会根据《联合国国际贸易法委员会国际商事仲裁示范法》或者《尼日利亚仲裁和调解法》，约定临时仲裁方式进行仲裁。在极少数的尼日利亚当事人、选择机构仲裁的情况下，当事人会选择在尼日利亚本土的仲裁机构进行机构仲裁，如英国皇家特许仲裁员协会尼日利亚分会，或者拉各斯区域商事仲裁中心等。

(一)争议解决方式及机构

如系商事交易(包括国内或国际交易),经当事人一致同意,争议解决方式为向尼日利亚法院提起诉讼的,绝大部分案件由州立高等法院受理。尼日利亚一个联邦制国家,由 36 个州及联邦首都区阿布贾组成。1999 年《尼日利亚联邦共和国宪法》(修订版)规定,在各州及首都区设立一个高等法院。同时,宪法还设立了联邦高等法院,该法院对特定事项享有管辖权。合同履行地或应履行地所在的州的高等法院对该合同纠纷享有管辖权。但是,如果纠纷涉及房地产,则房地产所在州的高等法院对此纠纷享有管辖权。如果尼日利亚联邦政府及其派出机构为诉讼当事人,或者争议涉及尼日利亚联邦政府行政管理作为与不作为的,联邦高等法院拥有管辖权。

尼日利亚常见商业纠纷仲裁机构包括:
① 拉各斯多元化门户法院(www.lagosmultidoor.org.ng);
② 英国皇家特许仲裁员协会(CIArb 尼日利亚分会)(www.ciarbnigeria.org);
③ ICC 国际商会(www.iccwbo.org);
④ 国际投资争端解决中心(icsid.worldbank.org);
⑤ 英国伦敦国际仲裁院(www.lcia.org);
⑥ 拉各斯区域商事仲裁中心(www.rcicalagos.org)。

在尼日利亚,最常用的替代性争议解决方式为仲裁与调解。

(二)适用法律

法律适用由争议的性质和争议双方的具体情况而决定。在商事争议中,常用法律规定如下:
① 《尼日利亚联邦共和国宪法》(修订)(1999 年);
② 《公司和相关事务法》;
③ 《投资与证券法》;
④ 《时效法》;
⑤ 《货物买卖法》;
⑥ 《仲裁与调解法》;
⑦ 《州高等法院规则》;
⑧ 《联邦高等法院规则》;
⑨ 《公司清算规则》;
⑩ 《公司章程》;
⑪ 《证券交易委员会规则》;
⑫ 《尼日利亚证券交易所规则》。

当当事人选择外国法律作为准据法时,尼日利亚法院一般会尊重当事人的选择。但是,尼日利亚最高法院同时也认为,当事人选择的准据法并非绝对适用,必须符合"真实、善意、合理"原则才有效,同时,如果要选择外国法作为准据法,该外国法应与合同的实际情况存在关联性。符合上述条件的前提下,当事人有权自由选择准据法。

八、其他

(一)反商业贿赂

1. 反贿赂法律法规概况

(1)《尼日利亚联邦共和国宪法》(1999 年),2011 年修订(以下简称《宪法》)

《宪法》附件五"行为规范",禁止公务人员履行其职责过程中通过其作为或不作为,为自己或他人谋取、收受任何形式的财产或利益;

(2)《腐败犯罪及其他相关犯罪法》(2000 年,以下简称《腐败犯罪法》)

这部法律包含诸多向公务人员行贿的相关条款。该法适用对象为:被他人指使行贿的人,或代他人从事行贿的人,包括政府官员、公共机构成员、政党及其分支机构的成员、政府组织或私有组织的工作人员、雇员或代理人等,上述主体的相关腐败行为,根据本法相关规定构成犯罪。对于尼日利亚公民、被授予尼日利亚永久居民身份的人在尼日利亚境外实施的相关行为,如同时违反尼日利亚和行为地相关法律的,也将依据《腐败犯罪法》进行定罪量刑。

如果向公务人员提供"好处"导致发生法律明文禁止的行为的,此提供"好处"的行为将构成犯罪。根据《腐败犯罪法》,所谓"好处",包括金钱、捐赠、礼物、物权、物权相关权益,以及给予或承诺给予的任何其他形式的类似好处,并意图影响收受好处的人履行或不履行其有关职责,还包括相关授权行为、各种形式的报酬、无条件或附条件地给予或承诺给予、代为清偿债务、免除债务或相关义务、放弃债权等。《腐败犯罪法》还进一步规定,行为人为了签订相关合同、获得有关许可执照或从相关政府部门谋取任何其他好处,而向相关部门公务人员提供财物的,此行为也属于腐败行为。同样,基于帮助或影响相关合同的履行、采购等,而收受或索要好处的公务人员,此行为亦属于腐败行为。此外,该法还规定公务员和个人均有义务依法举报相关腐败犯罪行为。

(3)《刑法》(2004年《尼日利亚联邦法律》第C38章)

该法规定,公务人员利用职权作为或不作为相关事务之之前或之后,为自己或为他人索取、收受或试图收受财物的行为,将构成腐败罪(重罪),可判处7年有期徒刑。《刑法》规定,任何人向公务人员或公务人员指定的第三方,承诺给予、提供、授予、促成或企图采购任何财产或利益的,将同样被认定为共构成腐败罪(重罪),可判处7年有期徒刑。关于索贿行为,《刑法》规定任何公务人员在履行职务过程中,收受任何超出其工资范围报酬的,将被认定为重罪,可判处3年有期徒刑。

(4)《经济和金融犯罪委员会法》(2004年《尼日利亚联邦法律》第E1章)

根据该法设立的经济和金融犯罪委员会,负责调查经济和金融的相关犯罪。该法将"经济和金融犯罪"定义为非暴力性犯罪,即个人、组织为牟取非法利益而从事的非法活动,包括欺诈、贩毒、洗钱、贪污、贿赂、抢劫行为,以及各种形式的腐败贿赂、非法武器交易、走私、人口贩卖、雇佣和使用童工、非法原油采集、非法采矿、逃税、外汇欺诈行为(包括伪造货币)、窃取知识产权、盗版、滥用公开市场、倾倒有毒废物和禁止物等。该法还规定了一些其他金融犯罪行为,如银行或其他金融机构的职员实施的金融犯罪行为,恐怖主义犯罪以及其他经济和金融相关犯罪等。关于经济和金融类犯罪,该法还规定,如明知是犯罪所得,任何人不得掩饰、隐瞒该收益,不得将犯罪所得从尼日利亚转出,也不得转移给其他相关人员。

2. 主管部门

尼日利亚负责监督反贿赂的部门是:

① 反腐败和相关犯罪独立委员会。这是一个依据《腐败犯罪法》建立的12人委员会,负责监督《腐败犯罪法》的实施。该委员会可以调查《腐败犯罪法》下的任何犯罪行为,以及其他尼日利亚法律规定腐败犯罪行为。

② 经济和金融犯罪委员会。《经济和金融委员会法》授权该委员会打击经济和金融犯罪,负责预防、调查、指控和惩罚经济和金融犯罪,并负责实施其他法律法规中关于"经济和金融犯罪"的有关规定(包括贿赂犯罪)。《经济和金融委员会法》也赋予了其广泛的调查和自由处罚权,如通过处以超过犯罪最高处罚金额的款项、进行辩诉交易。

3. 惩处措施

《刑法》第98A条规定,任何人向公务人员或公务人员指定的第三方,给予承诺、提供、授予、促成或企图采购任何财产或利益的,将同样被认定为共构成腐败罪(重罪),可判处7年有期徒刑。关于索贿行为,《刑法》规定任何公务人员在履行职务过程中,收受任何超出其工资范围报酬的,将被认定为重罪,可判处3年有期徒刑。

《腐败犯罪法》规定:公务人员利用职权作为或不作为相关事务之之前或之后,为自己或为他人索取、接受或试图接受财物的行为,将构成腐败罪(重罪),可判处7年有期徒刑。该法进一步规定,向公务人员或其他提供或许诺帮助的人提供、授予财产或利益的人,为寻求公务人员帮助,亦可判处7年有期徒刑。此外,《腐败犯罪法》还规定,如果违反某些法律明令禁止的行为(如在公务员的协助下,获得批准合同、奖励、认证或任何有利事项)而给予公务员好处,此行为被认定为犯罪。如果公务人员或其他人员未依法举报贿赂行为的,此行为亦会被认定为犯罪,并可判处一定刑期,并处或单处罚金。

《经济和金融犯罪委员会法》第18条规定,对经济和金融犯罪处以2～3年有期徒刑,除监禁刑之外,本法还规定犯罪人应支付等同于犯罪所得金额的罚金。此外,该法规定的惩罚还有没收资产(包括尼日利亚境内和境外的资产)、冻结犯罪嫌疑人的银行账户。《经济和金融犯罪委员会法》第23条进一步规定,如果行为人构成本法规定的相关罪行,其护照将被尼日利亚联邦政府没收,直至其服刑期满,或总统特赦后才予以返还。

(二)工程承包

1. 许可制度

2007年第14号《政府采购法》规定了相关采购主体采购有关货物、服务和资产处置的行为。采购主体包括:尼日利亚联邦政府的采购代理机构;采购资金中至少有35%是联邦政府从综合收入基金中拨款的其他采购主体。

《政府采购法》设立了政府采购管理局,该局负责监管所有采购主体的采购行为。

《政府采购法》要求所有的货物和服务采购必须公开招标。关于资产处置活动,如果处置的是特许基础设施,除了满足该法的要求外,投标程序还必须满足2005年《基础设施特许经营监督管理委员会法》,根据该法,所有的基础设施特别许可须获得联邦执行委员会的批准。公共采购还应遵守政府采购管理局所发布的相关规定,包括《采购程序手册》和《货物和服务政府采购规则》。

《政府采购法》仅适用于与联邦政府相关的采购机构;不适用于私营部门的采购,也不适用于36个州政府。此外,一些州已经制定了当地的采购法。

外国公司若想参与政府采购,其必须在当地设立法人实体,通过该实体来执行项目。该公司可以是外国公司的全资子公司。如未在本国设立公司,外国公司不能在尼日利亚开展业务,除非总统予以特许。

2. 禁止领域

尼日利亚国民和外籍人士、外资公司,禁止投资下列领域:
① 武器和弹药的生产;
② 麻醉药品和精神药品的生产和交易;
③ 军事及准军事服装、装备的生产,包括尼日利亚警察部队、海关部门、移民局、监狱部门等单位的服装、装备;
④ 联邦执行委员决定的其他禁止投资领域。

涉及国防或国家安全的特殊物品、工程和服务的采购,除非事先得到总统的批准,否则不属于《政府采购法》的范围。

3. 招投标

采购主体应适用的采购方法/程序,取决于采购的性质、规模、是否能在当地采购、成本、紧迫性等多种因素。根据政府采购管理局规定的采购标准,如采购项目的价值超过政府采购管理局规定的标准的,需提供相当于投标价2%的投标保证金,投标保证金可由信誉良好的银行提供保函。所有的采购合同,中标人均应支付履约保证金,履约保证金的支付是采购人员支付动员费的前提条件。履约保证金应至少为合同总额的10%或等同于动员费的金额,以较高者为准。

采购方式有三种:公开邀请招标;特殊的受限制情况下的采购方式,包括招标程序、询价或直接采购;意向书。

(1)邀请招标

国内邀请招标:如国内投标人的实力和竞争力使低于一定价值的某个采购项目对外国人无吸引力,或采购货物和服务的国内采购价远低于国际市场价,上述情况下会采用国内邀请招标;如果是较大型的采购项目,国际邀请招标是首选方法。

投标邀请函须为书面形式，或采用相关招标文件规定的其他形式，由有相应授权的人员签字确认，并置于密封信封内。投标文件须用英文制作，存放于安全的防篡改投标箱中。采购主体收到投标文件时应出具收据，注明投标文件送达的日期和时间。采购主体将对投标文件进行评审，评估投标文件是否符合招标文件中规定的最低资格条件，是否按照招标文件的要求编制投标文件，是否对招标文件提出的实质性要求和条件作出响应，以及总体上是否有条理等。如果招标项目是采购货物和服务，将选择成本最低的投标人为中标人。

（2）特殊的受限制情况下的采购方法

招标程序适用于采购主体无法明确拟采购商品或服务的具体要求时；询价程序中，投标价不得超过招标控制价；直接采购程序适用于以下三种情形：在货物、服务只能在特定的供应商或承包商处获得，供应商或承包商对商品、项目或服务享有专属权，且无其他可替代选项存在，存在紧急需求。

投标文件根据采购主体预先设定的标准进行评议，同时，每项标准的权重、标准适用方式，亦应由采购主体预先设定。

（3）意向书

此种采购程序适用于拟采购的服务具体、准确，特别是在采购合同是以调研、实验、研究、开发为目的时。

Nigeria

Authors: Ken Etim, Toba, Ozofu 'Latunde Ogiemudia, Mary Ekemezie
Translators: Xie Xianghui, Zhao Rongrong

I. Overview

A. Overview of Nigeria's Political, Economic, Social and Legal Environment

a. Key Socio-economic Indicators

Available demographic data in Nigeria confirms the country's status as a global economic frontier, with opportunity of high rates of returns on investments. Latest country data include:

• Population of 182 million people as at 2017 more than half of whom are youths below age 30[1].
• Population projected to hit 400 million and surpass that of the United States of America by 2050[2].
• Largest market for consumer goods and services on the African continent and projected to remain Africa's largest consumer market by 2025[3].
• Highest number of internet users on the African continent and very high mobile telecoms penetration rate[4]. There are a total number of 98,391,456 internet and mobile telecoms subscribers in Nigeria as at December 2017, representing 50.2% of total population. This statistics has been corroborated by the Internet World Statistics (IWS).
• Largest producer of crude oil in Africa[5] and 13th in the world (2015).
• Largest proven natural gas reserves in Africa and ninth (9th) in the world[6].
• Large deposit of diverse solid mineral resources – Nigeria is rich in solid minerals with verse deposits of about 44 different non-oil minerals spread across the length and breadth of the country[7].
• Uncultivated vast arable land – Since 1990, about 82 million hectares out of Nigeria's total land area of 91, 0770 hectares has been found arable but only about 42 percent of this has been cultivated[8].
• Africa's regional economic hub – Lagos, one of Nigeria's most populated States and a rising mega city is home to many international businesses and commercial activities.[9]

b. Geography, Culture & Politics

Nigeria is a land of rich and diverse cultures, over 250 ethnic groups, a wide array of religions and sophisticated visual arts. Nigerian classic arts consist of mainly sculptures which were excavated at different sites in the country.[10]

With several bourgeoning cities, Nigeria, many times rated as the home of some of the happiest people

---

[1] National Population Commission (NPC), Nigeria, May 2017 – http://population.gov.ng/nigerias-population-now-182-million-npc/.
[2] United Nations: "World Population Prospects, the 2012 Revision" (June 2013 Report) – http://www.un.org/en/development/desa/publications/world-population-prospects-the-2012-revision.html.
[3] McKinsey Global Institute: "Lions on the move II: Realizing the potential of Africa's economies", September 2016 https://www.mckinsey.com/global-themes/middle-east-and-africa/lions-on-the-move-realizing-the-potential-of-africas-economies.
[4] Nigerian Communication Commission (NCC) – https://www.ncc.gov.ng/stakeholder/statistics-reports/industry-overview#view-graphs-tables-5.See also, report by Internet World Statistics (IWS): "Africa 2018 Population and Internet Users Statistics" – https://www.internetworldstats.com/stats1.htm.
[5] African Vault: "Top 20 Oil Producing Countries in Africa" – https://www.africanvault.com/oil-producing-countries-in-africa/
[6] World Energy Council: "Gas in Nigeria" – https://www.worldenergy.org/data/resources/country/nigeria/gas/.
[7] Ministry of Mines and Steel Development, Nigeria, 2016: "Roadmap for the Growth and Development of the Nigerian Mining Industry" – http://www.minesandsteel.gov.ng/wp-content/uploads/2016/09/Nigeria_Mining_Growth_Roadmap_Final.pdf.
[8] Facts About Nigeria (FAN): "Agriculture in Nigeria" – https://total-facts-about-nigeria.com/agriculture-in-nigeria.html.
[9] The World Bank: "Global Economic prospects: Sub-Saharan Africa", January 2018 – http://www.worldbank.org/en/region/afr/brief/global-economic-prospects-sub-saharan-africa-2018.See also, Quartz Africa: "Lagos is Africa's 7th largest economy and is about to get bigger with its first oil finds" – https://qz.com/676819/lagos-is-africas-7th-largest-economy-and-is-about-to-get-bigger-with-its-first-oil-finds/.
[10] Federal Ministry of Information and Culture, Nigeria – https://fmic.gov.ng/culture/.

on earth[1], is also expectedly home to diverse forms of entertainment: exciting music, joyous dance, rich foods and drinks, and theater. Nollywood is the third largest film producer in the world after US' Hollywood and India's Bollywood. Widely regarded as "The Heart of African Music", Nigeria has always been at the vanguard of world music and has produced many global music stars with a worldwide following such as the Late Fela Ransome (Anikulapo) Kuti.[2]

Fast gaining attraction as a tourist haven, the country parades many and great tourist destinations and the tourism industry in Nigeria benefits from attractive incentives having been declared a preferred sector by the Government. The cuisine of Nigeria has its roots in the nine thousand year old African traditions and some European influences.[3]

Located at the extreme inner corner of the Gulf of Guinea on the west coast of Africa, Nigeria occupies an area of 923,768 sq.km, which is bordered by lake Chad in the northeast, by Cameroon in the east, by the Atlantic Ocean in the south, by the Republic of Benin in the west, and by Niger Republic in the northwest, and having a total boundary length of 4,900 km, of which 853 km is coastline[4]; Nigeria's geographical features position her as an important international trade route and a strategic place of interest to the Silk Road Economic Belt and the 21st-Century Maritime Silk Road.

A constitutional, multi-party and liberal democracy, Nigeria has a relatively peaceful and stable political space. Since 1999 when it returned to civil rule, after a military interregnum in its government, the country has become a political reference point for other African countries; having successively and peacefully transited from one national government to another and from one political party to an opposition party.

Nigeria's foreign policy is greatly influenced by her resolve to attain national development within a prosperous and peaceful international community of nations, by maintaining friendly ties with most countries of the world as an active State party to many bilateral, multilateral and global treaties. The Constitution of Nigeria[5], which is the nation's grund norm and mother of all its laws, prescribes the country's foreign policy objectives[6] as:

(i) Promotion and protection of the national interest;

(ii) Promotion of African integration and support for African unity;

(iii) Promotion of international co-operation for the consolidation of universal peace and mutual respect among all nations and elimination of discrimination in all its manifestations;

(iv) Respect for international law and treaty obligations as well as the seeking of settlement of international disputes by negotiation, mediation, conciliation, arbitration and adjudication; and

(v) Promotion of a just world economic order.

c. Legal Landscape

Nigeria has an efficient and functional judiciary, vibrant legal profession and a legal system predicated upon the Rule of Law and international best practices. The Nigerian legal system is a body or rules from diverse and mixed sources, which include domestic statutes enacted or foreign laws and treaties domesticated in the country by the Legislature; case law (judicial authorities or decisions of superior courts of records); and Received English Law.

The country's legal and regulatory framework has, over the years, been attuned to foreign investments through provisions supporting liberalization; private ownership of properties; opening up vital sectors of the economy to private sector players, including foreigners; establishing quality incentives to industries; and forging cross-border, reciprocal legal and diplomatic alliances with other countries of the world.

Nigeria has entered into many bilateral and multilateral agreements with other countries on many areas of mutual interest and cooperation, such as avoidance of double taxation; trade promotion and protection; judicial agreement on extradition; transfer of sentenced persons; and mutual legal assistance on criminal and commercial matters, among others. For instance, in August 2017, President Muhammadu Buhari of Nigeria signed nine treaties with other countries namely: (i) Agreement on Mutual Legal Assistance in Criminal Matters, with The United Arab Emirates (UAE); (ii) Agreement on Mutual Legal Assistance in Civil and Commercial Matters, with The UAE; (iii) Agreement on the Transfer of Sentenced Persons, with The UAE; (iv) Extradition Treaty, with The UAE;

---

[1] Nigerians were in 2010 rated as the happiest people on earth.See "Gall up 2010 Global Emotions Report" - Gallup 2010 Global Emotions Report @ www.http://news.gallup.com/reports.

[2] The Economist (November 9th 2012): "Nigerian music: The immortal Fela Kuti" – https://www.economist.com/blogs/baobab/2012/11/nigerian-music.

[3] Federal Ministry of Information and Culture, supra.

[4] ENCYCLopedia.com: "Nigeria" – https://www.encyclopedia.com/places/africa/nigeria-political-geography/nigeria.

[5] Constitution of the Federal Republic of Nigeria, 1999 (as amended).

[6] Ibid, section 19.

(v) Charter for the Lake Chad Basin between Nigeria, Cameroun, Central African Republic, Libya, Niger and the Republic of Chad; (vi) African Tax Admin Agreement on Mutual Assistance in Tax Matters; (vii) World Intellectual Property Organisation Performances and Phonograms Treaty; (viii) Agreement on the World Intellectual Property Organisation Treaty on Audio-Visual Performances; and (ix) Marrakesh Treaty to Facilitate Access to Published Works for Persons, who are blind, visually impaired or otherwise.①

The Nigerian Legislature is constantly working in collaboration with the Executive to ensure that all treaties signed with other countries are domesticated in Nigeria, for them to be applicable and enforceable in the country as required by the Constitution.② In furtherance of this constitutional requirement, President Muhammadu Buhari of Nigeria assented on 26 January, 2018 to the "Avoidance of Double Taxation Agreement between the Federal Republic of Nigeria and the Kingdom of Spain (Domestication and Enforcement) Act, 2018" earlier passed by the Legislature.③

Private individual right to work or do legitimate businesses, is a corollary of the right to private acquisition and ownership of property; which is one of the fundamental human rights enshrined in the Constitution of Nigeria. The Courts in Nigeria are empowered to adjudicate on matters relating to the breach of any of these rights in the country. Specifically, any person alleging the breach of any of his rights in the country may apply to a High Court to seek redress④. There are also specialized courts / tribunals in Nigeria having the jurisdiction to decide on exclusive areas of law such as securities and investments⑤; labour and industrial relations⑥; and tax disputes⑦ etc.

B. China–Nigeria Cooperation Under The Belt and Road Project

China–Nigeria diplomatic ties have existed for close to half a century, with many mutual benefits accrued to each country. The two countries also share a lot of similarities: Whilst China is the most populous country in Asia and the world, Nigeria is the most populous country in Africa. China remains the largest economy in Asia and Nigeria the largest economy in Africa. Both China and Nigeria boast of rich cultural heritages dating back to centuries and are of strategic interest to other world and regional powers. Incidentally, they also share the same National Day of October 1.

Beyond the similarities, China and Nigeria have remained trade, economic and development partners for nearly fifty years on a win-win basis, and Nigeria has proven to be an ideal partner for propagating the Belt and Road's five major goals⑧ of Policy Coordination, Facilities Connectivity, Unimpeded Trade, Financial Integration, and People-to-People Bond.

In deepening its vision of shared growth, openness and regional economic cooperation, China is reportedly looking to push forward the implementation of the Belt and Road construction in Africa, and support the continent in implementing its Agenda 2063 and the 2030 Agenda for Sustainable Development, as well as planning to focus in the next few years on importing $10 trillion worth of goods and services and foreign investment reaching $750 billion, and outbound tourism with 700 million travelers.⑨ Nigeria as the Africa's regional power is poised to cooperate with China in delivering the promises of shared growth to the continent.

Chinese technologies, innovation and finance are meeting with Nigeria's abundant natural resources endowment, cheap labour, large market and exquisite hospitality to deliver critical infrastructure. Infrastructure projects such as the Abuja Light Rail, Lagos Rail Mass Transit System, Abuja-Kaduna Railway, Manbilla Power Project, Lekki Deep Seaport, and the Lagos-Calabar Coastal Railway are some of the products of the China-

---

① The Guardian: "Buhari tightens noose on graft war, signs extradition, economic treaties" –https://guardian.ng/news/buhari-tightens-noose-on-graft-war-signs-extradition-economic-treaties/.
② Ibid, section 12.
③ See Deloitte Nigeria's Tax Alert, January 30, 2018 – https://blog.deloitte.com.ng/nigeria-signs-double-tax-treaty-with-spain-into-law/
④ Section 46, Constitution of the Federal Republic of Nigeria, supra.
⑤ Investments and Securities Tribunal (IST) established under sections 274 – 297, Investments and Securities Act, 2007.
⑥ National Industrial Court of Nigeria (NICN) established under section 254 of the Constitution of the Federal Republic of Nigeria 1999 (as amended).
⑦ Tax Appeal Tribunal (TAT) established in accordance with section 59(1) of the Federal Inland Revenue Service (Establishment) Act, 2007.
⑧ See the Belt and Road's "Cooperation Priorities" in the "Vision and Actions on Jointly Building Silk Road Economic Belt and 21st-Century Maritime Silk Road" – a joint publication of the National Development and Reform Commission, Ministry of Foreign Affairs, and Ministry of Commerce of the People's Republic of China, March 2015.Source: Economic and Commercial Counsellor's Office of the Embassy of the People's Republic of China in the Federal Republic of Nigeria – http://nigeria2.mofcom.gov.cn/article/chinanews/201504/20150400936317.shtml.
⑨ Chao Xiaoliang, Consul-General of the People's Republic of China in Lagos: See Vanguard, November 9, 2017 – https://www.vanguardngr.com/2017/11/china-trade-volume-nigeria-hits-8-94bn/.

Nigeria development cooperation in recent times. There has also been mutually beneficial cooperation in the areas of Trade, Information Technology, Agriculture and Culture[1].

China-Nigeria bilateral trade reached $13.78 billion in 2017[2] on the back of continuous bilateral trade and economic agreements between the two countries. In 2016, China and Nigeria negotiated a currency swap deal to allow trading between the two to be done directly in their local currencies without any need for the Dollar, and enabling the Renminbi (Yuan) to flow freely within the Nigerian banking system. The Nigerian Government few years ago converted a sizeable percentage of its foreign reserve from the Dollar to Yuan in a bid to reduce the dependence of the Nigerian economy on the Dollar and improve on its trade with China.

On the international scene, Nigeria has always recognized China's foreign policy and global aspirations. In conjunction with other developing countries in Africa, Asia, and Latin America, Nigeria stood up to outside pressure on the "One Policy of China", and fully supported the People's Republic of China in securing its legitimate seat in the United Nations Security Council[3].

With the history of the Chinese Admiral Zheng He leading a fleet of 300 ships to Africa in the 15th Century, following which numerous friendship seeds have since then been planted in the hearts of both Chinese and African people, Africa has both natural and traditional connection with the Belt and Road Initiative[4] and Nigeria holds the promise of being the gateway to the continent.

Through platforms such as the Forum on China-Africa Cooperation (FOCAC) and several diplomatic and mutually beneficial alliances, Nigeria, as Africa's preferred investments destination, presents a unique opportunity of aiding implementation of the Belt and Road's important aspiration to connect Asian, European and African countries more closely for shared prosperity.

II. Investment

A. Market Access

a. Department Supervising Investment

The primary agencies responsible for supervising investment in Nigeria are:

a) Securities and Exchange Commission (SEC)

This is the apex regulatory institution of the Nigeria capital market which operates under the overall supervision of the Ministry of Finance. The SEC, among other functions, regulates the capital market through issuance of rules and guidelines on various forms of investment available in the country with a view to protecting investors, develops the capital market in order to enhance its allocative efficiency, and pave the way for a private sector led economy.[5]

b) Central Bank of Nigeria (CBN)

The CBN is the apex regulator in the Nigerian financial system and is in charge of the overall control and administration of the monetary and financial sector policies of the Federal Government of Nigeria (FGN). By its mandate, the CBN not only regulates all banks and other financial institutions (OFIs) operating in the economy but also issues the legal tender currency in Nigeria; promotes a sound financial system by monitoring and keeping records of the amount of money in circulation; maintains the country's external reserve; and controls the credit, foreign trade, and foreign exchange (forex) regimes in Nigeria[6].

A foreign investor will require capital to operate a business enterprise in Nigeria. In the process of doing business in Nigeria, foreign investors who incorporate Nigerian companies, or make equity investments into Nigerian companies, or advance loans to local associates / subsidiaries, have had to transfer investment capital into the country.

---

[1] "Nigeria: Beyond sharing National Day with China", Interview by Chao Xiaoliang, Consul-General of the People's Republic of China in Lagos: See Vanguard, October 1, 2016 – https://www.vanguardngr.com/2016/10/nigeria-beyond-sharing-national-day-with-china/.
[2] Chao Xiaoliang, Consul-General of the People's Republic of China in Lagos: See Vanguard, February 7, 2018 – https://www.vanguardngr.com/2018/02/china-nigeria-bilateral-trade-hit-n4-97-trillion-2017/.
[3] "Nigeria: Beyond sharing National Day with China", Interview by Chao Xiaoliang, supra.
[4] Chao Xiaoliang: "The Belt and Road: New Opportunities for China-Nigeria Cooperation", Consulate-General of the People's Republic of China in Lagos, April 1, 2017 – 01 April, 2017.Source: Website of the Consulate-General of the Peoples' Republic of China in Lagos – http://lagos.china-consulate.org/eng/xwfb/zxhd/t1450672.htm.
[5] SEC Nigeria – www.sec.gov.ng/about.
[6] CBN – www.cbn.gov.ng/AboutCBN.

Foreign Capital, under the Nigerian law means "convertible currency, plant, machinery, equipment, spare parts, raw materials and other business assets, other than goodwill, that are brought into Nigeria with no initial disbursement of Nigerian foreign exchange and are intended for the production of goods and services related to an enterprise to which the Nigerian Investment Promotion Commission (NIPC) Act applies".[1]

Hence, the law requires that such investor should import the needed capital into the country through an authorised dealer licensed by the CBN[2]. The authorised dealer through which the capital for investment is imported is obligated to issue within 24 hours of the importation, a Certificate of Capital Importation (CCI) to the investor and within 48 hours thereafter, make returns to the CBN as the banking and forex regulator[3]. The CCI entitles an investor to open a foreign currency domiciliary account with any authorised dealer and also to open a special non-resident Naira account, as well as guarantees unconditional transferability and repatriation of funds (both capital and earnings) by an investor upon exit from Nigeria[4].

c) Nigerian Investment Promotion Commission (NIPC)

The NIPC is the agency set up by the FGN to attract foreign investments into the country. It advices the Government on policy matters, including fiscal measures, designed to promote industrialisation of Nigeria and the general development of the economy. It coordinates, monitors, and encourages the establishment and operation of all investment promotion activities in the country by providing business entities with the necessary assistance and guidance needed to grow.

The NIPC liaises between investors and relevant government departments, ministries and agencies (MDAs); institutional lenders; and other authorities within the investment industry. Part of NIPC's functions is the dissemination of up-to-date information on incentives available to investors, as well as provision of support services to both prospective and existing investors[5].

Upon incorporation but before the commencement of business, a foreign investor is required to register with the NIPC in order to qualify for benefiting from certain incentives available to business enterprises in Nigeria, including tax holiday, ease of repatriation of funds upon exit from the country, as well as protection of investment and special status designation where eligible[6].

A Certificate of Registration is issued by the NIPC to a business entity within fourteen (14) days of registration where all relevant registration requirements have been duly completed and submitted[7]. An application made to the NIPC for the registration of a business entity is required to be accompanied some documents which include, company's incorporation documents; shareholding structure; joint venture, shareholders' or partnership agreement; and letter of authority, where applicable.

To further enhance the objectives of the NIPC, the Government has created a One-Stop-Investment-Center (OSIC) at the NIPC as a way of enhancing the ease of doing business and facilitating investments in Nigeria.

The OSIC is an investment facilitation mechanism which brings relevant government Agencies to one location, coordinated and streamlined, to provide efficient and transparent services to investors. It provides investors with a single place to pick up all documents and approvals that are statutorily needed to set up an investment project in Nigeria. The aims of OSIC include the removal of obstacles and unnecessary bureaucracy faced by investors in setting up and running of businesses. It provides statistical data and information on the Nigerian economy, investment climate, legal and regulatory framework as well as sector and industry specific information to aid existing and prospective investors in making informed business decisions.

The range of services offered to investors at the OSIC covers:

• General information and data on the Nigerian economy to facilitate informed investment decisions.

• Prompt granting of business entry approvals, permit and authorization to enable investors to set up an investment project.

• Facilitates post-entry approvals, licences and sector-specific permits with statutory government agencies with extant regulatory mandate.

• General facilitation with all government agencies in respect of investment projects on behalf of investors.

• General advisory services on unlimited and profitable investment opportunities in Nigeria including matching investors' requirements with opportunities available in Nigeria's 36 States and FCT.

---

[1] Section 31, Nigerian Investment Promotion Commission Act, Cap N117, Laws of the Federation of Nigeria 2004.
[2] Section 15(1), Foreign Exchange (Monitoring and Miscellaneous Provisions) Act, Cap F34, Laws of the Federation of Nigeria 2004.
[3] Ibid, section 15(2).
[4] Ibid, sections 13 & 15(4).See Rule 408(2), SEC Consolidated Rule 2013 @ http://sec.gov.ng/sec-nigerias-consolidated-rules-and-regulations-as-at-2013/.
[5] NIPC – http://www.nipc.gov.ng/about.html.
[6] Section 20(1), Nigerian Investment Promotion Commission Act, supra.
[7] Ibid, section 20(2).

The following can be processed and obtained at the OSIC without having to visit different regulatory agencies separately[1]:
- Company incorporation and registration;
- Business permit and registration;
- Tax registration / Clearance;
- Work permits and other Immigration facilities;
- Facilitation of Customs clearance for investment projects;
- Information and data on Nigeria's economic sectors and industry;
- Familiarization on Nigeria's regulatory environment;
- Sorting out of any administrative barriers confronting local and foreign investors.

d) Nigerian Office for Technology Acquisition and Promotion (NOTAP)

NOTAP is the agency of the FGN saddled with the responsibilities of evaluation and registration of technology transfer agreements (TTAs); promotion of intellectual property (IP); technology advisory and support services etc. Where the object to be transferred is a foreign technology i.e.technical expertise, plant, machinery, engineering supply, training facilities, trade mark & patent rights etc., the commercial contract or agreement in respect of such a foreign technology is required by law to be registered with NOTAP not later than sixty days from the execution or conclusion of the contract[2].

The NOTAP Act stipulates circumstances under which a technology (capital) transfer agreement will not be registered. These include where the technology to be transferred is freely available in Nigeria and where the consideration is not commensurate with the technology acquired or to be acquired. Similarly, contracts or agreements in which the transferee is obliged to submit to a foreign jurisdiction in the case of any disputes arising from the contract or agreement are not registrable in Nigeria.

b. Laws and Regulations of Investment Industry

The legal and regulatory regimes governing investments in the Nigerian economy include the following:

a) Companies and Allied Matters Act (CAMA), 1990[3]

This is the statute that governs incorporation of business entities in Nigeria and regulates their operations right from commencement of business through to liquidation. It prescribes the periodic statutory filings which business organizations are expected to make (such as Annual Returns), and established the Corporate Affairs Commission ("CAC") as the agency of Government in charge of the regulation of the formation and management of companies in Nigeria.[4]

b) Companies Regulation 2012[5]

The Companies Regulation 2012 is a body of rules made pursuant to the CAMA[6] and operated by the CAC. The regulation codifies some established practices and conventions, not properly addressed by the substantive law and prescribes the forms and standards of the statutory requirements for company incorporation, management and dissolution.

c) Investments and Securities Act (ISA), 2007[7]

The ISA establishes the SEC as the apex regulatory authority in the Nigerian capital market and empowers it to make rules and regulations governing investment and securities business in the country, especially in the areas of mergers, acquisitions and take-over, as well as collective investment schemes. It also licenses capital market operators in Nigeria.

d) SEC Rules[8]

The rules governing investments in the Nigerian economy are issued and applied by the SEC. There are SEC Codes of Corporate Governance / Conduct for regulated entities as well as SEC Rules on Fixed Income Securities; Fund / Portfolio Managers; Capital Market Operators; Trading in Securities; Global Depository Receipts (GDRs);

---

[1] NIPC OSIC – http://www.nipc.gov.ng/onestop.html.
[2] Section 5(2), National Office for Technology Acquisition and Promotion (NOTAP) Act, Cap.N 62, Laws of the Federation of Nigeria 2004.
[3] Cap.C20, Laws of the Federation of Nigeria, 2004.
[4] CAC – http://new.cac.gov.ng/home/about-us/.
[5] See http://new.cac.gov.ng/home/wp-content/uploads/2013/11/Companies_Regulations_As_Ammended.pdf and http://new.cac.gov.ng/home/wp-content/uploads/2017/04/Amendment-to-Companies-Regulation-2012.pdf.
[6] Sections 16, 585 and 609, CAMA.
[7] SEC, ISA – http://sec.gov.ng/investment-and-securities-act/.
[8] SEC Rules & Codes – http://sec.gov.ng/regulation/rules-codes/.

Collective Investment Scheme (CIS); Infrastructure Funds; Bonds; Mergers & Acquisitions (M&A) among others.[1]

e) Central Bank of Nigeria Act[2]

The CBN Act established the CBN and empowers it to regulate currency matters and issue legal tender in Nigeria; maintains external reserve and promote monetary stability and a sound financial system in the country. Further to this, the CBN regulates the amount of money in circulation and the inflow, investment, and outflow of foreign capital in the country.

f) Banks and Other Financial Institutions Act[3]

The BOFIA empowers the CBN as the regulator for the non-bank financial industry, and operations of all Other Financial Institutions (OFIs) in the country; such as licensing, management, structure, liquidation etc.

g) Foreign Exchange (Monitoring and Miscellaneous Provisions) Act[4]

The forex Act established an autonomous forex market in Nigeria to provide for the monitoring and supervision of the transactions conducted in the market and regulates the inflow of foreign capital into the country for investment purposes.

h) Monetary, Credit, Foreign Trade and Exchange Policy Guidelines[5]

This guidelines prescribe the directions which the country's policies will follow in any particular year in terms of monetary measures, credit, foreign trade, and forex management. It largely shapes the level of foreign capital inflow into the country in any given financial year.

i) Other CBN Circulars and Guidelines[6]

CBN regulations on foreign trade, forex, and investment etc.are often clarified in Circulars and Guidelines issued on specific matters. Implementation of these Circulars and Guidelines determines to a great extent the inflow or outflow of foreign capital. There have been Circulars on almost all regulatory issues in the Nigerian financial and investment landscape ranging from access to the forex market; registration of imported forex; repatriation of foreign capital and allowable investments.

j) National Office for Technology Acquisition and promotion (NOTAP) Act[7]

NOTAP Act established NOTAP as the agency for the registration of technology transfer agreements and of intellectual property ("IP") in Nigeria. The Act empowers NOTAP to prescribe application fees for the registration of transferred technologies and provide for penalties in cases of default.[8] Where a relevant contract or agreement is not presented for registration by NOTAP within 30 days from the date of execution of the agreement, the delay attracts a fine by NOTAP.[9]

k) Nigerian Investment Promotion Council (NIPC) Act[10]

NIPC Act established the NIPC to encourage and promote investment in the Nigerian economy and empowers it in this connection to administer incentives to enterprises registered and operating in Nigeria; designate certain investments as "Priority areas" deserving of special incentives; and facilitate repatriation of foreign capital with proceeds from Nigeria unhindered as well as providing guarantee against expropriation of foreign enterprises[11].

l) Federal Inland Revenue Service (Establishment) Act[12]

The FIRS Act established the Federal Inland Revenue Service and empowers it to assess and collect revenues accruable to the Government of the Federation. In this connection, the FIRS Act provides that the objective of the FIRS shall be to control and administer the different taxes and laws specified in the statute or any other law made by the National Assembly or other regulations made pursuant to the statute and to account to the Government for all taxes collected.[13] Essentially, these include all laws specifying one form of tax or the other which business enterprises are expected to pay for doing business in Nigeria.

---

[1] Ibid.
[2] Central Bank of Nigeria (Establishment) Act, 2007.
[3] Cap B3, Laws of the Federation of Nigeria, 2004.
[4] Foreign Exchange (Monitoring and Miscellaneous Provisions) Act, Cap F34, Laws of the Federation of Nigeria 2004.
[5] CBN – https://www.cbn.gov.ng/documents/Monetarycreditguide.asp.
[6] CBN, "All Circulars" – https://www.cbn.gov.ng/documents/circulars.asp.
[7] National Office for Technology Acquisition and Promotion (NOTAP) Act, supra.
[8] Ibid, section 20.
[9] NOTAP, "Schedule of Applicable Fees for Registration of Technology Transfer Agreements" – http://notap.gov.ng/sites/default/files/schedule_of_applicable_fees_for_registration_of_technology_transfer_agreements.pdf.
[10] Nigerian Investment Promotion Act, supra.
[11] Ibid, sections 22 – 25.
[12] Federal Inland Revenue Service (Establishment Act) No.57 of 2007.
[13] Ibid, section 2.

c. Forms of Investment

Foreign investors willing to invest in the Nigerian economy can make their investments either in the form of Foreign Direct Investment (FDI), Foreign Portfolio Investment (FPI), or International Commercial Loans and Official Flows. Whichever form an investor chooses to use, the inflow of foreign capital for the investment must be duly registered with the appropriate authorities as earlier stated and CCI obtained in that regard.

d. Standards of Market Access and Examination

After a foreign investor has duly obtained a CCI and registered with the NIPC as may be required, it is free to invest in any enterprise or security in Nigeria with all the benefits, incentives, and guarantees earlier stated in place[1]. However, where it is required by law to incorporate a company, a foreign investor will have to do this before commencing business. In certain industries or enterprises, there are sector specific regulators which prescribe the standards of entry and are empowered to issue permit or license to a foreign investor to commence operation, after all given requirements have been duly complied with[2]. In addition to obtaining the sector specific operating licenses, all enterprises in Nigeria are required to register with the FIRS and obtain a Tax Identification Number (TIN) as a condition precedent to commencing business.

B. Foreign Exchange Regulation

a. Department Supervising Foreign Exchange

The primary agency responsible for supervising the foreign exchange market in Nigeria is the Central Bank of Nigeria (CBN).

b. Brief Introduction of Laws and Regulations of Foreign Exchange

The primary statute governing foreign exchange (forex) in Nigeria is the Foreign Exchange (Monitoring and Miscellaneous Provisions) Act[3]. The Act liberalised the forex market in Nigeria with the introduction of an Autonomous Foreign Exchange Market ("AFEM") in 1995, for the sale of forex to end-users by the CBN, through selected authorized dealers at market determined exchange rates. In addition, Bureaux-de-Change were licensed and accorded the status of authorized buyers and sellers of forex to provide access to small users of forex and enlarge the officially recognised forex market. Exchange rates in the Bureaux de Change are market determined. Scarcity in the official sector and bureaucratic procedures necessitated the growth and development of the parallel market. The forex market was further liberalized in October, 1999 with the introduction of an Inter-bank Foreign Exchange Market ("IFEM"). However, harsh economic situations precipitated by the persistent fall in international oil prices in the years following the forex market liberalization affected the value of the local currency, put a strain on external reserves and raised inflationary pressures; necessitating the reversal to forex control and adoption of a pegged / official exchange rate by the CBN for some years.

In June 2016, with the launch of a "Revised Guidelines for the Operation of the Nigerian Inter-bank Foreign Exchange Market[4]", the CBN went back to liberalization of the Nigerian forex market but with periodic interventions to maintain stability, by introducing a single autonomous forex market for all end-users; non-deliverable, over-the-counter (OTC) forex futures as hedging products in the IFEM; and maintaining a previous ban on some forty one (41) items[5] from accessing the official forex market in Nigeria. Letters of Credit cannot be established in respect of the 41 banned items except for those earlier established before the June 2015 ban[6]. To further boost liquidity in the forex market and ensure timely execution and settlement of forex trades for eligible transactions in Nigeria, the CBN, among many other initiatives, established the Investors' and Exporters FX Window[7] in 2017. Stipulated eligible transactions benefiting from this special window include loan repayments, interest payments, dividend / income remittances, capital repatriation, bills for collection and others miscellaneous payments specified in the CBN Foreign Exchange Manual.

---

[1] Foreign Exchange (Monitoring and Miscellaneous Provisions) Act, supra, at section 15.
[2] For instance, a foreign investor with interest in banking will have to comply with specific regulations issued by the CBN and be duly licensed before it can commence operation. There are corresponding regulators/licensors in other industries.
[3] Supra.
[4] The CBN's "Revised Guidelines for the Operation of the Nigerian Inter-bank Foreign Exchange Market" is accessible @ https://www.cbn.gov.ng/out/2016/ccd/revised%20guidelines%20for%20flexible%20exchange%20rate%20marketjune%202016%20v1.pdf.
[5] The 41 items not valid for forex allocation in Nigeria as at the time of preparing this Guide can be accessed @ https://www.cbn.gov.ng/Out/2015/CCD/tedcircular062015.pdf.
[6] CBN Circular – https://www.cbn.gov.ng/Out/2015/TED/TED.FEM.FPC.GEN.01.021.pdf.
[7] CBN Circular for the "Establishment of Investors' & Exporters' FX Window" is accessible @ https://www.cbn.gov.ng/out/2017/fmd/establishment%20of%20investors%27%20&%20exporters%27%20fx%20window.pdf.

c. Requirements of Foreign Exchange Management for Foreign Enterprises

Foreign enterprises are required to import their foreign capital through a CBN-licensed authorized dealer and obtained a CCI as earlier stated. After this, a foreign investor may open, maintain and operate a domiciliary account designated in an internationally convertible foreign currency with the authorised dealer through which the capital was imported or with any other banks. The law protects a foreign investor who has duly complied with the statutory requirement for capital importation from forceful disclosure of the source of the foreign currency deposited in his domiciliary account or accounts, except where expressly required by law. The capital so imported is also statutorily protected from seizure, forfeiture or expropriation by the Government[1]. The general management of imported foreign capital is as stipulated by the CBN from time to time in Circulars and Guidelines[2].

C. Financing

a. Main Financial Institutions

The main financial institutions operating in Nigeria include:
- Central Bank of Nigeria (CBN) – Apex regulator for the financial system;
- Commercial Banks;
- Bank of Industry;
- Nigerian Export-Import Bank;
- Bank of Agriculture;
- Other Financial Institutions (OFIs): Primary Mortgage Banks (PMBs), Nigeria Mortgage Refinance Company (NMRC), Discount Houses, Development Finance Institutions, Finance Houses, Bureaux-De-Change, Micro Finance Banks ("MFBs") etc;
- Insurance Companies;
- Nigerian Agricultural Insurance Corporation.

b. Financing Conditions for Foreign Enterprises

The financing conditions for foreign enterprises in Nigeria are as stated earlier. In most cases, foreign investors act as the lenders to Nigerian enterprises and usually will be required to import their capital through an authorized dealer, obtain a CCI of the transfer, and ensure compliance with the investment, business and operational regulatory environment.

D. Land Policy

a. Brief Introduction of Land-Related Laws and Regulations

The major land policy in Nigeria is provided in the Land Use Act of 1978[3] which is to the effect that all lands in any State of the federation is held by the Governor of the State on trust for the people Nigeria and administer same for their benefit (mainly in the allocation of land to individuals and organisations; for residential, agricultural, commercial and other purposes and collecting rents in relation thereto). The Land Use Act (LUA) generally governs the ownership and use of, as well as the general administration of land, in Nigeria. Section 1[4] of the LUA vests title to all land within the urban territory of each State (with the exception of land vested in the Federal Government or its agencies) solely in the Governor of the relevant State (Lands within the rural territory of a State are vested in the Local Governments under section 2[5] of the LUA). With the enactment of the LUA, the highest interest that anyone (individuals or companies) can have in land is a "Right of Occupancy", which is tantamount to a leasehold interest usually for a period not exceeding 99 years.

The Governor of a State is empowered by virtue of section 5(1)(a)[6] of the LUA to grant the Right of Occupancy, which is evidenced by the issuance of a certificate of occupancy (C of O). Any subsequent transactions in respect of the land (which is the subject of the Right of Occupancy), must be with the consent of the Governor of the State where the land is situate.

By virtue of the provisions of the LUA, no transactions affecting land in Nigeria either by way of assignment,

---

[1] Foreign Exchange (Monitoring and Miscellaneous Provisions) Act, Supra – section 17.
[2] Ibid, section 20.See also, CBN's Revised Guidelines for the Operation of the Nigerian Inter-bank Foreign Exchange Market" – https://www.cbn.gov.ng/out/2016/ccd/revised%20guidelines%20for%20flexible%20exchange%20rate%20marketjune%202016%20v1.pdf.
[3] Cap L5, Laws of the Federation of Nigeria 2004.
[4] Ibid.
[5] Ibid.
[6] Ibid.

mortgage, transfer of possession, sublease or otherwise howsoever, shall be carried out without first obtaining the Consent of the Governor of the concerned State[1]. Any transaction done, or any instrument which purports to confer on, or vest any interest or right over land in any person in contravention of these provisions is null and void[2]. However, the Supreme Court of Nigeria has held that such transactions concluded without obtaining the requisite Governor's Consent is not void but merely inchoate[3] but it is important to note that investors may not be able to enforce a mortgage, charge, or any form of securities created through inchoate land transactions in Nigeria. All States of the federation have their respective land registration laws which, in addition to the LUA, govern the administration of real property transactions within their boundaries. In Lagos State (Nigeria's commercial capital and financial centre), the registration of title to land (with the connected purposes) is governed by the Lagos State Lands Registration Law, 2015. Salient provisions of the Lagos Lands Law are as follows:

a) The mode of transfer of interests in land, sub-lease or mortgage is by deed. Such transfer shall be deemed complete after the deed has been filed for registration at the Land Registry.

b) All deeds by which sub-leases, mortgages and dealings in land are effected are registrable documents

c) Registrable documents are mandated to be registered within sixty (60) days after obtaining the Governor's Consent (where applicable) on them

d) A Power of Attorney authorising a third party to deal in land is a registrable document

e) Land Certificates shall be issued, containing the details of all transactions relating to land, which have been registered as required and the Land Certificates shall be prima facie evidence of title

f) A registered holder of land has power to dispose or deal with it and create any interest or right over it, subject to obtaining the required Governor's Consent

Perfection of title involves three main stages: (i) obtaining Governor's Consent; (ii) stamping the relevant transaction document and payment of Stamp Duty; and (iii) registration of the transaction document at the relevant Lands Registry. The procedures making up these three main stages are currently being undertaken in Lagos State with a 30-Day Guideline (a 10-step procedure that seeks to achieve registration of interest in land within 30 days to improve the ease of doing business in the State and in Nigeria.

It is important also for investors to know that while title to a land is vested in the Governor of the State where the land is located, the laws of the country vests total ownership and control of all minerals, mineral oils and natural gas in, under or upon any land, territorial waters and the Exclusive Economic Zone of Nigeria in the Federal Government[4].

b. Rules of land Acquisition for Foreign Enterprises

Land acquisition for foreign enterprises in Nigeria is guided by the provisions of the Constitution of the Federal Republic of Nigeria, 1999 (as amended); Land Use Act (LUA); Land Registration Law of the State where the relevant land is located; and the Nigerian Minerals and Mining Act, 2007 and others.

Essentially, foreign entities seeking to do businesses in Nigeria can legally acquire lands subject to varying local constraints on the types of leases they may hold. In Lagos State, lands are allocated by the State Government to foreign companies and individuals for a maximum tenor of twenty five (25) years[5]. In practice however, this stipulation is often not strictly enforced. Of particular importance to foreign investors is the fact that banks and other financial institutions usually require real property as security for loans. This makes it very vital for a corporate entity to always obtain the Certificate of Occupancy on its land / real property as this is usually required to be produced before the mandatory Governor's Consent will be granted in respect of any transaction for the transfer of interest in land.

E. The Establishment and Dissolution of Companies

a. Forms of Enterprises

The forms of enterprises available to investors in Nigeria are: sole proprietorship, partnership, and incorporated companies. Incorporated companies can either be Private Limited Liability Companies or Public Limited Liability Companies. A foreign investors interested in setting up a non-profit organisation is required to register either a Company Limited by Guarantee or Incorporated Trustees depending on the purpose for which the entity is to be established.

---

[1] Ibid, sections 21 and 22.
[2] Ibid, section 26.
[3] Awojugbagbe Light Industries Ltd.Vs.P.N.Chinukwe & Anor [1995] 5 NWLR [Pt.390] 409.
[4] Constitution of the Federal Republic of Nigeria, 1999 (as amended) and Nigerian Minerals and Mining Act, 2007.
[5] By virtue of the Acquisition of Lands by Aliens Law, Cap 2, Laws of Lagos State 1994 [Section 1(i)(a) and 2(1) thereof].

The commonest form of enterprises used by investors in Nigeria is the limited liability company because of the advantage of being a separate legal entity from its promoters / shareholders. Investors are not personally liable for any liability incurred by a Limited Liability Company except to the amount paid on the shares. The legal personality of the company also ensures that no restriction exists to bar a foreign investor who wants to liquidate his interest in a registered company in Nigeria.

The minimum number of persons to form a company in Nigeria shall be two. Though a private company has a limit of fifty members, there is no maximum number of members in a public company.

Another common form of enterprise by foreign investors in Nigeria, particularly private equity (PE) funds is Limited Partnership. There is no federal law regulating the registration of limited partnerships in the country and CAMA only provides for the registration of business names. However, private equity limited partnerships are typically registered at the CAC as business names. In Lagos State however, there is a limited partnership registry which was established pursuant to the Partnership Law of Lagos State[①].

b. Procedure of Establishment

The following are the procedures for incorporating business entities in Nigeria:

a) Reservation of Proposed Name

The first step towards incorporating a company in Nigeria is to conduct an "availability search" at the CAC to confirm that the desired name for the company is available for use, i.e., that the said name is not identical or similar to the name of an existing company or any existing trademark or trade name or otherwise unacceptable to the CAC. Usually, two (2) or three (3) alternative names are submitted for the availability search and where available, same will be reserved for an initial period of sixty (60) days which can be renewed for further sixty (60) day periods. During the reservation period, no other company can be registered with the reserved name or any other name which, in the opinion of the CAC, is identical or similar to the said reserved name.

b) Objects of the Company

A foreign investor or entity may engage in any business in Nigeria except for enterprises involved in the production of arms and ammunitions; production and dealing in narcotic drugs and psychotropic substances; and the production of military and para-military wears and accouterment. Where the proposed object of the company includes rendering professional services, the CAC may require a proficiency certificate of the applicant before such an object is registered.

c) Incorporation Documents

Where a name has been approved and reserved by an applicant, the following documents are required to be submitted with the CAC Forms of Incorporation:

(i) Memorandum and Articles of Association (Mem Arts):

The Memorandum is the Constitution document of the Company, which sets out its main objects whilst the Articles regulate its internal governance and administrative procedures. The MemArts must be subscribed to by at least two (2) entities (individuals or companies). The CAC, in December 2008, introduced a standard form for MemArts, which essentially adopts the MemArts contained in the schedule to CAMA. Promoters of companies are however allowed to add an extra page to the Articles, which will set out any particular provisions considered imperative for the Company.

The MemArts must be subscribed to by at least two (2) entities (individuals and or companies), both of whom / which can be non-Nigerians and whom / which must jointly take up a minimum of twenty five percent (25%) of the Company's authorised share capital. Each individual subscriber must submit a recognised form of identification such as a copy of the data page of his / her international passport, national driver's license or the national identity card or a certificate of incorporation in the case of a corporate subscriber.

Where any of the proposed promoters of a new company is an incorporated entity, the CAC requires that such promoter must be represented by an individual, who will sign the incorporation documents, in addition to affixing that promoter's common seal thereto. A resolution of the board of directors of such promoter authorizing it to become a member of the proposed company and nominating the individual who will sign the incorporation documents and or represent it on the board of directors of the proposed company, is also required to be filed together with the incorporation documents with the CAC. The resolution must be printed on the promoter's stationery, signed by its directors, and have its common seal affixed thereon. The CAC may also require a certificate of proficiency where the Company seeks to provide professional or consultancy services.

(ii) Statement of Authorised Share Capital and Return of Allotment of Shares (Form CAC 2):

This form will contain the details of the company's authorised, issued and paid-up share capital (please see our advice in Section "Share Capital" below regarding the statutory requirements on share capital).

---

① Cap P21, Laws of Lagos State 2003 (as amended).

(iii) Particulars of Directors (Form CAC 7):

The names, addresses and job descriptions of the directors of the proposed company, who must be at least two (2) individuals, are set out in this form. The directors need not be Nigerians but must be at least eighteen (18) years old. This must be submitted with a recognised form of identification of the directors, a copy of the data page of each director's international passport, national driver's license or national identity card will suffice. Where any of the directors is a foreigner resident in Nigeria, evidence of residence permit must also be submitted to the CAC.

(iv) Notice of registered office address (Form CAC 3):

Every company is required to have a registered office address in Nigeria at the time of its incorporation.

(v) Particulars of the Company Secretary (Form CAC 2.1):

Every company incorporated in Nigeria is required to have a Company Secretary.[1]

(vi) Declaration of Compliance with the Requirements of CAMA (Form CAC 4):

This form is a statutory declaration to be made by a legal practitioner attesting that the statutory requirements for the registration of the Nigerian company have been duly complied with.

d) Share Capital

(i) Authorised Share Capital:

Pursuant to the CAMA, the minimum authorised share capital for a private company is ₦10,000 (Ten Thousand Naira) whilst a public company must have a minimum authorised share capital of ₦500,000 (Five Hundred Thousand Naira). However, where any of the subscribers to the company's MemArts is a foreign entity or individual, the company's authorised share capital must be a minimum of ₦10,000,000 (Ten Million Naira) as prescribed by the NIPC.

(ii) Issued Share Capital:

At incorporation and at every point in time during its existence, a company's issued share capital must not be less than 25% of its authorised share capital. In other words, at least 25% of the company's authorised share capital must be taken up by its shareholders. Generally, there are no restrictions under Nigerian law, preventing a foreign entity from "wholly-owning" a Nigerian company. However, there are certain industry-specific restrictions which preclude some categories of Nigerian companies from being "wholly-owned" by foreigners. For example, any company seeking to register a vessel under the Coastal and Inland Shipping (Cabotage) Act[2] must be 60% owned by Nigerians. It is important to note that Section 18 of CAMA requires every Nigerian company to have a minimum of two shareholders (who need not be Nigerians). Foreign nationals are however required to obtain a business registration certificate and a business permit before undertaking any form of business in Nigeria.

(iii) Paid-Up Share Capital:

There is no statutory requirement that any minimum amount of a company's issued share capital must be paid up.

e) Official Fees

The statutory fees payable upon incorporation of a company limited by shares is assessed based on its authorized share capital and these include:

(i) Stamp duties – 0.75% of the authorised share capital which is payable to the Federal Inland Revenue Service.

(ii) CAC filing fees – 1%[3] of the authorised share capital which is payable to the CAC.

(iii) Approximately ₦11,000 (Eleven Thousand Naira) which is payable for obtaining certified true copies of the MemArts and Forms CAC 2, 3, 7 and 2.1 from the CAC.

The incorporation process can typically be concluded within a period of about fourteen (14) business days from the date on which all official fees have been paid and all relevant documents are filed with the CAC.

c. Routes and Requirements of Dissolution

There are different routes through which corporate business enterprises can be dissolved in Nigeria. Dissolution is one of the consequences of insolvency, and pursuant to the provisions of section 401 of CAMA, a company may be wound up on ground of insolvency by the court, voluntarily by members or creditors of the company, or under the supervision of the court. It can also be the result of regulatory sanction by the CAC.

The CAMA and the Companies Winding up Rules (CWU Rules) are the relevant legislation and regulations that govern corporate insolvency proceedings in Nigeria. The bulk of the framework of Nigeria Insolvency regime is contained in part XIV (14), XV (15) and XVI (16) of CAMA which makes provision for Receivership and Manager, Winding up of companies, Arrangement and Compromise respectively.

---

[1] Section 293, CAMA.
[2] Cap C51, Laws of the Federation of Nigeria 2004.
[3] This fee is assessed at 2% for public companies.

a) Winding Up by Court

By Section 408 of CAMA, a Company may be wound up by the Court on the following grounds:

(i) the company has by special resolution resolved that the company be wound up by the court;

(ii) default is made in delivering the statutory report to the Commission or in holding the statutory meeting;

(iii) the number of members is reduced below two;

(iv) the company is unable to pay its debts; or

(v) the court is of opinion that it is just and equitable that the company should be wound up.

It must be noted that in relation to 408 (iv) above, a Company is deemed to be insolvent if it is indebted to its creditors:

(i) in a sum exceeding 2,000 Naira and is unable to pay same upon service of three weeks' statutory notice on it;

(ii) upon execution of judgment against and it is returned unsatisfied in whole or in part; or

(iii) where the court considers the liability of the company and is satisfied that it is unable to pay its debts.

Where the petition is presented on the ground that the company is unable to pay its debt, the winding up proceeding is filed in the court for an order of winding up to be made by the Court and the Petitioner in a winding up proceeding must show that the petition is brought bona fide and based on any one or more of the grounds stated above. Further, by the provisions of section 410 of CAMA, any or all of the following persons may file a petition for the winding up of the company by the court, separately or jointly:

(i) the company;

(ii) a creditor (This includes a contingent or prospective creditor of the company, and by Section 410(2)(c) of CAMA, the court would not hear a winding up petition presented by a contingent or prospective creditor until sufficient security for costs has been given and a prima facie case for winding up has been established to the satisfaction of the court);

(iii) the official receiver (who shall be the Deputy Chief Registrar of the Federal High Court or an officer so designated by the Chief Judge of the Federal High Court, for the purpose of winding up of the company)[1];

(iv) a contributory[2];

(v) a trustee in bankruptcy to or a personal representative of a creditor or contributory; and

(vi) the Corporate Affairs Commission (CAC).

The court also has the powers to appoint an official receiver and a liquidator for the purposes of conducting the winding up. A Minority Shareholder qualifies as a Contributory under the provisions of CAMA and accordingly, an application can be made by the Minority Shareholder to court for the winding up of the Company by the Court on the basis that it is just and equitable that the Company be wound up.

By the combined effect of Sections 407 to 410 of CAMA and Sections 15 to 41 of CWU Rules, the procedure for winding up of companies, by the court is as follows:

(i) Filing of a Petition for Winding by the Minority Shareholder;

(ii) Filing of an Affidavit verifying the Petition;

(iii) Obtain an Order by the Court for advertisement of the Petition in a daily newspaper and Gazette for fifteen (15) clear days before the date of hearing;

(iv) Advertisement of the Petition stating name and address of the petitioner and petitioner's solicitor;

(v) Hearing of the Petition and making of winding up order;

(vi) Court Registrar shall on the same day or not later than five (5) days after the making of the order, send to the Official Receiver, a Notice informing him that the order has been pronounced;

(vii) Three (3) copies of the order sealed shall be sent to the Official Receiver[3] who will then serve same on the CAC;

(viii) Delivery of two (2) copies of Statement of Affairs of the company to the Official Receiver by the person authorized or asked to produce same. One (1) copy will be verified by an Affidavit and same will be filed with the Court Registrar, by the Official Receiver;

(ix) Appointment of liquidator by the Court;

(x) Advertisement of the appointment of a liquidator in the Gazette and two newspapers and delivery of copies to the CAC;

(xi) Winding up by the liquidator;

(xii) Application to Court and granting of an order dissolving the Company;

---

[1] Section 419(1), CAMA.

[2] A contributory is any person who is liable to contribute to the assets of a company in the event of its being wound up.

[3] This is the Deputy Chief Registrar of the Federal High Court or an officer designated for the purpose by the Chief Judge of the Federal High Court.

(xiii) Delivery of the dissolution order to the CAC within fourteen (14) days.

Once the Company is fully wound-up and dissolved, it loses its status as a legal entity and ceases to exist in law. It should however be noted however that the Court has a discretion whether or not to authorize the winding up of the Company and as such, can approve the winding up; or refuse the application for winding up; or approve the same with additional requirements other than the ones stated above.

b) Voluntary Winding Up

A company may be wound up when the period (if any) fixed for the duration of the company by its articles, expires, or the event (if any) occurs, on the occurrence of which the articles provided that the company is to be dissolved and the company, in general meeting, has passed a resolution requiring the company to be wound up voluntarily. A lso, a company may be voluntarily wound up if the company resolves by special resolution that the company be wound up voluntarily. The winding-up process may be implemented by way of members' / shareholders' voluntary winding-up proceedings (the "Liquidation"), in accordance with the provisions of the CAMA and the Liquidation process will essentially involve the following steps:

(i) Preparation of a Declaration of Solvency, to be issued by its directors, confirming that the Company is able to pay all its outstanding debts and other liabilities (if any);

(ii) Preparation of a special resolution to be passed by the shareholders, at a general meeting to be called, approving the winding-up of the Company;

(iii) Appointment of a liquidator by the shareholders (this can be done at the same general meeting where the winding-up is approved);

(iv) Winding-up of the affairs of the Company by the liquidator (that is, the gathering of the Company's assets, ascertaining and verifying it's outstanding liabilities and discharging it's liabilities to its creditors);

(v) Convening of a final meeting of the shareholders of the Company, at which the liquidator will present a final report (in relation to the winding-up process) and the final accounts of the Company, both for approval by the shareholders;

(vi) Registration of the liquidator's final report and final accounts with the CAC; and

(vii) Dissolution of the Company and striking-off its name from the companies' register, by the CAC [this will occur three (3) months after the registration of the liquidator's final report and final accounts with the CAC].

It should be noted that the effect of winding up, is that from the commencement of winding up, the company ceases to carry on business. Also within 14 days after a resolution for winding up has been passed, the notice of the resolution has to be advertised in the Gazette or two daily newspapers and to the Commission.

c) Winding Up Under the Supervision of the Court

Regarding winding up under the supervision of the court, if a company passes a resolution for voluntary winding up, upon petition[1] by any of the persons entitled to bring a petition for winding up by the court, the court may order that the voluntary winding up shall continue but subject to the supervision of the court. The effect of this type of winding up is that it is deemed to be a petition for winding up by the court. Also, Section 519 (1) of CAMA provides that in all matters relating to winding up of company, the court can order for a meeting of the creditors to be called and it shall have regard to individual debt. After completion of winding up, officers of the court are expected to make returns to the commission.

The CAC can also strike out the name of the Company from its registers, if the company no longer carries on business. However, an aggrieved member may within 20 years apply for restating of the name of the company on the register.[2]

It is worthy to note that typically, mandatorily preferred interests will rank ahead of the claims of secured creditors in insolvency. Where a company is being wound up, CAMA prescribes a regime of priorities[3] which must guide the liquidator in the distribution of assets of the company. The various priorities may be classified as follows:

(i) Costs and expenses of winding up;

(ii) Local rates and charges, Pay-As-You-Earn tax deductions, assessed taxes, land tax, property or income tax due from the company;

(iii) Deductions under the National Provident Fund Act;

(iv) All wages and salaries of workmen in respect of services rendered to the company;

(v) All accrued holiday remuneration becoming payable to any clerk, servant, workman or laborer on the termination of his employment as a result of the winding up order or resolution;

---

[1] A petition for winding up subject to the supervision of the court operates for most purposes as a petition for winding up by the court (Sections 487 and 490(2) CAMA).

[2] Section 525(6) of CAMA.

[3] Section 494 of CAMA.

(vi) All amounts due in respect of any compensation or liability for compensation under the Employee Compensation Act, accrued before the commencement of winding up;

(vii) Debts (secured creditors have priority over unsecured ones);

(viii) Distribution of net assets to members according to their rights and interests in the company, subject to any contrary provisions in the Articles of Association.

Subject to the aforementioned statutorily preferred payments, all unsecured creditors would be treated pari passu during insolvency proceedings.[1]

d) Arrangement or Compromise

Arrangement or compromise is a recognized mode of business combination or restructuring and provisions on them are contained in Part XVI of CAMA. The arrangement regime in Section 538 allows a company to pass a special resolution for the voluntary liquidation of the company, and to appoint a liquidator who is mandated to sell its assets to another company. The issue of consideration is usually settled by the shareholders of the company to be liquidated being allocated shares in the transferee company.

Section 539 of CAMA allows for a compromise and arrangement between a company and its creditors or members (or any class thereof). The procedure takes the form of an application by the company to the court for a court-ordered meeting. Pursuant to the grant of the court order, the notice of meeting is sent and the notice shall be accompanied with a statement, and any material interest of the directors and debenture holders i.e. how the arrangement would affect the directors or the denture holders (any advertisement must capture these aforementioned statements). If authorization is granted, the meeting is held.

At the court-ordered meeting, the scheme must be approved by a majority vote representing at least three-quarters (by value) of the shares of members (or a class thereof) or the interests of creditors (or a class thereof). Section 539(2) further envisages the possibility of a compromise or arrangement being referred to the SEC, which must then appoint one or more inspectors to investigate the fairness of the compromise or arrangement and file a written report with the court. If the court is satisfied on the question of fairness, it may give its approval and make the scheme binding. In addition to the above mentioned, a certified true copy (CTC) of the scheme sanctioning the scheme by court shall be delivered to the CAC, and the order is not to be effective until the CTC of the order is so delivered to the CAC for registration.[2]

F. Mergers and Acquisition

The key legislation governing Mergers and Acquisitions (M&A) in Nigeria is the Investments and Securities Act, 2007. Transactions are regulated primarily by the Rules and Regulations issued by the SEC[3]. Where the target company is listed on a securities exchange, the Exchange Rules will apply.[4]

All operations of companies in Nigeria (business combinations inclusive) are also subject to the CAMA[5] and the regulations made pursuant to it – Companies Regulation 2012[6]. Stamp duties are also required to be paid on M&A documents under the Stamp Duties Act. Depending on which sector of the economy the combining companies belong, additional laws and rules may apply. There are industry-specific statutes and regulations in such sectors as banking, insurance, telecommunications, electric power, broadcasting, oil & gas etc. which may impact M&A transactions pertaining to them.

The main regulatory authority for M&A in Nigeria is the SEC, which reviews and grants approval for all business combinations. The taxes payable (stamp duties inclusive) on M&A transactions are administered by the FIRS while the CAC enforces compliance with the Companies Regulation 2012 for the combining companies.

In accordance with statutory provisions, the Federal High Court makes orders, directing pre-merger meetings between the combining companies and sanctioning the resulting mergers. Others, as the circumstances of each case may determine, are the Nigerian Stock Exchange (NSE) or any other applicable securities exchange and sector-specific regulators such as the CBN and National Insurance Commission (NAICOM) among others.

Merger is defined by the ISA as any amalgamation of the undertakings or any part of the undertakings or interest of two or more companies and one or more corporate bodies[7] while Acquisition means the takeover by one company of sufficient shares in another company to give the acquiring company control over that other

---

[1] Section 480, CAMA.
[2] Essentials of Corporate Law Practice in Nigeria by Nelson C.S.Ogbuanya.
[3] SEC Rules – SEC Rules & Codes – http://sec.gov.ng/regulation/rules-codes/.
[4] The Rules Book of the NSE – http://www.nse.com.ng/regulation-site/Pages/The-Rulebook-of-The-NSE.aspx.
[5] Cap C20, Laws of the Federation of Nigeria, 2004.
[6] Supra, see note 39.
[7] Section 119.

company.[1]

Thresholds and Categories of Mergers:

The SEC prescribes the thresholds of mergers in the Nigerian market and has powers to review from time to time what amounts to a small, intermediate, and large merger.[2] The legal requirements for M&A transactions under Nigerian law include the following[3]:

(i) The intending companies are required, either alone or together, to apply to the Federal High Court (FHC);

(ii) The FHC makes orders for separate meetings of the intending companies for the purpose of approving the scheme of merger or acquisition;

(iii) Members of each company holding three quarters of the total shares of the company are required to consent to the scheme of by a Resolution;

(iv) The Consent given is thereafter referred to the SEC for approval;

(v) Upon obtaining SEC's approval to the proposed merger / scheme, the parties or one of them is required to apply to the FHC for judicial sanction of the scheme;

(vi) The sanction of the FHC is thereafter forwarded to the CAC within seven (7) days of the Court Order;

(vii) The FHC Order is also required to be published in two government gazettes and in at least one National Newspaper.

In addition to the foregoing, the ISA and SEC Rules further prescribes penalty for default in obtaining the required approvals[4]. The approval is usually given where the SEC is satisfied that:

(i) The merger or acquisition, whether directly or indirectly of the whole or any part of the equity or other share capital or of the assets of another company, is not likely to cause substantial restraint of competition or tend to create monopoly in any line of business enterprise;

(ii) The use of such shares by voting or granting proxies or otherwise will not cause substantial restraint of competition or tend to create monopoly in any line of business enterprise; and

(iii) Where though it appears like the proposed merger is to restrain competition, one of the parties to the merger has proved that it is failing.

The thresholds prescribed by the SEC for merger are as set below:

(i) Small Merger

The lower threshold for a small merger is below 1 million Naira of either combined assets or turnover of the merging companies.

(ii) Intermediate Merger

The intermediate threshold is between 1 million Naira and 5 million Naira of either combined assets or turnover of the merging companies.

(iii) Large Merger

The upper threshold for a large merger is above 5 million Naira of either combined assets or turnover of the merging companies.

G. Competition Regulation

a. Department Supervising Competition Regulation

Competition regulation in the Nigerian market is primarily within the purview of SEC. The ISA empowers the SEC as the agency to give approval to all forms of business combination (merger, acquisition, or take-over) and to ensure that schemes of merger or any proposed acquisition or take over is not calculated to destroy competition or gain unfair market advantage. Other regulators in competition-prone sectors such as telecoms, banking, and insurance etc. have industry-specific mechanisms for checking anti-competition practices.

b. Brief Introduction of Competition Law

There is no separate Competition / Antitrust Law in Nigeria at the moment and what appears to be the country's first giant step towards enacting a legislation on Competition is found in the Federal Competition and Consumer Protection Bill, 2015 already passed by the Senate of the Federal Republic of Nigeria but awaiting concurrent passage by the Federal House of Representatives. Competition in Nigeria is presently governed by the provisions in the ISA preventing business arrangements which tend to create monopoly, unfair market practices or abuse of a dominant position.

---

[1] SEC Rule 227.
[2] ISA, supra @ section 120.
[3] Section 591, CAMA. See also, section 100, ISA.
[4] Ibid, ISA.

Any form of business combination undertaken to substantially prevent or lessen competition is prohibited and as such, will not be given the statutory approval by the SEC; except where such anti-competition scheme will result in any technological efficiency or other pro-competitive gain which will be greater than, and off-set, the effects of any prevention or lessening of competition that may result or is likely to result from the merger; or that such competition-lessening arrangement is justifiable on substantial public interest grounds.[1]

In determining whether or not a merger is likely to substantially prevent or lessen competition, the SEC has the mandate to assess the strength of competition in the relevant market, and the probability that the company, in the market after the merger, will behave competitively or co-operatively, taking into account any factor that is relevant to competition in that market[2], including:

(i) The actual and potential level of import competition in the market;
(ii) The ease of entry into the market, including tariff and regulatory barriers;
(iii) The level and trends of concentration, and history of collusion, in the market;
(iv) The degree of countervailing power in the market;
(v) The dynamic characteristics of the market, including growth, innovation, and product differentiation;
(vi) The nature and extent of vertical integration in the market;
(vii) Whether the business or part of the business of a party to the merger or proposed merger has failed or is likely to fail; and
(viii) Whether the merger will result in the removal of an effective competitor.

In competition-prone sectors, business arrangements that create unfair market advantage like monopoly or abuse of a dominant position are usually not allowed by the sector-specific regulator[3]. Also, before schemes for business combination (merger, acquisition or take-over) are submitted to the SEC for approval, sector regulators usually scrutinize them for any underlining anti-competition motives and may withhold consent to such schemes, such that they are not eligible for submission to the SEC.

c. Measures Regulating Competition

Some of the measures presently regulating competition in Nigeria are the regulatory regimes for checking anti-competition practices such as price-fixing, bid-rigging, sponsoring false or misleading information about a competitor, creating monopoly, and abusing a dominant market position.

Apart from the mandate of the SEC to prevent business arrangements not favorable to heathy competition in any sector of the economy, internal regulatory framework in form of Circulars, Guidelines and Regulations have been used by industry regulators to prohibit anti-competition practices.

In the Nigerian telecoms industry for instance, NCC as the regulator maintains fair competition. By section 4(d) of the Nigerian Communications Act (NCA)[4], the NCC has responsibility for promoting fair competition in the communications industry and protecting communications services and facilities providers from misuse of market power or anti-competitive and unfair practices by other service or facilities providers or equipment suppliers. Similarly, by section 90 of the NCA, the NCC has the exclusive competence to determine, pronounce upon, administer, monitor and enforce compliance of all persons with competition laws and regulations, whether of a general or specific nature, as it relates to the industry. Specifically with respect to ensuring that competition continues to exist in the industry, section 91(1) of the NCA prohibits a licensee from engaging in any conduct which has the purpose or effect of substantially lessening competition in any aspect of the Nigerian communications market.

Section 91(3) of the NCA, on its part, prohibits licensees from entering into agreements or arrangements which provide for rate fixing, market sharing, or any boycotting of a competitor, supplier or licensee, whilst section 91(4) of the NCA prohibits licensees from requiring any person that acquires communications products or services, to acquire any other product or service, either from the licensee or another person, or directing them not to acquire any other product or service either from the licensee or another person. Lastly, section 92(1) allows the NCC to determine whether a licensee is in a dominant position in any aspect of the Nigerian communications market.

Sections 91(2) and 92(2) of the NCA separately empower the NCC to publish guidelines and regulations which clarify the meaning of "substantial lessening of competition" in the Nigerian communications market and how it shall apply the test of "dominant position" to licensees, respectively. In furtherance of the referenced sections 91(2) and 92(2) of the NCA, the NCC issued the Competition Regulations which, amongst others, outline the standards and procedures which the NCC will apply in determining whether a particular conduct constitutes substantial

---

[1] section 121(1), CAMA.
[2] Ibid, section 121(2), CAMA.
[3] Such as the CBN in the banking industry or the NAICOM in the insurance industry or the National Broadcasting Commission (NBC) in the broadcast industry.
[4] No.19 of 2003.

lessening of competition for the purposes of the NCA, as well as whether a licensee has a dominant position in one or more communications markets.

H. Tax

a. Tax Regimes and Rules

The tax environment in Nigeria is currently shaped by the National Tax Policy 2017 (NTP). The NTP, among other objectives:

(i) Guides the operation and review of the tax system;
(ii) Provides the basis for future tax legislation and administration;
(iii) Serves as a point of reference for all stakeholders on taxation;
(iv) Provides benchmark on which stakeholders shall be held accountable; and
(v) Provides clarity on the roles and responsibilities of Stakeholders in the tax System.

As envisioned by the NTP, all existing and future taxes are expected to conform to the following fundamental features[1]:

(i) Equity and Fairness – The tax system in Nigeria should be fair, equitable and devoid of discrimination and payment should be in accordance to ability of the taxpayers.

(ii) Simplicity, Certainty and Clarity – Tax laws and administrative processes should be simple, clear and easy to understand.

(iii) Convenience – The time and manner for the fulfilment of tax obligations shall take into account the convenience of taxpayers and avoid undue difficulties.

(iv) Low Compliance Cost – The financial and economic cost of compliance to the taxpayer should be kept to the barest minimum.

(v) Low Cost of Administration – Tax Administration in Nigeria should be efficient and cost-effective in line with international best practices.

(vi) Flexibility – Taxation should be flexible and dynamic to respond to changing circumstances in the economy in a manner that does not retard economic activities.

(vii) Sustainability – The tax system should promote sustainable revenue, economic growth and development. There should be a synergy between tax policies and other economic policies of government.

b. Main Categories and Rates of Tax

a) Companies Income Tax

Under the Companies Income Tax Act (CITA), Cap C21, LFN 2004, (as amended by the Companies Income Tax Amendment Act No.11 of 2007), a tax at the rate of thirty percent (30%) is imposed on the income of a company incorporated in Nigeria, after the deduction of all allowable expenses, losses and capital allowances.

Every company assessable to tax under the CITA must prepare and file on a self-assessment basis, with the FIRS, audited accounts and income tax computations within 6 months after the end of the accounting period. However, in the case of new companies, the returns are to be filed within 18 months, from the date of incorporation, or 6 months after its first accounting period, whichever occurs first.

b) Education Tax

Pursuant to the Education Tax Act Cap E4 LFN 2004, every company incorporated in Nigeria is obliged to pay 2% of its assessable profit as Education Tax.

c) Industrial Training Fund (ITF)

The Industrial Training Fund Act CAP I9, LFN 2004 (the "IDTF Act") (as amended by the Industrial Training Fund Amendment Act, 2011) establishes the Industrial Training Fund (the "Fund"). The purpose of the Fund is to promote the acquisition of relevant skills in industry or commerce with a view to generating a pool of indigenous manpower to satisfy the needs of the economy. Every employer that is liable under the ITF Act must contribute one (1) percent of the amount of its annual payroll to the Fund. Employers that are liable to make contributions under the Fund are:

(i) Employers having five (5) or more employees in their establishment;
(ii) Employers who have less than five (5) employees but having a turnover of fifty N50 million and above per annum;
(iii) Suppliers, Contractors or Consultants who bid for contracts from any federal government agency or parastatals or private companies; and
(iv) Companies operating in the free trade zone which seeks for approval for Expatriate Quota or makes use

---

[1] "Guiding Principles of Nigeria Tax System", Approval of the Revised National Tax Policy by the Federal Executive Council, Federal Ministry of Finance, 1st February, 2017 – http://www.finance.gov.ng/.

of any custom services.

In the determination of the contributions to be made to the Fund, all employees including those who work part time and temporary employees are included in the assessment. Further, all the allowances and entitlements paid to such employees within or outside Nigeria are calculated when considering the total payroll of an employer.

The IDTF Act further imposes a duty on employers to provide training for their indigenous staff with a view to improving their job related skills. Furthermore, the IDTF Act provides that the Fund's Council may make a refund of up to 50% of the amount paid by an employer where it is satisfied that its training program is adequate.

Failure to make contributions within the stipulated period in a calendar year attracts a penalty of five per cent (5%) of the amount unpaid for each month or part of a month after the date on which payments should have been made.

d) Information Technology Tax

Pursuant to the National Information Technology Development Agency Act No.31 of 2007 a tax of 1% of profits before tax is chargeable on the income of the underlisted companies with a turnover of N100 million and above:

(i) GSM service providers and all telecommunications companies;
(ii) Cyber companies and internet providers;
(iii) Pension managers and pension related companies;
(iv) Banks and other financial institutions; and
(v) Insurance companies.

e) Personal Income Tax

The income of employees is subject to tax levied at progressive rates as detailed in the table below. The Personal Income Tax Act (PITA) Cap P8, LFN 2004 establishes a Pay-As-You-Earn (PAYE) system whereby employers are required to act as agents of the tax authorities for the purpose of collecting and remitting taxes on salaries due to their employees. PAYE taxes are required to be remitted within fourteen (14) days after the month of deduction. At the end of every year, the employer is required to submit all the tax deduction cards and employer's remittance card (Form G).

First ₦ 300,000	7%
Next ₦ 300,000	11%
Next ₦ 500,000	15%
Next ₦ 500,000	19%
Next ₦ 1,600,000	21%
Above ₦ 3,200,000	24%

The summary of the tax deducted from each employee would be shown on the employer's annual Declaration Form (Form H1) and submitted to the tax authority. This should be done on or before January 30 of the following year.

f) Withholding Tax

The Nigerian tax laws (CITA and PITA) provide that where any payment on which withholding tax should be deducted is due from one person to another, the person making the payment is expected to deduct tax at the applicable rate and remit the tax deducted to the relevant tax authority within a reasonable period, not later than 30 days after deduction. Some of the activities and services on which withholding taxes are deductible and the current applicable rates are as follows:

Transactions	Companies	Individuals
Dividend, interest & rent	10%	10%
Royalties	10%	5%
Hire of equipment, motor vehicles, plants, and machinery	10%	10%
Commission, consultancy, technical and management fees, legal fees, audit fees, and other professional fees	10%	5%
Construction	5%	5%
All types of contracts and agency arrangements, other than sales in the ordinary course of business	5%	5%
Directors' fees	N/A	10%

The rate of withholding tax on dividend, interest and royalty is reduced to 7.5% when paid to a recipient resident in a country with which Nigeria has a double taxation treaty.

g) Capital Gains Tax

Capital gains tax is levied on capital gains accruing to a taxable person upon disposal of assets, irrespective of whether the asset is situated in Nigeria or not. The tax is applicable to all companies, including pioneer companies and all individuals and non-corporate bodies. The rate of tax is currently 10%.

h) Transfer Pricing

Generally, there are no restrictions applicable to conducting business via the use of affiliated companies outside Nigeria. However such transactions may be regarded as transfer pricing and thus caught by the Income Tax (Transfer Pricing) Regulations 2012 (Transfer Pricing Regulations). Transfer pricing occurs whenever two companies which are part of the same multinational group trade with each other, usually through the instrumentality of a Service-Level Agreements (SLA).

Regulation 3 of the Transfer Pricing Regulations provides that the Transfer Pricing Regulations shall apply to transactions between connected taxable persons carried on in a manner not consistent with the arm's length principle and includes; (i) sale and purchase of goods and services; (ii) sales, purchase or lease of tangible assets; (iii) transfer, purchase or use of intangible assets; (iv). provision of services; (v) lending or borrowing of money; (vi) manufacturing arrangement; and (vii) any transaction which may affect profit and loss or any other matter incidental to, connected with, or pertaining to the transactions referred to in (i) to (vi) above.

The Transfer Pricing Regulations is intended to guard against transactions not contracted on arm's length basis with "connected taxable persons". These are persons one of whom either has control over the other or related with each other or both of whom are controlled by some other person, engaging in transactions which in the opinion of the tax authorities have not been made on terms which might fairly have been expected to have been made by persons engaged in the same or similar activities dealing with one another at arm's length.

Basically, the goal of the FIRS is to ensure that the transactions between the affiliated companies are conducted in line with the arm's length principle. In determining whether the result of a transaction or series of transactions is consistent with the arm's length principle, the FIRS will apply one of the following transfer pricing methods— (i) the Comparable Uncontrolled Price Method (ii) the Resale Price Method; (iii) the Cost Plus Method; (iv) the Transactional Net Margin Method; or (v) the Transactional Profit Split Method. The determination of whether there has been a breach of the arm's length principle or what transfer pricing method to apply is determined on a case by case basis.

c. Tax Declaration and Preference

Tax declaration is made by taxpayers in a prescribed form and submitted to the FIRS for assessment and payment on a periodic basis, usually annually. The CITA provides for the taxation of profits of companies (other than oil companies) in Nigeria. For this reason, all companies assessable to tax under CITA must register with the FIRS and obtain a Tax Identification Number (TIN). The TIN must be reflected on all returns filed or correspondence exchanged with the FIRS. This registration is undertaken immediately after the incorporation process.

For the purpose of PAYE, every employer is required to register with the zonal office of the tax authority in the State where its place of business is located. This registration is undertaken immediately after the incorporation process.

Value Added Tax (VAT) is imposed under the Value Added Tax Act Cap V1, LFN 2004 (as amended by the Value Added Tax Amendment Act No.12 of 2007) (VATA). Under the VATA, all manufacturers are required to register with the FIRS within six (6) months of commencement of business.

I. Securities

a. Brief Introduction of Securities-Related Laws and Regulations

Investment in securities is regulated in Nigeria by the ISA and the various SEC Rules on investment[1]. The SEC Consolidated Rules 2013[2] make provisions regulating all forms of investment in Nigeria, including Foreign Investments and Cross-border Securities Transactions[3] and define foreign investments as any investment in

---

[1] Rules made pursuant to section 313 of the ISA.
[2] SEC Consolidated Rules contains a total number of 602 Rules on different modes of capital market investments together with Codes of Conducts applicable to persons and transactions in the market – http://sec.gov.ng/sec-nigerias-consolidated-rules-and-regulations-as-at-2013/.
[3] Ibid, Part H.

securities involving foreign capital importation made by a foreign person (corporate body or individual) or by any Nigerian resident outside the country. According to the Consolidated Rules, foreign investors shall include foreign institutional investors such as pension funds, unit trust funds, investment trust funds, institutional portfolio managers, nominee companies, asset management companies, or any other corporate body as well as individual investors who are foreigners and Nigerians resident abroad who are investing with foreign currency. In the same manner, the Consolidated Rules bring all transactions in securities traded on the primary and secondary market (equities, Government stocks, industrial loan stocks, bonds, unit trusts, investment trusts, derivatives or any other securities registered by the SEC) under the class of investments within its regulatory purview.[1]

Other securities-related laws in Nigeria include the following together with rules and regulations made pursuant to them:

• Investments and Securities Act (ISA), 2007;
• Companies and Allied Matters Act, 1990 (Cap C20, Laws of the Federation of Nigeria 2004);
• Central Bank of Nigeria (Establishment) Act, 2007;
• Banks and other Financial Institutions Act (BOFIA), No.25 of 1991 (Cap B3, Laws of the Federation of Nigeria 2004);
• Nigerian Investment Promotion Commission (NIPC) Act, No.16 of 1995 (Cap N117, Laws of the Federation of Nigeria 2004); and
• Foreign Exchange (Monitoring and Miscellaneous Provisions) Act, No.17 of 1995 (Cap F34, Laws of the Federation of Nigeria 2004).

b. Supervision and Regulation of Securities Market

The laws mentioned above collectively provide the framework for supervising and regulating the securities market in Nigeria. The ISA established the SEC as the apex regulatory authority for the Nigerian capital market and therefore supervises all dealings in securities. The SEC carries out its supervisory roles in conjunction with the other regulators within the financial system as prescribed by relevant legislation. For instance, the SEC, CBN, and NIPC work in collaboration to regulate capital importation into Nigeria and ensure that foreign investors obtain Certificate of Capital Importation (CCI) for capital transferred into Nigeria for investment purposes, in order to be able to safely invest same in securities, money market instruments or any enterprises in Nigeria; benefit from incentives; enjoy investment protection and seamlessly repatriate their capital with proceeds at the time of exiting the country.[2]

c. Requirements for Engagement in Securities Trading for Foreign Enterprises

Foreign enterprises desirous of investing in securities trading in Nigeria shall comply with all legislation guiding the foreign exchange market, foreign capital importation, incorporation of business, tax payment, as well as registration with all relevant regulators. They are also required to make their investment through capital market operators registered by the SEC[3]. Essentially, registration will be required with the: CBN (through the authorized dealer to process CCI for the investor); Nigerian Immigration Service (for processing of Resident and Business Permits); and the NIPC.

J. Preference and Protection of Investment

a. The Structure of Preference Policies

Preference is given to enterprises or industries which the NIPC has designated as the "Priority areas" of investment in Nigeria. Applicable incentives and benefits, which are in conformity with Government policy, are prescribed for these industries in Guidelines issued by the NIPC. Some of the various investment incentives provided under the relevant laws and regulations include tax holidays; tax credits; capital allowances; investment allowances; tax exemptions; duty drawback; subsidies; export expansion grants; export development funds; double taxation reliefs; and investment promotion and protection agreements, among others. The following have been given preference in Nigeria according to NIPC declaration[4]:

• Infant Industry—Industries in their infant stages are granted Pioneer Status in Nigeria. This is a tax holiday granted to an industry aimed at enabling the industry concerned to make a reasonable level of profit within its formative years. The profit so made is expected to be ploughed back into the business to engender growth.

---

[1] Ibid, section 405.
[2] Sections 15 and 26, Foreign Exchange (Monitoring and Miscellaneous Provisions) Act, supra; Rule 408, SEC Consolidated Rules 2013, supra; and sections 21 and 24, NIPC Act, supra.
[3] Rule 406(2), SEC Consolidated Rules 2013, ibid.
[4] NIPC – http://www.nipc.gov.ng/investment.html.

Pioneer Status is granted for a period of up to five years (that is, an initial three (3) year period beginning from the date of first production, which may be extended for a further period of two (2) years for companies carrying on business in the priority sectors of the Nigerian economy). To qualify for the grant of Pioneer Status, a joint venture company or a wholly foreign-owned company must have a minimum share capital of Ten Million Naira (N10 million) and incure a capital expenditure of not less than Five Million Naira (N5 million) whilst that of qualified indigenous company should not be less than One Hundred and Fifty Thousand Naira (N150, 000.00). An applicant company is required to pay to the NIPC a service charge of two per cent (2%) of the applicant company's estimated savings. In addition, an application in respect of Pioneer Status must be submitted within one year of the commencement of commercial production by the applicant company, otherwise the application will be time-barred[1]. The legal framework for Pioneer Status comprises the Industrial Development (Income Tax Relief) Act[2] (the IDITR Act) and the Pioneer Status Incentive Regulations 2014 (the IDITR Regulations). Pursuant to the IDITR Act, the Federal Executive Council may declare an industry to be a pioneer industry and any product of the industry to be a pioneer product, if it is satisfied that: (i) the industry is not being carried on in Nigeria; (ii) the industry is not being carried on in Nigeria on a scale suitable to the economy; (iii) there are favourable prospects of further development of the industry in Nigeria; and (iv) it is expedient in the public interest to encourage the development or establishment of the industry in Nigeria by declaring it to be a pioneer industry.

• Exemption from taxes is also granted to companies' profits in respect of goods exported from Nigeria, provided the proceeds are repatriated to Nigeria and used exclusively for purchase of raw materials, plants equipment and spare parts.

• Exclusion from taxes is granted to the profits of companies whose supplies are exclusively from input to the manufacturing of products for exports.

• All new industrial undertakings including foreign companies and individual operating in an Export Processing Zone (EPZ) are allowed full tax holidays for three consecutive years.

• As a means of encouraging industrial technology, companies and other organizations that engage in research and development activities for commercialization enjoy 20% investment tax credit on their qualifying expenditure.

• Dividends distributed by unit in Nigeria are free of tax and no withholding tax is deducted therefrom since such incomes have already suffered tax in the first instance.

• All companies engaged wholly in fabrication of tools, spare parts and simple machinery for local consumption and export are to enjoy 25% investment tax credit on their qualifying capital expenditure while any tax payer who purchases locally manufactured plants and machinery are similarly entitled to 15% investment tax credit on such fixed assets bought for use.

• In-plant Training—This is applicable to industrial establishments that have set up in-plant training facilities. Such industries enjoy a two percent tax concession for a period of five years.

• Investment in Infrastructure—This is a form of incentive granted to industries that provide facilities that ordinarily should have been provided by the government. Such facilities include access roads, pipe borne water and electricity. Twenty percent (20%) of the cost of providing these infrastructural facilities, where they do not exist, is tax deductible.

• Labour Intensive Mode of Production—Industries with high labour / capital ratio are entitled to tax concessions in Nigeria. These are industries with plants, equipment and machinery, which essentially are operated with minimal automation. Where there is automation, such automation should not be more than one process in the course of production. The rate is graduated in such a way that an industry employing 1,000 persons or more will enjoy 15 percent tax concession, while an industry employing 200 will enjoy 7 percent and those employing 100 will enjoy 6 percent and so on.

• Local Value Added—This is a 10% tax concession for five (5) years applicable essentially to engineering industries in Nigeria whose production inputs are some finished imported products. The concession is aimed at encouraging local fabrication rather than the mere assembly of completely knocked down parts.

• Re-investment Allowance—This incentive is granted in Nigeria to companies engaged in manufacturing which incur qualifying capital expenditure for the purposes of approved expansion etc. The incentive is in the form of a generalized allowance of capital expenditure incurred by companies for the following: expansion of production capacity; modernization of production facilities; and diversification into related products.

• Minimum Local Raw Materials Utilization—This is a tax credit of 20% granted for five years to industries in Nigeria that attain the minimum level of local raw material sourcing and utilization. The minimum levels of local raw

---

[1] NIPC – http://www.nipc.gov.ng/investment.html.
[2] Cap.I7, Laws of the Federation of Nigeria, 2004.

materials sourcing and utilization by sectors are: Agro-allied – 70%; Engineering – 60%; Chemicals – 60%; and Petrochemicals – 70%.

b. Support for Specific Industries

There are certain industry-specific incentives provided in Nigeria, particularly to those operating within designated priority areas of investment. The following are some of the industry-related support[①] given to investors:

a) Agriculture

Investors in the agricultural and agro-allied industries enjoy the following incentives:

(i) Full and unrestricted (100%) capital allowance for companies in the agro-allied business;

(ii) The payments of minimum tax by companies that make small or no profits at all do not apply to agro-allied business;

(iii) Agro-allied plant and equipment enjoy enhanced capital allowances of up to 50%;

(iv) Processing of agricultural produce is an industry granted pioneer status hence granted 100% tax-free period of 5 years;

(v) All agricultural projects involved in processing of agricultural produce, as well as machinery and equipment used in the processing of agricultural and agro-allied products enjoy 1% duty;

(vi) The Agricultural Credit Guarantee Scheme Fund (ACGSF), administered by the CBN, provides guarantee to all loans granted by commercial banks for agricultural production and processing, up to 75% of any amount in default;

(vii) Companies and investors who borrow from banks under the ACGS for the purpose of cassava production and processing, and who repay their loans on schedule, benefit from Interest Drawback Program Fund which entitles them to 60% repayment of interest paid on their loan.

b) Solid Minerals

The following incentives are available in the solid minerals sector:

(i) 3 to 5 years tax holiday;

(ii) Low income tax of between 20% and 30%;

(iii) Deferred royalty payments depending on the magnitude of the investment and the strategic nature of the project;

(iv) Possible capitalization of expenditure on exploration and surveys;

(v) Extension of infrastructure such as roads and electricity to mining sites;

(vi) The holder of a mining lease shall, where qualified, be entitled to the following:

• Depreciation or capital allowance of 75% of the certified true capital expenditure incurred in the year of investment and 50% in subsequent years;

• Investment allowance of 5%;

• Exemption from payment of customs & import duties;

• Expatriate quota & resident permit for approved expatriate personnel;

• In addition to roll-over relief under the capital gains tax (CGT), companies replacing their plants and machinery are to enjoy a once-and-for-all 95% capital allowance in the first year with 5% retention value until the assets is disposed while 15% will be granted for replacement of an asset.

c) Petroleum

The incentives in this sector are granted to companies that are into joint ventures with the Nigerian National Petroleum Corporation (NNPC) and have signed Memorandum of Understanding (MoU). The incentives are:

• Accelerated capital allowance (Tax Depreciation) which enables capital allowance to be carried forward indefinitely. This is granted on qualifying capital expenditure (QCE) at a flat rate of 20% annually (19% in the fifth year and the balance is retained in the books until the QCE is disposed);

• Dividends paid out of income derived from petroleum operations are exempted from withholding tax;[②]

• Graduated Royalty Rate of 10% approved for oil companies in Deep Offshore operations (ranging from 0% to 12% depending on the water depth of operation).

d) Gas

In view of the enormous potentials in this sector, Government has approved the following fiscal incentives:

(i) Gas Production Phase

• Applicable tax rate is the same as the company income tax (CIT);

• Capital allowance at the rate of 20% per annum in the first four years, 19% in the fifth year and the remaining 1% in the books

---

① Cap.17, Laws of the Federation of Nigeria, 2004.
② Section 60, Petroleum Profits Tax (Amendment) Act of 2007 (PPTA).

• Investment Tax Credit (ITC) at the current rate of 5%;
• Royalty at the rate of 7% onshore and 5% offshore
(ii) Gas Transmission and Distribution
• Capital allowance as in production phase above;
• Tax rate as in production phase;
• Tax holiday under Pioneer Status[①]
(iii) LNG Projects
• Applicable tax rate under Petroleum Profit Tax (PPT) is 45%;
• Capital allowance is 33% per year on-straight line basis in the first three years with 1% remaining in the books;
• Investment Tax Credit of 10% Royalty, 7% on-shore, and 5% off-shore tax deductible.
(iv) Gas Exploitation (Upstream Operation)
Fiscal arrangements are reviewed as follows:
• All investments necessary to separate oil from gas from reserves into suitable product is considered part of the oil field development;
• Capital investment facilities to deliver associated gas in usable form at utilization or transfer points will be treated for fiscal purposes as part of the capital investment for oil development;
• Capital allowances, operating expenses and basis for assessment will be subjected to the provisions of the Petroleum Profit Tax Act and the revised MoU.
(v) Gas Utilisation (Downstream Operation)
• Companies engaged in gas utilization are to be subjected to the provisions of the Companies Income Tax Act (CITA);
• An initial tax free period of three (3) years renewable for two (2) additional years;
• Accelerated capital allowances after the tax-free period in the form of annual allowance of 90% (with 10% retention) for investment in plant and machinery, and
• An additional investment allowance of 15%, which shall not reduce the value of the asset.
(vi) Additional incentives approved by the Government to support the gas industry are in the following areas
• All gas developmental projects, including those engaged in power generation, liquid plants, fertilizer plants, gas distribution / transmission pipelines are taxed under the provisions of Companies Income Tax (CITA) and not the Petroleum Profit Tax;
• All fiscal incentives under the gas utilization downstream operations since 1997 are to be extended to industrial projects that use gas i.e.power plants, gas to liquids plants, fertilizer plants, gas distribution / transmission plants;
• The initial tax holiday is to be extended from three years to five years;
• Gas is transferred at 0% PPT 0% Royalty;
• Investment capital allowance is increased from 5% to 15%;
• Interest payment on loans for gas project is tax deductible, provided that prior approval of the Federal Minister of Finance was obtained before taking the loan; and
• All dividends distributed during the tax holiday are exempted from tax.
e) Telecommunications
Government provides non-fiscal incentives to private investors in addition to a tariff structure that ensures that investors recover their investment over a reasonable period of time, bearing in mind the need for differential tariffs between urban and rural areas. The tariff structure as approved by the regulatory authority, the Nigerian Communication Commission, also provides adequate cross-subsidy between the profitable trunk and local calls of the urban and non-profitable operation of the rural areas. Other incentives in place are:
• Manufacture / installation of telecommunications related equipment is granted pioneer status and a result, enjoy 3 to 5 years tax holiday;
• Taxes and duties do not exceed those charged on essential electrical goods.
f) Energy (Electricity)
Among the incentives put in place by the Government to encourage investors in the power sector:
• Tax holiday of 3 – 5 years is granted to companies that manufacture transformers, meters, control panels, switch gears, cable and other electrical related equipment, which products / industries are granted pioneer status;
• Power plants using gas are assessed under the CIT at a reduced rate.

[①] Gas manufacture and distribution are identified as pioneer industries by the Federal Republic of Nigeria's Official Gazette No.63, Vol.102, issued on May 27, 2015.

g) Tourism

The following incentives have been put in place to encourage domestic and foreign investors' participation in the tourism industry in Nigeria:

• The tourism sector was accorded preferred sector status in 1999. This makes the sector qualify for incentives (available to similar sectors of the economy) such as tax holiday, longer years of moratorium and import duty exemption on tourism related equipment;

• Provision of basic infrastructure like road, water, electricity, communications etc., to centre of attraction some states have specific areas as tourism development zones thereby making acquisition of land easier;

• Provision of land for tourism development at concessional rates;

• Availability of soft loans with long period of moratorium.

h) Transport

The following incentives are in place to encourage investment in the sector:

• Ship building, repairs and maintenance of vessels, boat, barges, diving and underwater engineering services, aircraft maintenance and manufacturing are industries granted pioneer status and therefore enjoy 3 -5 years tax holiday depending on location.

i) Investment in Economically Disadvantaged Areas

• Without prejudice to the provision of the pioneer status enabling law, a pioneer industry sited in economically disadvantaged Local Government Area in Nigeria is entitled to 100% tax holiday for seven (7) years and an additional 5% capital depreciation allowance over and above the initial capital depreciation allowance.[1]

c. Special Economic Areas

For the purpose of encouraging rapid industrial and local content development, attracting foreign direct investment and promoting public-private-partnership for economic development (especially in export-orientated industries), the Nigerian government has designated certain areas as free zones or export processing zones where enterprises enjoy exemption from taxes on their profits and other fiscal incentives and benefit from economies of scale and concentration of infrastructure.

a) Nigeria Export Processing Zones

Section 2 of the Nigeria Export Processing Zones Act (NEPZ Act), 1992[2] establishes the Nigeria Export Processing Authority (the "NEPZA") as the agency charged, under Section 4 of the NEPZ Act, with general administration, supervision and coordination of the activities within Export Processing Zones (EPZ) in Nigeria. The President is empowered (under Section 1 of NEPZ Act), on the recommendation of the NEPZA, to designate any area in Nigeria as an EPZ.

b) Oil and Gas Free Zone

There is also the Oil and Gas Free Zone Onne, Rivers State (OGFZ) administered by the Oil and Gas Free Zone Authority (the "OGFZA"), which was created by the Oil and Gas Export Free Zone Act (OGFZ Act), 1996[3]. OGFZ Act provides for incentives to oil & gas companies operating within the OGFZ, as well as companies providing services and supplying equipment to such oil & gas companies within the OGFZ. The regulatory and operational guidelines applicable within the OGFZ are similar to those applicable in other (general) EPZs, save that while the former is created specifically for oil and gas businesses, the latter cater for the development of multiple industries.

c) Incentives Available to Investors in the Zones

Registration of enterprises within the zones is generally easier and faster while residence and work permits for expatriates are seamlessly processed and obtained. Also, procedures for customs clearing of cargoes in the OGFZ are without the usual bureaucratic hassles experienced by shippers and operators at the regular ports.[4]

Some of the other incentives enjoyed within the OGFZ include exemption of "Form M" prior to shipment; possibility of breaking bulk goods into smaller units to be repackaged, sold and even exhibited; exemption from payment of customs duty on goods exported from, and consumed within the OGFZ; exemption from import and export licences for investors; exemption from Personal Income Tax payment; 100% repatriation of capital and profit; and no pre-shipment inspection for goods imported into the free zone.[5]

Notably also, foreign exchange regulations are relaxed within the zones In this connection, the CBN in a 2016

---

[1] Ibid.
[2] Cap N107, Laws of the Federation of Nigeria 2004.
[3] Cap O5, Laws of the Federation of Nigeria 2004.
[4] Banwo and Ighodalo: "Doing Business in Nigeria: Some of the Incentives Available to Investors", Grey Matter, December 2015 – http://www.banwo-ighodalo.com/grey-matter/doing-business-in-nigeria-some-of-the-incentives-available-to-investors?leaf=3.
[5] Ibid.

regulation[1] makes provisions for seamless foreign exchange transactions in all free trade / export processing zones in Nigeria.

Specifically, the Government has made following incentives available to investors in the zones:
• Complete tax holiday for all Federal, State and Local Government taxes, rates, custom duties and levies;
• One-stop approval for all permits, operating licenses and incorporation papers;
• Duty-free, tax-free import of raw materials for goods destined for re-export;
• Duty-free introduction of capital goods, consumer goods, components, machinery, equipment and furniture;
• Permission to sell 100% ;of manufactured, assembled or imported goods into the domestic Nigerian Market;
• When selling into the domestic market, the amount of import duty on goods manufactured in the free zones is calculated on the basis of the value of the raw materials or components used in assembly not the finished product;
• 100% foreign ownership of investments;
• 100% repatriation of capital, profits and dividends;
• Waiver of all import and export licenses;
• Waiver on all expatriate quotas for companies operating in the zones;
• Prohibition of strikes and lockouts; and
• Rent-free land during the first 6 months of construction.

d. Investment Protection

a) Bilateral Investment Promotion and Protection Agreement (IPPA)

As part of additional effort to foster foreign investors' confidence in the Nigeria economy, the FGN has entered into bilateral investment promotion and protection agreements (IPPAs) with some of the countries that do business with Nigeria[2]. The IPPA helps to guarantee the safety of the investments of the contracting parties in the event of war, revolution, expropriation or nationalization. It also guarantees investors the transfer of interests, dividends, profits and other incomes as well as compensation for dispossession or loss. To this end, Nigeria has concluded and signed IPPAs with: France, United Kingdom, Netherlands, Romania, Switzerland, Spain, South Africa, and others. With negotiations on IPPAs ongoing and at various stages of completion with the United States of America, Belgium, Sweden, Russian Federation, and others.

b) Liberalisation of Ownership Structure

The government in repealing the Nigerian Enterprises Promotion Act of 1972 (as amended), and promulgating the Nigerian Investment Promotion Commission Act of 1995 has liberalized the ownerships structure of business in Nigeria. The implication of this is that foreigners can now own 100% shares in any company as opposed to the earlier arrangement of 60%-40% in favour of Nigerians.

c) Repatriation of Profit

Under the provisions of the Foreign Exchange (Monitoring & Miscellaneous) Provision Act[3] and the NIPC Act[4], foreign investors are free to repatriate their profits and dividends net of taxes through an authorized dealer in freely convertible currency.

d) Guarantee Against Expropriation

The NIPC Act guarantees that no enterprise shall be nationalized or expropriated by any government in Nigeria and neither shall any person who owns (whether wholly or in part) the capital of any enterprise be compelled by law to surrender his interest in the capital to any other person.[5] In Nigeria and in most jurisdictions, prohibitions with respect to expropriation are generally subject to qualifications in relation to non-discriminatory measures in respect of which adequate compensation is paid to the national / investor. This prohibition is however subject to the qualifications[6] that any expropriation measures must:

(i) be in the public interest and under due process of law;

(ii) not be discriminatory or contrary to any express undertaking of the FGN;

(iii) be accompanied by provision for the payment of just compensation representing the genuine value of the affected investment; and

(iv) not restrict affected investors' access to the court for the purpose of determining the appropriate amount of compensation to which they may be entitled.

---

[1] CBN: "Guidelines for Banking Operations in the Free Zones in Nigeria, February 2016" – https://www.cbn.gov.ng/Out/2016/BPSD/GUIDELINES%20FOR%20BANKING%20OPERATIONS%20IN%20THE%20FREE%20ZONES.pdf.
[2] NIPC – http://www.nipc.gov.ng/investment.html.
[3] Section 15(4).
[4] See also sections 24 and 25, NIPC Act, supra.
[5] Ibid, section 25(1).
[6] Ibid, section 25(2).

III. Trade

A. Department Supervising Trade

The Federal Ministry of Industry, Trade and Investment (the "Ministry"), in conjunction with the Federal Ministry of Finance and the Central Bank of Nigeria, is primarily responsible for formulating and implementing trade policies in Nigeria. In carrying out its duties, the Ministry consults with other governmental agencies including the Nigerian Export Promotion Council, Nigeria Investment Promotion Commission, Nigeria Customs Service (NCS), Bureau of Public Enterprises, and organisations in the private sector such as the National Association of Chambers of Commerce, Industry Mines and Agriculture, Organised Private Sector and Nigeria Employers' Consultative Association.

B. Brief Introduction of Trade Laws and Regulations

The primary laws that regulate trade in Nigeria are:

(i) Companies and Allied Matters Act[1], which sets out the framework for corporate and unincorporated businesses and charities operating in Nigeria;

(ii) Customs and Excise Management Act (CEMA)[2], which regulates the management and collection of duties of customs and excise;

(iii) Foreign Exchange (Monitoring and Miscellaneous Provisions) Act[3], which establishes an autonomous foreign exchange market and provides for the monitoring and supervision of the transactions conducted in the Nigerian foreign exchange market;

(iv) Nigerian Investment Promotion Commission Act[4], which established the Nigerian Investment Promotion Commission to encourage and promote investment in the Nigerian economy;

(v) Nigerian Export Promotion Council Act[5], which established the Nigerian Export Promotion Council, the agency responsible for the regulation, promotion, recording and monitoring of export trade in Nigeria and the implementation of Nigeria's export policies and strategies;

(vi) Nigeria Export-Import Bank Act[6], which established the Nigerian Export-Import Bank, that is primarily responsible for the provision of export credit guarantee and export credit insurance facilities;

(vii) Nigeria Export Processing Zones Act[7], established the Nigeria Export Processing Zones Authority (NEPZA), the agency responsible for the establishment, licensing, regulation and operation of free zones and the supervision and co-ordination of the functions of various public sector and private sector organisations operating within free zones in Nigeria;

(viii) Standards Organisation of Nigeria Act[8], which established the Standard Organisation of Nigeria, Nigeria's major standardisation organisation;

(ix) Coastal and Inland Shipping (Cabotage) Act[9], which regulates the use of foreign owned or manned vessels for coastal trade in Nigeria;

(x) Export (Incentives and Miscellaneous Provisions) Act[10], which provides for various incentives to exporters of locally manufactured goods;

(xi) Nigerian Ports Authority Act[11], which established the Nigerian Ports Authority which governs and operates the ports of Nigeria;

(xii) Nigerian Maritime Administration and Safety Agency Act[12], which provides for the promotion of maritime safety and security, protection in the maritime environment, shipping registration and commercial shipping,

---

[1] The Companies and Allied Matters Act, Chapter C20, Laws of the Federal Republic of Nigeria, 2004.
[2] Customs & Excise Management Act 2004 Chapter C44 Laws of the Federal Republic of Nigeria, 2004.
[3] Foreign Exchange [Monitoring and [Miscellaneous Provisions] Act Chapter F35 Laws of the Federal Republic of Nigeria, 2004.
[4] Nigerian Investment Promotion Commission Act Chapter N117 Laws of the Federal Republic of Nigeria 2004.
[5] Nigerian Export Promotion Council Act, Chapter 306, C44 Laws of the Federal Republic of Nigeria, 1990 as amended by Act No.64 of 1992.
[6] Nigeria Export-Import Bank Act No.38, 1991.
[7] Nigeria Export Processing Zones Act, Chapter N107, Laws of the Federal Republic of Nigeria 2004.
[8] Standards Organisation of Nigeria Act, 2015 ACT No 14, which repealed the Standards Organisation of Nigeria Act, Chapter S9 Laws of the Federal Republic of Nigeria, 2004.
[9] Coastal and Inland Shipping (Cabotage) Act, No.5, 2003.
[10] Export (Incentives and Miscellaneous Provisions) Act, Chapter E19, Laws of the Federal Republic of Nigeria, 2004.
[11] Nigerian Ports Authority Act, Chapter N126, Laws of the Federal Republic of Nigeria, 2004.
[12] Nigerian Maritime Administration and Safety Agency Act.

maritime labour and the establishment of the Nigerian Maritime Administration and Safety Agency; and

(xiii) National Agency For Food and Drug Administration and Control Act[1], which established the National Agency For Food and Drug Administration and Control ("NAFDAC"), the agency that regulates and controls the manufacture, importation, exportation, distribution, advertisement, sale and use of food, drugs, cosmetics, chemicals, detergents, medical devices and packaged water in Nigeria.

C. Trade Management

See section A above.

D. The Inspection and Quarantine of Import and Export Commodities

The inspection and quarantine of imports and exports is carried out by the Nigerian Customs Service, the Ministry of Agriculture and the National Agency for Food and Drug Administration and Control.

a. Nigerian Customs Service

Under the Nigerian Custom Service's ("NCS") guidelines on importation of goods, all imports into the country must be accompanied by certain documents including the combined certificate of value and origin (CCVO), the final / commercial invoice, the packing list, bill of lading, manufacturers certificate of production and where applicable, laboratory test certificates. Goods that do not comply with the guidelines laid out by the NCS are liable to seizure upon arrival. Goods listed in the import and export prohibition list cannot be imported into, or exported from Nigeria. Some prohibited imports are frozen poultry, cocoa butter, powder and cakes, spaghetti / noodles, fruit juice in retail packs, water, hand beer and stout, bagged cement and mosquito repellents. Prohibited exports include timber, raw hides and skins, scrap metal, unprocessed rubber latex and rubber lumps, artefacts and antiquities, wildlife animals classified as endangered species and their products.

b. Nigeria Agricultural Quarantine Service

The Nigeria Agriculture Quarantine Service ("NAQS") is responsible for protecting the agricultural economy of Nigeria and for the issuance of import permits and sanitary and phytosanitary certificates for the importation of plants, animals and aquatic resources.

Plants and plant products are subject to inspection upon and must be accompanied by an import permit and where applicable, the phytosanitary certificate of country of export. If the inspection is satisfactory, a phytosanitary inspected and released certificate is issued. If, however, the report of the investigation is unsatisfactory, the imported plant / plant products will be subjected to:

(i) laboratory tests;
(ii) appropriate treatment for disinfection / disinfestation;
(iii) re-exportation;
(iv) confiscation; or
(v) destruction by a means to be specified at the importer's expense.

Any person that wishes to export or re-export of plants or plant products from or through Nigeria must obtain a phytosanitary certificate.

Animals or animal products that are sought to be imported into Nigeria must be inspected upon arrival at the Nigerian ports. Live animals are sent to the quarantine stations for observation and suspected animal products are tested.

Persons that wish to export animals or animal products require an export permit.

c. The National Agency For Food & Drug Administration & Control (NAFDAC)

Any person that proposes to import food, drugs, cosmetics, medical devices, bottled water and chemicals (Regulated Products) into Nigeria, is required to register such products with NAFDAC. Registration of a product with the NAFDAC is evidenced by the issuance of a product registration certificate.

E. Customs Management

The NCS is primarily responsible for customs management in Nigeria which includes the collection of customs and excise revenue (import / excise duties and other taxes / levies). The import duty ranges from 0% to 35% of the value of the goods while import levy ranges from 0% to 70% of the value of the goods. Value added tax is payable on imported goods at the rate of 5%.

---

[1] National Agency For Food and Drug Administration and Control Act, Chapter N1, Laws of the Federal Republic of Nigeria 2004.

IV. Labour

A. Brief Introduction of Labour Laws and Regulations

The principal law that regulates the employment of persons in Nigeria is the Labour Act, Chapter L1, Laws of the Federation of Nigeria 2004 (the "Labour Act"), as well as the principles of Nigerian case law based on judicial precedent. This statute and the body of laws operate against the backdrop of the Constitution of the Federal Republic of Nigeria 1999 as amended (the "Constitution") and any provisions that are inconsistent with the provisions of the Constitution are void. The Labour Act is, however, limited in its scope of application and only applies to "Workers" who are defined in the Act, as employees who perform manual labour or clerical work. The relationship between an employer and an employee who is not a "Worker" (such as employees who exercise administrative, executive, technical or professional functions) is, therefore, primarily regulated by the relevant contract of employment and the principles of Nigerian case law. Based on the foregoing, it could be said from a legal perspective, that there are two broad categories of employees in Nigeria, namely "Workers" (as defined in the Labour Act) and other employees who exercise administrative, executive, technical or professional functions ("Non-Workers").

Although the terms and conditions prescribed in the Labour Act strictly speaking should only apply to Workers, in practice, it is not unusual for employers to use the Labour Act as a benchmark for determining the minimum terms of employment of Non-Workers such as when trying to determine issues such as maternity leave and notice periods for terminating contracts of employment.

Notwithstanding the category of an employee, the contract of employment may include any additional terms that are incorporated by reference to a staff handbook, conditions of service manual, or any other document. Where employees are part of trade unions that have entered into any collective bargaining agreement ("CBA") with an employer, the terms of employment of such employees would also be regulated by the provisions of the CBA, if such provisions are incorporated into the employment contract.

The following laws also regulate the employment relationship in Nigeria:

(i) Pension Reform Act 2014, which regulates the contributory pension scheme;

(ii) Employees' Compensation Act 2010, which regulates the payment of compensating to employees that suffer occupational diseases or sustain injuries arising from accidents at workplace or in the course of employment;

(iii) Personal Income Tax Act (as amended) (PIT)[1], which regulates the taxation of employees' remuneration and employers obligations with respect to the deduction and remittance of taxes;

(iv) The National Health Insurance Scheme Act[2], which established the national health insurance scheme. The scheme is aimed at providing easy access to healthcare for all Nigerians at an affordable cost through various prepayment systems;

(v) Industrial Training Fund Act (as amended) (ITFA)[3], which requires employers to contribute 1% of their annual payroll to the Industrial Training Fund created by the ITFA. The ITFA is applicable to every employer that has either five or more employees or an annual turnover of not less than ₦50million (approximately US$ 143,000);

(vi) National Housing Fund Act[4], which established the National Housing Fund and imposes an obligation on employers to deduct 2.5% of the monthly salary of its employees and to remit the sums deducted to the Federal Mortgage Bank of Nigeria as its employees' contribution to the National Housing Fund;

(vii) Trade Unions Act 2004 as amended by the Trade Union (Amendment) Act 2005[5], which regulates the operation, membership and the activities of trade unions in Nigeria;

(viii) Immigration Act 2015 which regulates the employment of foreign nationals; and

(ix) HIV and AIDS (Anti-Discrimination) Act 2014, which regulates the employment of persons living with HIV and AIDS and prescribes employers obligations to such employees.

In addition to the federal statutes listed above, employers are also required to comply with any relevant laws made by the government of the state where such employer operates.

---

[1] Personal Income Tax Act (Chapter P8 LFN 2004, as amended by the Personal Income Tax (Amendment) Act 2011.
[2] National Health Insurance Scheme Act, Chapter N42, LFN 2004.
[3] Industrial Training Fund Act, Chapter I9 LFN 2004.
[4] National Housing Fund, Chapter N45 Laws of the Federal Republic of Nigeria 2004.
[5] Trade Unions Act, Chapter T14 Laws of the Federal Republic of Nigeria 2004 as amended by the Trade Union (Amendment) Act 2005.

B. Requirements of Employing Foreign Employees

a. Work Permit

The Immigration Act requires any person in Nigeria that intends to employ a foreign national to apply to the Comptroller-General of Immigration for permission to employ such person(s) and no such person shall be employed without the permission of the Comptroller- General of Immigration. In practice, this permission which is the authorisation required by a company that intends to employ foreigners, is referred to as an expatriate quota and is issued by the Federal Ministry of the Interior (FMI). The expatriate quota permits a company to employ expatriates to specifically approved job designations, and also specifies the duration that such employment is permitted. The expatriate quota is issued to the company and not the expatriate, as such when the expatriate leaves the company, the position reverts to the company and the company may employ another expatriate in the same position for as long as the quota position remains valid.

Expatriate quotas are granted on a temporary basis, usually for a period of 2 (two) years in the first instance, and may be renewed up to five times or for a period not exceeding 10 (ten) years in exceptional circumstances. The exact number of expatriate quota positions granted will depend on the nature of a company's activities. The Nigerian Government has a policy of encouraging the employment and training of Nigerians and, therefore, the renewal of a quota position is usually dependent on showing that at least 2 (two) Nigerian employees have understudied the expatriate.

It is possible for companies to obtain a "permanent until reviewed" (PUR) quota. A PUR quota position is normally given in respect of chief executive officers of such companies. A fee payable in convertible foreign currency is charged for the grant of a PUR quota. A PUR quota will only be issued after a company has been in operation for over 2 (two) years and has applied for and utilised expatriate quota positions.

Where a prospective employer requires the services of an expatriate to provide specialised skilled services for short periods of time (between 1 to 6 months), and the employer does not have an expatriate quota, the employer may apply for a temporary work permit (TWP) on behalf of such expatriate. An expatriate who has been granted a TWP will not be required to obtain any other further immigration permits or approvals for the duration of the TWP. A TWP is valid for three months and may be extended for another period of three months.

In addition to the expatriate quota, the company is also required to obtain residence and work permits from the Nigerian Immigration Service (NIS) in respect of all its foreign employees (other than a national of any of the countries comprising the Economic Community of West African States (ECOWAS). This permit is referred to as the Combined Expatriate Residence Permit and Aliens Card (CERPAC Card). It allows a non-Nigerian to reside in Nigeria and carry out an approved activity as specified in the permit. A CERPAC is also required for a dependent to accompany an expatriate. The CERPAC Card is valid for 12 (twelve) months at a time and may be renewed at its expiration.

b. Application Procedure

a) Expatriate Quota Approval: The application is made to the Permanent Secretary, Ministry of Interior by the Nigerian company. In support of the application, the company shall submit the following documents: (i) duly completed application form; (ii) bankers reference; (iii) evidence of acquisition of office premises, machinery and equipment; (iv) Certificate of Capital Importation (the evidence of importation of foreign capital) in Nigeria; (v) qualifications and positions to be occupied by the expatriates, including the proposed salaries of the expatriates; (vi) the training programme for the company's Nigerian employees; (vii) the company's current tax clearance certificate and VAT registration certificate, and such other documents as the Ministry may require. Following the payment by the applicant company of the relevant fees, the Ministry will process the application and issue the expatriate quota approval within three to four months from submission of the application.

b) Temporary Work Permit: The Nigerian company submits an application letter to the Comptroller General of the NIS, together with a copy of the data page of the expatriate's passport and such supporting documents as the NIS may require including copies of the Nigerian company's certificate of incorporation and memorandum and articles of association. The NIS would approve the application within two to three weeks of the submission of the application. The TWP is valid for three months and upon expiry of the first TWP, the Nigerian company may submit an application, on behalf of the expatriate, for an extension of the TWP for another three months. The grant of the second TWP is subject to the discretion of the NIS which discretion is exercised judiciously.

c) Combined Expatriate Resident Permit and Aliens Card (CERPAC): The Nigerian company must have obtained expatriate quota approval and the foreign national must have obtained a subject-to-regularisation (STR) visa in his country of residence. The application must be submitted within three months from the date on which the expatriate arrives in Nigeria. Although the obligation to apply for a CERPAC is that of the expatriate, in practice, the company submits the application on the expatriate's behalf. An application letter addressed to the Comptroller General of the NIS, together with the expatriate's international passport, the STR visa and such other documents as the NIS may required is submitted in support of the application. The official cost of a CERPAC is about US$1,200 and the process could be completed within one to two weeks.

c. Social Insurance

Nigeria does not have a system of a social insurance. A contributory pension scheme came into effect on 1st January 2005, and is currently administered under the framework of the Pension Reform Act 2014. Under the Pension Reform Act 2014, every employer that has fifteen or more employees is required to contribute at least 10% of an employee's salary, while the employee contributes 8%, bring the total contribution to 18% of the employee's monthly salary. Within seven days from the day on which the employee was paid his / her salary, the employer is obliged to remit the total contribution of 18% (the employer deducts the employee's portion of the contribution at source) and remit the monies to the employee's retirement savings account, held with a pension fund administrator of the employee's choice. An employer's obligation in this respect is limited to Nigerian citizens, as expatriates are not required to enroll in the scheme, unless such expatriate elects to participate in the scheme.

Employers are also required by the Pension Reform Act 2014 to obtain life insurance cover for all their employees, of a value that is at least three times the annual emoluments of all the employees.

C. Exit and Entry

a. Visa Types

The categories of visas available to expatriates desirous of traveling to Nigeria for various reasons & purposes are:

(i) Transit Visa: Transit visas are required by citizens of all countries who wish to enter Nigeria in order to transit to another destination outside the country. Nationals of the countries comprising the Economic Community of West African States (ECOWAS) and nationals of other countries that have visa abolition agreements with Nigeria do not require this visa to enter Nigeria.

(ii) Tourist Visa: Tourist visas are required by citizens of all countries who wish to enter Nigeria for tourism purposes and to visit family and friends. ECOWAS nationals and nationals of other countries that have visa abolition agreements with Nigeria do not require this visa to enter Nigeria.

(iii) Business Visa: Business visas are issued to foreign nationals wishing to travel to Nigeria on a temporary basis in order to attend meetings, conferences and engage in other business activities. Persons who enter into Nigeria on business visas are prohibited from engaging in any form of employment in Nigeria. ECOWAS nationals and nationals of other countries that have visa abolition agreements with Nigeria do not require this visa to enter Nigeria.

(iv) Subject-to-Regularisation (STR) Visa: This is the visa that is required for an expatriate employee who has been offered employment by a Nigerian company and who wishes to take up such employment. The expatriate is required to apply for a STR visa from the Nigerian Embassy / High Commission in their country of usual residence to enable them to enter Nigeria for the purpose of taking up employment. After obtaining the STR visa, the expatriate can travel to Nigeria and on arrival will have a period of three months to regularise their immigration status by obtaining a Combined Expatriate Residence Permit & Alien Card, the approval document which evidences that the expatriate can reside and take up employment in Nigeria.

(v) Diplomatic Visa: These visas are granted to visiting heads of states, top government officials, accredited diplomats, holders of United Nations / International Agencies Diplomatic Passport and Laisser Passez.

b. Restrictions for Exit and Entry

The restrictions are as follows:

(i) Transit Visa: A transit visa is valid for 48 hours if obtained on arrival, and for 7 days if obtained from a Nigerian foreign mission prior to arrival in Nigeria.

(ii) Tourist Visa: A tourist visa is valid for 90 days.

(iii) Business Visa: A business visa is valid for 90 days and may be extended (where necessary) at the sole discretion of the NIS.

(iv) STR Visa: STR visas are valid for three months (within which period the relevant expatriates are required to regularise their immigration status by obtaining a CERPAC).

(v) Diplomatic Visa: A diplomatic visa is valid for 90 days.

D. Trade Union and Labour Organisations

The Trade Unions Act[1] (the "TUA"), regulates the operation, membership and the activities of trade unions

---

[1] Trade Unions Act, chapter T14, Laws of the Federation of Nigeria 2004 as amended by the Trade Union (Amendment) Act 2005.

in Nigeria. In Nigeria, trade unions are actively involved in negotiating collective bargaining agreements ("CBA") on behalf of their members and the terms of such agreements usually form part of the contracts of employment of their members. The TUA provides that for the purposes of collective bargaining, all registered unions represented in the employment of an employer shall constitute an electoral college to elect members who will represent their union in negotiations with the employer.

The rights of trade unions in Nigeria include the rights to:

(i) negotiate the terms and conditions of employment with employers on behalf of employees who are members of the trade union;

(ii) embark on an industrial strike action;

(iii) engage in peaceful picketing; and

(iv) be informed by an employer of the reasons for and the extent of any proposed redundancy(ies), if any of the employees likely to affected are members of a trade union.

E. Labour Disputes

a. Trade Disputes

The principal legislation governing trade disputes in Nigeria is the Trade Disputes Act[1]. In order for there to be a valid trade dispute:

(i) there must be a dispute which must involve a trade and it must be between employers and workers, or amongst the workers; and

(ii) the dispute must be connected with the employment or non-employment or terms of employment or physical condition of work of any person.[2]

The term "worker" as defined under the Trade Disputes Act is broader than the definition of the term in the Labour Act, and applies to "any employee, that is to say any public officer or any individual (other than a public officer) who has entered into or works under a contract with an employer, whether the contract is for manual labour, clerical work or otherwise, express or implied, oral or in writing, and whether it is a contract of service or of apprenticeship".

The mechanism for resolving a trade dispute under the Trade Disputes Act comprises the following steps:

a) Internal settlement mechanism: The disputing parties are required to first attempt to settle their dispute if there is an agreed means for settlement of disputes e.g.in accordance with the provisions of a collective agreement. This process ensures that grievances are settled through negotiations between the disputing parties.

b) Mediation: This mechanism is adopted where the disputing parties are unable to settle the dispute using the internal settlement mechanism or where no such means of settlement exists. The parties are required to meet to resolve the dispute amicably under the supervision of a mediator mutually agreed upon and appointed by the parties.

c) Ministerial intervention: If mediation fails, the matter is referred to the Minister in charge of labour ("the Minister") within three days of the expiration of the period for resolving the dispute by mediation. The Minister may direct the parties to take further steps to resolve the conflict but if the deadlock continues without resolution, the Minister shall, within 14 (fourteen) days, refer the matter for conciliation.

d) Conciliation: If a settlement of the dispute is not reached within seven days of the appointment of a conciliator or if, after attempting negotiation with the parties, the conciliator is satisfied that he will not be able to bring about a settlement by means thereof, the conciliator must report that fact to the Minister.

e) Industrial Arbitration Panel: Within 14 (fourteen) days of receipt of the conciliator's report notifying him of the failure of the conciliation process, the Minister shall refer the dispute for settlement to the Industrial Arbitration Panel (the "IAP") and the IAP chairman shall constitute an arbitration tribunal. The arbitral tribunal is obliged to make its award within 21 (twenty-one) days of its constitution, or such longer period as the Minister may allow and shall forward a copy of the award to the Minister without communicating the award to the affected parties. Upon receipt of the arbitral tribunal's award, the Minister shall, where he does not consider it necessary to refer the award back to the tribunal for reconsideration, issue a notice to the parties that (i) sets out the award(s), (ii) specifies a time of not more than 7 (seven) days from the publication of the notice, within which any party may give notice of its objection to the award to the Minister, and (iii) states that the Minister will confirm the award if he does not receive a notice of objection to the award within the prescribed timeline and in the manner specified in the notice. If no notice of objection to the award is given to the Minister, the Minister shall publish a notice confirming

---

[1] Trade Disputes Act, chapter T8, Laws of the Federation of Nigeria 2004.
[2] NURTW v.Ogbodo (1998) 2 N.W.L.R (Pt.537) at 189.

the award in the Federal Gazette and the award shall be binding on the employers and workers to whom it relates.

f) Reference to the National Industrial Court of Nigeria: Where any or both parties reject the arbitral tribunal's award, and issues a notice of objection to the Minister, the Minister shall immediately refer the dispute to the National Industrial Court of Nigeria (NICN). The NICN's judgment on the matter is binding on the parties and an appeal of its judgment can only be heard by the Court of Appeal. The Court of Appeal's decision on any such appeal is final, and the parties shall be obliged to comply with the provisions of the judgement of the Court of Appeal.

b. Disputes Involving Employees Other Than Trade Disputes

The NICN is vested with exclusive jurisdiction in respect of civil and criminal matters relating to labour including trade unions and industrial relations; environment and conditions of work; health, safety and welfare of the workforce and matters of industrial relations. All disputes arising from the employment relationship, other than trade disputes, are instituted at the NICN. Appeals from decisions of the NICN go to the Court of Appeal and the decision of the Court of Appeal, on any appeal arising from any civil jurisdiction of the NICN is final. However, appeals from decisions of the NICN in respect of criminal cases can be made to the apex court of Nigeria, the Supreme Court. A judge of the NICN may, however, refer any matter instituted at the NICN to the Alternative Dispute Resolution Centre established within the NICN, for amicable settlement through conciliation or mediation. Where parties are unable to settle their disputes through the mediation or conciliation process, the NICN would hear the matter in accordance with its rules.

V. Intellectual Property

A. Brief Introduction of IP Laws and Regulations

There are two classes of Intellectual Property ("IP") in Nigeria: Copyright and Industrial Property. Industrial Property is a broad heading that covers trademarks, patents and industrial designs. IP rights are protected under the following legislation:

(i) Copyright Act (Chapter C28) Laws of the Federation of Nigeria 2004 (the "Copyright Act"), with respect to copyright and neighbouring rights;

(ii) Trademarks Act (Chapter T13) Laws of the Federation of Nigeria 2004 (the "Trademarks Act") and the Trademark Regulations 1967, with respect to trademarks; and

(iii) Patent and Designs Act (Chapter P2) Laws of the Federation of Nigeria 2004 (the "PDA") and the Patent Rules 1971, with respect to patent and industrial designs.

These legislation define the extent of protection, the procedure for registration (where required), enforcement, and other miscellaneous matters.

B. Copyright

Copyright does not require registration. A work eligible for copyright is automatically protected upon creation. Although copyright holders are encouraged to notify the Nigerian Copyright Commission of their copyright under the Copyright Notification Scheme, this procedure was introduced for record-keeping purposes, and does not amount to registration.

C. Patent Application

A patent is a monopoly granted in respect of an invention. Under the PDA, for an invention to be registrable as a patent, it must be new or constitute an improvement upon a patented invention and must also result from inventive activity and be capable of industrial application.

To register a patent, an application should be made to the Patents and Designs Registry (the "Registry") to register the invention. This application is required to be supported by the following documents / information:

(i) the full name and address and, if that address is outside Nigeria, and address for service in Nigeria;

(ii) a description of the relevant invention with any appropriate plans and drawings. In this regard, the description is required to disclose the invention in a manner sufficiently clear and complete for the invention to be put into effect by a person skilled in the art or field of knowledge to which the invention relates;

(iii) a claim or claims i.e.a detailed description of the functions or uses to which the invention may be applied which shall not go beyond the limits of the said description;

(iv) where the applicant is not the actual inventor, a declaration signed by the true inventor requesting that he be mentioned as such in the patent and giving his name and address;

(vi) power of attorney / authorisation of agent, authorising the agent in Nigeria to file and process the application on behalf of the applicant; and

(vii) such other matter as may be prescribed by the Registry.

If the registrar is satisfied that the above requirements have been met, and upon payment of the prescribed fees, a patent will be granted in respect of the invention.

D. Trademark Registration

Section 67 of the Trade Marks Act defines a "trade mark" as:

"a mark used or proposed to be used in relation to goods for the purpose of indicating, or so as to indicate, a connection in the course of trade between the goods and some person having the right either as proprietor or as registered user to use the mark, whether with or without any indication of the identity of that person".

The procedure for the registration of a trademark is set out below:

a) A trademark clearance search is conducted at the Nigerian Trademarks Registry (the "Trademarks Registry"), in order to determine whether the trademark is available for registration (i.e.whether or not the mark has already been registered);

b) If the trademark is available, an application is then made to the Trademarks Registry to register the trademark. This application must be supported with the following documents / information:

(i) he full name(s), nationality and physical address of the applicant;

(ii) copies of the proposed trade mark / logo;

(iii) the full range of goods / services to be covered by the proposed trade mark; and

(iv) power of attorney / authorisation of agent, authorising the agent in Nigeria to file and process the application on behalf of the applicant.

The classification of goods for the purpose of registration of trademarks in Nigeria is governed by Section 5 and the Fourth Schedule of the Trademarks Regulations made pursuant to the Trademarks Act. There are currently 45 classes in which a trademark may be registered. Nigerian law only confers trademark protection in respect of specific classes in which a trademark has been registered in relation to specific goods, therefore, a trademark infringement would not be deemed to have arisen in respect of classes in which a trademark has not been registered.

c) Following the submission of an application for registration of a trademark, the registrar of trademarks confirms receipt of the application by issuing an official acknowledgment letter. The registrar will thereafter, consider the application and conduct a search of the registry's records to confirm that no similar mark has been accepted or registered previously.

d) If the registrar is satisfied that no similar mark has been accepted / registered, the registrar will issue a letter of acceptance indicating that the trademark has been accepted for registration. If, however, the registrar determines that a similar trademark has already been accepted or registered, the registrar will issue a letter of refusal of the application, which sets out the reasons for the refusal.

e) After the issuance of the letter of acceptance, the trademark will be published in the trademarks journal. For a period of 2 (two) months after the mark is published in the trademarks journal, the public is free to raise any objections they may have to the registration of the trademark. If within those 2 (two) months no objections are received by the Registrar (or no objections are sustained), the Registrar will issue the applicant with a certificate of registration of the trademark. If, however, objections are filed within the period, these objections would have to be resolved prior to the registration. In order to resolve such objections, the applicant is obliged to respond to the objections. The content of the response would depend on the nature of the objection filed.

E. Measures for IP Protection

Apart from the registration of intellectual property rights at the relevant registries where applicable, the various IP laws stipulate mechanisms for the enforcement of rights of the IP owners.

a. Industrial Property (i.e.Trademarks, Patents and Industrial Designs)

The essential benefit of registration of an industrial property right is that it confers on the proprietor the right to institute proceedings in the Federal High Court for infringement of the proprietor's exclusive right in the industrial property, and the carrying out of any action that conflicts with the rights granted to such proprietor.

Available reliefs include damages, injunction and account for any profits. As an interim measure before the commencement of the trial, an anton piller order can be granted to enable the proprietor, with the aid of the court bailiffs and law enforcement agents, to enter the premises of the defendant and seize the infringing products.

b. Copyright

Similar to the proprietor of an industrial property right, a copyright owner may institute an action in the Federal High Court for infringement of copyright. A copyright owner is also entitled to seek interim and interlocutory reliefs already discussed above. Section 17(1) of the Copyright Act also entitles the owner of a copyright to institute an action for breach of a statutory duty against a party infringing the owner's exclusive right in the copyright.

The making, selling, distribution, importation etc.of an infringing copy of a work covered by copyright is a criminal offence punishable with a term of imprisonment, or a fine, or both, under the Copyright Act. The Copyright Act also provides that both criminal and civil actions may be taken simultaneously in respect of the same infringement.

VI. Environmental Protection

A. Department Supervising Environmental Protection

The National Environmental Standards and Regulations Enforcement Agency ("NESREA") is the principal agency that is responsible for protecting and developing the environment, enforcing environmental laws, regulations and standards and deterring people, industries and organisations from polluting and degrading the environment.

The Department of Petroleum Resources (DPR) is responsible for the enforcement of environmental regulations relating to the oil and gas sector because the oil and gas sector is specifically excluded from the scope of NESREA's responsibilities.

B. Brief Introduction of Laws and Regulations of Environmental Protection

The relevant laws and regulations are:

a) National Environmental Standards and Regulations Enforcement Agency (Establishment) Act of 2007 (the NESREA Act) – This is the principal Nigerian legislation for the protection of the environment and the law that established the NESREA. The NESREA Act deals with issues such as emissions to air, ground and water, noise pollution, reduction and elimination of pollution and other forms of environmental degradation of Nigeria's air, land and water, ozone protection, water quality standards, effluent limitations, environmental sanitation, public health, land resources, watershed quality and the discharge of hazardous substances in harmful quantities into the air upon the land and waters of Nigeria.

b) Environmental Impact Assessment Act Chapter E12 Laws of the Federation of Nigeria 2004 (EIA Act)— Under the EIA Act, individuals, firms or agencies are prohibited from undertaking or authorising any projects or activities without the prior consideration, at an early stage, of the environmental effects of such projects and activities. In addition, the proponent of the project or activity is required to conduct an environmental impact assessment in respect of the project or activity. The EIA Act also specifies the matters that must, at a minimum, be addressed in the EIA, and these include the following:

(i) a description of the proposed activity and the environment likely to be affected by the activities, including specific information necessary in order to identify and assess the environmental effect of the proposed activities;

(ii) an assessment of the likely or potential environmental impact of the proposed activity and the alternatives, including the direct or indirect cumulative, short-term and long-term effects of the potential impact;

(iii) an identification and description of the available measures for mitigating or addressing the environmental impact of the proposed activity together with an assessment of the proposed measures; and

(iv) an indication of the knowledge gaps and uncertainties encountered in collating the required information and of any areas outside Nigeria that may be affected by the proposed activity or its alternatives.

c) Regulations issued by the NESREA - Sections 7(h) and (j) of the NESREA Act empowers NESREA to enforce, through compliance monitoring, environmental regulations and standards relating to noise, air, land, the seas, oceans and other water bodies and environmental control measures through registration, licensing and permitting systems. In the exercise of its powers, NESREA has issued numerous regulations including:

(i) National Environmental (Wetlands, River Banks and Lake Shores) Regulations, 2009 which provide for the conservation & wise use of wetlands & their resources in Nigeria;

(ii) National Environmental (Sanitation and Wastes Control) Regulations 2009 which provides the legal framework for the adoption of sustainable and environment friendly practices in environmental sanitation and waste management to minimize pollution;

(iii) National Environmental (Permitting and Licensing System) Regulations, 2009, the provisions of which seek to enable the consistent application of environmental laws, regulations and standards in all sectors of the economy and geographical region;

(iv) National Environmental (Desertification Control and Drought Mitigation) Regulations, 2010 which seeks to provide an effective and pragmatic regulatory framework for the sustainable use of all areas already affected by desertification and the protection of vulnerable lands;

(v) National Environmental (Protection of Endangered Species in International Trade) Regulations, 2010 which seeks to protect species of endangered wildlife.

C. Evaluation of Environmental Protection

The NESREA and the DPR seek to ensure that they carry out their obligations to protect and preserve the environment and there is a general awareness and increased compliance levels from the citizenry.

VII. Dispute Resolution

The most common forms of dispute resolution in Nigeria are litigation and arbitration. Arbitration is either ad hoc or institutional. Transactions involving international counter-parties typically provide for institutional arbitration under the International Chamber of Commerce Rules, the London Court of International Arbitration Rules, or the Rules of the Chartered Institute of Arbitrators (UK).

Transactions involving only Nigerian parties tend to provide for ad hoc arbitration under the UNCITRAL Model Law on International Commercial Arbitration or the Nigerian Arbitration and Conciliation Act. In the few cases where contracts involving Nigerian parties provide for institutional arbitration, the parties tend to choose local Nigerian arbitration institutions such as the Chartered Institute of Arbitrators (UK) Nigerian Branch or the Lagos Regional Centre for International Commercial Arbitration.

A. Methods and Bodies of Dispute Resolution

With regard to transactions (local or international), where parties have agreed to submit their disputes to Nigerian courts, most of the cases are filed in the state high courts. Nigeria is a federation comprised of 36 states and the federal capital territory, Abuja. The 1999 Constitution of the Federal Republic of Nigeria (as amended) creates a high court for each state and the federal capital territory. The Constitution also creates the Federal High Court with jurisdiction over specific subject matter. The state where the contract is implemented or ought to be performed will determine the high court that will have jurisdiction over the contractual dispute. However, where the dispute relates to real property, it is the high court of the state where the asset is located that would have jurisdiction over the dispute. Where the Federal Government of Nigeria (FGN) or any of its agencies is a party to the proceedings or where the dispute relates to the executive, administrative or managerial action or inaction of the FGN, the Federal High Court would have jurisdiction.

The arbitration institutions commonly used to settle commercial disputes in Nigeria are:

(i) Lagos Multidoor Courthouse (www.lagosmultidoor.org.ng);
(ii) Chartered Institute of Arbitrators, UK (Nigerian Branch) (www.ciarbnigeria.org);
(iii) International Chamber of Commerce (ICC) (www.iccwbo.org);
(iv) International Centre for Settlement of Investment Disputes (ICSID) (https://icsid.worldbank.org);
(v) London Court of International Arbitration (LCIA) (www.lcia.org);
(vi) Lagos Regional Centre for International Commercial Arbitration.(www.rcicalagos.org).

The most commonly used Alternative Dispute Resolution (ADR) methods in Nigeria are arbitration and mediation.

B. Application of Laws

The applicable laws to govern a dispute resolution are determined by the nature of the dispute, and the status of the parties. However, in a commercial dispute, the following laws / rules are generally applicable:

(i) Constitution of the Federal Republic of Nigeria (1999) (as amended);
(ii) Companies and Allied Matters Act;
(iii) Investments and Securities Act;
(iv) Limitation Act;
(v) Sale of Goods Act;
(vi) Arbitration and Conciliation Act;
(vii) The State High Court Rules;

(viii) Federal High Court Rules;
(ix) Companies Winding-Up Rules;
(x) Companies Regulations;
(xi) Securities and Exchange Commission Rules; and
(xii) Nigerian Stock Exchange Rules etc.

Where parties choose a foreign law as the governing law of their transaction, the attitude of the Nigerian court has, generally, been to hold parties to their bargains. The Nigerian Supreme Court has, however, held that the parties' choice of law is not conclusive and that, to be effective, the choice of law must be "real, genuine, bona fide, and reasonable". The foreign law chosen by parties as the proper law of their contract must have some relationship to, and connection with, the realities of the contract considered as a whole. Subject to these qualifications, parties are free to choose a governing law of their choice.

VIII. Others

A. Section on Anti-bribery

a. Brief Introduction of Anti-bribery Laws and Regulations

[Drafting note: We have amended the phrase "Anti-commercial bribery" to "Anti-bribery" as the latter is the proper expression for this term.]

a) The Constitution of the Federal Republic of Nigeria 1999 as amended in 2011 (Constitution)

The Fifth Schedule to the Constitution (the Code of Conduct) prohibits public officers from accepting property or benefits of any kind for himself or for any other person, because of anything done or omitted to be done in the discharge of official duties.

b) The Corrupt Practices and other Related Offences Act 2000

This law contains broad provisions in relation to corrupt offers to public officers. The Act applies to any person employed by or acting for another and includes any governmental official, member of a public body or any political party any sub-contractor or any official, employee or agent of a public or private organisation and criminalises any corrupt act by any of these persons. The Corrupt Practices Act also applies to actions taken outside Nigeria by citizens of Nigeria and persons that have been granted permanent residence in Nigeria, in circumstances where the actions would be a contravention of Nigerian law and the law of the place where the act took place.

The Act criminalises the giving or offer of anything of value that constitutes "gratification", where such gratification is given in furtherance of a proscribed act. "Gratification" is defined under the Act to include money, donations, gifts, property or interest in property or any similar advantage given or promised to any person with intent to influence such a person in the performance or non-performance of his duties; any agreement to give empowerment; any valuable consideration of any kind; any offer, undertaking or promise whether conditional or unconditional; any payment, release, discharge or liquidation of any loans or other obligation or the writing off of any loan. The Corrupt Practices Act goes further to provide that payments, promises or the giving of anything of value to an official by a person holding or seeking to obtain a contract, licence, permit or anything whatsoever from a government department in which the official is employed is presumed to have been received such corruptly. The same offence arises in respect of a public officer that solicits or accepts any consideration from any person as an inducement to or reward for the public officer's assistance or influence in the execution or procurement of any contract or sub-contract. The Act also imposes a duty on both public officers and private individuals to report offences under the Act.

c) The Criminal Code Act, Chapter C38, Laws of the Federation of Nigeria 2004 (the Criminal Code Act)

The Criminal Code Act provides that any public official who corruptly asks for or receives or attempts to receive or obtain any property of any kind for himself or for another either before or after he does or omits to do anything in his official capacity is guilty of the felony of official corruption and liable to imprisonment for seven years. Under the Criminal Code Act, any person, who corruptly gives, promises, offers, confers, procures or attempts to procure any property or benefit of any kind to, on, or for a public officer or another party at the insistence of the public officer is guilty of a felony of official corruption and liable to imprisonment for seven years. In relation to extortion, the Criminal Code Act provides that any public officer who takes or accepts any reward beyond his emoluments, for the performance of his duty, is guilty of a felony and liable to imprisonment for three years.

d) The Economic and Financial Crimes Commission (Establishment) Act, Chapter E1, Laws of the Federation of Nigeria 2004 (EFCC Act)

The Economic and Financial Crimes Commission established under the EFCC Act is responsible for investigating all offences relating to economic and financial crimes. The Act defines "economic and financial crimes" as the non-violent criminal and illicit activity committed with the objective of earning wealth illegally, either individually or in a group or organised manner and includes any form of fraud, narcotic drug trafficking, money laundering, embezzlement, bribery, looting and any form of corrupt malpractices, illegal arms deal, smuggling, human trafficking and child labour, illegal oil bunkering and illegal mining, tax evasion, foreign exchange malpractices including counterfeiting of currency, theft of intellectual property and piracy, open market abuse, dumping of toxic wastes and prohibited goods, etc. Other offences created by the EFCC Act include those relating to financial malpractices by an official of a bank or any other financial institution; offences relating to the commission of acts of terrorism and offences relating to economic and financial crimes. In relation to the offence described as an "economic and financial crime", the EFCC Act prohibits anyone from concealing, removing from Nigeria or transferring to nominees, the proceeds of an economic and financial crime, on behalf of another, with the knowledge that such proceeds are as a result of criminal conduct by the principal.

b. Department Supervising Anti-bribery in Nigeria

The departments supervising anti-bribery in Nigeria are:

(i) The Independent Corrupt Practices and other related Offences Commission (ICPC): This is a 12-member commission established by the Corrupt Practices Act with authority to oversee the implementation of the provisions of Corrupt Practices Act. The ICPC can investigate the commission of any offence under the Corrupt Practices Act or the breach of any other Nigerian law which prohibits corruption.

(ii) The Economic and Financial Crimes Commission: The EFCC Act mandates the EFCC to combat financial and economic crimes. The EFCC is authorised to prevent, investigate, prosecute and penalise economic and financial crimes and is charged with the responsibility of enforcing the provisions of other laws and regulations relating to economic and financial crimes which includes bribery. The EFCC Act also gives the EFCC extensive investigative and discretionary powers to compound any offence by accepting money exceeding the maximum amount for which any person may be liable if convicted for the offence.

c. Punitive Actions

The Criminal Code Act: Section 98A of the Criminal Code Act provides that any person, who corruptly gives, promises, offers, confers, procures or attempts to procure any property or benefit of any kind to, on, or for a public officer or another party at the insistence of the public officer is guilty of the felony of official corruption and liable to imprisonment for seven years. In relation to extortion, the Criminal Code Act provides that any public officer who takes or accepts any reward beyond his emoluments, for the performance of his duty, is guilty of a felony and liable to imprisonment for three years.

The Corrupt Practices Act: The Corrupt Practices Act provides that any person who corruptly asks for or receives or attempts to receive or obtain any property of any kind for himself or for another, either before or after he does or omits to do anything in his official capacity, is guilty of an offence of official corruption and is liable to imprisonment for seven years. The Act further prescribes a seven-year term of imprisonment for any person that corruptly gives, or confers any property or benefit to, or on a public officer or on any other person or who offers or promises to do so, because of any act or favour to be done or shown by a public officer. In addition, the Corrupt Practices Act criminalises the giving or offer of "gratification", by any person to any public officer, where such gratification is given as an inducement or reward for certain prescribed acts which include aiding in procuring the grant of any contract, award, recognition or advantage in favour of any person. The Act also penalises the failure to report a bribery transaction by a public officer or private individual with a term of imprisonment and / or a fine.

The Economic and Financial Crimes Commission (Establishment) Act: Section 18 of this Act imposes a term of imprisonment of two to three years for economic and financial crimes. In addition to the term of imprisonment, the Act also requires convicted persons to pay a fine equivalent to the value of the proceeds of the crime. Other sanctions imposed under the EFCC Act include the forfeiture of assets (both within and outside Nigeria), and the freezing of bank accounts maintained by a person accused of the commission of a financial crime. Section 23 of the EFCC Act further provides that where a person is convicted of an offence under the EFCC Act, his passport shall be forfeited to the Federal Government of Nigeria and will not be returned to him until he has served any sentence served on him or the President grants him a pardon.

B. Project Contracting

a. Permission System

The Public Procurement Act No.14 of 2007 ("PPA") regulates the procurement of goods and works and disposals of assets by procuring entities (i.e. agencies of the Federal Government of Nigeria and all entities that derive at least 35% of the funds appropriated or proposed to be appropriated for any type of procurement described in the PPA, from the Federal Government's share of the Consolidated Revenue Fund).

The PPA also established the Bureau of Public Procurement ("BPP"), the agency that is responsible for overseeing the procurement activities of all the procuring entities.

The PPA requires that all procurement of goods and works must be conducted by open competitive bidding. In relation to disposals of assets by procuring entities, where the disposal involves the concession of any infrastructure, in addition to complying with the requirements of the PPA, the bid process must comply with the Infrastructure Concession Regulatory Commission (Establishment, etc) Act, 2005 (the "ICRC Act"). The ICRC Act requires that all proposed concessions must be approved by the Federal Executive Council ("FEC"). In addition to the PPA and the ICRC Act, public procurement is subject to the provisions of regulations issued by the BPP including the Procurement Procedure Manual and the Public Procurement Regulations for Goods and Works.

The PPA only applies to agencies that are connected with the Federal Government; it does not apply to the private sector or to the 36 states of the Federation. Some states have, however, enacted their own procurement laws.

Foreign companies that wish to participate in a public procurement process must have incorporated a local entity through which the project will be executed. The local entity could be a wholly owned subsidiary. This is because foreign companies are not allowed to carry on business in Nigeria without first incorporating a local company in Nigeria, unless a waiver is granted by the President.

b. Prohibited Areas

Nigerian nationals and foreign nationals including companies with foreign shareholders are prohibited from investing in the following sectors:

(i) the production of arms and ammunition;

(ii) the production of and dealing in narcotic drugs and psychotropic substances;

(iii) the production of military and para-military wears and accoutrement, including those of the Nigerian Police Force, and the Nigeria Customs Service, Nigeria Immigration Service and Nigeria Prison Services;

(iv) such other items as the Federal Executive Council may, from time to time, determine.

The procurements of special goods, works and services involving national defence or national security are exempted from the purview of the PPA unless the prior approval of the President has been obtained.

c. Invitation to Bid and Bidding

The procurement method / procedure that is adopted by the procuring entity would depend on the nature and size of the procurement, local availability and cost of goods and services and the urgency with which the goods and services to be procured are required. Subject to thresholds set by the BPP, all procurements valued in excess of the sums prescribed by the BPP require a bid security of up to 2% of the bid price by way of a bank guarantee issued by a reputable bank acceptable to the procuring entity. A performance guarantee is a precondition for the award of any procurement contract upon which a mobilisation fee is to be paid. This guarantee shall be for a sum that is at least 10% of the contract value or an amount equivalent to the mobilisation fee, whichever is higher.

There are three different procedures for procurements: open invitation to bid; special and restricted methods of procurement which could be by way of a tendering process, request for quotations or direct procurement; and expressions of interest to provide services for ascertained needs (procurement of consultants).

a) Open invitation to bid

A national competitive bidding is adopted where the capability and competitiveness of local bidders make it unattractive for foreign bidders to compete for contracts below a certain value and where the goods and works are available locally at prices significantly below those in the international markets. On the other hand, international competitive bidding is the preferred method of procurement for larger contracts.

An invitation to bid for a contract must be submitted in writing or in any other format stipulated in the relevant tender documents, signed by an official authorised to bind the bidder to a contract and placed in a sealed envelope. The bid must be in English language and deposited in a secured tamper-proof bid-box. The procuring entity shall issue a receipt showing the date and time the bid was delivered. The bids are examined to determine if they meet the minimum eligibility requirements stipulated in the solicitation documents, executed properly, are substantially responsive to the bidding documents and are generally in order. Qualifying bids are evaluated in order to determine and select the lowest evaluated responsive bid. Where the bid is relation to procurement of goods and services, the lowest cost bidder will be selected.

b) Special and restricted methods of procurement

A tendering process could be where it is not feasible for the procuring entity to formulate detailed specifications for the goods or services required. A request for quotation can only be made if the value of the goods or works does not exceed any thresholds specified in the procurement regulations. Direct procurements are done where the goods, works and services are only available from a particular supplier or contractor, or if a particular supplier or contractor has exclusive rights in respect of the goods, works or services, and no reasonable alternative exists or there is an urgent need.

The proposals are evaluated on the basis of criteria previously set by the procuring entity, which shall also prescribe the weight to be accorded to each criterion and the manner in which these criteria are applied.

c) Expressions of interest

This procurement process is adopted where the services to be procured are precise and ascertainable, and especially when the contract is for the purpose of research, an experiment, a study or development.

巴勒斯坦

作者：Sharhabeel Yousef Al Zaeem、Khaled Sharhabeel Al Zaeem
译者：蓝斐、罗静

一、概述

（一）历史背景

第一次世界大战结束前，巴勒斯坦地区一直是奥斯曼帝国的一部分，适用奥斯曼法律法规。1919年，巴勒斯坦地区受英国托管，英国修改了部分法律法规。这种情况一直持续到了第二次世界大战结束。此后巴勒斯坦地区分裂为三部分：

第一部分：逾70%的巴勒斯坦地区地区被归入"以色列"；

第二部分：巴勒斯坦地区西南的小部分地区现为"加沙地带"；

第三部分：巴勒斯坦地区中东部地区（即"约旦河西岸地区"）。

之后，1950年，约旦河西岸地区被侵占，成为了约旦王国的一部分，因此开始适用约旦的法律法规，并废除了1948年前的法律。在加沙地带，埃及政府宣称其仅享有治理权，并不享有领土及主权，因此包括1871年《奥斯曼民法典》在内的所有法律法规仍旧适用。

1967年以色列占领加沙地带和约旦河西岸地区后，军事法令对这两处地区的法律有一定的影响，但没有改变基本的法律体系。

1994年奥斯陆和平谈判后，巴勒斯坦自治政府废除了大部分的军事法令，因此约旦河西岸地区仍适用约旦法律，加沙地带仍适用奥斯曼法律或英国法律。巴勒斯坦自治政府立法委员会开始颁布普适法，尝试统一两个地区的法律和司法体系。

2007年发生了政治派别分裂，约旦河西岸地区紧急政府主席开始通过主席令变更现有法律并颁布新的法律，而加沙地带自治政府也是这样做的，因此现在两个地区的法律体系存在众多的差异。

（二）巴勒斯坦人口

1. 巴勒斯坦世界人口分布

截至2016年底，巴勒斯坦世界总人口约为1 270万人，其中约488万人居住于巴勒斯坦，约153万人居住于以色列，约559万人居住于阿拉伯国家，约69.6万人居住于其他国家。[①]

2. 约旦河西岸地区巴勒斯坦人口

截至2016年底，居住于约旦河西岸地区的巴勒斯坦人口约为297万人。巴勒斯坦的人口中有41.9%为难民，其中26%的难民居于约旦河西岸地区，66.7%的难民居于加沙地带。

3. 加沙地带巴勒斯坦人口

截至2016年底，居住于加沙地带巴勒斯坦人口约为191万人。

（三）巴勒斯坦劳动力概况

1. 巴勒斯坦劳动力

2016年第三季度约旦河西岸地区劳动力人口为851 300人。

2016年第三季度加沙地带劳动力人口为505 000人。

约旦河西岸地区劳动力参与率为45.7%，加沙地带为46.7%，巴勒斯坦的男女劳动力的参与率相差

---

① 参见巴勒斯坦中央统计局2016年数据。

悬殊，男性劳动力参与率为72.3%，女性劳动力参与率仅为19.2%。[①]

2. 巴勒斯坦劳动力人口失业比例

2016年第三季度加沙地带劳动力人口失业比例为43.2%，而同期约旦河西岸地区失业比例为19.6%。

3. 私营企业员工薪酬

在约旦河西岸地区，约19.2%的私营企业员工的薪酬低于月最低工资标准，他们的月平均工资为1 050新谢克尔。

在加沙地带，有78%的私营企业员工薪酬低于月最低工资标准，月平均工资为745新谢克尔。

4. 2016年第三季度约旦河西岸地区就业状况

- 65.6%的从业人员是授薪员工；
- 19.7%的从业人员是自由职业者；
- 6.1%的从业人员是无薪酬的家庭成员；
- 8.6%的从业人员是雇主。

5. 2016年第三季度加沙地带就业状况

- 78.6%的从业人员是授薪员工；
- 13.0%的从业人员是自由职业者；
- 4.0%的从业人员是无薪酬的家庭成员；
- 4.4%的从业人员是雇主。

（四）巴勒斯坦法院体系

巴勒斯坦法院体系如下[②]：

1. 高等宪法法院

高等宪法法院由一位院长，一位副院长及七位法官组成。开庭需要至少一位院长及六位法官组成合议庭，并经多数投票作出决定。

2. 普通法院

（1）高等法院

高等法院由一位院长，一位或多位副院长及适当人数的法官组成。其包括：

① 上诉庭

上诉庭对以下案件行使管辖权：

- 由上诉法院提交的重罪案件、疑难民事案件及非穆斯林人身地位案件；
- 由一审法院提交的其有权上诉至高等法院的案件；
- 依据的事实发生重大变更的案件；
- 涉及其他法律的案件。

② 审判庭

- 与选举相关的诉讼案件；
- 利害相关方提起的关于终局行政裁决、命令、判决注销企业案件中涉及公法人（包括专业联合企业）的人员及财产案件；
- 关于要求释放被非法拘留者的申请；
- 关于公职人员任职、升职、加薪、薪酬、调任、退休、纪律处分、裁员、解雇及所有其他人事方面的纠纷；
- 行政机关依法应履行职责却不作为案件；
- 所有的行政纠纷；
- 未正式立案却违法发布禁令或传票且为正义必需判决的案件；

---

① 参见巴勒斯坦中央统计局2016年7月数据。
② 2001年第5号法律《司法组织法》，2002年第1号法律《司法机关法》。

- 其他依法应由其审理的案件。

（2）上诉法院

上诉法院应由一位院长及足够人数的法官组成。

上诉法院有权审查就一审法院作出的判决和决定向其提出的上诉。

（3）一审法院

一审法院应由一位院长及适当人数的法官组成。

（4）地方法庭

地方法庭由一名法官独任行使行政控制权。

3. 伊斯兰教法庭及宗教法庭

处理所有与穆斯林身份地位的相关事件。

4. 军事法庭

- 高级军事法庭；
- 私人军事法庭；
- 永久军事法庭；
- 中央军事法庭；
- 地区军事法庭。

阿拉伯语是法庭官方语言。不会说阿拉伯语的当事人或证人应通过翻译人员向法庭陈述事实。

（五）"一带一路"倡议下与中国企业合作的现状与方向

2017年11月30日，巴勒斯坦自治政府与中国政府签署了两国之间自由贸易谅解备忘录。

在巴勒斯坦总理哈姆达拉先生与中国驻巴勒斯坦大使陈兴忠先生的陪同下，巴勒斯坦国民经济部部长欧黛博士与中国商务部副部长王受文先生签署了自由贸易谅解备忘录。

因此在"一带一路"倡议下，巴勒斯坦与中国企业已建立了强有力的经济基础。

二、投资

（一）市场准入

1. 投资监管部门

（1）巴勒斯坦投资促进局（PIPA）

1998年，依据1998年第一号法律《投资促进法》，PIPA作为一个独立部门成立。这部法律尽最大可能地为投资者们提供了与投资相关的激励、推动和保证，通过建立一个不存在官僚主义和纠纷的投资环境，使投资者在巴勒斯坦取得独特且成果丰硕的投资。PIPA的成立，表明了巴勒斯坦政府的招商引资决心，用政策鼓励私营企业经营，打造一个适当的投资环境。

PIPA董事会由11名成员组成——4名私营企业代表，7名公众代表。国民经济部部长担任董事会主席（即现任部长欧黛），财政部代表担任副主席。

PIPA向投资者提供了许多必要的帮助，包括通过PIPA的一站式服务获得所有必需的许可证。投资支持部门提供了有关在巴勒斯坦投资机会、支出及出资等的最新信息及数据。

PIPA提供给投资者的不仅仅是法律赋予的鼓励及帮助，PIPA的后期服务部门也提供了大量的便利。为现有投资者提供服务及协助，以便帮助他们在解决项目设立时可能遇到的任何问题。调控可能影响当前良好投资环境的现行法律法规也是PIPA的职责之一。[①]

（2）巴勒斯坦工业园区及自由工业区管理局（PIEFZA）

PIEFZA具有以下作用：

① 制定巴勒斯坦工业园区及自由工业区的总体建设发展策略；

---

① The Palestinian Investment Promotion Agency's website.

② 就巴勒斯坦工业园区及自由工业区的建设、发展和管理事项向部长理事会建言献策；
③ 接受以建立工业项目为目的工业园区及自由工业区的申请，并将该申请提交到部长理事会；
④ 审查各方关于在工业园区和／或自由工业区工作许可的申请，向投资者发放自由工业区营业许可；
⑤ 直接或通过推销商开发工业园区和自由工业区；
⑥ 制定工业园区和自由工业区发展规划；
⑦ 建设工业园区和自由工业区或第三方所需的公共设施；
⑧ 确定该机构向工业园区和自由工业区提供服务的费用及征收规则；
⑨ 在不违反本法规定的前提下，签订合同、接受帮助及捐助；
⑩ 批准该机构的年度总预算，并告知相关部门；
⑪ 挑选推销商并与其签约；
⑫ 监督工业园区和自由工业区的表现与发展，并公布相关报告；
⑬ 尽力执行依据本法所签订的地方或区域协议。

（3）巴勒斯坦资本市场管理局（PCMA）

PCMA 是依据 2004 年第十三号法律建立的自治机构。其管辖范围包括证券、保险、金融抵押、金融租赁行业及其他非银行金融机构。

（4）巴勒斯坦标准测量所

该机构成立于 1994 年，自 1997 年开始运作。它是负责颁布巴勒斯坦标准的唯一机构，并被外界看作巴勒斯坦融入全球统一标准体系的关键机构。

2. 投资行业的相关法律法规

（1）1998 年第一号法律《投资促进法》及其修正案（加沙地带和约旦河西岸地区）

依据本法，巴勒斯坦或非巴勒斯坦公司或投资者享有的直接或间接的权利包括：

第二十二条　企业的固定资产享有下列免税额：

① 若 PIPA 核准一批企业的固定资产可以在其设定的期限内进口，则在 PIPA 规定的期限内免征关税；PIPA 可根据投资的性质和规模适当延长这一免税期限；

② 自生产和投资开始之日，在 PIPA 设定的生产或投资期限内，经 PIPA 批准的不超过企业固定资产 15% 价值的进口零配件免征关税；

③ 若 PIPA 认定企业生产能力提高，因扩大投资增加的企业固定资产应免征关税；

④ 若因原产国或运输的原因导致固定资产价值增长，则增值部分应免征关税。

第二十三条　经管理局批准的已依法取得营业许可的项目，应通过下列方式获得本法所定的奖励：

① 介于 10 万到 100 万美元的投资，在生产或进行运作后 5 年内免交所得税，并在免税期满后的 8 年内享有 10% 的净收入名义税率；

② 介于 100 万到 500 万美元的投资，在生产或进行运作后 5 年内免交所得税，并在免税期满后的 12 年内享有 10% 的净收入名义税率；

③ 500 万美元以上的投资，在生产或进行运作后 5 年内免交所得税，并在免税期满后的 16 年内享有 10% 的净收入名义税率；

④ 经管理局提议，部长董事会决议批准的定性重大私人项目，在生产或进行运作后 5 年内免交所得税，并在免税期满后的 20 年内享有 10% 的净收入名义税率。

第二十四条

① 若项目的工作范围、地理位置涉及公共利益、促进出口额增加、增加就业岗位、刺激社会发展，则经管理局提议、部长理事会决议批准，可以再增加累积不超过 5 年的免税期。

② 那些设立在工业区、偏远区或受定居点威胁的区域的项目可以指定免税期限。新工业区、偏远区或近居民区的范围应由部长理事会决议确定。

③ 不论何时，若机械、设备、供应品等超过 60% 的部分是来自本地，则项目的免税期应再额外增加 2 年。土地和建筑物的投资不应包括在这一比例中，管理局有权设定这个比例。

④ 政府可以给予国内投资者最优惠的政策或提供特殊奖励或保障。

第二十七条　对于现有项目的扩大，根据第 24 条中提到的由董事会在扩大项目开始生产时批准的资本投资价值，适用10%的名义税率征收所得税。此处的"扩大"是指增加新的固定资产的资本，而该固定资产的增加能反映项目中产品和服务产能的增加，或者制造用于替代进口的产品或提供新的服务或活动。

第二十八条 在第22条和第23条中所规定的免税期届满后，项目盈利应在原始资金的10%范围内免交所得税。依据本法规定，公开募股超过总股份40%的股份公司，前段所述的免税额度应为股东份额的20%名义税率。

第三十五条 已取得营业许可的项目所有人有权进行任何工业或出口活动，也可以进行许可范围内的其他活动。

第三十六条 若当地市场有类似的产品且在当地市场销售的产品所需的原材料适用海关费用和税收，则已取得营业许可的项目所有人可在当地市场销售不超过其项目总额20%的产品。

第三十七条 在自由工业区中已取得营业许可的项目所必需的商品和货物，当储存到仓库中时就应当被视为已进口到自由工业区。

第三十八条 从国外进口到自由工业区的所有的商品、原材料、必需品、机械和运输工具在自由工业区或其中的任何工业项目中使用时，都应免交关税及其他附加税。

第三十九条 进口至自由工业区的来自巴勒斯坦其他区域的本国货物或产品不受任何既有政策、税费或费用的限制。

第四十条 所有出口到境外的自由工业区内加工的货物或产品不受出口、出境税收或其他税收的法规措施限制。

第四十二条 除了其他法律保证的其他权利，取得营业许可的项目所有者可以自由调整产品的价格，可以在国内外购置必需的服务或货物，也可以自由处置项目的销售。

（2）2015年部长理事会《关于促进投资的第四号决议》（约旦河西岸地区）

第十条

① 促进局董事会可以依据政府发展规划确定的土地开发的优先顺序对巴勒斯坦土地进行分级。出于公共利益的考虑，需要对土地分级情况进行定期审查。

② 出于地理位置、当地出口额的巨大贡献、就业增加、推动发展、传播国际文化等公共利益项目的考虑，经部长理事会批准，董事会被授权为这些项目的协议提供除税收之外的其他奖励。

③ 在获得部长理事会的批准后，所有的官方机构和相关方都应坚持执行协议项下的奖励条款。

④ 激励协议可包括提供资源支持，基础设施服务及政府土地。

⑤ 促进局董事会在其权力范围内可被授权并无需部长理事会批准对已取得许可的投资项目进行物流和技术激励，例如培训和康复服务、职业经验建立、市场营销、参加本地和世界级博览会。

⑥ 大部分的激励合同应在官方公告上进行刊登，若协议已经得到批准，则刊登公告不是其生效的条件之一。

（3）2011年部长理事会《关于不动产投资的第一百七十四号决议》（加沙地带）

第四条 本决议所提及的不动产项目或其分项目应享有巴勒斯坦《不动产投资法》及其修正案所规定的免税及激励权益。投资者不得将政府土地抵押来为其项目融资。

第八条

① 一旦项目完成并交付政府部门在不动产项目中的份额，则政府部门将与相关方合作对分配给投资者的土地项目进行登记。

② 在不违反上述第1款的前提下，在投资者依据商定的时间表向有关部门交付每阶段项目份额后，应当允许该投资者根据项目进度对土地分阶段登记（阶段性所有权）。

第九条 在投资截止日前，项目若已运作，应提供给投资者每月项目价值5%的补贴。

第十条 阿拉伯或外国投资者应依据以下条款获准在巴勒斯坦拥有土地：

① 当地的巴勒斯坦合伙人至少持有51%的项目资产；

② 履行协议的所有条件；

③ 同意遵守巴勒斯坦法规；

④ 获得巴勒斯坦部长理事会的许可。

3. 投资形式

（1）《投资促进法》规定的投资领域

第三条　除特别法禁止，投资者可以依据本法对巴勒斯坦任何经济领域的项目进行投资。

第四条　投资项目应享有本法所提供的免税政策及优惠条件。除下列部门和领域需要征得部长理事会的批准外，其他所有投资领域都适用本法：

① 制造、分销武器、弹药或其零部件；
② 航空行业，包括机场；
③ 电力生产和分配；
④ 石油及其衍生物的再加工；
⑤ 垃圾和固体废物回收；
⑥ 电信；
⑦ 广播电视机构。

（2）巴勒斯坦投资促进局投资领域包括：

① 可再生能源；
② 信息通信技术；
③ 餐饮行业；
④ 纺织品和服装；
⑤ 旅游业；
⑥ 制药业；
⑦ 采石；
⑧ 农业；
⑨ 教育部门；
⑩ 建筑和房地产开发部门；
⑪ 证券业务。

4. 市场准入和审查标准

（1）如何在巴勒斯坦开展业务

巴勒斯坦投资促进局规定，外国投资者应按照下列步骤在巴勒斯坦开展经营：

- 注册企业（国民经济部）；
- 在增值税部门和所得税部门注册（财政部）；
- 在相关部门获得项目所需许可证；
- 在巴勒斯坦投资促进局获得投资登记和确认证书。

（2）1998年第十号法律《关于自由工业用地及园区的相关规定》

第三十条　在自由工业区从事工业活动必须取得在某个自由工业区作业的授权许可证书。

第三十一条　项目所有人向部门总经理申请获取自由工业区许可证书，总经理自收到申请后1个月内转交至董事会。董事会在收到申请后两周内进行处理，若拒绝申请应提供充分的理由。

第三十四条　自由工业区许可证书仅向巴勒斯坦境内在自由工业区作业的个人或机构颁发。

第四十三条　许可项目所有人应遵守下列规定：

① 不得从事本法第35条规定之外的其他业务。业务类型可依据相关部门的批准进行更改。
② 应相关部门要求提交任何文件、记录或账目以作统计。
③ 遵守自由工业区的一切规章制度，在自由工业区内提供安保。
④ 当企业家决定清算终结项目，应当在清算完成前3个月向PIEFZA机构提交书面通知。

第四十四条　项目所有人应自停工之日起6个月内无条件完成项目清算。若所有人在期限内没有完成清算，相关部门有权配合海关部门一起拍卖该项目，若项目上负有债务，应从拍卖价格中扣除，剩余金额应退还至所有人个人账户。

（二）外汇管理

1. 外汇监管部门

巴勒斯坦货币局负责外汇监管。

1997 年第 2 号法律第 61 条关于巴勒斯坦货币部的规定：

① 除国家货币外，所有其他货币均为外币；

② 依据《外汇管制法》和《货币交易法》，货币局应负责：

- 制定有关外汇管理的规章制度；
- 授予和撤销外汇经销商的经营许可。

2. 外国企业外汇管理要求

对于资金的进出口没有任何限制，可以以任何货币支付款项汇回本国。

居民和非居民均可持有任何币种的银行账户。

1998 年第十号法律《关于自由工业园区的相关规定》

第四十五条　在自由工业区内持有和交易外币不受任何限制，所有外币都可从自由工业区流入巴勒斯坦的任何地区，反之亦然。

第四十六条　自由工业区内的银行或其经批准的分支机构可以接受任何自然人或法人的任何外币，并为其开设账户。存款人有权在不受任何限制的情况下使用账户里的任何外币。

（三）金融融资

1. 主要金融机构

（1）负责金融机构的部门

① 巴勒斯坦货币部

货币部旨在保证银行业的平稳，维持货币稳定，并根据国家机构相关政策促进巴勒斯坦经济增长。它享有授予银行业务所需许可的专有权。

② 巴勒斯坦资本市场管理局（PCMA）

巴勒斯坦资本市场管理局依据 2004 年第十三号法律成立的自治机构，由 7 名成员组成的董事会管理。其管辖范围包括证券、保险、金融抵押、金融租赁以及其他非银行金融业务等领域。在过去的几年里，PCMA 主持着巴勒斯坦公司治理国家委员会的工作。

PCMA 在最近几年进行了大量关于改善内部工作环境的项目，并加强与公众的信息传播。

（2）1997 年第二号法律《关于巴勒斯坦货币部的规定》

巴勒斯坦货币部的权力包括：

① 发行、管理和维护货币部的债券，向个人、银行或其他方购买或发售债券，以实现其货币政策；

② 进行相关交易；

③ 向银行或其分支机构授予许可证，批准办事处的合并、关闭、开张及撤销执照；

④ 出售动产或不动产以支付到期债券；

⑤ 购买、租赁、出售和维护部门的建筑及设施；

⑥ 依据货币信用法来规范、控制、监督、保护流通中的银行票据和硬币；

⑦ 对所提供的服务进行适当收费；

⑧ 终止所有在本法颁布前进行的违反本法的活动。

第四十条

① 依据本法规定，只有在货币局颁发许可证后才能从事银行业务。经许可的银行应在货币局登记注册。许可决定应在官方公告报纸进行刊登。

② 货币局应制定相关规章制度。这些规章制度应经理事会提议后经国民政府主席决定后颁布，并在官方公告报纸进行刊登。

③ 前款规定设立的银行，如期经营期限不少于 3 年，则应依据该规定进行调整。货币局应提供相应的调整措施。

（3）2004年第十三号法律《关于PCMA的规定》

第三条　PCMA的目标、责任和职能：

资本市场部旨在创造适当环境，实现资本稳定增长，组织、发展和监控巴勒斯坦资本市场，保护投资者权益。为了实现这些目标，资本市场部应依据本法执行下列规定：

① 监督：
- 保证证券市场的正常运行；
- 保险业；
- 融资租赁业；
- 抵押贷款业。

② 组织、监测、监督非银行金融机构（包括证券交易所、非银行金融服务所）业务。
③ 发布关于非银行金融机构的所有数据和信息。
④ 监控非银行金融组织的发展以确保其业务的合法、合规性。

第二十五条　与其他部门合作
① 资本市场部应与巴勒斯坦从事监督管理金融机构的其他公共部门合作；
② 各部门、事业单位及政府单位工作人员应依法履行职责；
③ 资本市场部可参与处理关于证券市场监管的国家及国际组织业务。

（4）PCMA参与组织

巴勒斯坦资本市场部是下列组织的成员：
- 国际证监会组织（IOSCO）；
- 国际保险监督协会（IAIS）；
- 阿拉伯保险联合会，总部在埃及；
- 阿拉伯证券联盟（创始成员），总部在阿布扎比；
- 国际住房金融联盟（IUHF）；
- 儿童青少年金融国际（CYFI）；
- 国际金融教育网络（INFE）。

2. 外国企业融资条件

第五十五条　货币部在与财政部协调下，可以作为中间部门，按照《一般预算法》的规定向受益人提供来自国际金融机构和外国政府的资金。

第六十九条
① 巴勒斯坦货币部可通过向有资质的经济机构收集必要信息和数据来履行职责。
② 货币局应通过一项特别法，来划定其收集的信息和数据类型，提交信息和数据的第三方应一并提交信息的收集方式及保密形式。

（四）土地政策

1. 土地相关法律法规概况

（1）巴勒斯坦土地体制框架

巴勒斯坦土地部（PLA）成立于2002年。它现在是巴勒斯坦管控土地的唯一机构。巴勒斯坦相关法律规定，司法部的土地登记部门及房屋部的测量部门应归入土地部。巴勒斯坦相关法律规定，土地部的职权范围应由特别法规定，这一特别法尚未颁布。土地部现在是巴勒斯坦一个完全独立的土地维护机关。

巴勒斯坦土地部的任务是通过各地方及官方机构测量和登记的方式，保护土地财产权利及其他附随权利。其任务还包括处理土地划界争议，保护并妥善处置公共土地和财产。

国家土地处置：自1994年起，国家土地有多种处置方式，包括向建设、农业及旅游业的个人投资公司分配，向用于住房建设的个人分配。这些处置方式有许多问题产生，例如违法用地、向第三方出售土地、暗箱分配土地，这些行为都会导致纠纷。

（2）土地分级

宗教或慈善用地（Waqf）：土地所有者因宗教及慈善目的而捐献的土地，据说该类土地归神所有。这类土地由 Mutwally（即照料或者负责的人）管理。

完整所有权土地（Mulk）：土地所有者拥有绝对所有权的土地。

使用权可私有化的国有土地（Miri）：最终所有权归国家，但个人可以购买其使用权的土地。

国有土地（Metruke）：国家因公共利益而保留的土地。

废地（Mawat）：位于城镇外的、不具有生产能力的土地。这类土地已经不复存在。

公共用地（Public Land）：这一概念是由英国托管地引入的，受限于政府控制或者因公共目的而取得的土地。

（3）与土地相关的法律和规章
- 1993 年第七十八号法律 修订的《土地法》；
- 1928 年第九号法律《土地财产权力解决机制》；
- 2012 年第二十四号法律《民法》；
- 2001 年第二号法律《民商事诉讼法法典》；
- 1936 年第二十八号法律《城市规划法》；
- 2001 年第四号法律《民商事诉讼证据法》。

2. 外国企业获得土地的规定

（1）土地强制收购的方式和强制收购令的范围

需要特别注意，根据在加沙地带优先适用的法律，特别是被 1946 年第三十四号和四十六号法律修订的 1943 年第二十四号法律，尤其是其中的第 3 条和第 6 条授予最高执行官（如今该项权力由总统或总统授权的人行使）收购任何土地的所有权、占有权、地役权或在其上或据此能占有该等土地的其他任何权力。这项权力可以通过为公共目的收购土地或为公共使用征收土地。由两部法律规范该等行为：

① 1936 年第二十八号《城市规划法》

该法是由英国托管地政府签发。该法包含了政府为公共目的而进行征用行为的条文。这部法律目前仍然具有强制力。

② 1943 年的《土地（为公共目的收购）法令》（约旦河西岸地区和加沙地带）

该法由英国托管地政府签发，用于非市政目的，该法授予总执行官为公共使用而征用土地的权力。

收购定义为：因公共管理而授予其在提供公平赔偿作为对价的前提下，因公共利益而强制剥夺不动产所有者权力的特权。

需要注意的是，总统或总统授权的人具有前述英国托管地政府法律和规章授予的最高执行官的全部权力。

（2）2002 年《基本法》第 21 条的规定如下：

① 巴勒斯坦经济体系是建立在自由市场经济的原则上。执行分支可以依法设立公众公司；

② 经济活动的自由是有保障的。法律应当界定管理其监督权和相应的限制的规则；

③ 私人财产，包括不动产和动产受到保护，除根据法律或司法裁定因公共利益并给予合理赔偿的情况外，不得被征收征用；

④ 没收、征用应当依据司法裁定。

（3）土地争议

只要争议的不动产在巴勒斯坦境内而不论争议各方的国籍，巴勒斯坦普通法院有权审理所有与不动产、土地相关的所有纠纷和权利主张。

（五）企业的设立和解散

1964 年第十二号法律《公司法》及其修正案（约旦河西岸地区）

2012 年第七号法律《公司法》（加沙地带）

2012 年第七号法律《公司法》（加沙地带）规定的企业形式如下：

1. 普通合伙

（1）普通合伙的形式和注册
① 普通合伙是由 2～20 个自然人组成；
② 合伙人至少年满 18 周岁；
③ 普通合伙的合伙人应具有商人的全部行为能力并以合伙企业的名义从事商业活动。

（2）注册程序
申请注册合伙企业应当向官员递交申请书、全体合伙人签署的合伙协议原件和在官员面前亲自或授权他人签署的声明。声明也可以在公证员或律师面前签署。合伙协议及其备忘录应当包含：
① 合伙企业地址和交易名称，如有；
② 合伙人姓名、国籍、年龄及地址；
③ 合伙企业主要办公地址；
④ 合伙企业资本和合伙人份额；
⑤ 合伙企业目标；
⑥ 合伙期间，如有约定；
⑦ 被授权管理、代表合伙企业签署文件和行使权利的合伙人（们）的姓名；
⑧ 合伙人死亡、破产或不适格的合伙企业的状况；
⑨ 其他合伙人同意的声明。
官员应当自收到注册申请之日起 15 个工作日内批准合伙企业的注册。
合伙企业可以在多个地方设立分支机构。

（3）普通合伙的解散
普通合伙出现下列任一情形应予解散：
① 当全体合伙人同意解散合伙或同意与其他普通合伙合并的；
② 全体合伙人一致同意合伙协议约定原合伙期限或延长的合伙期限到期的；
③ 合伙企业设立目标完成的；
④ 只剩一名合伙人的；
⑤ 宣称合伙企业破产的，该合伙企业的破产导致合伙人的破产；
⑥ 除非剩余合伙人一致同意根据合伙协议保留合伙企业的，一个合伙人宣称破产或在法律上不适格的；
⑦ 法庭命令解散合伙的；
⑧ 根据官员决议取消合伙企业注册的。

2. 有限合伙

（1）合伙的形式和注册
有限合伙有两类股东组成，他们的名字应在合伙协议中列明：
① 普通合伙人：他们负责管理和运营合伙企业。他们以其全部私人财产对合伙企业的债务和责任承担连带责任。
② 有限合伙人：仅向合伙企业出资，但不享有管理和运营合伙企业的权利，他们的责任以其在合伙企业资本中所占的份额为限。
有限合伙的注册和清算与普通合伙相同。

（2）合资
合资类似于两人或两人以上组成的协会的商业运营组织。其中一名成员应当负责合伙的运营并明示地与他人进行交易。合资受限于各成员的特殊约定。
合资本身不是一个独立的法人实体并不受限于注册和许可。

3. 有限责任公司

（1）有限责任公司的形式和注册
• 有限责任公司有 2～50 名股东。每一股东以其出资额为限对公司的债务、义务和亏损承担责任。

- 经官员合理推荐，部长可允许注册一人有限责任公司。
- 有限责任公司的注册资本不得少于 50 000 约旦第纳尔（约合 70 500 美元），被分割为不少于 1 第纳尔的等额股份。但如果多个合伙人共同持有股份，无论何种原因，这些合伙人应当从中推选 1 名合伙人代表他们。如果合伙人不能达成一致或不能在他们成为合伙人之日起 30 日内完成推选，则公司经理或管理委员会有权从他们中推选人员作为他们的代表。
- 股东不能以劳务形式向公司出资。
- 有限责任公司不得公开认购股份或通过认购股份增加资本或借贷，也不得公开发行股份或可转换债券。

（2）注册程序

① 申请注册有限责任公司应按照批准的格式向官员提交申请书、公司章程、备忘录，并且在官员、官员授权的人、公证员或律师面前签署前述文件。

② 有限责任公司的备忘录应载明下列事项：
- 公司名称、目标和主要办事机构所在地；
- 股东名称、国籍和地址；
- 注册资本金总额和每个股东的股份；
- 关于股份数额、种类和持有股份的股东姓名和股份的估值的声明；
- 管理委员会的股东超过 7 人。

③ 公司章程必须包含上述②的全部信息及下列信息

管理公司的方式、管理委员会人员、他们的权力和关于管理委员会在借款、不动产抵押及提供担保方面的权力限制；
- 公司股份的转让条件、程序和转让的书面形式；
- 利润分配和损失承担的方式；
- 股东大会、法定人数、形成决议的法定人数和股东会程序；
- 关于公司清算的规则和程序；
- 其他股东设定或官员要求的附加信息。

（3）有限责任公司的管理

公司应当由经理或董事会管理，该董事会成员应当为 2~7 人，根据公司章程其任期不得超过 4 年。董事会应当选举主席和副主席。

经理和董事会在公司章程特别规定的限制内，享有管理公司的全部权力。

（4）有限责任公司的解散

有限责任公司应当根据临时股东会决议自愿清算或根据法律或法院命令强制解散。存在下列情形，有限责任公司应当自愿解散：
- 公司终止期限届满；
- 公司设立时的目标得以实现或没有实现的可能；
- 执行临时股东会决议解散或清算公司。

当总检察长或官员向法庭提交声明申请对公司强制清算时，有限责任公司应当强制清算：
- 公司严重违反法律和公司章程的；
- 公司没有履行职能的；
- 公司没有合法或正当理由停止营业一年的；
- 公司亏损超过其注册资本的 75% 的。

4. 股份有限合伙（Limited Partnership in Shares）

（1）股份有限合伙包含两类合伙人：
- 普通合伙人：普通合伙人不少于 2 人，以个人财产对合伙企业债务和义务承担责任。
- 有限合伙人：有限合伙人不少于 3 人，每位合伙人应当以持有的股份数额对合伙企业债务和义务承担责任。

股份有限合伙的出资额不少于 10 万约旦第纳尔。

（2）股份有限合伙的管理

股份有限合伙由一个或多个普通合伙人管理。

（3）股份有限合伙的清算

股份有限合伙应当以合伙企业章程决定的方式进行解散或清算。否则，其应当按照有限合伙的相关规定进行。

5. 持股公司

（1）公众持股公司应至少有2名发起人

公众持股公司应当永久存续，但如公司以完成某项商业为设立目标，而该目标完成时公司应予结束。

（2）持股公司类型

① 控股公司：控股公司是一个控制一个或多个子公司管理金融事务的公众持股公司。

② 对冲基金公司（联合投资公司）：该类公司的目标应当限定为以自有基金或第三方基金投资不同类型的证券及根据证券法组织其业务。

③ 离岸公司（豁免公司）：是指虽然在巴勒斯坦注册但在巴勒斯坦境外从事业务的公司。

（3）注册程序

公司发起人应当设立发起人委员会，发起人委员会应当由2～5人组成，委员会成员应负责在有权部门注册的流程。

发起人委员会应当向官员提交申请的同时，提交下列文件：

- 公司章程；
- 公司备忘录；
- 公司发起人姓名、名称；
- 监督设立流程的发起人委员会成员姓名。

持股公司的章程和备忘录应当包含下列信息：

- 公司名称；
- 主要办事机构；
- 公司目标；
- 公司发起人姓名、名称、国籍、地址、认购的股份；
- 注册资本和实际认缴的部分；
- 关于股份种类的声明和股份价值（如有）；
- 公司的财务年度。

（4）公众持股公司的管理

公众持股公司的管理被授予董事会，董事会成员为3～13人，由公司章程确定。

董事会主席可委任经理并决定其职权。董事会根据公司章程享有管理公司的全部权力。

（5）公众持股公司的解散

公众持股公司（或者）根据临时股东会决议解散（或者）根据法庭的命令或法律强制解散。存在下列情形，公众持股公司应当解散：

- 公司终止期限届满；
- 公司设立时的目标得以实现或没有实现的可能；
- 执行临时股东会决议解散或清算公司。

当总检察长或官员向法庭提交声明申请对公司强制清算时，公众持股公司应当强制清算：

- 公司严重违反法律和公司章程的；
- 公司没有履行职能的；
- 公司没有合法或正当理由停止营业一年的；
- 公司亏损超过其注册资本的75%的。

6. 外国公司

（1）在巴勒斯坦境内运营的外国公司

经营性外国公司是指一个公司或实体注册在巴勒斯坦境外且其主要经营机构在其他国家，则该公司国籍为非巴勒斯坦。外国公司或机构不得在巴勒斯坦境内从事任何商业业务，除非其依法取得许可后按照规定进行登记。

（2）非在巴勒斯坦境内运营的外国公司

非在巴勒斯坦运营的外国公司是指，在巴勒斯坦设有区域办公室或代表处，但其运营行为均发生于巴勒斯坦境外的，其区域办公室和代表处仅用于管理其运营行为和与总部合作的公司。

非在巴勒斯坦运营的外国公司禁止在巴勒斯坦境内从事任何经营和商业活动，包括运营商业机构和中介，否则其将被取消注册并负责赔偿因此对他人造成的损失和损害。

在非在巴勒斯坦运营的外国公司中，巴勒斯坦籍的雇员不少于总雇员的半数。

（3）外国公司在巴列斯坦注册分支机构的法律要求

- 一份章程及阿拉伯文翻译件（章程及翻译件均需巴勒斯坦在当地的代表处认证）；
- 一份章程细则及阿拉伯文翻译件（细则及翻译件均需巴勒斯坦在当地的代表处认证）；
- 一份登记证书阿拉伯文翻译件（证书及翻译件均需巴勒斯坦在当地的代表处认证）；
- 由律师（公司代理人）代为完成的申请并提交给国家经济部；
- 向本所提交的从事登记业务的授权委托书（授权委托书需经巴勒斯坦在当地的代表处认证）；
- 公司签发的授权其职员在加沙地区管理公司运营的授权委托书（授权委托书需经巴勒斯坦在当地的代表处认证）；
- 公司董事会成员的个人身份证件或护照复制件；
- 公司分支机构在加沙经营场所的租赁合同或买卖合同。

（4）外国公司分支机构在巴勒斯坦开立银行账户的法律要求

- 分支机构在巴勒斯坦的注册证书；
- 公司据以要求在银行开立账户的公司董事会决议和银行账户签字人名单；
- 公司董事会授权某人管理账户的授权；
- 账户签字人和管理人的护照。

（六）收购兼并

根据合伙协议并遵从公司注册和公司变更的法律程序，普通合伙和有限合伙可以互相转化。

根据法律规定，有限责任公司和股份有限合伙可以转化为持股公司。申请转化应当向官员提交申请及下述文件：

① 公司股东（或合伙人）会议批准公司形式转化的决议；

② 基于公司状况的经济和金融研究而得出的公司形式转换的理由和原因，及转换完成后的当年公司状况的变化；

③ 如果公司的平均年净利润不少于公司实缴注册资本的15%，则需要申请公司形式转换前连续3年的年度资产负债表；

④ 公司注册资本已经全部实缴的声明；

⑤ 公司预估其财产和责任的声明书。

1. 公司合并

如果希望合并的公司的目标是一致且相互补充的，上述公司的合并应当通过下列任一方式完成：

① 与一家或多家其他公司合并的成为并购方，被并购公司应当消失，其公司主体也将不复存在；

② 与一家或多家公司合并而设立作为合并结果的新的公司，则公司和公司主体都将不复存在；

③ 外国公司在巴勒斯坦的分支机构和代理与以本次合并为目的设立的巴勒斯坦公司合并的，前述分支机构和代理应当消失，其公司主体也将不复存在。

并购中的被并购方及其股东和并购方应当免于缴纳因并购或其结果产生的所有税费。

2.《投资法》规定的投资项目受限于收购兼并因根据投资法规定而获得投资激励

第二十九条

① 只要项目按照已有项目继续运营，则项目获益的投资激励可以适当的全部转让给新的所有者而没有任何限制。

② 只要新的项目所有者按照已有项目继续运营，则新的项目所有者可以享受投资激励。

第三十条　合并、混合公司和重组及分立公司或形式转化的公司应当享有在合并、分立、变换前已经享受的豁免直到它的豁免终止。合并、分立和变化不应当产生新的税收豁免。

第三十三条　如果激励政策进行修订，因激励政策受益的项目应当有权在修订后的激励政策或修订前有效的激励政策中选择适用对其最有利的。

第三十四条　如果项目在享受豁免期间从一个发展区域转移到另一发展区域，只要通知了主管当局，则该项目应当在剩余的期限内为了豁免之目的享受类似的豁免。

（七）税收

1. 税收管理体制和规则

（1）巴勒斯坦管理税收的部门

① 财政部；

② 所得税主管机关；

③ 增值税主管机关。

（2）税收法律和法规

① 2011 年第八号法律《关于所得税及其修正的法令》（约旦河西岸地区）；

② 2004 年第十七号《所得税法》（加沙地区）。

2. 主要的税收类别和税率

（1）个人所得税

① 纳税人注册

从事经营和投资活动的自然人有义务自其开始投资和从事经营活动之日起向税务部门登记。

② 税务年度

纳税人的税务责任以日历年为基础计算。

③ 税项和税率

巴勒斯坦居民税率如下：

年度所得税（约旦河西岸地区/单位：新以色列谢克尔）

- 年度收入为 1～40 000 谢克尔的税率为 5%；
- 年度收入为 40 001～80 000 谢克尔的税率为 10%；
- 年度收入超过 80 000 谢克尔的税率为 15%。

年度所得税（加沙地区/单位：美元）

- 年度收入为 1～10 000 美元的税率为 8%；
- 年度收入为 10 001～16 000 美元的税率为 12%；
- 年度收入超过 16 000 美元的税率为 16%。

（2）公司所得税税率

- 居所：如果一个公司注册在巴勒斯坦境内或其在巴勒斯坦境内进行管理活动则被视为纳税居民。
- 巴勒斯坦公司的经营基本使用 15% 的所得税税率。
- 寿险公司适用降低为 5% 的税率。
- 电讯公司和享有特权或垄断的公司适用 20% 的税率。
- 亏损、设备折旧和经营费在计算所得税是被考虑在内。

（3）增值税

增值税是以消费为基础设立在货物销售、服务提供和进口的税种，税率为 16%。

关于公司向增值税和所得税主管部门注册的要求：
- 公司注册登记证复印件；
- 公司注册摘要；
- 公司在巴勒斯坦经营场所的租赁合同；
- 公司授权人的护照；
- 公司活动和运营的简介；
- 公司账户信息；
- 公司税收豁免的复印件。

（4）公司税务声明和意向

① 有义务提交税务声明的类别
- 每一纳税人应当提交由资料和必要信息支持的税务声明，且声明和其他信息受限于评估人的审查。
- 根据所适用的投资立法规定享受所得税豁免的人应当提交税务声明。
- 公司的清算人应当以书面形式通知税务部门开始清算程序的时间并证明公司税务责任的金额，同时还应当代表公司提交税务声明陈述公司正在进行清算且其有义务在税务到期后尽快支付。
- 部长根据董事的推荐，可签发指示允许某些类别的自然人豁免提交税务声明。

② 提交税务声明的日期

每个纳税人有义务在税务期间结束后的 4 个月内提交纳税声明，载明纳税人的毛收入、抵扣、净收入、豁免、可纳税收入和相应税务期间的税务责任。

在指定期限提交纳税声明及附件的纳税人针对到期的税额可被授予如下进一步的税收折扣：
- 如果税务声明是在税务期间结束后 1 个月提交且在当月或声明涵盖的纳税期间已经完成纳税的，可享受 4% 的折扣；
- 如果税务声明是在税务期间结束后第 2 或第 3 个月提交且在前述第 3 个月末前或声明涵盖的纳税期间已经完成纳税的，可享受 2% 的折扣。

③ 税务声明附件

纳税人需要与声明共同提交下列附件：
- 纳税年度的最终账目复制件；
- 具有资格的审计师资格证书和经该审计师批准的以纳税为目的修订报告复制件；

有义务保存准确账目的普通公司和个人应当根据所适用的法律和规章以纳税为目的附带最终账目和修订报告。

上述提到的纳税人之外的其他纳税人应当在其纳税报告中明确可纳税净收入并提交简短声明说明他们在纳税期间的收入和花费。

（八）证券交易

当巴勒斯坦证券交易所作为私人公司于 1995 年设立时，证券业务在巴勒斯坦出现。除提供监管、交易、交割和转让证券的最新电子系统外，巴勒斯坦证券交易所从设立之初便开始提供一整套用于组织巴勒斯坦证券工作的规则和规章。证券交易所自设立之日至 2005 年资本市场管理局设立前归财政部管理。

2004 年第十二号法律《证券法》和第十三号法律《资本市场管理局法》[①] 签发

2010 年 2 月为回应公开透明原则以及实现公司的优化治理，巴列斯坦证券交易所经资本市场管理局许可变更为公众持股公司。

1. 有关证券的法律和法规简介

（1）2004 年第十二号《证券法》

根据 2004 年第十二号法律《证券法》和第十三号法律《资本市场管理局法》，巴勒斯坦证券业务包括下列由资本市场管理局监管和控制的实体：

---

① 参见 http://www.pcma.ps/portal/english/Securities/Pages/Sector-Overview.aspx。

- 巴勒斯坦交易所和登记结算中心；
- 公众持股公司；
- 巴勒斯坦交易所成员证券公司；
- 金融执业者；
- 投资基金。

（2）法律范围

法律适用于：
- 证券交易所、授权成员和从事证券交易的人的活动及经资本市场管理局授权的任何新型活动；
- 在其中的证券发行及交易；
- 证券公司、投资顾问、金融经理、投资者、证券专家、登记结算中心、基金管理人、托管服务、发行人、主要持有人和任何主管当局授权的活动适用本法。

（3）证券的含义
- 证券意味着经主管当局批准的所有权和债权工具，而无论其是国内或国外。
- 证券包括：股份和债券；
- 根据投资计划发行的投资单位；
- 包括可转换股份和债券、销售和购买选择权合同在内的衍生品；
- 期货和商品。

（4）登记证券的所有权

证券在登记中心登记不视为登记中心或证券交易所占有该证券。

外国证券在取得主管部门批准并按规定在外国中心登记的，中心可以作为该外国证券的登记人。

（5）许可要求

任何人在从事证券中间人业务或成为金融投资顾问前，应当取得主管部门的许可并在证券交易所登记。

持有许可的证券公司可以从事投顾问业务而无需取得附加许可，但是投资顾问在未取得附加许可的情况下，禁止从事任何只有证券公司才能开展的业务。

任何个人在作为基金管理顾问或其他证券执业人员从事业务前，必须从主管当局取得许可并在证券交易所注册。

禁止证券公司或投资顾问雇佣任何人作为基金管理人、金融顾问或在证券交易所执业的专业人员，除非该人已经取得主管当局的许可并在证券交易所注册。

主管当局应当签发指引，说明取得许可的程序、适格条件和最低注册资本要求、财务状况、管理、职业和技术要求。

主管当局可以授权证券交易所为申请取得从事基金顾问、财务顾问、证券从业人员颁发许可，并准备和监督作为许可先决条件的考试。

主管当局可以授权证券交易所确保这些个人在许可的期间拥有所需的资格和能力。

证券交易所可以要求主管当局暂停或取消证券交易所、投资顾问或其他基金管理人、财务顾问和证券从业人员在证券行业的许可，只要该要求是合理的。

2. 监督和管理证券市场

证券业务是在2005年依据2004年第十二号法律《证券法》和第十三号法律《资本市场管理局法》设立的，由巴勒斯坦资本市场管理局监督管理，目的是规范、监督和发展证券业务及其他非银行金融因素。

证券业务包括股份在巴勒斯坦证券交易所挂牌的公司，他们中的绝大多数是盈利的。这些公司被分为五大类经济因素：银行和金融服务、保险、投资、工业和服务。股票使用约旦第纳尔和美元进行交易。

如何在巴勒斯坦向证券业务投资：

① 在一家有资质的中介开立账户；

② 以电话、传真或电子邮件的方式向中介设定买卖指令；

③ 可进行网上交易。

3. 外国公司从事证券交易的要求

根据巴勒斯坦证券交易所的指引，一个公司开立账户要求提供下列文件（原件的真实复制件）：
- 公司注册登记证；
- 章程；
- 章程细则；
- 公司授权签字人的个人身份证明；
- 发送给中介的带有公司抬头纸的信函，说明公司授权签字人的姓名；
- 填妥中介的交易开户申请；
- 任何巴勒斯坦证券交易所要求提供的任何文件。

所有上述文件应当以阿拉伯文或英文填写，否则文件应由司法部有资质且宣誓过的翻译人员翻译成阿拉伯文。

（九）投资优惠和投资保护

1. 优惠政策的框架

没有关于优惠政策的特别法律、法规或指令。其他法律法规中的相关规定有：

（1）1998年第一号法律《投资促进法》

第六条
- 任何投资者都不应因任何理由而被排除使用依据本法授予的特权。
- 国家主管当局可以根据双边或多边贸易协定，或者国家主管当局与其他国家在不歧视第三方权利和适用互惠原则的条件下签订的投资协议，依国籍对投资者授予"最优惠地位"。

① 对特定产业和区域的支持

在出口产品不少于总产品的30%且根据特殊规章标准制作，同时，增加免税期不超过3年的前提下，主管当局可以给予出口导向型项目特殊的豁免。

② 海关和税收的特殊豁免
- 为宾馆和医院而进口的家具应当豁免关税和其他税（种）；
- 为旅游项目，包括宾馆，而进口的电力和电子器械及设备应当豁免关税和其他税（种）；
- 为医院而进口的电力和电子器械和设备应当豁免关税和其他税（种）；
- 宾馆和医院项目应当就其购买家具、装备、电力和电子器械和装备以及为现代化和创新而所需供给，享受每5年一次额外豁免，只要它们被认可进入巴勒斯坦或从签发批准购买清单和数量之日起2年内被使用到项目中。

第四十三条　除下列例外之外，所有的投资应当享受本法所给予的激励：商业项目、保险、不动产（开发项目除外）、银行、货币兑换公司、任何金融机构（只有不动产抵押除外）。

（2）2017年部长理事会第六号法律《关于规范以鼓励投资为目的的在可再生能源技术领域的激励打包合同的决定》（约旦河西岸地区）

第四条　电站激励措施

电站：任何使用可再生资源发电的电站，包括建筑物、设施、附属土地和为此目的而使用的机器设备。

在经批准的区域实施的容量不少1百万瓦特的电站，应当享受下列激励：

第一阶段：自电站运营之日起7年内，所得税为零。
第二阶段：第一阶段结束之日起5年内，所得税税率为5%；
第三阶段：第二阶段结束之日起3年内，所得税税率为10%；
第三阶段结束后，所得税依据当时适用且有效的税率计算。

2. 巴勒斯坦特殊投资区

- 杰里科工业和农业区；

- 加沙工业区；
- 伯利恒工业区；
- 杰宁工业区。

3. 投资保护

1998 年第一号法律《投资促进法》

第七条　除根据法院裁判外，项目不得被国有化或征用，资金也不得被限制、查封、冻结、征用或者处置。

第八条　项目的不动产所有权不得被全部或部分征用，除非根据法律公共利益而为之，且需要以赔偿在市场价值基础上确定的不动产价值和因征用而遭受的全部损失为对价。

第九条　除主管当局根据本法有关规定撤销项目批准外，非经采用主管当局意见，其他主管部门无权全部或部分撤销因项目使用而授予不动产的许可，主管当局应当自被要求发表意见之日起最多 7 日内明确提出。除非由于法律原因或公共利益，许可证不得取消；若取消，则应基于不歧视的方式，并向受到损害的投资者提供所有合法手段，以通过法院主张其因取消许可而遭受的损失。

第十条　在遵守本法第十一条之规定且遵循自由市场经济的前提下，国家主管当局确保所有投资者将其金融资源转移除巴勒斯坦，包括资本、利润、股息和资本收益、工资、利息、债权支付、管理费、技术协助及其他费用和因征收、取消许可、法庭决定、仲裁裁决和任何其他形式的支付或金融资源。

投资者可以依当时在市场上现行有效且占主导的汇率，自由地用投资者可接受的货币将其金融资源转移出巴勒斯坦。

第十一条　如果下列限制情形适用投资者，则国家主管部门可以对投资者转移金融资源或部分金融资源予以限制：
- 巴勒斯坦破产法和其他为保护债权人权利的巴勒斯坦法律；
- 巴勒斯坦关于证券发行和交易的法律；
- 巴勒斯坦刑法；
- 巴勒斯坦税法；
- 巴勒斯坦关于现金转移通知或者其他货币工具的法律；
- 巴勒斯坦法院或仲裁机构作出的禁止令或最后判决。

三、贸易

（一）贸易监管部门

国民经济贸易部贸易总局和过境处由三个部门组成：
- 贸易部；
- 过境处；
- 专利和商业机构。

（二）巴勒斯坦标准和测量机构

1. 贸易法律法规简介
- 1996 年第十二号《商法》（约旦河西岸地区）；
- 2014 年第二号《商法》（加沙地带）；
- 2000 年第六号巴勒斯坦《标准和测量法》；
- 2000 年的第二号有关规范商业机构工作的法律。

2. 贸易管理

（1）贸易部有下列职权：
- 就所有与贸易和口岸有关的运营和战略问题提出建议；

- 跟踪出口程序；
- 跟进并签发出口许可证；
- 执行对外贸易协议；
- 为进口流程提供一切所需文件及许可证。

（2）专利和商业机构具有以下职权：
- 注册专利、商标和商业机构；
- 保护有关专利、商标和商业机构的权利；
- 处理有关专利、商标和商业机构的争议。

（3）巴勒斯坦标准和测量机构具有以下职权：
- 拟定并通过与商品、材料、服务和其他物品有关的巴勒斯坦标准和测量标准，审查、修订、替换或公布相关标准和测量标准。该机构的职权范围不包括人用和兽用药物、疫苗和血清；
- 开发国家测量系统；
- 除校准和调整测量工具外，统一和开发测量方法；
- 签发委员会批准的合格标志和证书；
- 采用国家主要计量基准对测量工具进行校准，以便在测量工具上加盖印章或贴上标签；
- 批准合格和专门对商品和其他材料进行测试和分析的测试及校准范围，以适用相关标准和测量；
- 批准产品标签；
- 与地方政府机构和科研机构合作，以实现该机构的目标并履行其职能职责；
- 支持和鼓励在经批准的测试和检验实验室进行与标准、测量和质量控制有关的研究，并举办与该机构工作范围有关的培训班和方案；
- 与阿拉伯、区域和国际机构签订关于相互承认合格标志和证书的协定，但此类协定必须包括一项关于先前和继续测试协定所载材料的协定，以确保协定确认符合已通过的技术标准和条件；
- 与在标准和测量领域工作的阿拉伯、区域和国际机构合作和协调，并加入这些机构；
- 出版和分发与该机构或其他阿拉伯、区域或国际有关机构发布的标准和测量有关的出版物。

（三）注册商业机构

任何商业代理必须在所有有关各方签署协议之日起3个月内，在登记处登记所有商业代理协议。

（四）商业机构协议中应履行的条款

商业机构的协议必须以书面形式记录，并必须包括以下信息：
- 代理人的姓名、年龄、国籍、商号和居住地（住所）；如果代理人是公司，则必须包括其注册号码；
- 授予人的名称（姓名）、年龄、国籍、商号和居住地（住所）；
- 该协议的生效日期和期限必须涵盖所有巴勒斯坦的地区；
- 该协议所涵盖的产品；
- 支付给商业代理的销售佣金价值；
- 承诺为汽车、机器、电机或电气和电子设备和设备提供足够的配件和必要的维修；
- 商品或服务商标和专利；
- 代理人与授予人商定的任何其他条款。

（五）进出口商品的检验和检疫

国民经济部贸易总局与过境处具有以下职权：
- 控制过境点商品进出口的流动；
- 控制和检查过境点商品的流动；
- 适用巴勒斯坦关于商业机构的标准和衡量及保护的法律。

（六）海关管理

1962年第一号法律《海关法》及其修正案规定，所有进口到巴勒斯坦的商品均须缴纳关税。除按照本条例或其他法律之规定或者任何协定予以豁免外，应当按照关税征收关税。

四、劳动

（一）劳动法律法规简介

- 2000年第七号法律《劳动法》（加沙地带和约旦河西岸地区）。
- 劳动部和部长会议决定（约41项决定）。这些决定大部分涉及2000年第七号法律《劳动法》条款。
- 2016年关于社会保障的第六号法令（约旦河西岸地区）。

1. 基本定义

雇主：每一个自然人或法人或其代表，雇用一人或多人，应支付劳动报酬。
雇员：每个自然人为雇主工作以换取劳动报酬，并应在其工作期间接受雇主的管理和监督。
短期工作：工作的性质、实施的性质和完成需要有限定的期限。
临时工作：偶然条件下需要的工作，其完成时间不超过3个月。
季节性工作：在每年的周期性季节中实施和完成的每项工作。
基本工资：雇主支付给劳动者的现金和/或实物报酬，以换取其为雇主工作。任何种类的加薪和津贴均不包括在内。
薪金：全额薪金，即加薪和津贴的基本工资。

2. 个人劳动合同

个人劳动合同应当是雇主与雇员之间在有限的或者无限的时间内或者为完成特定的工作而订立的明确或者默示的书面或者口头协议，根据该协议，劳动者应当承诺为雇主的利益和在其管理和监督下从事工作；雇主应承诺支付与劳动者商定的工资。

3. 劳动合同的最长期限

同一雇主有期限的劳动合同的最长期限不得超过连续2年，包括续订的情况。如果劳动合同包括续约期限，合同将被视为无限期。

4. 试用期

劳动合同可以实行试用期，期限为3个月，同一用人单位只能实行一次。

5. 个人劳动合同期满

个人劳动合同在下列情形中任何一种情况下均应终止：
① 经双方同意。
② 在短期的、临时的或季节性的工作期满时。
③ 试用期内任何一方的意愿。
④ 根据雇员的意愿，只要提前以书面形式通知到雇主：
 • 如果雇员以前每个月都按月领取薪水，则需要提前1个月的时间；
 • 如果雇员过去以每天或每周或基于计件或佣金的方式赚取工资，则需要提前1周的时间。
⑤ 根据医务委员会发布的医疗报告，雇员死亡，或其受到感染而导致疾病或残疾、致使其无法工作的时间超过6个月，并且雇员的职业能力和新的健康状况不胜任空缺职位。

6. 不经通知终止劳动合同

雇员有下列行为之一的，雇主有权不经通知单方面终止劳动合同，同时保留雇主对雇员进行剩余索取的权力：
① 假冒他人向雇主提交虚假证件或文件；

② 雇员确实因疏忽所犯错误，造成雇主的严重损失，但雇主应在知晓的 48 小时内向主管当局报告该事件；

③ 雇员虽已收到适当的形式的警告，却仍多次违反劳动部批准的或者书面指示有关劳动安全、工人卫生的规定；

④ 如果雇员在同一年度内无正当理由连续旷工超过 7 天，或累计超过 15 天缺席，前提是前一种情况劳动者在旷工 3 天内被以书面形式提出警告，在后一种情况下为 10 天内；

⑤ 雇员虽已收到适当形式的警告，但仍未履行其在工作合同规定的义务；

⑥ 泄露与工作有关的秘密，可能造成严重损害；

⑦ 雇员因违反荣誉、信任或社会公德的罪行和违法行为最终判决成立；

⑧ 雇员在工作时间内处于醉酒状态或受消耗麻醉药物影响，应受法律惩处；

⑨ 以殴打或蔑视雇主或其代表或其直属经理的方式进行攻击。

7. 因技术原因或损失而终止劳动合同

因根据法律或亏损有必要减少雇员数量时，雇主可以终止劳动合同，但前提是，雇员有权得到通知并被支付劳动期满的补偿金，且雇员得到通知。

8. 劳动终止的补偿金

工作满 1 年的雇员，有权获得终止劳动补偿金，其数额为雇员在工作中所获得 1 个月的工资，以最后 1 个月的工资为标准，但不计额外工作时间。

9. 计件工作的劳动终止的补偿金

服务期届满的报酬和任意解雇劳动者的补偿金，应按最后 1 年期间的月平均工资，通过计件或佣金计算。

10. 不正当终止劳动关系的惩罚（仲裁驳回）

除维护其所有其他合法权利外，雇员每工作 1 年应有权获得 2 个月工资的任意解雇报酬，但前不得超过 2 年的工资。

11. 辞职致劳动终止的补偿金

- 如果雇员工作期限不满 5 年，其有权获得劳动终止的补偿金的 1/3。
- 如果雇员工作期限为 5 至 10 年，则其有权获得劳动终止的补偿金的 2/3。
- 如果雇员工作期限满 9 年或 10 年以上，则其有权获得全部劳动终止的补偿金。

12. 定期合同劳动者的权利

定期劳动合同的雇员，包括临时工合同或者季节性劳动合同的雇员，在类似情况下享有与无限期劳动合同规定的雇员相同的权利和义务，同时应参考与有限、临时和季节性工作有关的规定。

13. 工作时间

每周实际工作时间应不超过 45 小时。

危险职业或危害健康的职业以及夜间工作的每日工作时间应减少至少 1 小时。这类职业应由部长与雇主和雇员的有关组织商议后作出界定。

考虑到雇员不能连续工作 5 小时，因此每日工作时间必须包括一段或多段时间供雇员休息（总计不超过 1 小时）。

14. 额外的工作时间（加班）

生产方可同意每周不超过 12 小时的额外工作时间。

每增加 1 小时工作时间，应向雇员支付 1.5 小时的报酬。

15. 每周假日

每周五为休息日，除非由于工作的利益需要另安排一天作为定期休息日。

16. 年假

- 雇员有权享受带薪年假，职工假期为每年 2 周，从事有害职业或有害健康的工作，以及已在该单位工作满 5 年的职工享有 3 周的带薪年假。
- 雇员不得放弃年假。
- 根据生产双方的协议，年假可以分割。
- 年假累计不得超过 2 年。

17. 宗教节日及法定假日

雇员有权在宗教节日及法定假日期间休带薪假，但不得从年假中扣除。

18. 朝圣宗教假期

因执行朝圣宗教任务（前往沙特阿拉伯麦加市圣地朝圣），在单位工作满 5 年的雇员有权享受带薪假，应一次性给予职工不少于两周假期。

19. 死亡或意外因由的请假

- 如果亲属发生二级死亡，雇员享有 3 天的带薪假期，且该假期不得从其年假中扣除。
- 每年雇员可因某一特定原因缺勤 10 天，从年假中扣除，但一次请假的连续天数不得超过 3 天。

20. 病假

根据医务委员会的报告，雇员有权在一年内享受 14 天的全薪病假及另外 14 天的半薪病假。

21. 职业安全卫生

就业单位应公布职业安全和卫生指示以及经劳动部批准的处罚细则。此类指示应张贴在就业单位的醒目位置。

22. 性别歧视

严禁性别歧视。

23. 产假

（1）分娩前就职超过 180 天的处于工作状态的妇女有权休 10 周带薪产假，其中包括分娩后至少 6 周的带薪产假。

（2）不得因上文第（1）款所述休假而解雇处于工作状态的妇女，除非证明她在此期间受雇于另一职业。

24. 最低工资限额

2012 年部长理事会第 11 号决定：

雇员的工资不得低于法定最低工资限额。

据巴勒斯坦劳动部称，最低工资为 1 450 新谢克尔（约合 400 美元）。

每日的最低工资为 65 新谢克尔（约 18.5 美元）。

每小时最低工资为 8.5 新谢克尔（约合 2.4 美元）。

25. 劳动监察

根据《劳动法》，劳动部长应设立一个由足够多具有学术和专业资格的视察员组成的委员会，称为"劳动监察委员会"，并根据该法颁布的条例贯彻执行本法的规定。

劳动监察委员会成员在行使职责时应享有司法警察的权力。

（二）雇用外国员工的规定

1. 工作许可

劳动部有权为非巴勒斯坦人颁发在巴勒斯坦工作的许可证。禁止雇主在确认获得上述许可证之前，以直接方式或通过第三方雇用任何非巴勒斯坦雇员。

应当指出，《劳动法》的规定也适用于外国雇员。

2. 申请程序

- 获得巴勒斯坦内政部批准；

- 获得巴勒斯坦劳动部批准。

3. 社会保险

（1）工伤和职业病

雇主必须为其在巴勒斯坦许可方工作的职员提供工伤保险。

（2）雇主对工伤事故责任

发生工伤时，雇主必须履行下列义务：

- 向伤者提供必要的急救，并将其送往最近的（医疗）治疗中心；
- 当发生任何损伤导致雇员死亡或造成身体伤害而无法继续工作时，立即向警方报告；
- 从事故发生之日起48小时内，通知卫生部和保险公司书面处理每一件工伤事故。应交给受伤者一份通知副本。

雇主应负责下列事项：

- 在受伤雇员痊愈之前对其进行治疗，并支付所有临时治疗费用，包括康复服务和必需品；
- 所有因损害而产生的开支应由雇主承担，即使他们援引第三方的赔偿责任。

（三）出入境

1. 签证类型

请注意，目前没有进入巴勒斯坦领土的具体签证类型。进入巴勒斯坦的情况如下：

（1）约旦河西岸地区

- 阿伦比桥：（在以色列控制下，位于约旦和西岸之间）经约旦进入约旦河西岸地区。
- 从以色列（本·古里安机场）出发：经以色列过境到约旦河西岸地区。

（2）加沙地带

① 拉法过境点：经埃及过境加沙地带。该过境点每3~4个月开放2~3天（每年总计约12天），据估计，每一天的乘客人数为500~700人。

② 埃雷兹过境点（在以色列控制下的加沙和以色列之间的过境点）。

- 阿伦比桥：经约旦过境到西岸，然后经埃雷兹过境点过境加沙。
- 从以色列（本·古里安机场）出发：过境到以色列，然后经埃雷兹过境点过境加沙。

（3）投资者访问巴勒斯坦许可证

巴勒斯坦投资促进局（PIPA）可以给予投资者访问许可证，以便进入巴勒斯坦领土，详情如下：

① 签发投资者访问许可证的规定

- 护照的扫描副本（有效期至少6个月）；
- 个人照片；
- 巴勒斯坦有关机构的配套文件（如果投资者已在其公司注册或在巴勒斯坦机构投资）；
- 关于潜在投资的概述；
- 以往任何投资（巴勒斯坦境内或境外）摘要；
- 财产概述（巴勒斯坦境内或境外）；
- 预计访问日期；
- 联系方式。

② 申请投资者访问许可证的程序

根据PIPA的要求，投资者需要一封求职信，其中包括拟议投资的摘要和附件清单。然后，这些文件连同求职信应在预计访问日期的45天前提交给PIPA。此外，此类请求可于PIPA的网站（http://www.pipa.ps/elogin.php）提交。

2. 出入境限制

通过过境点进入以色列控制下的加沙地带和约旦河西岸地区需经以色列当局批准。

（四）工会和劳工组织

1. 建立工会组织

根据该法的规定，雇员和雇主有权组成专业的工会组织，以维护其权益。

2. 巴勒斯坦工业联合会

巴勒斯坦工业联合会的目标是支持巴勒斯坦民族工业，并通过以下方式保护它们免遭倾销和不公平竞争：

- 通过引导国内外投资，引进现代产业体系，发展民族工业。
- 通过专门的工会，根据工业生产的类型对工业活动进行管制，并向它们提供必要的支持。
- 努力提高国家工业产品竞争力。

（五）劳动争议

1. 劳动争议费用

劳动者在劳动诉讼中免缴司法费用，因为他们是因劳动终止的工资、休假和报酬、工伤赔偿或任意解雇有关的争议而提出的诉讼。

2. 利于员工的特别规定

本法规定的条款应表明不得免除职工权利的最低限额。凡劳动关系中存在特别规定的，对雇员有利的本法的规定或特别规定条款均适用于雇员。

3. 集体劳动争议

集体劳动争议是一个或多个雇主与雇员或其群体之间为集体利益而产生的纠纷。

五、知识产权

（一）知识产权法律法规简介

1938 年第三十五号《商标法令》（加沙地带）

1952 年第一号《商标细则》（约旦河西岸地区）

商标：指在商品上或与商品有关而使用或拟使用的标志，目的是表明该等商标的所有人凭借制造、选择、核证或要约出售且属该商标所有人的商品。

商标部门：从属国家经济部的一个部门，负责商标注册和管理过程。

注册记录：所有商标的记录应包括所有注册商标及其所有人的名称、地址和说明、转让和移交通知、免责声明、条件、限制以及与不时规定的商标有关的其他事项。

注册官：被任命为国家经济部商标部门负责人的官员。

（二）商标注册

1. 商标注册过程包括以下三个阶段：

（1）填写商标申请：本阶段包括向注册官提交一份申请，其中包括提交商标所需的所有信息和要求，包括：

- 商标所有人的名称；
- 商标所有人的商标地址；
- 商标类别；
- 商标名称，如果商标是一个图案的，将通过电子邮件发送（标明是黑白的还是彩色的）；
- 由商标所有人签署并盖章的有效授权书，该授权书必须是合法的且经过公证的。

（2）公示：商标在官方公告上公布（大约 6 至 9 个月）之后，就有机会对任何已公布的商标提出异议。从商标在官方公告上公布之日起，可提出异议的期限为 3 个月。

（3）最终注册：商标所有人（代理人）在 3 个月的反诉期限届满后，可以要求取得商标的最终注册证书。

2. 可注册为商标的标志
- 能够注册的商标必须由具有鲜明特征的字符、图案、标志或其组合组成；
- 就本条而言，"独特"指经修改以区分商标所有人的商品与其他人的商品；
- 注册官或法院在决定商标是否合适时，如属实际使用的商标，可考虑该使用人在多大程度上使该商标对其注册或拟予注册的商品事实上具有独特之处；
- 商标可全部或部分局限于一种或多种特定颜色，而在这种情况下，须由注册官或法院考虑以决定该商标的独特性质。如在不限颜色的情况下注册商标，则该商标须当做已注册所有颜色；
- 商标必须就特定商品或商品类别注册；
- 就任何商品所属的类别而产生的任何问题，均须由注册官决定，且其决定即为最终决定。

3. 不能注册为商标的标志
- 巴勒斯坦或国王陛下或外国的公共徽章、王冠、标记或勋章，除非经主管当局授权；
- 官方标志或具有官方保证的标志，除非由拥有或控制该商标的主管当局提出或授权；
- 代表王室的武器、皇冠、与其极为相似的武器、王冠、国旗、"皇室"字样或者其他旨在使人认为申请人享有王室资助或者授权的文字、字母或图案；
- 出现以下字句的标志："专利""专利的""由皇室英皇制诰"（"皇室字样专利"）、"注册""注册图案""版权""冒牌即伪造"或具有类似效力的字句；
- 损害或者可能损害社会秩序、道德或者故意欺骗社会的商标；或者鼓励不公平贸易竞争或者含有虚假原产地标志的商标；
- 由贸易中常用的数字、字母或文字组成的标志，以区分或描述商品或商品类别，或直接提及其性质或质量；其普通含义为地理或姓氏的文字，除非以特殊或特别方式表示；但本款所载任何规定均不得视为禁止注册本段所述具有特殊性质的商标；
- 与宗教意义完全相同或类似的标志；
- 标志是或包含或几乎类似于欺骗某人的申述、名称或商号，或法人团体或社团的名称，但如已取得相关人员的同意，则不受此限；如属最近去世的人，则注册官可要求其法律代表同意。
- 与已登记在册的不同所有者的商标或商品说明相同的商标，或者与该商标极为相似以致被认为欺骗的商标。

4. 更换代理人的规定
由商标所有人将有效的委托书签字盖章，并应经合法化和公证。

5. 商标在有效期届满之前/之后续期的规定
- 商标的名称及编号；
- 由商标所有人在有效的委托书上签字盖章，并应经合法化和公证。

6. 商标更名规定
- 经签字、盖章、合法的商标名称变更证明；
- 由商标所有人在有效的委托书上签字盖章，并应经合法化和公证。

7. 变更商标地址的规定
- 经签字、盖章、合法的商标地址变更证明；
- 由商标所有人在有效的委托书上签字盖章，并应经合法化和公证。

8. 商标检索的规定
- 商标类别；
- 如果商标是一个图案（标明是黑白的还是彩色的），将通过电子邮件发送商标或标志的名称。

9. 对转让备案的规定

- 由商标所有人签署并盖章的有效授权书，必须按照所附草案予以合法化和公证；
- 转让协议。

10. 商标注册的有效性

- 注册商标的有效期为 7 年，自申请之日起计算；
- 7 年后，应当将商标注册续展。续展后的有效期为 14 年。

11. 多类别注册

请注意，巴勒斯坦的商标法不允许多类别注册，也就是说，如果一个商标需要注册两个以上的类别，则应在每一个类别中单独申请注册商标。

12. 三维商标归档

在加沙地带无法将三维商标归档，但可在工业设计申请中详细说明这一点。

（二）专利申请

专利申请所需文件：

- 经公证的授权书；
- 由发明人和希望登记发明的人，或发明人和其他人作为原籍国的发明人签署的经公证的宣誓书；
- 以阿拉伯语和英语对该发明的品质和保护要素进行解释的说明；
- 经合法化及公证的专利副本；
- 该发明图纸或图表的副本（如有）。

（三）知识产权保护措施

第九条　商品的名称或说明

凡商标上出现任何商品的名称或说明，注册官可拒绝将该商标注册在除了如此指定或说明的商品以外的任何商品上。凡任何商品的名称或说明出现在商标上，而其使用的名称或描述有所不同，注册官可准许该商标的名称或说明注册在除这些命名或说明之外的商品，申请人在其申请中应对不同的名称或说明进行声明。

第二十六条　商标所有人的权利

在符合注册的任何因素和条件的前提下，商标所有人的注册，如属有效，须给予该人在该商标注册所涉商品上或与该商品有关的专用权：

如果同一商品的同一（或实质上相同）商标的注册所有人为两人或两人以上，则该商标的专用权（除非其各自权利已由注册官和最高法院作出界定）均不得由其中任何一人享有。但在其他方面，该等人所享有的权利，须与其为该商标的唯一注册所有人相同。

第二十九条　注册成为有效性的原始证据

在所有与注册商标有关的法律程序中，注册为该商标所有人的人，即为该商标的原始注册及所有其之后的转让及移交的有效性的原始证据。

第三十四条　未注册的商标

任何人均无权提起诉讼，以追讨未在巴勒斯坦注册的商标的损害赔偿。

六、环境保护

（一）环境保护监督部门

环境质量管理局：政府部门中负责执行和实施 1999 年第七号法律《环境法》条款，与其他专业实体在该方面协调合作的部门。

根据 2005 年第 273 号部长理事会决议，旅游和文物部已被指定为环境质量管理局的董事会成员。

根据 2005 年第 321 号部长理事会决议，国民经济部已被指定为环境质量管理局的董事会成员。

(二) 环境保护法律法规简介

1. 1999 年第七号法律《环境法》

1999 年通过并颁布了 1999 年第七号法律《环境法》,该法授权环境部执行和实施该法的规定。

2002 年,根据第六号总统令成立环境质量管理局。根据该法令,由环境质量管理局承担环境部的任务和责任。

2. 关于修订 1999 年第七号法律《环境法》的 2013 年第十一号法令

第三条 凡原法律(1999 年第七号法律《环境法》)规定的环境事务部名称和环境事务部长头衔,应分别改为"环境质量管理局"和"环境质量管理局主席"。

3. 1999 年第七号法律《环境法》中一些与投资项目相关的条款

第六条 专门机构应与环境事务部协调制定土地利用公共政策,使土地得到最佳利用,并应保护自然资源和具有特殊自然特征的地区,同时要保护环境。

第七条 该部门应与其他专门机构协调制定国家固体废物管理综合计划,包括确定固体废物处置的方式和地点,并监督地方议会执行该计划。

第十二条 任何人无权制造、存储、分发、使用、处理或处置任何有害物质或废弃物,无论是固体、液体或气体,除非此类处理过程符合该部门与其他专门机构制定的规定、说明和规范。

第十六条 该部门应与专门机构协调建立适应采矿、采石活动、碎石、矿山和采石场的环境条件,以保护环境免受环境污染的危害,并保护自然资源。

第十八条 禁止冲积可耕土地或运输土壤用于农业以外的目的。如果土地平整,或其土壤运输用于农业改良、保持其肥沃或根据专门机构颁布的条款和限制进行建设,则不应视为冲积土壤。

第十九条 该部门应与专门机构协调制定标准以规范空气中可能对公共卫生、社会福利和环境造成危害或破坏的污染物比例;

每个设在巴勒斯坦的设施都应遵守这些标准;每个现有设施应按照符合这些标准的方式进行必要的更改,期限不超过 3 年。

第二十条 每一设施所有者应采取一切手段,确保职工和设施周边居民在符合职业安全和健康条件的情况下,免受工作场所内或外的任何污染物的泄漏或排放。

第二十五条 该部门应与专门机构协调制定标准、说明和条件以减少不同活动产生的环境滋扰;此外,每个设施所有者、实体或个人不得对他人造成滋扰。

第三十四条 除非获得环境部的环保批文,否则禁止采取任何可能影响海滩自然径迹的行动,或进行海岸工程和海洋工程建设。

第三十九条 所有获准开展挖掘或勘探活动、生产或制造原油、提取或开采油田和其他海洋自然资源的国家、国际公司和机构应遵守环境条款。

第四十六条 授权任何设施时,专门机构应努力避免环境危害,鼓励采用对环境危害较小的物质和操作的项目,并在经济发展的基础上优先重视此类项目。

第四十七条 该部门应与专门机构协调合作,确定活动和项目在得到许可之前须获得环境许可,并允许在限制区建立这些项目。

第四十八条 专门机构不得为本法第四十七条规定的项目或设施,或其他活动发放或更新许可证,除非获得该部门的环境许可。

第五十三条 不同项目和活动的所有者须允许环境规划和任何其他专门机构的检查人员履行其职能,并按照该法的规定向他们提供他们认为必要的信息和数据。

(三) 环境保护评估

第五十条 该部门应与专门机构协调监测各机构、项目和活动,确保其符合为保护环境和重要资源规定的要求、标准和说明,符合该部门与其他机构颁布的本法律的规定。

第七十八条 该部门应与其他专门机构配合制定应对计划,对抗环境灾害。

第七十九条 该部门应与专门机构协调进行环境监测以收集不同环境要素的信息,并编制综合报告提交给专门机构。

第八十条　根据部长的提议，部长内阁应颁布执行本法所必需的执行条例。

（四）违反《环境法》条款的处罚

第五十九条　任何设施所有人或经营人对其拥有或经营设施的环境提供错误或误导信息的，应处以6个月以下的监禁和不超过2 000约旦第纳尔或同等价值的其他合法流通货币的罚款，或处以其中一项进行处罚。

（五）国际法在环境保护方面的适用

第七十五条　为了执行本法或其他任何国际公约中巴勒斯坦参与部分关于环境的有关规定，该部门应与地方专门机构协调与签署国合作交流科技信息，整合联合环境研究领域的项目，制定并实施联合合作项目，以预防或减少环境污染，并就此方面以各种形式相互援助。

第七十六条　任何自然人或法人因行动或疏忽而与本法或巴勒斯坦参与的任何国际公约规定相悖而造成环境损害的，除承担本法说明的刑事责任外，还应支付适当赔偿。

第七十七条　根据该法规定，国际和区域公约、条款以及巴勒斯坦参与的专门国际实体的规定、或其他在巴勒斯坦领土实行的与环境有关法律应被视为对该法的补充，除非另有规定。

七、争议解决

（一）争议解决的方法和机构

1. 解决争议的方法

① 普通法院：巴勒斯坦主管法院有权调查由任何一方提交法院的双方之间出现的任何纠纷。

② 仲裁：解释如下文。

2. 2000年第三号法律《仲裁法》

根据仲裁法律对仲裁进行分类

第三条　就本法而言，仲裁：

如果不是国际贸易问题，并且发生在巴勒斯坦，应为地方仲裁。

在下列情况中，如果冲突涉及经济、贸易或民事问题，应为国际仲裁：

（1）仲裁当事人订立仲裁协议时，当事人的总部设在不同的国家。当事人有多个业务中心的，应当将其总部界定为与仲裁协议联系更密切的中心。当事人没有业务中心的，应当考虑其居住地。

（2）如果仲裁协议中包含的冲突问题与多个国家相关联。

（3）如果仲裁各方的业务总部在仲裁协议签署后位于同一国家，且下列中心之一设在另一国家。

- 仲裁协议规定的仲裁地点或者说明的仲裁地点；
- 各方贸易或合同关系中重要部分的执行中心；
- 与冲突中的问题联系最密切的地方。

如果发生在巴勒斯坦以外的地方，则为国外仲裁。

如果不是由专门仲裁机构组织的仲裁，则为特殊仲裁。

如果是通过专门从事仲裁和监督的机构执行（无论该机构在巴勒斯坦境内还是境外），则为机构仲裁。

3. 组成仲裁小组

第八条　仲裁小组应由一名或多名仲裁员经各方同意组成。

如果未就组成仲裁小组达成协议，则各方应各选择一名仲裁员，且这些仲裁员应选择一名主仲裁员，除非各方同意另行规定。

4. 仲裁程序

第二十条　仲裁小组在冲突发生并接受当事人之间的仲裁后，即开始运作。

第二十一条 若仲裁双方对仲裁地点持不同意见，仲裁小组应考虑冲突情节和对成员地点的适宜性确定仲裁地点；仲裁小组可在其认为合适的任何其他地点举行一次或多次会议。

第二十二条 除非双方另有协议，仲裁应以阿拉伯语进行。在多种语言的情况下，仲裁小组应规定所要采用的语言。

仲裁小组可要求任何一方提交翻译成阿拉伯文或规定采用的任何语言的书面文件。

如果冲突各方的语言种类繁多，仲裁小组可能会使用经过认证的翻译员。

第三十条 仲裁小组可根据任何一方的要求或自行决定，在其确定的任何事项上指定一名或多名专家，在这种情况下，各方须向该专家提交与此相关的任何材料或文件。

第三十一条 仲裁小组应将专家报告副本送交当事各方，同时提供机会在为此目的举行的一次会议之前向专家小组提问。

任何一方均有权请一位或多位专家就仲裁小组指定的专家报告中涉及的事项发表意见。

第三十四条 仲裁小组可以决定迫使当事人支付其认为合适的任何款项以支付仲裁产生的费用，前提是仲裁协议明确规定可以接受该原则。如果当事人或其中任何一方未能向仲裁小组支付赔偿金，仲裁小组可要求主管法院就此作出裁决。

（二）法律适用

1. 2000 年第三号法律《仲裁法》

第二条 在不损害本法第四条规定的情况下，本法的规定应适用于享有法定资格行使权利的自然人或法人之间的仲裁，无论冲突的法律关系主体是何种性质，同时应考虑巴勒斯坦为缔约成员国的国际协定。

第四条 本法的规定不适用于下列事项：
（1）与巴勒斯坦公共秩序有关的问题。
（2）法律调解无法解决的问题。
（3）与个人身份有关的纠纷。

第十九条 国际仲裁各方可就冲突情况下适用的法律达成协议。如无此种协议，仲裁小组应适用巴勒斯坦法律。

如果国际仲裁在巴勒斯坦进行，而且当事各方未能就适用的法律达成协议，则应适用关于适用巴勒斯坦法律中法律冲突的法规，同时考虑到各方规定的巴勒斯坦法律的适用范围，否则不得适用税收法律。在所有情况下，仲裁小组应考虑适用于冲突各方之间关系的惯例。

第四十七条 主管法院批准仲裁决定后，仲裁裁决应具有与法院裁决相同的权力和效力，并应按照适用程序执行任何法院作出的任何裁决或决定。

第四十八条 拒绝国外仲裁裁决或决定的情况

考虑到巴勒斯坦遵守的国际协定和在巴勒斯坦生效的法律，主管法院即使经自身审议，也可在下列两种情况中的任何一种情况下拒绝执行外国仲裁裁决或决定：
（1）如果违反巴勒斯坦的公共秩序；
（2）如果不符合在巴勒斯坦适用的国际条约和协定。

2. 2005 年第二十三号法律《执行法》

执行国外官员的判决、裁决、决议和令状。

第三十六条 可就在外国发出的判决、决定和命令发出命令，这些判决、决定和命令在巴勒斯坦按照该国为执行其中的巴勒斯坦判决、决定和命令而规定的相同条件执行，但不得违背巴勒斯坦法律或损害最高国家利益。

执行在外国发出的判决、决定和命令的命令，应通过向原讼法庭提出诉讼进行请求，在原讼法庭的管辖范围内，必须执行该等判决、决定和命令，但该等判决、决定和命令须经主管当局以适当形式核证。

第三十七条 除非对下列情况进行核查，否则执行令不得执行：

（1）巴勒斯坦国法院不完全有权裁决已作出判决、裁决或命令的争端，作出裁决的外国法院根据其法律规定的国际司法管辖权规则，有权裁决争端。

（2）该判决、决定或命令具有按照发出判决的法院的法律作出判决的命令的效力。

（3）判决、决定或决议与巴勒斯坦法院事先发布的判决、决定或决议并不矛盾，并且不包括任何违反巴勒斯坦公共秩序或道德的行为。

第三十八条 第三十六条和第三十七条规定应根据仲裁员在外国发布的判决执行的条件是该判决已通过案件的审理，并可根据有效的巴勒斯坦《仲裁法》仲裁。

第三十九条 若国外拟定的可执行官方令状与巴勒斯坦的可执行官方令状的认可条件相同并符合对等原则，则可以签发。

有关执行命令的申请应提交至该执行管辖范围内的一审法院院长。

在核实令状的官方性质和可执行性等所要求的条件符合完成执行国的法律之后，且其不得违反巴勒斯坦公共秩序或道德，执行令方可执行。

八、其他

（一）《投资促进法》中纠纷的解决

第三十九条 本部分规定适用于投资者与国家主管部门当局之间就《投资促进法》规定的权利和义务发生的纠纷。

第四十条 当投资者或国家主管部门认为双方之间存在纠纷时，任何一方可根据条例规定的程序要求举行谈判。涉及纠纷的任何一方在诉诸本条（b）款解决纠纷的规定之前可以要求举行谈判。

如果谈判未能在规定期限内解决纠纷，双方中的任何一方可将纠纷提交至：
- 条例规定的独立和有约束力的仲裁机构；
- 巴勒斯坦法院。

（二）项目合同

相关法律有《关于政府工程投标》的1999年第六号法律与《关于公共采购系统》的2014年第五号部长理事会决定。

1. 中央招标专业委员会

署长担任主席的中央招标专业委员会应由以下4个领域的相关人员组成，该委员会的总部应设在中央招标部门，并可在与投标有关的部门举行会议：
- 政府建筑领域；
- 水利、灌溉、污水和水坝领域；
- 公路、交通和采矿领域；
- 电子机械和通信工程领域。

2. 执行工程和服务的方法

下列工程和服务应采用以下方法之一执行：

（1）公开招标：采取公开、平等、竞争自由的原则，无论是本地还是国际招标。

（2）通过邀请发盘的方式进行招标，即向至少3名承包商或顾问发出特别邀请函。

（3）在特别加急或特殊情况下直接签约。

（4）直接执行：即由该部门通过其设备和工作人员执行。

3. 公共工程或技术服务投标应遵守的规则

- 应通过在当地报纸上刊登广告的方式公布招标，但不得宣布任何投标或作出任何授标，除非有财务拨款可以支持该行动或通过内阁会议的决议得到财政部门对此的承诺。
- 采取竞争原则，以主管当局认为适当的方式为符合资格的各方提供平等机会实施工程或提供技术服务，适当给予承包商和顾问足够的时间来研究招标文件并提交符合工程或技术服务要求性质的报盘。

- 中标时，应遵守符合招标条件和最适合价格的最佳报盘，并考虑在规定期限内完成所需质量的程度和执行的可能性，以及承包商或顾问根据条件和规格进行所需工作的能力程度。
- 制定规定，要求工程中使用当地材料和工业产品的投标条件和规格符合批准，并且避免向任何行业定义商业名称。
- 所有协议和合同条款均应使用阿拉伯语，但规格、版面、技术报告和信函可采用英文书写。此外，合同可以翻译成英文，但优先采用阿拉伯语。
- 制定合同条件时应遵守现行的法律、法规和说明，并且不得要求免除任何法律规定的任何财务承诺，除非在签署合同前得到部长理事会的批准。
- 如果当地承包商符合政府工作项目所需条件，则优先考虑当地承包商。
- 国外公司应遵守巴勒斯坦现行的相关法律法规。

4. 投标的统一条件

各部门在执行与其有关的工程和技术服务时，应当对招标采用统一的条件，但应在合同的特定条件下提供任何修改或补充条件。

（三）招标及投标

1. 招标的主要内容

- 请求投标方的名称；
- 所需规格（草图、图表、图纸和任何其他说明）；
- 通知及通用条款；
- 投标提案（技术方面和财务方面）；
- 请求投标方的特殊条件；
- 指定投标的地址；
- 指定投标的截止日期及方法；
- 有关招标主题的专用附件，可能包括补充条款。

2. 文书语言

所有投标文件和资格预审文件，包括合同文件，可采用阿拉伯文或英文，如为国际招标文件，则应采用英文。

投标人应当以招标文件中规定的语言准备投标。投标人提交的非阿拉伯文或非英文书写的证明文件和印刷材料应进行翻译。

Palestine

Authors: Sharhabeel Yousef Al Zaeem、Khaled Sharhabeel Al Zaeem
Translators: William Lan, Luo Jing

I. Overview

A. Historical Background

Palestine was part of the Ottoman Empire until the end of First World War, all the Ottoman laws and regulations were applicable thereof. In 1919, Palestine was placed under the British Mandate where some of the laws start to be amended by the British High Commissioner. The situation continues until the end of the Second World War where Palestine was divided into three different jurisdictions.
(i) First jurisdiction: more than 70% of the historical Palestine fall under what is so called Israel;
(ii) Second jurisdiction: small strip in the southern west of Palestine called the Gaza Strip;
(iii) Third jurisdiction: the eastern mid part of Palestine (West Bank).
Following that, in 1950 West Bank was annexed by Jordan and formed a part of the Jordanian Kingdom, therefore all laws and regulations of Jordan became applicable therein revoking all the previous laws that were applicable pre 1948.
In Gaza Strip, the Egyptian Administration announced that they are only want to administer the Gaza Strip and they have no territorial or sovereign claims, hence all previous laws and regulations continued to be applicable including (Al Majalla) which is the Ottoman Civil Code of 1871.
The situation change a bit after 1967 when both jurisdictions fall under Israeli Occupation, some military orders were promulgated by the Military Governor, but it didn't alter or change the basis of the legal system of both jurisdictions.
In 1994 after Oslo Accords, the Palestinian Authority revoked most of the military orders, thus the Jordanian laws were applicable in West Bank and the Ottoman / British laws applicable in the Gaza Strip. The Legislative Council of the Palestinian Authority started to issue new laws to be applicable in both jurisdictions in an attempt to unify the legal and judicial systems of both jurisdictions.
The situation continues until 2007 when the political division took place. As a result, the President in West Bank started to issue presidential decrees altering some laws and promulgating some others, while the de facto authority in Gaza started to do the same, hence today there are many differences between the two systems.

B. Population in Palestine

a. Population of Palestinians in the World

The projected number of Palestinians in the world at the end of 2016 is 12.70 million, of whom 4.88 million are in State of Palestine, 1.53 million in 1948 Territory, 5.59 million in Arab countries and around 696 thousand in foreign countries[①].

b. Number of Palestinians in West Bank

The projected number of Palestinians living in West Bank at the end of 2016 is around 2.97 million. Palestinian refugees make up 41.9% of the Palestinian population in State of Palestine: 26.0% of them in the West Bank and 66.7% in Gaza Strip.

c. Number of Palestinians in Gaza Strip

The projected number of Palestinians living in Gaza Strip at the end of 2016 is 1.91 million.

C. Labour Force in Palestine

a. The Labour Force in Palestine

The number of persons participating in the labour force in the West Bank in the 3rd quarter of 2016 was 851,300.

---

① Palestinian Central Bureau of Statistics, 2016.

The number of persons participating in the labour force in the Gaza Strip in the 3rd quarter of 2016 was 505,000.

The labour force participation rate in the West Bank was 45.7% and 46.7% in Gaza Strip, the gap in the participation rate between males and females in Palestine still very big where it reached 72.3% for males compared with 19.2% for females.[①]

b. The Unemployment Rate Among Labour Force Participants in Palestine

The unemployment rate in Gaza Strip was 43.2% compared with 19.6% in the West Bank in the 3rd quarter 2016.

c. Wage of Employees in the Private Sector

In the West Bank about 19.2% of wage employees in the private sector received less than minimum monthly wage with average monthly wage 1,050 NIS.

In Gaza Strip the percentage of wage employees in the private sector who received less than the minimum monthly wage was 78.0% with average monthly wage 745 NIS.

d. Employment Status in the 3rd Quarter 2016 in West Bank

- 65.6% of employed persons are wage employees;
- 19.7% of employed persons are self- employed;
- 6.1% of employed persons are unpaid family members;
- 8.6% of employed persons are employers.

e. Employment Status in the 3rd Quarter 2016 in Gaza Strip

- 78.6% of employed persons are wage employees;
- 13.0% of employed persons are self- employed;
- 4.0% of employed persons are unpaid family members;
- 4.4% of employed persons are employers.

D. The Structure of Courts in Palestine

The structure of courts in Palestine can be described as follow[②]:

a. High Constitutional Court

This court comprises of a President and a deputy for him and seven judges. The court shall convene before a panel of a president and six judges at least and shall issue its decisions with a majority vote.

b. Regular Courts

a) High Court

The High Court shall be comprised of a President, one or more Vice-Presidents and a sufficient number of Judges. It consists of:

(i) The Court of Cassation

The court of cassation exercises jurisdiction over:

• Challenges raised to it from courts of appeal in felony and civil cases and Personal Status matters for non-Muslims;

• Challenges raised to it from courts of first instance in their appellate capacity;

• Matters related to changing the terms of reference of a case;

• Any claims raised to it by virtue of any other law.

(ii) The High Court of Justice

• Challenges related to elections;

• Requests presented by interested parties for the cancellation of final administrative regulations, regimes and decrees touching on persons or on the assets of public legal persons, including professional syndicates;

• Applications in the nature of motions opposing imprisonment which entail the issuance of orders to release persons who are illegally detained;

• Disputes related to public employees in respect of appointments, promotions, raises, salaries, transfers, retirement, disciplinary measures, layoffs, dismissal and all matters related to personnel affairs;

• The refusal or abstention by the administrative authority to take any decision it is held to take pursuant to the provisions of laws or regulations in force;

• All administrative disputes;

---

① Palestinian Central Bureau of Statistics, July 2016.
② Law of Judicial Organization No.(5) of 2001, LAW NO.(1) Of 2002 On The Judicial Authority.

• Matters which are not court cases or trials but merely injunctions or summons outside the jurisdiction of any court and which must be adjudicated in the interest of justice;
• Any other matter raised to it pursuant to the provisions of law.

b) Courts of Appeal

Each Court of Appeal shall consist of a President and a sufficient number of Judges

The courts of appeal are competent to review appeals filed before them in respect of judgments and decisions rendered by the courts of first instance in their capacity as courts of initial jurisdiction.

c) Courts of First Instance

Each Court of First Instance shall be comprised of a President and a sufficient number of Judges.

d) Magistrate Courts

The Magistrate court is composed of a single judge who exercises administrative control thereover.

c. Sharia and Religious Courts

Handles all the matters related to PERSONAL STATUS of Muslims.

d. Military Court

- High Military Court;
- Private Military Court;
- Permanente Military Court;
- Central Military Court;
- Field Military Court.

Arabic shall be the official language used in courts. The court shall hear the statements of non-Arabic speaking litigants or witnesses through a sworn interpreter.

E. The Status and Direction of the Cooperation with Chinese Enterprises Under the B&R

On 30 November 2017, the Palestinian Authority (PA) and the government of China signed a "memorandum of understanding" on free trade between the two countries on Thursday.

The Palestinian Minister of National Economy, Dr.Abeer Odeh, and the Deputy Chinese Minister of Commerce, Mr.Wang Shouwen, signed the memorandum of understanding on free trade in the presence of Prime Minister Mr.Rami Hamdallah and China's ambassador to Palestine, Mr.Chen Xingzhong.

Accordingly, there is a strong economical basis for the cooperation with the Chinese enterprises under the Belt and Road Initiative.

II. Investment

A. Market Access

a. Department Supervising Investment

a) The Palestinian Investment Promotion Agency (PIPA)

PIPA was established in 1998 as an independent agency, pursuant to the promulgation of the Investment Promotion Law "Law Number (1) for the year 1998". This law provided investors with all possible incentives, progression and assurances to make their investment in Palestine a unique and fruitful investment through creating an economic environment clear of bureaucracy and complications. PIPA reflects the Palestinian Authority vision and its policies to promote the private sector and to define an appropriate investment environment.

PIPA Board of Directors is composed of 11 members; 4 members represent the private sector and the remaining 7 represent the public sector. Minister of National Economy chairs the board of directors (currently Dr.Abeer Odeh) and representative of the Ministry of Finance acts as vice- chairman.

PIPA offer investors the necessary information to start an investment including providing assistance in obtaining all necessary licenses through PIPA's one-stop-shop. The investment support unit offers updated information and data related to investment opportunities, expenditure and funding in Palestine.

The relationship between PIPA and investors do not end with the awarding of all the incentives and advantages that the law offer, however the relationship is continuous through PIPA's After Care Unit. Many services and assistance are offered to current investors to solve any problems they might face while establishing their projects. Part of PIPA's role is to monitor the existing regulations and laws that may affect the healthy investment environment.[①]

b) Palestinian Industrial Estate and Free Zone Authority (PIEFZA)

It has the competence over the following functions:

(i) Formulate an overall general policy for the establishment and development of the industrial estates and free industrial zones in Palestine.

(ii) Submit proposals, plans and recommendations to the Council of Ministers with respect to the establishment, development and management of any industrial estate or free industrial zone in Palestine.

(iii) Accept and receive applications for the establishment of industrial estates and free industrial zones for the purpose of establishing industrial projects and transmit same with its recommendations to the Council of Ministers.

(iv) Review the applications of the various parties concerning the licensing for work in an industrial estate and/or a free industrial zone and granting of certificates of the free industrial zone to investors.

(v) Develop the industrial estates and free industrial zones directly or through promoters.

(vi) Prepare the plans and programs pertaining to the development and progress of the industrial estates and free industrial zones.

(vii) Establish the public utilities which are required for the industrial estates and free industrial zones by itself or through third parties.

(viii) Fix the fees in consideration of the services provided by the Institution to the industrial estates and free industrial zones as well as the rules of its collection vide a law.

(ix) Conclude the contracts and agreements as well as accept the assistances and grants offered to it in a manner which is not in contradiction with the provisions of this law.

(x) Approve the annual general budget of the institution and transmit same to the concerned parties for due adoption.

(xi) Selection of promoters and conclude contracts with them.

(xii) Supervise the performance and development of the industrial estates and free industrial zones as well as publish the reports pertaining thereto.

(xiii) Endeavor to implement the local and regional agreements concluded in respect of any of the matters stated in this law.

c) The Palestine Capital Market Authority (PCMA)

It was established as an autonomous agency by law No.(13) of the year (2004). Its jurisdiction encompasses securities, insurance, financial mortgage and financial leasing sectors, along with any other non-banking financial institutions.

d) Palestine Standards and Measurements Institute

It was established in 1994 and started operations in 1997. It is considered the sole body responsible for issuing Palestinian standards, and recognized by the both locally and internationally as the focal point for Palestinian participation in the global system of harmonized standards.

b. Laws and Regulations of Investment Industry

a) The Investment Promotion Law No.(1) for the Year 1998 and Its Amendments (Gaza and West Bank)

The rights that Palestinian and non-Palestinian companies / investors would own (directly or indirectly) after making an investment project in Palestine under this law:

Article (22)

The fixed assets of the Enterprise shall receive the following exemptions:

(i) The fixed assets of the Enterprise shall be exempted from customs, provided that they are brought in or imported within the period set by the Agency when it approved the list of the fixed assets; the Agency may extend this period if the nature and size of the investment requires so.

(ii) Spare parts imported by the Enterprise shall be exempt from customs duties provided that their value does not exceed 15% of the fixed assets and, so long as, they are brought in or used by the Enterprise within the period set by the Agency commencing from the date of production or investment start-up and pursuant to a decision by the Agency approving the list and quantity of spare parts.

(iii) The fixed assets of the Enterprise required for enlarging, developing, or upgrading the Investment shall be exempt from customs duties if the Agency determines that they increase the productive capacity of the Investment.

(iv) A price increase in the value of fixed assets shall be exempt from customs duties if the increase in value was caused by a rise in prices at the country of origin or as a result of an increase in the cost of shipping or change in the price of transformation.

---

① The Palestinian Investment Promotion Agency's website.

Article (23)

The projects approved by the Authority and which have obtained the licenses required under the law shall be granted the incentives mentioned in this law in the following manner:

(i) Any investment with a value from one hundred thousand up to less than one million Dollars shall be granted an exemption from income tax when it becomes due for a period of five years beginning from the date of commencement of production or carrying on the activity and shall be subject to an income tax on the net profit at a nominal rate of 10% for an additional period of (8) years.

(ii) Any investment with a value from one million to five million Dollars shall be granted an exemption from income tax when it becomes due for a period of five years beginning from the date of commencement of production or carrying on the activity and shall be subject to income tax on the net profit at a nominal rate of 10% for an additional period of (12) years.

(iii) Any investment with value of five million Dollars and above shall be granted an exemption from income tax when it becomes due for a period of five years beginning from the date of commencement of production or carrying on the activity and shall be subject to income tax on the net profit at a nominal value of 10% for an additional period of (16) years.

(iv) The qualitative and capital private projects for the determination of which a resolution by the Council of Ministers is issued upon the Authority's proposal shall be granted an exemption of income tax when it becomes due for a period of five (5) years beginning from the date of commencement of production or carrying on of the activity and shall be subject to income tax on the net profit at a nominal rate of 10% for an additional period of twenty (20) years.

Article (24)

(i) It shall be permissible, by a resolution of the Council of Ministers, upon the recommendation of Authority, to extend the exemptions for another period or periods to a maximum of five (5) years if such is called for by public interest in accordance with the project's scope of work, its geographic location, extent of its contribution to the increase of exports, creation of employment opportunities and stimulation of the wheel of development.

(ii) It is possible to specify the periods of exemption in respect of the projects which are set up within the industrial or remote areas or the areas which are threatened with settlements. A resolution shall be issued by the Council of Ministers to specify the new industrial, remote or threatened areas.

(iii) In all cases, the period of exemption for the projects shall be increased by two additional years if the ratio of local components in the machines, equipment and supplies exceed (60%). The invested funds in lands and buildings shall not be included in this percentage and the Authority shall be the competent authority for determining this percentage.

(iv) The National Authority may grant a most favored treatment or determine special incentives or guarantees to the national investor.

Article (27)

An income tax at a 10% nominal rate shall apply on the expansions in the existing projects according to the value of the capital investments mentioned under Article (24) which are approved by the Board of Directors as of the date of commencement of production of such expansions or its carrying on the activity. The expansion means the increase in the capital which is utilized in adding new fixed capital assets that realize an increase in the project's production capacity of the commodities and services or manufacturing in what he used to import or for the purpose of producing or providing new services or activities.

Article (28)

Profits distributed by the project shall be exempted from income tax at the rate of 10% of the original value of the financier's share in the project's capital after the expiry of the period of exemption provided for under articles (22) and (23). The exemption referred to in the foregoing paragraph shall be at the rate of 20% of the nominal value of the shareholder's share in the project's capital which is established by the application of the provisions of this law in the form of the shareholding company which issues its shares for public subscription and the subscription therein amounts to no less than 40% of its capital.

Article (35)

The licensed project owner shall have the right to carry out any industrial or export activity as well as any additional activities including the services within the licensed limits.

Article (36)

The licensed project owner may sell a maximum of 20% of the production of his project in the local market provided that all materials included in the manufacture of this production which is sold in the local market shall be subject to the customs fees and taxes should there be found in the local market a similar local production.

Article (37)

All the necessary commodities and goods which are required for use by a licensed project in the free industrial area and are stored in the warehouse, of the Customs Department shall be treated as if they are imported into the free industrial zone.

Article (38)

All goods, materials, provisions, machinery and means of transport which are imported from abroad into the free industrial zone for the purpose of using same within the free industrial zone or in any industrial project therein shall be exempted from customs fees and other fees attached thereto.

Article (39)

The local goods and products which are imported to the free industrial zone from all the other Palestinian territories shall not be subject to any established measures, taxes or fees.

Article (40)

All goods and products processed in the free industrial zones which are exported abroad shall not be subject to the rules and measures which are legally established for export, outgoing tax as well as other taxes.

Article (42)

In addition to any other rights which are guaranteed in any other law, the project owners who are licensed shall be free to fix the prices of their production and services as well as procure the services and goods necessary to them from within the country or abroad as well as freedom of disposal for the sale of their projects.

b) Resolution of the Council of Ministers No.4 of the Year 2015 Regarding the Encouragement of Investment (West Bank)

Article (10)

(i)The board of directors of the agency may classify the Palestinian lands according to the development priorities in accordance with the governmental development plans. These classifications are regularly reviewed whenever necessary based on the public interest.

(ii)In the strategic projects for public interest, and in accordance with the requirements of geographical location or the extent of the strategic contribution in the increment of the local exports or job creation or to support the wheel of development or to transfer knowledge on the national level or to support search and development, the board of directors will be authorized to enter into contract in which he grant the project additional incentives in addition to the tax incentives aiming to empower and support this project, and to encourage it according to the terms and conditions of this contract provided that this contract shall be presented to the council of ministers to obtain their approvals and enacted the bulk of incentives under it.

(iii)After acquiring the approval of the council of ministers, all the official governmental references and the competent parties shall adhere to implement the terms of the bulk of incentives contract all that concerns him.

(iv)The incentives contract may include providing support resources, infrastructure services and governmental lands.

(v)The board of directors of the agency, at its own discretion and abilities, shall be authorized and without referring to the council of ministers to provide incentives with logistical and technical nature like training and rehabilitation services, experience building, marketing, participation in the exhibitions on the local and international level for the investment projects which are eligible to benefit from bulk of incentives contract and others within the regulations and standards issued by the board of director of the agency.

(vi)The bulk of incentives contract shall be published in the official Gazette provided that the publication shall not be considered a condition to enforce it as long as it has the approval of council of minister.

c) Resolution of the Council of Ministers No.174 of the Year 2011 Regarding the Real Estate Investment (Gaza)

Article (4)

Real Estate projects or its branches mentioned in this resolution shall enjoy exemptions and incentives stipulated in the law of encouragement of Real Estate Investment in Palestine and its amendments. The Investor shall not mortgage the governmental land for the process of financing his project.

Article (8)

(i) The ministry, in coordination with the concerned bodies, shall register the land allocate to the investor's project once the completion and handing the share of the ministry in the real estate project.

(ii) Without prejudice to article 1 above, it should be allowed to register the land for the investor on concurrent stages with the stages of performing the project after handing the share of the ministry of each phase of the project according to agreed upon timetable (ownership on phases).

Article (9)

It should be allowed to grant the investor in case of performing the project before the deadline a reward at. 5% of the project's value for each month before the deadline.

Article (10)

The Arab or foreign investor shall be allowed to own land in Palestine in accordance with the following terms:
(i) To have a local Palestinian partner who owns at least 51% of the project's value;
(ii) To carry out all the conditions of the contract;
(iii) To acknowledge to subject to the Palestinian regulations and commit to them;
(iv) To acquire a permission from the Palestinian Council of Ministers.

C. Forms of Investment

a) Article (3) of the Investment Promotion Law

The investor may, pursuant to the provisions of this law, invest in projects of any sector of the Palestinian economy unless it is prohibited by special laws.

b) Article (4) of the Investment Promotion Law

The projects shall enjoy the exemptions and advantages provided for in this law. This applies to all fields of investment with the exception of the sectors and fields which require an approval in advance from the Council of Ministers prior to commencing therewith, namely:
(i) Manufacturing and distribution of arms and ammunition or spare parts thereof;
(ii) Aviation industries, including airports;
(iii) Production and distribution of electricity;
(iv) Re-processing of petroleum and its derivatives;
(v) Recycling of garbage and solid waste;
(vi) Tele-communications;
(vii) Radio and Television Authority.

c) The Fields of Investment in Palestine According to Palestine Investment Promotion Agency (PIPA) Include:
(i) Renewable energy;
(ii) The information and communication technology;
(iii) Food and beverage industry;
(iv) Textiles and Garment;
(v) Tourism sector;
(vi) Drugs and pharmaceuticals;
(vii) Stone and Marble;
(viii) Agriculture;
(ix) Education sector;
(x) Construction and real estate development sector;
(xi) The Palestine Securities Sector.

d. Standards of Market Access and Examination

a) How to Start a Business in Palestine

According to the Palestine Investment Promotion Agency, the foreign investor shall go through the following steps to start a business in Palestine:
- Registering a business (Ministry of National Economy);
- Registering in Value Added Tax Department and Income Tax Department (Ministry of Finance);
- Obtaining the required licenses from the appropriate ministries in regard to the project;
- Obtaining investment registration and confirmation certificate from the Palestine Investment Promotion Agency.

b) Related Articles of Law No.(10) for the Year 1998 Regarding Free Industrial Estates and Areas

Article (30)

No party may carry out any industrial activity within the free industrial area except by a certificate of the free industrial zone which authorizes it to work in a single free industrial zone.

Article (31)

The applications for the obtaining of free industrial zone certificates from the projects owners to the Director General of the Institution who will transmit it to the Board of Directors within a maximum period of one month from the date thereof. The Board of Directors should finalize the applications submitted thereto within two weeks from the date of its presentation and in the event of rejection, it should be justified.

Article (34)

The free industrial zone certificate shall be granted only to the persons or institutions registered in Palestine and whose object is to work in the free industrial zone.

Article (43)

The licensed project owner shall undertake the following:

(i) Restrict their activities which are shown in the license established by the certificate of the free industrial zone granted to each of them or any additional activity as per article (35) of this law. The type of activity may be amended in the area subsequent to the PIEFZA's approval thereon.

(ii) Submit any documents, records, or accounts to the Institution if requested to do so for the purpose of carrying out any statistical activities.

(iii) Comply with any instructions or regulations formulated for running the free industrial zones or to observe the order and provide security within the free industrial area.

(iv) Notify the Institution (PIEFZA) in writing of the entrepreneur's decision to liquidate and finalize his project three months prior to the implementation of the liquidation or finalization decision.

Article (44)

The project owner should liquidate his project from the free industrial zone within six months from the date of suspension of work without justification. If he fails to do so, the Institution shall have the right, in coordination with the Customs Department, following the lapse of the said period, to sell it through auction where all the obligations and debts consequent on the project, if any, shall be deducted from the price and the balance shall be transferred to the personal account thereof.

B. Foreign Exchange Regulation

a. Department Supervising Foreign Exchange

The Palestinian Monetary Authority is the department which is responsible of supervising the foreign exchange.

Article (61) of Law no.2 of 1997 regarding the Palestinian Monetary Authority

(i) Save the national currency, all other currencies shall be regarded as foreign currencies.

(ii) According to the Foreign Currency Control Law and the Money Exchange Law, the Monetary Authority shall be responsible for:

- Formulating the regulations and instructions which regulate dealing with the foreign currency;
- Granting and revoking the licenses of dealers in foreign currency.

b. Requirements of Foreign Exchange Management for Foreign Enterprises

Please note that there are no restrictions on the import and export of capital and the repatriation payments can be made in any currency.

It should be noted that both residents and non-residents can hold bank account in any currency.

Related Articles of Law No.10 for the Year 1998 Regarding Free Industrial Estates and Areas

Article (45)

The dealing in foreign currency or keeping it within the free industrial zone shall not be subject to any restrictions and any foreign currency may be brought in from the free industrial zone to any part in the other Palestinian territories or vice versa.

Article (46)

The banks or its approved branches in the free industrial zone may accept payment in any foreign currencies from any natural or corporate person and open accounts in these currencies in the names of depositors. The depositors shall have the right to utilize the balances of these accounts in foreign currency without any restrictions.

C. Financing

a. Main Financial Institutions

a) Department Responsible About Financial Institutions

(i) The Palestinian Monetary Authority

The Monetary Authority aims at guaranteeing the soundness of the banking activity, maintaining monetary stability and encouraging the economic growth in Palestine in accordance with the general policy of the National Authority.

It has the exclusive right to grant the required licenses in regard to banking activities.

(ii) Palestine Capital Market Authority

The Palestine Capital Market Authority was established as an autonomous agency by law no.(13) of the year (2004). It is governed by a Board of Directors composed of seven members. Its jurisdiction encompasses securities, insurance, financial mortgage and financial leasing sectors, along with any other non-banking financial institutions. In the past years the PCMA chaired the National Committee for Corporate Governance in Palestine.

During the past years PCMA embarked on a number of projects aimed at improving the internal working environment as well as enhancing the dissemination of information to the public.

b) Law No.2 of 1997 Regarding the Palestinian Monetary Authority

Powers of the Palestinian Monetary Authority

(i) Issue, manage and maintain bonds on behalf of the Monetary Authority, purchase from and sell to individuals, banks and other parties in order to realize its monetary policy.

(ii) Make transfers related to its activities.

(iii) Grant licenses to banks or branches thereof and approves the merger, closure or opening of offices or withdraws the licenses thereof.

(iv) Sell movable property or real estate inured to it as a payment of due debts.

(v) Purchase, lease, sell and maintain buildings and equipment thereof.

(vi) Regulate, control, supervise, protect and manage bank notes and coins in circulation in accordance with the Monetary and Credit Law.

(vii) Impose the appropriate fees for any kind of services provided by it.

(viii) Terminate all operations and activities which were carried out before the promulgation of this law and which contravene with the provisions of this law.

Article (40)

(i) With due observance of the provisions of this law, no banking operations may be carried out except after licensing same by the Monetary Authority. The licensed banks shall be registered in the register provided for this purpose by the Monetary Authority. The licensing decision shall be published in the official gazette.

(ii) The Monetary Authority shall lay down the necessary regulations and instructions thereto. These regulations and instructions shall be issued under a decision by the President of the National Authority upon the recommendation of the Board and shall be published in the official gazette.

(iii) The banks existing upon the operation of the regulations and instructions referred to in the previous paragraph should reconcile their situations according to such regulations and instructions during the period fixed by it provided that such period is not less than three years. The Monetary Authority shall specify the measures relating thereto.

c) Capital Market Authority Law No.(13) for the Year 2004

Article (3) the objectives, duties and capacity of Palestinian Capital Market Authority (PCMA):

The authority aims to create suitable environment to accomplish capital stability and growth, and to organize, develop and monitor the capital market in Palestine, in addition to protecting the rights of the investors. In order to accomplish these objectives, the authority shall perform the following in accordance with the provisions of the law:

(i) Supervise the following:
- The securities market to ensure the proper conduct of the market;
- Insurance enterprises;
- The financial leasing enterprises;
- Mortgage finance enterprises.

(ii) Organizing, monitoring and supervising the activities of non-banking financial entities including securities exchange, and non-banking financial services.

(iii) Organize the release of any data or information related to the non-banking financial sector.

(iv) Monitor the development of non-banking financial organizations to ensure the precision of its business.

Article (25)

Cooperation with other authorities:

(i) The authority shall cooperate with other public authorities engaged in supervision and regulation of financial institutions and their operations in Palestine.

(ii) All persons and employees working at the ministries, public institutions and governmental departments shall comply with the authority's request for information necessary to carry out its duties and activities in accordance with the provisions of this law and its regulations.

(iii) The authority may be a member and to participate in the businesses of national and international organizations dealing with the regulation of securities markets.

d) Memberships of PCMA

The Palestinian Capital Market Authority is a member in the following organizations:
- The International Organization of Securities Commissions (IOSCO);
- International Association of Insurance Supervisors (IAIS);
- Arab General Union of Insurance, based in Egypt;

- A founding member of the Union of Arab Securities Authorities, based in Abu Dhabi;
- International Union for Housing Finance (IUHF);
- Child & Youth Finance International (CYFI);
- International Network on Financial Education (INFE).

b. Financing Conditions for Foreign Enterprises

Article (55)

The Monetary Authority, in coordination with the Ministry of Finance, may act as a intermediary to deliver the funds provided by the international financing institutions and foreign governments to the beneficiaries in accordance with the provisions of the General Budget Law.

Article (69)

(i) The Palestinian Monetary Authority shall collect from the qualified bodies and economic agents the information and statistics necessary for achieving its goals and carrying out its functions.

(ii) The Monetary Authority shall specify, by a special regulation, the type of the necessary information and statistics, the form in which such information should be provided to it and the parties which shall undertake its supply with the information and the secrecy of the information submitted to it.

D. Land Policy

a. Brief Introduction of Land-Related Laws and Regulations

a) Institutional Framework Regulating Palestinian Land

The Palestinian Land Authority (PLA) was established in 2002. It is now the sole institution for the administration and control of lands in Palestine. Article 2 of the Decree states that land registration departments at the Ministry of Justice and the Surveying Departments of the Ministry of Housing should be placed under the Land Authority. Article 5 of the Decree affirms that the jurisdiction and mandates of the Land Authority should be determined by a specific law, which has not yet been enacted. The Land Authority is now a completely independent institution for the upkeep of land in Palestine.

The mission of the Palestinian Land Authority is to preserve land, property titles and other ensuing rights of citizens and government, as well as civic and official institutions through survey and registration in the Land Registry. Its mission also includes resolution of disputes over land demarcation, and the preservation and proper disposal of public land and property

State Land Disposal: Since 1994, state land has been disposed in various ways including through allocations to private investment companies in the construction, agriculture and tourism sectors and allocations to individuals for the purposes of house construction. Some problems have been witnessed in these allocations like use of land for other than agreed purposes or sold to other parties or allocations made using unclear criteria and have led to disputes.

b) Classification of Lands:

Waqf: These lands are devoted by the owner (s) for pious or charitable purposes and it is said to be in the implied ownership of the Almighty. It is administered by the Mutwally (caretaker or person-in-charge).

Mulk: This kind of land is in absolute ownership of the proprietor.

Miri: The Raqaba (ultimate ownership) of this land lies with the state but the tesarruf (utilization) of this land can be bought by individuals.

Metruke: These were state lands left over for public use.

Mawat: These were dead or unproductive lands situated outside the towns. This category of land is no more present in Palestine.

Public Land: This category of land was introduced by the British Mandate and comprised of lands which are subject to the control of the Government or which are acquired for public purpose.

c) Land-related Laws and Regulations
- Amended Lands Law No.(78) for the year 1933;
- Settlement of Land Property Rights no.(9) for the year 1928;
- Palestinian Civil Law No.(24) for the year 2012;
- The Code of Civil and Commercial Procedure No.(2) for the year 2001;
- City planning law no.28 of 1936;
- The Law of Evidence in Civil and Commercial MattersNo.4 of 2001.

b. Rules of Land Acquisition for Foreign Enterprises

a) The Manner in Which Land Can be Compulsorily Acquired and the Scope of Compulsory Orders

Please note that according to the prevailing laws in Gaza, particularly law no.24 for the year 1943 as amended by law no.34 and 46 for the year of 1946, particularly article no.3 and 6 grant to the High Commissioner (nowadays this authority has been transferred to the President or any other person authorized by him) to acquire the ownership, possession and easement on any land or any other right thereon or thereover also can grant possession of such land.

This can be done through land acquisition for public purposes or expropriation for public utility. There are two laws that regulate this:

(i) City Planning Law No.28 of 1936

It was issued by the British Mandate. It includes articles regarding the expropriation for public utility as a part of the activities and practice of local authorities. This law is still enforceable till now.

(ii) Land (Acquisition for Public Purposes) Ordinance, 1943(West Bank and Gaza)

It was issued by the British Mandate, and it is for non municipal purposes. This law granted the General Commissioner for the expropriation for public utility.

Acquisition is defined as: a privilege for the management that grant it to compulsorily deprive the owner from his real estate for the public interest in consideration for fair compensation

It should be noted that that the President or any person authorized by him has all the authorities of High Commissioner that were mentioned in the British Mandate Laws and Regulations

b) Article 21 of the Basic Law for the Year 2002 States the Following:

(i) The economic system in Palestine shall be based on the principles of a free market economy. The executive branch may establish public companies that shall be regulated by a law.

(ii) Freedom of economic activity is guaranteed. The law shall define the rules governing its supervision and their limits.

(iii) Private property, both real estate and movable assets, shall be protected and may not be expropriated except in the public interest and for fair compensation in accordance with the law or pursuant to a judicial ruling.

(iv) Confiscation shall be in accordance with a judicial ruling.

c) Land Disputes

The Palestinian regular courts are authorized to look into all the disputes and claim related to real estates and lands in Palestine regardless the nationality of the disputing parties as long as the real estate is in Palestine.

E. The Establishment and Dissolution of Companies

Companies Law No.12 for the year 1964 and its amendments (West Bank)
Companies Law No.7 for the year 2012 (Gaza Strip)
The forms of companies according to the Companies Law No.7 for the year 2012 (Gaza Strip) are as follow:

a. General Partnership

a) Formation and Registration of General Partnership Company

(i) A general partnership shall consist of a number of natural persons, of not less than two and not more than twenty.

(ii) The partner shall be at least eighteen years of age.

(iii) A partner in the general partnership will acquire the capacity of the merchant and shall be considered as practicing the commercial business in the name of the partnership.

b) Registration Procedures

The application for registration shall be submitted to the Controller, together with the original partnership agreement, signed by all the partners, and with a statement signed by each of them before the Controller or the person authorized by him in writing. This statement may be signed before the Notary Public or a licensed lawyer. The partnership agreement and its memorandum must include the following:

(i) Address of the partnership and its trade name, if any;
(ii) Name of partners, nationality, age and address of each of them;
(iii) Head office of the partnership;
(iv) The partnership capital and each partner's share therein;
(v) Objectives of the partnership;
(vi) Duration of partnership, if limited;
(vii) Name of partner or names of partners authorized to manage and sign on behalf of the partnership and their powers;
(viii) The position of the partnership in event of the death of any or of all its partners, his bankruptcy or incompetence;
(ix) Any other statements as agreed upon between partners.

The Controller shall approve the registration of the partnership within fifteen days from the date of the submission of the registration application.

The general partnership company may establish branches in several places.

c) Dissolution of General Partnership

A general partnership shall be dissolved in any of the following circumstances:

(i) When all partners agree on the dissolution of the partnership or on its merger with another general partnership;

(ii) Expiration of the partnership's term whether it is its original term or the extended term per the agreement of all partners;

(iii) Completion of the objective for which it was formed;

(iv) When only one partner remains in the partnership;

(v) Declaring the partnership bankrupt in which case this will result in a consequent bankruptcy of the partners;

(vi) Declaring one of the partners as bankrupt or legally incompetent unless all remaining partners decide to keep the partnership between themselves in accordance with the partnership agreement;

(vii) Dissolution of the partnership by a court order;

(viii) Canceling the registration of the partnership upon the Controller's resolution.

b. Limited Partnership

a) Formation and Registration of General Partnership Company

A limited partnership is formed of two categories of partners whose names should be listed in the partnership agreement:

(i) General Partners: they are responsible for the management and operations of the partnership. They are also jointly and severally liable for all the partnership's debts and liabilities with their private properties.

(ii) Limited Partners: they are the partners who contribute to the capital of the partnership without having the right to manage the partnership or to carry out its operations and the liability of each one of them is limited to his share in the capital of the partnership.

The provisions of registration and dissolution of General Partnership apply to Limited Partnership.

b) Joint Venture

A joint venture is a commercial undertaking organized as an association of two persons or more. One partner shall carry out the operations of the Joint Venture and shall deal expressly with the others. The joint venture as such is limited to the special relationship between the partners.

A joint venture is not a separate legal entity and is not subject to the provisions and procedures of registration and licensing.

c. Limited Liability Company

a) Formation and Registration of Limited Liability Company

• The limited liability company is composed of two persons, at least, and doesn't exceed 50 persons. The liability of any partner therein for its debts, obligations and losses shall be in proportion to his shareholding in its capital.

• Upon a justifiable recommendation by the Controller the Minister may register a limited liability company composed of one person only.

• The capital of the limited liability company shall not be less than 50,000 Jordanian Dinars (about 70,500 USD) and shall be divided into indivisible shares of equal value of not less than one Dinar. However should more than one partner jointly own such shares, for any reason, the partners must select one person from amongst them to represent them with the company. But if the partners do not come to an agreement or do not make that election within thirty days from the date they become partners in such share, then they shall be represented by the person elected from amongst them by the company's manager or its management committee.

• The partner's share shall not be a work provided by him / her to the company.

• A limited liability company may not offer its shares for public subscription, increase its capital or borrow by subscription and shall not have the right to issue shares or negotiable corporate bonds.

b) Registration Procedures

(i) The application to incorporate the limited liability company shall be submitted to the Controller along with the company's memorandum and articles of association on the approved forms for this purpose, and shall be signed before the Controller, before any person delegated in writing by the Controller, before a notary public or before a licensed lawyer.

(ii) The limited liability company's memorandum shall incorporate the following particulars:

• Name of the company, its objectives and its head office;

• Names of the partners, their nationalities and address of each of them;

- Amount of capital and the shares of each partner therein;
- Statement of the capital's share or shares in kind, name of the partner who presented such shares and their estimated values;
- The controlling board of the number of partners exceed 7 members.

(iii) the articles of association of the limited liability company must include the information provided for in paragraph (ii) above in addition to the following information:
- The manner of managing the company, number of management committee, their powers and the limits of the powers of the management committee in borrowing, mortgaging the real estates owned by the company and presenting guarantees in its name;
- Conditions for transferring the shares in the company and the procedures to be followed in that respect and the form of writing the transfer;
- The manner of distributing the profits and losses to the partners;
- Meetings of the company's general assembly, its legal quorum, and the quorum needed for taking decisions thereby and procedures to be followed for holding the said meetings;
- Rules and procedures pertaining to the liquidation of the company;
- Any other additional information furnished by the partners or requested by the Controller.

c) Management of Limited Liability Company
- The company shall be managed by a manager or board of directors whose members shall not be less than two and not more than seven as provided for in the company's articles of association for a period of not more than four years. The board of directors shall elect a chairman and a deputy chairman.
- The manager of the limited liability company or its board of director shall have full power to manage the company within the limits specified by its articles of association.

d) Dissolution of Limited Liability Company
The limited liability company shall be liquidated either voluntarily, per a resolution adopted by its extraordinary general assembly, or manadatorily by a conclusive and final court order or in accordance with this law.

The limited liability company shall be voluntarily liquidated in any of the following circumstances:
- Upon the expiry of the specified period of the company;
- Upon fully achieving the objectives for which the company was established, or due to the impossibility of achieving these objectives;
- In execution of a resolution adopted by the extraordinary general assembly to dissolve or to liquidate the company.

The limited liability company shall be manadatorily liquidated in case an application for mandatory liquidation submitted to the court per a statement of claim by the Attorney General, or by the Controller in the following two cases:
- Should the company commit serious violations of the law or of its articles of association;
- Should the company fail to fulfill its commitments;
- Should the company suspend its operations for one year without a legal or justified cause;
- Should the losses of the company exceed 75% of its capital.

d. Limited Partnership in Shares

a) A limited Partnership in Shares is Composed of the Following Two Categories of Partners
- General Partners: The number of general partners shall not be less than two and they shall be liable for the partnership's debts and obligations in their personal property;
- Limited Partners: The number of limited partners shall not be less than three and each partner shall be liable for the company's debts and obligations in proportion to his shareholding.

The capital of the limited partnership in share shall not be less than one hundred thousand Jordanian Dinars.

b) Management of Limited Partnership in Shares
The limited partnership in shares shall be managed by one or more general partners.

c) Liquidation of Limited Partnership in Shares
The limited partnership in shares shall be dissolved and liquidated in the manner determined by the partnership's articles of associations otherwise it shall be subject to the provisions for the liquidation of the limited partnership company.

e. Shareholding Company

a) A public Shareholding Company Shall Consist of a Number of Promoters of not Less than Two
The duration of the public shareholding company shall be unlimited unless the objectives thereof is to carry out certain business in which case the duration thereof shall end upon the completion of that business.

b) Types of Shareholding Company

(i) Holding Companies: A holding company is a public shareholding company which undertakes to control the financial administrative matter of one or more companies called subsidiary companies.

(ii) Mutual Fund Companies (Joint Investment Company): The objectives of such company shall be confined to investment of its funds and of third parties funds in securities of different types and organize its business in accordance with the provisions of securities law.

(iii) Offshore Company (Exempt Company): a company which is registered in Palestine and carries out its operations outside the Palestine.

c) Registration Procedures

The promoters of the company shall elect a committee which is called "Promoters Committee" which shall consist of a number not less than two and not to exceed five days which shall be responsible for the procedures of registering the company at the competent departments.

The application for the formation of the company shall be submitted by the committee to the Controller accompanied by the following:

- The company's articles of association;
- Its memorandum of association;
- Names of promoters of the company;
- Names of a committee of promoters who shall supervise the formation procedures.

The shareholding company's articles of association and memorandum of association should include the following information:

- Name of the company;
- Its head office;
- Objectives of the company;
- Names of company's promoters, their nationalities, elected domicile and the number of shares subscribed for;
- The authorized capital of the company and the portion actually subscribed for;
- A statement of the in kind shares of the company, if any and the value thereof;
- The fiscal year of the company.

d) The Management of a Public Shareholding Company

The management of a public shareholding company is entrusted to a board of directors whose members shall not be less than three and not more than thirteen as determined by the company's articles of association.

The chairman of the board of directors may appoint a manger for the company and determines the powers.

The board of directors or the manager shall have the full powers to manage the company in accordance with the articles of association.

e) Dissolution of Public Shareholding Company

The Public Shareholding Company shall be liquidated either voluntarily, per a resolution adopted by its extraordinary general assembly, or manadatorily by a conclusive and final court order or in accordance with this law.

The Public Shareholding Company shall be voluntarily liquidated in any of the following circumstances:

- Upon the expiry of the specified period of the company;
- Upon fully achieving the objectives for which the company was established, or due to the impossibility of achieving these objectives;
- In execution of a resolution adopted by the extraordinary general assembly to dissolve or to liquidate the company.

The Public Shareholding Company shall be manadatorily liquidated in case an application for mandatory liquidation submitted to the court per a statement of claim by the Attorney General, or by the Controller in the following two cases:

- Should the company commit serious violations of the law or of its articles of association;
- Should the company fail to fulfill its commitments;
- Should the company suspend its operations for one year without a legal or justified cause;
- Should the losses of the company exceed 75% of its capital.

f. Foreign Companies

a) Foreign Companies Operating in Palestine

An operating foreign company means a company or a body which is registered outside Palestine, and its head office is in another state, and its nationality is considered non-Palestinian.

A foreign company or body may not exercise any commercial business in Palestine unless it is registered in accordance with the provisions of this law after obtaining the permits to operate pursuant to the applicable laws and regulations.

b) Foreign Companies not-operating in Palestine

A company which has a regional office or representative office in Palestine, for operations that it conducts outside Palestine, with the aim of using such a regional or representative office for managing its operations and coordinating them with its headquarters.

A non-resident foreign company is prohibited from carrying out any business or commercial activity inside Palestine, including the operations of commercial agents and middlemen, otherwise it will suffer the penalty of canceling its registration and will be responsible for compensation of any loss or damage it may have caused to others

The number of the Palestinian employees in a non-operating foreign company in Palestine should not be less than half of the total of the company's employees.

c) The Legal Requirements to Register a Branch of a Foreign Company in Palestine
• One authenticated copy Articles of Association translated into Arabic (both the original and the translation should be authenticated from the Palestinian representation office).
• One authenticated copy of the by-laws translated into Arabic (both the original and the translation should be authenticated from the Palestinian representation office).
• A copy of the authenticated registration certificate of the company, translated into Arabic (both the original and the translation should be authenticated from the Palestinian representation office).
• A Request which shall be completed by the lawyer (company's attorney) and submitted to the Ministry of National Economy.
• A POA from the company to our firm to follow up the registration in Gaza (the POA should also be authenticated at the Palestinian representation office).
• A POA from the company to one of its staff who shall be in charge of to managing the company's operations in Gaza (the POA should also be authenticated at the Palestinian representation office).
• A Copy of the personal ID or passport for each the members of the Board of the Company.
• A Lease contract or an ownership deed of the Branch's premises in Gaza.

d) The Legal Requirements to Open a Bank account for Branch of a Foreign Company in Palestine
• Registration certificate of the branch of Palestine
• Decision from the Company's Board to open the Branch in the Bank which you decide upon, along with the list of the names upon signatories.
• An authorization from the board of directors to the person who manages the account.
• The Passports of the signatories / managers of the accounts.

F. Merger and Acquisition

General partnership may be transformed to limited partnership which may also transformed to general partnership with the agreement of all partners and by following the legal procedures for the registration of the company and registration of the changes effected thereto.

A limited liability company and the limited partnership in shares may be transformed to Shareholding Company pursuant to the provisions stipulated in this law. The application shall be submitted to the Controller, and to which the following documents are to be attached:

(i) A resolution of the general assembly of the company approving the transformation;

(ii) The reasons and justification for the transformation based on an economic and financial study of the company's status, and how that during such year shall status will be after the transformation;

(iii) An annual balance sheet for the last three consecutive years preceding the application for transformation, provided that the average annual net profit shall not be less that 15% of the company's paid up capital;

(iv) A statement that the company's capital is paid up in full;

(v) A statement by the company indicating the preliminary assessments of the value of its assets and liabilities.

a. Merger of Companies

Merger of the above mentioned companies shall be accomplished by any one of the following methods, provided that the objectives of the companies wishing to merger shall be identical or complementary:

(i) By the merger of one company or more with another company called the (Merging Company), and the merged company or companies shall disappear and the corporate entity of each of them shall no longer exist;

(ii) By the merger of two companies or more to form a new company, which will be the result of the merger, and the companies and the corporate entity of each of them shall no longer exist;

(iii) By the merger of branches and agencies of foreign companies operating in Palestine, with an existing Palestinian company, which will be formed for this purpose, and the said branches and agencies shall disappear and the corporate entity of each of them shall no longer exist.

The merged company, along with its shareholders and the merging company resulting from the merger, shall be exempted from all taxes and fees due on the merger or as a result thereof.

b. Investment Project Subject to Merger or Acquisition Benefiting from the Investment Incentives According to the Investment Law

Article (29)

(i) The project benefiting from the investment incentives may be duly transferred in full to a new owner without any restrictions as long as it continues to operate the project as an existing investment.

(ii) The new owner of a transferred project may benefit from the investment incentives as long as he operates the project as an existing investment.

Article (30)

The merging and amalgamating companies and installations as well as the companies that are split or their legal form changed shall enjoy the exemptions established thereto before merger, splitting or changing the legal form until the expiry of its period of exemption. The merger, splitting or changing of the legal form shall not entail any new tax exemptions.

Article (33)

If any amendment has been introduced on the incentives, the projects benefiting from the incentives shall have the option of either selecting the incentives provided for in the amendment or make use of the incentives in force prior to the amendment, whichever are more favorable.

Article (34)

If the project has been transferred from a development area to another development area during the period of the granted exemption, it shall be treated for the purposes of exemption during the remaining period similar to the development projects transferred to provided that the Authority is notified thereof.

G. Tax

a. Tax Regime and Rules

a) Departments Supervising Tax in Palestine
(i) Ministry of Finance;
(ii) Income Tax Authority;
(iii) Value Added Tax (VAT) Authority.
b) Tax Law and Regulations
(i) A Law by Decree No.(8) of 2011 on Income Tax and its amendments (West Bank);
(ii) The Law of Income Tax no.(17) of 2004 (Gaza Strip).

b. Main Categories and Rates of Tax

a) Individual Income Tax Rates
b) Taxpayer Registration
A person who practices business or investment activity shall be obliged to register with the Department from the date of conducting the activity or operating the business.
c) Tax Annuity
The tax liability of the taxpayer is calculated on the basis of the calendar year.
d) Tax Brackets and Rates
The tax rates payable by Palestinian residents are as follows:
Annual Income Tax (West Bank, Currency: New Israeli Shekel)
(i) From 1 to 40,000 NIS (5%);
(ii) From 40,001 to 80,000 NIS (10%);
(iii) In excess of 80,000 NIS (15%).
Annual Income Tax (Gaza Strip, Currency: United States Dollar)
(i) From 1 – 10,000 USD (8%);
(ii) From 10,001 – 16,000 USD (12%);
(iii) Above that (16%).
e) Company Income Tax Rate
• Residence: a company is resident if it is incorporate in Palestine or managed or managed and controlled in Palestine.
• Palestinian companies and businesses are primarily subject to a 15% tax on their income.
• Life insurance companies are subject to a reduced rate of 5%.
• Telecommunication companies and companies that enjoy specific privileges or monopolies are subject to a

20% tax on income.
  · Losses, equipment depreciation, and business expenses are also included into the calculation of taxes.
  f) Value Added Tax (VAT)
  VAT is a consumption-based tax imposed on the sale of goods and the provisions of services and on imports at the rate of 16%.
  Requirements for registering a company at Valued Added Tax Department and Income Tax Department:
  · Copy of the registration certificate of the company;
  · Extract of the company registration;
  · Lease contract of the company's premises in Palestine;
  · Passport/s of the company authorized person/s;
  · Short description of the company's activities and operations;
  · Bank account details of the company;
  · Copy of any tax exemptions granted to the company.
  g) Tax Declaration and Preference
  (i) Categories obliged to submit the tax declaration
  · Every taxpayer shall submit a tax declaration supported by documents and the necessary information and the declaration and other information shall be subject to scrutiny by the assessor;
  · The persons whose incomes are tax-exempted according to the applicable investment legislations shall submit the tax declaration;
  · The liquidator of a company shall inform the Department in writing of the beginning of liquidation procedures to specify and prove the amount of tax liability of the company, and shall submit a tax declaration on behalf of the company he/she is liquidating and he / she shall be obliged to pay the tax as soon as it is due;
  · The Minister, upon the recommendation of the Director, may issue instructions through which certain categories of natural persons are exempted from submitting the declaration stipulated in this article.
  (ii) Date for Submitting the Tax Declaration
  Every taxpayer is obliged to submit the tax declaration within four months following the end of the tax period, specifying the details of the taxpayer's gross income, deductions, net income, exemptions, taxable income and tax liability for the tax period.
  The taxpayer who submits the tax declaration and its attachments within the specified period shall be granted a promotional discount for the due tax balance that is to be paid as follows:
  · 4% discount if the declaration submitted during the first month following the tax period and settlement of the tax within this month or within tax periods covered in the declaration;
  · 2% discount if the declaration submitted during the second or third month following the tax period and settlement of the tax until the end of the third month or within tax periods covered in the declaration.
  (iii) Tax Declaration Attachments
  The taxpayer shall submit the following documents along with the declaration as follow:
  · A copy of the final accounts for the tax year;
  · Certificate by the certified auditor and a copy of amendments report for the purposes of income tax approved by the certified auditor;
  · Ordinary companies and persons who are obliged to keep accurate accounts shall attach a copy of the final accounts and amendments report for the tax purposes according to the applicable laws and regulations;
  · Taxpayers, other than the taxpayers mentioned in paragraph (a) above shall clarify in their tax declaration their net taxable income with a brief statement of their earnings and expenses for the tax period.

H. Securities

The securities sector in Palestine emerged in 1995 when the Palestine Securities Exchange was set up as a private company, it has provided, from the onset, a set of rules and regulations that organized the work of the securities sector in Palestine, in addition to the latest electronic systems for monitoring, trading, settlement and transfer of securities. It was subject to the supervision of the Palestinian Ministry of Finance since its establishment until 2005 when the Palestine Capital Market Authority was set up.

The year 2004 witnessed the issuance of the Securities Law No.12 and the Law of the Capital Market Authority No.13 for the year 2004.[1]

In February 2010 and as a respond to the principles of transparency and good governance the Palestine securities exchange became a public shareholding company licensed from the PCMA.

---

[1] http://www.pcma.ps/portal/english/Securities/Pages/Sector-Overview.aspx.

a. Brief Introduction of Securities-Related Laws and Regulations

a) Securities Law No.12 for the Year 2004

In accordance with the Securities Law No."12" and the Capital Market Authority Law No."13" for the year 2004, Palestine Securities sector consists of the following bodies supervised and controlled by the PCMA. These are as follows:

- Palestine Exchange and the Centre of Depository and settlement;
- Public-shareholding companies;
- Securities companies members of the Palestine Exchange;
- Financial professionals;
- Investment funds.

b) Scope of Law

This Law applies to:

- The activities of the Securities Exchanges, authorized members, those dealing in securities and any new activities authorized by the Capital Market Authority;
- Issuance and offering of securities and trading therein;
- Securities companies, investment advisors, financial manager, investors, securities experts, depositary and settlement Centers, fund managers, custody services, issuers, major holders and any activity authorized by the Authority pursuant to this Law.

c) Meaning of Securities

Securities means ownership rights or debt instrument whether domestic or foreign which the Authority approves.

Securities include, specially:

- Shares and bonds;
- Investment units issued by investment schemes;
- Derivatives including convertible shares and bonds, sale or purchase option contracts;
- Futures and commodities.

d) Ownership of Deposited Securities

The securities deposited at the Center are not considered possessions of the Center or the Securities Exchange.

The Center may serve as a depository for foreign securities if these securities were properly registered at a foreign Center after obtaining the Authority's approval.

e) Licensing Requirements

Any person must obtain a license from the Authority and register at the Securities Exchange before engaging in the practice of securities intermediation or as a financial investment Advisor.

The licensed securities company may perform the tasks of the investment Advisor without obtaining an additional license, but it is prohibited for the investment Advisor to carry out any of the tasks exclusive to the securities company without an additional license.

Any individual must obtain a license from the Authority and register at the Securities Exchange prior to practicing his activity as a fund administrator Advisor, or any other professional in securities.

It is prohibited for any securities company or investment Advisor to employee any person as a fund administrator or financial Advisor or professional dealing in securities exchange unless he/she has been licensed by the Authority and has registered at the Securities Exchange.

The Authority shall issue instructions that specify the licensing procedures, qualifications requirements, and the minimal capital requirement, financial position, management, professional and technical qualifications. The Authority has the right to specify the different requirements for each activity.

The Authority may authorize the Securities Exchange to certify the qualifications of those applying to obtain licenses to operate as a fund administrator, financial Advisor, or professional dealing in securities, and to prepare and administer any tests required as a prerequisite for licensing.

The Authority may authorize the Securities Exchange to ensure that these individuals still enjoy the required capacity during the duration of the licensing period.

The Securities Exchange may request the Authority to suspend or revoke the license of a Securities Exchange, an investment Advisor, or any fund administrator, financial Advisor or professional in securities provided that the request is justified.

b. Supervision and Regulation of Securities Market

The securities sector is supervised by the Palestine Capital Market Authority (PCMA) which was established in 2005 as a result of the securities law No.12 and the Capital Market Authority law No.13 of 2004, to regulate, oversee, and develop the securities sector along with other non-banking financial sectors.

The securities sector includes shares of companies listed on PEX, the grand majority of which are profitable. They are classified into five economic sectors: banking and financial services, insurance, investment, industry, and services. Shares trade in Jordanian dinars and in US dollars.[①]

How to invest in securities sector in Palestine?
(i) Open an account with one of the licensed local brokers;
(ii) Set buy / sell orders through the broker either via phone, Fax or Email;
(iii) Internet trading is available.

c. Requirements for Engagement in Securities Trading for Foreign Enterprises

According to the instructions of Palestine Exchange, the following documents are required to open an account for a company as follow (true copy of the original):
- Company registration certificate;
- Articles of association;
- By-Law;
- Personal identification of the authorized signatories of the company;
- Letter on the company's headed paper sent to the broker stating the name/s of the authorized signatories;
- Completing the trading account opening application of the broker;
- Any further documents required by the Palestine Exchange.

All the above mentioned documents shall be either in Arabic or English languages, otherwise the documents shall be translated into Arabic by a licensed sworn translator from eh Ministry of Justice.

I. Preference and Protection of Investment

a. The Structure of Preference Policies

There are no specific laws or regulations or instructions in regard to preference polices. Below, we state the most similar articles of

a) Investment Promotion Law No. 1 for the Year 1998

Article (6)

• No investor shall be excluded on any grounds whatsoever from enjoying the privileges granted in accordance with the provisions of this law.

• The National Authority may grant a "most favored status" treatment to investors on the basis of nationality pursuant to bilateral or multilateral trade or investment agreements which the National Authority may conclude with other States without prejudice to the rights of third parties and with due observance to the principle of reciprocity.

(i) Support for specific industries and regions

The Authority may grant exceptional exemptions to the export-oriented projects, provided that the production destined for export shall not be less than 30% of its total production, provided that the same is made according to the criterion of a special regulation and that the period of the additional exemption may not exceed three years.

(ii) Special exemptions from customs and taxes

• The furniture imported for hotels and hospitals shall be exempted from customs duties and taxes;

• The electrical and electronic appliances and equipment imported for tourist projects, including hotels, shall be exempted from customs duties and taxes;

• The electrical and electronic appliances and equipment imported for hospital projects shall be exempted from customs duties and taxes;

• The hotel and hospital projects shall be granted additional exemptions from the customs and taxes on its purchases of furniture, furnishings, electrical and electronic appliances and equipment as well as supplies for the purposes of modernization and renovation once every five (5) years provided that they are admitted into Palestine or used in the project within two (2) years from the date of issue of a decision approving the purchasing lists and quantities.

Article (43)

All investments shall enjoy the incentives granted by this law with the exception of: Commercial projects, insurance, real estate (with the exception of development projects), banks, money exchange companies, any financial institution (with the exclusive exception of the real estate mortgage).

b) Decision of the Council of Ministers No. 6 of 2017 On the Regulation of Incentive Package Contract for the Purpose of Encouragement of Investment in the Employment of Renewable Energy Technologies (West Bank)

---

① Palestinian Investment Promotion Agency.

Article (4) Power Station Incentives

Power Station: Any station that uses renewable energy resources to produce electricity. It includes buildings and facilities, affiliated lands, and machines and equipment used for this purpose

Power stations with capacity no less than (1) Megawatt, that are implemented within the Approved Areas shall benefit from the following incentives:

• Phase 1: income tax shall be imposed with (0%) for seven years, as of the date of operation of the power station;

• Phase 2: income tax shall be imposed with (5%) for five years, starting from the end of Phase 1;

• Phase 3: income tax shall be imposed with (10%) for three years, starting from the end of Phase 2;

• After the end of phase 3, income tax shall be calculated based on the applicable and in effect rates.

b. Special Investment Zones in Palestine

• The industrial and agricultural zone of Jericho;
• The Industrial zone of Gaza;
• The Industrial zone of Bethlehem;
• The Industrial zone of Jenin.

c. Investment Protection

Article (7)

The projects may not be nationalized or confiscated nor the funds thereof be attached, seized, frozen, confiscated or dealt with except through the courts of law.

Article (8)

The real estate ownership of projects may not be expropriated in whole or in part except for public interest according to the law in consideration of a fair compensation for the value of the real estate on the basis of the market value thereof and other losses which might be sustained as a result of the expropriation.

Article (9)

In the cases other than those in which the Authority may revoke the approval on the project in accordance with the provisions of this law, no other administrative authority may revoke the license of utilizing the real estates which were licensed for utilization by the project, in whole or in part, except after taking the opinion of the Authority. The Authority should express its opinion in this respect within a maximum period of seven days from the date it was requested to do so. The license may not be cancelled except with due to legal reasons or for the sake of public interest and on the basis of none discriminative manner as well as provide all legal means to the prejudiced investor to claim compensation for the losses he sustained as a consequence of cancellation of the license through the courts of law.

Article (10)

With due observance to the provisions of Article (11) of this law and in pursuance with the free market economics, the National Authority guarantees to all investors the unrestricted transfer of all their financial resources outside Palestine including the capital, profits, dividends and capital profits, wages, and salaries, interest, debt payments, management fees, technical assistance, other fees and compensation money for expropriation, cancellation of licenses, courts of law decisions, arbitration awards and any other form of payments or financial resources. The investor may freely transfer all the financial resources outside Palestine at the rate of exchange in force and prevailing in the market at the time of transfer and in a transferable currency acceptable to the investor.

Article (11)

The National Authority may place restrictions on the transfer of the financial resources or part thereof if any of the following restrictions apply on an investor:

• Palestinian bankruptcy laws and other laws which aim at protecting the rights of the creditors;
• Palestinian laws related to the issue of, trading or dealing in securities;
• Palestinian criminal or penal laws;
• Palestinian tax laws;
• Palestinian laws relating to the notification of currency transfers or other monetary instruments;
• Prohibiting orders or final judgments issued by the Palestinian Courts of law or arbitration bodies.

III. Trade

A. Department Supervising Trade

The General Administration of Trade and Crossings at the Ministry of National Economy which consists of

three departments
- Trade Department
- Crossings Department
- Patent and Commercial Agencies

B. The Palestinian Standards and Measurements Institute

a. Brief Introduction of Trade Laws and Regulations
- The commercial law no.12 for the year 1966 (West Bank);
- The commercial law no.2 for the year 2014 (Gaza Strip);
- Palestinian standards and measurements law no.(6) of 2000;
- Law No. 2 for the year 2000 regarding regulation of the work of commercial agents.

b. Trade Management
a) The Trade Department has the following functions and powers:
- Providing advice about all the operational and strategically matters related to trade and crossings;
- Following up the exporting procedures;
- Following up and issuing the exporting licenses;
- Working as observe for external commercial agreement;
- Facilitating and providing all the required documents and licenses for the importing process.

b) The Patent and Commercial Agencies has the following functions and powers:
- Registering patents, trademarks and commercial agencies;
- Protecting the rights pertaining to patents, trademarks and commercial agencies;
- Handling disputes pertaining to patents, trademarks and commercial agencies.

c) The Palestinian Standards and Measurements Institute has the following functions and powers:
- Prepare and adopt the Palestinian standards and measurements related to goods, materials, services and other items and reviewing such standards and measurements and amending or replacing in addition to publishing them. Human and veterinary medications, vaccines and serums shall be excluded from the Institutes' scope of powers and functions;
- Developing a national measurement system;
- Unifying and developing the measurement methods in addition to calibrating and adjusting the measurement tools;
- Issuing the conformity marks and certificates which are approved by the Board;
- Adopting the national main measurement references for the calibration of measurement tools in order to stamp or brand them;
- Approving the testing and calibration laps which are qualified and specialized in conducting the tests and analyses on goods and other materials in order to apply the related standards and measurements;
- Approving the products' labels;
- Cooperation with the local governmental bodies and scientific institutions in order to achieve the Institute's goals and carry out its functions and duties;
- Support and encourage the research conducted in the approved testing and examination labs in areas related to standards, measurements and quality control, in addition to holding training sessions and programs related to the Institutes scope of work;
- Enter into agreements with Arab, regional and international agencies, related to the mutual recognition of conformity marks and certificates, provided that such agreements include an agreement on the previous and continuing testing of the material included in the agreement, in order to make sure that it confirms with adopted technical standards and conditions;
- Cooperating and coordinating with Arab, regional and international institutions which work in the standard and measurements field and joining such institutions;
- Publish and distribute the publications related to standards and measurements issued by the Institute or other Arab, regional or international related bodies.

C. Registering Commercial Agency

Any commercial agent must register every commercial agency agreement in the registry within a period not exceeding three months after signature of the agreements by all concerned parties.

D. Terms to be Fulfilled in Commercial Agencies Agreements

The agreement on commercial agencies must be documented in writing and must include the following information:
- Name, age, citizenship, trade name and residence of the agent; if the agent is a company, its registration number must be included;
- Name, age, citizenship, trade name and residence of grantor;
- Date of commencement and duration of the agreement, which must include all of Palestine;
- Products covered by the agreement;
- The value of sale commission payable to the commercial agent;
- Commitment to supply sufficient accessories and provide necessary maintenance for cars, machines, motors or electric and electronic device and equipment;
- Trademarks of goods or services and patents;
- Any other terms agreed upon between the agent and grantor.

E. The Inspection and Quarantine of Import and Export Commodities

The Crossings Department at the General Administration of Trade and Crossings at the Ministry of National Economy has the following functions and powers:
- Controlling the movement in the crossings in regard to exporting and importing of goods;
- Controlling and inspecting the movement of goods in the crossings;
- Applying the Palestinian laws in regards to standards and measurement and protection of commercial agencies.

F. Customs Management

Law no.1 of 1962 The Customs and Excise Law and its amendments
- All the Goods which are imported into Palestine shall be subject to customs duties. Such duties shall be collected according to the tariff, except what had been exempted from such duties according to the provisions of this or any other law or according to the provisions of any agreement.

IV. Labour

A. Brief Introduction of Labour Laws and Regulations

- Labour Law No.7 for the year 2000 (Gaza and West Bank);
- Decisions issued by the Ministry of Labour and the Council of Ministers (about 41 decisions). Most of these decisions pertain to articles of Labor Law No.7 for the year 2000;
- Law by Decree No.(6) for the year 2016 regarding Social Security (West Bank).

a. Basic Definitions

The employer: Each natural or legal person or a representative thereof who employs one or more person(s) in return for a salary.

The worker: Each natural person who performs a work for the employer in return for a salary and shall be, during his or her performance of the work, under his or her management and supervision.

The temporary work: The work, the nature of the implementation and accomplishment of which necessitates a limited period.

The casual work: The work that is required by contingent necessities and the period of the accomplishment of which does not exceed three months.

The seasonal work: Each work that is implemented and accomplished during periodical annual seasons.

The basic wage: The agreed cash and / or in-kind payment which the employer pays to the worker in return for his or her work. Increments and allowances of any type whatsoever shall not be included thereunder.

The salary: The full salary, which is the basic salary to which the increments and allowances are added.

b. The Individual Work Contract

The individual work contract shall be an explicit or implicit written or verbal agreement that is concluded between an employer and a worker for a limited or unlimited period of time or for the accomplishment of a specified work, in accordance with which the worker shall undertake to perform a work for the benefit of the employer and under his or her management and supervision, and in which the employer shall undertake to pay the wage agreed upon to the worker.

c. Maximum Duration of the Work Contract

The maximum duration of the work contract of a limited period for the same employer must not exceed two consecutive years, including the cases of renewal.

In case the work contract, including renewal periods, the contract will be considered for unlimited period.

d. Probationary Period

The work contract may commence with a probationary period, the duration of which is three months, and it may not be repeated from more than once at the same employer.

e. Expiration of the Individual Work Contract

The individual work contract shall expire in any of the following cases:
(i) Upon agreement of both parties.
(ii) By the expiration of its duration in the casual, temporary or seasonal works.
(iii) Upon the wish of either party during the probationary period.
(iv) Upon the wish of the worker, provided that the employer is notified in writing prior to the leave:
• by one month in case he or she used to earn his or her salary on a monthly basis;
• by one week in case he or she used to earn his or her salary on a daily or weekly basis or based on piecework or commission.
(v) By the death of the worker or his or her being infected with an illness or disability that disables him or her from work for a period of time exceeding six months based upon a medical report issued by the Medical Committee and a vacant position that suits his or her occupational capabilities and new health condition is unavailable.

f. Terminating Work Contract Without Notice

The employer shall be entitled to terminate the work contract unilaterally without a notice along with preserving his or her right to demand all rights from the worker when he or she commits any of the following contraventions:

(i) His or her impersonation of a personality other than his or hers or submission of false certificates or documents to the employer.

(ii) His or her committing of an error due to a confirmed negligence from which a grave loss is caused to the employer, provided that the employer reports the incident to the competent authorities within forty eight hours from the time on which its occurrence comes to his or her knowledge.

(iii) His or her repeating of the infringement of the bylaw of the installation which is approved by the Ministry of Labour or the written directives pertaining to the work safety and workers' hygiene despite his or her being warned thereby in due form.

(iv) His or her being absent without an acceptable excuse for a period of more than seven consecutive days, or more than fifteen sporadic days within the same year, provided that he or she was warned in writing following an absence of three days in the former case or ten days in the latter case.

(v) The worker's non-fulfillment of the obligations due by him or her under the work contract although he or she has been warned thereof in due form.

(vi) His or her revealing of the secrets related to the work, which may cause a grave damage.

(vii) His or her being convicted by a final judgement of a crime or misdemeanor that violates honor, trust or public morale.

(viii) His or her being present during the working hours in a state of inebriation or affected by a consumed narcotic drug, which is punishable by Law.

(ix) His or her assault by means of beating or contempt against the employer or his or her representative or against his or her immediate manager.

g. Terminating the Work Contract for Technical Reasons or a Loss

The employer may terminate the work contract for technical reasons or a loss that has necessitated the reduction of the number of workers, provided that the worker maintains his or her right in the reimbursement for the notice and remuneration of the expiration of service, on condition that the Ministry is ;notified thereof.

h. End of Service Benefits

The worker who has completed a year at work shall be entitled to a remuneration of the end of service, the amount of which shall be a salary of one month for each year he or she spent at work on the basis of the last salary which he or she earned without counting of the extra working hours. For such purpose, the fractions of the year shall be calculated.

i. End of Service Benefits for Piecework

The remuneration of the expiration of service and the compensation for the arbitrary dismissal of the worker shall be calculated by piecework or by commission on the basis of the average of his or her monthly salary during the period of the last year.

j. Payment for Unjustified Rermination (Arbitral Dismissal)

In addition to maintaining all his or her other legal rights, the worker shall be entitled to a compensation for his or her being dismissed arbitrarily in the amount of the salary of two months for each year he or she spends at work, provided that the compensation does not exceed his or her salary for a period of two years.

k. End of Service Benefits in Case of Resignation

- If the employee spent less than five years at work, then he / she is entitled to one third of the end of service benefits.
- If the employee spent five to ten years at work, then he / she is entitled to two thirds of the end of service benefits.
- If the employee spent ten years or more at work, then he / she is entitled to full end of service benefits.

l. Rights of Workers of Limited Contract

Workers under work contracts of limited periods, including workers under a casual work contract or seasonal work contract, shall enjoy the same rights and same obligations to which workers under work contracts of unlimited periods are subject under similar circumstances, taking into consideration the provisions pertaining to the work for a limited, casual and seasonal period.

m. Working Hours

The actual working hours per week shall be no more than forty five hours.

The daily working hours shall be reduced by at least one hour in the hazardous occupations or those damaging health as well as at night work. Such occupations shall be defined in a decision from the Minister, after consultation with the concerned organisations of employers and workers.

Daily working hours must include one or more period(s), the total of which shall not exceed one hour, for the repose of the worker taking into consideration that the worker does not work for five consecutive hours.

n. Extra Working Hours (overtime)

The parties to production may agree to extra working hours that do not exceed twelve hours a week.
A remuneration of an hour and a half shall be paid to the worker for each extra working hour.

o. Weekly Holiday

Friday is the weekly holiday unless the interest of the work requires the allocation of another day on a regular basis.

p. Annual Leaves

- The worker shall be entitled to a paid annual leave, the duration of which is two weeks per year at work and three weeks for the work in hazardous occupations or those damaging health as well as for those who have spent five years at the installation.
- The worker may not relinquish the annual leave.
- Based upon the agreement between the parties to production, the annual leave may be partitioned.
- The annual leaves may not be accumulated for over two years

q. Religious and Official Holidays

The worker shall have the right to a paid leave on religious and official holidays, which are not to be counted from among the annual leaves.

r. Hajj Religious Leave

The worker, who has spent five years at the installation, shall be entitled to a paid leave, the duration of which is not less than two weeks for performance of the Hajj religious duty [pilgrimage to the Holy Shrines in the city of Mecca in Saudi Arabia] to be granted to him or her once.

s. Leave in Case of Death or Contingent Cause

- The worker shall be entitled to a paid leave for a period of three days in the event of the death of one of his or her relatives up to the second degree. It shall not be counted from his or her annual leave.
- The worker may be absent from work for a demonstrated contingent cause for a period of ten days a year to be counted from the annual leave, provided that it does not exceed three consecutive three days on the one

occasion.

t. Sick Leave

Based upon a report from the Medical Committee, the worker shall be entitled to a paid sick leave, the period of which is fourteen days, within the one year. It shall be [taken] with half of the salary for another period of fourteen days.

u. Occupational Safety and Hygiene

The installation shall issue forth instructions on occupational safety and hygiene as well as bylaw of penalties, which is approved by the Ministry. Such instructions shall be posted on visible places at the installation.

v. Discrimination Between Men and Women

The discrimination between men and women shall be prohibited.

w. Maternity Leave

(i) The working woman who has spent at work prior to each delivery a period of one hundred and eighty days shall have the right to a paid maternity leave for a period of ten weeks, including at least six weeks after the delivery.

(ii) The working woman may not be dismissed due to the leave mentioned in Paragraph (1) above unless it is demonstrated that she was employed in another occupation during it

x. The Minimum Wage Limit

Decision of Council of Ministers No.11 for the year 2012 regarding the minimum wage limit in all areas of the Palestinian National Authority:

The wage of the worker may not be less than the legally approved minimum wage limit.
The minimum wage according to the Palestinian ministry of Labour is NIS 1,450 (about US$ 400).
The minimum wage for daily worker is NIS 65 (about US$ 18.5)
The minimum wage for hour is NIS 8.5 (about US$ 2.4)

y. Labour Inspection

Under this Law, the Minister shall establish a commission to be named the "The Commission of Labour Inspection" from an adequate number of inspectors as well as those qualified academically and professionally to follow up on the enforcement of the provisions of this Law and the regulations issued forth in accordance with it.

The members on the Commission on Labour Inspection shall enjoy in the exercise of their duties the powers of the Judicial Police.

B. Requirements of Employing Foreign Employees

a. Wark Permit

The Ministry shall be entitled to grant a license to work in Palestine for non-Palestinians. The employer shall be prohibited from employing, in a direct manner or by means of a third party, any non-Palestinian worker prior to the confirmation of obtaining the license mentioned above.

It should be noted that the provisions of the Labor Law apply also to the foreign employees.

b. Application Procedure

- Obtaining approval from the Israeli authorities;
- Obtaining approval from the Palestinian Ministry of Interior;
- Obtaining approval from the Palestinian Ministry of Labour.

c. Social Insurance

a) Work Injuries and Occupational Diseases
The employer must insure all his or her workers against work injuries at the licensed parties in Palestine.
b) Duties of employer upon the occurrence of a work injury
Upon the occurrence of a work injury, the employer must perform the following:
• Offer necessary first medical aid to the injured and transport him or her to the nearest centre for [medical] treatment;
• Report to the Police immediately upon the occurrence of any injury that leads to the death of a worker or causes a physical damage that prevents him or her from continuing to work;
• Notify the Ministry as well as the insurer in writing of each work injury within 48 hours from its occurrence. The injured shall be handed a copy of the notification.

The employer shall be responsible for the following:
- Treatment of the injured worker until he or she is cured as well as cover all expedient treatment expenses, including rehabilitation services and requisites;
- All entitlements resulting from the injury even if they invoke the liability of a third party.

C. Exit and Entry

a. Visa Types

Please note that currently no specific visa types to enter the Palestinian territories. The entry to Palestine would be described as follow:

a) West Bank
- Allenby Bridge (Allenby Bridge between Jordan and West Bank under the control of Israel) to cross to West Bank via Jordan.
- From Israel (Ben Gurion Airport): to cross to West Bank via Israel.

b) Gaza Strip
- Rafah Crossing: to cross to Gaza via Egypt. This crossing is opened for two-three days each three-four months (about 12 days per a year) The number of passengers each days is estimated 500 – 700 (about 2000 for each opening). It should be noted that there are about 32,000 registered passengers who want to leave from Rafah crossing, in addition to the emergency illness cases;
- Erez Crossing (crossing between Gaza and Israel under the control of Israel);
- Allenby Bridge: to cross to West Bank via Jordan and then to cross to Gaza via Erez crossing;
- From Israel (Ben Gurion Airport): to cross to Israel and then to cross to Gaza via Erez crossing.

c) Investor Visit Permit to Palestine

The Palestinian Investment Promotion Agency (PIPA) can arrange for granting an investor visit permit to enter the Palestinian territories as described below.

(i) Requirements for Issuing Investor Visit Permit
- Scanned copy of the Passport (valid for 6 months, at least).
- Personal photo.
- Supportive documents from a relevant Palestinian body (if the investor already registered his company or investment in the Palestinian institutions).
- Overview of the potential investment.
- Summary of any previous investments (inside or outside Palestine).
- Summary of properties (inside or outside Palestine).
- Proposed date of the visit.
- Contact information.

(ii) Process of requesting Investor Visit Permit

According the requirements Palestinian Investment Promotion Agency (PIPA), the investor needs to a covering letter which includes a summary of proposed investment and a list of the attachments. Then, these documents along with the covering letter shall be submitted to PIPA 45 days prior the proposed date of the visit. Additional, such request can be submitted via PIPA's website (http://www.pipa.ps/elogin.php).

b. Restrictions for Exit and Entry

The approval of entry to Gaza and West Bank thorough crossings under the Israeli control subject to the approval of the Israeli authorities.

D. Trade Union and Labour Organizations

a. Composing Union Organizations

In accordance with the provisions of the Law, the workers and employers shall have the right to compose union organizations on a professional basis with the aim to sponsor their interests and defend their rights.

b. The Palestinian Federation of Industries

The Palestinian Federation of Industries aims to support the Palestinian national industries and protect them against dumping and unfair competition via the following:
- Development of the national industries by orienting domestic and foreign investments and introducing modern industrial systems;
- Regulating of industrial activity in accordance with the type of industrial production through specialized unions and provide them with the necessary support;

- Endeavor to raise the competitiveness of the national industrial products.

E. Labour Disputes

a. Costs for Labour Disputes

Workers shall be exempted from the judicial fees in the labour actions at law, which they lodge as a result of a dispute related to salaries, leaves, and remunerations of the end of service, indemnities for work injury or arbitrary dismissal of the worker.

b. Special Regulations in Favor of Employees

The provisions prescribed under this Law shall represent the minimum limit of the rights of workers which may not be waived. Wherever a special regulation on work relations exists, the provisions under this Law or the provisions under the special regulation, any of which is better for the worker, shall be applicable to workers.

c. Collective Labour Dispute

The collective labour dispute shall be a dispute which arises between one or more employer(s) and workers or a group thereof over a collective interest.

V. Intellectual Property

A. Brief Introduction of IP Laws and Regulations

Trade Marks Ordinance No.35 of 1938 (Gaza)
The Trademarks By-Law No. 1 for the year 1952 (West Bank)
Trademark: means a mark used or proposed to be used upon or in connection with goods for the purpose of indicating that they are the goods of the proprietor of such trade mark by virtue of manufacture, selection, certification dealing with or offering for sale.
Trademarks Department: a department at the Ministry of National Economy which is responsible for managing the process of registering and administrating trademarks.
Register: a record called of all the trademarks wherein shall be entered all registered trademarks with the names, addresses and descriptions of their proprietors, notifications of assignments and transmissions, disclaimers, conditions, limitations and such other matters relating to such trademarks as may from time to time be prescribed.
Registrar: the person who is appointed to be in charge of the of the trademarks department at the Ministry of National Economy.

B. Trademark Registration

a. The Process of Registering a Trademark Includes the Following Three Phases:

a) Filing a trademark application: this phase includes submitting an application to the registrar with all the information and requirements necessary to file a trademarks, including:
- The Trademarks owner's name.
- The Trademarks owner's address of the trademark.
- Class of the trademark.
- Name of the trademark "logo to be sent by email if the trademark is a design" (specifying if it is black and white or in colors).
- A valid Power of attorney signed and sealed by the owner of the trademark to our office and it must be both legalized and notarized.

b) Publication: trademarks are published in the official gazette after (6 – 9 months, approximately) whereby the chance of filing opposition against any published trademark is available. The opposition period is three months as from the date of publishing the trademark in the official gazette.

c) Finial registration: after the expiry of the three months period for filing oppositions, the trademark owner (agent) can request to obtain the final registration certificate of a trademark.

b. Marks Capable of Registration as Trademarks

- Trademarks capable of registration must consist of characters, devices or marks or combinations thereof which have a distinctive character.

- For the purposes of this section "distinctive" shall mean adapted to distinguish the goods of the proprietor of the trade marks from those of other persons.
- In determining whether a trade mark is so adapted, the registrar or the court may, in the case of a trade mark in actual use, take into consideration the extent to which such user has rendered such trade mark in fact distinctive for goods with respect to which it is registered or proposed to be registered.
- A trade mark may be limited in whole or in part to one or more specified colours, and in such case the fact that it is so limited shall be taken into consideration by the registrar or court having to decide on the distinctive character of such trade mark. If and so far as a trade mark is registered without limitation of colour it shall be deemed to be registered for all colours.
- A trade mark must be registered in respect of particular goods or classes of goods.
- Any question arising as to the class within which any goods fall shall be determined by the registrar, whose decision shall be final.

c. Marks not Capable of Registration as Trademarks

- public armorial bearings, crests, insignia, or decorations of Palestine or of His Majesty's Dominions or Foreign States or nations, unless authorized by the competent authorities.
- official hall marks or signs indicating an official warranty; unless put forward or authorized by the competent authority owning or controlling the mark.
- representations of royal arms or royal crests, or arms or crests so nearly resembling them as to lead to mistake, or of national flags, or the word "royal" or any other words, letters, or devices calculated to lead persons to think that the applicant has royal patronage or authorisation.
- marks in which the following words appear: "Patent", "Patented", "By Royal Letters Patent", "Registered", "Registered design", "Copyright", "To counterfeit this is forgery" or words to like effect.
- marks which are or may be injurious to public order or morality or which are calculated to deceive the public; or marks which encourage unfair trade competition, or contain false indications of origin.
- marks consisting of figures, letters or words which are in common use in trade to distinguish or describe goods or classes of goods or which bear direct reference to their character or quality; words whose ordinary signification is geographical or a surname, unless represented in a special or particular manner: provided that nothing herein contained shall be deemed to prohibit the registration of marks of the nature described in this paragraph which have a distinctive character.
- marks identical with or similar to emblems of exclusively religious significance.
- marks which are or contain, or which so nearly resemble as to be calculated to deceive, the representation, name or the trade name of a person, or the name of a body corporate or of an association, unless the consent of the person or persons concerned has been obtained; in the case of persons recently dead the registrar may call for consents from their legal representatives.
- A mark identical with one belonging to a different proprietor which is already on the register, in respect of such goods or description of goods, or so nearly resembling such trade mark as to be calculated to deceive.

d. Requirements for Change of Agent

A valid Power of attorney signed and sealed by the owner of the trademark to our office and it must be legalized and notarized.

e. Requirements for Renewal of Trademark Before/After the Expiration Date

- The trademark name and number
- A valid Power of attorney signed and sealed by the owner of the trademark to our office and it must be legalized and notarized.

f. Requirements for Changing the Name of Trademark

- A certificate proving the change of name of the trademark signed, sealed and legalized.
- A valid Power of attorney signed and sealed by the owner of the trademark to our office and it must be legalized and notarized

g. Requirements for Changing the Address of Trademark

- A certificate proving the change of address of the trademark signed, sealed and legalized.
- A valid Power of attorney signed and sealed by the owner of the trademark to our office and it must be legalized and notarized.

h. Requirements for Search for Trademark

-class of the trademark

-name of the trademark or logo to be sent by email if the trademark is a design (specifying if it is black and white or in colors).

i. Requirements for Recordal of Assignment

- A valid Power of attorney signed and sealed by the owner of the trademark to our office and it must be legalized and notarized "as per the attached draft".
- the deed of assignment.

j. Validity of a Trademark Registration

- The trademark registration shall be valid for a period of 7 years as from the application date.
- After 7 years, the trademark registration shall be renewed. Such renewal shall be valid for a period of 14 years.

k. Registering in More than One Class

Please note that the trademarks law in Palestine doesn't allow multiple class registration, which means that if a trademark needs to be registered in more than one class, a separate application shall be submitted to register the trademark in each class.

l. Filing 3D Trademarks

Filling a 3D trademark would not be possible in Gaza, however, such can be described in detail within an application for an industrial design.

C. Patent Application

Required documents in patent application:
- A notarized power of attorney.
- Notarized affidavit signed by the inventor and the person who wants to register the invention, or by the inventor and others as inventors in the country of origin.
- Explanatory description of the invention qualities and protection elements in both languages Arabic & English.
- Legalized and notarized copy of the patent.
- Copy of drawings or charts of the invention (if available).

D. Measures for IP Protection

Article (9) Name or description of goods

Where the name or a description of any goods appears on a trade mark the registrar may refuse to register such mark in respect of any goods other than the goods so named or described. Where the name or description of any goods appears on a trade mark, which name or description in use varies, the registrar may permit the registration of the mark with the name or description upon it for goods other than those named or described, the applicant stating in his application that the name or description varies.

Article (26) Rights of proprietor of trade mark

Subject to any limitations and conditions entered upon the register, the registration of a person as proprietor of a trade mark shall, if valid, give to such person the right to the exclusive use of such trade mark upon or in connection with the goods in respect of which it is registered: Provided always that where two or more persons are registered proprietors of the same (or substantially the same) trade mark in respect of the same goods, no rights of exclusive user of such trade mark shall (except so far as their respective rights shall have been defined by the registrar or by the Supreme Court sitting as a High Court of Justice) be acquired by any one of such persons as against any other by the registration thereof, but each of such persons shall otherwise have the same rights as if he were the sole registered proprietor thereof.

Article (29) Registration to be prima facie evidence of validity

In all legal proceedings relating to a registered trademark the fact that a person is registered as proprietor of such trade mark shall be prima facie evidence of the validity of the original registration of such trade mark and all subsequent assignments and transmissions of the same.

Article (34) Unregistered trade mark

No person shall be entitled to institute any proceedings to recover damages for the infringement of a trademark not registered in Palestine.

VI. Environmental Protection

A. Department Supervising Environmental Protection

Environment Quality Authority: it is the governmental department which is responsible to implement and apply the provisions Environment Law no.7 of 1999 and to cooperate with other specialized entities in this regard.

The Ministry of Tourism and Antiquities has been assigned to be a member of the board of directors of the Environment Quality Authority in accordance with the Council of Ministers Decision no.(273) for the year 2005.

The Ministry of National Economy has been assigned to be a member of the board of directors of the Environment Quality Authority in accordance with the Council of Ministers Decision no.(321) for the year 2005.

B. Brief introduction of Laws and Regulations of Environmental Protection

a. Environment Law No.7 of 1999

In 1999, the Environment Law no.7 of 1999 was passed and promulgated. This law has authorized the Ministry of Environment to implement and apply the provisions of this law.

In 2002, Environment Quality Authority has been established under the presidential decree no.(6) for the year 2002. According to this decree, the tasks and responsibilities of the Ministry of Environment were allocated to the Environment Quality Authority.

b. Law by Decree No.11 of 2013 Regarding the Amendment of Environment Law No.7 of 1999

Article (3)

The titles of Ministry of Environment Affairs and Minister of Environment Affairs wherever it stipulated in the original law (environment law no.7 of 1999) shall be replaced by the titles "Environment Quality Authority" and "Chairman of Environment Quality Authority".

c. Some of the Articles in Environment Law No.7 of 1999 that Would Be Relevant to Investment Projects:

Article (6)

The specialized agencies, in coordination with The Ministry, shall devise the public policy for land uses taking into account the best use thereof and the protection of natural resources and areas with special natural characteristics as well as the conservation of the environment.

Article (7)

The Ministry, in coordination with other specialized agencies, shall set a comprehensive plan for solid waste management on the national level, including the ways and the designation of sites for solid waste disposal as will as the supervision to implement this plan by the local councils.

Article (12)

No person shall be authorized to manufacture, store, distribute, use; treat, or dispose any hazardous substance or waste whether it was solid, liquid, or gas, unless such a process is in compliance with the regulations, instructions and norms specified by The Ministry, in coordination with the specialized agencies.

Article (16)

The Ministry, in coordination with the specialized agencies, shall set up the environmental conditions compatible for mining, quarrying activities, rubbles, mines and stone quarrying places in a manner that ensures both the protection of the environment against the hazards of environmental pollution; and the preservation of natural resources.

Article (18)

It is forbidden to drift arable lands or transport its soil in order to use it for purposes other than farming. It shall not be considered as drifting if the land is leveled, or its soil is transported to be improved agriculturally or preserve its fertility or build on it in compliance with the terms and restrictions enacted by the specialized agencies.

Article (19)

The Ministry, in cooperation with the specialized agencies, shall specify standards to regulate the percentage of pollutants in the air which may cause harm or damage to public health, social welfare and the environment;

Each facility, which will be established in Palestine, shall abide to these standards; every existing facility shall make necessary changes in a manner that makes it conform to these standards within a period, which does not exceed three years.

Article (20)

Every facility owner shall provide all means to ensure the necessary protection for workers and the neighbors of the facility, in compliance with the conditions of occupational safety and health, against any leak or emission of pollutants in or out the working place.

Article (25)
The Ministry, in cooperation with the specialized agencies, shall work on establishing standards, instructions and conditions to reduce environmental nuisance generated by different activities; in addition, every facility owner, entity or individual shall be forbidden to cause any nuisance to the others.

Article (34)
It shall be forbidden to perform any action, which may affect the natural track of the beach, or adjust it inside or far from the sea unless an environmental approval is obtained from the Ministry.

Article (39)
All national and international companies and agencies authorized to undertake digging or exploration activities, or to produce or manufacture crude oil, or to extract or exploit oil fields and other marine natural sources, shall abide to the environmental conditions.

Article (46)
When authorizing any facility, the specialized agencies shall work on to avoid environmental hazards, by encouraging transferring to the projects that use substances and operations less harmful on the environment, and by giving priority to such projects on the basis of economic development.

Article (47)
The Ministry, in coordination with the specialized agencies, shall determine the activities and projects that have to obtain an environmental approval before being licensed, similarly, the projects are allowed to be established in the restricted areas.

Article (48)
The Specialized Agencies are not allowed to issue licenses for establishing projects or facilities, or licenses for any other activities specified in article (47) in this Law, or to renew them unless an environmental approval is obtained from the Ministry.

Article (53)
The owners of the different projects and activities have to allow the inspectors of the Environmental Planning and any other specialized agencies to conduct their functions, and provide them with the information and data that they see necessary in compliance with the provisions of this law.

C. Evaluation of Environmental Protection

Article (50)
The Ministry, in coordination with the specialized agencies, shall monitor the variant institutions, projects and activities to ensure their compliance with the requirements, standards and instructions prescribed for protecting the environment and the vital resources, in compliance with the provisions of this law, which are enacted by the ministry and the other agencies.

Article (78)
The Ministry, in conjunction with the other specialized agencies, shall prepare emergency plans to combat environmental disasters.

Article (79)
The Ministry, in cooperation with specialized agencies shall perform environmental monitoring in order to gather information about the different environmental elements and shall prepare comprehensive reports to be submitted to the specialized agencies.

Article (80)
Upon suggestion from The Minister, the Ministerial Cabinet shall issue the Executive Regulation, which is necessary for the enforcement of the provisions of this law.

D. Penalties of Violating the Provisions of the Environment Law

Article (59)
Any facility owner or operator provides incorrect or misleading information regarding the environmental aspects of the facility he owns or operates, shall be penalized by imprisonment of a period does not exceed six months and a fine of not more than two thousand Jordanian Dinars or the equivalent thereof in the legally circulated currency, or one of them.

E. Application of International Laws in Regard to Environmental Protection

Article (75)
In order to implement the provisions of this law or any other international conventions, regarding environment, of which Palestine is a part, the Ministry in coordination with the local specialized agencies shall cooperate with

the signatory countries to exchange scientific and technical information, coordinate programs in the field of joint environmental research, set and implement joint cooperation programs to prevent or reduce environmental pollution and exchange various forms of assistance in this regard.

Article (76)

Any natural or juridical person who causes environmental harm as a result of action or omission in contradiction with the provisions of this law or any international convention of which Palestine is a part, shall be compelled to the payment of convenient compensations in addition to the penal liability explicated in this law.

Article (77)

According to the provisions of this law, International and Regional conventions, treaties as well as the provisions of the specialized international entities of which Palestine is a part, or any other laws related to the environment which are in effect in the Palestinian territories, shall be considered complementary to this law, unless otherwise is provided.

VII. Dispute Resolution

A. Methods and Bodies of Dispute Resolution

a. Methods of Solving Disputes

1.Regular Courts: the competent Palestinian courts are authorized to look into any disputes arise between the parties and brought to the courts by either party.

2.Arbitration: Explained below

Law on Arbitration No (3) for the year 2000

b.Classification of Arbitration According to the Arbitration Law

Article (3)

For the purposes of this law, arbitration shall be:

Local if it is not a matter of international trade and is taking place in Palestine

International if the issues at conflict related to economic, trade or civil issues in the following cases:

a) If the headquarters of the parties in arbitration are in different countries in the time of conclusion of the agreement on arbitration. If any of the parties has several business centers, his headquarters shall be defined as the center that is more closely linked to the agreement on arbitration. If any of the parties has no business center, his place of residence shall be considered.

b) If the issues at conflict included in the agreement on arbitration are linked to more than one country.

c) If the headquarters for the business of each of the parties in arbitration are in the same country upon signature of the agreement on arbitration and that one of the following centers is located in another country.

• the location to make the arbitration as is specified in the agreement on arbitration or as is explained the manner of specification thereof;

• the center for the implementation of an essential part of the commitments arising from the trade or contractual relation between the parties;

• the place that is most linked to the issues at conflict.

Foreign if it takes place outside Palestine.

Special if it is not organized by an institution specialized in arbitration.

Institutional if it is performed via any organization specialized in arbitration and the supervision thereof whether it be in or outside Palestine.

c. Forming Arbitration Panel

Article (8)

An arbitration panel shall be formed of one or more arbitrators with agreement of parties.

If there is no agreement on the formation of a panel for arbitration, each party shall choose an arbitrator and the arbitrators shall choose a casting arbitrator unless the parties agree to proceed otherwise.

d. Arbitration Procedures

Article (20)

The arbitration panel shall start operation upon referral of the conflict thereto and its acceptance to arbitration between the parties.

Article (21)
If the arbitration parties do not agree on the place for arbitration, it shall take place in the place determined by the arbitration panel taking into consideration the circumstances of the conflict and the suitability of the place for members; the arbitration panel may hold one or more sessions in any other place it deems fit.

Article (22)
Arbitration shall take place in Arabic unless the parties agree otherwise. In case of multiplicity of languages, the arbitration panel shall set the language (s) to adopt.

The arbitration panel may request from any of the parties to submit written documents translated into Arabic or in any of the languages adopted thereby.

The arbitration panel may have recourse to a certified translator in case of multiplicity of languages of the parties in conflict.

Article (30)
The arbitration panel may upon request of any of the parties or by its own decision appoint one or more experts in any matter it determines, in which case each party must submit to such expert any information or document related to this matter.

Article (31)
a) The arbitration panel shall send a copy of the expert's report to all of the parties while providing for an opportunity to question the expert before the arbitration panel in a session set for this purpose.

b) Every party shall have the right to call one or more experts to give their opinion on the matters dealt with in the report of the expert assigned by the arbitration panel.

Article (34)
The arbitration panel may decide to oblige the parties to payment of any sums it deems fit to cover the expenses incurred by the arbitration provided that the agreement on arbitration states clearly that this principle is acceptable. If the parties or any thereof fails to pay the sums due to the arbitration panel, the panel may request the competent court to issue a ruling therefor.

B. Application of laws

a. Law on Arbitration No.(3) for the Year 2000

Article (2)
Without jeopardizing the provisions of Article (4) of this law, the provisions of this law shall apply in arbitration between natural or legal persons who enjoy legal capacity to hold rights regardless of the nature of the legal relation subject of the conflict, while taking into consideration the international agreements in which Palestine is a signatory member.

Article (4)
The provisions of this law shall not apply to the following matters:
a) Issues related to public order in Palestine.
b) Issues that cannot be solved by conciliation by law
c) Disputes related to personal status.

Article (19)
Parties in international arbitration may agree on the law to be applicable in case of conflict. In the absence of such agreement, the arbitration panel shall apply the Palestinian law.

In case of international arbitration taking place in Palestine and that the parties do not reach agreement on the law to be applicable, statute rules referred to on regulations regarding conflict in application of laws in the Palestinian law shall apply, taking into consideration that the rules of revenue cannot apply unless they stipulate for application of the Palestinian law. In all cases, the arbitration panel shall take into consideration the customs applicable to the relation between the parties in conflict.

Article (47)
After ratification of the arbitration decision by the competent court, it shall have the same power and effect as court decisions and shall be implemented in the manner used to implement any ruling or decision emanating from any court in compliance with the applicable procedures.

Article (48)
Cases of refusing a foreign arbitration decision

Taking into consideration the international agreements adhered by Palestine and the laws in effect in Palestine, the competent court may, even upon its own consideration, refuse to implement a foreign arbitration decision in any of the two following cases:

a) if the decision violates public order in Palestine;

b) if the decision is not conform to the international treaties and agreements applicable in Palestine.

The Law of Execution No (23) for the Year 2005

b. The Execution of the Foreign Official Judgments, Decisions, Orders and Writs

Article (36)

An order may be issued forth in regard of the judgments, decisions and orders issued forth in a foreign country to be executed in Palestine under the selfsame conditions prescribed in such country for the execution of the Palestinian judgments, decisions and orders therein, provided that they do not contradict the Palestinian Laws or cause damage to the supreme national interest.

The order to execute the judgments, decisions and orders issued forth in a foreign country shall be requested through an action to be submitted before the Court of First Instance, within the jurisdiction of which the execution is to required, provided that the such judgments, decisions and orders are certified by the competent authorities in due form.

Article (37)

The order concerning execution may not take place except following the verification of the following:

a) That the courts of the State of Palestine are not solely competent of the adjudication of the dispute regarding which the judgement, decision or order has been issued forth, and that the foreign courts which issued it forth are competent thereof in conformity with the Rules of International Judicial Jurisdiction established in their Law.

b) That the judgement, decision or order has possessed the force of the order that has been judged in conformity with the law of the court which has issued it forth.

c) That the judgement, decision or order does not contradict a judgement, decision or order that had been issued in advance by a Palestinian court and that it does not include any contraventions of the public order or morals in Palestine.

Article (38)

The provisions of Articles (36) and (37) shall be enforced upon the judgements of arbitrators issued in a foreign country, on the condition that the judgement has been passed in a case, in which arbitration is allowable in pursuance of the provisions of the effective Palestinian Law of Arbitration.

Article (39)

An order may be issued forth to execute the executable official writs which are drawn up in a foreign country under the same conditions established in the law of such country for the execution of the executable official writs which are drawn up in Palestine.

The application concerning the order of execution shall be submitted to Head of the Court of First Instance, within the jurisdiction of which execution is wanted.

The order of execution may not take place except following the verification of the fulfillment of the required conditions such as the official nature of the writ and its executability in accordance with the law of the country in which it was completed, and that it is void of contraventions of the public order or morals in Palestine.

VIII. Others

A. Settlement of Disputes in the Investment Promotion Law

Article (39)

The provisions contained in this part shall apply to the disputes that arise between the investors and the National Authority in respect of the rights and duties provided for in the Investment Law.

Article (40)

When the investor or National Authority believes that a dispute has arisen between them, either of them can request the holding of negotiations in accordance with the proceedings specified in the regulations. Either party to the dispute may request the holding of negotiations prior to its resorting to the settlement of disputes provided for under paragraph (b) of this article.

If the negotiations fail to settle the dispute during the time span specified in the regulations, either of the two parties may refer the dispute to:

- An independent and binding arbitration as stipulated by the regulations;
- The Palestinian Courts.

B. Project Contracting

Law No.(6) For the Year 1999 Concerning Tenders For Governmental Works
Decision of Council of Ministers no.(5) for the year 2014 regarding the Public Procurement System.

a. Specialized Central Tenders Committee

A specialized central tenders committee under the chairmanship of the Director shall be formed for every one of the following four fields and the headquarters of such committees shall be in the Central Tenders Department and it may hold its meetings in the Department concerned with the tender:
- Government buildings field;
- Water, irrigation, sewage and dams field;
- Roads, transportation and mining field;
- Electro-mechanic and communication works field.

b. Methods of Executing the Works and Services

The following works and services shall be executed in one of the following methods:

a) Public tenders: They are those which take the principle of publicity, equality and freedom of competition and are either local or international.

b) The tenders through the method of invitation of offers that is by addressing special invitations to a minimum number of three contractors or consultants

c) Direct contracting in urgent special or exceptional cases

d) Direct Execution: Is the execution which is carried out by the Ministry through its equipment and staff.

c. Rules Should be Observed in Regard to Tenders for Public Works or Technical Services

- The issue of the tender shall be made vide an advertisement in the local newspapers provided that the announcement of the issue of any tender or making any award is not made unless the financial appropriations are available for its execution or there is a commitment for providing same from the financing authority by a resolution of the Council of Ministers.

- Apply the principle of competition and provide equal opportunities to the qualified parties to execute the works or provide the technical services in the manner deemed proper by the competent authority with due observance of giving sufficient period to the contractors and consultants to study the tender documents and submit the offers that are consistent with the required nature of works or technical services.

- Comply, upon the award of the tender, with the best offers which meet the conditions of tender invitation and most suitable prices with due observance to the degree of the required quality and the possibility of execution within the fixed period and the extent of capability of the contractor or consultant to carry out the required work according to the conditions and specifications.

- Place a provision in the conditions of tenders and specifications on the use of local materials and industrial products in the works as long as they comply with the approved specifications coupled with the requirement to avoid the defining of the commercial names to any industry.

- All the agreements and contractual conditions should be in the Arabic language but the specifications, layouts, technical reports and correspondence may be in the English language. Also, the contracts may be translated into the English language provided that the Arabic language shall prevail in the contract.

- Comply with the laws, regulations and instructions in force upon formulating the contractual conditions and not to provide for the exemption from any financial commitment which is imposed by any legislation except after the approval of the Council of Ministers of the exemption prior to the signing of the contract.

- Give the priority in governmental work projects to local contractors if they meet the required conditions.
- The foreign companies should observe the relevant laws and regulations in force in Palestine

d. Unified General Conditions for the Tenders

Every department should, upon the execution of works and technical services pertaining thereto, adopt the unified general conditions for the tenders provided that any amendments or additional conditions should be provided for in the particular conditions of the contract.

C. Invitation to Bid and Bidding

a. Main Elements in Invitation to Tender

- Name of the party requesting the tender;
- Required specifications (sketches, diagrams, drawings and any other clarifications;
- Instructions and general conditions;

- Tender proposals (Technical and financial);
- Special conditions from the party requesting the tender;
- Specifying the address to where the tender shall be submitted;
- Specifying the deadline and method of submitting the tender;
- Special annexed in relation to the tender subject which may include additional conditions.

b. Language of Documents

All tender documents and prequalification documents, including contract documents, may be in Arabic or English, and in the case of international tenders, they shall be in English.

The bidder shall prepare the bid in the language specified in the tender documents. The supporting documents and printed materials submitted by the bidder and not written in Arabic or English shall be translated.

巴拿马

作者：Alejandro Ferrer、Eloy Alfaro B.、Diego Anguizola
译者：涂崇禹、赵浚锡

一、概述

(一) 政治、经济、社会和法律环境概述

巴拿马领土面积约为 77 082 平方公里，其中包括临近加勒比海和太平洋的 2 857 公里的海岸线。政治上，它分为 10 个省和 5 个主要的原住民地区。[①] 巴拿马实行民主总统制，实行三权分立，即：行政机关、立法机关和司法机关。

行政机关由巴拿马总统领导。总统连同副总统由公众直接投票选举产生，任期 5 年，期间没有紧急改选的权力。行政机关的核心是由巴拿马总统任命的 15 位部长所共同组成的内阁顾问（Consejo de Gabinete）。其他重要的行政机关包括一些政府机构，比如银行监管局、证券市场监管局、消费者保护和维护公平竞争局和巴拿马运河管理局。立法机关是由实行一院制的"国民大会"组成，有 71 名成员，经与总统选举同时进行的公众投票选举产生，任期 5 年。司法机关的最高级别法院是最高法院，由 9 名地方法官组成，他们均由巴拿马总统提名并经国民大会确认。

巴拿马欢迎来自世界各地的投资，由于其位于中美洲地峡最薄处，也处于西半球进出便利的中心位置，所以在历史上一直以来都是商业和物流中心。巴拿马的经济虽然多样化，但是以服务业为导向，旅游业和巴拿马运河服务被视为每年重要的收入来源。2017 年巴拿马国内生产总值约为 61.382 亿美元，与上一年相比增长 6.2%。[②] 来自产品销售和服务提供的收入为 401.769 亿美元，与上一年相比增长了 5.4%。

2016 年巴拿马的人口估计为 4 034 119 人，其中绝大部分集中在巴拿马省。大多数巴拿马人是天主教徒，其他几个宗教群体在历史上一直和平地生活在巴拿马。

此外，巴拿马的官方语言是西班牙语。但是，在金融服务和旅游行业熟练掌握英语对巴拿马人而言很常见。另外，一些大型企业的高级雇员以及顶级事务所的法律和会计专业人员一般会熟练掌握和流利地使用英语。

自 20 世纪 90 年代初以来巴拿马一直是一个稳定的民主国家，并自 1997 年以来一直是世界贸易组织的成员。巴拿马不仅是许多双边贸易协定的成员国，包括与美国、加拿大、墨西哥、新加坡、智利和秘鲁签订的协议；特别地，巴拿马也是与其他中美洲国家签署的多边条约中的成员国。

(二) "一带一路"框架下与中国企业合作的现状和方向

尽管巴拿马和中国目前没有双边贸易协定，但巴拿马和中国政府正考虑达成自由贸易协定。代表巴拿马负责指导国际贸易谈判的政府部门是工商部。

[①] 十个省分别是：Bocas del Toro、Coclé、Colón、Chiriquí、Darién、Los Santos、Herrera、Panamá、Panamá Oeste 和 Veraguas。五个主要原住民地区分别是：Guna Yala、Guna Madugandi、Guna Wargandi、Embera Wounan 和 Ngäbe-Bugle。
[②] 参见 Contraloría General de la República, Instituto Nacional de Estadística y Censo, Avances de Cifras del Producto Interno Bruto de la República (Año 2017)。

二、投资

(一) 市场准入

1. 投资主管部门

巴拿马没有专门主管投资的部门或机构。但是，巴拿马政府通过隶属于巴拿马工商部的"巴拿马招商及出口促进局"（Agency for Investment Attraction and Export Promotion of Panama，PROINVEX），便利有关对巴拿马所具优势、战略部门和特殊鼓励措施信息的分享，实施强有力地招商引资，并积极参与促进前述目标实现的重大活动。①

2. 投资行业法律法规

巴拿马没有具体法律规定了直接投资的一般架构。但是，外国投资者及企业具有与本地投资者及企业同等的权利和义务，除宪法和巴拿马法律规定的限制条件以外没有其他限制。我们将在下文进一步讨论这些限制条件。②

下述法律规定了在某些经济部门实施的重要鼓励措施，或旨在促进某些行业部门或公司类型发展的措施：

- 《跨国公司总部法》（Sedes de Empresas Multinacionales 或简称 SEM）。2007 年第 41 号法令确立了跨国公司总部设立和运营的特别制度。该法的主要目标是促进投资、就业和技术转让，吸引跨国公司提供由该法明确的服务项目，同时也吸引其他公司组建自身的经济集团。依照法律，跨国公司总部将受益于重要的免税、劳动和移民福利措施。

- 《自由贸易区法律》。自由贸易区受 2011 年第 32 号法令管辖，并被限定为由专门划定的、为世界各地投资人在巴拿马设立公司而具备必要基础设施、运营组织和行政管理功能的免税企业区。自由贸易区旨在从事包括商品生产、服务及先进技术提供、科学调查、高等教育、物流服务、环境服务、卫生保健及一般公共服务。自由贸易区可在全国任何地区建立，享有不同税收和劳动福利优惠措施。

- 《巴拿马—太平洋特别经济区法》。2004 年第 41 号法令创设了巴拿马—太平洋特别经济区。经济区位于巴拿马太平洋海岸，作为特别自由贸易区拥有自己的法律、税务、海关、劳动和移民制度，经济区按照 2004 年第 41 号法令的规定从事相关活动。许多优惠措施与根据 2011 年第 32 号法令规定提供给自由贸易区的优惠措施类似。

- 《科隆自由贸易区法》。2016 年第 8 号法令批准了科隆自由贸易区的重组，旨在使其适应国际贸易新趋势和机遇，同时建立一个确保其在该地区优势地位的法律抓手。根据 2016 年第 8 号法令，组成科隆自由贸易区的区域将被视为免税区，施行特殊的法律、税务和移民制度，在该自由贸易区可从事该法中规定的活动。

- 《石油自由贸易区法》。1987 年第 8 号法令为石油自由贸易区建立了一个特殊的制度，自由贸易区里没有任何税收。一般而言，在这些自由贸易区内，公司能够进口、再出口、储存、交易以及向巴拿马国内外市场和 / 或经巴拿马运河过境的船只出售石油衍生产品。

- 《呼叫中心法》。根据 2001 年第 54 号法令，任何经公共事业管理局（Autoridad Nacional de los Servicios Públicos）正式授权的人士可以运营呼叫中心并依据 2011 年第 32 号法令的规定享受给予自由贸易区经营企业的税收鼓励优惠。

- 《旅游法》。1994 年第 8 号法令规范了巴拿马的旅游活动，建立了对诸如旅馆、饭店、夜总会、会议中心、公寓、机场、生态旅游以及其他旅游项目的鼓励和优惠措施。

- 《知识之城法》。1998 年第 6 号法令批准了称为"知识之城"的项目。该项目通过给予不同税收优惠和移民政策促进在某特定领域的教育和科学调研活动。

- 《电影产业法》。2012 年第 16 号法令为在巴拿马从事电影制作活动创设了特殊制度，主要为在巴拿马从事此类活动的个人或公司确立了税收优惠和特殊的移民规则，这些个人或公司必须在"电影

---

① 参见 PROINVEX 网站（英文）：http://proinvex.mici.gob.pa/。
② 参见 1998 年第 54 号法令，第 2 条。

及音像行业鼓励措施国家登记处"进行登记注册。

• 《投资法律稳定法》。1994年第54号法令规定：投资额超过200万美元及以上数额的某些投资活动可以在10年以内一直适用投资发生时已施行的法律、税法、关税和劳动法等法律法规。此类投资通常必须在2年以内完成，并且投资人必须在"商业金融部投资登记处"（Investment Register of the Ministry of Commerce and Finance）进行注册登记。此类投资活动涉及领域包括：旅游业，工业，农产品出口，采矿，出口加工区，商业自由贸易区，石油自由贸易区，石油及天然气精炼、储存和运输，电信，建筑，港口建设，铁路建设以及电力的发电、配电和传输。

3. 投资类型

没有一般预先设定的投资类型。但是，实际上大多数在巴拿马市场上发生的投资通常属于外资直接投资类型，典型的有购买私人持股公司的股权或者购买土地。

另一方面，投资于在证券市场监管局注册的公众持股公司，无论是通过购买债券或是股票，实践中并不常见。

值得注意的是，根据《投资法律稳定法》的规定，十年稳定保护期仅适用于投资额超过200万美元及以上数额的投资。

4. 市场准入和检验标准

外国投资人在巴拿马通常具有与本地投资人及企业同等的权利和义务，除宪法和巴拿马法律规定的限制条件以外没有其他限制。一些主要限制如下：

（1）零售

一般情况下，可以在巴拿马从事零售的是：
• 因出生在巴拿马而取得巴拿马国籍的公民；
• 通过入籍程序成为巴拿马籍公民并满3年时间；
• 在1972年宪法正式生效时通过入籍程序成为巴拿马籍公民，或巴拿马籍公民的丈夫或妻子，或有一名巴拿马籍公民小孩的任何个人；
• 1972年宪法生效时曾经是零售业务法定所有人的任何外国人或外国实体；
• 无论注册地在何处但作为法定所有人具有上述人员的任何实体。

（2）购置土地

除大使馆用地外，外国政府或政府机构不得购置土地。外国个人或实体不得购置距边界10公里范围以内的土地。

对巴拿马所属岛屿领土，只有出于特定的开发目的才可以购置，条件是：
• 特定的岛屿范围不属于战略性区域或是保留区域；
• 特定的岛屿范围已被宣布为特别开发区域并已有与其利用相关的立法。

（3）公共服务

除法律另有规定外，公用事业服务公司的大部分股权，必须由巴拿马籍人员持有。

（4）石油和烃类品公司

对石油、烃类品或天然气的销售、提炼、运输、储存、销售、出口和勘探拥有行政特许权的外国公司必须在巴拿马拥有本地机构。

（5）采矿

外国政府不允许被授予采矿特许权。

（6）商业捕鱼

在巴拿马对以销售为目的的商业捕鱼也有不同限制条件，仅限于巴拿马公民或巴拿马公民拥有的实体。其他类似的限制条件适用于从事商业捕鱼船舶的所有权方面。

（7）巴拿马航空公司

只有巴拿马公民才能在巴拿马提供航空运输服务。巴拿马航空公司已发行股份中的至少51%必须由巴拿马人持有。如果公司只提供在巴拿马境内的运输服务，则这一比例不得少于60%。

(二) 外汇管理

巴拿马没有外汇管制。并且,自 1904 年以来美元可作为法定货币自由流通并可与巴拿马官方货币巴波亚(Balboa)互换使用。①

1. 外汇主管部门

巴拿马没有从事外汇管制的主管部门。

2. 外汇法律法规简介

巴拿马没有外汇管制的法律法规。

3. 对外国企业的外汇管理要求

巴拿马没有外汇管制要求。

(三) 融资

1. 主要金融机构

(1) 银行

银行是巴拿马主要的金融参与者。银行由 1998 年第 9 号法令《银行法》规制,并受巴拿马银行监管局(Superintendence of Banks of Panama)监督。

《银行法》规定,只有获得巴拿马银行监管局颁发的银行业执照的实体才可以在巴拿马从事或开展来自巴拿马的银行业务。银行业务主要指通过吸收存款或其他经巴拿马银行监管局或银行实务规定的方式从公众或金融机构处获取资源以发放贷款、从事投资或任何其他由巴拿马银行监管局许可的交易。

有三种类型的银行执照。①普通执照:允许相关银行在巴拿马国内或国外无区别地从事银行业务;②国际执照:允许相关银行通过在巴拿马设立的办公室指挥完成海外交易或将在海外产生影响的交易;③代表处执照:允许一家外国银行在巴拿马设立一个代表处。

申请普通执照的银行必须有最低实收资本金 1 000 万美元,而申请国际执照的最低实收资本金要求是 300 万美元。此外,银行还有其他最低储备金要求。

目前②在巴拿马共有 48 家银行持有普通执照,27 家持有国际执照,13 家持有代表处执照。

(2) 保险公司

保险公司在巴拿马也是重要的金融参与者。保险公司由 2012 年第 12 号法令《保险法》规制,并受"巴拿马保险和再保险监管局"(Superintendence of Insurance and Reinsurance of Panama)监管。

《保险法》规定,所有以任何形式开展保险业务为目的的实体以及以开展保险业务为目的而发行债券的行为均应接受"巴拿马保险和再保险监管局"的监管、事先授权、管理、规制并受其监督。

另外,《保险法》要求所有居住在巴拿马境内的实体、企业或个人取得的保险单,对位于巴拿马境内的资产或个人有关的风险提供的保险应由在巴拿马取得许可证的保险公司签发。该要求不适用于某些情况,特别是当:①国际条约或协定(巴拿马是参与方)另有规定时;②保险单涉及在巴拿马未提供保险的风险;③在巴拿马获得许可证的保险公司拒绝提供保险后,获得相应的保险变得不可行。

获准在巴拿马经营的保险公司必须维持最低 500 万美元的实收资本金。另外,保险公司还有其他最低准备金要求。

目前③有超过 25 家保险公司在巴拿马运营。

(3) 券商和投资顾问

券商和投资顾问作为金融参与者也发挥着重要的作用。《证券法》规定,只有经过证券市场监管局(Securities Market Superintendence)许可的人士才有资格在巴拿马共和国从事专业活动或开展来自巴拿

---

① 在巴拿马,美元与巴波亚 1∶1 等值互换。此外,巴波亚仅以硬币形式发行(1 分、5 分、10 分、25 分和 50 分),因此只有相应面额的美元钞票被用作纸币。
② 截至 2018 年 3 月 7 日。
③ 截至 2018 年 3 月 7 日。

马的专业活动。

券商从事买卖证券或金融票据的业务，作为他们专业服务的一部分也可以从事提供和开立投资账户的业务。

另外，投资顾问是指那些专业从事向他人提供有关决定投资、买卖证券或金融票据价格适当性咨询意见的实体，或指那些从事准备并在 Forex 上发布有关证券研究、报告和意见的专业实体。投资顾问不包括会计师、律师、教授或其他专业人士，他们的投资意见只是在从事本专业时附带产生；同时也不包括编辑、制片人、记者、作家、评论员或者传媒人员，只要这些人士是出于他们的工作或职位需要在所述传媒中只表达标准或观点，但同时没有通过从其表达标准或观点所依据的证券中直接或间接地获取利益，也没有就此获取特定的佣金或款项支付。

目前[①]在巴拿马共有 79 家实体获准经营券商业务，其中的 24 家是银行或银行的分支机构。此外，总共有 52 家实体获准担任投资顾问。

2. 外资企业融资条件

国内企业和外资企业适用同样的融资条件。但是，需要注意的是巴拿马银行相对于其他国家而言倾向于对开设银行账户设置非常严格的要求。

另外，所有的金融机构都必须遵守法律和某些规则要求实施的"了解你的客户"（know-your-client, KYC）和尽职调查政策，包括向"预防资金洗钱罪财务分析部"报告可疑交易。

（四）土地政策

1. 土地法律法规概况

与土地有关的规定大多见于具有市民传统特征的巴拿马《民法典》。法典将所有的财产权利划分为动产和不动产，土地所有权被认为是一项不动产权利。土地所有权为其权利人提供了处分（dominio）、占有（posesión）、使用（uso）和收益（goce）的权利。

在巴拿马购置任何土地之前，重要的是要核实在该土地之上附着的任何地役权（servidumbres）、用益权（usufructs），或在其之上负担的任何义务，比如抵押权或司法留置权。同样重要的是要了解由所有人授予的任何租约；承租人在新的土地所有人对所购置土地有关的租约事先知情的情况下，或者该租约已在公共登记处登记，则该承租人有权对购置土地施加限制条件。

最后，在巴拿马购置土地之前，重要的是要了解任何财产利用是否符合任何现行的规划法律规定并了解任何根据特殊的财产制度可适用于所购置土地的现行特殊规定，比如"平行财产"（Horizontal Property）制度（通常适用于住宅楼、商务写字楼和居住社区项目）。

2. 外资企业购置土地规定

在巴拿马，土地通过在公共登记处对法定所有权（通常是一份售地契约）登记备案予以转让，并且一般来讲任何个人或私营实体无论是何国籍都可以购置土地。但是，外国个人或实体不可以购置距巴拿马边境线 10 公里范围以内的土地。

对所属岛屿领土，只有为了特定的开发目的才可以购置，条件是：
- 特定的岛屿范围不属于战略性区域或是保留区域；
- 特定的岛屿范围已被宣布为特别开发区域并已有与其利用相关的立法。

除大使馆外，任何外国政府或外国政府机构不得购置土地。

（五）公司的设立与解散

1. 企业形式

尽管在巴拿马有多种类型的法律实体可用于开展业务（比如普通合伙、有限合伙、股份有限公司、有限责任公司），但通常绝大多数属于以下三种类型之一：股份有限公司（sociedades anónimas）、有限责任公司（sociedades de responsabilidad limitada）和外资公司（sociedades extranjeras）。

---

① 截至 2018 年 3 月 7 日。

（1）股份有限公司和有限责任公司

巴拿马式股份有限公司受 1927 年 2 月 26 日施行的第 32 号法令规制，也是在巴拿马最常见的法定实体，部分原因在于其简单性和灵活性。自该法令颁布施行以来几乎未作过修改。

巴拿马式有限责任公司则受 2009 年 1 月 9 日施行的第 4 号法令规制，该法令对自 1966 年以来就此类公司实施的法律制度进行了更新。

近期更新后，这两种类型的实体现在非常类似：

• 简单的内部治理结构。两者都有类似的内部治理结构（从治理结构上讲，公司所有人在最上层，公司管理层在中间，公司执行人员在底部）：

股份有限公司	有限责任公司
股东	份额持有人
董事（管理层）	管理人（管理层）
执行人员	执行人员

• 独立人格和继承财产。两者均具有独立的法律人格和财产，因此能够以自身名义行使权利和承担义务。

• 有限责任。其股东或合伙人对公司债务不承担个人无限责任，只对自己还未支付的股本金或份额资金负责。

• 灵活的组织文件。两者都允许公司文件和其他组织文件就法无禁止的任何事项作出规范，包括不同类别的股份或份额，以及确立在转让股份或份额情况下的优先权。

• 灵活的会议规则。除非另有规定，两者都允许自己的股东或合伙人以及董事、经理人能够在世界的任何地方或通过电子方式召开会议。

• 允许书面决议。两者都允许无需召开会议即可通过书面决议。

• 不限制所有者人数。两者都没有限制公司类型可以设定的股东或份额持有人的人数。

两种巴拿马式公司结构的两个主要区别是：

• 所有者最少人数要求。巴拿马式股份有限公司可以只有 1 位股东，巴拿马式有限责任公司则最少需要有 2 位份额持有者。但是，对每位份额持有人持有份额数量没有最低数量的要求。

• 所有者的身份。巴拿马式股份有限公司股东的身份不用公开登记（由股份有限公司私下记录在其股东名册之中），但巴拿马式有限责任公司份额持有者的身份必须包含在提交给公共登记处的文件当中并予以公开登记。

最后，重要的是要注意即便巴拿马式有限责任公司并不像巴拿马式股份有限公司那样得到普遍使用，但是通常外资企业为了在其他一些管辖区获取特别税收待遇——如果可行的话，有时会选择有限责任公司形式。不过，后者取决于其他管辖区具体的税收规定。

值得注意的是在巴拿马还有另外一种经常使用的法定实体形式，即私人基金（Fundación de Interés Privado）。但是，该实体形式主要用于财产规划目的。

（2）外资公司

外资企业可以在巴拿马成立"外资公司"作为注册在海外的企业分支或实体的扩展机构，因此这些公司的结构是根据其注册地法律的规定设立。但是，外资公司需要向公共登记处提交这些文件：

• 已更新的组织机构文件；

• 宣布将用于在巴拿马开展业务而投入资金数额的最后声明副本；

• 以及由企业注册地相对应的登记机构颁发的证明该企业已正式注册成立的资信证明。

上述文件在提交登记之前必须是已经合法化的文件，并且如果是使用西班牙文之外的语言，则必须翻译后再提交。

未在巴拿马注册登记为外资公司的外资企业分支机构不可以在巴拿马法院或其他司法机构提起司法程序或其他类型的诉讼，但是却可以被提起诉讼或者处以罚金。

2. 设立程序

设立巴拿马式股份有限公司或有限责任公司的程序相对简单，简要而言，公司设立文件必须出示给公证员并将文件转录成公共证书，然后将该证书在公共登记处进行登记注册。登记完成设立程序即告结束。整个程序一般是 3～5 个工作日。

我们进一步提供有关公司设立所需文件内容细节，如下：

（1）巴拿马式股份有限公司

巴拿马式股份有限公司的成立文件和公司章程（pacto social）必须至少包括以下信息：

- 股份有限公司章程股份认购人的名称和地址。认购人在公证员面前出示设立文件并将文件转录成公共证书。认购人必须明确他们将认购的股份数量，认购数量至少为一股。但是实际操作中，这仅仅被视为一种形式，律师事务所为实现认购股份通常以办公人员或为此目的所设公司之名义来充当认购人，然后他们转让认购权利，这样就可以向任何可以成为股东成员的人发行股份。

- 股份有限公司名称。股份有限公司的名称不可以与另一个现有股份有限公司的名称过于类似；另外，该名称必须包括指名该法律实体是股份有限公司（通常缩写为"S. A."）的用语。公共登记处提供名称可用性验证并且收取少量费用提供保留名称的选择性服务。

- 股份有限公司的目标（目的）。必须说明股份有限公司设立的目的。巴拿马法律并不禁止股份有限公司设置广泛的目标，实践中绝大多数股份有限公司常常列明自己的特定目的并在最后以宽泛的用语来表明股份有限公司可以从事任何法律允许的行为。

- 授权资本。股份有限公司必须说明它要发行的股份总数量以及面值，如果可以的话还需说明发行无面值股份的数额。股份可以记名形式或无记名形式发行。如果是以无记名形式发行股份，则必须载明公司愿意接受股份托管制度的内容，这将使得授权保管人占有和托管无记名的股份。授权托管人必须是获得许可的金融机构、信托或持证律师。

- 不同类别的股份（如适用）。可以设置不同类别的股份（普通股，优先股等）；如果设置，则公司章程必须进一步注明它们的数量、名称、特权、投票权和限制条件。

- 每位认购人获得的股份数量。每位认购人必须至少认购一股。（见前述"股份有限公司章程股份认购人的名称和地址"内容。）

- 股份有限公司地址。实际上，大多数股份有限公司没有提供详细的地址，有时只会记载股份有限公司设有办事处的城市。如果股份有限公司在巴拿马有业务，通过运营通知（商业许可证）公众可以知道股份有限公司的详细地址。

- 股份有限公司存续时间。大多数股份有限公司的存续时间被确定为"无限期"或"永久"。

- 董事人数和地址。股份有限公司至少要有 3 名董事。董事不需要是股份有限公司股东。法人实体可以被任命为董事。

- 总裁、秘书和出纳。所有股份有限公司都必须指定一位总裁、一名秘书和一名出纳作为办公人员。因此，这些人员在股份有限公司成立时就应指定。

- 驻地代理人。所有股份有限公司在巴拿马都必须有驻地代理人，代理人可以是巴拿马执业律师或律师事务所。

（2）巴拿马式有限责任公司

巴拿马式有限责任公司的成立文件和公司章程必须至少包括以下信息：

- 有限责任公司名称。有限责任公司的名称不可以与另一个现存的有限责任公司的名称过于类似；另外，该名称必须包括指名该法律实体是"有限责任"（通常缩写为"S. de R. L."）的用词。公共登记处提供名称可用性验证并且收取少量费用提供保留名称的选择性服务。

- 公司章程中授予人和合伙人的姓名及地址。与股份有限公司不同的是，向公证人提交公司注册文件的人是授予人，而不是认购人。此外，公司章程内容应载明合伙人姓名及地址。

- 有限责任公司地址。实际上，大多数有限责任公司没有提供详细的地址，有时只会记载有限责任公司设有办事处的城市。如果有限责任公司在巴拿马有业务，公众可以通过运营通知（商业许可证）获知公司的详细地址。

- 有限责任公司的期限。大多数有限责任公司的存续期间被设置为"无限期"或"永久"。

- 有限责任公司的目标（目的）。必须说明有限责任公司设立的目的。巴拿马法律并不禁止有限责任公司设置广泛的目标，实践中绝大多数公司常常列明自己的特定目的并在最后以宽泛的用语来表明公司可以从事任何法律允许的行为。
- 授权资本。必须注明有限责任公司发行的资本份额总数以及它们的面值。
- 担任管理人的单个人士或多位人士。有限责任公司至少需要 1 名管理人。管理人士不需要是合伙人。法人实体可以被指定为管理人。
- 一位或多位办公人员。有限责任公司不必像股份有限公司那样设置总裁、秘书和出纳。但实际上，大多数有限责任公司通常会任命担任此类工作的相应人员。
- 驻地代理人。所有公司在巴拿马都必须有驻地代理人，代理人可以是巴拿马执业律师或律师事务所。

须重点注意的是一般形式的公司，包括巴拿马式股份有限公司和有限责任公司每年必须支付 300 美元的特许税（Tasa Única）。

3. 解散程序及要求

巴拿马式股份有限公司的解散要求其股东通过股份有限公司解散决议，公司应事先通知召开会议并以股东多数投票表决通过解散决议。如果全体股东均出席会议或被代理出席会议，则可以不用提前发出通知。或者，如果所有具有表决权的股东以书面形式同意解散，比如由全体股东签署的书面决议书，则也不需要举行会议。

股东大会的会议记录必须由总裁和公司秘书签署。会议记录必须经过公证并随后在巴拿马公共注册处予以登记，并在当地报纸上发布解散公告。

根据 1927 年第 32 号法令《公司法》，股份有限公司解散之后继续存续 3 年，目的是以公司名义提起诉讼或就针对公司提起的诉讼进行应诉，或者使公司能够结算业务、处分和转让财产以及分配其股本，但是公司不得继续从事为运营之目的开展的业务。

董事应作为股份有限公司受托人全权处理公司事务，清收未偿债务，出售及转让各类财产，在股东之间分配资金和财产；他们有权以股份有限公司的名义起诉并追讨债务和财产，也有权就股份有限公司以公司名义所欠债务代表股份有限公司应诉。

在解散过程中，公司开始"清算"程序。如果公司在解散时没有任何资产或负债，或者在解散决议通过时公司已经偿付了所有债务并分配了剩余资产，则该解散决议可以声明公司自解散会议结束时被视为已完成清算。如果是这种情况，则不需要采取进一步措施，清算程序可视为已经完成。

但是，如果公司在解散时还没有偿付债务和分配资产，那么它应该履行这一程序，一旦完成该程序，公司股东或份额持有人必须事后通过决议，表明清算程序已经进行并完成，然后这个决议必须在公共注册处进行公证和登记。

（六）并购

虽然公司考虑收购或合并事宜一般需要提前批准或通知，但某些经济并购可能被竞争条例规定可能所禁止。

另外，如果目标公司是受管制市场的一部分（比如电信、电力、银行和保险市场），则相关的并购将最有可能需获得相关市场监管机构的事先批准或通知程序。

最后，重要的是要注意对在证券市场监管局注册的发行人股份发出的公开购买要约（收购要约），可能会导致一定比例的具有投票权的股份被收购，这将要求该要约收购应遵守 1999 年第 1 号法令《证券法》规定的特定程序，涉及通知及披露与要约有关的信息。

（七）竞争管制

巴拿马的竞争管制可以追溯到 1996 年，当时根据 1996 年第 29 号法令成立了"自由竞争和消费者事务委员会"（CLICAC），这就建立了保护竞争的监管框架。竞争法主要是依据 2007 年第 45 号法令《消费者保护和维护公平竞争法》制定。

1. 竞争管制主管机构

监督竞争管制行为的政府机构是"消费者保护和维护公平竞争局"（ACODECO），它是CLICAC的继承机构。

2. 竞争法概况

《消费者保护和维护公平竞争法》一概禁止任何限制、减少、损害、阻止或以任何其他方式妨碍自由经济竞争和自由参与商品或服务的生产、分配、供应或者销售的任何行为、协议或做法。

巴拿马的竞争法主要分为"垄断行为"和"经济集中"。

（1）垄断行为

垄断行为分为绝对垄断行为和相对垄断行为。

绝对垄断行为被定义为在当前或潜在竞争者之间存在的任何行为、联合、安排、协议或合约，或者是通过合谋一致实施的行为，具有以下目的或效果：

- 固定、操纵、组合、同意或强制执行商品或服务的销售或购买价格，或另行为此目的交换信息。
- 同意承担仅生产、加工、分销或推销有限数量商品的义务，或同意提供有限数量或不经常提供服务的义务。
- 通过指定的或可指定的客户、供应商、次数或空间对现时或未来的商品及服务细分市场进行划分、分配、转让、同意或施以强制义务。
- 为最大化利益，就框架协议、反向拍卖、公共资产拍卖而建立、同意或协同竞价，或阻碍参与向公众开放的投标以及参与其他任何与政府达成合约的形式。

在另一方面，相对垄断行为通常被定义为那些减少或阻碍自由竞争或者经济主体自由参与竞争的做法，只有当经济主体单独或联合对相关市场①具有实质性权力②的时候才会被认为是具有侵害性。

更具体而言，相对垄断行为包括为了非理性地排挤其他市场主体、非理性地阻碍它们进入市场、或者为了一个或多个经济主体行为非理性地创设排他性优势而在下列情况下实施的单方面行为、联合、安排、协议或合约：

- 在非竞争对手之间，根据人员类型、地理区域或就特定时间段对商品或服务固定价格、强制义务或进行独家销售的行为，包括对客户或供应商的划分、分配或转让以及在一定时间内强制规定不生产或分销商品或服务的义务。
- 制造商、生产商或供应商为销售商品或提供服务实施强制价格或固定价格以及施加其他条件。
- 以购买、收购、出售或提供通常不同的或可辨别的，或以互惠为基础的附加商品或服务为条件的销售或交易。
- 以禁止使用、获取、出售或提供由第三方生产、加工、分销或经销的商品或服务为条件的销售或交易。
- 由拒绝向某些客户出售或提供通常可获得并向他人提供的那些商品或服务构成的单方面行为，除非该行为对客户来讲违反了客户与经济主体的合同义务，或者是根据以往同客户的经验存在很高的退货或商品损坏索赔可能性。

---

① 以下因素与确定"相关市场"有关：
- 将商品或服务替换为本地或外国的其他商品或服务的可能性，以及消费者寻找替代品的能力。
- 考虑到运输成本、关税或非关税限制，各经济主体或其协会施加的限制条件以及为相关市场供应的时间，在巴拿马或外国境内分销商品、其投入品、零部件或替代品的成本费用。
- 消费者进入其他市场的成本和可能性。
- 限制消费者获取其他供应源或限制供应商获取其他消费者的管制。
- 创新动态。

② 以下因素与确定经济主体是否具有"实质性权力"有关：
- 经济主体参与相关市场以及其在相关市场单方面限定价格或限制市场供应的能力，无须竞争者能够有效或潜在地抵制此类能力为条件。
- 进入相关市场的障碍以及预期可能会改变其他来自竞争对手的障碍和供应的因素。
- 竞争对手的存在和力量。
- 经济主体及其竞争者获得投入的可能性。
- 经济主体最近的行为。

- 与若干经济主体一致行动，或鼓励他们向客户或供应商施加压力以阻止客户参与特定行为、施加谴责或强迫此类客户以某种方式行事。
- 当某经济主体实施倾向于损害竞争者或将竞争者挤出相关市场、或者阻止潜在竞争者进入市场的任何掠夺行为时，该经济主体不合理地期望竞争者停止竞争或者离开市场，将使自己实现可靠的盈利，同时也具有了实质性市场权力或者垄断地位。
- 购买所有生产、分销或销售商品或服务的行为，目的是从其后续销售中获利或倾向于支持第三方生产、分销或销售此类商品或服务。
- 一般来说，任何不合理的损害或妨碍自由经济竞争或自由参与生产、加工、分销、供应或销售商品或服务的行为。

（2）经济集中

经济集中被定义为由供应商、客户和其他竞争者相互之间以公司、合伙组织、股票、配额、信托基金、机构或者一般资产方式组合起来实施的并购、获取控制权以及任何其他行为。

经济集中可以不合理地减少、限制、损害或阻止与相同、相似或者实质相关的商品或服务有关的自由经济竞争。该概念不包括关于特定项目的合资，也不包括对市场或竞争不产生有害影响的经济集中。另外，连续亏损的经济主体或者处于即将退出市场的经济主体也许可以获得豁免，但是前提是该经济主体（没有成功地）与不是竞争对手的买家联系。

参与经济集中的经济机构可以要求ACODECO对潜在的经济集中中将会产生的效果进行"事先验证"。这种机制对于参与经济集中中的各方来说充当了安全港，因为该机制在经济集中发生后3年内都可以接受质询。

如果ACODECO认为，根据经过验证的垄断效果不禁止实行经济集中，相应的经济集中将免于接受ACODECO将来关于垄断效果验证的质询（当然，除非提供了虚假或不完整的信息）。

3. 管制竞争的措施

绝对垄断行为被认为是无效的，并且即使这些行为尚未实施完毕或其垄断效果尚未发生，违法的经济主体也可能受到制裁。

除了绝对垄断行为的受影响方能够针对实施侵害行为方发起民事诉讼之外，ACODECO可以对绝对垄断行为采取的措施包括：
- 最高为100万美元的罚款；
- 强制按照因违法行为造成的损害赔偿数额的3倍支付赔偿金的义务；
- 在全国性报纸上公告相关经济参与方的违规行为和对相关参与方实施的制裁；
- 对于反复违法行为，由ACODECO向工商部提出撤销经济主体经营许可证的请求。

可以对相对垄断行为采取的措施包括：
- 最高为25万美元的罚款；
- 强制按照因违法行为造成的损害赔偿数额的3倍支付赔偿金的义务；
- 在全国性报纸上公告相关经济参与方的违规行为和对相关参与方实施的制裁；
- 对于反复违法行为，由ACODECO向工商部提出撤销经济主体经营许可证的请求。

另外需要重点注意的是，个人涉及与公共承包合约有关的价格限制行为可能被处以6个月至2年的监禁。

对于接受质询的经济集中行为，ACODECO可以认为其有效同时不采取任何进一步措施，或认为其在采取某些措施后有效，或者完全禁止。ACODECO可以强制施加某些措施作为经济集中行为有效的条件，这包括：
- 放弃从事某种行为；
- 出售某些资产或股份；
- 修改、转让或淘汰某些生产线；
- 修改或删除包含在待执行协议中的某些条款；
- 使得生产或物流能力可供其他竞争者使用；
- 保证向消费者转移利益。

(八) 税务

1. 税制和规则

巴拿马的税制主要基于"领土原则",这意味着只有国内活动产生的收入或在巴拿马境内完成的收入才会缴纳所得税。

在巴拿马从事业务默认的"纳税期"是从日历年的 1 月 1 日至 12 月 31 日。然而,可以根据业务性质和公司的经营情况向国家税务局(Dirección General de Ingresos)提出申请特别纳税期的许可。

2. 主要税种和税率

税 种	税 率
增值税	标准税率:7%
公司所得税	统一税率:25%
海外汇款代扣所得税 (指向在巴拿马以外的个人或公司住所地作出的支付,这些支付是为了获得对在巴拿马境内个人或公司有益的服务或行为)	适用税率,适用于汇出总金额的 50% (当付款的受益人在巴拿马登记为纳税人时不需要代扣税)
资本利得税	出售股份所得:10% (由购买者代扣销售价格的 5% 作为预缴税款付给税务机关) 财产出售所得:10% (由购买者代扣销售价格的 3% 作为预缴税款付给税务机关)
不动产转让税	统一税率:2%
不动产税	税率范围从 0% 到 1%,取决于财产类型(例如住宅、商业不动产、工业不动产等)
股息税	巴拿马来源收入:10% 外来收入:5%
运营通知税 (仅适用于拥有商业许可证的公司)	统一税率:净值的 2% 或 60 000 美元(以较低者为准)
附加税 (适用于公司不分配收益或分配收益少于公司相应财务年度净收入 40% 的情况)	标准税率:4%
社会保障缴付费用	社会保障雇主负担比例:12.25% 社会保障雇员负担比例:9.75% 教育保险雇主负担比例:1.50% 教育保险员工负担比例:1.25%

3. 纳税申报与优惠

公司必须在每个纳税年度之后的 3 月 31 日之前提交年度纳税申报表。但是,公司可以提出延长 30 天的请求。在巴拿马不需缴纳所得税的公司(比如在巴拿马不从事创收活动或业务的公司)则不需要提交所得税纳税申报表。

(九) 证券

1. 证券相关法律法规概况

1999 年第 1 号法令《证券法》是规范巴拿马证券市场的主要法律,证券市场监管局是其主要管理机构。《证券法》主要规范证券公开发行和证券市场参与者。

证券被定义为:

任何债券、可转让商业所有权或公司债、股份(包括库存股)、在托管账户中确认的交易权、参股份额、所有权证书、信托证明、存款证明、抵押债券、权证或任何其他通常被承认为证券或由监管机构认定为证券的票据或权利。

但不包括：

• 由银行向客户签发的作为其通常所提供之银行服务组成部分的代表银行义务的不可转让凭证，比如不可转让的存款证明。此例外不包括由银行机构签发的可转让银行承兑汇票或可转让商业有价证券。

• 保险单、本值证明以及由保险公司签发的类似契约。

• 任何其他由证券监管机构认定为不是证券的票据、凭证或认股权。

下列证券在销售之前必须在证券市场监管局注册：

• 根据《证券法》规定必须"公开发行"并且不是另行获得注册豁免的证券；

• 住所在巴拿马的证券发行人其有 50 位以上的股东在巴拿马定居，这些权益所有人至少拥有发行人 10% 的实缴注册资本；

• 在巴拿马证券交易所上市的证券。

作为一般规则，在巴拿马做公开发行必须在证券市场监管局进行登记，除非另行获得豁免。《证券法》规定，向居住在巴拿马的人士提出的任何要约或作出的销售在巴拿马共和国应视为公开发行。以下公开发行获得豁免：

• 豁免证券的发行，包括政府发行债券以及由巴拿马作为成员的国际组织发行的证券。

• 考虑私人配售的发行，即向不超过 25 人发行证券并在 1 年内发行证券对象的人数总共不超过 10 人。

• 向机构投资者发行，由于机构投资者在证券市场的经验，他们具有知识和财务能力无须《证券法》的保护来评估和承担投资风险（例如投资银行）。

• 公司转让发行，包括：为了扩大发行人的股本而针对发行人现有股东作出的股份发行；分配股利；发行人公司重组、解散、清算或合并；以及行使先前由发行人授予的权利或选择权。

• 在特定范围内专门针对发行人的员工、管理人员或董事作出的发行。

证券市场参与者包括：证券交易所（当前[①]只有巴拿马证券交易所）、票据清算机构（当前[②]只有拉丁美洲中部交易所）、券商机构、经纪人、投资顾问、分析师、信用评级机构和发行人。除发行人必须履行重要的注册和持续披露信息要求外，大多数其他市场参与者需取得证券市场监管局颁发的执照。

2. 证券市场的监管

作为负责监管证券市场的机构，证券市场监管局有权发布市场参与者在从事相应活动前必须遵循的具体规定。

最重要的相关规定之一是第 7-2017 号协定，它规定了证券登记程序，列明了在相关的证券发行说明书中发行人必须披露的信息以及需要提交给证券市场监管局的文件，这些文件将提供给潜在投资人使用。

3. 外资公司参与证券交易的要求

只有获得由证券市场监管局颁发的相应许可证的机构才可以协助个人或机构买卖符合《证券法》规定的公开发行的证券，或者提供与这些证券有关的专业建议。

专门代表第三方或以自身名义购买和出售证券或金融票据的机构必须拥有券商经纪牌照。另外，专门为证券或金融票据投资提供咨询服务的机构必须取得投资顾问许可证。

（十）优惠及投资保护

1. 优惠政策框架

享有投资鼓励措施或施行特殊法律制度的行业绝大多数时候关注以下四个方面中的某个或某几个方面，它们是：税务、劳动、海关、移民。此外，在这些行业中根据其从事的受鼓励活动的性质，同时为了满足要求的特定利益，投资金额就变得更重要。例如，《投资法律稳定法》体现的法律稳定利益

---

① 截至 2018 年 3 月 7 日。
② 截至 2018 年 3 月 7 日。

只适用于投资金额不少于 200 万美元的行业。

对于在巴拿马设立跨国公司总部（SEM）的公司而言，这些公司必须证明申请许可证的公司是属于总资产最少为 2 亿美元的经济集团的一部分，并且需要进一步提供公司将在巴拿马雇用的职员人数。

上述内容反映了设立这些鼓励措施背后的主要目的之一，就是将更多的资源引入巴拿马经济体，同时增加巴拿马人的就业。

2. 支持特定行业和地区

享有投资鼓励措施的行业包括：旅游业、工业活动、农产品出口、采矿、出口加工区、商业自由贸易区、石油自由贸易区、石油及天然气精炼、储存和运输、电信、建筑、港口开发、铁路建设以及发电、配电和传输。

3. 特别经济区

（1）巴拿马—太平洋特别经济区

巴拿马—太平洋特别经济区（以下简称"巴—太经济区"）是一个施行特殊法律、税收、海关、劳动和商业制度的经济区，位于阿赖汉地区（前身是霍华德空军基地），其根据 2004 年第 41 号法令设立，旨在通过商品、服务和资本的流动和自由迁移来吸引和促进投资。

巴—太经济区由"伦敦 & 地区"开发商管理。经济区负责执行和规范制度的政府机构是巴拿马—太平洋特别经济区管理局。

任何在巴—太经济区的个人或设立的公司都可以开展任何类型的商业活动，一般而言，巴—太经济区没有任何限制措施。除非法律就公共卫生、公共安全、公共秩序事项以及对国际商品或其他特别经济区生产商品的展示厅设置有明确禁止性规定。

但是，在经济区重点受益的商业活动（"受鼓励的活动"）主要如下：

- 向巴拿马共和国境外的个人或实体（离岸服务）提供服务。
- 巴—太经济区设立的公司之间出售或转让股份。
- 出售非巴—太经济区内生产的商品、在途商品或销往外国的商品。
- 向使用巴拿马机场并飞往外国机场的飞机出售非巴—太经济区内生产的商品包括提供一般服务。
- 提供与航空和机场有关的服务。
- 高技术产品、配件和零件的生产以及加工、制造、组装活动，或者利用高科技加工技术制造产品、部件和零件。
- 多式运输和物流服务，以及销售非巴—太经济区内生产并运往国外的商品。
- 提供呼叫中心服务；处理、存储、传输、转发数据和数字信息；无线电、电视、音频、视频和/或数据信号的连接；用于内部网和互联网的资源和数字化应用研发；管理在巴—太经济区设立的联系用户办事处或在巴拿马境外建立的办事处；向在巴—太经济区内设立的公司或在巴拿马境外设立的公司提供受知识产权法或工业产权法规保护的高附加值服务。
- 商品或其他商业货物的进口、出口和转口业务，包括并不进入巴拿马领土商品的再开票业务以及物流和多式联运服务。

在巴—太经济区内开展受鼓励活动公司可以享有的主要税收优惠是：

- 免除与受鼓励活动有关的所得税和进口税。
- 无论分配收入是来源于巴拿马还是境外均适用税率为 5% 的股息税和 2% 的附加税（不分配收入时适用）。这是对来源于巴拿马收入通常税率为 10% 的股息税和 4% 的附加税的减免。
- 对资本净值最小为 100 美元以及最大为 5 万美元的公司适用 0.5% 的年度税率。

2004 年第 41 号法令规定了一些重要的劳动和移民优惠措施，包括：

- 对支付额外工作小时报酬适用 25% 的统一税率。
- 建立灵活的休假制度。
- 公司可以在假日继续营业。
- 提供签证一站式窗口服务。
- 可提供特别签证。

（2）科隆自由贸易区

1948年6月17日颁布的第18号法令在科隆省建立了名为"科隆自由贸易区"的自治国家实体，施行特殊的法律、税务、海关和商事制度。该法最近被2016年第8号法令取代，第8号法令重组了科隆自由贸易区。

在科隆自由贸易区内从事的业务主要是产自不同国家商品及货物的进出口以及为大量商业和物流活动提供的服务和设施，比如对来自世界各地的产品提供进口、仓储、组装、重新装箱和再出口服务。

适用的主要税收优惠措施：

- 对来自离岸业务的收入没有所得税。
- 对无论是进入自由国际贸易区、停留在贸易区还是从贸易区出口的商品和其他货物一概免于征税、免于交纳其他税费（无论是全国性的还是其他性质的），包括免除任何形式的领事手续费。
- 无论分配收入是来源于巴拿马还是境外均适用税率为5%的股息税。
- 对资本净值最小为100美元以及最大为5万美元的公司适用0.5%的年度税率。

（3）自由贸易区

2011年，与出口加工区有关的1992年第25号法令已被2011年4月5日施行的第32号法令《自由贸易区法》所取代。后者是一部涵盖范围更为广泛的法律，它为设立于这些区域并开展不同业务（大多数是出口导向）的公司创设了特别税收制度。

自由贸易区的主要目标是为客户提供激励机制，以便使他们在国际市场上具有很高水平的竞争力。从地域上讲，自由贸易区可以建立在巴拿马境内的任何地方。自由贸易区可以是私有的、国有的或两者共同所有。

（4）发起人和运营商

根据《自由贸易区法》的规定，开发和拥有一个自由贸易区的公司是发起人，它好比与相应的自由贸易区融为一体。

发起人免征所得税和增值税（VAT）。发起人也可以担任"运营商"，负责自由贸易区的指导、管理和运营。发起人享有与自由贸易区用户（见以下"自由贸易区用户"内容）相同的豁免，此外他们享有与租赁有关的所得税和增值税豁免。

（5）自由贸易区用户

在自由贸易区内设立的开展业务活动的公司被视为自由贸易区的"用户"。自由贸易区法律允许为以下类型用户建立自由贸易区：

- 物流服务公司；
- 成品和半成品加工公司；
- 装配公司（通过装配原材料或半成品生产成品或半成品）；
- 制造公司（通过制造原材料或半成品生产货物）；
- 服务公司（向自由贸易区内或其他自由贸易区的离岸客户）提供服务；
- 高科技公司（硬件、软件、数据中心）；
- 航空和机场相关服务公司；
- 一般服务公司（在自由贸易区内提供的个人服务，如餐厅、洗衣店、药店、美容院、健身房、银行等）；
- 环境服务公司；
- 高级教育中心；
- 科研中心；
- 专门的卫生服务中心。

作为一般规则，2011年第32号法令规定对在自由贸易区设立的用户开展的下列业务活动免征直接和间接税：

由在自由贸易区内设立的公司从事的涉及动产与不动产的任何活动、经营、交易、处理和转让，建筑设备及物资的购买，公司运营所需的原材料、机器、工具、配件、物资或任何所需的货物及服务的购买，应免于缴付任何直接或间接的国税、公司分摊费用、权利费用及征费。它们也被免除"运营通知"执照税。

但是，作为上述规则的例外情况，根据自由贸易区特别税制，下列税/费款项的缴付仍然适用：
- 不论其来源为何，5%的股息税和2%的附加税（只在收入未分配时）。这是对普通税制下10%股息税和4%附加税的减税。
- 对公司净值最低为100美元，最高为5万美元的公司，按公司净值的0.5%缴纳年度税。
- 消费税（选择性消费）税。①
- 利息赔偿特殊基金（FECI）②，但由银行存款担保的贷款除外。
- 社会保险缴款。
- 汇款代扣代缴税（实际税率12.5%），适用于支付服务费、特许权费和向外国供应商支付的佣金。但是，只有在这些服务、特许权或佣金是以产生收益为目的时才需缴税，并且需扣除与此类服务、特许权或佣金相关的费用。

（6）在巴拿马设立的自由贸易区包括（括号内为发起人）：
- 海富自由贸易区（苏卡萨房地产公司，股份有限公司）；
- 伊斯拉玛格丽塔自由贸易区（伊斯拉玛格丽塔开发公司）；
- 国有戴维斯自由贸易区（退伍军人管理局）；
- 阿尔布鲁克自由贸易区（阿尔布鲁克出口加工区，股份有限公司）；
- 马培斯加/科罗萨尔自由贸易区（马培斯加加工厂，股份有限公司）；
- 奇尼布热自由贸易区（迪塞尔专家，股份有限公司）；
- 西班牙自由贸易区（西班牙伊比利亚美洲，股份有限公司）；
- 欧聚自由贸易区（欧聚，股份有限公司）；
- 美洲自由贸易区（莫罗乔，股份有限公司）；
- 科隆海事投资人自由贸易区（科隆海事投资人，股份有限公司）；
- 巴—太出口自由贸易区（巴太出口，股份有限公司）；
- 惠普自由贸易区（巴拿马惠普全球服务，股份有限公司）；
- 地峡自由贸易区（地峡自由贸易区，股份有限公司）；
- 高宝迪尤自由贸易区（高宝迪尤，股份有限公司）；
- 佛拉莫科自由贸易区（弗朗西斯科·哈维尔·莫拉莱斯·戈保德）；
- 托库门国际机场物流贸易区（托库门国际机场，股份有限公司）。

4. 投资保护

如前文所述，《投资法律稳定法》规定，在某些业务中投资额在200万美元或以上的投资可以在10年以内一直适用投资发生时已施行的法律、税法、关税和劳动法等法律法规。

此类投资通常必须在2年内完成，并且投资者必须在工商部投资登记处登记。

三、贸易

（一）贸易监管部门

1. 国内贸易

国内贸易，即巴拿马境内的商品和服务的销售，一般由工商部进行监管。不同类型的商品、服务或相关经济活动可能会受到不同政府部门的进一步管理。根据2007年第5号法令规定，工商部是负责向在巴拿马开展商业活动的企业发放营业执照（经营许可）的部门。

---

① 适用于某些特定物品，比如苏打水（5%），啤酒、葡萄酒和蒸馏酒（0.045美元每度/公升）、游艇、喷气式飞机和直升机（10%）、珠宝和枪械（5%），赌博门票（5.5%）。
② FECI 代表 Fondo Especial de Compensación de Intereses，翻译过来是"利息赔偿特殊基金"，指一项对本地授予超过5 000美元的某些个人和商业贷款额外征收1%利息的特别税。税收收入被用于补贴某些优惠抵押贷款和支持在农业领域里的其他政府机构。

2. 国际贸易

国际贸易，即商品服务进口或从巴拿马出口至他国，同样由工商部进行监管，但主要由海关条例和国际条约等法律法规进行规范，适用法规取决于具体的情况和因素，如货物或原料的类型、产地、目的地、货物或原料在巴拿马可能进行的加工、适用的条约、进口至经济特区（或从特区出口）等。

（二）贸易法律法规概况

1. 国内贸易

巴拿马的公司一般必须先获得营业执照，称为"经营许可"，方可开展商业或工业活动。该许可由工商部通过巴拿马创业（系统 PanamaEmprende）发放，该系统可通过其门户网站（www.panamaemprende.gob.pa）进行访问。

如果企业的商业活动属于管制行业或管制市场，其将成为"受监管活动"，企业很可能需要事先得到相应行业或市场监管部门的批准。受监管活动比如：

（1）酒精饮料销售；
（2）公用行业服务（例如供水服务、供电服务和电信服务）；
（3）金融服务（银行、信托、保险、再保险、金融企业及投资顾问）；
（4）药品销售；
（5）医疗健康服务；
（6）武器和弹药销售；
（7）私人安保服务。

一般来说，任何可能对公众健康、环境或国家安全带来风险的活动都将作为受监管活动。

其他部分已有提到在巴拿马经营工商业普遍适用的法律法规（参见"投资""劳动"和"知识产权"部分），但尚未涉及消费者保护法，就此在这个部分作简要讨论。

最终产品和服务的消费者是地方消费者法律法规的主要受益者。该领域的主要法律是2007年第41号法令《消费者保护和竞争保护法》。该法律规定的卖方义务包括：

（1）清楚并真实地告知提供的产品或服务的特性，例如其性质、成分、含量、重量、产地、有效期、毒性、预防措施、价格和其他判定条件。对于需要警告和采取预防措施的药品、农用化工产品、有毒产品和食品，必须使用西班牙语标注。
（2）提供如何正确使用产品的说明，并告知与健康或危害相关的使用风险。
（3）告知消费者任何适用于产品或服务的保障及相关条款。
（4）当零部件或者备件系二手件时告知消费者。
（5）如在巴拿马无法获得零部件、备件或技术服务，且该信息与产品有关，需告知消费者。
（6）如存在产品维修义务，且该义务在合理期限内未履行时，需承担其维修责任。
（7）告知消费者产品退货或损坏索赔的截止期限。
（8）为产品或服务开具发票，标明卖方税号（"registro único de contribuyente"，简称 RUC）、产品及服务的描述以及运送或交付日期。
（9）关于销售的任何特殊条款。

制造商、进口商、经销商或供应商（如适用）对产品和服务的适用性、质量、广告准确性、标签的真实性以及包装或标签上标明的产品内容和保质期都承担相应责任。

2. 国际贸易

国际贸易受工商部的监督，由国家国际商务谈判部门、国家国际商务谈判与商业保护局及外贸部副部长负责。此外，国家海关总署（Autoridad Nacional de Aduanas）作为监督机构负责巴拿马的货物进口。

国际贸易主要受当地法律法规以及适用的国际条约的约束，具体处理办法根据不同因素而定。相关因素包括：货物种类或材料及其分类、原产地、目的地、进口货物是否在巴拿马经过变更、适用条约、货物或材料是否进口至（或出口）巴拿马海关区域内或者经济特区内的海关关区。

（三）贸易管理

1. 国内贸易

国内贸易和工业一般处于工商部的监管下，其国内工商部副部长参与一系列国家贸易管理活动，职责包括通过巴拿马创业系统发放经营许可。

2. 国际贸易

在工商部部门机构中，国家国际商务谈判部门代表巴拿马参与条约谈判协商，国家国际商务谈判与商业保护局则参与国际贸易条约的管理。这两个机关都由国际商务谈判部副部长进行监管。

此外，外贸部副部长也具有促进投资和出口的职能。

（四）进出口商品的检验检疫

对进出口商品的检验和检疫（如适用）根据商品种类而定，在这里不作详细说明。但需要注意的是，某些种类的商品有特殊的检疫规定，如食品、植物以及活体动物。

巴拿马食品安全管理局（Autoridad Panameña de Seguridad de Alimentos，简称 AUPSA）是负责管理巴拿马食品进口的机构。

（五）海关管理

一般来说，任何公司进口其产品或原材料至巴拿马关税区，都必须缴纳相应关税。作为世界贸易组织（WTO）的成员国，巴拿马根据最惠国贸易待遇原则，默认采取"普通关税"，主要含巴拿马通常对其他国家的产品或原材料采用的相应关税。

巴拿马目前[1]采用的普通关税参照世界海关组织《商品名称及编码协调制度》第六修正案，该修正案经由 2016 年第 35 号法令通过。

然而，例外是，如果巴拿马与原产国之间就进口的产品或原材料存在关税协议，则相应关税适用此协议内容。但在此种情况下，必须确定产品是否符合条约中关税优惠政策的要求。（该要求常见于相应条约中"原产地规则"一节）

如果产品或原材料符合要求并有列入条约，则必须适用相应关税。（常见于"国家清单"部分）

在出口方面，如果巴拿马作为成品原产地，没有与进口国达成关税协议，则该国通常对该产品采用本国的"普通关税"。

四、劳动

（一）劳动法律法规概况

1. 雇佣关系

巴拿马的雇佣关系主要依据《劳动法》进行规范，该法在巴拿马全境适用。雇佣关系正式生效需要签订书面协议（其副本必须向劳动与劳动力发展部提交并盖章）。要注意的是，在存在法律隶属[2]或经济依赖[3]的情况下提供劳动服务时，法律承认其雇佣关系。

2. 工作期限

关于工作期限，雇员可被无固定期限（无限期）雇佣，有固定期限（有限期）雇佣，或以完成一定的工作为期限雇佣。当没有书面合同时，则认定为无固定期限雇佣。此外，有固定期限合同规定的雇佣期限不得超过 1 年；如涉及特殊的技术，规定的雇佣期限不得超过 3 年。但是，对于通常认为是

---

[1] 截至 2018 年 3 月 10 日。
[2] 法律隶属关系包括雇员在服务或劳动时，由雇主或其代表对雇员实施的，或可能行使的指导或控制。
[3] 当提供服务或劳动的人（无论是由个人或实体直接或间接接受，或是他的活动所得）得到的报酬构成此人的唯一或主要收入来源时，就存在经济依赖。这种情况同时发生在当提供服务或工作的人没有经济自主权，并且在经济上与雇主的活动形式相关联时。

永久性的职位,不会采取固定期限雇佣的方式。

3. 最低工资、休息、休假以及第十三个月

工资标准要受政府批准的最低工资标准约束,该标准的制定参考劳动服务地区的经济情况和地理位置。目前,基于上述经济和地理因素,最低工资大多在每小时1.53～4.45美元之间。

巴拿马的雇员同样有权每周休息1天,日期由雇主与雇员共同商议决定。但是,除了某些特定职业(如从事药房、酒店和餐馆工作)外,一般情况下雇主必须选择星期日作为相应休息日。

关于休假时间,巴拿马的雇员有权每工作11个月休假30天(每年约休假1个月)。

需要注意的是,在巴拿马,雇主必须向雇员发放一笔特殊的津贴,称为"第十三个月",相当于雇主每年额外支付雇员一个月的工资,分三期支付(每年4月15日、8月15日和12月15日)。

4. 节假日

以下是巴拿马的法定带薪节假日:1月1日(元旦)、1月9日(烈士节)、星期二狂欢节、基督受难日、5月1日(劳动节)、11月3日(独立日)、11月5日(巩固独立成果日)、11月10日(独立呐喊日)、11月28日(自西班牙独立日)、12月8日(母亲节)、12月25日(圣诞节)。

5. 雇员工作班次与延长工作时间补贴

以工作起止时间划分,巴拿马的劳动制度将雇员工作班次分为以下三类:

(1)日班,工作时间在早上6点至下午6点之间(日间时段),每天工作时长限制8小时,每周限制48小时;

(2)夜班,工作时间在下午6点至早上6点之间(夜间时段),每天工作时长限制7小时,每周限制42小时;

(3)混合班次,工作时间自日间(夜间)某一时刻起至夜间(日间)某一时刻结束,每天工作时长限制7.5小时,每周限制45小时。

加班时长每天不得超过3小时,每周不得超过9小时。以班次及工作时段划分,一般劳动制度规定以下几种加班费计算标准:

(1)加班时长与日班相关,并且加班时间在日间时段的,必须额外支付25%的工资作为加班费;

(2)加班时长与日班相关,并且加班时间在夜间时段的,必须额外支付50%的工资作为加班费;

(3)加班时长与夜班相关,或从夜间时段开始混合班次工作的,必须额外支付75%的工资作为加班费。

在一般的劳动制度下,雇员在休息日工作的必须额外支付其50%的工资作为加班费,在法定休假节日工作的,则必须额外支付其150%的工资作为加班费。此外,如果工作周时间短于6天,则可能适用较低的加班费标准。

6. 雇佣关系终止

雇佣关系不因合同期满或完成约定的工作为期限而终止的,可由雇员辞职终止、雇主单方终止、双方协议终止、雇员死亡或雇主死亡(当死亡导致无法继续雇佣时)终止。不得以法律规定以外的原因与服务2年以上的雇员终止合同。

值得注意的是,如果合同规定雇员有3个月试用期,试用期内雇员可以被无理由解雇,雇主无需对此承担责任。

7. 缴纳社会保障金

巴拿马的一般劳动制度在巴拿马境内具有强制适用的效力。巴拿马的《社会保障计划法》和2005年第51号法令规定,雇主与雇员必须按照雇员"工资"的一定比例缴纳社会保障金,其中"工资"包括:

(1)佣金;

(2)假期;

(3)奖金;

(4)日津贴(如果是经常性补贴并且超过月薪的25%);

（5）生产补贴（如超过月薪的 50%）；
（6）代理费用。

以下是当前适用于雇主与雇员的社会保险费率：

	雇主	雇员（雇主代缴）
社会保障	12.25%	9.75%
教育险	1.50%	1.25%
第十三个月	10.75%	7.25%

8. 离职基金

雇主有义务设立离职补偿金（fondo de cesantía），主要为资历赔偿（prima de antigüedad）及补偿金（indemnización）（如雇员无故被辞退或因故辞职），以支付雇员离职福利。

（二）雇用外籍雇员的要求

巴拿马的企业中，巴拿马公民、与巴拿马公民结婚的外国人以及在巴拿马居住至少 10 年的外国人总人数必须至少占所有正式员工人数的 90%（即外籍正式员工一般不超过 10%）。外籍专业人员或技术人员可占全体员工人数的 15%。企业员工少于 10 人的可临时雇用至少一名外籍员工。

值得注意的是，以上比例限制（外籍雇员所占的最大比例）同样适用于企业支付的总工资。因此，一家企业支付给外籍员工的总工资不能超过该企业总薪酬的 10%。

1. 工作许可证

外籍雇员必须获得劳动与劳动力发展部发放的工作许可。

岗位要求的工作许可类型将根据具体情况而有所不同，例如：

（1）"10% 工作许可证"，适用于外籍正式员工；
（2）"15% 工作许可证"，适用于外籍专业人员或技术人员；
（3）"无限期工作许可证"，适用于在巴拿马居住至少 10 年的外籍人士；
（4）"婚姻工作许可证"，适用于与巴拿马公民结婚的外籍人士；
（5）"特定国家工作许可证"，适用于一些特定国家（德国、阿根廷、巴西、智利、西班牙、美国、墨西哥、葡萄牙、英国、乌拉圭和瑞士等）；
（6）"外籍专业工作许可证"，适用于具有本科或研究生学历的外籍专业人士，其职业不受宪法或法律的限制（某些专业的工作岗位受限，如法学、医学、土木工程、建筑学）。

10% 和 15% 的工作许可证经两步可升至"无限期工作许可证"。第一步，工作许可证被授予 2 年的；第二步，被授予无固定期限工作许可证。

需注意的是：

（1）一般来说，工作许可证有效期为 1 年，但可续期；
（2）有外籍员工的企业必须符合雇用外籍人员的要求（外籍正式员工一般不超过全体员工的 10%，外国专业人员或技术人员不超过 15%）；
（3）因工作许可证有效期为 1 年，外籍员工的雇佣合同必须为固定期限合同，外籍人士在巴拿马居住 10 年以上的情况除外，这种情况下可发放无限期工作许可证。

2. 申请程序

工作许可证需要通过执业律师向劳动与劳动力发展部申请。许可证的批准通常需要大约 5～6 个月。

3. 社会保险

参见"（一）7. 缴纳社会保障金"部分。

（三）出入境

1. 签证类型

法律规定"劳工"或"就业"的移民签证属于临时居民类别（也称为10%、15%以及马拉喀什签证）。这类签证停留期为1年，可延长至6年。

签证审批程序可能需要12～15个月，将会被授予的停留期是1年，一旦劳动与劳动力发展部批准相应的工作许可后，签证停留期可以延长至6年。

2. 出入境限制

出入境的限制因不同签证类型而异，但一般情况下，一旦签证获批，最主要的限制就是签证停留期。

（四）工会与劳工组织

雇员有权成为工会的一员。并且，有意加入者不少于40名的有组织的雇员团体可以在一个商业组织内建立工会。在此种情况下，工会委员会成员享有工会豁免权，因此除非有特殊原因，其雇佣合同不得被该商业组织接触。

需要注意的是，根据《劳动法》相关规定，所有从工会和商业组织间的集体协议受益的雇员，即便不是工会会员，也都必须向工会支付费用。

所有工会都有罢工的宪法权利。但是，需要工会首先与雇主进行谈判，谈判时间不超过11周，谈判过程有劳动与劳动力发展部的人员介入，罢工才能被视作合法。如果双方达成和解，则罢工可能不会进行。

（五）劳动争议

所有劳动争议或诉求主要由两个特别争议解决机构进行审理和裁决：

（1）调解和裁决委员会（Juntas de Conciliación y Decisión），该委员会拥有裁定下列事项的专属管辖权：

① 违法解除雇佣关系的诉求；

② 任何涉及金额达到1 500美元的诉求；

③ 国内雇员任何性质或金额的诉求。

（2）劳动部门特别法庭（Juzgados Seccionales de Trabajo），有权对调解和裁决委员会无法裁定的所有其他劳动争议作出裁决：

① 涉及未支付工资、工作时长及其他既得权利索赔的诉求；

② 涉及雇员死亡相关权利要求索赔的诉求；

③ 雇员因故辞职。

所有涉及工会的劳动争议都由劳动与劳动力发展部下属劳动局进行监督。

五、知识产权

（一）知识产权法律及法规概况

2012年第61号法令《工业产权法》是巴拿马在规范诸如发明、实用新型、服务商标、注册商标、地理标志、原产地及等级证明和工商业机密等广泛范围的知识产权方面的主要立法。另外，2012年第64号法令《著作权法》是规范作者权利（版权）之主要法律。

1. 发明

受专利保护的发明，是指任何可能在实践中用以解决实际技术问题的想法，可能包含产品或者工艺。可以申请专利的发明必须新颖、具有创造性并能在工业中应用。

发明新颖性的条件是尚未有与之相关的现有技术（在该发明之前已有的技术）。本文中的"现有技术"包括在专利申请日之前在世界上任何地方通过有形出版物、口头披露、销售或贸易、使用或以其他方式向公众披露或提供过的任何技术，或者在其优先权日之前已经有类似专利申请的技术。

根据发明人自己的披露，或者由于针对发明人的滥用信托权、合同违约或者违法行为而被披露，安全港条款在专利申请日前（或在另一类似申请的优先权日之前）的12个月内保护发明人。

若对于通常被认为应精通相应技术的人员而言，发明并非明显来源于，也无证据表明其来源于现有技术的，该发明被认为是具有创造性。

最后，当一项发明的对象可以被制造出来，或可以被工业利用，或者用于任何活动（例如工艺、矿业、渔业或服务业）时，该发明被认为是具有工业实用性。

被授予专利者将享有禁止第三人从事下列行为的权利：①产品方面，制造产品、提供产品或以其他方式进口、保存产品以销售或使用；②工艺方面，使用该工艺或使用该工艺直接生产上述①中任何产品的行为。

专利的授予期限为20年，自申请日起算。若专利被成功授予，专利所有人可向在专利申请过程正在进行中且为公众所知悉时使用该专利的第三人索赔。

2. 产品及服务标记

依据《工业产权法》规定，产品或服务标记是标志、文字、或这些元素的结合或其他方式，使商业产品或服务特定化（或可识别）。标记可能包括：文字或文字的组合，包括识别人体的词汇；图片、图形、符号及图样，字母和数字以及上述不同元素的组合；三维形状，包括包装材料、包装风格、产品的形状或其表现形式及全息照片；在不同组合情况下的色彩；以及声音、气味和味道。

可能无法注册的标记，包括：

① 简单表述产品或服务类型，或已成为描述产品的常用术语或通称的；

② 可能造成消费者误解或混淆的，例如对标记的属性或相对应产品或服务的错误指示；

③ 与其他相同类型产品或服务的标记相同或相似，而且此种相似可能导致大众对产品、服务或来源产生误解、混淆或错误认识的；

④ 与已经在巴拿马驰名的产品或服务标记相同或相似的，无论该驰名产品或服务标记是否已注册。

产品或服务标记的权利系通过对其使用而获得。然而，标记的注册授予其所有人独有使用权，因此禁止他人使用相应产品或服务标记，包括：

① 禁止他人使用相应的标记制造、打印或复制标签、信头、包装及其他标识、包装或工艺，如果上述标记明显被用于与已注册的产品或服务标记相关的同类产品或服务上；

② 将标记用于类似产品的标记或包装上，并可能导致大众对与该产品有高度关联的产品产生误解或混淆的；

③ 在商业中非法使用与注册商标类似的标记，可能对注册商标的所有权人造成损害，特别是当产品或服务标记的显著性被削弱，或注册商标的商业价值下降时；

④ 将特定产品或者服务标记与相同或类似的另一个标记进行比较，唯一目的是为了削弱特定产品或服务标记的独特性或降低其商业价值的。

3. 工业和商业秘密

关于工业及商业秘密，《工业产权法》规定，任何人因雇佣或工作获得信息的，该等信息的秘密性已经受到保护，不得在未经该人同意的情况下予以披露。

任何人因其工作成果、雇佣关系、工作岗位、履行规定或商业关系而能够接触到工业或商业秘密的，该等信息的秘密已经受到保护，其不得将这些秘密用于个人的商业目的，在未经保密信息所有人或授权用户同意时，不得无故泄露这些机密。违反本条款的，受侵害人有权要求立即停止披露相关的机密并索取损害赔偿。

需要注意的是，希望进一步保护其工业或商业秘密的公司，通常会与经常接触此类信息的董事或关键人员签订保密协议。

4. 著作权（版权）

在《著作权法》中，作者对其工作成果（作品）享有著作人身权及财产权。工作成果是指以任何形式出版或复制的在文学、艺术或科学领域内的任何原创知识创造成果，即使该出版或复制形式不为人所知。工作成果的例子包括：

① 以书籍、杂志、传单形式表达的书面知识创造成果，以及通过传统信件、标识或标记进行的任何工作；

② 会议、演讲及其他包含口头表述作品的成果；

③ 具备或不具备歌词的乐曲；

④ 电影、照片及任何视听作品；

⑤ 建筑作品、地图、蓝图及其他与地理学、地貌学、建筑学或科学相关的作品；

⑥ 软件程序。

在作品上体现本人的名字、签名或符号以确定其作者身份的人被视为作品的作者。此外，除非有反证，作者的权利存在于其作品之上。

对于匿名作品，或是以笔名创作的作品而言，出版的个人或实体可在作者身份不明的情况下临时行使任何保护作品所必要的权利。对于基于已经存在的作品的演绎作品，作者在原有作品上享有的权利不受影响。

著作权中的财产权由以下几部分组成：①修改作品的权利，包含执行或授权翻译、改编、编配及其他对作品的转换；②复制作品的权利，包含任何利用任何形式或程序直接修改作品的行为；③作品的发行权，包含授权或拒绝以销售或者任何其他传播方式向公众发行作品拷贝的权利；④通过任何大众传播方式向公众公开作品的权利，例如通过互联网、电报，或任意其他相似方式。

著作权在作者在世期间及其死后 70 年内有效，作者继承人享有权利的期限与该期限相同。就合著者的情况而言，70 年的期限自最后一名作者死亡之日起计算。

就集体作品，即由多名作者依照个人或公司的安排或指示完成的各自署名的作品而言，作者权将自该作品首次出版之日起 70 年内有效。

在著作权有效期间的计算上，值得注意的是该期间自某一作者去世或作品第一次出版之日的下一年份的 1 月 1 日起计算。

（二）专利申请

专利申请必须通过 1 名执业律师提出，并附以下材料：

① 知识产权登记处总理事会（DIGERPI）的专利申请表；

② 一份描述性备忘录及摘要；

③ 关于申请的专利内基本元素的明确保护要求；

④ 相应的图纸；

⑤ 发明人姓名及地址的说明（另外，若发明人未提交申请，则需附上申请人姓名及地址的说明，以及支持该人申请专利权的文件）；

⑥ 证明申请费已经支付的收据；

⑦ 授权委托书。

自申请提出时起，发明的描述必须足够完整和清晰，以便在领域有技术经验的人能够无需对其进行不必要的审查即可对其进行评估。

DIGERPI 收到下述最低要求文件之日应被视为申请提交之日：

① 申请人的姓名及住址；

② 初步说明该发明的描述文件；

③ 就专利的基本要素提出的包括一个或多个明确保护请求的初步说明文件；

④ 证明申请费已经支付的收据。

（三）产品或服务标记的注册

商标的注册申请必须由一位执业律师提起并附下列材料提交：

（1）标明以下内容的 DIGERPI 的专利申请表：
- 申请人姓名、住址及国籍的阐述（若申请人为公司，则另外需要公司注册证书）；
- 律师的姓名及住址；
- （若申请人居住在国外）在巴拿马的住址，以便送达与注册相关的行政和司法通知；
- 标记的名称及／或设计；
- 按《尼斯协议》进行相应分类的与标记相关的产品或服务；
- 优先权请求（如有）。

（2）授权委托书。

（3）标记草图两份、标记翻译一份、标记音译一份、及／或支持优先权请求的文件（如适用）。

（4）用声明或意图使用声明。

（5）证明申请费已经支付的收据。

（四）保护知识产权的措施

《工业产权法》为与专利侵权争端及与产品和服务标记有关的侵权争端提供了特殊的程序，该程序应由相应的法院／法庭所遵循。

六、环境保护

（一）环境保护监管部门

环境部（MiAMBIENTE）主管环境保护，其职责包括：①制定环境质量保护与控制办法；②发布推进《国家环境政策》实施的技术、行政命令和规章；③保护其管辖范围内的自然资源以防止环境退化；④实施环境法；⑤规定环境影响研究的必要研究范围和研究条件，并提供相关方面的指导；⑥评估环境影响研究成果和相关资料；⑦审批自然资源相关的许可证、特许权及授权。

巴拿马水产资源管理局（ARAP）负责渔业与水产养殖相关法律的实施，其职责还包括保证水生资源合理、可持续、有保障利用，保护相关生态系统，以及与环境部（MiAMBIENTE）及其他地方实体共同协调监测渔业和水产养殖活动地区的水质。

（二）环境保护法律法规概况

1998 年第 41 号法令奠定了巴拿马环境保护的法律框架。其最重要的一项规定关系到外国潜在投资者在巴拿马进行活动或投资项目时，可能会涉及的环境风险。这项规定要求在性质、特点、影响、位置或资源的使用等方面可能对环境造成风险的活动、工作或项目须通过环境影响评估（EIA）。

需要注意的是规定将环境影响评价分为三类（Ⅰ类、Ⅱ类和Ⅲ类），评估结果取决于相应的活动、工作或项目将为环境带来的潜在风险。

2008 年第 41 号法令规定 EIA 评估由在环境部注册的环境进行。在进行评估时，环境专家将根据特定活动可能带来的环境风险，评估其 EIA 评价类别，并提出可降低环境风险的措施。

（三）环境保护评估

巴拿马是《联合国气候变化框架公约》《京都议定书》的成员国之一，也是最早批准《巴黎协定》的国家之一。

七、争议解决

(一)争议解决方式和机构

1. 司法程序

巴拿马民商事性质的司法程序一般是由《民事诉讼法》中所规定的程序规则进行规制。这些程序分为：

① 审判程序，更细致分为：
- 普通诉讼程序；
- 口头程序；
- 简易诉讼程序。

② 非诉讼程序，指原则上无对抗（对抗方面大部分都会通过简易诉讼程序解决）。最值得注意的是，该分类包含继承诉讼程序。

③ 执行程序，最值得注意的是，包含"抵押执行程序"，即抵押物的执行程序以及"质押执行程序"。

在实践中，大部分带有民商事性质的争端是通过审判程序解决的，而这其中绝大部分使用的是普通诉讼程序。除法律另有规定的外，所有程序都适用两审制，二审程序通常允许当事人对一审法院（下级法院）的判决向上级法院提出上诉。

需要注意的是，巴拿马的法律体系是大陆法系传统（非普通法系传统），法官直接监督证据收集过程。先前由同一法院作出的判决，甚至是先前由上级法院作出的判决都不能约束审判法庭。审判法庭在实践中有时会理所当然地遵从本院先前作出的或是上级法院作出的判决，特别是在适用的法律条款已经经常且一致地用于相似问题时，该判决被视为地方判例。

然而，需要注意的是，即使与其他在实践中严格其法律体系的大陆体系传统不同，巴拿马的法律制度也倾向于不严格遵守其大陆法系法律制度。当法律条款对特定问题规定不够明确时，法院同等采纳当地知名学者著作中的观点，有时候采纳的是西班牙或哥伦比亚学者的著作中的观点（《民法典》中若干规定来源于西班牙和哥伦比亚民法典，或者有与其相似的条款）。

（1）普通诉讼程序

任何具有对抗性的事项，且没有考虑特别程序时，可以适用普通诉讼程序作出判决，因此这属于一般的诉讼类型。即使需要考虑适用特别程序，潜在的原告也可以选择使用普通诉讼程序解决争议。

普通诉讼程序中标的价值大于 250 美元小于 5 000 美元的称为"小额程序"，由地方法院法官主持审判。标的达到或超过 5 000 美元的普通诉讼程序称为"大额程序"，由巡回法院法官主持审判。

普通诉讼程序的大额程序要求诉状必须以书面形式通过律师提交。普通诉讼程序各审级的时限往往比大额程序的时限要长。例如，被告在接到通知后将有 10 个工作日而不是 5 个工作日的时间来答辩。

在实践中，普通诉讼程序的大额程序每一审级都往往持续 2 年时间。因此，如果就一审法院的判决提出上诉，则争议通常将持续大约 4 年时间。

需要注意的是有些裁决可能通过特别上诉程序上诉至巴拿马最高法院，通过撤销原判的令状，最高法院可以撤销或维持原判。如果巴拿马最高法院决定维持原判，该判决将被维持且不得再次上诉。然而，如果巴拿马最高法院决定撤销原判决，案件可能审查案件的实体问题，并撤销原判或者将原判决发回重审或改判。

特别上诉程序案件一旦被受理，无论适用实体法还是程序法，申请人必须遵循严格的程序，并提供原审判决存在严重错误的有力证据，无论是实体法上诉，还是程序法上诉。被成功受理的撤销原判上诉案件通常审理两年时间。

（2）口头程序

口头程序适用于以下情形的特殊程序：①与交通事故相关，且损失超过 5 000 美元的民事诉求；②与公司股东会或董事会决议相关的上诉，或与私营实体的股东会或董事会决议违反法律或公司章程有关的上诉；③与政府发行的债券或商业产权的宣告无效或者位置变更有关而产生的争议。然而需要注意的是，当事人可以自愿以提交认证文件（例如公证文书）的方式将其他类型诉求以口头程序方式提交。

尽管口头程序往往比普通诉讼程序用时更短，但也更不正式一些。实践中这些程序类型通常并不作为争议解决方法。

（3）简易诉讼程序

简易诉讼程序是适用于多种特定诉求的特别程序，包括：

① 与地役权、共有财产的分割或出售、禁令和其他占有程序有关的诉求；

② 在非诉程序中产生的异议或争议；

③ 与租赁、陆上运输货物、寄存物品和托管有关的诉求；

④ 与特定专业收费相关的诉求（律师、医生、会计师、建筑师、工程师及其他需要执照才能从业的专业人员）；

⑤ 共有权诉求；

⑥ 与抵押贷款的发放和特定抵押条款修改有关的诉求；

⑦ 特定协议须强制遵守法定程序的诉求（例如不动产销售要求协议应当是证书形式）；

⑧ 取得时效诉求。

简易诉讼程序往往比普通诉讼程序用时更短（例如，被告在收到通知后有5个工作日的时间来答辩）。尽管简易诉讼程序在实践中并不如普通诉讼程序那般常见，但作为争议解决方式，比听证程序更常用。

（4）参与司法程序的机构

对于参与司法程序的机构，下面，按从高级到低级的顺序对其架构和体系进行介绍：

① 巴拿马最高法院。巴拿马最高法院共有9名大法官，目前由4个法庭组成，每个法庭配有3名法官。法庭分别为：

- 第一法庭，管辖民事和商事纠纷；
- 第二法庭，管辖刑事案件；
- 第三法庭，管辖劳动纠纷和行政纠纷；
- 第四法庭，管辖某些特定事项，特别是向律师颁发执照、对外国判决的认可（通过称为"认可证书"程序）。需要注意的是，每一个法庭都由一名法官主持，而主持第一、第二、第三法庭的法官共同组成第四法庭。最后，9名法官对某些特定事项，特别是带宪法性质的事项将采取9名法官全体出庭审理的方案。

② 高级法庭。高级法庭作为上诉法庭，管辖范围通常覆盖了在巴拿马领土范围内的不同司法区。与民商事纠纷相关的高级法庭共有5个：第一司法区第一高级法庭，享有在巴拿马省、科隆省、达里恩省及圣巴拉斯原住民地区的民事纠纷管辖权；第一司法区第三高级法庭，享有对一些特殊事项，包括垄断行为、消费者保护、知识产权、代理和分销关系及不公平竞争的管辖权；第二司法区高级法庭，享有在科克莱省和贝拉瓜斯省的民事纠纷管辖权；第三司法区高级法庭，享有在奇里基省和博卡斯德尔托罗省的民事纠纷管辖权；第四司法区高级法庭，享有在埃雷拉省和洛圣都省的民事纠纷管辖权。

③ 巡回法官。每个区都配有数名巡回法官，负责绝大多数的一审案件，其中绝大部分在巴拿马进行的案件都是普通诉讼程序案件的大额诉讼。

④ 地方法官。地方法官通常在小额程序的普通诉讼程序范围内判决案件，这些案件涉及的诉求标的小于5 000美元。

最后，需要注意的是还有处理其他纠纷的专门法庭（例如，消费者保护、劳工、及家事纠纷），也适用特别的程序规则。

2. 替代性纠纷解决机制

（1）仲裁程序

相对于司法程序，仲裁程序成本更高。然而仲裁的审理期限通常更短，因此与争议解决的用时长短有关的潜在成本也是重要的考虑因素。在涉及高额诉求的商业交易领域纠纷中，越来越多的当事人选择仲裁。

在巴拿马，仲裁程序由 2013 年第 131 号法令《仲裁法》规定。然而，该法所规定的程序规则，往往更具有概括性和补充性，而且仲裁通常根据当事人选择适用的仲裁中心的仲裁规则进行而不需要根据《仲裁法》的规定（与证据、指控及作出裁决的截止期限相关的规则除外）。

巴拿马主要的仲裁中心是"巴拿马调解和仲裁中心"（CeCAP），CeCAP 规则中规定的程序概述如下：

① 申请将争议提交仲裁的当事人（如果双方通过"仲裁条款"的方式达成一致），必须向 CeCAP 的仲裁总秘书处提交仲裁申请书，仲裁申请书中必须描述争议的性质、事实、仲裁请求及支持仲裁请求的全部证据。仲裁申请人还必须指定其选择的仲裁员。

② CeCAP 仲裁总秘书处在确认 CeCAP 有管辖权后，书面通知被申请人，并给予被申请人 10 个工作日的时间进行答辩，提供所有支持其答辩意见的证据，并指定其选择的仲裁员。（在此期间内，被告可提出反请求，若被告提出反请求，CeCAP 将通知申请人，申请人将获得 10 个工作日的时间对反请求提出答辩意见，并提供所有证据支持其答辩意见）。

③ 若双方无法就第三名仲裁员达成合意，双方选定的仲裁员可在 30 个工作日内共同选定第三名仲裁员。如果选定的仲裁员之间无法达成合意，CeCAP 将在 CeCAP 仲裁员名单中抽签指定第三名仲裁员。

④ 仲裁员必须在收到任命通知的 5 个工作日内以书面方式就其是否接受任命作出回复，并声明将公正独立作出裁决。与衡平法仲裁（根据公平原则作出仲裁裁决）的情形不同，如果系普通法仲裁（根据明确法律规定作出仲裁裁决），则该仲裁裁决必须由律师仲裁员作出。

⑤ CeCAP 必须在仲裁庭组成时通知双方当事人，并告知仲裁所需费用。若被申请人未在 5 个工作日内支付其应付部分的费用，则申请人必须在另 5 个工作日内支付该费用，否则仲裁程序将不会进行。后者支付仲裁费用的行为不妨碍仲裁庭事后裁定败诉方支付全部或部分仲裁费用。

⑥ 在确认仲裁费用已经支付后的 15 日内举行听证会，当事人双方与仲裁员可以讨论有关仲裁协议、仲裁程序、仲裁请求、争议事项、证据规则和适用法律及其他问题。听证会上也可能提出对仲裁管辖权的异议。

⑦ 在听证会上，仲裁庭必须确认将要采纳的证据及需要进一步审查的证据。除双方当事人另有约定，需要进一步审查的证据必须在 20 个工作日内审查完毕。

⑧ 证据听证阶段结束后，CeCAP 仲裁总秘书处已经将所有证据听证记录在案，仲裁庭将传唤双方当事人进行最后陈述。当事人可以就最后答辩是以书面方式、口头方式或者是以二者结合的方式进行与仲裁庭达成一致。

⑨ 根据 CeCAP 规则，最终陈述阶段结束后，仲裁庭必须在 2 个月内作出仲裁裁决，该期限可以延长 1 个月。当事人双方可以就期限的继续延长达成合意；然而实践中仲裁程序的期限（自仲裁程序开始之日至仲裁裁决作出之日）一般不超过 1 年。

⑩ 仲裁规则也确立了申请临时救济措施的可能性。然而临时救济措施最终需要法庭或司法部门的协助（如无该等协助即表明当事人放弃仲裁管辖权）。

（2）调解程序

巴拿马的调解程序由 1999 年第五号法令调整。当事人双方除同意仲裁外还同意进行调解的，必须先进行调解。然而，由于调解并不要求当事人双方就争议问题达成有约束力的协议，因此如果调解程序没有达成具有约束力的协议，当事人双方往往会进入仲裁程序。

（二）法律的适用

在巴拿马司法实践中大部分司法程序涉及实体问题的事项都需要适用巴拿马法律。当事人选择另一法域的法律作为适用法律，如果选择的法律不违反公序良俗的规定，原则上在巴拿马将被认定为有效且可以适用。此外，在某些特定事项上当事人不得选择放弃适用巴拿马法律，例如涉及巴拿马境内土地权利的事项。

八、其他

(一) 反商业贿赂

1. 反商业贿赂法律法规简介

巴拿马的各种反腐败法律法规关注有关反腐败的不同事项。本部分着重于以下三个方面：信息透明度、公务员职业规范和反洗钱。

（1）信息透明度

公共机构或者不参与公共设施服务的私人实体的信息透明度，主要由2002年第5号法令《信息透明度法》规定，该法规定个人有权从上述主体获得信息，除非该等信息被认定为"机密信息"或"限制公开"。

机密信息是指政府拥有的个人医疗数据或心理数据、个人隐私、犯罪记录或警察记录、个人通信、个人电话通话以及未达法定年龄人（未成年人）的信息。

限制公开的信息是指政府拥有的按照其各自职能依法提供给各机构或公务员的信息。此类信息包括：有关国家安全的信息、工商业机密、作为职能规范披露给公共机构的信息和公诉人发布的有关未决诉讼的信息。

（2）《公务员职业伦理法》

任何一级公务员均须遵守《公务员职业伦理法》和适用于特定政府部门或政府机构的道德守则。

值得注意的是，《公务员职业伦理法》作为一般规则，规定公务员不得以索取或收受金钱、礼品、福利、便利、利益或者获得其他好处为目的，利用职权或者职务上的影响加快、推迟或者阻止与其职能有关的工作。

其他法律，例如政府采购法律，规定了未包含在《公务员职业伦理法》中的特定规则。需要注意的是，巴拿马《宪法》还要求每个公务员就其所继承的财产和财务状况作出宣誓声明。

（3）反洗钱

2015第23号法令《反洗钱法》是巴拿马最主要的反洗钱法律。反洗钱法确立了特定实体或专业人士需遵守的"了解你的客户"要求（KYC要求），包括要求其客户提供某些特定信息的义务。

受《反洗钱法》管制的实体或专业人士同时承担报告它们遇到的可疑的、可能涉及洗钱或资助恐怖主义的责任。

以下特定实体或专业人士都在承担报告义务的范围内：

① 金融义务实体（例如银行、保险公司、经纪自营商及提供信托服务的公司）；

② 非金融义务实体（例如设立在科隆自由贸易区、巴拿马—太平洋地区及任何自由贸易区内的公司）。

③ 受监管的专业人士（例如房地产经纪人及提供注册代理服务的律师事务所）。

银行监管局、保险和再保险监管局及证券市场监管局等监管机构对《反洗钱法》的条款进行细化，适用于各自监管下的实体。

（4）国际条约

巴拿马是《美洲反腐败公约》的缔约国，同时也是《联合国反腐败公约》的缔约国。

2. 反商业贿赂监管部门

履行反腐败监管义务的主要政府部门为国家权力透明度及信息公开局（ANTAI）、财务分析局（UAF）及公共部。

3. 惩罚措施

最近《反洗钱法》及2015年第34号法令完善了《刑法》中有关恐怖主义、资助恐怖主义、反洗钱方面的规定，并增加了关于违禁品和海关欺诈的章节。

值得注意的是，收受的资金可合理预见地来源于包括国际贿赂、公务员腐败、恐怖主义、资助恐怖主义、违禁品或海关欺诈等犯罪活动，或掩盖其非法来源的，将被判处5～12年有期徒刑。

(二)工程承包

1. 许可制度

若项目中涉及一项受监管活动,承包该项目的公司必须拥有适用的监管许可证。值得注意的是,涉及建筑工程的项目必须委托拥有执照并在工程与建筑技术委员会注册的公司。此外,大多数特定规模的项目也需要通过环境影响评估(详见上文"六、环境保护"部分)。

2. 禁止领域

对于建设工程,除了任何适用的地区限制或其他基于地理位置和工程类型的限制外,巴拿马的特定地区要求承包人在施工前遵守严格的规定。例如,环境保护部门(巴拿马环境卫生部)发布了关于国家公园等保护区在内的特殊规定。

3. 招标投标

私人实体之间的工程承包不受特定法律约束,而是适用承包的一般规则,且招标邀请和投标邀请取决于发出与自己签订合同邀请的公司。

从另一方面来说,公共实体的工程承包则受 2006 年第 22 号法令《政府采购法》的约束。具体而言,《政府采购法》适用于:政府一方的公开招投标和政府采购,政府持有 51% 以上股份的公司和涉及公共资金使用的合同,具体包括:①收购或租赁政府资产;②实施公共工程;③政府资产处置;④提供服务;⑤资产经营和管理,以及特别法未规定的行政许可。

Panama

Authors: Alejandro Ferrer, Eloy Alfaro B., Diego Anguizola
Translators: Tu Chongyu, Zhao Junxi

I. Overview

A. General Introduction to The Political, Economic, Social and Legal Environment of The Country Receiving Investment

Panama's territory has approximately 77,082 square kilometers, including 2,857 kilometers of coastline on both the Caribbean Sea and the Pacific Ocean. It is divided, politically, into ten provinces and five main indigenous regions.[①] Panama has a democratic presidential system, structurally composed of three branches: the Executive Branch, a Legislative Branch, and the Judicial Branch.

The Executive Branch is headed by the President of Panama, who is elected by direct popular, vote along with a Vice-President, for a five-year term with no immediate reelection option. Key to the Executive Branch are also the (15) Ministers appointed by the President of Panama, who together compose the Cabinet Counsel (Consejo de Gabinete). Other important parts of the Executive Branch include several government agencies, such as the Superintendence of Banks, the Superintendence of the Securities Market, the Consumer Protection and Defense of Competition Authority, and the Panama Canal Authority. The Legislative Branch is structured as a unicameral chamber called the 'National Assembly', composed of seventy-one (71) members elected by popular vote in parallel with the Presidential election, for a five-year term. The Judicial Branch's court of highest hierarchy is the Supreme Court of Justice, composed of nine (9) magistrates, who are appointed by the President of Panama subject to confirmation by the National Assembly.

Panama welcomes investment, from anywhere in the world, and has been historically a business and logistics focus point, due to its accessible and central location in the Western Hemisphere, which is at the thinnest part of the Central American Isthmus. Panama's economy, although diversified, is service-oriented, with the tourism sector and Panama Canal services being considered important sources of revenue every year. GDP for the year 2017 was estimated at US$61,38.2 million, reflecting a growth of 6.2% from the previous year.[②] Revenue derived from the sales of products and services in Panama accounted for US$40,176.9 million, reflecting a grown of 5.4% from the previous year.

Panama's population for the year 2016 was estimated at 4,034,119, with a substantial portion concentrated in the Province of Panama. The majority of Panamanians are Catholic Christians, and several other population groups with other religions have peacefully lived in Panama throughout its history.

Furthermore, Panama's official language is Spanish. However, it is usual for Panamanians in the financial services and tourism industries to have some proficiency in English. Furthermore, several upper-level employees of large businesses, as well as legal and accounting professionals at top level firms, will usually be proficient or fluent in English.

Panama has had a stable democracy since the early 1990's, and a been a member of the World Trade Organization since 1997. Panama is also member of several bilateral trade agreements, including agreements with the United States, Canada, Mexico, Singapore, Chile, and Peru. Notably, Panama is also part of a multilateral treaty with other Central American countries.

B. The Status and Direction of Cooperation with Chinese Enterprises under B&R

Although Panama and China do not presently have a bilateral trade agreement, the governments of Panama and China are currently contemplating negotiations with a view to entering into a Free Trade Agreement. The government department responsible for directing international trade negotiations on behalf of Panama is the Ministry of Commerce and Industries.

---

① Provinces: Bocas del Toro, Coclé, Colón, Chiriquí, Darién, Los Santos, Herrera, Panamá, Panamá Oeste, and Veraguas. Indigenous regions: Guna Yala, Guna Madugandi, Guna Wargandi, Embera Wounan, and Ngäbe-Bugle.
② Contraloría General de la República, Instituto Nacional de Estadística y Censo, Avances de Cifras del Producto Interno Bruto de la República (Año 2017).

II. Investment

A. Market Access

a. Department Supervising Investment

Panama has no department or agency in charge of supervising investment. However, through its Agency for Investment Attraction and Export Promotion of Panama (PROINVEX), of the Ministry of Commerce and Industries, the Government is strongly involved in attracting and promoting investment, by facilitating information about the advantages of Panama, strategic sectors, special incentives, and actively participating in special events that further these objectives.[1]

b. Laws and Regulations of Investment Industry

Panama has no specific law that lays down a general framework of direct investment. However, foreign investors and businesses have the same rights and obligations as local investors and businesses, with no restrictions other than those established by the Constitution and Panamanian laws (we discuss these restrictions further below).[2]

The following laws establish important incentives in certain sectors of the economy, or otherwise promote certain types of industries or companies:

• Law of Multinational Companies Headquarters (Sedes de Empresas Multinacionales, or SEMs). The special regime for the establishment and operation of the Headquarters for Multinational Companies was created by Law 41 of 2007. The main objective of this law is to promote investment, employment, and transfer of technology, attracting multinational companies that would supply the services indicated by such law, as well as other companies forming part of their own economic group. In accordance with the law, the Headquarters for Multinational Companies will benefit from important tax exemptions, as well as labor and immigration benefits.

• Law of Free Zones. Free Zones are governed by Law 32 of 2011, and defined as free enterprise zones specifically delimited, with the infrastructure, operational organization, and administrative management necessary for the establishment of companies from around the world. The activities contemplated include the production of goods, services, and advanced technology; scientific investigation; higher education; logistics services; environmental services; healthcare services, and general services. Free Zones may be established in any part of the national territory, and enjoy various tax and labor benefits.

• Law of the Panama-Pacific Special Economic Area. Law 41 of 2004 created the Panama-Pacific Special Economic Area, a specific area located on the Pacific coast of Panama, as a special free zone, with its own legal, tax, customs, labor and immigration regime, wherein the activities described under Law 41 would be carried out. Many of the benefits are similar to those offered to Free Zones under Law 32 of 2011.

• Law of the Colon Free Zone. Law 8 of 2016 approved the reorganization of the Colon Free Zone, with the objective of adapting it to the new tendencies and opportunities provided by international trade, and at the same time establishing a legal tool that will ensure its positioning in the region. According to Law 8 of 2016, the areas that make up the Colon Free Zone will be considered zones free of taxes, with a legal, tax and special immigration regime, within which the activities described in such law could be carried out.

• Law of Petroleum Free Zones. Through Law 8 of 1987, a special regime was established for petroleum free zones, within which no taxes are incurred. In general, in these free zones, the companies can import, re-export, store, trade and sell petroleum derived products to the domestic Panamanian market, abroad and / or to vessels in transit in the Panama Canal.

• Law of Call Centers. In accordance with Law 54 of 2001, any person duly authorized by the Public Utilities Authority (Autoridad Nacional de los Servicios Públicos) may operate call centers, benefiting from tax incentives granted to companies operating within Free Zones, according to the stipulations of Law 32 of 2011.

• Law of Tourism. Law 8 of 1994 regulates touristic activities in Panama, establishing incentives and benefits for tourism projects such as hotels, restaurants, nightclubs, convention centers, condominiums, airports, ecological tourism, among others.

• Law of the City of Knowledge. Decree Law 6 of 1998 approved the project called "City of Knowledge", which promotes educational and scientific investigation within a specific area, by the granting of various tax and immigration benefits.

• Law of Film Industry. Law 16 of 2012 creates a special regime for film-making activities in Panama, mainly establishing tax benefits and a special immigration rules for individuals or companies engaging in these activities,

---

[1] See PROINVEX website (available in English): http://proinvex.mici.gob.pa/.
[2] See Law 54 of 1998, Art. 2.

who must be registered with the National Register of Incentives to the Cinematographic and Audiovisual Industry.

• Law of Legal Stability of Investments. Law 54 of 1994 provides that investments of US$2,000,000.00, or more, in certain activities may be subjected, for a period of ten (10) years, to the same legal, tax, customs, and labor laws that were in place at the time of the investment. The investment must generally be made within a period of two (2) years, and the investor must be registered with the Investment Register of the Ministry of Commerce and Finance. The activities include: tourism; industrial activities; export of agricultural products; mining; processing zones for export; commercial free zones; petroleum free zones; petroleum or natural gas refining, storage, and transport; telecommunications; construction; port development; railway developments; and electric power generation, distribution and transmission.

c. Forms of Investment

There are no general pre-established categories of investment. In practice, however, most investments in the Panamanian market are usually of the foreign-direct investment type, typically involving the purchase of equity in privately-held companies, or the purchase of land.

On the other hand, investments in publicly-held companies, registered before the Superintendence of the Securities Market, whether such investments are made through the purchase of debt or equity, are less frequent in practice.

It is important to note that, under the Law of Legal Stability of Investments, the 10-year stability protection only applies to investments of US$2,000,000.00 or more.

d. Standards of Market Access and Examination

Foreign investors in Panama generally have the same rights and obligations as local investors and businesses do, with no restrictions other than those established by the Constitution and Panamanian laws. We list below some of the main restrictions:

a) Retail Sales

Retails sales in Panama may, in general, only be carried by:

• Panamanian nationals by birth;

• Panamanian nationals by naturalization, after three years;

• An individual who, by the time the 1972 Constitution came into force, was a naturalized Panamanian national, the husband or wife of a Panamanian national, or an individual with children from a Panamanian national;

• A foreign individual or foreign entity who was the legal owner of retail sales business by the time the 1972 Constitution came into force; and

• An entity, regardless of its place of incorporation, if has as legal owners the persons mentioned above.

b) Acquisition of Land

Land may not be acquired by a foreign government, or a foreign government entity, except in the case of embassies. Land located less than 10 kilometers from the border may not be acquired by foreigner individuals or entities.

Regarding insular territory, it may only be acquired for specific development purposes, provided:

• the specific insular area is not considered a strategic area, or a reserved area, and

• the specific insular area has been declared an area of special development, and legislation has been dictated relating to its use.

c) Public Services

A majority of the share ownership in companies that provide public utility services must be owned by Panamanians, except where the law expressly provides otherwise.

d) Petroleum and Hydrocarbon Companies

Foreign companies who have administrative concessions for the sale, refinement, transportation, storage, marketing, exportation and exploration of petroleum, hydrocarbons, or natural gas, must have local presence in Panama.

e) Mining

Foreign governments may not be granted mining concessions.

f) Commercial Fishing

Commercial fishing for sale in Panama also has several restrictions is limited to Panamanian nationals or entities owned by Panamanian nationals. Other similar restrictions apply to ownership of vessels engaged in the commercial fishing.

g) Airlines based in Panama

Only Panamanian nationals may render air transportation based in Panama. At least fifty-one percent (51%) of the shares issued and outstanding in a Panamanian airline company must be owned by Panamanians. If the company is only dedicated to are transportation within Panama, such percentage may not be less than sixty-percent (60%).

B. Foreign Exchange Regulation

Panama has no foreign exchange controls. Moreover, the U.S. Dollar circulates freely as a legal tender, since 1904, interchangeably[①] with Panama's official tender, the Balboa.

a. Department Supervising Foreign Exchange

There is no department supervising foreign exchange control.

b. Brief Introduction of Laws and Regulations of Foreign Exchange

There are no laws or regulations of foreign exchange control.

c. Requirements of Foreign Exchange Management for Foreign Enterprises

There are no requirements of foreign exchange control.

C. Financing

a. Main Financial Institutions

a) Banks

Banks are the main financial participants in Panama. Banks are regulated by Law Decree 9 of 1998 (the "Banking Law"), and supervised by the Superintendence of Banks.

The Banking Law provides that only entities with a banking license issued by the Superintendence of Banks may engage in banking business in or from Panama. Banking business is defined, principally, as the taking of resources from the public or financial institutions, by means of the acceptance of deposits or any other means as dictated by the Superintendence of Banks or banking practices, to grant loans, make investments, or any other transactions as determined by the Superintendence of Banks.

There are three types of banking licenses: (i) a general license, which allows the corresponding bank to engage in banking business in Panama or abroad, indistinctively; (ii) an international license, which allows the corresponding bank to direct, from an office established in Panama, transactions which are completed or which will have their effect abroad, and (iii) a representation license, which allows a foreign bank to establish a representation office in the Republic of Panama.

Banks applying for a general license must have a minimum paid-in capital of US$10,000,000, while entities applying for an international license must have a minimum paid-in capital of US$ 3,000,000. Additionally, banks have other minimum reserve requirements.

Currently[②] in Panama, there is a total of forty-eight (48) banks holding a general license, a total of twenty-seven (27) holding an international license, and a total of thirteen (13) holding a representation license.

b) Insurance Companies

Insurance companies are also important financial participants in Panama. Insurance companies are regulated by Law 12 of 2012 (the "Insurance Law"), and supervised by the Superintendence of Insurance and Reinsurance.

The Insurance Law provides that all entities that have as a purpose the carrying out of insurance operations, in any of its forms, and the issuing of bonds, shall be under the control, prior authorization, supervision, regulation, and oversight of the Superintendence of Insurance and Reinsurance.

Furthermore, the Insurance Law requires all insurance policies obtained by entities, businesses, or individuals domiciled in the Republic of Panama, covering risks related to assets or persons located in Panama, to be issued by insurance companies licensed in Panama. This requirement will not apply in certain situations, notably, when (i) an international treaty or agreement (to which Panama is a party) establishes otherwise; (ii) when the insurance policy relates to risks not covered in the Republic of Panama; and (iii) when obtaining the corresponding coverage becomes unfeasible, after a rejection on the part of Panama-licensed insurance companies.

Insurance companies licensed to operate in Panama must maintain a minimum paid-in capital of US$5,000,000. Additionally, insurance companies have other minimum reserve requirements.

Over twenty-five (25) insurance companies currently[③] operate in Panama.

c) Broker-Dealer Houses and Investment Advisors

---

① The U.S. Dollar has a 1:1 equivalency to the Balboa in Panama. Moreover, the Balboa is only issued in coin format (1 cent, 5 cents, 10 cents, 25 cents, and 50 cents), and therefore only U.S. Dollar bills, in their several denominations, are used as paper currency.
② March 7, 2018.
③ March 7, 2018.

Broker-Dealer Houses, and Investment Advisors, also play an important role as financial participants. The Securities Law provides that only persons licensed by the Superintendence of the Securities Market are entitled to exercise those professional activities in or from the Republic of Panama.

Broker-Dealer Houses are engaged in the business of purchasing and selling securities or financial instruments, and may, as part of their profession, engage in offering and opening investment accounts.

Investment Advisors, on the other hand, are entities who professionally engage in the business of advising others with respect to the determination of the price of securities of the advisability of investing, purchasing or selling securities or financial instruments, or who are engaged in preparing and publishing studies or reports regarding securities and advice on Forex. This does not include accountants, lawyers, professors or other professionals whose investment advice is merely incidental in the exercise of their profession, nor to an editor, producer, journalist, writer, commentator, or communication media employee, provided that said person communicates only criteria or opinions as part of their job or position in said communication media, and have not acquire an interest, directly or indirectly, in the securities upon which they express their criteria or opinions, nor a special commission or payment for these.

Currently[①] in Panama, there is a total of seventy-nine (79) entities licensed to act as Broker-Dealer Houses, twenty-four (24) of which are banks or subsidiaries of banks. Furthermore, there is a total of fifty-two (52) entities licensed to act as Investment Advisors.

b. Financing Conditions for Foreign Enterprises

The same financing conditions apply to national and foreign companies. However, it is important to note that banks in Panama tends to have, relative to other countries, very strict requirements for opening bank accounts.

In addition, all financing institutions must comply with know-your-client and due diligence policies imposed by the law and certain regulations, including the reporting of suspicious transactions to the Financial Analysis Unit for the Prevention of the Crimes of Capital Laundering.

D. Land Policy

a. Brief Introduction of Land-Related Laws and Regulations

Land-related provisions are mostly found in Panama's Civil Code, of civilian tradition, which classifies all property rights into either 'movables' or 'immovables', with ownership in land falling being considered an immovable. The right of ownership over land provides its holder the right of disposition (dominio), possession (posesión), use (uso), and enjoyment (goce) of such land.

Prior to acquiring land in Panama, it is important to verify any applicable easements (servidumbres), usufructs, or encumbrances over such land, such as a mortgage or a judicial lien. It is also important to know of any leases granted by the owner; to the extent the new owner has knowledge of a lease prior to acquisition, or such lease is registered at the Public Registry Office, the lessee's rights may also impose limitations.

Finally, prior to acquiring land in Panama, it is important to know any if the use that will be given to the property conforms to any applicable zoning laws, and to be aware of any special rules that may also apply by the property being subject to a special property regime, such as the 'Horizontal Property' regime (usually, residential buildings, business office buildings, and residential community projects).

b. Rules of Land Acquisition for Foreign Enterprises

Land in Panama is transferred through the recordation of legal title (usually, a sale deed) in the Public Registry, and may generally be acquired by any individuals or private entities, regardless of nationality. However, land located less than 10 kilometers from the border may not be acquired by foreigner individuals or entities.

Regarding insular territory, it may only be acquired for specific development purposes, provided:
• the specific insular area is not considered a strategic area, or a reserved area; and
• the specific insular area has been declared an area of special development, and legislation has been dictated relating to its use.

Land may not be acquired by a foreign government, or a foreign government entity, except in the case of embassies.

E. The Establishment and Dissolution of Companies

a. The Forms of Enterprises

Although there are several types of legal entities that may be used for conducting business in Panama (e.g.,

---

① March 7, 2018.

general partnership, limited partnership, corporation, limited liability companies), usually most of them fall into one of the following three categories: corporations (sociedades anónimas), limited liability companies (sociedades de responsabilidad limitada), and foreign companies (sociedades extranjeras).

a) Corporations and Limited Liability Companies

Panamanian companies are governed by Law 32 of 26 February 1927, and are the most commonly used legal entity in Panama, partly due to their simplicity and flexibility, which has accounted for almost no amendments to such law since its enactment.

Panamanian limited liability companies, on the other hand, are governed by Law 4 of 9 January 2009, which updated the legal regime that was in place for such type of legal entity, dating from 1966.

As a result of the relatively recent update, the two types of entities are very similar nowadays:

• Simple internal governance structure. Both have a similar internal governance structure (hierarchically: owners at the top, management at the middle, and executive officers at the bottom):

Corporation	Limited Liability Company
Shareholders	Quota holders
Directors (management)	Administrators (management)
Officers	Officers

• Separate personhood and patrimony. Both have personhood and a patrimony of their own, and can therefore exercise rights and assume obligations on their own.

• Limited liability. their shareholders or partners are not personally liable for the obligations of the corporation, only for the unpaid part of their shares or quotas.

• Flexible organizational documents. Both allow the incorporation documents and other organizational documents to regulate any aspect not prohibited by law, including different classes of shares or quotas, as well as the establishment of preferential rights in the event of a transfer of shares or quotas.

• Flexible meeting rules. Both allow, unless otherwise established, their shareholders or partners, as well as their directors or managers, to hold meetings in any part of the world or through electronic means.

• Written resolutions are allowed. both allow for the possibility of passing written resolutions, without having to hold a meeting.

• No limit on the number of owners. neither limits the number of shareholders or quota holders the type of corporation may have.

Two main differences between the two types of Panamanian structures are:

• Minimum number of owners. While Panamanian companies may have one shareholder, Panamanian limited liability companies require a minimum of two quota holders. However, there is no minimum number of quotas each quota holder must have.

• Identity of owners. While the identity of the shareholders of a Panamanian corporation is not of public record (it is kept privately by the corporation, in its shareholder register), the identity of the quota holders of a Panamanian limited liability corporation must be included in the documents filed in the Public Registry Office, and therefore of public record.

Finally, it is important to note that, even though Panamanian limited liability companies are not as commonly used in Panama to conduct business as corporations, foreign businesses sometimes opt for a limited liability company structure for purposes of special tax treatment in some other jurisdiction, if applicable. The latter will depend, however, on the specific tax regulations of the other jurisdiction.

It is worth noting that there is another type of legal entity that is commonly used in Panama, the Private Interest Foundation (Fundación de Interés Privado). However, it is mostly used for estate planning purposes.

b) Foreign Companies

Foreign companies may establish in Panama as a "foreign company" (sociedad extranjera), which are considered as a branch or extension of the entity as incorporated abroad, and therefore the structure of these companies is that which is contemplated under the laws of its place of incorporation. However, foreign branches are required to file at the Public Registry Office: their organizational documents, updated; a copy of their last statement, with a declaration of the amount that will be used for business in Panama; and a good standing certificate from the corresponding registration office at its place of incorporation, certifying that the company is duly incorporated. These documents must be legalized prior to proceeding with their filing, and further translated if presented in some language other than Spanish.

Foreign branches that engage in operations in Panama without registering as a foreign company, may not file judicial or other types of proceedings before Panamanian courts or entities, but may instead be sued or sanctioned with fines.

b. The Procedure of Establishment

The process of establishing a Panamanian corporation or a limited liability company is relatively simple, and can be summarized as follows: the incorporation documents must be presented before a Notary Public and transcribed into a public deed, which is then registered at the Public Registry Office. Once registration is completed, the process ends. The timeframe is usually 3-5 business days.

Below we provide further details relating to the content of the corresponding incorporation documents.

a) Panamanian Corporation

The incorporation document of Panamanian corporations, the Articles of Incorporation (pacto social), must include at least the following information:

• Names and addresses of the subscribers of the Articles of Incorporation. Subscribers act as the persons who appear before the Notary Public to provide the incorporation documents to be transcribed into public deed. The subscribers must indicate how many shares they will "subscribe", which must be at least one share each. In practice, however, this is treated as a mere formality, and law firms usually act as subscribers through office personnel or companies created for such purpose, and their right to "subscribe" shares is then assigned, such that all shares may be issued to the whomever the shareholders shall be.

• Name of the corporation. The name of the corporation may not closely resemble that of another existing corporation; additionally, the name must include language suggesting that the legal entity is a corporation (usually, the abbreviation 'S.A.'). The Public Registry Office offers the option of verifying the availability of a name, and having it reserved for a small fee.

• The objects (purposes) of the corporation. The purposes for which corporation will exist must be indicated. Panamanian law does not forbid corporations to include broad objects, and in practice, most often corporations will list its specific purposes, and as a final item, include broad language indicating that the corporation may carry out any acts permitted by law.

• The authorized capital. The number of total shares the corporation may issue, must be indicated, as well as their par value and, if applicable, the number of shares with no par value. Shares may be issue in registered form or bearer form. If issued in bearer form, however, specific language must be included to the effect that the corporation will be subject to a custody regime, which will require the bearer shares to be in the possession and custody of an authorized custodian, who must be a licensed financial entity, a licensed trust, or a licensed attorney.

• Different classes of shares (if applicable). Different classes of shares may be established (common, preferential, etc.); if so, the Articles of Incorporation must further indicate their number, designation, privileges, voting rights, and restrictions.

• The number of shares each subscriber will take. At least one share must be subscribed by each subscriber. (See 'Names and addresses of the subscribers of the Articles of Incorporations', above.)

• The address of the corporation. In practice, most corporations do not provide a detailed address, and sometimes will only indicate the city where the corporation has its offices. If the corporation has operations in Panama, a detailed address is available to the public through the operations notice (the commercial license).

• The duration of the corporation. The duration of most corporations is established as 'indefinite' or 'perpetual'.

• The number of directors and their addresses. Corporations are required to have at least three directors. Directors are not required to be shareholders. Legal entities may be appointed as directors.

• President, Secretary, and Treasurer. All corporations are required to have, as officers, a President, a Secretary, and a Treasurer. Accordingly, these should be appointed upon incorporation.

• Resident Agent. All corporations are required to have a Resident Agent in Panama, who may be a Panama-licensed attorney or law firm.

b) Panamanian Limited Liability Companies

The incorporation document of Panamanian limited liability companies, the Articles of Organization (pacto social), must include at least the following information:

• Name of the limited liability company. The name of the limited liability company may not closely resemble that of another existing limited liability company; additionally, the name must include language suggesting that the legal entity is a limited liability (usually, the abbreviation 'S. de R.L.'). The Public Registry Office offers the option of verifying the availability of a name, and having it reserved for a small fee.

• Names and addresses of the grantors of the Articles of Organization, and of the partners. Different from corporations, the persons who appear before the notary public to provide the incorporation documents are grantors, and not 'subscribers'. Additionally, the Articles of Organization will require the Articles of Organization will require the names and addresses of the partners to be included.

• The address of the limited liability company. In practice, most limited liability companies do not provide a detailed address, and sometimes will only indicate the city where the limited liability company has its offices. If the limited liability corporation has operations in Panama, a detailed address is available to the public through the operations notice (the commercial license).

• The duration of the limited liability company. The duration of most limited liability companies is established as 'indefinite' or 'perpetual'.

• The objects (purposes) of the limited liability company. The purposes for which limited liability company will exist must be indicated. Panamanian law does not forbid limited liability companies to include broad objects, and in practice, most often these types of legal entities will list its specific purposes, and as a final item, include broad language indicating that the limited liability corporation may carry out any acts permitted by law.

• The authorized capital. The number of total participation quotas the limited liability may issue, must be indicated, as well as their par value.

• The person or persons who will act as administrator. A limited liability company requires at least one (1) administrator. Administrators are not required to be partners. Legal entities may be appointed as administrators.

• One or more officers. Limited liability companies are not required to have a President, a Secretary, and a Treasurer, as corporations do. However, in practice, most limited liability companies usually appoint persons to act as such.

• Resident Agent. All corporations are required to have a Resident Agent in Panama, who may be a Panama-licensed attorney or law firm.

It is important to note that companies in general, including corporations and limited liability companies, must pay an Franchise Tax (Tasa Única) of US$300, annually.

c. Routes and Requirements of Dissolution

The dissolution of a Panamanian corporation requires its shareholders to adopt a resolution to dissolve the corporation, by a majority of votes at a meeting duly held with prior notice. If all the shareholders are present or represented at the meeting, prior notice may be waived. Alternatively, if all the shareholders with a right to vote provide their consent in writing, i.e., by written resolution executed by all the shareholders, the holding of a meeting is not required.

The minutes of the shareholders' meeting must be executed by the President and the Secretary of the corporation. The minutes must be notarized and later registered at the Public Registry in Panama, and a notice of dissolution published in a local newspaper.

Under Law 32 of 1927 (the "Law of Corporations"), after dissolution, the corporation generally continues for a term of three (3) years for the purpose of prosecuting or defending suits by or against the corporation or enabling it to settle its business and dispose of and convey its property and to divide its capital stock, but not for the purpose of continuing the business for which the corporation was organized.

The directors shall act as trustees for the corporation with full power to settle the affairs, collect the outstanding debts, sell and convey the property of every kind, and divide the monies and property among the stockholders, after paying the debts of the corporation; and they shall have authority to sue for, in the name of the corporation, and recover debts and property and to be sued in its name for debts owing by the corporation.

With dissolution, the process of 'liquidation' of a company starts. If the company has no assets or liabilities at the time of dissolution, or if whatever debts have already been paid and the remaining assets distributed, by the time the dissolution resolution is adopted, such resolution may indicate that the company will be deemed liquidated by the end of the meeting. If such is the case, no further step is required for liquidation to be deemed complete.

If, however, the company has not engaged in the payment of its debts and the distribution of its assets upon dissolution, then it should engage in such process and, once completed, the shareholders or quota holders must afterwards adopt a resolution stating that liquidation has taken place, and such resolution must then be notarized and registered at the Public Registry Office.

F. Merger and Acquisition

Although companies contemplating an acquisition or a merger are generally not subject to prior authorization or notification, certain economic acquisitions or mergers may be prohibited under competition regulation (see 'Competition regulation', below).

Additionally, if the target company is part of a regulated market (for example, the telecommunications, electricity, banking, and insurance markets), the corresponding acquisition or merger will most likely be subject to prior authorization or notification from the relevant market regulator.

Finally, it is important to note that public offers for the purchase of shares in an issuer registered before the Superintendence of the Securities Market (a 'tender offer'), which may result in a certain percentage of voting stock being acquired, will require a specific process to be followed, pursuant to Decree Law 1 of 1999 (the "Securities Law"), involving notification and disclosure of information relating to the offer.

G. Competition Regulation

Competition regulation in Panama dates back to 1996, when the government agency called the Commission on Free Competition and Consumer Affairs (the "CLICAC") was created under Law 29 of 1996, which established a regulatory framework for the defense of competition. Competition law is regulated under principally under Law 45 of 2007 (the "Law of Consumer Protection and Defense of Competition").

a. Department Supervising Competition Regulation

The government agency supervising competition regulation is the Consumer Protection and Defense of Competition Authority (the "ACODECO"), the CLICAC's successor entity.

b. Brief Introduction of Competition Law

Law 45 of 2007 (the "Law of Consumer Protection and Defense of Competition") prohibits, in general, any act, agreement, or practice that restricts, diminishes, harms, prevents, or in any other way hinders free economic competition and the free engagement in the production, distribution, supply or marketing of goods or services.

Competition law in Panama is mainly divided into 'Monopolistic Practices' and 'Economic Concentrations'.

a) Monopolistic Practices

Monopolistic practices are divided into absolute monopolistic practices and relative monopolistic practices.

Absolute monopolistic practices are defined as any act, combination, arrangement, agreement, or contract, between current or potential competitors, among themselves or through acts in consort, which have the following purposes or effects:

• Fixing, manipulating, coordinating, agreeing, or imposing the sales or purchase price of goods or services, or otherwise exchanging information for such purposes.

• Agreeing the obligation to produce, process, distribute or market only a limited quantity of goods, or to provide services in a limited amount or unfrequently.

• Dividing, distributing, assigning, agreeing, or imposing parts or segments of an existing or future market of goods and services, through specified or specifiable clients, suppliers, times or spaces.

• Establishing, agreeing, or coordinating bids, or the refrainment from participations in bids open to the public, for best value, for a framework agreement, reverse auctions, auctions of public assets, as well as any other forms of contracting with the government.

Relative monopolistic practices, on the other hand, are generally defined as those practices that diminish or hinder free competition, or the free engagement of economic agents, and which are considered infringing only when the economic agent or agents have 'substantial power'[1], individually or collectively, over the 'pertinent market'[2].

Relative monopolistic practices consist, more specifically, of unilateral acts, combinations, arrangements, agreements or contracts with the object or purpose of irrationally forcing out other market agents, irrationally preventing their access, or irrationally creating exclusive advantages in favor of one or more economic agents, in the following situations:

---

[1] The following factors are relevant for determining whether an economic agent has 'substantial power':

• The economic agent's participation in the pertinent market, and its capacity to fix prices unilaterally or restrict the supply in the pertinent market, without competitors being able to, effectively or potentially, counter such capacity.

• The existence of entry barriers to the pertinent market, and of factors that anticipatorily may alter the barriers and supply from other competitors.

• The existence and power of competitors.

• The possibility of access, on the part of the economic agents and its competitors, to inputs.

• The economic agent's recent behavior.

[2] The following factors are relevant for determining the 'pertinent market':

• The possibility of substituting goods or services for others, whether local or foreign, and the capability of consumers to find substitutes.

• The costs of distribution of the good, its inputs, its parts, or its substitutes, in Panamanian or foreign territory, considering transportation costs, tariff duties or non-tariff restrictions, restrictions imposed by economic agents or its associations, as well as the time required to provide the pertinent market with supply.

• Costs and possibilities of consumers accessing other markets.

• Regulatory restrictions that limit the access of consumers to other sources of supply, or the access of suppliers to other consumers.

• Innovation dynamics.

• Between non-competitors, the fixing, imposition, or exclusive distribution, of goods or services based on the types of persons, geographic area, or for a specified period of time, including the division, distribution, or assigning of clients or suppliers, as well as imposing obligations not to produce or distribute goods or services for a certain period of time.

• The imposition, or fixing, of prices and other conditions, on the part of the manufacturer, the producer, or the supplier, for the resale of goods or services.

• The sale or transaction that is contingent to buying, acquiring, selling, or providing an additional good or service, usually different or discernible, or based on reciprocity.

• The sale or transaction conditioned upon refraining from using, acquiring, selling, or providing the goods or services produced, processed, distributed, or marketed by a third-party.

• The unilateral action consisting of refusing to sell or provide, to certain clients, those goods or services usually available and offered to others, except where there would be a breach of contractual obligations on the part of the client vis-à-vis the economic agent, or except where, based on prior experiences with the client, there exists a high possibility of returns or of damaged merchandise claims.

• The acting in consort with several economic agents, or encouraging of these, to exert pressure on a client or provider, with the purpose of dissuading the client from engaging in a specific conduct, applying reprimands, or forcing such client to act in a certain way.

• Any predatory act by an economic agent, that tends to cause damages or force out a competitor from the pertinent market, or that prevents a potential competitor from entering the market, when it is unreasonable to expect that the economic agent will profit safe when the competitor stops competing or leaves the market, and economic agent is left with substantial power or a monopolistic stance.

• The act of buying up all production, distribution or sales of goods or services, with the purpose of obtaining a profit in their later sale or tending to favor a third party in the production, distribution, or sale of such goods or services.

• In general, any act that unreasonable harms or hinders free economic competition or the free engagement in the free engagement in the production, processing, distribution, supply or marketing of goods or services.

b) Economic Concentrations

Economic concentrations are defined as the merger, acquisition of control, or any other act whereby companies, partnerships, stocks, quota shares, trusts, establishments, or assets in general, are combined by suppliers, clients, and other competitors, among themselves.

Economic concentrations that may unreasonably diminish, restrict, harm or prevent free economic competition in relation to the same, similar, or substantially related, goods or services. The concept does not include a joint venture regarding a specific project, or economic concentrations that will not have harmful effects on the market or on competition. Additionally, an economic agent with continuous losses, or on the verge of leaving the market, may be exempted; provided, however, it (unsuccessfully) approached buyers who were not competitors.

Economic agents who engage in economic concentrations may request ACODECO for a 'prior verification' of the effects the potential economic concentration will have. This mechanism acts as a safe-harbor for parties engaging in economic concentrations, which may be challenged up to three years after economic concentration takes place.

If the ACODECO deems that, based on the verified effects, the economic concentration is not prohibited, the corresponding economic concentration is protected from future challenges from ACODECO regarding the verified effects (except, of course, where false or incomplete information was presented).

c. Measures Regulating Competition

Acts considered to be absolute monopolistic practices are considered null and void, and infringing economic agents may be sanctioned even when these practices have not been perfected or its effects have not taken place.

In addition to the affected parties being able to file civil claims against the infringing entity, measures that may be taken by ACODECO against absolute monopolistic practices include:

- Monetary fine up to US$1,000,000.
- Obligation to pay three (3) times the amount of damages and harms caused by the illicit act.
- Public release, in a nationwide newspaper, of the violation and the sanction imposed on the corresponding economic actor.
- Upon repetitive conduct, a request, on the part of ACODECO to the Ministry of Commerce and Industries, to revoke the economic agent's operating license.

Measures that may be taken against relative monopolistic practices include:

- Monetary fine up to US$250,000.
- Obligation to pay three (3) times the amount of damages and harms caused by the illicit act.

- Public release, in a nationwide newspaper, of the violation and the sanction imposed on the corresponding economic actor.
- Upon repetitive conduct, a request, on the part of ACODECO to the Ministry of Commerce and Industries, to revoke the economic agent's operating license.

It is important to note, additionally, that individuals who engage in price fixing relating to public contracting, may be subject to imprisonment from 6 months to 2 years.

Regarding economic concentrations challenged, ACODECO may deem these valid without any further measures, valid but conditioned to certain measures, or completely prohibited. Examples of measures ACODECO may impose, as conditions to an economic concentration's validity, include:
- Abstaining from carrying out a certain conduct.
- Sale of certain assets or shares.
- Modification, transfer, or elimination, of certain production lines.
- Modification or elimination of certain provisions included in the agreements to be executed.
- Making the production or logistics capacity available to other competitors.
- Guaranteeing the transfer of benefits to consumers.

H. Tax

a. Tax Regime and Rules

Panama's tax regime is mainly based on the 'principle of territoriality', which implies that only income generated by domestic activities, or carried out in the territory of the Republic of Panama, will be subject to income tax.

Panama's default 'tax period' for businesses operating in Panama is the calendar year, going from January 1st to December 31st. However, authorization may be sought from the General Revenue Office (Dirección General de Ingresos) for a special tax period to apply, based on the nature of the business and the company's operations.

b. Main Categories and Rates of Tax

Tax	Tax Rate
Value Added-Tax	Standard rate – 7%
Corporate Income Tax	Uniform rate – 25%
Withholding Tax on Remittances Abroad (Payments sent to individuals or companies domiciles outside of Panama, which are paid in exchange for a service or action benefiting individuals or companies located in Panama)	Rate of applicable tax, applied to 50% of amount to be remitted (Withholding will not be required when the beneficiary of the payment registers as a taxpayer in Panama)
Capital Gains Tax	Sale of shares – 10% (5% of sales price must be withheld by purchaser and remitted to the tax authorities as an advance payment) Sale of property – 10% (3% of sales price must be withheld by purchaser and remitted to the tax authorities as an advance payment)
Transfer of Immovable Property Tax	Uniform rate – 2%
Immovable Property Tax	Rates range from 0% to 1%, depending on the type of property (e.g., residential, commercial, industrial, etc.)
Dividends tax	Panama-sourced income – 10% Foreign-sourced income – 5%
Operations notice Tax (Only applies to companies that have a commercial license.)	Uniform rate – 2% of net worth or US$60,000 (whichever is lower)

(continued)

Tax	Tax Rate
Supplementary Tax (Applies when a company does not distribute earnings, or distributes earnings but these account for less than 40% of net income for the corresponding fiscal year)	Standard rate – 4%
Social Security Contributions	Social Security Employer – 12.25% Social Security Employee – 9.75% Education Insurance Employer – 1.50% Education Insurance Employee – 1.25%

c. Tax Declaration and Preference

Companies must file an annual tax return by March 31st of the year following the tax period. However, an extension of thirty (30) days may be requested. Companies not subject to income tax in Panama (e.g., companies with no income-generating activities or operations in Panama), are not required to file income tax returns.

I. Securities

a. Brief Introduction of Securities-Related Laws and Regulations

Decree Law 1 of 1999 (the "Securities Law") is the main law that regulates the securities market in Panama, and the supervising agency is the Superintendence of the Securities Market. The securities law mainly regulates public offers of securities, and securities market participants.

A security is defined as:

Any bond, negotiable commercial title or debenture, share (including treasury shares), trading right recognized in a custody account, participation quota, certificate of title, trust certificate, deposit certificate, mortgage bond, warrant or any other instrument or right usually recognized as a security or a security determined as such by the Superintendence.

It does not include the following:

- Non‐negotiable certificates or titles that represent obligations, issued by banks to its customers as a part of its usually offered banking services, such as non‐negotiable certificates of deposit. This exception does not include negotiable bank acceptances or negotiable commercial securities issued by banking institutions.

- Insurance policies, certificates of capitalization, and similar obligations issued by insurance companies.

- Any other instruments, titles or rights, which have been determined by the Superintendence as not being securities.

The following securities must be registered with the Superintendence of the Securities Market prior to their sale:

- securities that are the subject of a 'public offer' under the Securities Law, and not otherwise exempted from registration;

- securities of issuers domiciled in Panama which have fifty (50) or more shareholders domiciled in Panama, who are beneficial owners of at least ten percent (10%) of the paid-in capital of said issuer; and

- securities listed in a securities exchange in Panama.

As a general rule, public offers in the Republic of Panama must be registered with the Superintendence of the Securities Market, unless otherwise exempted. The Securities Law establishes that any offer or sale made to persons domiciled in Panama shall be considered public offers in the Republic of Panama. The following offers are exempted:

- Offers of exempted securities, which includes government-issued securities, as well as securities issued by international organizations in which Panama is a part of;

- Offers considered private placements, that is, offers of securities made to no more than twenty-five (25) persons, and that together result in a sale to no more than ten (10) persons, in a one-year period;

- Offers to institutional investors, who, due to their experience in the securities market, have the knowledge and financial capacity to evaluate and undertake investment risks without the protection of the Securities Law (e.g., investment banks);

- Offers considered corporate transfers, including (i) an offer of shares with the purpose of increasing the issuers capital, when such offer is directed to the issuer's existing shareholders, (ii) share dividends, (iii) the corporate reorganization, dissolution, liquidation or merger of the issuer; and (iv) the exercise of rights or options previously granted by the issuer; and

- Offers made exclusively to employees, officers, or directors of the issuer, within certain parameters.

Securities market participants include the following: securities exchanges (currently[①], only the Bolsa de Valores de Panamá), clearing-houses (currently[②], only the Central Latinoamericana de Valores), broker-dealer houses, brokers, investment advisors, analysts, credit rating entities, and issuers. Except for issuers, who must fulfill important registration and on-going disclosure of information requirements, most other market participants will require a license issued by the Superintendence of the Securities Market.

b. Supervision and Regulation of Securities Market

The Superintendence of the Securities Market, as the entity in charge of supervising the securities market, has powers to issue specific regulations which market participants must follow prior to engaging in their corresponding activities.

One of the most relevant of these regulations is Agreement No. 7-2017, which regulates the process of registration of securities, and lays out the information that must be disclosed by issuers in the corresponding prospectus of the security to be offered, as well as all the documentation that needs to be presented to the Superintendence of the Securities Market, and which will be available to prospective investors.

c. Requirements for Engagement in Securities Trading for Foreign Enterprises

Only entities that have obtained the corresponding license issued by the Superintendence of the Securities Market may assist individuals or entities with the sale or purchase of securities which are the object of 'public offer' under the Securities Law, or with professional advice in relation to these securities.

Entities dedicated to purchasing and selling securities or financial instruments, on behalf of third parties or on their own, must have a broker-dealer house license. On the other hand, entities dedicated to advising regarding investments in securities or financial instruments, on the other hand, are required to have an investment advisor license.

J. Preference and Protection of Investment

a. The Structure of Preference Policies

Industries that have investment incentives or a special legal regime, will most often focus on one or more of four aspects: tax, labor, customs, and / or immigration. Additionally, by the very nature of the activities incentivized within those industries, investments tend to be of significance, and for certain specific benefits sometimes required. For example, the stability benefit contemplated under the Law of Legal Stability of Investments, is only available to those who make an investment of US$2,000,000.00 or more.

In the case of companies that establish in Panama a Multinational Company Headquarter (or SEM), these must demonstrate that the company seeking license is part of a corporate group that has a minimum of US$200,000,000 in assets, and they're furthermore required to provide statistics on how many employees the company will have in Panama.

What is mentioned above reflects one of the main objectives found behind creating these incentives, which is that of bringing more resources into the Panamanian economy, and increasing employment for Panamanians.

b. Support for Specific Industries and Regions

Industries that have investment incentives include: tourism; industrial activities; export of agricultural products; mining; processing zones for export; commercial free zones; petroleum free zones; petroleum or natural gas refining, storage, and transport; telecommunications; construction; port development; railway developments; and electric power generation, distribution and transmission.

c. Special Economic Areas

a) Panama-Pacific Special Economic Area

The Panama-Pacific Special Economic Area (the "Panama-Pacific Area") is an area with a special legal, tax, customs, labor and business regime, located in the district of Arraiján (former Howard Air Base), and created through the Law 41 of 2004, to attract and promote investments through the flow and free movement of goods, services and capital.

The Panama-Pacific Area is managed by London & Regional, as Developer. The government agency in charge of the implementation and regulation of the regime is the Panama-Pacific Special Economic Area Agency.

Any person or corporation establishing within the Panama-Pacifico may be able to carry out any type of

---

① March 7, 2018.
② March 7, 2018.

commercial activity, since, in general terms, there are no exceptions, unless there is an express prohibition established by law, in matters of public health, safety and public order, and the express prohibition of display rooms of products that are commercialized internationally or at other special economic areas.

However, the main benefits are applicable to the activities that we summarize below (the "Incentivized Activities"):

• The provision of services to individuals or entities located outside the territory of the Republic of Panama (offshore services).

• The sale or transfer of shares between companies established in the Panama-Pacific Area.

• The sale of merchandise not manufactured in the Panama-Pacific Area, in transit or destined to foreign countries.

• The sale of products not manufactured in the Panama-Pacific Area, as well as services in general, to aircraft that use airports in Panama, destined for foreign airports.

• The provision of services related to aviation and airports.

• The manufacture of high technology products, components, and parts, as well as the activities of processing, manufacturing, assembly, or manufacturing products, components, and parts in using high technology processes.

• The multimodal and logistics services, as well as sales of merchandise not manufactured in the Panama-Pacific Area, destined to foreign countries.

• The provision of call center services; processing, storage, transmission and retransmission of data and digital information; the connection of radio, television, audio, video and / or data signals; research and development of resources and digital applications for use in Intranet and Internet networks; the administration of offices to users within the Panama-Pacific Area or established outside the territory of the Republic of Panama; the provision of high value-added services protected by intellectual or industrial property regulations, provided to companies established within the Panama-Pacific Area or to companies established outside the territory of the Republic of Panama.

• The activities of import, export and re-export of merchandise and other commercial goods, including the activities of re-invoicing of merchandise that does not enter the Panamanian territory, as well as those of logistics and multimodal services.

Among the principal tax benefits available to companies carrying out an Incentivized Activity within the Panama-Pacific Area, are:

• Exemption from Income Tax and Importation Tax, in relation to the Incentivized Activity.

• Dividends Tax, of 5%, whether earnings distributed are from Panama-source or foreign-source income, and a Supplementary Tax of 2% (applies if earnings are not distributed). (This is a reduced tax from the general rate of 10% for Panama-source dividends, and a 4% Supplementary Tax.)

• Annual tax of 0.5% over the net worth of the company, with a minimum of US$100.00 and a maximum of US$50,000.00.

Law 41 of 2004 provides some important labor and immigration benefits, including:

• 25% uniform rate for payment of extra hours.
• Flexibility in establishing rest days.
• Companies may continue operations during holidays.
• One-Stop-Window Service for obtaining visas.
• Special types of visas available.

b) Colon Free Zone

Decree Law No. 18 of June 17, 1948 established a special legal, tax, customs and business regime, as an Autonomous State Entity know as Colon Free Zone, in the Province of Colon. Such law was recently subrogated by Law 8 of 2016, which reorganized the Colon Free Zone.

Operations within the Colon Free Zone consist mainly on import and export of merchandise and goods from different countries, as well as services and facilities offered by the Free Zone, for a wide array of commercial and logistics activities, such as importing, storing, assembling, re-packing and re-exporting products from all over the world.

Among the principal tax benefits available are:

• No Income Tax on profits obtained from offshore operations.

• Merchandise and other commercial goods are generally exempt from payment of taxes, charges or other tax contributions, national or otherwise, including consular fees of any kind, whether for their introduction to Areas of Free International Trade, or their remanence therein, or their export.

• Dividends Tax, of 5%, whether earnings distributed are from Panama-source or foreign-source income.

• Annual tax of 0.5% over the net worth of the company, with a minimum of US$100.00 and a maximum of US$50,000.00.

c) Free Trade Zones

In 2011, Law 25 of 1992, the law in place related to export processing zones was, replaced by Law No. 32 of April 5, 2011 (the "Law of Free Trade Zones"), a more expansive law, which established a special tax regime for companies located in these zones and carrying one of several activities (export-oriented, mostly).

The main objective of Free Trade Zones is to provide users incentives so that these can achieve high levels of competitiveness in the international markets. Geographically, FTZs may be established anywhere in the territory of Panama. Free Trade Zones may be privately owned, state owned, or both privately and state owned.

d) Promoters and Operators

A company that develops and owns an Free Trade Zone is a 'Promoter' under the Law of Free Trade Zones, which is assimilated with owning the corresponding Free Trade Zone.

Promoters are exempt from Income Tax, and from Value-Added Tax (VAT). Promoters may also act as 'Operators', in charge of the direction, administration, and operation of the Free Trade Zone. Promoters have the same exemptions as Free Trade Zone Users (see 'Free Trade Zone Users', below) and, in addition, they have exemptions from Income Tax and VAT in relation to leases.

e) Free Trade Zone Users

Companies established within a Free Trade Zone to carry out their business activities are considered 'users' of the Free Trade Zone. The Law of Free Trade Zones allows the establishment of Free Trade Zones for following categories of users:

- logistics services companies;
- finished and semi-finished goods processing companies;
- assembly companies (production of finished or semi-finished goods through assembly of raw inputs or semi-finished goods);
- manufacturing companies (production of goods, through manufacture of raw inputs or semi-finished goods)
- services companies (to clients offshore, inside the FTZ, or in another FTZ);
- high technology companies (hardware, software, data center);
- aviation and airport related services companies;
- general services companies (personal services offered within the FTZ, e.g., restaurants, laundries, pharmacies, beauty parlors, gyms, banks, etc.);
- environmental services companies;
- superior education centers;
- scientific research centers; and
- specialized health services centers.

Law No. 32 establishes, as a general rule, that activities carried out by users established in a Free Trade Zone are exempt from direct and indirect taxes:

any activity, operation, transaction, processing and transfer of movable and immovable property, purchase of construction equipment and supplies, raw materials, machinery, tools, accessories, supplies, and any good or service required for their operations, carried out by the companies established within the free zones, shall be exempt from any direct or indirect national taxes, contributions, rates, rights and levies. They will also be exempt from the [operations notice] license tax.

However, as an exception to the above rule, under the Free Trade Zone special tax regime, payment of the following listed taxes / contributions would still apply:

- Dividends Tax, of 5%, whether earnings distributed are from Panama-source or foreign-source income, and a Supplementary Tax of 2% (applies if earnings are not distributed). (This is a reduced tax from the general rate of 10% for Panama-source dividends, and a 4% Supplementary Tax.)
- Annual tax of 0.5% over the net worth of the company, with a minimum of US$100.00 and a maximum of US$50,000.00.
- Excise (Selective Consumption) Tax.[1]
- FECI[2], but not in the case of loans secured with bank deposits.
- Social Security contributions.
- Withholding Tax on Remittances (12.5% effective tax rate). This tax applies regarding payment for services,

---

[1] Applies over certain specified items, such as sodas [5%]; beer, wine, and liquor [US$0.045 per every alcohol percentage point/litter]; recreational boats, jet-skies, and helicopters [10%]; jewelry and firearms [5%]; and gambling tickets [5.5%].

[2] FECI stands for Fondo Especial de Compensación de Intereses, which translates to 'Compensation of Interests Special Fund', and refers to a special tax levied as an additional 1% interest on certain personal and commercial loans granted locally over US$5,000.00. The tax proceeds are used to fund subsidies of certain preferential mortgage loans, nd to support other government entities in the area of agriculture.

royalties, and commissions paid to foreign providers. However, payment is only required to the extent such services, royalties, or commissions are for income-production purposes and a deduction is taken regarding expenses related to such services, royalties, or commissions.

 f)Free Trade Zones established in Panama include (promoter indicated)
 ·Zona Franca Panexport (Inmobiliaria SUCASA, S.A.);
 ·Zona Franca Isla Margarita (Isla Margarita Development, Inc.);
 ·Zona Franca Estatal Davis (Unidad Administrativa de Bienes Revertidos);
 ·Zona Franca de Albrook (Zona Procesadora de Exportación Albrook, S.A.);
 ·Zona Franca Marpesca / Corozal (Procesadora Marpesca, S.A.);
 ·Zona Franca Chilibre (Expert Diesel, S.A.);
 ·Zona Franca Espanam (Espanam Iberoamérica, S.A.);
 ·Zona Franca Eurofusion (Eurofusion, S.A.);
 · Zona Franca de las Américas (Mi Morocho, S.A.);
 · Zona Franca Colon Maritime Investor (Colón Maritime Investor, S.A.);
 · Zona Franca Export Pacific Panamá (Export Pacific Panamá, S.A.);
 · Zona Franca Hewlett Packard (Hewlett Packard Global Services Panamá, S.A.);
 · Zona Franca del Istmo (Zona Franca del Istmo, S.A.);
 · Zona Franca Cobol Due (Cobol Due, S.A.);
 · Zona Franca Framorco (Francisco Javier Morales Gerbaud);
 · Zona Logística del Aeropuerto de Tocumen (Aeropuerto Internacional de Tocumen, S.A.).

d. Investment Protection

As mentioned already, the Law of Legal Stability of Investments provides that investments of US$2,000,000.00, or more, in certain activities may be subjected, for a period of ten (10) years, to the same legal, tax, customs, and labor laws that were in place at the time of the investment.

The investment must generally be made within a period of two (2) years, and the investor must be registered with the Investment Register of the Ministry of Commerce and Finance.

III. Trade

A. Department Supervising Trade

a. National Trade

Trade at the national level, as referring to the sale of goods and services within Panama, is supervised at a general level by the Ministry of Commerce and Industries. Depending on the types of goods, services, or the economic activities involved, these could be subject to further supervision of a different government entity. The Ministry of Commerce and Industries is the entity responsible for issuing commercial licenses (operation notices) to businesses carrying out business activities in Panama, under Law 5 of 2007.

b. International Trade

Trade at the international level, as referring to the import and export of goods and services in or from Panama, is also supervised by the Ministry of Commerce and Industries, but mainly governed by applicable laws and regulations, such as customs provisions and international treaties, and will vary depending on the specific circumstances, as well as several factors (for example, types of goods or materials, place of origin, place of destination, any changes the goods or materials may undergo in Panama, applicable treaties, if location is to be imported to [or exported from] a special economic zone, etc.).

B. Brief Introduction of Trade Laws and Regulations

a. National Trade

In general, for a company to establish commercial or industrial operations in Panama, it must first obtain a commercial license, called an 'operations notice' (aviso de operación), issued by the Ministry of Commerce and Industries, through the PanamaEmprende system, which may be accessed through its web portal (www.panamaemprende.gob.pa).

If the type of commercial activity to be carried is within a regulated industry or market, and therefore considered a 'regulated activity', the corresponding company will most likely require prior authorization from the

corresponding industry or market regulator. Examples of regulated activities include:
- Sales of alcoholic beverages.
- Public utility services (for example, water, electricity, and telephone services).
- Financial services (banking, trustee services, insurance, re-insurance, financial enterprises, and investment advising).
- Sale of pharmaceutical products.
- Health services.
- Sales of weapons and ammunitions.
- Private security services.

In general, also, any activities that may impose a risk to the public's health, the environment, or national security, are considered regulated activities.

Although we already address, in other sections, laws and regulations of general relevance to anyone carrying out commercial or industrial operations in Panama (see 'Investment', 'Labor,' and 'Intellectual Property' sections), we do not discuss consumer protection laws elsewhere. We therefore include a brief discussion here.

Consumers of final products and services are the main beneficiaries of local consumer laws and regulations. The main law in this area is Law 41 of 2007 (the Law of Consumer Protection and Defense of Competition). Some of the obligations imposed on sellers under such law include:

- Informing clearly and truthfully about the characteristics of the product or service offered, such as its nature, composition, content, weight, origin, expiration date, toxicity, precautions, the price, and any other determining condition. The language must necessarily be Spanish, in the case of pharmaceuticals, agrochemicals, toxic products, and food products that require warning or precautions.
- Providing instructions on proper use of the product, and information on any health or hazard risks.
- Informing the consumer about any applicable warranties applicable to the products or services and the specific conditions of these.
- Informing the consumer whenever some parts or spare parts are used parts.
- Informing the consumer of the non-availability of parts, spare parts, or technical services in Panama, and that are related to the product.
- Assuming responsibility when there is an obligation to repair, and such obligation has not been satisfied within a reasonable time.
- Informing the consumer of any applicable deadlines for making returns or damage clams regarding the product.
- Issuing invoices for the product or service, indicating the seller's tax identification number (called the 'registro único de contribuyente', or also RUC), a description of the goods or services, the price, and the date of delivery or provision.
- Any special conditions applicable to the sale.

Manufacturers, importers, distributors, or suppliers, as applicable, are also responsible for the suitability, quality, veracity of advertising, and authenticity of the labels on the products and services, as well as for the content and shelf life of the product as indicated on the packaging or label.

b. International Trade

International trade falls under the supervision of the Ministry of Commerce and Industries, through the National Directorate of International Commercial Negotiations, the National Directorate of Administration of International Commercial Negotiations and Commercial Defense, and the Vice Ministry of Foreign Trade. Additionally, it is important to note that the agency in the agency in charge of supervising the introduction of goods into Panama is the National Customs Authority (Autoridad Nacional de Aduanas).

International trade is mainly governed by local laws and regulations, as well as any applicable international treaties, and the specific treatment will vary depending on different factors. Some of the relevant factors include: the type of good or material and its classification, place of origin, place of destination, whether the goods or materials imported underwent any change in Panama, applicable treaties, and whether the good or material will be imported to (or exported from) Panama's customs territory or a customs area within a special economic area.

C. Trade Management

a. National Trade

National Trade and Industries, at a general level, falls under the supervision of the Ministry of Commerce and Industries, though its Vice Ministry of Interior Commerce and Industries, which is involved in several national trade management activities, including the issuance of operations notices through the PanamaEmprende system.

b. International Trade

Within the structure of the Ministry of Commerce and Industries, the National Directorate of Administration of International Commercial Negotiations is involved in treaty negotiations on behalf of Panama, while the National Directorate of International Commercial Negotiations and Commercial Defense is involved in management of international trade treaties. Both of these directorates fall under the supervision of the Vice Minister of International Commercial Negotiations.

The Vice Ministry of Foreign Trade, on the other hand, is involved in the promotion of investments and exports.

D. The Inspection and Quarantine of Import and Export Commodities

Inspection, and quarantine (if applicable), of import and export commodities will vary depending on the type of commodity. Although we do not go into detail here, it is important to note that certain types of commodities have special quarantine provisions, including foods, plants, and live animals.

The Panamanian Food Safety Authority (Autoridad Panameña de Seguridad de Alimentos, or AUPSA) is the agency generally in charge of foods that are imported to the territory of Panama.

E. Customs Management

As a general rule, any company that imports a product or raw material into Panama's tax territory, must pay the corresponding tariffs. Being a member country of the World Trade Organization (WTO), Panama will default to its 'general tariff', based on the principle of the Most Favored Nation, mainly consisting of the corresponding tariff that Panama would normally apply to the specific product or raw material from other countries in general.

General tariffs currently[1] applied by Panama are found in the Sixth Amendment to the Nomenclature of the Harmonized System of Designation and Codification of Goods of the World Customs Organization (the "Harmonized System"), adopted by Decree Law 35 of 2016.

Exceptionally, however, if Panama has a treaty with the country of origin relating to the products or raw material which is the object of importation, it will apply such corresponding treaty. In that case, however, it must be determined if the requirements established in said treaty are met, so that the product receives preferential tariff treatment. (Such requirements will usually be established in a section called 'Rules of Origin', in the corresponding treaty.)

If the product or raw material complies with such requirements, and the product or raw material is included among those categorized by the treaty, then the corresponding tariff must be applied (usually located in a section called 'Country List').

In the case of exports, if Panama is considered the country of origin of the finished product, and Panama does not have a treaty with the country of destination, said country will usually apply its own 'general tariff' relative to said product.

IV. Labour

A. Brief Introduction of Labor Laws and Regulations

a. Employment Relationship

Employment relationships in Panama are mainly governed by the Labor Code, which is of general application in all of Panama's territory. Employment relationships require to be formalized through a written agreement (a copy of which must be presented and stamped by the Ministry of Labor and Workforce Development). It is important to note, however, that an employment relationship will be presumed whenever services are rendered under conditions of juridical subordination[2] or economic dependence[3].

---

[1] March 10, 2018.
[2] Juridical subordination consists of the direction or control exercised, or that may be exercised, by the employer or its representatives, with regards to the employee, in the execution of the service or work.
[3] Economic dependence exists when the retribution received by the person rendering the service or works (whether received directly or indirectly by an individual or entity, or as a consequence of his activity) constitutes the only or main source of income for such person. It also exists when the person rendering the service or work does not have economic autonomy, and is economically bound to the type of activity advanced by the employer.

b. Duration

Regarding duration, employees may be hired (a) for an undefined (unlimited) period, (b) a defined (limited) period, or (c) for a specific work. When no written contract exists, an undefined period is presumed. Furthermore, an employment for a defined period may not exceed one (1) year, unless it involves special technical skills, in which case the defined period may not exceed three (3) years. Defined period employments, however, may not be established for a position which is normally considered to be permanent.

c. Minimum Wage, Rest Day, Vacations and Thirteenth Month

Wages are subject to a minimum wage table approved by the government, which considers the economic activity and geographic area where the services are rendered. Presently, depending on these factors, minimum wages mostly fall between US$1.53 and US$4.45 per hour.

Employees in Panama also have a right to one (1) day of rest every week, to be agreed to by the employer and employee. However, except with regards to certain activities (for example, pharmacies, hotels and restaurants), employers in general must give preference to Sunday as the corresponding rest day.

Regarding vacation time, employees in Panama have a right to thirty (30) days of vacation for every eleven (11) months of work (approximately a month of vacation per year).

It is important to note that, in Panama, employers must pay their employees a special bonus called the 'thirteenth month', which consists of payment of an extra month of salary every year, to be paid in three installments (April 15th, August 15th, and December 15th).

d. Holidays

The following are paid holidays in Panama: January 1st (New Year's Day); January 9th (Martyr's Day); Carnival Tuesday; Good Friday; May 1st (Labor Day); November 3rd (Secession from Colombia); November 5th (Secession Consolidation); November 10th (Call for Independence from Spain); November 28th (Independence from Spain); December 8th (Mother's Day); and December 25th (Christmas Day).

e. Employee Work Shift and Compensation for Extra Hours

Panama's labor regime places an employee's shift into one of three categories, depending on when the work shift begins and ends:

- if agreed to begin and end sometime between 6:00 a.m. and 6:00 p.m. (the "Day Block"), it is considered a 'day shift', limited to eight (8) hours per day and forty-eight (48) hours per week;
- if agreed to start and end sometime between 6:00 p.m. and 6:00 a.m. (the "Night Block"), it is limited to seven (7) hours per day and forty-two (42) hours per week; and
- if agreed to begin sometime in the Day Block and end sometime in the Night Block (Day Block), or vice versa, it is considered a 'mixed shift', limited to seven and a half (7.5) hours per day and forty-five (45) hours per week.

Extra hours worked may not exceed more than three (3) hours per day, nor more than nine (9) extra hours per week. Regarding payment of extra hours, the general labor regime establishes the following premium rates, depending the type of shift and time block:

- extra hours related to a day shift and inside the Day Block, must be paid at a 25% premium;
- extra hours related to a day shift, and inside the Night Block, must be paid at 50% premium;
- extra hours related to a night shift, or mixed shift starting in the Night Block, must be paid at a 75% premium.

Under the general labor regime, an employee's work during a rest day must be compensated at a 50% premium, but if such day falls on a National Holiday, then the employee must be compensated at a 150% premium. On the other hand, when the work week is set to be shorter than six (6) days, lower premium rates may apply.

f. Termination

Employment relationships not otherwise terminating by reason of expiration of duration, or completion of the special work contracted, may be terminated by resignation on the part of the employee, unilateral termination on the part of the employer, mutual consent, the employee's death, or death or the employer (when such death results in continuation of employment being precluded). Employees with two (2) or more years of rendering services may not be terminated without cause established by law.

It is important to note that employees are subject to a three (3) month probationary term if so stipulated in the contract; they could be dismissed without cause within such term with no responsibility for the employer.

g. Social Security Contributions

Panama's general labor regime is of robust application in Panama's territory. Panama's Social Security Program Law, Law No. 51 of 2005, establishes that the employer and employee are required to pay social security contributions, based on a percentage of an employee's 'salary', which includes:

a) commissions;
b) vacations;
c) bonuses;
d) per diem, if recurrent and exceeding 25% of monthly salary;
e) production premiums, if exceeding 50% of monthly salary; and
f) representation expenses.

The following social contribution rates currently apply to the employer and the employee:

	Employer	Employee (Employer-withheld)
Social Security	12.25%	9.75%
Education Insurance	1.50%	1.25%
Thirteenth Month	10.75%	7.25%

h. Severance Fund

Employers are obligated to establish a severance fund (fondo de cesantía), with a view to complying with payment of termination benefits applicable to employees, mainly, a seniority premium (prima de antigüedad), and compensation (indemnización) if the employee was terminated without cause or if the employee resigned with cause.

B. Requirements of Employing Foreign Employees

Companies in Panama are required to hire persons of Panamanian nationality, or foreigners married to Panamanians or with at least ten (10) years of residence in Panama, who must make up at least 90% of all regular employees (i.e., generally, no more than 10% of regular employees may be foreign employees). Foreign specialized or technical employees, however, may make up to 15% of all employees. Companies with fewer than ten (10) workers, however, may temporarily hire at least one foreign employee.

It is important to note that these percentage limits (of maximum foreign employees) also apply to the total salaries paid by the company. Accordingly, a company with regular foreign employees may not pay more than 10% of such company's total salaries to these.

a. Work Permit

Foreign employees are required to have a work permit issued by the Ministry of Labor and Workforce Development.

The type of work permit requested will vary, depending on the situation, for example:
- the '10% Work Permit', will apply to foreign regular employees;
- the '15% Work Permit', will apply to foreign specialized or technical employees;
- the 'Undefined-Term Work Permit', will apply to foreigners with at least ten (10) years of residence in Panama, and
- the 'Married-to-Panamanian Work Permit', will apply to foreigners married to Panamanians.
- the 'Specific-Countries Work Permit', will apply to foreigners from certain specific countries with which Panama has established a special relationship (Germany, Argentina, Brazil, Chile, Spain, United States, Mexico, Portugal, United Kingdom, Uruguay, and Switzerland, among others); and
- the 'Foreign-Professional Work Permit', will apply to foreign professional with undergraduate or graduate degrees, provided the specific profession is not otherwise limited by the Constitution or laws (restrictions exist regarding certain professional sectors, such as, law, medicine, civil engineering, and architecture).

There 10% and 15% Work Permits are both characterized for leading up to an 'Undefined Term Work Permit', albeit in two stages. The first, where the Work Permit is granted for two (2) years. The second, where the Work permit is granted for an undefined period of time.

It is important to note that:
- generally, work permits are valid for one (1) year, but these may be renewed;
- companies with foreign employees must comply with the requirements of employing foreign personnel (generally, no more than 10% of all employees, if foreign regular employee, nor more than 15%, if foreign specialized or technical employees);
- the employment contract for foreign employees must be for a defined term (i.e., not exceeding one year), since work permits are valid only up to one (1) year, except in the case of foreigners with more than ten (10) years

of residence in Panama, in which case indefinite work permits may be issued.

b. Application Procedure

Work permits must be requested to the Ministry of Labor and Workforce development, through licensed attorneys. Approval or denial of these permits usually takes about five (5) to six (6) months.

c. Social Insurance

(See Section Ag, Social Security Contributions.)

C. Exit and Entry

a. Visa Types

The immigration categories regulated by our legislation as 'labor' or 'employment' visas are contemplated under the category of temporary residents (also known as the 10%, 15%, and Marrakech visas). These types of visas are granted for periods of one year, and are renewable for up to six (6) years.

The process of obtaining these visas may take between 12 to 15 months, and will be granted for a period of one (1) year, once the corresponding work permit is approved by the Ministry of Labor and Workforce Development. Furthermore, and may be renewed up to six (6) years.

b. Restrictions for Exit and Entry

Restrictions for exit and entry will vary from one visa type to another, but generally, once a visa is approved, the key restriction is the length of time the visa is granted for.

D. Trade Union and Labor Organizations

Employees have a right to become part of a trade union. Furthermore, an organized group of employees with a minimum of forty (40) interested persons may create a trade union within a business organization. In such case, the members of the board of such union will have trade union immunity, and therefore may not be terminated by the business organization except for limited causes.

It is important to note that, according to the Labor Code, all employees who benefit from a collective agreement between the trade union and the business organization, must pay union fees, even if the employee is not a member of the trade union.

All unions have the constitutional right to strike. However, for the corresponding strike to be considered legal, union are required to first enter into negotiations with their employer, for a period not exceeding eleven (11) weeks, such negotiations involving the presence of persons from the Ministry of Labor and Workforce Development. If an agreement is reached between the corresponding union and the employer, a strike may not proceed.

E. Labor Dispute

All labor disputes or claims present by employees are mainly reviewed and decided by two special dispute solving bodies:
• Boards of Conciliation and Decision (Juntas de Conciliación y Decisión), which have exclusive jurisdiction to decide the following matters:
• Complaints of unjustified dismissals;
• Complaints of any means that are up to US$ 1,500;
• Complaints of any nature or amount by domestic employees;
• Labor Sectional Tribunals (Juzgados Seccionales de Trabajo), which have jurisdiction to decide all other labor matters not decided by the Boards of Conciliation and Decisions, including;
• Claims regarding unpaid salary, extraordinary hours, and acquired rights;
• Claims regarding payment of acquired rights, in relation to death of the corresponding employee;
• Employee resignations with cause.

All labor disputes involving unions are overseen by the Labor Directorate, of the Ministry of Labor and Workforce Development.

V. Intellectual Property

A. Brief Introduction of IP Laws and Regulations

Law 61 of 2012 (the "Law of Industrial Property") is the principal legislation in Panama regulating a broad range of intellectual property rights, such as inventions, utility models, service marks, trademarks, geographical indications, denominations of origin, as well as industrial and commercial secrets. Law 64 of 2012 (the "Law of Authors' Rights"), on the other hand, is the principal legislation regulating authors' rights (copyrights).

a. Inventions

Inventions, protected through patents, are defined as any idea that may be applied in practice to solve an established technical problem, and may consist of a product or process. To be patentable, inventions must be new, must involve inventive activity, and must be susceptible of industrial application.

An invention is considered new when, in relation to it, there is no 'precedence in the state of its technique' (anterioridad en el estado de su técnica). State of its technique, in this context, comprises everything that has been disclosed or made accessible to the public, anywhere in the world, though a tangible publication, oral disclosure, sale or trade, use, or any other means, prior to the date of presentation of the patent application (or, if applicable, prior to its date of priority vis-a-vis another similar application).

There is a safe harbor provision, however, protecting investors within a twelve (12) month period prior to the patent application date (or, if applicable, prior to its date of priority vis-a-vis another similar application), in regards to disclosures made by the inventor himself, or from disclosures that arise from an abuse of trust, a contractual breach, or from an illicit act against the inventor.

An invention is considered to involve inventive activity if, for a person normally versed in the corresponding technical matter, the invention is not obvious nor evidently derived from the state of its technique.

Finally, an invention is considered susceptible of industrial application when its object may be produced or used for an industry or activity of any type (for example, crafts, mining, fishing or services).

A person who is granted a patent, will have a right to prohibit third persons from doing any of the following: (i) regarding products, manufacturing the product, offering it for sale or use, or otherwise importing or keeping it in store for these purposes, and (ii) regarding a process, use the process, or carrying out any act under 'i' regarding a product that directly results from such process.

Patents are granted for a twenty (20) year period from the time the application was made. If the patent is successfully granted, the holder of the patent may claim damages from third persons who used the patent during the time when the patent application process was still ongoing and known to the public.

b. Product and Service Marks

Under the Law of Industrial Property, a product or service mark is any sign, word, or combinations of these elements or any other means that, through its characters, may be susceptible of individualizing (or identifying) a commercial product or service. Marks may include: words, or combinations of words, including those that identify persons; images, figures, symbols, and graphics; letters, numbers, and combinations, when composed of distinctive elements; three-dimensional shapes, including wrappings, packaging, the shape of a product or its presentation and holograms; colors, in their different combinations; as well as sounds, smells or tastes.

Marks that may not be registered, however, include:

• Those that simply describe the type of product or service, or which have become the usual or generic term for describing the type of product or service.

• Those that may lead consumers in general to error or confusion, such as those that have false indications of the nature or quality of the corresponding product or services.

• Those that are identical or similar to other marks used for the same types of products or services, when such similarity is likely to lead the general public to errors, confusion, or mistakes regarding those products or services, or their source.

• Those that are identical or similar to a product or service mark that is already famous in Panama, regardless of whether such product or service mark is registered.

The right to a product or service mark is obtained through its use. Registration of the mark, however, grants its owner exclusive use over it and, consequently, the right to prohibit other persons from using the corresponding product or service mark, including:

• Prohibiting others from manufacturing, printing, or reproducing labels, letterheads, wrappings and other means of identification, wrapping, or conditioning, with the corresponding mark, when it is evident that these will be used in relation to the same products or services covered by the registered product or service mark.

• Applying the mark to the labels or wrappings of a similar product, which may lead the general public to error or confusion in connection with the product that is covered by the product mark, or a high degree of association to it.

• Using in commerce a distinctive or sign that is similar to the registered mark, which may, without justification, cause a detriment to the owner of the registered mark, particularly, when the distinctiveness of the product or service mark is weakened, or the commercial value of the registered mark decreases.

• Using, with respect to a specific product or service mark, terms of comparison with another mark for identical or similar product, with the sole purpose of weakening the product or service mark's distinctiveness, or lowering its commercial value.

c. Industrial and Commercial Secrets

In relation to industrial and commercial secrets, the Law of Industrial Property establishes that information obtained by any person because of its employment or work, whose confidentiality has been prevented, must refrain from revealing it without the consent of such person.

Article 87

Any person who, because of his work, employment, position, position, performance of his provision or business relationship, has access to an industrial or commercial secret, whose confidentiality has been prevented, shall refrain from using it for his own commercial purposes, without revealing it without just cause and without the consent of the person who keeps said secret, or of the authorized user. The infraction of this provision will give the right to request the immediate suspension of the disclosure of said secret and the compensation of damages.

It is important to note that companies wishing to further protect their industrial or commercial secrets usually do so through confidentiality agreements with directors or key personnel with regular access to this type of information.

d. Authors' Rights (Copyrights)

Under the Law of Authors' Rights, authors have moral and patrimonial rights over their work (obra). A work is defined as any original intellectual creation in the literary, artistic, or scientific domain, susceptible of being published or reproduced in any form, even if such form is not known. Examples of works include:

• Intellectual creations expressed in writing, such as books, magazines, leaflets, and any work exteriorized through conventional letters, signs, or marks.

• Conferences, speeches, and other works consisting of works expressed orally.

• Musical compositions, with or without lyrics.

• Films, photographs, and any audiovisual works.

• Architechtural works, maps, blueprints, and other works related to geography, topography, architecture, or the sciences.

• Software programs.

The author of a work is presumed to be the person whose name, signature, or symbol appears on the work identifying him as such. Furthermore, unless proven otherwise, it is presumed that the authors' rights over the work subsist in regards with such work.

In the case of anonymous works, or works authored under a pseudonym, the individual or entity that publishes may exercise temporarily any rights necessary to protect such work during the time when the identity of the author remains unknown. In the case of derivative works, which are works based on a prior existing work, the rights of the author over the original work are not affected.

Patrimonial rights are composed of: (i) the right to modify the work, which consists of the exclusive right to carry out or authorize translations, adaptations, arrangements, and other transformations of the work; (ii) the right to reproduce the work, which consists of any act directed to the fixing the work through any form or process; (iii) the right to distribute the work, which consist of the right to authorize or reject the distribution of copies of the work to the public, through sale or any other form of transmission; and (iv) the right to communicate such work to the public, through any forms of transmission to the public, for example, through the internet, cable, or any other similar means.

Authors' rights remain valid for the period comprising the life of the author plus seventy (70) years after such person's death, remaining during that time with the authors' successors. In the case of co-authors, the period of seventy (70) years starts to run from the time of death of the last co-author who died.

In the case of collective works, which are works created by several authors under the initiative or direction of one individual or company that later publishes such work under its own name, authors' rights will be valid for a period of seventy (70) years from the time the work was first published.

For purposes of computation of time, it is important to note that the periods of validity that follow the death of an author or date the work was first published, will run from January 1st of the year that follows the corresponding event.

B. Patent Application

Patent applications must be presented through a licensed-attorney, with the following:
• Patent application form of the General Directorate of the Intellectual Property Registrar (DIGERPI).
• A descriptive memo, and a summary.

- Precise claims for protection regarding the essential elements of the patent sought.
- The corresponding drawings.
- Indication of the name and address of the inventor (in addition, if the inventor is not submitting the application, indication of the name and address of the applicant, and document supporting the right of such person to request the patent).
- Receipt evidencing payment of application fees.
- Power-of-Attorney.

The description of the invention must be, from the time the application is presented, sufficiently complete and clear to the effect that someone with technical experience in the subject matter may be able to evaluate it, without the need to resort to unnecessary examination.

The date or presentation of the application shall be established as the date when the DIGERPI received the following minimum requirements:
- The name and address of the applicant.
- A document that, prima facie, provides a description of the invention.
- A document that, prima facie, has one or more precise claims for protection regarding the essential elements of the patent sought.
- Receipt evidencing payment of application fees.

C. Product or Service Mark Registration

Trademark registration applications must be presented through a licensed-attorney, with the following:
a) Registration form of the DIGERPI, indicating:
- Indication of the name, address, and nationality of the applicant (if applicant is a company, additionally, a certification of incorporation).
- Name and address of the attorney.
- Address in Panama (if the applicant resides abroad), for purposes of administrative and judicial notification in relation to the registration.
- Mark denomination and / or design.
- The products or services related to the mark, in accordance with the corresponding classification under the Nice Agreement.
- Claim of priority right, if applicable.

b) Power-of-Attorney.

c) If applicable, two sketches of the mark; a translation of the mark; a transliteration of the mark; and / or document supporting a claim of priority right.

d) A declaration of use or, alternatively, a declaration of intent to use.

e) Receipt evidencing payment of application fees.

D. Measures for IP Protection

Law of Industrial Property provides a special process for disputes related to patent infringement, as well as infringement relating to product and service marks, which must be followed by the corresponding judicial court.

VI. Environmental Protection

A. Department Supervising Environmental Protection

The department in charge of supervising environmental protection is the Ministry of Environment (MiAMBIENTE), which has among its duties the following: adopting rules for environmental quality protection and control; issuing technical and administrative orders and rules that advance the National Environmental Policy; protecting natural resources within its jurisdiction, in order to prevent environmental degradation; enforcing compliance of environmental laws; dictating the scope and terms the environmental impact studies must have, and providing guidance relating to these; evaluating environmental impact studies and related documents; and issuing permits, concessions, and authorizations regarding natural resources.

The Aquatic Resources Authority of Panama (ARAP), however, is tasked with enforcing compliance with laws related to fishing and aquaculture, and has among its duties the rational, sustainable and responsible use of aquatic resources and the protection of related ecosystems. It is also responsible for monitoring the water quality where fishing and aquaculture activities are carried out, in coordination with MiAMBIENTE and other local entities.

B. Brief Introduction of Laws and Regulations of Environmental Protection

Law 41 of 1998 established a regulatory framework for the protection of the environment in Panama. Among the most important provisions relevant to potential foreign investors interested in undertaking an activity or project in Panama possibly involving environmental considerations, is the requirement of an approved Environmental Impact Assessment (EIA), applicable to activities, works, or projects which, by their nature, characteristics, effects, location or resources, may generate environmental risk.

It is important to note that the regulation contemplates three categories of EIA (Category I, Category II and Category III), the determination of which will depend on the potential risk imposed on the environment by the corresponding activity, work or project.

Law 41 of 2008 requires EIAs to be prepared by environmental experts, duly registered with MiAMBIENTE. In their preparation of the corresponding EIA, the environmental expert will, among other things, measure the environmental risk that the specific activity may impose, asses the applicable EIA category, and propose any mitigation measures.

C. Evaluation of Environmental Protection

Panama is a member of the United Nations Framework Convention on Climate Change, the Kyoto Protocol, and was among the first countries to ratify the Paris Agreement.

VII. Dispute Resolution

A. Methods and Bodies of Dispute Resolution

a. Judicial Proceedings

Judicial proceedings in Panama, of a civil or commercial nature, are governed generally by procedural rules found in the Code of Civil Procedure. These proceedings are categorized into:
 (i) Proceedings of Cognizance (Procesos de Conocimiento), further categorized into:
 • Ordinary Proceedings
 • Oral Proceedings
 • Summary Proceedings
 (ii) Non-Contentious Proceedings (Procesos No Contenciosos), which are in principle non-adversarial (however, adversarial aspects will mainly be solved through Summary Proceedings). Most notably, this category includes Inheritance Proceedings (Procesos Sucesorios).
 (iii) Execution Proceedings (Procesos de Ejecución), which, most notably, include 'Mortgage Execution Proceedings' (Procesos Ejecutivos Hipotecarios), which are proceedings for the execution of mortgages, and 'Pledge Execution Proceedings' (Procesos Ejecutivos Prendarios).

In practice, most disputes of a civil or commercial nature are solved through Proceedings of Cognizance, with the overwhelming majority of these being Ordinary Proceedings. Except as otherwise specified by law, all proceedings allow for two instances, the second instance usually allowing parties to appeal the decision of the court of first instance (the lower court) to a court that is higher in hierarchy.

It is important to note that, Panama's legal system being of civilian tradition (e.g., and not of the common law tradition), the process of evidence gathering is directly supervised by the judge. Additionally, prior decisions from the same court, or even prior decisions from a higher-ranked court, do not bind the deciding court. The deciding court, of course, in practice will sometimes follow its own prior decisions, or those of a higher-ranked court, particularly where applicable provisions have been applied to a similar matter with frequency and consistency, regarded as local jurisprudence.

However, it is important to note that, even in relation to other systems of civilian tradition, where the system's jurisprudence is closely followed in practice, the Panamanian legal system tends not to follow its own jurisprudence very closely, and when legal provisions are not very clear on a certain matter, courts will equally resort to publications of local well-known scholars, and sometimes from Spanish or Colombian scholars (the language of several provisions in the Civil Code have their source, or resemble, similar provisions in the civil codes of Spain and Colombia).

 a) Ordinary Proceedings
Any matter that is adversarial, and for which no special type of proceedings is contemplated, may be decided through an Ordinary Proceeding, therefor a general type of proceeding. Even where a special proceeding is

contemplated, the prospective plaintiff may opt for the matter being decided through an Ordinary Proceeding.

Ordinary Proceedings for claims over US$250, which do not exceed US$5,000, are called 'Proceedings of Minor Amount' (Procesos de Menor Cuantía), and are conducted by Municipal Judges (Jueces Municipales). Proceedings for claims of US$5,000 or more, on the other hand, are called 'Proceedings of Mayor Amount' (Procesos de Mayor Cuantía), and are conducted by Circuit Judges (Jueces de Circuito).

Ordinary Proceedings of Mayor Amount require the complaint to be presented in writing, though an attorney. The timeframes for different stages of the process tend to be longer than those for Orginary Proceedings of Mayor Amount. For example, the defendant will have ten (10) business days to answer the complaint upon being notified, as opposed to five (5) business days.

In practice, Ordinary Proceedings of Mayor Amount will usually last approximately two (2) years for each instance. Accordingly, if the court of first instance's decision is appealed, the dispute will usually last approximately four (4) years.

It is important to note that some decisions may be submitted to a special type of challenge before the Supreme Court of Justice of Panama, through a writ (recurso) called Cassation (Casación), which allow such court to either nullify (casar) or not nullify (no casar) the decision. If the Supreme Court of Justice of Panama decides not to nullify the decision, the decision will stand and will not be subject to any further challenge. However, if the Supreme Court of Justice of Panama decides to nullify the decision, it may go into the substance of the decision, and affirm, reverse, remand, or modify such decision.

For this special type of challenge to be first admitted, the applicant must comply with strict formalities, and have a strong basis for alleging severe errors, whether in the application of substantive law (Casación en el fondo), or in the application of procedural law (Casación en la forma). Cassation challenges that are successfully admitted will usually last approximately two (2) years.

b) Oral Proceedings

Oral Proceedings are special proceedings applicable to: (i) civil claims regarding car accidents, where damages exceed US$5,000; (ii) challenges regarding resolutions of the Shareholders or the Board of Directors of a corporation, or resolutions of other type of private entities, where such resolutions are contrary to law or the organizational documents; (iii) disputes that may arise in relation to the resposition or annulment of commercial titles or bonds issued by the government. It is important to note, however, that parties may voluntarily to submit to Oral Proceedings other types of claims, through 'authenticated document' (e.g., a notarized document).

Although Oral Proceedings generally involve shorter terms than Ordinary Proceedings, and tend to be less formal. In practice, however, these types of proceedings are not very usual as a dispute resolution method.

c) Summary Proceedings

Summary Proceedings are special proceedings applicable several specific claims, including:

• Claims regarding easements (servidumbres), division or sale of co-owned property, injunctions (interdictos) and other possessory proceedings.

• Oppositions or controversies that arise within a Non-Contentious Proceedings.

• Claims regarding leases, transportation of goods through land, deposit, and mandates.

• Claims regarding payment of fees of certain types of professionals (attorneys, medics, accountants, architects, engineers, and other professionals which require a license to practice).

• Co-ownership claims.

• Claims regarding the release of a mortgage, or certain modifications to the mortgage terms.

• Claims to enforce compliance with formalities required by law for certain agreements (e.g., sales of immovable property require the agreement to be in deed form).

• Acquisitive prescription claims.

Summary Proceedings generally involve shorter terms than Ordinary Proceedings (e.g., the defendant will have five [5] business days to answer the complaint, upon being notified). Although Summary Proceedings are not as usual in practice (as Ordinary Proceedings are), they are more usual than Oral Proceedings as a dispute resolution method.

d) The Bodies Involed in Judicial Proceedings

Regarding the bodies involved in judicial proceedings, we proceed to describe these and their structure, from higher to lower rank in hierarchy:

(i) The Supreme Court of Justice of Panama. The Supreme Court of Justice of Panama has a total of nine (9) magistrates, and is currently composed of four (4) chambers, with three (3) three judges allocated to each of these:

• the First Chamber (Sala Primera), with jurisdiction over civil and commercial matters;

• the Second Chamber (Sala Segunda), with jurisdiction over criminal matters;

• the Third Chamber (Sala Tercera), with jurisdiction over labor matters and administrative law matters; and

• the Fourth Chamber (Sala Cuarta), which oversees certain specific matters, notably, licensing of attorneys, the recognition of foreign decisions (through a process called 'exequatur'). It is important to note that each chamber is presided by one (1) judge, with the presiding judges of the First, Second, and Third Chambers all three being the justices who make up the Fourth Chamber. Finally, the nine (9) justices act 'en-banc' (en pleno) regarding certain matters, most notably, matters of a constitutional nature.

(ii) The Superior Tribunals. Superior Tribunals act as courts of appeal, and usually cover different judicial 'districts' in the territory of the Republic of Panama. There are five (5) Superior Tribunals that are relevant for civil and commercial matters: the First Superior Tribunal of the First Judicial District, which has jurisdiction over civil matters in the provinces of Panama, Colon, Darien, and the indigenous area of San Blas; the Third Superior Tribunal of the First Judicial District, which has jurisdiction over several special matters, including monopolistic practices, consumer protection, intellectual property, agency and distribution relationships, and unfair competition; the Superior Tribunal of the Second Judicial District, which has jurisdiction over civil matters in the provinces of Coclé and Veraguas; the Superior Tribunal of the Third Judicial District, which has jurisdiction over civil matters in the provinces of Chiriquí and Bocas del Toro; and the Superior Tribunal of the Fourth Judicial District, which has jurisdiction over civil matters in the provinces of Herrera and Los Santos.

(iii) Circuit Judges. For every district there are several 'circuit' judges, which account for the vast majority of courts of first instance, with the majority of these proceedings in Panama being Ordinary Proceedings of Mayor Amount.

(iv) Municipal Judges. Municipal judges generally decide over claims within the context of Ordinary Proceedings of Minor Amount, which involve claims under US$5,000.

Finally, it is important to note that there are other specialized tribunals for other matters (for example, consumer protection, labor, and family matters), also including special procedural rules.

b. Alternative Dispute Resolution

a) Arbitration Proceedings

Arbitration proceedings tend to be more costly than judicial proceedings. However, matters submitted to arbitration are generally decided within a shorter timeframe, hence the potential costs associated with longer timeframes of dispute resolution will be important to consider. Arbitration is increasingly becoming the method of choice for disputes that arise in the context of commercial transactions involving high-value claims.

In Panama, arbitration proceedings are governed by Law 131 of 2013 (the "Arbitration Law"). The procedural rules established by this law, however, tend to be of a general and suppletory nature, and very often arbitration proceedings may be carried out mostly with reference to the rules of the applicable arbitration center chosen by the parties, without the need to resort to those established in Law 131 of 2013 (except for rules regarding evidence, allegations, and deadlines for issuing the award).

The arbitration center primarily used in Panama is the Center for Conciliation and Arbitration of Panama (CeCAP). The procedure established in the CeCAP regulation can be summarized as follows:

(i) The party requesting submitting the dispute to arbitration (provided arbitration has been agreed to, usually through an 'arbitration clause'), must file an arbitration complaint addressed to the General Secretariat of Arbitration of CeCAP, in which it must describe the nature of the dispute, the facts, the claims and, in addition, all evidence that supports the claims. The plaintiff must also designate the arbitrator he has chosen.

(ii) The General Secretariat of Arbitration of the CeCAP, upon verifying competence of the CeCAP, will notify the demand by means of a notice to the defendant, granting defendant a term of ten (10) business days to answer the demand, provide all evidence supporting his defense, and designating the arbitrator he has chosen. (During this period, the defendant may file a counterclaim. If so, the CeCAP will notify the plaintiff, who will in turn have a period of ten (10) business days to answer the counterclaim and provide all evidence supporting his defense.)

(iii) If the parties do not agree on a third arbitrator, the arbitrators themselves may appoint such third arbitrator within a period of thirty (30) business days. If the arbitrators chosen by the parties do not agree, the third arbitrator may be appointed by CeCAP, though a draw process of arbitrators that are included in a list of arbitrators of CeCAP.

(iv) The arbitrators must communicate their acceptance in writing within a period of five (5) business days after being notified of their appointment, making a declaration of impartiality and independence. If it is an arbitration in law (en derecho), as opposed to an arbitration in equity (en equidad), the arbitrators must be attorneys.

(v) CeCAP must notify the parties when the arbitration tribunal is constituted and, in addition, of the arbitration expenses. If the defendant does not pay his part of the expenses within the term of five (5) business days, the claimant must do so within an additional period of five (5) business days, or otherwise the proceedings will not proceed. The latter is without prejudice to the power of the arbitration tribunal to later condemn the losing to pay all or part of the arbitration expenses.

(vi) Within fifteen (15) days following the confirmation of payment of the arbitration expenses, a hearing is held where the parties and the arbitrators may discuss the arbitration agreement, the procedure, the claims, any controversial issues, evidentiary rules, and applicable law, among others. In this hearing, it is also possible to challenge the jurisdiction of the arbitration tribunal.

(vii) At the hearing, the court must decide on the evidence that will be admitted, and those that require further examination. Evidence requiring further examination, must be examined (practicadas) within twenty (20) business days, unless the parties agree otherwise.

(viii) Once the evidentiary stage has concluded, with the CeCAP General Arbitration Secretariat having transcribed all the evidentiary hearings, the arbitration tribunal will summon the parties to present their final pleadings. The parties may agree, with the arbitration tribunal, on how the final pleadings will be presented, whether in writing, orally, a combination of both.

(ix) Once final pleadings are completed, the arbitration tribunal must issue the arbitration award within a period of two (2) months, which may be extended one (1) additional month under CeCAP rules. However, the parties may agree on a more extensive timeframe; in practice, however, it is usual for the length of arbitration proceedings (from the time such proceedings start, to the time a decision is issued) not to exceed one (1) year.

(x) Our arbitration rules also establish the possibility of requesting precautionary measures. These, however, will ultimately require the assistance of a tribunal or judge from the judicial branch (without such assistance implying a waiver of the arbitration tribunal's jurisdiction).

b) Mediation Proceedings

Mediation proceedings in Panama are governed by Decree Law 5 of 1999. Parties who, in addition to arbitration, have agreed to mediation, must first undergo mediation. However, since mediation does not require the parties to reach a binding agreement in relation to the dispute, if no binding agreement results from the mediation proceedings, the parties will usually proceed to arbitration proceedings.

B. Application of Laws

Most all judicial proceedings in Panamanian judicial practice involve matters governed by Panama law as the applicable law for substantive matters. To the extent the parties have chosen the laws of another jurisdiction as their applicable law, however, such choice of law, in principle, would be recognized as valid and enforceable in Panama, provided such choice of law does not go against public order provisions. Additionally, there are certain matters as to which the interested parties may not deviate from Panamanian law, e.g., matters related to rights over land located in Panama.

VIII. Others

A. Anti-commercial Bribery

a. Brief Introduction of Anti-commercial Bribery Laws and Regulations

Panama's anti-corruption laws and regulations focus on different subject matters related to these types of laws and regulations. We focus on three of these subject matters: transparency of information, code of ethics for public servants, and anti-money laundering (AML).

a) Transparency of Information

Regarding transparency of information from public entities, or from private entities engaged exclusively in public utility services, the main law is Law 5 of 2002 (the "Law of Transparency"), which establishes the right of every person to request information from these entities, except when such information is considered 'confidential information' or 'of restricted access'.

Confidential information is defined as information in the government's possession regarding a person's medical or psychological data, intimacies of individuals, criminal or police record, their correspondence, their telephone conversations, and information regarding persons who have not reach the legal age (minors).

Information of restricted access is defined as information in the government's possession, which has been provided to the agencies or public servants based on their functions under the law. Examples of such type of information include the following: information regarding national security; commercial or industrial secrets, disclosed to public entities in their capacity as regulators; and information regarding ongoing proceedings brought forth by the Public Ministry.

b) The Uniform Code of Ethics for Public Servants

All public servants in general, regardless of their hierarchy, are subject to the Uniform Code of Ethics for

Public Servants, as well as any applicable ethics code adopted within the public servant's specific government department or government agency.

As a general rule, notably, the Uniform Code of Ethics establishes that public servants may not request or accept money, gifts, benefits, favors, promises, or any other advantages for purposes of accelerating, delaying, or refraining from doing tasks in relation to their functions; for purposes of influencing another public servant in such regard; or where such items had not been received except by reason of the public office which the public servant holds.

There are also other specific rules not included in ethics codes, but that nonetheless refer or relate to ethical conduct, and found in other bodies of law, for example, in the law applicable to Public Contracting. It is important to note, in addition, that Panama's Constitution requires every public servant to provide a sworn statement regarding his patrimony and financial situation.

c) AML

Law 23 of 2015 (the "AML Law") is the main Anti-Money Laundering law in Panama. The AML Law establishes general know-your-client (KYC) requirements that must be followed by specific categories of entities or professionals, including the obligation to request from their clients the provision of some specific information.

Entities or professionals subject to Law 23 of 2015 also have a general obligation to report suspicion activities they come across with, and which may be related to money laundering or terrorism financing.

There are general categories, each contemplating specific entities or professionals within such category:

• Financial Obligated Entities (for example, Banks, Insurance Companies, Broker-Dealer Houses, and companies that provide trustee services).

• Non-Financial Obligated Entities (for example, companies established in the Colon Free Zone, the Panama-Pacific Area, and in a Free Trade Zone).

• Professionals Subject to Supervision (for example, real estate brokers, and law firms that provide registered agent services).

Regulators, such as the Superintendence of Banks, the Superintendence of Insurance and Reinsurance, and the Securities Market Superintendence, also have specific rules that regulate in further detail the provisions of Law 23 of 2015, as applied to entities under their supervision.

d) International Treaties

It is important to note that Panama is a party to the Inter-American Convention Against Corruption, as well as the United Nations Convention Against Corruption.

b. Department Supervising Anti-commercial Bribery

The principal governmental departments or agencies exercising general oversight regarding anti-corruption are the National Authority of Transparency and Access to Information (ANTAI), the Financial Analysis Unit (UAF), and the Public Ministry.

c. Punitive Actions

Laws 10 and 34 of 2015 recently strengthened provisions of the Criminal Code regarding terrorism, financing of terrorism, AML, and added a chapter on contraband and customs fraud.

Notably, receipt of funds reasonably foreseen to have their source in several criminal activities – including international bribery, corruption of public servants, terrorism, financing of terrorism, contraband, or customs fraud – for the purposes of concealing their illicit origin, are sanctioned with prison from 5 to 12 years.

B. Project Contracting

a. Permission System

To the extent the project involves a regulated activity, the contracting company engaging in such activity must have any applicable regulatory permits. Notably, where construction works are involved, the project must engage companies that are duly licensed and registered with the Technical Board of Engineering and Architecture (Junta Técnica de Ingeniería y Arquitectura). Furthermore, most projects of a certain scale will also require an approved EIA (see 'Environmental protection' section, above).

b. Prohibited Areas

Regarding construction works, in addition to any applicable zoning restrictions or other limitations based on the geographic area or the types of works, certain areas in Panama will require contractors to follow strict guidelines prior to engaging in construction works. For example, there are special guidelines issued by the environmental protection agency, MiAMBIENTE, regarding protected áreas, many national parks included among these.

c. Invitation to Bid and Bidding

Project contracting among private entities are not governed by a specific law; instead, general rules of contracting will apply, and invitation to bid and bidding will depend on the company that invites others to bid for a contract with such company.

Project contracting with public entities, on the other hand, is in general subject to Law 22 of 2006 (the "Public Contracting Law"). Specifically, the Public Contracting Law applies to public bids and public contracting on the part of the government, as well as companies where the government owns 51% or more of the shares, as well as contracts that involve use of public funds for (i) the acquisition or lease of government assets; (ii) the execution of public works; (iii) the disposition of assets of the government; (iv) the provision of services; (v) operation and management of assets; and administrative concessions not otherwise regulated under special laws.

秘鲁

作者：Viviana Garcia、Guillermo Ferrero、José Antonio Olaechea、Vladimir Popov

译者：江家喜、吴凯

一、概述

（一）政治、经济、社会和法律环境概述

秘鲁是一个多元的国家，坐落在南美洲中部，领土面积为1 285 216平方公里，人口为31 826 018人。该国主要语言为西班牙语；此外还有克丘亚语、艾马拉语和其他具有官方地位的土著语言。商务领域大部分说英语。

秘鲁是多党制的宪政民主共和国，总统既是国家元首又是政府首脑。此外，应当注意秘鲁政府分为以下三个独立系统：

- 立法机关：为一院制国会，由130位代表组成，每届任期5年，按各地区人口比例选举。主要职能是批准法律（包括但不限于成文法、条例）和条约。
- 司法机关：由全国司法委员会选举的法官组成。
- 行政机关：它由总统组成。负责国家的日常管理，职能包括根据法律规定执行政策，以及在对外关系中代表国家。

秘鲁货币是索尔（PEN），实行自由浮动的汇率制度。

从经济方面来看，秘鲁在信用评级机构享有投资级地位。在过去15年里，国内生产总值（GDP）以高于拉美地区平均值的增长率连续增长。

近年来，由于秘鲁政府采取的经济政策负责任并具有延续性，秘鲁经济增长的主要来源一直是私人投资。

（二）"一带一路"下与中国企业合作的现状和趋势

为了创造更有竞争力的市场和更多的机会，秘鲁与世界各国有各种的商业一体化政策。

秘鲁与中国签署了很多商业协议，其中包括《自由贸易协定》；该协定自2010年3月1日起生效。该协定的目的是消除两国间在贸易和投资上可能出现的障碍。

中国已经把自己定位为秘鲁的顶级商业伙伴。秘鲁根据协定出口的若干主要产品是铜和铜矿，价值大约5 468 000 000美元。这个数字代表了秘鲁2016年传统出口总量的67%。受协定积极影响的其他产业包括渔业产业（食用鱼粉），由此产生的第三大出口产品出口金额为714 000 000美元。

因此，秘鲁与中国都得益于两国之间的贸易协定，并且该协定使得秘鲁的产品在世界最重要和最相关的市场占有一席之地。

二、投资

（一）市场准入

1. 投资监管部门

秘鲁的外国投资监管部门是私人投资促进局（Proinversión）。它是一个隶属于经济财政部的公共机构，负责执行促进私人投资的政策。

私人投资促进局负责给当地或外国的投资者提供信息和指导服务，也根据国家的政治经济计划，为私人投资提供蓝图，实施监控。

2. 投资产业法律法规

在秘鲁，关于外国投资的主要法律如下：①第 662 号法令，批准了《外国投资的法律稳定计划》；②第 757 号法令，批准了《私人投资发展的法律框架》；③第 162-92-EF 号最高法令，批准了《私人投资保证制度条例》；④《一般公司法》（第 26887 号法律）。

3. 投资方式

外商投资可以根据任何秘鲁法律认可的商业法律形式自由投资，具体有以下方式：

- 外商直接投资，作为股权投资；
- 向合作经营企业投资；
- 向秘鲁境内的货物和财产投资；
- 组合投资；
- 无形技术投资；
- 任何其他有利于秘鲁发展的投资方式。

另一种被广泛提倡的私人投资方式是通过执行与公共基础设施、公共服务、财产、公司和其他政府项目有关的项目实施。因此，一种有效的投资方式是通过公私合作项目实施，前者来自国家实体（政府部门的、地区政府的或地方政府的），而后者来自私人投资者。

关于前述内容，值得注意的是第 1012 号法令创建了公私合作（PPP）的法律框架及其实施条例。该法对有关项目进行了分类，分为自我支持型或共同出资型。这些主要通过特许经营制度实施；也就是说，特许经营者通常负责设计、融资、建设、运行和维护公共基础设施或服务。

4. 准入条件和审查

秘鲁的法律框架对投资行业是稳定且具有吸引力的。因此，当外国投资者进入秘鲁市场时，应该注意以下内容：

- 《秘鲁宪法》保证平等对待秘鲁投资者和外国投资者；
- 有关制度建立在自由竞争机制之上；
- 资本自由转移；
- 可以自由进入金融产业（境内和境外融资）；
- 宪法保证对私人财产的维护和保护；
- 收购国有公司股份没有额外或不同要求；
- 大多数的经济领域准入几乎都没有限制。

秘鲁并不限制外国人成为秘鲁企业的拥有者。尽管如此，也有例外情况，在某些行业可能存在某些明文限制。以下将说明若干此等限制：

- 外国公司或个人不能直接或间接收购或拥有位于国际边界 50 公里以内的矿山、土地、水、燃料、森林或能源。与此类似，在边境 50 公里以内的地区投资，以及投资弹药、武器和炸药行业必须经过相应政府机构的事先批准。
- 关于广播服务、空运和海运、银行和金融行业，秘鲁的法律框架规定这些活动仅对秘鲁投资者开放，或至少要求秘鲁投资者拥有大多数股权。

本国和外国投资者在秘鲁投资不需要经过任何事先批准。但是，一旦实施投资，外国投资者可能需要在私人投资促进局登记该项投资。该登记使得投资者有权向境外转移其投资的全部资本、设备等，并有权在进行外汇交易时，使用更优惠的汇率。

（二）外汇管理

1. 外汇主管部门

秘鲁《宪法》保障拥有和处理外币自由，因此秘鲁没有外汇兑换控制或外汇管制。尽管如此，值得注意的是秘鲁中央储备银行（Banco Central de Reserva del Perú）有权根据市场平均兑换汇率确定官方的货币兑换汇率。此官方汇率适用于公共机构（秘鲁公共登记局和税务机关）的有关程序。

2. 外汇法律法规概况

对于版税、红利和资本没有限制,仅对汇款到海外的利润,需要支付所得税。这意味着,公司应当向税务机关代扣代缴相应数额。为确保其投资,强烈推荐投资者在私人投资促进局进行外国投资登记。

3. 外国企业外汇管理要求

出口商和进口商可以在开放市场上自由交易,且不需要通过秘鲁中央储备银行进行外汇交易。因此,没有对外国企业的外汇管理要求。

(三) 融资

1. 主要金融机构

根据秘鲁法律,以下是秘鲁主要的金融机构:

(1) 银行、保险和 AFP 监管局(Superintendencia de Banca, Seguros y AFP, SBS):是根据公法组建的宪法自治机构,其目的是保护金融和保险系统的公共利益。为此,该机构通过执行监管有关从业人员和法律实体活动的法律、法规和规章,确保该机构监管下的从业人员和法律实体在经济和财务方面的稳健。该机构也负责防止和侦查洗钱和资助恐怖主义的活动。

银行、保险和 AFP 监管局受《秘鲁银行法》(第 26702 号法律)的规制。

(2) 证券市场监管局(Superintendencia de Mercado de Valores, SMV):是隶属于经济和财政部的专业技术机构,通过其管制、监督和促进功能,保护投资者,并确保其监管下的市场的效率和透明以及为上述目的定价的适当性和信息传播。

证券市场监管局的职能如下:

- 制定规章,监管证券市场、产品市场和资金支付系统。
- 确保个人和公司合法参与证券市场、产品市场和资金支付系统。受银行、保险和 AFP 监管局监管的自然人和法人在参与由证券市场监管局监管的证券市场时,也受证券市场监管局的监管。
- 促进和研究证券市场、产品市场和资金支付系统。
- 监督所有国际审计准则合规。

(3) 秘鲁中央储备银行:是自治的法律实体,其目的是管制货币供应,管理国际储备,发行纸币及硬币,并就国家财政提供报告。根据秘鲁《宪法》,中央储备银行目的之一是保持货币稳定。

2. 外国企业融资条件

根据秘鲁《银行法》(第 26702 号法律),外国投资应受到与本国资本相同的对待,除非相关事项在国际协定中另有规定。与此类似,当根据秘鲁《宪法》公共利益受到影响的时候,银行、保险和 AFP 监管局也将考虑基于互惠原则产生的标准。

除此之外,第 26702 号法律规定,所有要从事其监管范围内的业务的人,皆应获得银行、保险和 AFP 监管局的事先批准。如果没有相应的批准,所有人皆不得:

- 从事金融系统的任何公司的业务,具体指不论以存款、兑换或其他形式,从第三方收取或筹集资金,通常将此等资源用作投资、贷款或以任何合同形式的资金供应;
- 参与金融系统的任何公司的业务,以自己名义授予保险或以保险公司经纪人身份活动,以及进行其他辅助活动;
- 广告宣传其从事前述禁止从事的交易和服务;
- 使用任何措辞,误导公众认为其从事只有经由银行、保险和 AFP 监管局的事先批准且在其监管下才能从事的业务活动。

因此,据上所述,法人或个人如果没有取得批准而从事以下活动,即已发生上述违规行为:

- 邀请公众直接或间接投保,或邀请保险公司雇佣他们作为保险经纪人;
- 邀请公众在任何机制下提供资金,或获得贷款或融资;
- 主要为实现前述目的,通过任何方式做广告。

在银行和金融领域,对国内和国外投资者的某些限制应当值得加以注意。根据第 26702 号法律,此等限制适用于对"金融或保险系统的公司"的投资。因此，此等限制适用于授权的金融中介（或其需要授权的分支机构）、授权的再保险或保险公司（及其分支机构），以及保险中介或辅助机构。这些公司皆应获得银行、保险和 AFP 监管局的批准。

根据秘鲁《民法典》的规定，融资协议的利率受到限制。这意味着，延期偿付性或补偿性传统利息的最高利率由秘鲁中央储备银行规定。如果超过规定利率，则会导致债务人要求返还超付金额或抵扣本金。但是，传统利息或延期偿付利息的最高利率并不适用于经正当授权在其范围内经营的银行系统的实体或根据外国法律进行的融资。

应加以说明的是，对于外国投资、个人或国内公司并没有最低资本金的要求，但银行、保险和 AFP 监管局和证券市场监管局监管的某些活动除外。此等活动需要公司符合最低股本要求，其方可从事金融活动或参与资本市场活动。

最后，要通过公开发行融资，还需要符合特定要求。此等要求规定在秘鲁《银行法》中。有关细节请见稍后部分。

（四）土地政策

1. 土地法律法规概况

在秘鲁，对财产（动产和不动产）的权利被称为"物权"。秘鲁法律制度承认特定或有限数量的物权。也就是说，人（自然人、法人，内国人、外国人）只能行使法律明确承认的不动产权利，不能通过私人主体间的合同或协议创设现行有效法律未曾明确承认过的新的不动产权利。

另一方面，不动产权的拥有人没有义务在公共登记处登记其获得的物权。然而，不登记是存在风险的：那些保持物权登记在其名下的人可以再次向第三方转让，或为金融机构利益将其作为货币贷款的抵押物抵押。在这些情况下，如果第三方将其权利登记，或金融机构将其作为抵押物登记，这些权利将优先于未登记的权利。因此，即使不动产权登记不是强制性的，为避免发生意外，建议取得物权时在公共登记处进行登记。为了能够进行登记，取得物权的合同必须进行公证。公证人是国家指定的官员，其职能就是在文件获得登记前，证明文件是真实的，并且给予文件公信力。

不动产权具有最长有效期。除了财产权是永久的（除非其所有人决定转让）外，其他不动产权利（例如地表权、用益物权、使用权等）存在有效期的限制，不能被个体排除。例如，地表权的最长时效是 99 年，而对于用益物权，当所有权人是法人（公司）时，该权利不能超过 30 年。

财产权是法律制度为个人承认的最重要的权利，因为其给予个人最大限度的权能（使用、享有、处置、修缮、限定使用、设置负担等），其受到宪法保护。正是在这个意义上，秘鲁《宪法》第 70 条规定任何人（自然人、法人，内国人或外国人）不得被剥夺财产权。

然而，同样的条款也承认对这种财产权保护的例外，这就是征收。在这方面，根据秘鲁《宪法》第 70 条规定，要征收需满足一些要求：①必须为国家安全或公共需要所需；②必须为法律明确规定允许；③受影响的所有权人必须获得赔偿金，其金额除包含财产价值外，还必须包括对所遭受最终损害的补偿。

除此之外，秘鲁《宪法》承认受到征收影响的所有权人如果认为所涉财产价值高于赔偿，有权向司法法院起诉，质疑国家所承认的赔偿金额。

与此类似，秘鲁《宪法》和秘鲁《民法典》要求财产权的行使不得侵犯公共利益，且须在法律的限度内。在这个意义上，关于财产权行使可能有四种主要管制：

① 城市开发；
② 规划；
③ 城建参数；
④ 建筑管理。

城市开发即是通过建设道路、分配水资源和收集排水、分配能源和公共照明，以及建设轨道和人行道，将乡村土地（也就是说，农业和畜牧业活动的土地）转变为城市土地的过程。执行此过程是为财产所有权人配置城市型活动的基本要求。

规划，从另一方面来说，是一系列包含在城市开发计划中的城市规划技术规范，其根据城市的物理的、经济的和社会的需求管理土地使用，为城市住房、娱乐、保护和设备划分活动区域，也为工业生产、贸易、交通和通信划分活动区域。为了解特定财产上的规划类型，有必要在省级市政当局办理规划和道路证明；此等证明有效期为3年，明确在特定财产上可以进行的活动类型。

城建参数是设定建筑项目必须具有特点的技术规范。此等参数显示宗地可建维度、建筑系数、每公顷的居民净密度、建筑物的高度、取水量、空置区域的百分比、停车场数量以及其他所有权人欲实施一项新工程或改造一个既存建筑所必须遵守的条件。为了解一个特定财产分配的参数，有必要到地区市政当局办理城建参数证明，有效期是3年。

最后，所有权人在自己财产上建设，必须要取得地区市政当局的事先批准，即建筑许可。没有此许可，不得建造或施工。建筑许可由市政当局在审查所有权人提交的技术档案后核发；该技术档案由一系列描述建筑施工必要特征、要求和规格的文件组成。一旦建设完成，市政当局会评估实际建筑是否符合技术档案概要；如果符合，则通过决议，同意相关建设，承认其合法性。

2. 外国企业获得土地的规定

对外国人拥有和／或占有不动产没有一般性的限制性规定。尽管如此，秘鲁《宪法》规定外国公民和／或法律实体不能直接或间接购买或拥有位于国际边界50公里以内的土地，除了在特定情况下，即因为公共需要，国家允许其获得此等财产。此等例外决定必须由部长会议以最高法令形式批准。

除此限制外，对宗地所有者是外国人在行使财产权利时没有其他限制。正是在这个意义上，秘鲁《宪法》第71条规定，无论外国人是个人还是法律实体，其与秘鲁人行使财产权利时的条件相同，在任何情况下不得引用豁免或外交保护。

最后，尽管所有权人在财产权利上拥有所有权能，秘鲁《民法典》不允许其限制处置权或设置负担权。也就是说，所有权人不得为任何人利益，同意其将不会出售财产或将财产设定为抵押物（无论短期或长期），因为此等协议在法律上视为完全无效。对于所有其他权能（除了上述处置和设置负担外），所有权人可以暂时自行限制。

（五）企业设立与解散

1. 企业形式

在各种企业形式中，以下是投资者最广泛使用的类型：

- 股份公司（Sociedad Anónima，S.A.）：以股东出资额为限承担责任。因此，股东没有责任用其个人财产为公司还债。
- 封闭式公司（Sociedad Anónima Cerrada，S.A.C.）：尽管主要受公司规则的管理，其亦需要遵守一些特殊法规。它最多只能有20个股东，不是必须要设立董事会，所有管理所要求的义务和权力皆授予总经理和其他被任命的代表。
- 开放式公司（Sociedad Anónima Abierta，S.A.A.）：这种类型的公司来源于法律授权，而不是股东协议。它①向公众发行股份或可转化为股份的债务；②有超过750个股东；并且③在资本市场公共登记处将所有代表其股本的已发行股票上市。
- 有限责任公司（Sociedad Comercial de Responsabilidad Limitada，S.R.L.）：合伙人以出资额为限承担责任。最少得有2个合伙人，可以是个人或法人，最多可以有20个合伙人。

根据秘鲁法律，公司的股本由股份或股东的出资额代表，可以是现金或实物。股东大会是公司的最高决策机构。

此外，外国公司可以在秘鲁设立办事机构，作为其总部的延伸，用其处理行政、经济和政治事务，尽管它在一些管理方面有自主权。总部通过绝大多数决定并承担办事机构的所有责任。为能适当运行，他们需要有足够授权且住所在秘鲁的常设法定代表人。

2. 设立程序

在秘鲁设立公司实体的程序通常相似。以下是设立公司的程序：

- 首先，需要确认拟定公司名称可以使用；
- 其次，拟定公司文件，缴存公司股本（货币或非货币出资，如货物）；

- 再次，必须取得公开契据，以便提交给秘鲁公共登记处；
- 复次，一旦完成前述步骤，公司必须在税务机关，即 SUNAT（Superintendencia Nacional de Aduanasy de Administración Tributaria）登记，以获得"纳税识别号"（RUC）；
- 最后，公司登记簿必须经公证人公证。

整个过程可能持续达 5 周时间。另外，没有最低资本要求。尽管如此，大多数有限公司的起始资本是 S / 100 000。重要的是，根据秘鲁法律，为了设立新的公司，已发行股本必须被认购且至少 25% 数额得到支付。

另外，如果公司由外国和位于秘鲁以外的投资人组成，则此等投资人必须提供外交部门确认或领事部门认证的授权委托书，具体要看该国是否参加了《关于国际私法的海牙会议》。

3. 解散程序及要求

根据《一般公司法》(第 26887 号法律)，基于以下任何一项原因，公司可以解散：

- 公司经营期限届满，除非已经经过批准延期并在公共登记处登记；
- 实现公司目的、长期不能实现公司目的，或显著难以实现公司目的；
- 公司股东会议持续不能履行职能；
- 亏损使得公司净资产少于实缴资本的三分之一，除非损失已得到弥补或实缴资本已有很大增加或减少；
- 债权人会议依据相关法律通过决议，或者破产；
- 合伙人数额不足，且 6 个月内未能补足；
- 最高法院根据第 410 条规定通过决议；
- 股东 / 投资人大会同意，无需法律或法定事由；
- 法律确定的、公司章程、公司规章制度或在公司登记的合伙人协议中考虑的其他事由。

此外，法律规定了召开会议的程序，以通过解散协议或应适用的合适措施。一旦决议通过，决议必须按法律规定连续三次进行公告，然后向公共登记处提出登记要求。随后，公司一旦确认解散，清算程序即开始。公司的财产被分配完毕时，将在公共登记处登记注销。在此之后，公司注销需通过书面文件向税务机关（SUNAT）告知。

（六）合并与收购

《一般公司法》(第 26887 号法律)规定，合并是两个或两个以上公司合并形成一个单独公司的程序，须符合现行法律的所有要求。

合并有两种类型：①两个或两个以上公司合并形成一个新公司，导致参与合并的公司法律人格消灭，其资产完全转移到新公司；②一个既存的公司收购一个或一个以上公司，导致被收购的公司法律人格消灭。在此情形下，收购的公司承接所有资产。视具体情况，这两种情形都会导致因为合并而不再存在的公司的股东或合伙人获得收购公司或新公司的股份或份额。

实施合并需要满足若干要求，具体如下：

- 合并协议符合法律和公司章程的规定。
- 每个公司的董事会必须批准合并协议的文本。赞成票比例必须达到绝对多数。如果公司没有董事会，则批准必须经大多数负责公司管理的人员通过。
- 必须符合法律规定的特定标准，且此等标准必须成为合并协议内容的一部分。
- 合并协议一旦起草完毕，必须召集大会讨论。注意召集需符合特定召集要求。
- 当合并获得批准，将设立一个使合并生效的共同日期，但合并需以秘鲁公共登记处登记公开契据为条件。此等登记将导致被合并或被收购的公司注销。
- 由于合并不再存在的公司必须在合并生效前制定资产负债表，且该表须由相应机构批准。
- 合并协议必须根据法律规定公布条款。
- 清算过程中的公司合并，必须在转换前先撤销解散协议，如果公司财产还没有分配给合伙人。

应该指出的是，《电气产业反垄断和寡头垄断法》(第 26876 号法律) 及其实施条例规定了在该市场合并、收购的前置批准程序要求，具体与动力的传输、生产和分配活动有关。

关于公司的收购，根据秘鲁法律，可以通过收购资产（具体规定在销售和购买协议中）和根据《一般公司法》（第 26887 号法律）收购股权。需要签署相应的协议，并且收购需通知到公司。总而言之，收购私人公司是没有限制的，除非涉及若干特定行业（例如，银行和金融行业等）。

此外，收购上市公司的股份应符合证券市场监管局规定的特定要求［例如，收购股份必须通过证券中介，或在利马证券交易所（Lima Stock Exchange）进行，该交易所为秘鲁唯一的证券交易所］。

除此之外，目前正在起草《公司合并与收购条例》，其目的是促进竞争，以使消费者、供应商以及总体市场受益。

（七）竞争管制

1. 竞争管制主管机构

国家自由竞争保卫和知识产权保护局（INDECOPI）是秘鲁负责控制市场适当运行和竞争活动效率的专门公共机构。为确保国家竞争管制得到遵守，该机构对公司和其他市场参与者具有多重监督和制裁职能。

2. 竞争法概况

秘鲁竞争法框架主要由两部分法律构成：

（1）第 1034 号法令，即《关于压制反竞争行为法》（"LD 1034"）。

LD 1034 基本上是一部反垄断法。该法的目的是在秘鲁市场促进和维护竞争，追查可能损害市场运行的反竞争行为，不管该行为在哪个国家和行业实施。

根据该法，反竞争行为可以分成两种不同类型：

① 滥用支配地位：在这种情况下，一家公司试图排除其他竞争者，使其获得（或维持）市场支配地位。被指控的垄断者必须在经准确界定的产品或服务市场中拥有足够的权力，以至于其他竞争者没有机会阻止它。

除其他情况外，捆绑销售，拒绝与其他代理商交易，以及推行独家或竞业禁止协议（当它们不合理时）皆被认为是滥用支配地位的行为。

② 独立企业间为削弱合法竞争的共谋协议（卡特尔）：卡特尔联合起来操纵定价，限制生产，在他们之间分配客户或划分市场（除其他情况外），避免自然竞争。

作为一般规则，在相同层级市场链运营的公司之间的卡特尔一概属于非法。但在不同层级市场链形成的共谋（例如生产商和经销商之间的协议）须经过分析才可以决定其合法性。十分类似的是，要惩罚此类行为，至少得有一个涉案的市场参与者必须在相关市场拥有支配地位。

根据两种禁止类型分析此类行为：

① 本身违法规则，即不需要进一步调查行为对市场的影响或参与行为的个体的意图。在这种情况下，相关部门仅仅通过证明行为的发生就可以决定存在违反反垄断管制行为。如前文所述，处于相同层级市场链的公司之间的卡特尔一般即根据此规则进行审查，且总是被认定是非法的。

② 理性规则，即要求分析这种做法是促进还是抑制市场竞争。要处罚此类违法行为，INDECOPI 不仅必须证明行为的发生，也应证明行为对（或本来可能对）市场竞争和消费者福利带来的消极影响。滥用市场支配地位的行为即根据理性原则进行分析。

LD 1034 规定，反竞争行为不属于刑事犯罪，不受刑事责任追究。

需要指出的是，竞争管制并不是对合并收购的控制。只有电力市场公司实施集中运营，且集中程度超过一定标准，才需要取得反垄断部门的事先批准。在其他市场兼并时并不要求这种事先批准。

到目前为止，国会中有几项旨在引进合并前通知制度的动议；此等动议在秘鲁医药市场的几次可以导致垄断的兼并之后变得更为相关。这些项目目前还处于国会委员会的讨论之中，等待辩论和批准。

（2）第 1044 号立法法令，即《反不公平竞争法》（"LD 1044"）。

LD 1044 旨在压制任何客观违背在市场中公司必须遵守的诚信义务的不公平竞争行为；这种不公平竞争行为可能通过不道德的商业行为损害消费者或企业。该法范围涵盖参与国内市场并可能试图获得不公平竞争优势的所有经济主体。

"不公平竞争行为"的定义相当广泛,适用于任何商业活动,不管他们采取什么形式和使用什么手段来加以实施(包括广告)。因此,任何暗示非法阻碍其他公司(损害其在市场上的地位)的行为,皆可能将被认定不公平。

另一方面,LD 1044 规定,认定不公平竞争行为,要考虑以下条件:
① 不要求证明有意识或有意愿实现行为;
② 不需要核实不公平行为对市场已造成有效损害的后果(行为的损害后果可以是潜在的);
③ 不要求受不公平行为影响的主体与违法者之间有直接竞争关系。
常见的不公平竞争行为例子包括侵犯职业秘密、盗用商业信誉、误导性模仿和欺骗性广告等。
不公平竞争行为不构成刑事犯罪。

(3)竞争管制措施

LD 1034 对违反反垄断管制的公司规定了经济罚款,罚款可以是 1 UIT① 直至超过 1000 UIT②,具体取决于侵害的严重性。INDECOPI 也有权惩罚公司的董事会成员,如果他们对促进反不正当行为有直接责任。对董事的经济罚款最高可达 100 UIT。

另一方面,违反不公平竞争管制(LD 1044)可适用自 1 UIT 至 700 UIT 的经济罚款。

(八)税收

1. 税收体系与制度

在秘鲁,主管税务机关是国家海关和税务监管局(Superintendencia Nacional de Aduanas y de Administración Tributaria),其为隶属于经济与财政部的一个专业技术机构。它建立了税务、海关事务以及它的内部组织的法律框架。

税收制度将适用于那些被认定为在该国居住的个人。另一方面,如果外国人在 12 个月的期间内在秘鲁停留时间超过 180 天,那么他们也符合居住要件。从这个意义上说,他们将为他们的全球收入纳税;此等收入包括源自外国的任何收入。

与此类似,在征税时,在秘鲁设立或组成的公司将被认定为居住在秘鲁。此等公司包括实体在国外设立但在秘鲁运营的任何代理机构、办事机构或任何其他常设机构。应该指出的是,只有此等代理机构、办事机构或其他常设机构在秘鲁产生的收入,才会向秘鲁报税。

2. 主要税种及税率

(1)企业所得税

以下法律实体被认为居住在秘鲁:在秘鲁设立的法律实体,以及归属于不在秘鲁居住的个人或法律实体在秘鲁设立的办事机构、代理机构及其他永久性经营机构。关于后者,仅对其源自秘鲁的收入征税。

企业所得税根据总收入扣减产生总收入的费用后,适用 29.5% 的税率计算确定。也就是说,根据公司年度净回报决定,而不考虑公司的结构。

此外,公司间实施利润分成的,税率为 5%,除非受益人为另一个居住在秘鲁的法律实体。

直接或间接地与避税地居民交易产生的费用,在申报所得税时,不得抵扣费用。

公司被要求预缴税款,预缴金额根据《所得税法》规定的计算当月净收入的两个制度之一确定。

财务年度从 1 月 1 日开始,到 12 月 31 日结束,没有例外。在每个财务年度结束时计算年度税收。预缴税款从余额中扣除,而差额则作为结算支付支付,并附到包含年末余额的纳税申报表上。这种结算支付和纳税申报需要在财务年度结束后 3 个月内完成。

纳税人获得的净收入可以根据以下两种制度抵扣损失:
① 在接下来的 4 个财务年度获得的收入中抵扣损失(直到抵扣完所有金额);
② 在本财务年度获得的净收入中抵扣 50%,没有时间限制。
会计账簿、记录和其他税务会计信息必须在法定时限内作相应保存。

---

① UIT: Unidad Impositiva Tributaria. 经济和财政部规定 2018 年 1 UIT 的价值是 S/4 150。
② 罚款不能超过侵害主体或其经济集团总收入的 12%。

（2）增值税（VAT）

销售税（VAT）是在商业周期的不同阶段对每笔交易的增值征收的一种税。适用税率：18%（包括2%的市政促进税）。

在秘鲁，销售税在下列操作中征收：
- 出售动产；
- 提供服务；
- 使用服务；
- 履行施工合同；
- 首次销售直接由施工者建造的不动产；
- 进口货物。

《销售税法》包含若干豁免，主要包括：公司重组所产生的资产转让、个人或不从事法定商业活动的法律实体所进行的旧货转让。

纳税人是从事应税活动的人，也就是销售货物、提供服务、进口有关货物等的人。

增值税遵循贷方/借方制度；根据这一制度，采购支付的增值税（进项税）用来抵消销售的增值税（销项税）。

（3）净资产临时税（ITAN）

净资产临时税是根据资产负债表对公司的净资产进行征税。如果净资产超过100万索尔（307 692美元），则超出部分以0.4%税率征税。

公司可以从所得税（IT）中扣除已支付的净资产临时税金额。

（4）金融交易税

对以本国货币和外国货币进行的银行交易征收的税收。

适用的税率是交易价值的0.005%。金融交易税为所得税目的可以扣除。

（5）不动产税（Impuesto Predial）

对所有权人申报的不动产的总价值征收的一种税收。纳税人是每年1月1日前登记在册的不动产所有人。

本税收按以下累进表计算：

不动产价值	税率
15 UIT 及以下	0.2%
15～60 UIT 之间	0.6%
超过 60 UIT	1.0%

（*）1 UIT（纳税单位）在2018年等于S/4 150。

（6）Alcabala税

在购买不动产时征收该项税收。税率为3%，税基为房地产价值。

（7）其他地方税收

（8）交通工具所有权税

其对车辆和船只征税。

（9）市政税

该税率应该由拥有不动产和从当地市政当局提供的公共服务中受益的人支付。一些市政税包括以下服务：街道清洁、垃圾收集、公园和绿地的维护、巡逻警卫等。税收金额根据提供的公共服务的有效成本计算。

（10）市政许可

其为为开办商业、工业或服务设施取得市政许可而支付的税率。

3. 纳税申报和优惠

秘鲁法规确立了某些税收优惠，以总体上鼓励包括外国投资在内的投资。这些优惠可以在稳定协议和秘鲁工业的各产业中找到。请参阅"（十）投资优惠及保护"部分；该部分对此话题将有更广泛讨论。

（九）证券

1. 证券法律法规概况

根据秘鲁法律，证券是一种可自由交易的工具，它们批量发行，给予持有者债权、财产权利或所有权，或对发行人的资本、利润或股权的权利。

主要的证券相关法律法规如下：

- 第 093-2002-EF 号最高法令，批准了《证券市场法》；
- 第 27287 号法律，批准了《证券法》；
- 第 862 号立法法令，批准了《投资基金和管理公司法》；
- 第 26126 号行政命令，批准了《公司和证券监督委员会组织法》；
- 第 29440 号法律，批准了《支付系统和证券清算法》，该法的实施条例经第 027-2012-SMV/01 号 SMV 决议批准；
- 第 141-1998 号 CONASEV 决议，批准了《首次公开发行和证券销售实施条例》（自 1998 年起生效）；
- 第 26702 号法律，批准了《银行法》。

2. 证券市场监管

根据第 093-2002-EF 号最高法令，公司监管和证券监督委员会（Comisión Nacional Supervisora de Empresas y Valores，CONASEV），即现在的证券市场监督局（SMV），是负责监督上述法律及其执行的公共机构。

此外，在证券交易方面提供管制规则的另一个实体是利马证券交易所。该所是秘鲁的证券交易所，其内部监管规则应遵从证券交易和发行规则。

在此方面，应该注意到另一个实体，即 CAVALI（Registro Central de Valores y Liquidaciones），其负责创建、维护和发展国家证券市场的基础设施。

3. 外国企业从事证券交易的要求

根据《资本市场法》，公开发行证券需受到特定法律条文的约束，包括向证券市场监督局详细说明和注册招股说明书。通常向 100 人或更多的人（数字可以少于 100，取决于具体案件）发售，即为公开发行，尽管这应该逐案审查。尽管如此，如果发行只针对机构投资者，则不受上述限制的约束，因为它可视为非公开发行。同理，如果证券发行为 S / 250 000 或更多，该发行也不被认为是公开发行。

（十）投资优惠及保护

1. 优惠政策框架

税收稳定协议：承诺在本国投资的投资者和公司可以与秘鲁政府达成协议，以保证在协议签署时生效的基本规则（包括某些税收规则）随着时间推移仍保持不变。一旦此等协议被签署，国家也不能单方面修改，使得投资者在合理的期限内对其在秘鲁投资有关的规则能够得到确定。

2. 对特定行业和地区的支持

秘鲁的法规规定了某些税收激励机制，以在总体上鼓励包括外国投资在内的投资：

- 农业税制：本税制适用于种植庄稼和 / 或饲养动物的公司，但属于林业活动的除外。此外，从事农工业活动的公司也适用该税制，只要他们在利马省外使用农产品。

  优惠：所得税税率降低至 15%，等等。

- 亚马逊税制：适用于位于亚马逊地区的从事下列经济活动的公司：①农业；②水产养殖业；

③渔业；④旅游业；等等。

优惠：①所得税税率可以低至 10%、5% 和 0%；并且②位于亚马逊地区的公司在亚马逊地区销售商品和服务也免征增值税。

- 提前退增值税税制：本税制授予公司权利，在一个项目进入生产阶段前，退取在进口和／或当地采购商品和服务时支付的增值税；退税随后可以用在与秘鲁政府签署的投资合同项下的项目执行中。

要适用这一税制，公司必须满足以下要求：

- 与秘鲁政府签署投资合同；
- 项目要求 2 年或更长时间的生产阶段；
- 承诺投资金额不少于 5 000 000 美元。该金额不包括增值税。
- 主管政府部门已核发部门决议。

3. 特殊经济地区

秘鲁经济传统上以采矿业的显著地位和对金融部门的大力支持而闻名。然而，秘鲁也有各种各样的经济活动，这些活动不断得到扩大，并已延伸到国际市场：

- 农业产业：在过去的 10 年中，秘鲁对这一产业的参与在成倍增加。秘鲁公司是世界上第二大甘蔗生产商、世界上第三大芦笋和橄榄生产商，且即将成为国际市场上第一大鳄梨生产商；等等。秘鲁在最重要的市场中还有季节性窗口。
- 渔业产业：秘鲁最终受益于物种多样性和有利于水产养殖业发展的气候条件。因此，秘鲁是世界上第一大鱼油和鱼粉生产国。
- 纺织产业：秘鲁的产品之一——皮玛棉，是世界上最受好评的纤维之一。此外，秘鲁是最好的南美洲骆驼（也就是羊驼和骆马）纤维的主要生产商之一。
- 矿业产业：秘鲁拥有世界上最大的白银储量，同时拥有一些最重要的铜和锌储量。它也是为数不多的拥有非金属矿藏的国家之一。
- 能源产业：因为水和天然气资源的广泛易得性，秘鲁拥有巨大的能源潜力，使得该国的电力需求不断增长。
- 房地产产业：经济的显著增长促进了对住房、购物中心、商业办公室、酒店和娱乐休闲场所的更大需求。对房地产的需求极大地促进了对该产业的投资。因此，随着 2014 年总额超过 100 亿美元的基础设施项目的开标结束，秘鲁的房地产产业将会得到蓬勃发展。

4. 投资保护

（1）对外国投资者没有限制

秘鲁《宪法》对特定行业的外国所有权和外国投资没有设置任何绝对限制。从这个意义上说，外国个人或公司与秘鲁投资者具有相同的地位，并得到相同条件的对待。

此外，根据秘鲁《宪法》，财产权利不受侵犯，除非在特殊情况下，经支付公平赔偿，其中包括对最终损害的补偿，才允许征用财产。

尽管有以上规定，外国公司或个人不能直接或间接购买或拥有位于国际边界 50 公里以内的矿山、土地、森林、水、燃料或能源，除非在某些情况下，由于公共需要，经部长会议批准，他们可以取得此等财产。

此外，第 162-92-EF 最高法令允许外国投资者根据秘鲁《宪法》、法律和条约从事他们选择的任何经济活动。但是，根据第 757 号立法法令，在保留的自然保护区内进行活动和制造战争武器，不包括在内。

必须注意的是，对外国投资者，只有少数具体立法批准的限制。例如，下列领域存在一定限制：①广播服务；②空运和海运。因为这些活动是专门为秘鲁投资者保留的，或者另行要求秘鲁投资者持多数股权的。

（2）国际条约

在过去的几十年中，秘鲁大幅增加了对国际组织中的参与，以便立足于国际市场并吸引外国投资。以下是秘鲁作为成员国的主要国际条约组织的名单：

- 安第斯共同体（Comunidad Andina，CAN）：秘鲁早在 1969 年就加入了该组织，当时只有几个南美国家决定签署《卡塔赫纳条约》。目前该组织的成员国是玻利维亚、哥伦比亚和厄瓜多尔。该组织为所有成员国提供自由贸易优惠。

- 世界贸易组织（WTO）：秘鲁自 1995 年 WTO 成立即为其成员方。该组织拥有超过 160 个成员方，是一个允许世界各国政府就贸易协定进行谈判的论坛。
- 拉丁美洲一体化协会（Asociación Latinoamericana de Integración，ALADI）：该组织拥有 13 个成员国（即阿根廷、玻利维亚、巴西、智利、哥伦比亚、古巴、厄瓜多尔、墨西哥、巴拿马、巴拉圭、秘鲁、乌拉圭和委内瑞拉），成员国在相互之间的交易中享受优惠关税。

此外，秘鲁还与不属于安第斯共同体或拉丁美洲一体化协会的国家签署了多项自由贸易协定，例如：

- 与美国的《贸易促进协议》，自 2009 年 2 月 1 日起生效。
- 与加拿大的《自由贸易协定》，自 2009 年 8 月 1 日起生效。
- 与智利的《自由贸易协定》，自 2009 年 3 月 1 日起生效。
- 与哥斯达黎加的《自由贸易协定》，自 2013 年 6 月 1 日起生效。
- 与巴拿马的《自由贸易协定》，自 2012 年 5 月 1 日起生效。
- 与欧盟的《自由贸易协定》，自 2013 年 3 月 1 日起生效。
- 与欧洲自由贸易协会的《自由贸易协定》，自 2012 年 7 月 1 日起生效。
- 与中国的《自由贸易协定》，自 2010 年 3 月 1 日起生效。

三、贸易

（一）贸易监管部门

国家对外贸易和旅游部（Ministerio del Comercio Exterior y Turismo）负责执行、协调和监督外贸政策。

国家对外贸易和旅游部在其权限范围内制定关于开展对外贸易活动的条例，并使商品的进出口免受禁令或关税限制等影响。同时，该部门负责对其发布的监管制度的遵守履行情况进行监督，并在监管制度得到适用的情况下，在其管辖权范围内作出制裁措施并予以实施。

在该部门基本组织结构的框架内，其部长负责制定该部门在国家层面的政策，结合政府的总体政策予以执行并监督其实施情况。部长可以将上述权力委托给副部长，由后者按其要求履行。

（二）贸易法律法规简介

过去 20 年的实践经验证明，秘鲁对本地和外国投资均是友好的。秘鲁政府确保秘鲁《宪法》以及有关规则和条例支持有利于开放市场的原则，使有兴趣的潜在投资者可在秘鲁开展项目。

秘鲁的外商投资制度受第 662 号法令——《外国投资促进法》和第 757 号法令——《私人投资框架法》的调整，这两部法律分别于 1991 年 9 月 9 日和 1991 年 11 月 13 日颁布，均受 1992 年 10 月 12 日颁布的第 162-92-EF 号最高法令的管辖。

为鼓励外资流入，第 662 号法令创设了稳定的税务与法律、有效的外汇及非歧视性国民待遇机制以保障外国投资者利益。

第 757 号法令包含为在所有经济领域增加私人投资所需的规定，包括消除所有阻碍经济发展和限制私营部门自由活动的法律及行政壁垒、扭曲措施，使公司之间在私营领域开展竞争等。该法律还制定了与税收有关的基本规定、保护投资者免受任意变化带来的影响。

1991 年 9 月 11 日，秘鲁颁布第 668 号法令，建立了秘鲁对外贸易体系的基本法律制度，确保将贸易自由作为国家发展的必要条件。该法令为外汇的使用和处置，以及以单一汇率自由兑换本国货币提供了法律保障。

第 1053 号法令，即现行有效的《一般贸易法》，确立了海关服务对促进对外贸易具有重要作用的总体原则。该法令的宗旨在于使商品进出口手续更加便捷。

(三)贸易管理

1. 自由贸易区

秘鲁有以下自由贸易区：Tacna 自由区（Zofra Tacna）和特殊开发区：位于 Matarani、Paita 和 Ilo。从关税的角度而言，这些区域被认为处于秘鲁境外。因此，对于进入自由贸易区和特殊开发区的所有货物，均适用特殊的税收制度。

自由贸易区和特殊开发区为在自由贸易区和特殊开发区从事工业活动、农业综合经营、组装和服务业务的公司提供了税收和关税优惠（例如机器的包装、贴标、维护和/或整修、呼叫中心活动、软件开发等）。

2. 协定

到目前为止，秘鲁参加诸多的区域和多边贸易协定，为其出口业务和商业部门的发展创造了很多机会。

其近期签署的协定如下：

（1）多边协定

世界贸易组织（WTO）：世界贸易组织是处理世界各国之间贸易规则的国际组织。因此，世界贸易组织有关反倾销、反补贴的规则适用于秘鲁。

（2）区域性协定

安第斯共同体（CAN）——包括玻利维亚、哥伦比亚、厄瓜多尔和秘鲁。秘鲁目前是由秘鲁、哥伦比亚、玻利维亚和厄瓜多尔组成的安第斯共同体（CAN）的成员。这些国家之间的贸易可享受关税减免，并共同构成自由贸易区。

（3）双边协议

秘鲁已同下列国家或组织签署了双边协议：

- 澳大利亚；
- 加拿大；
- 智利；
- 中国；
- 哥斯达黎加；
- 古巴；
- 欧洲自由贸易联盟（EFTA）——瑞士、冰岛、列支敦士登和挪威；
- 欧盟；
- 日本；
- 墨西哥；
- 巴拿马；
- 新加坡；
- 韩国；
- 南方共同市场（MERCOSUR）——阿根廷、巴西、巴拉圭和乌拉圭；
- 泰国；
- 美国；
- 委内瑞拉。

（4）其他组织的成员

秘鲁也是亚太经济合作论坛（APEC）的成员。该协议致力于商业交易的扩大和多样化，以及取消影响商品和服务互惠交易的关税和非关税限制。

最后，在 2017 年，世界贸易组织的《贸易便利化协定》（AFC）生效。当中与外贸相关的措施简化了与商品清关有关的程序，减少了商品流动的环节，并促进控制实体作出决策的平等性。

（四）进出口商品的检验和检疫

秘鲁国家海关税收监督管理局（Superintendencia Nacional de Aduanas y de Administración Tributaria，SUNAT）是秘鲁海关主管部门。

尽管如此，秘鲁并没有一个单一的机构来检验农产品、限定或禁运品在卫生方面的要求，因为对于进入秘鲁的每种产品，都指定了一个相应的机构。例如：

- 任何进入该国的植物或植物产品都必须由国家农业食品质量卫生局（Servicio Nacional de Sanidad y Calidad Agroalimentaria，SENASA）在获授权的外部控制办公室（Puestos de Control Externo，PCCE）进行检验。

国家农业食品质量卫生局是专门负责颁布旨在预防、控制或根除病虫害的强制性植物检疫措施和动物园检疫措施的主管部门。

国家农业食品质量卫生局将批准并公布该国的检疫性有害生物和须申报的疾病清单，并实行有利于提高通报程序的效率的机制。国家农业食品质量卫生局是该国拟订病虫害官方报告的主管部门。

- 国家自然资源研究所（Instituto Nacional de Recursos Naturales，INRENA）：负责管理野生动植物濒危物种的出入境。
- 秘鲁国家竞争和知识产权保护局（Instituto Nacional de Defensa de la Competencia y de la Protección de la Propiedad Intelectual，Indecopi）和环境健康总局（Dirección General de Salúd Ambiental，DIGESA）负责监控进口商品的标签是否符合商业化所需的全部必要法律信息。环境健康总局是在进口时检验产品的标签要求的主管部门，而秘鲁国家竞争和知识产权保护局是在进口产品在秘鲁境内商业化之后，监管标签要求的主管部门；随后产品将会被本国化（一旦海关主管部门向进口商批准放行商品，商品将被本国化）。

（五）海关管理

管理海关事务的主要法律法规是根据第 1053 号法令批准的《秘鲁关税总则》（CGL）及由第 010-2009-EF 号最高法令批准的条例（CGLR）。① 这些法律法规调整 SUNAT 与涉及海关辖区内商品入境、停留和出境的自然人及法人之间的法律关系，即关税和海关违法行为。

以下，我们将简要介绍海关分派的通关模式以及进出口流程。

1. 进口程序

（1）将商品分配到进口流程的模式和期限

为了将商品分配到"进口消费品系统"，须履行某些义务，例如电子传送报关单（Declaración Aduanera de Mercancías，DAM）。

有关的商品可以按照以下模式被分配到进口消费品系统：

- 预先分派：在运输工具到达前 15 个日历日内提交报关单（DAM）。一旦该期限届满，有关商品将会被提交至特殊分派。②
- 紧急分派：在运输工具到达前 15 个日历日直至从卸货完成次日起的 7 个日历日内提交报关单（DAM）。
- 特殊分派：在卸货完成次日起的 30 个日历日内提交报关单（DAM）。

（2）适用于进口的税收制度

特定的进口商品（通过进口消费品系统要求）通常需要支付进口关税。关税的具体金额因商品类型而异。

① 从价税

从价税按照有关商品的成本、保险费和运费（CIF）价值征收。根据国内法，现行税率分别为：0%、4%、6% 和 11%。③

---

① 参见海关当局的官方网页：http:// www.sunat.gob.pe/orientacionaduanera/index.html。
② 本程序已经第 063-2010-SUNAT-A 号海关协议通过。
③ 第 342-2016-EF 号最高法令。

如基于商品的原产国,适用特定的自由贸易协定(FTA),则这些税率可以降至 0%。

② 从量税 —— 价格水平体系

价格水平体系适用于某些农产品的进口,例如大米、黄玉米、牛奶和糖。当有关商品的国际价格低于某一水平时,该系统会征收额外的从量税;而当该等价格高于某一水平时,该系统会给予关税折扣[①],具体将根据从量税表格确定。

③ 增值税

增值税(VAT)由第 055-99-EF 号最高法令(VATL)批准的《增值税和消费税法》的统一文本以及由第 29-94-EF 号最高法令(VATR)批准的条例进行调整。

VAT 按进口商品的 CIF 价格加上关税和其他税费的 18% 征收。

④ 消费税

消费税(ET)也由 VATL 和 VATR 调整。消费税适用于某些商品的进口,例如燃料、软饮料、车辆、酒精饮料(酒、啤酒和皮斯科白兰地酒等)和香烟。税率因有关商品的类型而异。

(3)与进口消费品报关单(DAM)一起提交的文件

作为一般规则,进口商品需要将以下文件与报关单(DAM)一并提交[②]:

① 原始发票;
② 运输单据(提单或空运单);
③ 商品运输保险单据;
④ 主管部门签发的授权;
⑤ 根据进口性质需要提交的其他文件。

2. 出口程序

为了将商品分配到出口系统,须履行一定的义务,例如电子传输报关单(DAM)。

(1)适用于出口的税收制度

在秘鲁,出口商品不适用海关关税、消费税或增值税。

(2)与出口报关单(DAM)一起提交的文件

作为一般规则,以下文件需要与报关单(DAM)一起提交:

① 简化出口报表;
② 原始发票;
③ 原产地证明;
④ 商品运输保险单据;
⑤ 根据出口性质需要提供的其他文件。

四、劳动

(一)劳动法律法规简介

秘鲁的劳动事宜主要由第 728 号立法法令——《劳动生产力和竞争力法》(以下简称《劳动法》)(该法经第 003-97-TR 号最高法令批准)的唯一统一文本及根据该法颁布的条例调整。《劳动法》由劳动与就业促进部(Ministerio del Trabajo y Promoción del Empleo)及下设机构(即劳动局)负责执行,与劳动有关的诉讼由秘鲁地方法院管辖。

《劳动法》调整劳动关系的各个方面,包括但不限于档案保管、工资和法定福利的支付、工作时间和休假、服务期终止时的福利、内部管理以及劳动管理中的劳动安全和健康、劳动检查和劳动关系的终止。

《劳动法》适用于在秘鲁工作的所有员工,无论其是本国员工还是非本国员工,以及是否在私营部门工作。但是,政府公共服务部门的员工、军队成员、警察以及类似人员不在《劳动法》的适用范

---

① CGLT 的规定(CGLR)及第 10-2015-SUNAT SC0000 号监管决议。
② CGLR 第 60 条。

围内。

《劳动法》规定了秘鲁私营企业员工的最低权利和保障，且基于劳动权利不可剥夺和不可放弃的特征，该法规定，雇主与员工之间的任何影响、限制或剥夺员工权利的协议都是无效的。

此外，员工亦不能放弃或转让法律规定的权利和保证。

根据《劳动法》，当实际情况与劳动合同的规定不一致时，应以实际情况为准。

（二）雇用外籍员工的规定

1. 工作许可证

在秘鲁工作的外国员工根据劳动局先前批准的劳动协议，有权享有与秘鲁公民相同的劳动权利和福利。雇主雇用的外籍员工人数可达到其总员工人数的 20%，但外籍员工的薪酬不得超过企业工资总额的 30%。外籍员工的劳动合同必须采用书面形式，且期限固定，最长为 3 年。该等合同可以按相同的期限连续续约。

但是，雇主在下列情况下可以要求免除上述雇用外籍员工的限制：
- 专业或技术人员；
- 参与新设企业活动或企业重组的管理人员和/或一般人员。

同样，下列情形也不受外籍员工雇用手续或限制条件的约束：
- 具有秘鲁配偶、祖先、后代或兄弟的外国人；
- 享有移民签证的外国人；
- 原籍国签订了互惠的劳动或双重国籍协议的外国人。

2. 申请程序

与外籍员工签订的劳动合同必须提交给劳动局审批。审批过程不超过 5 个工作日（如果需要额外信息，则不超过 3 周）。劳动局对劳动协议的批准并不意味着该外籍员工可以开始工作。除此之外，其还需要获得国家移民局（Superintendencia Nacional de Migraciones）批准的签证。

3. 社会保险

（1）秘鲁国民和非秘鲁国民

社会保险服务包括医疗保险和养老基金，由第 22482 号法令创设的秘鲁社会保险及医疗保险（Seguro Social de Salud del Perú，EsSalud）以及由第 26790 号法律批准的《社会保险现代化法》调整。上述法律规定的规则适用于所有员工或人员——无论其是秘鲁国民还是非秘鲁国民。对于非秘鲁国民，必须由相关主管部门向非秘鲁国民的员工签发外国人身份证（Carné de Extranjería），且其根据形成的劳动关系提供服务的公司必须在该国正式注册成立。该等员工应在开始工作的第一天内在公司的工资单上登记。该要求也适用于 EsSalud 的用途，即出于养老基金的目的，相关登记可以在工作开始后的 10 天内完成。

企业主、自由职业者、承包商、自雇职业者等未达成劳动关系的人员（因此未在当地公司的工资单上登记），不论其国籍如何，都不在秘鲁社会保险范围之内。

采用公共医疗保险形式的社会保险，适用于与当地公司具有劳动关系的秘鲁国民和持有外国身份证的非秘鲁国民，两者均有权免费享受指定医院和相关医院的医疗服务。社保医疗保险要求雇主按每位员工每月工资总额的 9% 强制缴费。

秘鲁的养老基金系统包括由政府养老基金办公室（Oficina de Normalización Previsional，ONP）负责的全国养老金系统，以及由现有养老基金管理公司（Administradoras de Fondos de Pensiones，AFP）管理的私人养老金系统。适用的员工有权选择缴费的系统。对任何养老金系统适用的员工均必须支付，且雇主必须按相应的比例从员工的月薪中扣缴。

（2）外籍雇员

如前所述，对于未通过在该国正式注册成立的当地公司形成劳动关系而取得外国人身份证的非秘鲁国民，其不在秘鲁社会保险系统的范围之内，其中包括医疗保险和养老基金。

（三）出入境

根据秘鲁有关外国人的法律规定，所有进入秘鲁的外国个人在该国驻留期间应具有适当的移民身份或签证。

1. 签证类型

根据申请人的国籍，可向秘鲁驻外国领事馆或国家移民局提交签证申请。

希望进入和/或留在秘鲁的外国个人必须持有有效护照（至少6个月有效期）或类似文件以及相应的签证（如果需要的话）。外国公民可以凭下述任何一种签证或移民身份进入秘鲁：

临时	旅游
	国际条约
	商务
	艺术家或运动员
	专员
	派遣员工
	培训/临时调查
	商务
	临时派遣员工
	乘务员
	记者
居住	外交
	领事
	派遣员工
	官员
	合作
	交换人员
	调查
	政治庇护
	人道主义
	宗教
	学生
	员工
	独立签证持有者
	食利者
	家庭
	延误
	培训
	移民
	国际条约

国家移民局对签证的批准可能需要约 45 个工作日。签证的种类如下：
- 临时签证：允许外国公民入境和停留最多 90 天（可延长）；
- 居住签证：允许外国公民入境和停留 1 年。

临时签证和居住签证将按照上表根据个人的移民身份签发。根据秘鲁《移民法》确定的最常见的签证或移民身份类型如下：

（1）旅游签证

对进入秘鲁的外国公民签发的临时签证，不可用于居留目的，只可用于观光、休闲活动等。该签证不允许个人在该国进行有报酬的或其他营利活动。中国公民可免于申请该类签证，如其可证明：①持有至少 6 个月有效期至美国、英国、澳大利亚或任何申根区国家成员的签证；或②具有美国、加拿大、英国、澳大利亚或申根区任何国家成员的永久居留权。

（2）商务签证

对进入该国的外国公民签发的临时签证，不可用于居留，只可进行商业性质的安排或相关活动。持续期为 183 天，在 365 天内累计，不可延长。中国公民可免于申请该类签证，如其可证明：①持有至少 6 个月有效期至美国、英国、澳大利亚或任何申根区国家成员的签证；或②具有美国、加拿大、英国、澳大利亚或申根区任何国家成员的永久居留权。

（3）派遣员工签证

该类签证可以在临时或居住类别的基础上签发给进入该国的公民，以开展由其外雇主所委托的与工作有关的活动，并且在有限和限定的时间内执行特定任务或职能，或者需要专业、商业、技术或高度专业知识的工作。持有该等签证的个人不得进行有报酬的或其他营利活动，也不得获取秘鲁来源的收入，仅可以从其雇主处获得收入。该类签证的持续期为 365 天。

（4）居住员工签证

居住员工签证适用于进入秘鲁的外国公民，其根据先前劳动局批准的劳动合同提供服务。

（5）培训签证

对进入秘鲁的外国公民签发的签证，以便在秘鲁政府认可的教育机构或中心学习。除非这些外国公民获得国家移民局授予的特别工作许可，否则不得获取秘鲁来源的收入。

一旦居住签证获得批准，外国公民必须在国家移民局外国人登记中心登记，并获得相应的外国人身份证。当外国个人在秘鲁时，必须随身携带其外国人身份证。

2. 出入境限制

对违反秘鲁移民法律法规的行为，例如在该国的停留时间超过了签发的签证所准许的时间等，可以处以罚款、强制出境、取消居留、取消居住签证和/或驱逐出境。

（四）工会和劳动组织

秘鲁《宪法》保护员工参加工会、集体谈判和罢工的权利。

1. 工会

加入工会是自愿的。如果要成为工会会员，员工必须在企业工作或参与和相关类型的工会对应的活动、专业或职业。除非公司章程另有规定，否则管理人员和高级员工不得成为工会会员。员工的最低人数取决于工会的类型。如要成立并存续，一个公司工会必须至少有 20 名员工；其他类型的工会（即活动工会、同业工会或各种职业工会）至少需要 50 名员工。雇主可以从员工的月薪中扣除其工会费用，但须经有关员工明确授权。

2. 工会保护

一般而言，工会法律保护工会成员及其代表免受解雇，并保证在欠缺充分证明的合理理由或雇员未同意的情况下，员工不会被调职到雇主公司的其他岗位。如果相同公司内的岗位变更不影响员工作为工会代表的职能，则不需要取得员工同意。

3. 谈判

当工会会员直接（在公司层面谈判的情况下）或通过劳动局（在工会层面谈判的情况下）向雇主

提交其诉求清单时，则会发起集体谈判。诉求清单必须经工会大会批准，并且必须在获得该等批准后的 2 个月内提交给雇主。

4. 集体谈判协议

集体谈判是旨在规范工资、生产率和其他工作条件的协商，其一方为一个或多个工会组织，或者在不存在工会组织的情况下，则为经明确授权或为此等目的选举产生的员工代表；另一方则是雇主、一群雇主或多个雇主组织。

集体谈判的结果对于同意该等结果的各方以及此后加入工会组织的员工具有约束力。

（五）劳动争议

目前，国内的劳动争议由第 29497 号法律——《劳动程序法》调整。无论劳动关系是以何种形式终止的，关于未支付报酬和 / 或合法福利的诉讼时效为 4 年，从劳动关系终止后的第二天起算。对与建立或终止劳动关系的异议有关事项的诉讼时效一般为 30 个日历日，从相关事件发生的次日起算。员工希望就任何上述方面进行索赔，可以直接向劳动法院提起诉讼。

秘鲁劳动诉讼程序的模式基本上是口头的；尽管诉讼应以书面形式提出，在诉讼程序中当事方将会被要求在程序的各个阶段以口头形式证实索赔请求或答辩意见，（视情况而定）以及支持其答辩意见的证据。

劳动诉讼程序的进程或发展将取决于索赔请求的性质；但一般而言，其是由员工提起诉讼而发起，随后相关的法院将会决定是否可以受理。如果索赔被法院确定受理，雇主则会被通知诉讼的内容，以便其按受理法院许可的期限和条件进行答辩。在向雇主通知诉讼的同时，法院还将会设定并通知雇主调解听证会举行的日期和地点。

由于秘鲁的劳动诉讼程序模式鼓励各当事方达成和解，因此设置了调解听证阶段，以便雇主可以向员工或前员工提出并达成和解协议，终止劳动诉讼程序。在某些情况下，法官会建议双方达成协议。如果当事方达成和解协议，法院会宣布终止劳动诉讼程序。

同时，法官可以在此听证会上审查被告是否已经对诉讼进行了答辩；如果该诉讼请求是单纯的法律问题，或者这是一个事实争议，则没有必要采取任何复杂的证据或抗辩方式。在这种情况下，法官可能会要求当事方证实其主张，并且可能据此作出最终裁决。

如果当事方之间未达成和解，法院将会确定举行判决听证会的日期。在此阶段，当事方应支持和证实其诉讼请求和答辩意见，并解释和说明其证据如何适用于案件。任何有关程序性例外的补充行为、复杂证据等也将在本次听证会中进行评估。

根据诉讼程序的性质，法院可以决定在听证会上当庭或者在听证会结束后 5 个工作日内作出最终裁决。如当事方不同意裁决，可按特定的期限和条件提起上诉。同样，如果当事方不同意上诉的裁决，按特定的期限和条件可以提起最终的上诉（严格限于诉讼的形式方面的问题）。

五、知识产权

（一）知识产权法律法规简介

秘鲁的知识产权（IP）法律涵盖：专利、保护证书、实用新型、工业品外观设计、商业秘密、商标、商号、原产地名称等。秘鲁是多个国际和区域公约（组织）的成员国，例如《保护工业产权巴黎公约》《伯尔尼版权公约》《里斯本原产地名称协定》、世界知识产权组织（WIPO）、《商标和商务保护泛美公约》《与贸易有关的知识产权协定》（TRIPs）、《建立世界贸易组织（WTO）协定》和《专利合作条约》（PCT）等。

为了遵守美国与秘鲁之间签署的《自由贸易协定》，秘鲁立法引入了一些变化。这些细则仅在某些方面对原来的立法进行了补充，基本原则均得以保留。由于秘鲁也是安第斯共同体的成员，将由第 486 号决议和第 1075 号法令（《知识产权法》）裁定知识产权。此外，版权管理事项由安第斯共同体第 351 号决议和第 822 号立法法令（《版权法》）规定。

秘鲁国家竞争和知识产权保护局是负责知识产权、版权、消费者保护条例、不正当竞争等的国家主管部门。

(二) 专利申请

秘鲁的专利保护由第 486 号决议（安第斯共同体①关于知识产权的法律）和《知识产权法》（包括对前述决议的补充规定）进行规制。其专利管理涵盖了发明专利、实用新型、集成电路和工业品外观设计专利。

此外，秘鲁是《专利合作条约》(PCT) 的签署国，该条约在国际上提供了一套统一的程序，用于提交、检索和审查保护发明的申请以及提供特殊技术服务。

《专利合作条约》于 2009 年 6 月 6 日对秘鲁生效。《专利合作条约》系统由缔约国之间的统一专利申请程序组成，从而使申请人无须在需要保护发明的每个国家发起不同的程序。因此，根据该条约提交的任何申请将会被视为"国际申请"。

专利注册所赋予权利的保护期限为 20 年。在该期限之后，专利不能续期。一旦该期限结束，专利将会进入公共领域。

在秘鲁的专利保护需要向秘鲁国家竞争和知识产权保护局发明与新技术司提交申请，以进行注册。专利注册过程至少需要 3 年或 4 年。

秘鲁国家竞争和知识产权保护局应对所有技术领域的发明授予专利，无论是商品还是工艺，只要其是新颖的，具有创造性并且在工业上适用。如要申请专利，应将申请提交至发明与新技术司，并附上发明人的请求书，其中包括申请人或提交申请的人员的信息、发明的完整说明以及规定费用的付款凭证。

假设发明人符合所有法律要求，发明与新技术司将在 18 个月内正式公布申请摘要。因此，申请在该段时间内处于保密状态。在公布之日起 60 天内，任何具有合法权益的人员可以提交（仅一次）正当理由，对发明的专利性提出异议。根据申请，上述的期限可给予 60 天的延期。专利申请人在收到通知后有 60 天的时间来解决任何索赔或提交所需的文件。上述的期限可给予 60 天延期。如果最终审查结果是有利的，则将会授予专利。无论是否有人提出异议，申请人可以在申请公布后 6 个月内要求对发明的专利性进行审查。

秘鲁国家竞争和知识产权保护局将注册申请划分为以下类别：
- 专利和新发明注册申请；
- 工业品外观设计专利注册申请；
- 集成电路布图设计注册申请；
- 植物新品种权证书注册申请；
- 实用新型注册申请。

(三) 商标注册

根据第 486 号决议和《知识产权法》，秘鲁的商标保护需要通过向秘鲁国家竞争和知识产权保护局显著性标志司提交登记注册申请。该规定还涵盖了商号、标语和原产地名称以及集体商标的保护。除了众所周知的显著性标志外，未注册的商标都不受保护，无论其用途为何。

秘鲁还遵循并使用第 11 版商品和服务尼斯分类。

商标程序应提交申请，并应符合显著性标志司所确定的所有正式条件，其中包括以下内容：
- 申请人的身份信息（如果是自然人）或与法人的识别信息；
- 指明可用于登记注册的标志种类；
- 指明申请人想要区分的产品或服务，及其根据国际尼斯分类的类别；
- 在该意义上，可以注册商业名称、标语、集体商标和证明商标；
- 授权委托书（不需要公证）。

---

① 秘鲁、玻利维亚、厄瓜多尔和哥伦比亚均加入了安第斯条约组织。四国在知识产权保护上适用相同的法律。

自收到申请之日起10个工作日内，商标管理局将审查申请是否符合主要的前提条件，如果申请人符合所有的前提条件，商标管理局将在官方商标公报上公布该商标。如果申请人不符合上述要求，商标管理局将给予其10个工作日以修改任何遗漏。一旦符合所有必要条件，在公布日期之后的30个工作日内，任何具有合法权益的人员可以提交（仅一次）有效的异议，以拒绝商标注册。

商标登记注册自申请获批准之日起10年内有效，并可以每10年期连续无限次续展。

（四）版权保护

根据安第斯共同体第351号决议以及根据第1076号法令颁布的《版权法》及其修正案，版权保护适用于书籍、小册子、杂志、讲座、演说、演讲稿、教学解释、音乐作品、电影作品、戏剧作品、编舞艺术、哑剧作品、视听作品、应用艺术作品和美术作品、草稿、素描、雕塑、版画、印刷物、建筑作品、照片、插图、地图、平面图、与地理、地形、建筑或科学相关的塑料作品、口号和短语、计算机软件、新闻文章、新闻报道、社论、评论、翻译和改编等。秘鲁国家竞争和知识产权保护局是版权主管部门，有权决定采取预防措施，例如没收和检查，并对侵权行为实施处罚。

此外，秘鲁还是《保护文学和艺术作品伯尔尼公约》的成员，因此，它还为该公约的成员国提供保护。

与商标不同，版权即使未注册，也受到保护；根据《保护文学和艺术作品伯尔尼公约》，版权是声明性的，但登记注册可使版权对抗第三方。

（五）知识产权保护措施

作为执行措施，知识产权持有人可以采取以下法律行动，例如：
- 对商标申请提出异议；
- 提起侵权诉讼；
- 要求采取预防措施，包括销毁侵权材料、停止侵权行为等；
- 请求主管部门进行检查。

在该意义上，秘鲁知识产权条例允许知识产权持有人通过对可能的侵权人提起侵权诉讼来保护其知识产权。秘鲁商标管理局有权对侵权人实施制裁和最高达194 532美元（大约）的罚款，并责令停止侵权行为。

边境措施：第043-2009-SUNAT-A号决议批准了有关边界措施要求的建议（INTA-IT-00.08）。边境措施包括秘鲁海关主管部门与秘鲁国家竞争和知识产权保护局之间的信息系统，通过建立知识产权权利人的登记，阻止侵犯知识产权的产品以商业为目的地进入秘鲁境内。

该登记是自愿的，并应呈交给海关主管部门。对于假冒产品，甚至可以对可能的侵权人提起刑事诉讼。从该意义上说，不仅可以在行政层面上还可以在刑事层面上作出制裁。

六、环境保护

（一）环境保护监督部门

环境部（Ministerio del Ambiente）是秘鲁环境主管部门，该部门主管国家环境管理系统，其主要职能是通过保护和恢复环境生态系统和自然资源，致力于促进环境的可持续性发展。

环境评估监管局（Organismo de Evaluación y Fiscalización Ambiental，OEFA）是国家环境评估和监督系统的指导实体，负责评估、监督和审核秘鲁国内环境法律的遵守情况。

（二）环境保护法律法规简介

《普通环境法》（第28611号法律）确立了环境权利和义务的一般制度。根据该法律，任何易造成环境损害的生产活动，在开展之前都需要经过环境评估，并得到主管部门批准。

上述评估必须包含活动对环境造成的所有可能后果，以及申请人计划避免或将这些损害减少到可容忍水平的方法。这些水平因行业而异，并且越来越多的行业正在受到监管。另外，这些限制可以根据某些因素而变化，例如地点；因此，通常有必要在当地进行适当的调查。

一项非常重要的法规是第 1278 号立法法令，其批准了《固体废物综合管理法》，并取代了 2000 年发布的第 27314 号法律——《固体废物普通法》。该法规适用于所有的生产部门，并包括了与固体废物的收集、储存、处理、运输和出口相关的活动。

（三）环境保护的评估

在过去的 20 年中，秘鲁经济的增长速度非常迅速。该增长基于与采矿、天然气、石油和农业等相关的活动。

上述活动与自然资源的开发密切相关，并且由于其特点和性质，对环境构成了潜在威胁。

秘鲁政府和社会一直在应对保护自然资源的挑战，着眼于当地农村和当地社区，并以长期、可持续的方式利用自然资源。

政府非常积极地治理环境事宜，以确保秘鲁自然资源的保护；然而，由于秘鲁有着大量崎岖不平及个别交通不便利的领土，主管部门不一定能够时时执行并监督有关的法律及其遵守情况。

尽管如此，秘鲁政府一直致力于寻找新的方法和管理手段来保护环境，且同时促进私人投资。

七、争议解决

（一）争议解决的方法和机构

1. 秘鲁的成文法制度和司法系统

秘鲁基于其民法对其所有领土推行实施统一的法律制度。秘鲁的法律制度以民法原则（包括成文法）为基础，由此，在秘鲁，宪法具有最高级别，其次是法律和立法法令，排在第三位的是由行政部门颁布的最高法令等。

秘鲁司法系统划分为 34 个司法辖区和 3 个主要的法院和法官级别。首先，位于利马的最高法院（Corte Suprema）在全国拥有管辖权。其次，34 个司法地区的高等法院（Corte Superior）是各区的最高法院。再次，是根据不同的专业所组成的初级法官。最后，是农村地区的治安法官以及和平法官。

秘鲁司法系统的诉讼程序为两审制。这意味着下级法院作出的判决可以通过上诉，由高等法院进行审查。一般来说，大多数民事和商事审判由初级法官裁决，当事方可以向所在的司法辖区的高等法院提出上诉。此后，在高等法院作出判决之后，当事方只能就涉及以下的事项提出最终的上诉：①直接影响有争议的判决的违反法律的问题；②目的不明的撤销司法先例。作为最高上诉法院，最高法院的裁决可以撤销、改判或维持先前的判决。

2. 宪法法庭

秘鲁宪法通过宪法法庭（Tribunal Constitucional）保护个人的基本权利和自由，宪法法庭是一个自主实体，对与维护被当局或其他公民所侵害的宪法权利有关的法律诉求有管辖权。此外，宪法法庭负责主管法律的合宪性审查。

宪法法庭由国会指定的 7 名成员组成。

3. 仲裁

秘鲁的仲裁受第 1071 号立法法令的管辖。几乎所有的争议都可以进行仲裁，但涉及刑法、家事和公共利益事项、工业产权、破产程序等争议的情况除外。

一旦当事方签署了仲裁协议，法院就不能再对该事项作出裁决。

在秘鲁，仲裁可以分为两类：良心仲裁和法律仲裁。两者之间的主要区别在于：在第一类情况下，仲裁员根据自己对该事项的认知和理解进行裁决；而在第二类情况下，仲裁员依据法律作出裁决。此外，对于良心仲裁，仲裁员可以是任何自然人、国民或外国人；而对于法律仲裁，仲裁员必须是在秘鲁律师协会（Colegio de Abogados）注册的律师。

如果仲裁纠纷中的当事方约定临时仲裁，则可以就仲裁地点和仲裁程序达成一致。否则，如果当事方将纠纷提交至仲裁机构，例如利马商会，则适用该机构的规则。除非当事方在协议中另有规定，否则仲裁庭将按过半数仲裁员的一致意见运作。仲裁庭的决定和裁决应以过半数仲裁员的投票结果为基础。仲裁庭主席有权投上决定性的一票。

仲裁裁决具有既判效力，一旦通知，当事方必须遵守。可通过司法系统中的地区法院强制执行裁决。

如果不服仲裁裁决的，唯一的救济办法是向司法机关申请撤销裁决。仅在仲裁违反法律规定的适当程序时，才可以启动撤销仲裁裁决的程序。

撤销申请必须向仲裁地的高等法院提起。只有当高等法院判决仲裁裁决完全或部分无效时，才可以提出最终上诉。

（二）法律的适用问题

在商业诉讼情况下，在起诉之前，诉讼当事方必须完成有关的诉前要求，包括履行额外的司法调解程序。额外的司法调解程序必须在秘鲁司法部授权的调解中心进行。调解人召集当事方进行调解听证会。如果当事方未达成协议或被邀请方经两次传唤未到庭，则索赔方可以提起诉讼。

仲裁则不需要经过上述的调解程序。

向司法机关提起的商业诉讼由《民事诉讼法》调整，而仲裁程序则由第1017号立法法令调整。

仲裁裁决可以自行执行，但如果当事方认为有必要使用公共力量来执行仲裁裁决，则可以启动执行仲裁裁决的司法程序。

另外，只要不违反秘鲁的法律法规，可以在秘鲁执行外国判决。外国判决要获得秘鲁法院的承认，必须遵守有关的执行程序。

八、其他

（一）反商业贿赂

1. 反商业贿赂法律法规简介

涉及至少一名公职人员或公务员的贿赂行为由刑法制裁。根据秘鲁现行立法，私人之间的腐败行为不被视为犯罪。秘鲁的反腐败法包括：《刑法典》，其规定全面禁止贿赂公职人员；《公职人员道德守则》，其禁止公职人员收受贿赂；第023-2011-PCM号最高法令，其规定了对收受贿赂的公职人员的行政处罚。

根据秘鲁《刑法典》的规定，贿赂是指：

- 向公职人员或公务员提供任何好处、款项、捐赠、利益或承诺给予利益，以使其作出或不作出一项行为，从而违反其职责；
- 向公职人员或公务员提供任何好处、款项、捐赠、利益或承诺给予利益，以使其实施一项本身为其工作一部分且不违背其职责的行为。

秘鲁《刑法典》对接受或索要贿赂的公职人员和给予或提供非法利益的私人个人进行制裁。

历史上，秘鲁的司法制度只追究个人的刑事责任，但从2018年1月开始，新的法律制度已经生效。该新法律规定了对法人实体（公司）的自主刑事责任，如果法人实体（公司）直接或间接参与了主动贿赂、特定主动贿赂、跨国贿赂、洗钱和恐怖主义金融案件。根据该规定，参与到上述罪行的实体将面临起诉和可能的定罪，除非其能够证明其在指控的犯罪行为发生之前已经采取了有效的全面合规措施，以便不触犯上述罪行。

《刑法典》规定了秘鲁的刑事犯罪行为，并提供了一般规则，如共同犯罪，其适用于所有秘鲁公民及所有在秘鲁和海外针对该国犯罪的外国公民。

《刑法典》中包含11项不同的与贿赂有关的犯罪。根据具体情况，触犯贿赂罪的公职人员的最低刑期为4年，最长为15年。《刑法典》还包括对触犯腐败犯罪的公职人员的其他制裁，例如取消公职人员的工作资格。

2. 反商业贿赂监督部门

公共部（Ministerio Público）是负责起诉包括贿赂在内的所有犯罪的机关。专责调查腐败案件的特别检察官办公室于多年前被建立，其直接参与起诉这些案件。

公共部在进行初步调查的过程中会得到警方的支持（其也设有专门的反腐部门）。在公共部提出指控后，案件将由司法系统的刑事法院审理。

公共部受理来自私人、单位以及公共机关如审计总署、国会、州检察官部门等机构的刑事举报。

最后，新《刑事诉讼法》已经生效，其适用于全国范围的腐败案件。

3. 惩罚措施

贿赂罪将被判处 3 年到 15 年不等的有期徒刑。

对各种贿赂犯罪的最高刑罚如下：

① 公职人员为违反其职责行事而实施被动贿赂犯罪（接受或接收贿赂），处以 8 年有期徒刑；

② 公职人员违反其职责（直接或间接要求）贿赂而实施被动贿赂犯罪，处以 8 年有期徒刑；

③ 公职人员通过利用其职务获取非法利益而实施被动贿赂犯罪，处以 10 年有期徒刑；

④ 对于跨国贿赂，处以 8 年有期徒刑；

⑤ 为了从事不违背其职责的行为，或对于其已经完成的行为，公职人员实施被动贿赂犯罪（接受或收受贿赂），处以 8 年有期徒刑；

⑥ 为了从事不违背其职责的行为，或对于其已经完成的行为，公职人员实施被动贿赂犯罪（索要贿赂），处以 8 年有期徒刑；

⑦ 仲裁员、检察官、公共专家、行政法庭成员或类似人员实施被动贿赂犯罪（接受贿赂），以影响其决定，处以 15 年有期徒刑；

⑧ 仲裁员、检察官、公共专家、行政法庭成员或类似人员实施被动贿赂犯罪（索要贿赂），以影响其决定，处以 15 年有期徒刑；

⑨ 国家警察人员实施被动贿赂犯罪（接受、收取或要求贿赂），以违背其职责行事，处以 10 年有期徒刑；

⑩ 国家警察人员通过利用其职务获取非法利益而实施被动贿赂犯罪，处以 12 年有期徒刑；

⑪ 国家警察人员通过接受或接收贿赂而履行其职责，实施被动贿赂犯罪，处以 7 年有期徒刑；

⑫ 国家警察人员通过接受贿赂以便按照其职责行事，实施被动贿赂犯罪，则会被处以 8 年有期徒刑；

⑬ 司法辅助人员实施被动贿赂犯罪，处以 8 年有期徒刑；

⑭ 实施主动贿赂（向公职人员提供、承诺或给予非法利益）犯罪，以使公职人员违反其职责行事的人员，处以 6 年有期徒刑；

⑮ 实施主动贿赂（向公职人员提供、承诺或给予非法利益）犯罪，以使公职人员从事不违反其职责行为的人员，处以 5 年有期徒刑；

⑯ 对于主动跨国贿赂者，处以 8 年有期徒刑；

⑰ 为影响其决定而向仲裁员、检察官、公共专家、行政法庭成员或类似人员提供、承诺或给予非法利益而实施主动贿赂犯罪者，则会被处以 8 年有期徒刑；

⑱ 为影响其决定而向司法助理、证人、官方翻译人员或类似人员提供、承诺或给予非法利益而实施主动贿赂犯罪者，处以 8 年有期徒刑；

⑲ 对实施主动贿赂犯罪的律师或律师事务所的人员，处以 8 年有期徒刑；

⑳ 实施主动贿赂犯罪，向国家警察人员提供、承诺或给予非法利益，以使其违反职责作出或不作出某行为的人员，处以 8 年有期徒刑；

㉑ 国家警察人员通过利用其职务获取非法利益而实施主动贿赂犯罪，处以 6 年有期徒刑。

最后，如果腐败案件所涉及的人员配合调查，则可以根据法律获得宽大处理。根据第 27378 号法律第 4 节，宽大措施包括：①免于刑罚；②在法定最低限度以下处以罚款；③缓刑；等等。给予的具体宽大措施将取决于其提供信息的质量。

(二) 项目合同

秘鲁项目合同分为 2 个主要系统：①政府采购系统；②政府和社会资本合作（PPP）合同系统。这两个系统适用不同的规定，并回应着不同的需求。政府采购系统下的项目一般是为了满足特定的政府机构的具体需求，并且通常是标准化的合同；而 PPP 合同系统适用于更大型和 / 或更复杂的合同，其中包括公共服务、大型基础设施项目、公共交通和类似项目。

此外，在这两大系统之外还有一些其他类型的项目合同。

1. 政府采购

政府采购法作为一般规则，适用于所有以公共资金（财政资金和通过政府机构募集的资金）出资的合同。该系统包括一系列合同，从为政府机构采购设备到建设和维护基础设施的较大型合同（只要其不属于 PPP 的一部分）。

政府采购系统受第 30225 号法律以及根据该法律制定的最高法令 350-2015-EF 调整，并由政府采购合同监管机构（Organismo Supervisor de Contrataciones del Estado，OSCE）监督。政府采购合同监管机构还发布了具体指令，以确定第 30225 号法律和第 350-2015-EF号最高法令的适用规则。

（1）登记

为了参加政府采购系统的竞标，投标人必须在国家供应商登记处（Registro Nacional de Proveedores，RNP）进行登记。可以为外国、本地、有永久住所和无永久住所的实体进行登记。根据待登记的实体的活动，登记处分为 4 个主要部分，即"服务供应商登记处""商品供应商登记处""工程承包商登记处"和"工程咨询登记处"。一个实体可以在上述数个或所有注册处进行登记。

（2）投标邀请书和招标

该过程有如下所述的数个阶段：

• 投标邀请书和征求建议书

一旦相应的政府机构按照内部批准在公共采购系统下启动招标过程，投标邀请书和征求建议书（RFP）将在电子政府采购系统（Sistema Electrónico de Contrataciones del Estado，SEACE）内发布。如果投标邀请书和条件由政府机构发布，则会是一个网页。

• 征求建议书意见

一旦发布征求建议书，潜在的投标人可在规定的期限内提交关于征求建议书的问题和意见。在政府机构回答问题和意见后，这些回复将被整合到征求建议书中，并发布新的经过整合的征求建议书。应注意，在该阶段不能对所需的服务、商品或工程的基本特征作出重大更改。

• 投标书的提交

在完成前面的阶段之后，投标书将在招标日期提交给政府机构。根据过程的类型，文件的提交可以通过公证人进行的公开行为或私人行为。一旦审查文件和投标人合格，则会评估建议书并授标。不符合资格的投标人可以向相应的政府机构或政府采购合同监管机构公共采购法庭（Tribunal de Contrataciones del Estado）提出异议（取决于合同的价值）。

• 合同的最终确定

在合同授予后，中标人必须向承包政府机构提交特定文件和履约保函。一旦提交了所有文件和履约保函，即可签订合同。

2. PPP 合同

PPP 合同由第 1224 号立法法令管理，并由第 410-2015-EF 号最高法令进一步制定。负责 PPP 项目的主要实体为 ProInversion，但是，只要不违反上述一般规定，基层和地区政府也有权发布具体规定。

PPP 项目在特许协议中具体化。

适用法规将 PPP 项目分为两大类：①自己出资；②共同出资。

（1）自己出资的 PPP

在自己出资的 PPP 项目中，政府机构不提供直接或间接资金或有保证。这意味着特许权获得者通过用户支付的使用费来收回投资，例如在被称为"Metropolitano"的利马 BRT 公交系统的情况下，特许权获得者通过销售可充值卡以及用户的充值来收回投资。

（2）共同出资的 PPP

共同出资的 PPP 项目具有来自政府机构的直接付款或来自政府机构的或有保证。由于这些项目需要使用公共资金，因而常被保留用于最大和更复杂的项目，并且程序涉及更多的先前研究，因为这些项目必须由涉及的政府机构宣布为可行，并且需要公共预算中的相应拨款。

根据共同出资或自己出资的资格以及项目的规模，授予 PPP 项目的过程由 ProInversion 或相应的地方或地区政府进行。

可通过公开倡议招标或私人倡议方式进入 PPP 流程：

① 公开倡议

一旦获得先前的批准，相应的实体有权进行招标。

• 投标文件和征求建议书的邀请和发布

相应的实体邀请投标并发布所有相关的投标研究和文件，以及进入付款金额、征求建议书和特许权合同项目。

• 征求建议书意见和特许权合同

在投标文件发布后，潜在投标人提交其有关征求建议书和特许权合同的问题、意见和修改建议。一旦对问题、意见和修改进行了审查，相应的实体会发布其回应，并继续整合征求建议书和特许权合同。

应注意，在这种情况下，可以提出数轮的意见。

• 先前的意见

应注意，为了使投标有效，一旦发布了最终版本的特许权合同，必须获得经济财政部的赞同意见。

• 投标和授标

一旦确定了投标的最终文件并获得了经济财政部的赞同意见，应按照预定日期和时间公开提交投标书，并且在资格审核和评标之后，进行授标。

应注意，资格预审阶段是可能的，但并不总是适用。

通过提交保证金，未中标者有权对结果提出异议。

• 合同的最终确定

一旦授标并且提起异议的期限届满（或异议已解决），在提交相应的截止文件（包括履约保函）之后，合同将在预定日期正式签署生效。

② 私人倡议

进入 PPP 项目的另一种方式是提交私人倡议请求。这意味着私营公司可以向政府机构提议执行 PPP 项目。该请求的提交具有一定的规则，结果可以是公开招标程序或直接授标。

• 私人倡议请求的提交

根据项目的规模和特点，向 ProInversion 或当地或地区政府提交请求。

中央政府自己出资的私人倡议和共同出资的私人倡议应提交至 ProInversion。

地方和地区政府自己出资的私人倡议应直接提交给相应的实体。

• 评估

一旦进行了提交并符合正式要求，私人倡议将遵循所有相关实体和经济财政部的批准程序。对于共同出资的项目，还必须声明可行性。

• 利益关系声明

如果私人倡议通过了所有必要的批准，则可作利益关系声明。并且，提议者必须公布并提交相应的保证金。

一旦公布了利益关系声明，将会为第三方提供 90 个日历日来提交利益关系说明以及保证金。

• 直接授标或公开招标

如果第三方表示对该项目感兴趣，则会启动公开招标程序，并且提议者在未能中标的情况下有权要求第二轮招标。

如果没有第三方表示对该项目感兴趣，则向私人倡议的提议者直接授标。

- 合同的最终确定

一旦通过公开投标或直接授标方式获得项目,在提交所需的截止文件和履约保函之后,签订合同。

应注意,在截止日期后的 3 年期限内,对特许权合同的修改仅限于重大错误的纠正,在截止后使合同修改具有必要性的事件或执行合同所需的具体修改。

上述限制阻止了"银行可担保性修改",在近些年来,这在秘鲁是常见的。这也意味着在提交建议书时,项目必须具有银行可担保性,因为在截止后的 3 年期限内,不得做出重大修改。

3. 其他合同类型

秘鲁法规规定了不受公共采购或 PPP 法律约束的某些类型的合同。主要包括:①由世界银行或类似组织等国际实体资助的合同;②由军事实体作出的军备收购;③税收项目的执行。

这些合同受特定法规[①]或融资实体所定义的规则管辖。

在执行税收项目的具体情况下,如果具有社会重要性的某些项目由私人投资者执行,然后给予税收优惠,这属于私人与公共实体之间的特殊协作制度。这些项目通过与具体实体达成协议来具体化,并且不包括在一般公共采购或 PPP 规定之中。

近年来,政府作出重大努力来宣传和推广税收项目协议模式,以作为发展地方和区域项目并对人口产生积极影响的替代方案。

---

① 涉及国际金融的合同由各特定的金融机构指令调整,军事机构合同受第 1128 号法令与第 005-2013-DE 号最高法令调整;执行税收项目受第 29230 号法律、第 036-2017-EF 号最高法令及第 1250 号法令调整。

Peru

Authors: Viviana Garcia, Guillermo Ferrero, José Antonio Olaechea, Vladimir Popov
Translators: Eric J. Jiang, Raymond Wu

I. Overview

A. General Introduction to the Political, Economic, Social and Legal Environment of the Country Receiving Investment

The Republic of Peru is a diverse country located on the centre of South America with an extension of 1,285,216 km^2 and an estimated population of 31,826,018 up to 2017.

The main language in the country is Spanish, along with Quechua, Aymara and other indigenous languages that have official status, with the majority of the business sector speaking English.

Peru has a constitutional democratic republic with a multiparty system, where the President is both the head of state and of government. Additionally, it should be noted that the government is divided into the following three independent systems:

• Legislature: it is represented by a unicameral Congress of one hundred and thirty (130) representatives, which are elected for a five-year term and proportionally to each region's population. Their main function is to approve laws (Statues, Regulations, among others.) and treaties;
• Judiciary: it is comprised by judges elected by the Judiciary National Counci;
• Executive: it is comprised by the President. It is responsible for the day to day management of the State, it executes policies in accordance with the law, and represents the nation in their foreign relations, among others.

Peruvian currency is the Sol (PEN) and interacts in a free-floating managed exchange rate regime.

Economically, Peru has obtained Investment-grade status from credit rating agencies and its GDP over the past fifteen (15) years has demonstrated a consecutive growth at rates higher that the average region of Latin America.

Throughout the latest years, the leading indicator of Peruvian growth has been private investment, granted its responsible economic policy and its contribution towards its continuity.

B. The Status and Direction of the Cooperation with Chinese Enterprises Under the B&R

Peru has various commercial integration policies with countries all over the world, in order to create a more competitive market and have more opportunities.

Among the commercial agreements that have been entered into by Peru with China is the Free Trade Agreement, which is currently in force since March 01, 2010. Its purpose is to eliminate the obstacles that may arise regarding trade and investment matters between both countries.

China is a strategic country that has positioned itself as one of our top commercial partners. Some of the main products that we have exported regarding the agreement is copper and its concentrates with an approximate value of US$ 5, 468 million. This cipher represented 67% of our total traditional exportations for the year of 2016. Among other sectors that have also been positively affected by the agreement is the fisheries sector (fish flour) resulting in the third product exported for an amount of US$ 714 million.

Thus, it can be appreciated that the Trade Agreement between Peru and China has resulted extremely beneficial for both countries and has made Peru position its products in one of the most important and relevant markets worldwide.

II. Investment

A. Market Access

a. Department Supervising Investment

The Peruvian regulatory authority in foreign investment is Proinversión (Private Investment Promotion

Agency), a public entity attached to the Ministry of Economy and Finance, which is responsible for the execution of policies regarding the promotion of private investment.

Proinversión provides information and orientation services towards investors (local or foreign), as well as contributing and monitoring an attractive landscape for private investment in accordance to the country´s political and economic plans.

b. Laws and Regulations of Investment Industry

The main laws related to foreign investments in Peru are the following: (i) Legislative Decree No.662, which approves the Legal Stability Scheme for Foreign Investments; (ii) Legislative Decree No.757, which approves the Framework Law for the Development of Private Investments; (iii) Supreme Decree No.162-92-EF, which approves the Regulations on Private Investment Guarantee Regimes; and, (iv) General Corporations Law (Law No.26887).

c. Forms of Investment

Foreign investments can be made freely under any of the business legal forms that are recognizes by our laws, and under the following models:
- Direct Foreign Investment, as contributions to the capital stock;
- Contributions to the development of contractual joint ventures;
- Investments in goods and property located within Peruvian territory;
- Portfolio Investments;
- Intangible technology contributions; and,
- Any other mode of investment that contributes to the development of Peru.

Another widely promoted form for private investment is through the execution of projects related to public infrastructure, public services, assets, companies and other Government projects. Thus, an effective way of participating is through public and private initiatives, the prior being from State Entities (Ministry's, Regional Governments or Local Governments) and the latter being made by private investors.

With regards to the aforementioned, it should be noted that Legislative Decree No.1012 establishes the Framework Law for Public-Private Partnerships (PPP) and its Regulation. There, we have the classifications for the projects, them being either self-sustained or co-financed. These are mainly executed under the concession system, which implies that the concessionaire is usually responsible for the design, financing, construction, operation and maintenance of the public infrastructure or service.

d. Standards of Market Access and Examination

Our legal framework is stable and attractive for the investment industry. Thus, the following are items foreign investors should bear in mind when entering our market:
- The Peruvian Constitution guarantees equal treatment towards both Peruvian and foreign investors;
- We are based on a free competition system;
- There is free transfer of capital;
- We have free access to financial sectors (internal and external financing);
- Our Constitution guarantees for maintaining and protecting private property;
- There are no additional or different requirements to acquire shares from national corporations;
- Practically unrestricted access to most economic sectors.

There are no limits nor restrictions for a foreigner to become the holder of a business in Peru. Notwithstanding the aforementioned, there are exceptional cases in which certain limitations are stated depending on the industry. Hereunder, we will state some of them:
- Foreign companies or individuals cannot purchase or own mines, land, water, fuel, forests or energy sources, both directly or indirectly, which are within fifty (50) kilometres from international borders. Likewise, investment in areas within fifty (50) kilometres of the frontiers, ammunition, weapons and explosive industries shall require the prior approval from the corresponding government agency;
- Regarding broadcasting services, air and maritime transportation, banking and finance sectors, our legal framework establishes that these activities are exclusive to Peruvian investors or require at least a majority stake by Peruvian investors.

National and foreign investors do not require any prior authorization in order to invest in Peru. However, once the investment has been performed, then the foreign investor could register said investment before Proinversión. This registration allows the investor the right to transfer abroad, the whole of their capitals from their investments, utilities, among others, as well as to acquire the right to use an exchange rate more favourable in the moment of effectuating an exchange transaction.

B. Foreign Exchange Regulation

a. Department Supervising Foreign Exchange

The Peruvian Constitution guarantees freedom to hold and dispose of foreign currency, thus there is no foreign exchange control or currency regulations. Nonetheless, it should be noted that the Peruvian Central Reserve Bank (Banco Central de Reserva del Perú) is the authority that establishes the official currency exchange rate following the market average exchange rate. This official rate is applied to procedures before public entities (Peruvian Public Registry and Tax Authority).

b. Brief Introduction of Laws and Regulations of Foreign Exchange

There are no restrictions regarding royalties, dividends and capital, only regarding the remittance of profits abroad, which are subject to the payment of income taxes. This means that the company shall withhold and pay to the Tax Authority the corresponding amounts. Investors are highly recommended to register foreign investment with Proinversión, in order to secure their investment.

c. Requirements of Foreign Exchange Management for Foreign Enterprises

Exporters and importers can conduct transactions freely on the open market and are not required to channel foreign exchange transactions through the Central Reserve Bank of Peru. Therefore, there are no requirements for foreign exchange management regarding foreign enterprises.

C. Financing

a. Main Financial Institutions

According to Peruvian law, hereunder are the main financial institutions:

a) Superintendency of Banking, Insurance and AFP (Superintendencia de Banca, Seguros y AFP—SBS): is a constitutionally autonomous institution organized under public law, whose purpose is to protect the interest of the public in the financial and insurance systems. In order to do so, they guarantee economic and financial soundness of individuals and legal entities under its control by enforcing the legal, regulatory and statutory provisions governing their activities. It is also in charge of preventing and detecting money laundering and financing of terrorism.

The Superintendency of Banking, Insurance and AFP is regulated in the Peruvian Banking Law (Law No.26702).

b) Superintendency of Securities Markets (Superintendencia de Mercado de Valores - SMV): is a specialized technical entity attached to the Ministry of Economy and Finance, that protects investors and ensures the efficiency and transparency of markets under its oversight, appropriate price making and dissemination of information for the purposes aforementioned, through its regulatory, oversight and promotion functions.

The functions of the Superintendency of Securities Markets are as follows:

• To introduce regulations governing the securities market, the products market and the collective funds system.

• To ensure the individuals and corporations participating in the securities market, the products market and the collective funds system comply with the law. Both natural and legal persons that are subject to the oversight of the Superintendency of Banking, Insurance and AFP are also subject to oversight by the Superintendency of Securities Markets regarding their participation in the securities market under the Superintendency of Securities Markets oversight.

• To promote and study the securities market, the products market and the collective funds system.

• Supervise the compliance of all international auditing standards.

c) Peruvian Central Reserve Bank (Banco Central de Reserva del Perú): is a legal entity with autonomy, whose purpose is to regulate the money supply, administer the international reserves, issue notes and coins and report on the nations finances. According to the Peruvian Constitution, the Central Reserve Bank has as a purpose to preserve money stability.

b. Financing Conditions for Foreign Enterprises

According to the Peruvian Banking Law (Law No.26702), foreign investment in companies shall have the same treatment as local capital, subject to international agreements related to the matter, if applicable. Likewise, the Superintendency of Banking, Insurance and AFP, if it corresponds, will consider criteria inspired in the principle of reciprocity when public interest results affected in accordance to the provisions of the Peruvian Constitution.

In addition, Law No.26702 establishes that for all of the persons who operate under the scope of its regulation, then shall require a prior authorization from the Superintendency of Banking, Insurance and AFP. In case they do

not have the corresponding authorization, then they are forbidden to:
• Engage in the business of companies of the financial system, specifically to receive or collect funds from third parties either in deposit, exchange or any other form and usually to place those resources as investment, loans or provision of funds under any contractual modality.
• Take part in the business of companies of the financial system, that grants insurance coverage on its own and acts as a broker for insurance companies, as well as other complementary activities.
• Advertise that it performs transactions and services being prohibited to perform by virtue of the preceding items.
• Use any wording that would induce the public in thinking the business carries out activities which can only be performed if you have the authorization of the Superintendency of Banking, Insurance and AFP and are under its supervision.

Therefore, given the aforementioned, either a legal person or an individual has incurred in the mentioned infractions while not having the authorization required, if they have an establishment that:
• Invites the public to either directly or indirectly contract insurance coverage or invites insurance companies to hire their services for brokerage;
• Invites the public to provide money under any type of mechanism, or to obtain loans or financing;
• Mostly advertises through any means with the purpose of accomplishing the aforementioned.

In the banking and finance sector, there are certain restrictions on investment by domestic and foreign investors that should be noted. In accordance to Law No.26702, the restrictions are applied to investments made in "corporations of the financial or insurance systems". Consequently, these apply to authorized financial intermediary (or their subsidiary which required authorization) and authorized reinsurance or insurance company (as well as their subsidiary), and to insurance intermediary or auxiliary. These companies shall be authorized by the Superintendency of Banking, Insurance and AFP.

Under the Peruvian Civil Code, there are limitations on the interest rate for financing agreements. This means that the maximum rate for moratorium or compensatory conventional interest is set by the Peruvian Central Reserve Bank. If the rate is exceeded, then that would result the debtor requiring the refund the excess payment made or the imputation of said amount towards the capital. However, the maximum rates of conventional and moratorium interests will not apply to the entities of the banking system duly authorized to operate under that scope or for financing made under foreign law.

It should be stated that there are no minimum capital requirements for foreign investments, individuals or national corporations, except for some activities regulated under the Superintendency of Banking, Insurance and AFP and the Superintendency of Securities Market. These activities require a minimum capital stock for the companies in order to execute financial activities or participate in capital market activities.

Finally, in order to finance through a public offering, then there are certain requirements that shall be complied with. These requirements are established in the Peruvian Banking Law. Refer to Section I literal c) for more details on the matter.

D. Land Policy

a. Brief Introduction of Land-Related Laws and Regulations

In Peru, the rights that are exercised over assets (movable and immovable) are called „right in rem". The Peruvian legal system recognizes a closed or limited number of real rights. That is, persons (natural and legal, national and foreign) can only exercise the real rights that the law expressly recognizes, not being feasible that through a contract or agreement between private parties a new real right is created that is not previously and expressly recognized in any law currently in force.

On the other hand, the holder of a real right is not obliged to register its acquisition in the Public Registries. However, if it does not do so, there is a risk that those who keep the property registered in their favor may dispose of it again in favor of a third party or may affect it as a collateral of a monetary loan for the benefit of a financial institution. In these cases, if the third party registers his right or the financial institution that received it as a collateral does the same, these rights will have preference over the one that was not registered. Therefore, even when the registration of the real right is not mandatory, it is recommended that all acquisitions be registered in Public Registries to avoid this type of contingencies. To be able to make this registration, the contract by which the real right is acquired must be celebrated before a Notary Public, which is the official designated by the State and whose function is to authenticate and give public faith on the documents before they enter the Registry.

Real rights have maximum terms of validity. Apart from the property right, which is perpetual (unless its owner decides to transfer it), the other real rights (such as surface usufruct, use, etc.) have validity limits that cannot be overcome by individuals. For example, the maximum term for the surface right is ninety-nine (99) years, while for the usufruct, when its owner is a legal person (a company), the right cannot exceed thirty (30) years.

Regarding the property right, which is the most important right that the legal system recognizes in favor of a person, for it grants him the maximum of possible faculties (use, enjoyment, disposition, edification, affectation in use, encumbrance, etc.), it is protected at a constitutional level. In this sense, article 70 of the Constitution states that no one (natural, legal, national or foreign) can be deprived of their property.

However, the same rule recognizes an exception to this protection of the property right, and such is the case of expropriation. In this regard, and in accordance with article 70 of the Constitution, a certain number of requirements must be fulfilled for said figure to proceed: (i) it must be justified by a national security or public necessity (ii) the permission to expropriate must be declared in a law; and (iii) the affected owner must be paid with a compensation, which in addition to contain the value of the property, must include compensation for the eventual damage suffered.

In addition to this, the Constitution recognizes the owner affected by the expropriation the right to bring a claim before the Judicial Court to question the compensation amount that the State has recognized in his favor, if it considers that the value of the property is greater.

Likewise, the Constitution and the Civil Code require that the property right be exercised in harmony with the common good and within the limits of the law. In this sense, it is possible to find four major types of regulations linked to the exercise of property:

(i) Urban Development;
(ii) Zoning;
(iii) Urbanistic parameters; and,
(iv) Building Control.

Urban development is the process by which a rustic land (that is, one destined for agricultural and livestock activities) is converted into an urban land, through the execution of works of accessibility, water distribution and collection of drainage, distribution of energy and public lighting, tracks and sidewalks. Carrying out this process is an essential requirement for the owner of a property to allocate the same to urban-type activities.

Zoning, on the other hand, is the set of urban planning technical norms contained in the Urban Development Plan that regulates land use according to the physical, economic and social demands of the city, to locate activities for the purpose of housing, recreation, protection and equipment; as well as industrial production, trade, transport and communications. In order to know the type of zoning assigned to a specific property, it is necessary to process a Zoning and Roads Certificate before the Provincial Municipality, which has a validity of three (3) years and establishes the type of activity that can be carried out in a specific property.

The urbanistic and building parameters are the technical provisions that establish the characteristics that a building project must have. They indicate the dimensions of the lot that can be built, the building coefficient, the net density of inhabitants per hectare, the height of the building, the withdrawals, the percentage of free area, the number of parking lots and other conditions that must be respected by the owner who wishes to execute a new work or modify an existing building. In order to know the parameters assigned to a specific property, it is necessary to process before the District Municipality a Certificate of Urbanistic and Building Parameters, which has a validity of three (3) years.

Finally, so that the owner can build on his property, must have a prior authorization issued by the District Municipality, called building license. No construction or work can be carried out without this authorization. This license is the result of the review of the technical file presented by the owner made by the Municipality, which is made up of a set of documents that determine the characteristics, requirements and specifications necessary for the execution of the building. Once the construction is completed, the Municipality evaluates whether the actual construction is related to the outline contained in the technical file; if so, the Municipality grants its consent to the construction by means of a resolution, which recognizes legality in it.

b. Rules of Land Acquisition for Foreign Enterprises

There are no general restrictions on foreign ownership and / or occupation of real estate. Notwithstanding, the Constitution establishes that foreign citizens and / or legal entities cannot purchase or own, whether directly or indirectly, land which is located within fifty (50) kilometers from international borders, except in certain cases, when due to public necessity, the State allows them to acquire those properties. Such decision must be issued by means of a Supreme Decree approved by the Council of Ministers.

Apart from this limitation, there is no other restriction on the exercise of the property right due to the fact that the owner of the domain is a foreigner. In this sense, article 71 of the Constitution states that regarding the exercise of the property right, foreigners, whether individuals or legal entities, are in the same condition as Peruvians, without in any case invoking exception or diplomatic protection.

Finally, although the owner has in his favor all the possible faculties on his property right, the Civil Code does not allow him to limit the powers of disposal and encumbrance. That is, the owner cannot agree to the benefit of anyone that he will not sell the property nor give it as a collateral (either for a short or long period of time), because such agreements are considered null and void by law. All other faculties (with the exception of disposal and encumbrance, as already stated) the owner can temporarily self-limit them.

E. The Establishment and Dissolution of Companies

a. The Forms of Enterprises

From the various forms of enterprises, the following corporations are the most widely used ones by investors:
- Corporations (Sociedad Anónima or S.A.): the liability is limited to capital contributions of each of its members. Thus, shareholders are not responsible for paying corporate debt with their own assets.
- Closely Held Corporation (Sociedad Anónima Cerrada or S.A.C.): although it mainly is governed by the rules of the S.A., it has some special regulations it must comply with. It may only have up to twenty (20) shareholders, the Board of Directors is optional and all of the obligations and powers that are required for its administration will be granted to the General Manager and any other appointed representative.
- Open Corporation (Sociedad Anónima Abierta or S.A.A.): this type of corporation generally originates from a legal mandate, rather than by a shareholders' agreement. It (i) does a primary public offer of shares or obligations that can convert to shares; (ii) has more than seven hundred and fifty (750) shareholders; and, (iii) lists all off shares that represent their capital stock in the Capital Markets Public Registry.
- Limited Liability Company (Sociedad Comercial de Responsabilidad Limitada or S.R.L.): the liability of the partners is limited to capital contributions of each of its members. There is a minimum of two (2) partners which can either be individuals or legal persons and the maximum number is of twenty (20).

According to Peruvian law, the capital stock of corporations is represented by the shares and by shareholders' contributions, which can be either in cash or in kind. The General Shareholders' Meeting is the supreme decision-making body in the company.

Moreover, foreign companies can establish branch offices in Peru which is an extension of the Main Office and will depend on it for administrative, economic and political matters, although it does have some autonomy in some of its management aspects. Being the Main Office the one that adopts the vast majority of decisions, they assume full responsibility for the obligations of the branch. They are required to have a permanent legal representative with sufficient powers of attorney in order to function properly and that is domiciled in Peru.

b. The Procedure of Establishment

The procedure to establish corporate entities in Peru are commonly similar. Hereunder, are the procedures to follow in order to incorporate a corporation:
- First, you must confirm the availability of the intended corporate name.
- Secondly, the corporate documents must be elaborated and the deposit of the capital stock must be done (either by monetary or non-monetary contributions such as goods).
- Consequently, the Public Deed must be granted in order to submit it before the Peruvian Public Registry.
- Once the previous steps are done, the company must be registered before the tax authority, which is SUNAT (Superintendencia Nacional de Aduanas y de Administración Tributaria), in order to obtain a "Tax Identification Number" (RUC).
- Finally, the corporate books of the company must be legalized before a Notary Public.

The whole process can last, approximately, up to five (5) weeks. Additionally, there is not a minimum amount required for the capital stock. Nevertheless, the majority of companies are incorporated with an initial capital of S/ 1,000.00. It is important to consider that according to Peruvian law, the issued capital stock must be subscribed and paid in at least 25% of its total amount in order to incorporate a new company.

Additionally, if the constituent is foreign and located outside of Peru, then they shall provide the powers of attorney duly apostilled or by Consulate, depending if the country is subscribed to The Hague Conference on Private International Law.

c. Routes and Requirements of Dissolution

According to the General Corporations Law (Law No.26887), a company is dissolved for any of the following reasons:
- Expiry of term, operating in full right, except if an extension was previously approved and recorded in the Public Registry;
- Conclusion of its purpose, non-fulfilment of its purpose over a long period of time or a notable impossibility to fulfil it;
- Continuous inactivity of Shareholders' Meeting;

• Losses that reduce the net assets to an amount smaller than on third (1/3) if the paid capital, except if the losses are reimbursed or the capital paid is increased or reduced by a considerably big amount;

• Agreement of the creditor assembly, adopted in accordance with the pertinent law, or bankruptcy;

• A lack of plurality of partners and if such plurality is not re-established within a six (6) month period;

• Resolution adopted by the Supreme Court, in conformity with Article 410;

• Agreement of the general board, without the need of legal or statutory cause; and,

• Any other cause established in the law or considered in the articles of incorporation, in the bylaws or in a partner agreement registered with the company.

Additionally, the Law establishes the procedure to call for a meeting in order to adopt the dissolution agreement or the appropriate measures applicable. Once the matter is settled, the agreement must be published for three consecutive times in accordance to the provisions of the Law and then submit a registration request before the Public Registry. As a result, upon dissolving the company, the process for the liquidation will begin. When the company or companies' assets have been distributed, the extinction will be recorded in the Public Registry. Right after, the extinction shall be communicated through a written document to the Tax Authority (SUNAT).

F. Merger and Acquisition

The General Corporations Law (Law No.26887) regulates mergers as the process by which two or more companies join to form a single one, complying with all of the requirements prescribed by the present law.

There are two types of mergers: (i) when two or more companies join in order to create a new incorporated company, which causes the extinction of the legal personality of the incorporated company and the complete transfer of their assets to the new company; or, (ii) the takeover of one or more companies by an existing one, which results in the extinction of the legal personality of the company or companies being taken over. In this case, the company that takes over assumes all of the assets. Both of these circumstances result in giving the shareholders or the partners of the companies that no longer exist due to the merger, shares or holdings as shareholders or partners in the company taking over or of the new company, as applicable.

There are certain requirements in order to carry out a merger, as indicated hereafter:

• The Merger Agreement must be in accordance to the provisions established by law and the bylaws of the companies involved.

• The Board of Directors of each company involved must approve the text of the merger project. The votes in favour must be by the absolute majority of their members. If the company does not have this body, then the approval must be made by the majority of the people in charge of the companies' administration.

• The law establishes certain criteria that must be complied with and that shall be part of the content of the merger project.

• Once the merger project is drafted, then a general meeting or assembly must be called to deliberate over it. Bear in minds there are certain requirements to comply with for the call.

• When the approval of the merger project is agreed upon, then a common date for the merger will be established for it to enter into force. However, the merger is conditioned by the registration of the public deed in the Peruvian Public Registry. This registration will result in the extinction of the companies incorporated or taken over.

• The companies that as a result of the merger no longer exist must elaborate a balance sheet before the day that the merger enters into force and it has to be approved by the corresponding body.

• Regarding the merger agreements, they must be published accordingly to law for the established terms.

• For the merger of companies in liquidation, then the dissolution agreement must be revoked previous to the transformation, provided that the company´s assets are not yet distributed among its partners.

It should be noted that there is an Antitrust and Oligopoly Law in the Electric Sector (Law No.26876) and its Regulation, which establishes the requirement of a prior approval procedure applicable to mergers and acquisitions in such market, specifically in the activities of transmission, generation and distribution of energy.

In regard to the acquisition of companies, according to Peruvian Law it can be made through the purchase of assets (formalized in a sales and purchase agreement) and the purchase of shares under the General Corporations Law (Law No.26887). The corresponding agreement will be subscribed and the acquisition will be communicated to the company. In general, there are no restrictions for the acquisitions of private companies, unless of certain specific industries (e.g.Banking & Finance, among others). Moreover, the purchase of shares of companies that list their shares in the Securities Markets shall comply with certain requirements established by the Superintendency of Securities Market (e.g.the acquisition of shares must be made through a stock intermediary, or in the Lima Stock Exchange, which is the only stock exchange in Peru).

Additionally, there is currently a draft law for the Regulation of Corporate Mergers and Acquisitions Act. Its objective is to promote competition in order to benefit consumers, suppliers and, in general, the market.

G. Competition Regulation

a. Department Supervising Competition Regulation

The National Institute for the Defense of Free Competition and the Protection of Intellectual Property (INDECOPI) is the Peruvian specialized public agency in charge of controlling the proper functioning of the market and the efficiency of the competitive process. This institution has multiple supervisory and sanctioning faculties over Companies and other agents of the market to enforce compliance of the national competition regulation

b. Brief Introduction of Competition Law

The Peruvian competition legal framework is ruled by two main bodies of law:

a) Legislative Decree No.1034, Law on Repression of Anticompetitive Behaviors ("LD 1034")

LD 1034 is essentially an antitrust law. The purpose of this law is to promote and maintain competition within the Peruvian market, pursuing anticompetitive conducts that could harm its operation, regardless of the country and the sector in which these conducts are carried out.

According to this regulation, anticompetitive practices can be catalogued under two different modalities:

(i) Abuse of a dominant position: In this scenario, one company seeks to exclude other competitors, allowing it to obtain (or preserve) a dominant position in the market. The alleged monopolist must possess sufficient power in an accurately defined market for its products or services, to the point that the competitors have no chance of stopping it.

Bundle sales; the refuse of doing business with another agent; and the imposition of exclusive or non-competition agreements (when they are not reasonable) are considered -among others- as abusive practices of dominant position.

(ii) Collusion agreements between independent companies to undermine legitimate competition (cartels): Cartels join forces to fix prices, limit production, distribute clients or share markets between them (among other practices), avoiding natural competition.

As a rule, cartels between companies that operate in the same level of the market chain are always illegal. However, collusions performed in a different level of the market chain (such as agreements between manufacturers and dealers) must be analyzed to determine its legality. Likewise, to punish this type of conducts at least one of the involved agents must first have a dominant position in the relevant market.

These conducts are analyzed under two types of prohibitions:

(i) Per se rule, which requires no further inquiry into the effects of the practice on the market or the intentions of those individuals who engaged in the conduct. In this scenario, the authority determines that there is a breach of the antitrust regulation merely by proving that the conduct occurred. As stated before, cartels between companies of the same level in the market chain are subject to this rule in general, and will always be considered illegal.

(ii) Rule of reason, which requires analyzing whether the practice promotes or suppresses market competition. To punish the breach INDECOPI must not only prove that the conduct occurred, but it should also demonstrate that it has (or could have) negative effects on the market competition and the welfare of the consumers. Practices of abuse of dominant position are analyzed under the Rule of Reason.

LD 1034 states that anticompetitive conducts do not qualify as criminal offenses and are not subject to criminal liability.

It is important to point out that competition regulation does not establish a control over mergers and acquisitions. Prior approval from the antitrust authority is only required in concentration operations executed by companies of the electrical market, if the operation surpasses a certain legal threshold. This authorization is not required in other markets.

To date there are several initiatives in the Congress that aim to regulate a general pre-merger notification system, which has become more relevant after the execution of several acquisitions in the pharmaceutical market of Peru, which could lead to a possible monopoly. These projects are currently being discussed in the committees of the Congress, and are pending of debate and approval.

b) Legislative Decree No.1044, Law on Suppression of Unfair Competition ("LD 1044")

LD 1044 aims to suppress any unfair competition practice that objectively violates the duty of good faith that companies must observe in the market, which may cause harm to consumers or enterprises through unethical commercial behaviours. The scope of this law covers all economic agents that participate in the national market that may attempt to gain unfair competitive advantages.

The definition of "unfair competition practice" is quite broad and applies to any commercial activity, regardless of the form they adopt and the means used to carry them out (including advertisement). Therefore, any act that implies an illegitimate obstruction of other companies (damaging their position in the market) would be deemed as unfair.

On the other hand, LD 1044 states the following conditions to consider that a practice qualifies as unfair competition:

(i) It is not required to prove conscience or will about the realization of the conduct.

(ii) It is not necessary to verify an effective damage in the market as a consequence of the unfair conduct (the harmful effects of the behaviour could be potential).

(iii) No direct competitive relationship between the agent affected by the unfair conduct and the offender is required.

Frequent examples of unfair competition acts are breach of professional secrets, misappropriation of commercial reputation, misleading imitations and deceptive advertisement, among others.

Unfair competition acts do not qualify as criminal offenses.

c. Measures Regulating Competition

LD 1034 does establish a scale of economic fines for Companies that violate the antitrust regulation, which may vary between 1 UIT[①] and more than 1000 UIT[②], depending of the severity of the infringement. INDECOPI is also empowered to sanction the members of the Board of Directors of a Company if they are directly liable for the promotion of the anticompetitive practice. The economic fines for Directors may reach up to 100 UIT.

On the other hand, infringements to unfair competition regulation (LD 1044) are subject to economic fines that range between 1 UIT and 700 UIT.

H. Tax

a. Tax Regime and Rules

In Peru, the competent tax authority is the National Superintendency of Customs and Tax Administration (Superintendencia Nacional de Aduanas y de Administración Tributaria), a technical specialized organism attached to the Ministry of Economy and Finance. It establishes a legal framework in tax and customs matters, as well as its internal organization.

The tax regime will be applied to individuals who are considered domiciled in the country. On the other hand, foreigners qualify as domiciled if they have stayed in the country for more than one hundred and eighty (180) days during a 12-month period. In this sense, they will pay taxes on their worldwide income, which include any income that comes from foreign sources.

Likewise, companies that are established or incorporated in Peru will be considered as domiciled for tax purposes. These companies include an agency, a branch or any other permanent establishments whose entities were incorporated abroad but which operate in Peru. It should be noted that only the income generated in Peru by the agency, branch or other permanent establishment will be subject to taxation.

b. Main Categories and Rates of Tax

a) Corporate Income Tax

The following legal entities are considered domiciled in Peru: legal entities incorporated in Peru, as well as branch offices, agencies, and other permanent businesses in Peru belonging to individuals or legal entities which are not domiciled in the country. With respect to the latter, tax is only levied upon Peruvian source income.

Corporate Income Tax is determined by applying a rate of 29.5% on the total amount of this income minus expenses incurred in generating it, i.e. on net returns obtained by the companies on an annual basis irrespective of their company structure.

Moreover, profit sharing carried out by companies is taxed with a tax rate of 5%, except when the beneficiary is another domiciled legal entity.

Expenses derived from transactions carried out directly or indirectly with residents of tax havens are not accepted as deductible expenses for income tax purposes.

Companies are required to make tax pre-payments, which are determined using one of the two systems established by Income Tax Law regarding net income obtained during the month.

The fiscal year begins on January 1 and ends on December 31, with no exceptions. At the end of each fiscal year, the annual tax is calculated. Pre-payments are deducted from the balance and the difference is paid as a regularization payment attached to the tax return statement containing the end-of-year balance. This regularization payment and the tax return need to be completed within 3 months of fiscal year end.

Net income obtained by taxpayers can be offset against losses under two systems:

(i) Charging the losses (until exhausting the amount) against the income obtained in the following four

---

① UIT: Unidad Impositiva Tributaria. The Ministry of Economy and Finance has established that the value of 1 UIT for the period of 2018 is of S/ 4,150.00.

② The fine cannot exceed the 12% of the gross income received by the offender or its economic group.

(4) fiscal years; or,

(ii) Charging the losses against 50% of the net income obtained in the fiscal year, without time limits.

Accounting ledgers, records, and other tax accounting information must be kept during statute of limitation period, as appropriate.

b) Value Added Tax (VAT)

The Sales Tax (VAT) is a tax levied upon value added in each transaction at various stages of the business cycle. Applicable rate: 18% (including 2% Municipal Promotion Tax).

The Sales Tax is levied upon the following operations in Peru:
- Sale of personal property;
- The provision of services;
- The use of services;
- Construction contracts performed;
- The first sale of real property built directly by constructors;
- The import of goods.

Sales Tax Law contains a number of exemptions; among the main ones: the transfer of assets carried out as a consequence of company restructuring, the transfer of used goods carried out by individuals or legal entities who do not perform any legal business activity, among others.

The Taxpayer is the person performing the taxable activity, i.e.who sells goods and provides services, imports affected goods, among others.

The VAT follows the debit / credit system, under which the VAT paid upon acquisitions (input tax) is offset against the VAT of the sale (output tax).

c) Temporary Tax on Net Assets (ITAN)

The Temporary Tax on Net Assets taxes the net assets of the companies according to their balance sheets. If the value of the net assets exceeds one million Soles (US$ 307,692.00), the excess amount is taxed with 0.4%.

The company can deduct the amount payed for the ITAN from the IT.

d) Financial Transactions Tax

Tax levied on bank transactions in national and foreign currency.

The applicable rate is 0.005% on the value of the transaction. The Financial Transaction Tax is deductible for Income Tax purposes.

e) Real Estate Property Tax (Impuesto Predial)

Tax applied on the total value of the real estate declared by the owner. The taxpayer is the real estate owner registered by January 1st of each year.

The tax is calculated according to the following cumulative scale:

Real State Value	Tax Rate
Up to 15 UIT	0.2%
More than 15 UIT and up to 60 UIT	0.6%
More than 60 UIT	1.0%

(*) 1 UIT (Tax Unit) is equivalent to S/4,150.00 for 2018.

f) Alcabala Tax

This tax is levied on the acquisition of real property. The tax rate is 3% and the tax base is the real estate value.

g) Other local taxes

h) Vehicle ownership tax

It levies vehicles and ships

i) Municipal taxes

It is a rate that should be paid by people who own real property and who benefit from the public services rendered by the local Municipality. Some of the municipal taxes include the following services: street cleaning, garbage collection, maintenance of parks and green areas, patrolling guards, etc. The amount of taxes is based in the effective cost of the public services rendered.

j) Municipal license

It is the rate paid in order to obtain the municipal authorization required for opening a commercial, industrial or service establishment.

c. Tax Declaration and Preference

Peruvian regulation establishes certain tax preferences in order to encourage investment in general, including foreign investment. These preferences can be noticed in stability agreements and in various sectors of our industry. Please refer to Section J literal a, which gives a broader approach to the matter.

I. Securities

a. Brief Introduction of Securities-related Laws and Regulations

According to Peruvian law, securities are freely tradable instruments which are issued in bulk, that grant their holders credit, property rights or ownership, or rights over the issuer's capital, profits or equity.

The main securities-related laws and regulations are the following:
- Supreme Decree No.093-2002-EF, which approves the Securities Markets Law;
- Law No.27287, which approves the Securities Act;
- Legislative Decree No.862, which approves the Investment Funds and Management Companies Act;
- Executive Order No.26126, which approves the Organic Law of the Supervising Commission of Companies and Securities;
- Law No.29440, which approves the Payment Systems and Liquidation of Securities and its Regulation approved by Resolution SMV No.027-2012-SMV/01;
- Resolution CONASEV No.141-1998, which approves the Regulations for the Initial Public Offerings and Sales of Securities (in force since 1998);
- Law No. 26702, which approves the Peruvian Banking Law.

b. Supervision and Regulation of Securities Market

According to Supreme Decree No. 093-2002-EF, the Supervising of Companies and Securities National Commission (Comisión Nacional Supervisora de Empresas y Valores – CONASEV) now called the Superintendency of Securities Markets (SMV) is the public institution in charge of the supervision of the mentioned law, as well as its enforcement.

Furthermore, another entity which provides regulation in terms of security trading is the Lima Stock Exchange. This is stock exchange house in Peru, were its internal regulation is subject to the regulations that govern the trading and offering of securities.

Another entity that should be noted in this regard is CAVALI (Registro Central de Valores y Liquidaciones), which is in charge of the creation, maintenance and development of the infrastructure of the national securities markets.

c. Requirements for Engagement in Securities Trading for Foreign Enterprises

In accordance to the Capital Markets Law, the Public Offering of Securities is subject to certain legal provisions, which include the elaboration and registration of a prospectus before the SMV. An offer will qualify as public usually if it is directed towards one hundred (100) or more people (the number can be fewer than of one hundred, it will depend on the concrete case), although this should be reviewed on a case to case basis. Nonetheless, if an offering is only directed towards Institutional Investors it is not subject to the restriction above mentioned, as it qualifies as a private offering. Likewise, if the offer of securities is of S/ 250,000.00 or more, then such offer will not be considered as public either.

J. Preference and Protection of Investment

a. The Structure of Preference Policies

Tax stability agreements: Investors and corporations committed to invest in the country can enter into an agreement with the Peruvian Government in order to guarantee that the basic rules (including certain tax rules) in force at the moment of the execution of the agreement will remain the same over time. Once these agreements have been executed, they cannot be unilaterally modified by the State, allowing the investors to have certainty as to the rules governing their investment in Peru during a reasonable term.

b. Support for Specific Industries and Regions

Peruvian regulation established certain tax incentive schemes in order to encourage investment in general, which includes foreign investment:
- Agrarian regime: This regime is applicable to companies that grow crops and / or breeding of animals, except for activities considered to be part of the forest industry. Also, companies that carry out agro-industrial activities will be under this regime, provided that they use agricultural products outside the province of Lima.

Benefits: Income Tax rate is reduced to 15%; among others.

• Amazon regime: Applicable to companies located in the Amazon region and which perform the following economic activities: (i) agriculture; (ii) aquaculture; (iii) fishing; (iv) tourism, among others.

Benefits: (i) Income Tax rates can be as low as 10%, 5% and 0%; and, (ii) companies located in the Amazon also are exempted from VAT from the sale of goods and services made into the Amazon region.

• Early Recovery of VAT Regime: This regime grants the right to recover VAT paid in the import and / or local acquisition of goods or services in the pre-productive stage of a project, which can later be used in the execution of a project regulated under an investment contract entered into with the Peruvian Government.

In order to qualify for this regime, companies must meet the following requirements:

• Enter into an investment contract with the Peruvian Government;
• Such project will require an equal or greater productive stage of two (2) years;
• An investment commitment of no less than US$ 5'000,000.00.This amount does not include the VAT;
• A Ministerial Resolution issued by the competent Ministry.

c. Special Economic Areas

Traditionally, the Peruvian economy has been known for the prominent role of the mining industry and the strong support of its financial sector. However, the country also holds a diversified range of economic activities which are constantly expanding and reaching out to international markets:

• Agribusiness Sector: Peruvian participation in this sector has multiplied in the past decade. Our companies are the second sugarcane producers in the world, third asparagus and olives producers worldwide, and are about to become the first producers of avocados in the international market; among others. We must also add the Seasonal windows in the most important markets.

• Fishing Sector: Peru is finally benefitting from the diversity of species and favourable climate conditions for the development of aquaculture. As a result, Peru is the first producer in the world of fish oil and fishmeal.

• Textile Sector: One of our products, pima cotton, is one of the most highly-appraised fibres in the world. Also, Peru is one of the leading producers of the finest fibres of South American camelids (i.e.alpaca and vicuña).

• Mining Sector: Peru has the largest silver reserves worldwide, as well as holding some of the most significant copper and zinc reserves. It is also one of the few countries with non-metallic mineral deposits.

• Energy Sector: Peru has great energy potential because of the wide availability of water and natural gas resources which have allowed an increasing electricity demand in the country.

• Real Estate Sector: The significant growth of the economy is promoting greater demand for housing, shopping malls, commercial offices, hotels and recreational houses. Demand for real estate has vastly boosted investment in this sector. Therefore, the real estate sector in Peru will be booming with infrastructure projects tendered out in 2014, which together amount over US$10 billion.

d. Investment Protection

• No restrictions to foreign investors

The Constitution of Peru does not establish any absolute restriction on foreign ownership and investment in specific industry sectors. In that sense, foreign individuals or companies and Peruvian investors have the same status and shall be treated under the same conditions.

Furthermore, according to the Constitution of Peru, the property right is inviolable except under exceptional circumstances, when expropriation shall be allowed only if payment of a fair indemnification, which includes a compensation for eventual damages, is made.

Notwithstanding the above mentioned, foreign companies or individuals cannot purchase or own mines, land, forests, water, fuel or energy sources, whether directly or indirectly, within fifty (50) kilometers from international borders, except in certain cases, when due to public necessity, they are specifically allowed to acquire such properties by means of a Supreme Decree approved by the Council of Ministers.

Moreover, Supreme Decree No.162-92-EF authorizes foreign investors to carry out any economic activity of their choice in compliance with the Peruvian Constitution, Laws and Treaties. However, activities that are going to be developed in reserved natural protected areas and the manufacturing of war weapons are not included in this consideration, pursuant to Legislative Decree No.757.

It must be noted that only few restrictions approved by specific legislation applies to foreign investment. For example, there are some restrictions which apply to: (i) broadcasting services; and, (ii) air and maritime transportation; since these activities are reserved exclusively for Peruvian investors or otherwise require a majority stake by Peruvian investors.

• International treaties

In the past few decades, Peru has significantly increased its participation in international organizations in order to position itself in the international market and attract foreign investment. Following is a list of the main international treaty organizations in which Peru is a member:

- Andean Community (Comunidad Andina — CAN): Peru joined this organization back in 1969, when a few South American countries decided to execute the Cartagena Treaty. Current state members are Bolivia, Colombia and Ecuador. This organization provides free-trade benefits to all state members.

- World Trade Organization (WTO): Peru became a member of the WTO since its creation in 1995. This organization, which has over 160 members, is a forum which allows governments worldwide to negotiate trade agreements.

- Latin American Integration Association (Asociación Latinoamericana de Integración—ALADI): This organization has 13 state members (Argentina, Bolivia, Brazil, Chile, Colombia, Cuba, Ecuador, México, Panama, Paraguay, Peru, Uruguay and Venezuela) which can benefit from preferential tariffs in transactions held among each other.

Also, Peru has signed various free-trade agreements with countries which are not part of the CAN or ALADI, such as:
- Trade Promotion Agreement with USA, in force since February 1st, 2009;
- Free-trade Agreement with Canada, in force since August 1st, 2009;
- Free-trade Agreement with Chile, in force since March 1st, 2009;
- Free-trade Agreement with Costa Rica, in force since June 1st, 2013;
- Free-trade Agreement with Panama, in force since May 1st, 2012;
- Free-trade Agreement with the European Union, in force since March 1st, 2013;
- Free-trade Agreement with the European Free Trade Association, in force since July 1st, 2012;
- Free-trade Agreement with the People´s Republic of China, in force since March 1st, 2010.

III. Trade

A. Department Supervising Trade

The Ministry of Foreign Trade and Tourism (Ministerio del Comercio Exterior y Turismo) is the entity in charge of executing, coordinating and supervising foreign trade policies.

The Ministry of Foreign Trade and Tourism, within the framework of its powers, establishes the regulations for the development of foreign trade activities without prohibitions or tariff restrictions that affect the import or export of goods. Likewise, it supervises compliance with the regulatory framework issued, establishing sanctions and imposing them, if applicable, within the scope of its jurisdiction.

Within the framework of the basic organizational structure of the Ministry, it is the responsibility of the Minister to formulate the national policies in his sector and to execute and supervise their application in harmony with the general policy of the government. The Minister may delegate the aforementioned powers to the Vice Minister, who shall fulfill them on request.

B. Brief Introduction of Trade Laws and Regulations

The practical experience of the past two decades has proven Peru to be friendly to both local and foreign investment. The Peruvian Government has ensured that the Peruvian Constitution and the relevant rules and regulations endorse principles favorable to an open market for potential investors interested in developing projects in Peru.

Peru's foreign investment regime is governed by Legislative Decree 662, the Foreign Investment Promotion Law, and Legislative Decree 757, Framework Law for Private Investment, published on September 9, 1991 and November 13, 1991, respectively. Both laws are regulated by Supreme Decree 162-92-EF of October 12, 1992.

Legislative Decree 662 created mechanisms to guarantee foreign investors with tax and legal stability; availability of foreign currency; and nondiscriminatory treatment between national and foreign investors, to stimulate flows of foreign capital.

Legislative Decree 757 contains provisions required for growth of private investment in all economic sectors, including the elimination of all legal and administrative barriers and distortions blocking economic development and restricting free private initiative, leaving competition to the companies in the private sector. It also established basic provisions regarding taxes, protecting investors from arbitrary changes.

On September 11, 1991, Legislative Decree 668 was enacted, becoming the legal framework of Peru's foreign trade system, guaranteeing trade liberty as an essential condition for the country development. This legislative decree guarantees the use and disposal of foreign currency, as well as the free convertibility of the national currency at a single exchange rate.

The Legislative Decree 1053, the General Trade Law in force, establishes as a general principle, that customs services are essential to facilitate foreign trade. The purpose of this Law is to make more expeditious the procedures of import and export of goods.

C. Trade Management

a. Free Trade Zone

Peru has the following Free Trade Zones: Tacna Free Zone (Zofra Tacna) and Especial Development Zones: located in Matarani, Paita and Ilo.

For customs purposes these zones are considered to be outside of Peruvian territory. Consequently, a special tax regime is applied for all the goods entering into the Free Trade Zone and Especial Development Zones. Currently, Zofra Tacna this zone is considered a strategic access point for South American and Asia-Pacific markets.

The Free Trade Zone and Especial Development Zones offers tax and customs benefits for companies performing industrial activities, agribusiness, assembly and services carried out in the Free Trade Zones and Especial Development Zones (e.g.packing, labeling, maintenance and / or refurbishment of machinery, call center activities, software development, between others).

b. Treaties

On to date, Peru has a wide range of regional and multilateral trade agreements, which generate opportunities for the development of our exportable offer and the business sector.

Recently, the Ministry has signed the following treaties:

a) Multilateral Agreements

World Trade Organization (WTO): The World Trade Organization (WTO) which deals with the rules that govern trade in countries around the world. Accordingly, the WTO rules on anti-dumping, subsidies and countervailing measures are applicable in the country.

b) Regional Agreements

Andean Community of Nations (CAN) — Bolivia, Colombia, Ecuador, and Peru: Similarly, Peru is currently a member of the Andean Community (CAN), made up by Peru, Colombia, Bolivia and Ecuador. Trade between these countries has a total tariff reduction constituting a Free Trade area.

c) Bilateral Agreements

Peru has signed Bilateral Agreements with the following countries:
- Australia;
- Canada;
- Chile;
- China;
- Costa Rica;
- Cuba;
- European Free Trade Association (EFTA) — Switzerland, Iceland, Liechtenstein, and Norway;
- European Union;
- Japan;
- Mexico;
- Panama;
- Singapore;
- South Korea;
- Southern Common Market (MERCOSUR) — Argentina, Brazil, Paraguay, and Uruguay;
- Thailand;
- United States;
- Venezuela.

d) Other memberships

Peru it is also a member of the Asia - Pacific Economic Cooperation Forum (APEC). This agreement seeks the expansion and diversification of commercial exchange and the elimination of tariff and non-tariff restrictions that affect the reciprocal exchange of goods and services.

Finally, on 2017, the Agreement on Trade Facilitation (AFC) of the World Trade Organization (WTO) entered into force. The measures linked to foreign trade, streamline and simplify the procedures related to the clearance of goods, reduce the flow of goods and generate equality in the decisions of the control entities.

D. The Inspection and Quarantine of Import and Export Commodities

National Superintendence of Customs and Tax Administration (Superintendencia Nacional de Aduanas y de Administración Tributaria — SUNAT) is the Peruvian Customs Authority.

Nevertheless, in Peru there is no unique body that verifies the sanitary requirements of agricultural products or of restricted or prohibited goods, given that there is an agency assigned to each type of product that enters to Peru. For example:

• Any plant or plant-based product that enters the country must be inspected by the National Service of Health and Agro-Food Quality (Servicio Nacional de Sanidad y Calidad Agroalimentaria—SENASA) in the authorized External Control Offices (Puestos de Control Externo—PCCE).

SENASA is the authority with exclusive competence to issue mandatory phyto-sanitary and zoo-sanitary measures aimed at the prevention, control or eradication of pests and diseases.

SENASA will approve and publish the list of quarantine pests and notifiable diseases for the country, and will implement mechanisms to strengthen an efficient notification process. SENASA is the competent authority in the country that elaborates the official report of pests and diseases.

• National Institute of Natural Resources (Instituto Nacional de Recursos Naturales—INRENA): Regulates the entry and exit of endangered species of wild flora and fauna.

• The National Institute for the Defense of Competition and Protection of Intellectual Property (Instituto Nacional de Defensa de la Competencia y de la Protección de la Propiedad Intelectual—Indecopi) and the General Directorate of Environmental Health (Dirección General de Salúd Ambiental—DIGESA) are entitled to control whether the label complies with all the legal information necessary for the commercialization of the imported goods. DIGESA is the competent authority that verifies the labelling requirements of the products at the moment of the import, while Indecopi is the competent authority that supervises the labelling requirements once the imported products are commercialized in the Peruvian territory; immediately afterwards they are nationalized (the merchandise is nationalized once the Customs Authority grants the release of the goods to the importer).

E. Customs Management

The main regulatory body in customs matters is the Peruvian Customs General Law approved by Legislative Decree 1053 (CGL) and its Regulations approved by Supreme Decree 010-2009-EF (CGLR).[1] These rules regulates the legal relationship established between SUNAT and natural and legal persons, who intervene in the entry, stay, and exit of goods to, within and from the customs territory, respectively, the customs regimes and customs infractions.

Below, we will detail briefly the customs modalities for customs dispatch and the export and import regimes.

a. Import Procedure

a) Modalities and Deadlines for Assigning the Goods to Import Regime

For assigning merchandises to the "import for consumption regime" certain formal obligations shall be fulfilled, for example, the electronic transmission of the Customs Declaration (Declaración Aduanera de Mercancías — DAM).

The goods can be assigned to the import for consumption regime under the following modalities:

• In the advance dispatch: By filing the DAM within the term of fifteen (15) calendar days before the arrival of the transport. Once this period has expired, the merchandise will be submitted to the exceptional dispatch.[2]

• In the urgent dispatch: By filing the DAM within the term of fifteen (15) calendar days before the arrival of the transport until seven (7) calendar days counted from the following day the unload is finished.

• In the exceptional dispatch: By filing the DAM within the term of thirty (30) calendar days counted from the following day the unload is finished.

b) Tax Regime Applicable to Imports

Definitive imports (requested through import for consumption regime) are generally subject to the payment of import duties. The exact amount of duties varies depending on the type of merchandise.

(i) Ad Valorem Duties

Ad valorem duties are levied on the cost, insurance and freight (CIF) value of the goods concerned. Current

---

[1] You can also see the Customs Authority's official webpage: http://www.sunat.gob.pe/orientacionaduanera/index.html.
[2] This procedure was approved through the Customs Resolution 063-2010-SUNAT-A.

tax rates, according to domestic law, are: 0%, 4%, 6% and 11%[1].

These rates can be reduced up to 0% depending if certain Free Trade Agreement (FTA) is applicable due to the country of origin of the goods.

(ii) Specific Duties — System of Price Levels

The System of Price Levels applies to imports of certain agricultural products such as rice, yellow corn, milk and sugar. The system imposes additional specific custom duties when international prices are below a certain level and discounts on the customs duties when such prices are above certain level, as determined in specific customs tables.[2]

(iii) Value Added Tax

Value added tax (VAT) is regulated by the Single Unified Text of the Value Added Tax and Excise Tax Law, approved by Supreme Decree 055-99-EF (VATL) and the Regulations approved by Supreme Decree 29-94-EF (VATR).

VAT is imposed at the rate of 18% on the CIF value of imported goods plus tariffs and other customs duties.

(iv) Excise Tax

Excise tax (ET) is also regulated by the VATL and the VATR.ET is levied on the importation of certain goods, such as fuel, soft drinks, vehicles, alcoholic drinks (for example, wine, beer and pisco) and cigarettes. Rates vary depending on the type of goods concerned.

c) Documents Filed with the Import for Consumption DAM

As a general rule, the following documents are required for the importation of merchandises, together with the DAM:[3]

(i) Original invoice;
(ii) Transportation Document (Bill of Lading or Airway Bill);
(iii) Insurance document for merchandise transportation;
(iv) Authorizations issued by the competent sector; and
(v) Other documents required according to the nature of the import.

b. Export Procedure

For assigning merchandises, to the export regime certain formalities obligations shall be fulfilled, for example, the electronic transmission of the Customs statement (DAM).

a) Tax Regime Applicable to Exports

In Peru, exports are not subject to Customs Duties, ET or VAT.

b) Documents Filed with the Export DAM

As a general rule, the following documents are required together with the export DAM[4]:

(i) Simplified Export Statement;
(ii) Original invoice;
(iii) Certificate of origin;
(iv) Insurance document for merchandise transportation; and
(v) Other documents required due to the nature of the export.

IV. Labour

A. Brief Introduction of Labour Laws and Regulations

Labour matters in Peru are primarily governed by Sole Unified Text of Legislative Decree 728, Law of Labour Productivity and Competitiveness, approved by Supreme Decree 003-97-TR (Labour Law), together with regulations promulgated under that law. The Labour Law is enforced by the Ministry of Labour and Promotion of Employment (Ministerio del Trabajo y Promoción del Empleo) and its entities (Labour Authority), and labour-related litigation is competence of local Peruvian courts.

The Labour Law governs all aspects of employment relationships, which includes, but is not limited to the maintenance of records, payment of wages and legal benefits, hours of work and leave, end of service benefits, internal regulations, as well as the safety and health at work regulations, labour inspections and the termination of

---

[1] Supreme Decree 342-2016-EF.
[2] Supreme Decree 115-2001-EF.
[3] Regulations under the CGL (CGLR), art.60; and Resolution of Superintendence 10-2015-SUNAT 5C0000.
[4] CGLR, art.60.

employment relationships.

The Labour Law applies to all employees working in Peru, whether national or non-national, within the private sector regime. Note that employees of the Government within departments that constitute public services, members of the armed forces, police, and similar; are exempt from the scope of the Labour Law.

The Labour Law sets out the minimum rights and guarantees granted to private sector employees in Peru to the effect that any agreement between an employer and an employee that affects, restricts or denies employee rights is void, considering the inalienable and non-renounceable character of labour rights.

In addition, an employee cannot waive or assign the rights and guarantees provided by the law.

Under the Labour Law, when the facts are in conflict with the provisions of an employment agreement the facts will prevail over the terms of the agreement.

B. Requirements of Employing Foreign Employees

a. Work Permit

Foreign employees who are in Peru under labor agreements previously approved by the Labor Authority are entitled to the same labor rights and benefits as Peruvian citizens. Employers are able to hire foreign employees to the extent of up to 20% of their total work force, provided the remuneration of such employees does not exceed 30% of total payroll. Foreign labor agreements must be in writing and for fixed-terms of up to three years. Such agreements may be renewed successively for equal periods.

However, employers may request an exemption from these limitations on the employment of foreigners in the case of —among others-:
- Specialized professional or technical personnel; and,
- Management and / or general personnel involved in a new corporate activity, or in the case of corporate restructuring.

Similarly, the following cases—among others—are not subjected to the formalities or limitations for hiring foreign employees:
- Foreigners who have Peruvian spouse, ascendants, descendants or brothers;
- Foreigners enjoying immigrant visas;
- Foreigners whose country of origin has reciprocal labour or dual citizenship agreements.

b. Application Procedure

Labor agreements — with foreign employees — must be submitted for approval to the Labor Authority. The approval process does not take more than five working days (or three weeks in cases where additional information is required). The Labor Authority's approval of a labor agreement is not sufficient for a foreign employee to commence work. The foreign employee will also need to obtain a visa approved by the National Migration Office (Superintendencia Nacional de Migraciones) before being able to work.

c. Social Insurance

a) Peruvian Nationals and Non-Peruvian Nationals

Social Security services, which comprehend both health insurances and pension funds are governed by the Peruvian Social Security Health Insurance (Seguro Social de Salud del Perú — EsSalud) created by Decree Law 22482, as well as the Law for the Modernization of Social Security, approved by Law 26790. Rules set forth in these mentioned laws are applicable for all employees or personnel — whether Peruvian nationals or non-Peruvian, in which case, it is mandatory that these latter have been issued a Foreign ID card (Carné de Extranjería) by the relevant authority — rendering services under a labor relationship with a local company that must be duly incorporated in the country. Such employees shall be registered in the payrolls of the company within the first day of commencement of employment. This term is also applicable for purposes of EsSalud, being that for purposes of pension funds, the registry may be done within the following ten days as of the commencement of employment.

Business owners, freelancers, contractors, self-employed professionals, among other kind of personnel that is not within a labor relationship; and therefore, not registered in the local company's payroll, are excluded from the scope of the Peruvian Social Security, regardless of their nationality.

Social insurance in the form of public healthcare EsSalud is available for Peruvian nationals and non-Peruvian nationals holding a Foreign ID card, as consequence of a labor relationship with a local company, both of which are entitled to free access to the assigned and relevant hospitals. EsSalud comprehends a mandatory contribution of the employer and equals to the 9% of the gross monthly remuneration of each employee.

Pension fund system in Peru includes a National Pension System which is under the responsibility of the Government Pension Fund Office (Oficina de Normalización Previsional — ONP); and, the Private Pension

System which is managed by the existing Pension Fund Management Companies (Administradoras de Fondos de Pensiones — AFP). Applicable employees are entitled to choosing which system to contribute. Contribution to any of the Pension Systems is paid by each applicable employee mandatorily and the employer must withhold the corresponding percentage from the employee's monthly salary.

b) Foreign Expatriates

As mentioned in previous points, non-Peruvian nationals that do not have a Foreign ID card as consequence of a labor relationship with a local company that is duly incorporated in the country, are excluded from the scope of the Peruvian Social Security system, which includes both health insurance and pension funds.

C. Exit and Entry

The Peruvian laws on foreigners, requires all foreign individuals entering Peru to hold the appropriate migratory status or visa during while they remain in the country.

a. Visa Types

Depending on the nationality of the applicant, visa applications may be filed with the Peruvian Consulate abroad or the National Migration Office.

Foreign individuals wishing to enter and / or to stay in Peru must have a valid passport (minimum of six months of validity) or similar document; and, the corresponding visa, if required. Foreign citizens may be admitted into Peru under any of the following visas or migratory statuses:

Temporary	Tourist
	International Agreements
	Business
	Artist or Athletes
	Special
	Detached Employee
	Training/Temporary Investigation
	Business
	Detached Employee Temporary
	Crew Member
	Journalist
Resident	Diplomatic
	Consular
	Detached Employee
	Official
	Cooperating
	Exchange
	Investigation
	Political Asylum
	Humanitarian
	Religious
	Student

(Continued)

Resident	Employee
	Independent
	Rentier
	Family
	Suspended
	Training
	Immigrant
	International Agreements

Approval of a visa by the National Migration Office may take up to approximately 45 business days. Visas may be classified as follows:
- Temporary: admission and stay of the foreign citizen is authorized for up to 90 days (extendible); or
- Resident: admission and stay of the foreign citizen is authorized for periods of one year.

Temporary and resident visas are granted based on the migratory status of the individual, according to the chart above. The most common types of visa or migratory status established by the Peruvian immigration law are described below:

a) Tourist Visa

Temporary visa granted to foreign citizens who enter Peru not to take up residence, but for sightseeing, recreational activities and the like. The visa does not allow an individual to perform remunerated or other for-profit activities in the country. Chinese citizens are exempted from requesting this type of visa, to the extent that these latter demonstrate (i) being holders of a visa with a minimum validity of six months to the United States of America, Great Britain, Australia or any country member of Schengen community; or, (ii) being holders of a permanent residence to the United States of America, Canada, Great Britain, Australia or any country member of Schengen community.

b) Business Visa

Temporary visa addressed to foreign citizens who enter into the country not to take up residence but to conduct arrangements of a business nature or related activities. The period of permanence is 183 days, cumulative during a period of 365 days, which cannot be extended. Chinese citizens are exempted from requesting this type of visa, to the extent that these latter demonstrate (i) being holders of a visa with a minimum validity of six months to the United States of America, Great Britain, Australia or any country member of Schengen community; or, (ii) being holders of a permanent residence to the United States of America, Canada, Great Britain, Australia or any country member of Schengen community.

c) Detached Employee Visa

This type of visa can be given on a temporary or resident basis and is granted to those citizens who enter the country to carry out work-related activities commissioned by their employer abroad, and for a limited and defined period to perform a specific task or function, or a job that requires professional, commercial, technical or highly specialized knowledge. Individuals holding such visa are not allowed to perform remunerated or other for-profit activities, or to receive income from Peruvian sources, other than the income they receive from their employer. The period of permanence is 365 days.

d) Resident Employee Visa

Resident visa applicable to foreign citizens entering Peru to provide their personal services under an employment agreement previously approved by the Labor Authority.

e) Training Visa

Visa granted to foreign citizens entering Peru for purposes of studying in educational institutions or centers recognized by the Peruvian Government. Such individuals are not allowed to receive income from Peruvian sources, except when the foreign citizens have received special permission to work granted by the National Migration Office.

Once the resident visa has been approved, the foreign citizen is required to register before the Central Register of Foreigners at the National Migration Office and will be granted the relevant Foreign ID. Foreign individuals must carry their Foreign ID card with them at all times while they are in Peru.

b. Restrictions for Exit and Entry

Non-compliance with Peruvian immigration laws and regulations, such as the stay in the country exceeding the time permitted by the granted visa, among others, is punishable with monetary fines, compulsory exit, cancellation of stay, cancellation of residence visa and / or expulsion.

D. Trade Union and Labour Organizations

Employee rights to join unions, collective bargaining and strike are protected under the Peruvian Constitution.

a. Unions

Union affiliation is voluntary. To be a member of a union, an employee must work in an enterprise or be involved in an activity, profession or occupation that corresponds to the type of union concerned. Managers and executive employees are not allowed to be members of unions, unless otherwise established by the by-laws of the company. The minimum number of employees depends on the type of union. To be constituted and subsist, a Company Union must have a minimum of 20 employees; other types of unions (i.e., an Activity Union, a Guild Union, or Various Occupations Union) require a minimum of 50 employees. Employers may deduct union fees from the monthly salary of their employees, provided they are expressly authorized to do so by the employees concerned.

b. Union Immunity

In general terms, union laws protects union members and their representatives from dismissal and guarantees that they will not be transferred to other establishments of the employer company, without a duly proven fair reason or without the employees' acceptance. Employee acceptance is not required when a change of establishment within the same company does not interfere with an employee's function as a union representative.

c. Negotiation

Collective bargaining begins with the submission of a list of claims by the unionized employees to the employer (in the case of company level bargaining) or through the Labor Authority (in the case of union level bargaining). The list of claims must be approved by the Union's General Assembly and must be submitted to the employer within two months after such approval.

d. Collective Bargaining Agreements

Collective bargaining is the agreement aimed at regulating wages, productivity and other working conditions, between: on one side, one or more trade union organizations, or, in their absence, representatives of the employees, expressly authorized and elected for such purpose; and, on the other side, an employer, a group of employers or a number of employer organizations.

The results of collective bargaining are mandatory for the parties that agree to it and for the employees that join the union at a later date.

E. Labour Disputes

Currently, labour disputes across the country are governed by Law 29497— Procedural Labour Law. The statute of limitation for claims of employees related to the non-payment of the remunerations and / or legal benefits is equal to four years as of the following day of the termination of the labor relationship, regardless of the form of termination of the same. Forfeiture of the action for matters related to the objection of the development or termination of the labor relationship is equal, normally, to thirty calendar days as of the following day of the applicable event. Employees desiring to claim any of the mentioned aspects may proceed with the filing of a lawsuit directly before the Labour Courts.

Labour procedures model in Peru are fundamentally oral; notwithstanding that the lawsuit should be filed in written, parties within a procedure will be asked to substantiate the claim or statement of defence, as the case may be, as well as the evidence supporting these latter, orally in each of the phases of the procedure.

Labour procedures progress or development will depend on the nature of the claim; but, generally, it is initiated by the filing of the claim of the employee, following which the applicable Court will determine if admissible or not. Where the claim is determined to be admissible, the applicable employer will be notified of the content of the lawsuit, in order for this latter to reply it, within the term and conditions granted by the applicable Court. Along with the notification of the lawsuit to the employer, the Court also sets and notifies the employer of the date where the Conciliation Hearing will take place.

Since our Labour procedure model encourages the parties to reach a settlement, the Conciliation Hearing stage has been set, so that employers may be able to propose employees or ex-employees an agreement and have the labour procedure coming to an end. In certain cases, Judges themselves suggest the parties to reach an agreement. Where the parties agree on a settlement, the Court declares the termination of the labour procedure.

Similarly, the Judge may verify within the same Hearing, whether there has been a reply to the lawsuit or not, if the claim is a matter of pure law; or, that being an issue of fact, there is no need to act any complex evidence or means of defense, in which cases, the Judge may require the parties to substantiate their pleadings, at whose term, the final ruling, may be issued.

If no settlement between the parties has been fixed, the applicable Court will have to set a date in which the Judgement Hearing takes place. At this opportunity, parties are required to support and substantiate their claims and statements of defense, as well as, to explain and show how their evidence are applicable to the case. Any supplementary act related to procedural exceptions, complex evidence and the like will be also be evaluated within this hearing.

Depending on the nature of the procedure, the applicable Court may decide on issuing the final ruling within the hearing; or, following five working days from the hearing. In the events where parties do not agree with the ruling, an appeal action may be filed to the extent that certain terms and conditions are met. Similarly, where the applicable parties do not agree with the ruling solving the appeal action, a cassation appeal may be filed to the extent that certain terms and conditions are met, that strictly relate to formal aspects of the action.

V. Intellectual Property

A. Brief Introduction of IP Laws and Regulations

Intellectual Property ("IP") laws in Peru cover: patents, certificates of protection, utility models, industrial designs, industrial secrets, trademarks, trade names, and appellations of origin, among others. Peru is member of multiple international and regional conventions such as: the Paris Convention for the Protection of Industrial Property, The Bern Convention for Copyrights, the Lisbon Agreement for Appellation of Origins, the World Intellectual Property Organization (WIPO), the Inter-American Convention for Trademark and Commercial Protection, the Agreement on Trade Related Aspects of Intellectual Property Rights (TRIPs), the Agreement Establishing the World Trade Organization (WTO), and the Patent Cooperation Treaty (PCT), among others.

In order to comply with the Free Trade Agreement signed between the United States of America and Peru, some changes were introduced in the Peruvian legislation. These rulings are only complementary in some aspects, the fundamentals are preserved. As Peru is also a member of the Andean Community, Intellectual Property will be ruled by Decision 486 and Legislative Decree 1075 (Intellectual Property Law). Additionally, Copyrights regulation is established in, Decision 351 of the Andean Community and by Legislative Decree 822 (Copyright Law).

Indecopi is the national office in charge of intellectual property rights, copyrights, consumer protection regulations, unfair competition, among others.

B. Patent Application

Patent protection in Peru is regulated under Decision 486 (Andean Community[1] Legislation on IP) and the Intellectual Property Law, that includes complementary dispositions to the decision. Regarding patent regulation, it covers inventive patents, utility models, integrated circuits and industrial designs.

Additionally as Peru is a signatory to the Patent Cooperation Treaty (PCT) which provides a unified procedure for the filing, searching, and examination of applications for the protection of inventions and for rendering special technical services internationally.

The PCT entered in force for Peru on June 6, 2009. The PCT system consists of a unified application procedure for a patent among the Contracting States, thereby enabling the applicant to avoid having to begin a different process in each country in which protection for the invention is desired. Hence, any application filed under this treaty will be considered an "international application."

The protection of the right that is granted by the patent registration lasts 20 years. After this period it is not possible to renew the patent. Once the term is over, the patent will enter in the public domain.

Protection of a patent in Peru is subject to its registration by filing an application before the Inventions and New Technologies Direction of Indecopi. The registration process for patents takes at least three or four years.

Indecopi shall grant patents for inventions, whether of goods or of processes, in all areas of technology, provided that they are new, involve an inventive step and are industrially applicable.

To apply for a patent, the application is submitted to the Inventions and New Technologies Direction with the inventor's petition, which includes among others, the data identifying the applicant or person filing the application, a full description of the invention, and the proof of payment of the prescribed fees.

Assuming the inventor complies with all the legal requirements, the Inventions and New Technologies

---

[1] Peru, Bolivia, Ecuador and Colombia are part of the Andean Community Pact.These four countries share the same legislation on Intellectual Property protection.

Directions will officially publish a summary of the application within 18 months. Thus, the application will be kept secret for that time. Within a period of sixty days following the date of publication, any person with a legitimate interest may, for one time only, submit valid reasons for contesting the patentability of the invention. An extended sixty day period may be granted upon request. The patent applicant will have sixty days following the notification to discharge any claim or file the required documentation. An extended sixty day period may be granted. If the findings of the final examination are favorable, the patent will be granted. The applicant may request an examination be made of the patentability of the invention within six months after publication of the application, regardless of whether or not any objections have been filed.

Indecopi divides the application for the registration as follows:
- Application for the registry of the Patents and New Inventions;
- Application for the registry of Industrial Design;
- Application for the registry of an Integrated Circuit Layout Design;
- Application for the registry of a Plant Variety Certificate of Obtainer;
- Application for the registry of Utility Models.

C. Trademark Registration

According to Decision 486 and the Intellectual Property Law the protection of a trademark, in Peru, is subject to its registration by filing an application before the Distinctive Signs Direction at Indecopi. Such regulation also covers the protection of tradenames, slogans, and denominations of origin, and collective trademarks. Unregistered trademarks, with the only exception of well-known distinctive signs, have no protection no matter its use.

Peru also follows and utilizes the Nize classification of goods and services as per the 11th Edition.

The trademark procedure consists on the filing of an application that should comply with all the formal conditions established by the Distinctive Signs Direction, which includes the following:
- Applicant's identification information if it is a natural person or identification information related to the legal entity.
- Indicate the kind of sign which is available for registration.
- Indicate the products or services that the applicant wants to distinguish, and the class thereof according to the international nice classification.
- In this sense, one could register a commercial name, slogan, collective trademarks and certification marks.
- Power of attorney (no legalization is required).

Within ten working days from the day the application was received, the Trademark Office will examine the application for compliance with the main requisites, if the applicant complies with all the requisites, the trademark office will publish the trademark in the official trademark gazette. If he / she does not comply with the mentioned requisites, the trademark office will grant ten working days in order to amend any omissions. Once all the requisites are complied, within a period of thirty working days following the publication date, any person having a legitimate interest, for one time only, may file a valid opposition that could result in the denial of the trademark registration.

The trademark registration is valid for ten years from the date the application was granted, and can be renewed indefinitely for consecutive ten years periods.

D. Copyright Protection

Pursuant to Decision 351 of the Andean Community and the Copyright Law and its amendments introduced by Legislative Decree 1076, copyright protection is available for books, pamphlets, magazines, lectures, addresses, speeches, didactic explanations, musical composition, cinematographic works, dramatic works, choreographic art, mimed works, audiovisual work, work of applied art and work of fine art, rough drafts, drawings, sculptures, lithographs, prints, architectural works, photographs, illustrations, maps, plans, plastic work relating to geography, topography, architecture, or the sciences, slogans and phrases, computer software, journalistic articles, press reports, editorials, comments, translations, and adaptations, among others. Indecopi is the copyright authority and has the power to dictate precautionary measures, such as confiscations and inspections, and to impose sanctions for infringements.

Additionally Peru is also a member of the Bern Convention for the Protection of literary and artistic works, in this sense it also provides protection to the country members of the convention.

Unlike trademarks, copyrights are protected even if they are not registered; they are declarative, according to Bern Convention, but the registration makes the copyrights opposable to third parties.

E. Measures for IP Protection

As enforcements measures, IP holder can use the following legal actions such as:
• File oppositions against trademark applications;
• Initiate infringement actions;
• Request precautionary measures consisting on the destruction of the infringing materials, cease of the infringing acts among others; and
• Request inspective visits of the authority.

In this sense the Peruvian IP regulations let the IP right holders, to enforce their protection over their IP rights, by the initiation of claims for infringement actions against possible infringers. The Peruvian Trademark Authority is authorized to apply sanctions and fines to infringer's up to USD 194,532 (approximately) and the cease of the infringement acts.

Frontier Measures: Resolution 043-2009-SUNAT-A approved the instructions for the request of measures on frontier (INTA-IT-00.08). Measures on frontier consists of a system of information between Peruvian Customs Authority and INDECOPI, by creating a registry of IP rights owners, in order to stop the entrance into Peruvian territory of products that may infringe IP rights, as long as such goods are entering for commercial purposes.

This registry is voluntary, and should be addressed to the Customs Authority. Even criminal actions can be initiated for counterfeiting products, against possible infringers. In this sense, sanctions cannot only be on an administrative but on a criminal level.

VI. Environmental Protection

A. Department Supervising Environmental Protection

The Ministry of Environment (Ministerio del Ambiente) is the Peruvian environmental authority, this entity is in charge of the national environmental management system and its main functions are focused in promoting environmental sustainability by preserving, protecting, recovering and securing the environment ecosystems and natural resources.

The Agency for Assessment and Environmental Control (Organismo de Evaluación y Fiscalización Ambiental – OEFA) is the guiding entity of the national environmental assessment and supervisory system and is responsible for the evaluation, supervision and auditing of the compliance with environmental laws in Peru.

B. Brief Introduction of Laws and Regulations of Environmental Protection

Under the General Environmental Law, Law 28611, which establishes the general regime of environmental rights and obligations, any productive activity that is susceptible of causing environmental damage requires an environmental assessment approved by the authority before the activity is started.

Said assessment must contain all the possible consequences of the activity on the environment and the ways in which the petitioner plans to avoid or reduce these damages to tolerable levels. These levels vary from sector to sector, and progressively more sectors are being regulated. Additionally, these limits can vary depending on certain factors such as the place; thus, it is always necessary to do the appropriate investigations at the local level.

A very important regulation is also the Legislative Decree 1278 which approves the Law on the Integral Management of Solid Waste and replaces Law 27314: General Law of Solid Waste published in the year 2000. This regulation is applicable to all the productive sectors and includes activities related to internment, storage, treatment, transport and export of solid waste.

C. Evaluation of Environmental Protection

During the last 20 years Peruvian economy has grown at a very fast pace. This growth has been grounded in activities related to mining, gas, oil, and agriculture, among others.

The above-mentioned activities are heavily related to the exploitation of natural resources and, due to their characteristics and nature, pose a potential threat to the environment.

The Peruvian government and society has taken the challenge of preserving its natural resources, taking into consideration local rural and native communities and at the same time exploiting them in a sustainable manner within a long-term perspective.

The government has ruled environmental matters very actively to assure the protection of Peruvian natural resources; however, because of Peru´s big rugged and sometimes isolated territory, it is not always possible for the authorities to apply and monitor compliance of the law.

Notwithstanding the above mentioned, the Peruvian government is always looking forward to find new ways and regulations to protect the environment, and at the same time, promote the private investments.

VII. Dispute Resolution

A. Methods and Bodies of Dispute Resolution

a. Civil Law System and the Judiciary in the Republic of Peru

The Republic of Peru has a unitary legal system for all its territory based on the civil law. The Peruvian legal system is founded upon civil law principles including codification, following this, the Constitution in Peru has the highest rank, followed by Laws and Legislative Decrees, in a third place the Supreme Decrees issued by the Executive Branch and so on.

The Peruvian Judiciary System is organized and divided in 34 judicial districts and three main levels of courts and judges. First, the Supreme Court (Corte Suprema) located in Lima which has jurisdiction in the entire country. Second, the Superior Courts (Corte Superior) which are the highest courts in every of the 34 judicial districts. Third, lower judges organized according to different specializations, and finally judges of peace in law and judges of peace in rural areas.

The procedure in the Peruvian justice system guarantees two instances. This means that the judgment issued by a lower court may be reviewed, through an appeal, by the Superior Court. Generally, most of the civil and commercial trials are resolved by the lower judges, and the parties can appeal to the Superior Court of the judicial district where the judicial case is in process. Consequently, after the judgment in a Superior Court, parties are able to file a petition of Cassation only in matters related to; (i) Law infringement that directly affects the contested decision and (ii) Unmotivated withdrawal of judicial precedent. The Supreme Court works as cassation court and its decision can annul, reverse or validate a previous judgment.

b. The Constitutional Tribunal

The Peruvian Constitution safeguards the individual fundamental rights and liberties through the Constitutional Tribunal (Tribunal Constitucional), which is an autonomous entity with jurisdiction over legal actions regarding the protection of a constitutional right violated by the authorities or by another citizen. Also, the Constitutional Tribunal is in charge of controlling the constitutionality of the laws.

The Constitutional Tribunal is composed by seven members, designed by the Congress.

c. Arbitration

Arbitration in Peru is governed by the legislative Decree 1071. Almost all disputes can be subject to arbitration, except the ones involving controversies such as criminal law, family and public interest matters, industrial property, bankruptcy proceedings, etc.

Once the parties have signed an arbitration agreement, a court of the Judiciary can no longer rule on the matter.

In Peru arbitration can be of two types: conscience arbitration and law arbitration. The main difference between them is that in the first case the arbitrators rule a proceeding according to their own knowledge and understanding of the matter, while in the second, the arbitrator bases its award on the laws. Also, the conscience arbitration the arbitrator can be any natural person, national or foreign, whereas for law arbitration, the arbitrator must necessarily be a lawyer registered in a Peruvian Bar Association (Colegio de Abogados).

The Parties in an arbitral dispute can agree on the place of arbitration and in arbitration proceeding if they pact Ad-hoc arbitration. Otherwise, if the parties refer to an arbitration institution, like the Lima Commerce Chamber, the rules of such institution are applicable. Unless the parties stated otherwise in their agreement, the arbitration tribunal will operate with the concurrence of the majority of the arbiters appointed. Resolutions and the award should be based on the vote of the majority of the arbiters. The president of the arbitration tribunal has the decisive vote.

The arbitral awards have the authority of res judicata and the parties are forced to comply with it, once notified. The enforcement of an award is made through a district court in the Judiciary system.

Against the arbitral award, there is only one remedy, which is the annulment claim before the judiciary. The annulment recourse only proceeds because of infringements to the due process of law.

The annulment claim must be filed before the Superior Court of the jurisdiction where the arbitration took place. The Superior Court decision may only be challenged with a cassation claim only when the award was declared totally or partially null and void.

B. Application of Laws

In case of commercial litigation, before filing a case before the Judiciary, litigants must complete a pre-judicial requirement consisting in a process of extra judicial conciliation. The extra judicial conciliation must be held before a conciliation center authorized by the Justice Ministry of Peru. The conciliator summons the parties to a conciliation hearing. If the parties do not reach an agreement or if the invited party does not attend to two citations, the claiming party will be able to file the claim.

For arbitration is not necessary to pass through the conciliation process.

Commercial proceedings before the Judiciary are governed by the Civil Procedural Code, while arbitration proceedings are governed by the Legislative Decree 1017.

An arbitration award is executable by itself, however, if a party considers necessary to use the public force to execute the arbitration award, it is possible to initiate a judicial process of execution of an arbitration award.

Also, foreign judgments are executable in Peru as long as they do not breach Peruvian laws. For a foreign judgment to be recognized by Peruvian courts, an execuatur procedure must be followed.

VIII. Others

A. Anti-commercial Bribery

a. Brief Introduction of Anti-commercial Bribery Laws and Regulations

Peruvian criminal law sanctions bribery acts involving at least one public official or public servant, since according to current Peruvian legislation corruption acts between privates is not considered a crime. Peruvian anti-corruption law includes: the Criminal Code, which establishes a general prohibition on bribery of public officials; the Ethics Code for Public Service, which prohibits receipt of bribes by public officials; and Supreme Decree 023-2011-PCM, which establishes administrative sanctions for public officers who receive bribes.

Under the provisions of the Criminal Code, a bribe is:

• any offer, payment, donation, benefit or promise to confer a benefit to a public official or public servant in order to obtain the public official to commit or omit an act in breach of his duties;

• any offer, payment, donation, benefit or promise to confer a benefit to a public official or public servant in order to obtain the public official to carry out an act that is part of his work without breaching his duties;

The Peruvian Criminal Code sanctions both the Public Official that accepts or that requests a bribe and the private individual that offers or provides the illegal benefit.

Historically Peru has had a juridical system that recognized criminal liability only to individuals, however recently, starting January 2018 a new legal system has entered in force. This new legislation establishes autonomous criminal liability to juridical entities (corporations) if they are directly or indirectly involved in a case of active bribery, specific active bribery, transnational bribery, money laundry and terrorism financial. Under this regulation, entities involved in the aforementioned crimes will face prosecution and potential conviction except if they are able to demonstrate that they had in force a full compliance program designated to avoid the commission of the crimes listed above before the alleged crime was committed.

The Criminal Code establishes criminal offences in Peru and provides general rules, such as the Rule of Complicity, which are applicable to all Peruvian citizens and all foreign citizens that commit crimes in Peru and overseas against the country.

The Criminal Code includes eleven different bribery-related crimes. Depending on the circumstances, the minimum term of imprisonment for a public official who commits a bribery crime is four years and the maximum is fifteen years. The Criminal Code also includes other kind of sanctions against public officials who unlawfully commit corruption crimes, such as disqualification from work as a public official.

b. Department Supervising Anti-commercial Bribery

The Public Ministry (Ministerio Público) is the entity in charge of the prosecution of all crimes including bribery. Specialized prosecutor´s office dedicated to investigate corruption cases were created years ago and are directly involved in the prosecution of those cases.

The Public Ministry receives the support of the Police (also having a specialized Anti-Corruption Division) to carry out preliminary investigations. After the Public Ministry files an accusation, the resolution of the case lies on the Criminal Courts of the Judiciary system.

The Public Ministry receives criminal complaints from private individuals and entities as well as from public institutions such as the General Comptroller, Congress, state attorney, etc.

Finally, the New Criminal Proceedings Code is in force nation-wide for corruption cases.

c. Punitive Actions

Bribery is sanctioned with imprisonment that ranges from three to fifteen years of imprisonment.

The maximum penalties for bribery offences are as follows:

(i) 8 years of imprisonment for passive bribery committed (accepting or receiving) by a public official in order to act in violation of his duties;

(ii) 8 years of imprisonment for passive bribery committed by a public official (requesting directly or indirectly) in violation of his duties;

(iii) 10 years of imprisonment for passive bribery committed by a public official by conditioning to carry out his duties to an illegal benefit;

(iv) 8 years of imprisonment for transnational bribery;

(v) 8 years of imprisonment for passive bribery (accepting or receiving) by a public official in order to act without breaching his duties or for an act already carried out;

(vi) 8 years of imprisonment for passive bribery by a public official (requesting) in order to act without breaching his duties or for an act already carried out;

(vii) 15 years of imprisonment for an Arbitrator, Prosecutor, public expert, member of an administrative court or similar for passive bribery (accepting a bribe) in order to influence in his decision;

(viii) 15 years of imprisonment for an Arbitrator, Prosecutor, public expert, member of an administrative court or similar for passive bribery (requesting a bribe) in order to influence in his decision;

(ix) 10 years of imprisonment for passive bribery by a member of the National Police (by accepting, receiving or requesting) in order to act in violation of his duties;

(x) 12 years of imprisonment for passive bribery by a member of the National Police by conditioning to carry out his duties to an illegal benefit;

(xi) 7 years of imprisonment for passive bribery by a member of the National Police by accepting or receiving a bribe in order to act complying his duties;

(xii) 8 years of imprisonment for passive bribery by a member of the National Police by accepting a bribe in order to act complying his duties;

(xiii) 8 years of imprisonment for passive bribery by a jurisdictional auxiliary;

(xiv) 6 years of imprisonment for he who commits active bribery (offering promising or giving an illegal benefit to a Public Official) in order to get him to conduct acts in violation of his duties;

(xv) 5 years of imprisonment for he who commits active bribery (offering promising or giving an illegal benefit to a Public Official) in order to get him to act without violation of his duties;

(xvi) 8 years of imprisonment for active transnational bribery;

(xvii) 8 years of imprisonment for he who commits active bribery by offering, promising or giving an illegal benefit to an Arbitrator, Prosecutor, public expert, member of an administrative court or equivalent in order to influence in his decision;

(xviii) 8 years of imprisonment for he who commits active bribery by offering, promising or giving an illegal benefit to a jurisdictional assistant, witness, official translator or equivalent in order to influence in his decision;

(xix) 8 years of imprisonment for a lawyer or member of a law firm that commits active bribery;

(xx) 8 years of imprisonment for he who commits active bribery by offering, promising of giving an illegal benefit to a member of the National Police in order to obtain him to carry out or omit acts in violation of his duties;

(xxi) 6 years of imprisonment for active bribery by a member of the National Police in order to obtain him to carry out his duties to an illegal benefit.

Finally, persons involved in corruption cases who cooperate in the investigation are able to obtain some benefits under the law. Pursuant to the section 4 of Law 27378, these benefits include: (i) exemption from the penalty; (ii) imposition of a penalty under the legal minimum; (iii) suspension of the penalty, etc. The benefit to be granted will depend upon the quality of information.

B. Project Contracting

Peruvian Project contracting is divided into two major systems: (i) the Public Procurement System; and (ii) the Public Private Partnership (PPP) contracting. The two systems are subject to different regulations and respond to different needs. While the projects under the Public Procurement System are made generally to cover specific needs of certain government entities and are usually standardized contracts, the PPP contracting system is destined for larger and / or more complex contracts, which include public services, large infrastructure projects, public transportation, and similar projects.

In addition, there some other types of project contracting which are excluded from both regulations.

a. Public Procurement

Public Procurement laws apply, as a general rule, to all contracts financed with public funds (fiscal funds and funds generated by the activities of public entities). This system includes a wide range of contracts, from acquisition of equipment for public entities, to larger contracts to build and maintain infrastructure (as long as it is not part of a PPP).

The Public Procurement System is governed by Law 30225 which is further developed by Supreme Decree 350-2015-EF, and supervised by the Public Procurement Contracting Supervising Organism (Organismo Supervisor de Contrataciones del Estado — OSCE). The OSCE also issues specific directives that establish rules of application of the Law 30225 and Supreme Decree 350-2015-EF.

a) Registration

In order to participate in a bid under the Public Procurement System, the bidder must be registered in the National Provider Registry (Registro Nacional de Proveedores— RNP). The registration can be done for foreign, local, domiciled and non-domiciled entities. The registry is divided into 4 main sections depending on the activities of the entities to be registered, which are "Service Provider Registry", "Goods Provider Registry", "Works Contractor Registry" and "Works Consulting Registry". A single entity can be registered in several or all the registries mentioned above.

b) Invitation to Bid and Bidding

The process has several stages as described below:

• Invitation to bid and Request for Proposals

Once the corresponding public entity has followed the internal approvals to initiate a bidding process under the Public Procurement System, an invitation to bid and the Request for Proposals (RFP) is published in the Electronic Public Procurement System (Sistema Electrónico de Contrataciones del Estado — SEACE), which is a webpage were the bid invitations and conditions are published by the public entities.

• Comments to the RFP

Once the RFP is published, the potential bidders are given a term to submit questions and comments to the RFP. After the questions and comments are responded by the public entity, these responses are integrated to the RFP and a new Integrated RPF is published. Note that, no major changes to the fundamental characteristics of the required services, goods or works can be made at this stage.

• Submission of Bids

After the previous stages are completed, bids are submitted to the public entity in the bidding date. Depending on the type of process, the submission may be in a public act with a notary, or a private act. Once the documents are reviewed and the bidders are qualified, the proposals are evaluated and the award is granted. A disqualified bidder may challenge the decision before the corresponding public entity or the Public Procurement Tribunal (Tribunal de Contrataciones del Estado) of the OSCE (depending on the value of the contract).

• Finalising the contract

After the contract is awarded, the winner must submit certain documents and a performance bond to the contracting public entity. Once all the documents and the performance bond are submitted, the contract is signed.

b. PPPs

The PPP contracts are regulated by Legislative Decree 1224 and further developed by Supreme Decree 410-2015-EF. The main entity in charge of PPP projects is ProInversion, however, local and regional governments also have authority to issue specific regulations as long as they not contravene the mentioned general regulations.

The PPP projects are materialised in concession agreements.

The applicable regulation classifies PPP projects in two main categories: (a) self-sustained and (b) co-financed.

a) Self-sustained PPPs

The self-sustained projects are PPPs where the public entities do not provide direct or indirect finance or contingent guarantees. This means that the concessionaire recovers the investment through the payment of tariffs by the users, for example, in the case of the BRT system of Lima known as Metropolitano, the concessionaires recover the investments through the sale of rechargeable cards and the recharges made by the users.

b) Co-financed PPPs

Co-financed PPP projects have direct payments from the public entities or have contingent guarantees from the public entities. As these projects require the use of public funds, they are reserved usually for the largest and more complex projects, and the procedures involve more previous studies, as they must be declared feasible by the involved public entities, and require the corresponding provisions in the public budgets.

Depending on the qualification as co-financed or self-sustained and the magnitude of the projects, the process of granting the PPP project is either conducted by ProInversion, or the corresponding local or regional government.

Access to a PPP process can be obtained either through a public initiative bidding or a private inititative:

(i) Public Initiative Invitation to Bid and Bidding

Once the previous approvals are obtained, the corresponding entity is entitled to call for the bid.

- Call and publication of bid documents and RFP

The corresponding entity calls for a bid and publishes all relevant studies and documents for the bid, as well as the entry payment amount, the RFP and a project of the concession contract.

- Comments to the RFP and concession contract

Following the publication of the bid documents, the potential bidders submit their questions, comments and amendment proposals to the RFP and the concession contract. Once the questions, comments and amendments are reviewed, the entity publishes its responses and proceeds to integrate the RFP and concession contract.

Note that there can be several rounds of comments in this case.

- Previous opinion

Note that for the bid to be valid, once the final version of the concession contract is published, a favourable opinion of the Ministry of Economy and Finance must be obtained.

- Submission of bids and award

Once the final documents of the bid are defined and the favourable opinion of the Ministry of Economy and Finance obtained, the bids are submitted on the scheduled day and hour in a public act and, after the qualification and evaluation, the award is granted.

Note that a pre-qualification stage is possible but not always applicable.

The losing bidders have the right to challenge the results submitting a guaranty bond.

- Finalising the contract

Once the award is granted and the term to challenge has expired (or the challenge resolved), the contract will be executed on the scheduled date, with the submission of the corresponding closing documents including a performance bond.

(ii) Private Initiative

An alternative way to access a PPP project is to submit a private initiative request. This means that a private company can propose the public entities the execution of a PPP project. The submission of the request has certain rules and can end in a public bidding process or a direct award.

- Submission of a private initiative request

Depending of the magnitude and characteristics of the project, the submission of the request is made either to ProInversion or to the local or regional government.

Self-sustained private initiatives of central government competence and co-financed private initiatives are submitted to ProInversion.

Self-sustained private initiatives of local and regional governments are submitted before the corresponding entities directly.

- Evaluation

Once the submission is made and the formal requirements are complied with, the private initiative follows a process of approvals of all involved entities and the Ministry of Economy and Finance. For co-financed projects, a declaration of feasibility must be also made.

- Declaration of interest

If the private initiative passes all required approvals, it is declared of interest and the proponent must publish it and submit the corresponding guaranty bond.

Once the declaration of interest is published, a 90 calendar day window is opened for third parties to submit their expressions of interests accompanied with a guaranty bond.

- Direct award or public bidding

If a third party expresses interest in the project, a public bidding processes is opened with the right of the proponent to a second round of biddings in case he loses.

If no third party expresses interest, a direct award is granted to the proponent of the private initiative.

- Finalising the contract

Once the project is awarded either in a public bid or by direct award, the contract is signed with the previous submission of the required closing documents and the performance bond.

Note that within a three year period from the closing date, amendments to the concession contract are only allowed to correct material errors, events that occur after closing that generate a vital need to amend the contract, or specific operational amendments required to execute the contract.

The restriction mentioned above prevents "bankability amendments" which were common in Peru in previous years. This also means that the project must be bankable at the submission of proposals, as no material amendments will be possible within a three year period from the closing.

c. Other Contracting Schemes

Peruvian regulations establish certain type of contracting that is not subject to public procurement or PPP laws. The main cases include (i) Contracts financed by international entities such as the World Bank or similar; (ii) acquisitions of armament made by the military entities; and (iii) execution of projects for taxes.

These contracts are governed either by specific regulations[1] or the rules defined by the financing entity.

In the specific case of execution of projects for taxes, it is a special regime of collaboration between private and public entities were certain projects of social importance are executed by a private investor and then discounted from its taxes. These projects are materialized in agreements with the specific entities and are excluded from the general public procurement or PPP regulations.

In recent years, the Government has put an important effort to publicize and promote the modality of projects for taxes agreements as an alternative to develop local and regional projects and generate a positive impact in the population.

---

[1] The contracts with international financing are regulated by the directives of each specific financing entity; the contracts of the military forces are regulated by Legislative Decree 1128 and Supreme Decree 005-2013-DE; the execution of projects for taxes is regulated by Law 29230, Supreme Decree 036-2017-EF, and Legislative Decree 1250.

斯洛文尼亚

作者：Uroš Ilić、Katarina Škrbec、Tatjana Andoljsek、Klemen Mir
译者：王秀娟、曹平

一、概述

（一）总体介绍

斯洛文尼亚是一个与奥地利、意大利、克罗地亚和匈牙利接壤的中欧国家。该国于1992年6月宣布独立，2004年成为欧盟（EU）的正式成员，2007年接受欧元为本国货币，并于同年成为申根区国家。1992年，斯洛文尼亚成为联合国会员国、欧洲安全与合作组织成员国，1993年加入欧洲委员会，并最终于2010年成为经济发展与合作组织（以下简称"经合组织"）成员国。

斯洛文尼亚是一个地域统一、不可分割的民主议会制共和国，拥有"不完全的两院制"。下议院（国民议会或"Državni zbor"）拥有立法权，而上议院（国民协商会或"Državni svet"）则监督下议院的工作。国民议会由90名代表组成，其中2个职位留给意大利族和匈牙利族的代表。

斯洛文尼亚总统是国家元首和武装部队总司令，每5年由大选直接选举产生。总统提名首相，首相在国民议会选出后组成政府，政府由国民议会批准（选举）成立。政府拥有广泛的行政权力，包括：确定执行法律和其他规定的政策；制定提交议会审议的立法提案、财政预算和其他条例；通过二级立法和执行法律的其他条例等。

斯洛文尼亚法律制度属于大陆法系。由于斯洛文尼亚历史上属于奥匈帝国，因此受到日耳曼法律体系的强烈影响。"法院法"[①]规定了斯洛文尼亚法院的管辖权和组成。普通法院（即一般管辖法院）包含初审民事和刑事两种不同类型的法院（43个县法院和11个地区法院）。此外还有高等法院（4个）和最高法院两级上诉法院。在某些情况下，裁决可能由宪法法院审查。除一般民事和刑事法院外，还有若干具有专门管辖权的法院，这些法院拥有属事管辖权而非属人管辖权。专业法院是劳动和社会法院（高等劳动和社会法院是上诉法院）和行政法院（作为上诉法院）。法官在履行其司法职能时是独立的，并享有终身任职资格。

斯洛文尼亚是最成功的转型国家之一，但受到世界经济危机和欧元区危机的极大影响。过去几年，斯洛文尼亚的国内消费、出口和投资不断增长，经济持续强劲发展。改善企业资产负债表和信贷条件有望推动投资增长。预计2018年斯洛文尼亚GDP增长率将达到4.2%，高于欧盟平均水平2.3%。[②]

由于具备重要的战略地位、完善的交通系统以及高学历、高技术的劳动力，斯洛文尼亚对外国投资者极具吸引力。不足之处主要在于存在官僚主义风气和不完善的劳动保障立法。斯洛文尼亚经济以出口为导向，其主要行业包括汽车行业（如KLS Ljubno、Adria Mobil、Revoz）、化学材料和药品（如Henkel Maribor、Krka、Lek），电气和电子行业（如Interblock、Kolektor、Iskratel），信息通信技术（如Telemach、Telekom、Slovenije），物流配送（如科佩尔港、斯洛文尼亚铁路、BTC、卢布尔雅娜约热•普奇马克机场），金属加工（如Danfoss Trata、Acroni）和木材加工（如Lesonit、Merkscha）。

（二）在"一带一路"的倡议下，与中国企业合作的现状及趋势

斯洛文尼亚强烈支持中国"一带一路"的倡议，特别是"16+1"的机制。斯洛文尼亚政府希望进

[①] 斯洛文尼亚《法院法》《斯洛文尼亚政府公报》Nos.19/1994, 45/1995, 38/1999, 26/1999 - ZPP, 28/2000, 26/2001 - PZ, 67/2002 - ZSS-D, 110/2002 - ZDT-B, 56/2002 - ZJU, 73/2004, 72/2005, 127/2006, 49/2006 - ZVPSBNO, 67/2007, 45/2008, 96/2009, 86/2010 - ZJNepS, 33/2011, 75/2012, 63/2013, 17/2015, 23/2017 – ZSSve。

[②] 参见https://ec.europa.eu/info/sites/info/files/economy-finance/ecfin_forecast_winter_0718_sl_en.pdf，访问日期：2018年2月9日。

一步加强在农业、汽车制造、旅游和冬季运动等领域的中斯合作。[1] 2018年2月2日，斯洛文尼亚和中国在北京签署了基础设施合作备忘录。备忘录的重点是海上运输和铁路、高速公路和物流的发展。[2] 斯洛文尼亚希望将其现有的运输系统与"一带一路"倡议下穿越斯洛文尼亚的运输走廊连接起来。这条走廊由地中海走廊和阿尔卑斯—巴尔干走廊组成。地中海走廊从乌克兰经匈牙利到斯洛文尼亚，经意大利、法国和西班牙，已经是欧洲TEN-T网络的组成部分。阿尔卑斯—巴尔干走廊从奥地利经斯洛文尼亚到克罗地亚、塞尔维亚、保加利亚和土耳其。[3]

二、投资

（一）市场准入

1. 投资监管部门

经济发展和技术部下属的企业发展部、国际化部、外国投资部和技术部（核心机构）等公共机构为斯洛文尼亚的国际化和投资提供了便利。

2. 投资行业法律法规

斯洛文尼亚没有具体的法律规范鼓励外国投资，但政府鼓励外国投资，而且在过去几年中，斯洛文尼亚银行的数据显示，外国投资也在不断增长。[4]

根据政府五年计划，《促进外商直接投资和企业国际化法案》[5]制定了与促进外商对内直接投资和国际化相关的政府措施。[6] 目前正在采用一项新的"投资激励法案"，以激励战略投资（向加工或服务行业4 000万欧元和400个工作岗位，向研发行业提供2 000万欧元和200个工作岗位），简化获得所有必要权限的流程（如环境、建设），并推出更加清晰明了的投资激励体系。其重点是可持续发展、环境保护和社会责任。[7]

斯洛文尼亚的私有化仍在进行，投标过程对外国投资者开放。政府列举了15家国有企业的名单，这些公司将在未来几年内私有化。

3. 投资方式

斯洛文尼亚的投资者大多选择投资股票、债权（不良债务）和房地产。另一个对国内外投资者有吸引力的是政府和社会资本合作（PPP），国内外投资者通过与国家、政府或其他公共实体签订特许协议，以获得提供经济或其他公共服务或公共利益活动的特许或专属权。在斯洛文尼亚的外国直接投资可以以多种方式进行，实践中通常包括在斯洛文尼亚开设分支机构，收购现有的斯洛文尼亚公司，或与斯洛文尼亚公司建立合资企业。

4. 准入条件及审查

外国投资者可以享受国民待遇或最惠国待遇，并可以按照欧盟和经合组织的原则自由进入市场。银行和保险部门、空运和海运以及游戏业有某些限制（需要斯洛文尼亚银行或保险监督机构批准）。[8]

---

① 中华人民共和国中央人民政府：《中国承诺在"一带一路"下与斯洛文尼亚进一步开展合作》，载http://english.gov.cn/state_council/vice_premiers/2017/04/16/content_281475628112971.htm，访问日期：2018年2月19日。
② 参见《斯洛文尼亚和中国签署基础设施合作备忘录》，载https://english.sta.si/2478366/slovenia-and-china-sign-memorandum-on-infrastructure-coop，访问日期：2018年2月19日。
③ 参见《斯洛文尼亚和中国签署基础设施合作备忘录》，载《斯洛文尼亚时报》，http://www.sloveniatimes.com/slovenia-and-china-sign-memorandum-on-infrastructure-coop，访问日期：2018年2月21日。
④ 参见斯洛文尼亚银行：《斯洛文尼亚宏观经济预测》，2017年12月，载https://bankaslovenije.blob.core.windows.net/publication-files/gdgfnNehiggfP_macroeconomic-projections-for-slovenia-december-2017.pdf，访问日期：2018年2月10日。
⑤ 参见《促进外商直接投资和企业国际化法》(ZSTNIIP)，由《斯洛文尼亚政府公报》发布，Nos.86/2004, 78/2006, 11/2011, 57/2012, 17/2015。
⑥ 参见《2015—2020年国际化计划》，载http://www.mgrt.gov.si/fileadmin/mgrt.gov.si/pageuploads/SEKTOR_ZA_INTERNACIONALIZACIJO/ANG/Program_INTER_2015-2020_koncna_EN-_FINAL.pdf，访问日期：2018年2月7日。
⑦ 参见http://www.vlada.si/en/media_room/government_press_releases/press_release/article/156th_regular_session_of_the_government_of_the_republic_of_slovenia_60628/，访问日期2018年2月7日。
⑧ 外国投资制度参见https://www.investslovenia.org/fileadmin/dokumenti/is/CMSR_dokumenti/Investment_Regime_SPIRIT_2016_August.pdf，访问日期：2018年2月18日。

外国公司和外商独资公司与国内公司享有同等的权利和义务，但房地产所有权的取得存在例外（见下文）；然而，一旦外国公司拥有不动产，它将受到与在斯洛文尼亚注册的公司相同的法律制度的约束。

根据《宪法》的规定，任何人（国内的或外国的自然人、法人）的财产只有在符合法律规定的条件并有货币或实物补偿的公共利益（例如建造公共基础设施）的情况下才能被征用。①征收包括直接和间接征收措施。

（二）外汇管理

1. 外汇监管部门

斯洛文尼亚银行负责外汇兑换业务的授权，并参照银行业规定，对外汇经营者进行监管。海关当局监督从国内转入和转出的现金的性质和数量。②

2. 外汇法律法规简介

外汇制度全面放开，受《外汇法》监管。③

货币兑换业务可由持有斯洛文尼亚银行签发的有效授权的货币兑换经营者和银行或储蓄银行执行，这些银行根据《规范银行法》提供对外支付的交易服务，包括货币兑换业务。运营商必须使用斯洛文尼亚银行的汇率，允许斯洛文尼亚银行访问，并报告可能发生的状态变化。

3. 外资企业外汇管理要求

斯洛文尼亚完全遵守《国际货币基金协定》第8条的规定，这是不歧视和不受限制的货币自由兑换的法律依据。④外国企业的外汇管理不受具体立法的约束，因此实现了自由化。居民和非居民拥有的流动资金转移不受限制。⑤利润的返还是免费的，但仍然征收税收之债。《反洗钱和资助恐怖主义法》⑥规定了一些报告和鉴定方面的安全措施，如果超过1万欧元，海关当局可以没收流入国内未申报的现金。⑦

（三）融资

1. 主要金融机构

斯洛文尼亚最重要的金融机构是斯洛文尼亚银行，它是直接对国民议会负责的独立法人。⑧斯洛文尼亚银行实施欧元区货币政策、监管外汇业务、监管银行和储蓄银行的运行，并负责保持银行系统的一般流动性。金融机构主要受欧盟法律管辖，即欧洲议会第572/2013号条例和关于信贷机构和投资公司审慎性要求以及理事会修订的第648/2012号条例。⑨

银行业、金融业和其他类似业务受到《银行法》⑩的严格约束，并受到斯洛文尼亚银行的严格监督。⑪信用机构可以以股份有限公司的形式，也可以以欧洲股份有限责任公司的形式设立作为银行或储

---

① 参见斯洛文尼亚《宪法》，《斯洛文尼亚政府公报》Nos.33/91-I, 42/97, 66/2000, 24/03, 69/04, 68/06, 47/13, 75/16, Art.69。
② 参见斯洛文尼亚《外汇法》(ZDP-2)，《斯洛文尼亚政府公报》Nos.16/2008, 85/2009, 109/2012, Arts.11-14。欧洲议会和理事会关于信贷机构和投资公司审慎性要求的第572/2013号条例修订了第648/2012号条例。
③ 参见斯洛文尼亚《外汇法》(ZDP-2)，《斯洛文尼亚政府公报》(Official Gazette RS) Nos.16/2008, 85/2009, 109/2012。
④ 国际货币基金组织:《2016年汇兑安排与汇兑限制年报》，载 https://www.imf.org/en/Publications/Annual-Report-on-Exchange-Arrangements-and-Exchange-Restrictions/Issues/2017/01/25/Annual-Report-on-Exchange-Arrangements-and-Exchange-Restrictions-2016-43741，访问日期：2018年2月21日。
⑤ 根据《外汇法》(ZDP-2)，居民纳税人是指：①斯洛文尼亚境内成立并从事营利活动的公司和其他法人，不包括其在世界其他地区的分支机构；②从事营利活动并在斯洛文尼亚法院登记处登记的外国公司的分支机构；③在斯洛文尼亚注册或永久居住的从事注册商业活动的独资商人和个人；④在斯洛文尼亚永久居留的自然人和在斯洛文尼亚至少有6个月的有效居留证临时居留的自然人，不包括在外交和领事馆工作的外国公民和他们的家庭成员；⑤洛尼亚共和国在世界其他地区由国家资产供资的外交人员、领事人员和其他代表，受雇于这些代表处的斯洛文尼亚公民及其家属。除此之外他人都被视为非居民。
⑥ 参见《反洗钱和资助恐怖主义法》(ZPPDFT-1)，斯洛文尼亚第68/16号政府公报，第44条。
⑦ 参见斯洛文尼亚《外汇法》，斯洛文尼亚政府第16/2008、85/2009、109/2012号公报，第11—14条。欧洲议会和理事会关于信贷机构和投资公司审慎性要求的第572/2013号条例修订了第648/2012号条例，详见欧盟《官方公报》L 176/1。
⑧ 参见斯洛文尼亚《宪法》(URS)，第152条。
⑨ 欧洲议会和理事会关于信贷机构和投资公司审慎性要求的第572/2013号条例修订了第648/2012号条例，欧盟《官方公报》L 176/1。
⑩ 参见斯洛文尼亚《银行法》(ZBan-2)，斯洛文尼亚第25/15、44/16、77/16、41/17号政府公报。
⑪ 参见斯洛文尼亚《银行法》(ZBan-2)，第5条。

蓄银行。外国银行可以在斯洛文尼亚设立分行，将其作为一个正规的信贷机构运营。公司治理、风险管理、公司状态变化和银行业的类似关键领域的业务受到斯洛文尼亚银行严格监管和监督。

斯洛文尼亚的银行业具有较高的集中度。① 该国最大的银行NLB（新星卢布尔雅那银行）是国有企业②，约占1/4的市场份额。③ 第二大银行NKBM（马里博银行）和其他外资银行约占50%的市场份额。④ 目前，斯洛文尼亚有12家银行、3家储蓄银行和3家欧洲经济区分支机构获得斯洛文尼亚银行的授权提供银行服务、共同认可的服务和在斯洛文尼亚提供额外的金融服务。⑤

银行业在斯洛文尼亚的金融体系中占主导地位，在2013年占金融资产约77%的市场份额。⑥ 保险公司和养老基金以及其他金融中介机构等金融机构从业者⑦，下文将依次讨论。后者中，隐形银行部门（主要包括投资基金和租赁公司）已逐渐达到金融系统总资产的8%。⑧ 此外，其他非银行信贷渠道也变得更为重要，如企业对企业贷款和内部资金转移。⑨

斯洛文尼亚的保险业与银行业一样，高度集中。4家最大的保险公司占据了大约78%的保险市场。⑩ 保险和再保险业务受《保险法》⑪的管辖，并以透明、勤勉、风险管理和监管为原则开展业务。⑫ 再保险业务由保险监督机构执行。保险业务可以由斯洛文尼亚法人开展，该法人需获得保险监管机构的授权；或由外国企业——通过分支机构或直接——根据《保险法》的具体规定开展。一家保险公司的设立形式可以是股份有限责任公司、欧洲股份有限责任公司或相互保险公司。⑬ 一般来说，保险公司可以人寿保险集团或非人寿保险集团开展保险业务，但已取得上述立法要求开展两组保险业务授权的公司（即所谓的综合保险公司）可以在两个领域内开展业务。

斯洛文尼亚实行三支柱的养老金制度。根据互惠和团结的原则，第一支柱由强制性的雇员捐款提供资金，由斯洛文尼亚养老金和伤残保险研究所管理。⑭ 第二支柱适用于同一投保人，分为强制附加保险和个人或集体性质的自愿附加保险。这些捐款是在特别基金中收集的，这些基金受国家管制（例如规定的最低回报率），并享受税收优惠。第三个支柱完全是自愿的，不依赖于个人的工作地位，也不受国家的管制。

投资基金受到《投资基金和管理公司法》⑮的管制，可作为集体投资可转让证券（UCITS）⑯或替代投资基金（AIF）⑰而设立。

如上所述，隐形银行部门的另一个重要角色是专门的金融机构—租赁公司。⑱ 资产租赁是银行法规

---

① 参见 https://www.export.gov/article?id=Slovenia-Efficient-Capital-Markets，访问日期：2018年2月25日。
② 2017年底出售NLB的部分国家股权是经欧盟委员会批准的国家对NLB提供重要援助的关键承诺之一。参见 http://europa.eu/rapid/press-release_IP-18-482_en.htm，访问日期：2018年2月25日。
③ 参见《NLB银行2017年第3季度报告》，2017年9月，载 https://www.nlb.si/financna-porocila-2017，访问日期：2018年2月25日。
④ 参见 http://www.zbs-giz.si/zdruzenje-bank.asp?StructureId=480，访问日期：2018年2月25日。
⑤ 受到监管的机构参见：https://www.bsi.si/en/financial-stability/institutions-under-supervision (10.2.2018)。
⑥ 参见UMAR《2013年经济挑战：斯洛文尼亚金融危机对信贷市场的影响》（2013年），第50页。
⑦ 参见经合组织：《斯洛文尼亚：金融体系回顾》，2011年10月，第12页。
⑧ 参见经合组织：《斯洛文尼亚2017年经济调查：概览》，第33页，载 http://www.oecd.org/eco/surveys/Slovenia-2017-OECD-economic-survey-overview.pdf，访问时间：2018年2月27日。
⑨ 同上注。
⑩ 参见保险监督管理局：《2016年保险业务状况年度报告》，第23页，载 https://www.a-zn.si/wp-content/uploads/letno_porocilo-2016.pdf，访问时间：2018年2月27日。
⑪ 参见《斯洛文尼亚保险法》斯洛文尼亚政府第93/15号公报。
⑫ 参见《保险法》(2011)，第6—7页，载 http://www.mizs.gov.si/fileadmin/mizs.gov.si/pageuploads/podrocje/ss/Gradiva_ESS/UNISVET/UNISVET_68ET_Zavarovalno_Ciglic.pdf，访问时间：2018年2月10日。
⑬ 再保险事业不允许采用第一种组织形式。
⑭ 关于斯洛文尼亚养老金和伤残保险研究所，参见，https://www.zpiz.si/cms/?ids=contenten&inf=484，访问时间：2018年2月9日。
⑮ 参见《斯洛文尼亚投资基金和管理公司法》，《斯洛文尼亚政府公报》Nos.31/15, 81/15, 77/16。
⑯ UCITS是一种开放式的向公众募集资金的证券，其唯一目标是根据风险分散原则投资于证券或其他流动金融资产。UCITS可根据持有人的要求变现或支付。UCITS可由授权的管理公司以共同基金或伞形基金的形式建立。管理公司可以公共有限公司、欧洲公司或公共有限责任公司的方式设立。
⑰ 所有不符合UCITS标准的投资基金都是AIF，AIF可以公开或非公开地募集资本，并由另类投资基金经理（AIFM）管理，即以管理一个或多个AIF为业务的法人。AIFM的名单由证券市场机构保存，并受《另类投资基金管理人法案》（斯洛文尼亚第32/15号政府公报）监管。
⑱ 许多斯洛文尼亚银行通过其子公司开展作为非核心业务的租赁业务。

定的一种特殊类型的金融服务，需要斯洛文尼亚银行的授权。

监管金融票据市场的独立法人是1994年成立的证券市场管理机构（SMA）。该机构监管投资公司、卢布尔雅那证券交易所、中央证券清算公司（KDD）、投资基金和管理公司，并与斯洛文尼亚银行分担监管某些银行和投资服务的职责。其任务和职能范围包括金融机构的业务授权、授权资格的控股和公司收购的授权，在公开发行证券时批准招股说明书，控制金融机构，保存某些登记册并批准证券交易所规则。[1]

2. 外资企业融资条件

斯洛文尼亚对外国企业的融资没有特殊要求。《金融票据市场法》[2]要求在公开发行证券（包括债券）时公布招股说明书，但该法规定的要求同样适用于外国和国内企业。

根据《反洗钱和资助恐怖主义法》[3]而制定的欧盟2015/849号关于防范利用金融系统洗钱和资助恐怖活动指令，要求银行和其他金融机构在接收、移交、交换、保管、处置资金或其他财产以及缔结业务关系时，采取措施以防止和打击洗钱活动和资助恐怖主义活动。

预防措施包括"了解你的顾客"检查，如个人识别和最终受益人的身份验证。当一家公司（外国或国内）希望在斯洛文尼亚开立一个银行账户或一个交易账户时，最终的实际受益人信息是必要的。如果外国公司通过分支机构开展业务，母子公司的身份将受到检查。国内法人和外国法人的斯洛文尼亚分支机构必须收集最终受益人的信息，并将此信息报告给斯洛文尼亚商业登记处。最终受益人名册已公开发布至2018年1月。

（四）土地政策

1. 土地法律法规简介

斯洛文尼亚房地产法基本原则都包含在《财产法》[4]中，而其他规范土地的重要法律是《土地登记法》[5]《房地产登记法》[6]《农业土地法》[7]《住房法》[8]《公寓买方保护法》[9]和《独栋建筑法》。

土地产权法典详细列举了法人可获得的物权清单[10]：

- 所有权（lastninska pravica）；
- 抵押权（zastavna pravica）；
- 地役权（služnost）；
- 留置权（pravica stvarnega bremena）；
- 建筑权（stavbna pravica）。

物权属于对世权，但必须进行土地登记注册才具有法律效力。土地登记册中的数据是公开的，人人都可以获取。[11]除物权之外，土地登记册还包括其他有关财产的信息，例如法律诉讼通知。

所有权是主要且最广泛的产权。它不受时间和条件的限制，包括占有、收益、使用和处置的权利。两个或两个以上的人对可分割的财产的所有权被称为按份共有（在不可分割的财产上，即共同共有）。而财产共有权是一种特殊类型的所有权，其中一个单位的固定所有权制度必然与共同区域的共同所有

---

[1] 关于证券市场监管机构，参见 http://www.a-tvp.si/Eng/Default.aspx?id=1，访问日期：2018年2月10日。
[2] 参见《金融工具市场法》，《斯洛文尼亚政府公报》Nos.67/2007, 100/2007., 69/2008, 40/2009, 88/2010, 78/2011, 55/2012, 105/2012 - ZBan-1J, 63/2013 - ZS-K, 30/2016, 44/2016 - ZRPPB, 9/2017。
[3] 参见《斯洛文尼亚反洗钱和资助恐怖主义法》，《斯洛文尼亚政府公报》No.68/16, Art.44。
[4] 参见《斯洛文尼亚财产法》，《斯洛文尼亚政府公报》Nos.87/2002, 91/2013。
[5] 参见《斯洛文尼亚土地登记法》，《斯洛文尼亚政府公报》Nos.58/2003, 45/2008, 37/2008 - ZST-1, 28/2009, 25/2011, 14/2015 - ZUUJFO, 23/2017 - ZDOdv, 69/2017。
[6] 参见《斯洛文尼亚农业土地法》，《斯洛文尼亚政府公报》Nos.71/11, 58/12, 27/16, 27/17 - ZKme-1D, 79/17。
[7] 参见《斯洛文尼亚房地产记录法》，《斯洛文尼亚政府公报》Nos.47/06, 65/07，斯洛文尼亚宪法法院判决 79/12, 61/17 – ZAID。
[8] 参见《斯洛文尼亚住房法》，《斯洛文尼亚政府公报》Nos.69/03, 18/04 – ZVKSES, 47/06 – ZEN, 45/08 – ZVEtL, 57/08, 62/10 – ZUPJS, 56/11，斯洛文尼亚宪法法院判决 87/11, 40/12 – ZUJF, 14/17, 27/17。
[9] 参见《斯洛文尼亚土地产权法》，《斯洛文尼亚政府公报》No.18/04。
[10] 参见斯洛文尼亚《财产法》，第2条。
[11] 参见斯洛文尼亚《财产法》，第10条。

权（如一幢公寓内的大厅）相结合。

2. 外资企业获得土地的规定

根据《宪法》，外国主体可在法律规定的条件或国民议会批准的条约条件下取得房地产的所有权。[①] 后者适用于欧盟公民，欧洲自由贸易联盟和经合组织成员国的公民可以在与斯洛文尼亚公民同等条件下购买房地产，对于欧盟候选国的公民，他们可以在互惠的条件下取得房地产。[②] 其他国家的公民和公司（例如中国和俄罗斯）只能通过继承和在互惠条件下获得斯洛文尼亚的不动产。[③] 国民待遇原则确保外国公司享有与本国公司相同的所有权。

无论情况如何严峻，俄罗斯和中国的公民和公司都是斯洛文尼亚最常见的外国房地产买家。[④] 斯洛文尼亚和平的环境和在欧洲的中心位置，中国人在斯洛文尼亚主要投资于适合出租的房地产，而俄罗斯人则经常在斯洛文尼亚购买自用的房地产。[⑤] 购买行为通常通过在斯洛文尼亚设立一家公司进行。

（五）企业设立与解散

商业公司的法律地位、设立和经营规则受《公司法》[⑥] 管辖。斯洛文尼亚的法律体系以企业所有者是否对公司承担有限责任将企业分为有限责任公司和合伙企业。公司设立的目的是为了在市场上进行各种各样的营利活动，但法律明确禁止的除外。

所有公司经法院登记注册后取得法人资格，作为合法实体，可以获得权利、承担义务、拥有动产和不动产，并可以提起诉讼和被起诉。公司以其全部资产（与股东以其出资额为限承担有限责任不同）对外承担责任，但某些侵权行为和违法行为可能引发对法人人格的否认和公司成员的连带责任。公司的经营由管理层（如董事、管理委员会或董事会[⑦]）领导。

在斯洛文尼亚从事营利活动的外国公司与在斯洛文尼亚注册的公司有同等的权利和义务。外国公司的地位根据公司所属国的法律确定。外国公司（在欧盟成员国注册的公司适用某些例外情况）可以通过其国际母公司或附属公司的分支机构在斯洛文尼亚进行营利活动，该机构是独立的法人实体。斯洛文尼亚《公司法》关于公司的经营活动、公司名称、注册办事处、委任状和商业秘密等规定比照适用于分支机构。外国公司代表可向法院申请在注册登记簿上注册或注销分支机构。[⑧] 根据斯洛文尼亚《公司法》成立的独立子公司可以是有限责任公司或股份有限公司，但需有在外国法项下注册的母公司。

1. 企业形式

（1）合伙公司

无限责任公司（družba z neomejeno odgovornostjo）由两个或两个以上的人以其全部财产为公司承担责任。股东在合伙协议中约定设立公司，并规定股东之间的关系。公司设立无最低注册资本要求，股东通常出资相等，并根据出资比例分红或承担损失。股东有权并有义务管理和代表公司。[⑨]

有限合伙公司（komanditna družba）是根据两个或两个以上的人所达成的合伙协议设立的公司，其股东中至少有一个以其个人所有财产对公司承担责任（普通合伙人，komplementar）且至少一个股东不为公司的责任负责（有限合伙人，komanditist）。普通合伙人有权管理和代表公司，由有限合伙人监

---

① 参见斯洛文尼亚《宪法》（URS），第68条。
② 参见http://www.mp.gov.si/si/delovna_podrocja/direktorat_za_civilno_pravo/sektor_za_civilno_pravo/pridobivanje_lastninske_pravice_tujcev_na_nepremicninah_v_republiki_sloveniji/，访问时间：2018年2月10日。
③ 斯洛文尼亚《继承法》，《斯洛文尼亚政府公报》Nos.št.15/76, 23/78.13/94 – ZN, 40/94 – decision of the Constitutional Court RS, 117/00, 斯洛文尼亚宪法法院判决 67/01, 83/01 – OZ, 73/04 – ZN-C, 31/13, 63/16, Art.6.
④ 参见https://pro.finance.si/8857134，访问日期：2018年2月10日。
⑤ 参见http://www.bidom.si/novice/prodaja-nepremicnin-tujcem-ruski-angleski-trg/245，访问日期：2018年2月10日。
⑥ 参见斯洛文尼亚《公司法》，《斯洛文尼亚政府公报》Nos.42/2006, 60/2006., 26/2007 – ZSDU-B, 33/2007 – ZSReg-B, 67/2007-ZTFI, 10/2008, 68/2008, 42/2009, 33/2011, 91/2011, 100/2011, 32/2012, 57/2012, 44/2013, 斯洛文尼亚宪法法院判决 82/2013, 55/2015, 15/2017, art.1.
⑦ 也就是说，就欧盟公司而言，如果提供服务是暂时性的［与在斯洛文尼亚常规性、定期性或持续性经营相反，在这种情况下，必须建立斯洛文尼亚分公司或外国（欧盟）公司的子公司］，则不需要进行注册。
⑧ 参见斯洛文尼亚《公司法》(ZGD-1)，第八部分。
⑨ 参见斯洛文尼亚《公司法》(ZGD-1)，第III/1部分。

督。① 除另有规定外，无限责任公司规则适用于有限合伙企业。

（2）有限责任公司

有限责任公司（družba z omejeno odgovornostjo）由一个或多个的国内或国外的自然人或法人作为公司股东发起成立。有限责任公司以全体股东签署书面或电子形式的公证书或其他形式的合伙协议的方式设立。该公司的股本最低为 7 500 欧元，由股东出资（以现金或实物提供）构成，其价值可能有所不同，但平均每名股东至少出资 50 欧元。

公司管理受合伙协议约束。最重大的决定，如任命、解雇和监督董事，通过年度报告，以及对股东权益的划分和终止，都是股东通过表决程序在股东大会上作出的。一个或多个董事负责管理公司并在其职权范围内代表公司，董事在任何时候都可以被股东大会决议解雇。

（3）股份有限公司

股份有限公司（delniška družba）的股本形式为股票（证券）。最低股本为 25 000 欧元，可分为面值和非面值股票。面值股票中所列的最低金额，或每一个无面值股份的股本金额，必须为 1 欧元或其倍数。

每个股份有限公司可选择一级或两级的公司管治制度。在一级制中，股东指定并监督管理公司业务的董事会。在双层体系中，管理职能与监督职能分离。股东选举监事会，监事会任命和监督管理委员会。管理委员会由一名或多名成员（董事）组成，负责管理。管理人员或监事会成员因违反职责而对公司负有连带责任，除非他们能证明自己公正而认真地履行职责。必要时或法律有规定时，管理层负责召集股东召开股东大会决定公司的重要决策，包括年度报告的通过、监事会的任命和罢免、公司的清算或重组、可分配利润分配、章程修改、增加和减少注册股本，以及公司审计机关的任命。不过，尽管股份有限公司和有限责任公司均仅需其成员对公司承担有限责任（限于公司股权认购的范围），但是在成本效率和公司治理机制的灵活性方面，有限责任公司可能是一个更具吸引力的选择。

（4）股份有限合伙公司

股份有限合伙公司（komanditna delniška družba）由至少有 5 人签署的公司章程确定。在这种合伙关系中，至少有一个股东以其全部资产（普通合伙人）对公司债务承担责任，有限股东不承担公司对债权人的责任。普通合伙人在股东大会上的投票权与他们认购股本的比例成正比。

（5）欧洲股份有限公司

欧洲股份有限公司（Societas Europea, evropska delniška družba）是一种特殊类型的公司，根据欧盟关于欧洲公司章程（SE）的第 2157/2001 条成立。欧洲股份有限公司建立的先决条件是公司注册地和总部在同一个欧盟国家，最低资本为 120 000 欧元，并有公司员工参与制定公司管理的协议。其他要求可能因国家而异。在斯洛文尼亚，欧洲股份有限公司的管理规则作了必要的变通。②

2. 设立程序

来自欧盟、欧共体和瑞士联邦的个人和企业可以在斯洛文尼亚无限制地按照固定的程序设立公司。第三国国民也可以，但他们可能需要获得商业签证或其他类型的签证才能进入斯洛文尼亚。③

成立一家公司之前，非本地居民必须通过税收管理办公室获得斯洛文尼亚税收账号。要注册一家公司，必须确定一个公司的名称、法定代表、主要场所和经营范围。一般来说，原始股东（们）在公证处签合同，提供必要的股本，并在法院登记册上登记，取得公司法人资格。登记程序按照法院登记法律实体法进行。④ 股份有限公司也可以免费在"VEM"网点或通过"VEM"网站注册。⑤

3. 解散方式及要求

公司的解散可以是自愿的，也可以是强制的。这两种程序都是相同的流程，即资产变现、公司债

---

① 参见斯洛文尼亚《公司法》(ZGD-1)，第 III/2 部分。
② 参见斯洛文尼亚《公司法》(ZGD-1)，第五部分。
③ 非欧盟国家国民如何在斯洛文尼亚创业，参见 http://eugo.gov.si/en/starting/how-can-non-eu-nationals-start-a-business-in-slovenia/，访问日期：2018 年 2 月 13 日。
④ 斯洛文尼亚法院登记法律实体法，《斯洛文尼亚政府公报》Nos.13/1994, 31/2000 - ZP-L, 91/2005, 42/2006 - ZGD-1, 33/2007, 93/2007, 65/2008, 49/2009, 82/2013 - ZGD-1H, 17/2015, 54/2017。
⑤ e-VEM 网站访问地址：http://evem.gov.si/evem/drzavljani/zacetna.evem，访问日期：2018 年 2 月 13 日。

务清偿、公司股东剩余资产的分割以及公司从法院登记簿上除名。自愿清算由公司成员或股东发起，受公司法管辖；强制清算由法院领导，并受到金融法、破产程序法和强制清算法的规范。① 各种类型公司的清算原因已在公司法中详细列明。

金融业务法，破产程序法和强制清算法也规定了破产公司解散的破产程序。该程序基于共同满意和公平分配原则，由法院监督。法院指定破产管理人，负责对公司资产进行最有利的管理，并对破产财产中的优先权利、普通债权和从属债权给予合理的处分。关于终止的司法决定作出，破产程序结束。公司清算在终止决定进入法院登记册后生效。

（六）合并收购

斯洛文尼亚并购条例的基础包括《公司法》和《收购法》②。前者是概括性的，规范各种形式的公司、公司治理和相关人员的权利和义务关系。后者调整收购程序适用于上述列举的获准在受监管市场交易的斯洛文尼亚股份有限公司，以及至少有 250 名股东或公司权益总额不低于 400 万欧元的非公开交易的公司。

《收购法》区分自愿和强制性收购要约。在这两种情况下，都主张向所有证券持有人公开提出要约，受要约人可能获得出让的部分或全部证券。③ 当一个人（单独或与其他合作的人一起）达到该公司 1/3 的表决权门槛时，公司必须进行强制收购。每获得 10% 的表决权，收购要约义务就会增加，直到在收购完成和要约义务都结束后，最终获得 75% 的表决权。④ 未能履行强制性收购要约要求的，收购方所有表决权将被中止，并面临罚款甚至需对此造成的损害承担赔偿责任。⑤ 当收购门槛尚未达到时，要约人可以选择自愿收购要约。⑥

一般而言，收购程序分为三个主要阶段⑦：

（1）在收购之前，要约人向作为目标企业的管理机关和斯洛文尼亚竞争保护机构的证券市场管理机构（SMA）宣布收购意向；

（2）在获得了 SMA 的收购要约授权后，要约人可以在公告收购意向后的 10 至 30 天内，附随招股说明书公开公告要约；

（3）最后，接受要约的期限是 28 到 60 天。

与收购有关的少数股东的特殊权利和义务载于《公司法》。通过强制排除程序，股东大会根据持股 90% 以上股东（即主要股东）的提议，决议将剩余股份转让给主要股东，以获得适当补偿。⑧ 反之，小股东可以要求主股东在出售过程中购买剩余股份。⑨

近来，政府刺激私有化的举措，特别是政府集合了 15 家待售的国有上市企业的名单，极大地活跃了斯洛文尼亚的并购活动。为了独立于政府所有者，斯洛文尼亚的国有企业由斯洛文尼亚主权控股公司（SSH）管理，其性质是管理股份有限公司并负责管理斯洛文尼亚国有资产。《斯洛文尼亚产权法》⑩ 明确了三类资产中国家股的最低比例、战略资产的最低国家股（50% 股和具有一票否决权），重要资产（25% 股和具有一票否决权）和投资组合的资产（没有最低份额，自由配置）。国有资产的处置可以通过公开招标、公开拍卖或者公开发行等方式进行。⑪

---

① 相关财务业务参见《破产程序和强制终止法》,《斯洛文尼亚政府公报》Nos.126/2007, 40/2009, 59/2009, 52/2010, 106/2010 - ORZFPPIPP21, 26/2011, 47/2011 – ORZFPPIPP21-1, 87/2011 – ZPUOOD, 23/2012 – odl.US, 48/2012 – decision of the Constitutional Court RS, 47/2013, 100/2013, 10/2015 – popr., 27/2016, 31/2016 – odl.US, 38/2016 – odl.US, 63/2016 – ZD-C.
② 斯洛文尼亚《收购法》,《斯洛文尼亚政府公报》Nos.79/2006, 67/2007 - ZTFI, 1/2008, 68/2008, 35/2011 - ORZPre75, 55/2011, 斯洛文尼亚宪法法院判决 105/2011 - odl.US, 10/2012, 22/2012, 斯洛文尼亚宪法法院判决 38/2012, 47/2013 - ZFPPIPP-E, 56/2013, 63/2013 - ZS-K, 25/2014, 75/2015。
③ 参见斯洛文尼亚《收购法》(ZPre-1), 第 11 条。
④ 参见斯洛文尼亚《收购法》(ZPre-1), 第 12 条。
⑤ 参见斯洛文尼亚《收购法》(ZPre-1), 第 63 条。
⑥ 参见斯洛文尼亚《收购法》(ZPre-1), 第 13 条。
⑦ 参见斯洛文尼亚《收购法》(ZPre-1), 第 24—41 条。
⑧ 参见斯洛文尼亚《公司法》(ZGD-1), 第 384 条。
⑨ 参见斯洛文尼亚《公司法》(ZGD-1), 第 389 条。
⑩ 参见斯洛文尼亚《产权法》(ZSDH-1),《斯洛文尼亚政府公报》。
⑪ 参见斯洛文尼亚《产权法》(ZSDH-1), 第 10—16 条。

(七) 竞争条例

1. 竞争管制主管机构

负责监督和执行竞争管制的主管机关是斯洛文尼亚竞争保护办公室（CPA）。它于2013年成立，取代前斯洛文尼亚竞争保护办公室并作为一个独立的行政机关运行。[①]

2. 竞争法概况

斯洛文尼亚的竞争法依据《宪法》第74条制定，并受到欧盟法律的重大影响，其中包括反托拉斯条例、合并控制和国家援助等内容。[②]规制竞争的核心法律是《防止限制竞争法》[③]，分为实体法和程序法两部分，并规定了竞争保护机构的各种执法和监督程序。

斯洛文尼亚的反垄断政策体现了《欧盟运作条约》（TFEU）第101、102条的规定。首先，它宣布经营者之间、经营者协会之间订立的关于避免、限制或破坏斯洛文尼亚的市场竞争的协议或一致行动协议无效。[④]这个一般规则不适用的情形是那些次要的（微量豁免）协议或对技术和经济进步有积极影响同时与消费者公平分享收益的协议（集体豁免）。其次，禁止处于市场支配地位的一个或几个企业在斯洛文尼亚境内的全部或特定区域滥用市场支配地位。[⑤]拥有市场支配地位是指该企业在很大程度上具备独立于竞争对手，拥有影响客户或消费者的能力，因此一个企业在斯洛文尼亚市场份额超过40%也被推定为拥有市场支配地位。

经营者集中规则以《欧共体并购条例》为基础。[⑥]经营者集中是指由于合并、收购或合资企业的建立而导致的控制权的持续变化。[⑦]通过一个特殊的通知程序，CPA对每个经营者的集中行为进行评估，以确定其是否妨碍有效竞争或者不符合竞争规则。[⑧]

总的来说，TFEU第107条禁止任何国家援助破坏或者威胁破坏欧盟内部的市场竞争。国家援助是指国家公共当局有选择地对企业进行的任何形式的优势支持。[⑨]斯洛文尼亚政府可例外地根据《为困难企业和合作社提供援助和重组方案法》给予国家援助。[⑩]该法旨在确保企业经营和就业的长期连续性。陷入经营困难的，对国家、特定区域或者行业具有重要作用的公司或企业，可能会获得国家以信用贷款、补贴、担保或投资的形式进行的援助。财政部根据《国家援助监督法》[⑪]监督国家拨款。它可以给予与欧盟法律相一致的国家援助，向欧盟委员会通报这种援助，并保留所有国家授予援助企业的名单。

3. 竞争规制措施

竞争规制可公开或私下执行。公共执法主要由竞争保护机构在市场情况表明可能存在限制性措施时依职权启动。当明确发生侵犯竞争的行为时，竞争保护机构会作出停止侵权的决定，通常是由侵权方处理一部分或全部业务。当没有发现违规时，程序将被终止。

通常，经营者集中程序是事前性质的，从向CPA发出集中通知开始，这也触发了集中行为的暂时

---

① 参见 http://www.varstvo-konkurence.si/en/about-the-agency/，访问日期：2018年2月13日。
② 参见 http://ec.europa.eu/competition/index_en.html，访问日期：2018年2月15日。
③ 参见斯洛文尼亚《防止限制竞争法》(ZPOmK-1)，《斯洛文尼亚政府公报》Nos.36/08, 40/09, 26/11, 87/11, 57/12, 39/13, 斯洛文尼亚宪法法院判决 63/13 – ZS-K, 33/14, 76/15, 23/17。
④ 参见斯洛文尼亚《防止限制竞争法》(ZPOmK-1)，第6条。
⑤ 参见斯洛文尼亚《防止限制竞争法》(ZPOMK-1)，第9条。
⑥ 参见2004年1月20日《欧盟理事会条例》(EC)第139/2004号，关于控制企业集中（EC并购条例），欧盟官方公报 L 24/1。
⑦ 参见斯洛文尼亚《防止限制竞争法》(ZPOmK-1)，第10条。
⑧ 斯洛文尼亚《防止限制竞争法》(ZPOmK-1)，第41条；关于CPA的通知程序参见 http://www.varstvo-konkurence.si/en/concentrations-of-undertakings/notification-procedure/，访问日期：2018年2月15日。根据斯洛文尼亚《防止限制竞争法》，如果出现以下情况，则需要通知：(1)上一个业务年度斯洛文尼亚市场上所有相关企业的总年度营业额连同集团内的其他企业的总营业额超过3500万欧元；(2)上一个业务年度，斯洛文尼亚市场目标公司的年营业额连同集团内的其他业务超过100万欧元。此外，如果集中度未达到上述标准，但由于集中而导致相关企业（包括关联企业）共同在斯洛文尼亚市场上获得超过60%的市场份额，相关企业必须通知管理局，管理局可以在15天内要求他们通知这种集中。尽管如此，如果欧盟委员会根据经修订的《欧盟理事会条例》(EC)第139/2004号（ECMR）进行评估，则无需通知。
⑨ 参见 http://ec.europa.eu/competition/state_aid/overview/index_en.html，访问日期：2018年2月15日。
⑩ 参见《为困难企业和合作社提供援助和重组方案法》(ZPRPGDZT)，《斯洛文尼亚政府公报》No.5/17。
⑪ 参见《国家援助监督法》(ZSDrP)，《斯洛文尼亚政府公报》No.37/04。

中止。一般来说，CPA 会在 60 个工作日内宣布集中行为是否符合竞争规则。

在这个程序中，参与集中的公司可采取某些主动措施。也就是说，这些公司在通知 CPA 之前，必须先采取某些补救措施，以消除竞争侵权风险。如果公司提出的措施能充分减少风险，CPA 将终止程序。此外，在宽大处理原则下，企业联合的成员在发现企业非法联合时，向当局披露有关现有企业联合或合作的信息，可获豁免或减少罚款。①

CPA 的决定可以通过比照适用行政纠纷规则进行司法审查。此外，最严重的侵犯行为可能构成《刑法》②所界定的"非法限制竞争罪"。

2017 年《防止竞争法》第 2014/104 号指令实施，以加强对私人竞争执法的可能性，这是对公共竞争的补充。私人实体可通过民事司法程序要求赔偿因违反反垄断法而遭受的损害。修订后的立法引入了一种选择，即在一个案件中加入由同一违法行为引起的不同法律诉讼，并便利先前难度较高的证据收集。法院可以命令被告、CPA 和其他有关方面披露相关信息和文件，但保密的商业信息受到保护。据预测，这些变化将增加斯洛文尼亚私人竞争执法程序，而这些程序在过去相对较简单。③

（八）税收

1. 税收体系与制度

斯洛文尼亚将税收法律制度分为三大类即直接所得税、直接财产税、间接税（详见表 1）。一般的实质性和程序性税收规则载于《征税程序法》④，但有关个人所得税的细节由具体法规界定。⑤

直接所得税	直接财产税	间接税
• 个人所得税法 • 工资税法案 • 合同工作税 • 企业所得税法 • 关于在研究和开发投资中申请减免税收的规则 • 对某些农产品过度库存的征收法 • 社会保险法 • 经济区法 • 征收吨税法案 • 关于衍生产品处置利润的税法	• 遗产和赠与税法 • 水船税法 • 民事税法 • 对传统赌博游戏所得税 • 银行资产负债表税法 • 不动产质量估价法	• 增值税法 • 消费税法 • 不动产交易税法 • 博彩税法 • 保险合同税法 • 金融服务税法

斯洛文尼亚的所有税都是由财政部主管的税务局征收的。每一个应纳税者的税收都是基于财务管理局保存在计算机中和统一税务登记册中收集的数据。财政部的税务登记涉及各种类别的纳税者，包括在法院登记注册运营商、具有永久居留权或暂时居住在斯洛文尼亚的个人、在斯洛文尼亚从事业务的有席位或无席位的法人和自然人，以及没有法律人格的国外协会的个人。这些主体都有一个独一无二的纳税人识别号。税务登记可以依职权登记或根据申请进行。希望通过分支机构在斯洛文尼亚开展业务的外国公司必须在斯洛文尼亚记录其活动，而欧盟注册公司可以直接经营。但是，所有没有税务识别号的公司必须在其业务开始之前申请一个纳税识别号。⑥

---

① 斯洛文尼亚《防止限制竞争法》(ZPOmK-1)，第 76 条。
② 斯洛文尼亚《刑法》(KZ-1)，《斯洛文尼亚政府公报》Nos.55/2008, 66/2008, 39/2009, 55/2009，斯洛文尼亚宪法法院判决 91/2011, 54/2015, 38/2016, 27/2017, Art.225。
③ 参见 https://svetkapitala.delo.si/mnenja/pot-do-odskodnine-zaradi-krsitev-konkurencnih-pravil-je-po-novem-lazja-2412?meta_refresh=true，访问日期：2018 年 2 月 22 日。
④ 斯洛文尼亚《征税程序法》(ZDavP-2)，《斯洛文尼亚政府公报》，Nos.117/2006, 24/2008 - ZDDKIS, 125/2008, 85/2009, 110/2009, 1/2010., 43/2010, 97/2010, 24/2012 - ZDDPO-2G, 24/2012 - ZDoh-2I, 32/2012, 94/2012, 101/2013-ZDavNepr, 111/2013, 22/2014, 斯洛文尼亚宪法法院判决 40/2014 - ZIN-B, 25/2014 - ZFU, 90/2014, 95/2014 - ZUJF-C, 23/2015 - ZDoh-2O, 23/2015 - ZDDPO-2L, 91/2015, 63/2016, 69/2017。
⑤ 斯洛文尼亚财政部关于税和关税的规定，参见 http://www.mf.gov.si/en/areas_of_work/taxes_and_customs/taxes_and_custom_duties/，访问日期：2018 年 2 月 15 日。
⑥ 关于斯洛文尼亚财务管理、税务登记和税号，参见：http://www.fu.gov.si/en/taxes_and_other_duties/work_with_us/entry_into_the_tax_register_and_tax_number/，访问日期：2018 年 2 月 15 日。

2. 主要税赋和税率

（1）增值税

增值税是一种由增值税法[1]调整的一般性间接消费税。增值税法[2]附录一中规定的所有特定货物和服务供应均以标准税率 22% 或减免税率 9.5% 的税率支付增值税。除某些从事特定活动的公司外，所有公司都应缴纳增值税，包括每年营业额低于 50 000 欧元的小企业，以及出口产品的公司。

（2）企业所得税

应缴纳企业所得税的纳税人有国内法人、外国法律实体和没有法人资格的外国协会。《企业所得税法》[3]要求对税务居民的全球收入征税（比如注册所在地或实际管理机构所在地在斯洛文尼亚的公司），而非居民支付的所得税仅对其在斯洛文尼亚或通过他们的斯洛文尼亚办公场所产生的收入课税。[4]

企业所得税的一般税率是 19%，此外，《企业所得税法》在该税基的基础上准予不同科目的扣除项，即税前扣除研发支出（成本的 100%）、投资成本（投资总额的 40%），特定群体工人就业补贴（对工人的工资的 20%、45% 或 70%），自愿补充的养老保险金额（保险费），以及企业对外捐款（收入的 0.3%）。[5]

（3）个人所得税

个人所得税受《个人所得税法》[6]的规制，适用于六类个人收入，即就业收入、经营收入、基本农业和林业收入、租金收入、特许权使用费收入以及资本收入。主动收入类征税按照 16%、27%、34%、39% 或 50% 的累进税率进行，而被动收入类征税按照 25% 的扁平税率[7]进行。资本收益类税率取决于持有期，每 5 年下降 5%。

3. 纳税申报与优惠

税收程序是一种特殊的行政程序，主要由《征税程序法》和《一般行政程序法》[8]所调整。一般来说，纳税债务是在纳税申报或税务裁定中计算的。

纳税申报需要自我评估，纳税义务人必须在规定的纳税期内纳税申报。该申报必须通过电子商务税收方式发送或到税务局现场书面及时提交。未及时申报或者申报错误的纳税义务人，可以处以罚款和利息。纳税申报期限届满后，纳税义务人意识到存在违规行为的，可以主动报告并立即补缴税款，避免面临惩罚性措施。

税务裁定是税务行政部门按照纳税申报程序、税务稽查程序和其他涉税程序发布的一种特殊类型的行政行为。在纳税申报程序中，纳税义务人向税务机关报告计算纳税义务所需的信息[9]，而税务稽查程序则是税务机关在税务程序中面对可能出现违法的行为时所采取的一种特殊的行政程序。

该法没有为外国自然人和法人提供任何特别的税收优惠制度；但是，它们有资格获得国内实体享有的所有税务减免和奖励。

---

[1] 参见斯洛文尼亚《增值税法》(ZDDV-1)，《斯洛文尼亚政府公报》Nos.117/2006, 52/2007, 33/2009, 85/2009, 85/2010, 18/2011, 78/2011, 38/2012, 40/2012 - ZUJF, 83/2012, 14/2013, 46/2013 - ZIPRS1314-A, 101/2013 - ZIPRS1415, 86/2014, 90/2015。
[2] 参见斯洛文尼亚《增值税法》(ZDDV-1)，第 41 条。
[3] 参见斯洛文尼亚《企业所得税法》(ZDDPO-2)，《斯洛文尼亚政府公报》Nos.117/06, 56/08, 76/08, 5/09, 96/09, 110/09 – ZDavP-2B, 43/10, 59/11, 24/12, 30/12, 94/12, 81/13, 50/14, 23/15, 82/15, 68/16, 69/17。
[4] 参见斯洛文尼亚《企业所得税法》，第 4、5 条。
[5] 参见斯洛文尼亚《企业所得税法》，第 55—59 条。
[6] 参见斯洛文尼亚《所得税法》(ZDoh-2)，《斯洛文尼亚政府公报》Nos.117/2006, 90/2007, 119/2007, 10/2008, 92/2008, 78/2008, 125/2008, 119/2008, 20/2009, 104/2009, 10/2010, 20/2010, 43/2010, 106/2010, 103/2010, 9/2011 - ZUKD-1, 105/2011, 9/2012，斯洛文尼亚宪法法院裁决，24/2012, 30/2012, 40/2012 - ZUJF, 75/2012, 94/2012, 102/2012, 52/2013，斯洛文尼亚宪法法院裁决，96/2013, 108/2013, 29/2014，斯洛文尼亚宪法法院裁决，50/2014, 94/2014, 23/2015, 55/2015, 102/2015 - ZUJF-E, 104/2015, 63/2016, 69/2017。
[7] 斯洛文尼亚《所得税法》，第 122 条。
[8] 一般行政程序法 (ZUP)，《斯洛文尼亚政府公告》Nos.80/1999, 70/2000, 52/2002, 73/2004, 119/2005, 105/2006 - ZUS-1, 126/2007, 65/2008, 8/2010, 82/2013。
[9] 企业所得税由计税人计算和支付。上一个营业年度的纳税申报必须在当前营业年度的 3 个月内提交，必须向税务管理机关公布并且在接下来的几年内不能更改。预付税款按月分期支付。

(九) 证券交易

1. 证券法律法规简介

证券市场受各种法律法规的管制,特别是《金融工具市场法》《信托投资和管理公司法》《投资基金经理法》《收购法》和《证券法》。前面的章节未详细讨论的法律和法规将在下文中依次介绍。

《金融票据市场法》界定了金融工具市场的主要参与者以及他们的权利和义务、证券类型以及证券公开发行的一些基本规则。在有组织的市场上,可通过卢布尔雅那证券交易所或通过授权机构在证券交易所以外进行证券交易。未经证券市场管理机构(SMA)核准的适当招股说明书,禁止公开发行证券。招股书的内容及其产生的程序载于《金融工具市场法》和《收购法》。

唯一有组织的证券市场是在斯洛文尼亚的卢布尔雅那证券交易所(LJSE)。卢布尔雅那证券交易所的规则[1]界定市场结构的基础上市金融票据的类型和质量,即根据股票市场、债券市场和结构性产品市场,以及证券交易的具体程序来确定的。

记账式证券受《记账证券法》管辖。记账证券的收购、缺失和转移通过记账证券中央登记机关进行,电脑化的记账证券记录是他们的权利和义务,以及持有和抵押情况的凭证。[2]该登记由中央国债登记清算公司(KDD)进行。中央国债登记清算公司是股份有限责任公司[3],其创始人和大股东是银行、证券公司、基金管理公司、政府基金和发行人。[4]

允许银行和其他市场参与者短期获得担保资金或贷款的证券金融交易受《欧盟条例》2015/2365"关于证券融资交易和再利用的透明度以及相关国内法实施情况"的管制。[5]该条例增加了机构间的透明度和协作性。在斯洛文尼亚,实施上述欧盟立法的主管机构是斯洛文尼亚银行、证券市场管理机构和保险监督机构。

2. 证券市场监督

斯洛文尼亚资本市场由证券市场监管机构监管。SMA 是一个独立的法律实体,其宗旨是维持一个安全、透明和高效的金融证券交易市场。SMA 每年向国民议会报告,其运作完全由税收供资,其职能由审计法院监督。[6]

3. 外资企业参与证券交易要求

根据《金融工具市场法》,第三方国家实体参与证券市场交易比较困难。第三方国家发行人、要约人打算公开发行证券,或者申请将该发行人的证券获准在证券交易所交易,只能通过中间人进行操作。因此,第三方国家实体必须委托经授权的投资公司进行与证券有关的业务。所选择的投资公司对履行债务和违反这些义务所产生的任何损害负有连带责任。[7]

如果发行人的招股说明书符合国际标准,包括国际证券委员会组织的标准,并按照欧盟第2003/71号指令或欧共体的标准编制,第三方国家发行人的招股说明书可能会获得批准。

外商投资企业可通过已被 SMA 授权的斯洛文尼亚分支机构在斯洛文尼亚证券市场进行交易。母公司可能需要在斯洛文尼亚存入一定数额的资金,作为解决斯洛文尼亚交易所产生债务的担保。该分支机构只能行使经 SMA 授权批准的活动。[8]

---

[1] 参见《卢布尔雅那证券交易所规则》和《斯洛文尼亚政府公告》,Nos.88/10, 89/11, 71/12, 84/12, 44/13, 81/13, 10/14, 80/14, 88/15, 32/16, 67/16, 5/17, 63/17, 76/17。
[2] 参见《非物质化证券法》(ZNVP-1),《斯洛文尼亚政府公告》,Nos.75/15, 74/16 – ORZNVP48, 5/17。
[3] 中央证券清算公司简介,参见 https://www-en.kdd.si/about_kdd,访问日期:2018年2月18日。
[4] 根据公开数据,SSH 约20%将要售出的资产构成 KDD 股权份额的一部分,参见 https://www.sdh.si/en-gb/sale-of-assets. 访问日期:2018年2月21日。
[5] 《证券融资和再利用交易的透明度》,《斯洛文尼亚政府公报》,No.55/17。
[6] 证券市场管理机构简介,参见 http://www.atvp.si/Eng/Default.aspx?id=71,访问日期:2018年2月18日。
[7] 参见《金融工具市场法》(ZTFI),第86、87条。
[8] 参见《金融工具市场法》(ZTFI),第182、185条。

（十）投资优惠及保护

1. 优惠政策框架

斯洛文尼亚政府一直致力于为投资者创造一个普遍有利的环境。斯洛文尼亚正在发展成为一个环保、物流和研发中心，并向新投资者和已经在斯洛文尼亚投资的投资者提供了一些奖励。财政激励措施包括有利的折旧免税额和摊销率、投资和研发的税收减免，以及结转前一会计期间损失的可能性。财政奖励包括区域援助计划和各种就业激励措施[1]（例如，承担雇主支付的社会捐助、税收奖励、计划雇用失业人员的雇主可以向当地就业办公室申请提供免费的培训和再培训）。其他奖励措施也可在国家和市一级获得；特别是后者的奖励措施是根据具体情况确定的。[2]

2. 行业与地区鼓励

2014年3月，欧盟委员会批准斯洛文尼亚2014—2020年区域援助地图来支持投资，这将有助于区域发展。[3] 区域援助地图覆盖斯洛文尼亚全境，分为两个区域。"A"（斯洛文尼亚东部）地区的财政奖励是企业合格费用的25%、35%或45%，而在"C"（斯洛文尼亚西部）地区的这些奖励是10%、20%或30%。[4]

此外，受经济危机影响特别严重，而且失业率高于斯洛文尼亚其他地区的4个地区，斯洛文尼亚可能受益于临时发展援助措施。这些措施针对的是具有增长潜力的公司，主要是帮助它们进入国外市场。4个符合条件的地区是地域较广的马里博尔市，普利科姆地区、特尔博夫列镇、赫拉斯特尼克镇、拉代切镇和波科皮杰地区。[5]

3. 特殊经济区域

根据《经济区法》[6]，政府可同意一个或多个国内法律实体设立经济区，从事金融、工业或零售性质的经济活动。一个经济区的建立和运行依赖于当地或所属地区的立法，可能需要一定的税收、就业和基础设施激励措施。外国企业如果在斯洛文尼亚注册并取得创始人的许可就可以在经济区内经营。

欧盟第952/2013号条例和《欧洲联盟海关法实施法》[7]允许设立特别自由区，便利贸易，简化海关手续。自由区有两种类型：第一类区域有海关围栏，货物由海关放置和监督；第二类区域与海关仓库的情况相似，货物须申报。[8] 在斯洛文尼亚设立自由贸易区必须得到政府的批准，并通知欧盟委员会，在指定的自由贸易区建设需要得到海关当局的批准。目前，在斯洛文尼亚唯一的保税区是科佩尔港。

4. 投资保护

截至2018年底，斯洛文尼亚共有34项双边投资条约生效，规定了"国民待遇条款""最惠国条款""公平与公正待遇"和"非歧视性征收措施"等标准国际法的保护措施。[9] 斯洛文尼亚和中国[10]之间的双边投资协定签署于1993年9月13日并于1995年1月生效。[11] 斯洛文尼亚生效的双边投资协定如

---

[1] 参见《财政奖励政策》，载 https://www.ess.gov.si/delodajalci/financne_spodbude/ugodnosti_pri_zaposlovanju，访问日期：2018年2月21日。
[2] 参见 https://www.investslovenia.org/business-environment/incentives/，访问日期：2018年2月21日。
[3] 参见 http://ec.europa.eu/competition/state_aid/cases/251276/251276_1548895_58_2.pdf，访问日期：2018年2月19日。
[4] 参见 https://www.investslovenia.org/business-environment/incentives/，访问日期：2018年2月21日。
[5] 参见 https://www.investslovenia.org/business-environment/incentives/，访问日期：2018年2月18日。
[6] 参见《经济区法》(ZEC)，《斯洛文尼亚政府公报》No.35/10。请注意，该法目前只规范经济区内截至2013年12月31日的经济活动，但修正后的经济区法延长了这一期限。
[7] 《欧盟海关法实施法》(ZICZEU)，《斯洛文尼亚政府公报》，No.32/16。
[8] 参见 https://ec.europa.eu/taxation_customs/business/customs-procedures/what-is-exportation/free-zones_en，访问日期：2018年2月18日。
[9] 例如，《土耳其和斯洛文尼亚关于促进和保护投资的协定》，参见 http://investmentpolicyhub.unctad.org/Download/TreatyFile/2274，访问日期：2018年2月21日；新加坡共和国政府和斯洛文尼亚共和国政府关于相互促进和保护投资的协定，参见 http://investmentpolicyhub.unctad.org/Download/TreatyFile/3535，访问日期：2018年2月21日。
[10] 双边投资条约清单，参见 https://view.officeapps.live.com/op/view.aspx?src=http%3A%2F%2Fwww.mgrt.gov.si%2Ffileadmin%2Fmgrt.gov.si%2Fpageuploads%2FSEKTOR_ZA_INTERNACIONALIZACIJO%2Fpredlogi_in_veljavni_predpisi%2FBilateral_Investment_Treaties.-list.doc，访问日期：2018年2月19日。
[11] 《中华人民共和国政府和斯洛文尼亚共和国政府关于鼓励和相互保护投资的协定》，参见 http://investmentpolicyhub.unctad.org/Download/TreatyFile/779，访问日期：2018年2月19日。

下[①]:

国家	签署日	生效日
阿尔巴尼亚	1997年10月23日	2000年3月22日
奥地利	2001年3月7日	2002年2月1日
比利时—卢森堡经济联盟	1999年2月1日	2002年1月14日
波斯尼亚和黑塞哥维那	2001年5月30日	2002年7月1日
保加利亚	1998年6月30日	2000年11月26日
中国	1993年9月13日	1995年1月1日
克罗地亚	1997年12月12日	2004年7月8日
丹麦	1999年5月12日	2002年3月30日
埃及	1998年10月28日	2000年2月07日
芬兰	1998年6月1日	2000年6月03日
法国	1998年2月11日	2000年8月5日
德国	1993年10月28日	1998年7月18日
希腊	1997年5月29日	2000年2月11日
匈牙利	1996年10月15日	2000年6月9日
科威特	2002年4月26日	2004年7月28日
立陶宛	1998年10月13日	2002年5月15日
马其顿	1996年6月5日	1999年9月21日
马耳他	2001年3月15日	2001年11月6日
摩尔多瓦	2003年4月10日	2004年6月01日
荷兰	1996年9月24日	1998年8月01日
波兰	1996年6月28日	2000年3月31日
葡萄牙	1997年5月14日	2000年5月4日
罗马尼亚	1996年1月24日	1996年11月24日
塞尔维亚	2002年6月18日	2004年5月1日
新加坡	1999年1月25日	2000年9月8日
斯洛伐克	1993年7月28日	1996年3月28日
西班牙	1998年7月15日	2000年4月3日
瑞典	1999年10月5日	2001年5月12日
瑞士	1995年11月9日	1997年3月20日
泰国	2000年2月18日	2002年10月20日
土耳其	2004年3月23日	2006年6月19日
乌克兰	1999年3月30日	2000年6月1日
英国	1996年7月3日	1999年3月27日
乌兹别克斯坦	2003年10月7日	2004年5月18日

[①] 参见 http://investmentpolicyhub.unctad.org/IIA/CountryBits/192,访问日期：2018年2月23日。

三、贸易

（一）贸易监管部门

斯洛文尼亚的贸易及贸易政策的主管部门是经济发展和技术部，该部门在商品和服务的自由流动、全国质量技术基础设施（认证、度量和标准化）、公司法、消费者权益保护、知识产权及竞争保护领域适用欧洲及本国的政策和立法，以适应市场和商品储备要求，并有效控制价格、商业活动和物流。

斯洛文尼亚财政部和财政管理局（FURS）共同构成了财政与税务管理的核心机构。斯洛文尼亚财政管理局的主要职能包括评估、计算、征收税款及关税，货物清关，财务监管，财务调查，进出欧盟的现金管制，扣押物的存放、销售和销毁、没收，对涉及安全和人民生命健康保护，动物、植物、环境保护以及文化遗产保护，对知识产权保护等采取特别措施的商品进行排查、销毁和没收，控制此类商品的入境、运输和转移，采取商业政策措施，实施对外贸易和农业政策措施等。市场监察局是斯洛文尼亚另一个重要的监管主体，主要负责监督消费者权益保护、产品安全、贸易、餐饮、工艺品、服务、价格、旅游、竞争保护、版权等领域的立法执行。

斯洛文尼亚工商协会作为一个非政府组织，是欧洲商会和国际商会（ICC）的成员，在斯洛文尼亚国内是最具影响力的商业协会。

（二）贸易法律法规简介

斯洛文尼亚法律体系包括三个层面的法律和法规。按照等级划分（除宪法外），依次为国际条约、欧盟法规、国内立法，其中欧盟法规优先于国内立法。欧盟在关税同盟领域拥有专属权利，《欧盟条约》根据《欧盟运作条约》的规则，为内部市场运作制定了必要的竞争条例，为使用欧元作为流通货币的成员国制定了货币政策，在共同渔业政策和共同商业政策下建立了海洋生物资源保护政策，其他领域则采取共同享有或成员国独立控制（例如，税法领域）。而斯洛文尼亚在自己的法律法规中大量采用了欧盟法的规定。

对于贸易各方面管理最重要的法律有：
- 《义务法典》(《斯洛文尼亚官方公报》，第 97/07 号)；
- 《公司法》(《斯洛文尼亚官方公报》，第 65/09 号，第 33/11 号，第 91/11 号，第 32/12 号，第 57/12 号，第 44/13 号)；
- 《执行欧盟海关立法》(《斯洛文尼亚官方公报》，第 32/16 号)；
- 《消费者权益保护法》(《斯洛文尼亚官方公报》，第 98/04 号)；
- 《避免限制竞争法》(《斯洛文尼亚官方公报》，第 36/08 号，第 40/09 号，第 26/11 号，第 87/11 号，第 57/12 号，第 39/13 号，第 63/13 号，第 33/14 号，第 76/15 号和第 23/17 号)；
- 《检查法》(《斯洛文尼亚官方公报》，第 42/07 号，第 40/14 号)；
- 《电子商务和电子签名法》(《斯洛文尼亚官方公报》，第 98/04 号，第 61/06 号和第 46/14 号)；
- 《电子商务市场法》(《斯洛文尼亚官方公报》，第 24/08 号，第 47/15 号)；
- 《贸易法》(《斯洛文尼亚官方公报》，第 24/08 号，第 47/15 号)。

（三）贸易管理

1. 一般贸易规则和不正当竞争

贸易规则和条例，如最低技术条件、贸易地点、价格指示、产品标签等，受国家立法的各种法律法规限制，同时也受欧盟立法的直接规定。对贸易管理最主要的法律有《义务法典》（一般民法规则和对特殊合同类型的规定，包括商事主体的具体规则）、《公司法》（公司和类似法律实体的合并和运营）、《消费者权益保护法》（给消费者和终端用户提供商品和服务的具体要求）、《贸易法》和《产品安全法》。

进入斯洛文尼亚市场的外国企业家可以在斯洛文尼亚国内成立公司或注册一个分支机构，也可以在国外运营，还可以与当地分销商签约合作。外国公民和法律实体在具备与斯洛文尼亚公民和法律实体相同条件的情况下可以成立公司。最为常见的公司形式是有限责任公司，最低股本为 7 500 欧元。其他常见的公司类型包括有限公司、无限责任公司、有限合伙和个体公司（无法人主体地位）。公司注册过程非常方便快捷。但所有的注册文件都需要由经认证的翻译人员翻译为斯洛文尼亚语。

所有产品进入斯洛文尼亚零售市场必须符合《消费者权益保护法》，要求公司必须使用斯洛文尼亚语言（某些地区使用匈牙利语和意大利语）与消费者开展业务。《斯洛文尼亚公共用语法》（《斯洛文尼亚官方公报》，第 86/04 号和第 8/10 号）对此进行了更为具体的规定。产品声明必须采用斯洛文尼亚语，并且必须包含产品信息、产品特性和使用说明，也可使用常见且易理解的图片和符号。

只有被证实安全的产品才能进入市场。根据各种法律法规规定，各种类型的产品都需要有产品标识。一般来说，所有食品都有一个相同的最低标准，必须满足这些标准后才能投放市场（产品上必须明确说明：产品名称、配料清单、净含量、到期日期等）。欧盟关于产品的申报和标准斯洛文尼亚也同样适用。所有产品必须配备 CE 认证书和相关文件。

斯洛文尼亚立法中关于不正当竞争的规定和相关措施与欧盟一致。《防止限制竞争法》明确规定禁止不正当竞争，禁止一切损害或可能损害其他公司的商业活动。如果有造成损害的行为，可以根据《义务法典》的规定提起诉讼。此外，如果可能的话，受影响实体可以要求停止不正当竞争活动，销毁侵权过程中使用的物品并消除影响。

2. 电子贸易和消费者保护

斯洛文尼亚的《电子商务市场法》对电子贸易进行了规范。本法适用于信息技术服务的提供者，即在斯洛文尼亚注册办事处的个人或其他法律组织，他们针对用户的具体要求通过电子设备提供远程服务并收取费用。斯洛文尼亚法律也规定了一些例外情形，这些例外与服务提供者的注册办事处无关。这些例外包括知识产权、基金投资广告、消费者合同中的合同义务、特殊形式的不动产权利。《电子商务和电子签名法》是对《电子商务市场法》的补充，它对电子或数字运营及电子商务和公共程序中电子签名的使用分别作出了规定。

斯洛文尼亚《消费者权益保护法》执行了欧盟大部分重要的指令，例如理事会指令中关于产品缺陷责任的规定和管理条款，以及消费者合同中的不公平条款的规定等。《消费者权益保护法》的条款适用于所有的消费者合同，该法规定了缔结远程协议的最低法律要求，以及在缔结这些协定之前需要提供哪些必要的信息。值得注意的是，某些消费者合同，例如消费者贷款和信贷协议受其他专门立法的约束。

（四）进出口商品检验检疫

在《欧盟海关法典》（UCC）一般授权下，进入欧盟关税区的商品有时可能受到海关的管制。本法典的适用下，所有商品除受到公共道德、公共政策或公共安全等的约束，还应符合保护人类生命健康，保护动植物，保护环境，保护具有艺术、历史或考古价值的国宝，保护工业或商业财产，包括控制前体药物、控制某些侵犯知识产权的物品、控制货币，以及实施渔业养护和管理措施和商业政策措施的要求。商品必须接受监管以决定是否通关，在没有海关当局的允许下不得转移。非欧盟商品在海关状态发生变化之前，或从欧盟关税区中取出前或销毁前，均受海关的监管。

海关当局在认为有必要时，可能采取所有海关控制措施，包括货物检查，抽样检查，验证申报中提供的信息，检查文件的真实性，审查商业实体的账目和其他记录，检查车辆、乘客、行李或乘客携带的商品或其他物品。

（五）海关管理

1. 适用法律和国际协议的概况

（1）海关法

斯洛文尼亚作为欧盟成员国之一，同时作为《欧盟运作条约》的签约方，完全执行欧盟的海关政策。在此领域最重要的法律是欧盟议会和欧盟理事会在 2013 年 10 月 9 日制定的《欧盟海关法典》（2013/952 号）。斯洛文尼亚采用了该法典并制定了《执行欧共体海关规定法案》（《斯洛文尼亚官方公报》，第 32/16 号）。欧盟在海关和关税方面的法律还包括欧盟议会和欧盟理事会制定的欧盟第

2016/1037 号和第 2016/1036 号法律，对成员国在非成员国采取反补贴和反倾销措施进行保护。

（2）关税

斯洛文尼亚使用"欧盟产品分类系统"，该系统对所有产品均按照关税代码进行分类，其中载有进出口税率和其他征税的信息，并列明保护措施（例如，反倾销），对外贸易统计，进出口手续要求和其他免税要求。"欧盟系统"有以下三个组成部分：

• 协调制度（HS——世界海关组织制定的术语）；
• 欧盟综合术语（CN——欧盟八位编码系统，包括欧盟进一步细分的 HS 码）；
• 综合关税（TARIC）提供适用于欧盟特定商品的所有贸易政策和关税措施的信息（例如，中止关税、反倾销税等）。包含欧盟综合术语的八位编码，并在此基础上新增两位。

（3）自由贸易协定和双边协定

斯洛文尼亚作为一个主权国家，与中国已经签订了 7 个双边协议：《经济贸易协议》(1993)、《科学技术合作协议》《科学文化教育合作协议》《鼓励和相互保护投资协议》《经济合作协议》(2007)、《国防领域合作协议》《避免双重征税和防止偷税漏税协定》。

2. 海关管理和程序

《欧盟海关法典》对所有的海关管理及程序都作了一般规定。根据原产国的不同或产品种类的差异，涉及的程序也有所不同。有关特定产品的更准确具体的信息（包括所需表格、标签等）可以通过输入特定的综合术语编码、原产地和目的地来获得（表格可在 http://trade.ec.europa.eu/tradehelp/ 获取）。产品的原产国证书可由斯洛文尼亚商会、贸易商会或海关当局签发。

（1）进口程序

进入欧盟关税区的货物需要在欧盟入境处的首个海关办事处通过入境摘要报关单（ENS）预先提交货物信息。进入欧盟关税区的货物进入欧盟即受到海关监管，并可能受到海关管制（可能受到禁止和限制）。

进入欧盟关税区的商品必须具有入境摘要报关单。然后货物处于临时存放状态（最多不超过 90 天），受海关监管，直至被置于下列海关程序或直至该商品再出口：

• 准予自由流通；当商品符合进入欧盟的条件时，将被准予自由流通；
• 特殊程序；商品可能会进入以下特殊程序。

① 转运，包括对外转运或对内转运：

对外转运：非欧盟商品可能在欧盟关税区内从一个地点转移到另一个地点，而不征收进口关税；

对内转运：欧盟商品可能在欧盟关税区内从一个地点通过关税区外的国家或地区转移到另一关税区地点，海关状态不因此发生改变。

② 仓储，包括海关监管仓库和自由区。

海关监管仓库：非欧盟货物可以存放在海关监管（在"海关监管仓库"）或海关当局授权的任何场所和地方，不需要缴纳进口关税和与货物进口相关的其他费用，不受商业政策措施限制。

自由区：成员国可以将欧盟关税区的某些地点指定为自由区。这是欧盟关税区内的特殊区域，免收进口关税和其他费用（例如，国内税），不受其他商业措施的限制，直到经批准进入下一个海关程序或再出口为止。货物也可能经过简单的加工或再包装。

③ 特殊程序，包括暂时入境和最终使用程序。

暂时入境：准备转口的非欧盟货物可能在欧盟关税区内进入特殊程序，全部或部分免除进口税，并且不需要支付其他费用如内部税，且不受商业政策措施的影响。该程序只能使用于不加工或不发生改变的货物，货物可在此程序内最长停留 2 年。

最终用途：货物可免税放行或因其具体用途而降低税率。

④ 加工，包括内加工和外加工。

内加工：货物进口到欧盟之后在欧盟内进行一次或多次加工，不征收进口税和其他税收，也不受商业政策措施的约束。海关当局会指定办理内加工程序的具体期限。若产品加工完成后最终未能出口，应缴纳相应的税收，采取相应的措施。

外加工：欧盟货物暂时出口至欧盟关税区外进行加工操作。这些经加工的货物可以自由流通，免收或部分免收进口税。

欲从海关当局获得处理或使用货物的许可，需提交"欧盟统一报关单"（SAD），所有的欧盟成员国均使用"欧盟统一报关单"进行报关，欧盟现在正在建立海关的全部电子化系统。海关当局使用进口货物的价值作为评估税额的要素之一，大部分关税和增值税都是按照申报货物价值的百分比表示的，在货物进入欧盟之前必须先支付这些税款。

欧共体综合关税（TARIC）将货物做了标识，以适用欧盟的所有贸易政策及关税措施（例如，中止税收，反倾销税等）。该标识由欧盟综合术语的八位编码及新增的另外两位代码组成。下列进口税可能被征收：

- 进口税（欧盟）：关税、反倾销税和反补贴税。
- 国家税收：增值税（VAT）、消费税、各种环保税收（例如液体燃烧产生的二氧化碳征收的税）、机动车辆税（MVT）、机动车辆附加税（AMVT）。

世界贸易组织在其多个协定中承认其成员国有权对不公平贸易采取反对措施，欧盟据此采取的贸易防御手段中有以下三个不同之处：

- 监督措施不是限制进口的手段，而是欧盟成员国当局为达到监管目的签发进口许可证的一种强制性制度。这些措施主要适用于一些农产品、纺织品和钢铁产品。
- 对某些产品采取限量进口，是为保护欧洲生产商免受大量低价进口商品的侵害。
- 根据不同情况，对欧盟内可能受到损失或威胁的产业采取保护措施。包括对某些进口产品采取的临时或紧急限制。这些措施可以根据欧盟成员国的请求而实施，也可以由欧盟委员会自己启动，但不能由该行业直接提出。这些措施都必须遵守WTO的《保障措施协议》。

（2）出口程序

除少数例外情况，离开欧盟关税区的货物必须办理出口程序。所有的出口措施必须合法有序，例如：出口限制、出口监管及农产品出口退税。

出口程序原则上分为两个阶段：

① 首先，出口商/报关员出示货物和出口申报单，必要时，需要其所在地区或货物包装和装载地海关的授权或许可证。

② 若因行政原因无法执行上述条款，可以向有相关权力的海关进行出口申报。（在有正当理由时，可以向其他海关进行出口申报）。

如果不适用简化程序，出口申报可以使用"欧盟统一报关单"或电子申报。货物出口时要与申报时出示的货物和出口报关单相符，然后向出口海关出示货物并提交申报单副本，货物经查验后与申报单单货相符即可放行。

通过铁路运输、公路运输、空运和海运的出口货物，将运输合同中起运地的海关办事处作为出口海关，然后运往第三国（港口、机场或火车站）。出口海关在"统一报关单"副本的第三联或其他类似的可替代文件上盖章，然后返还给申报人或其代表人（这可以作为出口证明，免除增值税和消费税）。虽然申报出口的货物受海关的监管，但由于欧盟货物可以在欧盟关税区内自由流通，因此海关不对程序的完成情况进行监督（例如，在出口海关处出示的货物和申报单），处于海关程序下具有经济影响的非欧盟货物再出口的，需要办理出口程序。

四、劳动

（一）劳动法律法规简介

雇佣关系中适用以下法律法规：

（1）《雇佣关系法》（《斯洛文尼亚官方公报》，第21/13号，第78/13号，第47/15号，第33/16号，第52/16号和第15/17号）；

（2）《工作健康和安全法》（《斯洛文尼亚官方公报》，第43/11号）；

（3）《社会保障法》（《斯洛文尼亚官方公报》，第5/96号，第18/96号，第34/96号，第87/97号，第3/98号，第7/98号，第106/99号，第81/00号，第97/01号，第62/10号，第40/12号，第96/12号，

第 91/13 号，第 99/13 号和第 26/14 号）；

（4）《劳动市场管理法》(《斯洛文尼亚官方公报》，第 80/10 号，第 40/12 号，第 21/13 号，第 63/13 号，第 100/13 号，第 32/14 号，第 47/15 号和第 55/17 号）及目前部分有效的《防止失业的雇佣和保险法》(《斯洛文尼亚官方公报》，第 107/06 号，第 114/06 号，第 59/07 号，第 51/10 号，第 80/10 号和第 95/14 号）；

（5）《养老金和残疾保险法》(《斯洛文尼亚官方公报》，第 96/12 号，第 39/13 号，第 99/13 号，第 101/13 号，第 44/14 号，第 85/14 号，第 95/14 号，第 90/15 号，第 102/15 号，第 23/17 号，第 40/17 号和第 65/17 号）；

（6）《个人所得税法》(《斯洛文尼亚官方公报》，第 13/11 号，第 9/12 号，第 24/12 号，第 30/12 号，第 40/12 号，第 75/12 号，第 94/12 号，第 52/13 号，第 96/13 号，第 29/14 号，第 50/14 号，第 23/15 号，第 55/15 号，第 69/17 号，第 63/16 号）；

（7）《最低工资法》(《斯洛文尼亚官方公报》，第 13/10 号和第 92/15 号）；

（8）《外国公民雇佣和工作法案》(《斯洛文尼亚官方公报》，第 1/18 号）；

（9）《劳资协议法》(《斯洛文尼亚官方公报》，第 43/06 号和第 45/08 号）；

（10）《员工参与管理法》(《斯洛文尼亚官方公报》，第 42/07 号和第 45/08 号）；

（11）《工会代表法》(《斯洛文尼亚官方公报》，第 13/93 号）。

斯洛文尼亚雇佣关系均适用欧盟的指令和法律。

《雇佣关系法》是劳工关系和雇佣关系方面的主要法律，该法规定了雇佣中的所有权利和义务。个别行业的权利和义务由集体协议进一步进行约定。

（二）外籍员工的聘用要求

1. 劳动力的市场准入

斯洛文尼亚根据原籍国为欧盟成员国、非欧盟成员国分别对外籍工人采取两级管理体系。

（1）欧盟成员国公民

欧盟成员国公民（包括欧洲经济区公民）可以自由进入斯洛文尼亚劳动市场，不需要取得特殊的工作许可。他们与斯洛文尼亚公民具有同等的就业权利。但从 2018 年年中开始，斯洛文尼亚对克罗地亚公民设定了一些限制。在开始工作前雇主有义务在签订雇佣合同 8 日内为雇员办理养老保险、残疾保险、健康保险和失业保险登记。值得注意的是，根据斯洛文尼亚法律规定，任何欧盟成员国雇主派遣至斯洛文尼亚的员工（借调人员和被指定人员）有权要求最低工作条件和就业条件。

（2）非欧盟成员国公民

非欧盟成员国公民进入斯洛文尼亚劳动市场或停留在斯洛文尼亚工作，均需要工作许可证和居住许可证。由雇主申请外籍员工在特定雇主（申请人）处工作，然后颁发工作许可证。在法律规定的情况下，外籍工人也可以自己申请个人工作许可证，申请人有权在该工作许可证允许的时间内自由选择职业、工作和雇主。斯洛文尼亚就业服务局负责发放工作许可证。

2. 工作许可证和就业许可证的类型

单独工作许可证适用范围：工作、就业、自主创业、调派员工、派遣员工、派驻员工、外籍人员培训、提供个人服务、在一个日历年内从事代理工作超过 90 天，或季节性农业工作超过 90 天的。

3. 申请程序

斯洛文尼亚从 2015 年开始使用单独就业居住许可证。申请人（雇主为首次雇用的员工申请或符合条件的雇员）必须向本土行政部或外交机关、领事机关申请单独就业居住许可证。行政部门管理许可证申请程序，需要有斯洛文尼亚的就业服务局（SEE）审核批准，如果条件符合相关工作或职业类型的法律要求，将被授予许可证。外籍人员申请单独就业居住许可证只需要填写一份申请表。单独就业居住许可证将作为身份证进行发放。

4. 非欧盟成员国公民的就业条件

在斯洛文尼亚连续合法居住 1 年以上的外国人（除非他在商业登记中登记为可以进行独立活动的

人）可以申请自主创业许可证。

满足以下条件可以颁发单独就业居住许可证：
- 在失业人员中没有可以填补空缺职位的合适人员的；
- 雇主为其活动进行了合法登记并实际开展经营活动的（在申请前6个月全职雇用了至少1位非成员国公民，或个人注册社会保险达6个月的，或申请前6个月雇主向斯洛文尼亚银行存入10 000欧元营业收入的）；
- 雇主缴纳了所有的税款和关税；
- 雇员可以填补职位空缺；
- 雇佣合同原件附在申请书上。

对于登记不满6个月的雇主，需证明其在商业活动中投资了至少50 000欧元。

5. 管理费用和取得单独就业居住许可证的时间

管理费用大约为100欧元。许可证的取得从提交申请（或完成申请）之日起通常需要2个月。首次单独工作许可证在雇佣合同期内签发的，最多不超过1年，1年到期之前可以申请延长。

6. 社会保险

斯洛文尼亚强制雇员缴纳社会保险，雇主和雇员根据工资总额支付固定百分比的社会保险费。社会保险包括养老金险、残疾险、健康险、失业险和父母险。雇主按照雇员薪资总额的16.10%为雇员缴纳社会保险（不包含在薪资内），其中6.56%为健康险，8.85%为养老险，父母险、失业险、意外险占0.69%。雇员个人按照薪资总额的22.10%缴纳社会保险（不包含在薪资内），其中6.36%为健康险，15.5%为养老险，父母险、失业险、意外险占0.24%。

7. 雇佣总成本

斯洛文尼亚的雇佣成本由以下部分组成：薪资、社会保险缴费和工作成本相关的补偿（工作中的交通费、营养费和差旅费）。除普通工资外，斯洛文尼亚雇主每年应一次性向雇员支付假期津贴，以斯洛文尼亚的月平均工资为支付标准。

（三）出入境

1. 签证类型

进入斯洛文尼亚必须持有合法护照、居住许可证或签证（在原籍国取得）。

（1）居住许可证

外籍人员想要在斯洛文尼亚工作需要获得单独就业居住许可证。并需要向相关的行政部或斯洛文尼亚大使馆提交以下资料进行申请：

① 近期照片一张；
② 合法有效的护照复印件；
③ 健康保险缴纳证明（从申请之日到开始在斯洛文尼亚工作或居住期间）；
④ 具备生活能力的证明（资金证明）；
⑤ 原籍国的警方记录；
⑥ 双方签字的雇佣合同（原件）；
⑦ 雇主要求的受教育证明或资格证明，其他证明（需注意，某些文凭或资质证明可能需要斯洛文尼亚的相关单位进行认证）；
⑧ 居住或停留在斯洛文尼亚的证明。

（2）暂时居住证和永久居住证

首次申请居住证的非欧盟成员国公民取得的是最多不超过1年的暂时居住证。在暂时居住证到期前可以申请延长。外籍公民在斯洛文尼亚取得居住证合法居住5年以上，可以申请永久居住证。

（3）签证

《外国人法》根据欧盟的签证规则采用了三种签证：

① 机场过境签证（A类签证）

A 类签证是为必须在指定机场的国际中转区停留或等待几小时，以乘坐下一班飞机的旅客颁发的签证。如果旅客必须过夜等待，他们不能在中转区之外住宿。

② 短期签证（C 类签证）

C 类签证持有人根据签证的有效期，可以在申根国家（申根区）居住。根据签证申请人的目的，符合以下情况可以获得此种签证：

• 一次入境签证仅允许签证持有人在一段时间内进入申根国家（申根区）一次。一旦离开所进入的申根区，即使签证还在有效期内，也无法再次使用。

• 两次入境签证与上述签证政策相同，只是可以两次进入申根区。在签证有效期内可以进入申根区，并在离开之后再次进入。当第二次离开申根区后，签证失效。

• 多次入境签证允许其持有者随时进出申根区。但是这种签证只允许其持有者在半年内停留在申根区最多不超过 90 天，从进入申根成员国之日起开始起算。

③ 长期签证（D 类签证）

D 类签证只适用于准备在申根国家学习、工作或长期居住的人。这种签证只适用于那些因为特定目的需要在一定时间内居住在申根国家，之后便返回自己国家的人，且只能入境一次。同时，这种签证允许持有者在申根国家内随意进出，而不需要办理其他的签证。

2. 出入境限制

申请人申请居住许可证或签证失败的原因包括但不限于以下情况：怀疑外籍人员不会居住在斯洛文尼亚；外籍人员被禁止进入斯洛文尼亚；有理由怀疑外籍人员在许可证或签证到期时拒不离开斯洛文尼亚；该外籍人员可能会对斯洛文尼亚产生威胁；为取得居住许可证而结婚的外籍人员；以及其他法律规定的情形。

（四）工会及劳工组织

斯洛文尼亚宪法赋予公民组织和参与工会的权利，不论国有企业还是私有企业都可以组建工会。法律没有对组建工会的最低人数及企业规模进行限制。

根据《工会代表法》规定，斯洛文尼亚已经成立了约 50 个代表性工会。工会是集体协议的签约方，参与公共机构的谈判，保障劳动者的安全和社会保障。

（五）劳动争议

劳动争议由专门的劳动社会法院进行审理。劳动者权利受到侵害向法院提起诉讼不需要支付任何费用。劳动法规定劳动就业相关的索赔必须在终止劳动关系之后 5 年内提出。

法院在审理之前都会先询问争议双方是否可以调解。如果同意调解，双方可以在调解员的组织下进行调解。相对于漫长的诉讼程序而言，调解是快速有效解决争议的办法。如果当事人无法达成调解协议，法院将启动诉讼程序。

社会保险相关的争议也由劳动社会法院处理。劳动社会法院处理社会保险、赔偿金、残疾保险、养老金保险等相关的问题。

五、知识产权

（一）知识产权相关法律法规概况

斯洛文尼亚的知识产权法律体系由国际、欧洲和国内立法的规范组成。斯洛文尼亚宪法准予直接使用知识产权相关的国际条约，该领域现行的国际条约有 23 个。欧盟对知识产权的某些方面也有相应的规定，主要是在版权、生物科技发明专利、工业设计某些领域、商标领域。该领域所有的欧盟指令都已经在斯洛文尼亚国内的知识产权法中被采纳，而欧盟在该领域的法律也可直接使用。斯洛文尼亚在该领域现行适用的国际条约和欧盟法律在 http://www.uil-sipo.si/uil/dodatno/koristni-viri/zakonodaja/mednarodne-pogodbe/ 网站上可以获取。

斯洛文尼亚国家立法中将知识产权分为版权和工业产权两大领域，因此有两部法律对这两个领域分别作了规定：
- 《工业产权法》(《斯洛文尼亚官方公报》第51/06和第100/13号)；
- 《版权法》(《斯洛文尼亚官方公报》第16/07号，第68/08号，第110/13号，第56/15号和第63/16号)。

根据性质的不同，特殊的知识产权由以下法律分别进行了规定：
- 《集成电路布图设计保护法》(《斯洛文尼亚官方公报》第81/06号)；
- 《工业产权相关就业法》(《斯洛文尼亚官方公报》第15/07号)。

1. 工业产权

（1）《工业产权法》中规定的权利

- 专利权：专利权是向发明人授予的一项权利，该发明人可以是在各个领域内发明新的、具有创造性的、可以被工业运用的技术。专利权是其所有人/持有人的一项专有权利，以保护专利权人不受任何第三方对该项发明制造、使用、销售、进口等行为的侵害。专利权赋予发明人对任何未经同意利用该项发明的人有采取法律措施和进行索赔的权利。

- 短期专利权：《工业产权法》中规定了一项特殊的"短期专利"，这与德国等一些其他国家的实用新型专利相类似。对一些新型的、易用于工业的创造性发明成果可以授予短期专利权，短期专利权自申请日起算满10年即终止，且不能授予程序类、植物种类、动物种类发明或发现。

- 工业设计专利：工业设计专利是对产品本身的线条、轮廓、颜色、形状、质地和/或材料构成的部分或整体的外观进行的保护。包括工业产品和手工艺品，以及可以进行组装的零部件、包装、图形符号和印刷字体，但不包括计算机程序。经注册的工业设计赋予其所有人排除任何第三人未经同意而使用的权力。对于不新颖、不具有独创性、违反公共道德、含有《巴黎公约》第6条之三所包含的官方标志或只是产品本身的外观形式或功能、不需要进行加工的这类产品不能授予工业设计专利。

- 商标：商标是一个可以区分不同商品或服务的标志或标志的组合，可以由文字、人名、数字、字母、图形元素、三维图像、商品形状或外包装形状，结合颜色的任何组合而成。对于缺乏显著特征、仅具有描述性、只是商品的形状或包装、具有误导性、只是习惯用语、违反公共道德秩序、含有《巴黎公约》第6条之三的官方标志、含有酒的产地暗示但并非原产于该地区的这类产品不能注册商标。

- 地理标识：根据斯洛文尼亚《工业产权法》注册的地理标识是指识别某一产品来源于某领土内某一地区或地方的标志，该产品的特定质量、声誉或其他特征主要归因于其地理来源。某种产品的名称由于在贸易过程中长期使用而为大众所熟知，该名称暗示了产品的原产地，也可以注册成为地理标识。根据《农业法》和《红酒法》的规定，可以指代农产品、葡萄酒、葡萄或葡萄酒制作的其他食品的地理标识也可以被注册。

- 补充保护认证：产品发明专利期满后，可以给予补充保护认证书。作为对产品在投入商业使用之前为取得官方授权所消耗的专利期的补偿。此处的"产品"是指药品或植物保护产品的活性成分或活性成分的组合。补充保护认证书在基本的专利期限届满后立即生效，申请基本专利到首次获得准予投入市场（包括欧盟成员国、挪威、冰岛和列支敦士登）的时间前5年即为补充保护认证书的期限。补充保护认证书的最长保护期限为5年，从其生效之日起计算。补充保护认证书在欧盟的第469/2009号和第1610/96号（包括其修改内容）法律中有相关规定，斯洛文尼亚直接适用了补充保护认证书的相关规定。

（2）互联网域名

《工业产权法》中没有对互联网域名进行规定，域名注册所依据的是所有者与注册服务商之间的合同关系，因此域名注册不会对所有者/持有者的绝对权利进行扩展。互联网域名只有获得与商标、版权、个人名称、公司名称等同样的保护的时候才能具有绝对的权利。互联网域名注册采用注册原则和申请在先原则，先注册域名的人比后注册的人具有优先权，无论该域名是否与他们的公司名称相符。在某些情况下，在涉及知识产权侵权时，知识产权持有人可请求域名持有人转让域名。因此，将名字作为域名以此获得商标保护是非常有必要的。同时，需要注意的是，域名注册（与商标相反）不受域名类型的限制，可以在全球进行使用。

2. 版权

斯洛文尼亚《版权法》规定了文学作品、科学和艺术作品的作者和表演者、唱片公司、电影制作人、广播组织、出版商和数据库制造商（相关）的权利。前述版权保护的主体，包括以任何形式表现的文学、科学和艺术领域的个人智力创作。版权赋予作者一种与作品不可分割的权利，由此产生一种排他的个人权利（精神权利——首次发表权、承认作者身份权、保护作品完整权、收回已发表的作品权等），排他的经济权（经济权利——复制权、分配权、出租权、公开表演权、公开传播权等），以及作者的其他权利（作者的其他权利——使用权、转移权、转售权、公开出租权等）。

斯洛文尼亚在知识产权的保护上，赋予外国法人和自然人与本国自然人和法人同等的权利。

（二）专利申请

在斯洛文尼亚申请专利首先应该向知识产权局递交专利申请表。申请表可以用任何国家的文字填写，内容包含至少一项请求的权利，并且同意知识产权局用斯洛文尼亚语、英语、法语或德语与申请人进行联系。斯洛文尼亚知识产权局随后会要求申请人在3个月内提交一份以斯洛文尼亚语翻译的申请表。申请公布前，斯洛文尼亚知识产权局只对专利申请进行形式上的审查，不对其新颖性、工业实用性和创造性进行审查。在专利授予第9年届满前需要专利持有人提交一套完整的专利审查文件，以证明该专利具有有效性（更多详细信息请看下文）。斯洛文尼亚对专利申请表的形式没有具体的要求，只要符合《专利使用条约》（PCT）或《欧洲专利公约实施条例》即满足了所有的形式要件。

专利申请有几个必要的要素：请求授予专利；对发明已知的数据和存在的问题及解决方案和不完善的地方进行描述；请求对发明专利权进行保护（一句话描述）；对发明的本质进行简要描述，必要时需要绘制图纸；接受费用；如果有填写申请的代表，同意向其代表授予专利权。

申请人提交专利申请或要求优先权后18个月没有对发明进行实质性（新颖性）审查即视为专利申请成功。专利权期限一般从申请之日起计算为20年。

若外国自然人或法人在斯洛文尼亚既没有居住地，也没有真实有效的工商业机构，必须有一个在斯洛文尼亚知识产权局注册的当地代表人或专利代理人。外国申请人在申请优先权或收到知识产权局办理程序的相关通知时，应填写申请表、形成申请时间、支付费用、提交首次申请表的副本。没有代表的，需要提供一个在斯洛文尼亚范围内知识产权局可以与之联系的地址。

斯洛文尼亚专利授予有以下注意事项：所有的专利授予，在第9年届满前需要提供一套完整的审查报告，以确保其符合专利性标准（例如，新颖性、创造性和工业实用性）。同一项发明若被欧洲专利局授予一项或多项专利，最好有一个斯洛文尼亚语的专利授予翻译版本。如果一项欧洲专利没有提交专利申请表，但由《专利使用条约》第32条下享有国际初审地位的相关机构或签订了相关条约的其他有关专利局进行实质审查或授予，用斯洛文尼亚语对该项专利授予进行翻译，也可以被认可。如果没有及时提交完整的专利性审查报告，专利的有效期在第10年失效。斯洛文尼亚专利所有人或持有人若想起诉第三人专利侵权，必须在此之前提交完整的专利审查报告。

斯洛文尼亚专利申请也可以根据其所签署的国际条约进行申请，即《专利使用条约》（指定欧洲专利局）和《欧洲专利公约》。一旦被授予欧洲专利，可以根据这两个条约获得在斯洛文尼亚的专利权。

（三）商标注册

注册斯洛文尼亚商标应首先向斯洛文尼亚知识产权局提出商标注册申请。国家商标申请表可以用任何国家的文字填写，内容包含至少一项请求的权利，并且允许知识产权局用斯洛文尼亚语、英语、法语或德语与申请人进行联系。斯洛文尼亚知识产权局随后会要求申请人在3个月内提交一份以斯洛文尼亚语翻译的申请表。知识产权局将首先进行形式审查，随后进行绝对拒绝情形的审查，如果存在这样的情形，将给予申请人一次说明的机会。如注册申请被接受，将会公布在知识产权局的官方期刊上，如果该商标已经存在，其所有人可以在3个月内提出异议。商标注册后，专用权限为10年，之后每10年缴纳一次续期费。申请人可以根据《商标国际注册马德里协定》和《马德里议定书》在斯洛文尼亚提交商标注册申请。斯洛文尼亚商标作为欧共体商标（CTM）受欧盟知识产权局的保护。

对于缺乏显著特征、仅具有描述性、只是商品的形状或包装、具有误导性、只是习惯用语、违反公共道德秩序、含有《巴黎公约》第6条之三的官方标志、含有葡萄酒的地理标志暗示但并非原产于该地区的这类产品不能注册商标。国际申请适用与国内申请相同的程序（应当拒绝的情形审查和异议）。

与专利申请类似，外国自然人或法人在斯洛文尼亚既没有居住地，也没有真实有效的工商业机构，必须有一个在斯洛文尼亚知识产权局注册的当地代表人或专利代理人。但是外国申请人在申请优先权或收到知识产权局办理程序的相关通知时，应填写申请表、形成申请时间、支付费用、提交首次申请表的副本。没有代表的，需要提供一个在斯洛文尼亚范围内知识产权局可以与之联系的地址。

在斯洛文尼亚知识产权局注册的商标，商标持有人或所有人的权利只在斯洛文尼亚受到保护，但在斯洛文尼亚申请的国家商标在国外受6个月优先权保护。根据《商标国际注册马德里协定》和《马德里议定书》，斯洛文尼亚商标可以用作申请国际注册商标的基础。

商标注册申请有以下要求：商标注册请求；商标保护请求；请求使用某标记作为商标保护的商品或服务的清单（商品或服务必须按照尼斯分类方法进行分类）。同一商标可以在一种或多种商品或服务中受到保护。

（四）知识产权保护措施

斯洛文尼亚知识产权局无权采取知识产权执法的相关措施（它只能与执行此类措施的其他机构进行合作）。权利持有人可以选择民事、刑事或行政措施。律师或斯洛文尼亚专利代理人、商标代理人、设计代理人可以为权利人提供帮助。

1. 民事措施

卢布尔雅那地方法院对与知识产权有关的争端享有专属管辖权。权利人可以向上述法院就侵权行为提起民事诉讼，并要求停止侵权、回收已经投入市场的侵权货物、销毁侵权货物、赔偿损失、公布法院判决（也属于对侵犯版权及相关权利可采取的民事制裁）。有关知识产权的初步禁令和临时措施也可以提交给该法院。

2. 刑事措施

警察机关、检察院、地方刑事法院有权采取刑事措施。侵犯知识产权也可以构成刑事犯罪。《斯洛文尼亚刑法典》(《斯洛文尼亚官方公报》第50/12号，第6/16号，第54/15号，第38/16号和第27/17号）将若干知识产权滥用的行为定义为刑事犯罪，例如未经授权擅自使用他人的公司名称、商标、地理标志、工业品外观设计或商品特殊标志，或者将这些标志进行组合形成自己的标志。此外，未经授权使用他人的专利权、补充保护认证书和集成电路布图注册的作品也构成刑事犯罪。根据《刑法典》的规定，侵犯版权包括侵犯精神权利（未经授权进行发表、展示、表演或散布和损毁）和侵犯物质权利（未经授权使用具有版权的作品或其样本）。刑事处罚包括罚款及8年以下的监禁，并且所有未经授权使用的物品、工具和设备都将被没收。法人在触犯相关规定时也将受到刑事处罚。刑事犯罪都是依职权起诉，但版权例外，对版权侵权人的起诉都是由受害人提出。

3. 行政措施

由斯洛文尼亚财政部执行行政措施。海关当局按照欧洲议会和欧盟理事会第608/2013（EU）号规则，第1352/2013号委员会实施细则，《欧盟海关法典》第952/2013条例（在斯洛文尼亚直接适用）以及斯洛文尼亚海关执行欧盟知识产权规定的规定（《斯洛文尼亚官方公报》第29/16号）。

如果海关当局在执行任务期间发现涉嫌侵犯某种知识产权的货物，可对此进行暂扣，并通知货物的所有人和该权利的所有人。在货物暂扣期间，知识产权所有人必须决定是否对侵权行为提起诉讼，而货物所有人必须决定是否坚持该货物没有侵犯知识产权的陈述，海关当局将根据他们的决定采取下一步行动。如果权利持有人决定提起诉讼的，该货物将被扣留等待法院的最终裁决。如法院裁决侵权，该货物将被销毁；如法院最终认定不侵权的，货物将被放行。海关当局将根据权利持有人的申请或依职权采取措施。对知识产权侵权的起诉时效为1年，向海关总署提出。如果请求获得支持，海关总署将通知所有海关办事处，这些海关办事处根据支持采取行动。

如果货物所有人没有对海关当局的扣押通知作出回应，或者权利持有人与货物所有人达成一致意见时，可以在没有法院裁决的情况下直接对货物进行销毁。如果可以明显看出货物属于假冒品或盗版，海关可以依职权直接进行销毁。

六、环境保护

（一）环境保护部门监督

斯洛文尼亚环境和空间部有权进行环保管理，并负责为斯洛文尼亚人民提供一个适合居住的生活环境，通过合理利用自然资源，实现经济的可持续发展。斯洛文尼亚环保局网站上会随时对天气、水、空气、地震、气候变化、自然环境保护相关的预测、分析和报告进行公布。环保局启动了一些国内外项目，同时还负责水资源的管理（消除对水的不利影响，确保水质和保护生物多样性），有权进行环保登记、作出环境许可决定，并进行公开公告。该局负责制作环保报告并在环境信息观测网进行公布，同时向欧洲环保局进行报告。

斯洛文尼亚环境和空间部监察局有权独立自主地对环保领域的法律执行进行检查监督。

斯洛文尼亚核安全管理部负责环保管理、监督和发展，防止电离辐射污染，对核材料和设备进行保护，防止核武器扩散，保护核产品。除此之外，它还负责对环境的放射性状态进行监测，对核损害赔偿责任法律进行执行，履行监管职责，履行国际义务，负责国际数据的交换。斯洛文尼亚符合所有辐射防护和核安全标准。

斯洛文尼亚水利部是水资源管理和发展相关规定的执行部门。其目标是建立水资源综合管理系统（以斯洛文尼亚的水资源作为发展对象，充分考虑空间规划中的水容量，减少对生命、健康和公民财产的威胁），囊括国家、地区和区域性河流。水利部还建立了水籍，其中包括水域、供水设施清单。

（二）与环境保护相关法律法规概况

欧盟环保相关法律在斯洛文尼亚直接适用，并且大部分被转化为各种环境保护法律法规。

① 环境保护领域最主要的法律是2004年制定通过的《环境保护法》（《斯洛文尼亚官方公报》第39/06号，第49/06号，第66/06号；宪法法院的决定，第33/07号，第57/08号，第70/08号，第108/09号，第48/12号，第57/12号，第92/13号，第56/15号，第102/15号，第30/16号和第61/17号）。它将环境保护作为可持续发展的重要组成部分，并确定了环境保护基本原则、环境保护措施、环境监测和环境信息、环境保护的经济和金融手段、公共环境保护服务以及其他与环境保护有关的问题。斯洛文尼亚目前正在制定新的"环境保护法"，旨在加强对欧盟立法的遵守，特别是欧洲经济委员会制定的《奥胡斯公约》。

② 《水资源法》（《斯洛文尼亚官方公报》第67/02号，第2/04号；第41/04号；其他法律，第57/08号，第57/12号，第100/13号，第40/14号和第56/15号）管理海洋水域、内陆水域和地下水以及水生和沿海土地，其中包括水保护、水资源管理和用水决策。该法还规定了水、水设施和设备领域的公共产品和公共服务以及与水有关的其他问题。

③ 《废物法令》（《斯洛文尼亚官方公报》第37/15号和第69/15号）旨在保护环境和人类健康，防止或减少废物产生带来的不利影响。它还根据欧盟相关指令和条例的要求，减少使用自然资源造成的影响和提高自然资源使用率。

④ 《自然保护法》（《斯洛文尼亚官方公报》第96/04号，第61/06号；第8/10号；第46/14号）确立了保护生物多样性的措施和保护自然价值体系，以促进对自然资源的保护。

⑤ 《生态保护区和大陆架法》（《斯洛文尼亚官方公报》第93/05号）公布了生态保护区，并按照国际法的规定行使其在大陆架上的主权权利。

⑥ 《转基因有机体管理法》（《斯洛文尼亚官方公报》第23/05号，第21/10号和第90/12号）与欧盟第2009/41号和第2001/18指令一致，规定了对转基因作物（GMOs）的管理措施，预防和减少对环境的不利影响，尤其是对生物多样性和人类健康的保护，禁止转基因作物进入自然环境或将转基因作物投入市场。该法还要求执行欧洲议会和理事会制定的第1830/2003号条例。

⑦《防电离辐射和核安全法》(《斯洛文尼亚官方公报》第102/04号)规定了对电离辐射的防护,尽可能少地使用电离辐射以减少电离辐射对人类健康造成的影响,减少生活环境中放射性污染,同时允许开发、生产和使用辐射源并实施辐射活动。为获取核能产生的辐射源,本法要求采取核安全措施和使用核材料的特别保护措施。

⑧《自然资源恢复法》(《斯洛文尼亚官方公报》第114/05号,第90/07号,第102/07号,第40/12号,第17/14号)规定了当发生自然灾害并对农业造成影响后,用于灾后重建的预算资金的使用条件和方式。

(三)环境保护评估

斯洛文尼亚自2004年5月年加入欧盟以来,致力于将其法律(包括环境保护法在内)与欧盟立法协调一致。欧盟委员会对斯洛文尼亚执行欧洲环境法的情况进行审查,并形成了《欧盟环境实施审查国家报告》——2017年的报告上指出,斯洛文尼亚拥有丰富多样的自然资源,是Natura 2000自然保护区网络陆地覆盖面积最大的国家,是欧洲森林覆盖率最高的国家之一。

从对欧盟环境立法遵守的角度看,斯洛文尼亚仍然有相当多的环境侵权案件。根据欧盟委员会的报告,斯洛文尼亚在环境方面的主要挑战在于精简规划和环境评估有关的法律,确保欧盟环境立法得到执行,同时减轻行政负担和投资障碍;保持较大的Natura 2000自然保护区网络覆盖面积和给予废水投资的优先权,实现斯洛文尼亚入盟条约的义务。斯洛文尼亚在空气质量方面也存在较大的问题,有几个地区的臭氧浓度相关数据依然无法达到标准值,长期目标尚未实现,并且可吸入颗粒物(PM10)日平均最高浓度时常过高。斯洛文尼亚需要关闭一些野外废弃物填埋场,注意退化土地的恢复。

然而,斯洛文尼亚在城市垃圾回收方面是做得最好的国家之一,在卢布尔雅那拥有最先进的废物管理中心,斯洛文尼亚也是环境税收最多的国家之一。斯洛文尼亚的饮用水具有很高的软度,洗浴水也达到了高质量的标准。

七、争议解决

(一)解决争议的机构和方式

斯洛文尼亚争议解决方式除了传统的诉讼之外,还有调解和仲裁。

1.诉讼

诉讼适用《民事诉讼法》,斯洛文尼亚法院民事法律程序是对抗式的,法官作为中立的中间人,根据当事人向法院提交的意见作出决定,并带有一些调查制度的成分。诉讼主体为原告、被告、法官,其中法官有权作出裁决。法官只能在请求的范围内作出裁决,当事人必须陈述他们的主张及所依据的事实和理由,并提出证据来证明这些事实。原告适用必要性原则自主决定是否起诉,没有机构可以对不遵守民事法律关系的行为主动提起诉讼。法院的管辖权原则上由被告住所地决定,但当事人另有约定的除外。

斯洛文尼亚法官适用《民事诉讼法》作出裁决,只有在极少数情况该裁决为最终裁决(例如,财产保护)。但在程序存在问题时,通常会作出最终裁决(如,原告人不按照法院的要求提交起诉资料而法院不予受理的)。

当事人享有法律救济的权利,一般可以在判决送达之日起30日内对一审判决提起上诉。当程序违法、事实认定错误、不完整或法律适用错误时,二审法院有权作出公正完整的裁决。如果判决是终局判决,且已经生效,当事人可以使用某些特殊的法律进行救济。

斯洛文尼亚常规司法制度被分为三个等级。第一个层级,普通法院分为民事、刑事、执行、保险和其他法院。这些法院根据所管辖案件的重要性被进一步划分为44个县级法院(管辖轻微犯罪和小型民事案件)和11个地区法院(其他所有案件)。

第二个层级,4个高级法院内设多个部门,例如商事、清算、民事、刑事和家事部门。此外,还设有两类专业法院:劳动和社会法院与行政诉讼法院,具有高等法院的地位。这些法庭审理一审上诉案件。

最高上诉法院是位于首都卢布尔雅那的最高法院,负责统一全国判例,通常只审理涉及法律适用相关的上诉案件,具有民事、刑事、商事、行政、劳动和社会事务案件的管辖权。最高法院为第三级审理法院,通常审理特殊法律救济案件。这种特殊的法律救济方式只有当存在实体法律问题和严重程序违法时可采取。此外,最高法院还处理下级法院之间的管辖权争议和案件移送问题的争议。

斯洛文尼亚宪法法院与普通司法机构分离。它是保护宪法、法律、人权和基本自由的最高权力机构。

2. 仲裁

适用《仲裁法》(《斯洛文尼亚官方公报》第45/08号)。受斯洛文尼亚法律和其他政府实体法律约束的自然人或法人,可以对任何货币或财产产生的争议达成仲裁协议。其他争议只有在双方可以达成和解时才能达成仲裁协议。仲裁协议可以以合同中的仲裁条款或独立协议的形式达成,但必须以书面形式订立。

仲裁和诉讼是相互排斥的,在缔结仲裁协议时双方同意将争议提交仲裁,从而排除了法院对案件的管辖权。在仲裁过程中,双方可以就争议进行友好协商解决,协商不成的,仲裁员将作出仲裁裁决。与司法程序不同,仲裁允许协议双方就仲裁程序中的许多细节(例如程序的保密性)达成一致,并根据自己的意愿进行调整。通过仲裁解决纠纷通常比诉讼程序更快,且更专业,因为仲裁员具备专业领域的专业资格。仲裁裁决对双方具有约束力,当事人无法进行上诉。

为解决争议,当事人可以组成临时仲裁(专为个别案件组成的仲裁)或机构仲裁。斯洛文尼亚工商会有一个常设仲裁机构,同时还有一些专业的仲裁机构。值得注意的是,超过40%的案件在常设仲裁机构进行仲裁前都对一些国际因素存在争议。

3. 调解

与诉讼程序相比,调解程序更少受到程序规则的限制。适用《民商事案件调解法案》(《斯洛文尼亚官方公报》第56/08号),《替代诉讼解决争议法》(《斯洛文尼亚官方公报》第97/09号和第40/12号)等相关规定。立法只规定了基本原则和程序规则,而真正的程序主要取决于当事人的自愿。调解是当事人各方通过中立的第三方调解自愿和平地解决冲突的过程。适用调解的各方当事人具有同等的权利,可以平等地进行陈述声明,双方就争议的解决达成调解协议。当事人可以就调解的程序达成一致协议,如无法达成协议的,调解员将根据案件具体情况、各方当事人的意愿并快速有效得解决争议选定调解程序。

斯洛文尼亚的调解具有与法院判决及相关法律程序同等的效力,但完全独立于法院及法院程序。与仲裁方式不同,调解员不能就争议作出裁决,只有当各方当事人协商一致达成解决方案时,争议才能得到解决。调解通常有中立第三方提供帮助,程序具有非正式性,在保密性、速度及成本上都具有优势。争议各方可以就争议处理方案协商一致并以公正记录的方式进行草拟或根据解决方案参照法院裁决书或仲裁裁决书进行拟定。仲裁裁决对各方当事人具有终局效力,对其提起诉讼要以撤销仲裁裁决为前提。

调解如果是在法院的组织下进行,斯洛文尼亚地区法院具有管辖权。法院调解的期限为3个月,调解的请求期限不计算在调解程序中。

斯洛文尼亚多数调解员加入了调解员协会,调解机构加入了调解机构协会。实践中,越来越多的争议都通过调解得到解决。统计数据显示,2017年有2608个案件申请调解,其中有337个案件调解成功。

(二)法律适用

斯洛文尼亚作为欧盟成员国,直接受欧盟法律的约束,欧盟法律大多被纳入其立法之中。

1. 诉讼

民事诉讼程序在《民事诉讼法》(《斯洛文尼亚官方公报》第73/07号,第45/08号;第45/08号,第111/08号,第57/09号,第12/10号,第50/10号,第107/10号,第75/12号,第40/13号,第92/13号,第 10/14 号，第 48/15 号，第 6/17 号；斯洛文尼亚宪法法院的所有裁决第 10/17 号）中作出了规定。除了一些由特殊法院或机构处理的争议，本法规定了自然人或法人之间的个人和家庭关系、财产关系以及其他民事法律关系相关争议管辖法院适用的程序。

斯洛文尼亚个人、家庭、劳动、社会、财产和其他民事法律关系的纠纷中，如果涉及国际因素，除了适用欧盟相关条例外，还应适用《国际私法》和《程序法》（《斯洛文尼亚官方公报》第 56/99 号和第 45/08 号）。

2. 仲裁

仲裁程序适用的基本法律是《仲裁法》（《斯洛文尼亚官方公报》第 45/08 号），本法适用于斯洛文尼亚的仲裁案件，无论当事人为本国人还是外国人。

3. 调解

斯洛文尼亚的调解案件适用《民商事案件调解法案》（《斯洛文尼亚官方公报》第 56/08 号）和《替代诉讼解决争议法》（《斯洛文尼亚官方公报》第 97/09 号和第 40/12 号；其他法律）。

八、其他

（一）反商业贿赂

斯洛文尼亚的政治腐败问题和挪用公款现象较为严重。根据 2017 年公布的全球清廉指数（该指数根据国家公共部门的腐败程度进行划分），斯洛文尼亚在欧洲和中亚地区 180 个国家中排第 34 位。根据透明国际 2013 年公布的全球贪污趋势指数，政治党派是斯洛文尼亚最腐败的机构，紧随其后的是议会、司法机构和政府官员。与透明国际 2012 年公布的数据相比没有任何改善。公共资金的不合理、不透明使用导致斯洛文尼亚的腐败现象严重。

1. 反腐败相关法律法规概况

斯洛文尼亚在腐败和贿赂方面除了国内法，还直接适用欧盟条例并将其纳入本国法律体系中。长期以来，斯洛文尼亚内部涉及腐败有关的法律只有《刑法典》，其对构成腐败的刑事犯罪进行了定义。直到 2004 年才通过了有关腐败的特别法案；作为国家反腐败决议和国家防止腐败委员会的议事规则，是一项特别的法案，通过以下实施细则具体执行。

①《反腐败法》（《斯洛文尼亚官方公报》第 69/11 号）作为反腐败方面主要的法律，旨在加强执法力度、防止腐败、预防并解决利益冲突，规定了提高透明度的方法和措施。本法所指的"腐败"是指公共及私立部门的官员或负责人违反强制规定，为自己或他人谋利。

②《刑法典》（《斯洛文尼亚官方公报》第 50/12 号，第 6/16 号，第 54/15 号，第 38/16 号和第 27/17 号）建立了减少腐败、行贿、受贿和洗钱等其他违法行为的法律框架。

③《法人刑事犯罪责任法案》（《斯洛文尼亚官方公报》第 98/04 号，第 65/08 号和第 57/12 号）制定了法人及其管理人的法律责任；

④ 斯洛文尼亚《关于防止腐败的决议》（《斯洛文尼亚官方公报》第 85/04 号）通过实现某些目标在个人和社会创造一个高水平的反腐败文化。

⑤《政府计划》增强 2017—2019 年持续引导提高公共部门机构、公职人员、官员和其他雇员的工作廉洁度，提高公共部门活动的透明度。

⑥《防止洗钱和恐怖主义融资法》（《斯洛文尼亚官方公报》第 68/16 号）规定了侦查和预防洗钱的措施、主管部门和程序，并规定了对执行相关规定情况的检查。斯洛文尼亚设有最终实益拥有者登记处（UBOR），以确保对实际所有人进行适当披露，防止商业贿赂和洗钱。UBOR 是一个数据库，其中收集了有关实际所有者的数据，以确保商业实体所有权结构的透明度，并防止商业实体被洗钱和恐怖主义融资滥用。因此，每个商业实体必须在 UBOR 中认证并注册其实际所有人，该实际所有人通常是直接或间接持有总公司 25% 以上股份的个人。

⑦《对公职人员收受礼物的规定》（《斯洛文尼亚官方公报》第 53/10 号和第 73/10 号）对公职人员执行公务中收受的礼物制定清单，并对礼物的处置管理进行了规定，对收受礼物相关的禁止、限制等

执行问题进行了规定。

⑧《防腐败委员会程序规则》(《斯洛文尼亚官方公报》第 24/12 号）规定了防腐败委员会作为一个独立自主的国家机构，在行使防止公共部门腐败及利益冲突、增加透明度法律职权方面的特别程序。

2. 反商业贿赂监督部门

（1）政府机构

斯洛文尼亚共和国防腐败委员会（CPC）是一个有权防止和查办公共部门腐败、违反诚信道德行为的独立国家机构，不隶属于任何其他国家机构或部门，不受行政机关或立法机关的直接指示。防腐败委员会（CPC）不属于执法部门，也不属于诉讼部门，其人员不具有一般警察的职能。但其有权查看金融文件或其他文件（即使具有保密性），询问公务员和政府官员，行使行政调查和行政程序，指导其他执法机构（如，反洗钱局和税务局等）在其权限范围内收集信息和证据。

（2）非政府组织

透明国际（TI）是一个非政府和非营利组织，具有公共行政部的地位。从 2009 年起，透明国际在斯洛文尼亚设有分会。透明国际发表《全球腐败年度报告》，发布腐败新闻并进行分析，指出国际和国家发展趋势，对各区域进行研究报告，并给出了一个腐败指数，包括 CPI（清廉指数）和 BPI（行贿指数）。

3. 惩罚措施

（1）商业相关

斯洛文尼亚《刑法典》明确界定了以下属于腐败行为的刑事犯罪：非法接受礼物，非法馈赠，滥用职权，受贿，行贿，为达到非法目的给予利益、赠送礼物使得官方作为或不作为的行为。这些犯罪可处以罚款和/或 8 年以下的监禁。

《刑法典》惩罚商业行为中任何与索取或接受回扣、礼物或利益有关的活动。对经济活动中作出承诺、送礼、给予未经授权的奖励、给予其他财产性利益的行为将采取惩罚措施。所有接受的礼物、回扣或其他利益都将予以没收。

（2）公共部门和政府相关

《刑法典》对政府官员的行贿、受贿行为进行了规定。公职人员或政府官员索取或者收受请托人的回扣、礼物及其他财产利益后，本应行使其职能而不行使或不应行使某职能而行使的行为，或其他滥用职权的行为，或作为代表向公职人员、政府官员行贿的人员，将被处以 1 年以上 8 年以下的监禁并处罚金。公职人员或政府官员索取或者收受请托人的回扣、礼物及其他财产利益后，本应行使其职能而不行使或不应行使某职能而行使的行为，或其他滥用职权的行为，或作为行贿的中间人，将被处以 1 年以上 5 年以下的监禁。所有行贿的财物将处以没收。

（3）公开招标和与公共机构的协议

与斯洛文尼亚任何公共机构签订的合同均应包含一项反腐败条款。如果合同条款中有为促成合同的缔结或不按合同约定履行义务，向公共机构或其代表或中间人的账户提供或承诺提供任何利益的条款，将导致合同无效。

（4）法人构成刑事犯罪的责任承担

如果某人经管理层授权或命令或因管理层的管理不当，代表法人从事违法犯罪活动，法人从该违法犯罪活动中获得利益，法人构成刑事犯罪。对法人实施的制裁包括罚款、扣押财物和取消法人资格。

（二）工程承包

斯洛文尼亚公共采购系统一般适用《公共采购法》(《斯洛文尼亚官方公报》第 91/15 号），该法规定了政府采购和招标项目的采购程序，欧盟相关指令也被该法采用。根据该法，"公共采购"是指一个或多个商业实体与一个或多个承包实体之间，为完成工程、提供货物或提供服务而订立的以经济利润为目的的书面合同。工程发包机构在符合政府采购条件时，可适用以下八个程序：公开程序、限制程序、竞争性对话、创新合作、竞争性谈判、谈判公开程序、非事先公开的谈判程序和小额采购程序。这些程序在《公共采购法》中有进一步的详细介绍，它们之间存在巨大的差异。

此外,《国防和安全公共采购法》(《斯洛文尼亚官方公报》第 90/12 号,第 90/14 号;其他法律和第 52/16 号)规定了在国防和安全领域采购货物、服务和工程中发包机构与投标人的义务。

《公共采购程序法》(《斯洛文尼亚官方公报》第 43/11 号,第 60/11 号;其他法律,第 63 号)规定了对供应商、用户、公共利益的保护,以及对采购程序进行了规定。

1. 许可制度

"被允许的投标"是指投标人提交的投标符合参与条件,不存在应被拒绝的情形。投标人必须满足发包机构的所有要求和需求,且必须在规定的时间进行投标,不能有任何勾结串通的行为。在不存在低价竞标而且投标价格不超过发包机构可承受范围的情况下,投标可能被接受。发包机构必须确保同等对待公共采购各个阶段的投标人,除了法律特别规定外,任何企业均可在其经营范围内参与投标。发包机构可以为个别投标制定特殊的许可。投标人可以单独投标,也可以作为一个组合或临时团体联合投标,但每个投标实体必须满足个别条件。

2. 禁止投标

被有关主管部门列在负面清单上的企业,在特定时间内不能进行投标。企业在最近 5 年有触犯已有的 43 个刑事犯罪之一、有未纳税的情况或未承担缴纳社保的情况或未提交雇佣相关的资料,在最近 3 年因工资支付问题被罚款两次以上的,不能参与公共投标。被禁止投标的企业,其代表人或管理人员均不能进行投标。

3. 招标和投标

必须按照规定以公开透明的方式选择投标人。如前所述,公共采购的各种程序大有不同,但以下程序被普遍适用。发包机构应首先预估合同的价值并启动签订合同的程序。然后在公共采购门户网站上公布公共采购文件,包括公共采购合同的草案。有意向的投标人可以根据已公布的合同通知提交所需文件。标书可以提交纸质版,也可以通过官方网站 https://ejn.gov.si/ 提交。投标的最短期限为公开招标之日起 35 天,但情况紧急,可以缩短为 15 天。在符合既定的要求和条件的情况下,发包机构选取报价低的投标,但不得选择低价竞标的投标人。确定中标人之后,发包机构必须公布中标通知至少 30 天。

规定的公共采购类型有如下几种:公开招标,有限投标,竞争对话,创新合作,竞争谈判投标,公开或非公开谈判招标,低价投标。所有公开投标都将在公共采购局的官方网站(http://www.djn.mju.gov.si/)进行公布。发包机构有权决定开标的时间和地点,以及公开招标的标准,包括担保的银行。除非招标人另有规定,开标应当是公开的。对已接受的投标进行评估,然后决定中标人,并向所有的投标人公布中标结果。在中标人作出最终决定后签订合同。

(三)其他规定

《推动外国直接投资和企业国际化法案》(《斯洛文尼亚官方公报》第 107/06 号,第 11/11 号,第 57/12 号和第 17/15 号)对外商直接投资进行了规定,本法采用了欧盟相关条例,对推动外商直接投资和企业国际化制定了目标,并对活动开展、措施采取和主管机构进行了规定。

斯洛文尼亚成立了企业、创新、旅游、发展和投资事务局(SPIRIT),在线上和线下为外国投资者提供信息、咨询等服务。

在斯洛文尼亚开展业务的公司具有与其本国公司同等的权利、义务和责任。个人和各类经济组织有权开展商业活动。个人通常以独资经营者的身份从事经营活动,但企业可以有不同的形式:最常见的是有限责任公司和有限公司。非斯洛文尼亚居民在开展商业活动前必须取得斯洛文尼亚的税号。斯洛文尼亚《公司法》(《斯洛文尼亚官方公报》第 65/09 号,第 33/11 号,第 91/11 号,第 32/12 号,第 57/12 号,第 44/13 号;宪法法院的判决第 82/13 号,第 55/15 号 和第 15/17 号)与欧盟立法完全一致,对公司的建立、管理和组织进行了规范。

Slovenia

Authors: Uroš Ilić, Katarina Škrbec, Tatjana Andoljsek, Klemen Mir
Translators: Wang Xiujuan (Jansy Wang), Richard Cao

I. Overview

A. General Introduction

Slovenia is a central European country bordering Austria, Italy, Croatia and Hungary. It declared its independence in June 1992, became a full member of the European Union (EU) in 2004, adopted EURO as its currency in 2007, and entered the Schengen area in the same year. In 1992, Slovenia became a member of the United Nations and a participating state of the Organization for Security and Co-operation in Europe, joined the Council of Europe in 1993, and finally became a member state of the Organisation for Economic Development and Cooperation (OECD) in 2010.

Slovenia is a territorially unified and indivisible democratic parliamentary republic with an "incomplete bicameral system". The lower chamber (the National Assembly or "Državni zbor") is vested with legislative power while the upper chamber (the National Council or "Državni svet") supervises the work of the lower chamber. The National Assembly is composed of 90 deputies, of which two posts are reserved for the representatives of Italian and Hungarian minorities.

The President of the Republic is the head of state and the Commander-in-Chief of the armed forces and is directly elected by general elections every five years. The President nominates the Prime Minister who, after having been elected by the National Assembly, forms the Government, which is then approved (elected) by the National Assembly as well. The Government has extensive executive powers, including determination of the policy of execution of the laws and other regulations; proposals of legislation, the budget and other regulations to be adopted by the Parliament; adoption of secondary legislation and other regulations for the execution of laws, etc.

Slovenian legal system is a part of continental legal systems with a strong influence of Germanic legal orders due to Slovenia's historical inclusion in the Austro-Hungarian Empire. The Courts Act[1] regulates the jurisdiction and composition of Courts in Slovenia. Regular courts (i.e.courts of general jurisdiction) are civil and criminal courts of two different kinds at the first instance (43 County courts and 11 District courts) and with two stages of appeal, High courts (4) and the Supreme Court of the Republic of Slovenia. In some cases, the rulings may be examined by the Constitutional Court. Beside the general civil and criminal courts there are several courts of specialized jurisdiction that have jurisdiction ratione materiae and not ratione personae. Specialized courts are Labour and social courts (with the High Labour-Social Court at the appellate level) and Administrative Court (which acts as an appeal court). Judges are independent in the performance of their judicial function and hold a permanent mandate.

Slovenia is one of the most successful transition countries, but has been considerably affected by the world economic crisis and Eurozone crisis. In the past several years, strong and constant economic growth returned as a result of increased domestic consumption, exports and investment. Improved corporate balance sheets and credit conditions are expected to further the growth of investment and the GDP growth is forecast to reach 4.2% in 2018, well above the EU average of 2.3%.[2]

Slovenia is attractive for foreign investors due to its strategic position, well developed transport system, and highly-educated and skilled labour force. Some drawbacks include bureaucratic troubles, and employment legislation. Slovenian economy is export-oriented and its main industries include automotive industry (e.g.KLS Ljubno, Adria Mobil, Revoz), chemicals and pharmaceuticals (e.g.Henkel Maribor, Krka, Lek), electric and electronic industry (e.g.Interblock, Kolektor, Iskratel), ICT (e.g.Telemach, Telekom Slovenije), logistics and

---

[1] Sl.Zakon o Sodiščih (ZS), Official Gazette of RS Nos.19/1994, 45/1995, 38/1999, 26/1999 - ZPP, 28/2000, 26/2001 - PZ, 67/2002 - ZSS-D, 110/2002 - ZDT-B, 56/2002 - ZJU, 73/2004, 72/2005, 127/2006, 49/2006 - ZVPSBNO, 67/2007, 45/2008, 96/2009, 86/2010 - ZJNepS, 33/2011, 75/2012, 63/2013, 17/2015, 23/2017 – ZSSve.

[2] Slovenia: Balanced Growth Path, URL: https://ec.europa.eu/info/sites/info/files/economy-finance/ecfin_forecast_winter_0718_sl_en.pdf (9.2.2018).

distribution (e.g.Port of Koper, Slovenian Railways, BTC, Aerodrom Ljubljana), metalworking (e.g.Danfoss Trata, Acroni), and wood-processing (e.g.Lesonit, Merkscha).

B. The Status and Direction of the Cooperation with Chinese Enterprises Under the B&R

Slovenia strongly supports the Chinese "Belt & Road Initiative", especially through the "China + 16" mechanism. The Government of Slovenia would like to further increase the Sino-Slovenian cooperation, inter alia in the fields of agriculture, auto manufacturing, tourism and winter sports.[1] On 2 February 2018, Slovenia and China signed a memorandum on infrastructure cooperation in Beijing. The memorandum focuses on the sea transport and the development of railways, motorways and logistics.[2] Slovenia aspires to connect its existing transport system with transport corridors of the B&R Initiative which cross Slovenia, namely the Mediterranean corridor, running from Ukraine via Hungary to Slovenia, Italy, France and Spain, which is already a part of the European TEN-T network, and the Alpine-Balkan corridor, running from Austria via Slovenia on to Croatia, Serbia, Bulgaria and Turkey.[3]

II. Investment

A. Market Access

a. Department Supervising Investment

Internationalization and investment in the Republic of Slovenia are facilitated by the Public Agency for Entrepreneurship, Internationalization, Foreign Investments and Technology (SPIRIT Agency), which falls under the Ministry of Economic Development and Technology.

b. Laws and Regulations of Investment Industry

There are no specific laws regulating foreign investment, however foreign investments are encouraged by the Government and have been strongly increasing in the past several years according to the Bank of Slovenia.[4]

The Promotion of Foreign Direct Investment and the Internationalisation of Enterprises Act[5] lays down measures of the State related to the promotion of inward direct foreign investment and the internationalisation in accordance with the five-year governmental plan.[6] A new Investment Incentives Act is currently in the process of adoption to define strategic investments (40 million EUR and 400 jobs in processing or services industry, 20 million EUR and 200 jobs in research and development industry), simplify the process to obtain all necessary permissions (e.g.environmental, construction), and introduce a more coherent investment incentives system with an emphasis on sustainable development, environment and social responsibility.[7]

The privatization in Slovenia is still ongoing, and the bidding process is open to foreign investors. The government prepared a list of 15 state-owned companies, which will be put on sale in the following years.

c. Forms of Investment

Investors in Slovenia mostly opt for investments in equity, claims (distressed debt) and real estate. Another attractive opportunity for domestic and foreign investors alike are public-private partnerships where special or exclusive rights to provide economic or other public services or activities in public interest are awarded through a concession agreement with the Government, municipality or other public entity. Foreign direct investments

---

[1] The State Council of the People/s Republic of China, China pledges further cooperation with Slovenia under Belt and Road Initiative URL: http://english.gov.cn/state_council/vice_premiers/2017/04/16/content_281475628112971.htm (19.2.2018).
[2] Slovenska Tiskovna Agencija, Slovenia and China sign memorandum of infrastructure coop, URL: https://english.sta.si/2478366/slovenia-and-china-sign-memorandum-on-infrastructure-coop (19.2.2018).
[3] The Slovenia Times, Slovenia and China sign memorandum on infrastructure coop, URL: http://www.sloveniatimes.com/slovenia-and-china-sign-memorandum-on-infrastructure-coop (21.2.2018).
[4] Bank of Slovenia, Macroeconomic Projections for Slovenia – December 2017, URL: https://bankaslovenije.blob.core.windows.net/publication-files/gdgfnNehiggffP_macroeconomic-projections-for-slovenia-december-2017.pdf (10.2.2018).
[5] Zakon o spodbujanju tujih neposrednih investicij in internacionalizacije podjetij (ZSTNIIP), Official Gazette of RS, Nos.86/2004, 78/2006, 11/2011, 57/2012, 17/2015.
[6] See Programme For Internationalisation 2015–2020, URL: http://www.mgrt.gov.si/fileadmin/mgrt.gov.si/pageuploads/SEKTOR_ZA_INTERNACIONALIZACIJO/ANG/Program_INTER_2015-2020_koncna_EN-_FINAL.pdf (7.2.2018).
[7] 156th regular session of the Government of the Republic of Slovenia, URL: http://www.vlada.si/en/media_room/government_press_releases/press_release/article/156th_regular_session_of_the_government_of_the_republic_of_slovenia_60628/ (7.2.2018).

in Slovenia can be made in a variety of ways; in practice, they commonly include the opening of a Slovene subsidiary, acquiring a controlling interest in an existing Slovene company, or by means of a joint venture with a Slovene company.

d. Standards of Market Access and Examination

Foreign investors are afforded national treatment or the most-favoured nation treatment and can access the market freely in accordance with the principles of the EU and the OECD. Certain limitations apply in the banking and insurance sectors (Bank of Slovenia or Insurance Supervision Agency approval is needed), air and maritime transport, and game of chance industry.[1] Companies with a share of foreign capital and companies fully owned by foreigners that are registered in Slovenia have equal rights and obligations as domestic companies. An exception applies to the real estate ownership acquisition (see below); nevertheless, once a foreign company owns real property it is subject to the same legal regime as companies incorporated in Slovenia.

According to the Constitution, expropriation of any person (natural or legal, domestic or foreign) is allowed only if it is in the public interest (e.g.construction of public infrastructure), under the conditions established by law and against monetary or in-kind compensation.[2] Expropriation is understood so as to include direct and indirect expropriation measures.

B. Foreign Exchange Regulation

a. Department Supervising Foreign Exchange

The Bank of Slovenia manages authorizations to perform currency exchange operations and conducts supervision of foreign exchange operators, mutatis mutandis using the banking sector regulations. The customs authority supervises the nature and quantity of cash transferred to and from the Community.[3]

b. Brief Introduction of Laws and Regulations of Foreign Exchange

Foreign exchange regime is fully liberalized and regulated by the Foreign Exchange Act[4].

Currency exchange operations can be performed by currency exchange operators holding a valid authorisation issued by the Bank of Slovenia, and banks or savings banks which, in accordance with the act regulating banking, provide the service of trading in foreign means of payment, including currency exchange operations. Operators must use exchange rates of the Bank of Slovenia, allow access to the Bank of Slovenia, and report on possible status changes.

c. Requirements of Foreign Exchange Management for Foreign Enterprises

Slovenia fully adheres to the Article VIII of Articles of Agreement of the International Monetary Fund, which is the legal basis for a non-discriminatory and free of restrictions currency convertibility.[5] The foreign exchange management for foreign enterprises is not governed by specific legislation and is thus liberalized. There are no restrictions to current and capital transfers owned by residents or non-residents.[6] Repatriation of profits is free, but the tax debt ought to be settled. Certain security measures in terms of reporting and identification are in place by

---

[1] Foreign investment regime, URL: https://www.investslovenia.org/fileadmin/dokumenti/is/CMSR_dokumenti/Investment_Regime_SPIRIT_2016_August.pdf (18.2.2018).
[2] Sl.Ustava Republike Slovenije (URS), Official Gazette of RS Nos.33/91-I, 42/97, 66/2000, 24/03, 69/04, 68/06, 47/13, 75/16, Art.69.
[3] Sl.Zakon o deviznem poslovanju (ZDP-2), Official Gazette RS Nos.16/2008, 85/2009, 109/2012, Arts.11-14.Regulation No.572/2013 of the European Parliament and of the Council on prudential requirements for credit institutions and investment firms amending Regulation No.648/2012, Official Journal of the EU L 176/1.
[4] Sl.Zakon o deviznem poslovanju (ZDP-2), Official Gazette RS Nos.16/2008, 85/2009, 109/2012.
[5] IMF, Annual Report on Exchange Arrangements and Exchange Restrictions 2016, URL: https://www.imf.org/en/Publications/Annual-Report-on-Exchange-Arrangements-and-Exchange-Restrictions/Issues/2017/01/25/Annual-Report-on-Exchange-Arrangements-and-Exchange-Restrictions-2016-43741 (21.2.2018), p.64.
[6] Residents according to the Foreign Exchange Act (ZDP-2, Article 2) are:1.companies and other legal persons established in the Republic of Slovenia that pursue profit-making activities, other than their branches in the rest of the world;2.branches of foreign companies that pursue profit-making activities and are registered in the Court Register in the Republic of Slovenia;3.sole traders and individuals pursuing registered business activities as a profession with a registered office or permanent residence in the Republic of Slovenia;4.natural persons with permanent residence in the Republic of Slovenia and natural persons temporarily resident in the Republic of Slovenia on the basis of a valid residence permit issued for at least six months (hereinafter: individuals), other than foreign citizens employed at diplomatic and consular offices and members of their families;5.diplomatic personnel, consular personnel and other representatives of the Republic of Slovenia in the rest of the world financed from the budget, Slovenian citizens employed at such representative offices and their family members.Everyone else is deemed a non-resident.

the Prevention of Money Laundering and Terrorist Financing Act[1] and the customs authority may seize undeclared cash import to the Community if exceeding 10.000 EUR.[2]

C. Financing

a. Main Financial Institutions

The most important financial institution is the Bank of Slovenia, which is an independent legal person directly accountable to the National Assembly.[3] The Bank of Slovenia implements Eurozone monetary policy, supervises foreign exchange operations, regulates functioning of banks and savings banks and is responsible for the system's general liquidity. Financial institutions are mainly governed by the EU law, namely the Regulation No.572/2013 of the European Parliament and of the Council on prudential requirements for credit institutions and investment firms amending Regulation No.648/2012[4].

Banking, financial and other similar operations are defined in the Banking Act[5] and strictly supervised by the Bank of Slovenia.[6] A credit institution may be established as bank or savings bank, either as a public limited company, or a European public limited liability company. A foreign bank may establish a branch in Slovenia through which it operates as a regular credit institution. Corporate governance, risk management, status changes and similar pressing fields of banking business are stringently regulated and supervised.

The banking sector in Slovenia is marked by a relatively high degree of concentration.[7] The country's largest bank, NLB (Nova Ljubljanska Banka), which is state-owned,[8] accounts for approximately one-quarter of the market share.[9] The second largest, NKBM (Nova Kreditna banka Maribor), and other foreign-owned banks account for almost 50 per cent.[10] At the present time, twelve banks, three savings banks, and three EEA branches are granted the Bank of Slovenia authorisation to provide banking services, mutually recognised services and additional financial services in Slovenia.[11]

Whereas the banking sector dominates the Slovenia's financial system, accounting for approximately 77 % of financial assets in 2013,[12] other actors include insurers and pension funds, as well as other financial intermediaries,[13] which will be addressed in turn below. Among the latter, the shadow banking sector (primarily including investment funds and leasing companies) has gradually reached an estimated 8 % of the financial system's total assets.[14] Additionally, other non-bank credit channels have become more important, such as business-to-business loans and internal funds.[15]

The insurance sector in Slovenia is, similarly to the banking sector, highly concentrated as four largest insurance companies dominate approximately 78 % of the insurance market.[16] Insurance and reinsurance business is governed by the Insurance Act[17] and funded on the principles of transparency, diligence, risk management and

---

[1] Prevention of Money Laundering and Terrorist Financing Act [Zakon o preprečevanju pranja denarja in financiranja terorizma (ZPPDFT-1)], Official Gazette RS, No.68/16, Art.44.
[2] Sl.Zakon o deviznem poslovanju (ZDP-2), Official Gazette RS Nos.16/2008, 85/2009, 109/2012, Arts.11-14.Regulation No.572/2013 of the European Parliament and of the Council on prudential requirements for credit institutions and investment firms amending Regulation No.648/2012, Official Journal of the EU L 176/1.
[3] URS, Art 152.
[4] Regulation No.572/2013 of the European Parliament and of the Council on prudential requirements for credit institutions and investment firms amending Regulation No.648/2012, Official Journal of European Union L 176/1.
[5] Sl.Zakon o bančništvu (ZBan-2), Official Gazette of RS Nos.25/15, 44/16 – ZRPPB, 77/16 – ZCKR, 41/17).
[6] ZBan-2, Art.5.
[7] https://www.export.gov/article?id=Slovenia-Efficient-Capital-Markets (25.2.2018).
[8] The partial sale of the State shareholding in NLB by the end of 2017 was one of the key commitments based on which the European Commission approved a significant State aid to NLB.http://europa.eu/rapid/press-release_IP-18-482_en.htm (25.2.2018).
[9] NLB, Intrayear report for Q3 2017, September 2017, https://www.nlb.si/financna-porocila-2017 (25.2.2018).
[10] http://www.zbs-giz.si/zdruzenje-bank.asp?StructureId=480 (25.2.2018).
[11] Institutions under supervision, URL: https://www.bsi.si/en/financial-stability/institutions-under-supervision (10.2.2018).
[12] UMAR, Ekonomski izzivi 2013: Vpliv finančne krize na kreditni trg v Sloveniji (2013), p.50.
[13] OECD, Slovenia: Review of the Financial System, October 2011, p.12.
[14] OECD, Economic Survey of Slovenia 2017: Overview, p.33.Available at http://www.oecd.org/eco/surveys/Slovenia-2017-OECD-economic-survey-overview.pdf (27.2.2018).
[15] Ibid.
[16] Insurance Supervision Agency, Annual Report on the Status of Insurance Business 2016, p.23.Available at: https://www.a-zn.si/wp-content/uploads/letno_porocilo-2016.pdf (27.2.2018).
[17] Sl.Zakon o zavarovalništvu (ZZavar-1) Official Gazette RS, No.93/15.

supervision.[1] The latter is performed by the Insurance Supervision Agency. The insurance operations may be conducted by a Slovenian legal entity, which has obtained authorisation of the Insurance Supervision Agency, or by a foreign enterprise – either through a branch or directly – based on specific conditions set out by the Insurance Act. An insurance undertaking may be established as a public limited liability company, a European public limited liability company, or a mutual insurance company.[2] Generally, an insurance undertaking may conduct insurance business in either life insurance group or non-life insurance group, however undertakings that have obtained the authorization to conduct insurance business in both groups in accordance with the former legislation (the so-called composite insurance companies) are allowed to continue their business in both groups.

Slovenia runs a three-pillar pensions system. Based on the principles of reciprocity and solidarity, the first pillar is financed by compulsory contributions of employees and managed by the Pensions and Disability Insurance Institute of Slovenia.[3] The second pillar applies to same insured persons and is divided into mandatory additional insurance and voluntary additional insurance of individual or collective nature. The contributions are collected in special funds, which are subject to State regulation (e.g.prescribed minimum rate of return) and tax incentives. The third pillar is entirely voluntary, independent of the person's working status and not regulated by the State.

Investment funds are governed by the Investment Funds and Management Companies Act[4] and may be established as undertakings for collective investment in transferable securities (UCITS)[5] or as alternative investment funds (AIF)[6].

As mentioned above, another important actor in the shadow banking sector are specialised financial institutions – leasing companies.[7] Leasing of assets is a special type of financial service regulated by the Banking Act for which an authorization by the Bank of Slovenia is required.

The independent legal entity in charge of supervising the financial instruments market is the Securities Market Agency (SMA) established in 1994. The SMA supervises investment firms, the Ljubljana Stock Exchange, the Central Securities Clearing Corporation (KDD), investment funds, and management companies, and shares responsibility with the Bank of Slovenia for supervision of certain banking and investment services. Its tasks and competencies include authorizing operations of financial institutions, authorizing acquisitions of a qualifying holding and takeovers of companies, ratifications of a prospectus when publicly offering securities, controlling financial institutions, keeping certain registers, and giving consent to the stock exchange rules.[8]

b. Financing Conditions for Foreign Enterprises

There are no special conditions in relation to financing of foreign enterprises. The Financial Instruments Market Act[9] requires the publication of a prospectus when publicly offering securities (including bonds), however conditions set forth by the act apply equally to foreign and domestic enterprises.

Pursuant to the Prevention of Money Laundering and Terrorist Financing Act[10] which implements the EU Directive 2015/849 on the prevention of the use of the financial system for the purposes of money laundering or terrorist financing, banks and other financial institutions are required to exercise measures for detection and prevention of money laundering and financing of terrorist activities when receiving, handing over, exchanging, safekeeping, disposing of or handling monies or other property and in concluding business relationships.

Preventive measures include "know your customer" checks, such as personal identification and authentication

---

[1] Ciglič, Zavarovalno pravo (Insurance law), (2011), URL: http://www.mizs.gov.si/fileadmin/mizs.gov.si/pageuploads/podrocje/ss/Gradiva_ESS/UNISVET/UNISVET_68ET_Zavarovalno_Ciglic.pdf (10.2.2018), pp.6-7.
[2] The first organisational form is not allowed for the reinsurance undertakings.
[3] About the Institute, URL: https://www.zpiz.si/cms/?ids=contenten&inf=484 (9.2.2018).
[4] Sl.Zakon o investicijskih skladih in družbah za upravljanje (ZISDU-3), Official Gazette of RS Nos.31/15, 81/15, 77/16.
[5] An UCITS is an open-end investment fund raising capital from the public, with the sole object of investment in securities or in other liquid financial assets in compliance with the principle of risk-spreading.The units of UCITS may be realized or paid out at the request of holders.UCITSs may be established by authorized management companies in form of mutual funds or umbrella funds. Management companies may be organized as public limited companies, European companies or as public limited-liability companies.
[6] All investment funds that do not fulfil the UCITS criteria are AIFs.AIFs may collect the capital publicly or non-publicly and are managed by the alternative investment funds managers (AIFMs), i.e.legal persons whose regular business is managing one or more AIFs.List of AIFMs is kept by the Securities Market Agency and regulated by the Alternative Investment Fund Managers Act [Sl.Zakon o upravljavcih alternativnih investicijskih skladov (ZUAIS), Official Gazette of RS No.32/15].
[7] Many Slovene banks perform leasing through their subsidiaries as a non-core activity.
[8] About the Agency, URL: http://www.a-tvp.si/Eng/Default.aspx?id=1 (10.2.2018).
[9] Sl.Zakon o trgu finančnih instrumentov (ZTFI), Official Gazette RS Nos.67/2007, 100/2007, 69/2008, 40/2009, 88/2010, 78/2011, 55/2012, 105/2012 - ZBan-1J, 63/2013 - ZS-K, 30/2016, 44/2016 - ZRPPB, 9/2017.
[10] Prevention of Money Laundering and Terrorist Financing Act [Zakon o preprečevanju pranja denarja in financiranja terorizma (ZPPDFT-1)], Official Gazette RS, No.68/16, Art.44.

of the ultimate beneficial owner. The ultimate beneficial owner information is for example necessary when a company (either foreign or domestic) wishes to open a bank account or a trading account in Slovenia. If a foreign company conducts business through a branch, the identity of both the mother and the branch company is checked. Domestic legal entities and Slovenian branches of foreign entities must collect information on ultimate beneficial owners and report this information to the Slovenian Business Register. The register of ultimate beneficial owners is publicly available as of January 2018.

D. Land Policy

a. Brief Introduction of Land-Related Laws and Regulations

Foundational principles of Slovenian real estate law are contained in the Law Property Code[1], while other important acts regulating land are the Land Register Act[2], the Real-Estate Recording Act[3], the Agricultural Land Act[4], the Housing Act[5], and the Protection of Buyers of Apartments and Single Occupancy Buildings Act[6].

The Land Property Code contains an exhaustive list of in rem rights that can be obtained by legal entities:[7]
-ownership ("lastninska pravica")
-pledge ("zastavna pravica")
-servitudes ("služnost")
-encumbrance ("pravica stvarnega bremena"), and
-building right ("stavbna pravica").

The in rem rights are of an erga omnes nature, but must be registered in the Land Register to have legal effect. The data in the Land Register is publicly available and can be relied on by everybody.[8] In addition to the in rem rights, the Land Register contains some other relevant information regarding property, for example a notice of legal action.

Main and the most extensive property right is ownership. It is not limited by time or conditions and includes the rights of possession, enjoyment, use, and disposal. Ownership by two or more persons on a divided property is called co-ownership (on an undivided property, a joint ownership exists instead), while a condominium is a special type of ownership where regular ownership regime over a unit is necessarily coupled with a joint ownership over common areas (e.g.halls in a block of flats).

b. Rules of Land Acquisition for Foreign Enterprises

According to the Constitution, foreign subjects may acquire ownership rights over real estate under conditions provided by law or by a treaty ratified by the National assembly.[9] The latter applies to citizens of the EU, EFTA and OECD member states who may acquire real estate under same conditions as Slovenian citizens, and to citizens of the EU candidate countries who may acquire real estate under the condition of reciprocity.[10] Citizens of other countries and companies with seats in these countries (including for example the People's Republic of China and the Russian Federation) may acquire real estate in Slovenia only through inheritance and under the additional condition of reciprocity.[11] The principle of national treatment ensures that foreign companies enjoy the same ownership rights as domestic companies.

Regardless of rather stringent conditions, Russian and Chinese citizens and companies are among most

---

① Sl.Stvarnopravni zakonik (SPZ), Official Gazette of RS Nos.87/2002, 91/2013.
② Sl, Zakon o zmljiški knjigi (ZZK-1), Official Gazette of RS Nos.58/2003, 45/2008, 37/2008 - ZST-1, 28/2009, 25/2011, 14/2015 - ZUUJFO, 23/2017 - ZDOdv, 69/2017.
③ Sl.Zakon o evidentiranju nepremičnin (ZEN), Official Gazette of RS Nos.47/06, 65/07 – decision of the Constitutional Court of RS, 79/12 – decision of the Constitutional Court of RS, 61/17 – ZAID.
④ Sl.Zakon o kmetijskih zemljiščih (ZKZ), Official Gazette of RS Nos.71/11, 58/12, 27/16, 27/17 – ZKme-1D, 79/17.
⑤ Sl.Stanovanjski zakon (SZ-1), Official Gazette of RS Nos.69/03, 18/04 – ZVKSES, 47/06 – ZEN, 45/08 – ZVEtL, 57/08, 62/10 – ZUPJS, 56/11 – decision of the Constitutional Court of RS, 87/11, 40/12 – ZUJF, 14/17 – decision of the Constitutional Court of RS, 27/17.
⑥ Sl.Zakon o varstvu kupcev stanovanj in enostanovanjskih stavb (ZVKSES), Official Gazette of RS No.18/04.
⑦ SPZ, Art.2.
⑧ SPZ, Art.10.
⑨ URS, Art.68.
⑩ Sl.Pridobivanje lastninske pravice tujcev na nepremičninah v republiki sloveniji (Real estate acquisition in RS by foreigners), URL: http://www.mp.gov.si/si/delovna_podrocja/direktorat_za_civilno_pravo/sektor_za_civilno_pravo/pridobivanje_lastninske_pravice_tujcev_na_nepremicninah_v_republiki_sloveniji/ (10.2.2018).
⑪ Sl.Zakon o dedovanju (ZD), Official Gazette RS, Nos.št.15/76, 23/78.13/94 – ZN, 40/94 – decision of the Constitutional Court RS, 117/00 – decision of the Constitutional Court RS, 67/01, 83/01 – OZ, 73/04 – ZN-C, 31/13 – decision of the Constitutional Court RS in 63/16, Art.6.

common foreign real estate buyers in Slovenia.[1] The Chinese mostly invest in the real estate suitable for renting out, while the Russians frequently purchase real estate in Slovenia for personal use due to peaceful environment and Slovenia's central location in Europe.[2] The purchases are usually conducted through the establishment of a company with a seat in Slovenia.

E. The Establishment and Dissolution of Companies

Corporate status, establishment, and operation rules of commercial enterprises are governed by the Companies Act.[3] Slovenian legal order separates between partnership companies and companies limited by shares – most importantly distinguished by the liability of their shareholders (or the lack thereof) for the company's liabilities. Companies are established with the purpose of pursuing a profitable activity on the market as their sole activity. These activities may be of all kinds, unless the law specifically prohibits commercialization of an activity.

All companies obtain their legal personality upon the entry into the Court Register and are, as legal entities, allowed to acquire rights, assume obligations, own movable and immovable property, and may sue and be sued. The company is responsible for its liabilities with all its assets (unlike the owners of a company limited by shares), however certain abuses and legal violations may trigger the disregard of legal personality and subsequent responsibility of company members. Company's operations are led by the management (directors, management board or board of directors, as the case may be).

Foreign companies pursuing profitable activity in Slovenia have equal rights, liabilities and obligations as companies with a seat registered in Slovenia. The status of a foreign-owned company is considered under the law of the country under which the company is incorporated. A foreign company (with certain exceptions applicable to companies incorporated in EU member states[4]) may conduct a profitable activity in Slovenia through a branch office, which is dependent on its international mother company, or a subsidiary, which is considered an independent legal entity. The provisions of the Companies Act regarding activities, corporate name, registered office, power of procuration and trade secrets apply mutatis mutandis to the branch office. The entry and deleting of a branch office from the Court Register may be requested by the representative of a foreign company.[5] A subsidiary company is an independent company established under Slovenian corporate law as a Limited Liability Company or a Public Limited Company, but has a parent company registered under the foreign law.

a. The Forms of Enterprises

a) Partnership Companies

Unlimited Liability Company ("družba z neomejeno odgovornostjo") consists of two or more persons who assume liability for the company's obligations with all their assets. Shareholders establish the company and regulate relations between them in the partnership agreement. There is no minimum share capital requirement for the establishment and shareholders usually make equal capital contributions based on which the distribution of capital and loss is allocated to them each year. Shareholders are entitled and obliged to manage and represent the company.[6]

Limited partnership ("komanditna družba") is established by the partnership agreement by two or more persons in which at least one of the shareholders is liable for the liabilities of the company with all his or her assets (a general partner, "komplementar") and at least one shareholder is not liable for the liabilities of the company (a limited partner, "komanditist"). The general partner is entitled to manage and represent the company and is supervised by the limited partner.[7] Unless stipulated otherwise, the rules governing unlimited liability companies are applicable mutatis mutandis to limited partnerships.

b) Companies Limited by Shares

A Limited Liability Company ("družba z omejeno odgovornostjo") is founded by one or more, domestic or

---

[1] Sl.Rusi, Nemci, Angleži in Kitajci najbolj zagreti za naše nepremičnine (Russians, Germans, English and Chinese are most enthusiastic about Slovenian real estate), URL: https://pro.finance.si/8857134 (10.2.2018).

[2] Sl.Prodaja nepremičin tujcem (Selling real estate to foreigners), URL: http://www.bidom.si/novice/prodaja-nepremicnin-tujcem-ruski-angleski-trg/245 (10.2.2018).

[3] Sl.Zakon o gospodarskih družbah (ZGD-1), Official Gazette RS, Nos.42/2006, 60/2006., 26/2007 - ZSDU-B, 33/2007 - ZSReg-B, 67/2007 - ZTFI, 10/2008, 68/2008, 42/2009, 33/2011, 91/2011, 100/2011 - skl.US, 32/2012, 57/2012, 44/2013 - decision of the Constitutional Court RS, 82/2013, 55/2015, 15/2017, art.1.

[4] Namely, in respect of EU companies, no registration is required if the provision of services is temporary (as opposed to regular, periodical or continuous pursuit of activity in Slovenia – in which case a Slovene branch or a subsidiary of a foreign (EU) company has to be established).

[5] ZGD-1, Part VIII.

[6] ZGD-1, Part III/1.

[7] ZGD-1, Part III/2.

foreign natural or legal persons who become shareholders upon the company's establishment. The company is formed by a partnership agreement in the form of notarial deed or a special form, in paper or electronic format, which must be signed by all members. The company's share capital in the minimum amount of 7500 EUR is made of shareholders' contributions (provided either in cash or in kind) the value of which may differ, but must at least equal 50 EUR per each shareholder.

Corporate governance is governed by the partnership agreement. The most important decisions, such as the appointment, discharge and supervision of directors, the adoption of the annual report, and the division and termination of shareholdings, are taken by the shareholders at the general meeting through the voting procedure. A company has one or more directors who manage and represent the company at their own responsibility and may generally be dismissed by the general meeting at any time.

c) Public Limited Company

A Public Limited Company ("delniška družba") has its share capital divided into shares (securities). The minimum share capital is 25,000 EUR and can be divided in either nominal value or non-par value shares. The lowest amount stated in the nominal value shares or, as the case may be, the amount in the share capital belonging to each no-par value share, has to be 1 EUR or multiples thereof.

Each Public Limited Company may choose between a one-tier or two-tier system of corporate governance. In the one-tier system shareholders appoint the board of directors who manage and supervise the company's business. In the two-tier system the function of management and that of supervision are separated. Shareholders elect the supervisory board, which appoints and supervises the management board. The management board consists of one or more members (directors) and is responsible for the management. Members of the management or supervisory board are jointly and severally liable to the company for damage arising from violation of their duties unless they can demonstrate that they fulfilled their duties fairly and conscientiously. When necessary or required by the law, the management calls a general meeting of shareholders who are responsible for taking important decisions regarding the company, including the adoption of the annual report, the appointment and dismissal of the supervisory board, winding-up and corporate restructuring of the company, the appropriation of distributable profit, amendments to the articles of association, measures to increase and reduce share capital, and the appointment of the auditor. Nevertheless, whereas both Public Limited Company and Limited Liability Company afford their members limited liability (restricted to their equity contributions in the company), a Limited Liability Company may represent a more attractive choice in terms of cost efficiency and flexibility of corporate governance in comparison to the Public Limited Company.

d) Partnership Limited by Shares

Partnership limited by shares ("komanditna delniška družba") is established by the articles of association, which must be signed by at least five persons. In this partnership, at least one shareholder assumes responsibility for the company's liabilities with all his or her assets (general partner), and the limited shareholders do not assume any responsibility for the company's liabilities to the creditors. The general partners have voting rights at the general meeting in proportion to their participation in the share capital.

e) European Public Limited Company

European Public Limited Company (Societas Europea, "evropska delniška družba") is a specific type of company regulated by the EU Regulation 2157/2001 on the Statute for a European company (SE). Prerequisites for the establishment of Societas Europaea are a registered office and a head office in a same EU country, presence in other EU countries, a minimum capital of 120.000 EUR, and an agreement on employee participation in the company's bodies. Other requirements may vary between states. In Slovenia rules governing regular Public Limited Companies are applied mutatis mutandis.[1]

b. The Procedure of Establishment

Individuals and enterprises from the EU, EEC and Swiss Confederation may establish a company in Slovenia following a regular procedure without limitations. The same rule applies to third-country nationals; however, they may need to obtain a business or other type of visa to be able to enter and return to Slovenia.[2]

Before starting a company, non-residents must obtain a Slovenian tax number through the Tax administration office. To register a company, it is necessary to define a company's name, its representatives, head office, and activities. In general, founder or founders establish a company by signing a contract at a notary, providing the necessary share capital, and registering the company in the Court Register, by which a company obtains a legal

---

[1] ZGD-1, Part V.
[2] How can non-EU nationals start a business in Slovenia?, URL: http://eugo.gov.si/en/starting/how-can-non-eu-nationals-start-a-business-in-slovenia/ (13.2.2018).

personality. The registration procedure is described in the Court Register of Legal Entities Act.[1] A Public Limited Company may also be established at the "VEM" office or via the "VEM" e-point, which is free of charge.[2]

c. Routes and Requirements of Dissolution

Dissolution of a solvent company may be voluntary or mandatory. Both procedures follow the same idea, i.e.realization of assets, payment of company's debts, division of remaining assets among company's shareholders, and the deletion of the company from the Court Register. Voluntary liquidation is initiated by the company members or shareholders and governed by the Companies Act, while the mandatory liquidation is led by the Court and regulated in the Financial Operations, Insolvency Proceedings and Compulsory Winding-up Act[3]. Most frequent reasons for a winding-up of different types of companies are listed in the Companies Act.

The Financial Operations, Insolvency Proceedings and Compulsory Winding-up Act also defines the bankruptcy proceeding for a dissolution of an insolvent company. The proceeding is based on the principles of joint satisfaction and equitable distribution and is supervised by the Court. The Court appoints the bankruptcy administrator who is responsible for the most advantageous management of company's assets and subsequent satisfaction of preferential, ordinary, and subordinate claims from the bankruptcy estate. The bankruptcy proceeding is finalized with a judicial decision on the termination; the winding-up of a company is effective upon the entry of the termination decision in the Court Register.

F. Merger and Acquisition

Foundations of M&A regulation in Slovenia are contained in the Companies Act and in the Takeovers Act[4]. The former is general and governs various forms of companies, corporate governance, and rights and obligations of the persons involved. The latter regulates the takeover procedure and is applicable to the listed Slovenian Public Limited Companies that are admitted to trading on a regulated market, as well as to non-publicly traded companies which have at least 250 shareholders or a total equity of at least 4 million EUR.

The Takeovers Act differentiates between voluntary and mandatory takeover bid, where they both stand for a public offer made to all holders of securities that may result in the acquisition of some or all securities subject to the offer by the offeror.[5] A mandatory takeover bid is required when a person (either alone or together with other persons acting in concert with such person) reaches the threshold of one third of voting rights of the company in question. For acquirement of each additional 10% of voting rights the takeover bid obligation is renewed, up until the attainment of 75% of voting rights when the takeover is complete and the bidding obligation ceases altogether.[6] Failure to fulfil the mandatory takeover bid requirement is sanctioned by the suspension of all voting rights of the acquirer, possible fines or even liability for damage caused.[7] An offeror may opt for a voluntary takeover bid when the takeover threshold has not been reached.[8]

In general, the takeover procedure consists of three main stages:[9]

(i) Prior to the takeover bid, the offeror announces a takeover intention to the Securities Market Agency (SMA), the management of the targeted company, and the Slovenian Competition Protection Agency;

(ii) Having obtained the SMA's authorisation for takeover bid, the offeror may publicly announce the bid with the accompanying prospectus 10 to 30 days after the announcement of the takeover intention;

(iii) Finally, the deadline for the acceptance of the takeover bid is 28 to 60 days.

Special rights and obligations pertaining to minority shareholders in case of takeovers are contained in the Companies Act. In a squeeze-out procedure, the general meeting, following the proposal of the shareholder who reached 90% of the share capital (i.e.main shareholder), decides to transfer the remaining shares to the main

---

[1] Sl.Zakon sodnem registru (ZSReg), Official Gazette RS, Nos.13/1994, 31/2000 - ZP-L, 91/2005, 42/2006 - ZGD-1, 33/2007, 93/2007, 65/2008, 49/2009, 82/2013 - ZGD-1H, 17/2015, 54/2017.

[2] Sl.Portal e-VEM, URL: http://evem.gov.si/evem/drzavljani/zacetna.evem (13.2.2018).

[3] Sl.Zakon o finančnem poslovanju, postopkih zaradi insolventnosti in prisilnem prenehanju (ZFPPIPP), Official Gazette RS, Nos.126/2007, 40/2009, 59/2009, 52/2010, 106/2010 - ORZFPPIPP21, 26/2011, 47/2011 - ORZFPPIPP21-1, 87/2011 - ZPUOOD, 23/2012 - odl.US, 48/2012 – decision of the Constitutional Court RS, 47/2013, 100/2013, 10/2015 - popr., 27/2016, 31/2016 - odl.US, 38/2016 - odl.US, 63/2016 - ZD-C.

[4] Sl.Zakon o prevzemih (ZPre-1), Official Gazette of RS Nos.79/2006, 67/2007 - ZTFI, 1/2008, 68/2008, 35/2011 - ORZPre75, 55/2011 - decision of the Constitutional Court of RS, 105/2011 - odl.US, 10/2012, 22/2012 – decision of the Constitutional Court of RS, 38/2012, 47/2013 - ZFPPIPP-E, 56/2013, 63/2013 - ZS-K, 25/2014, 75/2015.

[5] ZPre-1, Art.11.

[6] ZPre-1, Art.12.

[7] ZPre-1, Art.63.

[8] ZPre-1, Art.13.

[9] ZPre-1, Arts.24-41.

shareholder against an appropriate compensation.① Conversely, the minority shareholders may request that the main shareholder purchases their remaining shares in a sell-out procedure.②

Lately, the M&A flows in Slovenia have been influenced by the strengthened privatisation efforts stimulated by the government, inter alia by assembling the list of 15 state-owned companies ready for sale. In order to attain independence from the government as the owner, state-owned companies are managed by the Slovenian Sovereign Holding (SSH), which functions as regular Public Limited Company and is inter alia responsible for the management of the assets of the Slovene State. The Slovenian Sovereign Holding Act③ determines the minimum state share for each of the three types of assets i.e.strategic assets (50% share plus one vote), important assets (25% share plus one vote), and portfolio assets (no minimum share, free disposition). Disposition of state assets may be conducted through a public tender, public auction, public call, or public offering.④

G. Competition Regulation

a. Department Supervising Competition Regulation

The authority responsible for the supervision and enforcement of competition regulation is the Slovenian Competition Protection Agency (CPA). It was established in 2013 to replace the former Slovenian Competition Protection Office and is organized as an independent administrative authority.⑤

b. Brief Introduction of Competition Law

The competition legislation in Slovenia is enacted on the basis of Article 74 of the Constitution and is heavily influenced by the EU law, which includes antitrust regulations, merger controls and State aid.⑥ The central legal act governing competition is the Prevention of the Restriction of Competition Act⑦ divided into substantive and procedural part, which defines various enforcement and supervision procedures pursued by the CPA.

Slovenian antitrust policy reflects Articles 101 and 102 of the Treaty of the Functioning of the EU (TFEU). Firstly, it declares as null and void restrictive agreements between undertakings, decisions by associations of undertakings, and concerted practices of undertakings, which have as their object or effect the prevention, restriction or distortion of competition in Slovenia.⑧ This general rule is not applied when an agreement is of minor importance (de minimis exemption) or positively affects the technical and economic progress, while affording a fair share of benefits to consumers (block exemption). Secondly, the abuse of dominant position by one or several undertakings in the whole or substantial part of Slovenian territory is prohibited.⑨ Dominant position is defined as the ability to act in a significant degree independently of competitors, clients or consumers and is presumed when the share of an undertaking on Slovenian market exceeds 40%.

Concentrations regulations are based on the EC Merger Regulation.⑩ A concentration is defined as a lasting change of control due to a merger, acquisition, or a creation of a joint venture.⑪ Through a special notification procedure, the CPA evaluates each concentration to determine whether it could impede the effective competition and be thus incompatible with competition rules.⑫

---

① ZGD-1, Art.384.
② ZGD-1, Art.389.
③ Sl.Zakon o Slovenskem državnem holdingu (ZSDH-1), Official Gazette of RS.
④ ZSDH-1, Arts.10-16.
⑤ Slovenian Competition Protection Agency, URL: http://www.varstvo-konkurence.si/en/about-the-agency/ (13.2.2018).
⑥ European Commission, Competition, URL: http://ec.europa.eu/competition/index_en.html (15.2.2018).
⑦ Sl.Zakon o preprečevanju omejevanja konkurence (ZPOmK-1), Official Gazette RS Nos.36/08, 40/09, 26/11, 87/11, 57/12, 39/13–decision of the Constitutional Court RS, 63/13 – ZS-K, 33/14, 76/15, 23/17.
⑧ ZPOmK-1, Art.6.
⑨ ZPOMK-1, Art.9.
⑩ Council Regulation (EC) No.139/2004 of 20 January 2004 on the control of concentrations between undertakings (the EC Merger Regulation), Official Journal of the EU L 24/1.
⑪ ZPOmK-1, Art.10.
⑫ ZPOmK-1, Art.41; CPA, Notification procedure, URL: http://www.varstvo-konkurence.si/en/concentrations-of-undertakings/notification-procedure/ (15.2.2018).Pursuant to ZPOmK-1 the notification is required if: (i) the combined aggregate annual turnover of all the undertakings concerned, together with other undertakings in group, exceeds EUR 35 million in the Slovenian market in the preceding business year; and (ii) the annual turnover of the target, together with other undertakings in group, exceeds EUR 1 million in the Slovenian market in the preceding business year.In addition, if the concentration does not reach the above stated thresholds, but the undertakings concerned, including affiliated undertakings, as a result of the concentration jointly achieve more than 60 percent market share in the Slovenian market, undertakings concerned have to inform the Agency of such concentration and the Agency can within 15 days request that they notify this concentration.Nevertheless, s concentration need not be notified if it is to be appraised by the European Commission in accordance with the Council Regulation (EC) No.139 / 2004 (the ECMR) as amended.

In general, Article 107 of the TFEU prohibits any state aid which distorts or threatens to distort competition in the EU internal market. State aid stands for any form of advantage conferred on a selective basis to undertakings by national public authorities.[1] The Government of Slovenia may inter alia grant state aid pursuant to the Act Governing Rescue and Restructuring Aid for Companies and Cooperatives in Difficulty[2]. The act aims at ensuring a long-term continuity of business operation and employment of the population. Companies and cooperatives in trouble that hold an important systemic role in the national, regional or sectorial development may receive an aid in the form of a credit, a subsidy, a guarantee or a capital investment. The Ministry of Finance supervises state aid allocation according to the Monitoring of State Aids Act[3]. It may grant state aid which is compatible with the EU law, notifies such an aid to the European Commission for approval and keeps a list of all awarded state aids.

c. Measures Regulating Competition

Competition regulations can be enforced publicly or privately. Public enforcement is primarily in hands of the CPA, which initiates a procedure ex officio when circumstances indicate possible restrictive practices. When an infringement of competition is established, the CPA issues a decision to terminate the infringement, most often by the disposal of a part or whole of a business by the infringing party. The procedure is terminated by an order when no violation is found.

The usual concentrations procedure is of ex ante nature and is commenced by the notification of a concentration to the CPA, which also triggers a temporary suspension of the concentration implementation. As a rule, the CPA declares a concentration compatible or incompatible with competition rules within 60 working days.

Certain own-initiative measures are available to the companies involved in such proceedings. Namely, an undertaking that is subject to procedure before the CPA may propose certain commitments or remedies to eliminate competition infringement risks. If proposed measures adequately abate the risk, the CPA terminates the procedure. Furthermore, under the leniency program members of cartels that disclose information regarding existing cartels to the authorities or cooperate when a cartel is discovered, may be granted immunity or reduction of fines.[4]

CPA's decisions may be judicially reviewed by mutatis mutandis application of the administrative disputes rules. Additionally, most severe violations may constitute a crime of "unlawful restriction of competition" as defined by the Criminal Code[5].

In 2017, the Directive 2014/104/EU was implemented in the Prevention of the Restriction of Competition Act to enhance the possibility of private competition enforcement, which is complementary to the public one. A private entity may seek compensation for damages suffered as a result of antitrust violations through a civil judicial proceeding. The amended legislation introduces an option to join in one case different legal actions arising from the same violation, and facilitates the previously challenging collection of evidence. A court can order the disclosure of relevant information and documentation from the defendant, the CPA, and other concerned parties, with confidential business information nevertheless being protected. It is predicted that these changes will increase the number of private competition enforcement proceedings in Slovenia, which have been relatively scarce in the past.[6]

H. Tax

a. Tax Regime and Rules

Slovenian legal system classifies taxes into three main categories i.e.direct taxes on income, direct taxes on property, and indirect taxes. General substantive and procedural taxation rules are contained in the Tax Procedure

---

[1] URL: http://ec.europa.eu/competition/state_aid/overview/index_en.html (15.2.2018).
[2] Sl.Zakon o pomoči za reševanje in prestrukturiranje gospodarskih družb in zadrug v težavah (ZPRPGDZT), Official Gazette of RS No.5/17.
[3] Sl.Zakon o spremljanju državnih pomoči (ZSDrP), Official Gazette Rs, No.37/04.
[4] ZPOmK-1, Art.76.
[5] Sl.Kazenski zakonik (KZ-1), Official Gazette of RS Nos.55/2008, 66/2008, 39/2009, 55/2009 – decision of the Constitutional Court of RS, 91/2011, 54/2015, 38/2016, 27/2017, Art.225.
[6] Krdžić, Pot do odškodnine zaradi kršitev konkurenčnih pravil je po novem lažja, URL: https://svetkapitala.delo.si/mnenja/pot-do-odskodnine-zaradi-krsitev-konkurencnih-pravil-je-po-novem-lazja-2412?meta_refresh=true (22.2.2018).

Act[1], however the details pertaining to individual taxes are defined by specific acts.

Direct taxes on income	Direct taxes on property	Indirect taxes
- Personal Income Tax Act - Payroll Tax Act - Contractual work tax - Corporate Income Tax Act - Rules on claiming tax relief for investments in research and development - Stock-Taking and Levies On Excess Stocks of Some Agricultural Products Act - Social Security Contributions Act - Social Security Contributions Act - Economic Zones Act - Act on Tonnage Tax - Law on tax on profit from disposal of derivatives	- Inheritance and Gift Taxation Act - Water Vessel Tax Act - Civil Tax Act - Act on Taxation of Winnings from Conventional Games of Chance - Bank Balance Sheet Tax Act - Real Property Mass Valuation Act	- Value Added Tax Act - Excise Duty Act - Real Property Transaction Tax Act - Gaming Tax Act - Insurance Contracts Tax Act - Financial Services Tax Act

Table 1: Acts regulating taxes in three main categories[2]

All taxes in Slovenia are collected by the Tax Administration working under the auspices of the Ministry of Finance. Taxation of every taxable person is based on the data collected in the computerized and uniform Tax Register kept by the Financial Administration. The Tax Register includes various categories of taxable persons, including for example operators registered in the Court Register, individuals with a permanent or temporary residence in Slovenia, legal and natural persons with or without a seat in Slovenia that perform business in Slovenia, and foreign associations of persons without legal personality, whereby each of these persons receives a unique Tax Identification number. The Entry into the Tax Register may be done ex officio or upon request. Foreign companies that wish to perform business in Slovenia through a branch are required to register their activity in Slovenia, while the EU registered companies may operate directly; however, all companies that do not have their Tax Identification number must apply for one prior to starting their business operations.[3]

b. Main Categories and Rates of Tax

a) Value Added Tax

Value Added Tax (VAT) is a general, indirect consumption tax governed by the Value Added Tax Act[4]. VAT is payable on all supplies of goods and services either at the standard rate of 22% or at the reduced rate of 9.5%, which is applicable to specific goods and services defined in the Addendum I to the Value Added Tax Act.[5] VAT is payable by all companies except for certain companies that engage in specifically defined activities, by small businesses with an annual turnover below 50.000 EUR, and by companies dealing with products for export.

b) Corporate Income Tax

Persons subject to the corporate income tax are domestic legal entities, foreign legal entities, and foreign associations of persons without a legal personality. The Corporate Income Tax Act[6] requires taxation on a worldwide income for tax residents (i.e.companies with a registered seat or a place of effective management in Slovenia), while non-residents pay income tax only on the income generated in Slovenia or through their Slovenian office.[7]

---

[1] Sl.Zakon o davčnem postopku (ZDavP-2), Official Gazette of RS, Nos.117/2006, 24/2008 - ZDDKIS, 125/2008, 85/2009, 110/2009, 1/2010., 43/2010, 97/2010, 24/2012 - ZDDPO-2G, 24/2012 - ZDoh-2I, 32/2012, 94/2012, 101/2013 - ZDavNepr, 111/2013, 22/2014 – decision f the Constitutional Court of R, 40/2014 - ZIN-B, 25/2014 - ZFU, 90/2014, 95/2014 - ZUJF-C, 23/2015 - ZDoh-2O, 23/2015 - ZDDPO-2L, 91/2015, 63/2016, 69/2017.

[2] Ministry of Finance of RS, Taxes and custom duties, URL: http://www.mf.gov.si/en/areas_of_work/taxes_and_customs/taxes_and_custom_duties/ (15.2.2018).

[3] Financial Administration RS, Entry into the Tax register and tax number, URL: http://www.fu.gov.si/en/taxes_and_other_duties/work_with_us/entry_into_the_tax_register_and_tax_number/ (15.2.2018).

[4] Sl.Zakon o davku na dodano vrednost (ZDDV-1), Official Gazette of RS Nos.117/2006, 52/2007, 33/2009, 85/2009, 85/2010, 18/2011, 78/2011, 38/2012, 40/2012 - ZUJF, 83/2012, 14/2013, 46/2013 - ZIPRS1314-A, 101/2013 - ZIPRS1415, 86/2014, 90/2015.

[5] ZDDV-1, Art.41.

[6] Sl.Zakon o davku od dohodkov pravnih oseb (ZDDPO-2), Official Gazette of RS Nos.117/06, 56/08, 76/08, 5/09, 96/09, 110/09 – ZDavP-2B, 43/10, 59/11, 24/12, 30/12, 94/12, 81/13, 50/14, 23/15, 82/15, 68/16, 69/17.

[7] ZDDPO-2, Arts.4,5,.

The general tax rate is 19% and additionally, the Corporate Income Tax Act grants different deductions of the tax base i.e.tax deduction for research and development (100% of the expense), for investment (40% of the invested amount), for employment of certain groups of workers (20%, 45% or 70% of the worker's salary), for voluntary supplementary pension insurance (paid premiums), and for donations (0.3% of the income).[1]

c) Personal Income Tax

Personal Income Tax is regulated by the Personal Income Tax Act[2] and is applicable to six categories of individual's income i.e.income from employment, business income, income from basic agriculture and forestry, income from rental income and royalties, and income from capital. Active income categories are taxed aggregately at the progressive tax rate of 16%, 27%, 34%, 39% or 50%, while the passive income categories are taxed cedularly at the flat 25% rate.[3] For capital gains, the rate depends on the holding period and decreases for 5% every five years.

c. Tax Declaration and Preference

Tax procedure is a special type of administrative procedure, which is primarily regulated by the Tax Procedure Act and subsidiary by the General Administrative Procedure Act[4]. In general, tax debt is calculated in the tax declaration or in a tax ruling.

Tax declaration is a result of the self-assessment procedure in which a taxable person is required to file a tax declaration for the given tax period. The declaration must be filed in time either through the e-point "E-davki" or sent to the Tax Administration in physical form. Taxable person that fails to file the declaration in time, or files an erroneous declaration may be subject to fines and interests. After the expiry of the tax declaration deadline, a taxable person that is aware of irregularities may voluntarily report such irregularities and immediately pay its tax debt in order to avoid punitive measures.

A tax ruling is a special type of administrative decision, issued by the Tax Administration following the tax return procedure, the tax inspection procedure and some other tax-related procedures. In the tax return procedure, a taxable person reports to the Tax Administration the necessary information to calculate the tax debt,[5] while the tax inspection procedure is a special type of administrative procedure pursued by the Tax Administration when there may be irregularities in the tax procedure.

The legislation does not provide any special tax regimes for foreign natural and legal persons; however, they are eligible for all tax reliefs and incentives available to domestic entities.

I. Securities

a. Brief Introduction of Securities-Related Laws and Regulations

Securities market is regulated by various acts; inter alia the Financial Instruments Market Act, the Investment Trusts and Management Companies Act, the Act on Alternative Investment Fund Managers, the Takeovers Act, and the Book Entry Securities Act. The laws and regulations which have not been discussed in more detail in the preceding chapters will be introduced in turn below.

The Financial Instruments Market Act defines crucial actors on the financial instruments market, their rights and obligations, types of securities, and some fundamental rules with regard to public offerings of securities. The sale of securities is possible on the organized market through the Ljubljana Stock Exchange or outside the stock exchange through authorized agencies. Public offering of securities is prohibited without issuing the appropriate prospectus pre-approved by the Securities Market Agency (SMA). The content of the prospectus, as well the procedure of its creation are contained in the Financial Instruments Market Act and the Takeovers Act.

The only organized securities market in Slovenia is the Ljubljana Stock Exchange (LJSE). The Ljubljana Stock

---

[1] ZDDPO-2, Arts.55-59.
[2] Sl.Zakon o dohodnini (ZDoh-2), Official Gazette of RS Nos.117/2006, 90/2007, 119/2007, 10/2008, 92/2008, 78/2008, 125/2008, 119/2008, 20/2009, 104/2009, 10/2010, 13/2010, 20/2010, 43/2010, 106/2010, 103/2010, 9/2011 - ZUKD-1, 105/2011, 9/2012 – decision of the Constitutional Court of RS, 24/2012, 30/2012, 40/2012 - ZUJF, 75/2012, 94/2012, 102/2012, 52/2013 - decision of the Constitutional Court of RS, 96/2013, 108/2013, 29/2014 - decision of the Constitutional Court of RS, 50/2014, 94/2014, 23/2015, 55/2015, 102/2015 - ZUJF-E, 104/2015, 63/2016, 69/2017.
[3] ZDoh-2, Art.122.
[4] Sl.Zakon o splošnem upravnem postopku (ZUP), Official Gazette of RS Nos.80/1999, 70/2000, 52/2002, 73/2004, 119/2005, 105/2006 - ZUS-1, 126/2007, 65/2008, 8/2010, 82/2013.
[5] The corporate income tax is calculated and paid by a taxable person.Tax return must be submitted within three months of the current business year for the previous business year, which must be announced to the Tax Administration and cannot be changed in next several years.Tax prepayments are paid in monthly instalments.

Exchange Rules[1] define market structure, which is based on the type and quality of listed financial instruments i.e.equity market, bond market, and structured product market, and the detailed procedure of the securities trade.

The book-entry securities are governed by the Book Entry Securities Act. The acquisition, deletion, and transfer of book-entry securities are facilitated by the Central Register of book-entry securities, a computerised record of book-entry securities, rights and liabilities arising from them, their holders and encumbrances.[2] The register is managed by the Central Securities Clearing Corporation (KDD), [3] which is a Public Limited Company whose founders and shareholders are banks, stockbroking firms, fund management companies, government funds and issuers.[4]

Securities financial transactions that allow banks and other market participants to access secured funding or lending on a short term are regulated by the EU Regulation 2015/2365 on the transparency of securities financing transactions and of reuse and by the appertaining implementing domestic act.[5] The regulation increases the transparency and collaboration between institutions. In Slovenia, the competent authorities under the aforementioned EU legislation are the Bank of Slovenia, the SMA and the Insurance Supervision Agency.

b. Supervision and Regulation of Securities Market

The capital market in Slovenia is supervised by the Securities Market Agency (SMA). The SMA is an independent legal entity with the mission of maintaining a safe, transparent, and efficient market in financial instruments. The SMA annually reports to the National Assembly, its operations are fully funded from taxes, and its functioning is supervised by the Court of Auditors.[6]

c. Requirements for Engagement in Securities Trading for Foreign Enterprises

According to the Financial Instruments Market Act, trading in securities market is more difficult for third-country entities. A third-country issuer, offeror intending to offer such issuer's securities or an applicant for the admission of such issuer's securities to trading on the stock exchange is only allowed to operate through the intermediary. Hence, a third-country entity must authorize an authorized investment firm to conduct its securities related businesses. The chosen investment firm is jointly and severally liable for the fulfilment of obligations and for any damages arising from the violation of these obligations.[7]

The SMA may approve a prospectus of a third-country issuer if it is drawn according to international standards, including the standards of the International Organisation of Securities Commissions, and if such an approval is in line with the EU Directive 2003/71/EC.

Foreign investment companies may operate in Slovenian securities market through a Slovenian branch, which has received an authorization of SMA. A mother company may be required to deposit a certain amount of money in Slovenia as a guarantee for settlements of liabilities arising from transactions in Slovenia. A branch may only exercise activities approved in the SMA authorization.[8]

J. Preference and Protection of Investment

a. The Structure of Preference Policies

The creation of a generally favourable environment for investors has been a priority for the Government. Slovenia is being developed as a green, logistics, and R&D hub and several incentives are offered to new investors as well as to those already running operations in Slovenia. Fiscal incentives include favourable depreciation allowances and amortization rates, tax reliefs for investments and R&D, and a possibility to carry forward the loss of the previous accounting period. Financial incentives include regional aid program (see next

---

[1] Sl.Pravila borze, Official Gazette of RS, Nos.88/10, 89/11, 71/12, 84/12, 44/13, 81/13, 10/14, 80/14, 88/15, 32/16, 67/16, 5/17, 63/17, 76/17.
[2] Sl.Zakon o nematerializiranih vrednostnih papirjih (ZNVP-1), Official Gazette of RS, Nos.75/15, 74/16 – ORZNVP48, 5/17.
[3] About the Central Securities Clearing Corporation, URL: https://www-en.kdd.si/about_kdd (18.2.2018).
[4] According to the publicly available data, almost 20% of SSH's assets that will be sold, form part of the KDD's equity share; SSH, Disposition of Assets and Sale of SOEs, URL: https://www.sdh.si/en-gb/sale-of-assets (21.2.2018).
[5] Sl.Zakon o izvajanju Uredbe (EU) o preglednosti poslov financiranja z vrednostnimi papirji in ponovne uporabe (ZIUPVP), Official Gazette of RS, No.55/17.
[6] SMA, Presentation of the Agency, URL: http://www.atvp.si/Eng/Default.aspx?id=71 (18.2.2018).
[7] ZTFI, Arts.86, 87.
[8] ZTFI, Arts.182-185.

sub-point) and various employment incentives[1] (e.g., covering social contributions paid by the employer, tax incentives, employers who intend to hire unemployed persons may apply for free training and retraining provided by local employment offices). Other incentives are available at the national and municipal level; especially the latter are negotiated on a case-by-case basis.[2]

b. Support for Specific Industries and Regions

In March 2014, the European Commission approved the Slovenian regional aid map 2014-2020 to support investment that would contribute to the regional development.[3] The regional aid map covers the whole territory of Slovenia, which is separated into two areas. The financial incentives in the area "a" (eastern Slovenia) are 25%, 35% or 45% of eligible costs of enterprises, while these incentives in area "c" (western Slovenia) are 10%, 20% or 30%.[4]

Additionally, four areas of Slovenia that were particularly affected by the economic crisis and still suffer from higher unemployment rates than other areas of Slovenia, may benefit from temporary development support measures. These measures are aimed at companies with growth potential, mostly to help them reach foreign markets. The four eligible areas are the City of Maribor with wider surroundings, Prekmurje region, towns of Trbovlje, Hrastnik, and Radeče, and Pokolpje region.[5]

c. Special Economic Areas

In accordance with the Economic Zones Act[6], the Government may grant consent to one or more domestic legal entities for the establishment of an economic zone to perform economic activities of financial, industrial or retail nature. Establishment and operation of an economic zone depends on the local or regional legislation, and may entail certain tax, employment, and infrastructural incentives. Foreign enterprises may operate in economic zones if they are registered in Slovenia and obtain a permission of the founder.

The EU Regulation No.952/2013 and the Act Implementing the Customs Legislation of the European Union[7] enable the establishment of special free zones to facilitate trading and customs formalities. There are two types of free zones. Type I zones have a perimeter fence where goods are placed and supervised by the customs, while type II zones are under similar conditions as customs warehouses where goods must be declared.[8] Establishment of a free zone in Slovenia must be approved by the Government and notified to the European Commission, construction in the designated free zone requires an approval by the customs authority. Currently, the only free zone in Slovenia is the Port of Koper.

d. Investment Protection

As of 2018, there are 34 Bilateral Investment Treaties in force for Slovenia, which guarantee the standard international law protection such as the national treatment clause, the most favoured nation clause, fair and equitable treatment, and the non-discriminatory expropriation measures.[9] The BIT between Slovenia and the People's Republic of China[10] was signed 13 September 1993 an entered into force in January 1995.[11]

---

[1] Sl.Finančne spodbude (Financial incentives), URL: https://www.ess.gov.si/delodajalci/financne_spodbude/ugodnosti_pri_zaposlovanju (21.2.2018).
[2] Incentives, URL: https://www.investslovenia.org/business-environment/incentives/ (21.2.2018).
[3] European Commission, State Aid No.Sa.38060 (2013/N) – Republic Of Slovenia – Regional Aid Map 2014-2020, URL: http://ec.europa.eu/competition/state_aid/cases/251276/251276_1548895_58_2.pdf (19.2.2018).
[4] Incentives, URL: https://www.investslovenia.org/business-environment/incentives/ (19.2.2018).
[5] Incentives, URL: https://www.investslovenia.org/business-environment/incentives/ (18.2.2018).
[6] Sl.Zakon o ekonomskih conah (ZEC), Official Gazette of RS, No.35/10.Please note that the current wording of this Act only guarantees the pursuit of economic activity in the economic zones until 31 December 2013.In the past, however, this duration has been extended by amendments to the Economic Zones Act.
[7] Sl.Zakon o izvajanju carinske zakonodaje Evropske unije (ZICZEU), Official Gazette of RS, No.32/16.
[8] European Commission, Free zones, URL: https://ec.europa.eu/taxation_customs/business/customs-procedures/what-is-exportation/free-zones_en (18.2.2018).
[9] e.g.Agreement Between the Republic of Turkey and the Rebuplic of Slovenia On the Promotion and Protection of Investments, URL: http://investmentpolicyhub.unctad.org/Download/TreatyFile/2274 (21.2.2 2018); Agreement between the Government of the Republic of Singapore and the Government of the Republic Of Slovenia on the Mutual Promotion and Protection of Investments, URL: http://investmentpolicyhub.unctad.org/Download/TreatyFile/3535 (21.2.2018);
[10] List of bilateral investment treaties, URL: https://view.officeapps.live.com/op/view.aspx?src=http%3A%2F%2Fwww.mgrt.gov.si%2Ffileadmin%2Fmgrt.gov.si%2Fpageuploads%2FSEKTOR_ZA_INTERNACIONALIZACIJO%2Fpredlogi__in_veljavni_predpisi%2FBilateral_Investment_Treaties.-list.doc (19.2.2018).
[11] Agreement between the Government of the People's Republic of China and the Government of the Republic of Slovenia concerning the encouragement and reciprocal protection of investments, URL: http://investmentpolicyhub.unctad.org/Download/TreatyFile/779 (19.2.2018).

Partners	Date of signature	Date of entry into force
Albania	23/10/1997	22/03/2000
Austria	07/03/2001	01/02/2002
Belgium-Luxembourg Economic Union	01/02/1999	14/01/2002
Bosnia and Herzegovina	30/05/2001	01/07/2002
Bulgaria	30/06/1998	26/11/2000
China	13/09/1993	01/01/1995
Croatia	12/12/1997	08/07/2004
Denmark	12/05/1999	30/03/2002
Egypt	28/10/1998	07/02/2000
Finland	01/06/1998	03/06/2000
France	11/02/1998	05/08/2000
Germany	28/10/1993	18/07/1998
Greece	29/05/1997	11/02/2000
Hungary	15/10/1996	09/06/2000
Kuwait	26/04/2002	28/07/2004
Lithuania	13/10/1998	15/05/2002
Macedonia, The former Yugoslav Republic of	05/06/1996	21/09/1999
Malta	15/03/2001	06/11/2001
Moldova, Republic of	10/04/2003	01/06/2004
Netherlands	24/09/1996	01/08/1998
Poland	28/06/1996	31/03/2000
Portugal	14/05/1997	04/05/2000
Romania	24/01/1996	24/11/1996
Serbia	18/06/2002	01/05/2004
Singapore	25/01/1999	08/09/2000
Slovakia	28/07/1993	28/03/1996
Spain	15/07/1998	03/04/2000
Sweden	05/10/1999	12/05/2001
Switzerland	09/11/1995	20/03/1997
Thailand	18/02/2000	20/10/2002
Turkey	23/03/2004	19/06/2006
Ukraine	30/03/1999	01/06/2000
United Kingdom	03/07/1996	27/03/1999
Uzbekistan	07/10/2003	18/05/2004

Table 2: Bilateral investment treaties in force for Slovenia[1]

---

[1] UNCTAD, Slovenia, URL: http://investmentpolicyhub.unctad.org/IIA/CountryBits/192 (23.2.2018).

III. Trade

A. Department Supervising Trade

The competent authority for trade and trade policy is the Ministry of Economic Development and Technology. It prepares and implements the European and national policy and legislation in the field of the free movement of goods and services, the national technical infrastructure of quality (accreditation, metrics, and standardization), company law, consumer protection, intellectual property and competition protection, supply for the market and the commodity reserves, control of prices and trading activity and mailing.

The Finance Ministry together with the Financial Administration of the Republic of Slovenia (FURS) forms a backbone of finance and tax administration. FURS's tasks include assessment, calculation and collection of taxes and duties, customs clearance of goods, financial supervision, financial investigation, cash controls on entering or leaving the EU, storage, sale and destruction of seized, confiscated, abandoned or found goods and supervision of destruction of goods control of admission, removal and transit of goods subject to special measures due to interests of the safety and protection of the health and lives of people, animals, plants, environmental protection, as well as protection of the cultural heritage, intellectual property and commercial policy measures, implementation of foreign trade and common agriculture policy measures in the competence of the Financial Administration, etc. Another key supervisory body is the Slovene Market Inspectorate, who is responsible for surveillance of execution of Slovene legislation on areas of consumer protection, product safety, trade, catering, crafts, services, pricing, tourism, competition protection and copyrights.

As far as non-governmental bodies are concerned the largest and most influential economic association in Slovenia is the Chamber of Commerce and Industry, which is a member of Eurochambres (the European Association of Chambers of Commerce and Industry) and the International Chamber of Commerce (ICC).

B. Brief Introduction of Trade Laws and Regulations

Slovene legal system comprises three levels of law and regulations. Hierarchically (with the exception of the Constitution itself) international treaty laws and the legislation of the European Union (EU) have priority over national laws. As far as EU laws are concerned according to the Treaty of the functioning of the European Union, the Union has exclusive competencies in the areas of customs union, establishing of the competition rules necessary for the functioning of the internal market, monetary policy for the Member States whose currency is the Euro, conservation of marine biological resources under the common fisheries policy and the common commercial policy, whilst other areas are either under shared competences or are in the exclusive domain of the member state (such as taxation laws). Slovenia has in most cases implemented the EU laws into its local laws and regulations.

The most important laws which regulate various aspects of trade are:
- Obligations Code (Official gazette of the RS, no.97/07);
- Companies Act (Official gazette of the RS, no.65/09, 33/11, 91/11, 32/12, 57/12, 44/13);
- Act Implementing the Customs Legislation of the European Union (Official gazette of the RS, no.32/16);
- Consumer Protection Act (Official gazette of the RS, no.98/04);
- Prevention of Restriction of Competition Act (Official gazette of the RS, no.36/08, 40/09, 26/11, 87/11, 57/12, 39/13 – dec.CC, 63/13 – ZS-K, 33/14, 76/15 and 23/17);
- Inspection Act (Official gazette of the RS, no.43/07, 40/14);
- Electronic Business and Electronic Signature Act (Official gazette of the RS, no.98/04 61/06 – ZEPT and 46/14);
- Electronic Commerce Market Act (Official gazette of the RS no.96/09 and 19/15);
- Trade Act (Official gazette of the RS, no.24/08, 47/15).

C. Trade Management

a. General Trade Requirements and Unfair Competition

Trade rules and regulations, such as minimal technical conditions, place of trade, price indication, labeling of products etc., are regulated by different laws and regulations of the national legislation as well as directly by the EU legislation. The most important Slovene laws regulating trade rules and conditions are Obligations Code (general civil law rules and specific contract types, including specific rules for commercial subjects), Companies Act (incorporation and operations of companies and similar legal entities), Consumer Protection Act (specific requirements regarding sales of goods and services in business to consumer or end users), Trade Act and General Product Safety Act.

Foreign entrepreneurs entering the Slovene market can establish a domestic company or register a branch office in Slovenia or they can operate from abroad, or they can contract a local distributor. Foreign nationals or foreign legal entities respectively can incorporate companies under the same conditions as Slovene nationals or Slovene legal entities. The most frequent company form is a limited liability company (d.o.o.) with a minimum share capital of EUR 7,500. Other most common types of companies include public limited company (d.d.), unlimited liability company (d.n.o.), limited partnership (k.d.), and sole proprietor (s.p.– no legal entity status). The process of incorporation is quick and straight forward. All documents required for incorporation have to be translated into Slovene language by a certified translator.

All products entering the Slovene retail market must comply with the Consumer Protection Act, which specifies that companies have to conduct business with consumers in Slovene language (in certain areas also in Hungarian or Italian). This is further regulated by provisions of the Public Use of the Slovene Language Act (Official gazette of RS no.86/04 and 8/10). Product declarations have to be in Slovene language and have to include product information, characteristics of the product and usage instructions. Generally understandable symbols and pictures may also be used.

Only products that are proven to be safe may enter the market. Various rules and regulations are in place for product labeling depending on the type of the product in question. In general, all food products have a common minimal standard that has to be met in order for the product to be placed on the market (he following needs to be clearly stated on the product: name of the product, list of ingredients, net quantity, expiration date, etc.). EU rules on product declarations and criteria apply in Slovenia as well. All products must be equipped with CE conformity declarations and related documents.

Slovene legislation is in line with the EU rules on unfair competition and related practices. Unfair competition is prohibited by provisions of the Prevention of Restriction of Competition Act. All market activities contrary to good business practices which and cause or may cause damage to other companies are forbidden. If such acts cause damage, a lawsuit can be filed under the general rules of the Obligations Code. Additionally, the affected entity can request further prohibition of unfair competition activities, destruction of objects used in the process and elimination of the consequences, if possible.

b. Electronic Trade and Consumer Protection

Electronic trade in Slovenia is regulated by the Electronic Commerce Market Act. Application of this regulation is generally limited to the providers of information technology services i.e.every person or legal entity with a registered office in Slovenia which provides services at a distance for a fee, through electronic equipment at the personal request of service users. Certain exceptions apply which allow enforcement of limitations under Slovene law, regardless of the registered office of the service provider. These exceptions cover areas such as intellectual property rights, advertising of investment funds, contract obligations in the consumer contracts, validity of contracts regarding rights on real estates which require special form, etc. The Electronic Business and Electronic Signature Act supplements the aforementioned Electronic Commerce Market Act. It regulates electronic or digital operations and the use of digital signature in electronic commerce and public procedures respectively.

The Slovene Consumer Protection Act has implemented all EU's most important directives such as Council Directive on the approximation of the laws, regulations and administrative provisions of the Member States concerning liability for defective products, Council Directive on unfair terms in consumer contracts etc. Provisions of the Consumer Protection Act apply to all business to consumer contracts and can`t be legally excluded from such contracts. Accordingly, provisions regulating minimum legal requirements for concluding long-distance agreements, providing of necessary information prior to the conclusion of these agreements, and alike, also apply. It is important to note that certain consumer contracts, in particular consumer loans and credit agreements are subject of additional specialized legislation.

D. The Inspection and Quarantine of Import and Export Commodities

The Union Customs Code (UCC) grants general authorization under which goods brought into the customs territory of the European Union are occasionally subject to customs supervision and may be subject to customs controls. Where applicable, all goods are subject to such prohibitions and restrictions as are justified on grounds of, inter alia, public morality, public policy or public security, the protection of the health and life of humans, animals or plants, the protection of the environment, the protection of national treasures possessing artistic, historic or archaeological value and the protection of industrial or commercial property, including controls on drug precursors, goods infringing certain intellectual property rights and cash, as well as to the implementation of fishery conservation and management measures and of commercial policy measures. Goods remain under supervision for as long as is necessary to determine their customs status and may not be removed therefrom without the permission of the customs authorities. Non-Union goods remain under customs supervision until their customs status is changed, or they are taken out of the customs territory of the Union or until they are destroyed.

Customs authority may perform all customs control measures they deem necessary, including inspection of goods, sampling, verifying the information given in declaration, as well as checking the authenticity of documents, examining the accounts and other records of business entities, inspection of vehicles, passengers luggage or other commodities that persons carry with them or on them.

E. Customs Management

a. Overview of the Applicable Law and International Agreements

a) Customs Law

Slovenia, as a member state of the European Union and a contracting party to the Treaty of the functioning of the European Union, has transferred its authority regarding legislating competencies in the area of customs to the European Union. The most important piece of legislation in this area is Regulation (EU) No 952/2013 of the European parliament and of the Council of 9 October 2013 laying down the Union Customs Code. Slovenia has adopted these rules with the Act Implementing the Customs Legislation of the European Union (Official Gazette of RS no.32/16). Further relevant EU regulations on customs and duties are Regulation (EU) No 2016/1037 of the European parliament and of the Council on protection against subsidized imports from countries not members of the European Union and Regulation (EU) No 2016/1036 of the European parliament and of the Council on protection against dumped imports from countries not members of the European Union.

b) Customs Tariff

Slovenia uses the "EU Product classification system" under which all products are classified under a tariff code that carries information on duty rates and other levies on imports and exports, any applicable protective measures (e.g.anti-dumping), external trade statistics and import and export formalities and other non-tariff requirements. The EU classification system consists of three integrated components:

- The Harmonized System (HS - nomenclature developed by the World Customs Organization)
- The Combined Nomenclature (CN - EU's eight-digit coding system, comprising the HS codes with further EU subdivisions)
- The Integrated Tariff (TARIC) provides information on all trade policy and tariff measures applicable to specific goods in the EU (e.g.temporary suspension of duties, antidumping duties, etc). It comprises the eight-digit code of the combined nomenclature plus two additional digits (TARIC subheadings).

c) Free Trade Agreements and Bilateral Agreements

Slovenia, as a sovereign country, has seven bilateral agreements in power with the People's Republic of China: the Agreement on Trade and Economic Cooperation (1993), the Agreement on Scientific and Technological Cooperation, the Agreement on Cooperation in Education, Culture and Science, the Agreement concerning the Encouragement and Reciprocal Protection of Investments, the Agreement on Economic Cooperation (2007), the Agreement concerning the Co-operation in the Defense Field, the Agreement for the Avoidance of Double Taxation and the Prevention of Fiscal Evasion with respect to Taxes on Income.

b. Customs Management and Procedures

Regulation (EU) No 952/2013 (the Union Customs Code) lays down general rules and regulations on all customs management and procedures. Procedures may vary depending on the country of origin or depending on the type of product. More precise information about specific requirements for a certain product (including required forms, labels etc.) can be accessed by introducing the specific Combined Nomenclature code, the country of origin and the Member State of destination (form available on http://trade.ec.europa.eu/tradehelp/).Certificate for product's country of origin can be issued by the Slovene Chamber of Commerce, Chamber of Trade or by customs authorities.

a) Import Procedures

A carrier of goods entering the customs territory of the EU needs to submit advance cargo information in the first customs office at the entry to the EU through the Entry Summary declaration (ENS). Goods brought into the customs territory of the European Union are subject to customs supervision from the time of their entry and may be subject to customs controls (where applicable, they are subject to prohibitions and restrictions).

Goods imported into the EU customs territory must be accompanied by a summary declaration. Goods are then placed under the temporary storage situation (not exceeding 90 days in any case), which means that they are stored under customs supervision until they are placed under any of the following customs procedures or until they are re-exported:

- Release for free circulation; goods are "released for free circulation" when the conditions relating to importation into the EU have been duly;

- Special procedures; goods may be placed under any of the following categories of special procedures:

(i) Transit, which includes external and internal transit:

External transit: non-Union goods may be moved from one point to another within the customs territory of the Union without being subject to import duties,

Internal transit: Union goods may be moved from one point to another within the customs territory of the Union, passing through a country or territory outside that customs territory, without any change in their customs status.

(ii) Storage, which comprises customs warehousing and free zones:

Customs warehousing: non-Union goods may be stored in premises or any other location authorized by the customs authorities and under customs supervision ('customs warehouses') without being subject to import duties, other charges related to the import of the goods and commercial policy measures.

Free zones: Member States may designate parts of the customs territory of the Union as free zones. They are special areas within the customs territory of the Union where goods can be introduced free of import duties, other charges (i.e.internal taxes) and commercial policy measures, until they are either assigned another approved customs procedure or re-exported. Goods may also undergo simple operations such as processing and re-packing.

(iii) Specific use, which comprises temporary admission and end-use:

Temporary admission: non-Union goods intended for re-export may be subject to specific use in the customs territory of the Union, with total or partial relief from import duty, and without being subject to other charges like internal taxes and commercial policy measures. This procedure may only be used provided that the goods are not intended to undergo any change. The maximum period during which goods may remain under this procedure is 2 years.

End-use: goods may be released for free circulation under a duty exemption or at a reduced rate of duty on account of their specific use.

(iv) Processing, which comprises inward and outward processing:

Inward processing: goods are imported into the Union in order to be used in the customs territory of the Union in one or more processing operations, without being subject to import duties, taxes and commercial policy measures. The customs authorities shall specify the period within which the inward processing procedure is to be discharged. Where finished products are not finally exported, these shall be subject to the appropriate duties and measures

Outward processing: Union goods may be temporarily exported from the customs territory of the Union in order to undergo processing operations. The processed products resulting from those goods may be released for free circulation with total or partial relief from import duties.

The placing of the goods under any customs approved treatment or use is done using the Single Administrative Document – SAD, which is a common form used by all EU Member States whereas a fully electronic customs environment is created. Customs authorities use the value of imported goods as one of the elements to assess the amount of duty (customs debt), which has to be paid before goods can enter the EU, since most customs duties and VAT are expressed as a percentage of the value of the goods being declared.

The Integrated Tariff of the European Communities (TARIC) identifies goods with a view to include all trade policy and tariff measures applicable in the EU (such as temporary suspension of duties, antidumping duties, etc.). Its structure is based on the 8-digit code of the CN and on two additional digits. The following import duties may be charged:

- Import duties (EU): customs, anti-dumping and countervailing duty

- National duties: value added tax (VAT), excise duty, various environmental duties (for example duty on CO_2 emissions from liquid fuels), motor vehicle tax (MVT), additional motor vehicle tax (AMVT)

There are some exceptions where the EU implements Trade Defence Instruments designed in accordance with several WTO agreements which recognize the right of its members to counter the unfair trade practices. The instruments set by the EU are the following:

- Surveillance measures are not import restrictive instruments but a system of mandatory import licenses issued by the EU Member States' authorities for monitoring purposes. These measures are applied principally on some agricultural, textile and steel products.

- Quantitative Limits on imports of some products originating from certain third countries are aimed to protect European producers against harmful mass importations at a very low price.

- Safeguard measures are applied on a case-by-case basis to imports which cause or threaten to cause damage to the EU industry. They consist in the temporary and emergency restriction of some specific imports. The procedure to impose these measures can be started either at the request of a Member State or at the European

Commission's own initiative; however industry cannot directly lodge a request. Nevertheless, these measures must anyhow respect the WTO Agreement on Safeguards.

b) Export Procedures

The export procedure has to be carried out for community goods leaving the EC customs territory except for a very few exceptions. This is due to the fact that this procedure must ensure the correct application of all export measures, e.g.: export restrictions and surveillance measures, and payment of export refunds for agricultural products.

The export procedure foresees, in principle, two stages:

(i) First the exporter / declarant presents the goods, his export declaration and, where necessary, his export authorization or license at the customs office responsible for the place where he is established or where the goods are packed or loaded for export

(ii) if, for administrative reasons, this provision cannot be applied, the export declaration may be lodged with any customs office which is competent for the operation in question (Finally, an export declaration may also be accepted by a customs office other than that normally responsible, provided there are duly justified good

If no simplified procedure is used, the export declaration is made on the Single Administrative Document (SAD) or its electronic equivalent. The customs office to which the goods and the export declaration have been presented releases the goods for export on condition that they leave the EC customs territory in the same condition as when the declaration was accepted. Subsequently, the goods and a copy of the export declaration are presented to the customs office of exit which satisfies itself that the goods presented correspond to those declared and supervises their physical departure.

In the case of goods exported by rail, post, air or sea, the customs office of exit may be the office competent for the place where the goods are taken over under a single transport contract for transport to a third country (e.g.port, airport, railway station). The customs office of exit endorses copy No 3 of the SAD or any other document replacing it and returns it to the declarant or his representative (this serves as proof of export and can be used for exemption from VAT and excise duty). Though goods declared for export are under customs supervision, completion of the procedure (i.e.presentation of the goods and the declaration at the customs office of exit) is not monitored by customs, given that Community goods can move freely throughout the customs territory. Where non-Community goods placed under a customs procedure with economic impact are re-exported, the formalities for the export procedure apply.

IV. Labour

A. Brief Introduction of Labour Laws and Regulations

The following laws apply to employment relationships:

(i) Employment Relationship Act (Official Gazette of the Republic of Slovenia no.21/13, 78/13 – corr., 47/15 – ZZSDT, 33/16 – PZ-F, 52/16 and 15/17 – dec.CC);

(ii) Health and Safety at Work Act (Official Gazette of the Republic of Slovenia no.43/11);

(iii) Social Security Contributions Act (Official Gazette of the Republic of Slovenia no.5/96, 18/96 – ZDavP, 34/96, 87/97 – ZDavP-A, 3/98, 7/98 – dec.CC, 106/99 – ZPIZ-1, 81/00 – ZPSV-C, 97/01 – ZSDP, 97/01, 62/10 – dec CC, 40/12 – ZUJF, 96/12 – ZPIZ-2, 91/13 – ZZVZZ-M, 99/13 – ZSVarPre-C and 26/14 – ZSDP-1);

(iv) Labour Market Regulation Act (Official Gazette of the Republic of Slovenia no.80/10, 40/12 – ZUJF, 21/13, 63/13, 100/13, 32/14 – ZPDZC-1, 47/15 – ZZSDT and 55/17), together with partially valid Employment and Insurance Against Unemployment Act (Official Gazette of the Republic of Slovenia no.107/06, 114/06 – ZUTPG, 59/07 – ZŠtip, 51/10 – dec CC, 80/10 – ZUTD and 95/14 – ZUJF-C);

(v) Pension and Disability Insurance Act (Official Gazette of the Republic of Slovenia no 96/12, 39/13, 99/13 – ZSVarPre-C, 101/13 – ZIPRS1415, 44/14 – ORZPIZ206, 85/14 – ZUJF-B, 95/14 – ZUJF-C, 90/15 – ZIUPTD, 102/15, 23/17, 40/17 and 65/17);

(vi) Personal Income Tax Act (Official Gazette of the Republic of Slovenia no.13/11, 9/12 – dec.CC, 24/12, 30/12, 40/12 – ZUJF, 75/12, 94/12, 52/13 – dec.CC, 96/13, 29/14 – dec.CC, 50/14, 23/15, 55/15, 63/16 in 69/17);

(vii) Minimum Wage Act (Official Gazette of the Republic of Slovenia no.13/10 and 92/15);

(viii) Employment, Self-employment and Work of Foreigners Act (Official Gazette of the Republic of Slovenia no.1/18);

(ix) Collective Agreements Act (Official Gazette of the Republic of Slovenia no.43/06 and 45/08 - ZArbit);

(x) Worker Participation in Management Act (Official Gazette of the Republic of Slovenia no.42/07 and 45/08 –

ZArbit);

(xi) Act on Representative Trade Unions Act (Official Gazette of the Republic of Slovenia no.13/93).

Please note that all EU Directives and EU Regulations in the area of employment relationship also apply in Slovenia as an EU member state.

The key act regulating labour and/or employment relationships is the Employment Relationship Act which governs and regulates all rights and obligations arising from or in connection with the employment. Certain rights and obligations are further determined by respective collective agreement for individual industries

B. Requirements of Employing Foreign Employees

a. Access to Slovene Labour Market

Slovenia has introduced a two tier system regulating work of foreigners, depending on the country of origin: EU nationals and non-EU nationals / third country nationals respectively.

(i) EU Nationals

EU Nationals (including nationals from the EEA (European Economic Area) have free access to the labour market in Slovenia meaning they do not require a special work permit to enter the Slovene labour market. They can apply for job vacancies under equal conditions as Slovene nationals. Certain limitations are in place for Croatian nationals until middle of 2018. Before commencing work employer is obligated to register the EU national into the obligatory pension, invalidity, health and unemployment insurance within 8 days of the date of signing the employment contract. Please note that any EU nationals sent to work in Slovenia by their foreign employer (seconded workers or assignees) has a right to minimal working and employment conditions pursuant to Slovene regulations.

(ii) Non-EU Nationals

Non-EU nationals require a work permit and a residence permit to access the Slovene labour market and reside in Slovenia for work. Work permits shall be issued upon an application of the employer for an employment permit or a permit for work enabling a foreigner to work or be employed by a specific employer – the applicant. In legally stipulated cases a worker may apply for a personal work permit which enables the applicant to freely select the employment, work or employer during the duration term of the permit. Work permits are issued by the Employment Service of Slovenia.

b. Types of Employment or Work Permits

Single permit approval may be issued for the following: employment, self-employment and work, seconded or posted workers, training or further training courses for foreign nationals, individual foreign national services, agent working longer than 90 days in a calendar year, or seasonal work in farming exceeding 90 days.

c. Application Procedure

Slovenia has introduced a single work and residence permit in 2015. Applicants (employers for first time employees or employees fulfilling conditions) have to submit their single permit application at an administrative unit or at the diplomatic or consular office in their home country. The single permit procedure, managed by administrative units, requires the ESS (Employment Service of Slovenia)'s approval, which is granted if legal conditions are met for specific type of work or employment. A foreigner files a single application for both employment and work and residence permit. Upon approval a single employment or work and residence permit is issued in a form of an ID card.

d. Conditions for Employment of Non-EU Nationals

A foreigner may apply for self-employment permit after legally residing in Slovenia continuously for one year (unless he / she is registered as a person carrying out independent activity in the business register).

Single employment permit is issued if the following conditions are met (cumulatively):

- if there are no suitable candidates for the job vacancy in the register of unemployed persons;
- if the employer is validly registered for its activity and has demonstrated active operations (it has employed at least one person for full time in the period of 6 months prior to the application, or the individual has been registered with social security for six months or that the employer has received business revenue of at least EUR 10,000 to its Slovene bank account during each of the last six months prior to the application);
- the employer has settled and paid all taxes and duties;
- the employee fulfil job vacancy conditions; and
- the original employment contract is enclosed to the application.

Alternatively employers not yet registered for a period of six months have to demonstrate they have invested a minimum of EUR 50,000 into its business activity.

e. Administrative Fees and Time to Obtain a Single Permit

The administrative fee amounts to approximately EUR 100. A permit is generally issued within two months from the date of the application (or from the date when the application is completed). The first single permit is issued for the duration of the employment contract but for maximum one year. After this the single permit may be prolonged providing the application is filed before the expiry of the first single permit.

f. Social Insurance

Slovenia has introduced the obligatory social security scheme for all employees. Employer and employee pay fix percentage social security contributions based on the gross salary amount. Obligatory social security comprises pension, disability, health, unemployment and parental insurance. The employer pays social security contributions in the total amount 16.10 % of the gross salary (in addition to the gross salary), of which 6.56 % for health insurance, 8.85 % for pension insurance and total of 0.69 % for parental, unemployment and accident insurance. The employee pays social security contributions in the total amount 22.10 % of the gross salary (in addition to the gross salary), of which 6.36 % for health insurance, 15.50 % for pension insurance and total of 0.24% for parental, and unemployment insurance.

g. Total Cost of Employment

The total cost of employment in Slovenia comprises the following costs: gross salary, employer's social security contributions and obligatory reimbursement of work related costs (transport to and from work, nourishment during work, business trip costs). In addition to regular salaries the employer is obliged to pay to the employee each year a one-time vacation allowance in the amount of average monthly salary in Slovenia.

C. Exit and entry

a. Visa Types

Entry into Slovenia is only possible with a valid passport and a valid residence permit or a visa (depending on the country of origin).

a) Residence Permit

A foreigner wishing to work in Slovenia has to obtain a single permit comprising both work and residence permit. The following documentation must be submitted with the application to the competent Administration Unit or the Slovene embassy abroad:

(i) a recent photo;
(ii) certified copy of the passport;
(iii) proof of health insurance (for the period from the date of application to the commencement of employment and / or residence in Slovenia;
(iv) proof of sufficient means for living (proof of funds);
(v) police record form the country of origin;
(vi) employment contract signed by both parties (in original);
(vii) proof of education and / or qualifications required by the employer, proof of other conditions (please note foreign degrees and / or titles education might need to be recognised by competent Slovene bodies in certain cases);
(viii) proof of residence / accommodation during stay in Slovenia.

b) Temporary and Permanent Residence Permit

First residence permit for a non-EU national is issued as a temporary residence permit for a maximum of one year. A new residence permit may be requested before the expiration of the term of the first temporary residence permit. After a foreigner legally resides in Slovenia for a minimum of five years on the basis of a residence permit, he / she may file an application for a permanent residence permit.

c) Visas

Slovenia's Foreigners Act has introduced three types of visas pursuant to the EU Visa Code:

(i) Transit Visa (Visa A)

Visa A is destined for the travellers that have to stop and wait for several hours for their next flight, in the international transit area of the designated airport. However, if planned to wait overnight, these travelers cannot accommodate in any place else except the transit area.

(ii) Short-Term Visa (Visa C)

Visa C allows its holder to reside in a Schengen Country (Schengen Area) for a certain period of time depending on the visa validity. This particular category, according to the holder's purpose of the travel can be obtained in a form of:

- Single-entry visa allows its holder to enter a Schengen country (Schengen Area) only once for the certain period of time. Once you leave the certain Schengen Area you entered the visa validity expires, even if the time period allowed to stay in the Schengen Area is not over yet.

- Double-entry visa applies for the same policy as above mentioned, however you are allowed to enter the Schengen Area twice, meaning that for the certain period of time permitted by your visa you can enter the Schengen Zone, leave and enter again without any problems. Once you are out of the country for the second time the visa expires.

- Multiple-entry visa allows its holder to go in and out of the Schengen Area as pleased. However, this visa allows its holder to stay in a Schengen Zone for maximum 90 days within half the year, starting from the day one crosses the border between a Schengen member country and the non-Schengen member country.

(iii) Long-Term Visa (Visa D)

Visa D is granted to the certain individuals who are to be studying, working or permanently residing in one of the Schengen countries. The national visa can be of a single entry, granted to the people who are in need of residing in the Schengen country for a certain period of time and for a sole purpose after which they shall return to their country. On the other hand a multi-entry national visa is also granted for certain individuals, allowing its holder to travel in and out of this Schengen country as he / she pleases and also travel throughout the whole Schengen Area without additional visa requirements.

b. Restrictions for Exit and Entry

A residence permit or a visa is not issued to a foreigner that fails to fulfil legal conditions, including, but not limited to, in the case of suspicion that the foreigner will not reside in Slovenia, he / she was forbidden to enter Slovenia, there are reasons to believe the foreigner would not leave Slovenia upon expiry of a permit or a visa, the foreigner is considered to be a threat for Slovenia, there is suspicion that a marriage was concluded only for the purpose of obtaining a residence permit and in other cases determined by the law.

D. Trade Union and Labour Organizations

Slovenia has implemented a constitutional right to organise and partake in trade unions. Unions are organised in both public and private sector. There are no rules about minimum number of employees or the size of employer when it comes to organisation of an union.

There are approximately 50 representative unions which are organised pursuant to the Act on Representative Trade Unions. Representative unions are parties to collective agreements, participate in negotiations with public bodies and ensure safety and social security of employees.

E. Labour Disputes

Labour disputes are resolved by special Labour and Social Courts. Employee's right are rather well protected and an employee has no obligation to pay any court fee in order to commence a proceeding for a breach of his / her rights. Labour legislation determines deadlines for filing claims related to employment with a general statute of limitations of five years from the termination of employment.

Before each court proceeding parties are asked whether they agree with a mediation as an alternative manner of solving disputes. If they agree, they commence mediation under supervision of a mediator. Mediation is a short and mostly efficient procedure aimed at removing the need to lengthy court proceedings. Should parties not reach an agreement during mediation, the court will commence its proceedings.

All social security issues are also resolved by the specialised Labour and Social Courts. These courts resolve issues of social security insurance, compensation, disability and pension as well as other social security rights.

V. Intellectual Property

A. Brief Introduction of IP Laws and Regulations

The intellectual property legal framework in Slovenia is regulated by international, European and national legislation. According to the Slovene Constitution ratified international treaties are used directly and currently (February 2018) there are 23 valid international treaties in this field. Certain IP fields are also regulated on EU level, mainly some areas of copyright law, patenting of the biotechnical inventions and certain areas regarding industrial designs and trademarks. It is important to point out, that all of the European directives have been implemented in the national IP laws, while European regulations (slo: Evropska uredba) are used directly. An up to date list of all applicable international treaties and EU regulations is available on http://www.uil-sipo.si/uil/dodatno/koristni-viri/zakonodaja/mednarodne-pogodbe/

The Slovene national legislation follows the traditional separation of IP rights into copyright rights and industrial property rights and accordingly, there are two main pieces of legislation that regulate this field:

- Industrial Property Act (slo: Zakon o industrijski lastnini, the Official Gazette of the RS No.51/06 and 100/13)

- Copyright and Related Rights' Act (slo: Zakon o avtorski in sorodnih pravicah, the Official Gazette of the RS No.16/07, 68/08, 110/13, 56/15 and 63/16)

Certain aspects of intellectual property are, due to their specific nature, regulated separately:

- Protection of Topographies of Integrated Circuits Act (slo: Zakon o varstvu topografije polprevodniških vezij, the Official Gazette of the RS No.81/06).

- Employment Related Industrial Property Rights Act (slo: Zakon o izumih iz delovnega razmerja, the Official Gazette of the RS No.15/07).

a. Industrial Property

a) According to the Slovene Industrial Property Act the following rights can be granted

- Patent: A patent is defined as a right, granted for any inventions, in all fields of technology, which are new, involve an inventive step and are susceptible of industrial application. A patent right confers upon its holder / owner an exclusive right to prevent third parties not having the owner's consent from acts of making, using, offering for sale, selling, or importing for these purposes the invention protected by the patent. A patent also confers the right to take legal action against any person exploiting the patented invention without the owner's consent, as well as the right to claim damages.

- Short-Term Patent: the Slovene Industrial Property Act provides a specific type of protection of inventions called a "short-term patent" which to a large extent corresponds to utility model protection as known for example in Germany as well as in some other countries. A short-term patent may be granted for inventions which are new, susceptible of industrial application and are the result of a creative effort. The maximum term of a short-term patent is ten years starting from its application date, however it cannot be granted for processes, botanical species or animal breeds.

- Industrial Design: an industrial design protects an outward appearance of the whole or a part of a product, resulting from features of, in particular, lines, contours, colours, shape, texture and / or materials of the product itself and / or its ornamentation. A product is any industrial or handy craft item, including parts intended to be assembled into a complex item, packaging, get-up, graphic symbols and typographic typefaces, but excluding computer programs. A registered industrial design confers upon its owner an exclusive right to use it as well as a right to prevent any third party not having the owner's / holder's consent from using it. Industrial design cannot be registered if it is not new or does not have an individual character, if it is contrary to public order or morality or contains official symbols covered by Article 6ter of the Paris Convention, or if it subsists in features of appearance of a product, which are solely dictated by its technical function and must not necessarily be reproduced in their exact form and dimension.

- Trademarks: a trademark is any sign, or any combination of signs, capable of distinguishing the goods or services of one undertaking from those of another undertaking and capable of being graphically represented, in particular words, including personal names, letters, numerals, figurative elements, three dimensional images, including the shape of goods or of their packaging, combination of colours as well as any combination of such signs. A trademark cannot be registered if it is devoid of any distinctive character, merely descriptive, exclusively the shape of goods or their packaging, misleading, customary in the current language, contrary to public order or morality, official symbol covered by Article 6ter of the Paris Convention, or if it contains or consists of a geographical indication for wines or spirits, where the trademark relates to wines or spirits not having their origin.

- Geographical Indications: geographical indications eligible for registration under the Slovene Industrial Property Act are indications which identify a good as originating in a territory, or a region or a locality in that territory, where a given quality, reputation or other characteristic of the good is essentially attributable to its geographical origin. The name of a good, which has become generally known through long-term use in the course of trade as the name indicating that the good originates in a specific place or region, is also registrable as a geographical indication. Geographical indications for agricultural products and foodstaffs as well as for wines and other products obtained from grapes or wine are eligible for registration under the Agriculture Act and Wine Act.

- Supplementary Protection Certificates: Supplementary protection certificates can be granted after the expiry of a patent for the invention, provided that the subject-matter of the patent is a product, a process to obtain the product or an application of the product, for which an official authorization is needed prior to commercial exploitation. 'Product' in this event means an active ingredient or a combination of active ingredients of a medicinal product or a plant protection product. Supplementary protection certificate takes effect immediately after the expiry of the basic patent for a period equal to the period which elapsed between the date on which the application for a basic patent was filed and the date of the first authorization to place the product on the market in the Community (EC Member States, Norway, Iceland and Liechtenstein), reduced by a period of five years. However, the duration of the certificate may not exceed five years from the date on which it takes effect. A supplementary protection certificate is regulated at the EU level with the regulations (EC) no.469/2009 and no.1610/96 (including all of their subsequent amendments) which are directly applicable for supplementary protection certificates in Slovenia.

b) Internet Domains

Internet domains are not regulated under the Industrial Property Act. A domain registration does not extend absolute rights to its owner / holder as it is based on a contractual relationship between the owner and the registrar. Referral to absolute rights is possible only if a domain name is also protected by or based on a trademark, copyright, personal name, company name etc. Regarding domain registration the "prior tempore, potior ure" principle is utilized, which means that the person who registers the domain first, has advantage over the person who wishes to register the same domain later, regardless of the fact whether the domain name matches their (for example) company name. In certain cases it is possible for the / an IP rights holder to request the domain transfer from the domain holder, usually because of an intellectual property rights' violation. That is also why it is highly recommendable that the name used as a domain name is additionally protected with a trademark. It is also important to note that a domain name (contrary to a trademark) registration is not subject to registration classes but has global usage.

b. Copyright and Related Rights

The Slovene Copyright and Related Rights Act regulates rights of authors with respect to their works of literature, science and art (copyright) and rights of performers, producers of phonograms, film producers, broadcasting organizations, publishers and makers of databases (related rights). According to the before mentioned act copyright works, which are the subject of copyright protection are individual intellectual creations in the domain of literature, science, and art, which are expressed in any mode. Copyright rights grant the author an indivisible right to a work, from which emanate exclusive personal powers (moral rights - right to the first disclosure, right to recognition of authorship, right to integrity of the work and right to withdrawal), exclusive economic powers (economic rights - right of reproduction, right of distribution, rental right, right of public performance, right of public transmission, etc.), and other powers of the author (other rights of the author - right of access and of delivery, resale right, public lending right, etc.).

With respect to intellectual property rights' protection in Slovenia it is important to note that foreign natural persons and legal entities have the same rights as domestic natural persons and legal entities.

B. Patent Application

Filling a patent application with the Slovene Intellectual Property Office represents an initiation of the procedure. The application may be filed in any foreign language, provided that it includes at least an indication of the right, which is requested, and an indication allowing the applicant to be contacted by the Office, in the Slovene, English, French or German language. The Office then invites the applicant to submit (within three months) the translation of the application in the Slovene language. Prior to the application publication, the patent application is examined only as to formal requirements. The Slovene Intellectual Property Office does not examine novelty, industrial application and inventive step of the invention. A full patentability examination however needs to be submitted by any national Slovene patent holder before expiry of the ninth year of patent validity, to upkeep the validity of the patent (for more please see further below). There are no specific national requirements when drafting a patent application. If the application is made according to the Regulations under the Patent Cooperation Treaty (PCT) or Implementing Regulations to the European Patent Convention it fulfills all formal requirements.

A patent application has a few obligatory elements: a request for the grant of right, a description of the invention with the demonstration of the problem and data regarding known solutions and their imperfections, one or more patent claims for the protection of the invention (written In one sentence), short abstract about the essence of the invention, drawings if necessary, receipt of the paid fee and authorization to the representative if the application was filed through the representative.

Patents are granted without a substantive (novelty) examination 18 months after the application filing date or the date of the claimed priority. The protection conferred by the Slovene patent is limited to 20 years starting from the application filing date.

Foreign natural and legal persons having neither residence nor real and effective industrial or commercial establishment in Slovenia must have a local representative, patent agent registered with the Slovene Intellectual Property Office. However, foreign applicants may file applications, perform acts relating to the establishment of the filing date, pay fees, file copies of first applications when claiming the right of priority and receive notifications by the Office relating to those proceedings, without a representative, provided that they communicate to the Office an address for correspondence which is in the territory of Slovenia.

Concerning the national patent procedure please kindly note the following: for any granted national Slovene patent, a full examination report confirming that patentability criteria (i.e.novelty, inventive step and industrial applicability) were met, must be submitted before the end of the ninth year of such patent's validity. This can preferably be either a Slovene translation of one or more European patents granted for the same invention by the European Patent Office or, if no application for a European patent has been filed for the same invention, a Slovene translation of a patent for the same invention, granted, following substantive examination, by another authority which, under Article 32 of the PCT, enjoys the status of International Preliminary Examining Authority, or by any other patent office with which a relevant treaty has been concluded. If such full patentability examination report is not submitted in due time, the validity of the patent irrevocably lapses after the tenth year. A patent owner / holder of a Slovene national patent, who intends to sue a third person for patent infringement, can only do so provided that the full patent examination report was submitted latest when filing the suit or before.

An application for a patent in Slovenia can also be filed under one of two international agreements which Slovenia is party to, namely under the Patent Cooperation Treaty, where one should designate the European Patent Office, or under the European Patent Convention. Both systems enable the applications to enter the national phase in Slovenia once the European patent has been granted.

C. Trademark Registration

The procedure of a national trademark registration starts by filling a national trademark application with the Slovene Intellectual Property Office. A national trademark application may be filed in a foreign language, provided that it includes at least an indication of the right, which is requested, and an indication allowing the applicant to be contacted by the Office, in the Slovene, English, French or German language. The Office then invites the applicant to submit, within three months, the translation of the application in the Slovene language. The application is first examined as to formal requirements, which is followed by an examination for absolute grounds for refusal. If the latter exist, the Office gives the applicant an opportunity to make observations. If the trademark is accepted for registration, the application is published in the Official Journal of the Slovene Intellectual Property Office to allow owners of an earlier trademark to oppose, within three months, the registration. If no opposition is filed or it has been refused, the trademark is registered. The trademark registration is valid for 10 years, and can be renewed each subsequent 10 years' period upon payment of the renewal fee. An application for the registration of a trademark in Slovenia can also be filed under the WIPO Madrid Agreement and Madrid Protocol which Slovenia is party to. A trademark for Slovenia can also be protected via the European Union Intellectual Property Office as a Community Trademark (CTM) valid throughout the entire European Union.

A sign cannot be registered as a trademark if it is devoid of any distinctive character, merely descriptive, represents exclusively the shape of goods or their packaging, is misleading, is customary in the current language, is contrary to public order or morality, represents an official symbol covered by Article 6ter of the Paris Convention, or if it contains or consists of a geographical indication for wines or spirits, where the trademark relates to wines or spirits not having this origin. International applications are subject to the same procedure (examination on absolute grounds for refusal and the possibility of filing the opposition) as when the applications are filed nationally.

Similar to patent applications, foreign natural and legal persons having neither residence nor real and effective industrial or commercial establishment in Slovenia must have a local trademark representative, registered with the Slovene Intellectual Property Office. However, foreign applicants may file applications, perform acts relating to the establishment of the filing date, pay fees, file copies of first applications when claiming the right of priority and receive notifications by the Office relating to those proceedings, without a representative, provided that they communicate to the Office an address for correspondence which is in the territory of Slovenia.

Registering a trademark with the Slovene Intellectual Property Office protects the applicant's / holder's rights in Slovenia only. But the filing date of a Slovene national trademark application can be used as a priority date for the trademark application when applying up to six months later for protection abroad. It can also be used as the basis of an application for an international registration under conditions set up by the WIPO Madrid Agreement or Madrid Protocol.

A trademark application has a few obligatory elements: request for trademark registration, the sign the protection is requested for, the list of goods and/or services for which the sign is to be protected as a trademark (goods and / or services must be classified according to the Nice classification). A trademark may be protected with respect to one or more types of goods and / or services.

D. Measures for IP Protection

Slovene Intellectual Property Office is not competent to take measures related to enforcement of intellectual property rights (it only cooperates with other bodies authorized to carry out such measures). Rights' holders can choose between civil, criminal (penal) or administrative measures. They can be provided legal assistance by lawyers / attorneys and, in certain cases, patent, trademark and design agents (representatives) registered with the Slovene Intellectual Property Office.

a. Civil Measures

District Court of Ljubljana has exclusive jurisdiction over disputes related to intellectual property rights. With the mentioned court the right holder may institute civil proceedings with respect to infringement(s) of its rights and request prohibition of infringement, recall of infringing goods from channels of commerce, destruction of infringing goods, compensation for damage, publication of the court's judgment, in cases of copyright and related rights infringement also a civil sanction). Preliminary injunctions and provisional measures with respect to intellectual property rights' infringements can also be lodged with the same above named court.

b. Criminal Measures

Criminal measures are within the competence of the police, Office of the State Prosecutor and local criminal courts. Infringements of intellectual property rights may also represent criminal offences. The Slovene Penal Code (the Official Gazette RS, No.50/12, 6/16 – corr., 54/15, 38/16 and 27/17) defines several events of intellectual property rights' misuses as criminal offences, such as an unauthorized use of someone else's company name, trademark, geographical indications, industrial designs or special marks for goods or incorporation of particular features of those marks, as its own. Furthermore, criminal offences are also an unauthorized usage of someone else's invention protected by a patent or supplementary protection certificate or registered topography of integrated circuit. With respect to copyright rights the Penal Code defines as criminal offences breaches of copyright moral rights (publishing, presenting, performing or transmitting and disfigurement, infringement and any other unauthorized breaches of someone else's copyright work), breaches of material copyright rights (unauthorized usage of one or more copyright works or its samples) and breaches of copyright related rights (unauthorized reproduction, lending, public presenting and related). Criminal sanctions range from a fine to imprisonment up to 8 years, while all products made on the basis of unauthorized usage as well as all the objects, tools and devices used in this process, are seized. Legal entities are also criminally liable when committing the mentioned criminal offences. Prosecution proceedings in connection with the mentioned criminal offences are initiated ex officio, the exception being criminal offence of copyright infringement, where the prosecution of the perpetrator of such criminal offence is initiated on the proposal by the injured party.

c. Administrative Measures

Administrative measures are carried out by the Financial Administration of the Republic of Slovenia. The Customs Authorities (acting within the framework of the Financial Administration of the RS) when enforcing intellectual property rights act based on the EU Regulation Nr.608/2013 on enforcement of intellectual property from the side of customs' authorities, the Implementing EU Regulation Nr.1352/2013, the EU Regulation Nr.952/2013 on Community Customs' Code (all directly applicable in Slovenia) as well as the Slovene Regulation on the exercising of the EU Regulation enforcement of intellectual property from the side of customs' authorities (the Official Gazette RS, Nr.29/16).

If, during performance of their tasks, customs authorities discover goods suspected of infringing a certain intellectual property right they may temporary detain such goods, of which they notify the right holder and the owner of the goods. During the period of detention of goods, the right holder must decide whether to lodge a lawsuit for infringement of the right or not, while the owner of the goods must decide whether to persist or not in its statement that the goods do not infringe the intellectual property right. Further actions of the customs authorities depend on these decisions. If the right holder lodges a lawsuit, the goods shall be confiscated until the final decision of the court, and after the court's decision establishing an infringement of the right becomes final, the goods, as a rule, shall be destroyed. In the event the right holder is unsuccessful in court, the goods are released. Actions by customs authorities are initiated upon request of the right holder or ex officio. A general request for prosecution of goods infringing a specific intellectual property right, which is valid for one year, can be lodged with the General Customs Directorate. If the request is granted / approved, the General Customs Directorate notifies all customs offices accordingly, who act upon such approved request.

Destruction of suspended goods is also possible without a court decision when the owner of the goods does not respond to the notification by the customs authority on temporary detention of goods or if so agreed upon between the owner of the goods and the right holder (a shortened procedure is in place). The proceedings are initiated ex officio by customs authority when the latter establishes that the goods are evidently counterfeit or pirated.

VI. Environmental Protection

A. Department Supervising Environmental Protection

The Ministry of the Environment and Spatial Planning of the Republic of Slovenia is competent for environmental protection in Slovenia. Its competence is to provide a healthy living environment for all inhabitants and residents of the Republic of Slovenia and to promote and coordinate efforts towards sustainable development, which is based on rational and economical use of natural resources.

The Environmental Agency of the Republic of Slovenia runs a website / operates an IT system where current data, forecasts, analyses and reports on the weather, water, air, earthquakes, climate change, environmental protection and nature is published. The Agency runs several domestic and international projects and is competent for managing water resources (eliminating adverse effects on water, ensuring water quality and conserving biodiversity). It is competent for the Environmental Protection Register, adopts decisions on environmental consent and publishes public announcements. It also issues environment reports available on the EIONET network and reports to the European Environment Agency.

The Inspectorate of the Republic of Slovenia for the Environment and Spatial Planning performs inspection supervision over the implementation or compliance with regulations in this field. It operates autonomously and independently.

The Administration of the Republic of Slovenia for Nuclear Safety inter alia performs professional, administrative, supervisory and development tasks of environmental protection against ionizing radiation, physical protection of nuclear materials and facilities, non-proliferation of nuclear weapons and protection of nuclear goods. Additionally, it monitors the state of radioactivity of the environment, the implementation of regulations in the area of liability for nuclear damage, tasks of inspection supervision, fulfills international obligations and performs tasks of international data exchange. Slovenia is in line with all modern standards for radiation protection and nuclear safety.

The Water Directorate of the Republic of Slovenia performs professional, administrative and development tasks in the field of water management in accordance with regulations. Its goal is to establish a water management system that enables an integrated management (to exploit the water potential of Slovenia as a development opportunity, to take into account water capacity in spatial planning and to reduce the threat to the lives, health and personal property of the citizens). The system of integrated water management is organized at national level and by river basins at regional and local level. The Directorate also established the Water Cadastre which consists of an inventory of waters, water facilities and installations.

B. Brief Introduction of Laws and Regulations of Environmental Protection

EU law is directly applicable in Slovenia and is mostly transposed into its various laws regulating environmental protection.

(i) The key law regulating this area is the Environmental Protection Act adopted in 2004 (Official Gazette of the Republic of Slovenia, no.39/06, 49/06 – other law, 66/06 – the decision of the Constitutional Court, 33/07 – other law, 57/08 – other law, 70/08, 108/09, 108/09 – other law, 48/12, 57/12, 92/13, 56/15, 102/15, 30/16 and 61/17 – other law). It regulates environment protection as an essential part of sustainable development and defines the basic principles of environmental protection, environmental protection measures, environmental monitoring and environmental information, economic and financial instruments for environmental protection, public environmental protection services and other questions related to environmental protection. Currently, a new Environmental Protection Act is under preparation aimed at increasing the compliance with EU legislation, especially with the UNECE Aarhus Convention.

(ii) The Waters Act (Official Gazette of the Republic of Slovenia, no.67/02, 2/04 – other law, 41/04 – other law, 57/08, 57/12, 100/13, 40/14 and 56/15) regulates the management of the sea, inland waters and groundwater as well as aquatic and coastal land, which includes water protection, water management and decision making on water use. This Act also regulates public goods and public services in the fields of water, water facilities and installations, as well as other issues related to waters.

(iii) Decree on waste (Official Gazette of the Republic of Slovenia, no.37/15 and 69/15) with the aim to protect the environment and human health regulates the prevention or reduction of the harmful effects of waste generation and management. It also regulates the reduction of the overall impact of the use of natural resources and improvement of the efficiency of the use of natural resources in accordance with relevant EU Directives and

Regulations.

(iv) The Nature Conservation Act (Official Gazette of the Republic of Slovenia, no.96/04, 61/06 – other law, 8/10 – other law and 46/14) establishes measures for the conservation of biodiversity and a system for the protection of natural values in order to contribute to the conservation of nature.

(v) The Act Declaring the Ecological Protection Zone and Continental Shelf of the Republic of Slovenia (Official Gazette of the Republic of Slovenia, no.93/05) proclaims ecological protection zone and regulates the exercise of its sovereign rights on the continental shelf in accordance with international law. The Republic of Slovenia has its own continental shelf in which it exercises its sovereign rights in accordance with international law.

(vi) The Management of Genetically Modified Organisms Act (Official Gazette of the Republic of Slovenia, no.23/05, 21/10 and 90/12 – other law) in accordance with Directive (EC) 2009/41 and Directive (EC) 2001/18 regulates the management of genetically modified organisms (GMOs) and sets out measures to prevent and reduce the potential adverse effects on the environment especially with regard to biodiversity conservation and human health which could occur when working with GMOs in closed systems, deliberately releasing GMOs into the environment or placing of products on the market. This Act also regulates the implementation of Regulation (EC) No.1830/2003 of the European Parliament and Council.

(vii) The Ionizing Radiation Protection and Nuclear Safety Act (Official Gazette of the Republic of Slovenia, no.102/04) regulates the protection against ionizing radiation in order to minimize damage to human health and radioactive contamination of the living environment due to ionizing radiation of the use of ionizing radiation sources to the smallest possible extent, while at the same time allowing the development, production and use of radiation sources and the implementation of radiation activities. For radiation source intended for the acquisition of nuclear energy, this Act regulates the implementation of nuclear safety measures and special safeguards in case of the use of nuclear materials.

(viii) The Natural Disaster Recovery Act (Official Gazette of the Republic of Slovenia, no.114/05, 90/07, 102/07, 40/12 – other law and 17/14) determines the conditions and manners of using the funds of the budget of the Republic of Slovenia when eliminating consequences of natural disasters and allocating them in order to ensure assistance to those affected by natural disasters and when in eliminating the consequences of damage to agriculture due to natural disasters

C. Evaluation of Environmental Protection

As a Member State of the European Union since May 2014, the Republic of Slovenia is committed to harmonize its laws with the EU legislation. Accordingly its goal is that its environmental protection regulation complies with EU regulations. The implementation of EU environment protection in Slovenia has been reviewed by the European Commission, which issued the EU Environmental Implementation Review Country Report - Slovenia on this topic in 2017 which remarked that Slovenia has a diverse and rich natural environment and the biggest share of land area covered by Natura 2000 network and is one of the most forested countries in Europe.

Looking at the compliance with EU environmental legislation one can see that Slovenia still has a relatively large number of environmental infringement cases. According to the EC Report, the main challenges are streamlining the legal framework related to planning and environmental assessments by ensuring that EU environmental legislation is respected while reducing administrative burdens and investment barriers; preserving the extensive Natura 2000 network and giving priority to waste-water investments and thus fulfilling Slovenia's Accession Treaty obligations. Slovenia is also facing challenges in the area of air quality. The target value and long-term objectives related to the ozone concentration in several air quality zones have not yet been achieved and the share of particulate matter's (PM10) in daily limit concentration is occasionally still too high. Slovenia also needs to pay attention to the closure of some, especially wild, landfills and the rehabilitation of degraded areas.

However, Slovenia is one of the best performing State in terms of municipal waste recycling with its state-of-the-art regional waste management center in Ljubljana and boasts one of the highest contributions of revenues from environmental tax. It has a very high degree of compliance in the field of drinking water and achieves high quality of bathing waters.

VII. Dispute Resolution

A. Methods and Bodies of Dispute Resolution

Slovene legislation provides a traditional litigation proceeding and out-of-court alternatives (mediation and arbitration) for the dispute resolution.

a. Litigation

The civil legal procedure of Slovenian courts is characterized as being adversarial, where judges act as neutral intermediaries and render their decision on the basis of parties' submissions to the court with some elements of inquisitorial systems. The subjects of litigation are the plaintiff, the defendant and the judge who decides on the dispute as the authority. The judge can only decide within the limits of the filed claim and the parties must state all facts on which their claims are based and propose evidences to prove these facts. The principle of dispensability applies, where the plaintiff himself decides whether to file a lawsuit or not, as there is no specific state body that would prosecute those who do not respect civil law relations. The territorial jurisdiction of the court is in principle determined by the defendant's domicile but parties may exceptionally agree otherwise.

Provisions of the Slovene Contentious Civil Procedure Act apply. The court may issue a judgment or a decision. A decision is issued only in some rare cases as a final decision (e.g.protection of property), but is always issued if the procedure has deficiencies (eg by rejecting the lawsuit if the claimant fails to complete the application on request of the court).

Parties have the right to a legal remedy, meaning they can file an appeal against the first instance judgment, generally within 30 days from the service of the judgment. The judgment may be challenged due to substantial violations of the provisions of civil procedure, erroneous or incomplete finding of the facts and misapplication of the substantive law. The court of second instance is competent to decide on timely, complete, allowed and justified appeal. It can then annul the judgment and decide on the matter or return the case to the first instance court. After the judgment is final and binding, the parties may file extraordinary legal remedies in certain cases prescribed by the law.

The regular judicial system in Slovenia is hierarchically divided in three instances. On the first instance, regular courts are divided into civil, criminal, enforcement, insurance and some other courts. These courts are then upon the importance of cases before them further divided into 44 district courts (for minor offences and small civil cases) and 11 regional courts (for all other cases).

On the second instance, there are four higher courts with internal organizational units such as the commercial, liquidation, civil, criminal and family law department. Besides, specialized courts that comprise labour and social court and administrative court has the status of a higher court. These courts hear appeals against first instance decisions.

The highest court of appeal is the Supreme Court, located in the capital city Ljubljana, which is responsible for the uniform jurisprudence and thus normally only hear appeals concerning the proper application of law. It has jurisdiction in civil, criminal, commercial, administrative, labour and social affairs. The Supreme Court is normally a third instance court, which means that it deals primarily with the so-called extraordinary legal remedies. These remedies may be filed only where there are questions of substantive law and in case of most serious violations of the procedure. In addition, the Supreme Court also decides on disputes on jurisdiction between lower courts and on the transfer of jurisdiction to another court in individual cases.

The Constitutional Court of Slovenia is separated from the regular judiciary system. It is the highest authority, competent for protection of constitutionality, legality, human rights and basic freedoms.

b. Arbitration

The Slovene Arbitration Act (the Official Gazette RS No.45/08) applies. An arbitration agreement may be concluded by any natural or legal person, including the Republic of Slovenia and other entities governed by public law. The subject of an arbitration agreement may be any monetary/property claim. Other claims may be subject of an arbitration agreement only if the parties can reach a settlement with respect to such claim(s). The arbitration agreement may take the form of an arbitration clause in a contract or a form of an independent agreement, however it must always be concluded in writing.

Arbitration and litigation are mutually exclusive, meaning that with a conclusion of an arbitration agreement the parties agree to refer the dispute to arbitration and thereby exclude the jurisdiction of the court. In arbitration, the parties can reach an amicable solution to the dispute; if they fail to do so, the arbitrators decide on the dispute. Unlike the judicial process, arbitration allows parties to agree on a number of details on the course of the procedure (e.g.the secrecy of the procedure) and thus adjust it to their own wishes. Solving the dispute by arbitration is usually faster and more professional than the court procedure since the arbitrators are professionally qualified for the particular field. Also, the issued arbitrator's decision is binding, meaning that appeal is normally not possible.

For the purposes of resolving their dispute the parties may form an ad hoc arbitration (arbitration designed specifically for an individual case) or turn to an institutional arbitration. A permanent general institutional arbitration operates in the Chamber of Commerce and Industry of Slovenia, but there are also some specialized arbitrations in Slovenia. It is noted that more than 40% of all cases before Permanent Arbitration are disputed with an international element.

c. Mediation

In comparison with legal proceedings, mediation is much less limited by procedural rules. Mediation in Civil and Commercial Matters Act (the Official Gazette RS Nr.56/08), Act on Alternative Dispute Resolution in Judicial Matters (the Official Gazette RS Nr.97/09 and 40/12) and some related ones apply. Legislation regulates only the basic principles and procedural rules, otherwise the procedure is largely adapted to the needs of clients. Mediation is a process in which parties try to reach a peaceful resolution of the conflict on a voluntary basis through a neutral third party, a mediator. The parties to the mediation procedure are equal and must each have the right to make declarations. In order to reach a solution they must conclude an agreement on the settlement of the dispute. The parties may agree on the course of the procedure, but if they fail to do so the mediator shall conduct the procedure by taking into account all the circumstances of the case, possible wishes of the parties and the need for a quick and lasting solution to the dispute.

In Slovenia, mediation may take place as a court adjudicated or a court-linked program, but it can also be conducted entirely independently from the court and court proceedings. Unlike arbitration, the mediator cannot decide on the dispute, the dispute may be resolved only if the parties reach a consensual solution. The advantages of mediation are normally the help of a neutral third party, informal nature of the procedure, its confidentiality and speed, as well as low price. The parties may agree that a dispute settlement agreement is drawn up in the form of a directly enforceable notarial record, a court settlement or an arbitration award based on a settlement. An arbitral award has the effect of a final judgment between the parties and can be challenged before the court only with an action for annulment of an arbitration award.

When mediation is conducted in conjunction with the courts, the competent bodies are the regional courts are in Slovenia. In mediation programs in courts, mediation is limited to a period of 3 months and the limitation period for a claim which is the subject of mediation is not running during mediation process.

In Slovenia, many mediators are joined in the Association of Mediators of Slovenia and mediation organizations are joined in the MEDIOS Association. In practice, a growing number of disputes are being resolved by mediation. Statistic data show that there has been 2608 cases offered in mediation in regional courts of which 337 cases were successfully completed in 2017.

B. Application of laws

Slovenia is as a member of the European Union directly bound to the EU law, which is mostly transposed into its legislation.

a. Litigation

The civil litigation proceeding is regulated by the Contentious Civil Procedure Act (Official Gazette of the Republic of Slovenia, no.73/07, 45/08 – other law, 45/08, 111/08, 57/09, 12/10, 50/10, 107/10, 75/12, 40/13, 92/13, 10/14, 48/15, 6/17 – all decisions of the Slovenian Constitutional Court and 10/17). This Act sets out the rules of procedure for the competent court to act in disputes arising from personal and family relations, as well as in disputes arising from property and other civil law relationships of natural and legal persons, unless one of the disputes in question is under the jurisdiction of a specialized court or another organ.

Where there is an international element in personal, family, labour, social, property and other civil law relationships, the rules of the Private International Law and Procedure Act (Official Gazette of the Republic of Slovenia, no.56/99 and 45/08 – other law) apply in addition to relevant EU Regulations in this field that are binding on Slovenia.

b. Arbitration

The basic rules of the arbitration procedure are governed by the Arbitration Act (Official Gazette of the Republic of Slovenia, no.45/08). This Act applies to arbitrations established in the Republic of Slovenia, irrespective of whether the parties to the proceedings are domestic or foreign persons.

c. Mediation

In Slovenia mediation is regulated by the Mediation in Civil and Commercial Matters Act (Official Gazette of the RS, no.56/08) and the Act on Alternative Dispute Resolution in Judicial Matters (Official Gazette of the Republic of Slovenia, no.97/09 and 40/12 – other law).

VIII. Others

A. Anti–commercial Bribery

Political corruption and the diversion of public funds are major concerns in Slovenia. According to the Corruption Perceptions Index 2017 which classifies countries according to corruption of the public sector, Slovenia in ranked as the 34th country between 180 countries in the region of Europe and Central Asia. Further, according to Transparency International's Global Corruption Barometer 2013, political parties rank as the most corrupt institution in Slovenia, closely followed by Parliament, the judiciary and public officials. The Transparency International Slovenia report also that since 2012, no significant progress was made in this field. Corruption in Slovenia is also supposed to be greatly affected by unreasonable and non-transparent use of public funds affects.

a. Brief Introduction of Anti-commercial Bribery Laws and Regulations

In addition to internal laws in the field of bribery and thus corruption, the EU regulation directly applies and is generally transposed into Slovenia's legal system. As far as internal Acts are concerned, for a long time the only Act regulating corruption in Slovenia was the Criminal Code that defined criminal offenses with elements of corruption. It was only in 2004 that special legal acts on corruption were adopted; a special law, the national anti-corruption resolution and the rules of procedure of the State Commission for the Prevention of Corruption, followed by various implementing regulations based on adopted legal acts.

(i) The Integrity and Prevention of Corruption Act (Official Gazette of the RS, no.69/11) with the aim of strengthening the functioning of the rule of law, preventing corruption and preventing and resolving conflicts of interest, defines measures and methods for enhancing integrity and transparency, is the main legal act in the field of corruption. Under this Act, "corruption" is any violation of obligatory conduct of official and responsible persons in the public or private sector in order to gain benefit for themselves or for others.

(ii) The Criminal Code (Official Gazette of the RS, no.50/12, 6/16, 54/15, 38/16 and 27/17) establishes the legal framework to mitigate corruption, passive and active bribery and money laundering, among other offences.

(iii) The Liability of Legal Persons for Criminal Offences Act (Official Gazette of the Republic of Slovenia no.98/04, 65/08 and 57/12) established rules for determining legal liability of legal persons and their managers;

(iv) The Resolution on the prevention of corruption in the Republic of Slovenia (Official Gazette of the RS, no.85/04) applies, which basic purpose is to create an appropriately high level of anti-corruption culture on personal and general social level through the realization of the certain goals.

(v) The Government program of the Republic of Slovenia for strengthening the integrity and transparency 2017-2019 introduces continuous work to improve the integrity of institutions, public officials, officials and other employees in the public sector, and increase transparency in public sector activities.

(vi) The Prevention of Money Laundering and Terrorist Financing Act (Official Gazette of the RS, no.68/16) sets out measures, competent authorities and procedures for the detection and prevention of money laundering and regulates the inspection of the implementation of its provisions. The Ultimate Beneficial Owners Register (UBOR) was recently established in Slovenia in order to ensure proper disclosure of actual owners and prevent commercial bribery and money laundering. UBOR is a database in which data on actual owners are collected in order to ensure the transparency of ownership structures of business entities and to prevent abuse of business entities for money laundering and terrorist financing. Accordingly, every business entity must identify and register in the UBOR its actual owner, who is generally an individual person who holds directly or indirectly more than 25% of the shares of the ultimate parent company.

(vii) Rules on limitations and duties of officials regarding the acceptance of gifts (Official Gazette of the RS, no.53/10 and 73/10) regulates the manner of disposing of gifts, the management and the content of the list of gifts received by functionaries in connection with the performance of the function, as well as other implementation issues related to prohibitions, restrictions and duties of officials in accepting gifts.

(viii) The Rules of Procedure of the Commission for the Prevention of Corruption (Official Gazette of the RS, no.24/12) regulate the organization and operation of the Commission for the Prevention of Corruption of the Republic of Slovenia as an autonomous and independent state body and specifies the procedures by which the commission implements its legal tasks in the areas of prevention and restraint of corruption, conflicts of interests, strengthening of integrity and transparency of the public sector and the rule of law.

b. Department Supervising Anti-commercial Bribery

a) State Authorities

The Commission for the Prevention of Corruption of the Republic of Slovenia (CPC) is an independent state body with a mandate in the field of preventing and investigating corruption, breaches of ethics and integrity of public office. The CPC is independent, not subordinate to any other state institution or ministry and does not receive direct instructions from the executive or the legislature. The CPC is not part of the law enforcement or prosecution system of Slovenia and its employees do not have typical police powers. They do, however, have broad legal powers to access and subpoena financial and other documents (notwithstanding the confidentiality level), question public servants and officials, conduct administrative investigations and proceedings and instruct different law enforcement bodies (e.g.Anti-money laundering Office, Tax Administration ...) to gather additional information and evidence within the limits of their authority. The CPC can also issue fines for different violations (sanctions can be appealed to the Court).

b) Non-Governmental Organisations

Transparency International (TI) Slovenia is a non-governmental and non-profit organization with a status in the public interest of the Ministry of Public Administration. Since 2009, it has been part of the international Transparency International network. TI issues the annual publication "Global Corruption Report", which publishes news and analysis of corruption, international and national trends on its incidence, regional reports and results of various research, and presents empirical indicators of corruption, including the CPI (The Corruption Perceptions Index Index) and BPI (Bribe Payers Index Bribe Index).

c. Punitive Actions

a) Commercial Relations

Criminal offenses which are also corrupt practices are specifically defined by the Criminal Code of the Republic of Slovenia as follows: illicit acceptance of gifts, illicit gift giving, abuse of official position or official rights, taking a bribe, giving a bribe, accepting benefits for illegal cooperation to achieve or not achieve any official act, giving gifts for illegal cooperation to achieve or not achieve any official act. These offences are punishable by a fine and / or imprisonment of up to eight years.

As far as commercial relations are concerned, the Penal Code punishes any activity relating to requesting or accepting an award or a gift or a benefit. It further punishes any activity relating to a promise, offer, or giving an unauthorised award, gift or any other property benefit to a person performing an economic activity. All accepted or given gifts, awards or other benefits shall be seized.

b) Relations with Public Bodies and Officials

The Penal Code punishes any activity of public officials relating to accepting or giving a bribe. An official or a public officer who requests or agrees to accept for himself or any third person an award, gift or other property benefit, or a promise or offer for such benefit, in order to perform an official act within the scope of his official duties which should not be performed, or not to perform an official act which should or could be performed, or make other abuse of his position, or whoever serves as an agent for the purpose of bribing an official, shall be sentenced to imprisonment for not less than one and not more than eight years and punished by a fine. An official or a public officer who requests or agrees to accept for himself or any third person an award, gift or other property benefit, or a promise or offer for such benefit, in order to perform an official act within the scope of his official duties which should or could be performed, or not to perform an official act which should not be performed, or make other use of his position, or whoever intermediates in such a bribery of the official, shall be sentenced to imprisonment for not less than one and not more than five years. All bribes are seized.

c) Public Tenders and Contract with Public Bodies

All contracts concluded with any public body in Slovenia shall include an anticorruption clause which shall cause any contract to be null and void in the event that any person on behalf of or for the account of the other contracting party promises, offers or gives any unauthorized benefit to any representative or intermediary of a public sector body or organization in order to win a contract, to conclude a contract under favourable terms or to omit due control over the performance of contractual obligations.

d) Responsibility of Legal persons for Criminal Offences

A legal person is responsible for any criminal offence committed by a person on behalf or for the account or for the benefit of such legal person, if such criminal offense constitutes execution of illegal or unlawful resolution, order or approval by its management, if its management influenced the perpetrator or enabled him / her to commit such offence, if a legal persons obtains illegal or unlawful benefit from such criminal offence or if its management omitted is due supervision. Sanctions that can be imposed against a legal person include amongst others a monetary fine, seizure of property and termination of a legal person.

B. Project Contracting

The Slovene public procurement system is generally governed by the Public Procurement Act (Official Gazette of the RS, no.91/15) lays down rules on public procurement procedures carried out by contracting authorities in connection with public procurement and project design contests. Also, the relevant EU directives are transposed into Slovenia's legal order by this Act. "Public procurement" under this Act means a contract for pecuniary interest concluded in writing between one or more business entities and one or more contracting entities whose object is the execution of works, the supply of goods or the provision of services. The contracting authority may, in the manner and under the conditions set, for the award of a public procurement apply the eight following procedures: open procedure, restricted procedure, competitive dialogue, innovation partnership, competitive negotiated procedure, negotiated procedure with publication, negotiated procedure without prior publication and the procedure for low-value procurement. These procedures are further described in the Public Procurement Act and vary greatly.

Additionally, the Public Procurement for Defence and Security Act (Official Gazette of the Republic of Slovenia, no.90/12, 90/14 – other law and 52/16) defines the obligatory conduct of contracting authorities and bidders in the procurement of goods, services and works in the defense and security field.

The legal protection of providers, subscribers and the public interest, including legal protection in procurement procedures is regulated in the Legal Protection in Public Procurement Procedures Act (Official Gazette of the RS, no.43/11, 60/11 – other law, 63/13, 90/14 – other law and 60/17).

a. Permission System

A "Permitted bid" is a bid submitted by the bidder, for which there are no grounds for exclusion and which meet the conditions for participation. The bidder needs to meet all needs and demands of the contracting authority, the bid must be received in a timely manner and unauthorized collusion or corruption has not been proven to it. The bid is concerned as permitted also if the contracting authority does not consider it unusually low but at the same time the set price does not exceed funds of the contracting authority. The contracting authority must ensure that there is no distinction between bidders at all stages of the public procurement procedure and that they are treated equally. Any commercial entity may participate in public tenders unless it is excluded in accordance with specific legal provisions. Entity may only perform activities within the scope of its registered business activity. Contracting authority may stipulate special permits or similar conditions for individual public tender. Bidders may bid individually or as a group or a temporary syndicate but each entity has to fulfil required individual conditions.

b. Excluding Bidders

Entities listed on a negative reference list maintained by the competent ministry are prohibited from bidding within the specified time period. Any entity which has committed any of the 43 listed criminal offences, has unpaid due tax or social security liabilities, has failed to file required employment forms during the last 5 years or has received two fines during the last three years due to payment of salaries shall be excluded from the public tender. Prohibition to bid is extended to the commercial entity, its legal representatives and its managers.

c. Invitation to Bid and Bidding

A bidder must be selected in a transparent manner and according to the prescribed procedure, which must always be public. As mentioned above, the procedures for public procurement vary greatly. Most often, the following procedure apply. The contracting authority firstly calculates the estimated value of the contract and initiate the procedure for awarding a public contract. Then, it publishes in the public procurement portal the procurement documentation which also contains a draft of the public procurement contract. Interested bidders may submit their offer with all required information from the published contract notices. A bid is submitted on paper or through the official webpage https://ejn.gov.si/.Minimum time period to receive bids is 35 days from the date of publication of the public tender, but a shorter 15 days period may be used if urgent. Where the bid complies with the set requirements and conditions, the contracting authority submits a public procurement on the basis of the most economically advantageous bid, but must reject an abnormally low bid. After the decision of the execution of public procurement, the contracting authority must publish the award notice in no later than 30 days.

The following type of public procurements are regulated: open tender, limited tender, competition dialogue, partnership for innovations, competitive tender with negotiations, tender with negotiations with or without publication, tender of smaller value. All public tenders are published on the official web page of the Public Procurement Directorate (http://www.djn.mju.gov.si/). The contracting authority determines the place and time for opening bids as well as all criteria of the public tender, including bank guarantees. Bid opening is public, unless determined otherwise by the public tender. Protocol of opening is prepared. Accepted bids are then assessed and a winning bid is announced and all candidates are notified of results. A contract is signed when the decision on the winning bid becomes final.

C. Others

Foreign direct investment is regulated in the Promotion of Foreign Direct Investment and the Internationalisation of Enterprises Act (Official Gazette, no.107/06, 11/11, 57/12 and 17/15) which sets goals, activities, measures and organization of the state in the areas of promotion of foreign direct foreign investment and internationalization of companies in the Republic of Slovenia and transposes relevant EU Regulations.

In this field, the Slovene Public Agency for the Promotion of Entrepreneurship, Innovation, Development, Investment and Tourism (SPIRIT) is the main public agency that offers information, consulting and other services for foreign investors, both personally and via the online portal for foreign investors.

Foreign companies conducting business in Slovenia have the same rights, obligations, and responsibilities as domestic companies. An individual or business in a variety of different legal and organizational forms may perform economic activities. Individuals most often operate as sole traders; however, legal entities may establish different forms of businesses: the most common are the limited liability company (d.o.o.) and public limited company (d.d.). Non-residents of the Republic of Slovenia have to obtain a Slovene tax number before starting the process of establishing a business. Slovenia's Companies Act (Official Gazette of the RS, no.65/09, 33/11, 91/11, 32/12, 57/12, 44/13 – the decision of the Constitutional Court, 82/13, 55/15 and 15/17), which is fully harmonized with EU legislation, regulates the establishment, management, and organization of companies.

南非

作者：Kenny Chiu、Wil Huang、Wendy Shih
译者：俞毓斌、周争平

一、概述

（一）政治、经济、社会与法律环境概述

南非是一个宪政国家，宪法是其最高法律。法治观念已深深植根于南非的政治，其法律体系深受罗马－荷兰法和英国普通法的影响。自 1994 年起，固有法或习惯法的作用也被充分认可，习惯法在南非的法律体系中赢得了其应有的位置。

南非根据其宪法实行立法、司法、行政三权分立制度，三者根据宪法各负其责并互相制衡，以确保各个职能在行使的同时能互相监督，各项权力能互相制衡。南非政府从上到下也分为中央政府、省政府及地方／市政府三级。虽然南非不实行联邦制，但其省政府和地方政府可以在不与上级政府制定的法规相冲突的前提下自行制定其地方法规。省级及地方级政府亦自行负责其管辖区域内的行政管理。

在政治方面，近十年来，南非在一些涉及高层政治人物的丑闻事件中，对腐败官员的判决，显示了南非法院保持司法独立，并勇于作出正确的判决，表明南非政府对法治的坚守，使大家对未来充满信心。南非的法律体系承继自罗马－荷兰法和英国法律体系，拥有坚实的法律基础，这些坚实的基础时至今日依然是其民主制度的重要基石，本文将从商事方面对此进行介绍。

在经济方面，2016 年南非货币兰特对美元的汇率跌至历史最低位，同时评级机构将南非评级降至接近垃圾级。在西里尔•拉马福萨于 2018 年 2 月 15 日当选南非总统后，兰特对美元汇率走强至近 3 年的最高点。执政党和新总统承诺即将进行积极的改革，使得投资者对南非的信心逐渐恢复。

在社会方面，南非目前正在与近 30 年来最严重的旱灾作斗争。自 2016 年起多个省份的旱情已有不同程度的缓解，但还有几个省份依然遭受着旱情的严重打击，其中包括西开普省、东开普省及北开普省。最重要的是，南非政府发放的社会救助金已高达社会发展全部预算 1.6 亿南非兰特中的 94.3%。尽管存在这些问题，南非人民还是对国家的潜力保持乐观积极的态度，他们中的一些人甚至注意到国外投资正蜂拥进入这个国家。因而本文述及的政策及监管框架将持续促进南非的可持续发展。

（二）"一带一路"背景下与中国企业合作的现状及趋势

融资、电力和基础设施领域的重大工程，包括技术、电信、制造业、消费品及零售将是未来几年"一带一路"倡议所关注的焦点。双方合作目标也包括促进相互投资领域的扩展，深化双方在农业、林业、渔业、农业机械制造及农产品加工方面合作，及促进双方在海产品、深海渔业、海洋工程技术、环保产业及海洋旅游业方面的合作。南非向中国企业提供符合"一带一路"倡议精神的水产业、农用工业、海洋经济、可再生能源、海产食品及海洋旅游业方面的投资机会。

中国和南非于 2015 年 12 月签署了《共建丝绸之路经济带和 21 世纪海上丝绸之路谅解备忘录》。该备忘录也意在创造良好机遇供两国之间相互学习，实现商品、技术、资本和人力资源等方面更好的交流和融合。中国目前是南非最大的贸易伙伴。这种关系不仅有利于促进两国之间的双边贸易和投资，也将为中非关系的转型注入新动力，为中国和非洲国家提供经济发展机会，有助于在非洲推动"一带一路"倡议。

因此，预期今后将会有许多投资进入南非，伴随而来的也将有大量的基础设施建设和贸易增长。2014 年，中国政府设立丝路基金以引领"一带一路"倡议的投资。2014 年丝路基金拥有资金规模为 400 亿美元，2017 年，惠誉国际的报告显示其投资规模已达 9000 亿美元。基础设施建设和贸易必将在"一带一路"倡议中成为主角。

二、投资

(一) 市场准入

1. 投资主管部门

贸易工业部（以下简称"贸工部"）是负责促进南非经济发展的政府部门，它的任务是建立一个能促进发展，加强与主要经济体之间的贸易和投资联系，并能支持非洲区域经济一体化和发展合作的多边贸易体系。贸工部也在符合南非国际关系及合作协议的目标市场建设贸易与投资关系，并与省级投资促进机构合作从事投资及出口的促进工作。该部门职责范围还包括国际贸易、消费者保护及推动南非黑人经济振兴政策落实。

2. 投资行业规定

2015年《投资保护法案》规定了对投资者及其投资的保护，以平衡适用于所有投资者的权利与义务。《投资保护法案》第7节规定所有投资均须遵守南非法律，并强调该法案本身并未赋予国外投资者或未来的国外投资者在南非投资的权利。但《投资保护法案》规定在同等条件下外国投资者及其投资应享有与南非国内投资者同等的待遇；南非必须在其资源和能力许可的条件下，根据国际习惯法的最低标准向外国投资者及其投资提供与南非通常向国内投资者提供的同等水平的实体安全保护；投资者根据南非《宪法》第25节的规定对资产拥有财产权利；外国投资者（就某项投资）可以在遵守南非税收和其他适用法律的前提下撤回投资。

《投资保护法案》也确认了采取措施（如"黑人经济振兴政策"）保护南非因歧视原因历史性地处于弱势的人士或群体或帮助他们发展的义务。"黑人"经济振兴政策是政府的一个重大政策和社会经济过程，其目标是通过显著增加管理、拥有和控制国家经济的"黑人"数量及显著减少收入的不平等来帮助南非的经济转型。此处的"黑人"是一个通称，包括非洲黑人、有色人种、印度裔，并且按规定仅限在1994年之前已成为南非公民的"黑人"。黑人经济振兴政策在诸多方面促进了"黑人"经济发展而被称为"broad-based"。

2003年《广义基础的黑人经济振兴法案》和其后续的修改或修正案（以下统称《黑人经济振兴法案》）及《广义基础的黑人经济振兴法案良好实践准则》（以下简称《良好实践准则》）对"黑人"经济振兴政策作出了规定。《良好实践准则》中规定的目标并非强制性的，但《黑人经济振兴法案》和《良好实践准则》通过直接或间接的激励机制来发挥作用。在直接的激励机制下，如果一家企业的相当一部分业务是依赖于与政府或半国营集团之间的合同而取得的，或该企业从事的业务须取得政府颁发的许可证、配额或其他许可，则该企业须遵守《良好实践准则》。在间接激励机制下，如果政府、半国营的公司和越来越多的大公司在其采购和其他政策下要求作为其供应商的企业须具有《黑人经济振兴法案》规定的情形或性质，供应商会受到《黑人经济振兴法案》的规制。《黑人经济振兴法案》也得到许多其他形式立法的支持并与其相互协调发挥作用，包括1998年《平等雇佣法》、1998年《技能提高法》、2000年《优惠采购政策框架法案》及其他。

其他规定或可能影响投资的重要立法包括（但不限于）2008年《公司法》、1961年《外汇管理条例》《约翰内斯堡证券交易所规则》、1998年《竞争法》及包括其他与各行业相关的立法。

3. 投资方式及市场准入标准

外国公司可以在南非设立全资的分支机构（外国公司）或成立子公司（或全资或合资），不要求公司的股东或董事是南非居民（对于个人也不要求其是南非居民）。

外国投资如涉及有关国家利益的领域（例如采矿业、电信、国家安全），则有附加限制及/或附加许可证要求，部分领域（例如金融服务、银行业、博彩业）须遵守附加规定。

(二) 外汇管理

1. 外汇主管部门

南非通过南非储备银行的金融监控部和"外汇授权经纪商"实施其外汇管制。外汇授权经纪商是南非储备银行授权代其监督管理资本进出南非的商业银行或一些外国银行的分支机构，是唯一获许为南非居民进行离岸货币交易的机构。

2. 外汇法律法规概况

南非现行的《外汇管制规则》是1961年12月1日颁布的，并不定期进行修改。政府还根据《外汇管制规则》颁布《命令和规则》，现行的《命令和规则》是1961年12月1日颁布的，并不定期进行修改。《命令和规则》中包含各种命令、规则、豁免、格式及程序安排。金融监控部也会发布通知就外汇管制的现有的或新的问题向公众公告监管部门的最新规定。《外汇授权经纪商货币及外汇指南》包含了适用于外汇授权经纪商可能自行及/或代表客户从事的外汇交易的许可和条件、相关管理责任细节及金融监控部报告要求。

3. 外资企业外汇管理要求

所有南非居民和国内公司都应遵守外汇管制。位于南非境内的子公司与南非境外的母公司之间的外汇事项视为居民与非居民之间的外汇交易，因此须取得金融监控部的核准。

对于涉及非居民或非居民在其中享有利益的外汇交易，在某些情形中须取得金融监控部的核准：

（1）受管制证券的批注

根据《外汇管制规则》第14条规则，非经金融监控部许可，任何人均不得取得或处置"受管制证券"。"受管制证券"是指任何以非居民的名义登记的，或其所有人为非居民的或非居民于其中享有利益的证券。对于受管制证券的取得或处置的管制是通过对非居民所拥有的或非居民在其中享有利益的证券进行批注来实施的。这种批注的效果是确保在非居民处置其利益时，相应的款项能够转移到国外或转账至非居民的账户。

（2）外来贷款和利息

从境外取得的贷款称为外来贷款。在引入境外贷款之时，其可能对外支付利息的利率及支付条件就必须取得金融监控部或外汇授权经纪商的核准。贷款的本金部分的偿还条款也必须事先取得外汇管制方面的核准。贷款收取的利率必须在规定的范围之内。

（3）股息的汇付

股息可以汇给非居民股东，只要其股票上如前面所述注明"非居民"。金融监控部或外汇授权经纪商在授权汇付股息之前将会要求公司提供文件（如经审计的财务报表）证明公司有盈利。

（4）特许权使用费、许可费和专利费的汇付

南非居民向非居民支付特许权使用费、许可费或专利费的协议必须事先取得外汇管制方面的核准。向非南非居民汇出产品制造方面的特许权使用费须经贸工部核准。其他种类的特许权使用费的对外支付须经金融监控部的核准。最低特许权使用费或预付特许权使用费的支付一般无法取得核准。

（5）管理费的汇付

南非居民向非居民支付管理费必须取得外汇管制方面的核准。非居民向居民提供的服务费必须合理。

一般来说，根据外汇管制的规定，对进入南非的外汇金额没有限制，但对于汇出南非的外汇金额则是有限制的。

（三）金融

1. 主要金融机构

南非储备银行是南非的中央银行。南非储备银行负责管理南非的货币及银行体系（包括制定和执行货币政策、必要时向银行提供流动性及担任现金储备保管人），并进而负责南非银行的管理和监督。

金融市场的主要参与者是各个银行（包括商业银行和一些外国银行的分支机构）。银行的业务包括接受公众存款、招揽存款或为存款做广告、对资金或因资金（来自接受存款）赚取的利息或其他收入的使用以及其他各种活动。

2. 外资企业融资条件

（1）对国外贷款方的限制：发放贷款

除了由金融监控部执行的外汇管制规定外，对于跨境贷款并无重大障碍。非经金融监控部事先核准，南非居民不得向非南非居民借贷。并且，如果该贷款被认定为在南非构成影响，则应适用2005年第34号法案《国家信贷法》，国外贷款方将被要求根据《国家信贷法》登记为授信方。

（2）对国外贷款方的限制：提供担保

担保在南非是普通使用的。如果是南非国内实体为非南非居民实体或为非南非居民实体的债务提供担保，则须事先经金融监控部核准。对于贷款中的担保，如果担保方是与借款方有关联或相互关联的，该等担保将构成2008年《公司法》第44节规定的"财务援助"。除非根据股东们最近两年内通过的特别决议，并且董事会确定公司提供该等财务援助后仍随即能满足偿付能力和流动性测试，否则董事会不得批准该等财务援助。并且，董事会必须确认将提供的该等财务援助（对于该公司）是公平合理的。此外，董事会还必须确保提供该等财务援助符合其公司章程规定的所有相关条件或限制。

（四）土地政策

1. 土地法律法规概况

南非关于不动产的法律框架形成了关于财产所有权的明确全面的立法框架。适用于土地转让与登记的法律首先是1937年《地契登记法》及其规章。还有许多其他法规规定土地的所有权及转让，但实质上，南非对土地所有权并无限制，任何自然人或法人均可拥有土地。实际的土地所有权属于所有权人而非国家。

根据土地调查，南非的各个省份在各个地契登记处设立了地产登记簿。地产登记簿均编制了索引，而且现在可以使用电子方式查询，房地契原件和其他文件已被数字化。地契登记处设立在相关政府部门之下，由总契据登记官掌管。由于有明确的调查系统为基础，地产登记簿非常准确，形成了非常明确的土地登记形式。

对土地所有权的证明是地契登记处出具的地契，其上记载了所有权人的详细信息和持有该土地的条件。持有该土地的条件通常是由地方管理部门和私人协议设定的。如果所有权未在地契登记处登记，则该所有权很可能未转移。在地契登记处的登记亦证明土地所有权的转移。

在南非可以根据1986年《区分所有权法》取得建筑物中的单元的所有权。这种单元被称为区分所有权单元，根据在地籍测量局局长处登记的地籍测量员编制的区分所有权方案，区分所有权单元登记于地契登记处。《地契登记法》和《区分所有权法》构成了地产所有者之间转让所有权的环境及立法框架。

产权根据宪法获得保护。除非依据普遍适用的法律进行征收并给予经受损害方同意或法院认可的补偿，否则宪法中的《权利法案》限制对地产的剥夺。补偿必须是合理公平的，通常应考虑遵循公允价值原则。南非持续进行土地偿还，虽然也有几片城市土地涉及未解决的土地权利要求，但土地权利要求主要是针对农村土地而非城市土地。这会对涉及位于有权属争议的土地上的物业投资造成影响。

在南非，所有地产的取得均应适用1949年《财产转让税法》。就财产转让税而言，此处的"财产"系指土地及其附着物，包括土地物权、矿产权、在"住宅地产公司"的股权或利益或"巨额证券（share-block）公司"的股权。一般规则是，所有人（包括公司、封闭式公司及信托）取得财产的转让税是基于购买价格按浮动比例支付的，其中900 000兰特之内的部分无须缴纳转让税（目的是为了支持购买低值地产）。如果地产的卖方为增值税目的注册的卖方，则应缴纳15%的增值税而非转让税。在某些情形下，取得商业用地有可能适用零税率的增值税。

2. 外国投资者获得土地规定

南非对外国投资者取得土地并无限制。外国公司如要在南非取得土地，必须根据2008年《公司法》的规定登记为外国公司。

非居民必须先取得南非储备银行的核准才能将其出售的南非不动产或出售持有南非不动产的公司股权所取得的收入汇到南非境外；取得南非储备银行核准的条件之一是所有税收须均已缴纳。作为非南非居民的卖方就待确定的税款向南非税务署支付一定的预提金额，现行的预提税率对个人是7.5%，对公司是10%，对信托是15%，但纳税人有可能因为相关的国际条约享受税收豁免。

（五）企业设立与解散

1. 企业形式

对有兴趣在南非设立企业的投资者而言，设立企业的形式可以有多种选择，选择设立何种形式的企业取决于多个因素，包括对有限责任的要求和税务方面的考虑。可供外国投资者选择的主要企业形式有：
- 个人责任公司（注册）；
- 私人有限责任公司（有限责任）；
- 境外公司（分支机构）；
- 上市公司（有限责任）；
- 合伙；
- 个体经营者；
- 业务/交易信托。

2. 设立程序

2008年《公司法》认可两类主要的公司，即"营利性公司"和"非营利性公司"。营利性公司包括国有公司、私人公司（该类公司的章程和公司注册备忘录必须规定禁止向公众发行股份）、个人责任公司（该类公司的董事与公司要对合同之债承担连带责任）及上市公司。

成立私人公司或个人责任公司涉及公司名称的预留、提交公司注册备忘录（公司章程）、审计师代表公司行事的书面同意（如有）、公司注册地址通知及提交董事登记册。公司设立程序本身平均需要一至两个月的时间，但是这很大程度上取决于企业和知识产权委员会进行该登记所需的时间。

在南非设立登记境外公司分支机构必须向企业和知识产权委员会提交经公证的母公司章程。境外公司必须遵守《公司法》，如被要求，须指定一位南非的审计师，并提交法定申报表。该类公司无须任命境内的董事会，只需指定一位居住于南非的人负责接受任何程序或通知的送达；公司须保存与在当地运营有关的、与对境内公司的要求类似的会计记录。

合伙不是一个区别于组成该合伙的人员的法律实体，包括在涉及所得税时亦是如此。但在考虑增值税时，合伙视为一个独立的个体，因此须以其自己的名义登记为销售者。普通合伙中的每个成员均对合伙的债务和义务承担连带责任。

个体经营者不构成独立的法律人格，不能永久承继，亦不是有限责任。个体经营在设立方面并无程序上的要求，可以用所有者的名义经营，也可以用一个虚拟的名称或用商号来经营。

业务信托的设立须向南非高等法院主事官递交信托契约。信托仅在某些目的下取得独立的法律人格，如税务和永久承继目的，这些通常会在信托契约中进行约定。信托资产的所有权归属于受托人，受托人最多不得超过20人。信托可以达到承担有限责任的目的。信托适用1988年《信托财产管理法》。

3. 解散方式及要求

根据南非法律，公司或任何第三方可以申请注销一个商业实体。但如要进行注销程序，该公司必须已经停止开展业务并且不具有资产，或因为资产不足，公司或封闭式公司已无被清算的合理可能性。因此公司提交的申请文件必须包括证实此种状态的证明文件及必要的支持文件（包括完税证明或南非税务署出具的确认公司没有未缴款项的任何其他书面确认文件）。如果公司连续两次或更多次未递交年度申报表，企业和知识产权委员会也可能会将公司注销。

（六）合并收购

在南非公开兼并收购活动适用的主要法律法规如下：

（1）2008年《公司法》，该法规范南非的所有收购及公开并购。《公司法》及其规章包含了被称为"收购规则"的规范收购和并购的规定。

（2）2004年第36号法案《证券服务法》，除其他方面的规定外，该法规范了内幕交易和市场滥用行为。

（3）下列情形适用约翰内斯堡证券交易所有限公司执行的约翰内斯堡证券交易所上市要求：

① 如出价者或目标股票属约翰内斯堡上市公司，则遵守约翰内斯堡证券交易所的上市要求，如所提出的对价（及/或稀释结果）超过该出价人的总市值的25%，则该并购必须经出价人的股东批准；或

② 作为报价对价一部分而发行的新股必须在约翰内斯堡证券交易所上市。

（4）1998年《竞争法》（南非《反垄断法》）。

根据具体情况，每个兼并收购的执行可能还需要取得诸如下列监管机构的核准：收购监管委员会、约翰内斯堡证券交易所、竞争监管部门、南非储备银行及其他特定产业（例如银行业、采矿业及通信业）的监管机构。

取得上市公司控制权的传统方式是向其股东提出全面要约及协议安排。《公司法》在南非法律上首次引入了一种法定合并机制进行交易，自2011年5月1日起生效。已有一些合并是根据此法定合并机制完成的。

（七）竞争管制

1. 竞争管制主管机构

南非竞争管制主管机构包括竞争委员会、竞争裁判庭、竞争上诉法院、最高上诉法院及宪法法院。竞争委员会负责调查和评估企业合并及被禁止的行为；竞争裁判庭实质上是审理竞争法案件的一审法院；竞争上诉法院是指定的审理竞争法上诉案件的法院；最高上诉法院被授权审理对竞争上诉法院审理的案件的上诉；宪法法院负责审理竞争法案件中涉及宪法的事项。

2. 竞争法概况

南非拥有基于最佳国际实践发展而来的健全的竞争法制度。其经济体系主要基于自由市场原则，但如同大多数发达经济体一样，竞争是受管控的。1998年《竞争法》是南非管控竞争秩序的核心制度。

1998年《竞争法》的首要目标是保证有效、公平、活跃的市场竞争。该法循欧盟、美国及加拿大的模式，极大地强化了竞争主管机构的权力，规定了对反竞争行为、限制行为（如固定价格、掠夺性定价及串通投标）及公司滥用市场支配地位行为的种种禁止性规定。1998年《竞争法》也对某些企业兼并收购规定了通告和事先许可程序，并对违反规定的行为制定了重大的处罚措施。它的效力范围不仅限于南非境内，既适用于南非境内的经济活动，也适用于会对南非造成影响的经济活动。

3. 竞争管制措施

1998年《竞争法》授权竞争裁判庭对被禁止的行为作出各种命令，其中包括对被禁止的行为颁布禁令或宣布该等协议部分或全部无效。当一方须基于合理条件供应或销售货物或提供服务给竞争者以停止被禁止的行为或当竞争者要求基于合理条件使用关键设施时，主管机构可以颁布更严格的命令。

竞争裁判庭作出的更常见的命令之一是行政处罚令。竞争主管机构对违法者作出不超过涉案各方在南非年营业额及他们在前一财政年度从南非出口额10%的罚金（罚款）处罚。

4. 限制横向限制竞争行为

1998年《竞争法》限制企业形成横向限制竞争的关系，即限制竞争者之间从事形成限制竞争的行为。某些行为是1998年《竞争法》完全禁止的，被称为本身违法或自动禁止行为。这类行为被视为"不可以申辩的行为"，任何从事此类行为的公司都无权就自己参与此类被禁止的行为提出申辩或辩护。这类行为包括企业间直接或间接固定购买、销售价格或任何其他贸易条件，企业间通过分配顾客、供应商、区域及/或特定商品或服务的方式分割市场，或企业间串通投标行为，包括竞争者之间的压制投标、轮流投标及补充投标。

5. 限制纵向限制竞争行为

"纵向关系"是一种存在于供应链不同层级的上下游企业之间的关系。1998年《竞争法》会权衡

大多数的纵向限制竞争行为和上文强调过的合理性检测规则，允许被指控其协议及行为违反该法限制纵向限制竞争规定的企业就其行为有提升技术、提高效率或其他有利于竞争的益处进行申辩。纵向限制竞争行为中唯一属于本身违法的绝对禁止行为是制定最低转售价格。

制定最低转售价格是指上游供应商试图规定或控制其供应的货物或服务的转售价格，并采取措施来执行或维持其规定的转售价格，以减少竞争。这并不意味着企业不可以建议最低的转售价格。只要该等建议对该等货物或服务的转售并无约束力，并且在该等产品上清楚地表明其仅为建议，则该等建议是1998年《竞争法》所允许的。

（八）税收

1. 税收体系与制度

（1）南非税务署和主要立法

南非税务署管理范围涉及广泛的税收立法事宜，包括不定期修订的1962年《所得税法》、1991年《增值税法》、2011年《税收管理法》、1964年《关税和消费税法》和2013年《就业税收优惠法》。

（2）计税基础

南非居民应就其来源于全球范围的所得纳税，非居民仅就其来源于南非或视为来自南非的收入纳税。《所得税法》对"居民"做了定义。个人符合如下标准时，将被视为南非的税收居民：①是南非的普通居民；②5年内其本人身处南非的天数达到规定。如根据南非与另一国家订立的双重征税协议，某人被视为完全是该另一国的居民，则该双重征税协议将优先于南非国内法适用。如果该个体不是自然人，根据《所得税法》的定义，任何在南非注册、设立或组成的，或有效管理地在南非的，即属于居民纳税人，在此情形下，双重征税协议也将优先于南非国内法适用。

（3）税种

南非的税收宽泛地分为直接税和间接税。直接税由纳税人直接向政府缴纳，而间接税是对产品或服务的供应所征收的税。直接税包括所得税、股息红利税、资本利得税、房地产遗产税、某些种类的预提税及赠与税。间接税包括增值税、证券交易税、财产转让税、关税及消费税。

2. 主要税赋与税率

（1）所得税

所得税是应纳税所得支付的正常税。

① 个人和特别信托

对个人征收的税率是按浮动比例设定的，应纳税所得越高，则纳税越多。现行税率为应税所得的18%至45%。

② 公司

公司的税率为应税所得的28%。境外公司在南非的分支机构就该非居民或分支机构的应税所得纳税也适用28%的税率。

③ 信托

信托统一租用的税率为45%。

（2）股息红利税

南非公司决议向终极股东派发股息红利时，如果股东不是法人或不是南非居民，则须缴纳股息红利税。对于任何自2017年2月22日起支付的股息红利（不考虑决议派发股息红利的日期），现行税率是20%，除非其有可适用税收豁免或税率降低的情形（例如可适用双重征税协议）。

（3）资本得利税

个人、公司或信托在处置资产时应缴纳资本得利税。资产是指任何性质的财产（无论是动产或不动产），包括对该等财产、有形或无形资产（不包括货币，但包括任何主要由黄金或铂金制成的铸币）或存在于其上的任何性质的权利或利益。

个人或特别信托应将其资本利得的40%计为应税所得，因而实际税率为18%。其他的法律实体（例如公司及其他信托）应将其资本利得的80%计为应税所得，因此公司的最高实际税率为22.4%，而信托则为 36%。

（4）房地产遗产税

通常居住在南非的人死亡后，对其全球的资产统一按 20% 征税。应税金额允许做一些扣除，最主要的是允许一般性扣除 350 万兰特。南非与莱索托、瑞典、英国、美国和津巴布韦之间拥有双重遗产税协议。对于非南非居民而言，遗产税仅针对其位于南非的遗产征收。

（5）赠与税

对于没有对价或对价低于市价的财产处置，统一适用 20% 税率的赠与税。非南非居民不适用此税种。上市公司的赠与可根据规定获得豁免。慈善性赠与本身不可扣税，除非其是赠与公益组织并符合一些其他条件，或其可以纳入《所得税法》一般扣减条款的范围内。

（6）增值税

南非适用的增值税体系接近于英国和新西兰的体系。在南非经营的企业销售货物或提供服务应按 15% 的税率缴纳增值税，该税率也适用于进口的货物和一些服务。该 15% 的税率存在一些豁免、例外、扣减和调整的情形。

很少有供应品可免除增值税，最值得注意的例外是某些对价采取利息形式支付的金融服务。大多数收取手续费的金融服务都应缴纳增值税。南非出口的货物及离岸提供的服务或向非南非居民提供的服务的增值税通常是零。

（7）证券交易税

2007 年《证券交易税法》规定，自 2008 年 7 月 1 日起，任何证券的所有交易都应缴纳证券交易税。应缴纳的证券交易税的税率为 0.25%。（在一般情况下，以证券转让对价的金额或市场价值为基数。）

（8）财产转让税

在南非，所有不动产的取得都适用 1949 年《财产转让税法》。自然人、公司及信托取得不动产纳转让税时适用累进税率，最高税率为 13%。若转让适用 15% 的增值税时，则不再征收财产转让税。

（9）关税

进口到南非的货物应缴纳税率不等的关税。根据 1964 年《关税和消费税法》的规定，货物从视为进口时起即产生纳税责任。纳税责任由船舶船长、飞机驾驶员、其他交通工具的承运人、集装箱营运商、仓库营运商或分拆业务运营商承担，直至货物适当地入境并合法交付至进口商，其后纳税责任转由进口商承担。

南非与欧盟、欧洲自由贸易协会及南部非洲发展共同体之间有自由贸易协议，对于来自这些区域的货物提供优惠关税税率。南非也是南部非洲关税联盟的成员，该联盟成员间的贸易免征关税。

（10）消费税

南非对某些本地生产的货物征收消费税，如果同样的货物是进口的（如酒、香烟、香水、电视机等），则征收等量的关税。

3. 纳税申报与优惠

每年南非税务署都会公布其报税季节，即个人须申报及/或提交其所得税申报表的期间。对于企业所得税，每个注册纳税人须在财政年度结束后 12 个月内提交所得税申报表。除了每年的申报表，每个公司还应提交临时报税表，当年的前 6 个月内须提交第一份临时报税表，当年年底提交第二份临时报税表，且其中必须包含对当期已取得或将取得的总应税所得的预估。提交报税表时应同时缴纳税款。第三笔补足款可以在年底过后 6 个月支付。申报表可以电子方式提交，或在纳税人注册地的南非税务署分支机构人工提交。其他种类的税应在规定的期间申报，否则可能会遭受处罚。例如，财产转让税应在取得财产后 6 个月内缴纳，如逾期未缴，则每个月的利息按每年 10% 计算。

（九）证券交易

1. 证券相关法律法规概况

南非拥有高度成熟的资本市场，监管良好。除了 2008 年《公司法》外，证券方面主要的立法包括：一是 2012 年《金融市场法》，该法取代了 2004 年《证券服务法》，对证券（例如股票或其他证券投资工具）服务作出规定，目的是增强相关方面对南非金融市场的信心，促进对受规范人员和客户的保护，减少系统风险并提升南非证券的国际竞争力；二是 2004 年《金融咨询和中介服务法》，该法的施行是为了在金融服务业推广良好和适当的商业行为，并协助改善公司管治和提升市场信心。

2. 证券市场监管

金融服务委员会是根据 1990 年《金融服务委员会法》设立的一个独立机构，负责监管非银行金融服务业，包括短期及长期保险、公司、集合投资计划（单位信托及股票市场），以及财务顾问及 / 或经纪。2004 年《金融咨询和中介服务法》和 2001 年《金融情报中心法》扩大了金融服务委员会的职权范围，将银行业的市场行为和打击金融犯罪（如洗钱、逃税和恐怖主义筹资活动）都包括在内。

南非储备银行（SARB）的银行监管部门负责银行的管制和监督。约翰内斯堡股票交易所有限公司对金融服务委员会（FSB）负责，在股票交易中监督被授权的使用者，包括会计、交易和保管活动。

3. 外资企业参与证券交易的要求

任何南非居民进行注册在非居民名下（或非居民是所有者或享有权益）的证券（包括无论是私人公司或是公众公司的股份、股票等）交易时，这些证券证都必须由 FinServ（金融监管部门）和 / 或被授权经销商批注为"非居民"，以便允许交易收入转移至国外（比如转移至一位非居民的银行账户中）。

特定产业（包括广播业、银行业和保险业）受到有关立法调整，严格禁止或在未经相关部门同意的前提下，外国买家持有超过一定份额的股票。

（十）投资优惠和保护

1. 优惠政策的结构

2015《投资保护法案》（PIA）建立起了投资运行的总体框架。本质上，PIA 承认外国投资的必要性以及共和国宪法中纳入的原则。它试图整合《宪法》的价值并将其体现投资活动中。投资被定义为：

（1）投资者依据南非的法律建立、取得或扩张任何合法企业，在一段合理时间内投入具有经济价值的资源，以期获取利润；

（2）持有或收购企业的股份、债权或其他所有者工具；或

（3）持有、收购或兼并在南非外建立的企业，这一持有、收购和兼并对前述第（1）项和第（2）项所规定的投资产生影响。[①]

同样重要的是，尽管 PIA 规定了引导投资的整体结构，但这仍然取决于政府或依照相关宪法、法律规定的国家机构提供具体细节，即特定的投资将被哪些部门引导。PIA 奉行的重要价值如下：

（1）在处理国内外所有投资时促进公平的行政待遇；

（2）所有投资，无论是在国内的还是国外，在类似情形下，都必须被平等对待而无偏袒；

（3）国内外投资的实体安全必须一致；

（4）根据南非《宪法》，投资者享有财产权；

（5）外国投资者可在遵守税法或其他法律的情况下调回资金。

受到不法侵害的外国投资者可以要求相关政府部门通过任命一名调解员来协助解决争议。

2. 包括投资保护在内的对特定行业和地区的支持

自 2015 年 12 月 PIA 颁布以来的两年内，特定行业和地区的发展缓慢。一般制造业、汽车业、水产养殖业、商业流程服务业、纺织业和其他行业在各自领域的投资保护方面所制定的政策均进展缓慢。[②] 南非政府已经汇集了各种投资激励措施，旨在促进不同行业的未来成长。

对于上述各行业领域而言，政府都有各种旨在激励和保护该行业投资的各类合适的方案。所有方案、对行业保护的支持等都必须遵守 PIA 的规定。

---

① 参见 2015 年《投资保护法案》第 2 章。
② 参见南非政府官方激励计划门户网站 http://www.investmentincentives.co.za/。

激励发展和管理部门负责管理DTI（贸易工业部）的激励计划，并且作为实现特定发展目标的回报向企业提供该激励计划。以下是DTI提供的部分激励计划：

（1）121税收激励

121税收激励政策为资本投资以及涉及棕地投资和绿地投资的培训提供支持。优先地位的棕地投资可以享受高达5.5亿兰特的投资津贴，优先地位的绿地投资可以享受高达9亿兰特的投资津贴。投资者也可以申请培训津贴，最高可以从全职雇员应税收入中扣除3.6万兰特。在优先项目的情况下，最高可以从应税收入中扣除3 000万兰特。

（2）农产品加工支持计划（APSS）

APSS只适用于农产品加工企业及深加工企业（农业企业），在为期两年的投资期内，提供20%～30%成本分摊金，最高可达2 000万兰特，这笔资金可用于投资成本的组合。DTI可能考虑授予达到经济效益标准的项目10%的额外资金，经济效益标准包括就业、转型、地理扩散和本地采购，等等。

（3）汽车投资计划（AIS）

AIS的目标是通过对新的或者替代模型和部件的投资，加强和扩大汽车产业，增强工厂的产量、维持就业以及加强汽车价值链。涉及生产性资产的，AIS目前会提供免税资金资助，针对符合条件的投资，资助比例为投资价值的20%；针对符合条件的由DTI批准的部件制造和模具公司的投资，资助比例为投资价值的25%。对于满足某些经济要求，例如具体增加每个工厂单位产量和增加营业额以及对目前在南非没有生产制造的部件的项目，可提供5%至10%的额外免税资金资助。

（4）重要基础设施项目（CIP）

CIP是一项成本分摊激励措施。其适用于被核准的申请者或者完成可被证实的里程碑事件的基础设施项目，或经DTI批准的项目。CIP的要求之一是，基础设施对投资来说必须是重要的（换句话说，没有此类投资，基础设施的运行效益不能达到最佳）。CIP提供的补助金占全部合格基础设施发展费用的10%～30%，但最高不超过5 000万兰特（满足特定经济效益标准）。

（5）服装及纺织竞争力提升计划（CTCIP）

CTCIP旨在提高南非服装、纺织、鞋类、皮革和皮革制品、制造商和设计者在全球市场上的竞争力。此项激励项目资助大中小型公司的竞争力提升活动，否则这些公司就无法为干预活动提供资金，鼓励供应商和消费者组织对制造企业的干预（一种价值链方法）。在项目实施期间，成本分摊补贴计划可高达合格项目的75%，并在项目执行期间累计不超过2 500万兰特，或者在不同阶段采取不同的成本分摊比例，比如第一年100%的初始投资，在往后几年会采取不同的成本分摊比例（通常是更低的比例）。

（6）制造业投资项目（MIP）

MIP对本国和外资实体提供可偿还的现金补助。投资补助金可高达合格投资成本价值的30%。这些投资成本用于机械、设备、商用车辆、土地和建筑以及建立新生产设施和扩大现有生产设施，提升现有服装和纺织生产设施的生产力。

（7）工业创新支持计划（SPII）

SPII旨在促进南非科技发展，通过提供高达500万兰特的财政援助，用于开发创新产品。SPII特别致力于开发阶段，开始于基础研究的结束，结束于生产原型的产生之前。为满足合格标准，申请者必须证明开发行为代表了技术上的重大进步，并且后续生产会在南非国内进行。

（8）战略伙伴项目（SPP）

SPP通过鼓励商业以加强《最佳行为准则》中的《进入和供应商开发》（ESD）来支持"黑人经济振兴"政策，通过鼓励大型私营企业和政府间的伙伴关系，在合作伙伴的供应链和以可持续的方式成为产品制造商和服务供应商的部门中，支持和发展中小型企业。SPP作为政府与战略伙伴间成本分摊的基础，在3年期间内，基础设施和商业发展服务的补助金，每一财政年度最高可达1500万兰特。其同样向制造业项目提供50∶50的成本分摊支持，向支持制造业供应链相关服务的项目提供70:30的成本分摊支持。

3. 经济特区

2014 年《经济特区法》（SEZA）确立了调整该国规定经济特区的整体框架。目前，全国有 5 个运行中的经济特区，分别是科尔加 IDZ（大都会纳尔逊曼德拉湾），理查兹湾 IDZ，东伦敦 IDZ，萨尔达尼亚湾 IDZ 和德班（Dube）贸易港。目前在贸易工业部还有其他经济特区申请未决。经济特区咨询委员会（SEZAB）是负责管理、监督和实施南非经济特区政策和战略的监管机构。SEZAB 依据 SEZA 规定享有权力并承担责任。

在指定的经济特区内开展业务的激励措施由各经济特区的规则决定，并不会在全国范围内使用同一标准。主要原因是每个经济特区都有义务在各自的地方政府辖区内推动特定的经济活动和各类产业发展。因此，这些激励措施将针对特定行业中的参与者，这些行业是当地政府力图促进的。任何经济特区的所有规则必须符合 PIA 规定的价值和框架。

三、贸易

（一）管理和监督贸易的部门

DTI 与一些专门的监管和促进金融发展的代理和机构（称为"贸易和工业机构理事会"）紧密合作，以管理、监督和促进贸易，提升外国对该国的直接投资水平，扩大南非商品和服务的出口市场；并为建立技能、技术和基础设施平台作出贡献，使得企业可以在这一经济中有所获益。监管机构包括但不限于：CIPC（公司与知识产权协会），公司法庭，国家消费者法庭，国家信用调节机构，国家博彩委员会，国家奖券委员会，国家消费者委员会，以及负责标准化、质量保证和认证的机构，包括但不限于：国家强制性规范管理机构、南非国家认证体系、南非标准局和南非国家计量学院。

南非国际贸易管理委员会（ITAC）是根据 2002 年《国际贸易管理法》（以下简称"ITA 法"）成立的。ITAC 的核心职能是：海关关税调查、贸易救济和进出口管制。

（二）贸易法律法规简介

ITA 法的目的是通过建立一个符合 ITA 法和非洲南部关税联盟协定的有效的国际贸易管理体系，以促进经济增长和发展，并提高南非和共同关税联盟地区的收入、投资和就业。部门可以依据宪法或其他相关法律规定的程序和要求，在公报上发布贸易政策声明或指令。

（三）贸易管理

DTI 的目标之一是促进贸易和投资关系。它通过鼓励出口并与现有贸易伙伴和快速增长的新兴市场建立合作协议来实现这一目标。南非政府还建立了经济特区（SEZs）项目，吸引外商直接投资和出口增值商品。经济特区是为特别关注的经济活动留出的国内地理指定地区，并通过通常以与该国其他地区不同的特殊安排（可能包括法律）和系统来支持它。根据 2014 年第 16 号《特别经济区法案》中的定义，经济特区可能是指向特定行业的或者是多产品的。许多激励措施可用于确保经济特区的增长、创收、就业机会增加、吸引外国直接投资和维持国际竞争力。

（四）海关管理

1. 海关立法

1964 年的《海关和消费税法》于 1965 年 1 月 1 日生效，(该法)对于海关和消费税事宜均予以规定。关税修正案在以下法律和政策框架中获得制定：ITA 法（《国际贸易管理法》），关税调查条例和国际贸易协定，双边、多边和区域协定。2014 年《海关管制法》、2014 年《海关税法》和 2014 年《海关和消费税法修正案》已于 2014 年 7 月发布在政府公报中，这些法案在总统确认生效日期后方可生效。

2. 海关办事处

南非目前有 37 个海关办事处，包括海、陆、空港口，以及 4 个集中处理中心，有关工作人员参与并致力于如下活动：在确保合规的同时促进合法贸易和旅游业；控制和核算所有进出口；收取国家应得的全部收入；管理具体的行业计划、贸易措施、国际协议和其他国际义务；通过执法行动消除走私和其他违法行为；代表其他有权执行此类法律的机关对禁止和限制货物的进出口实施管制。

3. 进口

货物可以通过各种运输方式抵达南非：航空、海运、公路、铁路或邮政。进口商必须向海关申报他们带入南非的货物种类、使用的运输方式和持有某些（和被限制）货物的进口许可证，未能提供必要的许可证可能会被加以处罚。该种许可证仅对指定类别和国家的货物有效。特定类别和被限制货物所需的进口许可证需从贸易和工业部的进口和出口管制处负责人处获得。这些类别的数量已经减少，但大多数二手／旧货物仍须获得相应许可。

4. 出口

对南非离境货物的管制被认为是海关的核心职能之一，因为关键的经济决策是基于贸易数据作出的，因此 SARS（南非税务署）必须准确记录出口业绩。出口报关由海关进行处理并保存，以便记录和贸易统计，如果海关要求，任何其他文件（关于出口货物，包括运输单据）应被出示。现行立法和政策要求特定文件，即表格上的一些特定内容，例如检验结果、邮戳日期和签字，需经过批注，才视为真正完成。特殊许可、许可证等证书可能也需要出示，海关官员会仔细检查所有出口文件，以确保各项法律、法规和规则获得遵守。必须指出的是，某些货物将需要出口许可证，此类许可证必须在清关时取得。出口许可的申请须向 ITAC 作出，并且在某些情况下，申请可能需要来自其他部门的支持文件，具体取决于所涉及的产品。

四、劳动

（一）劳动法律法规简介

调整南非雇佣关系的主要法律是：① 1995 年颁布的《劳动关系法》（LRA），该法规定了在不公平解雇和不平等劳动关系中对雇员的保护，同时规定了对雇主与雇员之间纠纷的解决机制，还包括处理罢工、停工以及调解雇主与工会之间的关系；② 1997 年《基本就业条件法》（BCEA），规定了雇员的最低雇佣条件，除了一些例外情况，如为慈善机构工作的无偿志愿者。这些最低条款和条件适用于任何雇佣合同，除非双方协商或者其他法律规定了更有利的条款，又或者该条款依据 BCEA 的变更或豁免条款被排除在外。

特定部门或行业的最低条款和条件通常是被单独规定的，可能通过特定行业设立的谈判委员会来制定（如果协议是由雇主代表和工会之间谈判达成）或由劳动部长（通常在咨询利害相关方之后）所在部门决定制定部门细则。

南非雇佣法律对于落入其管辖范围内的任何雇员均强制性适用。因此，其适用于在南非工作的外国公民。即使外国人在这里非法工作，情况也是如此。南非雇佣法律通常不适用于在国外工作的国民。但是，其可能会适用于借调期间临时在国外工作的南非国民，特别是如果雇佣合同规定了这一点。

在雇佣关系存续过程中或在雇佣关系结束以后都可以限制雇员的活动。这可以通过协议来实现，或者是雇佣合同，或者是独立的限制性协议。如果雇员了解了商业秘密和机密信息或者他们拥有有价值的客户关系，而雇主对这些享有所有者权益，则可以限制雇员在劳动合同终止后的一段合理时期内及地理区域内禁止为雇主的竞争者工作。这些协议是有效的。然而当雇主寻求执行限制条款时，法院保有是否执行这些限制条款的自由裁量权。如果在特定案件中，执行限制条款是不合理的，或者违背了公共利益，法院可以决定不予执行。雇员有责任举证证明此类协议是不合理的且不应当被执行。

（二）雇用外籍雇员的要求

1. 工作许可和申请程序

外国人应当依照规定的方式向其原籍国或经常居住地的南非领事馆申请工作许可。在特殊情况下，如果需要在南非境内申请，该外国人应当通过签证便利服务亲自递交工作许可的任何申请。此后申请必须提交给这些领事馆，而不是提交给民政部。在申请中必须写上在境内申请的正当理由。

一个外国人不允许同时持有一个以上的许可证。只要每个外国雇员持有适当的工作许可证，那么公司可雇用持有不同类别工作许可证的外国人而不受人数限制。工作许可的其中一项要求是说明公司雇用外国人而不是南非公民或永久居民的动机。

2002年《移民法》规定了工作许可的各种类别。

第11（2）条访问签证/许可证被视为一次性、不可延长的签证/许可证，以解决在有限的时间里短期或紧急需要的工作，这种签证类型并不能被视为工作许可。那些"免签"的外国人（包括澳大利亚、加拿大、欧洲、英国和美国国民）可以亲自到最近的领事馆办理允许的工作访问签证。该外国人在离开的至少一周以前，确认不能申请工作许可证的原因和该短期工作是必要、紧急的原因。

根据《移民法》第19（2）条的规定，另一类是一般工作许可。这个过程很繁琐，但一般工作许可证的最大优点是有效期可以长达5年。新法规增强了劳动部在审批过程中的作用。劳动部负责颁发证书，以证明：

- 尽管经过尽职调查，雇主一直无法找到具有与该申请人具有相同资质和技能或经验的南非公民或永久居民；
- 申请人具有符合工作要求的资质或可被证明的技能和经验；
- 工资不低于一般水平，雇佣合同符合劳动标准；
- 雇佣合同符合劳动标准，并以签证批准为条件。

劳动部的职能已得到广泛的延伸（之前的职能是负责证明薪酬以及向外国人提供的就业条款和条件与从事类似职位的南非人提供的条件相同）。

尽管没有清单规定必须提交给劳动部的证明文件包括哪些文件，劳动部表明需要完成对劳动力市场进行尽职调查以确保在相关职位提供给外籍人士之前，南非公民已经获得了应有的机会。为了寻求批准申请，并评估该公司在雇用南非公民方面所尽到的努力，它将考虑到以下几点：

- 以报纸印刷广告和其他广告、招聘方式（例如网络广告等）的形式在相关位置投放广告（新规定没有规定广告投放的位置，但似乎劳动部仍将坚持在全国印刷媒体上进行广告宣传，以确认已经进行了合适的劳动力市场测试）；
- 私营雇佣代理机构的报告，作为已进行劳动调查的书面证据；
- 南非公民候选人已经进行了有关职位的面试，面试记录体现出任命外国人的理由或当地人未被任命的原因；
- 最后，劳动部表示，希望所有就业机会都可以被登记在当地劳动中心的就业服务数据库中，并根据收到的申请，详细说明后续的招聘过程。

公司内部转移工作许可证可以发给就职于在南非境内的分支机构的外国人，子公司或具有隶属关系的外国人以及那些因工作需要而在当地工作的外国人。公司内部转移工作许可证的有效期最长为4年，不可延期。公司内部工作许可的要求是最简单和最容易达到的。

根据《移民法》第21条的规定，希望聘用一些外国工人的公司也可以申请企业许可证。企业许可证适用于打算在一些特定职位雇用外国人的企业申请人。法规还规定，为了获得企业许可证，该企业必须证明其雇用的人中至少60%是南非人。公司许可证的有效期最长为3年。工人不能在南非更新或申请更改地位。

关键技能工作签证会发给符合关键技能列表中列出的最低资格和经验的外国人，该关键技能列表尚未发布。除此之外，申请人必须提交经认证的专业团体、董事会或理事会的书面确认，其中包括技能、资质和获得资质后的工作经历、法律要求的专业注册申请证明以及南非资格认证机构的评估。技能许可证的有效期限不得超过5年。

2. 失业保险基金

雇主和雇员都必须每月向失业保险基金缴款，（该基金）为个人提供失业救济金。雇主和雇员各自必须贡献1%的员工薪酬。计算基数最高为每月14 872兰特。对于在南非完成任务后将从南非遣返的外国雇员，这些缴款不是必需的。

（三）工会和劳工组织

《宪法》第 23 条保护雇员组建和参加工会以及参加工会的合法活动的权利。第 23 条还保护雇主组建和参加雇主组织的合法活动的权利。宪法也特别重视保护结社自由。LRA 进一步强调，将保护和赋予这些基本权利以具体内容。

LRA 的第 4 和第 5 部分力求保护雇员的结社自由权利。根据这些条款为员工提供的保护不仅对雇主有效，而且对任何可能侵犯此类权利的人都有效。同样的，除此之外，每位员工均有权参与组建工会或工会联合会，并加入符合其组织章程的工会。此外，工会成员有权根据其工会章程参与其合法活动，包括选举办公室负责人、工作人员和工会代表，以及被选举和聘用为办公室负责人，任职并履行该职位。同样，隶属于工会联盟的工会成员有权根据该联合会的章程参加活动和选举，并参加选举和任职。

LRA 的第 6 和第 7 部分保护雇主享有结社自由的权利，类似于上述给予雇员的权利。

工会和雇主组织享有 LRA 第 8 条的某些权利。这些权利包括确定自己的组织法和规则的权利，以及选举办公室负责人、工作人员和工会代表的权利。工会和雇主组织也有权计划和组织他们自己的管理和合法活动，参加联合会的组建或参加工会联合会或雇主组织联合会。

组织权利在工会与雇主或雇主组织建立集体谈判关系方面也很重要。为了能够有效地与雇主谈判，工会需要会员。为了招募会员并代表他们的利益，工会需要进入雇主的场所与会员保持联系。工会可能还希望雇主直接从支付给员工的报酬中扣除工会的会员费，可能还希望提名和选举某些员工在工作场所代表工会的利益。同样的，组织权利有助于工会在工作场所建立存在感，从而奠定与雇主进行集体谈判关系的基础。

需要强调的是，只有注册的工会才能依据 LRA 行使组织权利。LRA 不强迫工会和雇主组织进行登记，但鼓励这些联盟这样做。这是通过 LRA 将大部分权利仅赋予注册工会来实现的。只有经过注册的工会才能行使组织权利，包括签订 LRA 所规定的集体协议，申请设立谈判委员会或法定理事会，申请成立工作场所讨论会，授权其成员在和解、调解和仲裁委员会（CCMA）的程序中代表其成员。然而，注册并不是进行受保护的罢工行动的先决条件。

（四）劳动纠纷

所有劳动纠纷首先由 CCMA 或相关交易谈判委员会进行调解，以力图解决纠纷。

未解决的纠纷，根据纠纷的性质，由相关交易谈判委员会、CCMA 或劳动法院决定。有关解雇伤残或解雇不当行为、不公正劳工措施、推定解雇和单一性裁员的争议由相关交易谈判委员会或 CCMA 进行仲裁。

其他裁员、歧视纠纷和罢工纠纷由劳动法庭裁决。

根据宪法，雇员拥有不被不公正解雇的权利，这也被纳入南非 LRA 当中。雇主只能以涉及雇员的行为或能力或雇主的运营要求的公平理由而解雇（雇员）。

雇主有责任证明解雇是出于公平原因。所有涉嫌不公平解雇的争议都必须提交给 CCMA 进行调解（除非存在一个具有管辖权的交易谈判委员会）。若无法调解解决，CCMA 将裁决涉及行为或能力的争议，劳动法院裁定涉及业务原因的解雇争议（除非只有一名员工被裁减，在这种情况下，该员工可以选择由 CCMA 仲裁）。

针对不公平解雇的救济措施是：恢复原来的岗位，重新聘用到相似的岗位，或补偿最高 12 个月的工资（如果解雇系《劳动关系法》规定的法定不公平情形，则补偿 24 个月的工资）。如果不公平只涉及程序，则救济措施仅限于经济补偿。

五、知识产权

（一）知识产权法简介

1993 年商标法和普通法，源自于罗马–荷兰法的一般原则，共同构成了南非涉及商标的法律基础。

普通法认为非法竞争是一种普遍的不法行为，其有多种形式，其中一种是仿冒侵权。商标法并没有改变普通法，事实上，在某些情况下，它承认并确认了这些原则。

各类知识产权的许可在南非都是允许的，受法规或普通法管制。可以授予独占、独家或非排他性的许可。在某些情况下，例如就版权而言，独占许可必须是书面的，且须由许可方或代表许可方签署才有效。

南非专利法很大程度上建立在英国专利法的基础上，而且专利法院经常依赖英国的判例法来作出决定。根据1978年的南非《专利法》，在贸易、工业或农业领域具有实用性，并且新颖又非常见的发明可以获得专利保护。"国际新颖性"概念的运用意味着，为在南非获得专利，作为专利申请标的物的发明，在专利申请日之前，且在世界任何地方，未通过使用或描述被投入公共领域，或被公众所知。

1993年《设计法案》在南非引入了一种现代化、具有创新性的知识产权保护。一项专利保护一项新发明，以及它的制造方式或功能，而一个注册设计保护一件物品的新颖外观。注册设计特别为图纸或照片所示的工业用品形状和外观提供保护。

专有技术和商业秘密与技术或商业保密信息有关，并在普通法下受保护。这类知识产权可包括研制或商业开发产品所需的任何非专利的、保密的信息，并延伸到思想、概念、方法、流程、配方、技术、发明、发现、数据、公式或规范。保护的关键在于维护信息的保密性。如果信息被披露或落入公共领域，其将不再受法律保护。因此，建议遵循严格的规则，以确保信息保密，例如，将文件标记为"机密"，并确保任何接触到机密文件的人员签署严格的保密协议。

在外国知识产权被许可给南非实体或个人使用并获得权利使用费的情况下，这种安排需要 SARB（南非储备银行）根据南非外汇管制条例事先批准。

（二）专利申请

南非是《巴黎公约》的成员国之一，也是《专利合作条约》的签署国，这意味着南非专利局已经完全融入了国际专利注册系统和程序。因此，南非专利权可以作为向其他地区扩展保护的基础，同样，外国专利权也可以扩展到南非。

南非是一个没有审查的国家，不会对专利申请中所描述的发明的有效性或可专利性进行调查。审查只是形式。（有关部门）在申请提出后6至8个月内受理申请，且必须在专利杂志上刊登公告。登记证书将于其后签发，但发布日期被视为专利的授予日期。不可对专利申请提出反对意见，但可申请撤销授予的专利。

专利权赋予专利权人权利以阻止他人在南非制造、使用、行使或处置或允许处置或进口该项发明。在南非，专利保护期限为20年，自提交完整描述之日起计算，前提是专利授予3年之后每年支付必要的更新费用。20年的保护期限不能获得延期。

（三）商标注册

商标法将"标志"定义为任何能够以图形方式表示的符号，包括装置、名称、签名、文字、字母、数字、形状、轮廓、图案、装饰、颜色、容器或任何以上形式的组合。为了作为商标受到保护，这样的符号或标志必须与其使用或拟使用的有关商品或服务有区别。不能区分的标志以及在相关贸易中经常使用或描述性的或通用的标志，不能作为商标注册，或者已经注册的，应从注册系统中移除。

南非根据商品与服务尼斯分类，将商品和服务划分为45个不同的类别，包括34个商品类别和11个服务类别。目前在南非法律上没有规定多类商标的申请，因此商标必须在每一种权益类别中分别注册。

南非是巴黎公约的缔约国，因此在南非可以主张申请优先权，前提是申请人在其他公约国就相同商标首次提出注册申请之日起6个月内，又在南非提交申请。根据南非《商标法》，商标申请可能因第三方就相同或者易混淆商标的在先使用或注册或者其他相关的原因被驳回，包括申请注册的商标不具有显著性。

商标一经注册，经商标权人申请，10年期满后可以续展10年。在南非，无需为商标续展注册而证明其使用情况。

(四)知识产权保护措施

注册商标的权利人有权阻止未经授权的第三方在相同或类似的商品或服务领域使用相同或者类似(易混淆)商标。或者,如果是著名商标,在未经授权的第三方可能不正当利用或损害该注册商标的独特字符或声誉的情况下,权利人有权阻止该等行为。

在未经授权的情况下,制造、使用或处置发明专利是一种侵犯专利权的行为。该索赔应首先确定该发明的确切范围,然后对其侵权行为进行调查,以确定其是否属于该范围。侵权诉讼可通过申请或传票提起,并在专利法院审理。被告或者被申请人可以辩称,被诉行为不属于专利的权利要求范围,也可以提出撤销该专利的反诉。胜诉专利权人可以要求申请禁令、损害赔偿和补偿维权成本。需要注意的是,除非得到豁免,否则在专利授予之日起的 9 个月内,不能进行侵权诉讼。

六、环境保护

(一)环境保护监管部门

负责在全国范围内执行环境立法的是环境事务署(DEA)。DEA 负责国家一级的环境许可和废弃物管理许可,这些许可必须进行基本的评估或环境影响评估(EIAS)。在颁发这类许可的过程中,DEA 会考虑其他专业环境部门的建议。

另一个国家级的重要监管机构是水务和公共卫生部门(DWS)。DWS 负责颁发所有与用水有关的许可证,包括从水源取水和向南非的水源排放污染物。

矿产资源部(DMR)管理采矿业。DMR 的主要职能是管理矿产和能源的问题。该职能的一部分要求 DMR 对新的或现有的采矿工程进行环境影响评估和环境管理计划规范,并且有关当局根据 2008 年《国家环境管理修正法案》中规定的过渡性规定以及 2008 年《矿产与石油资源开发修正法案》的规定为采矿工程颁发环境许可。

(二)环境保护法律法规简介

享有不损害自身健康或福祉的环境权,是宪法确立的基本权利,并得到环境立法的支持,该立法旨在保护环境,同时以适用于发展中国家的条款追求可持续的经济增长。主要法规是 1998 年的《国家环境管理法》(NEMA)。这部法规:

- 在影响环境的事项上提供合作治理和决策;
- 基于可持续发展和综合环境管理的最佳国际原则;
- 列出多类需进行基本评估或全面环境影响评估才能获得环境许可的活动;
- 授予环境管理检查员执行各环境法的广泛权力;
- 规定对环境的一般"谨慎注意义务",即每个人都有责任避免污染和环境退化。在履行环境保护责任时,民事主体和政府都应遵守该义务。

此外,NEMA 还颁布了一些具有实质意义的具体的环境管理法规,以规范与环境保护相关的各方面。例如:

- 国家环境管理——《生物多样性法案》;
- 国家环境管理——《保护区法案》;
- 国家环境管理——《空气质量法案》;
- 国家环境管理——《废物法案》。

环境权利和义务也可通过南非普通法来实施,南非法主要以罗马-荷兰法为基础。然而,一些英国法概念已被引入到南非法中,例如,环境背景下的妨害制度。

七、争议解决

(一) 司法系统和法院层级

宪法将南非的司法权赋予法院。根据宪法对法院结构进行合理化在立法上仍然是一个问题，需要指出的是，目前的法院结构在某种程度上仍然反映了 1994 年以前的情况。法院结构由三级法院组成，分别是最高法院、高等法院和初级法院。

宪法法院和最高上诉法院是最高法院。这两个法院都是最终上诉法院，但在宪法问题上，可针对最高上诉法院的裁决向宪法法院提起上诉。

高等法院由省和地方部门的高等法院和其他专门法院组成，如税务法院、竞争上诉法院、劳动法院和劳动上诉法院、土地求偿法院、选举法院、离婚法院和衡平法院（其中有些情况是特别指定的治安法院/下级法院）。高级法院有审查刑事和民事的上诉案件的管辖权。

初级法院由区域和地方治安法院组成。地方治安法院既有民事管辖权也有刑事管辖权，而区域治安法院只有刑事管辖权。地方治安法院的民事管辖权特别受到财产价值或争议索赔金额的限制。

所有法院的裁决对当事方有约束力，包括相关的政府。应注意的是，遵循先例的规则适用于南非法律，因此特定层级的法院将受到更高层级法院的法律论证或先例的约束。

(二) 仲裁

由于南非的所有法院都有案底记录，并对公众开放。诉讼当事人可能更喜欢可替代（诉讼）的能够根据客户的具体需要量身定制的私人争议解决程序，例如仲裁。

关于南非仲裁的主要立法是 1965 年的《仲裁法》。该法管辖国内和国际仲裁程序。尽管如此，需要指出的是，1977 年《承认及执行外国仲裁裁决公约》具体规定了外国仲裁裁决在南非的执行。

除刑事事项、地位事项和婚姻事项外的任何其他事项，均可由有关各方通过协议提交仲裁解决。

希望将问题提交仲裁的各方将签订仲裁协议，以规定与仲裁进行和裁决有关的条款和依据。当事人可以自行选择或通过他人代表其选择仲裁员。仲裁员是具有相关专业知识、独立公正的裁决者，负责监督仲裁程序并最终发布支持某一方当事人的仲裁裁决。

仲裁裁决的约束力不来源于仲裁员的权力，而来源于当事人提交的受约束的仲裁协议。

像南部非洲仲裁基金会（the Arbitration Foundation of Southern Africa）这样的组织可以管理仲裁，协助任命一位合适的仲裁员，并提供仲裁程序所依据的规则。

应该指出的是，仲裁不能完全排除法院的管辖权。尽管当事人将争议提交仲裁，法院可能会在发布临时禁令或执行仲裁裁决时介入。

八、其他

(一) 反商业贿赂

1. 反商业贿赂法律法规简介

南非是旨在打击腐败的一些国际协议和公约的缔约方。其中一个例子是南部非洲发展共同体反腐败议定书。根据这些不同的议定书和公约，南非有义务采取各种措施来杜绝腐败。根据这些义务，南非已经通过了各种反腐败立法。主要的反腐败法是 2004 年《防止和打击腐败活动法》(PRECCA)。它特别设立一项义务，即有关部门应报告腐败交易和登记投标违规者。

PRECCA 设置了一个涵盖广泛内容的一般腐败罪。它也为某些特定的腐败活动设定了相应的罪名。该法适用于公共和私营部门（不同于美国的《反海外腐败法》）。

一般而言，如果一个人直接或间接地接受或主动接受另一人的贿赂，或者给予或同意向任何其他人行贿，那么他就触犯了 PRECCA 所规定的腐败罪。这种给予或接受（贿赂）必须是为了促使另一方以不正当的方式行事、履行其个人的义务而发生。

PRECCA 不区分涉及公共实体或政府官员的腐败与涉及私人或实体的腐败。PRECCA 的处罚适用于公共和私人腐败。

2. 反商业贿赂监督部门

就执法而言，南非警察局是南非的主要执法机构。对于任何报告涉嫌腐败行为或任何其他犯罪，均可向南非警察局报警。

国家检察机关（NPA）设有专门的商业犯罪部门，拥有专业的商业犯罪检察官和专门的商业犯罪法庭。2010 年，全国检察总长发布了一项优先指控腐败的指令。NPA 是南非的中央检察机关，有权代表国家提起刑事诉讼。

3. 惩罚性措施

一般而言，如果有人被判定有腐败罪，下列法院可以进行下列裁判：
- 高等法院可因腐败判处一个人（包括一家公司的董事）罚金或长达终身的监禁；
- 区域法院可因腐败判处一个人（包括一家公司的董事）罚金或不超过 18 年的监禁；
- 治安法院可因腐败判处一个人（包括一家公司的董事）罚金或不超过 5 年的监禁。

传统而言，南非法院认为欺诈和腐败是严重罪行，15 年或以上的监禁判决并不少见。

（二）项目合同

1. 许可系统

一个项目所对应的政府监管部门与该项目的所涉及的性质有很大关联。常常参与项目融资行业监管的政府部门包括以下几个（仅举几例）：
- 水务和公共卫生部；
- 能源部；
- 贸易与工业部；
- 环境事务部；
- 财政部；
- 交通部；
- 矿产资源部；
- 农业、林业和渔业部。

在上述政府部门中，可能还设有一些附属机构负责特定领域的监管，这些附属机构可能会要求获取额外的许可。

2. 禁止领域

南非力图创造一个有吸引力的投资环境，并持续发展对投资者广泛有利的监管框架。一般来说，外资公司对一家南非项目公司的所有权没有限制。然而，项目公司基于某一特定项目或招标项目运营（视具体情况），该项目要求可能会对项目公司外资所有权有某些限制，并可能要求该项目公司在一定程度上由南非公民持有。

此处值得一提的是，政府的"黑人经济振兴政策"。B-BBEE 政策与《宪法》第 217 条第 2 款（允许在公共采购背景下为历史上处于不利地位的人优先分配）相一致，并在 2003 年《黑人经济振兴法案》中被定义为"通过多元化复合型的社会经济战略赋予包括妇女、工人、儿童、残疾人和农村居民在内的所有黑人经济权力"。这一点的重要性体现在，南非项目公司中的通常都会要求有 B-BBEE 公司的参与。

（三）公私伙伴关系

1. 公私伙伴关系法律法规简介

在南非，没有一项单独法案专门处理公司伙伴关系，然而，在省市和国家层级上，有大量立法和法规与公司伙伴关系（PPP）有关，这取决于交易的性质、交易方和 PPP 计划的具体产业和部门。

尽管如上，1999 年第 1 号《公共财政管理法案》（PFMA）和《国家财政部第 16 号条例》仍然值得专门一提。PFMA 的目的在于规范国家政府和省级政府的财政管理行为；确保政府所有的财政收入、支出、资产和负债得到有效管理；规定给政府中财政管理人员的责任；提供与之相关的事项。PFMA 在采购程序、有关政府实体借款的限制方面为 PPP 交易设定了明确的要求。

《国家财政部第 16 号条例》特别而详细地规定了公司伙伴关系的各个方面，包括预期有关的方面，包括但不限于获取财政部的批准，可行性研究（确定 PPP 是否符合该机构的最佳利益），在向任何潜在投标人发布前批准采购文件，PPP 协议的管理和修正。

2. 对公共实体的限制

根据 PFMA 第 66（1）条，公共实体不应借款或提供担保，或者进行任何有可能涉及未来财政承诺交易，除非被 PFMA 和其他与 PFMA 不冲突的立法授权此类借款、担保或交易。根据第 66（3）条，PFMA 允许出资人通过其董事会构进行借款或提供担保或进行前述交易。

PFMA 第 54 条要求计划参与以下交易的公共实体提前通知国家财政局，并且就该交易获得相关部长的书面批准：

- 建立或参与建立公司；
- 参与重大合伙、信托、合资企业或类似安排；
- 收购或处置公司的重大股权；
- 收购或处置重大资产；
- 开始和停止重大商业活动；
- 在重大合伙、信托、非法人合资企业或类似安排中权益性质和占比发生重大改变。

（四）消费者保护

2009 年第 68 号《消费者保护法案》（CPA）适用于可能导致特定交易的商品和服务的销售，和发生在南非境内，在供应商和消费者正常商业活动中提供商品和服务的交易，以及交易下的商品和服务本身。重要的是，CPA 为特许经营合同下的特许经营人提供重要保护。

CPA 适用于：

- 商品和服务被销售或供应给该国时；
- 消费者是法人，且在交易时其资产价值或年销售额等于或超过部长规定的临界值（目前为 200 万南非兰特）；
- 2005 年第 34 号《国家信贷法案》规定下的信贷协定，但依协议提供的商品和服务不被排除在 CPA 的范围外；
- 雇佣合同；
- 1995 年第 66 号《劳动关系法案》和《宪法》中定义的集体谈判或集体协议；
- 交易落入经相关管理机构申请并获部长批准的全行业豁免范围内。

CPA 的核心是 8 项消费者权利。这些权利有：平等进入消费者市场的权利；隐私权；选择权；披露和信息权；公正和负责的市场营销权；诚实和公平交易权；公正和合理的条款和条件权；公允价值、良好品质和安全权。CPA 致力于通过给予消费者一般知情权、易于理解的信息权，要求强制披露价格和交易记录条款来改善信息披露。

CPA 促进公平和负责的广告和市场营销，并且禁止进行诱导性的和消极选择的市场营销。它规制着促销活动、竞争和忠诚项目。根据 CPA 的规定，广告不能是错误的或是误导性的，并且供应商不得与缺乏行为能力的人订立协议。另外，CPA 规制商号的使用。出于公共管制的需要，供应商不得以未注册的名称展开经营、宣传、推广活动，或提供任何商品和服务。

违反 CPA 的规定可以触发各类惩罚，从收到要求合规的通知到征收罚款和刑事处罚。违反 CPA 的合同条款可能会依据违反的程度被认定为无效。

（五）信息技术法

在南非，信息技术（IT）部门没有受到严格的监管。然而，有生效的法律法规规制了信息技术的元素，比如电子商务、隐私和数据保护以及信息获取。网上信息一般不受法案规制，除了一些具体的领域，比如网上赌博和儿童色情。普通法的保护适用于在网上发布诽谤材料。

1. 电子商务

在南非，电子商务受到 2002 年《电子通信和交易法案》（ECTA）的规制。ECTA 大部分基于《联合国贸易法委员会示范法》，规制电子交易、数字签名、身份验证和加密、隐私和数据保护、网络环境下的消费者保护，以及在其系统上传输的第三方内容基础设施和通信服务提供者的责任。

2. 隐私和数据保护

隐私权受《宪法》的保护，约束国家、自然人和法人。然而，南非目前尚未有生效的具体的隐私和数据保护立法，法院依赖于已经建立的普通法规定的个人的人身、自由、名誉、尊严和隐私权来处理隐私法有关问题。

ECTA 设立了基本的指导原则来保护通过电子交易获得的个人信息。数据控制者可以自愿遵守这些指导原则，然而，如果其这样做了，则他们必须遵守 ECTA 中有关数据隐私的所有规定。ECTA 指导原则包括要求数据控制者在收集、整理、处理和披露数据主体的个人信息时必须获得数据所有者的书面许可。

3. 信息的获得

2000 年第 2 号《信息获取促进法案》（PAIA）完善了宪法规定的获取信息的权利。PAIA 允许获取公共主体拥有的记录以及为行使和保护权利获取私人部门享有的信息。

所有公共机构（比如国家部门和国家级、省级和地区级政府管理机构）通常在收到请求 30 日内必须提供公众要求的记录，除非未遵循正当程序或者有法律规定的拒绝理由。PAIA 规定，可以拒绝获取以下公共机构记录的请求：

- 第三方的私人信息；
- 南非税务署的特定记录；
- 第三方的商业和保密信息；
- 损害个人人身安全的信息；
- 享有法定特权的记录；
- 有关国防、证券、国际关系、南非经济和财政福利的记录；
- 第三方的研究信息；
- 有关公共机构运行的记录；
- 无意义的或无理的索取信息的请求。

尽管有这些禁止规定，但如果一项纪录①揭露了实质性违反任何法律或即将到来的严重的公共安全或环境风险的证据，和②公共利益高于披露造成的危害，它就必须被披露。

私有主体仅会在其记录是用于行使或保护任何权利，PIPA 中规定的程序性要求被满足以及不存在法定拒绝理由的情况下，被要求向公众披露其记录。私有主体拒绝披露的理由同公共机构的拒绝理由相似。再次强调，当公共利益高于披露造成的伤害时，这些拒绝理由可以被推翻。

所有公共机构和私有主体都需要编制一份手册，详细说明该主体所持有的记录的主题和类别。在 PAIA 的规定下，违反则构成刑事犯罪。

（六）矿业及矿产资源法

作为矿产权利的管理人，矿产资源部（DMR）部长可以授予、发布和拒绝勘测许可、探矿和采矿权。申请必须按照 2002 年第 8 号《矿产及石油资源开发法》（MPRDA）规定的方式提出。

DMR 的地区经理在各自省份内，接受和处理勘测许可、探矿和采矿权的申请，这些申请以"先到先受理"（first-come first-served）的方式处理，部长有义务授予首先提交申请的一方勘测许可、探矿和采矿权，前提是他们必须符合包括《采矿宪章》规定在内的所有要求。部长可以基于以下原因自由裁量拒绝授予一项勘测和/或采矿权：授予这项权利会造成排他行为，妨碍公平竞争或者造成在申请者控制下的矿产资源的集中。

拥有探矿权的人享有排他地申请并被授予探矿权续期的权利，以及在其享有探矿权的区域内申请并被授予一项矿物的采矿权的权利。同样，拥有采矿权的人享有排他地在其首次采矿权规定的矿物和区域范围内申请和被授予此项采矿权续期的权利。

MPRDA 第 11 章禁止在未经部长书面同意的情况下，转让探矿权和采矿权，或基于此类权利享有的利益，或拥有该权利的公司或相近公司的控制利益，或在这些权益上设置权益负担。上市公司控制权益的变更不受本规定的约束。一项探矿权在此项权利规定的时间范围内有效，最高不超过 5 年。一项采矿权在此权利规定的时间范围内有效，最高不超过 30 年。根据特定条款和条件，MPRDA 分别规定了勘探和采矿权的续期。

South Africa

Authors: Kenny Chiu, Wil Huang, Wendy Shih
Translators: Rubin Yu, Daivd Zhou

I. Overview

A. General Introduction to the Political, Economic, Social and Legal Environment of South Africa

The Republic of South Africa is a constitutional state with the Constitution as the supreme law of the country. The rule of law is deeply entrenched in South African politics with its legal system being heavily influenced by Roman Dutch and English common law jurisprudence. Since 1994, the role of indigenous or customary law has also been well recognised and had since earned its rightly place within the South African legal structure.

The Constitution divides the government into three different spheres, being the legislature, judiciary and the executive. Each has a specific role and limited powers of the others under the Constitution to ensure that the State functions with additional oversight capacity so that a balance in government is achieved. The government is also divided up into three different tiers with the national government on top, followed by the provincial governments, and lastly by the local governments / municipalities. Although South Africa is not a federal system, it is possible for the provincial and local government to make its own by-laws which should not be in conflict with a government tier which is higher. Provincial and local governments are also in charge of their own administration in their own jurisdiction.

Politically, the country has, in recent years, had a number of political scandals involving some of its top politicians and private individuals. However, what can really be described as the silver lining in South African current affairs in the past decade is the independence of the courts and focus on the rule of law. Court rulings against corrupt officials are clear signs that South African courts remain independent and fearless in making the right decisions. Inheriting the Roman-Dutch and English legal systems, the South African legal system has strong foundations on which to build on. These foundations have remained strong in our legal system today which still remains a prominent cornerstone of the democracy. This publication will introduce specific commercial aspects of it.

Economically, the country saw the Rand tank against the dollar to its worst level in 2016 and was downgraded by ratings agencies where it is hanging just above junk status. Following the election of Cyril Ramaphosa as the President of South Africa on 15 February 2018, the Rand strengthened to a three-year high against the dollar. Positive reforms are on the horizon as promised by the ruling party and the President and investor confidence in the country is slowly returning to previous levels.

Socially, the country is currently struggling against the worst drought the country has seen in 30 years. Several provinces have recovered to varying extents since 2016 but a few are still hard hit by the drought, including the Western, Eastern and Northern Cape. On top of it all, social grants made by the South African government amounts to 94.3% of the total social development budget of ZAR160-million. Despite these issues, South Africans remain upbeat and positive about the potential of the country, some have even observed foreign investments piling in to enter the country. It is thus the policies and regulatory frameworks discussed in this paper which will count and promote a continuous and sustainable growth.

B. The Status and Direction of the Cooperation with Chinese Enterprises Under the Belt and Road Initiative

Financing opportunities, major projects in the power and infrastructure sector, which include technology, telecommunications, manufacturing, consumer goods and retail, will all become the main focus and role in the Belt and Road Initiative in the coming years. It also aims to promote expansion of mutual investment areas, deepen cooperation in agriculture, forestry, fisheries, agricultural machinery manufacturing and farm produce processing and to promote cooperation in marine-product, deep-sea fishing, ocean engineering technology, environmental protection industry and marine tourism. South Africa provides Chinese enterprises the investment opportunities in aquaculture, agro-industry, ocean economic, renewable energy, sea food and marine tourism. Those are in line with the Belt and Road Initiative.

China and South Africa signed a memorandum of understanding ("MoU") in December 2015 to jointly build the "Silk Road Economic Belt and the 21st Century Maritime Silk Road". The MoU also aims to create opportunities for mutual learning and to realise the better exchange and integration of goods, technology, capital and personnel between the two countries. China is currently South Africa's largest trading partner. This relationship will not only be favourable to boosting bilateral trade and investment between the two countries, but will also infuse a new momentum to the transformation of Sino-African relations and provide economic development opportunities between China and the African countries. It will also help promote the Belt and Road Initiative in Africa.

As a result, a lot of investment is expected to roll in together with infrastructure development and growth in trade. In 2014, The Silk Road Fund was set up by the Chinese government to lead the investment arm of the initiative. The Silk Road Fund had a fund value of USD40-billion back in 2014. In 2017, Fitch reported that USD900-billion in projects is already underway. Infrastructure development and trade will certainly take centre stage in the Belt and Road Initiative.

II. Investment

A. Market Access

a. Department Supervising Investment

The Department of Trade and Industry ("DTI") is the government department responsible for promoting economic development in South Africa. The DTI is tasked to build a multilateral trading system that facilitates development, strengthens trade and investment links with key economies, and which supports African regional economic integration and development cooperation. The DTI also builds on trade and investment relations, and in partnership with the Provincial Investment Promotion Agencies undertakes investment and export promotion activities in targeted markets that are aligned to South Africa's international relations and cooperation agreements. It is also involved in regulating international trade and consumer protection and promoting Black Economic Empowerment ("BEE") in South Africa.

b. Laws and Regulations of Investment Industry

The Protection of Investment Act, 2015 provides for the protection of investors and their investments so as to achieve a balance of rights and obligations that apply to all investors. Section 7 of the Protection of Investment Act states that all investment must be established in compliance with the laws of South Africa, and emphasises the fact that the Act itself does not create a right for a foreign investor or prospective foreign investor to establish an investment in South Africa. However, the Protection of Investment Act provides that foreign investors and their investments must not be treated less favorably than South African investors in like circumstances, and South Africa must accord foreign investors and their investments a level of physical security as may be generally provided to domestic investors in accordance with minimum standards of customary international law and subject to available resources and capacity, investors have the right to property in terms of section 25 of the Constitution of the Republic of South Africa, and that a foreign investor may (in respect of an investment) repatriate funds subject to taxation and other applicable legislation.

The Protection of Investment Act also recognises the obligation to take measures to protect or advance persons, or categories of persons, historically disadvantaged in South Africa due to discrimination (for example, BEE). BEE is a prominent government policy and socio-economic process which seeks to contribute to the economic transformation of South Africa by bringing about significant increases in the number of "black people" that manage, own and control the country's economy, and by bringing about significant decreases in income inequalities. "Black people" is a generic term which means black Africans, Coloureds and Indians and included provisions to ensure that they must have been South African citizens prior to 1994. BEE is said to be broad-based when it contributes to the economic development of black persons over a range of specified BEE elements.

BEE is regulated by the Broad-Based Black Economic Empowerment Act, 2003, as amended and / or amendment acts (collectively, the "BEE Acts"), and the Codes of Good Practice on Broad-Based BEE ("Codes"). It is not mandatory to comply with the BEE targets provided for in the Codes; however, the BEE Acts and Codes operate through the mechanism of direct and indirect incentives to comply. Directly, an enterprise will effectively have to comply with the Codes if it relies on government or parastatal contracts for a substantial part of its business, or if it relies on government to issue licences, quotas or other permissions to carry on its business. Indirectly, an enterprise will be exposed to BEE if the government, parastatals and increasingly, large corporate firms in general, have procurement and other policies in place which dictate that their suppliers should have a particular BEE status or characteristic. The BEE legislation is supported and functions in conjunction with various other forms of legislation, including the Employment Equity Act,1998, Skills Development Act, 1998, Preferential Procurement Policy Framework Act, 2000 and others.

Other significant legislation that regulates or may affect investment includes (but is not limited to) the Companies Act, 2008, Exchange Control Regulation, 1961, the Johannesburg Stock Exchange Rules, the Competition Act, 1998 and including other industries-related legislation.

c. Forms of Investment and Standards of Market Access

Foreign companies are entitled to establish wholly owned branches (external companies) or incorporate subsidiaries (whether wholly or partially owned) in South Africa. There is no requirement that any of the shareholders or directors of a company must be resident in South Africa (nor be a citizen in the case of individuals).

There are additional restrictions on foreign ownership and / or additional licensing requirements for sectors of national interest, (such as mining, telecommunications, national security) and certain sectors (such as financial services, banking, gaming) are subject to additional regulation.

B. Foreign Exchange Regulation

a. Department Supervising Foreign Exchange

South Africa has exchange controls which are administered by the Financial Surveillance Department ("FinSurv") of the South African Reserve Bank ("SARB") and "authorised dealers". Authorised dealers are merely commercial banks and some branches of foreign banks that SARB has delegated power to oversee and regulate the inflow and outflow of capital in South Africa on its behalf and are the only entities permitted to effect an offshore currency transaction for a South African resident.

b. Brief Introduction of Laws and Regulations of Foreign Exchange

The current set of Exchange Control Regulations was promulgated on 1 December 1961 and amended from time to time. Orders and Rules get issued under the Exchange Control Regulations and the current set was published on 1 December 1961, and amended from time to time. The Orders and Rules contain various orders, rules, exemptions, forms and procedural arrangements. The FinSurv also issues circulars to update the public regarding any existing or new issues relating to exchange control. The "Currency and Exchanges Manual for Authorised Dealers" contains the permissions and conditions applicable to transactions in foreign exchange that may be undertaken by Authorised Dealers and / or on behalf of clients, details of related administrative responsibilities as well as the FinSurv reporting requirements.

c. Requirements of Foreign Exchange Management for Foreign Enterprises

All South African residents and domestic companies are subject to exchange control. Transactions between a subsidiary in South Africa and its holding company outside South Africa are regarded as being between a resident and non-resident, and are therefore subject to the approval of the FinSurv.

In regard to transactions involving a non-resident, or in which a non-resident has an interest, FinSurv approval may be required in certain instances:

a) Endorsement of Controlled Securities

In terms of Regulation 14 of the Exchange Control Regulations, no person may acquire or dispose of a "controlled security" without the permission of the FinSurv. "Controlled security" is defined as any security that is registered in the name of a non-resident, or of which a non-resident is the owner, or in which a non-resident has an interest. The control over the acquisition or disposal of controlled securities is exercised by endorsing the securities owned by non-residents or in which non-residents have an interest. The effect of this endorsement is to ensure that in the event of a disposal by the non-resident of its interest, the payment may be transferred abroad or credited to a non-resident account.

b) Inward Foreign Loan and Interest

When money is borrowed from abroad, the loan itself is known as inward foreign loan. The rate and terms at which interest may be remitted must be approved either by FinSurv or an authorised dealer at the time of introduction of the loan. Prior exchange control approval for the terms of repayment of the capital portion of the loan is also required. The interest rate charged on the funding must fall within certain prescribed limits.

c) Remittance of Dividends

Dividends may be transferred to non-resident shareholders provided the shares have been endorsed "non-resident" as described above. FinSurv or authorised dealers will require documentary proof that the company has profits (e.g. audited financial statements) before authorising the remittance of the dividends.

d) Remittance of Royalties, Licence Fees and Patent Fees

Any agreement between a resident and non-resident to the effect that the resident would pay royalties, licence fees or patent fees requires prior exchange control approval. The payment of royalties to a non-resident for the manufacture of goods in South Africa must be approved by the Department of Trade and Industry. The payment of other royalties is approved by FinSurv. Approval will generally not be granted for the payment of minimum royalties or upfront royalties.

e) Remittance of Management Fees

Exchange control approval is required for any payment of a management or administration fee by a resident to a non-resident. The amount paid must be reasonable in relation to the services provided by the non-resident to resident.

Generally speaking, under the exchange control regulations there are no limitations as to how much money can be brought into South Africa, but there are limitations on the amount of money that can be transferred out of South Africa.

C. Financing

a. Main Financial Institutions

The South African Reserve Bank ("SARB") is the central bank of the Republic of South Africa. The SARB is responsible for the management of the South African money and banking system (which includes the formulation and implementation of monetary policy, provides liquidity to banks when necessary and acts as custodian of cash reserves) and is furthermore, responsible for bank regulation and supervision in South Africa.

The main participants in the financial market are the banks (inclusive of commercial banks and some branches of foreign banks). The business of a bank includes the acceptance of deposits from the general public, the soliciting of or advertising for deposits, the utilisation of money, or of the interest or other income earned on money (accepted by way of deposit) and various other activities.

b. Financing Conditions for Foreign Enterprises

a) Foreign Lender Restrictions: Granting Loans

There are no significant impediments on cross-border lending other than exchange-control regulation which is administered by FinSurv. No South African resident may incur an obligation to a non-resident except with FinSurv's approval, which must be obtained in advance. In addition, the National Credit Act No. 34 of 2005 ("NCA") would be applicable where the loan could be said to "have an effect within the Republic" of South Africa and foreign lenders would then be required to register as credit provider under the NCA.

b) Foreign Lender Restrictions: Granting of Security

Guarantees are commonly used in South Africa. The prior approval of the FinSurv would be required if any guarantee is given by a local entity in favour of a non-resident entity or for the obligations of a non-resident entity. Where guarantees are used in loan transactions and the guarantor is a company related or inter-related to the borrower, such guarantees would constitute "financial assistance" in terms of section 44 of the Companies Act, 2008. The board may not authorise financial assistance other than pursuant to a special resolution of the shareholders, adopted within the previous two years and the board being satisfied that immediately after providing the financial assistance, the company would satisfy the solvency and liquidity test. Furthermore, the board must be satisfied that the financial assistance to be provided will be fair and reasonable (to the company). In addition, the board must ensure that any conditions or restrictions respecting the granting of financial assistance set out in the company's memorandum of incorporation have been satisfied.

D. Land Policy

a. Brief Introduction of Land-Related Laws and Regulations

A statutory legal framework for real estate in South Africa gives rise to a definite and comprehensive legislative framework within which property is owned. The law applicable to the transfer and registration of land, is, in the first instance, the Deeds Registries Act,1937, together with its regulations. There are a number of other statutes that govern the ownership and transfer of land, but in essence, there is no restriction on ownership of land in South Africa and any natural person or juristic person may own land. Actual ownership therefore vests in the owner and not the state.

Pursuant to the land survey, property registers have been established in the various Deeds Registries within the different Provinces of South Africa. Those registers are properly indexed and are now accessible electronically, the originals of title deeds and other documentation having been digitised. The deeds registries are established under the relevant government department, and all fall under a chief registrar of deeds. Given the definite underlying survey system, the property registers are very accurate and create a definite form of land registration.

All ownership of land is recorded in a deeds registry.

Ownership of land is evidenced by a title deed issued by the deeds registry, which will record the owner's details and the conditions under which the land is held. These conditions are normally imposed by local authorities and by private agreement. If ownership is not registered in a deeds registry, then it is most likely that ownership of the property has not passed. Transfer of ownership of property is also evidenced by registration in the deeds registry.

It is possible to own units in buildings through the Sectional Titles Act,1986. These are known as sectional title units, and are registered in a deeds registry, by reference to a sectional title plan, prepared by a surveyor registered with the Surveyor General. Both the Deeds Registries Act and the Sectional Titles Act create the environment and legislative framework within which properties are transferred from one party to another.

Property rights are protected in the Constitution. The Bill of Rights in the Constitution restricts the deprivation of property, except in the case of expropriation in terms of a law of general application, and then must be subject to compensation, which must be agreed by the affected persons or approved by a court. That compensation must be just and equitable and generally requires that regard be given to the fair-value principle. The land restitution process continues in South Africa, and land claims have been made mostly in respect of rural property and not to urban property, although there are certain tracts of urban property that are subject to outstanding land claims. This has had an effect on investment in properties subject to land claims.

All acquisition of property in South Africa is subject to the Transfer Duty Act,1949. The term "property" for the purpose of transfer duty means land and fixtures and includes real rights in land, rights to minerals, a share or interest in a "residential property company" or a share in a share-block company. As a general rule, transfer duty is payable at a sliding scale for acquisition by all persons (including companies, close corporations and trusts) where no transfer duty is payable for the first ZAR900 000 of the purchase price (this is to assist in the purchase of lower-value properties). If the seller of the property is a registered vendor for VAT purposes, then VAT at 15% is payable and not transfer duty. Under certain circumstances the acquisition of a business premises maybe subject to zero-rated VAT.

b. Rules of Land Acquisition for Foreign Investors

There is no restriction on foreign investors acquiring property in South Africa. For foreign companies to acquire property in South Africa, they must register as an external company in terms of the Companies Act, 2008.

Before the proceeds of the sale of immovable property in South Africa or shares in a company owning South African immovable property may be remitted abroad by a non-resident, SARB approval is required, and one of the requirements for approval is that all taxes must have been paid. A withholding amount is payable to the South African Revenue Services ("SARS") pending determination of the tax liability by the non-resident seller to the SARS. The current rates are 7.5% for individuals 10% for companies and 15% for trusts. Treaty relief may be available to taxpayers in terms of international treaties.

E. The Establishment and Dissolution of Companies

a. The Forms of Investment Vehicles

There are various investment vehicles available to investors interested in setting up a business in South Africa. The decision as to which is appropriate will depend on numerous factors, including the need for limited liability and tax considerations. The main entities available for foreign investment are:
- Personal liability company (incorporated);
- Private limited liability company (proprietary limited);
- External company (branch office);
- Public company (limited);
- Partnership;
- Sole trader; and
- Business / trading trust.

b. The Procedure of Establishment

Two main categories of companies are recognised in the Companies Act, 2008. These are the "profit company" and the "non-profit company". A profit company will include state-owned companies, privately owned companies (in terms of which the company's constitutional document, the memorandum of incorporation ("MOI") must prohibit the offer of shares to the public), personal liability companies (in terms of which the directors and the company are jointly and severally liable for contractual debts) and public companies.

The incorporation of a private company or personal liability company involves the reservation of a company name, the filling of the MOI of the company (the constitution of a company), written consent of auditors to act for the company (if any), notice of the company's registered office and the submission of a register of directors. The process of incorporation itself takes on average one to two months however this is largely dependent on the time taken by the Companies and Intellectual Property Commission ("CIPC") to effect the registration.

In respect to the incorporation of a branch office (external company), a notarially certified copy of the memorandum and articles or association (constitutional documents) of the parent company must be filed with CIPC to effect registration. External companies must comply with the Companies Act by appointing a South African auditor if required to do so, and by submitting statutory returns. There is no need to appoint a local board of directors, but simply one person residing in South Africa to accept service of any process and notices; and accounting records similar to those prescribed for local companies must be kept in respect of the local operations.

A partnership is not a legal entity distinct from the persons comprising the partnership, including for income tax purposes. However, for value-added tax ("VAT") purposes, a partnership is a person and therefore registers as a vendor in its own name. Every partner in a general partnership is liable jointly and severally for all the debts and obligations of the partnership.

A sole proprietorship does not give rise to separate legal personality, perpetual succession or limited liability. There are no formalities required to set up the sole proprietorship, and can be operated under the name of its owner or it can do business under a fictitious (trading) name.

A business trust is constituted by the lodgement of a deed of trust with the Master of the High Court of South Africa. Trusts obtain separate legal personality only for certain purposes, such as for taxation and perpetual succession, which is usually provided for in the deed of trust. Ownership of the trust assets vests in the trustees who are limited to a maximum of 20 persons. Limited liability can be achieved via the business trust. Trusts are regulated by the Trust Property Control Act, 1988.

c. Routes and Requirements of Dissolution

Under South African law, a company or any other third party may apply for a business entity to be deregistered. However, to embark on the deregistration process, the company must have ceased to carry on business and have no assets or, because of the inadequacy of its assets, there is no reasonable probability of the company or close corporation being liquidated. Therefore, documentary proof confirming such statements and necessary supporting documents (including tax clearance certificate or any other written confirmation from SARS that no tax liability is outstanding) must be submitted as part of the application. When two or more successive annual returns are outstanding, the CIPC may also deregister the corporation.

F. Merger and Acquisition

The main laws and regulations which govern the conduct of public merger and acquisition activity in South Africa are the following:

a) the Companies Act, 2008, which regulates all takeover and public merger and acquisition ("M&A") activity in South Africa. The Companies Act and the regulations thereto contain provisions regulating takeovers and mergers, which are known as the Takeover Regulations;

b) the Security Services Act 36 of 2004 regulates, inter alia, insider trading and market abuse;

c) the Listings Requirements of the Johannesburg Stock Exchange ("JSE") operated by the JSE Limited apply if:

(i) the bidder's or target shares are listed on the JSE, under the Listings Requirements, the bidder's shareholders must approve an acquisition if the offer consideration (and / or dilutionary effect) is larger than 25% of the market capitalisation of the bidder; or

(ii) any new shares being offered as part of the bid consideration are to be listed on the JSE,

d) the Competition Act, 1998 (South African anti-trust law).

Depending on the circumstances, the implementation of each M&A may need to be approved by, among others, regulatory authorities such as the Takeovers Regulation Panel, the JSE, the competition authorities, the SARB and other industry-specific regulators (for example, in the banking, mining and communications industries).

The traditional methods of acquiring control of public companies have been the general offer to shareholders and the scheme of arrangement. The Companies Act has, with effect from 1 May 2011, introduced for the first time in South African law a statutory merger mechanism for effecting transactions. In this regard, certain mergers have been effected pursuant to the statutory merger provisions.

G. Competition Regulations

a. Department Supervising Competition Regulation

The South African competition authorities include the Competition Commission (the "Commission") which is responsible for investigating and evaluating mergers and prohibited practices; the Competition Tribunal (the "Tribunal") which is essentially the court of first instance in adjudicating competition law matters; the Competition Appeal Court (the "CAC") which is the designated appellate authority for competition law matters; the Supreme Court of Appeal (the "SCA") which is authorised to hear appeals from the CAC and the Constitutional Court, which is empowered to hear constitutional issues arising from competition law cases.

b. Brief Introduction of Competition Law

South Africa has a well-developed and regulated competition regime based on best international practice. Its economic system is predominantly based on free market principles, however, as in most developed economies, competition is controlled. In South Africa the Competition Act of 1998, ("Competition Act") is the predominant mechanism which aims to keep competition in check.

The overarching aim of the Competition Act is to ensure effective, fair and vigorous competition in the market. The Competition Act substantially strengthened the previous powers of the competition authorities along the lines of the European Union, United States and Canadian models. The Competition Act provides for various prohibitions of anti-competitive conduct, restrictive practices (such as price fixing, predatory pricing and collusive tendering) and abuses by dominant firms. The Competition Act also entails a notification and prior approval procedure for certain mergers and acquisitions, and carries significant penalties for contraventions. It reaches beyond South Africa, applying to economic activity both within and having an effect within the country.

c. Measures Regulating Competition

The Competition Act empowers the Tribunal to make various orders in relation to prohibited practices. Among these, the Tribunal may interdict a prohibited practice, or declare a part or the whole of such an agreement to be void. More onerous orders may be made where a party is required to supply or distribute goods or services to a competitor on terms reasonably required to end a prohibited practice, or where access to an essential facility (on reasonable terms) may be required for competitors.

One of the more common orders that the Tribunal may impose is that of an administrative penalty. Competition authorities may impose on the transgressors an administrative penalty (fine) not exceeding 10% of the parties' annual turnover in South Africa and their exports from South Africa for the preceding financial year.

d. Restrictive Horizontal Practices

The Competition Act restricts the ability of firms in a horizontal relationship, that is, a relationship between competitors, to engage in conduct that constitutes a prohibited practice. Certain practices are prohibited outright by the Competition Act, and are known as per se or automatically prohibited practices. This kind of conduct is viewed as being "non-defensible", in that any firms engaged in such conduct are not entitled to give a justification or defence for participating in the prohibited behaviour. These include where firms directly or indirectly fix a purchase or selling price or any other trading condition; market division between firms, whereby customers, suppliers, territories and / or specific types of goods or services are allocated amongst the firms; or where firms engage in collusive tendering, which includes the suppression of bids, or the rotation of bids and complementary tendering among competitors.

e. Restrictive Vertical Practices

A "vertical relationship" is one that exists between parties operating at different levels of a supply chain. The Competition Act weighs most restrictive vertical practices against the rule of reason test highlighted above. Thus, the Competition Act allows for the justification by entities accused of contravening the restrictive vertical practice provisions of the Competition Act of their agreements and practices, if they result in technological, efficiency or other pro-competitive gains that outweigh their anti-competitive effects. The only per se prohibition with regard to vertical practices is that of minimum resale price maintenance.

Minimum resale price maintenance occurs when an upstream supplier attempts to regulate or control the resale price of goods or services that it supplies, and implements measures to enforce or maintain the prescribed resale price, thereby reducing competition. This does not mean that there cannot be a recommended minimum resale price. As long as that recommendation is not binding on the sale of the product or service, and it appears clearly on the product itself that it is simply a recommendation, it is allowed in terms of the Competition Act.

H. Tax

a. Tax Regime and Rules

a) South African Revenue Service and Primary Legislation

SARS administers a wide range of tax legislation, which includes the Income Tax Act,1962, the Value-Added Tax Act, 1991, the Tax Administration Act, 2011, the Customs and Excise Act, 1964 and the Employment Tax

Incentives Act, 2013, as amended.

b) Basis of Taxation

South Africa taxes residents on their world-wide income, whereas non-residents are taxed only on income sourced in South Africa or deemed to be from a source in South Africa. The Income Tax Act defines the term "resident". An individual will be regarded as a resident in South Africa if such person is either ordinarily resident in South Africa or qualifies in terms of a physical presence test based on the number of days such individual is present in South Africa over a period of five years. Where a person is deemed to be exclusively a resident of another country in terms of a double taxation agreement concluded between such country and South Africa, the double taxation agreement will override the domestic law. With regard to persons other than natural persons, a resident is defined in the Income Tax Act as any person that is incorporated, established or formed in South Africa or which has its place of effective management in South Africa. The provision of a double taxation agreement may similarly override the domestic law in this respect.

c) Types of Taxes

Taxes in South Africa are broadly classified as direct tax and indirect tax. Direct taxes are taxes paid by the taxpayer directly to the government whereas indirect taxes are taxes levied on the supply of goods and services. Examples of direct taxes are income tax, dividends tax, capital gains tax, estate duty, certain types of withholding tax and donations tax. Examples of indirect taxes are value-added tax, securities transfer tax, transfer duty, and customs and exercise duty.

b. Main Categories and Rates of Tax

a) Income Tax

Income tax is the normal tax which is paid on your taxable income.

(i) Individuals and special trusts

The rate of tax levied on an individual is set on a sliding scale which results in the tax increasing as taxable income increases. The rate currently starts from 18% to 45% of the taxable income.

(ii) Companies

The corporate tax rate is 28% of taxable income. The income of South African branches of foreign companies is also taxed at a rate of 28% of taxable income derived by such non-resident or branch.

(iii) Trusts

Trusts are taxed at a flat rate of 45%.

b) Dividends Tax

Dividend tax is payable in respect of dividends declared to the ultimate shareholders of a South African company, if such shareholders are non-corporates or non-residents. The rate is currently 20% for any dividend paid on or after 22 February 2017 (irrespective of declaration date), unless an exemption or reduced rate is applicable (for example by an applicable double taxation agreement).

c) Capital gains Tax ("CGT")

This tax applies to individuals, companies and trusts and is payable on the disposal of an asset. An asset is property of whatever nature (movable or immovable), including rights or interest of whatever nature to or in such property, tangible or intangible assets, excluding currency but including any coin made mainly from gold or platinum.

Individuals and special trusts are required to include 40% of their capital gain in their taxable income, which gives an effective CGT tax rate of 18%. Other legal entities (for example, companies and other trusts) are required to include 80% of the capital gain in their taxable income. The maximum effective CGT tax rates as a result of these inclusions are that the companies would pay 22.4% and trusts 36%.

d) Estate Duty

For persons ordinarily resident in South Africa at the date of death, duty is levied at a flat rate of 20% on world-wide assets. The dutiable amount is determined after allowing certain deductions, the principal one being a general abatement of R3.5 million. South Africa has double death duty tax agreements with Lesotho, Sweden, the United Kingdom, the USA and Zimbabwe. In the case of a non-resident, estate duty in South Africa is payable only on the non-resident's South African estate.

e) Donations Tax

Donations tax at a flat rate of 20% is charged on dispositions of property for no or for inadequate consideration. Non-residents are not subject to this tax and an exemption exists in respect of donations by public companies as defined. Charitable donations per se are not deductible for tax purposes unless they are made to public benefit organisations and certain other requirements are met, or unless they can be brought within the ambit of the general deduction provisions of the Income Tax Act.

f) Value-added Tax ("VAT")

A Value-added tax system, similar to that of the United Kingdom and New Zealand, applies in South Africa. The rate of 15% is charged on the supply by any vendor of goods and services within South Africa while conducting an enterprise in South Africa and also applies to imported goods and certain services. The imposition of 15% is subject to certain exemptions, exceptions, deductions and adjustments.

Few supplies are exempt from VAT, the most notable exclusion being certain financial services, where the consideration for the service takes the form of interest. Most fee-based financial services are subject to VAT. Goods exported from South Africa and services rendered offshore or rendered to non-residents of South Africa are generally zero-rated for VAT.

g) Securities Transfer Tax

The Securities Transfer Tax Act, 2007 provides for the levying of a securities transfer tax in respect of every transfer of any security on or after 1 July 2008. Securities transfer tax will be payable at a rate of 0.25% (in the normal course of events, on the amount or market value of the consideration for the transfer of the security).

h) Transfer Duty

All acquisition of immovable property in South Africa is subject to the Transfer Duty Act, 1949. Transfer duty is charged at a progressive rate to a maximum of 13% in the case of immovable property acquired by natural persons, corporations and trusts. The duty is not charged where the transfer of the property is subject to VAT at 15%.

i) Customs Duty

Customs duty at various rates is payable on certain goods imported into South Africa. In terms of the Customs and Excise Act, 1964, duty liability arises from the time the goods are deemed to have been imported. Liability rests on the master of the ship, the pilot of the aircraft, the carrier of any other vehicle, the container operator, the depot operator or degrouping operator until due entry and lawful delivery of the goods to the importer, when liability transfers to the importer.

South Africa has free trade agreements with the European Union, European Free Trade Association and Southern African Development Community that offers preferential customs duty rates on goods originating in these territories. South Africa is also a member of the Southern African Customs Union in terms of which trade between the members are customs duty free.

j) Excise Duty

Excise duty is charged on certain locally produced goods and an equivalent duty, referred to as a customs duty, is charged on the same goods if imported, for example: alcohol, cigarettes, perfumes, television sets etc.

c. Tax Declaration and Preference

Every year, SARS announces its tax season which is the period that an individual is required to declare and / or submit its income tax returns. In terms of corporate income tax, every registered taxpayer is required to submit a return of income twelve months after the end of the financial year. In addition to annual returns, every company is required to submit provisional tax returns, the first of these returns is required to be submitted six months from the start of the year, and the second at year end, and must contain an estimate of the total taxable income earned or to be earned for that period. Payment of the tax must accompany the return. A third "top-up" payment may be made six months after year-end. Returns can be submitted electronically via e-filing or manually at a SARS branch where the taxpayer is registered. The other types of tax are to be declared within the prescribed period, failure to do so may attract penalties. For example transfer duty is payable within six months from the date of acquisition of the property, and if the transfer duty is not paid within this period, interest calculated at 10% per annum for each completed month.

I. Securities

a. Brief Introduction of Securities-Related Laws and Regulations

South Africa has highly sophisticated capital markets which are well-regulated. The primary pieces of legislation in addition to the Companies Act, 2008 are the Financial Market Act, 2012, which replaced the Securities Services Act, 2004 and which regulates securities (for example shares or other instruments) services and is aimed at increasing confidence in the South African financial markets, promoting the protection of regulated persons and clients, reducing systemic risk and promoting the international competitiveness of securities in South Africa ("Financial Market Act"); and the Financial Advisory and Intermediary Services Act, 2004 ("FAIS"), which was introduced to promote good and proper business practices in the financial services industry and to contribute to improving corporate governance and market confidence.

b. Supervision and Regulation of Securities Market

The Financial Services Board ("FSB") is an independent institution established in terms of the Financial

Services Board Act, 1990 and is responsible for the regulation and supervision of non-banking financial services industries, which includes short-term and long-term insurance, companies, schemes, collective investment schemes (unit trusts and stock market) as well as financial advisors and / or brokers. FAIS and the Financial Intelligence Centre Act, 2001 have expanded the mandate of the FSB to include aspects of market conduct in the banking industry as well as to combat financial crime (such as money laundering, tax evasion and terrorist financing activities).

The Bank Supervision Department of the SARB is responsible for the regulation and supervision of banks, and the JSE Limited is responsible to the FSB for the supervision of authorised users on the stock exchange, including the accounting, trading and custody activities.

c. Requirements for Engagement in Securities Trading for Foreign Enterprises

Any transactions by residents in any securities [inclusive of shares (whether in a private or public company), stocks etc.)] registered in the name of a non-resident (or which a non-resident is the owner or holds an interest), then such securities certificates must be endorsed "non-resident" by FinServ and / or authorised dealers so as to allow the sale proceeds to be transferred abroad (for example into a non-resident bank account).

Certain industries (including broadcasting, banking and insurance) have legislation applicable to them which precludes foreign buyers from holding above a threshold stake at all or without obtaining the consent of the relevant minister.

J. Preference and Protection of Investment

a. The Structure of Preference Policies

The Protection of Investment Act, 2015 ("PIA") sets out an overarching framework whereby investments are channelled. In essence, the PIA recognises the need for foreign investment as well as the principles enshrined in the Constitution of the Republic. It attempts to merge the values on the Constitution and condenses it into a structure dealing with investments. Investments are defined as:

(i) "any lawful enterprise established, acquired or expanded by an investor in accordance with the laws of the Republic, committing resources of economic value over a reasonable period of time, in anticipation of profit;

(ii) the holding or acquisition of shares, debentures or other ownership instruments of such an enterprise; or

(iii) the holding, acquisition or merger by such an enterprise with another enterprise outside the Republic to the extent that such holding, acquisition or merger with another enterprise outside the Republic, has an effect on an investment contemplated by paragraphs (i) and (ii) in the Republic."[1]

What is also important to note is that although the PIA provides for the overall structure in which investments are to be channelled, it is still up to government or any organ of state in accordance with the Constitution and applicable legislation to provide the details in which sector specific investments are channelled. The important values enshrined by the PIA are as follows:

(i) the promotion of a fair administrative treatment in dealing with all investments, domestic or foreign;

(ii) all investments, be it domestic or foreign, must be treated equally on grounds that do not favour either in like circumstances;

(iii) physical security of both foreign and domestic investment must be the same;

(iv) investors have the right to property in terms of the Constitution of the Republic of South Africa;

(v) foreign investors may in circumstances repatriate funds subject to taxation and other applicable legislation.

Aggrieved foreign investors may request the relevant government department to facilitate the resolution of the dispute by the appointment of a mediator.

b. Support for Specific Industries and Regions including the Protection of Investments

It has been two years since the promulgation of the PIA in December 2015, but development has been slow in specific industries and regions. General manufacturing, automotive industry, aquaculture, business process services, textiles, and additional industries have all made slow progress in putting in policies in protecting investment in their section.[2] The South African government has put together various investment incentives that will hopefully grow the different industries in the future.

For each industry sector mentioned above, the government has in place various programmes which aims at incentivising and protecting investments in that sector. All programmes, support to industries protections, and the

---

[1] Section 2 of the Protection of Investment Act 22 of 2015.
[2] See the official portal for South African Government Incentive Schemes at http://www.investmentincentives.co.za/industry-specific-incentives.

like would all have to subject to the PIA.

The DTI incentives are managed by the Incentive Development and Administration Division and are offered to enterprises in return for specific developmental objectives. Below is just a few incentive schemes offered by the DTI:

a) 121 Tax Incentive:

The 121 tax incentive offers support for both capital investment and training in respect of Brownfield investments as well as Greenfield investments. The investment allowance for Brownfield investment with preferred status can be as high as R550 million and Greenfield Investment with preferred status as high as R900 million. Training allowance can also be applied for, with up to R36 000 may be deducted from full time employee's taxable income; and a maximum of R30 million may be deducted from taxable income in the case of a preferred project.

b) Agro-Processing Support Scheme (APSS)

The APSS is a scheme only available to the agro-processing / beneficiation (agri-business) enterprises and offers a 20% to a 30% cost-sharing grant to a maximum of R20 million over a two-year investment period which grant may be utilised on a combination of investment costs. An additional 10% grant for projects that meet all economic benefit criteria such as employment, transformation, geographic spread and local procurement may be considered by the DTI.

c) Automotive Investment Scheme (AIS)

The objective of AIS is to strengthen and expand the automotive sector through investment in a new and / or replacement models and components with the aim of increasing plant production volumes, sustain employment and / or strengthen the automotive value chain. In respect of productive assets the AIS currently provides for a non-taxable cash grant of twenty percent (20%) of the value of qualifying investment and twenty five percent (25%) of the value of qualifying investment in productive assets by component manufactures and tooling companies as approved by the DTI. An additional non-taxable cash grant of five to ten percent (5%-10%) may be made available for projects that fulfils certain economic requirements, and / or can demonstrate a specified increase in unit production per plant and increase in turnover and manufacturing of components that are currently not being manufactured in South Africa.

d) Critical Infrastructure Programme (CIP)

CIP is alike a cost-sharing incentive. It is available to the approved applicant / s or infrastructure project / s upon the completion of verifiable milestones or as may be approved by DTI. One of the requirement of CIP is that the infrastructure must be deemed "critical" to the investment (in other words, without such investment the said infrastructure would not operate optimally). The CIP offers a grant of between 10% to 30% of the total qualifying infrastructural development costs, but is limited to a maximum of R50 million (upon achieving certain economic benefit criteria).

e) Clothing and Textile Competitiveness Improvement Programme (CTCIP)

The CTCIP is a programme that aims to improve the competitiveness of South African based clothing, textile, footwear, leather and leather goods manufacturers and designers in the global market. The incentive programme subsidises competitiveness improvement activities in small, medium-sized and large companies that would otherwise not be able to finance these interventions, and encourage interventions that include supplier and / or customer organisations to these manufacturing entities (a value chain approach). The cost-sharing grant incentive can be as high as 75% of the qualifying project limited to a cumulative ceiling of R25 million over the period of programme implementation, alternatively be of different cost sharing percentage but in phases (i.e. initial investment grant of 100% for the first year, where after it becomes a different cost sharing percentage (often lower percentages) for the remaining years).

f) Manufacturing Investment Programme (MIP)

The MIP works like a reimbursable cash grant for both local- and foreign-owned entities. The investment grant can be as high as 30% of the value of qualifying investment costs in machinery, equipment, commercial vehicles, land and buildings, required for establishing a new production facility; expanding an existing production facility; or upgrading production capability in an existing clothing and textile production facility.

g) Support Programme for Industrial Innovation (SPII)

The SPII is a programme intended to promote technology development in South Africa, by providing financial assistance of up to R5 million for the development of innovative products and / or processes. SPII is focussed specifically on the development phase, which begins at the conclusion of basic research and ends at the point when a pre-production prototype has been produced. To meet the qualifying criteria, the applicant must be able to show that the development will represent significant advance in technology and subsequent production must take place within South Africa.

h) Strategic Partnership Programme (SPP)

The SPP is a programme to support Broad-Based Black Economic Empowerment (B-BBEE) policy through encouraging businesses to strengthen the element of Enter and Supplier Development (ESD) of the Codes of Good Practice by encouraging partnership between large private sector enterprises and Government to support and develop Small and Medium-sized enterprise within the partner's supply chain or sector to be manufacturers of goods and suppliers of services in a sustainable manner. SPP works like a cost-sharing basis between Government and the strategic partner(s) for infrastructure and business development services with grant approval capped at a maximum of R15 million per financial year over a three year period. It also offers a cost-sharing support of 50 : 50 towards manufacturing projects and 70 : 30 for projects that support manufacturing supply chain related services.

c. Special Economic Areas

The Special Economic Zones Act, 2014 ("SEZA") deals with the overall framework regulating special economic zones in the country. Currently, there are five operating special economic zones across the country, namely Coega IDZ (Nelson Mandela Bay Metropolitan Municipality), Richards Bay IDZ (Richards Bay), East London IDZ (East London), Saldanha Bay IDZ (Saldanha Bay), and Dube TradePort (Durban). There are also additional special economic zone application pending before the Minister responsible for trade and industry. The regulatory body responsible for the regulation, monitoring and implementing special economic zone policies and strategies in South Africa is the Special Economic Zones Advisory Board ("SEZAB"). The SEZAB has prescribed powers and responsibilities in terms of SEZA.

The incentives in operating a business within a designated special economic zone are determined by the rules of each special economic zone and will not be standard across the country. The main reason for this is that each special economic zone has the obligation to promote specific economic activities and types of industry within their respective local government. The incentives would therefore target those entrants placed in the industries which the local government seeks to promote. All rules of any special economic zone would have to be compliant with the values and framework as set by PIA.

III. Trade

A. Department Regulating and Supervising Trade

The Department of Trade and Industry ("DTI"), together with a group of specialised, regulatory and financial development agencies and institutions (known as the Council of Trade and Industry Institutions) work close together to regulate, supervise and promote trade, so as to increase the levels of foreign direct investment into the country, expand market access opportunities for the exportation of South African goods and services; and contribute towards building skills, technology and infrastructure platforms in the economy from which enterprises can benefit. A few examples of the regulatory institutions include, but are not limited to: the CIPC, Companies Tribunal, National Consumer Tribunal, National Credit Regulator, National Gambling Board, National Lotteries Commission, National Consumer Commission and the institutions that are responsible for standardization, quality assurance and accreditation include, but are not limited to: National Regulator for Compulsory Specifications, South African National Accreditation System, South African Bureau of Standards and National Metrology Institute of South Africa.

The International Trade Administration Commission of South Africa ("ITAC") was established in terms of the International Trade Administration Act, 2002 (the "ITA Act"). The core functions of ITAC are: customs tariff investigations, trade remedies and import and export control.

B. Brief Introduction of Trade Laws and Regulations

The object of the ITA Act is to foster economic growth and development in order to raise incomes and promote investment and employment in South Africa and within the Common Customs Union Area by establishing an efficient and effective system for the administration of international trade subject to the ITA Act and the Southern African Customs Union Agreement. The Minister may by notice in the Gazette and in accordance with procedures and requirements established by the Constitution or any other relevant law, issue Trade Policy Statements or Directives.

C. Trade Management

One of DTI's objectives is to advance trade and investment relations. It achieves this by encouraging exports and establishing collaborative agreements with existing trading partners and dynamic fast-growing emerging markets. The South African government also established the Special Economic Zones ("SEZs") programme to attract Foreign Direct Investment and export value-added commodities. SEZs are geographically designated areas of a country set aside for specifically targeted economic activities, supported through special arrangements (that may include laws) and systems that are often different from those that apply in the rest of the country. SEZs may be sector-specific or multi-product as defined in the Special Economic Zone Act No. 16 of 2014. A number of incentives are available to ensure SEZs growth, revenue generation, creation of jobs, attraction of Foreign Direct Investment and international competitiveness.

D. Customs Management

a. Customs Legislation

The Customs and Excise Act, 1964 came into effect on 1 January 1965 ("Customs and Excise Act"), and both customs and excise matters are provided for in the same legislation. The legal and policy framework within which customs duty amendments are made include: (i) the ITA Act, the Tariff Investigations Regulations, and International Trade Agreements, Bilateral, Multilateral and Regional Agreements. The Customs Control Act, 2014, Customs Duty Act, 2014, and the Customs and Excise Amendment Act, 2014, were published in the government gazettes in July 2014, and these Acts will only come into effect on a date yet to be determined by the President.

b. Customs Office

There are currently 37 customs offices in South Africa, including sea, land and air ports, as well as four centralised processing centres, with officers involved in a number of activities aimed at: facilitating legitimate trade and travel while ensuring compliance; controlling and accounting for all imports and exports; collecting all revenue due to the State; administering specific industry schemes, trade measures, international protocols and other international obligations; eradicating smuggling and other transgressions through enforcement action; and enforcing controls on the importation and exportation of prohibited and restricted goods on behalf of other authorities administering such laws.

c. Imports

Goods may arrive in South Africa in various modes of transport: air, sea, road, rail or post. The importer must declare to customs what they have brought into South Africa, the mode of transport used and be in possession of import licences for certain (and restricted) items, and failure to produce the necessary permit could result in the imposition of penalties. The permit is only valid in respect of the goods of the class and country specified. Import permits required for specific categories of restricted goods are obtainable from the Director of Import and Export Control at the Department of Trade and Industry. These categories have been reduced, but still must be obtained for most used / second-hand items.

d. Exports

The control of goods leaving South Africa is considered one of the core functions of customs, as key economic decisions are based on trade statistics and it is therefore imperative that SARS accurately records export performance. The export declaration is processed by customs and kept for record and trade statistics purposes and any other documents (about the goods exported, including the transport documents) should be produced if required by customs. Current legislation and policy requires specific documents to be endorsed, which could entail the completion of required fields on a form such as findings of an examination, date stamping and signing. Special permits / licences / certificates may also be required, and customs officers will peruse all export documents in order to ensure compliance with the various laws, regulations and rules. It must be noted that certain goods will require an export permit, which must be produced at the time of clearance. Application for export permits must be made to the ITAC and in certain instances, the applications require support documentation from other departments, depending on the product in question.

IV. Labour

A. Brief Introduction of Labour Laws and Regulations

The main laws governing the employment relationship in South Africa are the (i) Labour Relations Act, 1995 ("LRA") which governs protections for employees against unfair dismissal and unfair labour practices in employment, and regulates the resolution of disputes between employers and employees, as well as strikes, lockouts and the relationship between employers and trade unions; (ii) Basic Conditions of Employment Act, 1997 ("BCEA") which sets minimum conditions of employment for employees, with a few exclusions such as unpaid volunteers working for a charity. These minimum terms and conditions apply to any contract of employment unless either a more favourable term has been negotiated or is provided for in another law; or a term has been excluded under the BCEA's variation or exemption provisions.

Minimum terms and conditions for specific sectors or industries are often regulated separately, either through bargaining councils set up for specific industries (if agreements are negotiated between representative employers and unions) and sectoral determinations (sector-specific rules) published by the Minister for Labour (usually after consultation with all interested parties).

South African employment laws are mandatory for any employees that fall within their jurisdiction. Therefore, they apply to foreign nationals working in South Africa. This is the case even if the foreign nationals are working here illegally. South African employment laws generally do not apply to nationals working abroad. However, they may apply to a South African national who works abroad temporarily on secondment, especially if the employment contract provides for this.

It is possible to restrict an employee's activities during employment and after the employment relationship is terminated. This is done by agreement, in either the employment contract; or a separate restraint of trade agreement. Employees can be restricted from working for a competitor within a reasonable period and geographical area after their contracts are terminated, if they have been exposed to trade secrets and confidential information or they hold valuable client relationships over which the employer has a proprietary interest. These agreements are valid. However, when the employer seeks to enforce restraint provisions, the courts retain a discretion as to whether or not to enforce the restraints and they will not enforce them if, in a particular case, such enforcement would be contrary to the public interest or unreasonable. The onus is on the employee to show that an agreement is unreasonable and should not be enforced.

B. Requirements of Employing Foreign Employees

a. Work Permit and Application Procedure

A foreign national is obliged to obtain a work permit by applying in the prescribed manner to the South African consular office in the foreign national's country of origin or ordinary residence. In exceptional cases, where it is necessary to apply within South Africa, a foreign national is obliged to personally submit any application for a work permit via visa facilitation services. Applications must henceforth be submitted to these offices rather than to the offices of home affairs. Good cause must be shown for the application being brought locally.

A foreign national is not permitted to hold more than one permit at a time. A company may employ an unlimited number of foreign nationals who all hold different categories of work permit, provided that each foreign employee holds the appropriate work permit. One of the requirements of a work permit includes a motivation from the company regarding the reasons for employing a foreign national rather than a South African citizen or permanent resident.

There are various categories of work permits provided for in the Immigration Act, 2002 (the "Immigration Act").

A section 11(2) visitor's visa / permit is considered as a one-off, non-renewable visa / permit that addresses an immediate short-term or urgent need for a limited duration of work activity that cannot be met by an application for a work permit. Those foreign nationals who are "visa exempt" (which includes Australian, Canadian, European, United Kingdom and United States nationals) are permitted to obtain a visitor's visa with permission to conduct work by applying in person at their closest consular offices, at least a week prior to the foreign national's departure, to confirm why the foreign national cannot apply for a work permit and the reasons why the limited duration work is necessary and urgent.

Another category is a general work permit in terms of section 19(2) of the Immigration Act. The process is cumbersome, but the greatest advantage of a general work permit is that it can be issued for up to five years. The new regulations amplify the role of the Department of Labour in the approval process. The Department of Labour is charged with issuing a certificate that confirms that:

• despite a diligent search the employer has been unable to find a South African citizen or permanent resident with qualifications and skills or experience equivalent to those of the applicant;

• the applicant has qualifications or proven skills and experience in line with the job offer;

• the salary is not inferior, the contract of employment is in line with labour standards; and

• that the contract of employment is in line with labour standards and is conditional upon approval of the visa.

The role of the Department of Labour (which has historically been to certify that the remuneration, as well as the terms and conditions of employment offered to the foreign national, are equal to those offered to South Africans occupying similar positions) has been extensively extended.

Although there is no prescribed list of documents that must be submitted to the Department of Labour for it to base its findings on, the Department of Labour has indicated that it is tasked with satisfying itself that a due and diligent search of the labour market has been made to ensure that South Africans who can fill the identified expat roles have been given due opportunity before the role is filled by an expat, in order to recommend approval of an application and that, in conducting its evaluation of the company's efforts to employ South Africans in the role, it will have regard, inter alia, to the following:

• advertising of the relevant positions in the form of newspaper print advertisements and other methods of advertising and recruitment such as online advertisements, etc. (the new regulations do not prescribe advertisement of the position but it appears that the Department of Labour will still insist on advertising in the national print media in order to satisfy itself that a proper labour market test has been performed);

• a private employment agency report as written evidence of the labour search from a private recruitment agency;

• to the extent that South African candidates may have been interviewed for the roles concerned, interview notes indicating the rationale for appointment of the foreign national or the reasons for locals not being appointed; and

• finally, the Department of Labour has also indicated that it wants all opportunities to be registered with the local labour centre on the employment services database, and, depending on the applications received, a detailed account of the recruitment process that ensued.

An intra-company transfer work permit may be issued to a foreign national who is employed abroad by a business operating in the Republic in a branch, subsidiary or affiliate relationship, and who by reason of his or her employment is required to work in the Republic. The maximum of validity of an intra-company transfer work visa was increased to four years and is not renewable. The requirements for the intra-company work permit are the simplest and easiest to obtain.

A company wishing to employ a number of foreign workers may also apply for a corporate permit in terms of section 21 of the Immigration Act. Corporate permits are suited to corporate applicants who intend to employ a number of foreign nationals in specific positions. The regulations also propose that in order to qualify for a corporate permit, a company must demonstrate that at least 60% of its employees are South African. The corporate permit can be issued for a maximum of three years. Workers cannot renew or apply for a change of status in South Africa.

The critical skills work visa category will be issued to foreign nationals who meet the minimum qualifications and experience listed on the critical skills list, which has yet to be published. Applicants must submit, inter alia, written confirmation from the accredited professional body, board or council of the skills, qualifications and post-qualification work experience, proof of application for professional registration if required in law and evaluation by the South African Qualifications Authority. The critical skills permit can be granted for a period not exceeding five years.

b. Unemployment Insurance Fund

Both the employer and the employee must make monthly contributions to the unemployment insurance fund, which provides unemployment benefits to individuals. The employer and employee must each contribute 1% of the employee's remuneration (that is, a total contribution of 2%). Remuneration for this purpose is limited to a maximum of ZAR14,872 a month. These contributions are not required in relation to foreign employees who will be repatriated from South Africa at the completion of their South African assignment.

C. Trade Union and Labour Organizations

Section 23 of the Constitution protects the rights of employees to form and join a trade union and to participate in the lawful activities and programmes of such a trade union. Section 23 also protects the rights of employers to form and join employer's organisations and to participate in the lawful activities and programmes of an employer's organisation. The Constitution also places particular importance on the protection of freedom of association. The LRA further emphasises, protects and gives concrete content to these fundamental rights.

Sections 4 and 5 of the LRA seek to protect employees' rights to freedom of association. The protections afforded to employees in terms of these sections are effective not only against employers but against anyone who may infringe such rights. As such, every employee has, inter alia, the right to participate in forming a trade union or trade union federation and to join a union subject to its constitution. Furthermore, union members have the right, subject to their union's constitution, to participate in its lawful activities, including the election of office bearers, officials and union representatives, standing for election as office bearers, officials or union representatives and, if so elected or appointed, holding office and carrying out the functions of that position. Similarly, members of unions belonging to a federation of unions have the right, subject to the constitution of that federation, to participate in activities and elections and to stand for elections and hold office.

Sections 6 and 7 of the LRA protect employers' rights to freedom of association similar to those granted to employees as abovementioned.

Trade unions and employer's organisations have certain rights in terms of section 8 of the LRA. These rights include, inter alia, the right to determine their own constitutions and rules and to hold elections for office bearers, officials and representatives. Trade unions and employer's organisations also have the right to plan and organise their own administration and lawful activities, to participate in forming federations or to join a federation of trade unions or federations of employers' organisations.

Organisational rights are also important in making it possible for a trade union to establish a collective bargaining relationship with an employer or an employer's organisation. In order to be able to effectively bargain with the employer, the trade unions needs members. To recruit members and to represent their interests, a trade union needs to have access to the employer's premises to keep in contact with the members. The union may also want the employer to deduct trade union subscriptions directly from the remuneration paid to employees, and it may want to nominate and elect certain employees to represent union interests in the workplace. As such, organisational rights assist a union in building up a presence in the workplace and thereby laying the foundation of a collective bargaining relationship with the employer.

It is in this regard, it is important to emphasise that only a registered trade union can exercise organisational rights in terms of the LRA. The LRA does not compel trade unions and employer's organisations to register, but it encourages these coalitions to do so. It does this by granting most of the rights set out in the LRA only to registered unions. As such, only registered trade unions may exercise organisational rights, conclude collective agreements as defined in the LRA, apply for the establishment of a bargaining council or a statutory council, apply for the establishment of a workplace forum, authorise a picket by their members and represent members at the Commission for Conciliation, Mediation and Arbitration ("CCMA") proceedings. Registration is not, however, a prerequisite for protected strike action.

D. Labour Disputes

All labour disputes are first conciliated by the CCMA or relevant bargaining council in an attempt to settle the dispute.

Unresolved disputes are determined either by the relevant bargaining council, CCMA or the Labour Court depending on the nature of the dispute. Disputes regarding dismissals for incapacity, misconduct, unfair labour practices, constructive dismissal and single retrenchments are arbitrated by the relevant bargaining council or the CCMA.

Other retrenchments, discrimination disputes and strike disputes are adjudicated by the Labour Court.

Employees have a right under the Constitution not to be unfairly dismissed, which is incorporated into the LRA. An employer can only dismiss for a fair reason related to the employee's conduct or capacity or the employer's operational requirements.

The employer has the burden of proving that a dismissal was for a fair reason. All alleged unfair dismissal disputes must be referred to the CCMA (unless there is a bargaining council with jurisdiction) for conciliation. If unresolved, the CCMA arbitrates disputes relating to conduct or capacity, and the Labour Court adjudicates dismissals for operational reasons (unless only one employee was made redundant, in which case this employee can elect to have the dispute arbitrated by the CCMA).

The remedies against unfair dismissal are: reinstatement, re-employment or compensation up to a maximum of 12-months' pay (or 24-months' pay if the dismissal was automatically unfair as defined in the LRA). If the unfairness relates only to procedure, the remedy is limited to compensation.

V. Intellectual Property

A. Brief Introduction of IP Laws

The Trade Marks Act, 1993 ("Trade Marks Act") and the common law, which is derived from the general principles of the Roman-Dutch law, together form the basis of the law relating to trade marks in South Africa. The common law recognises a general delict of unlawful competition, which has a variety of forms, one being the delict of passing-off. The Trade Marks Act has not changed the common law, in fact, in some instances it recognises and confirms those principles.

Licensing of all types of intellectual property is permitted in South Africa and is regulated either by statute or by the common law. Intellectual property may be licensed on an exclusive, sole or non-exclusive basis. In certain instances, such as in the case of copyright, in order to be valid, an exclusive licence must be in writing and signed by, or on behalf of, the licensor.

South African patent law is largely based on the United Kingdom Patents Act and the Court of the Commissioner of Patents often relies on British case law in making decisions. In terms of the South African Patents Act, 1978, patent protection may be obtained for inventions which are new and non-obvious, and which are capable of use in the fields of trade, industry or agriculture. The concept of "international novelty" is applied meaning that, in order to be patentable in South Africa, the invention forming the subject matter of the patent application cannot have been put into the public domain, by use or description, or have been otherwise known, anywhere in the world, prior to the application date of the patent.

The Designs Act, 1993 introduced a modern and innovative type of intellectual property protection in South Africa. While a patent protects a new invention and how it is made or functions, a registered design protects the novel appearance of an article. Registered designs afford protection specifically for the shape and appearance of an industrial article, as represented in drawings or photographs.

Know-how and trade secrets relate to confidential information of a technical or business nature and enjoy protection under the common law. This category of intellectual property can include any unpatented, secret information necessary to develop or commercially exploit products, and extends to ideas, concepts, methods, processes, recipes, techniques, inventions, discoveries, data, formulae or specifications. The key to protection lies in maintaining the confidentiality of the information. If the information is disclosed or falls into the public domain, legal protection will be lost. It is therefore advisable to adhere to strict protocols to ensure that the information remains confidential, for instance, by marking documents as being "confidential" and ensuring that any persons given access to confidential documents sign a stringent non-disclosure agreement.

In instances where foreign-owned intellectual property is licensed to a South African entity or person in return for payment of a royalty, such an arrangement would be subject to prior approval by the SARB in terms of South African exchange control regulations.

B. Patent Application

South Africa is a member of the Paris Convention and is also a signatory to the Patent Cooperation Treaty, which means that the South African Patent Office is fully integrated into conventional international patent registration systems and procedures. South African patents can therefore be used as a basis for extending protection to other territories, and, similarly, foreign patents can be extended to South Africa.

South Africa is a non-examining country which means that no investigation is carried out into the validity or patentability of the invention described in the patent specification of a patent application. Examination is to formalities only. Acceptance of the application takes place six to eight months after filing and must be advertised in the Patent Journal. The certificate of registration will be issued thereafter but the publication date is regarded as the grant date of the patent. It is not possible to oppose a patent application, but applications can be made to revoke granted patents.

A granted patent gives the patentee the right to prevent others from making, using, exercising or disposing of, or offering to dispose of, or importing the invention, in South Africa. Patent protection endures for twenty years from the date of lodging the complete specification in South Africa, provided that the requisite renewals are paid annually after the third anniversary. It is not possible to obtain an extension of the twenty-year period.

C. Trademark Registration

The Trade Marks Act defines a "mark" as any sign capable of being represented graphically, including a device, name, signature, word, letter, numeral, shape, configuration, pattern, ornamentation, colour or container for goods or any combination of these. In order to be protectable as a trade mark, such a sign or mark has to be distinctive of the goods or services in relation to which it is used, or proposed to be used. Marks that are not capable of so distinguishing; marks that are commonly used in the relevant trade or which are descriptive or generic, are not registrable as trade marks or, if registered, are liable to be removed from the register.

South Africa follows the Nice Classification of Goods and Services in terms of which goods and services are classified into 45 different classes. There are 34 goods classes and eleven service classes. There is currently no provision in South African law for filing multi-class trade mark applications, therefore a trade mark must be registered separately in each class of interest.

South Africa is a signatory to the Paris Convention and it is therefore possible to claim priority for applications filed in South Africa, provided that they are filed within six months of the filing date of a prior application for the same trade mark in any other Convention country. In terms of the South African Trade Marks Act, a trade mark application may be opposed on the basis of a third party's prior use or registration of an identical or confusingly similar trade mark or on a number of other relative grounds, including that the trade mark sought to be registered is not distinctive.

Once registered, a trade mark may, at the instance of the proprietor, be renewed after ten years for further periods of ten years. It is not required to adduce evidence of use in order to renew a trade mark registration in South Africa.

D. Measures for IP Protection

Proprietors of registered trade marks are entitled to prevent the unauthorised use of the same or confusingly similar trade mark by third parties in respect of the same or similar goods or services or, if the trade mark is well-known, they are entitled to prevent the unauthorised use of a trade mark by a third party, where such use is likely to take unfair advantage of, or be detrimental to the distinctive character or repute of, the registered trade mark.

It is an infringement of a patent to make, use or dispose of the invention without authorisation. The claims are first interpreted to ascertain the exact scope of the invention and the alleged infringement is then investigated to determine whether it falls within that scope. Action for infringement may be brought by way of application or summons and is heard in the Court of the Commissioner of Patents. The defendant or respondent may argue that the activity complained of does not fall within the scope of the claims and may also include a counterclaim for revocation of the patent. A successful patentee can be awarded an interdict, damages and costs. It should be noted that infringement proceedings cannot be instituted until nine months after the sealing date of the patent, unless condonation is obtained.

VI. Environmental Protection

A. Department Supervising Environmental Protection

The authority with the primary responsibility for enforcing environmental legislation nationally is the Department of Environmental Affairs ("DEA"). The DEA is responsible at a national level for environmental authorisations and waste management licences where basic assessment or environmental impact assessment ("EIAs") must be undertaken. In issuing such authorisations, the DEA takes into consideration other specialist environmental departments' recommendations.

Another important regulator at a national level is the Department of Water Affairs and Sanitation ("DWS"). The DWS is responsible for issuing all licences relating to the use of water, which includes taking water from a water resource and the discharge of pollutants into South Africa's water resources.

The Department of Minerals Resources ("DMR") regulates the mining industry. The DMR's main function is to regulate matters concerning minerals and energy. Part of this function requires the DMR to regulate EIAs and environmental management plans in respect of new or existing the mining activities and is the relevant authority to approve environmental authorisations for mining activities in accordance with the transitional provisions provided for in the National Environmental Management Amendment Act, 2008, as read with the Mineral and. Petroleum Resources Development Amendment Act, 2008.

B. Brief Introduction of Laws and Regulations of Environmental Protection

The right to an environment that is not harmful to one's health or well-being is entrenched as a fundamental right in the Constitution and is supported by environmental legislation that aims to protect the environment while pursuing sustainable economic growth on terms applicable to a developing nation. The main statute is the National Environmental Management Act, 1998 ("NEMA"). This statute:

• provides for cooperative governance and decision-making in matters affecting the environment;
• is based on best international principles of sustainable development and integrated environmental management;
• contains various listed activities that require either a basic assessment or a full scoping and environmental impact assessment in order to obtain an environmental authorisation;
• grants wide powers to environmental management inspectors to enforce various environmental laws; and
• contains a general "duty of care" to the environment, which means that every person has the duty to avoid pollution and environmental degradation. Both civil parties and the government rely on this when enforcing environmental obligations.

The NEMA is, in addition, enabling in nature and specific environmental management acts have been enacted to regulate various sectors of the environment. For example, the:

• National Environmental Management Biodiversity Act;
• National Environmental Management Protected Areas Act;
• National Environmental Management Air Quality Act;

• National Environmental Management Waste Act.

Environmental rights and duties can also be enforced through South African common law, which is mainly based on Roman-Dutch law. However, some English law concepts have been imported into South African law such as, in an environmental context, the law of nuisance.

VII. Dispute Resolution

A. Judicial System and Court Hierarchy

The Constitution vests the judicial authority of South Africa in the courts. The rationalisation of the court structures in terms of the Constitution is a matter still before the legislature and it is to be noted that the structure to date still reflects to some extent that of the pre 1994 period. The court structure consists of three tiers of courts these are the apex courts, superior courts and inferior courts.

The apex courts are the Constitutional Court and the Supreme Court of Appeal. Both courts are courts of final appeal save that in the case of constitutional matters an appeal may be brought in the Constitutional Court against a ruling of the Supreme Court of Appeal.

The superior courts consist of the High Courts (provincial and local divisions) and other specialised courts such as tax courts, the Competition Appeal Court, Labour Court and Labour Appeal Court, land claims court, electoral court, divorce courts and equality courts (which in some instances are specially designated magistrates courts / inferior courts). Superior courts have both review and appellate jurisdiction in criminal and civil matters.

The inferior courts consist of regional and district magistrates' courts. District magistrates' courts have both civil and criminal jurisdiction while regional magistrates have only criminal jurisdiction. The civil jurisdiction of the district magistrates courts are constrained among other things by the value of the property or claim in dispute.

The decisions of all courts are binding on the parties including, where relevant, the government. It should be further be noted that the rule of stare decisis is applicable in South African law and accordingly courts of particular tiers will be bound by the legal reasoning or precedent of higher ranking courts.

B. Arbitration

As all courts in South Africa are courts of record and open to the public a litigant may prefer an alternative private adjudicative process that can be tailored to the client's specific needs, such as arbitration.

The primary legislation governing arbitrations in South Africa is the Arbitration Act, 1965. This Act governs both domestic and international arbitration proceedings although it is to be noted that the Recognition and Enforcement of Foreign Arbitral Awards Act, 1977 governs specifically the enforcement of foreign arbitral awards in South Africa.

Any matters save for criminal matters, matters of status and matrimonial matters may be referred to arbitration by agreement between the parties concerned.

Parties wishing to refer a matter to arbitration will enter into an arbitration agreement governing the terms and basis on which the arbitration will proceed and conclude. The parties may elect or have an arbitrator chosen on their behalf. An arbitrator is an independent impartial adjudicator with the relevant expertise who will oversee the process of the arbitration and ultimately issue an award in favour of one of the parties.

An arbitration award is considered binding not by any special authority of the arbitrator but rather by the agreement of the parties to submit to binding arbitration.

Organisations such as the Arbitration Foundation of Southern Africa may be approached to administer an arbitration and assist with the appointment of an appropriate arbitrator as well as provide rules in terms of which the arbitration process will be run.

It is to be noted that arbitrations do not serve to completely exclude the jurisdiction of the courts. Notwithstanding the submission of a dispute to arbitration, courts may be approached for interim interdicts and the enforcement of an arbitral award.

VIII. Others

A. Anti-commercial Bribery

a. Brief Introduction of Anti-commercial Bribery Laws and Regulations

South Africa is party to a number of international agreements and conventions aimed at combating corruption.

An example of these is the Southern African Development Community Protocol against Corruption. Arising from these various protocols and conventions, South Africa has obligations to take various steps to stamp out corruption. In line with these obligations, South Africa has passed various pieces of anti-corruption legislation. The main anti-corruption law is the Prevention and Combating of Corrupt Activities Act, 2004 ("PRECCA"). It introduced, inter alia, a duty to report corrupt transactions and the creation of a register for tender defaulters.

PRECCA creates a general offence of corruption that is extremely broadly defined. It also criminalises certain specified corrupt activities. The Act applies to both the public and private sector (unlike the USA Foreign Corrupt Practices Act).

Generally speaking, a person is guilty of an offence in terms of PRECCA if he or she directly or indirectly accepts or offers to accept a gratification (as defined) from another person, or gives or agrees to give a gratification to any other person to his or her benefit, or that of another. The giving or acceptance must be done in order to induce the other party to act in an improper manner, in the performance of that individual's duties.

PRECCA does not differentiate between corruption involving public entities or government officials and corruption involving private individuals or entities. PRECCA's penalties apply to both public and private corruption.

b. Department Supervising Anti-commercial Bribery

As far as enforcement is concerned, the South African Police Service is the primary law enforcement body in South Africa. It is the first port of call for anybody wishing to report a suspected act of corruption, or indeed any other crime.

The National Prosecuting Authority (NPA) has a specialised commercial crimes unit, with specialised commercial crime prosecutors and specialised commercial crime courts. In 2010, the National Director of Public Prosecutions issued a directive prioritising the prosecution of corruption. The NPA is South Africa's centralised prosecuting authority, and has the power to initiate criminal proceedings on behalf of the State.

c. Punitive Actions

In general, if one is convicted of the offence of corruption the following courts can impose the following sentences:
- the High Court can sentence a person (including a company's directors) convicted of corruption to a fine or to imprisonment up to a period of imprisonment for life;
- the regional court can sentence a person (including a company's directors) convicted of corruption to a fine or to imprisonment for a period not exceeding 18 years;
- the magistrates court can sentence a person (including a company's directors) convicted of corruption to a fine or to imprisonment for a period not exceeding five years.

Traditionally, South African courts have viewed convictions for fraud and corruption as serious, and sentences of 15 years or more are not uncommon.

B. Project Contracting

a. Permission System

The relevance of any government department to a project is largely dependent on the nature of the project in question. Government departments that are common role players in the project finance industry include the following (to name a few):
- the Department of Water Affairs and Sanitation;
- the Department of Energy;
- the Department of Trade and Industry;
- the Department of Environmental Affairs;
- the Department of Finance;
- the Department of Transport;
- the Department of Mineral Resources; and
- the Department of Agriculture, Forestry and Fisheries.

Within the above-mentioned government departments, there may be additional bodies that have been established to act as functionaries and regulators within the specific sector and from which approvals or other participation may be required.

b. Prohibited Areas

South Africa seeks to create an attractive climate for investment and has continued to develop the regulatory framework that is broadly favourable to an investor. Generally speaking, there are no restrictions on a foreign company having ownership in a South African project company. However, the requirements of a specific project or tender under which the project company will operate (as the case may be), may place certain foreign ownership restrictions on the project company and require that the project company is held, to some extent, by South African citizens.

Important to mention in this regard, is the government's Broad-Based Black Economic Empowerment ("B-BBEE") Policy. The B-BBEE Policy is consistent with section 217(2) of the Constitution (which permits the allocation of preferences for historically disadvantaged persons in the public procurement context) and is defined in the Broad-Based Black Economic Empowerment Act, 2003, as 'the empowerment of all black people including women, workers, youth, people with disabilities and people living in rural areas through diverse but integrated socio-economic strategies […]'. The importance of this is that the participation of B-BBEE companies in South African project companies is often a requirement.

C. Public-Private Partnership

a. Brief Introduction of Public-Private Partnership Laws and Regulations

In South Africa there is no single act dealing specifically with public-private partnerships, however there is a vast array of legislation and regulations, on both a municipal and national level, that may be relevant to public-private partnership (PPP) transactions, depending on the nature of the transaction, the parties and the specific industry or sector for which the PPP is planned.

Notwithstanding the above, the Public Finance Management Act No. 1 of 1999 (PFMA) and National Treasury Regulation 16 require special mention. The PFMA's purpose is to regulate financial management in the national government and provincial governments; to ensure that all revenue, expenditure, assets and liabilities of those governments are managed efficiently and effectively; to provide for the responsibilities of persons entrusted with financial management in those governments; and to provide for matters connected therewith. The PFMA sets out clear requirements in respect of PPP transactions in terms of, inter alia, procurement procedures and restrictions in respect of borrowing monies by certain government entities.

National Treasury Regulation 16 deals specifically and in detail with various aspects of public-private partnerships and pertinent aspects related thereto, including but not limited to, obtaining Treasury approval, feasibility studies (to determine whether the PPP is in the best interests of the institution), approval of procurement documentation before its issuance to any prospective bidders, the management and amendment of PPP agreements.

b. Limitations on Public Entity

In terms of section 66(1) of the PFMA, a public entity may not borrow money or issue a guarantee, indemnity or security, or enter into any other transaction that binds or may bind that institution to any future financial commitment unless such borrowing, guarantee, indemnity, security or other transaction is authorised by the PFMA and by other legislation not in conflict with the PFMA. In terms of section 66(3), the PFMA authorises the sponsor to borrow money or issue a guarantee, indemnity or security, or enter into any other transaction that binds or may bind the sponsor to any future financial commitment through its accounting authority, which in sponsor's case is the board of directors.

Section 54 of the PFMA obliges a public entity that plans to enter into any of the following transactions to notify the National Treasury in advance and to seek the written approval of the relevant minister for such a transaction as:

- establishment or participation in the establishment of a company;
- participation in a significant partnership, trust, unincorporated joint venture or similar arrangement;
- acquisition or disposal of a significant shareholding in a company;
- acquisition or disposal of a significant asset;
- commencement or cessation of a significant business activity; and
- a significant change in the nature or extent of its interest in a significant partnership, trust, unincorporated joint venture or similar arrangement.

D. Consumer Protection

The Consumer Protection Act 68 of 2009 (CPA) applies to the promotion of goods and services that could lead to certain transactions, as well as to most transactions occurring within South Africa for the supply of goods and services concluded in the ordinary course of business between suppliers and consumers, and to the goods and services themselves once the transaction has been concluded. Importantly, the CPA provides significant protections to franchisees under franchise agreements.

The CPA applies:
- where goods and services are promoted or supplied to the State;
- where a consumer is a juristic person whose asset value or annual turnover, at the time of transaction, equals or exceeds a threshold value determined by the Minister (currently R2 million);
- to credit agreements under the National Credit Act 34 of 2005 (NCA), but goods and services provided under the agreement are not excluded from the ambit of the CPA;
- to employment contracts;
- to collective bargaining and collective agreements as defined in the Labour Relations Act 66 of 1995 and the Constitution; and
- if the transaction falls within an industry-wide exemption granted by the Minister on application by the relevant regulatory authority.

The CPA is centred around eight consumer rights. These rights are the right to: equal access to the consumer market; privacy; choice; disclosure and information; fair and responsible marketing; honest and fair dealing; fair, just and reasonable terms and conditions; fair value, good quality and safety. The CPA seeks to improve disclosure by, inter alia, giving consumers the right to information in plain, easily understandable language; requiring the compulsory display of prices and the provision of transaction records.

The CPA promotes fair and responsible advertising and marketing and prohibits bait and negative option marketing. It regulates promotions, competitions and loyalty programmes. In terms of the CPA, advertising must not be false or misleading and suppliers may not enter into agreements with persons who lack legal capacity. Furthermore, the CPA regulates the use of business names. A supplier must not carry on business, advertise, promote, or supply any goods or services under any name not registered in terms of a public regulation.

A failure to comply with the provisions of the CPA attracts various sanctions, commencing with compliance notices and leading to the imposition of fines and criminal penalties. Contractual provisions in contravention of the CPA may be declared null and void to the extent of non-compliance.

E. Information Technology Law

The information technology ("IT") sector is not heavily regulated in South Africa. However, there are legislative enactments in force that regulate elements of IT such as e-commerce, privacy and data protection and access to information. Information over the internet is not generally regulated by statute, except in relation to specific areas such as online gambling and child pornography. Common law protections exist in relation to defamatory material that is published online.

a. E-commerce

E-commerce in South Africa is governed by the Electronic Communications and Transactions Act, 2002 (the "ECTA"). The ECTA is based largely on the UNCITRAL model law, and regulates electronic transactions, digital signatures, authentication and cryptography, privacy and data protection, consumer protection in the online environment, and the liability of infrastructure and connectivity providers for third party content that is transmitted over their systems.

b. Privacy and Data Protection

The right to privacy is protected in the Constitution, which binds the state, natural and juristic persons. However, there is currently no specific privacy or data protection legislation in force in South Africa, and the courts rely on the established common law rights of every person to physical integrity, freedom, reputation, dignity and privacy to deal with privacy law related issues.

The ECTA sets out basic guidelines for the protection of personal information obtained through electronic transactions. Data controllers may subscribe to these guidelines voluntarily, however, if they do, then they must adhere to all the data privacy stipulations in the ECTA. The ECTA guidelines include the requirement for data controllers to obtain the express written permission of the data subject for the collection, collation, processing or disclosure of the data subject's personal information.

c. Access to Information

The Promotion of Access to Information Act 2 of 2000 (PAIA) gives effect to the constitutionally enshrined right of access to information. The PAIA allows for access to records held by public bodies and information held by the private sector which is required for the exercise or protection of rights.

All public bodies (such as departments of state and government administrations in the national, provincial and local arms of government) must supply copies of records that have been requested by the public, generally within thirty days of receiving the request, unless the proper procedure has not been followed or a statutory ground of refusal exists. Access to the following records of a public body can be refused under the PAIA:

- personal information about third parties;
- certain records of the South African Revenue Service;
- commercial and confidential information of third parties;
- information endangering the physical safety of individuals;
- legally privileged records;
- records relating to the defence, security, international relations, economy and financial welfare of South Africa;
- the research information of third parties;
- records relating to the operations of public bodies; and
- frivolous or vexatious requests for information.

In spite of these prohibitions, a record must be disclosed if (i) it reveals evidence of a substantial contravention of any law or an imminent and serious public safety or environmental risk and (ii) the public interest outweighs the harm caused by the disclosure.

A private body is only required to disclose copies of its records to the public on request if that record is required for the exercise or protection of any right, the procedural requirements set out in the PAIA are met and no statutory grounds of refusal exist. The grounds of refusal for private bodies are similar to those for public bodies. Again, the grounds of refusal can be overridden if the public interest outweighs the harm caused by the disclosure.

All public and private bodies are required to produce a manual detailing the subjects and categories of records that are held by that body. Under the PAIA, It is a criminal offence not to do this.

F. Mining and Mineral Law

Through the Minister (the "Minister") of the Department of Mineral Resources (the "DMR"), the state, as custodian of all mineral rights, may on application grant, issue and refuse inter alia, reconnaissance permits, prospecting and mining rights. Applications for titles are made in the manner and form prescribed by the Mineral and Petroleum Resources Development Act No. 28 of 2002 (MPRDA).

The regional managers of the DMR, based in the respective provinces of the country, receive and process applications for reconnaissance permits, prospecting and mining rights. These applications are processed on a first-come first-served basis, in that the Minister is obliged to grant a prospecting or mining right to the party that submitted its application first, provided they comply with all the requirements including the provisions of the Mining Charter.The Minister is empowered to refuse the granting of a prospecting and / or mining right if, in the discretion of the Minister, the granting of such right will result in an exclusionary act, prevent fair competition or result in the concentration of the mineral resources under the control of such applicant.

The holder of prospecting rights has an exclusive right to apply and to be granted the renewal of a prospecting right and the right to apply for and to be granted a mining right for the mineral and area in respect of which he holds a prospecting right. Similarly, the holder of a mining right has an exclusive right to apply for and be granted the renewal of such mining right for the mineral and area in respect of which the initial mining right was granted.

Section 11 of the MPRDA, prohibits the transfer and encumbrance of prospecting and mining rights or an interest in any such right, or a controlling interest in a company or close corporation that holds such right without the written consent of the Minister. Change of controlling interest in a listed company is excluded from this requirement. A prospecting right is valid for the period prescribed in such right, which period may not exceed five years. A mining right is valid for the period specified in such right, which period may not exceed thirty years. The MPRDA provides for the renewal of prospecting and mining rights respectively, subject to certain terms and conditions.

东帝汶

作者：Rui Botica Santos、Paulo Oliveira
译者：谭伟华、杨振发

一、概述

（一）简介

东帝汶曾被称为东方帝汶岛，曾属于葡萄牙的海外殖民地，随后成为印度尼西亚的省。随着 2002 年《宪法》的颁布，东帝汶取得了独立主权实现了独立，成为东方国家中唯一的葡语国家。东帝汶是最年轻的东南亚国家之一，同时也是在 21 世纪内独立的第一个国家。

东帝汶与印度尼西亚接壤，南隔帝汶海与澳大利亚相望，包括帝汶岛东部和西部北海岸的欧库西地区以及附近的阿陶罗岛和东端的雅库岛。

由于本国政治动荡导致的冲突和不稳定，东帝汶的独立之路十分艰难。该国在 16 世纪首次被葡萄牙帝国殖民化。1975 年，东帝汶脱离了葡萄牙的殖民统治，并在同年独立后被印度尼西亚侵略和占领。1999 年，在联合国的支持下，东帝汶宣布脱离印度尼西亚取得独立。2002 年 5 月 20 日，在经过了由联合国牵头的临时行政管理时期之后，东帝汶成为 21 世纪的第一个新的独立主权国家。

独立后，东帝汶逐渐获得了安定、稳定的环境。在公共支出和大型石油天然气储备收入的推动下，2013 年东帝汶的国民收入取得显著增长，成为世界上国内生产总值（GDP）增长率排名第六的国家。

尽管如此，东帝汶在重建成为一个现代化国家的过程中，仍然经历了一段艰难而复杂的时期。由于政府面临着严峻的政治、经济和社会挑战，该国在发展中仅优先实现了一些短期事项。解决就业不足的问题，重建安全机构，加强公共部门的职能以及发展非石油经济都是东帝汶面临着的长期挑战。

东帝汶向外国投资者开放，且近年来政府进行了一系列结构性改革，旨在进一步开放经济和改善商业监管环境。

（二）基本数据

面积：14 874 平方公里
人口：1 291 358（2017 年）
国内生产总值（GDP）：83.64 亿美元（2014 年）
首都：帝力
官方语言：德顿语、葡萄牙语、16 种土著语言。印度尼西亚语和英语为商业语言。
气候：东帝汶高温多雨，无寒暑季节变化，有两个明显的季节，6 月到 10 月为旱季，11 月到 5 月为雨季，平均气温 30 摄氏度。
时区：东九区
货币：美元
主要民族：南岛人（马来-波利尼西亚人），巴布亚人和小部分华人
宗教：大部分人口信奉天主教，也包括小部分新教徒和逊尼派穆斯林群体
东帝汶划分为 13 个省，包括 65 个县、443 个乡和超过 2200 个村。省包括：

- 阿伊莱乌省（Aileu）
- 阿伊纳罗省（Ainaro）
- 包考省（Baucau）
- 博博纳罗省（Bobonaro）
- 科瓦利马省（Cova-Lima）

- 帝力省（Dili）
- 埃尔梅拉省（Ermera）
- 劳滕省（Lautém）
- 利基萨省（Liquiçá）
- 马纳图托省（Manatuto）
- 马努法伊省（Manufahi）
- 欧库西省（Oecussi）
- 维克克省（Viqueque）

（三）政治和法律制度

东帝汶民主共和国，简称东帝汶，是一个统一、法治、自由、平等、保障个人隐私和选举权的半总统制民主共和国。作为一个正在发展的年轻国家，东帝汶正在尽最大的努力建立有效的立法、行政和司法机构，起草法律、法规以及完善政府职能。①

东帝汶国民议会实行一院制，代表全体公民行使制定法律、监督政府和政治决策权。②议会议员由选民直接选举产生，每届任期5年。

在葡萄牙模式影响下的半总统制政体中，共和国总统是国家元首，总理是政府首脑，领导国民议会。

共和国总统由全民公投选出，任期5年，总统为国家象征，同时担任国家军队总司令，有权否决立法，任命国家总理，解散议会，并召开全国选举。

政府由总理、各部部长和国务秘书组成，各部部长和国务秘书由共和国总统根据总理的提议任命。政府负责执行国家政策，是全国最高行政机构。

东帝汶《宪法》规定，"总理人选应当由议会多数派的政党或政党联盟指定，并由共和国总统在与国民议会中的政党协商后任命"③。

代议制民主依靠政党得以实现。议会中的主要政党包括：
- 民主党，简称PD（Democratic Party）
- 革新阵线党（Frenti-Mudança）
- 东帝汶全国重建大会党，简称CNRT（National Congress for Timorese Reconstruction）
- 东帝汶独立革命阵线，简称革阵（Revolutionary Front of Independent East Timor）（FRETILIN）

东帝汶具有独立的司法体制，法院具有独立审判权，只服从于宪法和法律审理案件，不受其他行政机关的干涉。

关于法律，"东帝汶的司法制度以印度尼西亚的法律法规、联合国过渡行政当局通过的法案和独立后的东帝汶立法为基础。该国正在对其立法进行审查，以协调法律体系，但尚未对不同法律体系中相互重叠的法律进行整改。所有新颁布的立法都采用葡萄牙语，并以民法法系为基础"④。

（四）商业和经济环境

东帝汶拥有巨大的石油和天然气储量，其经济主要依靠石油和天然气产业。然而，能源并不是东帝汶国内唯一丰富的自然资源，其他产业发展也极具潜力，例如农业（即咖啡和檀香木）、矿产业、渔业、可再生能源业与旅游业。

尽管历史上及独立后的早期发展阶段的东帝汶动荡不安，但东帝汶现在的经济相对稳定自由。如上所述，东帝汶在"2011—2030年战略发展计划"之后颁布了一系列旨在进一步实现经济自由化和改善商业监管环境的结构性改革的政策。

东帝汶于2012年修改了《劳动法》，使得劳动合同制度更加规范，更大程度地保障劳动者的权益。

---

① https://www.state.gov/e/eb/rls/othr/ics/2017/eap/269858.htm。
② 东帝汶《宪法》第92条。
③ 东帝汶《宪法》第106.1条。
④ https://www.state.gov/e/eb/rls/othr/ics/2017/eap/269858.htm。

此外，国家在教育方面的投资、葡萄牙语的推广、社会保障方面的改革（包括培训及构建）做出应有的贡献。

一些措施的出台简化了行政程序，降低行政成本，减轻公民和企业的负担。东帝汶已将工作时间（天数）由 147 个工作日降低到 103 个工作日，成本从 5% 降至 4.5%，也降低了企业设立所需的最低注册资本。

《个人投资法》（2017 年第 15 号法律）是"政府努力促进私营部门经济吸引外国投资的一部分"。为确保"国家投资立法与东南亚国家联盟全面投资协定的规定相一致，促使东帝汶成为协定成员国"，该法律鼓励私人对国家进行投资，其中包括根据投资的性质和投资地而享有的 5 至 10 年的免税期。

政府也在投资新建基础设施和物流，即道路、港口和机场，以促进商业发展和吸引外国投资。

目前，东帝汶在 2018 年世界银行商业经商环境排名的 190 个国家中位列第 178 位。根据该排名，合同履行（190 位）、注册财产（187 位）、信贷（167 位）和破产处理（169 位）是东帝汶经济的瓶颈。

（五）经济统计

根据国际货币基金组织的统计数据，东帝汶的国内生产总值（GDP）为 62 亿美元（2017 年估值），人均国内生产总值（PPP）为 5 000 美元（2017 年估值）。按照行业划分，工业占总体国内生产总值的 57.8%，其次是服务业和农业，分别占 31.3% 和 9.4%（2017 年估值）。

关于贸易平衡，2016 年东帝汶出口总额 2 000 万美元，而进口总额为 5.586 亿美元（2016 年估值）。出口主要为石油、咖啡、檀香和大理石，进口主要为食品、汽油、煤油和机械。东帝汶的主要贸易伙伴是印度尼西亚、澳大利亚、中国、新加坡、马拉西亚、葡萄牙和德国。

2016 年，东帝汶的外国直接投资存量（FDI）为 3.46 亿美元。

该国劳动人口数量为 286 700 人（2016 年度），其中 64% 从事农业，10% 从事工业，26% 从事服务业（2010 年度）。失业率为 4.4%（2014 年度）。

2017 年预算收入总计 3 亿美元，支出 22 亿美元。税收和其他收入相当于 GDP 的 11%（2017 年度）。

2017 年，通货膨胀率为 1.3%，公共赤字（政府净贷款/借款占 GDP 的百分比）为-18%。

（六）石油和天然气

东帝汶只有一个油田，就财政收入而言，东帝汶每个月都在提炼价值约一亿美元的石油，这意味着每天大约三百到四百万美元。

东帝汶的主要油田是 Bayu-Undan，位于联合石油开发区（JPDA），这个区域跨越了东帝汶和澳大利亚之间的海上边界，两国共享石油资源。这个油田预计将成为 2025 年前国家的主要收入来源。另外一个油田 Kitan 包含约 3 450 万桶石油的储量。

2008 年，东帝汶政府成立了 ANP（国家石油管理局），为管理东帝汶专属管辖区和联合石油开发区（JPDA）的部门。

世界银行支持政府建立具有国际竞争力的石油体制。东帝汶宣布加入采掘业透明度行动计划，该计划的目的在于增加各国政府和企业在资源管理方面的责任。作为达到该计划标准的唯一一个第三世界国家，东帝汶为其他发展中国家设定了透明度和问责制的标准。

为了管理石油产业的收入，东帝汶政府创建了一个石油基金。根据《石油基金法》（2005 年第 9 号法律），所有有关石油产业的收入都必须存入该基金，该基金将用于投资国际金融市场，其收益为东帝汶全体公民享有。银行和支付管理局负责该基金的业务管理，根据计划和财政部长商定的投资授权进行。

财政部长代表政府负责石油基金的整体管理和投资战略。在履行上述职责时，东帝汶中央银行成立了石油基金管理部，该部门由执行主任领导，执行主任对省长负责，投资部门负责投资管理，风险管理部门负责绩效评估和风险监控。

从广义上说，石油基金是一个考虑了公民长期利益的有助于健全财政政策的工具。关于"花多少钱和存多少钱"都是由国家财政预算做出的，政府的所有优先事项都是互相权衡的。

(七)自然资源和经济潜力

正如所强调的那样,东帝汶政府一直致力于使经济活动多样化,减少本国对石油、天然气产业的依赖。以下是投资者可能感兴趣的一些事例。

1. 矿产

除石油和天然气外,东帝汶还拥有其他自然资源,如矿产(金属:金、锰、铜,非金属:沙石),这些资源的开采在能源和建筑业之间可能会有所不同。

在 Vemasse 和 Soibada 南部发现了铜矿和方铅矿。金矿分布于苏尔河、Lacló do Sul 和 Clerac 河以及 Faluberliu(Manufahi 区)。

锰是最常见的矿物之一,尽管过去在 Vemasse、Baucau、Baguia 和 Uatucarbau 的开采被认为没有足够的赢利。

煤矿分布在 Viqueque(Uatolari)和 Baucau(Baguia)地区。

关于具有建造潜力的矿产,帝力地区有丰富的闪长岩、大理石和片岩。帝力和马纳图托有粘土资源。

石灰岩主要分布在 Maubisse 地区,具有巨大潜力的热能源位于山区(Bobonaro、Ermera、Viqueque 和 Baucau 地区)。矿山和采石场的勘探和开采需要事先得到政府许可。

2. 可再生能源

东帝汶蕴含大量的水资源,降雨充沛,表明其具有地下蕴藏水资源和生物质的潜力。其他有潜力的待开发资源是风能、太阳能、波浪能和地热。

3. 渔业

东帝汶有着丰富的海洋资源,其自然条件有利于贝类、爬行动物、甲壳类动物、鱼类和哺乳动物的生长繁育。该地区金枪鱼的产量丰富,同时还包括鳄鱼、鱿鱼、鳕鱼、鲭鱼、鲨鱼、龙虾、蟹、牡蛎、海龟和红梭鱼,河里还有虾和鳗鱼。

4. 旅游业

由于国家的自然风光(从热带海滩、清澈的海水和丰富的海洋生物,到有温带气候的山区),都为旅游业提供了良好的机遇。此外,东帝汶在亚太地区享有优越的地理位置,经济发达的地区和新兴的动态经济体可能为东帝汶旅游业带来新的市场机遇。

根据国家旅游政策,东帝汶政府计划到 2030 年每年外国旅游业收入达到 1 亿 5 000 万美元(按 2016 的价格计算),不包括运输经营者的收入(机票费和轮渡费),以及每年有 200 000 名国际游客(平均逗留时间为 4 天)。

(八)基础设施

基础设施的发展是东帝汶政府战略发展计划中所述的一个重要优先事项,在政策政策框架中,基础设施的目标是在 2020 年完成高质量的国家基础设施。每年约 10 亿美元的公共收入将投入于基础设施建设。

1. 道路

主要的道路系统包括两条贯穿南北的重要公路以及五条连接上述两条重要公路的道路。

政府的首要任务是修复和修缮 90% 的现有道路,以提高其安全性并使其达到国际标准。

道路建设将从首都帝力周边地区开始,第二阶段将进入其他地区,以改善人们出行,增加货物流通率。

亚洲开发基金(ADF)支持路网升级项目,该项目将升级东帝汶最繁忙的两条道路及改善通往印度尼西亚的主要西路连接线。

2. 港口

东帝汶拥有建立海上运输网络的最佳条件,相较于其他竞争国家,东帝汶在石油勘探和地理位置上具有巨大的优势。

目前，只有帝力才有能力发送和接收大型货物集装箱，并且仅有一艘名为柏林纳克索马的用于将人们运送到阿塔罗岛和 Oé-cussi 的渡轮。但是，政府承认帝力港对于流通货物和人员增加而言还是太小了。

因此，根据 NSDP（国家战略发展计划）的未来实施情况，港口设施将迁移至蒂巴尔港，帝力港将仅用于旅游目的。蒂巴尔港也位于北部海岸，将部分天然气输送到国内。

3. 航空运输

目前东帝汶帝力国际机场的运营航空公司是仅有鸽航、胜安航空、汶航和巴达维亚航空。每天仅限于几班航班。该机场跑道从 1 850 米扩建到 2 500 米，并新建了一个航站楼计划将该机场变成一个具有国际标准的现代化机场，预计到 2020 年可容纳 100 万乘客。

政府将利用 PPP 模式选择一名私人开发商，签订为期 25 年的 BFO（建设—融资—经营）协议。该项目将通过石油基金资助。国际金融公司被政府选为交易顾问，该项目的第一阶段近期已启动。有三个用于国际航班的机场——包考（第二大城市），苏艾和乌库西，都只用于国内航班。

4. 电信网络

东帝汶电信提供有关所有固定电话和移动电话服务的独家系统。政府已宣布对电信进行公开招标，选定的公司包括来自拥有 6 100 万订户及拥有近 1.7 亿用户，越南公司 Viettel Global Investment JSC 及 PT Telekomunikasi Indonesia International（Telin）。

东帝汶准备发展电信产业，目的是引入竞争和降低费率，提高覆盖率，并且继续努力改善农村和城市电力的接入条件，特别是在向本国供电的电厂现代化之后，是开发低压电站综合安装系统的基础。

5. 电力

2003 年第 13 号法令的实施奠定了国家电力系统（ENS）的基础，为政府制定战略发展 ENS 提供了条件。为了创造一个均衡的结构，政府已采取重大步骤，实施通用的电力分配制度，建设下列发电站：

- Central Electric Hera，中速生产：7 × 17 MW；容量：119.5 兆瓦。
- Beatno 发电站，速度：8 × 17 MW；容量：136.6 兆瓦
- 大约 715km 的 150kv 输电线；
- 地区首府的九个分站；
- 帝力的一个控制中心。

（九）"一带一路"倡议下与中国企业合作的现状和方向

作为亚洲邻国，中国与东帝汶有着良好的友谊关系。自 2002 年新东帝汶初期以来，两国建立了外交关系。这些年来，作为贸易邻国，中国在东帝汶的投资只增不减。

据中国香港贸易发展委员会称，"根据中国商务部的统计数据，中国在该国的投资一直在增长，2010 年至 2015 年的累计外商直接投资从 750 万美元猛增至 1 亿美元"。

2014 年，中国成为东帝汶第三大商品供应国，仅次于印度尼西亚和新加坡，出口额为 4100 万美元。

"近年来，中国为东帝汶外交部、国防部、东帝汶国防军以及总统府建造了办公大楼。1000 多名东帝汶公务员已经访问了中国并进行培训，成千上万的中国技术人员在最新的农业方法、城市规划、旅游和其他领域指导了他们的同行。"[①] 2009 年至 2016 年，中国公司在东帝汶的建筑合同金额超过 5.25 亿美元。[②]

中国也是国际援助的重要援助国，并自 2011 年以来向东帝汶提供了 7 700 万美元的援助。[③]

毫无疑问，这一成功的合作关系在 "丝绸之路经济带和 21 世纪海上丝绸之路" 下有很大的发展空间。东帝汶在太平洋地区，澳大利亚和印度尼西亚之间的战略位置，以及拥有开阔的海域，深水海域

---

① https://thediplomat.com/2016/11/is-chinas-influence-in-timor-leste-rising/.
② https://thediplomat.com/2016/11/is-chinas-influence-in-timor-leste-rising/.
③ https://thediplomat.com/2016/11/is-chinas-influence-in-timor-leste-rising/.

和完美的航行条件这一事实，使得本国有利于从该计划中受益。

二、投资

（一）市场准入

1. 投资监督部门

由 2015 年第 45 号法令设立的投资和出口促进局是负责东帝汶投资的政府机构，隶属于国家私营部门秘书处（SEAPRI）。

投资和出口促进局与外国投资者达成协议，为其在国内投资提供激励措施和特殊条件。

该机构的目标是促进和支持潜在投资者在东帝汶进行投资，并协助外国公司确定在东帝汶出现的大量商业机会中的项目[1]。

投资和出口促进局的活动得到了一个名为 IADE（Instituto de Apoio ao Desenvolvimento Empresarial）的机构的支持，该机构的创建旨在提供相关信息以及指导和咨询，以帮助公司决定投资地和投资时间。

总的来说，IADE 可以通过建立生产者和卖家之间的联系、进行市场调查、确定尚待探索的业务领域以及提供公开招标和信贷贷款方面的协助来协助公司。

2. 投资业法律法规

对东帝汶的投资受 2017 年第 15 号法令的约束，《私人投资法》和 2018 年第 2 号政府法令的管制，这些法律法规规定了对新投资的财政和海关激励措施，以及对私人投资的特殊激励措施。

法律投资框架的主要目的是：
- 创造税收和关税优惠；
- 为东帝汶创造有利的投资条件；
- 支持依法确定的某些地区的发展；
- 保证投资者的诉权，以保障他们的合法权益。

3. 投资形式

投资或再投资可能包括以下内容：
- 根据东帝汶现行法律的条款成立公司；
- 收购商业公司的部分或全部股权，参与增加资本或实现额外注资；
- 修改与企业所有权和管理有关的合同，农业，工业和商业性质的场所，房地产综合体和其他旨在用于发展经济活动的设施或设备；
- 投资者向其参与的商业公司提供的银行贷款或供应的资金或与同一企业中的利润和股息再投资有关的任何贷款；
- 为该公司购买或进口有利于该项目的货物或资本设备，包括承包相应的保险；
- 以独家实现投资或再投资的方式获得或进口有利于原料或半成品的产品；
- 向公司免费转让工业机密，版权，工业产权，商标特色标志或法律承认的任何其他知识产权。

须达到最低投资金额才可获得投资激励：
- 国内投资者 50 000 美元；
- 外国投资者 500 000 美元；
- 国内人境外投资者的合作经营协议或法律允许的其他形式：250 000 美元（其中国内者须持有 75%以上的股权）。

4. 市场准入和审查标准

如前所述，投资和出口促进局是负责谈判并向投资者提供奖励和福利的机构。福利和奖励可以通过"福利宣言"或"特别投资协议"的形式进行谈判和授予，详情如下。

---

[1] http://www.investtimor-leste.com/?q=node/4。

（1）福利宣言

"福利宣言"是一份有确认福利的投资者的文件。申请和发布"福利宣言"的处理比"特别投资协议"更为简单。

投资者须向投资和出口促进局的执行董事提交申请及以下资料以获得福利宣言：
- 表格（规例附件 I）；
- 参与公司及投资的个人身份证复印件（国家投资者）；
- 投资者商业登记证书复印件；
- 授予法律规定的工作签证和文件（最多 5 份）；
- 商业计划。

该申请将被转交给投资和出口促进局的主管部门进行初步分析。

负责处理流程的部门需于 6 个工作日内将文件副本发送给国家土地管理局（负责出租国有资产）和移民服务局（负责批准签证）。

一旦收到文件，国家土地管理局和移民局自收到文件起 6 个工作日内发表意见。若仍未作出决定，则视为批准该申请。

批准后，投资和出口促进局执行董事向监管机构发送信息报告，建议通过投资者的申请。

监管机构应于 6 个工作日内签署并向投资和出口促进局退回申报表。

一旦收到申报表，就会将其发放给投资者，并将副本发送给国家土地局和移民服务局。

福利宣言应列出核准投资项目下给予投资者的税收优惠以及各自的授予期限。

在下列情况下，可以撤销福利宣言：
- 投资金额与投资的实际价值不符；
- 在项目未启动时，出于投资者的原因，在发布利益声明后的 1 年内；
- 通过解散或清算公司；
- 通过宣布投资者或公司破产；
- 合并或收购与该项目相关的商业公司。

（2）特别投资协议

特别投资协议是例外情况，须事先与政府协商，仅适用于规模或性质或其经济、社会、环境或技术影响可能给国家带来重大利益的投资项目。在这种情况下，除了正常的福利外，政府可以提供和给予除税收优惠以外的更多优惠政策。

为达成特别投资协议，投资者必须向投资和出口促进局的执行董事提交申请，并提供以下资料：
- 表格（规例附件 I）；
- 参与公司和投资活动的个人身份证复印件（国家投资者）；
- 投资者商业登记证书复印件；
- 申请授予法律规定的工作签证和文件（最多 5 份）；
- 商业计划；
- 一份说明文件列明达成特别投资协议的意向以及项目在战略发展计划框架内可能带来的经济、社会、环境和技术方面的重大影响。

投资和出口促进局执行董事收到请求后，将其转交主管部门进行申请初步分析。该部门在收到请求后的 5 个工作日内确定需要咨询的主要政府实体和相关部门，并将文件副本发送给主管当局。

监督机构必须在收到文件后的 10 个工作日内安排与东帝汶贸易投资公司进行会议，初步讨论投资建议。会议结束后，投资和出口促进局主管部门将有关文件的副本发送给主要政府实体和有关部门，这些部门需要 20 个工作日的时间对投资建议发表意见。

批准后，特别投资协议草案提交政府进行分析，并经政府决议批准，明确说明协议的理由及其适用的特殊制度。

特殊投资协议因其中一方当事人的违反合同约定或协议规定的其他原因，可以由双方协议终止。

（二）外汇管理

1. 外汇监督部门

请参阅"外汇法律法规简介"部分。

2. 外汇相关规定

东帝汶的官方货币是美元，这有助于资金的转入与转出。

到目前为止，东帝汶没有货币管制，也没有汇款政策，但"东帝汶中央银行对 5 000 美元以上的进口或出口货物实行报告制度，并且当总和超过 10 000 美元需要明确授权"①。

除此要求外，银行还可以根据"交易超过一定金额以遵守本国反洗钱法规"实行报告制度。②

尽管如此，根据 2017 年第 15 号法律，外国投资者有权自由将资金转移到国外（例如：利润和股息、资本、收入、补偿、支付）以及将资金金额转换为外币（通过银行系统）。

3. 外国企业的外汇管理要求

请参阅"外汇法律法规简介"部分。

（三）金融

1. 主要国家金融机构

除了根据东帝汶货币政策设立的公立银行——东帝汶中央银行及根据 2011 年第 5 号法律设立的支付系统、金融机构，还有以下银行同时在东帝汶经营：

- 大西洋银行——BNU，Caixa Geral deDepósitos 集团；
- 东帝汶国家商业银行——BNCTL；
- 澳大利亚和新西兰的澳新银行；
- 印度尼西亚人民银行；
- 印度尼西亚曼边利银行。

与以上机构一起，三家保险公司获得东帝汶国家商业银行许可并在该国运营：

- 东帝汶国家保险公司；
- 东帝汶联邦保险，SA；
- 金光保险，SA。

2. 境外投资者面临的金融环境

在东帝汶获得银行信贷是有限制的。困难来自多方面，包括银行体系规模仍然较小，企业生产力低下以及在现行法律体系下不可能提供真正的担保。

为克服这些困难，东帝汶政府通过 2017 年第 23 号法令，为中小企业建立了信用担保体系。在这个体系中，按照法律规定，国家至多可承担 70% 的贷款风险。小型企业是指雇用 6 至 20 名工人的企业，中型企业是指雇用 21 至 50 名工人的企业。

但是，该制度不适用于外国公司，仅适用于根据东帝汶法律成立和注册的公司，其中至少 75% 的有表决权的股份是由拥有东帝汶国籍个人直接或间接持有的。

（四）土地政策

1. 土地相关法律法规简介

东帝汶的土地政策仍处于早期阶段。在 2017 年之前，没有关于土地和房产登记的政策或法律，导致房地产权利和所有权陷入不稳定和混乱。因为没有发放具有公信力的财产凭证给房产持有人，导致就同一房产的所有权问题引发争议。

为了解决这个问题，议会于 6 月 5 日批准了 2017 年的第 13 号法律，建立了"界定财产所有权特

---

① https://www.state.gov/e/eb/rls/othr/ics/2017/eap/269858.htm。
② https://www.state.gov/e/eb/rls/othr/ics/2017/eap/269858.htm。

别制度",以期处理关于东帝汶财产所有权正规化和承认的问题。

目前,这些房产正在由国土局、国家土地房产目录和登记服务指南(DNTPSC),通过地籍调查和土地登记系统进行调整,并提供有关房地产法律状况的官方信息,结合房屋持有人发放凭证并建立一个安全和透明的房地产市场。

没有具体的法律规定关于征收问题。然而,宪法规定"只有在支付适当的补偿金的情况下,才允许征收或征用私有财产以维护公共利益"①。

2. 外国企业征地规则

根据议会于6月5日批准的2017年第13号法律,只有东帝汶国民,完全由东帝汶国民完全组建的东帝汶法人实体或其资本完全属于国民,当地社区和非营利法人实体的东帝汶法人实体可拥有财产所有权。

实际上,宪法上的限制是禁止外国人或外国法人拥有土地和拥有房地产权利。

尽管如此,外国投资者可以通过长期租赁获得土地——国家资产最长可达50年,在这个过程中投资和出口促进局可以提供援助。

(五)公司的设立和解散

1. 公司的形式

根据2017年第10号法律《公司法》的规定,东帝汶有两种企业形式:有限责任公司和股份公司。

(1)有限责任公司

在东帝汶,有限责任公司是股东人数2~30人的公司,即公司不少于两个合伙人/股东,也不超过30个。顾名思义,社会资产可用于偿还公司负债。

这些公司的名称必须由所有或一个合伙人/股东的名称或签名,或使用特定名称,或由以上两个要素结合(可使用缩写),用"有限"或缩写"Lda"。

股本由合伙人自由设定,但必须始终对应于份额的总和。公司的章程必须规定每个合伙人/股东的股本。

在这种类型的公司中,每个配额的面值应等于或大于1美元,并为1美元的倍数。份额只能由股东分期支付。

资金存款可能推迟至等于或大于5 000美元的现金存款配额名义值的一半。在主管部门规定的日期内,配额的推迟不超过3年。

如果合伙人/股东未出资,其他股东应按比例完成拖欠的出资。未完成出资股东的份额由出资的股东持有,即出资股东的份额由其原先持有的份额加上未出资股东的份额。未出资股东丧失恢复出资以获得股权的权利。

(2)股份公司

股份公司是指公司资本由股份组成的公司。股东人数不得少于3人,资本金不得少于50 000美元。在这种类型的公司中,所有股票都是有实名的、不可分割的,而股东的责任仅限于其所认购的股份价值。

这些公司的名称是由一个或几个股东的名称、签名或通过特定名称或通过这两个要素的会议形成的,无论是否有缩写,但应包括"sociedadeanónima"或缩写为"SA"结尾。

股份公司在未认购其全部股本且支付少于25%的情况下不会被注册成立。不存在延期支付的情况。

股份分为普通股和优先股;普通股被赋予投票权和存在可分配利润的股息,优先股不赋予投票权,但赋予优先股股息和优先偿还权以分担结算余额。

允许公开认购的公司合并。

2. 设立程序

任何希望在东帝汶开展业务的公司网站都必须按照国内法成立,并在SERVE——企业家注册和认

---

① https://www.state.gov/e/eb/rls/othr/ics/2017/eap/269858.htm。

证服务上注册，司法部下设的"一站式服务"由商业部、工业部和环境部负责，具体"负责公司独资经营者的注册，以及核实和宣传其合法身份，具备胜任能力，批准公司名称，以及组织和管理商业登记数据库"。在 SERVE 可以获得商业注册，申请商业许可并获得税号（TIN）。

根据关于商业登记的 2017 年第 16 号法律，在东帝汶成立公司需要四个步骤：
- 选择公司形式并注入最低资本；
- 注册公司名称，提交公司章程，申请 TIN（纳税人编号）并获得最终注册编号（CRC-Número Únicoda Empresa）以及由 SERVE 和 AEA（营业执照）认证的公司注册证书；
- 在 SERVE 上发布章程；
- 获得公司印章；

一般申请设立所需的文件是：
- 申请注册的表格；
- 原公司住所地的证明（仅适用于分公司）；
- 大会会议纪要，决定将公司设立在东帝汶或设立公司分支机构；
- 遵守法律规定；
- 股本证明；
- 股东身份信息；
- 至少 1 名董事有东帝汶的居住证明；
- 公司职位的接受函（董事，秘书等）；
- 所在地的地图；
- 公司法定代理人的授权书（如有）；
- 授权主管部门发布的活动（如有）。

在公开认购公司股份的情况下，项目必须与以下内容一起提交给 SERVE：
- 章程的整体设计，严格规范公司的目标；
- 拟用于公开认购的股份数量及其性质和面值以及发行溢价（如有）；
- 认购期限和信用机构可以达到的期限。

制造大会会议的期限：
- 根据真实完整的数据，并考虑到报告中已知的情况和预测，对公司发展进行为期 3 年技术、经济和财务预测研究，以便及时使对认购感兴趣的任何人清楚了解；
- 认购时的认购资本金额，完成剩余资金支付的截止日期以及公司不构成的情况下恢复该资金的截止日期。

在石油、采矿、食品和饮料等被认为具有中等或高风险的经营领域，特定立法中规定了许可制度，并且可能需要特别许可。

法律分支机构和子公司的设立程序如下：
为了注册在东帝汶或国外设立的商业公司的分公司或其他公司当地形式，需要下列文件：
- 分支机构的行为或其他当地形式的代表性，并参考其位置；
- 确定法定代表人，不确定授权范围；
- 法定代表人和法人团体其他持有人的身份证明文件；
- 所选代表聘用职位的签署声明。

对于设有注册办事处、总部或海外能有效管理的机构（即分支机构、代理机构或其他形式的代表处）的公司，可以适用下列注册义务，但不影响法律规定的其他义务：
- 常设代表的创建和注销；
- 任命和确定法定代表人的职责；
- 确定常驻代表机构的资金分配；
- 适用时，指定法定代表人为经理或律师。

对于总部在国外的东帝汶常驻代表机构的注册，需要提供以下文件：
- 根据原注册所在地国法律，证明商业公司存在的证明，对于在国外发布的任何文件，强制其在原籍国东帝汶大使馆合法化，并将其翻译成东帝汶官方语言（葡萄牙语或德顿语）；
- 最新的公司章程；
- 在东帝汶建立代表权的审议情况，并提及资本分配情况；
- 审议其代表的名称；
- 公司机构代表和其他成员的身份证件（如有）；
- 代表和其他法人团体成员的接受函（如有）；
- 东帝汶常设代表的所在地地图。

3. 公司解散的程序

在东帝汶，公司可以被解散：
- 通过合伙人/股东的决议；
- 持续时间到期；
- 停止经营活动超过3年；
- 连续12个月以上未开展任何活动，未正式声明停止其经营活动；
- 主体资格的灭失；
- 如果在45天内按照修改章程所规定的条款对不合法或超越其目的事项不能作出修改；
- 年度账目中核实，该公司的净值低于股本的一半；
- 在司法裁判决定解散。

解散具有启动公司清算的效力。

一旦公司解散，董事必须在60天内向股东批准在解散登记日报告的库存、资产负债表和损益表。

一旦账目得到股东的批准，未成为清算人的管理人员必须向其提供公司的所有文件、书籍、纸制材料、录音、录像、资金或资产。

如果在解散时公司没有债务，股东可以立即开始分配剩余财产。在解散时尚未到期的税务债务并不排除分配，但所有成员都是共同承担共同连带责任，无论他们以任何方式提存他们估计的用于支付此尚未到期的税务、债务的款项。

一旦最终账目获得批准，资产（扣除结算费用和尚未到期的税务或注册性质的债务）由合伙人按照公司章程规定的条款分摊。

清算人必须在15日内申请注销清算结束程序，并且必须附上所提交的文件。

根据本法或破产程序的条款，该公司被视为在清算结束登记之日已经解散。

一旦清算结束并且公司被撤销，原股东应以其从公司清算资产中所获财产为限对公司清算承担连带责任。

（六）并购

1. 合并授权

- 通过将一家或多家公司的资产全部转让给另一家公司并将其归属于该股份或配额股东的股东之下；
- 通过组建一家新公司，合并后的公司的资产在全球转让，新公司的股份归属于这些公司的合伙人。

预期合并的公司应共同编制一份合并项目计划，其中包含：
- 与所有参与公司有关的公司中合并的公司形式、原因、条件和目标；
- 每家公司的名称、注册办事处、资本和注册号码；
- 其中一家公司持有另一家公司的股份；
- 经过特别组织的中介公司的资产负债表，显示将转移给收购公司或新公司的资产和负债的价值；
- 归属于被合并公司股东或拟合并公司股东的股份或配额以及归属于同一股东的现金金额，具体说明股权交换比率。

2. 合并注册后

- 被合并后的公司将被取消，或者在组建新公司的情况下，将所有合并的公司转让给收购公司或新公司；
- 已解散公司的成员成为收购公司或新公司的成员。

董事、监事及公司的秘书负责公司财务状况的审查及合并事宜，并且若违反了谨慎义务，将对公司的债权人、合伙人承担连带责任。

除了所列明的例外情况，上述条款应适用于被其他股东显名/隐名持有股份的公司并购的所有公司由其股份或股份为唯一所有人的另一家公司直接或以其名义注册成立。在这种情况下，关于股份交换的条款，公司合并报告条款以及责任条款都不适用。

3. 分立

公司可能会分立：
- 分离部分资产以组建另一家公司；
- 解散和分割其资产，最终每个部分会构成一个新的公司；
- 分离或分解部分资产，将其资产分为两部分或更多，将其与现有公司或其他公司的部分资产合并，或者以相同的流程和相同目的进行分解。

公司的管理层将被拆分，或者在合并的情况下，参与公司的主管部门必须共同编制一个部门的草案，除了以下信息，还应包括其他必要的操作设想：

- 所有参与公司分立的形式、原因、条件和目标；
- 各公司的名称、注册办事处、资本金额和税号；
- 其中一家公司注入另一家公司的资本；
- 将要转移给收购公司或新公司的资产的完整清单以及资产价值；
- 在分拆的情况下，每家参与公司按照第108（1）d）条准备的资产负债表；
- 兼并公司或新公司的股权与公司股东所持有的现金总值（特别是持股比例及合伙基础）应剥离开；
- 分拆产生的公司股份类别（如匿名）以及这些股票交付的日期；
- 新公司授予参与分配的日期以及与其权利有关的信息；
- 由剥离公司向拥有特殊权利的被剥离公司股东所担保的权利；
- 对收购公司章程或新公司章程草案进行修改的草案；
- 保护债权人权利的措施；
- 保护非会员参与公司利润分配权的措施；
- 因与雇员签订雇佣合同而产生的公司或合作公司的合同职位的归属情况，这些合同并未因分割而消失。

分立的公司对因公司分立行为而产生的债务承担连带责任。
从分立中受益的公司，以受益的范围为限，对公司分立登记前的债务承担连带责任。
即使公司正在清算，分立也可能发生。
有关合并的规定适用于分立公司，并进行必要的适应性调整。

（七）反不正当竞争

尚未颁布竞争法，没有负责监督不正当竞争的部门与竞争管理措施。

（八）税收

1. 税制和规则

2008年第8号法律为《税收和关税法》，是东帝汶的主要税法。该法由石油业务的具体条例和印度尼西亚税法加以补充，因为国家在其组成之前根据东帝汶政府1999年/1号条例通过了印度尼西亚税法，并修正了东帝汶过渡政府2000年第18号条例，并未被撤销，并在适用时保持有效。

如前所述，石油业务有特殊的税收制度。例如，JPDA 的 Bayu-Undan 油田拥有从许多方面建立起来的财政和法律制度，包括印度尼西亚法律，东帝汶过渡当局条例，特定于 Baya-Undan 的立法以及实施的合同安排。

该国正在进行税收改革。改革的目的是改善税收和海关管理，降低企业成本，改进制度并增强可预测性、效率、完整性及透明度。其中包括与东盟地区的企业和个人收入相比，降低税率的计划，并建立增值税信用体系以确保税收不仅仅依靠商业。

2. 主要税种和税率

在东帝汶，主要税种和税率分别是：
- 个人所得税：0% 至 10%；
- 公司所得税：10%；
- 工资所得税：0% 至 10%；
- 服务税：每月超过 500 美元的营业额的 5%；
- 销售税：进口产品的 2.5%；
- 进口关税：进口产品的 2.5%；
- 消费税：税率取决于产品种类。

3. 纳税申报和优惠

① 所得税

东帝汶居民对其在全世界范围内的收入/利润承担纳税义务，而非居民则只对其来源于东帝汶境内的收入/利润缴纳税款。从法律概念上讲，居民法人是指在东帝汶成立、组织或设立的法人。法人包括许多实体类型，如公司、合伙企业、信托公司、政府机构和非公司协会。

应纳税的营业利润是基于净利润计算的，即应纳税所得额是指收入总收益（包括国内和国外）和允许的扣除额之间的差额。营业收入包括营业活动收益、资产转让或债务清偿。此外，在某些类型的收入受制于预提税，这些收入被排除在应纳税所得额之外。

在法律上，总收入为：
- 业务收入；
- 财产性收入；
- 彩票奖项或奖金；
- 退税；
- 以任何名义或形式增加经济能力的其他数额，其可由纳税人用于消费或增加纳税人的财富，而非工资所得税。

免税收入包括：
- 任何援助或捐赠，只要其捐赠者和受赠人不具有任何商业、所有权或控制权关系；
- 从直系亲属或宗教、教育、慈善组织或合作组织中获得的礼物，其捐赠者或受赠人没有任何商业关系、所有权或控制权；
- 遗产；
- 法人以股份或出资方式获得的资产（包括现金）；
- 在健康、事故、生命或教育保险方面，由保险公司支付给自然人的款项；
- 股息；
- 由雇主或雇员向经批准的养老基金支付的任何款项；
- 经批准的养老基金所得的收入。

所得税的税率为：
- 在一个居民自然人的情况下，从 0 美元至 6000 美元的利率为 0%，超过 6000 美元的利率为 10%；
- 在非居民自然人的情况下，利率为 10%；
- 在法人的情况下，利率为 10%。

一个法律实体向东帝汶和国外政党双方支付的某些款项将按以下方式扣缴税款：
- 特许权使用费：10%；
- 租金（土地和建筑）：10%；
- 奖金/奖赏：10%；
- 建设/建筑活动：2%；
- 建设咨询服务：4%；
- 航空或海运：2.64%；
- 采矿和采矿相关活动：4.5%。

只有在向个人支付特许权使用费时，特许权使用费（如：版税）和租金的税率才适用于最终税率的预提，此费用不适用于企业实体。奖品和奖金需要缴纳最终税。至于剩余款项，收款人可以选择向税务机关提交通知函，以支付不受制于最终税的服务费。

受法律约束的，允许扣除：
- 在进行应纳税业务活动时发生的财产转让或者债务清偿所造成的损失；
- 总收入中计入其他金额的支出；
- 对资产处置的任何损失，除第1点所涉及的资产外，均由个人账户持有；
- 对经批准的养老基金的捐赠；
- 可疑债券。

为了尽量减少对国际重复征税居民的影响，他们获得国外利润和收入的同时，也可以获得国外税收抵免。

每一位纳税义务人应当以应计制核算所得税。年度总营业额低于10万美元的纳税人，可以按现金或应计制计算所得税。

纳税人须于纳税年度结束后第三个月的最后一天，向银行及支付当局或税务机关指定的另一个单位，提供一份完整的纳税年度纳税申报表。纳税义务人从事经营活动的所得税形式由纳税人的损益表、资产负债表和纳税年度的现金流量表组成。

个人或法人在上一纳税年度总营业额超过100万美元应按月缴纳所得税。分期付款的金额是纳税人当月总营业额的0.5%。在此情况下，上一纳税年度总营业额为100万美元或以下的，应按季度分期缴纳所得税。在纳税年度的第三、第六、第九、第十二个月的最后一日应支付所得税，分期付款的期限为3个月。每笔款项的数额占纳税人本季度总营业额的0.5%。所得税的分期缴付应在其所述期间结束后的第15天支付。

②工资所得税

工资所得税是指雇员在东帝汶就业时所获得的应纳税工资。在东帝汶，就业是指服务于东帝汶或受雇于东帝汶政府的雇员在该国或其他地方执行的服务。工资所得税按累进税率从0%到10%，按工资数额计算。

以下工资为免税工资：
- 法律所规定的免除税收官方职责的工资；
- 外籍员工的工资。
- 受雇于外国政府，其工资只需在受雇国缴纳所得税；
- 联合国或其专门机构雇员的工资；

雇员在东帝汶就业的，应扣缴工资所得税。如果一名员工缴纳了正确的工资所得税，其将不会对工资所得税产生进一步的负担。

为了达到报告的目的，雇主应在一个日历月结束后的第15天向银行和支付管理局或税务机关指定的另一个实体完成交付：
- 由税务机关规定的已完成的工资所得税扣缴形式；
- 当月扣缴的工资所得税。

此外，雇主须按其所涉及的纳税年度终了后的3月最后一日，向银行及支付管理局或由税务机关指定的另一实体，按税务总局规定的年度工资所得税预扣税信息表完成相关的纳税义务。

③ 服务税

服务税是根据一个人对提供"指定服务"的总体考虑而征收的，即：
- 酒店服务；
- 餐厅和酒吧服务；
- 电信服务。

若这类服务源自东帝汶，则在东帝汶提供服务。

每月营业额低于 500 美元的人员的服务税税率为 0%，每月营业额超过 500 美元的服务税税率为 5%。

在东帝汶，有责任缴纳服务税的人应在一个日历月结束后的第 15 天向银行及支付管理局或税务机关指定的另一实体缴纳服务税。

- 税务总局规定的完整的服务税清单；
- 提供指定服务的人应在当月所收到的总费用中的全部应缴税款。

此外，一个有缴纳服务税义务的人应向银行及支付管理局或由税务机关指定的另一实体，在随后的几个月内，提供已填妥的服务税表，无论是否须在随后的数月缴付服务税。

④ 营业税

一般来说，当纳税人将任何应税货物进口到东帝汶时，就会对应税货物征收营业税。营业税是按货物完税价格的 2.5% 计算的，包括货物进口时应缴纳的进口税和消费税。

营业税的支付方式与进口关税相同。

⑤ 进口关税

进口关税是对所有货物（特别豁免除外）的进口货物征收 2.5% 的关税。海关价值是货物的公平市场价值，包括成本、保险费和运费（CIF）。

由个人从另一地区随身携带抵达东帝汶的物品可以免征进口关税，即：
- 每人 200 支香烟和 2.5 升饮料；
- 价值 300 美元的非商业性质的专属个人使用或享受或作为礼物的物品，根据货物的性质和数量分析表明他们不是基于商业目的进口或拟进口的；
- 除珠宝以外的非商业性质的商品，仅供旅客个人使用或享受并由旅客随身携带的物品；
- 在东帝汶居住的前居民的家庭效应将永久居住在东帝汶。

除个人物品外，免征进口税：
- 1961 年《维也纳外交关系公约》和 1963 年《领事关系》豁免的项目；
- 《联合国特权和豁免公约》豁免的项目；
- 《专门机构特权和豁免公约》豁免的项目；
- 在相同的出口条件下再进口的货物；
- 在注册登记的慈善机构进口的除酒精或烟草以外的商品，根据东帝汶法律进行登记的慈善组织，该商品基于人道主义援助和救济、教育或卫生保健的慈善目的；
- 进口商按照规定的方式已提供进口关税的担保的临时进口货物；
- 婴儿配方奶粉，专门针对一岁以下的婴儿，可以在冲泡加工之后，以液体的形式食用，并提供与母乳相似的营养；
- 卫生棉条和卫生巾。

进口关税在进口时支付。

⑥ 消费税

已注册登记的制造商将货物从仓库移出，以供在东帝汶消费或是进口到东帝汶的货物征收消费税。利率变化取决于应税商品。在其他方面，被认为是应税货物的有：
- 啤酒；
- 葡萄酒、苦艾酒和其他发酵饮料；
- 乙醇（除变性和其他含酒精的饮料以外）；
- 烟草及相关产品；

- 汽油、柴油及其他石油产品；
- 消费税超过7万美元的小型车，；
- 武器和弹药；
- 打火机；
- 吸烟管道；
- 休闲艇和私人飞机。

注册制造商不用缴纳消费税的情形：
- 在出厂前被火灾或其他自然因素破坏；
- 在制造商的仓库中已经变质或损坏，并以符合税务管理的方式进行了安全处理。

任何希望在东帝汶制造和销售货物的人，必须按照既定程序和满足一定的要求，在税务局注册登记成为上述货物的生产者。

注册登记的生产者应在日历月结束后第15天向银行及支付机构或者税务机关指定的其他单位缴纳税款：
- 税务总局规定的完整的消费税税单；
- 在该日历月期间，从制造商的仓库中取出的应税货物的消费税。

此外，根据上述条款，任何有缴纳消费税义务的人在随后的几个月应向银行和支付管理局或由税务机关指定的另一个实体完成纳税义务。

如果在东帝汶境内进口或制造的货物，被已登记的生产者用作生产其他货物的原料，税务当局可以就这类货物给予部分豁免。

对进口货物的消费税按照相同的程序征收进口关税。

⑦ 印花税

在东帝汶税法中没有印花税。

⑧ 增值税

总体来说，在东帝汶税法中没有增值税（VAT）。

但就石油业而言，应指出在东帝汶的税法中有一个特别的规定，允许对这些产业征收增值税。这一特殊制度还允许根据《帝汶海条约》在联合石油开发区内征收石油业增值税。

综上所述，政府计划引入增值税（VAT），促使东帝汶成为出口免税区，并以此来吸引制造业和其他行业的出口导向型投资。

⑨ 双重课税协议

东帝汶与葡萄牙达成了取消重复征税的协议，与中国澳门特别行政区的类似协议也在进行中。

（九）证券

1. 相关证券法律法规概述

"东帝汶没有股票市场。对证券投资没有已知范围。"[①]

2. 证券市场监管

参见"相关证券法律法规概述"部分。

3. 外国企业从事证券交易业务的要求

参见"相关证券法律法规概述"部分。

（十）投资优惠和保护

1. 优惠政策的结构

在东帝汶，持有利益申报或已签订特别投资协定的投资者可享受100%免征所得税和服务税：
- 从项目开始之日起5年（利益申报的日期）：在帝力市以内进行的部分或全部投资。
- 从项目开始之日起8年（利益申报的日期）：在帝力市以外进行的部分或全部投资/再投资。

---

① 美国国务院《2017年投资环境报表》，参见 https://www.state.gov/e/eb/rls/othr/ics/2017/eap/269858.htm。

- 从项目开始之日起 10 年（利益申报的日期）：在欧库西－安贝诺（Oé-Cusse Ambeno）和阿陶罗岛（Ataúro）以内进行的部分或全部投资 / 再投资。

在同一期间内，上述投资者可以对用于投资或再投资项目中建设或管理的所有商品和设备 100% 免缴销售税和进口关税。此外，考虑到每个活动部门以及在清关后的转售条件，法律还规定了资本货物和设备的种类和数量免征与进口有关的关税。

不受益于豁免的情况：
- 对进口到东帝汶的商品征收选择性消费税，对东帝汶出口的商品免征进口关税。
- 对工资征税：在一个依赖和应税的雇佣关系的框架内，将其所有薪酬视为工资收益。
- 租金税：根据租赁协议收取的租金。

法律为投资者提供的其他利益包括：
- 关于国有房地产，可与国家签订为期 50 年的租赁协议，甚至可续期最长 100 年；
- 向符合投资项目的监督、指导或技术职能的工人或雇员发放 5 份工作签证。

2. 支持特定行业和地区

正如先前所述，激励可能根据投资区域的不同而有所不同。根据《私人投资法》，政府倾向于对不发达地区在一定时期内提供税收优惠政策，如下：
- 在帝力市内 5 年；
- 在帝力市外 8 年；
- 在特别的社会市场经济特区（SSMEZ）的欧库西－安贝诺和阿陶罗岛 10 年。

3. 特殊经济区

东帝汶有两个经济特区：一个是在印度尼西亚的欧库西－安贝诺，另一个是离帝力市非常近的阿陶罗岛。这两个领域都被第 2014 年第 3 号法令视为特殊的社会市场经济特区（SSMEZ），具有行政和财务自主权，二者都有独立的财政、独立的税收制度、专属的采购制度、专属的金融市场和专属的海关制度。

阿陶罗岛是以旅游性质而设立的特别行政区，而欧库西－安贝诺区域则是以贸易和工业为支柱，并因为它本身所具有的突出商业潜力从而吸引了大量的基础设施投资。

欧库西－安贝诺在其领土范围内，将免征关税和尊重社会市场经济原则作为其经济增长的一种模式。该区域的经济性目标是：
- 发展商业化农业；
- 建立符合职业伦理金融中心；
- 建立自由贸易区；
- 发展旅游业；
- 建立一个国际化气候变化研究中心；
- 创建一个绿色生态研究中心；
- 实施和发展进出口工业活动。①

为该区域设立了一个特别发展基金，意在为战略型社会和经济项目提供资金，包括道路基础设施、港口和机场、供水和卫生设施、能源和电信分销网络以及医院和其他社会性旅游基础设施。在计划的项目中，发电厂、一些道路、灌溉系统、诊所和一座桥已竣工。在其他正在进行的项目中，机场预计将于 2018 年底竣工，且目前正在建设一座酒店。

4. 投资保护

外国投资者在东帝汶享有下列权利和保障：
- 除土地所有权和最低投资价值外，国内外均享有平等待遇；
- 享有诉诸法院的权利；
- 保护私人财产（根据宪法的限制性规定）。有必要对投资者的全部或者部分财产进行征用或征收

---

① 6 月 18 日颁布的第 3/2014 号法令，第 5 条。

的，国家必须基于法律规定对其给予公平的补偿；
- 具有进口产品及设备和出口产品的权利；
- 具有依靠国内外信贷的权利；
- 将资金自由转移到国外（例如：利润和股息、资本、收入、补偿、支付款）和兑换外币（通过银行系统）的权利；
- 雇用外国工人的权利；
- 对专业、银行业和商业秘密的权利；
- 投资者有权保护他们所注册的实用新型专利以及在知识产权条款下保护的商标、标识、名称或标志等信息；
- 在受益人履行义务的前提下，法律所规定的特权和税收优惠直到投资期限届满时才可撤销或减少；
- 政府推动与尽可能多的国家建立国际协议，以避免国际重复征税；
- 外国投资者有权在东帝汶获得纳税证明。

三、贸易

（一）部门监管贸易

负责东帝汶贸易的政府机构是财政部。

（二）贸易法律法规概述

最主要的贸易法律是第 14/2017 号法令《海关代码》，它制定了东帝汶在与其他国家进行商业交流时海关政策措施所适用的法律规定。此外，其他主要法规包括第 08/2006 号法令《关税条例》，第 09/2003 号法令《海关的职责和能力条例》，第 09/2006 号法令《制造烟草制品条例》，第 10/2003 号法令《旅客的海关管制条例》及第 21/2003 号法令《检疫管理条例》。

贸易体制正在进行改革，一系列旨在通过简化和规范全球惯例过程来提高海关效率的活动将得到实施，例如：
- 根据国际最优标准，将海关程序代码现代化。
- 根据东盟标准，更新东帝汶所有商品的国际编码。引入 ASYCUDA 世界，使 IT 系统更现代化，从而规范进口货物的流程并进一步加强海关的完整性。
- 通过提供经纪人培训来提高行业服务水平。
- 通过自我评估流程来简化货物清关。
- 通过对进口商进行高级管理来提高企业信心。
- 通过为官员提供专业培训以协助合法的决策。
- 通过制定标准操作程序为决策提供确定性。
- 根据海关程序代码来开发和实施海关人员培训和能力建设战略。
- 在关键的软件平台（如 IFMIS 服务、ASYCUDA 世界、税务管理 IT 系统和 PBS）之间实现一个完整的实时接口/集成。
- 加强海关机场和陆地边境货运业务。
- 改进海关争议解决流程。[1]

在 2017 年年末，东帝汶成为世界贸易组织（WTO）的观察者，这是成为成员国重要的一步，这一立场将有助于该国"向其他国家提供重要的保证，以确保该国进口的规范和标准被遵守"（例如，植物检疫措施）[2]，并提出"与其他成员国解决贸易争端的机制"[3]。

---

① 参见 https://www.mof.gov.tl/frc_menu/trade-facilitation/customs-reform-to-facilitate-trade/?lang=en。
② 参见 https://www.mof.gov.tl/frc_menu/trade-facilitation/becoming-a-member-of-the-wto/?lang=en。
③ 参见 https://www.mof.gov.tl/frc_menu/trade-facilitation/becoming-a-member-of-the-wto/?lang=en。

（三）贸易管理

在东帝汶，有一个"全国单一窗口"的贸易管理系统。它是"一个海关入口，贸易商可以提交所有与贸易有关的文件，并可通过单一电子网关获取有关贸易的所有相关信息，帮助处理和清关"。该门户将海关当局与所有处理人员或货物流动的政府机构联系起来，包括税收、移民、检疫、卫生、运输、农业、渔业、外交和中央银行。[1]

（四）进出口商品检验检疫

根据颁布的《第21/2003号法令》，一些生物制品及相关货物进入东帝汶境内须接受检验检疫，即活体动物、肉类和肉制品、活鱼、鲜鱼和冷冻鱼产品、奶制品、蛋制品、蜂蜜制品、动物毛发、牛皮制品及其他动物产品、活植物、植物材料和花卉、新鲜蔬菜和蔬菜产品、谷类产品、坚果及其制品、乳制品、家畜饲料和木材产品。

东帝汶的检疫服务机构负责监督和实施关于卫生控制的程序，从国家领土到另一种植物、动物和产品的衍生品的进出口，以及其他项目，包括制定植物检疫或卫生证书动物的规定、进口和前程序的检疫措施以及从一个地区到另一个地区的进口、出口或移动的实际授权，出口和签发及动物园和植物检疫证书的说明、害虫和检疫的定义、费用和成本的确定、侵权和处罚的建立的程序[2]。

（五）海关管理

海关总署（DCG）是负责货物在进入国家领土时管理和征收关税和费用的机构。

DGC有以下任务：

- 根据政府的方案和部长发布的上级指导方针，确保国家政策在其范围内的实施和综合执行；
- 对进入国家领土的商品和运输工具，以及在财政行为下存放商品的场所进行管理，并确保货物向海关出示的海关手续，并在清关时向海关提供货物的海关手续；
- 开展研究，起草法律法规，并根据其目标制定操作规则和技术；
- 参与有关关税、营业税、消费税税收政策的定义和管理，确保在其职责范围内的任何税收、费用或支付的结算和征收；
- 规范适用于自然人和资产流动的海关制度，包括入境、居留、过境或离开海关，并审核其申请；
- 根据法律对港口、机场和国家边境的人员和资产进行海关核查；
- 打击逃税和欺诈，以及走私、越界和非法贩运毒品、武器和其他违禁物品，并与其他国家机构和国际组织合作打击这些活动。[3]

四、劳动

（一）劳动法律法规概述

2012年第4法令《劳动法典》是规范东帝汶就业关系的法律。

根据该法律，雇佣合同可以采用不定期合同或者固定期限合同的形式，最好以书面形式订立。但是，在未签订书面劳动合同或者合同中无明确期限的情况下，应当视为不定期合同。

定期合同在下列情况下自动转为无定期合同：

- 同等条件下，与同一员工在第一份合同终止前90天内又签订一项新的固定期限合同；
- 合同期限应超过3年，包括续签的合同。

该法律的主要原则之一是对员工的保护，因此，法律赋予员工很多权利且若无正当理由，解雇工人是被禁止的，但也可能基于市场、技术和结构上的原因终止雇佣合同。

其中，员工的权利包括：

---

[1] 参见 https://www.mof.gov.tl/frc_menu/trade-facilitation/national-single-window/?lang=en。
[2] 12月31日颁布的第21/2003号法令。
[3] 参见 https://www.mof.gov.tl/about-the-ministry/organisation-structure-roles-and-people/generals-directorate/general-diretore-customs/?lang=en。

- 正常工作时间不应超过每天 8 小时或每周超过 44 小时；
- 在工作日，加班工资是正常工资的 50%，周末和节假日是 100%；
- 员工每年至少享有 12 天的带薪假期；
- 雇主终止合同可能是由于员工严重的不当行为或市场、技术或结构发生了变化；
- 被控非法解雇的案件，必须在接到解雇通知后 60 天内由法院宣布；
- 产假为 12 周；
- 最低工作年龄为 15 岁；
- 最低工资为 115 美元每周。

该法律还提到了外国雇员的身份，与外国雇员签订的合同应为书面形式且由主管机关书面授权。

（二）雇用外国雇员的要求

1. 工作许可

根据 2003 年第 09 号法律《移民和庇护法》，工作许可证旨在授权持证人进入一国国家领土，临时去从事一项作为雇员或独立的工作人员的职业性活动，工作许可专门允许持证人去执行他签证授权的专业行动，并且允许最长不超过一年的停留时间及适用于一次或多次入境。

2. 申请手续

居留许可申请将提交给入境事务处并由国家职业培训和就业秘书处批准。要获得居留证，申请人必须满足下面的要求：

- 拥有有效的居留签证；
- 若被权威机构所知，没有作为被签证拒绝的隐藏的阻碍；
- 在东帝汶境内。

审核申请之后，移民局通过借助于面试的方式结束这一进程，这一过程大约需要到 2 个月时间。

3. 社会保障

根据东帝汶《宪法》规定的条件，2016 年 11 月 14 日通过的第 2016 年第 12 号法律确定了缴费型社会保障计划，缴费型社会保障制度必须包含以下内容：

- 整个私营部门，即所有按照"劳动法"规定有固定或无期限雇佣合同的员工；
- 整个公共部门，即所有在国家有偿履行职能的人员；
- 雇主。

另一方面，可选择性的包含这些计划：

- 个体企业家；
- 自我雇佣；
- 公司的经理和经管人；
- 家政从业人员。

根据社会保障缴费方案收取的费用，旨在确保工人在某些偶然事件中有权享受的福利，即下面这些部分：

- 产假津贴；
- 亲子津贴；
- 领养津贴；
- 怀孕期间的临床风险补贴；
- 终止妊娠补助；
- 死亡补助金；
- 殡葬补助费用；
- 生存年金；
- 绝对残疾养恤金；
- 相对残疾养恤金；

- 老年津贴；
- 工伤事故赔偿。

在这种情况下，为了系统的组织和成本计算，雇主必须：
- 在服务处注册并去登记或在登记工作人员信息下，为他们获取适用终身的各自的NISS（社会安全识别号码）；
- 提供和更新信息；
- 发布每月报酬声明（DR）；
- 支付每月保险费。

缴纳保险费的数额是通过将缴费税基数（BIC）乘以缴费税（TC）得出，其中：
- BIC是总薪酬（工资）总额加上其他永久的月薪，其包含了每年/13个月的津贴、夜间工作的补偿工资、特殊职业的额外补贴，但不包括在可变的计算中，例如，来源于每日的津贴、加班费、餐费补助和其他额外的补贴中得出的总的数额。
- TC设置成10%的比例，分开在雇主和工人之间，分别达到6%和4%，到2020年，缴费率的可能性被考虑在其中，作为社会保障体系的持续性担保的一种方式。

由于其创造的复杂且重大的职责所赋，法律为私营部门的雇主规定了一个适应的过渡时期。

这一时期是分阶段的，一直延伸至2026年，在这个阶段，有10个或更少工人的公司，只要本土员工至少占到60%，就有权享受过渡期所负义务的折扣，即享受根据条款仅仅需支付一定比例的税费：
- 2017年和2018年：70%；
- 2019年和2020年：50%；
- 2021年和2022年：30%；
- 2023年和2024年：20%；
- 2025年和2026年：10%。

（三）出入境

1. 签证种类

在东帝汶，有六种方式的签证：
- 旅游和商务签证；
- 过境签证；
- 学习签证；
- 文化签证；
- 工作签证；
- 建立居住地的签证。

2. 出入境限制

任何国籍的旅客如果抵达帝力国际机场或帝力海港，可以在抵达时办理旅游或商务签证，落地签证包含单次入境的30日停留。

只有印度尼西亚和葡萄牙的国民可以在抵达陆地边境时获得签证或入境许可，所有其他国籍的人在进入陆路口岸前都必须申请"签证申请授权书"。

（四）工会和劳工组织

在东帝汶，没有歧视或需要事先授权，所有工人和雇主都可以以促进和维护其权益为目的而设立和加入组织，同时不得强迫工人参加、不加入或停止加入工会组织。

在开展工作时，工会和雇主组织的目标应该是：
- 促进和维护会员的权益；
- 与政府合作制定和实施劳工政策规定的目标；
- 行使集体谈判的权利；

- 在执行法律和集体协议规定方面与劳动监察局合作；
- 依法参与劳动立法的过程。

（五）劳动争议

在劳资纠纷方面，法律规定了"个人劳动纠纷将在诉诸法庭之前，强制进行调解"，除非当此争议关系到由于雇主原因违法解决雇佣合同或由雇佣者以基于市场、技术或结构原因结束合同的。

在涉及仲裁的问题上，诉诸仲裁源于自愿，并且"可能由相关方提出要求或者其中一方提出要求，在这种情况下，如果另一方接受或者不愿意诉诸仲裁，则需要宣告"。

如果调解失败并且双方都选择不去诉诸仲裁，将可能根据民事诉讼法的规定启动司法劳工纠纷。

通常情况下，劳工纠纷始于劳动合同的终止，劳动合同的终止依据第45—57条的规定，并可以采用以下情形：

- 合同已到期；
- 双方协议约定；
- 员工终止合同；
- 雇主以正当理由解雇雇员；
- 公司用市场、技术或结构性原因结束。

劳动合同终止的前两种情形都是建立在双方同意基础上的，很少或者根本没有空间引发争议。

雇员向雇主提出对终止劳动合同的质疑期为接到通知之日起的60天内，但并不妨碍其诉诸调解组织可能性。

如果雇员指出的正当理由被宣告无效，则雇主有权就造成的损害得到补偿。

最常见的劳资纠纷出现在雇员不接受雇主终止合同，因为合同的终止必须在公司裁员的情况下才有正当理由，或者由于公司的经济可行性受到损害，导致公司的市场、技术或结构原因无法维持致使雇佣合同终止。对于这两个情形下的合同终止，都有一些严格的程序需要遵守，因为法律禁止没有正当理由的解雇。

如果员工因正当理由而被解雇，则程序应以约束性的程序开始，该程序应在雇主（或其代表）发现违规行为发生之日起的最多20天内编写和启动。之后，雇员有权在服务日期后的10天内以书面形式提出其申辩意见，并可提供任何为其申辩所证明的证据（例如，目前的文件，要求举行听证会和其他必要步骤）。

如果用人单位在约束性程序开始后的6个月内未通知员工最终决定，解雇的可能性将过期。雇员有权对作出的决定提出上诉，并且尽管有诉诸仲裁或司法程序的权利，他也可以要求中介和调解机关的干预，以解决冲突。

对于因市场、技术或结构原因而终止合同的，只有在用人单位减少工作期限和中止聘用合同之后才可以采用。采取这些措施后，雇主必须以书面形式向受影响的雇员和其代表（如适用）传达其意图，并将副本转交给中介和调解服务部门，并且必须在5天内与员工或他们的代表谈判，以便就终止程序达成协议。

当谈判过程结束时，如果双方没有就避免合同终止达成协议，雇主将书面向每位员工（如适用），向代表委员会和调解服务机构作出终止雇佣决定的书面文件，文件中明确说明终止依据的理由、终止日期和将收到的补偿金额。

五、知识产权

（一）知识产权法律法规简介

东帝汶《宪法》第60条规定保护文学、科学和艺术作品，国家议会已批准加入世界知识产权组织的公约。

但是，国家没有关于知识产权保护的具体法律。

在知识产权法最终获得批准之前，保护国内商标、标识、徽章和专利的唯一选择是在当地报纸上发布警示声明，声称拥有知识产权。

一般而言，警示通知应说明知识产权持有者的名称和地址，以及相关知识产权的说明。在专利的情况下，需要摘要，并且在设计的情况下，设计的形状是必需的。

一旦发布警告通知，假定第三方已知晓所涉及的知识产权的所有权，并建议定期（每两年）重新发布警戒通知，以防止知识产权侵权。

关于商标，在发布警告通知警示申明后，应通知商业主管部门（SERVE）警告，如果导致与特定公司发生冲突或混淆，则不能批准类似商标。

考虑到已提交给议会的法律草案，一旦知识产权法最终获得批准，则根据警戒说明所保护的名称、商标、徽标和徽记以及专利将在注册程序中排列优先顺序。

（二）专利申请

参见"知识产权法律法规简介"部分。

（三）商标注册

参见"知识产权法律法规简介"部分。

（四）知识产权保护措施

参见"知识产权法律法规简介"部分。

六、环境保护

（一）环境保护监督部门

东帝汶环境保护监督部门为国家污染控制和环境影响管理局（NDPCEI）。

（二）环境保护法律法规简介

"东帝汶宪法明确规定了保护环境的重要性，该国是与环境管理相关的若干国际公约的缔约方，并已签署和批准了《联合国防治荒漠化公约》（UNCCD；2003年8月），《联合国气候变化框架公约》（UNFCCC；2006年10月）和《联合国生物多样性公约》（UNCBD；2006年10月）。东帝汶也签署了《联合国气候变化框架公约》《京都议定书》，表达了对减少全球气候变化的承诺。

2012年第26号法令规定了环境基本规则，而2011年第05/2011号环境许可法令（ELL）构建了东帝汶的环境法律框架。还有其他未决的法律和法规，包括生物多样性法律。

环境许可法令（ELL）规定环境影响评估和许可制度。根据ELL，可能影响环境的项目或活动的发起者或活动者需要进行环境评估。

除法律要求外，国家污染控制和环境影响管理局NDPCEI还不时发布准则，并更好地适用于国际惯例。

需要注意的是，采矿，石油和天然气等活动可能需要特殊许可。

（三）评估环境保护

请参考"环境保护法律法规简介"部分。

七、争议解决

（一）解决争端的方法和机构

由于历史原因，即由于葡萄牙人和葡萄牙的顾问在独立时所带来的影响，东帝汶的法律是以民法体系为基础的。

民事纠纷通常是通过国内法院系统处理的，而这种系统并不总是适合当前的要求。

该国建立了一审法院和上诉法院。然而，法院目前只在 13 个地区中的 4 个地区开展工作，大多数地方案件都是通过当地社区的传统和东帝汶司法机制处理的。宪法和立法中预计设立的其他法院，例如专门税务法院尚未建立。

替代性争端解决办法与东帝汶传统司法系统一致，但尚未制定正式制度。部长理事会于 2016 年 12 月批准了《仲裁、调解以及和解法》，作为财政改革努力的一部分，但该部法律尚未获得议会的批准。

（二）法律的适用

包括警察、检察官和法院在内的司法系统仍在发展并且人员配备不足。

2015 年 12 月，政府成立了立法改革与司法部门委员会，其任务是推荐法律改革，评估法律如何实施以及协调立法。正如该国战略发展计划所规定的那样，该委员会将审查和完善法律文书以确保权利、自由和保障以及法律的准入，使立法更接近民主理想和符合东帝汶公民的实际需求。

八、其他

（一）反商业贿赂

1. 反商业贿赂法律法规简介

东帝汶已经批准了《联合国反腐败公约》，该公约已在该国直接适用。

关于腐败的主要法律是第 19/2009 号法令和确定有关罪行的《刑法》以及第 8/2009 号法令，该法律创建并且管理反腐败委员会。

2. 部门监督反商业贿赂

反腐败委员会是负责执行现行有关反腐败和反贿赂立法的机构。该委员会具有专门和独立的刑事警察的地位，反腐败委员会有权要求任何人以直接或间接的方式对正在进行的调查予以配合。此外，一般的合作义务不仅针对反腐败委员会，也是对法院的一般合作义务。

3. 惩罚性措施

大多数犯罪和非法活动都与公共代理人或公共的和 / 或政治角色本人所获得的报酬、人情、礼金或任何其他类型的好处有关。

《刑法》规定如下行为是一项罪行，并分别处以下罚款：

- 因非法行为而被动腐败判处 3 至 15 年徒刑；
- 对于合法行为被动腐败判处 3 年有期徒刑或罚款；
- 主动腐败判处 3 至 10 年有期徒刑；
- 贪污判处 3 至 10 年有期徒刑；
- 滥用公共物质资源和设施判处 2 年有期徒刑；
- 滥用权力判处 1 至 4 年有期徒刑；
- 非法获取公共财物判处 2 至 8 年有期徒刑。

此外，对这些非法行为的惩罚可能涉及民事制裁，即根据民法典的一般规定在赔偿责任方面计算受影响方的赔偿义务。

（二）项目合同

1. 许可制度

第 11/2005 号法令规定了政府官员在代表东帝汶政府购买货物、服务或工程时必须执行的采购程序。

根据法律规定，"公共合同应被理解为双边议价措施，其中至少有一方是公法上的法人，这些方式的目的是为了满足公共采购的公开需求由政府当局发起"。

根据本法律条款签订的公共合同可以根据其目的不同，可以：
- 提供货物；
- 提供服务；
- 执行作品。

出于公共利益的原因，合同可根据主管当局或公共服务部门特别授予的授权，将特定或专有权归属于某些货物、工程或服务。

下列机关有权批准或签署公共合同：
- 总理，针对于价值等于或高于100万美元（100万美元）的合同；
- 规划和财务部长；
- 合同委员会；
- 主权机构、部长和国务秘书以及根据各自组织法的条款负责人；
- 由各主权机构和部长及国务秘书各自明确任命和授权的负责人；
- 自治部门，公共当局和其他拥有行政和财政自主权的机构负责人；
- 其他国家资本份额超过50%的法人，虽然不具有商业性质，但追求公共目标；
- 所有受国家预算限制或大部分由其资助的其他机构和公共服务。

主要招标流程是：
- 要求报价；
- 公开招标；
- 全国公开招标；
- 国际公开招标；
- 资格预审有限；
- 限制投标；
- 通过谈判程序；
- 通过独家采购和常备报价协议进行采购。

2. 禁止私人投资领域

邮政服务、公共通信、受保护的自然区域以及武器生产和分配是为国家预留的区域，私人公司不得介入。

3. 招标邀请和投标

对政府的总体结果的最佳评估是考虑到所有相关的"整个生命周期"成本和收益：这是每种商品、服务或作品超过其预期使用寿命的全部成本——而不仅仅是在采购方面。政府采购决策应以"物有所值"为基础，这需要对成本、收益和替代结果进行比较。

（三）其他

除此之外，东帝汶是以下国际组织及机构的成员国：国际货币基金组织（IMF），联合国（提供了行政、经济发展、安全培训和治理支持），联合国贸易及发展会议（UNCTAD），教科文组织，工发组织，非洲，加勒比和太平洋地区国家集团（ACP），亚洲开发银行，东盟观察员国，葡语国家联盟，粮农组织，国际金融公司，国际刑警组织，太平洋岛屿论坛国观察员国和亚洲发展基金成员，亚洲发展基金是亚洲开发银行（亚行）支持东帝汶活动的主要资金来源。

"东帝汶尚未通过经合组织，世贸组织或贸发会议进行任何投资的政策审查。东帝汶于2016年被接纳为世贸组织的观察员，加入世贸组织的工作组于2016年12月成立。东帝汶正在根据世贸组织的要求，重新启动设计和启动财政和经济改革，其中包括有关私人投资的新法律，出口促进，商业公司，制裁，税收和增值税（VAT）。东帝汶的政治稳定为企业发展提供了机会。商业正在增加，政府正在资助额外的公共服务和大型公共工程项目。除石油和天然气部门外，服务业、旅游业、农业和基础设施行业还存在投资机会。虽然政府致力于改善其关键部门的服务，但挑战依然存在。官僚效率低下，基础设施瓶颈，缺乏地方融资选择，缺乏不动产法和其他基本立法，政府程序实施存在不确定性，人力资源严重缺乏、渎职行为，利益冲突和腐败显著的挑战。"[1]

---

[1] https://www.state.gov/e/eb/rls/othr/ics/2017/eap/269858.htm.

Timor-Leste

Authors: Rui Botica Santos, Paulo Oliveira
Translators: Tell Tan, Yang Zhenfa

I. Overview

A. Introduction

Timor-Leste, formerly known as East Timor, once Portuguese ultra-marine territory and later Indonesian province, consolidated its independence and achieved its sovereignty with the promulgation of its Constitution in 2002, becoming the only Lusophone state in Eastern World and one of the youngest states in the world, the youngest in Southeast Asia and the first to become independent in 21 century.

The Country borders Indonesia and is located northwest of Australia in the Lesser Sunda Islands at the eastern end of the Indonesian archipelago, comprising part of the island of Timor, which lies to the north of the Timor Sea, as well as the enclave of Oecussi (Ambeno) on the northwest portion of the island of Timor, and the islands of Pulau Atauro and Pulau Jaco.

Timor-Leste achieved independence with difficulty due to civil and political turmoil, conflict and instability. The country was first colonized by the Portuguese Empire in the 16th century. In 1975, the Portuguese decolonized Timor-Leste and, in the same year, right after became independent, the Country was invaded and occupied by Indonesia. In 1999, with the support of the United Nations, Timor-Leste declared its independence from Indonesia. On May 20 of 2002, after a transitional administration period leaded by the United Nations, Timor-Leste was (re)born as the first new sovereign state of the 21st century.

Since then, the Country became safe, stable and richer. Driven by public expenditure and the revenues from its large and oil and gas reserves, Timor-Leste has grown significantly, registering, in 2013, the sixth higher rate of Gross Domestic Product – GDP growth in the World.

Notwithstanding, the country has undergone a difficult and complex process aiming to rebuild the country into a modern state. It has achieved some of its short-term priorities, but the Government faces immediate and serious political, economic and social challenges. Long-term challenges are tackling employment and underemployment, rebuilding the security institutions, strengthening the institutional capacity of the public sector and developing a non-petroleum economy.

Timor-Leste is open to foreign investments and the Government has released in recent years a significant set of structural reforms aimed at further liberalization of the economy and the improvement of the regulatory environment for business.

B. General Facts

Area: 14.874 km²[1]
Population: 1.291.358 (Estimated in 2017[2])
GDP: US$ 8,364 billion (Estimated in 2014[3])
Capital: Dili
Official Languages: Tétum and Portuguese. 16 indigenous languages are also spoken. Indonesian and English are the business languages.
Climate: The climate of East Timor is regular all year, tropical hot and humid and has two distinct seasons, dry - from June to October and rainy - from November to May with an average temperature of 30° Celsius.
Time zone: UTC+09
Currency: US Dollar
Main Ethnic Groups: Austronesian (Malayo-Polynesian), Papuan and small Chinese community.
Religion: The majority of the population is Catholic. There are also small Protestant and Sunni Muslim

---

[1] Central Intelligence Agency (CIA). CIA World Factbook.
[2] Central Intelligence Agency (CIA). CIA World Factbook.
[3] International Monetary Fund. World Economic Outlook Database.

communities.

Timor-Leste is divided into 13 districts, which are subdivided into 65 administrative posts, 443 villages (sucos) and more than 2.200 hamlets (aldeias). The districts are:
- Aileu
- Ainaro
- Baucau
- Bobonaro
- Cova Lima
- Dili
- Ermera
- Lautém
- Liquiçá
- Manatuto
- Manufahi
- Oecusse
- Viqueque

C. Political and Legal System

Timor-Leste, officially Democratic Republic of Timor-Leste, is a unitary semi-presidential representative democratic republic, based in the universal, free, direct, equal, secret and personal suffrage and governed by the rule of law. As a young nation in process of building, Timor-Leste is making "considerable effort to establish effective legislative, executive, and judicial institutions, draft laws and regulations, and build government personnel capacity[1]".

The National Parliament, a unicameral assembly, represents the Timorese people amd is "vested with legislative supervisory and political decision making powers[2]", whose members are is elected by popular vote for a five-year term.

In its semi-presidential regime, inspired in the Portuguese model, the head of state is the President of Republic and the head of government is the Prime Minister, who leads the National Parliament.

The president of the Republic of Timor-Leste is elected by popular vote for a five-year term and plays a largely symbolic role, but is the commander in chief of the military and is able to veto legislation, appoint the Prime Minister, dissolve parliament and call national elections.

The Government, formed by the Prime Minister and the Ministers and the Secretaries of State – appointed by the President of the Republic following proposal by the Prime Minister – is responsible for conducting and executing the general policy of the country and is the supreme organ of Public Administration.

According to the Constitution of the Democratic Republic of Timor-Leste, "the Prime Minister shall be designated by the political party or alliance of political parties with parliamentary majority and shall be appointed by the President of the Republic, after consultation with the political parties sitting in the National Parliament[3]".

The representative democracy relies on political parties. The main ones, only political parties in Parliament, are:
- Democratic Party or PD;
- Frenti-Mudança;
- National Congress for Timorese Reconstruction or CNRT;
- Revolutionary Front of Independent Timor-Leste or FRETILIN.

The Country has a judiciary system with independent courts, whose decisions are subject only to the Constitution and the law and shall be binding and prevail over the decisions of any other authority.

Regarding the law, "Timor-Leste has a legal system is based on a mix of Indonesian laws and regulations, acts passed by the United Nations Transitional Administration, and post-independence Timorese legislation. The country is working on a review of its legislation to harmonize the system, but has yet to undergo a comprehensive overhaul of the overlapping yet disparate systems. All new legislation is enacted in Portuguese and is based on the civil law tradition[4]".

---

[1] U.S. Department of State. 2017 Investment Climate Statements. https://www.state.gov/e/eb/rls/othr/ics/2017/eap/269858.htm.
[2] Constitution of the Democratic Republic of Timor-Leste, Article 92.
[3] Constitution of the Democratic Republic of Timor-Leste, Article 106, 1.
[4] U.S. Department of State. https://www.state.gov/e/eb/rls/othr/ics/2017/eap/269858.htm.

D. Business and Economic Environment

Timor-Leste has huge reserves of oil and gas, being its economy based on the oil and gas sector. However, these are not the only abundant natural resources in the Country, and others sectors are growing and have great potential, such as agriculture, namely coffee and sandalwood, mining, fisheries, renewable energy and tourism.

Despite its turmoil past and its early stage of development, Timor-Leste has a stable and free economy. As mentioned, the Country, following its Strategic Development Plan 2011-2030, has released a significant set of structural reforms aimed at further liberalization of the economy and the improvement of the regulatory environment for business.

In 2012 the Labor Law was improved with more consolidated and complete specifications about the labor contracts system establishing better conditions and protection to the employees. The investment on education and promotion of Portuguese language together with the reforms on social security in terms of training and formation are a proper contribute to the development of the country.

Some measures are simplifying procedures and reducing administrative costs were implemented making citizens and businesses everyday life easier. Timor-Leste has reduced the time (days) from 147 to 103, the costs from 5% to 4.5% and the minimum capital required to start a business.

The new Private Investment Law (Law 15/2017) is "part of the Government's effort to promote the private sector of the economy and to create conditions to attract foreign investment[1]". The law offers incentives to private investment in the Country, including tax holidays from five to ten years, depending on the nature and location of the investment, and aims to ensure that "the national legislation on investment will act in accordance with guidelines issued by the Association of Southeast Asian Nations Comprehensive Investment Agreement, to facilitate the accession of Timor-Leste to the organization[2]".

The Government is also investing directly and promoting investments in basic infrastructure and logistics, namely roads, ports and airports, as a way to facilitate business and attract and enhance foreign investments.

Currently, Timor-Leste ranks #178 among 190 countries in the World Bank Doing Business Ranking 2018. According to the ranking, enforcing contracts (position 190), registering property (position 187), getting credit (position 167) and resolving insolvency (position 169)[3] are the bottle necks of Timor-Leste's economy.

E. Economic Statistics

According to the International Monetary Fund – IMF, the Gross Domestic Product – GDP (Purchasing Power Parity – PPP) of Timor-Leste is USD 6.2 billion (2017, estimate)[4], making the GDP per capita (PPP)[5] USD 5,000 (2017, estimate). By sector, industry represents 57.8% of the GDP, followed by services with 31.3% and agriculture with 9.4% (2017 estimate)[6].

Regarding trading balance, total exports amounted to USD 20 million in 2016[7], while total imports totaled USD 558.6 million (2016 estimate[8]). Exports are composed mainly by oil, coffee, sandalwood and marble, whereas imports are food, gasoline, kerosene, machinery. The Country main trade partners are Indonesia, Australia, China, Singapore, Malaysia, Portugal and Germany.

Foreign Direct Investment (FDI) stocks in Timor-Leste amounted to USD 346 million in 2016[9].

The labor force of the Country relies on 286,700 people (2016 est.), of which 64% works on agriculture, 10% in industry and 26% in services (2010)[10]. Unemployment rate is 4.4% (2014 est.)[11].

Budget revenues totaled $300 million in 2017 and expenditures $2.2 billion[12]. Taxes and other revenues correspond to 11% of GDP (2017 est.)[13].

---

[1] Council of Ministers. Press Release of the meeting of July 19th, 2016.
[2] Council of Ministers. Press Release of the meeting of July 19th, 2016.
[3] World Bank. Doing Business 2018.
[4] IMF World Economic Outlook 2016.
[5] IMF World Economic Outlook 2016.
[6] Central Intelligence Agency (CIA). CIA World Factbook.
[7] Central Intelligence Agency (CIA). CIA World Factbook.
[8] Central Intelligence Agency (CIA). CIA World Factbook.
[9] IMF World Economic Outlook 2016.
[10] Central Intelligence Agency (CIA). CIA World Factbook.
[11] Central Intelligence Agency (CIA). CIA World Factbook.
[12] Central Intelligence Agency (CIA). CIA World Factbook.
[13] Central Intelligence Agency (CIA). CIA World Factbook.

Inflation in 2017 was 1.3%[1] and public deficit (general government net lending / borrowing as a % of GDP) was -18% in 2017[2].

F. Oil & Gas

In terms of revenues, with only one oil field, Timor-Leste is managing to extract oil worth around one hundred million dollars per month. This means around three to four million dollars a day.

The main oil field in East Timor is the Bayu-Undan located in the Joint Petroleum Development Area (JPDA), an area encompassing the maritime boundary between Timor-Leste and Australia where revenues from oil are shared. This field shall continue to be a source of income until the year 2025. An additional field, Kitan, contains about 34.5 million barrels of oil.

In 2008, the Timorese government created the ANP (National Petroleum Authority) to regulate the sector in the Timor-Leste exclusive jurisdictional areas and in the Joint Petroleum Development Area (JPDA).

The World Bank supported the government in establishing a petroleum regime that is internationally competitive. Timor-Leste was declared compatible with the international Extractive Industries Transparency Initiative, which aims to increase the accountability of governments and companies in resource management throughout the world. As only the third World Bank member country to achieve this status, Timor-Leste has set benchmarks for other developing countries in transparency and accountability in this regard.

In order to manage the revenues from oil sector, the Government created a Petroleum Fund. According to the Petroleum Fund Law (Law nº 9/2005), all petroleum and related revenues must be paid into the Fund, with balance of the fund being invested in international financial markets for the benefit of the present and future generations of Timor-Leste citizens. The operational management of the fund is the responsibility of the Banking and Payments Authority, carried out under an investment mandate agreed with the Minister of Planning and Finance.

The Government, represented by the Minister of Finance, is responsible for the overall management and investment strategy of the Petroleum Fund.

In executing its responsibility, the Central Bank of Timor-Leste established the Petroleum Fund Management Department. The Department is headed by an Executive Director accountable to the Governor, and comprises an Investment Division with responsibility for investment management, and a Risk Management Division responsible for performance measurement and to monitor and manage risks.

In very broad terms, the Petroleum Fund is a tool that contributes to sound fiscal policy, where appropriate consideration is given to the log-term interest of Timorese citizens. The decision on "how much to spend and how much to save (i.e. spend later)" is done in the state budget where all the government's priorities are weighed against each other.

G. Natural Resources and Economic Potential

As highlighted, the Timorese Government has been making efforts to diversify the economic activity in order to make the country less dependent of the oil and gas resources. The following are some examples of sectors with potential interest for investors.

a. Minerals

Beyond oil and gas, Timor-Leste has other natural resources like minerals (metallic – gold, manganese, copper and non-metallic – sand and stones), which exploitation could vary between the energy and construction industry.

There are copper and galena located in south of Vemasse and Soibada. Gold deposits were spotted by the rivers Sue, Lacló do Sul and Clerac, as well as in Faluberliu (district of Manufahi).

Manganese is one of the most common minerals, although its exploitation in the mines of Vemasse, Baucau, Baguia and Uatucarbau were considered not profitable enough in the past.

Coal deposits were found in Viqueque (Uatolari) and Baucau (Baguia).

Regarding minerals with potential for the construction, diorite, marble, and schist are abundant in the district of Dili. Clay can be found in Dili and Manatuto.

Limestones can be found mainly in the Maubisse area and thermal resources of high potential are located in the mountains (districts of Bobonaro, Ermera, Viqueque and Baucau).

The prospection and exploitation of mines and quarries are subject to prior licencing awarded by the government.

---

[1] IMF World Economic Outlook 2016.
[2] IMF World Economic Outlook 2016.

b. Renewable energies

The extensive hydro network and the high records of rain indicate a good potential of mainly underground hydric resources, and biomass. Other potentially interesting areas, yet to be developed, are the wind, solar, wave and geothermic energies production.

c. Fisheries

The natural conditions favor the rich Timorese marine ecosystem of shellfish, reptiles, crustaceans, fish and mammals. Tuna, being of high potential in the region, is abundant, as well as corvinas, squids, soles, hakes, mackerel, sharks, lobsters, crabs, oysters, turtles, bonitos, and red mullets In the rivers one can find shrimps and eels.

d. Tourism

Due to the natural beauty of the country (from tropical beaches, with clear waters and rich in marine life, to mountain areas with temperate climates), the tourism sector presents good opportunities. In addition, Timor-Leste's has a privileged location in the Asia-Pacific region, a region with strong developed economies and emerging dynamic economies that may constitute clear emitting markets for Timor-Leste's tourism sector.

Under the National Tourism Policy, the Government of Timor-Leste intends to reach USD 150 million (at 2016 prices) by 2030 in annual revenues from foreign tourism, not including transport operators' revenues (air fares and ferry charges), as well as 200,000 international visitors annually, with an average stay of four days.

H. Infrastructure

The development of infrastructures is a key priority of the government as outlined in its Strategic development Plan, in which policy framework it targets quality national infrastructures in place by 2020. Around USD 1 bilion per year of public revenues will be invested in fundamental projects.

a. Roadways

The main road system consists of two cost roads along the north and south costs, as well as five roads that cross the country and connect with the two cost roads.

The main priorities of the Government are to rehabilitate and repair 90% of the existing roads to upgrade their safety and bring them up to international standards.

There will be high investments in the roadways starting with the connections around Díli and in a second phase in the districts in order to increase and improve the efficiently of circulation of people and goods.

The Asian Development Fund (ADF) has supported the Road Network Upgrading Project that will upgrade two of the busiest roads in Timor-Leste and improve the main western road link to Indonesia.

b. Ports

Timor-Leste has best conditions to establish networks of sea transportation which along with the oil exploration and its geographical position is a huge advantage against competitor countries.

Presently, only Díli has the capacity to send and receive big cargo containers and has a ferry called Berlin Nakroma which is used to essentially transport people to Ataúro Island and to Oé-cussi. However, the government acknowledges that Díli Harbor is becoming too small for the increase of goods and people circulating.

Therefore according to the future implementation of the NSDP (National Strategic Development Plan) the port facilities will be relocated to Tibar and Dili Harbor will be used solely for tourism purposes. The port of Tíbar is also situated on the north coast, transferring part of the gas to the country.

c. Air Transport

The only companies that presently operate the Presidente Nicolau Lobato International Airport are Merpati, Silkair, AirTimor and Batavia, limited to a few flights per day. The extension of this airport's runway from 1850 to 2500 meters, and the construction of a new terminal, are planned to turn this facility into a modern airport, of international standards, with capacity for one million passengers by 2020.

According to the Government, a private developer will be selected under a PPP (Public / Private Partnership) agreement for a Build, Finance and Operate concession contract expected to last 25 years. This project will be funded through the Petroleum Fund. IFC was selected by the government to be the Transaction Adviser and the first phase of this project was recently launched. There are three airfields – Baucau (2nd largest city), Suai and Oecussi, all used merely for domestic flights.

d. Telecommunications Network

Timor Telecom provides an exclusive system regarding all landline and mobile phone services. The Government has announced a public tender for the telecommunications and the selected companies were Viettel

Global Investment JSC (from Vietnam) which for instance has 61 million subscribers with networks with nearly 170 million people and also the PT Telekomunikasi Indonesia International (Telin).

The country is ready to develop this sector aiming to bring in competition and lower rates, better reach and a Following national efforts to improve the conditions of accessing to electricity for rural and urban populations, especially after this modernization of power plants that supply the country, is fundamental to develop an integrated national system of installation of low voltage stations.

e. Electricity

The implementation of the Decree-Law 13/2003 which establishes the basis of the Electricity National System (ENS) delivered competences to the Government to set up strategic lines for the development of ENS. In order to create a homogeneous structure and in addition, the Government has taken significant steps towards implementing a universal distribution system of electricity through the construction of:

- Central Electric Hera, medium speed production - 7 x 17 MW; capacity - 119.5 MW.
- Beatno Power Station, speed - 8 x 17 MW; capacity - 136.6 MW
- 150kV transmission line with approximately 715km;
- Nine sub-stations in the district capitals;
- A control center in Dili.

I. The Status and Direction of the Cooperation with Chinese Enterprises Under the B&R

As Asian neighbors, China and Timor-Leste have a good relation of friendship. Diplomatic ties were established between the two countries since the early days of the new Timor-Leste, in 2002. Through all of these years, the friendship as the Chinese investments in Timor-Leste only grew.

According to the Hong Kong Trade Development Council of China, "China's investment in the country has been growing, with cumulative FDI between 2010 and 2015 soaring from US$7.5 million to US$100.3 million based on statistics of China's Ministry of Commerce".

In 2014, China became Timor-Leste's third largest provider of goods, after Indonesia and Singapore, exporting USD 41 million.

"In recent years, China has built office buildings for Timor-Leste's Ministry of Foreign Affairs, Ministry of Defense, and the Timor-Leste Defense Force, as well as the Presidential Palace. More than one thousand Timorese civil servants have visited China for training, while thousands of Chinese technicians have tutored their counterparts on the latest agricultural methods, urban planning, tourism, and other areas[1]". Between 2009 and 2016 Chinese companies construction contracts in Timor-Leste amounted to more than USD 525 million[2].

China is also an important source of aid and has provided $77 million in aid to Timor-Leste since 2011[3].

Undoubtedly, this successful partnership has a lot to grow under the 'Silk Road Economic Beit and the 21st-Century Maritime Silk Road'. Timor-Leste's strategic location in the Pacific, between Australia and Indonesia, as well as the fact that is wide open to the sea and has deep waters and perfect conditions for navigation, are characteristics that makes the country well positioned to benefit from the program.

II. Investment

A. Market Access

a. Department Supervising Investment

TradeInvest Timor-Leste, I.P., Investment and Export Promotion Agency, established by the Decree-Law 45/2015, is the government body responsible for investments in Timor-Leste, under the State Secretary of Private Sector (SEAPRI).

TradeInvest negotiates agreements with foreign investors, granting them incentives and special conditions and benefits to invest in the country.

The Agency's' goal "is to facilitate and support potential investor locate in Timor-Leste and assist foreign companies in identifying projects in the vast array of business opportunities that are emerging in Timor-Leste[4]".

---

[1] https://thediplomat.com/2016/11/is-chinas-influence-in-timor-leste-rising/.
[2] https://thediplomat.com/2016/11/is-chinas-influence-in-timor-leste-rising/.
[3] https://thediplomat.com/2016/11/is-chinas-influence-in-timor-leste-rising/.
[4] TradeInvest's web site, "About TradeInvest": http://www.investtimor-leste.com/?q=node/4.

TradeInvest's activity is complemented by an institution called IADE (Instituto de Apoio ao Desenvolvimento Empresarial), which was created with a view to provide relevant information as well as guidance and counseling that can help companies decide where to invest, when invest or even what to invest.

In general terms, IADE can assist companies by establishing a link between the producer and the seller, by doing market researches, by identifying business areas yet to be explored and by providing assistance in Public tenders and credit loans.

b. Laws and Regulations of Investment Industry

Investments in Timor-Leste are regulated by Law 15/2017, the Private Investment Law, and the Government Decree 2/2018, establishing, among other provisions, fiscal and customs incentives for new investments, as well as special incentives for private investments.

The main purposes of the legal investment framework are:
- To create tax and customs benefits and advantages;
- To create favorable investment conditions in Timor-Leste;
- To support the development of certain regions determined by Law;
- To guarantee to the investors access to the courts in order to protect the defense of their legitimate rights and interests.

c. Forms of Investment

Investment or reinvestment may consist of the following:
- Creation or increase of a company, under the terms of the law in force for Timor-Leste;
- Acquisition of part or all of the shareholdings of a commercial company, participation in the increase of its capital or realization of additional capital contributions;
- To celebrate and amend contracts related to the ownership and management of companies, establishments of agricultural, industrial and commercial character, real estate complexes and other facilities or equipment that are aimed to be used in the development of economic activities;
- Financial resources from bank loans or supplies made by an investor to a commercial company where it participates or any loans related to reinvestment of profits and dividends in the same enterprise;
- Acquisition or importation in favor of the company of good or capital equipment allocated to the project, including the contracting of the respective insurance;
- Acquisition or importation in favor material or semi-processed goods for exclusive realization of the investment or reinvestment;
- Free transfer to the company of industrial secrets, copyright, industrial property rights, trade mark distinctive signs, or any other intellectual property rights that are recognized by law.

The minimum investment values, in order to obtain investment incentives, are:
- USD 50,000.00 (Fifty thousand US dollars), for national investors;
- USD 500,000.00 (Five hundred thousand US dollars), for foreign investors;
- USD 250,000.00 in the case of joint venture association agreements or legally admissible partnerships between foreign and domestic investors, in which they control at least 75% of the equity interest of the companies.

d. Standards of Market Access and Examination

As mentioned, TradeInvest is the body responsible for negotiating and granting incentives and benefits to investors. Benefits and incentives may be negotiated and granted under the form of a "Declaration of Benefits" or a "Special Investment Agreement", both detailed in the following.

a) Declaration of Benefits:

The Declaration of Benefit is a document issued in favor of the investor in which the benefits are acknowledged. The processing of application and issuance of the Declaration of Benefits is simpler than that for Special Investments Agreement.

In order to obtain the Declaration of Benefits, the investor must submit a proper request to the Executive Director of TradeInvest together with:
- Form (Annex I of the Regulation);
- Copy of the ID of the persons incorporated into the company and participating in the investment (national investors);
- Copy of certificate of commercial registration of the investor;
- Request for the granting of a maximum of 5 work visas and documents required by law;
- Business plan.

The request is forwarded to the competent department of TradeInvest TL, I.P., for a preliminary analysis.

Within 6 working days, the department responsible for the process sends a copy of the documentation to the

National Directorate of Lands (responsible for renting state properties) and Immigration Services (responsible for granting visas).

Once received the documentation, the National Directorate of Lands and the Immigration Services, have 6 working days to issue an opinion. In the absence of a reply, the opinion is considered to be favourable.

After a favourable opinion, the Executive Director of TradeInvest sends an information report to the supervisory authority, recommending the issuance of the declaration of benefits in favour of the investor.

The supervisory authority has 6 working days to sign and return the declaration of benefits to TradeInvest.

Once received the declaration of benefits, it is delivered to the investor and a copy sent to the National Directorate of Lands and to the Immigration Services.

The declaration of benefits shall list the tax benefits granted to the investor under the approved investment project, as well as the respective granting period.

The Declaration of Benefits may be revoked in the following situations:
• When the amount for the investment does not correspond to the actual value of the investment;
• When the project is not initiated, for reasons attributable to the investor, within 1 year from the issuance of the benefits declaration;
• By dissolution or liquidation of the company;
• By declaration of bankruptcy of the investor or company;
• By merger or acquisition of a commercial company associated with the project.

b) Special Investment Agreement

Special Investment Agreements are exceptional and subject to prior negotiation with the Government, being applicable only to investment projects which, because of their size or nature, or their economic, social, environmental or technological impact, may be of great national interest. In this case, besides the regular benefits, the Government may offer and grant more benefits other than tax benefits.

In order to conclude a Special Investment Agreement, the investor must submit a proper request to the Executive Director of TradeInvest together with:
• Form (Annex I of the Regulation);
• Copy of the ID of the persons incorporated into the company and participating in the investment (national investors);
• Copy of certificate of commercial registration of the investor;
• Request for the granting of a maximum of 5 work visas and documents required by law;
• Business plan.
• A document identifying the reasons why the investor intends to conclude the special investment agreement, as well as economic, social, environmental and technological impact that may be of great national interest within the framework of the Strategic Development Plan.

After receiving the request, the Executive Director of TradeInvest forwards it to the competent department for the preliminary analysis of the application. This department, identifies the main governmental entities and respective departments that shall be consulted and sends a copy of the documentation to the competent authority within 5 working days from the receipt of the request.

The supervisory authority must, within 10 working days from the reception of the documentation, arrange a meeting with TradeInvest Timor-Leste for a preliminary discussion of the investment proposal. After this meeting, the competent department of TradeInvest sends a copy of the relevant documentation to the main governmental entities and respective departments that are to be consulted, which have a term of 20 working days to issue an opinion on the investment proposal.

Upon a favourable opinion, the draft of the special investment agreement is submitted to the Government for analysis, and shall be approved by Government Resolution, expressly indicating the reasons justifying the agreement and the special regime by which it is governed.

A Special Investment Agreement may be terminated by agreement of both parties, for the definitive default of one of the parties or for any other causes provided for in the respective agreement.

B. Foreign Exchange Regulation

a. Department Supervising Foreign Exchange

Please see section b.

b. Brief introduction of Laws and Regulations of Foreign Exchange

The official currency of Timor-Leste is the US dollar, which facilitates transferring of funds from and to abroad.

Until now, there is no currency control in Timor-Leste, nor policies governing remittances, but is worth to mention that "the Central Bank of Timor-Leste imposes reporting requirements for the importation or exportation of cash above USD 5,000 and requires explicit authorization for sums in excess of USD 10,000[1]".

In addition to this requirements, other reporting obligations may be imposed by banks in "transactions above a certain amount in order to comply with home-country anti-money laundering regulations[2]".

Notwithstanding, foreign investors, under the Law 15/2017, the Private Investment Law, have the right to free transfer of funds to abroad (ex.: profits and dividends; capital; income; compensation; payments) and conversion of amounts into foreign currency (via the banking system).

c. Requirements of Foreign Exchange Management for Foreign Enterprises

Please see section b.

C. Financing

a. Main Financial Institutions

Besides the Central Bank of Timor-Leste – BCTL – a public bank with authority over the monetary policy, payment system and financial institutions, created and regulated by the Law 5/2011 –, the following banks operate in Timor-Leste:
- Banco Nacional Ultramarino – BNU, Caixa Geral de Depósitos Group, from Portugal;
- Banco Nacional de Comércio de Timor-Leste – BNCTL, from Timor-Leste;
- Australia and New Zealand Banking Group – ANZ, from Australia and New Zealand;
- Bank Rakyat, from Indonesia; and
- Bank Mandiri, from Indonesia.

Along with those institutions, three insurance companies are licensed by BCTL and operate in the country:
- National Insurance Timor–Leste, SA;
- Federal Insurance Timor, SA;
- Sinarmas Insurance, SA.

b. Financing Conditions for Foreign Enterprises

Access to bank credit in Timor-Leste is limited. The difficulties stem from a number of factors, including the still small size of the banking system, low business productivity and the impossibility of providing real guarantees under the current legal system.

As a way to mitigate these difficulties, the Government of Timor-Leste, through Decree-Law no. 23/2017, created a Credit Guarantee System for small and medium-sized enterprises. In this system, the State shares the risk of lending with commercial banks up to a maximum of 70% of the loans granted that meet the legal requirements established. For law purposes, small enterprises are those that employ between 6 and 20 Workers and medium-sized enterprises that employ between 21 and 50 workers

The system, however, is not applicable to foreign companies and applies only to companies incorporated and registered under Timorese law in which at least 75% of the voting shares are directly or indirectly held by individuals of Timorese nationality.

D. Land Policy

a. Brief Introduction of Land-Related Laws and Regulations

Timor-Leste´s land policy is in its early stages. Until 2017, there was no policy or law about lands and properties registration, fact that caused instability and confusion regarding real estate rights and ownership, since property holders could not have public property deeds, leading to different claims over the same property.

In order to solve this problem, the Parliament approved the Law 13/2017 of 5 June, establishing a "Special Regime for the Ownership Definition of Property", with a view to address a process of regularization and recognition of property ownership in Timor-Leste.

Now, the properties are being regularized by a National Bureau, the National Directory of Land, Property and Registering Services – DNTPSC, through a cadastral survey and a land registration system with official information on the legal status of real estate, allowing the granting of public property deeds to legitimate owners and the formation of a safe and transparent real estate market.

Concerning expropriation, there is no specific law. The Constitution, however, "permit the expropriation or

---

[1] U.S. Department of State. https://www.state.gov/e/eb/rls/othr/ics/2017/eap/269858.htm.
[2] U.S. Department of State. https://www.state.gov/e/eb/rls/othr/ics/2017/eap/269858.htm.

requisition of private property in the public interest only if just proper compensation is paid[①]".

b. Rules of Land Acquisition for Foreign Enterprises

According to the Law 13/2017 of 5 June, only Timorese nationals, Timorese legal entities exclusively constituted by Timorese nationals or whose capital is entirely and exclusively owned by nationals, local communities and non-profit legal entities may hold title to property.

In fact, there is a constitutional limitation that prohibits foreign persons or foreign legal entities from owning land and have real estate rights.

Notwithstanding, foreigners investors may have access to land through long-term leases - up to 50-year for state owned properties, renewable for more 50 (2 x 25), in which process TradeInvest can provide assistance.

E. The Establishment and Dissolution of Companies

a. The Forms of Enterprises

According to the Law nº 10/2017, Companies' Act, there are two forms of enterprises in Timor-Leste: limited liability companies and joint stock companies

a) Limited Liability Companies

In Timor-Leste, limited liability companies are those whose capital is divided into a minimum of two and a maximum of thirty quotas, i.e., it may not have less than two partners / shareholders nor more than thirty. As its denomination suggests, only the social assets shall respond to the creditors for the debts of the company.

The name of these companies must be formed, with or without an acronym, by the name or signature of all or one of the partners / shareholders, or by a particular name, or even by the meeting of both these elements, concluding, in any case, with the word "Limited" or by the abbreviation "Lda.".

The share capital is freely set by the partners, but must always correspond to the sum of the nominal values of the quotas. The company's articles of association must specify the share capital of each partner / shareholder.

In this type of company, the nominal value of each quota shall be equal to or greater than USD 1 and shall constitute a multiple of one. A quota may only be divided by the effect of partial amortization, partial assignment, sharing or division among joint owners.

The deposit of capital may be deferred up to half the nominal value of the quotas for cash deposits equal to or greater than USD 5,000. The quotas may only be deferred for a period not exceeding three years, for a date fixed determined by the competent authority.

If a partner / shareholder does not punctually pay its quota, the other partners are required, in proportion to their quotas but jointly and severally with the company, to perform the partner / shareholder in arrears. The quota, in its entirety, shall belong to the shareholders who hold the defaulting party, in proportion as they do so, being for this purpose divided and added to their quotas. The member who loses the quota under this terms is not entitled to recover the amounts already paid for the quota.

b) Joint Stock Companies

Joint stock companies are those whose capital is divided into shares represented by securities. It may not have less than three shareholders and its capital may not be less than USD 50,000. In this type of company, all shares are nominative and indivisible and the shareholder's liability is limited to the value of the shares it subscribes to.

The name of these companies is formed, with or without an acronym, by the name or signature of one or some of the shareholders or by a particular name, or by the meeting of both these elements, but shall include in any case the expression "sociedade anónima" or the abbreviation "S.A." at the end.

Joint stock companies may not be incorporated without subscribing the whole of its share capital and paying up at least 25%. There is no deferral on the deposit of capital.

Shares may be common or preferred; the common shares confer the right to vote and the dividend of distributable profits, and the preferred shares do not confer voting rights but confer the right to a priority dividend and priority reimbursement in the sharing of the settlement balance.

The incorporation of companies with public subscription is allowed.

b. The Procedure of Establishment

Any company that wishes to operate in Timor-Leste must be incorporated in accordance with domestic law and shall be registered at SERVE – Services for Registration and Verification of Entrepreneurs – an "One-Stop-Shop" under the authority the Ministry of Justice, Ministry of Finance and by the Ministry of Commerce, Industry

---

① U.S. Department of State. https://www.state.gov/e/eb/rls/othr/ics/2017/eap/269858.htm.

and Environment, "responsible for the registration of companies an sole traders, as well for the verification and publicity of their legal status, with competency, to approve company's name, as well as to organize and manage the business registration data base". At SERVE it is possible to obtain the business registration, apply for a commercial license and get the Tax Identification Number (TIN).

According to the Decree-Law 16/2017 on Business Registration, four steps are required to set up a company in Timor-Leste. Basically, the steps are:
- Choose the for form of company and Deposit minimum capital at the Bank;
- Register the company's name, file the company's statutes, apply for a TIN (Tax Payer Number) and obtain the final registration number (CRC- Número Único da Empresa) and the certificate of incorporation certified by SERVE and AEA (business license);
- Publish statutes at SERVE;
- Obtain a company stamp.

In general terms, the required documents are:
- Form requesting the registration;
- Proof of existence in the country of origin (only for company's branch);
- Minutes of the meeting of the General Assembly deciding to incorporate a company in Timor-Leste or to create a company's branch;
- By-laws;
- Proof of the Capital Stock;
- Identification of the shareholders;
- Proof of residence in Timor-Leste of at least one of the Directors;
- Letter of Acceptance for the Company's Positions (Directors, Secretary, etc.);
- Map of localization;
- Power of attorney to the company's legal representative (if applicable);
- Authorization for the activity issued by the competent Ministry (if applicable).

In the case of incorporation of companies with public subscription, a project must be submitted to SERVE together with:
- The integral design of the statutes, with strict specification of the object of the company;
- The number of shares intended for public subscription as well as their nature and nominal value and the issue premium, if any;
- The term of the subscription and the credit institutions where it can be made;
The term within which the constituent assembly will meet;
- A three-year forecast technical, economic and financial study of the evolution of the company, based on true and complete data and taking into account the known circumstances and forecasts available in the report, in order to duly clarify any interested in the subscription;
- The amount of the subscribed capital to be effected at the time of subscription, the deadlines for realizing the remainder, as well as the deadline for restitution of that amount in case the company does not constitute.

In areas of activity that are considered of medium or high risk such as petroleum, mining, food & beverages etc., the licensing has its own regulations in specific legislation and special licenses may be required.

The procedure of establishment for Legal Branch Office and Subsidiary

In order to register a Branch or other local form of a commercial company established in Timor-Leste or abroad, the following documents are required:
- Constitution act of the branch or of another local form of representation, with reference of its location;
- Determination of the official representative, with a mention to the recognized powers;
- ID Documents of the official representative and other holders of the corporate bodies, when applicable;
- Endorsement statement of the position engaged by the chosen representative;

In the case of Companies with a registered office, head office or effective management abroad (i.e. branches, agencies or other forms of representation), the following registration obligations, without prejudice to others established by law, may apply:
- The creation and extinction of permanent representation;
- Appointment and conclusion of duties of the legal representative;
- Determination of capital allocation to the activity of a permanent representation;
- The appointment of the legal representative as manager or attorney, when applicable;

For the registration of a permanent representation in Timor-Leste of a company headquartered abroad, the following documents are required:
- Proof of existence of the commercial company, according to the law of the country of origin. For any

document issued abroad, it is mandatory its legalization before the Timorese Embassy of the country of origin, as well as its translation to a Timorese official language (Portuguese or Tetum);
- Up to date articles of association;
- Deliberation of the creation of representation in Timor-Leste, with mention of the capital allocation;
- Deliberation of the designation of its representative;
- ID documents of the representatives and other members of the corporate bodies, if applicable;
- Acceptance letters of the representatives and other members of the corporate bodies, if applicable;
- Location map of the permanent representation in Timor-Leste;

c. Routes and Requirements of Dissolution

In Timor-Leste, societies can be dissolved:
- by resolution of the partners / shareholders;
- by the expiry of the duration period;
- For the suspension of the activity for a period exceeding three years;
- For not exercising any activity for a period of more than twelve consecutive months, without its activity being duly suspended;
- by the extinction of its object;
- for the unlawfulness or supervening impossibility of its object if, within a period of forty-five days, it is not resolved to alter it, in accordance with the terms established for the amendment of the statutes;
- as it is verified, from the accounts for the year, that the net worth of the company is less than half the value of the share capital;
- by judicial decision that determines the dissolution.

The dissolution has the effect of entering the company in liquidation.

Once the company is dissolved, the directors must submit to the shareholders' approval, within 60 days, the inventory, the balance sheet and the profit and loss account reported at the date of registration of the dissolution.

Once the accounts have been approved by the members, the administrators who do not become liquidators must deliver to them all documents, books, papers, records, money or assets of the company.

If, at the time of the dissolution, the company does not have any debts, the shareholders can immediately proceed to the sharing of social assets. Debts of a tax nature which have not yet been due at the time of dissolution do not preclude sharing, but all the members are unlimited and jointly liable for these debts, although they reserve in any way the sums they estimate for their payment.

Once the final accounts have been approved, the assets, net of settlement costs and debts of a tax or registration nature not yet due, are shared between the partners in the terms set forth in the articles of association.

The liquidators must request at SERVE the registration of the decision to close the liquidation within a period of fifteen days, and must have it accompanied by the referred documents.

The company is considered extinct on the date of registration of the closing of the liquidation, under the terms of this law or in insolvency proceedings.

Once the liquidation is closed and the company is extinguished, the former shareholders are jointly and severally liable for the liability of the company that was not considered in the liquidation until the amount they have received in exchange for the liquidation balance.

F. Merger and Acquisition

Mergers are authorized:
- by means of the global transfer of the assets of one or more companies to another and the attribution to the shareholders of those of shares or quotas of this one;
- by means of the constitution of a new company, to which the assets of the merged companies are transferred globally, and the shares of the new company are attributed to the partners of these companies.

Companies wishing to merge shall jointly prepare a merger project containing:
- The modality, reasons, conditions and objectives of the merger, in relation to all the participating companies;
- the name, registered office, capital and registration number of each company;
- The participation that one of the companies has in the capital of another;
- Balance sheets of the intervening companies, specially organized, showing the value of the assets and liabilities to be transferred to the acquiring company or to the new company;
- The shares or quotas to be attributed to the shareholders of the company to be merged or of the companies to be merged and the cash amounts to be attributed to the same shareholders, specifying the exchange ratio of the shareholdings;

Upon the registration of the merger:
- The merged companies are extinguished or, in the case of the formation of a new company, all merged companies, transmitting their rights and obligations to the acquiring company or to the new company;
- The members of the extinct companies become members of the acquiring company or of the new company.

The directors, members of the supervisory board or the sole supervisor and the secretary of each of the participating companies are jointly and severally liable for damages caused by the merger of the company and its partners and creditors if they have not observed the diligence of a prudent and orderly manager in the verification of the financial position of the companies and in the conclusion of the merger.

The provisions of the previous articles shall apply, with the exceptions set forth in the following paragraphs, to the incorporation by another company of whose shares or shares is the sole holder, directly or on its behalf but in his own name. In this case, the provisions regarding the exchange of shares, the reports of the corporate bodies of the merged company and the liability of these bodies are not applicable.

Companies may spin-off:
- to highlight part of its assets in order to form another company;
- to dissolve and divide up its assets, each of the resulting parts being intended to constitute a new company;
- to highlight parts of its assets or to dissolve it, dividing its assets into two or more parts, to merge them with existing companies or parts of the assets of other companies, separated by the same processes and for the same purpose.

The companies resulting from the spin-off may be of a different type from the spun-off company.

The management of the company to be split up or, in the case of a merger, the administrations of the participating companies must, jointly, to prepare a draft of a division, which includes, in addition to other elements necessary or convenient for the perfect knowledge of the operation envisaged:
- The modality, reasons, conditions and objectives of the spin-off for all participating companies;
- The name, registered office, capital amount and tax identification number of each company;
- The participation that one of the companies has in the capital of another;
- The complete listing of the assets to be transmitted to the acquiring company or to the new company, and the values attributed to them;
- In the case of a spin-off, the balance sheet of each of the participating companies, prepared in accordance with Article 108 (1) d);
- The shares or shares of the acquiring company or the new company and, if applicable, the cash sums attributed to the shareholders of the company to be spun off, specifying the exchange ratio of the shares and the bases of this relationship;
- The categories of shares of the companies resulting from the spin-off, when these are anonymous, and the dates from which these shares are delivered;
- the date from which the new participations grant the right to participate in profits, as well as any particularities relating to this right;
- The rights guaranteed by the companies resulting from the spin-off to the shareholders of the spun-off company holding special rights;
- Draft changes to be made to the statutes of the acquiring company or the draft articles of incorporation of the new company;
- measures to protect the rights of creditors;
- Measures to protect the right of non-members to participate in the company's profits;
- The attribution of the contractual position of the company or companies involved, arising from contracts of employment concluded with their employees, which are not extinguished by virtue of the split.

The spun-off company is jointly and severally liable for debts which, as a result of the spin-off, have been attributed to the acquiring company or to the new company.

The companies benefiting from the entries resulting from the spin-off are jointly and severally liable, up to the value of those entries, for the debts of the spun-off company prior to the registration of the spin-off.

The spin-off may take place even if the company is in liquidation.

The provisions relating to the merger are applicable to the spin-off of companies, with the necessary adaptations.

G. Competition Regulation

A competition law is yet to be established and there is no entity responsible for supervising competition regulation and competition regulating measures.

H. Tax

a. Tax Regime and Rules

The law Nº. 8/2008, Taxes and Duties Act, is the main tax law of Timor-Leste. This law is complemented by specific regulations for petroleum operations and by Indonesian Tax Law, as the Country, prior to its constitution, adopted the Indonesian tax law in accordance with UNTAET Regulation No.1999/1 with amendment of UNTAET Regulation 2000/18, which was not revoked and remains in force when applicable.

As mentioned, petroleum operations have a special regime of taxation. Bayu-Undan Field, for example, in the JPDA, has a fiscal and legal regime constructed from many sources, including Indonesian law, UNTAET Regulations, legislation specific to the Bayu-Undan Field and contractual arrangements implemented.

A tax reform is under way in the country. The aim of the reform is to improve tax and customs administrations, reduce costs for businesses, improve systems and create predictability, efficiency, integrity and transparency. Among this reforms is the plan to reduce tax rates compared to those in the ASEAN region for corporate income and personal incomes and create a VAT credit system to ensure that taxes do not stick to businesses.

b. Main Categories and Rates of Tax

In Timor-Leste, the main categories of tax and its respective rates are:
- Personal income tax: from 0 to 10%;
- Company income tax: 10%;
- Wage income tax: from 0 to 10%;
- Services tax: 5% for monthly turnovers exceeding USD 500;
- Sales tax: 2.5% on the imported product;
- Import Duties: 2.5% on the imported product;
- Excise tax: rate depends on the product.

c. Tax Declaration and Preference

a) Income Tax

Timor-Leste residents are taxable on world-wide income / profits, while non-resident are taxable on Timor-Leste sourced income / profits only. For the purpose of the law, resident legal persons are those incorporated, formed, organized or established in Timor-Leste. Legal persons include a vast range of entities such as companies, partnerships, trusts, governmental institutions and unincorporated associations.

Taxable business profits are computed on the basis of net profit, being that taxable income is the difference between the gross income, whether domestic or foreign sourced, and the allowable deductions. Business income includes gains from business activities and the alienation of assets or the discharged of indebtedness. Additionally, where certain types of income are subject to withholding tax which is final, such income is excluded from taxable income.

For law purposes, are considered as gross income:
- business income;
- property income;
- lottery prizes or awards;
- refund of a tax payment previously deducted as an expense; and
- any other amount that increases economic capacity, in whatever name or form, which can be used by the taxpayer for consumption or to increase the wealth of the taxpayer, other than wages subject to wages income tax.

And is considered as exempt income:
- any aid or donations, provided the donor and donee do not have any business, ownership, or control relationship;
- gifts received by relatives within one degree of direct lineage, or by a religious, educational, or charitable organization, or a co-operative, provided that the donor or donee does not have any business relation, ownership, or control;
- inheritances;
- assets (including cash) received by a legal person in exchange for shares or capital contribution;
- an amount paid by an insurance company to a natural person in connection with health, accident, life, or education insurance;
- dividends;
- any contribution paid by an employer or employee to an approved pension fund;
- income derived by an approved pension fund.

The rates for Income Tax are:

- in the case of a resident natural person, from $0 to $6,000 the rate is 0%, in excess of $6,000 the rate is 10%;
- in the case of a non-resident natural person 10%;
- in the case of a legal person 10%.

Certain payments made by a legal entity both to Timorese and foreign parties are subject to withholding tax as follows:
- Royalties – 10%;
- Rent (Land and Buildings) – 10%;
- Prizes and Winnings – 10%;
- Construction / Building Activities – 2%;
- Construction Consulting Services – 4%;
- Air or Sea Transportation – 2.64%;
- Mining and Mining Support Services – 4.5%.

The tax rates applicable to royalties and rent are only subject to a withholding at a final tax rate if we are in the presence of royalty payments to individuals, as opposed to corporate entities. Prizes and Winnings are always subject to a final tax. As for the remain payments, the income recipient can elect to have these payments for services not subject to a final tax, by submitting a notification letter to the tax authority.

Subject to the law, deductions are allowed for:
- expenditures to the extent incurred, and losses on the alienation of assets or the discharge of indebtedness incurred in the conduct of a taxable business activity;
- expenditures incurred in deriving any other amounts included in gross income;
- any loss on disposal of an asset, other than an asset covered on the first point, held on personal account;
- contributions to an approved pension fund; and
- doubtful debts

In order to minimize the effect of double taxation residents who receive foreign sourced profits and income, can receive credits for foreign taxes suffered.

Every income taxpayer shall account for income tax on an accrual basis. An income taxpayer whose annual gross turnover is less than USD 100,000 may account for income tax on either a cash or accrual basis.

Income taxpayers are required to deliver a completed income tax form for a tax year to the Banking and Payments Authority or another entity nominated by the Tax Administration not later than the last day of the third month after the end of the tax year. The income tax form of an income taxpayer conducting business activities shall be accompanied by the taxpayer's income statement, balance sheet, and cash flow statement for the tax year.

Individual or legal persons whose total turnover for the previous tax year is more than USD 1 million shall pay monthly instalments of income tax for a tax year. The amount of each instalment is 0.5% of the taxpayer's total turnover for the month. In its turn, those whose total turnover for the previous tax year is $1 million or less shall pay quarterly instalments of income tax for the year. Instalments shall be payable for the three-month period ending on the last day of the third, sixth, ninth, and twelfth months of the tax year. The amount of each instalment is 0.5% of the taxpayer's total turnover for the quarter. Instalments of income tax are payable by the 15th day after the end of the period to which they relate.

b) Wage Income Tax

Wage income tax is imposed on taxable wages received by an employee in respect of employment in Timor-Leste, where employment means services performed in Timor-Leste or services performed by an employee of the Government of Timor-Leste whether performed in the country or elsewhere. Wage income taxes are due in accordance with a progressive rate from 0 to 10% as per as the wage amount.

The following wages are exempt wages:
- wages received for official duties that are exempt from taxation under the Law;
- wages of an employee who is a citizen of a foreign country received in the

employee's capacity as a public servant of the government of a foreign country, provided the wages are subject to income tax in that country;
- wages of an employee who is an employee of the United Nations or its specialized agencies;

An employer paying taxable wages in respect of employment in Timor-Leste shall withhold wage income tax from those wages. An employee who receives wages that have been correctly subject to wage income tax has no further liability with respect to wage income tax imposed on those wages.

For the purpose of reporting, the employer shall deliver to the Banking and Payments Authority or another entity nominated by the Tax Administration by the fifteenth day after the end of a calendar month:

• a completed wage income tax withholding form as prescribed by the Tax Administration; and
• any wage income tax withheld in that month.

In addition, employers shall deliver to the Banking and Payments Authority or another entity nominated by the Tax Administration a completed annual wage income tax withholding information form as prescribed by the Tax Administration by the last day of March following the end of the tax year to which it relates.

c) Services Tax

Services taxes are imposed on the gross consideration received by a person for the provision of "designated services" namely:

• Hotel services;
• Restaurant and bar services;
• Telecommunications services.

Services are provided in Timor-Leste if such services originate in Timor-Leste.

The rate of services tax applicable to persons with a monthly turnover of designated services of less than USD 500 is 0% with a rate of 5% applicable where monthly turnover exceeds USD 500.

A person providing designated services in Timor-Leste who is liable to pay services tax shall deliver to the Banking and Payments Authority or another entity nominated by the Tax Administration by the fifteenth day after the end of a calendar month:

• a completed services tax form as prescribed by the Tax Administration; and
• any services tax payable on the gross consideration received in the month by the person for the provision of designated services.

In addition, a person who has had a liability to pay services tax in respect of any month shall deliver to the Banking and Payments Authority or another entity nominated by the Tax Administration a completed services tax form for subsequent months whether or not services tax is payable in subsequent months.

d) Sales Tax

As a general rule, sales tax is imposed on the value of the taxable goods whenever a taxpayer imports any taxable goods into Timor-Leste. Sales tax is calculated at 2.5% of the customs value of the goods, including any import duty and excise tax payable on the importation of the goods.

The payment of sales tax follows the same procedure for the payment of import duty.

e) Import Duty

Import Duty is imposed on the import of all goods (except those specifically exempt) at a 2.5% rate of the customs value of the goods. The customs value is the fair market value of the goods including cost, insurance and freight (CIF).

Goods accompany a person arriving in Timor-Leste from another territory are exempt from import duty, namely:

• two hundred (200) cigarettes and two and one half (2.5) litres of excisable beverages per person;
• goods up to a value of US $300 of a non-commercial nature that are exclusively for the personal use or enjoyment of travellers or goods intended as gifts, when the nature and quantity of the goods indicate that they are not imported for, or intended to be imported for, commercial purposes;
• goods of a non-commercial nature, other than jewellery, that are exclusively for the personal use or enjoyment of travellers and that are brought into Timor-Leste by travellers in accompanying luggage or carried on or about the travellers' bodies;
• household effects accompanying former residents of Timor-Leste returning to reside in Timor-Leste on a permanent basis.

In addition to personal items, are exempt from import duty:

• items exempted under the Vienna Conventions on Diplomatic Relations of 1961 and Consular Relations of 1963;
• items exempted under the Convention on the Privileges and Immunities of the United Nations;
• items exempted under the Convention on the Privileges and Immunities of the Specialized Agencies;
• goods re-imported in the same condition in which they were exported;
• goods, other than alcohol or tobacco imported by registered charitable organizations, being charitable organizations that have registered under any law of Timor-Leste that has been promulgated for that purpose, if the goods are to be used for charitable purposes of humanitarian assistance and relief, education or health care;
• goods for temporary admission, if the importer has provided security for import duty in the prescribed manner;
• baby formulas that are specially designed for babies under one (1) year of age so that after preparation they are consumed in a liquid form and provide the health benefits of human milk;

• tampons and sanitary napkins.

The import duty is payable at the time of import.

f) Excise Tax

Excise tax is imposed on excisable goods removed from a warehouse by a registered manufacturer for consumption in Timor-Leste; or excisable goods imported into Timor-Leste.

Rates varies depending on the excisable good. Among others, are considered excisable goods:
• Beer;
• Wine, vermouth and other fermented beverages;
• Ethyl alcohol (other than denatured and other alcoholic beverages;
• Tobacco and related products;
• Gasoline, diesel fuel and other petroleum products;
• Small passenger vehicles with an excise value exceeding USD 70,000;
• Arms and ammunition;
• Cigarette lighters;
• Smoking pipes;
• Leisure boats and private aircraft.

No excise tax is payable by a registered manufacturer in respect of excisable goods:
• destroyed by fire or other natural cause prior to removal from the manufacturer's warehouse; or
• that have deteriorated or have been damaged in storage in the manufacturer's warehouse, and which are securely disposed of in a manner satisfactory to the Tax Administration.

Any person wishing to manufacture and sell excisable goods in Timor-Leste will have to register as producer of said goods by way of a request submitted to the Tax Administration, following a given procedure and fulfilling certain requirements.

A registered producer shall submit to the Banking and Payments Authority or another entity nominated by the Tax Administration by the fifteenth day after the end of a calendar month:
• a completed excise tax form as prescribed by the Tax Administration;
• any excise tax payable on excisable goods that have been removed from the manufacturer's warehouse during that calendar month.

In addition, any person required to pay excise tax under the mentioned terms with respect to a given month shall submit to the Banking and Payments Authority or another entity nominated by the Tax Administration a completed excise tax form for subsequent months, whether or not excise tax is payable in subsequent month.

If excisable goods, whether imported or manufactured in Timor-Leste, are intended to be used by the registered producer as raw materials for the manufacture of other excisable goods, the Tax Administration may, in respect of such goods, give a partial exemption.

The payment of excise tax on imported goods follows the same procedure for the payment of import duty.

g) Stamp Duty

There is no stamp duty in Timor-Leste tax law.

h) Value added Tax

In general terms, there is no Value Added Tax (VAT) in Timor-Leste tax law.

However, regarding petroleum operations, it should be noted that Timor-Leste's tax law has a special regime that allows VAT on those operations. This special regime also allows VAT on petroleum operations in the Joint Petroleum Development Area, in accordance with the Timor Sea Treaty.

As mentioned, the Government plans to introduce a Value Added Tax (VAT) in order to make Timor-Leste an export-free zone and attract export-oriented investment in the manufacturing, manufacturing and other sectors.

i) Double Taxation Agreements

Timor-Leste has an agreement with Portugal for the elimination of double taxation. A similar agreement with Macau (China) is under way.

I. Securities

a. Brief Introduction of Securities-Related Laws and Regulations

"Timor-Leste does not have a stock market. There are no known restrictions on portfolio investment." [1]

b. Supervision and Regulation of Securities Market

Please see section a.

---

[1] U.S. Department of State. 2017 Investment Climate Statements. https://www.state.gov/e/eb/rls/othr/ics/2017/eap/269858.htm.

c. **Requirements for Engagement in Securities Trading for Foreign Enterprises**

Please see section a.

J. Preference and Protection of Investment

a. The Structure of Preference Policies

In Timor-Leste, investors who hold a declaration of benefits or concluded a special investment agreement may benefit from 100% exemption of income tax and services tax for:

• 5 (five) years from the commencement date of the project (the date of the benefits declaration) – investment total or parcially carried out in the municipality of Dili.

• 8 (eight) years from the commencement date of the project (the date of the benefits declaration) – if the investment / reinvestment is totally or parcially carried out outside Dili's municipality.

• 10 (ten) years from the commencement date of the project (the date of the benefits declaration) - investment / reinvestment totally or parcially carried out in the Oé-Cusse Ambeno and Ataúro.

Mentioned investors may also benefit, for the same period, from 100% exemption of sales tax and import duties over all goods and equipment used in the construction or management of the investment or reinvestment projects. In addition, the law foresees the categories and quantities of capital goods and equipment exempt from paying customs duties related to the import, considering each activity sector, as well as the resale conditions after its customs clearance.

It is worth to mention that do not benefit from exemption:

• Selective consumption tax - levied on goods imported to Timor-Leste and exempt from import duty; goods exported from Timor-Leste.

• Tax on wages - levied on all remuneration received as wages in the framework of a dependent and taxable employment relationship.

• Rental tax – levied on the rents pay that are result from a lease agreement.

Other benefits provided for in the law for investors include:

• possibility to enter into a lease agreement with the State (for state-owned real estate) for a period of 50 years, renewable until the maximum limit of 100 years;

• granting of five work visas for workers or employees qualified for supervisory, directing or technical functions appropriate to the investment project.

b. Support for Specific Industries and Regions

As previously mentioned, incentives may vary according to the region where the investment is made. Favouring less developed areas, the Government, in accordance with the Private Investment Law, offers tax benefits for a certain period of time as the following:

• 5 years in the municipality of Díli;
• 8 years outside the municipality of Díli; and
• 10 years in the Special Social Market Economy Zones (SSMEZ) of Oé-Cussi Ambeno and Atauro Island.

c. Special Economic Areas

Timor-Leste has two special economic areas: Oé-cusse Ambeno, an enclave in Indonesia, and Ataúro, an island very close to Díli. Both areas are considered by the Law nº. 3/2014 as Special Social Market Economy Zones (SSMEZ) and have administrative and financial autonomy, which means that both have independent finances, independent tax system, own procurement system, own financial market and own customs system.

While Ataúro Island was established as special zone to be a pole of a tourist nature, the area of Oé-cusse Ambeno was designed to be a trade and industrial pole and has attracted large investments in infrastructure. For its potential must be highlighted.

Oé-cusse Ambeno offers, in its own territorial limits, exemption from payment of customs duties and respect for the principles of the social market economy as a model of economic growth. The Region's objectives, of an economic nature, are:

• Development of commercial agriculture;
• Creation of an ethical financial center;
• Creation of a free trade zone;
• Increase in tourism;
• Creation of a center for international studies and research on climate change;
• Creation of a center of green research;

• Implement and develop industrial activities, for export and import[①].

A Special Development Fund is set for the region, which is intended to finance the implementation of strategic social and economic projects, including road infrastructures, ports and airports, water and sanitation facilities, energy and telecommunication distribution networks, as well as hospitals and other social and tourism infrastructures. Of the planned projects, the electric power plant, some roads, irrigation systems, a clinic and a bridge are already completed. Among other ongoing projects, the airport is expected to be completed by the end of 2018 and a hotel is under construction.

d. Investment Protection

Foreign investors have the following rights and guarantees in Timor-Leste:

• Equal treatment for domestic and foreign, except with regard to land ownership and on the minimum investment values;

• Right of access to the courts;

• Protection of private property (in accordance with the limits laid down in the Constitution. In cases where it is necessary to resort to requisition or expropriation for public use of all or part of the property of an investor, the State must compensate the fairly promoter and under the law);

• The right to import goods and equipment and export of products produced;

• The right to recourse to domestic and foreign credit;

• The right to free transfer of funds to abroad (ex.: profits and dividends; capital; income; compensation; payments) and conversion of amounts into foreign currency (via the banking system);

• Right to employment of foreign workers;

• Right to professional, banking and commercial secrecy.

• Investors have the right to the protection of patents or utility models registered by them as authors, as well as trademarks, logos, names or emblems of establishment and other information protected under the terms of intellectual property.

• The special and tax benefits foreseen in the Law cannot be revoked or decreased until the term of the investment period, provided that the beneficiary obligations are fulfilled.

• The Government promotes the establishment of international agreements with the large possible number of countries in order to avoid international double taxation.

• The foreign investor is entitled to receive the payment taxes proof in Timor-Leste.

III. Trade

A. Department Supervising Trade

The Government body responsible for trade in Timor-Leste is the Minister of Finance.

B. Brief Introduction of Trade Laws and Regulations

The most relevant law for trade is the Decree-Law 14/2017 – "Customs Code", which establishes the legal provisions that regulates the application of customs policy measures within the framework of the commercial exchanges with other countries. In addition, other major regulations include, the Decree Law 08/2006, on regulation of customs duties, the Decree Law 09/2003, on customs duties and competencies, the Decree Law 09/2006, on manufactured tobacco products, the Decree Law 10/2003, on custom control for travelers and the Decree Law 21/2003, on quarentine management.

The trade system is under reform and a set of activities designed to increase the efficiency of Customs by simplifying and standardizing processes to global practice is to be implemented, such as:

• "Modernise the Customs Procedures Code in line with international best practice.

• Updating Timor-Leste's international coding for all goods in line with ASEAN standards. Introducing ASYCUDA World; modernising IT systems to facilitate the process of importing goods as well as strengthening the integrity of customs.

• Delivering broker's training to improve industry service.

• Having self-assessment processes to simplify the clearance of goods.

• Having advanced rulings for importers to improve business confidence.

---

① Law no. 3/2014, of 18 June, Article 5.

• Delivering specialised training for officers to assist lawful decision making.
• Developing Standard Operating Procedures to provide certainty in decisions.
• Developing and implementing a training and capacity building strategy for customs officers based on the Customs Procedures Code.
• Implementing a full real time interface / integration between key software platforms such as IFMIS SERVE, ASYCUDA World, the tax administration IT system and PBS.
• Strengthening Customs airport and land border cargo operations.
• Improving the dispute resolution process in Customs[1].

Recently, in late 2017, Timor-Leste became an observer of World Trade Organization – WTO, which is an important step to become a member, position that would help the country "to give to other countries important guarantees in terms of the norms and standards (for example, phytosanitary measures) that imports into the country must follow[2]", and to bring "a mechanism for solving trade disputes with other member countries[3]".

C. Trade Management

In Timor-Leste there is a "National Single Window" system for trade management. It is "a customs portal where traders can submit all documents relating to trade and can access all relevant information regarding trade via a single electronic gateway, helping processing and clearance. The portal connects the Customs Authority with all government agencies that deal with the movement of people or goods, including tax, immigration, quarantine, health, transport, agriculture, fisheries, foreign affairs and the Central Bank[3]".

D. The Inspection and Quarantine of Import and Export Commodities

In accordance with the Decree Law 21/2003, some bio products and related cargo entering Timor-Leste are subject to inspection and quarantine, namely live animals, meat and meat products, live fish, fresh fish and frozen fish Products, milk products, egg products and honey products, animal hair, rawhide products and other animal products, live plants, plant material and flowers, fresh vegetables and vegetable products, cereal Products, nuts and its products, dairy products, livestock feed and timber products.

The Serviço de Quarentena de Timor-Leste is the body responsible for supervising and applying the rules of quarentine and "procedures relating to health control over the import, export or movement of a health district from the national territory to another of plants, animals and products derivatives, as well as other items, including the rules of on the preparation of the phytosanitary or health certificate animal, quarantine measures of post-importation and pre-procedures and the practical authorizations for the import, export or movement of from one district to another, an indication of the points of export and the issuing and zoo and phytosanitary certificates, the definition of pests and quarantine, the determination of fees and costs, the establishment of infringements and penalties[5]".

E. Customs Management

The Directorate-General for Customs – DCG is the body responsible for administering and collecting customs taxes and fees upon entering the national territory. The DGC has the following tasks:

• Ensure the implementation and integrated execution of the national policy for the areas under its scope, in accordance with the Government's programme and with the superior guidelines issued by the Minister;
• Exert control over commodities and means of transportation that enter the national territory and over places where commodities under fiscal action are stored, as well as ensure compliance with the customs formalities required for the presentation of commodities to customs and give a customs destination to commodities upon customs clearance;
• Carry out studies, draft legislation and regulations and set operation rules and techniques in accordance with its goals;
• Participate in the definition and management of the tax policy concerning customs rights, sales tax and excise tax, ensuring the settlement and collection of any taxes, fees or payments under its responsibility;
• Regulate the customs regimes applicable to the movement of people and assets, in terms of entering, staying, transiting or leaving the customs territory, and look after their application;

---

[1] https://www.mof.gov.tl/frc_menu/trade-facilitation/customs-reform-to-facilitate-trade/?lang=en.
[2] https://www.mof.gov.tl/frc_menu/trade-facilitation/becoming-a-member-of-the-wto/?lang=en.
[3] https://www.mof.gov.tl/frc_menu/trade-facilitation/becoming-a-member-of-the-wto/?lang=en.
[4] https://www.mof.gov.tl/frc_menu/trade-facilitation/national-single-window/?lang=en.
[5] Decree-Law no. 21/2003, of 31 December.

• Exert customs verification over people and assets at the ports, airports and national borders, in accordance with the law;
• Combat tax evasion and fraud, as well as the smuggling, straying and illicit trafficking of narcotics, weapons and other forbidden items, and collaborate with other national and international bodies in the fight against these activities[1].

IV. Labor

A. Brief Introduction of Labour Laws and Regulations

The Law n°. 4/2012, Labor Code, is the law that governs employment relations in Timor-Leste.

According to the law, an employment contract can adopt the form of an indefinite term contract or of a fixed term contract, and shall preferably be executed in writing. However, in those cases where the labor contract is not written or does not establish a term, it shall be considered as an indefinite term contract.

Also fixed term contracts shall be automatically converted into indefinite term contracts when:
• A new fixed term contract is executed under the same conditions, with the same employee, 90 days before the termination of the first contract and the execution of the second contract;
• The term of the contract shall exceed three years, including renewals.

One of the main principles of the Law is the protection of the employee, therefore several rights are granted to workers and dismissal without just cause is forbidden, although it is possible to terminate the employment contract due to market, technological and structural reasons since justified.

Among others, the rights of employees include:
• Normal working hours shall not be more than 8 hours a day or more than 44 hours per week.
• Overtime is paid at 50% of the normal wage on weekdays and 100% on weekends and holidays.
• Workers are entitled to a minimum number of 12 leave days per year.
• Contract termination by the employer may be justified by serious employee misconduct or by market, technological or structural justifications.
• Alleged cases of wrongful dismissal must be declared by the courts within 60 days of the notification of dismissal.
• The maternity leave is of 12 weeks.
• The minimum working age is 15 years old.
• The minimum wage is USD 115.00.

The law also makes reference to the status of foreign employees mentioning that contracts entered into with foreign employees shall be written and authorized by the competent authority.

B. Requirements of Employing Foreign Employees

a. Work Permit

According to the Law 09/2003, Immigration and Asylum Act, a work permit is intended to authorize the bearer thereof to enter the national territory, on a temporary basis, to carry out a professional activity as an employee or independent worker. A work permit exclusively allows the bearer thereof to carry out the professional activity which he or she claimed for the granting of the visa and allows a length of stay of up to one year and is valid for one or multiple entries[2].

b. Application Procedure

Applications for authorization of residence shall be submitted to the Immigration Department and be approved by the Secretary of State of Professional Training and Employment.

To be granted residence the applicant must meet the following requirements:
• Possess a valid visa for establishing residence;
• No hidden hindrances for visa denial if known by the competent authorities;
• Actual presence in the national territory

After review the application, the Immigration Department concludes the process by means of an interview.

---

[1] https://www.mof.gov.tl/about-the-ministry/organisation-structure-roles-and-people/generals-directorate/general-diretore-customs/?lang=en.
[2] Law 09/2003, Article 36.

The procedure can take approximately up to 2 months.

c. Social Insurance

Law no. 12/2016, of 14 November, established, under the terms established in the Constitution of the Democratic Republic of Timor-Leste and in the context of the progressive organization of a social security system, the contributory social security scheme.

The following must be covered by the contributory social security scheme:
- The entire private sector, i.e. all workers who have an employment contract for a fixed or indefinite term, in accordance with the Labor Law[①];
- All public sector, i.e. all those who perform paid functions in the State;
- Employers.

On the other hand, they are optionally covered by the scheme:
- Individual entrepreneurs;
- Self-employed;
- Managers and managers of companies;
- Domestic workers.

The contributions collected under the contributory scheme of social security aim to ensure the payment of benefits to which workers are entitled in certain eventualities, namely the following:
- Maternity allowance;
- Paternity allowance;
- Adoption allowance;
- Clinical risk benefit during pregnancy;
- Discontinuation of pregnancy allowance;
- Death grant;
- Refund funeral expenses;
- Survival pension;
- Absolute disability pension;
- Relative disability pension;
- Old Age Pension;
- Work accident allowence.

In this sense, for the organization and costing of the system, Employers must:
- To register and register the workers at their service, for the attribution of their respective NISS (Social Security Identification Number) for life;
- Provide and update information;
- Deliver monthly Remuneration Statement (DR);
- Pay the monthly contributions.

The amount of the contribution to be paid is obtained by multiplying the Contribution Tax Base (BIC) by the Contributory Tax (TC), where:
- BIC is the Gross Compensation (salary) gross plus other permanent monthly salaries paid as salary increase, which includes the 13th month / annual allowance, supplementary salary for night work, additional for special careers. It is not included in the calculation of this variable, for example, the amounts derived from per diem allowances, overtime, food allowance and other extra subsidies;
- TC is a rate set at 10%, divided between employers and workers at the rate of 6% and 4%, respectively. From 2020, the possibility of the contributory rate is considered, as a way of guaranteeing the sustainability of the social security system.

The law, because of the complexity and volume and importance of the obligations it creates, provides for a transitional period of adaptation for employers in the private sector.

The period is phased and extends until 2026, during which companies with 10 or fewer workers, provided that at least 60% of these workers are nationals, are entitled to a discount on their obligations, paying only a percentage of the tax rate to their following terms:
- 70% in 2017 and 2018;
- 50% in 2019 and 2020;
- 30% in 2021 and 2022;
- 20% in 2023 and 2024;

---

① Foreign workers working temporarily in Timor-Leste are also covered by the Social Security scheme. However, if they prove that they are covered and discounted to another system in another country, they are exempt for a period of 10 years.

• 10% in 2025 and 2026.

C. Exit and Entry

a. Visa Types

In Timor-Leste, there are six types of Visa:
• Class I (Tourism & Business) visa;
• Class II (Transit) visa;
• Class III (Study) visa;
• Class IV (Cultural) visa;
• Work Visa;
• Visa to Establish Residence.

b. Restrictions for Exit and Entry

Travellers of any nationality may obtain a Tourist & Business Visa on arrival if arriving at Dili International Airport or Dili Seaport. Visas on arrival are granted for 30 days stay, single entry.

Only nationals of Indonesia and Portugal may obtain a visa or entry clearance on arrival at a land border. All other nationalities are required to apply for a "Visa application Authorisation" prior to entering at a land border crossing[1].

D. Trade Union and Labour Organizations

In Timor-Leste, all workers and employers, without discrimination or need for prior authorization, may set up and join organizations for the purpose of promoting and defending their rights and interests. No worker shall be compelled to join, not to join, or cease to join a trade union organization.

In the exercise of their activities, trade unions' and employers' organizations shall aim at:
• Promoting and defending the rights and interests of their members;
• Collaborating with the Government in the development and fulfillment of the objectives provided for in the labor policy;
• Exercising the right to collective negotiation;
• Collaborating with the Labor Inspectorate as regards the enforcement of the rules provided by law and the collective agreement;
• Participating in the process of preparation of labor legislation, pursuant to the law.

E. Labour Disputes

In the context of labor disputes, the law establishes that "the individual labour disputes shall be mandatorily submitted to conciliation and mediation before resorting to courts", except when the dispute concerns the unlawfulness of a termination of an employment contract with just cause by the employer or by the employee and of a termination based on market, technological or structural reasons.

In what concerns arbitration, resort to it is voluntary, and "may result of a request of the involved parties, or by request of one of the parties, in which case the other party is notified to declare if he / she accepts or not resort to arbitration".

If Conciliation fails and both parties choose not to resort to arbitration, it will be necessary to initiate a judicial labor dispute that arises under the laws of civil procedure.

Usually, labor disputes begin with the termination of an employment contract.

The termination of an employment contract is regulated in articles 45 to 57 of the Law 4/2012 and may adopt the following terms:
• Expiration;
• Agreement between the parties;
• Termination of the contract by the employee;
• Employee's dismissal with just cause;
• Termination for market, technological or structural reasons of the company or the establishment.

Both the first two terms for employment termination are quite consensual, leaving little or no space for any dispute to take place.

The termination of the contract by the employee can be challenged by the employer within the period of 60

---

[1] http://migracao.gov.tl/html/sub0301.php.

days from the date of notification, without prejudice to the possibility of appealing to the Services of Mediation and Conciliation.

If the just cause indicated by the employee is declared unfounded, the employer has the right to be compensated for the damages caused.

The most usual labor disputes appear when the termination of the contract by the employer it's not accepted by the employee, as the termination of the contract must be justified by just cause in case of employee dismissal, or by the impossibility of maintaining the employment contract without impair the economic viability of the company in case of termination for market, technological or structural reasons of the company or the establishment. For both these terms of contract termination there are some strict procedures that need to be followed due to the prohibition to dismiss without just cause.

In case of employee's dismissal with just cause the process begins with a Disciplinary procedure that shall be written and initiated in the maximum period of 20 days after the date in which the employer (or his / her representative) discovers the violation. Afterwards, the employee has the right to present his / her defence in writing within a period of 10 days after the date of service, and may present any proof that he / she acknowledge is necessary for his / hers defense (e.g. present documents, require a hearing and other necessary steps).

If the final decision is not served to the employee within 6 months after the beginning of the disciplinary procedures the possibility of dismissal will expire. An employee has the right to appeal from the decision taken, he / she may also request the intervention of the mediation and conciliation organs in order to solve the conflict, notwithstanding the right to resort to arbitration or judicial proceedings.

As for the termination of contract for market, technological or structural reasons, it is only possible after the employer has resorted to the reduction of working periods and suspension of the employment contract. After those measures an employer must communicate his / her intention in writing to the affected employees and to his / her representatives (if applicable), and shall forward a copy to the Service of Mediation and Conciliation and must begin within 5 days the negotiations with the employees or with their representatives in order to reach an agreement regarding the termination procedure.

When the negotiation process is concluded without the parties reaching an agreement on avoiding the termination, the employer will communicate in writing to each employee (if applicable), to the representative commission and to the Services of Mediation and Conciliation, the decision to terminate the employment contract with clearly indicating the grounds on which the termination is based, the date of termination and the amount of compensation to be received.

V. Intellectual Property

A. Brief Introduction of IP Laws and Regulations

Section 60 of Timor-Leste's constitution provides for the protection of literary, scientific, and artistic work and the National Parliament has ratified the convention establishing the World Intellectual Property Organization (WIPO), the United Nations agency charged with the protection of intellectual property.

The Country, however, has no specific law on protection of intellectual property rights.

Until an Intellectual Property Law is finally approved, the only option for protection of trademarks, logos, insignias and patents in the Country is the publication of Cautionary Notices in the local newspaper claiming the ownership over the intellectual property.

In general terms, the Cautionary Notice should state the name and address of the holder of the intellectual property right, as well as a description of the relevant intellectual property. In the case of a patent, an abstract is required, and in the case of a design, the shape of the design is required.

Once the Cautionary Notice is published, it is assumed that third parties are aware of the ownership of the intellectual property at issue. The republication of Cautionary notices is recommended at regular intervals (every two years) to prevent intellectual property infringement.

Regarding trademarks, it is also important, after publishing the cautionary notice, to notify the commercial authority (SERVE) warning that similar trademarks cannot be approved if lead to conflicts or confusion with a particular company.

Considering the legal drafts that have been presented to the Parliament, once the Law on Intellectual Property is finally approved, the names, trademarks, logos and insignias and patents protected under the Cautionary Notes will be prioritized upon the registration procedure.

B. Patent Application

Please see section A.

C. Trademark Registration

Please see section A.

D. Measures for IP Protection

Please see section A.

VI. Enviromental Protection

A. Department Supervising Environmental Protection

National Directorate of Pollution Control and Environmental Impact (NDPCEI).

B. Brief Introduction of Laws and Regulations of Environmental Protection

"The Constitution of Timor-Leste has clearly established the importance of protecting the environment and the country is party to several international conventions that are relevant to environmental management and has signed and ratified the United Nations Convention to Combat Desertification (UNCCD; August 2003), the UN Framework Convention on Climate Change (UNFCCC; Oct. 2006) and the UN Convention on Biodiversity (UNCBD; Oct. 2006). Timor-Leste also has signed the Kyoto Protocol to the UNFCCC, expressing its commitment to reduce global climate change.

The Decree Law 26/2012 sets the environmental basic rules, while the Decree Law 05/2011 on Environmental Licensing Law (ELL) completes the environmental legal framework of Timor-Leste. There are other pending laws and regulations, including a biodiversity law.

The ELL implements a system of environmental impact assessment and licensing. Under the ELL, proponents of projects or activities that may impact the environment are required to undertake a process of environmental assessment.

In addition to the legal requirements NDPCEI also issues guidelines from time to time and refers to best international practice.

It is important to note that activities such as mining and oil and gas may require special licenses[1]".

C. Evaluation of Environmental Protection

Please see section B.

VII. Dispute Resolution

A. Methods and Bodies of Dispute Resolution

By historical reasons, namely the influence brought about by the Portuguese as well as the Portuguese consultants in this country dating from its independence, Timor-Leste law is based on the Civil Law system.

Civil disputes are generally handled through the domestic court system, which is not always properly equipped for the demands that are currently placed upon it.

The country has established courts of first instance and a court of appeal. However, courts currently operate only in four of the thirteen districts, and most cases at the local level are handled through traditional and ancient Timorese justice mechanisms of the local communities. Additional courts foreseen in the Constitution and legislation, such as specialized tax courts, have not yet been established.

Alternative dispute resolution is consistent with Timorese traditional justice systems, but there is no formal system yet in place. The Council of Ministers approved the Arbitration, Mediation, and Conciliation Law in December 2016 as part of the fiscal reform efforts, but the law has not yet received parliamentary approval[2].

---

[1] https://www.adb.org/sites/default/files/project-document/190291/50211-001-iee-01_0.pdf.
[2] https://www.state.gov/e/eb/rls/othr/ics/2017/eap/269858.htm.

B. Application of Laws

The justice system – police, prosecutors, and courts – are still evolving and short-staffed.

In December 2015, the government established a Legislative Reform and Justice Sector Commission which has the mission to recommend law reform, evaluate how laws are being implemented, and harmonize legislation. As stipulated in the country's strategic development plan, the commission will review and improve the legal instruments ensuring protection of rights, liberties and guarantees, as well as access to the law, bringing legislation closer to the democratic ideals and the citizens of Timor-Leste[①].

VIII. Others

A. Anti-commercial Bribery

a. Brief Introduction of Anti-commercial Bribery Laws and Regulations

Timor-Leste has ratified the United Nations Convention against Corruption and such Convention has direct application in the country.

The main laws on corruption are the Decree-Law no. 19/2009, the "Criminal Code", which defines and establishes related crimes, and the Law 8/2009, which creates and regulates the Anti-Corruption Commission;

b. Department Supervising Anti-commercial Bribery

The Anti-Corruption Commission is the body responsible to enforce the existent legislation regarding anti-corruption and anti-bribery. This Commission has the status of a specialized and independent Criminal Police and powers to act in any manner in matter directly or indirectly related to corruption or bribery matters.

The Commission has the powers to request anyone to collaborate, directly or indirectly with any ongoing investigation. Also, there is a general obligation to collaborate, not only with the Commission, but also with the Courts.

c. Punitive Actions

The majority of crimes and illegal activities are related to payments, favors, gifts or any other kind of advantages given to, or taken by, public agents or holders of public and / or political roles.

The Criminal Code so provides to be a crime the following, with the respective penalties:
- Passive corruption for an illicit act means, penalty 3 to 15 years imprisonment;
- Passive corruption for a licit act means, penalty 3 years imprisonment or a fine;
- Active corruption means, penalty 3 to 10 years imprisonment;
- Embezzlement means, penalty 3 to 10 years imprisonment;
- Misuse of public material resources and facilities means, penalty 2 years imprisonment;
- Abuse of power, penalty 1 to 4 years imprisonment;
- Financial participation in public affairs means, penalty 2 to 8 years imprisonment;

Also, the punishment of those illicit conducts may involve civil sanctions, namely the obligation to compensate the affected party(ies), calculated under the general provisions of Civil Code in terms of liability, compensating.

B. Project Contracting

a. Permission System

The Decree Law 11/2005 sets out the procurement processes which must be carried out by government officers when purchasing goods, services or works on behalf of the Government of Timor-Leste.

According to the law, "a public contract shall be understood as the bilateral bargain measure, in which at least one of the parties is a legal person governed by public law, the purpose of such measure being to meet the public needs of a public procurement procedure initiated by a competent authority".

Public contracts entered into under the terms of this legal diploma may, depending on their object, be:
- For the provision of goods;
- For the provision of services;
- For the execution of works.

For reasons of public interest, contracts may be awarded with special or exclusive rights being attributed

---

① https://www.state.gov/e/eb/rls/othr/ics/2017/eap/269858.htm.

to certain goods, works or services in accordance with authorizations specifically granted by the competent authorities or Public Service.

The following authorities shall have the powers to approve or sign public contracts:

• The Prime Minister, for contracts of a value equal to or higher than 1,000,000 USD (one million United States dollars);

• The Minister of Planning and Finance;

• The Contracts Committee;

• The heads of sovereign bodies, Ministers and Secretaries of State, under the terms of their respective organic laws;

• Those heads expressly appointed and authorised by the respective heads of the sovereign bodies and by Ministers and Secretaries of State;

• The heads of the Autonomous Services, public authorities and other bodies with administrative and financial autonomy;

• Other legal persons with a share of State capital of over 50% (fifty percent) which, albeit not of a business nature, pursue eminently public aims;

• All other bodies and Public Services subject to the limits of the State Budget or which are mostly financed by it.

The key tender processes are:
• Request for quotes
• Public tendering
• National public tender
• International public tender
• Limited tender by pre-qualification
• Restricted tenders
• Procedure by negotiation, and
• Procurement by sole sourcing and standing offer agreement[①].

b. Prohibited Areas

Postal services, public communications, protected natural areas and weapons production and distribution are areas reserved for the state and cannot be explored by private companies.

c. Invitation to Bid and Bidding

An assessment of the best net overall outcome for government is to take account of all relevant 'whole of life' costs and benefits: that is the full cost of each good, service, or works over its expected useful life – not just at time of purchase. Decisions on government procurement should be made on the basis of 'value for money' which requires a comparison of costs, benefits and alternative outcomes[②].

C. Others

Among others, Timor-Leste is a member of the International Monetary Fund (IMF), United Nations (administration, economy development, security training and governance support), UNCTAD, UNESCO, UNIDO, African, Caribbean and Pacific States (ACP), Asian Development Bank (ADB), ASEAN (observer), CPLP, FAO, International Finance Corporation (IFC), Interpol, Pacific Islands Forum - PIF (observer), and Asian Development Fund (ADF), the latter being the main source of funding for activities in Timor-Leste supported by the Asian Development Bank (ADB).

"Timor-Leste has not yet conducted any investment policy reviews through OECD, WTO, or UNCTAD. Timor-Leste was accepted as an observer to the WTO in 2016, and its Working Party for accession to the WTO was established in December 2016. The country is in the process of designing and adopting fiscal and economic reform that include new laws on private investment, export promotion, commercial companies, sanctions, taxation, and the value-added tax (VAT). Timor-Leste's political stability has given opportunities for business to grow. Commerce is increasing and the government is funding additional public services and larger public works projects. Other than the oil and gas sector, investment opportunities exist in the service, tourism, agriculture, and infrastructure sectors. While the government is committed to improving its services in critical sectors, challenges remain. Bureaucratic inefficiency, infrastructure bottlenecks, a paucity of local financing options, the absence of a real property law and

---

① https://www.mof.gov.tl/government-procurement/guide-to-government-procurement/tender-processes-and-tender-documents/?lang=en.

② https://www.mof.gov.tl/government-procurement/guide-to-government-procurement/tender-bid-evaluation/?lang=en.

other essential legislation, uncertain implementation of government procedures, significant deficiencies in human capacity, and perceptions of malfeasance, conflicts of interest, and corruption are the notable challenges[①]".

[①] U.S. Department of State. https://www.state.gov/e/eb/rls/othr/ics/2017/eap/269858.htm.

土库曼斯坦

作者：Atabek Sharipov、Sabina Saparova、Gulnur Nurkeyeva
译者：徐玲、李志强

一、概述

（一）政治、经济、社会与法律环境概述

土库曼斯坦是一个位于中亚西南部，1991年10月27日获得主权的国家。土库曼斯坦与伊朗、阿富汗、哈萨克斯坦、乌兹别克斯坦接壤并与阿塞拜疆、俄罗斯通过里海隔海相望。

全国划分为5个州（welayat）：阿哈尔州、巴尔坎州、达绍古兹州、列巴普州和马雷州。土库曼斯坦的首都阿什哈巴德市的地位等同于州，而州由众多行政区（"etrap"）、市、新区组成。

土库曼斯坦坚持中立的外交政策，与其他国家保持和平发展关系。根据联合国大会决议（1995年12月12日），它享有永久中立国地位。换言之，该国未曾参与军事冲突、缔结军事联盟或允许外国军队和军事基地在其领土驻扎。

土库曼斯坦政府实行总统共和制。国家结构基于分权原则成立。土库曼斯坦的立法机构是拥有125名议员的议会（Mejlis）。行政职能由国家总统领导的部长内阁行使。最高法院行使司法权力。此外，土库曼斯坦还设有一个代表人民利益的额外立法机构人民委员会（Halk Maslakhaty）。

作为政治中立管辖区，土库曼斯坦政局稳定。在独立后的最初十几年里，议会由一个政党——土库曼斯坦民主党控制，是由土库曼斯坦第一任总统萨帕尔穆拉特·尼亚佐夫领导的，其一直管理这个国家直至2006年。此后，现任总统别尔德穆哈梅多夫创立了工业企业家党和农业党。这三个政党均在议会有席位，并掌握大多数选票。

多年来，土库曼斯坦一直保持其国内生产总值（GDP）和其他宏观经济指标的高增长率。因此，2017年第一季度的结果显示其GDP增长率为6.2%。在工业领域，这一指标增长了1.8%，建筑领域增长了4.4%，交通和通信领域增长了10.8%，贸易领域增长了10.4%，农业领域增长了3.4%，服务领域增长了10.8%。

土库曼斯坦以其大量的碳氢化合物资源储备（天然气和石油）而闻名。截至目前，该国拥有世界第四大天然气储量（位列俄罗斯、伊朗和卡塔尔之后）。根据《土库曼斯坦2012—2016年石油、油气田、化工和渔业发展规划》，在此期间该国的石油总产量为5 590万吨、天然气总产量为4 487亿立方米。

目前，土库曼斯坦向中国出口天然气（土库曼斯坦—乌兹别克斯坦—哈萨克斯坦—中国天然气管道），产能高达400亿立方米。值得关注的是，土库曼斯坦还完成了位于马雷州的"Galkynysh"气矿床第一期工程的开发。该气矿床为增加天然气出口量提供了更多的机会。随着土库曼斯坦—阿富汗—巴基斯坦—印度（TAPI）天然气管道在建工程的完成，土库曼斯坦将实现燃气供应路线多样化，并进入东南亚的替代能源市场。

土库曼斯坦是化工行业矿物原料主要的储藏地之一。在该国列巴普州的科伊坚达格地区，发现了不同类型的矿物质（硫、磷酸盐、岩盐、石膏、锶原料、天青石、多金属、石灰石和其他矿物）。

土库曼斯坦是中亚第二大棉花生产国（仅次于乌兹别克斯坦）和世界第九大棉花生产国（位列土耳其、美国、印度、中国、巴基斯坦、巴西、澳大利亚和乌兹别克斯坦之后），也是众所周知的中亚主要的棉花出口国之一。超过70%的棉产品被出口到美国、加拿大、德国、英国、意大利、土耳其、中国和乌克兰等国家。国际著名品牌如彪马、宜家、巴适卡、诺帝卡、莎莉、Casual Wear、沃尔玛、杰西潘尼等都是土库曼斯坦棉花的主要购买者。一般来说，土库曼斯坦通过其商品原料交易所用拍卖方式销售棉花。目前，在土库曼斯坦有超过70多家企业从事纺织业经营，并提供了超过3万个就业机会。

(二)"一带一路"倡议下与中国企业合作的现状及趋势

土库曼斯坦和中国在 1992 年建交。双方的战略合作伙伴关系始于 2013 年。2013 年,两国签署了三个重要文件,以促进进一步合作:
- 《友好合作条约》;
- 《关于发展和深化战略伙伴关系的联合宣言》;
- 《关于通过〈中华人民共和国和土库曼斯坦战略伙伴关系发展规划(2014 年至 2018 年)〉的声明》。

土库曼斯坦和中国在不同领域长期合作期间,签订了众多的条约和协议:
- 《关于加强天然气稳定合作协定》;
- 《土库曼斯坦—中国管道安全和稳定运营协定》;
- 《经济技术合作协定》;
- 《土库曼斯坦国有银行对外经济活动银行和中国进出口银行的合作协议》;
- 《关于鼓励和相互保护投资协定》;
- 《中华人民共和国陕西省人民政府与土库曼斯坦阿哈尔州政府经贸、科技和文化合作协议书》;
- 《中华人民共和国山东省人民政府与土库曼斯坦列巴普州政府经贸、科技和文化合作协议书》;
- 《西安市与马雷市建立友好城市关系协议书》;
- 《关于土库曼纳巴特市和日照市之间建立友好城市关系协议书》;
- 《文化交流合作框架协定》;
- 《马育种领域合作框架协定》;
- 《关于交通运输领域合作基本原则谅解备忘录》;
- 《农业合作谅解备忘录》。

土库曼斯坦坚定地致力于增进"一带一路"倡议下两国之间的合作,特别是在天然气和石油生产及改善运输业结构等领域。

中国石油天然气集团公司(以下简称"中石油")作为土库曼斯坦的首要商业合作伙伴,自 1994 年起就一直在土库曼斯坦市场开展经营活动。自 2007 年起,中石油一直在进行"Bagtyyarlyk"矿床的勘探开发,该矿床被视为土库曼斯坦—中国跨国天然气管道的原料基地。

另一个大型的投资项目,是中石油和派特法石油工程公司就一个大型气矿床"Galkynysh"实施的联合勘探。该矿床与"Yashlar"和"Garakol"矿床天然气储藏量合计达到 27.4 万亿立方米,被认为是世界上最大的陆上气矿床。

中国国家开发银行是国际发展融资提供者中的领导者,为土库曼斯坦提供了许多必要的投资,在支持和加速土库曼斯坦发展的同时,增大了当地的工业和商业体量。

二、投资

(一)市场准入

1. 投资监管部门

2006 年,直属于土库曼斯坦总统的国家外国投资管理局被撤销。其职能划归土库曼斯坦财政经济部。

目前,土库曼斯坦财政经济部下属的法律实体和投资项目国家注册管理局,负责规范该国的投资活动、投资项目登记和促进外国及地方投资。

土库曼斯坦工商会在吸引外商直接投资和现代技术引进、创造有利的商业环境等方面发挥了重要作用,是土库曼斯坦推广外国企业和商业宣传的有效平台。

2. 投资行业法律规定

土库曼斯坦投资监管领域的两个主要法规为《投资活动法》(第 698-XII 号文件,1992 年 5 月 19 日)

与《外国投资法》(第184-III号文件，2008年3月3日)。它们界定了投资主管机构的权利范围，确立了投资项目的国家鉴定及注册程序，并列出了向外国投资者提供的激励、保障和特权。法律将投资活动定义为：
- 个人、经济组织、团体及合伙企业、宗教组织以及其他法律实体进行的投资，不论其所有权结构为何；
- 土库曼斯坦公共及地方主管机关使用国家预算资金进行的国家投资；
- 外国国家、法律实体和个人以及无国籍人士进行的境外投资；
- 土库曼斯坦和外国政府、法律实体和个人进行的联合投资。

土库曼斯坦《油气资源法》(第208-III号文件，2008年8月20日)特别适用于油气产业的投资活动，列举了外国投资者在这一领域可以缔结的协议类型（产量分成协议、特许权协议、联合经营协议和其他服务协议）。

2017年，土库曼斯坦通过的《自由经济区法》(第620-V号文件)，旨在在本国创造新的自由经济区以吸引外国投资者。通过建立自由经济区，政府为外国投资者建立了特殊的法律制度，为他们提供了特定的税收和海关激励，并简化了业务办理流程。

其他促进投资的法律、法规包括《创新活动法》(第106-V号文件，2014年8月16日)、《外国特许权法》(第859-XII号文件，1993年10月1日)及《创业活动法》(第863-XII号文件，1993年10月1日)。

例如，土库曼斯坦《创新活动法》明确提出，法律实体及个人可以参与的创新活动和土库曼斯坦法律允许批准设立的组织类型有：科技中心、创业园区、创新中心、技术转移中心、创新基金和创业组织。土库曼斯坦法律规定，公司从事创新活动可以取得一定的特权和福利。

土库曼斯坦的《外国特许权法》为拟在土库曼斯坦开展经营的外国公司和个人，就涉及获取国家许可的程序创建了一个监管框架。特许权是指基于特许协议，有偿向外国公司和个人提供地块、自然资源矿床、企业和其他财产。特许权的提供建立在竞争的基础上。竞争程序的条款和条件由土库曼斯坦的部长内阁制定。特许权所有者有权开展勘探工作，勘探及经营自然资源矿床及开展土库曼斯坦法律许可范围内的其他类型的商业活动。

此外，土库曼斯坦已与英国、瑞士、俄罗斯联邦、罗马尼亚、西班牙、斯洛伐克、德国、法国、中国、巴林、乌兹别克斯坦、比利时、亚美尼亚、埃及、格鲁吉亚、印度、土耳其、乌克兰、印度尼西亚、意大利、以色列、卢森堡、伊朗、巴基斯坦、塔吉克斯坦、阿拉伯联合酋长国及马来西亚签署了双边投资协定。这些双边投资协定旨在通过减少政治风险来促进外国投资。双边投资协定保护一个协定成员国在另一个协定成员国领土上的投资不被征收和征用，并确立了外国投资的公平待遇原则。

3. 投资方式

土库曼斯坦《投资活动法》规定，投资包括所有类型的财产和有价值的知识性权益，例如：
- 货币、特别银行存款、股权、股票和其他证券；
- 动产和不动产（建筑物、设备和其他物质资产）；
- 因版权、技术诀窍和其他有价值的知识性权益产生的财产权；
- 土地和其他自然资源的使用权，以及其他财产权；
- 其他有价物。

外国公司或个人可以进行下列形式的投资：
- 与土库曼斯坦企业和个人合作，设立参股企业；
- 设立外商独资企业、外国公司的分支机构和/或收购现有企业；
- 购买动产和不动产；
- 提供贷款；
- 取得土库曼斯坦法律规定的财产权及非财产性权利。

4. 市场准入条件及审查

土库曼斯坦法律对外国投资没有限制，但是对外国投资者施加了特定的义务：

- 向财政主管机关申报投资额和来源；
- 取得必要的施工执照和许可证；
- 在抗震、防火和爆炸安全、卫生、生态和城镇规划要求的准则和规则的合规方面，获得投资项目国家鉴定局的结论性意见。

外商投资企业及其分支机构需要在土库曼斯坦财政经济部下属的法律实体和投资项目国家注册管理局进行注册登记。提交的登记文件需由外交部（负责审核外国官方机构提供文件的合法性）、财政经济部及国家安全局（负责审核财务状况和商业信誉）共同审核。

应该关注的是，为了保障国家的宪法制度及确保土库曼斯坦的国家安全，土库曼斯坦政府可采取"一事一议"的方式就某些特定行业对外国投资者予以限制。

（二）外汇管理规定

1. 外汇监管部门

土库曼斯坦中央银行是负责国家货币信贷政策、货币调控、发展和强化该国的银行体系和金融服务业及确保国家货币——土库曼马纳特（TMT）稳定的有权主管机关。

中央银行具有下列职能：
- 进行所有类型的银行业务；
- 发展土库曼斯坦的银行体系；
- 组织国家货币流通；
- 实施有效统一的国家货币和信贷政策；
- 保证国家支付系统的有效运行；
- 调控其他银行的业务；
- 监控价格稳定；
- 采取措施防止洗钱；
- 确定外国货币的官方汇率；
- 发行货币；
- 根据土库曼斯坦法律规定进行货币管理和调控；
- 建立国家货币储备及其他有价物的储备；
- 信贷机构登记和银行业务的许可；
- 对财政经济部、信贷机构和其他客户的账户进行维护；
- 保持土库曼斯坦国际储备（黄金和货币资产）；
- 管理在土库曼斯坦注册的信贷机构的会计和财务报告系统；
- 确立银行账户开立和银行业务开展的一般规则；
- 接受外国代理银行和其他贷款机构的存款。

为了履行其职能，中央银行可以发布法令（通常以官方指令的形式），该法令对土库曼斯坦所有信贷机构、国家机关和法律实体或个人均为强制性的。

2. 外汇法律、法规概况

土库曼斯坦《对外经济关系货币调控法》（第 230-IV 号文件，2011 年 10 月 1 日）是规范土库曼斯坦外汇问题的一个主要的法律文件。该法明确了货币管制的原则，并规定了在该国允许的货币交易类型。同时，该法也旨在保护参与外汇业务的居民和非居民的利益。

外汇问题部分受制于以下法律、法规的约束：《中央银行法》（第 167-IV 号文件，2011 年 3 月 25 日）、《信贷组织和银行法》（第 168-IV 号文件，2011 年 3 月 25 日）及《土库曼斯坦境内货币经营法》（第 5490 号总统令，2002 年 1 月 7 日）。

2008 年，土库曼斯坦政府曾经尝试改革国家的金融服务业，取消了对外汇交易的限制，统一汇率以及对国家货币重新计价。

3. 外资企业外汇管理要求

外汇要求适用于外资企业和本地企业。

外汇交易是按官方和市场汇率进行的。官方汇率是由土库曼斯坦中央银行根据市场汇率的平均值确定的。所有类型的货币交易，包括涉及土库曼斯坦法律规定的税收、关税及其他强制性支付款缴纳的业务，均按照官方汇率执行。

而市场汇率取决于土库曼斯坦外汇市场的供求关系。这种汇率是用于外汇交易的。应注意的是，根据《对外经济关系货币调控法》的规定，居民和非居民只能通过经授权的银行及其外汇办事处购买及出售外币。

（三）金融融资

1. 主要金融机构

土库曼斯坦金融市场的主要参与者是土库曼斯坦中央银行和商业银行。至今为止，大约有12家商业银行在土库曼斯坦开展运营：国有银行对外经济活动银行、国有商业银行"Turkmenbashi"、国有商业银行"Turkmenistan"、国有商业银行"Presidentbank"、国有商业银行"Dayhanbank"、国有商业银行"Halkbank"、土库曼斯坦国家开发银行、股份制商业银行"Senegat"、股份制商业银行"Rysgal"、土库曼斯坦—土耳其股份制商业银行、国际股份制商业银行"Garagym"及其伊朗分行"Saderat"。

股份制商业银行"Rysgal"是土库曼斯坦第一家私营银行。它于2011年在库尔班古力·别尔德穆哈梅多夫总统颁发的关于发展该国私营经济的政令下设立。目前，该银行遵照中央银行颁发的许可证开展经营。

Dayhan bank是一家国有商业银行，主要从事提供农业贷款的业务。最初该银行专注于为工农业提供融资。自2012以来，开始向建设、交通、通信和信息技术领域的投资项目提供融资。该行还就个人住房建设提供贷款。

国有商业银行"Turkmenbashi"是土库曼斯坦最早的银行之一，曾数次更名。在苏联时代，它被称为"Turkmenpromstroybank"。苏联解体后，该行更名为"Investbank"。2000年，国有商业银行"Turkmenbashi"取代了"Investbank"这个名称。该行主要专注于为土库曼斯坦的工业提供融资。

国有银行对外经济活动银行成立于1992年，是为了发展和加强对外经济关系和吸引外资贷款而设立的。该行是土库曼斯坦政府在国际资本市场的代理人。

国有商业银行"Halkbank"（人民银行）成立于1991年，在全国的所有州均有分支机构。它为当地居民提供了广泛的服务。

国有商业银行"Presidentbank"于2000年在总统萨帕尔穆拉特·尼亚佐夫关于执行向从事出口活动的私营制造商提供贷款的国家政策的政令下设立。

股份制商业银行"Senegat"是第一个开始向中小企业提供融资支持的银行。该行的客户是私营企业家、各类法律实体、中小企业、合资公司和外国公司。

2. 外资企业融资要求

土库曼斯坦金融监管规定同样适用于国外公司。外国投资者可以以任何形式（如通过缴付注册资本，以信贷或贷款等方式）向当地公司和外商投资企业提供金融支持。但是，在一笔超过10 000美元（往来交易）的交易中，当地法律实体与外国法律实体之间的信贷和贷款［以信贷（现金）和延期付款/预付款的形式］必须在土库曼斯坦中央银行登记。

（四）土地政策

1. 土地法律、法规概况

土库曼斯坦《土地法》（第243-II号文件，2004年10月25日）是土库曼斯坦规范土地分配的主要规定。该法列举了该国现有的土地类别，并规定了购买和租赁土地的强制性要求。

另外，土库曼斯坦在2017年11月25日通过了新的《国家土地管理法》（第656-V号文件）。本法规定了土库曼斯坦的土地管理局负责维护国家土地的地籍，即一个关于土地自然、经济和法律特征、分类和定性及其地理位置和大小，以及土地所有人、土地使用权人和土地承租人对土地的分配情况的统一的信息记录系统。

《土地法》规定了七种土地类型：
- 农业用地；
- 林地；
- 水资源储备用地；
- 国家储备用地；
- 住宅用地（城市、城镇和农业社区）；
- 工业用地；
- 娱乐用地和保留地。

2. 外国企业获得土地的规定

《土地法》对外国企业取得土地单独进行了规定。首先，土库曼斯坦全部土地均为国有。只有土库曼斯坦公民可以拥有土库曼斯坦的土地所有权。外国企业和个人、国际组织和其他国家仅可在签订租赁协议的基础上使用土库曼斯坦的土地。

拟在土库曼斯坦租用土地的外国公司或者个人，应当向部长内阁提出申请。在取得部长内阁的同意性结论意见后，国家环境保护和土地资源委员会及其区域分支机构可以向外国公司或者个人提供土地。

《土地法》第20条对地块的使用用途进行了一定限制。外国公司和个人、国际组织和其他国家在土库曼斯坦使用土地仅限于：建设或其他非农业目的；临时设施的安置。

（五）公司的设立和解散

1. 企业形式

根据土库曼斯坦《企业法》（第28-II号文件，2000年6月15日）的规定，在土库曼斯坦可以设立七种类型的企业：
- 国有企业；
- 个体企业；
- 合作企业；
- 合资公司；
- 公共组织企业；
- 经济团体；
- 股份公司。

所有的法律实体均无设立期限限制，且有名称、住所及印章。其可以自身的名义拥有独立的资产，取得并行使财产权及自身的非财产性权利，并可在当地法院担任原告或被告。

外国投资者首选的企业形式是外商独资设立的私营企业、合资公司、经济团体、代表处和分支机构。在土库曼斯坦，代表处和分支机构被界定为外国法律实体独立的分支。需要注意的是，按照土库曼斯坦的法律，代表处和分支机构不具有法律实体资格。

（1）国有企业

国有企业是由政府全额出资的法律实体，可拥有、使用和处置分配给其的资产。国有企业承担有限责任，其职能由公司章程确立。

国有企业是基于或由于部长内阁或其他国家机关颁发的命令而设立的。为此，当地主管机关将颁发特别政府法令或决议来确定新成立的国有企业的注册资本的规模和业务经营类型。国有企业通常设立并经营战略性工业领域的业务，例如电力、运输、建筑材料、陆上油气的生产和精炼。

（2）个体企业

个体企业由一个个人设立并仅归属该个人所有。个体企业的所有者对企业承担无限责任。个体企业的经营活动由其章程规定。个体企业的最低注册资本是最低工资的25倍，相当于5 000美元。

个体企业应当由其所有者管理。但是,个体企业的所有者有权根据协议将其职能委托(外包)给指定的人(经理或董事)。

(3)合作企业

合作企业是一种以成员参与人数为基础的企业形式。合作企业的资产是由其成员以收入或财产和其他不受限制的资源作为出资形成的。合作企业的最低注册资本是最低工资的50倍,相当于10 000美元。

合作企业由企业成员大会进行管理。合作企业的成员就该企业的义务承担有限责任。

(4)合资公司

合资公司可以由境内外的法律实体和个人注册成立。合资公司是基于创办人签署的设立协议而设立。另外,土库曼斯坦法律规定每一个合资公司的创办人出资额至少应占公司注册资本的10%。合资公司的最低注册资本是最低工资的100倍,相当于20 000美元。合资公司是有限责任企业,由创办人大会进行管理。

(5)公共组织企业

公共组织企业是由宗教组织、非政府组织、慈善团体或其他公共组织设立的企业。公共组织企业的宗旨应以创立组织的目的为基础。公共组织企业的最低注册资本是最低工资的100倍,相当于20 000美元。

(6)经济团体

经济团体通常由两个或多个法律实体或个人以创收为目的而设立。经济团体根据其创办人签署的合同设立。经济团体的最低注册资本是最低工资的100倍,相当于20 000美元。经济团体的资产由创办人的股权构成。创办人大会是经济团体的管理机构。创办人在其缴纳的注册资本范围内对公司承担有限责任。

(7)股份公司

股份公司是股份归属股东(法律实体及个人)所有的法律实体。股份公司独立且区别于其股东,享有自身的股本及资产。股份公司有两种设立形式:公众股份公司和非公众股份公司。公众股份公司可以不征得其他股东同意向公众公开募集股份。非公众股份公司仅能向有资格的个人或法律实体出售股权。非公众股份公司原股东较之有资格的个人或法律实体而言,具有优先购买权。非公众股份公司的股东人数最多为50人,而公众股份公司并没有人数限制。股份公司的最低注册资本是最低工资的200倍,相当于40 000美元。

(8)分支机构和代表处

法律实体有权设立分支机构和代表处。母公司管理代表机构和分支机构的经营活动。代表机构不能从事与企业相关的活动,但是分支机构可以在土库曼斯坦法律限制范围内开展商业活动。分支机构更像是一个代理机构而非独立的公司,其被视作母公司的延伸。

2. 公司设立的程序

公司的设立程序是由下列法律规定的:《企业法》(第28-II号文件,2000年6月15日)、《股份公司法》(第400-1号文件,1999年12月23日)以及《法律实体国家登记》(第11896号总统令,2011年11月11日)。

从实务经验上来讲,外国投资者最优选的企业设立形式是合资公司和股份公司。因此,本部分将讨论两者的注册流程。

法律实体需向土库曼斯坦经济财政部下属的法律实体和投资项目国家注册管理局(以下简称"国家注册局")及其各州分部申请登记。

(1)合资公司

合资公司在国家注册局注册。登记注册合资公司,创办人应提交以下文件用以注册主管机关审核:

- 包含业务类型和创办人的信息的申请表;
- 创办人关于设立合资公司的决定;
- 设立协议和公司章程一式两份,分别为俄语和土库曼语;
- 合资公司投资方案;

- 合资公司在土库曼斯坦的负责人的个人信息表、3 cm × 4 cm 照片及护照复印件；
- 经土库曼斯坦大使馆或外交部公证的外国投资者的设立文件；
- 经土库曼斯坦大使馆或外交部公证的外国投资者注册证明；
- 经土库曼斯坦大使馆或外交部公证的外国投资者的财务报告；
- 当地主管机关出具可使用的法定地址的确认书；
- 证明已实缴合资公司 50% 的注册资本的银行声明；
- 确认缴纳注册费用的银行收据。

（2）股份公司

拟设立股份公司的个人及法律实体需向国家注册局提交上述文件。一旦注册，股份公司可以永久经营，且有充分的资格在土库曼斯坦从事任何商业活动（包括需要许可证的经营类型）。

需要注意的是，根据土库曼斯坦《特殊活动类型许可法》（第 202 号文件，2008 年 6 月 25 日）的规定，一些活动需取得许可证。公司通常需要被授予通用的许可证（即不限于特定项目）。所有签发的许可证均不可转让。

在特殊经济区内（自由创业经济区、国家旅游区等）运营的公司无须取得许可证即可开展许可经营活动。

3. 公司解散的程序和要求

（1）概述

多数土库曼斯坦的法律、法规均对公司解散和清算有规定，包括《破产法》（第 861-XII 号文件，1993 年 10 月 1 日）、《股份公司法》（第 400-1 号文件，1999 年 12 月 23 日）、《投资活动法》（第 698-XII 号文件，1992 年 5 月 19 日）及《外国投资法》（第 184-III 号文件，2008 年 3 月 3 日）。

清算分为自愿性（基于创办人的决定）和强制性（基于法院的决定）。如发生以下情形，法律实体将被迫启动清算程序：

- 破产；
- 因违反土库曼斯坦有关法律实体登记相关法律的规定，登记证书被吊销；
- 无照经营（针对许可经营类的活动）或开展禁止经营的业务类型；
- 屡次违反土库曼斯坦法律的规定开展经营；
- 土库曼斯坦法律规定的其他情形。

此外，清算可在下列情况下进行：注册证书到期、公司注册资本大幅减少或公司重组。

（2）公司解散的监管

公司的创办人可以决定发起自愿清算，并可以选择清算人和拟进行清算的期间。应当注意的是，启动自愿清算，公司需征得其债权人的事先同意。

在强制清算的情形下，经济法院将启动清算程序并指定清算人：

- 终止与公司雇员的劳动合同；
- 通知清算公司的债权人；
- 进行公司资产的盘点（对公司的资产和产品进行评估，获得应收款，并与债权人签署和解案）；
- 准备拟向税务机关提交的报告；
- 在大众媒体上刊登清算公告。

（3）清算的最后阶段

完成上述步骤后，清算人应当注销公司的银行账户，向国家档案局进行公司文件的备案。从这个阶段起，公司将被视作已按照《破产法》第 34 条的规定完成清算，并被排除在法律实体统一国家登记册之外。

（六）公司兼并与收购

1. 收购兼并法律、法规

兼并和收购的法律尚未发展完善，故该流程是政府和总统以法令和决议的形式作出批准来推进。

这些问题在《企业法》《投资活动法》和《外国投资法》中进行了部分规定。土库曼斯坦法律对于外资并购的程序或标准没有明确的规定。一般情况下，公司在涉及国有企业或国家参股企业的并购活动中，应当取得有关国家部门的批准。

2. 收购兼并程序

土库曼斯坦法律承认企业兼并重整的概念。《企业法》第52条就前述概念定义如下：

（1）兼并是由两个或多个企业，在其资产完全合并的基础上，通过建立一个新企业的方式实施。参与兼并的企业在停止经营活动的同时，其权利和义务依据转让行为转让给新成立的企业。

（2）重整是由一个或数个企业，通过将其财产纳入重整企业的资产，进而实施重整。同时，被纳入企业应当停止其作为独立法律实体的经营活动，其权利和义务根据转让行为转让给重整企业。设立文件应进行组织结构变更。

被纳入企业在重整企业的注册资本的单独股份比例，可根据重整的具体条件进行变更。

（3）基于兼并或重整的决定或合同，合并实体签署新的设立协议，批准新注册企业的章程，并选举其执行和管理机构。

（七）竞争法

1. 竞争法的监管部门

目前土库曼斯坦没有竞争监管部门。

土库曼斯坦的前反垄断委员会于1995年依据第2057号总统令（1995年1月11日）被撤销。

2. 竞争法简介

土库曼斯坦没有制定反垄断法律、法规。但是，有关反垄断和竞争的一些问题部分规制于《民法》《刑法》《外国投资法》和《贸易活动法》。

此外，为了阻止垄断行为，《国家支持中小企业法》（第57-IV号文件，2009年8月15日）第17条对公共机关施加了一定的限制。因此，公共机关不能：

① 颁布法令和/或执行限制中小企业权利或利益的行动；

② 订立的协议或采取的一致行动可能导致：

- 提高价格导致市场不公平竞争；
- 按区域原则、销售量或按已变现产品（成品、服务）的范围划分市场；
- 对中小企业的市场准入施加限制。

3. 规制反垄断的措施

违反竞争法律可能导致土库曼斯坦法项下的行政和刑事责任。建立并维持或高或低的垄断价格，垄断企业通过一致行动限制竞争以及限制市场准入，将被视为严重违反当地的反垄断法规。上述违法行为将被处以罚款或刑期为1至3年的监禁。

（八）税收

1. 税收制度和规则

截至2004年10月25日，税收问题主要由土库曼斯坦《税法》（第245-II号文件）调整。国家税制有两个层级。根据《预算制度法》（第121-1号文件，1996年6月18日）的规定，税收在中央和地方预算之间进行分配。

此外，土库曼斯坦已加入一些双重征税条约，这些条约是与以下国家缔结的：奥地利、法国、印度、巴基斯坦、乌克兰、亚美尼亚、英国、伊朗、俄罗斯、美国、白俄罗斯、德国、日本、斯洛伐克、乌兹别克斯坦、比利时、格鲁吉亚、哈萨克斯坦、土耳其。

2. 主要税种和税率

根据《税法》的规定，公司受限于土库曼斯坦法律规定的下列主要税种和强制性支付款项：

税种	税率	纳税人
企业所得税	居民企业所得税税率为 8% 包括外国公司分支机构在内的其他法律实体的税率为 20%	土库曼斯坦居民法律实体 通过常驻代表处或者分支机构在土库曼斯坦经营的非居民法律实体
增值税（VAT）	增值税税率通常为 15% 从事土库曼斯坦《油气资源法》项下业务的承包商和分包商，在从事与石油和天然气工业有关的部分工程中免征增值税	法律实体，包括外国公司的分支机构 创业者个人
财产税	财产税的税率为应税资产账面价值的 1%	法律实体——财产所有人
地下资源税	对于天然气和伴生气的提取，地下资源税税率为 22% 对于原油产品的提取，地下资源税税率为 10% 对于开采其他矿产，地下资源税税率为 0% 到 50%	仅当法律实体从底土中提取矿产时才会产生地下资源税
个人所得税	个人所得税税率为 10%	土库曼斯坦居民个人 在土库曼斯坦取得收入的非居民个人
消费税	根据消费产品的不同，消费税税率从 10% 到 100%	消费产品的制造商和 / 或销售商
城市、乡镇和农业社区发展的特殊费用	创业者个人的特殊费用费率为总收入的 0.3% 其他个人的特殊费用费率为 2 马纳特 / 月 农业企业的特殊费用费率是利润的 0.5% 其他法律实体的特殊费用费率是利润的 1%	法律实体 土库曼斯坦居民个人 创业者个人
养老基金缴纳	缴费比率是各员工工资的 20%	由外国公司法律实体及其分支机构代其员工缴纳

3. 税务的申报和优惠

纳税申报表和申报手续的完成需经国家税务局和财政经济部的批准。一经国家机构成功登记，实体需向国家税务局登记以取得纳税证明和"商业识别号"。大部分实体需向各州国家税务机关申报并提交纳税申报表。

政府提供的优惠和激励旨在支持中小企业。涉及中小企业的税收豁免主要包括财产税和增值税的豁免。针对教育机构、残疾人组织、卫生和宗教组织的投资项目免征企业所得税和财产税。

在自由经济区经营的公司也享有一定的税收激励。例如，外国投资者在土库曼斯坦旅游区（国家旅游区"Avaza"）开展活动免征增值税、财产税和企业所得税。

（九）证券

1. 证券相关法律、法规简介

2011 年通过了《2012—2016 年发展土库曼斯坦证券市场国家计划》。发展计划由三个阶段组成，旨在吸引外国投资、集中资本以及经济部门和商业实体之间的合理再分配。

2014 年，政府正式通过新版《证券市场法》（第 139-V 号文件）。该法规定了土库曼斯坦境内证券发行和流通的基本原则，证券交易所活动的主要规定，同时规定了证券市场参与者之间的法律关系。股份公司的证券发行规定于《股份公司法》（第 400-I 号文件，1999 年 12 月 23 日）。

此外，2015 年土库曼斯坦总统发布了《证券市场职业活动许可令》。在土库曼斯坦，对涉及经纪活动（金融中介）、证券管理活动、结算业务、托管业务、维持证券持有人登记活动及股票交易活动的证券市场业务实行强制许可。

发展计划的最后阶段已于 2016 年开始，其标志是完成了为将成熟的证券市场纳入国际金融市场体系创造条件的工作。《公债发行、变现和再融资的总统令》（2015 年 12 月）规定了期限 5 年以上的公债的发行，该等债券可向所有法律实体出售，不论法律实体的所有权结构如何，在土库曼斯坦经营的外国法律实体亦包括在内。

2. 证券市场的监管

财政经济部是土库曼斯坦监管证券市场、监督和许可证券市场特定业务的国家有权主管机关。

3. 外国企业参与证券交易的要求

《证券市场法》规定有价证券可以由依据土库曼斯坦法律合法登记的法律实体或公共机构发行。在土库曼斯坦发行证券，外国公司必须设立一家当地公司（例如封闭型或开放型股份公司）。股份公司发行证券，须经土库曼斯坦经济财政部进行国家登记。所发行的证券信息应当被记录在全国统一的证券登记簿中。股份公司完成前述登记时，可以采用各种分配方案进行证券发行：①面向其股东；②面向预先确定的个人或公司；③面向无数量限制的个人和公司。

外国公司发行的证券可被准许在土库曼斯坦进行分配。然而，部长内阁可以为该等证券的分配设立年度配额。

（十）投资优惠与保护

1. 优惠政策框架

外国投资者在土库曼斯坦可获得的经济激励规定于《外国投资法》（第184-III号文件，2008年3月3日）。在土库曼斯坦境内外商投资企业工作的外籍个人及其家庭成员，可以获得不少于1年的多次签证。

另外，作为外国投资者对外商投资企业注册资本的出资而进口到土库曼斯坦的财产，可以免征进口税和关税。在实现投资项目的框架内，就进口财产可以执行简化的通关程序。

以自由兑换货币出资而占到当地公司注册资本30%以上的外国投资者，在初始投资回收的一定期间内，可以免于缴纳股息税，公司自身免征所得税。部长内阁可根据投资项目的类型一事一议地给予额外的税收激励。

在自由经济区（例如国家旅游区"Avaza"）内经营的外国投资者被给予最优惠的条件。国家旅游区"Avaza"是根据总统法令第8855号文件的规定，于2007年在里海东岸建立。根据该法令的规定，从事"Avaza"建设及在"Avaza"内实施投资项目的法律实体的国家登记是免费的。此外，在"Avaza"工作的外国专家可以获得入境签证并适用简化手续，无须支付领事签证费和登记费。最后，中央银行担保外国投资者在"Avaza"内基于提供服务所获得的净利润可转化为可兑换货币。

外商投资企业（外商投资的可自由兑换货币出资额不少于30%）有权出口等值于外国投资者在注册资本中所占股份的自有产品（成品、服务），而不需要授权机关所颁发的许可证书。

此外，外商投资企业可以在不需要许可证的情形下为其自身经济活动而进口产品（货物、服务）。

2. 特定产业支持

土库曼斯坦以其庞大的天然气和石油矿床而闻名，因而特别重视该等领域的投资项目。土库曼斯坦在经营液化石油气发电站（LPG发电站）的同时，当前正在开发两座气变液设施（GTL发电站）。土库曼斯坦计划吸引外国投资者对该等领域进行进一步投资。

土库曼斯坦是中亚地区最大的棉花生产国之一，近期已就加大对当地纺织加工能力的投资作出了积极努力，以将原材料转化为制成品并提高国家的出口潜力。2012年，总统通过了《2012—2016年纺织产业发展计划》。该计划旨在与外国证券交易所建立业务关系，进一步发展中小型公司，增加土库曼斯坦的出口潜力及吸引对该等产业的外商投资。政府还计划对现有棉花生产企业进行升级改造和建设新设施。

此外，土库曼斯坦正计划发展该国的化学、建设、农业产业以及管道网络。

3. 特殊经济区

土库曼斯坦的《自由创业经济区法》（第893号文件）于1993年生效。位于自由创业经济区（以下简称"自创区"）的公司被授予一定的税收、海关和财政福利。自创区内建立了简化的进出口业务制度。进口至自创区或从自创区出口的货物免予征收关税。在自创区内经营的公司3年内无须为使用土地支付租赁费。此外，政府保证外国投资者在支付完所有的税款后，其可将利润自由汇出。目前，土库曼斯坦有10个自创区：Ekerem-Hazar, Ashgabat-Anew, Saragt, Ashgabat International Airport, Mary-

Bayramaly、Turkmenabat-Seydi、Ashgabat-Abadan、Dashoguz Airport、Bakharly-Serdar 和 Gulneshli。

2017 年 10 月 9 日土库曼斯坦政府正式通过《自由经济区法》(第 620-V 号文件)。该法计划，至 2030 年，建立起 23 个自由经济区（以下简称"自经区"）。拟建自经区的目标主要是吸引外国投资者和先进技术以使资源得到有效利用。法律规定在土库曼斯坦可以设立以下类型的自经区：

- 自由贸易区和出口区；
- 工业和生产区，包括工业园区；
- 科技园区；
- 提供金融、银行、旅游娱乐、信息和其他类型服务的专门区域；
- 运输和物流区；
- 农—工业区；
- 综合区。

4. 投资保护

土库曼斯坦境内外国投资者的权益受到《外国投资法》和《投资活动法》的保护。土库曼斯坦法下的投资保护包括：

- 外商投资企业中的外籍个人、代表和雇员（以下简称"外企人员"）有在土库曼斯坦自由行动的权利，并可获得多次入境签证；
- 外国投资者和外资人员可以开设本币和外币银行账户，且汇回在土库曼斯坦境内获得的利润不受任何限制；
- 外国投资者的知识产权受到土库曼知识产权法的保护；
- 在投资活动终止的情况下，外国投资者有权自由收回其基于投资活动所获得的资产；
- 在国有化或征用的情况下，外国投资者有权要求对其资产进行全额补偿。

三、贸易

（一）部门监督贸易

由于两个部委（对外经济关系部和贸易资源部）的合并，土库曼斯坦贸易和对外经济关系部于 1998 年成立。该部是负责管理贸易活动和国家对外经济关系发展的最高权力机构。

此外，该部还管理与土库曼斯坦消费者保护有关的问题。该部有自己的分支，国家贸易管制处负责审查贸易标准和规范遵守情况、市场价格形成的正确性和产品质量，并防止低质量产品进入国内市场。

（二）贸易法规简介

2016 年 3 月 26 日通过了新版《贸易活动法》(第 370-V 号)。该法规定的在贸易管制领域的国家政策的目的是：①为贸易发展创造有利条件；②确保货物流通稳定；③贸易基础设施的发展和商品质量的服务提供；④支持本土商品生产者；⑤确保消费者权益的保护。

由于某些类型的贸易活动需要获得许可（例如批发贸易），这样的问题适用于 2008 年 6 月 25 日颁布的第 202 号《特殊活动类型许可法》和《民法》。

保护消费者权益是该国贸易法的重要组成部分。这方面的主要文件是 2017 年 6 月 3 日发布的第 565-V 号法律和 2016 年 11 月 23 日发布的第 479-V 号法令（新版）。

（三）贸易管理

《贸易活动法》规定了土库曼斯坦贸易活动组织的最低要求和土库曼斯坦贸易活动的许可，产品的认证和标签。该法管理远程交易和拍卖的组织情况，并处理不公平竞争问题。

根据土库曼斯坦的法律，贸易活动的主要类型是批发贸易、零售贸易、公共餐饮组织和提供与货物销售有关的服务。根据交易市场的规模，市场分为小型（500 平方米以下）、中型（1 000 平方米以下）和大型（超过 1 000 平方米）。

在国内市场上销售的产品必须经过认证并符合当地标准和要求。产品标签应以土库曼语和俄语提供（以及作为其他选项，也可用英语或其他语言）。某些类别的产品（酒精和烟草产品）需要用消费税标签强制标注。

希望从事贸易的外国公司需要设立当地公司或分支机构并获得相关许可证。另一种选择是，外国公司可以与当地公司签订代理或分销合同，根据该合同，后者将作为外国公司的代理商或分销商在土库曼斯坦销售。

（四）进出口商品的检验检疫

土库曼斯坦没有针对进出口商品检验检疫的具体规定。所有从土库曼斯坦进口或出口的产品均按照一般既定程序进行海关清关和海关监管。

此外，大多数类型的进出口交易均须在土库曼斯坦国家商品和原材料交易所注册。在注册合同时，各方均应支付相当于交易金额总额 0.2% 的费用（居民以土库曼马纳特支付，非居民以美元支付）。

（五）海关管理

土库曼斯坦国家海关是被授权执行海关监管领域国家政策的指定机构。该部门由中央行政办公室和 6 个地区海关组成。阿什哈巴德市、阿勒哈尔、巴尔干、列巴普、达什奥古兹和玛丽地区的海关办事处对通过土库曼斯坦边境的货物实施海关监管和清关。此外，在土库曼斯坦有 50 个关税和检查点。

所有通过土库曼斯坦国家边界的货物和车辆均按照土库曼斯坦《海关法》规定的程序进行海关清关和海关管制。为执行清关，需缴纳以下税款和费用：①关税；②税（增值税、消费税）；③海关费用（清关费、海关支持费和/或存储费）。申请人必须向海关当局提供关于通过边境货物的可靠且最新的信息。以下文件应与海关申报一起提交：

- 进口或出口合同；
- 商业文件（发票、装箱单等）；
- 交通运输（海运）文件；
- 相关许可证、执照和证书；
- 确认货物来源的文件；
- 支付（结算）文件；
- 确认申报的报关金额的文件。

土库曼斯坦建立了以下类型的海关制度：

- 货物自由流通；
- 出口；
- 海关转运；
- 关境内加工货物；
- 加工货物的自由流通；
- 在关境外加工货物；
- 临时进口；
- 临时出口；
- 海关仓库；
- 免税贸易；
- 免费报关区（免费仓库）；
- 复进口；
- 复出口；
- 货损；
- 放弃本国有利的原则。

四、劳动

(一) 劳动法律、法规简介

2009年4月18日的土库曼斯坦《劳工法》(第29-IV号) 为所有主要与就业有关的事宜提供监管保障,并规定雇佣合同各方的强制性条件,雇员可获得的担保和社会福利,雇主和雇员的相互权利和义务,对孕妇、有子女的妇女和未成年人的就业限制,工作时间,工作安全以及与终止雇佣合同有关的问题。

其他与劳动有关的事项受以下法律文件的约束:
- 2012年10月19日颁布的第340-IV号《人口社会保护法》;
- 2016年7月18日颁布的第411-V号《人口就业法》;
- 2013年11月9日颁布的第443-IV号《关于工会及其权利和活动保证的法律》;
- 2005年2月1日颁布的第5-III号法律《保障青年的工作权利》;
- 2011年3月26日颁布的第169-1号《关于土库曼斯坦外国公民法律地位的法律》;
- 2012年3月31日颁布的第287-IV号《国家养老保险法》;
- 2005年7月13日颁布的第7367号《关于临时雇用外国公民的总统令》;
- 2005年7月13日颁布的总统令《关于土库曼斯坦关于外国人登记的国家服务》(第7367号);
- 2003年2月21日颁布的总统令《关于土库曼斯坦外国公民入境、出境和逗留》(第6135号);
- 2007年5月22日颁布的总统令《商务旅行费用》(第8629号);
- 2000年11月27日颁布的总统令《关于土库曼斯坦雇员——公民的工作就业记录》(第4970号);
- 2000年1月31日颁布的总统令《关于在高风险生产设施工作的雇员的强制性人身保险》(第4550号);
- 1999年1月15日颁布的总统令《关于雇员受伤或职业病造成的损害赔偿》(第4039号)。

(二) 聘用外籍员工的要求

1. 工作许可证

《关于暂时雇用外国公民》的总统令规定了在土库曼斯坦境内的外籍雇员的就业程序。寻求聘用外籍雇员的当地雇主必须申请特别许可证(以下简称"工作许可证")。未经土库曼斯坦就业机构批准(该批准文件以下简称"确认书"),外籍人士可能无法在土库曼斯坦就业。该确认书是针对每名外籍员工发放的,当地雇主有义务代表未来的外籍员工去向该机构申请。

有两个主要的国家机构管理外国公民的就业及发放工作许可证和确认书:
- 临时聘用外国公民监督委员会(以下简称"委员会");
- 国家外国公民登记局(以下简称"登记局")。

2. 申请程序

为了领取许可证和确认书,雇主应向登记局提交以下文件:
- 申请书;
- 雇主工作人员名单;
- 雇主设立文件的副本;
- 雇主的国家注册证书;
- 税务机关关于没有拖欠税款的函件;
- 与外籍员工签订的劳动合同初稿;
- 确认外国员工专业程度和显示符合资格要求的文件;
- 有照片的外籍员工简历;
- 外籍员工的无艾滋病证书;
- 确认支付国家费用的收据。

包含所有必要文件的申请应先提交给登记局,然后提交给委员会批准。委员会在1个月内作出最终决定，然后由登记局发放工作许可证和确认书。

一般来说，工作许可证和确认书的期限为1年。到期后，工作许可证和确认书期限延长，最长延期期限为1年。聘用外籍雇员的雇主每月为该外籍雇员支付25美元的费用。

雇用外籍人士的当地雇主必须确保任何雇主的员工结构中外国劳动力的比例不超过30%。登记局必须根据土库曼斯坦法律密切监测当地所有雇主的合规情况。

3. 社会保险

土库曼斯坦的社会保护体系包括以下组成部分：
- 养老保险；
- 社会福利制度。

在土库曼斯坦，养老保险有强制性和自愿性两种类型。根据《劳动法》的规定，本地雇主必须确保雇员获得土库曼斯坦养老基金（支付员工总报酬的20%形成）的强制养老金和保险费。员工也可以自愿缴纳该基金，因为这些缴费可能会增加未来养老金的规模（占其薪金的2%或更多）。

《国家养老保险法》列举了几种养老金。退休金在达到一定的年龄条件时支付。军人和飞行员有权享受长期服务养老金，在高风险生产设施工作的雇员有权享受专业养老金。此外，残疾养老金支付给因某种残疾而无法工作的个人。此外，幸存者养老金将给失去负担家计者但又没有生存能力的人。

根据《人口社会保护法》设立的土库曼斯坦社会福利制度包括以下几种福利：
（1）临时伤残津贴；
（2）产妇津贴；
（3）育儿津贴；
（4）伤残津贴；
（5）赋予伟大爱国战争参与者妻子的津贴；
（6）国家社会补贴。

（三）出境和入境

1. 签证类型

外国公民和无国籍人士可根据入境签证进入和留在土库曼斯坦领土。签发签证并延长其有效期由以下机关操作：
- 在土库曼斯坦境内——由外交部根据签证发放监督委员会的决定；
- 在土库曼斯坦境外——通过驻外国的土库曼斯坦的外交和领事代表。

签证的类型			
1	外交签证（DP）	7	旅游签证（TU）
2	公务签证（OF）	8	过境签证（TR）
3	商务签证（BS）	9	医疗签证（HL）
4	工作签证（WP）	10	驾驶员签证（DR）
5	私人签证（PR）	11	出境签证（EX）
6	学生签证（ST）		

希望聘用外籍人士的公司需要向外交部提交以下文件：
- 用土库曼语写的申请；
- 雇主设立文件的公证副本；
- 税务机关关于没有拖欠税款的正式函件；
- 外籍员工护照复印件。

上述文件在1个月内由外交审查完毕。审查完毕后，外国雇员获得入境签证。根据雇主的支持函，外国公民可获得多次入境签证。

另外，外国公民也需办理一定的注册手续。在土库曼斯坦停留超过 5 天的外国人必须在抵达后的 3 天内向登记局或其地区分区（取决于外国公民将居住的地区）进行登记。

2. 出入境限制

违反留在土库曼斯坦规定的外国公民可能会受到某些限制（驱逐出境、禁止入境等）。包括未遵守注册要求、缺乏有效文件（入境签证、工作许可证等）、在停留期满后仍不出境，以及不遵守通过土库曼斯坦过境的规则。

（四）工会和劳工组织

根据土库曼斯坦的法律，员工有权参加工会。《劳动法》第 17 章和《工会、工会权利与工会活动保障法》规定了工会的作用和法律地位。该法确立了以下工会类型：

- 由在一家公司工作的员工组成的基层工会；
- 由在同一行业中经营的若干公司的雇员组成的行业工会（例如银行业、农业等）；
- 可以在土库曼斯坦每个地区建立的地域工会。

土库曼斯坦现有的所有工会都是土库曼斯坦工会组织（一个官方政治组织）的成员。工会组织可以参加议会的会议。本组织成员在土库曼斯坦议会占有 33 个席位。

无论类型如何，所有工会均须在司法部进行国家注册。登记工会时，下列文件应提交给司法部：

- 工会管理机构所有成员签署的申请；
- 工会章程两份；
- 工会会员会议记录；
- 有关工会管理权力和工会地点的信息；
- 支付国家注册费的收据。

工会会员是自愿的。每个员工独立决定他是否加入工会。

工会代表和保护雇员与公共当局及雇主关系中的社会、经济和劳工权益。工会有广泛的谈判能力，他们可以参与准备设置劳动协议、员工与雇主之间的集体协议、公司的内部劳动规定和其他劳动文件。此外，他们还可以在当地法院提出索赔，以保护雇员的利益。

（五）劳资纠纷

根据土库曼斯坦法律，劳动争议可以通过以下方式解决：①工作中的劳工纠纷委员会；②工会；③具有一般管辖权的地方法院。《劳动法》第 16 章规定了解决劳动争议的程序。

员工人数超过 15 人的公司有资格根据土库曼斯坦法律成立劳工纠纷委员会，其成员将由公司的雇员选举产生。2013 年 9 月 21 日，司法部通过了《劳工纠纷委员会示范条例》，对此类委员会的活动提供了详细指导。

如果雇主和雇员之间有任何分歧，后者可向劳工纠纷委员会提出申请。自提交申请之日起 10 日内，劳工纠纷委员会有义务解决争议并作出决定。如果员工对劳工纠纷委员会的决定不满意，他也可以向工会提出请求，或者在没有工会的情况下向当地法院提出请求。

某些类别的劳动争议专属于一般管辖法院管辖，包括：①恢复工作；②对雇员造成的伤害或职业病的赔偿；③对强迫失业期的赔偿；④无理拒绝雇用的纠纷。还应该指出的是，向劳动关系索赔法院提出申请的劳动者可以免交法院费用。

五、知识产权

（一）知识产权法律、法规简介

土库曼斯坦拥有完善的知识产权保护法律体系，并在 2017 年通过了几项法律。2017 年 11 月 4 日，议会通过了两项新的法律文件：《关于发明的法律保护的法律》（第 629-V 号）和《关于工业模型的法律保护的法律》(第 630-V 号)。这些法律取代了以前的《专利法》(1993 年 10 月 1 日)。新法律提及了土库曼斯坦签署的国际条约,并包括规定发明和工业模型国际保护的条款。

土库曼斯坦在版权法、商标和专利注册以及知识产权保护领域的其他主要文件如下:
- 1998 年 7 月 17 日第 294-I 号土库曼斯坦《民事法典》;
- 2008 年 10 月 23 日颁布的第 221-III 号《关于商标、服务标志和货物产地法》;
- 2012 年 1 月 10 日第 257-IV 号《版权和相关权法》;
- 1992 年 9 月 30 日第 755-XII 号《关于科学知识产权的法律》;
- 1994 年 9 月 23 日第 964-XII 号《关于算法、电子计算机程序、数据库和综合微电路拓扑的法律保护》;
- 2011 年 8 月 4 日第 207-IV 号《关于选育育种结果的法律保护》。

此外,土库曼斯坦已加入若干国际条约,如:
- 《建立世界知识产权组织公约》;
- 《保护工业产权巴黎公约》;
- 《专利合作条约》;
- 《欧亚专利公约》;
- 《商标国际注册马德里协定有关议定书》;
- 《国际专利分类斯特拉斯堡协定》;
- 《建立工业品外观设计国际分类洛迦诺协定》;
- 《关于国际货物和货物分类的尼斯协定》;
- 《建立商标图形要素国际分类维也纳协定》。

(二)专利申请

1. 发明专利

专利局(Turkmenpatent)是财政和经济部的一个专门部门,是负责在国家发明登记册中登记发明以及在该国发布专利的主管机关。

申请发明专利是由发明人(或多位作者)、他的雇主(如果发明是由一名雇员在履行其公务中完成)或其继任者向专利局提交的。申请应采用土库曼语(或应附土库曼语翻译)。此类申请应包含以下信息:
- 有关发明作者(作者)和他的居住地的信息;
- 发明的详细描述;
- 发明的公式;
- 与发明相关的图纸和其他材料;
- 载明发明的简要描述的报告。

如果申请是由申请人的代表或官方专利代理人提交的,则应提交委托书给专利局。

在收到包含所有相关文件的申请后,专利局会进行专家考核。基于考核结果,专利局颁发发明专利。该专利从向专利局提交申请之日起 20 年内有效。应该提到的是,需在专利有效期内按年度支付一笔国家费用。

根据 1993 年《保护工业产权巴黎公约》的规定,申请人可对一项发明享有优先权利。此外,专利局也可发布根据 1994 年《欧亚专利公约》提起申请的专利。

2. 工业模型专利

工业模型专利的申请也向专利局提交。申请中应包含以下信息:
- 关于工业模型的发明人(作者)及其居住地的信息;
- 提供展示工业模型外观完整画面的工业模型图片;
- 绘制工业模型的总体视图、人类工程学方案、精制图;
- 工业模型的简要描述。

若申请是由申请人的代表或官方专利代理人提出的,则申请方应向土库曼斯坦提交授权委托书。

基于考核结果,土库曼斯坦专利局可以颁发工业模型专利,该专利最初 5 年有效。专利有效期的最长期限为 15 年,但每 5 年申请人需要支付其延期的国家费用。

(三)商标注册

商标保护通过注册获得。《关于商标、服务标志和货物产地法》规定了商标注册的详细程序。注册申请必须由申请人或其代理人或根据授权书行事的专利代理人向专利局提出。注册一项商标的国家费用为 250 美元。外国个人和法人实体需要通过专利代理人申请。

申请过程包括正式审查、独特性审查和先前商标搜索。基于审查结果,专利局颁发商标注册证书,并在专利局公告中公布注册商标信息。

该证书自注册之日起有效期为 10 年,并可通过续期申请延长。续期请求可在商标到期日前的 6 个月内提出。延长有效期的国家费用为 500 美元。

如果商标从签发证书之日起 3 年内未使用,或者连续 3 年未使用,可能会被取消。

(四)知识产权保护措施

知识产权权利人有权按照《民法典》和其他相关法律、法规的规定在权利受侵犯时寻求法律保护。索赔人可向当地有关法院申请:

- 承认对其知识产权对象拥有的权利;
- 防止侵犯知识产权的行为;
- 对因非法使用知识产权对象(可能包括对精神损害的赔偿)造成的损害进行赔偿;
- 扣押侵犯知识产权过程中使用的设备或材料。

索赔人还可以要求法院在大众媒体上公布其决定,以防止未来的侵权行为。法院也可以决定没收侵权货物。

专利权人可以在他应当知道其权利遭受侵犯之日起 3 年内提出申诉。

侵犯知识产权在土库曼斯坦将导致行政和刑事责任。根据法院的判决,侵权人可能会被拘留最多 15 天或者罚款。重复的违规行为会导致更高的罚款或最高 2 年的矫正惩罚。

六、环境保护

(一)环境保护监督部门

国家环境保护和土地资源委员会于 2016 年由环境保护部和国土资源部两个机构重组后成立。

目前国家环境保护和土地资源委员会(以下简称"委员会")是国家在环境保护和合理利用土地资源领域的国家最高权力机构。委员会在土库曼斯坦所有地区设有分支机构。

委员会制定并实施环境保护领域的国家统一政策,参与起草法律、法规,协调该领域其他公共部门的活动。委员会对国家的自然资源进行评估和登记,并负责国家对动植物、水土资源的登记入册工作。它还组织国家对自然资源利用情况的监测,保护珍稀濒危动植物物种。

委员会决定使用自然资源的缴费率,并确定污染物的允许排放量的限制。此外,委员会及其分支机构负责处理与违反环境保护法律和赔偿法律的实体和个人对环境造成的损害有关的问题。

委员会颁布进出口动植物物种的许可证。此外,它还可以批准向土库曼斯坦进口/出口臭氧消耗物质。

(二)涉及环境保护的法律、法规简介

关于保护环境,合理利用自然资源,保护濒危动植物物种的法律行为包括以下内容:

- 2016 年 10 月 15 日颁布的第 456-V 号土库曼斯坦《水法典》;
- 2011 年 3 月 25 日颁布的第 166-1 号土库曼斯坦《林业法典》;
- 2014 年 3 月 1 日颁布的第 40-V 号《关于保护自然的法律》;
- 2009 年 8 月 15 日颁布的第 53-IV 号《关于保护臭氧层的法律》;

- 2016 年 3 月 26 日颁布的第 366-V 号《关于保护大气层的法律》；
- 2017 年 6 月 3 日颁布的第 569-V 号《生态安全法》；
- 2016 年 6 月 18 日颁布的第 413-V 号《植物保护法》；
- 2014 年 12 月 20 日颁布的第 160-V 号《底土法》；
- 2013 年 3 月 2 日的颁布的第 375-IV 号《动物法》；
- 2012 年 3 月 31 日颁布的第 286-IV 号《自然保护区法》；
- 2011 年 5 月 21 日颁布的第 197-1 号《关于渔业和水生生物资源保护》。

此外，土库曼斯坦已经在环境保护领域批准了下列国际条约和公约：
- 《世界气象组织公约》；
- 《保护臭氧层维也纳公约》；
- 《关于消耗臭氧层物质的蒙特利尔议定书》；
- 《联合国气候变化框架公约》；
- 《联合国防治荒漠化公约》；
- 《生物多样性公约》；
- 《控制危险废物越境转移及其处置巴塞尔公约》；
- 《联合国气候变化框架公约的京都议定书》。

土库曼斯坦根据双边条约和协定和独联体国家、土耳其、伊朗和印度进行环境和水文气象信息的区域交流。

（三）评估环境保护

土库曼斯坦的环境法律、法规正在进行持续审查和更新，以确保符合关键性的国际环境保护标准。但是，某些区域环境问题继续引起重大关注。

由于该国位于温带沙漠地区，具有强烈的大陆性气候，夏季炎热干燥，冬季寒冷，特别容易受到气候变化的影响。土库曼斯坦面临着若干影响当地居民福利和健康的严峻生态问题。

1. 荒漠化

荒漠化是土库曼斯坦的主要生态问题。约有 80% 的土库曼斯坦领土被卡拉库姆沙漠覆盖。荒漠化是由于农业集约化发展、大规模建设项目和石油天然气工业的快速发展所导致的。咸海的规模缩减也对土库曼斯坦的环境造成重要影响，导致大面积海床暴露在地面而受到风蚀。来自咸海的沙尘包含盐、肥料和杀虫剂，并且会危害人体健康。

2. 盐渍化

新土地的开发和农业生产的增长对该国的土壤产生了不良影响。该国将近 90% 的水资源用于灌溉。过去数十年里，水质急剧下降，因此用于灌溉的水往往不符合国家水中所含矿物成分相关标准，氯化物和硫酸盐的含量超过了允许的标准。这些因素导致土库曼斯坦一半以上农业用地盐渍化。

3. 污染

排放到大气、土壤和水中的污染程度在过去几年中迅速增加。主要造成污染的企业是从事天然气、石油、化工、工程和建筑行业的企业。在土库曼斯坦的城市，污染是由车辆排放造成的。

由于大多数石油和天然气公司位于里海沿岸地区，因此里海作为该国的一个大型水库也受到严重污染。

七、争议解决

（一）纠纷解决的方法和机构

1. 诉讼

土库曼斯坦最常见的争端解决方法是在当地法院进行诉讼。目前该国的司法系统是根据 2014 年 11

月8日颁布的第134-V号《法院法》设立的。对当地法律的修正导致废除了最高经济法院，其职能转交土库曼斯坦最高法院。

该法规定，民事、刑事、家庭、土地，劳工和军事案件由地区法院管理（初审），区域法院（上诉案件）和最高法院的刑事和民事专门小组作为监督法庭。应该指出的是，1997年政府废除了军事法庭，因此军事案件属于一般管辖法院的职权范围。

此外，商事案件由仲裁法院和区域法院处理（初审）以及最高法院的商业小组（在上诉案件中）处理。某些类别的商业纠纷属于仲裁法庭的专属管辖范围：

- 其中一方是外国法人或外国公民的争议；
- 公司破产纠纷；
- 有关请求撤销中央机构颁布的与土库曼斯坦现行法律冲突的违规法律；
- 被告位于该国不同地区的争议。

以上处理商事纠纷的仲裁法院和地区法院，均属于司法系统的法院。

由于仲裁法院只设在阿什哈巴德市，因此会对位于该地以外的公司造成一定的不便。对于总部设在首都以外的公司，在仲裁法院进行争议解决就会变成一个漫长而昂贵的过程。

仲裁程序受2015年8月18日第260-V号《民事诉讼法》、2009年4月18日第28-IV号《刑事诉讼法》和2000年12月19日第52-II号《仲裁程序法》管辖。

上述法律规定，外国法律实体拥有与土库曼斯坦对应方相同的程序权利和义务。争议在提交申请之日起2个月内由法院审理。根据审理结果，法院将作出决定，该决定将在10日内生效。

任何法院的决定可以在生效之前向上诉法院提出上诉，并且可以由监督法院进行审查（决定生效后）。

但是，案件审理期限可能超过2个月。在实践中，某些商业纠纷（特别是投资纠纷）的诉讼持续了数年。

2. 仲裁

在土库曼斯坦经营的公司也可以使用替代争议解决机制并适用于仲裁法庭。这些法院依照2014年8月16日颁布的第101-V号《国际商事仲裁法》执行。

仲裁法庭审理个人和法律实体的纠纷。土库曼斯坦仲裁法庭的显著特点是：

① 只有在仲裁协议有效的情况下，仲裁法庭才可以考虑争议。
② 仲裁法庭解决：

- 一方当事人在位于土库曼斯坦境外的外贸活动过程中产生的合同纠纷；
- 在土库曼斯坦境内设立外商投资企业和国际组织的纠纷。

③ 根据任何一方的请求，土库曼斯坦最高法院可以撤销违反仲裁程序规则的仲裁法庭裁决。

如果公司有意将争议提交至仲裁，则应在与交易对方签订的合同中设置仲裁条款或签订单独的仲裁协议。

土库曼斯坦有一个永久的仲裁机构——土库曼斯坦工商会仲裁法庭（以下简称"CCI"）。CCI下的仲裁法庭解决有关外贸和其他国际经济关系引起的契约和其他民法问题的争议。

在土库曼斯坦商品交易所获得认可的公司可以根据2014年3月1日发布的第38-V号《货物、原材料和外汇交易法》向商品交易所仲裁委员会提出上诉。该仲裁委员会为贸易商之间的纠纷提供调解机制。该仲裁委员会的职权和职能由商品交易所根据土库曼斯坦法律确定。如果其中一方不同意仲裁委员会的决定，有权向土库曼斯坦的阿比特拉兹法院提出申请。

各方也可以选择向国际仲裁机构（伦敦国际仲裁院、国际商令仲裁院、解决投资争端国际中心等）提交争议。

（二）适用法律

由于土库曼斯坦被视为大陆法系国家，地方法院参考政府、总统和其他立法机构通过的法律。因此，法院在开展活动时主要以土库曼斯坦法律的规定为指导，其中包括拥有最高层级法律效力的宪法、规定特定法律领域的法规以及定期修订的单行法律、法规。

大陆法系国家的法院依据既定的法律行事，因此不具有立法权力，也无权制定新的法律规则，但法院在解释和适用法律行为方面拥有很大的自由。

《仲裁程序法》规定，如果违反或不当使用实体法，地方法院的决定可能被撤销。因此，法院努力遵循统一的方式来解释和适用法律。此外，最高法院还定期分析下级法院的做法并提出旨在便利法院行事的决议。最高法院的决议向地方法院提供了解决各方面争议的详细指导。这些决议不针对某一起案件，而被认为是基于对数十起案件进行分析得出的法院实践的全面查证结果。

土库曼斯坦没有制定适用外国法的法律。土库曼斯坦法律规定，在土库曼斯坦签署的国际协定有明确规定的情况下，地方法院可以适用外国法律。在没有多边或双边国际条约的情况下，法院将适用当地法律。

土库曼斯坦在执行外国法院决定和仲裁裁决方面的实践以及立法均是不完善的。2014年11月8日颁布的第135-V号《执行程序法》规定，外国法院决定和仲裁裁决的执行应根据国际协议和当地法律执行。

根据一般规定，外国法院的决定或仲裁裁决的强制执行始于向当地有关法院提出执行请求。《民事诉讼法》规定，外国法院关于民事事宜的决定可以在决定生效之日起3年内在土库曼斯坦执行。这些决定是在互惠原则的基础上执行的。此外，土库曼斯坦于1993年1月22日成为《明斯克民事、家庭、刑事法律援助条约》的缔约方，有义务承认和执行独联体国家有关法院的决定。土库曼斯坦还加入了独联体国家1992年10月9日签署的《基辅商事活动相关争议解决条约》，并承诺执行独联体国家法院签发的关于商业事宜的决定。

土库曼斯坦的电子管理系统正处于发展的初期阶段，没有公开公共数据库向大众公开在土库曼斯坦法院执行的决定。

还有一点需要提及的是，土库曼斯坦尚未批准1958年《承认及执行外国仲裁裁决公约》。因此，公司和个人在土库曼斯坦执行国际仲裁裁决可能会遇到一些困难。土库曼斯坦法院在审理与仲裁裁决的承认和执行有关的案件时没有统一的处理方法。

八、其他

（一）反商业贿赂

1. 反商业贿赂法律、法规简介

在成为主权国家的初期，反腐监管在该国并不发达。但在过去10年中，政府为改善当地反腐败法作出了巨大努力。2014年3月1日，土库曼斯坦通过了第35-V号法律《反腐败法》，这是该领域的主要法案，旨在防止和禁止所有层级的政府贿赂行为。

公职人员遵守反腐败法律的义务由2016年3月26日颁布的第363-V号法律和2016年3月26日颁布的第364-V号《公职人员道德与行为法》确定。这些法律规定了公职人员的义务，并规定了可接受行为的界限。

此外，2010年5月10日颁布的土库曼斯坦《刑法典》（第104-IV号）列举了对违反反腐败法律的违法行为的惩罚，例如罚款、监禁等。

2. 反商业贿赂监督

土库曼斯坦没有单独负责防止腐败的机构。《反腐败法》要求所有公共当局在其能力范围内防止和打击腐败。

根据《反腐败法》的规定，预防、侦查和惩罚反腐败行为主要由检察官办公室、内政部和土库曼斯坦国家安全局执行。税务和边防服务以及其他金融机构也负责打击腐败。

2017年6月，政府成立了国家打击经济犯罪服务机构，这是一个新的国家机构，将在反腐监管领域与其他机构协调合作。该机构参与解决腐败计划、制定和实施消除和预防措施。此外，它还有权调查对国家造成经济损害的罪行。

3. 惩罚性行为

《刑法典》界定了主动和被动类型的贿赂。根据土库曼斯坦法律，贿赂的定义是行贿者为获取回报向公职人员提供金钱、证券、贵重物品、财产、财产权或与财产有关的服务。

依据《公职人员道德行为法》相关规定，公职人员不应寻求或接受任何形式的不正当利益，以影响公职或职能的履行或不履行。因此，公职人员不得从个人和法人实体收到任何礼物（金钱或实物）。

但是，土库曼斯坦法律只有一个例外。公职人员可以接受与礼宾活动、商务旅行和其他官方活动有关的礼物。在这种情况下，他们有义务将这些礼物上交国家纳入国库。

（1）被动贿赂

公职人员接受贿赂将导致以下刑事责任：

- 强制在某州/地区居住5～8年，并剥夺获得某些职位或从事某些活动的权利3年，不论有无没收财产；
- 监禁长达8年，剥夺获得某些职位的权利或从事某些活动3年，不论有无没收财产。

屡次犯罪、由一群人犯罪、一名公职负责人参与犯罪或伴随敲诈勒索的犯罪行为将导致以下更严厉的惩罚：

- 强制在某州/地区居住8～15年的义务，不论有无没收财产；
- 监禁长达15年，剥夺占有某些职位的权利或从事某些活动3年，不论有无没收财产。

如果公职人员接受大量贿赂（超过100倍最低平均工资），可能会被监禁10～20年。

（2）主动贿赂

主动行贿的人（即向公职人员行贿）将导致以下刑事责任：

- 不论有无没收财产，监禁3～5年；
- 重复犯罪：5年至10年监禁。

（3）贿赂中的中间人

根据土库曼斯坦法律，贿赂犯罪中作为中间人的人员也应承担责任，因为在贿赂中提供中间服务被认为与贿赂本身一样危险。贿赂犯罪中的中间人可能被判处2～10年监禁（或因屡犯判10年）。

（二）项目合同

土库曼斯坦的公共采购体系一直是近期公共部门改革的目标领域。2014年12月，土库曼斯坦政府通过了一项新的《关于为国家需求提供货物、执行工作和提供服务的投标法》（第158-V号）（以下简称《投标法》），以促进国家经济发展、提高公共采购部门的商业竞争环境和增加当地生产量。

《投标法》为投标过程提供了一个总体框架，从发布招标，准备投标文件，投标初步评估到谈判和签订合同。它界定了所有投标人的权利和义务以及投标委员会的资格。此外，《投标法》还详细列明了适用于投标公司的资格标准。

应该指出的是，石油和天然气行业的公共采购由2008年8月20日的《关于碳氢化合物资源》（第208-III号）进行管理。

此外，2016年2月，土库曼斯坦总统签署了第14602号决议《关于对预算消费者的货物、工程、服务供应商的招标和选择》。本文件完全符合《投标法》的规定，并详细介绍了投标过程。

目前上述文件被视为土库曼斯坦公共采购领域的主要法律文件。

1. 许可制度

任何外国或当地公司都可以参加在土库曼斯坦境内举行的招标活动。

如符合《投标法》规定的以下资格要求，任何公司都可参与投标程序：

- 投标人具有符合土库曼斯坦法律要求的全部法律能力和相关执照、证书和许可证；
- 投标人应具有技术和专业能力，并具备履行投标义务所需的经验、财务资源和设备；
- 投标人应具有偿付能力并且没有拖欠税款；
- 投标人不应为破产人、不得处于破产、清算或充足的过程中；
- 投标人不应该是有利益冲突的人。

因此，如果不符合上述任一要求，投标人就不能参与投标。

投标公司（包括本地和外国）及其中介机构无须通过注册来参与投标过程。只要投标公司符合《投标法》规定的资格标准，就可以自由参与投标。

但是，在招投标完成且宣告获胜者后，可能需要在当地注册设立一家公司或常驻代表机构。如果投标义务包括在土库曼斯坦境内开展需要获得许可的活动，则投标的获胜者有义务注册当地公司并申请相关许可。

此外，如果非居民公司在土库曼斯坦的任何后续 12 个月内从事商业活动超过 45 个日历日，则应向当地税务机关注册一家常驻代表机构。考虑到土库曼斯坦可能会对一些包含在投标义务中的活动征税，外国公司可能需根据土库曼斯坦法律要求注册一家常驻代表机构。

2. 禁止规定

《投标法》第 15 条（利益冲突）列出了不能参加投标的人员名单。首先，该法规定，实际担任公职人员的个人不能作为潜在供应商或承包商参与投标。

此外，下列人员不得参加投标（特别是组织招标）：
- 与任何供应商或承包商有密切关系的个人——个人或法人实体的代表或员工；
- 在招标公告发布之前的 3 年内，作为参与投标的任何供应商或承包商的雇员的个人。

3. 招标邀请和投标

《投标法》规定，招投标可以组织成为两种类型：不限制参与者数量；限制参与者数量。

以下情况下，参与投标者是有数量限制的：
- 招投标需审查和评估大量投标书，其费用与提供的货物、执行的工作或提供的服务的价值不相称；
- 由于其技术复杂性或专业性质，货物、工程或服务仅能被有限数量的潜在供应商（承包商）所提供；
- 针对具有国家重要性的对象进行招标。

在初始阶段，招标的组织者发出邀请，向潜在供应商或承包商投标（或在大众媒体上公布投标条件的信息），并向他们提供招标文件。招标的组织者创建至少由 5 人构成的招标委员会。该委员会接收并登记投标书，对其进行评估，进而最终决定中标人。

Turkmenistan

Authors: Atabek Sharipov, Sabina Saparova, Gulnur Nurkeyeva
Translators: Xu Ling, Li Zhiqiang (Jack Li)

I. Overview

A. General Introduction to the Political, Economic, Social and Legal Environment of Turkmenistan

Turkmenistan is a state located in the south-west of Central Asia, which became sovereign on 27 October 1991. Turkmenistan borders with Iran, Afghanistan, Kazakhstan, Uzbekistan, and with Azerbaijan and Russia through the Caspian Sea.

The country is divided into five regions ("welayat"): Ahhal, Balkan, Dashoguz, Lebap and Mary. The capital of Turkmenistan, Ashgabat, has a status of region. In its turn, those regions consist of numerous districts ("etrap"), cities and settlements.

Turkmenistan holds a neutral foreign policy and develops peaceful relations with other countries. Its declaration of "permanent neutrality" was formally recognized by the Resolution of UN General Assembly (dated 12 December 1995). That is to say, the country has not participated in military conflicts, entered military alliances, and provided its territory for foreign troops and military bases.

Turkmenistan's form of government is a presidential republic. Its state structure is based on the principle of separation of powers. The legislative authority of Turkmenistan is a Parliament ("Mejlis") with 125 deputies. Executive functions are carried out by the Cabinet of Ministers headed by the President of the country. Judicial authority is exercised by the Supreme Court. Also, Turkmenistan has an additional legislative body, Halk Maslakhaty (People's Council), which represents interests of the country's population.

As a politically neutral jurisdiction, Turkmenistan remains a stable state. During the first decades of its independence, the Parliament was dominated by one political party, the Democratic Party of Turkmenistan. It was headed by first President of Turkmenistan Saparmurat Niyazov who ruled the country until 2006. After that, the current President Gurbanguly Berdimuhamedov created the Party of Industrialists and Entrepreneurs as well as Agricultural Party. These three parties are represented in the country's Parliament and have the majority of votes.

Over the years, Turkmenistan has maintained high growth rates of its gross domestic product (GDP) and other macroeconomic indicators. Thus, the results of the first quarter of 2017 shows that the GDP growth rate was 6.2 percent. In the industrial sector this indicator increased by 1.8 percent, in construction - 4.4 percent, in transport and communication sector - 10.8 percent, in trade - 10.4 percent, in agriculture - 3.4 percent, and in the services sector–10.8 percent.

Turkmenistan is known for its large deposits of hydrocarbon resources (natural gas and oil). As of today, the country has the world's fourth largest reserves of gas (after Russia, Iran and Qatar). According to "The Program for the Development of Oil and Gas Complex, Chemical Industry and Fisheries of Turkmenistan for 2012-2016", the total volume of oil produced in the country during this period was 55.9 million tons and natural gas – 448.7 billion cubic meters.

Currently, Turkmenistan exports natural gas to China (Turkmenistan-Uzbekistan-Kazakhstan-China gas pipeline) with a capacity of up to 40 billion cubic meters. It should be noted that Turkmenistan also finished the first stage of the development of the "Galkynysh" gas deposit located in Mary region. This deposit gives an additional opportunity to increase natural gas exports volumes. With completion of the ongoing construction of gas pipeline through Afghanistan to Pakistan and then to India (TAPI), Turkmenistan will diversify its gas supply routes and gain access to alternative energy markets in South East Asia.

Turkmenistan occupies one of the leading places in the reserves of mineral raw materials for the chemical industry. Different types of minerals were found in Koytendag district of the Lebap region of the country (sulfur, phosphate, rock salt, gypsum, strontium raw material, celestine, polymetals, limestone and other minerals).

Turkmenistan is the second largest cotton producer in the Central Asia (after Uzbekistan) and the ninth largest producer in the world (after Turkey, United States, India, China, Pakistan, Brazil, Australia and Uzbekistan). It is also known as one of the leading cotton exporters in the Central Asia. More than 70 % of cotton products are exported to the USA, Canada, Germany, the United Kingdom, Italy, Turkey, China, Ukraine and etc. The famous international brands such as Puma, Ikea, Bershka, Nautika, Sara Lee, Casual Wear, Wal-Mart, JP Penney and others are among the main purchasers of Turkmenistan's cotton. As a general rule, the country sells its cotton through auctions in its Commodity and Raw Materials Exchange. Currently, there are more than 70 enterprises operating in textile industry and providing more than 30 thousands of people with jobs in Turkmenistan.

B. The Status and Direction of the Cooperation with Chinese Enterprises Under The B&R

Turkmenistan and China established diplomatic relations in 1992. Their strategic partnership began in 2013. This year was marked by the signing of three important documents aimed at further cooperation between the countries:
• Treaty of Friendship and Cooperation;
• Joint Declaration on Development and Deepening of the Strategic Partnership;
• Declaration on Adoption of the Development Plan for the Strategic Partnership for 2014-2018.

During the years of long-term cooperation Turkmenistan and China signed numerous treaties and agreements in different spheres:
• Agreement on Deepening Stable Cooperation in Natural Gas Sector;
• Agreement on Safe and Stable Operation of the Turkmenistan-China Pipeline;
• Agreement on Economic and Technical Cooperation;
• Agreement on Cooperation between the State Bank for Foreign Economic Relations of Turkmenistan and the Export-Import Bank of China;
• Agreement for the Promotion and Reciprocal Protection of Investments;
• Agreement on Trade-Economic, Scientific-Technical and Cultural Cooperation between the Administration of Akhal Province of Turkmenistan and the People's Government of Shaanxi Province of China;
• Agreement on Trade-Economic, Scientific-Technical and Cultural Cooperation between the Administration of Lebap Province of Turkmenistan and the People's Government of Shandong Province of China;
• Agreement on Establishment of Sister-City Relations between the Cities of Xi'an and Mary;
• Agreement on Establishment of Sister-City Relations between the Cities of Turkmenabat and Jizhao;
• Framework Agreement on Further Cooperation in the Sphere of Culture;
• Framework Agreement on Cooperation in the Sphere of Horse Breeding;
• Memorandum of Understanding on the Basic Principles of Cooperation in the Sphere of Transport;
• Memorandum of Understanding on Cooperation in Agriculture.

Turkmenistan is strongly committed to improving cooperation between the countries under the Belt and Road initiative in such spheres as natural gas and oil production and improvement of transportation structure.

The leading business partners of Turkmenistan, Chinese National Petroleum Corporation ("CNPC"), has been operating in Turkmen market since 1994. Starting from 2007 CNPC has been conducting exploration and development of "Bagtyyarlyk" deposit which is considered as the raw material base for the transnational Turkmenistan-China gas pipeline.

Another major investment project, implemented jointly by CNPC and Petrofac, is the exploration of a large gas deposit "Galkynysh". This deposit together with "Yashlar" and "Garakol" deposits has 27.4 trillion cubic meters of gas and is considered as the world's largest onshore gas deposit.

China Development Bank is in the leading group of international development financiers bringing much needed investment to support and accelerate Turkmenistan's growth and strengthen local industrial and business capacity.

II. Investment

A. Market Access

a. Department Supervising Investment

In 2006 the State Service of Foreign Investments under the President of Turkmenistan was abolished. Its functions were transferred to the Ministry of Finance and Economy of Turkmenistan.

Currently, the Department of State Registration of Legal Entities and Investment Projects under the Ministry of Finance and Economy of Turkmenistan is responsible for regulation of investment activity in the country, registration of investment projects and promotion of foreign and local investments.

Turkmenistan's Trade and Industry Chamber also plays an important role in facilitating entry of direct foreign investment and modern technology and creating enabling business environment, acts as an effective platform for promotion of foreign businesses and business advocacy in Turkmenistan.

b. Laws and Regulations of Investment Industry

Two main documents in the sphere of investment regulation in Turkmenistan are Law "On Investment Activity" No.698-XII dated 19 May 1992 and Law "On Foreign Investments" No.184-III dated 3 March 2008. They define the competency of investment-regulating authorities, establish the procedure of state expertise and registration of investment projects and list incentives, guarantees and privileges provided to foreign investors. The Laws define investment activity as:

• investments made by individuals, economic associations, societies and partnerships, religious organizations and other legal entities irrespective of their ownership structure;

• state investments made by public and local authorities of Turkmenistan from state budget funds;

• foreign investments made by foreign states, legal entities and individuals as well as by stateless persons;

• joint investment made by Turkmen and foreign states, legal entities and individuals.

Law of Turkmenistan "On Hydrocarbon Resources" No.208-III dated 20 August 2008 separately regulates investment activities in oil and gas industries and lists types of agreements concluded in this field by foreign investors (production-sharing agreements, concession agreements, joint operation agreements and other service agreements).

In 2017 Turkmenistan adopted Law "On Free Economic Zones" No.620-V aimed at creation of new free economic zones in the country and attraction of foreign investments. By establishment of free economic zones the Government creates a special legal regime for foreign investors and provides them with certain tax and customs incentives as well as simplifies procedures of business conduction.

Other laws and regulations in the sphere of investment promotion are Law "On Innovation Activity" No.106-V dated 16 August 2014, Law "On Foreign Concessions" No.859-XII dated 1 October 1993 and Law "On Entrepreneurship Activities" No.863-XII dated 1 October 1993.

For example, the Law of Turkmenistan "On Innovation Activity" provides specific reference to the types of legal entities and individuals which are entitled to be engaged in innovation activity and granted incorporation under Turkmen laws: scientific and technological centers, business incubator zones, innovation centers, technology transfer centers, innovation funds and venture organizations. Companies engaged in innovation activity are afforded certain privileges and benefits under Turkmen laws.

Law of Turkmenistan "On Foreign Concessions" creates a regulatory framework for the process involving provision of state permits for foreign companies and individuals wishing to operate in Turkmenistan. A concession is defined as fee-based provision of land plots, deposits of natural resources, enterprises and other property to foreign companies and individuals on the basis of concession agreements. Concessions are provided on a competitive basis. The terms and conditions of the competition process are established by the Cabinet of Ministers of Turkmenistan. Concession owners have the right to engage in exploration works, explore and operate deposits of natural resources and carry out other types of business activities to the extent permitted by Turkmen laws.

In addition, Turkmenistan has signed bilateral investment treaties with the United Kingdom, Switzerland, Russian Federation, Romania, Spain, Slovakia, Germany, France, China, Bahrain, Uzbekistan, Belgium, Armenia, Egypt, Georgia, India, Turkey, Ukraine, Indonesia, Italy, Israel, Luxembourg, Iran, Pakistan, Tajikistan, the United Arab Emirates and Malaysia. These bilateral agreements are aimed at stimulating foreign investments by reducing political risks. They protect investments of one member state of the agreement in the territory of another member state from expropriation and confiscation, and establish the principle of fair treatment of foreign investments.

c. Forms of Investment

Law of Turkmenistan "On Investment Activity" establishes that an investment includes all types of property and intellectual values such as:

• money, special bank deposits, shares, stocks and other securities;

• movable and immovable property (buildings, equipment and other material assets);

• property rights arising from copyright, know-how and other intellectual values;

• right to use land and other natural resources, as well as other property rights;

• other values.

A foreign company or individual could make investments in the following forms:

• share participation in enterprises in cooperation with Turkmen companies and individuals;

• establishment of companies wholly owned by foreign investors, branches of foreign companies and / or purchase of existing enterprises;

• purchase of movable and immovable property;

- provision of loans;
- acquisition of property and non-property rights under Turkmen laws.

d. Standards of Market Access and Examination

Turkmen laws contain no restrictions in relation to foreign investments. However, certain obligations are imposed on foreign investors:
- to provide financial authorities with declaration of volume and sources of an investment;
- to obtain necessary licenses and permits for construction;
- to obtain the conclusion of the State Expertise of Investment Projects in terms of compliance with the norms and rules of seismic resistance, fire and explosion safety, sanitary and hygienic, ecological and town-planning requirements.

Enterprises with foreign investments and their branches are registered with the Department of State Registration of Legal Entities and Investment Projects under the Ministry of Finance and Economy of Turkmenistan. Documents submitted for the registration are considered jointly by the Ministry of Foreign Affairs (for the legality of the submitted documents issued by the official bodies of foreign states), the Ministry of Finance and Economy and the Ministry of National Security (for confirmation of financial status and business reputation).

It should be noted that restrictions for foreign investors could be established by the Turkmen Government on case-by-case basis in certain industries in order to protect the constitutional system of the country and ensure the security of Turkmenistan.

B. Foreign Exchange Regulation

a. Department Supervising Foreign Exchange

Central Bank of Turkmenistan is the competent regulatory authority responsible for state monetary and credit policy, currency regulation and control, development and strengthening of the country's banking system and financial services sector and ensuring stability of national currency – Turkmen manat (TMT).

Central Bank has the following functions:
- carries out all types of banking operations;
- develops Turkmenistan's banking system;
- organizes cash circulation in the country;
- conducts an effective unified state monetary and credit policy;
- ensures the effective functioning of the country's payment system;
- controls the activities of other banks;
- monitors the price stability;
- takes measures for the prevention of money laundering;
- establishes official rates of foreign currencies;
- issues currency notes;
- carries out currency regulation and currency control in accordance with Turkmen laws;
- creates state reserves of currency notes and other valuables;
- registers credit institutions as well as licensing of banking activities;
- maintains the accounts of the Ministry of Finance and Economy, credit institutions and other clients;
- maintains international reserves of Turkmenistan (gold and currency assets);
- regulates the accounting and financial reporting system in credit institutions registered in Turkmenistan;
- establishes general rules for opening bank accounts and conducting bank operations;
- accepts deposits from foreign correspondent banks and other lending institutions.

To perform its functions, the Central Bank can issue legislative acts (usually in the form of official instructions), which are obligatory for all credit institutions, state bodies and all legal entities / individuals in Turkmenistan.

b. Brief Introduction of Laws and Regulations of Foreign Exchange

Law of Turkmenistan "On Currency Control of Foreign Economic Relations" No.230-IV dated 1 October 2011 is a main legal document regulating foreign exchange issues in Turkmenistan. The Law establishes the principles of currency regulation and defines types of currency transactions permitted in the country. Also it is aimed at protecting interests of residents and non-residents involved in foreign exchange operations.

Foreign exchange issues are partly regulated by Law "On Central Bank" No.167-IV dated 25 March 2011, Law "On Credit Organizations and Banking" No.168-IV dated 25 March 2011 and Presidential Decree "On Foreign Currency Operations in the Territory of Turkmenistan" No.5490 dated 7 January 2002.

In 2008 the Government made some attempts to reform the financial services sector of the country. It removed limits on foreign exchange transactions, unified exchange rate and redenominated the national currency.

c. Requirements of Foreign Exchange Management for Foreign Enterprises

Foreign exchange requirements are applicable to both foreign and local enterprises.

Foreign exchange transactions are made at the official and market exchange rates. The official exchange rate is established by the Central Bank of Turkmenistan on the basis of the averaged value of the market exchange rate. All types of currency transactions including operations related to the payment of taxes, customs and other mandatory payments established by Turkmen laws are carried out at the official exchange rate.

In its turn, the market exchange rate is determined on the basis of supply and demand in the foreign exchange market of Turkmenistan. This exchange rate is used for exchange transactions. It should be noted that in accordance with Law "On Currency Control" residents and non-residents could buy and sell foreign currency only through authorized banks and their exchange offices.

C. Financing

a. Main Financing Institutions

Main participants in Turkmenistan's financial market are the Central Bank of Turkmenistan and commercial banks. As of today, there are approximately 12 commercial banks operating in Turkmenistan: State Bank of Foreign Economic Relations, State Commercial Bank "Turkmenbashi", State Commercial Bank "Turkmenistan", State Commercial Bank "Presidentbank", State Commercial Bank "Dayhanbank", State Commercial Bank "Halk bank", State Development Bank of Turkmenistan, Joint-Stock Commercial Bank "Senegat", Joint-Stock Commercial Bank "Rysgal", Turkmen—Turkish Joint-Stock Commercial Bank, International Joint-Stock Commercial Bank "Garagym" and branch of the Iran Bank "Saderat".

Joint-Stock Commercial Bank "Rysgal" is the first private bank in Turkmenistan. It was established in 2011 under the Decree of the President Gurbanguly Berdimuhamedov to develop the country's private sector. Currently the bank operates in accordance with a license issued by the Central Bank.

State Commercial Bank "Dayhan" is a state-owned commercial bank engaged primarily in the provision of agricultural loans. Initially the bank focused on financing the agro-industrial sector. However, since 2012 it began to finance investment projects in construction, transportation, communication and information technology spheres. The bank also provides loan for the construction of individual residential buildings.

State Commercial Bank "Turkmenbashi" is one of the oldest banks in the country. It changed its name several times. In Soviet era it was called "Turkmenpromstroybank". After the collapse of the USSR, the bank was renamed – "Investbank". And, finally, in 2000 "Investbank" was replaced by State Commercial Bank "Turkmenbashi". The bank mainly focuses on financing the industrial sector of Turkmenistan.

State Bank of Foreign Economic Relations was established in 1992 for the development and strengthening of foreign economic relations and attraction of foreign investment loans. The bank acts as an agent for the Government on international capital markets.

State Commercial Bank "Halk Bank" (People's Bank) was established in 1991 and has branches in all regions of the country. It provides a wide range of services to the local population.

State Commercial Bank "Presidentbank" was established in 2000 under the Decree of the President Saparmurat Turkmenbashi to implement the state policy in the field of the provisions of loans to private manufacturers engaged in export activities.

Joint-Stock Commercial Bank "Senegat" is one of the first banks that began to provide financial support to small and medium business enterprises. The clients of the bank are private entrepreneurs, all types of legal entities, small and medium companies, joint venture companies as well as foreign companies.

b. Financing Conditions for Foreign Enterprises

Financial regulation in Turkmenistan equally apply to foreign and domestic companies. A foreign investor may provide financial assistance to local companies and enterprises with foreign investments in any form (e.g.through contribution to the charter capital, in form of credit or loan and etc.). However, credits and loans (both in the form of credit (cash) and in the form of deferred payment / prepayment) between a local legal entity and foreign legal entity in a transaction which exceeds 10,000 US Dollars (incoming and outgoing transactions) must be registered with the Central Bank of Turkmenistan.

D. Land Policy

a. Brief Introduction of Land-Related Laws and Regulations

Land Code of Turkmenistan No.243-II dated 25 October 2004 is the main document regulating the allotment of land plots in Turkmenistan. The Code lists categories of land plots existing in the country and establishes mandatory requirements for its purchase and rent.

In addition, a new edition of Law "On State Land Service" No.656-V was adopted on 25 November 2017. This Law regulates the activities of Turkmenistan's Land Service which is responsible for maintaining the state land cadaster, a unified system of documented information on the natural, economic and legal regimes, categories and qualitative characteristics of land plots, their location and size, as well as their distribution by landowners, land users and land tenants.

The Land Code establishes that there are seven types of land plots:
- agricultural land;
- forest land;
- water reserve land;
- state reserve land;
- residential area (cities, towns and rural settlements);
- industrial land;
- recreational land and reservations.

b. Rules of Land acquisition for Foreign Enterprises

Land acquisition for foreign enterprises is separately regulated by the Land Code. To start with, all land in Turkmenistan is state-owned. Only citizens of Turkmenistan may own a land plot in Turkmenistan. Foreign companies and individuals, foreign countries and international organizations may use land plots in Turkmenistan only on the basis of land rental agreement.

Foreign companies or individuals intending to rent a land plot in Turkmenistan should apply to the Cabinet of Ministers. On the basis of a positive conclusion of the Cabinet of Ministers the State Committee on Environment Protection and Land Resources and its territorial subdivisions provide a foreign company or individual with a land plot.

Article 20 of the Land Code establishes certain limitations on the use of land plots. Foreign companies and individuals, foreign countries and international organizations must use land plots in Turkmenistan only for (i) construction or other non-agricultural purposes and (ii) placement of temporary facilities.

E. Establishment and Dissolution of Companies

a. The Forms of Enterprises

Seven types of enterprises could be established in Turkmenistan in accordance with Law "On Enterprises" No.28-II dated 15 June 2000:
- State Enterprise;
- Individual Enterprise;
- Co-operative Enterprise;
- Joint-Venture Company (JVC);
- Public Organisation Enterprise;
- Economic Society;
- Joint-Stock Company (JSC).

All legal entities are established for unlimited period of time and have their own name, legal address and stamp. They can own separate assets, acquire and exercise property and personal non-property rights under their own name, and act as a claimant or defendant in local courts.

The most preferred forms of enterprises used by foreign investors are individual enterprises with 100% foreign owned capital, JVC, economic societies, representative offices and branches. Representative offices and branches are defined as a separate subdivision of a foreign legal entity in Turkmenistan. Please note that representative offices and branches are not considered as legal entities under Turkmen laws.

a) State Enterprise

A state enterprise is a legal entity that is fully funded by the government, which can own, use and dispose property of assigned to it. State enterprises have limited liability and their functions are defined in their charter.

A state enterprise is incorporated on the basis or by virtue of an order issued by the Cabinet of Ministers or other state authorities. To this end, a special government decree or resolution issued by local authorities shall determine the size of charter capital and types of business operation of a newly incorporated state enterprise. State enterprises are typically incorporated and operate in such strategic industry sectors as power, transportation, construction materials, onshore hydrocarbon production and refining.

b) Individual Enterprise

An individual enterprise is established by and belongs to one individual only. An owner of an individual enterprise bears unlimited liability. The activities of an individual enterprise are governed by its charter. The charter capital threshold for an individual enterprise is 25 minimum wages which equals to USD 5,000.

An individual enterprise shall be managed as a rule by its owner. However, the owner could delegate (contract out) its functions to a designated person (manager, director) on a contractual basis.

c) Co-operative Enterprise

A co-operative enterprise is considered as a form of enterprise that is based on participation of number of members. Property of a co-operative enterprise is accumulated by contributions of its members in the form of income or property and other unrestricted sources. The charter capital threshold for a co-operative enterprise is 50 minimum wages which equals to USD 10,000.

A co-operative enterprise is governed by general meetings of its members. Members of a co-operative enterprise bear limited liability in relation to enterprise's obligations.

d) Joint-Venture Company (JVC)

A Joint-Venture Company can be incorporated by local and foreign legal entities and individuals. A JVC is incorporated on the basis of foundation agreement signed by its founders. Moreover, under Turkmen laws each founder of a JVC should own at least 10 per cent of the company's charter capital. The charter capital threshold for a JVC is 100 minimum wages which equals to USD 20,000. A JVC is limited liability enterprise which is governed by general meeting of its founders.

e) Public Organization Enterprise

A Public Organization Enterprise is formed by religious, non-governmental, charity or other public organizations. Purpose of this organization should be based on the goals of incorporating organizations. The minimum charter capital for a public organization entity is 100 minimum wages which equals to USD 20,000.

f) Economic Society

An Economic Society is typically incorporated by two or more legal entities or individuals for the purposes of generating income. An Economic Society is incorporated by an agreement, which is signed by the founders. The threshold for charter capital of an Economic Society is 100 minimum wages which equals to USD 20,000. An Economic Society's property consists of shares of its founders. Governing body is the general meeting of its founders. The liability of founders in the company is limited to the amount of their contributions to the charter capital.

g) Joint-Stock Company (JSC)

A Joint-Stock Company is a legal entity whose stocks are owned by its shareholders: legal entities and individuals. A JSC is separate and distinct from its shareholders and has its own share capital and property. A JSC can be established in two forms: public and private. A public JSC can offer shares to the public without agreeing it with others shareholders. A private JSC is restricted to sell its shares only to entitled individuals / legal entities. Shareholders of a private JSC have a preferential right of purchasing shares prior to entitled individuals / legal entities. The maximum number of shareholders in a private JSC is 50, whereas in a public JSC it is unlimited. The threshold for charter capital of a JSC is 200 minimum wages which equals to USD 40,000.

h) Branches and Representative Offices

Legal entities have the right to establish branches and representative offices. Parent companies regulate the activities of representative offices and branches. Representative offices cannot engage in entrepreneurial activity. In its turn, branches can carry out commercial activity with certain restrictions set by Turkmen laws. Branches act more like an agency than as a separate company and are considered as an extension of the parent company.

b. The Procedure of Establishment

The procedure of companies' incorporation is regulated by Law "On Enterprises" No.28-II dated 15 June 2000, Law "On Joint-Stock Companies" No.400-1 dated 23 December 1999 and Presidential Decree "On State Registration of Legal Entities" No.11896 dated 11 November 2011.

From practical experience the most preferred forms of legal entities chosen by foreign investors are JVC and JSC. Therefore, this section will discuss registration process for both of them.

Legal entities are registered with the Department of State Registration of Legal Entities and Investment Projects under the Ministry of Economy and Finance (hereinafter – "the Department of State Registration") and its regional sub-divisions.

a) JVC

Joint-Venture Companies are registered by the Department of State Registration. To register a JVC, a founder(s) should submit the followings documents for review and examination of the registering authority:

• application that includes types of business and information on a founder(s);

• decision of a founder(s) on formation of JVC;

• foundation agreement and charter signed in two copies in Russian and Turkmen languages;

- investment project of a JVC;
- personal information form of JVC's head in Turkmenistan, 3x4 cm photos and a copy of passport;
- foundation documents of a foreign investor(s) notarized by Turkmenistan's embassy or the Ministry of Foreign Affairs;
- certificate of registration of a foreign investor(s) notarized by Turkmenistan's embassy or the Ministry of Foreign Affairs;
- financial report of a foreign investor(s) notarized by Turkmenistan's embassy or the Ministry of Foreign Affairs;
- confirmation on availability of legal address issued by the local authorities;
- bank statement confirming 50 percent payment of the charter capital of JVC;
- bank receipt confirming the payment of registration fee.

b) JSC

Individuals and legal entities intending to establish a JSC should submit the above-mentioned documents to the Department of State Registration. Once registered, JSC may operate unlimited period of time and has full capacity to engage in any commercial operations (including the types of operations which require license) in Turkmenistan.

Please note that some activities are subject to licensing in accordance with Law of Turkmenistan "On Licensing of Certain Types of Activities" No.202 dated 25 June 2008. Companies are typically granted with a general license (i.e.not limited to a specific project). All issued licenses are non-transferable.

Companies operating in a special economic zone (economic zone of free entrepreneurship, national touristic zone, etc.) may carry out licensable activity without obtaining a license.

c. Routes and Requirements of Dissolution

a) General

Dissolution and liquidation of companies are governed by a number of Turkmenistan laws and regulations, including Law "On Bankruptcy" No.861-XII dated 1 October 1993, Law "On Joint-Stock Companies" No.400-1 dated 23 December 1999, "On Investment Activity" No.698-XII dated 19 May 1992 and Law "On Foreign Investments" No.184-III dated 3 March 2008.

Liquidation can be voluntary (on the basis of the founders' decision) and involuntary (due to the court decision). Legal entities are forced to start liquidation process in case of:
- bankruptcy;
- suspension of certificate due to violation of Turkmen laws on registration of legal entities;
- carrying out business without license (for licensed types of activities), or carrying out prohibited types of business;
- carrying out business with repeated violations of Turkmen laws;
- in other cases, established by Turkmen laws.

Moreover, liquidation can take place in the following cases: expiry of the certificate of registration, significant decrease of a company's charter capital or in case of a company's reorganization.

b) Regulators in Dissolution Process

Voluntary liquidation is initiated by the decision of company's founders, by which they choose a liquidator and define the intended term of liquidation. It should be noted that to start a voluntary liquidation a company must obtain prior consent of its creditors.

In case of involuntary liquidation, economic courts initiate the process of liquidation and assign a liquidator which:
- terminates labour contracts with a company's employees;
- informs creditors of a company on the liquidation;
- carries out inventory of a company' assets (conduct an evaluation of assets and products of a company, obtain receivables and sign reconciliation acts with creditors);
- prepares reports to tax authorities;
- publishes the announcement on the liquidation in mass media.

c) Final stages of Liquidation

After the abovementioned steps are completed, the liquidator shall proceed with closing of the company's bank accounts and filing a company's documentation with the State Archive. From this stage a company is considered as liquidated in accordance with Article 34 of Law "On Bankruptcy" and excluded from the Consolidated State Register of Legal Entities.

F. Merger and Acquisition

a. Governing Legislation

Merger and acquisition laws are not well developed so the process involves government and presidential approvals in the form of decrees and resolutions. These issues are partly regulated by Laws "On Enterprises", "On Investment Activity" and "On Foreign Investments". Turkmen laws are silent on the procedures or standards regarding mergers via foreign investment. Under the general rule a company should obtain relevant state approvals in the case of merger or acquisition involving enterprises with state ownership or shareholding.

b. Process of Merger and Acquisition

Turkmen laws recognize the concept of merger and consolidation of enterprise. Article 52 of Law "On Enterprises" defines them as follows:

• Merge of two or several enterprises is carried out by means of creation of a new enterprise on the basis of full association of their property. The enterprises participating in merger cease their activity. At the same time their rights and obligations pass to the newly incorporated enterprise according to the transfer act.

• Consolidation of one or several enterprises to other enterprise is carried out by inclusion of their property to the property of consolidated enterprise. At the same time the joining enterprises cease their activity as sole legal entities, and their rights and obligations pass to the consolidated enterprise according to the transfer act. Constituent changes should be made in the foundation documents.

The ratio of individual shares in the charter capital of the joining enterprises may change according to the specific conditions of consolidation.

• On the basis of the decision or the contract on merger / consolidation, merging entities sign new foundation agreement, approve the charter of newly incorporated enterprise and elect its executive and managing authorities.

G. Competition Regulation

a. Department Supervising Competition Regulation

Currently there is no department supervising competition regulation in Turkmenistan.

The former Anti-Monopoly Committee of Turkmenistan was abolished in 1995 according to Presidential Decree No.2057 dated 11 January 1995.

b. Brief Introduction to Competition Law

Turkmenistan does not have developed anti-monopoly laws and regulations. However anti-monopoly and competition issues are partly covered by the Civil Code, Criminal Code, Law "On Foreign Investments" and Law "On Trade Activity".

Further, Article 17 of Law "On State Support to Small and Medium Enterprises" No.57-IV dated 15 August 2009 imposes certain restrictions on public authorities aimed at prevention of monopolistic activity. Thus, public authorities cannot:

(i) enact acts and / or perform actions that limit rights or interests of small and medium enterprises.

(ii) make agreements or take coordinated actions which could lead to:

• increase of prices that causes unfair competition in the market;

• division of the market by the territorial principle, sales volume, or by the range of the realized goods (works, services);

• restrictions imposed on small and medium enterprises in relation to the access to the market.

c. Measures Regulating Competition

Violation of competition laws could lead to administrative and criminal liability under Turkmen laws. Establishment and maintenance of monopolistically high or low prices, restriction of competition through coordinated actions of monopolist companies as well as restriction of access to the market are considered as severe violation of local anti-monopoly laws. Such violations may result in a fine or imprisonment for a term of one to three years.

H. Tax

a. Tax Regime and Rules

Taxation issues are mainly regulated by Tax Code of Turkmenistan No.245-II as of 25 October 2004. Taxation system of the country has two levels. Taxes are distributed between centralized and local budgets according to the Law "On Budget System" No.121-1 dated 18 June 1996.

In addition, Turkmenistan has joined to the several double tax treaties concluded with the following countries:

Austria	France	India	Pakistan	Ukraine
Armenia	Great Britain	Iran	Russia	USA
Belarus	Germany	Japan	Slovakia	Uzbekistan
Belgium	Georgia	Kazakhstan	Turkey	

b. Main Categories and Rates of Taxes

Under the Tax Code companies are subject to the following principal taxes and mandatory payments established under the Turkmen laws:

Tax	Tax Rate	Taxpayer
Corporate Income Tax	Rate of corporate income tax for residents is 8% Rate for other legal entities including branches of foreign companies is 20%	Legal entities-residents of Turkmenistan Legal entities-non-residents operating in Turkmenistan through a permanent representation or branch
Value Added Tax (VAT)	General rate of value added tax is 15% Contractors and sub-contractors involved in operations provided for in the Law of Turkmenistan "On Hydrocarbon Resources" are exempted from paying the VAT in part of works relating to oil and gas industry.	Legal entities, including branches of foreign companies Individuals-entrepreneurs
Property Tax	The rate of property tax is set at 1% of the book value of taxable assets.	Legal entities – owners of property
Subsoil Tax	For extraction of natural and associated gas, the rate of subsoil tax is 22% For extraction of crude oil products, the rate of subsoil tax is 10% For mining other minerals, the rate of subsoil tax is from 0% to 50%	Subsoil tax arises only at extraction of minerals from the subsoil by legal entities
Personal Income Tax	The rate of personal income tax is set at 10%	Individuals-residents of Turkmenistan Individuals-non-residents receiving income in Turkmenistan
Excise Tax	Excise tax rates vary from 10% to 100% depending on the type of excisable goods.	Manufacturers and / or sellers of excisable goods
Special fee for development of the territories of cities, town and rural settlements	The rate of the special fee for individuals-entrepreneurs is 0.3 % of gross income The rate of the special fee for other individuals is TMT 2 per month The rate of the special fee for agricultural enterprises is 0.5% of profit The rate of the special fee for other legal entities – 1% of profit	Legal entities Individuals-residents of Turkmenistan Individuals-entrepreneurs
Contributions to the Pension Fund	The rate of the contributions is 20% of the salaries of respective employees	Legal entities and branches of foreign companies in respect of their employees

c. Tax Declaration and Preference

Tax declaration submission form and completion process are approved by the State Tax Service and the Ministry of Finance and Economy. Upon successful registration with the state authorities, entities are required to register with the State Tax Service to acquire a tax certificate and "Business Identification Number". Most of the entities obliged to carry out and submit tax declaration to regional state tax authorities.

Preferences and incentives are aimed to support small and medium size enterprises. Tax exemptions involving small and medium size enterprises cover mainly property and value added tax. Investment projects targeting educational institutions, disabled persons organizations, health and religious organizations are exempt from corporate income tax and property tax.

Companies operating in free economic zones are also granted certain tax incentives. For example, foreign investors carrying out their activity in Turkmen tourist zones (national Tourist Zone "Avaza") are exempt from value added tax, property tax and corporate income tax.

I. Securities

a. Brief introduction of Securities-Related Laws and Regulations

2011 was marked by adoption of the State Program for the Development of Securities Market in Turkmenistan for 2012-2016. The Development Program consists of three phases and is aimed at attracting foreign investments, concentration of capital and its rational redistribution between economic sectors and business entities.

In 2014 the Government adopted a new edition of Law "On Securities Market" No.139-V. The Law defines common principles for the issuance and circulation of securities in the territory of Turkmenistan, main provisions of stock exchanges' activities, and also regulates legal relations among players of the securities market. Issuance of securities by joint-stock companies is regulated by Law "On Joint-Stock Companies" No.400-I dated 23 December 1999.

Further, in 2015 the President of Turkmenistan issued the Decree "On Licensing of Professional Activities in Securities Market". Securities market operations involving brokerage activity (financial intermediation), securities management activities, clearing, custody business, activity on maintaining the register of securities holders and stock exchange activities are subject to mandatory licensing in Turkmenistan.

The final phase of the Development Program has started in 2016 and is marked by completion of works on creation of conditions for joining full-fledged securities market to the system of international financial markets. Presidential Decree "On Issuance, Realization and Refunding of Public Bonds" dated December 2015 regulates the issuance of public bonds for a term of up to five years and their sale to all legal entities regardless of ownership structure, including foreign legal entities operating in Turkmenistan.

b. Supervision and Regulation of Securities Market

The Ministry of Finance and Economy is the competent state authority with regulatory oversight for securities market, monitoring and licensing certain operations in the securities market in Turkmenistan.

c. Requirements for Engaging in Securities Trading for Foreign Enterprises

The Law "On Securities Market" establishes that securities can be issued by (i) legal entities duly registered in accordance with Turkmen laws and (ii) public authorities. To issue securities in Turkmenistan a foreign company will be required to establish a local company (e.g.joint-stock company of closed or open type). The issuance of securities by joint-stock companies is subject to state registration with the Ministry of Economy and Finance of Turkmenistan. Information on the securities issued should be included to the Unified State Register of Securities. On completion of such registration a joint-stock company may place securities using various schemes of distribution (i) among its shareholders, (ii) to predetermined individuals / companies or (iii) to unlimited number of individuals / companies.

Securities issued by foreign companies are admitted for distribution in Turkmenistan. However, the Cabinet of Ministers may establish annual quotas for the admission of such securities.

J. Preference and Protection of Investment

a. The Structure of Preference Policies

Economic incentives available to foreign investors in Turkmenistan are captured and defined by Law "On Foreign Investments" No.184-III dated 3 March 2008. First of all, foreign individuals working in enterprises with foreign investments in the territory of Turkmenistan as well as their family members may obtain multiple visas for a period not less than one year.

Further, property imported into Turkmenistan as a foreign investor's contribution to the charter capital of enterprises with foreign investments is exempt from import tax and customs duty. Import of property within the framework of realization of investment projects is carried out under the simplified procedure of customs clearance.

A foreign investor contributing in excess of 30% to the charter capital of the local company in freely convertible currency, may for a period of recovering his initial investments be exempt from tax on dividends, and the company itself – from income tax. Depending on the type of investment project the Cabinet of Ministers may also grant additional tax incentives on a case-by-case basis.

The most favorable conditions are provided to foreign investors operating in the territory of free economic zones (e.g.in National Tourist Zone "Avaza"). The National Tourist Zone "Avaza" was established in 2007 under the Presidential Decree No.8855 on the east coast of the Caspian Sea. Under this Decree the state registration of legal entities engaged in construction of "Avaza" and investment projects implemented in the territory of "Avaza" is made on a free basis, without charging registration fees. Further, foreign specialists working in "Avaza" could obtain entry visas and work in a simplified order without charging consular and registration fees. And, finally, the Central Bank guarantees the free conversion of foreign investors' net profit earned as a result of rendering services in the territory of "Avaza" into freely convertible currency.

Companies having foreign investments in their charter capital (not less than 30% in freely convertible currency) have the right to export own products (works, services) without a license on the basis of a certificate issued by an authorized authority in an amount equal to a foreign investor's share in the charter capital.

In addition, companies with foreign participation may import products (goods, services) for their own economic activities without a license.

b. Support for Specific Industries

Known for its large gas and oil deposits, Turkmenistan attaches particular importance to investment projects in the sector. Turkmenistan operates liquefied petroleum gas plants (LPG plants) and is currently in the process of developing two gas-to-liquid facilities (GTL plants). The country plans to attract further foreign investments in this sector.

Turkmenistan is one of the largest cotton producers in the region and has recently made active effort to step up investment in its local textile processing capacity to convert the raw material into finished goods and boost the country's export potential. In 2012 the President has adopted the Program for the Development of Textile Industry for 2012-2016. The Program is aimed at establishing business relations with foreign stock exchanges, further development of small and medium companies, increase of export potential of Turkmenistan and attraction of foreign investment into the industry. The Government also plans to upgrade the existing cotton-producing enterprises and build new facilities.

In addition, Turkmenistan is planning to develop chemical, construction and agriculture industries as well as pipeline networks in the country.

c. Special Economic Areas

Law "On Economic Zones of Free Entrepreneurship" No.893 was enacted in Turkmenistan in 1993. Companies located in Economic Zones of Free Entrepreneurship (hereinafter – "EZEE") are granted with certain tax, custom and financial benefits. The simplified regime of export-import operations is established in the territory of EZEE. Goods imported to or exported from the territory of EZEE are exempt from the payment of customs duties. Companies operating in EZEE are not required to pay rental fees for the use of land for three years. In addition, the Government guarantees free repatriation of profits of foreign investors after the payment by the latter of all applicable taxes. As of today there are ten EZEE in Turkmenistan: Ekerem-Hazar, Ashgabat-Anew, Saragt, Ashgabat International Airport, Mary-Bayramaly, Turkmenabat-Seydi, Ashgabat-Abadan, Dashoguz Airport, Bakharly-Serdar and Gulneshli.

On 9 October 2017 the Government of Turkmenistan adopted Law "On Free Economic Zones" No.620-V. It is planned to create up to 23 Free Economic Zones (hereinafter – "FEZ") to 2023. The main goal of future FEZs is to attract foreign investors and advanced technologies for the efficient use of resources. The Law states that the following types of FEZ could be established in Turkmenistan:

- free trade zones and export zones;
- industrial and production zones, including industrial parks;
- technological parks;
- zones specialized in the provision of financial, banking, tourist-recreational, informational and other types of services;
- transport and logistics zones;
- agro-industrial zones; and
- complex zones.

d. Investment Protection

Laws "On Foreign Investments" and "On Investment Activities" guarantee the protection of foreign investors' rights and interests in the territory of Turkmenistan. Investment protection under Turkmen laws includes the following:

- Foreign individuals, representatives and employees of enterprises with foreign investments (hereinafter –

"EFI") have the right of freedom of movement in Turkmenistan and may obtain multiple-entry visas;
• Foreign investors and EFIs may open bank accounts in local and foreign currency and repatriate profit earned in the territory of Turkmenistan without any restrictions;
• Intellectual property rights of foreign investors are protected under Turkmen IP laws;
• In case of termination of its investment activity a foreign investor has the right to free return of its assets received as a result of investment activity;
• In case of nationalization or requisition a foreign investor has right to full compensation of its assets.

III. Trade

A. Department Supervising Trade

As a result of merger of two ministries (Ministry of Foreign Economic Relations and Ministry of trade and resources) the Ministry of Trade and Foreign Economic Relations of Turkmenistan was established in 1998. The Ministry is the supreme authority responsible for regulation of trade activities and development of foreign economic relations of the country. In addition the Ministry administers issues related to consumers' protection in Turkmenistan.

The Ministry has its own structural subdivision, State Trade Control Service, which examines the compliance with standards and norms of trade, correctness of price formation in markets, quality of products and prevents the entry of low-quality products to the domestic market.

B. Brief Introduction of Trade Laws and Regulations

A new edition of the Law "On Trade Activity" was adopted on 26 March 2016 (No.370-V). The Law sets out the state policy in the field of trade regulation is aimed at: (i) creation of favorable conditions for the development of trade; (ii) ensuring a stable system of goods circulation; (iii) development of trade infrastructure and provision of quality trade services, (iv) support for homegrown commodity producers and (v) ensuring the protection of consumers' rights.

As certain types of trade activity are subject to licensing (e.g.wholesale trade), the same issues are governed by Law "On Licensing of Certain Types of Activities" No.202 dated 25 June 2008 and the Civil Code.

Protection of consumers' rights is an important part of the country's trade laws. Main documents in this sphere are Law "On Consumer Society" No.565-V dated 3 June 2017 and Law "On Food Safety" No.479-V dated 23 November 2016 (new edition).

C. Trade Management

Law "On Trade Activity" establishes minimal requirements for organization and licensing of trade activity in Turkmenistan, certification and labelling of products. The Law regulates the organization of remote trade and auctions and also deals with unfair competition issues.

Under Turkmen laws main types of trade activity are wholesale trade, retail trade, organization of public catering and provision of services related to sale of goods. Depending on its size, marketplaces are classified as small (up to 500 square meters), medium (up to 1000 square meters) and large (more than 1000 square meters).

Products for sale on domestic market are subject to certification and compliance with local standards and requirements. Labelling of products should be provided in Turkmen and Russian languages (and, as an option, in English or other languages). Certain categories of products (alcohol and tobacco products) are subject to mandatory labelling with excise stamps.

Foreign companies wishing to engage in trade are required to establish a local company or a branch and acquire relevant license. As an option a foreign company may enter into an agency or distribution contract with a local company, under which the latter will act as a foreign company's agent or distributor for sales in Turkmenistan.

D. The Inspection and Quarantine of Import and Export Commodities

There are no specific rules on inspection and quarantine of import / export commodities. All products imported to or exported from Turkmenistan are subject to customs clearance and customs control in accordance with the generally established procedure.

In addition, most types of import & export transactions are subject to registration with the State Commodity and Raw Materials Exchange of Turkmenistan. To register the contract, each party is required to pay a fee equal to 0.2% of the total transaction amount (residents pay in Turkmen Manats, non-residents – in US Dollars).

E. Customs Management

The State Customs Service of Turkmenistan is the designated authority mandated to implement the state policy in the field of customs regulation. The Service consists of central administrative office and 6 regional customs offices. Customs control and customs clearance of goods passing through the border of Turkmenistan is carried out by customs offices in Ashgabat city, Ahhal, Balkan, Lebap, Dashoguz and Mary regions. In addition, 50 customs posts and check-points operate in Turkmenistan.

All goods and vehicles crossing the state border of Turkmenistan are subject to customs clearance and customs control pursuant to the procedure established by the Customs Code of Turkmenistan. For the performance of customs clearance the following shall apply: (i) customs duty, (ii) taxes (VAT, excise tax) and (iii) customs fees (fee for customs clearance, fee for customs support and / or fee for storage). Applicants must provide customs authorities with reliable and up-to-date information on goods crossing the border. The following documents should be submitted along with the customs declaration:
- Import or export contract;
- Commercial documents (invoice, packing list etc.);
- Transportation (shipping) documents;
- Relevant permits, licenses and certificates;
- Documents confirming the origin of goods;
- Payment (settlement) documents;
- Documents confirming the declared customs value.

The following types of customs regimes are established in the country:
- Release into free circulation;
- Export;
- Customs transit;
- Processing of goods in customs territory;
- Processing of goods for free circulation;
- Processing of goods outside customs territory;
- Temporary import;
- Temporary export;
- Customs warehouse;
- Duty free trade;
- Free customs zone (free warehouse);
- Re-import;
- Re-export;
- Destruction of goods;
- Abandoning in favour of the state.

IV. Labour

A. Brief Introduction of Labour Laws and Regulations

Labour Code of Turkmenistan No.29-IV dated 18 April 2009 provides regulatory umbrella for all major employment related matters and reflects mandatory conditions applicable to parties of the employment contract, guarantees and social benefits available to employees, mutual rights and obligations of an employer and an employee, certain restrictions on employment of pregnant women, women with children and juveniles, working time, work safety and issues related to termination of employment contracts.

Other labour-related matters are regulated by the following legal documents:
- Code On Social Protection of Population" No.340-IV dated 19 October 2012;
- Law "On Employment of Population" No.411-V dated 18 July 2016;
- Law "On Trade Unions, Their Rights and Guarantees of Their Activity" No.443-IV dated 9 November 2013;
- Law "On Guarantees of Rights of Youth to Work" No.5-III dated 1 February 2005;
- Law "On Legal Status of Foreign Citizens in Turkmenistan" No.169-IV dated 26 March 2011;
- Law "On State Pension Insurance" No.287-IV dated 31 March 2012;
- Presidential Decree "On Employment of Foreign Citizens on a Temporary Basis" No.7367 dated 13 July 2005;
- Presidential Decree "On State Service of Turkmenistan on Registration of Foreign Employees" No.7367

dated 13 July 2005;
• Presidential Decree "On Entry, Departure and Stay of Foreign Citizens in Turkmenistan" No.6135 dated 21 February 2003;
• Presidential Decree "On Business Trip Expenses" No.8629 dated 22 May 2007;
• Presidential Decree "On Work Employment Records of Employees-Citizens of Turkmenistan" No.4970 dated 27 November 2000;
• Presidential Decree "On Compulsory Personal Insurance of Employees Working in High Risk Production Facilities" No.4550 dated 31 January 2000;
• Presidential Decree "On Compensation of Damage Caused to An Employee by An Injury or Occupational Disease" No.4039 dated 15 January 1999.

B. Requirements of Employing Foreign Employees

a. Work Permit

Presidential Decree "On Employment of Foreign Citizens on a Temporary Basis" regulates the employment process involving foreign employees in the territory of Turkmenistan. Local employers seeking to engage foreign labour must apply for a special Permit for attracting foreign individuals (hereinafter – "the Work Permit"). Foreign nations may not be granted employment in Turkmenistan unless cleared by Agency for employment in Turkmenistan (hereinafter – "the Confirmation"). The Confirmation is issued for each foreign employee and it is the local employer that has the burden to apply on behalf of the prospective foreign employee with the Agency.

There are two main state agencies regulating the employment of foreign citizens and issuing Permits and Confirmations:
• Commission of Supervision over the Employment of Foreign Citizens on a Temporary Basis (hereinafter – "the Commission");
• State Agency on Registration of Foreign Citizens (hereinafter – "the Agency").

b. Application Procedure

To receive the Permit and the Confirmation, an employer shall submit the following documents to the Agency:
• Application;
• List of an employer's staff;
• Copies of an employer's foundation documents;
• Certificate of state registration of an employer;
• Official letter from tax authorities on absence of tax arrears;
• Draft labour agreement with a foreign employee;
• Documents confirming the specialization of a foreign employee and compliance with qualification requirements;
• A foreign employee's curriculum vitae with photograph;
• A foreign employee's HIV-free certificate;
• Receipt confirming the payment of a state fee.

Applications with all necessary documents are submitted to the Agency, which then submits the documents to the Commission's approval. The Commission makes the final decision within one-month period, which is then used by the Agency to issue (i) the Permit and (ii) the Confirmation.

As a general rule the Permit and the Confirmation are issued for a period of one year. After the expiration these documents may be prolonged for a term of up to one year. An employer hiring a foreign employee pays a state fee of USD 25 for each month of employment of such foreign employee.

Local employers engaging foreign labour must ensure that the proportion of foreign workforce does not exceed 30% in anyone employer's staff structure. The Agency are required to under Turkmen law to closely monitor compliance by all local employers.

c. Social Insurance

Social protection system of Turkmenistan consists of the following components:
• pension insurance;
• social benefits system.

Pension insurance is of the two types in Turkmenistan mandatory and voluntary. Local employers are required under Labour Code to ensure mandatory pension and insurance contribution for its employees with the Pension Fund of Turkmenistan (20% of the aggregate remuneration paid to employees). Employees could also make voluntary contributions to this Fund since such contributions may increase the size of future pension (from 2% or more from their salaries).

The Law "On State Pension Insurance" lists several types of pensions. Retirement pensions are paid upon reaching certain age limitation. Military servants and pilots are entitled to long-service pension and employees working in high-risk production facilities have the right to professional pension. Further, disability pensions are paid to individuals who are unable to work due to certain disability. And, finally, survivor pension will be paid to dependent family members left without a breadwinner.

Social benefits system of Turkmenistan established by the Code of Social Protection of Population includes the following types of benefits:
- Temporary disability allowance;
- Maternity allowance;
- Childcare allowance;
- Disability allowance;
- Allowance assigned to wives of the Great Patriotic War's participant;
- State social allowance.

C. Exit and Entry

a. Visa Types

Foreign citizens and stateless persons may enter and stay in the territory of Turkmenistan on the basis of entry visas. Issuance of visas and extension of their validity is performed:
- in the territory of Turkmenistan – by the Ministry of Foreign Affairs (hereinafter – "the MFA") based on the decision of the Commission on Supervision of Visas Issuance;
- outside Turkmenistan – by diplomatic and consular representations of Turkmenistan located in foreign countries.

		Types of visas		
1	Diplomatic visa (DP)	7	Tourist visa (TU)
2	Official visa (OF)	8	Transit visa (TR)
3	Business visa (BS)	9	Medical visa (HL)
4	Work visa (WP)	10	Driver's visa (DR)
5	Private visa (PR)	11	Exit visa (EX)
6	Student visa (ST)		

Companies wishing to engage foreign nationals are required to submit the following documents to the MFA:
- application made in Turkmen language;
- notarized copies of an employer's foundation documents;
- official letter from tax authorities on absence of tax arrears;
- copy of a foreign employee's passport.

Documents are reviewed by the MFA within one-month period. As a result of such review, a foreign employee receives an entry visa. Pursuant to an employer's supporting letter foreign citizen may receive multiple entry visas.

In addition, a foreign citizen is subject to certain registration requirements. Foreigners staying in Turkmenistan for a period longer than five days must register with the State Agency of Registration of Foreign Citizens or its regional sub-divisions (depending on the region where a foreign citizen will be living) within three days upon their arrival.

b. Restrictions for Exit and Entry

Certain restrictions (deportation, prohibition of entry and etc.) may be imposed on foreign citizens for violation of the rules for staying in Turkmenistan. It includes non-compliance with registration requirements, absence of valid documents (entry visa, work permit and etc.), evasion of departure after the expiration of the stay period as well as non-observance of the rules for transit passage through the territory of Turkmenistan.

D. Trade Unions and Labour Organizations

Under Turkmen laws employees are entitled to join trade unions. The role and legal status of trade unions are specified in Chapter 17 of the Labour Code and the Law "On Trade Unions, Their Rights and Guarantees of Their Activity". The Law establishes the following types of trade unions:
- primary trade unions formed by employees working in one company;

• industrial trade unions formed by employees of several companies operating in the same industry (e.g.in banking sector, agriculture and etc.);
• territorial trade unions that could be establishes in each region of Turkmenistan.

All trade unions existing in Turkmenistan are members of Trade Unions Organization of Turkmenistan (an official political organization). Trade Unions Organization may participate in the Parliament's sessions. Members of the Organization occupy 33 seats in Turkmenistan's Parliament.

Regardless of the type, all trade unions are subject to state registration with the Ministry of Justice. For registration of a trade union the following documents should be submitted to the Ministry:
• application signed by all members of trade union's managing authority;
• the Charter of a trade union in two copies;
• minutes of trade union's members meeting;
• information on trade union's managing authority and location of a trade union;
• receipt on payment of state fee for registration.

Membership in a trade union is voluntary. Each employee decides independently whether he / she wants to join a trade union.

Trade unions represent and protect social, economic, labour rights and interests of employees in relations with public authorities and employers. Trade unions have broad bargaining power; they can participate in preparation of labour agreements, collective agreements concluded between employees and an employer, internal labour regulations of a company and other labour documents. In addition they can raise a claim in a local court to protect interests of employees.

E. Labour Disputes

Under Turkmen laws labour disputes could be resolved by (i) a labour disputes commission at work, (i) a trade union or (ii) a local court of general jurisdiction. The procedure for settlement of labour disputes is set out in Chapter 16 of the Labour Code.

Companies with the number of staff exceeding 15 are entitled under Turkmen law to form a labour disputes commission, whose members will be elected by a company's employees. On 21 September 2013 the Ministry of Justice adopted Model Regulation on Labour Dispute Commission that provides a detailed guidance on the activities of such commissions.

In the event of any disagreement between an employer and an employee, the latter may apply to a labour disputes commission. Within 10 days from the date of submission of the application, the commission is obliged to resolve the dispute and make a decision. In case an employee is not satisfied with the commission's decision, he / she may also apply to a trade union or, in absence of a trade union, to a local court.

Certain categories of labour disputes fall within the exclusive competence of courts of general jurisdiction. They include disputes (i) on reinstatement in a job, (ii) on compensation of an injury or occupational disease caused to an employee, (iii) on compensation for a period of forced unemployment, and (iv) on groundless refusal of employment. It also should be noted that an employee applying to a court with a claim arising from labour relations is exempted from payment of court's fees.

V. Intellectual property

A. Brief Introduction on IP Laws and Regulations

Turkmenistan has well-developed system of IP protection laws with several recently adopted laws. On 4 November 2017 the Parliament adopted two new legal documents: Law "On Legal Protection of Inventions" No.629-V and Law "On Legal Protection of Industrial Models" No.630-V. These Laws replaced the former Patent Law (dated 1 October 1993). New Laws provide references to international treaties signed by Turkmenistan and include provisions regulating international protection of inventions and industrial models.

Other major documents in the sphere of copyright laws, registration of trademarks and patents, and protection of IP rights in Turkmenistan are:
• Civil Code of Turkmenistan No.294-I dated 17 July 1998;
• Law "On Trademarks, Service Marks and Place of Goods' Origin" No.221-III dated 23 October 2008;
• Law "On Copyright and Related Rights" No.257-IV dated 10 January 2012;
• Law "On Scientific Intellectual Property" No.755-XII dated 30 September 1992;
• Law "On Legal Protection of Algorithms, Electronic Computer Programs, Databases and Topologies of

Integrated Microcircuits" No.964-XII dated 23 September 1994;
- Law "On Legal Protection of Selective Breeding Results" No.207-IV dated 4 August 2011.

In addition Turkmenistan has joined several international treaties such as:
- Convention Establishing the World Intellectual Property Organization;
- Paris Convention for the Protection of Industrial Property;
- Patent Cooperation Treaty;
- Eurasian Patent Convention;
- Protocol Relating to the Madrid Agreement Concerning the International Registration of Marks;
- Strasbourg Agreement Concerning the International Patent Classification;
- Locarno Agreement Establishing an International Classification for Industrial Design;
- Nice Agreement Concerning the International Classification of Goods and Services for the Purposes of the Registration of Marks;
- Vienna Agreement Establishing an International Classification of the Figurative Elements of Marks.

B. Patent Application

a. Patent for Inventions

Turkmenpatent, a special department of the Ministry of Finance and Economy, is the competent Turkmen authority with the remit to register inventions in the State Register of Inventions and issuance of patents in Turkmenistan.

An application for the issuance of a patent for invention is filed with Turkmenpatent by an author (authors), his / her employer (if an invention was made by an employee in connection with the performance of his / her official duties) or their successors. The application should be made in Turkmen language (or should be accompanied with translation to Turkmen language). Such application should contain the following information:
- Information on author (authors) of an invention and his / her place of residence;
- Detailed description of an invention;
- Formula of an invention;
- Drawings and other materials related to an invention;
- Report providing a brief description of an invention.

If the application is filed by an applicant's representative or official patent agent, Power of Attorney should be submitted to Turkmenpatent.

After the receipt of the application with all relevant documents Turkmenpatent carries out expert examinations. On the results of examinations Turkmenpatent issues a patent for invention. The patent will be valid for 20 years from the date of filing an application to Turkmenpatent. It should be mentioned that a state fee is paid on an annual basis for each year of patent's validity period.

The applicant may have priory right for an invention in accordance with Paris Convention for the Protection of Industrial Property 1993. Also Turkmenpatent may issue a patent on the basis of the application made in accordance with Eurasian Patent Convention 1994.

b. Patent for Industrial Models

An application for the issuance of a patent for industrial model is also filed to Turkmenpatent. The following information should be included in the application:
- Information on author (authors) of an industrial model and his / her place of residence;
- Images of an industrial model providing a complete picture of an industrial model's appearance;
- Drawing of the general view of an industrial model, ergonomic scheme, confection map;
- Brief description of an industrial model.

Power of Attorney should be provided for an applicant's representatives or patent agents.

On the results of examinations Turkmenpatent can issue a patent for industrial model that will be valid for initial 5 years. The maximum duration of the patent's validity period is 15 years, however, each five years an applicant should pay a state fee for its prolongation.

C. Trademark Registration

Trademark protection is obtained by registration. The Law "On Trademarks, Service Marks and Place of Goods' Origin" sets out the detailed procedure for trademark registration. An application for registration must be filed with Turkmenpatent either by the applicant or his / her representative or patent agent acting on the basis of power of attorney. State fee for registration of a trademark equals to USD 250. Foreign individuals and legal entities are required to apply through patent agents.

The application process includes a formal examination, examination of distinctiveness and search for prior trademarks. On the results of such examination, the Patent Office issues a Certificate of Trademark Registration and publishes information on registered trademark in the Patent Office Bulletin.

The Certificate is valid for 10 years from the date of registration and can be extended through a request for renewal. This renewal request can be filed within six months prior to the expiration date of the trademark. State fee for the extension of the validity period is USD 500.

If the trademark was not in use within 3 years from the date of issued Certificate or has not been used later for a continuous period of 3 years, it may be subject to cancellation.

D. Measures for IP Protection

Holders of IP rights are entitled to seek legal protection in the event of any infringement upon their rights in a manner prescribed by the Civil Code and other related laws and regulations. The claimant may apply to the relevant local court:

(i) on recognition of his / her right for an IP object;

(ii) on prevention of actions violating IP rights;

(iii) on compensation for damages caused by an unlawful use of IP objects (which may include compensation for moral damage);

(iv) on seizure of equipment or materials used in course of violation of IP rights;

The person could also ask the court to publish its decision in mass media in order to prevent future infringements. The court also may decide to confiscate infringing goods.

Patent holders may file a claim within three years from the day when he / she should have known about the violation of his / her right.

Violation of IP rights leads to administrative and criminal liability in Turkmenistan. At the discretion of the court the infringer may be arrested for a period of up to 15 days or pay fine. Repeated violation results in a higher amount of fine or correctional work for a period of up to 2 years.

VI. Environmental Protection

A. Department Supervising Environmental Protection

The State Committee for Environmental Protection and Land Resources was established in 2016 following reorganization of two former institutions: the Ministry of Environment Protection and the Land Resources Service.

Currently the State Committee for Environmental Protection and Land Resources is the supreme authority administering state policy in the area of environmental protection and rational use of land resources. The Committee has its sub-divisions in all regions of Turkmenistan.

The Committee is involved in drafting laws and regulations, develops and implements the unified state policy in the area of environment protection and coordinates activities of other public authorities engaged in the same field. It makes an assessment and registration of the country's natural resources and maintains state cadasters of flora and fauna objects, water and land resources. It also organizes the state monitoring of the use of natural resources and protects rare and endangered species of plants and animals.

The Committee approves payments rates for the use of natural resources and establishes limitations on the amount of permitted emissions of pollutants into the environment. Also the Committee and its sub-divisions deal with issues related to violation of environment protection laws and compensation of damages caused to the environment by legal entities and individuals.

The Committee issues permits for import / export of flora and fauna objects. In addition, it can grant permits for import / export of ozone-depleting substances into Turkmenistan.

B. Brief Introduction on Laws and Regulations Involving Environmental Protection

Legal acts governing the protection of environment, rational use of natural resources, preservation of endangered species of plants and animals, include the following:

- Water Code of Turkmenistan No.456-V s of 15 October 2016;
- Forestry Code of Turkmenistan No.166-IV dated 25 March 2011;
- Law "On Nature Protection" No.40-V dated 1 March 2014;
- Law "On Protection of Ozone Layer" No.53-IV dated 15 August 2009;
- Law "On Protection of the Atmosphere" No.366-V dated 26 March 2016;

- Law "On Ecological Safety" No.569-V dated 3 June 2017;
- Law "On Plant Protection" No.413-V dated 18 June 2016;
- Law "On Subsoil" No.160-V dated 20 December 2014;
- Law "On Animals" No.375-IV dated 2 March 2013;
- Law "On Protected Natural Areas" No.286-IV dated 31 March 2012;
- Law "On Fisheries and Conservation of Aquatic Biological Resources" No.197-IV dated 21 may 2011;

In addition, Turkmenistan has ratified the following international treaties and conventions in the sphere of environment protection:
- Convention of the World Meteorological Organization;
- Vienna Convention for the Protection of the Ozone Layer;
- Montreal Protocol on Substances that Deplete the Ozone Layer;
- United Nations Framework Convention on Climate Change;
- United Nations Convention to Combat Desertification;
- Convention on Biological Diversity;
- Basel Convention on the Control of Transboundary Movements of hazardous Wastes and Their Disposal;
- Kyoto Protocol to United Nations Framework Convention on Climate Change.

Turkmenistan participates in the regional exchange of information on the environment and hydrometeorology with the CIS countries, Turkey, Iran and India on the basis of bilateral treaties and agreements.

C. Evaluation of Environmental Protection

Local environmental laws and regulations are under permanent review and update to ensure compliance with key international environment protection standards. However, certain regional environment issues continue to give a cause for major concern.

As the country lies in the zone of extratropical deserts and has strong continental climate characterized by dry, hot summers and frosty winters, it is very vulnerable to climatic changes. Turkmenistan faces several ecological problems affecting the welfare and health of local population.

a. Desertification

Desertification is the main ecological problem of Turkmenistan. About 80% of Turkmenistan's territory is covered by Karakum Desert. Desertification is caused by an intensive agriculture development, realization of high-scale construction projects and rapid development of oil and gas industry. Shrinking of Aral Sea also affects the environment of Turkmenistan in the major way and leads to the emergence of vast areas of the former seabed exposed to wind erosion. Dust coming from the Aral Sea consists of salts, fertilizers and pesticides and is dangerous to people's health.

b. Salinization

The development of new lands and the growth of agricultural production negatively affect the country's soil. Almost 90% of the country's water resources are used for irrigation. The quality of water in the last decades declined sharply and, consequently, water used for irrigation often does not comply with state standards for the level of mineralization. The content of chlorides and sulfates exceeds the permissible standards. These factors cause salinization of more than a half of agricultural land in Turkmenistan.

c. Pollutions

The level of pollutions emitted into the air, soil and water is increased rapidly in the last years. The main polluters are enterprises operating in gas, oil, chemical, engineering and construction industries. In the cities of Turkmenistan pollution is caused by emissions from vehicles.

Caspian Sea being a large water reservoir of the country also suffers from high volumes of pollutions as the majority of oil and gas companies are located in the coastal zone.

VII. Dispute Resolution

A. Methods and Bodies of Dispute Resolution

a. Litigation

The most common method of dispute resolution in Turkmenistan is litigation at local courts. Current judicial system of the country was established by Law "On Court" No.134-V dated 8 November 2014. Amendments to local laws led to the abolishment of the Supreme Economic Courts whose functions were transferred to the Supreme Court of Turkmenistan.

The Law defines that civil, criminal, family, land, labour and military cases are administered by district courts (at the first instance), regional courts (at the appeal instance) and the Supreme Court's criminal and civil panels acting as a court of supervision. It should be noted that in 1997 the Government abolished military courts, therefore military cases fall within the competence of the courts of general jurisdiction.

Further, commercial cases are handled by the Arbitration court and regional courts (at the first instance), and the Supreme Court's commercial panel (at the appellate instance). Certain categories of commercial disputes fall within the exclusive jurisdiction of the Arbitration court:

• Disputes where one of the parties is a foreign legal entity / foreign citizen;
• Disputes on insolvency of companies;
• Disputes on annulment of acts of non-normative nature issued by central bodies, that do not comply with normative legal acts of Turkmenistan;
• Disputes where the defendants are located in different regions of the country.

Despite the name Arbitration court and regional courts dealing with commercial disputes, these are purely judiciary courts.

As Arbitration court resides only in Ashgabat city it causes certain inconvenience for companies located outside the city. For companies headquartered outside the capital dispute resolution proceeding at the Arbitration court become a long and expensive exercise.

Arbitration proceedings are governed by Civil Procedure Code No.260-V dated 18 August 2015, Criminal Procedure Code No.28-IV dated 18 April 2009 and Code of Arbitration Procedure No.52-II dated 19 December 2000.

The abovementioned Codes establish that foreign legal entities have the same procedural rights and duties as their Turkmen counterparts. Disputes are considered by courts within a period of two months from the date of submission of a claim. On the results of hearing the court makes a decision that becomes effective within ten-day period.

Any court decision may be appealed to the cassation court (before the decision becomes effective) and may be reviewed by the court of supervision (after the decision becomes effective).

However, the length of the period of case examination may exceed two months. In practice the proceedings of certain commercial disputes (in particular, investment disputes) have lasted several years.

b. Arbitration

Companies operating in Turkmenistan may also use alternative dispute resolution mechanisms and apply to arbitration courts. These courts act in accordance with Law "On International Commercial Arbitration" No.101-V dated 16 August 2014.

Arbitration courts hear disputes of individuals and legal entities. The distinctive features of arbitration courts in Turkmenistan are:

(i) Dispute may be considered by an arbitration court only if there is an arbitration agreement;
(ii) Arbitration courts solve:

• contractual disputes arising in the course of foreign trade activity where one of the parties is located outside Turkmenistan, and
• disputes of companies with foreign investments and international organizations established in the territory of Turkmenistan;

(iii) Upon request of any of the parties, arbitration court's decision can be cancelled by the Supreme Court of Turkmenistan in case of violation of arbitration procedural rules.

If a company intends to submit disputes to arbitration, it should insert an arbitration clause into contracts with counterparties or conclude a separate arbitration agreement.

Turkmenistan has a permanent arbitration institution – Arbitration Court under the Chamber of Commerce and Industry of Turkmenistan (hereinafter – "the CCI"). The Arbitration Court under the CCI resolves disputes concerning contractual and other civil law issues arising from foreign trade and other international economic relations.

Companies accredited at the Commodity Exchange of Turkmenistan could appeal to the Arbitration Committee of the Commodity Exchange in accordance with Law "On Commodity and Raw Materials Exchange and Exchange Trade" No.38-V dated 1 March 2014. The Arbitration Committee provides conciliation services to traders. The competence and functions of the Arbitration Committee are determined by the Commodity Exchange in accordance with Turkmen laws. If one of the parties does not agree with the decision of the Arbitration Committee it has the right to apply to the Arbitrazh court of Turkmenistan.

Parties may also choose to submit a dispute to international arbitration institutions (LCIA, ICC, ICSID etc).

B. Application of Laws

As Turkmenistan is considered as civil law country, local courts refer to written statutory acts adopted by the Government, the President and other legislative bodies. Therefore in carrying out its activities, the courts are mainly guided by Turkmen laws' provisions that include the Constitution having highest legal force in the hierarchy of legislative acts, codes regulating particular areas of law, and separate laws and regulations amended on regular basis.

Courts in civil law countries act on the basis of established laws, therefore they are not endowed with legislative powers and have no right to create new rules of law, but courts have great freedom in interpreting the applicable legal acts.

Code of Arbitration Procedure establishes that decisions of local courts may be annulled in case of violation or improper use of substantive laws. Thus, courts endeavors to follow the unified approach to the interpretation and application of laws. In addition the Supreme Court regularly analyses lower courts' practice and issues resolutions aiming at facilitation of courts activities. Resolutions of the Supreme Court provide local courts with a detailed guidance on the settlement of disputes in various spheres. These resolutions do not refer to a separate case; they are considered as a comprehensive survey of courts' practice, which is based on the analysis of dozens of cases.

Application of foreign countries' laws is not developed in Turkmenistan. Turkmen laws establish that local courts may apply foreign countries' laws if it is expressly stated in an international agreement concluded by Turkmenistan. In absence of multilateral or bilateral international treaties, the courts will apply local laws.

Turkmenistan's practice in enforcement of foreign courts' decisions and arbitral awards and, consequently, legislation is this sphere is not well developed. Law "On Enforcement Proceeding" No.135-V dated 8 November 2014 establishes that enforcement of foreign courts' decisions and arbitral awards shall be performed in accordance with international agreements and local laws.

Under the general rule compulsory enforcement of foreign court's decision or arbitral award starts by filing a petition for enforcement with the relevant local court. Civil Procedure Code provides that foreign courts' decisions on civil matters may be enforced in Turkmenistan within three years from the effective date of the decisions. These decisions are enforced on the basis of reciprocity principle. Further, Turkmenistan being a party to Minsk Convention on Legal Assistance in Civil, Family and Criminal Cases dated 22 January 1993 is obliged to recognize and enforce the decisions of the relevant court of the CIS countries. Turkmenistan also joined Kiev Convention on Resolution of Disputes Related to Commercial Activity dated 9 October 1992 concluded between the CIS countries and made a commitment to enforce decisions on commercial matters issued by courts of the CIS countries.

Turkmenistan's electronic governance system is in the early stages of development, there is no open-access public database of courts' decisions enforced in Turkmenistan.

Another point to mention is that Turkmenistan has not ratified the Convention on the Recognition and Enforcement of Foreign Arbitration Awards dated 1958. Therefore, companies and individuals may face certain difficulties with the enforcement of international arbitral awards in Turkmenistan. Turkmen courts do not have a unified methodology for considering cases connected with the recognition and enforcement of arbitral awards.

VIII. Others

A. Anti-commercial Bribery

a. Brief Introduction of Anti-commercial Bribery Laws and Regulations

During the early years of sovereignty anti-corruption regulations were not well-developed in the country. However, in the last decade the Government made great efforts to improve local anti-corruption laws. On 1 March 2014 it adopted Law "On Combatting Corruption" No.35-V, the main legislative act in this field, which prevents and prohibits bribes at all governmental levels.

Obligations of public officials to comply with anti-corruption laws are established by Law "On State Service" No.363-V dated 26 March 2016 and Law "On Ethics and Behavior of Public Officers" No.364-V dated 26 March 2016. These Laws specifies obligations of public officials and sets the limits of acceptable behavior.

In addition, Criminal Code of Turkmenistan No.104-IV dated 10 May 2010 lists certain penalties for violation of anti-corruption laws such as fine, imprisonment and etc.

b. Department Supervising Anti-commercial Bribery

There is no authority solely responsible for prevention of corruption. Law "On Combatting Corruption" obliges all public authorities to prevent and fight against corruption within the limits of their competence.

Prevention, detection and punishment under anti-corruption laws are performed mainly by the Prosecutor's office, the Ministry of Internal Affairs and the National Security Service of Turkmenistan. Tax and border guard services as well as other financial authorities are also responsible for combatting corruption.

On June 2017 the Government established the State Service for Combatting Economic Crimes, a new state authority that will coordinate activities of other authorities in the field of anti-corruption regulation. This Service is involved in unraveling corruption schemes, develop and implement measures for their elimination and prevention. In addition, it has the remit to investigate crimes causing economic damage to the state.

c. Punitive Actions

The Criminal Code recognizes active and passive types of bribery. Under Turkmen laws bribe is defined as money, securities, valuables, property, property rights or property-related services given to a public official in return of assistance to a briber.

Provisions of the Law "On Ethics and Behavior of Public Officers" establishes that public officials should not seek or accept any form of improper benefit in expectation of influencing the performance or non-performance of official duties or functions. Therefore, public officials are prohibited to receive any gifts (money or actual items) from individuals and legal entities.

However, Turkmen laws provide one exception. Public officials can receive gifts in connection with protocol events, business trips and other official events. In this case, they are obliged to transfer such gifts to the state budget.

a) Passive bribery

Acceptance of a bribe by a public official lead to criminal liability:

• imposition of an obligation to reside in certain region / district for a period of five to eight years with deprivation of the right to occupy certain positions or engage in certain activities for up to three years with/without confiscation of a property.

• imprisonment for up to eight years with deprivation of the right to occupy certain positions or engage in certain activities for up to three years with/without confiscation of a property.

The crime committed (i) repeatedly, (ii) by group of persons, (iii) by a public official holding a responsible position or (iv) accompanied with extortion lead to more severe punishment:

• imposition of an obligation to reside in certain region/district for a period of eight to fifteen years with with/without confiscation of a property;

• imprisonment for up to fifteen years with deprivation of the right to occupy certain positions or engage in certain activities for up to three years with/without confiscation of a property.

If a public official accepts a bribe in large amounts (exceeding 100 minimum average wages) it may be imprisoned for a period of ten to twenty years.

b) Active

Active bribery (i.e.provision of bribes to public officials) entails the following:

• imprisonment from three to five years with/without confiscation of a property;

• imprisonment from five to ten years for repeated crime.

c) Mediation in Bribery

Persons who acted as an intermediary in the crime are also liable under Turkmen laws as mediation in bribery is considered as dangerous as the crime of bribery itself. A person found liable for mediation in bribery may be sentenced for imprisonment of two to ten years (or up to ten years for repeated crime).

B. Project Contracting

The public procurement system in Turkmenistan has been the target area of recent public sector reforms. In December 2014 the Government of Turkmenistan adopted a new Law "On Tenders for the Supply of Goods, Execution of Works and Provision of Services for State Needs" No.158-V (hereinafter – "Law on Tenders") in order to promote development of the national economy, improve business competitive environment in public procurement sector and increase the volumes of local production.

The Law on Tenders provides an overall framework for the tender process, from issuing a tender, preparation of tender documentation and initial evaluation of tender bids to negotiations and contract signing. It defines rights and obligations of all tender participants as well as the competency of the tender commission. In addition, the Law on Tenders gives an exhaustive list of qualification criteria applicable to bidding companies.

It should be noted that public procurement in oil and gas sectors is separately regulated by Law "On Hydrocarbon Resources" No.208-III dated 20 August 2008.

Further, in February 2016 the President of Turkmenistan signed Resolution No.14602 "On Tenders and Choice of Suppliers of Goods, Works, Services for Budgetary Consumers". This document fully complies with the provisions of the Law on Tenders and gives a detailed step-by-step description of tendering process.

At the present time the abovementioned documents are considered as the main legal acts in the sphere of public procurement in Turkmenistan.

a. Permission System

Any foreign or local company may participate in a tender held in the territory of Turkmenistan.

Any company may be eligible to engage in a tender process subject to the below qualification requirements as set out in the Law on Tenders:

• bidder has full legal capacity and relevant licenses, certificates and permits required in accordance with Turkmenistan laws;

• bidder should be technically and professionally competent and have necessary experience, financial resources and equipment to fulfill tender obligations;

• bidder should be solvent and have no tax arrears;

• bidder should not be bankrupt and not be in the process of bankruptcy, liquidation or reorganization;

• bidder should not be a person in respect of whom there is a conflict of interest.

Consequently, a failure to comply with any of above-mentioned requirements deprives a bidder from participation in a tender.

Bidding companies (both local and foreign) as well as their intermediaries are not obliged to register to participate in tendering process. As long as bidding company comply with qualification criteria set out in the Law on Tenders, it can freely engage in a tender.

However, the necessity to register a local company or a permanent representation may arise after the completion of a tender and announcement of the winner.

In case the tender obligations include the performance of activities in the territory of Turkmenistan that are subject to licensing, the winner of the tender is obliged to register a local company and apply for the relevant license.

Further, if a non-resident company is engaged in business operations in Turkmenistan for more than 45 calendar days within any subsequent 12-month period, it should register a permanent representation with local tax authorities. Considering that some activities comprising tender obligations may be taxed in Turkmenistan, a foreign company may qualify under Turkmen law requirement for registering a permanent representation.

b. Prohibited Areas

Article 15 of the Law on Tenders (Conflict of interest) provides a list of persons who cannot participate in a tender. First of all, the Law establishes that individuals who are actually working as public officials cannot participate in tenders as potential suppliers/contractors.

Further, the following persons cannot participate in a tender (especially organize a tender):

• individuals who are in close relationship with any supplier/contractor –an individual or a legal entity's representative/employee;

• individuals who has been working as an employee of any supplier/contractor participating in a tender within three years preceding the moment of publication of a tender notice.

c. Invitation to Bid and Bidding

Law on Tenders establishes that tenders could be organized: (i) for unlimited number of participants or (ii) for limited number of participants.

Tenders with limited participation are organized in the following cases:

• costs for review and evaluation a large number of bids are not commensurate with the value of the goods supplied, works performed or services provided;

• goods, works or services, due to their technical complexity or specialized nature, are available only to a limited number of potential suppliers (contractors);

• a tender is conducted in relation to objects of national importance.

At the initial stage an organizer of a tender sends invitations to bid to prospective suppliers/contractors (or publishes information on a tender conditions in mass media) and acquaints them with tender documentation. An organizer of a tender creates a tender commission of at least five people. This commission receives and registers tender bids, evaluates them and makes a final decision on the selection of successful bidder.

委内瑞拉

作者：Fulvio Italiani、Roberto Mas
译者：赖向东、许智慧

一、概述

（一）政治

委内瑞拉是位于南美洲北加勒比海岸的联邦共和国，由23个州、首都地区、联邦属地和300多个市组成。加拉加斯是委内瑞拉首都、最大的城市和政府所在地。2016年委内瑞拉人口大约3150万，官方语言是西班牙语。

委内瑞拉政府有三个级别：联邦、州和市。国家政治结构由1999年制定、2009年修订的《宪法》确立。中央政府分为行政、立法、司法、公民和选举部门。

总统是国家首脑、政府首脑和军队首脑。总统由普选产生，任期6年，可以连任。所有行政权力都集中于总统。总统还有如下权力：①否决国民大会通过的法律；②颁布和法律同等地位的法令；③颁布对法律和法令进行补充的规章。

其他的行政领导人包括执行副总统、各部部长（不包括司法部部长）、司法部部长[①]和某些执行部门领导。执行副总统和部长们由总统任免，直接或间接向总统汇报。总统、执行副总统和部长不定期会见部长理事会来批准某些事项。

国家立法部门是国民议会。国民议会只有一个分庭，其成员由普选产生，任期5年，可连任。国民议会有权制定法律，然后由委内瑞拉总统颁布并在官方公报中予以公布之后生效。2017年5月，委内瑞拉总统呼吁选举全国制宪大会修改宪法。全国制宪大会被赋予改革国家、建立新的法律框架和起草新的宪法的权力。2017年7月30日，545名全国制宪大会成员被选出。全国制宪大会于2017年8月成立后，颁布了一项法令，宣布全国制宪大会及其立法行为至高无上，并将所有其他实体和政府部门置于其宪法权限之下。

司法权归属于委内瑞拉最高法院和各下级法院。最高法院是最后的上诉法院。它有权取消与宪法或法律相抵触的行政或立法部门的法律、法规和其他行为或决定。最高法院的法官由立法部门任命，任期12年。最高法院设有6个分庭，其中包括负责解释宪法的宪法分庭。委内瑞拉法院体系是一个国家体系；没有州法院，但各州都有国家法院。法院的司法管辖区分为民事、商业、劳工、税务、行政、刑事和家事等主题。

公民部门由三个实体组成：①促进和监督保护人权的巡视员；②促进公正司法和司法程序的检察官办公室；③监测和控制政府资产、收入和公共债务管理的审计长。每个实体的负责人由立法部门任命，任期7年。

选举部门负责监督选举进程、竞选筹资和竞选广告。选举部门通过全国选举委员会运作。全国选举委员会负责人和董事会由立法部门任命。

在州和市两级，政府分为行政（州长和市长）和立法部门（州议会和市议会）。各州实际上没有征税权力，但它们可能会对非贵金属和非国家保留的矿物征税。市政当局有权颁布当地法律，并对营业收入征收营业税，并批准城市和其他人口中心的建设项目。

委内瑞拉中央银行是该国的货币管理机构。中央银行和财政部长共同制定主要的货币政策指导方针和法规。中央银行负责印刷货币、持有和管理委内瑞拉的外汇储备，与财政部长一起设定官方汇率，调节利率，并设定当地银行的准备金要求。

[①] 司法部部长是共和国首席法律长官。

（二）经济

委内瑞拉的官方货币是玻利瓦尔。委内瑞拉有严格的外汇管制限制，严格限制本币兑换外币。只有通过中央银行和财政部长颁布的外汇管理条例规定的系统才能购买外汇。参考汇率每日由中央银行公布。

委内瑞拉是石油输出国组织（欧佩克）的成员，是世界上最大的石油生产国和出口国之一。截至 2016 年 12 月 31 日，委内瑞拉估计已探明的原油储量总计达 3 020 亿桶（其中包括奥里诺科油区约 2 610 亿桶重和特稠油原油）。[①] 委内瑞拉的所有碳氢化合物储量都归共和国所有。该国的原油勘探、生产和出口都由委内瑞拉国内生产总值的最大贡献者、国有石油天然气集团 Petróleosde Venezuela, S.A.（PDVSA）及其子公司负责。委内瑞拉经济在很大程度上取决于石油收入。

PDVSA 控股一系列石油和天然气公司。PDVSA 是拉丁美洲最大的垂直一体化石油公司，也是全球最大的垂直一体化石油公司之一。根据委内瑞拉《碳氢化合物法》，委内瑞拉政府保留勘探和开发碳氢化合物及其衍生物有关的每项活动的权力。私营石油公司可能通过参与持有少数股份合资企业从事石油项目，而 PDVSA 直接或间接持有多数股权。PDVSA 及其子公司受石油部的监督。

委内瑞拉公司（CVG）是 1960 年成立的一家自治机构。CVG 是一家从事铝、铁、钢、黄金和其他行业的公司的非营业性控股实体。CVG 的使命是持续开发丰富的铝土矿、铁矿和黄金矿藏以及其他贵金属，并促进圭亚那地区的整体发展。

Fondo de Desarrollo Nacional（FONDEN）是国家发展基金，用于资助委内瑞拉的基础设施、社会和发展项目。FONDEN 由中央银行提供资金。FONDEN 的资金来源还有根据委内瑞拉石油暴利税法支付的款项，根据此法，委内瑞拉的石油出口商（PDVSA 及其子公司，包括石油合资公司）必须支付对石油价格征收的特别税款。存入 FONDEN 的款项通常用于资助委内瑞拉国内的重大基础设施项目。

2016 年 2 月，政府创建了国家战略开发区"Arco Minero del Orinoco"，目的是促进该国黄金和其他矿产品，如铝土矿、铜和钻石的生产。Orinoco 矿区位于奥里诺科河以南，面积约 112 000 平方公里。矿业发展部负责 Orinoco 采矿带的采矿活动。

2018 年 2 月，为促进"公民直接参与的独立，透明的数字经济"，委内瑞拉政府推出了石油主权加密货币"Petro"。Petro 将在区块链平台上运营，并将在人与人之间或在投资组合间交换。Petro 将用于购买商品或服务，并可通过数字货币兑换法定货币和其他加密货币。

委内瑞拉的经济在 2016 年收缩了 16.5%。[②] 预计 2018 年国内生产总值将下降约 15%（自 2013 年以来 GDP 累计下降近 50%）。[③] PDVSA 的原油产量在过去几年一直在下降。2018 年 1 月产量平均为 160 万桶，而 2017 年平均为 190 万桶，2016 年为 220 万桶，2015 年为 240 万桶。[④] 截至 2017 年 11 月 30 日，中央银行持有的外汇储备平均为 97 亿美元，而 2014 年 12 月 31 日则为 221 亿美元。截至 2016 年 12 月 31 日，国际收支赤字为 68 亿美元。[⑤]

委内瑞拉政府负责提供大部分基本公共服务，包括电力、水、家庭和工业液化石油气、卫生和教育，同时也是食品的主要进口商和分销商。国家直接或间接控制或拥有在委内瑞拉经济各行业和行业（包括碳氢化合物，采矿，电信，食品，交通和汽车）经营的大量公共实体和公司的 50% 或更多股权。每个委内瑞拉国营公司都由一个部长监督。

（三）法律

委内瑞拉是大陆法系国家，这意味着法律和法规优先于法院的判例。除最高法院宪法法庭作出的某些判决外，委内瑞拉法院的判决不具约束力。

委内瑞拉法律结构由：①《宪法》；②立法部门颁布的法律和委内瑞拉总统颁布的法令；③委内

---

① 委内瑞拉 2016 年财政年度向美国证券交易委员会年报告递交的表 18-K 附件 D。
② 同上注。
③ Alejandro Werner，"拉丁美洲的美国和加勒比 2018：经济复苏的决策"，载国际货币基金组织博客，访问时间：2018 年 1 月 25 日。
④ 石油输出国组织 2018 年 2 月和 2016 年 1 月的月度石油市场报告。
⑤ 委内瑞拉 2016 年财政年度向美国证券交易委员会年报告递交的表 18-K 附件 D。

瑞拉总统颁布的法规；④决议和国家行政部门或其他官员发布的其他普遍适用的规定组成。①

委内瑞拉《民法典》和《商业法典》规定适用于商业和合同的一般规则。总体而言，除非对委内瑞拉的公共政策构成不当影响，否则《民法典》和《商业法典》的规定可以被合同取代或修改。这意味着委内瑞拉的合同通常可以按照自身的条款执行，除非合同中的条款与委内瑞拉公共政策相抵触。

（四）与中国企业的合作现状

中国和委内瑞拉于 1974 年建立外交关系。

中国是委内瑞拉最重要的战略、经济和贸易伙伴之一。中国和委内瑞拉签署了大量合作协议和谅解备忘录，用于在能源、石油、技术、贸易、基础设施、农业、教育、文化和体育等领域开展具体项目合作。

2001 年，中委两国签署了设立中委高层委员会的谅解备忘录。委员会负责制定、执行和监督两国合作项目、方案和提案。自成立以来，委员会定期在中国和委内瑞拉举行会议，评估活跃项目取得的进展，有时会签署更多的合作文书，并讨论新的投资机会。2007 年，中国和委内瑞拉签署了设立名为中委合作基金（Fondo Financiamiento Conjunto Chino-Venezolano）的联合投资基金的协议，以资助委内瑞拉几个经济地区的社会经济项目，总额为 40 亿美元。②

中国和委内瑞拉是避免双重征税综合条约的缔约国。

两国经济关系和合作在过去二十年中有了显著增长。2015 年，中国占委内瑞拉出口总额的 16.7% 和进口总额的 18.5%，2013 年分别为 8.1% 和 13.6%。③ 近十年来，中国向委内瑞拉提供的融资超过 500 亿美元。

二、投资

（一）市场准入

1. 投资监管部门

委内瑞拉对外贸易部是负责集中注册委内瑞拉公司的外国投资登记以及技术援助、分销和技术转让协议的部门。对于能源、矿业、银行和电信等特定领域，负责登记外资的机构是相应地区的相关部门（例如石油部登记石油项目，财政部登记银行和保险项目）。

外贸部负责：①促进外国投资和向委内瑞拉转让技术；②批准、拒绝、更新和记录外国投资和技术转让协议；③组织、管理和集中管理外国投资登记处；④审计和控制外国投资和技术转让协定；⑤就外国投资返回境外发表意见。

2. 投资行业的法律法规

在委内瑞拉的外国投资受外国投资法和下位法规管辖。外国投资法的主要目的是：①促进生产性外国投资；②确保外国投资将技术带入委内瑞拉，取代进口并促进出口；③创造良好、公平和生产性的就业机会；④增加和改善获得外国融资、外汇和新市场的机会；⑤吸引能够在委内瑞拉非传统经济领域创汇的外国投资。

外国投资必须符合外国投资法规定的条件。只有投资超过 800 000 欧元或 6 500 000 元人民币（或等值外币）才有资格获得外商投资注册。外国投资者必须在委内瑞拉境内停留至少两年，才有权将其全部或部分投资资金或在委内瑞拉出售所得资金汇回本国。一旦其投资目的得以实现，外国投资者有权汇出从其注册和新增的投资中获得的股息。只有在不可抗力或特殊经济情况下，国家主管才有权减

---

① 委内瑞拉法律框架还包括国家法律和市政条例。
② 其他协议包括：(1) 原油、农业和电信领域的 2009 合作协定；(2) 在委内瑞拉奥里诺科重油带开发重质原油 2010 和 2011 的合资协议；(3) 改善委内瑞拉主要的铝冶炼厂 2011 美元贷款 4 亿 300 万协议；(4) 2013 协议为 Las Cristinas 金矿项目的开发挖掘地图和计划 2013 协议；(5) 关于中型和重型卡车厂建设、轮胎制造厂及 Orinoquia 电信合资企业扩张的 2015 协议；(6) 增加中国的石油产品和原油生产和贸易，并形成一个新的合资公司，发展中国炼油厂加工委内瑞拉原油之 2016 协议；(7) 促进铁矿石、铝矾土和铝生产之 2017 合作协定；及 (8) 中国提供总额 150 亿美元的贷款给予委内瑞拉总体经济支持和为原油项目融资之 2017 协议。
③ 委内瑞拉 2016 年财政年度向美国证券交易委员会年报告递交的表 18-K 附件 D。

少这一比例。

外国投资登记是通过中央银行获取外汇以汇回股息、分支机构利润、销售投资收益、清算公司资本或减少资本所需的文件之一。然而实际上，由于委内瑞拉实行严格外汇管制制度，将委内瑞拉玻利瓦尔兑换成外币以换取现金的可能性非常有限。

3. 投资形式

外国投资有两种类型：外国直接投资和投资组合投资。外国直接投资是对当地公司的股权进行投资，参与公司资本等于或大于10%。投资组合投资是对当地公司股票或配额的投资，代表股权参与率低于10%。

投资形式可以有如下方式：①外币；②有形或有形资产（工业厂房、设备、原材料或中间产品）；③无形资产（商标、专利、其他知识产权以及技术援助，条件是此类无形资产在非关联实体之间转让，相关合同在委内瑞拉知识产权监管机构进行登记，权利转让涉及将无形资产的所有权有效转让）；④通过资本再投资。

在委内瑞拉的外国投资须遵守外国投资者与接受投资的实体（国家或公共，私人或合资公司）之间的投资合同条款。投资合同规定投资类型、投资目的、价值和投资所在国的地区、合同期限、融资条件以及与投资相关的任何其他条款。

委内瑞拉是几个税收协定以及双边投资保护条约的缔约方。

4. 市场准入的标准和检验

除了在国家主管部门确定的对国家经济和社会发展具有战略意义的领域进行的投资以外，外国投资法保证外国投资者及其投资与本国投资者的地位一致。

露天电视、无线电广播、西班牙语报纸、国家航空运输和法律规定的专业服务等行业只开放给本国投资者拥有或控制的公司。有些行业，如上游石油工业，是委内瑞拉政府保留行业，外国投资者只能以小股东身份通过与共和国或其他委内瑞拉国有公司的合资公司参与。

此外，对一些被视为公共利益的行业进行投资需要相应监管机构的特别行政许可（如电信，银行，保险，发电、输电、配电，供水和勘探以及开采某些矿物）。

（二）外汇管理

1. 外汇主管部门

中央银行是委内瑞拉的货币管理机构，是负责监督外汇谈判和贸易的实体，并与财政部一起设定官方汇率，并规定与委内瑞拉外汇体系有关的各个方面。中央银行由委内瑞拉《中央银行法》授权，对委内瑞拉玻利瓦尔的自由兑换制定限制。

委内瑞拉政府成立了外贸国家中心，与中央银行和财政部协调制定并实施政府的外汇管理、出口、进口和离岸投资政策。

2. 外汇法律法规概况

委内瑞拉的外汇交易受《外汇管理法》、中央银行和财政部长联合颁布的外汇管理法规和中央银行颁布的规定管辖。

委内瑞拉外汇管制制度严格限制私人公司和个人将玻利瓦尔转换为外币。目前，只能通过以下系统或市场进行外币买卖：① Cencoex；② Dicom 系统；③零售市场（operaciones al menudeo）；④证券市场。目前，所有四个系统或市场都对购买外币有严格限制。

Cencoex 控制私人实体获得批准的进口食品、药品和原材料的外币购买。Dicom 系统是一种外币拍卖机制，由中央银行管理和控制，并向希望购买或出售外币的私营部门实体和个人开放。①

委内瑞拉的官方汇率被称为"Dicom 汇率"，由中央银行公布。通常，Dicom 利率会根据 Dicom 系统中每次外币拍卖的结果（通常每周一次）而波动。委内瑞拉的所有官方外汇交易均以当时的 Dicom 利率结算。

---

① DICOM 系统给私人公司（每月）和个人（每季度）可以购买的外汇设立限制。

3. 外资企业的外汇管理要求

国家和委内瑞拉国有公司可以通过法规或特别许可证在中央银行授权的范围内以外币进行支付。除了某些类型的交易（如买卖房地产）之外，私人公司还可以以外币进行支付，并在本地和离岸银行账户中持有外币。私人公司持有的外币可以：①在离岸银行账户中保持（除下文所述外）；②用于在委内瑞拉或国外以外币进行支付；③通过现有外汇体系将可用资金自愿转换为当地货币。

委内瑞拉商品和服务出口商可以扣留出口产品获得的外汇收入的80%，并用它支付与其活动有关的费用和任何其他支出。其余的20%必须出售给中央银行。私营部门货物出口商可以从这种20%中扣除作为流动资金出资的数额，用以购买对其出口活动至关重要的原材料、用品、固定资产和其他货物。

（三）金融融资

1. 主要金融机构

主要职责为控制通货膨胀并维持委内瑞拉玻利瓦尔稳定的中央银行，和当地银行（公共和私人）以及保险公司是委内瑞拉金融市场的主要参与者。

委内瑞拉银行受《银行业机构法》《金融体系法》以及中央银行和委内瑞拉银行业监管机构（Sudeban）的监管。一般而言，委内瑞拉银行有权获得存款、贷款、发行信用卡和借记卡、充当受托人（受托人）并发行债券或担保。

委内瑞拉保险公司受到《保险活动法》《金融体系法》以及委内瑞拉保险业监管机构（Sudeaseg）的监管。保险公司也有权发行债券或担保。

委内瑞拉银行市场是一个专业银行机构、存款和信贷组合高度集中的市场。截至2016年年底，在委内瑞拉经营的银行中几乎有75%是全能银行。委内瑞拉十大银行占该国银行资产的80%以上，而五大银行集中了近70%的存款。委内瑞拉国家银行是委内瑞拉最大的银行。

委内瑞拉有31家银行：6家是国有银行，25家是私人银行。外资参与委内瑞拉银行业和保险业的规模很小。

委内瑞拉有约50家保险公司和5家再保险公司。外资参与委内瑞拉保险业的情况也很少。

2. 外资企业融资条件

外资企业有特殊的融资条件。

由于目前的外汇管制制度限制了委内瑞拉公司将玻利瓦尔转换为外币的能力，公共或私人银行的本币融资实际上是唯一可用的资金来源。由于通胀水平和银行对现金流的偏好，3年以上的融资难以获得，本地银行市场主要用于每月摊销。在实践中，借款人几乎无法从银行市场获得大笔贷款。银行市场上银团贷款工具的使用越来越频繁，利率随之变得非常具有吸引力，因为它们是负实际利率（即大幅低于通货膨胀率），并且利息支出可以全额抵扣所得税。尽管当地货币贷款的期限通常较短，但对于蓝筹公司来说，滚存债务目前不成问题。

委内瑞拉的银行通常需要将大部分信贷组合分配给关键经济领域，如住房、农业、旅游业和制造业。

（四）土地政策

1. 土地法律法规概况

委内瑞拉房地产的所有权、购买、销售和发展主要受《民法典》《公共登记和公证法》《国土安全法》《市级区划法》、市级区划规定（ordenanzas dezonificación）以及安全和防卫安全区的法律及其下的条例监管。

委内瑞拉的房地产交易很常见，它们经常被用来对付高通胀率和外汇管制的影响。然而，委内瑞拉房地产市场的活跃程度低于拉丁美洲的其他市场，并且以国内交易为主，主要是由于政治和经济不稳定以及随之而来的外国投资的减少。在委内瑞拉，公开上市的不动产投资信托和不动产经营公司不活跃。

不动产的转让在向相应的公共登记处登记转让契据之后有效。在该国大部分地区，特别是在城市地区，由公共登记处负责房地产所有权和交易登记。公共登记处的房地产申报显示房地产的位置、面积、所有权和产权负担。房地产的转让需要支付注册税和费用。房地产销售者必须支付销售价格0.5%

的预付所得税,销售者可以对其应缴的年度所得税进行抵扣,并且可以要求退还预付的超额所得税(尽管实际上不可能获得这种退款)。

城市房地产须按地方市政当局划定的房地产价值征收城市房地产税。城市房地产税每年征收一次,税率通常很低。

委内瑞拉租赁法对住宅、商业和办公室租赁条款有一定的限制。

2. 外资企业获得土地的规则

一般来说,外国个人和企业(以及由他们拥有或控制的委内瑞拉公司)有权在委内瑞拉拥有、出租、转让、出售或以其他方式转让不动产。但是,外国人必须:①在通过任何方式获得位于委内瑞拉政府指定区域内作为安全区域或与水体相邻的区域内的财产时,通知国防部;②在获得国防授权之后取得位于委内瑞拉国际边界附近的土地,或开始在该土地上建设。①

(五)企业设立与关闭

1. 企业形式

外国投资者在委内瑞拉开展业务有如下选择:①公司;②有限责任公司;③普通合伙;④有限合伙;⑤股份有限合伙企业;⑥外国实体的分支机构;⑦财团。在本文中,"公司"一词可用于上述任何选项,包括分支机构、公司或任何合伙企业,但不包括财团。

(1)公司

委内瑞拉公司是外国投资者在委内瑞拉经营的最常见的实体形式。公司由股东拥有,是一个独立于股东的独立法人实体。公司简称为 C.A. 或 S.A.。②

公司股东的责任仅限于支付该股东拥有股份的面值(及溢价,如有)。一般规则下,公司的股东对公司的义务不承担责任。

公司在委托人所在地的委内瑞拉商业注册处注册公司章程。商业登记处中可用的任何名称都可以用于公司,其后是首字母 S.A. 或 C.A.。

公司至少需要由两名股东组成,但公司成立后可由一名股东全资拥有。公司必须拥有规定的或认可的资本("注册资本")。③公司的注册资本可以现金或实物支付。④所述资金的现金支付必须由委内瑞拉银行账户中的本币存款支付。在某些情况下,例如石油合资公司,允许以外币支付所规定的资本。

注册资本以股票形式表示(不记名股票不被允许)。所有股票面值必须以玻利瓦尔计价。公司可以发行不同类别的股票,包括优先股。所有权和股份转让由公司保存的股东账簿中的注释证明。⑤

股东大会是公司的最高权力机构。每位股东均有权亲自出席股东大会或根据授权委托书(代理人)派第三方代理出席。除非章程中另有规定,否则每份股份均有一个投票权。股东会议可以在委内瑞拉或国外举行。法定人数和多数人的规则通常由公司的章程规定。

以下事项需要股东大会的批准:①批准年度资产负债表;②任免董事;③任命和解雇法定审计员;④预期解散;⑤延长公司期限;⑥与另一实体合并;⑦出售全部或绝大部分公司资产;⑧增加注册资本;⑨减少注册资本;⑩目的的改变;⑪派发股息;⑫回购股份;⑬补充亏损;⑭发行债券;⑮由公司向其董事提起司法索赔;⑯修改章程。涉及该公司的任何其他事宜均可提交给股东大会,并且章程可能对需要股东批准的其他事宜作出规定。

董事负责管理或监督公司的管理。公司必须至少有一名董事。⑥公司章程可以授予公司的高级管理人员,如执行总裁,总经理,财务总监,司法代表等广泛的或有限的代表权和管理权。⑦

---

① 委内瑞拉国土安全法律及下位法规。
② 除名字之外,C.A. 公司和 S.A. 公司没有区别。
③ 虽然没有法定最低资本要求,但每一个委内瑞拉商业登记处根据个案规定了最低的资本要求。
④ 在现金支付的情况下,至少 20% 的法定资本必须由股东在股东大会会议记录中批准公司成立时支付。
⑤ 股票也可以用证书来表示,但不要求必须签发股票证书。
⑥ 一些商业登记处要求至少有一名董事为委内瑞拉公民或持有工作或商业签证的外国人,而一些商业登记处要求所有董事要么是委内瑞拉公民,要么是持有工作或商务签证的外国人。
⑦ 如果章程没有明文规定,公司也可以指定或通过授权委托书授予高管人员权力。

董事对公司的义务和责任不承担个人责任，但如果他们违反董事的职责，则需要对公司和第三方承担责任。董事的任期由公司章程规定，董事只能由公司的股东大会撤销。①

公司必须至少有一名由股东大会任命的法定审计师。②法定审计师每年必须编制年度资产负债表和公司账目报告，提交给股东大会。如果法定审计师发现公司管理不规范，则有权召开股东大会。

公司的会计年度为 12 个月，不需要与日历年度相匹配。

股息只能用流动资金和已收利润支付，并且反映在公司股东大会批准的年度资产负债表中。股息必须经股东大会批准，除非章程中另有规定，股息将按比例分配给股东。

- 有限责任公司（SRL）

委内瑞拉有限责任公司是一种很少使用的形式，因为其规定的资本目前不能超过 2 000 玻利瓦尔（不到 1 美元）。有限责任公司的成员像股东一样享有有限责任。有限责任公司的资本由配额表示。如果某成员转让所拥有的配额，其他成员享有优先购买配额的权利，并且将配额转让给第三方，需要获得有限责任公司资本的 3/4 的批准。

- 普通合伙（SNV）

委内瑞拉的普通合伙企业（Sociedad en Nombre Colectivo 或 SNC）由合伙人拥有。合伙人对普通合伙企业的任何债务、义务和责任承担连带责任（无限责任）。普通合伙必须至少有两个合伙人。商业登记处目前接受法人实体（包括外国公司）为普通合伙人的合伙人。合伙人的出资额不以股份为代表。合伙权益的转让需要其他合伙人的批准。

- 有限合伙（SCS）

委内瑞拉有限合伙企业（Sociedad en Comandita Simple 或 SCS）由至少一个普通合伙人和至少一个有限合伙人组成。普通合伙人对有限合伙的债务、义务和责任承担连带责任，而有限责任合伙人的责任仅限于他们同意为有限合伙出资的金额。

- 股份有限合伙企业（SCA）

委内瑞拉股份有限合伙企业（Sociedad en Comandita por Acciones 或 SCA）与有限合伙企业类似，此处有限合伙人的股权以股份为代表，有限合伙人的制度类似于公司股东。

- 分支机构

外国实体可以在委内瑞拉设立分支机构。分支机构并不是独立的法人实体。因此，外国公司（总公司）将承担分公司的所有义务。

分支机构必须在住所所在地的商业登记处登记。外国投资者可以选择分支机构的住所所在地进行登记。通常用于分支机构的名称与外国公司（总公司）或其缩写名称相同，后跟 Sucursal Venezuela（即委内瑞拉分行）。

该分支机构必须至少有 1 名代表。除了出售或转让业务的权力（除非此权力明确授予该代表），分支机构全权代表和管理分行。对代表权力的任何限制都不能对抗第三方。③

总部必须为分支机构分配资本（以下简称"分支机构资本"）。分支机构资本并不构成总公司的有限责任。④分支机构资本必须由总行以现金或实物形式支付。

（2）财团

财团不是一个独立的法律实体，而是几个人（财团成员）之间签订的执行特定项目的合同。

2. 成立程序

（1）设立公司的步骤

以下是对设立公司的步骤的描述（组建普通合伙企业、有限责任公司和有限合伙企业需要类似的步骤）⑤：

---

① 董事无论何时因任何原因，甚至在任期届满之前，均可以被解职。
② 法定审计师必须是委内瑞拉的公共会计师或管理人员。
③ 如果分支机构代表不是委内瑞拉公民，他需要获得工作或商务签证才能在委内瑞拉公证人或登记处面前代表分公司签署文件。
④ 虽然没有适用于分公司资本的法定最低资本要求，但委内瑞拉商业登记处根据个案规定了最低分公司的资本要求。
⑤ 商业登记处经常修改公司成立的要求。

① 向委内瑞拉商业登记处查询该公司使用的名称的可用性，并在可能的情况下预留；

② 向商业登记处提交以下文件：授权委托书委托授权一名或多名人士登记公司，在委内瑞拉当局开立银行账户并代表股东和公司；股东章程；委内瑞拉银行发出的信函，确认收到资金支付或类似证明；法团的公司章程，包括董事及法定核数师的姓名；由被指定为公司的法定审计员（comisario）的人签署的接受书①；

③ 当上述所有文件均齐备，委内瑞拉银行账户已经开设，资金现金付款已存入在委内瑞拉的银行账户（或已获得类似证明），委内瑞拉银行发出证明现金付款的信件或已获得捐款的证据，以及已经支付所有注册费用处理完毕之后，公司在商业登记处的注册一般需要两周时间；

④ 公司注册完成后，必须在委内瑞拉的报纸上公布注册副本；

⑤ 公司必须购买公司账簿并由商业登记处加以封存；

⑥ 根据章程发行的股票记录在公司股东簿中，如果需要的话出具股票证明。

注册成立后，公司必须申请执行公司特定业务所需的注册、批准、许可证（如税务登记，市政许可、社会保障、就业获得机构、住房捐款、国家公共承包商登记、进口许可证和环境许可证）。

（2）设立分支机构的步骤

以下是在委内瑞拉注册外国公司分支机构的步骤说明：

① 向委内瑞拉商业登记处查询分支机构可用的名称，并预留（如有的话）；

② 向商务登记机关提交下列文件：

- 外国公司（总行）主管法人机构批准开立和注册分支机构并指定分支机构代表人的决议；
- 授权一名或多名人士在委内瑞拉开设分行并颁布开设分行的银行账户的授权书；
- 总公司章程；
- 关于外国公司的成立和运作的法律的副本；
- 委内瑞拉银行发出的确认收到现金支付或类似证明的信件。②

③ 当上述所有文件均齐备，委内瑞拉银行账户已经开设，资金现金付款已存入在委内瑞拉的银行账户或已获得类似证明，委内瑞拉银行发出证明现金付款的信件或类似证明，以及已经支付所有注册费用处理完毕之后，分支机构在商业登记处的注册一般需要两周时间；

④ 分支机构注册完成后，必须在委内瑞拉的报纸上公布注册文本；

⑤ 购买会计账簿，并由商业登记机关予以封存。

3. 解散方式及要求

公司的预期解散必须经股东大会批准。公司解散后（无论是预计还是期满），股东大会必须指定一名或多名清算人，负责清算资产并支付公司债务。清算要求支付或清偿所有债务。除非章程中另有规定，一旦所有债务支付或清算完毕，股东有权按比例收取剩余资产或超出公司负债的资金。公司股东对清算法律公司的税务负债承担连带责任，直至法定时效期满为止。

如果公司停止付款（即无法在到期时偿还债务），任何债权人都可以向主管委员会请求破产公司宣布破产（非自愿破产）。此外，公司董事在停止支付（自愿破产）的情况下必须向委内瑞拉主管法院申请破产声明。如果破产，①被宣布为疏忽或欺诈，并且在某些其他情况下，公司的董事可能会面临刑事责任；②公司在暂停期间（或者在由破产法院确定的停止付款的日期10日之前）的交易可能无效或可撤销。③

---

① 委内瑞拉境外形成的授权文件必须经公证或认证，并由委内瑞拉注册翻译人员译成西班牙语。委内瑞拉是《取消外国公文认证要求公约》(《海牙公约》) 的签字国。

② 同上注。

③ 破产法官拥有广泛的自由裁量权确定停止付款日期，前提是，破产法官最多可以回溯停止付款期至破产宣告前两年。根据《商业法》第945条，债务人在停止付款期的下列交易无效：①无对价的资产（动产或不动产）转让（赠与）；②用债务人的资产给予担保（或其他优先付款）停止付款期之前发生的债务；③未到期债务的支付；及④如果债务应当用现金支付，用现金或流通票据以外的任何方式支付到期债务。根据《商业法》第946条，如果收款人或其他交易当事人在支付或交易时明知债务人处于停止付款期，支付到期债务或以停止付款期起始后的对价进行的所有其他交易可以被宣布无效。

（六）合并收购

目前委内瑞拉的并购活动水平适中。在过去的几年中，委内瑞拉的子公司被外国投资者向高风险偏好的投资者以极具吸引力的价格销售。影响委内瑞拉并购活动水平的主要因素是政府监管、外汇管制以及政治经济环境和前景。制造业、金融业和石油天然气行业在未来几年可能会有大量的并购活动。如果政府为投资者提供足够的法律保护（包括通过国际仲裁解决争端），在不远的将来，与委内瑞拉政府合资的石油和天然气公司（私人或国有）的小股东投资规模也可望增加。

收购可能为股票交易或资产交易。股票购买是最简单和最常见的收购方式。如果潜在购买者特别关注公司的重大非税务或劳务实际情况或有负债，则应考虑购买资产。在资产交易中必须考虑批量销售条例以及特殊税收和劳动条例。

一般而言，委内瑞拉的并购交易与其他司法管辖区的交易类似，即：①签署保密协议和无约束力或有约束力的意向书；②尽职调查；③谈判股票或资产购买协议；④签署协议；⑤交易的披露；⑥要约收购程序（就上市公司而言）；⑦交易结束。

购买协议通常包含其他司法管辖区中的并购交易中常有的陈述和保证、赔偿和结束条件。考虑到监管环境快速变化，融资完成条件通常是卖方和买方之间漫长谈判的主要内容。在许多情况下，如果不需要特别的监管批准，签署即视为完成。与普通法国家不同的是，在委内瑞拉（与其他拉丁美洲司法管辖区一样），购买协议通常由买方与目标公司的股东签订，而不是目标公司本身。

委内瑞拉的上市公司非常少。其中一些公司在现有的国际标准下已经实施（或者不时继续实施）针对敌对收购的传统防御措施。

公司与另一实体合并需要股东大会的批准。合并的完成需要等待3个月。在此期间，公司的债权人可能会反对合并。有反对的情况下，合并不能完成，除非异议在当事人之间解决或由法院驳回。作为合并的结果，股东丧失撤回权，除非合并导致公司目的发生变化。委内瑞拉法律不允许"挤压兼并"（即未经受影响股东同意，合并取消股份换取现金）。

监管部门的批准适用于某些受监管的行业，如电信、石油和天然气、银行和保险。

（七）竞争规范

1. 监管竞争的部门

反垄断主管部门是负责监督和执行反托拉斯法规则和条例的委内瑞拉实体。

2. 竞争法的简单介绍

《反托拉斯法》于2014年11月26日颁布。它替代了1992年的《竞争法》，但基本上保留了相同的原则和禁令。其他反托拉斯法规包括：①《竞争法》下的第2条规定（即所谓的合并条例）；②关于经济集中度的指导性数据；③合并准则。

《反托拉斯法》旨在通过禁止和惩罚垄断和寡头垄断商业惯例，控制地位，企业合并和任何其他反竞争或欺诈行为来促进，保护和规范委内瑞拉的公平竞争。《反托拉斯法》涵盖了在委内瑞拉从事经济活动的个人和公营或私营实体，本地和外国的营利性或非营利性实体，但不包括战略上市公司和合资企业。

3. 规范竞争的方法

根据目前的反托拉斯法律和法规，向委内瑞拉反托拉斯监管机构提交反托拉斯文件不是强制性的，除非交易涉及电信公司或某些其他受监管公司。未申报本身并不构成对委内瑞拉竞争法的违反，对不申报不予处罚。但是，如果未申报交易影响了竞争，反垄断主管部门可以在交易结束后开始调查。第三方（即竞争对手）也可以要求反托拉斯监管机构开展调查。《反垄断法》对调查的时间限制在反垄断监管机构或有关第三方反对交易之后一年内。

作为一般规则，反托拉斯法禁止任何阻止、限制、扭曲或限制经济竞争的行为、惯例、协议、合同或决定，包括：①在市场上限制或阻碍实体，产品或服务的获取的任何行为；②限制反托拉斯法涵盖的实体之间的经济竞争或导致其中任何一方拒绝或限制购买或出售商品或服务的任何行为；③操纵生产、分配、贸易、技术开发和投资等要素以损害经济竞争的行为；④限制或防止经济竞争的任何协议；⑤相关协议，包括：直接或间接确定商品和服务价格；限制生产、分销、贸易和技术开发；限制创新、研发投资；在竞争者中分销市场，地区，行业或供应商；为类似服务采用不同条件使竞争对手处于不利地位；将合同的执行条件限制在与合同目的无关的绩效中；创造或加强市场控制地位的经济集中度。[1]

一个或多个实体滥用本地市场的控制地位也是被禁止的。控制地位包括经济活动由单一实体或同时作为买方和卖方的一组实体之间进行；或两个或两个以上实体之间不存在有效竞争。根据《反托拉斯法》，在货物和服务的生产、分销和交易中不诚实，欺骗性和误导性的做法也受到惩罚。不诚实做法定义为：①虚假广告；②产品模拟或模仿；③商业贿赂；④违反法律和法规扩大市场占有的情况。

（八）税务

1. 税收规定

委内瑞拉对居民公司和个人的全球收入征收所得税，累计税率高达34%。外国公司的分支机构按委内瑞拉应占所得缴纳所得税，税率最高达34%。非居民公司或个人委内瑞拉所得税按来源于委内瑞拉境内的收入课税。

委内瑞拉所得税是通过从年度总收入中减去成本和可允许的扣除额（即薪金、利息、摊销、折旧、技术援助和任何"创造收入的正常和必要"费用）计算得出的净应税收入。正常和必要的支出可以被扣除。

外国和国内损失可以结转3年，最高抵消纳税人每年应纳税所得额的25%。损失不能抵免以前年度应税所得。损失可以在所有权变更后仍然存在。

外国公司的委内瑞拉分支机构被视为常设机构。常设机构对其活动产生的所得征税。单独的独立实体的常设机构产生的收入归于常设机构。常设机构的费用，包括执行和一般行政费用允许扣除。分支机构向其总部及其关联公司支付的利息、技术协助费或特许权使用费不可扣除，但支付给其他实体的利息、费用和特许权使用费可以扣除。

委内瑞拉所得税法律和法规包含了基于公平原则的转让定价规则，并根据1995年经济合作与发展组织（以下简称"经合组织"）转让定价指导原则建立模型，强制执行转让定价文件和备案要求，并包含具体的预先定价协议条款。

根据委内瑞拉的资本弱化规则，只要不超过1∶1的债务权益比率，关联方债务的利息就可以用于税务抵扣。

委内瑞拉制定了反递延规则，居民对在低税收国家组织的外国实体和其他投资的直接或间接控制权益有披露义务，并对其进行管理或控制。

对所得税和其他委内瑞拉税种进行税务审计和罚款的法定时效为6年。如果纳税人未能提交适用的纳税申报表，法定时效将延长至10年。

公司和财团必须在注册或开始活动后的第一个月内向委内瑞拉税务信息注册机构注册。这一要求也适用于公司的董事和股东或合伙人以及分支机构的代表和总部。

2. 主要税种和税率

国家级别的税务机关（或有权收税和其他款项的实体）包括：①委内瑞拉国家税务机关（Seniat），负责收取所得税、增值税、礼品税和关税；②负责收取与雇员培训和教育相关的工资税的部门或教育合作机构；③国家住房和居所银行，负责收取房屋和居所税；④负责为失业或裁员紧急情况征收工资社会保障税的部门或社会保障机构；⑤全国反毒组织（ONA）或国家反毒品组织；⑥Fonacit或国家科学、技术和创新基金。所有税务机关或实体都有广泛的权力进行调查、审计和评估，实施处罚，采取预防措施或责令暂时停止违反相应税收义务的活动。

主要税种和税率有：

---

[1] 中小企业不受这些禁止限制。

税 种	税 率
公司所得税	• 分为三档 　- 2000 课税单位以下为 15%[①] 　- 2000 以上至 3000 课税单位为 22% 　- 3000 课税单位以上为 34% • 银行、金融或保险业：40% 单一税率 • 石油公司：净利润的 50% • 矿业：净利润的 60%（由政府认定的具备"国家利益"的特殊项目按常规税率征税）
对非居民的境外支付预扣税	• 股息：34%[②] • 资本利得：34%[③] • 银行利息[④]：44.95% • 其他利息：总款项的 95% 征收 34% • 特许经营权费：总款项 90% 征收 34% • 技术支持：总款项 30% 征收 30% • 职业服务：总款项 90% 征收 34%
中委协议下对非居民的境外支付预扣税	• 股息：如果是股东直接控制分配实体资本至少 10% 的公司，则为 5%。在所有其他情况下为 10%。 • 银行利息：最多 5% • 其他利息：10% • 特许经营权费：10%
增值税[⑤]	• 标准税率：12% • 出口产品或服务：0%
首次出资，公司增资或分支机构分配资本的印花税	• 1% 至 2%
金融交易税[⑥]	• 标准税率：0.75% • 外汇交易税：0%
市政经济活动税[⑦]	• 各市自定
礼品税[⑧]	• 最高 55%
国家反毒品附加[⑨]	• 净利润的 1%
国家科学技术创新基金附加[⑩]	• 总收入的 0.5% 至 2%

---

① 纳税单位是每年由委内瑞拉税务局确定的计量价值。
② 由委内瑞拉居民公司、有限责任公司或股份有限责任合伙公司向非居民股东或合伙人支付股息，财务收入超过应纳税所得额部分，按 34% 征收股息税（"红利税"）。股息税由公司代扣。委内瑞拉居民公司从其他委内瑞拉公司收到的股息分配中支付股息不受股息税的约束。外国法人实体的分支机构对其所得税纳"视同股息税"，按财务收入超过该分支机构应纳税所得额的 34% 的统一税率征收。如果分支机构将在委内瑞拉获得的视同股息税金额再投资于委内瑞拉并保持投资 5 年，享受视同股息税豁免。
③ 出售或其他处置（除通过委内瑞拉证券交易所以外）公司股份和股份有限合伙制所获得的资本收益将被视为源自委内瑞拉的收入。须缴税应课税资本利得的股份持有人须填写委内瑞拉所得税申报表，且有权要求退还因此类收益而超额支付的税款（尽管几乎不可能获得这种退款）。实物支付不受扣缴，但适用资本利得所得税。
④ 向非居民实体支付利息须扣缴所得税，但贷款人必须报告所收到的利息，并支付相应的所得税。共和国发行债券的利息支出免征所得税，不适用扣缴义务。
⑤ 增值税适用于整个分销链中所有商品和服务的销售。增值税纳税人在购买商品和服务时被收取增值税（进项税额）。反过来，他们须在其商品和服务的销售环节收取增值税（销项税），有效地将增值税税负传递给最终消费者。增值税税负（销项税减去进项税）按月由纳税人支付给委内瑞拉财政。豪华车、摩托车、珠宝等奢侈品还须缴纳附加增值税。免征增值税的产品包括食品、医药、电话、家用电和家用天然气等。增值税不适用于金融和保险服务。
⑥ 指定为特别纳税人的实体须：①通过委内瑞拉银行系统支付的款项；②通过以新代旧、抵销和/或债务减免清偿的债务交纳金融交易税。
⑦ 就商业活动征收的市政税由地方市政当局按毛收入征收（不允许扣除）。
⑧ 捐赠位于委内瑞拉的资产根据受益人和赠与人之间的关系一般须交纳委内瑞拉赠与税。
⑨ 有 50 个或更多工人的商业或工业企业必须根据他们的净收入支付一定的国家反毒品附加税，按年计算和缴付。
⑩ 根据所开展的业务活动的类型，总收入超过 100 000 个纳税单位的公司就其总收入交纳国家科学技术创新基金附加税。本税按年计算和缴付。

（续表）

国家体育基金附加①	• 净利润的 1%
社会保障机构附加②	• 雇主税率：①每名员工工资，或②每名雇员按城镇最低工资（以下简称"Ivss 工资基数"）计算的 5 倍，其中较低者的 9%，10% 或 11%。 • 雇员税率：Ivss 工资基数的 4%
教育机构附加③	• 雇主税率：总薪水、工资、支出和所有报销（包括偶然支出）的 2% • 雇员税率：分红的 0.5%
房屋附加④	• 雇主税率：每个雇员每月工资的 2% • 雇员税率：月工资的 1%
失业和裁员附加⑤	• 雇主税率：Ivss 工资基数的 2% • 雇员税率：Ivss 工资基数的 0.5%

3. 税务申报和优惠

所得税纳税期为 12 个月。公司的纳税时间由章程规定。纳税年度可以是日历年度或任何 12 个月期间。所得税申报表必须在纳税人纳税年度结束后的 3 个月内提交。没有规定定期审计周期。

委内瑞拉与奥地利、巴巴多斯、白俄罗斯、比利时、巴西、加拿大、中国、古巴、捷克、丹麦、法国、德国、印度尼西亚、伊朗、意大利、韩国、科威特、马来西亚、荷兰、挪威、巴勒斯坦、葡萄牙、卡塔尔、俄罗斯、西班牙、瑞典、瑞士、特立尼达和多巴哥、阿拉伯联合酋长国、英国、美国和越南签署了避免双重征税的条约。

委内瑞拉总统在部长理事会上，在财政措施的范围内，可以根据委内瑞拉经济的地区状况、部门状况或临时情况对特别重要的部门完全或部分免除所得税。

（九）证券

1. 证券相关法律法规的简要介绍

委内瑞拉的资本市场按市值和交易量计算非常小。它受：①证券市场法（Ley del Mercado de Valores）及其下的法规；②公共证券交易法（Ley de la BolsaPúblicade Valores）；③证券存管法（Ley de Caja de Valores）；④集体投资法（Ley de Entidades de Inversion Colectiva）的管辖。

股票已在委内瑞拉证券交易所公开上市或委托上市的公司，受国家证券监管机构 [Superintendencia Nacional de Valores（Sunaval）] 的监管。

目前在委内瑞拉有三家证券交易所。它们是：①加拉加斯证券交易所（Bolsa de Valores de Caracas），一家成立于 1947 年的私营证券交易所；②二百周年纪念公众证券交易所（Bolsa Pública de Valores Bicentenaria），2010 年成立的公共和私营证券交易所；③委内瑞拉农产品和货物交换所（委内瑞拉农业生物技术委员会），1999 年成立的一个谈判稻米、高粱和玉米等农业衍生品的交流中心。

在委内瑞拉公开发售股票需要根据《公开发售条例》提交（经 Sunaval 批准的）招股说明书。

在一次或多次交易中，直接或间接收购委内瑞拉上市公司的控股权必须通过公开收购要约进行，所有股东都可以（但不要求）按平等条款和条件（强制性投标规则）出售其股票。

上市公司必须在扣除所得税和法定准备金并抵销任何累计亏损后，从每个财政年度的净利润中分配股息给其股东。不低于 25% 的股息必须以现金方式分配。支付上市公司董事会成员的本财年净利润，扣除税收和法定准备金后，不得超过该利润的 10%。如上所述，在派发股息之前不能支付这种款项。

---

① 总收入超过 20 000 个纳税单位的公司须就其净收入缴纳国家体育基金附加税，本税是按年计算和缴付。
② 雇主和雇员必须向社会保障机构缴纳相应税费。对雇主来说，适用率（9%、10% 或 11%）取决于业务活动的风险程度（风险越高，百分比越高）。员工应缴部分由雇主代扣代缴。本税是按月缴付的。
③ 雇员和雇用 5 人或更多员工的雇主须缴纳教育机构附加税。员工应缴部分由雇主代扣代缴。本税由雇主每季度前 5 日支付。
④ 雇主和雇员必须缴纳房屋附加税。员工应缴部分由雇主代扣代缴。房屋附加税按月缴纳。
⑤ 雇主和雇员必须就失业或裁员风险向社会保障机构支付相应份额。员工应支付部分由用人单位代扣，按月支付。

委内瑞拉上市公司须遵守报告要求，包括向 Sunaval 提交经审计的年度财务报表、年度报告、未经审计的季度财务报表、与在 Sunaval 上注册的证券的价格或交易有影响的实质性的信息、关于股息的信息、公司与董事会成员或其主要股东及其股东之间有任何利益的公司之间的交易、关于某些股东会议召集的信息、补充资料、增加或减少资本、出售重大公司资产、公司目的的变更、公司转型或合并、预期清算、上述事项中的章程变更等。

2. 证券市场的监管

证券市场由 Sunaval 监管。

3. 外国企业证券交易的要求

委内瑞拉证券市场没有关于外国企业交易的具体规定。国内实体和外国企业都遵守委内瑞拉证券交易法规的规定。

（十）优先投资和保护

1. 优先政策结构

外国投资法将"优先投资"定义为国家行政部门对该国经济和社会发展给予优惠的部门所作的投资。优先投资可能会获得比其他投资更有利的收益和激励。其他投资如果符合以下几个目标，也可以享受有利的条件：①部分或全部利润再投资；②出口非传统商品或服务；③技术转移到委内瑞拉；④与委内瑞拉科学和技术机构进行的培训活动和技术研究；⑤发展生产性供应链；⑥大额投资；⑦持久投资；⑧进口替代；⑨工作岗位提供。

有利的条件可能包括税收减免、加速摊销、关税豁免、免税、特殊信贷条件、公共服务特殊税率、政府管理的投入和/或原材料的优惠准入、税收稳定性以及任何其他由总统宣布的有利条件。

2. 对特殊行业的支持

2016 年，国家行政部门创建了奥里诺科采矿带，这是一个国家战略开发区，位于玻利瓦尔州，占地 112 000 平方公里，计划按照可持续和尊重环境的做法开发该地区的矿产储量。①

3. 特别经济区

根据本土社会生产发展的整体区域化法律，委内瑞拉总统有权建立特别经济区（SEA），以吸引外国和国内投资，促进特定地区的经济、工业和商业发展。

特别经济区受益于特殊的税收和海关优惠措施，如所得税和增值税豁免。2014 年，政府在 Falcón 州创建了 ParaguanáSEA，在 Táchira 州创建了 UreñaSEA。ParaguanáSEA 的设立是为了促进技术、信息和电信领域的区域发展。UreñaSEA 旨在促进纺织、鞋类、林业、农业、汽车和金属机械行业。②

委内瑞拉自由贸易区法律（Ley de Zonas Franca）规定建立和运营自由贸易区和自由港。自由贸易区和自由港免除大部分进出口关税。委内瑞拉政府在 Falcón 州的 Paraguaná 半岛，苏利亚州的 Atuja 以及梅里达州的 Libertador，CampoElías，Sucre 和 Santos Marquina 市创建了自由贸易区（文化和科技产品）。在玛格丽塔岛（Nueva Esparta 州的一部分）和玻利瓦尔州的 Santa Elena de Uairen 创建了自由港。

4. 投资保护

委内瑞拉与阿根廷、巴巴多斯、白俄罗斯、比利时、卢森堡、加拿大、智利、哥斯达黎加、古巴、捷克、丹麦、厄瓜多尔、法国、德国、伊朗、立陶宛、巴拉圭、秘鲁、葡萄牙、俄罗斯、西班牙、瑞典、瑞士、英国、乌拉圭和越南签署了双边投资条约。委内瑞拉和中国之间没有双边投资条约。

双边投资条约下的外国投资不受东道国的某些政府行为的影响，例如征用或国有化。委内瑞拉于 2012 年退出《关于解决国家与其他国家国民之间投资争端公约》（ICSID 公约）。然而，退出 ICSID 公约并未排除利用国际争端解决方式来解决未来投资争议。双边投资条约就在国际仲裁中解决与委内瑞

---

① 委内瑞拉与中国、加拿大和刚果运营商签署了开发该区的特许协议。
② 2015 年委内瑞拉和中国签署了关于委内瑞拉经济特区合作框架协议。

拉的投资争端的可能性提供保证。[①] 委内瑞拉签署的大部分双边投资协定都包含根据贸易法委员会的[②]仲裁规则和国际投资争端解决中心的附加便利规则提供选择仲裁的条款。

三、贸易

(一) 贸易主管部门

委内瑞拉负责贸易监管的机构为财政部，渔业部、粮食部、对外贸易部、委内瑞拉国税及海关权力部门给予配合。

(二) 贸易法律法规概况

委内瑞拉自 1990 年 8 月 31 日成为《关税和贸易总协定》(GATT) 的协议方，系世界贸易组织 (WTO) 成员。委内瑞拉也是拉丁美洲一体化协会 (ALADI) 的成员。

委内瑞拉 2011 年 4 月正式退出安第斯条约组织 (CAN)。退出后，委内瑞拉与除秘鲁外的所有安第斯条约组织成员国——玻利维亚、哥伦比亚和厄瓜多尔签订了一系列双边关税协议。与哥伦比亚的双边协议系最后一个签署。

委内瑞拉 2004 年成为以促进成员国之间自由贸易为宗旨的区域贸易集团及关税联盟南美共同市场 (阿根廷、巴西、玻利维亚、巴拉圭、乌拉圭及委内瑞拉)[③] 的准成员。2016 年 12 月，南美共同市场中止了委内瑞拉在集团的成员身份。委内瑞拉对成员身份中止提出异议，并已经根据南美共同市场内部规则就此申请争议解决。

如前所述，委内瑞拉与中国就特定项目和领域的发展已经签署众多合作协议及备忘。

委内瑞拉颁布的其他立法包括：①规定进出口和在委内瑞拉境内之运输法律框架的《海关法》及其实施细则，以及关税和海关规则；②旨在防止和惩戒夹带走私的《反走私法》；③为防止倾销进口确定政策和指导的《反倾销法》。

(三) 贸易管理

进口货物需要通过国家对外贸易中心外汇支付价款，在货物装运前必须获得国家对外贸易中心签发的购汇许可 (AAD)。进口货物进入境内后，将被签发购汇结算授权 (ALD)。所有通过国家对外贸易中心进口的主要商品一般均要求取得无生产证明和生产不足证明。一般说来，其他进口 (通过使用经其他换汇渠道获得的外汇或进口商在境外银行存放的外汇支付价款的进口) 根据一般国际贸易实践进行。《国际商会国际贸易术语解释通则》被委内瑞拉公司广泛适于国际贸易。

因对等原则的适用，特定商品或某些国家的产品的进口可能受到限制。

尽管出口商是增值税的纳税主体，但适用税率为零。

委内瑞拉法律虑及退税机制，允许出口商就出口产品生产过程中使用原料直接交付的关税获得退税。但是，获得退税许可的程序繁杂，退税遭遇政府的长时间延误。

(四) 进出口商品检验检疫

某些商品的进口需要提前获得资质、许可、质量证明、授权、产地证明，如卫生部和／或农业部签发的卫生证明，或国防部签发的许可。进口健康产品、化妆品、食品需要在卫生部注册登记。许可程序虽然漫长 (大约 3～6 月)，但比较透明和常规。

大部分农产品进口要求食品部、农业部签发的卫生和植物检疫证 (SPS)。农业部签发动植物产品和半成品植物检疫证，食品部签发许可和执照，卫生部负责所有国内产品和进口加工产品的注册登记。

---

① 根据委内瑞拉《外国投资法》，外国投资受委内瑞拉法院管辖。法律人士讨论外国投资法是否排除了仲裁解决投资争端的可能性。
② 1966 年联合国大会成立的联合国国际贸易法委员会 (UNCITRAL)。
③ 2012 年委内瑞拉成为南美共同市场的正式成员。根据《南美共同市场公约》，委内瑞拉为适用南美共同市场的规则和共同关税，有 4 年过渡期限。

在原产地未注册登记的食品不得进口到委内瑞拉。

某些商品出口（如基本食物清单的某些产品、特定金属、战略物资、放射性产品及化肥）要求提前获得出口执照。某些其他商品（其中包括黄金、可可、咖啡、水果、蔬菜、花卉及某些药品）需要特别许可和/或注册登记。出口的其他要求还包括农产品的卫生许可、动物源产品卫生许可证、蔬菜植物检疫证书、原产地文件证明、该出口产品在国内有效生产的文件。

（五）海关管理

委内瑞拉在大部分委内瑞拉入境口岸实行海关电脑管理系统，在货物到达时评估、应付和交付进口税。

进口前，进口商必须根据委内瑞拉海关列表提交进口舱单，同时出示与进口商品所匹配的特定证明、许可证及执照。海关列表规定了与进口舱单一起提交财政部国家技术标准质量监督机构签发的登记证的义务。该义务只适用于委内瑞拉标准委员会强制标准、技术规范调整，或二者均调整的商品。海关列表也包括受标准委员会调控的进口商品和国家运输名录。

所有在入境口岸提示的商品必须在到港5天内向委内瑞拉税务局正式申报。海关规则明确规定收货人为货主并对所有海关费用负责。

只有经注册的海关代理机构有权进行海关程序。

进口要求将国外货物引入委内瑞拉海关辖区并最终使用或消费。例如，如果国外货物进入委内瑞拉海关辖区的期间只为一定时间段，这种操作将被归类为临时准入。①

外国商品国有化指外国商品引入委内瑞拉接受海关机构管辖的过程。这一过程的结果是，进口商品可以脱离海关辖区并在委内瑞拉使用或消费。外国商品国有化过程一般包括以下阶段：①货物到达委内瑞拉海关（作为到达的一部分，运输方必须通知收货人货物已经到达）；②海岸查验文件以确保所有海关申报支持文件正确完整；③实物和书面审查，其中包括确定适用于货物的法律制度（作为这个程序的一部分，海关对货物实质审查以便确认其性质、产地、状态、品质及价值与申报内容相符。作为审查结果，海关签发相应已支付关税、费、其他税的表格）；④支付关税、费、其他税；⑤对进口货物予以放行。所有符合上述外国商品国有化程序的进口货物转化成为国有货物。

委内瑞拉海关要求所有文件用西班牙语书写。上述文件一般要求提供：商业发票、提单货空运单、装箱单、产地证明及若需要，还需提供特别证书或许可。

进口需要交纳从价关税。关税根据适用于进口货物的海关估价准则确定，并在从价税的基础上征收（即：进口货物价值的一定比例）。此外，进口货物须按货物价值交付增值税及相应的关税、其他税，货物到达有权核定征收进口税的国家海关的主要辖区时应支付进口税。②

在原产国被补贴或者在委内瑞拉倾销的进口货物，根据反倾销法将被征收反倾销或补偿性关税。任何在委内瑞拉生产类似货物的人，可以要求反倾销和补贴委员会对进口货物进行调查。③

关税不适用于出口。然而，出口商必须遵守所有需要使用海关代理人的行政海关手续。矿物出口须获得运输证明。

四、劳动

（一）劳动法律法规概况

委内瑞拉劳工法保护劳动者，规定最低福利，保证劳动者权利不被剥夺或放弃，并强制适用于所有劳动关系。《劳动法》于2012年修订。

劳动事务中的主要法律框架包括：①《劳动法》；②《劳动法》下的实施细则；③《工作场所健

---

① 海关法和规则允许对临时进口货物，不收取关税或增值税。进口商必须向海关部门（国家税局）申请进口许可，提交特定信息，包括申请的原因、进口商的情况、进口货物的详细情况证明货物的使用和特性。
② 为避免因关税分类不当而遭受惩罚，进口商应在进口前从海关当局获得产品的适当关税分类。
③ 反倾销和补贴委员会如果确定存在倾销或导致或可能导致对类似产品的国内生产造成重大损害的补贴将征收反倾销或补偿性关税。

康与安全法》；④《工作场所健康与安全法》下的实施细则；⑤《劳动法》下关于对工作时间的规定。

雇佣关系受委内瑞拉劳动法律和条例、具体劳动合同、雇主实施的福利计划和相应的集体谈判协议的规定约束。

委内瑞拉政府自 2002 年以来实行劳工冻结政策，据此，不经劳工部事先授权，不得解雇雇员。虽然劳工冻结在理论上是暂时的，但国家行政部门自 2002 以来一直在不断续展该政策。最后一次延期是在 2015 年 12 月 28 日颁布的，为期 3 年。除高级管理人员外，劳工冻结涵盖所有雇员。

只有在特殊情况下，劳工部才允许解雇。因此，作为一般规则，在与雇员的协议中雇主必须保证通过提供额外的终止付款（除了法定福利）换取其雇员自愿离职。引起劳动合同终止的其他事项包括辞职、有原因辞职、不可抗力和协议终止。

在雇佣终止的情况下，雇员在大多数情况下有权获得：①遣散费（如有原因辞职，雇员有权领取双倍遣散费；②累积休假每日一天工资；③最后一个工作年度，每个假日一天工资；④应计未付假期奖金；⑤过去一年就业月份的假期奖金；⑥过去一年就业期间的利润分配；⑦根据公司福利和薪酬计划的其他累积福利。

《劳动法》规定了为委内瑞拉公司工作的外国人的数量限制。一般来说，雇用 10 名或更多雇员的公司至少有 90% 的工人是委内瑞拉公民，付给外籍工人的工资不得超过公司员工工资总额的 20%。

（二）外国人在当地工作规定

1. 工作许可

一个非委内瑞拉国民需要劳工部签发的工作签证和工作许可证才能在委内瑞拉工作。工作许可证和工作签证只能由雇主申请。下列人员不需要工作许可证：①从事国际科学项目研究的科学家；②与从事新闻活动的国际媒体的有关记者和其他雇员；③依据国际合作和技术援助条约提供服务的人员；④从事为期不满 90 天的科学或学术活动的专业人员和技术人员；⑤科学家、专业人员、技术人员和其他专门人员到委内瑞拉培训其他职工，或者进行为期不足 90 天的临时活动；⑥艺术家和职业运动员。

2. 申请程序

雇主必须先向委内瑞拉劳工部申请工作许可证，然后从委内瑞拉驻原籍国大使馆领事处申请工作签证。

雇主必须提交：①工作许可申请表；②至少尚有 6 个月有效期的雇员护照复印件；③经委内瑞拉公证机构公证的聘用机构签发的聘用函件（也就是说，聘用机构总部必须在委内瑞拉）[①]；④西班牙语简历；⑤证明申请人专业培训或专业资格的文件；⑥医疗证明；⑦刑事背景检查证明。

劳工部可要求提供其他文件以支持雇主的申请。

3. 社会保险

由于非委内瑞拉国民有权享有与国民相同的权利，雇主须在社会保障机构登记外籍雇员。

（三）出入境管理

1. 签证类型

与外国雇员有关的主要签证类型是：

（1）商务签证（TR-L 签证），针对计划进入委内瑞拉从事商业、金融或其他盈利性法律活动或与其经营业务相关交易行为的非移民个体商人、高管、公司代表、微型企业家；

（2）工作签证（TR-L 签证），它允许外国公民在委内瑞拉受聘工作。为确立雇佣合同关系，雇主必须在委内瑞拉合法存在（须在委内瑞拉注册设立并注册登记）。

所涉国家如果是委内瑞拉参加的规定签证免签的条约或公约的成员，签证会有不同要求。

---

① 该聘用函件必须注明雇佣合同期限、雇员遣返成本、职位、工作时间、薪金和劳动福利。该聘用函件还必须指出，外籍员工将在整个雇佣合同中培训委内瑞拉工人，雇佣合同将受委内瑞拉法律管辖。

2. 出入境限制

商务签证的有效期为 1 年,允许持续停留 180 天,多次往返。这种签证必须在委内瑞拉驻原籍国大使馆领事处申请。

工作签证的期限为 1 年,允许永久停留相同期限,多次往返。这种签证必须在委内瑞拉驻原籍国大使馆领事处申请。

(四) 工会与劳工组织

根据《劳动法》,工人和雇主有权组织和成立工会。建立工会至少需要 20 名职工。根据委内瑞拉劳动法律,工会有两种基本类型:①公司范围工会,该等工会由一个公司内职工组织设立;②行业工会,该等工会由一个行业内职工组织设立,不论职工属于哪个公司及承担什么职务。在某些情况下,工人可以行使集体谈判协议的权利,并诉诸集体行动,包括罢工。

雇主应设立职工理事会。职工必须选举 3 至 7 名雇员组成职工理事会。在这些成员中,必须有 1 名妇女、1 名 15 岁至 35 岁的人士和 1 名国家民兵成员。

(五) 劳动争议

劳动争议在委内瑞拉很普遍。委内瑞拉的劳工法律和法规旨在保护雇员,法院和当局一般都同情雇员。

委内瑞拉劳工法律和法规给予职工的保护包括:①委内瑞拉政府制定了最低工资标准;②劳工冻结,根据相关规定,非因经主管劳工当局事先认可的原因,不得对雇员解雇、降职或调转;③劳工部可以反对裁员;④解雇职工需要支付额外的赔偿金。

员工遣散费索付时效规定为自终止雇佣之日起 10 年,其他福利自终止雇佣之日起 5 年;工伤事故和职业病要求的法定时效为自事故或疾病确认后起 5 年。

员工可诉诸劳动法院或劳动监察部门解决劳资纠纷。

五、知识产权

(一) 知识产权法律法规概况

在委内瑞拉,商标和专利的所有权、使用和注册主要由:①《保护工业产权巴黎公约》(1883 年);②世界贸易组织《与贸易有关的知识产权协定》(TRIPs)(1994 年);③委内瑞拉《工业产权法》(1956 年) 调整。

版权受 1993 委内瑞拉《版权法》(1993 年)、版权法规、《保护文学与艺术作品伯尔尼公约》及《世界版权公约》保护。

(二) 申请专利

专利在知识产权自主服务 (SAPI) 系统注册,该机构受财政部监督。发明、实用新型和外观设计在委内瑞拉受到保护。发明、实用新型和外观设计专利权被授权的期限为 5 年或 10 年 (根据申请人的请求)。专利申请向知识产权自主服务提出,由其审查,其后发表在委内瑞拉《工业产权公报》以便第三方提出异议。如无人提出异议 (或异议被驳回),则在有关行政程序完成后予以核准。

(三) 注册商标

商标注册也向知识产权自主服务提出。与专利申请相同,经审查后发表在委内瑞拉《工业产权公报》以便第三方提出异议。如无人提出异议则授予商标注册权。商标权期限为 15 年,期满以 15 年为时长延长。

(四) 保护知识产权措施

商标权和专利权可以通过民事和刑事诉讼程序获得保护。

六、环境保护

(一)环境保护主管部门

环境部是主要负责监督环境保护的机构。地方市政当局在其相应管辖区内拥有一定环境执法权限。

(二)环境保护法律法规概况

委内瑞拉环境保护法律法规包括：①《环保法》及其细则；②《环境刑法》；③《危险物质法》；④《社会、自然和技术风险管理法》；⑤《植物多样性管理法》；⑥《水资源法》；⑦《水资源与空气质量法》；⑧包含《水体和液体流出物或排放物的分类和质量控制条例》的第883号法令；⑨包含《空气质量和空气污染管制条例》的第638号法令；⑩环境管理部门颁布的条例。

此外，委内瑞拉还签署了五十多项多边环境保护条约，包括：①《保护臭氧层维也纳公约》(1985年)；②《关于消耗臭氧层物质的蒙特利尔议定书》(1989年)；③《联合国气候变化框架公约》(1994年)、《京都议定书》(2005年)，及《关于气候变化的巴黎协定》(2016年)；④《石油污染防备、应对和合作国际公约》(1994年)；⑤《关于在大加勒比区域打击石油泄漏合作议定书》(1985年)；⑥《西半球自然保护和野生生物保护公约》(1940年)。

根据环境法律，在城市或农村地区发展的任何项目都必须遵守足以对环境造成退化活动的环境评估程序。这种程序要求公司或出资人就项目的社会、文化或环境影响评估(EIA)[①]进行准备。根据环境影响评估分析、环境项目的位置和对环境的干预或影响程度，环境部可以发布三种不同的环境授权：①占有土地授权(AOT)；②影响自然资源授权(AARN)；③一个对环境和社会文化影响研究的技术认证(也被称为AT)。环境授权将规定适用于项目所有阶段的条款和条件。

在批准的项目实施前，需要向环境部提交履约保证金，办理民事责任和对可能发生的环境事故赔偿保险。

单位和个人参与使用、处理或生产有害物质、材料或废料，或参与对空气排放气体和颗粒，向河流、湖泊或污水管网排放废液，或涉及危险物质和危险废物的活动，在参与活动前必须向环境部对环境构成损害事项注册处(RACDA)注册登记。

对向空气中排放气体和颗粒活动负有责任的公司必须遵守《技术规则》中规定的空气质量限值，并按环境部的授权，每年或每两年提供一次排放量读数。

向河流、湖泊或污水管网进行液体排放的公司必须调整排放量，以符合技术法规中规定的质量参数，通常每3个月需要提供排放量读数。

处理危险材料和废物的公司必须遵守《危险材料和废物环境法》中规定的义务，包括：①制订使用、储存、处理和处置危险废物，减少生产的合规措施计划；②制订应急计划，防止和应对与危险废物有关的事件或事故；③控制危险废物的数量和种类、存在和储存风险。

对噪音负有责任的公司必须将噪音排放量调整到相关技术法规所规定的限度之内。相关法律对于固定和移动源产生的噪音污染均有技术规定。

关于环境的犯罪，《环境刑法》规定对环境和自然资源造成不利影响的行为或不作为作出刑事和民事处罚(罚款和监禁)。如果认定公司及职员、董事或股东参与造成环境损害，可以对其实施制裁。

危害环境罪包括：①危害生物多样性犯罪；②使水资源、土壤、地形景观及自然与野生生物退化变质、损坏、毁损等犯罪；③危害环境质量的犯罪(大气、固体废物、有害物质、放射性物质和噪声污染、汽油等运输过程中对水域的污染等)。

(三)环境保护评估

尽管拥有一个详尽的环境法律体系，委内瑞拉环境保护部门环境执法却是缓慢而且不系统的。许多环境法规已经过时，达不到国际标准。

一些最关键的环境问题包括未经授权的采矿作业、石油污染水和土壤、城市和工业污染、非法砍

---

① 根据《宪法》第129条的规定，对生态系统足以造成损害的所有活动都必须进行事前环境和社会文化影响评估。

伐森林、废物和垃圾填埋管理、将污水排入湖泊和河流以及城市和工业废料处理等。

七、争议解决

(一) 争议解决方式及机构

1. 诉讼

委内瑞拉法院系统是联邦体系。委内瑞拉没有州法院。最高级别法院是委内瑞拉最高法院，由6个庭组成：宪法庭、社会事务上诉庭、民事上诉庭、刑事庭、选举事务庭和政治行政庭。每个庭由5名法官组成，但宪法法庭由7名法官组成。

民事和商业纠纷由初审法院审理，就初审法院的判决可以向二审法院提出上诉。有些案件如上诉案件或有关宪法保护案件可由最高法院审理。

委内瑞拉民商事诉讼按照《民事诉讼法》进行。商业案件是以书面形式进行的。诉求、答辩、质证程序、证据阶段和动议均以书面文件呈示。在委内瑞拉商事业案件中，除非法官决定口头听证或动议，否则没有听证程序。法官可以签发临时救济决定，即判前措施、禁令或扣押。

非委内瑞拉管辖权的选择是合法和有效的，但涉及在委内瑞拉境内的不动产、家庭事务和其他事项的争端除外。

2. 仲裁、和解和调解

根据《国际私法》和《商事仲裁法》的规定，仲裁条款及由此形成的仲裁裁决在委内瑞拉可强制执行。

委内瑞拉是联合国《承认及执行外国仲裁裁决公约》(又称《纽约公约》)的缔约国，该公约于1958年在纽约联合国总部通过。

外国仲裁员在境外作出的仲裁裁决可以根据《委内瑞拉商业仲裁法》第48条在委内瑞拉法院针对仲裁对方（包括个人）提起执行，法院对外国仲裁裁决的理由不予过问的前提是：①外国仲裁裁决仅涉及私法或商法问题；②外国仲裁裁决与委内瑞拉境内不动产的利益无关；③提交仲裁的事项不涉及禁止和解的事项，也不涉及违反委内瑞拉公共政策基本原则的事项；④仲裁裁决在执行程序之前未被中止、废除或取代；⑤合法组成的仲裁庭就仲裁程序正式送达被申请人，有足够的时间在仲裁讼程序中抗辩，且通常得到程序上的保障确保其能够行使抗辩权；⑥仲裁庭的组成和仲裁程序符合仲裁地有关管辖的法律规定。

两个主要地方仲裁中心是委内瑞拉仲裁和调解商务中心（CEDCA）及加拉加斯商会仲裁中心（CCC）。

调解与和解是宪法承认和鼓励的有效替代纠纷解决方法。CEDCA与CCC规定提供调解或和解程序规则，使冲突各方在诉诸仲裁之前以友好方式解决争端。

(二) 适用法律

合同受缔约方协议、委内瑞拉法律的强制性规则和《民法典》和《贸易法》中未被缔约方协议取代的规定调整。选择适用外国法一般情况下合法并具有法律约束力。根据《民法典》，合同的执行和解释必须遵循善意原则。

八、其他

(一) 反商业贿赂

1. 反商业贿赂法律法规概况

委内瑞拉的反贿赂法律法规包括：①《反腐败法》；②《反有组织犯罪和资助恐怖主义罪法》；③委内瑞拉《刑法典》。委内瑞拉也是联合国《反腐败公约》（UNCAC）、《美洲反腐败公约》、联合国《打击跨国有组织犯罪公约》的缔约国。

反贿赂法是委内瑞拉反腐败规定的主要来源。法律的目的是为了维护公共财产和保障公共资源的正确和透明的管理。

反贿赂法律适用于个人、公共和私人的法律实体、地方公职人员和社区组织。

反贿赂法律对行贿、尝试受贿、非法敛财、贪污以及其他可能造成公共财产损失的行为给予刑罚处罚。贿赂外国官员的行为也会受到反贿赂法的惩罚（虽然其下没有定义"外国官员"）。作为联合国《反腐败公约》的缔约国，委内瑞拉将协助国外反腐机关调查外国贿赂案件。

2. 反商业贿赂主管部门

国家反腐败局创建于2014年11月，是负责实施反贿赂法的机构，监督公共实体或私人实体遵守反贿赂法的情况，调查腐败犯罪。反贪局在防止、打击和调查腐败行为方面与总审计长办公室（GCO）、总检察长办公室（GPPO）、国家有组织犯罪和资助恐怖主义局密切合作。总检察长办公室负责起诉和处理刑事案件（包括腐败案件）。

3. 惩处措施

根据反贿赂法惩处的一些最相关的犯罪行为包括：

（1）贿赂委内瑞拉公职人员（行贿），可处以1至4年监禁，并可获得高达贿赂额50%的贿赂罚金；

（2）委内瑞拉公职人员接收贿赂（收受贿赂），可处以3至7年监禁，并可获得高达贿赂额50%的贿赂罚金；

（3）行贿未遂（贿赂公职人员不成功），可判处6个月至2年监禁；

（4）贿赂外国公职人员（承诺或实际向外国官员提供好处或不当得利，以换取其履行职责的行为（或不履行），可处以6至12年监禁；

（5）贪污公共资产，可判处3至10年的监禁，并处贪污额20%到60%的罚金。

（二）工程承包

1. 许可制度

作为一般原则，为政府机构采购货物、提供服务和完成工程的合同须遵守：①购置公共物品、服务和工程的法律规定；②《政府采购法》及其细则的规定。为本部分的目的，笔者使用术语"政府机构"用以突出指代委内瑞拉政府、国有机构和国家直接或间接持有控股的合资企业。

根据《政府采购法》，政府机构获取货物、工程或服务必须选用《政府采购法》规定的方式，与下述有关或与之订立的合同除外：①专业和金融服务；②不动产取得；③艺术、文化或科学作品取得；④承包商与政府实体之间的商业或战略联盟；⑤政府机构需要的重要基本公共服务（电力、煤气、电话、互联网）；⑥公共部门、国有公司和集体；⑦紧急状态时获取货物、服务或工程；⑧粮食、药物和基本必要服务购买；⑨利用政府机构小额现金购买货物和服务；⑩为国家安全而购置货物、服务和工程等，这些采购合同可以直接由政府实体最高权力部门授予。

此外，在国际合作条约框架内订立的合同、与根据国际协定组建的公司订立的合同、聘用合同、不动产租赁合同及有关体育、艺术、科学或学术赞助等合同不受《政府采购法》的调整。

一般而言，希望向政府机构提供货物、完成工程或提供服务的公司必须在委内瑞拉国家承包商登记处（RNC）[①]登记并取得资格。有些情况下无需取得资格。登记必须每年更新，但登记不应适用于上述不受政府采购法调整的合同。

公司参加国际公开招标、无需选用规定方式的采购合同以及通过直接邀请被挑选的非注册公司和个人等不需要资质。

2. 禁止领域

外国投资受限制领域清单见"市场准入的标准和检验"部分。

[①] 国家承包商登记处根据评估承包商财务能力的特定公式决定是否授予承包商参与政府采购合同的资质。

3. 招投标

政府机构使用下列方法之一选择承包商：

（1）公开招标

邀请所有有兴趣的当地或外国实体或个人参加公开招标程序。在以下情况下政府机构必须采用公开招标或国际公开招标方式选择承包商：①采购货物时，货物的估计合同金额超过20 000个纳税单位；②采购服务时估算合同额大于30 000个纳税单位；③采购工程时估算合同额大于50 000个纳税单位。①

（2）限制投标

根据技术、财务和法律能力，直接邀请至少5名承包商投标的一种选择方法。在以下情况下政府机构可以采用限制招标选择办法：①采购货物时货物的估计合同金额大于5 000个纳税单位，但少于20 000个纳税单位；②采购服务时估计合同额大于10 000个纳税单位但少于30 000个纳税单位；③采购工程时估计合同额大于20 000个纳税单位但少于50 000个纳税单位。

（3）价格协商

小额合同要求至少向三个承包商询价。下述情况下政府机构可以采用价格协商：①采购货物时货物的估计合同金额小于5 000个纳税单位；②采购服务时估计合同额小于10 000个纳税单位；③采购工程时估计合同额小于20 000个纳税单位。

（4）直接签署

例外情况下，无论合同金额如何，只要政府实体的最高权力部门认为合理，政府机构有权在如下情况下直接签署合同，包括：

- 采购政府机构连续生产所需的货物、服务或工程，使用其他选择方法造成延误可能会严重影响政府机构连续生产；
- 当某一特定的技术、服务或工程的技术条件不适合竞争或需要使用这种选择方法；
- 由于存在承包商同意投标或政府机构邀请投标的特殊条件，无法使用其他选择方法；
- 已证实的紧急情况下；
- 对经提前终止合同的工程、货物或服务采购，使用其他选择方法可能对政府实体不利；
- 其他选择方法可能泄露政府机实体密或商业战略的货物、服务或工作的采购。

（三）石油

1. 石油法律制度简介

勘探、开发、提炼、工业化、运输、储存和商业化碳氢化合物及其副产品以及这些活动所需的工程受委内瑞拉《碳氢化合物法》的管辖。与石油有关的气态烃的提取（称为"伴生气体"）也受碳氢化合物定律的调整。

根据《碳氢化合物法》，与寻找油气储藏及其开采、收集和初始运输和储存有关的所有活动（上游活动或"主要活动"）均保留给委内瑞拉政府，政府可以：①直接；②通过全资国有实体；③通过委内瑞拉政府拥有超过50%股权控股的合资公司（EMS）进行上述活动。

外国投资者只能通过在委内瑞拉政府直接或间接拥有多数利益控股的合资公司中占有少数股份参与上游或初始活动。外国投资者一般有权在董事会中拥有少数股东代表，在股东层面上通常享有一定的否决权。参与委内瑞拉政府拥有超过50%股权的控股合资公司，需要获得多个政府机构批准证书，而且政府一般需要向政府支付签约金并接受某些其他附加特殊条件。

合资公司必须将其生产的碳氢化合物出售给委内瑞拉石油公司（PDVSA）的关联公司，而不是自己使用，除非：①碳氢化合物作为许可费交付给国家；②委内瑞拉石油公司或其关联公司不接受的伴生气。合资公司可以直接在国际市场销售升级后的原油（合资公司在奥里诺科重油带项目生产的）。②

合资公司拥有国有公司的资质，因此必须遵守一些公法领域法律法规，包括政府采购法律法规、预算法、融资法、反贿赂法、金融管制法规等。

---

① 纳税单位是由委内瑞拉国家税局确定一个衡量值。
② 奥里诺科重油带位于委内瑞拉的奥里诺科河北部的一片区域，此处拥有世界最大的石油储藏。

由委内瑞拉政府或国有独资实体拥有的用于在委内瑞拉精炼碳氢化合物和主要运输石油产品和天然气的所有设施和现有工程，其扩建和修改都保留给国家。然而，天然烃和烃类副产品的新炼制活动可：①由委内瑞拉政府直接进行；②由委内瑞拉政府通过全资国有实体进行；③通过委内瑞拉政府直接或间接参与及私营部门以任何比例参与（这可能包括EMS）的混合公司进行；④由私营公司进行。[①]

天然碳氢化合物的商业化，以及通过总统令由国家保留经销权的碳氢化合物产品的国内或国际销售只能由国有实体进行。液体燃料的商业化也保留给国家。未经总统法令由国家保留经销权的其他碳氢化合物产品的商业销售可以由私营公司进行。

2. 石油税制

下文概述了委内瑞拉适用于包括合资公司在内的石油公司的税收，在前述税收部分之外：

- 提取碳氢化合物总量30%的许可税，可以用实物或现金支付，由委内瑞拉政府选择。对熟油藏或从奥利诺科河开采的超重原油，委内瑞拉政府可将30%降低至20%。《暴利税法》规定许可税的计算价格最多不超过每桶80美元。一个合资公司设立的特殊条件可造成额外许可税。

- 以每平方公里100个税率单位或按比例计算的地表税（这项税是根据非生产特许区确定的，5年内每年增加2%，以后每年增加5%）。

- 相当于其经营过程中消耗的每立方米油气产品价值10%的燃油消费税，以销售给最终消费者的价格计算。如果该产品未在国内市场销售，则由石油部核算。

- 一般消费税税率介于最终消费者支付价格的30%至50%之间，适用于在委内瑞拉国内市场销售的每公升碳氢化合物衍生产品；消费税税率每年确定；该税在来源上扣缴。

- 以从油田开采的所有液态碳氢化合物的价值的1/3计算（与计算许可税的基础相同）开采税。纳税人可从需要交付的本税款项中扣除已付许可税（或作为额外许可税或每年应支付的款项之预付款，但只能扣除支付的上期预付款）。在某些情况下，委内瑞拉政府可以降低这一税收至20%。《暴利税法》规定开采税的计算价格最多不超过每桶80美元。

- 按从委内瑞拉港口出口的所有碳氢化合物的价值（以这些碳氢化合物的销售价格为基础）0.1%计收的出口登记税。《暴利税法》规定出口登记税的计算价格最多不超过每桶80美元。

- 从事开采碳氢化合物（不包括非关联气体）和相关活动的公司，如炼油和运输业，按净收入的50%的税率交纳所得税；然而，专门从事提炼碳氢化合物或升级重质和超重质原油的公司按正常的公司税率（即最高税率为34%）交纳。鉴于这两个独立的税收制度的存在，政府和外国企业正在考虑通过形成一个超稠油生产合资公司（适用50%的石油税制）和一个炼制营销的合资公司（适用34%普通税率）的分体商业模式（不是一个集成的项目）架构某些奥里诺科重油带项目，以提高工程经济效益。对一定的奥里诺科重油带项目，政府已同意一个有利的扣除、摊销和亏损递延所得税制度。

- 根据委内瑞拉国家预算价格与委内瑞拉石油篮子国际平均价格的差额而制定的针对"非常"和"过高"价格的暴利税。这个税是由销售天然或升级的液态烃和副产品的出口商和向委内瑞拉石油公司及其关联公司出售天然或升级液态烃和副产品的合资公司交纳。然而，《暴利税法》规定了下列情况下可以免除纳税义务：①向委内瑞拉石油公司及其关联属公司出售天然或升级液态烃和副产品的合资公司从事新油田开发项目，或增加石油部宣布的正在进行的项目中的开采计划，但合资公司尚未收回这些项目的总投资；②在国际合作或融资协定框架内的出口。

- 合资公司设立的特殊条件通常要求支付相当于1%税前利润的社会投资费以及支付特许费、税款和其他税款后，财政支出达不到毛利润50%以上时触发的所谓的"影子税"，因此，合资公司必须支付这个数值和财政支出之间的差额。"影子税"每年支付一次，然而，对某些奥里诺科重油带项目，政府认可从早期生产到生产升级开始的积累"影子税"。

- 石油公司不是市政商业税的纳税人，但某些城市有时会试图对它们征税。

- 某些奥里诺科重油带项目，如果不能在一定时间内收回投资，委内瑞拉政府同意特许费和税款的减收并给予额外的税收优惠。

---

① 提炼天然碳氢化合物需要获得委内瑞拉石油部颁发的许可证。精炼许可证的最高期限为25年，最长可延长15年。

Venezuela

Authors: Fulvio Italiani, Roberto Mas
Translators: Tony (Xiangdong) Lai, Xu Zhihui

I. Overview

A. Political

The Bolivarian Republic of Venezuela ("Venezuela" or the "Republic") is a federal republic situated on the northern (Caribbean) coast of South America. Venezuela is divided into 23 states, the Capital District, the federal dependencies and more than 300 municipalities. The city of Caracas is Venezuela's capital, its largest city and the seat of government. Venezuela's estimated population in 2016 was 31.5 million and the official language is Spanish.

The Venezuelan government is divided into three levels: federal, state and municipal. The political structure of Venezuela is set forth in the Constitution enacted in 1999 and amended in 2009. At the national level, the government is divided into executive, legislative, judicial, civic and electoral branches.

The president of Venezuela is the head of state, head of the national executive branch, and the commander-in-chief of Venezuela's armed forces. The president is elected by universal suffrage for a term of six years, and can be reelected for unlimited terms. All executive powers are vested in the president. The president is entitled to: (a) veto laws passed by the Venezuelan National Assembly; (b) issue decrees with the same force of the laws issued by the National Assembly (known as law decrees or decretos leyes), if so authorized by the legislative branch; (c) issue regulations (reglamentos) which further develop the provisions of laws or law decrees.

The other authorities of the executive branch are the executive vice president, the ministers, the Attorney General and the heads of certain agencies of the national executive branch.[①] The executive vice president and the ministers are appointed and removed by the president and directly or indirectly report to the president. The president, the executive vice president and the ministers from time to time meet in the council of ministers (Consejo de Ministros) to approve certain matters.

The national legislative branch is vested in the National Assembly (Asamblea Nacional). The National Assembly has only one chamber, and its members (diputados) are elected by universal suffrage for terms of five years, and may be reelected for unlimited five-year terms. The National Assembly is empowered to enact laws, which require the promulgation of the Venezuelan president and its publication in the official gazette to become effective. In May 2017, the Venezuelan president called for the election of a National Constituent Assembly (Asamblea Nacional Constituyente or "ANC") to revise the Constitution. The ANC is entrusted with the power to transform the State, create a new legal framework and draft a new constitution. On July 30, 2017, 545 constituent members where elected to the ANC. After its installation in August 2017, the ANC issued a decree proclaiming the supremacy of the ANC and of its legislative acts, and subordinating all other entities and branches of government to its constitutional authority.

The judicial branch is vested in the Venezuelan Supreme Tribunal (Tribunal Supremo de Justicia) and in various lower tribunals. The Supreme Tribunal is the final court of appeals. It has the power to void laws, regulations, and other acts or decisions of the executive or legislative branches that conflict with the Constitution or the laws. Justices of the Supreme Tribunal are appointed by the legislative branch for twelve-year terms. The Supreme Tribunal has six chambers, including the Constitutional Chamber in charge of interpreting the Constitution. The Venezuelan court system is a national system; there are no state courts, but there are national courts sitting in each respective state. The jurisdictions of courts are divided by subject matter: civil, commercial, labor, tax, administrative, criminal and family, among others.

The civic branch is comprised of three entities: (a) the Ombusman (Defensoría del Pueblo), which promotes and monitors the protection of human rights; (b) the Prosecutor's Office (Ministerio Público), which promotes the fair administration of justice and judicial processes; (c) the Comptroller (Contraloría General de la República), which monitors and controls the administration of the Government's assets, revenues and public debt. The head of

---

① The Attorney General (Procurador General de la República) is the chief legal counsel of the Republic.

each of these entities is appointed by the legislative branch for seven-year terms.

The electoral branch is responsible for monitoring electoral processes, campaign financing and campaign advertising. The electoral branch operates through the National Electoral Council. The head and board of directors of the National Electoral Council are appointed by the legislative branch.

At the state and municipal levels, the government is divided in the executive (governor and mayor) and legislative branches (state legislative and municipal councils). States have virtually no taxing power but they may create taxes on non-precious metals and minerals that are not reserved to the State. Municipalities are empowered to issue local laws (ordinances or ordenanzas) and levy business tax on gross income and to approve construction projects in cities and other population centers.

Venezuela's Central Bank (Banco Central de Venezuela or BCV) is the country's monetary authority. The Central Bank, together with the Finance Minister, sets key monetary policy guidelines and regulations. The Central Bank is in charge of printing the currency, holding and managing Venezuela's foreign currency reserves, setting the official foreign exchange rate together with the Finance Minister, regulating interest rates, and setting local bank's reserve requirements.

B. Economic

The Venezuelan official currency is the Bolivar. Venezuela has strict exchange control restrictions that significantly limit the ability to convert local currency into foreign currency. The purchase of foreign currency can only be made through the systems set up by the foreign exchange regulations (convenios cambiarios) issued by the Central Bank and the Finance Minister. The reference forex rate is published daily by the Central Bank.

Venezuela, a member of the Organization of the Petroleum Exporting Countries (OPEC), is one of the world's largest oil producers and exporters. As of December 31, 2016, Venezuela had estimated proven crude oil reserves totaling 302 billion barrels (including an estimated 261 billion barrels of heavy and extra-heavy crude oil in the Orinoco Oil Belt).[1] All of Venezuela's hydrocarbon reserves are owned by the Republic. The country's crude oil exploration, production and exportation is in charge of Petróleos de Venezuela, S.A.(PDVSA) and its subsidiaries, the state-owned oil and gas conglomerate and the single largest contributor to Venezuela's GDP. Venezuela's economy heavily depends on oil revenues.

PDVSA is the holding company for a group of oil and gas companies. PDVSA is the largest vertically integrated oil company in Latin America and one of the largest vertically integrated oil companies in the world. Under the Venezuelan hydrocarbons law, every activity relating to the exploration and exploitation of hydrocarbons and their derivatives is reserved to the Venezuelan government. Private oil companies may engage in oil projects through a minority participation in joint ventures (empresas mixtas) where PDVSA directly or indirectly holds a majority equity interest. PDVSA and its subsidiaries are under the supervision of the Petroleum Ministry (Ministerio del Poder Popular de Petróleo).

The Corporación Venezolana de Guayana (CVG) is an autonomous institute created back in 1960. CVG is a non-operating holding entity of a group of companies engaged in the aluminum, iron, steel, gold and other industries. CVG's mission is to sustainably exploit the abundant reserves of bauxite, iron, and gold, as well as other precious metals in, and to promote the overall development of, the Guayana region.

The Fondo de Desarrollo Nacional (FONDEN) is a national development fund created by the Republic to finance infrastructure, social and development projects in Venezuela. Fonden is financed via contributions made by the Central Bank. Fonden also receives contributions paid under the Venezuelan oil windfall tax law, pursuant to which oil exporters in Venezuela (PDVSA and its subsidiaries, including the oil joint venture companies) must pay a special contribution levied over the price of the oil. Amounts deposited in Fonden are normally used to fund major infrastructure projects in all areas of the Venezuelan economy.

On February 2016, the government created the National Strategic Development Zone "Arco Minero del Orinoco" ("Orinoco Mining Belt"), for the purpose of boosting the country's production of gold and other minerals such as bauxite, copper, and diamond. The Orinoco Mining Belt is an area of approximately 112,000 square kilometers, located south of the Orinoco river. The Ministry for Mining Development (Ministerio del Poder Popular de Desarrollo Minero Ecológico) is the entity in charge of mining activities in the Orinoco Mining Belt.

On February 2018, in an effort to promote an "independent, transparent digital economy, open to direct citizen participation", the Venezuelan government launch an oil-backed sovereign cryptocurrency known as the "Petro". The Petro will operate on a blockchain platform and will be exchanged from person to person or from portfolio to portfolio. The Petro will be used for the purchase goods or services, and will be redeemable for fiat money and

---

[1] Bolivarian Republic of Venezuela.Exhibit D to the Annual Report on Form 18-K to the United States Securities and Exchange Commission for the fiscal year ended December 31, 2016.

other cryptocurrencies through digital currency exchanges.

Venezuela's economy contracted 16.5% in 2016.① GDP is projected to fall around 15% in 2018 (a cumulative GDP decline of almost 50% since 2013).② PDVSA's crude oil production has been declining over the last years. Production averaged 1.6 million bpd in January 2018, compared to an average 1.9 million bpd in 2017, 2.2 million bpd in 2016 and 2.4 million bpd in 2015.③ Foreign exchange reserves held by the Central Bank as of November 30, 2017 averaged US$9.7 billion, compared to US$22.1 billion in December 31, 2014. For the year ended December 31, 2016, the overall balance of payments recorded a deficit of US$6.8 billion.④

The Venezuelan Government is responsible for the supply of most basic public services, including electricity, water, domestic and industrial LPG, health and education, and is also a major importer and distributor of food products. The Republic directly or indirectly controls or owns 50% or more of the equity of a significant number of public entities and corporations operating in various sectors and industries of the Venezuelan economy, including hydrocarbons, mining, telecommunications, food, transportation, and automobile. Each Venezuelan state-owned company is under the supervision of a minister (ministro de adscripción o tutela).

C. Legal

Venezuela is a civil law country, meaning that laws and regulations take preference over court precedents. Except for certain decisions rendered by the Constitutional Chamber of the Supreme Tribunal, Venezuelan court decisions are not binding.

The Venezuelan regulatory framework is set forth in: (a) the Constitution; (b) the laws enacted by the legislative branch and the law-decrees issued by the Venezuelan president; (c) the regulations issued by the Venezuelan president; (d) the resolutions and other provisions of general application issued by the ministries or other officers of the national executive branch.⑤

The general rules applicable to business and contracts are set forth in the Venezuelan civil code (Código Civil) and the code of commerce (Código de Comercio). Overall, the provisions of the civil code and the code of commerce can be superseded or modified by contract, unless the matter constitutes Venezuelan public policy. This means that contracts in Venezuela are generally enforceable in accordance with their own terms unless a provision in a contract is contrary to Venezuelan public policy.

D. The Status and Direction of the Cooperation with Chinese Enterprises

Diplomatic relations between Venezuela and the People's Republic of China ("China") date back to 1974.

China is one of the most important strategic, economic and trading partners of Venezuela. China and Venezuela have concluded a significant number of cooperation agreements and memorandums of understanding for the development of specific projects in areas such as energy, petroleum, technology, trade, infrastructure, agriculture, education, culture and sports.

In 2001, China and Venezuela signed the memorandum of understanding for the creation of the Mixed Venezuela-China High Level Committee, in charge of the formulation, execution and monitoring of cooperation projects, programs and proposals between the two countries. Since its formation, the committee has met regularly in Venezuela and China to evaluate the progress made in the active projects, sometimes sign additional cooperation instruments, and debate new investment opportunities. In 2007, China and Venezuela signed agreements for the creation of a joint investment fund known as the Sino-Venezuelan Joint Fund (Fondo Financiamiento Conjunto Chino-Venezolano), to finance socio-economic projects in several economic areas in Venezuela through a credit facility in the aggregate amount of US$4.0 billion.⑥

---

① Bolivarian Republic of Venezuela, Annual Report, Exhibit D.
② Alejandro Werner, "Latin America and the Caribbean in 2018: An Economic Recovery in the Making", IMF Blog, January 25, 2018.
③ OPEC's Monthly Oil Market Report for February 2018 and January 2016.
④ Bolivarian Republic of Venezuela, Annual Report, Exhibit D.
⑤ The Venezuelan legal framework also includes the state laws and the municipal ordinances.
⑥ Other agreements include: (a) the 2009 cooperation agreements in the areas of crude oil, agriculture and telecommunications; (b) the 2010 and 2011 joint venture agreements to develop heavy crude oil in the Venezuelan Orinoco Belt; (c) the 2011 agreement for a US$403 million loan to improve Venezuela's primary aluminum smelters; (d) the 2013 agreements to create a mining map and plan for the development of Las Cristinas gold project; (e) the 2015 agreements for the construction of a factory for medium and heavy trucks, a factory for tire manufacturing, and the expansion of the Orinoquia telecommunications joint venture; (f) the 2016 agreements to increase crude oil production and trade in petroleum products with China, and form a new joint venture to develop a refinery in China to process Venezuelan crude oil; (g) the 2016 agreements to increase crude oil production in Venezuela and trade in petroleum products with China; (h) the 2017 cooperation agreements to boost production of iron ore, bauxite and aluminum; (i) the 2017 agreements for an aggregate of US$15 billion loan facilities from China, for general economic support and financing of crude oil projects.

China and Venezuela are parties to a comprehensive treaty for the avoidance of double taxation.

The economic relation and cooperation between both countries has grown significantly in the last two decades. In 2015, China accounted for 16.7% of Venezuela's total exports and 18.5% of its total imports,[1] compared to 8.1% and 13.6% respectively in 2013.[2] In the last decade, China has provided financings to Venezuela in excess of US$50 billion.

II. Investment

A. Market Access

a. Department Supervising Investment

The Venezuelan Foreign Trade Ministry (Ministerio del Poder Popular para el Comercio Exterior e Inversión Internacional) is the entity in charge of centralizing the registration of foreign investments made into Venezuelan companies, as well as technical assistance, distribution and technology transfer agreements. For certain areas, such as energy, mining, banking and telecommunications, the entity responsible of registering foreign investments is the ministry of the corresponding area (for instance, the Petroleum Ministry for oil projects, the Finance Ministry for banking and insurance).

The Foreign Trade Ministry is in charge of: (a) promoting foreign investments and the transfer of technology into Venezuela; (b) approving, rejecting, updating and recording foreign investments and technological transfer agreements; (c) organizing, managing and centralizing the registry of foreign investments (registro de inversion extranjera); (d) auditing and exercising control over foreign investments and technological transfer agreements; and (e) issuing opinions regarding the repatriation of foreign investments.

b. Laws and Regulations of Investment Industry

Foreign investment in Venezuela is governed by the foreign investment law (Ley de Inversión Extranjera Productiva) and regulations thereunder. The main purposes of the foreign investment law are: (a) to promote productive foreign investments; (b) to guarantee that foreign investments bring technology into Venezuela, replace imports and promote exports; (c) to create decent, fair and productive jobs; (d) to increase and improve access to foreign financing, foreign currency and new markets; (e) to attract foreign investments able to generate foreign currency in non-traditional areas of the Venezuelan economy.

Foreign investments must comply with the conditions set forth in the foreign investment law. Only investments in excess of Eur 800,000 or CNY 6,500,000 (or their equivalent in another foreign currency) are eligible to obtain foreign investment registration. Foreign investments must remain in Venezuela for at least two years before the foreign investors are entitled to repatriate all or a portion of the capital invested or the proceeds received from the sale in Venezuela of their investments. Once the purpose of their investments has been fulfilled, foreign investors are entitled to repatriate all of the proven dividends obtained from their registered and updated Venezuelan investment. The national executive is entitled to reduce this percentage only in the event of force majeure or extraordinary economic circumstances.

Registration of foreign investments is one of the documents required to obtain foreign currency through the Central Bank to repatriate dividends, branch profits, proceeds from sales of investment, liquidation of the company or capital reductions. In practice, however, due to a strictly regulated exchange control system in Venezuela, the possibility to convert Venezuelan bolivars into foreign currency for cash repatriations is very limited.

c. Forms of Investment

There are two types of foreign investments: direct foreign investments and portfolio investments. Direct foreign investments are investments made into the equity of the local company and representing a participation equal to or greater than 10% of the capital of the company. Portfolio investments are investments in the shares or quotas of the local company and representing an equity participation of less than 10%.

Either form of investment may be made: (a) in foreign currency; (b) in tangible or physical assets (industrial plants, equipment, raw materials or intermediate products); (c) in intangible assets (trademarks, patents, other intellectual property, and technical assistance, provided that such intangible assets are transferred between non-related entities, the relevant contract is registered with the Venezuelan intellectual property regulator and the assignment of rights involves the effective transfer of ownership over the intangible assets); (d) via capital

---

[1] Economist Intelligence Unit.
[2] Bolivarian Republic of Venezuela, Annual Report, Exhibit D.

reinvestments.

Foreign investments in Venezuela are subject to the provisions of the investment contract to be entered between the foreign investor and the entity receiving the investment (the State or the public, private or joint venture company). The investment contract will set forth the type of investment, its purpose, value and the area of the country where the investment will be made, as well as the term of the contract, any financing conditions and any other provision relevant to the investment.

Venezuela is a party to several tax treaties as well as bilateral investment protection treaties.

d. Standards of Market Access and Examination

With the exception of investments made in areas determined by the national executive to be of strategic importance for the nation's economic and social development, the foreign investment law guarantees that foreign investors and their investments will be treated as favorably as the Republic treats the investments made by Venezuelan investors.

The only areas reserved to companies owned or controlled by Venezuelan investors are open-air television, radio broadcasting, newspapers in Spanish, national air transportation, and professional services regulated by law. There are some areas, such as the upstream oil industry, that are reserved to the Venezuelan government, in which foreign investors may participate only through minority participations in joint venture companies with the Republic or other Venezuelan state-owned companies.

Furthermore, investments in some industries considered of public interests require special administrative license from the corresponding regulatory entity (such as telecommunications, banking, insurance, electric generation, transmission, distribution, water supply and exploration and extraction of certain minerals).

B. Foreign Exchange Regulation

a. Department Supervising Foreign Exchange

The Central Bank is Venezuela's monetary authority and, as such, is the entity in charge of overseeing the negotiation and trade of foreign currencies, and together with the Finance Ministry, sets the official foreign exchange rate and regulates every aspect related to Venezuela's foreign exchange system. The Central Bank is authorized by the Venezuelan central bank law to establish limitations or restrictions to the free convertibility of the Venezuelan bolivar.

The Venezuelan government created the foreign trade national center [Centro Nacional de Comercio Exterior (Cencoex)] to develop and implement, in coordination with the Central Bank and the Finance Ministry, the government's policies on foreign exchange management, export, import and offshore investments.

b. Brief Introduction of Laws and Regulations of Foreign Exchange

Foreign exchange transactions in Venezuela are governed by the provisions of the foreign exchange regime law, the foreign exchange regulations (convenios cambiarios) jointly issued by the Central Bank and the Finance Minister, and the regulations issued by Cencoex and the Central Bank.

The Venezuelan exchange control regime significantly restricts the ability of private companies and individuals to convert bolivars into foreign currency. Currently, the sale and purchase of foreign currency can only be made through the following systems or markets: (a) Cencoex; (b) the Dicom system; (c) the retail market (operaciones al menudeo); (d) the securities market. All four systems or markets currently pose significant limitations to the purchase of foreign currency.

Cencoex controls the purchase of foreign currency by private entities for the import of previously approved food, medicine and raw material items. The Dicom system is a foreign currency auction mechanism, managed and controlled by the Central Bank and opened to private sector entities and individuals looking to buy or sell foreign currency.[1]

The official foreign exchange rate in Venezuela, known as the "Dicom rate", is published by the Central Bank. Normally, the Dicom rate fluctuates depending on the results of every foreign currency auction held in the Dicom system (usually once a week). All official foreign exchange transactions in Venezuela are settled at the prevailing Dicom Rate.

c. Requirements of Foreign Exchange Management for Foreign Enterprises

The Republic and the Venezuelan state-owned companies can make payments in foreign currency to the extent authorized by the Central Bank by regulation or special permit. Except for certain types of transactions,

---

[1] The Dicom system adds restrictions to the monthy (companies) or quaterly (individuals) amounts of foreign currency that private companies and individuals are authorized to purchase.

such as purchase and sale of real estate, private companies can also make payments in foreign currency and hold foreign currency in local and offshore bank accounts. Foreign currency held by private companies can be: (a) maintained in offshore bank accounts (except as described below); (b) used to make payments in foreign currency in Venezuela or abroad; (c) voluntarily converted into local currency through the available foreign exchange systems.

Venezuelan exporters of goods and services are authorized to withhold up to 80% of the foreign currency income obtained from exports made, and use it to pay for expenses and any other expenditures related to their activities. The remaining 20% must be sold to the Central Bank. Private sector exporters of goods are authorized to deduct from such 20% the amounts contributed as working capital through the purchase of raw materials, supplies, fixed assets and other goods essential to their export activities.

C. Financing

a. Main Financial Institutions

Together with the Central Bank, whose principal role is to control inflation and maintain the stability of the Venezuelan bolivar, local banks (both public and private) and insurance companies are the main players in the Venezuelan financial market.

Venezuelan banks are subject to the banking sector institutions law (Ley de Instituciones del Sector Bancario), the national financial system law (Ley Orgánica del Sistema Financiero Nacional), and the regulations and supervision of the Central Bank and the Venezuelan banking superintendent (Sudeban). In general, Venezuelan banks are authorized to take deposits, make loans, issue credit and debit cards, act as trustees (fiduciario) and issue bonds or guarantees (fianzas).

Venezuelan insurance companies are subject to the insurance activity law (Ley de la Actividad Aseguradora), the financial system law, and the regulations and supervision of the Venezuelan insurance activity superintendent (Sudeaseg). Insurance companies are also authorized to issue bonds or guarantees.

The Venezuelan bank market is highly concentrated in terms of specialized banking institutions, deposits and credit portfolios. By the end of 2016, almost 75% of the banks operating in Venezuela were universal banks. The ten largest banks in Venezuela account for more than 80% of the country's bank assets, while the five largest concentrate almost 70% of deposits. Banco de Venezuela, a state-owned bank, is the single largest bank in Venezuela.

There are 31 banks in Venezuela; six are state-owned banks and 25 are private banks. Foreign investment involvement in the Venezuelan banking and insurance industry is small.

There are approximately 50 insurance companies and five reinsurance companies operating in Venezuela. Foreign investment involvement in the Venezuelan insurance industry is also marginal.

b. Financing Conditions for Foreign Enterprises

There are no special financing conditions for foreign enterprises.

Local currency financing by public or private banks is practically the only source available since the current foreign exchange control regime restricts the ability of Venezuelan companies to convert bolivars into foreign currency. It is difficult to obtain financing beyond three years and the local bank market is used to monthly amortizations. This is due to inflation levels and the banks' preference for cash flow. In practice, borrowers have little access to large loan facilities in the bank market, where the use of syndicated loan facilities is becoming more frequent, rates are extremely attractive because they are negative real interest rates (i.e., substantially below inflation) and interest expenses are fully deductible for income tax purposes. Although local currency loans typically have short durations, rollover debts are currently not a problem for blue chip companies.

Venezuelan banks are generally required to allocate substantial portions of their credit portfolios to pivotal economic areas such as housing, agriculture, tourism and manufacturing at subsidized rates.

D. Land Policy

a. Brief Introduction of Land-Related Laws and Regulations

The ownership, purchase, sale and development of real estate in Venezuela is governed primarily by the civil code and the public registries and notaries law (Ley de Registros y del Notariado), and also by the homeland security law (Ley Orgánica de Seguridad de la Nación), the municipal branch law (Ley Orgánica del Poder Público Municipal), the municipal zoning regulations (ordenanzas de zonificación), and the law for the security and defense of the security areas (Ley Orgánica de Seguridad y Defensa sobre las Zonas de Seguridad) and regulations thereunder.

Real estate transactions are common in Venezuela as they are often used as a way to counter the effects of high inflation rates and foreign exchange controls. However, the Venezuelan real estate market is less active than other markets in Latin America and it is marked by domestic deals, mainly because of political and economic instability and the consequent reduction of foreign investment. Publicly traded REITs and REOCs are not active in Venezuela.

Transfer of real estate is effected by registration of a deed of transfer with the corresponding public registry office. There are public registry offices in charge of registration of real estate ownership and transactions in most parts of the country, especially in urban areas. Real estate filings in public registry offices show the location, area, ownership and encumbrances of the real estate. Transfer of real estate triggers the payment of registration taxes and expenses. Sellers of real estate must pay an advance income tax of 0.5% of the sale price, which the seller may credit against its yearly income tax payable and will be able to claim a refund for advance income taxes paid in excess (although it is practically impossible to obtain such refund).

Urban real estate is subject to a municipal tax on urban real estate levied by local municipalities on the value of the real estate. The tax on urban real estate is levied on a yearly basis and rates are generally immaterial.

Venezuelan leasing laws contain certain restrictions on the terms of residential, commercial and office leases.

b. Rules of Land Acquisition for Foreign Enterprises

In general, foreign individuals and enterprises (as well as Venezuelan companies owned or controlled by them) are entitled to own, lease, assign, sale or otherwise transfer real property in Venezuela. However, foreigners are required to (a) notify the Defense Ministry if they acquire, by any means, a property located within an area designated by the Venezuelan government as a security zone or in line adjacent to a water body, within 90 days from the date of the acquisition, or (b) obtain an authorization from the Defense Ministry to acquire property located adjacent to the international borders of Venezuela, or initiate construction in such property.①

E. The Establishment and Dissolution of Companies

a. The Forms of Enterprises

The options available to foreign investors to set up business in Venezuela are (a) the corporation; (b) the limited liability company; (c) the general partnership; (d) the limited partnership; (e) the stock limited partnership; (f) the branch of a foreign entity, and (g) the consortium. In this guide the term "company" is used to indistinctively refer to any of the options above, including the branch, the corporation or any of the partnerships, but excluding the consortium.

a) The Corporation (SA or CA)

The Venezuelan corporation is the most common form of entity used by foreign investors to do business in Venezuela. The corporation is owned by shareholders and is a legal entity separate and distinct from its shareholders. The corporation is indistinctively known as compañía anónima (C.A.) or sociedad anónima (S.A.).②

The liability of the shareholders of a corporation is limited to the payment of the nominal value (and premium, if any) of the shares such shareholder owns. As a general rule, the shareholders of the corporation are not liable for the obligations of the corporation.

Corporation are incorporated with the registration of its articles of incorporation and bylaws with a Venezuelan commercial registry office in the city of domicile of the corporation. Any name available in the commercial registry may be used for the corporation, followed by the initials S.A.or C.A.

Corporations need to be incorporated by at least two shareholders, but after incorporation they can be wholly owned by one shareholder. Corporations must have a stated or subscribed capital ("stated capital").③ The stated capital of the corporation can be paid in cash or in kind.④ Cash payments of the stated capital must be made by a deposit in bolivars in a Venezuelan bank account. Payment of stated capital in foreign currency is allowed in certain cases, such as the oil joint venture companies.

The stated capital is represented by shares (bearer shares are not permitted). All shares must have a par value denominated in bolivars. The corporation can issue different classes of shares, including preferred shares. Ownership and transfers of shares is evidenced by notations made in the book of shareholders kept by the

---

① Venezuelan homeland security law and regulations thereunder.
② Other than the name, there is no difference between a compañía anónima (C.A.) or a sociedad anónima (S.A.).
③ Although there are no statutory minimum capital requirements, each Venezuelan commercial registry sets forth a minimum stated capital requirement on a case-by-case basis.
④ In case of payment in cash, at least 20% of the stated capital must be paid-in by the shareholders at the time of registration of the minutes of shareholders' meeting approving the incorporation of the corporation.

corporation.①

The shareholders' meeting is the maximum authority of the corporation. Each shareholder is entitled to attend shareholders' meetings in person or be represented by a third party under a power of attorney (proxy). Unless otherwise provided in the bylaws, each share entitles its holder to one vote at the meeting. Shareholder's meetings can be held in Venezuela or abroad. Quorum and majorities rules are normally set forth in the bylaws of the corporation.

The following matters require the approval of the shareholders' meeting of the corporation: (a) approval of annual balance sheets; (b) appointment and removal of directors; (c) appointment and removal of statutory auditors; (d) anticipated dissolution; (e) extension of corporate term; (f) merger with or into another entity; (g) sale of all or substantially all the corporate assets; (h) increase of stated capital; (i) reduction of stated capital; (j) change of purpose; (k) declaration of dividends; (l) repurchase of shares; (m) replenishment of losses; (n) issuance of bonds; (o) bring by the corporation of judicial claims against its directors; (p) amendment to the bylaws. Any other matter involving the corporation can be submitted to the shareholders' meeting, and the bylaws may require shareholders' approval for other matters.

The directors are in charge of managing or overseeing the management of the corporation. Corporations must have at least one director.② The articles of incorporation and bylaws may provide for officers of the corporation, such as an executive president, a general manager, a financial officer, a judicial representative, etc., and grant them broad or limited powers of representation and management.③

Directors are not personally liable for the obligations and liabilities of the corporation, but they are liable to the corporation and to third parties in case they breach their duties as directors. Directors are appointed for the term set forth in the articles of incorporation and bylaws and can only be removed by the shareholders' meeting of the corporation.④

A corporation must have at least one statutory auditor (comisario) to be appointed by the shareholders' meeting.⑤ Each year, the statutory auditor must prepare a report on the annual balance sheet and accounts of the corporation to be submitted to the regular shareholders' meeting. The statutory auditor is entitled to call a shareholders' meeting if he finds irregularities in the management of the corporation.

The fiscal year of a corporation is a period of 12 months, and does not need to match the calendar year.

Dividends can be paid only out of liquid and collected profits reflected in the annual balance sheet approved by a shareholders' meeting of the corporation. Dividends must be approved by the shareholders' meeting and unless otherwise provided in the bylaws, dividends are distributed to the shareholders on a pro-rata basis.

(i) The Limited Liability Company (SRL)

The Venezuelan limited liability company (sociedad de responsabilidad limitada or SRL) is a form seldom used, since its stated capital cannot currently exceed Bs.2,000 (less than one US$). The members of the limited liability company enjoy limited liability like the shareholders of the corporation. The capital of the limited liability company is represented by quotas. In case of transfer of a quota owned by a member, the other members have a preferential right to acquire such quota, and the transfer of the quota to third parties requires the approval of 3/4 of the limited liability company's capital.

(ii) The General Partnership (SNV)

The Venezuelan general partnership (sociedad en nombre colectivo or SNC) is owned by partners. The partners are jointly and severally liable for any debts, obligations and liabilities of the general partnership (unlimited liability). The general partnership must have at least two partners. Commercial registries currently accept that legal entities (including foreign companies) be partners of a general partnership. The capital contributions of the partners are not represented by shares. The transfer of partnership interests requires the approval of the other partners.

(iii) The Limited partnership (SCS)

The Venezuelan limited partnership (sociedad en comandita simple or SCS) is owned by at least one general partner (socio comanditante) and at least one limited partner (socio comanditario). The general partners are jointly and severally liable for the debts, obligations and liabilities of the limited partnership, whereas the liability of the limited partners is limited to the amount they agree to contribute to the limited partnership.

---

① Shares can also be represented in certificates, but the issuance of share certificates is not required.
② Some commercial registry offices require that at least one director be either a Venezuelan citizen or a foreigner holding a working or business visa, and some commercial registry offices require all directors to be either Venezuelan citizens or foreigners holding working or business visas.
③ The corporation may also appoint these officers or grant them powers pursuant to powers of attorney even if the bylaws do not expressly provide for such officers.
④ Directors can be removed with or without cause, at any time, even before the expiration of their term.
⑤ The statutory auditor must be a Venezuelan public accountant or administrator.

(iv) The Stock Limited Partnership (SCA)

The Venezuelan stock limited partnership (sociedad en comandita por acciones or SCA) is similar to the limited partnership, except that the limited partners' equity interest is represented by shares, and the regime of the limited partners is similar to that applicable to the shareholders of a corporation.

(v) The Branch

Foreign entities can set up a branch in Venezuela. The registration of the branch does not result in a separate legal entity being formed in Venezuela. Therefore, the foreign company (head office) will be liable for all the obligations assumed by the branch.

The branch must be registered with a commercial registry located in the city of domicile of the branch. The foreign investor can choose the domicile of the branch. The name generally used for the branch is the same name of the foreign company (head office) or its abbreviation followed by the expression Sucursal Venezuela (which means Venezuelan branch).

The branch must have at least one representative. The branch representative will have full powers to represent and manage the branch, except for the power to sell or transfer the business (unless such power is expressly granted to the representative). Any limitations to the powers of the representative are not effective against third parties.①

The head office must assign a capital to the branch (capital asignado or "branch capital"). The branch capital does not constitute a limitation of the liability for the head office.② The branch capital must be paid by the head office either in cash or in kind.

b) The Consortium

A consortium (consorcio) is not a separate legal entity, but a contract between several persons (consortium members) to carry out a specific project.

b. The Procedure of Establishment

- Steps to set up a corporation

The following is a description of the steps to set up a corporation (similar steps are required for the formation of the general partnership, the limited liability company and the limited partnerships)③:

a) check with the Venezuelan commercial registry the availability of the name to be used for the corporation, and reserve it if available;

b) file the following documents with the commercial registry office: (i) power of attorney authorizing one or more individuals to register the corporation, open the bank account and represent the shareholders and the corporation before Venezuelan authorities; (ii) articles of incorporation and bylaws of the shareholders; (iii) letter issued by the Venezuelan bank acknowledging receipt of payment of the capital, or evidence of contribution in kind; (iv) articles of incorporation and bylaws of the corporation, including the name of the directors and the statutory auditor; and, (v) letter of acceptance signed by the person to be appointed as statutory auditor (comisario) of the company;④

c) registration of the corporation with the commercial registry generally takes two weeks once: (i) all the documents referred to above are available; (ii) the Venezuelan bank account is opened; (iii) the payment in cash of the capital is deposited in the Venezuelan bank account (or the contribution in kind has been completed); (iv) the Venezuelan bank issues the letter evidencing the cash payment, or evidence of the contribution is obtained; (v) all registration fees and expenses are paid;

d) once the registration of the corporation is completed, a copy of the registration must be published in a Venezuelan newspaper;

e) the corporation must purchase the corporate books and have them sealed by the commercial registry office; and

f) the shares issued pursuant to the bylaws are recorded in the book of shareholders of the corporation, and if desired share certificates are issued.

---

① If the branch representative is not a Venezuelan citizen, he or she may have to obtain a working or business visa in order to sign documents on behalf of the branch before public notaries or registries in Venezuela.

② Although there are no statutory minimum capital requirements applicable to the branch capital, the Venezuelan commercial registry sets forth a minimum branch capital requirement on a case-by-case basis.

③ Commercial registry offices change the requirements to incorporate companies frequently.

④ Documents granted abroad must be either legalized or apostilled if granted outside Venezuela, and translated into Spanish by a Venezuelan-registered translator.Documents such as the power of attorney may be drafted in two languages to avoid the need of translation.Venezuela is a signatory to the Hague Convention Abolishing the Requirement of Legalisation for Foreign Public Documents (the Apostille Convention).

After incorporation, the company must seek the registrations, approvals, licenses and permits required to carry out the specific business of the company (such as, tax registration, municipal license, social security, employment capacitation institute, housing contributions, national registry of public contractors, import licenses and environmental permits)

• Steps to domicile a branch

The following is a description of the steps to register a branch of a foreign company in Venezuela:

a) check with the Venezuelan commercial registry the availability of the name to be used for the branch, and reserve it if available;

b) file the following documents with the commercial registry office: (i) resolution of the competent corporate body of the foreign company (head office) approving the opening and registration of the branch and appointing the branch representative; (ii) power of attorney authorizing one or more individuals to open and register the branch and open the branch's bank account in Venezuela; (iii) articles of incorporation and bylaws of the head office; (iv) a copy of the laws governing the incorporation and functioning of the foreign company; (v) letter issued by the Venezuelan bank acknowledging the receipt of payment in cash of the branch capital or evidence of contribution in kind;[1]

c) registration of the Venezuelan branch with the commercial registry generally takes two weeks once: (i) all the documents referred to above are available; (ii) the Venezuelan bank account is opened; (iii) the Venezuelan bank issues the letter evidencing payment in cash, or evidence of the contribution is obtained; (iv) all registration fees and expenses are paid;

d) once the registration of the branch is completed, a copy of the registration must be published in a Venezuelan newspaper;

e) purchase the accounting books and have them sealed by the commercial registry.

c. Routes and Requirements of Dissolution

Anticipated dissolution of the corporation must be approved by the shareholders' meeting. Upon the dissolution of the corporation (either anticipated or for expiration of its term), the shareholders' meeting must appoint one or more liquidators that will carry out the liquidation of the assets and payment of the liabilities of the corporation. Liquidation requires payment or settlement of all liabilities. Once all the liabilities are paid or settled, the shareholders are entitled to receive the remaining assets or funds in excess of the liabilities of the corporation, on a pro rata basis, unless otherwise provided in the bylaws. The shareholders of the corporation are jointly and severally liable for the tax liabilities of the liquidated corporation until the expiration of the statute of limitation.

If a corporation incurs in cessation of payments (i.e., inability to pay debts when they become due), any creditor may request from the competent Venezuelan court the declaration of bankruptcy of the corporation (involuntary bankruptcy). In addition, the directors of the corporation must request the declaration of bankruptcy from the competent Venezuelan court in case of cessation of payments (voluntary bankruptcy). In case of bankruptcy: (a) directors of the corporation may face criminal liability if the bankruptcy is declared negligent or fraudulent and in certain other cases; (b) certain transactions made by the corporation during the suspect period (or ten days before the date on which the cessation of payment has occurred, as determined by the bankruptcy court), may be void or voidable.[2]

F. Merger and Acquisition

The current level of M&A activity in Venezuela is moderate. In the last couple of years there has been a surge of sales of Venezuelan subsidiaries by its foreign investors at attractive prices to investors with high risk appetite. The main factors influencing the level of M&A activity in Venezuela are governmental regulations, exchange control restrictions and political and economic environment and prospects. Manufacturing, financial and the oil and gas industries are likely to have the most M&A activity in the following years. Provided that the government offers

---

[1] See preceding footnote.

[2] The bankruptcy judge has broad discretion to set the suspect period date, provided, however, that the bankruptcy judge can backdate the suspect period date only up to a maximum of two years prior to the bankruptcy declaration. Under article 945 of the code of commerce, the following transactions of the debtor are null and void if made during the suspect period: (a) transfers of assets (movable assets or real estate) with no consideration for the debtor (gifts); (b) granting of security (or other preferences in payment) on assets of the debtor to secure debt incurred before the suspect period; (c) payments of non-matured debt; and (d) payments of matured debt made in any matter other than cash or negotiable instruments, if the debt was payable in cash. Under article 946 of the code of commerce, other payments of matured debt by the debtor or all other transactions with consideration made after the date of cessation of payments are voidable if the payees or other parties to such transactions had knowledge of the cessation of payments of the debtor at the time of such payments or transactions.

investors adequate levels of legal protection (including settlement of disputes by international arbitration), minority investments by oil and gas companies (private or state-owned) in joint ventures with the Venezuelan government can also be expected to increase in the near future.

The acquisition may be structured as a stock or as an asset transaction. The stock purchase is the simplest and most common method of acquisition. An asset purchase should be considered if the potential purchaser is particularly concerned with a major non-tax or labor actual or contingent liability of the company. Bulk sale regulations, as well as special tax and labor regulations, must be taken into account in asset transactions.

In general, M&A transactions in Venezuela are conducted in a fashion similar to those in other jurisdictions, namely: (a) the signing of confidentiality agreements and non-binding or binding letters of intent; (b) due diligence investigation; (c) negotiation of stock or asset purchase agreement; (d) signing of the agreement; (e) disclosure of the transaction; (f) tender offer process (in case of publicly listed companies); (g) closing of the transaction.

The purchase agreement generally contains representation and warranties, indemnification and closing conditions customary for M&A transactions in other jurisdictions. The conditions for closing are frequently the subject of lengthy negotiations between seller and purchaser given the rapidly changing regulatory environment. In many cases, and provided that no special regulatory approval is required, signing and closing occurs simultaneously. One particular difference from common law countries is that in Venezuela (like other Latin American jurisdictions) the purchase agreement is generally signed between the purchaser and the shareholder or shareholders of the target company, instead of the target company itself.

There are very few publicly listed companies in Venezuela. Several of these companies have implemented (or, from time to time, continue to implement) traditional defenses against hostile takeovers in line with existing international standards, such as repurchases, poison pills and supermajority provisions, among other measures.

Mergers of a company with or into another entity require the approval of the shareholders' meeting. Consummation of the merger is subject to a three-month waiting period. During such period, creditors of the corporation may oppose to the merger. In the event of opposition, the merger cannot be consummated unless the opposition is settled between the parties or dismissed by a court. Shareholders do not have withdrawal rights as a result of a merger, unless the merger results in the change of corporate purpose of the corporation. Venezuelan law does not permit "squeeze out mergers" (i.e., the cancellation of shares as a result of a merger in exchange for cash without the consent of the affected shareholder).

Regulatory approvals apply on certain regulated sectors, such as telecommunications, oil and gas, banking and insurance.

G. Competition Regulation

a. Department Supervising Competition Regulation

The antitrust superintendent (Superintendencia Antimonopolio) is the Venezuelan entity in charge of supervising and enforcing the rules and regulations of the antitrust law (Ley Antimonopolio).

b. Brief Introduction of Competition Law

The antitrust law was enacted on November 26, 2014. It replaced the competition law of 1992 but essentially preserves the same principles and prohibitions. Other antitrust regulations include: (a) regulation number 2 under the competition law (the so-called merger regulation); (b) instructive number 3 on economic concentrations; (c) the merger guidelines.

The antitrust law is aimed at promoting, protecting and regulating fair competition in Venezuela by proscribing and punishing monopolistic and oligopolistic business practices, positions of control, businesses combinations and any other anticompetitive or fraudulent practice. Individuals and public or private entities, whether local or foreign, for-profit or nonprofit, carrying out economic activities in Venezuela are covered by the antitrust law. Strategic public companies and joint ventures (empresas mixtas) are excluded.

c. Measures Regulating Competition

Under current antitrust law and regulations, antitrust filing with the Venezuela's antitrust superintendent is not mandatory, unless the transaction involves a telecom company or certain other regulated companies. The lack of notification would not constitute by itself a violation of the Venezuelan competition law and there are no penalties for not filing. However, the antitrust superintendent may open an investigation after the closing of the transaction if it deems that a transaction not notified affects competition in Venezuela. Third parties (i.e., competitors) may request the antitrust superintendent to open an investigation. There is a statute of limitations of one year after the closing for the antitrust superintendent or interested third parties to oppose the transaction.

As a general rule, the antitrust law bans any conduct, practice, agreement, contract or decision that prevents, restricts, distorts or restrains economic competition, including: (a) any action that restricts or obstructs the access or permanency of entities, products or services in the market; (b) any action that restricts economic competition between the entities covered by the antitrust law, or causes any of them to reject or restrict the purchase or sale of goods or services; (c) any action to manipulate elements of production, distribution, trade, technological development and investments, in order to harm economic competition; (d) any agreement that restricts or prevents economic competition; (e) any agreement or arranged practice that: (i) directly or indirectly sets the price of goods and services; (ii) limits production, distribution, trade and technological development; (iii) restricts innovation, research and development investments; (iv) distributes markets, territories, industries or suppliers among competitors; (v) applies different conditions to similar services in order to place a competitor in disadvantage; (vi) conditions the execution of a contract to performances not related to the purpose of the contract; (f) economic concentrations that create or strengthen a controlling position in the market.[1]

Abuse of a controlling position in the local market by one or more entities is also prohibited. An entity has a controlling position when: (a) an economic activity is performed by a single entity or between a group of entities acting as buyer and seller at the same time; (b) there is no effective competition between two or more entities. Disloyal, deceitful and misleading practices in the production, distribution and trade of goods and services are also punishable under the antitrust law. A disloyal practice is defined as: (a) false advertising; (b) product simulation or imitation; (c) commercial bribe; (d) the violation of laws and regulations to prevail in the market.

H. Tax

a. Tax Regime and Rules

Venezuelan resident companies and individuals are subject to income tax on their worldwide income at a progressive tax rate of up to 34%. A branch of a foreign company is subject to income tax on its Venezuelan attributable income at a progressive tax rate of up to 34%. Non-resident companies or individuals are subject to Venezuelan income tax on their Venezuelan source income.

Venezuelan income tax is levied on net taxable income, calculated by subtracting the costs and allowable deductions (i.e., salaries, interest, amortization, depreciation, technical assistance and any expense that is "normal and necessary" to generate income) from annual gross revenue. Expenses that are considered normal and necessary to produce income may be deducted.

Foreign and domestic losses may be carried forward for three years and offset up to 25% of the taxpayer's yearly taxable income. Losses may not be carried back. Losses can survive a change of ownership.

Venezuelan branches of foreign companies are considered a permanent establishment. The permanent establishment is taxed on income attributable to the permanent establishment's activities. Income which the permanent establishment might be expected to make if it will be a separate and distinct entity is attributable to the permanent establishment. Deductions of expenses incurred for the purpose of the permanent establishment are allowed, including executive and general administrative expenses. Interest, technical assistance fees or royalty payments made by a branch to its head office and its affiliates are not deductible, but interest, fees and royalties paid to other entities are deductible.

The Venezuelan income tax law and regulations thereunder contain transfer pricing rules which are based on the arm's length principle, and are modeled after the 1995 OECD transfer pricing guidelines, imposing transfer pricing documentation and filing requirements and containing specific advance pricing agreements provisions.

Under the Venezuelan thin capitalization rules, interest on related party debt will be deductible for tax purposes provided a 1:1 debt-to-equity ratio is not exceeded.

Venezuela has anti-deferral rules that require reporting of income and imposes disclosure obligations on Venezuelan residents with direct or indirect controlled interests in foreign entities and other investments organized, located or resident in low tax jurisdictions when a resident exercises management or control over such investments.

The statute of limitations for tax audits and imposing fines for income tax and other Venezuelan taxes is six years. The statute of limitations is increased to ten years if the taxpayer failed to file the applicable tax return.

Companies and consortia must be registered with the Venezuelan tax information registry (Registro de Información Fiscal) within the first month after incorporation or commencement of activities. This requirement also applies to the directors and shareholders or partners of the companies and to the branch's representative and its head office.

b. Main Categories and Rates of Tax

The tax authorities (or entities with power to collect taxes and other contributions) at the national level are:

---

[1] Small and mid-size companies are excluded from this prohibition.

(a) the Servicio Nacional Integrado de Administración Aduanera y Tributaria (Seniat), the Venezuelan national tax authority, in charge of collecting income tax, value added taxes, gift tax and custom duties; (b) the Instituto de Capacitación y Educación Socialista (Inces) or institute of educational cooperation, in charge of collecting payroll taxes relating to training and education of employees; (c) Banco Nacional de Vivienda y Habitat Banavih or national bank for housing and habitat, in charge of collecting payroll taxes for housing and habitat; (d) the Instituto Venezolano de los Seguros Sociales (Ivss) or social security institute, in charge of collecting payroll social security taxes and taxes for unemployment or layoff contingency; (e) the Organización Nacional Antidrogas (ONA) or national organization against drugs; (f) the Fondo Nacional de Ciencia, Tecnología e Innovación (Fonacit) or national fund of science, technology and innovation. All tax authorities or entities have broad powers to make investigations, audits and assessments, to impose penalties, to take preventive measures or to order temporary suspension of activities for violations of the corresponding tax obligations.

The main categories and tax rates are:

Tax	Tax Rate
Corporate income tax	• The schedule of income tax rates contains three rate-brackets: - 15% on taxable income up to 2,000 tax units; - 22% on additional taxable income up to 3,000 tax units; and - 34% on taxable income above 3,000 tax units. • Banking, financial or insurance - 40% flat rate. • Oil companies - 50% tax rate on net income. • Mining - 60% tax rate on net income (except for specific projects considered by the government to be "of national interest" which are taxed at the regular rate).
Withholding tax on outbound payments to non-residents	• Dividends - 34% • Capital gains - 34% • Interests (banks) - 4.95% • Interests (others) - 34% on 95% of the payment. • Royalties - 34% on 90% of the gross payment • Technical Assistance - 34% on 30% of the gross payment. • Professional services - 34% on 90% of the gross payment.
Withholding tax on outbound payments to non-residents under the Venezuela – China DTT	• Dividends - 5% if the shareholder is a corporation that directly controls at least 10% of the capital of the distributing entity.10% in all other cases. • Interests (banks) - maximum of 5% • Interests (others) - 10% • Royalties - 10%
Value added tax	• Standard rate - 12%. • Exports of goods or services - 0%.

① The tax unit is a value for measurement set by the Venezuelan tax administration (Seniat) every year.
② Dividends paid by a Venezuelan resident corporation, limited liability company or stock limited partnership to a nonresident shareholder or partner are subject to a dividend tax levied at a flat rate of 34% of the amount by which financial earnings exceed net taxable income of the company paying the dividend (the "dividend tax"). The dividend tax is collected through a withholding tax at the company level.Dividends paid by a Venezuelan resident company out of dividend distributions received from other Venezuelan companies are not subject to the dividend tax.The branch of foreign legal entities is subject to a "deemed dividend tax" on their earnings, levied at a flat rate of 34% of the amount by which financial earnings exceed net taxable income of the branch.The deemed dividend tax is exempted if the branch reinvests in Venezuela the amount subject to the deemed dividends tax and the investment is maintained in Venezuela for five years.
③ Capital gains obtained from the sale or other disposition (other than through a Venezuelan stock exchange) of shares of corporations and stock limited partnerships will be considered Venezuelan source income. Holders of shares with taxable capital gains realized will be required to file a Venezuelan income tax return, and will be able to claim a refund for taxes withheld in excess due with respect to such gains (although it is practically impossible to obtain such refund). Payments in kind are not subject to withholding, but the income tax on the capital gain will be applicable.
④ Interest payments made to non-resident entities are subject to an income tax withholding. Payments in kind are not subject to withholding, but the lender must report the interest payment received and pay the applicable income tax.Interest payments on bonds issued by the Republic are exempted from income tax and no withholding is applicable.

(continued)

Tax	Tax Rate
Stamp tax on initial capital contribution and increase of stated capital of companies, or assigned capital of branches	• 1% to 2% of the capital contribution or increase.
Financial transactions tax	• Standard rate - 0.75%. • Foreign currency transactions rate - 0%.
Municipal tax on economic activities	• Depends on the municipality.
Gift tax	• Up to 55%.
Contribution to the national organization against drugs (ONA)	• 1% tax rate on net income.
Contribution to the national fund of science, technology and innovation (Fonacit)	• Rates range from 0.5% to 2% of gross revenue.
Contribution to the national sports fund	• 1% tax rate on net income.
Contribution to the social security institute (Ivss)	• Employer rate - 9, 10 or 11% of the lower of (i) each employee's salary, and (ii) five times the minimum monthly urban salary for each employee (the "Ivss Salary Base"). • Employee rate - 4% of the Ivss Salary Base.
Contribution to the institute of educational cooperation (Inces)	• Employer rate - 2% of total wages, salaries, daily payments and remunerations of any kind (excluding occasional payments). • Employees rate - 0.5% of their profit sharing (utilidades).
Housing contribution (Banavih)	• Employer rate - 2% of monthly integral salary of each employee. • Employee rate - 1% of monthly integral salary.
Unemployment or layoff contribution (paro forzoso)	• Employer rate - 2% of Ivss Salary Base. • Employee rate - 0.5% of Ivss Salary Base.

c. Tax Declaration and Preference

The tax period for income tax purposes is 12 months. The tax period of a company is set forth in the bylaws.

---

① VAT applies to sales of all goods and services throughout the chain of distribution.VAT taxpayers are charged VAT on all their purchases of goods and services (input credits).In turn they have to charge and collect VAT in their sales of goods and services (output debits), effectively passing down the VAT to the end consumers. VAT liability (excess of output debits over input credits) is paid monthly by tax payers to the Venezuelan treasure. There is an additional surcharge VAT on certain luxury items such as luxury cars, motorcycles and jewelry. Exemptions from VAT include certain items such as food, medicine, telephone, domestic electricity and domestic natural gas.VAT does not apply to financial and insurance services
② Entities designated as special taxpayers are charged FTT on (i) payments made through the Venezuelan bank system, and (ii) the settlement of debts by means of novation, setoff and/or debt reliefs.
③ Municipal tax on business activities is levied by local municipalities on gross revenue (no deductions allowed).
④ Donations or gifts of assets located in Venezuela are generally subject to the Venezuelan gift tax applicable in accordance with the relationship between the beneficiaries of the gift and the donor.
⑤ Commercial or industrial businesses with 50 or more workers must pay a special contribution to the ONA on their net income. This tax is calculated and paid annually.
⑥ Companies generating gross revenues in excess of 100,000 tax units must pay a special contribution to Fonacit on their gross revenues, depending on the type of business activity carried out. This tax is calculated and paid annually.
⑦ Companies generating net profits in excess of 20,000 tax units must pay a special contribution to the National Sports Fund on their net profits. This tax is calculated and paid annually.
⑧ Employers and employees must pay contributions to the Ivss.For the employer, the applicable rate (9, 10 or 11%) depends on the level of risk of the business activities (the higher the risk, the higher the percentage). Employees' contributions are withheld by the employer and paid to Ivss.Ivss contributions are paid on a monthly basis.
⑨ Employees and employers with five or more employees must pay contributions to Inces. Employees' contributions are withheld by the employer and paid to Inces. Inces contributions are paid by the employer within the first five days of each quarter.
⑩ Employers and employees must pay contributions to Banavih. Employees' contributions are withheld by the employer and paid to Banavih. Banavih contributions are paid on a monthly basis.
⑪ Employers and employees must pay contributions to Ivss for unemployment or layoff contingency.Employee's contributions are withheld by the employer and paid to Ivss. Contributions are paid on a monthly basis.

The tax year of a taxpayer may coincide with the calendar year or with any 12-month period. Income tax returns must be filed within three months following the end of the tax year of the taxpayer. There are no regular routine audit cycles.

Venezuela has signed treaties for the avoidance of double taxation with Austria, Barbados, Belarus, Belgium, Brazil, Canada, China, Cuba, the Czech Republic, Denmark, France, Germany, Indonesia, Iran, Italy, Korea, Kuwait, Malaysia, the Netherlands, Norway, Palestine, Portugal, Qatar, Russia, Spain, Sweden, Switzerland, Trinidad and Tobago, the United Arab Emirates, the United Kingdom, the United States and Vietnam.

The Venezuelan president, in the council of ministers, within the measures of fiscal policy required pursuant to the regional, sectorial or temporary situation of the Venezuelan economy, may totally or partially exempt from Venezuelan income tax the earnings obtained by sectors considered of particular importance.

I. Securities

a. Brief Introduction of Securities-Related Laws and Regulations

Venezuela's capital market is very small in terms of market capitalization and trading volume. It is governed by: (a) the securities markets law (Ley del Mercado de Valores) and regulations thereunder; (b) the public stock exchange law (Ley de la Bolsa Pública de Valores); (c) the securities depository law (Ley de Caja de Valores); (d) the entities of collective investment law (Ley de Entidades de Inversion Colectiva).

Companies whose shares have been publicly offered in Venezuela or have been listed on a Venezuelan stock exchange (listed companies) become subject to the national securities superintendent [Superintendencia Nacional de Valores (Sunaval)], Venezuela's securities commission.

Currently there are three stock exchanges operating in Venezuela. These are: (a) the Caracas stock exchange (Bolsa de Valores de Caracas), a private sector securities exchange founded in 1947; (b) the bicentennial public stock exchange (Bolsa Pública de Valores Bicentenaria); a public and private sector securities exchange founded in 2010; (c) the Venezuelan agricultural products and goods exchange (Bolsa de Productos e Insumos Agropecuarios de Venezuela), an exchange founded in 1999 for the purpose of facilitating the negotiation of agricultural derivatives, including rice, sorghum and corn.

The public offering of shares in Venezuela requires the preparation and filing with (and approval by) Sunaval of a prospectus pursuant to the public offering regulations and forms.

The direct or indirect acquisition of a controlling stake of a Venezuelan listed company in one or several transactions must be made by public tender offer made pursuant to the public tender offer regulations where all the shareholders can (but are not required to) sell their shares on equal terms and conditions (mandatory tender rule).

Listed companies must distribute dividends to their shareholders out of net profits obtain in each fiscal year, after deduction of income taxes and legal reserves and after offsetting any accumulated losses. Not less than 25% of the dividends approved must be distributed in cash. Payments to board members of listed companies as participation in the net profits of the fiscal year may not exceed 10% of such profits after deduction of tax and legal reserves. Such participation cannot be paid before the payment of dividend as described above.

Venezuelan listed companies are subject to reporting requirements, including filing with Sunaval of audited annual financial statements, annual reports, unaudited quarterly financial statements, information that is material for the price or trading of the securities registered with the Sunaval, information on dividends, information on transactions between the company and the members of the board of directors or its principal shareholders and companies on which such shareholders have any interest, information on the call of certain shareholders' meetings, information on replenishment, increase or reduction of capital, sale of a substantial portion of the assets of the company, change of corporate purpose, transformation or merger, anticipated liquidation, change of bylaws in the mentioned matters, etc.

b. Supervision and Regulation of Securities Market

The Venezuelan securities market is supervised by Sunaval.

c. Requirements for Engagement in Securities Trading for Foreign Enterprises

There are not specific rules governing transactions in the Venezuelan securities market by foreign enterprises. Both domestic entities and foreign enterprises are subject to the rules of the Venezuelan securities laws and regulations thereunder.

J. Preference and Protection of Investment

a. The Structure of Preference Policies

The foreign investment law defines "preferred investments" as investments made in the sectors that the national executive branch defines as preferential for the economic and social development of the country. Preferred investments may obtain more favorable benefits and incentives with respect to other investments. Other investments can enjoy favorable conditions provided that the investment meets several of the following objectives: (a) partial or complete reinvestment of profits; (b) export of non-traditional goods or services; (c) technology transfer into Venezuela; (d) training activities and technological research with Venezuelan science and technology institutions; (e) development of productive supply chains; (f) significant investment amounts; (g) permanence of the investment; (h) substitution of imports; (i) job generation.

Favorable conditions may include tax deductions, accelerated amortization, tariff exemptions, tax exemptions, special credit conditions, special rates in public services, preferential access to inputs and / or raw materials managed by the government, tax stability, and any other favorable condition granted by the Venezuelan president.

b. Support for Specific Industries and Regions

In 2016, the national executive branch created the Orinoco mining belt, a national strategic development zone comprising 112,000 square kilometers in the State of Bolivar, to exploit the region's mineral reserves in accordance with sustainable practices and respect for the environment.[1]

c. Special Economic Areas

Under the law of integral regionalization for the socio-productive development of the homeland (Ley de Regionalización Integral para el Desarrollo Socioproductivo de la Patria), the Venezuelan president is authorized to create special economic areas ("SEAs") to promote economic, industrial and commercial development of selected regions by attracting foreign and domestic investments.

SEAs will benefit from special tax and customs incentives such as income tax and VAT exemptions. In 2014, the government created the Paraguaná SEA in the Falcón State, and the Ureña SEA in the Táchira State. The Paraguaná SEA was created to promote sub-regional development in the technological, informatics and telecommunication areas. The Ureña SEA is intended to promote textile, footwear, forestry, agricultural, automotive and metal-mechanical sectors.[2]

The Venezuelan free trade zone law (Ley de Zonas Franca) provides for the creation and operation of free trade areas and free ports. Free areas and free ports are exempted from most import and export duties. The Venezuelan government has created free trade areas in the Paraguaná Peninsula in the Falcón State, Atuja in the Zulia State, and in the municipalities of Libertador, Campo Elías, Sucre, and Santos Marquina in the Mérida State (for cultural, scientific and technological goods). Free ports have been created in the Margarita island (part of the Nueva Esparta State), and in Santa Elena de Uairen in the Bolívar State.

d. Investment Protection

Venezuela has bilateral investment treaties ("BITs") with Argentina, Barbados, Belarus, Belgium and Luxembourg, Canada, Chile, Costa Rica, Cuba, Czech Republic, Denmark, Ecuador, France, Germany, Iran, Lithuania, Paraguay, Peru, Portugal, the Russian Federation, Spain, Sweden, Switzerland, the United Kingdom, Uruguay, and Vietnam. There is no BIT in place between Venezuelan and China.

Foreign investments under BITs are protected against certain government actions of the host country, including expropriations or nationalizations. Venezuela withdrew from the Convention on the Settlement of Investment Disputes between States and Nationals of Other States ("ICSID Convention") in 2012. However, the withdrawal from the ICSID Convention does not foreclose international dispute resolution for future investment disputes. BIT protections include the possibility to resolve investment disputes with Venezuela in international arbitration.[3] The majority of the BITs signed by Venezuela provide a choice for arbitration under the UNCITRAL arbitration rules[4] and the ICSID's Additional Facility rules.

---

[1] The Republic signed agreements with operators from China, Canada and the Republic of Congo to exploit concessions in the region.
[2] In 2015, Venezuela and China signed a Framework Agreement for Cooperation on Special Economic Zones in Venezuela.
[3] Pursuant to the Venezuelan foreign investment law, foreign investments are subject to the jurisdiction of Venezuela courts. There is discussion among legal analysts on whether the foreign investment law excludes the possibility of arbitration for the resolution of investment disputes.
[4] The United Nations Commission on International Trade Law (UNCITRAL), established by the United Nations General Assembly in 1966.

III. Trade

A. Department Supervising Trade

The Venezuelan entity in charge of supervising trade is the Finance Ministry, in coordination with the Ministry of Fisheries, the Ministry of Food and the Ministry of Foreign Trade, and with Seniat, the Venezuelan national tax and customs authority.

B. Brief Introduction of Trade Laws and Regulations

Venezuela is a contracting party to the General Agreement on Tariff and Trade (GATT) since August 31, 1990, and is a member of the World Trade Organization (WTO). Venezuela is also a member of the Latin American Integration Association (ALADI).

Venezuela officially exited the Andean Community of Nations (Comunidad Andina de Naciones) ("CAN") in April 2011. Following its departure, Venezuela formed a series of bilateral tariff agreements with CAN members Bolivia, Colombia and Ecuador - all except Peru. The bilateral agreement with Colombia (Acuerdo de Alcance Parcial) was the most recent.

Venezuela became an associate member of Mercosur in 2004, a regional trading bloc and customs union promoting free trade among its member countries (Argentina, Brazil, Bolivia, Paraguay, Uruguay and Venezuela).[1] In December 2016, Mercosur suspended Venezuela's membership in the bloc. Venezuela has disputed the suspension and has filed a request for dispute resolution under Mercosur's internal rules.

As mentioned above, Venezuelan and China have signed a significant number of cooperation agreements and MOUs for the development of specific projects and sectors.

Additional trade legislation issued by Venezuela include: (a) the customs law (Ley Orgánica de Aduanas) and regulations thereunder, which provide the regulatory framework for the import, export and transport of goods in Venezuela, as well as the tariff and customs regulations; (b) the anti-smuggling law (Ley sobre el Delito de Contrabando) aimed at preventing and sanctioning contraband and smuggling; (c) the anti-dumping law (Ley sobre Prácticas Desleales del Comercio Internacional) which provides the policies and guidelines for the prevention of imports made under dumping conditions.

C. Trade Management

In case of imports intended to be paid with the purchase of foreign currency through Cencoex, before the dispatch of the import Cencoex must have issued the authorization of acquisition of foreign currency (autorización de adquisición de divisas or "AAD"). An authorization of settlement of the purchase of foreign currency (autorización de liquidación de divisas or "ALD") will be issued after nationalization of the import. Certificates of non-production and certificates of insufficient production are normally required for almost all primary goods imported through Cencoex. In general, other imports (those intended to be paid using foreign currency obtained through other exchange systems, or held by the importer in offshore banks) are concluded under regular international trade practices. Incoterms are widely used in international trade by Venezuelan companies.

Restrictions may be imposed on the importation of certain products or on products from certain countries as a response to reciprocal treatment.

Exports are deemed to be sales for income tax purposes. Although exporters are subject to the VAT, the applicable tax rate is zero.

Venezuelan laws contemplate a drawback mechanism that would allow the reimbursement of custom duties levied on goods used in the production process of goods to be exported and which have been paid directly by the exporter; however, the process to obtain the drawback certificates is cumbersome and the government incurs in significant delays in making the disbursement.

D. The Inspection and Quarantine of Import and Export Commodities

Imports of certain products may require a prior license, permit, certificate of quality, delegation, certificates of origin, such as a health permit from the Health Ministry and / or the Agriculture Ministry, or a license from the Defense Ministry. Registration with the Health Ministry is required to be able to import health products, cosmetics and foodstuffs. The approval process, though lengthy (approximately three to six months), is relatively transparent

---

[1] Venezuela was accepted as a full member of Mercosur in 2012. According to the Mercosur protocol, the Republic had four years to adopt the rules and common tariffs of the bloc.

and routine.

Sanitary and phytosanitary ("SPS") certificates from the Food and the Agriculture Ministries are required for most agricultural imports. Agriculture Ministry issues SPS permits for imported products and sub-products of plant or animal origin; Food Ministry issues import permits and licenses; and the Health Ministry grants food registration for all domestic and imported processed food products. Foods not registered in the country of origin cannot be registered in Venezuela.

Certain exports (such as certain components of the basic food list, certain metals, strategic products, radioactive products, and fertilizers) are subject to prior export license. Certain other products (gold, cocoa, coffee, fruit, vegetables, flowers, and certain drugs, among others) are subject to special permits and / or registrations. Other requirements for exports include health permits for agricultural products, sanitation permits for animal origin products; phytosanitary certificate for vegetable products, and a certificate of origin, which documents that the product exported has effectively been manufactured in the country.

E. Customs Management

Venezuela has implemented the customs computerized system (Sidunea) in the majority of Venezuelan ports of entry. Import duties are assessed, due and payable at time of arrival.

Prior to the importation, the importer must present, along with the import manifest, certain permits, certificates, and licenses corresponding to the merchandise to be imported, according to the Venezuelan customs schedule. The customs schedule provides for the obligation to submit, together with the import manifest, the certificate of registration issued by the autonomous service for standardization, quality, metrology and technical regulations (Sencamer) of the Finance Ministry. This obligation only applies to the goods that are subject to mandatory standards of Covenin (Venezuela's standards agency), technical regulations, or both. The customs schedule also includes a list of the goods for importation and national transit that are subject to Covenin standards.

All imported goods presented at the ports of entry must be officially declared to the Venezuelan tax authority (Seniat) within five days of arrival. Customs regulations stipulate that the consignee is the owner of the shipment and is responsible for all custom payments.

Only registered custom agencies are entitled to conduct customs procedures.

An import requires the introduction of foreign goods into the Venezuelan customs territory for definitive use or consumption. If, for example, foreign goods are brought into the Venezuelan customs territory but only for a specified period of time, this operation would be categorized as a temporary admission.[①]

The nationalization of foreign goods is the process whereby such goods are introduced in Venezuela and are submitted to the jurisdiction of the customs authorities. As a result of this process, the imported goods may leave the customs territory and may be used or consumed in Venezuela. The nationalization process generally encompasses the following stages: (a) arrival of the goods to a Venezuelan customs (as part of the arrival, the carrier must notify the consignee that the goods have arrived); (b) verification of documents by the customs to ensure that all of the documents supporting the customs declaration are correct and sufficient; (c) physical and documentary examination, which consists in determining the legal regime applicable to the goods (as part of this stage, the customs physically inspects the goods to confirm that the nature, origin, condition, quantity and value of the goods are in accordance with the particulars furnished in the declaration; as a result of the examination, the customs issue the corresponding forms required to pay the applicable customs duties, fees and taxes); (d) payment of the customs duties, fees and taxes; (e) release of the imported goods. All imported goods that comply with the nationalization process mentioned above become nationalized goods.

Venezuelan customs require all documents to be in Spanish language. The following documents are normally required: commercial invoice, bill of lading or airway bill, packing list, certificate of origin, and special certificates or permits when required.

Imports are subject to ad valorem customs tax. Customs duties are determined according to the custom valuation code applicable to the goods to be imported and are imposed on an ad valorem basis (i.e., as a percentage of the value of the imported goods). Additionally, imports are subject to VAT on the value of the goods and the applicable custom taxes, tariffs and duties. The import duties will be caused as of the date of arrival of the

---

[①] The customs law and its regulations allow the import of goods on a temporary basis without being subject to customs duties or VAT. The importer must request authorization for temporary import from the customs authority (Seniat), providing certain information, including reason of the request, information about the importer, detailed description of the goods indicating the use to be given to them and their characteristics.

goods to the primary zone of any national custom able to carry out the operation.[1]

Imported goods subsidized in the country of origin or dumped in Venezuela are subject to anti-dumping or compensatory duties under the anti-dumping law. Any person that produces similar goods in Venezuela may request an investigation of imported goods by the anti-dumping and subsidies commission ("CASS").[2]

Customs duties are not applied to exports. However, exporters must comply with all administrative customs formalities which require the use of a customs agent. Exports of minerals are subject to the issuance of transport certificate.

IV. Labour

A. Brief Introduction to Labour Laws and Regulations

Venezuela labour laws grant protection for workers and set forth minimum benefits and guarantees that may not be waived by the parties and are of mandatory application to all labour relationships. The labour law was amended in 2012.

The main legal framework in labour matters consists of: (a) the labour law (Ley del Trabajo, los Trabajadores y las Trabajadoras); (b) labour regulation under the labor law (Reglamento de la Ley Orgánica del Trabajo); (c) the workplace health and safety law (Ley Orgánica de Prevención, Condiciones y Medio Ambiente de Trabajo); (d) regulation under the workplace health and safety law (Reglamento Parcial de la Ley Orgánica de Prevención, Condiciones y Medio Ambiente de Trabajo); (e) regulation under the labour law on worktime (Reglamento Parcial de la Ley Orgánica del Trabajo sobre el Tiempo de Trabajo).

The employment relationship is governed by the provisions set forth in the Venezuelan labour laws and regulations, the individual labour contracts, the benefits plans implemented by the employer and the applicable collective bargaining agreements.

The Venezuelan government has imposed a labour freeze since 2002, whereby employees cannot be dismissed without the previous authorization from the Labour Ministry. Although labor freezes are theoretically intended to be temporary, the national executive branch has been extending them continuously since 2002. The last extension was enacted on December 28, 2015 for three years. The labour freeze covers all employees except for top-level management.

Only in exceptional cases does the Labor Ministry grant authorization for dismissal. Therefore, as a general rule, employers must secure voluntary departures in agreement with its employees, by offering enhanced termination payments (in addition to the statutory benefits) in exchange for their resignation. Other causes of employment termination include resignation (renuncia injustificada), resignation for cause (renuncia justificada), force majeure and agreement to terminate.

In case of employment termination, the employee will in most cases be entitled to: (a) severance payments (prestaciones sociales) (in case of resignation for cause, the employee is entitled to receive double severance payments); (b) a day of salary for each day of accrued vacation (vacaciones vencidas y no disfrutadas); (c) a day of salary for each day of vacation for the months worked during the last year of employment (vacaciones fraccionadas); (d) accrued and not paid vacation bonus (bono vacacional vencido y no pagado); (e) vacation bonus for the months worked during the last year of employment (bono vacacional fraccionado); (f) profit sharing for the months worked during the last year of employment (utilidades fraccionadas); (g) any other accumulated benefit under the company's benefits and compensation plan.

The labour law provides limitations regarding the number of foreign nationals working for Venezuelan companies. As a general rule, at least 90% of the workers of a company employing 10 or more employees must be Venezuelan citizens, and payments made to the foreign workers must not exceed 20% of the company's total payroll.

B. Requirements of Employing Foreign Employees

a. Work Permit

A non-Venezuelan national requires a work visa and a work permit issued by the Labour Ministry to work

---

[1] In order to avoid penalties caused by an improper tariff classification, importers should obtain the product's proper customs tariff classification from the customs authorities prior to importation.

[2] The CASS will establish anti-dumping or compensatory duties if it determines that there is dumping or that subsidies that cause or threaten to cause a major impairment to domestic production of similar goods have been granted.Anti-dumping or compensatory duties expire five years after the effective date.

as an employee in Venezuela. The work permit and the work visa can only be applied for by the employer. The following employees do not require a work permit: (a) scientists that perform studies as part of an international scientific mission; (b) journalists and other employees related to international media accredited for the performance of news activities; (c) employees who render services as part of an international treaty of cooperation and technical assistance; (d) professionals and technicians that will perform scientific or academic activities for less than 90 days; (e) scientists, professionals, technicians, experts and other specialized personnel who visit Venezuela to train other employees or to perform temporary activities for a period of less than 90 days; and (f) artists and professional sports players.

b. Application Procedure

Employers must first apply for a work permit from the Labour Ministry in Venezuela, and then apply for the work visa from the consular section of the Venezuelan embassy in the country of origin of the applicant.

Employers are required to submit: (a) an application form for the work permit; (b) copy of the worker's passport with at least six months' validity; (c) job offer issued by the hiring organization (i.e., the hiring organization must have its head office in Venezuela), notarized by a Venezuelan notary;[①] (d) curriculum vitae in the Spanish language; (e) documents that certify the applicant's professional training or professional qualification; (f) medical certificate; (g) criminal background check certificate.

The Labour Ministry may request additional documents to support the application.

c. Social Insurance

Because non-Venezuelan nationals are entitled to the same rights as nationals, employers are required to register foreign employees at the social security institute.

C. Exit and Entry

a. Visa Types

The main types of visa, relevant to foreign employees are:

(1) the business visa (TR-N visa), which is intended for traders, executives, company representatives, micro-entrepreneurs, who are non-migrants, and is meant for individuals who will enter Venezuela to perform commercial and financial or any other lucrative legal activity or transaction related to their business affairs; and

(2) the work visa (TR-L visa), which allows foreign nationals to work under an employment relationship in Venezuela. The employer must have legal presence in Venezuela (incorporation and registry requirements in Venezuela would have to be fulfilled) in order to engage in the employment contract.

Visa requirements may vary if the country involved is party to a treaty or convention with Venezuela, stipulating visa exemptions.

b. Restrictions for Exit and Entry

The business visa has a duration of one year and allows permanent stay for up to 180 days, with multiple entries into the country. This type of visa must be applied for at the consular section of the Venezuelan embassy in the country of origin of the applicant.

The work visa has a duration of one year and allows permanent stay for the same period, with multiple entries into the country. This type of visa must be applied for at the Consular Section of the Venezuelan embassy in the country of origin of the applicant.

D. Trade Union and Labour Organizations

Pursuant to the labour law, workers and employers are entitled to organize and incorporate unions. A minimum of 20 workers is required to form a union. There are two basic types of unions under Venezuelan labor laws: (a) company-wide unions that organize workers of a single company, and (b) industry-wide unions that organize workers in an entire industry regardless of the company they belong to and the position they hold. Under certain conditions, the workers may exercise their right to negotiate collective bargaining agreements and to resort to collective conflicts, including strikes.

Employers are also required to set up a workers' council. Workers must elect between three and seven employees to form the workers' council. Among those members there must be a woman, an individual aged 15 to 35 and a member of the national militia.

---

① The job offer must indicate the duration of the employment contract, costs of repatriation of the worker, position, working hours, salary and labour benefits. The job offer must also state that the foreign worker will train Venezuelan workers throughout the employment contract and that the employment contract will be governed by Venezuelan laws.

E. Labour Disputes

Labor claims are common in Venezuela. Venezuelan labour laws and regulations are designed to protect employees, and courts and authorities are generally sympathetic to employees.

Protections granted to workers by Venezuela's labour laws and regulations include: (a) the minimum wage is set by the Venezuelan government; (b) labour freeze pursuant to which workers with workers cannot be dismissed, demoted or moved, without a cause, previously qualified as such by the competent labor authorities; (c) the Labour Ministry may oppose to layoffs; (d) dismissal of a worker requires payment of additional compensation.

The statute of limitations for labour claims regarding severance payment is ten years from the date of employment termination, five years for labor claims regarding the payment of any other labour benefits from the date of employment termination; and the statute of limitations for work-related accidents and illness is five years from the date the accident or illness was certified.

Workers may resort to the labour courts or the labour inspectorate to settle labour disputes.

V. Intellectual Property

A. Brief Introduction of IP Laws and Regulations

The ownership, use and registration of trademarks and patents in Venezuela is governed mainly by: (a) the 1883 Paris Convention for the Protection of Industrial Property (the Paris Convention); (b) the 1994 World Trade Organization-Agreement on Trade-Related Aspects of Intellectual Property Rights (TRIPS); (c) the Venezuela industrial property law of 1956 (Ley de Propiedad Industrial).

Copyright is protected under the 1993 Venezuelan copyright law (Ley sobre el Derecho de Autor), its regulations, the Bern Convention, and the Universal Copyright Convention. Copyright law protects creative work such as literary, artistic and scientific creations, including computer software.

B. Patent Application

Patents are registered with the autonomous service of intellectual property (Servicio Autónomo de la Propiedad Intelectual or "Sapi"), an entity under the supervision of the Finance Ministry. Inventions, utility models and industrial designs are subject to protection in Venezuela. Inventions, utility models and industrial design patents are granted for a term of five or ten years (as requested by the filer). Patent applications are filed with Sapi, reviewed and later published in the Venezuelan industrial property bulletin to allow for third party opposition. If no opposition is made (or if an opposition is dismissed), the application is approved after completion of the relevant administrative procedure.

C. Trademark Registration

Trademark registrations are also filed with Sapi. Like the patent application process, the trademark application is filed, reviewed and published to allow opposition from third parties. If no opposition is made the trademark is granted. Trademarks are granted for a term of 15 years and may be renewed for successive 15-year periods.

D. Measures for IP Protection

Trademarks and patent rights can be enforced through civil and criminal actions.

VI. Environmental Protection

A. Department Supervising Environmental Protection

The Ministry of Environment is the entity mainly responsible of supervising environment protection. Local municipalities have some limited enforcement authority within their corresponding jurisdictions.

B. Brief Introduction of Laws and Regulations of Environmental Protection

Environmental protection laws and regulations in Venezuela include: (a) the environmental law (Ley Orgánica del Ambiente) and regulations thereunder; (b) the environmental criminal law (Ley Penal del Ambiente); (c) the dangerous substances law (Ley de Sustancias Peligrosas); (d) the socio-natural and technological risk management law (Ley de Gestión Integral de Riesgos Socionaturales y Tecnológicos); (e) the biological diversity management law; (f) the water resources law (Ley de Aguas); (g) the water resources and air quality law (Ley de Calidad de las Aguas y del Aire); (h) Decree number 883 containing the regulations for the classification and quality control of water bodies and liquid effluents or discharges (Normas para la Clasificación y el Control de la Calidad de los Cuerpos de Agua y Vertidos o Efluentes Líquidos); (i) Decree number 638 containing the regulations on air quality and air pollution control (Normas sobre la Calidad del Aire y Control de la Contaminación Atmosférica); (j) the regulations issued by the environmental authorities.

In addition, Venezuela has signed more than 50 multilateral environmental protection treaties, including: (a) the Vienna Convention for the Protection of the Ozone Layer (1985); (b) the Montreal Protocol on Substances that Deplete the Ozone Layer; (c) the United Nations Framework Convention on Climate Change (1994), the Kyoto Protocol (2005), and the Paris Agreement (2016) on climate change; (d) the International Convention on Oil Pollution Preparedness, Response and Co-operation (1994); (e) the Protocol Concerning Co-operation in Combating Oil Spills in the Wider Caribbean Region (1985); (f) the Convention on Nature Protection and Wild Life Preservation in the Western Hemisphere (1940).

Under the environmental law, any project to be developed in urban or rural areas must comply with a procedure of environmental assessment of activities capable of causing degradation to the environment. Such procedure requires the preparation by the company or the entity sponsoring the project of a social, cultural or environmental impact assessment (the "EIA").[1] Upon the analysis of the EIA, and depending on the location of the project and the level of intervention or affectation to the environment, the Ministry of Environment may issue one of three different environmental authorizations: (a) an authorization to occupy land (autorización para ocupación del territorio, also known as "AOT"); (b) an authorization to affect natural resources (autorización para la afectación de recursos naturales, also known as "AARN"), or (c) a technical certification of the environmental and socio-cultural impact study (acreditación técnica, also known as "AT"). The environmental authorization will provide the terms and conditions applicable to all the stages of the project.

Before implementation of the approved project, the company will need to post a performance bond in favor of the Ministry of Environment, as well as insurance for civil responsibility and for indemnification for possible environmental accidents.

Entities and individuals involved in the use, handling or generation of hazardous substances, materials or waste, or in activities that emit gas and particles into the air, generate liquid discharges into rivers, lakes or sewage networks, or involve hazardous materials and hazardous waste, are required to obtain registration with the Ministry of Environment's registry of activities capable to degrading the environment (RACDA) before initiating such activities.

Companies responsible for activities that emit gas and particles into the air are required to comply with air-quality limits established in the technical rules and perform readings of its emissions every year, or every two years if authorized by the Ministry of Environment.

Companies generating liquid discharges into rivers, lakes or sewage networks must adjust their discharges to comply with the quality parameters set forth in the technical regulations, and are normally required to perform readings of its effluents every three months.

Companies handling hazardous materials and waste are subject to the compliance with the obligations set forth in the environmental law on hazardous materials and waste, including the obligation to: (a) file a compliance plan with measures to mobilize, store, process and dispose of the hazardous waste and to minimize its production; (b) have a contingency plan to prevent and respond to incidents or accidents related to hazardous waste; (c) have a control of the amounts and types of hazardous waste, types and risks that they present and of their storage.

Companies responsible for creating noise must adjust their noise emissions to the limits established by the applicable technical regulations. There are technical regulations for noise pollution produced by both fixed and mobile sources.

Regarding crimes against the environment, the environmental criminal law provides for criminal and civil penalties (fines and imprisonment) for actions or omissions that adversely affect the environment and natural resources. Sanctions may be imposed on both the company and its officers, directors or shareholders, if determined to have been involved in causing the environmental damage.

Crimes against the environment include: (a) crimes against biological diversity; (b) crimes involving degradation, alteration, deterioration and other damages to: (i) water resources, (ii) soil, topography and landscape, and (iii) nature and wild life; (c) crimes against environmental quality (atmosphere, solid waste,

---

[1] Pursuant to article 129 of the Constitution, every activity capable of causing damage to the ecosystem must be previously accompanied by an environmental and socio-cultural impact assessment.

hazardous substance, radioactive materials and noise pollution, pollution of waters during transportation of oil, etc.)

C. Evaluation of Environmental Protection

Despite having an extensive environmental legal framework, enforcement of environmental laws by the Venezuelan environmental authorities is slow and often spasmodic. Many environmental regulations are outdated and fail to meet international standards.

Some of the most critical environmental issues include unauthorized mining operations, oil pollution of water and soil, urban and industrial pollution, illegal deforestation, waste and landfill management, sewage pollution into lakes and rivers, and urban and industrial waste disposal.

VII. Dispute Resolution

A. Methods and Bodies of Dispute Resolution

a. Litigation

The Venezuelan court system is a federal court system. There are no state courts in Venezuela. The highest ranking court is the Venezuelan Supreme Tribunal (Tribunal Supremo de Justicia), which is comprised of six chambers: the constitutional chamber, the social cassation chamber, the civil cassation chamber, the criminal chamber, the electoral chamber and the political-administrative chamber. Each chamber is composed of five justices, except for the constitutional chamber which is composed by seven.

Civil and commercial claims are heard by first instance courts. Decisions of first instance courts can be appealed with the second instance courts. In some cases, extraordinary actions, such as casación or amparo constucional, can be brought before the Supreme Tribunal.

Venezuelan civil and commercial procedure is conducted under the code of civil procedure (Código de Procedimiento Civil). Commercial cases are conducted in written form. The claim, the answer, interlocutory proceedings, evidentiary stage and motions are presented in writing. There are no oral motions or hearings in Venezuelan commercial cases unless the judge orders an oral hearing or motion. Judges can issue provisional remedies, i.e., pre-judgment attachments, injunctions, or seizures.

Choice of non-Venezuelan jurisdiction is legal and enforceable, except for disputes relating to real property located in Venezuela, family matters and other matters.

b. Arbitration, Conciliation and Mediation

Arbitration clauses and awards arising therefrom are enforceable in Venezuela in accordance with the provisions and conditions of the private international law statute (Ley de Derecho Internacional Privado) and the commercial arbitration law (Ley de Arbitraje Comercial).

Venezuela is a party to the United Nation's Convention on the Recognition and Enforcement of Foreign Arbitral Awards, adopted in 1958 at the United Nations headquarters in New York (New York Convention).

An arbitration award rendered by arbitrators abroad would be enforceable against a counterparty (including individuals) in the courts of Venezuela pursuant to article 48 of the Venezuelan commercial arbitration law without a review of the merits of the foreign arbitral award, provided that: (a) the foreign arbitration award concerns matters of private civil or commercial law only, (b) the foreign arbitration award does not relate to real property interests over real property located in Venezuela; (c) the matter submitted to arbitration does not relate to a subject matter in which no settlement is allowed, and does not relate to a subject matter that violates essential principles of Venezuelan public policy; (d) the arbitral award has not been suspended, annulled or superseded prior to the enforcement proceedings, (e) the defendant has been duly served of the arbitration proceedings by a duly incorporated arbitration panel, with sufficient time to appear in the proceedings and has been generally granted with procedural guarantees that secure a reasonable possibility of defense; (f) the incorporation of the arbitration tribunal and the arbitration procedure have complied with the laws of the jurisdiction where the arbitration has been conducted.

The two main local arbitration centers are the Venezuelan business center of arbitration and conciliation (Centro Empresarial de Conciliación y Arbitraje or CEDCA), and the arbitration center of the Caracas chamber of commerce (Cámara de Comercio de Caracas or CCC).

Conciliation and mediation are recognized and promoted by the Constitution as a valid alternative dispute resolution method. The arbitration rules of CEDCA and the CCC provide regulations on conciliation or mediation procedures as an amicable way to settle a dispute that can be used by the parties to the conflict before resorting to arbitration.

B. Application of Laws

Contracts are governed by the agreements reached by the parties, by the mandatory rules of Venezuelan law and by the supplementary rules set forth in the civil code and the code of commerce which are not superseded by the parties. Choice of foreign law to govern contract is generally legal and binding. Pursuant to the civil code, contracts must be carried out and interpreted in good faith.

VIII. Others

A. Anti-commercial Bribery

a. Brief Introduction of Anti-commercial Bribery Laws and Regulations

Venezuela's anti-bribery laws and regulations include: (a) the anti-bribery law (Ley Contra la Corrupción); (b) the law against organized crime and the financing of terrorism (Ley Orgánica Contra la Delincuencia Organizada y Financiamiento al Terrorismo); (c) the Venezuelan criminal code (Código Penal). Venezuela is also a signatory to the United Nations Convention against Corruption (UNCAC), the Inter-American Convention against Corruption, and the United Nations Convention against Transnational Organized Crime.

The anti-bribery law is the primary source of regulations against corruption in Venezuela. The purpose of the law is to safeguard public patrimony and guarantee the correct and transparent management of public resources.

The anti-bribery law applies to individuals, public and private legal entities, local public officers (funcionarios públicos), and communal organizations.

The anti-bribery law criminalizes bribery, attempted bribery, illicit enrichment, embezzlement, and other actions capable of causing damage to the public patrimony. The act of bribing a foreign officer is also punishable under the anti-bribery law (although the term "foreign officer" is not defined therein). As a signatory to the UNCAC, Venezuela will assist foreign anti-corruption authorities in investigating foreign bribery cases.

b. Department Supervising Anti-commercial Bribery

The national anti-corruption bureau (Cuerpo Nacional Contra la Corrupción), created in November 2014 is the entity in charge of enforcing anti-bribery regulations, supervising compliance by public or private entities, and investigating corruption offenses. The anti-corruption bureau works in close coordination with the General Comptroller's Office (Contraloría General de la República) (GCO), the General Public Prosecutor's Office (Ministerio Público) (GPPO), the National Organized Crime and Financing of Terrorism Unit, and the specialized police units, in preventing, combating and investigating corruption violations. The GPPO is responsible for prosecuting and handling criminal cases (including corruption cases).

c. Punitive Actions

Some of the most relevant criminal acts punishable under the anti-bribery law include:

a) active bribery of a Venezuelan public official (the giving of a bribe), is punishable by one to four years of imprisonment, and a fine of up to 50% of the bribe;

b) passive bribery of a Venezuelan public official (the taking of a bribe), is punishable by three to seven years of imprisonment, and a fine of up to 50% of the bribe;

c) attempted bribery (unsuccessful effort to bribe a public official), is punishable by six months to two years of imprisonment;

d) bribery of a foreign public official (the act of promising or actually giving a benefit or undue profit to a foreign official in exchange for the performance (or lack of performance) of his duties), is punishable by six to twelve 12 years of imprisonment; and

e) embezzlement of public assets, is punishable by three to ten years of imprisonment, and a fine of 20% to 60% of the value of the assets embezzled.

B. Project Contracting

a. Permission System

As a general rule, contracts for the sale of goods to, the rendering of services to, and the execution of works for, government entities are subject to the provisions of (a) the law for the acquisition of public goods, services and works, and (b) the public procurement law (Ley de Contrataciones Públicas) and regulations thereunder. For the purpose of this section, we use the term "government entities" to indistinctively refer to the Venezuelan government, the state-owned entities and the joint ventures where the State directly or indirectly holds a controlling interest.

Pursuant to the public procurement law, the acquisition of goods, works or services to government entities must be awarded using the selection methods (modalidades de contratación) provided in the public procurement law, with the exception of procurement contracts for, related to, or entered with: (a) professional and financial services; (b) the acquisition of real estate; (c) the acquisition of artistic, literacy or scientific works; (d) commercial or strategic alliances between contractor and the government entity; (e) basic public services essential to the government entity (electricity, gas, telephone, internet); (f) public sector entities, state-owned companies and communes; (g) the acquisition of goods, services or works whenever a state of emergency is in effect; (h) the acquisition of food, medicines and services of basic necessity (primera necesidad); (i) the acquisition of goods and services using the government entity's petty cash; (j) the acquisition of goods, services and works for the purpose of national security. These procurement contracts can be awarded directly by the government entity's highest authority (maxima autoridad contratante).

In addition, contracts entered into within the framework of international cooperation treaties, contracts with companies incorporated pursuant to international agreements, employment contracts (servicios laborales), contracts for the lease of real estate, and contracts for sport, artistic, scientific or academic sponsorships are excluded from the scope of application of the public procurement law.

As a general rule, companies wishing to supply goods, perform works or supply services to government entities are required to register with, and obtain qualification from, the Venezuelan national contractors registry (Registro Nacional de Contratistas) (RNC).[1] Certain exemptions apply. Registration must be updated annually and should not apply to excluded contracts listed above.

Qualification is not required in the case of companies participating in international open bids (concurso abierto anunciado internacionalmente), procurement contracts excluded from the use of selection methods, and non-domiciled companies and individuals selected using the direct solicitation method (contratacion directa), among others.

b. Prohibited Areas

See section (d) of the "Investment" chapter of this guide for a list of the areas where foreign investment is restricted.

c. Invitation to Bid and Bidding

Selection of contractors is made by the government entity using one of the following selection methods:

a) Open tender (Concurso abierto)

A public bidding process where all local or foreign entities or individuals interested in participating are invited to submit a bid. The government entity must use the open tender or the international open tender selection method for: (i) the acquisition of goods when the estimated contract amount if greater than 20,000 tax units; (ii) the procurement of services when the estimated contract amount is greater than 30,000 tax units; (iii) the procurement of works when the estimated contract amount is greater than 50,000 tax units.[2]

b) Restricted tender (Concurso cerrado)

A selection method in which at least five contractors are personally invited to bid, based on their technical, financial and legal capabilities. The government entity can use the restricted tendering for: (i) the acquisition of goods when the estimated contract amount is greater than 5,000 tax units but less than 20,000 tax units; (ii) the procurement of services when the estimated contract amount is greater than 10,000 tax units but less than 30,000 tax units; (iii) the procurement of works when the estimated contract amount is greater than 20,000 tax units but less than 50,000 tax units.

c) Price consultation (Consulta de precios)

A selection method used for small value contracts, in which price quotes are requested to at least three contractors. The government entity may use the quotation method for: (a) the acquisition of goods when the estimated contract amount is less than 5,000 tax units; (b) the procurement of services when the estimated contract amount is less than 10,000 tax units; (c) the procurement of works when the estimated contract amount is less than 20,000 tax units.

d) Direct award (Contratacion directa)

Exceptionally, and regardless of the contract amount but provided that the government entity's highest

---

[1] RNC qualifies contractors based on specific formulas that evaluate contractor's financial capacity to engage in public procurement.
[2] The tax unit is a value for measurement set by the Venezuelan tax administration (Seniat) every year

authority satisfactorily justifies it, the government entity is entitled to directly award a contract in several cases, including:

• procurement of goods, services or works required for the continuity of the government entity's production, which otherwise could be seriously affected by delays in the use of other selection methods;

• when the technical conditions of a particular good, service or work excludes the change of competition or requires the use of this selection method;

• when it is not possible to use another selection method due to the special conditions under which the contractors agree to bid or the government entity invites to tender;

• in the case of a proven emergency (emergencia comprobada);

• procurement of works, goods or services governed by contracts terminated in advance, where the use of another selection method could be detrimental to the governmental entity; and

• procurement of goods, services or works for which another selection method could compromise the government entity's secrets or commercial strategies.

C. Oil

a. Brief Introduction to the Oil Legal Regime

Exploration, exploitation, refining, industrialization, transportation, storage and commercialization of hydrocarbons and its by-products and the works required for these activities are governed by the Venezuelan hydrocarbons law. Extraction of gaseous hydrocarbons associated to petroleum (known as "associated gas") is also governed by the hydrocarbons law.

Under the hydrocarbons law, all activities relating to exploration in search of hydrocarbon reservoirs and its extraction, collection and initial transportation and storage ("upstream" or "primary activities") are reserved to the government of Venezuela, which may undertake such activities: (a) directly; (b) through wholly-owned state entities; (c) through joint venture companies (empresas mixtas) controlled by the Venezuelan government through an equity participation of more than 50% ("EMs").

Foreign investors can participate in upstream or primary activities only through a minority equity ownership in EMs where the Venezuelan government directly or indirectly holds a majority interest. Foreign investors are generally entitled to have a minority representation in the EM's board of directors and are normally given certain veto rights at the shareholders' level. Participation in an EM requires the issuance of several governmental approvals and the government generally requires the payment of a signing bonus to the Republic and certain other special advantages.

EMs must sell all the hydrocarbons produced and not consumed by them to an affiliate of Petróleos de Venezuela, S.A.(PDVSA), except for: (a) hydrocarbons delivered to the Republic as payment in kind of the royalty; (b) the associated gas that PDVSA or its affiliate does not accept to receive. Upgraded crude oil (produced by EMs in the Orinoco Belt projects) can be sold directly by the EMs in the international markets.[1]

EMs qualify as state-owned companies and as such are subject to several public-sector laws and regulations, including public procurement laws and regulations, budget laws, financing laws, anti-bribery laws, financial controls, etc.

All facilities and existing works, its expansions and modifications, owned by Venezuela or by wholly-owned state entities, engaged in the refining of hydrocarbons in Venezuela and in the main transport of oil products and gas, are reserved to the Republic. However, new refining activities of both natural hydrocarbons and hydrocarbon by-products can be carried out: (a) directly by the Venezuelan government; (b) by the Venezuelan government through wholly-owned state entities; (c) through mixed companies with the direct or indirect participation of the Venezuelan government and the participation of the private sector in any proportion (this may include EMs); (d) by private companies.[2]

National or international commercialization of natural hydrocarbons, as well as hydrocarbon by-products which commercialization has been reserved to the Republic by Presidential decree, can only be carried out by state-owned entities. Commercialization of liquid fuels is also reserved to the Republic. Commercialization of other hydrocarbons by-products not reserved to the Republic by presidential decree can be carried out by private companies.

---

[1] The Orinoco Belt (Faja Petrolifera del Orinoco) is an area located north of the Orinoco River in Venezuela, where the largest oil deposits in the world lie.

[2] Refining of natural hydrocarbons requires a license issued by the Venezuelan Petroleum Ministry.Refining licenses have a 25-year maximum term, renewable for a maximum of 15 years.

b. Oil Tax Regime

Set forth below is a summary of the Venezuelan taxes applicable to oil companies, including oil EMs (additional to those described in the tax section above):

• Royalty (regalía) levied at a 30% rate on the volume of extracted hydrocarbons, which can be paid in kind or in cash, at the option of the Venezuelan government. The 30% rate can be reduced by the Venezuelan government to 20% in case of mature reservoirs or extra-heavy crude oil from the Orinoco Belt. The windfall profits tax law caps the price for calculation of the royalty at US$80 per barrel. The special conditions for the creation of an EM may contemplate additional royalties.

• Surface tax (impuesto superficial) calculated at the annual rate of 100 tax units per each square kilometer or fraction thereof (this tax is determined based on the concession area not under production, with an annual increase of 2% for five years and 5% in subsequent years).

• Fuel consumption tax (impuesto de consumo propio), equivalent to 10% of the value of each cubic meter of hydrocarbon-derived product consumed as fuel oil in their operations, calculated based on the final sale price to the final consumer and if such product is not sold in the national market, calculated by the Petroleum Ministry.

• General consumption tax determined at a rate ranging between 30% and 50% of the price paid by the final consumer and applicable to each liter of hydrocarbon-derived product sold in the Venezuelan domestic market; the consumption tax rate is determined annually; this tax is withheld at source.

• Extraction tax (impuesto de extracción) calculated at a rate of one third of the value of all the liquid hydrocarbons extracted from an oil field (from the same base established for royalty calculation); the taxpayer may deduct from the amount to be paid for this tax, the amount paid as royalty (or as additional royalty or as special advantage payable annually, but only for the periods subsequent to the payment of such annual special advantage); this tax can be reduced by the Venezuelan government in certain cases up to a minimum of 20%; the windfall profits tax law caps the price for calculation of the extraction tax at US$80 per barrel.

• Export registration tax calculated at a rate of one thousandth (0.1%) of the value of all hydrocarbons exported from a port in Venezuela (based on the sales prices of these hydrocarbons); the windfall profits tax law caps the price for calculation of the export registration tax at US$80 per barrel.

• Companies engaged in the exploitation of hydrocarbons (excluding non-associated gas) and related activities, such as refining and transport are subject to Venezuelan income tax at a flat rate of 50% of net income; however, companies exclusively engaged in the refining of hydrocarbons or the upgrading of heavy and extra-heavy crude oil are subject to the normal corporate tax rate (i.e., a maximum tax rate of 34% on income). Given the existence of these two separate tax regimes, the government and foreign companies are considering to structure certain Orinoco Belt projects on a disintegrated business model (instead of a fully-integrated project) to improve the economy of the project by forming an EM of production of extra-heavy crude (subject to the oil taxation regime of 50%) and an EM of refining and marketing of products (subject to the ordinary tax regime of up to 34%). In certain Orinoco Belt projects, the government has agreed to a favorable deduction, amortization and loss carry-forward regime for income tax purposes.

• Windfall profits tax for "extraordinary" and "exorbitant" prices, which are based on the difference between prices in the Venezuelan national budget and the monthly average of international prices of the basket of Venezuelan hydrocarbons. This tax is payable by exporters of natural or upgraded liquid hydrocarbons and by-products and by EMs that sell natural or upgraded liquid hydrocarbons and by-products to PDVSA and its affiliates; however, the windfall tax law provides for certain exemptions for: (a) EMs that sell natural or upgraded liquid hydrocarbons and by-products to PDVSA and its affiliates that are engaged in projects of development of new oil fields, or increase the production of exploitation plans in ongoing projects declared as such by the Petroleum Ministry, provided that EMs have not recovered their total investment in said projects; (b) exports in the framework of international cooperation or financing agreements.

• The special conditions for the creation of EMs generally provide for a social investment payment equal to 1% of their earnings before taxes, and the so-called "shadow tax" (or ventaja especial) triggered in case the fiscal take does not reach at least 50% of gross profits after applying royalties, taxes and other levies; thus, the EM must pay the difference between this threshold and the fiscal take. The "shadow tax" is payable annually; however, in certain Orinoco Belt projects, the government agreed to the accumulation of the "shadow tax" from early production until the start of production of the upgrader.

• Oil companies are not subject to municipal business taxes, but certain municipalities from time to time attempt to tax them.

• In certain Orinoco Belt projects, the Venezuelan government has agreed to the reduction of royalties and taxes and the granting of additional tax incentives if the investments cannot be recovered within a certain timeframe.

津巴布韦

作者：Terence Hussein、Paresh Ranchhod、Sara Nyaradzo Moyo、Shorai Rutendo Chidemo
译者：刘兴燕、王红燕

一、概述①

津巴布韦位于非洲南部地区的中心，占据有利的地理位置，并已成为区域贸易和内陆运输中心。该国有利的地理位置使其成为南非的投资中心。津巴布韦被视为未来几年提供高投资回报的非洲国家之一。

津巴布韦是一个资源丰富、和平的国家，是通往非洲南部的门户，战略地位于非洲南部的中心地带，与赞比亚、莫桑比克、南非和博茨瓦纳为邻。这个国家处于南北走廊中部，将所有南部非洲的物流、铁路、道路、电力和电信联系起来。津巴布韦拥有近 1 400 万人口，拥有温带气候和季节性降雨。

津巴布韦拥有强大的高等教育体系，人力资本基础雄厚。津巴布韦致力于改善经营环境，并专注于巩固投资政策，并在以制造业、农业、采矿业、能源、旅游基础设施和服务为主的各领域提供各种投资机会。

多币种制度的采用有效地结束了津巴布韦元作为交易媒介的使用。当前使用的主要货币是美元和南非兰特（ZAR），英镑、博茨瓦纳普拉和欧元也是法定货币，虽然它们的使用程度比美元和 ZAR 稍低。

政府通过财政部表示，多货币制度将在可预见的将来保持不变。

政府已采取措施和激励政策，吸引外资进入几个经济部门。

本指南的这一方面涵盖适用于津巴布韦投资的法律和法规。本报告仅为法律摘要。

二、投资

（一）市场准入

津巴布韦政府在创造有利的商业环境以转变经济和吸引外国直接投资方面取得了进展。政府为持续这样做，宣布将在今年第一季度颁布 13 项法律，通过解决外国投资者以前提出的疑虑，创造有利的投资环境。这些法案中包括《国家竞争力委员会法案》《司法法修正案》和《商店许可修正案》。②

正是在这种背景下，政府于 2018 年 1 月 18 日发布了投资政策声明。③投资指南概述了该国的投资政策战略；并展示经济中可用的投资机会，包括但不限于农业、矿业、制造业、旅游业、信息通信与技术以及基础设施发展等。该准则是政府为努力解决本国面临的国内挑战（经济增长缓慢、公司关闭、现金危机、高失业率等）的一部分。④

1. 投资指南摘要

投资指导方针确定了政府致力于建立以合理投资原则和国际最佳实践（如不歧视、有效保护财产、透明度和高标准治理）为基础的经济的决心。政府承诺遵守双边、区域和国际协定下的法律义务。此外，政府已承诺在 6 个月内完善与调整投资法律框架使其与国际标准保持一致。在这方面，政府自 2018 年 3 月起修订了《本土化和经济赋权法》⑤，仅将钻石和铂金行业的本土化率限制在 51% 和 49%。

---

① 参见津巴布韦政府：《2017 年津巴布韦投资指南》。
② 参见津巴布韦政府：《津巴布韦投资指南和机遇》，2018 年 1 月。
③ 同上注。
④ 同上注。
⑤ 参见第 14:33 章。

津巴布韦正在3个战略地区推行《经济特区法》①，以建立经济特区（SEZ）。经济特区旨在通过为合格投资提供特殊激励措施来吸引投资，增加出口，并促进增值和增效。同时意在通过向投资者提供有竞争力的财政和非财政激励措施，促进对经济战略部门的投资，振兴重点行业。与促进投资相关的还有政府的目标是加强投资的体制框架，减少针对投资入境和设立企业的官僚程序。②

2. 投资法规

津巴布韦有几部适用于投资的立法：
- 《宪法》③；
- 《证券交易法》④；
- 《集体投资计划法》⑤；
- 《投资管理局法》⑥。

（1）宪法

根据《宪法》第2节和第71节的规定，《宪法》赋予私人投资免遭无偿征收的法律保护。此外，津巴布韦是保证有效的投资保护和争议解决的国际条约的签署国。其中包括MIGA、OPIC、ICSID、UNICITRAL，《承认及执行外国仲裁裁决公约》⑦。此外，津巴布韦还与包括中国在内的许多国家达成了多项双边投资保护协定（BIPPA），与中国签署的双边协议迄今仍然有效并保护中国和津巴布韦公民的利益。

（2）证券交易法⑧

《证券交易法》规定了控制和监管证券投资的若干方面。该法规的具体规定将出现在本报告的其他地方进行描述。根据该法第4（1）（a）条规定的目标，证券委员会旨在维持高水平的投资者保护。

（3）投资管理局法⑨

该法规定了津巴布韦投资管理局（ZIA）的设立和职能，津巴布韦投资管理局是负责推动、促进、管理和协调国内外投资的投资促进机构。

根据该法案，外国投资者必须从ZIA获得投资许可证，这将使投资者能够获得津巴布韦法律规定的激励和保护。派发股息和偿还贷款、税收、出口便利和外汇管制以及进口关税配额时也需要许可证。该许可证在ZIA委员会确定的特定期限内有效，并可申请延期。⑩

申请投资许可证的要求如下⑪：
- 不可退还的法定申请费；
- 一份完整的ZIA申请表格；
- 公司注册文件；
- 股东和/或董事的官方名单和简介；
- 业务计划或可行性研究；
- 财务证明（项目融资的证据可以以银行对账单、银行确认函、确认的银行贷款、其他已确认的信贷措施和/或设备/机器中提供）；
- 许可证发放费。

一旦投资许可证颁发后，投资者就可以申请居住和工作许可证，以及其运营地区所需的其他许可证，以使立即开始运营。

---

① 参见第14:34章。
② 参见津巴布韦政府：《津巴布韦投资指南和机遇》，2018年1月。
③ 2013年第20号修正案。
④ 参见第24:25章。
⑤ 参见第24:19章。
⑥ 参见第14:30章。
⑦ 参见津巴布韦政府：《2017年津巴布韦投资指南》。
⑧ 参见第24:25章。
⑨ 参见第14:30章。
⑩ 参见津巴布韦政府：《2017年津巴布韦投资指南》。
⑪ 同上注。

3. 投资形式

津巴布韦的三个外国投资主要切入点是：津巴布韦投资局（ZIA），津巴布韦证券交易所（ZSE）以及与政府公司或实体的合资安排。

津巴布韦投资局（ZIA）是该国的投资促进机构，旨在促进和为外国直接投资和地方投资提供便利。根据《合资企业法》①，外国投资者可能与政府成立合资企业。该法旨在通过制定关于公私合作伙伴关系的规则，为执行合资协议提供指导方针，从而促进投资。

外国投资者可以在津巴布韦的任何部门进行投资，但需要批准的保留部门除外②：

- 农业/林业；
- 运输；
- 零售/批发贸易，包括分销；
- 理发店和美容院；
- 商业摄影；
- 职业中介；
- 地产代理；
- 代客服务；
- 粮食磨坊产品；
- 在矿产部门，需要本土参与的唯一资源与钻石和铂金有关。

津巴布韦证券交易所（ZSE）为通过股票市场向当地经济注入外国证券投资（FPI）提供了另一种途径。目前在 ZSE 上有来自各经济领域的约 59 个有效柜台，包括采矿、农业、旅游、服务和制造业。外国人购买 ZSE 股票必须通过正常的银行渠道转入外币。购买股份不得超过总股本的 40%，单一投资者的购买不得超过发行股份的 10%。

4. 市场准入及检测标准

津巴布韦标准协会（SAZ）是津巴布韦的国家标准组织。SAZ 代表津巴布韦在 ISO、IEC 扩展国家计划、SADCSTAN 和 Comesa 标准协调委员会中积极参与这些组织的标准化计划。越来越多的国际和地区标准被作为国家标准采用，以确保国家标准不与区域和国际贸易伙伴的标准相冲突。2010 年发布的标准中有 24% 是采用 ISO 标准。③

SAZ 是 ISO 的成员，也通过了南非国家认证系统的认证。津巴布韦生产或进口到津巴布韦的产品必须经过 SAZ 检验，进口货物必须在进入津巴布韦之前由国际检验集团代表政府进行预检。海关和商标法规还禁止进口侵犯商标和专利法的产品，并对进口、销售或分销侵权产品实施处罚。④

（二）外汇管制

1. 部门监督外汇

根据《外汇管制法》⑤，总统拥有广泛的权威和权力，可以监管有关黄金、货币、证券、交易所交易、津巴布韦资产进出口、财产清算转移、与债务有关的付款和交易等全部事务。

该法于 1965 年颁布，迄今仍然有效。在颁布时，它旨在控制、限制和管理货币、黄金和罗得西亚价值资产的流入和流出。⑥该法在 1980 年津巴布韦获得独立后仍然有效，并在 2009 年继续进行重大修订，当时津巴布韦当地货币因恶性通货膨胀而被非货币化并被美国、南非、博茨瓦纳、英国和欧盟的货币所取代。随后许多其他国际货币在津巴布韦被列为法定货币，包括人民币和印度卢比。目前有 11 种国际货币在津巴布韦被确认为法定货币。此外还有债券货币，一种当地货币单位，自 2016 年 5 月起以有限的规模推出，并由津巴布韦《储备银行修正法案》确定为法定货币从 2016 年 10 月 30 日起

---

① 参见第 22:22 章。
② 2013 年和 2014 年在津巴布韦做生意 - Grant Thornton。
③ www.iso.org/member/308829.html.
④ www.iso.org/member/308829.html.
⑤ 参见第 22:05 章。
⑥ 1980 年独立前的国家名称。

生效。①

津巴布韦储备银行根据津巴布韦《储备银行法》②设立，是一家法人机构，中央外汇管制机构拥有管理津巴布韦外汇交易、黄金、铂金和钻石交易相关事宜的权力。储备银行依次授权15个"授权经销商"执行津巴布韦有关外汇管制立法的规定。③授权经销商实质上是商业银行和金融机构，为津巴布韦的公众提供银行服务。

储备银行外汇管理司负责妥善核算津巴布韦国际收支平衡状况活期账户的情况④，并执行《外汇管制条例》，《外汇管制（一般）法令》⑤和根据外汇管制条例发布的任何储备银行指令的规定。储备银行对财政部长负责，力求执行和规范政府部委和政府的政策。

2. 津巴布韦外汇法律法规简介

储备银行通过授权经销商执行《外汇管制法》及其相关附属条例颁布的规定，其中最重要的是《外汇管制条例》和《外汇管制（一般）法令》。

在《外汇管制法》方面，津巴布韦总统有权管理与黄金、货币、证券、交易所交易、津巴布韦进出口贸易、与债务有关的付款和交易的所有事宜。该法案授权总统颁布法规，禁止和规范与上述财产有关的交易，并授权人员进行货币交易业务。

但是，该法还规定了证明某人没有违反该法的义务，并对任何不遵守该法或条例规定的人施加严厉的处罚。该法还规定了域外适用的条款。根据2009年实施的第5（3）条，对违反该法或其条例的处罚可包括支付等于所处理的外币或资产的价值的罚款，不超过10年的监禁或并处罚款和监禁，以及处理和没收所处理的资产或财产的价值的最多三倍的经济处罚（该法第7条）。

尽管津巴布韦目前在津巴布韦承认11种国际货币为通用的法定货币，除非获得储备银行外汇管制的批准，1996年《外汇管制条例》通常限制和禁止黄金、外汇、证券和债务交易。这些条例的效力是限制未获得事先外汇管制批准的用从津巴布韦获得的资金支付津巴布韦境外的金额、债务或义务。由于条例没有被废除或修改，它们仍然有效。

1996年的《外汇管制（一般）法令》自1996年以来一直没有大幅度修改，并寻求调整和限制津巴布韦可汇出的外币，批准可用于支付服务费、企业汇款、假期津贴、借记卡的外币汇出金额、费用和专业费用、医疗费用和教育费用。该法令还将任何津巴布韦实体的股份或股票的外资所有权限制为股份或股票总值的40%，并规定授权交易商在处理外币支付审批时的责任。虽然该法令在许多方面已经过时，但在撤销或修改之前仍然有效。

从2016年10月开始，津巴布韦《储备银行修正法案》⑥在法律上认可津巴布韦债券货币为法定货币。债券货币从2016年5月开始作为出口激励措施给予所有出口商，出口商有权获得因此给津巴布韦带来的所有外汇收入的5%作为奖励（对初级矿物出口商的激励限制为2.5%）。奖励以债券货币支付并记入出口商的银行账户。债券货币是根据储备银行于2016年5月发行的《外汇管制指令》引入的，指示债券货币被视为可替代货币，并以面值与美元交易。

2017年颁布了更具体的规定，以防止个人和实体持有现金金额，并对债券货币与金额高于债券面值的10%其他货币的交易进行惩罚[《外汇管制（修正）令》]⑦。这些规定在废除或修改之前一直有效。

3. 外国企业的外汇管理要求

根据上述有关津巴布韦外汇交易的法律规定，所有进入津巴布韦的外国资金都必须通过津巴布韦授权经销商开设的账户。如果资金投资于津巴布韦的一家企业，这种投资的资本部分（如果包含货币资源）必须取得投资许可证，以保护外国投资者的利益，并使得投资所得利润能够转移至本国。如果

---

① 2017年第1号法令。
② 参见第22:15章。
③ 根据外汇管制条例 S.I.109/1996。
④ 1996年法定文书第109号。
⑤ 1996年法定文书第110号。
⑥ 2017年第1号。
⑦ 2017年法定文书第122A号。

企业要从外部借款，贷款工具必须在资金进入津巴布韦之前在授权经销商处进行注册以获得批准。授权经销商的批准限额为 2 000 万美元，任何超过此数额的贷款都需要获得储备银行的批准。津巴布韦的资产可以抵押贷款，包括获得储备银行批准的矿产。批准的目的是支付贷款人贷款的资金和利息，并确定贷款条款对借款人不是繁重或惩罚性的。在这方面，储备银行参考了关于利率、期限以及可能对外国贷款征收的其他费用的指导方针。

由于最近对外国投资法律进行了修订，任何外国实体或个人现在都可以拥有津巴布韦任何企业 100% 的股权，不包括钻石和铂金或经济储备部门。该批准是通过津巴布韦投资管理局向申请人颁发的投资许可证获得的。

投入企业或作为贷款进入津巴布韦的资金不符合获得债券货币出口激励的资格。

（三）融资

在津巴布韦，商业银行通常被储备银行指定为授权经销商。"授权经销商"指：

① 津巴布韦储备银行；

② 储备银行通过命令宣布为授权经销商的任何商业银行或承兑银行或其他任何类别的银行。[①]

授权经销商可以不经外部贷款协调委员会（ELCC）的批准，处理最高达 2000 万美元的外部贷款和/或贸易信贷。ELCC 是一个负责审查外国贷款申请的委员会。所有超过规定限额的外部贷款申请都必须提交给储备银行进行 ELCC 批准。

所有的外部贷款和/或贸易信贷必须按照现有的 ELCC 指导方针进行处理。授权经销商必须向外汇管制机构提交月度退款（EC 模式贷款）。

（1）授权经销商借贷

① 居民

授权经销商可以转贷给个人和公司以满足活期账户和国内资金需求，而无需事先征得外汇管制的许可。但是，任何符合资本账户义务的贷款都需要特定的外汇管制批准。授权经销商必须进行尽职调查，并采用审慎贷款方式向个人和企业发放贷款。

② 非居民

未经外汇管制批准，个人不得从授权交易商处借款。非居民控制的公司可以在当地借款以 1∶1 的比例为股东资金提供营运资金，也就是说，他们可以借到的总额不得超过股东的资金。

③ 外汇管制涉及股东资金、已发行股本、股份溢价、资本/收入储备、股东贷款和留存收益。但是，这种借款需要事先获得外汇管制批准。[②]

（2）银行

津巴布韦注册银行机构名单：

① 商业银行

- 农业银行；
- BancABC 有限公司；
- 巴克莱津巴布韦银行有限公司；
- CBZ 银行有限公司；
- 生态银行津巴布韦有限公司；
- FBC 银行有限公司；
- MBCA 银行有限公司；
- Metbank 有限公司；
- NMB 银行有限公司；
- 津巴布韦斯坦比克银行有限公司；
- 渣打银行津巴布韦有限公司；

---

① 参见 1996 年《外汇管制条例》第 2 节，1996 年法定文书第 109 号。
② 参见津巴布韦储备银行发布的《外汇管制指引》第 5 节。

- 管家银行有限公司；
- ZB 银行。

② 投资银行

Tetrad 投资银行有限公司。

③ 建设社团
- CABS；
- FBC 建筑协会；
- 全国建筑协会；
- ZB 建筑协会。

④ 储蓄银行

人民储蓄银行。

⑤ 发展机构

津巴布韦基础设施发展银行（IBDZ）。

（3）中小企业发展公司（SMEDCO）

根据《银行法》①申请银行执照，并应遵守银行业法规《第 01-2004 / BSD 号指引：公司治理和第 07-2014 / BSD 号审计准则》②的适当性与诚信评估标准。

微型金融机构也在津巴布韦成立，其主要目标是放贷。根据《小额信贷法》③向津巴布韦储备银行提出申请。津巴布韦目前有 189 家微型金融机构。

（四）土地政策

在津巴布韦，包括土地在内的所有财产都受到《宪法》第 71 条的保护。

私人拥有的城市地区土地属于在契约登记处登记的所有权契据，并赋予土地所有者土地的实际权利。登记权利在《契据登记法》④中得到承认并赋予法律效力。农村的农业用地主要由国家持有，宗地由传统酋长监督。根据《宪法》第 72 条的规定，国家对农业用地（不包括城市土地、公有土地或乡镇土地）享有绝对权力并且出于农业用途、土地重整或者安置目的，国家可以强制征收土地而无需给予补偿。国家强制征收土地的权力由《土地征用法》⑤第 5 条予以确认，该法允许征收当局在向土地所有人发布通知时申报土地。唯一可以向国家索赔的是在征收前对土地所作的改进。根据《宪法》第 72 条的规定，一旦农地被强制征收，该土地的所有权契据被视为取消，土地由国家所有。没有法律授权的国有土地的占有或占用构成违法行为。国有土地只能按国家许可或租赁的方式占用。

私人土地出售、抵押、出租或处置而无需国家事先批准。公有土地不得出售或处置，占有权归入占用人的家族后代。

目前，只要通过正规的银行渠道将资金带入津巴布韦，外国企业就可以获得城市土地。外国企业不得收购农业用地、公有土地或国有土地。

（五）公司的建立和解散

（1）公司法
- 津巴布韦的公司法律主要受不定期修订的《公司法》⑥管辖；⑦
- 津巴布韦的普通法在津巴布韦的公司法律中起着非常重要的作用，主要依据罗马－荷兰法律；
- 津巴布韦的公司法主要以英国法律为基础；

---

① 参见第 24:20 章。
② 参见 2000 年法定文书第 205 号。
③ 参见第 24:29 章。
④ 参见第 20:05 章。
⑤ 参见第 20:10 章。
⑥ 参见第 24:03 章。
⑦ "公司和其他商业实体法案"，2018 年已起草并且尚未通过。如果它被批准并通过，它将取代目前的公司法（第 24:03 章）和《私营企业法案》（第 24 章第 11 节）。

- 津巴布韦公司法由公司法和法规编纂和管理，也受津巴布韦、英国和南非的各种司法裁决的管辖。

（2）津巴布韦公司/协会的类型
- 私人公司；
- 上市公司；
- 担保有限公司；
- 私营企业；
- 独资经营企业；
- 合伙企业；
- 合作公司。

（3）私人公司[1]

私人公司[（Prt）Ltd]不得向公众募集股份，且通常不需要向公司注册处提交年度财务报告。私人公司的人数限制为最多50位股东，以及员工股东。

私人公司的股本规模没有法定限制，但对人数有限制。

私人公司有权在注册后立即开始业务，而上市公司不能这样做，除非已符合该法案规定的有关公司设立的所有条款，且注册服务机构已证明公司有权开始业务。

私人公司有权任命自己选择的董事，即使是任命那些没有持有公司股份的人。

（4）上市公司[2]
- 上市公司将"有限公司"（Ltd）作为其名称中的最后一个词；
- 上市公司必须向公司注册处提交年度财务报告，并受公众监督；
- 上市公司需要接受审计；
- 上市公司可能会寻求在津巴布韦证券交易所上市并向公众发售股票，此类要约必须附有招股说明书，在提出要约之前，必须向公司注册处提交并注册；
- 上市公司的成员人数没有限制；
- 由于上市公司有权向公众提供股票，所以投资者的权利受到该法案的保护。

（5）担保有限公司
- 这是为慈善而创立的公司，其目的是为了公众的利益而存在；
- 其目的不是为其成员创造利润，并禁止向其成员支付股息；
- 在第26条中，如果部长认为该协会符合该条款的规定，他可以将该协会注册为公司而不必使用名称末尾的（Limited）字样；
- 公司注册处应相应注册公司；
- 这类公司的成员的责任仅限于他们保证在清盘公司时所提供的金额；
- 担保有限公司享有公司的所有特权，并遵守其义务。

（6）私营企业公司

这些是私人公司的简化版本，并且在同一个办公室登记，但由于其性质，他们对事务的处理有简化的规则。

（7）独资企业
- 独资企业是指个人承担单一无限责任的商业组织；
- 任何来自企业的收入都被视为所有者的税收收入，因为此类企业不被视为法律实体。

（8）合伙企业[3]
- 与独资企业一样，对合伙企业的立法控制很少；
- 企业的性质可能意味着合作关系将落入具体的监管法规中，例如咨询工程师和公共会计师；
- 除了指定的专业协会，如医生、特许会计师、律师和工程师之外，盈利合伙一般限于最多20位

---

① 参见《公司法》第33条。
② 参见《公司法》第24:03章。
③ 参见《公司法》第6节。

合伙人；
- 通常情况下，合伙人对合伙企业的所有债务承担连带责任，前提是合伙人是以合伙人的名义和权利发生的；
- 目前在津巴布韦尚无有关建立有限责任合伙制的法律规定；
- 在投资者能够提供资金、技术和技术专业知识以及管理大规模运营的能力的情况下，可以根据《合资企业法》①设立与国家和半国营企业的合资经营。

（9）合作社②
- 这种形式的商业实体最适合小规模的农业、采矿和渔业部门，这些实体是根据合作社法案（第24:05章）设立的；
- 实体的主要目标是提供便利农产品或牲畜的生产或市场或向其成员销售商品的服务；
- 此类形式限制了股份的转让，只有一类普通股。

（10）公司组建

公司和其他商业企业受到《公司法》③的监管。公司经在司法部的公司注册处注册成立，其名称必须获得批准，并且至少有一名股东签署的公司组织章程大纲，才能注册生效。公司章程要求以原始形式提交，说明公司的目标和成员的权利，并规定成立时至少有两名董事。一经接受，公司注册处处长会给予注册证明书作为注册证明。

股份由公司成员以公司出具的持股证明形式持有，股份可根据公司章程转让。

（11）解散

公司可以由成员自行清盘（自动清盘——第242条）或债权人在公司未能履行其债务时清盘（强制清盘——第206条）。

清盘程序需向高等法院提出申请，解释清盘情况及委任高等法院主事官批准的临时清盘人监管清盘程序的情况。

临时清盘人需要评估针对该公司的债权，批准合法债权并确定债权人的债权可以全部或部分清偿的方法。

（六）并购及竞争规则

津巴布韦《竞争法》④，于1998年生效。

津巴布韦的竞争法规由竞争与关税委员会（CTC）根据《竞争法》调整。该法旨在促进和维持津巴布韦经济的公平竞争，规定了预防和控制限制性做法，规范兼并，防止和控制垄断情况，禁止不公平贸易做法。

竞争法涵盖反竞争协议（横向和纵向协议）、滥用支配地位和反竞争性兼并和收购。

《竞争法》考虑了大多数限制性做法以及使用"合理规则"方法进行的所有兼并。该法中的一些限制性做法被称为"不公平的商业行为"，本身是禁止的。

《竞争法》适用于津巴布韦境内或在津巴布韦境内发生影响的所有经济活动。通常不适用该法的知识产权包括根据《植物育种者权利法》⑤《工业品外观设计法》⑥《版权和邻接权法》⑦《专利法》⑧和《商标法》⑨获得的知识产权。

如果国家参与商品的生产和销售，该法也对国家具有约束力。该法的兼并控制条款的效力优先于任何行业监管机构在审议和批准兼并和收购方面的权力。因此，委员会对于任何合格合并具有最终授

---

① 参见第22:22章。
② 参见《公司法》第36—45节。
③ 参见第24:03章。
④ 参见第14:28章。
⑤ 参见第18:16章。
⑥ 参见第26:05章。
⑦ 参见第26:02章。
⑧ 参见第26:03章。
⑨ 参见第26:04章。

权的权力。①

该法的阈值规则有效地排除了中小企业的适用。该法案仅禁止那些高度限制竞争的限制性做法。也只有那些达到规定门槛,因而必须通知委员会审查合并和收购,以及那些大幅度阻止或减少可能被禁止的竞争才适用该法。津巴布韦竞争委员会是一个自治组织,它不会将任何竞争决定提交给津巴布韦的任何其他当局。②

出于执法目的,委员会针对任何反竞争做法发出的命令可以向津巴布韦高等法院提出,作为高等法院的命令进行登记,以使其具有高等法院民事判决的效力。针对委员会的任何决定可以向行政法院提出上诉。③

在该地区,津巴布韦是南部非洲发展共同体(SAPC)与东部和南部非洲共同市场(CDMESA)的成员。在东南非共同市场中,津巴布韦竞争管理局积极参与制定和通过区域竞争政策和法律,并派代表参加区域竞争委员会。津巴布韦和其他东南非共同市场成员国的区域竞争政策和法律有利于他们处理具有跨国性质的限制性商业惯例。④

津巴布韦竞争管理局也是南部和东部非洲竞争论坛(SEACF)的创始成员之一,该论坛也旨在促进和加强该地区竞争管理机构之间的合作。⑤

(七)税收

1. 税收制度和规则

对来自津巴布韦的贸易过程中产生的所有收入或来自津巴布韦的收入征收所得税。来自贸易业务,有收入的就业和投资的收入须缴纳不同的税率。关于津巴布韦税收的主要立法规定包含在《所得税法》(经财政法修订),《资本利得税法》《海关税法》和《增值税法》中。津巴布韦税务局是一个独立的实体,负责税务管理,向财政部长负责。

地方当局和法定机构征收了一些附加税、特许权使用费和法定费用,但这些费用通常是基于使用和本地化的,而不是普遍适用的。特许权使用费是从所提取的矿物中收取的,根据所提取的矿物的不同,从1%到10%不等。

在所得税方面,法律规定对来自津巴布韦的贸易过程中的收入和投资收益征税。所得税是对个人、公司、信托和合伙关系的收入征收的。对实体征收所得税的原则是考虑到在津巴布韦产生的(《所得税法》第8至12节)在评估期间(每年1月至12月)除去资本收入后累计的总收入,并允许在产生收入和津贴时扣除(《所得税法》第15条)以确定需要征税的净收入。公司的所得税申报表必须在财政年度结束后的当年4月30日之前提交。一年内发生的税收损失可以结转6年。

但是,季度支付日期系统(QPD)要求企业在评估年度评估其潜在的利润,并在特定日期按比例将可能的部分税款交给津巴布韦税务局:3月25日(潜在税收的10%),6月25日(潜在税收的25%),9月25日(潜在税收的30%)和12月20日(潜在税收的35%)。

资本利得税根据《资本利得税法》对出售"特定资产"即土地和建筑物,出售有价证券,剥夺土地权和采矿权以及转让商标、专利、工业品外观设计和其他知识产权。除非在津巴布韦税务局批准的有限情况下延期或免除税款,否则任何处置特定资产都会导致纳税费用。

增值税是对消费征收的间接税,并在销售应税货物和服务时收取。年度交易额超过60 000美元的注册运营商被征收税款,并通过评估运营商在该期间的月销售总额和税额(销项税额),扣除运营商在同一个月的总购买额以及运营商支付的税额(进项税额)进行计算。差额构成运营商应付的增值税或津巴布韦税务局退还的应付退税。运营商在接下来的月份的第25天前必须提交月度退货。

对从津巴布韦出口的货物或免税或零税率的特定基本商品不征收增值税。

---

① 参见《津巴布韦竞争政策法律概述》,津巴布韦竞争和关税委员会主任兼首席执行官亚历山大•库布巴先生在第三届年度竞争委员会竞争法庭和曼德拉研究所竞争法、经济和政策研讨会上的发言,2009年9月3日至4日。
② 同上注。
③ 同上注。
④ 同上注。
⑤ 同上注。

对进口到津巴布韦的进口货物根据《海关法》征收关税和增值税。以投资为目的设备的进口免征关税。该法由津巴布韦税务局管理，根据产品的类型、描述和来源，按照进口产品的详细类别收取关税。对津巴布韦生产的某些类别的产品（如酒精饮料）征收消费税，并根据财政部长确定的并在《财政法》中公布的税率计算。

2. 主要税种和税率

员工的所得税按照定期收入，"即用即付"（PAYE）方式征收。税率因员工收入而异，最高收入员工的税率可增至40%。

企业、信托、合伙企业和商业组织需要按下列税率纳税：

来自贸易或投资的收入	利润的25%，加上3%的税收（Aids征费）
来自公司、合伙或信托的收入	利润的25%，加上3%的税收（Aids征费）
持牌投资者的收入（前5年）	利润的0%
持牌投资者的收入（后5年）	利润的25%
特别采矿租赁持有人	利润的15%
公司从事采矿业务	利润的25%
BOT/BOOT批准的项目（前5年）	利润的0%
BOT/BOOT批准的项目（第5年）	利润的15%
工业园区开发商（前5年）	利润的0%
工业园区开发商（后5年）	利润的25%
经批准区旅游经营者（前5年）	利润的0%
经批准区旅游经营者（后5年）	利润的25%
出口30%～41%产出的制造商	利润的20%
出口41%～51%产出的制造商	利润的17.5%
出口51%产出的制造商	利润的15%

经济特区经营者在头5年的经营活动中无需缴纳所得税，此后根据2017年《财务法》第12/13条第3款，按照利润的15%交纳所得税。

对于未在交易所上市的公司，股息收益要按照15%缴纳所得税，交易所上市公司的股息税率为10%。

从银行机构赚取的利息需缴纳15%的预扣税，而从其他活动赚取的利息需要缴纳税率为25%。

对出售特定资产征收的资本利得税按以下税率征税：

就2009年3月1日前购入并于2009年3月1日后出售的特定资产而言，资本利得税按指定资产处置价值的5%征收。

对于2009年3月1日后收购和出售的特定资产，税率为资本收益的20%（即资产被收购和出售的价格之间的差额）。

注册运营商对商品或服务的销售征收增值税的税率为15%。

关税根据附属法规中公布的关税征收，并由财政部长根据法定文书定期修改。

津巴布韦根据2016年第8号公告已经和中国签署的双重征税协议，以避免双重征税和防止偷漏税，其效果通常是允许各种收入来源的国家通常对这些收入以及利润征收一般税，以最大商定的百分比为准。①

（八）证券

1. 证券相关法律法规简介

津巴布韦有关证券的法规主要受《证券交易法》②管制，该法还设立了津巴布韦证券交易委员会（SECZ）用来监管证券交易，保护投资者权益，鼓励资本市场发展及授予从事证券业务许可证。根据《证券法》第 118 条的规定，证券交易委员会有权制定法规来落实其法定目标。该法还规定了证券交易所的注册、券商的许可以及交易所的管理和监管。如果注册投资实体宣布资不抵债，SECZ 还拥有投资者保护基金以提供货币救济。但是，该基金不能支付超过基金价值 10% 的赔偿金。

《资产管理法》③规定了涉及资产管理业务的实体和人员的行为，即将客户的资产投资于货币市场、认可的证券交易所和其他投资，以确保客户的利益。资产经理必须在 SECZ 的首席执行官进行登记（第 5 节）。该法还规定，资产管理人可能被迫投资特定的规定资产，前提是这些投资不超过基金投资组合的 40%（第 12 节）。

目前，津巴布韦证券交易所是上市证券交易的唯一注册证券交易所。该交易所上市的柜台数量相对较少，市值也相应较小。证券交易所公布自己的上市要求，其业务受 SECZ 监管。

金融证券交易所（私人）有限公司是根据《证券（其他交易平台）规则》注册为其他交易平台的实体。

《集体投资计划法》④涵盖了建立投资计划，使参与者能够整合资源，并在不涉及日常活动的情况下分享或获得收购、持有、管理和处置财产的收入或利润（第 3 节）。这种方案需要在 SECZ 进行登记（分类为内部计划、外部计划和专业计划）（第 5 节）。

2. 外国公司证券交易要求

希望从事证券交易的外国公司需要在当地注册并向 SECZ 申请注册。

外国公司持有任何上市证券的股份或股票目前仅限于已发行证券的 40%，单个外国投资者在上市公司持有的证券的最高数额为已发行证券的 10%。

外国投资者可以认购高达 100% 的任何由资金资助转入外汇的初级债券。外国投资者也可以在二级市场上购买和出售债券，并且可以在未经储备银行批准的情况下进行因撤资所产生的资金汇款。

（九）投资的优惠和保护

上述报告的内容已经提到了投资优惠和投资保护。

三、贸易

（一）贸易监管部门

"贸易"指两国之间交换一定价值的进出口货物及服务。在津巴布韦，贸易由外事及国际贸易部和工商部监管。

一些关于贸易的实际功能由法定机构管理，包括：

1. 代表政府征税的津巴布韦税务局

具体征收如下税收项目：
① 关税和消费税：分别依据《关税和消费税法案》⑤以及其相关法规对进口货物和本地产品征税；
② 附加税：对于 5 年以上进口车辆征税；

---

① 参见 2016 年第 8 号公告《中华人民共和国政府和津巴布韦共和国政府对所得避免的重征税和偷税漏税的协定》。
② 参见第 24:25 章。
③ 参见第 24:26 章。
④ 参见第 24:19 章。
⑤ 参见第 23:02 章。

③ 增值税：根据《增值税法案》及其相关法律法规①对货物及服务消费征税；
④ 所得税：对来源于贸易的收入征税；
⑤ 矿区使用费：根据《矿藏法案》②。

2. 根据《竞争法案》③设立的竞争及关税委员会

该委员会行使如下职权：
① 对于与本地产业提供的商品及服务形成竞争关系的进口商品及服务征税；
② 对被本地产业所使用的进口商品及服务降低税收；
③ 为了制止不公平交易实施立法或者行政措施；
④ 向政府提供技术援助，以便与其他国家达成协议，以造福当地工业。
委员会同时还通过对进口到津巴布韦的货物征税来管理和执行反倾销措施。

3. 与贸易有关的协议

津巴布韦也是许多贸易协定的缔约国，在这些协定中，它对其贸易规则和条例作出了承诺。这种成员关系和其国内法律，影响和支配了其与其他国家的贸易行为。津巴布韦作为缔约国一方的主要协议包括：
①《建立东部和南部非洲共同市场协定》（COMESA 协定）；
②《南部非洲发展共同体条约》。
津巴布韦还与包括马来西亚（1994 年的法定文书第 139 号）、阿根廷（2001 年的法定文书）和德国（1981 年的法定文书第 926 号）在内的一些国家缔结了双边投资保护协定。

（二）贸易法律法规概要

关于津巴布韦的贸易法规可分为四个部分，即：
① 宪法；
② 议会制定的国内法律；
③ 法定文书；
④ 国际协议。
尽管在国内法律的条款中有与国际贸易相似的条款，与在津巴布韦从事进口和出口货物的任何人有关的法令如下：

1. 宪法

2013 年津巴布韦宪法修正案（第 20 号）第 64 节在法律规定的范围内，确立了选择和进行任何交易的权利。第 71 项规定有权获得、持有、占有、使用、转让、抵押、租赁或处置所有形式的财产，无论是单独的还是与他人共有的。此外，宪法第 34 节规定："国家必须确保津巴布韦作为缔约国的所有国际公约、条约和协定都纳入国内法。"
以上条款同样适用于国际贸易条约和协定。

2. 相关法规

（1）《关税和消费税法案》④
该法案规定了货物合法地进口并出口到津巴布韦的方式。它还指导货物如何分类，以及如何征收反倾销和反补贴税。该法同时还规定了为了税收目的的计算价值的方法。
（2）竞争法案⑤
该法案涉及商业竞争的规则，特别是关于货物贸易某些特定关税的维持。该法案还以反补贴和反倾销税的形式实施处罚。

---

① 参见第 23:12 章。
② 参见第 21:05 章。
③ 参见第 14:28 章。
④ 参见第 23:02 章。
⑤ 参见第 14:28 章。

（3）货物控制法案[①]

该法案规定了确立了对津巴布韦某些商品的进口和出口的控制。它还规定了限制出口以实现配额的目的。

3. 规章

（1）《海关及消费税（一般）规例》（2001年法定文书第154号）

该规定管理货物进出津巴布韦的货物进口和出口。尤其是其规定了如下程序：

① 通过进口进入津巴布韦的货物；
② 特定运输方式进口货物的特殊条件；
③ 不同类型货物的清关程序；
④ 某些特定货物在进口时引起退税或减税的情况；
⑤ 货物出口清关。

（2）关税和消费税（入境及路线口岸）令（2002年法定文书第14号）

这些法规规定了津巴布韦的入境口岸和入境口岸的开放时间。

（3）关税和消费税（关税）公告（2012年法定文书第112号）

公告列举了对于每一进口货物到期应缴纳的税款。同时还列明了关于这种产品的详尽描述。它规定了按数量和产地计算的每一种产品应缴纳的税款。关税和附加税的税率取决于该产品是否来自COMESA国家、SADC国家或任何其他贸易协定国家。

（4）《管制货物（矿物及金属出口）法规，1979（RGN 247/1979）》《管制货物（进出口）（商业）法规，1974（RGN 766/1974）》《控制货物（进出口）（农业）法规，2007年法定文书137号》。

该法规规定了从津巴布韦进口和出口的矿物、某些商品和农产品，以及从津巴布韦到根据这些法规的规定持有许可证的人。

（5）《竞争（反倾销及反补贴税）（调查）法规》（2002年法定文书第266号）

该法规规定了部长可以对进口到津巴布韦的货物征收反补贴税的方式。该法规还为那些被认为已从出口国家获得补贴的商品提供了指导意见，批准了对其征收反补贴税。该法规还授权部长对某些商品征收反倾销税，并界定为倾销的商品。

4. 国际协定

（1）《关税和消费税（东、南非洲共同市场）法规》（暂停）（2000年法定文书第244号）。

这些法规规定，按照《COMESA条约》第48条的规定，遵守《COMESA条约》附件四规定的原产地规则，对在成员国境内生产或制造的货物暂停征收关税。

（2）《关税及消费税（南部非洲发展共同体）法规》（暂停）（2002年法定文书第345号）。

该法规规定，在南部非洲共同体成员国领土内生产或制造的货物暂停关税。

（3）《SADC（差异化报价）法规》（2007年法定文书第188号）。

该法规暂停对海关关税法第二部分中出现的货物征收关税，并在本条例附表二所列的标题或副标题下进行分类，足以使该等关税降低到本法规所规定的有效税率。

（4）《关税和消费税（欧共体和东部和南部非洲经济伙伴协定）（暂停）（市场准入）法规》，2016年法定文书第117号。

根据《经济伙伴协议》（EPA），该法规暂停了对从欧洲共同体进口的货物征收关税。这些货物必须在欧洲共同体领土内种植、生产或制造，并遵守《第一议定书》中规定的原产地规则。

（三）贸易管理

1. 进口

根据1974年《货物（进出口）（商业）法规》，任何进口货物到津巴布韦的人，都必须取得公开一般进口许可证或一项专门授予出口这些特定货物的许可证。

---

① 参见第14:05章。

大多数货物根据公开一般进口许可证（OGIL）分类，不需要特定的进口许可证。需要特定进口许可证的货物，按政府不时发出的公告分类，最新的为《货物管制（公开一般进口许可证）（第 2 号）修订公告》（2016 年第 8 号）及《货物管制（公开一般进口许可证）（修订）公告》（2017 年第 5 号）。

在进口结算时，需要下列文件：
① 报关单（表格 21）；
② 供应商发票；
③ 出口国家的出口或过境单据；
④ 提单；
⑤ 价值声明表格；
⑥ 铁路通知书；
⑦ 港口费用发票；
⑧ 代理/进口商的工作表；
⑨ 原始许可证、许可证、免税证、返利信、价值裁定（如适用的情况下）。

进口许可证的申请向负责贸易部门部长提出，必须包含以下内容：
① 进口商的公司简介，说明其业务范围；
② 进口产品说明；
③ 税费代码；
④ 进口数量；
⑤ 产品各单位的采购价格，包括其售价；
⑥ 进口货物的总价值；
⑦ 货物的原产地；
⑧ 从当地供应商采购货物的原因；
⑨ 进口商注册证书，反映公司董事的表格 CR14、税务清关证明和标准发展基金征费收据复印件；
⑩ 形式发票。

某些货物的进口许可证需要从相关的部委或部门获得。例如，有害物质只能通过环境管理机构（EMA）颁发的许可证进口。同样，进口药品需要津巴布韦药品监督管理局（MCAZ）颁发的许可证。这些信息通常是津巴布韦税务局在通关过程中使用的。

2. 出口

任何打算从津巴布韦出口货物的人都必须取得公开一般出口许可证或许可证，这取决于出口货物的分类。

如果海关官员要求出示发票和其他有关出口货物的文件，每个出口商都应交出这些文件，并允许海关官员检查货物。

根据《海关税务法》的规定，如果任何货物的出口受到任何法律规定的限制或控制，这些货物只能按照该法令的规定出口。

出口货物的清关所需文件为：
① 已填妥的表格（CD1）；
② 报关单（表格 21）；
③ 货物的发货通知单；
④ 商业发票和装箱单；
⑤ 外国货物的出口许可证和必要时的过境许可证。

还需要向海关官员支付清关费。如果货物要出口到 COMESA 或 SADC 的任何成员国，则需填写第 30 号表格。货物必须在海关人员作出评估后 10 天内出口。

对出口的限制包括没有农业部的健康证明活的动物（没有有效的狂犬病疫苗接种证明和兽医证书）和植物及植物材料。

（四）进出口商品检验检疫

根据《关税和消费税法》而言，如果需要对货物进行检验，进口商必须自费和自担风险卸货并重新装载这些货物，将其移到官员指示的任何地点或从官员指示的任何地点移除。所有费用由进口商承担。

每一个入境口岸都有检查人员，他们有权：
① 审查并制作与任何进出口货物有关的记录的摘录和副本；
② 要求任何进口商或出口商，对有关该货物的任何记录作出解释；
③ 在检查人员看来可能违反的记录，其可以节选并删除任何记录；
④ 未经付款，任何商品的任何样品或样品在检验后，应立即取出。

当任何货物被检验员扣押时，应发出收据。扣押的货物被保存在政府仓库，直到导致扣押货物的条件得到补救。

根据《海关和消费税法》的规定，津巴布韦税局官员应被允许进入抵达或即将离开津巴布韦任何船只、火车或车辆，以确定该船、火车或车辆的货物是否合法运输。

（五）海关管理

在到达任何入境口岸时，要求每个人都应向海关申报他们所拥有的货物。其目的是查明货物是否应缴纳关税，以及是否有禁止进口或出口的规定。

1. 进口

关税是根据进口货物进入津巴布韦境内前的成本、保险费和运费（CIF）的价格计算。在津巴布韦境内的保险和运费被排除在征税价值之外（VDP）。进口货物的到岸价格是指在津巴布韦境外发生的货物成本、保险、运费和其他费用的总和。

为了结算货物，需要一张报关表。这可以通过津巴布韦税务局的海关数据自动化系统（ASYCUDA）提交，该系统是一个在线的货物清关系统。津巴布韦税务局要求所有的支持文档都作为附件在线提交。

当进口货物时，需要进口商的税务清关证明，而在没有相同的情况下，在其他应交关税的基础上加征 10% 的关税。税款是以通过进口局账产直接存入津巴布韦税务局银行账户的方式支付的。

一旦所有的文件已经提交和处理，进口的批准以交付释放订单的形式给出。这允许进口商从承运人或扣押地点取回他的货物。如果需要检查货物，则签发检查令并进行检查以核实数量、分类、来源、价值或任何需要澄清的方面。之后，必须提供两套纸质文件以便最终释放货物。

2. 出口

根据《关税和消费税法》第54（5）项，每一个出口商都必须出示所有发票和其他与出口货物有关的单据，并在出口前，由海关人员检查出口货物。

在出口前，还须向海关官员提供一份入报关单。当货物从津巴布韦出口时，不应支付任何关税，但是清关费用将会到期应付。

在 ASYCUDA 世界体系中，通过与进口相同的方式提交一份报关单（表格21）。此外，必须提交下列文件：
① 从商业银行获得的外汇管制表格 CD1；
② 供应商的发票；
③ 托运单；
④ 出口许可证／许可证副本。

四、劳动

（一）劳动法律法规简要介绍

劳动法规范雇主和雇员的关系。它规范在工作场所基于自愿产生的法律关系。津巴布韦劳动法主要基于立法，更准确来说，在 2013 年津巴布韦《宪法修正案》（第 20 号）、国会法案和授权立法中，普通法只是次要的劳动法律渊源，并且在成文法中无具体规定时适用。

《宪法》是津巴布韦的最高法律，任何与其相抵触的法律都被认为是无效的。《宪法》第 4 章是"权利宣言"，规定了与劳动法有关的各种权利，例如免于奴役的自由（第 54 条）；免受强迫劳动的自由（第 55 条）；平等和不歧视的权利（第 56 条）；行业、贸易或职业自由（第 64 条）和公平听证的权利（第 69 条）。最重要的是，第 65 条专门为劳工权利提供了关于公平和安全的劳动实践、标准和支付公平合理的工资的权利；成立和加入工会的权利；参与集体行动，包括罢工权；有权参加集体谈判，妇女有权享有至少 3 个月的带薪产假。《宪法》第 172 条创设了劳工法院，该法院对劳动法事项具有排他性管辖权。

《劳动法》（第 28:01 章）是调整劳动关系的主要法令。按照《劳动法》第 2A(1) 条的规定，该法的目的是提升工作场所的社会正义和民主，除其他外，确保公正、有效和迅速解决争端和不公平的劳工行为。第 2A(2) 条要求的最终能确保达成第 2A 条第 (1) 款所述的目的的方式解释该法，而第 2A(3) 条则规定，该法应优先于与之不一致的任何其他法令。该法对雇佣关系提供了更详细的规定，适用于除《宪法》明确排除的雇佣关系之外（如公共服务和纪律部队）的所有工人和雇主。《劳动公约》的详细标题还要求该法对津巴布韦根据国际法所承担的义务，特别是津巴布韦批准的国际劳工组织公约。

《劳动法》还规定制定附属法例，例如法定的集体谈判协议。这些是根据《劳动法》第 74 条进行的集体谈判所产生的协议。集体谈判协议对其注册的行业内的所有雇主和雇员都具有约束力。他们提供了更详细的规定，并就工资率和工作时间等就业问题提供最低标准。《劳动法》第 101 条进一步规定了《劳动法规（全国就业守则）》（2006 年法定文书第 15 号）的贯彻，该法规提供了一种模范法典，提供了在工作场所进行纪律处分的程序。《行为守则》的规定对没有注册行为准则的雇佣关系具有约束力。

《劳动法》必须与其他现有规范就业的附属法例一起阅读，例如《国家社会保障局法》（第 17:04 章）和《养恤金及其他福利法》（第 16:01 章）和其他条例。所有在津巴布韦的雇主都有义务向国家社会保障管理局（《事故预防和工人补偿计划》1990 年的法定文书第 68 号）和国家社会保障局（《养恤金和其他福利计划》，1994 年法定文书第 146A 号）作出贡献。雇员也要缴税（薪酬计划中，该税通常直接从雇员的工资中扣除）。从健康和安全的角度来看，尘肺的法案（第 15:08 章）、《工厂和工作法案》（第 14:08 章）和《辐射保护法案》（第 15:15 章）可能会对有关工作场所安全法的问题进行监管。

（二）聘用外籍员工的要求

《移民法》（第 4:02 章）规定了津巴布韦出入境的要求。该法设立了首席移民官和移民局官员的职位，他们被授权执行该法案的条款和附属法例。

1. 工作许可

（1）临时就业许可证

在津巴布韦工作，外国人可能需要临时就业证。根据保留《移民法规》（1998 年法定文书第 195 号）第 22 条，可以向外国人发放临时就业证，以便在 5 年内为在津巴布韦注册的组织或公司工作，无论是否从中获取报酬。该许可证效力也可延及许可证持有人的配偶和子女在同一时期居住在津巴布韦。临时就业证持有人的配偶或子女，如欲在津巴布韦工作，须另行申请临时就业许可证。

根据该法第 23 条的规定，如果许可证持有人未能从事雇佣工作或停止受雇，或在未能从事或停止从事许可证规定的职业，临时就业许可证就不再有效。许可证的签发条件是，许可证持有人及所有获授权随持证人进入津巴布韦的人士应在许可证规定的期限届满前离开津巴布韦。许可证持有人须在离开津巴布韦前向入境事务官员交出许可证。总入境事务官员有权自行处理任何其他附加情形。

（2）其他许可

根据条例第 16 条，总入境事务官可向任何满足如下条件的人士签发居留许可证：

① 持有临时就业证；

② 在津巴布韦居住连续不少于 5 年；或在其临时就业证到期日前 6 个月内申请居住证，而且在其临时就业证到期日前已在津巴布韦居住连续 5 年。

还可以向拥有大量财产并准备在不从事任何职业的情况下在津巴布韦进行大量投资的人颁发居住

许可证。根据法规第 17 条规定，永久居留证不得向任何人签发，除非其在津投资给津巴布韦投资机构批准的项目有 1 000 000 美元或更多的投资，或者在其他项目上有 3 000 000 美元或者更多的投资并且在其目前持有的居留证到期日之前在津巴布韦已居住满 3 年的，又或是在与一位津巴布韦善意合伙人共同经营的合伙企业中已投入 100 000 美元或更多的资本设备并且在其目前持有的居留许可证上到期日前已经在津居住不少于 3 年的专业人员或技术人员。

2. 申请程序

临时就业许可证申请应向入境事务处提出。雇主必须向负责人提出申请，以聘用外籍人士，并附下列材料：

- 不予退还的法定费用为 500 美元；
- 申请人填写的居住证申请表；
- 未来雇主提供的在津巴布韦工作的雇佣信，表明申请人的就业能力、薪水和服务条件；
- 未来雇主的信，要求临时雇佣许可说明所需要的期限；
- 在拟议的职业中有资格和经验的英文书面证据，经认证的学历、文凭、证书和奖状；
- 两张最近拍摄的申请人的完整护照尺寸照片（两张照片都应作为申请人的真实肖像在背面进行认证）；
- 申请人出生证明的核证副本；
- 结婚证的核证副本（如有）。

3. 社会保险

国家社会保障基金（NSSA）为国家社会保障养老金制度提供支持。NSSA 是一个法人团体，由《NSSA 法》授权管理社会保障制度，尤其是老年福利和补助金、幸存者的福利和津贴以及工伤赔偿金。其对于任何在津巴布韦就业（贸易或其他职业）的已满 16 岁未满 60 岁的普通市民或居民应在 NSSA 注册并以员工身份缴纳费用［国家社会保障退休金和其他福利计划（救济金标准）公告书第 4 节（1993 年法定文书 393 号）］是强制的义务。向 NSSA 注册其单位和员工信息是雇主应尽的义务，雇员和雇主应当通过 NSSA 缴纳保险费用。

（三）出入境

1. 签证种类

根据《移民法案》第 31 条，移民官员对于持有满足上述条件的并且不超过 6 个月的有效的入境许可证的外国访客的旅行证件的认可有自由裁量权。根据《移民法案》第 42 条的规定，旅客入境证明书须符合下列条件：

- 持有证书的人应将其在津巴布韦的地址告知移民官员，并将地址的任何更改通知给该官员；
- 在未经首席入境事务官允许的情况下，持有该证书的人不得采取任何与他进入津巴布韦的目的不一致或与之相反的行动或行为；
- 除非事先获得许可，否则持有该等证书的人不得从事任何职业；
- 证书持有者应在证书上注明的日期当天或之前离开津巴布韦无需缴纳费用，除非由首席入境事务官员授权的移民官员批准该证书的有效期延长；
- 一旦证书持有者已离开该国，该证书将不再有效。

2. 入境和离境限制

（1）入境限制

《移民法》对进入津巴布韦进行了一定的限制。按照第 12 条的规定，进入津巴布韦的每个人都必须向移民官员出示自己的证件并出示他们的旅行证件。在第 13 条中，16 岁以下的未成年人，还须由一名成年人陪同，该成年人持有一份发给该人的有效旅行证件。第 14 条还建立了一份名单，名单上的人被视为禁止进入津巴布韦的人，除非首席入境事务官给予特别许可。该名单包括任何受感染患有特定疾病的人，除非他拥有进入和留在津巴布韦的许可证，并遵守许可证条件。被禁止的人还包括妓女或同性恋者或以其为生活来源，或有意接受或已接受卖淫或同性恋的收入的人。

（2）离境限制

《移民法》第 25、26 条也对离开津巴布韦进行了限制。任何离开津巴布韦的人都必须出示旅行证件。16 岁及以下的未成年人必须由另一个持有有效旅行证件的成年人士陪同。

（四）贸易联盟和工会组织

1. 贸易联盟

根据《劳动法》第 27 条，雇员有权成立工会并成为工会成员。这项权利也受到《宪法》第 65(2) 条的保护。一旦成立工会，就不需要登记。然而，《劳动法》第 30 条对未登记的工会规定了某些限制，例如禁止他们在劳工法庭上代表其成员。另一方面，登记的工会享有一些利益，例如他们有权向有关当局或劳工法院提出交涉，并有权以自己的名义起诉和应诉。此外，雇主有义务为此目的提供合理的设施。

雇主须从雇员的薪金中扣除工会会费。最重要的是，工会具有自动被雇主认可作为雇员的谈判代理人的自动权利。雇主拒绝与工会谈判被认为是不公平的劳动实践。

在津巴布韦有许多行业特定的注册工会，还有两个总工会，即津巴布韦工会联盟（ZCTU）和津巴布韦工会联合会（ZFTU），他们意在为所有雇员的利益而行动。

2. 雇主联合组织

根据《劳动法》第 27 条，任何雇主团体均可组成雇主组织，任何雇主组织均可组成联盟。第 28 条要求雇主组织在其成立之日起 6 个月内制定章程。除其他事项外，章程还必须规定本组织的权力和职能以及成员资格。雇主的组织可以是注册的，也可以是未注册的。然而，《劳工法》第 30 条对未登记的雇主组织作了某些限制，例如禁止他们在劳工法庭代表其成员的组织。另一方面，已登记的雇主组织享有一些利益，例如有权向当局或劳工法院提出交涉，并有权以自己的名义起诉和应诉。

3. 工人委员会

除了组建工会和有成为其成员的权利外，《劳动法》第 23 条赋予雇员在工作场所内选举工人委员会的权利，以及在任何影响其权利和利益的事项中代表他们的权利。与工会不同的是，工人委员会并没有被授予团体法人资格，因此他们不能以自己的名义起诉或应诉。

4. 工作委员会

《劳动法》第 25A 条要求在每一机构中成立工作委员会，并在该委员会中选举出代表除管理人员以外的雇员的工人委员会。这是由代表雇主和工人委员会的相等数目的成员组成的双方机构。其主要职能是促进和维持员工的有效参与，确保员工的合作与信任。

5. 就业委员会

这是一个由注册工会和注册的雇主组织在一个行业建立的跨团体机构。《劳工法》第 56 条允许任何雇主、注册雇主组织或该等组织的联合会或工会或工会联合会设立自愿就业委员会。就业委员会的主要职能是协助其成员达成集体谈判协议，该协议对所有成员都有约束力。

（五）劳动争议

《劳动法》第 2 条将争议定义为与任何有关就业的问题有关的争议，该争议由该法案调整。《劳工法》还规定了若干争端解决办法，包括但不限于调解、仲裁、裁决、集体谈判以及集体工作行动的参与，如停工和罢工行动。

1. 集体谈判和罢工

《劳动法》第 76 条对在津巴布韦进行集体谈判作出规定。集体谈判可以延伸到所有在雇主、某些雇主或雇主组织之间作为其中一方，一个或多个工人工会作为另一方，双方之间的谈判。它的作用是确定工作条件、雇用期限和对雇主和雇员之间关系的规定。根据《劳工法》第 25 条，一项集体谈判协定在性质上是有约束力的，必须本着诚意进行谈判，并自愿签订。

双方谈判陷入僵局产生争议后，根据《劳动法》第 13 部分规定的集体工作行动权利处理。津巴布韦《宪法》还为集体工作行动提供保护。根据《宪法》第65（3）条，每位员工都有权参与集体工作，包括罢工、静坐或采取其他类似的一级行动的权利。但是，法律对行使这项权利也作出了限制。

2. 调解

这是一种一名劳工官员或有关就业理事会的指定代理人通过调解和事实调查来解决劳资纠纷的当事人之间的争端的方法。《劳动法》第93条规定，除争议双方将该事项提交仲裁外，所有劳动争议都必须进行调解。它的期限为30天，在此期间，必须由劳工事务官员解决该问题，以确保当事各方达成和解，或在不解决问题的情况下，出具一份没有解决的证明。

3. 仲裁

仲裁可以是自愿的，也可以是强制性的。根据《劳动法》第93(5)条，只有在利益争端和调解失败且劳工事务官员出具了没有解决的证明的情况下，仲裁才是强制性的。在这个事件中，仲裁员将根据对事实和法律的认定作出裁决。

4. 裁定

仲裁裁决或劳工官员的裁决并非终局裁决，可在劳动法院于2018年《劳动法》规定的指定时限内提起上诉或复议。在调解期间，当劳工官员在调解期后未签发未解决争议证明，或已签发无和解证书，但未将该事项提交强制仲裁，劳动法院将作为初审法院。只有在存在法律问题时，才有可能向劳动法庭上诉，而且应向最高法院提出。在涉及宪法问题的地方，宪法法院将有权审理该案件。

五、知识产权

（一）知识产权法律法规简介

除著作权无需登记外，津巴布韦法律承认的知识产权都需要在津巴布韦知识产权局（ZIPO）、非洲知识产权组织（ARIPO）或在马德里国际商标体系（以下简称"马德里系统"）进行注册后才能受到保护对抗第三人。

津巴布韦承认并保护下列知识产权：
- 《版权及相邻权利法》下的版权及相邻权利（第26:05章）；
- 《工业设计法》规定的工业设计相关权利（第26:02章）；
- 《集成电路布置图设计法》下的集成电路布置图（第26:07章）；
- 《地理标识法》下的地理标识（第26:06章）；
- 《专利法》下的专利权（第26:03章）；
- 《商标法案》下的商标（第26:04章）。

ZIPO的主要职能是对以上所列知识产权进行注册，并维护注册登记，以及转让、许可、续展、注册用户和其他权利转让的记录。

上述各项知识产权法规授权知识产权的登记官裁定异议、要求撤销和注销登记，以及其他知识产权纠纷的权利。对登记官的裁定可向知识产权法庭或津巴布韦高等法院提出上诉。

津巴布韦是非洲区域知识产权组织（ARIPO）的成员，是一些知识产权公约、议定书和条约的缔约国。其中包括《哈拉雷关于专利和工业设计的议定书》《班殊尔商标协议》《马德里议定书》《专利合作条约》（PCT）。

ZIPO对于津巴布韦人来说，是希望通过马德里体系获得国际注册的一个办事处，并且是PCT下的受理处。

ARIPO是一家总部设在津巴布韦哈拉雷的区域性知识产权组织。ARIPO是在1976年由几个非洲国家根据《卢萨卡协定》设立的，目标是建立共同的服务和机构，以调解、协调和发展影响其成员的知识产权活动。

ARIPO代表其成员国根据各种协议下登记和管理知识产权，即：
- 《哈拉雷关于专利和工业设计的协议》，授权ARIPO授予专利并注册工业设计和实用新型；
- 《班殊尔商标协议》；

- 《斯瓦科普蒙德协议》保护传统知识和民间传说的表达；
- 保护新品种植物的阿鲁沙议定书。

APIPO 目前有 19 个成员国。其中 18 个国家可以在哈拉雷议定书下指定。这些国家包括博茨瓦纳、冈比亚、加纳、肯尼亚、莱索托、利比里亚、马拉维、莫桑比克、纳米比亚、卢旺达、圣多美和普林西比、塞拉利昂、苏丹、斯威士兰、乌干达、坦桑尼亚、赞比亚和津巴布韦。可以在班珠尔议定书下指定的会员国有：博茨瓦纳、莱索托、利比里亚、马拉维、纳米比亚、斯威士兰、乌干达、坦桑尼亚和津巴布韦。索马里是 ARIPO 的成员，但它并不是任何 ARIPO 协议的缔约国。

ARIPO 体系的主要优势是，它为本地、地区和国际知识产权所有者提供申请的便利，通过电子方式只需提交一个申请就可以在 1 个或 18 个 ARIPO 成员国中的多个国家获得批准和注册。

ARIPO 登记的权利在强制许可、丧失、为公共利益而使用、取消或无效等方面受成员国法律的制约。

如果知识产权在某会员国内被侵犯或有争议，登记的所有人或独家被许可人或登记的使用权人可采取侵犯知识产权的应对措施。

（二）专利申请

《专利法案》（第 20:03 章）允许符合专利性标准的创新的注册和保护，即符合新颖性、创造性和实用性的标准。

根据《专利法案》第 2A 条，津巴布韦专利法不允许对下列创性进行注册：就有关人类或动物的诊断、治疗或手术方法；除了微生物外的植物或动物；用于生产植物或动物的生物过程，而不是微生物的过程；能被用作食品或药物的物质，但需是已知成分的混合物，且只含有已知成分；生产这种物质的过程。

如果其使用可能危及公共秩序或公共安全，鼓励无礼、不道德或反社会的行为；危害人类、动物、植物的生命或者健康；或对环境造成严重损害的发明也不能获得专利（第 13 条）。

1. 申请要求

根据《专利法案》第 7 条的规定，提交专利申请，并在津巴布韦取得注册的日期的最低要求如下：

- 专利申请必须以英文的规定形式提交。申请必须披露申请人的全名、实际地址、国籍，并由申请人或授权代表签字。它还必须提供为津巴布韦境内服务的地址。
- 不居住在津巴布韦的申请人必须通过授权书授权在津巴布韦任命一名合格的代表。文件不需要认证或公证，但必须签名。签名人必须填写完整的姓名和名称。
- 申请人的代表必须是一名有权在津巴布韦从事法律执业的人或有权在津巴布韦执业的注册专利代理人。
- 必须披露发明者的全名、国籍和实际地址。
- 申请必须附有完整或临时的说明，说明申请人在津巴布韦拥有本发明，并在适当的情况下证明其所有权。
- 在 ZIPO 申请专利申请时，需要提交正式的申请费。

完整的说明书必须在提交专利申请的 12 个月内提交，否则申请被视为被放弃［第 8（4）条］。

2. 审查

津巴布韦不提供对专利申请的实质性审查。审查是为了评估是否符合正式的文件要求。《专利法》第 15 条要求专利注册处处长在申请日起 18 个月内审查并在适当的情况下，接受完整的说明书，否则该申请将被视为失效。在专利注册处处长拒绝专利申请的情况下，申请人可向知识产权法庭或津巴布韦高等法院提出上诉。

3. 异议和注册

《专利法案》第 17 条规定，利害关系人应在《津巴布韦工业产权杂志》刊登公告之日起 3 个月内，对注册处处长接受专利申请提出异议。除非有异议或上诉程序，在接受完整的说明书的公告之日起 3 个月内，就可以要求对已接受的专利的注册证书进行盖章和签发。

4. 专利保护期间

国家发明专利和津巴布韦的 ARIPO 专利的期限从申请日起 20 年（第 25 条）。

（三）商标注册

《商标法案》（第 26:04 章）作出了在津巴布韦注册商标的规定。为进行注册，商标必须具有鲜明的特点，并且能够区分于他人进行贸易的同一类商品或服务中使用或建议使用商标。

1. 申请要求

根据《商标法》和《商标条例》（2005 年第 170 号法令）的规定，在津巴布韦注册商标申请的最低要求如下：

- 以英文规定的格式填写的申请表。申请必须披露申请人的全名、实际地址、国籍。还必须提供津巴布韦境内服务的地址；
- 需要申请的商标细节和适当的商品/服务和国际类别；
- 必须签署的委托书。它不需要认证或公证。但是，签字人必须填写完整的姓名和名称；
- 10 个打印且标记好的原始高质量样本，除非该标记只有一个单词或由普通字母组成的几个单词（最大尺寸 70mm x 70mm）；
- 如果标记/设备是彩色的，则需要使用颜色限制条款的描述，在必要的情况下使用 Pantone 颜色代码来指定准确的颜色；
- 如主张公约优先权，可将该商标的第一个外国申请的核证副本连同适用的英文翻译一起提交（在提交申请的 3 个月内）；
- 关于该标记是否已在津巴布韦使用或保留将来使用的建议；
- 如果标记是用英语以外的语言描述的，则需要该语言对其意义和细节（以及对任何外国字符的音译和意义，如汉字进行翻译）；
- 申请人不打算使用商标的，可以在提交申请时同时指定注册用户，否则注册用户可以在注册后指定。

2. 审查

审查申请是否符合手续、可登记性和是否与在先的登记相冲突。ZIPO 平均需要 3 到 5 个月的时间来审核申请并出具审查报告。

一旦有条件接受通知中规定的条件已被书面同意，或反对通知书已被否决，ZIPO 将发出要求支付公告费用的接受表格。

3. 公告及异议

一旦申请被刊登在《津巴布韦工业产权杂志》上，任何利害关系人都可以在杂志发表后的 2 个月内对该申请提出异议。如果提出异议，商标申请就不能进行注册，直到异议方撤回或最终支持商标申请人。异议期满未提出异议的，申请人可以提交签发注册证书的申请，并由 ZIPO 签发证书。

4. 商标保护期

国内商标根据《班珠尔商标协议》注册的 ARIPO 商标以及《马德里议定书》规定的商标的有限期限为从提交日起 10 年。在全国范围内提交的公约申请的期限是自公约国提交文件之日起计算的。到期后可续期 10 年。

5. 公约协议

在班珠尔和马德里议定书下注册的商标具有同样的效力，并享有与在本国注册的商标相同的保护。但是在班珠尔和马德里协议分别于 2010 年 9 月 10 日和 2016 年 7 月 1 日被国内立法化之前，在津巴布韦注册的商标，该商标所有人不享有生效的之前发生的侵犯商标权的赔偿或其他救济措施的权利。

（四）知识产权保护措施

《专利法》和《商标法》为侵犯注册专利和商标提供民事、刑事和海关救济措施。

1. 民事救济

侵犯知识产权的民事诉讼可以在知识产权法庭、高等法院或地方法院（受管辖权限制）之前，由注册的所有人或独家被许可人或注册使用人提出。

未经专利权人的授权和同意，在津巴布韦被制造、使用、提供处理、处理、进口和行使专利权和效力的行为均构成对专利权的侵犯。如果专利与一种新物质有关，同一化学成分和构成的任何物质都应被认为是通过专利过程产生的。

《商标法》不允许对未注册商标的侵权行为采取行动。但是，未注册商标的所有者可以就不正当竞争或者将商品或者服务冒充他人的商品或者服务提起诉讼。

《商标法》还承认和保护相似的国外商标。相似商标的国外持有者可以申请知识产权法庭或者有管辖权的法庭作出裁决，禁止在津巴布韦使用构成或主体部分构成复制、仿冒或翻译外国相似商标的商标方商标与以下相关时：

（1）商品或服务所使用商标与外国相似商标下的商品或服务完全相同或类似，而在津巴布韦，该相似的外国标志是众所周知的，这种使用可能会欺骗或引起混淆；

（2）与商品或服务相似的外国商标不相似，如果：

① 使用与这些商品或服务有关的商标，能表明他们与相似的外国商标的经营者之间有联系；

② 相似的外国商标所有者的利益可能会受到这种使用的损害；

③ 相似的外国商标已在公约国家注册为商标。

相似外国商标所有者提起侵权诉讼，一个月内必须在津巴布韦申请注册该商标。

在津巴布韦，侵犯注册专利和商标的补救措施包括安东·皮莱（Anton Piller）命令、禁令、损害赔偿、交付和交出账户，以及任何其他专利侵权的其他补救措施。控告人在计算损害赔偿金额方面有困难，可以根据使用专利或商标的合理使用费来评估损害赔偿。

2. 刑事救济

刑事犯罪包括：

- 伪造注册商标；
- 将注册商标错误地应用于商品或服务；
- 为伪造或用于伪造、注册商标而制造模具、模块、机器或其他工具；
- 制作任何该商标的复制品或仿制品，或导致欺骗或混淆的类似标志；
- 进口任何仿制品、复制品或可以呈现商标的东西，而非适用于该商标的商品。

对侵犯注册专利和商标的刑事制裁包括没收财产、罚款和监禁。

3. 海关备案

《商标法》进一步规定禁止进口或出口假冒商标商品。

"假冒商标商品"一词定义为任何未经授权使用注册商标的下列商品：

(a) 与注册商标相同；或

(b) 不能从主要方面与注册商标加以区分；从而侵犯了注册商标所有者的权利。

对于他人申请禁止货物进出口时，海关总署认为满足条件并且申请人提供相应保证金，可以禁止此类假冒商品进出津巴布韦10个工作日，并在该期限内，注册商标的所有人必须向知识产权法庭或法院提起诉讼，要求指示海关署长禁止假冒商品的进口和出口，具体视情况而定。

只要法庭或法院的命令有效地阻止了假冒商品的进口或出口，所涉货物是被禁止的货物，不得从津巴布韦进口或出口。

六、环境保护

环境和环境保护的重要性在津巴布韦最高法律——津巴布韦《宪法》《2013年修正案（第20号）》中得到承认，即根据《宪法》第73条：

（1）每个人都有权享有：

① 对无害于其健康或福祉的环境；

②通过合理的立法和其他措施，为当代和后代的利益使环境得到保护：
- 防止污染和生态退化；
- 促进节约；
- 在促进经济和社会发展的同时，确保生态可持续发展和利用自然资源。

（2）国家必须在现有资源的范围内采取合理的立法和其他措施，以逐步实现本节所规定的权利。

（一）环境保护监督

《环境管理条例》（第 20:27 章）是监管环境保护的关键立法。它由气候生态部部长管理，其职责包括促进、协调、监测和保护环境。该部长还可以对任何对环境造成损害的人进行处罚，并有责任确保对造成环境损害负责的人员或机构将承担补救的费用。

《环境管理法》设立了环境管理委员会（EMA），该机构的职责在《环境管理法》第 10 条中列出，包括制定空气、水、土壤、噪音、振动、辐射和废物管理的质量标准。该机构负责制定国家计划、环境管理计划和地方环境管理行动计划的指导方针，并对废物的收集、处置、处理和回收进行管理和监测。它还规定任何污染物或有害物质排放到环境中，并以登记册的形式记录根据《环境管理法》发出的所有许可证和执照。

EMA 有权通过示范法在地方当局管辖范围内建立环境管理办法和出具书面命令，要求相关人员执行命令中指定或采用等措施来保护环境。在开始实施《环境管理法》附表一所载的活动之前，公司须取得环境影响评估，而环境管理委员会则负责监管、监察、复核及批准环境影响评估。

在进行影响评估后，EMA 还对活动进行定期的环境审计，以确保其执行符合《环境管理法》的要求。

此外，根据《区域、城镇和乡村规划法》（第 29:12 章），区域规划委员会、市议会、镇议会、农村区议会和地方委员会也负责监督环境保护。他们制定和执行调节土地使用的政策，并在各自的规划领域内保护和改善自然环境。

（二）环境保护的法律法规概要

如上所述，津巴布韦《宪法》第 73 条明确规定了环境保护。《宪法》要求通过包括防止污染和生态退化、促进节约、确保生态可持续发展和利用自然资源、同时促进经济和社会发展的方法来实现这种保护。

此外，《环境管理法》附表一（第 2、97 条）列出了需要环境影响评估的项目。这些包括房地产开发项目；工业活动；采矿、采石、石油生产储存和分配等基础设施项目；以及发电和输电。

《环境管理法》第 97 条指明上述列明的项目不能执行，除非环境管理机构总负责人在相关责任人根据本法案规定提交环境评估报告后，签发一份环境评估报告的证明，证书有效且由机构总负责人签发的证书事项符合规定。在违反《环境管理法》第 97 条的情况下实施一项工程，是可能被处以罚款和监禁的刑事处罚。该法还规定了某些许可证的要求，包括污水排放许可证、废气排放许可证、废弃物许可证以及农药和有毒物质的登记。

除了以上所讨论的《环境管理法》外，还有其他立法对特定行业相关环境问题作出规定。《区域、城镇和乡村规划法》规定了在地方当局管辖范围内进行的活动。《矿山和矿物法》（第 21:05 章）规定了与采矿和采矿有关活动相关的环境问题。尤其是，根据第 237 条，采矿计划必须由采矿专员考虑环境保护并给予批准后方可进行。

《水资源法》（第 20:24 章）规定了水资源的开发和利用。该法规定了保护环境和防止和控制水污染的相关内容。《水资源法》要求任何人抽象为满足基本要求（家庭人员需求，动物生活需求，为私人使用和浸水槽制造砖）以外的基地目的而抽取水资源的，必须按照第 32 节规定从相关领域的流域管理委员会获得许可。应从采矿专员那里获得了用于采矿的许可证。

《公园和野生生物法》（第 20:14 章）规定建立国家公园、植物保护区、植物园、鸟兽类保护区、狩猎区和休闲公园。该法令限制或禁止在受保护区域内的某些活动，包括打猎；采摘或破坏植物以及车队旅游（第 24 和 29 条）；勘探和采矿（第 119 条）。《森林法》（第 19:05 章）规定了国家森林的管理、控制和经营、保护私人森林、树木和林产品、砍伐和砍伐木材用于采矿和焚烧植被(《森林法》第 37、41、45、56 节和第 8 部分)。禁止砍伐、砍伐、伤害或破坏该法附表三列明的森林及其产品和保留土地。

就农业而言,也有立法规定可以使用哪些化学品和肥料,以确保健康和安全以及环境保护。《肥料、农场饲料和救济法》(第 18:12 章)、《肥料条例》(1972 年罗德西亚政府第 669 号公告)规定了农业生产、许可和使用化肥的要求。

津巴布韦也是许多关于保护环境国际条约的签署国。例如《国际重要湿地特别是水禽栖息地公约》(《拉姆萨尔公约》)。该条约承认湿地作为水资源管理机构的基本生态功能,以及作为特有动植物群的栖息地。它试图通过人力和经济发展来减少对湿地的侵蚀和损失。根据《拉姆萨尔公约》,若干湿地被指定为具有国际重要性的湿地,因此国际上要求国家促进它们的保护。禁止任何扰乱指定湿地生态系统的开发活动。

在津巴布韦开展业务活动的公司必须遵守各种环境法律和条例,因此,潜在的企业主必须获得全面的法律意见,包括所有与他们所考虑的活动有关的法律。

(三)环境保护评估

作为环境管理机构的环境保护部负责制定和执行环境保护法例和标准。这包括维持和执行环境影响评估政策、国家防火战略、有害物质使用和处理、生态系统保护和废物管理的准则的责任。环境保护部亦提供化验服务、专业服务及紧急服务,以应对意外或溢漏。

EMA 通过三个主要单位来运作,即环境质量局、生态系统保护局和质量实验室。环境质量局负责环境达标检查、取样和测试各种资源,以核实质量和派生标准,制定和审查适用于各种环境质量数据库的预期用途和维护的环境质量标准。它包括空气质量科、有害物质及物品管制科、液体及废水科及固体废物管理科。

生态系统保护局负责环境影响评估,它定义、量化和评价人类活动对生态系统的潜在和已知影响,以及必须实施的缓解措施,以减少对生态系统的不良影响并提升积极方面的影响。环境影响评估用于确定一个项目是否应该继续进行,以及以何种方式进行。《环境管理法》的第十一部分要求项目开发人员聘请独立顾问进行环境影响评估。环境管理计划必须连同所要求的表格和规定的费用一起提交给环境管理机构。该机构的检查员将视察该地区,审查环境管理计划并选择接受该项目,或有限制接受或直接拒绝项目。该机构通过质量实验室服务局提供实验室服务。

七、争议解决

在津巴布韦,解决争端的主要途径是通过对抗式诉讼和替代争端解决机制(ADR),即仲裁、调解和和解。

(一)争议解决的方法和机构

争端可以通过法院系统的对抗式诉讼或通过上述三种形式的 ADR 方式来解决。

1. 诉讼

诉讼是解决纠纷的最常用手段。这涉及向法院寻求法律裁定。2013 年津巴布韦《宪法》第 162 节规定设立下列法院:
- 宪法法院;
- 最高法院;
- 高等法院;
- 行政法院;
- 劳动法院;
- 治安法庭;
- 习惯法法庭。

还有根据《议会法》设立的其他法庭。

此外,根据《宪法》第 162(3)条的规定,议会通过法律设立了包括小额索偿法院、知识产权法庭、水务法院、财政上诉法院和所得税上诉特别法庭等各种专门法庭。每个法院都有规则来规范其中的程序。

一旦事项已经由法庭裁决并且法令已经作出,如有必要胜诉方可以继续执行,但是此法令只能通过向高等法院执行官或法庭信使申请完成。

(1)宪法法院

《宪法》第 167 条规定,宪法法院是津巴布韦涉及宪法事项的最高法院。它只处理一些引起宪法问题的事项,例如立法的合宪性和基本权利和自由的执行,以及它的决定对所有其他法院都有约束力。根据上述章节,诉讼人可以直接通过下级法院的转介或就《宪法》第 175 条规定的宪法事项根据下级法院的上诉通知,直接向宪法法院提出上诉。宪法法院可以作为初审法院,作为上诉法院,并作为与宪法声明有关的确认法庭,开庭审理宪法事项。宪法法院还负责确认下级法院作出的宣布一项条款违反宪法的决定。

某些事项属于宪法法院的专属管辖范围。《宪法法院规则》(2016 年法定文书)第 61 号第 21 条规定,诉讼当事人可以在某些情况下直接向法院提起诉讼,例如:

① 下级法院或较小管辖区的转介;
② 议会或总统是否未能履行宪法义务的决定;
③ 根据《宪法》第 175(3)条提出的上诉,反对关于任何法律的宪法效力或无效的命令;
④ 个人的自由受到威胁。

宪法法院还负责确认任何声明的合宪性问题。《宪法法院规则》第 31(1)条规定,如果违宪声明是由宪法法院以外的法院作出的,作出该声明的法院的登记员或书记员必须在作出决定的 14 天内向宪法法院的登记员提交包括法院裁定在内的程序记录以便宪法法院进行确认。

上述情形是宪法法院在当事人没有主动上诉的情况下可以直接接受诉讼的唯一情况。《宪法法院规则》第 32(2)条规定,如果一方当事人对下级法院或法庭关于宪法事项的裁定不满,希望可以上诉至宪法法院,则该方应在裁定作出的 15 日之内,向宪法法院登记员提出上诉请求。

(2)最高法院

根据《最高法院法》第 21 条(第 7 章 13 节)的规定,最高法院作为终审法院有权审理上诉的任何和所有事项。它可以审理包括宪法事项在内的任何问题。然而,就宪法事项而言,终审法院是宪法法院。

一般来说,向最高法院提出上诉的时间是在收到判决之日的 15 天之内。根据《最高法院法》第 22 条,最高法院有权确认、修改、更改或驳回上诉或作出合适判决。它也可能要求重新审判或启动新的诉讼。

在某些情况下上诉至最高法院,可能需要获得许可。《高等法院法》第 43 条(第 7:05 章)规定,当一方当事人想要上诉时,必须获得高等法院上诉许可:

① 允许审判中上诉的时间延长的裁定;
② 高等法院法官拒绝简易判决的申请,并无条件允许被告进行辩护;
③ 由当事人同意的命令或仅由法律决定由法院自行决定的费用的命令;
④ 中间裁定或裁决。

《劳动法》第 92F 条(第 28:01 章)规定,任何希望对劳动法院的任何裁决提出上诉的受侵害的一方,应向审理该事项的法官或向劳动法院的任何其他法官提出上诉申请,以获得许可。

若上述申请被高等法院或劳工法院审理法官驳回,受侵害的一方可以根据《最高法院法》第 19 条的规定直接向最高法院提起上诉,根据 1964 年《最高法院规则》第 19(1)条规定,受侵害的一方必须在上诉被驳回之日其 10 日内向最高法院提出。

(3)高等法院

高等法院既是初审法院也是审理来自地方法院或任何类似的法院案件的上诉法院。《宪法》第 171 节的规定赋予了高等法院的审理所有案件的初审管辖权,这一地位进一步体现在《高等法院法》第 13

节（第 7:06 章）中。所有源自地方法院的民事上诉均由等高法院审理，一些来自其他下级法院或法庭的上诉也由高等法院审理。若立法有特别规定，例如《商标法案》（第 26:04 章）和《专利法案》（第 26:02 章）。根据《高等法院法》第 26 条规定，高等法院对其所有的下级法院的诉讼程序具有固有的审查权力。

如果下级法院在审理中适用法律错误，受害一方也可以提起上诉。这需要考虑到作出判决的法律依据是否准确。但是，审查申请涉及下级法院或法庭据以作出裁决的程序是否合法，例如这种主审法官的偏见导致的不正当行为。

（4）行政法院

行政法院是一个专门法院，它只审理上诉案件或审查行政机关的事项。《行政司法法》第 2 节（第 10:28 章）对行政机构进行了如下界定：

- 一名官员、雇员、成员、委员会、理事会或委员会或地方政府或半国营集团；
- 根据指派或任何法律法规规定的理事会和委员会；
- 国家部长或副部长；
- 任何被授权执行或行使行政权力或职责的人或机构。

行政法院是法规的产物，因此在其管辖范围是有限的。行政法院根据《行政司法法》第 4 节和《行政法院法》第 4 节（第 7:01 章）行使其司法管辖权，行政法院有权受理行政机关提出的上诉或审查事项。

例如，根据国家社会保障法案（第 17:04 章）赋权的国家社会保障行政管理部门，根据《矿业和矿产法》（第 21:05 章）赋权的采矿事务委员会，根据《环境管理法》（第 20:27 章）赋权的环境管理机构，根据《农村协议法案》（第 29:13 章）或《城市议会法案》（第 29:15 章）赋权的农村或城市委员会，当事人对行政机关的决定感到不满的，可以向行政法院提出上诉或者申请复议。

如果行政机构的法律没有明确规定针对该行政机关行政行为的上诉或申请行政复议的时间期限或程序，那么上述适用于 1980 年的《法政法院（多种上诉）规则》，申请行政复议适用于 1971 年的《高等法院规则》。《行政法院（多种上诉）规则》第 5 条规定，当事人应在法院作出决定之日起在 30 天内提出上诉。《高等法院规则》第 256 条规定，当事人可以在行政机关终止程序之日起 8 个星期内提起复议。

（5）劳动法院

劳动法院亦是法规的产物，其管辖范围仅限于《劳动法》第 89 条规定的事项（第 28:01 章）。《劳动法》第 89(1) 条规定劳动法院可行使下列职能：

- 根据《劳动法》或任何其他法令，审理和终止申请和上诉；
- 根据《劳动法》的规定，审理和裁定部长所提到的事项；
- 当劳动法院认为在有利的情况下将争端提交劳工事务官、指定代理人或由劳动法院指定的人来调解劳资纠纷；
- 从仲裁员名册中任命一名仲裁员，以审理和裁定申请；
- 《劳动法》或任何其他法令规定的事项。

此外，根据《劳动法》第 92EE 条，劳动法院有具体的审查权力如下：

① 根据本法和任何其他法律的规定，在劳动法院作出的任何诉讼或裁决或与之有关的决定的依据均可在劳动法院作出复审。

- 仲裁员或者仲裁机构没有管辖权的；
- 仲裁员或仲裁机构与案件有利害关系，存在偏见、恶意或腐败现象。
- 仲裁机构的决定或仲裁程序或裁决所涉及的事项的严重违规。

② 第①款内的任何内容均不得影响任何与审查程序或下级法院、法庭或当局的决定有关的其他法律。

需谨慎注意的是，不同于其他民事案件中根据惯例法案（第 8:11 章）中的惯例，劳动法中的惯例是由《劳动法》第 94 条加以规定的，其规定与劳动法相关的惯例从案件发生之日起或者诉讼当事人知晓不公平的劳动行为时起算 2 年。

劳动争议当事人因其雇主、劳工官员、仲裁员、国家就业委员会或任何其他法庭的决定而受到侵害的，他可向劳动法院提出上诉或提出复议申请，视情况而定。根据2017年《劳动法院规则》第19(1)条的规定，当事人可从其收到决议、裁定、指导、判决的日期起21天内提出上诉。关于复议的申请，《劳动法院规则》第20(1)条规定，应在法庭程序结束之日起21天内提交对审查法庭决定的复议申请。

（6）地方法院

地方法院由刑事法庭和民事法庭组成。刑事案件取决于国家，在提交给警察部门之后，由国家检察机关决定是否追究刑事责任。

地方法院的民事管辖权由《地方法院法》第11条（第7:10章）规定，并与地理管辖权、行为原因和案件的财产价值有关。每一个地方法院对该地方行政区划内任何从事商业活动的人或合伙企业都具有地理上的管辖权。如果诉讼的原因完全在该法院的管辖范围内，法院对在该法院提起诉讼的人也有管辖权。

一件案件的财产价值在决定法院是否有管辖权方面起着一定的作用。但是，当事各方有权就地方法院的管辖权达成协议，或放弃其财产主张的一部分，以确保该事项属于地方法院的管辖范围。财产限额是在《地方法院（民事管辖权）（货币限制）规则》（2012年法定文书第163号）中规定的，地方法院的财产管辖权一般为最高价值为10 000美元，或根据案件情况在5 000美元上下浮动。

《地方法院法》第14条规定了地方法院没有管辖权的事项。这些内容包括关于根据《婚姻法》（第5:11章）解除婚姻关系的事项，因智力情况影响个人地位、对遗嘱的解释和效力以及永久沉默的法令。

2. 替代争议解决机制

如上所述，在津巴布韦有三种ADR的方式，即仲裁、调解和和解。每种方式将在下面讨论。

（1）仲裁

本迪克斯在《南非的劳资关系》（2010年第5版）第619—620页指出，仲裁需要任命第三方（仲裁员）来裁决争端，并公平地作出决定。仲裁员听取双方的意见，是最终的决策者。他的决定对双方都有约束力。

津巴布韦是《承认及执行外国仲裁裁决公约》的签署国，该公约为缔约国承认和执行仲裁裁决提供了条件，前提是，裁决是由缔约国作出的。根据公约，津巴布韦通过了《联合国国际贸易法委员会示范仲裁法》，并通过制定《仲裁法》将这一规则国内化。因此，《仲裁法》规定了仲裁纠纷的裁决应遵循的程序。

通常情况下，合同双方约定仲裁解决纠纷。这些条款被称为"仲裁条款"。该条款可以指定仲裁员，以及在与任命仲裁员有关的分歧时将采取什么行动。如果双方未做约定，或双方不能达成协议的，则可以通过商业仲裁中心，任命一名仲裁员来审理此事。裁定作出后一方当事人对其不满意时，根据《仲裁法》第34条的规定，该方在收到裁决之日起3个月内向高等法院申请撤销该仲裁裁决。

在双边投资条约中出现争议的地方，可以根据《国际投资争端解决中心（ICSID）公约》的规定，通过仲裁解决。该公约也已经通过《仲裁国际投资争端法》（第7:03章）进行了国内化。公约设立了国际投资争端解决中心，负责审理与国际投资争端有关的事项，并规定了在仲裁过程中应遵循的规则和程序。津巴布韦是公约的缔约国，因此也受到同样的约束。《仲裁国际投资争端法》为ICSID裁决的登记和执行提供了可能。

《劳动法》第93(5)(a)条指出，只有在涉及利益争议的情况下，才可通过仲裁解决劳工问题。根据《劳动法》第63(3b)条的规定，由国家就业委员会指定的代理人可以担任在其特定中产生的劳资纠纷的仲裁员。

仲裁裁决在性质上是有约束力的，为了裁决所支持一方的执行目的，要求进行登记。《仲裁法》第35条规定高等法院对裁决进行登记。一经登记，该裁决就成为法院的命令，并可根据《仲裁法》第36条申请执行。

（2）调解

Bendix（supra）616描述，当独立的第三方介入一场纠纷，并试图促成和解时，即为调解。在调解中，调解员扮演一个积极的角色，他试图通过建议各方，充当中间人，并提出可能的解决办法来促成和解。调解人不能强迫当事人和解，也不能对当事人作出有约束力的决定。在津巴布韦，一些法律从业者和退休法官提供调解服务，但没有相关的立法。

（3）和解

和解是指设立一个讨论会，在该讨论会中，争端各方可以聚在一起，试图解决他们之间的分歧。在津巴布韦，这种解决争端的方式主要用于劳工事务。根据《劳动法》第93条的规定，在劳工事务官员和国家就业委员会接到申诉之后，必须首先通过和解程序。但是，如果双方不能友好地解决该问题，则可以参照《劳动法》第93(5)条提出或作出裁决。

（4）外国判决和裁决的登记

根据《承认及执行外国仲裁裁决公约》和《仲裁法》的规定，外国仲裁裁决经登记可予以执行。外国的判决必须按照《民事事项（互助）法》第5条的规定进行登记（第8:02章）。外国的判决必须由指定国家的法院作出。判决债权人应当自作出判决之日起6年内，或者在裁定上诉或者复审后，向有管辖权的法院申请登记。这类申请将以具体法院指定的形式提出。

根据《民事事项（互助）（指定国家）令》（1998年法律文书第65号）的附表和第八章只有下列国家的判决可根据上文第5节的规定进行登记：
- 澳大利亚；
- 多米尼克；
- 德国；
- 加纳；
- 葡萄牙；
- 南非；
- 意大利；
- 赞比亚；
- 斯洛伐克；
- 保加利亚。

但是，如果一方当事人试图执行一个非指定的国家的判决，同样的情况也不排除。《民事事项（互助）法》第25条规定，该法案是附加的，不限制任何其他有关承认和执行外国判决的法律。根据习惯法，当事人可以申请外国判决的登记。根据Jones v Krok 1995 (1) SA 677(A)在685 B-E段的规定，申请登记外国判决的适用要求如下：
- 作出判决的法院有权受理该案件；
- 判决是终局的，其效力是决定性的，并没有被废除；
- 承认和执行判决不会违反公共政策；
- 不以欺诈手段取得判决的；
- 判决不涉及执行外国的刑法或税法；
- 该判决的执行并未被任何法律所排除。

（二）法律适用

津巴布韦最高效力法是2013年津巴布韦《宪法》。所有其他法律都服从于宪法，如果其他法律与宪法相抵触或不反映宪法规定的价值观和权利，与宪法抵触部分是非法的和无效的，也可以被宣布为无效。法院体系维护宪法，并确保所有的法律都是一致的。

津巴布韦的其他法律渊源包括成文法和普通法。案例法也得到了说明和发展。成文法是指津巴布韦议会制定的法律和条例。

津巴布韦的普通法主要是罗马-荷兰法。然而，在某些情况下，适用英国普通法，例如合同法和保险法。当争端出现时，法院适用相同的情况，除非当事人通过合同约定了适用于他们的争端的法律制度。例如，各方可能决定，德国的法律将适用于其协议的内容，而《高等法院法》第49条规定的任何适应的官方语言均为英语。当事人要求使用不同语言的，必要时必须有翻译，且必须出庭。除非有明文规定，所有向法院提交的文件都应该是英文的。

解决争端的一般原则是，提出主张的一方负责举证。在民事案件中，举证责任是一种可能性的平衡，因此，这个人必须提供足够的证据来说服法院他们有权得到他们所主张的东西。

在法律诉讼程序中，纠纷中的当事人可以为自己辩护，也可以委托一名根据《法律从业人员法》（第27:07章）正式注册，并持有津巴布韦法律协会颁发的有效执业证书的法律从业人员进行辩护。然而，工会有权代表其成员参加劳动事务。法人（例如公司）在高级法院和上级法院的诉讼中必须由法律从业人员代表。

尽管根据《法律从业人员法》规定津巴布韦法律协会可能在特定情况下会向外国律师颁布有限的执业证书，但外国律师不得在津巴布韦法院代理当事人。只有来自互惠国的外国法律从业人员才有资格获得限定时间内有效的执业证书。

八、其他

（一）反商业贿赂

在津巴布韦的反贿赂行动受2013年《津巴布韦宪法修正案》(第20号)、《宪法》和其他立法的制约，如《反腐败法》（第9:16章）、《反腐败委员会法》（2004年）、《刑法典》（第9:23章）和《反腐败委员会法》（第9:22章）。

1. 反贿赂法律法规

（1）《刑法典》

在津巴布韦，贿赂和腐败是《刑法典》第9章的犯罪行为。

贿赂在《刑法典》第170条中进行了定义。根据《刑法典》第170（1）条规定，行为人可能通过两种方式构成贿赂罪。第一种方式是代理人无偿收取礼物或报酬作为开展与其业务相关行为的诱因或者回报，而且，在其开展业务时明知或意识到礼物或报酬并非按照协议或约定应得的。第二种方式是第三人给予或同意给予代理人礼物或报酬作为开展与其业务相关行为的诱因或者回报，而且，代理人在其开展业务时明知或意识到礼物或报酬并非按照协议或约定应得的。

《刑法》第169节定义了任何一个人受雇于或代理另一个人的任何能力，包括一个公司的董事或秘书，一个董事会的成员或负责管理一个法人团体和公职人员的事务或业务的机构的成员。委托人被定义为代理人的雇主或代理人所代理的任何其他人。

《刑法典》第170(2)条还规定了可反驳的推定，即在下列情况下贿赂已发生：

① 代理人已经取得或同意获得或请求任何礼物或报酬，无论是为自己或为他人；

② 一个人已经给予，同意给予或提供任何礼物或给代理人，无论是为代理本人，或为另一个人或任何其他与代理人达成协议的人。

《刑法典》并没有提供腐败的定义，但涉及腐败行为的犯罪在刑法第9部分中予以处理。例如，在第171条中，任何代理人，就其委托人的事务或业务而言，故意使用含有虚假陈述并有意欺骗其委托人的文件，构成腐败使用虚假文件罪。第172条规定，在进行与他的当事人的主要事务相关的交易中，故意不向其当事人披露交易的全部本质对其进行欺骗，犯有腐败隐瞒事务罪。

《刑法典》第174条还将滥用职权视为公职人员的罪行。这是公职人员在行使他的职能时，例如故意做与其职能背道而驰的行为或者与其作为一名公职人员的职责不相符合的行为，或者为了对任何人示好或恶待某人而疏于其职责工作为一定行为。

（2）反腐败法[①]

《反腐败法》（第9:16章）的目的是为防止腐败和调查任何有关不诚实或腐败和相关问题的指控提供法律依据。该法第6节授权司法部长、法律和议会事务部长或总统指定的任何部长，以确定涉嫌参与腐败行为的人。第6节规定，部长在有合理依据下，怀疑任何人已经接受了好处或利益，违反预防腐败行为或《刑法典》第九章，特定宣称该人是一个可疑的人，并启动对该人事务的调查。第7节授

---

① 参见第9:16章。

权部长任命调查人员进行同样的工作,并可以限制对某一特定人员的交易。

第10条禁止特定人在未经指定的调查人员批准的情况下从事某些行为。这些行为包括:

① 支出或以任何方式处理财产;
② 订立任何处置任何财产的合同;
③ 在任何银行或金融机构经营任何账户;
④ 增加债务或对其财产造成不利影响;
⑤ 担任公司董事或合伙企业的合伙人;
⑥ 履行作为公司或合伙企业的代理人的任何行为。

2. 监督反商业贿赂的部门

(1) 反腐败委员会

《宪法》第254条设立了津巴布韦反腐败委员会,该委员会有权调查和揭露公共和私营部门的腐败案件,打击腐败、盗窃、滥用职权和在公共和私人部门中任何不当行为,如贿赂(第255条)。反腐败委员会的任务是接收和考虑公众的投诉,并就其认为有必要的投诉采取行动。反腐败委员会是由反腐败委员会授权成立的。该法第3条规定,委员会是法人团体,可以以自己的名义起诉和应诉。

(2) 警察的职责

根据《宪法》的规定,警察部门负责侦查、调查和预防犯罪。《宪法》第219(2)条要求警务部门行使其与任何可能由法律设立的机构合作的职能,以侦查、调查和防止特定类别的罪行,例如反腐败委员会。反腐败委员会与警务处合作,负责调查和揭发贪污案件。

根据第255(e)条的规定,反腐败委员会有权责成警务处处长调查涉嫌贪污的个案,并向反腐败委员会报告任何此类调查的结果。警务部门亦须在执行《刑法》第九章所引致的贿赂及贪污法例的执行过程中,实施调查和拘捕。

(3) 国家检察机关

根据《宪法》第258条,国家检察机关负责代表国家提起和开展刑事诉讼,并履行对此类起诉所必要或附带的任何职能。警方和反腐败委员会均须将贪污及贿赂事宜提交国家检控机关处理。《反腐败委员会法》第12条规定了在警察和反腐败委员会行使其权力时发生冲突的情况下,总检察长有权介入并且指导双方当事人依其观点行事以解决冲突。

3. 惩罚措施

依照《刑法典》第170节的规定,行贿是一种犯罪,惩罚该类犯罪行为时罚款不超过14级(目前5 000美元)或不超过犯罪所得或犯罪支出的3倍,两者以高者论,或处以不超过20年监禁或罚款和监禁同时适用。

《刑法典》第171条将带有贿赂意图使用虚假文件规定为犯罪,其刑罚最多不超过14级罚款或20年监禁,或两者并罚,第172条将腐败的对委托人隐藏交易规定为犯罪,其刑罚也是最多不超过14级罚款或20年监禁,或两者并罚。第174条规定在滥用职权的情况下,最多处以不超过14级罚款或20年监禁,或两者并罚。

洗钱和犯罪收益法(第9章24节)允许没收犯罪使用的物品或资金。

(二)工程承包

1. 许可体系

在到津巴布韦运营之前,公司必须获得各种监管机构的许可。根据项目的性质和实施的形式,将适用不同的法律。

由承包机构(已签订合同或正在考虑订立合资协议的任何部门、政府部门或公共实体)和一家私营公司通过合资协议执行的项目,由《合资企业法》(第22:22章)规定。

具体来说,《合资企业法》规定了投资者或开发者在特定期限内代表合同方履行承包方的职能的项目,并通过下列方式收取效益:来自国会批准的基金,由承包机构通过贷款获得的基金,用户征收,从项目或任何组合取得的收入[第2(2)节]。此外,合同相对方应对其履行职能所产生的风险承担责任，公共资源可以转让或让相同相对方使用。

《合资企业法》第 3 节创建了合资企业局，其责任包括审核提交给它的项目提案和评估承包机构是否能够负担，是否能够带来利润，是否能够将技术、运营和金融风险以最佳方式转移给交易对手以及是否存在竞争力。合资企业局向合资委员会提供项目建议，合资委员会的职能包括确认所有项目均符合相关合资企业政策中规定的国家优先事项，并就是否批准或拒绝合资企业局提交的项目提案向内阁提出建议（该法第 4 节）。

根据《合资企业法》第 8 节，承包机构若想参与联合经营，可通过公共广告的方式表达意向，除非已有指定项目及指定交易对方并已对合资企业局披露。在进行可行性研究后，将其提交给合资企业局。如果合资企业局批准了可行性研究，其将被要求上交项目建议书和模板协议。然后，合资企业局将向委员会提交项目提案，委员会应就此向内阁提出建议。

除上述内容外，《合资企业法》还规定了包括与合资合同、适用法律、争议解决、可行性研究、投标、主动收购、合资项目类型和合资协议类型有关的其他技术方面。投资者必须寻求与他们所寻求的具体项目有关的全面法律意见和技术意见。

任何外国实体收购股份或证券的投资，或在津巴布韦境外设立付款义务的任何投资，都需要根据《外汇管制法》的第四部分和第五部分获得外汇管制的批准（第 22:05 章）。通过授权的交易商（注册商业银行）向外汇管理局（作为财政部长或津巴布韦储备银行）申请外汇管制审批。

此外，投资者进入津巴布韦需要获得津巴布韦投资局（ZIA）根据《津巴布韦投资局法》（第 14:30）颁发的投资许可证。《津巴布韦投资管理局法》第 9 节规定了投资许可证的申请，并要求外国投资者向津巴布韦投资局按照规定格式提交申请，并缴纳相应费用（若有）以及提交投资局要求的其他文件。

根据《津巴布韦投资管理局法》第 14 条，核准投资许可证的因素包括：可以转化为津巴布韦及其人民的利益的技能和技术的程度；拟进行的投资将在多大程度上创造就业机会和发展人力资源；对当地原材料的使用和处理的程度；与项目有关的可兑换外币转移到津巴布韦的价值；拟进行的投资可能对环境和当地经济的现有产业产生的影响。

ZIA 还将规定投资许可证的有效期，在到期之前必须续期。如果投资者未能实施投资，他必须在其意识到无法进行投资情况后 30 天内通知 ZIA。未经当局批准，不得转让的牌照。

虽然投资许可证并非强制性要求，但《津巴布韦投资管理局法》规定，工业和国际贸易部长可向投资许可证持有人（第 24 条）公布激励措施，其中可能包括与税收有关的激励措施，或政府招投标门槛。

2. 禁止的区域

在津巴布韦没有明确禁止外国企业和外国投资者的投资领域，但是津巴布韦《投资机构法》规定投资部门可通过颁布法规的方式规定本国和外国投资区域；指定专门为国内投资者保留的经济部门，以促进国内投资者公平参与经济；禁止出口指定的原材料，规定在出口前对原材料进行增效的方式或者程度；并规定投资许可证申请人提交的投资建议的出口导向程度。建议投资者就在津巴布韦进行投资和经营所需的许可取得全面的咨询意见，并在项目承包之前了解限制事项。

《本土化和经济赋权法》（第 14:33 章）规定了进一步的限制，该法案是推动津巴布韦本土人权力的。该法规定，任何年营业额或拥有资产总额达 120 万美元的公司，必须由津巴布韦本土居民持有至少 51% 的股份。获豁免的商业部门的详情，会不时修订。为保证津巴布韦妇女、法定年龄以下的青少年以及《残疾人法》（第 17:01 章）规定的残疾人的利益，政府可就《本土化和经济赋权法》采取特别措施。负责本土化和经济赋权的国务大臣可规定，通过低于 51% 的股份或比控制比例更低的比例，可以实现对《本土化和经济赋权法》的遵守，并为这种遵守提供延长的时间期限。

根据《本土化和经济赋权（一般）规例》第 3 条，2010 年的法定文书 21 号，在开始营业的 5 年内，在上述规定时间范围内的公司，必须提交本土化实施计划，由国家部长批准，以进行本土化和经济赋权。在收到相同的计划后 45 天内，部长必须批准或否决该计划。如果在 90 天内没有收到书面答复，该计划被视为批准。根据《本土化和经济赋权法》第 3(6) 条，部长们也可以考虑本土化实施计划，并对企业进行本土化和经济赋权评级。此外，在 2016 年 9 月出版的《政府公告》（GN9/2016）中，在与部长和国家本土化和经济赋权委员会（NIEEB）的协商后，津巴布韦投资局可以将本土化计划与投资许可证一起审议。

在业务方的书面要求下，部长将发出一份合规证明书，并将其转交给国家的本土化和经济赋权委员会，以便列入规定的登记册［第3(8)条］。如果业务进行或被要求遵守任何规定的条件，部长可向该业务发出临时证书，而不是最终的证书，完成后，部长应签发最终证书。

2017年12月，在预算演讲期间，政府宣布了修改《本土化和经济赋权法》的计划，除钻石和铂金行业外，将外国投资的本地所有权要求排除在外。2018年"财政法"草案于2018年1月19日公布，提出了拟议的修正案。然而，时至本文撰写之日，该法案尚未提交议会，也没有法律效力。

3. 工程承包

（1）政府招投标项目

根据《公共采购和国有资产处置法》（第22:23章）规定，采购实体（即政府部门、法定机构、国家控股企业、农村或地方议会、和国家之间建立伙伴关系与合资企业）办理采购商品和服务事宜。

该法规定的采购条款受津巴布韦采购管理部门的管辖。管理部门是根据《公共采购和国有资产处置法》第5条设立的。该法第6条规定的职权范围包括：

① 确保以透明、公平、诚实、具成本效益、有竞争力和符合该法的方式进行公共采购；

② 监督采购实体和公共采购制度，以确保遵守该法，并对采购实体和公共采购制度实施电子手段监测和监督；

③ 就该法的解释和实施发出技术准则和指导；

④ 编制与公共采购有关的标准文件和模板，并使采购实体保持记录和编制报告；

⑤ 应请求，向采购实体提供意见和协助。

（2）投标的方法

根据该法第30(1)条的规定，必须在所有情况下采用竞争性投标方法，但须遵守下文所述的某些例外情况。在不适用竞争性投标的情况下，需要获得主管部门授权的书面说明。

在该法第38条中，在竞争性招标过程中，在政府公报和在津巴布韦全国流通的报纸上刊登招标文件。所有适合和合格的投标人均可在不受歧视的情况下提交投标书，并对所有投标人采用相同的标准进行评估。

招标文件应包含以下内容：

① 采购实体的身份和地址；

② 对采购的描述，包括货物或服务的交货地点、任何建筑工程的地点以及提供采购要求的时间；

③ 如何获得投标文件（如适用）、资格预审文件以及应付的价格（如有）；

④ 必须提交投标或申请资格预审的地点和时间。

（3）不适用竞争性投标方法的情形

不适用竞争性投标方法的情形，规定于该法的第32—34条：

① 按该法第32条规定的限制投标方式。

该程序适用于由采购实体选出或邀请的投标人：

- 考虑大量投标的时间和成本与采购要求的估计价值不成比例；
- 在规定期限内发生紧急情况的；
- 合同的估价不超过规定的阈值。

② 按照该法第33条规定的直接采购方法。

这是采购实体在没有收到其他投标人投标的情况下，从一个投标人或供应商那里获得其要求的方式。该方法应用于以下情形：

- 对竞争性招标程序没有作出响应性投标；
- 由于技术或艺术原因，或与保护专有权有关的原因，本合同只能由某一特定供应商履行，不存在合理的选择范围或替代；
- 由于不可归因于采购实体或其不能预见的极端紧急事项，无法按时通过招标程序满足要求；
- 采购实体从该研究所采购样机或第一件产品或服务，并要求制定特定采购合同进行研究、试验、研究或原始开发。

③ 根据该法第 34 条提出的报价要求。

在这一过程中，采购实体从信誉良好的供应商处获得至少三种竞争性报价，而采购要求低于规定的标准。

（4）投标方应满足的标准

投标人通常被允许在不受国籍与条件限制的情况下参与政府项目招标，但具体的限制可能会不时产生。按照该法第 38(e) 条的规定，每一份投标文件都包含必须由每个投标方满足的独特要求，任何投标方都必须满足某些标准，以投标任何政府合同。根据《法案》第 28(2) 条，该标准如下：

① 他们符合特定的道德标准；

② 具有进入采购合同程序的法律能力；

③ 他们不处于破产状态、清算状态，受司法管理状态或不是由法院或司法官员管理；

④ 在开始采购程序之前的 5 年内，招标方及其任何一名员工都没有因为职业行为或做虚假陈述歪曲事实而被定罪；

⑤ 任何其他标准将证明投标人拥有专业技术资格和能力、财务资源、设备和其他物理设施、管理能力、经验、商业信誉，需要执行采购合同的人员。

获得授权的人可以选择一个津巴布韦投标人，只要这种要求在招标的邀请中明确表述。除非招标文件中另有规定，否则当局须以最低价格接受投标。

（5）注册为投标人或承包商

根据《公共采购和国有资产处置法》（2018 年法定文书第 5 号）第 4 条以及相关规定，潜在投标人或承包商可在由采购机构维持的数据库上登记。机构邀请有意投标者和承建商在政府宪报、全国性报纸及网站上登载。

就同一规例第 4(4) 条而言，申请列入注册投标人及承建商名单必须包括以下内容：

① 在公司的情况下，公司的章程大纲、章程或其他组织文件，连同公司的注册证书、董事名单、总公司和当地的实际地址和详细说明，显示出津巴布韦人和外国股份的相应比例；

② 在合伙企业、集团或其他业务实体的情况下，合伙企业、集团或其他业务实体的合伙协议或显示合伙关系的其他组织文件，以及其合伙人或控制人或经理，其总部和当地办公室的地址，以及显示津巴布韦和外国人对于合伙企业、集团或实体的控制程度；

③ 就个人而言，需有详细的履历和资格证明。

根据该法第 28 条的规定，任何注册投标人或承建商均有资格参与并对政府引导的投标项目进行投标。

Zimbabwe

Authors: Terence Hussein, Paresh Ranchhod, Sara Nyaradzo Moyo, Shorai Rutendo Chidemo
Translators: Liu Xingyan, Grace Wang

I. Overview[1]

Zimbabwe is strategically positioned in the centre of the southern Africa region and has emerged as a centre for regional trade and landlocked transport. The country is well positioned to be the investment centre of southern Africa. Zimbabwe has been viewed as one of the African countries offering high return on investments within the coming years.

Zimbabwe is a resource rich and peaceful country that is a gateway to Southern Africa and is strategically placed at the heart of Southern Africa with Zambia, Mozambique, South Africa and Botswana at its borders. The country is at the spine of the North–South Corridor which interlinks all Southern African logistics, railways, roads, power and telecommunication. With a population of approximate 14 million citizens Zimbabwe is blessed with a temperate climate and seasonal rainfall.

Zimbabwe has a strong tertiary education system with a highly skilled and competent human capital base. Zimbabwe is committed to improve the conditions for doing business and has focused on the consolidation of its investment policies and now offers a variety of investment opportunities in various sectors mainly manufacturing, agriculture, mining, energy, tourism infrastructure and services.

The introduction of a multi-currency system effectively ended the use of the Zimbabwean dollar as a medium of exchange. The main currency in use is the USD, with the South African Rand (ZAR). The GBP, Botswana Pula and Euro are also legal tender, although they are used to a lesser extent than the USD and ZAR.

The Government, through the Ministry of Finance has indicated that the multi- currency regime will remain in place in the foreseeable future.

The Government has put in measures and incentives to attract foreign investment in several sectors of the economy.

This aspect of the guide covers the laws and regulations applicable to Zimbabwe in relation to investment. This report is a summary of the laws only.

II. Investment

A. Market Access

The Government of Zimbabwe has made strides towards creating a conducive business environment to transform the economy and attract Foreign Direct Investment. The Government in keeping with this has made a pronouncement that 13 laws will be promulgated in the first quarter of the year to create a conducive investment climate by addressing concerns previously raised by foreign investors. Some of the Bills include the National Competitiveness Commission Bill, Judiciary Laws Amendment Bill and the Shop Licences Amendment Bill.[2]

It is in this context that the Government has launched its investment policy statement[3] on 18 January 2018. The Investment Guidelines outline the country's investment policy strategy; and showcase investment opportunities available in the economy including, among others, agriculture, mining, manufacturing, tourism, information communication and technology, and infrastructure development. The Guidelines are issued as part of government efforts to address domestic challenges facing the country (poor economic growth, company closures, cash crisis, high levels of unemployment etc).[4]

---

[1] Investment in Zimbabwe, Handbook 2017, published by the Government of Zimbabwe.
[2] Investment Guidelines and Opportunities in Zimbabwe, January 2018- Government of Zimbabwe.
[3] Investment Guidelines and Opportunities in Zimbabwe, January 2018- Government of Zimbabwe.
[4] Investment Guidelines and Opportunities in Zimbabwe, January 2018- Government of Zimbabwe.

a. Summary of the Investment Guidelines

The Investment Guidelines affirm the Government's commitment to build an economy founded on sound investment principles and international best practices (such as non-discrimination, effective protection of property, transparency and high standards of governance). The Government pledges to comply with its legal obligations under bilateral, regional and international agreements. Further, the Government has committed itself to modernise and align its legal framework for investment with international standards within six months. In this regard, the Government has since March 2018 amended the Indigenisation and Economic Empowerment Act[1] by confining the 51/49 percent indigenisation threshold to diamond and platinum sectors only.

The establishment of Special Economic Zones (SEZ) in terms of the Special Economic Zone Act[2] is being pursued in 3 strategic locations in Zimbabwe. SEZs are aimed at attracting investments, increasing exports, and promoting value addition and beneficiation by offering special incentives to qualifying investments. It is also meant to promote investment in the strategic sectors of the economy to revitalize key industries through providing competitive fiscal and non- fiscal incentives to investors. Also relevant to investment promotion is the Government's aim to strengthen the institutional framework for investment, and reduce the bureaucratic procedures for investment entry and establishment.[3]

b. Investment Regulations in Zimbabwe

Zimbabwe has several pieces of legislation that are applicable to investment
- The Constitution of Zimbabwe[4]
- Securities & Exchange Act[5]
- Collective Investment Schemes Act[6]
- Zimbabwe Investment Authority Act[7]

a) The Constitution

The Constitution guarantees legal protection of private investment against expropriation without compensation in terms of Sections 2 and 71 of the Constitution. In addition, Zimbabwe is a signatory to international treaties that guarantee effective investment protection and dispute resolution. These include–the MIGA, OPIC, ICSID, UNICITRAL, New York Convention on the enforcement of foreign Arbitral awards.[8] Moreover, Zimbabwe has entered into several Bilateral Investment Protection Agreements (BIPPA) including with the People's Republic of China, which to date remains valid and protect the interests of citizens of both China and Zimbabwe.

b) Securities & Exchange Act[9]

The Securities Act governs a number of aspects amongst which is the control and regulation of investment in securities. Details of this legislation appear elsewhere in this report.

In terms of the objectives set out in section 4 (1) (a) of the Act, the Securities Commission aims to maintain high levels of investor protection.

c) Zimbabwe Investment Authority Act[10]

This Act governs the establishment and functions of the Zimbabwe Investment Authority (ZIA) which is the investment promotion agency responsible for promoting, facilitating, regulating and coordinating both domestic and foreign invesments.

In terms of the Act, a foreign investor is required to obtain an investment license from ZIA and this will enable the investor to access incentives and protection under Zimbabwe laws. The license is also required for purposes of repatriation of dividends and loan repayments, taxation, export facilitation and exchange controls and import tariff dispensation. The license is valid for a specific period determined by the ZIA board, and renewable on application.[11]

The requirements for an application for an investment licence are as follows[12]:

---

[1] Chapter 14:33.
[2] Chapter 14:34.
[3] Investment Guidelines and Opportunities in Zimbabwe, January 2018- Government of Zimbabwe.
[4] Amendment No. 20 of 2013.
[5] Chapter 24:25.
[6] Chapter 24:19.
[7] Chapter 14:30.
[8] Investment in Zimbabwe Handbook 2017, Published by the Government of Zimbabwe.
[9] Chapter 24:25.
[10] Chapter 14:30.
[11] Investment in Zimbabwe Handbook 2017, Published by the Government of Zimbabwe.
[12] Investment in Zimbabwe Handbook 2017, Published by the Government of Zimbabwe.

• A non-refundable statutory application fee;
• A fully-completed ZIA Application Form;
• Company registration documents;
• Official list and profiles of Shareholders and / or Directors;
• Business plan or feasibility study;
• Proof of finance (the evidence of project finance may be provided in either bank statements, confirmation letter from a bank, confirmed bank loans, other confirmed credit facilities and or equipment / machinery)
• Licence issuance fee.

Once an investment licence has been issued, the investor can then apply for residence and work permits, and other licences required in their area of operation to immediately commence operations.

c. Forms of Investment

Zimbabwe's three main entry points for foreign investment are; the Zimbabwe Investment Authority (ZIA), Zimbabwe Stock Exchange (ZSE) and in joint venture arrangements with Government corporations or entities.

The Zimbabwe Investment Authority (ZIA) is the country's investment promotion body set up to promote and facilitate both foreign direct investment and local investment. Foreign investors may enter into joint ventures with the Government in terms of the Joint Ventures Act.[①] The Act seeks to promote investment by providing guidelines for the implementation of Joint Venture Agreements through establishing rules governing public-private partnerships.

Foreign investors are able to invest in any sector in Zimbabwe, except in reserved sectors where approval is necessary[②] :
• Agriculture / Forestry;
• Transportation;
• Retail / Wholesale trade, including distribution;
• Barber shops, hairdressing and beauty salons;
• Commercial photography;
• Employment agencies;
• Estate agencies;
• Valet services;
• Grain mill products;
• In the minerals sector the only resources which require Indigenous involvement are those relating to diamonds and platinum.

The Zimbabwe Stock Exchange (ZSE) provides an alternative avenue for Foreign Portfolio Investment (FPI) injection into the local economy through the stock market. There are currently approximately 59 active counters listed on the ZSE from various sectors of the economy including mining, agriculture, tourism, services and manufacturing. The purchase of shares on the ZSE by foreigners must be financed by an inward transfer of foreign currency through normal banking channels. The purchase of shares must not exceed 40% of the total equity and a single investor's purchase must not exceed 10% of the shares on offer.

d. Standards of Market Access and Examination

The Standards Association of Zimbabwe (SAZ) is the National Standards Body for Zimbabwe. SAZ represents Zimbabwe in ISO, IEC Country Affiliate Programme, SADCSTAN and Comesa Standards Harmonization Committee and actively participates in these organizations' standardization programmes. Increasingly international and regional standards are adopted as national standards to ensure national standards do not conflict with those of regional and international trade partners. 24% of standards published in 2010 were ISO standards adoptions.[③]

SAZ, which is a member of the ISO, is also accredited by the South African National Accreditation System. Products manufactured or imported into Zimbabwe are subject to examination by the SAZ and imports are required to be pre-examined by Bureau Veritas on behalf of Government prior to entry into Zimbabwe. Customs and Trademark regulations also prohibit the importation of products that seek to infringe trademark and patent laws and impose penalties for the importation, sale or distribution of infringing products.[④]

---

① Chapter 22:22.
② Doing Business in Zimbabwe 2013 and 2014- Grant Thornton.
③ www.iso.org/member/308829.html.
④ www.iso.org/member/308829.html.

B. Foreign Exchange Regulation

a. Department Supervising Foreign Exchange

In terms of the Exchange Control Act[1] the President has the broad authority and power to regulate all matters relating to gold, currency, securities, exchange transactions, the import and export of assets from Zimbabwe, the transfer of settlement of property, payments and transactions relating to debts.

The Act was promulgated in 1965 and remains in force to date. When promulgated it was intended to control, restrict and manage the movement in and export of currency, gold and assets of value from Rhodesia.[2] The Act remained in force after 1980 when Zimbabwe attained independence and continued with significant amendments in 2009 when the local currency of Zimbabwe was demonetized as a result of hyperinflation and replaced by the currency of the United States of America, South Africa, Botswana, the United Kingdom and the European Union. A number of other international currencies were subsequently included as legal tender in Zimbabwe, including the Yuan and Indian Rupee. There are presently 11 international currencies that are recognized as legal tender in Zimbabwe, in addition to Bond currency, a local currency unit which was introduced on a limited scale from May 2016 and given legal effect as a currency in terms of the Reserve Bank of Zimbabwe Amendment Act[3] operative from 30 October 2016.

The Reserve Bank of Zimbabwe, established in terms of the Reserve Bank of Zimbabwe Act[4], is a body corporate and the central Exchange Control authority vested with the powers to regulate all matters relating to foreign exchange dealings, gold, platinum and diamond dealings in Zimbabwe. The Reserve Bank in turn has, by order[5], authorised 15 "authorised dealers" to implement the provisions of the legislation relating to exchange controls in Zimbabwe. Authorised dealers are in essence commercial banks and financial institutions that provide banking services to the public in Zimbabwe.

The Reserve Bank Exchange Control Division is charged with the responsibility for the proper accounting of the current account of the Balance of Payments position in Zimbabwe and implements the provisions of the Exchange Control Regulations[6], and Exchange Control (General Order)[7] and any Reserve Bank Directives issued in terms of the Exchange Control Regulations. The Reserve Bank is responsible to the Minister of Finance and seeks to carry out and regulate the policies of the Ministry and Government.

b. Brief Introduction to the Laws and Regulations of Foreign Currency in Zimbabwe

The Reserve Bank, through authorised dealers, implements the provisions of the Exchange Control Act, and the subsidiary regulations promulgated in terms thereof, the most significant being the Exchange Control Regulations and the Exchange Control (General) Order.

In terms of the Exchange Control Act, the President of Zimbabwe has the power to regulate all matters relating to dealings in gold, currency, securities, exchange transactions, imports and exports into and from Zimbabwe, payments and transactions relating to debts. The Act empowers the President to issue regulations to prohibit and regulate transactions in relation to the aforesaid property and to license persons to carry on the business of dealing in currency.

However, the Act also places the onus of proving that a person has not committed any offence in terms of the Act and imposes severe penalties for any person failing to comply with the provisions of the Act or regulations. The Act also makes provision for extra-territorial application. In terms of Section 5(3) introduced in 2009 the penalties imposed for contravening the Act or its regulations can include payment of fines equal to the value of the foreign currency or asset dealt in, a period of imprisonment not exceeding 10 years, or both such fine and imprisonment and a further financial penalty of up to three times the value of the asset dealt with and forfeiture of the asset or property dealt with (Section 7 of the Act).

Notwithstanding that Zimbabwe currently recognizes 11 international currencies as legal tender for all purposes in Zimbabwe, the Exchange Control Regulations of 1996 generally restrict and prohibit dealings in gold, foreign currency, securities and debts except with exchange control approval granted by the Reserve Bank. The effect of these Regulations is to restrict the payment of amounts, debts or obligations outside Zimbabwe from funds derived in Zimbabwe without prior exchange control approval. As the Regulations have not been repealed or

---

[1] Chapter 22:05.
[2] The name of the country before independence in 1980.
[3] Act No. 1 of 2017.
[4] Chapter 22:15.
[5] In terms of Exchange Control Regulations S.I. 109/1996.
[6] Statutory Instrument 109/1996.
[7] Statutory Instrument 110/1996.

amended, they remain in force.

The Exchange Control (General) Order of 1996 similarly has not been amended substantially since 1996 and seeks to regulate and restrict the amounts of foreign currency that may be remitted, with approval, from Zimbabwe for service payments, corporate remittances, holiday allowances, debit cards, fees and professional charges, medical expenses and education costs. The Order also restricts foreign ownership of shares or stocks in any Zimbabwean entity to 40 percent of the aggregate value of the shares or stocks and sets out the responsibilities of authorised dealers in processing approvals for payments in foreign currency. While the Order is outdated in many respects, it remains in force until repealed or amended.

With effect from October 2016, the Reserve Bank of Zimbabwe Amendment Act[1] gave legal recognition to the introduction of Bond currency in Zimbabwe as legal tender. The Bond currency was introduced as an export incentive from May 2016 to all exporters, who are entitled to an incentive of 5 percent on all foreign currency proceeds brought into Zimbabwe (the incentive is limited to 2.5 percent to exporters of primary minerals). The incentive is payable in Bond currency and credited to the exporter's bank account. The Bond currency was introduced in terms of the Exchange Control Directive RR86 issued by the Reserve Bank in May 2016 which directed that the Bond currency be regarded as fungible and trade at par value to the United States dollar.

In 2017, further regulations were promulgated to prevent the holding of cash amounts by individuals and entities and to penalise dealings in Bond currency against other currencies at a premium of more than 10 percent of the par value of Bond currency (Exchange Control (Amendment) Order.[2] These regulations remain in force until repealed or amended.

c. Requirements of Foreign Exchange Management for Foreign Enterprises

In terms of the aforesaid law relating to foreign exchange dealings in Zimbabwe, all foreign funds into Zimbabwe are required to be brought in via accounts opened with authorised dealers in Zimbabwe. If funds are being invested in an enterprise in Zimbabwe, the capital portion of such investment, if it comprises currency resources, must be brought in in terms of an Investment Licence to protect the interests of the foreign investor and enable the repatriation of profits accrued from the investment. If the enterprise is to borrow funds from an external source, the loan instrument must be registered with an authorised dealer for approval prior to the funds entering Zimbabwe. The limit for approvals by authorised dealers is US$ 20 million and any loans in excess of this amount require approval from the Reserve Bank. Loans may be secured against assets in Zimbabwe, including minerals with Reserve Bank approval. The approval is to enable the remittance of capital and interest payments on the loan to the Lender and to determine that the terms of the loan are not onerous or punitive on the borrower. In this regard, the Reserve Bank makes reference to guidelines on the rates on interest, tenor, and other charges that may be levied on foreign loans.

Due to the recent amendment of the laws regarding foreign investment, any foreign entity or person may now own 100 percent of the shareholding of any enterprise in Zimbabwe, excluding diamonds and platinum or in the reserves sectors of the economy. This approval is attained in terms of an Investment Licence issued to an applicant by the Zimbabwe Investment Authority.

Funds invested into an enterprise or brought in as loans into Zimbabwe do not qualify to receive the export incentive of Bond currency.

C. Financing

In Zimbabwe commercial banks are generally designated as authorised dealers by the Reserve Bank. "Authorised dealer" means;

a. The Reserve Bank of Zimbabwe

b. Any commercial bank or accepting house, or any class thereof, which the Reserve Bank, by order declares to be an authorised dealer for the purposes of the Exchange Control Regulations[3]

Authorised Dealers can process external loans and / or trade credits of up to USD 20 million without prior External Loans Coordinating Committee (ELCC) approval. The ELCC is a Committee responsible for vetting foreign loan applications. All applications for external loans in excess of the stipulated threshold must be submitted to the Reserve Bank for ELCC approval.

All external loans and / or trade credits must be processed in line with the existing ELCC guidelines. Authorised Dealers are required to submit a monthly return (EC Form Loans) to Exchange Control authority.

---

[1] No.1 of 2017.
[2] SI 122 A of 2017.
[3] Defined in Section 2 of the Exchange Control Regulations, 1996, S.I. 109 of 1996.

a) Lending by authorised dealers

(i) To Residents

Authorised Dealers can on-lend to individuals and corporates to meet current account and domestic funding requirements without seeking prior permission from Exchange Control. However, any lending to meet capital account obligations requires specific Exchange Control approval. Authorised Dealers are required to exercise due diligence and apply prudential lending practices in advancing loans to individuals and corporates.

(ii) Non-resident

Individuals may not borrow from Authorised Dealers without prior Exchange Control approval. Non-resident controlled companies may borrow locally to finance working capital on ratio of 1:1 with shareholders' funds, that is, the total amount they can borrow may not exceed their shareholders' funds.

(iii) Exchange Control regards shareholders' funds to include; issued share capital; share premium; capital / revenue reserves; shareholders' loans; and retained earnings. Such borrowing shall however, require prior Exchange Control authority.①

b) Banks

List of Registered Banking Institutions in Zimbabwe:

(i) Commercial Banks:
- Agribank;
- BancABC Limited;
- Barclays Bank of Zimbabwe Limited;
- CBZ Bank Limited;
- Ecobank Zimbabwe Limited;
- FBC Bank Limited;
- MBCA Bank Limited;
- Metbank Limited;
- NMB Bank Limited;
- Stanbic Bank Zimbabwe Limited;
- Standard Chartered Bank Zimbabwe Limited;
- Steward Bank Limited;
- ZB Bank.

(ii) Merchant Banks:
- Tetrad Investment Bank Limited.

(iii) Building Societies:
- CABS;
- FBC Building Society;
- National Building Society;
- ZB Building Society;

(iv) Savings Bank:
- People's Own Savings Bank;

(v) Development Institutions:
- Infrastructure Development Bank of Zimbabwe (IBDZ).

c) Small and Medium Enterprises Development Corporation (SMEDCO)

An application for a banking licence is made in terms of the Banking Act② and should comply with the Banking Regulations③, Guideline No. 01-2004 / BSD: Corporate Governance, and Prudential Standards No. 07-2014 / BSD: Fitness & Probity Assessment Criteria.

Micro-financing institutions have also been established in Zimbabwe and the main objective of these is money lending. Applications are made in terms of the Microfinance Act④ and through the Reserve Bank of Zimbabwe. There are currently 189 micro-financing institutions in Zimbabwe.

D. Land Policy

In Zimbabwe all property, including land is protected in terms of Section 71 of the Constitution.

Land in urban areas that is privately owned is held under title deeds which are registered in the Deeds

---

① Extracted from Section 5 Exchange Control Guidelines issued by the Reserve Bank of Zimbabwe.
② Chapter 24:20.
③ Statutory Instrument 205 of 2000.
④ Chapter 24:29.

Registry and confer real rights in the land to the owner thereof. The rights of registration are recognised and given legal effect in the Deeds Registries Act①. Rural agricultural land is primarily held by the State and ancestral lands are overseen by traditional chiefs. In terms of Section 72 of the Constitution, the State has the overriding right in respect of agricultural land (which excludes urban land, communal land or township land) to compulsorily acquire the land and any permanent improvement or crops thereon for agricultural purposes, land reorganisation or settlement purposes without compensation. The right of the State to compulsorily acquire land is confirmed in terms of Section 5 of the Land Acquisition Act② which permits the acquiring authority to declare land as being acquired on publication of a notice to the land holder. The only compensation claimable from the State relates to improvements made on the land, prior to acquisition. In terms of Section 72 of the Constitution, once agricultural land is compulsorily acquired, the title deeds to that land are deemed cancelled and title vests in the State. The possession or occupation of State land without lawful authority constitutes an offence in terms of the law. State land may only be occupied in terms of a permit or lease granted by the State.

Private land may be sold, encumbered, leased or disposed of without prior approval from the State. Communal land may not be sold or disposed of and the right of occupation thereto reposes in the family descendants of the occupant.

Presently, foreign enterprises may acquire urban land, provided funds are brought into Zimbabwe via formal banking channels. Foreign entitites may not acquire agricultural land, communal land or State land.

E. Establishment and Dissolution of Companies

a) Company Law

• Company law in Zimbabwe is largely governed by the Companies Act③ which has been amended from time to time.④

• Common law in Zimbabwe plays a very vital role in Zimbabwe's company laws and is mainly based on Roman Dutch law.

• The Companies Act in Zimbabwe is mainly premised on English law.

• Zimbabwean Company Law is codified and governed by the Companies Act and the regulations. It is also governed by the various judicial decisions from Zimbabwe, England and South Africa

b) Types of Companies / Associations in Zimbabwe

• private company;
• public company;
• company limited by guarantee;
• private business corporations;
• sole proprietors;
• partnerships;
• Co-operative companies.

c) Private Companies⑤

A private company, denoted by the words (Private) Limited [abbreviated "(Pvt) Ltd"], may not offer shares to the public and is not generally required to file annual financial reports with the Registrar of Companies. Membership of a private company is restricted to a maximum of 50 shareholders, plus employee-shareholders.

There are no statutory limitations on the size of the share capital of private companies, the limitation is, however, on the size of membership.

Private Company has the right to commence business as soon as it is registered whereas a public company cannot do so unless all provisions of the Act in respect of starting a company has been complied with and Registrar has certified that the company is entitled to start business.

Private companies have the right to appoint directors of its own choice, even those who do not hold any shares in the company.

d) Public Companies⑥

• A Public company has "Limited" (abbreviated "Ltd") as the last word in its name.

---

① chapter 20:05.
② chapter 20:10.
③ Chapter 24:03.
④ A Companies and other business entities Bill, 2018 has been drafted and is yet to be passed. If it is approved and passed it will replace the current Companies Act (Chapter 24:03) and the Private Business Corporations Act (Chapter 24:11).
⑤ Section 33 of the Companies Act.
⑥ Companies Act (Chapter 24:03).

- A public company must file its annual financial report with the Registrar of Companies, where it is open to public scrutiny.
- Public companies are required to be audited.
- Public companies may seek a listing on the Zimbabwe Stock Exchange and offer shares to the public. Such an offer must be accompanied by a prospectus which must, prior to making the offer, be lodged with and registered by the Registrar of Companies.
- There is no limit on the size of membership of a public company.
- Because the public company is entitled to offer shares to the public, the rights of investors are sought to be protected in terms of the Act.

e) Company Limited by Guarantee

- This is a company created for a charitable purpose which exist for purposes which are in the interest of the public.
- It is not intended to generate profit for its members and prohibits payment of dividend to its members.
- In terms section 26 if the Minister is satisfied that the association complied with the provision of that section, he may license the registration of the association as a company without using the word (limited) at the end of its name.
- Registrar of companies shall register the company accordingly.
- Liability of the members of such a company is limited to the amounts they guaranteed to contribute on winding up of the company.
- A company limited by guarantee enjoys all privileges of a company and is subject to the obligations thereof.

f) Private Business Corporations

- These are simplified versions of private companies and are registered in the same office. However, by their nature they have simplified rules for the conduct of their affairs.

g) Sole Proprietorships

- Sole proprietorship refers to a business organisation for which an individual has sole and unlimited liability.
- Any income derived from the business is regard as the owner's income for tax purposes, since the business is not regarded as a legal entity.

h) Partnerships[1]

- As with sole proprietorship, there is little legislative control on partnerships.
- The nature of the business may mean that a partnership will fall under specific regulatory statutes as, for example, in the case of consulting engineers and public accountants.
- Profit-making partnerships are generally restricted to a maximum of 20 partners, except for designated professional associations such as doctors, chartered accountants, lawyers and engineers.
- Normally, partners are jointly and severally liable for all debts of a partnership, provided they were incurred in the name of and with the authority of the partnership.
- Presently no legislation exists for the establishment of Limited Liability Partnerships in Zimbabwe.
- Joint ventures with the State and parastatals may be pursued in terms of the Joint Venture Act[2] in circumstances where the investor is able to provide funding, technical and technological expertise and the ability to manage large scale operations.

i) Co-operatives[3]

- This form of business entity is most appropriate for the small scale farming, mining and fishing sectors. Such entities are formed in terms of the Co-operative Societies Act (Chapter 24:05).
- The entities' main objective is to provide a service facilitating the production or market of agricultural produce or livestock or the sale of goods to its members.
- It restricts the transfer of its shares and has only one class of ordinary shares.

j) Company Formation

Companies and other commercial enterprises are regulated by the Companies Act.[4] A company is established by registration in the Registrar of Companies, a division of the Ministry of Justice. The name of the entity is required to be approved and a minimum of one shareholder must subscribe to the memorandum of association for the registration to be effected. The articles and memorandum of association are required to be filed in original form setting out the objects of the company and the rights of members and providing for the appointment of at least two

---

[1] Section 6 of the Companies Act.
[2] Chapter 22:22.
[3] Sections 36 to 45 of the Companies Act.
[4] Chapter 24:03.

directors at incorporation. Upon acceptance, the Registrar of companies issues a certificate of registration as proof of incorporation.

Shares are held by members in the form of share certificates issued by the company and shares may be transferred in terms of the Articles of Association.

k) Dissolution

Companies may be wound up either by members themselves (voluntary winding up-Section 242) or by creditors whose debts the company has failed to discharge (compulsory winding up-Section 206)

The winding up process requires an application made to the High Court to explain the circumstances for the winding up and the appointment of a provisional liquidator approved by the Master of the High Court to oversee the winding up process to finality.

The provisional liquidator is required to assess claims against the company, approve legitimate claims and determine a method by which creditors claims may be settled either wholly or in part.

F. Merger and Acquisition and Competition Regulations in Zimbabwe

Zimbabwe's competition law enshrined in the Competition Act[1], came into force in 1998.

Competition law in Zimbabwe is regulated by the Competition and Tariff Commission (CTC) through the Competition Act. The purpose of the Act is to promote and maintain fair competition in the economy of Zimbabwe, provide for prevention and control of restrictive practices, regulate mergers and prevent and control monopoly situations and prohibit unfair trade practices.

The competition law covers anti-competitive agreements (both horizontal and vertical agreements); abuse of dominant position; and anti-competitive mergers and acquisitions.

The Act provides for the consideration of most restrictive practices and all mergers using the 'rule of reason' approach. Some restrictive practices, termed 'unfair business practices' in the Act, are per se prohibited.

The Competition Act applies to all economic activities within or having an effect within Zimbabwe. Intellectual property rights generally excluded from the application of the Act include those acquired under the Plant Breeders Rights Act[2] the Copyright & Neighbouring Rights Act[3] the Industrial Designs Act[4]; the Patents Act[5]; and the Trade Marks Act.[6]

The Act also binds the State to the extent that the State is involved in the manufacture and distribution of commodities. The merger control provisions of the Act override any powers given to any sector regulator in considering and approving mergers and acquisitions. Accordingly, the Commission grants the final authorisation of any qualifying merger.[7]

The threshold rule in the Act effectively exempts small and medium-sized enterprises from its application. The Act only prohibits those restrictive practices that restrict competition to a material degree. It is also only those mergers and acquisitions that fall within the prescribed threshold that have to be notified to the Commission for examination, and those that substantially prevent or lessen competition that can be disallowed. The Competition Commission of Zimbabwe is an autonomous body that does not refer any of its competition decisions to any other authority in Zimbabwe.[8]

For enforcement purposes, orders made by the Commission against any anti-competitive practices can be lodged with the High Court of Zimbabwe for registration as an order of the High Court to enable it to have the effect of a civil judgment of the High Court. Appeals against any decision of the Commission are made to the

---

[1] Chapter 14:28.
[2] Chapter 18:16.
[3] Chapter 26:05.
[4] Chapter 26:02.
[5] Chapter 26:03.
[6] Chapter 26:04.
[7] Overview of Competition Policy and Law in Zimbabwe- Presentation by Mr Alexander J Kububa, Director and Chief Executive Officer of the Competition and Tariff Commission of Zimbabwe at the Third Annual Competition Commission, Competition Tribunal And Mandela Institute Conference On Competition Law, Economics And Policy In South Africa-Pretoria, South Africa: 3–4 September 2009.
[8] Overview of Competition Policy and Law in Zimbabwe- Presentation by Mr Alexander J Kububa, Director and Chief Executive Officer of the Competition and Tariff Commission of Zimbabwe at the Third Annual Competition Commission, Competition Tribunal And Mandela Institute Conference On Competition Law, Economics And Policy In South Africa-Pretoria, South Africa: 3–4 September 2009.

Administrative Court.[1]

In the region, Zimbabwe is a member of both the Southern African Development Community (SADC) and the Common Market for Eastern and Southern Africa (COMESA). Under COMESA, the competition authority of Zimbabwe actively participated in the formulation and adoption of a regional competition policy and law, and is represented on the Regional Competition Commission. The regional competition policy and law benefit Zimbabwe, and other COMESA member States, in that they can deal with restrictive business practices of a cross-border nature.[2]

The Zimbabwean competition authority is also a founding member of the Southern and Eastern African Competition Forum (SEACF), which also aims at fostering and increasing cooperation among the region's competition authorities.[3]

G. Tax

a. Tax Regime and Rules

Income tax is levied on all income derived in the course of trade from a source in Zimbabwe or deemed to be from a source in Zimbabwe. Income from trading operations, gainful employment and investment is subject to taxation at various rates of tax. The main legislative provisions regarding taxation in Zimbabwe are encompassed in the Income Tax Act (as amended by the Finance Act), the Capital Gains Tax Act, the Customs and Excise Act and Value Added Tax Act. The administration of taxes is reposed in the Zimbabwe Revenue Authority, an independent entity, answerable to the Minister of Finance.

There are a number of additional levies, royalties and statutory charges that are levied by local authorities and statutory authorities, but these are usually use-based and localised, rather than of general application. Royalties are charged on minerals extracted and vary from between 1 percent to 10 percent depending on the mineral extracted.

In respect of income tax, the law provides for the taxation of income and investment proceeds in the course of trade from a source considered to be in Zimbabwe. Income tax is levied on income of individuals, corporations, trusts and partnerships. The principle for levying income tax in respect of artificial entities is to have regard to the gross income accrued during the period of assessment (January to December of each year), excluding capital receipts, from a source in Zimbabwe (sections 8 to 12 of the Income Tax Act) and after allowing for deductions incurred in the production of income (section 15 of the Income Tax Act) and allowances to determine the net income that is subject to taxation. Income tax returns for corporations are required to be filed by the 30th April of the year following the end of the financial year. Tax losses incurred in one year may be carried forward for a period of 6 years.

However, a system of Quarterly Payment Dates (QPD) requires that corporates assess their potential profit during the year of assessment and remit portions of the likely tax to the Zimbabwe Revenue Authority on the 25th March (10 percent of the potential tax), 25th June (25 percent of the potential tax), 25th September (30 percent of the potential tax) and 20th December (35 percent of the potential tax).

Capital Gains Tax is levied in terms of the Capital Gains Tax Act on the disposal of "specified assets", namely, land and buildings thereon, the sale of marketable securities, the cession of rights in land and mining claims and the transfer of rights in trademarks, patents, industrial designs and other intellectual property. The tax is assessed on the basis that any disposal of a specified asset attracts the tax charge, unless the tax is deferred or exempt in limited circumstances approved by the Zimbabwe Revenue Authority.

Value Added Tax is an indirect tax imposed on consumption and is charged on the sale of taxable goods and services. The tax is levied by registered operators whose annual trade turnover exceeds US$ 60 000.00 and is

---

[1] Overview of Competition Policy and Law In Zimbabwe- Presentation by Mr Alexander J Kububa, Director and Chief Executive Officer of the Competition and Tariff Commission of Zimbabwe at the third annual Competition Commission, Competition Tribunal And Mandela Institute Conference On Competition Law, Economics And Policy In South Africa-Pretoria, South Africa: 3–4 September 2009.

[2] Overview Of Competition Policy And Law In Zimbabwe- Presentation by Mr Alexander J Kububa, Director and Chief Executive Officer of the Competition and Tariff Commission of Zimbabwe at the Third Annual Competition Commission, Competition Tribunal And Mandela Institute Conference On Competition Law, Economics And Policy In South Africa-Pretoria, South Africa: 3–4 September 2009

[3] Overview Of Competition Policy And Law In Zimbabwe- Presentation by Mr Alexander J Kububa, Director and Chief Executive Officer of the Competition and Tariff Commission of Zimbabwe at the Third Annual Competition Commission, Competition Tribunal And Mandela Institute Conference On Competition Law, Economics And Policy In South Africa-Pretoria, South Africa: 3–4 September 2009.

calculated by assessing the total monthly sales and the tax charged during that period by the operator (Output tax) and deducting the operator's total purchases for the same month and the tax paid thereon by the operator (input tax). The difference constitutes the Value Added Tax payable by the operator or the refund due to it from the Zimbabwe Revenue Authority. Monthly returns are required to be filed by the operator by the 25th day of the month following.

Value Added Tax is not levied on goods exported from Zimbabwe, or on specified basic commodities which are exempt or zero-rated.

Customs duties and Value Added Tax are levied on imports brought into Zimbabwe and charged in terms of the Customs & Excise Act Ch. The importation of capital equipment for the purpose of investment is exempt from customs duty. The Act is administered by the Zimbabwe Revenue Authority and the tariff are charged on particulars classes of imported products based on the type, description and origin of the products. Excise duties are levied on certain categories of products produced in Zimbabwe, such as alcoholic beverages, and are based on rates determined by the Minister of Finance and published in the Finance Act.

b. Main Categories of Tax and Rates of Tax

Income tax for employees is levied on a Pay-as-You-Earn (PAYE) levied on periodic earnings. The rates of tax are vary on the earnings of employees and increase up to 40 percent for the highest earning employees.

Corporates, trusts, partnerships and business organisations are subject to tax at the following rates:

Income from trade or investment	25 percent of profits, plus 3 percent of tax paid (Aids Levy)
Income from company, partnership or trust	25 percent of profits, plus 3 percent of tax paid (Aids Levy)
Income of a Licenced Investor (first 5 years)	0 percent on profits
Income of LIcenced Investor (after 5th year)	25 percent of profits
Holder of Special Mining Lease	15 percent of profits
Company engaged in mining operations	25 percent of profits
BOT / BOOT approved project (first 5 years)	0 percent
BOT / BBOT approved project (second 5 years)	15 percent of profits
Industrial Park Developer (first 5 years)	0 percent
Industrial Park Developer (after 5th year)	25 percent of profits
Tourism operator in Approved Zone (first 5 years)	0 percent
Tourism operator in Approved Zone (after 5th year)	25 percent of profits
Manufacturer who exports 30-41% of output	20 percent of profits
Manufacturer who exports between 41% -51%	17.5 percent of profits
Manufacturer who exports more than 51%	15 percent of profits

Operators in Special Economic Zones are not subject to income tax for the first 5 years of operations, and thereafter are subject to 15 percent tax on profits in terms of Section 3 of the Finance Act of 2017 par 12/13.

Dividends are subject to tax at the rate of 15 percent in respect of companies not listed on the Stock Exchange, and at a rate of 10 percent for dividends from companies listed on the Stock Exchange.

Interest earned from banking institutions attracts withholding tax of 15 percent, while interest earned from other activities is subject to tax at the rate of 25 percent.

Capital Gains Tax levied on the disposal of specified assets is subject to tax at the following rates:

In respect of specified assets acquired before 1 March 2009 and disposed of after 1 March 2009, Capital Gains Tax is levied at 5 percent of the value at which the specified asset is disposed of.

In respect of specified assets acquired and disposed of after 1 March 2009, the tax rate is 20 percent of the capital gain (being the difference between the price at which the asset was acquired and disposed of).

Value Added Tax on the sale of goods or services by a registered operator is levied at the rate of 15 percent.

Customs duties are levied according to tariffs published in subsidiary legislation and are amended periodically by the Minister of Finance by statutory instruments.

Zimbabwe has entered into a Double Taxation Agreement under proclamation 8 of 2016 for the avoidance of Double Tax and prevention of fiscal evasion, the effect of which is generally to permit the State in which the various heads of income are earned to generally tax such income and profits, subject to maximum agreed percentages. [1]

---

[1] Attached in Proclamation 8 of 2016 in relation to the Double Taxation Agreement between China and Zimbabwe.

H. Securities

a. Introduction to Securities- related Laws and Regulations

The law relating to securities in Zimbabwe is regulated primarily by the Securities & Exchange Act[1] in terms of which the Securities & Exchange Commission of Zimbabwe (SECZ) is established to regulate the trade in securities, protect investor rights, encourage development of capital markets and license persons to conduct business in securities. In terms of Section 118 of the Securities Act, the Commission is empowered to make rules to give effect to its statutory objectives. The Act also provides for the registration of securities exchanges, the licensing of brokers and the management and regulation of exchanges. The SECZ also maintains an Investor Protection Fund to provide monetary relief in the event that a registered investment entity is declared insolvent. However, the fund cannot pay out compensation in excess of 10 percent of the value of the fund.

The Asset Management Act[2] regulates the conduct of entities and persons involved in the business of asset management, which is to invest the property of clients in money markets, recognized stock exchanges and other investments to secure profits for clients. Asset managers are required to be registered with the Chief Executive Officer of the SECZ (Section 5). The Act also provides that asset managers may be compelled to invest in specified prescribed assets, provided that such investments does not exceed 40 percent of the fund's portfolio (Section 12).

Zimbabwe Stock Exchange–Currently the only registered stock exchange for the trading of listed securities. The number of counters listed on this exchange is relatively small and market capitalization is correspondingly small. The stock exchange publishes its own listing requirements and its operations are subject to oversight by SECZ.

The Financial Securities Exchange (Private) Limited is an entity registered as an alternative trading platform in terms of the Securities (Alternative Trading Platform) Rules S.I. 100/2016.

Collective Investment Schemes Act[3], which covers the establishment of investment schemes that enable participants to pool resources as a whole and share or receive income or profits from the acquisition, holding, management and disposal of property in circumstances where they are not involved in the day-to-day control of operations (Section 3). Registration of such schemes, classified as internal schemes, external schemes and professional schemes, are required to be made to the SECZ (Section 5).

b. Requirement for Securities Trading for Foreign Companies

Foreign companies that wish to engage in securities trading will be required to incorporate locally and seek registration with the SECZ.

The holding of shares or stocks by foreign companies of any listed securities is presently restricted to 40 percent of the securities in issue and the maximum amount of securities that a single foreign investor may hold in a listed entity is 10 percent of the securities in issue.

Foreign investors may subscribe for up to 100 percent of any primary issue of bonds funded by the inward transfer of foreign currency. Foreign investors may also acquire and sell bonds on the secondary market and remittance of funds arising from disinvestment may be made without prior Reserve Bank approval.

I. Preference and Protection of Investment

Reference to preference and protection of investments has already been made in the content of the report above.

III. Trade

A. Department Supervising Trade

Trade relates to the importation and exportation of goods and services between two countries in exchange of some consideration of value. Trade in Zimbabwe is supervised by the Ministry of Foreign Affairs & International Trade and the Ministry of Industry & Commerce.

Some of the practical functions relating to trade are administered by statutory bodies including:

---

[1] Chapter 24:25.
[2] Chapter 24:26.
[3] Chapter 24:19.

a) The Zimbabwe Revenue Authority which collects revenue on behalf of the Government. Specifically it collects the following:

(i) Customs Duty and Excise Duty: these are taxes levied on imported goods and locally manufactured goods respectively, in terms of the Customs and Excise Act (Chapter 23:02) and its regulations;

(ii) Surtax–levied on imported vehicles older than five years

(iii) Value Added Tax (VAT), which is levied on consumption of goods and services in terms of the Value Added Tax Act [Chapter 23:12] and its regulations;

(iv) Income Tax, levied on income earned from trade;

(v) Mining Royalties–charged in terms of the Mines and Minerals Act (Chapter 21:05).

b) The Competition and Tariff Commission, established in terms of the Competition Act (Chapter 14:28). The Commission carries out the following duties:

(i) Raising of tariff charges on imported commodities or services that compete with commodities or services provided by local industry;

(ii) Lowering of tariff charges on imported commodities or services that are used by local industry;

(iii) Implementation of legislative or administrative measures for the purpose of countering unfair trade practices; and

(iv) Technical assistance to Government in the conclusion of arrangements with other countries for the benefit of local industry.

The Commission also manages and implements the Anti-Dumping policy which levies duty on certain goods imported into Zimbabwe.

c) Zimbabwe is also a state party to a number of trade agreements in which it has made commitments in relation to its rules and regulations of trade. Such membership, coupled with its own domestic laws, influences and governs the conduct of trade with other countries. The main trade agreements that Zimbabwe is a party to are:

(i) The Agreement Establishing the Common Market for Eastern and Southern Africa (COMESA Treaty); and

(ii) The Treaty of the Southern African Development Community.

Zimbabwe has also concluded Bilateral Investment Protection Agreements (BIPAs) with a number of countries including Malaysia (Statutory Instrument 139 of 1994), Argentina (Statutory Instrument 45 of 2001) and Germany (Statutory Instrument 926 of 1981).

B. Brief Introduction of Trade Laws and Regulations

The regulation of trade in Zimbabwe can be broken into four parts namely:
a) The Constitution;
b) Domestic laws enacted by parliament;
c) Statutory instruments; and
d) International agreements.

Although a number of domestic laws have in their provisions a semblance of international trade, the enactments most relevant to anyone engaged in the importation and exportation of goods in Zimbabwe are as follows:

a. The Constitution

Section 64 of the Constitution of Zimbabwe Amendment (No. 20), 2013 ("the Constitution") entrenches the right to choose and carry on any trade subject to regulation by law. Section 71 provides for the right to acquire, hold, occupy, use, transfer, hypothecate, lease or dispose of all forms of property, either individually or in association with others. In addition, Section 34 of the Constitution provides that:

"The State must ensure that all international conventions, treaties and agreements to which Zimbabwe is a party are incorporated into domestic law".

The above provision would apply to international trade treaties and agreements.

b. Relevant Statutes

a) Customs & Excise Act (Chapter 23:02)

The Act provides for the manner that goods are lawfully imported and exported into Zimbabwe. It also directs how goods are classified and how anti-dumping and countervailing duties are imposed. The Act also provides how value for the purposes of duty is calculated.

b) Competition Act (Chapter 14:28)

This Act deals with the regulation of competition in commerce and specifically with regards to trade provides for the maintenance of certain tariffs on goods. The Act also imposes penalties in the form of countervailing and anti-dumping duties.

c) Control of Goods Act (Chapter 14:05)

The Act establishes the control of the importation and exportation of certain goods in Zimbabwe. It also provides for restrictions on exportation for the purposes of rationing.

c. Regulations

a) Customs and Excise (General) Regulations, Statutory Instrument 154 of 2001

These regulations govern the importation and exportation of goods into and out of Zimbabwe. In particular, they provide the procedures for:

(i) the entry of goods into Zimbabwe on importation;
(ii) the special conditions for the importation of goods by way of specific modes of transport;
(iii) clearance procedure for different types of goods;
(iv) instances where certain goods attract rebate or refund of duty upon importation;
(v) clearance of goods for export.

b) Customs and Excise (Ports of Entry and Routes) Order, Statutory Instrument 14 of 2002

These regulations provide the ports of entry in Zimbabwe and the hours that those ports of entry are open.

c) Customs and Excise (Tariff) Notice, Statutory Instrument 112 of 2012

This notice lists the duty payable for each imported product. It also provides a comprehensive description of such products. It specifies the duty payable for each product calculated on the basis of quantity and origin. The rate of duty and surtax payable is dependent on whether the product is imported from a COMESA country, a SADC country or any other Trade Agreement.

d) Control of Goods (Export of Minerals and Metals) Regulations, 1979 (RGN 247/1979); Control of Goods (Import and Export) (Commerce) Regulations, 1974 (RGN 766/1974); and Control of Goods (Import and Export) (Agriculture) Regulations, Statutory Instrument 137 of 2007

These regulations govern the importation and exportation of minerals, certain commercial goods and agricultural goods to and from Zimbabwe to holders of licenses issued in terms of the regulations.

e) Competition (Anti-Dumping and Countervailing Duty) (Investigation) Regulations, 2002 (Statutory Instrument 266 of 2002)

These regulations provide for the manner that the Minister may impose countervailing duties on goods imported into Zimbabwe. The regulations also provide a guideline on those goods that are deemed to have received a subsidy from the export country warranting the imposition of a countervailing duty. The regulations also empower the Minister to impose anti- dumping duty on certain goods and define those goods deemed to have been dumped.

d. International Agreements

a) Customs and Excise (Common Market For Eastern and Southern Africa) (Suspension) Regulations, Statutory Instrument 244 of 2000

These regulations provide for the suspension of duty on goods produced or manufactured in the territory of the Member States which comply with the rules of origin set out in Annex IV of the COMESA Treaty, as read with Article 48 of the COMESA Treaty.

b) Customs & Excise (Southern Africa Development Community) (Suspension) Regulations, Statutory Instrument 345 of 2002

These regulations provide for the suspension of duty on goods produced or manufactured in territory of member states of SADC.

c) SADC (Differentiated Offer) Regulations, Statutory Instrument 188 of 2007

These regulations suspend the duties on goods appearing in Part II of the customs tariff, and which are classified under the heading or subheading shown in Schedule II of these regulations to the extent sufficient to reduce such duties to the effective rates shown in the regulations.

d) Customs and Excise (European Community (EC) and Eastern and Southern Africa (ESA) States Economic Partnership Agreement) (Suspension) (Market Access Offer) Regulations, Statutory Instrument 117 of 2016

These regulations suspend duty on goods imported from the European Community under the Economic Partnership Agreement (EPA). Such goods must be grown, produced or manufactured in the territory of the European Community and in compliance with the Rules of Origin set out in Protocol 1 to the EPA.

C. Trade Management

a. Import

In terms of the Control of Goods (Import and Export) (Commerce) Regulations, 1974, any person importing goods into Zimbabwe is required to do so either by way of an Open General Import License or a license specifically awarded for the export of those specific goods.

Most goods are classified under the Open General Import License (OGIL) and do not require a specific license to import. Those goods that require a specific license for importation are classified under notices issued by government from time to time, the latest being the Control of Goods (Open General Import License) (No. 2) Amendment Notice, 2016 (No. 8) and the Control of Goods (Open General Import Licence) (Amendment) Notice, 2017 (No.5).

When clearing imports, the following documentation is required:
a) Bill of Entry (Form 21);
b) Suppliers invoices;
c) Export or Transit Bill of Entry from the country of export;
d) Bill of Lading;
e) Value Declaration Forms;
f) Rail Advice Note;
g) Port Charges Invoices;
h) Agent / Importer's Worksheet;
i) Original Permits, Licences, Duty Free Certificates, Rebate Letters, Value Rulings (where applicable).

An application for an import license is made to the Secretary of the Ministry responsible for trade and must contain the following:
a) Company profile of the importer indicating its line of business;
b) Description of the product for importation;
c) Tariff code;
d) The quantities to be imported;
e) The purchase price of each unit of the product including its selling price;
f) Total value of the imported consignment;
g) Country of origin for the goods;
h) Reasons for importing vis a vis sourcing the goods from a local supplier;
i) The importer's Certificate of Incorporation, CR14 reflecting company directors, tax clearance certificate and copy of Standard Development Fund Levy receipt; and
j) Proforma invoice.

Licenses for the importation of certain goods are obtainable from the relevant line ministry or department. As an example, any hazardous material can only be imported upon a license being issued by the Environmental Management Agency (EMA). Likewise, the importation of medicines requires a license from the Medicines Control Authority of Zimbabwe (MCAZ). This information is usually availed by ZIMRA during clearance procedures.

b. Export

Any person intending to export goods from Zimbabwe is required to do so either through an Open General Export License or a license, depending on the classification of the goods for export.

If requested by a customs officer to produce invoices and other documents related to the goods for exportation, every exporter shall hand over such documents and shall permit the customs officer to inspect the goods if so requested.

According to the Customs & Excise Act, if the exportation of any goods is restricted or controlled by any enactment, such goods shall only be exported in conformity with the provisions of such enactment.

Documents required for the clearing of goods for export are:
a) A duly completed CD1 Form;
b) Bill of Entry Form 21;
c) Instruction for Despatch of Goods Form;
d) Commercial Invoice and Packing list;
e) Export Licence for foreign goods and transit permits where necessary.

Payment to the customs officer of a clearance fee is also required. If the goods are to be exported to any member country of COMESA or SADC then Form No. 30 is to be filled in. The goods must be exported within ten days of an assessment being made by the customs officer.

Restrictions on exports include live animals (without a valid Rabies Vaccination Certificate and Veterinary Certificate) and plants and plant material without a Health Certificate from the Ministry of Agriculture.

D. The Inspection and Quarantine of Import and Export Commodities

In terms of the Customs & Excise Act, if required to avail goods for inspection, an importer must at his own expense and risk unload and reload such goods, remove them to or from any place indicated by the officer. All charges for such inspection are borne by the importer.

There are inspectors stationed at every port of entry that have the powers to:

a) examine and make extracts from and copies of records relating to any goods imported or exported in terms of any license;

b) demand from any importer or exporter an explanation of any entries in any records concerning the goods in question;

c) seize and remove any records which, in his opinion, may afford evidence of a contravention of these regulations; or

d) seize and remove, without payment, any sample or specimen of any goods after inspection.

Whenever any goods are seized by an inspector, a receipt shall be issued. Seized goods are kept in a Government warehouse until conditions that led to the seizure of the goods have been remedied.

According to the Customs & Excise Act, a ZIMRA officer shall be permitted to enter any ship, train or vehicle arriving in or about to depart from Zimbabwe for the purposes of ascertaining whether or not goods in such ship, train or vehicle are being transported lawfully.

E. Customs Management

Upon arrival at any port of entry, it is a requirement that every person avail themselves to the customs office for declaration of any goods they may have in their possession. The purpose is to ascertain whether or not the goods attract any duty and whether there is any prohibition on their import or export.

a. Import

Duty is calculated on the basis of Cost, Insurance and Freight (CIF) value of the imported goods up to the point of entry into Zimbabwe. Insurance and Freight inside Zimbabwe is excluded from the Value for Duty Purposes (VDP). The CIF value of the imported goods is an aggregate of the cost of goods, insurance, freight and any other charges incurred outside Zimbabwe.

For the purposes of clearing the goods, a Bill of Entry form is required. This can be submitted electronically under ZIMRA's Automated System for Customs Data (ASYCUDA) system, a web based system for clearance of goods. ZIMRA requires that all supporting documents be submitted online as attachments.

When importing goods, the tax clearance certificate of the importer is required and in the absence of the same, 10% duty is levied on top of any other payable duty. Duty is paid by way of direct deposits into ZIMRA's bank account, which deposit is credited to the importer's account.

Once all documents have been submitted and processed, an approval for the importation is given in the form of a Delivery Release Order. This allows the importer to collect his or her goods from the carrier or place of detention. If there is need to inspect the goods, an Examination Order is issued and an inspection carried out to verify the quantities, classification, origin, values or any aspect that needs clarification. After assessment, two sets of documents in hard copy must be submitted for final release of the goods.

b. Export

In terms of Section 54(5) of the Customs & Excise Act, every exporter is required to produce for inspection all invoices and other documents relating to any goods entered for export in terms of this section and shall cause the goods for export to be examined by a customs officer before exportation.

Before export, a bill of entry is also required to be furnished to a Customs Officer. There is no duty payable whenever goods are exported from Zimbabwe, however clearance fees will be due and payable.

A Bill of Entry (Form 21) is lodged through the ASYCUDA World System in the same manner as for imports. In addition, the following documents must be submitted:

a) Exchange Control CD1 forms which are obtained from commercial banks;

b) Suppliers' invoices;

c) Consignment notes; and

d) If applicable, copies of Export Permits/Licences.

IV. Labour

A. Brief Introduction of Labour Laws and Regulations

Labour law concerns the relationship between master and servant. It is the law governing the voluntary relationships arising from the workplace. Labour law in Zimbabwe is mainly founded in legislation, more specifically, in the Constitution of Zimbabwe Amendment (No. 20), 2013, Acts of Parliament and delegated legislation. Common law is a secondary source of labour law in Zimbabwe, and is applicable where there is no specific provision in legislation.

The Constitution is the supreme law in Zimbabwe and any law in contravention with its provisions is considered to be a nullity. Chapter 4 of the Constitution, being the Declaration of Rights, provides for various rights relating to labour law such as freedom from slavery and servitude (Section 54); freedom from forced or compulsory labour (Section 55); the right to equality and non-discrimination (Section 56); freedom of profession, trade or occupation (Section 64) and the right to a fair hearing (Section 69). Above all else, Section 65 exclusively provides for labour rights in regard to the right to fair and safe labour practices, standards and to be paid a fair and reasonable wage; right to form and join a trade union; right to participate in collective job action including the right to strike; right to engage in collective bargaining and women's right to a paid maternity leave for a period of at least three months. Section 172 of the Constitution establishes the Labour Court, which has exclusive jurisdiction over labour law matters.

The Labour Act [Chapter 28:01]is the principal Act governing labour. In terms of Section 2A(1) of theAct, the purpose of the Act is to advance social justice and democracy in the workplaceby, among other things, securing the just, effective and expeditious resolution of disputes and unfair labour practices. Section 2A(2) requires that the Act be construed in such manner as best ensures the attainment of the purpose referred to under Section 2A(1), while Section 2A(3) stipulates that the Act shall prevail over any other enactment inconsistent with it. The Act provides a more detailed regulation of the employment relationship and it is applicable to all workers and employers other than those expressly excluded by the Constitution(such as the Public Service and disciplined forces). The long title of the Labour Actalso requires the Act to give effect to Zimbabwe's obligations under International Law, and in particular to the International Labour Organization Conventions ("the ILO Conventions"), which conventions Zimbabwe has ratified.

The Labour Act also provides for the enactment of subsidiary legislation such as statutory collective bargaining agreements. These are agreements arising from collective bargaining undertaken in terms of Section 74 of the Labour Act. Collective bargaining agreements are binding on all employers and employees in the industry for which they are registered. They provide for a more detailed regulation and provide minimum standardswith regard to employment issues such as wage rates and working hours. Section 101 of the Labour Act further provides for the promulgation of Labour (National Employment Code of Conduct) Regulations, Statutory Instrument 15 of 2006 which provides a model code which provides the procedures for carrying out disciplinary action in the work place. The provisions of the code of conduct are binding on employment relationships in the absence of a registered code of conduct.

The Labour Act must be read with other applicable subsidiary legislation which impact on employment, such as the National Social Security Authority Act [Chapter 17:04] ("NSSA Act") andthe Pensions and Other Benefits Act [Chapter 16:01] and the regulations made thereunder. All employers in Zimbabwe are obliged to contribute to the National Social Security Authority (Accident Prevention and Workers' Compensation Scheme) Statutory Instrument 68 of 1990 and the National Social Security Authority (Pension and Other Benefits Scheme)Statutory Instrument 146A of 1994. Employees are also taxed [which tax is usually deducted directly from the employee's salary under the Pay As You Earn scheme (PAYE)]. From a health and safety perspective, thePneumoconiosis Act [Chapter 15:08], Factories and Works Act[Chapter 14:08] and the Radiation Protection Act [Chapter 15:15] may regulate issues regarding work place safety law.

B. Requirements of Employing Foreign Employees

The Immigration Act (Chapter 4:02) regulates the entry into and departure of persons from Zimbabwe. It establishes the posts of Chief Immigration Officer and immigration officers who are empowered to administer the provisions of the Act and the subsidiary legislation.

a. Work Permit

a) Temporary Employment Permit

To work in Zimbabwe, a foreign person may require a temporary employment permit. In terms of Section 22 of the Immigration Regulations, Statutory 1nstrument 195 of 1998 ("the Regulations"), a temporary employment permit can be issued to foreigners to work, either paid or unpaid, for an organization or company registered in Zimbabwefor a period not exceeding five years. This permit may also be extended to the spouse and children of the permit holder to reside in Zimbabwe for the same period. A spouse or child of a temporary employment permit holder will be required to apply for their own temporary employment permit if they intend to work in Zimbabwe.

In terms of Section 23 of the Regulations, a temporary employment permit ceases to be valid if the permit holder fails to take up employment with, or ceases to be employed by, the employer or fails to engage, or ceases to be engaged, in the occupation specified in the permit. The permit is also issued on the condition that the permit holder and all persons authorised to enter Zimbabwe with him or her shall leave Zimbabwe on or before the expiry of the period stated in the permit. The permit holder is required to surrender the permit to an Immigration Officer before leaving Zimbabwe. The Chief Immigration Officer has the discretion to fix any other additional conditions to the permit.

b) Other Permits

In terms of Section 16 of the Regulations, a Chief Immigration Officer may issue a residence permit to any person who:

(i) holds a temporary employment permit; and

(ii) has been resident in Zimbabwe for a continuous period of not less than 5 years; or where he applies for a residence permit within 6 months before the date of expiry of his temporary employment permit, will on the date of such expiry, have been resident in Zimbabwe for a continuous period of 5 years.

A residence permit may also be issued to a person who possesses substantial financial means and is prepared to invest substantially in Zimbabwe without engaging in any occupation. In terms of Section 17 of the Regulations, a permanent resident permit may not be issued unless a person has transferred US$1 000 000.00 or more into Zimbabwe for the purposes of an investment project approved by the Zimbabwe Investment Authority, or has invested US$300 000.00 or more and will have been resident in Zimbabwe for not less than 3 years on the date of the expiry of the residence permit currently held or has invested US$100 000.00 or more in capital equipment in a joint venture with a bona fide Zimbabwean partner and is a professional or technical person who will have been a resident in Zimbabwe for not less than 3 years on the date of expiry of the residence permit currently held by him.

b. Application Procedure

A temporary employment permit application is filed with the Immigration Department. The employer must lodge an application to engage a foreign national to the Principal Director, accompanied by the following:

- A non-refundable statutory fee of US$500.00;
- Residence permit application forms completed by the applicant;
- Letter of offer of employment in Zimbabwe by prospective employer indicating the capacity in which applicant is to be employed and salary and conditions of service;
- Letter from prospective employer requesting the temporary employment permit stating the period required;
- Documentary evidence in English of qualifications and experience in the proposed occupation i.e., certified copied of degrees, diplomas, certificates and testimonials;
- Two recently taken full face passport size photos of the applicant. (Both should be certified at the back as a true likeness of the applicant);
- Certified copy of the applicant's birth certificate;
- Certified copy of marriage certificate (if applicable).

c. Social Insurance

The National Social Security Pension Scheme is provided for by the National Social Security Authority (NSSA). NSSA is a body corporate, empowered by the NSSA Act to administer social security schemes, more particularly, old age benefits and grants, survivor's benefits and grants as well as employment injury benefits. It is compulsory for any person who is working in a profession, trade or occupation, is a citizen of or ordinarily resident in Zimbabwe and has attained the age of sixteen years but has not attained the age of sixty years to register with NSSA and contribute as an employee [Section 4 of the National Social Security Authority Pension & Other Benefits Scheme (Rates of Benefits) Notice, Statutory Instrument 393 of 1993]. It is the employer's obligation to register itself and its employees with NSSA. It is also a requirement that both the employer and employee contribute to the schemes available through NSSA.

C. Exit and Entry

a. Visa Types

In terms of Section 31 of the Immigration Act, an immigration officer has the discretion to endorse the travel document of an alien with a visitor's entry certificate which shall be subject to the prescribed conditions and valid for the period stated therein, which shall not exceed 6 months in the first instance. In terms of Section 42 of the Regulations, a visitor's entry certificate is subject to the following conditions:

- The holder of the certificate shall give his address in Zimbabwe to an immigration officer and notify in writing any change of address to such an officer;
- That the holder of the certificate shall not, without the permission of the Chief Immigration Officer, commit

any act or conduct himself in any manner which is inconsistent with or contrary to the purpose for which he was admitted to Zimbabwe;

• That the holder of such certificate shall not engage in any occupation unless he has previously obtained a permit authorizing him to do so;

• That the holder of the certificate shall, without expense to the State, leave Zimbabwe on or before the date stated in the certificate unless an extension of the validity of the certificate has been endorsed thereon by an immigration officer authorized for the purpose by the Chief Immigration Officer; and

• That the certificate shall cease to be valid once the holder of the certificate has made exit from the country.

b. Restrictions on Exit and Entry

a) Restrictions on Entry

The Immigration Act places certain restrictions on entry into Zimbabwe. In terms of Section 12, every person entering Zimbabwe is required to present themselves to an immigration officer and produce their travel documents. In terms of Section 13, minors aged 16years and below are, in addition, required to be accompanied by an adult who is in possession of a valid travel document issued to that other person. Section 14 also establishes a list of persons who are regarded as prohibited persons who are not allowed to enter into Zimbabwe unless special permission is granted by the Chief Immigration Officer. This list includes any person who is infected or afflicted with or suffering from aprescribed disease, unless he is in possession of a permit to enter and remain in Zimbabwe issued upon conditions fixed in the permit and complies with suchconditions or any person convicted of a crime in Zimbabwe. A prohibited person also includes any person who is a prostitute or homosexual or lives or has lived on, or knowingly receives or has received, any part of the earnings of prostitution or homosexuality.

b) Restrictions on Exit

Sections 25 and 26 of the Immigration Act also place restrictions on exit out of Zimbabwe. Any person departing from Zimbabwe is required to produce travel documents. Minors aged 16 and below are further required to be accompanied by another person who is in possession of a valid travel document issued to that other person.

D. Trade Union and Labour Organizations

a. Trade Unions

In terms of Section 27 of the Labour Act, employees have the right to form and a member of a trade union. This right is also protected under section 65(2) of the Constitution. A trade union once formed is not required to be registered. Section 30 of the Labour Act, however, places certain restrictions on unregistered trade unions such as prohibiting them from representing their members in the Labour Court. Registered trade unions are on the other hand, provided with a number of benefits such as their entitlement to make representations to determining authorities or to the Labour Court and the right to be sued and to sue in its own name. Furthermore, an employer is obliged to grant reasonable facilities for this purpose.

An employer is required to deduct Trade Union dues from the member employee's salary. Most importantly, trade unions are afforded the automatic right to be recognized by an employer as a bargaining agent for the employee members. Refusal by the employer to negotiate with a trade union is considered to be an unfair labour practice.

There are a number of industry specific registered trade unions in Zimbabwe, as well as two general trade unions, namely Zimbabwe Congress of Trade Unions (ZCTU) and Zimbabwe Federation of Trade Unions (ZFTU) who purport to act in the interests of all employees.

b. Employers' Organisations

In terms of Section 27 of the Labour Act, any group of employers may form an employers' organization and any group of employers' organizations may form a federation. Section 28 requires an employers' organization to adopt a constitution within 6 months of its formation. The constitution is required to provide for, among other things, the powers and functions of the organization as well as the qualification for membership. An employers' organization can either be registered or unregistered. Section 30 of the Labour Act, however, places certain restrictions on unregistered employers' organizations such as prohibiting them from representing their members in the Labour Court. Registered Employers' organizations are on the other hand, provided with a number of benefits such as their entitlement to make representations to determining authorities or to the Labour Court and has the right to be sued and to sue in its own name.

c. Workers' Committees

Further to the employees' right to form and be a member of a trade union, Section 23 of the Labour Act affords employees the right to elect a workers' committee within the work place to represent them in any matter affecting their rights and interests. Unlike trade unions, workers' committees are, however, not granted body corporate status and therefore they cannot be sued or sue in their own name.

d. Works Councils

Section 25A of the Labour Act requires a works council to be formed in every establishment in which a workers' committee representing employees other than managerial employees has been elected. This is a bipartite body composed of an equal number of members representing the employer and the workers' committee. Its main function is to promote and maintain the effective participation of the employees and to secure their co-operation and trust.

e. Employment Council

This is a bipartisan body established by the registered trade union and registered employers' organizations in an industry. Section 56 of the Labour Act allows for the establishment of voluntary employment councils by any employer, registered employers' organization or federation of such organizations or registered trade union or federation of such trade unions. The main function of an employment council is to assist its members in the conclusion of a collective bargaining agreement, binding on all its members.

E. Labour Disputes

Section 2 of the Labour Act defines a dispute as a dispute relating to any matter concerning employment which is governed by the Act. The Labour Act also prescribes to a number of dispute resolution methods including but not limited to conciliation, arbitration, adjudication, collective bargaining as well as the engagement of collective job action such as lock outs and strike action.

a. Collective Bargaining and Strike Action

Section 76 of the Labour Act provides for collective bargaining in Zimbabwe. Collective bargaining extends to all negotiations which take place between an employer, a group of employers or employer's organization on the one hand, and one or more workers unions on the other. Its role is in the determination of working conditions, terms of employment and the regulation of relations between the employers and employees. In terms of Section 25 of the Labour Act, a collective bargaining agreement is binding in nature and must be negotiated in good faith and entered into voluntarily.

A deadlock in the negotiations becomes a dispute which is dealt with in terms of the collective job action mechanisms provided for in terms of Part XIII of the Labour Act. Collective job action is also provided constitutional protection in Zimbabwe. In terms of Section 65(3) of the Constitution, every employee has the right to participate in collective job action, including the right to strike, sit in, and withdraw their labour and to take other similar concerted action. The law however places restrictions on the exercise of this right in order to maintain essential services.

b. Conciliation

This is a method whereby a labour officer, or designated agent of the relevant employment council, through mediation and fact-finding attempts to resolve a dispute between parties to a labour dispute. Section 93 of the Labour Act makes conciliation compulsory for all labour disputes whatever their nature except where parties to the dispute refer the matter to arbitration. It is given a time span of 30 (thirty) days wherein the labour officer is required to resolve the matter by either ensuring that the parties enter a settlement, or in the event of non-settlement, issue out a certificate on no settlement.

c. Arbitration

Arbitration may either be voluntary or compulsory. In terms of section 93 (5) of the Labour Act, arbitration is compulsory only in a dispute of interest and when conciliation has failed and the labour officer has issued out a certificate of no settlement. In this event, the arbitrator is expected to make a ruling on his findings.

d. Adjudication

An arbitral award or ruling of a labour officer is not final and can be appealed or reviewed in the Labour Court within the specified timelines set out in the Labour Court Rules, 2018. The Labour Court also acts as a court of first instance where a labour officer fails to issue a certificate of no settlement after the period allowed at conciliation or, having issued a certificate of no settlement, fails to refer the matter to compulsory arbitration. An appeal from the Labour Court is only possible on a question of law and lies to the Supreme Court. Where a constitutional matter is involved, the Constitutional Court will have jurisdiction to hear the matter.

V. Intellectual Property

A. Brief Introduction of IP Laws and Regulations

Zimbabwean law recognises a number of intellectual property rights and, with the exception of copyright which is not a registered right, requires formal registration of same in the Zimbabwe Intellectual Property Office ("ZIPO"), the African Regional Intellectual Property Organisation ("ARIPO") or under the Madrid International Trademark System ("Madrid System") before such rights can be protected and enforced against third parties in Zimbabwe.

Zimbabwe recognises and protects the following intellectual property:
• Copyright and Neighbouring Rights under the Copyright and Neighbouring Rights Act (Chapter 26:05);
• Industrial Designs under the Industrial Designs Act (Chapter 26:02);
• Integrated Circuit Lay-Out Designs under the Integrated Circuit Lay-Out Designs Act (Chapter 26:07);
• Geographical Indications under the Geographical Indicates Act (Chapter 26:06);
• Patents under the Patents Act (Chapter 26:03);
• Plant Breeders Rights under the Plant Breeders Act (Chapter 18:16);
• Trade Marks under the Trade Marks Act (Chapter 26:04).

ZIPO's main functions are to register the above listed intellectual property and maintain the Registers in respect thereof as well as the recordal of assignments, licenses, renewals, registered users and other transfers of rights.

The various intellectual property statutes mentioned above empower the Registrars of the different intellectual property rights to adjudicate oppositions, requests for revocation and expungement of registrations, and other intellectual property disputes as prescribed therein. The Registrars' decisions can be appealed to the Intellectual Property Tribunal or the High Court of Zimbabwe.

Zimbabwe is a member of the African Regional Intellectual Property Organisation ("ARIPO") and party to a number of intellectual property conventions, protocols and treaties. These include among others the Harare Protocol on Patents and Industrial Designs, the Banjul Protocol on Marks, the Madrid Protocol and the Patent Cooperation Treaty ("PCT").

ZIPO acts as an office of origin for persons in Zimbabwe wishing to obtain international registrations through the Madrid system; and acts as a receiving office under the PCT.

ARIPO is a regional intellectual property organization headquartered in Harare, Zimbabwe. ARIPO was established in 1976 under the Lusaka Agreement by several African countries with the objective of, among other things establishing common services and organs for the coordination, harmonisation and development of the intellectual property activities affecting its members.

ARIPO registers and administers intellectual property rights on behalf of its member states under various Protocols, namely:
• the Harare Protocol on Patents and Industrial Designs and which empowers ARIPO to grant patents and to register industrial designs and utility models;
• the Banjul Protocol on Marks;
• the Swakopmund Protocol on the Protection of Traditional Knowledge and Expressions of Folklore;
• the Arusha Protocol for the Protection of New Varieties of Plants.

ARIPO currently has 19 member states. 18 of these states may be designated under the Harare Protocol. These are Botswana, The Gambia, Ghana, Kenya, Lesotho, Liberia, Malawi, Mozambique, Namibia, Rwanda, Sao Tome and Principe, Sierra Leone, Sudan, Swaziland, Uganda, Tanzania, Zambia and Zimbabwe. The member states which may be designated under the Banjul Protocol are: Botswana, Lesotho, Liberia, Malawi, Namibia, Sao Tome and Principle, Swaziland, Uganda, Tanzania and Zimbabwe. Somalia is a member of ARIPO, however it is not a party to any of the ARIPO Protocols.

The main advantage of the ARIPO system is that it enables local, regional and international proprietors of intellectual property the convenience of filing, electronically, a single application for the registration of any one of the intellectual property rights it is empowered to grant or register in one or more of the 18 ARIPO member states.

ARIPO registered rights are subject to the national laws of member states on compulsory licences, forfeiture, cancellation, use of in the public interest, cancellation or invalidation.

Actions for infringement of ARIPO registered rights are available to the registered proprietor or exclusive licensee or registered user in the member state within which such intellectual property rights are being infringed or contested.

B. Patent Application

The Patents Act [Chapter 20:03] permits the registration and protection of innovations that meet the criteria for patentability, namely, absolute novelty, inventiveness and industrial applicability.

Zimbabwean patent law under Section 2A of the Patents Act does not permit the registration of innovations relating to to diagnostic, therapeutic or surgical methods for the treatment of human beings or animals; plants or animals, other than microorganisms; essentially biological processes for the production of plants or animals other than microbiological processes; substances capable of being used as food or medicine which is a mixture of known ingredients possessing only the aggregate of the known properties of the ingredients; and processes producing such substances.

Inventions will also not be patentable if their use is likely to endanger public order or public safety; encourage offensive, immoral or anti-social behaviour; endanger human, animal or plant life or health; or promote serious prejudice to the environment (Section 13).

a. Filing Requirements

The minimum requirements for filing a patent application, as set out in Section 7 of the Patents Act, and obtaining filing date in Zimbabwe are as follows:
- A patent application is required to be filed in the prescribed form in English. The application must disclose the full name, physical address, nationality and state of incorporation of the applicant and be signed by the applicant or an authorised representative. It must also provide an address for service within Zimbabwe;
- An applicant not residing in Zimbabwe is required to appoint a qualified representative in Zimbabwe by Power of Attorney. The document need not need be legalised or notarized, it must be simply signed. The signatory must however state full names and designation held;
- The applicant's representative must be a person entitled to practise as a legal practitioner in Zimbabwe or a person entitled to practise as a registered patent agent in Zimbabwe;
- The full name, nationality and physical address of the inventor must be disclosed;
- The application must be accompanied by a complete or provisional specification and a declaration that the applicant owns the invention in respect of Zimbabwe, and where applicable proof of such title;
- Official filing fees are required to be made on lodgement of the patent application in ZIPO.

The complete specification must be lodged within twelve months of the filing of the patent application,failing which the application is deemed to be abandoned [Section 8(4) of the Regulations].

b. Examination

Zimbabwe does not provide for substantive examination of patent applications. Examination is conducted to assess compliance with formal filing requirements only. Section 15 of thePatentsAct requires the Registrar of Patents to examine and where appropriate, to accept the complete specification for grant, within 18 months from the filing date, failing which the application shall be deemed to have lapsed. In the case of refusal of a patent application by the Registrar of Patents, an appeal may be made to the Intellectual Property Tribunal or to the High Court of Zimbabwe.

c. Opposition and Registration

Section 17 of the Patents Act provides for interested parties to oppose the Registrar's acceptance of a patent application within 3 months of the date of advertisement in the Zimbabwe Industrial Property Journal. Unless there are opposition or appeal procedures the sealing and issuance of a registration certificate for a patent which has been accepted for grant can be requested within 3 months from the date of advertisement of acceptance of the complete specification.

d. Duration of Patents

The term of national patents of invention and ARIPO patents designating Zimbabwe is 20 years calculated from the filing date (Section 25).

C. Trade Mark Registration

The Trade Marks Act [Chapter 26:04] governs the registration of trademarks in Zimbabwe. To be registrable, a trademark must be distinctive and capable of distinguishing the goods or services in relation to which the mark is used or proposed to be used, from the same kind of goods or services connected in the course of trade with any other person.

a. Filing Requirements

The minimum requirements for filing a trademark application in Zimbabwe, as set out in Trade Marks Act and

Trade Marks Regulations, Statutory Instrument 170 of 2005, are:
  • An application in the prescribed form in English. The application must disclose the full name, physical address, nationality and state of incorporation of the applicant. It must also provide an address for service within Zimbabwe;
  • Details of the mark to be applied for and the appropriate goods / services and international class;
  • Power of Attorney which must be simply signed. It does not need to be legalised or notarized. The signatory must however state full names and designation held;
  • 10 printed original good quality specimens of the mark except where it is a word or words in plain letters (maximum size 70mm x 70mm);
  • If the mark / device is in colour, the wording of the colour limitation clause is required, specifying the precise colours to be claimed using Pantone colour codes where necessary;
  • A certified copy of the first foreign application for the trademark, if applicable, together with an English translation where applicable, if Convention Priority is claimed (within 3 months of filing);
  • Advice as to whether the mark is already being used in Zimbabwe or is proposed to be used in the future;
  • If the mark is in a language other than English, a translation of the meaning and details of the language to which it belongs (and a transliteration and the meaning of any foreign characters, for example Chinese characters);
  • Where the applicant does not have an intention to use the mark, it may appoint a registered user simultaneously when filing the application, otherwise a registered user may be appointed after registration.

b. Examination

Applications are examined as to compliance with formalities, registrability and conflict with prior registrations. ZIPO takes an average of 3 to 5 months to examine applications and to issue examination reports.

Once the conditions stipulated in a notice of conditional acceptance have been agreed to in writing or the objections in a notice of objection have been overcome, ZIPO will issue an acceptance form calling for payment of advertisement fees.

c. Publication and Opposition

Once an application is advertised in the Zimbabwe Industrial Property Journal, any interested person may enter opposition to the application within 2 months of the date of publication in the Journal. If opposition is filed, a trademark application cannot proceed to registration until the opposition has been withdrawn or finalised in favour of the trademark applicant. If no opposition is filed by the expiry of the opposition period, application for issuance of the registration certificate is submitted and the certificate issued by ZIPO.

d. Duration of Trademarks

The term of a national trade mark or an ARIPO mark registered under the Banjul Protocol on Marks or a mark registered under the Madrid Protocol is 10 years calculated from the filing date. The term of Convention applications filed nationally is calculated from the date of filing in the Convention country. The registration can be renewed for periods of 10 years thereafter.

e. Convention Arrangements

Trademarks registered under the Banjul and Madrid Protocols have the same effect and are afforded the same protection as marks registered nationally. However, with regards marks which were registered in Zimbabwe prior to the domestication of the Banjul and Madrid Protocols on 10 September 2010 and 1 July 2016 respectively, the proprietor of such marks is not entitled to damages or any other remedy for infringement of copyright in the mark which took place before the effective date.

D. Measures for IP Protection

The Patents Act and the Trade Marks Act provide civil, criminal and customs remedies for infringement of registered patents and trademarks.

a. Civil Remedies

Civil action for infringement may be brought before the Intellectual Property Tribunal, the High Court or the Magistrates Court (subject to jurisdictional limits) by the registered proprietor or exclusive licensee or registered user.

A registered patent is infringed by the making, using, offering to dispose of, disposing of, importing and exercising any rights and effects of a patent in Zimbabwe without the authority and consent of the holder of the patent. If the patent relates to a new substance, any substance of the same chemical composition and constitution shall be deemed to have been produced by the patented process.

The Trade Marks Act does not permit action for infringement of unregistered trademarks. However the proprietor of an unregistered trademark may bring action for unlawful competition or for passing off goods or services as the goods or services of another person.

The Trade Marks Act additionally recognises and protects familiar foreign marks. The proprietor of a familiar foreign mark may apply to the Intellectual Property Tribunal or a court of competent jurisdiction for an order prohibiting the use in Zimbabwe of a trade mark which constitutes, or the essential part of which constitutes, the reproduction, imitation or translation of the familiar foreign mark where the trademark is being used in relation to:

(a) goods or services which are identical or similar to the goods or services in respect of which the familiar foreign mark is well known in Zimbabwe, where such use is likely to deceive or cause confusion; or

(b) goods or services which are not similar to those in respect of which the familiar foreign mark is well known in Zimbabwe, if:

(i) the use of the trade mark in relation to those goods or services would indicate a connection between them and the proprietor of the familiar foreign mark; and

(ii) the interests of the proprietor of the familiar foreign mark are likely to be injured by such use; and

(iii) the familiar foreign mark is registered as a trade mark in the Convention country concerned.

Where the proprietor of a foreign familiar mark institutes infringement proceedings, it is however required to apply for registration of such mark in Zimbabwe within one month of instituting the infringement proceedings.

In Zimbabwe the remedies for infringement of registered patents and trade marks include Anton Piller orders, interdicts, damages, delivery up and rendering of accounts and all such other remedies as are otherwise available for infringement of any other proprietary right. Where the complainant has difficulty in calculating the quantum of damages suffered, the damages may be assessed in terms of the reasonable royalty that would have been levied for the use of the patent or trade mark.

b. Criminal Remedies

Criminal offences include

• forging a registered trademark;

• falsely applying a registered mark to goods or in relation to services;

• making a die, block, machine or other instrument for the purpose of forging or being used to forge, a registered trademark;

• making any reproductions, replicas of that trademark or, a mark so nearly resembling as to deceive or confuse;

• importing any reproductions, replicas or representations of that trademark otherwise than on goods to which applied.

Criminal sanctions for infringement of registered patents and trade marks include forfeiture, monetary fines and imprisonment.

c. Customs Recordal

The Trade Marks Act further provides for the prohibition of the importation or exportation of counterfeit trade mark goods.

The term 'counterfeit trademark goods' is defined as any goods which bear without authorization a trademark which:

a) is identical to a registered mark; or

b) cannot be distinguished in its essential aspects from a registered trademark; and thereby infringes the rights of the proprietor of the registered trademark:

Where on application the Director of Customs and Excise is satisfied as to the merits of a request for goods to be declared prohibited goods, s/he may, on provision of security in such form and such amount as s/he may request, prohibit the importation or exportation of such counterfeit goods into or out of Zimbabwe for a period of 10 working days and within that period the proprietor of the registered trademark is required to institute proceedings in the Intellectual Property Tribunal or a court seeking an order directing the Director of Customs and Excise to prevent the importation and exportation of the counterfeit goods, as the case may be.

As long as an order by the Tribunal or a court is in force preventing the importation or exportation of counterfeit goods, the goods in question are prohibited goods and may not be imported into or exported from, Zimbabwe.

VI. Environmental Protection

The importance of the environment and environmental protection is recognised in the supreme law of Zimbabwe, namely the Constitution of Zimbabwe, Amendment (No. 20) Act 1 of 2013. In accordance with Section 73 of the Constitution:

a. Every Person Has the Right:

a) to an environment that is not harmful to their health or well-being; and

b) to have the environment protected for the benefit of present and future generations, through reasonable legislative and other measures that:

(i) prevent pollution and ecological degradation;

(iii) promote conservation; and

(iv) secure ecologically sustainable development and use of natural resources while promoting economic and social development.

b. The State must take reasonable legislative and other measures, within the limits of the resources available to it, to achieve the progressive realisation of the rights set out in this section.

A. Department Supervising Environmental Protection

The Environmental Management Act (Chapter 20:27) is the key piece of legislation that regulates environmental protection. It is administered by the Minister of Environment, Water and Climate whose functions and duties include promoting, co-coordinating, monitoringand protecting the environment. The Minister can also impose penalties on any persons who cause harm to the environment and has the responsibility to ensure that persons or institutions that are responsible for causing environmental harm will meet the cost of remedying that harm.

The Environmental Management Actestablishes the Environmental Management Agency ("EMA"), whose functions are set out in Section 10 of the Environmental Management Act, and include the formulation of quality standards on air, water, soil, noise, vibration, radiation and waste management. The Agency is responsible for developing guidelines for the preparation of the National Plan, environmental management plans and local environmental management action plans and regulating and monitoring the collection, disposal, treatment and recycling of waste. It also regulates the discharge or emission of any pollutant or hazardous substance into the environment and keeps records in the form of registers of all licences and permits issued under the Environmental Management Act.

EMA has the authority to make model by-laws and to establish measures for the management of the environment within the jurisdiction of the local authorities and to serve written orders on any persons requiring them to undertake or adopt such measures as are specified in the orders to protect the environment. Prior to embarking on the activities set out in the First Schedule of the Environmental Management Act, companies are required to obtain environmental impact assessments and EMA is responsible for the regulation, monitoring, reviewing, and approval of the environmental impact assessments.

After the impact assessments are conducted, EMA also carries out periodic environment audits of the activities to ensure that that their implementation complies with the requirements of the Environmental Management Act.

In addition, in terms of the Regional, Town and Country Planning Act[Chapter 29:12], regional planning councils, municipal councils, town councils, rural district councils and local boards arealso responsible for supervising environment protection. They formulate and implement policies that regulate land use and the conservation and improvement of the physical environment in their respective planning areas.

B. Brief Introduction of Laws and Regulations of Environmental Protection

As set out above, the Constitution of Zimbabweexpressly provides for environmental protection inSection 73. The Constitution requires such protection to be effected through methods that include the prevention of pollution and ecological degradation, the promotion of conservation, securing ecologically sustainable development and use of natural resources while promoting economic and social development.

In addition, the First Schedule (Sections 2 and 97) of the Environmental Management Act lists the projects that require environmental impact assessment. These include housing developments; industrial activities;infrastructure projects such as mining, quarrying and petroleum production storage and distribution; and power generation and transmission.

Section 97 of the Environmental Management Act provides that the projects listed above must not be implemented unless the Director-General of the Environmental Management Agency has issued a certificate of the environmental impact assessment following the submission of an environmental impact assessment report in terms of the Act, the certificate remains valid and the conditions imposed by the Director-General in regard to the issue of the certificate are complied with. Implementing a project in contravention of Section 97 of theEnvironmental Management Act is a criminal offence that may attract a fine and imprisonment. The Act also provides requirements for certain licences, including effluents discharge licence, emission licence, waste licence and registration of pesticides and toxic substances.

Apart from the Environmental Management Actdiscussed above, there is other legislation which regulates environmental factors relating to specific industries or sectors. The Regional, Town and Country Planning Act regulates activities conducted within the jurisdiction of local authorities. The Mines and Minerals Act [Chapter 21:05] regulates environmental issues associated with mining and mining related activities. In particular, in terms of Section 237, a mining plan must be approved by the mining commissioner who shall take environmental protection into account.

The Water Act (Chapter 20:24) regulates the development and utilisation of water resources. It provides for the protection of the environment and the prevention and control of water pollution. The Water Act requires any person abstracting water for any purpose other than primary purposes (domestic human needs, support of animal life, making of bricks for private use and dip tanks) to do so in terms of a permit from the catchment council for the area concerned, as set out in Section 32. A permit to use water for mining purposes is obtained from the mining commissioner.

The Parks and Wild Life Act (Chapter 20:14) provides for the establishment of national parks, botanical reserves, botanical gardens, sanctuaries, safari areas and recreational parks. The Act restricts or prohibits certain activities within the protected areas, including hunting; picking or destroying plants; and having convoys travel through the same (Sections 24 and 29) as well prohibiting prospecting and mining (Section 119). The Forest Act[Chapter 19:05] regulates the administration, control and management of State forests, the protection of private forests, trees and forest produce, the cutting and taking of timber for mining purposes andthe burning of vegetation (Section 37, 41, 45, 56 and Part VIII of the Forest Act). The Act prohibitscutting, felling, injuring or destroying any forest produce from certain forests and reserved land specified in the Third Schedule of the Act.

From an agricultural perspective, there is also legislation governing which chemicals and fertilizers may be utilized, to ensure health and safety as well as environment protection. The Fertilizers, Farm Feeds and Remedies Act (Chapter 18:12) and the Fertilizers Regulations, 1972 (Rhodesia Government Notice No. 669 of 1972)set out the requirements for making, licensing and using fertilizers for farming.

The State is also a signatory to various international treaties that protect the environment. An example is the Convention on Wetlands of International Importance Especially as Waterfowl Habitat ("the Ramsar Convention"). The treaty recognizes the fundamental ecological functions of wetlands as regulators of water regimes and as habitats supporting a characteristic flora and fauna. It seeks to curtail the encroachment on and loss of wetlands through human and economic development. Several wetlands were designated Wetlands of International Importance under the Ramsar Convention therefore internationally obligating the State to promote their conservation. Any development activity that upsets the ecosystem of designated wetlands is prohibited.

There are various environmental laws and regulations that must be complied with by companies conducting business activities in Zimbabwe, prospective business owners must thus obtain comprehensive legal advice covering all the laws relating to the activities that they contemplate.

C. Evaluation of Environmental Protection

The Environmental Management Agency's Environmental Protection Department has the mandate of setting up and enforcing environmental legislation and standards. This includes the responsibility for maintaining and enforcing the Environmental Impact Assessment policy, national fire strategy, hazardous substances use and handling, guidelines for ecosystems protection and waste management. The Department also provides laboratory services, specialist services and emergency services in the event of an accident or spillage.

EMA operates through three main units namely the Environmental Quality Unit, the Ecosystems Protection Unit and the Quality Laboratory. The Environmental Quality Unit is responsible for environmental compliance inspections, sampling and testing various resources to verify quality and deviations from standards, setting and reviewing environmental quality standards that are suitable for the intended use and maintenance of various environmental quality databases. It comprises of the air quality section, hazardous substances and articles control section, water and effluent section and solid waste management section.

The Ecosystems Protection Unit is responsible for Environmental Impact Assessments which define, quantify and evaluate the potential and known impacts of human activities on ecosystems and the mitigation measures that must be implemented to reduce negative impacts while enhancing the positive. The Environmental Impact Assessment is used to determine whether a project should proceed and in what manner. Part XI of the Act requires a project developer to engage an independent consultant to undertake the Environmental Impact Assessment. An Environmental Management Plan must be presented to the Agency together with required forms and prescribed fees. Inspectors from the Agency will then inspect the area, review the Environmental Management Plan and accept the project as it is, accept it with restrictions or reject it. The Agency provides laboratory services through the Quality Laboratory Services Unit.

VII. Dispute Resolution

The primary avenues of dispute resolution in Zimbabwe is through adversarial litigation and Alternative Dispute Resolution (ADR), which takes the form of arbitration, mediation and conciliation.

A. Methods and Bodies of Dispute Resolution

Disputes may be resolved either byadversarial litigation through the court system or through any of the three forms of ADR set out above.

a. Litigation

Litigation is the most utilised means of dispute resolution. This involves approaching a court of law for a determination. Section 162 of the Constitution of Zimbabwe, 2013 provides for the establishment of the following Courts:

- The Constitutional Court;
- The Supreme Court;
- The High Court;
- The Administrative Court;
- The Labour Court;
- The Magistrates Courts;
- The Customary Law Courts; and
- Any other court established in terms of an Act of Parliament.

In addition, in accordance with Section 162 (viii)of the Constitution, Parliament has established various specialised courts through its enactments including the Small Claims Court, the Intellectual Property Tribunal, the Water Court, the Fiscal Appeal Court and the Special Court for Income Tax Appeals. Each court has rules that govern the procedure to be adopted therein.

Once a matter has been determined by a court and an order is made, the party in whose favour the order was made may proceed with execution of the order, if necessary, execution of an order can, however, only be done through the Sheriff of the High Court or the Messenger of Court as applicable.

a) The Constitutional Court

Section 167 of the Constitution provides that the Constitutional Court is the highest court of law in Zimbabwe in respect of all constitutional matters. It deals exclusively with matters that raise constitutional issues, such as the constitutionality of legislation and enforcement of fundamental rights and freedoms, and its decisions are binding on all other courts. In accordance with the aforementioned section, litigants may approach the Constitutional Court directly, through referral from a lower court or through an appeal noted from a lower court on a constitutional matter under Section 175 of the Constitution. The Constitutional Court can sit and hear constitutional matters as a court of first instance, as a court of appeal, and as a court of confirmation in relation to constitutional declarations. The Constitutional Court is also responsible for the confirmation of decisions made by a lower court that declare a provision unconstitutional.

There are certain matters that are within the exclusive jurisdiction of the Constitutional Court. Rule 21 of the Constitutional Court Rules, Statutory Instrument 61 of 2016 provides that litigants may approach the Court directly in the certain instances such as:

(i) Referrals from a court of lesser jurisdiction;
(ii) Determinations on whether Parliament or the President has failed to fulfil a constitutional obligation;
(iii) Appeals in terms of Section 175 (3) of the Constitution against an order concerning the constitutional validity or invalidity of any law; and
(iv) Where the liberty of an individual is at stake.

The Constitutional Court is also tasked with confirming any declarations relating to the constitutional validity of legislation. Rule 31 (1) of the Constitutional Court Rules provides that where a declaration of constitutional invalidity is made by a court other than the Constitutional Court, the Registrar or Clerk of the lower court must, within 14 days of the making of such order, file with the Registrar of the Constitutional Court a copy of the record of proceedings including the court order for confirmation.

The above positions are the only instances in which the Constitutional Court can be approached without first seeking leave to appeal. Rule 32 (2) of the Constitutional Court Rules provides that where a party to proceedings in a subordinate court or tribunal is aggrieved by the decision of the same on a constitutional matter and wishes to appeal against it to the Constitutional Court, the aggrieved party must within 15 days of the decision file with the Registrar of the Court an application for leave to appeal.

b) The Supreme Court

The Supreme Court is exclusively a court of appeal with jurisdiction to hear any and all matters on appeal as the final court of appeal in accordance with Section 21of the Supreme Court Act [Chapter 7:13]. It can hear any matters including constitutional matters. However, in respect of the latter, the final court of appeal is the Constitutional Court.

Generally, the time to note an appeal with the Supreme Court is within 15 days of the handing down of the judgment one wishes to appeal against. In accordance with Section 22 of the Supreme Court Act the Supreme Court is entitled to confirm, amend, vary or set aside the judgment which is appealed against or to grant any order it deems fit. It may also order that a new trial or fresh proceedings be held.

In certain instances, it may be necessary to obtain the leave of the court aquo to note an appeal with the Supreme Court. In respect of matters emanating from the High Court, Section 43 of the High Court Act [Chapter 7:05] provides that leave to appeal must be sought from the High Court when a party wishes to appeal against:

(i) An order allowing an extension of time for appealing from a judgment;

(ii) An order of a High Court judge refusing an application for summary judgment and granting of unconditional leave to defend an action;

(iii) An order by consent of the parties or an order against costs only which by law is left to the discretion of the Court; and

(iv) An interlocutory order or judgment.

Section 92F of the Labour Act [Chapter 28:01] provides that any aggrieved party who wishes to appeal against any decision of the Labour Court shall make an application for leave to appeal to the judge who presided over the matter or to any other judge of the Labour Court.

In the event that leave to appeal is refused by the presiding judge in the High Court or Labour Court, an aggrieved party may make an application for leave to appeal directly to the Supreme Court in terms of Section 19 of the Supreme Court Act. Where such an application is to be made, Rule 19 (1) of the Supreme Court Rules, 1964 provides that it must be done within 10 days of the date when leave to appeal was refused.

c) The High Court

The High Court is a court of first instance as well as an appeals court for matters originating from the Magistrates Court or any court of similar standing. It derives its original jurisdiction to hear any and all matters from Section 171 of the Constitution. This position is further embodied in Section 13 of the High Court Act [Chapter 7:06]. All civil appeals emanating from the Magistrates Court lie with the High Court. An appeal from other lower courts or tribunals may lie with the High Court where the empowering legislation specifically provides for the same, for example under the Trade Marks Act [Chapter 26:04] and under the Patents Act [Chapter 26:02]. It also has inherent review powers over proceedings of all tribunals subordinate to it in terms of Section 26 of the High Court Act.

An appeal may be noted by an aggrieved party where the lower court or tribunal erred in law in making its decision. It involves consideration of the merits of a matter to determine whether the decision was correctly arrived at. An application for review, however, involves a challenge of a lower court or tribunal's decision based on a procedural irregularity or illegality in the conduct of proceedings. An example of such irregularity is bias on the part of the presiding officer.

d) The Administrative Court

The Administrative Court is a specialised court in that it only hears matters on appeal or review from an administrative body. Section 2 of the Administrative Justice Act [Chapter 10:28] defines an administrative body as follows:

- An officer, employee, member, committee, council, or board of the State or a local authority or parastatal; or
- A committee or board appointed by or in terms of any legislation;
- A Minister or Deputy Minister of the State;
- Any other person or body authorised by any enactment to exercise or perform any administrative power or duty.

The Court is a creature of statute and as such is limited in its jurisdiction. It exercises its jurisdiction in accordance with Section 4 of theAdministrative Justice Act and Section 4 of Administrative Court Act [Chapter 7:01] which entitles the Court to entertain matters on appeal or review from administrative bodies.

Examples of Administrative Authorities are the National Social Security Authority governed by the National Social Security Authority Act [Chapter 17:04], Mining Affairs Board which derives its powers from the Mines and Minerals Act [Chapter 21:05], the Environmental Management Agency which derives its power from the Environmental Management Act [Chapter 20:27], any Rural or City Council which derives its power from the Rural Councils Act [Chapter 29:13] or the Urban Councils Act [Chapter 29:15]. Where a party is aggrieved by a decision of an administrative authority, such a party is entitled to note an appeal or file an application for review with the Administrative Court.

Where the Act that regulates the Administrative Authority does not specify the time period or procedure to be adopted in appealing or applying for the review of a decision by the same, the Administrative Court (Miscellaneous Appeals) Rules, 1980 apply to appeals and the High Court Rules, 1971 apply to reviews. Rule 5 of the Administrative Court (Miscellaneous Appeals) Rules gives a party 30 days within which to note an appeal which time is reckoned from the date that the decision was given. In respect of reviews, Rule 256 of the High Court Rules gives a party 8 weeks from the date of the termination of proceedings by the Administrative Authority to file an application for review.

e) The Labour Court

The Labour Court is also creature of statute and its jurisdiction is limited to matters provided for in Section 89 of the Labour Act [Chapter 28:01]. Section 89 (1) of the Labour Act provides that the Labour Court may exercise the following functions:

• Hearing and determining applications and appeals in terms of the Labour Act or any other enactment; and

• Hearing and determining matters referred to it by the line Minister in terms of the Labour Act; and

• Referring a dispute to a labour officer, designated agent or a person appointed by the Labour Court to conciliate the dispute where the Labour Court considers it expedient to do so;

• Appointing an arbitrator from the panel of arbitrators to hear and determine an application; and / or

• Doing any other things as may be assigned to it in terms of the Labour Act or any other enactment.

In addition, under Section 92EE of the Labour Act, the Labour Court has specific powers of review which are as follows:

(i) Subject to this Act and any other law, the grounds on which any proceedings or decision conducted or made in connection with is Act may be brought on review before the Labour Court shall be:

• absence of jurisdiction on the part of the arbitrator or adjudicating authority concerned;

• interest in the cause, bias, malice or corruption on the part of the arbitrator or adjudicating authority concerned;

• gross irregularity in the proceedings or the decision of the arbitrator or adjudicating authority concerned.

(ii) Nothing in subsection (1) shall affect any other law relating to the review of proceedings or decisions of inferior courts, tribunals or authorities.

It is prudent to note that unlike in other civil matters wherein prescription is determined by the Prescription Act [Chapter 8:11], prescription in labour matters is governed by Section 94 of the Labour Act which stipulates that the period for prescription in labour related matters is two years from the date when the dispute arose or the date on which the litigant became aware of an unfair labour practice.

Where a party to a labour dispute is aggrieved by a decision of his or her employer, a labour officer, arbitrator, National Employment Council or any other tribunal, he or she may note an appeal or file an application for review with the Labour Court, as the case may be. In noting an appeal, Rule 19 (1) of the Labour Court Rules, 2017 provides that a litigant is given 21 days from the date that he or she or it receives the decision, determination or direction or award within which to note an appeal. In respect of applications for review, Rule 20 (1) of the Labour Court Rules provides that an application for review of a decision from a tribunal should be filed within 21 days from the date when the proceedings in the tribunal were concluded.

f) The Magistrates Court

The Magistrates Courtscomprise ofcriminal courts and civil courts. Criminal matters are driven by the State, after a report of criminality is made to the Police Service. A prosecutor in the office of the National Prosecuting Authority will make the determination of whether to pursue criminal charges.

The MagistratesCourt's civil jurisdiction is regulated by Section 11 of the Magistrates Court Act [Chapter 7:10] and is related to geographical jurisdiction, cause of action and monetary value. Each Magistrates Court has geographical jurisdiction over any person or partnership that carries on business, is employed or resides within its province. The Court also has jurisdiction over persons who institute proceedings in that court where the cause of action arose wholly within that Court's province.

The monetary value of a matter plays a part in determining whether or not the Court has jurisdiction. However, parties are entitled to agree contractually to the jurisdiction of the Magistrates Court or to abandon a portion of their monetary claim to ensure that the matter falls within the Magistrates Court's monetary jurisdiction. The monetary limits are set out in the Magistrates Court (Civil Jurisdiction) (Monetary Limits) Rules, Statutory Instrument 163 of 2012 which stipulates that generally the monetary jurisdiction of the Magistrates Court is claims with a maximum value of US$10 000.00, or US$5 000.00 in cases founded on a liquid document.

Section 14 of the Magistrates Court Act provides for matters wherein the Magistrates Court does not have jurisdiction. These include matters pertaining to the dissolution of a marriage in terms of the Marriage Act [Chapter 5:11], matters affecting the status of a person in respect of mental capacity, the interpretation and validity of wills and decrees of perpetual silence.

b. Alternate Dispute Resolution

As stated briefly above, there are three methods of ADR that are used in Zimbabwe, namely arbitration, mediation, andconciliation. Each method will be discussed below.

a) Arbitration

Bendix in "Industrial Relations in South Africa" 5thed (2010) Juta: Cape Town at page 619-620 states that Arbitration entails appointing a third party ("the arbitrator") to adjudicate a dispute and make a determination on the same. The arbitrator hears submissions from both sides and is the final decision maker. His or her determination is binding on the parties.

Zimbabwe is a signatory to the Convention on the Recognition and Enforcement of Foreign Arbitral Awards which makes provision for the recognition and enforcement of arbitral awards in contracting states where an award is made by any state that is party to the treaty. Pursuant to the Convention, Zimbabwe adopted the United Nations Commission on International Trade Law (UNCITRAL) Model Arbitration Law and domesticated the same through the enactment of the Arbitration Act [Chapter 7:15]. The Arbitration Act therefore provides the procedure to be followed in the determination of the dispute by arbitration.

Typically, matters are decided through arbitration where the parties to a contract specify that disputes will be settled by arbitration. Such clauses are known as "Arbitration Clauses". The clause may specify who will be the arbitrator and what action will be taken in the event of a disagreement relating to the appointment of the arbitrator. Where an agreement is silent as to, or where parties cannot agreeon, the appointment of an arbitrator, the Commercial Arbitration Centre may be approached to appoint an arbitrator to preside over the matter. Where an award is made and a party is aggrieved by the award, Article 34 of the Arbitration Act provides that the aggrieved party may make an application to the High Court for the setting aside of the arbitral award within 3 months from the date when the party received the award.

Where a dispute arises in respect of bilateral investment treaties, the same is resolved through arbitration in accordance with the International Centre for Settlement of Investment Disputes (ICSID) Convention which has been domesticated through the Arbitration (International Investment Disputes) Act [Chapter 7:03]. The Convention established the ICSID, which adjudicates matters relating to international investment disputes and also set out the rules and procedure to be followed in the arbitration of the same. Zimbabwe is a party to the Convention and accordingly, is bound by the same. The Arbitration (International Investment Disputes) Act establishes provisions for the registration and enforcement of ICSID awards.

Section 93(5)(a) of the Labour Actsets out that labour matters can only be dealt with through arbitration where it involves a dispute of interest. Designated Agents from National Employment Councils can also sit as arbitrators in labour disputes that arise in their specified industries in terms of Section 63(3b) of the Labour Act.

Arbitral Awards are binding in nature but require registration in order for the party in whose favour the award was granted for enforcement purposes. Article 35 of the Arbitration Act provides for the registration of an award by the High Court. Once it has been registered, the award becomes an order of court and it may be enforced subject to Article 36 of the Arbitration Act.

b) Mediation

Bendix (supra) at 616 states thatmediation takes place when an independent third party intervenes in a dispute, in an attempt to induce a settlement. In mediation, the mediator plays an active role as he or she attempts to bring about a settlement by advising the parties, acting as an intermediary and suggesting possible solutions. The mediator cannot force the parties to settle nor can he or she make a binding decision for the parties. In Zimbabwe, certain legal practitioners and retired judges offer mediation services but there is no legislation relating to the same.

c) Conciliation

Conciliation refers to the establishment of a forum in which parties to a dispute may come together and engage in an attempt to settle their differences (Bendix (supra) at 616). In Zimbabwe, this form of dispute resolution is primarily utilised in labour matters. In terms of Section 93 of the Labour Act, matters before Labour Officers and National Employment Councils must first go through a conciliation process, after a complaint has been made. However, if the parties cannot settle the matter amicably, it is referred to or a Ruling may be made in terms of Section 93(5) of the Labour Act.

Registration of Foreign Judgments and Awards

Foreign arbitral awards are enforceable upon registration in accordance with the Convention on the

Recognition and Enforcement of Foreign Arbitral Awards and the Arbitration Act. Foreign judgments must be registered in terms of Section 5 of the Civil Matters (Mutual Assistance) Act [Chapter 8:02]. The foreign judgment must have been made by a court in a designated country. The judgment creditor must make an application for registration to the court with jurisdiction within 6 years from the date that the judgment was made or after the determination of an appeal or review as the case may be. Such application would be made in the form specified by the specific court.

In accordance with the Schedule to theCivil Matters (Mutual Assistance) (Designated Countries) Order, Chapter 8:02 Civil Matters (Mutual Assistance) (Designated Countries) Order, Statutory Instrument 65 of 1998, only judgments from the following countries may be registered in accordance with Section 5 mentioned above:
- Australia;
- Dominica;
- Germany;
- Ghana;
- Portugal;
- South Africa;
- Italy;
- Zambia;
- Slovak Republic; and
- Bulgaria.

However, where a party seeks to enforce a judgment from a non-designated country, the same is not precluded from doing so. Section 25 of the Civil Matters (Mutual Assistance) Act provides that the Act is additional to and does not limit any other law relating to the recognition and enforcement of foreign judgments. In accordance with the Common Law, a party may apply for the registration of a foreign judgment. The applicable requirements for an application for registration of a foreign judgment, as set out in Jones vKrok 1995 (1) SA 677(A) at 685 B-E are as follows:

(i) that the court which handed down the judgment had jurisdiction to entertain the matter;
(ii) that the judgment is final and conclusive in its effect and has not become superannuated;
(iii) that the recognition and enforcement of the judgment would not be contrary to public policy;
(iv) that the judgment was not obtained by fraudulent means;
(v) that the judgment does not involve the enforcement of a penal or revenue law of the foreign state; and
(vi) that enforcement of the judgment is not precluded by the provisions of any law.

B. Application of Laws

The supreme law of Zimbabwe is the Constitution of Zimbabwe, 2013. All other laws are subordinate to the Constitution and where the same contravene or do not reflect the values and rights set out in the Constitution they are unlawful and invalid to the extent of their contravention and can be declared the same. The courts system upholds the Constitution and ensures that all laws fall in line with the same.

The other sources of law in Zimbabwe include statute and common law. The same are clarified and developed case precedent. Statute law refers to the laws and regulations enacted by the Parliament of Zimbabwe.

The common law in Zimbabwe is primarily Roman-Dutch law. In certain instances, however, English common law applies, such as in respect of Contract law and Insurance law. The Courts apply the same when disputes arise unless the parties had contracted to have a different system of law apply to their disputes. For example, parties may decide that the law of Germany will apply to the substance of their agreement and any disputes arising therefromSection 49 of the High Court Act provides that the official language is English. Where a party wishes to use a different language, an interpreter must be engaged and must attend Court when necessary. All documents filed with the Court should be in English except where specifically provided for by an enactment.

The general principle in the resolution of disputes is that the onus to prove a claim rests on the person who makes the allegation. The burden of proof in civil matters is on a balance of probabilities, and as such that person must present sufficient evidence to persuade the Court that they are entitled to what they are claiming.

In legal proceedings, anatural person to a dispute may represent himself or herself in proceedings or may instruct a legal practitioner duly registered in terms of the Legal Practitioners Act [Chapter 27:07] and who holds a valid practicing certificate issued by the Law Society of Zimbabwe. However, Trade Unions are entitled to represent their members in labour matters. Juristic persons such as companies must be represented by a legal practitioner in the High Court and superior courts.

Foreign lawyers may not represent parties in Zimbabwean Courts, although limited practicing certificate from the Law Society of Zimbabwe may be issued in specific circumstances in terms of Section 7 of the Legal

Practitioners Act. The foreign legal practitioner must be from a reciprocating country to be eligible for the same and the practicing certificate will be given for a limited period of time.

VIII. Others

A. Anti-commercial Bribery

Anti-bribery efforts in Zimbabwe are governed by the Constitution of Zimbabwe Amendment (No. 20), 2013 ("the Constitution")as well as in other legislation such as thePrevention of Corruption Act [Chapter 9:16], the Anti-Corruption Commission Act (2004), Criminal Law (Codification & Reform) Act [Chapter 9:23] and the Anti-Corruption Commission Act [Chapter 9:22].

a. Anti-bribery Laws and Regulations

a) Criminal Law (Codification & Reform) Act

Bribery and corruption are criminal offences in Zimbabwe in terms of Chapter IX of the Criminal Law (Codification & Reform) Act ("the Criminal Code").

Bribery is defined in Section 170 of the Criminal Code. In terms of Section 170 (1) of the Criminal Code, there are two instances where a person is considered to have committed bribery. The first instance is where an agent freely receives a gift or consideration as an inducement or award for doing something in relation to his or her principal's business knowing or realizing that there is potential that the gift or consideration is not due to him or her in terms of any agreement that he or she has with his principal. The second instance is where a person gives or agrees to give an agent a gift or consideration as an inducement or award for doing something in relation to the business of the agent's principal knowing or realizing that there is potential that the gift or consideration is not due to the agent in terms of any agreement that he or she has with his principal.

Section 169 defines an agent as any person employed by or acting for another person in any capacity this includes a director or secretary of a company, a member of a board or authority responsible for administering the affairs or business of a body corporate and a public officer. A principal is defined as the employer of an agent or any other person for whom an agent acts.

Section 170 (2) of the Criminal Code also provides for the rebuttable presumption that bribery has occurred where it is proven that:

(i) An agent obtained, agreed to obtain or solicited any gift or consideration, whether for himself or herself or for another person; or

(ii) A person has given, agreed to give or offered any gift or consideration to an agent, whether it is for the agent himself or herself or for another person or any other person upon agreement with the agent.

The Criminal Code does not provide a definition for corruption, but crimes involving corrupt acts are dealt with under Part IX of the Criminal Code. For example, in terms of Section 171,any agent who, in connection with his principal's affairs or business uses a document which contains a false statement knowingly and with the intention to deceive his or her principal is guilty of corruptly using a false document. In terms of Section 172, any agent who, having carried out any transaction in connection with his or her principal's affairs, fails to disclose to the principal the full nature of the transaction knowingly and with the intention to deceive the principal is guilty of corruptly concealing a transaction from a principle.

Section 174 also criminalises the abuse of duty as a public officer. This is when a public officer, in the exercise of his or her functions as such, intentionally does anything that is contrary to or inconsistent with his or her duty as a public officer, or omits to do anything which it is his or her duty as a public officer to do for the purposes of showing favour or disfavour to any person.

b) Prevention of Corruption Act [Chapter 9:16]

The purpose of the Prevention of Corruption Act [Chapter 9:16]is to provide for the prevention of corruption and the investigation of any claims regarding dishonesty or corruption and related issues. Section 6 of the Act empowers the Minister of Justice, Legal & Parliamentary Affairs or any Minister so designated by the President, to identify persons who are suspected of engaging in corrupt acts. Section 6 stipulates that where the Minister, on reasonable grounds, suspects that any person has accepted a benefit or advantage in contravention of the Prevention of Corruption Act or Chapter IX of the Criminal Code, he or shemay declare that person to be a specified person and direct that an investigation be conducted into that person's affairs. Section 7 empowers the Minister to appoint investigators to conduct the same and may limit transactions with respect to a specified person.

Section 10 prohibits a specified person from undertaking certain acts without the approval of an investigator assigned to that specified person. These acts include:

(i) expending or in any way disposing of property; or
(ii) entering into any contract for the disposal of any property; or
(iii) operating any account with any bank or financial institution; or
(iv) increasing his indebtedness or adversely affecting his estate; or
(v) performing any acts as a director of a company or as partner in a partnership; or
(vi) performing any act as an agent of a company or partnership that is also a specified person.

b. Departments Supervising Anti-commercial Bribery

a) Anti-Corruption Commission

Section 254 of the Constitution establishes the Zimbabwe Anti-Corruption Commission which is empowered to investigate and expose cases of corruption in the public and private sectors, combat corruption, theft, abuse of power and any improper conduct in the public and private sectors such as bribery (Section 255). The Anti-Corruption Commission is mandated to receive and consider complaints from the public and take such action in regard to the complaints as it deems necessary. The Anti-Corruption Commission is empowered by the Anti-Corruption Commission Act [Chapter 9:22]. Section 3 of the Act sets out that the Commission is a body corporate, capable of suing and being sued in its own name.

b) The Police Service

In terms of the Constitution, the Police Service is responsible for detecting, investigating and preventing crime. Section 219 (2) requires the Police Service to exercise its functions in co-operation with any body which may be established by law for the purposes of detecting, investigating and preventing particular classes of offences, such as the Anti-Corruption Commission. The Anti-Corruption Commission works together with the Police Service in the conduct of its mandate to investigate and expose cases of corruption.

In terms of Section 255(e), the Anti-Corruption Commission is mandated to direct the Commissioner General of the Police to investigate cases of suspected corruption and report to the Anti-Corruption Commission on the results of any such investigation. The Police Service is also required to carry out its own investigations and arrests in the enforcement of the bribery and corruption laws arising from Chapter IX of the Criminal Code.

c) National Prosecuting Authority

In terms of Section 258 of the Constitution, the National Prosecuting Authority is responsible for instituting and undertaking criminal prosecutions on behalf of the State and discharging any functions that are necessary or incidental to such prosecutions. Both the Police Services and the Anti-Corruption Commission are required to refer corruption and bribery matters to the National Prosecuting Authority for prosecution. Section 12 of the Anti-Corruption Commission Act sets out that in the event of any conflict arising between the Police Services and the Anti-Corruption Commission in the exercise of their concurrent powers, Prosecutor-General, shall have the power to intervene and direct the parties to do anything that in his or her opinion must be done to resolve the conflict.

c. Punitive Actions

In accordance with Section 170 of the Criminal Code which stipulates that bribery is a crime, the penalty for committing the same isa fine not exceeding level fourteen (currently US$5 000.00) or not exceeding three times the value of any consideration obtained or given in the course of the crime, whichever is the greater, or imprisonment for a period not exceeding twenty years or both the fine and imprisonment.

Section 171 of the Criminal Codewhich criminalizes corruptly using a false document stipulates that the penalty of such a crime is a fine up to or exceeding level fourteen or imprisonment for period not exceeding 20 years or both. Section 172 which criminalizes corruptly concealing a transaction from a principal stipulates that the penalty of such a crime is a fine up to or exceeding level fourteen or imprisonment for period not exceeding 20 years or both. Section 174 in respect of abuse of office, the penalty is a fine up to or exceeding level thirteen or imprisonment for period not exceeding fifteen years or both.

The Money Laundering and Proceeds of Crime Act [Chapter 9:24] allows for the confiscation of goods or funds used in the commission of a crime.

B. Project Contracting

a. Permission System

Prior to operating in Zimbabwe, it is necessary for a company to obtain permission from various regulatory bodies. Depending on the nature of the project, and the form in which it is implemented, different laws will apply.

Projects that are implemented through a Joint Venture Agreement between a contracting authority (any Ministry, Government department or public entity which has entered into or is considering entering into a joint venture agreement) and a private company are regulated by the Joint Ventures Act [Chapter 22:22].

Specifically, the Joint Ventures Act regulates projects under which an investor or developer undertakes to perform a contracting authority's function on behalf of the contracting authority for a specified period and receives a benefit for performing the function by any of the following ways: compensation from funds appropriated by Parliament, funds obtained by way of loan by the contracting authority, user levies, revenue generated from the project or any combination thereof (Section 2(2) of the Act). Additionally, the counterparty is liable for the risks arising from the performance of its function and public resources may be transferred or made available to the counterparty.

Section 3 of the Joint Ventures Act establishes the Joint Venture Unit, whose responsibility it is to consider project proposals submitted to it and assess whether or not they are affordable to the contracting authority, they provide value for money, they provide for the optimum transfer of technical, operational and financial risks to the counterparty and they are competitive. The Unit makes recommendations on the project proposals to the to the Joint Venture Committee whose functions include ensuring that all projects are consistent with the national priorities specified in the relevant policy on joint ventures and to make recommendations to Cabinet as to whether to approve or reject project proposals submitted to it by the Unit (Section 4 of the Act).

Under Section 8 of the Act, a contracting authority wishing to enter into a joint venture invites expressions of interest in the project by means of a public advertisement unless it has already identified a proposed project with an identified counterparty and has disclosed that fact to the Joint Venture Unit. After feasibility study is undertaken, it is submitted to the Joint Venture Unit. If it approves the feasibility study, it prepares a request for the project proposal and a model agreement on the basis of the approved feasibility study. The Unit will then refer the project proposal to the Committee which shall make recommendations thereon to the Cabinet.

The Joint Ventures Act provides inter alia for other technical aspects relating with to the joint venture contract, governing law, dispute resolution, feasibility studies, tenders, unsolicited bids, types of joint venture projects and types of joint venture agreements. Investors must seek comprehensive legal and technical advice pertaining to the specific project that they seek to embark on.

Any investment which would result in the acquisition of shares or securities by a foreign entity, or which would create an obligation for payment to be made outside of Zimbabwe, requires Exchange Control approval in terms of Parts IV and V of the Exchange Control Act[Chapter 22:05]. Applications for Exchange Control approval are made through authorised dealers (registered commercial banks) to the Exchange Control Authority (being the Minister of Finance or the Reserve Bank of Zimbabwe).

In addition, investors into Zimbabwe may obtain an investment license issued by the Zimbabwe Investment Authority (ZIA) in terms of the Zimbabwe Investment Authority Act[Chapter 14:30]. Section 9 of the Zimbabwe Investment Authority Act regulates applications for investments licences and requires foreign investors to submit applications to the Zimbabwe Investment Authority in the prescribed form together with the prescribed fee, if any, and such documents as the Authority may require.

In terms of Section 14 of the Zimbabwe Investment Authority Act, factors considered in approval of an investment licence include; the extent to which skills and technology will be transferred for the benefit of Zimbabwe and its people; the extent to which the proposed investment will lead to the creation of employment opportunities and the development of human resources; the extent to which local raw materials will be utilised and beneficiated; the value of the convertible foreign currency transferred to Zimbabwe in connection with the project; the impact the proposed investment is likely to have on the environment and on existing industries in the local economy.

ZIA will also specify the period of validity of investment licence which must be renewed before it expires. If the investor fails to implement the investment, he or she must notify ZIA stating the reasons thereof, within 30 days of his or her becoming aware of the non-implementation of the investment. The licence in not transferable without prior approval of the Authority.

Whilst an investment licence is not a mandatory requirement, the Zimbabwe Investment Authority Act provides that the Minister of Industry and International Trade may publish incentives for holders of Investment Licences (section 24), which may include incentives relating to tax, or access to tenders by Governmental entities.

b. Prohibited Areas

There are no expressly prohibited investment areas for foreign companies and foreign investors however Section 25 of the Zimbabwe Investment Authority Act provides that the Minister may prescribe sectors for investment and may by notice in a statutory instrument specify the sectors of the economy available for investment by domestic and foreign investors; specify the sectors of the economy reserved exclusively for domestic investors for the purpose of promoting equitable participation in the economy by domestic investors; prohibit the export of specified raw materials, prescribe the manner in or extent to which any raw materials shall be beneficiated before export; and prescribe the degree of export orientation of investment proposals submitted by applicants for investment licences. It is advisable for investors to obtain comprehensive advice on the permits required for investing and operating in Zimbabwe, and the limitations thereof prior to project contracting.

Further limitations are prescribed by the Indigenisation & Economic Empowerment Act [Chapter 14:33] whichwas promulgated topromote empowerment of indigenous Zimbabweans. The Actrequires that any company with an annual turnover or which owns assets amounting to US$1 200 000.00, must have a minimum of 51% of its shares owned by indigenous Zimbabweans. Details of business sectors that are exempted are found in the Act as amended from time to time. The Government can specifically implement the Act for the benefit of indigenous Zimbabwean women, young persons under a prescribed age and disabled persons as defined in the Disabled Persons Act [Chapter 17:01]. The Minister of State for Indigenisation and Economic Empowerment may prescribe that compliance with the Indigenisation & Economic Empowerment Act can be achieved through a lesser share than 51% or a lesser interest than a controlling interest and afford extended time periods for such compliance.

In accordance with Section 3 of theIndigenisation and Economic Empowerment (General) Regulations, Statutory Instrument 21 of 2010, within 5 years of commencing business, a company falling within the threshold set out above, must submit an indigenisation implementation plan for approval by the Minister of State for Indigenisation and Economic Empowerment. The Minister is required to approve or reject the plan within 45 days. of having received the same. If no written response is received within 90 days, the plan is deemed approved. Under Section 3(6) of the Indigenisation and Economic Empowerment Act, Line Ministers may also consider indigenisation implementation plans and carry out indigenisation and economic empowerment ratings of businesses. In addition, under Government Notice (GN 9/2016), published in January 2016, provision was also made for indigenisation plans to be considered by ZIA in conjunction with an application for an Investment Licence, in consultation with Line Ministers and the National Indigenisation and Economic Empowerment Board (NIEEB).

At the written request of the business, the Minister will issue a certificate of compliance which must also be transmitted to the National Indigenisation and Economic Empowerment Board for inclusion in the prescribed register [Section 3(8) of the Act]. The Minister may issue a provisional certificate to the business in question instead of a final one if the business undertakes or is required to comply with any specified conditions, upon the fulfilment of which the line Minister shall issue a final certificate.

In December 2017, during the Budget Speech, the Government announced its plans to amend the Indigenisation & Economic Empowerment Act bypurging the local ownership requirement for foreign investment into the country, with the exception of the diamond and platinum sectors. The draft Finance Act of 2018, published as a Bill on 19 January 2018, set out the proposed amendments. However, as at the date of writing, the Bill has not been tabled before Parliament and does not have force of law.

c. Project Contracting

a) Invitation to Bid and Bidding for Government Projects

The procurement of goods and services by procuring entities (namely State Ministries, statutory bodies, companies in which the State has a controlling interest, rural or local councils, and partnerships and Joint Ventures between the State and any person), is dealt with in terms of the Public Procurement and Disposal of State Assets Act [Chapter 22:23] ("the Act").

The procurement provisions laid down in the Act are governed by the Procurement Regulatory Authority of Zimbabwe. The Authority was established in terms of Section 5 of the Act. The duties of the Authority as set out in Section 6 of the Act include, amongst others:

(i) to ensure that public procurement is effected in a manner that is transparent, fair, honest, cost-effective, competitive and in compliance with the Act;

(ii) to monitor and supervise procuring entities and the public procurement system in order to secure compliance with the Act, and to implement electronic means of monitoring and supervising procuring entities and the public procurement system;

(iii) to issue technical guidelines and instructions regarding the interpretation and implementation of the Act;

(iv) to prepare standard documents and templates to be used in connection with public procurement and to enable procuring entities to maintain records and prepare reports;

(v) on request, to give advice and assistance to procuring entities.

b) Method of Bidding

In terms of Section 30 (1) of the Act, a competitive bidding method must be applied in all instances, subject to certain exceptions described below. In an instance where competitive bidding is not applied, a written justification by the acquiring authority is required.

In terms of Section 38 of the Act, in a competitive bidding process, a bidding document is published once in the government gazette and in a newspaper with nationwide circulation in Zimbabwe. All eligible and qualified bidders are permitted without discrimination to submit their bids and assessment is carried out using the same criteria for all bidders.

The bidding document should contain the following:

(i) the identity and address of the procuring entity;

(ii) a description of the procurement, including the place of delivery of goods or services, the location of any construction works and the time within which the procurement requirement is to be provided;

(ii) how the bidding documents or, if applicable, the prequalification documents may be obtained and the price, if any, payable for them; and

(iv) the place at which and the time within which bids or applications to prequalify must be submitted.

c) Where Competitive Bidding May not be Applied

The instances where the competitive bidding method will not be applied are covered under Sections 32–34 of the Act where the following methods are preferred:

(i) The restricted bidding method, in terms of Section 32 of the Act.

• the time and cost of considering a large number of bids is disproportionate to the estimated value of the procurement requirement; or

• where urgency renders impracticable the prescribed time limit; and

• the contract has an estimated value that does not exceed the prescribed threshold.

(ii) The direct procurement method, in terms of Section 33 of the Act.

This is where a procuring entity procures its requirement from one bidder or supplier without having received bids from other bidders. This method is applied in the following instances:

• no responsive bids have been submitted in response to a competitive bidding procedure;

• where, for technical or artistic reasons, or for reasons connected with protection of exclusive rights, the contract can be performed only by a particular supplier and no reasonable alternative or substitute exists;

• where, for reasons of extreme urgency not attributable to and unforeseen by the procuring entity, the procurement requirement cannot be obtained in time by means of competitive bidding procedures;

(iv) where a procuring entity procures a prototype or a first product or service from aresearch institute which is then developed at its request for a particular procurement contract for research, experiment, study or original development.

d) The Request for Quotations, in Terms of Section 34 of the Act.

This is a process in which the procuring entity solicits at least three competitive quotations for its procurement requirement from reputable suppliers, and the procurement requirement is below the prescribed threshold.

Criteria to be met by bidders

Bidders are generally permitted to participate in the bidding for government projects without restriction as to nationality, subject to specific restrictions that may be imposed from time to time. In terms of Section 38(e) of the Act, each bidding document contains unique requirements that must be met by each bidder, certain criteria are required to be met by any bidders that bid for any government contract. In terms of Section 28(2) of the Act, such criteria are as follows:

• that they meet specified ethical standards;

• that they have the legal capacity to enter into the procurement contract;

• that they are not insolvent, in liquidation or under judicial management or their affairs are not being administered by a court or a judicial officer;

• that neither they nor any of their officers have, in the five years immediately preceding the initiation of the procurement proceedings been convicted in any country of an offence related to their professional conduct or the making of false statements or misrepresentations as to their qualifications;

• any other criteria that will demonstrate that the bidders possess the professional and technical qualifications and competence, financial resources, equipment and other physical facilities, managerial capability, experience, business reputation and personnel, needed to perform the procurement contract.

The acquiring authority is permitted to prefer a Zimbabwean bidder so long as such preference is clearly stated in the invitation to bid. The Authority is required to accept the tender with the lowest price, unless other criteria are specified in the solicitation documents.

e) Registration as a Bidder or Contractor

In terms of Section 4 of the Public Procurement and Disposal of Public Assets (General) Regulations, Statutory Instrument 5 of 2018 a prospective bidder or contractor may register on a database maintained by the Procurement Authority. The authority invites prospective bidders and contractors to register as such through publication in the Government Gazette, in national newspapers and on its website.

In terms of Section 4(4) of the same Regulations an application for inclusion on the list of registered bidders and contractors must contain the following:

• in the case of a company, the memorandum and articles of association or other constitutive document of the company, together with its certificate of incorporation, list of directors, head office and local physical address and particulars showing the relative extent of Zimbabwean and foreign shareholding of the company;

• in the case of a partnership, syndicate or other business entity, the partnership agreement or other constitutive document of the partnership, syndicate or entity, together with the list of partners or controlling members or managers, head office and local physical address and particulars showing the relative extent of Zimbabwean and foreign control of the partnership, syndicate or entity;

• in the case of an individual, a detailed curriculum vitae, and proof of qualifications.

Any bidder or contractor registered as such shall have the right to participate in and bid for any tender flighted by the government in terms of Section 28 of the Act.

附录
APPENDIX

黎巴嫩——撰稿人介绍 / Lebanon—Introduction to Authors

律所介绍 / Introduction to Law Firms

Badri and Salim El Meouchi 律师事务所

Badri and Salim El Meouchi 律师事务所于19世纪90年代在贝鲁特成立,为来自世界各地的客户服务。位于黎巴嫩和卡塔尔的律师事务所办事处向整个中东和北非地区提供法律服务。

该律所参与过一些复杂、广泛的交易。团队由大约40名精通普通法、民法和伊斯兰教法的法律专业人士组成。该律所经常为跨国公司提供"一站式"服务,为其在当地和跨司法管辖区的事务提供高价值、经济有效的全套法律解决方案。

The firm was founded in Beirut in the 1890s, and represents clients from all over the world, providing legal services throughout the MENA region, from its offices in Lebanon and Qatar.

The firm is involved in some of the complex, wide-ranging transactions. The team of around 40 legal professionals, is well versed in common law, civil law and Sharia'a (Islamic) law. The firm frequently acts for multinational companies as a "one-stop shop", providing high value, cost-effective turnkey legal solutions for local and multi-jurisdictional matters.

律师介绍 / Introduction to Lawyers

Chadia El Meouchi

Chadia 是律所的执行合伙人,她一直是公认的顶级公司和商业律师。她是纽约律师协会会员,且在北美和中东地区执业17年以上,并为客户提供包括并购、银行和金融、基金设立、资本市场、构建和重组、石油和天然气及项目融资在内的众多领域的咨询服务。

Chadia is the Managing Partner of the firm and has been consistently recognised as a leading corporate and commercial lawyer. She is member of the New York Bar and has practiced law in North America and the Middle East for over 17 years and advises clients in a large number of fields, including mergers and acquisitions, banking and finance, establishment of funds, capital markets, structuring and restructuring, oil and gas and project finance.

Carine Farran

Carine 是资深律师及交易实践小组的主管。她是魁北克律师协会的成员,曾在加拿大蒙特利尔的顶级律师事务所工作。她主要为客户提供银行和金融、石油和天然气、私人融资、商业事务、股东关系、跨境交易领域的咨询服务。

Carine is a senior associate and the director the transactional practice group. She is a member of the Quebec Bar and worked in leading law firms in Montreal, Canada. She advises clients in mainly the fields of banking and finance, oil and gas, private financing, commercial matters, shareholders relationships, cross-border transactions.

黎巴嫩——翻译及协调人介绍 / Lebanon–Introduction to Translators and Cooperators

律所介绍 / Introduction to Law Firms

广东卓信律师事务所

广东卓信律师事务所是中国华南地区大型综合性律师事务所之一，于1999年在中国广州成立，经多年发展，在业内声誉日隆，在全国聘有超过80名律师和专业人士为中外各类公司企业、政府机构和个人提供全方位的法律服务。卓信的服务领域包括公司法、民商法、并购、外商投资、国际贸易、房地产、劳动法、知识产权、家事法、政府采购、刑法、诉讼和仲裁等。

卓信先后被广州市司法局及广东省律师协会评为"广州市十佳律师事务所"和"2012—2016年度全省优秀律师事务所"，并入围《亚洲法律杂志》2017年及2018年汤森路透ALB中国法律大奖——"年度最佳中国南部律师事务所大奖"。

Zhuoxin Law Firm is one of the larger-scale comprehensive law firms in South China. Since its establishment in 1999 in Guangzhou, Zhuoxin has been gradually building recognition and renown in the legal field through years of development. With more than 80 lawyers and experts, Zhuoxin provides services in the various areas, such as corporate and commercial, mergers & acquisitions, foreign direct investment, international trade, real estate, employment and labor, intellectual property, family law, government contracts, criminal law, litigation and alternative dispute resolution, etc.

Zhuoxin was listed by Guangzhou Justice Bureau and Guangdong Lawyer Association as "Top 10 Law Firms in Guangdong Province" and "Elite Law Firm from the year 2012 to 2016" respectively. Furthermore, in 2017 and 2018, Zhuoxin was listed as the finalist of "China South Law Firm of the Year" for SQ Thomson Reuters ALB China Law Awards.

律师介绍 / Introduction to Lawyers

陈健斌

陈健斌律师自1994年中山大学法律系毕业后即进入律师行业，至今已执业超过20年，并有在英国、美国及西班牙留学及工作的经历。他的执业领域集中在外商直接投资、兼并与收购、对外投资、涉外重组、破产及清算、涉外诉讼及仲裁。陈律师先后于2016年及2017年入选国际知名法律媒体《商法》年度"法律精英100强"，并于2017年入选国际知名法律媒体汤森路透ALB"2017客户首选20强律师"。

Ever since Chen Jianbin graduated from Sun Yat-sen University with Bachelor of Law in 1994, Mr. Chen has endeavored in practice of law for more than 20 years, and has worked and studied in countries such as the UK, the US and Spain. He specializes in various areas, including FDI, M&A, outbound investment, foreign related restructuring, cross-border liquidation and foreign related litigation and arbitration. Mr.Chen has been selected as "China's Top 100 Lawyers" by China Business Law Journal in 2016 and 2017 respectively, and was also selected as "Top 20 Client Choice lawyer" by SSQ Thomson Reuters ALB in 2017.

律所介绍 / Introduction to Law Firms

北京高文律师事务所

北京高文律师事务所成立于2001年，在中国境内和境外设立有3家分所（上海、大连、合肥），17个办事处，总计拥有200余名律师、专家顾问和律师辅助人员。

高文致力于将专业分工与团队合作紧密结合。高文分设知识产权、公司、诉讼仲裁、刑事辩护、海事海商、银行与国际金融、房地产与建设工程、劳动与人力资源等专业部门，保证了高文律师在相关领域的专业化水平。同时，高文还秉承团队化工作模式，根据项目涉及的专业领域整合专家律师团队共同承办，并为客户提供极具专业性和建设性的解决方案。

高文代理了大量的有广泛社会影响的案例，其中多起案件荣获"最高法院十大案例""最高人民法院中国知识产权50典型案例""北京市十大外商知识产权保护案""北京市知识产权十大案例""国家知识产权局专利复审委十大案件"。

Beijing Globe-Law Law Firm was established in 2001. Headquartered in Beijing, Globe-Law now has branches in Shanghai, Dalian, and Hefei, along with its 17 offices worldwide. Globe-Law is now home to nearly 200 experienced lawyers and paralegals.

In providing services to clients, Globe-Law are firmly committed to the principle and spirit of specialization and teamwork. Globe-Law divide our team into several departments, including intellectual property, corporate, litigation and arbitration, criminal defense, maritime, banking and international finance, real estate and construction, labor and human resources, etc. Globe-Law will assign the case to a working team of professionals from various departments, optimizing personnel resources in order to provide the most professional, efficient, and quality legal service to meet our clients' needs.

Globe-Law's lawyers have resoundingly handled a number of cases with enormous social impact, including cases that marked as Top Ten Cases of The Supreme Court of China, 50 Typical Cases of IPR Infringement From The Supreme People's Court of China, Top Ten Cases of IPR Infringement In Beijing, Top Ten Cases of Patent Re-examination Board of SIPO, Top Ten Cases of IPR Infringement for Foreign Investors In Beijing, etc.

律师介绍 / Introduction to Lawyers

茆宇

茆宇，北京高文（合肥）律师事务所合伙人，曾赴新西兰交流学习。

茆宇律师执业达 20 年以上。早期以建设工程、房地产开发领域法律服务为主；目前以涉外、基金法律服务领域为主。

茆宇律师是中华全国律师协会涉外律师领军人才库成员，其选择的专业方向为跨境并购。

Yu Mao, as a partner of Beijing Globe-law(hefei) Law firm, has studied and communicated in the legal field of New Zealand.

The lawyer has been practicing for more than 20 years. In his early career, Mostly concentrated on field of construction and real estate; While at present, he is skilled on field of foreign related businesses and fund law.

Yu Mao, is one of the member of CILPA(China international legal professionals),and his professional field is about cross-border mergers and acquisitions.

立陶宛——撰稿人介绍 / Lithuania—Introduction to Authors

律所介绍 / Introduction to Law Firms

TGS Baltic 律师事务所

TGS Baltic 是波罗的海国家（立陶宛、拉脱维亚和爱沙尼亚）领先的提供全方位商业服务的律师事务所，目前在维尔纽斯（立陶宛）、里加（拉脱维亚）、塔林和塔尔图（爱沙尼亚）有 4 个办事处共 135 余名律师。自 20 世纪 90 年代初波罗的海国家恢复市场经济以来，TGS 专家一直为国际和国内客户提供咨询服务。该律所的专家律师拥有丰富的服务国内和国际业务以及政府部门的经验，与欧洲中央银行、欧洲投资银行、欧盟机构合作，并与顶级国际律师事务所协作。TGS Baltic 参与了几乎所有在波罗的海国家重新获得独立后完成的主要交易。该律所目前正在参与波罗的海地区最重要的战略能源和基础设施、企业和诉讼项目。TGS Baltic 在全球知名的法律评级机构中如钱伯斯欧洲、钱伯斯全球、Legal 500 以及 IFLR1000 持续高居榜首。

TGS Baltic 的使命不仅是成为该地区最好的法律专家，还要利用专业知识、经验和技能来支持其客户的业务或项目。越来越多的客户不断选择 TGS Baltic 来处理一些必须具有国际经验、提供过顶级法律服务并使客户信任的律所才能处理案件。TGS Baltic 与白俄罗斯 Vlasova Mikhel & Partners 律师事务所进行战略合作。此外，TGS Baltic 是国际律师网络（ILN）、TerraLex 全球网络以及欧洲律师协会（AEL）的独家成员。

TGS Baltic is a leading full-service commercial law firm in the Baltic States (Lithuania, Latvia, and Estonia) currently employing more than 135 lawyers in four offices in Vilnius (Lithuania), Riga (Latvia), Tallinn and Tartu (Estonia). TGS Baltic's experts have been advising international and domestic clients since the Baltic countries returned to a market economy in the early 1990s. The firm's experts have rich experience mix of serving local and international businesses, the public sector, working with the European Central Bank, the European Investment Bank, European Union institutions, collaborating with top-tier international law firms. TGS Baltic has been involved in almost all the major transactions that were completed in the Baltic States since they regained independence. The Firm is currently involved in the most important strategic energy and infrastructure, corporate and litigation projects in the Baltics. TGS Baltic is continuously highly ranked in prestigious international legal directories: Chambers Europe, Chambers Global, Legal 500, and IFLR1000.

TGS Baltic's mission is not only to be the best legal experts in the region but also to use the expertise, experience and skills to support the business of its clients. TGS Baltic is continuously selected by an increasing number of clients to handle cases where international experience, confidence and the track record of top-level law services is an absolute requirement. TGS Baltic is in strategic co-operation with law firm Vlasova Mikhel & Partners in Belarus. Furthermore, TGS Baltic is an exclusive member of the International Lawyers Network (ILN), the TerraLex Global Network as well as the Association of European Lawyers (AEL).

律师介绍 / Introduction to Lawyers

Vilius Bernatonis

Vilius Bernatonis 律师是 TGS Baltic 律师事务所的合伙人,同时是该所银行、金融及能源领域的团队负责人。多家全球知名的国际权威法律评级机构如 Legal 500、钱伯斯全球等,高度评价 Vilius Bernatonis 律师在能源、银行和金融、国际争端解决、企业和商业法领域的领先地位。

Vilius 经常担任仲裁员,也常作为代理人参与国内和国际仲裁活动。他因为在主要能源和基础设施项目中提供卓越的法律服务而闻名,主要包括欧盟第三能源一揽子计划的实施、AB Klaipėdos Nafta 液化天然气终端的建设、LitPol Link 和 NordBalt 战略电力跨境互联的实施。他一直参与立陶宛政府与俄罗斯天然气公司之间的一些仲裁争端;目前,Vilius 代表立陶宛政府与 Shearman & Sterling 律师事务所(巴黎办事处)共同合作参与与威立雅集团公司的仲裁。

Mr. Vilius Bernatonis is a Partner at TGS Baltic and the Head of Banking & Finance and Energy practice groups. The most authoritative and reputed international legal directories, like Legal 500, Chambers Global, etc., highly rank Vilius Bernatonis in energy, banking and finance, international dispute resolution, corporate, and commercial law. Vilius frequently acts as an arbitrator, also as a representative of parties in domestic and international arbitration proceedings. He is known for rendering exceptional legal services in major energy and infrastructure projects, inter alia, implementation of the EU Third Energy Package, construction of the LNG terminal by AB Klaipėdos Nafta, implementation of strategic electricity cross-border interconnections LitPol Link and NordBalt. He has been involved in a number of arbitration disputes between the Government of Lithuania and OAO Gazprom; currently Vilius represents the Lithuanian Government, in co-counsel with law firm Shearman & Sterling (Paris office), in the arbitration dispute against Veolia group companies.

Donatas Šliora

Donatas Šliora 先生是金融律师。他擅长银行金融、项目融资、航空和保险业务,他在金融和能源领域的重大国际仲裁方面经验丰富。Donatas 与当地和国际主要客户合作,就融资和航空交易以及金融机构提供有关电子货币、支付服务、P2P 借贷和众筹平台、加密货币等监管事宜的咨询。Donatas 最近的项目包括代表欧洲投资银行执行金融工程工具,担任 Valeant Pharmaceuticals International 的当地律师,负责重组现有的融资方案,包括定期贷款、循环贷款和附注,该方案融资额达 300 亿美元以上。Donatas 出版数篇文章,也是欧盟范围内关于适用保险合同法律的研究报告的合著者。

Mr. Donatas Šliora is a Banking & Finance lawyer. He specializes in banking and finance, project finance, aviation and insurance, he also has experience in major international arbitration cases in finance and energy sectors. Donatas works with major local and international clients advising on, inter alia, financing and aviation transactions, as well as financial institutions on regulatory matters pertaining to e-money, payment services, P2P lending and crowdfunding platforms, cryptocurrencies. Donatas' recent projects include representing the European Investment Bank on implementation of financial engineering instruments, acting as local counsel to Valeant Pharmaceuticals International in relation to restructuring the existing financing scheme consisting of term loans, revolving loans and notes pursuant to which financing in excess of USD 30 billion was received. Donatas is the author of a number of publications, as well as a co-author of the EU-wide study on the law applicable to insurance contracts.

律所介绍 / Introduction to Law Firms

Eversheds Saladžius 律师事务所

Eversheds Saladžius 律师事务所是 Eversheds Saladžius 国际的会员,是立陶宛同等规模律所中唯一的国际律师事务所。

Eversheds Saladžius 国际及其世界各地的办公室拥有超过 4000 名员工,在 32 个司法管辖区设置了 66 个国际办公室,涵盖欧洲中部、东部及西部,美国,中东的 7 个办公室及非洲的 7 个办公室(与 Eversheds Saladžius 非洲法律协会中 37 个律所网络紧密协作),属欧洲大陆律所之最,且在香港、新加坡、上海和北京也设有办公室。

Eversheds Saladžius 专注于商法的各个方面,并致力于为客户提供商业实践中高质量且积极的法律意见,提供值得期待的全套法律解决方案。

Eversheds Saladžius 主要从事商事法律服务,拥有以商业为导向的创新型执业者,在商法各个领域开展业务,包括银行与金融、公司与商法、公司重组、能源与基础设施项目、信息技术、知识产权、劳动法、争议解决、房地产及欧盟法律。

Eversheds Saladžius is a member firm of Eversheds International. Eversheds is the only international law firm of such size in Lithuania.

Eversheds Sutherland International and its worldwide offices have over 4,000 people providing services to the private and public sector business and finance community. Access to all these services is provided through 66 international offices in 32 jurisdictions. These include strategic locations across Central, Eastern and Western Europe; the United States; seven offices in the Middle East and seven offices in Africa working closely with a network of 37 firms in the Eversheds Africa Law Institute – the largest presence of any law firm on the continent. Eversheds also has operations in Hong Kong, Singapore, Shanghai and Beijing.

Law firm Eversheds Saladžius focuses on all aspects of business law. We are committed to providing clients with high quality, proactive legal advice in a practical and commercial context - advice that anticipates, challenges and provides complete legal solutions.

Eversheds Saladžius in Lithuania comprises business-oriented and innovative legal practitioners, practicing in all areas of business law, including banking and financial services, corporate and commercial law, corporate restructuring, energy and infrastructure projects, information technology, intellectual property, employment law, dispute resolution, real estate and EU law.

The law firm Eversheds Saladžius provides professional legal assistance to businesses and financiers, as well as governmental and state-owned entities in Lithuania. The Lithuanian and international clients of the law firm represent various industries such as financial services, industry, wholesale and retail trade, gas & oil, energy, real estate and construction, transport, telecommunications, information technology, pharmaceuticals and light industry.

律师介绍 / Introduction to Lawyers

Jonas Saladžius

Jonas Saladžius 是 Eversheds Saladžius 律所的管理合伙人，同时也是 Eversheds Sutherland 的董事会成员。Jonas 以优异的成绩取得了牛津大学工商管理学硕士学位，并在维尔纽斯大学获得法学硕士学位。Jonas 是立陶宛律师协会的理事会成员，也是国际法律协会的成员。Jonas 是立陶宛代表团在欧洲律师及法律协会的首席代表，他也在维尔纽斯大学法学院教授金融法。Jonas 曾是 PwC 税务及法律服务的负责人。他发表过许多法律文章、书籍，也经常在各类会议发表演讲。Jonas 专长于公司和商业领域，包括收购兼并、能源、银行与金融法。

Jonas Saladžius is the Managing Partner of law firm Eversheds Saladžius and a member of the Board of Eversheds Sutherland. Jonas obtained the Master of Business Administration degree (distinction) at University of Oxford and the Master of Laws degree at Vilnius University. Jonas is a member of the Council of the Lithuanian Bar Association and member of the International Bar Association. Jonas is a head of the Lithuanian delegation to CCBE (The Council of Bars and Law Societies of Europe). Jonas lectures finance law at Law Faculty of Vilnius University. His previous professional experience includes being Head of Tax and Legal Services of PwC. Jonas is an author of various legal articles and books and regularly delivers speeches at various conferences. Jonas specialises in corporate & commercial, including M&A, energy, banking and finance law.

Neringa Bubnaitytė

Neringa Bubnaitytė 是 Eversheds Saladžius 律所的高级律师，专门从事公司、商业、知识产权以及雇佣相关的法律，同时也着重研究能源、房地产以及其他基础设施建设方面相关法律。在其从事法律实践的 8 年内，她在国内及国际交易，特别是兼并和收购方面获得了广泛的经验和知识。在 2010 年加入 Eversheds Saladžius 之前，Neringa 曾在全球领先的国内及美国公司和公共机关任职。Neringa 是立陶宛律师协会以及立陶宛律师资格协会的成员。她在维尔纽斯大学获得了英语学学士学位及法律硕士学位。

Neringa Bubnaitytė is a Senior Associate at law firm Eversheds Saladžius and specialises in corporate, commercial, intellectual property, and employment law, with an increasing focus on energy, real estate and other infrastructure development sectors. During 8 years of legal practice, she acquired extensive experience and knowledge in local and international transactions, in particular in mergers and acquisitions. Prior to joining Eversheds Saladžius in 2010, Neringa worked for leading global corporations and public authorities both locally and in the U.S.A. Neringa is a member of the Lithuanian Bar Association and the Lithuanian Lawyers' Association. Neringa holds the Master of Laws degree from Vilnius University as well as a Bachelor's degree in English philology from the same university.

立陶宛——翻译及协调人介绍 / Lithuania—Introduction to Translators and Cooperators

律所介绍 / Introduction to Law Firms

金诚同达律师事务所

北京金诚同达律师事务所创立于 1992 年年底。今天，金诚同达已发展成为中国境内规模最大、最富活力的律师事务所之一。在诸多业务领域，金诚同达都已成为行业的领先者。各地区的分所与北京总所紧密合作，形成覆盖全国的网络，为客户提供广泛的法律服务，从公司、证券、金融、房地产、项目融资、基础建设、资产管理、保险、并购、税务、知识产权、反垄断、劳动法到外商投资、国际贸易、WTO 争端解决、商事仲裁诉讼等。金诚同达的客户包括政府部门、大型跨国公司、中央企业、国内外金融机构、保险公司、对冲基金、私募基金、风险投资基金、房地产企业、基础设施开发商、制造商、IT公司、高新技术产业、传媒娱乐业等。

多年来，金诚同达以其在中国各类法律事务中的各个领域内能够提供客户化的、综合战略性的和专业性的法律咨询服务而赢得客户的赞誉。

JT&N is widely recognized as one of the leading full-service law firms in China and Asia as a whole, with deep expertise across a broad spectrum of practice areas. Founded in 1992, JT&N has grown to become one of the largest and most respected law firms in China, with more than 450 highly qualified and talented attorneys in eight offices located in key urban centers across the country. The legal team is versatile and possesses excellent foreign language capabilities, ensuring that it is able to communicate and process cross-border transactions with fluency and skill. At JT&N, its mission is to provide tailored legal services that fully satisfy its clients' requirements, and to deliver our services efficiently, economically, and with the highest standard of performance.

Its reputation for excellence is substantiated by its extensive and prominent client base. It is honored to represent many leading international and domestic companies, including large and medium-sized state owned enterprises, publicly listed companies and private enterprises, multinational corporations, financial institutions, investment funds, as well as government authorities and many other organizations and individuals in need of legal services. Its clients conduct business in every major economic sector and, from years of experience, it has accrued deep insight into many industries and business models. Today, JT&N is uniquely prepared to understand and anticipate a clients' commercial interests, relevant legal requirements and help to reliably ensure efficient delivery of the highest quality legal services. For more than twenty years, JT&N has been continuously dedicated to providing legal services of the highest caliber to each of its many and varied clients, and it will continue to do so for many more years to come.

律师介绍 / Introduction to Lawyers

张云燕

张云燕律师是北京金诚同达律师事务所高级合伙人，合肥分所执行主任，全国青联委员，安徽省政协常委。曾入选中国律师排行榜100强，获得"安徽省优秀律师"称号。因个人涉外法律服务业绩突出，被司法部授予"律师个人三等功"，获得China Law and Practice 2017年"中国最佳争议解决"律师提名。

教育背景：中国社科院，金融博士（在读）；中国科技大学，高级工商管理硕士；安徽大学，法学硕士；中国政法大学，法律双学位；上海外国语大学，文学学士。

Ms. Zhang Yunyan is a senior partner with Beijing JT&N Law Firm, also the executive partner of its Hefei Office. Some of the social positions she held are: Committee Member, All-China Youth Federation; Committee Member, 10th and 11th Anhui Province Chinese People's Political Consultative Conference, 12th Standing Committee Member of Anhui Province Chinese People's Political Consultative Conference.

She has been selected as the top 100 lawyers in China and won the title of outstanding lawyer in Anhui. Because of her outstanding achievements in foreign-related legal services, she was awarded the Class-Three Merit for Individual Lawyers by the Ministry of Justice, and nominated as "China's Best Dispute Resolution" lawyer by China Law and Practice in 2017.

Academic background: B.A., Shanghai International Studies University; LL.B., China University of Political Science and Law; LL.M., Anhui University; EMBA, University of Science and Technology of China; Ph.D. Candidate (Finance), Chinese Academy of Social Sciences.

律所介绍 / Introduction to Law Firms

中伦律师事务所

中伦律师事务所创立于1993年，是中国司法部最早批准设立的合伙制律师事务所之一。经过数年快速、稳健的发展壮大，中伦已成为中国规模最大的综合性律师事务所之一。如今，中伦拥有290多名合伙人以及超过1900名专业人士，办公室分布在北京、上海、深圳、广州、武汉、成都、重庆、青岛、杭州、南京、东京、香港、伦敦、纽约、洛杉矶及旧金山16个城市，为全球60多个国家和地区提供市场领先和高质量的法律服务。

中伦的合伙人有极强的进取精神，他们投身一线，积极在交易及争议中为客户排忧解难。在过去数年中，受到钱伯斯亚太的行业指南肯定的中伦合伙人人数领先于其他任何一家中国律所。中伦不仅进取，而且还具有通力协作精神。中伦的合伙人结构合理，能够确保案件由案件所在领域内专业的团队接手。中伦的愿景是把中伦建成中国最好的律师事务所并积极投身于中国法治化的进程中。

Founded in 1993, Zhong Lun Law Firm was one of the first private law partnerships to receive approval from the Ministry of Justice. After years of rapid development and steady growth, today Zhong Lun is one of the largest full service law firms in China.

With over 290 partners and over 1900 professionals working in sixteen offices in Beijing, Shanghai, Shenzhen, Guangzhou, Wuhan, Chengdu, Chongqing, Qingdao, Hangzhou, Nanjing, Tokyo, Hong Kong, London, New York, Los Angeles and San Francisco, Zhong Lun is capable of providing clients with high-quality legal services in more than 60 countries across a wide range of industries and sectors through our specialized expertise and close teamwork.

With a strong entrepreneurial spirit, Zhong Lun partners join their clients at the front lines to actively resolve disputes and transactional issues. In recent years, the number of Zhong Lun partners recognized by Chambers Asia-Pacific industry guides has surpassed all other Chinese law firms. We also share a collaborative spirit and are structured to ensure that only the most appropriate professional team takes responsibility for your case. Zhong Lun's vision is to forge Zhong Lun into China's best law firm and to actively participate in the process of promoting the rule of law in China.

律师介绍 / Introduction to Lawyers

王勇

王勇律师是中伦律师事务所的合伙人，在中伦香港和广州办公室执业，具有中国、澳大利亚律师执照及中国香港律师资格，专业领域是"一带一路"境外投资和收购兼并业务。王律师曾协助众多中国企业的海外投资项目，他在处理大型、复杂、涉及多个司法管辖区法律的中国对外收购项目方面拥有特别丰富的实务操作经验，涉及众多行业领域。

Mr. Wayne Wang is a partner of Zhong Lun Law Firm and he practices in Zhong Lun's Hong Kong and Guangzhou offices. He is a dual admitted lawyer in PRC and Australia and he has Hong Kong(China) lawyer qualification. Mr. Wang specializes in "Belt and Road" investment and M&A. He has assisted in many overseas investment projects of PRC enterprises and he has extensive practical experience in dealing with large and complicated Chinese outbound acquisition projects involving multiple jurisdictions and industries.

马其顿——撰稿人介绍 / Macedonia–Introduction to Authors

律所介绍 / Introduction to Law Firms

Trpenoski 律师事务所

Trpenoski 律师事务所在马其顿名声出众，该律所被认为是马其顿近三十年来最好的律所之一。严格的用人标准、特殊的训练以及专业知识帮助 Trpenoski 成为众所周知的律所。

Trpenoski 被列为最专业的律所等级。Trpenoski 的律师服务全球的客户并帮助客户处理最复杂的诉讼、公司事务、重组以及税收与优惠方面的事务。Trpenoski 也在雇佣、投资基金以及资产方面提供顶级的服务。

Trpenoski 律师事务所为银行界的大多数机构提供服务，包括马其顿国家银行（中央银行）等机构。Trpenoski 律所的律师被指定为澳大利亚驻马其顿大使馆的法律顾问。

Law firm Trpenoskiis a stand-out name in the Macedonian market, which has been known as one of the premier law firms for nearly three decades.

The careful selection of employees, special training and professional knowledge helped turn the Law firm Trpenoski into an easily recognizable law firm.

Recognized by those covering the legal profession as best in class, Trpenoski's lawyers regularly advise clients globally on their most complex Litigation, Corporate, Restructuring, and Tax and Benefits matters. It also offers top-tier practices in employment, investment funds and property matters.

Law firm Trpenoski represents most of the banking sector, including National Bank (Central Bank) of Macedonia. Attorneys at law firm Trpenoski are designated legal counsel of Austrian embassy in Macedonia as well.

律师介绍 / Introduction to Lawyers

Bojana Paneva

Bojana Paneva 于 2013 年毕业于查士丁尼第一法学院，并在 2016 年 4 月份取得了民法硕士学位。

2013 年 9 月份以来，她加入 Trpenoski 律师事务所开始职业生涯。

2017 年，她通过了了律师资格考试并成为马其顿律师协会的一员。2017 年 6 月，她正式在 Trpenoski 律师事务所以律师身份执业。

她在民法、公司法以及贸易法领域有丰富经验。

她精通英语并可以说意大利语及法语。

Bojana Paneva graduated in 2013 from the Iustinianus Primus Faculty of Law, in Skopje, Republic of Macedonia and in April 2016 completed her LL.M in Civil law.

Since September 2013 she has professional engagement at the Trpenoski Law Firm.

In 2017, she passed the Bar exam and became a member of the Macedonian Bar Association. She is engaged as an Attorney at law at Trpenoski Law Firm since June 2017.

Her experience and engagement is mainly based in the field of civil, corporate and trade law.

She is highly proficient in English, and also speaks Italian and French language.

律所介绍 / Introduction to Law Firms

Karanović & Nikolić 律师事务所

Karanović & Nikolić 是东南欧领先的国际律师事务所，因律师工作质量和解决问题的商业方法而闻名。因参与了该地区许多较大和较复杂的交易，享有交易和企业/商业法律强所的声誉。团队由跨地区合作的100多名律师组成，可为投资者在众多区域和特定行业提供服务，为众多领先的公司、银行、投资者和政府机构在SEE地区开展业务提供咨询服务。由于其在塞尔维亚有业务机构，并与波斯尼亚和黑塞哥维那、克罗地亚、马其顿、黑山、斯洛文尼亚的律师长期合作，Karanović & Nikolić 的律师在这些司法管辖区内可以无缝工作，为客户提供服务，并能考虑到当地的特殊情况，以便在竞争条件下提供最佳的法律建议。

KKaranović & Nikolić is a leading international legal practice in South East Europe with a team composed of over 100 lawyers who cooperate together across the region. The team offers unrivalled regional and sector specific coverage to investors. It is one of the market leaders because of its dedication, quality legal service, and in-depth understanding of the needs of its clients.

By cooperating with more than 100 lawyers across the region, its original values remain an integral part of its philosophy and approach to client work. Lawyers practising in cooperation with Karanović & Nikolić have been involved in many of the large and complex transactions in the region and they take pride in their reputation as a transactional and corporate/commercial legal powerhouse.

Because they have a business presence in Serbia and a long standing cooperation with attorneys-at-law in Bosnia & Herzegovina, Croatia, Macedonia, Montenegro and Slovenia, lawyers associated with Karanović & Nikolić operate seamlessly across these jurisdictions, providing services to our clients and taking into consideration local particularities in order to provide the best legal advice under competitive terms.

They are practical and highly commercial, understanding that the commercial implications of their advice are often as important as the technical aspects. Renowned for the quality of work of the lawyers on their team and their commercial approach to solving problems, Karanović & Nikolić, in cooperation with qualified attorneys-at-law in each relevant jurisdiction, advises many of the leading companies, banks, investors and government institutions doing business in the SEE region.

律师介绍 / Introduction to Lawyers

Ljupka Noveska Andonova

Ljupka 是一名在马其顿执业的独立律师，与 Karanović & Nikolić 合作。她在银行和金融事务方面经验丰富，能为国内和国际客户提供服务。她还协助完成了一些项目融资和再融资任务以及其他与银行有关的事宜。Ljupka 经常为来自各行各业的客户提供企业和商业、并购、就业和税务建议，尤其是医疗保健和制药行业以及能源和基础设施行业。

Ljupka 毕业于 Ss. Cyril and Methodius 大学，获得最高荣誉，并于2013年在 Ss. Cyril and Methodius 大学以及法国斯特拉斯堡大学国际知识产权研究中心获得知识产权法硕士学位。

Ljupka 是马其顿律师协会、国际律师协会（IBA）成员，以及马其顿青年律师协会（MYLA）管理委员会主席。

Ljupka is an independent attorney at law, practicing in Macedonia in cooperation with Karanović & Nikolić. She is experienced in advising national and international clients on all aspects of banking and finance matters in Macedonia. She has also assisted in several project finance and refinancing mandates and other banking related matters. Ljupka regularly provides corporate and commercial, M&A, employment, and tax advice to clients from various industries, particularly from the sectors healthcare and pharmaceuticals, and energy and infrastructure.

Ljupka graduated with top honours from the University of Ss. Cyril and Methodius and went on to obtain her Master's Degree in intellectual property law in 2013 from the University of Ss. Cyril and Methodius and the Centre for International Intellectual Property

Studies at the University of Strasbourg, France.

Ljupka is a member of the Macedonian Bar Association, International Bar Association (IBA), and the president of the management board of Macedonian Young Lawyers Association (MYLA).

Veton Qoku

Veton Qoku 是一名在马其顿执业的独立律师，与 Karanović & Nikolić 合作。他在公司/商业部门工作，工作地点是马其顿。他的工作重心是大规模并购、能源和基础设施项目及项目融资，特别是在马其顿和阿尔巴尼亚。Veton Qoku 在汽车、电信、能源、采矿、基础设施、房地产、金融和医疗保健等行业经验丰富，能为客户提供良好咨询服务。

Veton Qoku 毕业于 Ss. Cyril and Methodius 大学，获得法学学士学位，并在斯科普里欧洲大学获得了商法硕士学位（LL.M.）。他是马其顿律师协会和国际律师协会的成员，并曾担任马其顿美国商会税务和法律委员会主席。

Veton is an independent attorney at law, practicing in Macedonia in cooperation with Karanović & Nikolić. He is active in the Corporate/Commercial department. Based in Macedonia, his particular focus is on large-scale M&A's, energy and infrastructure projects and project finance, particularly in Macedonia, and Albania. Veton's broad experience includes counselling clients in a variety of industries, including automotive, telecom, energy, mining, infrastructure, real estate, finance and healthcare.

Veton completed his LL.B. with honours from the University of Ss. Cyril and Methodius in Macedonia and completed a Masters of Business Law (LL.M.) at the European University in Skopje. He is a member of the Macedonian and International Bar Associations, and has served as the Chairman of the Tax and Legal Committee of the American Chamber of Commerce in Macedonia.

马其顿——翻译及协调人介绍 / Macedonia–Introduction to Translators and Cooperators

律所介绍 / Introduction to Law Firms

江苏高的律师事务所

江苏高的律师事务所是江苏省最大的创收过亿的律师事务所之一。自 2004 年起，江苏高的律师事务所连续 6 年被江苏省律师协会评为"优秀律师事务所"。2011 年，该所被中华全国律师协会授予"2008—2010 年度全国优秀律师事务所"的称号。

经过多年发展，江苏高的与美国、英国、德国、意大利等国家和中国香港等地区的律师事务所建立了广泛的业务合作关系，能够为客户提供覆盖境内外的法律服务。在外商投资、跨境投资与并购、国际贸易与海商以及涉外诉讼仲裁领域，该所均有着非常丰富的经验。

Jiangsu G&D Law is one of the largest law firms of Jiangsu province with more than one hundred million Yuan yearly income. Jiangsu G&D law firm had been awarded the tile of Outstanding law firm for 6 years since 2004. In 2011, our firm was ranked as one of the Best Chinese Law Firms of the Years 2008-2010 by the All China Lawyers Association.

After several years development, Jiangsu G&D law firm has built up extensive cooperation relationships with law firms in a number of major jurisdictions including Hong Kong(China), US, UK, German and Italy, which makes us capable of helping clients both locally and internationally. Jiangsu G&D Law firm is experienced in many aspects such as Foreign investment, Cross-border investment, Cross-border M&A, Foreign trade and Maritime and Foreign-related litigation and arbitration.

律师介绍 / Introduction to Law Firms

马笑匀

律师，高级合伙人。

中华全国律师协会涉外律师领军人才，中国国际经济贸易仲裁委员会仲裁员，江苏省十佳涉外律师，江苏省"一带一路"法律服务研究中心研究员，江苏企业国际化专家库专家，江苏省国际商会副会长。

曾经手数个大型跨境项目，包括国家领导人签约项目、发改委重点项目、江苏省十佳涉外法律服务案例等，为数家知名金融机构、国有企业、上市公司等提供法律服务。

专业领域：跨境投资，融资并购，国际商事仲裁。

The national leading foreign-related lawyer, Arbitrator of China International Economic and Trade Arbitration Commission, Top ten foreign lawyers in Jiangsu Province, Researcher of Jiangsu "Belt and Road" Legal Service Research Center, Expert of Jiangsu Enterprise Internationalization Expert Pool, Vice president of the International Chamber of Commerce.

Xiaoyun Ma has dealt with several big projects, including Projects signed in the presence of National leaders, Key projects of National Development and Reform Commission, Top ten legal service cases of Jiangsu Province etc. She also provides legal services for several well-known financial institutes, state-owned enterprises, listed companies etc.

Practice area: Cross-border Investment, Finance, M&A, International Business Arbitration.

律所介绍 / Introduction to Law Firms

江西友达律师事务所

江西友达律师事务所系经江西省司法厅批准成立的省直律师事务所，系一所以非诉讼法律服务和专门领域的诉讼服务为主，推行专业服务、团队合作服务模式的新型跨业律师事务所。本所致力于为客户提供包括但不限于常年法律顾问、涉外法律服务，企业并购、改制、资产重组，发行债券，招标投标，不良资产处置，房地产，知识产权等专项法律服务。服务优势在于律师均具备良好的法学教育背景、精湛的法律诉讼技巧、丰富的非诉法律服务经验和鲜明的专业服务特征。同时，本所系江西省内能提供全方位涉外法律服务的律师事务所之一。

Jiangxi youda law firm is a provincial law firm approved by the department of justice of jiangxi province. It is a new cross-industry law firm that mainly provides non-litigation legal services and litigation services in specialized fields, and carries out professional services and team cooperation services. The law firm is committed to providing customers with special legal services including but not limited to legal counsel, foreign-related legal services, merger and acquisition, restructuring, assets reorganization, bond issuance, tendering and bidding, disposal of non-performing assets, real estate, intellectual property and other special legal services. The advantage of the service lies in that lawyers all have a good background of law education, excellent legal litigation skills, rich non-litigation legal service experience and distinctive professional service characteristics. At the same time, the law firm is one of the law firms in jiangxi province that can provide comprehensive foreign legal services.

律师介绍 / Introduction to Lawyers

冯帆

冯帆律师，法学硕士，江西友达律师事务所主任，第十三届全国人大代表，江西省律师协会副会长。专业从事民商事法律服务，业务方向为重大争议解决、基金债券、并购重组以及涉外法律服务。2014年和2016年两度入选中华全国律师协会涉外律师领军人才培养项目赴西班牙和英国培训。执业以来，代理多起重大民商事案件，为当事人挽回损失逾10亿元。

Lawyer feng fan, master of law, director of jiangxi youda law firm, deputy to the 13th National People's Congress, vice president of jiangxi lawyers association. She specializes in civil and commercial legal services, including major dispute resolution, fund bond, merger and reorganization, and foreign-related legal services. In 2014 and 2016, she was selected into the "leading talent" training program for Chinese foreign lawyers twice, and went to Spain and the United Kingdom for training. Since her practice, she has represented a number of major civil and commercial cases to recover losses of more than $1 billion for the parties involved.

马耳他——撰稿人介绍 / Malta–Introduction to Authors

律所介绍 / Introduction to Law Firms

Mamo TCV 律师事务所

Mamo TCV 作为马耳他的顶级律所之一，在广泛的业务领域为客户提供深度和专业的法律服务。作为综合性的从事公司和商业律所，其致力于通过专业的建议和法律视角，为客户提供超值的法律服务。

该所拥有超过 50 名的律师和其他领域专业人员，持续为客户提供参考服务。

多年来，律所与客户建立了紧密联系，在客户面临复杂的商业和法律问题、尝试适应变化的市场和监管环境时，全程提供支持。

律所拥有宽广的执业领域、密切的客户关系、专业知识和经验丰富的业务部门以及高素质的成员，成为客户独一无二的选择。

过去几年，该所均位于 Legal 500、IFLR 1000、Martindale-Hubell、钱伯斯全球和钱伯斯欧洲的榜单前列。

该所是很多欧洲领先律所，特别是非英国律所在马耳他的首选合作方。律所通过国际律师合作网络在海外提供法律服务，涵盖广泛的法律领域。

Mamo TCV is one of Malta's top-tier law firms, with significant depth and expertise across a broad range of practice areas. As an integrated corporate and commercial legal practice, it prides itself on its service delivery. It always strives to exceed the expectations of clients as it provides them with the expert advice and legal insight.

With a team of over fifty lawyers and professionals from other disciplines, is is confident of its ability to continuously act as a point of reference for clients.

Over the years it has built strong relationships with clients and it remains committed to supporting them at all times as they face complex business and legal issues as well as they try to adapt to changing markets and regulatory landscapes.

Its broad areas of expertise, client relationships, sector-specific knowledge & expertise and the quality of its people make it a unique proposition to clients.

For the past years Mamo TCV has been top ranked by Legal 500, IFLR 1000, Martindale-Hubell, Chambers Global and Chambers Europe.

It has become the preferred correspondents in Malta for various, leading law firms based in Europe, particularly those operating out of the UK. It operates overseas through an international network of lawyers to cover a broad range of legal areas.

律师介绍 / Introduction to Lawyers

Joseph Camilleri

自 2003 年起在律所诉讼和替代争议解决部工作，主要负责民商事诉讼，包括银行金融、房地产、航运和航空业的资产追回。

他的业务领域还包括行政法，特别是政府采购、政府和社会资本合作和规划法。在该领域，他经常协助政府机构处理与起草招标文件、评标、中标后合同的履行相关的法律事务。他还经常代表公共和私营机构客户参加政府采购评审委员会的诉讼和高等法院的上诉程序。

在规划法领域，曾代理数家私营机构参加规划上诉案件，并在需要许可和授权的项目中与建筑师和建筑师事务所紧密合作。

曾代理外国银行在马耳他的债权催收程序，其中包括涉案金额为数百万美元的案件。

2016 年，成功代理客户参加马耳他少见的公司债权回收案件。

在上诉法院的采购案件中，代理被告马耳他政府机构并胜诉。

过去几年，参与一系列与交通和港口服务相关的大型合同的招标程序。

Since 2003, Joseph Camilleri has worked in the Litigation and Alternative Dispute Resolution department of the firm on assignments encompassing several aspects of civil and commercial litigation, including bank finance, real estate and asset recovery in the shipping and aviation industries.

Joseph also works in the administrative law sector, particularly in the fields of public procurement, private-public partnerships and planning law. In this regard he regularly assists Government entities in legal issues relating to the drafting of tender documents and in the evaluation of tenders, as well as in the implementation of contracts following awards. He also regularly represents clients – hailing both from the public and private sectors – in proceedings before the Public Procurement Review Board and in appeals before the Superior Courts.

In the field of planning law, Joseph has represented several clients in the private sector in planning appeals and has also worked closely with architects and architecture firms on projects requiring permits and authorisations.

In particular, Joseph represented foreign banks in asset repossession proceedings in Malta involving multi-million dollar claims.

In 2016, successfully represented a client in one of the very few company recovery proceedings ever filed in Malta.

Successfully defended Maltese Government authorities in procurement proceedings before the Court of Appeal.

In the past years, he has been involved in a number of tender proceedings related to major contracts relating to transport and port services.

Stephen Muscat

律所诉讼部合伙人，在民商事诉讼、仲裁等领域为企业和个人客户提供帮助。除了争议解决，他在民商法领域均有广泛涉猎。在执业过程中，为不同的客户处理各类问题，他的客户包括各领域内领导者、高净值人士，涉及行业包括批发和零售、建筑、服务、酒店、石油和其他工业。

某上市公司食品饮料行业领导者诉讼事务的唯一顾问。最近参与了一系列关于位于黄金开发地段的不动产取回的诉讼案件，法院作出有利于其客户的判决。

一起涉及身为液化石油气经销行业领导者的上市公司的诉讼案件的 Mamo TCV 首席律师。该公司最近获得一份里程碑式的判决，法院在判决中承认经营者对气罐的所有权，并可将同样的气罐投放到市场。

经常为行业中两家大公司（均为上市公司，其中一家持有更大的市场份额）代理保险索赔案件，主要涉及人身损害赔偿和签订保单时未披露重大事实所导致的免责。

Stephen Muscat is a partner in the litigation department within the firm, assisting a number of clients, both corporate and individuals within the commercial and civil law sphere involved in court-related, arbitration and other tribunals work. Apart from dispute-resolution work Stephen also practices extensively within the general commercial and civil law sphere. In his practice, Stephen regularly deals and dealt with a myriad of issues for a diverse portfolio of clients, some of which are leaders in their field and high-net individuals, operating within the wholesale and retail, construction, services, hotel, oil and other industries.

Sole and exclusive counsel in all litigation matters involving a public company which is the leader in the beverage and food industry. Stephen was recently involved in a series of court cases, concerning the recovery of immovable property in a prime site for development, which court cases were decided favourably for clients.

Lead counsel within Mamo TCV in all litigation matters involving another public company which is a leader in the distribution of liquefied petroleum gas (LPG) in cylinders and in bulk. The said public company recently obtained a landmark judgment in which the court recognised the ownership of the gas cylinders in favour of the operator who would have introduced the same gas cylinders on the market.

Regularly involved in insurance claims for two of the biggest players within the industry (both public companies and one of which enjoys the biggest market share), with special emphasis on personal injury claims and disclaimers bas.

Jonathan Abela Fiorentino

律所公司部高级律师，帮助外国和本地公司客户处理诉讼事宜，就民商事问题提供法律建议。在为众多本地和外国公司客户提供服务的过程中，积累了丰富的经验，特别是在民商事诉讼和知识产权法领域。

作为该等法人和实体客户的顾问，在诉讼前的阶段帮助客户尽量通过和解解决争议，在诉讼阶段负责起草必要的法律文书并代理客户参加庭审。

担任某国际社交游戏公司关于其游戏中多项知识产权被侵权案件的首席顾问，双方在诉讼前阶段达成了令人满意的和解。

担任某航运服务公司两个飞机租赁案件的律师，其中一个案件涉及终止租赁，另一个涉及服务费用的支付，案件均在进行中。

担任本地某知名珠宝公司的顾问，协助其处理各种法律问题，特别是涉及商法和合规性质的事宜。

参与本地某大型电信公司的广泛尽职调查，特别是对各类批发、零售、供货和支持协议的审核。

某国际建筑公司作为本地联合企业的成员从事一大型基础建设项目，本律师为该公司在项目中涉及的民商事法律事宜提供建议。

Jonathan Abela Fiorentino is a Senior Associate in the Corporate Department of the firm, assisting the firm's corporate foreign and local clients in litigation matters, as well as providing legal advice on general civil and commercial matters involving such clients. Having acted for various local and foreign corporate clients throughout his profession so far, Jonathan has gained extensive experience in the exercise of the legal profession, in particular in civil and commercial litigation and intellectual property law.

As counsel to such persons and entities, he assists clients throughout both the pre-litigation stage striving to settle and concluding disputes amicably, as well as during the litigation stage in drafting the necessary judicial acts and representing the client in the courts of law.

Lead counsel for an international social games company in a dispute concerning the breach of its various intellectual property rights in its games. The parties reached a favourable settlement at pre-litigation stage.

Counsel for a company operating in the aviation services industry in two separate actions concerning leases of aircraft for the termination of the lease in one case and payment of services in the other case. The cases are ongoing.

Retained as counsel for a well-established local company operating in the jewellery industry assisting it in the various legal matters it encounters, particularly matters of a commercial law and regulatory nature.

Participated in an extensive due diligence exercise of a large local company operating in the telecommunications industry, involving in particular the review of a myriad of wholesale, vendor and supply & support agreements.

Advising an international construction company forming part of a local consortium responsible for the construction of a major infra-structural project, on various general civil and commercial issues involving the project.

Christine Calleja

律所劳动法部高级律师。帮助众多本地和国际公司处理人力资源事宜，如合同起草、不公平解雇诉讼、营业转让和集体裁员、代理客户在马耳他劳资裁判庭和法庭出庭。她还以该领域的讲师身份参加人力资源行业的教育研讨会。

另外，作为诉讼部的成员，她擅长保险诉讼，代理马耳他的一家大型保险公司和个人原告处理保险相关事宜。

她帮助某大型保险公司与工会协商起草并达成集体合同；

她建议并协助客户进行与劳动相关的交易，如集体裁员和营业转让；

作为团队成员，她参与对一家上市公司全部股本的公开发行进行尽职调查，特别是与雇佣和人力资源相关的事宜；

作为团队的法律顾问，她在上诉法院的一宗与员工诚信义务相关的重要马耳他案件中胜诉；

她为一家行业领先的保险公司提供保险索赔方面的顾问服务。

Christine Calleja is a senior associate of the firm working in the employment law department. She has assisted various local and international companies in human resources matters, such as contract drafting, unfair dismissal claims, transfers of business and collective redundancies, as well as represented clients before the Maltese Industrial Tribunal and courts. Christine has also participated in educational seminars organised for the human resources industry as lecturer in this field.

Furthermore, forming part of the litigation team, Christine specialises in insurance claims, representing a major insurance company in Malta and also individual claimants in insurance related matters.

Assisted a major insurance company in negotiations with a trade union to draft and conclude its collective agreement;

Advised and assisted clients in relation to employment-related transactions such as collective redundancies and transfers of business;

Formed part of a team which carried out a due diligence exercise related to a public offer of the entire share capital of a listed entity, specifically in connection with employment and human resources matters.

Acted as legal counsel before the Court of Appeal in a team that won an important Maltese case relating to the fiduciary duties of employees;

Retained by a leading insurance company as counsel in relation to insurance claims.

马耳他——翻译及协调人介绍 / Malta–Introduction to Translators and Cooperators

律所介绍 / Introduction to Law Firms

江苏剑桥人律师事务所

江苏剑桥人律师事务所于 1996 年成立，在苏州市工业园区和吴江区设立办公室，聚集众多行业领军律师、行业骨干、行业新锐和海归精英人才。

剑桥人律师事务所设立公司治理、建筑房地产、证券金融、投资并购、知识产权、国际事务、家事法律与财富管理、政府法律事务、刑事风控、公司清算、争议解决等专业法律部，业务规模位居江苏省律师行业前列。

剑桥人律师事务所 4 次获得省级嘉奖，2011 年被授予"全国优秀律师事务所"称号。

Established in 1996 and having offices in both Suzhou Industrial Park and Wujiang District of Suzhou City, He & Partners Law Firm gathers lots of leading talents, backbones and overseas returnees of lawyers.

As a leading law firm of Jiangsu province, the Firm mainly deals with legal affairs in corporate governance, real estate and construction, finance and securities, family assets management, administrative issues, criminal risk control, liquidation and dispute solution.

The Firm has won four provincial awards, and was granted the title of "National Excellent Law Form" in 2011 by All China Lawyers Association.

律师介绍 / Introduction to Lawyers

刘志刚

江苏剑桥人律师事务所高级合伙人，国际事务部主任。

毕业于复旦大学，曾被公派至英国伦敦大学、美国马里兰大学、美国天普大学和英国 BPP 大学接受律师专业培训。专精于公司法律、国际贸易和投资法律、争议解决。中华全国律师协会涉外律师领军人才，苏州市领军型律师。

David Liu is the senior partner and the head of international legal affairs group of He & Partners.

David Liu started practicing law upon graduation from Fudan University, was thereafter sent abroad to London University, Maryland University, Temple University and BPP University for professional trainings. He is specialized in corporate law, international trade law, investment law and dispute solution.

He is among the Leading Talents of Chinese lawyers for foreign-related legal affairs and the Leading Talents of Suzhou lawyers.

律所介绍 / Introduction to Law Firms

广和律师事务所

广和律师事务所成立于1995年,是一家总部位于深圳的中国"十大规模律师事务所"(《亚洲法律杂志》2007)。被《2018钱伯斯亚太法律指南》评为"公司/商事"和"建设工程"两大领域亚太地区领先律师事务所,至今已连续第五年度蝉联该榜单。

广和律师事务所拥有多名精通英语、日语、法语等语种的律师,在跨境并购、海外工程建设、国际贸易争端解决等方面积累了丰富的经验。广和律师事务所不仅在纽约、多伦多、南美等地建立了分所,也与欧洲、非洲、东南亚等地的多家国际律师事务所建立了合作关系,能为客户提供全方位一站式的法律服务。

Established in 1995, Guangdong Guanghe Law Firm (GHLF) is the Top Ten Largest Firms in China (ALB 2007) with its headquarters based in Shenzhen. GHLF was again awarded as the Asia's Leading PRC Firm -Corporate/Commercial & Real Estate by Chambers Asia-Pacific Guidance (2018) which is the Fifth Consecutive Years for GHLF to be on the List.

GHLF has a group of lawyers who can use English, Japanese and French as the working languages. They have been accumulated rich experience in dealing with legal matters relating to Cross-border M&A, Overseas Engineering Construction, International Trade Dispute Settlement. Not only operated its overseas branches in New York, Toronto and South America, GHLF also built up cooperation relationships with lots of reputable international law firms from Europe, Africa and Southeast Asia which gives GHLF the competence to provide the full scales and one stop legal services for our Clients.

律师介绍 / Introduction to Lawyers

熊代琨

熊代琨律师毕业于西南政法大学,并获得英国威尔士大学国际商法专业硕士学位。她曾在境外执业,也曾在世界500强公司担任公司律师。

熊代琨律师拥有中国律师执业资格(1994年)及中国税务师执业资格(1998年),工作语言为中文(普通话和广东话)以及英文。

熊代琨律师从事律师业务二十多年来,在非诉法律事务领域积累了丰富的经验,尤其擅长于处理有关外商投资、跨境并购、企业法律风险防控等方面法律事务。

目前,熊代琨律师是广东广和律师事务所国际业务委员会负责人,也是广东省律师协会港澳台和外事工作委员会副主任以及前海"一带一路"法律服务联合会理事。

Xiong Daikun graduated from Southwest University of Political Science and Law, and holds an LLM in International Business Law from the University of Wales, UK. She has both practiced law overseas as well as working as an in-house lawyer in a Fortune 500 company.

Ms. Xiong is a registered & practicing lawyer (since 1994) and registered & practicing Tax Attorney (since 1998) in China. Her working language is Chinese (both Mandarin and Cantonese) and English.

Ms. Xiong has accumulated rich experience in non-litigation areas through more than 20 years of practice and specialises in matters relating to FDI, M&A and Legal Risk Prevention and Control.

Currently, Ms. Xiong is in charge of the International Business Committee of Guanghe Law Firm. She is also Vice Director of the Foreign Affairs Committee of Guangdong Lawyers Association as well as a Council Member of the Qianhai Belt & Road Legal Services Federation.

墨西哥——撰稿人介绍 / Mexico–Introduction to Authors

律所介绍 / Introduction to Law Firms

Galicia Abogados 律师事务所

Galicia Abogados 律师事务所于 1994 年成立。

Galicia Abogados 律所拥有超过 150 名律师的法律团队，执业领域超 18 个。钱伯斯将 Galicia Abogados 评为 2017 年 "拉丁美洲最佳律师事务所"；钱伯斯还于 2015 年和 2013 年将 Galicia Abogados 评定为 "墨西哥年度最佳律师事务所"，并将其评为下列领域的领先律所：银行和金融、公司/并购、能源及自然资源与项目。此外，Galicia Abogados 还获 IJ Global 颁发的 2017 年度 "拉丁美洲最佳本土律师事务所" 奖。

Galicia Abogados, S.C. was founded in 1994.

As of this date we have a legal team with more than 150 members and a multidisciplinary practice with more than 18 areas. Chambers and Partners recognized Galicia Abogados as "Best Firm in Latin America" for 2017; such publication has also recognized Galicia Abogados as "Mexico Law Firm of the Year" in 2015 and in 2013 and has ranked it as a leading firm in the following categories: Banking & Finance, Corporate/M&A, Energy & Natural Resources and Projects. In addition, Galicia Abogados was awarded "Best Local Law Firm in Latin America" for 2017 by IJ Global.

律师介绍 / Introduction to Lawyers

Manuel Galicia Romero

Manuel Galicia Romero 是墨西哥 Galicia Abogados 律师事务所的创始合伙人。他在信贷融资、私募和公开发行、联合投资、私有化交易、合资企业事务、并购和企业重组方面拥有丰富经验。他曾为地方、州和联邦政府及其他实体提供各类商业交易的咨询服务。

Galicia 律师作为对外贸易组织协调办公室的法律顾问参加了北欧自由贸易协定和欧盟自由贸易协定的谈判，并曾担任国家和国际组织的顾问。

Galicia 律师在国内和国际出版物中被认为是墨西哥最重要的事务型律师之一。

Manuel Galicia Romero is founding partner of the Mexican firm Galicia Abogados, S.C. He has broad experience in transactions with respect to credit facilities, private and public offerings, co-investments, privatizations, as well as advising corporations with respect to joint ventures in Mexico, mergers and acquisitions, and corporate restructurings. He has advised local, state and federal governments, as well as other governmental entities in diverse commercial transactions.

Mr. Galicia participated as legal advisor to the Coordinating Office of Foreign Trade Organizations in the negotiation of NAFTA and the Free Trade Agreement with the European Union and has served as advisor for national and international organizations.

Mr. Galicia has been recognized in national and international publications as one of the most important transactional lawyers in Mexico.

Juan Pablo Cervantes

Juan Pablo Cervantes 是 Galicia Abogados 律师事务所的律师。他的业务领域主要集中于银行与金融、并购、国际贸易和一般性公司事务。

Cervantes 律师负责律所的亚洲事务，并且是亚洲国家和墨西哥之间多个商业和投资协会的成员。

他曾就双边贸易协定的有关方面向不同的商会提供咨询意见，并同时就国际贸易协定和投资在拉丁美洲论坛上发言。

Juan Pablo Cervantes is counsel of Galicia Abogados, S.C. His professional practice is focused in banking and finance, M&A, international trade and general corporate matters.

Mr. Cervantes heads the firm's Asia practice and is member of various business and investment associations organized between Asian countries and Mexico.

He has advised different chambers of commerce in relevant aspects of bilateral trade agreements and has likewise participated as speakers in forums in Latin America regarding international trade agreements and investment.

墨西哥——翻译及协调人介绍 / Mexico–Introduction to Translators and Cooperators

律所介绍 / Introduction to Law Firms

福建旭丰律师事务所

福建旭丰律师事务所成立于 1995 年，是一家提供中国国内和国际法律服务的综合性律师事务所，曾获得包括"全国优秀律师事务所"称号在内的由中国司法部、中华全国律师协会及各级律师协会等评选的诸多荣誉。

律所为客户在公司、并购、破产重整、银行金融、证券与资本市场、房地产与建筑、国际贸易、知识产权保护的商业交易和争议解决领域提供优秀的解决方案。客户包括中国及世界知名的一些公司及基金。

Founded in 1995, Fujian Xufeng Law Firm LLP is a full-service law firm headquartered in Xiamen, China, and is recognized as one of the most prestigious legal service providers by the Ministry of Justice of the People's Republic of China, All China Lawyers Association, and other bar associations at various levels.

The firm provides cost-effective and first-class legal solutions and services to clients in corporate, M&As, restructuring and insolvency, banking and financing, securities and capital markets, real estate and construction, international trade, intellectual property, and dispute resolution. Working with some of the world's top-tier companies, investment banks, private equity firms and investors, it offers a full service in cross-border investment, covering corporate law, M&As, private equity, corporate governance and commercial work. Its clients include some of the largest funds and industrial companies in China and the rest of the world.

律师介绍 / Introduction to Lawyers

连铮

连铮律师是福建旭丰律师事务所副主任，擅长跨境并购、私募基金业务，在资本市场和知识产权领域也有广泛的经验，同时他为跨国公司在中国的投资及日常运营提供全面的法律服务，他的客户包括中国及世界知名的一些公司及基金。

连铮律师是福建省律师协会涉外专业委员会副主任，厦门市商务专家，厦门市商务局法律顾问。

Mr. Lian Zheng is a co-managing partner of Fujian Xufeng Law Firm LLP. Mr. Lian is an expert in cross-border M&A and private equity transactions, and he is also known for his extensive practice in capital markets and intellectual property law. Mr. Lian provides comprehensive services to multinational companies in regard to a complete range of investment activities and daily operational matters in China. Mr. Lian counts some of the largest funds and industrial companies in China and beyond among his clients.

Mr. Lian is Deputy Director of the Professional Committee of International Practices of the Fujian Bar Association. He is also a business expert of the Xiamen Municipal Government and the legal counsel to the Xiamen Bureau of Commerce.

律所介绍 / Introduction to Law Firms

北京德恒律师事务所

北京德恒律师事务所成立于 1993 年，现已发展成为中国规模最大的全方位律师事务所之一。德恒拥有广泛的客户群体和全球服务网络，在中国乃至全球 150 多个主要城市均设有分支机构和成员。

北京德恒律师事务所是中国最早具有从事证券、跨境投资、基础设施、破产管理、国内外专利诉讼法律服务资格的律师事务所之一。大部分德恒律师拥有硕士、博士学位，具有国内外立法、司法、行政机关，跨国公司、大型国企，金融证券机构的工作经验。

Deheng Law Offices was founded in 1993 and has grown into one of the largest full-service law firms in China. With a broad client base and a global service network with branches and associates both in China and over 150 major cities all over the world,

Deheng Law Offices was one of the earliest law firms in China to be qualified to render legal services in securities, cross-border investment, infrastructure, bankruptcy management, domestic and international patent prosecutions and other areas. Most of our professionals hold domestic or foreign LLM., J.D. or Ph.D. degrees, and have work experience in domestic and foreign legislatures, judicial organizations, government agencies, universities, research institutes, transnational companies, large scale state owned enterprises, and financial and securities institutions.

律师介绍 / Introduction to Lawyers

杨闰

杨闰律师是北京德恒（广州）律师事务所的合伙人，执业近 20 年，在公司、证券、国有资产、投融资法律服务等领域有丰富的经验，曾多次参与大型企业融资、并购、重组、合资项目。

在熟悉行业背景的前提下，杨闰律师善于从监管机构/企业法律风险防范等角度提供安全、务实、高效的法律解决方案。

Rene Yang is a partner of DeHeng Law (Guangzhou) Offices. She has practiced for nearly 20 years and has rich experience in the fields of corporate, securities, state-owned assets, investment and financing legal services. She has participated in many projects regarding finance, M&A, restructurings, joint venture of large-scale corporations.

Based on the familiarity with the industry, Ms. Yang is adept at providing safe, practical and efficient solutions from the perspective of regulatory institutions/corporate legal risk prevention.

摩尔多瓦——撰稿人介绍 / Moldova–Introduction to Authors

律所介绍 / Introduction to Law Firms

Turcan Cazac 律师事务所

成立于 1999 年，Turcan Cazac 是摩尔多瓦领先的律师事务所。根据钱伯斯和 Legal 500 的排名，该事务所连续 17 年处于第一等级。该事务所的客户既包括外国和跨国企业，也包括摩尔多瓦的战略性工业部门，如金融机构、能源、电信、汽车和农业。

该事务所致力于提升摩尔多瓦商业的法律环境，也同时活跃在摩尔多瓦商界。

Established in 1999, Turcan Cazac is the leading business law firm in Moldova. Turcan Cazac is a Band 1 firm in Moldova according to Chambers Global and Legal 500 directories for 17 consecutive years. The firm works with international clients from strategic industry sectors for Moldova, such as financial services, energy, telecommunications, automotive and agriculture.

The firm is an advocate of reform and improvement of the legal environment for doing business and an active member of the Moldovan business community.

律师介绍 / Introduction to Lawyers

Alexander Turcan

Alexander Turcan 是 Turcan Cazac 律师事务所的管理合伙人。

被钱伯斯全球评为 Eminent Practitioner（出色律师）；Legal 500 成员。

"Alexander Turcan 作为管理合伙人和执业律师，是摩尔多瓦最富经验的律师之一，其能够从市场的视野为客户提供战略性的意见。"（钱伯斯评论）

自 2011 年起 Turcan 律师成为是摩尔多瓦欧洲商会（www.eba.md）的董事会成员。

自 2013 年起，Turcan 律师担任摩尔多瓦律师协会在欧洲法律和律师协会（www.ccbe.eu）的代表。

Alexander 之前担任的各类社会职务包括：摩尔多瓦的美国商会（www.amcham.md）董事会成员；摩尔多瓦律师协会成员（2011—2015 年）。

曾参与 PMI 管理项目的培训，熟练使用英语、俄语和罗马尼亚语。

Managing Partner, Turcan Cazac Law Firm.

Chambers Global raking: Eminent Practitioner;

Member of The Legal 500 Hall of Fame.

Chambers Commentary (based on the Chambers research):

"Managing partner and eminent practitioner Alexander Turcan is one of the most experienced lawyers in Moldova. He lends his considerable market insight to clients in need of strategic advice."

Since 2011 Mr. Turcan is Member of the Board of Directors of the European Business Association in Moldova (www.eba.md).

Since 2013 Mr. Turcan is the representative of the Moldovan Bar at the Council of Bars and Law Societies of Europe (www.ccbe.eu).

Alexander's past community leadership positions include: member of the Board of Directors (2006-2012) of the American Chamber of Commerce in Moldova (www.amcham.md); member of the Board of the Moldovan Bar (2011-2015).

Trained in PMI Project Management. Fluent in English, Russian and Romanian.

律所介绍 / Introduction to Law Firms

ACI Partners 律师事务所

ACI Partners 是摩尔多瓦顶尖的律师事务所,业务合作关系遍布欧洲。ACI Partners 成立于 2006 年,源自安永会计师事务所的法务团队,能够提供优质法律服务并具有持续发展能力。ACI Partners 致力于为客户提供切实可靠的法律服务,体现在对法律的正确掌握,以及更全面维护客户利益。为更好地服务客户,ACI Partners 为每一位客户提供定制化服务,充分尊重客户的价值观,精益求精、尽职尽责地维护他们的权益,并提供满足客户需求的工作环境和数据系统。ACI Partners 不仅担任摩尔多瓦政府的法律顾问,还服务多家国际性和本地企业、国际性机构,参与过多起重大交易、工作和项目。通过成功办理一系列标志性的案例,ACI Partners 的律师赢得了客户的信任和广泛赞誉。ACI Partners 是钱伯斯、Legal 500 中位列第一的摩尔多瓦律师事务所,管理合伙人 Igor Odobescu 荣获最佳顾问律师。

ACI Partners is a leading law firm in Moldova with an expanding network of partners throughout Europe. ACI Partners was established in 2006 by separation of the legal business from Ernst & Young Moldova and as such it draws from the latter's long-acknowledged ability to offer competent advice. Its business strategy strives to deliver a solid and reliable service, going beyond merely grasping the law, which the clients may turn to whenever they need. In reaching this goal, ACI Partners employs a personalized approach to each client, showing a genuine respect for their values and unqualified commitment to their interests and needs, steadily investing in knowledge and data management and ensuring a working environment consistent with clients' quality demands and high expectations. ACI Partners has advised the Government of the Republic of Moldova, international and local businesses, international organizations, and other institutions on most challenging transactions, assignments and projects. In course of its activity its professionals have gained trust and earned high appreciation through a number of projects exemplary samples. ACI Partners is recommended as a Band 1 Law Firm in Moldova by Chambers&Partners and Legal500. Its Managing Partner, Igor Odobescu, is a member of the Best Lawyers Advisory Board.

律师介绍 / Introduction to Lawyers

Andrei Caciurenco

Andrei Caciurenco 是 ACI Partners 的创始合伙人之一,具有 17 年的丰富从业经验,在一系列复杂和重大交易中代理国际和本地投资人。Andrei Caciurenco 的执业领域涵盖外商投资、政府和社会资本合作、跨境交易等。在复杂商业交易中,Andrei Caciurenco 以擅长架构设计和审慎判断而著称。Andrei Caciurenco 在法律起草、法治改革、法律宣传、商业立法二次审议和评估等方面取得突出成绩,还是《电子商务法》《租赁法》《担保法》等立法起草工作组成员。

Andrei Caciurenco is a founding partner of ACI Partners and has 17 years of experience in representing international and local investors in a number of complex and challenging engagements. Andrei advises in projects related to foreign investments, public-private partnerships, cross-border deal structuring. Andrei has been praised for helping out businesses in complex deals when good structure and analysis are required, for well thought and successful trademark defence tactics, and exiting leonine contracts. Andrei has an outstanding record of legal reform activity. He has been a member of the Working Group of the Government for elaboration of the E-Commerce Law and authored Leasing Law and Mortgage Law in Moldova.

摩尔多瓦——翻译及协调人介绍 / Moldova–Introduction to Translators and Cooperators

律所介绍 / Introduction to Law Firms

上海市浦栋律师事务所

上海市浦栋律师事务所于 1992 年初创建,是上海较为领先的律师事务所之一。该所的律师均经过严格挑选,大部分律师都有在国内外著名法学院受教育,并在国外著名的律师事务所或跨国公司法律部从业的经历。该所在投资、国际贸易、公司、证券以及劳动人事法律事务方面具有丰富的经验。

Shanghai Pu Dong Law Office is one of the leading law firms based in Shanghai, established in early 1992. The lawyers of this office are selected from different law offices with special expertise and are guided by the principles of quality and cooperation, who are graduated in leading law schools and experienced in well-known international and domestic law firms or legal department of international companies. The firm is experienced in investment, international trade, corporate, securities and human resources.

律师介绍 / Introduction to Lawyers

卞栋樑

上海市浦栋律师事务所，合伙人。

工作语言为中英文。

专业领域为银行、融资租赁、公司并购、涉外商事仲裁、公司、劳动争议等。

2014年起担任上海市律师协会律师学院执业培训班讲师；2017年起担任上海市浦东新区专业人民调解中心特邀律师调解员。

自2004年开始从事律师行业以来，服务的客户涵盖医疗、航空、房地产、金融、影视娱乐、食品等多个行业和领域，特别是在为企业运营提供日常法律服务、为客户解决实际问题方面具备较强的专业水准。卞律师在金融、并购、企业合规、争议解决等方面为客户提供大量专业、有力的支持。

Shanghai Pudong Law Office; Partner.

Language: Chinese and English.

Banking, Finance Lease, M&A, Foreign-related Commercial Arbitration, Corporate, Labor Disputes, etc.

Lecturer of Shanghai Bar Association for Youth Lawyer since 2014; Guest mediator for Shanghai Pudong New Area People's Mediation Center since 2017.

Practice since 2004, Mr. Bian's clients cover medical, aero-service, real estate, finance, entertainment and foods, and is experienced in providing daily legal support and problem-solving for enterprises in operation. Mr. Bian also provides legal advice in finance, merger and acquisition, compliance and dispute settlement for clients.

律所介绍 / Introduction to Law Firms

新疆旭光律师事务所

新疆旭光律师事务所成立于1993年，是一家综合性律师执业机构。现有20名注册执业律师和10名律师助理，多年来保持健康、稳定地发展。执业律师富有敬业精神和丰富的从业经验，以良好的法律素养和娴熟的业务技能为当事人提供优质、迅捷的法律服务。经过长期的合作，各律师彼此之间配合默契，整体实力雄厚，具有解决各种疑难复杂法律问题的能力。

Xinjiang Xu Guang Law Firm was established in 1993, is a comprehensive legal professional institution. The firm has 20 practicing lawyers and 10 assistants, and has maintained a healthy and stable development over the years. The lawyers with rich professionalism and full of working experience will provide quality and efficient legal services with good legal literacy and highly skilled. After a long period of cooperation, the lawyers are working well together with a variety of difficulty to solve the complex legal problems.

律师介绍 / Introduction to Lawyers

李黎

李黎，二级律师，新疆旭光律师事务所副主任、合伙人。现任全国律师协会国际业务专业委员会委员、新疆律师协会国际业务专业委员会主任。李黎律师的执业领域涵盖涉外诉讼、仲裁、非诉法律服务。她以保护当事人合法权益为己任，运用丰富的职业经验和执业技巧，成功办理了大量的民商事案件。李黎律师的工作语言为中文和英文，为来自欧亚各国的外商提供优质高效的法律服务。

Lily Li, secondary lawyer, vice director and partner of Xinjiang Xu Guang Law Firm.

Now serves as member of international business committee of ACLA and director of international business committee of Xinjiang Lawyers Association. Her practicing area covers international litigation, arbitration and non-litigation practice. Aiming to achieve and maintain the client's legal rights and interests, with a wealth of practical experience and flexible approach, she has successfully settled a large number of civil and commercial disputes. Her working language is Chinese and English, and will serve the foreign clients from Europe and Asia with good and highly effective legal skills.

黑山——撰稿人介绍 / Montenegro–Introduction to Authors

律所介绍 / Introduction to Law Firms

Prelevic 律师事务所

Prelevic 律师事务所（PLF）1991 年设立，目前业已成为黑山最大的公司法律事务所之一。PLF 在黑山提供法律服务，特别是地方市场的法律服务。在通用法律框架咨询基础上，PLF 的长期地方服务为其获得了立法实践和个人行政诉讼全方位知识。PLF 代表了大量高净值客户，包括金融机构、房地产开发商、工业组装厂、石油商、非盈利组织、使领馆、公共设施机构，以及商务公司、国际及国家组织。在诉讼方面 PLF 也有出色业绩，代理客户在黑山各级法院进行诉讼。PLF 还为客户就在黑山商业活动提供税收、财务方面的法律服务。多少年以来，PLF 服务的领域涵盖了随着黑山商业环境、热门领域的迅速发展中的国家资源、企业的私有化、特许权、房地产交易、商业组织设立、环境保护、信用评级和海关及税务等问题。

Prelevic Law Firm (PLF) was formed in 1991 and has grown to become one of the largest corporate legal offices in Montenegro. PLF provides the legal services on the entire territory of Montenegro. It advises exclusively for the local markets. Above the consultancy of the general regulatory frameworks, its long-standing local presence has earned us a profound knowledge of the practice of legislative and individual administrative procedures. PLF bears strong reference to market participants from abroad intending to engage in Montenegro. PLF represents a broad spectrum of high-profile clients, including financial institutions, real estate developers, industrial complexes, petroleum concerns, non-profit organizations, embassies, public utilities, and commercial companies, international and national agencies. PLF has also an outstanding litigation practice, representing clients on all levels of Montenegrin courts. PLF offers its clients all the legal tax and accounting services required to conduct business in Montenegro. Over the years, PLF has advised in the areas of privatization of national resources and enterprises, concessions, real estate transactions, setting up businesses, environmental protection, credit facilities and custom and tax issues, all with a keen sensitivity to the rapid changes in the Montenegrin business environment.

律师介绍 / Introduction to Lawyers

Marko Ivković

Marko 于 2011 年加入 Prelevic 律师事务所。他在波德戈里察法学院学习，在德国汉堡大学获得硕士学位。Marko 先前服务于大型法律服务机构，在外商投资领域富有经验。Marko 是黑山律师协会会员，除了专业英语服务，他还被认可提供向法院德语翻译服务。Marko 经常协调事务所尽职调查团队，涉及合规、公司以及财务金融方面的问题；审查并购协议；取得合规许可等。

Marko joined Prelevic Law Firm in 2011. He studied at the Law Faculty in Podgorica and obtained a master degree at the University of Hamburg, Germany. Marko has previously served in one of the region's largest legal practices and is experienced in the advice for foreign investors. Marko is a member of the Montenegrin Bar Association and, apart from his professional command of English, is a certified court interpreter for the German language. Marko regularly coordinates our due diligence teams, and covers regulatory, corporate and financing issues; review of M&A agreements; obtaining regulatory approvals.

Savo Jasnić

Savo Jasnić 于 2012 年加入 Prelevic 律师事务所。2015 年，他在阿姆斯特丹大学获得法学硕士学位，专业为国际贸易投资法律。他的服务领域包括银行、公司、能源以及财产法律方面，特别是外商投资。他成功地代理一家黑山银行高管针对黑山政府向国际投资争端解决中心提交争议解决的动议。他已通过律师资格考试，现为黑山律师协会会员。

Savo Jasnić has been a member of Prelevic law firm since 2012. In 2015 he obtained LLM in International Investment and Trade Law from University of Amsterdam. He is advising in all matters of banking, corporate, energy and property law, with special focus on foreign investments. He advised a top executive of a bank in Montenegro on potential initiation of ICSID arbitration against Montenegro. He passed the BAR exam and is a member of BAR association of Montenegro.

律所介绍 / Introduction to Law Firms

Karanović & Nikolić 律师事务所

Karanović & Nikolić 律师事务所是一家在东南欧处于领先地位的国际性法律实践机构，整个团队由 100 多名律师组成，他们在该地区寻求合作，在投资者需求的特定区域和行业提供优质的法律服务。因为敬业、优质的法律服务以及对客户需求的深入理解，该律所成为市场的领导者之一。

通过与该地区上百名律师合作，律所将原始价值观有机地融入为客户工作的哲学和方法之中。与 Karanović & Nikolić 律师事务所合作的律师参与了该地区许多规模大、复杂的交易。该律所赢得了交易、公司 / 商业领域重要法律服务机构的声誉。

该律所在塞尔维亚设立机构，并与波斯尼亚黑塞哥维那、克罗地亚、马其顿、黑山和斯洛文尼亚的律师建立长期合作关系。与 Karanović & Nikolić 律师事务所有联系的律师在这些地区紧密合作，根据当地实际情况，以极具竞争力的方式，为客户提供最优的法律意见。

律所务实且高度商业化。Karanović & Nikolić 律师事务所与相关地区的优秀律师密切合作，为在该地区开展业务的众多领袖公司、银行、投资者和经商的政府机构提供咨询，并因团队律师工作质量和解决问题的商业方法而闻名。

Karanović & Nikolić is a leading international legal practice in South East Europe with a team composed of over 100 lawyers who cooperate together across the region. Its team offers unrivalled regional and sector specific coverage to investors. It is one of market leaders because of its dedication, quality legal service, and in-depth understanding of the needs of clients.

By cooperating with more than 100 lawyers across the region, its original values remain an integral part of its philosophy and approach to client work. Lawyers practising in cooperation with Karanović & Nikolić have been involved in many of the large and complex transactions in the region and they take pride in their reputation as a transactional and corporate/commercial legal powerhouse.

Because it has a business presence in Serbia and a long standing cooperation with attorneys-at-law in Bosnia & Herzegovina, Croatia, Macedonia, Montenegro and Slovenia, lawyers associated with Karanović & Nikolić operate seamlessly across these jurisdictions, providing services to its clients and taking into consideration local particularities in order to provide the best legal advice under competitive terms.

It is practical and highly commercial. Renowned for the quality of work of the lawyers on its team and its commercial approach to solving problems, Karanović & Nikolić, in cooperation with qualified attorneys-at-law in each relevant jurisdiction, advises many of the leading companies, banks, investors and government institutions doing business in the region.

律师介绍 / Introduction to Lawyers

Nikolina Kažić

Nikolina Kažić 是黑山的独立律师，与 Karanović & Nikolić 律师事务所合作。

她毕业于黑山大学法学院。她是黑山律师协会的注册律师，同时也是国际律师协会（IBA）的成员。

她为一些在黑山经营业务的国内和国际领袖公司提供咨询服务。她在能源领域有独特的经验，曾参与过黑山的一些具有里程碑意义的可再生能源和能源效率项目，并向该领域的利益相关方提供日常建议。Nikolina 还专业从事企业和商业、建筑、税收和就业领域的法律事务。

Nikolina is an independent Attorney at Law practicing in Montenegro in cooperation with Karanović & Nikolić.

She graduated from the University of Montenegro, Faculty of Law. She is a registered attorney at law in the Bar Association of Montenegro, and also a member of the International Bar Association (IBA).

Nikolina advised some of the leading domestic and international companies doing business in Montenegro. She has unique experience in the area of energy, having worked on some of the landmark renewable energy and energy efficiency projects in Montenegro, as well as providing day-to-day advice to the relevant stakeholders in the sector. Nikolina also specialises in corporate and commercial legal matters, construction legislation, taxation and employment.

Sonja Guzina

Sonja Guzina 是一名独立律师，与 Karanović & Nikolić 律师事务所合作。

她毕业于诺维萨德大学法学院，并获得了国际法硕士学位。她是伏伊伏丁那律师协会的注册律师，同时也是国际律师协会（IBA）的成员。

她专注于企业和商业事务，在企业和商业法律的各个领域为客户提供建议，包括并购、合资和公司重组。

她也是银行和金融实务组织的活跃成员，在广泛领域提供银行、金融相关事务的法律帮助，包括项目融资、跨境信贷及相关的担保、基础设施事务，以及再融资。

Sonja is an independent attorney at law practicing in cooperation with Karanović & Nikolić.

She graduated from University of Novi Sad, Faculty of Law, where she obtained her Masters' Degree in international law. She is a registered attorney at law in the Bar Association of Vojvodina, and also a member of the International Bar Association (IBA).

Sonja specialises in corporate and commercial matters, advising clients on all aspects of corporate and commercial law, including mergers and acquisitions, joint ventures, and corporate restructurings. Sonja is also an active member in the Banking & Finance Practice Group, providing legal assistance on a wide range of banking and finance related matters, including project finance, cross border credit transactions and related security, infrastructure transactions, and refinancing.

黑山——翻译及协调人介绍 / Montenegro–Introduction to Translators and Cooperators

律所介绍 / Introduction to Law Firms

国浩律师事务所

国浩律师事务所是中国最大的法律服务机构之一，中国投融资领域尤其是资本市场上最为专业的法律服务提供者之一，特别在跨境投资、海外并购等涉及中国企业"走出去"和"一带一路"相关法律服务方面，并积累了为跨境投资项目提供法律服务的丰富经验。迄今已为包括俄罗斯、蒙古、哈萨克斯坦、伊朗、印度、印度尼西亚、柬埔寨、越南、孟加拉、马来西亚、巴基斯坦、阿尔巴尼亚、新加坡等在内的许多"一带一路"沿线国家提供过法律服务，而由"国浩一带一路法律研究与服务中心"推出的"一带一路"沿线国家相关法律问题研究系列成果更是引起了业界的广泛关注。

Grandall Law Firm is one of the largest law firms in China, one of the most professional legal service providers in China in investment and financing area, and capital markets, in particular. It has remarkable advantage in providing legal service in cross-border investment, overseas merger and acquisition, and other projects relating to the Go Out Policy by Chinese Enterprises and the Initiatives of Belt and Road ("B&R"). Grandall has rendered services to a number of projects in the related B&R countries, covering Russia, Mongolia, Kazakhstan, Iran, India, Indonesia, Cambodia, Vietnam, Bangladesh, Malaysia, Pakistan, Albania and Singapore, etc. Moreover, the study concerning legal issues of the countries along the B&R made by Grandall B&R Legal Research and Service Center has drawn extensive attention in the industry in the world.

律师介绍 / Introduction to Lawyers

陈学斌

陈学斌是国浩律师（上海）事务所合伙人，一级律师，澳大利亚邦德大学法学博士。陈学斌律师从1984年起成为律师，现在是长三角地区侨商组织法律顾问委员会副主任、中华全国律协国际业务委员会委员、中国国际经济贸易仲裁委员会仲裁员、上海侨联法律顾问委员会委员。陈学斌律师曾被评为全国优秀律师，业务领域主要有跨境投资、金融服务、公司兼并收购、海事海商以及跨境交易等。

Dr. Chen Xuebin is a partner of Grandall Law Firm Shanghai Office, the First Class Lawyer, with SJD Degree from Bond University, Australia in 2003. Since 1984, he became a lawyer, and now he is the depute director of Legal Counsels' Committee for Overseas Chinese Businessmen Organization in Changjiang Triangle Area, a member of International Committee of All-China Lawyers' Association, an arbitrator of China International Economic and Trade Arbitration Commission, a member of Legal Counsels' Committee of Shanghai Federation of Returned Overseas. Dr. Chen was once awarded as one of the Best Lawyers in China. His main area is specialized in cross-border investment, finance legal services, corporate M&A, Maritime and various cross-border transactions.

律所介绍 / Introduction to Law Firms

锦天城律师事务所

锦天城律师事务所是一家提供全方位、高质量法律服务的律师事务所，办公室分布在上海、北京、深圳、杭州、苏州、南京、成都、重庆、太原、青岛、厦门、天津、济南、合肥、郑州、福州、南昌、西安、广州、香港、伦敦等国内外主要城市。

锦天城多次被中国司法部、律师协会及国际知名的法律媒体和权威机构（如钱伯斯、Legal 500、IFLR 1 000、Asia Law Profile、ALB）列为中国顶尖的法律服务提供者之一，居全国前列。

锦天城有执业律师2000多人，可以用中文、英文、日文、德文、法文等语言工作，许多律师拥有美国多州、英国、法国和日本等地的执业资格。

锦天城为其客户在公司、商业与并购、证券与资本市场、银行与金融、房地产与建筑、争议解决（诉讼与仲裁）、国际贸易、知识产权保护领域的商业交易和争议中，提供有效的解决方案。锦天城的客户遍及全国和全球，涉及大中型国有企业、事业单位、跨国集团、外商投资企业、民营企业、各类银行和金融机构等。

AllBright Law Firm, owing offices in domestic and overseas major cities as Shanghai, Beijing, Shenzhen, Hangzhou, Nanjing, Chengdu, Chongqing, Taiyuan, Qingdao, Xiamen, Tianjin, Jinan, Hefei, Zhengzhou, Fuzhou, Nanchang, Xi'an, Guangzhou, Hong Kong, London, etc., provides a comprehensive range of high-quality legal services.

Widely acknowledged as one of the top legal service providers by Ministry of Justice P.R.C., ACLA and numerous international legal media and institutions (e.g. Chambers and Partners, Legal 500, IFLR 1000, Asia Law Profile, ALB, etc.), AllBright Law Offices have been in the front rank of the country.

AllBright has approximately 2,000 lawyers, who can provide legal service in Chinese, English, Japanese, German, French and other languages. Many of the lawyers are admitted in the United States, the U.K., France, Japan and other foreign jurisdictions.

AllBright Law Offices provide cost-efficient legal solutions and services to clients in corporations, mergers and acquisitions, securities and capital markets, banking and financing, real estate and construction, dispute resolution(litigations and arbitrations), international trade, intellectual property and other practice areas. Its clients come from all over the country and the world, which include state-owned powerhouses, institutions, international groups, foreign invested enterprises, private enterprises, banks and financial institutions.

律师介绍 / Introduction to Lawyers

罗民

罗民律师是上海市锦天城（西安）律师事务所合伙人，现任西安市律师协会涉外委员会副主任。

罗律师入选中华全国律师协会涉外律师领军人才库和一带一路跨国律师人才库。经全国律师协会选拔，他参加涉外律师专项培训项目，并被选送欧洲留学、工作、考察。他在公司、并购、投融资及涉外诉讼方面具有广泛的经验。

Luo Min is a partner of Shanghai AllBright Law Firm Xi'an Office. Now he is the deputy director of Foreign-related Committee of Xi'an Lawyers Association.

Mr. Luo has been selected into "the Leading Talent Pool of Lawyers Specialized in Foreign-related Matters" and "the Talent Pool of Cross - border Lawyers for Belt and Road Initiative" by All China Lawyers Association. After rounds of selection, he was selected by All China Lawyers Association to participate in the special training project for lawyers specialized in foreign-related matters, and was sent to Europe to study ,work and investigate there. He owns extensive experience in the areas as company, mergers and acquisitions, investment, financing, foreign related litigation, etc.

摩洛哥——撰稿人介绍 / Morocco–Introduction to Authors

律所介绍 / Introduction to Law Firms

Hajji & Associés 律师事务所

Hajji & Associés 是摩洛哥一家独立的律师事务所，自 20 世纪 90 年代中期以来，已发展成为国际商法领域高水平的专业律所。

该所的业务活动涵盖国际金融、公司重组并购、能源和基础设施、市场准入计划、信息技术法律、商事诉讼和国际仲裁等具体领域。

该所实施现代化的管理方式，大多数律师完整掌握英语等三种语言，并具备法学博士学位。

目前该所雇员总数为 15 名，人员正在扩大。

此外，该所确保恪守职业秘密和独立有关的道德规范。

该所与大型国际律师事务所保持特殊的专业联系，他们经常通过该所的辅助来支持其客户在摩洛哥的投资项目。

一直以来，该所客户主要是外国的国际投资者，多为来自盎格鲁 - 撒克逊联盟的跨国公司。

该所在银行业、金融和资本市场、商事、公司和并购、争议解决和雇佣领域位列 Legal 500 第二等，在项目和公法领域位列第三等。

该所在普通商法领域亦位列钱伯斯第三等。

该所在 2015 年和 2016 年度连续获得"北非最佳律师事务所：摩洛哥"金奖，并于 2017 年获得"北非最佳律师事务所：摩洛哥"银奖。这些奖项由"领导人联盟"和名为"Décideurs"的法国杂志授予。

IJGlobal（全球基础设施和项目融资领域权威机构）发布的 2015 年度排行榜分析中，在中东和北非顶尖法律顾问排名中，该所还被列为中东北非唯一一家独立律师事务所。

Hajji & Associés is an independent Moroccan law firm which has developed, since the mid-nineties, high-level expertise in the international business law field.

The activities of the firm cover particular areas of international finance, company's restructuring and mergers and acquisitions, energy and infrastructure, market entry plans, IT law, commercial litigation and international arbitration.

The firm has implemented modern management methods. It is formed with a team of lawyers having high academic background with a level of doctoral studies in law with the complete knowledge of three languages including English.

The total number of employees of the firm is currently of 15 and is expanding.

In addition, Hajji & Associés ensure strict compliance with ethical rules on professional secrecy and independence.

The firm maintains privileged professional relationships with large international law firms who generally support their clients' investment projects in Morocco with the assistance of Hajji & Associés.

Historically, Hajji & Associés clientele has mainly been composed of foreign international investors – mainly multinational companies from Anglo-Saxon countries.

Hajji & Associés is ranked in Legal 500 as tier 2 in Banking, finance and capital markets, Commercial, corporate and M&A, Dispute resolution and Employment, and as tier 3 in Projects and public law.

Hajji & Associés is also ranked in Chambers and Partners as Band 3 in General Business Law.

Hajji & Associés has obtained the Gold Prize of "Best Law Firm in North Africa: Morocco" consecutively in 2015 and 2016 and the Silver Prize of "Best Law Firm in North Africa: Morocco" in 2017. These prizes are granted by Leaders League and by the French magazine "Décideurs".

Hajji & Associés was also listed as the only independent law firm in MENA in the MENA Top Legal Advisers ranking included in the League Tables Analysis issued by IJGlobal for 2015.

律师介绍 / Introduction to Lawyers

Amin Hajji

Amin Hajji 是一名法学博士，是毕业于法国图卢兹和摩洛哥卡萨布兰卡法律系公法学的商法律师。他在卡萨布兰卡有 20 年的律师执业经历并且是 Hajji & Associés 的创始合伙人。他还在卡萨布兰卡哈桑二世－艾因乔克法学院担任教授，讲授国际商法和商法的博士课程。他是卡萨布兰卡律师协会成员，专门从事银行法和金融法、航空法、能源法、公法、国际仲裁和诉讼等。他还是摩洛哥商法律师协会的创始成员，会讲阿拉伯语、法语和英语。

Amin Hajji is a juris doctor in Law and a business Lawyer graduated in public law at the Faculty of Law of Toulouse in France and of Casablanca in Morocco. He has twenty (20) years of experience as lawyer in Casablanca and he is the founding Partner of Hajji & Associés. He is also Professor at the faculty of Law of Casablanca Hassan II – Ain Chok: Doctoral studies in international Commercial Law and business Law. He is admitted before the Casablanca Bar Association. He specializes in Banking Law and Finance Law, Aviation Law, Energy Law, Public Law, International Arbitration and Litigation... He is founder member of the Moroccan Association of business lawyers. Amin speaks Arabic, French and English.

Nihma El Gachbour

Nihma El Gachbour 是 Hajji & Associés 的一名律师。她是卡萨布兰卡哈桑二世大学法学院商法学的在读博士生，并在撰写一篇关于房地产投资信托（Les organismes de placement collectif en immobilier）的金融法论文。她拥有卡萨布兰卡哈桑二世大学法学院商法学硕士学位，持有律师专业资格证书，是卡萨布兰卡律师协会成员，专门从事合同法、金融法（项目融资和资本市场）、劳动法、竞争法、民航法、信息隐私法领域的诉讼和非诉讼业务，会讲阿拉伯语、法语和英语。

Nihma El Gachbour is a lawyer at Hajji & Associés Law Firm. She is a PhD student in business law at Faculty of Law, University Hassan II-Casablanca and prepare a thesis in Finance Law regarding real estate investment trust "Les organismes de placement collectif en immobilier". She holds a Master degree in Business Law from Hassan II University-Faculty of Law of Casablanca, she is a holder of the professional proficiency certificate for attorney at law and member of Casablanca Bar. Nihma specializes in Contract Law, Finance Law (project finance & Capital Markets), Labor law, Competition law, Civil Aviation Law, Data Privacy Law and litigation. Nihma speaks Arabic, French and English.

Asmae El Khaier

Asmae El Khaier 是 Hajji & Associés 的一名律师，持有卡萨布兰卡哈桑二世大学法学院的商法硕士学位和法国图卢兹商学院的企业管理硕士学位，持有律师专业资格证书，是卡萨布兰卡律师协会成员，专门从事公司法、并购、银行法、金融法（项目融资和资本市场）、商法、劳动法、信息隐私法等领域的非诉讼业务以及国际仲裁和诉讼，会讲阿拉伯语、法语、英语和西班牙语。

Asmae El Khaier is a lawyer at Hajji & Associés Law Firm. She is a holder of a Master degree in Business Law from Hassan II University-Faculty of Law of Casablanca and a holder of a Master degree in entrepreneurship and business management from ESC-Toulouse (Toulouse Business School)- France. Asmae is a holder of the professional proficiency certificate for attorney at law and member of Casablanca Bar. Asmae specializes in Corporate Law, Mergers & Acquisitions, Banking Law, Finance Law (Project Finance & Capital Markets), Commercial Law, Labor Law, Data Privacy Law, International Arbitration and litigation. Asmae speaks Arabic, French, English and Spanish.

律所介绍 / Introduction to Law Firms

Benzakour 律师事务所

Benzakour 律师事务所（BLF）是 1968 年成立的摩洛哥商法领域主要的律师事务所，享誉摩洛哥，上游和下游业务将该所视为顶级律所之一。

该所在商法领域提供大量和全面的投资组合，尤其注重对外国投资和诉讼提供法律帮助。

该所主要业务领域有公司、合同、外商直接投资、航运／海商法、能源、航空、房地产、劳动法、税务、兼并控制／集中交易和诉讼：债务催收程序和仲裁。

该所擅长与多家外国律师事务所合作开展不同的项目，合作的律师事务所如：霍根·路伟，艾舍斯特，里德·史密斯等。

该所主要服务的客户如：美国进出口银行，摩洛哥皇家航空，谷歌等。

Benzakour Law firm (BLF) is a major Moroccan business law founded in 1968.

It is a prominent and very reputable firm in Morocco.

It is widely regarded as a top law firm acting in upstream and downstream sides.

The firm offers a large and full portfolio in business law, with a particular focus on assistance to foreign investment and litigation.

The main areas of practice are : corporate, contracts, foreign direct investment, shipping/maritime law, energy, aviation, real estate, labor law, tax, merger control/concentration and litigation:collection debt procedures and arbitration.

The firm is very well versed in working in different projects in collaboration with several foreign law firms, such as "Hogan Lovells", "Ashurst", "Reed Smith", "Simmons & Simmons", "Baker & McKenzie", "Shearman & Sterling", "Herbert Smith", "Clyde & Co", "Linklaters", "Clifford Chance", "Denton Wilde Sapte", "Stibbe", "Bredin Prat", "Cleary Gotieb", Sullivan & Cromwell, "The Eren Law Firm", "Morrison Cohen", " SJ Berwin", "Paul Hastings", "Simon et Associés".

The firm has been working for clients, such as: "Export and Import Bank of America: EXIM Bank, Royal Air Maroc, Air Lease Corporation, Google, Oetker, Alitalia, I.A.T.A, Club Med, Accor, Isuzu, Henkel, Diebold, Nokia Siemens", Danone, Alstom, "General Motors, New Look, Sumitomo, Columbia, Aeropuertos Argentina, Philip Morris, KT&G, Mapfre, Adidas, Travelclick, Oetker, ACWA, Fresenius Medical care, Power, Averda, Al Shafar General Contracting", "Endesa", "Sita", "SNCF International", "Aerolease", "Terex", Simba Toys, Teleperformance Intermediation, General Electric Healthcare, "AAR Corp", Can-Pack,Hermes,Technogym PGS, Acticall.

律师介绍 / Introduction to Lawyers

Rachid Benzakour

管理合伙人，顾问部和诉讼部负责人，深入参与对摩洛哥不同领域的外国投资的法律帮助服务：公司、商业、房地产、合同、劳动法、航空、航运、能源、汽车、烟草等。

摩洛哥（2000 年）全国律师资格考试 7000 名考生中排名第一，参与美国佛罗里达州盖恩斯维尔大学的交换项目（1999 年），获法国蒙彼利埃 Magistère DESS-DJCE 大学法学院的商法硕士学位（1998 年）。

工作语言为英语、法语、阿拉伯语和西班牙语。

写作文章：交易万事通（Getting the Deal Through）和全球法律集团（GLG）：《兼并控制——在摩洛哥的集中交易》；国际比较法指南：《航空法（2013 版）》，www.iclg.co.uk。

Managing Partner of the firm.

Responsible for the Consultancy Department and also Head of the Litigation Department.

Deeply involved in legal assistance to foreign investment in Morocco in different fields: corporate, commercial, real estate, contracts, labor law, aviation, shipping, energy, automotive, tobacco...

Ranked First (among 7000 candidates) in National Bar Exam Morocco (2000).

Exchange Program- University of Gainesville- Florida U.S.A (1999).

Masters Degree in Business Law- Magistère DESS-DJCE University of Montpellier, School of Law, France (1998).

He advises in English, French, Arabic and Spanish.

His articles: Getting the Deal Through et Global Legal Group GLG: Merger Control- concentrations in Morocco; The International Comparative Legal Guide to: Aviation Law 2013 Edition, www.iclg.co.uk.

摩洛哥——翻译及协调人介绍 / Morocco–Introduction to Translators and Cooperators

律所介绍 / Introduction to Law Firms

河南昌浩律师事务所

河南昌浩律师事务所成立于 1997 年，位于河南省省会郑州市。事务所拥有教育背景良好、业务能力出众、职业素养优秀的律师队伍，长期服务于国内大型企事业单位，并为来自美国、英国、澳大利亚、埃及、叙利亚等国的客户提供诉讼和非诉讼法律服务。

事务所采用公司化运行模式，实行扁平化、网格化和系统化管理。事务所内设数个综合业务团队，由不同领域的专业律师组成，业务各有侧重。团队成员律师分工明确，各司其职，负责处理专业事务。同时，通过团队律师间的紧密协作和团队间的横向联动，具备强大的处理综合性复杂业务的能力。事务所素以管理规范和诚信执业著称，以团队作战见长，能够为中外客户提供精准的法律服务。

Founded in 1997, Henan Changhao Lawyers (HCL) is located in Zhengzhou, the capital city of Henan Province. The firm has lawyers with good educational background, outstanding business skills and excellent professional quality, has long been serving for domestic large enterprises and government-affiliated institutions, and has been providing litigation and non-litigation legal services for foreign clients from the United States, Britain, Australia, Egypt, Syria and so on.

The firm adopts the operation mode of the company and implements flat, grid and systematic management. The firm has a number of integrated business teams, composed of professional lawyers in different fields whose businesses respectively focus on certain areas. Member lawyers of each team have clear division of labor, attend to their own duties and are responsible for dealing with professional affairs. Meanwhile, through the tight cooperation among the team lawyers and the horizontal linkage between the teams, the firm obtains the strong ability to handle comprehensive and complex businesses. The firm is known for its standardized management and good faith in practice, and is well known for its team operations, thus can provide accurate legal services for Chinese and foreign customers.

律师介绍 / Introduction to Lawyers

徐步林

河南昌浩律师事务所主任，一级律师，悉尼科技大学法学硕士，河南省优秀律师。河南省律师协会副会长，中华全国律师协会理事、国际委委员，河南省欧美同学会（河南省留学人员联谊会）副会长，郑州仲裁委仲裁员。

1993 年起执业，对国内法、普通法、国际商事法律和 WTO 规则有全面了解，曾代理美国和英国公司在中国的诉讼，曾参与国际投资和债权转让谈判及中英文法律文件的起草和审定。

Director of Henan Changhao Lawyers, Senior lawyer.
Master of Laws in University of Technology, Sydney (LLM. UTS).
Henan Excellent Lawyer Award.
Vice President of Henan Lawyers Association.
Director of the All-China Lawyers Association (ACLA).
Member of the International Committee of the ACLA.
Vice President of Henan Western Returned Scholars Association (Henan Overseas-Educated Scholars Association).
Arbitrator of the Zhengzhou Arbitration Commission.
Xu Bulin has been practicing since 1993 and has a comprehensive understanding of domestic law, common law, international commercial law and WTO rules. He has proceeded litigations in China as an attorney of companies of the United States and British, has participated in negotiations on international investment and debt transfer, and has undertaken the drafting and validation of Chinese and English legal documents.

律所介绍 / Introduction to Law Firms

北京高文律师事务所

北京高文律师事务所成立于 2001 年，在中国境内和境外设立有 3 家分所（上海、大连、合肥）、17 个办事处，总计拥有 200 余名律师、专家顾问和律师辅助人员。

高文致力于将专业分工与团队合作密切结合。高文分设知识产权、公司、诉讼仲裁、刑事辩护、海事海商、银行与国际金融、房地产与建设工程、劳动与人力资源等专业部门，保证了高文律师在相关领域的专业化水平。同时，高文还秉承团队化工作模式，根据项目涉及的专业领域整合专家律师团队共同承办，并为客户提供极具专业性和建设性的解决方案。

高文代理了大量的有广泛社会影响的案例，其中多起案件荣获"最高法院十大案例""最高人民法院中国知识产权 50 典型案例""北京市十大外商知识产权保护案""北京市知识产权十大案例""国家知识产权局专利复审委十大案件"等。

Beijing Globe-Law Law Firm was established in 2001. Headquartered in Beijing, Globe-Law now has branches in Shanghai, Dalian, and Hefei, along with its 17 offices worldwide. Globe-Law is now home to nearly 200 experienced lawyers and paralegals.

In providing services to clients, Globe-Law are firmly committed to the principle and spirit of specialization and teamwork. Globe-Law divide our team into several departments, including intellectual property, corporate, litigation and arbitration, criminal defense, maritime, banking and international finance, real estate and construction, labor and human resources, etc. Globe-Law will assign the case to a working team of professionals from various departments, optimizing personnel resources in order to provide the most professional, efficient, and quality legal service to meet our clients' needs.

Globe-Laws lawyers have resoundingly handled a number of cases with enormous social impact, including cases that marked as Top Ten Cases of The Supreme Court of China, 50 Typical Cases of IPR Infringement From The Supreme People's Court of China, Top Ten Cases of IPR Infringement In Beijing, Top Ten Cases of Patent Re-examination Board of SIPO, Top Ten Cases of IPR Infringement for Foreign Investors In Beijing, etc.

律师介绍 / Introduction to Lawyers

刘蓉

刘蓉律师是北京高文律师事务所合伙人，有着 15 年律师工作经验。2010 年，刘蓉律师被选为中国首届涉外律师领军人才，并赴德国、英国学习。

刘律师专注于海事纠纷及海外投资并购领域的法律服务。她常年为美国、斯里兰卡、巴西、摩洛哥等国家和中国香港等地区的企业提供法律服务。她还担任多家贸易公司、国有企业、港口、银行和金融公司的法律顾问。

Liu Rong is a partner of Beijing Globe-Law Law Firm, she has more than 15 years of working experience as a lawyer. In 2010, Lawyer Liu was chosen by Chinese Ministry of Justice to be the Chinese first batch of Leading Overseas Lawyers and was sent to study in German and England.

Lawyer Liu focus on the field of maritime disputes、legal services in overseas investment mergers and acquisitions. She has represented P&I、trade companies and ports handled numerous maritime disputes such as maritime transportation, contract of goods, maritime insurance, collision, shipbuilding and oil pollution cases. Lawyer Liu offers legal services to companies from different countries and regions such as Hong Kong（China）, America, Sri Lanka, Brazil and Morocco for many years. She also works as a legal counsel for Chinese trade companies, state-owned enterprise, ports, banks and financial companies.

新西兰——撰稿人介绍 / New Zealand–Introduction to Authors

律所介绍 / Introduction to Law Firms

Bell Gully 律师事务所

Bell Gully 是新西兰领先律师事务所。在奥克兰和惠灵顿设有办公室，在全国范围内提供全面综合的法律服务。

该所的团队由 43 位合伙人和 184 位律师组成，业务领域包括企业、财产、就业、金融服务、争议解决和税务等。

该所律师专业知识精湛，业务经验丰富，工作包括为客户极复杂、极具竞争力的项目和疑难案件提供咨询，及为客户的日常运营问题提供建议和协助。

作为一家独立的新西兰律师事务所，该所与世界领先的律师事务所、投资顾问、监管机构和公司合作，建立全球服务网络，为客户提供极佳国际服务。

Bell Gully 持续被独立法律目录《钱伯斯亚太》（Chambers Asia Pacific）、Legal 500 和 IFLR 1000 列为新西兰领先律师事务所。

Bell Gully is New Zealand's leading law firm. We operate as a fully integrated national practice with offices in Auckland and Wellington.

It have 43 partners and a team of 184 lawyers who combine market leading corporate, property, employment, financial services, dispute resolution and tax capability along with a wide array of specialist skills.

The firm's range of expertise and experience is extensive, and their work ranges from advising clients on the most complex and ambitious projects and difficult cases, to advising on, and assisting with, clients' day-to-day operational issues.

As an independent New Zealand law firm, they have built networks throughout the world with leading law firms, investment advisers, regulators and companies. This gives our clients access to international best practice.

Bell Gully is consistently ranking by independent legal directories Chambers Asia Pacific, The Legal 500 Asia Pacific and IFLR 1000 as New Zealand's leading law firm.

律师介绍 / Introduction to Lawyers

Chris Gordon

Chris 擅长企业和商业工作。他有超过 30 年的从事并购、合资企业、跨境投资、公司治理和合规、商业合同和竞争性招标等业务的经验。

Chris 还在能源、资源和基础设施方面有丰富的行业经验。在"钱伯斯亚太地区"2018 年的评比中，他在这些领域中名列前茅，并被称为"出色的领导人"，"Legal 500"2018 和"IFLR 1000"2018 也对他的并购工作给予了认可。作为 Bell Gully 律师事务所的前主席，Chris 在"2016 年新西兰法律奖"中获得了年度管理合伙人奖（超过 100 名员工）。

Chris specialises in corporate and commercial work. He has over 30 years' experience, which includes mergers and acquisitions, joint ventures, cross-border investment, corporate governance and compliance, commercial contracting and competitive tenders.

Chris also has significant industry expertise in energy, resources and infrastructure. He is ranked in these areas in Chambers Asia Pacific 2018 which describes Chris as "fantastic in a leadership role". The Legal 500 2018 and the IFLR1000 2018, which also ranks him for mergers and acquisitions work. Formerly Bell Gully's Chair, Chris won the Managing Partner of the Year (>100 Employees) award at the New Zealand Law Awards 2016.

Dean Alderton

Dean 对企业交易提供咨询，包括私募股权、并购交易、收购和 IPO。他在跨境交易咨询方面同样经验丰富。

Dean 于 2015 年被任命为合伙人。在此之前，他曾是 Dentons（大成）律师事务所迪拜办公室的公司合伙人，是悉尼 Gilbert + Tobin 律师事务所的高级律师。

Dean advises on corporate transactions including private equity and M&A transactions, takeovers and IPOs. He has extensive experience in advising on cross border transactions.

Dean was appointed a partner at the start of 2015. He was previously a corporate partner with Dentons in Dubai and a senior lawyer at Gilbert + Tobin in Sydney.

律所介绍 / Introduction to Law Firms

Russell McVeagh 律师事务所

Russell McVeagh 律师事务所是一个充满活力的专家平台，为客户的战略目标提供支持。该所被公认为新西兰领先律师事务所，致力于奋战在法律服务的最前沿。该所在奥克兰和惠灵顿办公室约有 350 名员工和合伙人，该所律师都是各自领域的佼佼者，其专业知识获得了国际认可。

该所的客户包括新西兰交易所的 11 家公司（共 15 家），新西兰的主要企业，包括众多能源和公用事业公司、所有的新西兰零售银行，以及新西兰规模最大的私营企业和上市公司。

该所的业务团队均为市场领导者，协助客户进行极复杂、极具挑战性和极引人注目的交易。即使没有囊括国内所有的重大交易，Russell McVeagh 律师事务所几乎涉足新西兰国内的所有交易（利益冲突案件除外）。

We are a dynamic network of specialists who are champions for our clients' strategic goals. Widely regarded as New Zealand's premier law firm, Russell McVeagh is committed to operating on the cutting edge of legal practice. We employ approximately 350 staff and partners across our Auckland and Wellington offices, our lawyers are the best in their fields and recognised internationally for their expertise.

The firm acts for 11 of the NZX 15 companies, and New Zealand's major corporates, including numerous energy and utilities companies, all of New Zealand's retail banks, and New Zealand's largest company and largest listed company.

All of our practice groups are respected as leaders in the market and we assist clients with their most complex, challenging and high-profile transactions. Russell McVeagh continues to be on almost every, if not all major transactions in the country (conflicts aside).

律师介绍 / Introduction to Lawyers

Dan Jones

Dan 为客户提供复杂的企业和商业法律问题咨询，经验丰富，专门从事证券法、并购、收购、上市规则和基金管理（包括 KiwiSaver 计划和养老金计划）。Dan 也就新西兰证券法要求的豁免、受托人许可和员工持股计划提供咨询。

Dan has extensive experience advising clients on complex corporate and commercial legal issues, specialising in securities law, mergers and acquisitions, takeovers, listing rules and funds management (including KiwiSaver and superannuation). Dan also advises on exemptions from New Zealand securities law requirements, trustee licensing and employee share schemes.

Mei Fern Johnson

Mei Fern 是 Russell McVeagh 的董事会成员，执业领域为企业和商业法，包括并购（含重组和合资企业）、石油和天然气、能源、技术和基础设施等专业领域。

Mei Fern 让客户深刻理解了其项目所在行业的适用监管框架，包括获得新西兰境外投资的监管许可。

她在利益相关者管理方面经验丰富，曾参与各种知名项目。她还在主要采购和招标过程中提供专家意见，包括参与政府项目投标。

Mei Fern 于 2000 年开始执业，是《能源监管与市场评述》（第 2 版）和《钱伯斯公司并购法律实务指导（2016）》两书中"新西兰"章节的合作人。

Mei Fern 是 Totum Limited（石油和天然气行业的服务提供软件）的顾问委员会成员，Russell McVeagh 创新委员会主席，同时也是 Global Women 和 "新西兰董事学会" 成员。

Mei Fern is a Russell McVeagh board member and practises in the areas of corporate and commercial law, including in the specialty areas of M&A (including restructuring and joint ventures), oil and gas, energy, technology, and infrastructure.

Mei Fern brings to clients a deep understanding of the applicable regulatory frameworks of the industries in which her projects are based, including obtaining regulatory consent for foreign investment in New Zealand.

She is experienced in stakeholder management, having worked on various high profile and sensitive projects. She also provides expert advice in major procurement and tendering processes, including responding to Government tender processes.

Mei Fern was admitted to practise in New Zealand in 2000. She co-authored the New Zealand chapters of The Energy Regulation and Markets Review (2nd ed) and Chambers Corporate M&A Legal Practice Guide 2016.

She is an advisory board member for Totum Limited (a software as a service provider in the oil and gas sector) and chairs Russell McVeagh's Innovation Committee. Mei Fern is also a member of Global Women and the Institute of Directors.

新西兰——翻译及协调人介绍 / New Zealand-Introduction to Translators and Cooperators

律所介绍 / Introduction to Law Firms

北京大成（深圳）律师事务所

大成是一家全球多中心的律师事务所，坚持超越自我，以客户需求为中心，始终如一地提供专业、全面、及时、高效便捷的服务，荣膺"Acritas 2015 全球顶尖 20 家精英品牌律所"称号。

北京大成（深圳）律师事务所目前有 200 余名执业律师，其中合伙人 80 名，执业律师中拥有海外留学背景或执业经验的近半数。目前已设立金融与资本市场部、公司与商业事务部、争议解决部、房地产与建设工程部以及知识产权部，共计 5 个专业部门。

Dentons is a global law firm. Being a top 20 firm on the Acritas 2015 Global Elite Brand Index, the Firm is committed to challenging the status quo in delivering consistent and uncompromising quality and value in new and inventive ways.

Beijing Dentons Law Offices, LLP (Shenzhen) currently has more than 200 lawyers, including 80 partners, and about half of them had studied or worked abroad before joining the firm. By now the firm consists of five departments, being finance and capital markets, corporate and commercial affairs, dispute resolution, real estate and construction engineering, and intellectual property.

Address: 3/F, 4/F, Block A, International Innovation Center, No.1006 Shennan Boulevard, Futian District, Shenzhen, P.R.China.

律师介绍 / Introduction to Lawyers

韦金记

韦金记为北京大成（深圳）律师事务所合伙人，具有中国、美国加利福尼亚州和纽约州的律师执业资格，毕业于美国佛罗里达大学，法学硕士（国际税法专业）。

韦律师拥有16年以上中国税务经验，主要处理与外商投资、境外投资、并购、企业重组、跨境交易以及跨国公司在中国经营运作有关的国内和国际税务事务，涉及税务咨询、税务筹划、转让定价、反避税、税务尽职调查、税务争议解决等。他已入选中华全国律师协会涉外律师领军人才库。

Wei Jinji (Glen) is a partner with Beijing Dentons Law Offices, LLP (Shenzhen) and admitted to practice law in China, California, and New York and holds an LL.M. degree in international taxation from the University of Florida.

Mr. Wei has more than 16 years of Chinese tax experience and focuses his practice on domestic and international tax matters related to inbound and outbound investments, mergers and acquisitions, corporate reorganizations, cross-border transactions, and multinationals' business operations in China, involving tax consulting, tax planning, transfer pricing, antiavoidance, tax due diligence, and tax dispute resolution, among others. Mr. Wei is one of the leading lawyers for foreign matters recognized by the All China Lawyers Association (ACLA).

律所介绍 / Introduction to Law Firms

上海段和段（成都）律师事务所

上海段和段（成都）律师事务所是在四川开平律师事务所基础上于2015年1月新组建而成。整合后成立的上海段和段（成都）律师事务所由造诣精深且经验丰富的律师组成，拥有一流的现代化办公场地，全体员工均坚持"高效和优质"的原则，倡导"诚实、严谨"的作风，奉行"委托人的利益高于一切"，为不同行业的客户提供优质的法律服务。

Shanghai Duan&Duan (Chengdu) Law Firm was founded in January 2015, on the basis of Sichuan Kaiping Law Firm. Newly merged Shanghai Duan&Duan (Chengdu) Law Firm is staffed with professional and experienced legal team. The office is furnished with first-class modern work equipment. ALL of our staff believe in the principles of high efficiency and high quality, in advocating with honesty and rigor, and pursuing the belief that the clients' interest comes first. Duan&Duan (Chengdu) lawyers have been providing legal services of high quality for clients from all circles of society.

律师介绍 / Introduction to Lawyers

辜超平

上海段和段（成都）律师事务所首席合伙人、主任，全国优秀律师，四川省律师协会副会长，成都市律师协会副会长，四川省建设厅首席法律顾问，国务院国资委中央企业总法律顾问备选人才，中华全国律师协会涉外领军人才库人才。

辜律师擅长办理外商投资、金融、合同、公司领域等民商事诉讼与非诉讼事务。主要业务领域是：外商投资、企业兼并、重组、产权转让、破产清算，并参与项目可行性论证及谈判。本科毕业于四川师范学院外语系，研究生先后毕业于四川大学历史文化学院、法学院，获历史学和法律双硕士。

Gu Chaoping is the senior partner & chief director of Shanghai Duan & Duan (Chengdu) Law Firm. Mr. Gu is also a National Outstanding Lawyer, vice chairman of Sichuan Province Lawyers Association, vice chairman of Chengdu Lawyers Association, the chief adviser of Sichuan Provincial Department of Construction, alternative legal adviser for enterprises owned by State-owned Assets Supervision and Administration Commission of the State Council, and one of the leading lawyers for foreign matters recognized by the ACLA.

Mr. Gu is proficient in civil and commercial litigation and non-litigation affairs in foreign investment, finance, contract and enterprise. The main practice areas of Mr. Gu are foreign investment, merger, reorganization, transfer of property rights, bankruptcy and liquidation, and demonstration and negotiation of project feasibility. He graduated from foreign language department of Sichuan Normal Institute and got two master's degrees in law and history from Sichuan University.

尼日利亚——撰稿人介绍 / Nigeria–Introduction to Authors

律所介绍 / Introduction to Law Firms

Banwo&Ighodalo（"B&I"）律师事务所

Banwo&Ighodalo（"B&I"）律师事务所成立于1991年2月1日，现如今已经从两人合伙所发展到由12名合伙人与70多名律师组成的律师事务所。该所擅长与上市公司和私营公司、政府、国内外投资者、金融机构、国际咨询公司等有关的业务。B&I律师事务所一直在银行、金融和资本市场、公司及并购、能源和自然资源、房地产和建筑、航运和运输业等领域保持一流水平，在商业纠纷解决领域有可以信赖的成功记录。该所的合伙人和部分律师被多个主要的国际法律评级机构选中入榜。

Banwo & Ighodalo（"B&I"）was established on February 1, 1991 and has today grown from a two-man practice to a twelve-man partnership with more than seventy lawyers. The Firm undertakes work for public and private companies, governments, Nigerian and foreign investors, financial institutions, foreign law firms and international consultancy firms. B&I is consistently listed as a 1st-tier law firm in Banking, Finance and Capital Markets; Commercial, Corporate and M&A; Energy and Natural Resources; Real Estate and Construction; Shipping and Transport; with a tested and dependable track record in Commercial Litigation. The Partners and some Associates of the Firm are ranked in several leading Nigerian and international legal directories.

律师介绍 / Introduction to Lawyers

Ken Etim

Ken是Banwo&Ighodalo律师事务所的管理合伙人。该所是一家在尼日利亚拉各斯和阿布贾都设有分所的综合性一流律师事务所。Ken曾获尼日利亚乌约大学法学学士学位，1991年获得律师执业证。他参与了本所大部分能源和自然资源交易以及基础设施项目。他是尼日利亚的公证人，还是尼日利亚律师协会商法分会能源及环境专业委员会副主任。他也是国际石油协调委员会和尼日利亚天然气协会的成员。

Ken is the Managing Partner of Banwo & Ighodalo, a leading first-class multi-disciplinary law firm with offices in Lagos and Abuja Nigeria. Ken obtained his law degree from the University of Uyo, and was admitted to the Nigerian Bar in 1991. He has been involved in most of the firm's energy and natural resources transactions, as well as infrastructure projects. He is a Notary Public for Nigeria, and is the Vice Chairman of the Energy & Environment Committee of the Nigerian Bar Association Section on Business Law (NBA-SBL). He is also a member of the Association of International Petroleum Negotiators and the Nigerian Gas Association.

Toba

Toba是Banwo&Ighodalo律师事务所的执业律师，他在保险行业工作10年后自2013年开始律师执业。他精通法律合规业务，对在尼日利亚经商涉及的法律法规十分熟悉。他是尼日利亚律师协会商法分会保险和年金专业委员会（NBA-SBL）的委员，他还在公司法以及诉讼法领域有着丰富的经验。他曾就读于埃基蒂联邦理工学院（商学）、拉各斯州立大学（学士）、尼日利亚法学院（法学学士）以及拉各斯大学（法学硕士）。

Toba is the Practice Support Lawyer (PSL) at Banwo & Ighodalo. He was called to the Nigerian Bar in 2013 after a 10-year stint in the insurance and pension industries. He has keen interest in regulatory compliance and is well versed in the legal and regulatory framework for doing business in Nigeria. A member of the Insurance and Pension Committee of the Nigerian Bar Association Section on Business Law (NBA-SBL), Toba also has considerable experience in corporate and commercial law practice and litigation. He studied at the Federal Polytechnic Ado-Ekiti (Business Studies); Lagos State University (LLB); Nigerian Law School (BL); and the University of Lagos (LLM).

律所介绍 / Introduction to Law Firms

Udo Udoma 和 Belo-Osagie 律师事务所

Udo Udoma 和 Belo-Osagie 律师事务所被誉为尼日利亚"魅力三角"（Magic Triangle）律师事务所之一，即该所是尼日利亚法律市场中拥有最高国际知名合伙人比例的律所之一。该所是一家专注于公司、商事法律服务的律师事务所，办公场所位于尼日利亚核心商区，并在加纳设有分所。该所与国内外的客户共同努力，开拓创新，帮助客户在尼日利亚国内外发展业务。

Udo Udoma and Belo-Osagie has been described in international rankings as one of Nigeria's "Magic Triangle" law firms – a description underscored by one of the highest ratios of internationally-recognised partners per firm in the Nigerian legal market. We are a full service corporate and commercial law firm with offices in Nigeria's key commercial centres and an affiliate in Ghana. We work with local and international clients to create and implement innovative solutions that are designed to facilitate business in Nigeria and beyond.

律师介绍 / Introduction to Lawyers

Ozofu 'Latunde Ogiemudia

Ozofu 律师是 Udo Udoma 和 Belo-Osagie 律师事务所合伙人，是企业法律顾问、私募股权和企业并购等团队成员，并与他人共同负责该所的法律援助事务。Ozofu 律师博学多才，为各个领域提供法律咨询，包括公司法和商法、私募股权、企业重组和兼并、劳动与就业等业务，并涉足诉讼和纠纷解决。Ozofu 律师是尼日利亚律师协会商法分会企业并购重组委员会副主任。

Ozofu is a partner in the firm's corporate advisory, private equity and mergers & acquisitions teams and co-heads the firm's pro bono practice. She is recognised as an extremely resourceful and versatile adviser and has advised on various areas of the law including corporate and commercial law, private equity, corporate re-structuring and mergers and acquisitions, regulatory compliance, labour and employment, company secretarial practice with a stint in litigation and dispute resolution. She is a Vice Chairman of the Nigerian Bar Association-Section on Business Law Committee on Mergers, Acquisitions and Corporate Restructurings.

Mary Ekemezie

Mary Ekemezie 律师是 Udo Udoma 和 Belo-Osagie 私募股权、企业并购、劳动就业以及企业法律顾问等团队的资深律师，为各种交易提供法律服务。Mary Ekemezie 律师具有丰富的执业经验，包括为私募股权基金和其他跨国投资者、运营商就股权投资和融资提供咨询服务，为参与企业并购的目标公司提供劳工法、工会法、劳动争议和劳工补偿等方面的咨询意见。Mary 是《世界银行女性商业和法律报告》的定期撰稿人，IFLR 2016 之《企业并购评论和法律实践——国际收购交易指南 2016》的合著者，同时也为《Bowmans 非洲指南——商业转移对就业的影响》撰稿。

Mary Ekemezie a Senior Associate in the firm's private equity, mergers and acquisitions, labour and employment and corporate advisory teams,and has been involved in various transactions across her practice areas.Her experience includes advising private equity funds and other multinational investors and operators on equity investments and financing in a range of sectors. She also advises target companies involved in mergers and acquisitions on issues relating to employment law as well as advising on trade union laws and trade disputes and the applicable compensation regime in the context of employment arrangements. Mary is a regular contributor to the World Bank's Women Business and Law Report.She co-authored the IFLR 2016 Mergers and Acquisition Review and the Practical Law-International Acquisitions Transaction Guide 2016 and contributed to the Bowmans Africa Guide-Employment Consequences of Business Transfer.

尼日利亚——翻译及协调人介绍 / Nigeria–Introduction to Translators and Cooperators

律所介绍 / Introduction to Law Firms

国浩律师事务所

国浩律师事务所成立于 1998 年，是中国最大的跨区域律师事务所之一，在投融资和争议解决领域提供极为专业的法律服务。国浩律师事务所在北京、上海、深圳、杭州、广州、昆明、天津、成都、宁波、福州、西安、南京、南宁、济南、重庆、苏州、长沙、太原、武汉、贵阳、乌鲁木齐、郑州、石家庄、香港、巴黎、马德里、硅谷、斯德哥尔摩设有分支机构。

国浩律师事务所现有 600 余名合伙人，90% 以上的合伙人具有博士、硕士学位和高级职称，其中多名合伙人为我国某一法律领域及相关专业的著名专家和学者。国浩律师事务所拥有执业律师、律师助理、律师秘书及支持保障人员逾 2700 人。

Grandall Law Firm (hereinafter referred to as "Grandall") was established in 1998 and is one of the largest trans-regional law firms in China, providing the most professional legal services in the field of investment, financing and dispute resolution. It has offices in Beijing, Shanghai, Shenzhen, Hangzhou, Guangzhou, Kunming, Tianjin, Chengdu, Ningbo, Fuzhou, Xi'an, Nanjing, Nanning, Jinan, Chongqing, Suzhou, Changsha, Taiyuan, Wuhan, Zhengzhou, Shijiazhuang, Hong Kong, Paris, Madrid, Silicon Valley and Stockholm.

Grandall currently has more than 600 partners. More than 90% of partners have doctoral, master's degree and senior professional titles. Many of them are renowned experts and scholars in a certain legal field and related fields in China. Grandall has more than 2,700 lawyers, assistant lawyers, lawyers' secretaries and support personnel.

律师介绍 / Introduction to Lawyers

谢湘辉

法学博士、高级律师，国浩律师（深圳）事务所高级合伙人。谢律师在英国皇家特许仲裁院、中国国际经济贸易仲裁委员会、广州仲裁委员会等多家海内外仲裁机构担任仲裁员。

谢律师擅长国际投资、国际贸易、知识产权、国际仲裁领域的法律事务，曾代理许多有重大影响的案件，受到全球媒体的关注。2016 年，谢律师被《亚洲法律杂志》评为"中国十五佳诉讼律师"。

PhD, senior lawyer, partner of Grandall Law Firm Shenzhen, arbitrator of CIA, CIETAC, Guangzhou Arbitration Commission and others.

Mr. Xie has expertise in the field of international investment, international trade and Intellectual Property, as well international commercial arbitration. He had represented his clients in many influential cases which were focused by global media. He was awarded by ALB as the Top 15 Litigation Lawyers in China in 2016.

律所介绍 / Introduction to Law Firms

广西欣和律师事务所

广西欣和律师事务所创立于 1998 年，是广西最大的综合性律师事务所之一，现有执业律师 70 余名，辅助人员 20 余名，总共超过 100 人，为客户提供包括民商诉讼、刑事诉讼、金融业务、涉外业务、房地产业务以及各类非诉业务等全面法律服务。

20 多年来，欣和律师事务所始终秉承"克己尽职，服务社会"的执业理念，坚持"专业团队、主动服务、资源整合、追求实效"的服务模式。该所经过 20 多年的不断发展和逐步壮大，已成为广西最具影响力的律所之一，深得当事人的赞誉和社会各界的认同，并多次荣获广西壮族自治区司法厅、广西壮族自治区律协授予的全区优秀律师事务所称号。

Guangxi Sunward Law Firm, founded in 1998, one of the biggest law firms in Guangxi with a total amount of over 100 persons, among whom over 70 are practicing lawyers and more than 20 are assistants.The Firm endeavours to provide comprehensive legal service for the clients, including civil litigation, criminal litigation, and all kinds of non-litigation legal services in commercial transactions such as financial business, foreign-related business, real estate business, etc.

The Firm's founding philosophy is "Try our best to provide the best legal services to our clients", adhere to the concept "Be Professional、Effective and Corporative". Through 20 years' constant development, the Firm has become one of most influential law firms in Guangxi Zhuang Autonomous Region, and won the title of "Outstanding Law Firm " awarded by the Department of justice and Lawyers Association Guangxi for many times.

律师介绍 / Introduction to Lawyers

赵荣蓉

赵荣蓉律师，法学硕士，广西欣和律师事务所合伙人，中华全国律师协会涉外律师领军人才库人员。主要从事业务领域：企业重组和并购、房地产开发、建设工程、金融和涉外法律服务，并同时担任多家大中型企业法律顾问。

Zhao Rongrong, Master of Law, partner of Guangxi Sunward Law Firm, listed in the Pool of the Top Foreign-related Lawyers of China National Lawyer's Association. She has advised on the following areas of the law: corporate re-structuring and mergers and acquisitions, real estate and constructions, acting as a legal counsel for many large and medium-sized enterprises.

巴勒斯坦——撰稿人介绍 / Palestine–Introduction to Authors

律所介绍 / Introduction to Law Firms

Al Zaeem & Associates 律师事务所

创建于 1987 年的 Al Zaeem & Associates 律师事务所是巴勒斯坦规模最大的商事律师事务所之一。该所因其擅长不同领域业务的律师和团队而赢得了良好的声誉。该所现有 14 名律师和 30 名行政和秘书人员，其中包括 2 名在约旦河西岸地区工作的律师。

Al Zaeem & Associates 律师事务所与其他国家的多家律师事务所建立了紧密的联系。同时，Al Zaeem & Associates 律师事务所是 Terralex 律师联盟（详见 www.terralex.org）在中东地区第一批的代表处之一。这种专业和文化的融合使 Al Zaeem & Associates 律师事务所能够同时理解本地客户和国际客户的需求。

自 1995 年至今，该所连续被钱伯斯评为巴勒斯坦最大的商事律师事务所。同时，Sharhabeel Al Zaeem 先生也被钱伯斯评选为巴勒斯坦优秀律师。

该所为众多的本地和国际公司、银行、非政府组织、国际非政府组织、非营利组织、半官方组织和个人提供法律服务。如需了解更多信息，请参见 www.alzaeem.ps。

Al Zaeem & Associates is one of the largest commercial law firm in Palestine, which has been established since 1987. The firm's reputation is built on the individual and collective strengths of its attorneys, each of whom specializes in a different area of work. Al Zaeem & Associates firm consists of 14 attorneys with thirty administrative and secretarial support staff including two associates in the West Bank.

The firm has forged close ties with other law firms in many countries. The firm is one of first representatives of Terralex (www.terralex.org) in the Middle East. This diverse mix of expertise and culture enables the firm to understand the needs and requirements of local and international clients.

The firm has been classified as the largest law firm in Palestine by ("Chambers Global" the world's leading lawyers) as from 1995 till today. In addition, Mr. Sharhabeel Al Zaeem has kept his classification as the best individual lawyer in Palestine.

The firm provides legal services to a wide range of local and international companies and banks, non-governmental organizations and international non- governmental organizations, not-profit institutions, semi-governmental organizations and individuals. For more complete list of clients, please visit our website www.alzaeem.ps.

律师介绍 / Introduction to Lawyers

Sharhabeel Yousef Al Zaeem

Al Zaeem 先生 1982 年毕业获法律学位，并具法律和政治学双硕士学位。在奥斯陆和平谈判和开罗宣言期间，他是巴勒斯坦代表团的法律顾问。

他被认为是拥有大量实践经验的巴勒斯坦杰出商事法律顾问。自 1995 年起他被包括钱伯斯在内的众多国际机构评定为一流律师。Al Zaeem 先生的执业领域包括：公司法、银行法、知识产权、诉讼、土地法、劳动法、税法、国际法、能源法、投资法、许可法、商业促进和替代争端解决。他在巴勒斯坦为许多各种类型的外国和本地企业提供顾问和代表服务。

Al Zaeem 先生是巴勒斯坦律师协会、美国律师协会、阿拉伯知识产权协会及耶鲁大学中东法律论坛的成员。

Mr. Al Zaeem graduated with a Law degree in 1982 and holds two master degrees in Law & Political Science. He was the legal consultant to the Palestinian delegation during the peace talks in Oslo and Cairo Accords.

He is recognized as the leading commercial law adviser in Palestine, with the largest private practice in Palestine. He is ranked first by many international agencies including Chambers Global since 1995. Mr. Al Zaeem areas of practice are: company law, banking law, intellectual property, litigation, land law, labor law, taxation law, international law, energy law, investment law, licenses, business development and alternative dispute resolution. He provides consultancies and representation services for a large majority of various foreign and local entities in Palestine.

Mr. Al Zaeem is a member at Palestinian Bar Association, American Bar Association, Arab Society for Intellectual Property and Yale Law School Middle East Legal Studies Seminar.

Khaled Sharhabeel Al Zaeem

Khaled Al Zaeem 先生，2013 年毕业于伦敦大学东方和非洲研究学院并获得法律学位，2018 年获得该学院的商法硕士学位。

在 Al Zaeem & Associates 律师事务所经过两年的训练后，Khaled Al Zaeem 先生 2015 年加入了该所的律师团队。在 2014 年的加沙冲突期间，他志愿为联合国近东巴勒斯坦难民救济和工程处工作，工作内容是为加沙司法部收集联合国边境检查而收集证人声明。之后他开始作为兼职法律助理为司法部工作。Khaled Al Zaeem 先生同时还兼任巴勒斯坦大学讲师。

Khaled Al Zaeem 先生主要业务领域是：商法、知识产权、劳动法和公司法。

Khaled Al Zaeem 先生是巴勒斯坦律师协会和国际律师协会成员。

Mr. Khaled Al Zaeem graduated with a Law degree from SOAS (School of Oriental and African Studies) University of London in 2013 and he got a master degree in Commercial Law from SOAS University of London in 2018.

He concluded his training at Al Zaeem & Associates Office for two years, and then joined the team of attorneys-at-law at the office in 2015. During Gaza conflict in 2014, he volunteered to work with UNRWA – Gaza Legal Department in collecting witness's statement for the UN Board of Inquiry, then he started to work as a part time Legal Assistant with the Legal Department. He also worked as a part time Lecturer at University of Palestine.

Mr. Al Zaeem is specialized in the following areas: Commercial Law, Intellectual Property, Labor Law and Corporate Law.

Mr. Al Zaeem is a member at Palestinian Bar Association and member of the International Bar Association.

巴勒斯坦——翻译及协调人介绍 / Palestine–Introduction to Translators and Cooperators

律所介绍 / Introduction to Law Firms

山东琴岛律师事务所

山东琴岛律师事务所于 1980 年 8 月在青岛市成立，是一家以资本市场、保险证券、公司事务、外商投资、刑事辩护、海事海商、知识产权、房地产、国际商务和人身损害民事赔偿等专业法律服务为特色的综合性律师事务所，业务范围广泛，囊括法律服务各专业领域。

总部设于青岛，在济南等地设有分支机构，执业律师 120 余人。

多年来，以突出的业绩获得各级各类荣誉数十项，其中国家级的有：全国五一劳动奖状、全国创建文明行业工作先进单位、司法部集体一等功、全国法律服务文明示范窗口、全国优秀律师事务所、司法部部级文明律师事务所等。琴岛法律服务得到社会各界的普遍认可，被授予青岛市"服务百佳""消费者放心满意服务""AAA 信誉等级"等多项荣誉，"琴岛"注册商标被认定为"山东省著名商标"和"青岛市著名商标"。

Founded in 1980, Qindao Law Firm ("Qindao") is the first law firm in Qingdao. It is a comprehensive law firm providing legal services in all fields covering capital market, insurance and securities, corporate affairs, foreign investment, criminal defense, maritime affairs, intellectual property, real estate, international commerce and personal injury claims.

With its head office in Qingdao, Qindao has branch offices in Jinan and other cities, employing around 120 practicing attorneys.

For many years, Qindao has been awarded dozens of honors for its outstanding performance, among which are: National May 1st Labor Award, Advanced Entity in Creating Civilized Trade Practice at the National Level, First-Class Commendation from Ministry of Justice, Show Window of Civilized Legal Services at the National Level, Excellent Law Firm at the National Level, and Civilized Law Firm at the Ministerial Level. Qindao's legal services have been generally acknowledged by various circles of the society and given various honors in Qingdao, including "Top 100 Service Providers", "Services Deserving Consumers' Reliance and Satisfaction", and "AAA Credibility Rating". Qindao as a registered trademark has been rated as "Well-known Trademark in Shandong Province" and "Well-known Trademark in Qingdao City".

律师介绍 / Introduction to Lawyers

蓝斐

蓝斐律师是山东琴岛律师事务所合伙人、执业律师，澳大利亚（昆士兰州）注册外国律师。他毕业于英国南安普顿大学，取得海商法硕士学位。他获得了"青岛市优秀律师"称号。蓝斐律师现为青岛仲裁委员会仲裁员、青岛市律师协会海事海商专业委员会副主任、青岛市律师协会对外交流委员会副主任。

蓝斐律师主要业务领域：涉外法律事务、公司法律事务、海事海商、金融法律事务等。他为多家企业提供常年法律顾问,并为多家银行及金融机构提供法律服务。执业期间蓝斐律师办理了大量的海事海商、金融类民事诉讼业务,具有丰富的诉讼经验。

Mr.Lan Fei is a partner of Shandong Qindao Law Firm, qualified lawyer in People's Republic of China, registered foreign lawyer in Queensland of Australia. Mr. Lan graduated from University of Southampton with master of maritime law. Mr. Lan has been awarded Qingdao Excellent Lawyer. He is currently an arbitrator of Qingdao Arbitration Committee, vice chairman of External Communication Committee of Qingdao Lawyer Association, vice chairman of Maritime and Admiralty Committee of Qingdao Lawyer Association.

His main practice fields include but not limit to foreign legal affairs, maritime affairs, corporate affairs, financial affairs and criminal defense. He serves as a long-term legal consultant for many companies and provides legal services for banks and financial institutions of Qingdao. During his practicing period, Mr. Lan participated in and handled numerous cases of maritime affairs and financial affairs.

律所介绍 / Introduction to Law Firms

北京市盈科律师事务所

北京市盈科律师事务所总部设在中国北京,是一家全球化和综合性的法律服务机构,是亚太地区规模最大的律师事务所之一,是 ALB 机构评选的 2017 年中国 30 强律师事务所之一。在中国大陆拥有 46 家办公室,盈科全球法律服务联盟已覆盖海外 53 个国家的 113 个国际城市。北京盈科(天津)律师事务所是总部设立的首家分所,是天津地区规模最大的律师事务所,客户涵盖了多家世界 500 强企业、政府及社会机构、国有企事业单位、金融机构及各类民营企业等。

As the one of largest law firm in the Asia-pacific region, Beijing Yingke Law Firm headquartered in Beijing, China, was a global and comprehensive legal services agency. Meanwhile, it was awarded as one of China's top 30 law firms by Asian Legal Business (ALB) in 2017. There are 46 offices in mainland China, and the global legal service alliance has covered 113 international cities in 53 overseas countries. Beijing Law Firm Tianjin Office is the first branch set up by the headquarters. As the largest law firm in Tianjin, its clients included a number of top 500 enterprises, government agencies, social institutions, state-owned enterprises, financial institutions, all kinds of private enterprises, etc...

律师介绍 / Introduction to Lawyers

罗静

罗静律师,北京盈科(天津)律师事务所高级合伙人、管委会成员,中华全国律师协会国际业务委员会委员、中华全国律师协会行政法专业委员会委员、中国国际贸易促进会商事调解员。2001 年起执业,专注于涉外商事、劳动法和行政诉讼并享有盛誉。罗静律师成功代理多起案件,被全国媒体所报道,努力以个案推动法治进程。

As the senior partner of Beijing Law Firm Tianjin Office, Luo Jing, lawyer is the member of cross-border issues committee of All China Lawyers Association (ACLA), the member of Administrative Law Committee of ACLA, the mediator of China Council for the Promotion of International Trade (CCPIT). Since 2001, she began her practice engaging in foreign trading affairs, labor law and administrative litigation and enjoyed a great reputation. A number of cases acted by Luo Jing, reported by the national media. Besides, she has been making g effort to promote the process of the rule of law with her case study.

巴拿马——撰稿人介绍 / Panama–Introduction to Authors

律所介绍 / Introduction to Law Firms

Alemán, Cordero, Galindo & Lee 律师事务所

Alemán, Cordero, Galindo & Lee 律师事务所在巴拿马是银行、并购、资本市场、能源、电信、诉讼、采矿、贸易和离岸业务等领域的顶级律所。该所的离岸业务受到其在世界各地办公室及在欧洲、亚洲、美国和拉丁美洲强大代理机构网络的支持。该所为来自各个行业的公司提供法律意见服务,其中包括全球财富 500 强企业。该所曾获得"巴拿马年度律师事务所""中美洲年度律师事务所"(钱伯斯)以及"巴拿马年度律师事务所"(IFLR)称号。

Alemán, Cordero, Galindo & Lee(Alcogal)is a firm widely recognized as a top tier firm in the areas of banking, M&A, capital markets, energy, telecommunications, litigation, mining, trade, and offshore. The firm's offshore practice is supported by its offices scattering around the world and also by a strong network of correspondents throughout Europe, Asia, the United States and Latin America. The firm provides legal advice to companies from various industries, which includes several Global Fortune 500 companies。 The firm was most recently credited with the title of Panama Law Firm of the Year(Chambers), Central American Law Firm of the Year* (Chambers), and Panama Law Firm of the Year (IFLR).

律师介绍 / Introduction to Lawyers

Alejandro Ferrer

Alejandro Ferrer 博士于 1998 年作为合伙人加入 Alemán, Cordero, Galindo & Lee, 是国际商事关系方面的资深律师，也是《巴拿马加入 WTO：对发展中国家加入世界贸易体系的影响》一书的作者。Ferrer 博士是钱伯斯、IFLR 1000 以及 Legal 500 认证律师，他拥有密歇根大学法学博士（S.J.D.）和法学硕士（LL.M.）学位，以及 Universidad Santa María La Antigua 大学法律和政治学学士学位，精通西班牙语、英语和法语。

Dr. Alejandro Ferrer joined Alemán, Cordero, Galindo & Lee in 1998 as a partner. He is considered as a resourceful advisor for international commercial relations, and is also the author of Accession of Panama to the WTO: Implications for Developing Countries Joining the World Trade System. Dr. Ferrer has been recognized as a leading lawyer by Chambers & Partners, IFLR1000, and Legal 500. Dr. Ferrer has a Doctor of the Science of Law (S.J.D.) and a Master of Laws (LL.M.) from the University of Michigan Law School, and a Bachelor of Law and Political Sciences from Universidad Santa María La Antigua. He is fluent in Spanish, English, and French.

Eloy Alfaro B.

Eloy Alfaro B. 先生于 2004 年加入 Alemán, Cordero, Galindo & Lee 律师事务所，2011 年成为该所合伙人，专业领域主要是在银行、资本市场、公司及并购、公开招标、特许经营以及房地产方面。Alfaro 先生已为数家国际银行和公司完成了跨境融资交易，以及为客户在重要的公开招标项目中提供顾问服务。Alfaro 先生拥有宾夕法尼亚大学法学院法学博士学位和哥伦比亚大学政治学学士学位，精通西班牙语和英语。

Eloy Alfaro B. joined Alemán Cordero Galindo & Lee and became a partner in 2011. His professional practice concentrates in banking, finance and capital markets, corporate and M&A, public bids and concession contracts, and real estate law. Mr. Alfaro has assisted several international banks and companies in cross-border financing transactions, and also advised clients in important public bid projects. Mr. Alfaro has a Juris Doctor from the University of Pennsylvania Law School, and a Bachelor of Arts in political science from Columbia University. He is fluent in Spanish and English.

Diego Anguizola

Diego Anguizola 自 2015 年起一直在 Alemán, Cordero, Galindo & Lee 律师事务所担任助理，业务领域包括离岸服务、公司和并购以及公开招标和特许权合同。Anguizola 先生已协助为数宗复杂的本地和跨境交易提供了顾问意见。Anguizola 先生拥有路易斯安那州立大学法学博士（J.D.）学位，Universidad Santa María la Antigua 大学法律和政治学学士学位，以及弗吉尼亚大学经济学和哲学学士学位，精通西班牙语和英语。

Diego Anguizola has been an associate at Alemán, Cordero, Galindo & Lee since 2015. His practice areas include offshore services, corporate and M&A, and public bids and concession contracts. Mr. Anguizola has helped advise in complex local and cross border transactions. Mr. Anguizola has a Juris Doctor (J.D.) from Louisiana State University, a Bachelor of Law and Political Sciences from Universidad Santa María la Antigua (Summa Cum Laude), and a Bachelor of Arts in Economics and Philosophy from the University of Virginia. He is fluent in Spanish and English.

巴拿马——翻译及协调人介绍 / Panama-Introduction to Translators and Cooperators

律所介绍 / Introduction to Law Firms

福建重宇合众律师事务所

福建重宇合众律师事务所成立于 2002 年 9 月 30 日，是"中律联盟"创始成员所及"TAGLAW"中国成员所。该所设有厦门总部及莆田、福州、泉州三个分所，年办理案件超过 5000 件。

该所的工作范围涉及各种新兴与疑难法律领域，其执业律师使用中英文双语服务，曾多次成功地为外国政府与世界知名机构在中国的投资与其他活动提供法律帮助，也曾为国内各级政府、各类企业单位、金融机构和个人包括弱势群体等提供全方位个性化的专业服务。

Founded on September 30, 2002, the Universal Legal Corp. of China ("ULC") is a charter member of "China Attorney's Network" and one of Chinese members of "TAGLAW" with its HO in Xiamen Special Economic Zone and three branch offices in Putian, Fuzhou and Quanzhou respectively, dealing with more than 5000 legal cases each year.

Due to its bilingual legal services covering all star-up and complex areas, ULC has successfully provided legal assistance for foreign governments and world-renowned institutions in their investments and other activities in China and also has furnished comprehensive and professional services for all levels of government and CPPCC, various types of enterprises, financial institutions and private individuals, including a number of vulnerable groups.

律师介绍 / Introduction to Lawyers

涂崇禹

福建重宇合众律师事务所首席合伙人，兼任中华全国律师协会宪法与人权专业委员会委员、中国案例法学研究会理事、中国国际贸易促进委员会调解中心调解员、福建省青年法律工作者协会副会长、福建省劳动法学研究会副会长、厦门大学法学院硕士生导师、福建农林大学校外研究生导师、厦门大学嘉庚学院副教授、厦门城市学院客座教授等；曾受聘担任 2017 金砖国家领导人厦门会晤全程法律顾问之总协调人，首批参加中国—欧盟法律与司法合作项目，获颁全国五一劳动奖章、全国维护职工权益杰出律师、全国同心·律师服务团优秀团员、中华全国律师协会涉外律师领军人才库成员等。

Mr. Tu Chongyu is the Chief Partner of the Universal Legal Corp. ("ULC") and also a Member of the Constitution & Human Rights Committee of ACLA, Council Member of China Case Law Society, Mediator of Mediation Center of CCPIT, Vice Chair of the Youth Lawyer Association of Fujian Province, Vice Chair of the Research Society on Labor Laws of Fujian Province, Supervisor of Postgraduate at Xiamen University School of Law, External Supervisor of Postgraduate at Fujian Agriculture and Forestry University, Associate Professor at Xiamen University TKK College, Guest Professor at Xiamen City University. Mr. Tu had hold the appointment as General Coordinator of Full Legal Advisors of 2017 BRICS Xiamen Summit, had also participated in the EU-China Legal and Judicial Cooperation Program and had been awarded the National Labor Medal, National Outstanding Lawyer for the Protection of Worker's Rights and Interests, Excellent Member of National Service Group of Tongxin Lawyers and is one of Chinese Leading Lawyers on International Pratice.

律所介绍 / Introduction to Law Firms

国浩律师事务所

国浩律师事务所成立于 1998 年，是中国最大的跨区域律师事务所之一，在投融资和争议解决领域提供极为专业的法律服务。国浩律师事务所在北京、上海、深圳、杭州、广州、昆明、天津、成都、宁波、福州、西安、南京、南宁、济南、重庆、苏州、长沙、太原、武汉、贵阳、乌鲁木齐、郑州、石家庄、香港、巴黎、马德里、硅谷、斯德哥尔摩设有分支机构。

国浩律师事务所现有 600 余名合伙人，90% 以上的合伙人具有博士、硕士学位和高级职称，其中多名合伙人为我国某一法律领域及相关专业的著名专家和学者。国浩律师事务所拥有执业律师、律师助理、律师秘书及支持保障人员逾 2700 人。

Grandall Law Firm (hereinafter referred to as "Grandall") was established in 1998 and is one of the largest trans-regional law firms in China, providing the most professional legal services in the field of investment, financing and dispute resolution. It has offices in Beijing, Shanghai, Shenzhen, Hangzhou, Guangzhou, Kunming, Tianjin, Chengdu, Ningbo, Fuzhou, Xi'an, Nanjing, Nanning, Jinan, Chongqing, Suzhou, Changsha, Taiyuan, Wuhan, Zhengzhou, Shijiazhuang, Hong Kong, Paris, Madrid, Silicon Valley and Stockholm.

Grandall currently has more than 600 partners. More than 90% of partners have doctoral, master's degree and senior professional titles. Many of them are renowned experts and scholars in a certain legal field and related fields in China. Grandall has more than 2,700 lawyers, assistant lawyers, lawyers' secretaries and support personnel.

律师介绍 / Introduction to Lawyers

赵浚锡

2013 年加入国浩律师（成都）事务所担任专职律师，执业领域为国际贸易、国际仲裁、公司、娱乐文化、商业地产项目的销售和租赁、商标知识产权、信托、融资及私募股权、反垄断、新能源与环保等，为客户代理民商及相关刑事案件。中华全国律师协会涉外律师领军人才库成员、成都市律师协会涉外法律专业委员会委员、成都市律师协会自贸区法律专业委员会委员和广西钦州仲裁委员会仲裁员，精通中文和英文。

Mr. Zhao Junxi joined in Grandall Law Firm (Chengdu Office) in 2013 as a Attorney-at-law. His professional practice concentrates in International Trade; International Business Arbitration; Corporate Counsel; Movie, Entertainment & Cultural; Sale & Lease of Commercial Real Estate Projects; Trademark IP; Trust, Financing, and Private Equity Industry Fund Operation; Competition and Anti-monopoly; New Energy and Environmental Protection; Acting on behalf of clients in foreign-related civil, commercial and penal litigious matters. He is a member of "Leading Talent" Among Foreign Related Lawyers of All China Lawyers Association, of the Professional Committee Concerning Foreign Affairs and Law of Chengdu Lawyers Association, of the Professional Committee Concerning FTZ Affairs and Law of Chengdu Lawyers Association and of Panel Arbitrators of Guanxi Qinzhou Arbitration Commission of China. Mr. Zhao is fluent in Chinese and English.

秘鲁——撰稿人介绍 / Peru–Introduction to Authors

律所介绍 / Introduction to Law Firms

Philippi Prietocarrizosa Ferrero DU & Uría 律师事务所

  Philippi Prietocarrizosa Ferrero DU & Uría（PPU）律师事务所是第一家主要伊比利亚美洲律师事务所。该所由智利的 Philippi，Yrarrázaval，Pulido & Brunner 律师事务所，哥伦比亚的 Prietocarrizosa 律师事务所和两家秘鲁律师事务所 Ferrero Abogados 和 Delmar Ugarte 合并而成。著名的西班牙和葡萄牙律师所 Uría Menéndez 在 2015 年也加入本所。

  该所在圣地亚哥（智利）、波哥大和巴兰基亚（哥伦比亚）和利马（秘鲁）皆设有办公室，律师业务覆盖 13 个领域。此外，Uría Menéndez 律师事务所将其在西班牙、葡萄牙、圣保罗、纽约、北京、伦敦和布鲁塞尔的办公室网络带进了该所。

  展望未来，该所寻求高效响应太平洋联盟国家（智利、哥伦比亚、墨西哥和秘鲁）不断增长的经济关系对专业服务的新的需求，并高效响应欧洲、亚洲和北美公司对拉丁美洲不断增加的兴趣带来的对专业服务的新的需求。

  该所主要业务领域是银行、金融和资本市场，基础建设与项目，公司法 / 并购，竞争法，争议解决，劳动法，能源法，采矿与自然资源，知识产权 / 生命科学，公法，税法与国际贸易法，电讯，房地产，以及私人客户与家庭法。

  Philippi Prietocarrizosa Ferrero DU & Uría (PPU) is the first major Ibero-American law firm. The firm is born from a merger between the Chilean Philippi, Yrarrázaval, Pulido & Brunner, Colombian Prietocarrizosa, and the two Peruvian firms Ferrero Abogados and Delmar Ugarte. The prestigious Spanish and Portuguese firm Uría Menéndez participates in the new firm since its inception in 2015.

  With offices in Santiago (Chile), Bogota and Barranquilla (Colombia), and Lima (Peru) PPU has lawyers in 13 practice areas. Additionally, Uría Menéndez brings its network of offices in Spain, Portugal, Sao Paulo, New York, Beijing, London, and Brussels to the partnership.

  Looking forward, the firm seeks to respond efficiently to new demands for professional services resulting from the growing economic relationship between the countries of the Pacific Alliance (Chile, Colombia, Mexico, and Peru), as well as a growing interest in Latin America by European, Asian, and North American companies.

  Among its main areas of practice are Banking, Finance and Capital Markets, Infrastructure and Projects, Corporate / M&A, Competition, Dispute Resolution, Labor, Energy, Mining and Natural Resources, Intellectual Property / Life Sciences, Public Law, Tax and International Trade, Telecommunications, Real Estate, as well as Private Clients and Family.

律师介绍 / Introduction to Lawyers

Viviana Garcia

  Viviana Garcia 律师在为亚洲公司，尤其是中国公司在秘鲁市场开拓与发展方面经验丰富。她是 PPU 律师事务所利马办公室亚洲业务的负责人，定期出差到中国。

  她在金融、油气、基础建设和运输等领域为客户提供咨询，并为中国机构在秘鲁设立公司提供咨询。她曾受邀到中国参加中国政府组织的几个项目，旨在促进中国与秘鲁的关系。

  她 1998 年获得秘鲁天主教大学法律学位，2002 年获得美国纽约大学公司法法律硕士学位。

  2013 年，Viviana 被《拉丁律师》杂志评为"在拉丁美洲律所工作的 50 大鼓舞人心女律师"。

  Viviana 现为秘鲁阿昂扎义务服务组织副会长，该组织由 17 家秘鲁律师事务所组成，致力于法律援助服务工作。

  Viviana has ample experience advising Asian companies, particularly from People's Republic of China, in its establishment and consolidation in the Peruvian market. She leads the Asian Desk in PPU's Lima office and regularly travels to China.

  She advises clients in several sectors such as financial, oil and gas, infrastructure and transportation, as well as in the incorporation of Chinese institutions in Peru. She has been invited to participate in several programs organized by the Chinese government in China, aimed to strengthen the relations with Perú.

She has a Law Degree from Pontificia Universidad Católica del Perú, Perú (1998), and an LLM in Corporate Law, by New York University (NYU), United States (2002).

In 2013, Viviana was considered by publication "Latin Lawyer" as one of the "50 Inspiring Women who practice Law in Latin American Law Firms".

Viviana is currently Vice President of the Peruvian Alianza Pro Bono, an organization of 17 Peruvian Law Firms committed to promoting among its members Pro Bono work.

Guillermo Ferrero

Guillermo Ferrero 律师具有美国（纽约州）和秘鲁律师执业许可。他在私人公司及上市公司公司事务、并购方面经验丰富，且曾分别代理买方与卖方。他也曾处理各种金融交易，包括各种发债项目（债券、短期凭证、可议付存证）、股权交易，中期综合贷款，租赁交易，资产证券化等。

他1996年获得秘鲁利马大学法律专业学士学位，2000年获得美国纽约大学公司法法律硕士学位，2003年获得英国剑桥大学工商管理硕士学位（获Violeta Aftalion奖毕业）。

他也积极从事学术活动。Guillermo曾为利马大学商法硕士班并购法教授，UPC研究生院公司法教授（2009—2016）（2010年获评最佳教授），秘鲁天主教大学商法II-公司与并购班公司融资法教授。他现为利马律师协会和纽约律师协会会员，以及国际分会秘鲁会长。

Guillermo is admitted to practice Law in United States (New York) and Peru. He has experience in corporate matters as mergers and acquisitions of private and listed companies, in which he has represented both sellers and buyers. He has also advised all kinds of financial transactions, including issuance programs of debt instruments (bonds, short-term instruments, negotiable certificate of deposit), equity issues, medium-term syndicated loans, leasing transactions, asset securitization, etc.

He has a Law Degree from Universidad de Lima, Peru (1996), a LLM in Corporate Law, New York University, United States (2000), and a MBA (Graduated with Violeta Aftalion Award), University of Cambridge, United Kingdom (2003).

Among his Academic experience Guillermo was a Professor of Mergers and Acquisitions, Master in Business Law, Universidad de Lima; Professor of Corporate Law, UPC – Post Graduate School (Distinguished as best law professor in 2010) (2009 – 2016), and Professor of Corporate Finance, Business Law II – Corporations and Mergers and Acquisitions, Pontificia Universidad Católica de Perú (2005 – 2016). Member of the Lima Bar Association and the New York Bar Association and President in Peru of the International Section.

律所介绍 / Introduction to Law Firms

Estudio Olaechea 律师事务所

Estudio Olaechea 律师事务所是一家全面服务的独立律师事务所，致力于提供高质量、有创造性及有效率的法律服务，重视每一个客户的需求。1878年成立后，该所现已发展成秘鲁最大律师事务所之一。该所极其强调律师执业道德和执业高标准。

该所律师曾代理买家、卖家、投资人、股东群体及财务顾问架构、协商和完成复杂商务事项。该所与银行、金融机构及工业界具有长期和珍贵的专业服务关系，代理过来自世界各地的客户。该所也通过成为Club de Abogados, Lex Mundi, The Interlex Group 及 Ius Laboris 这些独立律所联盟的秘鲁独家会员，与世界各地律师事务所建立了紧密的工作关系。

最后但尤为重要的是，该所致力于公益法律服务工作，曾被某专业杂志评为拉美第一公益服务律师事务所。该所为能向几个慈善、文化、体育及福利机构捐款而自豪。该所这个政策自该所成立即存在，已经保持了140年。

Estudio Olaechea is a full-service independent law firm committed to high quality, creative and efficient legal assistance sensitive to the particular needs of every individual client. Founded in 1878, Estudio Olaechea is among the largest law firms in Peru. The firm places great emphasis on ethical and high professional standards.

Estudio Olaechea's attorneys represent buyers, sellers, investors, shareholder groups and financial advisers in structuring, negotiating and consummating complex business matters. The firm has longstanding and valued professional relationships with banks, financial institutions and industries, representing customers from all around the world. The firm has established close working relationships with law firms from all over the world as the exclusive Peruvian member of Club de Abogados, Lex Mundi, The Interlex Group and Ius Laboris, global associations of independent law firms.

Finally, but not less important, our Firm is devoted to Pro-Bono matters, being ranked by a specialized publication as the first Pro-Bono Firm in Latin America. We are proud of our contribution to several charity, cultural, sportive, and welfare organizations. This policy was born together with the Firm and it is maintained through almost 140 years.

律师介绍 / Introduction to Lawyers

José Antonio Olaechea

　　José Antonio Olaechea 律师是 Estudio Olaechea 律师所的管理合伙人,毕业于秘鲁天主教大学法律及人文研究专业。

　　他具有 30 年律师从业经验,是一名非常活跃的利马律师协会会员,纽约律师协会秘鲁分会联席会长,以及国际律师协会秘鲁国别代表。他亦为几家秘鲁上市和非上市公司董事会成员,并自 2002 年起,担任利马驻丹麦总领事。

　　专长为民法、公司法、能源与采矿法。他在合同、反垄断、外商投资、资本市场以及并购方面也有丰富经验。

　　他曾发表无数法律文章,在国际上为钱伯斯、Legal 500、IFLR100、拉丁律师等所公认。

　　Managing Partner of Estudio Olaechea. Lawyer by the Pontificia Universidad Católica del Perú, graduated in Human Studies in the same university.

　　With more than 30 years of experience practicing law. He is an active member of the Lima Bar Association, Co-President of the Peru Chapter of the New York State Bar Association and representative of the country for the International Bar Association. Member of the Board of several Peruvian Companies listed and not listed shares, as well as Consul General of Denmark in Lima since 2002.

　　Specialized in Civil, Corporate Law, Energy and Mining Law. He has broad experience in Contracts, Antitrust, Foreign Investments, Capital Markets, and Mergers & Acquisitions.

　　Author of numerous legal articles and recognized internationally by legal publications such as Chambers & Partners, The Legal 500, IFLR100, Latin Lawyer, among others.

Vladimir Popov

　　Vladimir Popov 律师是 Estudio Olaechea 律师事务所的资深律师,专注于公司、并购、投资与基础建设领域。他毕业于秘鲁天主教大学法律系,是利马律师协会会员。

　　他在公私投资项目、与公共机构签约、开展 PPP 合同项目,以及并购方面,具有丰富的为公司服务的经验。

　　Senior Associate of the Corporate, M&A, Investment and Infrastructure areas of Estudio Olaechea, graduated from the Faculty of Law of the Pontificia Universidad Católica del Perú and member of the Lima Bar Association.

　　He has vast experience in advising companies on public and private investment projects, contracting with public entities, and developing contracts under the Public-Private Partnership scheme and in mergers and acquisitions.

秘鲁——翻译及协调人介绍 / Peru-Introduction to Translators and Cooperators

律所介绍 / Introduction to Law Firms

北京市时代九和律师事务所

　　北京市时代九和律师事务所是我国创立较早、服务全面、深入的大型律师事务所之一,前身为 1994 年成立的北京市时代律师事务所,以及稍后成立的北京市华地律师事务所和北京市九和律师事务所。2001 年,北京市时代律师事务所与北京市华地律师事务所为适应规模化、专业化需要,合并成立了提供全面商业法律服务的北京市时代华地律师事务所。2007 年年初,为了进一步扩大规模和提升专业层次,北京市时代华地律师事务所与北京市九和律师事务所合并成立了北京市时代九和律师事务所。经过两次合并后,该所的律师人数已达一百多名,业务收入已经昂然全国前列,业务规模不断扩大,成为中国知名律师事务所之一。该所在公司、证券、金融、融资、资本市场、房地产、诉讼仲裁、国际投资、国际贸易、海商海事、知识产权等领域拥有一流的专家级律师。

　　Jurisino Law Group is a large law firm offering comprehensive and thorough legal services to clients from within and outside China. Founded in 2001 by a merger between the Times Law Firm and the Highland Law Firm, both among the oldest private law firms in mainland China, and a further merger in 2007 between the Times Highland Law Firm and the Jusers Law Firm, With over 100 lawyers, Jurisino is distinguished by its expertise and reputation in capital markets, banking and financing, crossborder investment, international trade, marine and maritime law, land development, sports and entertainment, information technology, intellectual property, dispute settlement and many other areas of practice. For their unparalleled expertise and uncompromisable commitment to excellence, Jurisino lawyers have been known for many activities. One of Jurisino lawyers acted as the lead counsel for the Beijing Bidding Committee for the 2008 Olympics, another became an expert consultant to the Ministry of Commerce of the P.R. China in the WTO

Doha Round rules negotiation, and yet another led the Chinese legal profession for six years as the President of the All China Lawyers Association.

律师介绍 / Introduction to Lawyers

江家喜

江家喜律师为北京市时代九和律师事务所高级合伙人，具有中国、美国和加拿大律师执业许可证，北京大学法学学士和法学硕士、女王大学法律硕士、约克大学法律博士。主要从事公司治理、资本市场、国际投资、国际贸易、国际诉讼仲裁等业务。担任国际律师协会、中华全国律师协会、美国律师协会多个专业委员会，及国家律师学院客座教授等职务，已在公司治理、跨境投资、反倾销法、反垄断法等领域发表了多种中英文法律专著和专文。

Eric J. Jiang is a Senior Partner at Jurisino Law Group, based in Beijing. He is licensed to practise law in China, USA and Canada. He obtained an LL.B. and M. Jur. from Peking University, an LL.M. from Queen's University and a J.D. from York University. Currently he focuses on corporate governance, capital markets, mergers & acquisitions, cross-border investments, international trade and international arbitration. He serves in multiple positions at several specialized commitees of the International Bar Association, the All China Lawyers Association, and the American Bar Association, and is a Visiting Professor to the China National Lawyers College. He has many publications including A Practical Guide on Corporate Governance in China, "Towards A Truly Globalized Competition Initiative", "From TPP to 'Belt and Road': Some Thoughts on Establishing Institutional Supports", and "Ten Years After Accession to the WTO: Recent Developments in the Non-market Economy Issue".

律所介绍 / Introduction to Law Firms

广东恒益律师事务所

广东恒益律师事务所原名为"广州市对外经济律师事务所"，成立于1984年8月，是中国改革开放后首批成立的涉外专业律师事务所之一。

经过三十多年的发展，本所现已成为华南地区规模较大的综合性律师事务所之一，业务范围涵盖公司、金融、证券、知识产权、房地产、外商投资、国际贸易、反垄断、诉讼、仲裁等各个重要的法律服务领域，可为国内外客户提供全方位的法律服务。

该所多次受到政府主管部门和行业协会的表彰与肯定。1998年，该所荣获司法部授予的"部级文明律师事务所"称号。2005年，该所被中华全国律师协会评为"全国优秀律师事务所"。此外，该所更连续六年被广州市律师协会授予"规范管理奖"。国际著名的法律媒体Legal 500亦对该所予以肯定及推介。

GFE Law Office (the "Firm") used to known as Guangzhou Foreign Economic Law Office, which was founded on 28th August, 1984. In those days, the Firm was designated by the Ministry of Justice of China as one of the principal law firms in China practicing foreign-related legal affairs.

Over the years, the Firm has grown into one of the leading law firms in the South of China, which can provide full services for its domestic and foreign clients, including corporate, banking, securities, intellectual property, real property, FDI, international trade, antitrust and competition, litigation and arbitration.

The Firm is highly acknowledged and recommended by the authorities and bar associations in China. In 1998, the Firm was ranked by the Ministry of Justice as one of the 20 "Model Law Firms" in China. In 2005, the Firm was recognized as "Excellent Law Firm" in China by the All China Lawyers Association. Moreover, the Firm was granted Outstanding Management Award by Guangzhou Lawyers Association for consecutive 6 years. The Firm was also recommended by Legal 500 as one of the leading law firms in Guangzhou.

律师介绍 / Introduction to Lawyers

吴凯

吴凯律师是广东恒益律师事务所高级合伙人，现任广东省律师协会竞争与反垄断法律专业委员会副主任、广州市律师协会公平贸易法律业务专业委员会副主任。

吴凯律师为中山大学国际法硕士、英国格拉斯哥大学反垄断法硕士。

吴凯律师长期从事外商投资、企业并购、境外上市、公司法、反垄断法、商业诉讼、仲裁等领域的法律事务，执业经验丰富。

2013年，吴凯律师被评为中华全国律师协会"中国涉外律师领军人才"；2017年吴凯律师入选中华全国律师协会"一带一路"跨境律师人才库。

Mr. Raymond Wu is a senior partner of GFE Law Office in Guangzhou, China. Moreover, he is the Vice Director of Competition and Anti-trust Laws Committee under Guangdong Lawyers Association, Vice Director of Fair Trade Laws Committee under Guangzhou Lawyers Association in these days.

Mr. Wu obtained his LLM degree of International Competition Laws and Policies from Glasgow University in UK and Master Degree of International Laws from Zhong Shan University in China.

Mr. Wu mainly practices corporate and commercial laws. His specializations include FDI, M&A, overseas listing, antimonopoly legal affairs, general corporate legal affairs, commercial litigation and arbitration. He has extensive experience in advising domestic and foreign clients on their investments and transactions.

In 2013, Mr. Wu was elected as one of the leading Chinese lawyer talents practicing foreign related legal affairs by All China Lawyers Association（"ACLA"）; in 2017, he was enrolled to the "Belt and Road Cross-border Transaction Lawyers Pool" by ACLA.

斯洛文尼亚——撰稿人介绍 / Slovenia–Introduction to Authors

律所介绍 / Introduction to Law Firms

ODI 律师事务所

ODI 律师事务所是亚德里亚地区领先的律师事务所，拥有超过35位法律专家，可以为客户广泛的业务提供法律建议。

该律师事务所在斯洛文尼亚、塞尔维亚、克罗地亚和马其顿设有办公室，在罗马尼亚、波斯尼亚和黑山设立了专门办事处，并且与世界领先的国际律师事务所建立了战略伙伴关系，这使其处于优势地位。客户提供涉及某一地区的独立项目或交易，还是需要跨多个辖区的无缝协调，该律师事务所都能为整个地区广泛的项目和交易提供法律咨询。

该律师事务所的律师拥有国际培训知识，可以就企业与并购、银行与金融、商业、竞争与反垄断、争议解决、就业、能源与基础设施、交通运输、知识产权、公共部门、不动产、重组和破产、税务和技术、媒体和电信等广泛业务提供咨询。该律师事务所是世界银行的关联办公机构、世界正义项目法治指数的参考对象。该律师事务所的一些合伙人是国家法律考试的审查员，并且是司法部认可的执业讲师。

积极的态度、高标准的工作和专业的信誉帮助该律师事务所在所有实践领域发挥核心作用。该律师事务所的声誉得到了国际法律机构排名的认可：2018 年被"国际金融法律评论"评为顶级律所，2017 年被"Legal 500 EMEA"评为顶级律所，被"钱伯斯"评为欧洲顶级律所。

ODI Law Firm is a leading regional corporate law firm in the Adria region with over 35 legal experts providing legal advice regarding a wide spectrum of clients' operations.

ODI's offices in Slovenia, Serbia, Croatia and Macedonia, specialized desks for Romania, Bosnia and Montenegro and strategic partnerships with the world's leading international law firms put ODI in a unique position to provide legal advice in a wide range of projects and transactions throughout the region, irrespective of whether the engagement represents a discrete project or transaction in a single location or requires seamless coordination across multiple jurisdictions.

ODI draws on the knowledge of its internationally trained lawyers advising on a broad range of matters including corporate and M&A, banking & finance, commercial, competition and antitrust, dispute resolution, employment, energy & infrastructure, transport, intellectual property, public sector, real estate, restructuring and insolvency, tax and technology, media and telecommunications. It is the corresponding office for the World bank and referential office in the World Justice Project Rule of Law Index project. Some of its partners are examiners for the state legal exams and are licensed lecturers at the Ministry of Justice.

Its proactive approach, high standards of work and professional integrity have helped ODI in obtaining a central role in all practice areas. Its reputation is confirmed by the international legal directories rankings: IFLR 1000 Top Tier Firm 2018, The Legal 500 EMEA Top Tier 2017 and Chambers' Europe Leading Firm 2017.

律师介绍 / Introduction to Lawyers

Uroš Ilić

Uroš Ilić 律师是 ODI 律师事务所的管理合伙人和 ODI 交易部的主管。他是斯洛文尼亚唯一一位在公司法和破产法两方面都有专长的有资质的律师，在公司、企业并购、银行和金融以及重组方面拥有超过 15 年的经验。

Uroš Ilić 拥有丰富的跨境经验，领域扩展至所有行业。Uroš Ilić 的客户包括约克资本、B2 银行、VTB 银行、兴业银行、欧洲复兴开发银行、荷兰国际集团银行、Ambridge 保险、俄罗斯联邦储蓄银行、PEH、航空公司、国家银行和电信、区域蓝筹股等。

他被国际排名协会"钱伯斯"和"国际金融法律评论"评为斯洛文尼亚公司法和商法领域的领先律师。

Uroš Ilić is the Managing Partner of ODI Law Firm and ODI Head of the Transaction Division. He is the only certified attorney-at-law specialist in Slovenia in both, corporate and insolvency law and has over 15 years of experience in corporate/M&A, banking & finance and restructuring matters.

He has vast cross-border experience expanding across all industries and counts amongst his clients: York Capital, B2 Bank, VTB Bank, Société Générale, EBRD, ING Bank, Ambridge insurance, Sberbank, PE houses, airlines companies, national banks and telecoms, regional blue chips, etc.

He has been recognized by international ranking associations Chambers & Partners and IFLR 1000 as a leading lawyer in Slovenia in the fields of Corporate and Commercial Law.

Katarina Škrbec

Katarina Škrbec 律师，拥有法学硕士学位，ODI 企业并购组高级律师兼主管。除了定期协助客户并维护其在国内和跨境并购交易各个阶段的利益外，Katarina 还在交易过程的各个阶段（从项目计划到项目完成）引导客户。Katarina 在银行、金融和重组领域拥有丰富的经验。

Katarina Škrbec 曾代表不同的集团处理国内和跨境业务重组和重建，为债务人、债权人和机构债权人进行庭内和庭外重建，包括某些顶级的、在斯洛文尼亚破产实践中塑造标准和创造先例的交易。她的客户包括斯洛文尼亚的所有银行、斯洛文尼亚银行资产管理公司、航空公司、俄罗斯电信提供商 Mobile TeleSystems、荷兰 Eastern Horizon 集团、零售商 Tuš、碳交易公司 Belektron 等。

Katarina Škrbec, LL.M., is a Senior Associate and Head of ODI M&A group. In addition to regularly assisting clients and safeguarding their interests in all stages of domestic and cross-border M&A transactions, leading them through all stages of the transactional process, from planning to completion, Katarina has broad experience in banking & finance and restructuring.

She has represented different groups in connection with domestic and cross-border business reorganization and restructuring matters, acting for debtors, creditors, and institutional creditors in in- and out-of-court restructurings, including certain first-of-their-kind transactions that raise standards and set precedents in Slovene insolvency practice. Her clients include all Slovenian banks, Slovenian Bank Asset Management Company, airlines companies, Russian telecommunications provider Mobile TeleSystems, Eastern Horizon Group Netherlands, retailer Tuš, carbon trading company Belektron, etc.

律所介绍 / Introduction to Law Firms

Opam Law Slovenia 律师事务所

Opam Law Slovenia, OP Andoljsek 律师事务所位于斯洛文尼亚卢布尔雅那，为斯洛文尼亚国内和欧洲范围内的国际性企业及私营企业提供法律及税务方面的咨询服务。该律师事务所致力于为客户提供量身定制的服务，确保客户的需求得到最大的满足。信任、长期合作以及真诚沟通是我们工作的准则。该律师事务所侧重于提供国际和本地公司交易、知识产权、税收和合同框架方面的服务。同时，该律师事务所也提供欧盟法律和监管相关的咨询、合规和诉讼服务。

The law firm Opam Law Slovenia, OP Andoljsek d.o.o. from Ljubljana, Slovenia, provides legal and tax consulting services to both international corporate clients and privately owned entities active in Slovenia and in Europe. Opam Law Slovenia, OP Andoljsek provide tailor made services and take pride in assuring personal attention to each of our clients. Opam Law Slovenia, OP Andoljsek value trust, long-term cooperation and direct and open communication.

Opam Law Slovenia focuses on international and localised corporate transactions, intellectual property, taxation, and contractual frameworks. Opam Law Slovenia, OP Andoljsek also provide EU law and regulatory consulting, compliance and litigation services.

律师介绍 / Introduction to Lawyers

Tatjana Andoljsek

Tatjana Andoljsek, Opam Law Slovenia 律师事务所的创始合伙人，英国剑桥大学的法学硕士学位（LLM）和工商管理硕士学位（MBA），斯洛文尼亚律师协会会员和卢森堡律师协会成员。Tatjana 律师不仅具有制药行业背景，而且取得了剑桥硕士学位和国际工商管理硕士学位，其在国际交易、知识产权、公司法和商业法方面，及仲裁和诉讼中具有专业的业务水平。同时，Tatjana 律师精通包括英语、意大利语、德语和法语在内的七国语言。

The founding partner, Attorney Tatjana Andoljsek, LLM (Cambridge, UK), MBA, is member of the Slovenia and Luxembourg Bar. Tatjana's background in pharmaceutical industry and her Cambridge Masters and international MBA studies allow her to specialise in international transactions, intellectual property, corporate and business law aspects, and arbitration and litigation. Tatjana is fluent in 7 languages, including English, Italian, German and French.

Klemen Mir

Klemen Mir, Opam Law Slovenia 律师事务所税务合伙人，主要为客户运营提供国际和地方税务及财务方面的服务。他为两家最大的国际税务咨询公司提供国际税务和财务方面的全方位的咨询服务。Klemen 精通包括英语、法语和德语在内的六国语言。

Klemen Mir LL.B. is tax partner working on international and local tax and financial aspects of client operations. His work for two of the largest international tax consulting firms allows him to provide full scope international tax and financial services. Klemen is fluent in 6 languages, including English, French, and German.

斯洛文尼亚——翻译及协调人介绍 / Slovenia–Introduction to Translators and Cooperators

律所介绍 / Introduction to Law Firms

安杰律师事务所

安杰律师事务所是一家提供商业法律服务的综合性律师事务所，在境内外并购、私募股权投资、金融、反垄断与反不正当竞争、基础设施与项目融资、知识产权、争议解决、房地产与建设工程、证券与资本市场、能源和矿产资源、公司日常事务等领域有着丰富的法律服务经验和卓越的业绩。

安杰现有合伙人、高级顾问、执业律师及行政人员 300 多人。安杰的大多数合伙人具有在国外知名律师事务所工作或在海外长期学习的经历。部分合伙人、高级顾问曾经在中国相关部委、国际组织、司法机构任职。

安杰律师具有中国及亚洲、美洲、欧洲等其他国家从事律师工作的专业资格。安杰律师及其专业人士能用中文、英文、韩文、日文等语言为客户提供服务。

凭借着专业水平和卓越服务，安杰和安杰律师被钱伯斯（Chambers）、Who's Who Legal、Legal 500、ALB、中国商法等相关国际主流法律评级机构与专业刊物评定为专业领域的优秀中国律师和重点推荐律师。

AnJie Law Firm is a comprehensive law firm providing commercial legal services. Its practice areas include domestic and cross-border mergers and acquisitions, private equity investment, finance, antitrust and anti-unfair competition, infrastructure and project finance, intellectual property, dispute resolution, real estate and construction, securities and capital markets, energy and mining, and corporate governance and compliance. Anjie has vast experience in legal services and has achieved outstanding performance.

AnJie has more than 300 partners, senior counsels, lawyers and supporting staff. Most of AnJie's partners have practiced within leading international law firms, or have long-term overseas learning experience. Some of them have worked within national ministries of the People's Republic of China and within international organizations.

In addition to admissions to practice in China, Anjie's partners and senior counsels have obtained professional qualifications from America, Europe and other Asian countries. Anjie's lawyers and professionals are capable of providing legal services directly in Chinese, English, Korean and Japanese.

With professional standards and excellent service, AnJie and AnJie lawyers have been honored as excellent Chinese lawyers or are highly recommended by a number of international ranking institutions and legal journals, including Chambers, Who's Who Legal, Legal 500, Asian Legal Business, and the China Business Law Journal.

律师介绍 / Introduction to Lawyers

王秀娟

王秀娟律师，北京安杰律师事务所合伙人，中华全国律师协会涉外律师领军人才，国际律师联盟 UIA 国际私法委员会委员，美国天普大学比斯利法学院法学硕士，曾参加中国司法部和中华全国律师协会组织的"涉外律师领军人才"英国 BPP 大学国际商事仲裁境外培训项目。执业领域主要为国际商事仲裁和涉外诉讼业务，代理了在中国国际经济贸易仲裁委员会、北京仲裁委员会、上海仲裁委员会、国际商会仲裁院、新加坡国际仲裁中心等国际国内仲裁机构的大量国际商事争议案件，同时也为国内外客户提供常年法律顾问服务。

Wang Xiujuan (Jansy Wang), Partner of AnJie Law Firm, honored as "Leading talents of foreign-related lawyers" authorized by ACLA, a member of Private International Law Commission of UIA, LLM of Temple University Beasley School of Law. She has attended the international commercial arbitration training program in BPP University organized by Ministry of Justice and ACLA. Her practice areas focus on international commercial arbitration and cross-border litigation. She has represented clients in a number of domestic and international commercial disputes before CIETAC, BAC, SHAC, ICC, SIAC. She also provides corporate governance and compliance legal services for domestic and foreign clients.

律所介绍 / Introduction to Law Firms

重庆盛世文辉律师事务所

重庆盛世文辉律师事务所（以下简称"盛世文辉"）是合伙制律师事务所，成立于2002年2月。盛世文辉经过十余年的发展，已逐渐成为西南地区从事国际投资和外商投资法律服务的行业翘楚。盛世文辉是一家以指导国际投资和外企商事服务为龙头，以公司并购与重组、证券与资本融资、银行与金融、建筑工程与房地产、能源与自然资源、知识产权、劳资关系处理、争议解决、法律翻译为主业的综合性律师事务所。

Senswins Solicitors is a frequent recipient of industry recognition for its strength in litigation and high-stakes appellate work, its leadership in groundbreaking transactions and its depth in public policy, Senswins provides a comprehensive suite of services for global companies and local individuals. Its team of litigators, dealmakers, and policy lawyers and advisors collaborate with a single goal: the success of our clients. Founded in 2002 with the guiding vision that commitment, excellence and integrity drive success, the firm focuses on building lasting and mutually beneficial relationships with its clients. Through its global network of its partners the firm advises leading enterprises in a wide variety of industries, including communications and technology, mining, minerals and energy, and consumer goods and services on matters involving policy, trade, dispute resolution, transactions and project development activities in both mature and emerging markets.

律师介绍 / Introduction to Lawyers

曹平

专业领域为公司收购、兼并与重组，私募股权投资与风险投资，外商投资，能源和基础建设。

曹平律师作为英国驻重庆总领事馆在重庆的首位推荐律师，拥有中国项目在伦敦证券交易所成功上市的丰富经验，并曾在英国、中国香港大型律师事务所执业，擅长国际金融、海外上市、国内项目融资、贸易融资、典当、融资租赁等金融业务领域方面的法律服务；海外投资、离岸构架业务、国内矿产、能源、基础设施、房地产等项目投资业务方面的法律服务；行政机关、园区开发、外资引进等方面的法律服务。

As the primarily and first recommended lawyer of British General consulate stationed in Chongqing, Richard Cao has abundant experience in successful listing of Chinese projects in London Stock Exchange. He has practiced law in large-scale law firms of London and Hong Kong(China), expertised in offering legal service in such financial business areas as international finance, overseas listing, domestic project finance, trade finance, pawn, finance lease; and in such project investment business areas as foreign investment, offshore framework business, domestic minerals, energy, infrastructure, real estate; and in such other areas as dealing with administrative organs, park development and introduction of foreign capital.

南非——撰稿人介绍 / South Africa-Introduction to Authors

律所介绍 / Introduction to Law Firms

ENSafrica 律师事务所

ENSafrica是非洲最大的律师事务所，拥有超过600名从业人员和200多年的经验。该公司通过其在南部非洲、西非、东非和毛里求斯等地密切合作的办事处提供涵盖各商事领域的法律、税务、鉴证和知识产权等方面的专业服务。

ENSafrica is Africa's largest law firm with over 600 practitioners and more than 200 years of experience. The firm offers specialist expertise through its fully integrated offices across Southern, West and East Africa and Mauritius, which spans all commercial areas of law, tax, forensics and intellectual property.

律师介绍 / Introduction to Lawyers

Kenny Chiu

招君雄律师是南非 ENSafrica 律师事务所的合伙人，亚洲业务组的负责人。他本人拥有多年丰富的跨境并购交易和银行经验，并曾任职国际知名律师及会计师事务所，先后为众多跨国中资企业提供有关投资非洲的策略性咨询。他以丰富的经验为众多行业的交易提供全程帮助，包括基础设施、金融服务、矿业、房地产和媒体。

招君雄律师能流利使用普通话、广东话和英语。他广泛地访问过中国各地，对中国和非洲的商业以及社会、政治和文化问题有着广泛的实践经验和深入的了解。

招君雄律师是《法律时报》《商法和税务评论》《工程新闻》和《不带偏见》的定期撰稿人。

Kenny Chiu is an executive at ENSafrica. He heads up the firm's Asia Practice Group. Kenny has experience in banking and cross-border transactions and has advised international corporates, accounting and law firms on China – Africa strategy. Kenny has assisted in all phases of the transaction process and his experience spans a range of industries, including infrastructure, financial services, mining, real estate and media. Kenny speaks fluent Mandarin, Cantonese and English. He has travelled extensively to China and has broad practical experience and understanding of Chinese and African business, as well as social, political and cultural issues.

Kenny is the author of a number of articles and is a regular contributor for the Legal Times, Business Law and Tax Review, Engineering News and Without Prejudice.

Wil Huang

黄正祎律师是南非 ENSafrica 律师事务所亚洲业务组的资深律师，专注于建设、职业责任、企业拯救、职业责任和保险相关业务。他拥有为大建筑公司和咨询公司提供法律意见和诉讼辩护的经验。除此之外，黄正祎律师也曾作为团队成员为多家知名企业的企业拯救事宜提供服务。

关于公私营合资项目和再生能源电力生产采购计划，他为多家不同的国际 EPC 总承包提供投标、工程及项目执行的法律咨询。此外，他也代表全球最著名的通信技术公司之一，尤其是为其非洲区域的公司重组提供咨询。

黄正祎律师能使用流利的普通话和英语，对中国企业在非洲发展的需求及挑战拥有丰富经验，他也是 ENSafrica 律师事务所跨国咨询团队的成员之一，专注为中国企业在东非地区的发展提供咨询及意见。

Wil Huang is a senior associate at ENSafrica's Asia Practice Groupspecialises in construction, professional liability, business rescue and insurance related matters. Wil's experience includes the provision of advice and defence of actions brought against major construction companies and advisory firms. In addition to the above, Wil is part of team that is involved in a number of high profile business rescue matters.

Wil's commercial experience extends to acting for various international EPC contractors inpublic private partnership programs and bidding under the Renewable Energy Independent Power Producers Procurement Program. Wil also has experience in acting for one of the largest global telecommunications companies and in particular advising it on its corporate restructuring in Africa.

Wil is fluent in English and Chinese and has an in-depth understanding of Chinese businesses and their cultures. He works with numerous Asian clients and was instrumental in advising many of them in establishing a foothold in South Africa and other parts of the African continent. Wil is also part of our cross-border advisory team, focusing on China entry and expansion strategy in East Africa.

Wendy Shih

史秋禅律师是 ENSafrica 亚洲业务组的交易律师，拥有丰富的跨境并购、尽职调查、项目管理、合资经营、私募股权和其他与公司法相关的交易经验。她先后代表不同的上市和私人企业，服务经验遍及采矿、汽车、通信媒体、房地产发展、银行、航空及消费产品领域。

史秋禅律师能使用流利的普通话和英语，是其律师事务所跨国咨询团队的成员之一，对跨国企业在非洲所遭遇的文化、语言、惯例、经营上的挑战有深入的了解。此外，她也是南非高等法院的公证律师和房产过户律师。

Wendy Shih is an associate at ENSafrica's Asia Practice and has experience in cross-border mergers and acquisitions, due diligence investigations, project management, joint venture, private equity and other corporate transactions. She has acted for a diverse range of listed and unlisted clients inthe mining, automobiles, telecommunications, real estates, banking, aviation and consumer goods sectors.

Fluent in Chinese and English, Wendy is part of our cross-border advisory team and has an in-depth understanding on the cultural, linguistic, custom and business challenges facing cross-border companies doing business in Africa. She is also a Notary Public and Conveyancer of the High Court of South Africa.h.

南非——翻译及协调人介绍 / South Africa–Introduction to Translators and Cooperators

律所介绍 / Introduction to Law Firms

上海段和段律师事务所

上海段和段律师事务所成立于 1993 年，是中国改革开放后由中国留学生回国创办的第一家与国际接轨的知名综合性律师事务所，总部位于上海，设有公司部、国际投资贸易与反垄断部、证券金融部、知识产权部、房地产与建筑工程部、海事海商部、国内诉讼仲裁部、跨境争议解决部及民事法律部等多个专业部门，目前在国内外拥有将近 20 个办公室，曾被评为"司法部文明律师事务所""钱伯斯公司法／争议解决领域杰出律所"和《中国商法期刊》"年度最佳交易律师事务所"。

Founded in 1993 as the first renowned international law firm in China established by Chinese students with overseas studying experience after China's reform and opening up, Shanghai Duan&Duan Law Firm is a full service law firm headquartered in Shanghai providing services to international clients in a broad range of areas: Corporate, International Investment & Trade and Antitrust, Intellectual Property, Litigation, International Arbitration, Construction & Engineering, Real Estate, etc. With around twenty offices in and outside China, Duan&Duan has been top-ranked by Ministry of Justice of China, Chambers Global/Asia, Legal 500, China Business Law Journal etc.

律师介绍 / Introduction to Lawyers

俞毓斌

俞毓斌律师是上海段和段（厦门）律师事务所合伙人、中华全国律师协会涉外律师领军人才、福建省律协民商法律专业委员会副主任，民盟"一带一路"（福建）研究院研究员。

俞律师主要从事公司与证券、国际投资与贸易、国际争议解决等方面的专业法律服务，长期为国内外客户提供国内和涉外业务的建立、管理、运营、融资、重组与并购、上市及合规等方面的综合性法律服务。

2017 年，俞毓斌律师入选中华全国律师协会涉外律师领军人才 20 人赴美国培训项目，参加了美国国际法学会联合美国乔治敦大学在华盛顿特区举办的"跨国投资与国际贸易政策"培训，并在美国顶级律师事务所 Akin Gump Strauss Hauer& Feld LLP 学习相关的美国法律实务与律所管理。

Rubin Yu is the partner of Shanghai Duan&Duan (Xiamen) Law Firm, China National Leading International Lawyer Accredited by ACLA, Vice Director of Civil & Commercial Law Committee of Lawyers Association of Fujian Province, Research Fellow of Belt & Road (Fujian) Research Institute of China Democratic League.

Rubin's practicing areas are mainly Corporate & Securities, International Investment& Trade, International Dispute Resolution. He regularly advises international clients comprehensively on legal and regulatory matters related to the start-up, management, operation, financing, restructuring, M&A and stock listing of their business in and outside China. Rubin is fluent in Mandarin, English and Taiwanese.

In 2017, selected by All China Lawyers Association as one of the twenty Chinese lawyers, Rubin Yu successfully completed the Cross-border Investment and International Trade Policies Training Program given jointly by International Law Institute and Georgetown University in Washington D.C., the U.S. Meanwhile, Rubin also conducted internship in one of the U.S. top law firms, Akin Gump Strauss Hauer& Feld LLP, where he was trained on relevant U.S. legal practice and law firm management.

律所介绍 / Introduction to Law Firms

北京大成律师事务所

北京大成律师事务所（以下简称"大成"）成立于 1992 年，是中国成立最早、规模最大的合伙制律师事务所之一。2005—2010 年，大成连续六年被评为"全国优秀律师事务所"，并在《亚洲法律杂志》（ALB）"全国律师事务所规模 20 强"及"亚洲律师事务所规模 50 强"评比中连续多年排名第一。

2015 年，大成与全球十大律所之一的 Dentons 律师事务所正式合并。合并后的新律所在全球拥有逾 7300 名律师，服务超过 50 个国家，业务遍及加拿大、美国、欧洲、英国、中东、非洲、澳洲、拉丁美洲和加勒比海地区及整个亚太地区，为客户提供丰富的本土经验，帮助他们在各个地区开展业务或解决争议。大成律师事务所与 Dentons 律师事务所的合并，是中西方具影响力的著名律师事务所广泛、深入的合作，是律师服务体系世界范围内的创新，也是世界律师发展史上的一个重要里程碑。

Founded in 1992, Dacheng was one of the first partnership law firms in China and is now one of the largest. Dacheng began implementing its first five-year plan in 2004, and in 2007 the firm launched its strategy of building a global legal services network.

From 2005 to 2010, Dacheng was named an "Outstanding Law Firm in China" for six consecutive years, and topped Asian Legal Business' annual rankings of "ALB China Top 20 Largest Law Firms" and "ALB Asia Top 50 Largest Law Firms" for years.

In 2015, the gobol firm Dentons and Chinese firm Dacheng combined.

With more than 7,300 lawyers serving more than 50 countries, Dentons offers clients the benefit of quality experience in and of the communities in which they want to do business or resolve a dispute—from Canada and the United States across Europe, the United Kingdom, the Middle East and Africa, Australia, Latin America and the Caribbean and throughout the Asia Pacific region. Through broad and in-depth cooperation between the influential law firms from China and the West, Dentons is innovating the world's legal services sector and marking a milestone in the history of the global legal profession.

律师介绍 / Introduction to Lawyers

周争平

周争平律师，北京大成律师事务所高级合伙人、长沙分所涉外业务部主任，同时担任长沙市雨花区政协委员、仲裁员等社会职务，中华全国律师协会涉外领军人才，并参加了第五期英国培训工作。周律师的主要执业领域为公司治理、外商投资、跨境并购、诉讼与仲裁。周律师办理了大量的民商事诉讼与仲裁案件，包括一些涉外民事案件，为当事人挽回经济损失数十亿元。周律师曾为中车集团、博世中国、渣打银行、中联重科、三一重工、华菱集团、安赛乐米塔尔等多家世界500强企业提供过常年或包括企业合规、境外投融资、跨境并购等在内的专项法律服务。

David Zhou is a senior partner at Dentons and leads the foreign-related law department of the Changsha office. His business involves foreign investment and cross-border M&A, including the entrance and exit of foreign investment, M&A, and financing in China and investments and M&A by Chinese state-owned and private enterprises overseas.Mr. Zhou has provided professional, thorough legal services for the business development of numerous multinational enterprises in China, including Bosch, Standard Chartered Bank and Laureate Group, forcefully protecting the legitimate rights and interests of foreign businesses. As a project manager, Mr. Zhou has also assisted the overseas investments and M&A of a number of Hunan enterprises.

Mr. Zhou is a leader in the area of foreign-related law for the Hunan Lawyers Association, serving as a permanent legal advisor for the Chamber of Commerce, the Provincial Federation of Industry and Commerce and numerous other governments and institutions. He has led the overseas M&A business for a number of listed and private enterprises in Hunan.

东帝汶——撰稿人介绍 / Timor-Leste-Introduction to Authors

律所介绍 / Introduction to Law Firms

CRA Timor 律师事务所

CRA Timor 律师事务所成立于2006年1月，由名为 Coelho Ribeiro & Associados 的葡萄牙律师事务所的高级合伙人创办，是一家拥有三十多年丰富经验的葡萄牙律师事务所。

CRA Timor 致力于为有意对东帝汶投资的外国投资者提供最优质的法律咨询和解决方案，同时也支持国家政府、非政府机构和国际组织的投资。

在东帝汶，CRA Timor 可为本土及境外企业、公共和私营主体以及其他公共组织提供全方位的法律咨询服务。该所的法律服务包括为外国投资者提供翻译服务，为投资者选定投资地。该所可在所有业务领域内提供法律服务，为私营及公共实体提供日常法律咨询，包括内部咨询以及为公司从成立到解散过程中开展的所有业务活动提供法律服务。

CRA Timor 一直致力于成为东帝汶领先的国际律师事务所。

CRA Timor was founded on January 2006 by the senior partners of Coelho Ribeiro & Associados – CRA Portugal, a Portuguese Law Firm with a well established practice with over thirty years of experience in the legal profession.

Since CRA Timor's establishment in the territory onwards mission and main purpose is to provide the best legal advice and solutions to foreign investors interested in doing business in the Democratic Republic of Timor-Leste as well as supporting national governmental and non-governmental bodies and international organizations.

CRA Timor offers full-service legal advice in Timor-Leste to a high profile portfolio of Local and International Companies, public and private, as well as to all sorts of Public Entities. Its professional services also include translation services, representation and domiciliation services for foreign investors. CRA Timor performs legal services in all fields of activity, advising Private Companies and Public Entities on a daily basis, including in-house counseling, at all stages of their existence, since incorporation to closure, and in all legal fields of developing and implementing a successful activity.

CRA Timor was, has been and is committed to be a pioneer and the leading international Law firm in Timor-Leste.

律师介绍 / Introduction to Lawyers

Rui Botica Santos

葡萄牙 CRA 律师事务所（Coelho Ribeiro e Associados）合伙人（自 1998 年起）；东帝汶 CRA 律师事务所的创始合伙人；Coelho Ribeiro e Associados-Law 律师事务所合伙人（1993—1998）；马德里大学经济法律高级研究所国际运动法（LLM）专业硕士研究生班的受邀讲师（2007）；里斯本新星大学经济学院破产专业博士研究生班受邀讲师（2003—2007）及争端解决专业讲师（2004）；PortOil- Energia e Recursos Naturais，SA 的董事（2006 年起）；西班牙语公司电视电视频道副总裁（2002—2006）；Semanário Económico 报纸的合作者（1994—2004 年）；Somincor -Sociedade Mineira de Neves Corvo 公司的大会主席（自 2004 年起）；葡萄牙采矿公司 Pirites Alentejanas SA 董事（自 2006 年起）；葡萄牙公司集团总监（1992—1999）；里斯本市政厅旅游部法律顾问（1992—1993）；通用电气葡萄牙大会秘书（1993—2005）和通用电气葡萄牙总会会长（自 2006 年起）。

Professional Experience: Partner of CRA – Coelho Ribeiro e Associados – Portuguese Law Firm (since 1998); Founder Partner of CRA Timor – Timorese Law Firm; Associate of Coelho Ribeiro e Associados-Law Firm (1993-1998); Invited as Lecturer for the Master in International Sport Law (LLM) in Instituto Superior de derecho y Economia in association with the Compultense University of Madrid about Dispute Resolution Matters (2007); Invited as Lecturer for the post-graduation course in Nova Forum, Instituto de Formação de Executivos in the School of Economics at University Nova of Lisbon in Insolvency Subject (2003-2007) and Dispute Resolution Subject (2004); Director of PortOil – Energia e Recursos Naturais, SA (since 2006); Vice-President a TV Cable Channel-Spanish corporation (since 2002-2006); Collaborator of the newspaper "Semanário Económico" (1994-2004); Chairman of the General Meeting of Somincor – Sociedade Mineira de Neves Corvo, SA (since 2004); Director of the Portuguese mining Company Pirites Alentejanas SA (since 2006); Director of a Portuguese Companies Group in aggregates (1992-1999); Legal Advisor of Lisbon Town hall-Department of Tourism (1992-1993); Secretary of the General Meeting of General Electric Portugal (1993-2005) and Chairman of the General Meeting of General Electric Portugal, SA (since 2006).

Paulo Oliveira

专业经验：自 2016 年起担任 CRA 律师，曾在巴西、葡萄牙、东帝汶和中国（上海）工作。巴西圣卡塔琳娜区检察院法律顾问（2012—2015 年）。

学术教育：巴西科学院宪法（法学硕士）（巴西，2013 年）；Faculdade Cenecista de Joinville 法律学士（法学士）（巴西，2012 年）。

语言：葡萄牙语、英语、西班牙语。

成员资格：获准在巴西和东帝汶执业；巴西 BAR 协会（圣卡塔琳娜区）国际贸易委员会成员。

Professional Experience: Lawyer of CRA since 2016, with experience in Brazil, Portugal, Timor-Leste and China (Shanghai); Legal Advisor at the Brazilian Public Prosecution Office, District of Santa Catarina (2012-2015).

Academic Education: Master of Laws – Constitutional Law (LL.M.) in Academia Brasileira de Direito Constitucional (Brazil, 2013); Bachelor of Laws (LL.B.) in Faculdade Cenecista de Joinville (Brazil, 2012).

Languages: Portuguese; English; Spanish.

Memberships: Admitted to practice Law in Brazil and Timor-Leste; Member of the International Trade Commission of Brazilian BAR Association (District of Santa Catarina).

东帝汶——翻译及协调人介绍 / Timor-Leste-Introduction to Translators and Cooperators

律所介绍 / Introduction to Law Firms

德恒律师事务所

德恒律师事务所是中国规模最大的综合性律师事务所之一，1993 年 1 月创建于北京，1995 年更名为德恒律师事务所。除北京总部外，还在国内设立了 25 个分所，在纽约、海牙、巴黎等地建立了 6 个海外分所，并在境外设有 160 个分支与合作机构。自 2007 年起，德恒一直排名全国律所前三强（根据 ALB 排名）。

德恒的传统优势领域，包括国内外股票、债券的发行、承销、上市，投资基金，国内外企业分拆、购并，公司改制，资产重组、破产清偿、跨境融资投资、国际招投标、房地产开发经营、重大建设项目、国际工程、矿产能源、劳动保障、专利代理、知识产权保护等。

Deheng Law Offices, formerly known as China Law Office (CLO) until 1995, was founded on January 13, 1993 in Beijing. Since then the firm has grown to become one of the largest full-service law firms in China. Headquartered in Beijing, DeHeng Law Offices has a network of 25 domestic branches, 6 overseas offices in New York, the Hague, Paris, Brussels, Dubai and Chicago; and relationships with 160 overseas associated institutions. According to the ALB (Asian Legal Business) ranking, Deheng Law Offices has been ranked the TOP three law firms since 2007.

Deheng can provided services covering various areas including domestic and overseas issuance, underwriting, stocks and bonds issuance, investment funds, spin-offs and M&A of domestic and foreign enterprises, company and assets restructuring, bankruptcy liquidation, equity transaction, cross-border investment and financing, international bidding, real estate development and operation, key infrastructure projects, international projects, mining and energy, patent prosecution, Intellectual Property Protection etc.

律师介绍 / Introduction to Lawyers

谭伟华

谭伟华律师现任北京德恒（珠海）律师事务所执行主任、高级合伙人，珠海市律师协会涉外和海商海事委员会主任，具有中国律师资格和澳大利亚商标律师资格。谭律师在涉外、房地产、公司并购和知识产权等业务领域具有丰富的执业经验。2015年10月被司法部、中华全国律师协会选派至美国天普大学参加涉外律师领军人才培训计划。

Tell is currently the Executive Director and a senior partner of Deheng Law Offices(Zhuhai), and serve as the Director of the Foreign Investment and Maritime Law Committee of Lawyer Association of Zhuhai. As an experienced lawyer with solid legal theoretical knowledge and practice since 2002, Tell has extensive experience in dealing with foreign affairs, real estate, corporate mergers and acquisitions and intellectual property. In October 2015, Tell was nominated to study in Temple University of the United States for the "Leading Talent Foreign Lawyers Training Project" organized by the Ministry of Justice of China and the All China Lawyers Association (ACLA).

律所介绍 / Introduction to Law Firms

云南大韬律师事务所

云南大韬律师事务所是一家大型综合性律师事务所，总部设在昆明，拥有3家分所，是全省律师的实习基地之一。律所拥有上百名执业律师，均具有法学本科以上学历，其中法学博士6名、法学硕士十余名。律所的不少执业律师还曾从事过多年的公安、检察、法院等政法工作，以及国有企业经济管理工作，现担任多家国家机关、政府部门、大型企事业单位法律顾问，法院、检察院专家咨询顾问等。

Yunnan Datao Law Firm, a base of practice, is directly subordinated to the Justice Bureau of Yunnan Province. The firm has elegant office building, scientific management, strict case control system, advanced traffic and communicational instruments, besides, a website of its own. The firm has established several departments, such as Department of Criminal, Department of Civil and Commerce, Department of Real estate, Department of Intellectual property, Department of Finance and negotiable security, Department of Investment and Trade, Department of Investigating, Department of Non-litigious Legal Matters and so on. A group of excellent and capable attorney constitutes its law firm, among which the full-time ones are more than 100. Obtaining the bachelor degree or even more, all its attorneys were graduated from legal schools of domestic famous universities. Many of them were being employees in governmental department of political and legal matter, or have the experience of economical management. They are good at their special field of study, and capable of practical experience on lawsuits alike.

律师介绍 / Introduction to Lawyers

杨振发

杨振发，男，法学博士，昆明理工大学法学院副教授，东南亚法与国际法研究中心主任，加拿大北不列颠哥伦比亚大学进修生，云南大韬律师事务所兼职律师。中华全国律师协会涉外律师领军人才，云南省人民政府法制办英文法规审校专家。研究领域和执业领域包括国际法、东南亚国家法、跨境投资、并购。

Mr.Yang Zhenfa, male, Ph.D. at international law, the dean of Southeast Asia Nation Law and International Law Research Center and the Associate Professor of Law School, Kunming University of Science and Technology. Visiting scholar of UNBC, Canada; Expert Advisor for Yunnan provincial government; leading lawyer for foreign affairs selected by All China

Lawyers Association. The specialized researching and practicing Fields including international law, Southeast Asia Nation Law, Cross Border Investment; Funds M&A.

土库曼斯坦——撰稿人介绍 / Turkmenistan–Introduction to Authors

律所介绍 / Introduction to Law Firms

GRATA International 律师事务所

GRATA 成立于 1992 年，是专注于欧亚地区的最大区域性独立律师事务所之一，其设立有包括土库曼斯坦办事处在内的 17 家办事处。

作为深植于政治、法律和商业领域最具影响力的区域律师事务所之一，GRATA 在多种层面与各级政府和半政府机构及主要行业参与者保持着有效的工作关系和沟通渠道。

GRATA 的竞争优势在于最优的性价比和熟知当地的经商心态。客户可以通过向 GRATA 中国代表处咨询以获得其全球网络的服务。同时，GRATA 已经被多家国际领先的评级机构所认可。

Founded in 1992, GRATA International is one of the largest regional independent law firms focusing on Eurasia with 17 offices including Turkmenistan office.

As one of the most influential Regional law firms with deep roots in the political, legal and commercial circles, GRATA International maintains effective working relationships and communication channels with government and semi-governmental entities at various levels, as well as major industry players.

GRATA's competitive advantages include optimal price and quality ratio and understanding of the local mentality of doing business. Clients can gain access to the entire network by enquiring at China office of GRATA International.

GRATA International has been recognized by many leading international rating agencies.

律师介绍 / Introduction to Lawyers

Atabek Sharipov

Atabek 律师，GRATA 土库曼斯坦办事处负责人，专注于跨境并购和担保交易。

Atabek 律师曾参与包括中国—中亚天然气管道项目在内的数十亿美元的区域项目融资交易，该交易使得 GRATA 荣膺 ALB 2009 年度最佳项目融资交易大奖。Atabek 律师的执业能力获得了钱伯斯 2010、2011 及 2018 年版的认可。

Atabek is Head of Turkmenistan desk of GRATA International. He focuses on cross-border and secured transactions.

Atabek had been involved in multibillion regional project finance deals including under China – Central Asia Gas Pipeline Project for which GRATA International was awarded the Best Project Finance Deal of the Year by the ALB Law Awards 2009. Atabek has been recognised for his performance in Chambers and Partners 2010, 2011 and 2018 editions.

Sabina Saparova

Sabina，GRATA 律师，在国际私法、民法和一般商事领域有着丰富的从业经验。

Sabina 律师一直在为包括外国投资者在内的国际客户就土库曼斯坦不同领域的法律法规提供咨询意见，特别包括如下领域：公司、银行、劳动、竞争、知识产权、贸易、消费者保护、签证和投资法规。

Sabina Saparova is an Associate of GRATA International. She is experienced in international private law, civil law and general commercial law matters.

Sabina has been advising international clients including foreign investors on different aspects of Turkmenistan's laws and regulations in particular, among other things: corporate, banking, labour, competition, IP, trade, consumer protection, visa and investment regulations.

Gulnur Nurkeyeva

Gulnur Nurkeyeva 律师，GRATA 中国办事处负责人，负责 GRATA 所覆盖法域与中国相关的项目。

Gulnur 律师拥有超过 18 年的从业经验。Gulnur 律师获得北京大学的法学硕士学位。她在为中资企业，例如中铁、中化工、中建、中技公司、中冶集团、国家开发银行、中国进出口银行，提供哈萨克斯坦有关公司法、建设活动及并购交易等方面的法律服务具有丰富的经验。

Gulnur Nurkeyeva is Head of China desk of GRATA International, responsible for China Related projects in countries of GRATA International presence.

She has over 18 years of experience. Gulnur received her LL.M. from the Peking University (PRC).

She has extensive experience in advising Chinese Companies such as China Railway Construction, China National Chemical Engineering, China Construction, China National Technical Import & Export Corporation, Metallurgical Corporation of China, China Development Bank, China EXIM Bank etc, in Kazakh corporate law, construction activities and M&A transactions.

土库曼斯坦——翻译及协调人介绍 / Turkmenistan–Introduction to Translators and Cooperators

律所介绍 / Introduction to Law Firms

观韬中茂律师事务所

观韬中茂律师事务所（以下简称"观韬"）成立于 1994 年，总部设于中国北京。拥有 500 余名律师、100 余位合伙人，已发展成为中国优秀律师事务所之一。执业领域涉及资本市场、公司业务与并购、银行与金融等十几个业务领域。因其卓越表现，观韬被多个全球知名法律评级机构所推荐。

观韬设有 18 家办公室。通过与联盟所亚司特律师行的紧密合作，观韬可以在全球的平台上持之以恒地为国内及国际客户提供有价值的、全方位的法律服务。

Guantao Law Firm ("Guantao"), founded in 1994 and based in Beijing, has developed into one of the outstanding law firms in China with more than 500 lawyers and more than 100 partners. Its legal practice areas cover more than 10 business fields including capital markets, corporate/M&A, banking and finance, etc. Moreover, it has been recommended by many world-renowned legal professional rating agencies for its excellent performance.

Guantao has 18 offices. Through the close relationship with allied firm Ashurst LLP, Guantao endeavors to continue providing valuable and comprehensive legal services to domestic and international clients on a global platform.

律师介绍 / Introduction to Lawyers

徐玲

徐玲律师，观韬中茂律师事务所高级合伙人。擅长领域为跨境并购、境外上市、私募融资、外商直接投资，近年也涉足涉外商事仲裁和其他争议解决领域。牵头承办众多大型、复杂和具有影响力的跨境并购项目，入选中华全国律师协会涉外律师领军人才库，被多家国际知名法律评级机构评为领先律师和杰出律师。工作语言为英语、中文及德语。

Xu Ling is a senior partner in Guantao Law Firm. She specializes in cross-border M&A, overseas listing, private equity (PE) and foreign direct investment (FDI). In recent years, she begins to focus on international commercial arbitration and other dispute resolution. Ms. Xu has led a number of large-scale, complicated and significant deals on cross-border, and she has been selected as a member of the "Leading Talents" panel of the PRC lawyers practicing foreign-related business law by the All China Lawyers Association, and has been awarded the title of the leading lawyer and outstanding lawyer by many international renowned legal rating agencies. Her working Languages are English, Chinese and German.

律所介绍 / Introduction to Law Firms

金茂凯德律师事务所

金茂凯德律师事务所是上海市专业服务贸易重点单位，总部设在上海，并在北京、广州、香港、芜湖等地设有分所，事务所"一带一路"法律研究与服务中心已经在世界五大洲设有超过 50 个工作站。金茂凯德律师杰出的业务能力体现在全方位的法律服务上，如银行证券业务、资本市场、国际贸易、争议解决等领域。金茂凯德的合伙人均毕业于国内外著名的法律院校，多人被国际权威的法律评级杂志评为"亚洲领先律师"。

Jin Mao Partners is the key unit of Shanghai professional services trade. Jin Mao Partners has set up the branch office in Beijing, Guangzhou, Hong Kong and Wu Hu etc. Moreover, Jin Mao Partners has set up "Belt and Road" Legal Research and Service Center and already established more than 50 overseas stations in five continents.

The outstanding business capabilities of its lawyers have been embodied in overall legal services which including Bank Securities Business, Capital Markets, International Trade, Dispute Resolution etc. Partners of Jin Mao Partners all graduated from reputed law schools all over the world and several of whom were honored as "Asian Leading Lawyer" by an internationally prestigious legal rating magazine.

律师介绍 / Introduction to Lawyers

李志强

李志强为金茂凯德律师事务所创始合伙人、一级律师、仲裁员。1990起执业，担任环太平洋律师协会副主席、吉隆坡区域仲裁中心、上海国际仲裁中心、上海仲裁委员会、南京仲裁委员会仲裁员，上海行政复议委员会委员，黄浦政协常委，上海市"会议大使"。曾被评为上海律师涉外服务标兵、上海优秀青年律师、上海十大杰出青年。

Jack Li (Li Zhiqiang) is the Founding Partner of Jin Mao Partners, the First-grade lawyer and Arbitrator. Mr. Li commenced the legal practicing in 1990. Mr. Li is the Vice President of Inter-Pacific Bar Association, Arbitrator of Kuala Lumpur Regional Centre for Arbitration, Shanghai International Arbitration Center, Shanghai Arbitration Commission and Nanjing Arbitration Commission. Mr. Li is the legal advisor of Administrative Reconsideration Committee of Shanghai Municipal Government, Standing Committee Member of Shanghai Huangpu Political Consultative Conference, and Shanghai "Conference Ambassador".

委内瑞拉——撰稿人介绍 / Venezuela–Introduction to Authors

律所介绍 / Introduction to Law Firms

D'Empaire 律师事务所

D'Empaire 是委内瑞拉的顶级律师事务所之一。它在并购、证券、金融、税务和竞争法等业务领域享有良好的声誉。此外，D'Empaire 在能源、仲裁、诉讼、劳动和环保业务领域具有丰富的实践经验。D'Empaire 是处理经济和法律领域复杂事务的首选律师事务所。

钱伯斯法律评级机构分别于 2009 年、2010 年、2012 年、2015 年、2016 年和 2017 年授予 D'Empaire 第一届、第二届、第四届、第七届、第八届和第九届"拉美卓越奖"。在 2011 年和 2014 年，D'Empaire 与拉美其他 6 家顶级律师事务所一同被"钱伯斯拉美"授予"客户服务奖"，D'Empaire 是委内瑞拉第一家被授予此奖项的律师事务所。

2014 年，D'Empaire 被国际税收评估委员会（ITR）授予"2014 年度委内瑞拉税务事务所"。D'Empaire 也被"LATINLAWYER 250"，拉美顶级商业律师事务所，视为公司原动力。在"PLC Which Lawyer"法律评级项目中，D'Empaire 在竞争、劳动和税务多个领域被列为顶级律师事务所。D'Empaire 在能源、基础设施建设、金融和公司领域也被《国际金融法律评论》（IFLR 1000）列为顶级律师事务所。D'Empaire 的三位合伙人被"Latin Lawyer"列为委内瑞拉 40 岁以下的顶级律师。

D'Empaire 成立于 1972 年，由约 45 名律师组成。其客户包括跨国公司、委内瑞拉主要公司和国际投资银行。

D'Empaire is one of the leading Venezuelan law firms. It enjoys a reputation as the leading M&A, securities, finance, tax and competition law firm in Venezuela. In addition, D'Empaire has strong energy, arbitration, litigation, labor and environmental practices. D'Empaire is the law firm of choice for complex matters in all sectors of the economy and fields of law.

Chambers and Partners awarded D'Empaire with the distinction of Venezuelan Law Firm of 2009, 2010, 2012, 2015, 2016 and 2017 in the first, second, fourth, seventh, eighth and ninth edition of its Latin America Awards for Excellence. In 2011 and 2014, D'Empaire was recognized by Chambers Latin America with the "Client Service Award", together with six distinguished Latin American law firms. D'Empaire was the first Venezuelan law firm to receive this award.

In 2014, D'Empaire was awarded "Venezuelan Tax Firm of 2014" by International Tax Review (ITR). D'Empaire is also considered by LATINLAWYER 250 - Latin America's leading business law firms as a Corporate Powerhouse. D'Empaire is ranked as leading law firm by PLC Which Lawyer Venezuela in several areas, including competition, labor and tax. D'Empaire is also ranked as leading law firm by International Financial Law Review (IFLR 1000) in Energy and infrastructure and Financial and corporate. Three of our partners were considered as "top Venezuelan lawyers under 40" by Latin Lawyer.

D'Empaire was founded in 1972 and comprises approximately 45 lawyers. Its clients include multinationals, major Venezuelan companies and international investment banks.

律师介绍 / Introduction to Lawyers

Fulvio Italiani

Fulvio Italiani 在委内瑞拉是公认的企业和并购领域的顶级律师。他参与了过去几年委内瑞拉的大部分重大收购、融资、石油和天然气交易。

Fulvio Italiani 在 2013 年"钱伯斯拉美卓越奖"中荣获"法律职业杰出贡献"奖项。根据"钱伯斯"法律评级机构，Fulvio Italiani 能够获得这一著名奖项是基于他的业务技巧和法律经验，而 Fulvio Italiani 的这些工作能力对于投资于委内瑞拉这个具有挑战性经济环境的国内和跨国公司来说是非常有利的。

Fulvio Italiani 在成为 D'Empaire 合伙人之前，于 1993 年至 1996 年在世达国际律师事务所纽约办事处担任助理。Fulvio Italiani 曾于 1996 年在加拉加斯的安德烈斯贝洛天主教大学（Universidad Católica Andrés Bello, Caracas）学习法律，成绩优异，1990 年获得法学博士学位。Fulvio Italiani 精通西班牙语、英语和意大利语。

Fulvio Italiani is considered the leading corporate and M&A lawyer in Venezuela. He has participated in most of the significant acquisition, financing and oil and gas transactions taking place in Venezuela in the last years.

Fulvio was honored with the "Outstanding Contribution to the Legal Profession" award at the 2013 Chambers Latin America Awards for Excellence. According to Chambers & Partners, he was selected for the prestigious award in recognition of "his business skills and legal expertise which have been of great benefit to national and multinational companies investing in the challenging economic climate of Venezuela."

Before becoming a partner at D'Empaire, Fulvio Italiani worked as an associate at the New York office of Skadden, Arps, Slate, Meagher & Flom LLP from 1993 to 1996. He studied law at Universidad Católica Andrés Bello, Caracas (J.D. summa cum laude, 1990). He is fluent in Spanish, English and Italian.

Roberto Mas

Roberto Mas 于 2000 年在加拉加斯的安德烈斯贝洛天主教大学获得法学学位。2012 年加入 D'Empaire 之前，他曾任德勤在委内瑞拉的成员公司 Romero-Muci & Asociados 的高级助理。Roberto 在公司日常事务、石油的上下游交易、天然气事务、并购、外汇管制和房地产交易等方面拥有丰富的服务经验。他还为委内瑞拉的私人公司和高净值人士提供公司重组和税务规划方面的建议。Roberto 于 2014 年成为 D'Empaire 的非持股合伙人，并于 2018 年成为股权合伙人。他精通西班牙语和英语。

Roberto Mas received his law degree from Universidad Católica Andres Bello in 2000. Before joining D'Empaire in 2012, he worked as a Senior Associate at Romero-Muci & Asociados, a member firm of Deloitte in Venezuela. Roberto has extensive experience advising clients on general corporate matters, upstream and downstream oil and gas matters, mergers and acquisitions, foreign currency exchange control regulations and real estate deals in Venezuela. He also advises Venezuelan private companies and high-net-worth individuals on corporate restructurings and tax planning matters. Roberto became a non-equity partner at D'Empaire in 2014 and an equity partner in 2018. He is fluent in Spanish and English.

委内瑞拉——翻译及协调人介绍 / Venezuela–Introduction to Translators and Cooperators

律所介绍 / Introduction to Law Firms

隆安律师事务所

隆安律师事务所成立于 1992 年，总所设于北京，是中国最早的合伙制律师事务所之一，并于 2017 年成功改制为特殊普通合伙律师事务所。经过 26 年的发展，隆安已有执业律师八百余名、合伙人二百余名，在上海、深圳、广州等 20 个城市设有分所，在美国和欧洲拥有战略合作伙伴。

隆安曾为世界 500 强等大中型企业提供知识产权、资本市场及金融、公司项目、诉讼和仲裁等领域的法律服务。隆安多次被全国律师管理机构评为中国最优秀的律师事务所之一，成功入围《亚洲法律杂志》多项年度法律大奖，入选中国十佳成长律所，在亚洲最大 50 家律所及中国律所 30 强榜单均位列前十，亦在英国《律师》杂志亚太地区百强律所榜单及中国经营律所 30 强榜单中位居前列。

Established in 1992 and headquartered in Beijing, Longan Law Firm is one of the earliest privately owned law firms in China, and has been restructured into a firm in limited liability partnership in 2017. Longan has been looking to provide extraordinary, effective legal services to our clients, with diligence and integrity. After 26 years' development, Longan has grown into a large law firm with over 800 practicing lawyers and over 200 partners, with offices covering 20 cities including Shanghai, Shenzhen and Guangzhou, and has established strategic cooperation with large and renowned law firms throughout America and Europe. Longan, in the wave of globalisation, is going from strength to strength.

Many lawyers in Longan have graduated from prestigious domestic and foreign law schools with progressives and extensive experience. Some of them hold multiple certifies qualifying them to practice in China and other countries after years of legal practices in America, United Kingdom, and Japan.

In the past 26 years, Longan provided professional and premium legal services for numerous medium and large enterprises including those listed in the Fortune Global 500 in multiple fields including but not limited to intellectual property rights, capital market and finance, corporation projects, litigation and arbitration. Longan's overall strength won and evidenced by various awards and credentials. For many times, Longan has been rated as one of the most outstanding law firms by national lawyers administrative organisations, shortlisted in several annual legal awards of Asian Legal Business (ALB), ranked in ALB China Fast 10, and ranked top 10 in both the ALB Top 50 largest Asian Law Firms and ALB China Top 30 Law Firms. In addition, Longan has also ranked among the best in Top 100 Law Firms in Asian-Pacific Area and Top 30 Elite Law Firms in China by the Lawyer Magazine of Britain.

律师介绍 / Introduction to Lawyers

赖向东

赖向东律师，北京市隆安律师事务所高级合伙人、北京市隆安（深圳）律师事务所创始合伙人。现任中国国际经济贸易仲裁委员会、中国海事仲裁委员会和南京仲裁委仲裁员。广东省律师协会国际业务委员会副主任、深圳市律师协会理事。

赖向东律师在国际贸易法、跨境交易、知识产权、并购和外商投资等方面有较高的理论造诣和实务操作经验，从1986年起代理超过500宗各类涉及银行、保险、证券、公司、房地产、破产清算等诉讼、非诉和仲裁案件。

Tony (Xiangdong) Lai is the senior partner of Longan Law Firm, the Founding Partner of Longan Shenzhen Office. Mr. Lai is currently the listed in the Panel of Arbitrators with CIETAC , ACAS（the Arbitration Center Across the Strait) and Nanjing Arbitration Commission. He is serving as the vice-president of foreign related legal affair commission of Guangdong Bar Association and the Director of Shenzhen Bar Association.

Mr. Lai has particular expertise and substantial experience in international trade, cross-border transaction, IP, M&A and FIEs. Mr. Lai has been practicing law since 1986 and has dealt with over 500 pieces of variety cases involving banking, insurance, securities, corporate, real estate, bankruptcy and liquidation, litigation and arbitration.

律所介绍 / Introduction to Law Firms

北京市鼎业律师事务所

北京市鼎业律师事务所1996年由中华人民共和国司法部批准成立。总部设于北京，在河北、贵州、广西、四川和广东设有分支机构或派驻人员，与意大利、德国、美国、新加坡、印度等地相关律师事务所建立了紧密的合作关系。

合伙人均具有多年执业经历，大部分律师曾赴国外学习或研修法律，具有两种以上语言工作能力。

该所律师具有为国内外客户提供卓有成效法律服务的专业知识、经验和能力，为境内外客户提供公司、金融、境外投资、房地产、知识产权管理和跨境许可等领域的综合法律服务。

该所自成立以来，先后为国内外数百家著名公司、企业和其他机构提供上市、重组、知识产权或诉讼与仲裁代理等服务。

Established in 1996 with the earliest approval of the Ministry of Justice of the People's Republic of China, B.D.L International Law Firm is headquartered in Beijing, capital city of China, with direct offices or expatriate lawyers in Hebei, Guizhou, Guangxi, Sichuan he Guangdong. The firm has close cooperation with local law firms in New York, Geneva, Singapore, India and Africa.

B.D.L is comprised of 17 partners and 42 licensed lawyers. With many years practice as legal professional, all partners are experts with full professional knowledge, experience and expertise in their respective practice areas. Most of the lawyers have worked or received professional training abroad and can well use more than one language in their daily work.

B.D.L International Law Firm is a general law firm in its active development. It offers a full range of legal services and provides comprehensive and creative legal solutions to multinational and domestic clients in the fields of finance/ insurance, corporation/ security, construction, foreign investment, real estate, international business, intellectual property, litigation, arbitration etc.

Since its establishment, the firm has served hundreds of reputable domestic and off shore companies.

律师介绍 / Introduction to Lawyers

许智慧

许智慧律师,北京市鼎业律师事务所合伙人,中国政法大学法学学士、北京大学法学硕士,英国 Exeter 大学法学博士,曾担任广西律师协会副会长、中华全国律师协会副会长、中国女律师协会会长等职。1998 年被评为"全国优秀律师",2003—2012 年担任全国人大代表及公安部特约监督员。

许智慧律师 1993 年开始从事专业律师工作,曾担任多家中外知名企业的中国律师,其中包括荷兰卡地亚国际有限公司、意大利菲拉格慕公司、德国万宝龙公司、美国新百伦运动鞋公司、花花公子公司、永利集团、英国登喜路公司、印度电钢集团等。

许智慧律师主要业务领域包括国际投资、国际贸易、知识产权、公司购并、海洋运输、工程建设等。曾代理多起相关领域的商务谈判和争议解决。

Dr. Xu, Partner of B.D.L International Law Firm, LLB from China University of Political Science and Law, LLM from Beijing University Ph.D. in law from Exeter University, U.K.

Since 1995 Dr. Xu has held numerous important positions, including Vice-President of Guangxi Lawyers' Association, Vice-President of All China Lawyers' Association and President of the All China Female Lawyer's Association, as early as 1998 was named by the Ministry of Justice of China as the "Best lawyer in China". In 2003-2012 she was elected and acted as the deputy of the National People's Congress and supervisor of the Ministry of National Security.

Dr. Xu has been practicing as a professional lawyer since 1993. She has served as the legal counsel in China for many Chinese and overseas leading companies, including Cartier International N.V from Holland, Ferragamo from Italian, Montblanc Simplo GmbH from German, New Balance, Playboy and Wynn Resource from America, Alfred Dunhill from Britain, EletroSteel from India etc.

Dr. Xu's main practice areas cover international investment, international trade, intellectual property etc.

津巴布韦——撰稿人介绍 / Zimbabwe–Introduction to Authors

律所介绍 / Introduction to Law Firms

Hussein Ranchhod & Co. 律师事务所

律师事务所是过去 20 年来一直存在的注册律师事务所,位于津巴布韦的哈拉雷市。其为企业和知名人士提供利基市场服务。其在处理公司法律事务和高风险诉讼方面享有良好的声誉。

该律师事务所以代表哈拉雷市、津巴布韦政府、上市公司和国外客户等实体而闻名。其取得的成就之一是,自 2000 年至 2017 年以来,其一直保留代表津巴布韦前总统(包括官方和个人身份)以及其他政府部门。

该律师事务所已被钱伯斯全球列为津巴布韦仅有的 7 家认可的律所之一。

It is a registered firm of attorneys that has been in existence for the last 20 years. The firm is based in Harare, Zimbabwe. Is caters for a niche market of corporate and prominent individuals. The firm has built its formidable reputation on in its handling of corporate legal matters and high-stakes litigation.

The firm is renowned for having represented entities such as the City of Harare, the Government of Zimbabwe, listed corporations and foreign international clients. Amongst its achievements is the fact that it has been retained since the year 2000 to 2017 to represent the former President of Zimbabwe in his official and personal capacities, various Government ministries.

The firm has been listed by Chambers International, as one of only 7 recognised firms in Zimbabwe.

律师介绍 / Introduction to Lawyers

Terence Hussein

Terence 在 1992 年开始律师执业。他是国际律师协会以及津巴布韦律师协会的一名成员。

在他的职业生涯中,除在 2004—2005 年间担任哈拉雷市的委员外,Terence 还在多个委员会任职。

Terence 代表了大量津巴布韦知名客户,处理了许多备受关注的事情。

Terence started practice in 1992. He is a member of the International Bar Association and the Law Society of Zimbabwe.

As well as serving as Commissioner of the City of Harare between 2004 and 2005, Terence has sat on many Boards in his career.

Terence has represented and handled numerous high-profile matters for a clientele who read as the "who's who" of Zimbabwe.

Paresh Ranchhod

Paresh Ranchhod 在 1992 年加入 Shireen Ahmed & Associates 之前，一直在哈拉雷的 Atherstone & Cook 执业。他在商业、税收收购和兼并方面有丰富的经验。他的经验还包括转让、房地产开发并起草了大量的知识产权融资协议。

Paresh 代表英国、中国、南非和澳大利亚的投资者进行了各种关于铬、黄金、钻石、镍、煤国际交易，并定期前往中国、印度、南非、中东、西非和美国以确保这些交易的合法性和成功进行。

Began practice with Atherstone and Cook, Harare in 1992 before joining Shireen Ahmed & Associates. He has vast experience in commercial, tax acquisitions and mergers. His experience also extends to Conveyancing, Property Development and has drawn up numerous Intellectual Finance Agreements.

Paresh has structured various international transactions relating to chrome, gold, diamonds, nickel and coal on behalf of British, Chinese, South African and Australian investors, and has travelled regularly to China, India, South Africa, Middle East, West Africa and the United States to ensure the success and legality of such transactions.

律所介绍 / Introduction to Law Firms

Honey & Blanckenberg 律师事务所

Honey & Blanckenberg 是津巴布韦历史最悠久的律师事务所，在法律领域拥有 125 年的历史。该律师事务所参与了许多大型交易，并因其良好的声誉，代表了采矿、建筑、银行、电信、能源和农业等各个行业和领域的本地和国际实体和公司。

Honey & Blanckenberg 在全球钱伯斯指南（Global Chambers Guide）中享有国际排名，并且是 Nextlaw Global Referral Network 的成员。其个人合伙人和专业律师是许多专业机构包括津布韦专利和商标代理学院、国际律师协会和国际商标协会的成员。

Honey & Blanckenberg 是一家提供全面服务的律师事务所，涉及多个业务领域，包括但不限于知识产权、公司和商业、诉讼、不动产转让和合规。

Honey & Blanckenberg 致力于在具有挑战性的环境中提供专业服务，并且有多个部门为客户开展专业工作。

Honey & Blanckenberg is the oldest law firm in Zimbabwe with 125 years of experience in the legal field. The firm has been involved in several large transactions, and owing to its stellar reputation, represents local and international entities and companies across various sectors and fields such as mining, construction, banking, telecommunications, energy and agriculture.

Honey & Blanckenberg is internationally ranked in Global Chambers Guide and is a member of Nextlaw Global Referral Network. Its individual partners and professional assistants are members of a number of professional bodies including The Zimbabwe Institute of Patent and Trademark Agent, the International Bar Association and the International Trademark Association.

Honey & Blanckenberg is a full service law firm covering a number of practice areas, including but not limited to, Intellectual Property, Corporate and Commercial, Litigation, Conveyancing and Compliance.

Honey & Blanckenberg is dedicated to providing a professional service in a challenging environment and has a number of departments to carry out specialised work for clients.

律师介绍 / Introduction to Lawyers

Sara Nyaradzo Moyo

Sara 是一名知识产权律师，也是 Honey & Blanckenberg 的高级合伙人。

她领导 Honey & Blanckenberg 的知识产权部门，就津巴布韦知识产权法律和非洲地区知识产权组织的各个方面向当地和国际客户提供建议，包括民事和刑事执法和诉讼、海关救济措施以及对第三方申请提起异议。

她是许多专业知识产权组织的成员，其中包括国际律师协会和国际商标协会。

Sara is an IP Attorney and the senior Partner of Honey & Blanckenberg.

She heads the Intellectual Property Department at Honey & Blanckenberg and advises local and international clients on various aspects of intellectual property law in Zimbabwe and the African Regional Intellectual Property Organisation including civil and criminal enforcement and litigation, customs remedies and oppositions to third party filings.

She is a member of several professional intellectual property organisations including the International Bar Association and the International Trademark Association

Shorai Rutendo Chidemo

Shorai 是 Honey & Blanckenberg 公司与商业部的律师。她的执业领域包括起草合同、企业咨询和诉讼、商法、劳动法、信息技术和通信法、一般诉讼和人权法。她对国际贸易法、银行法、劳动法和债务追收特别感兴趣。

Shorai is an Associate in the Corporate & Commercial Department at Honey & Blanckenberg. Her areas of practice include drafting contracts, corporate advice and litigation, commercial law, labour law, IT and communication law, general litigation and human rights law. She has a particular interest in international trade law, banking law, labour law and debt collection.

津巴布韦——翻译及协调人介绍 / Zimbabwe–Introduction to Translators and Cooperators

律所介绍 / Introduction to Law Firms

北京市尚公律师事务所

北京市尚公律师事务所始创于 1996 年 5 月，是国内最早设立的大型合伙制律师事务所之一。历经二十余年的发展，尚公所已成为中国名列前茅的主要为机构（政府和企业）提供全方位综合民商事法律服务的规模化、综合性专业法律服务机构。尚公所现有执业律师和相关专业人员二百三十余名，分别专精于特定的法律专业领域。尚公致力的专业分工为客户提供充分、全面、精准的法律分析论证，提出优质切实的商业解决建议方案，提供最佳的目标实现方案、问题解决方案，全方位地向国内外客户提供优质高效的法律服务和支持。尚公所总部位于北京市东长安街，在上海、长春、硅谷、海南、昆明、杭州、烟台、西安等地设有分所和办公室，并与美国、英国、加拿大、澳大利亚等国家和中国香港等地区的多家律师事务所建立了长期稳定的战略合作关系。

Established in May 1996, S&P Law Firm is one of the earliest large partnership law firms in China. After development of two decades, S&P has become one of the top large-scale and comprehensive professional legal service providers, mainly offering all-around and comprehensive civil and commercial legal services to the institutes (government and enterprise alike).S&P has more than 230 practicing lawyers and other professionals who are specialized in specific legal areas. Thanks to the thorough division of work based on specialization, S&P lawyers can provide adequate, comprehensive and accurate legal analysis and demonstrations to the clients, fully exploit their professional skill, experience and social resources based on the specific information on the clients and matters entrusted by them to deliver quality and feasible commercial solutions to the attain the intended goals and address the relevant issues. Headquartered at Chang'an Plaza, No. 10 Chang An Street, Dongcheng District, Beijing. S&P has set up its branches in Shanghai, Changchun, Kunming, Hainan, Silicon Valley, Hangzhou and Yantai etc. and established long-term and stable strategic cooperative relationship with some laws firms in USA, UK, Canada, Australia and Hong Kong(China).

律师介绍 / Introduction to Lawyers

刘兴燕

刘兴燕律师，北京市尚公律师事务所管理委员会委员、高级合伙人。中华人民共和国执业律师，并通过美国纽约州律师执业考试。刘律师熟悉公司、金融、投资领域的法律实务，熟悉大型企业法律业务，擅长项目组织及谈判，代理重大经济纠纷案件的诉讼与仲裁，英文流畅。刘律师具有法律和金融专业跨学科理论和实践背景。刘兴燕律师于 2006 年赴美留学两年，2013 年入选中国涉外律师"领军人才"培养项目赴欧培训，对商业组织设立、基金业务、项目投融资并购及相关争议解决等法律实务有深入的了解和实践经验，并与许多国际律师建立了广泛的联系，是一名具有国际化视野的优秀律师。

Liu Xingyan is Senior Partner of S&P LAW FIRM. Liu Xingyan is an attorney experienced in advising foreign companies on Chinese legal matters as well as providing legal counsel to Chinese companies conducting business abroad. Well-equipped to represent both international and local corporations in Chinese courts, she has provided legal services to and litigated on behalf of some of the largest and best-known companies in China, including China Development Bank and Founder Group. Ms. Liu's practice also involves advising some of the largest banks in China on a broad range of matters, from bank regulatory to complex financing transactions. In addition to her practice in international litigation, Ms. Liu possesses excellent connections with large State-Owned Enterprises (SOEs), whom she has represented in their projects abroad.

Ms. Liu passed the PRC National Uniform Judicial Exam in 2002 and passed the New York State Bar in 2008.

律所介绍 / Introduction to Law Firms

中伦律师事务所

中伦律师事务所创立于 1993 年，是中国司法部最早批准设立的合伙制律师事务所之一。经过数年快速、稳健的发展壮大，中伦已成为中国规模最大的综合性律师事务所之一。如今，中伦拥有 290 多名合伙人以及超过 1500 名专业人士，办公室分布在北京、上海、深圳、广州、武汉、成都、重庆、青岛、杭州、南京、东京、香港、伦敦、纽约、洛杉矶及旧金山共计 16 个城市，业务范围遍及全球 60 多个国家和地区。通过合理的专业分工和紧密的团队合作，中伦有能力在各个领域为客户提供市场领先的高质量法律服务。中伦先后受邀加入 Terralex 和 World Law Group，成为其成员律所。这将助力中伦拓展更为广泛的境外法律服务联系渠道，搭建交流与合作平台，更加有效地为客户提供全球与全方位的法律服务。

Founded in 1993, Zhong Lun Law Firm was one of the first private law partnerships to receive approval from the Ministry of Justice. After years of rapid development and steady growth, today Zhong Lun is one of the largest full service law firms in China. With over 290 partners and over 1500 professionals working in sixteen offices in Beijing, Shanghai, Shenzhen, Guangzhou, Wuhan, Chengdu, Chongqing, Qingdao, Hangzhou, Nanjing, Tokyo, Hong Kong, London, New York, Los Angeles and San Francisco, Zhong Lun is capable of providing clients with high-quality legal services in more than 70 countries across a wide range of industries and sectors through our specialized expertise and close teamwork. Zhong Lun has been invited to join Terralex and World Law Group. This will expand our overseas networking strength and cooperation among law firms across the world, and enable us to provide our clients with more efficient, comprehensive and global legal services.

律师介绍 / Introduction to Lawyers

王红燕

王红燕律师，北京中伦（杭州）律师事务所权益合伙人，中国执业律师。王红燕律师熟悉国际投资、资本市场和知识产权，英文流畅。王律师入选全国律协涉外领军人才库、"一带一路战略建设项目跨境律师人才库"和中华全国律师协会推荐参加国际律师联盟 UIA 的 15 名中国律师之一，曾到比利时 DEWOL 律师事务所布鲁塞尔总所、美国摩根路易斯律师事务所（MORGAN LEWIS）休斯顿分所和西班牙嘉里盖斯律师事务所（GARRIGUES）马德里总所进行培训，与各国律师具有长期良好的合作关系。

Grace Wang is Partner and Attorney of Zhonglun Law Firm and is experienced in international investment, capital markets and intellectual property. She was elected be the member of ACLA (All China Lawyers Association) Foreign-related Leading Talents, member of Cross-border Lawyers of Strategic Construction Project of Belt and Road and one of the fifteen Chinese lawyers referred by ACLA to attend UIA (Union Internationale des Avocats) conference. She has trained at Brussel Office of De Wolf & Partners, Houston Office of Morgan, Lewis & Bockius, Madrid Office of J&A Garrigues and has a long-term good cooperation with the lawyers of various countries.